europe
on a shoestring

Sarah Johnstone, China Williams, Reuben Acciano, Fiona Adams, Sarah Andrews, Carolyn Bain, Joe Bindloss, Becca Blond, Terry Carter, Geert Cole, Lisa Dunford, Mark Elliott, Michael Grosberg, Paul Harding, Patrick Horton, Amy Karafin, Cathryn Kemp, Steve Kokker, John Lee, Alex Leviton, Leanne Logan, Vesna Maric, Amy Marr, Tom Masters, Craig McLachlan, Jeanne Oliver, Tom Parkinson, Fran Parnell, Josephine Quintero, Robert Reid, Miles Roddis, Simon Sellers, John Spelman, Lisa Steer-Guérard, Andrew Stone, Wendy Taylor, Mara Vorhees, Matt Warren, Richard Watkins, Neil Wilson

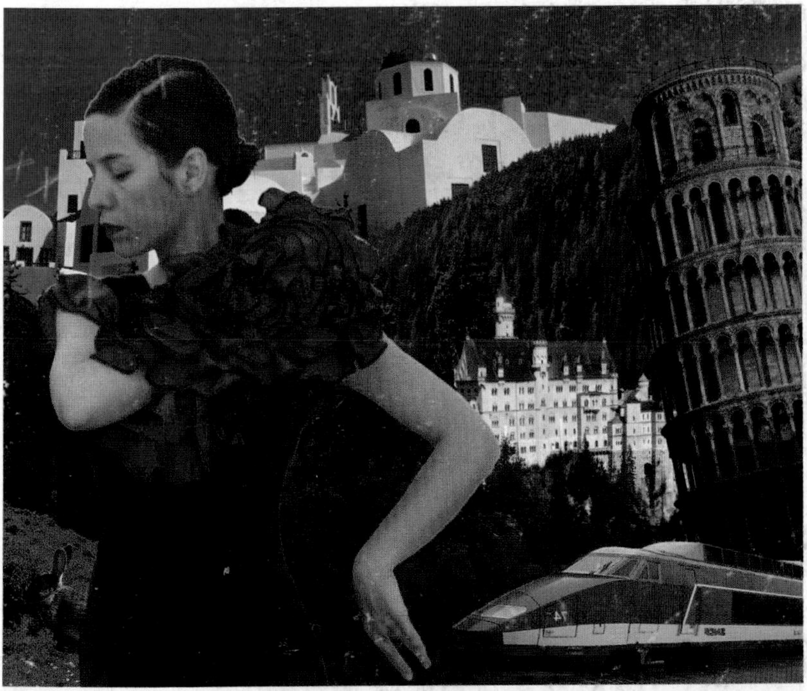

ICELAND (p588)
Hot springs, volcanoes and icecaps, this canvas was shaped by earth's bubbling core and purposely misnamed by the Vikings to deter visitors

BERGEN (p882)
A lush, relaxed city poised beside Norway's muscled fjords that grasp at the sea

AMSTERDAM (p845)
Like a tolerant parent, this classy city lets kids be kids without unnecessary meddling

SCOTTISH HIGHLANDS (p211)
Crumbling castles, nips of whisky and a haunting landscape sampled by ancestral pilgrims and rugged individualists

IRELAND (p602)
The Emerald Isle boasts Joyce haunts, rolling hills and convivial pubs, and, as they say, the Guinness really is tastier here

LONDON (p153)
Empire-building monarchs, dance-club heaven and Premier League football crown mighty Londontown

BELGIUM (p108)
Stuff your face on the planet's tastiest beer and chocolates

PARIS (p375)
Live a lusty life amidst these broad avenues lined with top-notch art museums and smoky cafés

SWISS ALPS (p1170)
Glacially carved sculptures drooled over by trekkers and skiers

BARCELONA (p1079)
Lisp into this modern art orgy filled with Gaudí, Picasso and Miró

ITALY (p640)
The easiest country to fall in love with and the hardest to leave

Responsible Travel

Overcrowded and littered beauty spots, the erosion of traditional cultures, ugly quick-fix tourist developments, fuel-burning flights and travellers behaving badly – if you thought Europe was immune to the destructive tendencies of tourism, think again. Millions of visitors each year have a huge impact on Europe's towns, countryside and people – often because they don't know or don't care about the consequences.

It doesn't have to be this way. Your stay can have a hugely beneficial effect, from jobs in local communities to a sustainable framework for conservation and preservation of Europe's wildlife and wild places. Ancient city centres are preserved and protected due to the money tourists bring to cities and towns throughout the continent. Donations and a thoughtful visit can help preserve the treasures taking your breath away on a daily basis.

It's not just your money, it's also your attitude that can really make a difference. While it isn't hard to make a better impression than some of the noisy, rude tourists you meet on the continent, you can go a step further and have a positive impact. With a dash of cultural sensitivity and a pinch of environmental concern, you can tread carefully without being a drag.

HOW YOU CAN HELP

- **Ask before you click** Get permission before taking someone's photo; sticking a camera in a person's face is universally rude. Learn to say 'May I take your picture?' in the language of every country you visit.
- **Be a smart shopper** Don't buy souvenirs or eat meals produced from endangered species or flora, including coral or some forest products. Try to buy crafts directly from the artisan. Support family businesses and hire knowledgeable and conscientious guides.
- **Don't be stingy** Be realistic about prices and treat bargaining like a flirtatious game rather than a test of wills. Tip when you can, and don't let hustlers and touts make you suspicious of everyone.
- **Don't litter** Don't leave rubbish out in the street – take your packaging home with you. Remember too that those cigarette butts belong in a rubbish bin, not snuffed out on the beach or flicked over the boat railing. Some countries offer recycling facilities, so use these where you can.
- **Learn the language** Take a course before leaving home or sign up for classes in the country. Your attempts will be rewarded with invitations, compliments and kindness.
- **Respect the local culture** Dress modestly, watch where you put your feet, and flash that beautiful smile. Treat religious centres, no matter how modest, like delicate treasures.

WEB RESOURCES

- **www.futureforests.com** Make your journey 'carbon neutral' with a donation to plant trees.
- **www.tourismconcern.org.uk** UK-based organisation dedicated to promoting ethical tourism.
- **www.transitionsabroad.com** Focuses on immersion and responsible travel.
- **www.eceat.nl** Dutch-based organisation facilitating farm stays.
- **www.wwf.org** Environmental conservation issues and links to national chapters.

BOOKS

For more on how not to dent the lands we visit (and listings of ecotour groups), read *The Good Alternative Travel Guide* (Tourism Concern) or Mark Mann's outstanding *The Community Tourism Guide*.

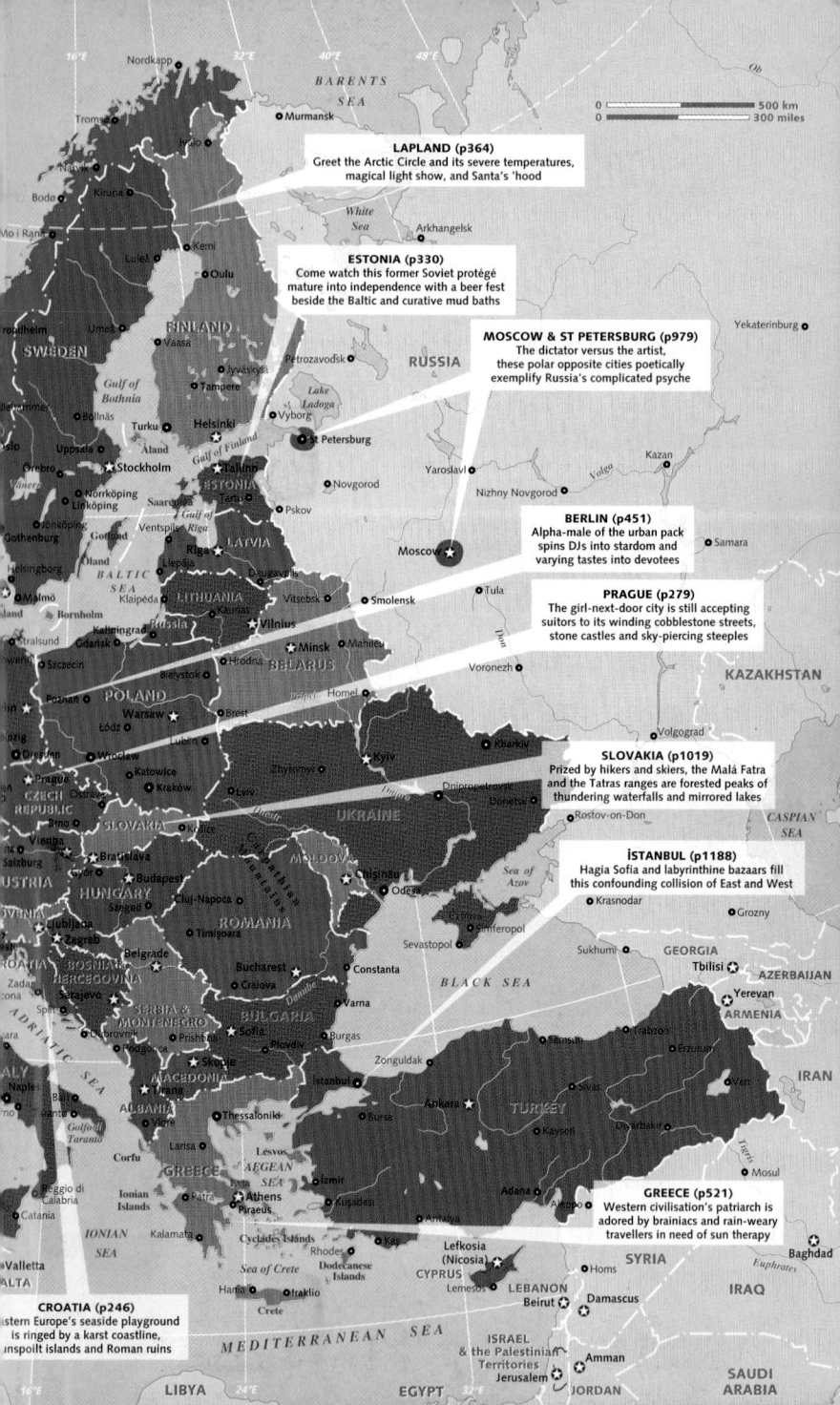

LAPLAND (p364)
Greet the Arctic Circle and its severe temperatures, magical light show, and Santa's 'hood

ESTONIA (p330)
Come watch this former Soviet protégé mature into independence with a beer fest beside the Baltic and curative mud baths

MOSCOW & ST PETERSBURG (p979)
The dictator versus the artist, these polar opposite cities poetically exemplify Russia's complicated psyche

BERLIN (p451)
Alpha-male of the urban pack spins DJs into stardom and varying tastes into devotees

PRAGUE (p279)
The girl-next-door city is still accepting suitors to its winding cobblestone streets, stone castles and sky-piercing steeples

SLOVAKIA (p1019)
Prized by hikers and skiers, the Malá Fatra and the Tatras ranges are forested peaks of thundering waterfalls and mirrored lakes

İSTANBUL (p1188)
Hagia Sofia and labyrinthine bazaars fill this confounding collision of East and West

GREECE (p521)
Western civilisation's patriarch is adored by brainiacs and rain-weary travellers in need of sun therapy

CROATIA (p246)
astern Europe's seaside playground is ringed by a karst coastline, nspoilt islands and Roman ruins

Contents

6

8

The Authors

SARAH JOHNSTON Coordinating Author, Austria, contributor to front chapters

Sarah has always found author bios difficult to take seriously, especially after the all-too-accurate piss-takes in *Molvania: A land untouched by modern dentistry*. Ouch. Having studied German (and journalism) at uni, she's now a freelance hack based in London, where she's previously worked for news agency Reuters, national newspapers and a host of magazines. She's been to Europe an awful lot, and she reckons that's more than any reader would want to know. Isn't it?

REUBEN ACCIANO   Italy

Trading his guitar for a backpack in 1998, Reuben trekked through Europe (but not Italy). That trip taught many truths; 'chemical memory' isn't a myth, you can thrive solely on pistachios, fruit, cheese and red wine, and never use Bulgarian train toilets. Ever. He inflicted his shoddy Flemish on the Dutch while researching Lonely Planet's *Netherlands* in 2003, after bussing around Italy on holiday. Reuben loves northern Italian pride; a subtler counterpoint to their southern cousins' explosive flamboyance.

FIONA ADAMS   Valencia, Andalucía, Balearic Islands, Spain

Fiona has lived and travelled in Africa and South America working as a freelance journalist and writer. Memorable adventures include piranha fishing in the Amazon, tango lessons in Buenos Aires and joining an expedition in search of Atlantis. She has a degree in archaeology and anthropology, a Masters in Latin American Studies and has worked on Lonely Planet editions of *South America on a Shoestring*, *Spain*, *Italy* and *Western Europe* and is the author of *Culture Shock! Argentina*. Fiona now lives in the Scottish Highlands.

SARAH ANDREWS   Madrid, Barcelona, Northern Spain

She grew up in North Carolina, but for the past five years Sarah has called Spain home. For this guide, she trekked across the northern half of Spain, developing an intimate relationship with Spain's railways and bus companies and discovering the greatest (and grimiest) corners of the Iberian peninsula. She won't pick a favourite spot, but Barcelona's gothic quarter, Santiago de Compostela's buzzing street scene and the elegant city of San Sebastián all rank highly on her best-of-Spain list.

CAROLYN BAIN   Malta, Sweden

Australian-born Carolyn once again fell in love with Europe's extremes during the research for this book, getting as much of a buzz from swimming in the Mediterranean as from crossing the Arctic Circle. Carolyn studied European history and languages, has lived in a few European countries and is the author or coauthor of Lonely Planet's *Malta*, *Sweden* and *Greece*. Her dream is for Lonely Planet to continue subsidising her search for the perfect Mediterranean island, and to visit every country in this book.

JOE BINDLOSS   Cyprus

Joe was born in Famagusta and refugeed to Lefkosia during the occupation in 1974. He now lives in the UK, but he still makes regular trips to Cyprus to see friends and family and enjoy fruit and vegetables that actually taste of something. Over the years, Joe has volunteered with sea turtles in the Akamas, gone rock-climbing in the Troodos and learned to cook *ofto kleftiko* (baked lamb) from refugee chefs on the Green Line.

BECCA BLOND — Liechtenstein, Switzerland

Becca and Switzerland became acquainted at an early age – she was born in Geneva. She moved to the States when she was very young and has slightly embarrassing childhood memories of wearing traditional Swiss alpine dresses to holiday functions, and fonder ones of family vacations in the Swiss Alps. Becca loves to travel on a budget: she's backpacked around much of Europe, southern Africa and parts of Asia. When not on the road she calls Boulder, Colorado, home.

TERRY CARTER — Greece

Terry's first visit to Greece was with a Greek-Australian friend returning to his local village in Rhodes for their annual festival. While still preferring to play the Turkish *saz* than the bouzouki, he now has a clear understanding on how making Greek coffee differs from cooking up a Turkish brew. And when not dreaming of hiding away in Monemvasia with a few good books, Terry is a freelance writer and designer based in Dubai.

GEERT COLE — Belgium, Luxembourg

Though now living in Australia, Geert regularly follows the call back to his native Belgium and home town Antwerp. Every year for the last decade, he has covered the length and breadth of Belgium and Luxembourg for various Lonely Planet titles, searching small villages for new things to see, combing cities for the best B&Bs and, of course, forever on the lookout for a fab new pub. Every trip reaffirms his essential belief – size matters not – Belgium is bigger than ever.

LISA DUNFORD — Hungary

Lisa has dreamed of Hungary ever since she learnt that it was the birthplace of her grandpa. While completing her BA in International Affairs, she was a part of one of the first study-abroad programmes in newly opened Hungary. She loved living in Budapest, and after college moved to nearby Bratislava, from where she took Hungarian classes. She continues to travel to Hungary every year to visit cousins and explore the land.

MARK ELLIOTT — Slovenia

A Belgium-based Brit, Mark is best known as a tourism specialist on Azerbaijan and the Caucasus. Mark has visited Eastern and central Europe repeatedly since childhood. In 1989, he joined Czechoslovakia's Velvet Revolution in Prague and stayed in the region, as an English teacher. His early visits to Slovenia included once arriving in Ljubljana by mistake when his Athens–London bus was hijacked by Metaxa smugglers. Mark has worked on many other travel guides including Lonely Planet's *Russia & Belarus*.

MICHAEL GROSBERG — Western Germany

Michael was raised in the Washington DC area, studied philosophy and then worked in Micronesia. After a long trip through Asia and across the US, he pursued journalism and NGO work in South Africa. Michael's interest in Germany began while doing graduate work. Wanting to combine book knowledge with actual experience, and having established a network of friends in Germany, he made several trips to the country. Post academia, he has taken many random jobs and currently teaches at university.

LISA STEER-GUÉRARD   London & Around, Southeast England, East England

Born in the Southeast and bred in South London, she now lives in Paris and regularly comes back to see what's new in her favourite English cities – London and Brighton. Lisa's ventures into travel started with Indonesia, on which she did a degree, studied with a Javanese *dukun* (traditional healer), met her French husband, worked as a UN election observer, and finally became a travel writer. Lisa has updated two guides on England, as well as writing articles and guidebooks on France and Southeast Asia.

PAUL HARDING   Finland

Paul first hit the road in Europe in the mid '90s. In several trips around the continent he has joined the *runtur* in Reykjavik, taken tea in Turkey, run with the bulls in Pamplona and met Santa in Lapland. In between he edited a London-based travel magazine and, as a writer for Lonely Planet, researched the latest editions of *Finland* and *Iceland*. Paul returned to Finland to indulge his growing appreciation of the sauna for this edition. He lives in Melbourne.

PATRICK HORTON   Bosnia & Hercegovina

Patrick, writer and photographer, was born with restless feet. He travelled extensively in his native Britain before hitting the around-the-world trail and ending up in Melbourne. His journeys lead him to regions including North Korea, Eritrea, East Timor, Tonga and Cuba. Some day he aims to find the longest railway journey. Patrick has had many photographs published with Lonely Planet and has contributed to Lonely Planet's *Australia*, *Ireland*, *Mediterranean Europe*, *Delhi*, and *Russia & Belarus* guides.

AMY KARAFIN   Ireland

Amy Karafin grew up on the USA's Jersey shore, where her curiosity about the horizon developed into a phobia of staying too long in one place. She spent many years behind desks in publishing houses in New York, leaving every job as soon as she had enough money for a trip, and finally decided to make a living on the road. She now lives in Dakar, Senegal, where she works as a freelance writer and translator in a little studio by the sea.

CATHRYN KEMP   Latvia, Lithuania, Romania, Moldova

Cathryn started travelling in 1990 when she studied art at the Moscow Institute of Architecture. Several trips through Russia and Ukraine later, and a passion for travel was born. Cathryn has worked on a number of Lonely Planet guides, including *Romania & Moldova* and *Estonia, Latvia & Lithuania* 3.

STEVE KOKKER   Estonia, Kaliningrad

Steve is a die-hard Eastern Europe lover. He has spent the majority of his time since 1996 living away from his native Montreal, basing himself in his father's homeland of Tallinn, Estonia, and trekking through the Baltic region, Russia and beyond. He has been writing and photographing for Lonely Planet since 1998.

JOHN LEE
Scotland, Northeast England

A British-born travel writer now living in Vancouver, John specialises in magazine and newspaper stories on the UK, Canada and fascinating spots around the world. His work has appeared in more than 60 publications, including the *Los Angeles Times*, Britain's *Observer*, *Prague Post* and *Travel+Leisure*. He regularly returns to Britain to gorge on Marmite and Curly-Wurlys. John also updated the Directory and Transport sections of the Britain chapter.

ALEX LEVITON
Southwest England, Central England, Northwest England, Wales

Most of Alex's life was spent either in California (LA, Humboldt County, San Francisco or getting a master's degree in journalism from UC Berkeley) or backpacking (often through Roman ruins). She's now a freelance writer living in a tobacco warehouse in Durham, North Carolina. After developing an addiction to scenic train journeys and scones and cream in 1994, she's visited Britain many times and hopes to hike the South West Coast Path next. Or at least stroll it. Between tea shops.

LEANNE LOGAN
Belgium, Luxembourg

After more than a decade of working with Lonely Planet, Leanne's connection to Belgium is as strong as to homeland Australia. She has scoured both countries more than 10 times, lived in Belgium for several years and now has a half-Flemish toddler Eleonor (who can already sling the guttural Flemish 'g'). A journalist by trade, Leanne has bounced by bike around Bruges, delved into the avant-garde in Antwerp, pub-crawled around Brussels and chilled-out in the Ardennes.

CRAIG MCLACHLAN
Greece

An adventurous Kiwi, Craig has walked the length of Japan, hiked around the 88 Sacred Temples of Shikoku, and climbed Japan's 100 Famous Mountains. He has been an author, pilot, hiking guide, interpreter and karate teacher. He has an MBA from the University of Hawaii, and has worked on Lonely Planet's *Japan* and *Hiking in Japan*. Craig presently runs Wilderness Adventures in Queenstown, New Zealand and was glad to accept his wife Yuriko's offer to carry the bags for his Greek research.

VESNA MARIC
Albania, Macedonia

Vesna Maric was born in Mostar, Bosnia and Hercegovina in 1976 and moved to Britain at the age of 16. She studied Czech Literature in London and lived in Prague for a year, before working for the BBC World Service for three and a half years. She has written magazine articles, produced radio features, and worked on short films, and she likes to photograph insignificant things. Her latest and, as she claims, most exciting project, was travelling to Albania and Macedonia for this Lonely Planet book.

AMY MARR
Rome & Around, Southern Italy, Sicily, Sardinia

Amy's love affair with Italy began with an early addiction to Sicilian-style pizza from Boston's North End. She went on to study Art History and Italian at Williams College and in Florence. After working as a business writer and PR director, she researched and led biking and hiking trips throughout Italy. Now a writer for magazines and a publisher of food and entertaining books, she lives in Marin County, CA. Amy has coauthored and contributed to a number of titles for Lonely Planet.

TOM MASTERS
Moscow, St Petersburg

A committed communist since the age of eight, Tom was a little disappointed to find Russia in the throes of avid capitalism by the time he finally got there in 1995. Since graduating from the University of London with a degree in Russian, Tom has returned many times, living in St Petersburg and working in the region. Despite living in London (having never adapted to the Russian winter), he finds himself back in Russia all the time and has also written Lonely Planet's *St Petersburg*.

JEANNE OLIVER
Croatia

Jeanne is a freelance journalist, born in New Jersey and living in the south of France. She has been visiting and writing about Croatia since 1996. Travelling the country by bus, boat, train and car, she's swum in its waters, hiked its trails and stuffed her backpack full of local cheese, homemade brandy and a handful of recipes to keep her going until the next trip. She's looking forward to eventually visiting every one of Croatia's islands, especially now she knows how to read the *Jadrolinija* schedule.

TOM PARKINSON
Berlin & Around, Eastern Germany, Turkey

Tom first visited Germany at the tender age of three, and was promptly involved in a road accident. Charmed, he studied German, spent a year working in Berlin, and has now written on both the country and the capital for Lonely Planet. Having lived in the second-biggest Turkish community in the world, it was only a matter of time before Tom graduated to the real thing, and he's now an apple tea addict as well as an avid Beşiktaş fan.

FRAN PARNELL
Iceland

Fran has worked as a cockroach-breeder, gun-runner and professional raconteur, and frequently invents work histories to hide her past as an Lonely Planet editor. After a childhood spent in Singapore and other humid hotspots, she has developed a passion for cold and empty places. This fact, combined with a handy degree in Anglo-Saxon, Norse & Celtic, meant that Iceland was the perfect choice for her first Lonely Planet assignment. Still pining for the fjords, Fran lives and works in West Yorkshire.

JOSEPHINE QUINTERO
Portugal

Born in England, Josephine started travelling in her teens, winding up in California where she gained an English degree from UC Berkeley and helped launch a food and wine magazine in the Napa Valley. Further travels took her to Kuwait where she was editor of the *Kuwaiti Digest* and briefly taken hostage during the Iraqi invasion. Shortly after Josephine moved to Seville, Spain, where she has side-stepped frequently into Portugal and come to know and love the country, the people and the custard tarts.

ROBERT REID
Bulgaria

Robert delved into old issues of *Soviet Life* as a teen to unveil the world of Eastern Europe. He minored in Russian at the University of Oklahoma, and – at last – studied in St Petersburg and talked about the Rolling Stones on Echo Moscow radio station in Moscow, before traipsing throughout Eastern Europe for several months. Bulgaria, with its Black Sea shores, Cyrillic pride, clunky communist-era hotels, and light(er) food, has always been a favourite. He lives in Brooklyn, New York.

MILES RODDIS
Andorra

Living in Valencia, Miles has lost count of the times he's nipped up to Andorra for a ski break – though never to shop. Or almost never; he'll confess, if pressed, to having once picked up a pair of cut-price walking poles and a snazzy shirt in Andorra la Vella. Andorra is also the starting point for the 23-day Pyrenean Traverse, a route he's twice trekked with enormous satisfaction. Miles has contributed to over 25 Lonely Planet titles, including guides, both general and walking, about Spain and France.

SIMON SELLERS
The Netherlands

A few years ago, freelance writer and editor Simon worked in London and used it as a base to explore the rest of Europe. During that time, he travelled to the Netherlands on a number of occasions. Later he worked as an editor at Lonely Planet before leaving to write full time. Based in Melbourne, Simon's work has appeared in major Australian newspapers as well as film and cultural magazines, and he is the founder of the online magazine *Sleepy Brain*. This is his second title for Lonely Planet.

JOHN SPELMAN
Norway

Making a career out of the generosity of others, John Spelman has spent too much time sleeping on his friends' floors in Oslo and beyond. When he's not busy interrupting otherwise happy marriages with his prostrate, slumbering body, John is usually drunk or hanging out with Norwegian architects. In his second life, John is a PhD student studying cultural landscapes and urbanism, some of them Norwegian. He currently resides in Charlottesville, Virginia.

ANDREW STONE
France, Denmark

Andrew's first experience of Southern France was as a schoolboy barely out of short trousers. A large extended French family (10 cousins) scattered around the country and an addiction to the country's wine and food ensures he remains a regular visitor. On visits to Denmark to see friends, he enjoys the pretty countryside and café culture, and feeds his interest in its rich Iron Age, Viking and Renaissance history.

WENDY TAYLOR
Belarus, Ukraine

Wendy has been a Slavophile ever since she read *Crime & Punishment*. By the time she was studying Slavic Languages & Literatures at UC Berkeley and Moscow State University, the Soviet Union was no more. After graduating, she had a year-long stint of working as an editor and writer in Moscow at the *Moscow Times* and other publications, and worked for two years as an editor for Lonely Planet before taking on authorial work. She has contributed to Lonely Planet's *Russia & Belarus* 3, amongst others.

MARA VORHEES
Morocco

On the first day of her first trip to Morocco, Mara called home in tears. She had been propositioned, harassed and followed – all on a stroll down Ave Mohammed V. Despite this initiation, she successfully produced her thesis. After working in international development and travelling in Spain and Morocco, she has since resorted to seeing and saving the world by other means. She has been lost and found in many medinas, drunk gallons of mint tea, and strolled down Ave Mohammed V in every town on the map.

MATT WARREN
Slovakia

Matt made his first foray into Eastern Europe as a schoolboy. After four months in Budapest, he hitched his way through Poland, the Czech Republic, Slovakia, Romania, Bulgaria and Turkey. As a UK-based journalist, he has subsequently worked in Eastern European destinations as diverse as Kaliningrad, Kosovo and Lithuania, and last year passed through again on his motorbike en route between Edinburgh and Istanbul. He has previously worked on many Lonely Planet titles including *Czech & Slovak Republics*.

RICHARD WATKINS
Poland

Born in Wales and a graduate of Oxford University, Richard's first paid job after leaving the academic world was teaching conversational English to college students in Bulgaria. Since then the travel bug has well and truly caught hold, and Richard has wandered the globe as a backpacker, English teacher and more recently, as a travel guidebook writer. Richard has written for several other Lonely Planet titles, including *Poland* and *Best of Prague*.

CHINA WILLIAMS
(contributor to front chapters, Directory, Transport)

Although her travels usually take her East, her undergraduate studies led her through the West, a tour from Plato to Kant, antiquity to modernity. She fondly remembers her college tour of Europe – trains, hostels, beer halls, and piazzas, back when the EU was just a twinkle in Brussels' eyes. Good times indeed. She now lives in Portland, Maine, with her husband Matt.

NEIL WILSON
Czech Republic

Neil first swung a rucksack on his back when he was 15, tramping the hills of Scotland, his home country. After working as a geologist, he pursued the life of a freelance writer and photographer. Since 1988 he has travelled in five continents and written around 40 travel and walking guides for various publishers. His first trip to the Czech Republic was in 1995, and he has been back many times, working recently on Lonely Planet's *Czech & Slovak Republics* and *Prague* guides.

CONTRIBUTING AUTHOR

Dr Caroline Evans wrote the Health chapter. Caroline studied medicine at the University of London and completed General Practice training in Cambridge. She is the medical advisor to Nomad Travel clinic, a private travel health clinic in London, and also a GP specialising in travel medicine. She has been an expedition doctor for Raleigh International Coral Cay expeditions.

Destination Europe

The headless statues of Cleopatra and Dioscrides found on Delos in the Cyclades (p546), Greece

Europe is a chameleon; its colours change rapidly. One day you can be on the cobbled streets of a medieval city, the next atop a snowcapped peak. Nowhere else greets you with such a swift succession of different languages and menu changes. With more than 30 national cultures on a modest landmass, Europe frequently dazzles even Europeans.

Dubbed a living museum for the way its past and present coexist, this wealthy continent offers the charms of quaint Amsterdam and Prague alongside the buzz of modern metropolises such as Berlin and London. Postmodern buildings such as the Guggenheim in Bilbao have quickly taken a place beside Barcelona's still unfinished Sagrada Família and older architectural icons like the ancient Parthenon.

Europe's appeal lies not just in an influential, often bloody past and a largely peaceful present, but also in its mix of culture and nature. Botticelli and Picasso masterpieces aren't far from the countryside or popular beaches. You can follow the footsteps of characters you read about in textbooks or blaze your own trail in the Alps. Whether you dream of experiencing the romance of Paris, absorbing the chaos of Istanbul or downing a few beers in Belgium, this multifaceted continent can satisfy your tastes.

Just as the EU has expanded east, so too has the traveller's itinerary and many formerly communist countries – even those outside of the EU – have been more open to tourism. The new colours that these destinations reveal, show how diverse the European cultural palette is, but for budget travellers there's a bonus. While Europe usually requires a longer, thicker shoestring than elsewhere, many of these recent hot locations are among the continent's cheapest.

MARTIN MOOS

Swimmers in Gellert Thermal Baths in Budapest (p571)

HIGHLIGHTS

BEST CLASSIC CITIES

Barcelona ■ Party around La Rambla, this medieval-modern Spanish hybrid, but Gaudí's Sagrada Família cathedral is the biggest treat (p1082)

Berlin ■ Feel the vibe around the German city's dozens of major new buildings and thrumming clubs (p451)

London ■ Tune into the new attitude of this British capital of street style at Tate Modern (p160)

Paris ■ Linger in one of the most romantic cities, with its Gothic Notre Dame, broad Champs-Elysées, France's best museums and relaxing cafés (p375)

Rome ■ Discover why the Vatican, the Colosseum and the Sistine Chapel truly make this Italy's Eternal City (p646)

BEST EASTERN EUROPEAN CITIES

Prague ■ Walk around the Czech Republic's capital and marvel at its fairytale architecture (p284)

Budapest ■ Take in this Hungarian city's magnificent skyline alongside the Danube, and enjoy the Turkish-era thermal baths (p571)

Tallinn ■ Estonia's capital was the first of several cities to be dubbed the 'new Prague'. Just try to avoid the English stag parties

Ljubljana ■ Take advantage of new low-cost flights and a groovy new central hostel, which have made the Slovenian capital backpacker-friendly (p1041)

Dubrovnik Enjoy Croatia's jewel: a magnificent walled city jutting out into the crystal-blue waters of the Adriatic Sea (p262)

NEIL SETCHFIELD

Interior of Reichstag, Parliament Building, Berlin (p451)

BEST NEW DISCOVERIES

Český Krumlov Immerse yourself in the huge backpacker scene in this pretty medieval Czech town (p297)

Kraków Wander through the Old Town's Gothic churches, the splendid Wawel Castle, the largest medieval town square in Europe, and the former Polish Jewish district of Kazimierz (p907)

Belgrade Cast off the hangover of war in Serbia with all-night barge parties (p1006)

Carpathian Mountains Ski on Romania's slopes: the newest and cheapest place to do so in Europe (p968)

Triglav National Park Catch a boat on Slovenia's Lake Bohinj, go rafting or paragliding in Bovec or simply hike (p1047)

BEST PARTY SPOTS

Amsterdam For those interested, spend time having fun the Dutch way in smoky, heady 'coffee shops' (p845)

Berlin & Munich Party in these German cities: Berlin for techno and all-night clubbing (p451); Munich for its enormous beer halls (p472)

Edinburgh Go where they know how to celebrate New Year's Eve (p202)

Ibiza Boogie the night away where this Spanish queen of the Balearic Islands still reigns (p1091)

Manchester Head for England's third-largest city for a more affordable clubbing mecca (p190)

Walkers on Pitzaler Joch (2996m) on the walking route of Otzaler Traverse, Tirol, Austria (p65)

BEST OUTDOOR EXPERIENCES

Chamonix ▪ Soak up the atmosphere in France's energetic ski village, which lies in the lee of Europe's highest peak, Mont Blanc (p421)

Tirol ▪ Be tempted by Austrian mountain trails, with free guided hikes in summer (p90)

Berner Oberland ▪ Hike in Switzerland's brilliant Jungfrau region and head for thrillseekers' heaven at Interlaken (p1177)

Vysoké Tatry ▪ Explore Slovakia's towering snowy mountains, crystal-blue lakes and waterfalls (p1029)

Scotland's Highlands & Islands ▪ Immerse yourself in wide empty spaces, heather and thistles (p211)

BEST BEACHES

Biarritz ▪ Be chic at France's stylish surf beaches and hunt out the cheap accommodation that exists here (p412)

Cyprus ▪ Enjoy unspoiled sandy beaches of the Akamas (p276) and Karpas (p277) peninsulas, where barely a soul can be seen

Greek Islands ▪ Start with the island of Santorini, Banana Beach on Skiathos or – for a party beach – Milopotas Beach in the Cyclades, but the real joy is discovering your own hideaway in the Cyclades (p546)

Costa de la Luz & San Sebastián ▪ Head to the Costa de la Luz for remote beaches (p1111) or sample Spain's best city beaches in San Sebastián (p1116)

Patara ▪ For perfect beach-bumming and turtle-watching, go to the place often rated the best beach on the Med (p1204)

ITINERARIES

Because there are so many options, decide which region you would like to concentrate on, then find the cheapest flight to one of its major cities. If you're set on the whirlwind tour, pick three or four cities (such as Paris, Amsterdam, Barcelona or Florence), then use these as a base for day trips into the country for more scenery. Unless otherwise noted, all travel in continental Europe is by train.

STORMING WESTERN EUROPE & MOROCCO

Castles, dance clubs, vineyards and medinas – don't allow a corner to go uncovered or a local beverage go unsampled.

Crash the club scene in **London** (p153), then proceed to romantic **Edinburgh** (p202), or the Loch Ness monster's 'hood near **Inverness** (p212). Set sail for **Belfast** (p630) before bussing to laid-back **Galway** (p625) and ferrying to the windswept **Aran Islands** (p627). Rejoin the modern world in **Dublin** (p608).

Hop on a ferry to castle-strewn **Wales** (p214) and then catch a train to **Stonehenge** (p177) before reaching France by tunnel.

Paris (p375) is a poetic start to a continental tour. To the east, **Strasbourg** (p391) is a regional rail hub. Southeast is the ski-bum town of **Chamonix** (p421) with its **Aiguille du Midi** (p421). Rail south to salty **Marseille** (p423) and permanently holidaying **Nice** (p429).

HOW LONG?
1-2 months
WHEN TO GO?
Jun-Aug; Sep-May
(high/low season)
BUDGET?
€50-70 per day

About 7000km; omit the British Isles if you're short on funds or time. Linger in the Spanish or French countryside, if you fancy yourself as an artist. And save a week for a Lost Generation escape to Morocco.

Barcelona (p1079) is Spain's exclamation point south of France. Zip up to Basque beauty **San Sebastián** (p1116), then to the Museo Guggenheim in **Bilbao** (p1117). Hug the coast to bustling **Santander** (p1120). Dive into the heart of the spirited nightlife in **Madrid** (p1062). Charge south to the Moorish empire of **Toledo** (p1076) and **Córdoba** (p1103). Catch a bullfight in **Seville** (p1099), sample fried fish in dishevelled **Cádiz** (p1111) or bake on the beaches of **Costa de la Luz** (p1111). Escape to Morocco (see below) on a slow boat. Or board a bus to the Islamic fortress, the Alhambra, in **Granada** (p1105) and depart by overnight train to vibrant **Valencia** (p1096).

From the southern tip of Spain ferry to hectic **Tangier** (p812) and bus to the **Rif Mountains** (p817). Continue by bus to imperial **Fès** (p831), blood-red **Marrakesh** (p824) and metropolitan **Casablanca** (p817). Return to Spain via the great limestone lump of **Gibraltar** (p1112).

Tasty custard tarts and safe streets reward a bus trip from Seville to **Lisbon** (p933), Portugal's breezy capital. Sidestep to gorgeous **Sintra** (p940), **Óbidos** (p946) and **Nazaré** (p946). Rent a car and drive north to **Porto** (p949).

CATALOGUING CENTRAL EUROPE

HOW LONG?
1-2 months
WHEN TO GO?
Jun-Aug; Sep-May
(high/low season)
BUDGET?
€50-70 per day

Efficient but scenic, these countries generally eat, live and play well in moderation.

From **Frankfurt** (p493), soar into the literary haunt of **Heidelberg** (p486) or explore the Brothers Grimm's Black Forest from **Freiburg** (p489). To the east is handsome **Munich** (p472), capital of Oktoberfest.

Saunter over to tidy **Zürich** (p1172) then make a beeline for the mountainous Jungfrau region and the popular base of **Interlaken** (p1177). With

About 3700km; devote a week to Germany and Switzerland, especially if you plan to hike in the Alps. Then spread the remaining time to the east and west depending on your budget and interests. To return with all your brain cells, spend only three days in Amsterdam.

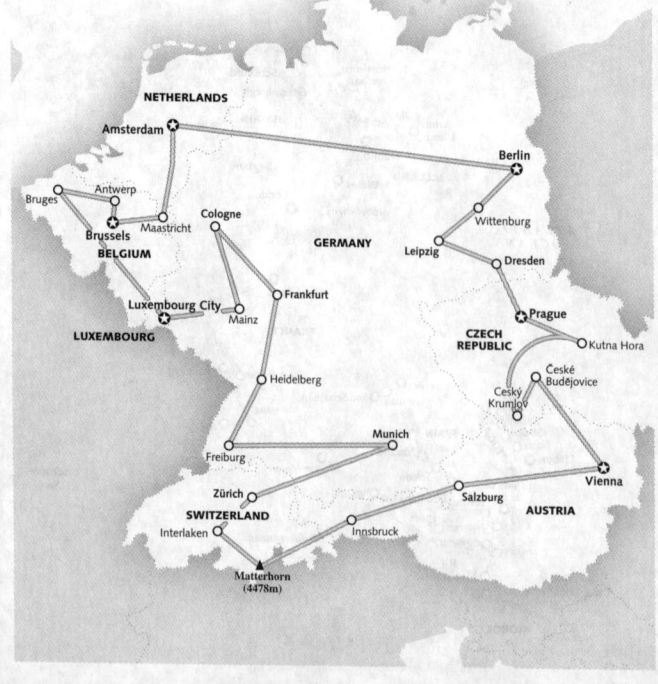

a few days to spare, head south to the A-list **Matterhorn** (p1170). A train crosses into the French Alps (see Storming Western Europe & Morocco, p21) from Geneva to Strasbourg.

Alternatively point the compass northeast to Austria's **Innsbruck** (p90) for skiing and hiking, or baroque **Salzburg** (p85). Then waltz into **Vienna** (p70).

Take a train to the Czech Republic to pay homage to **České Budějovice** (p296), the original home of Budvar (Budweiser) beer, close to the river in **Český Krumlov** (p297), or explore a silver mine in **Kutná Hora** (p293). Enjoy a tryst in darling **Prague** (p284) and go on to heady **Dresden** (p463), Bach's repose in **Leipzig** (p466) as well as Martin Luther's revolution in **Wittenberg** (p471). Give the old grey matter a rest in **Berlin** (p451).

Go to cannabis-friendly **Amsterdam** (p845) and clear the fog in old-world **Maastricht** (p862).

Fortify yourself in **Brussels** (p112). Head north to cosmopolitan **Antwerp** (p117) and medieval **Bruges** (p121), both historic outposts for the Flemish masters. Swing back into Germany through blue-blood **Luxembourg City** (p758). And complete the circle with a boat sojourn down the scenic Rhine Valley from wine-producing **Mainz** (p493) to Gothic **Cologne** (p498).

MEANDERING THROUGH MEDITERRANEAN EUROPE

Slip into the slow, easy pace of Europe's mellowed empires that now boast wine cheaper than water, ancient ruins and continuous blonde beaches.

Window-shop in **Milan** (p665), then be seduced by watery **Venice** (p671). Leap across the Adriatic to Bosnia and Hercegovina. Or stick to the boot

HOW LONG?
3 weeks - 2 months
WHEN TO GO?
Jun-Aug; Sep-May
(high/low season)
BUDGET?
€50-70 per day

About 5000km; weeks will slip away in this idyllic region. Allow at least a week each to bake on a Greek Isle, probe ancient Turkey or savour the atmosphere in Italy.

and ride the rails to charming **Florence** (p685); day-trip to **Pisa** (p692) and **Siena** (p693). Worship monumental **Rome** (p646), then get swept away by energetic **Naples** (p699) and peer into ill-fated **Pompeii** (p703).

Fate leads you to Greece via the dumpy ferry port of **Brindisi** (p706). Docking in **Patra** (p539), hop on a bus to the Byzantine pin-up city of **Mystras** (p540) and ancient heavyweight **Mycenae** (p540). Take the train to the ruins of Apollo's temple in **Corinth** (p539), and bus to venerable **Athens** (p528). By bus, consult the ruins of the oracle at **Delphi** (p538) before dipping south to **Piraeus** (p536) for an island-hopping expedition to buff **Mykonos** (p546), classic beauty **Naxos** (p548), or beach-bum **Ios** (p549). With more time, island-hop to marble-covered **Paros** (p547). Take a ferry to Mykonos and, from here, depart for volcanic **Santorini** (p550), encircled by dramatic cliffs, or visit **Iraklio** (p552) and charming **Hania** (p553) on Crete.

Set sail for Turkey via **Lesvos** (p558) to **Ayvalik** (p1198). Bus north along the Aegean coast to **Çanakkale** (p1197) and to the ruins of Troy or the Roman ruins of Ephesus in **Selçuk** (p1199). Continue by bus east along the Mediterranean coast to the Roman and Byzantine ruins in **Olympos** (p1205). From **Antalya** (p1206), set sail to **Cyprus** (p269), the mythical birthplace of Aphrodite. Return to the mainland and spin up to **Konya** (p1208), home of the whirling dervishes. Then bus into the wind-carved landscape of **Göreme** (p1209) before landing in legendary **Istanbul** (p1188), which is linked by train to Athens and Bucharest (see Exploring Eastern Europe & Russia, below). Note Eurail is not valid in Turkey.

EXPLORING EASTERN EUROPE & RUSSIA

Modern history has been cruel to this corner of the world, but the people are proud to show visitors the sweeter side of their homelands.

Come out of the 'cold' in **Moscow** (p983) and embrace abundant culture in **St Petersburg** (p991). Then poke around Estonia's **Tallinn** (p334) and the former-KGB cells at **Tartu** (p340).

HOW LONG?
3 weeks - 2 months

WHEN TO GO?
Jun-Aug; Sep-May
(high/low season)

BUDGET?
€30-50 per day

Bus to the ski slopes of Latvia's **Sigulda** (p730), former spy-central **Riga** (p724), or Lithuania's bewitching **Vilnius** (p743). Take the train to **Kaunas** (p748), a Mafioso hotbed, and the touching memorial at **Šiauliai** (p750). Bus to the seaport of **Klaipėda** (p750) and the Curonian Spit. Alternatively, train from Vilnius to Soviet-poster child **Minsk** (p101) in Belarus, Ukraine's **Kyiv** (p1220) or sassy **Lviv** (p1223).

Tour vibrant **Warsaw** (p901), then train south to historical **Kraków** (p907) and bus to sobering **Auschwitz** (p911). Trains run from Kraków to **Žilina** (p1028), on the doorstep of the Slovakian wilderness and to medieval **Levoča** (p1031). Head to **Bratislava** (p1023) for train connections to beautiful, cosmopolitan **Budapest** (p571).

Forge onward by bus to Romania's relaxed **Cluj-Napoca** (p962), and by train to the cobbled streets of **Sighişoara** (p972), baroque **Braşov** (p969) and castle-strewn **Râşnov** (p971). Sharpen your fangs at 'Dracula's' castle in **Bran** (p971) before heading south to Romania's capital, **Bucharest** (p962).

Ride the rails to picturesque **Veliko Târnovo** (p238) in Bulgaria, the Black Sea towns of **Varna** (p242) or **Sozopol** (p241). Then bus to must-see **Plovdiv** (p234), the amazing striped monastery at **Rila** (p234) and ascend to **Sofia** (p228), Europe's highest capital. Cruise the coastline to Istanbul or Athens (see Meandering through Mediterranean Europe, above).

Or head homeward through the barely touristed Balkans. Bus from Sofia to Macedonia's deep blue lake **Ohrid** (p772). Bus into Albania's **Tirana** (p49). Stumble off the tourist map by bus into Montenegro's **Durmitor National Park** (p1016) and **Cetinje** (p1015). Train or bus to **Sarajevo** (p136)

About 6000km; Russia's main cities deserve at least four days apiece. Spend a week and a half ricocheting south to Poland to assume a more relaxed pace of two weeks through the Adriatic beach towns, national parks and hillside villages. With more time, filter through the Balkans en route to Turkey or Greece.

in Bosnia-Hercegovina and medieval **Mostar** (p141). Saunter to Croatia's Adriatic coast for Agatha Christie's favourite, **Dubrovnik** (p262), or **Split** (p258). Ferry to sun-soaked **Hvar Island** (p260). Return to Sarajevo to catch a bus to the Serbian capital **Belgrade** (p1006) and a train north to **Novi Sad** (p1011), a lively university town.

Ride the rails to Croatian capital **Zagreb** (p251) and wind up in Slovenia's **Ljubljana** (p1041), a miniature Prague. Before whizzing into Austria (see Cataloguing Central Europe, p22), take day trips to idyllic **Bled** (p1048) and the **Bohinj Valley** (p1050).

SIMPLIFYING SCANDINAVIA

Fjords and forests, saunas and utopian socialism mind their manners in Europe's northernmost latitudes.

You can find lengthy layovers to **Iceland** (p588), a volcanic island full of hot springs and glaciers, Björk and whale meat.

Then fly to Denmark's **Copenhagen** (p304). Day-trip to Hamlet's 'Elsinore' Castle in **Helsingør** (p316), and the Viking ship museum in **Roskilde** (p316). Rail to cyclable **Odense** (p319), Hans Christian Andersen's hometown, and day-trip to the Renaissance **Egsekov Castle** (p319). Return to Copenhagen to train across the Baltic to Sweden's friendly **Malmö** (p1144), then swing by train to quiet **Lund** (p1146) before visiting the beautiful capital of **Stockholm** (p1131) and one of the 24,000 islands surrounding the city. Hop across the gulf to Finland's time-worn **Turku** (p358) and the intimate capital of **Helsinki** (p352), power north to a romantic region of lakes and forests surrounding **Kuopio** (p363) and cycle the bike paths of progressive **Oulu** (p364). Bus to Lapland's **Rovaniemi** (p364) for

HOW LONG?
2 weeks - 1 month
WHEN TO GO?
Jun-Aug; Sep-May
(high/low season)
HOW MUCH?
€70-90 per day

About 4400km; with Viking precision, you can 'sack' Scandinavia's capital cities in a week or more. Then spend a week or two trotting through pure, unfiltered nature, such as Norwegian fjords, Stockholm's archipelago or the Finnish lake region. Then reimmerse yourself in civilisation with a few days' rest.

a reindeer-sledding safari before bussing into Norway's **Bodø** (p890), an uninspiring jumping-off point for the spectacular **Lofoten islands** (p890) and their glacier-carved mountains shooting from the sea. Return to the mainland and jump a train that passes through Hell (a real town) en route to medieval **Trondheim** (p888), and visit the fjords of **Bergen** (p882) and scenic **Flåm** (p886). After receiving the Nobel Peace Prize in **Oslo** (p873) boat back to Copenhagen.

Getting Started

Of course, like all good Scouts, travellers should be prepared. What's less often said is that it's just as important to remain flexible. Build a little slack into your schedule, so that when a detour or little adventure presents itself you can grab what could be a once-in-a-lifetime opportunity.

This chapter gives information for the region as a whole; refer to the specific country chapters or the Europe Directory (p1227) for more details.

WHEN TO GO

Europe has one high season in summer and another in winter. Crowding is the main difficulty you'll encounter in the warmest months of June, July and particularly August. In some countries, like France and Italy, many shops and restaurants also close in August while locals take their own holiday.

See Climate Charts (p1232) for more information.

Global warming has meant a later start to the skiing season; often, decent snowfalls aren't recorded until January (or even February). December is still always busy in picturesque locations like Paris, Prague and any Austrian or German city with a quaint 'Christmas market'. Easter is another busy time.

You can find bargains by visiting traditionally 'summer' destinations such as Greece in winter, but beware that public transport might not be running so frequently, if at all. This can be true in some northern locations like Scotland and Scandinavia, where heavy snow and ice means services are seasonal.

For all the above reasons, it's often worth visiting in shoulder seasons, like late May/early June and September.

WHAT TO TAKE?

Packing light is the (often elusive) goal. A backpack that won't fit in luggage racks or hostel lockers is a drag, literally, and everyday essentials are widely available in most European cities. Still, it's sensible to make space for some of these:

- **Earplugs** Necessary unless you're a very heavy sleeper; a snoring dorm mate and traffic noise are almost inevitable at some point.

- **First-aid kit** Just the basics: some aspirin, sticking plasters, antiseptic cream, sun block and perhaps, if you have a delicate stomach, antidiarrhoea pills.

- **Mobile phone** Not only useful in emergencies and for staying in touch with the occasional SMS, it also doubles as an alarm clock. For technical specifications, see p1241.

- **Padlock** For hostel lockers and train luggage racks.

- **Photocopies** An absolute essential. Make two copies of your passport title page, visas, travellers cheque serial numbers and tickets, leaving one copy at home, and packing the other separately from the originals. Make a note somewhere safe of your credit card numbers.

- **Plastic bags** Just a couple to line your bag and keep the contents dry or to isolate dirty laundry.

- **Power adapter** Preferably with both a chunky UK plug and a Continental plug with two round prongs.

- **Rain gear** It *always* rains in some parts of Europe.

- **Small torch or flashlight** To prevent painful bumps in the night.

- **Swiss Army knife** Handy if opening tins and beer bottles; less handy if you accidentally leave it in your carry-on airline luggage – so don't.

COSTS & MONEY

Excluding transport costs, you can get by on about €50 to €70 in Western Europe. You might be able to squeak by on a little less in smaller towns and in Mediterranean Europe. Eastern Europe is probably the cheapest area, requiring a daily total of €30 to €50. Scandinavia is, if anything, more expensive than Western Europe. Switzerland also costs a premium.

The quickest way of getting foreign cash these days is to withdraw it direct from international ATMs in each new city. The best way to track such spending is to set up your account for online banking. Do this before you leave home and, on the road, remember to log off properly in Internet cafés. International transactions might take a few days to register on your statement.

For information, see Money (p1237) in the Europe Directory.

HOW MUCH FOR WESTERN EUROPE?

Camping €10-15

Hostel €15-30

Budget restaurant meal €10-20

Local transport (single fare) €2-3.50

Museum fees €5-12

One beer (500mL) €2-5

LIFE ON THE ROAD

Generally, travel goes smoother in orderly Europe. Dusty roads, buses that constantly break down and general chaos are only really found on the continent's outer fringes. Which is why Europe can make an ideal destination for a first-time trip.

More often than not, you'll roll into town on a train that's not too late (no guarantees in Britain, mind) and easily find a train station locker to store your backpack until you can check into your hostel at 5pm. A nearby tourist office will usually be on hand to help with anything this book can't provide.

More than in other parts of the world, sightseeing is dominated by churches and museums. But there are also spooky catacombs, cobblestoned streets and quaint houses in Europe's compact cities. And there are also places where being a visitor is all about hiking, cycling or perhaps even skiing.

10 TIPS TO STAY ON A BUDGET

- **Buddy up** Finding a travel partner slashes accommodation costs.

- **Spend more time East** Things still cost less in countries like the Czech Republic, Hungary, Poland and Slovakia.

- **Head for the countryside** Where the living is also cheaper.

- **Buy a rail pass** In Europe, travelling extensively without one is the transport equivalent of unprotected sex.

- **Overnight on trains** Sleeping in your seat or couchette on longer trips saves on a night's lodging.

- **Handwash clothes** Do your laundry in hostel and hotel sinks; even hostels that forbid it don't notice the odd item or two.

- **Invest in a phonecard** The cheaper alternative for calling home or within Europe.

- **Eat cheap** Buy food from street stalls or eat at informal, self-service places, where tipping doesn't even enter the equation.

- **Look up old mates** And don't be shy about being a (gracious) guest of friends of friends living in the countries you're visiting.

- **Become a couch surfer** Join www.couchsurfing.com, where residents let travellers stay with them for free.

> **WHOOPS!** *Sarah Johnstone*
>
> We all know to be careful when using ATMs. However, while I was dog-tired in Switzerland once, I walked off with my receipt only (which comes out first there) leaving Sfr200 cash sitting on the machine. Amazingly, the next customer ran 50m after me to return it – proving just how friendly Europe can be occasionally.

It sounds relatively effortless, but even in Europe a month-long holiday can start to feel like…work. So, pace yourself. Most of the time stay in hostels and go drinking with dorm mates. But try to treat yourself to your own room and a little privacy every two weeks or so.

There's a lot to see in Europe, but try to avoid the 'if-it's-Friday-it-must-be-Rome' syndrome. Plan extra time to rest up in one of your fantasy cities. Spending several days in one hostel also makes it easier to get to know people.

CONDUCT

One of the great delights of travelling in Europe is the way so many cultures live shoulder to shoulder. The differences can make your head spin – especially as you enter countries like Bulgaria where they nod their heads up and down to say 'no'.

Basics

Don't assume everyone understands English or will suddenly get it if you speak very loudly. Learn a few local phrases instead. 'Hello' and 'goodbye' are particularly useful in the many countries where it's customary to greet the proprietor when entering and leaving a shop, café or quiet bar. 'Thank you', 'please', 'sorry' and 'do you speak English?' are always good, too.

Watch the local customs for hand and body gestures. Be careful, for example, about raising your fingers to order two beers; even with your palm facing the bar staff, it's rude in some countries.

Public etiquette is helpful to know. If on foot, stay out of the bicycle-only paths in northern Europe. In Eastern Europe be more prepared to give up your seat to the elderly or infirm.

If introduced to a local, follow their cue. In some northern European countries, say Denmark or Germany, it's still common to shake hands with a stranger. In charming France, Spain or Italy, it doesn't matter if they don't know you from Adam, they'll still kiss you.

Dress

Europeans are among the planet's most dedicated followers of fashion, and in über-chic London, Paris, Milan and the like, scruffy clothing will give you away as a tourist. But equally, as long as you're not trying to get into trendy clubs, upmarket hotels or the opera, few will bat an eyelid at anything you wear in northern Europe. Away from the larger northern cities – and even in some of them, like Berlin – attitudes are more relaxed.

Snobbery can be more acute in southern and Eastern Europe. In the latter region, that's partly a result of nouveau riche attitudes and partly to do with old-fashioned pride in one's appearance.

All this said, the universal uniform of jeans, T-shirt and trainers will do for most daywear. If you're going clubbing, or somewhere posh, you can dress up a pair of everyday trousers with a funky top/formal shirt and shoes.

HOW MUCH FOR SCANDINAVIAN EUROPE?

Camping €10-20

Hostel €30-45

Budget restaurant meal €15-20

Local transport (single fare) €5-10

Museum fees €5-10

One beer (500mL) €6-10

HOW MUCH FOR EASTERN EUROPE?

Camping €5-8

Hostel €10-15

Budget restaurant meal €3-7

Local transport (single fare) €0.30-0.60

Museum fees €1-8

One beer (500mL) €0.80-2.50

10 MUST-SEE MOVIES

■ **All about My Mother** (Spain, 1999) Pedro Almodóvar's tribute to Barcelona, mothers and transvestites.

■ **Amélie** (France, 2001) An utterly charming Parisian fairy tale.

■ **À Bout de Souffle** (France, 1960) The last *mot* (word) in Gallic cool.

■ **Bicycle Thieves** (Italy, 1948) Haunting catch-22 situation in postwar Rome.

■ **Festen** (Denmark, 1998) Hand-held cameras and dark family secrets – the ultimate in naturalistic Dogma movies.

■ **Good Bye Lenin!** (Germany, 2003) Heart-warming comedy where Berliners pretend the wall never fell.

■ **The Seventh Seal** (Sweden, 1957) Death plays chess for a man's life in this Bergman classic.

■ **A Short Film about Killing** (Poland, 1988) Grim, but essential, communist-era masterpiece.

■ **Trainspotting** (UK, 1996) Scrappy heroin junkie eventually chooses life. Great soundtrack.

■ **Welcome to Sarajevo** (UK, 1997) Accessible, if sentimental, drama set in wartime Bosnia.

If you're hiking or cycling, obviously you'll need the appropriate clobber. Otherwise, hard-and-fast rules really only apply in places of worship; see below.

Giving Gifts

If you are invited to someone's home, bring them a gift, perhaps a bouquet of flowers or a bottle of wine. One of the hallmarks of a great trip is meeting kind people who help just when you've missed the last train or can't find a room for the night. Bring along a few region-specific gifts – like a magnet, key chain or postcard of your home town – to give to people on the road.

Meals

Habits are changing, but lunch, rather than dinner, remains the main meal in many parts of the Continent. With such rich and varied gastronomic traditions (see p36), Continental Europeans do tend to turn every sit-down meal into a social ritual. However, it's just as common to eat on the move – devouring everything from chips and mayonnaise in paper cones to hot dogs with mustard, pizza slices, spicy kebabs and gelati.

Religion

Be respectful in churches or other religious buildings. Refrain from using flash photography and keep your voice to a whisper, especially during Mass or other services. In mosques, women will be required to cover their heads with a scarf or similar; everyone has to remove their shoes. The same is still sometimes true in Christian churches in more pious countries, particularly in Eastern Europe.

READING UP

Rev up your wanderlust with witty travelogues such as Bill Bryson's *Neither Here nor There: Travels in Europe,* Tim Moore's *Continental Drifter* and Peter Moore's *The Wrong Way Home.* For a travel-literature classic, try Mark Twain's *A Tramp Abroad,* or mull over the meaning of it all with pop philosopher Alain de Botton's *The Art of Travel.* See p1231 for further details on each.

Snapshots

CURRENT EVENTS

Fireworks lit the night sky, Beethoven's *Ode to Joy* filled the air, and 75 million people celebrated as the clock struck midnight on 1 May 2004 and their 10 countries formally entered the EU. Six weeks later, it was another story. In historic, synchronised elections for the European Parliament in Strasbourg, more than 70% of new EU citizens didn't bother to vote.

Chalk that up as another case of *plus ça change* for European integration; the idea has always been underwritten by ambivalence.

The new members of the EU – Cyprus, the Czech Republic, Estonia, Latvia, Lithuania, Hungary, Malta, Poland, Slovakia and Slovenia – hope that joining the world's second-richest trading bloc will bring economic prosperity. That will take time. Few of the 15 older members have been willing to grant new EU citizens immediate equal rights to live and work wherever in Europe they choose.

Germany, the stalled economic motor at the continent's heart, is not expected to welcome migrant workers from Eastern European countries for the next seven years. Austria is expected to maintain restrictions for five. Only Ireland – itself transformed into a 'Celtic Tiger' by EU funding a decade ago – is welcoming migrants from new member states almost without reservation.

Economics is only one motivation for this stance by older EU states. Immigration is also a much-debated social issue, with far-right politicians gaining support in Austria, Belgium, Denmark, France and the Netherlands. In the UK, newspapers have fuelled racist fears with tales of Central European Roma people coming to steal jobs and – inimitable tabloid hype here – eat people's pets.

Statistically, Europe needs new blood. US secretary of defence Donald Rumsfeld was correct in one sense when he spoke of 'Old Europe'. Ageing populations mean looming labour shortages and pension shortfalls. By 2050 Italy is forecast to have only 1.5 workers for every pensioner, compared to eight in 1950.

Yet 'Fortress Europe' is still trying to pull up her drawbridges. The 2004 al-Qaeda–linked bombing of Madrid trains increased concerns about keeping out potential terrorists, but there's some evidence of overreaction. The UN has expressed concern about a rumoured scheme by the UK to use countries like Croatia as offshore immigration processing centres.

As politicians now face the enormous task of persuading voters to accept the newly drafted European Constitution in 2006, France and Germany stand united as the grand European project's driving force. Other EU nations, such as Denmark, Sweden and the UK, are less decided, still preferring to hang on to their own currency rather than adopt the widespread euro.

In this environment, being European only goes as far as each country wants. Nearly 250 years ago, the philosopher Jean Jacques Rousseau optimistically declared: 'There are no longer Frenchmen, Germans, and Spaniards, or even English, but only Europeans.' Don't try repeating that at the 2006 football World Cup in Germany.

Croatia, Bulgaria and Romania are negotiating to join the EU, possibly as early as 2007. Ultimately, Turkey would also like to join.

Tech-savvy Estonia has declared Internet access a basic human right.

HISTORY

'In the beginning, there was no Europe,' writes Professor Norman Davies in *Europe: A History*. In the beginning, all that existed was an unpopulated peninsula attached to the western edge of the world's largest landmass

---

TOP FIVE HISTORY READS

▪ Norman Davies' international bestseller *Europe: A History* is impressive in size, scope and balance, giving the continent's east and west an equal hearing.

▪ Manageably sized, readable and thought-provoking, *The Origins of the Second World War* is AJP Taylor's most celebrated work, but also the eminent historian's most controversial.

▪ *History of the Present: Essays, Sketches and Dispatches from Europe in the 1990s* by Timothy Garton Ash mixes eyewitness accounts with an analysis of momentous times in Central Europe.

▪ In *Imperium*, Ryszard Kapuscinski, Polish journalist extraordinaire, throws light on life behind the Iron Curtain in a way no Westerner ever could.

▪ Anthony Beevor made history sexy again with the doorstop-sized *Stalingrad* about one battle, two tyrants, more than one million poor soldiers and their countries.

(Asia). But after humanoid settlers arrived between 850,000 and 700,000 BC, Europe's temperate climate and unthreatening environment would make it the cradle of agriculture and the birthplace of great civilisations.

Evidence at Çatal Huyuk (7700–5700 BC) points to Turkey as one of the world's earliest sites of agriculture. However, it was in Greece and Rome that the continent's two great ancient societies arose. Greece (first emerging around 2000 BC) was renowned for its philosophers (Aristotle, Plato, Socrates) and democratic principles. Rome – boasting brilliant politicians, and writers like Cicero, Ovid and Virgil – spread its influence by military might. At its peak, the Roman Empire stretched from England to the Sahara and from Spain to Persia.

By the 4th century AD, both empires were in terminal decline. Greece had been swallowed by Macedonia's Alexander the Great, then by Rome itself in AD 146. Although Roman emperors in Constantinople hung on for another 1000 years, the empire's western half was toppled by Germanic tribes in 476.

This marked the start of the Middle Ages in Western Europe. In 768, conquering king Charlemagne grandly named his lands the 'Holy Roman Empire'. After this territory passed into the hands of Austrian Habsburgs in the 13th century, it became the continent's dominant political power. Elsewhere, an alliance of Christian nations repeatedly sent troops to reclaim the Holy Land from Islamic control. These unsuccessful 'Crusades' (1096–1291) unfortunately set the stage for centuries of skirmishes with the neighbouring Ottoman Empire as it took control of Asia Minor and parts of the Balkans from 1453 onwards.

Europe's grand reawakening also began in the mid-15th century, and the subsequent Renaissance, Reformation and French Revolution ushered in enormous social upheaval.

TIMELINE

508 BC: Democracy is introduced in ancient Athens

867: Viking Danes begin 200 years of seafaring raids on Britain

1512: Renaissance artist Michelangelo finishes painting the Sistine Chapel

1000BC   500BC   0 AD   500 1000   1200   1300   1400   1500 AD

753 BC: City of Rome is founded – in legend, by a she-wolf

476: The Roman Empire's west falls to Germanic tribes

1348: Bubonic plague sweeps Europe, killing 30% to 45% of the population

NAPOLEONIC COMPLEX

Myth surrounds Napoleon Bonaparte. In reality:

- He was Corsican and never fully mastered the French language.
- He was 168cm tall – not as short as generally believed.
- There's no evidence he ever told his wife, 'Not tonight, Josephine.'
- His Waterloo was in Belgium, not near a London train station.

The Renaissance fomented mainly artistic expression and ideas (see Art & Literature, p34 for greater detail). The Reformation was a question of religion. Challenging Catholic 'corruption' in 1517, German theologian Martin Luther established a breakaway branch of Christianity, Protestantism. Struggles between Catholics and Protestants flared during the Thirty Years' War (1618–48).

The French Revolution in 1789 was about political power, specifically the populace's attempt to wrest it from the monarchy. But in the ensuing vacuum, plucky general Napoleon Bonaparte (1769–1821) crowned himself emperor. Napoleon's efforts to colonise all Europe ended in defeat by the British at Waterloo in 1815, but the civil laws he introduced in France in 1804 would spread the revolutionary ideas of liberty and equality across the globe.

Having vanquished Napoleon, Britain became a major world player itself. With the invention of the steam engine, railways and factories, it unleashed the Industrial Revolution. Needing markets for goods, it and other European powers accelerated their colonisation of countries around the world, a process that had begun in the 16th century.

Meanwhile, the death throes of the Habsburg Empire (now called the Austro-Hungarian Empire) were about to rock the entire continent. Serbia was accused of backing the assassination of the heir to the Austro-Hungarian throne in 1914 and the battle between the two states developed into WWI. Crippled by a huge bill for reparations imposed at the war's end in 1918, Austria's humbled ally, Germany, proved susceptible to politician Adolf Hitler's nationalist rhetoric during the 1930s. Other nations watched as Nazi Germany annexed Austria and parts of Czechoslovakia, but its invasion of Poland in 1939 sparked WWII. During the final liberation of Europe in 1945, Allied troops from Britain, France, the USA and the USSR uncovered the full extent of the genocide that had occurred in Hitler's concentration camps for Jews, Roma and other 'degenerates'.

The Allies carved out spheres of influence on the continent, and Germany was divided to avoid its rising up again militarily. Differences in ideology between the Western powers and the communist USSR soon

1917: Russian Revolution kicks off, leading to the creation of the Soviet Union in 1922

1980: Solidarity workers' movement starts shaking up communist Poland

Present Day

1600 1700 1800   1900 1940 1950 1960 1970 1980 1990   2000   2002

1789: Queen Marie-Antoinette suggests French poor 'eat cake'; they revolt instead

1944: D-day landings begin France's liberation from Nazi Germany

1961: By the new Berlin Wall, JFK says he's 'ein Berliner' (a doughnut!)

2002: Twelve EU states adopt a common currency, the euro led to a stand-off. The USSR closed off its assigned sectors – East Germany, East Berlin and much of Eastern Europe – behind the figurative Iron Curtain. This 'Cold War' lasted until 1989 when the Berlin Wall fell. Germany was unified in 1990. A year later the USSR was dissolved. Czechoslovakia, Hungary, Poland and Bulgaria grasped multiparty democracy.

The downfall of the Eastern Bloc had a terrible effect in Yugoslavia, where nationalist leaders seized the chance to stir up political unrest and war: some of the young independent nations there are still recovering. For the most part, however, the end of the Cold War has brought a sense of peace to Europe. A sense of cooperation is proving slightly trickier to locate. The EU was formed in 1951 as a trade alliance and has developed fitfully into a political entity since. At this stage 12 members have adopted a common currency in 2002 and the initial signing of a European Constitution took place in October 2004.

PEOPLE & CULTURE
Art & Literature

Today it's considered slightly politically incorrect to promote Europe as 'the cradle of Western civilisation', but the continent's legacy to the world unquestionably includes some renowned paintings, as well as a fascinating array of philosophies.

After the prolific creativity of ancient Greek and Roman culture, the continent went through a fallow period – a kind of communal artistic block – during the early Middle Ages. Times were hard, mere survival was difficult enough and the church, the leading patron of the arts, wanted religious icons not realism.

But then in the 15th century a sea change occurred and European art came storming back with the Renaissance. The movement began slowly in the Italian city-states of Florence and Venice, with the rediscovery of Greco-Roman culture. Then it spread further afield over the next several centuries.

Leonardo da Vinci (1452–1519) and Michelangelo Buonarroti (1474–1564) led the Italian Renaissance; spurred on by Jan van Eyck (1390–1441) and other Flemish masters who led the Northern Renaissance in art.

The baroque period that followed in the 17th century, defined by Rembrandt and Peter Paul Rubens' ornate portraits, was also influenced by classic ideals. During the 18th century, Romantic painters (such as Eugène Delacroix and Francisco Goya) chose exultant political themes of liberty and great battles that eclipsed in reverence the old Christian allegories.

The late-19th-century impressionists (including Edgar Degas, Edouard Manet, Claude Monet and Pierre-Auguste Renoir) progressively moved away from realism, depicting ordinary people (instead of royalty) pursuing ordinary pursuits and using small disjointed brushstrokes to create an 'impression' of subject and light. Their worked segued into that of their successors, like Vincent van Gogh and Paul Gauguin.

Then in the 20th century came the Fauvists and the cubists. The Fauvists used colour to suggest figures and motion and are probably best represented by Henri Matisse. Among the Cubists was one Pablo Picasso, who went on to become almost a one-man art movement all to himself, abandoning perspective and drawing heavily on African and other native art to forge a style of wholly modernist painting. Following generations stripped away more elements of reality. In the 1930s, René Magritte, Joan Miró, Max Ernst, Salvador Dalí and Alberto Giacometti visually explored

Ode to Joy, the choral finale to Beethoven's Ninth Symphony, uses words by poet Friedrich Schiller to espouse universal brotherhood and has been adopted as the official EU anthem.

Fifty years old in 2005, the Eurovision Song Contest is watched by at least 300 million TV viewers annually. ABBA are still its best-known winner (in 1974).

dream themes and the subconscious. Sculpture was escorted into modernity by Auguste Rodin and later by Constantin Brancusi.

Contemporary European art often rebels against the barriers of 'good taste', using shock and wit as tools for making statements on politics, sexuality and social issues. Artists such as Germany's Katharina Fritsch, with her sculpture *Rat-King* of 13m-tall black rats, Britain's Jenny Saville with her immense nude portraits and Mark Quinn, known for his self-portrait sculpture made of his own refrigerated blood, are just a few examples.

For a stunning array of art, visit St Petersburg's Hermitage Museum (p994; www.hermitage museum.org), one of the world's best art galleries.

In the pantheon of European storytellers, the Greek epic poets (including Homer), dramatists (Aeschylus, Sophocles, Euripides) and philosophers (Plato, Aristotle) occupy revered positions. Rome's dominance of the continent impressed Latin as the voice of learning and literature (namely Virgil's *Aenid* and Plutarch's histories) until Geoffrey Chaucer *(The Canterbury Tales)*, Miguel de Cervantes *(Don Quixote)* and Dante Alighieri's *(La Divina Commedia)*, among others, fashioned their native tongues into epics.

Johann Gutenberg invented the printing press in 1450, which was to contribute to the spread of ideas during the Renaissance and the following Enlightenment (1650–1789), the so-called 'Age of Reason'. During this period, science and human logic for the first time took supremacy over religious belief as big-hitters like Voltaire (pro-rationalism)and Jean Jacques Rousseau (somewhat anti-) traded ideas across the divide.

Euro-pudding: Underwhelming pan-European film or TV show, often financed by state grants

The period building up to the Enlightenment was also a period of unbridled creativity in mathematics (eg Francis Bacon, René Descartes, Blaise Pascal), political theory (Niccolo Machiavelli) and theatre and poetry (William Shakespeare, Molière, John Milton).

Eurotrash: Kitschy, sex-obsessed, trailer-trash TV show of deliberately doubtful taste

With the advent of the machine age, the Romantics (eg Johann Wolfgang von Goethe, Aleksander Pushkin, Lord George Gordon Byron, John Keats, Percy Bysshe Shelley) bemoaned the severed ties with nature and looked to ancient Greece for guidance. Henrik Ibsen and Charles Baudelaire were also eminent literary figures in the 19th century. Here too, at the front door of modernity, philosophers including Friedrich Nietzsche dismantled the absolutes of morality and reality, and Sigmund Freud's theories opened a lid on the subconscious.

Euro-sceptic: Opponent, often rabid, of the EU and further integration

The modern age saw the rise of the novel from the character-driven stories of George Eliot, Jane Austen, the Brontë sisters, Charles Dickens, Thomas Hardy, Fyodor Dostoevsky, Leo Tolstoy and Thomas Mann to the literary experiments of James Joyce. In 1960s France, Jean-Paul Sartre and Albert Camus were the two leading lights of the existentialist movement. Many contemporary writers (like VS Naipul, Salman Rushdie, Milan Kundera, Zadie Smith, Monica Ali, Hanif Kureishi) wrestle with such modern problems as straddling two cultures, escaping political persecution, and balancing love and desire.

TEN CLASSIC EUROPEAN NOVELS

- *Anna Karenina* by Leo Tolstoy (1877)
- *Crime and Punishment* by Fyodor Dostoevsky (1866)
- *Death in Venice* by Thomas Mann (1912)
- *Don Quixote* by Miguel de Cervantes (1605)
- *Madame Bovary* by Gustave Flaubert (1857)
- *Oliver Twist* by Charles Dickens (1838)
- *Remembrance of Things Past* by Marcel Proust (1913)
- *The Outsider* by Albert Camus (1942)
- *The Trial* by Franz Kafka (1925)
- *Ulysses* by James Joyce (1904)

Food & Drink

Europeans take great pride in their different regional cuisines and it's no exaggeration to call the best of them exemplary. When modern nutritionists want to encourage us to adopt a healthy diet, two words often pass their lips: 'Mediterranean European'. After all, the fresh vegetables, seafood, olive oil and garlic ritually served up on the Med supposedly reduce heart-disease risk, help keep depression at bay and generally prolong life.

Even if you don't give a damn about your health, it's no sacrifice to eat like this, tucking into grilled sardines in Portugal, enjoying a fresh paella dish of seafood and rice in Spain, or snacking on vegetable, meat and seafood tapas. Surely sharing in the Spanish love of ham can't hurt too much, either?

Pasta generally tastes better in Italy, its country of origin, where homemade noodles are dished up with deliciously creamy sauces or cooked with oodles of garlic and tomatoes that have frequently just been picked. Each region has its own distinctive pasta (from *ziti* in Naples to *orecchiette* in Apulia). They know the right way to make pizza and polenta here too, and rustic Italian cooking also boasts healthy and tasty ingredients like truffles and white beans.

When the subject moves on to French cuisine, our nutritionists get confused. How can all the elaborate recipes, meat and rich cream sauces that define classic *haute cuisine* be good for the arteries? Yet the French have long dined on steak tartare, coq au vin, duck confit and goose-liver pâté without apparent harm. Indeed, they relish a mind-boggling array of cheeses – from the Normandy region's famous Camembert to the Dordogne's blue-veined Roquefort – and have a penchant for sweet crepes. Yet still they manage to have a low rate of heart disease.

The answer to this 'French paradox' lies not in the occasional foray into ratatouille (vegetable stew) or bouillabaisse (a seafood stew from Marseille), but in the national habit of enjoying a glass of red wine nightly. Quite right, too, with such excellent choices at their doorstep – from the busty Bordeaux and cocky Côte du Rhône reds to a bouquet of Loire Valley varietals.

Oh dear, we'd better leave the do-gooder nutritionists behind as we enter central and Eastern Europe – the land that calorie counting forgot. Modern Germans might have learnt to cut back just a little on the wurst (fatty sausages) and smoked pork of their traditional cuisine, but both dishes are still prominent in, say, the Czech Republic and Austria (which also makes a mean apple strudel). Moving closer to Hungary, you'll find goulash, plus a spice rack weighed down with paprika, poppy seeds, cinnamon and cumin.

It is possible to eat healthily in Slavic countries – if you stick to borsch (beet soup) or cabbage perhaps! But who can resist the *pierogi* (stuffed dumplings) that every country in the region claims to have invented? Fried, boiled or glazed with butter, they're filled with meat or mushrooms. Wash them down with a shot of neat Polish or Russian vodka.

Other European regions have their own specialities: the Swiss are known for fondue, rösti, chocolate and cheese, while Scandinavians favour salty 'roll mop' herrings. The Belgians are renowned for their mussels and chips as well as hundreds of varieties of beer made by monks, while Turkey and Greece share a penchant for lamb (as kebabs in Turkey or *gyros* in Greece), tangy cheeses like feta or *haloumi*, yogurt, hummus, aubergine (eggplant) and olives, all followed by honey-sweet baklava for dessert.

Serving food in courses was a Russian tradition that was widely adopted throughout Europe in the 19th century.

Ukraine boasts Europe's most unhealthy snack: *salo* (pure pig fat), which now also comes coated in chocolate. Scotland comes a close second by serving deep-fried Mars bars.

British food probably has the worst 'meat and three veg' reputation, and in parts of the country it's still unfortunately deserved. However, the larger cities boast just about every ethnic cuisine, and London, in particular, is awash with world-class chefs. Here, even old comfort food like bangers and mash or fish and chips are often given new twists (with, say, merguez sausages with mustard mash). If in doubt, order a curry. Its links to the Indian subcontinent mean this is something at which Britain excels.

Finally, of course, Europe is a brilliant spot for an alcoholic tipple, from the French wines, Russian vodka and Belgian beers already mentioned to German *Weissbier* ('white' wheat beer), world-famous Czech beers and Greece's aniseed liquor Ouzo. We'll leave you to explore that subject yourself; it's the most fun way. *Prost,* bottoms up, *nazdrave!*

Religion

Ironically, although they weren't particularly fond of them at the outset and fed early believers to the lions, the Romans did much to spread Christianity. Not only did this minority religion go with the Roman Empire as it spread across Europe, eventually Rome performed an about face; in AD 313 Emperor Constantine converted to Christianity and made it Rome's official religion.

When the Roman Empire fell in the west, the church's existing independent hierarchy of popes often assumed state power. In 1054 the church split over a theological debate on the Roman Catholic Church, which spread through most of Western Europe, as well as the Eastern Orthodox, in Asia Minor. The Roman Catholic Church dominated political, artistic and cultural life in Europe for nearly 500 years until the Protestant Reformation in the 1520s. Inspired by the teachings of Martin Luther, parts of Germany, Switzerland, Scotland, Hungary and England broke away from Rome, adopting Protestant tenets that assumed a variety of subsects (Lutherans, Evangelicals, Episcopalians).

Today traditionally Catholic countries like France have a large Muslim minority thanks to immigration from former African colonies. However, Islam (emerging in Saudi Arabia in the 7th century) has had a permanent presence in Europe and North Africa since the 12th century. That's due largely to military conquest, particularly of Spain and the Balkans.

During the infamous Spanish Inquisition (1478–1834), King Ferdinand and Queen Isabella tried to unite their country politically behind a Catholic national identity. Jews, Muslims and Protestants were systemically exiled or persecuted or both.

Sport

The running joke is that the English now regularly lose in sports they invented. This phenomenon is not just confined to cricket, where no other European country fields a national side, but extends to the continent's most popular pastime, football (soccer). England claims, perhaps tenuously, to be the birthplace of the 'beautiful game', because the rules were standardised here in the 19th century. However, England hasn't won a major tournament with a round football since 1966.

If 'football's coming home' is the fan's perennial catch cry, in 2006 in Europe it really is; the FIFA World Cup, the footballing equivalent of the Olympics, is being hosted by three-time winners Germany. But you don't have to have tickets to this big tournament; there's always the annual UEFA Champions League and UEFA Cup where you can watch the world's most famous players (David Beckham, Luis Figo, Thierry Henry, Cristiano Ronaldo) as the likes of Arsenal, Real Madrid, Chelsea, Manchester United, AC Milan and Juventus do battle. National leagues play the same October to May season.

Greece stunned everyone by becoming European football champions in 2004. The country, which had never won a major tournament before, holds the title until the next European Championship Cup (distinct from the annual league) in 2008.

Although the English also devised tennis, their players continually struggle – even on home turf at Wimbledon in London every June. Here,

---

TOP SPORTS WEBSITES

For more information on Euro sports, check out the following:

■ http://fifaworldcup.yahoo.com – Football World Cup 2006

■ www.uefa.com – UEFA European Football Association

■ www.wimbledon.org – Wimbledon

■ www.rolandgarros.org – French Tennis Open

■ www.torino2006.org – Winter Olympics 2006

■ www.letour.fr – Tour de France

■ www.bormio2005.com – World Skiing Championships

■ www.fis-ski.com – Skiing & Snowboarding World Cups

■ http://news.bbc.co.uk/sport – BBC Sport

Swiss, Russians, Belgians and Americans dominate. The French Open, Roland Garros, is held in Paris at the end of May. At least the English have fared better in rugby in recent years, where other heavyweight European teams are France, Ireland and Wales.

In 2004 the Olympics returned to its historic home, Athens (where they were first held in 776 BC). There's a good chance the 2012 Games will also be hosted on European soil, with Paris the bookmakers' favourite, and only one non-European city, New York, in contention.

However, you don't have to wait that long to see a European Olympics. The 2006 Winter Olympics will be held in Turin, Italy. The year before that, Italy hosts the Alpine World Skiing Championships, in Bormio.

Another huge draw is the annual Tour de France cycling race every July, but European sport isn't all about big-ticket events. Even if you're not particularly sports-minded, lesser pursuits like *boules* in a quiet French village, spear fishing off the Italian coast or diving off the Mostar Bridge in Bosnia provide interesting cultural insights.

ENVIRONMENT
The Land

Europe is often referred to as a continent, when it is more accurately a peninsula, which is surrounded on three sides by the Mediterranean Sea, Atlantic Ocean and the North Sea. Coastal Europe enjoys the moderating effects of the Gulf Stream, which brings moist warm air to a region that would otherwise suffer from extreme cold due to its latitude. Southern Europe is dry and sunny, while Central Europe is more variable.

In between the Baltic Sea and the spine of the Alps lies the European Plain, one of the greatest uninterrupted expanses on earth, stretching from the Pyrenees and the Atlantic coast to the Ural Mountains in Russia. This arable region of grassland and dense forests drains into the Rhine, Danube and Main.

Belting the centre of Europe, the Alps were carved by the retreating glaciers as ice ages passed and stretch from France to the Carpathian Mountains in Eastern Europe. Mont Blanc is Europe's tallest mountain at 4807m, followed by the Matterhorn at 4478m. The eastern range is significantly shorter than its western counterparts – Troglav in the Julian Alps is 2863m and Gerlach in the Tatras is 2655m. The Carpathians arc across seven countries from Austria to Ukraine and down to Romania. With an abundance of rainfall, the Carpathian Mountains is the primary spigot for the Danube and Vistula.

In the southern range is the Mediterranean area, with ready access to the sea and running along a volcanic range that was most active between

Europe has experienced 17 ice ages through its geologic history.

The coldest place in Europe is Vorkuta, Russia (average low -20°C), and the warmest is Seville, Spain (average high 29°C).

1628 BC (Thera) and AD 79 (Vesuvio), although Europe's largest live volcano, Mt Etna in Sicily, erupted most recently in 2001. The land is rocky and exhausted from mismanagement, although olive trees, cypress and grape vines thrive. Along the Dalmatian coast, karst shimmers like a jewel.

In the far north, the arctic fingers of Scandinavia dip into the northern Atlantic and the shallow North Sea. Fjords, steep cliffs and mud flats all prepare the continent to meet water.

Glaciers are responsible for much of the topography in Europe and still exist in the Alps and Scandinavia, despite climate change (see below). Most glaciers survive on the north-facing mountain slopes, which receive less direct sunlight throughout the year. Glaciers are born when layers of snow accumulate year after year and form solid ice blocks, some of which take on an ethereal blue colour. Switzerland's Aletsch Glacier is the largest on the continent.

Parts of Iceland look so out of this world, NASA sent Apollo astronauts to train there. The space agency is still studying the country in an effort to better understand Mars.

Wildlife & Plants

The Mediterranean forests are a range of corks (providing three-quarters of the world's cork supply) and holm oaks, cedars, pines as well as olive trees. The Mediterranean Sea has the world's second-highest percentage of native species, including the endangered monk seal. The Adriatic Sea shelters underwater pastures of the *Posidonia* seagrass, which is abundant with commercial fish.

The Carpathians are considered one of the last refuges of wilderness with healthy populations of brown bear, wolf and lynx, Imperial eagle and Ural owl, species that have all but disappeared elsewhere. The last population of Iberian lynx lives in the southwestern corner of Spain and Portugal.

The world's largest reed bed welcomes the Danube River into the Black Sea near Romania and Ukraine. More than half of the world's population of white pelicans, pygmy cormorants and red-breasted geese live here.

The northern Atlantic Ocean and North Sea provide unique habitats for sharks, seals and migratory birds. Rich blankets of kelp and seagrass, and cold-water coral reefs also inhabit the chilly waters.

Nature has left its mark in many spots, including: the Burren, Ireland (p624), the fjords of Norway (p882), Göreme, Turkey (p1209), Mont St-Michel, France (p400), and Pompeii, Italy (p703).

National Parks

The region's first national park was founded in Sweden in 1910. And today Sweden is sandwiched between Finland and Slovakia as the most forested countries in Europe – a coveted prize in an area where only 2% of Europe's existing forests are protected.

Underdeveloped Eastern Europe is regarded as the region's second chance to grow an environmentally friendly landscape (despite the small matter of Chornobyl!). Virgin forests in Belarus and Poland protect the last stand of forests that once stretched across the European Plain. Slovakia's Carpathian Mountains and Romania's rich natural diversity are protected as national parks.

Environmental Issues

Name all the big environmental problems related to densely populated areas and Europe suffers from them. Air and water pollution from industry are high in many regions, and approximately 56% of Europe has been deforested. Rivers have been dammed or straightened, resulting in destruction of wetlands, floodplains and forests, and in more loss of wildlife habitat. The once-abundant Mediterranean Sea has been over-fished and its role as a popular tourist destination puts additional stress on limited resources, like fresh water and open space. Homes and hotels crowd more than half the Mediterranean coast, clawing over each other for a water view.

In addition to this, Europe has had some singular issues to deal with. The world's worst nuclear disaster occurred at the Chornobyl reactor in 1986, and parts of the Ukrainian landside immediately around the reactor are still off limits. Thirteen years later, bombing of chemical factories during the Balkans conflict caused contamination of the already suffering Danube River basin. A year later, an accident at a gold-mining operation in Romania spilled 100 tonnes of cyanide into the river system.

Global warming is taking a toll, which was particularly evident during a summer heatwave in 2003. According to the Swiss Academy of Natural Sciences, Switzerland's glaciers retreated by up to 150m that year, causing landslides and the creation of new lake accumulations in the valleys.

During the same heatwave, forest fires in Portugal and elsewhere destroyed a total area four times the size of greater London, threatening wildlife and humans.

The EU has organised an international environmental agency to monitor threats and violations of member-signed mandates for land conservation, sustainable fishing and pollution reduction.

Festivals

Looking to party down in the Old World? If you attended just 10% of Europe's festivals, you'd be very tired indeed. Most countries take to the streets to celebrate major religious holidays like Christmas, the beginning of Lent and Easter. There are also pagan, saint's and harvest festivals that transform sleepy villages into folk parties. While we could never include all of the Continent's celebrations, here are some of our favourite events.

AIR GUITAR WORLD CHAMPIONSHIPS (FINLAND)
Late August; Oulu, northern Finland; www.omvf.net

Unleash the Hendrix inside you – without callusing your fingers. Bedroom rockers from around the world take the stage to show their proficiency in 'air' guitar, the cheapest instrument ever invented. Only people who've registered beforehand on the website can enter, but everyone can watch. Contestants must play two songs: one of their choosing and one selected by the judges. The winner receives a real-life guitar.

BASTILLE DAY (FRANCE)
14 July; Paris; www.paris.org

Vive la revolution! The French national holiday commemorates the beginning of the end for the French monarchy. Back on this date in 1789, the people got together, stormed the Bastille and released the prisoners. Fireworks at the Eiffel Tower, parties, dances and a military parade on the Champs-Élysées are the order of the day.

CASTLE PARTY (POLAND)
Late July; Bolkow, southwest Poland; www.castleparty.com

Huddle with the dark forces at the world's largest Goth festival. Staged in creepy Bolkow castle, the festival revolves around shock-rock bands playing to a crowd of 21st-century ghouls and goblins in white face paint, black clothing and industrial piercings. The easiest way to get to Bolkow is by bus from Wrocław.

COOPER'S HILL CHEESE-ROLLING CONTEST (BRITAIN)
Last Monday in May; Gloucestershire, England; www.cheese-rolling.co.uk

Dear Mum, please reconsider your outdated ban on playing with your food. Take this age-old contest, for example, where a 3kg wheel of cheese is hurled from the top of the hill and runners chase after it. Whoever catches it first wins. Silly? No, this is wholesome and nutritious fun.

FÈS FESTIVAL OF WORLD SACRED MUSIC (MOROCCO)
Late May to mid-June; Fès; www.fesfestival.com

At the beginning of the hot Moroccan summer, travellers cleanse their souls with moving performances of spiritual and religious music from around the world. Works from a wide range of traditions are presented over 10 uplifting days.

GALWAY ARTS FESTIVAL (IRELAND)
Mid to late July; Galway; www.galwayartsfestival.com

The biggest arts festival in Ireland is the perfect excuse for trekking across the Emerald Isle to this artistic university town. Big-name rock

DID YOU KNOW?
Originally a pagan festival marking the passage of winter into spring, Carnaval retains elements of fertility rituals, especially in the grotesque costumes, but was usurped by the Catholic calendar as the last gasp of excess before the Lenten season of abstinence. Famous Carnavals take place in Venice, Brussels and Nice.

acts, small-time street performers and pints of Guinness contribute to a Celtic good time.

GAY PRIDE PARADE (THE NETHERLANDS)
Early August; Amsterdam; www.amsterdampride.nl

One of Europe's gay capitals hosts the Continent's largest annual pride parade. It's also known as the 'canal parade', because outlandishly dressed participants literally float down the canals on, well, floats and boats. Celebrations include a film festival and nonstop partying; the leather-fetish party is among the tamer events…

GLASTONBURY FESTIVAL (BRITAIN)
Last weekend in June; Pilton, England; www.glastonburyfestivals.co.uk

The world's large 'greenfield' festival of music – and inevitably, given the predictablity English weather, mud – turns 35 in 2005. And what a long way it's come. Anybody who's anybody plays Glastonbury these days, from hip new art bands like Franz Ferdinand to established acts like Oasis and Paul McCartney. Blimey, even the English National Opera have performed Wagner's *Ride of the Valkyries* here (you know, the one from *Apocalypse Now*). If you want a break from the music, there are lots of stalls and tents where you can have your chakra balanced or just wash your clothes.

HOGMANAY (BRITAIN)
29 December-1 January; Edinburgh, Scotland; www.edinburghshogmanay.org
(operational Sep-Dec only)

All together now, 'Should auld acquaintance be forgot…' Scotland is home to the song dedicated to New Year's Eve, and, as long as the icy winter permits, it puts on a bloody good knees-up for the occasion. In Edinburgh, four days of revelry ring in the New Year, with processions, an excellent street party, fireworks, a concert and, of course, several thousand renditions of 'Auld Lang Syne'.

IL PALIO (ITALY)
2 July and 16 August; Siena, Tuscany; www.ilpaliodisiena.com

It seems folk in the Sienese districts of old used to fight a lot. One fine day in 1147, however, they decided to replace the bloodshed with a pony race; since then they've raced around Siena's Piazza del Campo twice a year, to the delight of multitudes. A parade introduces the race and a huge feast celebrates it afterwards.

INTERNATIONAL FESTIVAL OF FANTASY, THRILLER & SCIENCE FICTION FILM (BELGIUM)
Mid- to late March; Brussels; www.bifff.org

This is *the* most popular get-together for European fans of cult fantasy, thriller and science-fiction movies, doling out awards for such things as best android, best vampire and best special effects.

JAZZFEST BERLIN (GERMANY)
Late October or early November; Berlin; www.jazzfest-berlin.de

As avant-garde as its host city, this modern jazz festival pushes the definition of the genre beyond bebop. It's touted as one of Europe's most important events and draws international contributions from Japanese composers and electronica DJs. Concerts are held at different venues throughout the city.

LA TOMATINA (SPAIN)
Late August; Buñol; www.lahoya.net/tomatina

Throw 'em if you've got 'em at this citywide food fight. More than 20,000 revellers (open to the public) pelt each other with summer's juiciest fruit, the tomato, for one free-for-all hour in the tiny town of Buñol, near Valencia. Theories abound about the festival's origins: some say tomatoes first flew in 1945 during anti-Franco protests, others say it was just a simple fight between friends that engrossed nearby diners.

NOTTING HILL CARNIVAL (BRITAIN)
Last weekend in August; London, England; www.thecarnival.tv

This enormous Caribbean-flavoured carnival has had organisational issues in recent years, but it now seems back on track. Literally. Rerouting the 40-year-old parade has sorted out some crowding issues, for those of us who like our little luxuries like air to breathe. Enjoy the colourful floats, the steel bands and the fantastic Jamaican food stalls. Sunday is traditionally 'kids day' and thus quieter. On the Bank Holiday Monday, the fact becomes clear that this is one of Europe's biggest street parties.

OKTOBERFEST (GERMANY)
Mid-September to early October; Bavaria; www.oktoberfest.de

The first beer fest began as a celebration of the marriage of King Ludwig I to Princess Therese of Saxon-Hildburghausen on 12 October 1810. Today it has evolved into a celebration of all things Bavarian with revellers wandering from tent to tent in Munich, consuming millions of litres of beer and tonnes of pretzels, roasted meat and sausages.

ÕLLESUMMER (ESTONIA)
Early July; Tallinn; www.ollesummer.ee

The Baltics' largest beer festival is also the Continent's best budget surprise. Beer Summer is held on the Tallinn Song Festival Grounds, with stages focused on Estonian folk culture, international beers, local bands and even a petting zoo.

ORIGINAL MARATHON (GREECE)
Early November, Marathon to Athens; www.athensclassicmarathon.gr

The original marathon was run by Phidippides, an Athenian messenger who covered 24 (some say 26) miles delivering to Athens the news of a Greek victory over Persian invaders in the town of Marathon in 490 BC. The current marathon route is supposedly the exact route that Phidippides took, with the finish line in the Olympic Stadium (where the original Olympics were held). This is an open international marathon.

PRAGUE SPRING INTERNATIONAL MUSIC FESTIVAL (CZECH REPUBLIC)
Late May to mid-June; Prague; www.festival.cz

Possibly the best-value big-ticket festival in all of Europe, the Prague Spring International Music Festival is dedicated to the world's great orchestral works and kicks off each summer's classical music season. Leading international and national names attend.

ROSKILDE FESTIVAL (DENMARK)
Late June or early July; Roskilde; www.roskilde-festival.dk

Pretty much the same as Glastonbury, albeit with a slightly more grungy, gothy feel, Roskilde has big-name alternative bands, folk, soul and reggae.

Profits from the concert are donated to humanitarian aid organisations, and to support an environmental agenda, no glass or plastic bottles are allowed on site. Backpackers camp out in the town of Roskilde, near Copenhagen, and hang around as the festivities unfold.

RUNNING OF THE BULLS (SPAIN)
Early July; Pamplona (Iruña), Navarre; www.sanfermin.com
This is the big one, the one you see on TV, the one that macho-man Hemingway made famous in his novel *The Sun Also Rises*. Still a test of manliness, the bull run (the *Encierro*, which is just one of the events at the San Fermin festival) follows an 800m stretch through the narrow streets of Pamplona where for three heart-stopping minutes participants try to outrace a herd of pissed-off bulls. Everyone has a strategy for how to finish the race in one piece so as to enjoy the more sedate attractions like folk music, vespers and bacchanalia in honour of the saint who protects all those who escaped being gored.

ST PATRICK'S FESTIVAL (IRELAND)
Week leading up to 17 March; Dublin; www.stpatricksday.ie
In his homeland, the celebrations for St Patrick's 'falling asleep' (or death) last much longer than the day itself. In fact, there's almost a week's build-up to Dublin's famous St Patrick's Day parade on 17 March – and much of that week is spent drinking Guinness. Oh, all right, there are outdoor theatre performances, traditional music, dancing and lots of wearing of shamrock leaves, too. All is in honour of the patron saint of Ireland, who's often recognised as the most successful converter of the Celtic pagans to Christianity. Celebrations are held across the country, with popular parades in Cork, Armagh and Belfast.

STREET PARADE (SWITZERLAND)
Early August; Zürich; www.streetparade.ch
Zürich is one of Europe's techno capitals and – despite its banking reputation – pretty damn cool. So, when Street Parade's on, its streets are lined with hip kids ahead of the game and techno purists who complain about the commercialism of Berlin's Love Parade. The formula must be working; in 2003, Zürich's annual street party overtook both the Love Parade and the Notting Hill Carnival in size.

WIFE-CARRYING WORLD CHAMPIONSHIPS (FINLAND)
Early July; Sonkajärvi, central Finland; www.sonkajarvi.fi
Dragging around the old ball-and-chain takes on Olympic importance at this unusual foot race. The annual event covers 250m of obstacles, including a water course, all traversed by men carrying their wives on their backs. And the prize for completing the run first? Her weight in beer. (Do Finnish men choose a wife accordingly?) You aren't limited to your own wife; your burden can be anyone female, as long as she is older than 17. The race is believed to date back to the charming tradition of warriors stealing women away from neighbouring villages.

For a rundown of more festivals, visit www .whatsonwhen.com.

WORLD ROMA FESTIVAL KHAMORO (CZECH REPUBLIC)
Late May; Prague; www.khamoro.cz
Through music and dance, this festival highlights the little-known Roma culture and helps connect this maligned group with the Czech majority. Concerts are held in different venues throughout Prague, culminating in a richly orchestrated parade through the city's historic heart.

Albania

HIGHLIGHTS

- **Tirana** Bustling, dusty streets, communist relics, lush parks, cool bars (p49)
- **Butrint** Archaeological site in a delightful setting – lose yourself for hours among the ancient ruins and dream of past times (p55)
- **Gjirokastra** Misty steep cobbled streets, 200-year-old stone houses, brooding old castle (p54)

FAST FACTS

- **Area** 28,748 sq km
- **ATMs** There were none in Albania at the time of research
- **Budget** 2100 lekë per day
- **Capital** Tirana
- **Country codes** ☎ 355, international access code ☎ 00
- **Famous for** Ismail Kadare; beaches along the Adriatic and Ionian coasts
- **Head of State** President Alfred Moisiu
- **Languages** Albanian (Shqip), some Greek in the south
- **Money** Albanian lekë (A$1 = 75 lekë, CA$1 = 80 lekë, €1 = 129 lekë, ¥100 = 91 lekë, NZ$1 = 68 lekë, UK£1 = 192 lekë, US$1 = 105 lekë)

- **Phrases** *Përshëndetje* (hello), *mirupafshim* (goodbye)
- **Population** 3,582,205
- **Time** GMT/UTC + 1
- **Visas** None required for citizens of the EU, Australia, New Zealand, the US and Canada

TRAVEL HINTS

Always carry tissues, especially on long trips, as there is often no loo paper in the toilets. Buy food at local markets – it's good value and organic.

ROAMING ALBANIA

Start in Tirana city, before heading for the ruins at Butrint and the Gjirokastra castle. Finish up on the Ksamili beach near Saranda.

Sandy and pebbly beaches stretch all the way down the Adriatic and Ionian coasts and traditional villages perch on the majestic misty mountains. Labyrinthine streets snake through Gjirokastra, while its gloomy castle broods above the town. Apollonia and Butrint fascinate with classical ruins in rural settings that you won't want to leave.

Yet visiting Albania remains something only for the 'adventurous' and many people associate it with former isolation or remain deterred by stories of crime and poverty.

In reality, the visitor will find a warm and sincerely hospitable country, with fantastic nature and breathtaking mountain landscapes.

ALBANIA

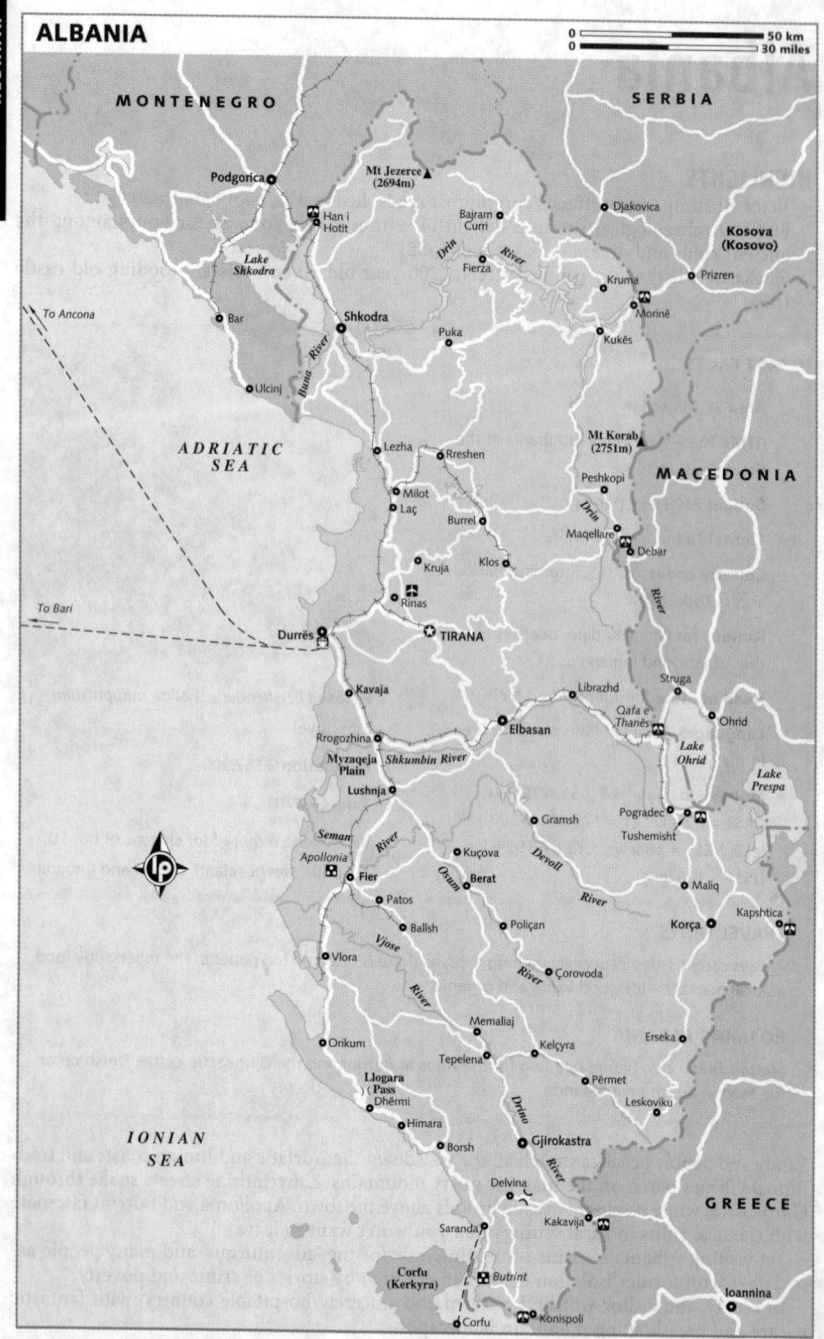

ALBANIA

0 ———————— 50 km
0 ———————— 30 miles

MONTENEGRO

SERBIA

Podgorica

Mt Jezerce
(2694m)

Bajram
Curri

Djakovica

Kosova
(Kosovo)

Han i
Hotit

Drini   River

Fierza

Kruma

Prizren

Lake
Shkodra

Bar

Shkodra

Buna   River

Puka

Kukës

Morinë

To Ancona

Ulcinj

ADRIATIC
SEA

Lezha

Rreshen

Mt Korab
(2751m)

MACEDONIA

Milot
Laç

Peshkopi

Burrel

Drin

Maqellarë

To Bari

Kruja

Klos

Debar

Rinas

Durrës

TIRANA

River

Kavaja

Librazhd

Struga

Rrogozhina

Elbasan

Qafa e
Thanës

Ohrid

Myzaqeja
Plain

Shkumbin River

Lake
Ohrid

Lushnja

Lake
Prespa

Seman

River

Gramsh

Pogradec

Apollonia

Kuçova

Tushemisht

Fier

Osum

Berat

Devoll

Patos

Poliçan

River

Maliq

Ballsh

Korça

Kapshtica

Vjosë

Vlora

River

Çorovoda

Orikum

River

Memaliaj

Kelçyra

Erseka

Tepelena

Përmet

Llogara
Pass

Dhërmi

Leskoviku

Drino

Himara

Gjirokastra

River

Borsh

IONIAN
SEA

Delvina

GREECE

Saranda

Kakavija

Corfu
(Kerkyra)

Butrint

Corfu

Konispoli

Ioannina

HISTORY

In the 2nd millennium BC, the Illyrians occupied the western Balkans and formed Illyria. Later, under the Greeks and then the Romans, Illyria enjoyed peace and prosperity. After Rome fell, invasions by migrating peoples forced ethnic Illyrians south.

In 1344 Albania was annexed by Serbia, then threatened by the Ottoman Turks and Venetians. From 1443 to 1468 the national hero Skënderbeg (George Kastrioti) successfully led Albanian resistance against the Turks. Eventually, though, the land fell to the Ottomans.

The late 19th and early 20th centuries saw Albanians in Kosovo struggling vainly for independence. In 1920 Ahmet Zogu became the ruler of Albania and declared himself King Zogu I, but his collaboration with Italy backfired in April 1939 when Mussolini invaded Albania. On 8 November 1941 the Albanian Communist Party was founded with Enver Hoxha (pronounced 'hoja') as first secretary (pronounced 'dictator').

In January 1946 the People's Republic of Albania was proclaimed, with Hoxha as president. At first Albania allied itself with Stalin's USSR, but in 1961 ended relations and realigned itself towards China. From 1966 to 1967 Albania experienced a Chinese-style cultural revolution. Agriculture was collectivised and organised religion banned.

Following Hoxha's death in 1985, Albania embarked on a programme of liberalisation and, after student demonstrations in December 1990, the government agreed to allow opposition parties. Party hardliners were purged and a programme of reforms was announced.

The March 1992 elections ended 47 years of communist rule. But a severe crisis developed in late 1996, when private pyramid investment schemes spectacularly collapsed. Around 70% of Albanians lost their savings,

---

READING UP

Ismail Kadare's atmospheric *Chronicle in Stone* (1971) and *Broken April* (1990) are a great source of information on Albanian traditions and history. Another good read is Edith Durham's *High Albania* (1909), and for rare insights into the communist times read Philip Ward's *Albania* (1983).

BUNKER LOVE

On the hillsides, beaches and most surfaces in Albania, you will notice small concrete domes with rectangular slits. Sometimes their presence will surprise you for they sprout in the least expected places. Meet the bunkers: Enver Hoxha's paranoid concrete legacy, built over 35 years, from 1950 to 1985.

These hard mushroom-like concoctions of concrete and iron were meant to repel the threat of foreign invasion. Indeed, Hoxha's chief engineer had to vouch for the strength of his creation by standing inside the prototype while it was bombarded by a tank. The shell-shocked engineer emerged unscathed and some 700,000 similar bunkers were built.

These days, the bunkers remain an indestructible reminder of a cruel regime. Locals try to make them 'blend in' by painting them, putting potted plants on them, or sometimes simply using them as their little love pads.

---

resulting in nationwide disturbances and violence. In spring 1999 Albania faced a crisis of a different sort – the influx of 465,000 war refugees from neighbouring Kosovo. While this put a tremendous strain on resources, the net effect has been positive. A substantial amount of international aid money has poured in, the service sector has grown and inflation has dropped.

Since 2002 the country has found itself in a kind of miniboom, with money being injected into construction projects and infrastructure.

PEOPLE & CULTURE

One of the best things about Albania is its people. Kind and warm, with an unquestioning generosity, they will go out of their way to help you. The traditional population breakdown is 95% Albanian, 3% Greek and 2% 'other' (Vlach, Roma, Serb and Bulgarian). Albanians are proud of their ancient Illyrian roots, and the country's romanised name comes from the Albanoi, an ancient Illyrian tribe.

When talking to your hosts, note that Albanians shake their heads sideways to say yes ('Po') and usually nod and 'tsk' to say no ('Jo').

Despite Tirana's youth being highly hip, traditional dress is still common in rural areas among the older generations, especially on Sunday and public holidays.

The *Kanun* is an ancient social law outlining most aspects of social behaviour, including the treatment of guests. Albanians are therefore very hospitable and will sometimes offer travellers free lodging and food. While payment may be acceptable sometimes, a small gift or a memento from home will often suffice.

TRANSPORT

GETTING THERE & AWAY
Air
Several airlines serve Tirana (see p52). It's usually cheaper, though, to fly into Greece or Italy and catch the ferry across.

DEPARTURE TAX

No matter how you enter Albania, you will have to pay a €10 charge. On leaving, there's another €10 fee if you fly out or €6 if you leave by sea. There is a US$1 daily tariff on vehicles, payable upon crossing the border out of the country.

Boat
The Italian company Adriatica di Navigazione offers ferry services to Durrës from Bari (US$60, 8½ hours, daily) and Ancona (US$85, 19 hours, four times a week). Cars cost US$90/100 respectively. Be prepared for increased prices in summer. Bicycles are carried free.

In Bari, ferry tickets can be purchased at **Agestea** (☎ 080-553 1555; agesteabari02@interbusiness .it; Via Liside 4) and in Ancona at **Maritime Agency Srl** (☎ 071-204 915; tickets.adn@maritime.it; Via XXIX Settembre 10). In Albania, tickets are sold by several travel agencies in Durrës or Tirana.

The fastest ferry connection between Bari and Durrës is via the passenger catamarans operated by **Quality Lines** (€130, 3½ hours). These high-speed vessels leave Durrës daily at 10am and 4.30pm. The Durrës agent can be contacted on ☎ 052-24 571.

See p55 for information on travel to and from Corfu and the port of Saranda.

Bus
Buses from Tirana to Thessaloniki (€35, 10 hours) leave at 6am daily from in front of **Albanian Interlines** (☎ 222 272; Bulevardi Zogu I). Buses to Athens (€50, 24 hours) also leave from here three times a week. Buses to Prishtina, Kosovo, leave daily from beside the Tirana International Hotel at 6pm (€30, 12 hours). For Macedonia, take the daily bus to Tetovo (also from here), and from Tetovo take a frequent local bus to Skopje.

Buses for Istanbul and Sofia leave from **Albtransport** (☎ 223 026; Rruga Mine Peza; ☯ 8am-4pm Mon-Fri). The Sofia bus (€35, 15 hours) leaves at 10am on Wednesday. Buses for Istanbul (€55, 24 hours) depart at 10am and 1pm on Monday, and go via Sofia.

Bringing a car or motorcycle to Albania is a risky business as theft and bad roads can be problems. Additionally, your insurance Green Card (p1252) might not cover Albania.

GETTING AROUND
Bus & Minibus
Most Albanians travel around in private *furgon* (minibuses) or larger buses. Bus and minibus activity starts at the crack of dawn and usually ceases by 2pm. They run frequently between Tirana and Durrës (38km), the last bus leaving at 5pm, but serve other towns north and south less frequently. You can catch a bus to Tirana from any town in Albania, whereas there may not always be direct buses between other places. Fares are low and tickets are rarely issued. Shared *furgon* leave when they are full or almost full. They usually cost more than the bus, but they're still cheap. Pay the driver or assistant when you get out.

City buses operate in Tirana, Durrës and Shkodra. They are crowded, so watch your possessions.

Car & Motorcycle
For car rental, **Hertz** (☎ 255 028; Rruga Ded Gjo Luli) has vehicles starting from €70 per day for an Opel Corsa and takes Visa payments. **Europcar** (☎ 246 192; Rruga e Durrësit, L.61) offers similar services.

Driving in Albania is only for those with nerves of steel as roads are often bad and kamikaze local drivers try to overtake on even the bendiest of roads.

Hitching

Lonely Planet does not recommend hitching, but should you try it, most people will take you if they possibly can. Cheap buses make hitching an emergency option only.

Train

It's incredibly cheap, but unless you have a lot of time and don't mind not having a toilet on board or any window panes, taking the train for any journey other than the Tirana–Durrës trip is not that great.

Daily passenger trains leave Tirana for Shkodra (3½ hours, 98km), Fier (4¼ hours), Ballsh (five hours) and Vlora (5½ hours). Seven trains a day also make the 1½-hour trip between Tirana and Durrës.

TIRANA (TIRANË)

☎ 042 / pop 440,000

Tirana is a city of dusty streets, shaded boulevards with elegant Italian 1930s architecture, street markets, beautiful mosques, rows of moneychangers, remnants of socialist-realist art and a fun nightlife. You will be surprised to see how different one street is from the next and to discover a small lake and a lush park at the city's edge. There's plenty to see and explore on foot, but do beware the gaping potholes as you stomp around Tirana's streets. You'll be happy to know that the city won't bleed your finances dry as other capitals might.

ORIENTATION

Tirana revolves around the busy central Skënderbeg Square (Sheshi Skënderbeg) from where various streets and boulevards dart off like dials. Running south is the shady Bulevardi Dëshmorët e Kombit, great for strolling and looking at the communist relics and near the trendy part of Blloku (The Block). Running north, Bulevardi Zogu I leads to the busy train and bus station where bus conductors shout out their destinations like market sellers. Most sights and services are within a few minutes' walk of Skënderbeg Square.

INFORMATION
Internet Access

Both of the following charge from 150 to 200 lekë per hour and offer printing:

GETTING INTO TOWN

All the incoming buses will drop you off at the bus and train station at the end of Bulevardi Zogu I, a five-minute walk north from the city centre. There is no public transport to the airport so you'll have to taxi it to and fro.

F@stech (☎ 251 947; Rruga Brigada e VIII; 🕐 8.30am-11pm) High stools bring you up to walled-in screens.

Interalb Internet (☎ 251 747; Rruga Dëshmorët e 4 Shkurtit, Pall 25/1; 🕐 8am-10pm) Plain computers and décor.

Medical Services

ABC Clinic (☎ 234 105; 360 Rruga Qemal Stafa; 🕐 Mon-Fri) Located opposite the 'New School', with English-speaking doctors.

All-night Pharmacy (☎ 222 241; Bulevardi Zogu I; 🕐 24hr) Situated just off Skënderbeg Square.

Money

While there are plenty of banks in Tirana, there were no international ATMs at the time of writing. Independent money exchangers operate on Skënderbeg Square and offer the same rates as banks.

National Savings Bank Branch (☎ 235 035; Hotel Rogner Europapark Tirana, Bulevardi Dëshmorët e Kombit; 🕐 10.30am-5pm Mon-Fri) Offers MasterCard advances, cashes US dollar, euro and sterling travellers cheques for 1% commission and exchanges cash.

Unioni Financiar Tiranë Exchange (☎ 234 979; Rruga Dëshmorët e 4 Shkurtit) Just south of the main post office, offers Western Union wire transfer services.

Post & Telephone

Main post office (☎ 228 262; Sheshi Çameria; 🕐 8am-8pm Mon-Fri) With adjacent telephone centre, on a street jutting west from Skënderbeg Square.

Telephone Centre (Bulevardi Zogu I) On the right-hand side, about 400m past Skënderbeg Square.

Tourist Information

As there is no official tourist office, you'll have to rely on travel agencies (see following).

EMERGENCY NUMBERS

- **Ambulance** ☎ 127
- **Fire** ☎ 128
- **Police** ☎ 129

TIRANA (TIRANË)

0 — 500 m
0 — 0.3 miles

A **B** **C** **D**

INFORMATION
ABC Clinic.................................1 D3
Albania Travel & Tours..............2 C4
All-night Pharmacy...................3 C4
Bulgarian Embassy....................4 B4
F@stech...................................5 C5
German Embassy.......................6 B4
Greek Embassy..........................7 B4
Interalb Internet......................8 C6
International Bookshop.........(see 27)
Macedonian Embassy.................9 C5
Main Post Office.....................10 C4
National Savings Bank Branch...11 C6
Serbia and Montenegro Embassy..12 B4
Telephone Centre....................13 C4
Turkish Embassy......................14 B4
UK Embassy.............................15 B4
Unioni Financiar Tiranë Exchange..16 C5
US Embassy.............................17 D6

SIGHTS & ACTIVITIES (p51)
Clock Tower.........................(see 19)
Congress Building....................18 C5
Et'hem Bey Mosque.................19 C4
Former Enver Hoxha Museum...20 C5
Former Residence of Enver Hoxha..21 C6
Former Sigurimi HQ..............(see 22)
Government Buildings..............22 C5
Hotel Dajti............................23 C5

National Art Gallery.................24 C5
National Bank Building.............25 C4
National Museum of History.....26 C4
Palace of Culture.....................27 C4
Prime Minister's Residence.......28 C6
Pyramid.............................(see 20)
Qemal Stafa Stadium................29 C6
Selman Stërmasi (Dinam) Stadium..30 B6
Skënderbeg Equestrian Statue...31 C4

SLEEPING (pp51–2)
Guva e Qetë...........................32 C5
Hotel Endri............................33 C6
Kalaja Hotel............................34 C5
Qëndra Stefan.........................35 D4
Tirana International Hotel.........36 C4

EATING (p52)
Food Market............................37 D4
Food Market............................38 C5
La Voglia................................39 C5
Pasticeri Francaise....................40 C5
Villa Ambassador.....................41 D6

DRINKING (p52)
Boom Boom Room....................42 B6

Buda Bar................................43 B6
Living Room Bar......................44 B5

ENTERTAINMENT (p52)
Academy of Arts......................45 C6
Rozafa Club............................46 C6

TRANSPORT (pp52–3)
Albanian Interlines..................47 C4
Albtransport...........................48 B4
Alitalia...............................(see 26)
Austrian Airlines..................(see 11)
Bus & Minibus Station for the South..49 A5
Bus & Minibus Station to Durrës &
    North................................50 C3
Bus Departure Point for Prishtina..51 C4
Europcar................................52 C4
Hertz....................................53 C4
Minibuses to Kruja, Lezha &
    Shkodra.............................54 A3
Olympic Airways......................55 C4
Swiss International Air Lines...(see 11)
Turkish Airlines...................(see 36)

OTHER
Tirana University.....................56 C6

Tirana In Your Pocket tells you what's hot and is available at bookshops and some of the larger kiosks for 300 lekë.

Travel Agencies

There are many of these, plus airline offices, on Rruga Mine Peza. However, not all operators speak English.

Albania Travel & Tours (☎ 32 983; fax 33 981; Rruga Durrësit 102; ☽ 8am-8pm Mon-Fri, 8am-2pm Sat & Sun) Good for arranging ferry tickets from Durrës (see p48) or booking private rooms.

SIGHTS

Skënderbeg Square is the best place to witness the daily goings-on, as kids in their orange plastic cars whiz past your ankles and real cars kick up the dust at the **equestrian statue of Skënderbeg** himself, on the southern side of the square. If you stop to examine the national hero's emblematic goat's-head helmet, you'll also catch sight of the minaret of one of the oldest buildings left in the city, the **Et'hem Bey mosque** (1789–1823), out of the corner of your eye. Behind the mosque is the tall **clock tower** (☎ 243 292; admission free; ☽ 9am-1pm & 4-6pm Mon, Wed & Sat), which you can climb to watch the square and its colourful Ferris wheel entertain the tiny Tiranans.

On the northern side of the square is the **National Museum of History** (admission 300 lekë; ☽ 8am-1pm Mon-Sat). This is the largest museum in Albania, holding most of the country's archaeological treasures. The fantastic **mosaic mural** *Albania* adorning the museum's façade shows Albanians victorious from Illyrian times through to WWII.

Take a look at the **Palace of Culture**, with a theatre, shops and art galleries to the east of the square and the large Italian red-brick **National Bank building** resting on three heavy square pillars to the west.

Stroll down the spacious tree-lined Bulevardi Dëshmorët e Kombit and take a break in **Hotel Dajti** for a whiff of Italian-1930s-meets-communism. Lush armchairs, low chandeliers and sunlight peeking through the ochre curtains will transport you to a different time.

Next door is Tirana's **National Art Gallery** (admission 200 lekë; ☽ 9am-1pm & 5-8pm Tue-Sun) where the garden is adorned with statues of proud partisans. See the astonishing exhibition of icons inside, by the renowned 16th-century master of colour Onufri.

A great place for a picnic or a break by the lake is the **Parku Kombëtar** (National Park) at the end of Bulevardi Dëshmorët e Kombit.

Communist Tirana

Built for the flamboyant fascist parades, Bulevardi Dëshmorët e Kombit, lined with pine and palm trees, was also the stomping ground of Albania's communist *Nomenklatura* (political elite).

Walking from Skënderbeg Square down Bulevardi Dëshmorët e Kombit, you will spot the now brightly painted **government buildings**, recognisable by their very serious military guards. Behind the last building on the left-hand side were the headquarters of the once much-feared Sigurimi, communist Albania's answer to the KGB.

Further down on the left, crossing the small Lana River bridge you'll see the sloping white-marble and glass walls of the **Pyramid**, aka the **former Enver Hoxha Museum** (1988), designed by Hoxha's daughter and son-in-law, and is now a disco and conference centre. Opposite and further down is the **Prime Minister's Residence** where Hoxha and cronies would stand and view military parades from the 2nd-floor balcony.

Follow Rruga Ismail Qemali, the street on the southern side of the Congress Building, and enter the once totally forbidden but now totally trendy **Blloku** – the former exclusive Communist Party elite hang-out closed to the public until 1991.

SLEEPING

One of the best money-saving options is renting a private room through Albania Travel & Tours (see above) for around 2600 lekë per person. Other travel agencies can also find you a private room.

Kalaja (☎ 250 000; Rruga Murat Toptani; s & d per person with shared bathroom 1000 lekë, with en suite 1500 lekë) This kitsch hotel has clean rooms with tiled floors, multicoloured linen and TVs. Some have balconies.

Hotel Endri (☎ 244 168, 229 334; Pall 27, fl 3 Apt 30, Rruga Vaso Pasha 27; dm US$20) Good value and located where all the action is, in Blloku. The 'hotel' is basically two sparkling-clean and new rooms in a run-down building, next to the owner Petrit Alikaj's apartment. Sturdy wooden doors and nice bathrooms with excellent showers.

ALBANIA

Guva e Qetë (☎ 235 491/440; fax 222 228; Murat Totani; s/d US$30/40) Hunter's lodge–style, with photos of tigers and other wild beasts on wooden walls, spacious rooms with TVs and new bathrooms.

Qëndra Stefan (Stephen Center; ☎ /fax 253 924; stephenc@icc.al.eu.org; Rruga Hoxha Tasim 1; s/d incl breakfast US$30/50) Airy, light *en suite* rooms with pressed white linen and a great rooftop terrace. Metres away from a nice fruit and vegetables market. Nonsmokers and non-drinkers only (see also Eating, below).

EATING

Cafés, bars, restaurants, markets and fast-food joints line Rruga Dëshmorët e 4 Shkurtit, the buzzing central street of the Blloku area.

Pasticeri Francaise (☎ 251 336; Rruga Dëshmorët e 4 Shkurtit 1; breakfast 200-300 lekë, lunch 400-500 lekë; ☽ 8am-10pm) A great breakfast spot, French-owned. Red walls and small lamps lighting individual tables give it an ooh-la-la feeling.

Qëndra Stefan (☎ 253 924; Rruga Hoxha Tasim 1; mains 300-400 lekë; ☽ 8am-10pm Mon-Sat; ✗) A friendly place for breakfast or Chinese and Mexican lunch.

La Voglia (☎ 228 678; Rruga Dëshmorët e 4 Shkurtit; pizza 350-400 lekë; ☽ 8am-11pm) In the small busy square off the street, serves some of the most delicious bruschettas and pizzas and makes great cappuccinos.

There is a fantastic food market off Rruga Abdyl Frasheri with organic fruit and vegetables and dairy products.

SPLURGE!

Villa Ambassador (☎ 069-202 4293; Rruga Themistokli Gërmenji; mains 500 lekë; ☽ noon-11.30pm) has a homely atmosphere, fantastic service and tasty Albanian meat and vegetarian dishes alike. This former embassy is among Tirana's best food choices.

DRINKING & CLUBBING

Living Room bar (☎ 242 481; BLvdGjergj Fishta, Pall Italiane 1; ☽ 24hr) One of the hippest places to drink'n'dance in Tirana, with an eclectic DJ on weekends and a good crowd. Cool lampshades and 1970s armchairs and sofas for you to lounge on when you're danced (or drunk) off your feet.

Buda Bar (☎ 068-205 8825; Rruga Ismail Qemali; ☽ 9am-late) All about a relaxed atmosphere, subdued lighting, incense burning and chaise lounges and armchairs.

Boom Boom Room (☎ 243 702; Gjin Bue Shpata; ☽ 7pm-2am) Caters for a smoky jazzy crowd with live performances most evenings.

The place to dance till dawn is **Rozafa Club** (Rruga Ismail Qemali; ☽ 8pm-late), next door to the Buda Bar. House, hard house and techno dominate the DJ repertoire.

ENTERTAINMENT

Pop concerts and other musical performances often take place in the Qemal Stafa Stadium near the university. Look out for street banners bearing details of upcoming events. The stadium also holds football matches every Saturday and Sunday afternoon.

For classical music performances go to the **Academy of Arts** (☎ 257 237; Sheshi Nene Teresa) opposite the National Museum of History.

GETTING THERE & AWAY
Air

Many of the airline offices are on Rruga Dur-rësit, off Skënderbeg Square. **Alitalia** (☎ 230 023; Skënderbeg Square) has an office behind the National Museum of History, and **Swiss International Air Lines** (☎ /fax 232 011) and **Austrian Airlines** (☎ /fax 374 355) are at Hotel Europa-park Tirana. **Olympic Airways** (☎ 228 960; Ve-Ve Business Centre, Bulevardi Zogu I) is 200m behind the Tirana International Hotel, and **Turkish Airlines** (☎ 234 185) is in the Tirana International Hotel.

Bus

The minibus system can seem pretty confusing at first. All minibuses going north (Kruja, Lezha, Shkodra) leave and drop off at the Zogu i Zi terminal just off Rruga Durrësit. If you are going south, your bus or minibus will leave from Rruga e Kavajës, west of Skënderbeg Square.

Main bus routes include the following: Berat (250 lekë, 3½ hours, 122km), Durrës (100 lekë, one hour, 38km), Fier (260 lekë, three hours, 113km), Gjirokastra (1000 lekë, eight hours, 232km), Kukës (1000 lekë, eight hours, 208km), Saranda (800 lekë, eight hours, 284km), Shkodra (300 lekë, 2½ hours, 116km) and Vlora (300 lekë, four hours, 147km). Minibuses are usually 40% to 50% more expensive than buses.

Train

Eight trains a day go to Durrës (55 lekë, one hour, 36km). Trains also depart for Shkodra (150 lekë, 3½ hours, twice daily) and Vlora (210 lekë, 5½ hours, twice daily).

GETTING AROUND

A taxi to/from the airport should cost about €30 or US$20. Taxi stands dot the city and charge 400 lekë for a ride inside Tirana (600 lekë at night). Make sure you reach an agreement with the driver before setting off. **Radio Taxi** (☎ 377 777), with 24-hour service, is particularly reliable.

AROUND TIRANA

DURRËS

☎ 052 / pop 85,000

Durrës, an ancient city and Albania's old capital, is also a city under construction. It has a long (10km) built-up beach stretching south where people stroll, play football and cool down in the shallow waters of the Adriatic. Unfortunately, cars also drive on the beach, which makes sunbathing something of a risky sport. Ancient remains, an interesting museum and good bus and train connections make Durrës a great base for archaeological exploration of places like Apollonia and Butrint.

Orientation

The town centre is easily covered on foot, although you might do well to get a taxi to any of the far ends of the beach. In the centre, the Xhamia e Madhe Durrës mosque can serve as a point of orientation: the archaeological attractions are immediately around it, the train and bus stations and the harbour are to the east, and on the hill top are the palace of King Ahmet Zogu and the lighthouse.

Information

Galaxy Internet Café (☎ 068-213 5637; Rruga Taulantia; per hr 200 lekë; ☼ 8am-11pm) On the main street.
Savings Bank of Albania (☼ 8am-2pm Mon-Fri) Across from the train station, changes travellers cheques and offers MasterCard advances for a 1% commission.

Sights

The newly built **Archaeological Museum** (admission 200 lekë; ☼ 8am-4pm Wed-Sun) on the waterfront is well-lit and its ground floor has artefacts from the Greek, Hellenistic and Roman periods. At the time of research the Byzantine collection was expected to open in 2004.

Beyond the museum are the 6th-century **Byzantine city walls**, built after the Visigoth invasion of AD 481 and supplemented by round Venetian towers in the 14th century.

Roam the vaults where the gladiators entered the arena and imagine the bloodthirsty lions in the impressive but neglected **Roman amphitheatre**. Built on the hillside just inside the city walls between the 1st and 2nd centuries AD, in its prime it had the capacity to seat 15,000 spectators.

On the hill top west of the amphitheatre stands the former **palace of King Ahmet Zogu**, which is not open to the public as it is a military area. It's a 20-minute walk to the top of the hill, but the views of the bay make it well worth the climb. A **lighthouse** stands on the next hill from where you can enjoy the royal views and check out the bunker constellation.

In the town centre you can find the small **Roman baths** directly behind Aleksandër Moisiu Theatre, on the central square. The large and not so graceful **Xhamia e Madhe Durrës** mosque on the square was erected with Egyptian aid in 1993, after the original one was destroyed in the earthquake of 1979.

Sleeping

Albania Travel & Tours (☎ 24 276; fax 25 450; Rruga Durrah; ☼ 8am-8pm) Near the port, they may be able to help arrange a private room given advance notice.

B&B Tedeschini (☎ 24 343, 068-224 6303; ipmcrsp@icc.al.eu.org; Dom Nikoll Kaçorri 5; dm US$15) This gracious, 19th-century former Italian consulate has airy rooms decorated with antique furniture, and portraits of consuls watch over you. From the square fronting the mosque, walk towards the restaurant Il Castello. Take the first right, then a quick left, then a quick right.

Hotel Mediteran (☎ /fax 24 319/27 074; Rruga Kolonel Thomson; dm €20) Perched on the corner of the city walls, this friendly family-run place has great views of monuments and the sea from some of its balconies.

Hotel Besani (☎ 068 203 5781; Skëmbi i Kavajës; s/d US$40/40) If the beach is your priority, this is one of the best choices among dozens of beach hotels. Seaview rooms are clean and comfortable. It's 1km south of the NATO base.

Eating & Drinking

Bar Torra (Rruga Kolonel Thomson; ⏰ 8am-midnight) Housed in a fortified tower, there are inside tables where cannon used to fire and a roof terrace for cheap al fresco eating and drinking. Order a panini for 100 lekë.

Bunker Blue, 1km south of the harbour, is the best food option in Durrës. This seafood taverna right on the beach has fresh and cheap fish at 350 lekë a plate.

Mondial Pizzeria (☎ 27 946; Rruga Taulantia; mains 400 lekë) A buzzing, popular little pizza and pasta joint, about 800m west of the city centre.

The place for coffee, cocktails or beer is **Bar Torra** (see above).

Entertainment

You could pay a visit to the **Aleksandër Moisiu Theatre** in the centre of Durrës. However its frequent theatrical productions are performed only in Albanian.

In the summer there are beach discos.

Getting There & Away

Albania's railway network centres on Durrës. Eight trains a day run to Tirana (55 lekë, one hour), two to Shkodra (150 lekë, 3½ hours) and two to Vlora (210 lekë, five hours) via Fier. Minibuses to Tirana (150 lekë, one hour) and buses (100 lekë, one hour) leave from beside the train station whenever they're full.

Numerous travel agencies along Rruga Durrah handle ferry bookings.

SOUTHERN ALBANIA

Sharp snowcapped mountain peaks, with wide green valleys zigzagged by rivers on one side and inviting white beach crescents touching the gentle blue sea on the other, make this visually the most exciting part of the country.

GJIROKASTRA (GJIROKASTËR)

☎ 084 / pop 24,500

The ancient town watches over the magnificent valley beneath it from rocky slopes and, climbing its steep cobbled streets, the traveller will be enchanted by the magic of Gjirokastra. Spend the night absorbing the life on its labyrinthine streets, where the pace is slow and suspended in the past, for an architectural feast of unique houses and the gloomy castle overlooking the town.

Sights

Gjirokastra's **19th-century houses** are a rare experience, for none are the same style. Houses like these cannot be found anywhere else in Albania or Europe. Despite their uniqueness, they do hold a common design characteristic: the number of their wings. Have a look inside the Kalemi hotel (see below) for a taste of old Albania and a peek at the interior of the houses. The city was given the status of a 'museum-city' because of its architectural heritage. The grey slate roofs blend into each other when seen from the front of the **castle** (admission 500 lekë; ⏰ 8am-8pm), the city's most dominant feature. Built from the 6th century AD onwards, this brooding giant was used as a prison by King Zog, the Nazis and the communists until 1971, when it became a museum. You can see the torture rooms, if you are that way inclined. There is also a weapons display in one of the dreary rooms inside the castle. A 1957 **US military spy-plane** displayed on the ramparts is a bizarre addition to the scene.

Sleeping & Eating

Kalemi (☎ /fax 467 260; Lagja Palorto; dm 4000 lekë) A cross between a hotel and a museum, this is the most authentic experience of old Albania, with old carved wood ceilings and stone fireplaces in the 1st-floor rooms. A delicious breakfast is included.

Guest House Haxhi Kotoni (☎ 35 26; Lagja Palorto 8, Rruga Bashkim Kokona; s/d 1500/2000 lekë) A cheaper option, with small but clean and comfy double rooms with bathroom, TV, heating and breakfast.

Argjiro (off Sheshi Çerçiz Topulli) This small homely restaurant offers tasty traditional dishes at 300 to 400 lekë.

Riçiola restaurant (☎ 069 255 3469; Lagja Palorto) If you want spectacular views of the castle and town, walk uphill or use the complimentary pick-up and drop-off service.

Getting There & Away

Buses to Gjirokastra depart from or stop on the main highway, 1.5km from the Old Town. Taxis can take you into town for about 200 lekë. Buses to Tirana (1000 lekë, eight hours) are fairly frequent; there are four a day to Saranda (300 lekë, 1½ hours). You'll need to take a taxi to get to the Greek border at Kakavija (1500 lekë, 30 minutes).

SARANDA (SARANDË)
☎ 0852 / pop 12,000

Horseshoe-shaped Saranda is a stone's throw from Corfu (38km) and a good point to cross into Albania from Greece. Its houses descend from the hillsides, small boats bob on the blue waters, people stroll up and down the relaxing promenade and the town boasts around 290 sunny days a year.

Information
Exchange Mario (☎ 23 61; Rruga Vangeli Gramoza) An alternative to the crowds of moneychangers near the central square.
Internet Café (Rruga 1 Maji; per hr 250 lekë)

Sights & Activities
Saranda is a great base for exploring the sights around it. Particularly impressive are the ancient ruins of the city of **Butrint** (☎ 46 00; admission 700 lekë; ☼ 8am-7.30pm), 18km south, the best and most extensive site of its kind in the Balkans. Lose yourself for a few hours among the well-preserved remains and discover the hidden mosaics under the sand. Butrint is believed to have been founded by the Trojans, but no evidence of this has been discovered. A cab there will cost around 2000 lekë.

The **Blue Eye spring** (Syri i Kalter), about 15km east of Saranda, is a hypnotic spring of deep blue water surrounded by electric blue edges like the iris of an eye. It feeds the Bistrica River and its depth is unknown. You can have lunch here under the oak trees.

A better bathing alternative to Saranda's beaches is the sandy **Ksamili beach** 17km south, with four small, dreamy islands within swimming distance.

Sleeping & Eating
Kaonia (☎ 2600/2608; Rruga 1 Maji; s/d 2000/3000 lekë) A lovely small hotel on the seafront with great beds, power showers, TVs and sea views.

Pizzeri Evangjelos (☎ 54 29; ne Shetitore; pizzas 350-600 lekë) Superb wood-oven pizzas are served up in the garden.

Getting There & Away
A daily ferry and hydrofoil service plies between Saranda and Corfu (€14 one-way). Call **Finikas Lines** (☎ 30 9-4485 3228) in Corfu

for schedules. The hydrofoil leaves Saranda at 10am.

Buses to Tirana (1000 lekë, eight hours) and Gjirokastra (300 lekë, 1½ hours) leave from Saranda's bus station four times daily.

FIER & APOLLONIA
☎ 0623 / pop 48,500

Fier is a large oil town on the Gjanica River, 89km south of Durrës. Its real attraction is the ruined city of ancient **Apollonia** (Pojan; admission 700 lekë; ☼ 9am-5pm), 12km west. The picturesque 3rd-century BC House of Mosaics, the 2nd-century AD elegant pillars, the façade of the city's administrative centre and the Byzantine monastery (note the gargoyles!) are spectacular.

ALBANIA DIRECTORY

ACCOMMODATION
Albania's accommodation is improving and there are a few good budget options as well as some quality mid-range and more pricey top-end places to lay your head.

DANGERS & ANNOYANCES
You are advised to avoid travelling in the far north of the country around Bajram Curri because of continuing instability in the neighbouring region. There might still be land mines near the northern border with Kosovo around Bajram Curri.

Don't flash money around. Some travellers report begging is a problem.

As Albania was closed for so long, most foreigners, especially black travellers, may encounter some curious stares.

Corrupt police may attempt to extort money from you. Strongly resist paying them anything without getting an official receipt. Always keep at least a copy of your passport with you.

EMBASSIES & CONSULATES
Embassies & Consulates in Albania
The following embassies are in Tirana:
Bulgaria (☎ 233 155; fax 232 272; Rruga Skënderbeg 12)
Germany (☎ 232 048; fax 233 497; Rruga Skënderbeg 8)
Greece (☎ 223 959; fax 234 443; Rruga Frederik Shiroka 3)
Macedonia (☎ 233 036; fax 232 514; Rruga Lekë Dukagjini 2)
Serbia and Montenegro (☎ 232 089; fax 223 042; Rruga e Durrësit 192/196)

Turkey (☎ 233 399; fax 232 719; Rruga E Kavajës 31)
UK (☎ 234 973; fax 247 697; Rruga Skënderbeg 12)
USA (☎ 247 285; fax 232 222; Rruga Elbasanit 103)

Albanian Embassies & Consulates Abroad

Canada (☎ 613-236 4114; fax 613-236 0804 130; Albert St, Ottawa, Ontario K1P 5G4)
Greece (☎ 21-0723 4412; fax 21-0723 1972; Karahristou 1, GR-114 21 Athens)
UK (☎ 020-7730 5709; fax 020-7828 8869; 24 Buckingham Gate, 2nd Floor, London SW1 E6LB)
USA (☎ 202-223 4942; fax 202-628 7342; 1511 K St NW, Washington, DC 20008)

GAY & LESBIAN TRAVELLERS

Homosexuality became legal in Albania early in 1995; however, attitudes are still highly conservative.

INTERNET RESOURCES

A good source of information on current events is www.frosina.org.

MONEY

Albanian banknotes come in denominations of 100, 200, 500 and 1000 lekë. There are 5, 10, 20 and 50 lekë coins. Notes issued after 1997 are smaller.

Everything can be paid for with lekë, however many hotel and transport prices in this chapter are quoted in US dollars or euros, both of which are readily accepted as alternative currencies.

Some banks will change US-dollar travellers cheques into US cash without commission. Travellers cheques (euro and US dollar) may be used at major hotels, but cash is preferred everywhere. You can change Sterling travellers cheques at Hotel Rogner Europapark Tirana. Credit cards are accepted only in larger hotels and travel agencies, and a few places in Tirana and Durrës will offer credit-card advances (usually for MasterCard, not Visa).

Every town has its free currency market, which usually operates on the street in front of the main post office or state bank. Be careful and make sure you count the money twice before tendering yours. The advantages are that you get a good rate and avoid the 1% bank commission.

In Albania, US dollars and euros are the favourite foreign currency. You cannot exchange Albanian currency outside of the country.

POST & TELEPHONE

There are few public mailboxes outside of main towns, but the number of modern post offices is on the rise.

Long-distance telephone calls made from main post offices are cheap. Phonecards are available in versions of 50 units (560 lekë), 100 units (980 lekë) and 200 units (1800 lekë).

The country code for Albania is ☎ 355. Albania's international access code is ☎ 00. Dial ☎ 124 for domestic directory assistance and ☎ 122 for international directory assistance.

Internet-access points now abound in Tirana, and most larger towns will have at least one place where you can surf the Web and print. Rates are generally low – 150 to 200 lekë an hour. Some Internet centres also offer cheap international phone connections.

VISAS

No visa is required for citizens of Australia, EU countries, New Zealand, the US and Canada. Citizens of all these countries, however, are required to pay an 'entry tax' at the border. The entry tax for most visitors is US$10. Israeli citizens pay US$30.

Upon arrival you will fill in an arrival and departure card. Keep the departure card, which may be stamped, with your passport and present it when you leave.

WOMEN TRAVELLERS

Albania is quite a safe country for women travellers, but it is important to be aware that outside Tirana it is mainly men who sit in bars and cafés in the evenings, while women generally stay at home. While the men are not threatening, it may feel strange to be the only woman in a bar, so it is advisable to travel in pairs and dress conservatively.

Andorra

HIGHLIGHTS

- **Trekking** Just about anywhere outside Andorra la Vella; pull on your boots and head up the valleys (p62)
- **Grandvalira** Shushing your way over these snowfields, by far the most extensive skiing area in all the Pyrenees (p62)
- **Caldea** Après-skiing or après-trekking, splashing out and splashing about in the warm waters of this space-age spa complex (p61)

FAST FACTS

- **Area** 464 sq km (that's 2½ times smaller than Paris)
- **ATMs** Available everywhere
- **Budget** €35-60
- **Capital** Andorra la Vella
- **Country codes** ☎ 376, international access code ☎ 00
- **Famous for** skiing, shopping and smuggling
- **Head of State** Marc Forné Molné
- **Languages** Catalan (but nearly everyone knows Spanish)
- **Money** Euro (AU$1 = €0.58, CA$1 = €0.64, ¥100 = €0.73, NZ$1 = €0.54, UK£1 = 1.45, US$1 = €0.81)
- **Phrases** *Hola* (hello), *adéu* (goodbye), *si us plau* (please), *gràcies* (thanks)

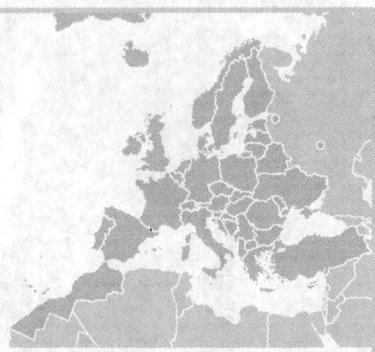

- **Population** 67,100
- **Time** GMT/UTC + 1
- **Visas** None required.

TRAVEL HINT

If you're planning a week or more in Andorra, skiing and summer walking packages (offered, for example, by all major UK tour operators) are much cheaper than going it alone.

ROAMING ANDORRA

To savour this mountain principality, you've got to pull on your walking boots and get out of Andorra la Vella, hub for all bus routes. On the other hand, if you're really pushed for time, study the bus timetable well and you can do what's significant in Andorra in a day.

Mention Andorra and many people will tell you with a grin or a grimace that it's all skiing and shopping. They might add that it's a one-road, one-town mini-state. And that its only highway cuts a swathe through its only town, Andorra la Vella – which in turn is little more than one vast traffic jam bordered by cut-price temples to human greed.

They're a bit right but mostly wrong. Shake yourself free of Andorra la Vella's clutching, commercial embrace, take one of the state's only three secondary roads and head for the hills. Although Andorra absorbs more than 11 million visitors each year (most of whom just pop in to shop), there are still areas where you can be alone.

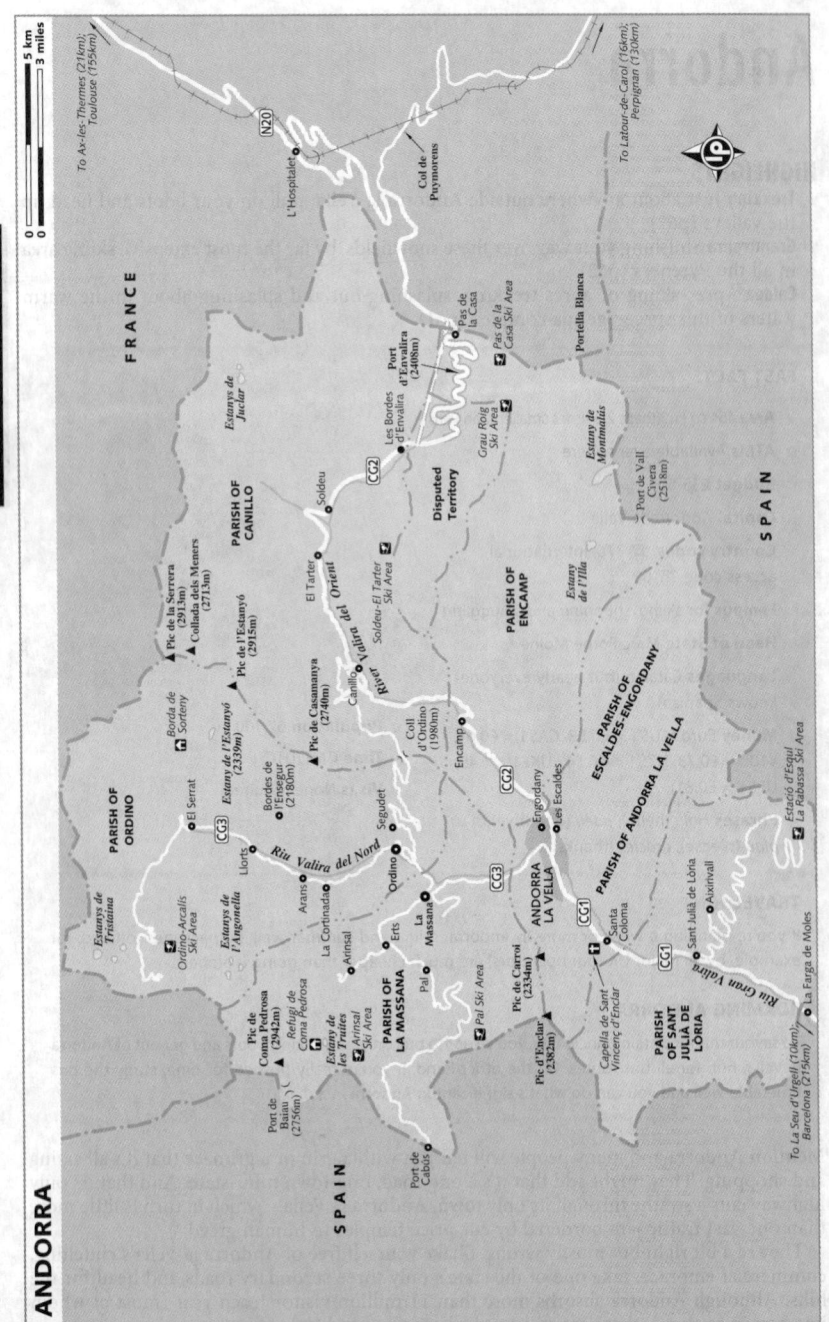

ANDORRA

0 — 5 km
0 — 3 miles

To Ax-les-Thermes (21km);
Toulouse (155km)

FRANCE

N20

L'Hospitalet

Col de
Puymorens

To Latour-de-Carol (16km;
Perpignan (130km)

Estanys de
Juclar

Pas de
la Casa

Port d'Envalira
(2408m)

Les Bordes
d'Envalira

Pas de la
Casa Ski Area

PARISH OF CANILLO

Soldeu

CG2

Grau Roig
Ski Area

Disputed
Territory

Portella Blanca

Estany de
Montmalús

SPAIN

Pic de la Serrera
(2913m)   Collada dels Meners
(2713m)

Pic de l'Estanyó
(2915m)

Borda de
Sorteny

El Tarter

Soldeu-El Tarter
Ski Area

Port de Vall
Civera (251km)

PARISH OF
ORDINO

El Serrat

CG3

Estany de l'Estanyó
(2339m)

Bordes de
l'Ensegur
(2180m)

Pic de Casamanya
(2740m)

Canillo

Valira del Orient

River

PARISH OF
ENCAMP

Estany
de l'Illa

Estanys de
Tristaina

Ordino-Arcalís
Ski Area

Llorts

Riu Valira del Nord

Arans

La Cortinada

Segudet

Coll
d'Ordino
(1980m)

Encamp

CG2

Estany de
l'Angonella

Ordino

CG3

Engordany

Les Escaldes

PARISH OF
ESCALDES-ENGORDANY

Pic de
Coma Pedrosa
(2942m)

Refugi de
Coma Pedrosa

Arinsal

La Massana

 Erts

PARISH OF
LA MASSANA

Arinsal
Ski Area

Pal

CG3

ANDORRA
LA VELLA

CG1

PARISH OF ANDORRA LA VELLA

Estany de
les Truites

Pal Ski Area

Pic de Carroi
(2334m)

Santa
Coloma

CG1

Sant Julià de Lòria

Auxivall

Port de
Baiau
(2759m)

Pic d'Enclar
(2382m)

Capella de Sant
Vincenç d'Enclar

PARISH OF
SANT JULIÀ DE
LÒRIA

Riu Gran Valira

SPAIN

Port de
Cabús

To La Seu d'Urgell (10km);
Barcelona (215km)

La Farga de Moles

Estació d'Esgui
La Rabassa Ski Area

SPAIN

Tucked into the Pyrenees between Spain's Catalonia region and France, Andorra has some of the most dramatic scenery and the best skiing in all the Pyrenees. Once the snows have melted, there's plenty of great walking, ranging from hands-in-pockets strolling to challenging day hikes.

HISTORY

Until as recently as 1993, Andorra was ruled, at least in name, by two 'princes': the Catholic bishop of La Seu d'Urgell, just over the Spanish border, and the French president himself (who inherited the job from France's pre-Revolutionary kings). Nowadays democratic Andorra is a 'parliamentary co-princedom', with the bishop and president remaining nominal joint heads of state.

PEOPLE & CULTURE

Andorrans make up less than 40% of the total population and are outnumbered by Spaniards. It's the only country in the world that has Catalan, which is related to both Spanish and French, as the state language. Younger Andorrans, especially in the capital and ski resorts, manage more than a smattering of English as well.

TRANSPORT

GETTING THERE & AWAY

You can only reach Andorra by road, unless you trek across the mountains (and hey, we're not entirely kidding; it's a magnificent way to drop in or out).

MIND HOW YOU GO

A law passed in 1999 made Catalan obligatory for all signage, publicity, restaurant menus, price lists and the like. But as tourism is the lifeblood of the country, most notices are also in Spanish, English and sometimes French.

However, though; we came across these Catalan-only signs, for which, with your safety in mind, we add the English equivalent!

■ *Perill: Zona Voladures* = Beware of Falling Stones

■ *Caiguda de Neu* = Watch Out for Snow Sliding from Roofs

■ *Risc Allaus* = Risk of Avalanche

Otherwise, jump when the locals jump.

To/From France

BUS

Autocars Nadal has two buses (€21, 3½ to four hours) on Wednesday, Friday and Sunday to/from Toulouse's bus station, while **Novatel Autocars** runs two minibuses daily (€28, 3½ hours) to/from Toulouse airport.

TRAIN

Take a train from Toulouse to L'Hospitalet (2¼ hours, three to eight daily). From L'Hospitalet, buses leave for Andorra la Vella at 7.35am and 7.45pm daily (€6.80). In the reverse direction, they leave the Andorran capital at the unholy hour of 5.45am, plus 5pm.

For the Mediterranean, trains go from Latour-de-Carol (see below) to Perpignan (€20.30, four hours, two to four daily).

To/From Spain

BUS

Autocars Nadal (☎ 805151; www.autocarsnadal.com) runs four to six buses to/from Barcelona's airport (€25, 3¾ hours, daily), calling by the city's Sants train station (€20, 3¼ hours).

Alsina Graells (☎ 827379) has five buses daily (€19.50, 3½ hours) between Barcelona's Estació del Nord and Andorra la Vella. Three are nonstop services.

Minibuses operated by **Novatel Autocars** (☎ 803789; www.andorrabybus.com) make four runs daily between Andorra la Vella's bus station and Barcelona airport.

Viatges Montmantell (☎ 807444; www.montman tell.com) runs three buses daily to/from Lleida and Andorra la Vella (€15, 2¾ hours) to connect with the Madrid-bound high-speed AVE train (a great experience in itself).

Hispano Andorrana (☎ 821372) runs hourly buses between La Seu d'Urgell, just across the border, and Andorra la Vella (€2.40, 40 minutes) and they arrive at the Plaça de Guillemó bus stop.

TRAIN

From Barcelona, five trains daily climb to the frontier terminus of Latour-de-Carol, from where buses leave for Andorra at 10.45am and 1.15pm daily.

ANDORRA

ANDORRA

GETTING AROUND
Bus

Buses run along Andorra's three main roads. Ask at any tourist office for the free leaflet giving current timetables for the eight bus routes, all radiating from the capital and run by **Cooperativa Interurbana** (☎ 806555).

Car & Motorcycle

The largely ignored speed limit is 40km/h in populated areas and 90km/h elsewhere. Two problems are the recklessness of local drivers and Andorra la Vella's horrendous traffic jams. Bypass the worst of the latter by taking the ring road round the south side of town.

Petrol in Andorra is about 25% cheaper than in Spain, so fill up before you leave.

ANDORRA LA VELLA

pop 25,500

Andorra la Vella (vey-yah, meaning 'old'), the capital and sole town of this tiny nation, is squeezed into the Riu Gran Valira Valley. Its main passion is flogging electronic and luxury goods to binge-shopping tourists, with a sideline in skiing.

ORIENTATION

Long-distance buses pull in at the bus station on Avinguda de Tarragona, right in the heart of town. Short-haul services for La Seu d'Urgell, just over the Spanish border, call by the stop on Plaça de Guillemó.

TOP FIVE ANDORRA

■ **Festival** The Día de Meritxell, patron saint of Andorra, is a vigorous country-wide celebration (8 September; p64)

■ **Walk** Arinsal (p63) up to Andorra's highest point, Pic de Coma Pedrosa

■ **Bar** La Borsa (p62) in Andorra la Vella

■ **Impressive Sight** The eight draught beer taps that welcome you to Cervesería l'Albadia (p62) in Andorra la Vella

■ **Ski run** Esquirol, a 4.5km blue run from top to bottom of the Soldeu slopes (p62)

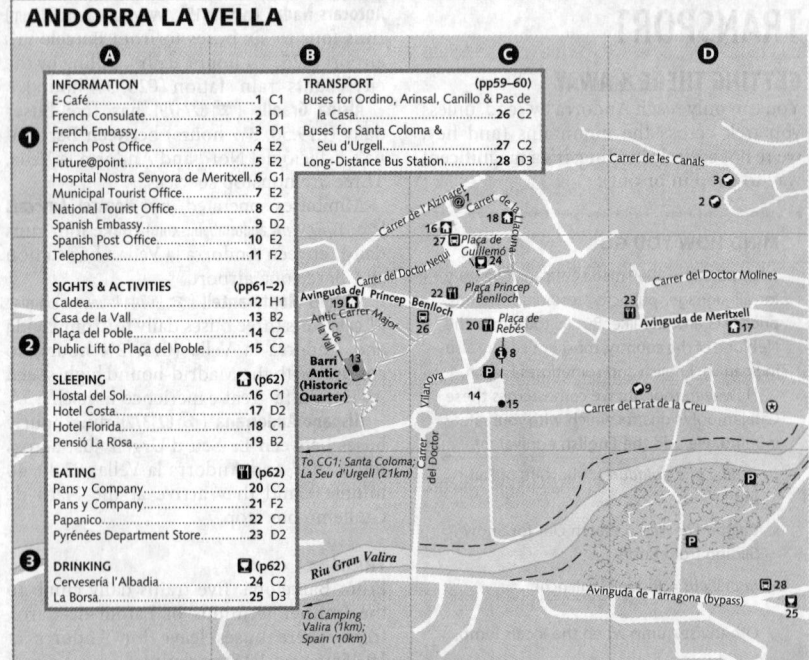

ANDORRA LA VELLA

Ⓐ	**Ⓑ**	**Ⓒ** **Ⓓ**

❶ INFORMATION
E-Café..1 C1
French Consulate.................................2 D1
French Embassy....................................3 D1
French Post Office...............................4 E2
Future@point.......................................5 E2
Hospital Nostra Senyora de Meritxell..6 G1
Municipal Tourist Office.....................7 C2
National Tourist Office........................8 C2
Spanish Embassy..................................9 D2
Spanish Post Office.............................10 E2
Telephones..11 F2

❷ SIGHTS & ACTIVITIES (pp61–2)
Caldea...12 H1
Casa de la Vall....................................13 B2
Plaça del Poble....................................14 C2
Public Lift to Plaça del Poble.............15 C2

SLEEPING 🏠 (p62)
Hostal del Sol.....................................16 C1
Hotel Costa...17 D2
Hotel Florida.......................................18 C1
Pensió La Rosa...................................19 B2

EATING 🍴 (p62)
Pans y Company.................................20 C2
Pans y Company.................................21 F2
Papanico...22 C2
Pyrénées Department Store................23 D2

❸ DRINKING 🍷 (p62)
Cervesería l'Albadia............................24 C2
La Borsa..25 D3

TRANSPORT (pp59–60)
Buses for Ordino, Arinsal, Canillo & Pas de la Casa.....................................26 C2
Buses for Santa Coloma & Seu d'Urgell......................................27 C2
Long-Distance Bus Station................28 D3

EMERGENCY NUMBERS

Ambulance, fire, police ☎ 112

Andorra la Vella runs along one main drag, whose name changes from Avinguda del Príncep Benlloch to Avinguda de Meritxell to Avinguda de Carlemany. The historic quarter is split by this busy road.

INFORMATION
Internet Access
E-Café (☎ 865677; Carrer l'Alzinaret 5; per hr €3; 🕙 9am-midnight Mon-Fri, 10am-midnight Sat)
Future@point (☎ 828202; Carrer de la Sardana 6; per hr €2.80; 🕙 10am-11pm Mon-Sat, 10am-10pm Sun)

Post & Telephone
French post office (La Poste; Carrer de Pere d'Urg 1; 🕙 8.30am-2.30pm Mon-Fri, 9am-noon Sat)
Spanish post office (Correus/Correos i Telègrafs; Carrer Joan Maragall 10; 🕙 8.30am-2.30pm Mon-Fri, 9.30am-1pm Sat)
There are several street-side telephones, but you'll find a battery of them along Carrer de la Borda, just off Avinguda de Meritxell.

Tourist Information
Municipal tourist office (☎ 827117; turisme@comuandorra.ad; Plaça de la Rotonda; 🕙 9am-9pm Jul-Aug, 9am-1pm & 3.30-7pm Mon-Sat, 9am-1pm Sun Sep-Jun) Carries all-Andorra information too.
National tourist office (☎ 820214; sindicatdiniciativa@andorra.ad; Carrer del Doctor Villanova s/n; 🕙 core hours 10am-1pm & 3-7pm Mon-Sat, 10am-1pm Sun) Just off Plaça de Rebés.

SIGHTS & ACTIVITIES
Caldea (☎ 800995; www.caldea.com; Parc de la Mola 10; adult/child €26/19.60; 🕙 core hours 10am-11pm, last entry 9pm) is Europe's largest spa complex, its lagoons, hot tubs and saunas are all fed by thermal springs – a great place for a splash and a splurge. Dunk yourself long enough and you can forgo showers for a week!

The small **historic quarter** (Barri Antic) was the heart of Andorra la Vella when the principality's capital was little more than a village.

Built in 1580 as a private home, the **Casa de la Vall** (House of the Valley) has been Andorra's parliament building since 1702. Downstairs is **El Tribunal de Corts**, the nation's only courtroom. The **Sala del Consell**, upstairs, must

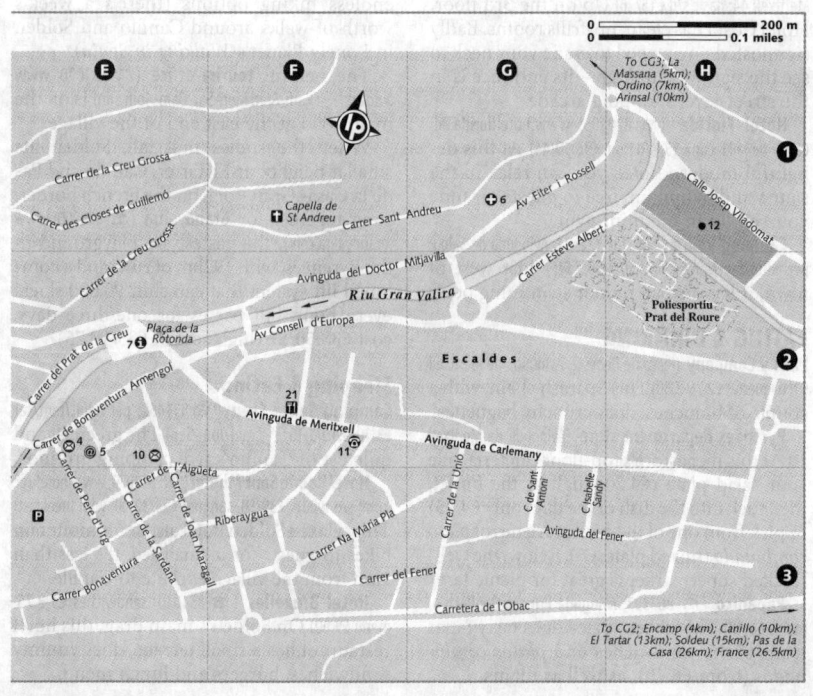

be the world's cosiest parliament chambers. There are **guided tours** (reservations ☎ 829129; admission free; ☺ 9.15am-1pm & 3-7pm Mon-Sat Dec-May, 9.15am-1pm & 3-7pm Mon-Sat, 10am-2pm Sun Jun-Nov) in a few languages, such as English. Book at least a week ahead in summer tobe included.

The **Plaça del Poble** occupies the roof of a modern government office building. It's a popular local evening gathering place.

If you've enough money left for **shopping**, you'll save on things like sports gear, photographic equipment, shoes and clothing, where prices are around 25% less than in Spain or France. Stock up on rock-bottom price booze and cigs before you leave.

SLEEPING

Hostal del Sol (☎ 823701; fax 822363; Plaça de Guillemó 3; s/d with shower €13.50/27) This family-run place has 12 spruce, great-value rooms and there are some cheap eateries in the square below.

Pensió La Rosa (☎ 821810; Antic Carrer Major 18; s/d €13/24) At the heart of the Barri Antic, La Rosa offers simple rooms with washbasin and has a couple of dorms (€72) that sleep six.

Hotel Costa (☎ 821439; fax 824867; Avinguda de Meritxell 44; basic s/d €15/26) Up on the 3rd floor, Hotel Costa has clean, no-frills rooms. Badly signposted – you need to crane your neck to see the sign way up high – its entrance is in the street-level shopping arcade.

Hotel Florida (☎ 820105; www.hotelflorida.ad; Carrer de la Llacuna 15; s/d from €36.50/44) At this delightful modern hotel, you can relax in the sauna and hammam, free to guests, or tone yourself up in the mini-gym.

Camping Valira (☎ /fax 722384; Avinguda de Salou; per adult/tent/car €4.50/4.50/4.50; ☒) Just west of town, it has a small indoor swimming pool.

EATING & DRINKING

Pans y Company (Plaça de Rebés 2; Avinguda de Meritxell 91; baguettes €2.75-3.60) This Spanish chain, with a couple of branches, does crunchy baguettes.

Pyrénées department store (Avinguda de Meritxell 21) At this megastore's top-floor cafeteria, pile your salad plate (€4.20) high at the buffet, then tuck into the dish of the day (only €4.25) or pick from one of the seven varieties of *plato combinado* (mixed plate; €6). Below, the well-stocked supermarket is great for picnic fare.

Papanico (☎ 867333; Avinguda Príncep Benlloch 4; mains €8-18) This cheery place does tasty tapas from €2.45, sandwiches and *platos combinados* (from €6.40), as well as mains.

La Borsa (Stock Exchange; ☎ 827657; Avinguda de Tarragona 36) Like a little flutter when you're drinking? At La Borsa, the price of each drink varies according to the night's consumption, so look at the electronic, computer-controlled screen as rates waver.

Cervesería l'Albadia (☎ 820825; Cap del Carrer 2) This is a place for serious beer drinkers, with over eight classics on draught and many more in the bottle.

GETTING THERE & AWAY

The bus stops and main bus station details are listed on p59.

AROUND ANDORRA

CANILLO & SOLDEU

Canillo, 10km northeast of Andorra la Vella, and Soldeu, 5km up the valley via CG2, are as complementary as summer and winter.

In summer **Canillo** (1500m) has canyon clambering, a *vía ferrata* climbing gully and climbing wall; the year-round Palau de Gel with its ice rink and pool; guided walks and endless hiking options (there's a week's worth of walks around Canillo and Soldeu in Lonely Planet's *Walking in Spain*).

The helpful **tourist office** (☎ 751090; www .vdc.ad; ☺ 8am-8pm Mon-Sat, 8am-4pm Sun) is on the main road at the east end of the village.

When the snows first fall, Soldeu, its smaller neighbour El Tarter, Canillo and Pas de la Casa–Grau Roig, on the French border, gang together for **Grandvalira** (☎ 808900; www .grandvalira.com), the vastest ski playground in the Pyrenees, with 192km of runs and a combined lift system that can shift 90,000 skiers every hour. Lift passes for one/three days, cost €33.50/87 (high season €35/90.75).

Sleeping & Eating

Camping Santa Creu (☎ 851462; per adult/tent/car €3.10/3.10/3.10; ☺ mid-Jun–Sep) The greenest and quietest of Canillo's five camping grounds.

Hotel Roc de Sant Miquel (☎ 851079; www.hotel-roc .com; s/d winter €39/58, summer €21/32, all with breakfast) This relaxed Soldeu hotel also rents mountain bikes to guests for a small fee. It's less than 1km from the village enroute to Canillo.

Hotel Bruxelles (☎ 851010; sandwiches €3-3.75, menu €9.90) On Soldeu's main drag, this hotel restaurant has a small terrace, does yummy sandwiches, burgers and lunch menu.

Slim Jim's (☎ 852567; ☺ 9am-5pm Jun-mid-Sep, 8.30am-11pm mid-Nov-Apr) This British-run place, one block from Soldeu's main street, does sandwiches, snacks and sizzling kebabs. It has four **Internet terminals** (per hr €6.70).

Entertainment

The music pounds on winter nights in Soldeu. **Pussy Cat** and its neighbour **Fat Albert** rock until far too late for impressive skiing next day, while **Avalanche** (☎ 852282) and, three doors away, **Aspen** (☎ 851974), have a live band at least twice a week.

Getting There & Around

Hourly buses run until 8pm from Andorra la Vella to Soldeu via Canillo and El Tarter. In winter there are free shuttle buses (just flash your ski pass) between Canillo and the two upper villages. Ask at any tourist office for the free leaflet giving current timetables for the eight bus routes, all radiating from the capital and run by **Cooperativa Interurbana** (☎ 806555).

ORDINO & AROUND

Despite recent development, Ordino, on highway CG3 8km north of Andorra la Vella, is a charming village, with most buildings still of local stone. At 1000m, it's a good starting point for summer activity holidays. The **tourist office** (☎ 737080; www.vallordino.com; ☺ 8am-7pm Mon-Sat, 9am-5pm Sun Jul-Sep, 9am-1pm & 3-7pm Mon-Sat, 9am-1pm Sun Oct-Jun) is beside the CG3.

Sights & Activities

Museu d'Areny i Plandolit (☎ 836908; adult/child €2.40/1.20; ☺ 9.30am-1.30pm & 3-6.30pm Tue-Sat, 10am-2pm Sun) is a 17th-century manor house with a richly furnished interior. In the same grounds is the far from nerdy **Museo Postal de Andorra** (Postal Museum; same hr & admission). It has a 15-minute audiovisual presentation (with English option) and stamps by the thousand, issued by France and Spain for Andorra.

The **Centre d'Interpretació de la Natura** (Nature Interpretation Centre; ☎ 837939; adult/student/child €3.70/1.85/free; ☺ 9.30am-1pm & 3.30-6pm Tue-Sat, 9.30am-1.30pm Sun) is a good multimedia introduction to Andorra's flora and fauna. A guided visit follows a 10-minute slide-video presentation (both with English option).

There are excellent **walking trails** around Ordino. Grab *Thirty-six Interesting Itineraries on the Paths of the Vall d'Ordino & the Parish of La Massana* (€2) from the tourist office.

Sleeping & Eating

Camping Borda d'Ansalonga (☎ 850374; www.camping ansalonga.com; per adult/tent/car €4/4/4; ☺ mid-Jun-Sep & Nov-Apr; ☒) A pretty site outside the village.

Restaurant Armengol (☎ 835977; mains €9-17; ☺ Jun-Apr) Has *menús* at €10.50 and €15 and also does a wide range of plentiful à la carte meat and fish dishes.

Bar Restaurant Quim (☎ 835645) Next door, it's friendly and more snacky, has a great range of tapas and does a filling midday *menú*.

Getting There & Away

Buses to/from Andorra la Vella run every half-hour from 7am to 9pm. Ask at any tourist office for the free leaflet giving current timetables for the eight bus routes, all radiating from the capital and run by **Cooperativa Interurbana** (☎ 806555).

ARINSAL

In winter, Arinsal, 10km northwest of Andorra la Vella and linked with the smaller ski station of Pal, has good skiing and snowboarding. The combined stations, which share a website (www.palarinsal.com), have 63km of pistes with a vertical drop of 1010m.

In summer, Arinsal is a good departure point for medium-grade mountain walks. From Aparthotel Crest on Arinsal's northern fringe, a trail leads northwest then west to **Estany de les Truites** (2260m), a lake. The steepish ascent takes around 1½ hours. It's another 1½ to two hours to bag **Pic de Coma Pedrosa** (2964m), Andorra's highest point.

Sleeping & Eating

Hostal Poblado (☎ 835122; hospoblado@andornet.ad; B&B per person €20, with bathroom €25; ☺ Dec-Oct; ☐) Right beside the cabin lift, it's handy for winter skiing and summer day walks and a great place to make contact with other skiers or walkers. There's a lively bar.

Camping Xixerella (☎ 836613; www.campingxixe rella.com; per adult/tent/car €4.20/4.20/4.20; ☺ Nov-Sep; ☒) Between Pal and Arinsal, this large, well-equipped site has an outdoor pool.

Refugi de la Fondue (☎ 839599; fondue dishes €13.50) Does cheese and meat fondues and, in summer, outdoor barbecues – a change from Arinsal's snack and sandwich joints.

ANDORRA

Restaurant el Moli (pasta & pizza €7-9.40) Pastas and pizzas and also more exotic fare.

Surf (see below) is another option, specialising in juicy Argentine grilled meat dishes (€7 to €13.20).

El Café Gourmet d'Arinsal (✹ mid-Jun–mid-May) does tasty snacks and also has an **Internet point** (per hr €4).

Entertainment
In winter, Arinsal fairly throbs after sunset. In summer, it can be almost mournful. When the snow's around, call by **Surf** (☎ 838069), near the base of the cabin lift – pub, dance venue and restaurant all rolled into one.

Getting There & Away
Five buses daily leave Andorra la Vella for Arinsal via La Massana. There are also around 15 local buses daily between La Massana and Arinsal.

In winter, a special ski bus runs six times daily between La Massana and Arinsal.

ANDORRA DIRECTORY

ACCOMMODATION
Tourist offices stock a free booklet, *Guia d'Allotjaments Turístics*. It's reliable, though the prices in it are only a guide. No bed comes cheap in Andorra. At the most modest end, expect to pay about €15 in a shared double. At the top end it's easy to climb well up into three figures.

There are no youth hostels, but there are plenty of camping grounds, many in beautiful surroundings. In high season, some hotels raise prices hugely and others don't take in independent travellers.

If you're trekking, ask at tourist offices for the free *Mapa de Refugis i Grans Recorreguts,* which marks and describes Andorra's 26 remote *refugis* (mountain refuges).

ACTIVITIES
Above the main valleys, it's attractive lake-dotted mountain country, good for skiing in winter and walking in summer. The largest and best slopes are the interconnecting runs of Grandvalira (see p62) in eastern Andorra. Others – Ordino-Arcalís, Arinsal and Pal – are a bit cheaper but often colder and windier. Ski passes cost €23.50 to €27.50 per day, depending on location and season;

downhill ski-gear is €8 to €11 per day, and snowboards €17 to €20.

In summer, you can rent mountain bikes in some resorts for around €18 a day.

But Andorra is, above all, for walkers. Both Ordino and Canillo or Soldeu make great bases and the trails, once you head out of the valley, will be all for you.

EMBASSIES & CONSULATES
Embassies & Consulates in Andorra
France and Spain maintain reciprocal missions in Andorra:

France (☎ 869396; Carrer les Canals 38-40)
Spain (☎ 800030; Carrer del Prat de la Creu 34)

Andorran Embassies Abroad
France (☎ 01 40 06 03 30; 30 rue d'Astorg, 75008 Paris)
Spain (☎ 91 431 74 53; Calle Alcalá 73, 28001 Madrid)

FESTIVALS & EVENTS
On 8 September, the Día de Meritxell, in honour of the patron saint of Andorra, is celebrated throughout the country.

INTERNET RESOURCES
www.andorra.ad For general info about Andorra
www.skiandorra.ad For skiing and practical wintertime info

POST
France and Spain operate separate systems with their own Andorran stamps, which you need only for international mail (letters within the country are delivered free).

TELEPHONE
Buy a *teletarja* (phonecard; €3 and €6 from tourist offices and kiosks). Off-peak times are 9pm to 8am, plus all day Sunday. You can't make a reverse-charge (collect) call from Andorra. The country code is ☎ 376 and the access code for international dialling from Andorra ☎ 00.

VISAS
Visas aren't necessary; the authorities figure that if Spain or France lets you in, that's good enough for them. But bring your passport or national ID card.

WORKING
You'll be up against strong competition from Chileans and Argentines working the northern winter in Andorra but you might pick up a ski-season bar or table-waiting job.

Austria

HIGHLIGHTS

- **Vienna** The capital is a cornucopia of impressive buildings, Habsburg treasures and art by Egon Schiele and Gustav Klimt (p70)
- **Salzburg** This picture-postcard baroque town has kitschy *Sound of Music* tours (p85)
- **Innsbruck** Skiing and snowboarding nearby are first-rate, and hiking in the surrounding mountains offers unforgettable views (p90)
- **Best journey** Grossglockner Hochalpenstrasse, the highway through the Hohe Tauern National Park, is among the world's most scenic (p94)
- **Off-the-beaten track** One of contemporary architecture's gems is the quirky, bubble-shaped Kunsthaus (Arts Centre) in Graz (p83)

FAST FACTS

- **Area** 83,870 sq km (less than one-third of Britain)
- **ATMs** Available everywhere
- **Budget** €40-50 per day
- **Capital** Vienna
- **Country codes** ☎ 43, international access code ☎ 00
- **Famous for** Apple strudel, Wiener Schnitzel, Adolf Hitler, Arnold Schwarzenegger and Freudian psychoanalysis
- **Head of State** President Heinz Fischer
- **Languages** German (Slovene, Croat and Hungarian are also official languages in some southern states)
- **Money** Euro (A$1 = €0.58, CA$1 = €0.64, ¥100 = €0.73, NZ$1 = €0.54, UK£1 = €1.45, US$1 = €0.81)

- **Phrases** *Grüss Gott* (hello), *servus* (hello and goodbye), *ba ba* (bye bye)
- **Population** 8.1 million
- **Time** GMT/UTC + 1
- **Visas** EU nationals don't need a visa. Most other nationalities can stay for up to 90 days in any half-year without a visa.

TRAVEL HINTS

Make lunch your main meal, when there are cheap *Tagesmenus* (daily specials/menus). Mention in conversation that you're from California and some locals *might* buy you a drink!

ROAMING AUSTRIA

Many backpackers arrive on a train from Zürich or Munich, stop at Salzburg, move on to Vienna and head straight to Eastern Europe. With more time, stop first in Innsbruck and later visit the Salzkammergut lakes district south of Salzburg. Graz makes a good budget stopover en route to Hungary or Slovenia.

AUSTRIA

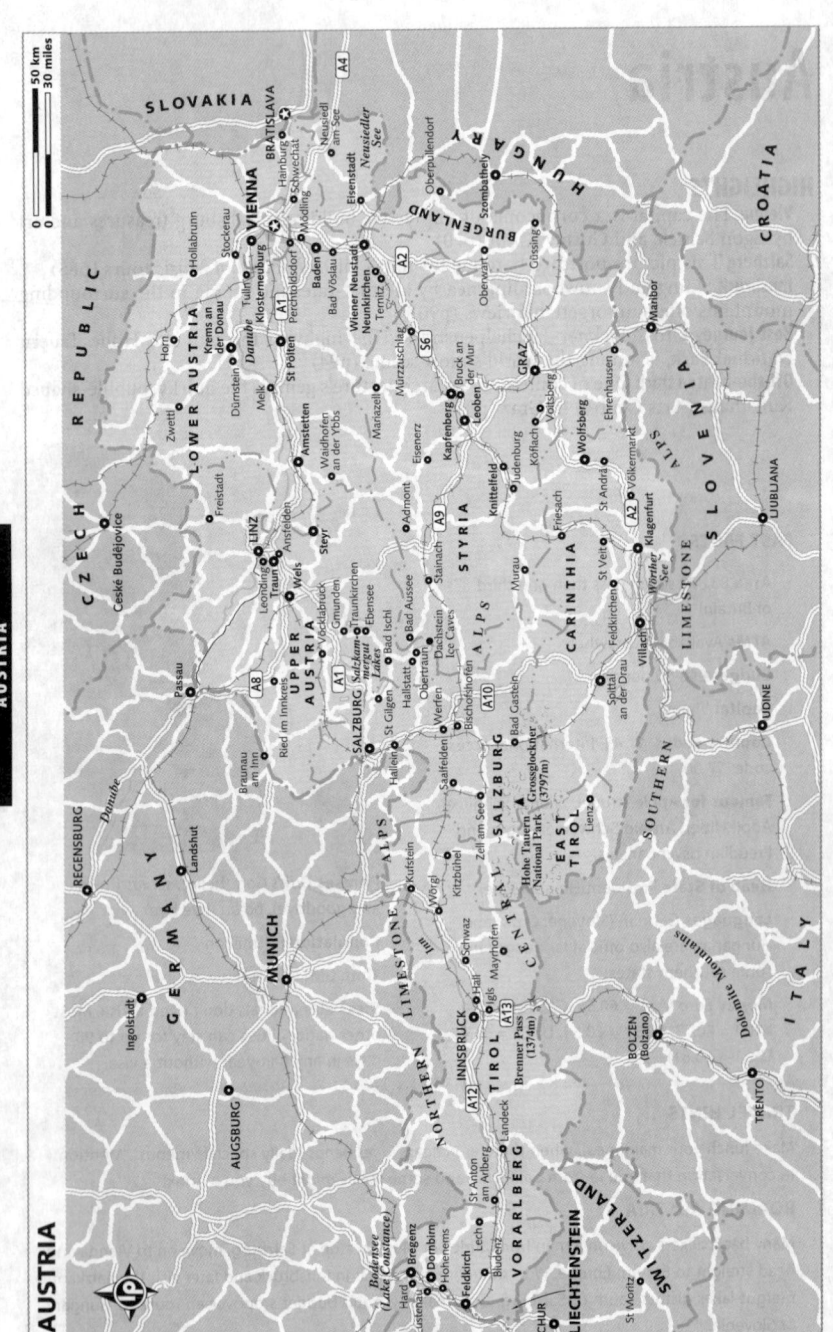

AUSTRIA

50 km
30 miles

SLOVAKIA

CZECH REPUBLIC

GERMANY

HUNGARY

CROATIA

SLOVENIA

ITALY

SWITZERLAND

LIECHTENSTEIN

BRATISLAVA
Hamburg
Schwechat
Neusiedl am See
Neusiedler See
Eisenstadt
VIENNA
Klosterneuburg
Stockerau
Oberpullendorf
Szombathely
BURGENLAND
Güssing
Oberwart
Hollabrunn
Tulln
Perchtoldsdorf
Mödling
Baden
Bad Vöslau
Wiener Neustadt
Neunkirchen
Ternitz
Mariazell
Mürzzuschlag
Bruck an der Mur
Kapfenberg
Leoben
GRAZ
Maribor
Horn
Krems an der Donau
St Pölten
Dürnstein
Melk
Danube
Amstetten
Waidhofen an der Ybbs
Eisenerz
LOWER AUSTRIA
Zwettl
Freistadt
LINZ
Enns
Leonding
Traun
Steyr
Wels
Admont
Knittelfeld
Judenburg
Köflach
Voitsberg
Ehrenhausen
Wolfsberg
St Andrä
Völkermarkt
STYRIA
Stainach
Murau
Feldkirchen
Friesach
St Veit
Klagenfurt
Wörther See
LIMESTONE ALPS
Ceské Budéjovice
Passau
Ried im Innkreis
UPPER AUSTRIA
Vöcklabruck
Gmunden
Traunkirchen
Bad Ischl
Bad Aussee
Ebensee
Hallstatt
Odertrann
Dachstein Ice Caves
Bischofshofen
Werfen
Salzkammergut
St Gilgen
SALZBURG
Hallein
CARINTHIA
St Veit
Spittal an der Drau
Villach
UDINE
Udine
Braunau am Inn
REGENSBURG
Landshut
Danube
MUNICH
Saalfelden
Zell am See
Bad Gastein
SALZBURG
Hohe Tauern National Park
Grossglockner (3797m)
EAST TIROL
Lienz
SOUTHERN
Ingolstadt
AUGSBURG
Kufstein
Wörgl
Kitzbühel
Mayrhofen
Schwaz
Hall
Igls
INNSBRUCK
CENTRAL ALPS
TIROL
Brenner Pass (1374m)
Inn
Landeck
Lech
St Anton am Arlberg
Bludenz
Feldkirch
Hohenems
Dornbirn
Bregenz
Hard
Lustenau
Bodensee (Lake Constance)
VORARLBERG
NORTHERN LIMESTONE ALPS
St Moritz
CHUR
BOLZEN (Bolzano)
TRENTO
Dolomite Mountains

A4
A1
A2
S6
A9
A2
A8
A10
A13
A12

LP

Although it likes to consider itself virtually twinned with California these days, Austria (Österreich) really couldn't be more different. And it's not just that Arnold Schwarzenegger's homeland offers mountains and snow instead of sun and surf. As a cultural bastion of 'old Europe', it still clings to its very un-Californian traditions of caffeine (coffee houses), cigarettes (everywhere) and calorific cuisine (schnitzel and apple strudel)!

Indeed, it's the country's seeming refusal to bow to the diktats of the modern world that attracts so many visitors, wooed by the historic treasures of the former Habsburg empire or by the sounds of Mozart and Strauss. Or they come for the Alps, which offer summer hikes and wintertime skiing.

However, even if baroque palaces, sparkling mountain vistas and Danube river cruises don't do it for you, Austria *does* have a forward-looking side, with the modern art Museums Quarter in Vienna and the architecturally adventurous Kunsthaus (Arts Centre) in Graz being just two examples.

HISTORY

Austria is a little nation with a big past. From 1278, it was the epicentre of the mighty Habsburg empire, stretching from Switzerland east into Ukraine, south to the Balkans and north to the Czech Republic, and one of Europe's dominant political players. However, by the 19th century, this increasingly unwieldy territory was starting to crack under the strain of nascent nationalism. In the 1866 Austro-Prussian War, the empire lost territory that was soon afterwards amalgamated into Germany. Following this, internal Hungarian politicians won their bid for equal status, forcing Austria-Hungary's creation.

The death knell came soon after Slavic separatists assassinated the heir to the throne, Archduke Franz Ferdinand, in Sarajevo on 28 June 1914. Austria-Hungary's resultant declaration of war on Serbia escalated into the 'Great War' (WWI); defeat in 1918 saw the empire broken up and today's small republic of Austria formed.

Nazis from neighbouring Germany assassinated Austrian Chancellor Dolfuss and installed a puppet regime in 1936, before the 1938 invasion. With Hitler, a native Austrian,

as German Chancellor, there was little resistance; a national referendum supported the two countries' *Anschluss* (Union).

Heavily bombed during WWII, Austria has since worked hard to be a good global citizen, proclaiming military neutrality in 1955 and in 1995 joining the EU. However, echoes of its fascist history regularly come back to haunt it. In the 1980s, rumours surfaced that President Kurt Waldheim had been involved in war crimes in WWII. In the late 1990s, other European nations briefly imposed sanctions when the far-right Freedom Party (FPÖ) and its controversial leader, Jörg Haider, joined the national government.

Haider remains on the scene but is no longer personally in the government, although Chancellor Wolfgang Schüssel of the People's Party, or ÖVP, continued to maintain a coalition with the FPÖ long after Haider's departure. In 2004 there was a tiny swing to the left when social democrat Heinz Fischer was narrowly elected the country's president – largely a figurehead role, compared with the chancellorship.

PEOPLE & CULTURE

Austrians don't enjoy the best reputation in Europe. Firstly, politicians like Jörg Haider add to a history of anti-Semitism to reinforce the notion that the country is very right-wing. Secondly, the people themselves are allegedly grumpy. However, Austria has relaxed a lot since the collapse of the Iron Curtain along its border more than 15 years ago. That last stereotype, in particular, is starting to lose its grip. Although 88.5% of the populace comes from an ethnic German background and 74% practise Catholicism, there are increasing numbers of Turkish, Bosnian and Serbian inhabitants.

READING UP

Graham Greene's evocative spy story *The Third Man* is set in Vienna, as is John Irving's *Setting Free the Bears*. Arthur Schnitzler's *Dream Story (Traumnovelle)* inspired – and is better than – the Stanley Kubrick film *Eyes Wide Shut*. Football fans might recognise Peter Handke's *The Goalie's Fear of the Penalty Kick (Der Angst des Tormanns beim Elfmeter)*.

Within the country, Vienna has always been a special case, mixing conservatism with decadence. The scene you might get at Viennese balls of grand old society dames flirting with drag queens aptly sums up the case. The capital's pervading humour, *Wiener Schmäh*, is quite ironic and cutting, but it is also charming.

SPORT

Ordinary Austrians are great lovers of the outdoors (see p95), and the country enjoys an international reputation in two disciplines particularly – mountaineering and skiing. Mountaineer Heinrich Harrer (born 1912) was among those who first conquered the infamously difficult north face of the Eiger in the Swiss Alps in 1938. Later, he spent *Seven Years in Tibet*. Reinhold Messner (born 1944) was the first man to climb Everest solo, among the first team to ascend Everest without oxygen and the first man to climb all the world's 14 mountains over 8000m.

Some of the biggest stars in competitive skiing in recent years have been Austrians, including Stephan Eberharter and Hermann Maier. The 'Herminator' nearly lost his leg in a motorbike accident in 2001, but made an amazing comeback to win the 2003/4 Super-G title.

ARTS

Beethoven, Brahms, Haydn, Mozart, Schubert and other European composers were drawn to Vienna by the Habsburgs' generous patronage during the 18th and 19th centuries. The waltz originated in the city, perfected by Johann Strauss junior (1825–99).

At the turn of the 20th century, Vienna was also a city of design and painting. The Austrian Secessionist movement, the local equivalent of Art Nouveau *(Jugendstil)*, turned out such talents as the painter Gustav Klimt and architect Otto Wagner. These were followed by the Expressionist painters Egon Schiele and Oskar Kokoschka, plus modernist architect Adolf Loos.

Today, Austria's fine musical tradition has headed in the direction of chilled, electronica and dub lounge, with names such as Kruder & Dorfmeister, Pulsinger & Tunakan, the Vienna Scientists and the Sofa Surfers.

Meanwhile, expat film director Michael Haneke has been garnering attention with suburban hostage-taking drama *Funny Games* (1997) and the twisted romance of *The Piano Teacher* (2001). The country's most famous TV export is the detective series *Inspector Rex (Kommisar Rex)*.

ENVIRONMENT

More than half of Austria is mountainous, with three chains running west to east: the Northern Limestone Alps, the Central Alps (which include the country's highest mountain, the 3797m Grossglockner) and the Southern Limestone Alps. The landscape around the Danube Valley in the northeast, and Graz to the southeast, is flat.

Only 3% of Austria's landmass is national park, but that does include the largest national park in the Alps, Hohe Tauern. Many species of alpine wildflowers are found here, while the bearded vulture and lyre-horned ibex were reintroduced in recent years. Marmots can be spotted in other national parks.

The Austrian people are highly environmentally conscious.

TRANSPORT

GETTING THERE & AWAY
Air

Austria is well served by low-cost airlines. **Ryanair** (☎ 0900 210 240; www.ryanair.com) flies from London to Graz, Klagenfurt, Linz and Salzburg, and **Air Berlin** (☎ 0820 400 011; www.airberlin .com) flies to Vienna from Germany. **Sky Europe** (☎ 01-998 555 55; www.skyeurope.com) flies to Croatia, France, Hungary, Italy and more.

However, its 'Vienna' airport is far from the city – in Slovakia, actually. To compete, the highly regarded national carrier **Austrian Airlines** (☎ 05-1789; www.aua.com) regularly offers special deals.

Boat

Hydrofoils run to Bratislava and Budapest from Vienna (see p75). Other boats go from Linz to Passau in Germany (see p80).

Bus

There are comprehensive bus services to Eastern European cities small and large – from the likes of Belgrade, Sofia and Warsaw, to Banja Luka, Mostar and Sarajevo. Other services go as far afield as England, the Baltic States, Germany, the Netherlands and Switzerland.

Vienna is the main departure point for services operated by **Eurolines** (www.eurolines .at in German), although some also leave from Salzburg and Graz as well as other provincial cities. For Eurolines departure information from Vienna, see p79.

Car & Motorcycle

Austria levies fees for its entire motorway network. Tourists must buy a 10-day pass (€7.60/4.30 for cars/motorcycles), a two-month pass (€21.80/10.90) or a yearly pass (€72.60/29) and clearly display the toll label *(Vignette)* on their vehicle. Passes are available at borders or from petrol stations. Otherwise, there's an on-the-spot fine of up to €220. For details, see www.oesag.at.

Hitching

Lonely Planet doesn't recommend hitching, as it is never entirely safe. If you must hitch, however, stay clear of the route from Salzburg to Munich, one of Europe's most difficult spots to get a lift.

Train

The main rail services in and out of the country include the route from Vienna's Westbahnhof to Munich, via Salzburg, Innsbruck and Bregenz. Most trains to the Czech Republic leave from Südbahnhof in Vienna, although to Ceský Krumlov it's easiest to travel from Linz. Express services to Italy go via Innsbruck or Villach; trains to Hungary and Slovenia are routed through Graz.

GETTING AROUND
Air

Austrian Airlines (www.aua.com) and its subsidiary, **Tyrolean Airlines** (www.tyrolean.at/e_index.htm), operate regular internal flights, but train, bus or car usually suffices in such a small country.

Bicycle

There are many national cycling paths. Private operators and hostels rent bikes; be prepared to pay anything from €7 to €10 a day. Vienna has cheap city bikes.

DEPARTURE TAX

Airport departure taxes for international flights are always included in the ticket price.

You can pay separately to take your bike on slow trains (€2.90/7.50/22.50 for a daily/weekly/monthly ticket); on fast trains, it costs €6.80 a day, if space allows. Booking is advisable.

Boat

Services along the Danube (see p80) are mainly pleasure cruises, but provide a leisurely, scenic way of getting from A to B.

Bus

Services are limited to less accessible regions, such as the Salzkammergut or Hohe Tauern National Park. Between major cities in environmentally friendly Austria, only train services exist.

For national bus information, call ☎ 01-711 01.

Car & Motorcycle

You'll require either an EU or an international driver's licence. All the multinational hire firms are here, but ask tourist offices about local agencies, which are usually cheaper. The minimum age for renting small cars is 19, or 25 for larger 'prestige' cars. Customers must have held a licence for at least a year. Many contracts forbid taking cars outside Austria, particularly into Eastern Europe.

Whether you hire a vehicle or bring your own, you must pay a tax to drive on motorways and affix a *Vignette* to your windscreen (see left).

Motorcyclists laws state that headlights must be switched on at all times. Crash helmets are compulsory.

Hitching

As well as being difficult to get a lift, it's illegal to hitchhike on Austrian motorways.

Train

The efficient state network, ÖBB, is supplemented by a few private lines. Eurail and Inter-Rail passes are valid on the former, but only sometimes on the latter. There is no supplement on Eurail and Inter-Rail passes for national travel on faster EC (Eurocity) and IC (Intercity) trains. Tickets purchased on the train cost about €3 extra. In this chapter, fares quoted are for 2nd class.

Combined Eurail passes are sometimes available for Austria and neighbouring countries; see p1256 for purchase details.

AUSTRIA

Within Austria, anyone can buy a Vorteils-card, which reduces fares by 45% and is valid for a year. At €19.90/99.90 under 26/over 26, it's of most interest to under-26s.

Nationwide train information is available by ringing ☎ 05-1717 (local rate).

VIENNA

☎ 01 / pop 1.6 million

If New York is the 'Big Apple', Vienna's the big wedding cake – a wonderfully rich indulgence packed with galleries and muse-ums. Marzipan-like buildings decorate the city's inner circular road, the Ringstrasse, but they're only the icing on a cultural treasure trove. The history of the Habsburg dynasty can be traced through the Hofburg (Imperial Palace) or Schloss Schönbrunn, while Art Nouveau artists Gustav Klimt and Egon Schiele are on show at the Seces-sion Building, Belvedere and the Leopold Museum.

Budget travellers may initially be intimi-dated by this city's diet of art, opera and clas-sical music, but its rich architectural history does leave scope for free sightseeing.

ORIENTATION

Many sights are in the *Innere Stadt* (inner city), encircled by the Danube Canal (Don-aukanal) to the northeast and broad boul-evards called the Ring or Ringstrasse.

In addresses, the number of a building *follows* the street name. Any number *before* the street name denotes the district, of which there are 23. District 01 (the *Innere Stadt*) is the most central. Generally, the higher the district number, the further out it is.

INFORMATION
Internet Access

Bignet (per 10/30 min €1.45/3.90; Map p76; ☎ 503 98 44; 01, Kärntner Strasse 61; Map p76; Theobaldgasse 19)

Haus Wien Energie (Map p72; ☎ 582 000; Mariahil-ferstrasse 63; free access)

Surfland Internetcafé (Map p76; ☎ 512 77 01; Krugerstrasse 10; €1.40, then €0.08 per min)

Medical Services

For out-of-hours dental treatment, call ☎ 512 20 78.

Allgemeines Krankenhaus (Map p72; ☎ 404 00; 09, Währinger Gürtel 18-20) General hospital.

EMERGENCY NUMBERS

- **Alpine Rescue** ☎ 140
- **Ambulance** ☎ 144
- **Doctor** ☎ 141 (after hours)
- **Fire** ☎ 122
- **Police** ☎ 133
- **Roadside Assistance** ☎ 120

Money

Train stations have extended hours for ex-changing money and there are ATMs all over the city.

Post

Other post offices open long hours are at Südbahnhof, Franz Josefs Bahnhof and Westbahnhof.

Main post office (Map p76; Hauptpost 1010; 01, Fleischmarkt 19; ☻ 24hr)

Tourist Information

Tourist-info Zentrum (Main Tourist Office; Map p76; ☎ 245 55; www.wien.info; 01, Am Albertinaplatz; ☻ 9am-7pm)

Information & hotel reservation counters Westbahnhof (☻ 8.30am-9pm); Airport (arrivals hall; ☻ 8.30am-9pm)

Jugend-Info Wien (Vienna Youth Information; Map p76; ☎ 17 99 inside Austria only; 01, Babenbergerstrasse 1; ☻ noon-7pm Mon-Sat) Can get various reduced-price tickets for 14- to 26-year-olds.

Travel Agencies

American Express (Map p76; ☎ 515 40; 01, Kärntner Strasse 21-23; ☻ 9am-5.30pm Mon-Fri, 9am-noon Sat)

STA Travel (Map p72; ☎ 401 48-0; 09,Garnisongasse 7; ☻ 9am-5.30pm Mon-Fri); (Map p76; ☎ 401 48-7000; 09, Türkenstrasse 6B); (Map p76; ☎ 502 43-0; 04, Karlsgasse 3)

SIGHTS & ACTIVITIES

Don't be overwhelmed by the cornucopia of things there is to see and do in Vienna; you can experience the best of these in a cou-ple of days. Commence at the **Stephansdom** (St Stephen's Cathedral; Map p76). Nearly every traveller does, for the 13th-century Gothic cathedral is situated at the city's heart. The tall, latticework spire and pat-terned roof are exceptional, but don't waste your time climbing the tower as the view is quite ordinary.

TOP FIVE AUSTRIA

- **Festival** The Christmas markets in Vienna and Salzburg (p96)
- **Walk** Guided mountain walks around Innsbruck (p92)
- **Beer hall** Augustiner Bräustübl, Salzburg (p88)
- **Impressive sight** from the Grossglockner Hochalpenstrasse (p94)
- **Best coffee house** Café Sperl, Vienna (p77)

Instead, head along **Graben**, past the nobbly **Plague Column**. At the end, turn left into **Kohlmarkt**, where you'll be greeted by the impressive sight of the **Hofburg** (Imperial Palace), the Habsburgs' city-centre base. Walk towards it and then wander around this large complex's nooks and crannies. There are several museums inside. If you're going to visit any, head for the **Kaiserappartements & 'Sissi' Museum** (Map p76; ☎ 535 75 75; adult/concession €7.50/5.90; ☼ 9am-5pm). Get the audio guide (free), because it's the strange life story of Empress Elisabeth ('Sissi'), wife of Kaiser Franz Josef, that's compelling here.

While in the neighbourhood, make a detour to the **Kaisergruft** (Imperial Vault; Map p76; 01, Neuer Markt/Tegetthofstrasse; adult/concession €4/1.50) where the remains of several Habsburgs, including Sissi, lie. Dead for more than a century, Sissi is still left fresh flowers by fans – an indication of the place's weird, cultish feel. *Six Feet Under*, indeed.

Now go back to the Hofburg and walk through it towards the Kunsthistorisches Museum and Museumsquartier.

Museums & Galleries

If you plan to see just one Viennese museum, the traditional choice has to be the **Oberes Belvedere** (Upper Belvedere; Map p72; ☎ 795 57-134; 03, Prinz Eugen Strasse 37; adult/concession €6/3; ☼ 10am-6pm Tue-Sun Apr-Oct, 10am-5pm Tue-Sun Nov-Mar). This baroque palace is home to Gustav Klimt's famous and beautiful *The Kiss* and *Judith,* and has a fine, manageably sized collection of Impressionist and other early-20th-century works. There's also an impressive view of Vienna over its French-style maintained gardens.

More central is the highly recommended **Museumsquartier** (Map p76; ☎ 523 04 31; 07, Museumsplatz 1). Architecturally stunning and modern, it's renowned for the **Leopold Museum** (Map p76; ☎ 525 70-0; adult/student €9/5.50; ☼ 10am-7pm Wed-Mon, 10am-9pm Fri), which houses the world's largest collection of Egon Schiele paintings, with some minor Klimts and Kokoschas. However, there's also the much-lauded **Museum Moderner Kunst, Stiftung Ludwig Wien** (Museum of Modern Art; Map p76; ☎ 525 00; adult/concession €8/6.50; ☼ 10am-6pm Tue & Wed, Fri-Sun, 10am-9pm Thu), an architecture centre, city art gallery and more.

It's claimed the **Kunsthistorisches Museum** (Map p76; ☎ 525 24-0; www.khm.at; 01, Maria Theresien-Platz; adult/concession €10/7.50; ☼ 10am-6pm Tue & Wed, Fri-Sun, 10am-10pm Thu) houses one of Europe's leading art collections. Given the works by Rubens, van Dyck, Holbein, Caravaggio, Peter Brueghel the Elder (including *Hunters in the Snow*), that's undoubtedly true. But this place can quickly give you museum fatigue with all its ornate ornaments, clocks, glassware and antiquities.

Other Museums & Galleries

Albertina (Map p76; ☎ 534 83-540; www.albertina.at; 01, Albertinaplatz 1A; adult/student €9/6.50; 10am-6pm Thu-Tue, 10am-9pm Wed) Albrecht Dürer's *Hare* and a few Michelangelos are joined by superbly curated modern exhibitions.

Haus der Musik (House of Music; Map p76; ☎ 516 48-51; www.hdm.at; 01, Seilerstätte 30; adult/concession €10/8.50; ☼ 10am-10pm) Make your own music in this mind-blowing array of interactive exhibits.

Sigmund Freud Museum (Map p76; ☎ 319 15 96; 09, Berggasse 19; admission €5; ☼ 9am-6pm Jul-Sep, 9am-5pm Oct-Jun) The former home of the father of psychoanalysis.

Notable Buildings

One cheap, restful way to get a quick overview of Vienna is to catch a tram (No 1 or No 2) around the Ringstrasse, passing buildings like the neo-Gothic **Rathaus**, the Greek Revival–style **Parliament**, the 19th-century **Burgtheater**, the Gothic **Votivkirche** and the **Postsparkasse** by Art Nouveau architect Otto Wagner. From the tram, you can even glimpse the baroque **Karlskirche** (St Charles' Church), set back from the Ringstrasse.

The Secessionist movement of the late 19th and early 20th century left a lasting impression on the city, with its Art Nouveau

AUSTRIA

VIENNA

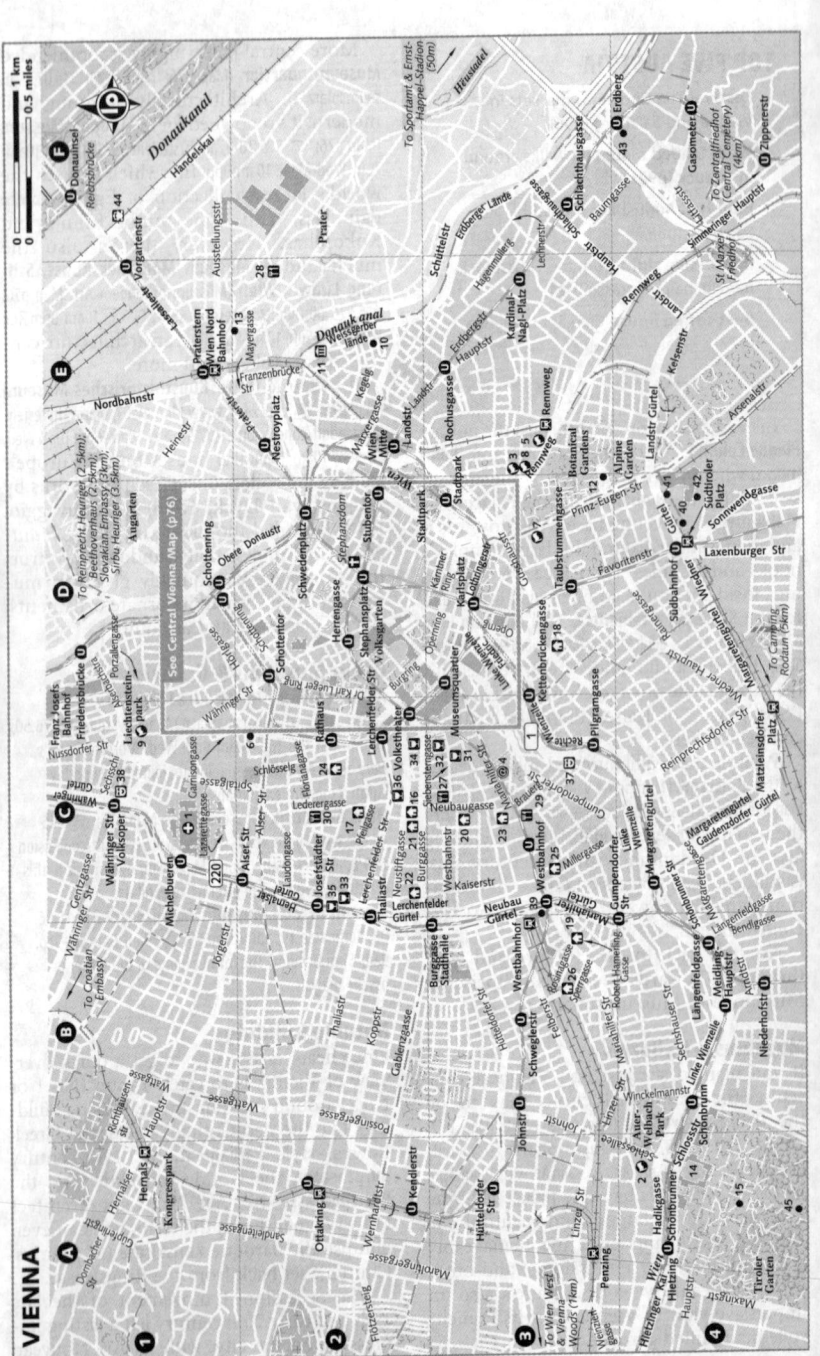

0   1 km
0   0.5 miles

Donauinsel
Reichsbrücke
Handelskai
Donaukanal

To Sportamt & Ernst-
Happel-Stadion (50m)
Gasometer
To Zentralfriedhof
(Central cemetery) (4km)
Zipererstr
Erdberg
43
St Marxer
Friedhof
To Camping
Rodaun (5km)

See Central Vienna Map (p76)

To Reinprecht-Heuriger (2.5km);
Beethovenhaus (2.5km);
Slovakian Embassy (3km);
Sirbu Heuriger (3.5km)

To Croatian
Embassy

To Wien West
& Vienna
Woods (1km)

Tiroler
Garten
45
14
15

architecture. The best example is the eponymous **Secession Building** (Map p76; ☎ 587 53 07; 01, Friedrichstrasse 12; adult/student €5.50/3; ☻ 10am-6pm Tue & Wed, Fri-Sun, 10am-8pm Thu), with an intricately woven gilt dome nicknamed the 'golden cabbage'. Inside is Klimt's enormous *Beethoven Frieze*.

Nearby, at Karlsplatz, are the unusually attractive train station entrances, or **Stadtbahn Pavilions**, by Otto Wagner. South of Secession, along Naschmarkt, are the decorated façades of Wagner's **Majolikahaus** and **Haus Linke Wienzeile** (Map p76; 01, Linke Wienzeile 38-40).

You can see the influence of Klimt, plus a little of Spain's Gaudí, on architect and artist Friedensreich Hundertwasser's **Kunsthaus Wien** (Map opposite; ☎ 712 04 91-0; 03, Untere Weissgerberstrasse 13; adult/concession €9/7, temporary exhibitions €15/12, half-price Mon; ☻ 10am-7pm). Nearby, on the corner of Löwengasse and Kegelgasse, there's a block of residential flats by Hundertwasser.

Schloss Schönbrunn
The Habsburgs' 1440-room summer palace, **Schloss Schönbrunn** (Map opposite; ☎ 811 13-0; 13, Schönbrunner Schlossstrasse 47; self-guided 22-/40-room tours adult €8/10.50, student €6.90/7.99; ☻ 8.30am-5pm Apr-Oct, 8.30am-4.30pm Nov-Mar), won't be to everyone's taste. On a sunny day, however, no opportunity should be missed to laze around its Versailles-like **gardens** (admission free). There's a **maze** (adult/concession €2.10/1.45) and similar attractions. Get there on U-Bahn No 4.

Riesenrad
Anyone who's seen the film *The Third Man* will recognise the **Riesenrad** (Giant Wheel; Map opposite; admission €7.50) in the Prater amusement park; it's where Orson Welles ad-libbed his immortal speech about peace, Switzerland and cuckoo clocks.

Cemeteries
Beethoven, Schubert, Brahms and Schönberg have memorial tombs in the atmospheric **Zentralfriedhof** (Central Cemetery; Map opposite; 11, Simmeringer Hauptstrasse 232-244), about 4km south of the centre. Mozart also has a monument here, but he is actually buried in the **St Marxer Friedhof** (Cemetery of St Mark; Map opposite; 03, Leberstrasse 6-8).

Naschmarkt
Saturday is the busiest day at this **market** (Map p76; 06, Linke Wienzeile; ☻ 6am-6pm Mon-Sat), when the week's food and clothes stalls are joined by a flea market. Curios and trinkets sit beside delicious produce from Austrian farms.

Water Sports
You can swim and sail in the stretches of water known as the Old Danube, located northeast of the Donaustadt island, and also in the the New Donau, which runs parallel to and just north of the Donaukanal (Danube Canal).

TOURS
The tourist office publishes a list of guided walks, *Wiener Spaziergänge*. **Vienna Walks** (☎ 774 89 01; http://viennawalks.tix.at) organises **Third Man tours** (adult/concession €16/13.50; ☻ 4pm Mon & Fri), including through the city's sewers.

It also has a **tour of Jewish Vienna** (adult/concession €11/10; ⊙ 1.30pm Mon).

Some boat operators (see p80) also conduct tours.

FESTIVALS & EVENTS

The **Wiener Festwochen** (Vienna Festival; Map p76; ☎ 589 22-22; www.festwochen.or.at) has a wide-ranging performing arts programme from mid-May to mid-June. Vienna's Marathon often coincides with Festwochen's start, and the city can be totally booked around that time.

At the end of June, look out for free rock, jazz and folk concerts in the **Donauinselfest**. Vienna's traditional Christmas market (*Christkindlmarkt*) takes place in front of the city hall between mid-November and 24 December.

SLEEPING

Vienna is difficult for budget travellers, so take care to book ahead, particularly in summer. **Tourist-info Zentrum** (Map p76; ☎ 245 55; www.wien.info; 01, Am Albertinaplatz; ⊙ 9am-7pm) and the **Information & hotel reservation counters** Westbahnhof (⊙ 8.30am-9pm); Airport (arrivals hall; ⊙ 8.30am-9pm) will book rooms (€2.90 to €4.50 commission).

Hostels

Hostel Ruthensteiner (Map p72; ☎ 893 42 02; www .hostelruthensteiner.com; 15, Robert Hamerling Gasse 24; dm €11.50-14, d €38; 🖳) The atmosphere at this hostel can change a bit. Sometimes it has a frat-house party atmosphere; at other times it's more low-key. Older four- to 10-bed dorms are supplemented by a small kitchenette and a nice courtyard garden where there's an 'Outback' summer dorm (€11).

Jugendherberge Myrthengasse (Map p72; ☎ 523 63 16; hostel@chello.at; 07, Myrthengasse 7; dm €15, d €34; ⊙ check-in 11am-4pm) This large hostel is well located in a student district, provides a similar level of accommodation to Ruthensteiner, but with four- to 6-bed dorms only.

Westend City Hostel (Map p72; ☎ 597 67 29; www.westendhostel.at; 6, Fügergasse 3; dm €17-19, s/d €40.50/49; 🖳) The weirdest thing behind the pale purple façade isn't the knowledge that this was once a bordello. It's the particle board–encased bathrooms in some of the co-ed dorms, which have extra mattresses on their mezzanine roof. Still, the place is well located and friendly.

Wombat's (Map p72; ☎ 897 23 36; www.wombats .at; 15, Grangasse 6; dm €19.50, d €49, with breakfast; 🖳) Top-flight comfort and cleanliness combine with a packed party bar to make Wombat's is hugely popular. The mixed-gender dorms have wooden bunk beds industrial-strength flooring, and modern bathrooms. Where the cool kids stay, if they remember to do something as terminally uncool as book.

Also recommended:
Believe It or Not (Map p72; ☎ 526 46 58; Apt 14, 07, Myrthengasse 10; dm €12.50) Small, intimate hostel.
Panda Hostel (Map p72; ☎ 522 53 53; 3rd fl, 07, Kaiserstrasse 77; dm €12.50) Cramped dorms, but friendly.
Brigittenau (Map p72; ☎ 332 82 94; jgh1200wien@chello.at; 20, Friedrich Engels Platz 24; dm from €15) Large HI hostel; take the U6 to Handelskai and then bus No 11A one stop.
Hütteldorf-Hacking (Map p72; ☎ 877 02 63; jgh@wigast.com; 13, Schlossberggasse 8; dm €16) Take the U4 to Hütteldorf; follow the Habikgasse exit.

Student Residences

These are available to tourists from 1 July to 30 September during the summer holidays. Central booking is available through two agencies.

There's **Academia** (☎ 401 76-55; www.academia -hotels.co.at), whose best of three options is **Gästehaus Pfeilgasse & Hotel Avis** (Map p72; 08, Pfeilgasse 4-6; s/d/tr €23/40/54, with bathroom €46/62/81).

The accommodation options at **Albertina Hotels** (☎ 512 74 93; www.albertina-hotels.at) include two new, quite central establishments:

Accordia (Map p72; 02, Grosse Schiffgasse 12; s/d €45/75) and **Haus Technik** (Map p72; 04, Schäffergasse 2; s/d €45/75).

Hotels & Pensions

Lauria (Map p72; ☎ 522 25 55; www.lauria-vienna .at; 3rd fl, 07, Kaiserstrasse 77; d/tr/quad from €46/63/80, with shower €60/75/92, apt €115, first night supplement €5) Great for those wanting privacy and autonomy, Lauria offers guests homey rooms, their own front-door key and access to a kitchen.

Pension Lehrerhaus (Map p72; ☎ 404 2358-100; www.lhv.at; 08, Lange Gasse 20; s/d from €27/49, with shower & toilet from €41/70) This boarding house for visiting academics offers a variety of rooms with or without private facilities. All are very modest but clean. Breakfast is not included.

Pension Hargita (Map p72; ☎ 526 19 28; 07, Andreasgasse 1; s/d from €33/46, with bathroom €50/62) Cheerful rooms in aqua blue or sunny yellow, spotless bathrooms and a charming owner make this one of Vienna's best budget options, even if there's no breakfast.

Hotel Kugel (Map p72; ☎ 523 33 55; www.hotel kugel.at; 07, Siebensterngasse 43; s/d from €33/45, with facilities from €50/66; ☺ closed mid-Jan–mid-Feb; **P**) The four-poster beds are appealing to some travellers, but the simpler rooms, without four posters or private bathrooms, offer great value. No credit cards.

Pension Dr Geissler (Map p76; ☎ 533 28 03; www .hotelpension.at; 01, Postgasse 14; s/d from €39/50, with private facilities from €65/88; **P**) Rooms here are either faux baroque or 1950s retro. It's handy because the airport bus leaves from nearby Schwedenplatz.

Hotel Post (Map p76; ☎ 515 83-0; www.hotel-post -wien.at; 01, Fleischmarkt 24; s/d €44/70, with bathroom €75/115; **P**) With parquet flooring in the rooms, long carpeted hallways and a decorative cast-iron lift, this central hotel feels like a formerly grand 19th-century boarding house.

Camping

Tourist offices list private rooms and offer a useful *Camping* pamphlet.

Wien West (Map p72; ☎ 914 23 14; www.wiencamp ing.at; 14, Hüttelbergstrasse 80; per adult/camp site Sep-Jun €5/3.50, Jul-Aug €6/3.50; ☺ closed Feb) On the edges of the Wienerwald forest, but just 20 minutes from town, this well-equipped site has modern facilities, **cabins** (2/4 people €27/37; ☺ Apr-Oct) and even a wireless Internet hot

spot. Take the U4 or the S-Bahn to Hütteldorf, then bus No 148 or 152.

Camping Rodaun (☎ /fax 888 41 54; 23, An der Au 2; per adult/camp site €5.50/4.50; ☺ Apr-Nov) There's a slightly more rural feel, and a lake, at this camping ground on a distant edge of the Wienerwald. Take the S1, S2 or S3 to Liesing, then Bus No 253, 254 or 255.

EATING

The most interesting cheap eats are found among the multicultural stalls, cafés and restaurants, all open Monday to Saturday, at the **Naschmarkt** (see p73). However, the usual university canteens exist, including the **Technical University Mensa** (Map p76; 04, Resselgasse 7-9; mains €3.20-4.80; ☺ 11am-2pm Mon-Fri) or **University Mensa** (Map p76; 7th fl, 01, Universitätsstrasse 7; mains €4.20-4.80; ☺ 11am-2pm Mon-Fri). While the latter is closed in July and August, its adjoining **café** (☺ 8am-3pm Mon-Fri) remains open. Do your after-hours grocery shopping at Franz Josefs Bahnhof or Westbahnhof.

Trzesniewski (sandwiches €0.80; ☺ Mon-Sat; Map p76; ☎ 512 32 91; 01, Dorotheergasse 1; Map p72; ☎ 596 42 91; 06, Mariahilferstrasse 95) At this stand-up café chain you can really feel like one of the Austrian Emperor's minions on the way home from the factory. Tiny open sandwiches featuring egg or fish are washed down with a tiny Pfiff beer.

Schnitzelwirt Schmidt (Map p72; ☎ 523 37 71; 07, Neubaugasse 52; schnitzels from €5.10; ☺ Mon-Sat) Fabulously grumpy waiters – who'll sometimes shout at you if you get in their way – plonk down huge Wiener Schnitzels on your table in this buzzing establishment. It's a true institution.

OH Pot, OH Pot (Map p76; ☎ 319 42 59; 09, Währinger Strasse 22; hot pots at lunch/dinner €6.20/8.20) This sweet Bohemian restaurant, painted in warm Mediterranean colours, serves decent hot pots (or stews) from around the world. They come with either soup or salad. From 3pm to 6pm prices drop to €4.90.

Ra'an (Map p76; ☎ 319 35 63; 09, Währinger Strasse 6-8; lunch €5.80, dinner €6.40-11.60) This cool noodle bar has sushi and rice dishes at lunch, served in cute cardboard boxes. At dinner, more elaborate Thai and Vietnamese dishes are served.

Ra'mien (Map pp76; ☎ 585 47 98; 06, Gumperndorferstrasse 9; mains from €6.80-15.50; ☺ Tue-Sun) Across town, Ra'an's sister establishment serves more straightforward noodle dishes.

AUSTRIA

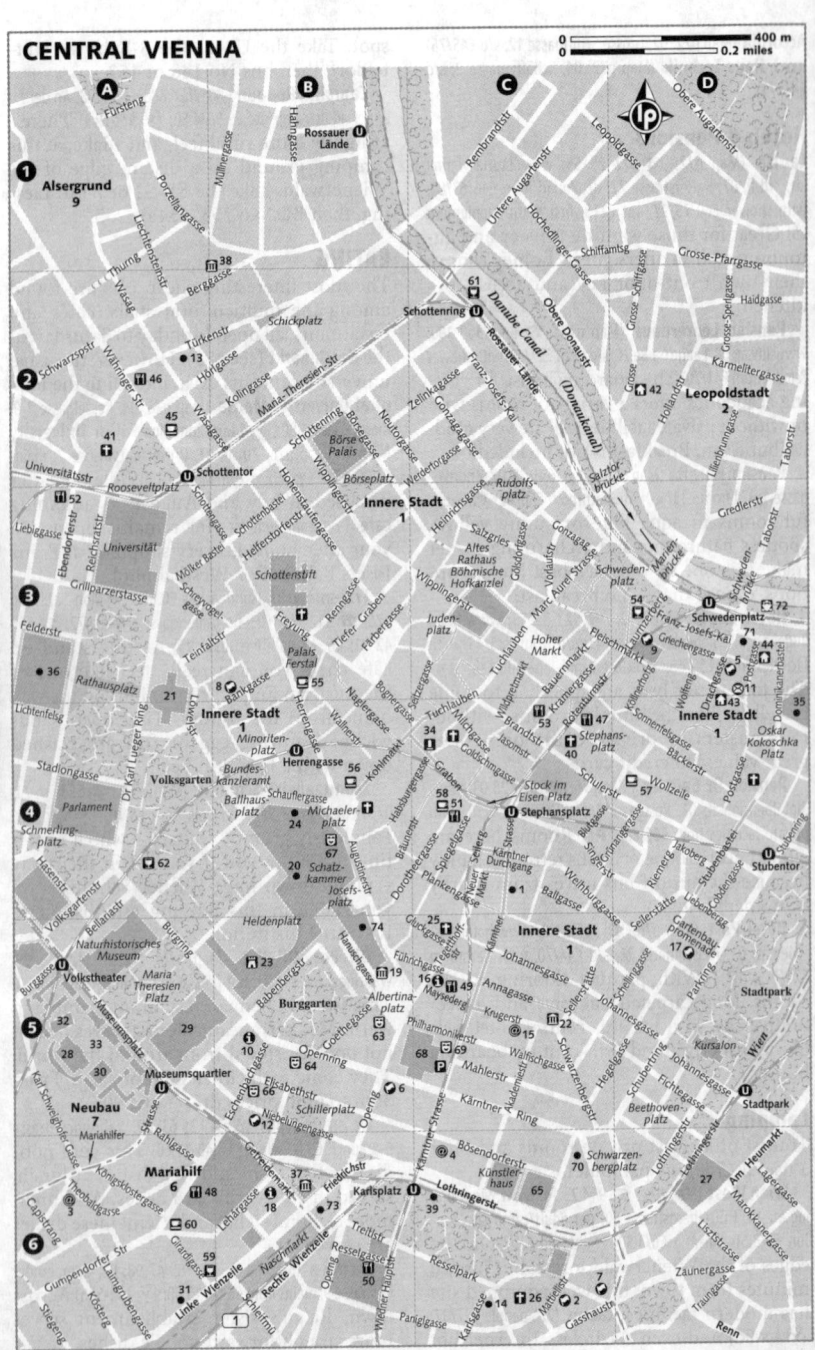

CENTRAL VIENNA

0 ——— 400 m
0 ——— 0.2 miles

A   **B**   **C**   **D**

Fürsteng.

Rossauer
Lände

1   Alsergrund
9

Hahngasse

Mühlgasse

Porzellangasse

Liechtensteinstr

Thurng.

Waag.

38

Berggasse

Schwarzsptr

Währinger Str

Türkenstr

13

Höfingasse

Kollingasse

Schickplatz

Leopoldsgasse

Untere Augartenstr

Obere Augartenstr

Rembrandtstr

Schiffamtg.

Grosse-Pfarrgasse

Haidgasse

2   46

45

41

61

Schottenring

Schottenring
Börsegasse

Maria-Theresien-Str

Zelinkagasse

Gonzagagasse

Neutorgasse

Rossauer Lände

Franz-Josefs-Kai

Karmelitergasse

42

Leopoldstadt
2

Lilienbrunngasse

Taborstr

Taborstr

Universitätsstr

Schottentor

Roosveltplatz

Hohenstaufengasse

Wipplingerstr

Börse
Palais

Börseplatz

Werdertorgasse

Salztor-
brücke

Rudolfs-
platz

Innere Stadt
1

52

Liebiggasse

Ebendorferstr

Reichratstr

Universität

Grillparzerstrasse

Schottengasse

Schottenbastei

Heßgasse

Heinrichsgasse

Salzgries

Altes
Rathaus
Böhmische
Hofkanzlei

Marc Aurel Strasse

Wipplingerstr

Gölsdorfgasse

Gonzagagasse

Schweden-
platz

Schwedenplatz

54

72

71

44

Felderstr

Rathausplatz

36

Lichtenfelsg

Dr Karl Lueger Ring

Schreyvogel-
gasse

Teinfaltstr

Melker Bastei

Schottenstift

Renngasse

Freyung

Tiefer Graben

Färbergasse

Judenplatz

Hoher
Markt

Tuchlauben

Judengasse

Fleischmarkt

Griechengasse

9

Postgasse

Dominikanerbastei

43

11

35

Oskar
Kokoschka
Platz

Innere Stadt
1

3

Palais
Ferstal

21

8

Bankgasse

55

Innere Stadt
1

Minoriten-
platz

Herrengasse

56

Löwelstr

Reitschulgasse

Renngasse

Naglergasse

Bognergasse

Seitzergasse

Wallnerstr

Kohlmarkt

Tuchlauben

Brandstätte

34

Bauernmarkt

Wildpretmarkt

Goldschmiedgasse

Jasomirgottstr

53

Kramergasse

Rotenturmstr

Bauernmarkt

47

Stephans-
platz

40

Sonnenfelsgasse

Bäckerstr

Wollzeile

57

Innere Stadt
1

Postgasse

Volksgarten

Bundes-
kanzleramt

Ballhausplatz

Schauflergasse

Michaeler-
platz

67

24

20

Schatz-
kammer
Josefs-
platz

Habsburgergasse

Dorotheergasse

Graben

Spiegelgasse

Seilergasse

Plankengasse

Neuer Markt

Kärntner
Durchgang

58

51

Stephansplatz

Stock im
Eisen Platz

Singerstr

Grünangergasse

Schulerstr

Weihburggasse

Rauhensteingasse

Riemergasse

Seilerstätte

Liebenberggasse

Jakobergasse

Stubentor

4

Parlament

Schmerling-
platz

62

Hasnerstr

Volksgartenstr

Bellariastr

Naturhistorisches
Museum

Volkstheater

Maria
Theresia
Platz

23

Heldenplatz

74

Burgring

Bumbergstr

Hanuschgasse

25

Führichgasse

19

16

49

Mayseder

Annagasse

Johannesgasse

22

15

Walfischgasse

Akademiestr

Ballgasse

1

Innere Stadt
1

Schellinggasse

Kärntner Ring

Seilerstätte

Coburgbastei

17

Cartenbau-
promenade

Stubenring

Stadtpark

5

32

28

33

30

Neubau
7

Mariahilfer

Museumsquartier

Maria-
hilfer Str

Museumsplatz

29

10

Getreidemarkt

Operngasse

Albertina-
platz

63

64

66

Elisabethstr

12

Nibelungengasse

Schillerplatz

Gauermanngasse

6

68

69

P

Mahlerstr

Kärntner Str

Philharmonikerstr

Krugerstr

Bösendorferstr

Künstler-
haus

4

Lothringerstr

65

70

Schwarzen-
bergplatz

Lothringerstr

27

Am Heumarkt

Beethoven-
platz

Schubertring

Lisztstrasse

Kursalon

Wien

Johannesgasse

Parkring

Stadtpark

6

Mariahilf
6

48

60

59

31

Linke Wienzeile

Rechte Wienzeile

Naschmarkt

Capistrang

Theobaldgasse

Gumpendorfer Str

Laimgrubengasse

Köstlerg.

Strohg.

Rahlgasse

Mariahilfer

Königsklosterg

Girardig.

Getreidemarkt

Lehárgasse

18

37

Friedrichstr

73

Karlsplatz

39

Wiedner Hauptstr

Operng.

Treitlstr

Resselgasse

Resselpark

Resselgasse

50

Paniglgasse

14

26

2

7

Karlsgasse

Mittersteig

Gusshausstr

Zäunergasse

Renn-

Mahlerstrasse

Trattnerg

Zentag.

Margaretenstrasse

1

Schweizerhaus (Map p72; ☎ 319 35 63; 02, Strasse des Ersten Mai 116; €5.40-17; ☺ Mon-Sat Mar-Oct) In this Prater Park institution, a rowdy crowd of international travellers wash down *hintere Schweinsstelze* (roasted pork hocks) and equally appealing goodies with enormous mugs of beer.

Wrenkh (Map opposite; ☎ 533 15 26; 01, Bauernmarkt 10; lunch menus €11) Sleek customers come to this up-market vegetarian restaurant for lip-smacking Mediterranean, Austrian and Asian fare. Not a mung bean in sight.

Also recommended:

Pizza Bizi (Map opposite; 01, Rotenturmstrasse 4; pizzas & pasta €5.40-5.80) Italian for those in a hurry.

Rosenberger Markt (Map opposite; 01, Maysedergasse 2; mains €6.20-7.80) Charmless but handy motorway-style restaurant with real value-for-money buffet.

Tunnel (Map p72; 08, Florianigasse 39; mains €5-11, lunch specials €4) Low-key student haunt.

Coffee Houses

The *Kaffeehaus* (coffee house) is an integral part of Viennese life. Everyone has a favourite. Try one of these:

Café Central (Map opposite; ☎ 533 37 63; 01, Herrengasse 14; ☺ closed Sun) A lot more commercialised than when Herr Trotsky drank here, but still with appealing vaulted ceilings and palms.

Café Demel (Map opposite; ☎ 535 1717-0; 01, Kohlmarkt 14) A bit posh to drink in, but the best for takeaway chocolate and cakes.

AUTHOR'S CHOICE

A bit like Goldilocks testing her porridge, we find some Viennese coffee houses too ornate and sterile, others too shabby and undistinguished. High-ceilinged **Café Sperl** (Map p72; 06, Gumpendorfer Strasse 11) is just right. With its scuffed but original 19th-century fittings and a cast of Bohemian patrons playing chess and reading the newspapers, it's exactly how you want a coffee house to be.

Café Diglas (Map opposite; ☎ 512 57 65; 01, Wollzeile 10) Ornate surroundings and a relaxed vibe.

Café Hawelka (Map opposite; 512 8230; 01, Dorotheergasse 6; ☺ closed Sun) Smoky, crowded, noisy, with nicotine-stained walls and arty regulars.

DRINKING
Bars

The area around Ruprechtsplatz, Seitenstettengasse and Rabensteig near Schwedenplatz is dubbed the **Bermudadreieck** (Bermuda Triangle; Map opposite) for the way drinkers disappear into its numerous pubs and clubs. Venues are lively and inexpensive, but not particularly atmospheric.

In summer, a stretch of Danube near the Reichsbrücke known as the **Copa Cagrana** (Map p72) comes alive with open-air bars, cafés and restaurants.

Centimeter (Map p76; ☎ 524 33 29; www
.centimeter.at; 07, Stiftgasse 4) This is the most conveniently located of a city-wide chain, in the
charming 'Spittelberg' area of cobbled streets,
bars and restored Biedermeier houses. It's a
rollicking establishment selling Austrian food
and lots of beer (sold by the centimetre).

7Sternbräu (Map p76; ☎ 523 61 57; 07, Siebensterngasse 17) A popular Styrian brewery, 7Stern
has an interesting range of brews, from hemp
beer to Prager Dunkel (dark Prague beer).

Shebeen (Map p76; ☎ 524 79 00; 07, Lerchenfelder-
strasse 45-47) English-speaking travellers and
expats alike come for the good food, relaxed
vibe and, occasionally, to watch major football matches on TV.

Café Stein (Map p72; ☎ 319 72 41; 09, Währinger
Strasse 6-8) This trendy student café-bar cum
diner has been an institution on the scene
for several years.

Das Möbel (Map p76; ☎ 524 94 97; 07, Burggasse 10)
Another Spittelberg hang-out, much cooler
than Centimeter, 'Furniture' is remarkable for
just that. It has cube stools, a circular ping-
pong table, quirky lamps and much more.

Rhiz (Map p76; ☎ 409 25 05; Lechenfelder Gürtel 37-
38) One of the bars lining the U-Bahn arches
near the Gürtel, this is a hip mecca of Vienna's electronic music scene.

Chelsea (Map p76; ☎ 407 93 09; Lechenfelder Gürtel 29-31) Along the same strip as Rhiz, this
is more underground, with frequent indie
bands or DJs.

Heurigen

In the suburbs to the north, south and west
of the city, you'll find Vienna's renowned
wine taverns (*Heurigen*). Selling 'new' wine
produced on the premises, plus food, they
have a lively atmosphere – and sometimes
strolling musicians wandering between
their outdoor picnic tables. Opening times
are approximately 4pm to 11pm, and wine
costs less than €2.50 a *Viertel* (0.25L).

The *Heurigen* areas of Nussdorf and Heiligenstadt are near the terminus of tram D.
In 1817 Beethoven lived in the **Beethoven-
haus** (19, Pfarrplatz 3, Heiligenstadt). Down the road
(bus No 38A from Heiligenstadt or tram
No 38 from the Ring) is Grinzing, an area
favoured by tour groups. There are several
Heurigen in a row where Cobenzlgasse and
Sandgasse meet, of which **Reinprecht** (☎ 320
14 71; 19, Coblenzgasse 22) is the best, even if still
rather touristy.

Alternatively, catch bus No 38A east to
the final stop at Kahlenberg and walk 15
minutes to **Sirbu** (☎ 320 59 28; 19, Kahlenberger
Strasse 210; ☷ Mon-Sat Apr-Oct), which has great
views of the Danube.

Many hostels now offer *Heurigen* excursions for about €45 to €50. It's a convenient
if relatively pricey way to visit.

CLUBBING

Check *Falter* for further listings. Although
closed at the time of research, the legendary
student party night every Friday in the ornate **Palais Eschenbach** (Map p76; Eschenbach Gasse
11) should have restarted by now.

Flex (Map p76; ☎ 533 75 25; Donaukanal, via Au-
gartenbrücke) Along a fairly urban-looking
stretch of the Danube Canal, Vienna's leading club buzzes every night, with visiting
or local bands and top-name DJs. There's
also a cool café area, where you can surf the
Internet and choose your own background
chill-out music from a massive sound archive of 700 CDs.

Volksgarten (Map p76; ☎ 533 05 18; 01, Burgring
1) This atmospheric 1950s building has recently been given a new high-tech dance
floor and retractable roof, but retains a traditional curved salon facing the Volksgarten
(People's Park) in which it's located. Friday and Saturday are the biggest nights. Be
warned that drinks are expensive.

Gay & Lesbian Venues

Rosa Lila Villa (Map p72; ☎ 586 81 50; 06, Linke Wienziele 102) The Ur-venue of Vienna's gay scene
is this pink-and-purple information centre
with popular bar and restaurant.

Café Savoy (Map p76; ☎ 586 73 48; 06, Linke Wienziele
36) This camped-up, olde-worlde café makes
for a prime people-watching spot during
Saturday's Naschmarkt (see p73). At other
times, the clientele is less mixed and more
male-oriented.

ENTERTAINMENT

Falter (€2.05) and the tourist office's *Vienna
Scene* have up-to-date listings.

Cinema

Burgkino (Map p76; ☎ 587 84 06; 01, Opernring 19)
Screenings every Friday evening and Sun-
day afternoon of *The Third Man* allow you
to revisit this classic film in the city where
it's set.

Classical Music

Staatsoper (State Opera; Map p76; ☎ 514 44-29 60; 01, Opernring 2; seats €5.50-220, standing room €3.70) Performances here are lavish, formal affairs, where you can watch Viennese high society in all its finery.

Volksoper (People's Opera; Map p72; ☎ 514 44-36 70; 09, Währinger Strasse 78; seats €17-75, standing room €1.50-24) Putting on more modern performances, the 'people's opera' is a little more relaxed in atmosphere.

You can buy tickets for both these venues, at little or no commission, at the **Bundestheaterkassen** (Map p76; ☎ 514 44-78 80; www .bundestheater.at; 01, Goethegasse 1) or **Wien Ticket** (Map p76; ☎ 588 85), in the hut by the Staatsoper. However, the cheapest deals are the standing-room tickets that go on sale at each venue an hour before the performance. You might need to queue three hours before that for major productions. An hour before curtain-up, unsold tickets also go on sale cheap (from €3.70) to students under 27 (student ID plus international student card necessary).

Musikverein (Map p76; ☎ 505 18 90; www.musik verein.at; 01, Bösendorferstrasse 12; seats €16-110, standing room €5-7) The opulent (unofficial) home of the world-class Vienna Philharmonic Orchestra is said to be acoustically perfect. Here, standing tickets can be bought three weeks in advance at the box office.

There are no performances in July and August. Ask the tourist office for details of free concerts at the Rathaus or in churches.

Lipizzaner Museum & Spanish Riding School

The famous Lipizzaner stallions strut their stuff in the **Spanish Riding School** (Map p76; tickets@srs.at; seats €45-145, standing room €24-25) near the Hofburg. Ask in the adjacent museum about seats. Same-day tickets can be bought for **training sessions** (€11.50; ☉ 10am-noon Tue-Sat Feb-Jun & Sep-Dec) or the weekly **final rehearsal** (€20; ☉ Fri or Sat).

Vienna Boys' Choir

The Wiener Sängerknaben perform weekly at the **Burgkapelle** (Music Chapel; Map p76; ☎ 533 99 27; hofmusikkapelle@asn-wien.ac.at; Swiss Courtyard, Hofburg; seats €5.50-30, standing room free; ☉ performances 9.15am Sun mid-Sep–Jun). Tickets are available on Friday, and from 8.15am Sunday before performances. They often put on shows in

the **Konzerthaus** (Map p76; ☎ 24 20 02; 03, Lotheringerstrasse 20; ☉ 3.30pm Fri May & Jun, Sep & Oct).

GETTING THERE & AWAY
Air

Vienna is a major hub between Western and Eastern Europe. Flights also leave to regional Austrian cities. Check with **Austrian Airlines** (Map p76; ☎ 05-17 89; www.aua.com; 01, Kärntner Ring 18).

Boat

In summer, hydrofoils travel east to Bratislava (one-way/return €22/33.50) and Budapest (€75/99). Book through **DDSG Blue Danube** (Map p76; ☎ 588 80-0; www.ddsg-blue-danube .at; 01, Friedrichstrasse 7) or **G Glaser** (Map p72; ☎ 726 08 20; www.members.aon.at/danube; 02, Handelskai 265). Both also offer slower ferry services westwards.

Bus

Bus operator **Eurolines** (www.eurolines.at) has a few locations. Most buses leave from its **Südbahnhof terminal** (Map p72; ☎ 796 85 52; 03, Arsenalstrasse; ☉ 7am-7pm), including those to Budapest (one-way/return €25.20/39, 3½ hours).

However, services to Bratislava (one-way/return €3.90/7.80, 1½ hours) leave from outside its other **Eurolines office** (Map p72; ☎ 798 29 00; 03, Erdbergstrasse 202; ☉ 7am-7pm).

Eurolines services to Prague (one-way/return €20/34, five hours) depart from a **third terminal** (☎ 93000-34305; 01, Rathausplatz 5).

Car & Motorcycle

The Gürtel is an outer ring road that joins up with the A22 on the north bank of the Danube and the A23 southeast of town. All the main road routes intersect with this system, including the A1 from Linz and Salzburg, and the A2 from Graz.

Train

Westbahnhof has trains to western Austria, plus Western and northern Europe. Some services to Salzburg continue to Munich and terminate in Paris (14½ hours total). To Zürich, there are two day trains (€77.70, nine hours) as well as one night train (same fare, plus charge for fold-down seat or couchette). Eight trains a day go to Budapest (€37.60, 3½ hours).

Südbahnhof has trains to Italy (eg Rome, via Venice and Florence), Slovakia, the Czech

Republic, Hungary and Poland, and southern Austria. Five trains daily go to Bratislava (€15.40, 1½ hours) and four to Prague (€40.70, five hours), with two continuing to Berlin (10 hours in total).

Wien-Mitte Bahnhof handles local trains only and Franz Josefs Bahnhof has local and regional trains.

For information, call ☎ 05-17 17.

GETTING AROUND
Underground (U-Bahn), tram, suburban train (S-Bahn) and bus routes are outlined in the free tourist office map.

All advance-purchase tickets must be slotted into the validation machines at the entrance to U-Bahn stations or on trams and buses. Singles cost €1.50 from automatic machines before you board; or €2 on-board.

Daily passes (Stunden-Netzkarte) cost €4/5 (8am to 8pm, valid for 24 hours from first use); one for three days costs €12 (valid for 72 hours).

You will need a Maestro debit card to use Vienna's cheap **city bikes** (☎ 0810 500 500; www.citybikewien.at in German; €2 deposit, bike rental free first hr, roughly €2 per hr afterwards). Check the website for locations.

THE DANUBE VALLEY

Terraced vineyards, ruined castles and medieval towns line the River Danube's most picturesque stretch between Krems and Melk.

Boats operate from early April to late October. **DDSG Blue Danube** (Map p76; ☎ 01-588 80-0; www.ddsg-blue-danube.at; 01, Friedrichstrasse 7, Vienna) has three departures daily (one daily in October) via the Wachau. From Me to Krems (1¾ hours downstream) or from Krems to Melk (three hours upstream) costs one-way/return €15.80/20.50. **Brandner** (☎ 07433-25 90-21; www.brandner.at) offers the same trips and prices.

Ardagger (☎ 07479-64 64-0; dsa@pgv.at) connects Linz and Krems three times a week in summer. **Wurm & Köck** (☎ 070-783 607; www.donauschiffahrt.de in German; Untere Donaulände 1, Linz) has services Tuesday to Sunday between Linz and Passau, in Germany (six hours), which stop in the Wachau. **G Glaser** (Map p72; ☎ 01-726 08 20; www.members.aon.at/danube; 02, Handelskai 265, Vienna) sails between Passau and Budapest, stopping at Krems and Melk.

Most operators carry bicycles without charge along these routes.

The Wachau stretch of the Danube Cycle Path is idyllic. Ask local tourist offices or visit www.radtouren.at/english.

KREMS AN DER DONAU
☎ 02732 / pop 23,000
As quaint as it is, Krems is really only a stop over on a Danube Valley trip. The **tourist office** (☎ 826 76; www.tiscover.com/krems; Kloster Und, Undstrasse 6; 9am-6pm Mon-Fri, 10am-noon & 1-5pm Sat, 10am-noon & 1-4pm Sun Apr-Oct) can provide accommodation details. There's riverside camping at **ÖAMTC Camping Krems** (☎ 844 55; Wiedengasse 7; per person €4.50, per tent €2.20-4.40, per car €3.65; Apr-Oct) and an HI **Jugendherberge** (☎ 834 52; Ringstrasse 77; dm €12.20, surcharge for stays under 3 nights €2.20; Apr-Oct). The **Gästehaus Einzinger** (☎ 823 16, fax 823 16-6; Steiner Landstrasse 82, Krems-Stein; s/d €36/52) has romantic, individually designed rooms around a plant-filled sunken courtyard (but precarious stairs).

The boat station (Schiffsstation) is a 20-minute walk west from the train station along Donaulände. Between three and five buses leave daily from outside the train station to Melk (€8.20, 65 minutes). Trains to Vienna (€10.50, one hour) leave regularly.

MELK
☎ 02752 / pop 6500
Featured in the epic medieval German poem Nibelungenlied and Umberto Eco's best-selling novel The Name of the Rose, Melk's impressive Benedictine monastery endures as a Wachau landmark of international acclaim.

Walk straight ahead from the train station along Bahnhofstrasse and turn right into Rathausplatz at the bottom of the hill, following the signs to the **tourist office** (☎ 523 07-410; melk@smaragd.at; Babenbergerstrasse 1; 9am-noon & 2-6pm Mon-Fri, 10am-2pm Sat Apr-Jun, Sep & Oct; 9am-7pm Mon-Sat, 10am-2pm Sun Jul & Aug; closed Nov-Mar).

Overlooking – and dominating – the town is the ornate golden abbey **Stift Melk** (☎ 555-232; www.stiftmelk.at; adult/student under 27 from €6.90/4.10, guided tours €1.60 extra; 9am-6pm May-Sep, 9am-5pm Oct-Apr, guided tours Nov-Mar only). Home to monks since the 11th century, today's building was erected in the 18th century after a devastating fire. It's an elaborate example of baroque architecture, lauded for its imposing marble hall and beautiful library.

The HI **Jugendherberge** (☎ 526 81; fax 542 57; Abt Karl Strasse 42; dm under/over 19s €12.20/15.70, surcharge for stays under 3 nights €2; ☺ Mar-Oct, check-in 5-9pm) To reach this modern hostel, take the second right into Abt Karl Strasse after leaving the train station. School groups often stay.

Gasthof Goldener Stern (☎ 522 14, fax 522 14-4; Sterngasse 17; s/d €22/44, with shower & toilet from €30/60) There are some cheaper 'student' rooms at this otherwise renovated guesthouse. The friendly owners have two dogs.

Camping Melk (sites per adult/tent/car €2.60/2.60 /1.90; ☺ Mar-Oct) On the west bank of the canal that joins the Danube. Reception is in the restaurant.

Boats leave from the canal by Pionierstrasse, 400m behind the monastery. Trains to Vienna Westbahnhof (€12, 70 to 90 minutes) are direct or via St Pölten.

LINZ

☎ 070 / pop 208,000

Poor Linz. Its small old town centre can't compete with Vienna or Salzburg. Its biggest claims to 'fame' are to having been Adolf Hitler's favourite town and having a cake – Linzer Torte – named after it. So it's carved its own niche by building a leading cyber centre and a stunning contemporary art gallery.

Information

INTERNET ACCESS

Ars Electronica Center (☎ 72 72-0; www.aec.at; Hauptstrasse 2; adult/student €6/3, free access; ☺ 9am-5pm Wed & Thu, 9am-9pm Fri, 10am-6pm Sat & Sun) See below for cyber centre review.

Bignet (☎ 7968 2010; Graben 17; per 30 min €3.70; ☺ 10am-midnight)

TOURIST INFORMATION

Tourist office (☎ 707 017-77; www.linz.at; Hauptplatz 1; ☺ 8am-7pm Mon-Fri, 10am-7pm Sat & Sun May-Oct; to 6pm daily Nov-Apr)

Sights & Activities

The **Lentos Kunstmuseum Linz** (☎ 7070 3600; www.lentos.at; Ernst Koref Promenade 1; adult/concession €6.50/4.50; ☺ 10am-6pm Wed-Mon, 10am-8pm Thu) is architecturally eye catching and artistically impressive. Behind its partially reflective glass façade lie works by Klimt, Schiele, Picasso, Matisse, Haring and Warhol.

Strapped to the ceiling in a virtual-reality headset at the **Ars Electronica Center** (☎ 72 72-0; www.aec.at; Hauptstrasse 2; adult/student €6/3; ☺ 9am-5pm Wed & Thu, 9am-9pm Fri, 10am-6pm Sat & Sun); you feel like you're 'flying' over Linz. You can also travel through space and time in the 'Cave' virtual environment or enjoy a drink in the **Sky Loft Media Bar** (☺ closed Sunday).

Linz has several famous festivals; see p96.

Sleeping

Jugendgästehaus (☎ 664 434; fax 664 434-75; Stanglhofweg 3; dm/s/d €15.50/19.58/26.08) In a leafy suburb, this large, modern hostel has dorms with bathroom attached. It's a 10- to 15-minute ride from town on bus No 17, 19 or 27.

Jugendherberge (☎ 782 720; zentral@jutel.at; Kapuzinerstrasse 14; dm under/over 19 €12/15; ☺ closed around Nov-Mar) Dorms in this more centrally located establishment are rather cramped. Reception keeps bewildering hours, so phone ahead.

Wilder Mann (☎ 656 078; wilder-mann@aon.at; Goethestrasse 14; s/d €28/48, with bathroom €35/55) Despite first impressions at this boarding house–style place, the rooms are reasonably comfy and the bathrooms clean. Try to avoid the top floor, where frosted-glass door panels let in hall light.

Camping is southeast of town at **Pichlinger See** (☎ 305 314; Wiener Bundesstrasse 937; per adult/ camp site €4/9.08; ☺ Apr-Oct).

Eating

Mangolds (Hauptplatz 3; salads per 100g from €1.13; ☺ Mon-Sat) This self-serve veggie canteen has lots of salads, accompanied by a daily choice of hot dishes.

Etagen Biesel (Domgasse 8; mains €6.70-12) The large 'thank-you' notes from previous customers immediately convey a lively, friendly atmosphere. Homey Austrian lunches and dinners are served among rustic décor.

Café Traximayr (☎ 773 353; Promenadestrasse 16; ☺ closed Sun) The menu of this elegant coffee house doesn't list Linzer Torte (a nutty sponge filled with strawberry jam), so just ask.

Getting There & Around

Ryanair (www.ryanair.com) flies daily from London Stansted to **Linz airport** (www.flughafen-linz .at). Linz is halfway between Salzburg (€17.70 by train) and Vienna (€23.50), both between 1¼ and two hours away. Trains go every day to Ceský Krumlov in the Czech Republic.

Around the city, it's €0.70 per journey or €3 for a day card. Some bus services stop early evening.

AUSTRIA

THE SOUTH

The two main southern states, Styria (Steiermark) and Carinthia (Kärnten), retain elements of Italian, Slovenian and Hungarian culture – unsurprisingly, as they have historical connections with all three of these countries.

GRAZ

☎ 0316 / pop 225,000

You have to love a city whose emblematic clock tower has its hands on back to front. Graz's jaunty medieval *Uhrturm* perches on Castle Hill above town, with a long hand marking the hours and a shorter minute hand. The mix-up rightly suggests that time is not the most important thing around here.

But alongside its laid-back provincial and university charm, the Styrian capital has an increasingly funky side. That's best demonstrated by its striking, blob-like Kunsthaus (Arts Centre) built during the city's reign as European Capital of Culture in 2003.

Orientation

Tram Nos 3, 6 and 14 run from the train station to the central Hauptplatz. Several streets radiate from this square, including café-lined Sporgasse and the main pedestrian thoroughfare, Herrengasse, which leads to Jakominiplatz, a major transport hub.

GRAZ

0 ——— 200 m
0 ——— 0.1 miles

INFORMATION	
Graz Tourismus	1 B3
Main Post Office	2 B4
Sit 'n Surf	3 C3

SIGHTS & ACTIVITIES	(p83)
Bell Tower	4 B1
Burg	5 C2
Clock Tower	6 B2
Farmers Market	7 D4
Garrison Museum	8 B1
Hofcafé Edegger-Tax	9 B2
Kunsthaus Graz	10 A3
Murinsel	11 A2

Schlossbergbahn	12 B1
Schlossberglift	13 B2
Stadtpfarrkirche	14 C3

EATING	(pp83–4)
Altsteirische Schmankerlstub'n	15 B2
Mangolds	16 A3

DRINKING	(p84)
Glöckl Bräu	17 C3
Parkhouse	18 C2

GETTING INTO TOWN

There's a Ryanair shuttle bus (€2.20, 20 minutes) from the airport to the train station. From here, take tram No 3 (€0.70) to the main square, Hauptplatz.

Information

INTERNET ACCESS

Sit 'n Surf (Hans Sachs Gasse; per 30 min €2.60; ☼ 8am-midnight)

POST

Main post office (Hauptpostamt 8010; Neutorgasse 46; ☼ 7.30am-8pm Mon-Fri, 8am-noon Sat)

TOURIST INFORMATION

Graz Tourismus (☎ 80 75-0; www.graztourismus.at; Herrengasse 16; ☼ 9am-6pm Mon-Sat, 10am-6pm Sun)
Tourist information counter (☎ 80 75-21; Hauptbahnhof; ☼ 8.30am-1pm & 2-5.30pm Mon-Wed & Fri, 8.30am-1pm & 2-6.30pm Thu)

Sights & Activities

Bring your camera; Graz's numerous free sights make it brilliant for those on a tight budget. Climb the 260 steps up the **Schlossberg** (Castle Hill) for an overview of the city and to explore the medieval **clock tower**, **bell tower**, **bastion** and **garrison museum** on top. Alternatively, you can ascend in the glass **Schlossberglift** hewn into the hill or take the **Schlossbergbahn** funicular railway (both €1.60).

From up here you've got great views of the bubble-shaped **Kunsthaus Graz** (☎ 8017 9200; www.kunsthausgraz.at; Lendkai 1; adult/student €6/2.50; ☼ 10am-6pm Tue & Wed, Fri-Sun, 10am-8pm Thu). Locals call this absolutely gob smacking, acrylic-coated modern building a 'friendly alien', but it's also been compared to a mutant bladder, a liver and a whale.

Equally fun is the glass, concrete and steel **Murinsel** (☼ 24hr, café 9am-11pm Sun-Wed, 9am-2am Thu-Sat), an artificial island in the River Mur. Shaped like an open seashell, its outer swirl is an amphitheatre, the inner sanctum a trendy café-bar.

Highlights in the old town centre include the **Burg complex** (Hofgasse); left of the door marked 'Stiege III', there's a **double-winding staircase** resembling a perspective-defying drawing by MC Escher. Take a look at the sculptured wood façade of **Hofcafé Edegger-Tax** (Hofgasse 8). The **Stadtpfarrkirche**

(Herrengasse 23) is (in)famous for the stained-glass window behind the altar depicting Hitler and Mussolini looking on as Jesus is tortured.

Graz's **farmers markets** (Kaiser-Franz-Josef Platz & Lendplatz; ☼ morning Mon-Sat) offer seasonal produce, sometimes including pussy willow and schnapps.

Sleeping

Jugendgästehaus & Jugendhotel (☎ 708 350; jgh .graz@jgh.at; Idlhofgasse 74; hostel dm/d €17/40, hotel d/f €47/80, first night surcharge €3; ☼ reception 7am-10pm Mon-Fri, 7-10am & 5-10pm Sat & Sun; **P** 💻) A deserved winner of a recent 'Best Austrian Hostel' award, this is ultra-modern and comfortable, with *en-suite* bedrooms, and spacious reception and restaurant areas in cheery Mediterranean colours.

Pension Steierstub'n (☎ 716 855; www.pension -graz.at; Lendplatz 8; s/d/tr from €37/66/99; **P**) The friendly young couple who own this Styrian charmer decorate the simple, modern rooms with fresh flowers and fruit – and place pumpkin seeds, rather than chocolates, on your pillow. There's free loan of bicycles.

Camping Central (☎ 378 51 02; fax 697 824; Martinhofstrasse 3; powered camp site for 1/2 people €13/20; ☼ Apr-Nov; 🏊) Beside the tree-shaded, trimmed lawn here there's a huge outdoor swimming pool (with a separate nudists' area). About 6km southwest of the centre, the ground also has excellent shower and laundry facilities. To get there, take bus No 32 from Jakominiplatz.

Also recommended:

Hotel Strasser (☎ 713 977; hotel@clicking.at; Eggenberger Gürtel 11; s/d from €26/42) Older, but spacious rooms.
Pension Jos (☎ 710 505; fax 710 406; Friedhofgasse14; s/d from €30/55) Small rooms decorated in sunny colours.

Eating

Cheap eats are available near the university, especially at the **Mensa Markt** (Schubertstrasse 2-4; menus €3.70-4.30). For an ultra-healthy and reasonably cheap vegetarian buffet, head to **Mangolds** (Griesgasse 11; salad per 100g from €1.05; ☼ 11am-8pm Mon-Fri, 11am-4pm Sat).

Pension Steierstub'n ((☎ 716 855; www.pension -graz.at; Lendplatz 8; mains €5.40-10.40) Those who aren't overnight guests (see above for accommodation review) should still make a detour for Steierstub'n's seasonal, regional specialities. In springtime, try the excellent

AUSTRIA

WHERE'S ARNIE?

Although Graz touts itself as Arnold Schwarzenegger's home town, there's little to commemorate the Californian 'gubernator' here. Two Russian artists have been trying to erect a Terminator statue in the city's Stadtpark. Without that, all that marks the bodybuilder-turned–movie star's existence in Graz is the Arnold Schwarzenegger Sports Stadium (and its paltry Schwarzenegger museum), to the south.

Vogerlsalat (green salad), dressed with egg, potatoes, tomatoes and oil made from pumpkin seeds.

Altsteirische Schmankerlstub'n (☎ 823 211; Sackstrasse 10; mains €7.50-16.50). Tucked down a passageway off Sackstrasse, this rustic place serves Styrian staples, including *Bauernschmaus* (roast pork with blood sausage, sauerkraut and dumplings) and *Ochsenfetzen* (beef strips with sour cream and roast potatoes). Nice, crispy polenta too.

Drinking

Murinsel (☎ 818 669; ♥ café-bar 9am-11pm Sun-Wed, 9am-2am Thu-Sat) With the aqua-blue interior fluorescent-lit at night, this shimmering river island is unique. So ignore the slight yuppie overtones and at least start the evening here. There are some DJ nights.

Parkhouse (☎ 827434; Stadtpark 2) For a less self-conscious vibe, join the friendly student-filled crowd at this atmospheric pavilion in the city park.

Graz's 'Bermudadreieck' (Bermuda Triangle) of drinking places is between Sporgasse, Färbergasse and Stempfergasse. **Glöckl Bräu** (☎ 814 781; Glockenspielplatz 2-3) does good, cheap beer and sausage snacks. There are other clusters of cool bars at the top of Sporgasse and behind the Kunsthaus.

Getting There & Around

Ryanair (www.ryanair.com) flies daily from London Stansted to **Graz airport** (☎ 290 20; www .flughafen-graz.at) daily. Direct IC trains to Vienna's Südbahnhof depart every two hours (€26.90, 2¾ hours). Trains depart every two hours to Salzburg (€36.50, 4¼ hours), either direct or changing at Bischofshofen. Two daily direct trains depart for Ljubljana (€34.30, four hours), and every hour or two

to Budapest via Szentgotthard and Szombathely (€55.20, 6½ hours). Trains to Klagenfurt (€27.70, three hours) go via Bruck an der Mur, roughly every two hours.

Public transport tickets cover trams, buses and transport up the castle hill. Singles/daily passes cost €1.60/3.20.

KLAGENFURT

☎ 0463 / pop 87,000

Klagenfurt's charm doesn't lie in the city itself – which is quite frankly dull – but in its location near the Wörthersee (lake) and the surrounding 'Austrian Riviera'. The capital of Carinthia (Kärnten), is the seat of power of Austria's most controversial politician, right-winger Jörg Haider.

The **tourist office** (☎ 537-22 23; www.info.klagen furt.at; Rathaus, Neuer Platz; ♥ 8am-8pm Mon-Fri, 10am-5pm Sat & Sun May-Sep; 8am-6.30pm Mon-Fri, 10am-3pm Sat & Sun Oct-Apr) is right in the centre, about 1km north of the train station. Walk down Bahnhofstrasse and then turn left into Paradiesergasse, or take Bus No 40, 41 or 42 to Heiligengeistplatz, right by Neuer Platz. For the Wörthersee, take bus No 10, 11, 12, 20, 21 or 22, all of which depart from Heiligengeistplatz.

The **Wörthersee**, 4km west of the centre, is warmed by subterranean thermal springs. In summer, you can swim or go boating. Steamers make circular tours; get details from **STW** (☎ 211 55; schifffahrt@stw.at). The **cycle path** around the lake is one of Austria's Top Ten. Ask at the tourist office for information or check www.austria-tourism.at.

Near the lake is the kitsch **Minimundus** (☎ 211 94-0; Villacher Strasse 241; adult/student €10/8.50; ♥ Apr-Oct), displaying more than 150 scale models of famous buildings.

Hotels downtown are unexpectedly expensive, so budget travellers usually stay near the lake, either at the well-equipped, family-friendly **Camping Strandbad** (☎ 211 69; fax 211 69-93; per adult/camp site €7/4) or the clean, modern **Jugendherberge** (☎ 230 020; jgh.klagenfurt@oejhv .or.at; Neckheimgasse 6; dm €17.50; dm as d €42; ♥ reception 7-11am & 5-10pm; P 🖵). Bus No 12 takes you to the closest stop for the hostel.

Out here, there's a **University Mensa** (Universitätsstrasse 90; mains from €4.20; ♥ 11am-2.30pm Mon-Fri). In town, you can get hot meals from the stalls in the **Benediktinerplatz market** (from €4) or from the brewery **Zum Augustin** (☎ 513 992; Pfarrhofgasse 2; mains €6.20-17.10).

Getting There & Away

Ryanair (www.ryanair.com) flies from London daily. Trains to Graz go via Bruck an der Mur, departing roughly every two hours (€27.70, five hours). Trains to western Austria, Italy and Germany go via Villach, 40 minutes away.

Bus drivers sell single tickets (€1.50). Daily passes cost €3.30. To the airport, take bus No 42. **Zweirad Impulse** (☎ 516 310) hires bikes.

SALZBURG

☎ 0662 / pop 145,000

The joke 'if it's baroque, don't fix it' would make a perfect motto for Salzburg; the picturesque old town nestled below steep hills looks much as it did when Mozart was born here, presenting postcard vistas from every angle. Ornate 17th-century buildings still line the narrow, cobbled streets beneath the landmark fortress, while manicured gardens surround the baroque Schloss Mirabell (Mirabell Palace).

Of course, in more recent times the surrounding hills have been alive to *The Sound of Music*, with movie locations in and around Salzburg, Austria's capital of kitsch.

ORIENTATION

The pedestrianised old town, with most attractions, is south of the River Salzach. On the north bank is the new town plus Mozart's Wohnhaus and Schloss Mirabell.

GETTING INTO TOWN

Bus No 2 goes to Salzburg airport from the train station. It's easy to walk from the train station into town.

INFORMATION
Internet Access

Prices are €1.50 to €1.80 for 10 minutes.
Bignet (☎ 841 470; Judengasse 5-7; ✆ 9am-11pm, 9am-midnight summer)
Cybar (☎ 844 822; Mozartplatz 5; ✆ 9am-10pm)
Piterfun (Ferdinand-Porsche-Strasse 7; ✆ 10am-10pm)

Laundry
Bubble Point Waschsalon (☎ 471 14 84; Karl Wurmb Strasse 2; ✆ 7am-11pm)

Money

There are ATMs around the train station and at the airport.
Train station currency exchange counter (✆ 8.30am-7pm Mon-Fri, 8.30am-2.30pm Sat)

Post
Main post office (Hauptpostamt 5010; Residenzplatz 9; ✆ 7am-7pm Mon-Fri, 8-10am Sat)

Tourist information

Commission for hotel reservations is €2.20, or €4 for three or more people.
Main tourist office (☎ 889 87-330 for information, ☎ 889 87-314 for hotels; www.salzburg.info; Mozartplatz 5; ✆ 9am-6pm May & Jun, Sep & Oct; 9am-7pm Dec, Jul & Aug; 9am-6pm Mon-Sat Nov & Jan-Apr)
Tourist information counter (Platform 2A, main train station; ✆ 9.15am-8pm Opening hours occasionally vary.

SIGHTS & ACTIVITIES

A Unesco World Heritage Site, Salzburg's old town is entrancing both at ground level and from the hills above.

Residenzplatz, with its horse fountain, is a good starting point. Head south to the **Dom** (Cathedral), with its bronze doors symbolising faith, hope and charity. From here, head west along Franziskanergasse and turn left into a courtyard for **St Peterskirche**. Among lovingly tended graves in this abbey's grounds is the entrance to the **Katakomben** (Catacombs; adult/student €1/0.70; ✆ 10.30am-5pm summer, 10.30am-3.30pm winter). The **Stift Nonnberg** (Nonnberg Abbey), where *The Sound of Music* first finds Maria, is back east of the **Festung Hohensalzburg**.

You can also walk along the crest of the hill behind the old town. Climb the steps from Toscanini Hof, behind the **Festival Halls**, or take the **Mönchsberg lift** (one-way/return €1.30/2.60) from Anton Neumayr Platz.

On the north side of the river, follow the stairs from Linzer Gasse 14 to the lookout at the **Kapuzinerkloster** (Capuchin Monastery).

Festung Hohensalzburg

The many archbishop-princes who ruled Salzburg lived in the **fortress** (☎ 842 430-11; www.salzburg-burgen.at; Mönchsberg 34; adult/concession for grounds only €3.60/3, with interiors & audio guide €7.20/6; ✆ 9am-6pm 15 Mar-14 Jun, 9am-7pm 15 Jun-14 Sep, 9am-5pm 15 Sep-14 Mar). The current incarnation dates from 1077 and houses ornate state rooms, torture chambers and museums.

AUSTRIA

AUSTRIA

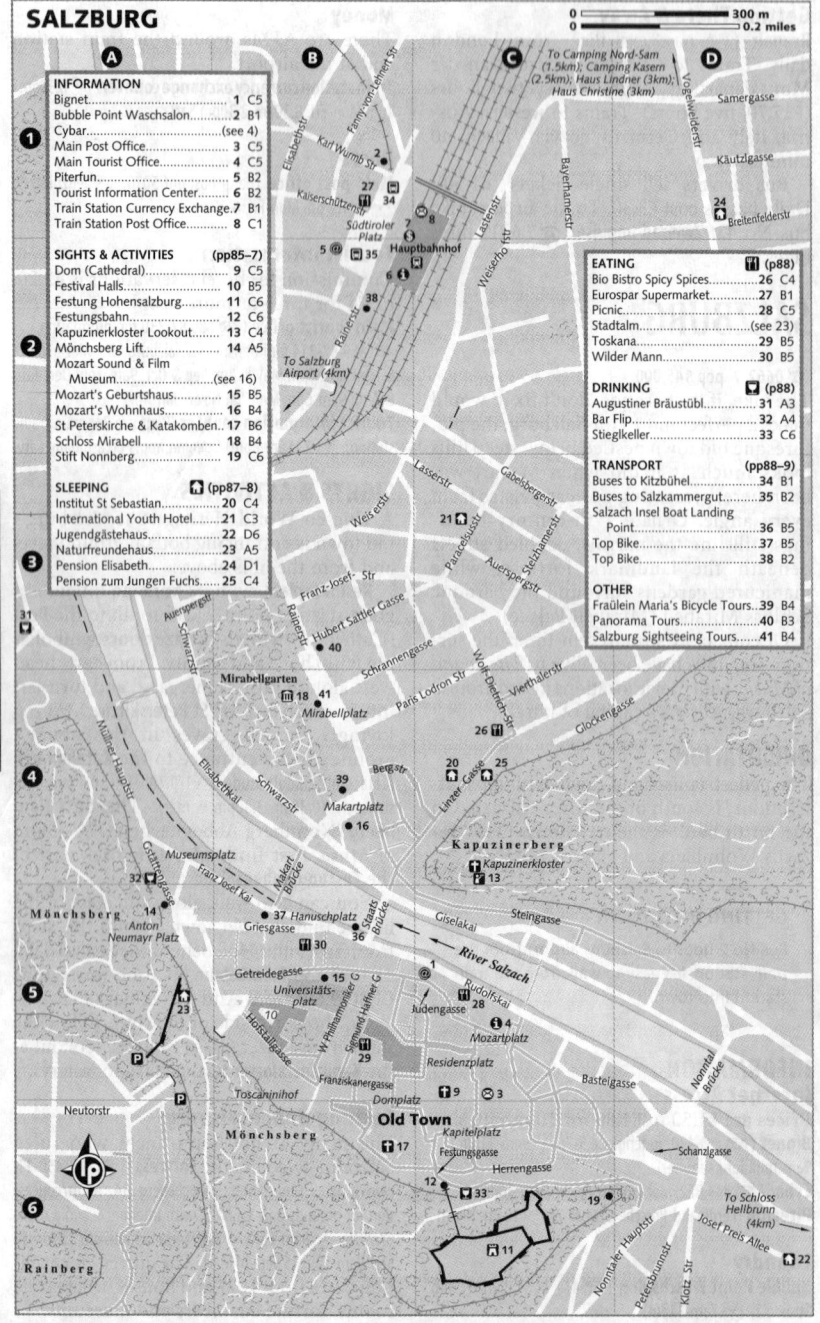

SALZBURG

0 — 300 m
0 — 0.2 miles

INFORMATION
Bignet.. 1 C5
Bubble Point Waschsalon.................. 2 B1
Cybar..(see 4)
Main Post Office.................................. 3 C5
Main Tourist Office............................. 4 C5
Piterfun... 5 B2
Tourist Information Center.................. 6 B2
Train Station Currency Exchange....... 7 B1
Train Station Post Office..................... 8 C1

SIGHTS & ACTIVITIES (pp85–7)
Dom (Cathedral).................................. 9 C5
Festival Halls....................................... 10 B5
Festung Hohensalzburg........................ 11 C6
Festungsbahn...................................... 12 C6
Kapuzinerkloster Lookout................... 13 C4
Mönchsberg Lift.................................. 14 A5
Mozart Sound & Film
   Museum.......................................(see 16)
Mozart's Geburtshaus......................... 15 B5
Mozart's Wohnhaus............................ 16 B4
St Peterskirche & Katakomben.......... 17 B6
Schloss Mirabell.................................. 18 B4
Stift Nonnberg.................................... 19 C6

SLEEPING (pp87–8)
Institut St Sebastian............................ 20 C4
International Youth Hotel..................... 21 C3
Jugendgästehaus................................. 22 D6
Naturfreundehaus............................... 23 A5
Pension Elisabeth................................ 24 D1
Pension zum Jungen Fuchs.................. 25 C4

EATING (p88)
Bio Bistro Spicy Spices......................... 26 C4
Eurospar Supermarket......................... 27 B1
Picnic... 28 C5
Stadtalm.......................................(see 23)
Toskana.. 29 B5
Wilder Mann....................................... 30 B5

DRINKING (p88)
Augustiner Bräustübl.......................... 31 A3
Bar Flip.. 32 A4
Stieglkeller... 33 C6

TRANSPORT (pp88–9)
Buses to Kitzbühel.............................. 34 B1
Buses to Salzkammergut...................... 35 B2
Salzach Insel Boat Landing
   Point.. 36 B5
Top Bike... 37 B5
Top Bike... 38 B2

OTHER
Fraülein Maria's Bicycle Tours............ 39 B4
Panorama Tours.................................. 40 B3
Salzburg Sightseeing Tours................. 41 B4

To Camping Nord-Sam
(1.5km); Camping Kasern
(2.5km); Haus Lindner (3km);
Haus Christine (3km)

It takes 15 minutes to walk up, or catch the funicular **Festungsbahn** (☎ 849 750; Festungsgasse 4; adult/concession one-way, incl admission to fortress grounds €5.60/5; ⓨ 9am-9pm May-Sep, 9am-5pm Oct-Apr).

Schloss Mirabell

The formal gardens, with their tulips, crocuses and Greek statues, are the main drawcard at this palace, built by the prince-archbishop Wolf Dietrich for his mistress in 1606. Standing at their western end and looking east towards the fortress gives you an iconic Salzburg view. Having featured in *The Sound of Music*, the gardens are now popular for weddings and open-air concerts.

Museums

Although Mozart is a major Salzburg attraction, the man himself couldn't wait to leave. Consequently, Mozart's **Geburtshaus** (Birthplace; ☎ 844 313; Getreidegasse 9; adult/concession €5.50/4.50; ⓨ 9am-6pm Sep-Jun, 9am-7pm Jul & Aug, last entry 30 min before closing) and his **Wohnhaus** (Residence; ☎ 874 227-40; Makartplatz 8; admission & ⓨ as for Geburtshaus) only cover his early years before he left town in 1780, aged 24. A combined ticket for both is €9 (concession €7). The more extensive Wohnhaus houses the **Mozart Sound & Film Museum** (admission free).

Ask the tourist office about secondary Salzburg museums.

TOURS
Sound of Music Tours

How much fun you have on these depends on entering into the kitsch, attitude necessary. Tours take three to four hours, mostly in neighbouring Salzkammergut.

Salzburg Sightseeing Tours (☎ 881 616) and **Panorama Tours** (☎ 874 029) both operate from Mirabellplatz, with €33 tours leaving at 9.30am and 2pm daily. Alternatively, you can get a €4 discount by waiting for the tours to pick you up at the HI **Jugendgästehaus** (☎ 842 670-0; jgh.salzburg@jgh.at; Josef Preis Allee 18), reviewed on the right, at 8.45am or 1.30pm; you don't need to be a hostel guest.

Fraülein Maria's Bicycle Tours (☎ 0646-342 6297; tours €16; ⓨ 9.30am mid-May–Sep) leave from the Makartplatz entrance to the Schloss Mirabell gardens, behind Hotel Bristol.

Boat Tours

In summer, **Salzburg Schiffahrt** (☎ 825 769-12) does 40- to 50-minute **round-trip river cruises**

(adult €11) and trips to **Schloss Hellbrunn** (adult €14; ⓨ 12.45pm year-round, 9.30am & 12.30pm Jul & Aug). Boats leave from the city side of the Makart Bridge at the Salzach Insel boat landing.

FESTIVALS & EVENTS

The famous **Salzburg Festival** (www.salzburgfestival.at) of classical music is held from late July to late August. Book online well in advance if you want cheap tickets. In 2006 Salzburg is having a huge bash for the 250th anniversary of Mozart's birth.

SLEEPING
Hostels

Naturfreundehaus (☎ /fax 841 729; Mönchsberg 19; dm €13.50; ⓨ mid-Apr–mid-Oct, 1am curfew) The dorms at this hill-top place are little more than glorified cupboards, but you wake to such amazing views (see p85 for directions on climbing the hill). There's the Stadtalm café here (see p88).

International Youth Hotel (YoHo; ☎ 879 649; www.yoho.at; Paracelsusstrasse 9; dm from €15, s/d/tr €27/40/54, incl 10-min shower daily; P ⌨) This relaxed party hostel boasts cheap beer and regular events, including daily screenings of *The Sound of Music*. But it charges for just about every extra – lockers (€0.50 to €1), breakfast (€1), deposit for sheets (€5) and, yup, even 10 minutes more in the shower (€0.50).

HI Jugendgästehaus (☎ 842 670-0; jgh.salzburg@jgh.at; Josef Preis Allee 18; dm from €13.90, with shower €18, d with facilities €36, surcharge for first night €2.50; ⓨ check-in from 11am, access to rooms from 1pm; P ⌨) This slightly more formal hostel has a bar and meals (€6). Try for a four-bed dorm or budget hotel–style twin on the upper floors; the eight-bed dorms without private facilities below feel a bit like a boarding school's.

Institut St Sebastian (☎ 871 386; www.st-sebastian-salzburg.at; Linzer Gasse 41; dm €17, s/d €29/48, with facilities €33/54) This central student abode has a nice communal feel. The church bells next door can be heard and dorms are a little cramped, but doubles and singles are pleasant and there's a kitchen. Go through the gate marked 'Feuerwache Bruderhof ' on Linzer Gasse.

Homestays

The tourist office doesn't cover the Kasern area, which has the best bargains. Alight at the Salzburg-Maria Plain train station on the main line.

Haus Lindner (☎ 456 681; info@haus-lindner.at; Panoramaweg 5; d/tr €30/45) Akin to staying at a friendly aunt's, this large and popular place has homey, comfortable rooms, serves breakfast and offers kitchen facilities.

Also recommended is **Haus Christine** (☎ 456 773; Panoramaweg 3; s/d/tr €15/30/45).

Hotels & Pensions

Pension Elisabeth (☎ 871 664; Vogelweiderstrasse 52; s/d from €35/42, with facilities from €44/66; **P**) Off the tiled halls and stairs, this small friendly budget hotel boasts well-lit rooms with white duvets, coloured upholstered chairs and wooden floors. Very IKEA. Catch bus No 15 to Breitenfelderstrasse. In July and August, it's 20% extra for single-night stays.

Pension zum Jungen Fuchs (☎ 875 496; Linzer Gasse 54; s/d/tr without breakfast €25.50/33.50/44) The cramped stairwell of this solid if unremarkable budget choice opens out into reasonably sized rooms.

Camping

Just north of the A1 Nord exit is **Camping Kasern** (☎ /fax 450 576; campingkasern@aon.at; Carl Zuckmayer Strasse 4; per adult/car/tent €4.50/3/3; ☯ Apr-Oct). **Camping Nord-Sam** (☎ 660 494; www .camping-nord-sam.com; Samstrasse 22A; per adult/car & tent €5.50/8; ☯ Easter, May-Sep) is slightly closer to town.

EATING

Bio Bistro Spicy Spices (☎ 870 712; Wolf-Dietrich-Strasse 1; mains €5.50) Go through a time warp back to the 1970s, where this compact restaurant serves 'holistic' Indian meals and salads, advertises self-help courses and sells herbal tea.

Picnic (Judengasse 15; mains €4.90-9.50; ☯ closed Tue Oct-Apr) This charming grotto of vintage advertising signs and plastic flowers is great for sandwiches and pizzas and keeps longer hours than most. Give the gratins a miss however.

Wilder Mann (in the passageway off Getreidegasse 20; mains €5.20-12; ☯ Mon-Fri) Traditional Austrian food is served in a friendly, bustling environment here. Tables, both inside and out, are often so packed it's almost impossible not to get chatting with fellow diners.

Stadtalm (☎ 841 729; Mönchsberg 19C; mains €5.50-9.90; ☯ 10am-5pm Tue-Sun Apr-Oct) The meals here are standard Germanic fare – wurst, Wiener schnitzel and *Züricher Geschnetzeltes* (veal in cream sauce) – but the look of the food

is completely overshadowed by fantastic hill-top views.

Some of the cheapest eats are available at the university *Mensa* **Toskana** (Sigmund Haffner Gasse 11; €3.50-4.20; ☯ 8.30am-5pm Mon-Thu, 8.30m-3pm Fri).

There are market stalls and fast-food stands on Universitätsplatz and Kapitelplatz. A **Eurospar supermarket** (☯ Mon-Sat) is opposite the train station.

DRINKING

Augustiner Bräustübl (☎ 431 246; Augustinergasse 4-6; ☯ 3-11pm Mon-Fri, 2.30-11pm Sat & Sun) It's Oktoberfest year-round at this huge hillside warren of beer halls. Well, perhaps it's not always *quite* so boisterous, but the local monks' brew – served in generously sized ceramic mugs – certainly keeps the huge crowd humming.

Stieglkeller (Festungsgasse 10; ☯ 10am-10pm Apr-Oct) Below the fortress, this beer hall's best feature is its terrace overlooking the town.

On weekend evenings, the crowds stream along **Rudolfskai**, Salzburg's most famous stretch of bars, clubs, Irish pubs and discos. However, most punters are barely out of, or still in, their teens.

Bar Flip (☎ 843 643; Gstättengasse 17) This dark, low-ceilinged bar is the popular student option among the small cluster of hip bars around Anton Neumayr Platz. Serving cocktails and cheap beer, it stays open until 4am on weekends (2am other nights).

GETTING THERE & AWAY

The **airport** (☎ 85 80-0; www.salzburg-airport.at) handles flights to European cities, including to London on low-cost **Ryanair** (www.ryanair.com).

Fast trains leave for Vienna (€36.50, 3¼ hours) via Linz each hour. The express service to Klagenfurt (€27.70, three hours) runs via Villach. The quickest way to Innsbruck (€29.50, two hours) is by the 'corridor' train through Germany, via Kufstein. There are regular trains to Munich (€25.80, two hours).

Bus services to the Salzkammergut region leave to the left of the main station exit. Destinations include Bad Ischl (€7.60, 1¾ hours). Other buses, including to Kitzbühel, depart from Südtiroler Platz, across from the train station post office. There are timetable boards at each departure point and a bus information office in the train station.

GETTING AROUND

Bus drivers sell singles for €1.70. Other tickets, including day passes (€3.20), must be bought from the automatic machines at major stops or *Tabak* shops.

Top Bike (☎ 0676-476 7259; www.topbike.at) rents bikes at the Intertreff Café, outside the train station, and on the main city bridge.

AROUND SALZBURG

HELLBRUNN

Ingenious trick fountains are the highlight at the 17th-century **Schloss Hellbrunn** (☎ 820 372-0; www.hellbrunn.at; Fürstenweg 37; adult/student €7.50/5.50; ☼ 9am-4.30pm Apr & Oct, 9am-5.30pm May, Jun & Sep, 9am-10pm Jul & Aug). So expect to get wet! Admission includes a palace tour; other parts of the garden (without fountains) are open year-round and free to visit.

City bus No 55 runs to Hellbrunn from the train station, via Rudolfskai. You can also catch a boat (see p87).

WERFEN

☎ 06468 / pop 3000

The world's largest accessible ice caves, the **Eisriesenwelt Höhle** (Giant Ice Caves; ☎ 56 46; www.eisriesenwelt.at; adult/concession with cable car up €17/15, without cable car €8/7; ☼ 1 May-26 Oct) house elaborate and beautiful ice formations. Take warm clothes as it gets cold during the 75-minute tour.

The **tourist office** (☎ 53 88; www.werfen.at; Markt 24; ☼ 9am-5pm Mon-Fri mid-Aug–mid-July, 9am-7pm Mon-Fri, 5-7pm Sat mid-Jul–mid-Aug) can provide further details.

Werfen can be reached from Salzburg by Hwy 10 or by train (€7.40, 50 minutes). A minibus (return €6.50) from the train station leads to the cave car park, where you can walk to the cable car (return adult/concession €9/8).

SALZKAMMERGUT

The Salzkammergut is Austria's Lakes District. An idyllic spot for hiking, water sports and even wintertime skiing, it boasts salt mines (for which it's named), ice caves, mountains and more than 80 lakes.

Bad Ischl is the region's transport hub, but Hallstatt is its true jewel.

ORIENTATION

Bad Ischl is the Salzkammergut's geographical centre. Hallstatt and the Dachstein ice caves lie to its south on the Hallstätter See (*See* means 'lake'). West of Bad Ischl is the Wolfgangsee, while the Attersee and popular Mondsee lie to the northeast.

INFORMATION

Salzkammergut Touristik (☎ 06132-240 00-0; www.salzkammergut.co.at; Götzstrasse 12, Bad Ischl; ☼ 9am-8pm)

GETTING AROUND

To get onto the regional railway lines through the Salzkammergut, you need to change at Attnang Puchheim on the Salzburg–Linz line. The track then connects Gmunden, Traunkirchen, Ebensee, Bad Ischl, Hallstatt and Obertraun. When you're travelling from a small, unstaffed station (*unbesetzter Bahnhof*), buy your ticket onboard; no surcharge applies.

Buses connect the region's towns and villages, though less frequently on weekends, and passenger boats ply the waters of the Attersee, Traunsee, Mondsee, Hallstätter See and Wolfgangsee.

HALLSTATT

☎ 06134 / pop 1150

There's evidence of human settlement at Hallstatt as long as 4500 years ago – and who wouldn't want to move into such a breathtaking location as early as possible? The village, now a Unesco World Heritage Site and somewhat touristy, clings to a steep mountainside beside a placid lake.

Orientation & Information

Seestrasse is the main street. Turn left from the ferry to reach the **tourist office** (☎ 82 08; hallstatt@inneres-salzkammergut.at; Seestrasse 169; ☼ 9am-noon & 1-5pm Mon-Fri year-round, 10am-5pm Sat May-Oct, 10am-2pm Sun Jul & Aug). The **post office** (Postamt 4830; Seestrasse 160) is around a bend in the road, and changes money.

Sights & Activities

Don't miss the macabre **Beinhaus** (Bone House; admission €1) near the village parish church; it contains rows of decorated skulls from the 15th century and later.

Salt mining was Hallstatt's principal activity for millennia, and a funicular (one-way/

return €5.50/7.50) goes uphill to the **Salzberg-werk** (Saltworks; ☎ 84 00; admission €14; 🕑 9am-4pm late Apr–early Sep, 9am-3.30pm mid-Sep–26 Oct). Near the mine, 2000 graves were discovered, dating from 1000 to 500 BC. There are two scenic hiking trails from here; ask the tourist office for details.

Around the lake at Obertraun are the **Dachstein Riesereishöhle** (Giant Ice Caves; admission €8, with Mammoth Cave €12.30; 🕑 early May–mid-Oct), including the arch-ceilinged, stone Mammoth Cave.

Sleeping & Eating
Some private rooms are only available during July and August; others require a minimum three-night stay. Ask at the tourist office.

For camping, there's **Campingplatz Krausner-Höll** (☎ 83 22; Lahn 201; per adult/tent/car €5.80/3.70 /2.90; 🕑 Apr-Oct). Tax is extra. There are two hostels. **Gasthaus zur Muhle** (☎ /fax 83 18; Kirchenweg 36; dm €15) is on the Hallstatt hillside overlooking the lake. Lots of independent travellers stay here, but with large dorms it is quite basic. The HI **Jugendherberge** (☎ 82 12; Salzbergstrasse 50; dm €15; 🕑 May-Oct, check-in 5-6pm), close to the Lamm bus station, is more expansive, but also usually full with groups in July and August.

Good restaurants include **Bräu Gasthof** (☎ 200 12; Seestrasse 120; mains €7.40-16; 🕑 May-Nov), for typical Austrian food in an old-fashioned atmosphere. Otherwise, try **Grüner Anger** (☎ 83 97; Lahn 10; mains €7-11.50) near the HI hostel.

Getting There & Away
About six buses a day run to/from Bad Ischl. You alight at 'Lahn', just south of the road tunnel. Services finish very early and the last guaranteed departure from Bad Ischl is 4.10pm. There are at least nine train services a day from Bad Ischl (€2.90, 50 minutes). The train station is across the lake from the village, but the ferry captain waits for trains to arrive before making the short crossing (€1.90). Though trains run later, the last ferry departs the train station at 6.30pm (leaving Hallstatt at just after 6pm).

TIROL

Tirol (sometimes spelt Tyrol) presents acres of quintessential Alpine scenery, with huge mountain ranges surrounding Innsbruck

(Tirol's capital), superb ski resorts, the Hohe Tauern National Park and the Grossglockner (3797m), Austria's highest peak.

INNSBRUCK
☎ 0512 / pop 111,000
Nearly everywhere you move in Innsbruck, majestic snowcapped mountains dominate your view. True, when you duck into the narrow, covered streets of the medieval town they sometimes disappear from sight. However, once you've seen the famous Golden Roof and re-emerge, there they are still. It's hard to resist the urge to get up high on an all-day mountainside hike.

Orientation
Innsbruck lies in the valley of the River Inn, scenically squeezed between the northern chain of the Alps and the Tuxer mountain range to the south. The town centre is compact, with the Hauptbahnhof only a 10-minute walk from the pedestrian-only, old town centre (Altstadt).

GETTING INTO TOWN

Bus Nos 600, 630 and 631 (€1.60) leave from outside the airport terminal for the train station and continue downtown to Hauptplatz or Jakominiplatz.

Information
INTERNET ACCESS
Bubble Point Waschsalon (☎ 565 007; www .bubblepoint.com in German; Brixner Strasse 1; per 30 min €1.50) Internet café and laundrette combined.

MONEY
There are various exchange bureaus and ATMS. Beware of the tourist office's hefty commission to exchange money.

POST
Main post office (Hauptpostamt 6010; Maximilianstrasse 2; 🕑 7am-9pm Mon-Fri, 7am-3pm Sat, 8am-7.30pm Sun)
Post office (Postamt 6020; Train station lower concourse; 🕑 7am-7.30pm)

TOURIST INFORMATION
The tourist office's free *Innsbruck Hallo!* has a map and lots of information.
Main tourist office (☎ 598 50 for general information, ☎ 53 56 for tickets & packages, ☎ 562 000-0 for hotel

reservations; www.innsbruck.info; Burggraben 3;
🕙 9am-6pm) Accommodation booking fee €3.
Tourist counter (Train station lower concourse,
🕙 7am-7pm)

Sights & Activities
OLD TOWN
The best thing to do among the warren of
streets and covered walkways in Innsbruck's
medieval town is simply to wander around
and soak up the atmosphere. Most people
usually start at the famous **Goldenes Dachl**
(Golden Roof). Built by Emperor Maximilian
I in the 16th century as a display of wealth, it
comprises 2657 gilded copper tiles.

The other attraction where crowds rightly
congregate is the **Hofkirche** (Imperial Church; ☎ 584

302; Universitätsstrasse 2; adult/student under 27 €2.20/1.45,
admission free Sun & holidays; 🕙 for visits 9am-5pm Mon-
Sat, before 8am, noon-3pm & after 5pm Sun), which
contains Maximilian's 'sarcophagus' (actually empty). You're now forbidden to touch
the 28 giant statues of Habsburgs around the
cask, but numerous inquisitive hands have
already polished parts of the dull bronze,
including Kaiser Rudolf's codpiece!

While in this neighbourhood, have a
wander through the pleasant **Hofgarten** city-
centre park.

Innsbruck offers other museums, but
most are eminently missable. If you're into
sparkle, at least the crystal-encrusted caves
of the **Swarovski Kristallwelten** (☎ 05224-510 80;
www.swarovski.com/kristallwelten; Kristallweltenstrasse 1;

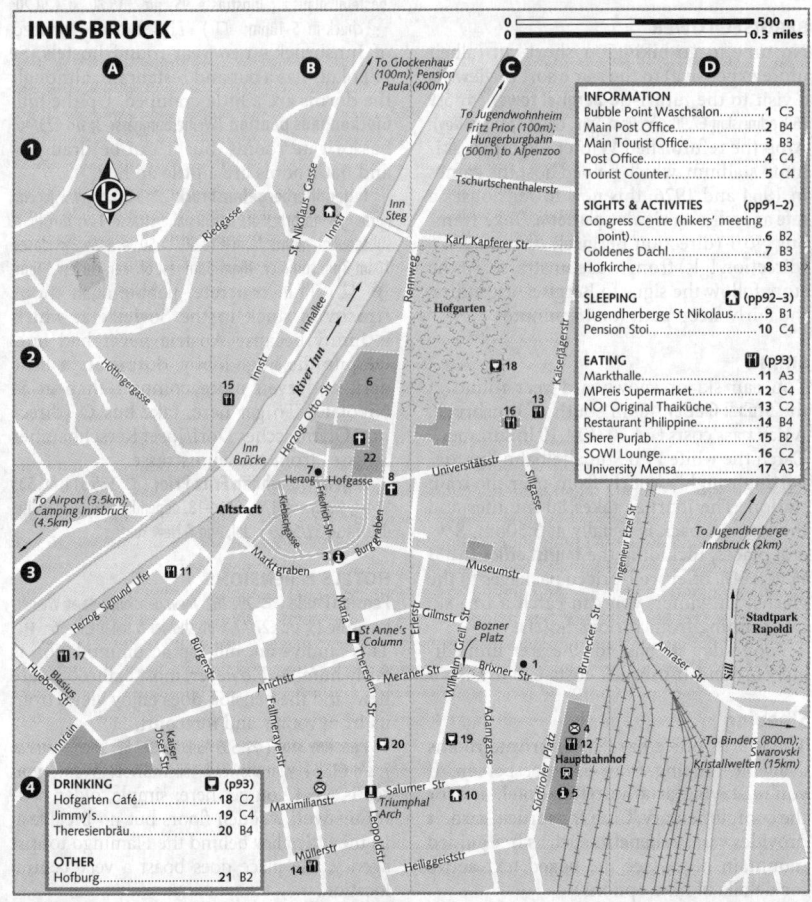

admission €8; ☼ 9am-6pm) are unique. Ask the tourist office to fill you in.

BERGISEL TOWER
No time to go hiking? A short cut (albeit more expensive) to the same sort of views is a visit to the futuristic **Bergisel tower** (☎ 589 259; admission €7.90; ☼ 9am-5pm, closes 6pm Jun-Nov). Atop the refurbished Winter Olympics ski-jump stadium, which helped host the games in 1964 and 1976, this new tower houses a **café** as well as a **viewing platform**. Take tram/bus No 1 (direction Bergisel) or tram No 6 (direction Igls) from Museumstrasse. At the stop, follow the signs to Bergisel, ascending the fairly steep path for 15 minutes.

SKIING
You can ski or snowboard year-round at the **Stubai Glacier** 40km south of Innsbruck. A day pass costs €34.50 (€24.10 in summer). Catch the white IVB Stubaitalbahn bus, departing roughly hourly from near the train station. The journey takes 80 minutes and the last bus back is usually at 5.30pm. Several places, including the **tourist office** (☎ 53 56; tours €49), offer well-priced packages to the glacier. In winter, you can catch a free ski bus running from various hotels.

A one-day ski pass for the area immediately around Innsbruck costs €20 to €26.

Sleeping
The tourist office has lists of private rooms available ranging from €20 per person. If you're staying at a hostel or hotel, ask for the complimentary 'Club Innsbruck' card. It provides various benefits such as free guided mountain hikes (see the boxed text above for details of hike options).

HOSTELS
Jugendherberge St Nikolaus (☎ 286 515; www .hostelnikolaus.at; Innstrasse 95; dm €15.80, d €20.20; ☼ check-in 5-10pm; 🖳) The better located of Innsbruck's two year-round hostels, St Nikolaus has a bar and restaurant, although the dorms are a little cramped. Up the hill, **Glockenhaus pension** (Weiherburggasse 3; s/d €23/46) has private rooms, but it can be draughty and bathrooms are a little ad hoc.

Jugendherberge Innsbruck (☎ 346179; www.jugend herberge-innsbruck.at; Reichenauerstrasse 147; dm first/subsequent nights from €14.50/11.50, d €46; ☼ closed 10am-3pm summer, 10am-5pm rest of year, curfew 11pm; 🅿 🖳) This concrete, pebble-dash monstrosity is stuck in the Soviet era, which is funny because Austria never had one. Despite the huge lobby, dorms are a little dark and even more compact than at St Nikolaus. To get here, take bus O (direction Olympisches Dorf/Josef Kerschbaumer Strasse) from Museumstrasse.

Jugendwohnheim Fritz Prior (☎ 585 814; fax 585 814-4; Rennweg 17B; s €14-18, depending on availability, d/tr/f €36/52/56; ☼ Jul, Aug & New Year)

HOTELS & PENSIONS
Pension Paula (☎ 292 262; www.pensionpaula.at; Weiher-burggasse 15; s/d €27/47, with shower & toilet €34/56; 🅿) This family-run, hill-top accommodation is fairly humble. However, most bathrooms are new, and the pension does enjoy views from its front rooms and forecourt.

Pension Stoi (☎ 585 434; fax 872 82; Salurner Strasse 7; s/d €32/51, with shower & toilet €37/58) What you see is what you get here: simple, older bedrooms with wooden floors but no breakfast. In the little alley behind the Flamingo tourist agency, the place does boast a very central location.

CAMPING

Camping Innsbruck Kranebitten (☎ 284 180; www .campinginnsbruck.com; Kranebitter Allee 214; per adult/ tent/car €5.35/3/3) In an idyllic location, west of town under the mountains, this year-round camping ground has a restaurant, bike rental and shuttle service into town.

Eating

There is an **MPreis Supermarket** (☺ 6am-9pm) in the train station and a large indoor food market by the river in **Markthalle** (Herzog Siegmund Ufer; ☺ Mon-Fri & Sat morning).

University Mensa (Herzog Sigmund Ufer 15; mains €3.90-5; ☺ 11am-2pm Mon-Thu, 11am-1.30pm Fri) The priceless views of the mountains surrounding Innsbruck are the real deal at this otherwise undistinguished student canteen.

SOWI lounge (Universitätsstrasse 15; mains from €3.20-5; ☺ 8am-5pm Mon-Thu, 10am-3pm Fri) Less scenic but with more appetising-looking food than the *Mensa*.

Otherwise, if you're looking for cheap eats, pop across the river to Innstrasse, which is lined with kebab shops, takeaway pizzerias and cut-price Indian restaurants, of which **Shere Purjab** (☎ 282 755; Innstrasse 19; mains €5.45-8.50) is probably the best.

Restaurant Philippine (☎ 589 157; Müllerstrasse 9; daily menus €6.80 & €7.80; ☺ 11.30am-2pm & 6.30-8pm Mon-Sat) Although it touts itself as a veggie outlet, this restaurant also serves fish.

NOI Original Thaiküche (☎ 589 777; Kaiserjäger-strasse 1; mains €4-11; ☺ lunch & dinner Mon-Fri, dinner Sat) Delicious Thai staples such as soups, noodle dishes and curries are served in this small restaurant. In summer, there are lots of outdoor tables with brightly coloured chairs.

Drinking

For further venues, try to pick up a copy of *Innsider*, found in cafés across town.

Jimmy's (☎ 570 473; Wilhelm Greil Strasse 17) Very cool, very industrial looking, Jimmy's is the hub of Innsbruck's hip nightlife. It features lots of metal and exposed stone, and a Buddha on the wall that oversees the proceedings.

Hofgarten Café (☎ 588 871; Rennweg 6A) Under the trees in summer, or in the spacious interior, this café-bar-restaurant in the middle of the palace gardens (despite the misleading address) remains a convivial and atmospheric place to carouse. Drinks are reasonably cheap.

Theresienbräu (☎ 587 580; Maria-Theresien Strasse 53) There's more of a beer barn than beer hall feel to this low-lit place, but the wide range of home-brews still pull the punters in.

Getting There & Away

Austrian Airlines (www.aua.com) has three flights a week from London Gatwick to **Innsbruck airport** (☎ 22 525).

Fast trains depart seven times a day for Bregenz (€25.10, 2¾ hours) and every two hours to Salzburg (€29.50, two hours). Regular express trains head north to Munich (via Kufstein; two hours) and south to Verona (3½ hours). Connections are hourly to Kitzbühel (€12.20, 1¼ hours). Rail-pass holders might need to pay a surcharge for travelling through Italy en route to Lienz. Check before boarding.

Long-distance bus departures were in a state of flux when we visited. Check the board outside the front door of the train station, or ask the tourist office in the train station for directions.

Heading south by car through the Brenner Pass to Italy, you'll hit the A13 toll road (€7.99). Toll-free Hwy 182 follows the same route, although is less scenic.

Getting Around

Single bus tickets cost €1.60; a 24-hour pass is €3.20. To the airport, take bus F, which leaves from opposite the main train station and passes through Maria Theresien Strasse. A taxi costs around €10.

KITZBÜHEL

☎ 05356 / pop 8200

Kitzbühel, a fashionable and prosperous winter resort offering excellent skiing, is renowned for the daring Hahnenkamm downhill ski race in January. In summer, dozens of hiking trails surround the town or you can swim in the Schwarzsee lake.

The **tourist office** (☎ 621 55-0; www.kitzbuehel.com; Hinterstadt 18; ☼ daily high season, Mon-Fri & Sat morning low season) is in the centre, about 1km from the train station (follow the signs). Ask here about homestays or other cheap accommodation, as Kitzbühel's hostel (Hotel Kaiser) now prefers only to take school groups.

Close to the train station is **Pension Hörl** (☎ /fax 631 44; Josef Pirchl Strasse 60; s/d €18/36, with shower & toilet €20/40). It's cheap, friendly and more comfortable than its jumble-sale décor first suggests. Alternatively, you can pitch your tent at **Campingplatz Schwarzsee** (☎ 628 06; Reither Strasse 24; ☼ year-round) by the lake.

Huberbräu Stüberl (☎ 656 77; Vorderstadt 18; mains €6.20-12.50) is a Kitzbühel 'must', although so many diners come for the Austrian food and beer that service can be pretty offhand.

Direct trains to Innsbruck (€12.20, one to two hours, depending on the service) only leave Kitzbühel every two hours or so, but there are hourly services to Wörgl, where you can change for Innsbruck. Trains to Salzburg (€20.80, two hours) leave roughly hourly. Slower trains stop at Kitzbühel-Hahnenkamm, which is closer to the centre than the main Kitzbühel stop.

Getting to Lienz by public transport is awkward. The train is slow and the bus is infrequent (€12.50, two hours). There are four bus departures Monday to Friday and two each on Saturday and Sunday.

LIENZ

☎ 04852 / pop 13,000

With the jagged Dolomite mountain ranges crowding its southern skyline, the capital of East Tirol makes a scenic staging point when travelling through the Hohe Tauern National Park (see following section).

Staff at the **tourist office** (☎ 652 65; www.lienz-tourismus.at; Europaplatz 1; ☼ 8am-6pm Mon-Fri, 9am-noon Sat, also Sun summer & winter high seasons) will find rooms free of charge, or you can use the hotel board (with free telephone) outside.

There is some downhill skiing nearby, but the area is more renowned for its cross-country skiing; Lienz fills up for the annual Dolomitenlauf cross-country skiing race in mid-January.

In summer, hiking is good in the mountains. The cable cars are closed in April, May, October and November.

Lienz has an excellent camping ground, **Comfort-Camping Falken** (☎ 640 22; Eichholz 7; per site with/without electricity €10.50/8, per adult €6; ☼ mid-Dec–Oct). Otherwise, try **Haus Egger** (☎ 720 98; Alleestrasse 33; s/d €14/28) or **Gästehaus Masnata** (☎ 655 36; Drahtzuggasse 4; apt per person around €19-20), both of which allow single-night stays.

There are ADEG supermarkets on Hauptplatz and Tiroler Platz. **Pick Nick Ossi** (☎ 710 91; Europaplatz 2; snacks €3-7) has a range of salads, pizzas and other fast food. There are lots of places to try regional dishes, such as **Adler-stüberl** (☎ 625 50; Andrä Kranz Gasse 5; mains from €7.80), which has daily specials.

Except for the 'corridor' route through Italy to Innsbruck, trains to the rest of Austria connect via Spittal Millstättersee to the east. Trains to Salzburg (€26.90) take at least three hours. Villach, between Spittal and Klagenfurt, is a main junction for rail routes to the south. To head south by car, you must first divert west or east along Hwy 100.

HOHE TAUERN NATIONAL PARK

The largest national park in the Alps (1786 sq km) is a hiking paradise where flora and fauna are protected. The park contains the **Gross-glockner** (3797m), Austria's highest mountain, which towers over the 10km-long Pasterze Glacier. The best viewing point is **Franz Josefs Höhe**, reached from Lienz by bus between mid-June and late September (round-trip fare €10.20, plus a €2.70 toll for the park).

Buses go via Heiligenblut, where there's also a HI **Jugendherberge** (☎ 04824-2259; Hof 36; ☼ mid-Dec–mid-Oct) and other accommodation available.

The **Grossglockner Hochalpenstrasse** (www.grossglockner.at), aka Hwy 107, through the park is considered one of the world's most scenic. The road winds upwards for 2000m past waterfalls, glaciers and Alpine meadows.

VORARLBERG

Vorarlberg is Austria's western panhandle. Angling down from the Alps to the shores of Lake Constance (Bodensee), it provides a convenient gateway to Germany, Liechtenstein or Switzerland.

The Arlberg region, shared by Vorarlberg and neighbouring Tirol, has some of the best skiing in Austria. St Anton am Arlberg is the largest resort. There are good medium to advanced runs here, as well as nursery slopes on Gampen and Kapall. The **tourist office** (☎ 05446-226 90; stantonamarlberg.com), on the main street, has details. Head diagonally left from the train station to find it.

A ski pass valid for St Anton and neighbouring St Christoph Lech, Zürs and Stuben costs €37 for one day and €171 for six.

Accommodation is mainly in a bewildering number of small B&Bs. Many budget places (prices from €29 per person in the winter high season) are booked months or even years in advance.

St Anton is on the main railway route between Bregenz (€14.30) and Innsbruck (€13.10), less than 1½ hours from both. It's close to the eastern entrance of the Arlberg Tunnel, the toll road connecting Vorarlberg and Tirol.

AUSTRIA DIRECTORY

ACCOMMODATION
Reservations are recommended at Christmas, Easter and during summer; they are binding on both sides.

If you pitch a tent outside an established camping ground you need the property owner's approval; on public land it's illegal. Outside Vienna, Tirol and protected areas, free camping is allowed in a campervan, but only if you don't set up equipment outside the van.

Hostels generally cost €13 to €20. If you want a break from dorms, many householders rent out rooms in their home (€15 to €30 per person). Ask the tourist office or look out for *Zimmer frei* (rooms vacant) signs. Prices quoted in this chapter are for the high summer season (or winter in ski resorts) and include all taxes and breakfast, unless otherwise stated.

ACTIVITIES
Austria has some of the world's best skiing and snowboarding, particularly in Tirol and Vorarlberg. Count on spending €20 to €38 for a daily ski pass (to ride the ski lifts). Rental generally starts at €15 for downhill equipment or €13 for cross-country skis; rates drop for multiple days.

Most tourist offices sell maps of hiking routes. Mountain paths have direction indicators and often markers indicating their level of difficulty. Those with a red-white-red marker mean you need sturdy hiking boots and a pole; a blue-white-blue marker indicates the need for mountaineering equipment. The **Austrian Alpine Club** (Österreichischer Alpenverein, ÖAV; ☎ 0512-587 828; office@alpenverein-ibk.at; Wilhelm Greil Strasse 15, A-6010 Innsbruck) maintains a list of alpine huts, for overnight stays.

Cycling is popular. Spas and swimming are too; Austrians will take any opportunity to get their kit off and get back to nature.

BUSINESS HOURS
Shops open 9am to 6pm Monday to Friday, and 9am to 1pm or 5pm on Saturday. However, grocery stores may open at 6am, and other shops don't close their doors until 7.30pm. In smaller cities, there's sometimes a two-hour lunch break.

Banks keep remarkably short hours, usually 9am to 12.30pm and 1.30pm to 3pm Monday to Friday, with 'late' (5.30pm) closing on Thursday.

CLIMATE
For climate description see p1231.

DANGERS & ANNOYANCES
Pickpockets work Vienna's two main train stations and pedestrian centre.

Take care in the mountains; helicopter rescue is expensive unless you are covered by insurance (assuming they find you in the first place).

EMBASSIES & CONSULATES
Embassies & Consulates in Austria
Only embassies (*Botschaften*) and consulates (*Konsulate*) in Vienna issue visas. In an emergency, you may be redirected to a limited-hours consulate in a nearer city.

Australia (Map p76; ☎ 01-506 74-0; www.australian -embassy.at; 04, Mattiellistrasse 2-4)

Canada (Map p76; ☎ 01-531 38-3000; www .kanada.at; 01, Laurenzerberg 2)

Croatia (☎ 01-484 8783-0; 17, Heubergg 10)

Czech Republic (☎ 01-894 3741; 14, Penzingerstrasse 11-13)

France (Map p76; ☎ 01-502 75-0; www .ambafrance-at.org; 04, Technikerstrasse 2)

Germany (Map p76; ☎ 01-711 54-0; 03, Metternichgasse 3)

Hungary (Map p76; ☎ 01-537 80-300; 01, Bankgasse 4-6)

Ireland (Map p76; ☎ 01-715 4246-0; 01, Rotenturmstrasse16-18)

Italy (Map p72; ☎ 01-712 5121-0; 03, Rennweg 27)

Netherlands (Map p76; ☎ 01-589 39; 01, Opernring 5)

New Zealand Honorary consul (☎ 01-318 85 05) Embassy is in Berlin (☎ 030-206 210).

Slovakia (☎ 01-318 9055-200; 19, Armbrustergasse 24)

Slovenia (Map p76; ☎ 01-586 1309; 01, Nibelungengasse 13)

Switzerland (Map p72; ☎ 01-795 05-0; 03, Prinz Eugen Strasse 7)

UK (Map p72; ☎ 01-716 13-0; www.british embassy.at; 03, Jaurèsgasse 12)

USA embassy (☎ 01-313 39-0; www.usembassy.at; 09, Boltzmanngasse 16); consulate (Map pp76; ☎ 512 58 35; 01, Gartenbaupromenade 2) For visas.

Austrian Embassies & Consulates Abroad

For a complete list visit www.ausland soesterreicher.at and click on 'Osterreich-ische Botschaften und Konsulate' under 'Kontakte'. Otherwise, you can contact the following:

Australia (☎ 02-6295 1533; www.austriaemb.org.au; 12 Talbot St, Forrest, ACT 2603)

Canada (☎ 613-789 1444; www.austro.org; 445 Wilbrod St, Ottawa, Ontario K1N 6M7)

France embassy (☎ 01 40 63 30 63; www.aussen ministerium.at/paris; 6 rue Fabert, 75007 Paris); consulate (☎ 01 40 63 30 90; 17 Ave de Villars, 75007 Paris)

Germany (☎ 030-202 870; www.oesterreichische -botschaft.de; Stauffenbergstrasse 1, Berlin D-10785)

Ireland (☎ 01-269 4577; dublin-ob@bmaa.gv.at; 93 Ailesbury Rd, Dublin 4)

Netherlands (☎ 70-324 5470; den-haag-ob@bmaa .gv.at; van Alkemadelaan 342, 2597 AS Den Haag)

New Zealand consulate (☎ 04-499 6393; diessl@ihug .co.nz; Level 2, Willbank House, 587 Willis St, Wellington)

UK (☎ 020-7235 3731; www.austria.org.uk; 18 Belgrave Mews West, London SW1X 8HU)

USA (☎ 202-895 6700; www.austria.org; 3524 Interna-tional Court NW, Washington, DC 20008)

FESTIVALS & EVENTS

The Austrian National Tourist Office web-site (www.austria-tourism.at) displays a comprehensive list, which you can access by clicking on 'Events'. The following are some of Austria's major festivals:

February
Fasching This Shrovetide carnival before Lent involves parties, waltzes and a parade.

May
Festwochen (Vienna) The Vienna Festival focuses on classical musical, theatre and other performing arts.

July
Bregenzer Festspiele (Bregenz) Opera with a difference – performed on a floating stage on Lake Constance.
Pflasterspektakel (Linz) Street performers' festival, especially popular with kids.
Salzburger Festspiele (Salzburg) Austria's leading clas-sical musical festival attracts major stars like Simon Rattle and Placido Domingo.

September
Ars Electronica Festival (Linz) This is a celebration of weird and wonderful technological art and computer music.
Bruckner Festival (Linz) This highbrow classical musical festival pays homage to native Linz son Bruckner.

November
Christmas Markets (particularly Vienna & Salzburg) Quaint stalls selling traditional decorations, foodstuffs, mulled wine and all manner of presents herald the arrival of the festive season.

December
Kaiserball (Vienna) The Imperial Ball kicks off Vienna's three-month season of balls, combining glamour and high society with camp decadence.
Krampus (Innsbruck and elsewhere) St Nicholas, his friend Krampus (Black Peter) and an array of masked creatures cause merriment and mischief, in a parade that harks back to pagan celebrations.

HOLIDAYS
New Year's Day 1 January
Epiphany 6 January
Easter Monday March/April
May Day 1 May
Ascension Five and a half weeks after Easter
Whit Monday Seven weeks after Easter
Corpus Christi 10 days after Whit Monday
Assumption of the Virgin Mary 15 August
National Day 26 October
All Saints' Day 1 November
Immaculate Conception 8 December
Christmas Day 25 December
Boxing Day 26 December

INTERNET RESOURCES

Train times and many fares are available from **Austrian Railways** (Österreiche Bundesbahnen, ÖBB; www.oebb.at). There's a list of cheap uni-versity canteens (*Mensas)*at www.mensen.at (in German).

LANGUAGE

Although they understand 'High' or received German, Austrians use different words and some even speak a dialect. They join their Bavarian cousins in forming the diminutive with 'erl' instead of the northern German 'chen'; when Austrians say *ein Bisserl*, they mean *ein Bisschen* (a little). Some time expressions are unique. *Heuer* means 'this year', and the first calendar month is *Jänner*, not *Januar*.

MONEY

The euro reigns, although you still hear references to its predecessor, the Schilling. Straight conversion of prices from Schilling to euro is the reason still for occasionally strange prices (eg for Post Office phonecards).

An approximate 10% tip is expected in restaurants. Pay it directly to the server; don't leave it on the table.

POST

Typical hours in smaller towns are 8am to noon and 2pm to 6pm Monday to Friday (money exchange to 5pm), and 8am to 11am Saturday, but a few main post offices in big cities are open daily till late, or even 24 hours. Stamps are also available in tobacco *(Tabak)* shops.

Postcards and standard letters (up to 20g) cost €0.55 within Austria and to Europe. Standard letters to other destinations cost €1.25. Heavier letters, up to 50g, can be sent either economy or priority, costing €1/1.10 to Europe and €1.25/1.75 to other destinations.

TELEPHONE

Don't worry if a telephone number you're given has only four digits, as many as nine or somewhere in between. The Austrian system often adds direct-dial (DW) extensions to the main number – after a hyphen. Thus, say ☎ 12 345 is a main number, ☎ 12 345-67 will be an extension, which could be a phone or fax. Mostly, a -0 gives you the switchboard operator.

The minimum tariff in phone boxes is €0.20. Some boxes only accept phonecards *(Telefon-Wertkarte)*, which can be bought from post offices in two denominations: €3.60 (face value €3.63) and €6.90 (face value €7.27).

Mobile phones in Austria operate on GSM 900/1800, which is compatible with other European countries and Australia, but not with the North American GSM 1900 system or the system used in Japan.

VISAS

Visas are not required for EU, US, Canadian, Australian or New Zealand citizens. Many other visitors may stay up to three months (six months for Japanese) without a visa. Most African and Arab nationals usually require a visa. There are no time limits for EU and Swiss nationals, but they should register with the police before taking up residency.

Seasonal work in ski resorts is the most obvious and readily available work option; even for this, non-EU nationals will need their prospective employer to apply for a work permit for them

Belarus Беларусь

HIGHLIGHTS

- **Minsk** Staunch Soviet architecture, eclectic restaurants and cosy cafés – it's communism with a cappuccino (p101)
- **Brest** Mellow pedestrian streets, colourful wooden homes and a WWII memorial of epic proportions (p104)
- **Best journey** Endless pastoral scenes and hobnobbing with natives on the train from Minsk to Brest (p104)

FAST FACTS

- **Area** 207,600 sq km (slightly smaller than the UK)
- **ATMs** At most banks, hotels and train stations
- **Budget** BYR108,000/US$50 per day
- **Capital** Minsk
- **Country Code** ☎ 375, international access code ☎ 8 + 10
- **Famous for** Dictatorial president Aleksandr Lukashenko
- **Head of State** President Aleksandr Lukashenko
- **Languages** Russian, Belarusian
- **Money** Belarusian rouble (A$1 = BR1576, CA$1 = BR1725, €1 = BR2673, ¥100 = BR1955, NZ$1 = BR1468, UK£1 = BR3871, US$1 = BR2175)

- **Phrases** *Dobree dzhen* (hello), *kalee laska* (please), *dzyahkooee* (thanks)
- **Population** 10.3 million
- **Time** GMT/UTC + 2
- **Visas** Most foreigners need a visa; arrange it in advance.

TRAVEL HINTS

Street vendors' fruit and veggies are tastier and cheaper than the shop-bought ones. Mandarins can be especially delicious!

ROAMING BELARUS

Minsk warrants at least two days; if you have a couple of days more, get to Brest to see the WWII memorial.

Typically, visitors to Belarus fall into three categories: people retracing their roots, human-rights workers and Slavophiles. But even if you don't fit into one of those categories, there's nothing stopping you from venturing here, a place unfairly shrouded in mystery and hearsay.

Architecturally, the capital city of Minsk is a testament to Soviet ideology, but it is also surprisingly westernised (and is even beginning to show a bit of a flashy side). And if you're going to see only one Soviet WWII memorial in your life, make it the epic Brest Fortress, only a five-hour train ride from Minsk.

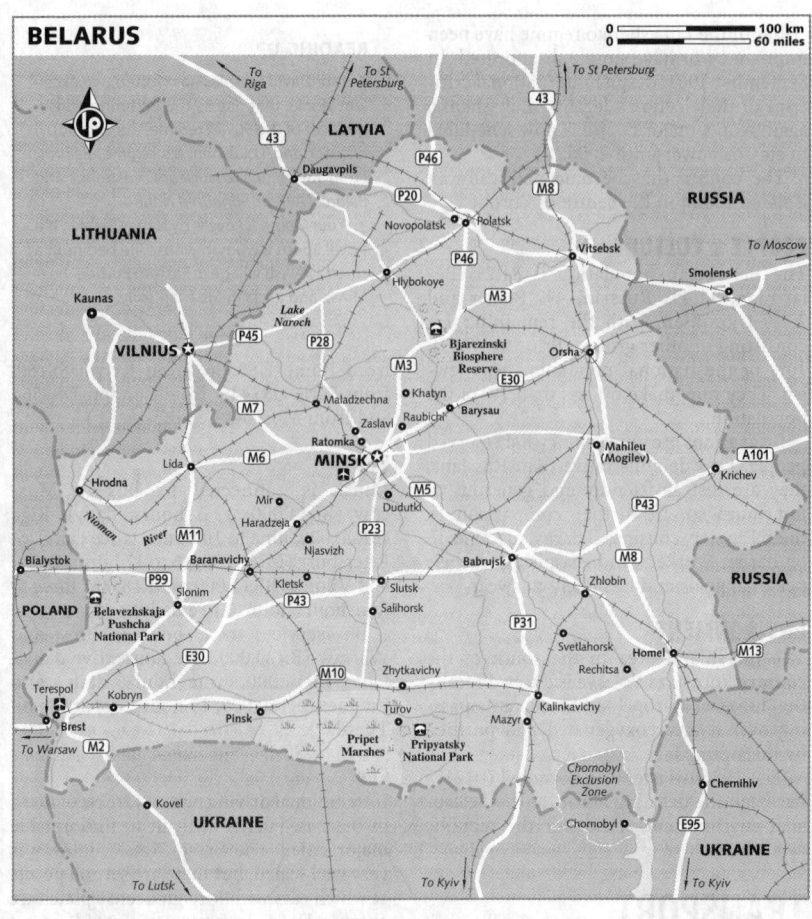

BELARUS

0 ⌷ 100 km
0 ⌷ 60 miles

To Riga
To St Petersburg
To St Petersburg
43
LATVIA
43
P46
Daugavpils
P20
RUSSIA
LITHUANIA
Novopolatsk
Polatsk
M8
P46
Vitsebsk
To Moscow
Kaunas
Hlybokoye
Smolensk
M3
Lake Naroch
P45
P28
Bjarezinski Biosphere Reserve
VILNIUS
M3
Orsha
M7
Maladzechna
Khatyn
E30
Raubichi
Barysau
Zaslaŭ
Ratomka
Mahileu (Mogilev)
A101
Lida
M6
MINSK
Krichev
Hrodna
Mir
M5
Nioman River
Haradzeja
Dudutki
P43
M11
Njasvizh
P23
Babrujsk
M8
Bialystok
Baranavichy
Zhlobin
RUSSIA
P99
Kletsk
Slutsk
POLAND
Slonim
P43
Salihorsk
Belavezhskaja Pushcha National Park
Svetlahorsk
P31
E30
M10
Zhytkavichy
Homel
M13
Terespol
Kobryn
Rechitsa
Brest
Pinsk
Turov
Kalinkavichy
To Warsaw M2
Pripet Marshes
Pripyatsky National Park
Mazyr
Chornobyl Exclusion Zone
Chernihiv
Kovel
UKRAINE
Chornobyl
E95
UKRAINE
To Lutsk
To Kyiv
To Kyiv

Don't make the common mistake of confusing the country's inscrutability with inaccessibility. Getting a visa isn't difficult (just do it in advance), and tourists will be untouched by the current government's repressive ways. Belarusians are delighted and flattered by foreign visitors, and fully deserve their reputation for being warm, interesting, cultured and well-spoken people.

HISTORY

Belarus has had an unhappy history. In the 1930s, under Stalin, Belarus saw purges in which hundreds of thousands were executed. During WWII, Nazi occupation was savage before the Red Army drove the Germans out of the country in 1944, with massive destruction on both sides. At least 25% of the Belarus population died from 1939 to 1945, many of them in the 200-plus concentration camps.

The 1986 disaster at Chornobyl, just over the border in Ukraine, left about a quarter of the country seriously contaminated, and its effects are still felt today.

On 25 August 1991 Belarus declared independence from the USSR. Since 1994, Belarus has been governed by Aleksandr Lukashenko. His leadership has been autocratic and authoritarian, and in 1996 he effectively made the entire government subservient to him. Numerous outspoken critics of the Lukashenko regime have been imprisoned or have simply disappeared. In September 2001, despite international criticism of the election's legality, Lukashenko again won a majority and is now scheduled to stay in power until 2006.

The country has become politically an isolated island in the centre of Europe.

PEOPLE & CULTURE

The Belarusian population is 81.2% Belarusian, 11.4% Russian, 4% Polish and 2.4% Ukrainian, with the remaining 1% consisting of other groups. Prior to WWII, 10% of the national population was Jewish. They now make up less than 1% of the population.

Belarusians are quiet, somewhat reserved people. Less demonstrative than Russians, they are just as friendly and generous, if not more so. In further comparison to their Russian cousins, Belarusians tend to be harder workers, more aspiring in their personal goals and less likely to swear.

ENVIRONMENT

The marshland area in the south of the country known as Polesye is dubbed locally the 'lungs of Europe', as air currents passing over it are reoxygenated and purified by the swamps.

The 1986 disaster at Chornobyl (p1217) has been the defining event for the Belarusian environment, if not for the republic as a whole.

TRANSPORT

GETTING THERE & AWAY

Air

Minsk-2 international airport (☎ 017-279 10 32) is about 40km east of Minsk. **Belavia** (B2; ☎ 017-210 41 00; www.belavia.by; vulitsa Njamiha 14, Minsk), Belarus' national airline, has direct connections to a number of European and US destinations. A return flight to Minsk from Berlin costs US$329, from Warsaw US$185,

from Rome US$396, from Kyiv US$160, from Paris US$445, from London US$564 and from Moscow US$165.

Bus

Minsk is connected by bus to Moscow (BR34,000, 13½ hours, daily), Rīga (BR40,000, nine to 10 hours, twice daily), St Petersburg (BR41,200, 16 to 17 hours, daily) and Vilnius (BR16,000 to BR18,000, three to four hours, four to five daily).

Bus services travel between Brest and Warsaw (BR20,000, five hours, five daily), Lviv (BR14,000, nine hours, daily) and Prague (BR160,000, 15 hours, departing on Tuesday).

Car

International driving permits are recognised in Belarus. Fuel is difficult to find outside major cities. The Brest–Minsk highway is very well sealed, but there are several points at which cars with foreign license plates are charged US$1. In future, this could extend to other highways.

Train

Train ticket prices are listed as *kupeyny/ platskartny* (see p1258). Three to six services a week leave for Berlin (BR224,000, 18 hours), and there are daily departures for Kaliningrad (BR56,000/36,000, 12 hours) and Kyiv (BR45,000/27,000, 12 hours). Other destinations include Lviv (BR43,000/27,000, 13½ hours, three to four weekly), Moscow (BR70,000/45,000, 10 to 11 hours, dozens daily), Prague (BR230,000, 11½ hours, daily), Rīga (BR100,000/70,000, 7½ hours, three to four weekly), St Petersburg (BR78,000/47,000, 16 hours, two to three daily), Vilnius (BR12,000, 4½ hours, daily) and Warsaw (BR90,000, 10 to 11 hours, three daily).

It's also possible to travel by train from Brest to Berlin (BR174,000, nine hours), with between three and six services a week. Brest is also only a train ride from Moscow (BR70,000/45,000, 12 to 15 hours, four daily) and St Petersburg (BR75,000/47,500, 20 hours, daily), Warsaw (BR53,000, three to five hours, twice daily) and Prague (BR191,210, 17½ hours, daily).

GETTING AROUND

Trains between major cities are moderately frequent and inexpensive – and the views are lovely. Buses are cheaper and more frequent though.

Rentals cost US$60 to US$120 a day. For car-rental companies in Minsk, see p104.

Hitching is never entirely safe in any country in the world, and Lonely Planet doesn't recommend it.

MINSK MIHCK

☎ 017 / pop 1.68 million

Belarus President Lukashenko runs a tight ship, and nowhere does it show better than in the capital.

Minsk is a strange city: it's extremely safe, squeaky clean, and super orderly, with none of the *bezobrazie* (gross behaviour) so prevalent in many large Russian and Ukrainian cities. It's the type of city in which you don't have to worry much about tripping over a huge crack in the pavement, getting caught in the crossfire of an old codger's farmer's blow, or becoming instant road kill when crossing a busy street.

In fact, the orderliness is at first refreshing, but it can also be disconcerting (note the ubiquitous police officers). Although democracy is quite suppressed in this country, capitalism isn't as much – which shows in the many Western-style restaurants and shops along the main thoroughfare. Still, for those of you who missed the opportunity to visit the USSR, it's true that Minsk provides a glimpse of what a model Soviet city would have been like.

ORIENTATION

Minsk's (try saying that 10 times fast) main thoroughfare, praspekt Francyska Skaryny,

---

EMERGENCY NUMBERS

- **Ambulance** ☎ 03
- **Fire** ☎ 01
- **Police** ☎ 02

---

extends over 11km from the train station to the outer city limits. After being obliterated during WWII, Minsk was rebuilt in the late 1940s and '50s, making a walk along Skaryny a vivid testament to Stalin's vision of grandeur.

INFORMATION

Hotels and banks have ATMs and currency exchange bureaus (there's a currency exchange at Minsk-2 airport, too). The ATMs at the train station offer US dollars.

Belintourist (☎ 226 98 40; www.belintourist.by; praspekt Masherava 19A; ⏱ 8am-1pm & 2-8pm Mon-Sat, 9am-5pm Sun & holidays) State-run. Good for visa support, advance hotel bookings (with a discount), Minsk and other kinds of tours, and trips to Mir, Njasvizh and Belavezhskaja Pushcha.

Beltelekom (☎ 217 11 05; 6 vulitsa Enhelsa; per hr BR1700 ; ⏱ 24 hr) Fax, phone and Internet.

EcoMedservices (☎ 220 45 81; vulitsa Tolstoho 4; ⏱ 24 hr) One of the only Western-style clinics.

Main Post Office (☎ 227 84 02; praspekt Francyska Skaryny 10; ⏱ 8am-8pm Mon-Fri, 10am-5pm Sat & Sun) Use Express Mail counter inside for faster delivery.

Soyuz Online (☎ 226 02 79; www.soyuzonline.by; vulitsa Krasnaarmejskaja 3; ⏱ 24 hr) Located in the Dom Ofitserov; this Internet café is through the door on the right.

Tsentralnaja Kniharnya (☎ 227 49 19; praspekt Francyska Skaryny 19; ⏱ 10am-8pm Mon-Fri, 10am-6pm Sat) Buy your very own Lukashenko poster at this bookshop.

GETTING INTO TOWN

If you're flying, chances are you'll be arriving at Minsk-2. A 40-minute taxi ride into town runs to US$25, but you'll be lucky to get it for under US$40. There are buses (BR2800, 90 minutes, hourly) that bring you to the central bus station, which is conveniently next to the train station and the ploshcha Nezalezhnastsi metro station. There are also regular minibuses that make the trip in under an hour and cost BR5000. If you arrive by train, you're already in town.

BELARUS

MINSK

0 _____ 1 km
0 _____ 0.5 miles

A   **B**   **C**   **D**

INFORMATION
Belintourist....................................1 A4
Beltelekom....................................2 C5
British Embassy............................3 C5
EcoMedservices...........................4 A6
French Embassy...........................5 B5
German Embassy..........................6 D4
Latvian Consulate.........................7 D3
Lithuanian Consulate....................8 D5
Main Post Office...........................9 B5
Polish Consulate..........................10 B3
Russian Consulate.......................11 A3
Soyuz Online...............................12 C5
Tsentralnaja Kniharnya................13 B5
Ukrainian Embassy & Consulate..14 B3
US Embassy.................................15 B3

SIGHTS & ACTIVITIES   (p103)
Former Residence of Lee Harvey
  Oswald.....................................16 C4

Island of Tears............................17 B4
KGB Headquarters........................18 B5
Museum of the Great Patriotic
  War..19 C5

SLEEPING   (p103)
40 Let Pobedy..............................20 D5
Hotel Express...............................21 B6
Hotel Sputnik...............................22 A6

EATING   (p103)
Express Krynitsa.......................(see 24)
Kafe U Franciska..........................23 B5
Planeta Sushi...............................24 B5
Taj...(see 22)

DRINKING   (p103)
London.....................................(see 24)
Rakovsky Brovar...........................25 B5
Stary Mensk.................................26 B5

ENTERTAINMENT   (p104)
Juravinka....................................27 C4
National Academic Opera & Ballet
  Theatre.....................................28 C4
Theatre Ticket Office....................29 B5

SHOPPING   (p104)
Suvenirnaja Lavka........................30 B4

TRANSPORT   (p104)
Avis...31 B3
Belavia..32 B5
Central Bus Station.......................33 B6
Hertz...34 A3
Train Ticket Office........................35 B5

OTHER
Palats Respubliki (Concert
  Venue).....................................36 C5

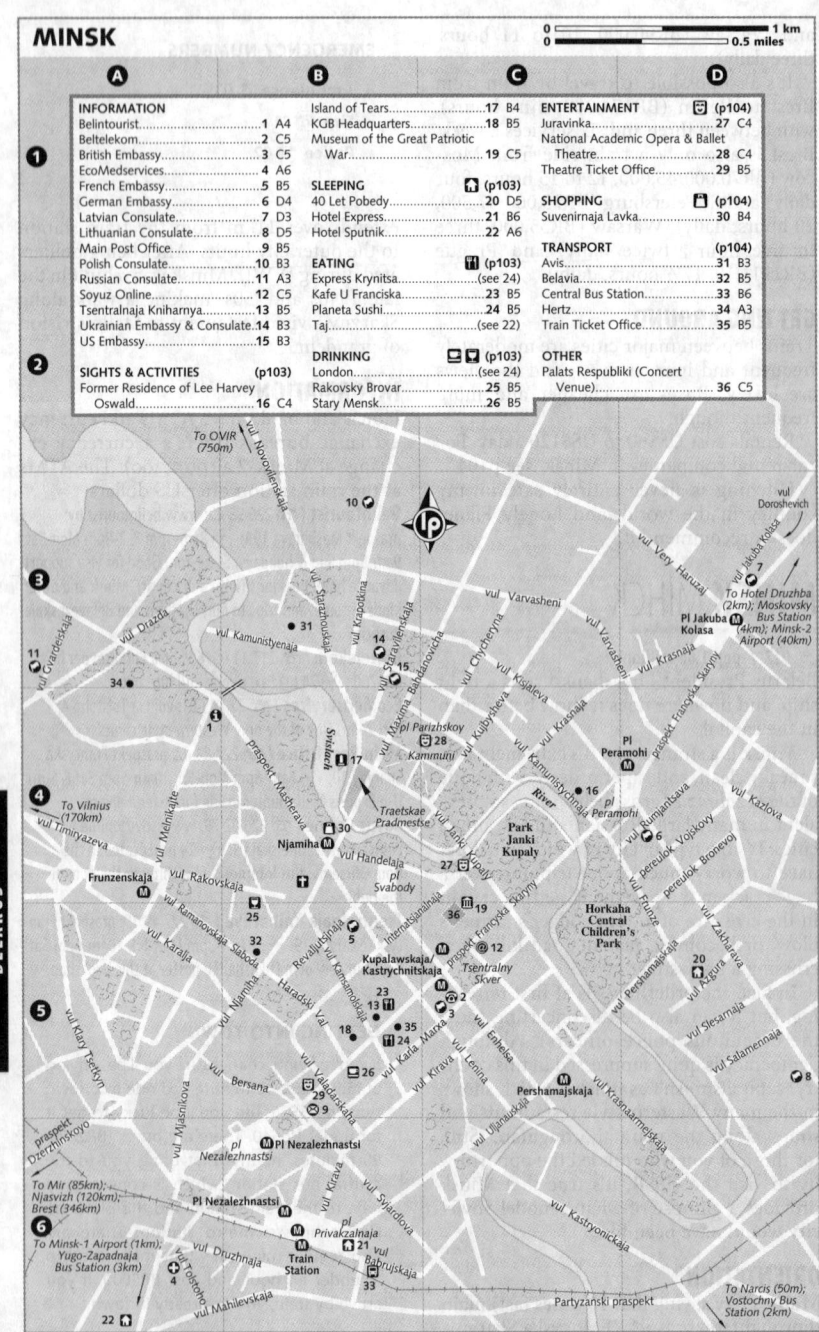

BELARUS

SIGHTS

The **Island of Tears** is an Afghanistan War memorial that's very evocative. On the other side of the bridge is the small 'old town', **Traetskae Pradmestse**. It's not actually old, it's just meant to look that way, but it has some decent restaurants. The **KGB Headquarters** are right on Skaryny (No 17).

Between vulitsa Enhelsa and vulitsa Janki Kupaly is a square that is still referred to by its Russian name, Oktyabrskaya ploshchad. **Palats Respubliki** is a dark, foreboding, newly constructed concert hall.

A fun, cheap way to spend the day is to tour the metro-stations. Get off at each stop and check out the glory of Soviet public transport. Vote on your favourite stations.

The heavy **Museum of the Great Patriotic War** (☎ 277 56 11; praspekt Francyska Skaryny 25A; admission BR3000; ☼ 10am-6pm Tue-Sun) demands time and energy, so be well rested before you visit, but don't miss it. Battle-scene dioramas and photos of death-camp victims and public hangings make the suffering and heroism of Belarus during WWII crystal clear, even though nothing's in English.

SLEEPING

There are no youth hostels in Belarus, and your chances of finding a private room are pretty slim. However, if you're staying a few days, consider renting an apartment (www.belarusrent.com) for just €14 to €55 a day – but it's a good idea to stay in a hotel at least one night for visa registration.

Hotel Sputnik (☎ 229 36 19; fax 207 83 30; vulitsa Brilevskaja 2; s US$26-40, d US$50-60; P) It's a bargain. The lobby is on the grim side, but the rooms are more spacious than in many pricier places. There's also a bonus cheap Indian restaurant with veggie dishes on site (see Taj p103). Bus No 100 (see p104) stops in front.

Inappropriately named alternatives to Hotel Sputnik include the following:

40 Let Pobedy (☎ 236 79 63; fax 236 73 13; vulitsa Azgura 3; s BR81,440, d BR58,330-150,000; P) The name means '40 Years of Victory', but the dingy rooms are nothing to celebrate.

Hotel Druzhba (☎ 226 24 81; vulitsa Tolbukhina 3; metro Park Chaljuskintsau; s & d US$40-50; P) The name means 'Friendship', but reception doesn't know the first thing about the word.

Hotel Express (☎ 225 64 63; ploshcha Privokzalnaja 4; s/d BR135,680/249,000; P) It's conveniently near the train station, but staff aren't in any special hurry to help.

EATING

Food stores are everywhere (look for the sign продукты).

Express Krynitsa (☎ 226 17 08; praspekt Francyska Skaryny 18; mains BR2,000-10,000; ☼ 11am-11pm) Real Soviet cafeteria-style eating – although quite a bit better and more modern than the old-school kind. Plus there are huge windows to sit by for people-watching.

Taj (☎ 229 35 92; vulitsa Brilevskaja 2; mains BR5000-16,000; ☼ 11am-midnight) Thank Krishna for Indian expats. Here, in the lobby of Hotel Sputnik, you'll find a big menu with lots of vegetarian choices, and there's live Indian music and dancing at 8pm. Service and décor are a little uptight, but that doesn't mean you have to be.

Planeta Sushi (☎ 210 56 45; praspekt Francyska Skaryny 18; sushi & mains BR600-104,000; ☼ noon-1am) *Wasabi* (spicy-hot horseradish paste) fans can't (and won't) miss this place, which also has *bento* (set meal in a box) lunches, *gyoza* (dumplings) and teriyaki dishes. A favourite is the salmon avocado roll (BR12,970). Book ahead, especially for weekend dinner.

Kafe U Francyska (☎ 222 48 02; praspekt Francyska Skaryny 19; mains BR10,000-40,000; ☼ 11am-11pm) Possibly the only place in Belarus that has 'tourist trap' written all over it. But there's an effigy of Francyska Skaryny himself to greet you (or scare you) at the bottom of the entry's stairs. Besides, where else can you get a metre of sausage? Or a metre of vodka shots, for that matter?

DRINKING

You'll see people drinking in public, but it's technically not OK, and you don't want to get on the bad side of local authorities.

Rakovsky Brovar (☎ 206 64 04; vulitsa Vitsebskaja 10; ☼ noon-midnight) This two-storey brewery–beer hall is the place to drink, although better and cheaper food can be had elsewhere. There are four house brews ranging from 11% to 13% alcohol, and one nonalcoholic selection (as if you care).

For hip cafés, head to **Stary Mensk** (☎ 289 14 00; praspekt Francyska Skaryny 14; ☼ 10am-11pm), a teeny-weeny enclave right on Skaryny that serves real coffee (no Nescafé, which makes a change in the former Soviet Union!) and some booze. Alternatively, try **London** (☎ 289 15 29; praspekt Francyska Skaryny 18; ☼ 10am-11pm), just like its Stary Mensk sister (same owner) but with a British bent in décor.

BELARUS

QUIRKY MINSK

Just across the bridge over the Svislach River, on the west bank, is the former residence of Lee Harvey Oswald (vulitsa Kamunistychnaja 4; bottom left apartment).

The alleged assassin of the US president John F Kennedy lived here for a couple of years in his early 20s. He arrived in Minsk in January 1960 after leaving the US Marines and defecting to the USSR. Once here, he truly went native: he got a job in a radio factory, married a Minsk woman, had a child and changed his name to Alek. But he returned to the United States and...you know the rest.

ENTERTAINMENT

If you like the performing arts, you're in for a treat. Some of the best ballet in Eastern Europe takes place in Minsk, and for peanuts. This is great for us, but think of what the artists must earn! (NB: The Russian word for artist is *khudozhnik*, from the word *khudo*, which means 'skinny' – ie 'poor').

To buy advance tickets or to find out what's on, head to the **theatre ticket office** (☎ 288 22 63; praspekt Francyska Skaryny 13; ☯ noon-5pm Sun & Mon, 9am-9pm Tue-Sat).

National Academic Opera & Ballet Theatre (☎ 234 06 52; ploshcha Parizhskoy Kamunni 1; BR2000-15,000) Some think the ballet here is better than at the Bolshoi in Moscow. The opera ain't bad either. Ticket prices are tragically low.

Juravinka (☎ 206 69 09; vulitsa Janki Kupaly 25; ☯ 2pm-5am Mon-Fri, 11am-6am Sat & Sun) It's not just a hotel, it's also a bowling alley (eight lanes). Friday is expat night.

SHOPPING

Suvenirnaja Lavka (☎ 234 54 51; vulitsa Maxima Bahdanovicha 9; ☯ 10am-7pm Mon-Fri, 10am-6pm Sat) This souvenir shop stocks straw crafts, wooden boxes and embroidered linens for dear ol' ma. And for pa, there's Belarusian vodka and *belavezhskaja* (a sort of herbal firewater).

GETTING THERE & AWAY
Bus

There is at least one bus daily (BR16,000 to BR19,000, five hours) to Brest. You can buy tickets at the **central bus station** (☎ 227 04 73; vulitsa Bobruiskaja 6; ☯ 5am-1am Mon-Fri, 5am-5pm Sat & Sun), by the train station, for any destination, but find out which of the four bus stations in Minsk you're departing from. Other stations:

Moskovsky (☎ 219 36 27; vulitsa Filimonava 61) Take the metro to Moskovskaja station.

Vostochny (☎ 248 58 21; vulitsa Vaneeva 34) From the train station, take bus 8, or trolleybus 20 or 30 and get off at Avtovokzal Vostochny.

Yugo-Zapadnaja (☎ 226 31 88; vulitsa Zheleznodorozhnaja 41) From the central bus station, take bus 1, 32 or 41 from vulitsa Druzhnaja and get off at Yugo-Zapadnaja Stantsija.

Car

Avis (☎ 234 79 90; belideal@avis.solo.by; vulitsa Staravilenskaja 15) and **Hertz** (☎ /fax 226 73 83; rent-car@mail.ru; vulitsa Masherava 15) both have offices in Minsk.

Train

There are three to four trains to and from Brest daily (*kupeyny/platskartny* BR23,000/17,000, 4½ hours). Tickets can be bought from the **train station** (☎ 005, 071-596 54 10) or the **train ticket office** (☎ 017-225 61 24; praspekt Francyska Skaryny 18; ☯ 9am-8pm Mon-Fri, 9am-7pm Sat & Sun), which sells advance tickets for both domestic and Commonwealth of Independent States (CIS) destinations.

GETTING AROUND

Bus No 100 comes every five to 15 minutes and plies praspekt Francyska Skaryny as far as you need to go. One ride on either the bus or metro costs BR250. Buy a ticket onboard, then punch it at one of the red buttons. Taxis can be hailed from the street by making a gesture as if you're dribbling a basketball (private cars will often stop, which is fine) or you can call a cab (☎ 061 or ☎ 007). State your destination and negotiate a price before getting in. The better your Russian, the better the price – even if you call – so have a local do it for you if you can.

AROUND BELARUS

BREST БРЭСТ
☎ 0162 / pop 300,000

Brest, sitting right next to Poland, is on one of the busiest road and rail border points in Eastern Europe. Aside from its laid-back pace, charming side streets and the friendliness of its locals, Brest will dazzle you with a true wonder of the Soviet era: Brest Fortress, an astounding war memorial.

The city was on the front line when Germany attacked the USSR on 22 June 1941. For its heroic defence, Brest was named one of the Soviet Union's 'Hero Cities' of WWII.

Central Brest is set up in a roughly grid-like formation. South of, and running parallel to, the train tracks is vulitsa Ordzhonikidze, which turns into vulitsa Brestskoy Kreposti as you go west. Further south are the east–west vulitsa Hoholja and praspekt Masherava. The latter runs north of the Mukhavets River and takes you west to the Brest Fortress. Major north–south streets, from west to east, are vulitsas Lenina, Karla Marxa, Kamsamolskaja Savetskaja, and vulitsa Kuybisheva – with vulitsa Savetskaja being the most major.

Information

Maps can be bought at most kiosks. There's an ATM and currency-exchange bureau at the train station.

Belpromstroi (ploshcha Lenina; 🕑 8.30am-7.30pm Mon-Fri, 8.30am-6.30pm Sat, 8.30am-5.30pm Sun) Currency exchange and Western Union; ATM outside near entrance.

Beltelekom (☎ 22 13 15; praspekt Masherava 21; 🕑 24 hr) Internet, phone calls and faxes.

Brest Intourist (☎ 22 19 00; int@brest.by; praspekt Masherava 15; 🕑 9am-6pm Mon-Fri) Staff speak English and can help you get to Belavezhskaja Pushcha.

Brest Fortress

If you are going to see only one Soviet WWII memorial in your life, make it **Brest Fortress** (☎ 20 41 09; praspekt Masherava; admission free; 🕑 8am-midnight). Epic monuments, solemn re-enactments and sombre music over loudspeakers pay tribute to the regiments who defended the fort for an astonishing month when the Germans invaded in 1941. Several museums and the oldest church in the city are inside. It's at the western end of praspekt Masherava, about a 20-minute walk from the centre.

The fascinating **Museum of Confiscated Art** (☎ 20 41 95; vulitsa Lenina 39; admission BR2100; 🕑 10am-5pm Tue-Sun) displays valuable art pieces – mostly breathtaking icons – that were seized by Brest border guards as they were being smuggled out of the country.

Trainspotter or no, you'll get a kick from the **Museum of Railway Technology** (☎ 27 47 64; praspekt Masherava 2; group tours BR20,000; 🕑 9am-5pm Wed-Sun). The price is good for up to 20 people. Even if you don't pay for the tour, you can see some classic choo-choos from the street.

Sleeping & Eating

Vesta Hotel (☎ 23 71 69; fax 23 78 39; vulitsa Krupskoi 16; s/d BR60,000/80,000) Commonly considered the best hotel in town; it's smaller and homier than the rest. You might even forget you're in the former Soviet Union (until you visit the onsite café, which is staffed by lazy men).

Hotel Bug (☎ 23 64 17; vulitsa Lenina 2; s/d BR60,000/100,000) It's named for the nearby river, not for its smaller, six-legged guests (the attached restaurant unfortunately shares the name). It's empty and not great value. On the other hand, it's palatial (if in a slatternly way) and near the train station, and the lobby sports a cool Soviet mural.

Also recommended, but hiding in the guise of unattractive Soviet concrete blocks, are **Hotel Belarus** (☎ 22 16 48; bresttourist@tut.by; vulitsa Shevchenko 6; s €22-26, d €36-41; P) and **Hotel Intourist** (☎ 20 20 82; int@brest.by; praspekt Masherava 15; s/d €21/36; P).

Well worth a splurge is **Jules Verne** (☎ 23 67 17; vulitsa Hoholja 29; mains BR5000-30,000; 🕑 noon-midnight). It's outrageously posh for the relatively humble prices, and the food (many veggie Indian dishes) is delicious.

All the hotels listed above have eateries.

Getting There & Away

Brest's **train station** (☎ 27 32 77) is on vulitsa Ordzhonikidze at the north end of town. There are connections to numerous destinations outside Belarus. From Brest to Minsk there is one service a day (BR17,200/12,500, 4½ to six hours).

The **bus station** (☎ 004 or 23 81 42) has services to Minsk (BR16,000 to BR19,000, five hours, daily).

BELARUS DIRECTORY

ACCOMMODATION

While accommodation standards in Belarus tend to be lower than in the West, they are still generally acceptable. Foreigners are charged more than Belarusians for rooms (as well as museums). Hotels don't have cooking facilities, but some have in-room fridges.

BELARUS

EMBASSIES & CONSULATES

See p107 for visa information.

Embassies & Consulates in Belarus

Embassies and consulates in Minsk.

France (☎ 210 28 68; fax 210 25 48; ploshcha Svabody 11)

Germany (☎ 288 17 52; fax 284 85 52; vulitsa Zakharava 26)

Latvia (☎ /fax 284 74 75; vulitsa Darashevicha 6A)

Lithuania (☎ 285 24 49; fax 234 72 00; vulitsa Zakharava 68)

Poland (☎ 283 23 10; fax 236 49 92; vulitsa Krapotkina 91A)

Russia (☎ 222 49 85; fax 250 36 64; vulitsa Gvardeiskaja 5A)

UK (☎ 210 59 20; vulitsa Karla Marxa 37)

Ukraine (☎ /fax 283 19 58; vulitsa Staravilenskaja 51)

USA (☎ 210 12 83; consularminsk@usembassy.minsk.by; vulitsa Staravilenskaja 46)

Belarusian Embassies & Consulates Abroad

Canada (☎ 613-233-99-94; fax 613-233-85-00; canada@belembassy.org; 130 Albert St, Suite 600, Ontario, K1P 5G4 Ottowa)

France (☎ 01-44 14 69 79; fax 01 44 14 69 70; france@belembassy.org; 38 blvd Suchet, 75016 Paris)

Germany (☎ 030-5 36 35 934; fax 5 36 35 924; info@belarus-botschaft.de; Am Treptower Park 32, 12435 Berlin)

Latvia (☎ 722 2560; fax 732 28 91; latvia@belembassy.org; Jezus baznicas iela 12, Riga 1050)

Lithuania (☎ 370-5 266 22 55; fax 223 33 22; 41 Muitine, Vilnius 2600)

Netherlands (☎ 31 70 363 1566; fax 364 0555; info@witrusland.com; Anna Paulownastraat 34, Den Haag 2518BE)

Poland (☎ 022-617 23 91; fax 617 84 41; poland@belembassy.org; Ul Atenska 67, 03-978 Warsaw)

Russia (☎ 095-924 70 95; fax 928 78 13; Armianansky pereulok 6, 101990 Moscow)

UK (☎ 090-6641 0140; fax 7361 0005; uk@belembassy.org; 6 Kensington Crt, London W8 5DL)

Ukraine (☎ 044-290 02 01; fax 290 34 13; belarus@visti.com; vulitsa Sichnevoho Povstannya 6, 252010 Kyiv)

USA (☎ 202-9861604; fax 986 1805; consular@belarusembassy.org; 1619 New Hampshire Ave NW, Washington, DC 20009)

FESTIVALS & EVENTS

The night of 6 July is a celebration with pagan roots called Kupalye, when young girls gather flowers and throw them into a river as a method of fortune telling. The Minsk Belarusian Musical Autumn in the last 10 days of November is a festival of folk and classical music and dance.

HOLIDAYS

New Year's Day 1 January
Orthodox Christmas 7 January
International Women's Day 8 March
Constitution Day 15 March
Catholic & Orthodox Easter March/April
International Labour Day 1 May
Victory Day 9 May
Independence Day 3 July
Dzyady (Memory) Day 2 November
Anniversary of the October Revolution 7 November
Catholic Christmas 25 December

INTERNET ACCESS

Pay in advance; when you're finished, your change (if any) is given. Access is about BR1700 per hour. Beltelekoms are in just about every city and are open 24 hours. The vast majority of hotels will not have Internet access, so if you are travelling with a laptop computer, make sure you have the necessary equipment to access the Internet from an Internet café. The Internet cafés are very reliable, ubiquitous and very cheap.

LANGUAGE

Belarusian is closely related to both Russian and Ukrainian. Today Russian dominates in nearly all aspects of social life and has been the second official language since 1995. While much of the signage is in Belarusian (street signs, inside train and bus stations, on museum displays), usage is indiscriminate.

MONEY

Belarusian roubles (BR) are also known as *zaichiki*, or 'rabbits', named after the one rouble note first issued in 1992, which featured a leaping rabbit. There is no coinage in Belarus, but notes range from five to 20,000 roubles – quite a span. If you're not confused by the wide variety of bunny money, you will be when you start to look at prices, especially at hotels, when the figures may be given in Belarusian roubles, euros or US dollars. Be prepared to do a little math.

For more information on costs and money, see Costs & Money p28.

POST

The word for post office is *pashtamt*. The best way to mail important, time-sensitive items is with the Express Mail Service (EMS), offered at most main post offices.

Poste restante is available in more expensive hotels in Minsk, and airmail to Western Europe takes about 10 days.

TELEPHONE & FAX

Long-distance calls and faxes can be completed from Beltelekom – most cities have a 24-hour office. To call, pay in advance, go to your assigned booth and hit the ответ button when the person you're calling answers.

To dial within Belarus, dial ☎ 8 (wait for tone) + city code + number. To dial abroad, dial ☎ 8 (wait for tone) + 10 + country code + city code + number. To phone Belarus from abroad, dial ☎ 375, followed by the city code and number.

TOURIST INFORMATION

Tourist offices in Belarus? Forget about it. But that's why you have this book, right? Also, travel agencies, which are abundant, can answer some of your questions.

VISAS

The visa regulations change frequently, so check www.belarusembassy.org for details and updates.

Most foreigners need a visa. Arranging one before you arrive in the country is essential: although you can get a visa at Minsk-2 airport, you will need to show an invitation or proof of a hotel reservation – and still, it's iffy, and not recommended.

There are four types of visas: transit, good for three days; visitor, if your invitation comes from an individual; tourist, issued if you have a hotel reservation; and business, if your invitation is from a business.

Transit visas aren't available at the border; they can be obtained at any Belarusian consulate upon presentation of tickets showing the final destination as outside Belarus. (Note that the possession of a valid Russian visa is not enough to serve as a transit visa for Belarus.) Tourist and visitor visas are issued for 30 days, while business visas are valid for 90 days and can be multi-entry.

Although it's rarely asked for, foreigners must possess medical insurance from a preapproved company. See www.belarus embassy.org for details.

Once you enter Belarus, your visa must be registered; hotels will do this. Keep the small bits of registration papers to show to customs upon departure. In theory, you'll be fined if you don't have them. In practice, these are rarely asked for.

Visitor visas must be registered within three days at **OVIR** (Minsk ☎ 017-288 71 02; vulitsa Orlovskaja 58; ⏲ 2-7pm Tue & Fri, 10am-1pm Wed, 9am-1pm Sat; Brest ☎ 0162-20 54 47; vulitsa Ostrovskaya 12; ⏲ 9am-1pm & 2-6pm Mon-Fri). OVIR is notoriously difficult; consider getting a tourist visa instead of a visitor visa, and register it at a hotel. Theoretically, you can also extend your visa at OVIR, but staff don't seem to know this, so it might be difficult – it could be easier to leave the country and get a new visa.

By far the simplest (but most expensive) way to get a visa is to apply through a travel agency. Alternatively, you can take a faxed confirmation from your hotel to the nearest Belarusian embassy and apply yourself.

These companies offer invitations (tourist and business) and visa advice:
Belarus Rent Service (www.belarusrent.com)
Belarus Tour Service (www.belarustravel.by)
Visa to Russia (www.visatorussia.com)

BELARUS

Belgium

HIGHLIGHTS

- **Brussels** Belgium's capital seduces with Art Nouveau architecture alongside surrealist art, great galleries and pubs galore (p112)
- **Bruges** A quaint medieval city that reels in travellers but is still a must-see (p121)
- **Chocolates** Forget fat, Belgium is praline paradise. The place to start is where it all began – at Neuhaus in Brussels' gorgeous Galeries St Hubert (p113)
- **Best journey** A whirlwind tour of Belgium's best cities including Brussels (p112), Antwerp (p117) and Ghent (p120) – will prime you to come back for more.
- **Off-the-beaten track** The Hautes Fagnes Nature Reserve is as wild and secluded as Belgium gets (p126)

FAST FACTS

- **Area** 30,000 sq km (about one third of Portugal)
- **ATMs** Widespread in the main cities, limited elsewhere
- **Budget** €35-40 per day
- **Capital** Brussels
- **Country codes** ☎ 32, international access code ☎ 00
- **Famous for** chocolate, Bruges and tennis stars Kim Clijsters and Justine Henin-Hardenne
- **Head of State** King Albert II
- **Languages** Flemish, French, German
- **Money** euro (A$1 = 0.58, CA$1 = €0.64, ¥100 = €0.73, NZ$1 = €0.54, UK£ = €1.45, US$1 = €0.81)
- **Phrases** Dag/bonjour (hello in Flemish/French), dag/au revoir (goodbye), dank U/merci (thanks), hoe veel kost het?/c'est combien? (how much is it?)

- **Population** 10.2 million
- **Time** GMT/UTC + 1
- **Visas** The citizens of many countries do not need visas to visit for up to three months.

TRAVEL HINTS

In restaurants, the 'dish of the day' (dagschotel in Flemish/plat du jour in French) is always good value. Train fares are 50% cheaper on weekends. Buy pralines from supermarket delicatessens rather than exclusive chocolateries.

ROAMING BELGIUM

Brussels' Grand Place, central Bruges and Antwerp's historic centre are all musts. Day-trip it to Ypres, then burrow down in the Ardennes.

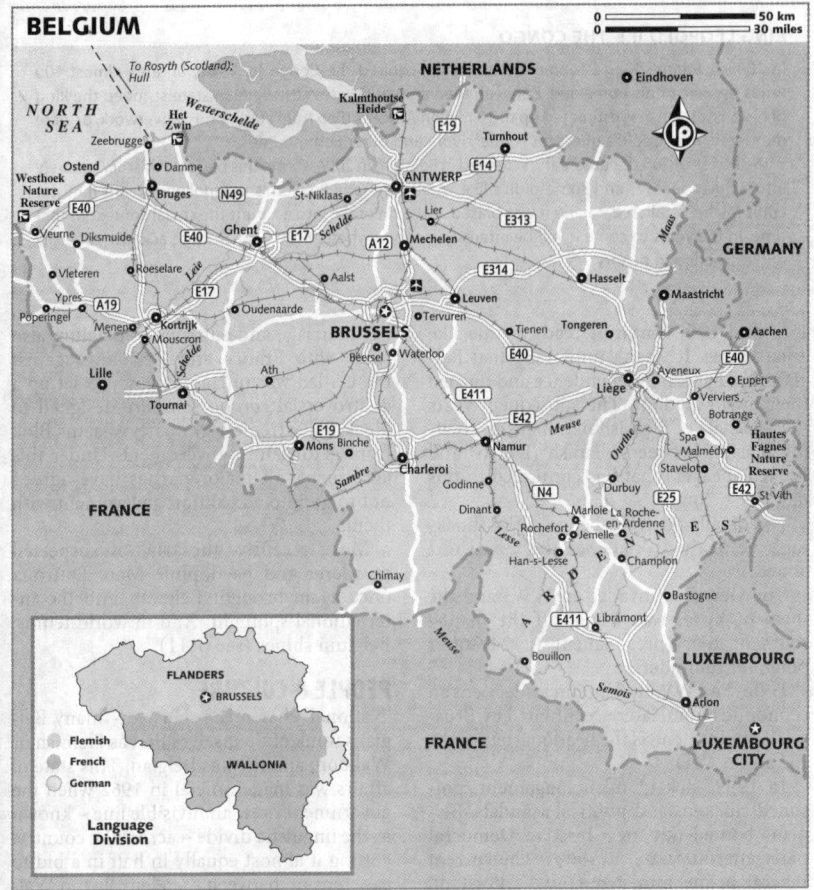

BELGIUM

To Rosyth (Scotland); Hull

NORTH SEA

NETHERLANDS

Eindhoven

Kalmthoutse Heide

Het Zwin

Westerschelde

Zeebrugge

Turnhout

Damme

ANTWERP

Ostend

Westhoek Nature Reserve

Bruges

St-Niklaas

Lier

Veurne Diksmuide

Ghent

Schelde

Mechelen

GERMANY

Roeselare

Aalst

Hasselt

Maastricht

Vleteren

Leuven

Ypres

Oudenaarde

Tervuren

Tienen

Tongeren

Aachen

Poperingel Menen Kortrijk Mouscron

BRUSSELS

Eupen

Lille

Ath

Beersel Waterloo

Liège

Verviers

Tournai

Botrange

FRANCE

Mons Binche

Namur

Spa

Hautes Fagnes Nature Reserve

Charleroi

Godinne

Durbuy

Malmédy

Stavelot

St Vith

Dinant

Rochefort Marloie La Roche-en-Ardenne

Chimay

Han-s-Lesse Jemelle

Champlon

Bastogne

Libramont

LUXEMBOURG

Bouillon

Semois

Arlon

FRANCE

LUXEMBOURG CITY

FLANDERS

BRUSSELS

Flemish
French
German

WALLONIA

Language Division

Belgium's a bizarre little place. Called 'Europe's most eccentric country' in one breath and 'boring' in the next, this is the place to come if you want something a bit offbeat.

Ruled for centuries by ever-changing European powers, België to the Flemish and La Belgique to the nation's French speakers only came into being in 1830. These days it's a bit like a teenager – world weary, unruly and avant-garde all rolled into one.

The country boasts one of Europe's richest art histories. From the passions of the Flemish Primitives to Gothic masterpieces, Art Nouveau jewels and strokes of surrealism, all are fabulously displayed.

To top it off, Belgians have a keen sense of the good things in life; they know how to eat well, they make some of the world's best beers and there's no need to introduce their chocolates.

HISTORY

Bruges, Ghent and Ypres were Belgium's first major cities, booming in the 13th and 14th centuries on the manufacturing and trading of cloth. Their craftspeople established powerful guilds (organisations to stringently control arts and crafts) whose elaborate guildhalls you'll see in many cities – the most famous are those on Brussels' Grand Place (see p113).

Sandwiched between the major European powers, Belgian history between the

KING LÉOPOLD II & THE CONGO

In 1885 Belgium's King Léopold II personally acquired the Congo in Africa, an area almost 100 times the size of his homeland. Between then and 1908, when the Belgian state stripped the king of his possession, it is estimated up to 10 million Africans died from starvation or overwork, or were murdered, in Léopold's quest for rubber, ivory and other commodities.

A BBC television documentary, screened in Belgium in 2004, shone this period of history squarely into Belgian faces – and some didn't like what they saw. Belgium's outspoken foreign minister Louis Michel retaliated, saying it was biased and didn't take into account the social context of that time. In the years to come it will be interesting to see whether the Belgian state acknowledges its darkest period in history.

15th and 19th centuries reads a little like a battle tale. It wasn't until 1830 that Belgians finally won independence and formed their own kingdom. The subsequent years saw the start of Flemish nationalism, creating tension between Flemish (Dutch) and French speakers that has continued to this day (see below).

For details on King Léopold II's shocking rule of the Congo, see the boxed text above.

The Germans invaded in WWI and the town of Ypres was wiped off the map – tours of the Ypres Salient (p124) offer poignant reminders.

Following WWII, Belgium underwent an economic boom, later accentuated by Brussels' appointment as the headquarters of the EU and NATO.

In 1999, sick of mismanagement, poisoned chickens and political scandals, Belgians booted out the Christian Democrat party after 40 years in power. The current Liberal prime minister, Guy Verhofstadt, leads a coalition government noted for robust foreign policies and new moral freedoms: it is the second country in the world (after the Netherlands) to legalise gay marriage and euthanasia. Belgium also sided with France and Germany against the US-led war in Iraq. It has also set up a controversial *cordon sanitaire* designed to block the extreme-right party Vlaams Blok from getting into government. Under this agreement, all major parties have agreed not to go into a coalition government with them.

More recently, the trial of suspected murderer and paedophile Marc Dutroux once again brought Belgium into the international spotlight. And in world tennis, Belgium shines (see p111).

PEOPLE & CULTURE

'National' character is elusive – many Belgians think of themselves first as Flemish or Walloon, and then as Belgian. This state of affairs was made official in 1962 when the government drew an invisible line – known as the linguistic divide – across the country, cutting it almost equally in half in a bid to ease tension between the Flemish and Walloon communities. To the north of the divide lies Flanders (Vlaanderen), whose Flemish speakers make up 60% of the population. South of the divide is Wallonia (La Wallonie), where French-speaking Walloons make up most – but not all – of the remainder. Left is a German-speaking enclave in the far east in an area known as the Eastern Cantons.

On top of all this there's Brussels. The only area in Belgium to be officially bilingual, the capital is predominantly French speaking, lies within Flanders but is governed separately. Brussels' population includes more than 100 nationalities, from Europeans through to Moroccans, Turks and Africans, the latter largely from the former Belgian colony of Congo.

READING UP

King Léopold's Ghost by Adam Hochschild investigates the atrocities committed in the Congo during Léopold II's reign and chronicles the small band of activists who fought his rule. *A Tall Man in a Low Land* is Harry Pearson's tale of family travel in Belgium, spotlighting the country's many idiosyncrasies. Belgium warrants two fun-filled chapters in Bill Bryson's European sojourn, *Neither Here nor There*.

BELGIUM

SPORT

If it wasn't for Kim Clijsters and Justine Henin-Hardenne, there'd be almost nothing to say here. But in 2003, Belgium's tennis aces became the world's top two women tennis players – a feat that no other country, except the USA, has managed.

Cycling is the only other sport to have sprouted an international hero. Grocer's son, Eddy Merckx, is revered as one of the greatest natural cyclists ever, winning the Tour de France five times in the 1960s and '70s.

ARTS

Belgium's rich art heritage began in Bruges in the late Middle Ages with the painters known as the Flemish Primitives. Their works greatly influenced the course of European art and, centuries later, they still astonish viewers. Key players included Jan van Eyck and Hans Memling; their paintings are best viewed at Bruges' Groeningemuseum (p123) and Memlingmuseum (p123), and also at Ghent's St Baafskathedraal (p120).

Antwerp held the cultural high ground during the 17th century, mainly due to Flemish baroque painter Pieter Paul Rubens. His famous altarpieces can be seen in the city's Onze Lieve Vrouwkathedraal (see p117).

Surrealism, a movement that developed in Paris in the 1920s, found fertile ground here. Works by René Magritte and Paul Delvaux are displayed at Brussels' Musées Royaux des Beaux-Arts (p113).

Not to be missed is Brussels' Art Nouveau architecture. Check out the Musée Horta (p113) and the Old England building (p113).

Inspector Maigret fans would know that Belgium celebrated the 100th anniversary of the birth of novelist Georges Simenon in 2003. The following year was the 75th anniversary of the birth of cartoon character Tintin by Georges Remi, aka Hergé.

The country's biggest export to Hollywood is the 'Muscles from Brussels', actor Jean-Claude Van Damme, who debuted in *Bloodsport* (1987) and does time in a Russian prison in his most recent film *In Hell* (2003).

ENVIRONMENT

Belgium's environmental picture is ugly and the scene is not getting rosier – in the 2003

TOP FIVE BELGIUM

- **Festival** 10 Days Off... (p130)
- **Walk** Around Antwerp's historic centre (p117)
- **Club** Fuse + Food club (p116)
- **Impressive sight** Brussels' Grand Place (p113)
- **Shop** Chocolate Shop Neuhaus (p113)

---

national elections, the country's two green parties were catapulted out of government. The only nationally protected reserve is the Hautes Fagnes Nature Reserve (see p126) in Wallonia. Water and noise pollution, urbanisation and waste management are the most pressing environmental issues.

TRANSPORT

GETTING THERE & AWAY

Air

There are two main international airports located in Belgium:

Brussels-Charleroi (☎ 07 125 12 11; www.charleroi-airport.com) Fifty kilometres south of Brussels near Charleroi. Shuttle buses connect the airport with Brussels' Gare du Midi train station.

Brussels National airport (☎ 02 753 42 21, flight information ☎ 0900 70 000; www.brusselsairport.be) Fourteen kilometres northeast of Brussels.

Airlines flying into Belgium include the following:

Aer Lingus (☎ 02 548 98 48; www.airlingus.com)

British Airways (☎ 02 717 32 17; www.britishairways.com)

Ryanair (☎ 0902 88 007; www.ryanair.com)

SN Brussels Airlines (☎ 070 35 11 11; www.flysn.com)

Virgin Express (☎ 070 35 36 37; www.virgin-express.com)

Boat

Hoverspeed (www.hoverspeed.com) runs a bus twice daily between Ostend in Belgium and Calais in France (€16 one-way, 1¼ hours) to connect with its ferry services out of Calais.

Two overnight car ferry services exist: **P&O** (www.poferries.com; Belgium ☎ 02 710 64 44; UK ☎ 0870-520 2020) Sails overnight from Zeebrugge in Belgium to Hull in the UK (14 hours).

BELGIUM

DEPARTURE TAX

Departure tax for airline passengers leaving Belgium is included in the plane ticket. There's no departure tax when leaving by sea.

Superfast Ferries (www.superfast.com; Belgium ☎ 050 25 22 52; UK ☎ 0870-234 08 70) Sails nightly between Zeebrugge in Belgium and Rosyth in Scotland (17½ hours).

Bus

Eurolines (www.eurolines.com; Brussels ☎ 02 274 13 50; Rue du Progrès 80; Antwerp ☎ 03 233 86 62; Van Straelenstraat 8; Ghent ☎ 09 220 90 24; Koningin Elisabethlaan 73; Liège ☎ 04 222 36 18; Rue des Guillemins 94) operates international bus services to and from Belgium. Services from Brussels (with one-way prices listed) include Amsterdam (€15, 3¾ hours, six daily), Frankfurt (€33, 5¼ hours, one daily), London (€42, 8½ hours, six daily) and Paris (€15, 3¾ hours, nine daily).

Car & Motorcycle

The main motorways into Belgium are the E19 from the Netherlands, the E40 from Germany, the E411 from Luxembourg, and the E17 and E19 from France. There are no controls at border crossings on these routes.

Hitching

TaxiStop (☎ 070 22 22 92; www.taxistop.be; Rue du Fossé aux Loups 28, Brussels) is an agency that matches long-distance travellers and drivers headed for the same destination for a reasonable fee.

Train

Eurostar (☎ 02 400 67 31; www.eurostar.com) operates trains between Brussels' Gare du Midi station and London's Waterloo station (2½ hours, 12 daily) through the Eurotunnel.

Thalys (www.thalys.com; ☎ 070 66 77 88) fast trains link various Belgian cities with destinations in France, the Netherlands and Germany. In Brussels, Thalys trains depart only from Gare du Midi. Thalys fares are cheaper on weekends and for trips booked well in advance. People aged 12 to 26 get a 50% discount.

GETTING AROUND
Bicycle

For details on cycling, see p129.

Car & Motorcycle

The **Touring Club de Belgique** (☎ 02 233 22 11; www.touring.be; Rue de la Loi 44, B-1040 Brussels) is Belgium's biggest motoring club. Road rules are easy to understand, though the peculiar give way to the right law takes getting used to. Motorways are toll-free. The speed limit is 50km/h in towns, 90km/h outside towns and 120km/h on motorways. The blood alcohol limit is 0.05%.

Train

Train is the best way to get around. Belgium built Continental Europe's first railway line in the 1830s and has since developed an extremely dense network. Trains are run by the **Belgische Spoorwegen/Société National des Chemins de Fer Belges** (Belgian Railways; ☎ 02 528 28 28; www.nmbs.be, www.sncf.be).

At weekends, return tickets to anywhere within Belgium are 50% cheaper than on weekdays. For day excursions, find discounted packages called B-Excursions. A rail pass to consider is Go Pass (€41.50), which gives 10 one-way trips anywhere in Belgium for under 26ers.

BRUSSELS (BRUSSEL, BRUXELLES)

pop 992,000

It's hard to fathom how Brussels got labelled 'boring'. In a city where fine food is mandatory, café culture common, Art Nouveau architecture prolific and the bizarre and surreal comfortably at home, how did anyone find it dull? It's true that for a long time Brussels didn't go out of its way to impress – it was, and still is, a secretive city.

ORIENTATION

The Grand Place, Brussels' imposing 15th-century market square, sits dead centre in the Petit Ring, a pentagon of boulevards enclosing central Brussels. The centre is divided into the Lower Town, comprising the medieval core and atmospheric quarters such as Ste Catherine, St Géry and the Marolles; and the Upper Town, home to major museums and chic shopping precincts based around the Sablon and Ave Louise. East of the Petit Ring is the EU's real-life Gotham City.

BELGIUM

INFORMATION

Internet Access

Concepts Telecom (inside Gare du Midi; Ave Fonsny; metro Gare du Midi; per hr €2; ☺ 9am-8.30pm Mon-Fri, 10am-7.30pm Sat)

Medical Services

Helpline (☎ 02 648 40 14) 24-hour assistance line run by Community Help Service.

Hôpital St Pierre (☎ 02 535 31 11, emergency ☎ 02 535 40 51; cnr Rue Haute & Rue de l'Abricotier; metro Porte de Hal) Central hospital offering 24-hour emergency assistance.

Money

Fortis Banque (☎ 02 289 05 70; Rue de la Colline 12; metro Gare Centrale; ☺ 9am-12.30pm & 1.30-4pm Mon-Fri) Just off the Grand Place; has a handy ATM.

Post

Main post office (☎ 02 226 21 11; 1st Fl, Centre Monnaie, Pl de la Monnaie; metro De Brouckère; ☺ 8am-6pm Mon-Fri, 9.30am-3pm Sat)

Tourist Offices

Belgian Tourist Information Centre (☎ 02 504 03 90; www.visitflanders.com, www.belgique-tourisme .net; Rue du Marché aux Herbes 63; metro Gare Centrale; ☺ 9am-6pm or 7pm Mon-Fri, 9am-1pm & 2-7pm Sat & Sun May-Oct, 9am-6pm Mon-Fri, 9am-1pm & 2-6pm Sat, 9am-1pm Sun Nov-Apr) Supplies national tourist information.

Brussels International (☎ 02 513 89 40; www.brus selsinternational.be; Grand Place; metro Gare Centrale; ☺ 9am-6pm Easter-Oct, 9am-6pm Mon-Sat, 10am-2pm Sun Nov-Dec, 9am-6pm Mon-Sat Jan-Easter) The city of Brussels tourist office is inside the town hall and usually crammed.

SIGHTS

Brussels' magnificent central square, **Grand Place**, tops the itinerary. Here the splendid Gothic-style **Hôtel de Ville** was the only building to escape bombardment by the French in 1695 – ironic considering that it was the target. The square's splendour is due largely to its antique frame of **guildhalls**.

Galeries St Hubert (Rue du Marché aux Herbes; metro Gare Centrale), one block northeast of the Grand Place, is a European first and a must visit. Opened in 1847, this *grande dame* of Brussels' shopping arcades contains an eclectic mix of cafés and traders including **Neuhaus** (☎ 02 512 63 59; Galerie de la Reine 25; metro Gare Centrale), a gorgeous chocolate shop

established in 1857 (it was thanks to Neuhaus' grandson that pralines were invented). Off one of the arcades is **Rue des Bouchers**, the capital's famous dining street – worth a wander if you're into dancing lobsters.

The **Musées Royaux des Beaux-Arts** (☎ 02 508 32 11; www.fine-arts-museum.be; Rue de la Régence 3; metro Gare Centrale; adult/concession €5/3.50; ☺ 10am-5pm Tue-Sun) houses Belgium's premier collections of ancient and modern art; walk up from the Lower Town.

The nearby **Musée des Instruments de Musique** (☎ 02 545 01 53; www.mim.fgov.be; Montagne de la Cour 2; metro Gare Centrale; adult/concession €5/3.50; ☺ 9.30am-5pm Tue, Wed & Fri, 9.30am-8pm Thu, 10am-5pm Sat & Sun) boasts one of the world's biggest collections of musical instruments. It's housed in the **Old England building**, an Art Nouveau showpiece and worth a look in itself.

A superb introduction to Art Nouveau is the **Musée Horta** (☎ 02 543 04 90; www.horta museum.be; Rue Américaine 25; metro Horta; admission €5; ☺ 2-5.30pm Tue-Sun). It occupies two adjoining houses in St Gilles that Horta designed in 1898. To get there take tram No

---

GETTING INTO TOWN

From Brussels National airport, take the Airport City Express train to Gare Centrale (€3, 20 minutes), Brussels' most central train station, from where it's five minutes by hoof to the Grand Place.

Travellers on Eurostar and Thalys trains arrive at Gare du Midi, 2.5km south of the Grand Place. You do not need to buy another train ticket to journey onto Gare Centrale – simply hop on a local train.

Eurolines buses deposit travellers at Gare du Nord, 1.5km north of the Grand Place; walk into town via Rue Neuve, or jump on a train to Gare Centrale.

BELGIUM

BRUSSELS

0 _____ 1 km
0 _____ 0.5 miles

Rue L Lepage
Rue du Rouleau
Place du Béguinage
Ste Catherine
Ste Catherine 24
Rue de Flandre
Rue de la Braie
Place de Brouckère
Rue Neuve
To Eurolines (600m); Gare du Nord 19
Rue des Sables 10
Blvd Pachéco
Botanique
Place Quetelet
To Centre Vincent Van Gogh (100m) 16
To Atomium (5.2km)
Rue Royale
Bisschofsheim
Place du Samedi
De Brouckère 38
7
Blvd de Berlaimont
Rue du Bois Sauvage
Rue de Ligne
Nord Rue du
To (Brussels National) Airport (14km)
Fleurs
St Géry
Rue des 6 Jetons
Bourse
Îlot Sacré
Place et Parvis Ste-Gudule
Saints Michel & Gudule Cathedral
Rue de Louvain
Rue du Congrès 32
Rue de l'Enseignement
Madou
Rue de la Croix de Fer
Blvd Maurice Lemonnier
Rue Ducale
Rue Hamer
Place Fontainas
See Enlargement
Gare Centrale
Gare Centrale
Rue Royale
Rue de la Loi
Parc
Rue Joseph II
Arts-Loi
Ave des Arts
5
Anneessens
Rue Terre Neuve
Rue du Poinçon
Place de la Vieille Halle aux Blés
Place de l'Albertine
Mont des Arts
Blvd de l'Empereur
Place de la Justice
Parc de Bruxelles
Rue Ducale
Blvd du Régent
9
1
Rue Guimard
To Musée Bruxellois de la Gueuze (400m)
Rue des Ursulines
Place de Dinant
17
Place de la Chapelle
Place du Grand Sablon
Sablon
14
15
Place des Palais
Palais Royal
Ave des Arts
Rue du Commerce
Rue de l'Industrie
Rue Montoyer
Square de Meeûs
8
To Eurolines (400m); Gare du Midi (500m)
Rue St-Ghislain
Rue des
Marolles
18
Place du Jeu de Balle
Rue Blaes
Square P Breughel
Place Poelaert
Rue Haute
26
Rue Ernest Allard
Rue de la Régence
Rue Bréderode
Place du Trône
Trône
Rue de Namur
Porte de Namur
Upper Town
Rue du Champ de Mars
Blvd de Waterloo
Rue Caroly
Rue du Luxembourg
Rue Blaes
Rue des Renards
Rue de Abricotier
6
Palais de Justice
Jardin d'Egmont
Ave de la Toison d'Or
Rue du Trône
Rue Londres
Rue Dublin
30
Rue Haute
Rue aux Laines
Place J Jacobs
Place Louise
Louise
To Café Belga (1km)
Rue E Solvay
25
Matonge
20
36
To Musée Horta (1.2km)
Place de la Monnaie
Rue de la Reine
Rue de l'Écuyer
Porte de Hal
Blvd de Waterloo
Ave de la Toison d'Or
Hôtel des Monnaies
Place J Dillens
Rue de l'Hôtel des Monnaies
21
Rue du Marché aux Poulets
Rue du Pont Devyn
Place de la Bourse
R Auguste Orts
Rue Crétyn
Impasse des Cadeaux
28
Galerie des Princes
Place de la Victoire
Place St-Géry
Rue J Van Praet
Bourse
Rue de la Bourse
Bourse
Rue Henry Maus
Rue au Beurre
Îlot Sacré
Galerie du Roi
27
35
37
11
Rue St-Géry
34
29
Rue des Pierres
Rue du Tabora
23
Rue du Marché aux Herbes
2
Horta
Rue de la Victoire
Rue des Teinturiers
Rue des Chartreux
Grand Place
3
12
4
Rue de la Colline
Blvd Anspach
33
Rue du Marché-au-Charbon
Rue du Midi
Rue des Brasseurs
Rue Charles Buls
22
Carr de l'Europe
Rue de Savoie
Rue de la Violette
Rue de l'Étuve
13
31
La Chapelle de la Madeleine

BELGIUM

91 or 92 from Place Louise in the Upper Town (metro Place Louise). The museum is 2.5km from the Grand Place.

Dedicated beer buffs must not miss the excellent **Musée Bruxellois de la Gueuze** (☎ 02 521 49 28; www.cantillon.be; Rue Gheude 56; metro Gare du Midi; adult/concession €3.50/3; ⌚ 9am-5pm Mon-Fri, 10am-5pm Sat), a working brewery located just a 10 to 15 minutes' stroll from Gare du Midi.

The **Centre Belge de la Bande Dessinée** (☎ 02 219 19 80; www.cbbd.be; Rue des Sables 20; metro Gare Centrale; adult/concession €6.20/5; ⌚ 10am-6pm Tue-Sun) tours the country's vibrant comic-strip culture. It's a 10-minute walk northeast from the Grand Place.

Two national symbols to consider viewing are the **Manneken Pis fountain** (cnr Rue de l'Étuve & Rue du Chêne; metro Gare Centrale) near the Grand Place, and the **Atomium** (☎ 02 475 47 77; Blvd du Centenaire; adult/concession €6/4.50; ⌚ 9am-7pm Jul-Aug, 10am-5pm Sep-Jun), a space-age leftover from the 1958 World Fair. Take the metro to Heysel or, more scenically, tram No 81 from *premetro* (a tram that runs underground for part of its journey) station De Brouckère.

SLEEPING

Brussels has all bases covered where sleeping is concerned.

Centre Vincent Van Gogh (☎ 02 217 01 58; chab@ ping.be; Rue Traversière 8; dm/s/tw €12/26.50/40, bedsheets €3.75; ✕ 🖳) This is Brussels' grooviest hostel and has clean, basic rooms and laid-back vibes but it's strictly for 17 to 35ers only. Some double rooms have private bathrooms (at no extra cost). It's 1.2km uphill from Gare Centrale or take the metro to Botanique.

Sleep Well (☎ 02 218 50 50; www.sleepwell.be; Rue du Damier 23; metro Rogier; dm/s/d/tr €15.75/26.50/48/64;

✕ 🖳) It's a bright, modern hostel-cum-hotel that's close to brash Rue Neuve, Brussels' pedestrianised shopping street. The central location makes it an excellent base for those wanting to pub crawl the night away.

Hôtel Galia (☎ 02 502 42 43; www.hotelgalia.com; Place du Jeu-de-Balle 15; metro Gare du Midi; s/d/tr €60/65/70; ✕) A no-frills hotel located on this famous bric-a-brac market square in the Marolles quarter, about 1.3km south of the Grand Place. The rooms are a decent size, and each has a tiny shower/toilet closet. Handy to plenty of cafés.

B&B Phileas Fogg (☎ 02 217 83 38; www.phileas fogg.be; Rue Van Bemmel 6; s/d/tr/f €75/85/100/120; ✕) Exotic B&B run by an exuberant young mother and avid traveller. All the rooms have bathrooms, though two share a toilet. The Blue room is a favourite. It's in St Josse; metro Madou is 400m away.

Beersel Camping (☎ 02 331 05 61; campingbeer sel@pandora.be; Steenweg op Ukkel 75; per adult/tent/car €3/2/1.35; ⌚ all year) Small ground south of Brussels in Beersel. Tram No 55 (direction Uccle) stops 3km away, from where you take bus UB (direction Halle).

Also recommended is **Breughel** (☎ 02 511 04 36; www.vjh.be; Rue du St Esprit 2; metro Gare Centrale; dm/s/d €16.75/25/40; ✕ 🖳), the most central of Brussels' three Hostelling International (HI) hostels, you'll find it on the edge of the Marolles.

EATING

As the capital of a nation of foodies, Brussels is over-endowed with quality eateries.

Taverne du Passage (☎ 02 512 37 31; Galerie de la Reine 30; metro Gare Centrale; mains €12-20; ⌚ noon-midnight Aug-May, closed Wed & Thu Jun-Jul) Consistently keen service and faithful Belgian meals are the pivotal points of this Brussels

BELGIUM

institution. Located in Galeries St Hubert, stepping through the draped doorway is like zapping away a century.

Le Perroquet (☎ 02 512 99 22; Rue Watteeu 31; metro Louise; light meals €8-10; 🕙 noon-1am) This Art Nouveau café in affluent Sablon makes a great pit stop after the nearby Musées Royaux des Beaux-Arts. Salads and stuffed pitas, including vegetarian options, are the mainstay.

L'Ultime Atome (☎ 02 513 48 84; Rue St Boniface 14; metro Porte de Namur; mains €9-16; 🕙 noon-midnight) This brasserie is one of a handful of great eateries on this Ixelles backstreet. The atmosphere hums.

Jacques (☎ 02 513 27 62; Quai aux Briques 44; metro Ste Catherine; mains €14-23; 🕙 lunch & dinner, closed Sun) One of many seafood restaurants in Ste Catherine. This one's down to earth and has been around for more than 60 years.

Da Kao (☎ 02 512 67 16; Rue Antoine Dansaert 38; metro Bourse; meals €5-10; 🕙 lunch & dinner Mon-Fri, noon-midnight Sat & Sun) As cheap as it gets in Brussels. This little Vietnamese restaurant with tacky décor but great food continues to hold out between designer boutiques and trendy eateries.

Also recommended:

African eateries (Rue Longue Vie; metro Porte de Namur) Casual Congolese cafés line up on this pedestrianised street in the Matongé quarter. Off-the-beaten track.

Frites/Pita (metro Gare Centrale) Pick from the swarm of places along Rue du Marché aux Fromages for *frites* (chips or fries) and pita.

GB Express (Rue au Beurre 25; metro Bourse; h 8am-10pm) Essentials sold at this little supermarket near the Grand Place.

DRINKING & CLUBBING

Café culture is ingrained in Brussels, and for those in search of more alcoholic refreshment, most streets in the city centre have at least one pub – Place St Géry is particularly well endowed.

À la Mort Subite (☎ 02 513 13 18; Rue Montagne aux Herbes Potagères 7; metro Gare Centrale; 🕙 10.30am-midnight; ✖) Long café with wood panelling, mirrored walls and brusque service. A must.

Falstaff (☎ 02 511 87 89; Rue Henri Maus 17; metro Bourse; 🕙 9am-midnight) Art Nouveau *grand café*, designed by Horta disciple, Houbion. Exotic world of mirrors, glass and fluidity.

Fuse + Food (☎ 02 511 97 89; www.fuse.be; Rue Blaes 208; metro Porte de Hal; admission free before 11pm,

depending on DJs €5-12; 🕙 10pm-7am Fri & Sat) The Marolles techno club that put Brussels on the international circuit. It recently merged with house club, Food.

Goupil le Fol (☎ 02 511 13 96; Rue de la Violette 22; metro Gare Centrale; 🕙 9pm-5am) Bastion of French *chanteuse*...you'll only hear the likes of Barbara, Édith Piaf and Brussels' own Jacques Brel in this kooky café.

Café Belga (☎ 02 640 35 08; Pl Flagey 18; 🕙 9.30am-2am Sun-Thu, to 3am Fri & Sat) Hippest of hip brasserie in Ixelles with a spacious interior and ample outdoor tables. Take tram No 81.

Tels Quels (☎ 02 512 32 34; www.telsquels.be; Rue du Marché au Charbon 81; metro Bourse; 🕙 from 5pm Sun-Tue, Thu & Fri, from 2pm Wed & Sat) Café-cum–info centre for Brussels' gay and lesbian community. Located on one of the city's prime nightlife streets.

Het Biercircus (☎ 02 218 00 34; Rue de l'Enseignement 89; metro Madou; 🕙 noon-2.30pm & 6pm-midnight Mon-Fri) This place is for serious beer buffs.

ENTERTAINMENT

The English-language magazine *Bulletin* has a 'What's On' guide with excellent entertainment coverage.

Arenberg Galeries (☎ 02 512 80 63 after 2pm; Galerie de la Reine 26; metro Gare Centrale) Remodelled Art Deco cinema located inside Galeries St Hubert. Foreign and art films are the staples.

AB (Ancienne Belgique; ☎ 02 548 24 00; www.abconcerts.be; Blvd Anspach 110; metro Bourse) AB, or Ancienne Belgique, is a great venue smack in the heart of town. The two auditoria accommodate international and home-grown bands.

La Monnaie/De Munt (☎ 02 227 12 00; www .demunt.be; Pl de la Monnaie; metro De Brouckère) Brussels' premier venue for opera, theatre and contemporary dance.

GETTING THERE & AWAY

Brussels is Belgium's international transport hub. For information on air services to Brussels, see p111 .

Details on rail services, including Eurostar and Thalys, are on p112. For details on Eurolines buses, see p112.

GETTING AROUND

Brussels' efficient public transport system is operated by **Société des Transports Intercommunaux de Bruxelles** (☎ 02 515 20 00; Rue l'Évêque

31); buses, trams and the metro run from about 5.30am to midnight.

AROUND BRUSSELS

WATERLOO
pop 28,900

Waterloo, the battleground where Napoleon was defeated and European history changed course in 1815, is 18km south of Brussels. Unless you're a war or history buff, it's staid. What's more, the sites are spread over several kilometres, making it tedious to get around on public transport (catch TEC bus W from Ave Fosny at Brussels' Gare du Midi train station; buy a €5.50 day card). Start at the **Office du Tourisme** (☎ 02 354 99 10; www.waterloo-tourisme.be; Chaussée de Bruxelles 218; 🕙 9.30am-6.30pm Apr-Sep, 10.30am-5pm Oct-Mar) in the village of Waterloo; bus W stops out the front.

FLANDERS

Belgium's northern region is flat ol' Flemish-speaking Flanders. Don't come here for geography – it's the history and the contemporary social scene that make Flanders great.

ANTWERP (ANTWERPEN, ANVERS)
pop 452,500

A city with attitude luring fashionistas, foodies and party queens alike, Antwerp is an essential stop. Worldly and seedy, historic and hip, Belgium's second-biggest city is currently basking in a third Golden Age that has made it one of Europe's most fashionable getaways. (On a different note, it's also the breeding ground for extreme-right party Vlaams Blok, which campaigns against immigrants.) Visit for the art and architecture, the avant-garde fashions or the dance scene that draws clubbers from far and wide.

Orientation

Antwerp's impressive train station, Centraal Station, is 1km east of the historic centre based around the Grote Markt and Groenplaats; to get to the centre walk along the Meir or take tram No 2 or 15 from *premetro* station Diamant below Centraal Station.

Information

ATMs KBC Bank (Eiermarkt) main post office (Groenplaats) branch post office (Pelikaanstraat) Fortis Bank (Wapper)

Branch tourist office (Koningin Astridplein 26; 🕙 9am-5.45pm Mon-Sat, 9am-4.45pm Sun) Outside the train station.

Main post office (☎ 03 202 69 11; Groenplaats 43; 🕙 9am-5pm Mon-Fri, 9am-noon Sat)

Main tourist office (☎ 03 232 01 03; www.visitant werpen.be; Grote Markt 13; 🕙 9am-5.45pm Mon-Sat, 9am-4.45pm Sun)

Sights

The heart of Antwerp is the **Grote Markt**, a vast, pedestrianised market square presided over by the impressive Renaissance-style **Stadhuis** and lined by **guildhalls**, most of which were reconstructed in the 19th century.

Antwerp's splendid **Onze Lieve Vrouwkathedraal** (☎ 03 213 99 40; Handschoenmarkt; adult/concession €2/1.50; 🕙 10am-5pm Mon-Fri, 10am-3pm Sat, 1-4pm Sun) is the largest and finest Gothic cathedral in Belgium (built 1352–1521). Its light interior houses four canvasses by Rubens.

The prestigious **Rubenshuis** (☎ 03 201 15 55; Wapper 9-11; adult/concession €5/2.50, free on Fri; 🕙 10am-5pm Tue-Sun) was the home and studio of Pieter Paul Rubens, northern Europe's greatest baroque artist.

The **Koninklijk Museum voor Schone Kunsten** (☎ 03 238 78 09; www.antwerpen.be/cultuur/kmska, with English version; Leopold De Waelplaats 1-9; adult/concession €5/4; 🕙 10am-5pm Tue-Sat, 10am-6pm Sun) houses an impressive collection of paintings dating from the Flemish Primitives to contemporary times. Take tram No 8 from Groenplaats or bus No 23 (direction Zuid) from Franklin Rooseveltplaats. The museum is 1.25km south of the Grote Markt.

Antwerp's much-celebrated Modemuseum, or **MoMu** (☎ 03 470 27 70; www.momu.be; Nationalestraat 28; adult/concession €7/4; 🕙 10am-6pm Tue-Sun), keeps firmly with the avant-garde, changing its exhibits every six months. To see what local designers are up to these days, wander down to **Walter** (☎ 03 213 26 44; St Antoniusstraat 12; 🕙 10am-6pm Mon-Sat), the shop of fashion guru Walter Van Beirendonck.

A block from the Grote Markt, next to the river, is a raised promenade known as **Zuiderterras**. Built decades ago alongside the city's main dock, it offers a great skyline view plus an essential pit stop (see Drinking, p119).

BELGIUM

BELGIUM

ANTWERP

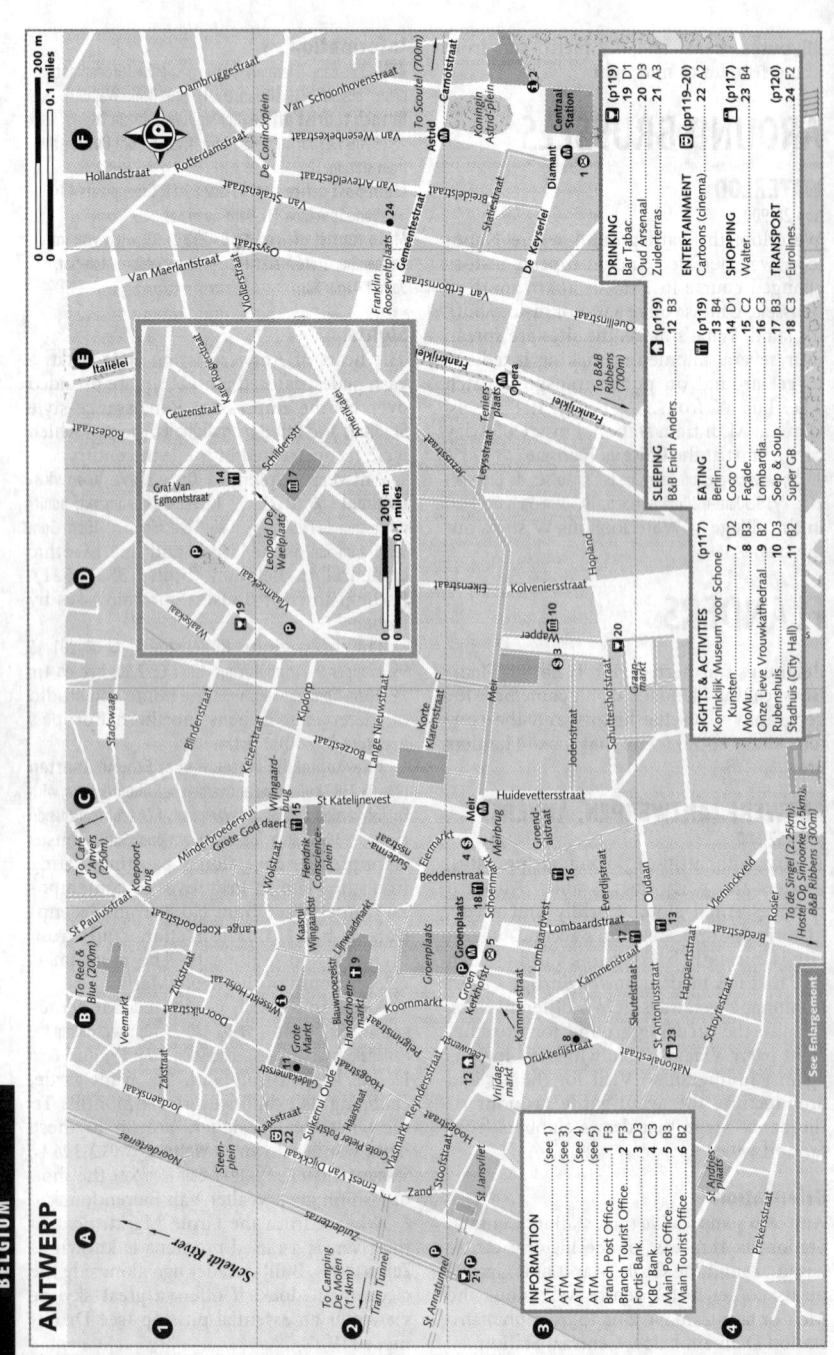

Scheldt River

200 m
0.1 miles

200 m
0.1 miles

See Enlargement

Sleeping

Scoutel (☎ 03 226 46 06; www.scoutel.be; Stoomstraat 3; dm €17, s/d 25 years & under €25/40, above 26 years €27/45; P ✗) Modern scouts' residence that welcomes travellers. Friendly staff and excellent location close to Centraal Station. The spartan modern rooms all have private bathrooms.

B&B Enich Anders (☎ 03 231 37 92; enich.anders@antwerpen.be; Leeuwenstraat 12; s/d/tr/f €45/50/65/80; ✗) A stone-sculptor's home that's superbly located and popular with independent types; if you don't mind things being a bit rough around the edges, this is your place. The rooms have small refrigerators and kitchenettes.

B&B Ribbens (☎ 03 248 15 39; www.bbantwerp .com; Justitiestraat 43; s/d/f Mon-Thu €42/50/75, Fri-Sun €50/60/85) Wooden floors and old-fashioned furniture are the salient features of this spacious and charming B&B. It's about 25 minutes' walk from the Grote Markt – to get there take bus No 290 (direction Hoboken) from Franklin Rooseveltplaats and get off at the 'Gerechtshof' stop.

Camping De Molen (☎ 03 219 81 79; Thonetlaan; per adult/tent/car €1.60/2.10/0.90; ✆ Apr-Sep) The pick of Antwerp's two camping grounds, located on the Linkeroever (Left Bank) of the Scheldt River; take bus No 81 or 82 (direction Linkeroever).

Also recommended is **Hostel Op Sinjoorke** (☎ 03 238 02 73; www.vjh.be; Eric Sasselaan 2; dm/s/d €13.75/24/38; ✆ closed Dec; ✗), an HI-affiliated hostel 3km south of the centre. To get there take tram No 2 (direction Hoboken).

Eating

Lombardia (☎ 03 233 68 19; Lombaardvest 78; light meals €4-8; ✆ 7.45am-6pm Mon-Sat) Legendary health-food shop-cum-café that has been around for three decades. The food's all *bio* (organic) and the décor's bizarre.

Berlin (☎ 03 227 11 01; Kleine Markt 1-3; mains €11-14; ✆ 7.30am-1am Mon-Thu, 9.30am-3am Fri-Sun) Spacious brasserie beneath the police tower in St Andries. Attracts an eclectic crowd from jeans-wearing teens to the old lady next door.

Façade (☎ 03 233 59 31; Hendrik Conscienceplein 18; mains €11-19; ✆ lunch Sat & Sun, dinner daily except Wed) Unpretentious restaurant that occupies a quaint pair of houses on one of the most delightful public squares in Antwerp. The French-Belgian cuisine is beautifully presented and prices are a snip.

Coco C. (☎ 03 216 96 43; Volkstraat 58; mains €18-20; ✆ lunch Mon-Fri, dinner daily) One of many restaurants in this part of Het Zuid. The décor and the food – Asian meets French – are the hippest of hip.

Also recommended:

Soep & Soup (☎ 03 707 28 05; Kammenstraat 89; small/large bowl €4.25/5.50; ✆ 11am-6.30pm Mon-Sat) Buzzing soup bar in trendy St Andries.

Super GB (Groenplaats; ✆ 8.30am-8pm) Supermarket in the Grand Bazar shopping centre.

Drinking

The only thing better in Antwerp than eating is drinking. Het Zuid (The South), commonly abbreviated as 't Zuid, is a popular nightlife quarter.

Oud Arsenaal (☎ 03 232 97 54; Pijpelincxstraat 4; ✆ 11am-midnight, closed Thu) Catch the city's most congenial brown café while it lasts. Beers are cheap and it's one of the few everyday pubs in Belgium to stock Westvleteren Trappist brews.

Zuiderterras (☎ 03 234 12 75; Ernest van Dijckkaai 37; ✆ 9am-midnight) Modern landmark café-restaurant at the southern end of the riverside promenade and designed by the city's eminent contemporary architect, bOb Van Reeth.

Bar Tabac (☎ 03 238 19 37; Waalsekaai 43; ✆ 8pm-7am daily, closed Mon Oct-Feb) Tiny bar that looks like it was plucked from obscurity in rural France and plonked in 't Zuid. The odd thing is, it's always packed.

Clubbing

One of the city's main dance parties is **Antwerp is Burning** (www.antwerpisburning.be), held towards the end of summer on open fields on the Linkeroever (Left Bank) of the Scheldt.

Café d'Anvers (☎ 03 226 38 70; www.cafe-d-anvers .com; Verversrui 15; ✆ 11pm-7.30am Fri & Sat) This legendary nightclub does funk and house, disco and soul in a refurbished church in the city's red-light district. Many of Belgium's top DJs started here.

Red & Blue (☎ 03 213 05 55; www.redandblue.be; Lange Schipperskapelstraat 11; ✆ 11pm-7am Sat) The biggest (and awarded best) gay nightclub in this corner of Europe, drawing a mixed crowd to house, techno, rap and soul.

Entertainment

Cinema buffs should head to **Cartoons** (☎ 03 232 96 32; Kaasstraat 4-6), where art-house movies and quality foreign films screen in three auditoriums.

For modern dance and theatre, there's **deSingel** (☎ 03 248 28 28; www.desingel.be; Desguinlei 25).

Getting There & Around

From **Centraal Station** (☎ 02 528 28 28), train connections include Brussels (€5.60, 35 minutes), Ghent (€7.20, 45 minutes) and Bruges (€11.40, 70 minutes).

For details on Eurolines buses, see p112.

De Lijn Antwerpen (☎ 070 22 02 00; Centraal Station; info kiosk ☽ 8am-4pm Mon-Fri) runs a good network of buses, trams and a *premetro*.

In summer, bikes can be hired from **De Windroos** (☎ 03 480 93 88; Steenplein 1A; rental per hr/day €2.50/12.50).

GHENT (GENT, GAND)
pop 228,000

Likeable Ghent is often overlooked on the art town hop between Brussels, Bruges and Antwerp. Compact and unpretentious, this lively university city has all the things that make Flemish towns great – historic architecture, fab restaurants and sublime chocolate shops – minus the crowds of Bruges and the attitude of Antwerp.

Orientation & Information

Ghent's main train station, St Pietersstation, is 2km south of the city centre based around the Korenmarkt – take tram No 1, 10, 11, 12 or 13 from the tunnel to the right as you exit the train station.

ATM (Post office, Maria Hendrikaplein) Opposite the train station.

Tourist office (☎ 09 266 52 32; www.visitgent.be; Botermarkt 17; ☽ 9.30am-6.30pm Apr-Oct, 9.30am-4.30pm Nov-Mar)

Sights

Though **St Baafskathedraal** (☎ 09 269 20 45; St Baafsplein; ☽ 8.30am-6pm) is unimpressive from the outside, formidable queues form to see the **Adoration of the Mystic Lamb** (adult/concession €3/2.50; ☽ 9.30am-5pm Mon-Sat, 1-5pm Sun Apr-Oct, 10.30am-4pm Mon-Sat, 1-4pm Sun Nov-Mar). This lavish representation of medieval religious thinking is one of the earliest-known oil paintings, executed in 1432 by Flemish Primitive artist Jan van Eyck and not to be missed.

The 14th-century **Belfort** (Botermarkt; admission €2; ☽ 10am-12.30pm & 2-5.30pm Easter–mid-Nov)

affords spectacular views of the city; there's a lift or stairs.

The **Gravensteen** (☎ 09 225 93 06; St Veerleplein; admission €5; ☽ 9am-6pm Apr-Sep, 9am-5pm Oct-Mar), smack in the heart of the city, belonged to the 12th-century counts of Flanders and is the quintessential castle.

Ghent's highly regarded **Stedelijk Museum voor Actuele Kunst** (☎ 09 221 17 03; www.smak.be; Citadelpark; admission €5; ☽ 10am-6pm Tue-Sun), better known as SMAK, contains works by Karel Appel, Pierre Alechinsky and Panamarenko – three of Belgium's best-known contemporary artists.

Sleeping & Eating

The old Patershol quarter is awash with ambient restaurants and pubs. The Vrijdagmarkt is another good nightlife spot.

De Draecke (☎ 09 233 70 50; www.vjh.be; St Widostraat 11; dm/tw €15.75/38; ✗) One of Belgium's best HI-affiliated hostels occupies a renovated warehouse smack in the heart of town. From the train station, take tram No 1, 10 or 11 to St Veerleplein.

B&B Henckens (☎ 09 224 34 05; www.bedandbreakfast-gent.be; Zwartezustersstraat 3; s/d/tr from €30/45/60; ✗) Homey B&B that was once part of an old cloister. The three guestrooms are done in rich colours and share one bathroom/toilet.

Chambre Plus (☎ 09 225 37 75; www.chambreplus.be; Hoogpoort 31; s/d/ste €65/80/140; ✗) Gorgeous B&B with a fab location on a pedestrianised street in the heart of town. The exotic rooms are complemented by convivial hosts and a gastronomic breakfast.

Souplounge (☎ 09 223 62 03; Zuivelbrugstraat 6; small/large soup €3/4.50; ☽ 10am-7pm) One of the new breed of modern soup kitchens and great for a light, fast meal.

Short Order (☎ 09 225 74 07; Hoogpoort 11; light meals €3-7; ☽ 11.30am-9pm Mon-Sat) Casual eatery pumping out loud music and big boxes of noodles, sushi or pasta. Good veggie burgers and fresh juices too.

Pakhuis (☎ 09 223 55 55; Schuurkenstraat 4; mains €14-25; ☽ noon-midnight, closed Sun) Huge brasserie-cum-restaurant occupying a restored textile warehouse on a dog-eared backstreet; draws young and old alike.

Getting There & Around

From **St Pietersstation** (☎ 02 528 28 28) trains run half-hourly to Antwerp (€7.20, 45 minutes), Bruges (€5, 20 minutes) and Brussels

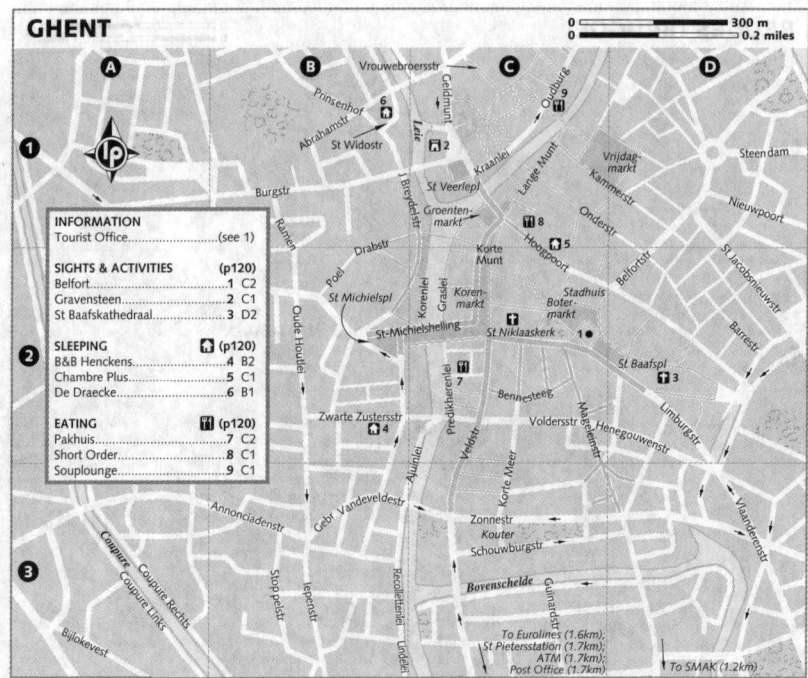

GHENT

0 ———————————— 300 m
0 ———————————— 0.2 miles

INFORMATION		
Tourist Office		(see 1)
SIGHTS & ACTIVITIES		**(p120)**
Belfort	1	C2
Gravensteen	2	C1
St Baafskathedraal	3	D2
SLEEPING		**(p120)**
B&B Henckens	4	B2
Chambre Plus	5	C1
De Draecke	6	B1
EATING		**(p120)**
Pakhuis	7	C2
Short Order	8	C1
Souplounge	9	C1

(€6.80, 45 minutes), and hourly to Ypres (€8.80, one hour).

For more details about Eurolines buses, see p112.

Public transport is operated by **De Lijn** (☎ 09 210 93 11), which has an info kiosk outside the train station. Bikes can be rented from the St Pietersstation (rental per day €9 plus deposit €12.50).

BRUGES (BRUGGE)
pop 117,000

Touristy, overcrowded and a tad fake. Preface any other city with these descriptions and it would be left for dead. Not Bruges. This medieval town is Belgium's most popular destination and, despite the crowds, it's not to be missed.

By the 14th century, Bruges was one of Europe's leading trade centres. But the following century, the waterway linking the city to the sea silted. Despite attempts to built a new canal, Bruges' economic lifeline was gone. Traders and townsfolk abandoned the city, leaving it suspended in time.

These days Bruges dreamily evokes a world long since gone. But its reputation as a perfectly preserved city is in part fabrication – much of the town was rebuilt in the 19th and 20th centuries to reflect medieval times.

Orientation & Information

Central Bruges fits neatly into an oval-shaped series of canals, at the core of which are two central squares, the Markt and the Burg. The main square, the Markt, is about 1.5km north of the train station; to get there just jump on any bus marked 'Centrum'.

ATM (Markt 5) Attached to the main post office.

Main post office (☎ 050 33 08 27; Markt 5; ☷ 9am-6pm Mon-Fri, 9.30am-noon Sat)

Toerisme Brugge (☎ 050 44 86 86; www.brugge.be; Burg 11; ☷ 9.30am-5pm Mon-Fri, 9.30am-noon & 2-5pm Sat & Sun) Tourist office.

Sights

Exploration of Bruges always starts at the historic **Markt**, the city's medieval core. Here rises Belgium's most famous **Belfort** (belfry; adult/concession €5/3; ☷ 9.30am-5pm Tue-Sun, last tickets sold 4.15pm); there are 366 steps to the top.

BELGIUM

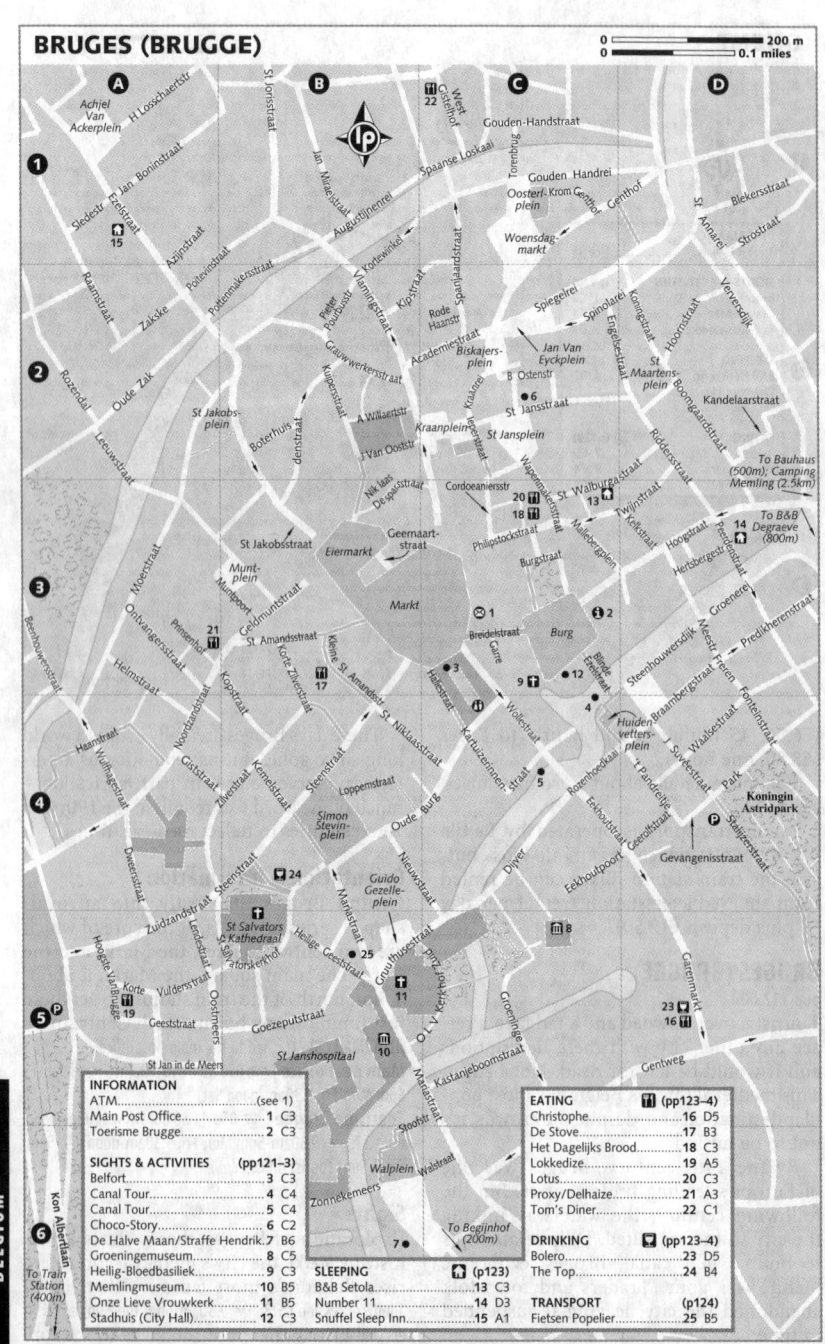

BRUGES (BRUGGE)

0 _____ 200 m
0 _____ 0.1 miles

INFORMATION
ATM.....................................(see 1)
Main Post Office.........................1 C3
Toerisme Brugge..........................2 C3

SIGHTS & ACTIVITIES (pp121–3)
Belfort..................................3 C3
Canal Tour...............................4 C4
Canal Tour...............................5 C4
Choco-Story..............................6 C2
De Halve Maan/Straffe Hendrik...7 B6
Groeningemuseum..........................8 C5
Heilig-Bloedbasiliek.....................9 C3
Memlingmuseum............................10 B5
Onze Lieve Vrouwkerk.....................11 B5
Stadhuis (City Hall).....................12 C3

SLEEPING (p123)
B&B Setola...............................13 C3
Number 11................................14 D3
Snuffel Sleep Inn........................15 A1

EATING (pp123–4)
Christophe...............................16 D5
De Stove.................................17 B3
Het Dagelijks Brood......................18 C3
Lokkedize................................19 A5
Lotus....................................20 C3
Proxy/Delhaize...........................21 A3
Tom's Diner..............................22 C1

DRINKING (pp123–4)
Bolero...................................23 D5
The Top..................................24 B4

TRANSPORT (p124)
Fietsen Popelier.........................25 B5

BELGIUM

The nearby **Burg** features Belgium's oldest **stadhuis** (city hall), along with the **Heilig-Bloedbasiliek** (Basilica of the Holy Blood; ☻ 9.30-11.50am & 2-5.50pm Apr-Sep, 10-11.50am & 2-3.50pm Oct-Mar), where a few coagulated drops of Christ's blood are kept and cherished.

Bruges' prized collection of art dating from the 14th to 21st centuries is housed in the small **Groeningemuseum** (☎ 050 44 87 50; Dijver 12; adult/concession €8/5; ☻ 9.30am-5pm Tue-Sun). Most notable is the section on Flemish Primitives.

The renowned **Memlingmuseum** (☎ 050 44 87 70; Mariastraat 38; adult/concession €8/5; ☻ 9.30am-5pm Tue-Sun) is home to a handful of masterpieces by Hans Memling, one of the early Flemish Primitives. Don't miss the reliquary of St Ursula – the attention to detail is stunning.

The **Onze Lieve Vrouwkerk** (Mariastraat; adult/concession €2.50/1.50; ☻ 9.30am-12.30pm & 1.30-5pm Tue-Sat, 1.30-5pm Sun), or Church of Our Lady, has one remarkable art treasure: Michelangelo's *Madonna and Child*. This small marble statue (1504) was the only work of art by Michelangelo to leave Italy in his lifetime.

The **begijnhof** (admission free; ☻ 9am-7pm Apr-Sep, 9am-6pm Oct-Mar) was home to a 13th-century religious community of unmarried or widowed women, known as *begijnen* (Beguines). A 10-minute walk south of the Markt, it's one of Bruges' quaintest spots and is unquestionably a must.

Bruges' newest attraction is **Choco-Story** (☎ 050 61 22 37; St Jansplein; admission €5; ☻ 10am-5pm), a museum devoted to telling the story of chocolate. It's well done.

De Halve Maan/Straffe Hendrik (☎ 050 33 26 97; Walplein 26; admission €3.70; ☻ 11am-4pm Apr-Sep, 11am-3pm Oct-Mar) is a family brewery offering crowded guided tours (45 minutes) that finish with a beer.

Tours

Canal tours (Steenhouwersdijk and Dijver; €5.20; ☻ 10am-6pm Mar–mid-Nov) Touristy but essential. Boats depart from jetties south of the Burg, and tours last 30 minutes.

Horse-drawn carriages (Markt; 5 passengers €27.50) Thirty-five minute trips departing from the Markt.

Quasimodo (☎ 0800 975 25; www.quasimodo.be; under/over 26 years €38/48) Bus day trips taking in either Bruges or Ypres (see p124).

Quasimundo (☎ 050 37 07 75; www.quasimundo.com; under/over 26 years €16/18; ☻ mid-Mar–mid-Oct) Excellent half-day bike tours; bookings necessary.

Sleeping

Snuffel Sleep In (☎ 050 33 31 33; www.snuffel.be; Ezelstraat 47-49; dm/d €11/30; ☒) Funky, unpretentious place that's been around for years and is the most alternative hostel in Bruges. The rooms are basic but original, the staff are friendly, and there's a kitchen and bar. From the train station take bus No 3 or 13.

Bauhaus (☎ 050 34 10 93; www.bauhaus.be; Langestraat 135; hostel section dm/d/tr €11/30/39, hotel section s/d/tr €24/36/51, breakfast €3) Big, bustling hostel with separate hotel section next door. A popular hang-out for young travellers, though the blue rooms hardly fuel the imagination. Take bus No 6 or 16 from the train station.

B&B Setola (☎ 050 33 49 77; www.bedandbreakfast-bruges.com; St Walburgastraat 12; s/d/tr/f €50/55/75/95, €10 extra for 1 night; ☒) Modern style comes to Bruges in this mansion dating from 1740. While the façade is historic, the three 2nd-floor guestrooms have crisp colours and cool vibes, and you'll be hard-pressed to get a better location or breakfast.

B&B Degraeve (☎ 050 34 57 11; www.stardekk.com/bedbreakfast; Kazernevest 32; s/d/tr €33/45/58) In a quiet, untouristed part of town and run by a zany woman who has filled the two spacious rooms with bizarre décor.

Camping Memling (☎ 050 35 58 45; www.camping-memling.be; Veltemweg 109; per adult/tent/car €4/4/4; ☻ all year) The quietest local camping ground, 2.5km east of town in St Kruis. Take bus No 11 from the train station.

Eating & Drinking

From cosy *estaminets* (taverns) to first-class restaurants, Bruges has all bases covered.

Tom's Diner (☎ 050 33 33 82; West Gistelhof 23; mains €10-15; ☻ 6.30pm-1am, closed Tue) To the north of town, a little way out of the tourist centre and all the better for it. Stylish food at very affordable prices. Locals love it.

Lokkedize (☎ 050 33 44 50; Korte Vuldersstraat 33; dishes €8-10; ☻ from 7pm Wed-Thu, from 6pm Fri-Sun) One of the city's most convivial cafés and a great spot for a late-night bite (kitchen open until midnight).

Het Dagelijks Brood (☎ 050 33 60 50; Philipstockstraat 21; snacks €5-11; ☻ 7am-6pm, closed Tue; ☒) Part of a national bakery-tearoom chain, with just one big table where you can eat salads or *boterhammen* (sandwiches).

De Stove (☎ 050 33 78 35; Kleine St Amandsstraat 4; mains €18-28; ☻ 11.30am-2.30pm Sat-Tue, 6-10pm

SPLURGE!

There's no mincing words, **Number 11** (☎ 050 33 06 75; www.number11.be; Peerdenstraat 11; d €115-140), while not cheap, is a stunner. The three rooms bathe in individual charm and harmoniously blend modern and medieval styles. Ask about the kookiest chandelier you'll ever see.

Fri-Tue, closed Wed & Thu) Charming restaurant tucked away on a pedestrianised lane. The eight tables are arranged around an old stove, the service is intimate and the food – fish specialities – is excellent.

The Top (St Salvatorskerkhof 5; ☽ from 9pm Tue-Sat, from 10pm Sun) Coolest bar in town; opens late and moves until morning.

Also recommended:

Lotus (☎ 050 33 10 78; Wapenmakerstraat 5; meals €9.20; ☽ 11.45am-2pm Mon-Sat) Excellent lunch-time vegetarian restaurant.

Christophe (☎ 050 34 48 92; Garenmarkt 34; mains €24; ☽ 7pm-1am Thu-Mon) Fab late-night bistro.

Bolero (☎ 050 33 81 11; Garenmarkt 32; ☽ 9pm-4am, closed Tue) The only gay and lesbian bar in town.

Proxy/Delhaize (Geldmuntstraat) Supermarket.

Getting There & Around

From Bruges' **train station** (☎ 02 528 28 28), trains run half-hourly to Brussels (€10.80, 60 minutes) and Ghent (€5, 20 minutes), and hourly to Antwerp (€11.40, 70 minutes). For Ypres (Ieper in Flemish; €9.30, two hours), you'll need to change in Kortrijk.

A small network of buses operated by **De Lijn** (☎ 059 56 53 53) covers destinations in and around Bruges.

Bruges is ideal for cyclists. Rent a bike from **Fietsen Popelier** (☎ 050 34 32 62; Mariastraat 26; rental per hr/half day/full day €3/6/9; ☽ 10am-6.30pm Sep-Jun, 10am-8pm Jul-Aug).

YPRES (IEPER)
pop 35,100

Ypres was the last bastion of Belgian territory unoccupied by the Germans in WWI. As such, this southwest corner was a barrier to a German advance towards the French coastal ports around Calais. More than 300,000 Allied soldiers were killed here during four years of fighting that left the medieval town flattened. Convincingly reconstructed, the town and its surrounds – the Ypres Salient – are now dotted with cemeteries and memorials. Unless you have a car, the best way to visit is by guided tour (see below). For more information there's the **Ypres Visitors Centre** (☎ 057 23 92 20; www .ieper.be; Lakenhalle, Grote Markt; ☽ 9am-6pm Mon-Fri, 10am-6pm Sat & Sun Apr-Sep, until 5pm Oct-Mar).

Sights

The town's hub, the **Grote Markt**, is dominated by the enormous **Lakenhalle** (Cloth Hall) with its 70m-high belfry.

On the 1st floor of the Lakenhalle is **In Flanders Fields Museum** (☎ 057 23 92 20; www .inflandersfields.be; Grote Markt 34; admission €7.50; ☽ 10am-6pm Apr-Sep, 10am-5pm Tue-Sun Oct-Mar), a moving testament to the wartime horrors experienced by ordinary people.

The **Menin Gate** (Meensestraat) is perhaps the saddest reminder of the town's past. The huge white gate is inscribed with the names of 54,896 British and Commonwealth troops who were lost in the quagmire of the trenches and who have no graves. Every evening at 8pm, traffic is halted while buglers sound the Last Post.

Tyne Cot Cemetery, the largest British Commonwealth war cemetery in the world, sits on a plateau about 8km northeast of Ypres. As cemeteries go, this one is hugely moving; in all, 11,956 soldiers are buried here.

Tours

Two companies offer good bus tours of the Ypres Salient. Book at least a day or two in advance:

Quasimodo (see Tours in Bruges, p123)

Salient Tours (☎ 057 21 46 57; tours@battlefields .freeserve.co.uk; 2½-4hr tours €15/21) Tours run daily except Wednesday, and there are none from December to February.

Sleeping & Eating

B&B Hortensia (☎ 057 21 24 06; www.guesthouse -ypres.be; Rijselsestraat 196; s/d €46/56) In the heart of town with modern, sober rooms. No fuss or bother.

Hotel Regina (☎ 057 21 88 88; www.hotelregina .be; Grote Markt 45; s €65-90, d €75-100) Smack on the Markt, this is Ypres' most atmospheric hotel. The cheaper rooms are old and ordinary; the most expensive ones are large and rustic.

Jeugdstadion (☎ 057 21 72 82; info@jeugdstadion .be; Leopoldlaan 16; per adult/tent/car €3/1.50/4.50;

mid-Mar–Oct) Basic camping ground attached to a youth centre, 900m southeast of the Grote Markt.

In het Klein Stadhuis (☎ 057 21 55 42; Grote Markt 32; mains €10-15; ☺ 10am-midnight, closed Sun Oct-May) Smooth, split-level café tucked away in a quaint guildhall next to the Stadhuis.

Getting There & Around

From Ypres **train station** (☎ 02 528 28 28) hourly trains go direct to Kortrijk (€4, 30 minutes) and Ghent (€8.80, one hour). For Brussels (€13.50, 1½ hours), Bruges (€9.30, two hours) and Antwerp (€15.10, two hours), change in Kortrijk.

WALLONIA

Wallonia, Belgium's French-speaking southern half, is a world away from the affluent Flemish art cities to the north. From intimate villages to industrial decay, forests to furnaces, this region offers both Belgium's most scenic and septic landscapes. For the former, burrow down in the Ardennes, where Wallonia's southeastern corner, where tranquil stone villages nestle next to ancient castles.

LIÈGE (LUIK)

pop 184,300

Visitors love or loathe Liège. This gritty city, sprawled along the Meuse River about 90km east of Brussels, is a place that takes time to know. Stay overnight and explore its excellent museums devoted to Walloon life, and its likely to win you over. For Simenon fans, this is Georges' birthplace and his primary place of homage (though there's little to see).

Orientation & Information

Liège's main train station, Gare Guillemins, is 2km south of Place St Lambert, the city's heart and main bus hub – to get there simply catch another train to the city's most central station, Gare du Palais.

The central district of town is strewn along the western bank of the Meuse River, which splits in two creating the island of Outremeuse.

Maison du Tourisme (☎ 04 237 92 92; www.liege.be; Place St Lambert 32; ☺ 9am-6pm Jun-Sep, 9.30am-5.30pm Oct-Mar) City tourist office.

Sights

A good starting place is **Montagne de Bueren** (Hors Château). This flight of 373 stairs leads up to a former citadel (now a hospital) and an excellent city panorama.

The excellent **Musée d'Art Réligieux et d'Art Mosan** (Museum of Religious Art and Art from the Meuse Valley; ☎ 04 221 42 25; Rue Mère Dieu; admission €3.80; ☺ 11am-6pm Tue-Sat, 11am-4pm Sun) is chock-full of well-preserved regional religious relics.

The **Musée de l'Art Wallon** (☎ 04 221 92 31; Féronstrée 86; admission €3.80; ☺ 1-6pm Tue-Sat, 11am-4.30pm Sun) accommodates art by French-speaking Belgians including surrealists René Magritte and Paul Delvaux.

Sleeping & Eating

Auberge de Jeunesse (☎ 04 344 56 89; liege@laj.be; Rue Georges Simenon 2; dm/s/d €15.75/24/38; ☒ ▣) Modern HI-affiliated hostel in Outremeuse; take bus No 4 from Gare Guillemins to Place St Lambert and change to bus No 18.

Hôtel Les Acteurs (☎ 04 223 00 80; www.lesacteurs.be; Rue des Urbanistes 10; s/d €50/60, breakfast €5) Comfy modern hotel which tries hard to be artistic. It's well located and bus No 1 or 4 stops about 200m away.

Les Dames Tartines (☎ 04 232 17 10; Rue des Mineurs 20; snacks €2-5; ☺ 9am-4pm Mon-Sat) A tiny snack bar that's well known for its filled baguette sandwiches.

Maharadja (☎ 04 223 23 94; Rue St-Jean-en-Isle 5; mains €13; ☺ noon-3pm and 6-9pm, closed Mon & Tue lunch) An Indian restaurant doing well-priced meals smack in the city's nightlife hub.

Getting There & Away

From **Gare Guillemins** (☎ 02 528 28 28), trains connect with Brussels (€11.40, one hour), Namur (€6.80, 50 minutes), Spa (€4, 50 minutes), Tongeren (€3.50, 30 minutes) and Luxembourg City (€26, 2½ hours).

For information on Eurolines buses, see p112.

AROUND LIÈGE
Tongeren

pop 29,700

Tongeren, 20km north of Liège in Flanders, is Belgium's oldest town. The original locals put up considerable resistance under the leadership of Ambiorix when the area was conquered by Roman troops in 15 BC. The slick **Gallo-Roman Museum** (☎ 012 67 03 30; www.limburg.be/gallo; Kielenstraat 15; adult/concession €5/4;

noon-5pm Mon, 9am-5pm Tue-Fri, 10am-6pm Sat & Sun) presents findings from these times.

Tongeren is also well known for its Sunday **antique market** (Veemarkt) and the elegant **Onze Lieve Vrouwbasiliek** (Grote Markt; 8am-noon & 1.30-5pm), or Basilica of Our Lady, currently undergoing archaeological excavation but still worth a visit.

For more information, head to the **tourist office** (☎ 012 39 02 55; www.tongeren.be; Stadhuisplein 9; 8.30am-noon & 1-4.30pm Mon-Fri, 10am-4pm Sat & Sun).

Spa

pop 10,500

There's no bursting its bubble. Spa, Europe's oldest health resort, has for centuries embraced royalty and the wealthy who came to drink, bathe and cure themselves in the mineral-rich waters that bubble forth here. In 2004 the town opened its spanking-new **Thermes de Spa** (☎ 087 77 25 60; www .thermesdespa.com; adult/child/concession €17/12/15; 9am-8pm Sun-Thu, 9am-10pm Fri & Sat), a hill-top complex reached by rack railway (steep mountain railway) that takes off near the tourist office.

Spa is 40km southeast of Liège and connected by regular trains (€3.90, 50 minutes). The **Office du Tourisme** (☎ 087 79 53 53; www.spa -info.be; Place Royale 41; 9am-6pm Mon-Fri, 10am-6pm Sat & Sun) can help with inquiries.

Hautes Fagnes Nature Reserve

The Hautes Fagnes, or High Fens, is a plateau of swampy heath, woods and wind-swept moors that sweeps over to Germany's Eifel hills. The area is popular with walkers and cyclists. Start a visit at the **Botrange Nature Centre** (☎ 080 44 03 00; www.ful.ac.be/hotes /cnatbotrange; Route de Botrange 131; 10am-6pm).

It takes at least 1¼ hours to arrive here on public transport from Liège – take the train to Verviers (€3.20, 20 minutes, hourly) and then bus No 390 (€2.40, 30 minutes, five daily) to Rocherath.

TOURNAI (DOORNIK)

pop 67,4000

Just 10km from the French border and 80km from Brussels, Tournai is one of Belgium's oldest cities. It enjoys a pleasant position on the Scheldt River (known as the Escaut in French) and has one of the country's finest cathedrals (currently being restored).

For more information, head to the **Office du Tourisme** (☎ 069 22 20 45; www.tournai.be; Vieux Marché aux Poteries 14; 8.30am-6pm Mon-Fri, 9.30am-noon & 2-5pm Sat, 10am-noon & 2.30-6pm Sun). It's in the centre of town about 900m from the train station – to get there head straight up Rue Royale.

Sights

The five towers of the striking but sober **Cathédrale Notre Dame** (Grand Place; admission free; 9.30am-noon & 2-6pm) have long been the trademark of Tournai's skyline. Pummelled by a freak tornado in 1999, major works to realign the towers are still under way, leaving much of the World Heritage–listed cathedral off limits to tourists.

Tournai's 72m-high **belfry** (☎ 069 22 20 45; Grand Place; admission €2; 10am-1pm & 2-5.30pm Tue-Sat, 11am-1pm & 2-6.30pm Sun) is Belgium's oldest, dating from 1188. Climb the 256 steps.

The **Musée des Beaux-Arts** (☎ 069 22 20 43; Enclos St Martin; admission €3; 9.30am-12.30pm & 2-5.30pm, closed Tue) is the city's little gem. Housed in a building designed by Victor Horta, it contains an enjoyable collection of paintings and sculptures by local, national and international artists.

Sleeping & Eating

Auberge de Jeunesse (☎ 069 21 61 36; www.laj.be; Rue St Martin 64; dm/s/d €13.75/24/38) Modern and pleasant hostel around the corner from the Musée des Beaux-Arts. It's a 20-minute walk from the train station – take bus No 4 (direction Baisieux).

Hôtel d'Alcantara (☎ 069 21 26 48; hotelalcantara@ hotmail.com; Rue des Bouchers St Jacques 2; s/d from €75/85) Not the most expensive hotel in town but certainly the most charming. Attentive service and 15 well-priced, modern rooms set behind a discreet courtyard.

Hôtel Tour St George (☎ 069 22 53 00; fax 069 22 50 35; Rue St Georges 2; s/d €20/28) Cheap as chips hotel in the heart of town. Don't expect much in the way of décor or service.

L'Écurie d'Ennetières (☎ 069 21 56 89; Ruelle d'Ennetières; mains €10-15; 11.30am-2.30pm & 6.30-10pm, closed Mon & Tue dinner) Occupies a renovated old building in the river quarter of town and does affordable French cuisine.

Getting There & Away

From Tournai's **train station** (☎ 02 528 28 28) there are regular trains to Brussels (€9.90, one hour) and Ypres (€7.20, one hour).

NAMUR (NAMEN)
pop 105,700

Namur is a great jumping-off point for exploring Wallonia's forested Ardennes. Some 60km southeast of Brussels, it's a picturesque town built at the confluence of the Meuse and Sambre Rivers and presided over by a citadel that, in times gone by, ranked as one of Europe's mightiest.

Orientation & Information

Place d'Armes is the town's nominal heart. To get there, turn left when you exit the station and follow Rue du Fer, the town's main shopping street, for about 800m.

Office du Tourisme (☎ 081 24 64 49; www.pays-de -namur.be; Sq de l'Europe Unie; ◷ 9.30am-6pm) Main tourist office, located near the train station.

Sights

Don't miss the **Trésor du Prieuré d'Oignies** (☎ 081 23 03 42; Rue Julie Billiart 17; admission €1.50; ◷ 10am-noon & 2-5pm Tue-Sat, 2-5pm Sun & Mon), a one-room hoard of exquisite Gothic treasures housed in a modern convent. Ring the bell to be taken on a guided tour by one of the nuns.

The **Musée Félicien Rops** (☎ 081 22 01 10; www .ciger.be/rops; Rue Fumal 12; admission €3; ◷ 10am-6pm Tue-Sun Sep-Jun, daily Jul-Aug) is devoted to works by the 19th-century Namur-born artist Félicien Rops (1833–98) who fondly illustrated erotic lifestyles and macabre scenes.

What remains of Namur's once-mighty **citadel** is slung high above the town on a rocky outcrop. It covers a huge area, and is most easily accessed by a **tourist train** (☎ 081 24 64 49; admission €1; ◷ 10am-5pm Jun–mid-Sep, closed Mon-Fri Apr & May), which departs hourly from the tourist office. Alternatively, you can walk up. The distances of trails vary; the shortest walk is 1km.

Sleeping & Eating

Auberge de Jeunesse (☎ 081 22 36 88; www.laj.be; Rue F Rops 8; dm/s/d €15.75/24/38; ◷ closed Jan–mid-Feb; ⊠ ▯) Attractive hostel located on the riverfront about 3km southwest of the train station. Bus 3 and 4, which both depart hourly from Place de la Station, stop nearby.

Hôtel Les Tanneurs (☎ 081 24 00 24; www.tan neurs.com; Rue des Tanneries 13; s €50-197, d €55-205, breakfast €8; ℗ ⊠ ▯) Unique hotel on a shabby street in the heart of town, which unites modern comfort with 17th-century charm. Book well ahead.

Brasserie Henry (☎ 081 22 02 04; Place St Aubain 3; mains €12-18; ◷ noon-midnight Mon-Thu, noon-1am Fri & Sat) Sociable brasserie and an institution among Namur's late-night diners.

Camping Les 4 Fils Aymon (☎ 081 58 02 94; Chaussée de Liège; per tent/caravan €6.50/12; ◷ closed Oct-Mar) Pleasant ground about 8km east of Namur – bus No 12 departs hourly from the bus station.

Getting There & Away

A major rail hub, Namur boasts a gleaming new **train station** (☎ 025 28 28 28). Regional connections include Brussels (€6.80, one hour, every 30 minutes), Dinant (€3.60, 30 minutes, hourly), Jemelle (€6.80, 40 minutes, hourly), Liège (€6.80, one hour, every 30 minutes) and Marloie (€6.20, 35 minutes, hourly).

Regional and local buses are operated by **TEC** (☎ 081 25 35 55; Place de la Station; ◷ 7am-7pm).

DINANT
pop 12,800

This distinctive town, 28km south of Namur, is one of the Ardennes' touristy hot spots. Pressed between rock and river, its bulbous cathedral, **Église Notre Dame** (Place Reine Astrid; admission free; ◷ 10am-6pm), competes for attention with the cliff-front **citadel** (☎ 082 22 36 70; Place Reine Astrid 3; admission €5.50; ◷ 10am-4pm Sat-Thu Oct-Mar, 10am-6pm Jul-Aug, closed Mon-Fri Jan). In summer the main thoroughfares through town are choked with traffic and the place feels hot and claustrophobic – good for a pit stop but there are better places deeper in the Ardennes to kick back.

The **tourist office** (☎ 082 22 28 70; www.dinant -tourisme.be; Ave Cadoux 8; ◷ 8.30am-7pm Mon-Fri, 9.30am-7pm Sat, 10am-6pm Sun) is on the opposite side of the river from the cathedral.

ROCHEFORT & HAN-SUR-LESSE
pop 23,000

As a base in the Ardennes, Rochefort is hard to beat. Together with its neighbour Han-sur-Lesse, 6km away, Rochefort is famed for the millennia-old underground limestone grottoes that attract visitors from all over Belgium. The caves at Han are the more spectacular of the two but Han itself is a tourist trap; stay in Rochefort and commute between towns.

The Rochefort **tourist office** (☎ 084 34 51 72; www.valdelesse.be; Rue de Behogne 5; ◷ 8am-6pm Mon-Fri, 9.30am-5pm Sat & Sun Jul-Aug, 8am-5pm Mon-Fri,

10am-5pm Sat, 10am-4pm Sun Sep-Jun) is in the centre of town.

Sights & Activities

The impressive **Grottes de Han** (☎ 084 37 72 13; Rue Lamotte 2; adult/child €11/6.50; ☑ 10am-noon & 1.30-5.30pm Apr-Oct, 11.30am-4pm Nov-Mar, closed Jan & Feb) is a series of caves a little way out of Han. A toy train chugs to the entrance and a barge brings you back. Rochefort's cave, **Grotte de Lorette** (☎ 084 21 20 80; Drève de Lorette; adult/child €7/4.50; ☑ 10.30am-4.30pm Apr-Oct), is smaller but also well worth seeing.

The area is a great base for **walking** and **cycling**. One trail for cyclists is **Le Ravel**, an 18km-long stretch of disused railway line linking Rochefort and the village of Houyet. Bikes can be rented in Rochefort from **Cycle Sport** (☎ 084 21 32 55; Rue de Behogne 59; rental per half/full day €15/20; ☑ 9.30am-noon & 1.30-7pm Mon-Sat, 9.30am-noon Sun).

Sleeping & Eating

The following options are all in Rochefort.

Le Vieux Moulin (☎ 084 21 46 04; www.giterochefort .be; Rue du Hableau 25; under/over 26 years €18/21; ☑ all year) Pleasant *gîte d'étape* (basic hostel-type dwelling) in the heart of town. The overnight price includes breakfast and one meal.

Hôtel La Fayette (☎ 084 21 42 73; www.hotellafayette .net; Rue Jacquet 87; s/d/tr/f from €37/42/60/70, breakfast €5, mains €10-20) Whitewashed hotel-restaurant that's yet to emerge from the '70s.

Camping Communal (☎ 084 21 19 00; Rue du Hableau; per adult/camp site €2/3; ☑ Easter-Oct) Next to the Lomme River immediately below the main part of town.

La Bella Italia (☎ 084 22 15 20; Rue de Behogne 50; pizzas €7.50-10; ☑ 11.45am-1pm & 6pm-midnight) Excellent wood-fired pizzas are served at this busy Italian restaurant in the heart of town.

Getting There & Away

To get to Rochefort from Namur, take the train to Jemelle (40 minutes, hourly) then the hourly bus No 29 to Rochefort (seven minutes), which continues on to Han (seven minutes).

LA ROCHE-EN-ARDENNE
pop 4100

La Roche is a vibrant little town, hidden in a deep valley, crowned by a ruined castle and surrounded by verdant hills. One of the Ardennes' most popular summer resorts, it hums with Belgian holiday-makers buying up big on smoked hams and getting into outdoor pursuits.

The **tourist office** (☎ 084 35 77 36; www.coeur delardenne.be; Place du Marché 15; ☑ 9am-5pm) is on the main street. Travellers arriving by bus will be dropped at Place du Bronze, the heart of town.

Sights & Activities

From the main street, steps head up to the ruins of La Roche's picture-postcard medieval **castle** (admission €3; ☑ 10am-noon & 2-5pm Apr-Oct, 1.30-4.30pm Mon-Fri, 10am-noon & 1.30-4.30pm Sat & Sun Nov-Mar). Perched on the crag above town, there's not actually much to see – a small museum is the focal point.

The most popular **kayaking excursion** involves a 25km paddle along the Ourthe River. Book through **Ardennes-Aventures** (☎ 084 41 19 00; Rue du Hadja 1; 4-6hr trips €20), next to the bridge at the northern end of town. It also hires **mountain bikes** (half/full day rentals €17/22) for exploring the many marked hiking/ biking trails that crisscross the surrounding hills.

Sleeping & Eating

Domaine des Olivettes (☎ 084 41 16 52; www.les olivettes.be; Chemin de Soeret 12; dm excl breakfast €12, s/d incl breakfast from €28/56) Hotel-cum-*auberge*-cum-equestrian centre, perched on a hill above town. The hotel rooms are pleasant; alternatively there's a separate *auberge* (hostel) with dormitory-style accommodation.

Hôtel Moulin de la Strument (☎ 084 41 15 07; www .strument.com; Petite Strument 62; s/d €64/71; ☑ closed Jan) La Roche's most agreeable hotel is nestled in a secluded wooded valley next to a babbling stream and is part of an old mill.

Camping Le Vieux Moulin (☎ 084 41 13 80; www.strument.com; Petite Strument 62; per adult/camp site €2.50/8; ☑ Easter–mid-Nov) Draped for what seems an eternity along a stream next to the Hôtel Moulin de la Strument. Great site.

Maison Bouillon et Fils (☎ 084 41 18 80; Place du Marché 9) Where but in the Belgian Ardennes would a butcher's shop have its own café? Dine in with an *assiette ardennaise* (plate of mixed local *charcuterie* – hams) for €9 or take away from this must-see *boucherie*.

Getting There & Away

Buses are the only form of public transport reaching La Roche. Coming from Namur, the nearest rail junction is Marloie, from where bus No 15 goes to La Roche (€1.80, 35 minutes, six daily). From Liège, get a train to Melreux and then the La Roche bus (€1.60, 30 minutes, seven daily).

BASTOGNE
pop 14,000

It was in Bastogne, close to the Luxembourg border, that thousands of soldiers and civilians died during WWII's Battle of the Bulge. Testament to these events is a huge, star-shaped **American memorial** on a hill 2km from Bastogne. The neighbouring **Bastogne Historical Centre** (☎ 061 21 14 13; Colline du Mardasson; admission €7.50; ⏰ 10am-4.30pm Feb-Apr & Oct-Dec, 9.30am-5pm May-Sep) recounts the battle.

The **Maison du Tourisme** (☎ 061 21 27 11; www .bastogne-tourisme.be; Place McAuliffe; ⏰ 9am-6pm mid-Jun–mid-Sep, 9am-5.30pm mid-Sep–mid-Jun) is in a conspicuous building in the heart of town.

Hôtel du Sud (☎ 061 21 11 14; www.hotel-du-sud.be; Rue du Marché 39; s/d €44/54) A block from Place McAuliffe, this hotel is the cheapest in town. Passes muster with clean if unexceptional rooms.

Camping de Renval (☎ 061 21 29 85; Route de Marché 148; per adult/camp site €5/15) This is the closest camping ground to town, about 1km from the tourist office.

To get to Bastogne, the closest rail junction is Libramont, from where bus No 163B departs every two hours (€1.80, 45 minutes).

BELGIUM DIRECTORY

ACCOMMODATION

Hostels (*jeugdherberg* in Flemish, *auberge de jeunesse* in French) affiliated with Hostelling International (HI) are easily found. Contact **Vlaamse Jeugdherbergcentrale** (☎ 03 232 72 18; www.jeugdherbergen.be; Van Stralenstraat 40, B-2060 Antwerp) for hostels in Flanders and **Les Auberges de Jeunesse** (☎ 02 219 56 76; www.laj.be; Rue de la Sablonnière 28, B-1000 Brussels) in Wallonia. There are also a few private hostels.

In rural areas, you'll occasionally come across *gîtes d'étapes*, basic hostel-style dwellings that welcome individual travellers.

B&Bs (*gastenkamers/chambres d'hôtes*) normally represent excellent value, with prices starting at €30/45 a single/double. Hotels start at similar rates, but at this price you'll get communal bathroom facilities.

Camping grounds are plentiful and at their best in Wallonia's Ardennes region.

ACTIVITIES
Cycling

Cycling is one of Belgium's national passions. In flat Flanders, many roads have dedicated cycle lanes. In Wallonia, the hilly terrain is favoured by mountain bike (VTT, or *vélo tout-terrain* in French; *terreinfiets* in Flemish) enthusiasts.

Bikes can be hired from private operators or from about 20 train stations for around €6/9 per half/full day. You may be required to pay a deposit (€12 to €20) and show your passport. They can also be taken on trains (one-way/return €4.20/7.20 to anywhere in Belgium).

Hiking

Hiking ranges from the easy terrain in Flanders to the more inspiring hills of the Ardennes. Local tourist offices have copious information about hiking paths and they sell regional hiking maps.

BUSINESS HOURS

Restaurants open from 11.30am to 3pm and 6.30pm to 11pm. Bars and cafés open when they want and close when the last customer leaves. Shops trade from 9am until 12.30pm and 2pm to 6pm Monday to Saturday. Many shops in major cities don't close for lunch, and many also open on Sunday. Banks open at 9am and close between 3.30pm and 5pm Monday to Friday.

EMBASSIES & CONSULATES
Embassies & Consulates in Belgium

The following diplomatic missions are all in Brussels:

Australia (☎ 02 286 05 00; fax 02 230 68 02; Rue Guimard 6, B-1040)

Canada (☎ 02 741 06 11; fax 02 741 06 43; Ave de Tervuren 2, B-1040)

France (☎ 02 548 87 11; fax 02 513 68 71; Rue Ducale 65, B-1000)

Germany (☎ 02 774 19 11; fax 02 772 36 92; Ave de Tervuren 190, B-1150)

Ireland (☎ 02 235 66 76; fax 02 235 66 71; Rue Wiertz 50, B-1050)

Luxembourg (☎ 02 735 57 00; fax 02 737 57 10; Ave de Cortenbergh 75, B-1000)

Netherlands (☎ 02 679 17 11; fax 02 679 17 75; Ave Herrmann-Debroux 48, B-1160)

BELGIUM

New Zealand (☎ 02 512 10 40; fax 02 513 48 56; 7th Fl, Sq de Meeus 1, B-1000)
UK (☎ 02 287 62 11; fax 02 287 63 55; Rue d'Arlon 85, B-1040)
USA (☎ 02 508 21 11; fax 02 511 27 25; Blvd du Régent 27, B-1000)

Belgian Embassies & Consulates Abroad

Australia (☎ 02-6273 2501; fax 02-6273 3392; 19 Arkana St, Yarralumla, Canberra, ACT 2600)
Canada (☎ 613-236 7267; fax 613-236 7882; Ste 820, Constitution Sq, 360 Albert St, Ottawa, ON K1R 7X7)
France (☎ 01 44 09 39 39; fax 01 47 54 07 64; rue de Tilsitt 9, F-75840 Paris Cedex 17)
Germany (☎ 49-3020 6420; fax 49-3020 642 200; Jägerstrasse 52-53, D-10117 Berlin)
Ireland (☎ 01-205 7100; fax 01-283 8488; 2 Shrewsbury Rd, Ballsbridge, Dublin 4)
Luxembourg (☎ 25 43 251; fax 45 42 82; Résidence Champagne, rue des Girondins 4, L-1626 Luxembourg City)
Netherlands (☎ 070-312 34 56; fax 070-364 55 79; Alexanderveld 97, NL-2585 DB Den Haag)
New Zealand (☎ 09-915 9150; fax 09-915 9151; Level 2, Orica House, cnr Kingdon & Carlton Gore St, Auckland SA 5071)
UK (☎ 020-7470 3700; fax 020-7259 6213; 103-105 Eaton Sq, London SW1 9AB)
USA (☎ 202-333 6900; fax 202-333 3079; 3330 Garfield St, NW, Washington, DC 2000)

FESTIVALS & EVENTS

The country buzzes with festivals. The following are a few of the highlights:
Brussels Jazz Marathon (www.brusselsjazzmarathon.be) The last weekend in May brings nonstop jazz to Brussels.
Couleur Café (www.couleurcafe.be) This world music event kicks off Brussels' summer festivities. Held over three days during the last weekend in June.
De Gentse Feesten (www.gentsefeesten.be) Ghent's annual 10-day festival shindig in mid-July transforms the city into a party of music and theatre. Includes **10 Days Off...** (www.10daysoff.be), one of Europe's main techno parties.
International Festival of Fantasy, Thriller & Science Fiction Film (www.bifff.org) Brussels' get-together for fans of cult fantasy, thriller and science-fiction movies. Held in March.

FOOD & DRINK

Belgians love food. They are reputed to dine out, on average, more than any other people in the world.

The national dish is *mosselen/moules* – mussels cooked in white wine and served in steaming cauldrons with a mountain of chips.

Meat and seafood are abundantly consumed, as are *frieten/frites* – chips or fries. Belgians swear they invented chips and, judging by the availability, it's a claim few would contest. Italian, Greek, Turkish and Portuguese cuisines thrive too. A few African eateries in Brussels reflect Belgium's colonial past. Many cafés and brasseries these days cater to vegetarian tastes (but not to vegans).

And then there's chocolate. Belgians have been quietly making some of the world's finest chocolate for well over a century. Filled chocolates, or pralines (prah-leens), are their forte.

On the drinking scene, beer rules. No country in the world boasts a brewing tradition as rich and diverse as Belgium. And nowhere will you find the quantity of quality beers offered by this little nation. Somewhere between 400 and 800 beers exist. Try a dark Trappist beer made by monks, golden nectars like Duvel (named after the devil himself), or the acquired taste of tangy, fruity *lambics* (beer unique to the Brussels region). For the latter, don't miss Brussels' Musée Bruxellois de la Gueuze (see p115).

HOLIDAYS

New Year's Day 1 January
Easter Monday March/April
Labour Day 1 May
Ascension Day 40th day after Easter
Whit Monday 7th Monday after Easter
Festival of the Flemish Community 11 July (Flanders only)
National Day 21 July
Assumption 15 August
Walloon Community 27 September (Wallonia only)
All Saints' Day 1 November
Armistice Day 11 November
Christmas Day 25 December

LANGUAGE

For details on the country's linguistic make-up, see People & Culture, p110.

MONEY

Banks are the best place to exchange money. Outside banking hours, exchange bureaus (*wisselkantoren* in Flemish, *bureaux d'échange* in French) operate at Brussels National airport and at main train stations. ATMs are widespread. Tipping is not obligatory as service and VAT (value-added tax) are included in hotel and restaurant prices.

POST

Some useful poste restante addresses include the following:

Poste Restante (Hoofdpostkantoor, Groenplaats, B-2000 Antwerp)

Poste Restante (Hoofdpostkantoor, Markt 5, B-8000 Bruges)

Poste Restante (Bureau de Poste Central, Centre Monnaie, B-1000 Brussels)

Post offices are generally open from 9am to 5pm weekdays and 9am to noon Saturday. Letters under 50g cost €0.60 within the EU, or €0.85 anywhere else.

TELEPHONE

Belgium's international country code is ☎ 32. To telephone abroad, the international access code is ☎ 00. For an international operator, call ☎ 1224.

Local phone calls are metered and cost a minimum of €0.25. Telephone numbers prefixed with 0900 or 070 are expensive pay-per-minute numbers. Numbers prefixed with 0800 are free calls. Those prefixed with 075, 0476 to 0479, 0486 and 0496 are mobile numbers.

VISAS

There are no entry requirements or restrictions on EU nationals visiting Belgium. The citizens of Australia, Canada, Israel, Japan, New Zealand and the USA do not need visas to visit the country as tourists for up to three months. Except for people from a few other European countries (such as Switzerland and Norway), everyone else must have a visa issued by a Belgian embassy or consulate.

Bosnia & Hercegovina

HIGHLIGHTS

- **Sarajevo** A revitalised city with a tumultuous history; the old Turkish quarter Baščaršija with ancient mosques, craft shops and cafés with proper Turkish coffee (p136)
- **Mostar** The beautiful, ancient bridge, a link between cultures, once destroyed and now rebuilt (p141)
- **Međugorje** A religious tourist resort where devout Catholics flock to visit the site of the Virgin Mary apparitions (p142)
- **Best journey** The train trip between Mostar and Sarajevo, chugging along the emerald Neretva River, then climbing the mountains via tunnels, viaducts and switchbacks (p142)
- **Off-the-beaten track** Bihać and the rolling green Una River sweeping through a rocky gorge, the location for rafting and kayaking (p141)

FAST FACTS

- **Area** 51,129 sq km (that's half a Cuba)
- **ATMs** Widespread in Sarajevo, sufficient in major towns
- **Budget** 80KM per day
- **Capital** Sarajevo
- **Country Code** ☎ 387
- **Heads of State** Presidents Dragan Čović (Croat), Borislav Paravac (Serb), Sulejman Tihić (Bosniak), each serving eight months on rotation
- **Famous for** 1984 Winter Olympics, bridge at Mostar
- **Languages** Bosnian, Croatian, Serbian
- **Money** Convertible mark (A$1 = 1.14KM, CA$1 = 1.26KM, €1 = 1.96KM, ¥100 = 1.43KM, NZ$1 = 1.07KM, UK£1 = 2.83KM, US$1 = 1.59KM)
- **Phrases** Zdravo (hello), hvala (thanks), molim (please), dovidjenja (goodbye)

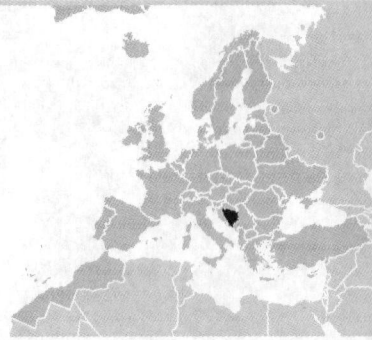

- **Population** 3.99 million (estimate)
- **Time** GMT + 1
- **Visas** Not required for citizens of most EU countries, Australia, New Zealand, Canada and the USA.

TRAVEL HINTS

Use the accommodation agencies for cheap sleeps, kill the hunger pangs for half a day with a wedge of *burek* (a layered meat pie) and get about cheaply on the country's extensive bus network.

ROAMING BOSNIA & HERCEGOVINA

Take a bus from the Croatian coast to Mostar, a side trip to Međugorje, then on to Sarajevo and exit to Croatia, Hungary or Serbia.

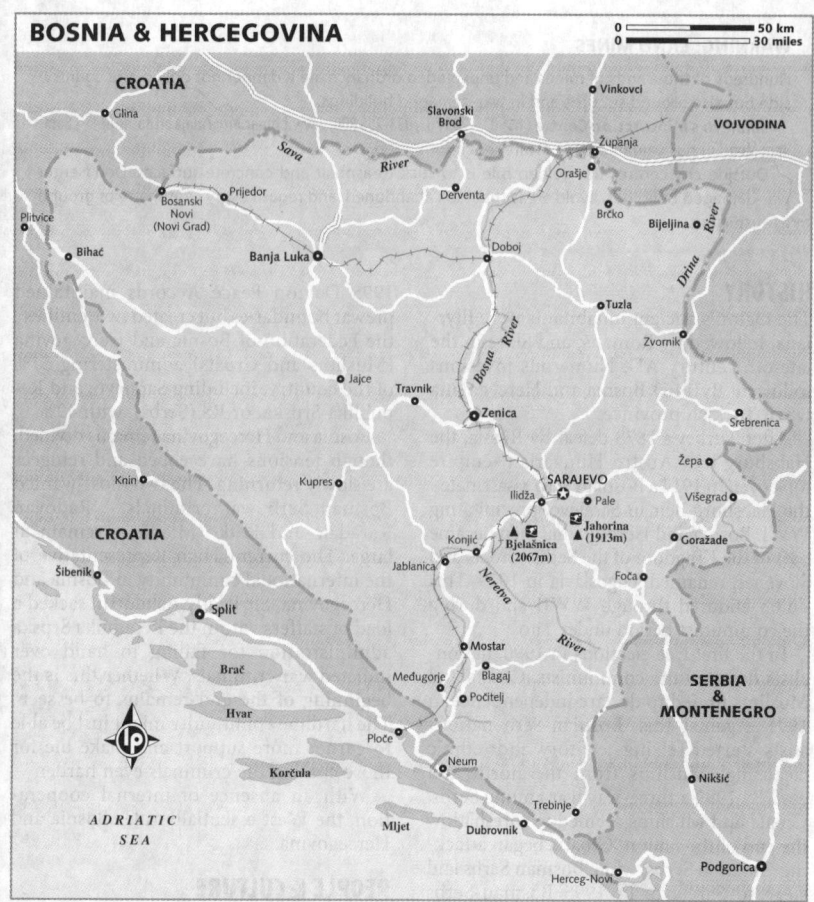

BOSNIA & HERCEGOVINA

| 0 | 50 km |
| 0 | 30 miles |

CROATIA

Clina

Slavonski Brod

Vinkovci

VOJVODINA

Sava River

Županja

Orašje

Plitvice

Bosanski Novi (Novi Grad)

Prijedor

Derventa

Brčko

Bijeljina

Bihać

Doboj

Banja Luka

Drina River

Tuzla

Zvornik

Jajce

Travnik

Bosna River

Zenica

Srebrenica

Žepa

Knin

Kupres

SARAJEVO

Ilidža

Pale

Višegrad

CROATIA

Konjic

Bjelašnica (2067m)

Jahorina (1913m)

Goražde

Šibenik

Jablanica

Neretva

Foča

Split

Brač

Mostar

River

Međugorje

Blagaj

SERBIA & MONTENEGRO

Hvar

Počitelj

Ploče

Neum

Korčula

Nikšić

ADRIATIC SEA

Trebinje

Mljet

Dubrovnik

Podgorica

Herceg-Novi

Magnificent mountain scenery etched by clear green rivers provides a backdrop to a combination of Eastern and Western cultures, which characterise this country. It has been a crossroads between Byzantine and Catholic Europe as well as between Turkish and Austro-Hungarian empires. It refers to both west and east. Such a medley has also produced a tolerant culture brimming in diversity. Sarajevo was the cultural epicentre of the old Yugoslavia; indicated by there being a Catholic cathedral, mosque, synagogue and Orthodox church standing within 150m of each other.

The country is most regularly conjured in people's minds for having hosted the 1984 Olympic Winter Games, and for the the heartwrenchingly cruel wars of the 1990s that practically destroyed the country. Fortunately Bosnia and Hercegovina is now on a progressive, albeit slow, road to recovery. Infrastructure is gradually being reintroduced and facilities developed. Visitors are now able to walk across the new 'old' bridge at Mostar, wander around the revitalised Baščaršija in Sarajevo, while white-water junkies are fortunate in having the splendid Una River at Bihać at their mercy for energetic kayaking and rafting thrills.

There's a vibrancy in the air, a cultural depth and a warmth for visitors, while Sarajevo is becoming a world-class tourist capital.

WARNING: LAND MINES

Hundreds of thousands of mines and unexploded ordnance are a danger not only in the country-side but also around suburbs and in war-damaged buildings.

Sarajevo's **Mine Action Centre** (☎ 033-209 762, 033-253 800; www.bhmac.org; Zmaja od Bosne 8; ⏲ 8am-4pm Mon-Fri) has valuable mine awareness information.

Outside city centres the golden rule is to stick to asphalt and concrete surfaces. Don't enter war-damaged buildings, avoid areas that look abandoned, and regard every centimetre of ground as suspicious.

HISTORY

The region's ancient inhabitants were Illyrians, followed by Romans, and Slavs in the late 6th century AD. Numerous invasions followed. By 1463 Bosnia and Hercegovina was a Turkish province.

After Turkey's 1878 defeat by Russia, the Habsburg-led Austro-Hungarian empire took over. In 1914 a Bosnian Serb assassinated the Habsburg heir in Sarajevo, precipitating WWI. Bosnia and Hercegovina then became part of the Kingdom of the Serbs, Croats and Slovenes, renamed Yugoslavia in 1929. This union endured through WWII and during the communist period under Tito.

In the first free elections in 1990, nationalists defeated the communists. Croats and Muslims united to declare independence in 1991. Against this, Bosnian-Serb nationalists started seizing territory and 'ethnic cleansing' Muslims from the north and east. By 1992 a three-way war among Serbs, Croats and Muslims seemed to foreshadow the end of the nation. Croatia began attacking Croatian Serbs, while Bosnian Serbs laid siege to Sarajevo. In 1995 Bosnian-Serbs slaughtered more than 7000 Muslims in the UN-protected 'safe' area of Srebrenica.

Battered by subsequent NATO air strikes, the Serbs entered peace talks. The resulting 1995 Dayton Peace Accords maintained prewar boundaries but created two 'entities', the Federation of Bosnia and Hercegovina (Muslims and Croats) administering 51% of the country, including Sarajevo; and Republika Srpska, or RS (Serbs), with 49%.

Bosnia and Hercegovina remains divided, though tensions have ebbed and refugees are slowly returning. The two most-wanted Bosnian Serb war criminals – Radovan Karadžić and Ratko Mladić – remain at large. The current High Representative of the international community in Bosnia and Hercegovina, Sir Paddy Ashdown, sacked a load of staffers within the Republika Srpska administration for failing to hand over indicted war criminals. Whether this is the beginning of the end remains to be seen. The hardline community might just be able to garner more support and make life for those chasing the criminals even harder.

With an absence of internal cooperation, the West essentially rules Bosnia and Hercegovina.

PEOPLE & CULTURE

Bosniaks (48% of the population) live mostly in the centre, Croats (14%) mainly in the south and west, and Serbs (37%) in Republika Srpska's north and east. Roma are the prominent minority.

Generally speaking, Croats are Catholic, Bosniaks Muslim and Serbs Orthodox. Bosnian, Croatian and Serbian are essentially the same language. The Federation officially uses the Latin alphabet; Republika Srpska officially uses Cyrillic. See the Language chapter (p1266).

ENVIRONMENT

Bosnia and Hercegovina is a mountainous country of 51,129 sq km in the central Balkans; just a toe of land connects it to the sea. A dry and arid south gives way to a central

---

READING UP

Read Noel Malcolm's *Bosnia: A Short History* to update and complement Rebecca West's classic 1941 *Black Lamb Grey Falcon*. Ivo Andric's fictional works, *Bridge over the Drina* and *Travnik Chronicles*, describes life under the Turks and Austro-Hungarians. Bosnian expat Aleksandar Hemon's (coined the new Nabokov) has written *The Question of Bruno*, which depicts surreal, childhood reminiscences.

mountainous core descending northwards to green rolling hills and flatlands.

Owing to its altitude, it gets hot in summer but quite chilly in winter; snowfall can last until April.

Main national parks are Sutjeska, with its remnants of 20,000-year-old primeval forests; and the Hutovo Blato wetlands, a prime bird sanctuary.

Mines and unexploded ordnance mean much of the country is out of reach but with local guides, visits are quite feasible. Leftover from war, these, the infrastructure damage, and industrial air pollution and rubbish disposal are large environmental problems.

TRANSPORT

GETTING THERE & AWAY
Air
Bosnia and Hercegovina's main airport, **Sarajevo** (☎ 033-289 100; www.sarajevo-airport.ba) is served by a few European airlines such as Austrian Airlines, Lufthansa and Adria Airways, which pick up at intercontinental hubs like London, Frankfurt and Vienna. No discount airlines fly into Bosnia and Hercegovina, but cheap flights to Dubrovnik in Croatia, followed by a bus trip into the country could be a possibility.

Air Bosnia, the national airline, is currently not operational.

Bus
Buses from Croatia travel to Sarajevo and Mostar. Buses from Serbia and Montenegro run to Banja Luka and the Sarajevo suburb of Lukavica (both in Republika Srpska).

Eurolines has bus services from Sarajevo to Munich (€54, 16 hours, daily), Amsterdam (€125, 32 hours, Tuesday, Thursday and Saturday) and Brussels (€105, 27 hours, Tuesday and Saturday).

Car & Motorcycle
There are no problems bringing in your own vehicle; a Green Card and International Driving Licence is all that's needed. Intercity roads are generally in good condition but cross-mountain routes can be narrow and winding, making for slower journeys than expected.

Seat belts must be worn and the tolerated alcohol in the blood limit is 0.05.

Train
A service travels from Ploče to Zagreb in Croatia via Mostar, Sarajevo and Banja Luka (30KM, 8½ hours, two daily); another connects Ploče and Sarajevo via Mostar (9KM, 2¾ hours, two daily).

A 10.25pm train runs from Sarajevo to Budapest (1st/2nd class 90/130KM, 11 hours, daily).

A 9.15pm train runs from Banja Luka to Belgrade (22.50KM, nine hours, daily).

GETTING AROUND
Bus
The bus network is comprehensive and reliable. Services between more distant towns can be infrequent.

Car & Motorcycle
Although travelling through beautiful countryside, narrow roads, hills and bends make for slow and challenging progress.

Local Transport
Taxis are readily available and cheap. Outside the big towns they may not have meters, so agree on a price before you set off.

DEPARTURE TAX
If not included in the ticket price, departure tax is €15.

BOSNIA & HERCEGOVINA

Train

There are far fewer trains than buses but they're more comfortable with better views of the countryside. Useful internal trains are between Sarajevo and Mostar (9KM, 2¾ hours, two daily) and Banja Luka (18.50KM, five hours, two daily). Trains from Banja Luka travel locally within Republika Srpska.

SARAJEVO

☎ 033 / pop 602,500

Sarajevo was once a society where Muslims, Serbs, Croats, Turks, Jews and others had peacefully coexisted. One of Europe's most eastern cities, it's retained the essence of a rich history in its mosques, markets and the picturesque bazaar of Baščaršija.

Despite the highly visible scars of war, Sarajevo is again bursting with energy. Rattling trams run around the city centre, innumerable cafés spread over the streets and locals spend leisurely evenings strolling down the main pedestrian street, Ferhadija. The energy poured into Bosnia and Hercegovina's recovery has made Sarajevo one of the fastest changing cities in Europe.

ORIENTATION

Sarajevo is ringed by hills with lower ground to the west making the main routes run east–west. From the airport, 13km to the southwest, the main road runs up to Ilidža then east through Novo Sarajevo, past the bus and train stations turn-off, and into the centre. Baščaršija occupies the east end of town.

INFORMATION
Bookshops

Buybook Radićeva (☎ 716 450; www.buybook.com .ba; Radićeva 4; ✆ 9am-10pm Mon-Sat, 10am-6pm Sun) Cheap English classics, books on the Balkans and an in-house café; Zelenih Beretki (☎ 712 000; Zelenih Beretki 8; ✆ 9am-10pm Mon-Sat) Art book specialists, English newspapers, CDs and Karabit Café (see p139).

Šahinpašić (☎ 220 111; www.btcsahinpasic.com; Mula Mustafe Bašeskije 1; ✆ 9am-8pm Mon-Sat, 10am-2pm Sun) English-language newspapers and magazines.

Internet Access

Albatros (☎ 555 483; Sagrdžije 27; per hr 3KM; ✆ 9am-midnight)

Click (☎ 236 914; Kundurdžiluk 1; per hr 3KM; ✆ 9am-11pm)

EMERGENCY NUMBERS

- **Emergency assistance** ☎ 124
- **Fire** ☎ 123
- **Police** ☎ 122
  (English speakers in major towns)

Left Luggage

Main bus station (1.50KM for 3hr, 0.50KM subsequent hr) Useful while you go into town to look for accommodation.

Medical Services

Ask your embassy for a list of private doctors. In an emergency, there are a couple of hospitals in town:

Koševo Hospital (☎ 297 000; Bolnička 25)

City Hospital (State Hospital; ☎ 285 100; Kranjčevića 12)

Money

There are ATMs all over the city; many banks change travellers cheques.

Turkish Ziraat Bank (☎ 720 209; Ferhadija 10; ✆ 8.30am-8pm Mon-Fri, 9am-noon Sat) ATM and cashes travellers cheques.

Post

Central Post Office (☎ 650 618; Obala Kulina Bana 8; ✆ 7am-8pm Mon-Sat) Counter 17 is for post; the others are for paying bills.

Telephone

Telephone Centre (Obala Kulina Bana 8; ✆ 7am-8pm) In the same building as the Central Post Office.

Tourist Information

Tourist Office (☎ 220 724, 532 606; www.sarajevo -tourism.com; Zelenih Beretki 22a; ✆ 9am-8pm Mon-Fri, 9am-4pm Sat, 10am-2pm Sun) A most helpful place with books, maps, brochures and ready answers.

Travel Agencies

Centrotrans (☎ 205 481; ferhadija16@hotmail.com; Ferhadija 16; ✆ 8am-8pm Mon-Fri, 8am-2pm Sat) Books international bus tickets.

Relax Tours (☎ 263 190; www.relaxtours.com; Zelenih Beretki 22; ✆ 9am-8pm Mon-Fri, 9am-5pm Sat) Books airline and ferry tickets.

SIGHTS & ACTIVITIES

The bustling old Turkish Quarter of Baščaršija is a labyrinth of polished cobble-stone laneways where, behind the tourist panache, Sarajevo keeps its soul. Lose yourself

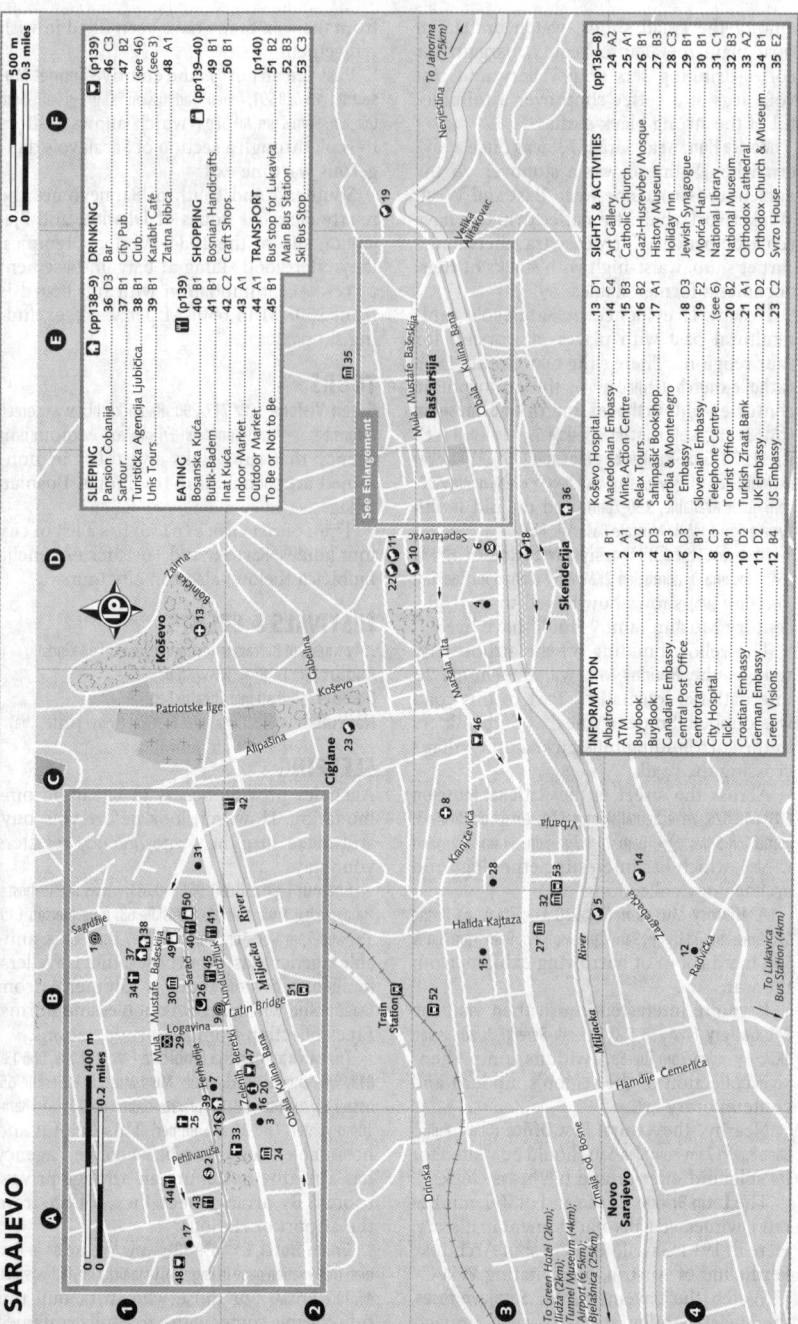

SARAJEVO

SLEEPING	**(pp138–9)**	**DRINKING**	**(p139)**
Pansion Cobanija	36 D3	Bar	46 B1
Sartour	37 B1	City Pub	47 B2
Turistička Agencija Ljubičica	38 B1	Club	(see 46)
Unis Tours	39 B1	Karabit Café	(see 3)
		Zlatna Ribica	48 A1
EATING	**(p139)**		
Bosanska Kuća	40 B1	**SHOPPING**	**(pp139–40)**
Butik-Bađem	41 B1	Bosnian Handicrafts	49 B1
Inat Kuća	42 C2	Craft Shops	50 B1
Indoor Market	43 A1		
Outdoor Market	44 A1	**TRANSPORT**	**(p140)**
To Be or Not to Be	45 B1	Bus stop for Lukavica	51 B2
		Main Bus Station	52 B3
		Ski Bus Stop	53 C3

INFORMATION		**SIGHTS & ACTIVITIES**	**(pp136–8)**
Albatros	1 B1	Art Gallery	24 A2
ATM	2 A1	Catholic Church	25 A1
BuyBook	3 A2	Gazi-Husrevbey Mosque	26 B1
BuyBook	4 D3	History Museum	27 B3
Canadian Embassy	5 B3	Holiday Inn	28 C3
Central Post Office	6 D3	Jewish Synagogue	29 B1
Centrotrans	7 B1	Morića Han	30 B1
City Hospital	8 C3	National Library	31 C1
Click	9 B1	National Museum	32 B3
Croatian Embassy	10 D2	Orthodox Cathedral	33 A2
German Embassy	11 D2	Orthodox Church & Museum	34 B1
Green Visions	12 B4	Svrzo House	35 E2
Koševo Hospital	13 D1		
Macedonian Embassy	14 C4		
Mine Action Centre	15 B3		
Relax Tours	16 B2		
Šahinpašić Bookshop	17 A1		
Serbia & Montenegro			
Embassy	18 D3		
Slovenian Embassy	19 F2		
Telephone Centre	(see 6)		
Tourist Office	20 B2		
Turkish Ziraat Bank	21 A1		
UK Embassy	22 D2		
US Embassy	23 C2		

among the small shops, watch craftsmen turn plain metal into beauty, bargain for coffee-drinking sets or jewellery and rest your legs at a coffee shop over a thimbleful of the strong black stuff.

Morića Han, near Saraći 73, was once a tavern when Sarajevo was a stopover on the ancient crossroads between East and West. Wickerwork chairs for coffee drinkers have replaced benches for weary travellers and a carpet shop, waist-high with stacks of rugs, occupies a former stables.

Nearby is evidence of Sarajevo's multicultural past with places of worship for four religions. There's the neo-Gothic 1889 **Catholic church** (Ferhadija bb); the atmospheric centuries-old **Orthodox church and museum** (☎ 534 783; Mula Mustafe Bašeskije 59; admission free); the 1531 **Gazi-Husrevbey Mosque** (☎ 532 144; Veliki Mudželeti 21; www.vakuf-gazi.ba; �9am-noon, 2.30-4pm guide available, 5.30-7pm); and the old **Jewish synagogue** (Mula Mustafe Bašeskije bb).

Just north of Baščaršija, **Svrzo House** (☎ 535 264; Glodžina 8; admission 2KM; �
10am-5pm Tue-Sat, 10am-1pm Sun) shows how a well-to-do 18th-century Muslim family would have lived.

The yellow building off the airport–city road is the **Holiday Inn**, wartime home to international journalists. Part of this road was dubbed 'Sniper's Alley' as Serb snipers in the surrounding hills picked off civilians crossing the road.

Across the street is the **National Museum** (☎ 668 026; www.zemaljskimuzej.ba; Zmaja od Bosne 3; admission 5KM; �
10am-2pm Tue-Sun, 11am-7pm Wed Jul-Sep), which has interesting ethnology and archaeology collections.

A **History Museum** (☎ 210 418; Zmaja od Bosne 5; admission 5KM; �9am-2pm Mon-Fri, 9am-1pm Sat & Sun) has a room of harrowing exhibits from the war.

If you're interested in art, then visit the **Art Gallery** (☎ 266 550; Zelenih Beretki 8; admission 2KM; �noon-2pm Tue-Sat), with its comprehensive collection of the region's modern and contemporary art.

Nearby, the **Central Post Office** (Obala Kulina Bana 8; �7am-8pm Mon-Sat) should be visited for its splendid interior and big brass clock.

The **Latin Bridge**, at the end of Zelenih Beretki, witnessed a pivotal moment in history. Here in 1914 Gavrilo Princip shot Archduke Ferdinand of Austria, precipitating WWI.

Watch the pavements for **Sarajevo roses**, the skeletal indentations of shell impacts

from the war. Some have been filled in with red cement.

Past the airport is the emotive **Tunnel Museum** (☎ 628 591; Tuneli 1; admission 5KM; �
9am-5pm Oct-Jun, 9am-7pm Jul-Sep), which allows visitors to walk through a section of Sarajevo's dangerous wartime exit.

Southeast and south of Sarajevo are the nearly deserted slopes of **Jahorina**, and **Bjelašnica**, site of the 1984 Winter Olympics; they offer good skiing at bargain-basement prices. Accommodation with full board is from 250KM to 650KM per week, excluding ski passes.

TOURS

Green Visions (☎ 717 290; Radnička bb; www.green visions.ba; �9am-5pm Mon-Fri) is an ecotourism agency that runs treks and tours in non-mined areas including traditional Bosnian villages.

The Tourist Office (p136) has a list of city tour guides; Sartour and Turistička Agencija Ljubičica (below) also run city tours.

FESTIVALS & EVENTS

July Nights of Baščaršija (cultural events of all kinds)
August Film Festival (www.sff.ba)
October International Theatre Festival
November International Jazz Festival (www.jazzfest.ba)

SLEEPING

Agencies provide access to cheap accommodation. However, look before you 'buy' and make sure the owner/agency registers your stay.

Sartour (☎ 238 680, 061 800 263; www.sartour-hostel -sarajevo.ba; Mula Mustafe Bašeskije 63; b per person €15; �9am-7pm Nov-Apr, 7am-8pm May-Oct) This amiable agency has a purpose-built travellers' hang-out hostel about a kilometre from Baščaršija with a mix of doubles and dorms. Free collection from airport or stations.

Turistička Agencija Ljubičica (☎ 232 109, 066 131 813, www.hostelljubicica.com; Mula Mustafe Bašeskije 65; hostel s/d/tr from €8-16, private rooms €6-20; �8am-10pm winter, 7am-11pm summer) This helpful and hospitable 'would you like a coffee?' agency has a nearby hostel or can arrange private rooms. By arrangement they collect from the airport or stations.

Green Hotel (☎ 639 701; www.green.co.ba in Bosnian (reservation page in English); Ustanička bb, Ilidža; s/d/tr 45/70.2/105KM) For those who work out, this tidy cheapie comes with a free fully equipped gym. The tram terminus is a 150m jog away with a 20-minute ride into Baščaršija.

Pansion Čobanija (☎ 441 749; fax 203 937; Čobanija 29; s/d 80/120KM) With a big open lounge and sink-into leather chairs, it's so homely it feels as if you're staying with friends. All rooms are different, with superior upstairs rooms; consider Room 202 with its neo-Art Deco mirrored furniture.

Other recommendations:

Unis Tours (☎ /fax 209 089; Ferhadija 16; s/d 42/74KM; ☺ 8am-7pm Mon-Fri, 9am-2pm Sat) Central private accommodation and hostels.

Relax Tours (☎ 263 190; www.relaxtours.com; Zelenih Beretki 22; rooms 50KM; ☺ 9am-8pm, 9am-5pm Sat) Hotel rooms including ski hotels.

EATING

The handy **outdoor market** (Mula Mustafe Bašeskije; ☺ 7am-4pm) overflows with fruit and vegetables; the **indoor market** across the street in the classical-style building sells dairy and meat products.

Bakeries for burek (try the peppery potato one) and pizza slices dot all the roads in the centre. For the ubiquitous cevapi (lamb and beef rolls in spongy bread), follow your nose.

Butik-Badem (☎ 533 135; Abadžiluk 12; ☺ 8am-11pm) Alternative snacks, such as yummy chocolate-coated pistachios, fruit bars and nuts, are on offer from this health food shop just downhill from the cobblestone square in Baščaršija.

Bosanska Kuća (☎ 237 320; Bravadžiluk 3; dishes 6-9KM; ☺ 24hr) 'Come eat,' says the waiter in national costume, inviting you into a restaurant promoting Bosnian traditional food and setting. A colour picture menu makes choosing easier; selections include kebabs, some grilled fish, or stuffed peppers or aubergines for vegetarians.

To Be or Not to Be (☎ 233 205; Čizmedžiluk 5; dishes 4-8KM; ☺ 11am-11pm) Grills, generous salads and tangy seafood dishes are the go here.

Inat Kuća (Spite House; ☎ 447 867; Velika Alifakovac 1; dishes 7-10KM; ☺ 8am-11pm) The restaurant was once across the river and when the authorities wanted to demolish it during the construction of the library, the owner insisted it be reconstructed here – hence the name. There's no spite in the offerings, though, which range from snacks such as kselo mlijelo (drinking yoghurt) and sticky baklava to a bowl of chips and beer or a full-blown grill.

> **GETTING INTO TOWN**
>
> Taxi (15KM) is the only way from the airport or get off at Ilidža (5KM) and transfer to tram No 3 for Baščaršija. Tram No 1 from the train and bus stations goes to Baščaršija.

In warm weather, the riverside terrace is the spot for a bit of afternoon relaxation.

DRINKING

Club (☎ 550 550; Maršala Tita 7; dishes 12-25KM; ☺ 10am-late) This hip and sassy basement joint grooves to DJ music or local bands on weekends. Different rooms cater for drinking, dancing or just chatting up under the seductive lighting, and a restaurant cooks up sizzling pizzas. It's a bit difficult to find, but it's the first door left after the entrance.

Bar (Maršala Tita 7; ☺ 7-3am) Listen to the music and hang out at this laid-back club with white deck chairs and bolsters under the trees.

Zlatna Ribica (☎ 215 369; Kaptol 5; ☺ 9am-late) A collision of aesthetics as baroque, fin de siecle Paris and Vienna, and Art Deco crash together in this warmly lit bar. Nature abhors a vacuum, and so does this bar's owner, who has filled every nook and cranny with knickknacks, creating a visual feast. Drinks come with a side plate of nuts and dried figs.

City Pub (☎ 299 916; Despićeva bb; dishes 6-9KM; ☺ 8am-late) A daytime café bar, with Lebanese and Mexican taste ticklers. At night it's a big music and drinking venue with local bands playing blues, jazz or rock most nights. This pub swings, and even the bouncers smile.

Karabit Café (☎ 712 000; Zelenih Beretki 8; ☺ 9am-10pm Mon-Sat, 10am-6pm Sun) Often the place to go when others are closed, you've had enough of them or you're out of ideas. Buy a book, read a magazine, sip a coffee and ponder the meaning of life.

SHOPPING

Baščaršija is the shopping magnet with small places specialising in enamelled and sculptured copper and brassware, jewellery, clothes and carpets.

Don't miss the Survival Map (15KM), a cartoon-like map of wartime Sarajevo, available in bookshops.

Bosnian Handicrafts (☎ 035-282 554; www.bosnianhandicrafts.com; Culhan 1; ☺ 8am-8pm Mon-Fri,

9am-7pm Sat, 10am-4pm Sun) In Baščaršija, this nonprofit organisation works with refugees, displaced people and rural women who produce colourful woven items.

GETTING THERE & AWAY
Bus
Sarajevo has two bus stations. Buses to Banja Luka leave from both. In winter a bus operates to the ski areas from a stop near the National Museum. The Tourist Office (see p136) always has a current bus schedule.

MAIN BUS STATION
Services from the **main bus station** (☎ 213 100; Put Života 8) serve all destinations outside Republika Srpska. Frequent buses go to Mostar (16KM return, 2½ hours, daily), Bihać (27KM, 6½ hours, three daily) and Banja Luka (21KM, five hours, two daily).

Buses run to Zagreb (€30, eight hours, three daily), Split (€30, eight hours, four daily) and Dubrovnik (€30, seven hours, daily, 7.15am).

LUKAVICA BUS STATION
The **Lukavica bus station** (☎ 057-677 377; Lukavica village) has buses to Belgrade (20KM, eight hours, six daily), Podgorica (€10, six hours, four daily) and Banja Luka (18.50KM, five hours, hourly).

For the Lukavica terminus, take trolleybus No 103 from Austrijski Trg to the last stop and walk 150m, or take a taxi.

Train
Services from the **train station** (☎ 655 330; Put Života 2) run to Mostar (9KM, three hours, two daily, 6.20am and 7pm) and Banja Luka (21KM, five hours, daily, 10.30am) with international services to Zagreb and Budapest (see p135).

GETTING AROUND
Sarajevo has an efficient tram service. Tram No 1 connects the stations and Baščaršija, tram No 3 Ilidža and Baščaršija, and tram No 4 Ilidža and the stations.

Buy tickets from a kiosk (1.20KM) or driver (1.50KM) and validate it in the machine on board. Buses and trolleybus tickets work the same way.

Sarajevo taxi meters begin at 2KM and charge about 1KM per kilometre. Call **Sarajevo Taxi** (☎ 1515).

AROUND BOSNIA & HERCEGOVINA

BANJA LUKA
☎ 051 / pop 200,000
The Republika Srpska capital is a good place for a breather and a look at 'RS' life. Down by the Vrbas River the large 16th-century **castle** is about the oldest thing around due to WWII bombardment and a 1969 earthquake. If you come across a bare patch of land in Banja Luka, it probably used to be one of the city's 16 destroyed mosques. Bosnian Serbs razed the **Ferhadija**, a famous mosque originally built in 1580 with the ransom money paid for an Austrian count.

Down a side alley, **Turistički Savez** (☎ 212 323; tursavbl@teol.net; Kralja Petra 113) has maps and brochures. Some staff speak a little English.

Sleeping & Eating
Hotel Bosna (☎ 215 775; Kralja Petra 97; s/d 67/104KM, renovated s/d 102/144KM) A grand hotel right in the heart of town with some perfectly adequate and cheap unrenovated rooms. It also has a big restaurant, bar and shops.

Hotel Vidović (☎ 217 217; fax 211 100; Kozarska 85; s/d 70/81KM; P ⊠) Down a leafy road a few kilometres from the centre, this hotel has clean, fresh rooms.

Kod Muje (☎ 358 492; snacks 2-5KM; ☼ 7am-11pm) A good cheap eatery but a bit hard to find. Head straight between the white theatre and park on Kralja Petra, over Bana Milosavljevica and down a laneway. A big fave with UN troops.

Master (☎ 317 444; Sime Solaje 7; dishes 8-12KM; ☼ 10am-midnight) If you're jaded by all that grilled meat, then try Mexican; the locals have certainly warmed to enchiladas, fajitas and a Corona beer or two.

Getting There & Away
The **train station** (☎ 300 752; Srpskih Boraca 17) and adjacent **bus station** (☎ 315 865; Prote N Kostića 38) are 3km north of the centre; a taxi should cost 5KM.

Buses run to Zagreb (23KM, seven hours, three daily), Sarajevo (23KM, five hours, seven daily) and Belgrade (23KM, seven hours, hourly). Buses run to Bihać (11KM, four hours, four daily).

Trains run once a day to Zagreb (4½ hours), Ljubljana (seven hours) and Sarajevo. A nightly train goes to Belgrade (see p135).

BIHAĆ

☎ 037 / pop 65,000

The attraction here is the wide and rolling Una River, interrupted occasionally by tumbling rapids. This is a kayaking and rafting centre, and the Una Regatta in July is three days of messing about in boats.

The **tourist office** (☎ 222 777; Dr Irfana Ljubijankica 13; ☽ 8am-4pm Mon-Fri) has information on river activities and accommodation possibilities.

Activities

The rafting season usually runs from March to October. Prices depend upon group numbers, distance and the difficulty factor of the trip.

Una Kiro Rafting (☎ 223 760, 061 192 338; www.una-kiro-rafting.com; Muse Ćazima Ćatića 1), based at Golubic 6km from Bihać, offers kayaking lessons, equipment and accommodation.

Una Rafting (Sport Bjeli; ☎ 223 502, 061 138 853; www.unarafting.com; rafting 40-80KM; Klokot, Pecikoviči bb) is another rafting and kayaking outfit.

Sleeping & Eating

Hut Aduna (☎ 310 487; Put 5 Korpusa; per adult 5KM; P) An under-the-trees *autocamp*, about 5km out of town between the Una River and the Sunce Hotel. Sites are powered and there's a toilet and shower block.

MB Lipovaća (☎ 351 620; mblip@bih.net.ba; Dr Irfana Ljubijankića 91; s/d/tr 32-45/80/120; P) About 2km out of town, this decent hotel has all the usual modcons although the cheaper singles are without TV.

Villa Una (☎ 311 393; Bihaćkih Branilaca 20; s/d 50/70; P) This sparkling private home with well-equipped rooms is centrally placed near the river and good value.

Express (☎ 332 380; Bosanska 5; dishes 3-5KM; ☽ 7am-10pm) Express by name, express by nature. Choose, point and eat heartily at this cafeteria near the post office.

Meno (☎ 311 511; Bihaćkih Branilaca 35; pizzas 5-10KM; ☽ 8am-11pm) The top place for pizza in town with a wide range of toppings and sizes. It's a takeaway place as well.

Getting There & Away

Bihać is best reached via Banja Luka. Services from the **bus station** (☎ 350 676; Put V Korpusa bb) are somewhat limited with two buses to Banja Luka and three to Sarajevo.

MOSTAR

☎ 036 / pop 94,000

Mostar, a beautiful medieval town, derives its name from the 16th-century gracefully arched bridge *(most)* that spans the emerald Neretva River. Destroyed in the war and now rebuilt it's also hopefully a symbol of reunification.

Visitors wander along cobblestone streets, visit 16th-century mosques and houses, browse through artisans' shops, or sip coffee with the locals on pavement cafés.

Information

Cob Net (☎ 555 301; Maršala Tita bb; per hr 1KM; ☽ 8am-10pm) Internet access.

Fortuna Travel Agency (☎ 552 197; www.fortuna.ba; Trg Ivana Krndelja 1; ☽ 8am-4.30pm Mon-Fri, 9am-1pm Sat) Helpful travel and accommodation information.

Tourist Office (☎ 397 350; Onešcukova bb; ☽ 9am-9pm Mon-Sat) West side of old bridge.

Zagrebačke Banka (☎ 312 120; Kardinala Stepinca 18; ☽ 8am-2.30pm Mon-Fri, 8am-noon Sat) All cards ATM, travellers cheque cashing.

Sights

The rebuilt **Stari Most** (Old Bridge), linking the refurbished **Kujundžiluk**, which extends on both sides of the river, is still the heart of the Old Town. Before the war, bridge-jumping was an annual event for young men to prove their bravery, impress their mates and attract the girls of the town. Nine men jumped off the bridge on 22 July 2004 as part of the reopening celebrations. Bridge-jumping will hopefully be restored as a yearly event.

Here among the cobblestone streets are small shops with curved tile roofs selling Turkish-style souvenirs or serving up plates of steaming cevapi.

Mostar's famous mosque, the 1557 **Karadžozbeg Mosque** (Braće Fejića) is being restored. Nearby, the 350-year-old **Turkish House** (☎ 550 677; Bišoevića 13; ☽ 9am-3pm Nov-Feb, 8am-8pm Mar-Oct) has colourful Turkish-style period furnishings.

The **Pavarotti Music Centre** (☎ 550 750; www.pavarottimusiccentre.com; Maršala Tita 179; ☽ 9am-10pm) is the hub of Mostar's cultural activities for young people with a variety of exhibitions and concerts.

BOSNIA & HERCEGOVINA

Sleeping & Eating

Fortuna Travel Agency (☎ 552 197; www.fortuna.ba; Trg Ivana Krndelja 1; per person 20-50KM; ☺ 8am-4.30pm Mon-Fri, 9am-1pm Sat) Arranges private accommodation.

Omer Lakiše (☎ 551 627; Mladena Balorde 21a; per room 20KM) Run by a retired professor with a smattering of English, this private house has eight beds in two rooms. Homeliness compensates for shared bathroom and full rooms.

Zdrava Hrana (☎ /fax 550 969; Trg 1 Maja 20; per person s/d/apt from 25-30KM, apt 35-55KM) Good for small groups. This *pansion* (pension) has some apartments with a basic kitchen but no implements for cooking. A DIY breakfast is possible or you can order breakfasts for 5KM. It's a bit of a leg-stretch uphill on the east side of the river.

Pizzeria abc (☎ 194 656; Braće Fejića 45; dishes 5-9KM; ☺ 8am-11pm Mon-Sat, noon-11pm Sun) Top notch for 25 varieties of pizza with a host of ingredients, including broccoli, sardines, Gorgonzola, veal and shrimp – but not on one pizza, unless you ask.

MM Restaurant (☎ 580 192; Mostarskeg Bataljona bb; meals 6-12KM; ☺ 8am-10pm Mon-Sat) Buffet presentation makes this a visitor-friendly feeding station. The food's lip-smacking good, with some veggie options.

Getting There & Away

The **bus station** (☎ 552 025; Trg I Krndelja 1) and **train station** (☎ 552 198) are adjacent.

Frequent buses run to Sarajevo, two to Split, two to Dubrovnik and one to Zagreb.

Buses to Međugorje (4KM, 40 minutes) go from the bus stop on Biskupa Cule near the Hotel Bevanda.

Two trains between Ploče and Sarajevo (9KM, 2¾ hours) stop in Mostar. The route is highly scenic involving several switchbacks to gain height over the mountains.

MEĐUGORJE

☎ 036 / pop 4300

In 1981, six teenagers in this dirt-poor mountain village claimed they'd seen the Virgin Mary, and Međugorje's instant economic boom began. Now the streets, without names and numbers, are awash with pilgrims, souvenir stands, travel agencies and *pansion*. Each 24 June the Međugorje **Walk of Peace** celebrates the anniversary of the apparition.

Pilgrims climb **Apparition Hill**, 1.5km out of town, where the Virgin was spotted, and **Mt Križerac** (Cross Mountain), 2.5km out of town, and pray at the Stations of the Cross. The routes are rough with angular rocks polished like marble. Walkers wear stout shoes; penitents go bare footed.

St James' Church is a hub of activity in town. There is an **information booth** (☎ 651 988; www .medjugorje.hr; ☺ 9am-6pm) beside the church that has daily schedules plus multilingual printings of the Virgin's monthly message.

You'd better believe it; you'll hear fluent Croatian in an Irish brogue at **Paddy Travel** (☎ 651 482; paddy@tel.net.ba; accommodation per person from €15; ☺ 9am-3pm Mon-Sat Nov-Mar, 9am-6pm Mon-Sat Apr-Oct), where you can book accommodation, change travellers cheques and organise day trips.

Vox Tours (☎ 650 771; vox.tours@tel.net.ba; accommodation from B&B/half board €20/26; ☺ 9am-5.30pm Mon-Fri, 9am-2pm Sat) is another useful travel and accommodation agency.

Pansion Zemo (☎ 651 878; www.medjugorjetravel .com/zemo; Kozine district; B&B/half board €9/14, per campsite €3), away from the town bustle, lies about 1km southeast of the church in village fields. Some rooms have bathrooms; others share.

Many visitors come up from the Croatian coast. **Globtour** (☎ 651393) runs buses between Međugorje and Split (18KM, 3½ hours) and Dubrovnik (18KM, three hours). Frequent local buses run to Mostar (4KM, 40 minutes).

BOSNIA & HERCEGOVINA DIRECTORY

ACCOMMODATION

Larger towns have a smattering of *pansion* that are humbler and more personable than hotels. Unless mentioned otherwise, breakfast is usually included in the rates.

ACTIVITIES

Outdoor activities are severely compromised by the presence of mines. Jahorina and Bjelašnica, Bosnia's ski resorts, are again open though; stay on the groomed ski runs as there are mines in the vicinity.

Rafting season runs from May to September. The Una River near Bihać is particularly popular.

Sarajevo's **Tourist Office** (☎ 220 724, 532 606; www.sarajevo-tourism.com; Zelenih Beretki 22a; ☺ 9am-8pm Mon-Fri, 9am-4pm Sat, 10am-2pm Sun) provides excellent advice about these activities.

BUSINESS HOURS
Official hours are 8am to 4pm Monday to Friday; banks open Saturday mornings. Shops are open longer hours and many open on Sunday.

EMBASSIES & CONSULATES
Embassies & Consulates in Bosnia and Hercegovina
The following embassies are in Sarajevo:

Canada (☎ 033-222 033; fax 222 038; Grbavička 4)
Croatia (☎ 033-444 331; fax 472 434; Mehmeda Spahe 16)
Germany (☎ 033-275 000; fax 652 978; Mejtaš Buka 11-13)
Macedonia (☎ /fax 033-206 004; Emerika Bluma 23)
Serbia and Montenegro (☎ 033-260 080; fax 221 469; Obala Maka Dizdara 3A)
Slovenia (☎ 033-271 260; fax 271 270; Bentbaša 7)
UK (☎ 033-444 429; www.britishembassy.ba; Tina Ujevića 8)
USA (☎ 033-445 700; www.usis.com.ba; Alipašina 43)

Bosnia and Hercegovina Embassies & Consulates Abroad
Australia (☎ 02-6232 4646; fax 6232 5554; 6 Beale Crs, Deakin ACT 2600)
Canada (☎ 613-236 0028; fax 236 1139; Suite 805, 130 Albert St, Ottawa, Ontario K1P 5G4)
Croatia Consulate (☎ 01-48 19 420; fax 48 19 418; Pavla Hatza 3, PP27, 10001 Zagreb)
Serbia and Montenegro (☎ 11-766 507; fax 329 1993; Milana Tankosića 8, 11000 Belgrade)
Slovenia (☎ 01-432 40 42; fax 432 22 30; Kolarjeva 26, 1000 Ljubljana)
UK (☎ 020-7373 0867; 5-7 Lexham Gardens, London W1R 3BF)
USA (☎ 202-337 1500; fax 337 1502; 2109 E St NW, Washington DC)

FOOD & DRINK
Alternatives to the ubiquitous burek for vegetarians include *sirnica* (cheese pie), *zeljanica* (spinach pie) or a variety of salads. *Cevapcici*, another favourite, is made of lamb and beef rolls tucked into a half-loaf of spongy somun bread. For dessert, try baklava or *tufahije* (apple cake).

Good wines include Žilavka (white) and Blatina (red), best sampled in Hercegovina's wineries. Sarajevo-brand beer is a good slurping beer.

HOLIDAYS
New Year's Day 1 January
Independence Day 1 March
May Day 1 May
National Statehood Day 25 November
Bajram Either February or November/December (depending on when the last day of Ramadan falls). The twice-yearly Muslim holiday is observed in some parts of the country. Easter and Christmas are observed but Orthodox and Catholic dates may not coincide.

MONEY
The convertible mark (KM) is tied to the euro at 1KM to €0.51129. Most places accept euros as well as convertible marks and sometimes list prices in euros.

Travellers cheques can be exchanged at banks in larger cities; ATMs have sprouted in all places mentioned in this chapter, taking all types of debit cards.

Tipping is customary in nice restaurants and taxis – round up the bill, or leave 1KM to 2KM extra.

POST
Post and telephone offices are usually combined. Poste-restante services are available at all cities in this chapter; letters should be addressed to: (Name), Poste Restante, (postcode), Bosnia and Hercegovina.

Postcodes are: Banja Luka 78101, Bihać 77000, Međugorje 88266, Mostar (Zapadni) 88000 and Sarajevo 7100.

TELEPHONE & FAX
International calls are cheapest from the post office; per-minute calls/per-page faxes are charged at 1.05/1.05/2.09KM to the UK/USA/Australia. It's the same cost for a minute of calling as it is for sending one page of fax.

Phone cards, bought from kiosks come in 50/100/200/500KM denominations. Republika Srpska has its own phone cards, which can't be used in the rest of the country and vice versa.

VISAS
No visas are required for citizens of most EU countries, Australia, New Zealand, Canada and the USA. For other countries and application requirements check the government website www.mvp.gov.ba.

Britain

HIGHLIGHTS

- **Tate Modern** Britain's best contemporary (and free) gallery will raise an eyebrow or two (p160)
- **Scottish Highlands** Scotland's most dramatic landscapes, made for ramblers (p210)
- **Durham Cathedral** The spectacular vaulted ceilings of Durham's fortress-like cathedral (p198)
- **Best journey** The picturesque train journey from Inverness to Kyle of Lochalsh (p212)
- **Off-the-beaten track** Brighton's North Laine, the place to haggle over a vintage A-Team T-shirt (p173)

FAST FACTS

- **Area** 93,000 sq miles (240,000 sq km; around the size of New Zealand)
- **ATMs** (known as cashpoints) Widespread outside banks and at supermarkets
- **Budget** £20-40 per day
- **Capital** London
- **Country codes** country code ☎ 44, international access code ☎ 0011
- **Famous for** Tea, football, the Royal Family
- **Head of State** Queen Elizabeth II
- **Languages** English, Gaelic, Welsh
- **Money** UK pound (A$1 = £0.40, CA$1 = £0.44, €1 = £0.69, ¥100 = £0.50, NZ$1 = £0.38, US$1 = £0.56)
- **Population** 58 million

- **Time** GMT/UTC + 0
- **Visas** £36/60, issued in advance by British overseas missions. Not required for citizens of US, EU and some Commonwealth countries.

TRAVEL HINTS

Check out restaurant early evening specials and bar happy hours, and buy food, drink and wine at supermarkets.

ROAMING BRITAIN

Head from Oxford's dreamy college spires to York's evocative Roman and Viking remains. Continue north to Edinburgh, Scotland's colourful capital, before travelling to the jaw-dropping Snowdonia region of Wales. Return to London and hit some of the world's greatest museums.

The world's 78th-largest nation has exerted more than its fair share of global influence. Britain once ruled 20% of the planet, sparked the Industrial Revolution and has produced enough cultural icons – including Shakespeare, Charles Dickens, the Beatles and Monty Python – to be forgiven for launching Marmite, bad hotel showers and the dysfunctional Royal Family on an unsuspecting world.

BRITAIN

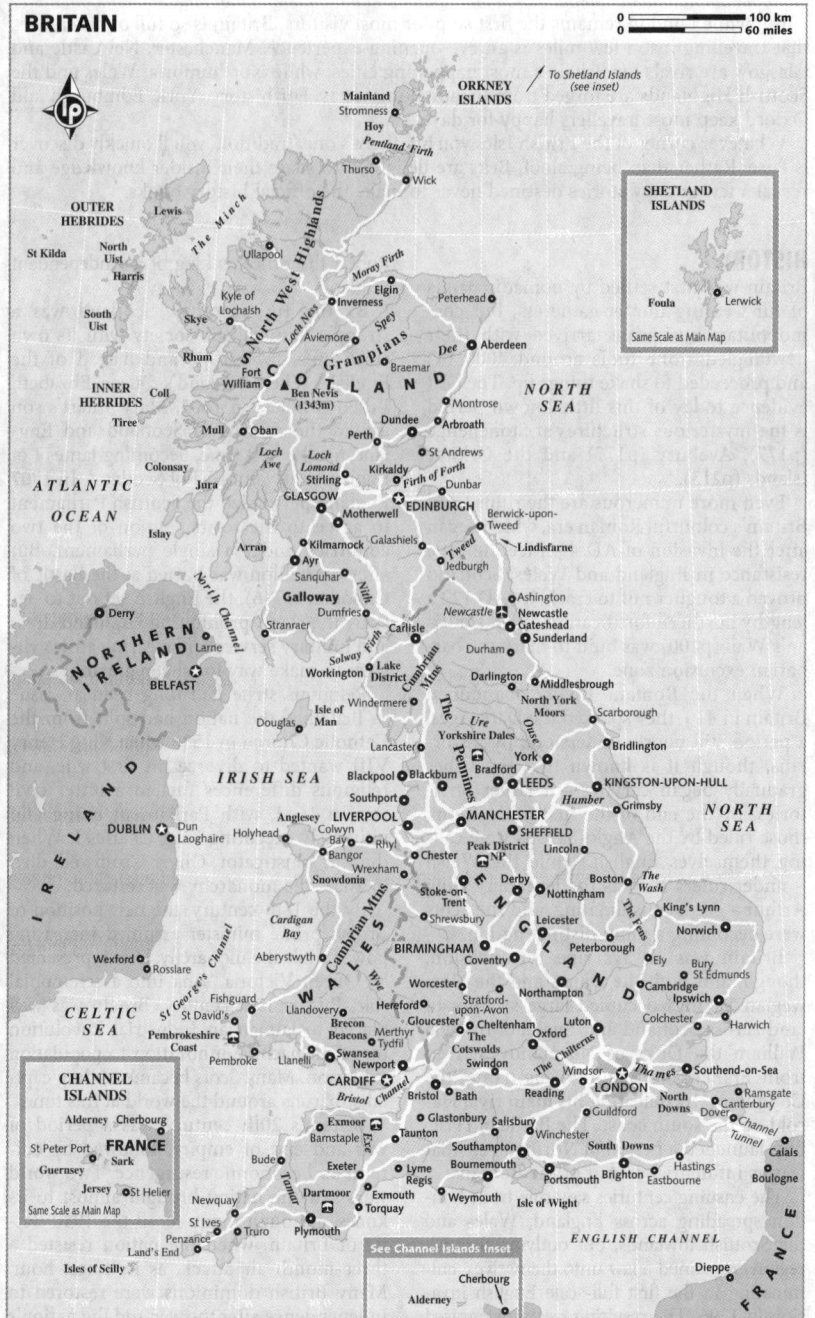

0   100 km
0   60 miles

BRITAIN

ORKNEY ISLANDS

To Shetland Islands (see inset)

Mainland
Stromness
Hoy
Pentland Firth
Thurso
Wick

SHETLAND ISLANDS

Foula
Lerwick

Same Scale as Main Map

OUTER HEBRIDES

Lewis

St Kilda
North Uist
Harris

South Uist

The Minch

Ullapool

NORTH WEST HIGHLANDS

Kyle of Lochalsh
Skye
Loch Ness
Elgin
Inverness
Moray Firth
Peterhead

Aviemore
Spey

Rhum

INNER HEBRIDES

Coll
Tiree
Mull
Oban

Dee
Aberdeen

SCOTLAND

Grampians
Braemar

Fort William
Ben Nevis
(1343m)

Montrose
Dundee
Arbroath

NORTH SEA

Loch Awe
Loch Lomond
Stirling
Perth
St Andrews

Colonsay
Jura
Islay

Kirkaldy
Firth of Forth
Dunbar

ATLANTIC OCEAN

GLASGOW
Motherwell
EDINBURGH

Arran
Kilmarnock
Ayr
Galashiels

Berwick-upon-Tweed

Tweed
Lindisfarne

North Channel

Sanquhar
Jedburgh

Galloway
Dumfries

Derry

Nith

NORTHERN IRELAND
Larne

Solway Firth
Carlisle

Ashington
Newcastle
Gateshead
Sunderland

BELFAST

Stranraer
Workington
Lake District
Cumbrian Mtns

Durham
Darlington
Middlesbrough

IRELAND

Douglas
Isle of Man

Windermere

North York Moors
Scarborough

IRISH SEA

Lancaster
The Pennines
Ure
Yorkshire Dales
Ouse

Bridlington

DUBLIN
Dun Laoghaire

Blackpool
Blackburn
Bradford
LEEDS
York

KINGSTON-UPON-HULL

Wexford
Rosslare

Southport

Anglesey
LIVERPOOL
MANCHESTER
Humber
Grimsby

Holyhead
Colwyn Bay
Rhyl
SHEFFIELD

NORTH SEA

Bangor
Chester
Peak District NP
Lincoln

Wrexham
Snowdonia
Stoke-on-Trent
Derby

Boston
The Wash

King's Lynn

Cardigan Bay
Shrewsbury
Nottingham
Leicester

Norwich

WALES
Cambrian Mtns
Aberystwyth
BIRMINGHAM
Coventry
Peterborough
Ely
Bury St Edmunds
Cambridge

CELTIC SEA

St George's Channel
Fishguard
St David's
Llandovery
Worcester
Stratford-upon-Avon
Northampton
Ipswich
Colchester
Harwich

Pembrokeshire Coast
Brecon Beacons
Merthyr Tydfil
Hereford
Gloucester
Cheltenham
Oxford
Luton

Pembroke
Llanelli
Swansea
Newport
The Cotswolds
Swindon
The Chilterns
Windsor
Thames
Southend-on-Sea

CARDIFF
Bristol
Bath
Reading
LONDON
Ramsgate
Canterbury

Bristol Channel
Glastonbury
Salisbury
Guildford
North Downs
Dover

CHANNEL ISLANDS

Alderney
Cherbourg
St Peter Port
FRANCE
Sark
Guernsey
Jersey
St Helier

Same Scale as Main Map

Exmoor
Barnstaple
Taunton
Southampton
Winchester
South Downs
Channel Tunnel
Calais

Bude
Exeter
Lyme Regis
Bournemouth
Portsmouth
Brighton
Hastings
Eastbourne
Boulogne

Newquay
Dartmoor
Exmouth
Weymouth
Isle of Wight

St Ives
Truro
Torquay

Penzance
Plymouth
ENGLAND

Land's End

Isles of Scilly

ENGLISH CHANNEL

Dieppe

FRANCE

See Channel Islands Inset

Cherbourg

Alderney

BRITAIN

But while London remains the first stop for most visitors, Britain is so full of differences that travelling just a few miles is an eye-opening experience. Manchester, Newcastle and Glasgow are rivals for Britain's most happening cities, while Northumbria, Wales and the Scottish Highlands are forged from breathtaking vistas. For history, York, Edinburgh and Oxford keep most travellers happy for days.

Whatever corner of the British Isles you hit, there's one 'tradition' you'll quickly discover is false. Rather than being aloof, Brits are delighted to share their insider knowledge and reveal a few gossipy stories destined never to make the official history books.

HISTORY

Britain was first settled by nomadic bands of fur-wearing hunter-gatherers, but cosmopolitan Europeans arrived with their newfangled stone tools around 4000 BC and proceeded to shake things up. The best evidence today of this little-known period is the mysterious structures at Stonehenge (p177), Avebury (p177) and the Orkney Islands (p213).

Even more numerous are the ruins from Britain's colourful Roman era, which began after the invasion of AD 43. Meeting little resistance in England and Wales, Scotland proved a tougher nut to crack; by AD 122 a lengthy northern fortification called Hadrian's Wall (p200) was built to mark the barbarian exclusion zone.

When the Romans finally abandoned Britain in 410, they sparked the Dark Ages, a period still poorly understood by historians, though it is known that the tribes gradually began carving out larger territories. By the end of the first millennium, those ruled by the Anglo-Saxons were calling themselves English, while the Welsh – under rulers such as the legendary King Arthur – were consolidating, and the Scots were becoming a more distinct nation.

Britain was always ripe for invasion, though, and both the Danes and the Norwegian Vikings occupied large swathes of land across Scotland and England. In 1066 William the Duke of Normandy arrived from France and acquired his name 'the Conqueror' by defeating his main rival Harold on the south coast. The Battle of Hastings launched a period of Norman rule that was as influential as that of the Romans.

The ensuing centuries saw rule from London spreading across England, Wales and the Scottish lowlands, but outlying Scottish regions remained a law unto themselves, culminating in the first full-scale English invasion in 1296. The resulting treaty recognised Robert the Bruce as king of an independent Scotland.

By the 16th century, Scotland was a strongly nationalistic society with its own close links to Europe and hatred of the English. When England's Queen Elizabeth I died childless in 1603, Mary Stuart's son united the crowns of Scotland and England for the first time, becoming James I of England and James VI of Scotland. In 1707 England persuaded the Scottish Parliament to agree to the formal union of the two countries under a single parliament. But after a rebellion was buried at the Battle of Culloden (1746), the English set out to destroy the clans, prohibiting Highland dress and military service and clearing entire villages to make way for sheep grazing.

Religious strife had long been an issue in Britain – the nation had split from the Catholic Church in 1536 when King Henry VIII wanted to divorce his first wife, and religious differences fuelled a bitter civil war in 1642, with Parliament rising and ultimately executing King Charles I. When the war's instigator, Oliver Cromwell, died in 1658, the monarchy was restored.

By the 18th century, the new position of British prime minister assumed increasing power while the monarchy, later represented by Queen Victoria, sank into a ceremonial role. By the 19th century, Britain was well placed to launch an Industrial Revolution that tied machine innovation to population explosion. Many Scots became leading capitalist-barons around the world at this time.

Britain's 20th century was a period of war and end of empire, followed by cultural and economic resurgence. Two world wars saw the nation brought almost to its knees, although many recall the 1940 Battle of Britain, when the nation resisted a three-month air attack, as its finest hour. Many British dominions were restored to independence after the war and the nation's manufacturing industries entered a period of painful decline.

By the 1990s, though, Britain had bounced back and entered the new millennium with one of the world's strongest economies; its role on the world stage has been exemplified by its 'special relationship' with the US and participation in recent military campaigns in Afghanistan and Iraq. Echoing a history of protest and political argument, millions of Brits took to the streets to protest their nation's involvement. The biggest protest may take place in 2005, when Prime Minister Tony Blair faces a testing general election in his attempt to win a third term in office.

PEOPLE & CULTURE

With 58 million people, Britain is one of the world's most densely populated nations. However, although sprawling mega-cities such as London, Birmingham and Manchester have cosmopolitan communities drawn from around the world, there are thousands of tiny villages and many regions where trees, sheep and hills easily outnumber people.

Surprisingly, there are myriad diverse regional identities in Britain: it's common to travel less than 50 miles (80km) and uncover a completely different accent with its own distinctive vocabulary. Southerners will tell you they don't understand a word uttered by the Geordies from the northeast, while Scots will happily tease the Welsh over the way they speak. Generally, this regional rivalry is

> **READING UP**
>
> For an insight into Britain's history and psyche try these: *The Isles: A History* (Norman Davies, 2000), *In Search of the Dark Ages* (Michael Wood, 2001), *Medieval Lives* (Terry Jones, 2004), *London: A Biography* (Peter Ackroyd, 2000), *Trainspotting* (Irvine Welsh, 1993), *England, England* (Julian Barnes, 1999), and *A History of Britain Volume 1-3* (Simon Schama, 2000-2003).

fairly friendly – although it's wise to avoid calling someone 'English' if they come from Scotland or Wales.

SPORT

The age-old joke that Brits invented most sports but can play few of them holds some resonance; you can count the number of current UK world tennis, boxing and hockey champions on the fingers of one badly mutilated hand. But Britain is passionate about sport – just pick up any newspaper and you'll see the football pages easily outnumber the business pages.

Many world-renowned events are held here, including Wimbledon (tennis), the British Open (golf) and Henley Regatta (rowing). But while cricket will always be part of England and rugby is close to the heart of many Welsh, it's football that defines the British nation like no other sport. Don't

TOP FIVE BRITAIN

■ **Festival** The Edinburgh Fringe Festival (p202) showcases wacky comedy and edgy theatre for those who like to combine pie-throwing slapstick with Samuel Beckett existentialism – sometimes in the same show.

■ **Walk** The 95-mile West Highland Way (p211) offers trekkers a microcosm of Scottish landscapes, from the craggy peaks of Ben Nevis to the brooding, glassy Loch Lomond. Along with walkers, red deer and eagles populate the route.

■ **Bar/Club Area** Manchester (p191) is Britain's nightlife capital, and dance fans can break into a sweat at throbbing mainstream mega-clubs or more intimate indie-flavoured faves. If you don't have a good time here, it's not gonna happen anywhere.

■ **Impressive sight** Experiencing a cold, misty sunrise over Leeds Castle (p173) is one of the best ways to sink into Britain's rich layer of history. Shout some suitable archaic battle cries to get yourself in the mood.

■ **Coastal stretch** The windswept stretch along the Pembrokeshire Coast Path (p216) takes in some of Britain's most achingly gorgeous curves. You'll soon be singing the praises of the lush valleys, verdant woods and wind-whacked cliff tops.

LIGHTS, CAMERA, ACTION...

While Hollywood often relies on fabricated sets to make its movies, British filmmakers can simply step outside. From rolling vistas untouched for centuries to unchanged Victorian streets, Britain is a giant outdoor movie set waiting to happen.

The Harry Potter series is the most prominent current user of British locations, with Hogwarts School of Witchcraft and Wizardry composed from interiors and exteriors of places including Gloucester Cathedral and Northumberland's Alnwick Castle. The most popular Potter site is Hogsmeade Station, played by the charming Goathland Station in the North Yorks Moors. London 'muggles' will also want to try and locate the movie's platform 9¾ at King's Cross Station. Other sites are more heavily disguised. Holywell Bay near Cornwall's Newquay doubled as a North Korean battlefield in James Bond's *Die Another Day*, while the opening battle scenes in *Gladiator*, supposedly set in Germany during Roman times, were shot near Farnham in Surrey. But even when the part demands it, Britain doesn't always get to play itself. Mel Gibson's Scottish epic *Braveheart* was partly shot in Ireland – although he made up for it by filming *Hamlet* in two brooding castles in Falkirk and Stonehaven.

Not surprisingly, London is England's movie location capital with recent shoots including *Elizabeth* (Tower of London), *Notting Hill* (have a guess) and *Lock Stock and Two Smoking Barrels* (Staples Market and Borough Market).

even think about calling it 'soccer' here. The English premiership competition, with teams like Arsenal and Manchester United, is arguably the world's best, while Scotland houses the giant Celtic and Rangers sparring partners. To understand the emotional pull of the game, take in the FA Cup Final in a pub and watch grown men weep.

RELIGION

In a recent census, 72% of Brits identified themselves as Christians, with Muslims being the second-biggest group at 3%. The remaining largest faiths are Hindu, Sikh, Jewish and Buddhist.

The main Christian denomination, the Church of England (C of E), became independent from Roman Catholicism in the 16th century. Led by the Archbishop of Canterbury, it has undergone a crisis of relevance in recent years; the church recently accepted the ordination of women priests and is struggling mightily with the question of gay ordination. North of the border, the Church of Scotland is independent from the Church of England, although its services are similar. The nation houses dozens of other Christian denominations, including Baptists, Methodists and Catholics – one in 10 Brits claim Catholicism as their faith.

ARTS

Theatre and literature are at the forefront of Britain's historic contribution to world cul-

ture, but important contemporary achievements include popular music and conceptual art.

Travelling in the footsteps of legendary English, Scottish or Welsh writers can be a highlight of any Brit visit. Walking through the cobbled streets of Canterbury is a reminder of Chaucer's ribald comedy, while strolling in the Scottish glens easily invokes the spirit of Robert Burns. Spirits of a different variety are available in the pubs of Wales, some of which inspired Dylan Thomas' evocative poetry.

A visit to Stratford-upon-Avon (p186) is also recommended. It's the historic home of the Bard, the world centre of Shakespeare performance and the home of the renowned Royal Shakespeare Company.

The nation's contribution to modern art has undergone a transformation in recent years, with cities like Glasgow, Manchester and London featuring some of the finest galleries in Europe. New developments such as the capital's Tate Modern (p160) and Newcastle's BALTIC (p199) have become dramatic and popular showcases for the latest artistic movements.

ENVIRONMENT

At less than 600 miles (966km) from north to south and under 300 miles (483km) at its widest point, Britain is roughly the same size as New Zealand or half the size of France. There is a huge variety of landscapes, including the Snowdonia mountains in northwest Wales, the Yorkshire Dales in England and the barren islands off Scotland.

Although the climate is mild and its annual rainfall unspectacular (35 inches/912mm), grey, overcast skies can make for depressing days any time of year. The average July temperature in London is 17.6°C (64°F), and the average January temperature is 4°C (39°F). Further north it's generally cooler. You're just as likely to enjoy fine weather in spring and autumn, so May to June and September to mid-October are the best times to visit.

The biggest environmental issue in many parts of the nation is house building. House prices are white hot in some areas as the number of houses – fewer and fewer homes have been built over the years – fails to meet demand. The government's belated response has been to announce a massive building programme on 'brown land' that has been farmed for centuries, with environmental groups up in arms.

Too crowded to have much wildlife, still Britain's hedgehogs – most famous for being run over on roads – are a common sight, even in urban settings where they commonly scavenge for food at night. Other night-time scavengers include foxes and badgers, although they are much warier of humans.

TRANSPORT

GETTING THERE & AWAY
Air
Britain is a busy transport hub with five airports serving London alone. The following are Britain's biggest international airports:

Aberdeen (☎ 0870 040 0006; www.baa.com/aberdeen)
Cardiff (☎ 01446-711111; www.cial.co.uk)
Edinburgh (☎ 0870 040 0007; www.baa.com/edinburgh)
Glasgow (☎ 0870 040 0008; www.baa.com/glasgow)
London Gatwick (☎ 0870 000 2468; www.baa.com/gatwick)

DEPARTURE TAX

Passengers flying from Britain need to pay an Air Passenger Duty. Those flying to other EU countries will pay £12 and those flying beyond will pay £24. This fee is usually 'hidden' in the cost of your ticket. There is no departure tax if you leave by boat or train.

London Heathrow (☎ 0870 0000 123; www.baa.com/heathrow)
London Luton (☎ 01582-405100; www.london-luton.co.uk)
London Stansted (☎ 0870 0000 303; www.baa.com/stansted)
Manchester (☎ 0161-489 3000; www.manairport.co.uk)
Southampton (☎ 020-7834 9449; www.baa.com/southampton)

Airlines flying to and from Britain include the following:

Aer Lingus (☎ 0845 973 7747; www.aerlingus.com)
Air Canada (☎ 0870 524 7226; www.aircanada.com)
Air France (☎ 0845 084 5111; www.airfrance.com)
American Airlines (☎ 0845 778 9789; www.aa.com)
British Airways (☎ 0845 773 3377; www.britishairways.co.uk)
British Midland (☎ 0870 607 0555; www.flybmi.com)
easyJet (☎ 0870 600 0000; www.easyjet.com)
KLM (☎ 0870 507 4074; www.klm.com)
Lufthansa (☎ 0845 773 7747; www.lufthansa.com)
Ryanair (☎ 0870 156 9569; www.ryanair.com)
Scandinavian Airlines (☎ 0845 6072 7727; www.sas.se)
Virgin Atlantourist office (☎ 0293-747 747; www.virgin-atlantic.com)

Boat
There's a bewildering array of car and passenger ferry and high-speed catamaran services between Britain and Europe, with prices changing rapidly to reflect the intense competition. Shop around for a bargain via operators' websites. The shortest crossing from mainland Europe is Calais to Dover on the English south coast. The following are among the main operators and some of the popular routes:

Brittany Ferries (☎ 0870 366 5333; www.brittany-ferries.com) Operates from France (Caen or St Malo to Portsmouth: six to nine hours, one to three daily; Cherbourg to Poole: three hours, one to three daily; and Roscoff to Plymouth: five hours, one to three daily) and from Spain (Santander to Plymouth: 24 hours, twice weekly).

DFDS Seaways (☎ 0870 533 3000; www.dfdsseaways.co.uk) Operates from Germany (Cuxhaven to Harwich: 16½ hours, every two days), the Netherlands (Amsterdam to Newcastle: 15 hours, one daily), Sweden (Gothenburg to Newcastle: 17 hours, twice weekly) and Denmark (Esbjerg to Harwich: 19½ hours, every two days).

Hoverspeed (☎ 0870 240 8070; www.hoverspeed.com) Operates from France (Calais to Dover: one hour, hourly).

P&O (☎ 0870 242 4999; www.poferries.com) Operates from France (Calais to Dover: 75 minutes, every 45 minutes; Cherbourg or Le Havre to Portsmouth: three to six hours, one to five daily). It also operates from Spain (Bilbao to Portsmouth: 31 hours, twice weekly) and from Ireland (Dublin to Liverpool: 7½ hours, twice daily).

Stena Line (☎ 0870 400 6798; www.stenaline.com) Operates from the Netherlands (Hook of Holland to Harwich: 3½ hours, three daily) and from Ireland (Dublin to Holyhead: 1½ to three hours, twice daily; and Rosslare to Fishguard: 3½ hours, six daily).

Superfast Ferries (☎ 0870 410 6040; www.superfast .com) Operates from Belgium (Zeebrugge to Rosyth near Edinburgh: 17½ hours, one daily).

Bus

Eurolines London (☎ 0870 514 3219; www.eurolines.com; 52 Grosvenor Gardens, Victoria, London SW1); Paris (☎ 01 49 72 48 00); Amsterdam (☎ 020-560 8788) Brussels (☎ 02-203 07 07); Frankfurt (☎ 069-790 32 40) Madrid (☎ 091-327 1381); Rome (☎ 06-884 08 40) services an enormous network of European destinations, including Ireland and Eastern Europe. Regular daily services to London arrive from cities including Amsterdam, Brussels, Frankfurt, Madrid, Paris and Rome. The company also operates six circular explorer routes, always starting and ending in London, the most popular of which is the London–Amsterdam–Brussels–Paris route (£62). Additionally, travellers leaving from London can purchase a Mini-Pass to visit two other cities (three in all) on a return trip back to London. There are six variations, costing from £55 to £75.

You can book tickets through any National Express office, including Victoria coach station in London (where Eurolines buses depart and arrive), and at many travel agencies.

Car & Motorcycle

You can bring a car to Britain via ferry or hovercraft services from several European nations or via the Channel Tunnel. See Train (below) for specific information on these options, and Car & Motorcycle (opposite) for information on driving in Britain. If renting, check with the company regarding insurance requirements and drop-off charges for travelling from Europe to Britain.

Train

Three options exist for travel between England and Europe: Eurostar, Eurotunnel or train–ferry connections. Travellers aged under 26 can pick up Billet International de Jeunesse (BIJ) tickets, which cut train fares by up to 50%. Various agents issue BIJ tickets in London.

The high-speed **Eurostar** (☎ 0870 5186 186; www.eurostar.com) passenger train travels between London and Paris or Brussels via the Channel Tunnel. There are stops in Ashford (England) and in Lille and Calais (France). The London terminal is at Waterloo station. There are up to 25 trains daily from Paris to London (one-way £29 to £149, 2¾ hours), and from eight to 12 trains daily between Brussels and London (one-way £29 to £149, 2½ hours). Holders of BritRail, Eurail and Euro passes are entitled to discounted fares.

Eurotunnel (☎ 0870 535 3535; www.eurotunnel .com) trains carry vehicles and their passengers or freight through the Channel Tunnel between Folkestone in the UK and Calais in France. The specially designed shuttle trains run 24 hours, departing up to four times an hour in each direction between 6am and 10pm, and hourly from 10pm to 6am. A car and passengers costs between £185 and £220, depending on day and time of travel.

Rail/ferry links involve trains at either end and a ferry or high-speed catamaran across the Channel. Trains arrive at London's Victoria, Liverpool St or Charing Cross stations from points across Europe and are usually much cheaper than travelling by Eurostar. Contact **Rail Europe** (☎ 0870 584 8848; www.rail europe.com) for information. Remember that Eurail passes are not valid in Britain.

GETTING AROUND

Britain's dense transport network diminishes to almost nothing in most remote areas and national parks where populations are low. But with some creative thinking, visitors can get almost anywhere via a combination of rail, road and cheap flights, with many areas crying out to be explored on foot or by bike. Rental cars are an option, but they are rarely cost-effective unless you're travelling in a group or to areas not well served by other transport options. Contact **Traveline** (☎ 0870 608 2608; www.traveline.org.uk) for information on air, train, coach, bus and ferry options in Britain. For Scotland-only transport options, check www.travelinescotland.com.

Your **International Student Identity Card** (www .isiccard.com) also qualifies you for discount travel passes – check bus (opposite) and train (p152) sections for details.

Air

No-frills airlines offer some of the best potential bargains for travelling around Britain – especially on the London to Scotland route – but you'll have to be flexible to get the best deals and factor in the cost of travelling to and from airports. There are often additional charges for credit-card bookings and ticket changes.

The following airlines operate domestic flights:

Air Scotland (☎ 0141-848 4990; www.airscotland.com)
bmibaby (☎ 0870 264 2229; www.bmibaby.com)
British Airways (☎ 0845 773 3377; www.british airways.co.uk)
British Midland (☎ 0870 607 0555; www.flybmi.com)
easyJet (☎ 0870 600 0000; www.easyjet.com)
Ryanair (☎ 0870 156 9569; www.ryanair.com)
ScotAirways (☎ 0870 606 0707; www.scotairways.co.uk)

Bicycle

Compact Britain is a bike-friendly destination. Keep in mind that many streets are narrow and you'll have to keep your wits about you as the cars whiz by. See p219 for further information.

Boat

For information on accessing Britain's extensive canal boat network, see p219. Ferries are an important part of Scotland's transportation network, with essential services linking islands such as Orkney, Skye and the Outer Hebrides to the mainland. The main operators include **Caledonian MacBrayne** (CalMac; ☎ 0870 565 0000; www.calmac .co.uk) and **Northlink Ferries** (☎ 0845 6000 449; www .northlinkferries.co.uk). CalMac offers a range of passes for those making multiple trips. See individual town, city and island listings for specific route and fare information.

Bus

Buses are the cheapest way to get around Britain, albeit slow, with many routes winding through several cities before reaching their destination. While local bus services run in each region, there's also a web of intercity buses – usually called coaches – that covers longer distances. It's worth making coach reservations in advance during July and August. This can be done online, by phone or at the ticket desk of main bus stations.

Since Britain's bus and coach system is substantially deregulated, several no-frills operators have emerged. These are worth checking out for a bargain if you enjoy sitting in a cramped and battered double-decker bus for several hours. See individual sections for sample bus and coach routes and fares.

Contact **Traveline** (☎ 0870 608 2608; www .traveline.org.uk) for bus and coach options throughout England, Scotland and Wales. Britain's largest coach operators include **National Express** (☎ 0870 580 8080; www.national express.com) and its subsidiary **Scottish Citylink** (☎ 0870 550 5050; www.citylink.co.uk). **Megabus** (☎ 01738-639095; www.megabus.com) is a popular no-frills provider with services between major cities, and **MacBackpackers** (☎ 0131-558 9900; www.macbackpackers.com) runs a jump-on, jump-off service linking several Scottish destinations. It's targeted at hostel-dwellers and costs £65 for up to one year of travel. **Silver Choice** (☎ 01355-230403; www.silverchoice travel.co.uk) also operates good-value services from London to Edinburgh and Glasgow.

BUS PASSES

The National Express Student/Young Persons Discount Coachcard (one year £10) provides discounts of up to 30% on all fares. It's available to 16- to 25-year-olds and all full-time students. There's a similar card for over-50s. Purchase one from any National Express agent using a passport (or an ISIC card for students). Discounts do not apply to travel in Scotland.

Scottish Citylink offers its own Young Person's Discount Card and 50+ Discount Card (£7), with 20% discount on most fares. UK students qualify for a free version of the card.

POSTBUS

Royal Mail postbuses provide a reliable service to remote areas and can be useful for wilderness hiking trips. For information and timetables, contact **customer service** (☎ 01246-546329; www.postbus.royalmail.com).

Car & Motorcycle

Often the quickest and most convenient way to travel around Britain is by car or motorcycle, particularly in remote areas. It can be a pain when you hit town: cars are often inconvenient in city centres and parking can be troublesome and expensive. Petrol is also expensive, especially compared to North America.

BRITAIN

DRIVING LICENCE

A foreign driving licence is valid in Britain for up to 12 months from your time of entry.

HIRE

Rental is expensive in Britain and it's often better to make arrangements in your home country for a fly/drive deal. Drivers are usually expected to be between the ages of 23 and 65, with special insurance conditions applying to those outside these limits.

Larger operators charge from around £120 per week for a small car (Ford Fiesta, Peugeot 106) but rates can vary considerably based on many factors including pick-up and drop-off locations, whether or not you're picking up on the weekend and how long you're renting for. Always ask for any special offers or mention that you're shopping around for the best rate. Tourist offices can also suggest favoured local rental companies. Major operators include the following:

Avis (☎ 0870 606 0100; www.avis.co.uk)
Budget (☎ 0845 606 6669; www.budget.co.uk)
Europcar (☎ 0870 607 5000; www.europcar.com)
Thrifty Car Rental (☎ 0870 066 0514; www.thrifty.co.uk)

ROAD RULES

The *Highway Code*, available in most bookshops, provides all the information you'll need about Britain's road rules. Vehicles drive on the left-hand side; seat belts are compulsory in the front seats (and also in the back, where fitted); the speed limit is 30mph (48km/h) in built-up areas, 60mph (96km/h) on single carriageways and 70mph (112km/h) on dual carriageways. Remember to give way to your right at roundabouts.

The maximum blood-alcohol level for driving is 35mg/100mL. A yellow line along the edge of a road indicates parking restrictions – look for a sign nearby for exact limits. Motorcyclists must wear helmets.

Train

Trains, especially with a travel pass purchased in your home country, are a competitive option: they're also quicker and often take you through Britain's best scenery. While the network is extensive, covering all cities and most towns, it can be difficult to use trains to reach remote areas. Investment from private companies means faster, more comfortable trains are being introduced but the ancient infrastructure means repairs to the rails are ongoing: don't be surprised to see services delayed for engineering work, particularly on weekends. When services are cancelled, replacement buses are provided. For information contact the **National Rail Enquiry Service** (☎ 0845 748 4950; www.nationalrail.co.uk).

CLASSES

There are a myriad of ticketing options for travelling by rail in Britain and the system can be quite complex. Call the National Rail Enquiry Service (above) for an explanation of the options. The main difference is that 1st-class tickets are up to 50% more expensive than standard-class tickets for travel in separate carriages on the same trains.

RESERVATIONS

Recommended for summer, peak times and popular routes, reservations can be made in advance at train stations or on the Web at www.thetrainline.com. The price you pay for a ticket generally depends upon the degree of flexibility you want, the availability of cheap tickets and any passes that you hold. Without a pass, the cheapest tickets must be bought at least a week in advance. There is a bewildering array of ticket options, including the following:

Apex For outward and return journeys (usually long-distance) on different days, these are the cheapest options. They must be booked at least 48 hours in advance and availability is limited.

Cheap Day Return For outward and return journeys on the same day (usually limited to travel after 9.30am); often costs little more than a one-way fare and is a great deal for day-trippers.

Saver Open return but travel during weekday peak times is not permitted.

SuperSaver Return ticket but with weekday peak time travel, Friday travel and holiday travel not allowed.

TRAIN PASSES

The Young Persons Railcard (£14), Seniors Railcard (£18) and Disabled Persons Railcard (£14) are each valid for 12 months and give a one-third discount on most trips in Britain. Check the options at www.railcard.co.uk; your application can be processed over the counter at main train stations. You'll need proof of age (passport, birth certificate or driving licence) for the Seniors and Young Persons Railcards (or proof of student enrolment) and proof of entitlement for the Disabled Persons Railcard.

The most convenient and, if you're planning to travel far and wide, the most cost-effective way to hit the rails is by purchasing a rail pass. **BritRail** (www.britrail .com) offers an excellent selection of passes. You must purchase them at home before you arrive in the UK – ask at your nearest British Tourist Authority (BTA) office (see p223 for contact details)– or from the **Britain & London Visitor Centre** (Map pp158-60; ☎ 020-7308 3838; 12 Regent St SW1; www.visitbritain .com; metro Piccadilly Circus; ☺ 9.30am-6.30pm Mon-Fri, 10am-4pm Sat & Sun). You simply have to show your pass (and sometimes your passport) on the train, thereby avoiding the confusing options and restrictions of most tickets. Remember your Eurail pass is not valid in Britain, so you'll need a separate BritRail pass here. Options include the popular BritRail Consecutive Pass (unlimited four- to 31-day passes from US$189 to $US605) and the BritRail Flexipass (four, eight or 15 days over a two-month period US$239 to US$519). There are cheaper, regional versions of these two passes, including the popular Days Out from London pass (two to seven days' travel US$59 to $US155), and all passes have 1st-class options for an additional US$100 to US$300.

ScotRail (☎ 0845 755 0033; www.scotrail.co.uk) offers a great range of passes for travel north of the border, and they can be purchased through BritRail or at train stations across the UK. The Freedom of Scotland pass (four days' travel out of eight, or eight days out of 15 £89 to £119) is the most convenient for many travellers. Among a range of additional passes, the Central Scotland Rover is popular. It allows unlimited travel for three days out of seven between Glasgow, Edinburgh, North Berwick, Stirling and Fife.

ENGLAND

With Scotland and Wales gaining increasing powers to run their own affairs, the idea of what it means to be English – as opposed to British – is being re-examined. For centuries, the English have buried their identity in that of greater Britain but English iconography is now more proudly displayed across the country than at any time since WWII. Trendy T-shirts with the heraldic three lions or the red cross of St George are commonly found in high street shops.

Following a crisis of confidence linked to its economic malaise in the 1970s and 1980s, many of England's cities and regions are more vibrant now than ever before, with several formerly depressed cities enjoying a cultural and economic renaissance. While London and Manchester are obviously buzzing, others such as Newcastle, Liverpool, Birmingham, Nottingham and Bristol are keen rivals for the title of 'most happening' English city.

LONDON

☎ 020 / pop 7.2 million

With familiar landmarks like Big Ben and the Tower of London, plus quintessential English traditions like afternoon tea, London has always seduced visitors with its rich history, architectural treasures and royal pomp. At the same time, the capital has often been the barometer of what's cool in music, fashion and the arts. In recent years with its reinvention of areas like the South Bank, London fizzes with a boundless creative energy that produces cutting-edge designers, a bristling music scene, a full-on club culture, and arts that are admired the world over.

However, London can be a massive tug on the purse strings. Save money by heading for the major museums and galleries, most of which are free, and if you get a sunny day, do as the locals do: buy some beer, park yourself in one of the many verdant spots, and watch everyone go pink with blissful abandon.

HISTORY

The Romans are credited with founding Londinium in AD 43. After they left, the city survived incursions of both the Saxons and Vikings. Fifty years before the Normans arrived, Edward the Confessor built his abbey and palace at Westminster. William the Conqueror raised the White Tower (part of the Tower of London) and confirmed the city's independence and right to self-government. Jacobean London was virtually destroyed, first by the Plague of 1665, and then the Great Fire of 1666. Still, by 1720 there were 750,000 inhabitants, and London, as the seat of Parliament and focal

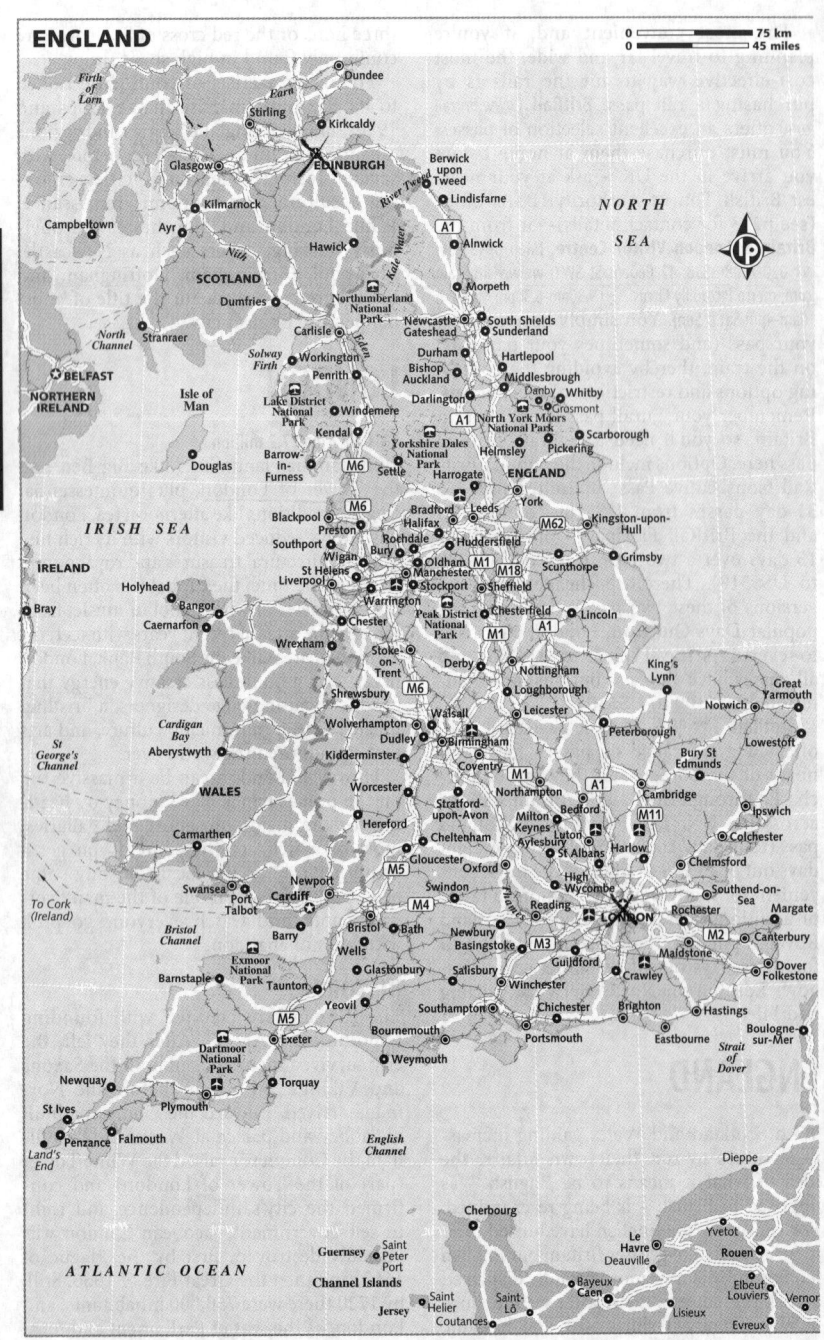

point for a growing empire, was becoming ever more important.

After WWII ugly housing and low-cost developments were laid on bombed sites. Some economic prosperity returned in the late 1950s, leading to the 'Swinging 60s' when London became the epicentre of all that was hip. In the '70s there was an economic downturn and the '80s saw Thatcher's policies create a canyon between rich and poor. Since then, even though the mid-90s notion of 'Cool Britannia' felt more like a New Labour marketing ploy, London has became a place to watch again.

In 2003 the mayor of London, Ken Livingstone, brought in controversial measures that improved the city's traffic problems and pushed for the revamping of Trafalgar Sq, which is now an occasional events venue and a gathering point for many a street protest. This, and the changing modern skyline propelled by the celebrated architect Norman Foster (Millennium bridge, the 'Gherkin' building etc), as well as the 2012 Olympic bid, reflects London's renewed vibrancy.

ORIENTATION

The city's main geographical feature is the Thames, which divides the city roughly into north and south. The London Underground system ('the tube'), although fairly decrepit and subject to delays, still manages to make this enormous city relatively accessible.

The heart of London, the crowded West End, is full of with pubs, restaurants, theatres, clubs, cinemas and shops. At its centre are the neighbourhoods of Soho and Covent Garden. It includes Trafalgar Sq and its National Galleries, intellectual Bloomsbury with the British Museum and University of London, and the fading grandeur of the Strand.

Southwest of this patch is Westminster and St James's, the traditional seats of parliamentary and royal power, where you'll find No 10 Downing St, the Houses of Parliament, Big Ben, Westminster Abbey and Buckingham Palace, behind which is the transport hub of Victoria. Added to the regal and political is the exclusive mix of glitzy Mayfair, chichi Chelsea, Hyde Park and the museum land of Kensington. Just west of here is Earl's Court, a ghetto of inexpensive hotels; and heading north is hip Notting Hill, home to the famous Carnival and Portobello market.

To the east of the West End is the commercial heart of London, simply known as the City; St Paul's Cathedral is the main attraction for visitors. Further east are the terminally cool Clerkenwell, Hoxton and Shoreditch of the multicultural East End, traditional home of the cockney. North of here are comfortably bohemian Islington and grungy Camden.

Across the Thames is the South Bank and Bankside, home to some of London's top attractions, including the London Eye, Tate Modern and the Globe Theatre. The neighbourhoods just south of here (like Borough and Bermondsey) are becoming another trendy hub.

GETTING INTO TOWN

Served by numerous low-cost flights, Stansted Airport lies 35 miles (56km) northeast of central London. The **Stansted Express** (www.stanstedexpress.com) goes to Liverpool St station (one-way/return £13/21, 45 minutes, every 15 to 30 minutes 5.30am to 11pm), stopping en route at Tottenham Hale on the Victoria Line of the tube. The **National Express Airport coach** (www.nationalexpress.com) goes to Victoria station (£10/15, one hour 40 minutes, every 15 minutes).

Gatwick Airport is 30 miles (48km) south of central London. You can get into town with the Gatwick Express train to Victoria station (£11/21.50, 30 minutes, every 15 minutes); or the National Express Airport coach, also to Victoria station (£6/11, one hour 20 minutes, hourly 7am to 11.30pm).

Heathrow Airport is 15 miles (24km) west of central London. You can get into the centre with the Heathrow Express train to Paddington station (£13/25, 15 minutes to Terminals 1, 2 & 3, 23 minutes to Terminal 4, every 15 minutes 5.10am to 11.40pm) or the tube (one-way £3.80, one hour, every two to eight minutes 5.30am to 11.30pm).

Eurostar passengers will arrive at Waterloo International (Map pp158–60), which is in the same station as Waterloo train and tube station. Coach travellers will arrive at Victoria coach station (Map pp158–60), Buckingham Palace Rd, about 10 minutes' walk south of Victoria train station.

Main line stations coming in from other parts of Britain interchange with the tube.

Maps

Pick up free maps at London Visitor Centres (below) or buy Lonely Planet's single-sheeted *London City Map*. The *London A-Z* is the definitive street guide and comes in a mini version.

INFORMATION
Bookshops

For a whole street of bookshops, head to Charing Cross Rd, which is filled with chain and specialist shops alike. Those listed below either focus on travel or have strong travel sections.

Borders (☎ 7379 8877; www.bordersstores.com; 120 Charing Cross Rd WC2; metro Tottenham Court Road) This American chain is a good all-rounder.

Stanford's (☎ 7836 1321; www.stanfords.co.uk; 12-14 Long Acre WC2; metro Covent Garden) One of the largest selections of maps, guides and travel literature in the world.

Travel Bookshop (☎ 7229 5260; www.travelbookshop .co.uk; 13 Blenheim Crescent W11; metro Ladbroke Grove) London's best 'boutique' travel bookshop has all the new travel guides as well as antiquarian gems.

Waterstone's (☎ 7851 2400; www.waterstones.co.uk; 203-6 Piccadilly W1; metro Piccadilly Circus) The biggest bookshop in Europe, with a superb travel section.

Internet Access

There are Internet cafés throughout the city. An inexpensive bet is the huge **easyInternet-café** (www.easyinternetcafe.com; per 20 min £1, per 1hr £1; ☯ 8am-midnight) outlets. Branches include:

Oxford St (Map pp158-60; 358 Oxford St W1; metro Bond St)

Tottenham Court Rd (Map pp158-60; 9-16 Tottenham Court Rd W1; metro Tottenham Court Rd)

Trafalgar Square (Map pp158-60; 7 Strand WC2; metro Charing Cross)

Victoria (Map pp158-60; 9-13 Wilton Rd SW1; metro Victoria)

Medical Services

NHS Direct (☎ 0845 4647; 24hr) Gives help with diagnosis, and information such as where the nearest 24-hour pharmacies are.

Hospitals with 24-hour accident and emergency departments include:

Charing Cross Hospital (☎ 8846 1234; Fulham Palace Rd W6; metro Hammersmith)

University College Hospital (Map pp158-60; ☎ 7387 9300; Grafton Way WC1; metro Euston Sq)

Money

Banks and ATMs abound across central London. All the airports have 24-hour *bureaux*

de changes, as well as ATMs. Reliable places to change money in town include:

American Express (Map pp158-60; ☎ 7484 9600; 30-31 Haymarket SW1; metro Piccadilly Circus; ☯ 9am-6pm Mon-Sat, 10am-5pm Sun)

Thomas Cook (Map pp158-60; ☎ 7853 6400; 30 St James's St SW1; metro Green Park; ☯ 8.30am-6pm Mon-Fri)

Post

Unless you (or the person writing to you) specify otherwise, poste restante mail sent to London ends up at the **Trafalgar Square Post Office** (Map pp158-60; ☎ 7484 9307; 24 William IV St WC2; metro Charing Cross; ☯ 8am-8pm Mon-Fri, 9am-8pm Sat). Mail will be held for four weeks; ID is required.

Telephone

The **Britain & London Visitor Centre** (see below) and **Internet Lounge** (Map pp164-5; ☎ 7370 1734; 24a Earl's Court Gardens SW5; metro Earl's Court; ☯ 9am-midnight) offer cheaper international calls than British Telecom.

Tourist Information

For comprehensive information on London check out **Visit London** (www.visitlondon.com).
Visitor centres include:

Britain & London Visitor Centre (Map pp158-60; www.visitbritain.com; 1 Regent St SW1; metro Piccadilly Circus; ☯ 9.30am-6.30pm Mon-Fri, 10am-4pm Sat & Sun) There are information desks here for London, England, Wales, Scotland and Ireland, as well as a map and guidebook shop. This is a walk-in only service.

Greenwich tourist office (☎ 0870 608 2000; Pepys House, 2 Cutty Sark Gardens SE10; Docklands Light Railway (DLR) Cutty Sark; ☯ 10am-5pm)

London Visitor Centre (Arrivals Hall, Waterloo International Terminal SE1; ☯ 8.30am-10.30pm)

Southwark tourist office (☎ 7357 9168; Vinopolis, 1 Bank End SE1; metro London Bridge; ☯ 10am-6pm Tue-Sun)

SIGHTS

London is brimming with fascinating ancient treasures, cutting-edge projects and quirky gems. Here we review a selection of sights, including the major museums, galleries, palaces and parks.

The West End
NATIONAL GALLERY ←

The **National Gallery** (Map pp158-60; ☎ 7747 2885; www.nationalgallery.org.uk; Trafalgar Sq WC2; metro Charing Cross; admission free; ☼ 10am-6pm Mon-Tue, Thu-Sun, 10am-9pm Wed, tours 11.30am & 2.30pm) is one of the largest galleries in the world, with more than 2000 Western European paintings spanning the 13th to 20th centuries. Seminal paintings from every important epoch in the history of art are here, including works by Leonardo da Vinci, Michelangelo, Van Gogh and Renoir.

NATIONAL PORTRAIT GALLERY

Around the corner, the **National Portrait Gallery** (Map pp158-60; ☎ 7306 0055; www.npg.org.uk; St Martin's Pl WC2; metro Charing Cross; admission free; ☼ 10am-6pm Mon-Wed, Sat & Sun, 10am-9pm Thu-Fri) is the place to put faces to the famous and infamous names of Britain's past and present. The ground floor is the most fun, focusing on contemporary figures from British popular culture.

BRITISH MUSEUM

Founded in 1753, the **British Museum** (Map pp158-60; ☎ 7323 8000; www.thebritishmuseum.ac.uk; Great Russell St WC1; metro Russell Sq; admission free, variety of free tours available; ☼ 10am-5.30pm Sat-Wed, 10am-8.30pm Thu-Fri) is one of the world's oldest and finest museums. Its anthropological wonders and the Egyptian, Mesopotamian, Greek and Roman antiquities are unparalleled. Marvel at the spectacular architecture of the Great Court – the largest covered public square in Europe – which opened in 2000.

St James's, Westminster & Pimlico
WESTMINSTER ABBEY

The rich history of **Westminster Abbey** (Map pp158-60; ☎ 7222 5152; www.westminster-abbey.org; Parliament Sq SW1; metro Westminster; adult/concession £7.50/5; ☼ 9.30am-4.45pm Mon-Tue & Thu-Fri, 9.30am-8pm Wed, 9.30am-2.45pm Sat, worship only Sun) started with Edward the Confessor building a church here in the 11th century. The coronation chair, where all but two monarchs since 1066 have been crowned, is behind the altar, and many greats – from Darwin to Chaucer – are buried here.

TATE BRITAIN

Built in 1897, the venerable **Tate Britain** (Map pp158-60; ☎ 7887 8000; www.tate.org.uk; Millbank SW1; metro Pimlico; admission free; ☼ 10am-5.50pm) has the definitive collection of British art from the 16th to the late 20th centuries. There is a boat service (one-way/day ticket £3.40/5, 18 minutes, every 40 minutes 10am to 5pm) to the Tate Modern (p160) from here, which also stops at the London Eye (p161).

BUCKINGHAM PALACE ←

Built in 1705 as Buckingham House for the duke of the same name, **Buckingham Palace** (Map pp158-60; ☎ 7766 7300; www.royal.gov .uk; Buckingham Palace Rd SW1; metro Victoria/Green Park; adult/concession £12.95/11; ☼ 9.30am-4.15pm 31 Jul-26 Sep, changing of the guard 11.30am Apr-Jun, alternate days Jul-Mar) has been the royal family's London lodgings since 1837. Nineteen lavishly furnished State Rooms are open to visitors in the summer, as well as the Picture Gallery and Throne Room, which features kitschy his-and-hers pink chairs initialled 'ER' and 'P'.

ST JAMES'S PARK

Bordering the Mall as it heads towards Buckingham Palace, **St James's Park** (Map pp158-60; ☎ 7930 1793; www.royalparks.gov.uk; The Mall SW1; metro St James's Park; ☼ 5am-dusk) has great vistas, including Buckingham Palace, and Whitehall to the south. The plentiful flowerbeds, large lake and waterfowl make this a lovely place to relax.

Kensington & Knightsbridge
VICTORIA & ALBERT MUSEUM

Dating from 3000 BC to the present day, the **Victoria & Albert Museum** (Map pp164-5; ☎ 7942 2000; www.vam.ac.uk; Cromwell Rd SW7; metro South Kensington; admission free; ☼ 10am-5.45pm Mon-Tue & Thu-Sun, 10am-10pm Wed) has the world's greatest collection of decorative arts. Spread over nearly 150 galleries, the rooms are filled with furniture to fashion and ceramics to sculpture.

NATURAL HISTORY MUSEUM

Lots of fascinating interactive exhibitions make the **Natural History Museum** (Map pp164-5; ☎ 7942 5000; www.nhm.ac.uk; Cromwell Rd SW7; metro South Kensington; admission free; ☼ 10am-5.30pm Mon-Sat, 11am-5.30pm Sun) a favourite for kids and adults alike. Highlights include the Darwin Centre, with specimens collected by Captain Cook; the dramatic earthquake experience; and the impressive dinosaur skeletons.

BRITAIN

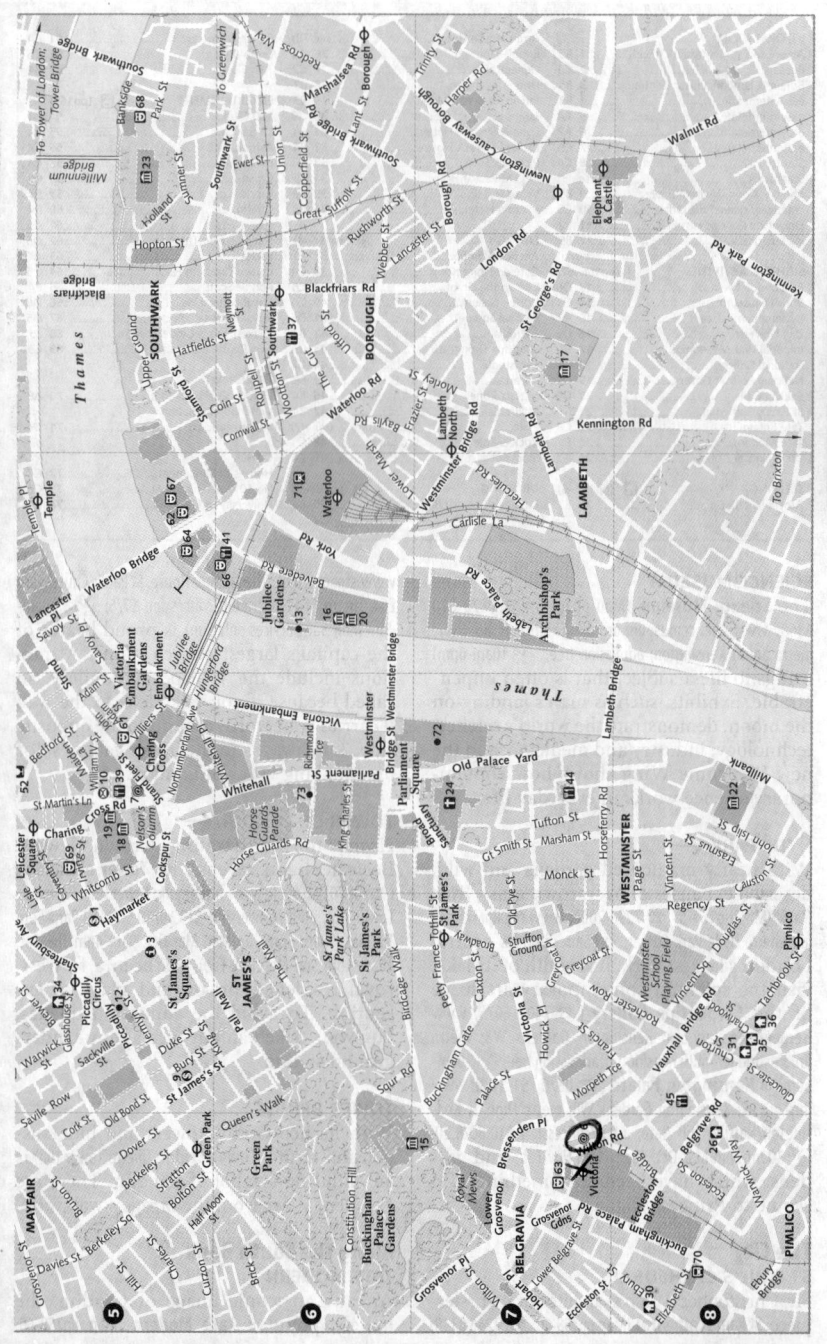

BRITAIN

SCIENCE MUSEUM

The **Science Museum** (Map pp164-5; ☎ 0870 870 4868; www.sciencemuseum.org.uk; Exhibition Rd SW7; metro South Kensington; admission free; ☿ 10am-6pm) brings to life a subject that is often impenetrable. Exhibits, such as man's landing on the moon, demonstrate the world's science, technology, industry and medicine; and the new Wellcome Wing shows how contemporary science works in everyday life.

HYDE PARK ←

With neatly manicured gardens and wild, deserted expanses of overgrown grass, **Hyde Park** (Map pp164-5; ☎ 7298 2000; www.royalparks.gov.uk; metro Hyde Park Corner; ☿ 5am-dusk) is central London's largest park. Just south of its lake, visit the splendid contemporary art space of the **Serpentine Gallery** (☎ 7402 6075; www.serpentinegallery.org; Kensington Gardens W8; metro Knightsbridge/South Kensington; admission free; ☿ 10am-6pm) or **Kensington Palace** (☎ 0870 751 5170; www.hrp.org.uk; Kensington Gardens W8; metro High St Kensington/Notting Hill Gate; adult/concession £10.80/8.20; ☿ 10am-5pm Mar-Oct, 10am-4pm Nov-Feb) and gardens, which have become something of a shrine to Princess Diana.

The City

ST PAUL'S CATHEDRAL

Sir Christopher Wren's architectural masterpiece, **St Paul's Cathedral** (Map pp158-60; ☎ 7246 8348; www.stpauls.co.uk; The Chapter House, St Paul's Churchyard EC4; metro St Paul's; adult/concession £7/6; ☿ 8.30am-4pm Mon-Sat, services only Sun) is proud bearer of the capital's largest church dome. Attractions include the Whispering Gallery, so called because if you talk close to the wall it carries your words around to the opposite side, 32m away; and the upper galleries, for breathtaking vistas of London.

TOWER OF LONDON ←

Home to the dazzling Crown Jewels, Beefeaters and ravens, the **Tower of London** (☎ 0870 756 6060; www.hrp.org.uk; Tower Hill EC3; metro Tower Hill; adult/concession £13.50/10.50; ☿ 9am-5pm Tue-Sat, 10am-5pm Sun-Mon Mar-Oct; 9am-4pm Tue-Sat, 10am-4pm Sun-Mon Nov-Feb) has been a fortress, royal residence, prison and place of execution. To avoid the admission queues, buy your tickets in advance at any Underground station.

TOWER BRIDGE

With its neo-Gothic towers and blue suspension struts, **Tower Bridge** (metro Tower Hill) is an enduring symbol of London. There are excellent views from the bridge's walkways.

Along the South Bank

TATE MODERN

Already an iconic image of London, the hugely popular **Tate Modern** (Map pp158-60;

☎ 7887 8008; www.tate.org.uk; Bankside SE1; metro Blackfriars/Southwark; admission free; ☼ 10am-6pm Sun-Thu, 10am-10pm Fri & Sat) houses 20th-century art in what was once an empty Bankside power station. The permanent collection, with artists ranging from Rothko to Lichtenstein, is arranged according to themes, eg Still Life, Object, Real Life. The **cafés** (levels 2 & 7; ☼ 10am-5.30pm Sun-Thu, 10am-9.30pm Fri & Sat) are renowned for their fabulous views over the Thames. There is a boat service (one-way/day ticket £3.40/5, 18 minutes, every 40 minutes 10am to 5pm) to Tate Britain (p157) from here, which also stops at the London Eye (below).

BRITISH AIRWAYS LONDON EYE
On a clear day from the **British Airways London Eye** (Map pp158-60; ☎ 0870 500 0600; www.ba-london eye.com; Jubilee Gardens, South Bank SE1; metro Waterloo; adult/concession £11.50/9; ☼ 10.30am-7pm Feb, Mar & Oct-Dec, 10.30am-8pm Apr, May & Sep, 10am-10pm Jun-Aug) you can see 25 miles (40km) in every direction. Offering great views, the glass-enclosed gondolas take 30 minutes to rotate completely. Buy tickets from the office behind the wheel, or better still, book ahead.

SAATCHI GALLERY
The **Saatchi Gallery** (Map pp158-60; ☎ 7823 2363; www.saatchi-gallery.co.uk; County Hall SE1; metro Waterloo/Westminster; adult/concession £8.75/6.75; ☼ 10am-7.15pm Sun-Thu, 10am-9.15pm Fri & Sat) is a roll call of the greatest hits of the so-called Young British Art (YBA) movement, where the works of Damien Hirst, Tracey Emin, Sarah Lucas and the like are on permanent display.

IMPERIAL WAR MUSEUM
Although there are lots of military hardware and interactive exhibits dealing with all aspects of the major wars (from spying to trench living), a large percentage of the **Imperial War Museum** (Map pp158-60; ☎ 7416 5339; www.iwm.org.uk; Lambeth Rd SE1; metro Lambeth North; admission free; ☼ 10am-6pm) deals with the human and social cost of conflict. There is a Tibetan Peace Garden to head to afterwards.

MILLENNIUM BRIDGE
Opened in 2000, the **Millennium Bridge** (Map pp158-60; metro St Paul's/Blackfriars) was closed after just three days when it began to sway alarmingly under the weight and movement of pedestrian traffic. Reopened 18 months

later, the elegant, 'blade of light' design now carries millions of people from St Paul's Cathedral on the north side of the river to Tate Modern on the south.

FASHION & TEXTILE MUSEUM
Dedicated to fashion from 1950 to the present day, the **Fashion & Textile Museum** (☎ 7403 0222; www.ftmlondon.org; 83 Bermondsey St SE1; metro London Bridge; adult/concession £6/4; ☼ 10am-4.15pm Tue-Sat, noon-4.15pm Sun) is clad in the signature colours – orange and pink – of its creator, the eccentric British designer Zandra Rhodes. The split-level interior holds brilliant temporary exhibitions, as well as a permanent collection of dresses by the likes of Christian Dior, Chanel, Ossie Clark and Mary Quant.

DALÍ UNIVERSE
Home to Europe's largest collection of Dalí, the **Dalí Universe** (Map pp158-60; ☎ 7620 2720; www.daliuniverse.com; County Hall, Riverside Building SE1; metro Waterloo/Westminster; adult/concession £8.50/7; ☼ 10am-5.30pm) has more than 500 works displayed, including his famous Mae West Lips Sofa and one of the Lobster Telephones.

JUBILEE BRIDGE
Reaching from the Embankment tube station to the Royal Festival Hall and London Eye, the pedestrian **Jubilee Bridge** (Map pp158-60; metro Embankment/Waterloo) has wonderful Thames views. Especially pretty at night, the white pylons look like they are floating in the air.

South London
GREENWICH WALKING TOUR
Greenwich can absorb the best part of a day and needs time to be fully explored. Take the Docklands Light Railway (DLR) to Cutty Sark or the train to Greenwich. Start with the beautiful **Cutty Sark** (☎ 8858 3445; www.cuttysark.org.uk; King William Walk SE10; adult/concession £4.25/3.25; ☼ 10am-5pm), the only surviving tea-and-wool clipper. Wander around the excellent **Greenwich market** (☼ 9.30am-5.30pm Thu-Sun), and then visit the **Queen's House** (☎ 8858 4422; www.nmm.ac.uk; Romney Rd SE10; admission free; ☼ 10am-6pm Jul & Aug, 10am-5pm Sep-Jun), designed in 1616 by Inigo Jones as a retreat for the wife of James I, Queen Anne of Denmark. Britain's famous naval traditions are covered in fascinating fashion at the **National Maritime Museum** (☎ 8858 4422; www.nmm.ac.uk; Romney Rd SE10;

BRITAIN

admission free; 🕙 10am-6pm Jul & Aug, 10am-5pm Sep-Jun). Climb the hill behind the museum to the **Royal Observatory** (☎ 8858 4422; www.nmm.ac.uk; Romney Rd SE10; admission free; 🕙 10am-6pm Jul & Aug, 10am-5pm Sep-Jun). A brass strip in the courtyard marks the Prime Meridian that divides the world into eastern and western hemispheres.

FESTIVALS & EVENTS

The following are popular festivals and events in London:

London Marathon (www.london-marathon.co.uk)
In April some 35,000 masochists cross London in the world's biggest road race from Greenwich Park to the Mall.
London Film Festival (National Film Theatre; www.lff.org.uk)
In October, see the best of British and international films before their cinema release.
New Year's Eve Celebration
Join the crowds and count down to midnight in Trafalgar Sq.
Notting Hill Carnival (www.thecarnival.tv)
Europe's biggest outdoor carnival over the August Bank Holiday weekend is a celebration of Caribbean London.
Pride Parade (www.pridelondon.org)
Gays and lesbians paint the town pink in this annual July parade.

SLEEPING

Staying in London is an expensive business whatever your budget. It's always best to book ahead, especially in summer. Visit London's **Accommodation Line** (☎ 7932 2020; www.visitlondonoffers.com) for some great deals (no booking fee). Alternatively, contact hotels directly with the information provided below.

For a full list of hostels in London contact the **Youth Hostels Association** (☎ 0870 770 6113; www.yha.org.uk) or the **YMCA** (☎ 8520 5599; www.ymca.org.uk), although most of the hostel details are covered here. A little pricier, student

---

SPLURGE!

Temporary home to everyone from the Sex Pistols to Johnny Depp and Kate Moss, the famous **Portobello Hotel** (☎ 7727 2777; www.portobello-hotel.co.uk; 22 Stanley Gardens W11; metro Notting Hill Gate; s/d from £120/160; ✕ 🐾 🖳) has been a firm favourite of rock and movie stars for years. There's a 24-hour bar to fuel guests on their merry way, and the individually decorated rooms (with themes like Morocco and Japan) are elegantly plush, loosely colonial and achingly cool.

---

accommodation or university halls of residence are let to nonstudents during the Easter and summer holidays. Contact ☎ 7995 7575 or ☎ 7107 5750, or check out www.lse.ac.uk /collections/vacations for information.

Unsurprisingly, renting is also expensive. To get abreast of current prices, consult the classifieds in *Loot*, *TNT*, *Time Out* and the *Evening Standard*'s Wednesday supplement *Homes & Property*.

Pimlico & Victoria

Victoria may not be the most attractive part of London, but the budget hotels are better value than those in Earl's Court. Pimlico is more residential, though convenient for the Tate Britain gallery at Millbank.

Victoria Hotel (Map pp158-60; ☎ 7834 3077; www.astorhostels.com; 71 Belgrave Rd SW1; metro Pimlico; dm £15-18; 🖳) This recently and funkily refurbished hostel has 60 beds so it's busy without being too impersonal. It's staffed by pausing travellers, has 24-hour reception, and is within easy walking distance of the Tate Britain and Westminster Abbey.

Brindle House Hotel (Map pp158-60; ☎ 7828 0057; www.brindlehousehotel.co.uk; 1 Warwick Pl North SW1; metro Victoria; B&B s/d £35/48, s/d/tr/q with shower £45/60/75/89) Recently refurbished with parquet floors and a lick of paint, the rooms are pristine but the *en suite* showers and toilets are rather squashed. Staff are helpful and friendly.

Luna & Simone Hotel (Map pp158-60; ☎ 7834 5897; www.lunasimonehotel.com; 47-49 Belgrave Rd SW1; metro Victoria; s £40, s/d/tr with shower £50/60/80; ✕ 🖳) In a road stuffed full of varying quality B&Bs, this is a shining example of good value simply done. The rooms have satellite TV, are bright, airy and spotlessly clean. A good, if pricier alternative is **Victor Hotel** (Map pp158-60; ☎ 7592 9853; www.victorhotel.co.uk; 51 Belgrave Rd SW1; metro Victoria; B&B s/d/tr with shower £70/90/135).

James House and **Cartref House** (Map pp158-60; ☎ 7730 7338; www.jamesandcartref.co.uk; 108 & 129 Ebury St SW1; metro Victoria; s/d/tr/q with shower £62/85/110/135; ✕ 🖳) The best in the street for the budget, these two B&Bs are across the street from each other. They are run by a very friendly couple with a good knowledge of Victoria, and have freshly decorated and clean rooms.

The West End & Covent Garden

Here you're in the centre of the action, but you pay for the convenience. Following are the best budget options:

Oxford St YHA (Map pp158-60; ☎ 7734 1618; oxfordst@yha.org.uk; 14 Noel St W1; metro Oxford Circus/Tottenham Court Rd; dm adult/YHA member £22.60/18.20, tw per person £26; ✗ 🖳) The most central of London's hostels is basic, clean, welcoming and loud. There is a large kitchen but no meals are served apart from a packed breakfast. There are laundry facilities and the majority of the 75 beds are twins.

Regent Palace Hotel (Map pp158-60; ☎ 0870 400 8703; www.regentpalacehotel.co.uk; Glasshouse St W1; metro Piccadilly Circus; s/d/tr from £64/89/99; ✗ 🖳) This central and inexpensive hotel is great for those arriving from Heathrow on the tube, and particularly convenient for sightseeing. But the rather frenetic ambience is not particularly relaxing.

Bloomsbury & Fitzrovia

Bloomsbury is an altogether more sedate, refined district at half the price of the West End.

The Generator (Map pp158-60; ☎ 7388 7666; www.the-generator.co.uk; Compton Pl, off 37 Tavistock Pl WC1; metro Russell Sq; B&B dm £12.50-17, s/tw/tr without bathroom £42/26.50/22.50; ✗ 🖳) One of the liveliest budget options in central London, this hostel has a bar that stays open to 2am, a movie lounge, pool table, safe-deposit boxes, laundry and canteen (£3 for pizza) but no kitchen. Booking is essential.

Pickwick Hall (Map pp158-60; ☎ 7323 4958; www.pickwickhall.co.uk; 7 Bedford Pl WC1; metro Holborn; dm/d £20/44; ✗ 🖳) A convenient stone's throw from the British Museum, this hostel offers basic, good-value accommodation. There's a kitchen, laundry and TV lounge.

Indian Student YMCA (Map pp158-60; ☎ 7387 0411; www.indianymca.org; 41 Fitzroy Sq W1; metro Warren St; dm/s/d £20/34/40, d with bathroom from £55; ✗ 🖳) For all nationalities and not just students, this YMCA has good-sized, clean rooms, a laundry and sports facilities. Prices include breakfast and a tasty curry dinner.

Hotel Cavendish (Map pp158-60; ☎ 7636 9079; www.hotelcavendish.com; 75 Gower St WC1; metro Goodge St; B&B s/d/tr/q £40/50/75/90; ✗) Run by a welcoming and friendly family, this hotel has simply furnished rooms with William Morris-style wallpapers. There is a cosy breakfast room filled with paintings of Bloomsbury writers and a pleasant walled garden. None of the rooms are *en suite* but facilities are conveniently right next to the rooms.

Arran House Hotel (Map pp158-60; ☎ 7636 2186; arran@dircon.co.uk; 77-79 Gower St WC1; metro Goodge St; dm £16-21, B&B s/d/tr £45/62/80, with bathroom £55/85/103; 🖳) This excellent-value, family-run hotel has lodgings ranging from spotlessly clean and airy dormitories to stylish and cosy doubles with Art Deco fireplaces. The rose garden is a pleasant bonus in the summer.

Arosfa (Map pp158-60; ☎ 7636 2115; 83 Gower St WC1; metro Goodge St; B&B s/d/tr/q £45/66/79/92; ✗) Arosfa (Welsh for 'a place to stay') reopened in late 2003 after a six-month renovation. All the rooms are now *en suite* and look much fresher with the new furniture, carpets and paint. There is a small garden open in the summer.

South Kensington & Earl's Court

South Kensington is close to the museums but Earl's Court offers the inexpensive options. The lower end of the Earl's Court hotel market can be appalling but you can usually tell instantly by the state of the hallway and the general atmosphere.

Earl's Court YHA (Map pp164-5; ☎ 7373 7083; earlscourt@yha.org.uk; 38 Bolton Gardens SW5; metro Earl's Court; dm adult/under-18 £19.50/17.20; ✗ 🖳) Set in a recently refurbished Victorian townhouse, this immaculate and spacious hostel has mainly four-bed dorms and very helpful staff. There is a well-equipped self-catering kitchen, large lounge and satellite TV, as well as a large courtyard garden.

Curzon House Hotel (Map pp164-5; ☎ 7581 2116; www.curzonhousehotel.co.uk; 58 Courtfield Gardens SW5; metro Gloucester Rd; B&B dm £15-17, s/d/tr £30/44/63) In a quiet square overlooking a pretty church, this hotel offers basic rooms (none *en suite*), a kitchen and a cable-TV room. The staff are some of the friendliest you'll meet.

Merlyn Court Hotel (Map pp164-5; ☎ 7370 1640; www.merlyncourthotel; 2 Barkston Gardens SW5; metro Earl's Court; B&B s/d/tr/q from £30/45/60/65, with shower £40/50/70/75; ✗) Near the tube, this hotel set in an Edwardian square has recently been freshened up. The décor is simple and the rooms have mainly three or four beds.

Philbeach Hotel (Map pp164-5; ☎ 7373 1244; www.philbeachhotel.freeserve.co.uk; 30-31 Philbeach Gardens SW5; metro Earl's Court; B&B s/d £50/63, with bathroom £59/81; 🖳) The Philbeach is one of London's few gay hotels. Set in the middle of a sweeping crescent, its 40 rooms are stylish and pristine. The on-site bar and Thai restaurant are both popular with the local gay crowd.

BRITAIN

BRITAIN

CENTRAL WEST LONDON

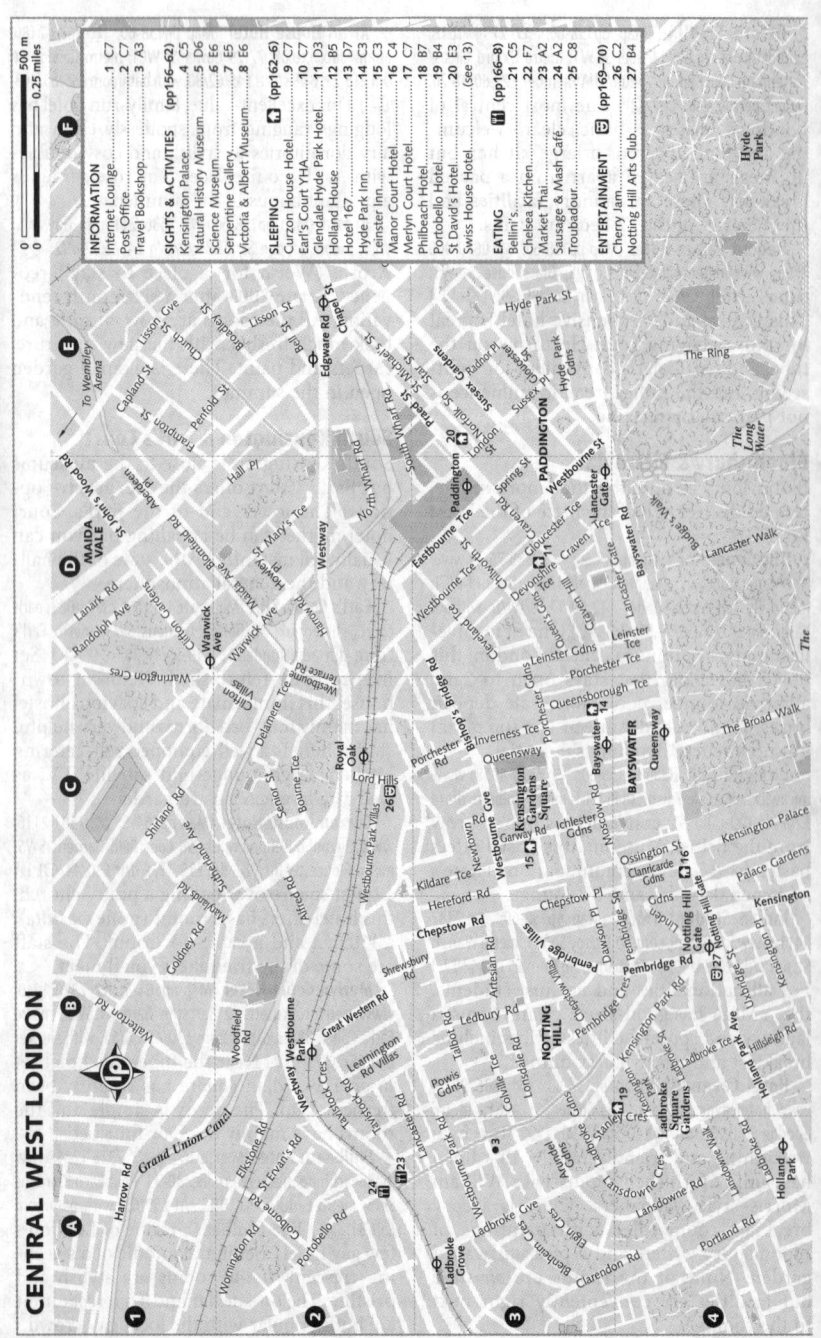

INFORMATION	
Internet Lounge.....................1	C7
Post Office............................2	C7
Travel Bookshop....................3	A3

SIGHTS & ACTIVITIES (pp156–62)	
Kensington Palace.................4	C5
Natural History Museum........5	D6
Science Museum...................6	E6
Serpentine Gallery...............7	E5
Victoria & Albert Museum.....8	E6

SLEEPING (pp162–6)	
Curzon House Hotel..............9	C7
Earl's Court YHA.................10	C7
Glendale Hyde Park Hotel....11	D3
Holland House....................12	B5
Hotel 167..........................13	D7
Hyde Park Inn....................14	C3
Leinster Inn......................15	C3
Manor Court Hotel..............16	C4
Merlyn Court Hotel.............17	C7
Philbeach Hotel.................18	B7
Portobello Hotel................19	B4
St David's Hotel.................20	E3
Swiss House Hotel...............(see 13)	

EATING (pp166–8)	
Bellini's...........................21	C5
Chelsea Kitchen.................22	F7
Market Thai......................23	A2
Sausage & Mash Café..........24	A2
Troubadour.......................25	C8

ENTERTAINMENT (pp169–70)	
Cherry Jam.......................26	C2
Notting Hill Arts Club..........27	B4

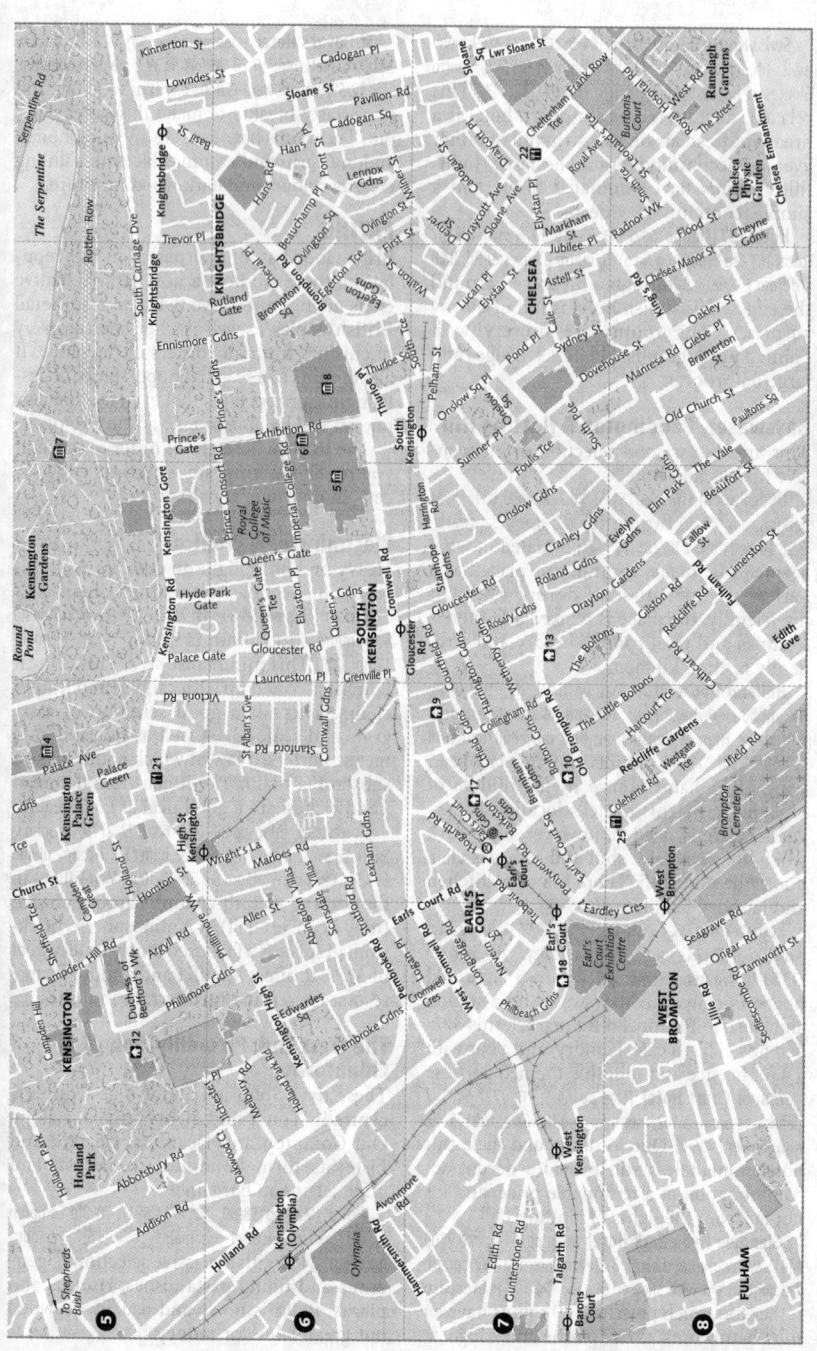

Swiss House Hotel (Map pp164-5; ☎ 7373 2769; www
.swiss-hh.demon.co.uk; 171 Old Brompton Rd SW5; metro
Gloucester Rd; B&B from s/d/tr/q £56/97/132/147) This
relaxed, uncluttered and modern hotel is a
breath of fresh air on this strip full of rather
average accommodation. The large, light-
filled rooms have laminated floors and a
simple, contemporary décor.

Hotel 167 (Map pp164-5; ☎ 7373 0672; www.hotel167
.com; 167 Old Brompton Rd SW5; metro Gloucester Rd; B&B
s/d from £72/90) Although a bit frayed around
the edges, this stylish hotel is full of quirky
surprises. The rooms are flowery with
painted photographs, old desks, fridges and
large bathrooms.

Bayswater, Paddington & Notting Hill
This area has a good selection of inexpensive hostels and hotels.

Hyde Park Inn (Map pp164-5; ☎ 7229 0000; www.hyde
parkinn.com; 48-50 Inverness Tce W2; metro Bayswater;
B&B 10-bed dm/s £10/28; ⊠ ⏻) Situated in what
seems to be hostel central, this place has a
variety of different-sized dorms. The staff
are friendly, the place is relaxed and there's
a games and pool room, laundry and a recently refitted kitchen.

Holland House YHA (Map pp164-5; ☎ 7937 0748;
hollandhouse@yha.org.uk; Holland Walk, Kensington
W8; metro High St Kensington; B&B dm adult/under-18
£21.60/19.30; ⊠ ⏻) Built into the Jacobean
wing of Holland House in the middle of
Holland Park, this hostel's location is gorgeous. Care is needed, however, after dark
when the park gates shut and access is via a
poorly lit side path. There is a café, kitchen
and laundry facilities.

Leinster Inn (Map pp164-5; ☎ 7229 9641; www.astor
hostels.com; 7-12 Leinster Sq W2; metro Bayswater; B&B dm
£13.50-18, s/d from £26/40; ⊠ ⏻) In a large, old
house northwest of Bayswater tube station
and close to Portobello Rd market, this 372-
bed hostel has a café, laundry, and a bar with
a 4am licence and monthly themed parties.

Manor Court Hotel (Map pp164-5; ☎ 7727 5407; 7
Clanricarde Gardens W2; metro Notting Hill Gate; s/d £25/40,
with shower £40/50) Due for a nip and tuck, this
hotel nonetheless still provides decent accommodation at a reasonable price, and it's
not far from the lights of Notting Hill.

Glendale Hyde Park Hotel (Map pp164-5; ☎ 7706
4441; www.ghphotel.com; 8 Devonshire Tce W2; metro
Paddington; s/d with shower £45/55; ⊠ ⏻) Despite
rather too much pastel, all 20 rooms have *en
suite* bathrooms, a TV, phone and fridge.

St David's Hotel (Map pp164-5; ☎ 7723 4963; www
.stdavidshotels.com; 16-20 Norfolk Sq W2; metro Paddington;
s/d £39/59, with shower £49/69) A warm welcome and
huge, tasty breakfasts make this hotel stand
out. The rooms have satellite TV and phones,
and are clean and comfortable with calming
creamy colours and dark wood furniture.

EATING
British food has long surpassed its dire reputation; there are now a host of imaginative
chefs giving innovative twists to traditional
British staples, as well as a bewildering array
of cuisines from all corners of the globe. It
all amounts to a feasting opportunity of gastronomic proportions that even the smallest
budget will be able to take advantage of.

The listings here are in order of price. If
you're self-catering, supermarkets and grocery shops are everywhere.

Westminster & Pimlico
Heavy on hotels, light on restaurants – this
area is for recliners rather than diners.

Kazan (Map pp158-60; ☎ 7233 7100; 93-94 Wilton Rd
SW1; metro Victoria; starters £3-5, mains £8-13; ☺ noon-
11pm; ⊠) This minimalist-style Turkish restaurant is cosied up with candles and leather
chairs. There is a good selection of tasty
grills and seafood, as well as hot and cold
mezze starters, a few of which could make a
substantial main. The lunch-time flatbread
'sandwiches' are a good deal at £3.55 each.

Footstool (Map pp158-60; ☎ 7222 2779; St John's,
Smith Sq SW1; metro Westminster; buffet £7, 2-course dinner
£13.50; ☺ 11am-2.45pm & 5.30-10.30pm Mon-Fri) Set in
the crypt of an 18th-century baroque church
(now a concert hall), this atmospheric, brick-
vaulted space is a favoured lunch-time retreat
of MPs. It offers a buffet and a more formal
restaurant serving Mediterranean dishes.

The West End: Piccadilly, Soho & Chinatown
These days Soho is London's gastronomic
centralis. You'll find plenty of choice along
Old Compton and Dean Sts. Gerrard and
Lisle Sts form London's Chinatown and
offer set-menu bargains.

Pollo (Map pp158-60; ☎ 7734 5917; 20 Old Compton
St W1; metro Leicester Sq; mains under £5; ☺ noon-
midnight; ⊠) With a massive selection of generous and filling pasta dishes, risottos and
pizzas, Pollo is noisy and usually crowded
but great value for money.

Stockpot (Map pp158-60; ☎ 7287 1066; 18 Old Compton St W1; metro Leicester Sq; mains £4-6; ⏰ 11.30am-midnight; ❌) Like Pollo next door, Stockpot is a London institution and one of the few places where you can get a three-course meal for under a tenner. Sturdy staples include the likes of spaghetti bolognese, beef stroganoff and steak.

Café de Hong Kong (Map pp158-60; ☎ 7534 9898; 47-49 Charing Cross Rd WC2; metro Leicester Sq; mains £4.20-6.50; ⏰ noon-11pm) If the traditional-style Cantonese restaurants with ducks hanging in the window put you off, then Café de HK is probably more up your street. It has brought Hong Kong café culture to London with its sleek and modern minimalist design and street hawker–style dishes.

Mildred's (Map pp158-60; ☎ 7494 1634; 45 Lexington St W1; mains £5.50-7.50; metro Oxford Circus/Piccadilly Circus; ⏰ noon-11pm Mon-Sat; ❌) This superb vegetarian/vegan restaurant serves generous portions of dishes like the virtuous organic energising detox salad and the more indulgent mushroom, tofu and ale pie. There are also naughty puddings and an impressive selection of organic wines. Takeaway available.

Masala Zone (Map pp158-60; ☎ 7287 9966; 9 Marshall St W1; metro Oxford Circus; mains £5.50-11.50; ⏰ noon-3pm & 5.30-11pm; ❌) The industrial, canteen-like design juxtaposed against terracotta walls and tribal Indian art fits perfectly with the modern Indian cuisine. Dishes range from street food, sandwiches and salads to thalis, noodle bowls and curries.

Covent Garden & the Strand

There is a huge choice of eateries around here. These are our favourites:

Food for Thought (Map pp158-60; ☎ 7836 0239; 31 Neal St WC2; metro Covent Garden; mains £3-6.50; ⏰ noon-8.15pm Mon-Sat, noon-4.45pm Sun; ❌ ❌) This cherished and tiny vegetarian institution serves huge portions of imaginative salads, crispy stir-fries, smooth curries and thick quiches. The menus change every day and food can be taken away.

Café in the Crypt (Map pp158-60; ☎ 7839 4342; St Martin-in-the-Fields, Duncannon St WC2; metro Charing Cross; mains £3.95-7.50; ⏰ noon-3pm daily, 5-7.30pm Mon-Wed & Sun, 5-10.30pm Thu-Sat) Right next to Trafalgar Sq, this cafeteria-style eatery set in the arched crypt of the St Martin-in-the-Fields church is the perfect place to rest weary bones and enjoy wholesome food. Expect a good choice of salads, Brit-

ish mains, proper puddings and teas and scones.

Rock & Sole Plaice (Map pp158-60; ☎ 7836 3785; 47 Endell St WC2; metro Covent Garden; fish & chips £8-9; ⏰ 11.30am-10pm Mon-Sat, noon-9pm Sun) Established in 1871, this landmark sit-down and takeaway chippy does fantastic cod, Dover sole, scotch salmon or tuna steak between perfectly crisp batter, along with tasty thick chips.

Bloomsbury

Due to the student contingent, Bloomsbury has a few reasonably priced places to eat.

Coffee Gallery (Map pp158-60; ☎ 7436 0455; 23 Museum St WC1; metro Tottenham Court Rd; mains £3-4; ⏰ 9am-6pm Mon-Fri, 9am-7pm Sat, 11am-7pm Sun; ❌) After the British Museum, drop in here and choose from the mainly organic and vegetarian pasta, salads and sandwiches.

Fitzrovia (Map pp158-60; ☎ 7636 2744; 29 Tottenham St W1; metro Goodge St; mains £3.60-9.20; ⏰ noon-3pm & 6-11pm) Just off Charlotte St, this hidden gem with slightly faded charm looks like it's been pulled out of an Italian village. Great-value, no-frills Italian dishes are served here, and it's filled with a mixture of older Bloomsbury locals and students.

South Bank & Bankside

Reflecting the development of the area, this part of town offers down-to-earth cafés and trendy gastropubs, as well as up-market refinement.

Festival Square (Map pp158-60; ☎ 7928 2228; ground flr, Royal Festival Hall, South Bank SE1; metro Waterloo; mains £5-10; ⏰ 8.30am-11pm Mon-Fri, 10am-11pm Sat, 10am-10pm Sun) With fresh and inventive modern European meals this contemporary café and bar is a handy pick-me-up point along the South Bank sightseeing strip.

Anchor & Hope (Map pp158-60; ☎ 7928 9898; 36 The Cut SE1; metro Southwark/Waterloo; mains £10-15; ⏰ noon-2.30pm & 6-10.30pm Tue-Sat, 6-10.30pm Mon) With mainly British fare, such as stuffed duck or Lancashire hotpot, the food here has received accolades galore, including the *Evening Standard*'s 2004 gastropub of the year award. There's a simple oak décor, relaxed atmosphere, and a good selection of cask ales and wines.

Chelsea, South Kensington & Earl's Court

All budgets are well catered for in these areas.

Chelsea Kitchen (Map pp164-5; ☎ 7589 1330; 98 King's Rd SW3; metro Sloane Sq; mains £3.30-5; ✆ 7am-11.45pm) The décor suggests trucker's café but the food suggests you've found a bargain. The varied menu includes the likes of French onion soup, lasagne and steak.

Troubadour (Map pp164-5; ☎ 7370 1434; www .troubadour.co.uk; 265 Old Brompton Rd SW5; metro Earl's Court; breakfast £3.25-6, mains £6.50-11; ✆ 9am-11pm) Bob Dylan and John Lennon have both performed here, and Troubadour remains a wonderfully relaxed bohemian hang-out decades later – great for just coffee, a reasonably priced, home-cooked meal or the live music that still plays most nights. It also has a deli next door.

Kensington & Knightsbridge

Cheap eats are few and far between around here.

Bellini's (Map pp164-5; ☎ 7937 5520; 47 Kensington Ct W8; metro High St Kensington; mains £8-16, 2-/3-course lunch £7.65/9.15; ✆ noon-11pm) This Italian restaurant with great pizza, pasta and meaty mains, has a few pavement tables and views of a flower-bedecked alley.

Notting Hill

Notting Hill is yet another good eat-out option, with everything from cheap takeaways to trendy restaurants, some quite quirky.

Sausage & Mash Café (Map pp164-5; ☎ 8968 8898; 268 Portobello Rd W10; metro Ladbroke Grove; mains £6-7; ✆ 11am-11pm) Entertainingly known as 'S&M', this place does an up-market version of an English favourite. There are 20 types of sausage to choose from (including vegetarian) and variations of mash and gravy.

Market Thai (Map pp164-5; ☎ 7460 8320; The Market Bar, 240 Portobello Rd W11; metro Ladbroke Grove; mains £5-8; ✆ noon-10.30pm) Set on the 1st floor of the Market Bar, its drippy white candles, carved arches and wrought-iron chairs make it feel way beyond the market crowds. Hospitable staff and fresh, delicately spiced Thai cuisine make for a delightful eating spot.

Islington

Islington is stuffed full of eateries, especially on Upper St.

Afghan Kitchen (☎ 7359 8019; 35 Islington Green N1; metro Angel; mains £4.50-6; ✆ noon-3.30pm & 5.30-11pm Tue-Sat) This tiny gem is known for its vegetarian concoctions (such as the scrumptious kidney bean, chickpea and potatoes cooked in yogurt, mint and lime) but the fish and meat dishes are equally as good. The décor is a calming pale green and light wood.

Elk in the Woods (☎ 7226 3535; 39 Camden Passage N1; metro Angel; breakfast £5, lunch £5-7, dinner £8-9; ✆ 10am-11pm) Set in the charming becobbled Camden passage, this cosy restaurant-bar with its standard lamps and flowered wallpaper attracts a jovial bohemian Islington crowd with its tasty and inexpensive modern European food.

East End

Brick Lane is lined with Indian and Bangladeshi restaurants of varying quality. Head to Hoxton for a more varied and pricey choice.

Brick Lane Beigel Bake (☎ 7729 0616; 159 Brick Lane E2; metro Shoreditch; filled bagels 70p-£1.30; ✆ 24hr) This café-deli provides the ultimate cure for late-night munchies. You won't find cheaper or fresher bagels anywhere else.

Preem (☎ 7247 0397; 120 Brick Lane E1; metro Aldgate East; mains £4-5; ✆ noon-2am) A Bengali favourite, this is one of the better restaurants found on the strip. Another recommended place is the modestly dressed **Le Taj** (☎ 7247 4210; 134 Brick Lane E1; metro Liverpool St; mains £5-10; ✆ 11.30am-midnight).

Greenwich

Greenwich's eateries are packed into a triangle formed by the Market, Greenwich Church St and Nelson Rd. The Cutty Sark DLR is the convenient station.

Bar du Musée (☎ 8858 4710; 17 Nelson Rd; mains £10.50-13; ✆ noon-midnight Mon-Thu, noon-1am Fri-Sun) More café than bar, this relaxed place serves well-executed French staples, as well as having a fantastic patisserie. Nibble on coffee and cakes in the new conservatory housing a lounge with comfy sofas.

DRINKING

From ancient and atmospheric taverns to slick DJ bars, London is awash in pubs and bars, all of which close at a puritanical 11pm (10.30pm Sunday).

Bradley's Spanish Bar (Map pp158-60; 44 Hanway St W1; metro Tottenham Court Rd) One of the most shabby, small and charming bars in London – downstairs is dimly lit with alcoves, red velvet seats and a bar; upstairs is similarly decorated with Spanish trinkets and has a wicked jukebox.

Lamb & Flag (Map pp158-60; Rose St WC2; metro Covent Garden or Leicester Sq) Manic just after office hours, it is loved by all for its family-like quality. Interesting, then, that it used to be called 'The Bucket of Blood'.

Coach & Horses (Map pp158-60; 29 Greek St W1; metro Leicester Sq) This small, busy boozer retains the atmosphere of old Soho bohemia with a regular clientele of soaks, writers, hacks and tourists.

George Inn (Talbot Yard, 77 Borough High St SE1; metro London Bridge/Borough) Dating from 1676, London's last surviving galleried coaching inn, with its low ceilings and dark-panelled rooms, is mentioned in Charles Dickens' *Little Dorrit*.

Bricklayers Arms (63 Charlotte Rd EC2; metro Old St) A determinedly down-to-earth stalwart of the Hoxton scene, it attracts an unpretentious but cool-looking, mid-to-late 20-something crowd.

Two Floors (Map pp158-60; 3 Kingly St W1; metro Oxford Circus/Piccadilly Circus) Attracting a mix of bohemian and trendy types, Two Floors always seems to be playing the music that you've just got into. Drinks are bottled beers and cocktails.

CLUBBING

Keep an eye on *Time Out* magazine to see what's hot and what's not on the cool London club scene. Admission prices vary from £3 to £10 between Sunday and Thursday, and £14 and £20 on Friday and Saturday. A selection of the best clubs include the following:

Fabric (Map pp158-60; ☎ 7336 8898; 77A Charterhouse St EC1; metro Barbican; ☯ 9.30pm-5am Fri & Sun, 10pm-7am Sat) Has a kidney-shaking 'sonic boom' dance floor.

93 Feet East (☎ 7247 3293; 150 Brick Lane E2; metro Liverpool St; ☯ 8pm-2am Thu-Sat) Attracts a typically cool Hoxton crowd.

Pacha (Map pp158-60; ☎ 7834 4440; Terminus Pl SW1; metro Victoria; ☯ 10pm-6am Fri & Sat) Head here for Balearic beats.

The Cross (Map pp158-60; ☎ 7837 0828; Goods Way Depot, York Way N1; metro King's Cross; ☯ 10.30pm-5am Fri & Sat, 10.30am-4pm Sun) Popular for its soulful funk and garage.

Cherry Jam (Map pp164-5; ☎ 7727 9950; 58 Porchester Rd W2; metro Royal Oak; ☯ 7pm-1.30am Thu-Sat) Club nights here range from Latin to deep-house, and there are also live bands and readings.

Gay & Lesbian Clubs

Ghetto (Map pp158-60; ☎ 7287 3726; 5-6 Falconberg Ct W1; metro Tottenham Court Rd; ☯ 10pm-3am Mon-Thu, from 10.30pm-3am Wed, 10.30pm-4.30am Fri & Sat) Attracts the fashionable glitterati.

Astoria (Map pp158-60; ☎ 7434 0044; 157 Charing Cross Rd WC2; metro Tottenham Court Rd; 10.30pm-4am Mon & Thu, 11pm-4am Fri, 10.30am-5am Sat) Plays mainly commercial beats.

Heaven (Map pp158-60; ☎ 7930 2020; Villiers St WC2; metro Embankment; ☯ 10.30pm-3am Mon & Wed, 10pm-3am Fri, 10pm-5am Sat) Is ever popular and has some mixed nights.

DTPM on Sunday night at superclub Fabric, and Fiction on Friday night at The Cross (see above) are good gay nights.

ENTERTAINMENT

By day and by night, London plays host to a lively, vibrant mix of welcome distractions. It's rich in contemporary and classical music, film, theatre and nightclubs. Buy a copy of *Time Out* (£2.35; every Wednesday), which lists and reviews everything going on in the capital.

Theatre

With the likes of Nicole Kidman and Dame Judi Dench having trod its boards, London's theatreland is an innovative and exciting place. At the same time, rip-roaring musicals are ever popular. Visit www.official londontheatre.co.uk to find out what's on and where. On the day of performance queue outside the **Tkts booth** (Map pp158-60; Leicester Sq; ☯ 10am-7pm Mon-Sat, noon-3pm Sun) to get discounted West End show tickets.

Royal National Theatre (Map pp158-60; ☎ 7452 3000; www.nationaltheatre.org.uk; South Bank SE1; metro Waterloo; £7-35) Britain's flagship theatre showcases a mix of classic and contemporary plays performed by excellent casts.

Shakespeare's Globe Theatre (Map pp158-60; ☎ 7401 9919; www.shakespeares-globe.org; 21 New Globe Walk SE1; metro London Bridge; standing room £5, seats £13-29; ☯ May-Sep) The Globe is the home of authentic Shakespearean theatre, not only in the sense that it's a near-perfect replica of the building Shakespeare himself worked in from 1598 to 1611, but because it also largely follows Elizabethan staging practices. Buy inexpensive standing tickets (for the mainly Shakespearean works) so you can emulate the 17th-century 'groundlings', who shouted and cajoled as they wished.

Cinemas

The choice of movies to watch in London is dazzling. For Hollywood blockbusters head to Leicester Square, or for a more eclectic choice try the **National Film Theatre** (Map pp158-60; ☎ 7928 3232; www.bfi.org.uk/showing/nft; South Bank Centre SE1; metro Waterloo), which screens an impressive range of classic, unusual, experimental and foreign films. In October, the **London Film Festival** (p162) is held here as well as in other venues around London, including Leicester Square.

Live Music

London's live rock and pop music scene with its hundreds of venues simply can't be beaten. Some of the major venues for live contemporary music include the **Brixton Academy** (☎ 7771 3000; 211 Stockwell Rd SW9; metro Brixton) and **Shepherds Bush Empire** (☎ 8354 3300; Shepherds Bush Green W12; metro Shepherds Bush). Smaller places with a more club-like atmosphere worth checking out (ring ahead to find out which bands are playing) include the following:

12 Bar Club (Map pp158-60; ☎ 7916 6989; 22 Denmark Pl WC2; metro Tottenham Court Rd)

Borderline (Map pp158-60; ☎ 7434 9592; Orange Yard, off Manette St WC2; metro Tottenham Court Rd)

Garage (☎ 7607 1818; 20-22 Highbury Corner N5; metro Highbury & Islington)

Notting Hill Arts Club (Map pp164-5; ☎ 7460 4459; 21 Notting Hill Gate W11; metro Notting Hill Gate)

Union Chapel (☎ 7226 1686; Compton Tce N1; metro Highbury/Islington).

If you're a jazz fan, keep your eye on **Ronnie Scott's** (Map pp158-60; ☎ 7439 0747; 47 Frith St W1; metro Leicester Sq), the **Jazz Café** (☎ 7916 6060; 5 Parkway NW1; metro Camden Town) and the **100 Club** (Map pp158-60; ☎ 7636 0933; 100 Oxford St W1; metro Tottenham Court Rd).

Major classical music venues include the **Barbican** (☎ 7638 8891; Silk St EC2; metro Moorgate/Barbican) and the **South Bank Centre** (Map pp158-60; ☎ 7960 4242; Belvedere Rd SE1; metro Waterloo) with its Royal Festival Hall, Queen Elizabeth Hall and Purcell Room.

GETTING THERE & AWAY

For details on getting into and out of London refer to p149.

GETTING AROUND
Public Transport

For information regarding the London bus, Underground, DLR or train networks contact Transport for London (TfL; ☎ 7222 1234; www.tfl .gov.uk) or go to the TfL centres at Victoria, Piccadilly Circus, Euston and Liverpool St stations and at Heathrow airport.

BUS & UNDERGROUND

Although traffic may make your journey longer than by Underground, buses have recently become a much cheaper transport option. Single tickets or one-day bus passes to anywhere in London cost £1 and £2.50 respectively. These prices include the comprehensive network of night buses that runs from or through Trafalgar Square (routes are denoted by the letter 'N'). There are machines next to all bus stops where you have to buy your ticket before boarding. Pick up a free bus map at a TfL centre.

Travelcards are the easiest option if you'll be using all public transport – they can be used on London trains, the DLR, buses and the tube. A Zones 1 and 2 day Travelcard costs £5.30 before 9.30am, £4.30 after. If you are staying for a week or longer, get an Oyster Card. It's an electronic card that you swipe over a yellow 'reader' each time you go through the ticket machine (Zones 1 and 2, one week £20.20).

Times of the last tube trains vary from 11.30pm to 12.30am, depending on the station and line.

DLR & TRAIN

The monorail-like, driverless Docklands Light Railway (DLR) links the City at Bank and Tower Gateway with Canary Wharf, Stratford, Beckton, Greenwich and Lewisham. Fares operate the same way as on the tube.

Trains are the primary means of transport to much of London's suburbia. All main line stations interchange with the tube, and you can use your Travelcard for any parts of the journey within London.

Taxi

The famous **London black cabs** (☎ 7272 0272; www.londonblackcabs.co.uk) can be hailed when the yellow 'for hire' sign is lit. They can carry five people but are not cheap. All fares are metered and drivers expect a tip of 10%.

Minicabs can carry four people and tend to be cheaper than the black cabs. Although they are only supposed to be hired by phone and need a licence to operate, hawkers abound in popular spots at night. Women, particularly if alone, are advised to steer clear. They're also unmetered, so make sure you barter hard on a price before you get in.

Small minicab companies are based in particular areas – ask a local for the name of a reputable company, or phone one of the large **24-hour minicab operations** (☎ 7387 8888, 7272 2222, 7272 3322, 8888 4444). Women could phone **Ladycabs** (☎ 7254 3501). Gays and lesbians can choose **Freedom Cars** (☎ 7734 1313).

AROUND LONDON

When the hubbub of the city gets too much, there are plenty of nearby respites to which you can escape. Places like Brighton (p173), Bath (p177), Oxford (p183) and Cambridge (p188) are within day-tripping distance. Closer to the city are the more royal options of Windsor and Eton.

Windsor & Eton
☎ 01753 / pop 31,000

One of three official residences of the Queen, **Windsor Castle** (☎ 020-7766 7304; www .royalresidences.com; adult/concession £12/10, half-price when State Apartments are closed; ☽ 9.45am-4pm Mar-Oct, 9.45am-3pm Nov-Feb, changing of the guard on alternate days 11am Mon-Sat Apr-Jun) has been home to English sovereigns for over 900 years. Attractions include the 14th-century St George's Chapel, which is the burial place of 10 monarchs (closed to visitors on Sunday), the amazing Queen Mary's Doll's House and the opulent State Apartments. The latter are closed when the royal family are in residence – phone to check. The Queen is at home when the Royal Standard is flying.

Eton College (☎ 671177; www.etoncollege.com; admission £3.80, 1hr tours £4.90; ☽ 10am-4.30pm 27 Mar-20 Apr & 3 Jul-7 Sep, 2-4.30pm 21 Apr-2 Jul & 8 Sep-3 Oct, tours 2.15pm & 3.15pm) is a short walk along Thames St and across the river. This famous public school has educated 18 prime ministers and a number of royals, the most recent being Princes William and Harry. Several buildings date from when Henry VI founded the school in the mid-15th century.

Trains go directly and twice hourly from London Waterloo to Windsor and Eton Riverside station (one-way/return £6.40/6.70, one hour).

SOUTHEAST ENGLAND

The Southeast is a region exceptionally rich in beauty and history and it caters to those unshakeable traditional images of England – picturesque villages with welcoming old pubs, spectacular coastlines, impressive castles and magnificent cathedrals. Yet the Southeast is not just about recapturing an England past and pastoral. Nowadays you'll find clubbing heaven in hip Brighton or fusion food under Winchester's Tudor beams.

The **South East England Tourist Board** (☎ 01892-540766; www.southeastengland.uk.com) has a comprehensive website on the region's attractions.

GETTING THERE & AROUND

There are plenty of fast, regular rail and bus services from London to the counties of Kent, East and West Sussex and Hampshire making it possible to see the main sights on day trips. For information on all public transport options in the region ring **Traveline** (☎ 0870 608 2608; www.traveline.org.uk). There is an interesting rail loop from London via Canterbury East, Dover, Ashford, Rye, Hastings, Battle (via Hastings), Brighton, Arundel, Portsmouth and Winchester, which can be cheaper using a BritRail SouthEast pass (see p152) if you are from overseas.

CANTERBURY
☎ 01227 / pop 46,000

Canterbury, with its charming medieval centre of cobbled streets and characterful buildings, is reigned over by the Gothic spires of its magnificent cathedral.

Canterbury Cathedral was the successor to the church that St Augustine built after he began converting the English to Christianity in AD 597; and it was here in 1170 that Archbishop Thomas à Becket was murdered by four of Henry II's knights during a dispute over the church's independence. An enormous cult grew up around the martyred Becket and Canterbury became the centre of one of the most important medieval pilgrimages in Europe, immortalised by Geoffrey Chaucer in the *Canterbury Tales*.

Orientation & Information

The two train stations are both a short walk from the centre. The bus station is just within the city walls at the eastern end of High St.

Public Library (☎ 463608; High St) Free Internet access but bookings required.

Visitor Information Centre (☎ 378100; www .canterbury.co.uk; 12-13 Sun St; ☼ 10am-4pm) Near the entrance to the cathedral.

Sights

Due to fires, the first church at **Canterbury Cathedral** (☎ 762862; www.canterbury-cathedral.org; adult/concession £4.50/3.50, tours £3.50/2.50; ☼ 9am-6.30pm Mon-Sat Easter-Sep, 9am-4.30pm Oct-Easter, 9am-2.30pm Sun all year) was rebuilt in 1070 by the Normans, and again in 1174 in an Early English Gothic style. A tour is recommended, as the cathedral is a treasure trove of associated stories. The one that has drawn pilgrims for centuries, and later tourists, was the brutal martyrdom of Becket.

At the **Roman Museum** (☎ 785575; www.canter bury-museums.co.uk; Butchery Lane; adult/concession £2.80/1.75; ☼ 10am-4pm Mon-Sat, 1.30-4.30pm Sun), built underground around the remnants of a Roman townhouse, you can visit the reconstructed Roman marketplace, handle artefacts and see the remains of a mosaic floor.

Sleeping

Kipps (☎ 786121; www.kipps-hostel.com; 40 Nunnery Fields; dm/s/d £13/18.50/32, ⓟ ✉ 🖳) This clean and friendly hostel south of the centre has a games room, tuck shop, kitchen, laundry facilities and garden.

Acacia Lodge & Tanglewood (☎ 769955; www.acacia lodge.com; 39-40 London Rd; s with shower £30-40, d with shower £42-55; ⓟ ✉) North of the centre, two 19th-century farm cottages have been converted into one welcoming and cosy B&B.

Tudor House (☎ 765650; 6 Best Lane; s £22-25, d £45-50; ⓟ) Set in a 450-year-old cottage this great-value B&B has traditional, flowery-style rooms, one of which opens onto the garden that backs onto the River Stour.

Eating

There's a **Safeway supermarket** (St George's Pl) before New Dover Rd.

Café St Pierre (☎ 456791; 41 St Peter's St; baguettes £3.50; ☼ 8am-6pm Mon-Sat, 9am-5.30pm Sun) This friendly French café has pastries, baguettes and quiches that come from France daily.

Olive Grove (☎ 764388; 12 Best Lane; mains £5.15-13.95; ☼ noon-10.30pm) This light-filled restaurant serves well-priced ciabatta, pizza, pasta and meat dishes.

Café des Amis du Mexique (☎ 464390; 95 St Dunstan's St; mains £4.95-12.95; ☼ noon-10.30pm Mon-Sat, noon-9.30pm Sun) This popular and colourful Mexican restaurant serves fantastic burritos, enchiladas and fajitas.

Drinking

Miller's Arms (☎ 456057; Mill Lane) and **Thomas Becket** (☎ 464384; 21 Best Lane) are both cosy, traditional pubs.

Bar 11 (☎ 478707; 11 Burgate) and **Ha Ha!** (☎ 379800; 7 St Margaret's St) have minimalist-style décor with a good range of beers, wines and cocktails.

Getting There & Away

National Express coaches leave from London Victoria to Canterbury (one-way/return £10/16, one hour 50 minutes, half-hourly). **Stagecoach East Kent's** (☎ 0870 243 3711) No 115 bus runs hourly (less on Sunday) from Canterbury to Dover (one-way/return £2.90/4.80, 30 minutes).

There are two train stations: Canterbury West, accessible from London's Charing Cross and Waterloo stations; and Canterbury East, reachable from London's Victoria station (one-way/return £17.30/19.60, 90 minutes, half-hourly). Trains operate between Canterbury East and Dover Priory (one-way £4.80, 30 minutes, hourly).

DOVER

☎ 01304 / pop 32,600

Dover is England's 'Gateway to Europe' and has two things going for it: the famous white cliffs and its spectacular medieval hill-top castle. The foreshore of Dover is basically an enormous vehicle ramp for the ferries.

Ferry departures are from the Eastern Docks (accessible by bus) below the castle. Dover Priory train station is off Folkestone Rd, just west of the town centre. The bus station is on Pencester Rd, north of Market Square.

The **Dover Visitor Centre** (☎ 205108; www.white cliffscountry.org.uk; Old Town Gaol, Biggin St; ☼ 9am-5.30pm) in the town centre has a ferry-booking service.

Sights

Dover Castle (☎ 211067; www.english-heritage.org.uk; adult/concession £8.50/6.40; ☼ 10am-6pm Apr-Sep, 10am-4pm Oct-Mar) is a well-preserved medieval fortress with spectacular views. The stunning tour of the **secret wartime tunnels** (incl in admission price; 50 min) covers the castle's history during WWII and takes you through the tunnels that burrow beneath it.

Dover Museum & Bronze Age Boat Gallery (☎ 201066; www.dovermuseum.co.uk; Market Sq; adult/concession £2/1.25; ☺ 10am-5.30pm Mon-Sat) covers Dover's history and houses the world's oldest boat (3600 years), discovered off the Dover coast in 1992.

Sleeping & Eating

Youth Hostel (☎ 202236; dover@yha.org.uk; 306 London Rd; B&B dm adult/under-18 £14.90/11.60; ☐) In a restored Georgian townhouse five minutes' walk from Market Sq, this hostel has a kitchen, café and garden.

East Lee Guest House (☎ 210176; www.eastlee .co.uk; 108 Maison Dieu Rd; s/d from £35/58; ✗) This pretty Victorian townhouse has opulent burgundy-and-gold furnishings and a friendly atmosphere.

Jermain's (☎ 205956; 18 Beaconsfield Rd; mains £4.50; ☺ 11.30am-2pm; ✗) Near the hostel, this restaurant has a range of traditional British lunches.

Cullin's Yard (☎ 211666; 11 Cambridge Rd; mains £6.50-19.80; ☺ noon-11pm) This rustic-style bistro specialises in seafood ranging from kippers to lobster.

Getting There & Around

See p149 for details of ferries to mainland Europe.

To Dover, National Express coaches leave hourly from London Victoria (one-way/return £9.50/10.50, 2¼ hours). Dover to Canterbury (30 minutes) costs one-way/return £2.90/4.80. Trains go from London Victoria and Charing Cross stations to Dover Priory (one-way/return £20.70/23.40, one hour 50 minutes, half-hourly).

The ferry companies run complimentary buses every 20 minutes between the docks and the train station.

LEEDS CASTLE

One of the world's most famous castles, **Leeds Castle** (☎ 01622-765400; www.leeds-castle.com; near Maidstone, Kent; castle & gardens: adult/concession £12.50/11, gardens only: £10/8.50; ☺ 10am-5pm Apr-Oct, 10am-3pm Nov-Mar) stands on two small islands in a lake, and is surrounded by woodlands, an aviary, and a hedge maze with a grotto in the centre. The castle is filled with medieval

furnishings, and there's a strange collection of antique dog collars.

National Express has a combined admission and travel ticket that leaves from Victoria coach station (it must be prebooked). It leaves at 9am and returns at 3.05pm (trip 90 minutes), and costs £16 Monday to Friday, and £18.50 Saturday, Sunday and bank holidays.

BRIGHTON & HOVE
☎ 01273 / pop 250,000

Brighton is a tantalising mix of the country's most popular seaside resort and one of its most innovative cities. Once a fishing village called Brighthelmstone and now a city named Brighton & Hove, its 7 miles (11km) of coastline and liberal persuasion have attracted an eclectic mix to its pebbly shores: from the 19th-century Prince Regent frolicking in his fantastical Pavilion to the clubbing crowd of the '60s immortalised in the film *Quadrophenia*.

Nowadays you'll find bohemians into environmental living and artistic pursuits, a large student population, a vivacious gay community and urban hipsters escaping the rat race. All have put their stamp throughout the city with its hedonistic nightlife, vibrant art scene, unusual shopping, and countless numbers of restaurants and cafés.

Orientation & Information

Brighton train station is a 15-minute walk north of the beach. The bus station is in Poole Valley, south of the Lanes.

Curve Internet (☎ 603031; 45 Gardner St; per hr £1.50; ☺ 10am-10pm Mon-Sat, 11am-8.30pm Sun) Above Curve Brasserie.

Visitor Information Centre (☎ 0906 711 2255; per min 50p; www.visitbrighton.com; 10 Bartholomew Sq; ☺ 9.30am-5pm) Has free listings magazines.

Sights

The area called **the Lanes** was the original fishing village of Brighton, and its maze of 17th-century narrow alleyways is crammed with a menagerie of shops, restaurants and bars. In the **North Laine** area, just above the Lanes, the atmosphere is more hip and bohemian with alternative therapy centres, cooperative cafés, vintage clothes shops and designer boutiques.

Built between 1815 and 1822 for the Prince Regent (later George IV), the **Royal**

Pavilion (☎ 290900; www.royalpavilion.co.uk; adult/concession £5.80/4, tours £1.25; ⏱ 9.30am-5pm Apr-Sep, 10am-4.30pm Oct-Mar, tours 11.30am & 2.30pm) is a fantasy of Asian exoticism mixed with English eccentricity. Not to be missed.

Brighton Museum & Art Gallery (☎ 290900; www.brighton.virtualmuseum.info; Royal Pavilion gardens; admission free; ⏱ 10am-7pm Tue, 10am-5pm Wed-Sat, 2-5pm Sun) has exhibitions devoted to subjects like fashion and style, 20th-century art and design, and Brighton's history.

Brighton Pier (☎ 609361; www.brightonpier.co.uk; Madeira Dr; admission free; ⏱ 9am-2am), the epitome of the British seaside, has fast food, amusement arcades and two new white-knuckle rides – tacky but lots of fun.

Courses

There are 32 English-language schools and a strong student support network in Brighton & Hove. Visit www.visitbrighton.com and click on 'Learning English' for more details.

Festivals & Events

Brighton Festival (☎ 292961; www.brighton-festival .org.uk) For the first three weeks in May Brighton hosts the largest arts festival outside Edinburgh. Much is free and in public spaces.

Brighton Pride (☎ 775939; www.brightonpride.org) Every August thousands of revellers dress to the nines and celebrate their sexual orientation in this flamboyant street festival.

Sleeping

Baggies Backpackers (☎ 733740; 33 Oriental Pl; dm/d £12/30, key deposit £5; ✗) By far the best hostel in Brighton, Baggies has a laid-back and cosy feel. The owner encourages a communal spirit and keeps the dorms spick and span.

Brighton Backpackers (☎ 777717; www.brighton backpackers.com; 75-76 Middle St; dm/dm with seafront annexe/d £11/12/30) Although this hostel has a cramped feel with its small dorms and narrow stairways, the funky murals and its good location almost make up for it.

Genevieve Hotel (☎ 681653; www.genevieve hotel.co.uk; 18 Madeira Pl; s £45, d £54-95; P ✗) Of the cluster of B&Bs in this area, this cosy, pristine establishment is the best. The large, airy rooms are great value and some have sea or pier views.

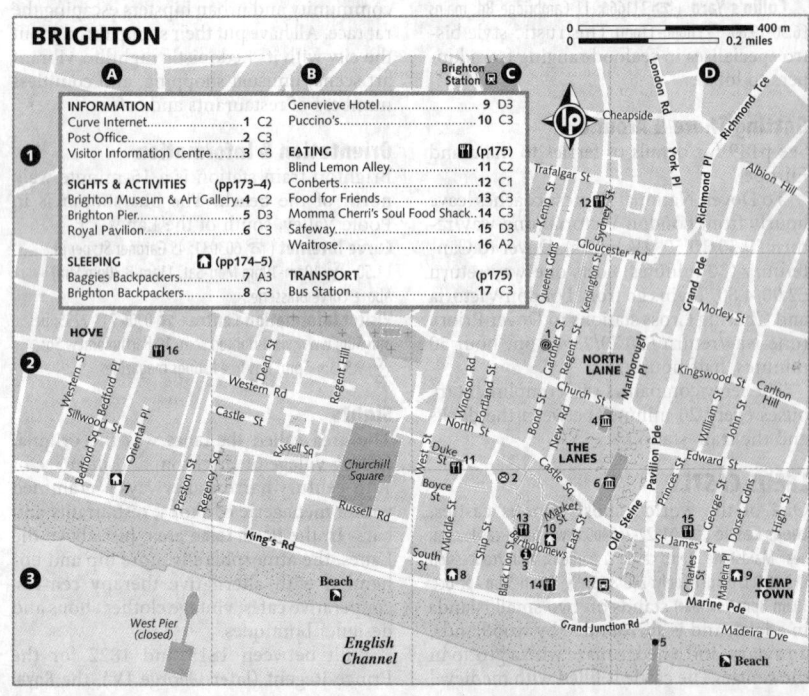

BRIGHTON

INFORMATION	
Curve Internet.....................1 C2	
Post Office..........................2 C3	
Visitor Information Centre........3 C3	
SIGHTS & ACTIVITIES (pp173-4)	
Brighton Museum & Art Gallery..4 C2	
Brighton Pier........................5 D3	
Royal Pavilion......................6 C3	
SLEEPING (pp174-5)	
Baggies Backpackers................7 A3	
Brighton Backpackers...............8 C3	

Genevieve Hotel.....................9 D3	
Puccino's...........................10 C3	
EATING (p175)	
Blind Lemon Alley..................11 C2	
Conberts...........................12 C1	
Food for Friends...................13 C3	
Momma Cherri's Soul Food Shack..14 C3	
Safeway...........................15 D3	
Waitrose..........................16 A2	
TRANSPORT (p175)	
Bus Station........................17 C3	

Puccino's (☎ 204656; 1 Bartholomews; per person £30; ☒) Above this café the owner runs two lovely B&B doubles. The rooms have wooden floors, pine furniture and ethnic rugs, as well as fold-up single futons.

Eating

For self-catering there's **Safeway** (St James's St) and **Waitrose** (Western Rd).

Conberts (☎ 625222; 16 Sydney St; sandwiches £1.95-3.75; ☽ 10am-6pm Mon-Sat, noon-4pm Sun) This two-level teashop serves such things as loose-leaf teas in beautiful vintage china and elegant cucumber sandwiches. The tiny resident dog called Pascale is adored, as is the Queen – her shrine is in the golden throne toilet.

Momma Cherri's Soul Food Shack (☎ 774545; 11 Little East St; mains £6.50-13; ☽ 6-11pm or midnight Mon-Tue & Thu-Fri, 11am-midnight Sat, 10.30am-8pm Sun) With a soundtrack of funky soul and a décor festooned with colour, this small American soul-food restaurant is about having fun and eating lots – try the New Orleans speciality jambalaya.

Food for Friends (☎ 202310; 17-18 Prince Albert St; mains £7.95-9.95; ☽ 11.30am-9.45pm Mon-Fri, 11am-10.15pm Sat & Sun) This light and airy café-style vegetarian restaurant serves delicious British, Mediterranean, Mexican and Indian dishes.

Blind Lemon Alley (☎ 205151; 41 Middle St; mains £8-14, 2-course lunch/3-course dinner £5.95/10.95; ☽ 12.30-11pm) Tuck into burgers, steaks and ribs in this intimate and informal restaurant. There is live blues and jazz on Sunday nights.

Drinking & Clubbing

The city brims with pubs and bars, as well as a wide choice of clubs with world-renowned DJs. For pubs head for the North Laine area, where there is a high density of trendy and more traditional drinking establishments. Most of the best clubs are in King's Rd Arches on the seafront. What's in vogue changes all the time so check the free magazines, *This Is Brighton* and *The Source*.

Brighton's vibrant gay and lesbian scene is well integrated throughout the city, although a concentration of bars and clubs are in Kemp Town (east of the Old Steine). To find out what's hot and what's not pick up the free *G Scene* and *3Sixty* magazines.

Getting There & Away

Megabus (www.megabus.com) offers one-way/return tickets from London to Brighton for

£1.50/3; there are two departures daily. National Express coaches leave hourly from London Victoria to Brighton (one-way/return £9/15, two hours). **National Express Airport** (☎ 0870 575 7747) runs coaches to Gatwick (one-way/return £6/9, 45 minutes), Heathrow (one-way/return £19.50/24.50, two hours) and Stansted (one-way/return £26/31, three hours 50 minutes) airports.

The quickest way to Brighton from London is the twice-hourly train service from Victoria station (one-way/return £15.90/21, 50 minutes). There are regular trains from Brighton to Portsmouth (one-way/return £12.80/17.60, 90 minutes), and to Canterbury and Dover.

PORTSMOUTH

☎ 02392 / pop 190,000

Portsmouth is the traditional home of the Royal Navy, whose ships once exported goods to far-flung corners of the British Empire. It's still a busy naval base, and the main attractions are the historic ships and museums of the Historic Dockyard.

Orientation & Information

The train and bus stations and ferry terminal for the Isle of Wight are a stone's throw from the Historic Dockyard and the **Visitor Information Centre** (☎ 826722; www.visitportsmouth .co.uk; The Hard; ☽ 9.30am-5.15pm Oct–end Mar).

The **Library** (☎ 819311; Civic Offices, Guildhall Sq; ☽ 9.30am-5pm Mon-Sat, 12.30-4pm Sun) has free Internet access. Bookings are required.

Sights

Portsmouth's centrepiece is the **Historic Dockyard** (☎ 861512; www.historicdockyard.co.uk; admission £14.85 incl all attractions; ☽ 10am-4.30pm). Exploring **HMS Victory**, Lord Nelson's flagship at the Battle of Trafalgar, is probably as close as you can get to time travel. **HMS Warrior** was the first all-iron warship. After 437 years underwater, the remains of Henry VIII's favourite ship, the **Mary Rose** can be viewed. Its time-capsule contents are in the **Mary Rose Museum**. The **Royal Navy Museum** presents the Navy's history, and the nearby **Actions Stations!** is a showcase of the modern navy.

Due to open in January 2005 is the 170m **Spinnaker Tower** (www.portsmouthand.co.uk/tower) at the shopping, eating and entertainment complex of Gunwharf Quays (just south of the Historic Dockyard). There will be lifts to the top for panoramic sea views.

Sleeping & Eating

Southsea Backpackers Lodge (☎ 832495; www.ports mouthbackpackers.co.uk; 4 Florence Rd, Southsea; dm £10, d £26-29; ✗ ▢) This hostel is comfortable and friendly with a satellite TV lounge and laundry facilities.

Sailmaker's Loft (☎ 823045; 5 Bath Sq; r per person £25; ✗ ▢) This recently renovated B&B is run by a retired merchant seaman who can tell you a lot about Portsmouth. There are views across the harbour.

Twigs (☎ 828316; 39 High St; sandwiches £1.50-3.75; ✤ 10am-5pm) Overlooking a pretty church, this is a pleasant place for a sandwich or coffee stop.

Getting There & Away

Megabus (www.megabus.com) offers one-way/ return tickets from London to Portsmouth for £1.50/3, with two departures daily. National Express has a coach service from London Victoria to Portsmouth (one-way/ return £12/17, 2½ hours, hourly).

Trains run from London Victoria and Waterloo stations (one-way/return £21/25.70, two hours) to Portsmouth. Two trains hourly go to Brighton (one-way/return £12.80/17.60, 90 minutes) and Winchester (one-way/return £7.30/7.60, 55 minutes).

See p149 for details of ferries to France and Spain. The Continental Ferryport is north of Flagship Portsmouth.

WINCHESTER

☎ 01962 / pop 38,000

Winchester is a beautiful cathedral city on the River Itchen, interspersed with water meadows. It has played an important role in the history of England, being both the capital of Saxon England and the seat of the powerful Bishops of Winchester from AD 670. Much of the present-day city dates from the 18th century, its main attraction being the stunning cathedral.

The train station is a 10-minute walk to the west of the centre, and the bus and coach station is on Broadway, directly opposite the **Visitor Information Centre** (☎ 840500; www .visitwinchester.co.uk; Guildhall, Broadway; ✤ 9.30am-5.30pm Mon-Sat, 11am-4pm Sun).

Winchester Cathedral (☎ 853224; www.winchester -cathedral.org.uk; The Close; adult/concession £3.50/3, free

1hr tours; ✤ 8.30am-5.30pm, tours: 10am-3pm Mon-Sat) is one of the most beautiful cathedrals in the country, a mixture of Norman, Early English and Gothic Perpendicular styles. Jane Austen's grave is in the northern aisle.

With its beginnings in 1382, **Winchester College** (☎ 621209; www.winchestercollege.org; College St) was the first of Britain's exclusive public schools. Explore it by **guided tour** (adult/ concession £3.50/3; ✤ 10.45am, noon, 2.15pm & 3.30pm).

Youth Hostel (☎ 0870 770 6092; winchester@yha .org.uk; 1 Water Lane; dm adult/under-18 £10.60/7.20) Set in a beautiful 18th-century water mill that spans the River Itchen, this hostel is in the heart of town.

La Bodega (☎ 864004; Great Minster St; mains £7-14; ✤ noon-2.30pm & 6.30-10.30pm Mon-Sat) This Italian restaurant serves excellent home-made pastas.

National Express coaches go to Winchester from London Victoria (one-way/return £11.50/16, two hours, every two hours). Trains depart twice hourly from London Waterloo (£19.90/23.30, 1¼ hours), Southampton (one-way £4, 30 minutes) and Portsmouth (one-way £7.30, 55 minutes).

SOUTHWEST ENGLAND

Every British culture has made its mark on the Southwest of England: the Bronze Age left Stonehenge, Avebury and prehistoric relics throughout Cornwall and Devon; the Iron Age left hill forts across Dartmoor; the Romans built some serious bathing facilities in Bath; the Georgians improved upon the aforementioned bathing facilities; and the transport revolution of the industrial age began with Victorian engineer Isambard Kingdom Brunel in places like Bristol.

GETTING AROUND

Try **Wilts & Dorset** (☎ 336855; www.wdbus.co.uk) for bus information throughout the region, including Avebury, Stonehenge, Bristol, Bath, Wells, Glastonbury or even the Cotswolds. Its Explorer ticket (£6) is great value.

Badgerline's Day Explorer (£5.70) accesses a good network of buses in Bristol, Somerset (Wells, Glastonbury), Gloucestershire (Gloucester via Bristol) and Wiltshire (Lacock, Bradford-on-Avon, Salisbury). Phone ☎ 0117 955 5111 or purchase the pass on any Badgerline, First Bus or Cityline bus.

SALISBURY

☎ 01722 / pop 40,000

Salisbury's medieval cathedral is second to none, but the town's appeal also lies in the fact that it has been holding markets every Tuesday and Saturday since 1361.

The town centre is a 10-minute walk from the train station – walk down the hill onto Fisherton St, directly into town. The bus station is just northeast of the **tourist office** (☎ 334956; visitorinfo@salisbury.gov.uk; Fish Row).

Beautiful **St Mary's Cathedral** (suggested donation £3.80) is built in a uniform style known as Early English (or Early Pointed). This period is characterised by the first pointed arches and flying buttresses, and has a rather austere feel. The cathedral owes its uniformity to the speed with which it was built. Between 1220 and 1258 over 70,000 tonnes of stone were piled up. The spire, at 123m, is the highest in Britain.

The adjacent **chapter house** is one of the most perfect achievements of Gothic architecture. There is plenty more to see in the **cathedral close**, including two houses that have been restored and two interesting museums.

Salisbury Youth Hostel (☎ 327572; salisbury@yha.org.uk; Milford Hill; adult/under-18 £14.90/11.60, d £33.80; P ☒ ☐) This attractive old building sits amid grassy surroundings, a five-minute walk from the city centre.

Griffin Cottage (☎ 328259; www.smoothhound.co.uk/hotels/griffinc.html; 10 St Edmund's Church St; d £45) A central and peaceful B&B that caters at breakfast to those on special diets.

Fisherton St, running from the centre to the train station, has Chinese, Thai, Indian and other restaurants. For outdoor dining April to October, head to the **Market Inn** (☎ 327923; Butcher Row; mains £2-6), a casual pub that serves light meals.

Getting There & Away

National Express has three buses a day from London via Heathrow to Salisbury (£12, three hours).

Salisbury is also linked by rail to London Waterloo station (one-way £24.40, 1½ hours, at least hourly), Portsmouth (one-way £11.60, 1¾ hours, hourly), Bath (one-way £10.40, 50 minutes, at least hourly) and Exeter (one-way £21.70, 1¾ hours, 11 daily).

STONEHENGE & AVEBURY

Stonehenge is a must on many itineraries. This pre-Celtic circle of stones can be dated to 2950 BC, and some are from as far away as the mystical Preseli mountains in Wales (now popular as a UFO-spotting site). Although linked to Druids and King Arthur, Stonehenge's original builders are still unknown. In any case, be prepared; while the stones are historically fascinating, they are a bit visually underwhelming, as thousands of tourists crowd around a roped-off corridor, shuffling their way out through the gift shop and the 'Stonehenge Kitchen'.

Stonehenge (☎ 01980-624715; adult/concession £5.20/3.90) is 2 miles west of Amesbury at the junction of the A303 and A344/A360, and 9 miles from Salisbury (the nearest station). Some feel that it's unnecessary to pay the entry fee because you can get a good view from the road. Tour companies visit Stonehenge from as far off as London or Bath, but the easiest way to get there using public transport is from Salisbury (bus No 3; £6 return, every 15 minutes) – there are guided double-decker buses in summer – or, better yet, buy an Explorer ticket in Salisbury (£6) and visit Avebury as well.

Avebury (between Calne and Marlborough, just off the A4) stands at the hub of a prehistoric complex of ceremonial sites, ancient avenues and burial chambers dating from 3500 BC. Things here are larger and more impressive than at Stonehenge, and it's possible to escape crowds if you visit outside summer weekends. In addition to an enormous stone circle, there's Silbury Hill (the largest constructed mound in Europe), West Kennet Long Barrow (a burial chamber) and a pretty village with an ancient church.

Avebury has a **tourist office** (☎ 01380-729408; alltic@kennet.gov.uk; Green St; ✆ 9am-5pm Wed-Sun).

Avebury is best reached on the Wilts & Dorset bus No 5 from Salisbury (one-way £4, 1½ hours, at least hourly) or by bus No 5, 6 or 49 from Swindon (one-way £1.80).

BATH

☎ 01225 / pop 86,000

Bath is historically, geographically and architecturally a quintessential English tourist destination. Combining Roman history with Georgian buildings in honey-coloured Bath stone, the town is practically a theme park of public spaces, museums, charming accommodation, shops and parks. Bath has been home to Celts, Druids, Romans, medieval monasteries, as well as to Georgian and Victorian high-society types.

Orientation & Information

Bath's train and bus stations are both just south of town near the river Avon. Most of the main sites and accommodation listed here are within walking distance of each other, contained in the boomerang-shaped Avon. Visit www.visitbath.co.uk for visitor information.

Click (☎ 481008; 13A Manvers St; per 20 min £1; ☼ 10am-10pm)

Tourist office (☎ 0870 4201278 accommodation, 0906 711 2000; per min 50p; Abbey Chambers, Abbey Churchyard;

☼ 9am-7pm Mon-Sat, 9am-6pm Sun mid-Jun–mid-Sep; 9am-5pm Mon-Sat, 9am-4pm Sun late Sep–early Jun)

Sights & Activities

Loads of Bath's most enjoyable activities are free. There is a **covered market** next to the **Guildhall**, and a maze of **passageways** just north of Abbey Churchyard. Free walking **tours** (10.30am & 2pm Mon-Fri, 10.30am Sat year-round, additional tours 7pm Tue, Fri & Sat May-Sep; contact tourist office for info) leave from outside the Pump Room (opposite), and a **flea market** is held on Saturday near the YMCA (opposite).

The **Roman Baths Museum** (☎ 477785; admission £9; ☼ 9am-5pm sep-Jun, 9am-9pm Jul & Aug) is a series of excavated passages and chambers beneath street level, taking in the sulphurous mineral

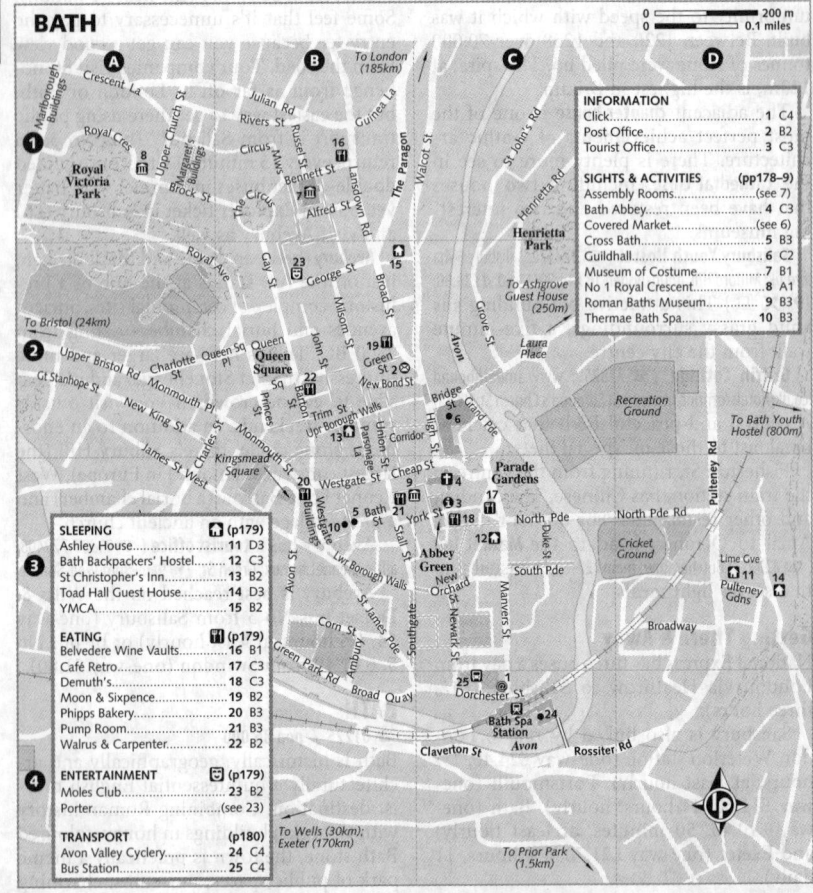

BATH

SPLURGE!

If you arrive in Bath exhausted from your travels, the **Thermae Bath Spa** (☎ 331234; www.thermaebathspa.com; Hot Bath St; 2hr/4hr/full day £19/29/45, treatments from £14; ⏰ 9am-10pm) is the perfect place for a pick-me-up. A ticket buys you a day of blissful swimming in the open-air rooftop thermal pool, taking a t'ai chi class or pampering yourself in the aromatherapy-infused steam rooms. If it's just a quick soak you're after, try the **Cross Bath** (per 1½hr £12) across the street.

springs (still flowing after all these years), the ancient central-heating system and the bath itself, which retains its Roman paving and lead base. Many of the treasures found here are on display in the museum. In the same square is the **Bath Abbey**. Built between 1499 and 1616, it boasts 56 stunning stained-glass windows depicting stages in the life of Christ.

Festivals & Events

Bath International Festival (☎ 463362; www.bathmusicfest.org.uk) is held from the last week of May to the first week of June.

Sleeping

HOSTELS

YMCA International House (☎ 325900; www.bathymca.co.uk; Broad St Pl; dm £11-13, s/d/tr/q with breakfast Sat & Sun £24/38/48/60, Mon-Fri lower; 💻) Tucked into a quiet corner, this most upscale of YMCAs is comfortable enough for just about anyone. Gym available at reduced rates, and £2 daily luggage storage.

Bath Youth Hostel (☎ 465674; bath@yha.org.uk; Bathwick Hill; adult/under-18 dm £11.80/8.50; P 💻) A good 25-minute walk from town, but the building's fine Italianate architecture and the views (try to snag one of the rooms facing town) may make it worth it. Breakfast is extra. To get there, hop on a Badgerline bus No 18 or 418.

Bath Backpackers' Hostel (☎ 446787; www.hostels.co.uk/bath; 13 Pierrepont St; dm/tw £12/30; 💻) Loved by some, hated by others, this hostel does better with the parties in its famed downstairs dungeon than in providing cleanliness or quiet.

St Christopher's Inn (☎ 020-7407 1856; 9 Green St; dm £15-18.50, d £46; 💻) Your grandparents will definitely *not* be staying here. Guests come here for the lively social scene and rollicking pub downstairs. Linens and breakfast included.

B&BS

Ashgrove Guesthouse (☎ 421911; 39 Bathwick St; s/d £30/50; P ⊠) Recently refurbished, this lovingly cared-for home away from home is a five-minute walk from town.

Also recommended:

Toad Hall Guest House (☎/fax 423254; 6 Lime St; s/d/f from £22/40/50; ⊠) A stone's throw from the train station.

Ashley House (☎ 425027; ashleybath@waitrose.com; 8 Pulteney Gardens; s/d/f £35/62/72; ⊠) Seven comfortable rooms with off-season discounts.

Eating & Drinking

Pump Room (☎ 444477; cream teas £9.75; ⏰ 9.30am-last orders 4pm) Pricey but undeniably Bath. Work on your pinkie-extending muscles as you sip tea and indulge in scones and clotted – as in clotted arteries – cream. The kindly staff allow those on a budget to split a cream tea.

Café Retro (☎ 339347; 18 York St; Aberdeen beef burgers £8, sandwiches £6) Try this place for a little '40s flair.

Walrus & Carpenter (☎ 314864; 28 Barton St; mains £10, sandwiches £6; ⏰ noon-2.30pm & 6-11pm) A funky eatery.

Phipps Bakery (☎ 462483; Kingsmead Sq; light lunches £4) Has excellent filled rolls, vegetable curries and spinach turnovers. There are several fast-food places in this area.

Demuth's (☎ 446059; 2 North Pde Passage; mains from £5-12; ⏰ 10am-10pm Sun-Fri, 9am-11pm Sat; ⊠) This place will please vegetarian gourmets, sweets lovers and adventurous children alike.

Moon & Sixpence (☎ 460962; 6A Broad St; 2-course lunch £5) A pleasant pub. Pubs are good bets for cheap evening meals, too.

Belvedere Wine Vaults (☎ 330264; www.belvederewinevaults.co.uk; 25 Belvedere; r £40-80; tapas £2.50-5; ⏰ dinner around 6-9.30pm, lunch Sun) This place offers it all: a large selection of wine and flavoured vodkas, tapas menu, nonsmoking bar, and even a few sleekly furnished guest rooms.

Entertainment

The Porter (☎ 424104; above Moles Club; ⏰ 11am-11pm Mon-Sat, noon-10.30pm Sun) and the **Moles Club** (☎ 404445; 14 George St; ⏰ 9pm-2am Sun-Thu, 9am-4am Fri & Sat) are the best spots in town to catch well-known live bands most nights, comedy Sunday nights, or get a pint just about any time.

Getting There & Around

BICYCLE

The Bristol & Bath Cycle Walkway is an excellent footpath and cycleway that follows the route of the disused railway. Bikes are available from **Avon Valley Cyclery** (☎ 442442; Bath train station; rental per half/full day £10/15, deposit required; 9am-5.30pm Mon-Sat).

BUS

National Express heads to London (£14.50, 3¼ hours, 11 daily), Portsmouth via Salisbury (£14.50, leaving 4.20pm to 7.15pm) and Oxford (£12, two hours, two daily).

Badgerline bus No X39 runs to/from Bristol (£3.60, 50 minutes, every 15 minutes).

Bus maps and timetables are available from the bus station. Call **Traveline** (☎ 0870 608 2608) for inquiries.

TRAIN

From Bath, it's faster but more expensive to London's Paddington station (£33 to £45, 1½ hours, at least hourly) and slower, cheaper and more scenic from Waterloo (£21.90, 2½ hours, 10 daily), changing in Salisbury (£10.40, 50 minutes). It's an easy connection to Cardiff (£11.90, 1¼ hours, hourly) and Bristol (£4.80, 15 minutes, half-hourly).

DARTMOOR NATIONAL PARK

Arthur Conan Doyle's *Hound of the Baskervilles* is set on the bewitching Dartmoor, the area as much a character in the book as Sherlock Holmes. Although the park is only about 25 miles (40km) from north to south and east to west, it encloses some of the wildest, bleakest country in England.

There are several small market towns surrounding the tableland, but the only village of any size on the moor is the ho-hum Princetown. Hiking is *de rigueur* here as trails crisscross the park, and views include dozens of archaeological ruins. Information is available from the **High Moorland Visitor Centre** (☎ 01822-890414; Princetown; ☒ 10am-5pm, 10am-4pm winter) or the **National Park Authority** (NPA; www.dartmoor-npa.gov.uk).

Most of Dartmoor is privately owned, but the owners of unenclosed moorland don't usually object to campers who keep to a simple code: don't camp on moorland enclosed by walls or within sight of roads or houses; don't stay on one site for more than two nights or near heavily trafficked

areas; and leave the site as you found it. Dial ☎ 01200-420102 for camping barn locations. Two beautifully situated hostels, **Bellever Youth Hostel** (☎ 0870 770 5692; bellever@yha .org.uk; dm £11.80; Ⓟ ☒) and **Steps Bridge Youth Hostel** (☎ 0870 770 6048; dm £9.30; Ⓟ) encourage public transport users by offering a £1 discount (take bus No 98 from Tavistock or No 82 going between Plymouth and Exeter).

Plume of Feathers (☎ 01822-890240; www.plume offeathers-dartmoor.co.uk; Princetown; camping £2.50-4, bunkhouse dm £5.50-7, s/d £17.50/35) is a jack-of-all-accommodation, boasting clean facilities for campers, comfortable guesthouse rooms, and a cheery pub and restaurant.

Getting There & Away

Exeter or Plymouth are the best starting points for the park. National Bus No 82 between Exeter and Plymouth runs three buses daily in summer but weekend services only in winter.

GLASTONBURY

☎ 01458 / pop 7000

Legends of King Arthur and Camelot and a link to Jesus' crown of thorns have tied Glastonbury to English mythology for millennia. Now it's a laid-back town that offers ample opportunity for chakra healing or Tarot readings, and plays host to one of the biggest and most famous music and arts festival in Europe.

The **tourist information centre** (☎ 832954; www .glastonburytic.co.uk; 9 High St, The Tribunal; ☒ 10am-5pm Sun-Thu, 10am-5.30pm Fri & Sat Apr-Sep) closes one hour earlier in winter. Free Internet access is available at the library.

At the **Abbey** (☎ 832267; adult/concession £3.50/3; ☒ 9.30am-6pm or dusk if earlier) you can't help but feel mystical on a hike up to the church-topped **tor**. Take the well-worn path from the top end of High St, or better yet, wander up one of the back routes.

Glastonbury Festival (☎ 832020; www.glaston buryfestivals.co.uk) is a three-day extravaganza of music, theatre, circus, mime, natural healing etc, with more than 1000 acts. The festival is in late June; admission is by advance ticket only (£119 for all three days).

Glastonbury Backpackers Hostel (☎ 833353; backpackers@glastonbury/online.com; Crown Hotel, 4 Market Pl; dm/d £10/30) Perfectly central, though it has a rather dodgy bar downstairs and apparently feels no need to employ a bathroom cleaner.

You won't be disappointed at **AppleTree House** (☎ 830803; www.appletreehouse.org.uk; s/d £30/60), whichever activity you choose – borrowing movies for your VCR, relaxing in the stone circle garden, or eating the homemade bread or chocolate and biscuits left in your room.

There are Badgerline buses from Bristol to Wells, Glastonbury and Street. Bus No 163 leaves every 15 minutes or so from Wells and continues to Bridgwater, from where there are buses to Minehead (for Exmoor).

EXETER

☎ 01392 / pop 102,000

Exeter has what one might call 'youthful exuberance'. Much of the city centre has been rebuilt since bombed in WWII and the university scene contributes to a café culture and thriving nightlife. It's a good starting point for Dartmoor and Cornwall.

Ask the **tourist office** (☎ 265700; www.exeter .gov.uk/visiting; Civic Centre, Paris St; ⊗ 9am-5pm Mon-Sat, Sun in summer only) about **walking tours**, many of which are free. Internet access is available at the central **library** (Castle St; 30 min free).

Exeter's **cathedral** is one of the most attractive in England, with two huge Norman towers surviving from the 11th century. From AD 50, when the Romans established the city, until the 19th century, Exeter was an important port, and the waterfront (including a large boat museum) is gradually being restored.

Exeter YHA (☎ 0870 770 5826; exeter@yha.org.uk; 47 Countess Wear Rd; dm/d £13.40/30.80; ⊗ year-round, closed Christmas; 🖳 🅿 ✗) This comfortable hostel is 2.5 miles (4km) southeast of the city towards Topsham, with welcoming and knowledgeable staff. From High St, catch minibus K or T (10 minutes) and ask for the Countess Wear post office. Camp sites are available.

Exeter Globe Backpackers (☎ 215521; www.exeter backpackers.co.uk; 71 Holloway St; dm/d £12/30; 🖳) In an 18th-century Georgian building, this has fabulously hot showers.

Exeter Phoenix Arts & Media Centre (☎ 667080; www.exeterphoenix.org.uk; Gandy St) Showcases the best the area has to offer: visual arts, theatre, music, comedy, even puppetry. Stay for a meal or drink at the fabulous Café Phoenix.

Getting There & Away

Nine buses a day run between London, Heathrow airport and Exeter (£20, four

hours). From Exeter there are frequent services to Plymouth (£6, 1¼ hours, every 90 minutes) and Penzance (£20.50, 4½ hours, three daily). For bus information phone **Traveline** (☎ 0870 608 2608) or **Stagecoach Devon** (☎ 01392-427711).

Exeter is at the hub of lines running from London's Waterloo and Paddington stations (£42, 3¼ hours, hourly), Bristol (£16.20, 1¾ hours, hourly), Salisbury (£21.70, 1¾ hours, 12 daily) and Penzance (£26.10, 3½ hours, approximately hourly). The 39-mile branch line to Barnstaple (£10.10, 1¼ hours, nine daily) gives good views of traditional Devon countryside.

For rail information phone ☎ 0845 748 4950.

EXMOOR NATIONAL PARK

Semi-wild ponies, red deer, picture-perfect English villages and hundreds of miles of walking trails are only a fraction of the reason to visit Exmoor. Horse riding, ocean vistas, farms, castles, wild flowers ... you could stay amused here for days.

Exmoor is accessible from Barnstaple (train from Exeter) and Taunton. There are five NPA visitor centres in and around the park, including **Dulverton** (☎ 01398-323841; Fore St; ⊗ year-round) and **Lynmouth** (☎ 01598-752509; The Esplanade; ⊗ Apr-Nov). It's also possible to get information from the tourist offices at Ilfracombe, Lynton and Minehead.

Sleeping

There are YHA hostels at **Ilfracombe** (☎ 0870 770 5878), **Minehead** (☎ 0870 770 5968), **Lynton** (☎ 0870 770 5942) and **Exford** (☎ 0870 770 5828), in the centre of the park. All close for part of the winter – either on Sunday or Monday or in January and February – so phone ahead.

Directly on the water, **Ocean Backpackers** (☎ 01271-867835; www.oceanbackpackers.co.uk; 29 St James Pl, Ilfracombe; dm/d £11/31) is a private hostel popular with surfers.

CORNISH COAST
Eden Project

Stroll from the rainforests of West Africa to a Mediterranean olive grove in minutes at the **Eden Project** (☎ 01726 811972; www.edenproject.com; Bodelva, St Austell; ⊗ 9.30am-6pm daily, 9.30am-8pm Tue-Thu late Jul–late Aug; admission family/adult/senior/student £30/12/9/6), where plant life becomes exciting. In additional to giant biomes (greenhouses), the Eden Project offers 90 exhibits and continual special events. Buses run from Newquay and St Austell (where the closest train stop is), or you can go by car or bike – follow the signposts on the A30, A390 or A391 4 miles (6.5km) east of St Austell.

Penzance
☎ 01736 / pop 20,000

Made famous by Gilbert & Sullivan's operetta *The Pirates of...* Penzance today is a sweet seaside resort with more landlubbers than peg-legged swashbucklers. As far west in England as you can get by train, it's a bit worn around the edges but the nearby beaches are superb. You can also catch a ferry to the Isles of Scilly (a rather serious nature preserve) or take in a performance at the incomparable Minack Theatre in Porthcurno (below).

INFORMATION
Pedals Bike Hire (☎ 251671; 17 Wharfside Shopping Centre; rental per day/week £10/50)
Tourist office (☎ 362207; pztic@penwith.gov.uk; ⌾ closed Sat afternoon & Sun off season)

SLEEPING & EATING
Castle Horneck YHA (☎ 362666; penzance@yha.org.uk; Castle Horneck, Alverton) Take bus No 5B or 6B from the train station to the Pirate Inn, from where it's a half-mile walk.

Penzance Backpackers (☎ 363836; www.pzback pack.com; Alexandra Rd; dm/d £10/24; 🖳) A short walk from the promenade and ocean, this hostel sometimes feels more like staying with a casual but unprepared friend. Buses go almost directly in front of the hostel to the Minack Theatre (below).

Zennor Backpackers & Café (☎ 01736 798307; www.cornwall-online.co.uk/zennor-backpackers/Welcome .html; The Old Chapel, Zennor; dm from £12, family rooms £40, breakfast £3-4.50) Spartan but beautifully situated. Take local bus No 8A from Penzance.

GETTING THERE & AWAY
National Express runs buses from Penzance to Newquay (£4.75, 1¾ hours, two daily) and to Plymouth, Exeter and London. Local bus No 8A goes to Zennor and St Ives every 40 minutes.

The train station is behind the tourist office. Trains go to London's Paddington station (£59, 5¼ hours, seven to eight direct trains daily) and Exeter (£19.90, three hours, 11 daily).

Land's End
☎ 01736

This most striking of English coastal settings would scare off even the heartiest pirate with treacherous oceans, jutting cliffs and a soul-sucking tourist threshold filled with tacky 'Last [Fill in the Blank] in Britain!' shops. Visitors who persevere will be greeted with a view of seemingly the entire Atlantic Ocean and miles of walking trails.

Whitesand's Lodge (☎ 871776; www.whitesands lodge.co.uk; Sennen village; dm £12.50, d with en suite in the guesthouse £50; 🅿 🖳) is a colourful hostel/guesthouse on the main road 2 miles before Land's End. It's the ultimate in relaxed holiday settings, with surf instruction, cosy log fires, a bar and restaurant, tent space and (this being Cornwall) yoga classes and spiritual workshops. Take bus No 1 or 1A from Penzance to get to the lodge or complex.

A Roman-styled amphitheatre carved out of granite and stone in the Cliffside is the setting for the **Minack Theatre** (☎ 810181; www.minack.com; Porthcurno; tours adult £3.20; ⌾ 9.30am-5.30pm Apr-Sep, 10am-4pm Oct-Mar, call as sometimes closed during the week; 🅿). If you're here during summer, don't leave without seeing a **performance** (tickets £4-7.50; ⌾ 8pm Mon, Tue & Thu, 2pm & 8pm Wed & Fri). First Bus runs a post-performance bus back to Penzance. Dress warmly.

St Ives
☎ 01736 / pop 9500

More compact than Penzance and quainter than Newquay is the adorable St Ives, a seaside resort town that doubles as an artists' colony. Visitors can spend several days enjoying beaches, narrow winding streets and a **Tate gallery** (☎ 01736 796226; www.tate.org.uk /stives; Porthmeor Beach; adult/concession/under-18, pensioner & Tate Gallery member £5.50/2.50/free; ⌾ 10am-5.30pm daily Mar-Oct, 10am-4.30pm Tue-Sun Nov-Feb). The **tourist office** (☎ 798309; www.stives-cornwall .co.uk; The Guildhall, Street-an-Pol; ⌾ year-round) is near the train station.

St Ives Backpackers (☎ 799444; www.backpack ers.co.uk/st-ives; Lower Stennack; dm depending on season £10.95-15.95) This busy hostel occupies a converted chapel and still has sensational stained glass. A free shuttle bus goes to the Newquay hostel (opposite).

Sunrise B&B (☎ 795407; 22 The Warren; s £22-30, d £48-54; ⌾ closed month after Easter, Oct & Nov; 🅿)

Features a fabulous breakfast (vegetarian available), patios and ocean views. Ask for the red balloon room.

Kynance Guest House (☎ 796636; enquiries@ kynance24.co.uk; The Warren; per adult £23; Ⓟ) Another good option next door to the Sunrise B&B.

Hub (☎ 799099; 4 The Wharf; dishes £2-7) The social centre of St Ives, for drinks or a meal.

Trains head to London's Paddington station (£60, 5½ hours, five daily) and Penzance (£2.90, 20 minutes direct or 40 minutes, 14 daily).

Newquay

☎ 01637 / pop 14,000

Britain's surf capital is the sort of deliciously tacky seaside resort town where one can eat candy floss and fish and chips while shopping for shell-related paraphernalia. After a day of soaking up sun and surf, indulge in the groovy nightlife scene. This is a great place to learn how to surf (see the Endless Summer Surf Lodge, below).

The **tourist office** (☎ 854020; info@newquay .co.uk; Marcus Hill; ☽ closed Sun off season) is near the bus station in the centre of town. Several surf shops on Fore St hire fibreglass boards and wetsuits, each around £6 per day.

Newquay has many independent hostels geared up for surfers.

Original Backpackers (☎ 874668; 16 Beachfield Ave; dm from £10) A great place to make new friends over a pint (or seven), and in an excellent central position overlooking Towan Beach.

St Christopher's Inn (☎ 020-7407 1856; www.st christophers.co.uk; 35 Fore St; dm £15-18.50, d £46; 🖳) Commanding a grand location overlooking Towan Beach, which you'll enjoy after a few hours in the lively bar, this has a rollicking atmosphere. During summer, guests are required to book a full week, starting Saturday, for £155, full cooked breakfast included.

Endless Summer Surf Lodge (☎ 851522; www .endlesssummersurflodge.com; 15-16 Mount Wise; per person £25; Ⓟ 🖳 🖳) Stay here or just enjoy the nightlife. With a sand-covered 1st floor and tiki bar where DJs spin almost every night, and its very own dive and surf school, this is a destination in itself.

There are four trains a day between Newquay and Par (£4.70, 45 minutes), which is on the London–Penzance line, and numerous buses to Truro.

CENTRAL ENGLAND

Several of England's most frequented towns – Oxford, Stratford-upon-Avon and the Cotswolds – draw those people interested in culture and natural beauty to the 'Heart of England'.

OXFORD

☎ 01865 / pop 134,000

The mix of foreign students, robe-clad dons and camera-flashing tourists makes this small city feel like a learned amusement park. Some sort of scholarly activity has been occuring here since 1069, with University, Balliol and Merton Colleges established between 1249 and 1264. Oxford has seen the education of many esteemed people, including Lewis Carroll, Christopher Wren and Mr Bean (Rowan Atkinson).

There is no one central university; instead, about 16,800 students attend 39 autonomous colleges. All teach the same 17 subjects but each has its own personality.

Orientation

The city centre is surrounded by rivers and streams on the eastern, southern and western sides, and can easily be covered on foot. Drivers will do best to leave cars at one of the Park 'n' Rides and take a bus into town.

Information

Budget (☎ 724884; budgetoxford@yahoo.co.uk; Osney Lane) Car rental.

Mic@s.com (per half-hour or less £1; ☽ 9am-11pm) High St (☎ 726364; 118 High St); Gloucester Green (☎ 726009; 91 Gloucester Green) Internet access.

Tourist office (☎ 726871; tic@oxford.gov.uk; 15-16 Broad St; ☽ 9.30am-6pm Mon-Sat, closes earlier winter, 10am-3.30pm Sun summer & bank holidays)

Sights & Activities

For comprehensive tourist information see www.visitoxford.org. Oxford University's website is at www.ox.ac.uk. In an unusual twist, many of Oxford's colleges charge admission, while most museums are free.

COLLEGES

Christ Church College (☎ 276150; admission £4) is perhaps the only university with a cathedral in its grounds. The current incarnation of Christ Church was founded by King Henry

VIII, among others. Most of the world will recognise its Great Hall as Harry Potter's Hogwarts Hall.

One of the richest Oxford colleges, **Magdalen College** (☎ 276000; adult/concession £3/2) has the most extensive and beautiful grounds, with a deer park, river walk, three quadrangles and superb lawns. This was CS Lewis' college and the setting for the film *Shadowlands*.

Merton College (☎ 276310; admission free; ☑ 2-4pm Mon-Fri, 10am-6pm Sat & Sun) is one of the three oldest colleges, dating to 1264. The present buildings mostly date from the 15th to 17th centuries. Check out the stained glass in its chapel.

Right on New College Lane is the **Bridge of Sighs**, modelled after the eponymous Venetian *Ponte de Sospiri* and connecting the two sides of Hertford College. Wren's **Sheldonian Theatre** (☎ 277299; Broad St; ☑ 10am-12.30pm & 2-4.30pm, 10am-12.30pm & 2-3.30pm winter, closed Sun) hosts Oxford graduations.

Other unmissable sights are the **University Church of St Mary the Virgin tower** (admission £1.60), the circular **Radcliffe Camera** (admission £1.50) and the **Bodleian Library** (☎ 277224). You're looking at a tiny fraction of the library; much of its 100 miles (161km) of storage space is underground, and it could take up to 24 hours to check a book out.

MUSEUMS

The **Ashmolean Museum** (☎ 278000; www.ashmol.ox .ac.uk; Beaumont St; admission free; ☑ 10am-5pm Tue-Sat,

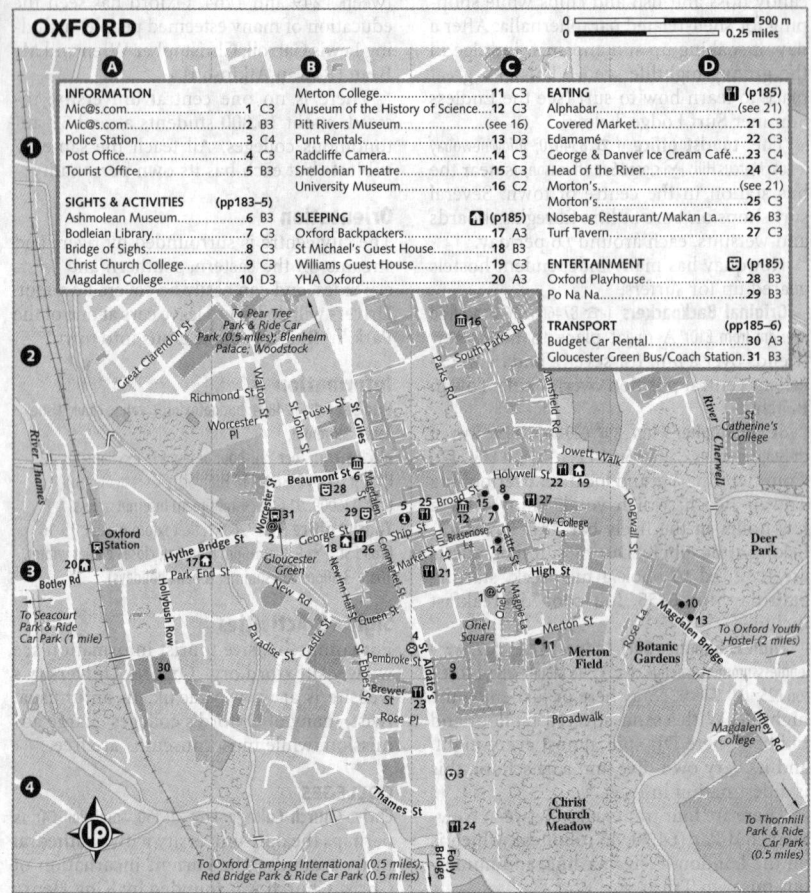

OXFORD

| | 0 _____ 500 m |
| | 0 _____ 0.25 miles |

| INFORMATION | |
| Mic@s.com.....................................1 C3 |
| Mic@s.com.....................................2 B3 |
| Police Station.................................3 C4 |
| Post Office.....................................4 C3 |
| Tourist Office.................................5 B3 |

| SIGHTS & ACTIVITIES (pp183–5) | |
| Ashmolean Museum.......................6 B3 |
| Bodleian Library............................7 C3 |
| Bridge of Sighs.............................8 C3 |
| Christ Church College...................9 C3 |
| Magdalen College.......................10 D3 |

| Merton College...........................11 C3 |
| Museum of the History of Science..12 C3 |
| Pitt Rivers Museum....................(see 16) |
| Punt Rentals...............................13 D3 |
| Radcliffe Camera.........................14 C3 |
| Sheldonian Theatre.....................15 C3 |
| University Museum......................16 C2 |

| SLEEPING ☐ (p185) | |
| Oxford Backpackers....................17 A3 |
| St Michael's Guest House............18 B3 |
| Williams Guest House..................19 C3 |
| YHA Oxford................................20 A3 |

| EATING ☐ (p185) | |
| Alphabar..................................(see 21) |
| Covered Market............................21 C3 |
| Edamamé....................................22 C3 |
| George & Danver Ice Cream Café...23 C4 |
| Head of the River.........................24 C4 |
| Morton's..................................(see 21) |
| Morton's.....................................25 C3 |
| Nosebag Restaurant/Makan La.......26 B3 |
| Turf Tavern..................................27 C3 |

| ENTERTAINMENT ☐ (p185) | |
| Oxford Playhouse.........................28 B3 |
| Po Na Na.....................................29 B3 |

| TRANSPORT (pp185–6) | |
| Budget Car Rental.........................30 A3 |
| Gloucester Green Bus/Coach Station.31 B3 |

SMART THINKING

Oxford has easy connections to both Gatwick and Heathrow. If you want a less hectic (and cheaper) alternative than staying in London, try staying in Oxford and catching a comfortable and direct half-hourly (Heathrow) or hourly (Gatwick) bus. Plan ahead as a return ticket costs only slightly more than a single.

2-5pm Sun) houses extensive displays of European art (including works by Raphael and Michelangelo) and Middle Eastern and Egyptian antiquities.

Also worthy are the **University Museum** (☎ 272950; Parks Rd; admission free; ✆ noon-5pm) and **Pitt Rivers Museum** (☎ 270927; through University Museum; admission free; ✆ noon-4.30pm Mon-Sat, 2-4.30pm Sun), filled with cool science stuff like shrunken heads, and paintings of dodo birds and dinosaurs.

The quirky **Museum of the History of Science** (☎ 277280; Broad St; admission free; ✆ noon-4pm Tue-Sat, 2-5pm Sun) displays Einstein's theory of relativity musings on a blackboard.

PUNTS

From May to September, punts and boats can be hired (per hour £10 to £12, £25 deposit) at Folly Bridge and Magdalen Bridge.

Sleeping

YHA Oxford (☎ 0870 770 5970; oxford@yha.org.uk; 2A Botley Rd; adult/under-18 dm £19.50/14.40, tw £46; ❑ ✗) This impeccably run hostel is well located in a new building directly behind the train station. It's deservedly popular, especially during holidays and summer, so book ahead.

Oxford Backpackers (☎ 721761; 9A Hythe Bridge St; 8- to 18-bed d £12, 4-bed d £13; ❑) This option is closer to town and has larger rooms.

Williams Guest House (☎ 721880; 14 Holywell St; s/d £35/50; Ⓟ ✗) Opposite New College, this place's panelled dining room and romantic fireplace add to the tranquil feel.

St Michael's Guest House (☎ 242101; 26 St Michael's St; s/d/f £35/55/66) This no-frills place is a block from Gloucester Green.

Oxford Camping International (☎ 244088; 426 Abingdon Rd; per adult/tent £4.45/4.50, backpackers incl camp site £4.15; Ⓟ) Roughly 3 miles (4.8km) south of the centre near the Park 'n' Ride car park, this site is open all year.

Eating

Turf Tavern (☎ 243235; 4 Bath Pl) This pub is a recommended watering hole dating from the 16th century and hidden away down an alley.

Head of the River (☎ 721600; Folly Bridge) Named for the victor in the annual inter-collegiate rowing regatta, it has an ideal location with a heated outdoor patio.

Edamamé (☎ 246916; 15 Holywell St; ✆ lunch Tue-Sun, dinner Thu-Sat) The current student hot spot, this hopping Japanese restaurant with communal tables offers excellent prices and beautiful presentation.

Nosebag Restaurant/Makan La (☎ 203222; 6 St Michael's St; soups £2.75, mains £6.25) With filling soups and a good range of vegetarian choices, the Asian-inspired downstairs restaurant serves up noodle and vegetable specialities, including a spicy mee goreng (£5).

George & Danver Ice Cream Café (✆ to midnight); 55 Little Clarendon St (☎ 516652); St Aldgate's (☎ 245592) Serves snacks, but come here for the to-die-for home-made Jersey ice cream.

For tasty baguettes, try **Morton's** (☎ 200860; 22 Broad St; sandwiches £2), which also has a branch in the **covered market** (✆ 8.30am-5.30pm Mon-Sat), with entrances on Market, Cornmarket and High Sts. A dozen places for sweets and takeaway are also found in the market, including the organic **Alphabar** (☎ 250499).

Entertainment

Leaflets and posters are plastered all over Oxford, announcing events throughout all 39 colleges.

Po Na Na (☎ 249171; 13 Magdalen St) This is a late-night bar–cum–club.

Oxford Playhouse (☎ 305305; Beaumont St) Sir John Gielgud and Dame Judi Dench have both graced the stage here. It has a mixed bag of theatre, dance and music.

Getting There & Away

BUS

Several bus companies leave Gloucester Green every few minutes for London 24 hours a day. Tickets cost around £9 and take 1¾ hours.

National Express heads to Bristol (£12.40, 1½ hours, hourly). From Bristol there are connections to Wales, Devon and Cornwall. Buses to Shrewsbury, North Wales, York and Durham go via frequent connections to Birmingham.

The Airline bus heads to Heathrow (one-way adult/senior £14/7, three-month return ticket £17/8.50, 70 minutes to the central bus terminal, 90 minutes to Terminal 4) at 2am, 4am, every half-hour from 4.30am to 10pm, and midnight. It leaves for Gatwick (one-way £21, three-month return ticket £24/12, two hours) at 2am, 4am, hourly from 5.15am to 8.15pm, 10pm and midnight. Pay on board with sterling, euros or US dollars.

Park 'n' Ride links 4000 parking spaces with the city centre.

TRAIN
Trains head to London's Paddington station (£14.90, one hour) about every 15 minutes. Oxford has frequent trains to Moreton-in-Marsh (£8.20, 35 minutes, 12 daily) for Stow in the Cotswolds, Bath (£16.20, 1¼ hours, at least hourly), and Bristol Temple Meads (£12.40, 1¾ hours, half-hourly), changing at Didcot Parkway. For train inquiries phone ☎ 0845 748 4950.

BLENHEIM PALACE
Legendary wartime prime minister Winston Churchill was born at **Blenheim Palace** (☎ 0870 060 2080; www.blenheimpalace.com; Woodstock; adult/concession £11/8.50; ⊙ house: 10.30am-5.30pm mid-Feb–mid-Dec, closed Mon-Tue Nov-Dec, park: 9am-4.45pm daily year-round). Home to the Duke of Marlborough (to whom Churchill was related), it's the archetypal grand English country home.

Catch a Stagecoach bus (Nos 20A-C) from Oxford's Gloucester Green or train station to the palace's entrance (return £3.70, at five and 35 minutes past the hour).

STRATFORD-UPON-AVON
☎ 01789 / pop 24,000
Stratford has become something of a Shakespeare factory, but lovers of Shakespeare and the theatre won't mind on account of the truly remarkable Royal Shakespeare Company (RSC) theatre and historical houses here.

Although it no longer has a permanent London home, the RSC has three theatres here and there's nearly always something on. Warwick, with its wonderful castle, is just to the north.

The **tourist office** (☎ 293127; www.shakespeare-country.co.uk; Bridgefoot; ⊙ 9am-6pm Mon-Sat, 10.30am-4.30pm Sun) has plenty of information about the sights and the numerous B&Bs. Five

museums filled with re-creations and the history behind William Shakespeare make up **Shakespeare Houses** (☎ 204016; adult/concession for all 6 locations £13/12; ⊙ call for opening hours).

Seeing a production by the **Royal Shakespeare Company** (☎ 0870 609 1110; www.rsc.org.uk; tickets £10-50; ⊙ box office 9.30am-8pm) should not be missed. Tickets are often available on the day of performance, but get in early. Stand-by tickets (£12) are available to students immediately before performances and there are almost always standing-room tickets (£5).

Sleeping & Eating
The **YHA Stratford** (☎ 0870 770 6052; stratford@yha.org.uk; Hemmingford House, Alveston; adult/under-18 with breakfast £17/12.30; P ⊒) is nearly 2 miles out of town. From the tourist office, cross Clopton Bridge and follow the B4086, or take bus No 18.

B&Bs are plentiful just west of the centre on Evesham Place, Grove Rd and Broad Walk. From the train station, turn right at the first traffic light and you'll find dozens of places, all fairly similar. Try the **Dylan** (☎ 204819; thedylan@lineone.net; 10 Evesham Pl; per person £25) or the **Carlton** (☎ 293548; 22 Evesham Pl; s/d from £22/45).

Sheep St has a fine selection of dining possibilities including the **Vintner** (☎ 297259; 4-5 Sheep St; afternoon tea £4-7, mains £9-16), a wine bar that serves Eastern-inspired dishes during the day. **Thespians** (☎ 267187; 27 Sheep St; mains £5-12) serves up delicious South Indian fare, with especially tasty vegetarian mains.

Getting There & Away
Direct trains go to London's Paddington station (£22.90, two hours, four to five daily), stopping in Oxford (£9, 1¼ hours). Otherwise, train services are patchy. Some trains to/from Bath, for instance, require three changes.

SPLURGE!

The best mid-range bet in town is the **White Swan** (☎ 297022; www.thewhiteswanstratford.co.uk; Rother St; s/d/f £60/80/130; P ✕), where you can enjoy soundproofed windows, 24-hour room service and well-appointed furnishings. Check in the off season or at the last minute for substantial discounts.

COTSWOLDS

Named after its rolling hills and ancient sheep structures, this rural swathe of central England boasts famous honey-coloured stone houses and manors, picturesque villages and gently sloping green meadows, crisscrossed by lazy rivers. Getting around by public transport can be difficult. The best base is Stow-on-the-Wold.

There are two useful tourist offices: the **Cirencester tourist office** (☎ 01285-654180; Market Pl) and **Stow-on-the-Wold tourist office** (☎ 01451-831082; The Square; ⊗ closed Sun off season).

Stow, as it is known, is one of the most impressive (and visited) towns in the Cotswolds. It's a terrific base if you don't have a vehicle, because several particularly beautiful villages, including the well-touristed Upper and Lower Slaughters, are within a day's walk or cycle ride.

YHA Stow-on-the-Wold (☎ 0870 770 6050; stow@yha.org.uk; The Square; adult/under-18 £13.40/9.30; 🖳) is extremely popular with families, with top-notch facilities. An alternative is **Limes Guest House** (☎ 830034; thelimes@zoom.co.uk; Evesham Rd; s/d £25/46; Ⓟ).

Trains from London's Paddington station reach Moreton-in-Marsh (£21.20, 1½ hours, 10 to 11 daily).

BIRMINGHAM
☎ 0121 / pop 969,000

Although Birmingham is England's second-largest city, it's not often thought of as a tourist destination. That's because it isn't. However, it's a transport hub, and the city is slowly transforming itself into a place where you wouldn't mind spending half a day. There are several museums and a beautiful **Jewellery Quarter**. The **tourist office** (☎ 693 6300; Victoria Sq; ⊗ daily) can help with visitor information.

Fans of Frodo, Gandalf and Middle Earth, head thee to the **Tolkien Trail** (www.tolkiensociety.org). JRR Tolkien grew up in the hamlet of Sarehole, which you can visit with a brochure using public transport (DaySaver £2.50) or by car. See Tolkien's boyhood haunts, as well as the inspiration for the Two Towers of Gondor and the Shire.

Try a balti restaurant for Birmingham's own version of Indian cooking. The original is **Royal Alfaisel** (☎ 449 5695; 136 Stoney Lane; buffet £5.95; ⊗ noon-midnight), or there are Balti zones cropping up around Ladypool St and in the Sparkhill area.

PEAK DISTRICT

Squeezed between the industrial Midlands to the south, Manchester to the west and Sheffield to the east, the Peak District seems an unlikely site for one of England's most beautiful regions. Even the name is misleading, being derived from the tribes who once lived here, not from the existence of any significant peaks (there are none!). Nonetheless, the 542-sq-mile (872-sq-km) Peak District National Park is a delight, particularly for walkers and cyclists.

Castleton and nearby Edale are popular villages on the border between the White and Dark Peaks. From Edale, the Pennine Way starts its 250-mile (402km) meander northwards. From the town of Castleton, the 25-mile Limestone Way is a superb day walk covering the length of the White Peak to Matlock. In addition, a number of disused railway lines in the White Peak have been redeveloped as walking and cycling routes, with strategically situated bicycle-rental outlets at old station sites.

There are National Park Information Centres at **Edale** (☎ 01433-670207), next to the train station; **Castleton** (☎ 01433-620679; Castle St); and **Bakewell** (☎ 01629-813227; Old Market Hall). For more details try www.peakdistrict.org or www.thepeakdistrict.info.

The regular Transpeak bus service cuts right across the Peak District from Nottingham and Derby to Manchester via Matlock, Bakewell and Buxton. Pick up a Derbyshire Wayfarer ticket (adult/concession £7.50/3.75) from any tourist office in the area, or call **Traveline** (⊗ 0870 6082608) for details.

EAST ENGLAND

A softer England is found in the eastern counties. Picturesque medieval market towns straddle a gently undulating landscape that is crisscrossed by waterways and marshland and bordered by some stunning coastlines. For comprehensive information on the region contact the **East of England Tourist Board** (☎ 0870 225 4800; www.visiteastofengland.com) or get its useful book *Great Days Out* (£4.50). Here we cover the most popular attraction, Cambridge.

BRITAIN

BRITAIN

CAMBRIDGE

☎ 01223 / pop 130,000

Home to one of the world's greatest universities, Cambridge is steeped in history and learning. The lofty academia, architectural beauty and gentle River Cam bordered by meadows (the Backs) give Cambridge a sense of agelessness and tranquillity surpassed by none. It's also a lively market town with its fair share of designer boutiques and trendy cafés.

The university began in the early 13th century, about a century later than its arch academic rival Oxford. The choir and chapel of King's College would be hard to beat in any city – they're indisputably among the highlights of any trip to England.

Orientation & Information

The bus station is in the centre of town, but the train station is a 20-minute walk to the southeast.

Cambridge Visitor Centre (☎ 0906 586 2526, per min 60p; www.visitcambridge.org; Wheeler St; ☺ 10am-5.30pm Mon-Sat, 11am-4pm Sun)

ITC Café (☎ 377358; 2 Wheeler St; per hr £1; ☺ 9am-9pm) Internet café opposite the visitor centre.

Sights

The main college opening hours are detailed below, but in general most are closed to visitors for the Easter term (mid-April to mid-June), and all are closed for exams (mid-May to mid-June). Times can change so verify with the **TIC** (☎ 322640; www.cambridge

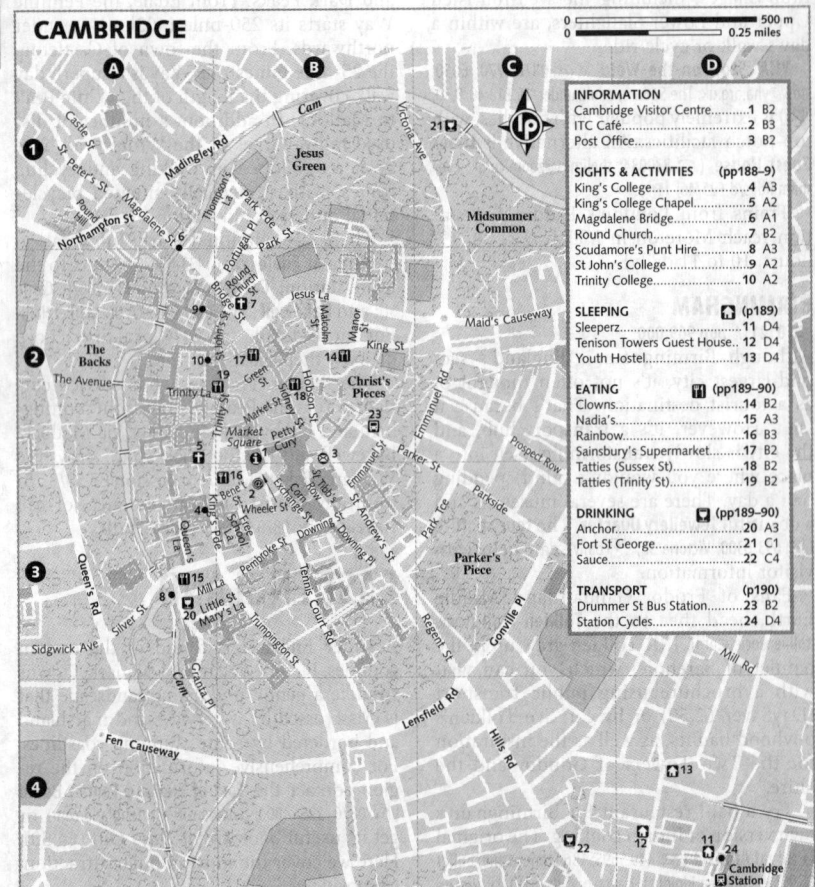

.gov.uk) or the university's **central information service** (☎ 337733).

What follows is a walking tour of some of the main sights.

Starting at **Magdalene Bridge**, walk south down Bridge St until you reach the unmistakable **Round Church** (adult/concession £1/50p; 🕙 10am-5pm Tue-Sat, 1-5pm Sun-Mon), one of only four surviving medieval round churches, dating from the 12th century. Turn right down St John's St (immediately across the road), which is named in honour of **St John's College** (☎ 338600; adult/concession £2.20/1.30; 🕙 10am-5pm March–end Oct) on the right.

Next door, **Trinity College** (☎ 338400; adult/concession £2/1; 🕙 10am-4.30pm, library noon-2pm Mon-Fri, closed 11–18 & 24 Jun) is one of the largest and most attractive colleges. It was established in 1546 by Henry VIII on the site of several earlier foundations. The Great Court, Cambridge's largest enclosed court, incorporates buildings from the 15th century. Beyond this is Nevile's Court and on its western side is Sir Christopher Wren's library, built in the 1680s.

Next comes Caius (pronounced keys) College, and then **King's College** (☎ 331100; adult/concession £4/3; 🕙 in term time: 9.30am-3.30pm Mon-Sat, 1.15-2.30pm Sun, choral service: 5.30pm Tue-Sat, 10.30am & 3.30pm Sun, out of term time: 9.30am-4.30pm Mon-Sat, 10am-5pm Sun, chapel open almost all year, grounds closed mid-Apr–mid-Jun). This is one of Europe's greatest buildings, with its perpendicular, late-Gothic style and famous **chapel**. The chapel was begun in 1446 by Henry VI but wasn't completed until 1545. Majestic as this building is from the outside, its interior, with its breathtaking scale, stunning stained glass and intricate fan vaulting, makes the greater impact. It's amazing when the choir sings.

Continue south on King's Pde and turn right onto Silver St (St Catherine's College is on the corner), which takes you down to the Cam where **punts** can be hired. **Scudamore's** (☎ 359750; www.scudamores.com; Granta Pl, Mill Lane; self-hire: per punt 1hr Mon-Fri £12, Sat & Sun £14, deposit Mon-Fri £60, Sat & Sun £70, tours: adult/concession per 45 min £12/10; 🕙 9am-dusk Apr-Sep, 10am-dusk Oct-Mar) has various punt stations along the Cam.

The **Cambridge Visitor Centre** (☎ 0906 586 2526, per min 60p; www.visitcambridge.org; Wheeler St; 🕙 10am-5.30pm Mon-Sat, 11am-4pm Sun) offers a punting tour as well as a wide variety of **walking tours** (☎ 457574; tours £5-8).

Festivals & Events
Held for three days at the end of July, the **Cambridge Folk Festival** (☎ 357851; www.cambridge folkfestival.co.uk; Cherry Hinton; tickets only: full festival £74, Fri/Sat/Sun £25/36/35, tickets & camping: £74 plus £33 per 2- to 3-berth tent) features British and overseas performers. There's a bus service to the site from Cambridge train station and the city centre.

Sleeping
The visitor centre has a **booking service** (☎ 457581; fee £3).

Youth Hostel (☎ 354601; cambridge@yha.org.uk; 97 Tenison Rd; adult/under-18 £16.50/12.40; 🖵) Near the train station, this hostel has a lounge, games rooms, café, kitchen and laundry facilities. Book ahead.

Tenison Towers Guest House (☎ 363924; www .cambridgecitytenisontowers.com; 148 Tenison Rd; B&B per person £25) Of the several B&Bs on this road, this is the best. Cosy and friendly, it has spotlessly clean rooms with blue and pine décor.

Sleeperz (☎ 304050; www.sleeperz.com; Station Rd; s/tw/d £35/45/55; 🅿) Right outside the train station in a converted railway warehouse, this great-value hotel has large, modern, minimalist-style rooms with spacious bathrooms. However, the hallways feel a bit hospital-like.

Eating & Drinking
There's a **Sainsbury's supermarket** (Sidney St).

Nadia's (☎ 568335; 16 Silver St; sandwiches £2; 🕙 8am-5pm) For a picnic on the Backs try the excellent-value rolls, baguettes, bagels and cakes here.

Clowns (☎ 355711; 54 King St; mains £3-6.50; 🕙 8am-midnight Mon-Sat, 8am-11pm Sun) Offering English breakfasts, toasted sandwiches and basic pasta dishes, this is a good place to refuel at a great low price. It has a jovial atmosphere and is popular with the students.

Tatties (baked potatoes £3-6; 🕙 8am-6pm Mon-Sat, 9am-5pm Sun) 15 Trinity St (☎ 357766); 11 Sussex St (☎ 323399) Sit down to baked potatoes stuffed with tempting fillings, as well as breakfasts, filled baguettes, salads and cakes.

Rainbow (☎ 321551; 9A King's Pde; mains £7-8; 10am-10pm Tue-Sat; 🚫) Opposite the King's College gates is this friendly vegetarian/vegan restaurant, with healthy dishes from around the world.

Fort St George (☎ 354327; Midsummer Common) In a lovely riverside spot this 16th-century pub is said to be the oldest on the Cam.

The Anchor (☎ 353554; Silver St) This pub has views over the River Cam with its willow trees and bobbing punts.

Sauce (☎ 360268; 3 Station Rd) This funky bar is popular with students and travellers.

Getting There & Around

Cambridge can easily be visited as a day trip from London or en route to the north.

From London Victoria there are hourly National Express coaches (one-way/return £9/15, two hours). **Stagecoach Express** (☎ 01865-772250) goes to Oxford hourly (£5.99, 3½ hours). **National Express Airport** (☎ 0870 575 7747) runs coaches to Stansted (one-way/return £8.50/10.50, one hour), Heathrow (one-way/return £23.50/29.50, 2½ hours) and Gatwick (one-way/return £27.50/33.50, 3½ hours) airports.

There are trains every half-hour from London's King's Cross and Liverpool St stations (one-way/return £16.40/21.70, one hour 20 minutes). If you want to go by train to Oxford or Bath, you'll have to return to London first.

Stagecoach Cambus (☎ 423578) operates buses around town from Drummer St, including bus No 1 from the train station to the town centre.

Bicycles can be hired from **Station Cycles** (☎ 307125; www.stationcycles.co.uk; Station Rd; rental per day £8; ☺ 9am-5pm Mon-Sat, 10am-4pm Sun Mar-Oct) just outside the train station.

NORTHWEST ENGLAND

The Northwest is attracting quite a bit of attention these days as cities such as Manchester and Liverpool become cultural capitals of England.

MANCHESTER

☎ 0161 / pop 390,000

Manchester's almost mythological nightlife earned the city for a brief, crazy time the moniker 'Madchester'. Following an IRA bombing in 1996 and the hosting of the Commonwealth Games in 2002, Manchester has been rebuilding for a greater future. The city centre is overflowing with shopping, public space, nightclubs and restaurants.

Orientation & Information

The University of Manchester lies to the south of the city centre (on Oxford St/Rd). To the west of the university is Moss Side, a ghetto with high unemployment and a thriving drug trade – keep clear. Victoria train station caps the city in the north. Try www.destinationmanchester.com for tourist information.

easyEverything (☎ 832 9200; St Anne's Sq)

Tourist office (☎ 234 3157; Town Hall Extension, Lloyd St, St Peter Sq; ☺ 10am-5.30pm Mon-Sat, 10.30am-4.30pm Sun & bank holidays) There are branches in Terminals 1 and 2 in the airport.

Sights & Activities

Get in touch with your supporter roots at the **Manchester United Football Museum & Tour** (☎ 0870 442 1994; www.manutd.com; Old Trafford stadium; admission £7.50). Hour-long tours run every 10 minutes and introduce fans to more information about Man United than the average person would ever, *ever* want to know. Call or email, as tour times depend on match days and times.

The **Lowry** is an eye-catching modern construction on Salford Quay. Two theatres and several galleries (one devoted to the Manchester-born LS Lowry, a twentieth-century artist known for his industrial landscapes often filled with simple but stylized match-stick figures) are encapsulated in the complex. The galleries are free to enter. Take the Metrolink to either Broadway or Harbour City.

Castlefield Urban Heritage Park is an extraordinary landscape made up of the remains of ancient Roman fortresses and newly constructed canalside footpaths, pubs, hotels and a YHA hostel. The area also takes in the excellent **Museum of Science & Industry** (☎ 832 2244; Liverpool Rd, Castlefield; admission free; ☺ 10am-5pm), where you'll discover that the history of fabric is actually interesting.

Sleeping & Eating

The tourist office can arrange accommodation for a £2.50 booking fee, plus a 10% deposit.

Hatters (☎ 236 9500; www.hattersgroup.com; 50 Newton St; dm £16-17; 🖳) In the city centre, equidistant from the train and coach stations, this hostel offers 200 beds, cheap high-speed Internet access (£1 per 30 minutes), a restaurant and laundry facilities.

YHA Manchester (☎ 839 9960; manchester@yha .org.uk; Potato Wharf, Castlefield; dm adults/under-18s £19.50/14.40) Across the road from the Museum of Science & Industry in the Castlefield area (well signposted), this has more than 140 beds and full facilities.

Rembrandt (☎ 236 1311; www.rembrandtman chester.com; 33 Sackville St; s/d/tr/q £35/40/45/50, en suite extra £10) In the heart of the gay village (see below), this inn has a fabulous bar and restaurant downstairs making it a genial, if not particularly quiet, place to stay.

The most distinctive restaurant zones are Chinatown in the city centre and Rusholme in the south, called the Curry Mile for its plethora of Indian restaurants, but cafés and restaurants cover the city centre as well.

Dimitri's (☎ 839 3319; Campfield Arcade; mains £4-8), near the YHA, is a hip place for tapas or a few drinks.

Earth Vegetarian Café (☎ 834 1996; 16-20 Turner St; mains £3-7), in the Northern Quarter, serves up an imaginative vegetarian selection.

Entertainment
There are several places to drink in Castlefield.

Barça (☎ 839 7099; Catalan Sq) Has outdoor seating for sunny days.

Two historic pubs are the **Old Wellington Inn** (☎ 830 1440), built in 1530, and **Sinclairs Oyster Bar** (2 Cathedral Gates) at the top of New Cathedral St, where you can get great cheap beer.

Manchester Academy (☎ 275 2930; 269 Oxford Rd) For live rock and pop, including big international acts, check out the academy, part of the University Students Union.

Roadhouse (☎ 237 9789; 8 Newton St) Indie bands play at the pulsating Roadhouse before they make it big.

Canal St is the centre of Manchester's enormous gay nightlife scene. There are more than 20 bars and clubs in the so-called 'gay village'.

Paradise Factory (☎ 273 5422; 114-116 Princess St) Cutting-edge club, with gay nights at the weekend.

Getting There & Away
There are numerous coach links with the rest of the country. National Express operates out of Chorlton St station in the city centre to pretty well anywhere you'll want to go, including London's Victoria station (return £25, 4½ hours, seven to nine daily)

and Edinburgh (£26.50, 6½ hours, about five daily).

Piccadilly is the main station for trains to and from the rest of the country; Victoria serves Halifax and Bradford. **Metrolink** (☎ 0845 748 4950) runs between the two stations. There are frequent services to London (£51.10, 2¾ hours, hourly) and Liverpool (£7.70, 45 minutes to one hour, three hourly).

CHESTER
☎ 01244 / pop 80,000
Chester's popularity comes from its Roman walls – the most complete in Britain – and its compact medieval shopping arcade. Whether listening to the town crier, taking a cruise on the Dee River or checking out the new excavations of the Roman amphitheatre (near the Chester Visitor Centre), all ages will find something to do.

Orientation & Information
Built in a bow formed by the River Dee, the walled centre is now surrounded by suburbs. The train station is a 15-minute walk from the city centre; go up City Rd, then turn right onto Foregate at the large roundabout.

Café Venue – The Crypt (☎ 350001; 34-40 Eastgate Rd; 9.30am-6pm Mon-Wed, 9.30am-7pm Thu, 9.30am-6.30pm Fri & Sat, 11am-5pm Sun) Internet access.

Chester Visitor Centre (☎ 351609; tis@chestercc.gov .uk; Vicar's Lane)

Tourist office (☎ 402111; www.chestercc.gov.uk; Town Hall) Just opposite the cathedral.

Sights & Activities
The present **Chester Cathedral** (☎ 324756; requested donation £2) was originally a Saxon Minster, and with its cloisters, showcases the most complete monastic complex in Britain.

The **Dewa Roman Experience** (☎ 343407; Pierpoint Lane; adult/concession £3.95/3.50; 9am-5pm) is an interactive museum. Its simulated archaeological dig and reconstruction of typical Roman street life is especially great for kids, but, honestly, who doesn't want to try on a set of Roman armour?

The Chester Visitor Centre can also keep you busy with guided walks, the excavation of the nearby Roman amphitheatre, ghost hunting and even a wall patrol with fully clad legionnaires.

Hear ye, hear ye, all photo-op seekers. Chester's **town criers** have been shouting cries since medieval times...although the ones about Welsh beheadings have lessened somewhat. Head thee to the Chester High Cross at the intersection of Eastgate, Northgate, Bridge and Watergate Sts at noon Tuesday to Saturday, May to August.

To meander lazily down the River Dee during the day or shake it to disco or the Beatles at night, head to **Showboats of Chester** (☎ 325394; Souters Lane; adult/senior & student £5-15/4-15, depending on length & cruise type), which offers trips from 30 minutes to 3½ hours.

Sleeping & Eating

Good-value B&Bs line Hoole Rd, the road into the city from the M53/M56 (check with the visitor centre).

YHA Chester (☎ 0870 770 5762; chester@yha.org.uk; 40 Hough Green; dm adult/under-18 £14.90/11.60; **P** ⊠ ▣) This charming and amiable hostel is in a large Victorian building, 1 mile from the centre, on the opposite side from the train station. Take bus No 3, 4, 4A or 16.

Chester Backpackers (☎ 400185; www.chester backpackers.co.uk; 67 Boughton St; dm/s/d £13/18.50/34; ▣) Five minutes from both the train station and the city centre. Most rooms have *en suite* and there's free left luggage.

Grove Villa (☎ 349713; grove.villa@tesco.net; 18 The Groves; s/d £23/46; **P** ⊠) Quietly situated not far from the city centre and next to the River Dee.

Café Venue – The Crypt (☎ 350001; 34-40 Eastgate Rd; sandwiches £3, salads £6; ☉ 9.30am-6pm Mon-Wed, 9.30am-7pm Thu, 9.30am-6.30pm Fri & Sat, 11am-5pm Sun) Built as a wine cellar around 1290, this cavernous venue is great for either a bite to eat, a few drinks or email checks (£1.50 for 30 minutes).

Getting There & Around

Chester has excellent transport connections, especially to and from North Wales.

National Express has numerous connections, including to Birmingham (£9.50, 2½ hours, four daily) and on to London (£16, 5½ hours), Manchester (£5.25, 1¼ hours, three daily), Liverpool (£5.75, one hour, four daily) and Llandudno (£8.25, 4.55pm to 6.35pm). For many destinations in the south or east, it's necessary to change at Birmingham; for the north, change at Manchester.

Local buses leave from Market Sq behind the town hall. For information ring **Chester City Transport** (☎ 602666).

Any bus from the station goes to the centre. There are numerous trains to Manchester (£9.50, one hour, hourly), Liverpool (£4.50, 40 minutes, half-hourly), Holyhead (£17.90, two hours, about hourly) via the North Wales coast for ferries to Ireland, Shrewsbury (£6, one hour, hourly in the morning) and London's Euston station (£51, 2½ to three hours, almost hourly, last one 7.30pm). Phone ☎ 0845 748 4950 for details.

LIVERPOOL
☎ 0151 / pop 510,000

When a city names its airport after its most famous son (the Liverpool John Lennon Airport), its dedication to music is evident. From the Beatles to Frankie Goes to Hollywood, Liverpool has seen the birth of more chart-topping bands than any other city in Britain.

Industrial decline and WWII bombing in the last century brought Liverpool its fair share of urban decay, unemployment and crime. However, Liverpool holds the title of European City of Culture for 2008. The place will be covered in scaffolding and cranes for the next several years and public transport is in flux, so watch as the city starts to shine.

Orientation & Information

The city is fairly compact but a fairly sizable hill adds a good walk between the Albert Dock and the city centre. You're advised to be a bit cautious in Liverpool. It's best to avoid dark side streets even in the city centre. Visit www.visitliverpool.com for tourist information.

Planet Electra (☎ 708 0303; 34-36 London Rd; per hr £2, 20% student discount; ☉ 10am-5.30pm Mon-Wed, 10am-7.30pm Thu & Fri, noon-5pm Sun) Internet access.

Tourist office (☎ 0906 680 6886, per min 50p; Queen Sq Centre; ☉ 9am-5.30pm Mon-Sat, 10.30am-4.30pm Sun) Also has a branch inside the Maritime Museum; both book accommodation.

Sights & Activities

A £100 million renovation has helped make **Albert Dock** (☎ 708 8854; all museums free; ☉ from 10am) Liverpool's deserved number one tourist attraction. It houses several outstanding museums, including the **Merseyside Maritime Museum** (☎ 478 4499; ☉ 10am-5pm), **Museum of Liverpool Life** (☎ 478 4080; ☉ 10am-5pm) and a **Tate Gallery Liverpool** (☎ 702 7400; ☉ Tue-Sun 10am-6pm, bank holiday Mon).

For those who equate Liverpool with the Beatles and don't mind a bit of kitsch, a Beatles bus tour might be just the thing. The **Magical Mystery Tour** (☎ 709 3285; tickets £11.95; ☼ tours leave 2.10pm daily from the main tourist office, 2.30pm from the Beatles Story, additional tours leave 11.40am/noon during summer, weekends & holidays) takes passengers by a brightly coloured bus to the actual Penny Lane, Strawberry Fields and where the banker never wore a mac in the pouring rain (very strange).

Sleeping

YHA Liverpool International (☎ 0870 770 5924 , 709 8888; liverpool@yha.org.uk; 25 Tabley St, at Wapping; dm adult/under-18 £19/14; ℗ 🖳) Right across the road from the Albert Dock, with all the best hostel amenities: complete restaurant with breakfast included, 24-hour access and laundry facilities.

Embassie Hostel (☎ 707 1089; www.embassie.com; 1 Falkner Sq; dm for 1st night £13.50, for subsequent nights £12.50) Named for its former life as the Venezuelan consulate, this converted hostel was a labour of love for its owners, an former backpacker and his father. They offer comfort, summer barbecues on the patio, and free coffee, tea and toast.

International Inn (☎ 709 8135; www.international inn.co.uk; 4 S Hunter St, off Hardman St; dm/tw £15/36; ℗ 🖳) Well equipped with a café, kitchen and games room, this is close to the centre.

Eating

There's a plethora of places to eat down Bold St in the city centre, but the restaurants at Albert Dock are geared towards fine dining.

Royal Liver Building diner (☎ 255 0192; Pier Head; light meals £2-4; ☼ 8am-3pm Mon-Fri) Its stained glass and gushing fountain create a memorable environment. Security will only allow diners – as opposed to sightseers – into the building.

Flannagan's Apple (☎ 231 1957; 18 Mathew St; pub meals £5) This renowned establishment is as proudly dank and smoky as Liverpool itself.

Entertainment

Wander around Mathew St and southwest to Bold, Seel and Slater Sts and you'll stumble upon an amazing array of clubs and pubs catering to every style you can imagine. A re-creation of the original music venue where the Beatles made their name, the **Cavern Club** (☎ 236 1964; 10 Mathew St), still attracts a big crowd when hosting live bands or DJs.

The founders of the now-closed scouse scenester club Cream have opened **Baby Cream** (☎ 01736 796226; www.babycream.co.uk; Atlantic Pavillion, Albert Dock), a club, bar and café purporting to be the hipper-than-thou place to be seen, drink and dance.

Getting There & Away

There are National Express services which connects Liverpool to most of the major towns, including London's Euston station (£20, 5¼ hours, four daily), Manchester (£5.25, 1½ hours, hourly) and Chester (£4.10, 45 minutes, half-hourly).

Direct trains head to London's Euston station (£51.10, three hours, hourly) and Chester (£4.10, 45 minutes, half-hourly).

Getting Around

Public transport in the region is coordinated by **Merseytravel** (☎ 236 7676). For day visitors, a Saveaway transport ticket (£3.20) covers zones B and E, which includes all city centre buses and the ferry.

The **ferry** (☎ 330 1444; adult/concession £2.40/1.85; ☼ tours hourly 10am-3pm Mon-Fri, 10am-6pm Sat & Sun) across the Mersey, started 800 years ago by Benedictine monks but made famous by Gerry & the Pacemakers, still offers one of the best views of Liverpool. Boats depart from Pier Head ferry terminal, just north of Albert Dock.

LAKE DISTRICT

There are two reasons to go to the Lake District: to do some serious rambling (also known as walking, hiking or trekking) amid jagged peaks, picturesque lakes, stone wall–enclosed meadows and sheep, or to do some serious village ambling among tea shops, stone cottages and souvenir shops. The 14-plus million visitors each year seem to be about divided.

This is Wordsworth country, and his houses – Dove Cottage at Grasmere and Rydal Mount, between Ambleside and Grasmere – are literary shrines.

Getting There & Away

National Express buses have direct connections from Windermere to Preston (£9.25, two hours, two daily) and Keswick to Birmingham (£29, 3½ hours, two daily).

For all public transport inquiries contact Traveline (☎ 0870 608 2608). There are several important bus services in the Lake District, including bus No 555, which runs about once an hour all year and links Lancaster with Carlisle via Kendal, Windermere, Ambleside, Grasmere and Keswick. No 599 is an open-top bus that runs during the summer between Windermere and Ambleside via Grasmere. No 505/506 runs from Ambleside to Coniston via Hawkshead. Ask about Day Ranger and Explorer tickets, as single tickets can be £3 apiece.

Windermere is at the end of a spur off the main railway line between London's Euston station and Glasgow. There are trains to London (£65.50, four hours, at least six daily) and Manchester (£12.55, two hours, 15 daily).

Getting Around

Walking or cycling are the best ways to get around, but bear in mind conditions can be treacherous and the going can be very, very steep. **Alexander Sports** (☎ 01539-488891; Main Rd, Windermere; rental per day £12) rents many sizes of bikes.

Windermere & Bowness
☎ 015394 / pop 8500

It's thanks to the railway that the Windermere/Bowness conglomerate is the largest tourist town in the Lake District. The two towns are quite strung out, with lakeside Bowness a 30-minute downhill walk from Windermere. The excellent **tourist office** (☎ 46499; Victoria St, Windermere; per 30 min £3) is near the train station at the northern end of town and offers Internet access.

Windermere is wall-to-wall B&Bs, which the tourist office can book for you.

Lake District Backpackers Lodge (☎ 46374 or 44725; www.lakedistrictbackpackers.co.uk; High St; dm £12.50) A comfortable hostel with free tea, coffee, bread and jam, it's imperative you call ahead for reservations any time of the year. It's just a short walk from the train station. The hostel runs an agency for live-in hotel jobs.

Windermere YHA (☎ 43543; High Cross, Bridge Lane, Troutbeck; dm adult/under-18 £11.80/8.50) Popular with families, this commands a scenic spot on Lake Windermere in the Troutbeck Valley. Two miles from the train station, numerous buses run past Troutbeck Bridge, and in summer the hostel sends a minibus to meet trains.

There's a healthy smattering of cafés and restaurants in both townships. **Bowness Kitchen** (☎ 45529; 4 Grosvenor Tce, Bowness) serves tasty toasted sandwiches for £3.

Grasmere
☎ 015394 / pop 2700

Grasmere is in a catch-22 situation. It's such a charming little village that continual streams of visitors arrive (many by tour bus) – making it less charming in the summer. Information can be found at the **tourist office** (☎ 35245; Red Bank Rd; ⏰ 9.30am-5.30pm). The homes of William Wordsworth are the major attractions here. **Dove Cottage & Museum** (☎ 35544; www .wordsworth.org.uk; adult/concession £5.95/5; ⏰ 9.30am-5.30pm) allows visitors to take a peek into the poet's belongings. South of Grasmere, it's accessible by bus 555 or 599 (in summer).

Grasmere Butterlip How YHA (☎ 35316; grasmere@yha.org.uk; Easedale Rd; dm adult/under-18 £13.40/9.30) is just north of the village. The lovely **How Foot Lodge** (☎ 35366; r from £22) is ideal for access to Dove Cottage, which is on the main A591 Kendal–Keswick Rd, just south of Grasmere village.

Keswick
☎ 017687 / pop 5000

Keswick isn't the most appealing Lake District village, but it's a good base for walking or lake adventures. The **tourist office** (☎ 72645), in the middle of the pedestrianised town centre, books accommodation and runs guided tours of the area. Check email at **U-Compute Cyber Café** (☎ 75127; 48 Main St) above the post office.

The **Youth Hostel** (☎ 72484; keswick@yha.org.uk; dm adult/under-18 £11.80/8.50) is a short walk down Station Rd from the tourist office and open most of the year. Station Rd has several B&Bs, most charging around £24 per person.

Kendal
☎ 01539 / pop 27,100

On the eastern outskirts of the Lake District National Park, Kendal is a lively town and has excellent public transport connections. The **tourist office** (☎ 725758; Highgate) is in the Town Hall.

Kendal Youth Hostel (☎ 724066; kendal@yha.org .uk; 118 Highgate; dm adult/under-18 £14.90/11.60; ⏰ daily mid-Apr–Aug, Tue-Sat Sep–early Apr) is right next door to the **Brewery**, a wonderful arts complex with a theatre, cinema and bar-bistro.

Kendal is on the branch railway line from Windermere to Oxenholme, with connections to Manchester, Lancaster and Barrow-in-Furness.

NORTHEAST ENGLAND

Rolling hills, craggy seafronts, turbulent history and some of England's most vibrant big cities – Northeast England is a region of rewarding contrasts. While many come to trek through three of the nation's best national parks, others come to explore Roman ruins or the world's finest cathedral architecture. The area's once-depressed industrial cities are also a great reason to visit, with a host of civic super-projects creating a renaissance in places that were on the scrap heap just a few years ago. For general information on visiting the region check www.visitnorthumbria.com and www.yorkshirevisitor.com.

YORK
☎ 01904 / pop 180,000
York wears its past on its sleeve and, since it's one of Britain's most historic cities, that works perfectly for visitors. An important settlement since Roman times, its spectacular Minster and medieval wall show that it was also a key ecclesiastical and political centre before it become an entrepreneurial hub of the Industrial Revolution. All this is celebrated in today's York, a bustling, tourist-friendly city that's perfect for exploring on foot.

Orientation
Although the city is relatively small, York's streets are a confusing medieval tangle. There are five major landmarks: the walkable 2.5-mile city wall; the Minster at the northern corner; Clifford's Tower, a 13th-century fortification and mound at the southern end; the River Ouse that cuts the centre in two; and the train station just outside the western corner.

Information
Gateway Internet Café-Bar (☎ 646446; 26 Swinegate; per 5 min 50p, per 30 min £2; 🕑 10am-8pm Mon-Wed, 10am-11pm Thu-Sat, noon-4pm Sun)
Tourist office (☎ 621756; www.thisisyork.co.uk/www .visityork.org; De Grey Rooms, Exhibition Sq; 🕑 9am-5pm Mon-Sat, 10am-4pm Sun Nov-Mar; 9am-6pm Mon-Sat, 10am-5pm Sun Apr-Oct)

Sights & Activities
Northern Europe's largest Gothic cathedral and the highlight of the city, **York Minster** (☎ 557216; Minster Yard; adult/concession £4.50/3; 🕑 9am-6.30pm Mon-Sat, noon-6.30pm Sun) is a treasure house of architecture and richly coloured stained glass, especially the giant **Great Eastern Window**. Take an audio tour of the **Undercroft** (adult/concession £3/2) for an atmospheric exploration of this evocative site that's been an important religious centre for 1400 years.

Housed in several former train sheds near the train station, the giant **National Railway Museum** (☎ 621261; Leeman Rd; admission free; 🕑 10am-6pm) is the home of dozens of legendary locomotives, each polished to a fine sheen. The **Great Hall** includes the record-breaking Mallard and the only Bullet Train outside Japan, while the **Station Hall** offers a glimpse of luxury with royal trains through the ages.

The kitschy **Richard III Museum** (☎ 634191; Monk Bar, Monkgate; adult/concession £2/1; 🕑 9.30am-4pm Nov-Feb, 9am-5pm Mar-Oct) puts one of Britain's looniest kings on trial for his various alleged crimes.

The Association of Voluntary Guides offers free two-hour **walking tours** (🕑 10.15am daily, plus 2.15pm Apr-Oct & 6.45pm Jun-Aug), departing across the street from the tourist office.

Sleeping
Locating a bed in York in the summer can be harder than finding a Brit with a tan. Avoid the tourist office's £3 accommodation booking fee by checking options online at www.roomcheck.co.uk/yk.

York International Youth Hostel (☎ 653147; york@yha.org.uk; 42 Water End, Clifton; dm £12.30-17; 🖥) This large and busy youth hostel is reached via a riverside footpath from the city centre. Rooms are mostly four-bed and there's a good café-bar and private garden.

York Youth Hotel (☎ 625904; www.yorkyouthhotel .com; 11-13 Bishophill Senior; dm £12-18) The popular York is in an impressive Georgian townhouse. It has some smaller dorms and family rooms, and there's a comfortable bar serving hearty pub grub.

York Backpackers (☎ 627720; www.yorkbackpackers .co.uk; 88-90 Micklegate; dm £13-14) This is the city's most sociable hostel, thanks to its lively bar and large dorms.

A gaggle of B&Bs cluster along Bootham Tce and Grosvenor Tce, just a few minutes' walk from the city centre. They're mostly expensive in the high season but good value the rest of the year, especially when you add in the greasy breakfast.

23 St Mary's (☎ 622738; www.23stmarys.co.uk; 23 St Mary's, Bootham; s/d £34/52) This has won awards for its high-level hospitality and is a popular spot with Lonely Planet readers. It has good-sized rooms bursting with character

and owners who are more than happy to help you plan your day out.

Arnot House (☎ 641966; www.arnothouseyork.co .uk; 17 Grosvenor Tce; s/d £60; ⊠) A cosy, well-located heritage B&B within walking distance of the Minster. Rooms are *en suite* (shower only) and some contain brass beds and other Victorian-style knick-knacks.

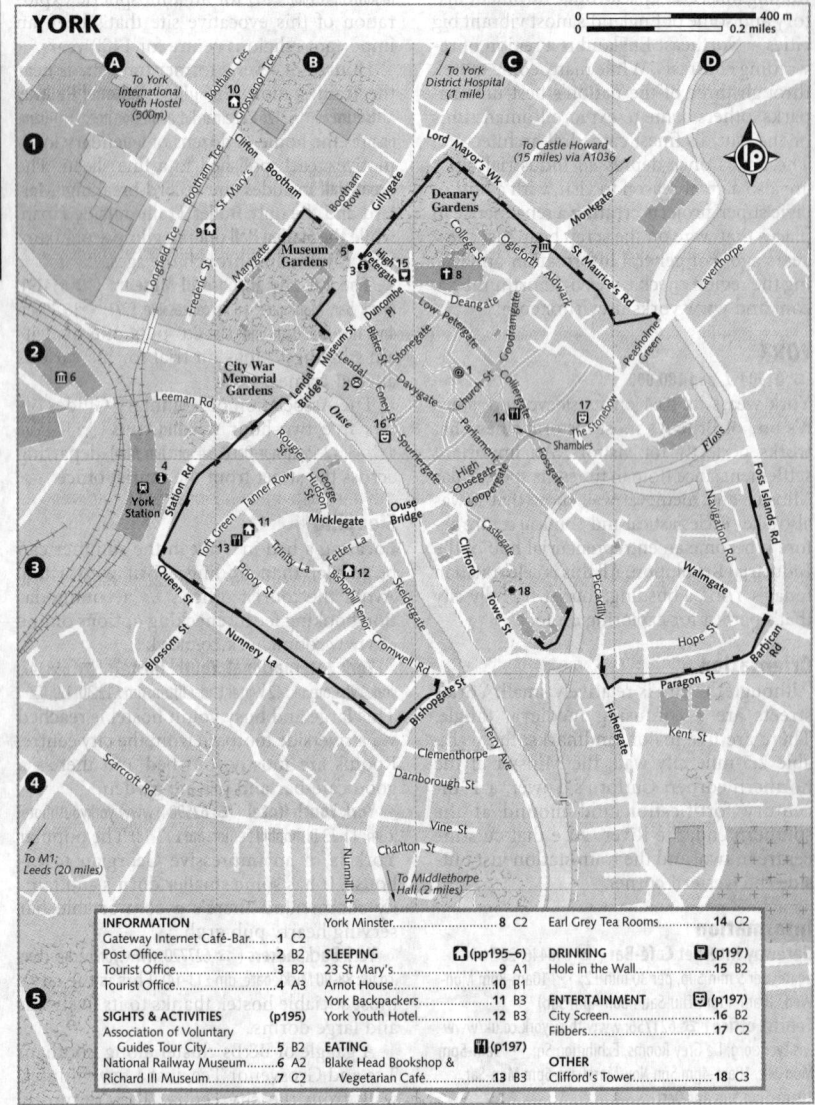

Eating & Drinking

Alongside the ubiquitous pie shops serving good-value stodge for those eating on the run, the grandmotherly ambience of the timber-framed **Earl Grey Tea Rooms** (☎ 654353; 13-14 The Shambles; tea & cake £3; ⏰ 9am-5pm) offers a good spot to relax while you write your postcards while knocking back a pot of strong Yorkshire tea.

Blake Head Bookshop & Vegetarian Café (☎ 623767; 104 Micklegate; mains £4.50; ⏰ 9.30am-5pm Mon-Sat, 10am-5pm Sun) Serves a wide array of vegan and vegetarian dishes and a heaping main course salad option that can't be beaten.

In the evening, a visit to one of the city's ancient pubs is recommended.

Hole in the Wall (☎ 634468; 10 High Petergate; mains £5-7) Among the best of the pubs, this attracts a comfortable mix of locals and visitors with its fine selection of regional tipples, including Yorkshire Terrier bitter. Its comfort-food menu stretches way beyond the usual pub selection, but the best deal is the curry night special where a beer and meal is £5.99.

Entertainment

York is not a nightlife hot spot; check the Friday edition of the *Evening Press* for entertainment listings.

Fibbers (☎ 651250; Stonebow House; admission £5-15; ⏰ 11am-1am Mon-Sat, noon-11pm Sun) This is the only live music venue worth a visit. It cranks up the ampage every night with new and up-and-coming bands.

City Screen (☎ 541144; 13-17 Coney St; tickets from £3.50) Has an eclectic mix of mainstream and art-house movies to keep the projectors rolling.

Getting There & Around

National Express buses arrive throughout the day from London (£22, five to seven hours). There are also six daily buses from Birmingham (£21.50, three to six hours) and four from Edinburgh (£28.50, six to eight hours). There are numerous daily trains from London's King's Cross (£69, two hours) and from Edinburgh (£56, 2½ hours).

A great city for getting lost on foot, York also has lots of cycle routes – ask at the tourist office for a network map. You can hire bikes from **Europcar** (☎ 656161; York train station; rental per day from £7.50).

NORTH YORK MOORS NATIONAL PARK

One of Britain's finest natural treasures, the **North York Moors** is 550 sq miles (885 sq km) of wild and wonderful terrain coloured by purple heather, craggy coastline and old stone farmhouses where long-haired sheep wander at will. It's the perfect spot for a dramatic *Wuthering Heights*–style run towards your sweetheart, but try not to fall over any escarpments or you'll ruin the moment.

Orientation & Information

The moors run east to west, from the craggy coastline to the gentle rolling hills and steep cliffs of Hambleton and Cleveland Hills. Pick up a copy of the tabloid-sized *Moors & Coast* (50p) from newsagents. With maps and information, it's the best-value park guide around.

There are several tourist offices in the area but the **Moors Centre** (☎ 01439-772737; Lodge Lane, Danby; ⏰ 10am-5pm Apr-Oct, 11am-4pm Nov-Dec & Mar, 11am-4pm Sat & Sun only Jan-Feb) is the best.

Activities

Walking is the best way to experience the park, and the 110-mile (177km) **Cleveland Way** from Helmsley to Filey will take you via as many of its hills and coastal vistas as you can handle. The steam trains of the **North Yorkshire Moors Railway** (NYMR; ☎ 01751-473799; one-day pass adult/concession £12.50/11; ⏰ Apr-Oct, with additional limited winter services) offer a more sedentary way to traverse the region, running the picturesque 18-mile between Pickering and Grosmont – look out for **Goathland Station**, transformed into Hogsmeade Station for the *Harry Potter* movies. The **Moor to Sea** (www.moortoseacycle.net) cycle route links Scarborough, Pickering and Whitby via 80 miles (128km) of forest tracks and old railway lines. Rent mountain bikes from **Trailways Cycle Hire** (☎ 01947-829207; day rates from £6.30) near Whitby, where hostel-style accommodation in the **old train station** (dm £19) is also available.

Sleeping

There are several camping grounds in the area but it is worth pitching your tent at **Foxholme Caravan Park** (☎ 771241; www.ukparks .co.uk/foxholme; Harome; camping £8.50-12.50; ⏰ Mar-Oct), which is only 4 miles (6.5km) from Helmsley.

Helmsley Youth Hostel (☎ 770433; helmsley@yha .org.uk; Carlton Lane; dm £10.60; ⏰ flexible) This is a friendly and popular backpacker option.

BRITAIN

Getting Around

The **Moorbus** (☎ 01845-597426; rover ticket £3; daily Jun-Sep, Sun Apr-Oct) services a network of stops throughout the region.

DURHAM

☎ 0191 / pop 90,000

With its winding medieval streets and dramatic skyline dominated by Britain's finest Norman cathedral, Durham is home to thousands of students at England's third-oldest university – they're the ones hanging around street corners with their long scarves and plummy accents.

There's free Internet access at **Clayport Library** (☎ 386 4003; Millennium Pl; ☼ 9.30am-7pm Mon-Fri, 9am-5pm Sat) but photo ID is required and there's a 30-minute limit at peak times. Across the street is the **tourist office** (☎ 384 3720; www.durhamtourism.co.uk; Millennium Pl; ☼ 9.30am-5.30pm Mon-Sat, 10am-4pm Sun).

Sights

Taking 40 years to finish, the magnificent **Durham Cathedral** (☎ 386 4266; Palace Green; admission free; ☼ 9.30am-6.15pm Mon-Sat, 12.30-5pm Sun, closes 8pm summer) is a landmark of solemn, rib-vaulted architecture, part church and part fortress. Climb the 218ft **tower** (admission £2.50) for spectacular city views or take an illuminating **history tour** (adult/concession £3.50/2.50; ☼ 11.30am & 2.30pm mid-Apr–mid-Sep). Nearby **Durham Castle** (☎ 333 3800; Palace Green; admission £3; ☼ 10am-12.30pm & 2-4.30pm Jul-Sep, extended at Easter & Christmas) was completed in 1072 and was the university's first home 800 years later.

Sleeping & Eating

Use the tourist office for its free accommodation booking service but be aware that vacancies are virtually nonexistent during June's university graduation. Outside term time, 11 **colleges** (☎ 334 5878; www.dur.ac.uk/conference_tourism; r per person from £20) offer rooms to visitors. The medieval **University College** is highly recommended. Otherwise, Durham's best deal is **Mrs Koltai** (☎ 386 2026; 10 Gilesgate; s £20).

Brown Sugar Bistro (☎ 386 5050; 81-83 New Elvet; mains £4-8; ☼ 7am-11pm) This is a former garage where you can still watch the cars go by. Heaped fried breakfasts – including a good selection of vegetarian options – are popular and it transforms throughout the day from coffee stop to sandwich bar and cosy evening lounge.

Numjai (☎ 386 2020; 19 Milburngate Shopping Centre; mains £7-11; ☼ 5-11pm) Plan for an early dinner stop at Durham's best restaurant, serving up Thai delicacies and sunset views of the River Wear. There's an early bird special from 5pm to 7pm, where you can sample two courses for £9.99.

Drinking

Locals take over the bars on North Rd at the weekend, while students and backpackers favour **Varsity** (☎ 384 6704; 46 Saddler St), a bright three-level pub offering a good beer selection, cheap food and a covered garden.

Entertainment

The city's friendliest dance floor is at the kitschy **Klute Nightclub** (☎ 386 9589; Elvet Bridge; admission £2.50-4.50), where students come to forget their exams.

Getting There & Around

National Express buses arrive from London (£25, six to eight hours, six daily) and Edinburgh (£20, four to five hours, three daily). The Arriva X1 service runs throughout the day from Newcastle, excluding Sunday. On the main London–Edinburgh line, trains arrive from London (£88, three hours) and Edinburgh (£37.50, two hours) throughout the day. Trains also arrive every few minutes from York (£17, 45 minutes).

The compact town centre is best explored on foot – it's hard to get lost with the cathedral looming permanently above. For local bus information call ☎ 0870 608 2608.

NEWCASTLE GATESHEAD

☎ 0191 / pop 470,000

These two Geordie cities now market themselves jointly but there's no denying that Newcastle-upon-Tyne gets the lion's share of attention. While the city lost its way during the decline of UK manufacturing in the 1970s and 1980s, the area is undergoing a mini cultural renaissance with new art centres, a swanky bar and restaurant scene and a kicking nightlife.

Orientation & Information

Newcastle's compact city centre is easy to navigate on foot. The central train and coach station is just south of the centre. Packed with chain stores, indoor markets and giant £1 shops (stock up on cheap bottled water and shampoo here), there's a surprising number of formidable 19th-century classical buildings, many of them heritage listed.

Tourist office (☎ 277 8000; www.visitnewcastlegates head.com; 132 Grainger St; ◷ 9.30am-5.30pm Mon-Sat, 10am-4pm Sun Jun-Sep)

Sights

A contemporary art centre housed in a former flourmill, **BALTIC** (☎ 478 1810; Gateshead Quay; admission free; ◷ 10am-7pm Mon-Sat, 10am-5pm Sun) is the North's answer to London's Tate Modern. While it scandalises some stuffy locals with occasional nude artworks, exhibitions change frequently and it's a great place to spend a couple of hours on a rainy day. It's reached from the Newcastle side of the river via the **Gateshead Millennium Bridge**, a curving movable pedestrian walkway that's a sci-fi artwork in itself.

Billing itself as a 'sexy' science museum, **Centre for Life** (☎ 243 8210; Times Sq; adult/concession £6.95/5.50; ◷ 10am-6pm Mon-Sat, 11am-6pm Sun) takes a refreshing, high-tech look at the natural science of genetics. Check out the simulator that takes you on a hair-raising taxi ride through Newcastle.

The most potent symbol of restored Northeast pride, the towering **Angel of the North** (☎ 478 4222; A1, Gateshead; admission free) sculpture was built from 200 tonnes of steel by artist Antony Gormley. The remarkable roadside landmark has a wingspan of 54m and has been embraced by locals.

Sleeping

Newcastle Youth Hostel (☎ 281 2570; newcastle@yha .org.uk; 107 Jesmond Rd; dm £11.80) Situated in an old brick townhouse, this is a five-minute walk from Jesmond metro station. The facilities are basic and there's nowhere to do laundry.

Northumbria University (☎ 227 4024; rc.conferen ces@northumbria.ac.uk; Ellison Tce; s £17-28.50; ◷ Jun-Sep) Offers summer accommodation in the city centre, when students are away. Most rooms are basic singles with shared bathrooms but *en suites* are also available for a few pounds extra. Rates include a cafeteria breakfast.

Bewick Hotel (☎ 477 1809; bewickhotel@hotmail .com; 145 Prince Consort Rd, Gateshead; B&B s/d £25/46) This B&B is 2 miles (3.2km) from the city centre in an end-of-terrace family house in a residential street. It's welcoming but on the quiet side.

Eating & Drinking

Many Newcastle restaurants ⬛⬛⬛ dinner specials. For food on the ▮▮▮ and sandwich shops are everywhere.▮▮

Café Blue (☎ 222 0371; 9 Higham Pl; mains ▮ ◷ 8am-6pm Mon-Sat) A low-cost fuel stop with surprisingly large breakfasts, this is also a great place to watch the world go by. A wide range of takeaway sandwiches is available.

Spice Cube (☎ 222 1181; The Gate, Newgate St; early evening 2-course dinner special £10.50; ◷ noon-2.30pm & 5.30-11.30pm Mon-Fri, noon-11.30pm Sat & Sun) The days of dodgy sitar muzak are long forgotten at this loungy reinvention of an Indian restaurant. The *nahari podina ghoust* (a tangy lamb and mint curry) is highly recommended and there are several worthwhile vegetarian options. The set lunch and dinner (before 7pm) specials are excellent value.

An atmospheric location in an old printworks adds to the warm yet modern Euro-ambience of **Paradiso Caffe Bar** (☎ 221 1240; 1 Market Lane; mains £5-17; ◷ 11am-10.30pm Mon-Fri, 12.30-3.30pm Sun) Grab a booth and take your time checking out the imaginative menu – the juicy fillet of pork stuffed with dates is perfect.

Drinking

Newcastle's pub scene has moved on from the days when the Bigg Market area was little more than an open-air vomitorium.

Popolo (☎ 232 8923; 82-84 Pilgrim St; ◷ 11am-1am) Away from the crowds, this is an excellent bar that's something of a Newcastle secret, so don't tell anyone about it. Large comfy chairs and two bars make this a good chill-out spot and the prices are reasonable. Good selection of international beers and lip-smacking cocktails.

Bob Trollop's (☎ 261 1037; Sandhill, Quayside) Among the trendy Quayside area's most popular pubs, Bob Trollop's has a wide regional beer selection and regular drinks specials for those who want to get blotto cheaply. The meals are good, too, including more vegetarian options than any pub in town.

Entertainment

The Geordies know how to party. Among their hip joints is **Foundation** (☎ 261 8985; Melbourne St; £8-10; ◷ 10pm-3am), where the music ranges from club classics to retro hip-hop and house and garage. Top UK club DJs are regularly scheduled but Monday night means school disco – indie style.

BRITAIN

entre for Life;
, four bars
trance, the
'80s techno
theme nights

Loc... the city centre, daily flights ...nternational Airport arrive from L... , Amsterdam and Paris, with other cities served on a less regular basis. Ferries also arrive at Royal Quays from Norway, Sweden and the Netherlands. See p149 for ferry details.

See p149 for ferry details.

National Express coaches arrive from many major UK cities, including (London (£24, 6½ hours) and Edinburgh (£11, 2½ hours), and there are frequent trains from Edinburgh (£33.50, 1¾ hours), London (£83, three hours) and York (£15.50, one hour).

The city centre is surprisingly easy to navigate on foot, and the excellent metro is quicker and more efficient than many local buses. Unlimited travel for one day is £3. For advice and information contact **Traveline** (☎ 0870 608 2608; www.traveline.org.uk).

NORTHUMBERLAND

With its haunting beauty and scattered population, Northumberland offers the chance to really get away from it all. But it's not just the breathtaking natural splendour that attracts visitors. There's almost an embarrassment of historic sites that speak of centuries of bloody conflict, mostly with the Scots. The horizon is full of the jagged remains of dozens of immense fortifications that look like old broken teeth.

The most significant is **Hadrian's Wall**. Brainchild of Roman Emperor Hadrian, it stretches for 73 miles (118km) from Newcastle to Bowness-on-Solway near Carlisle and was the northern frontier of the empire for almost 300 years. It was superseded in Norman times by dozens of castles and fortified houses, some of which remain intact. You'll stumble upon some of these by hiking in the wild and empty **Cheviot Hills**, although it's not a terrain for amateurs.

There are 15 tourist offices around Northumberland, each offering maps, accommodation booking and transport information. Some are quite small and open only seasonally, while **Alnwick** (☎ 01665-510665; 2 The Shambles) and **Hexham** (☎ 01434-652220; Wentworth Car Park) open year-round. Check www.visit northumberland.com for others.

Sleeping

Corbridge, Hexham, Haltwhistle and Brampton make ideal bases for exploring the region around Hadrian's Wall and are stuffed with B&Bs and YHA hostels.

Acomb Youth Hostel (☎ 01434-602864; acomb@ yha.org.uk; Main St; dm £8.20; ☺ Apr-Nov) A basic, converted stable about 2.5 miles (4km) north of Hexham. Catch bus number 880 from Hexham.

Once Brewed Youth Hostel (☎ 01434-344360; once brewed@yha.org.uk; Military Rd, Bardon Mill; dm £11.80; ☺ Feb-Nov, excl Sun/Mon Feb/Mar & Oct/Nov) Also basic, but next door to a tourist office, only 3 miles (4.8km) from Housesteads Roman Fort. Northumbria bus 685 (from Hexham or Haltwhistle stations) drops you at Henshaw.

Greenhead Youth Hostel (☎ 016977-47401; green head@yha.org.uk; Greenhead, Brampton; dm £10.60; ☺ Apr-Oct, flexible opening so call ahead) This charming chapel conversion boasts better facilities than most. It's 3 miles (4.8km) west of Haltwhistle station and is served by the trusty bus 685 and White Star bus 185 from Carlisle.

Getting There & Around

The Newcastle to Carlisle railway line has stations at Hexham, Haydon Bridge, Bardon Mill, Haltwhistle and Brampton, but not all trains stop at all stations. There are hourly bus services from Carlisle and Newcastle on No 685. From June to September the hail-and-ride Hadrian's Wall Bus links Hexham, Haltwhistle and Carlisle with all the main sites. Call **Hexham tourist office** (☎ 01434-652220) for information.

SCOTLAND

Craggy snowcapped mountains, sapphire-blue lochs and barren islands where seabirds easily outnumber the hardy locals: Scotland is dominated by huge swathes of picture-perfect wilderness. But alongside the dramatic Highlands and beautifully remote Orkney and Shetland Islands, there are also some world-class cities, dozens of appealing towns and a kaleidoscope of stone-hewn villages that look as if they've been around since the invention of the kilt.

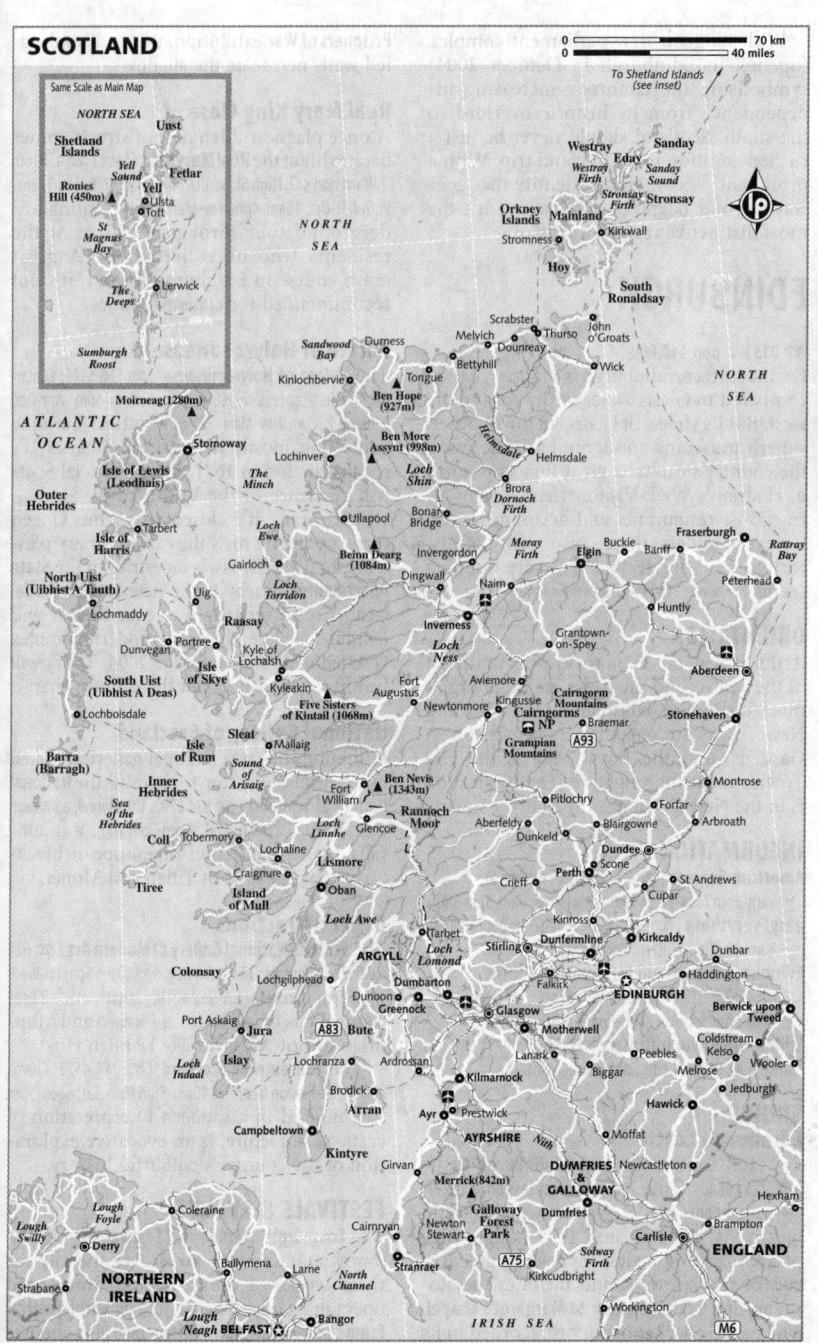

SCOTLAND

0 — 70 km
0 — 40 miles

To Shetland Islands
(see inset)

Same Scale as Main Map

NORTH SEA

Unst

Shetland
Islands

Yell
Sound
Fetlar

Ronies
Hill (450m) ▲
Yell
Ulsta
Toft

St
Magnus
Bay

The
Deeps

Lerwick

Sumburgh
Roost

ATLANTIC
OCEAN

Moirneag(1280m) ▲

Stornoway

Isle of Lewis
(Leodhais)

Outer
Hebrides

Tarbert

Isle of
Harris

North Uist
(Uibhist A'Tuath)

Lochmaddy

Dunvegan
Portree
Uig

Raasay

South Uist
(Uibhist A Deas)

Lochboisdale

Isle
of Skye

Kyle of
Lochalsh
Kyleakin

Sleat

Barra
(Barragh)

Isle
of Rum

Mallaig

Sound
of
Arisaig

Sea
of the
Hebrides

Coll

Inner
Hebrides

Tobermory

Tiree

Lochaline

Craignure
Lismore

Island
of Mull

Oban

Colonsay

Port Askaig

Jura

Islay

Loch
Indaal

Lochranza
Brodick

Arran

Campbeltown

Kintyre

Sandwood
Bay
Durness

Kinlochbervie

Ben Hope
(927m) ▲

Ben More
Assynt (998m) ▲

Lochinver

The
Minch

Loch
Shin

Loch
Ewe

Ullapool

Loch
Torridon

Gairloch

Beinn Dearg
(1084m) ▲

Melvich
Tongue

Bettyhill

Bonar
Bridge

Brora
Dornoch
Firth

Helmsdale

Thurso
Scrabster
Dounreay

John
o'Groats

Wick

NORTH
SEA

Invergordon

Dingwall

Nairn

Inverness

Loch
Ness

Moray
Firth

Elgin
Buckie
Banff

Fraserburgh

Rattray
Bay

Peterhead

Huntly

Fort
Augustus

Five Sisters
of Kintail (1068m)

Aviemore

Newtonmore
Kingussie

Grantown-
on-Spey

Cairngorm
Mountains
Cairngorms
NP
Braemar

Grampian
Mountains

A93

Aberdeen

Stonehaven

Ben Nevis
(1343m) ▲

Fort
William

Glencoe

Loch
Linnhe

Rannoch
Moor

Aberfeldy

Pitlochry

Dunkeld

Blairgowrie

Forfar

Montrose

Arbroath

Crieff

Perth
Scone

Dundee

St Andrews

Cupar

Loch
Awe

Tarbet

Loch
Lomond

ARGYLL

Lochgilphead

Dumbarton

Dunoon
Greenock

A83 Bute

Lochranza

Ardrossan

Kilmarnock

Ayr
Prestwick

AYRSHIRE

Girvan

Kinross

Stirling
Dunfermline

Kirkcaldy

Dunbar

Falkirk

EDINBURGH

Haddington

Glasgow
Motherwell

Lanark

Biggar

Peebles

Berwick upon
Tweed

Coldstream
Kelso
Wooler

Melrose

Jedburgh

Hawick

Moffat

Merrick(842m) ▲

Galloway
Forest
Park

DUMFRIES
&
GALLOWAY

Newcastleton

Hexham

Cairnryan

Newton
Stewart

Dumfries

Brampton

Lough
Foyle

Coleraine

Derry

Strabane

Ballymena

Larne

North
Channel

Stranraer

Kirkcudbright

Solway
Firth

A75

Carlisle

ENGLAND

Lough
Swilly

NORTHERN
IRELAND

Bangor

Lough
Neagh BELFAST

IRISH SEA

Workington

M6

Kirkwall

Orkney
Islands
Mainland

Stromness

Hoy

South
Ronaldsay

Westray
Westray
Firth
Eday

Sanday
Sanday
Sound

Stronsay
Firth
Stronsay

BRITAIN

With its giant new parliament complex (opened in Edinburgh in October 2004) symbolising the country's increasing independence from its historic overlord to the south, Scotland should never be just a rushed addition to an England trip. With a proud and vital national identity that goes way beyond bagpipes and haggis, it's the most distinctive region of Britain.

EDINBURGH

☎ 0131 / pop 440,000

On the surface, Edinburgh is a foppish dandy compared to Glasgow, its earthy rival to the west. But its streets of Georgian townhouses, superb museums and looming castle make the country's capital a great first stop north of Hadrian's Wall. Visitor-friendly, with attractions, restaurants and accommodation for every budget, there's also plenty of history to get your teeth into: every building seems to have its own ghost story.

ORIENTATION

Arthur's Seat, the 251m rocky peak southeast of the centre, and the castle are Edinburgh's most distinctive landmarks. The Old and New Towns are separated by Princes Street Gardens, and the Royal Mile is the Old Town's main thoroughfare. The bus station is in the New Town near St Andrew Square.

INFORMATION

American Express (☎ 718 2501; 69 George St; ☻ 9am-5pm Mon-Fri, 9.30am-5pm Wed, 9am-5pm Sat)
easyEverything (☎ 220 3580; 58 Rose St; per hr £1.60; ☻ 8am-10.30pm) Internet access.
Edinburgh & Scotland Information Centre (☎ 0845 225 5121; www.edinburgh.org; 3 Princes St; ☻ 9am-5pm Sep-Jun, 9am-8pm Jul & Aug)
Edinburgh Royal Infirmary (☎ 536 1000; 51 Little France Cres, Old Dalkeith Rd) Medical assistance.

SIGHTS
Edinburgh Castle

The hill-top complex of **Edinburgh Castle** (☎ 225 9846; Castle Hill; adult/concession £9.50/7; ☻ 9.30am-6pm Apr-Oct, 9.30am-5pm Nov-Mar) should be any visitor's first stop. It's a hodgepodge of architectural styles, representing centuries of myriad uses, and includes the Romanesque 11th-century **St Margaret's Chapel**. The castle's darker history is recorded in its

Prisoners of War exhibition, where disembodied wails permeate the shadows.

Real Mary King Close

A once plague-ridden nest of streets comes back to life at the **Real Mary King Close** (☎ 430160; 2 Warriston's Cl, High St; adult/concession £7/6; ☻ 10am-9pm Apr-Oct, 10am-4pm Nov-Mar), a fascinating underground tour through the lives of the residents who once lived here. A great crash course in Edinburgh history, it's not recommended for claustrophobes.

Palace of Holyroodhouse

The **Palace of Holyroodhouse** (☎ 556 5100; Canongate; adult/concession £8/6; ☻ 9.30am-6pm Apr-Oct, 9.30am-4.30pm Nov-Mar) is a beautiful baroque confection mostly dating from Charles II's reconstruction in 1671. It's the official Scottish residence of the British royal family – which means it's closed when the Queen turns up. Don't miss the extraordinary plaster ceiling and Brussels tapestries in the **State Apartments**. Nearby is the new **Scottish Parliament**. Controversially way over budget and behind schedule, this slick modern complex is scheduled to open in late 2004. Tours will be offered to visitors but there'll be a charge.

National Gallery of Scotland

Edinburgh has five national galleries, linked by a free bus. First stop for many is the **National Gallery of Scotland** (☎ 624 6200; The Mound; admission free; ☻ 10am-5pm Fri-Wed, 10am-7pm Thu), a beautifully housed collection of European blockbusters by the likes of Titian and Monet.

Other Attractions

The **Scottish National Gallery of Modern Art** (☎ 624 6200; 75 Belford Rd; admission free; ☻ 10am-5pm Fri-Wed, 10am-7pm Thu) has an eclectic 20th- and 21st-century mix of works from Picasso and Mondrian to Brit Art faves like Damien Hirst.

The **Museum of Scotland** (☎ 247 4422; Chambers St; admission free; ☻ 10am-5pm Mon-Sat, noon-5pm Sun), housed in a modern interpretation of castle architecture, is an evocative exploration of the country's colourful history.

FESTIVALS & EVENTS

The **Edinburgh International Festival** (☎ 473 2000; www.eif.co.uk) annually takes over the city for three weeks of music, dance, drama and opera in August. The edgier **Edinburgh Festival Fringe** (☎ 226 0026; www.edfringe.com) also chooses

CENTRAL EDINBURGH

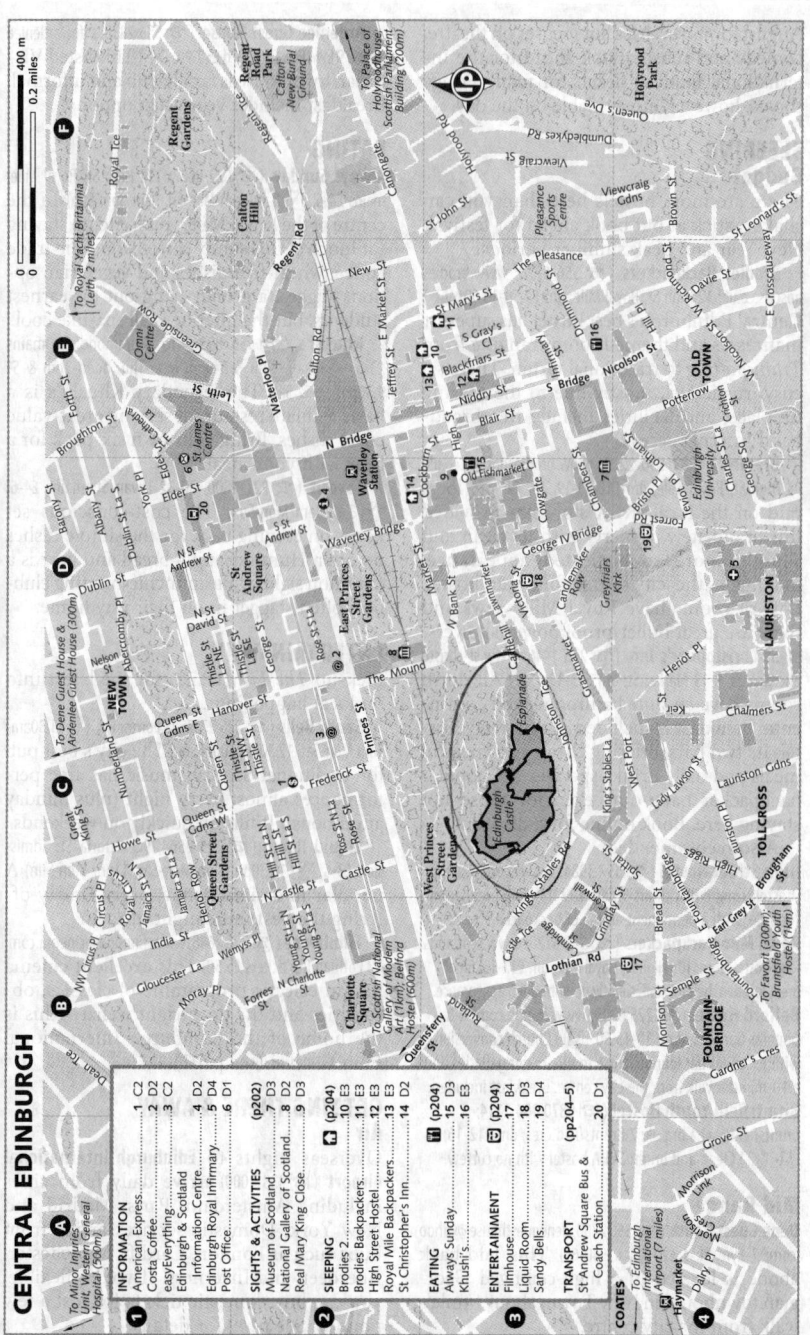

BRITAIN

0   400 m
0   0.2 miles

INFORMATION	
American Express...................	1 C2
Costa Coffee.........................	2 D2
easyEverything.....................	3 C2
Edinburgh & Scotland	
Information Centre...............	4 D2
Edinburgh Royal Infirmary......	5 D4
Post Office...........................	6 D1

SIGHTS & ACTIVITIES	(p202)
Museum of Scotland..............	7 D3
National Gallery of Scotland....	8 D2
Real Mary King Close.............	9 D3

SLEEPING	(p204)
Brodies 2..............................	10 E3
Brodies Backpackers..............	11 E3
High Street Hostel..................	12 E3
Royal Mile Backpackers..........	13 D2
St Christopher's Inn...............	14 D2

EATING	(p204)
Always Sunday......................	15 D3
Khushi's................................	16 E3

ENTERTAINMENT	(p204)
Filmhouse.............................	17 B4
Liquid Room..........................	18 D3
Sandy Bells...........................	19 D4

TRANSPORT	(pp204–5)
St Andrew Square Bus &	
Coach Station.......................	20 D1

August for its revelries but focuses on theatre, comedy and music. Book ahead for the International Festival; tickets for many Fringe shows, however, are available on the day.

SLEEPING
Budget

There are more hostels here than you can shake a stick at but book ahead for festival, New Year and peak summer periods.

Brodies Backpackers (☎ 556 6770; www.brodies hostels.co.uk; 12 High St, Royal Mile; dm £9.50-16.50; 🖳) Central Edinburgh's best hostel has superior mattresses and themed rooms ranging from *Trainspotting* to traditional tartan. There's a cosy, rustic feel, mostly due to the roaring fireplace, and facilities include free broadband Internet access.

Brodies 2 (☎ 556 2223; www.brodieshostels.co.uk; 93 High St, Royal Mile; dm £10.50-19.50; 🖳) A local raid on the local IKEA store has provided this brand-new property with its clean and slightly more sophisticated appearance, making it the city's first four-star hostel. Lots of rooms have Royal Mile views and there are great bullet-proof power showers.

St Christopher's Inn (☎ 226 1446; www.st-christo phers.co.uk; 9-13 Market St; dm £13-19; 🖳) All dorm rooms have *en suite* bathrooms and continental breakfast is included at this party hostel. Its two bars, offering cheap and cheerful meals and daily drinks specials, are popular backpacker hang-outs even for those not staying here. Book online for a discount.

Also recommended:

High Street Hostel (☎ 557 3984; www.scotlands-top -hostels.com; 8 Blackfriars St; dm £12-13) Ever popular and sociable, with a permanent aroma of backpackers' socks.

Royal Mile Backpackers (☎ 557 6120; www.scotlands -top-hostels.com; 105 High St, Royal Mile; dm £12-13) Small, great location, helpful staff, slightly downtrodden appearance.

Belford Hostel (☎ 225 6209; www.hoppo.com; 6-8 Douglas Gardens; dm £10-15.50; 🖳) Church conversion with excellent bar lounge. Close to two major galleries and a 10-minute walk from the city centre. Breakfast included.

Bruntsfield Youth Hostel (☎ 0870 004 1114; bruntsfield@syha.org.uk; 7 Bruntsfield Cres; dm £12-16; 🖳 ✖) Clean and bright SYHA hostel with no curfew.

Mid-Range

Dene Guest House (☎ 556 2700; deneguesthouse@yahoo .com; 7 Eyre Pl; s £20-35, d £40-65) This laid-back abode is located in a high-ceilinged Georgian townhouse in New Town, about 1 mile's walk from the city centre.

Ardenlee Guest House (☎ 556 2838; info@ardenlee .co.uk; 9 Eyre Pl; s £30-59, d £50-90; ✖) This listed Victorian townhouse is family-run and informal. Breakfast includes vegetarian options.

EATING

Always Sunday (☎ 622 0667; 170 High St, Royal Mile; mains £4-6; ☯ 8am-6pm Mon-Fri, 9am-6pm Sun) In the centre of the Royal Mile, you'll end up staying for lunch at this sunny coffee stop. Fair-trade coffee, wheat-free dishes and vegetarian options suggest a grungy hang-out for earnest students, but the interior is all spa-like cool.

Khushi's (☎ 556 8996; 16 Drummond St; mains £3-5; ☯ noon-3pm & 5-9pm Mon-Thu, noon-3pm & 5-9.30pm Fri & Sat) The legendary Khushi's is a basic Punjabi restaurant serving great-value curry dishes. Bring your own six-pack for a beer with your meal.

Favorit (☎ 221 1800; 30-32 Levan St; mains £4-6; ☯ 8am-3am Mon-Sun) The cost-conscious set keeps on coming back for the simple dishes on offer. Hummus, pitta bread and beer is a common sight, while munchie-hunting clubbers often stagger in on their way home.

ENTERTAINMENT

Pick-up *The List* (£2.20) for the latest info on local happenings.

Sandy Bells (☎ 225 2751; 25 Forrest Rd; ☯ 11.30am-1am Mon-Sat, 12.30-11.30pm Sun) The city's best pub for traditional Scottish music has free performances almost every night (plus Sunday afternoons). It fills up quickly on weekends.

Liquid Room (☎ 225 2564; 9C Victoria St; admission £3-5; ☯ 10.30pm-3am Mon-Sat, 11pm-3am Sun) A popular mid-sized venue, every Friday offering the best indie night in town.

Filmhouse (☎ 228 2688; www.filmhousecinema.com; 88 Lothian Rd; tickets £5.50) This excellent cinema has an eclectic programme of classics, obscurities and the downright weird – this is the home of the Edinburgh International Film Festival (see p202).

GETTING THERE & AWAY
Air

Overseas flights to **Edinburgh International Airport** (☎ 333 1000) arrive daily from cities including Amsterdam, Paris, Madrid and New York. Domestic services arrive from hubs such as London, Cardiff, Manchester, Aberdeen and Inverness. If you're flexible, you can buy domestic tickets for just a few pounds. See p149 for details.

Bus

National Express and Scottish Citylink services arrive from locations throughout the UK at St Andrew Sq bus and coach station. Citylink arrivals include Aberdeen (£15.40, 3¼ hours, hourly), Glasgow (£4, 1¼ hours, every 20 minutes) and Inverness (£15, four hours, hourly), while National Express services include London (£29, nine to 12 hours, seven daily), Newcastle (£14, three hours, three daily) and York (£28.50, 5½ to nine hours, four daily). **Megabus** (☎ 01738-639095; www.mega bus.com) runs from Glasgow (1½ hours), Dundee (two hours) and Perth (1½ hours), with fares from £1 (plus 50p booking fee).

Train

Up to 20 trains daily arrive from London's King's Cross (4½ to 5½ hours) but fares vary considerably (see p152). ScotRail runs two northern lines from Inverness (£32.90, 3½ hours) and Aberdeen (£32.90, 2½ hours), plus services every 15 minutes from Glasgow (£8.60, 45 minutes).

GETTING AROUND

Lothian Buses (www.lothianbuses.co.uk) operates an airport shuttle (one way £3.30/5, 30 minutes, every 10 to 15 minutes) from Waverley Bridge, just outside the train station, to the airport via the West End and Haymarket. Additional local services are operated by **First Edinburgh** (www.firstedinburgh .co.uk). Pick up a free *Edinburgh Travelmap* from the tourist office.

SOUTHERN SCOTLAND

The traditional buffer between the imperialist English and the Highland Scots, this region – the historic home of Robert Burns – is now a highly accessible tapestry of castles, stately piles, lush forest valleys and Scotland's largest city.

GLASGOW

☎ 0141 / pop 630,000

If Edinburgh is the historic heart of Scotland, Glasgow is its latter-day soul. Not as picturesque as its twee neighbour, it has an energy and vibrancy that can make a more rewarding visit for those delving beneath its edgier surface. Glasgow's reign as European city of culture in 1999 helped transform this maud-

lin industrial base into a metropolis boasting many museums and galleries, a lively arts scene and Scotland's best nightlife.

Orientation

The two main train stations (Central and Queen St), Buchanan St bus station and the tourist office are all within a couple of blocks of George Sq. Sauchiehall (sockyhall) St is a busy pedestrian mall with high street shops, pubs and restaurants. It connects with Buchanan St, another major thoroughfare.

Information

Gallery of Modern Art (☎ 229 1996; Queen St; 🕙 10am-5pm Mon-Thu & Sat, 11am-5pm Fri & Sun) Free Internet access in the basement library.
Glasgow Royal Infirmary (☎ 211 4000; 84-86 Castle St) Medical assistance.
Thomas Cook (☎ 207 3400; Central Station; 🕙 8.30am-5.30pm Mon-Fri, 9am-1pm Sat)
Tourist office (☎ 204 4400; www.seeglasgow.com; 11 George Sq; 🕙 9am-6pm Mon-Sat Oct-Apr; 9am-7pm Mon-Sat, 10am-6pm Sun May, Jun & Sep; 9am-8pm Mon-Sat, 10am-6pm Sun Jul & Aug)

Sights

GALLERY OF MODERN ART

Glasgow's **Gallery of Modern Art** (☎ 229 1996; Queen St; admission free; 🕙 10am-5pm Mon-Thu & Sat, 11am-5pm Fri & Sun) houses its highly accessible collection in a beautiful neoclassical building. Exhibits are designed to please both art lovers and those who would not normally set foot in a gallery, so humour is well represented.

ST MUNGO'S MUSEUM OF RELIGIOUS LIFE & ART

St Mungo's (☎ 553 2557; 2 Castle St; admission free; 🕙 10am-5pm Mon-Thu & Sat, 11am-5pm Fri & Sun) is a fascinating exploration of world religions that includes stained-glass windows, a magnificent bronze Shiva sculpture and Salvador Dalí's *Christ of St John of the Cross*. The **Gallery of Religious Life** illuminates disparate beliefs relating to birth, marriage and death.

GLASGOW NECROPOLIS

Looming above the nearby cathedral, Glasgow's **City of the Dead** (☎ 287 3961; Castle St; admission free; 🕙 dawn-dusk) is like no other cemetery in Scotland with its host of giant Victorian tombs built to house the great and good in the afterlife. A fascinating glimpse into the

GLASGOW

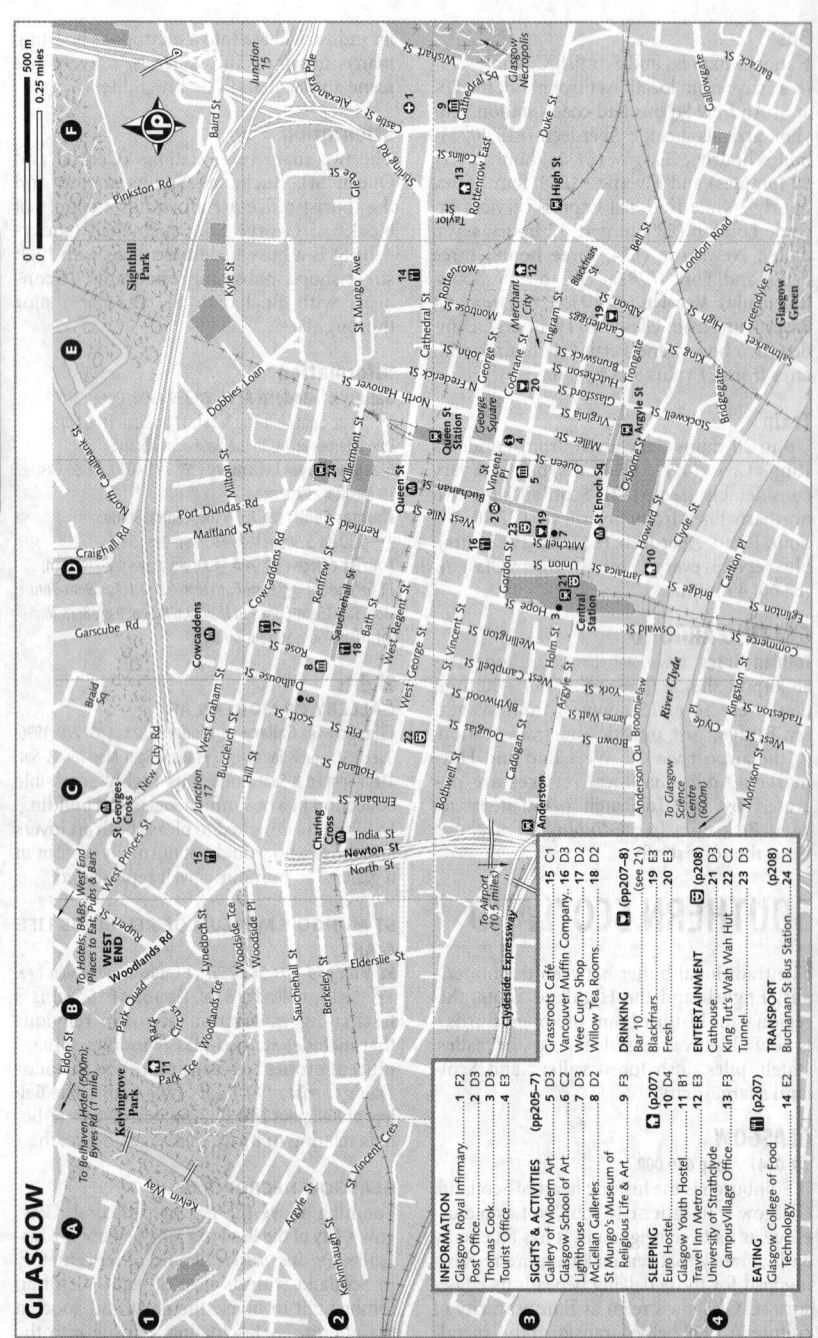

500 m
0.25 miles

BRITAIN

vanity of a bygone age, there are great city views from between crooked headstones.

THE LIGHTHOUSE

Exploring Scotland's unique contribution to contemporary architecture and design, the **Lighthouse** (☎ 221 6362; 11 Mitchell Lane; adult/concession £3/1.50; 🕙 10.30am-5pm Mon & Wed-Sat, 11am-5pm Tue, noon-5pm Sun) presents a kaleidoscope of revolving exhibitions on six modernised floors of the old Glasgow *Herald* newspaper offices. Celebrating the architect of the building, there's a permanent **Interpretation Centre** on the work of Glasgow design god Charles Rennie Mackintosh. See if you can spot any of his Art Nouveau cityscape flourishes around the area from the top-floor observation deck.

OTHER ATTRACTIONS

The **Glasgow Science Centre** (☎ 420 5000; Pacific Quay; admission £6.95; 🕙 10am-6pm) is a modern, hands-on science museum, while the **Glasgow School of Art** (☎ 353 4526; 167 Renfrew St; admission £5; 🕙 changeable, call ahead) is Mackintosh's greatest architectural achievement. The **McLellan Galleries** (☎ 565 4137; 270 Sauchiehall St; admission free; 🕙 10am-5pm Mon-Thu & Sat, 11am-5pm Fri & Sun) are currently housing art treasures from the Kelvingrove Art Gallery & Museum until 2006.

Sleeping

Euro Hostel (☎ 222 2828; www.euro-hostels.co.uk; 318 Clyde St; B&B £13.75-29; 🖳) Large, party-friendly hostel in a former student hall of residence. Twin, family and dorm rooms are *en suite* and prices are reduced depending on the number of guests per room. Good weekly rates and a 24-hour reception.

Glasgow Youth Hostel (☎ 0870 004 1119; 7-8 Park Tce; dm £13) Scheduled to reopen in summer 2004 after a fire in 2003, the city's only SYHA will have newly renovated facilities. It's always busy in summer, so book ahead.

Campus Village (☎ 553 1448; www.rescat.strath .ac.uk; Cathedral St; s & d £23-26; 🕙 Jun-Sep) A large, modern complex of student accommodation at the University of Strathclyde. Facilities are clean but basic with some rooms sharing bathrooms. Rates include breakfast.

Travel Inn Metro (☎ 0870 238 3320; glasgow.city .mti@whitbread.com; 187 George St; r £49.95) Brilliant location near George Sq for this cheery chain hotel. Family rooms with two beds and rooms for disabled guests are available at no extra cost, but book early.

Eating

Glasgow has some great cafés and some of Scotland's best restaurants. Check www .bestglasgowrestaurants.com.

Willow Tea Rooms (☎ 332 0521; 217 Sauchiehall St; lunches £3-6; 🕙 9am-5pm Mon-Sat, 11am-4.30pm Sun) Designed by Charles Rennie Mackintosh, this Art Nouveau café is packed at peak times so eat early or late to avoid the crowds. The afternoon tea is a local legend.

Wee Curry Shop (☎ 353 0777; 7 Buccleuch St; lunch £4.75; 🕙 noon-2pm Mon-Sat, 5.30-10.30pm Sat) Glasgow claims to be one of Britain's curry capitals and with this fabulous South Indian restaurant who can argue? With meals that would cost twice times as much elsewhere, the two-course £4.75 special is the city's best lunch deal.

Grassroots Café (☎ 333 0534; 93-97 St Georges Rd; mains £5-12; 🕙 10am-10pm) A laid-back vegetarian restaurant, its recommended comfort dishes include bangers and mash and some hearty daily soup specials. Try one of the organic beers –the delicious Lomond Gold's a winner.

Also recommended:

Vancouver Muffin Company (☎ 221 9253; 73 St Vincent St; mains £3-5; 🕙 8am-6pm Mon-Fri, 9am-6pm Sat, 10am-5pm Sun) Postcard-writing pit stop with great sandwiches to go.

Glasgow College of Food Technology (☎ 552 3751; 230 Cathedral St; mains from £3; 🕙 various hours daily) Restaurants staffed by students and open to the public.

Drinking

Glasgow has plenty of street cafés and is full of great pubs. Happy hour is *de rigueur* and often lasts longer.

Fresh (☎ 552 5532; 51-53 Cochrane St; juices & smoothies £2.50; 🕙 8am-7pm Mon-Fri, 9am-6pm Sat, 11am-6pm Sun) The centre's only fresh juice bar is a favourite haunt of Australian backpackers. Its Morning After beverage is recommended – an apple, orange, carrot and ginger concoction that removes all memory of the previous night's 10-pint booze-fest.

Blackfriars (☎ 552 5924; 36 Bell St; 🕙 noon-midnight Mon-Sat, 12.30pm-midnight Sun) Glasgow's best traditional pub attracts a healthy mix of locals, students and visitors. While some come for the giant meals (served until 7pm) or the live jazz, most are here for a few sociable beers.

Bar 10 (☎ 572 1448; 10 Mitchell Lane; 🕙 10am-midnight Mon-Sat, noon-midnight Sun) The brainchild of Ben Kelly, designer of Manchester's legendary Hacienda Club, this surprisingly unpretentious bar is superior to most of Glasgow's newer drinking holes. Capturing the essence of a metropolitan Euro-bar, there are drinks specials most nights.

Entertainment

Plug into what's on by picking up a copy of the *List* (£2.20).

King Tut's Wah Wah Hut (☎ 221 5279; 272A St Vincent St; 🕑 noon-midnight Mon-Sat, 6pm-midnight Sun) A deservedly popular live music pub where the early indie versions of Oasis and Radiohead started out. With shows every night, it also has good food with low-cost vegetarian options for those withered Morrissey fans.

For clubbers, the **Tunnel** (☎ 204 1000; 88 Mitchell St; admission £5; 🕑 11pm-3am Wed-Sat) is a mainstream good-time venue favouring house and trance where top UK DJs regularly appear. In contrast, the **Cathouse** (☎ 248 6606; 15 Union St; admission free-£5; 🕑 11pm-3am Thu & Sun, 10.30pm-3am Fri & Sat) is almost enough to make a Goth smile. This great alternative nightspot has two dance floors, the upper for hardcore mosh pit freaks, and an imaginative music selection that's almost matched by some of the wacky outfits on display.

Getting There & Away

AIR

Glasgow International Airport (☎ 887 1111) is 10 miles (16km) west of the city and receives flights from the UK and the rest of the world. Several no-frills airlines service domestic routes including easyJet, bmibaby and Ryanair (see p149 for details).

BUS

All long-distance buses arrive and depart from **Buchanan St bus station** (☎ 333 3708; Killermont St). **Silver Choice** (☎ 01355-230403; www .silverchoicetravel.co.uk) offers the best deal from London (£25, 8½ hours, one daily). National Express services arrive from London (single £29, 8½ to 10 hours, seven daily), Birmingham (£39.50, seven to nine hours) and York (£28.50, seven to 10 hours) among other destinations. **Scottish Citylink** (☎ 0870 550 5050; www.citylink.co.uk) arrivals include Edinburgh (£6, 1¼ hours), Stirling (£4, 45 minutes) and Inverness (£15.50, four hours). **Megabus** (☎ 01738-639095; www.megabus.com) runs from Edinburgh (1½ hours), Dundee (two to three hours) and Perth (two hours), with fares as low as £1 (plus 50p booking fee).

TRAIN

London Euston and London King's Cross trains arrive throughout the day but prices vary considerably (from £25) for the five-hour direct trip. **ScotRail** (☎ 0845 748 4950; www.scotrail.co.uk) operates the West Highland line north from Oban and Fort William, with direct links from Dundee (£21.60), Aberdeen (£32.90) and Inverness (£32.90). There are numerous trains from Edinburgh (£7.80 to £9, 50 minutes).

Getting Around

The No 905 shuttle (£3.30) service from Glasgow International Airport to Buchanan St bus station runs every 10 to 15 minutes throughout the week and half-hourly on weekends. The main operator on the city's extensive bus network is **First Glasgow** (☎ 423 6600; www.firstglasgow.com). For multiple trips, its FirstDay ticket allows unlimited all-day travel after 9.30am for £2.10.

There's also an efficient **SPT subway** (☎ 0870 608 2608; www.spt.co.uk) loop with 15 stops in the centre, west and south of the city. Tickets cost £1. For travel after 9.30am, there's an unlimited Discovery Ticket for £1.70.

SOUTHWEST SCOTLAND

Scotland's southwest corner has the region's mildest climate but it's a place of contrasts: from bare hills, moors and woodlands to ancient craggy coastlines. Ayrshire is immediately southwest of Glasgow, while Dumfries & Galloway covers the southern half. There are many notable historic and prehistoric sites linked by the **Solway Coast Heritage Trail**. You can find information and a route map via the Out & About button on the www.gretna-area.co.uk website.

The **Isle of Arran** offers perhaps the region's best walking country, with scenery including farmland dotted with sheep, rock-sheltered beaches, looming peaks such as **Goat Fell** and a coastal road that's perfect for cycling. The island's main **tourist office** (☎ 303774; www.ayrshire-arran.com; The Pier, Brodick; 🕑 9am-5pm Mon-Thu & Sat, 9am-7.30pm Fri, 10am-5pm Sun May-Sep; 9am-5pm Mon-Sat Oct-Apr) is in Brodick, along with a highly recommended **castle** (☎ 302202; admission £7; 🕑 11am-4.30pm Apr-Sep, 11am-3.30pm Oct). It's a magnificent 13th-century sandstone pile full of silver, porcelain and animal trophies. The nearby **Belvedere Guest House** (☎ 302397; stb@vision-unlimited.co.uk; Alma Rd; s & d £20-40) is a good B&B, while the closest **SYHA hostel** (☎ 0870 004 1140; dm £10.50-11; ☼ Mar-Oct) is 14 miles (22.5km) away in Lochranza.

Brodick is an hour's ferry ride from Ardrossan on the mainland (passenger/ car £4.70/33.50, four to six daily); **CalMac** (☎ 302166) operates the service. Six buses per day Monday to Saturday run from Brodick to Lochranza (£2, 45 minutes), with extra services around the island. Consider renting a bike from **Mini Golf Cycle Hire** (☎ 07968-024040; Shore Rd; rental per day £10).

CENTRAL SCOTLAND

An arm of land dividing the Scottish Lowlands and Highlands, Central Scotland includes some of the finest testaments to Scotland's rich military and ecclesiastical history. This is a great spot to get close to some spectacular castles – some blasted by age, others protected intact for the nation.

STIRLING

☎ 01786 / pop 45,000

With a fortress here since prehistoric times, Stirling has the most blood-drenched history of any Scottish city. On your way to the old town, take a detour to the **tourist office** (☎ 0870 720 0620; 41 Dumbarton Rd; ☼ year-round, various hours incl 9am-7.30pm Mon-Sat, 9.30am-6.30pm Sun Jul & Aug).

Stirling Castle (☎ 450000; adult/concession £8/6; ☼ 9.30am-6pm Apr-Oct, 9.30am-5pm Nov-Mar) rivals Edinburgh as Scotland's best castle. It's less crowded here, so it's easier to see yourself in centuries past. When the tourists have left for the day, head next door to the **Portcullis pub** (☎ 472290; Castle Wynd) for a wee dram.

Stirling Youth Hostel (☎ 0870 004 1149; St John St; dm £11.50-13.50; ☐) is one of Scotland's best SYHA properties, occupying a large old church building near the castle. The huge dining room/lounge area is a great hang-out, perfect for pulling up a chair for some inspiring postcard-writing views. Near the train station, the **Willy Wallace Hostel** (☎ 446773; www.willywallacehostel.com; 77 Murray Pl; dm £13) is cosy and welcoming.

Scottish Citylink buses arrive from Glasgow (£5, 45 minutes, hourly), Aberdeen (£14.50, 3½ hours, four daily) and Edinburgh (£6.20, one hour, three daily), while ScotRail trains arrive from Edinburgh (£5.50, 50 minutes, half-hourly), Glasgow

(£5.70, 40 minutes, every two hours) and Dundee (£12.70, 50 minutes).

ST ANDREWS

☎ 01334 / pop 14,200

St Andrews' history casts a long shadow over its cobbled streets. Scotland's former ecclesiastical capital, the ruins of a cavernous cathedral and a moody, seafront castle lurk on its outskirts, while the town's university, founded in 1410, is the country's oldest. Golfers flock here for the area's nine courses – especially the legendary Old Course, the sport's spiritual home.

Information

Costa Coffee (☎ 475986; 83 Market St; per 20 min £1; ☼ 8am-6pm Mon-Sat, 10am-1pm Sun) Internet access.

Tourist office (☎ 472021; www.visit-standrews.co.uk; 70 Market St; ☼ hours vary, incl Mon-Sat Oct-Mar, daily Apr-Sep)

Sights

Scotland's largest church, **St Andrews Cathedral** (☎ 472563; The Pends; joint admission with castle admission £4; ☼ 9.30am-6.30pm Apr-Sep, 9.30am-4.30pm Oct-Mar) was reduced to rubble during the Reformation in 1559. Half-eaten walls detail its past splendour while a visitor centre explains its turbulent history. A 12th-century tower offers spectacular views – look for the seals bobbing offshore. A short walk away is the ruined **St Andrews Castle** (☎ 477196; The Scores; admission & times as for the cathedral). Perched on coastal rocks, it's a great storm-watching spot.

Sleeping

Golf nuts monopolise the town's accommodation throughout the summer, so make peak bookings well in advance.

Craigtoun Meadows Holiday Park (☎ 475959; www.craigtounmeadows.co.uk; Mount Melville; camping from £12.50; ☼ Mar-Oct) The region's best camping ground is only 1 mile from town.

St Andrews Tourist Hostel (☎ 479911; www.eastgatehostel.com; St Mary's Pl; dm £11-16; ☼ 7am-11pm) This place is clean and friendly and only five minutes from the bus station.

Meade B&B (☎ 477350; 5 Albany Pl; r per person £20) Also a popular budget haunt but only has one room.

Almost every house along Murray Pl and Murray Park is a B&B, with off-season prices from £25.

Eating & Drinking

Eating Place (☎ 475671; 177-179 South St; mains £4-7; ☺ 9.30am-5pm Mon-Sat, 11am-5pm Sun) A good coffee stop with a bewildering selection of sweet and savoury Scottish pancakes.

Brambles Bistro (☎ 475380; 5 College St; mains £5-10; ☺ 9am-10pm) This charming eatery has hearty comfort food including good vegetarian options.

Central Bar (☎ 478296; Market St) The town's top pub, with a lip-smacking array of Scottish ales to keep locals and visitors merry.

Ma Bells (☎ 472611; 40 The Scores) This subterranean hot spot is where students and backpackers spend most of their drinking time.

Getting There & Around

Leuchars, the nearest train station (trains from Edinburgh, Dundee, Aberdeen, Inverness), is a £1.75 (No 96 or 99) bus ride away. **Stagecoach Fife** (☎ 01592-642394) runs buses from Edinburgh (£6, two hours, hourly) and Dundee (£2.70, 30 minutes, half-hourly). **Spokes** (☎ 477835; www.spokes cycles.com; 37 South St; ☺ 9am-5pm Mon-Sat) rents bikes from £6.50 per half day.

EASTERN HIGHLANDS

A warty nose jutting defiantly into the North Sea, the land between Perth and the Firth of Tay in the south and Inverness and Moray Firth in the north, is filled with a cornucopia of landscapes. From broad, deserted beaches and craggy cliffs teeming with seabirds to tiny stone fishing villages and the bare shoulders of the **Cairngorm Mountains**, it contains Scotland's newest national park, as well as Aberdeen, one of its biggest cities. Check out www.visithighlands.com for more information on this spectacular area.

ABERDEEN

☎ 01224 / pop 205,000

With almost every building constructed from granite, Scotland's third-largest city is a symphony in grey – shiny and almost silvery in the sun but dull and depressing when the blustery rain rolls in.

Aberdeen's Union St is the city's main thoroughfare. The train and bus stations are next to each other off Guild St, and the **tourist office** (☎ 288828; www.aberdeen-grampian.com; 23 Union St; ☺ 9am-7pm Mon-Sat, 10am-4pm Sun Jul & Aug, with various hours throughout the year) is on the

corner of Shiprow. The Old Town is 1 mile north of the centre.

Sights

Aberdeen Maritime Museum (☎ 337700; Shiprow; admission free; ☺ 10am-5pm Mon-Sat, noon-3pm Sun) is a fascinating exploration of the region's long association with the sea. There's plenty of touch-screen interaction and also a replica of a North Sea oil rig. The nonreplica **Provost Ross's House**, the city's third-oldest home, is also here.

Sleeping & Eating

SYHA Aberdeen Youth Hostel (☎ 0870 004 1100; 8 Queen's Rd; dm £11.50-13.50) The imposing (yes it's granite) youth hostel is 1 mile west of the train station. It's clean and welcoming but a bit too clinical to be truly cosy.

Clusters of B&Bs line Bon Accord St and Springbank Tce (both near the centre), including the recommended **Dunrovin Guest House** (☎ 586081; 186 Bon Accord St; s/d £23/37), where the hearty Scottish breakfast includes vegetarian options.

Books & Beans (☎ 646438; 22 Belmont St; ☺ 8.30am-5.30pm Mon-Wed, Fri & Sat, 8.30am-8pm Thu, 11am-4pm Sun) Offers fortifying coffees combined with second-hand books, poetry readings and vegetarian meals.

Prince of Wales (☎ 640597; 7 St Nicholas Lane; mains £5) For a cheap and cheerful lunch, head to the Prince of Wales, which pours some great Scottish ales to help the chips slip down.

Ashvale Fish Restaurant (☎ 596581; 42-48 Great Western Rd; mains £6-9, takeaway £3; ☺ 11.45am-11pm) Fresh fried fish is on the menu at this fish-and-chip joint of distinction.

Getting There & Away

Some 6 miles (9.5km) northeast of the city, **Aberdeen Airport** (☎ 722331) handles domestic and European flights. There are also regular but expensive **Loganair** (01856-872494; www.loganair .co.uk) services from Orkney and Shetland.

NorthLink Ferries (☎ 0845 600 0449; www.north linkferries.co.uk) services Orkney (passenger only from £14.75 one-way, car and passenger from £58.25 one-way, 10 to 12 hours, daily) and Shetland (passenger only from £19.75 one-way, car and passenger from £78.50 one-way, eight hours, three weekly).

National Express services arrive from London (£37.50, 12 hours, five daily) and frequent Scottish Citylink services roll in from Edinburgh (£8, three hours), Glasgow (£8, four hours) and other regions. Daily train services arrive from London's King's Cross (£98.90, 7½ hours), plus Scottish destinations including Dundee (£19.10, one hour) and Inverness (£19.90, 2¼ hours).

WESTERN HIGHLANDS

From Rannoch Moor to Fort William on the west coast, this is a wild and woolly region of mist-covered glens, ice-cold lochs and snow-frosted mountains, including Ben Nevis (1343m), Britain's highest peak. Fort William is the region's only town. The 95-mile (153km) **West Highland Way** between Fort William and Glasgow is a good hiking trail for moderately accomplished ramblers.

Fort William
☎ 01397 / pop 9500

An attractive base for exploring the mountains, Fort William is on the banks of Loch Linne. With a pedestrianised centre that's easily explored on foot, there's at least one of everything here – including shops, cafés, pubs and a **tourist office** (☎ 703781; www.discover -fortwilliam.com; Cameron Sq; ⊙ 9am-8pm Mon-Sat, 10am-6pm Sun).

The lively **Fort William Backpackers** (☎ 700711; www.scotlands-top-hostels.com; Alma Rd; dm £10-11; 🖳 ⊠) is a short walk from the bus and train stations and has impressive hillside views. **Bank Street Lodge** (☎ 700070; www.accommodation -fortwilliam.com; dm £10-12) has several room configurations and enjoys a more central location, while **St Andrew's Guesthouse** (☎ 703038; Fassifern Rd; r per person £18-24) retains many features from its former rectory days, including some stained-glass windows.

Scottish Citylink buses arrive from Glasgow (£11.80, three hours, four daily) and Edinburgh (£16.50, 3¼ hours, two daily). The impressive West Highland Railway runs from Glasgow (£18.70, 3¾ hours, three daily).

Oban
☎ 01631 / pop 8500

A summer holiday-maker hub, Oban is a traditional resort town combining pretty bayfront vistas with a raft of visitor amenities. The bus, train and ferry terminals are beside the harbour and the **tourist office** (☎ 563122; Argyll Sq; ⊙ Mon-Sat May-Sep) is in a former church nearby.

Oban Backpackers Lodge (☎ 562107; www.scotlands -top-hostels.com; Breadalbane St; dm £11-12; 🖳 ⊠) is less than 1 mile from the train station and has a welcoming ambience, including a hang-out-worthy lounge area. The SYHA **Oban Youth Hostel** (☎ 0870 004 1144; Corran Esplanade; dm £10.50-13; ⊠) is a little more institutional but has great views across the bay. There are several B&Bs along Corran Esplanade.

Scottish Citylink arrivals include Glasgow (£12.20, three hours, four daily) and Fort William (£7.60, 1½ hours, four daily). There are also three daily trains from Glasgow (£15.60, three hours). **CalMac** (☎ 566688; www.calmac.co.uk) ferries arrive from the Inner and Outer Hebrides.

NORTHERN HIGHLANDS & ISLANDS

While much of Scotland's outdoors is littered with crumbling castles, the Northern Highlands and Islands have uninhabited moors, glassy lochs and wind-buffeted coastal cliffs. Unfortunately, public transport outside the main centres can be as rare as a wild haggis sighting. Check in with the **Highlands of Scotland Tourist Board** (☎ 0845 225 5121; www.visit highlands.com) for travel advice.

THE CAIRNGORMS

The **Cairngorms** are as dramatic and demanding as any of the Scottish ranges, and the coastline, especially from Stonehaven to Buckie, is exceptional. With its excellent visitor amenities, **Aviemore** makes a good base – this is where hikers, bikers and climbers congregate to take on the Scottish outdoors, and it's the centre of the country's skiing and snowboarding action in winter. While the ski season traditionally runs from December until April, recent light snowfalls have seen closures as early as February. Check ski.visit scotland.com for the latest conditions.

The **Cairngorms National Park** (www.cairngorms .co.uk) doesn't rely on snow to show its visitors a good time. Combining wild mountain tundras and secluded ancient pinewoods, it's bursting with unique wildlife and lush colours year-round. **Aviemore Youth Hostel** (☎ 0870 004 1104; 25 Grampian Rd; dm £11.50-13; 🖳) is modern, well equipped and close to the tourist office.

BRITAIN

THE GREAT GLEN

A geological fault running from Fort William to Inverness, the Great Glen is the ruler-straight line that seems to slice right through the centre on maps of Scotland. It's long been used for navigation and as a route across country.

Inverness ✳

☎ 01463 / pop 44,000

The capital of the Highlands, Inverness has few attractions of its own but a stroll alongside the fast-moving River Ness is recommended. The **tourist office** (☎ 234353; www.inverness-scotland.com; Castle Wynd; ☼ 9am-8pm Mon-Sat, 9.30am-5pm Sun) has probably the best tourism bureau staff in Scotland. They can help with information on the entire Highlands and offer a currency exchange and Internet access terminal (£1 for 20 minutes).

No visit to Inverness is complete without a trek to **Loch Ness**, just 6 miles (9.5km) away by Citylink coach (return £6.90). Get off at **Urquart Castle** (☎ 01456-450551; adult/concession £6/4.50; ☼ 9.30am-6.30pm Apr-Sep, 9.30am-4.30pm Mon-Sat, 2-4.30pm Sun Oct-Mar) for some stunning views. If the weather's good, walk the 2 miles (3.2km) back to the bus stop in Drumnadrochit, where your search for Nessie can really begin. The better of the two Nessie exhibitions here is **Loch Ness 2000** (☎ 01456-450573; adult/concession £5.95/4.50; ☼ 9am-8pm Jul & Aug, 9am-6pm Jun & Sep, 9am-5.30pm Oct, 9.30am-5pm Easter-May, 10am-3.30pm Nov-Easter). It tells of the historic hunt for the scaly scallywag.

SLEEPING

Bazpackers Backpackers Hostel (☎ 717663; 4 Culduthel Rd; dm £9-11; ☐ ☒) Clean and compact with great views across the river. The homely feel is enhanced by a wood-burning stove and Poppy, the hostel cat.

Inverness Tourist Hostel (☎ 241962; 24 Rose St; dm £11-13; ☐) The town's newest backpacker option looks like an IKEA showroom, right down to the swanky fitted kitchen. Plus, there's a friendly band of staff.

Eastgate Backpackers Hostel (☎ 718756; www.eastgatehostel.com; 38 Eastgate; dm £9.50-13) A lively option with recently upgraded power showers and new metal bunks. With only 47 beds, it's quite small, until July and August when a 60-bed annexe is opened.

Also recommended:

Inverness Millburn Youth Hostel (☎ 0970 004 2227; Victoria Dr; dm £11.50-13.50; ☒) Large, modern property that's one of the SYHA's best.

Inverness Student Hotel (☎ 236556; inverness@scotlands-top-hostels.com; 8 Culduthel Rd; dm £10-12; ☐) Eclectic lounge and student house feel.

HoHo Hostel (☎ 221225; www.hohohostel.force9.co.uk; 23A High St; dm £8.90-9.90; ☐) Grunge comfort with free tea and coffee.

Bught Caravan Park & Campsite (☎ 236920; Bught Lane; camping £4.50-8) One mile southwest.

EATING & DRINKING

Castle Restaurant (☎ 230925; 41-43 Castle St; mains £4-7; ☼ 8am-8.30pm Mon-Sat) This cheap and cheery café serves heaping plates of comfort food providing enough fuel for a giant hike around the region. A backpacker favourite.

Hootannay Cèilidh Café Bar (☎ 233651; 67 Church St; ☼ noon-midnight) For a real Scottish knees-up, the Cèilidh can't be beaten. There's rip-roaring traditional music nightly on the ground floor and rock and comedy shows upstairs almost as regularly. Free entry throughout the week, there's a £2 charge, covering both floors, on Friday and Saturday.

GETTING THERE & AROUND

Inverness Airport (01667-464000) handles flights from London, Glasgow, Edinburgh, Orkney and Shetland, among others. National Express coach services arrive from London (£37.50, 13 hours, four daily), while Citylink buses arrive from Glasgow (£15.50, four hours, hourly), Edinburgh (£15.50, four hours, hourly) and other Scottish destinations.

There are several daily train services from London (£102, eight to 10 hours), along with services from Glasgow (£32.90, 3½ hours) and Edinburgh (£32.90, 3¼ hours). The picturesque Kyle of Lochalsh (£14.60, 2½ hours, two to four daily) line delivers passengers from the Isle of Skye bridge, while the line from Thurso (£13, 3½ hours, two to three daily) connects with the Orkney ferry.

Highland Country (☎ 710555) operates local buses. A Rover ticket costs £6 for unlimited one-day travel.

EAST COAST

A desolate region hardly touched by human habitation, the dominant natural feature here is the looming Sutherland mountain range. There are a few pretty coastal towns but most visitors make straight for the photo opportunity at John o'Groats.

John o'Groats
☎ 01955 / pop 510

For those who love tacky tourist traps, John o'Groats can't be beat. For the more sceptical, this spot is little more than an overdressed car park, even with its impressive sea views of Orkney. There are plenty of B&Bs here for those who want to stretch their souvenir shopping over a couple of days. Highland Country buses arrive from Wick (£2.30, 40 minutes, Monday to Saturday only, four services daily) and Thurso (£2.30, Monday to Saturday only, 40 minutes, five services daily).

NORTH & WEST COAST

The north coast from Dounreay to Ullapool is spectacular, with everything on a massive scale: vast emptiness, enormous lochs and giant mountains. Unreliable weather and limited public transport are the only drawbacks.

On the west coast, Ullapool is the jumping-off point for the Isle of Lewis; contact the **tourist office** (☎ 01854-612135; 6 Argyle St; ☼ daily Apr-Sep, Mon-Sat Oct, Mon-Fri Nov-Mar) for information. The coastline just keeps getting better round to Gairloch, along the incomparable Loch Maree and down to the Kyle of Lochalsh ('Kyle') and Skye. There's a **tourist office** (☎ 01599-534276; ☼ 9am-5.30pm Mon-Sat Easter-Oct) in Kyle, beside the seafront car park, but the nearest hostels are on Skye. Kyle can be reached by bus or train from Inverness and also by direct Citylink bus from Glasgow (£19.50, 5½ hours).

ISLE OF SKYE
pop 8850

Skye is a large, rugged island, 50 miles (80km) north to south and 25 miles (40km) east to west, ringed by stunning coastline and dominated by the magnificent Cuillin Hills. The main **tourist office** (☎ 01478-612137; Bayfield Rd) is in Portree.

The SYHA hostels most relevant to ferry users are at **Uig** (☎ 0870 004 1155; dm £10.50; ☼ Apr-Sep) for the Outer Hebrides (Western Isles) and **Armadale** (☎ 0870 004 1103; dm £10.50; ☼ Apr-Sep) for Mallaig.

Skye Backpackers (☎ 01599-534510; www.scotlands-top-hostels.com; Kyleakin; dm £10-12) The best independent hostel is this welcoming place a short walk from the Skye Bridge.

Rosedale Hotel (☎ 01478-613131; www.rosedalehotelskye.co.uk; Beaumont Cres; s £40-46, d £68-98) In Portree, this hotel is popular.

Portree House Hotel (☎ 01478-613713; Home Farm Rd; s £24-28, d £50-70) Also in Portree, and a great place for a good sleep and hearty meal.

The Skye Bridge toll costs between £5.70 and £11.40 per car. **CalMac** (☎ 0147-844248; www.calmac.co.uk) operates a ferry service from the mainland between Mallaig and Armadale (passenger £3, car £16.50, 30 minutes, eight daily). There's also a private Glenelg to Kylerhea service (☎ 01599-511302; www.skyeferry.co.uk) from mid-April to late October (pedestrian 70p, car and passengers £6).

OUTER HEBRIDES

The Outer Hebrides (Western Isles) are bleak and remote. The gale-force climate is fierce and it rains more than 250 days of the year. But many find the stark beauty and isolated world of the crofters captivating. Check out www.visithebrides.com for resources.

Lewis is reached by ferry from Ullapool, and its largest town, Stornoway, has a **tourist office** (☎ 01851-703088; 26 Cromwell St). On Harris (reached from Uig on Skye), the **tourist office** (☎ 01859-502011; Pier Rd) is in Tarbert. North Uist sports a **tourist office** (☎ 01876-50032) in Lochmaddy, while South Uist has a **tourist office** (☎ 01878-700286) in Barra.

ORKNEY ISLANDS
☎ 01856 / pop 19,250

Just 6 miles (9.5km) off the north coast, this magical group of islands is renowned for its dramatic coastal scenery, abundant marine bird life and plethora of prehistoric sites. Sixteen of the 70 Orkney Islands are actually inhabited, but Kirkwall is the major town and Stromness is the predominant port. Both of them are on Mainland, which is the largest island. Contact Kirkwall's **tourist office** (☎ 872856; 6 Broad St; ☼ Mon-Sat Oct-Apr, daily May-Sep) or visit www.visitorkney.com for pre-trip research.

Stenness, a short bus ride from Kirkwall or Stromness, is the most accessible spot for exploring prehistoric Orkney. Particularly recommended is **Maes Howe** (☎ 761606; admission £3; ☼ 9.30am-6.30pm Apr-Sep, 9.30am-4.30pm Mon-Sat, 2-4.30pm Sun Oct-Mar), a 5000-year-old earth-mound tomb. You can walk in and check out the engineering skills of the period and take a guided tour to find out more.

There's a good range of low-priced B&Bs in the area, especially on Mainland, and many small hostels dot the region. In Stromness, **Brown's Hostel** (☎ 850661; 45 Victoria St; dm £9-10) is popular and close to the ferry, while **Ness Caravan & Camping Park** (☎ 873535; camping £3.70-5.80) is a good option for tent-packers.

Getting There & Away

Loganair (☎ 0845 773 3377) has daily flights to Kirkwall from Aberdeen (£155, one hour) and Edinburgh (£186, 1¾ hours). **Northlink Ferries** (☎ 0845 600 0449; www.northlinkferries.co.uk) has routes from Aberdeen, Scrabster and the Shetlands, while **John o'Groats Ferries** (☎ 01955-611353; www.jogferry.co.uk) has a passenger-only run from the mainland.

Shetland Islands
☎ 01595 / pop 23,000

Sixty miles (97km) north of Orkney, the windswept, treeless Shetland Islands remained under Norse rule until 1469, when they were given to Scotland as part of a Danish princess' dowry. Visit www.shetland-tourism.co.uk for visitor information.

Bleaker than Orkney, Shetland is famous for its varied bird life, its rugged coastline and 4000-year-old archaeological heritage. There are 15 inhabited islands. Lerwick, the largest town on Mainland Shetland, is a base for the North Sea oilfields.

Contact the **tourist office** (☎ 693434; ☀ 8am-6pm Mon-Fri, 8am-4pm Sat, 10am-1pm Sun Apr-Sep, 9am-5pm Mon-Fri Oct) for information on B&Bs and camping barns, or stay at **Lerwick Youth Hostel** (☎ 692114; King Harald St; dm £11; ☀ mid-Apr–Sep).

Small ferries connect a handful of the smaller islands. **NorthLink Ferries** (☎ 01856-851144; www.northlinkferries.co.uk) runs services from Aberdeen to Lerwick and Kirkwall to Lerwick.

WALES (CYMRU)

Wales offers some of the best in outdoor adventures in Britain, with spectacular settings for hiking, cycling, surfing or just sunning on one of many beaches. In 1997 Wales voted in its first self-governing assembly in 600 years. The Welsh language is making a resurgence, especially in the North. There's an upbeat feel among the population and

young people are choosing to stay instead of head to bigger cities in Britain.

SOUTH WALES

Along with the traditional market town of Abergavenny, the southeast coast of Wales houses several historically fascinating spots.

Nestled in a beautiful valley is the breathtaking **Tintern Abbey** (☎ 051-562650; adult/£2.50/; ☀ 9.30am-6pm, shorter in winter), Cistercian ruins on a grand scale.

The **Big Pit** (☎ 01495-790311; admission free; ☀ 9.30am-5pm daily Mar-Oct, underground tours from 10am-3.30pm most days), near Blaenafon, closed as a coal mine in 1980. These days it gives you a chance to experience life underground, and the guided tours by former miners are highly recommended.

Cardiff (Caerdydd)
☎ 029 / pop 285,000

With a new stadium and the flourishing of the Cardiff Bay waterfront development, what was once thought of as a provincial backwater is becoming a destination in its own right. For information visit the **tourist office** (☎ 2022 7281; www.visitcardiff.info; The Hayes); free Internet access is available at **Cardiff Central Library** (☎ 2038 2116; Frederick St).

Cardiff Castle (☎ 2087 8100; Castle St) is worth seeing for its outrageous interior refurbishment. Revmped by the Victorians, it's more Hollywood than medieval. Nearby, the **National Museum & Gallery of Wales** (☎ 2039 7951; Cathays Park; admission free; ☀ 10am-5pm, closed nonbank holiday Mon) packs in everything Welsh but also includes one of the finest collections of impressionist art in Britain. The **Museum of Welsh Life** (☎ 2057 3500; St Fagan's; admission free; ☀ 10am-5pm), 5 miles (8km) from the centre, is a popular open-air attraction with reconstructed buildings and craft demonstrations.

The **YHA Cardiff** (☎ 0870 770 5750; cardiff@yha.uk; 2 Wedal Rd; dm £14.90) is in a hip student area; catch bus No 28 or 29. The lively **Cardiff Backpacker** (☎ 2034 5577; www.cardiffbackpacker.com; 98 Neville St, Riverside; dm from £15; P ⬚) is a five- to 10-minute walk from most sights in the city centre.

Famed Welsh singer Charlotte Church's mum runs the **Church Hotel** (☎ 340881; www.homepage.ntlworld.com/church.hotel; 126 Cathedral Rd; s/d/f from £25/45/55), or try the nearby **Town House** (☎ 2023 9399; www.thetownhousecardiff.co.uk; 70 Cathedral Rd; s/d £42.50/52.50; P).

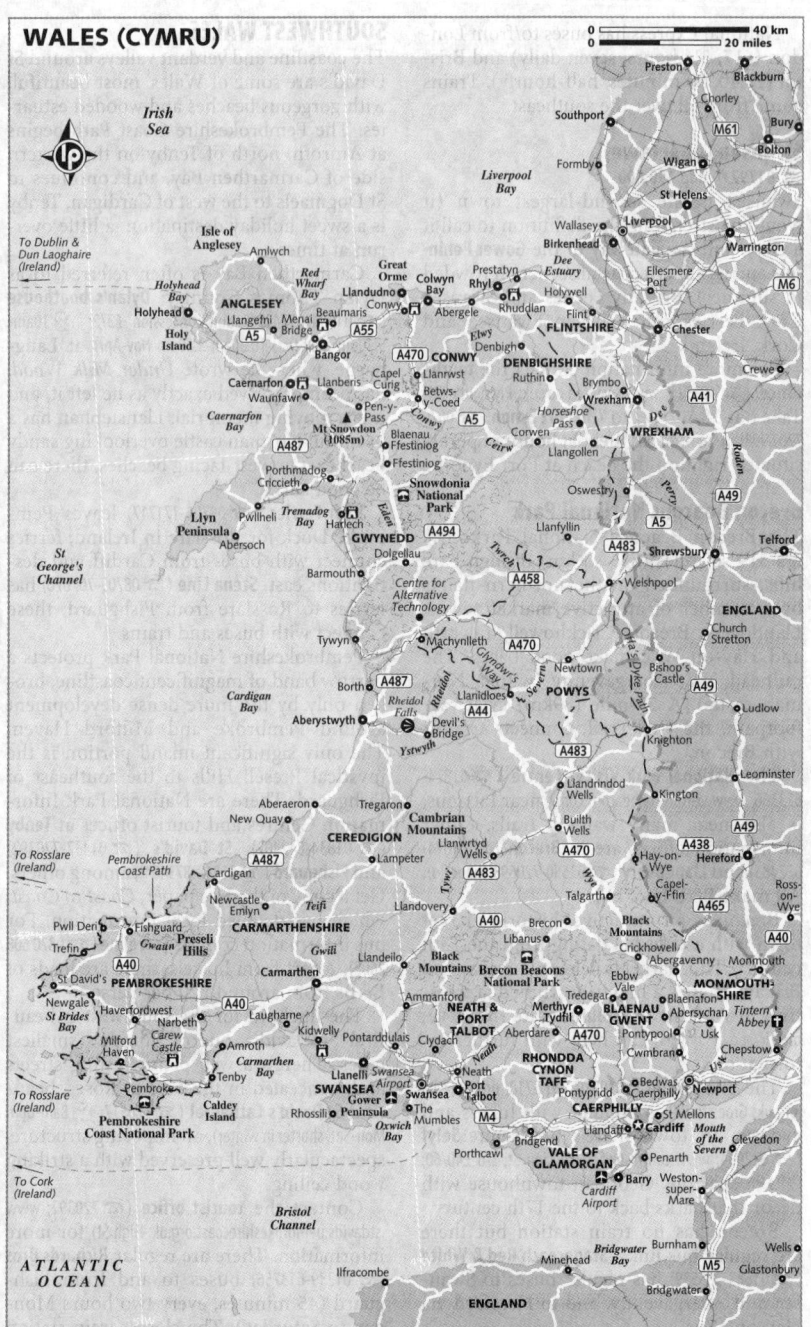

WALES (CYMRU)

BRITAIN

Irish
Sea

To Dublin &
Dun Laoghaire
(Ireland)

Isle of
Anglesey
Amlwch

Holyhead
Bay
Holyhead
Holy
Island

Llangefni
ANGLESEY
A5
Menai
Bridge
Beaumaris
Bangor
A55

Caernarfon
Llanberis
Caernarfon
Bay
Waunfawr
Pen-y-
Pass
Mt Snowdon
(1085m)
A487

Red
Wharf
Bay
Great
Orme
Llandudno
Colwyn
Bay
Conwy
Abergele
A470
Capel
Curig
Betws-
y-Coed
Blaenau
Ffestiniog
Ffestiniog

Prestatyn
Rhyl
Holywell
Elwy
Denbigh
CONWY
DENBIGHSHIRE
Llanrwst
A5
Conwy
Corwen
Cefni
Llangollen

Dee
Estuary
Flint
FLINTSHIRE
Ruthin
Brymbo
Horseshoe
Pass
WREXHAM
Wrexham

Liverpool
Bay

Southport
Formby

Wallasey
Birkenhead
Liverpool

Ellesmere
Port

Chester
A41

Crewe

Preston
Blackburn
Chorley
Bury
Bolton
M61
Wigan
St Helens
Warrington
M6

St
George's
Channel

Llyn
Peninsula
Pwllheli
Abersoch
Tremadog
Bay
Harlech
Criccieth
Porthmadog
GWYNEDD
Barmouth

Snowdonia
National
Park
A494
Dolgellau

Centre for
Alternative
Technology
Tywyn

Eden
Dysynni
Dwyfor

Glyndŵr's
Way

A483
Llanfyllin

Cerrig
A5
Oswestry

Berwyn
A458
Welshpool
Newtown
A470

Shrewsbury
Telford
ENGLAND
Church
Stretton
A49

Machynlleth
Borth
A487
Rheidol
Falls
Aberystwyth
Devil's
Bridge
Ystwyth

Cardigan
Bay

Rheidol
A44
Llanidloes
POWYS
Severn
A483

Offa's Dyke Path
Bishop's
Castle
Knighton
A49
Ludlow

Leominster

A487
Pembrokeshire
Coast Path
Cardigan
Newcastle
Emlyn

Aberaeron
New Quay
Tregaron
Lampeter

Cambrian
Mountains
Llanwrtyd
Wells

Llandrindod
Wells
Builth
Wells
A470
A438
Kington
Hereford
Ross-
on-
Wye
A49

To Rosslare
(Ireland)

Pwll Deri
Fishguard
Trefin
St David's
A40
Newgale
St Brides
Bay

Preseli
Hills
Gwaun
Teifi
Llandeilo
CARMARTHENSHIRE
Gwili
Carmarthen
Haverfordwest
Narbeth
Carew
Castle
Amroth
Tenby
Milford
Haven

Llandovery
Black
Mountains
A40
Brecon
Libanus
Brecon Beacons
National Park

Hay-on-
Wye
Talgarth
A483
Capel-
y-Ffin
Black
Mountains
A465
Crickhowell
Abergavenny
Monmouth
A40
MONMOUTH-
SHIRE

Laugharne
Kidwelly
Carmarthen
Bay
Llanelli
SWANSEA
Gower
Rhossili
Gower
Peninsula
The
Mumbles
Oxwich
Bay

Pontarddulais
Clydach
Swansea
Airport
Swansea
Neath
Port
Talbot
M4
Bridgend

Ammanford
NEATH &
PORT
TALBOT
Neath
Aberdare
RHONDDA
CYNON
TAFF
Pontypridd

Ebbw
Vale
Tredegar
Merthyr
Tydfil
A470
Cwmbran
Bedwas
Caerphilly
CAERPHILLY

Blaenafon
BLAENAU
GWENT
Abersychan
Pontypool
Usk
Newport

Tintern
Abbey
Chepstow

PEMBROKESHIRE

Pembroke
Caldey
Island
Pembrokeshire
Coast National Park

To Rosslare
(Ireland)

To Cork
(Ireland)

ATLANTIC
OCEAN

Porthcawl
Bristol
Channel

Ilfracombe

Llandaff
Cardiff
St Mellons
VALE OF
GLAMORGAN
Barry
Cardiff
Airport

Penarth
Mouth
of the
Severn
Clevedon

Weston-
super-
Mare

Bridgwater
Bay
Minehead
Bridgwater

Burnham
Wells
M5
Glastonbury

ENGLAND

CEREDIGION

0   40 km
0   20 miles

National Express has buses to/from London (£17, 3¼ hours, seven daily) and Bristol (£7.40, 50 minutes, half-hourly). Trains come from all over the southeast.

Swansea (Abertawe)
☎ 01792 / pop 190,000

Swansea is the second-largest town (it would be stretching the definition to call it a city), and the gateway to the **Gower Peninsula** and its superb coastal scenery (crowded in summer). Brittany Ferries and Swansea Cork Ferries run between Swansea and Cork, Ireland.

For more information contact the **tourist office** (☎ 468321; www.swansea.gov.uk; Plymouth St). Take bus 18A to get to **YHA Port Eynon** (☎ 0870 770 5998), a converted lifeboat house, superbly situated right on the beach at Port Eynon.

Brecon Beacons National Park
The Brecon Beacons National Park covers 519 sq miles (836 sq km) of high bare hills, surrounded on the northern flanks by a number of attractive market towns; Llandovery, Brecon, Crickhowell, Talgarth and Hay-on-Wye make good bases. The railhead is at Abergavenny (with a Norman castle). A 55-mile (89km) cycleway/footpath, the Taff Trail, connects Cardiff with Brecon.

The **National Park Visitor Centre** (☎ 01874-623366; www.visitbreconbeacons.com), near Libanus, is also near many walking trails. Other information offices are in **Brecon** (☎ 01874-622485) and **Llandovery** (☎ 01550-720693; Kings Rd). All make B&B bookings.

Brecon is an attractive, historic market town with a **cathedral** dating from the 13th century. The market is held on Tuesday and Friday. There's a highly acclaimed jazz festival in August. The **tourist office** (☎ 622485; brectic@powys.gov.uk) can help with further information.

The **YHA Brecon** (☎ 0870 770 5718; brecon@yha .org.uk; Groesffordd) is popular with hikers and cyclists. In town there's **B&B Cantre Selyf** (☎ 622904; www.cantreselyf.co.uk; Lion St; s/d £40/60; ✕), a spacious Georgian townhouse with décor that harks back to the 17th century.

Brecon has no train station but there are regular bus links. **Stagecoach Red & White** (☎ 01685-385539) has regular buses to Swansea and Abergavenny, and to Hereford via Hay-on-Wye.

SOUTHWEST WALES
The coastline and verdant valleys around St David's are some of Wales' most beautiful, with gorgeous beaches and wooded estuaries. The Pembrokeshire Coast Path begins at Amroth, north of Tenby on the western side of Carmarthen Bay, and continues to St Dogmaels to the west of Cardigan. Tenby is a sweet holiday destination, a little overrun at times.

Carmarthen Bay is often referred to as Dylan Thomas Country; **Dylan's boathouse** (☎ 01994-427420; adult/concession £3/2; ☼ 10am-5.30pm May-Oct, 10.30am-3.30pm Nov-Apr) at Laugharne, where he wrote *Under Milk Wood*, has been preserved exactly as he left it, and it is a moving memorial. Llanstephan has a beautiful Norman castle overlooking sandy beaches. On west-facing beaches, there can be good surf.

Irish Ferries (☎ 08705-171717) leaves Pembroke Dock for Rosslare in Ireland; ferries connect with buses from Cardiff and destinations east. **Stena Line** (☎ 08705-707070) has ferries to Rosslare from Fishguard; these connect with buses and trains.

Pembrokeshire National Park protects a narrow band of magnificent coastline, broken only by the more dense development around Pembroke and Milford Haven. The only significant inland portion is the mystical Preseli Hills to the southeast of Fishguard. There are National Park Information Centres and tourist offices at **Tenby** (☎ 01834-842402), **St David's** (☎ 01437-720392) and **Fishguard** (☎ 01348-873484), among others. Get a copy of the free paper, *Coast to Coast*, which has detailed local information. For bus information contact **Traveline** (☎ 0870 608 2608). Apart from hostels, there are loads of B&Bs from around £20 per person.

The linchpin for the southwest is beautiful St David's, one of Europe's smallest cities. There's a web of interesting streets and, concealed in the Vale of Roses, beautiful **St David's Cathedral** (☎ 720517; ☼ 8am-6pm Mon-Sat, shorter in winter), an imposing structure, spectacularly well preserved with a striking wood ceiling.

Contact the **tourist office** (☎ 720392; www .stdavids.pembrokeshirecoast.org.uk; High St) for more information. There are regular **Richards Bros** (☎ 01239-613756) buses to and from Fishguard (45 minutes, every two hours Monday to Saturday). The closest train station to St David's is Haverfordwest, from where bus No 411 runs hourly into town.

There are several handy **youth hostels**: near **St David's** (☎ 0870 770 6042); at **Trefin** (☎ 0870 770 6074), 11 miles (17.5km) from St David's; and the superb little **Pwll Deri** (☎ 0870 770 6004), on the cliffs 8 miles (13km) from Trefin and just over 4.5 miles (7km) from Fishguard.

Fishguard is on a beautiful bay and is a good base for outdoor adventure holidays. The train station and harbour (for ferries to Rosslare) are at Goodwick, a 20-minute walk from the town proper.

There's a **tourist office** (☎ 873484; fishguard@pembrokeshire.gov.uk; ☺ daily summer), but the **Hamilton Guest House & Backpackers Lodge** (☎ 874797; www.fishguard-backpackers.com; 21 Hamilton St; dm/d £12/30) is even more helpful. The owner knows the area well and can set you up with the best surfing or diving in the area. Be sure to enjoy the sauna.

MID-WALES

If you're driving through mid-Wales or would like to see an outstanding array of alternative energy sources and green technology, stop by the **Centre for Alternative Technology** (☎ 01654-702400; www.cat.org.uk; near Machynlleth; adult/concession £7.20/5.10 summer, £5.20/4.10 winter; ☺ 10am-5pm, closes 4pm winter). Anyone remotely interested in sustainable living and alternative energy will find a day's (or a week's) worth of exhibits and interactive displays. Courses and residential visits are available, and the centre holds many special events. It's a great place for kids. The centre is reachable by car, 3 miles (5km) north of Machynlleth on the A487 to Dolgellau, or by bus from the Machynlleth train station, accessible from Shrewsbury and Birmingham.

NORTH WALES
Llandudno

☎ 01492 / pop 22,000

This sweet Victorian holiday town somehow seems to keep some semblance of its 19th-century charm, although thousands upon thousands of visitors threaten its peacefulness. In summer, there's constant hustle and bustle along its crescent-shaped promenade and pier.

Llandudno is on its own peninsula between two sweeping beaches, and is dominated by the spectacular limestone headland, the **Great Orme**, with the mountains of Snowdonia as a backdrop. The Great Orme, with its tramway (£3.95), superb views and Bronze Age mine, is fascinating.

There are hundreds of guesthouses but it can be difficult to find somewhere in the peak July-August season. Contact the **tourist office** (☎ 876413; www.llandudno-tourism.co.uk; 1/2 Chapel St) for more information.

Snowdonia National Park

Popular with practically every sort of traveller, from mountain bike riders to families in caravans, Snowdonia offers a glut of activities for everyone. The most popular region is in the north around Mt Snowdon, at 1085m the highest peak in Britain south of the Scottish Highlands. Check www.visit snowdonia.info or www.snowdonia-npa.gov .uk for more information.

National Park Information Centres include those at **Betws-y-Coed** (☎ 01690-710426; ticbetws@hotmail.com), **Blaenau Ffestiniog** (☎ 01766-830360) and **Harlech** (☎ 01766-780658).

The beautiful, if crowded, hamlet of **Betws-y-Coed** is a lovely base from which to explore Snowdonia. The nearest hostel is **Capel Curig** (☎ 0870 770 5746), 5 miles (8km) west.

B&Bs and hotels are plentiful. The intimate **Henllys Guest House** (☎ 710534; www.jhaddy .freeserve.co.uk; Old Church Rd; r per person from £15) is a converted Victorian magistrate's court set next to the Conwy River.

Snowdon Sherpa buses (day ticket £3) run along the major mountain routes within the national park, with connections to Llandudno from Betws-y-Coed, to Caernarfon from Waunfawr, and to Caernarfon/Bangor from Llanberis.

In Llanberis, you can take the **Snowdon Mountain Railway** (☎ 0870 458 0033) for the ride to the top and back. The **tourist office** (☎ 870765; llanberis.tic@gwynedd.gov.uk; 41A High St) is helpful.

The best hostel in the area is the **Pen-y-Pass Youth Hostel** (☎ 0870 770 5990), 6 miles (9.5km) up the valley in a spectacular site at the start of one of the paths up Snowdon. **Pete's Eats** (☎ 870358) is a warm café opposite the tourist office where hikers swap information over large portions of healthy food. In the evenings, climbers hang out in the **Heights** (☎ 871179), a hotel with a pub and restaurant that even has its own climbing wall.

BRITAIN DIRECTORY

ACCOMMODATION

For most visitors to Britain, accommodation is their single biggest expense; even the cost of pitching your tent at a camping ground can be relatively high. Staying in hostels, university accommodation or B&Bs helps keep costs down, although not all B&Bs are budget-priced. In the mid-range, more characterful B&Bs share the bed with guesthouses, small hotels and a growing band of chain hotels offering good-quality, flat-rate rooms in and around city centres. Most towns and cities also have larger hotels, sometimes occupying grand converted castles or mansions, for a high-end splurge.

Remember that many tourist offices will search for and book accommodation for you ahead of your arrival if you tell them your budget and what you're looking for. The service is sometimes free but usually costs around £3.

B&Bs, Guesthouses & Hotels

A great British institution and often the best-value accommodation in town, B&Bs can range from £15 per person for a bedroom in a family home to more than £50 for a warm and fuzzy stay in a characterful old house that you won't want to leave. The common link is the heaping cooked breakfast that's intended to keep you fuelled until well into the afternoon. Solo travellers are unfortunately not well catered for in many B&Bs: single rooms are in short supply and can attract an ugly premium.

Guesthouses are a stepping stone between B&Bs and hotels. They're often large houses converted to resemble small hotels and prices range towards the higher end of the B&B scale.

Hotels can range from small-pub accommodation (£15 to £50) to a night of a luxury in a giant converted castle (upwards of £80). In between are a plethora of chains, including **Travelodge** (www.travelodge.co.uk), **Ibis** (www.ibishotel.com) and **Travel Inn** (www.travelinn.co.uk), providing good-value rooms for flat rates ranging from £39 to £69 per room per night. These are often located in city centres.

There are several competing grading systems for B&Bs, guesthouses and hotels, all of which are voluntary and some of which

are paid for. While tourist offices only recommend accommodation that pays them a fee to be listed, these are always of an acceptable standard and a safe bet when you arrive in an unfamiliar region.

Camping

Free camping is rarely possible, except in Scotland. There are hundreds of official camping grounds sites throughout Britain, with pitches usually running from £3 to £15 per night. *AA Caravan and Camping in Britain* (£9.99) is a comprehensive listing of these sites and is available in most bookshops.

Hostels

There are separate Youth Hostel Associations for **England & Wales** (☎ 0870 770 8868; www.yha.org.uk) and **Scotland** (☎ 0870 155 3255; www.syha.org.uk) but membership of one organisation gives you access to the other's accommodation. European Community residents can join in England for £14 (£7 for under-18s) or in Scotland for £6 (£2.50 for under-17s), while overseas visitors who are not members of a YHA in their home country can join after six nights' residency.

Dorm beds in YHA and SYHA hostels range from £7 to £16 per night and there's a free Book a Bed Ahead scheme, which is highly recommended in summer. Not all hostels are open throughout the year and some also have curfews and are closed during the day. Check the Web, call ahead for details or pick up the useful free brochures covering all English or Scottish hostels available from larger tourist offices.

There is also a growing number of independent hostels, particularly in large cities. Membership is not required and while dorms are still the norm, these hostels sometimes also offer good-value double or single rooms. Facilities and prices (typically from £8 to £23) vary widely: some are quiet and cosy while others are for serious party travellers. Check websites or pick up the useful *Independent Hostel Guide* (£4.95) from bookshops.

Rental Accommodation

Booking a self-catering, picture-postcard cottage in the British countryside can be one of the most cost-effective ways to experience a region. Prices, which start from £200 per week, are particularly appealing if you are travelling in a group of four or more. An online search will uncover dozens of rental agencies. **English Country Cottages** (☎ 01328-864041; www.english-country-cottages .co.uk) and **Cottages 4 You** (☎ 0870-078 2100; www .cottages4you.co.uk) are good starting places, but you can also order a free copy of *Self-catering Holiday Homes* from **Visit Britain** (www .visitbritain.com).

Universities

Many universities offer student accommodation to visitors during Christmas, Easter and summer holidays. Usually in basic, single study rooms, B&B here ranges from £17 to £35 per person. For more information, contact **Venuemasters** (☎ 0114-249 3090; www .venuemasters.com), which represents 100 British universities, or call campuses directly.

ACTIVITIES

Britain is a great destination for outdoor enthusiasts, from daredevil rock climbers to beach-bum surfer dudes and leisurely day hikers. There are clubs and associations across the land and useful brochures on many activities are available from **Visit Britain** (www.visitbritain.com/uk/outdoorbritain).

Cycling

Compact Britain is an excellent destination to explore by bike, but while not all cities are especially cycle-friendly, there are plenty of designated routes through some of the nation's best countryside. Popular cycle paths include the Yorkshire Dales Cycleway, the Trans-Pennine Trail and the challenging 1000-mile (1610km) Land's End to John o'Groats trail through western Britain. The **National Cycle Network** (☎ 0845 113 0065; www.sustrans.co.uk) administers a host of smaller routes, many of them one-day rides, and is actively expanding all the time. It can provide free maps and other resources. The **Cyclists Touring Club** (☎ 0870 873 0060; www.ctc.org .uk) is the leading national organisation for biking enthusiasts and can help with route information and general inquiries about cycling in Britain.

Hiring bikes is easy in many towns and cities, with prices typically ranging from £6 for a half-day to £60 for a week. Britain's roads are best cycled in spring or late summer – July and August can be very busy, so always book ahead for rentals. You can take your bike on many rail services but always call ahead to check because the regulations are complex and inconsistent. Bikes are welcome on many local buses but not on inter-city coaches operated by National Express or Citylink.

Hiking

Britain's cornucopia of picturesque terrains makes for great hiking country and there's an age-old tradition of experiencing the land on foot. Day hikes are a popular and accessible way to escape from the crowded cities and there are hundreds of longer routes, either marked or waiting to be created by adventurous travellers.

Popular hiking routes include the 191-mile (307km) **Coast to Coast Walk** (☎ 01609-882800; www.coast2coast.co.uk) which crosses three northern England national parks and the 84-mile (135km) **Dales Way** (☎ 01609-883881; www.thedalesway.co.uk) through Yorkshire's charming countryside. Other routes crisscross Exmoor National Park (p181) in Devon, Pembrokeshire National Park (p216) in Wales, and the highlands and islands of Scotland. Many of these are mentioned throughout this chapter.

The **Ramblers Association** (☎ 020-7339 8500; www.ramblers.org.uk) is a voluntary organisation with a wealth of experience and information on hiking and walking across Britain. It produces dozens of maps, guides and accommodation listings for local and visiting hoofers. **Visit Britain** (www.visitbritain.com/walking) also publishes a free folder of paths and trails.

Water Sports

Surrounded by water and dripping with lakes, lochs and canals, Britain offers a brimming bucketful of coastal and inland water-based activities.

Cornwall is England's surfing paradise, with ridable swells at more than 100 closely linked beaches, including Penhale, Droskyn and Holywell Bay. Scotland is also opening up to its surfing potential, with the north and west coasts proving particularly popular with visitors. The **British Surfing Association** (☎ 01637-876474; www.britsurf.org) should be your first stop for information and resources. Windsurfers can also check out their Brit-based options via the **Royal Yachting Association** (☎ 0845 345 0400; www.rya .org.uk).

BRITAIN

A 2000-mile (3220km) network of canals means that even budget travellers should consider the possibility of hiring a canal boat and cruising through Britain's inland waterways. If you hire a boat outside the high season, prices are quite reasonable, ranging from around £350 per week in April to £700 in August for a boat that sleeps four. Try **Hoseasons Holidays** (☎ 01502-501501; www .hoseasons.co.uk) and check in with the **Inland Waterways Association** (☎ 01923-711114; www .waterways.org.uk) for route information.

Britain has a rich naval history, so diving is also an eye-opening day out. With hundreds of shipwrecks strewn around the coast, some of the most popular wetsuit haunts are along the English south coast, where hapless medieval and WWII vessels reside together. The divable coast around St Abbs, Scotland's first marine nature reserve, is also popular. The **British Sub-Aqua Club** (☎ 0151-350 6200; www.bsac.com) offers courses and information for visiting divers.

BUSINESS HOURS

Standard office hours are 9am to 5pm Monday to Friday. Restaurants often open daily for lunch (11am to 3pm) then reopen for dinner (6pm to 10pm). Pubs typically operate 11am to 11pm Monday to Saturday and noon to 10.30pm Sunday, with some closing in the afternoon and others (particularly in Scotland) staying open later. Some late-opening pubs charge for entry. Shops open at least from 9am to 5pm Monday to Saturday, while a 10am to 4pm Sunday opening is also increasingly common with larger shops. Many also stay open late one night per week, usually Thursday or Friday. Some city-centre supermarkets open 24 hours.

CUSTOMS

There is no tax or duty on personal-use goods for those arriving in Britain from another EU country. Those under 17 are not allowed to import alcohol or tobacco, but others can bring in up to 3200 cigarettes, 10L of spirits, 90L of wine and 110L of beer. Those arriving from outside the EU can import up to 200 cigarettes, 1L of spirits, 2L of wine and £145 of other goods without paying tax or duty. Contact **HM Customs & Excise** (☎ 0845 010 9000; www.hmce.gov.uk) for more information.

DISABLED TRAVELLERS

While newer hotels, shops and attractions are wheelchair-friendly as a matter of course, there are many old buildings in Britain that are not. Wheelchair travellers are not well served by pubs, B&Bs and most public transit systems. The Travelodge and Travel Inn chains have well-designed rooms for disabled guests, particularly in their newer hotels, and many banks and ticket offices are fitted with hearing loops. The **Royal Association for Disability & Rehabilitation** (☎ 020-7250 3222; www.radar.org .uk) publishes an invaluable guide on disabled travel in Britain, while **Holiday Care** (☎ 0845 124 9971; www.holidaycare.org.uk) provides lists of checked and accredited disabled accommodation across the country.

EMBASSIES & CONSULATES
Embassies & Consulates in Britain

Countries with diplomatic representation in Britain include the following:

Australia high commission (☎ 020-7379 4334; www .australia.org.uk; Australia House, The Strand, London WC2B 4LA)

Canada high commission (☎ 020-7258 6600; Macdonald House, 1 Grosvenor Sq, London W1K 4AB)

France consulate general (☎ 020-7073 1200; www .ambafrance-uk.org; 21 Cromwell Rd, London SW7 2EN)

Germany embassy (☎ 020-7824 1300; www.german -embassy.org.uk; 23 Belgrave Sq, London SW1 8PZ)

Ireland embassy (☎ 020-7235 2171; 17 Grosvenor Pl, London SW1X 7HR)

Japan embassy (☎ 020-7465 6500; www.embjapan.org .uk; 101-104 Piccadilly, London W1J 7JT)

Netherlands embassy (☎ 020-7590 3200; www .netherlands-embassy.org.uk; 38 Hyde Park Gate, London SW7 5DP)

New Zealand high commission (☎ 020-7930 8422; www.nzembassy.com; New Zealand House, 80 Haymarket, London SW1Y 4TQ)

South Africa high commission (☎ 020-7451 7299; www .southafricahouse.com; South Africa House, Trafalgar Sq, London WC2N 5DP)

Spain consulate (☎ 020-7589 8989; 20 Draycott Pl, London SW3 2RZ)

USA embassy (☎ 020-7499 9000; www.usembassy.org .uk; 24 Grosvenor Sq, London W1A 1AE)

British Embassies & Consulates Abroad

British embassies and consulates abroad include the following:

Australia high commission (☎ 02-6270 6666; www .britaus.net; Commonwealth Ave, Yarralumla, ACT 2600)

Canada high commission (☎ 613-237 1530; www. britainincanada.org; 80 Elgin St, Ottawa, ON K1P 5K7)

France embassy (☎ 01 44 51 31 00; www.amb-grande
bretagne.fr; 35 rue du Faubourg St Honore, 75383 Paris)
Germany embassy (☎ 030-204570; www.britische
botschaft.de; Wilhelmstrasse 70, 10117 Berlin)
Ireland embassy (☎ 01-205 3700; www.britishembassy
.ie; 29 Merrion Rd, Ballsbridge, Dublin 4)
Japan embassy (☎ 03-5211 1100; www.uknow.or.jp;
1 Ichiban-cho, Chiyoda-ku, Tokyo 102-8381)
Netherlands embassy (☎ 070-4270 427; www.britain
.nl; Lange Voorhout 10, 2514 ED, Den Haag)
New Zealand high commission (☎ 04-924 2888; www
.britain.org.nz; 44 Hill St, Wellington 1)
South Africa high commission (☎ 012-421 7733; www
.britain.org.za; 255 Hill St, Arcadia, 0002 Pretoria)
USA embassy (☎ 202-588 6500; www.britainusa.com;
3100 Massachusetts Ave NW, Washington, DC 20008)

FESTIVAL & EVENTS

There are countless diverse special events
across Britain throughout the year, many
based on traditional customs initiated centuries ago.

January

Hogmanay (www.edinburghshogmanay.org) Huge New
Year street party in Edinburgh.
Chinese New Year (can be in February) Colourful London
parade.

March

Oxford/Cambridge University Boat Race Traditional
rowing face-off along the Thames.

April

London Marathon (www.london-marathon.co.uk) Giant
annual jog-a-thon.
Grand National (www.aintree.co.uk) Britain's top annual horse-racing event, held at Aintree, Liverpool.

May

English FA Cup Final Leading knock-out football club
competition. Held in Cardiff while London's Wembley
Stadium is rebuilt.
Cooper's Hill Cheese-Rolling Contest Competitors
chase a 3kg wheel of cheese down a hill.

June

Trooping the Colour The Queen's birthday is marked
with pomp and pageantry in London.
Lawn Tennis Championships (www.wimbledon.org)
World's leading tennis event, served up with strawberries
and cream, attracting the top tennis stars from around
the world.
Glastonbury Festival (www.glastonburyfestivals.co.uk)
Giant open-air music fest in Somerset.

July

Henley Royal Regatta (www.hrr.co.uk) Premier
rowing and posh social event in Henley-on-Thames,
Oxfordshire.

August

Edinburgh International Festival (www.eif.co.uk)
World's leading performance arts festival.
Edinburgh Fringe Festival (www.edfringe.com)
Comedy and avant-garde theatre dominates this alterna-
tive event.
Notting Hill Carnival (www.portowebbo.co.uk) Enor-
mous multicultural street parade in London.
Reading Festival (www.readingfestival.com) Popular
annual live music (and camping) fest in Berkshire.

September

Braemar Gathering Kilts and caber tossing attended
by the Queen (additional events held across Scotland June
to September).

October

Cheltenham Festival (www.cheltenhamfestivals.com)
Celebration of literature and books in the Cotswolds.

November

Guy Fawkes Night Bonfires and fireworks on the 5th
recall a failed antigovernment plot from the 1600s.
Lord Mayor's Show (www.lordmayorsshow.org) Giant
London street procession.

GAY & LESBIAN TRAVELLERS

Britain has an active and widespread gay
and lesbian scene with most major cities –
especially London, Brighton, Manchester,
Birmingham and Glasgow – having the
nightlife to prove it. Visit Britain operates
an excellent website of resources for gay
and lesbian travellers (www.gaybritain.org),
while the **Gay Britain Network** (www.gaybritain
.co.uk) website provides links to searchable
databases of clubs and bars and gay-friendly
travel options.

Gay Times, Britain's leading gay magazine, provides details of major happenings,
including the annual summer Pride event
in London. The **National Gay & Lesbian Switchboard** (☎ 020-7837 7324) provides a 24-hour
support service for residents and visitors
throughout Britain.

HOLIDAYS

While bank holidays affect most businesses
(increasingly excluding shops) in England
and Wales, they have less of an impact in

Scotland. The following are official public holidays in England and Wales:

New Year's Day 1 January
Easter (Good Friday to Easter Monday inclusive) March/April
First and last Monday in May
Last Monday in August
Christmas Day 25 December
Boxing Day 26 December

Scotland has fewer official holidays, although many towns set their own additional one-day holidays twice a year:

New Year 1 and 2 January
Easter (Good Friday to Easter Monday inclusive) March/April
Christmas Day 25 December

LANGUAGE

Britain has several regional languages, including Cornish, Welsh and, in Scotland, Gaelic. While everyone you will meet also speaks English, you should expect to see bilingual road signs and place names in many locations. There are also dozens of distinctive local accents and word choices that are unique to specific regions.

MEDIA
Newspapers & Magazines

Britain has a curious mix of some of the best and worst newspapers in the world. At the high-brow end, it's hard to beat the *Guardian, Telegraph, Times* and *Independent,* while the *Sun, Star* and *Mirror* continue to mine the bottom of the barrel. Blurring the old divide between the 'trashy tabloids' and the 'quality broadsheets', the *Independent* now publishes in the smaller format while the *Times* publishes in both large and small format editions. The tabloid *Sun,* complete with its topless Page Three Girl, remains Britain's top-selling newspaper. The magazine sector is equally diverse with *GQ, Vogue* and *Cosmopolitan* producing UK versions entirely different from their US counterparts.

MONEY

Britain is still holding out against adopting the euro, which is only accepted at some major tourist attractions and large hotels. The currency of choice here is the pound sterling (£), split among a variety of coins and banknotes each bearing the Queen's

image. Scotland also issues banknotes, which are legal tender on both sides of the border: if you have any trouble using them in England, exchange them at any bank. Most banks are open 9.30am to 4.30pm Monday to Friday, with major city centre branches staying open later and on Saturday mornings. For more information on costs and money see p28.

ATMs

It's not hard to find an ATM – usually called cashpoints – in Britain, where they're often located outside banks, building societies and large supermarkets. They accept a wide variety of cards, including Visa, MasterCard and American Express (Amex). Some cashpoints, particularly those in unusual locations like pubs, charge a £1 fee for withdrawals.

Credit Cards & Travellers Cheques

MasterCard and Visa are the most acceptable cards in Britain, with Amex and Diners Club not far behind. Thomas Cook and Amex travellers cheques are commonly used but don't rely on exchanging them at businesses since they are rarely accepted. Instead, bring large denomination cheques (in UK sterling) and cash them as needed at a Thomas Cook or Amex branch on your travels. Be aware that Amex offices are often located only in large cities. Banks will also change your cheques but will charge a small commission.

Exchanging Money

Be careful with *bureaux de change*: they may advertise good exchange rates but they frequently levy outrageous fees and commissions. The exchanges at airports are exceptions to the rule. They charge less than most banks and cash sterling travellers cheques for free. Always ask what the fees and commissions are before making a transaction.

POST

Most post offices are open 9am to 5pm Monday to Friday and to noon Saturday. Within the UK, 1st-class mail is quicker and more expensive (28p per letter) than 2nd-class mail (21p). Postcards sent overseas cost 40p (Europe) or 43p (outside Europe). Stamp vending machines are located outside some post offices.

STUDYING

There are thousands of language schools across Britain, not just the ones advertised on postcards handed out along London's Oxford St. Sadly, some are scams preying on impressionable wannabe-students. However, many schools belong to an accreditation scheme administered by the **British Council** (www.britishcouncil.org). It guarantees that teachers are properly trained and schools have the required facilities. **English in Britain** (www.englishinbritain.co.uk) provides a general introduction to the field, while the **Association of Recognised English Language Services** (www.arels.org.uk) is more specific about the classes and programmes on offer.

TELEPHONE

Call boxes are a common sight throughout Britain, although the beloved red telephone box has been largely usurped by a characterless steel and glass replacement. Most public payphones are operated by BT (British Telecom) and they take coins, credit cards, phonecards or a combination of all three. Coin phones do not give change and charge a minimum of 20p. Local calls are charged by time, while national calls are charged by time and distance: it's cheaper to call before 8am or after 6pm Monday to Friday or any time on weekends.

Mobile Phones

Codes for mobile phones usually begin with ☎ 07. Britain uses the GSM 900/18000 network, covering Europe, Australia and New Zealand. It's not generally compatible with North America. If you have a GSM phone, it's best to ask your service provider if it can be used in the UK. Consider buying a pay-as-you-go phone for as little as £50 for the duration of your visit.

Phone Codes

For international direct calls, dial ☎ 00 followed by the country code, area code (drop the first zero if there is one) and local number. Dial ☎ 155 for the international operator. For calls within Britain, dial ☎ 100 for operator assistance and ☎ 118500 for directory inquiries. The following are useful codes to know: ☎ 0800 – free call, ☎ 0845 – local rate call, ☎ 0870 – national rate call, ☎ 0891 – premium rate call

TOURIST INFORMATION

The British Tourist Authority now brands itself **Visit Britain** (www.visitbritain.com). Its website is stuffed with resources and it is ever eager to send brochures and information on request. **England** (www.visitengland.com), **Scotland** (www.visitscotland.com) and **Wales** (www.visitwales.com) also have dedicated tourism agencies. Britain has a good network of local tourist offices, although their opening hours and seasons vary widely. Some overseas Visit Britain contacts include the following:

Amsterdam (☎ 020-689 0002; britinfo.nl@bta.org.uk)
Auckland (☎ 09-3030 1446; bta.nz@bta.org.uk)
Dublin (☎ 01-670 8000; contactus@bta.org.uk)
New York (☎ 1 800 GO 2 BRITAIN; travelinfo@bta.org.uk)
Sydney (☎ 02-9377 4400; visitbritainaus@bta.org.uk)

VISAS

You don't need a visitor visa if you are a citizen of Australia, Canada, New Zealand, South Africa or the USA. Tourists are generally permitted to stay for up to six months, but are prohibited from working. The Working Holidaymaker scheme allows Commonwealth citizens aged 17 to 30 to live and work here for up to two years but arrangements must be made in advance via a British embassy overseas. Visiting full-time students from the USA are eligible to work in Britain for up to six months. Contact the **British North America Universities Club** (☎ 020-7251 3471; www.bunac.org.uk) for details. EU citizens can visit, live and work in Britain without a visa.

All other nationalities should apply for a visitor visa through their nearest British diplomatic mission. These currently cost £36 to £60. For more information, visit www.ukvisas.gov.uk.

Current worldwide security issues mean that immigration officials at all ports of entry are stricter than ever before. Be prepared to answer questions about your reasons for entering Britain and the date you expect to leave – show your outbound travel ticket if necessary.

Bulgaria България

HIGHLIGHTS

- **Veliko Târnovo** Medieval former capital atop a river bend, with biking, hiking, rock climbing and hill towns nearby, and a citadel right in town (p238)
- **Sofia** Bulgaria's humble modern capital sports the best bars and hostels; gravy comes in the form of a pet mountain, Mt Vitosha, just south (p228)
- **Plovdiv** Bursting with Roman ruins and cobbled paths, Plovdiv is Bulgaria's most relaxing city (p234)
- **Black Sea beaches** The stretch from historic Sozopol to Sinemorets is where Bulgarians go to avoid the resorts (p241)
- **Best journey** The 3km walk past (and atop) the sand-pyramid Pirin Mountains between Rozhen Monastery and the wine town of Melnik (p234)
- **Off-the-beaten track** The emptiest stretches of the Black Sea away from the resorts (south of Sozopol to wee Sinemorets) are Bulgaria's best (p240)

FAST FACTS

- **Area** 110,993 sq km (about one-third of Finland)
- **ATMs** Widespread, none in smallest towns (eg Sinemorets and Melnik)
- **Budget** 40-64lv per day
- **Capital** Sofia
- **Country code** ☎ 359, international access code ☎ 00
- **Famous for** Black Sea beaches, monasteries, yogurt
- **Heads of State** President Georgi Parvanov, Prime Minister Simeon Saxe-Coburg-Gotha
- **Language** Bulgarian
- **Money** leva (A$1 = 1.16lv, CA$1 = 1.26lv, €1 = 1.96lv, ¥100 = 1.43lv, NZ$1 = 1.08lv, UK£1 = 2.83lv, US$1 = 1.59lv)
- **Phrases** Zdrasti (hello), blagodariya (thank you), imati li..? (do you have..?), kolko

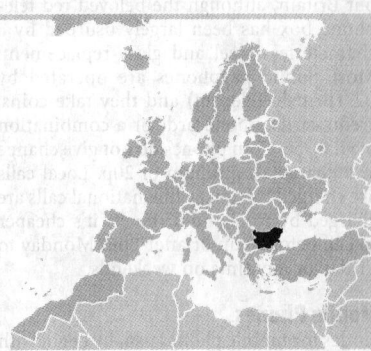

strubo? (how much?), oshte bira molya (another beer please)

- **Population** 7.97 million
- **Time** GMT/UTC + 2
- **Visas** Issued free on arrival for citizens of Australia, Canada, the EU, New Zealand, the USA and those of several other nations.

TRAVEL HINTS

Outside Sofia, Bulgaria has few hostels, so stay in private rooms (often 50% of the cost of a cheap hotel). As one Bulgarian warned, 'If you step on a frog, it'll rain', so keep away from anything that ribbets.

ROAMING BULGARIA

Start in Veliko Târnovo, off the track from Bucharest; go west via Plovdiv to Sofia and south into the mountains; or east from Veliko to the beach, based in Sozopol.

BULGARIA

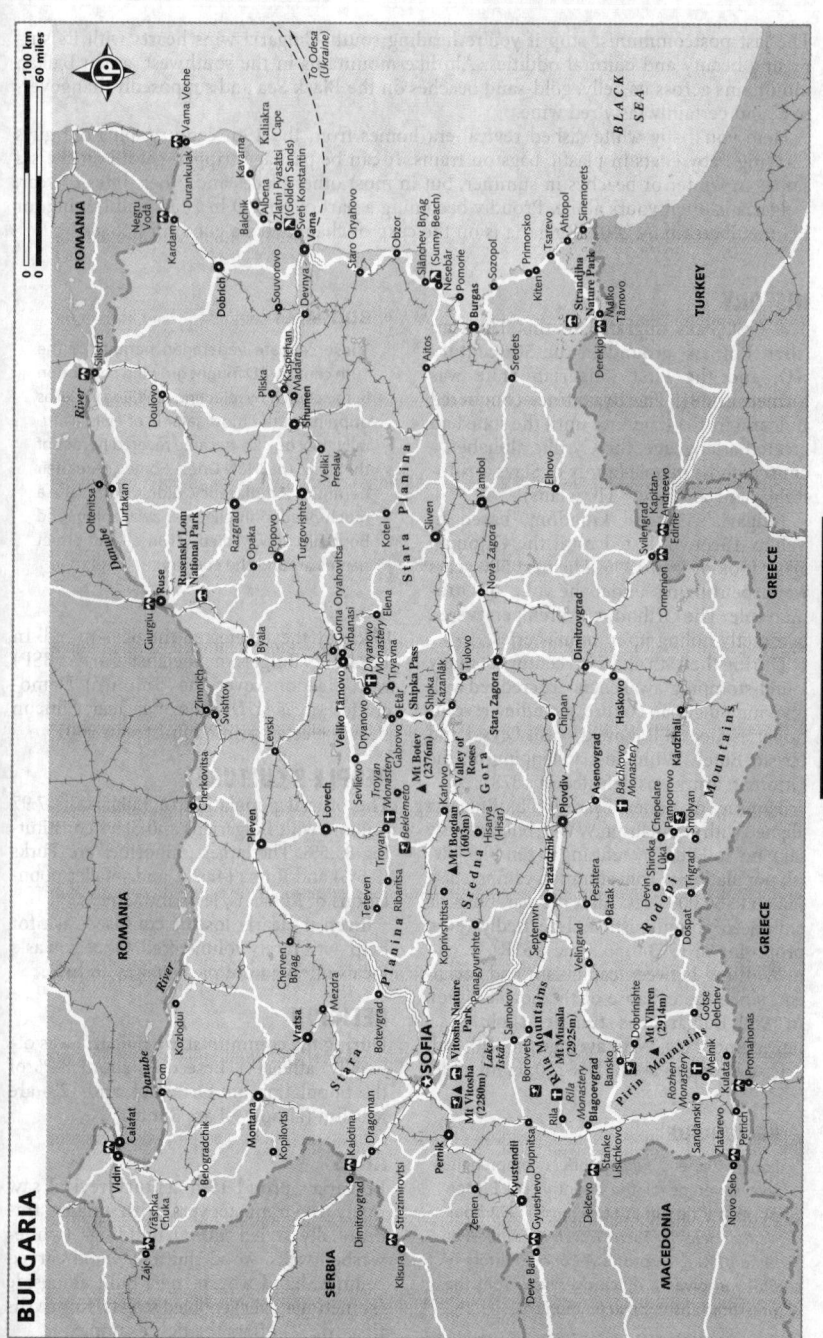

0 100 km
0 60 miles

BLACK SEA

To Odesa (Ukraine)

ROMANIA

TURKEY

GREECE

SERBIA

MACEDONIA

Vama Veche
Kaliakra Cape
Kavarna
Albena
Zlati Pyasatsi (Golden Sands)
Sveti Konstantin
Varna
Balchik
Durankulak
Negru Vodă
Kardam
Dobrich
Souvorovo
Devnya
Staro Oryahovo
Obzor
Slănchev Bryag (Sunny Beach)
Nesebăr
Pomorie
Burgas
Sozopol
Primorsko
Kiten
Tsarevo
Ahtopol
Sinemorets
Strandzha Nature Park
Malko Tărnovo
Silistra
Kaspichan
Madara
Pliska
Shumen
Dourlovo
Oltenitsa
Turtakan
Razgrad
Opaka
Popovo
Targovishte
Veliki Preslav
Rusenski Lom National Park
Ruse
Giurgiu
Byala
Gorna Oryahovitsa
Dryanovo Monastery
Arbanasi
Elena
Sliven
Atos
Siedets
Yambol
Elhovo
Svilengrad
Edirne
Ormenon
Kapitan-Andreevo
Derekoy
River Danube
Chervovitsa
Svishtov
Levski
Sevlievo
Veliko Tărnovo
Dryanovo
Troyan Monastery
Gabrovo
Tryavna
Bar
Shipka
Shipka Pass
Kazanlăk
Stara Zagora
Nova Zagora
Chirpan
Dimitrovgrad
Haskovo
Chipan
Zimnich
Pleven
Lovech
Teteven
Troyan
Ribaritsa
Mt Botev (2376m)
Beklemeto
Karlovo
Valley of Roses
Hisarya (Hisar)
Tulovo
Asenovgrad
Bachkovo Monastery
Kărdzhali
Stara Planina
Gora
Sredna
Kozlodui
Cherven Bryag
Mezra
Vratsa
Botevgrad
Kopivshtitsa
Panagyurishte
Septemvri
Pazardzhik
Plovdiv
Simporovo
Chepelare
Smolyan
Peshtera
Batak
Velingrad
Devin
Shiroki Lăka
Trigrad
Dospat
Zlatarevo
Mt Musala (2925m)
Mt Vihren (2914m)
Dobrinishte
Bansko
Rozhen Monastery
Gotse Delchev
Promahonas
Rila Mountains
Pirin Mountains
Rodopi Mountains
Mountains
Kalotina
Dragoman
Montana
Kopilovtsi
Belogradchik
Vidin
Vrăshka Chuka
Zaj
Calafat
Klisura
Strezimirovtsi
Pernik
Zemen
Kyustendil
Gyueshevo
Dupnitsa
Stanke Diitchkovo
Rila Monastery
Blagoevgrad
Mt Vitosha (2290m)
Vitosha Nature Park
Lake Iskăr
Samokov
Borovets
SOFIA
Deve Bair
Delčevo
Sandanski
Melnik
Kulata
Petrich
Novo Selo
Dimitrovgrad
Lom River
Lom

BULGARIA

The last postcommunist stop if you're heading south, Bulgaria wins hearts with its surprising beauty and cultural oddities: Alp-like mountains in the southwest, green Balkan mountains across its belly, gold-sand beaches on the Black Sea and supposedly 'hangover-free' and certainly tasty red wine.

Here you'll spy whitewashed revival-era homes from the 19th century, plus old guys carrying baby goats in plastic bags on trains. It can be package tripper–galore on the ski slopes in winter or beaches in summer, but in most other places and other times of year, Bulgaria is often yours alone. Proudly becoming a part of NATO in 2004, and hoping for EU membership by 2007, Bulgaria is on the cusp of change. It's a good time to go.

HISTORY

The first Slavs migrated to this Thracian (then Roman) ground in the 5th century AD, and the First Bulgarian State was formed in 681. The Byzantines conquered Bulgaria in 1014, but not until the state had created a language, the Cyrillic alphabet, a church and a people (a mix of Slavs, Proto-Bulgarians and a few Thracians).

Bulgaria's second kingdom, based in Veliko Târnovo, lasted until the Ottoman army took over in 1396. The next 500 years were spent living 'under the yoke' of Ottoman rule. The Orthodox church persevered by quietly holing up in monasteries.

During the 18th and 19th centuries, many laurel-stomping 'awakeners' are credited with reviving Bulgarian culture, including revolutionaries Georgi Rakovski, Vasil Levski and Hristo Botev. With Russia stepping in, the Ottoman army was defeated in 1878.

Hoping to annex Macedonia, Bulgaria aligned with Germany in WWII, but famously said 'no' to Hitler by refusing to send its Jewish population to concentration camps, sparing up to 50,000 lives. After the war, Bulgaria embraced communism full-heartedly (even proposing in 1973 to join the USSR).

Waffling between capitalism and socialism since the collapse of the Soviet Union in 1989, Bulgaria has stumbled slightly as a new democracy. With average monthly salaries dipping to about US$150, many older

> ### BOGOMILS
> These celibate vegetarian hermits of the 10th century AD fought growing corruption in the church by rejecting *anything* visual as dripping in the most satanic of evils. Naturally they quickly became revered heroes of their day: the 'Holy Ones'. Some argue their hermitic complacency didn't stimulate a much-needed intellectual awakening, and Bogomils slowly died off in all but street names around the country.

folks say they preferred the days in red. In 1994 the Bulgarian Socialist Party (BSP) won elections over the Union of Democratic Forces (UDF). Former Tsar, Simeon II, was elected prime minister in 2001.

PEOPLE & CULTURE

The official population of Bulgaria is 7.97 million, with Bulgarians and Slavs constituting 83.5%. The largest minorities are Turks (9.5%) and Roma (4.6%), and smaller populations of Russians, Jews and Greeks.

Even if clearly lost or confused, ask for help – it's rarely volunteered. Once you ask, locals often go out of their way to help.

RELIGION

During the communist era Bulgaria was officially 'atheist'. These days about 84% of the population are Orthodox and 12% are Muslim (almost all are Sunni).

ARTS

Bulgaria's proud 19th-century revival saw many town makeovers with quaint traditionally styled *kâshta* buildings (whitewashed walls, wood shutters, wood-carved ceilings, hand-woven rugs) built alongside (sometimes over) cobbled streets. Koprivshtitsa (p237) offers the best example.

> ### READING UP
> Lonely Planet's *Bulgaria* offers comprehensive coverage of the country. Bill Bryson pokes a little fun at Sofia in his 1992 book *Neither Here Nor There: Travels in Europe*. For history, RJ Crampton's *A Concise History of Bulgaria* gives a quick overview from the pre-Thracians to postcommunism.

'DA ILI NE?'

Bulgarians shake their head 'yes' and nod their head 'no'. Confusing at first, then fun. Just try to think that a shake is sweeping the floor clean ('yes, come in') and a nod is slamming shut a garage door ('no, go away'). If in doubt, ask 'Da ili ne?' (Yes or no?).

Bulgaria's most treasured art is on the walls of medieval monasteries and churches, such as the paintings by Zahari Zograf (1810–53) at Rila Monastery (p234).

The currently popular 'wedding music', aka *chalga* ('truck driver music'), is Turkish-sounding synth-pop with dumb lyrics. Essentially no-one in the country admits to liking Azis, a seriously flamboyant, sexually ambiguous *chalga* performer who sells more CDs than nearly any Bulgarian artist.

In recent years, Bulgarian folk singing has made a splash internationally. Every night you'll find folk music on a couple of Bulgarian radio stations or television channels.

ENVIRONMENT

Bulgaria lies in the heart of the Balkan Peninsula, stretching 502km from the Serbian border to the Black Sea.

The Stara Planina (Balkan Mountains) range stretches across central Bulgaria. In the southwest are three higher ranges – the Rila Mountains, Pirin Mountains and Rodopi Mountains. Bulgaria's Valley of Roses, around Kazanlâk, still produces most of the world's rose oil.

Although Bulgaria has some 56,000 kinds of living creatures, most visitors see little wildlife unless venturing deeper into the mountains, where they're likely to see bears, wild goats and deer.

Bulgaria maintains four national parks (Rila, Pirin, Rodopi and Central Balkans) and 10 nature parks.

TRANSPORT

GETTING THERE & AWAY
Air
Bulgaria's two most active airports are in Sofia (☎ 02-937 2211) and Varna (☎ 052-650 835), with summer charter flights reaching Burgas. There is no additional departure tax levied at the airport.

The airlines listed below fly to and from Bulgaria:

Aeroflot (☎ 02-937 3191; www.aeroflot.com)
Austria Air (☎ 02-980 2323; www.aua.com)
British Airways (☎ 02-945 9227, 02-937 3111; www.britishairways.com)
Bulgaria Air (☎ 02-937 3243, 02-865 9557; www.air.bg)
Czech Airlines (☎ 02-937 3175; www.cza.cz/en)
LOT Airlines (☎ 02-937 3161, 02-987 4562; www.lot.com)

Boat
You can ferry across the Danube River from Vidin or Ruse. In Varna, the ferry service to Odessa sometimes stops for a year off or so. Currently you can make the trip for about US$100 to US$120.

Bus
International tickets to the region (and beyond) are available at practically any bus station in the country. There's not one set price, so it's worth checking a couple of companies to find the cheapest fare.

Car & Motorcycle
Drivers pay a variable road tax (say you're going to the nearest big city) and €3 'disinfection fee' upon entering Bulgaria.

Train
Tickets for international trains can be bought at any **Rila Bureau** (www.bdz-rila.com/index-en.htm) or at some stations' dedicated ticket offices.

The daily *Trans-Balkan Express* (between Budapest and Thessaloniki, Greece) stops at Ruse, Gorna Oryahovitsa (near Veliko Târnovo), Sofia and Sandanski. A daily train connects Sofia with Belgrade and Istanbul.

The *Bulgaria Express* (between Sofia and Moscow) stops in Ruse and Pleven once weekly, or three times weekly in summer.

KEY BORDER CROSSINGS

Probably the most popular entry/exit is at the Ruse–Giurgiu border with Romania (en route to/from Bucharest); few buses cross the River Danube here, so most travellers go by train, enduring a 90-minute border check on both sides. Other key crossings are into Turkey, near Svilengrad or at Malko Târnovo–Derekoj near Burgas; and into Greece, south of Sofia at Kulata–Promahonas, and southeast of Plovdiv at Svilengrad–Ormenion.

BULGARIA

From mid-June through to September, a train service leaves Varna (and another Burgas) for Bucharest, Budapest, Bratislava and Prague. There is also a summer train connecting Bucharest with Sofia via Ruse and Gorna Oryahovitsa.

GETTING AROUND
Air
Hemus Air (☎ 02-981 8330; www.hemusair.bg) connects Sofia and Varna daily (one-way about €66), with extra flights in summer, when there are flights to Burgas (one-way about €40).

See p227 for airline contact information.

Bicycle
Traffic is relatively light outside the cities on many highways, but winding curves in the mountains and/or potholes anywhere can be obstacles.

Bulgaria has few bike-rental options (try Sofia, Koprivshtitsa and Veliko Târnovo), but most towns have bike shops that can make repairs or sell parts.

Bus
Unfortunately centralised information for schedules doesn't exist, and the schedules change frequently. This chapter lists the price and duration of a trip and the number of buses daily – *use these as a gauge only.*

Bigger bus stations have a confusing array of private bus booths advertising overlapping destinations. The public bus stops generally have a few windows and a list of timetables outside. In most cases, buses leave between around 7am and 6pm.

Most bus stations have a left-luggage service.

Car & Motorcycle
If you're 21 and have a driver's licence from your country, renting a car from a local agent can be a good way to beach hop or drive on mountain back roads (from €15 to €30 per day in bigger cities). **Penguin** (☎ 02-988 2163; penguin@einet.bg; Bldg 2, ul Moskovska 29, Sofia) allows some free drop-offs.

Train
Trains, all run by the Bulgarian State Railways (BDZh), are a bit cheaper than buses. *Ekspresen* (express) and *bârz* (fast) trains zip along at a speed akin to a bus, while the slow *pâtnicheski* (passenger) trains tinker along.

Listings in this chapter are for 2nd-class seats and off-season schedules. Check updated schedules at www.bdz.bg/eng/index _eng.htm.

Most Europe-wide rail passes can be purchased in Bulgaria, but they're not good value for getting around Bulgaria.

Bring food and water on board with you. Most train stations are signposted in Cyrillic. Nearly all train stations have left-luggage.

SOFIA СОФИЯ

☎ 02 / pop 1,114,000
With no real must-see attractions and a sometimes clunky layout, Sofia wins fans instead with hip happening bars and eateries, a gold-brick centre and the best 'pet' mountain (Mt Vitosha) any capital could ask for. Some visitors poking into its arty nooks stay for weeks.

Lived in by Thracians, Romans and now Bulgarians for up to 7000 years, Sofia was an outpost of 1200 residents when it became the nation's unlikely fourth capital in 1879.

ORIENTATION
Bul Maria Luisa runs from the train station to pl Sveta Nedelya; extending south of the

GETTING INTO TOWN

Sofia's main bus and train stations are across from each other, about 500m north of the start of the centre. Take tram No 1, 7 or 14 from outside the train station to central pl Sveta Nedelya. Buy a ticket from food stands inside the station; note that officials often check for validated tickets on this route.

Bus 84 connects the airport terminal with bul Vasil Levski, near Sofia University; and minibus 30 travels between the airport and bul Maria Luisa. Also, a booth at the airport operated by **OK Taxi** (☎ 973 2121) arranges metered cabs to the centre (about 8lv).

square is ritzy bul Vitosha, towards the National Palace of Culture (NDK). East of pl Sveta Nedelya, along ul Tsar Osvoboditel, are many government buildings, then a block north, pl Aleksander Nevski. Several city maps with transport routes are available.

INFORMATION
Bookshops
Dom na Knigata (☎ 981 7897; ul Graf Ignatiev; 🕑 8am-8pm Mon-Sat, 9am-6pm Sun) Messy racks of paperbacks in English and other languages.

Emergency
Police (☎ 116; 🕑 24hr; English-speaking operator ☎ 988 5239; 🕑 8am-6pm; French-speaking operator ☎ 982 3028; 🕑 8am-6pm)

Immigration
Immigration office (☎ 982 3316; bul Maria Luisa 48; 🕑 9am-12.30pm & 1.30-5pm Mon-Fri) Extends visas by three months for 200lv.

Internet Access
Quest (ul Trapezitsa 4; per hr 1.20lv; 🕑 24hr)

Medical Services
Poliklinika Torax (☎ 988 5259, 980 5791; bul Stamboliyski 57) Private clinic.

Money
Bulbank (Cnr ul Lavele & ul Todor Alexandrov; 🕑 8.30am-4.30pm Mon-Fri) Changes travellers cheques for €1.

Post
Central Post Office (☎ 980 4800; ul General Gurko; 🕑 varies widely)

Telephone
BTC (ul General Gurko; 🕑 24hr)

Tourist Information
National Tourism Information & Advertising Centre (☎ 987 9778; www.bulgariatravel.org; ul Sveta Sofia; 🕑 9am-5.30pm Mon-Fri) Brochures and English-speaking staff.

Travel Agencies
Aerotour MM (☎ 943 4900; www.aerotourmm.com; ul Shipka 34; 🕑 9am-7pm Mon-Fri) Arranges visas for Russia and former Soviet republics.

Orbita (☎ 987 9128; orbita@ttm.bg; bul Hristo Botev 48; 🕑 9am-5pm Mon-Fri) Issues student cards for 10lv.

Zig Zag (☎ 980 5102; www.zigzag.dir.bg; bul Stamboliyski 20V; 🕑 9am-6.30pm Mon-Fri) Super-helpful, English-language staff charge 5lv consultation fee to book

---

TOP FIVE BULGARIA

- **Festival** Varna's long Summer International Festival (p242)

- **Walk** Criss-cross the trails at Sofia's giant Mt Vitosha (p233)

- **Bar hopping** At Sofia's bizarre Studentski Grad (p232)

- **Medieval fort** Veliko Târnovo's Tsarevets Fortress (p239)

- **Hidden beach** Sinemorets (p241)

---

rooms, and give advice on hikes and activities around the country. Enter from ul Lavele.

Zip Limited (☎ 986 9260; ul Patriarh Evtimii 44; 🕑 9am-6pm Mon-Fri, 10.30am-2.30pm Sat) STA affiliate, can get student discounts on air fares.

SIGHTS & ACTIVITIES
Sofia's best attraction is actually outside the city: Mt Vitosha (p233).

Ploshad Aleksander Nevski
Gold domed and massive, **Aleksander Nevski Church** (pl Aleksander Nevski; admission free; 🕑 7am-7pm) is the city's focal point and the one Sofia sight you have to see. It was built between 1892 and 1912 and is named after a Swedish-born Russian warrior.

In the church's basement, the **Aleksander Nevski Crypt** (☎ 981 5775; adult/student 3/1.50lv; 🕑 10.30am-6.30pm Tue-Sun) features many national icons dating to the 5th century AD.

The nearby **National Gallery for Foreign Art** (ul 19 Fevruari; admission 1.50lv, free Sun; 🕑 11am-6.30pm Wed-Mon) hosts diverse international works on its walls, including a Rodin bust and some Monets.

Earthquake-battered **Sveta Sofia Church** (admission free; 🕑 7am-6pm or 7pm) inspired the name of the city.

Around Sofia City Garden
Facing this fountain-filled park is the former Royal Palace. It's now two museums, including the valuable **Ethnographical Museum** (☎ 988 1974; ul Tsar Osvoboditel; admission 3lv; 🕑 10am-5.30pm Tue-Sun Apr-Nov, 11am-3.30pm Dec-Mar), with a dozen rooms of well-explained exhibits on traditional Bulgarian architecture and costumes.

Across from the Party House (closed to public) is the President's Building (also closed

SOFIA

0 _____ 500 m
0 _____ 0.3 miles

INFORMATION
British Embassy.............................1 B3
BTC..2 B4
Bulbank...3 A3
Central Post Office.........................4 B4
Danish Embassy..............................5 D3
Dom na Knigata..............................6 B4
Hungarian Embassy.........................7 B6
Immigration Office..........................8 B2
National Tourism Information &
   Advertising Centre.......................9 A3
Polish Embassy.............................10 B6
Quest..11 A3
Turkish Embassy...........................12 C5
Zig Zag..13 A3
Zip Limited...................................14 A5

SIGHTS & ACTIVITIES   (pp229–31)
Aleksander Nevski Church..............15 C4
Aleksander Nevski Crypt...........(see 15)
Banya Bashi Mosque......................16 B3
Ethnographical Museum.................17 B3
National Gallery for Foreign Art.....18 D4
NDK (National Palace of Culture)....19 A6
Party House..................................20 B3
President's Building........................21 B3
Sveta Nedelya Cathedral................22 A3
Sveta Sofia Church........................23 C3

SLEEPING   (p231)
Art Hostel....................................24 A5
Hostel Kervan...............................25 C3
Hostel Mostel...............................26 A4
Hotel Enny...................................27 B2
Hotel Iskâr..................................28 B3
Hotel Maya..................................29 A3
Markela Accommodation Agency....30 B3
Red Star Hostel............................31 A4
Sofia Hostel.................................32 A3

EATING   (pp231–2)
Divaka..33 B5
Dream House...............................34 A4
Motto...35 C4
Oazis Supermarket........................36 B3
Trops Kâshta................................37 B2

DRINKING   (p232)
Blaze Club...................................38 C5
Hambara.....................................39 B5
Poison's......................................40 C5

ENTERTAINMENT   (p232)
Escape..41 B4
National Opera House....................42 C3
Odean...43 C5
Spartacus....................................44 D4
Swingin' Hall................................45 D6

SHOPPING   (p232)
Orion Ski Shop.............................46 A4
Souvenir Shop.........................(see 17)
Stenata......................................47 A3

TRANSPORT   (pp232–3)
MTT..48 B1
Penguin Travel.............................49 C3
Rila Bureau..................................50 B4

to the public), the site of the quite funny boot sole–slapping **changing of the guards**, staged on the hour during daylight hours.

Around Ploshad Sveta Nedelya
In the heart of pl Sveta Nedelya is well-lit, ornate **Sveta Nedelya Cathedral** (admission free; ☺ 7am-7pm), built between 1856 and 1863.

North on bul Maria Luisa is the unmistakable **Banya Bashi Mosque** (admission free; ☺ dawn-dusk).

One kilometre south of pl Sveta Nedelya is the huge 'viva-1981!' **NDK** (National Palace of Culture) complex, which smacks of its 1981 origins and has cafés, cinema and a viewing deck (the latter open most days).

COURSES
A branch of **Sofia University** (☎ 710 069; www .deo.uni-sofia.bg; ul Kosta Loulchev 27) offers Bulgarian-language (a three-week class costs €220) and traditional music and dance courses.

SLEEPING
Hostels
Most hostels lower the price if you stay a few days. Prices here include breakfast and are for summer; most drop by €1 or €2 in winter.

Art Hostel (☎ 987 0545; www.art-hostel.com; ul Angel Kânchev 21A; dm €10) This laid-back hostel gets its second name ('Usually we spend our time in the garden') because of its leafy courtyard out back. Past guests have helped transform small spaces into a cosy scene where travellers mix with arty locals. Emphasis: hanging out over sleeping.

Hostel Mostel (☎ 0889-223 296; www.hostelmostel .com; ul Denkoglu 2; dm €10, s/d with shared bathroom €12/15; ▣) Lovingly run by a Bulgarian couple who speak English and give rides from the train

---

REGISTRATION AT HOTELS
Technically you have to register your passport details with police every night during your stay in Bulgaria and show customs officials the documents upon leaving the country. Nearly all hotels and private accommodation agencies, even camping grounds, will do this automatically for you upon check-in. Try to be sure they do, though. Often border officials won't ask, but if they do, they can turn you back if you don't have the right documents.

---

station, this appealing new hostel has six- and eight-bed dorms, plus a private room. Lots of light, free Internet, lockers, cheap international calls plus loads of travel tips.

Other recommended hostels include the following:

Hostel Kervan (☎ 983 9428; www.kervanhostel.com; ul Rositza 3; dm €10) Clean, stylish and new. Rents bikes (€10 per day).

Red Star Hostel (☎ 986 3341; 3rd fl, ul Angel Kânchev 6; dm €10, r €13-15) Was set to open at time of writing.

Sofia Hostel (☎ 989 8582; ul Pozitano 16; dm €10) Bulgaria's first hostel has a family feel.

Homestays
The train station has an iffily run accommodation bureau; **EBP Tours** (☎ 931 1500; bul Maria Luisa; ☺ 6am-7pm Mon-Fri, 6am-4pm Sat & Sun), downstairs in the station (p233), finds private rooms for 20lv per person.

Markela Accommodation Agency (☎ 980 4925; www.markela.hit.bg; Room 103, ul Ekzarh Yosif 35; ☺ 8.30am-7.30pm Mon-Fri, 9.30am-4.30pm Sat & Sun) Central office finds single/double rooms for 20/30lv. Apartments start at 30lv; most are 50lv to 65lv.

Hotels
Hotel Enny (☎ 983 1649; ul Pop Bogomil 46; s without bathroom 20lv & 30lv, d 40lv, s with bathroom/bathroom & toilet 50/60lv, d 60/80lv) Quieter rooms with private bathroom are in the building behind. A café-bar courtyard is open in summer. The lone 20lv single is super small and fills quickly. All other rooms have TV. More budget options are on the other side of bul Maria Luisa.

Hotel Maya (☎ 989 4611; ul Trapezitsa 4; s/d 45/70lv) Clean and homey, this central guesthouse has rooms on either side of a rooftop courtyard overlooking the TsUM shopping centre. Private bathrooms are down the hall.

Hotel Iskâr (☎ 986 6750; ul Iskâr 11; r €25 & €37) Central location, with small but well-kept rooms. A bit quieter than other places. Cheaper rooms don't have TV and the private bathrooms are across the hall.

The train station's **Hotel Central** (☎ 931-1724; d 40lv) is for the desperate.

EATING
Appealing new places are popping up constantly – try between bul Vitosha and ul Rakovski. Cheap pizza slices and kebabs are hard to miss there.

Oazis Supermarket (bul Maria Luisa; ☻ 8.30am-8.30pm) Inside TsUM shopping centre.

Trops Kâshta (bul Maria Luisa 26; salads 1lv, mains 2-3lv; ☻ 8am-9pm) For cheap, fast point-and-eat cafeteria-style food, Trops is your new best comrade. This is one of several places serving Bulgarian stews and veggie dishes, and it's half-price after 8pm.

Dream House (ul Alabin 50A; mains 2-2.50lv; ☻ 11.30am-10pm) A dream for meatless dining, this cool-mint restaurant serves heaps of tasty soups and meals.

Divaka (ul William Gladstone 54; grills 1.10-3.90lv, mains 2-3.80lv; ☻ 24hr) This sprawling modern restaurant gets filled daily with happy Bulgarians looking for low-cost traditional fare – grilled meats, fish fillets, cheese-covered chips.

Motto (☎ 987 2723; ul Aksakov 18; pasta 5lv, mains 4.20-9lv; ☻ 9am-1am) Snazzy Sofians lounge after work, in this chic eatery with a courtyard. The jumbo burger (4lv) is as advertised.

DRINKING

Look for *Programata*'s free annual *Club Guide* for listings in English.

Poison's (ul Tsar Shishman 22; ☻ 10am-2am) This place has a shady outdoor space, which fills with 20-something locals.

Blaze Club (ul Slavyanska 36; ☻ 10am-3am) DJs a-spin, disco ball a-turns at this tiny hipster-hanging club with tri-level sitting areas.

Hambara (ul 6 Septemvri 22; ☻ 8pm-late) Low-key, candle-lit Hambara is unsigned and down a dark path.

A few kilometres south of the centre, **Studentski Grad** (Student Town) is literally that: an enclave of college students living in drab communist-era apartment blocks with the city's hippest cafés and bars below. Great for afternoon alfresco drinks. Get there by minibus No 7 from bul Maria Luisa or No 8 along ul Rakovski (one-way 1lv). City bus 94 leads from here to just south of Sofia University.

ENTERTAINMENT

Sofia Echo (www.sofiaecho.com) is a weekly English-language paper with entertainment listings (2.40lv – ouch!). Freebies include the monthly *Sofia City* (www.sofiacityguide.com) and weekly *Programata* (in Bulgarian only).

Odeon (☎ 989 2469; ul Patriarh Evtimii 1; tickets 1-3lv) This is Sofia's premier art-house cinema.

Escape (☎ 088-746 8064; ul Angel Kânchev 1; admission 2-3lv; ☻ 8.30pm-late) This is Sofia's big kids' favourite disco is.

Spartacus (☎ 088-955 1279; ☻ 6.30pm-late Tue-Thu, 11pm-late Fri & Sat) Bulgaria's first gay disco, at the underpass near Sofia University, is still going strong.

National Opera House (☎ 987 1366; ul Vrabcha 1) This opera house offers a treat with excellent ensembles.

Swingin' Hall (☎ 963 0696; bul Dragan Tsankov 8) Contemporary music (rock, jazz) is staged here most nights.

SHOPPING

Pavement vendors operating around pl Aleksander Nevski sell communist-era antiques (Soviet cameras!) and traditional crafts.

The **souvenir shop** (ul Tsar Osvoboditel; ☻ 9.30am-6pm) at the Ethnographical Museum is a catch-all of traditional Bulgarian knick-knacks.

Stenata (☎ 980 5491; ul Tsar Samuil 63; ☻ 9.30am-7pm Mon-Fri, 10am-5.30pm Sat) stocks hiking and rock-climbing gear.

Orion Ski Shop (☎ 986 4157; ul Pozitano; ☻ 10am-7.30pm Mon-Fri, 10am-4pm Sat) sells ski gear, including some second-hand stuff.

GETTING THERE & AWAY
Air
Hemus Air (☎ 02-981 8330; www.hemusair.bg) flies to Varna and to Burgas (in summer only). The departures terminal has an **information booth** (☎ 937 2211).

Bus
DOMESTIC BUSES
Sofia's sprawling **Central Bus Terminal** (behind the Princess Hotel) is the nation's most messy. At the time of research, the bus station was preparing to move to the train station's front; hopefully that will bring more order.

Generally it's possible to show up between 8am and 5pm or 6pm and get a bus to the following destinations within an hour or so: Burgas (15lv, 5½ hours), Plovdiv (8lv, two hours), Ruse (10lv to 12lv, 4½ hours), Varna (19lv, six hours) and Veliko Târnovo (10lv, 3½ hours). There's also a lone daily bus to Koprivshtitsa (5.50lv, 2½ hours).

From the **Zapad Bus Terminal** (aka Ovcha Kupel; ☎ 955 5362), there are nearly hourly buses to Bansko (5lv), and a daily bus to Rila town. Get to the terminal on bus No 260 from pl Ruski Pametnik or tram No 5 from pl Makedonia, which is west of the centre on ul Alabin.

INTERNATIONAL BUSES

Many bus companies sell tickets to bordering countries and beyond. Sample fares include: Athens (85lv, 12 to 13 hours, one or two daily Tuesday to Sunday), Belgrade (32lv to 58lv, nine hours, two daily), Bucharest (46lv to 50lv, 10 hours, three weekly), Istanbul (20lv, eight to 10 hours, nine daily) and Thessaloniki (28lv to 37lv, six to seven hours, two to six daily).

Get tickets at **MTT** (☎ 983 2665; www.skgt -bg.com; bul Maria Luisa 84; ⏲ 7.30am-8pm or later) or **EBP Tours** (☎ 931 1500; ⏲ 6am-7pm Mon-Fri, 6am-4pm Sat & Sun), downstairs at the train station.

Train

Sofia's **central train station** (bul Maria Luisa) lists departures and arrivals in English on a large computer screen on the main floor. Buy same-day tickets for Vidin, Ruse and Varna on the main floor; all other domestic destinations are downstairs. Advance tickets are available at another office downstairs.

International tickets can be purchased at the often-rude **Rila Bureau** (☎ 932 3346; ⏲ 7am-11.30pm) on the main floor, or at the helpful **centre office** (☎ 987 0777; ul General Gurko 5; ⏲ 7am-6.30pm Mon-Sat).

Sample off-season train fares include the following (there's sometimes an extra daily train or two in summer): Athens (63lv, 16½ hours, one daily), Belgrade (26lv, 8½ hours, one daily), Bucharest (35.50lv, 11½ hours, two daily), Burgas (11.10lv, 6½ to 7½ hours, four daily), Gorna Oryahovitsa (7.90lv, 4½ hours, 10 daily), Istanbul (36.50lv, 14½ hours, one daily), Koprivshtitsa (3.60lv, two to 2½ hours, four daily), Plovdiv (5lv, 2½ hours, 12 daily) and Varna (13.50lv, 7½ to 8½ hours, six daily).

GETTING AROUND
Car & Motorcycle

Penguin Travel (☎ 988 2163; penguin@einet.bg; Bldg 2, ul Moskovska 29; ⏲ 9.30am-6pm Mon-Fri, 9.30am-6pm Mon-Sat in summer) rents cars from €16 daily in summer. Also check **AutoJet** (www.rentacar.bg).

Public Transport

Sofia's trams, buses and metro line work on the same ticket system. A single ride is 0.50lv, a day pass is 2.10lv. Validate single-ride tickets once you board.

Minibuses ply many useful city routes at 1lv per ride.

The relatively new metro line reaches the western suburbs and is of little use to travellers. A new one, going southeast, was under construction at the time of research.

AROUND SOFIA

BOYANA БОЯНА

Now officially a part of Sofia, hillside Boyana has the capital's best museum (and highest entry fee), the **National Historical Museum** (☎ 955 7604; bul Okolovrusten Pat; adult/student 10/5lv, guide 10lv; ⏲ 9.30am-5.30pm). Treasured pieces include the world's oldest gold (4th millennium BC), and Thracian horse decorations. It's in a former presidential residence.

Built between the 11th and 19th centuries, the inside walls of the **Boyana Church** (☎ 959 0939; adult/student 10/5lv; ⏲ 9.30am-5pm), 1.5km south of the museum, have some 90 medieval frescoes, certainly among Bulgaria's finest.

Get to Boyana on minibus No 21, which goes southwest along bul Vasil Levski, passing the museum and close to the church.

VITOSHA ВИТОША

The feather in Sofia's cap is this mountain range south of the city. It's part of the Vitosha Nature Park, with ski runs operating from mid-December to April (Aleko is the main centre) and dozens of well-marked trails accessed by public bus or chairlifts.

Get the trail map *Vitosha Turisticheska Karta* (1:50,000) in Cyrillic (5lv) in Sofia.

Chairlifts are a popular way of getting up the mountains. **Dragalevtsi** (☎ 967 2511) is 2km up from the village; it's 2lv to take two lifts to Goli Vrâh mountain. More expensive **Simeonovo** sends gondolas to the peaks. It's 5lv to Aleko, a popular base for hikes and more ski lifts (€7 per day). Lifts tend to run all year, but sometimes take weekdays off in between seasons.

From Sofia's **Hladilnika bus stop** (ul Srebârna), near bul Cherni Vrâh), 2km south of the NDK, take bus No 122 to Simeonovo, and No 64 to Dragalevtsi or Boyana.

SOUTHERN BULGARIA

Bulgaria's mountainous southwest brims with rocky-topped peaks, scores of well-signed hiking trails and skiing (Bansko,

Borovets, Pamporovo). South of Sofia are the Alp-like Rila Mountains (www.rila nationalpark.org) and Pirin Mountains (www.pirin-np.com) near Greece. Just east are the culturally rich Rodopi Mountains. North, in the Thracian plain, is Plovdiv.

Drop by **Zig Zag** (☎ 980 5102; www.zigzag.dir.bg; bul Stamboliyski 20V; ☯ 9am-6.30pm Mon-Fri) in Sofia for tips on activities (p229).

RILA MONASTERY РИЛСКИ МАНАСТИР
☎ 07054

Set in a forested valley 120km south of Sofia, Bulgaria's most famous **monastery** (admission free; ☯ 6am-9pm or 10pm) is a frequent destination for day-trippers. It's near excellent hikes, but infrequent public transport makes it hard to do in a day trip independently. Day trips are €30 and up from Sofia. Try to avoid summer weekends.

Built in 927, and heavily restored in 1469, the monastery helped keep Bulgarian culture and language alive during the Ottoman rule.

The monastery's 300 monk cells fill four levels of colourful balconies, overlooking the mural-filled **Nativity Church**, built in the 1830s. Nearby, the **Ethnographical Museum** (adult/ student 5/3lv; ☯ 8.30am-4.30pm) houses woodwork pieces, including the ornate Rila Cross.

There are a couple of hotels and restaurants nearby, but it's best to stay in the monastery's simple **rooms** (☎ 2208; r with shared bathroom US$15). A sleeping bag is needed during winter.

Currently no direct buses connect Sofia and the monastery or Rila village, 22km west, which can be reached frequently from the nearby hubs of Dupnitsa and Blagoevgrad. Four daily buses leave Rila village for the monastery (1.20lv, 40 minutes). Rila village has an ATM and hotel but no taxis.

MELNIK МЕЛНИК
☎ 07437 / pop 275

Amid the jutting, 'sand pyramid' part of the Pirins, and only 15km from Greece, little Melnik is home to the country's best wine. (Locals claim it's 'hangover-free'.)

From the bus stop, roads run on either side of a (mostly dry) creek. Halfway along is a post office. There's no bank or ATM.

Slurp wine at the 250-year-old **Mitko Manolev Winery** (Shestaka; per glass 0.50lv), 350m east of the post office.

A remarkable 3km hiking trail leads between Melnik and the hill-top **Rozhen Monas-**

tery (suggested donation 2lv; ☯ 7am-9pm), 7km east by road. It's best to take a bus up (0.50lv, 20 minutes, three daily) and walk back.

Many private homes let out simple rooms with shared bathroom for as little as 8lv per person. Try up the hillsides. Or try a *mehana* (tavern); **Mehana Megdana** (☎ 088-866 6047; r per person with shared bathroom 8-10lv) is near the post office.

Four daily buses leave for Sandanski (1.70lv, 40 minutes), with direct connections to Sofia.

PLOVDIV ПЛОВДИВ
☎ 032 / pop 340,640

Super Plovdiv! Bulgaria's most appealing city, Plovdiv flares out its Roman guts, with crumbled walls and theatre seats spilling into view at nearly every turn in its compact centre and hilly Old Town.

Plovdiv was known as Philippopolis to the Romans in the 3rd century AD, but it was settled thousands of years beforehand by Thracians.

Orientation & Information

Plovdiv's train station and Yug Bus Terminal are about 600m southwest of the central pl Tsentralen, a 20-minute walk. From the square, the main pedestrian mall, ul Knyaz Aleksandâr, stretches 500m north to pl Dzhumaya. East from pl Dzhumaya, via ul Sâborna, is Old Town.

Bulbank (ul Ivan Vazov 4; ☯ 8.30am-4.30pm Mon-Fri)
Call Centre (ul Balkan; international calls per min 0.20lv; ☯ 10am-11pm)
Inter Jet Tours (☎ 653 001; www.interjet-bg.com; Knyaz Aleksandâr 35; ☯ 9am-5pm) Rents cars (from €16 daily during summer).
Speed (ul Knyaz Aleksandâr; per hr 1lv; ☯ 24hr) Internet access.
St Vrach Medical Centre (☎ 609 859; ul Hristo Botev 81; ☯ 8am-6pm)

Old Town

The **Ethnographical Museum** (☎ 625 654; ul Dr Chomakov 2; admission 4lv; ☯ 9am-noon & 2-5.30pm summer, 9am-noon & 2-5pm winter) consists of 22 rooms inside the Old Town's most striking building (built 1847), which is an added bonus to the country's finest ethnographical collection.

The **Theatre of Ancient Philippopolis** (admission 3lv; ☯ 9am-5.30pm summer, Wed-Sun winter) is the country's most impressive Roman ruin. An amphitheatre built in the 3rd century AD, it

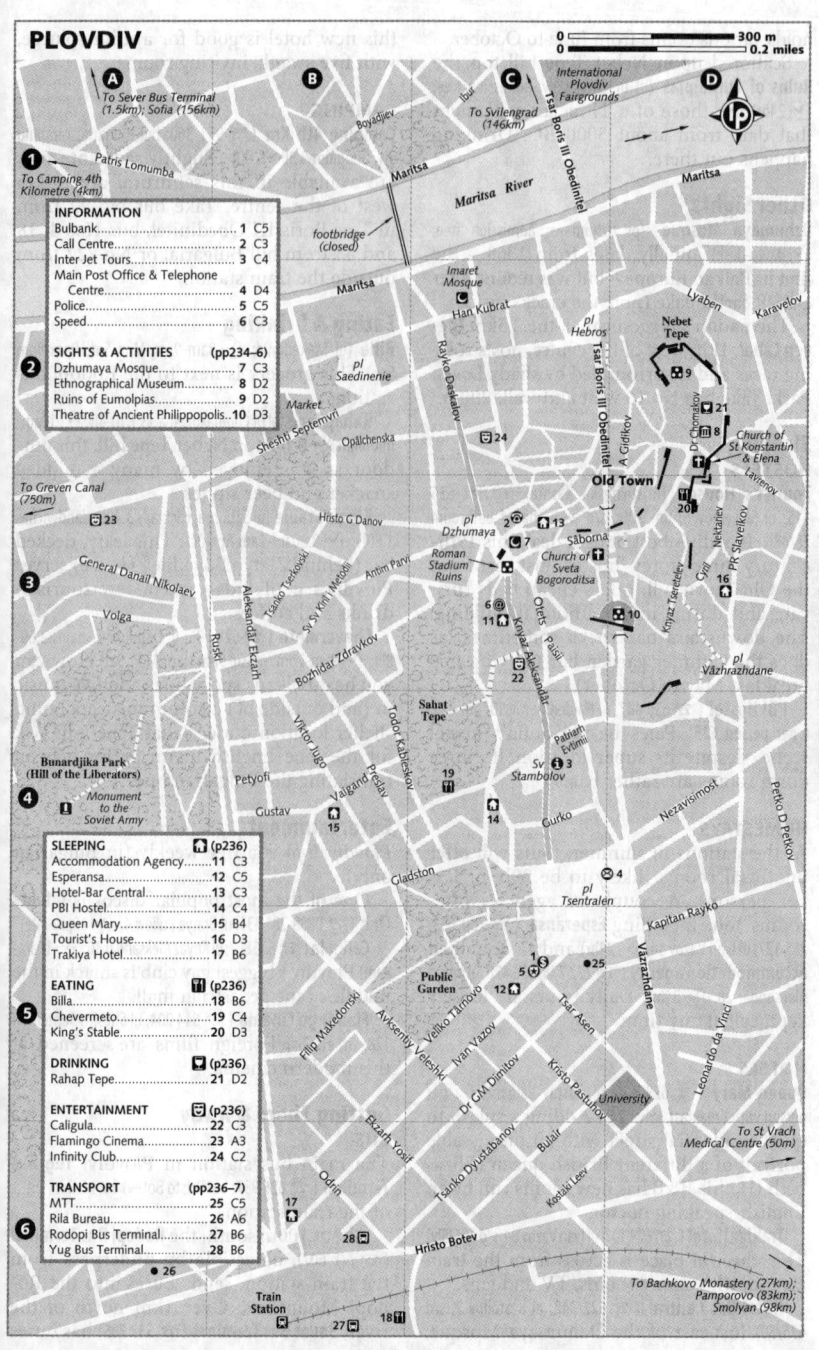

PLOVDIV

| 0 | 300 m |
| 0 | 0.2 miles |

To Sever Bus Terminal
(1.5km); Sofia (156km)

International
Plovdiv
Fairgrounds

To Svilengrad
(146km)

Patris Lomumba

To Camping 4th
Kilometre (4km)

Maritsa River

footbridge
(closed)

Imaret
Mosque

Han Kubrat

pl
Hebros

Nebet
Tepe

INFORMATION
Bulbank	1 C5
Call Centre	2 C3
Inter Jet Tours	3 C4
Main Post Office & Telephone	
Centre	4 D4
Police	5 C5
Speed	6 C3

SIGHTS & ACTIVITIES (pp234-6)
Dzhumaya Mosque	7 C3
Ethnographical Museum	8 D2
Ruins of Eumolpias	9 D2
Theatre of Ancient Philippopolis	10 D3

pl
Saedinenie

Market

Opălchenska

Church of
St Konstantin
& Elena

Old Town

pl
Dzhumaya

To Greven Canal
(750m)

Hristo G Danov

Roman
Stadium
Ruins

Church of
Sveta
Bogoroditsa

General Danail Nikolaev

Volga

Sahat
Tepe

pl
Vázrazhdane

Bunardjika Park
(Hill of the Liberators)

Monument
to the
Soviet Army

Petyofi

Gustav

Sv
Stambolov

Gurko

Nezavisimost

SLEEPING (p236)
Accommodation Agency	11 C3
Esperansa	12 C5
Hotel-Bar Central	13 C3
PBI Hostel	14 C4
Queen Mary	15 B4
Tourist's House	16 D3
Trakiya Hotel	17 B6

Cladston

pl
Tsentralen

Kapitan Rayko

EATING (p236)
Billa	18 B6
Chevermeto	19 C4
King's Stable	20 D3

DRINKING (p236)
| Rahap Tepe | 21 D2 |

Public
Garden

ENTERTAINMENT (p236)
Caligula	22 C3
Flamingo Cinema	23 A3
Infinity Club	24 C2

University

To St Vrach
Medical Centre (50m)

TRANSPORT (pp236-7)
MTT	25 C5
Rila Bureau	26 A6
Rodopi Bus Terminal	27 B6
Yug Bus Terminal	28 B6

Hristo Botev

To Bachkovo Monastery (27km);
Pamporovo (83km);
Smolyan (98km)

Train
Station

BULGARIA

holds various events from June to October.

Scattered upon Nebet Tepe hill top, the **Ruins of Eumolpias** (ul Dr Chomakov; admission free; 🕐 24hr) are those of a Thracian settlement that date from about 5000 BC. Drinking happens out there.

Other Sights

Dzhumaya Mosque (pl Dzhumaya; admission free; 🕐 dawn-dusk) initially dates from 1368 – the first in Balkan Europe – but was redone after a 1928 earthquake (note the cracks inside).

The nation's biggest canal, the 2.5km **Greven Canal**, 1km west of the centre, hosts rowing races and is surrounded by shady Loven Park. Take bus No 10 west and walk 200m.

Sleeping

HOSTELS

Tourist's House (Turisticheska Kâshta; ☎ /fax 635 115; ul Slaveikov 5; dm 20lv, s/d with shared bathroom 28/48lv) Plovdiv's best budget deal, this 19th-century three-storey 'hostel', just east from the Old Town hill, offers cheap beds (private and dorm) in a traditional building. The downstairs bar rocks sometimes, as does the summer garden bar (serving free breakfast May to October).

PBI Hostel (☎ 638 467; ul Naiden Gerov 13; dm €10, r per person €15) Pales beside Sofia's hostel scene, despite its super location. Its three dorm rooms are rather bare.

HOMESTAYS

At the stations in summer, touts will offer unofficial rooms (likely to be 20lv or less per person). A couple of agencies offer rooms too, including **Esperansa** (☎ 260 653, 265 127; ul Ivan Vazov 14; 🕐 24hr) and an unnamed **accommodation agency** (☎ 272 778, 632 428; ul Knyaz Aleksandâr 28; 🕐 24hr). Daily hours are loosely kept; call at any time.

HOTELS

Queen Mary (☎ 629 306; ul Gustav Vaigand 7; r per person with breakfast 15lv; 🔀) Adding a splash to quiet residential street with an unmissable portrait of a different British queen (Elizabeth II), this B&B has new rooms run by an English-speaking doctor.

Trakiya Hotel (☎ 624 101; ul Ivan Vazov 84; s/d 45/75lv) This cheerful place is across from the train station, with comfy rooms, TV and fans.

Hotel-Bar Central (☎ 622 348; ul K Stoilov 7; s/d €35/50) Just east of the Dzhumaya Mosque,

this new hotel is good for a mini-splurge, with five swank, inviting rooms.

CAMPING

Camping 4th Km (☎ 951 360; bul Bulgaria; camping 3lv, bungalows 30lv & 40lv) Slightly sad camp sites are available in this semirural area, 4km west of the centre. Take bus No 22 from ul Tsar Boris III Obedinitel, bus Nos 4, 18 and 44 from bul Bulgaria, or No 222 from outside the train station.

Eating & Drinking

Billa (ul Makedonia; 🕐 8am-9pm Mon-Sat, 9am-8pm Sun) This grocery is next to the Rodopi bus station.

Rahap Tepe (ul Dr Chomakov; snacks 1.10-4lv; 🕐 10am-midnight Apr-Oct) Atop Nebet Tepe hill, this outdoor spot is enjoyed by many a midday snacker and beer sipper.

King's Stable (ul Sâborna; cocktails 3.40lv, sandwiches 1.80lv; 🕐 8.30am-2am Apr-Oct) This leafy, decked bar (behind Zlatyo Boyadjiev House) serves Plovdiv's cool kids (and a few tourists) drinks and coffees.

Chevermeto (☎ 628 605; ul Dondukov; mains 2.60-8lv; 🕐 9am-2pm, music 9pm-4am Mon-Sat) How can you beat Balkans specialities and live music in (and outside of) a communist-era bomb shelter location under Sahat Tepe hill? Ask for the lone English menu or for help in translating the Bulgarian one.

Entertainment

Plovdiv Info is a free weekly (in Bulgarian only).

One of the most popular discos is **Infinity Club** (☎ 0888-281 431; ul Bratya Pulievi 4; 🕐 10pm-late).

Caligula (☎ 626 867; ul Knyaz Aleksandâr 30; 🕐 10am-8am) Plovdiv's biggest gay club is smack in the middle of the pedestrian mall.

Flamingo Cinema (☎ 644 004; ul Sheshti Septemvri 128; tickets 3lv) Foreign films are screened at this modern cinema.

Getting There & Away

BUS

The main bus station in Plovdiv, **Yug Bus Terminal** (☎ 626 937; bul Hristo Botev) is 100m east of the train station.

About 100m south, the **Rodopi Bus Terminal** (☎ 777 607), accessible by underpass from the train station, sends buses into the Rodopi Mountains. Over 1km north of the river, **Sever Bus Terminal** (☎ 553 705) has buses

BULGARIA

to Koprivshtitsa and Veliko Târnovo; get there by minibus No 4 from ul Tsar Boris III Obedinitel, or by taxi (about 1.50lv).

MTT (☎ 624 274; pl Tsentralen; ☽ daily), next to the Trimontium Hotel, sells international tickets.

The following are sample bus fares (buses leave from and arrive at Yug unless otherwise noted): Athens via Sofia (90lv, 15 hours, one to three daily), Burgas (15lv, four hours, two daily), Istanbul (30lv, six hours, six daily), Koprivshtitsa (with Sever; 5.50lv, two hours, one daily), Ruse (with Sever; 13lv, seven hours, one daily), Sofia (8lv, two hours, half-hourly 6am to 12.30pm and hourly 2pm to 8pm), Varna (15lv, seven hours, two daily) and Veliko Târnovo (10lv, 4½ hours, three daily, two daily with Sever).

TRAIN
Daily direct trains from the **train station** (☎ 622 732; bul Hristo Botev) include the following: Burgas (7.90lv, five hours, three to six daily), Istanbul (33lv to 49lv, 11 hours, one daily), Sofia (5lv, 2½ hours, 13 or 14 daily, every hour or two from 3am to 7.30pm), Varna (7lv, six hours, three daily) and Veliko Târnovo (4.80lv, five hours, two daily).

For international tickets, go to **Rila Bureau** (☎ 643 120; bul Hristo Botev 31A; ☽ 8am-6pm Mon-Fri, 8am-2pm Sat).

CENTRAL BULGARIA

Bulgaria's broad belly is pierced by the surprisingly high Stara Planina (Old Mountain) range (www.staraplanina.org), the local name of the Balkans. The mountains are bordered by plains, with windswept cities at certain access points. Many hiking paths (some of which can be cross-country skied or biked) lead to mountain huts.

KOPRIVSHTITSA КОПРИВШТИЦА
☎ 07184 / pop 2645

Nearly 400 19th-century buildings done up in revival style are the cake; cool temperatures in summer heat are the icing. And forested hikes in surrounding green hills, the ice cream on top. Tricky-to-reach Koprivshtitsa is a regular, kick-back treatsburg for those wishing to soak in a bit of yesteryear Bulgaria.

Koprivshtitsa was the setting-off point for the important (but failed) 20 April 1876 Up-

rising against the Turks. Big events include the uprising re-enactment (1 or 2 May) and Folklore Days Festival (mid-August).

Orientation & Information
The town spreads out for 1km along a creek. The bus stop is about 100m south of the centre, at pl 20 April. The train station (Gara Koprivshtitsa) is 9km north of town.

DSK Bank (☽ 8am-4pm Mon-Fri) Next to the bus station, has a 24-hour ATM.

Heroes Internet Agency (ul Hadzhi Nencho Palaveev 49; per hr 1.20lv; ☽ 9am-midnight)

Tourist office (☎ 2191; pl 20 April; ☽ 9am-6pm) Can arrange private stays, rents bikes and offers hiking info.

Sights
Koprivshtitsa is Bulgaria's revival-era capital; six of its 19th-century 'house museums' can be visited on a combination ticket (5lv to see all, or 3lv each). All have signs in English and are open about 9am to 5pm daily, with an alternating day off (see below). The six-pack includes the following list:

Benkovski House (ul Georgi Benkovski 5; ☽ closed Tue) Near an equestrian statue 400m southeast of the centre.

Debelyanov House (ul Dimcho Debelyanov 6; ☽ closed Mon)

Kableshkov House (ul Todor Kableshkov 8; ☽ closed Mon) Don't miss the photos of remarkable moustaches.

Karavelov House (ul Hadzhi Nencho Palaveev 39; ☽ closed Tue)

Lyutov House (aka Topalov House; ul Nikola Belovezhdov 2; ☽ closed Tue)

Oskelov House (ul Gereniloto 4; ☽ closed Mon)

Sleeping
The tourist office arranges private rooms from 20lv per person (most are 30lv); one cheapie is **Emi-98** (☎ 2245; ul Vekilova 9; r per person 20lv).

Voivodenets Hostel (☎ 2145; ul Vekilova 5; dm 8lv) Old home with nice sitting area but cramped rooms, with two to 10 beds in each. When full, the owners run another hostel too.

Hotel Panorama (☎ 2035; www.panoramata.com; ul Georgi Benkovski 40; s/d with breakfast €18/24) A super-friendly English-speaking family runs this hotel, with nice views of the south of town (worth the 300m walk from the bus stop).

Getting There & Away
Bus service is sadly infrequent. At the time of research, one daily bus connected Koprivshtitsa with Sofia (5.50lv, 2½ hours) and Plovdiv (5.50lv, 2½ hours).

BULGARIA

Four trains link Koprivshtitsa and Sofia (3.10lv, 1¾ to 2½ hours); one to Burgas (8.30lv, five hours); taxis and buses meet trains.

VELIKO TÂRNOVO ВЕЛИКО ТЪРНОВО
☎ 062 / pop 75,000

Just off the Bucharest–Istanbul tracks, this hilly medieval capital is a brilliant intro-duction to Bulgaria, with of-the-era homes leaning over a sharp S-shaped gorge split open by a snaking river, and the best damn citadel ruins in the country.

Orientation

From the train platform, a walkway heads northwest towards an underpass that leads

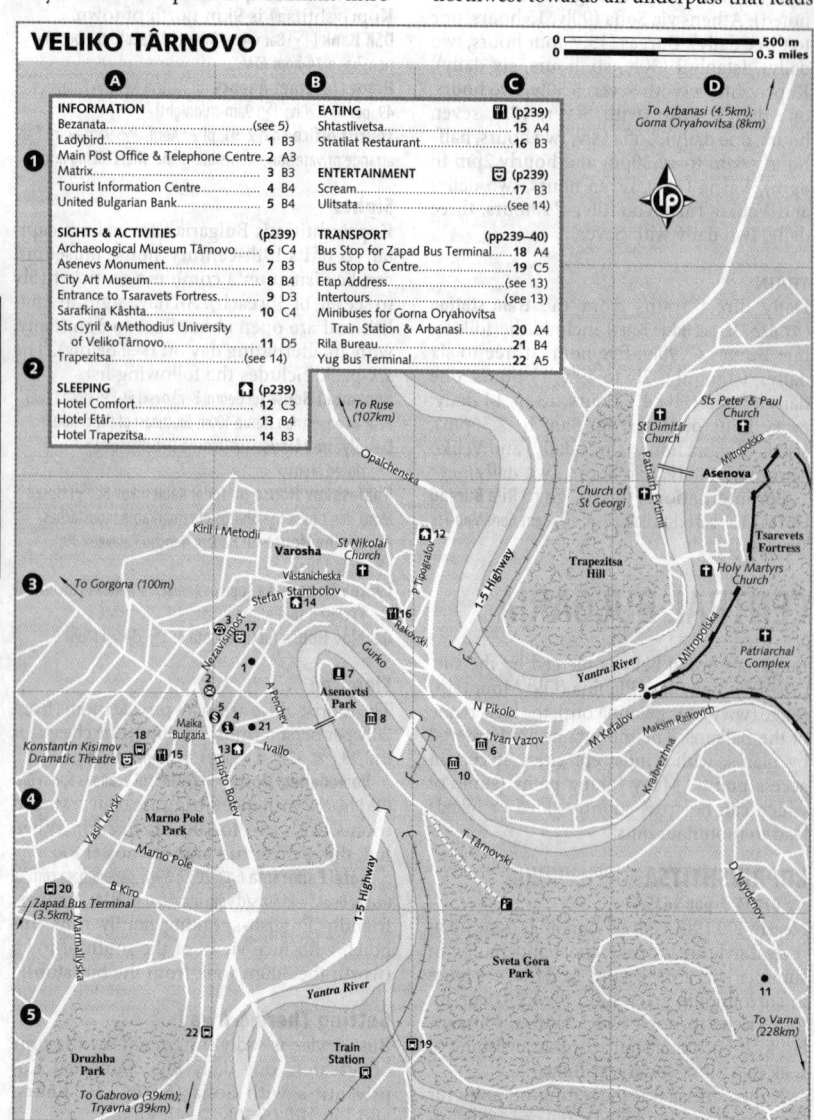

VELIKO TÂRNOVO

0 —— 500 m
0 —— 0.3 miles

INFORMATION
Bezanata...............................(see 5)
Ladybird....................................1 B3
Main Post Office & Telephone Centre..2 A3
Matrix.......................................3 B3
Tourist Information Centre............4 B4
United Bulgarian Bank...................5 B4

SIGHTS & ACTIVITIES (p239)
Archaeological Museum Târnovo......6 C4
Asenevs Monument.......................7 B3
City Art Museum..........................8 B4
Entrance to Tsaravets Fortress.........9 D3
Sarafkina Kâshta........................10 C4
Sts Cyril & Methodius University
  of VelikoTârnovo......................11 D5
Trapezitsa............................(see 14)

SLEEPING (p239)
Hotel Comfort..........................12 C3
Hotel Etâr...............................13 B4
Hotel Trapezitsa.......................14 B3

EATING (p239)
Shtastlivetsa...........................15 A4
Stratilat Restaurant...................16 B3

ENTERTAINMENT (p239)
Scream...................................17 B3
Ulitsata...............................(see 14)

TRANSPORT (pp239–40)
Bus Stop for Zapad Bus Terminal.....18 A4
Bus Stop to Centre.....................19 C5
Etap Address..........................(see 13)
Intertours.............................(see 13)
Minibuses for Gorna Oryahovitsa
  Train Station & Arbanasi............20 A4
Rila Bureau.............................21 B4
Yug Bus Terminal......................22 A5

To Arbanasi (4.5km);
Gorna Oryahovitsa (8km)

Sts Peter & Paul Church
St Dimitâr Church
Mitropolska
Asenova
To Ruse (107km)
Opalchenska
Church of St Georgi
Patriarh Evtimii
I-5 Highway
Trapezitsa Hill
Tsarevets Fortress
Holy Martyrs Church
Kiril i Metodii
Varosha
St Nikolai Church
Vâstanicheska
Stefan Stambolov
To Gorgona (100m)
Rakovski
Gurko
Yantra River
Patriarchal Complex
Nezavisimost
Asenovtsi Park
N Pikolo
Ivan Vazov
M Kefalov
Maksim Raikovich
Maika Bulgaria
A Penchev
Ivailo
Krabrehna
Konstantin Kisimov Dramatic Theatre
Hristo Botev
Marno Pole Park
Marno Pole
T Târnovski
Vasil Levski
I-5 Highway
B Kiro
Zapad Bus Terminal (3.5km)
Marmaliyska
Sveta Gora Park
D Naydenov
To Varna (228km)
Yantra River
Druzhba Park
Train Station
To Gabrovo (39km);
Tryavna (39km)

to ul Hristo Botev, near the Yug Bus Terminal. (Alternatively, you can catch several buses to the centre from in front of the train station.) From the bus station, it's an inclined walk up to pl Maika Bulgaria, where ul Vasil Levski heads west and the main crawl, ul Nezavisimost, heads east.

Information

Bezanata (ul Hristo Botev; per hr 0.50-0.90lv; 24hr) Nearly 80 computers in massive submarine-style café.

Ladybird (ul Hadzhi Dimitâr 25; 10am-6pm Mon-Sat, 10am-5pm Sun) Drop-off laundry service for about 3.50lv per bag.

Matrix (ul Nezavisimost; international calls per min 0.25lv; 24hr)

Tourist office (22 148; tic_vt@mobikom.com; ul Hristo Botev; 9am-6pm Mon-Sat Apr-Sep, closed Sat rest of year) English-speaking staff can arrange private accommodation, book rental cars for 25lv per day and sell regional maps (4lv).

United Bulgarian Bank (ul Hristo Botev; 8.30am-4.30pm Mon-Fri) Charges just 0.20lv to cash travellers cheques.

Tsarevets Fortress

About 1km from the centre, this mammoth **fortress** (admission 5lv; 8am-7pm Apr-Sep, 9am-5pm Oct-Mar) sits stoic and sprawling on a site shared over the centuries by Thracians, Romans and Byzantines. What's seen now – a triangular high-walled fortress with the remains of over 400 houses and 18 churches – was largely built between the 5th and 12th centuries.

The after-dark 40-minute **sound and light show** (636 828; admission 12lv) lights up the sky when enough tourists shell out 360lv (total), but can be watched for free outside the gates with ease.

Museums

Sarafkina Kâstha (ul Gurko 88; admission 4lv; 9am-noon & 1-6pm Mon-Fri) is a two-floor former banker's home from 1861 with a set-up sitting room upstairs and photos from the glory days.

Archaeological Museum Târnovo (601 528; ul Ivan Vazov; admission 4lv; 8am-noon & 1-6pm Tue-Sun Apr-Oct, 9am-5pm Tue-Sun Nov-Mar) has Roman ruins spilling out from its marbled stone walls. In 2003 it added the tomb of King Kaloyan, found recently in town.

City Art Museum (638 941; admission 3lv, free Thu; 10am-6pm Tue-Sun), facing town from behind the huge Asenevs Monument, hangs typical Veliko scenes downstairs and less predictable, mostly communist-era paintings upstairs.

Activities

Trapezitsa (635 823; www.trapezitca1902.com; ul Stefan Stambolov 79; 9am-6pm Mon-Fri) arranges rock-climbing trips.

Gorgona (601 400; www.gorgona-shop.com; ul Zelenka 2; rental per day 8lv; 10am-1pm & 2-7pm Mon-Fri, 10am-2pm Sat) rents mountain bikes.

Ask at the tourist office about **horse-riding** and **hiking** options in the area.

Courses

Sts Cyril & Methodius University (639 869; issblc@uni-vt.bg; ul Teodosi Tarnovski 2) offers Bulgarian-language classes (regularly in August); a two-week course starts from €190.

Sleeping & Eating

Touts offering private rooms (around 15lv per person) usually wait for buses and trains at the stations.

Hotel Trapezitsa (622 061; ul Stefan Stambolov 79; s/d 31/46lv, discount for students 3lv) This central and cheap hotel has 30 old but fine rooms with private bathroom. There's no TV. The price, not to mention gorge views from the back rooms, makes it Veliko's best deal.

Hotel Etâr (621 890; ul Ivailo 2; s/d 24/48lv, with private bathroom 30/60lv) This commie-era tower hotel has clean but stuffy rooms (about 80 in all); higher-up ones have fortress views.

Hotel Comfort (628 728; ul P Tipografov 5; r with breakfast €25-40;) Many of the hotel's dozen rooms have full-frontal views of the fortress and the light show, and a few have balconies. The enthusiastic owners will pay your taxi fare if you're coming from Veliko stations.

Stratilat Restaurant (ul Rakovski 11; sandwiches & pizza from 2lv; 24hr) A popular café – with its focus on drink and super desserts – has outdoor seating that fills quickly.

Shtastlivetsa (603 054; ul Marno Pole 7; mains 3.30-7.50lv; 10am-11pm) Traditional Bulgarian eatery that feels less contrived than some. Highlights on the big menu include Yugoslavian meat fingers and several egg dishes.

Entertainment

Ulitsata (ul Stefan Stambolov 79; draft beer 0.70lv; 7am-3am) is the local *biraria* (beerhouse) of choice, with a few choice balcony seats facing the gorge. The disco **Scream** (admission 1-2lv; 9pm-late) appeals to a rather scantily clad student base.

BULGARIA

Getting There & Away

BUS

From the **Yug Bus Terminal** (ul Hristo Botev), generally hourly buses en route to Sofia (10lv, three hours) and Varna (10lv, three hours) stop here. There are also roughly six daily buses to Ruse (5lv, two hours), two to Plovdiv (10lv, four hours), plus service to Gabrovo. Bus companies Etap Adress (domestic) and Intertours (international) have offices at **Hotel Etâr** (☎ 621 890; ul Ivailo 2).

TRAIN

Veliko's small train station sends about six daily trains to Ruse (4.30lv, 2½ to 3½ hours) and Tryavna (1.20lv, 1½ hours). A more useful train station is just 8.5km north at Gorna Oryahovitsa, where trains stop frequently between Sofia and Varna. Minibuses along ul Vasil Levski head there.

Buy international tickets at **Rila Bureau** (☎ 622 1330; ul Tsar Kolyan; ☯ 8am-noon & 1-4.30pm Mon-Fri).

AROUND VELIKO TÂRNOVO

Arbanasi

☎ 062 / pop 1500

Five kilometres from Veliko Târnovo, high-on-a-hill Arbanasi has stacks of old walled villas and taverns, plus outdoor cafés good for spending a beer-soaked afternoon watching the sunset discolour Veliko below.

The 16th-century **Nativity Church** (☎ 604 323; admission 4lv, guide 8lv; ☯ 9am-6pm Apr-Oct, 9am-5pm Nov-Mar), 200m west of the bus stop, was built ho-hum and low to dissuade the Ottomans from thinking it a place for (Orthodox) worship. Inside, it bursts with colourful murals.

Panorama (☎ 623 421; d 30lv & 40lv; P ☎) This simple, hillside hotel – about 400m west of the bus stop – has three rooms and a pool.

It's about 3lv or 4lv to reach Arbanasi by taxi from Veliko. Some Gorna Oryahovitsa–bound minibuses from ul Vasil Levski in Veliko stop in Arbanasi.

Tryavna

☎ 0677 / pop 12,200

As Bulgaria's ever-whittling woodcarving capital – with an old town centre, several museums and a church, plus revival-era shopfronts – Tryavna (39km south of Veliko) is an Arbanasi without so many tourists.

The Tryavna **tourist office** (☎ 2247; www.trya vna.bg; ul Angel Kânchev 22; ☯ 9am-noon & 2-5pm Mon-

Fri), 400m south of the train and bus stations, offers information on hikes, rents camping gear and arranges **private rooms** (per person 8lv to 15lv).

Up the west-side hill, **Kompleks Brâshlyan** (☎ 3019; bungalows 36lv, d 40-60lv) has great views.

Tryavna has half-hourly bus connections with Gabrovo (18km west). Nine daily trains go to/from Veliko Târnovo (2.50lv, 50 minutes).

BLACK SEA COAST

For most travellers (ie package tourists), the blue-green water and golden-sand beaches along the Black Sea coast *are* Bulgaria. Quieter pockets can be found on the south coast.

Most hotel prices raise their rates in June, again in July and August, then drop them a bit in September.

BURGAS БУРГАС

☎ 056 / pop 193,320

This Black Sea gateway is a rather sweaty port town with two big-time pedestrian malls and a so-so beach. However, it has frequent transport connections to better beaches nearby.

The pedestrianised ul Aleksandrovska runs north (across ul Bulair) from the train station and Yug Bus Terminal. At pl Svoboda it meets another pedestrian mall ul Bogoridi – the busier of the two – which extends east towards the beach.

Bulbank (ul Aleksandrovska; ☯ 8.30am-4pm Mon-Fri) has a 24-hour ATM. **SEANET** (ul Morska 40; per hr 1-1.60lv; ☯ 24hr) is just north of ul Bogoridi.

Sights

Burgas' **beach** is a 2km strip with barges passing by. Running alongside the beach is Maritime Park.

If it rains, there are a few museums in town; probably the best is the **Ethnographical Museum** (☎ 842 587; ul Slavyanska 69; adult/student 2/1lv; ☯ 8am-noon & 1-5pm Mon-Fri).

Hotel Bulgaria (pl Svoboda) houses a basement **public pool** (admission 5lv; ☯ 9am-10pm).

Sleeping & Eating

Dim-ant (☎ 840 779; dimant91@abv.bg; ul Tsar Simeon 15; ☯ 8.30am-8pm in summer, closed Sun other times) This place arranges rooms in Burgas and along the coast for about 10lv per person; an apartment for four is 40lv to 50lv.

Zornitsa Hotel (☎ 816 266; bloque 45, Zornitsa; tr with shared bathroom 30lv) This out-of-the-way communist-era high-rise dorm is 2km north of the train station. Each room has three beds. Take bus No 12A from the centre; it's behind the hospital, past the stadium.

Hotel Central (☎ 815 488; ul Ivailo 60; s/d 44/50lv) Dated rooms with fan, but the cheapest within a short walk of the centre. From ul Aleksandrovska, 450m north of pl Svoboda, head east for 400m on ul Tsar Boris.

Hotel Elite (☎ 845 779; ul Morska 35; s/d with breakfast 50/56lv; 🔀) Super-comfy rooms right off ul Bogodini.

Along the water are several **beach cafés**, open in summer.

BMS (ul Aleksandrovska; mains 3-3.50lv; 🕒 8am-10pm) Peppy pick-and-point cafeteria with good Bulgarian vittles and fluorescent lighting.

Nov Shanhai (☎ 843-105; ul Bogoridi 61; mains 2.50-6lv; 🕒 noon-midnight) Authentic Chinese restaurant at the eastern end of ul Bogoridi, with heaped veggie and meat dishes.

Getting There & Away

AIR
The airport north of town sees many charter flights in summer.

BUS
Most buses and microbuses use the convenient **Yug Bus Terminal** (near cnr ul Aleksandrovska & ul Bulair). Varna-bound buses from central Bulgaria, however, usually drop off Burgas passengers at the **Zapad Bus Terminal**, 2km north of centre. City bus No 4 connects the two.

Daily bus service from Yug connects Burgas with Sofia (13lv to 15lv, six hours, 10 daily), Plovdiv (10lv, four hours, two daily), several to Veliko Târnovo (10lv, four hours) and Varna (6lv to 7lv, 2½ hours, every 30 or 40 minutes).

South coast schedules swell in summer and trickle off in the low season. All year, buses leave half-hourly 6am to 8pm for Sozopol (2.10lv, 40 minutes) and Nesebâr (2.40lv, 50 minutes). A few daily buses go to Primorsko, Kiten and Ahtopol, with one continuing to Sinemorets (5.80lv, two hours). These often do *not* stop in Sozopol.

Kaleya (☎ 844 208; ul Bulair 11; 🕒 8am-6.30pm) can get you onto Istanbul-bound buses (35lv, seven hours), which leave a few times daily.

CAR
TS Travel (☎ 845 060; www.tstravel.net; ul Bulair 1; 🕒 9am-6pm Mon-Sat) rents out cars from €44 per day.

TRAIN
The train station sends buses to Sofia (11.10lv, seven to eight hours, seven daily) and Plovdiv (7.90lv, four to five hours, three daily). Usually one or two more trains make the trips in summer.

No direct international trains depart from Burgas, but you can buy tickets at the **Rila Bureau** (☎ 845 242; 🕒 8am-5pm Mon-Fri) in the train station.

SOUTHERN COAST

Sozopol Созопол
☎ 0550 / pop 5001

All things said, Sozopol is Bulgaria's Black Sea base of choice. It has two sandy beaches, a pretty island offshore and a stone-step historic centre on a jutting peninsula.

The bus stop, 31km south of Burgas, is roughly between the old town and inland new town (Harmanite). There are banks and Internet access in both areas.

Sea taxis out to 6.6-sq-km **St John's (Ivan) Island** are 20lv for the return trip (up to five people).

A summer accommodation agency near the bus stop books **private rooms** for about 20lv per person and up.

Hotel Radik (☎ 3706; ul Republikanska 4; r per person 15-25lv; 🔀) Just up the hill from the bus stop, a friendly elderly couple (no English) run this bright place with spotless rooms and a summer terrace bar.

Campers can head 4km south of town to **Kavatsi Camping** (☎ 22 261; camping 10lv, bungalows with bathroom 45lv) on the beach.

Buses and minibuses leave the **bus terminal** (ul Han Krum) for Burgas (2.10lv, 40 minutes, half-hourly 6am to 9pm) all year. In summer it's often possible to catch buses south.

South of Sozopol
The principal towns along this bay-to-bay linked stretch – Primorsko, Kiten, Ahtopol and far-off Sinemorets – access Bulgaria's best beaches. **Primorsko** is the liveliest but is also rather resorty. Most Bulgarians acknowledge that **Sinemorets**, 11km north of the (closed) Turkish border, has the finest stretch of sand (actually two). One hotel

BULGARIA

in Sinemorets is **Horizon** (☎ 0550-66 026; r 40lv), about 400m beyond the bus stop. See p240 for bus transport information from Burgas.

NESEBÂR НЕСЕБЪР

☎ 0554 / pop 9500

About 35km north of Burgas, historic but touristy Nesebâr sits out on a small rocky isthmus on the south end of the wide, practically perfect bay that's home to built-for-tourism **Sunny Beach** (Slânchev Bryag), 2km away. Nesebâr flaunts its centuries, dating back to when Thracians settled Mesembria here in 3000 BC.

Biochim Commercial Bank (ul Mesembria; ✹ 8.30am-12.15pm & 1-5.30pm Mon-Fri) cashes travellers cheques and has an ATM. Internet is available in Nesebâr's new town (about 1km west) all year.

Even the churched-out should stroll past Nesebâr's Byzantine-inspired ceramic disc–adorned **churches**, including the ruined 6th-century **basilica** (ul Mitropolitska).

Summer-run travel agencies book private rooms. See www.nesebar.com for a list of hotels. **Ekotour-BG** (☎ 43 200; ul Priboina), in the new town, arranges private rooms for around 10lv per person.

Hotel Toni (☎ 42 403; ul Kraybrezhna; r summer 55lv, off season 30-35lv; ✖) A dozen cosy rooms, some with north-facing balconies looking over the water. It's just past the St Georgi Hotel.

Around half-a-dozen daily buses (more in summer) head north to Varna (6lv, two hours) and more frequently to Burgas (2.10lv, 40 minutes). Buses run to Sunny Beach every 15 or 30 minutes, or else you can take a 30-minute walk there.

VARNA ВАРНА

☎ 052 / pop 314,540

Even without the Black Sea at its lip, Varna (with Roman ruins and one of the country's best museums) would be a Bulgarian highlight. Plus there are easy jaunts north and south to beaches, and not bad ones in town.

The renowned Varna Summer International Festival is held between May and October.

Varna was founded as Odessos by Greek sailors in the 6th century BC.

Orientation & Information

The train station is 650m south of central pl Nezavisimost, where pedestrian mall ul

Knyaz Boris I heads west to ul Slivnitsa, which goes southeast to seaside Primorski Park. The bus station is 2km north of the centre; take bus No 409 or 148.

Bulbank (ul Slivnitsa; ✹ 8.30am-4pm Mon-Fri) Changes travellers cheques, as do banks northeast of the train station.

Frag (pl Nezavisimost; per hr 0.50-1lv; ✹ 24hr) Internet café below the red opera building.

Peralnya (ul Voden; per load 2.50-4.30lv; ✹ 9am-7pm Mon-Fri, 9am-6pm Sat) Drop-off laundry service.

Top Tel (ul Filaret 9; international calls per min 0.35lv; ✹ 9am-9pm) Call centre 100m south of ul Knyaz Boris I.

Tourist office (☎ 602 907; www.tourexpo.bg; bul Tsar Osvoboditel 36; ✹ 9am-7pm Mon-Fri, 9am-1pm Sat) For regional info; the centre also rents cars from €28 per day.

Archaeological Museum

This large **museum** (ul Maria Luisa 41; adult/student 4/2lv; ✹ 10am-5pm Tue-Sun Apr-Sep, 10am-5pm Tue-Sat Oct-Mar) is one of Bulgaria's best. Housed in a former girls' school – a grand old two-storey – it is filled with more than 100,000 pieces from some 6000 years of the area's history, all remarkably well explained in English. Look out for the sculpted Thracian goatee.

Other Sights

The 8km-long **Primorski Park** is a leafy strolling ground, freckled with museums, a kiddie ride park, heroic statues and an endless array of popcorn vendors. Along its east side are a couple of beaches and several bars.

The leftovers of the 2nd-century AD **Roman Thermae** (cnr ul Khan Krum & San Stefano; adult/student 3/2lv; ✹ 10am-5pm May-Oct, Tue-Sat Nov-Apr), about 400m southeast of pl Nezavisimost, comprise the largest ruins in Bulgaria.

The greatest of Varna's many impressive churches is the mammoth onion-domed **Cathedral of the Assumption of the Virgin** (pl Mitropolitska Simeon; admission free; ✹ 7.30am-5.30pm Mon-Fri, 7.30am-6.30pm Sat & Sun), 200m northwest of pl Nezavisimost.

Sleeping

Both the bus and train stations have accommodation bureaus (with iffy hours in winter). Across from the train station, **Victorina** (☎ 603 541; Tsar Simeon 36; ✹ 7am-9pm daily Jun-Sep, 10am-6pm Mon-Fri Oct-May) arranges rooms from 20lv to 24lv.

Flag Hostel (☎ 648 877; flagvarna@yahoo.com; 1st fl, ul Opalchenska 25; dm 20lv) The Black Sea's first hostel – at last! – opened in summer 2004, with three six-bed rooms and an outside terrace in a modern building.

Hotel Relax (☎ 361 586; www.hotelrelax2.com; ul Stephan Karadja 22; r 35-50lv) This laid-back 14-room hotel has odds-and-ends furnishings, like the hilarious addition of an antique piano in one room. There's a garden bar in summer.

Cherno More Hotel (☎ 612 243; ul Slivnitsa 33; r with breakfast US$25-50; P 🔀) Most rooms at this central high-rise still wear decades-old scars, but the location is tops and the balcony sea views can't be beat.

Eating & Drinking

Chuchura (ul Dragoman 11; lunches 2.28-3lv, meats 2.50-6lv; ⏳ 11.30am-11.30pm) Just off the pedestrian mall, this revival-era tavern serves excellent Bulgarian meals. Anything grilled in the brick oven up front is super. Veggie options include rice-filled vine leaves covered in yogurt.

Nord (beach; fish 3-9lv; ⏳ 7am-4am) Open all year, Nord packs in them local young things for cold mugs of beer and plates of calamari and sprat.

Also at the beach is the disco **Exit** (follow the white footsteps).

Getting There & Away

AIR

Varna airport (☎ 650 835) is west of town. Bus No 409 goes there.

BUS

The **main bus terminal** (bul Vladislav Varenchik) sends buses to the following destinations: Athens (95lv, 26 hours, one daily), Burgas (7lv, two hours, every 30 or 40 minutes), Istanbul (40lv, 10 hours, two daily), Plovdiv (15lv, six hours, two daily), Ruse (8.40lv, four hours, two daily), Sofia (19lv, seven to eight hours, every 45 minutes) via Shumen and Veliko Târnovo), and Veliko Târnovo (8lv, four hours, every 45 minutes).

MICROBUS

The **microbus terminal** (Avtogara Mladost; ☎ 800 038; ul Knyaz Cherkazki), 200m west of the bus station, sends buses hourly to Burgas and Albena (2.50lv, 30 minutes), and less often to Nesebâr.

Microbuses also depart for Albena from ul Maria Luisa, 150m west of the Cathedral of the Assumption of the Virgin.

TRAIN

Direct trains from the **main train station** (bul Primorski) link Varna with Sofia (12.50lv, 8½ hours, six daily), Plovdiv (9.90lv, 6½ hours, three daily) and Ruse (6.90lv, four hours, two daily); there are also direct links to Bucharest in summer.

Buy international tickets at **Rila Bureau** (☎ 632 348; ul Preslav 13; ⏳ 8am-5.30pm Mon-Fri, 8am-3.30pm Sat), 150m east of the station.

NORTHERN COAST

Up from Varna are some up-market beach resorts that focus on rich package-trippers. All can be visited on day trips from Varna.

Get to **Sveti Konstantin** beach, 9km north, by bus No 8 from ul Maria Luisa.

Golden Sands (Zlatni Pyasâtsi), 18km north of Varna, has a 4km stretch of beach. Inland is the bizarre **Aladzha Monastery** (admission 2lv; ⏳ closed Mon year-round, Sun & Mon winter), a 50-minute walk (or a taxi ride) inland. City bus Nos 109, 209, 309 and 409 connect Golden Sands and Varna every 15 minutes from 6am to 11pm.

Albena is reached by hourly microbus from Varna, which is a 30-minute trip. **Gorska Feia** is a bungalow camping ground near the bus terminal.

BULGARIA DIRECTORY

ACCOMMODATION

Bulgaria's hostel scene is minimal outside Sofia, where there are more than half-a-dozen good ones. The Black Sea's first hostel opened in Varna (opposite).

Cheapest, then, is safe, clean homestays, found from the train-station touts, accommodation agencies (some open just in summer) or by posted 'stai pod naem' signs (rooms for rent). Families offering this type are used to travellers, so they respect your privacy. Rates go from 10lv to 20lv per person.

All hotel entries in this chapter include private bathroom and TV unless otherwise noted. Most have air-conditioning or fans; all have heating. Average rates are around 30lv for a single, 40lv for a double.

'Camping' for most Bulgarians means an area with side-by-side basic bungalows and a couple of spots to pitch a tent. Discreet camping outside official grounds is not technically legal but done.

Up in the mountains there are many *hizhas* (mountain huts) of varying condition. Many Bulgaria maps show their locations.

Quite a few of Bulgaria's 160 active monasteries let bare-bone rooms for as little as 10lv per night.

ACTIVITIES

The hiking options in Bulgaria's mountains abound (over 37,000km of hiking trails in all). Visit **Zig Zag** (☎ 980 5102; www.zigzag.dir.bg; bul Stamboliyski 20V) in Sofia, reviewed on p229, for trip info, tips and trail maps.

Bulgaria is gaining fame as a cheap downhill ski (and snowboarding) destination. Its three main resorts are in the southwest: Borovets, Bansko and Pamporovo. Lift tickets are 40lv to 50lv per day, rental gear 20lv to 40lv more. Mt Vitosha (p233), near Sofia, is cheaper. Package deals (look around in Sofia) will save money. Also check www .bulgariaski.com or, for lift-free, exciting trips, www.exploring-bg.com.

There's good rock climbing outside Veliko Târnovo (p239).

DANGERS & ANNOYANCES

Crime isn't unknown, but if you hold onto your bags at stations, you're not likely to have any problems. Cigarette smoke is a huge annoyance unless you like red eyes. Another annoyance is the incessant claims from many here that Roma will rob you blind.

DISCOUNT CARDS

Students can save 50% on ticket admission at most museums, and on air fares at some travel agents. In Sofia, **Orbita** (☎ 987 9128; orbita@ttm.bg; bul Hristo Botev 48; ☼ 9am-5pm Mon-Fri) issues student cards.

EMBASSIES & CONSULATES
Embassies & Consulates in Bulgaria
Australia consulate (☎ 02-946 1334; ul Trakia 37) Main office in Athens; call for hours.

Canada consulate (☎ 02-943 3704; ul Assen Zlatarov 11)

Denmark (☎ 02-980-0830; bul Dondukov 54; ☼ 9am-4pm Mon-Fri)

France consulate (☎ 02-946 1040; www.ambafrance -bg.org; ul Oborishte 21A; ☼ 9am-noon & 3-6pm Mon-Fri)

Germany (☎ 02-918-38-116; ul Frederic Joliot-Curie 25; ☼ 8am-5pm Mon-Thu, 8am-1.30pm Fri)

Greece consulate (☎ 02-946 1750; ul Evlogi Georgiev 103; ☼ 8.30am-4pm Mon-Fri)

Hungary (☎ 02-963 1135; ul 6 Septemvri 57; visas ☼ 9-11am Mon, Wed & Fri)

Ireland (☎ 02-981 2094; 4th fl, bul Stamboliyski 55)

Macedonia (☎ 02-701 560; ul Frederic Joliot-Curie 17)

Netherlands (☎ 02-816 0300; www.netherlands embassy.bg; ul Oborishte 15; ☼ 10am-noon Mon-Fri)

Poland (☎ 02-987 2610, visa info ☎ 981 8545; ul Han Krum 46; visas ☼ 9am-1pm Mon-Wed & Fri)

Romania consulate (☎ 02-973 3510; bul M Eminesku 1; visas ☼ 3-5pm Tue, 10am-noon Wed & Thu)

Russia (☎ 02-963 0914; bul Dragan Tsankov 28)

Turkey consulate (☎ 02-935 5500; bul Vasil Levski 80; ☼ 9.30am-1pm Mon-Fri)

UK (☎ 02-933 9222; www.british-embassy.bg; ul Moskovska 9; ☼ 8am-5pm Mon-Fri)

USA consulate (☎ 02-963 1391; www.usembassy.bg; ul Kapitan Andreev 1; ☼ 2-4pm Mon-Fri)

Bulgarian Embassies & Consulates Abroad
Australia (☎ 02-9327 7592; fax 9327 8067; 14 Carlotta Rd, Double Bay, NSW 2028)

Canada (☎ 613-789 3215; fax 789 3524; 325 Steward St, Ottawa, Ontario N1K6K5)

France (☎ 01 45 51 85 90; fax 01 45 51 18 68; www .bulgaria.com/embassy/france; 1 av Rapp, 75007 Paris)

Germany (☎ 030-201 0922; bbotscaft@myokay.net; Mauerstrasse 11, Berlin 10117)

Greece Athens (☎ 30-1-647 8105; fax 30-1-647 8130; 33 Stratigou Kallari St, 15452 Athens); Thessaloniki (☎ 031-829 210; Edmundo Abot 1, Thessaloniki)

Ireland (☎ 01-660 3229; fax 660 3915; 22 Burlington Rd, Dublin)

Israel (☎ 972-3-524 1798; fax 524 1798; 124 Rehov ibn Gavirol, 62308 Tel Aviv)

Macedonia (☎ 91-22 94 44; fax 11 61 39; 3 Zlatko Shnaider St, Skopje)

Netherlands (☎ 070-350 3051; www.embassy -bulgaria.nl; Duinroosweg 9, 2597 KJ The Hague)

Romania (☎ 01-230 2150 ; fax 230 7654; Str Rabat 5, sec 1, Bucharest)

Serbia (☎ 11-64 62 22; fax 64 10 80; 26 Birchaninova St, Belgrade)

Turkey Ankara (☎ 0312-426 7455; Atatürk Bulvari 124, Kavaklidere, Ankara); Mahallesi (☎ 0212-269 0478; fax 264 1011; Adnan Saygun Caddesi 44, Ulus, Mahallesi, Istanbul)

UK (☎ 020-7584 9400; www.bulgarianembassy.org.uk; 186-188 Queen's Gate, London SW7 5HL)

USA (☎ 202-387 0174; www.bulgaria-embassy.org; 1621 22nd St NW, Washington, DC 2008)

FESTIVALS & EVENTS

Bulgaria hosts many fascinating shindigs. City-run music and cultural events go all through summer. See listings in town sections.

As part of the national custom of Marten-itsa in March, most Bulgarians wear red-and-white figures made from yarn till they see a stork, when they tie the figure to a tree.

GAY & LESBIAN TRAVELLERS
Consensual homosexual sex is legal in Bulgaria. The best source for discos and bars is at www.bulgayria.com. **Bulgarian Gay Organization Gemini** (www.bgogemini.org) can help point out places to go, too.

HOLIDAYS
The following are official public holidays:
New Year's Day 1 January
Liberation Day (National Day) 3 March
Orthodox Easter Sunday & Monday (One week after Catholic/Protestant Easter) March/April
St George's Day 6 May
Cyrillic Alphabet Day 24 May
Unification (National Day) 6 September
Bulgarian Independence Day 22 September
National Revival Day 1 November
Christmas Day 25 December
Boxing Day 26 December

LANGUAGE
Almost everything is written in Cyrillic (even 'kseroks' for Xerox). Many Bulgarians know some Russian, German or English. See p1264 for a few useful words.

MONEY
The *leva* (lv) comprise 100 *stotinki*. It's been pegged to the euro (roughly 2:1) since January 2002. In touristy places and up-market hotels, many prices are quoted in euros, or sometimes US dollars. Prices in this chapter conform to quotes of individual businesses. Banknotes come in denominations of one, two, five, 10, 20 and 50 *leva* and coins in one, two, five, 10, 20 and 50 *stotinki*.

Exchanging Money
There is no problem changing money – foreign-exchange offices (many working non-stop) are in every city, town and at major attractions. US dollars, UK pounds and the euro are the best currencies to carry.

Foreigner Prices
Brace yourself for an official dual-pricing scheme, where foreigners pay double (or more) the local price at museums and hotels (only).

Travellers Cheques
American Express and Thomas Cook cheques can be cashed at almost all of the banks. Bulbank, the country's official bank, often charges the lowest commission rate – officially €1 per transaction (not per cheque).

POST
Sending a postcard to anywhere outside Bulgaria costs 0.32lv; letters up to 20g cost 0.83lv to Europe and 0.87lv outside Europe. Many post offices in bigger cities are open daily.

STUDYING
It's possibly to study Bulgarian in Sofia (p231) and Veliko Târnovo (p239). You can learn to play traditional Bulgarian music at a couple of schools, including the **Philip Kotev School** (☎ 2215; smu_k_l@mail.bg; ul Geori Zahariev 2, Kotel 8970), in Kotel.

TELEPHONE
At Bulgarian Telecommunications Centre (BTC), found inside or next to main post offices, you can make international calls for about 0.55lv per minute. It's cheaper to call from Internet cafés (as little as 0.20lv per minute). Mobika and BulFon telephone booths use *fonkarta* (phonecards).

To ring Bulgaria from abroad, dial the international access code, then ☎ 359, followed by the area code (minus the first zero), then the number.

To call direct out of Bulgaria, dial ☎ 00, then the country code.

Phone numbers tend to change often in Bulgaria.

VISAS
Currently citizens of Australia, Canada, Ireland, Israel, Japan, New Zealand, Poland, UK as well as USA can obtain a free 30-day tourist visa at any Bulgarian border, international airport or seaport. Other EU countries are able to get a 90-day tourist visas.

The easiest way to get a new visa is by leaving the country and returning the same or next day. It is also possible to pay 200lv for an extension at the **immigration office** (☎ 982 3316; bul Maria Luisa 48; 🕙 9am-12.30pm & 1.30-5pm Mon-Fri) in Sofia.

Also see Registration at Hotels (p231).

Croatia

HIGHLIGHTS

▪ **Dubrovnik** Glowing Renaissance architecture enclosed in a magnificent curtain of walls with dynamic nightlife and easy access to beaches. It's Croatia's crown jewel (p262)
▪ **Hvar Island** Lush greenery carpets the island, while the Old Town throbs with Croatia's sleekest bars. Diving, snorkelling or nude sunbathing – name your pleasure (p260)
▪ **Korčula Island** A walled old town built from stone fills a tiny peninsula, while forests and idyllic coves dot the island (p261)
▪ **Best journey** From Split, boat it to Hvar (p260), Korčula (p261) and on to Dubrovnik (p262), experiencing the best of the Dalmatian coast
▪ **Off-the-beaten track** Lokrum, where the pine trees shelter sunbathers and naturists cluster in discreet coves (p263)

FAST FACTS

▪ **Area** 56,538 sq km (about one quarter of Britain)

▪ **ATMs** Readily available in towns and transport hubs

▪ **Budget** 250KN per day

▪ **Capital** Zagreb

▪ **Country Code** ☎ 385

▪ **Famous for** Neckties, war, Tito

▪ **Language** Croatian

▪ **Money** Kuna (A$1 = 4.48KN, CA$1 = 4.88KN, €1 = 7.70KN, ¥100 = 5.56KN, NZ$1 = 4.16KN, UK£1 = 11.49KN, US$1 = 6.41)

▪ **Population** 4.5 million

▪ **Phrases** *Bog* (hello); *doviđenja* (goodbye); *hvala* (thanks); *pardon* (sorry)

▪ **Time** GMT/UTC + 1

▪ **Visas** None required for citizens of the EU, USA, Australia and Canada

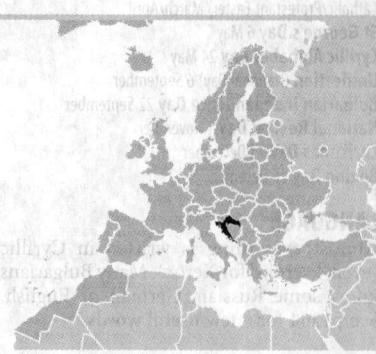

TRAVEL HINT

Watch out for sea urchins in shallow water!

ROAMING CROATIA

Start in Zagreb, head down to Pula, then follow the coast south hitting Zadar, Split, Hvar, Korčula and Dubrovnik.

Croatia is the Mediterranean's best-kept secret. Its lush islands, unspoilt fishing villages, beaches, lakes, waterfalls and walled cities were the star attraction of the former Yugoslavia before it split apart in 1991. The essential fabulousness of the country was forgotten as the region descended into war, but travellers are once again discovering its many treasures.

With 6000km of coastline winding around innumerable bays and almost 1100 islands offshore, there's a dream spot for every taste. The magnificent walled city of Dubrovnik, on

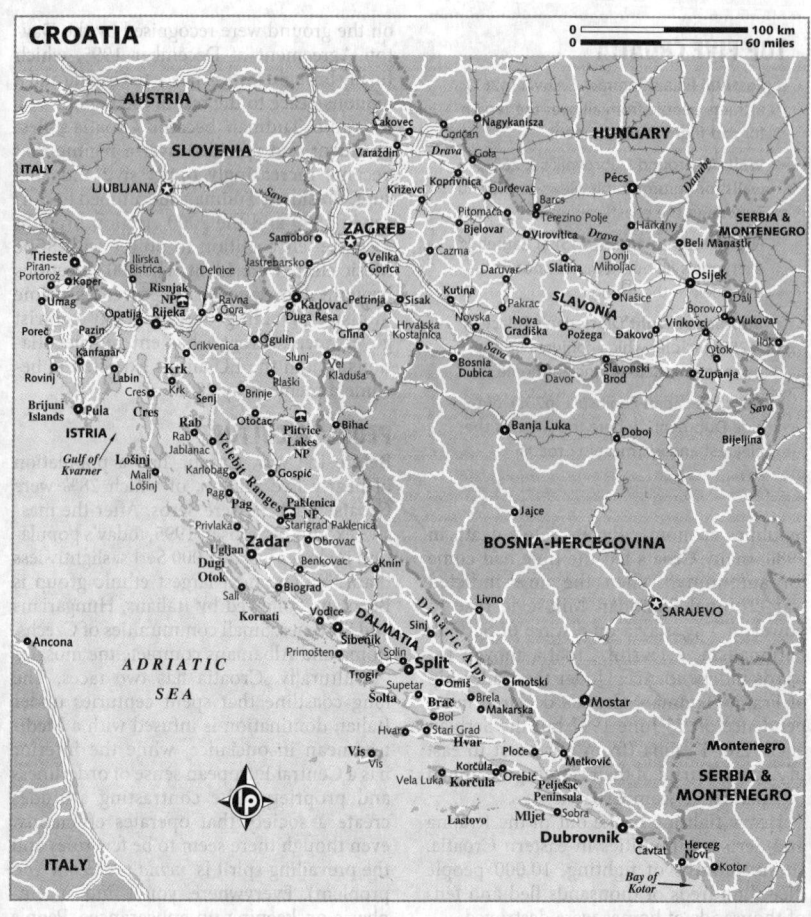

CROATIA

| 0 | 100 km |
| 0 | 60 miles |

the country's southern tip, is Croatia's crown jewel, with lovely Hvar and Korčula Islands within easy reach. Istria, on the north coast, is famous for its delicious food, rocky beaches and relaxed, Italian-influenced lifestyle. Austrian influence is most pronounced in Croatia's capital, Zagreb, a calm and gracious city. Yet wherever you go in Croatia, you'll find easygoing, tolerant people, accustomed to welcoming visitors and proud of the country they fought so hard to establish.

HISTORY

Modern Croatia is on the site of the ancient Roman province of Illyricum. Pula and Split were the two most important Roman towns. Slavs migrated into the region in the 7th century but political disarray tempted the Venetians to attack the coast. They established their first foothold on the coast in the 11th century and remained until Napoleon conquered Venice in 1797. In 1815 the Austro-Hungarian empire took control of Croatia, but with its defeat in WWI, Croatia became part of the Kingdom of Serbs, Croats and Slovenes (Yugoslavia). The Germans invaded in 1941 and tens of thousands of Croats joined the forces of Josip Broz, known as Maršal Tito.

After the war, Tito became prime minister of the new Yugoslav Federation. Croatia and Slovenia moved far ahead of the southern

TOP FIVE CROATIA

- **Festival** Pula's Summer Festival (p267) attracts people from all over the region for top-flight entertainment
- **Walk** All around Dubrovnik's (p263) walls for unforgettable views of the Old Town and the coast
- **Nightclub** Aquarius (p255) in Zagreb is everyone's favourite dance spot from the sleek to the grungy
- **Impressive sight** Diocletian's Palace (p259) in Split, which conjures up the bygone grandeur of ancient Rome
- **Beaches** Lapad Peninsula (p263), outside Dubrovnik, where the water is the clearest and warmest in Croatia

republics economically. By Tito's death in 1980, many Croats felt the time had come for autonomy. When the now indicted war criminal Slobodan Milošević rose to power in Yugoslavia on a wave of Serbian nationalism, a fearful Croatia moved towards independence. Under the leadership of Franjo Tuđman, Croatia declared independence on 25 June 1991 but the Serbian enclave of Krajina (from northeast to east of Zadar), fearful of their rights, proclaimed independence from Croatia.

Heavy fighting broke out in the Krajina and Serb communities in eastern Croatia. In six months of fighting, 10,000 people died, hundreds of thousands fled and tens of thousands of homes were destroyed.

A series of international peace plans halted the fighting until, in January 1993, the Croatian army suddenly launched an offensive in southern Krajina, recapturing much land. Their hold was consolidated in a new offensive launched on 1 May 1995, which essentially set Croatia's new borders. The facts

READING UP

The most comprehensive recent account of Croatian history is Marcus Tanner's *Croatia: A Nation Forged in War*. Misha Glenny's *The Fall of Yugoslavia* is an excellent account of the nationalistic yearnings and political infighting that tore apart the former Yugoslavia.

on the ground were recognised by the Dayton Agreement of December 1995, which finally brought lasting peace to Croatia and a tenuous peace to the rest of the region.

Franjo Tuđman became Croatia's first president and presided over a regime that became increasingly oppressive and corrupt. President Tuđman succumbed to cancer in 1999 and the 2000 election brought a centre-left coalition to power with Stipe Mesić elected president. The 2003 elections brought Ivo Sanader to power as prime minister presiding over a largely centrist government. Croatia has entered negotiations to join the EU and is expected to become a member by 2008.

PEOPLE & CULTURE

Before the war, Croatia had a population of nearly five million, of which 78% were Croats and 12% were Serbs. After the massive exodus of Serbs in 1995, today's population includes just 201,000 Serbs, slightly less than 5%. The next largest ethnic group is Bosnians, followed by Italians, Hungarians and Slovenes. Small communities of Czechs, Roma and Albanians complete the mosaic.

Culturally, Croatia has two faces. The long coastline that spent centuries under Italian domination is infused with a Mediterranean insouciance, while the interior has a Central European sense of orderliness and propriety. The contrasting attitudes create a society that operates efficiently, even though there seem to be few rules and the prevailing spirit is *'nema problema'* (no problem). Everywhere, you'll find an emphasis on keeping up appearances. People are well, if not flashily dressed and it pains Croatians to see dilapidation anywhere.

ARTS

Croatia's most famous artist is the sculptor Ivan Meštrović (1883–1962), whose work is seen in town squares throughout Croatia. Besides creating public monuments, Meštrović designed imposing buildings, such as the circular Croatian History Museum in Zagreb. Both his sculptures and architecture display the powerful classical restraint he learnt from the French sculptor Auguste Rodin. Meštrović's studio in Zagreb (p254) and his retirement home at Split (p258) have been made into galleries of his work. Another notable sculptor was Antun Augustinčić (1900–

79), who created the Monument to Peace in front of the UN building in New York.

In literature, Croatia's most important writer was the 20th-century novelist and playwright Miroslav Krleža. His most popular novels include *The Return of Philip Latinović* (1932) and *Banners* (1963).

ENVIRONMENT
Croatia has an incredibly diverse topography that runs from the Pannonian plains of Slavonia between the Sava, Drava and Danube Rivers, across hilly central Croatia to the Istrian Peninsula, then south through Dalmatia along the rugged Adriatic coast. Of Croatia's 1185 islands and islets, only 66 are inhabited. Although islands such as Korčula and Hvar are lush, many of the smaller islands are barren, with mountains that drop to the sea.

There are seven national parks and a generally high level of environmental consciousness among Croatians. The lack of heavy industry in Croatia has left the country largely free of industrial pollution.

TRANSPORT

GETTING THERE & AWAY
Air
The following are the major airlines flying into the country:

Adria Airways (JD; www.adria-airways.com; ☎ 01-48 10 011)
Aeroflot (SU; www.aeroflot.ru; ☎ 01-48 72 055)
Air Canada (AC; www.aircanada.ca; ☎ 01-48 22 033)
Air France (AF; www.airfrance.com; ☎ 01-48 37 100)
Alitalia (AZ; www.alitalia.it; ☎ 01-48 10 413)
Austrian Airlines (OS; www.aua.com; ☎ 062 65 900)
British Airways (BA; www.british-airways.com)
Croatia Airlines (OU; ☎ 01-48 19 633; www.croatiaair lines.hr; Zrinjevac 17, Zagreb) Croatia's national carrier and has recently increased its number of flights.
ČSA (OK; www.csa.cz; ☎ 01-48 73 301)
Delta Airlines (DL; www.delta.com; ☎ 01-48 78 760)
KLM-Northwest (KL; www.klm.com; ☎ 01-48 78 601)
Lot (LO; www.lot.com; ☎ 01 48 37 500)
Lufthansa (LH; www.lufthansa.com; ☎ 01-48 73 121)
MALEV Hungarian Airlines (MA; www.malev.hu; ☎ 01-48 36 935)
Turkish Airlines (TK; www.turkishairlines.com; ☎ 01-49 21 854)

Dubrovnik has an **international airport** (☎ 020-773 377; www.airport-dubrovnik.hr) located there.

Sea
Regular boats from several companies connect Croatia with Italy and Slovenia.

Jadrolinija (www.jadrolinija.hr; Riva 16; Ancona ☎ 071-20 71 465; Bari ☎ 080-52 75 439; Split ☎ 21 338 333; Zadar ☎ 23 25 0555; Dubrovnik ☎ 385 20 41800), Croatia's national boat line, runs car ferries from Ancona in Italy to Split (€44, 10 hours) and Zadar (€41, seven hours, up to four weekly in summer, weekly October to May), and a liner from Bari in Italy to Dubrovnik (€49, eight hours, up to four weekly in summer, weekly October to May).

Lošinska Plovidba (Koper ☎ 056-645 183, 66 45 181; Pristaniska 45; Pula ☎ 052-210 431, 211 878; Riva 14) runs boats connecting Koper in Slovenia with Pula (€9, 4½ hours) and Zadar (€23, 13½ hours).

SEM (www.sem-marina.hr; Split ☎ 21-338 292; Gat Sv Duje; Ancona ☎ 071-20 40 90) connects Ancona in Italy with Zadar and Split, continuing to Stari Grad (Hvar Island; two to four weekly).

SNAV (www.snav.com; Ancona ☎ 071-20 76 116; Naples ☎ 081-428 5555; Split ☎ 21 322 252) has a fast car ferry that links Pescara and Ancona, both in Italy, with Split (€73, 4½ hours), and Pescara with Hvar Island (€80, 3½ hours), as well as a passenger boat that connects Civitanova (Italy) and Ancona with Zadar (€70, 3¼ hours).

Adriatica Navigazione (www.adriatica.it; general information & bookings ☎ 081 317 2999; Venice ☎ 041-781 611; Ancona ☎ 071-20 74 334) connects Ancona and Split (weekly from July to August) and runs between Trieste and Rovinj (€15.49, 3½ hours, six weekly June to September).

Venezia Lines (☎ 041-52 22 568; www.venezialines .com; Santa Croce 518/A, Venezia 30135) runs a weekly boat from Venice to Pula (€45, three hours, April to October) and other coastal towns.

Archibugi (Ravenna ☎ 0544-422 682; archibugi@tin .it; Via Magazzini anteriori 27; Rijeka 051-325 540; travel .rijeka@transagent.hr; Verdijeva 6) runs a ferry from July to mid-September, connecting Ravenna to Rijeka (€40, eight hours, daily).

Bus
Eurolines runs buses to Zagreb from Vienna (€32, six hours, two daily). There are daily

DEPARTURE TAX

There is an embarkation tax of €3 from Italian ports.

connections from Sarajevo (€22, five hours) and Mostar (€10.65, three hours) to Dubrovnik; from Medugorje, Mostar and Sarajevo to Split (€15.50, seven hours); and from Sarajevo to Zagreb (€28, eight hours) and Rijeka (€33).

Deutsche Touring GmbH (☎ 069-790 350; www .deutsche-touring.com; Am Romerhof 17, Frankfurt) runs many buses from major German cities to Croatia. There are buses to Pula from Venice (€24, six hours, three daily) and Trieste (€14, 3¾ hours, three daily), Rijeka, Zadar, Split and Dubrovnik (€64, 15 hours, daily). Slovenia is well connected to the Istrian coast with buses from Ljubljana to Zagreb (3070SIT, three hours, two daily), Rijeka (2280SIT, 2½ hours, one daily) and Split (6550SIT, 10½ hours, one daily).

There's one bus a morning from Zagreb to Belgrade (€25.50, six hours). The border between Serbia and Montenegro and Croatia is open to visitors, allowing US, Australian, Canadian and UK citizens to enter visa-free.

There's a daily bus to the Montenegrin border at 11am, from where a Montenegro bus takes you to Herceg-Novi (60KN, two hours) and on to Kotor (100KN, 2½ hours) and Bar (130KN, three hours).

Car & Motorcycle

There are numerous border crossings to/ from Slovenia, Bosnia and Hercegovina, and Serbia and Montenegro.

Train

The *Ljubljana* express travels daily from Vienna to Rijeka (€65.50, 11½ hours, two daily) through Ljubljana, and the EuroCity *Croatia* travels from Vienna to Zagreb (€60.50, 6½ hours). Both travel via Maribor, Slovenia.

There's a weekend train from mid-June to August from Pula to Ljubljana (210KN, four hours).

There are trains from Munich to Zagreb (€70, nine hours, three daily) via Salzburg and Ljubljana, and a train from Berlin to Zagreb (€135, 16 hours, daily).

Trains from Zagreb to Budapest (€30, 6½ hours, four daily) also stop in Nagykanisza, the first main junction inside Hungary (€11). The price is the same for one-way and return-trip tickets.

Between Venice and Zagreb (€41, eight hours) there's also a daily connection via Ljubljana.

There are trains between Zagreb and Ljubljana (€23, 2¼ hours, 11 daily) and between Rijeka and Ljubljana (€25, three hours, four daily). Trains connect Zagreb with Belgrade (€17.50, six hours, five daily).

GETTING AROUND
Boat

Year-round Jadrolinija car ferries operate along the Bari–Rijeka–Dubrovnik coastal route, stopping at Zadar, Split and Hvar and Korčula Islands. Services are less frequent in winter. The most scenic section is Split to Dubrovnik, which all Jadrolinija ferries cover during the day. Ferries are a lot more comfortable than buses, though considerably more expensive. You must buy tickets in advance at an agency or Jadrolinija office, since they are not sold on board.

From Rejeka to Dubrovnik the deck fare costs €25 (there's a 20% reduction on the return portion of a return ticket). With a through ticket, deck passengers can have one port stopover if they notify the purser beforehand and have the ticket validated (which is cheaper than individual sector tickets).

Local ferries connect the bigger offshore islands with each other and the mainland.

Bus

At large bus stations, tickets must be purchased at the office; book ahead to ensure a seat. Tickets for buses that arrive from somewhere else are usually purchased from the conductor. Buy a one-way ticket only or you'll be locked into one company's schedule for the return.

Car & Motorcycle

Motorists require vehicle registration papers and the green insurance card (which proves drivers travelling through Europe have insurance that complies with the minimum insurance requirements of the places that they drive through) to enter Croatia. **Hrvatski Autoklub** (HAK; Croatian Auto Club) offers help and advice; contact the nationwide **HAK road assistance** (vučna služba; ☎ 987).

The large car-rental chains represented are Avis, Budget, Europcar and Hertz.

Hitching

Hitching is never entirely safe, and we don't recommend it. Hitchhiking in Croatia is undependable. You'll have better luck on the islands, but in the interior cars are small and usually full.

Local Transport

Zagreb has a well-developed tram system, as well as local buses, but in the rest of the country you'll only find buses. In major cities such as Rijeka, Split, Zadar and Dubrovnik, buses run every 20 minutes, and less often on Sunday. Small medieval towns along the coast are generally closed to traffic and have infrequent links to outlying suburbs.

Taxis are available in all cities and towns, but must be called or boarded at a taxi stand. Prices are high (meters start at 25KN).

Train

Train travel is about 15% cheaper than bus travel and often more comfortable, although slower. Local trains usually have only unreserved 2nd-class seats. Reservations may be required on express trains. 'Executive' trains have only 1st-class seats and are 40% more expensive than local trains.

ZAGREB

☎ 01 / pop 780,000

Zagreb is coming into its own as a destination that combines the best of Eastern and Western Europe. You can eat well and relatively cheaply, and then dance till dawn to the music of your choice. For daytime activities, you'll find that the stately Austro-Hungarian buildings of the lower town are dotted with a decent assortment of galleries, museums and fashionable boutiques. In the middle of it all is a long park with benches for picnicking and trees to nap under. A stroll through the charming little streets of the upper town is another pleasant way to while away an afternoon.

ORIENTATION

The city is divided into Lower Zagreb, where you'll find most shops, restaurants and businesses, and Upper Zagreb, defined by the two hills of Kaptol and Gradec. As you come out of the train station, you'll see a series of parks and pavilions directly in front of you and the twin neo-Gothic towers of the cathedral in the distance. Trg Jelačića, beyond the northern end of the parks, is the main city square.

INFORMATION
Internet Access

Art Net Club (☎ 45 58 471; Preradovićeva 25; per hr 20KN; ☽ 9am-11pm) Zagreb's flashiest cyber café hosts frequent concerts and performances.
Sublink (☎ 48 11 329; Teslina 12; per hr 20KN; ☽ 9am-10pm Mon-Sat, 3-10pm Sun) It was here first and has a comfortable setup.

Medical Services

KBC Rebro (☎ 23 88 888; Kišpatićeva 12; ☽ 24 hr) One kilometre east of the city, it provides emergency aid.

Money

There are ATMs at the bus and train stations and the airport, as well as numerous locations around town. Exchange bureaus at the bus and train stations change money with 1.5% commission. Both the banks in the train station and the bus station accept travellers cheques.
Atlas (☎ 48 13 933; www.atlas-croatia.com; Zrinjevac 17) The American Express representative in Zagreb.

Post

Main post office (Branimirova 4; ☽ 24 hr Mon-Sat, 1pm-midnight Sun) Holds poste restante mail. This post office is also the best place to make long-distance telephone calls and send packages.

GETTING INTO TOWN

The bus station is 1km east of the train station. Tram Nos 2 and 6 run from the bus station to the nearby train station, with No 6 continuing to Trg Jelačića. To walk to Trg Jelačića from the train station, head north for roughly 1km on the left side of the park. The airport is 17km southeast of town; take the Croatia Airlines bus (25KN) to the bus station.

CROATIA

ZAGREB

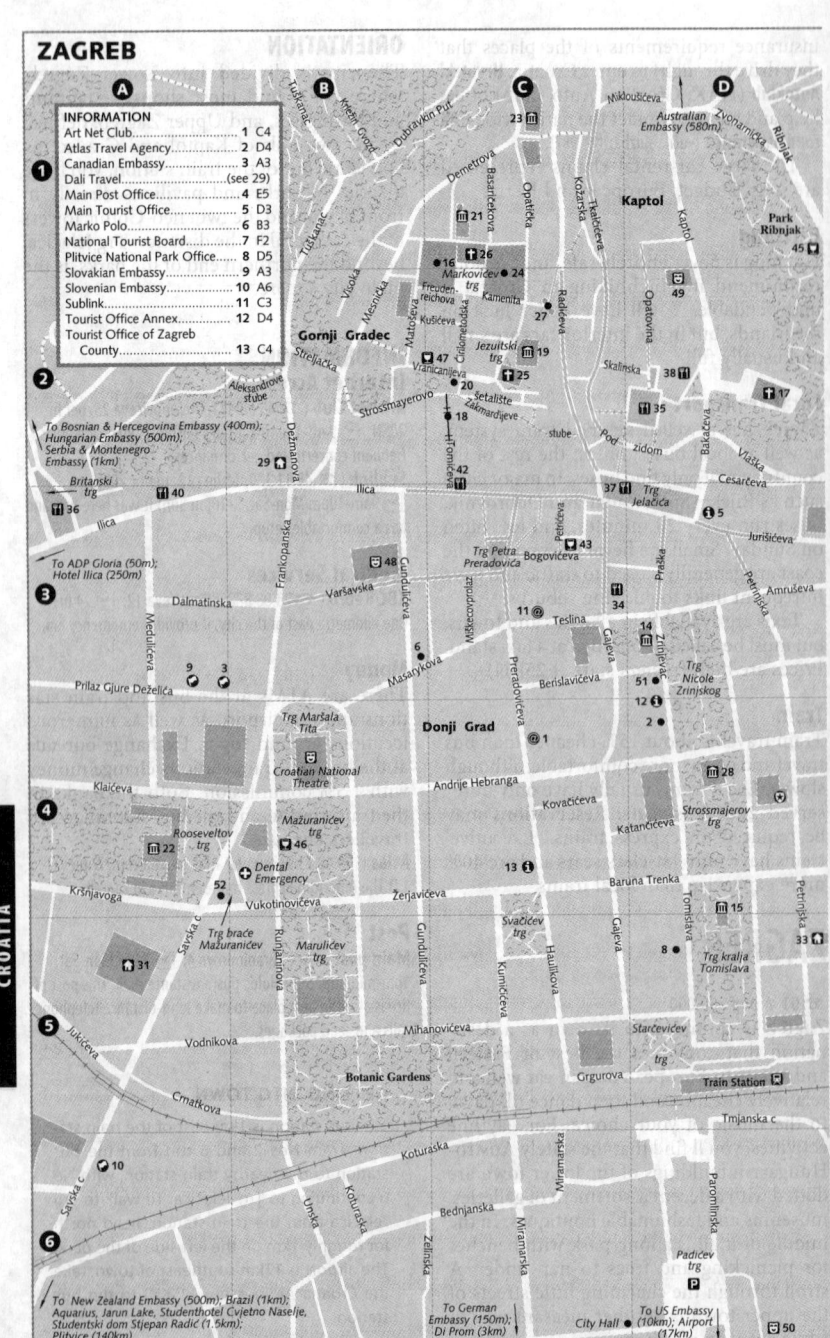

INFORMATION

Art Net Club..........................	1 C4
Atlas Travel Agency................	2 D4
Canadian Embassy..................	3 A3
Dali Travel...........................(see 29)
Main Post Office.....................	4 E5
Main Tourist Office.................	5 D3
Marko Polo..........................	6 B3
National Tourist Board.............	7 F2
Plitvice National Park Office.....	8 D5
Slovakian Embassy.................	9 A3
Slovenian Embassy.................	10 A6
Sublink...............................	11 C3
Tourist Office Annex...............	12 D4
Tourist Office of Zagreb County.........................	13 C4

To Bosnian & Hercegovina Embassy (400m); Hungarian Embassy (500m); Serbia & Montenegro Embassy (1km)

To ADP Gloria (50m); Hotel Ilica (250m)

To New Zealand Embassy (500m); Brazil (1km); Aquarius, Jarun Lake, Studenthotel Cvjetno Naselje, Studentski dom Stjepan Radić (1.5km); Plitvice (140km)

To German Embassy (150m); Di Prom (3km)

To US Embassy (10km); Airport (17km)

City Hall

Australian Embassy (580m)

Kaptol

Park Ribnjak

Gornji Gradec

Donji Grad

Croatian National Theatre

Botanic Gardens

Train Station

Dental Emergency

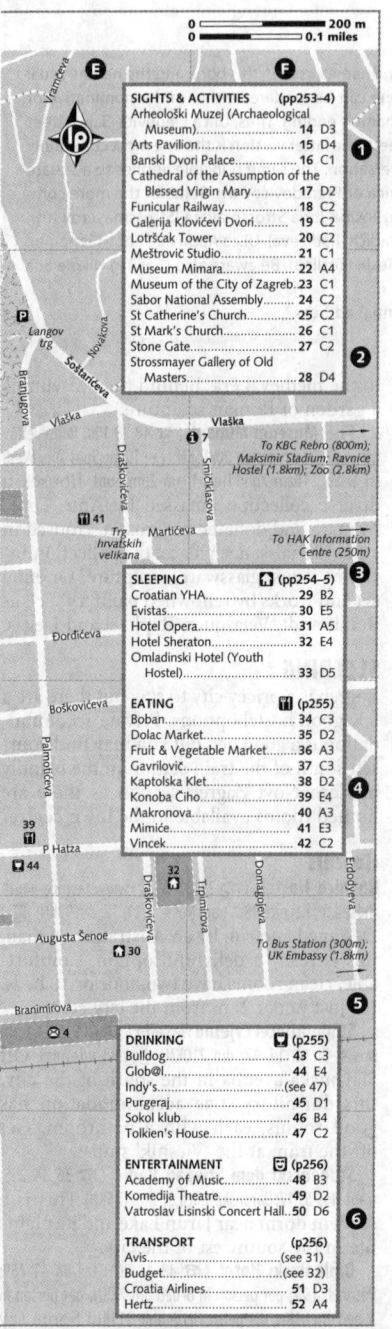

SIGHTS & ACTIVITIES (pp253–4)
Arheološki Muzej (Archaeological Museum).......... 14 D3
Arts Pavilion.......... 15 D4
Banski Dvori Palace.......... 16 C1
Cathedral of the Assumption of the Blessed Virgin Mary.......... 17 D2
Funicular Railway.......... 18 C2
Galerija Klovićevi Dvori.......... 19 C2
Lotršćak Tower.......... 20 C2
Meštrović Studio.......... 21 C1
Museum Mimara.......... 22 A4
Museum of the City of Zagreb.......... 23 C1
Sabor National Assembly.......... 24 C2
St Catherine's Church.......... 25 C2
St Mark's Church.......... 26 C1
Stone Gate.......... 27 C1
Strossmayer Gallery of Old Masters.......... 28 D4

SLEEPING (pp254–5)
Croatian YHA.......... 29 B2
Evistas.......... 30 E5
Hotel Opera.......... 31 A5
Hotel Sheraton.......... 32 E4
Omladinski Hotel (Youth Hostel).......... 33 D5

EATING (p255)
Boban.......... 34 C3
Dolac Market.......... 35 D2
Fruit & Vegetable Market.......... 36 A3
Gavrilović.......... 37 C3
Kaptolska Klet.......... 38 D2
Konoba Čiho.......... 39 E4
Makronova.......... 40 A3
Mimice.......... 41 E3
Vincek.......... 42 C2

DRINKING (p255)
Bulldog.......... 43 C3
Glob@l.......... 44 E4
Indy's.......... (see 47)
Purgeraj.......... 45 D1
Sokol klub.......... 46 B4
Tolkien's House.......... 47 C2

ENTERTAINMENT (p256)
Academy of Music.......... 48 B3
Komedija Theatre.......... 49 D2
Vatroslav Lisinski Concert Hall.......... 50 D6

TRANSPORT (p256)
Avis.......... (see 31)
Budget.......... (see 32)
Croatia Airlines.......... 51 D3
Hertz.......... 52 A4

Tourist Information
Croatian Auto Club (HAK) Information Centre
(☎ 46 40 800; Derenčinova 20) Helps motorists in need.
Main tourist office (☎ 48 14 051; www.zagreb-touristinfo.hr; Trg Jelačića 11; 8.30am-8pm Mon-Fri, 9am-5pm Sat, 10am-4pm Sun) Distributes city maps and free leaflets. It also sells the Zagreb Card, which costs 60KN and includes 72 hours of free transportation and a 50% discount on museums.
Marko Polo (☎ 48 15 216; Masarykova 24) Handles information and ticketing for Jadrolinija's coastal ferries.
Plitvice National Park Information Office (☎ 46 13 586; Trg Tomislava 19) Has details on Croatia's national parks.
Tourist office annex (☎ 49 21 645; Trg Zrinskoga 14; 9am-6pm Mon-Fri) Same services, but less brochures.
Tourist Office of Zagreb County (☎ 48 73 665; www.tzzz.hr; Preradovićeva 42; 8am-4pm Mon-Fri) Has information about attractions in the region outside Zagreb.

Travel Agencies
Dali Travel (☎ 48 47 472; hfhs-cms@zg.hinet.hr; Dežmanova 9; 9am-5pm Mon-Fri) The travel branch of the Croatian Youth Hostel Association (YHA), it can provide information on Hostelling International (HI) hostels throughout Croatia and make advance bookings. It also sells ISIC (International Student Identity Card) identification for 40KN.

SIGHTS
Kaptol
The twin neo-Gothic spires of the **Cathedral of the Assumption of the Blessed Virgin Mary** (☎ 48 14 727; 7am-7pm), built in 1899, contains elements from the medieval cathedral on its site, destroyed by an earthquake in 1880. Remnants include 13th-century frescoes, Renaissance pews, marble altars and a baroque pulpit. The baroque **Archiepiscopal Palace** surrounds the cathedral, as do 16th-century **fortifications** constructed when Zagreb was threatened by the Turks.

Gradec
From Ulica Radićeva 5, off Trg Jelačića, a pedestrian walkway called stube Ivana Zakmardija leads you to the **Lotršćak Tower** (11am-8pm Mon-Sat) and a **funicular railway** (3KN), constructed in 1888, which connects the lower and upper towns. To the right is the baroque **St Catherine's Church**, with Jezuitski trg beyond. The **Galerija Klovićevi Dvori** (☎ 48 51 926; Jezuitski trg 4; adult/student 20/10KN; 11am-7pm Tue-Sun) is Zagreb's premier exhibition hall. Further north and to the right is the 13th-century **Stone Gate**, with a painting of the Virgin.

STREET NAMES

In Zagreb you may notice a discrepancy between the names used in this book and the names you'll actually see on the street. In Croatian, a street name can be rendered either in the nominative or possessive case. The difference is apparent in the name's ending. Thus, Ulica Ljedevita Gaja (street of Ljudevita Gaja) becomes Gajeva ulica (Gaja's street). The latter version is the one most commonly seen on the street sign and used in everyday conversation. The same principle applies to a square *(trg)*, which can be rendered as Trg Petra Preradovića or Preradovićev trg. Some of the more common names are: Trg svetog Marka (Markov trg), Trg Josipa Jurja Strossmayera (Strossmayerov trg), Ulica Andrije Hebranga (Hebrangova), Ulica Pavla Radića (Radićeva), Ulica Augusta Šenoe (Šenoina), Ulica Ivana Tkalčića (Tkalčićeva) and Ulica Nikole Tesle (Teslina). Be aware also that Trg Nikole Sća Zrinskog is almost always called Zrinjevac.

For street addresses, 'bb' denotes a non-residential address.

The colourful painted-tile roof of the Gothic **St Mark's Church** (☎ 48 51 611; Markovićev trg; ☼ 11am-4pm & 5.30-7pm) marks the centre of Gradec. Inside are works by Ivan Meštrović, Croatia's most famous modern sculptor. On the eastern side of St Mark's is the **Sabor** (1908), Croatia's National Assembly. To the west of St Mark's is the 18th-century **Banski Dvori Palace**, the presidential palace.

Nearby is the former **Meštrović Studio** (☎ 48 51 123; Mletačka 8; adult/concession 20/10KN; ☼ 10am-6pm Tue-Fri, 10am-2pm Sat), which now presents an excellent collection of some 100 sculptures, drawings, lithographs and furniture created by the artist. Of the area's many museums, the most interesting is the **Museum of the City of Zagreb** (☎ 48 51 364; Opatička 20; adult/concession 20/10KN; ☼ 10am-6pm Tue-Fri, 10am-1pm Sat & Sun), with a scale model of old Gradec.

Lower Town

Zagreb really is a city of museums. There are four just in the parks between the train station and Trg Jelačića. The yellow **Arts Pavilion** (1897), across the park from the station, presents changing contemporary art exhibitions. The second building north, also in the park, houses the **Strossmayer Gallery of Old Masters** (☎ 48 95 115; adult/concession 20/15KN; ☼ 10am-1pm & 5-7pm Tue, 10am-1pm Wed-Sun), with paintings by great European painters from the 14th to 17th century. In the interior courtyard is the **Baška Slab** (1102), from the island of Krk, one of the oldest inscriptions in the Croatian language.

The **Arheološki Muzej** (Archaeological Museum; ☎ 48 73 101; Trg Nikole Zrinskog 19; adult/concession 20/10KN; ☼ 10am-5pm Tue-Fri, 10am-1pm Sat & Sun) has a fascinating and wide-ranging display of artefacts from prehistoric times through

to the medieval era. Behind the museum is a garden of Roman sculpture.

The **Museum Mimara** (☎ 48 28 100; Rooseveltov trg 5; adult/concession 20/15KN; ☼ 10am-5pm Tue, Wed, Fri & Sat; 10am-7pm Thu, 10am-2pm Sun) houses a diverse collection amassed by Ante Topić Mimara and donated to Croatia. Housed in a neo-Renaissance palace, the collection includes icons, glassware, sculpture, Oriental art and works by renowned painters such as Rembrandt, Velasquez, Raphael and Degas.

SLEEPING

Zagreb is a pricey city to stay but there are a few good hostel options. Private accommodation is a good bet, but you may find yourself south of the train station in the blandly modern Novi Zagreb section as there are limited rooms available in the town centre.

Hostels

Ravnice Hostel (☎ 23 32 325; www.ravnice-youth -hostel.hr; Ravnice 38D; tram Nos 4, 7, 11, 12; dm 99KN; ☐) Designed and run by an Australian woman, this is really a delightful option. Comfortable, clean rooms have two, four or 10 beds. It's just under 2km from the city centre.

Studenthotel Cvjetno Naselje (☎ 61 91 239; tram Nos 4, 5, 14, 16, 17; dm 210KN; ☼ mid-Jul–Aug) Off Slavonska avenija in the south of the city, this dormitory-style accommodation has good rooms, each with a bathroom. Get off the tram at the 'Vjesnik' stop.

Studentski dom Stjepan Radić (☎ 36 34 255; tram Nos 5, 17; Jarunska ulica 3; dm 125KN) This is a student dorm near Jarun Lake and its nightlife in the southwest of the city.

Omladinski Hotel (☎ 48 41 261; fax 48 41 269; Petrinjska 77; per person in 6-bed dm 73KN, per person in 3-bed dm 83KN, per person in double 211KN) Some say it's a dump. We prefer to call it an auditory and visual challenge with maintenance issues. At least it's in the centre of town.

Private Rooms

Agencies renting private rooms are closed Sunday and do not take telephone reservations. Prices run from about 170/220KN a single/double, and apartments cost at least 300KN per night. There's usually a surcharge for staying only one night.

Recommended agencies include **Evistas** (☎ 48 39 554; evistas@zg.tel.hr; Augusta Senoe 28; s 172-227KN, d 234-314KN, apt 364-835KN), closest to the train station; **ADP Gloria** (☎ 48 23 567; www.adp -glorija.com; Britanski trg 5); and **Di Prom** (☎ 65 50 039; fax 65 50 233; Trnsko 25A).

Hotels

Hotel Ilica (☎ 37 77 522; www.hotel-ilica.hr; Ilica 102; tram Nos 6,11, 12; s/d/tw/apt 349/449/549/749KN; P ⊠ ⊛) For small hotels, you can't do better than this stylish joint with comfortable rooms and friendly service.

EATING

What you've spent on lodging, you can save on meals in Zagreb; even the pricier places offer filling pasta or risotto starters for 30KN to 50KN.

Mimiće (Jurišićeva 21; mains 12-30KN; ☽ closed Sun) It's a local favourite and deservedly so. The fish is sure to be fresh because turnover is high, especially at noon when workers in the offices around Trg Jelaŏić turn out in droves for their lunch.

Boban (☎ 48 11 549; Gajeva 9; mains 30-50KN) This Italian restaurant-bar-café offers sophisticated food at good prices. It has an outdoor terrace and an indoor lounge and terrace that is popular with Zagreb yuppies. Try the gnocchi made from squid ink and topped with salmon sauce.

Kaptolska Klet (☎ 48 14 838; Kaptol 5; mains 55-70KN) This inviting space is comfortable for everyone from solo diners to groups of noisy backpackers. Although famous for its Zagreb specialities such as grilled meats, spit-roasted lamb, duck, pork and veal, as well as home-made sausages, it also turns out a nice platter of grilled vegetables and a vegetable loaf.

Makronova (☎ 48 47 115; Ilica 72; mains around 70KN; ☽ closed Sun) All very Zen and purely macrobiotic, and more than welcome for those of the vegetarian persuasion.

Konoba Čiho (☎ 48 17 060; Pavla Hatza 15; mains from 55KN) Tucked away downstairs, this cosy restaurant turns out a startling assortment of fish and seafood, grilled, fried and combined in delicious stews.

For dessert, slurp it up at **Vincek** (☎ 45 50 834; Ilica 18), famous for its ice cream.

For picking up yummy fresh produce there's a **fruit and vegetable market** (Britanski trg; ☽ 7am-3pm), **Dolac Market** (☽ 7am-2pm), which is up the steps from Trg Jelačića, continuing north along Opatovina, and **Gavrilović** (☽ closed Sun), near Dolac Market, for cheese, smoked meat and cold cuts.

DRINKING

The architecture may be sober but the nightlife definitely is not, especially as the weather warms up and Zagrebians take to the streets. Wander along Tkalčićeva in the upper town or along bar-lined Bogovićeva, just south of Trg Jelačića, which turns into prime meet-and-greet territory each evening. Tkalčićeva attracts a slightly funkier crowd.

Bulldog (☎ 48 17 393; Bogovićeva 6) Belgian beer loosens up a crowd of young execs, sales reps, gofers and expats.

Tolkien's House (☎ 48 51 776; Vranicanijeva 8) This place is decorated in the style of JRR Tolkien's books, it's very Frodo.

Indy's (☎ 48 52 053; Vranicanijeva 4) This friendly bar presents a dazzling assortment of juicy and fruity cocktails on an outdoor terrace.

Brazil (☎ 91 200 24 81; Veslačka bb) Parked on the Sava River, this bar on a boat refreshes a throng of thirsty revellers and offers occasional live music.

Glob@l (☎ 48 76 146; P Hatza 14) Gays and lesbians are more than welcome to take in the friendly, tolerant vibes at this café-bar.

CLUBBING

The dress code is relaxed in most Zagreb clubs but neatness counts. The cover charge is usually around 30KN.

Aquarius (☎ 36 40 231; Ljubeka bb; tram No 17) On Lake Jarun, this is the night temple of choice for Zagrebians of all ages and styles. The design cleverly includes an open-air terrace on the lake and the sound is usually house. Take the tram to the 'Jarun' stop.

Purgeraj (☎ 48 14 734; Park Ribnjak) A funky, relaxed space to listen to live rock, blues, rock-blues, blues-rock and country rock. You get the idea.

CROATIA

Sokol klub (☎ 48 28 510; Trg Maršala Tita 6) Across the street from the Ethnographic Museum, it's fashionable without being snooty and the dance floor is always packed.

ENTERTAINMENT

Zagreb is a happening city. Its theatres and concert halls present a great variety of programmes throughout the year. Many are listed in the monthly brochure *Zagreb Events & Performances*, which is available from the tourist office. If you feel like catching a flick, you'll be pleased that most English language films are shown in their original nondubbed version with subtitles.

Komedija Theatre (☎ 48 14 566; Kaptol 9) Near the cathedral, staging operettas and musicals.

Vatroslav Lisinski Concert Hall (ticket office ☎ 61 21 166; Trg Stjepana Radica 4; ☼ 9am-8pm Mon-Fri, 9am-2pm Sat) South of the train station, this prestigious venue holds regular symphony concerts.

Concerts also take place at the **Academy of Music** (☎ 48 30 822; Gundulićeva 6a), off Ilica.

GETTING THERE & AWAY

Croatia Airlines (☎ 01-48 19 633; www.croatiaairlines .hr; Zrinjevac 17, Zagreb) operates flights between Zagreb and Split (475KN, one hour, up to four daily). Rates are lower if you book in advance.

Bus

Zagreb's big, modern **bus station** (☎ 61 57 983; www.akz.hr in Croatian), 1km east of the train station, has a large, enclosed waiting room and a number of shops, including grocery shops. Buy most international tickets at window Nos 17 to 20. Buy an advance ticket at the station if you're travelling long distance.

Domestic buses depart from Zagreb to most major destinations in Croatia, including Dubrovnik (205KN to 401KN, 11 hours, seven daily), Korčula (195KN, 12 hours, daily), Pula (114KN to 161KN, four to six hours, 13 daily) and Split (112KN to 143KN, six to nine hours, 27 daily).

Train

Domestic trains depart from Zagreb to Pula (123KN, 5½ hours, two daily), Split (112KN to 143KN, 6 to 9 hours, 27 daily) and Zadar (97KN to 157KN, 4 to 5 hours, 20 daily).

Reservations are required on fast InterCity (IC) trains and there's a supplement that costs 5KN to 15KN for fast or express trains.

GETTING AROUND
To/From the Airport

The Croatia Airlines Bus (25KN) to Zagreb airport leaves from the bus station every half-hour or hour from about 5.30am to 7.30pm, depending on flights, and returns from the airport on about the same schedule. A taxi costs about 250KN.

Car

Major car-rental companies include **Budget Rent-a-Car** (☎ 45 54 936; Kneza Borne 2, Hotel Sheraton), **Avis Autotehna** (☎ 48 36 006; Kršnjavoga 1, Hotel Opera), and **Hertz** (☎ 48 46 777; Vukotinovićeva 1). These larger internationals usually charge about 250KN per day, while local companies usually have lower rates.

Public Transport

Buy tram tickets at newspaper kiosks for 6.50KN or from the driver for 8KN. You can use your ticket for transfers within 90 minutes, but only in one direction.

A *dnevna karta* (day ticket), valid on all public transport until 4am the next morning, is available for 18KN at most Vjesnik or Tisak news kiosks. Controls are frequent on the tram system, with fines that start at €30 for not having the proper ticket.

Taxi

Zagreb's taxi meters begin at 25KN and then ring up 8KN per kilometre. All day Sunday and other nights from 10pm to 5am there's a 20% surcharge.

ISTRIA (ISTRA)

The Istrian peninsula contains 3600 sq km of rolling hills and drowned valleys, plus 430km of bays, beaches and coves. Known for their tolerance, the Istrian people are as gentle as the landscape. Istria was a part of Italy from 1919 to 1947 and the Italian influence remains strong, especially in the cuisine. Lively Pula with its Roman ruins makes a good base from which to explore the fishing ports of Rovinj and Poreč.

PULA
☎ 052 / pop 58,600

Pula's star attraction is its Roman amphitheatre, which provides a splendid backdrop to the city's summer concerts. As the cultural and economic hub of Istria, there's always something going on in Pula. After wandering among the city's many Roman ruins, head out to the rocky beaches that dot the wooded peninsulas of Verudela or Premantura and rest up for some sizzling nightlife.

Orientation

If arriving by bus or train, you can easily walk to the town centre. The train station is near the water about 1km north of town. From the train station, follow the waterfront south for about 20 minutes to reach the Forum (where the tourist office is). The **bus station** (☎ 502 997; Istarske Brigade bb) is 500m northeast of the town centre. From the bus station, walk west about 10 minutes and turn left at Trg Na Mostu.

Information

You can exchange money in travel agencies or at any post office. There are many ATMs.

Arena Turist (☎ 529 400; www.arenaturist.hr; Splitska 1A; Hotel Riviera, Splitska 1) Finds private accommodation.

Atlas (☎ 393 040; atlas.pula@atlas.hr; Starih Statuta 1) Finds private accommodation and organises tours.

Enigma (☎ 381 615; Kandlerova 19; per hr 20KN) Internet access.

Jadroagent (☎ 210 431; jadroagent-pula@pu.hinet .hr; Riva 14) Has schedules and tickets for boats connecting Istria with Italy and the islands.

Main post office (Danteov trg 4; ⏰ to 8pm) Make long-distance calls from here.

Tourist office (☎ 219 197; www.pulainfo.hr; Forum 2; ⏰ 9am-8pm Mon-Sat, 10am-6pm Sun) With knowledgeable and friendly staff, it provides maps, brochures and schedules of upcoming events in Pula and around Istria.

Sights

Pula's most imposing sight is the 1st-century **Roman amphitheatre** (☎ 219 028; Flavijevska; adult/concession 16/8KN; ⏰ 8am-9pm Jun-Sep, 8.30am-4.30pm Oct-May), overlooking the harbour and northeast of the Old Town. Built entirely from local limestone, the amphitheatre was designed to host gladiatorial contests and could accommodate up to 20,000 spectators. The 30m-high outer wall is almost intact and contains two rows of 72 arches.

The **Arheološki Muzej** (Archaeological Museum; ☎ 218 603; Cararina 3; adult/concession 12/6KN; ⏰ 9am-7pm Mon-Sat, 10am-3pm Sun Jun-Sep, 9am-3pm Mon-Fri Oct-May), which presents archaeological finds from all over Istria, especially from the 2nd to 6th century AD, is on the hill opposite the bus station.

Even if you don't get into the museum, be sure to visit the large **sculpture garden** surrounding it and the **Roman theatre** behind the museum. The garden is entered through 2nd-century twin gates.

Along the street facing the bus station are **Roman walls** that mark the eastern boundary of old Pula. Follow these walls south and continue down Giardini to the **Triumphal Arch of Sergius** (27 BC). The street beyond the arch winds right around old Pula, changing names several times. Follow it to the ancient **Temple of Augustus** and the **old town hall** (1296).

The 17th-century **Venetian Citadel**, on a high hill in the centre of the Old Town, is worth the climb for the view.

Festivals & Events

Around the end of July a **Croatian film festival** is held in the amphitheatre, and there are pop, jazz and classical events, often with major international stars, throughout summer. Ask at the tourist office for the schedule and ticketing information.

Sleeping

Youth Hostel (☎ 391 133; pula@hfhs.hr; B&B/half board 110/142KN, camp site with breakfast 72KN, tent rental 10.50KN) Only 3km south of central Pula, this hostel overlooks a beach and is near one of the regions largest discos. Take the No 2 or 7 Verudela bus to the 'Piramida' stop, walk back to the first street, then turn left and look for the sign.

Arena Turist and Atlas will find private accommodation (see left), but there is little available in the town centre. Count on paying from 110KN for a double room and up to 430KN for an apartment.

Most hotel accommodation is outside town in the sprawling resorts on the Verudela Peninsula, which is about 6km southwest of the city centre.

Hotel Omir (☎ 210 614; fax 213 944; Dobricheva 6; s/d 424/550KN) Rooms are small but comfortable. Prices stay the same year-round.

Hotel Riviera (☎ 211 166; fax 211 166; Splitska ulica 1; s/d 437/715KN) Neither the service nor the comfort justifies the price (which eases in the low season) in this one-star hotel overlooking the harbour, but the large front rooms have a view of the water and the wide shady hotel terrace is a relaxing place for a drink.

CROATIA

Autocamp Stoja (☎ 387 144; fax 387 748; per adult/camp site & car 50/110KN; ☼ Apr-Oct) Three kilometres southwest of the city centre, Autocamp Stoja is on a shady promontory, with swimming possible off the rocks. Take bus No 1 to the Stoja terminus.

There are more camping grounds at Medulin and Premantura, coastal resorts southeast of Pula (take the buses heading southeast from town).

Eating

The best local restaurants are out of town, but the cheapest places are in the centre and the eating isn't bad. You'll have a number of choices along Kandlerova.

Jupiter (☎ 214 333; Castropola 38; mains from 25KN) This popular place serves up the best pizza in town, and the pasta is good too.

Splendid Self-Service (☎ 223 284; Trg I Svibnja 5; ☼ 9.30am-8.45pm) It's opposite the vegetable market and is simple and cheap.

Drinking & Clubbing

The streets of Flanatička, Kandlerova and Sergijevaca are excellent people-watching spots, and the Forum has several outdoor cafés that fill up in the early evening; the trendiest is café-gallery **Cvajner**, with a stunning, art-filled interior.

There's no shortage of nightlife at any time of the year. Pula is famous for its raves, usually held at two venues in Verudela: **Oasis** and **Fort Bourguignon**, keep an eye out for posters and flyers around town.

Entertainment

The amphitheatre hosts a full schedule of concerts in summer.

Getting There & Away

BOAT

In summer, Pula is connected with Mali Lošinj (73KN, 3½ hours, three weekly) and Zadar (112KN, eight hours, five weekly). The boats leave from Riva near Jadroagent.

BUS

The buses that travel to Rijeka (58KN, 2½ hours, 20 daily) are sometimes crowded, especially the eight that continue to Zagreb, so be sure to reserve a seat in advance. Going from Pula to Rijeka, be sure to sit on the right-hand side of the bus for a stunning view of the Gulf of Kvarner.

Other destinations for buses from Pula include Rovinj (23KN, 40 minutes, 18 daily), Poreč (32KN, one hour, 12 daily), Zagreb (121KN to 147KN, five hours, 11 daily), Zadar (161KN, seven hours, four daily), Split (215KN to 278KN, 10 hours, four daily) and Dubrovnik (366KN, 15 hours, one daily).

TRAIN

There are trains to Zagreb (123KN, 6½ hours, two daily), but you must board a bus for part of the trip.

Getting Around

The only city buses of use to visitors are bus No 1, which runs to the camping ground at Stoja, and bus Nos 2 and 7 to Verudela, which pass the youth hostel. Frequency varies from every 15 minutes to every 30 minutes, with services from 5am to 11.30pm daily. Tickets are sold at newsstands for 10KN and are good for two trips.

DALMATIA (DALMACIJA)

Whether your passion is history or hedonism, you'll find it in Dalmatia. Occupying the central 375km of Croatia's Adriatic coast, Dalmatia is rife with Roman ruins, spectacular beaches, old fishing ports, medieval architecture and unspoiled offshore islands. In the centre of it all is teeming Split, the city on the sea and best jumping-off point for Croatia's lushest islands.

SPLIT (SPALATO)

☎ 021 / pop 188,700

Split, the largest Croatian city on the Adriatic coast, achieved fame when the Roman emperor Diocletian (AD 245–313) had his retirement palace built here. Within the ancient walls of Diocletian's Palace rises a majestic cathedral, surrounded by a tangle of marble streets lined with shops and businesses. As the sun goes down, all Split turns out for a promenade along the harbour or a seat at one of the harbour-side cafés.

Orientation

The bus, train and ferry terminals are adjacent on the eastern side of the harbour, a short hop from the Old Town. Obala hrvatskog narodnog preporoda, the waterfront promenade, is your best reference point.

Information

Change money at travel agencies or the post office. ATM machines are around the bus and train stations. The Split Card (60KN), available from Turistička Zajednica and Turist Biro, offers free and discounted admissions to Split attractions.

Atlas (☎ 343 055; Nepotova 4) The American Express representative.

Daluma Travel (☎ 338 484; daluma-st@st.tel.hr; Obala Kneza Domagoja 1) Finds private accommodation.

Internet Games & Books (☎ 338 548; Obala Kneza Domagoja 3; per hr 35KN) Luggage storage, information for backpackers, used books and an Internet connection.

Mriža (☎ 321 320; Kružićeva 3; per hr 20KN) Internet access.

Main post office (Kralja Tomislava 9) Has a telephone centre (☉ 7am-9pm Mon-Sat).

Turist Biro (☎ 342 142; turist-biro-split@st.hinet.hr; Obala hrvatskog narodnog preporoda 12) Arranges private accommodation, and sells guidebooks and the Split Card.

Turistička Zajednica (☎ /fax 342 606; www.visitsplit .com; Peristyle; ☉ 9am-8.30pm Mon-Sat, 8am-1pm Sun) Has informational materials on Split and sells the Split Card.

Sights

The Old Town is a vast open-air museum. Dating from the third century AD, **Diocletian's Palace** (enter from Obala hrvatskog narodnog preporoda 22; admission free), facing the harbour, is one of the most imposing Roman ruins in existence. It was built as a strong rectangular fortress, with walls measuring 215m from east to west and 181m wide at the southernmost point and reinforced by towers. The imperial residence, temples and mausoleum were south of the main street, connecting the east and west gates. Its main features include the **Peristyle**, a picturesque colonnaded square; the open-area **Temple of Jupiter**, now a baptistry; and the **cathedral** (☉ 7am-noon, 4-7pm), originally Diocletian's mausoleum.

The west palace gate opens onto medieval Narodni trg, dominated by the 15th-century Venetian Gothic **old town hall**. Trg Braće Radića, between Narodni trg and the harbour, contains the surviving north tower of the 15th-century Venetian garrison castle, which once extended right to the water's edge. The east palace gate leads into the **market** area.

In the Middle Ages, the nobility and rich merchants built residences within the old palace walls; the **Papalić Palace** (Papalićeva 5) is now the town museum. Go through the north palace gate to see Ivan Meštrović's powerful **statue** (1929) of 10th-century Slavic religious leader Gregorius of Nin.

MUSEUMS & GALLERIES

The **town museum** (☎ 341 240; Papalićeva 5; adult/concession 10/5KN; ☉ 9am-noon & 5-8pm Tue-Fri, 10am-noon Sat & Sun Jun-Sep; 10am-5pm Tue-Fri, 10am-noon Sat & Sun Oct-May), east of Narodni trg, has a broad and well-displayed collection of artefacts, paintings, furniture and clothes from Split. Captions are in Croatian.

The **Arheološki Muzej** (Archaeological Museum; Zrinjsko-Frankopanska 25; adult/concession 10/5KN; ☉ 9am-noon & 5-8pm Tue-Fri, 9am-1pm Sat & Sun Jun-Sep; 9am-2pm Tue-Fri, 9am-1pm Sat & Sun Oct-May), north of town, is a fascinating supplement to your walk around Diocletian's Palace. The history of Split is traced from Illyrian times to the Middle Ages in chronological order, with explanations in English.

The finest art museum in Split is the **Meštrović Gallery** (Šetalište Ivana Meštrovića 46; adult/student 15/10KN; ☉ 9am-9pm Tue-Sun Jun-Sep; 9am-4pm Tue-Sat, 10am-3pm Sun Oct-May). You'll see a comprehensive, well-arranged collection of works by Ivan Meštrović, Croatia's premier modern sculptor, who built the gallery as his home from 1931 to 1939. Bus No 12 runs to the gallery, one kilometre west of the town centre, from Trg Republike every 40 minutes.

Sleeping & Eating

Hotels in Split are geared towards business travellers with deep pockets. For private rooms, you could go to one of the private accommodation agencies, but there are usually packs of women at the bus and train stations and ferry terminals ready to propose rooms to travellers. Prices rarely exceed 100KN for a room but you'll be sharing the bathroom with the proprietor.

Slavija (☎ 347 053; fax 344 062; Buvinova 3; r with/without bath 450/350KN) It has a great location in the Old Town but somewhat noisy rooms.

Bufet Fife (Obala Trumbićeva 11; mains from 30KN) Feast on Dalmatian home cooking side by side with the local fishermen.

Kod Joze (☎ 347 397; Sredmanuška 4; mains from 50KN) Slightly more upscale but still casual is this popular choice for a night out.

The enormous **supermarket-delicatessen** (Svačićeva 1) has a wide selection of meats and

CROATIA

cheeses for sandwiches. The **market** above Obala Lazerata has a wide array of fresh local produce.

Drinking

In summer, everyone starts the evening at one of the cafés along Obala hrvatskog narodnog preporoda and then heads to the Bačvice complex on the beach. This former public bathhouse offers restaurants, cafés, discos and venues for live rock and salsa.

Ghetto Klub (☎ 346 879; Dosud; ☽ 10am-midnight) Listen to jazz, trance or world music while sipping herbal tea or harder stuff in this funky café-bar.

Entertainment

Croatian National Theatre (☎ 515 999; Trg Gaje Bulata; best seats about 60KN) It's worth attending an opera or ballet performance for the architecture alone.

Getting There & Away

AIR

Split airport (☎ 021-203 506; www.spli-airport.hr) is used by **Croatia Airlines** (Obala hrvatskog narodnog preporoda 9) for daily flights to Zagreb (207kn, 45 minutes, daily).

The bus to Split airport (30KN) leaves from Obala Lazareta 3 about 90 minutes before flight times, or you can take bus No 37 from the bus station on Domovinskog (9.50KN for a two-zone ticket).

BOAT

Jadrolinija (☎ 355 399), located in the large ferry terminal opposite the bus station, handles the coastal ferry line to Hvar Island and operates year-round, stopping in Stari Grad (74KN, two to four weekly). However, the local car ferry is cheaper (32KN, 1½ hours), and there's a fast passenger boat to Hvar town (one hour) in July and August, as well as a passenger boat (24KN, two hours) that goes on to Vela Luka (35KN, 1¼ hours).

SEM (☎ 338 292) runs a catamaran between Vis and Split (26KN, 1 ½ hours, July and August).

For passenger ferries, buy tickets at the **Jadrolinija kiosk** (Obala Domagoja), near the train station.

Jadroagent (☎ 338 335), in the ferry terminal, represents Adriatica Navigazione for connections between Split and Ancona. There's also a **SEM agency** in the terminal selling tickets between Ancona and Split, Hvar Island and Vis, as well as **SNAV** (☎ 322 252), which has a connection to Ancona and Pescara (four hours). For information on connections to Italy, see p249.

BUS

Advance bus tickets are recommended. There are buses from the main bus station beside the harbour to Dubrovnik (72KN to 111KN, 4½ hours, 12 daily), Mostar 54KN to 65KN, four hours, four daily), Rijeka (161KN to 231KN, eight hours, 14 daily), Zadar (76KN to 89KN, three hours, 26 daily) and Zagreb (110KN to 154KN, eight hours, 27 daily).

TRAIN

There are services between Split and Zagreb (90KN to 131KN, eight to nine hours, four daily), and Split and Šibenik (33KN, 1½ hours, four daily).

HVAR ISLAND

☎ 021 / pop 12,600

Rapidly becoming the island of choice for a swanky international crowd, Hvar deserves the honour for it is the sunniest and greenest of Croatia's islands. Called the 'Croatian Madeira', Hvar receives 2724 hours of sunshine each year. The stunning interior is a panorama of lavender fields, peaceful villages and pine-covered slopes.

Hvar Town

Within the 13th-century walls of Medieval Hvar lie beautifully ornamented Gothic palaces and marble-paved traffic-free streets. A long seaside promenade dotted with small, rocky beaches, stretches from either end of the harbour. A few tasteful bars and cafés along the harbour are relaxing spots for people watching.

ORIENTATION & INFORMATION

Car ferries from Split deposit you in Stari Grad but local buses meet most ferries in summer for the trip to Hvar Town. The town centre is Trg Sv Stjepana, 100m west of the bus station. Passenger ferries tie up on Riva, the eastern quay, in front of Pelegrini Travel.

Mengola Travel (☎ 742 099; megola-hvar@st.tel.hr) Finds private accommodation.

Pelegrini Travel (☎ 742 250; kuzma.novak@st.tel.hr) Finds private accommodation.

Tourist office (☎ 742 977; www.hvar.hr; cnr Trg Sv Stjepana; 8am-1pm & 5-9pm Mon-Sat, 9am-noon Sun Jun-Sep; 8am-2pm Mon-Sat Oct-May) In the arsenal building.

SIGHTS

The flavour of medieval Hvar is best savoured on the backstreets of the Old Town. At each end of Hvar is a monastery with a prominent tower. The Dominican **Church of St Marko** at the head of the bay was largely destroyed by Turks in the 16th century, but you can visit the **Arheološki Muzej** (Archaeological Museum; admission 10KN; ☯ 10am-noon Jun-Sep) in the ruins.

At the southeastern end of Hvar, the interesting 15th-century Renaissance **Franciscan monastery** (☯ 10am-noon & 5-7pm Jun-Sep, plus Christmas week & Holy Week) has a collection of Venetian paintings in the church, and a **museum** (admission 10KN; ☯ 10am-noon & 5-7pm Mon-Sat Jun-Sep).

In the middle of Hvar is the imposing Gothic **arsenal**, its great arch visible from afar. Upstairs off the arsenal terrace is Hvar's prize, Europe's first **municipal theatre** (admission 10KN; ☯ 10am-noon & 5-7pm Jun-Sep), built in 1612. The theatre is not currently operating due to safety reasons.

On the hill top high above Hvar Town is a **Venetian fortress** (1551), well worth the climb for sweeping panoramic views.

For more activity, hop on a launch to the **Pakleni Islands**, famous for nude sunbathing.

SLEEPING

Accommodation is extremely tight in July and August. For private accommodation, try Mengola Travel or Pelegrini Travel (see opposite). Expect to pay from 160KN to 280KN in the town centre.

Jagoda & Ante Bracanović Guesthouse (☎ 741 416, ☎ 091 520 3796; virgilye@yahoo.com; Poviše Škole; s 100-120KN, d 190-220KN) This friendly place is close to the town centre and offers six spacious rooms with private bathrooms, balconies and kitchen access.

Slavija (☎ 741 820; fax 741 147; s/d from 465/700KN) This hotel is right on the harbour in town. Reservations are handled by **Sunčani Hvar** (☎ 741 026; www.suncanihvar.hr).

EATING

The pizzerias along the harbour offer predictable but inexpensive eating.

Bounty (☎ 742 565; mains from 60KN) Next to Mengola travel agency, this place is a long-time favourite.

Macondo (☎ 741 851; mains from 60KN) Head upstairs from the northern side of Trg Sv Stjepana for mouth-watering seafood.

Konoba Menego (☎ 742 036; mains around 40KN) On the stairway over the Benedictine convent, this is also a good choice.

The **grocery store** (Trg Sv Stjepana) is a viable restaurant alternative, and there's a **morning market** next to the bus station.

GETTING THERE & AWAY

The Jadrolinija ferries run from Rijeka to Stari Grad (152KN, 13 hours, two weekly) then from Stari Grad to Korčula (74KN, four hours, four weekly) and from Stari Grad to Dubrovnik (92KN, four hours, four weekly). The **Jadrolinija agency** (☎ 741 132), beside the landing, sells tickets.

Car ferries from Split call at Stari Grad (32KN, one hour, three daily, five daily in July and August), and there's an afternoon passenger boat from Split to Hvar Town (23KN) that goes on to Vela Luka on Korčula Island (22KN, one hour). Buses meet all ferries that dock at Stari Grad during July and August, but in winter it's best to check with a travel agency to ensure the bus (11KN) is running.

KORČULA ISLAND

☎ 020 / pop 16,200

Rich in vineyards and olive trees, Korčula was named Korkyra Melaina (Black Korčula) by the original Greek settlers because of its dense woods and plant life. Now it produces some of Croatia's finest wine, especially dessert wines made from the *grk* grape cultivated around Lumbarda. Local olive oil is another product worth seeking out.

Korčula Town

On a hilly peninsula jutting into the Adriatic sits Korčula, a striking walled town of round defensive towers and red-roofed houses. Resembling a miniature Dubrovnik, the gated, walled Old Town is crisscrossed by narrow stone streets designed to protect its inhabitants from the winds swirling around the peninsula. If you didn't plan a stop in Korčula, one look from the Jadrolinija ferry will make you regret it.

ORIENTATION & INFORMATION

The Jadrolinija ferry drops you off either in the west harbour next to the Hotel Korčula

CROATIA

or the east harbour next to Marko Polo Tours. The Old Town lies between the two harbours. Some car ferries land at Vela Luka on Korčula's western end and most are met by buses. The town bus station is 100m south of the town centre.

Atlas (☎ 711 231) Represents American Express, runs excursions and finds private accommodation.

Jadrolinija office (☎ 715 410) About 25m up from the west harbour.

Marko Polo Tours (☎ 715 400; marko-polo-tours@ du.tel.hr) On the east harbour. Finds private accommodation from 400KN and organises excursions.

Tourist office (☎ 715 701; www.korcula.net; Obala Franje Tuđmana bb; ✆ 8am-3pm & 5-9pm Mon-Sat, 8am-3pm Sun Jun-Sep; 8am-1pm & 5-9pm Mon-Sat Oct-May) On the west harbour. An excellent source of information.

SIGHTS
Other than following the circuit of the former city walls or walking along the shore, sightseeing in Korčula centres on Cathedral Square. The Gothic **Cathedral of St Mark** features two paintings by the Italian Renaissance master Jacopo Tintoretto (*Three Saints* on the altar and *Annunciation* to one side). The **treasury** (☎ 711 049; Trg Sv Marka Statuta; admission 10KN; ✆ 9am-7pm Jun-Aug), in the 14th-century Abbey Palace next to the cathedral, is worth a look. Even better is the **town museum** (☎ 711 420; Trg Sv Marka Statuta; admission 10KN; ✆ 9am-1.30pm Mon-Sat), in the 15th-century Gabriellis Palace opposite. It's said that Marco Polo was born in Korčula in 1254; for 5KN, you can climb the tower of what is believed to have been his house.

SLEEPING
The big hotels in Korčula are overpriced, but there is a wealth of guesthouses that offer clean, attractive rooms and friendly service. Atlas and Marko Polo Tours arrange private rooms (see above). Alternatively, you could try one of the following options.

Tarle (☎ 711 712; fax 711 243; Stalište Frana Kršinića; d with/without kitchen 270/210KN) Next to the Hotel Marko Polo, about 500m southeast of the bus station, this place has a pretty enclosed garden and attractive rooms with balconies.

Depolo (☎ 711 621; tereza.depolo@du.hinet.hr; d with/without sea view 240/200KN; 🅿 🅰) Closer to the Old Town in the residential neighbourhood of Sveti Nikola and 100m west of the bus station, this guesthouse has spiffy modern rooms.

Other guesthouses nearby for about the same price include **Peručić** (☎ /fax 711 458), with great balconies, and the homely **Ojdanić** (☎ 711 708; roko-taxi@du.hinet.hr). Ratko Ojdanić also has a water taxi and a lot of experience with **fishing trips** around the island.

EATING
Adio Mare (☎ 711 253; mains around 80KN) This place's charming maritime décor puts you in the mood for fish.

Marco Polo (☎ 715 077; mains from 40KN) The Italian-style fish and meat dishes are well prepared and the restaurant is open all year, feeding the locals.

Gradski Podrum (mains from 65KN) It serves up local specialities, such as Korčula-style fish boiled with potatoes and topped with tomato sauce.

There's a **supermarket** next to Marko Polo Tours.

ENTERTAINMENT
From May to September there's exciting **moreška sword dancing** (tickets 60KN) by the Old Town gate every Thursday at 9pm, more often in July and August. Atlas and Marko Polo Tours (see left) sell tickets.

GETTING THERE & AWAY
There is a bus to Dubrovnik (80KN, three hours, one daily) and Zagreb (195KN, 12 hours, one daily), and a bus to Sarajevo (150KN, eight hours, weekly).

The regular afternoon car ferry that goes between Split and Vela Luka (35KN, three hours) stops at Hvar Island (Hvar to Vela Luka 23KN, 45 minutes) most days. Buses link Korčula Town to Vela Luka (27KN, one hour, six daily), but services from Vela Luka are reduced on weekends.

DUBROVNIK

☎ 020 / pop 43,770

Whether you call it 'paradise on earth' (George Bernard Shaw) or merely 'the pearl of the Adriatic' (Lord Byron), Dubrovnik is clearly special. Enclosed in a curtain of stone walls, the town centre is radiant with the light reflected from its white marble paving stones. The narrow streets and graceful squares contain churches, monasteries, palaces and fountains ornamented with finely carved stone. Beyond the walls lie rocky beaches and the crystal-blue waters of the southern Adriatic.

The deliberate and militarily pointless shelling of Dubrovnik by the Yugoslav army in 1991 sent shockwaves through the international community. Now that the famous monuments have been rebuilt and resculpted, the streets paved and the clay roofs retiled, Dubrovnik looks better than ever.

Orientation

The Jadrolinija ferry terminal and the bus station are at Gruž, several kilometres northwest of the Old Town. There's a bus stop outside the gates to the Old Town with buses to Gruž harbour, Lapad and Cavtat. The main street in the Old Town is Placa, also called Stradun. Most accommodation is on the leafy Lapad Peninsula, west of the bus station.

Information

You can change money at any travel agency or post office. There are numerous ATMS in town, near the bus station and near the ferry terminal.

Atlas Pile Gate (☎ 442 574; Sv Đurđa 1); Old Town (☎ 323 609; Lučarica 1; Harbour (☎ 418 001; Gruška obala) In convenient locations Atlas is extremely helpful for general information as well as finding private accommodation. All excursions are run by the agency.

Dubrovnik Internet Centar (☎ 311 017; Ante Starčevića 7; per hr 20KN; ☺ 9am-9pm)

Dubrovnikturist (☎ 356 959; dubrovnikturist@net.hr; Put Republike 7) It's closest to the bus station for finding private accommodation, renting cars etc.

Gulliver (☎ 313 300; fax 419 119; Stjepana Radića 32) Near the Jadrolinija terminal, Gulliver finds private accommodation, changes money and rents cars and scooters.

Main post office (Cnr Široka & Od Puča, Old Town); Lapad (Kralja Zvonimira 21)

Tourist Information Centar (☎ 323 350; fax 323 351; Placa 1) Across from the Franciscan monastery in the Old Town, this centre is privately run and moderately helpful.

Turistička Zajednica (www.tzdubrovnik.hr) Pile Gate (☎ 427 591; Ante Starčevića 7; ☺ 8am-8pm Mon-Sat, 9am-noon Sun Jul-Aug; 9am-7pm Mon-Fri, 9am-1pm Sat Oct-May); Old Town (☎ 323 587; Miha Pracata bb); Harbour (☎ 417 983; Gruška obala bb) The branch outside Pile Gate has maps and the indispensable Dubrovnik Riviera guide. The Harbour branch has limited information.

Sights

You'll probably begin your visit at the bus stop outside **Pile Gate**. As you enter the city,

the Placa, Dubrovnik's wonderful pedestrian promenade, extends all the way to the clock tower at the other end of town. Just inside Pile Gate is the huge **Onofrio Fountain**, completed in 1438, and the **Franciscan monastery**, with a splendid cloister and the third-oldest functioning pharmacy, dating from 1391, in Europe. The **monastery museum** (adult/concession 10/5KN; ☺ 9am-5pm) presents a collection of liturgical objects, paintings and pharmacy equipment.

In front of the clock tower, at the eastern end of Placa, you'll find the **Orlando Column**, dating from 1419. On opposite sides of the Orlando are the 16th-century **Sponza Palace** (admission free; ☺ 8am-3pm Mon-Fri, 8am-1pm Sat) and **St Blaise's Church** (☺ for morning & late-afternoon Mass Mon-Sat), a lovely Italian baroque building.

At the end of the broad street called Pred Dvorom, beside St Blaise, is the baroque **Cathedral of the Assumption of the Virgin** (Poljana M. Drši a; ☺ for morning & late-afternoon Mass) and, between the two churches, the Gothic **Rector's Palace** (☎ 426 469; Ped Dvorom 3; adult/concession 15/7KN; ☺ 9am-2pm Mon-Sat Oct-May, 9am-5pm daily Jun-Sep), built in 1441.

As you proceed up Placa, make a detour to the **Museum of the Orthodox Church** (Od Puća 8; adult/concession 10/5KN; ☺ 9am-1pm Mon-Fri) for a look at a fascinating collection of 15th- to 19th-century icons.

By this time you'll be ready for a walk around the **city walls** (adult/concession 30/10KN; ☺ 9am-7pm), which have entrances just inside Pile Gate, across from the Dominican monastery and near Fort St John. These powerful walls are the finest in the world and Dubrovnik's main claim to fame. The views are great – this walk could be the high point of your visit.

Whichever way you go, you will notice the 14th-century **Dominican monastery** (adult/concession 10/5KN; ☺ 9am-6pm) in the northeastern corner of the city, whose forbidding fortress-like exterior shelters a rich trove of paintings from Dubrovnik's finest 15th- and 16th-century artists.

The closest beach to the Old Town, **Ploče**, is outside Ploče Gate. There are also hotel beaches on the **Lapad Peninsula**.

An even better option is to take the ferry (9am to 6pm) from the old port that shuttles half-hourly in summer to lush **Lokrum Island** (30KN return trip), a national park with a rocky

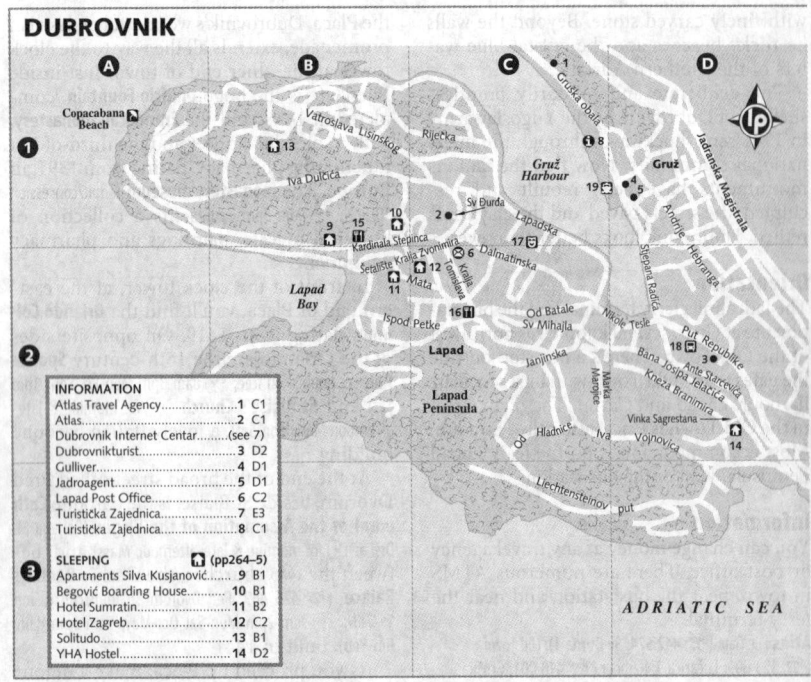

DUBROVNIK

INFORMATION
Atlas Travel Agency.................1 C1
Atlas..2 C1
Dubrovnik Internet Centar........(see 7)
Dubrovnikturist...........................3 D2
Gulliver.......................................4 D1
Jadroagent..................................5 D1
Lapad Post Office........................6 C2
Turistička Zajednica....................7 E3
Turistička Zajednica....................8 C1

SLEEPING (pp264–5)
Apartments Silva Kusjanović.......9 B1
Begović Boarding House..........10 B1
Hotel Sumratin.........................11 B2
Hotel Zagreb............................12 C2
Solitudo...................................13 B1
YHA Hostel...............................14 D2

ADRIATIC SEA

nudist beach, a botanical garden and the ruins of a medieval Benedictine monastery.

Festivals & Events

The **Dubrovnik Summer Festival** (www.dubrovnik -festival.hr), from mid-July to mid-August, is a major cultural event, with over 100 performances at different venues in the Old Town. The **Feast of St Blaise** (3 February) and **carnival** (February) are also celebrated.

Sleeping
HOSTELS

YHA Hostel (☎ 423 241; dubrovnik@hfhs.hr; Vinka Sagrestana 3; B&B/half board 95/140KN) It's not exactly restful but you'll have a lot of fun.

PRIVATE ROOMS

Private accommodation is generally the best option in Dubrovnik, but beware of the scramble of private owners at the bus station or Jadrolinija wharf. Some offer what they say they offer; others are rip-off artists. Be aware that most accommodation in the Old Town involves sharing the flat with the owner's family. The establishments listed

below are reputable and can often refer you to other places if they are full. All will meet you at the bus station if you call in advance. Otherwise, head to any of the travel agencies or Turistička Zajednica branches (see p263). Expect to pay about 200KN to 22OKN for a room in high season.

Apartments van Bloemen (☎ 323 433; ☎ 91 33 24 106; www.karmendu.tk; Bandureva 1; apt 750KN; ✗) This is the most personal and original accommodation, with a great location in the Old Town. All four apartments are beautifully decorated with original art. Three sleep three people comfortably.

Begović Boarding House (☎ 435 191; fax 452 752; Primorska 17; per person 110KN, with breakfast 30KN) A long-time favourite with our readers, this friendly place in Lapad has three rooms with shared bathroom and three apartments. There's also a terrace with a good view.

Apartments Silva Kusjanović (☎ 435 071, 98 244 639; antonia_du@hotmail.com; Kardinala Stepinća 62; per person 100KN) In Lapad, 'Sweet Silva' has four large apartments that can hold four to eight beds. All have terraces with gorgeous views and it's possible to barbecue.

CROATIA

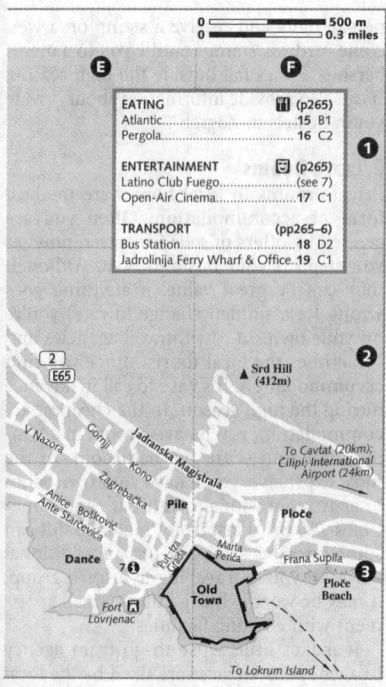

HOTELS

Hotel Sumratin (☎ 436 333; hot-sumratin@du.htnet.hr; Šetalište Kralja Zvonimira 31; s/d 355/600KN; Ⓟ) About 200m from the water, this calm hotel in Lapad offers good value for money.

Hotel Zagreb (☎ 436 146; hot-sumratin@du.htnet.hr; Šetalište Kralja Zvonimira 27; s/d 380/725KN) Nearby is this more old-fashioned place with a shady terrace and a garden.

CAMPING

Solitudo (☎ 448 200; Iva Dulčića 39; per adult/camp site 32/60KN) This pretty and newly renovated camping ground is within walking distance of the beach, north of Lapad Bay.

Eating

There are dozens of places to chow down in the Old Town, but there's not a great deal of variety. Pizza, pasta, pasta, pizza. Yawn.

Kamenice (☎ 421 499; Gundulićeva poljana 8; mains from 40KN) Portions are huge at this convivial hangout known for its mussels. Its terrace is on one of Dubrovnik's more scenic squares.

Express (☎ 329 994; M Kaboge 1; mains from 16KN) It's self-service but soups, salads, vegetables and desserts are freshly prepared and vegetarians will have an easy time assembling a meal.

Atlantic (Kardinala Stepinca 42; mains from 40KN) The homemade pasta and vegetarian lasagne in this Lapad restaurant are outstanding, even if the ambience is not terribly atmospheric.

Pergola (☎ 436 848; Kralja Tomislava 1; mains from 50KN) This is a consistently satisfying place with an outdoor terrace and good seafood.

Drinking

Bars have sprung up like mushrooms near the youth hostel, but these days thirsty young singles fill the cafés and terraces on Bunićeva.

Troubadur (☎ 412 154; Bunićeva 2) Live jazz every night, usually involving the owner, Marko, gives this cosy bar a joyous ambience that's rare anywhere.

Latino Club Fuego (Ante Starčevića 2) Despite the name, you'll find a gamut of dance music that includes techno and pop at this disco.

Entertainment

From mid-July to mid-August, Dubrovnik comes alive with music. Churches, squares and parks host folklore music and dancing, and a range of classical and jazz artists. See www.dubrovnik-festival.hr for the programme and reservations. There is also an open-air cinema in the Old Town on Za Rokum and one in Lapad on Kumičiča. Ask the tourist office for the schedule.

Getting There & Away

Daily flights to/from Zagreb are operated by **Croatia Airlines** (☎ 413 777; Brsalje 9). The fare runs is 400KN one way (one hour), higher in high season.

There are nonstop flights to Rome, London and Manchester from April to October.

BOAT

The Jadrolinija coastal ferry travels north to Hvar, Split, Zadar and Rijeka. **Jadrolinija** (☎ 418 000; Stjepjarta Radića 40) sells tickets and can provide information on coastal, international and local ferries. **Jadroagent** (☎ 419 009; fax 419 029; Stjepana Radića 32) handles ticketing for most international boats to/from Croatia.

BUS

Buses going daily from Dubrovnik include Korčula (80KN, three hours, one daily),

CROATIA

Mostar (77KN, three hours, two daily), Rijeka (300KN to 309KN, 12 hours, four daily), Split (100KN to 111KN, 4½ hours, 14 daily) and Zagreb (165KN to 199KN, 11 hours, seven daily).

During a busy summer season and on weekends, buses out of Dubrovnik can be crowded, so book a ticket well before the scheduled departure time.

Getting Around

The bus system in Dubrovnik is extensive and relatively efficient. Bus tickets cost 10KN (exact change only) if you buy from the driver and 8KN if you buy from Tisak news outlets. Bus Nos 4, 5, 6, 7b, and 9 travel to Lapad, and Nos 1a, 3, 7b and 8 travel to Gruz.

CROATIA DIRECTORY

ACCOMMODATION

Along the Croatian coast, accommodation is priced according to three different seasons. Generally October to May are the cheapest months, June and September are mid-priced, while the high season runs for a six-week period in July and August. Prices quoted in this chapter are for the high season, but do not include 'residence tax', which costs from about 4KN to 7.50KN depending on the location and the season. Deduct about 25% if you come in June, the beginning of July, and September; about 35% for May and October; and about 50% for all other times. Prices for Zagreb are constant all year. Many hotels on the coast close in winter.

Camping

Nearly 100 camping grounds are scattered along the Croatian coast. Most operate from mid-May to September only, although a few are open in April and October. In May and late September, call ahead to make sure the camping ground is open before beginning the long trek out.

Hostels

The **Croatian YHA** (☎ 01-48 47 472; www.hfhs.hr; travelsection@hfhs.hr; Dežmanova 9, Zagreb) operates youth hostels in Dubrovnik, Krk, Zadar, Zagreb and Pula open to YHA members. Nonmembers pay an additional 10KN per person daily and receive a stamp on a welcome card; six stamps entitle you to a membership. Prices fall outside the high season. It can also provide information about private youth hostels in Zagreb.

Private Rooms

Private rooms in local homes are the best form of accommodation. Often you are greeted by offers of *sobe* (private rooms) as you step off your bus and boat. Although they can be great value, if anything goes wrong (ie a sudden change in rate) you're on your own. In town, travel agencies and sometimes the local tourist office will find accommodation. It's wise to call in advance during the high season. In the cheapest accommodation, you'll have a room in a family home and share the bathroom. In the most expensive, you'll have your own room or apartment with a private bath and sometimes TV. Breakfast is not included but can sometimes be arranged for an additional 30KN. If you're travelling in a small group, it may be worthwhile getting a small apartment with cooking facilities.

It makes little sense to go from agency to agency since prices are fixed by the local tourist association. You'll pay a 30% surcharge for stays of less than four nights, and sometimes 50% or even 100% more for a one-night stay, although you may be able to get them to waive the surcharge if you arrive in the low season. Prices in this chapter assume a four-night stay in the high season.

Hotels

Hotels are ranked from one to five stars with the vast majority in the two- and three-star range. One-star hotels have at least a telephone in the room. Prices in this chapter are for the pricey six-week high season. Breakfast is included in hotel prices.

ACTIVITIES

The clear waters and varied underwater life of the Adriatic have led to a flourishing dive industry along the coast. The real speciality in Croatia is cave diving; night diving and wreck diving are also offered, and there are coral reefs in some places but in rather deep water. You must get a permit for a boat dive: go to the harbour captain in any port with your passport, diving certification card and 100KN. Permission is valid for a year. If you dive with a dive centre, they will take care of the paperwork. Most of the coastal resorts mentioned in this chapter have dive shops. See **Diving Croatia** (www.diving-hrs.hr) for contact information.

BUSINESS HOURS
Banking and post office hours are 7.30am to 7pm on weekdays and 8am to noon on Saturday. Many shops are open 8am to 7pm on weekdays and until 2pm on Saturday. Restaurants are usually open from noon to midnight daily. Bars and clubs open from 8pm or 9pm until about 2am. Along the coast, life is a little more relaxed; shops and offices frequently close around noon for an afternoon break and reopen around 4pm.

CUSTOMS
Travellers can bring their personal effects into the country, along with 1L of liquor, 1L of wine, 500g of coffee, 200 cigarettes and 50mL of perfume.

DANGERS & ANNOYANCES
Personal security, including theft, is not a problem but the former confrontation line between Croat and Federal forces is still undergoing de-mining operations. The hills behind Dubrovnik still contain some mines, so don't go wandering off on your own before checking with a local.

EMBASSIES & CONSULATES
Embassies & Consulates in Croatia
The following embassies and consulate are in Zagreb:
Australia (☎ 01-48 91 200; www.auembassy.hr; Kaptol Centar, Nova Ves 11)
Bosnia and Hercegovina (☎ 01-46 83 761; Torbarova 9)
Canada (☎ 01-48 81 200; zagreb@dfait-maeci.gc.ca; Prilaz Gjure Deželića 4)
Germany (☎ 01-61 58 105; www.deutschebotschaft-zagreb.hr; Avenija grada Vukovara 64)
Hungary (☎ 01-48 22 051; Pantovčak 128/I)
New Zealand Consulate (☎ 01-65 20 888; Avenija Dubrovnik 15)
Serbia & Montenegro (☎ 01-45 79 067; Pantovčak 245)
Slovakia (☎ 01-48 48 941; Prilaz Gjure Deželića 10)
Slovenia (☎ 01-63 11 000; Savska 41)
UK (☎ 01-60 09 100; Ivana Lučića 4)
USA (☎ 01-66 12 200; www.usembassy.hr; Ulica Thomasa Jeffersona 2)

Croatian Embassies & Consulates Abroad
Australia (☎ 02-6286 6988; 14 Jindalee Cres, O'Malley, ACT 2601)
Canada (☎ 613-562 7820; 229 Chapel St, Ottawa, Ontario K1N 7Y6)
Germany (☎ 030-219 15 514; Ahornstrasse 4, Berlin 10787)
New Zealand (☎ 09-836 5581; 131 Lincoln Rd, Henderson, Box 83200, Edmonton, Auckland)
South Africa (☎ 012-342 1206; 1160 Church St, 0083 Colbyn, Pretoria)
UK (☎ 020-7387 2022; 21 Conway St, London W1P 5HL)
USA (☎ 202-588 5899; www.croatiaemb.org; 2343 Massachusetts Ave NW, Washington, DC 20008)

FESTIVALS & EVENTS
Mardi Gras (February) The recently revived pre-Lent festival has gathered force in Croatia. The best is in Rijeka.
Pula Summer Festival (July–August) International pop and classical stars give concerts in the Roman Amphitheatre.
Dubrovnik Summer Festival (July–August) Devoted to classical music, this festival takes place in venues around town and showcases Croatian musicians.

HOLIDAYS
New Year's Day 1 January
Epiphany 6 January
Easter (Good Friday to Easter Monday inclusive) March/April
Labour Day 1 May
Corpus Christi 10 June
Day of Antifascist Resistance 22 June (marks the outbreak of resistance in 1941)
Statehood Day 25 June
Victory Day and National Thanksgiving Day 5 August
Feast of the Assumption 15 August
Independence Day 8 October
All Saints' Day 1 November
Christmas Day 25 December
Boxing Day 26 December

INTERNET ACCESS
Internet cafés are springing up everywhere. The going rate is about 20KN per hour, and connections are usually good.

MONEY
The currency is the kuna. Banknotes are in denominations of 500, 200, 100, 50, 20, 10 and 5. Each kuna is divided into 100 lipa in coins of 50, 20 and 10. Many places exchange money, all with similar rates. Exchange offices may deduct a commission of

1% to change cash or travellers cheques, but some banks do not. Hungarian currency is difficult to change in Croatia and Croatian currency can be difficult to exchange in some neighbouring countries.

Although they are widely accepted in up-scale places, don't count on credit cards to pay for private accommodation or meals in small restaurants. ATMs are available in most bus and train stations, airports, all major cities and most small towns. Many branches of Privredna Banka have ATMs that allow cash withdrawals on an American Express card.

A 22% Value Added Tax (VAT) is usually imposed upon most purchases and services, and is included in the price. If your purchases exceed 500KN in one shop you can claim a refund upon leaving the country. Ask the merchant for the paperwork, but don't be surprised if they don't have it.

For more information on costs and money, see p28.

POST

Mail sent to Poste Restante, 10000 Zagreb, Croatia, is held at the post office (open 24 hours) next to the Zagreb train station. A good coastal address to use is c/o Poste Restante, Main Post Office, 21000 Split, Croatia. If you have an American Express card, most Atlas travel agencies will hold your mail.

TELEPHONE

To call Croatia from abroad, dial your international access code, ☎ 385 (Croatia's country code), the area code (without the initial zero) and the local number. When calling from one region to another within

Croatia, use the initial zero. The international access code is ☎ 00. Dial ☎ 901 to place an operator-assisted call.

To make a phone call from Croatia, go to the main post office. You'll need a phonecard to use public telephones. Phonecards are sold according to impulsa (units), and you can buy cards of 25 (15KN), 50 (30KN), 100 (50KN) and 200 (100KN) units. These can be purchased at any post office and most tobacco shops and newspaper kiosks.

TOURIST INFORMATION

The **Croatian National Tourist Board** (☎ 45 56 455; www.htz.hr; Iblerov trg 10; Importanne Gallerija, 10000 Zagreb) is a good source of information. There are regional tourist offices that supervise tourist development, and municipal tourist offices that have free brochures and good information on local events. Some arrange private accommodation.

Croatian National Tourist Offices abroad include:

UK (☎ 020-8563 7979; info@cnto.freeserve.co.uk; 2 Lanchesters, 162-164 Fulham Palace Rd, London W6 9ER)
USA (☎ 212-279 8672; cntony@earthlink.net; Ste 4003, 350 Fifth Ave, New York, NY 10118)

VISAS

Visitors from Australia, Canada, New Zealand, the EU and the USA do not require a visa for stays of less than 90 days. For other nationalities, visas are issued free of charge at Croatian consulates. Croatian authorities require all foreigners to register with the local police when they first arrive in a new area of the country, but this is a routine matter that is normally handled by the hotel, hostel, camping ground or agency that organises your private accommodation.

Cyprus Κύπροσ, Kibris

HIGHLIGHTS

- **Greco-Roman ruins** Cyprus is full of them! There are the Pafos mosaics (p275) and Kourion, near Lemosos (p274), or Salamis in Northern Cyprus (p277)
- **Kantara Castle** Remote Crusader fortress, looming over the Mesaoria Plain in the northwest of the island (p277)
- **Best journey** Driving through the Troodos Massif, and stopping to see glorious Byzantine frescoes (p275)
- **Off-the-beaten track** The Akamas (p276) and Karpas (p277) peninsulas have shifting sands that barely see a soul

FAST FACTS

- **Area** 9250 sq km (about four Luxembourgs)
- **ATMs** Widespread; less common in Northern Cyprus
- **Budget** CY£20-40 per day
- **Capital** Lefkosia for the Republic; Lefkoşa for Northern Cyprus
- **Country Codes** Republic: ☎ 357; Northern Cyprus: ☎ 90 392
- **Famous for** Beaches, icons and *mezes* (multicoursed meals)
- **Head of State** Tassos Papadopoulos for the Republic; Rauf Denktash for Northern Cyprus
- **Languages** Greek for the Republic; Turkish for Northern Cyprus
- **Money** CY£/Euro (A$1 = CY£0.34/€0.58, CA$1 = CY£0.37/€0.64, CY£1 = €1.73, €1 = CY£0.58, ¥100 = CY£0.42/€0.73, NZ$1 =CY£0.32/€0.54, UK£1 = CY£0.83/€1.45, US$1 = CY£0.49/€0.81)

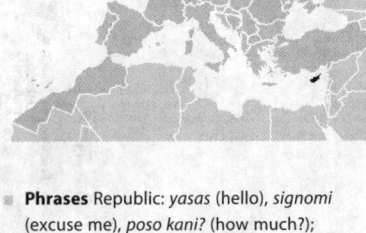

- **Phrases** Republic: *yasas* (hello), *signomi* (excuse me), *poso kani?* (how much?); Northern Cyprus: *merhaba* (hello), *affeders-iniz* (excuse me), *ne kadar?* (how much?)
- **Population** 802,500 (plus 120,000 Turkish settlers and soldiers in Northern Cyprus)
- **Time** GMT/UTC + 2
- **Visas** None required for most nationalities

TRAVEL HINTS

For a quick picnic anywhere in Cyprus, grab some village bread, *haloumi* (squeaky cheese), *lountza* (smoked ham) and juicy village oranges. Museums and monuments in the Republic are free to Europeans (no formal proof of nationality needed) on Sunday.

ROAMING CYPRUS

Starting in the republic, visit Pafos and Polis in the west and tour the monasteries of the Troodos Massif. Check out both sides of divided Lefkosia, and day-trip to Girne or Gazimağusa and the Karpas Peninsula in Northern Cyprus.

CYPRUS

50 km
30 miles

MEDITERRANEAN SEA

To Mersin (Turkey) (100km)

To Tasucu (Turkey) (60km)

To Tasucu (Turkey) (60km)

To Alanya (Turkey) (150km)

To Haifa (Israel) (170km)

To Rhodes (Greece) (400km); Piraeus (Greece) (800km)

Zafer Burnu (Cape Apostolos Andreas)

Dipkarpaz (Rizokarpaso)

Karpas Peninsula

Kantara

Cape Elaia

Famagusta Bay

Gazimağusa (Famagusta)

UN Buffer Zone

Ayia Napa

Salamis

NORTH CYPRUS

Mesoria Plain

Kythrea (Değirmenlik)

Protaras

Ercan Airport

Larnaka Bay

Larnaka

Larnaka International Airport

Korucam Burnu (Cape Kormakitis)

Akdeniz (Ayia Irini)

Kyrenia (Pentadactylos) Massif

Lefkoşa (Nicosia)

Lefkosia (Nicosia)

Girne (Kyrenia)

Bellapais

St Hilarion

Ledra Palace Checkpoint

Dhekelia UK Sovereign Base

Stavrovouni Monastery (689m)

Pano Lefkara

Governor's Beach

(Cruise Ship Route only)

Gazelyurt (Morfou)

Morfou Bay

UN Buffer Zone

Kato Pyrgos

REPUBLIC OF CYPRUS

Agros

Agios Nikolaos tis Stegis

Kakopetria

Olympus (1952m)

Platia Troodos

Troodos Massif

Lemesos (Limassol)

Kolossi

Salt Lake

Akrotiri Bay

Episkopi Bay

Akrotiri UK Sovereign Base

Kourion

(Cruise Ship Route only)

Kykkos Monastery

Kykkos (1318m)

Pedoulas

Archangelos

Omodos

Platres

Sanctuary of Apollon Ylatis

Pissouri

Aphrodite's Sanctuary

Kouklia

Hrysohou Bay

Polis

Latsi

Akamas Peninsula

Cape Arnaoutis

Baths of Aphrodite

Avakas Gorge

Tombs of the Kings

Coral Bay

Pafos International Airport

Pafos

Kato Pafos

CYPRUS

The third-largest island in the Mediterranean, Cyprus is famous as a package-tour destination, but there's plenty here for the shoestring traveller. This is the legendary birthplace of Aphrodite, who blessed the island with golden beaches and a laid-back, Mediterranean way of doing things.

Tourist development is concentrated around the coast but it's easy to escape the crowds by heading inland. History buffs swoon at the mention of Cyprus – you can't go more than a few miles in any direction without hitting a Roman ruin, Crusader castle or Byzantine monastery.

Cyprus has seen its share of troubles, and the northern part of the island has been occupied by Turkey since 1974. However, each year seems to bring the situation a little closer to resolution and the attractions speak for themselves. If you want a holiday with history, just follow in the footsteps of empire builders from Athens to Istanbul.

HISTORY

Blessed with natural resources but cursed with a strategic location, Cyprus has been a pawn in the games of empires since ancient times. Greek culture in Cyprus dates back to 2500BC, but the island was taken over by the Romans and then the Byzantines, who built churches and monasteries across the island.

Next came the Crusaders, whose castles are still evident on the island; the Franks, who erected Gothic cathedrals; and the Venetians, who built huge city walls around Lefkosia and Famagusta. This didn't stop the Ottomans, who invaded in 1571 and dominated the Cypriots for the next 300 years.

In 1878 Turkey sold Cyprus to Britain but the majority Greek Cypriot population demanded *enosis* – independence from British and Turkish rule and union with Greece. After years of intercommunal violence, Britain finally granted independence to Cyprus in August 1960.

On 15 July 1974 forces from mainland Greece launched a coup against the government of Archbishop Makarios III, killing hundreds of Turkish Cypriots. In response, Turkish forces occupied the northern third of the island, driving 180,000 Greek Cypriots from their homes and killing thousands more. About 65,000 Turkish Cypriots were displaced in the opposite direction before the UN partitioned the island in that same year.

Over the following decades, all traces of Greek culture were removed from the north. The area was flooded with settlers from mainland Turkey and hundreds of churches, monasteries and archaeological sites were plundered.

Despite a series of UN resolutions, Cyprus remains a divided island. In 2004 both sides were presented with a UN proposal for reunification in a referendum, but the agreement allowed Turkish settlers and troops to remain in Cyprus and limited the right of return for Greek Cypriot refugees. Perhaps unsurprisingly, the deal was accepted by 65% of Turkish Cypriots and rejected by 76% of Greek Cypriots. As a result, in May 2004 the southern Republic of Cyprus entered the European Union alone.

PEOPLE & CULTURE

Since partition, most Greek Cypriots live in the south. In the north, the Turkish Cypriot population is now heavily outnumbered by Anatolian settlers from the Turkish mainland.

Despite all the troubles, Cypriots on both sides of the line are friendly and law-abiding, if nationalistic. Family life and religion play a central role in society.

TOP FIVE CYPRUS

- **Festival** Kataklysmos Festival, 50 days after Easter in coastal towns
- **Walk** Strolling along Golden Beach, Karpas Peninsula (p277)
- **Club** Ayia Napa – if you have the energy, this tourist resort has tons of them! (p274)
- **Impressive sight** Archangelos Church in Pedoulas in the Troodos Massif (p275) or Kantara Castle in the northwest (p277)
- **Magnificent meze** Zanettos Taverna in Lefkosia, where the courses just keep on coming (p273)

READING UP

For an overview of the whole island, see Lonely Planet's *Cyprus* by Paul Hellander. To understand the glory that was undivided Cyprus, read Colin Thubron's *Journey into Cyprus* or Lawrence Durrell's *Bitter Lemons*. Brendan O'Malley and Ian Craig's *The Cyprus Conspiracy* explores US collusion in the partition of Cyprus.

RELIGION

More than 99% of the Northern Cyprus population is Sunni Muslim, while the south is 94% Greek Orthodox, with Roman Catholic, Maronite and Muslim minorities.

ARTS

The definitive art of Cyprus is the production of icons; you can see examples dating back to the Byzantine era in churches and monasteries in the Republic, particularly in the Troodos Massif (see p275). There are relics of Cyprus's architectural heritage all over the island.

ENVIRONMENT

Cyprus is divided by two mountain ranges: the Pentadactylos (Kyrenia) range in Northern Cyprus and the Troodos Massif in the centre of the Republic. On both sides of the divide, the construction of expat tourist villas is putting a huge strain on natural resources.

TRANSPORT

GETTING THERE & AWAY

Cyprus is a convenient gateway between Europe and the Middle East. Most travellers to Cyprus arrive by air, but there are also ferries to the north from Turkey.

Air

The Republic's international airports are at Larnaka and Pafos. There are scheduled and charter flights from Europe and the

DEPARTURE TAX

Varies with the destination and is included in the ticket price.

Middle East with **Cyprus Airways** (www.cyprusairways.com) and other carriers.

For information on transport between Lefkosia and Larnaka and Pafos airports, see p277 and p274 respectively. Flights to Ercan airport in Northern Cyprus start in Turkey. **Turkish Airlines** (TK; ☎ 227 1061; www.turkishairlines.com) and **Cyprus Turkish Airlines** (YK; ☎ 227 3820; www.kthy.net) are the main carriers. The main route from Ercan to Lefkoşa or Girne is by taxi.

Sea

Passenger services to the Republic's main port at Lemesos were temporarily suspended at the time of writing. Check with **Salamis Cruise Lines** (☎ 2586 0000), **Paradise Cruises** (☎ 2535 7604) or **Louis Cruise Centre** (☎ 2557 0000) to see if any of the cruise ships to Greece, Israel and Egypt are taking passengers again.

From Northern Cyprus there are several ferry routes to mainland Turkey. **Cyprus Turkish Shipping** (☎ 366 5786) has ferries between Gazimağusa and Mersin (€31.20, 12 hours, three weekly). **Fergün** (☎ 815 4993) and **Akgünler** (☎ 815 3510) both have daily ferries between Girne and Taşucu (€21.50, two to five hours). In summer, there is also a ferry to Alanya (€18.80, four to five hours, two weekly).

GETTING AROUND

Inexpensive buses link the major cities, except on Sunday. Shared taxis cover similar routes daily for similar prices.

Cheap car and motorbike rental is available in most towns. Most national driving licenses are valid in the Republic, but only British and international licenses are accepted in Northern Cyprus. Hire cars are not insured to cross the Green Line, separating the Republic of Cyprus from the north.

THE REPUBLIC OF CYPRUS

The Republic of Cyprus covers the southern 63% of the island and includes many of the most important historical sites. Uncontrolled development has reduced the charm of some seaside resorts, but the Troodos Massif and Akamas Peninsula are wonderfully unspoiled.

LEFKOSIA (SOUTH NICOSIA)
ΛΕΦΚΩΣΙΑ, LEFKOŞA

pop 208,900

The boundaries of the Greek Cypriot capital are dictated by the Green Line. Despite its troubles, Lefkosia is a friendly, laid-back place with good restaurants and museums, a lively art scene and a more genuinely Cypriot atmosphere than elsewhere on the coast.

The centre is Plateia Eleftherias by the city walls, from where Lidras St runs down to the Green Line. Most of the tourist attractions are tucked away in the nearby alleys of Laïki Yeitonia or around the old Famagusta gate.

Information

Several banks, the tourist office and post office are nearby Plateia Eleftherias. Cardphones are available on the square.

Cyprus Tourism Organisation (CTO; ☎ 2267 4264; Aristokyprou; ◷ 8.30am-4pm Mon-Fri, 8.30am-2pm Sat) In Laiki Yeitonia.

Kennedy Call Centre (☎ 2245 1020; Regina 60; per hr CY£1; ◷ 9am-10pm) Offers net access

Lefkosia General Hospital (☎ 2280 1400; Leoforos Nechrou). Dial ☎ 1402 for recorded information on late-night pharmacies.

Main Post Office (Konstantinou Palaiologou; ◷ 7.30am-1.30pm Mon-Fri, 3pm-5.30pm Thu)

Sights

Outside the walls near Pafos Gate, the excellent **Cyprus Museum** (☎ 2286 5888; Mouseiou 1; admission CY£1.50; ◷ 9am-5pm Mon-Sat, 10am-1pm Sun) has an incredible collection of pots, statues and treasures from ancient tombs, spanning 9000 years.

Off Lidras St in the old town, you'll find the interesting **Leventis Museum** (☎ 2266 1475; Ippokratous 17; admission free; ◷ 10am-4.30pm Tue-Sun)

CROSSING THE GREEN LINE

Depending on prevailing diplomatic relations, you can cross from the Republic into Northern Cyprus for day trips via the Ledra Palace checkpoint in Lefkosia. EU citizens only can also do a day trip in the opposite direction. You must show your passport and get a Turkish entry and exit stamp on a separate piece of paper – the border is open from 7am and you must return by midnight. The situation is volatile, so check with the tourist authorities before you attempt to cross.

---

dedicated to the history of Lefkosia. More east are the **Omeriye Mosque** and the 18th-century house of **Dragoman Hadjigeorgakis** (Patriachou Grigoriou; admission CY£0.75; ◷ 8.30am-3.30pm Mon-Fri) with traditional furnishings.

In the grounds of the Archbishop's Palace on Plateia Arhiepiskopou Kyprianou, **St John's Cathedral** (admission free; ◷ 9am-noon Mon-Sat, 2-4pm Mon-Fri) has wonderful 17th-century frescoes. Next door, the **Byzantine Museum** (admission CY£1; ◷ 9am-4.30pm Mon-Fri, 9am-1pm Sat) has a superb collection of icons, along with treasures from Northern Cyprus, recovered from around the world by international art police.

Sleeping & Eating

HI Hostel (☎ 9943 8360; Tefkrou 5; dm CY£5) Calm, friendly and full of cats, this no-frills hostel is about 1.5km from the centre in the new town, just off Themistokli Dervi.

Delphi Guest House (☎ 2266 5211; Kostaki Pantelidi 24; s/d with bathroom CY£12/15; ◉) Opposite Plateia Solomou bus stand, the Delphi has pokey but comfortable rooms overlooking the city walls.

Zanettos Taverna (☎ 2276 5501; Trikoupi 65; meze CY£7.50; ◷ closed Sun lunch) Packed with locals every night, Zanettos will ply you with meze dishes till you burst. The standard *meze* features souvlaki, seftalias, haloumi and keftedes (meatballs) amongst other local treats.

For cheap and tasty *seftalias* (pork and herb rissoles) and souvlaki, head to **Christakis** (☎ 2266 8537; Plateia Solomou; souvlaki CY£2-3; ◷ closed Sun) by the bus stand.

Drinking

Just south of the city walls, modernist **Zoo** (☎ 2245 8811; cnr Afroditis & Stasinou) attracts a party crowd on Friday and Saturday nights.

Entertainment

There are several cinemas that show international blockbusters that are close to Plateia Eleftherias. The CTO has information on theatrical performances.

Getting There & Away

Buses leave from several stands around the old city walls from Monday to Saturday; buy tickets on-board. **Intercity** (☎ 2266 5814; Plateia Solomou) has regular buses to Lemesos (CY£2, 1½ hours) and Larnaka (CY£2, one hour). **Nea Amoroza** (☎ 2693 6822; Constanza Bastion) and **Alepa** (☎ 2266 4636; Tripolis Bastion) both have a daily bus to Pafos (CY£3 to CY£4.50, 2½ hours). Buses and shared taxis take the same time to reach these destinations.

Solis (☎ 2266 6388; Tripolis Bastion) and **Lysos** (☎ 9941 4777; Tripolis Bastion) have buses going at noon to Polis (CY£6, 3½ hours), while **Eman** (☎ 2372 1321; Constanza Bastion) goes to Ayia Napa (CY£3, 1½ hours, daily, 3pm). For the Troodos Massif, **Zingas** (☎ 2295 2437; Leonidou 34) has an early morning weekday bus to Platres (CY£2.50, two hours) via Pedoulas, the depot is just south of Plateia Solomou.

Close to Podocataro Bastion, **Travel & Express** (☎ 7777 7474; Municipal Parking Space, Salaminos) has frequent service-taxis to Larnaka (CY£3.05) and Lemesos (CY£4.10).

For car hire, try **Petsas** (☎ 2266 2650; Kostaki Pantelidi 24; per day from CY£20) near Plateia Solomou.

LARNAKA ΛΑΡΝΑΚΑ

pop 73,200

Built over the ruins of Kition, Larnaka is the final resting place of two religious celebrities: Hala Sultan, the foster aunt of the prophet Mohammed; and Agios Lazaros, who rose from the dead in the Bible. It's now a busy little resort with a waterfront hotel strip and a quieter old town and Turkish district.

The **CTO** (☎ 2465 4322; Plateia Vasileos Pavlou; ☺ 8.15am-2.30pm & 3pm-6.15pm Mon-Fri, closed Wed pm, 8.15pm-1.15pm Sat) is at the northern end of town. **Alto Cafe** (☎ 2465 9625; Grigoriou Afxentiou; per hr CY£2; ☺ 10-2am) has Internet terminals.

In the old part of town, the ornate Byzantine **Church of St Lazaros** (Agiou Lazarou; admission free; ☺ 8am-12.30pm & 3.30-6.30pm) contains fabulous icons and the bones of Lazaros. The **Pierides Museum** (☎ 2481 4555; Zenonos Kitieos 4; admission CY£1; ☺ 9am-4pm Mon-Thu, 9am-1pm Fri-Sat) has an amazing collection of Cypriot artefacts.

Hala Sultan is buried at the peaceful **Hala Sultan Tekke**, a mosquelike shrine near the airport.

East of Larnaka are the package-tour resorts of **Ayia Napa** and **Protaras**, which have lively club scenes but no atmosphere.

Sleeping & Eating

HI Hostel (☎ 9993 5583; Nikolaou Rossou 27; dm/f CY£5/10) Attached to the Bekir Pasa mosque, this simple hostel isn't bad value, with single-sex dorms and family rooms that sleep four.

Onisillos Hotel (☎ 2465 1100; onisillos@cytanet.com.cy; Onisillos 17; s/d with bathroom CY£25/30; ✖) About 500m west of the fort in a quiet residential area, this homely two-star offers tidy rooms.

Prasino Amaxoudi (☎ 2462 2939; kebabs from CY£2) If you fancy a cheap bite on the hoof, grab a souvlaki, doner kebab or haloumi pitta from this place beside the mosque.

Militzis Restaurant (☎ 2465 5867; Piale Pasia 42; mains from CY£4) Packed with locals and tourists, Militzis offers fabulous *ofto kleftiko* (baked lamb) fresh from the clay oven.

Getting There & Away

Buses stop on the waterfront opposite the Four Lanterns hotel and run regularly to Ayia Napa (CY£1.80, 40 minutes), Protaras (CY£1.80, 45 minutes), Lefkosia (CY£2, one hour, not Sunday) and Lemesos (CY£2.50, not Sunday). **Travel & Express** (☎ 7777 7474) runs service-taxis to Lemesos (CY£3.60, one hour) and Lefkosia (CY£3). The journey to the airport takes 20 minutes. For the airport, you have the choice of a taxi (CY£5) or the No 22 and No 24 local buses (CY£0.60) from Erimou, near the junction with Vasilou Evagorou. Car hire firms have desks at the airport.

LEMESOS ΛΕΜΕΣΟΣ (LIMASOL)

pop 163,400

The Republic's second city, Lemesos is a major holiday resort and the main port. You can give the bland tourist strip running east along the waterfront a miss, but the old town is quite interesting.

The **CTO** (☎ 2536 2756; cnr Spyros Araouzou & Dimitriou Nikolaidi; ☺ 8.15am-2.30pm & 3pm-6.15pm Mon-Fri, 8.15am-1.30pm Sat, closed Wed afternoon) is on the waterfront, a few blocks east of the old harbour. **Travellers Tales** (☎ 2587 8340; Ayiou Andreou 4; per hr CY£1.50) offers Internet access.

All the sights in Lemesos are clustered around the old harbour. **Lemesos Castle Medieval Museum** (☎ 2253 0419; Eirinis; admission CY£1; ☺ 9am-5pm Mon-Sat, 10am-1pm Sun) displays Crusader gravestones, armour and old pots. For a steam bath, try the restored **Turkish baths**

(2 Loutron St; steam baths CY£5; ⊙ 2-10pm) close to the mosque.

About 19km towards Pafos are the extensive Greco-Roman ruins of **Kourion** (Curium; admission CY£1; ⊙ 8am-5.45pm). The nearby **Sanctuary of Apollon Ylatis** (admission CY£0.75) and **Kolossi Castle** (admission CY£0.75) are open similar hours.

There are a few old-fashioned guesthouses in the old port area. **Luxor Guest House** (☎ 2536 2265; Agiou Andreou 101; s CY£6-10, d CY£12) has enthusiastic staff, while its clean rooms come in various shapes and sizes.

Cheap eats are hard to come by – it's worth paying a bit more for the excellent Cypriot food at **Rizitiko** (☎ 6534 8769; Tzami 4; mains £3-7).

There are numerous bars and clubs on the tourist strip.

Getting There & Away

From Monday to Saturday, buses stop near the old market on Georgiou Gennadiou. **Intercity** (☎ 2266 5814) has frequent buses to Lefkosia (CY£2, 1½ hours), and buses from the old port roundabout to Larnaka (CY£2.50, one hour). **Troodos Mountain Bus** (☎ 2555 2220) has a weekday service to Platres (CY£2.50, two hours).

Alepa (☎ 9962 5027) has a single daily bus to Pafos (CY£2, 1½ hours) from Spyros Amaouzou. Local buses to the ruins at Kourion (CY£1.20, 20 minutes) leave from Lemesos Castle. **Travel & Express** (☎ 7777 7474) service-taxis run to Pafos (CY£3.30), Lefkosia (CY£4.10) and Larnaka (CY£3.60). Buses and taxis take the same amount of time.

TROÖDOS MASSIF ΤΡΟΟΔΟΣ

The last great wilderness in the Republic, the Troödos Massif provides fantastic walking country. Small winemaking villages and Byzantine monasteries are dotted among the pine trees.

The **CTO** (☎ 2542 1316; ⊙ 8.30am-4.30pm Mon-Fri, 8.30am-2.30pm Sat) is in the square at Platres, while Plateia Troodos has the **Troodos Visitor Centre** (☎ 2542 0144; admission CY£0.50; ⊙ 10am-4pm) with a nature museum and leaflets on walking trails.

Nearby, Pedoulas has a small **icon museum** and the tiny stone **Archangelos Church**, with awesome frescoes dating from 1474. Ask for the key is at a nearby signposted house. Another fine frescoed church is the 12th-century **Agios Nikolaos tis Stegis** on the road to Pedoulas, west of Kakopetria.

About 20km west of Pedoulas, the 12th-century **Kykkos Monastery** gets mobbed by tour groups, but the **museum** (☎ 2294 2736; admission CY£1.50; ⊙ 10am-4pm) has some fascinating religious paraphernalia.

Sleeping & Eating

The most convenient place to stay is in Platres.

Village Restaurant (☎ 2542 1741; Makariou; half board per person CY£10, meals CY£3-7) This place rents out cheap rooms and cooks up the best Cypriot food in town.

Minerva Hotel (☎ 2542 1731; Kaledonia 36; s/d CY£18/28; 🛇) A 10-minute walk uphill, the Minerva is decorated with Turkoman carpets and sits in a shady garden.

Getting There & Away

Hire car is the best and easiest way to get around, though there are infrequent buses between Platres and Plateia Troodos, Lefkosia and Lemesos.

From Lemesos, a service is run by **Troodos Mountain Bus** (☎ 2555 2220) that leaves for Platres and Plateia Troodos (CY£2.50, two hours) daily, except on Sunday. The return service leaves Platres at 8am. Weekday buses run from Lefkosia.

Rural taxis in Platres can ferry you around the monasteries. A taxi from Lemesos to Platres will cost around CY£25.

PAFOS ΠΑΦΟΣ (BAF)
pop 48,300

Pafos consists of laid-back Ano Pafos up on the hillside and tacky Kato Pafos down on the waterfront. It's very touristy but the historical treasures make up for a lot. The main **CTO** (☎ 2693 2841; Gladstonos 3; ⊙ 8.15am-2.30pm & 3pm-6pm Mon-Fri, 8.15am-1.30pm Sat, closed Wed afternoon) is in Ano Pafos. **Maroushia Internet** (☎ 2694 7240; Platia Kennedy 6; per hr CY£2) is on the main square in Ano Pafos.

Tourists mob the famous **Pafos Mosaics** (☎ 2694 0217; admission CY£1.50; ⊙ 8am-5pm) but the Roman mosaic floors are quite amazing. There are more Roman ruins in the grounds of **Chrysopolitissa Church**.

For a quieter historical experience, you can visit the 3rd-century BC **Tombs of the Kings** (☎ 2694 0295; admission CY£0.75; ⊙ 8.30am-7.30pm), about 2km north of Kato Pafos.

Sleeping & Eating

HI Hostel (☎ 2693 2588; Eleftheriou Venizelou 45; dm CY£4-5) This humble hostel is a long way north of Ano Pafos centre, off Evagora Pallikaridi.

Trianon Hotel (☎ 2693 2193; Arhiepiskopou Makariou III 99; s/d CY£5/12) Right on the main shopping street in Ano Pafos, it has simple rooms but the shared bathroom is off the kitchen and the toilet is off the lounge.

Nikos Tyrimos (☎ 2694 2846; Agapinoros 71; dishes CY£4-8) Inland from the tourist strip, halfway between Ano and Kato Pafos, Tyrimos cooks up all the wonders of the sea, to a mainly local clientele.

Getting There & Away

Monday to Saturday, **Alepa** (☎ 2693 4410; Nikodimou Mylona) runs one morning bus to Lefkosia (CY£3, 2½ hours) via Lemesos (CY£2, 1½). There are also regular local buses to Kato Pafos (CY£0.50, 15 minutes). **Nea Amaroza Co** (☎ 2693 6822; Evagora Pallikaridi 79) operates regular buses to Polis (CY£1.6, 45 minutes).

Travel & Express (☎ 7777 7474) runs servicetaxis to Lemesos (CY£3.30).

POLIS ΠΟΛΙΣ

Built over the ruins of ancient Marion, Polis retains much of the laid-back charm that first attracted holiday-makers to Cyprus. There's a **tourist office** (☎ 2632 2468; Vasileos Stasioikou 2; ☼ 9am-1pm & 2.30-5.30pm Sun-Tue, Thu & Fri, 9am-1pm Sat) and **museum** (☎ 2632 2955; Makariou III; admission CY£75; ☼ 8am-2pm Mon-Fri, 9am-5pm Sat) and you can hike to remote, empty **beaches** in the nearby Akamas Peninsula. Top **walks** include the Avakas Gorge on the south coast and the nature trails around the Baths of Aphrodite on the north coast.

The main square is packed with pavement cafés, and the self-catering apartments are a bargain – try the friendly **Lemon Garden** (☎ 2632 1443; Makariou III 12; s/d CY£15/28; 🔀 🗲) near the museum. The secluded garden pool is a lovely touch. The Polis **camping ground** (☎ 2681 5080; per adult/tent CY£1.50/2.50) is down on the beach.

Getting There & Away

Solis (☎ 2266 6388) and **Lysos** (☎ 9941 4777) buses to Lefkosia (CY£6, 3½ hours) leave from close to the tourist office at 5.30am (not Sunday). **Nea Amaroza Co** (☎ 2693 6822; Evagora Pallikaridi 79) operates regular buses between Pafos and Polis (CY£1.60, 45 minutes).

NORTHERN CYPRUS

The self-declared Turkish Republic of Northern Cyprus (TRNC) is recognised only by Turkey and occupies 37% of the island. So far, the north has seen only limited development but there are castles to explore and untouched beaches to kick back on.

LEFKOŞA (NORTH NICOSIA)
LEFKOŞA, ΛΕΦΚΩΣΙΑ
pop 39,180

The capital of Northern Cyprus occupies the northern half of divided Lefkosia. The old town is full of Frankish ruins, but it's more a place for a day trip than a longer stay. The only legal route between the north and south is the checkpoint by the Ledra Palace Hotel.

The well-preserved Kyrenia Gate contains the main **tourist office** (☎ 227 2994; Cumhuriyet Meydani; ☼ 9am-5pm Mon-Fri, 9am-2pm Sat) Girne Caddesi runs south to Atatürk Meydani (the main square) and the historic Selimiye quarter, which has banks and foreign exchange offices. There's a **post office** (Sarayönu Sokak; ☼ 7.30am-2pm daily, 3.30pm-6pm Mon) and slow 24-hour **Internet cafés** (Mediciye Sokak).

Just inside the walls, the **Mevlevi Museum** (☎ 227 1283; Girne Caddesi; admission €2.40; ☼ 9am-1pm & 2-4.45pm Mon-Fri) is devoted to a sect of whirling Sufi dervishes (Muslim mystics).

Further east, the Selimiye quarter is dominated by the ornate **Selimiye Mosque** (Kuyumkular Sokak), built as a Frankish cathedral between 1209 and 1326. Nearby are **Büyük Han** (Arasta Sokak), an old Ottoman inn; and the **Hamam** (Müftü Ziyai Sokak; ☼ 7am-10.30pm), where you can get a traditional steam bath and massage.

Sleeping & Eating

Accommodation is limited and the budget options are not recommended for solo female travellers. There are inexpensive, faded rooms at **Altin Pansiyon** (☎ 228 5049; Girne Caddesi 63; per person with bathroom €16.10).

Saray Hotel (☎ 228 3115; fax 228 4808; Atatürk Meydani; s/d with bathroom & TV €38.70/63.40; 🔀 🅿) This upmarket option offers tasteful rooms, right on the main square.

For food, you pretty much have a choice of kebabs or kebabs. The food is good and prices are reasonable at **Umutlar Restaurant** (☎ 227 3236; Girne Caddesi 51; kebabs from €1.60).

Getting There & Around

The bus station is north of the centre on Gazeteci Kemal Aşik Caddesi, but regular minibuses to Girne (€0.80) stop near the Kyrenia Gate, and to Gazimağusa (€1.30) leave from nearby Kaymakli Yolu Sokak.

Alternatively, **Kombos** (☎ 227 2929) has service-taxis to Girne from Mevlevi Tekke Sokak. A private taxi to Ercan airport will cost €10.75. For car hire, your best bet is **Sun Rent-a-Car** (☎ 227 2303; Abdi Ipekci Ave 10).

KYRENIA KEPHNEIA (GİRNE)

pop 14,200

Kyrenia is centred on a picturesque stone harbour that ends at a looming Byzantine castle, but the old town is rapidly being engulfed by villa developments. The **tourist office** (☎ 815 2145; ☯ 9am-5pm) is near the marina's waterfront at the west end of the harbour.

The main attraction is the **Kyrenia Castle & Shipwreck Museum** (☎ 815 2142; admission €4.80; ☯ 9am-7pm), which has sinister dungeons and the remains of a shipwreck from 3000 BC.

St Hilarion Castle (admission €2.40; ☯ 9am-5pm) looms over the highest ridge above Kyrenia, but you must drive through an army base to get there. Nearby are the Byzantine cathedral ruins at **Bellapais**.

Sleeping & Eating

Bingöl Guest House (☎ 815 2749; Efeler Sokak; per person €5.40) Down a quiet alley between the harbour and the main square, this place is as cheap as chips but the facilities are basic.

Erkenekon Hotel (☎ 815 4677; fax 815 6010; Efdal Akça Sokak; s/d €16/27; ☒) The family-run Erkenekon stands at the west end of the harbour and offers sea views.

For meals, you have the choice of the expensive waterfront restaurants on the harbour or the finger-licking kebab houses around Ramadan Cemil Meydani.

Getting There & Away

Buses and taxis leave from Ramadan Cemil Meydani (the main square) to Gazimağusa (€1.60, one hour) and Lefkoşa (€0.80, 30 minutes). See p272 for ferry services to Turkey. Town to the terminal is a €2.70 taxi ride.

NORTHWEST CYPRUS

In the northwest of the island, you'll find the sleepy walled city of **Gazimağusa** (Fama-gusta), which is dotted with ruined Frankish churches.

Buses and share-taxis run from Gazimağusa to/from Girne (€1.60, one hour, regular) and Lefkoşa (€1.30, one hour, half-hourly).

About 9km north of Gazimağusa are the rather unkempt Roman ruins of **Salamis** (admission €3.20; ☯ 7.30am-7.30pm), facing a popular sandy beach; a return taxi from Gazimağusa will cost €10.75.

For a taste of what Cyprus was like before partition, the remote **Karpas Peninsula** has incredible **beaches**, a handful of unmolested Greek Orthodox **monasteries** and the wonderful Crusader **Kantara Castle** (admission €2.40; ☯ 10am-6pm), which looms over the plains north of Gazimağusa. The finest beach is **Atinkum** (Golden Beach) on the south coast.

CYPRUS DIRECTORY

ACCOMMODATION

There are cheap hotels or guesthouses in most towns (charging €15 to €30 per night), plus several official camping grounds and youth hostels in Lefkosia, Pafos and Larnaka. Monasteries sometimes accept overnight guests for a donation. Prices for all accommodation options increase by 20-30% from June to August.

BUSINESS HOURS

As a general guide, banks are open from 8.30am to 12.30pm on weekdays, plus from 3.15pm to 4.45pm Monday afternoon, and government offices are open from 7.30am to 2.30pm on weekdays and 3pm to 6pm Thursday (Monday afternoon in Northern Cyprus). Shops close early on Wednesday and Saturday and all day Sunday. Restaurants serves lunch and dinner daily but snack places often close on Sunday.

EMBASSIES & CONSULATES

The Republic is represented worldwide while Northern Cyprus has just a few overseas offices.

Embassies & Consulates in Cyprus

REPUBLIC OF CYPRUS

Australia (☎ 2275 3001/3; Gonia Leoforou Stasinou & Annis Komninis 4, 2nd Flr, CY 1060 Lefkosia)
France (☎ 2277 9910/1; Ploutarchou 12, 2406 Egkomi, CY 1512 Lefkosia)

CYPRUS

Germany (☎ 2245 1145; Nikitara 10, 1080 Lefkosia, CY 1311 Lefkosia)

Greece (☎ 2268 0670; Leoforos Vyronos 8-10, CY 1513 Lefkosia)

UK (☎ 2286 1100; Alexandrou Palli, CY 1587 Lefkosia)

USA (☎ 2277 6400; cnrGonia Metochiou & Ploutarchou, Egkomi, CY 2407 Lefkosia)

NORTHERN CYPRUS

Australia (☎ 227 7332; Güner Türkmen Sokak 20, North Lefkoşa)

Germany (☎ 227 5161; 28 Kasım Sokak 15, North Lefkoşa)

Turkey (☎ 227 2314; Bedreddin Demirel Caddesi, North Lefkoşa)

UK (☎ 227 4938; Mehmet Akif Caddesi 23, North Lefkoşa)

USA (☎ 227 8295; Saran Sokak 6, K. Kaymakli, North Lefkoşa)

Cypriot Embassies & Consulates Abroad
REPUBLIC OF CYPRUS

Australia (☎ 02-6281 0832; 30 Beale Cres, Deakin, ACT 2600)

France (☎ 47 20 86 28; 23 rue Galilée, 75116 Paris)

Germany (☎ 30-30 868 30; Wallstrasse 27, D-10179 Berlin)

Greece (☎ 21-0723 2727; Irodotou 16, 10675 Athens)

Ireland (☎ 35-31 676 3060) 71 Lower Leeson St, Dublin 2)

UK (☎ 020-7499 8272; 93 Park St, London W1K 7ET)

USA (☎ 202-462 5772; 2211 R St Northwest, Washington, DC 20008-4082)

NORTHERN CYPRUS

Turkey (☎ 312-446 2920; Rabat Sokak 20, Gaziosmanpaşa, 06700 Ankara)

UK (☎ 020-7631 1920) 29 Bedford Sq, London WC1B 3EG)

USA (☎ 212-687 2350) 821 United Nations Plaza, 6th Flr, New York, NY-10017)

In other countries, contact the Turkish embassies for information.

HOLIDAYS
Holidays in the Republic are the same as those in Greece, with the addition of Greek Cypriot Day (1 April) and Cyprus Independence Day (1 October). Northern Cyprus observes Muslim holidays and a host of

national holidays. The **North Cyprus Tourism** (www.holidayinnorthcyprus.com) website has dates.

LANGUAGE
Cypriots on both sides of the divide usually speak some English, but settlers in the north tend to speak only Turkish. See the Language chapter (p1264).

MONEY
The Republic uses the Cyprus pound (CY£), while Northern Cyprus uses the Turkish Lira (TL). Due to exchange-rate fluctuations, prices in Northern Cyprus are given in euros. Foreign exchange is mainly handled by banks in the Republic and private exchange offices in Northern Cyprus. Both sides have international ATMs. For more information on costs and money, see p28.

POST
For post restante, stick to the main post offices in south and north Lefkosia. Mail to Northern Cyprus must be addressed to Mersin 10, Turkey, *not* Northern Cyprus.

TELEPHONE
In both the Republic and Northern Cyprus, payphones only take phonecards available from shops. To call Northern Cyprus from the Republic, dial ☎0139; to call the Republic from Northern Cyprus, dial ☎0123.

TOURIST INFORMATION
The **Cyprus Tourism Organisation** (www.cyprustourism.org) covers the Republic, while **North Cyprus Tourism** (www.holidayinnorthcyprus.com) covers Northern Cyprus.

VISAS
In both the Republic and Northern Cyprus, nationals of Australia, New Zealand, USA, Canada and European Economic Area countries can stay for up to three months without a visa. When entering the north, get the immigration stamp on a separate piece of paper.

Czech Republic

HIGHLIGHTS

- **Prague** A city rooted in art, architecture and existential angst (p284); an unforgettable journey despite the tourist crowds
- **Český Krumlov** Fairytale castle, medieval townscape and long summer days spent messing about on the river (p297)
- **Plzeň** The place to imbibe the wisdom of the brewer's art at the fountainhead of the world's finest beer (p295)

FAST FACTS

- **Area** 78,864 sq km (similar to Scotland or South Carolina)
- **ATMs** Widespread
- **Budget** 390-650Kč per day
- **Capital** Prague
- **Country code** ☎ 420
- **Famous for** Beer, ice hockey, Franz Kafka, Antonin Dvořák
- **Head of State** President Václav Klaus
- **Language** Czech
- **Money** Czech crown ($A1 = 18.51Kč, CA$1 = 20.20Kč, €1 = 31.38Kč, ¥100 = 23Kč, NZ$1 = 17.23Kč, UK£1 = 45.34Kč, US$1 = 25.42Kč)
- **Phrases** Dobrý den/ahoj (hello/informal); na shledanou (goodbye); děkuji (thank you); prominťě (excuse me)

- **Population** 10.2 million
- **Time** GMT/UTC + 1
- **Visas** None required for most travellers

TRAVEL HINTS

Find vastly cheaper food and beer simply by walking a few blocks away from tourist hotspots.

ROAMING THE CZECH REPUBLIC

Stop off in Plzeň for a brewery visit, then on to Prague for at least two or three days. Go south to hang out in Český Krumlov before heading for Vienna or Bratislava.

The Czech Republic is a country of fairytale castles, forests and fishponds, medieval towns and Renaissance chateaux. There's a rich heritage to explore – unravel Czech history and you'll get a deeper understanding of Europe as a whole – with the added bonus of the world's finest beer to lubricate debate. And at the centre of it all lies Prague, one of the most beautiful and cultured cities in the world.

No matter which direction you travel across Europe, you're sure to pass through the Czech Republic at some point. Landlocked deep in the heart of the continent, it has been fought over and occupied by its bigger neighbours for most of its history and only emerged

CZECH REPUBLIC

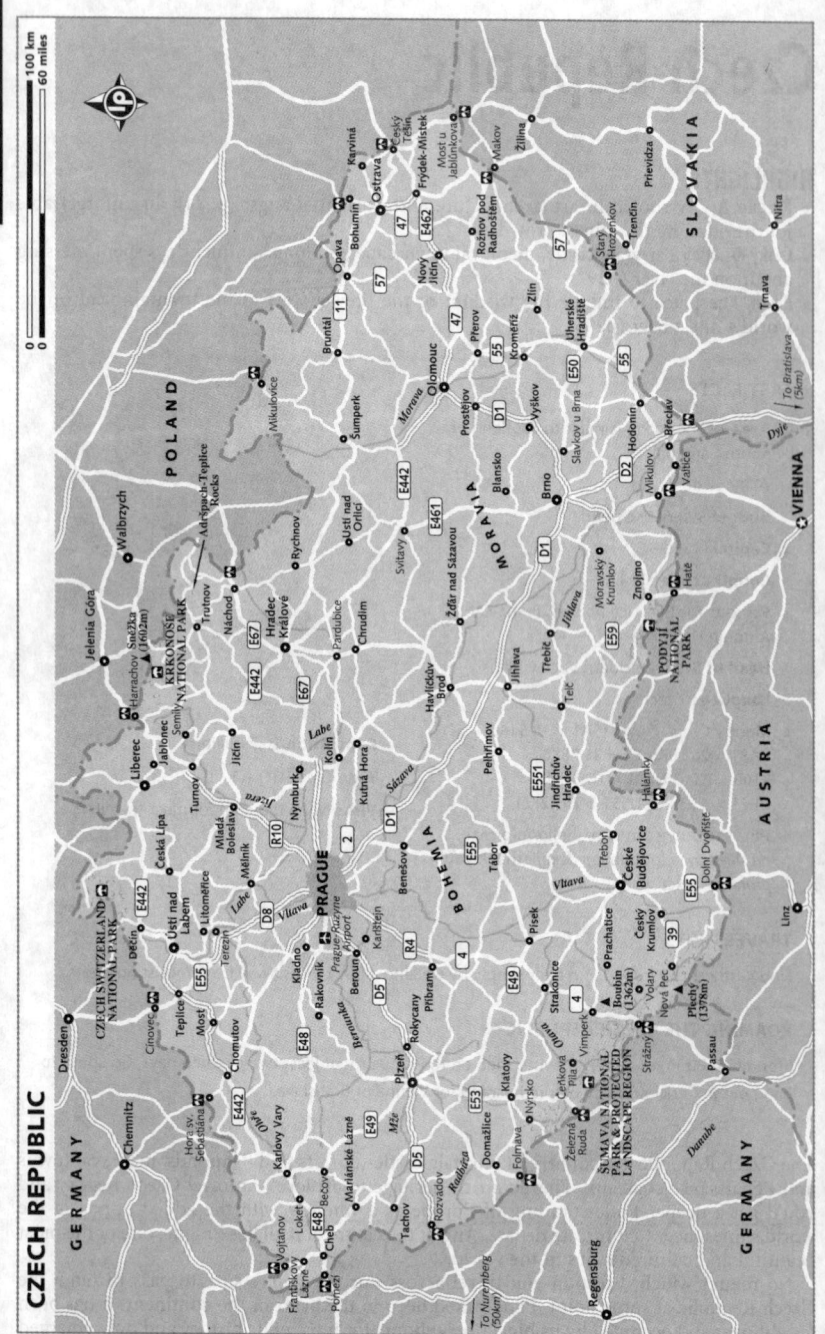

as a separate country in 1993. When it joined the EU in 2004, Czechs celebrated their return to the centre of a united Europe.

Czechs always hated being labelled 'eastern' Europeans. In fact, the watershed between Bohemia (the western two-thirds of the country) and Moravia marks the cultural divide between western and eastern Europe. To generalise: the beer-drinking Bohemians, like their Germanic neighbours to the west, are typically urban, industrious, sophisticated and introspective. Wine-loving Moravians, like their Slavic cousins to the east, are more rural, spontaneous, earthy and outgoing. Moravia's festivals celebrate folk music and dance, Bohemia's focus on classical music and film.

HISTORY

The Good King Wenceslas of Christmas carol fame was actually a prince, and the land he looked out over was Bohemia. This region, along with neighbouring Moravia, makes up the territory of the modern Czech Republic. Beatified as St Wenceslas (svatý Václav in Czech), he remains the country's patron saint.

Their location in the heart of Europe has seen the tides of war and imperial domination wash back and forth over Bohemia and Moravia for centuries. Many events in Czech history have had repercussions throughout the continent, from the hurling of two Habsburg councillors from a Prague Castle window in 1618 (the famous Defenestration of Prague), which sparked off the Thirty Years' War, to Hitler's annexation of the Sudetenland (the western borderlands of Czechoslovakia) in 1938, the event which triggered the final slide towards WWII.

The two 'Golden Ages' of Czech history were the rule of Charles IV (1346–78), who founded Prague's St Vitus Cathedral, built Charles Bridge and established Charles University; and the reign of Rudolf II (1576–1612), who made Prague the capital of the Habsburg Empire and drew many great artists, scholars and scientists to his court. Bohemia and Moravia remained under Habsburg dominion for the best part of 400 years.

The 20th century was notable for the 'years of eight'. Czechoslovakia was created after the fall of the Habsburg Empire in 1918, was occupied by the Nazis in 1938, and fell to a communist coup in 1948. And the hopeful 'Prague Spring', when censorship was relaxed and political prisoners were released, was crushed by the Soviet invasion of 1968.

The Velvet Revolution – the bloodless overthrow of the communist regime – however, didn't happen until 1989. It was soon followed by the Velvet Divorce of 1993, when Czechoslovakia split into separate Czech and Slovak republics, the former led by famous playwright and former political prisoner Václav Havel, whose term in office lasted until 2003.

PEOPLE & CULTURE

The Czech Republic is fairly homogeneous; 95% of the population are Czech and 3% are Slovak. There is a significant Roma population (0.3%), which is subject to widespread hostility and racist attitudes, and suffers from high levels of poverty and unemployment.

It is customary to say *dobrý den* (good day) when entering a shop, café or quiet bar, and *na shledanou* (goodbye) when leaving. If you are invited to a Czech home, bring fresh flowers and remember to remove your shoes when you enter the house.

ARTS

Famous Czech writers include that master of alienation, Franz Kafka (1883–1924; *The Trial; The Castle; Metamorphosis*); Milan Kundera (b. 1929; *The Book of Laughter and Forgetting; The Unbearable Lightness of Being*); and Bohumil Hrabal (1914–97; *I Served The King of England; The Little Town Where Time Stood Still*). And, of course, the playwright and ex-president Václav Havel (b. 1936).

Antonín Dvořák (1841–1904; *New World Symphony*) is the country's best-known composer, while the painter and designer Alfons Mucha (1860–1939), famous for his

---

READING UP

Readable histories (both Prague-oriented) with a personal touch include *The Coasts of Bohemia* by Derek Sayer and *Prague in Black and Gold* by Peter Demetz. For an insight into the paranoia of the communist era, read Milan Kundera's novel *The Joke*.

CZECH REPUBLIC

TOP FIVE CZECH REPUBLIC

- **Festival** Prague Spring (p289)
- **Walk** Strolling from Prague Castle (p285) to Staroměstské nám (Old Town Square; p288)
- **Bar/Club** U Zlatého Tygra (p291)
- **Impressive sight** Český Krumlov (p297)
- **Beer appreciation** České Budějovice (p296) or Plzeň (p295)

Art Nouveau posters, is the most widely known Czech artist. There are many accomplished Czech film directors, including Miloš Forman (b. 1932), best known for *One Flew Over The Cuckoo's Nest* (1975) and *Amadeus* (1984), and Jan Švankmajer, master of surrealism, whose most widely known film is *Otesánek* (*Little Otik*; 2000), based on a gruesome Czech fairy tale.

ENVIRONMENT

The Czech Republic consists of two low-lying river basins ringed by rounded, forest-clad hills. Acid rain caused by air pollution from intensive industry has damaged the forests in northern Bohemia and Moravia, but the situation has improved since the fall of communism; once-filthy rivers have also been cleaned up.

There is tension between the Czech government and non-nuclear Austria over the Temelín nuclear power station in South Bohemia. Austria threatened to block the Czech Republic's entry to the EU, but in 2004 the Czechs announced plans to expand the station.

TRANSPORT

GETTING THERE & AWAY

Air

The national carrier, **Czech Airlines** (ČSA; ☎ 220 104 620; www.csa.cz; V celnici 5, Nové Město), has direct flights to Prague from many European cities, the Middle East and North America.

The budget airline **easyJet** (www.easyjet.com) has direct flights to Prague from several British airports. **KLM** (☎ 233 090 933; www.klm .com) is also a good bet for low-cost flights to Prague via Amsterdam.

Bus

Prague's main international bus station is Úan Praha Florenc (Ústřední autobusové nádraží, or 'central bus station'), 600m north of the main train station. The peak season for bus travel is from mid-June to the end of September, when there are daily buses to major European cities; outside this season, frequency falls to two or three a week.

The following are the main international bus operators serving Prague:

Capital Express (☎ 220 870 368; www.capitalexpress.cz; U výstaviště 3, Holešovice; ✷ 8am-6pm Mon-Thu, 8am-5pm Fri) Five buses a week (daily in summer) from London to Prague and Brno via Plzeň. International Student Identity Card (ISIC) discount available.

Eurolines-Bohemia Euroexpress International (☎ 224 218 680; www.bei.cz; ÚAN Praha Florenc Bus Station, Křižíkova 4-6, Karlín) Buses to destinations all over Europe.

Eurolines-Sodeli CZ (☎ 224 239 318; www.eurolines.cz; Senovážné nám 6, Nové Město; ✷ 8am-6pm Mon-Fri) Buses to France, Spain, Switzerland and Poland.

Kingscourt Express (☎ 224 234 583; www.kce.cz; Havelská 8, Staré Město; ✷ 8am-6pm Mon-Fri, 8am-1pm Sat) Four buses a week (six in summer) from London to Prague and Brno via Plzeň.

Destinations from Prague include Amsterdam (2100Kč, 15 hours), Bratislava (320Kč, 4¾ hours), Brno (150Kč, 2½ hours), Budapest (1230Kč, 7¼ hours), Frankfurt (1250Kč, 8½ hours), London (1850Kč, 20 hours), Geneva (2280Kč, 15 hours), Paris (2180Kč, 15 hours), Salzburg (890Kč, 7½ hours), Vienna (600Kč, five hours), Warsaw (800Kč, 10½ hours) and Wrocław (670Kč, 4¾ hours).

Car & Motorcycle

Road rules are the same as in the rest of Europe; foreign driving licences are valid for up to 90 days. The legal blood alcohol limit is zero.

You will need to buy a motorway tax coupon (*nálepka*) – on sale at border crossings, petrol stations and post offices – in order to use Czech motorways (100/200Kč for 10 days/one month).

Train

International trains arrive at Prague's main **train station** (Praha-hlavní nádraží, or Praha hl. n; Wilsonova, Nove Mesto), or the outlying **Holešovice** (Praha Hol; Vrbenského, Holešovice) and **Smíchov** (Praha Smv; Nádražní, Smíchov) stations.

Prague and Brno lie on the main line from Berlin and Dresden to Bratislava and Budapest, and from Hamburg and Berlin to Vienna. Trains from Frankfurt and Munich pass through Nuremberg and Plzeň on the way to Prague. There are also daily express trains between Prague and Warsaw via Wrocław or Katowice.

Sample one-way fares to/from Prague include Berlin (1408Kč, five hours, one daily), Salzburg (1184Kč, eight hours, one daily), Frankfurt (1952Kč; 7½ hours, one daily), Bratislava (576Kč, 4½ hours, eight daily), Vienna (928Kč, 4½ hours, one daily), Kraków (896Kč, 8½ hours, one daily) and Warsaw (1152Kč, 9½ hours, one daily).

You can buy tickets in advance from Czech Railways (České dráhy, or ČD) ticket offices and various travel agencies. Seat reservations are compulsory on international trains. International tickets are valid for two months with unlimited stopovers. Inter-Rail (Zone D) passes are valid in the Czech Republic, but Eurail passes are not.

GETTING AROUND
Bus

Within the Czech Republic, buses are often faster, cheaper and more convenient than the train. Many bus routes have reduced frequency (or none) at weekends. You can check bus timetables on www.jizdnirady.cz. Buses occasionally leave early, so it's best to get to the station at least 15 minutes before the official departure time.

Bus ticketing at main stations such as Prague and Karlovy Vary is computerised, so you can often book a seat ahead and be sure of a comfortable trip. Way stations are rarely computerised and you must line up and pay the driver.

Car & Motorcycle

The main international car-rental chains all have offices in Prague. Small local companies offer better prices, but are less likely to have English-speaking staff – it's easier to book by email than by phone. Typical rates for a Škoda Felicia are around 700Kč a day including unlimited kilometres, Collision Damage Waiver and VAT. The following are reputable local companies:

Secco Car (☎ 220 802 361; www.seccocar.cz; Přístavní 39, Holešovice)

> **EMERGENCY NUMBERS**
>
> - **All emergencies** ☎ 112
> - **Ambulance** ☎ 155
> - **Automobile emergencies (ABA)** ☎ 1240
> - **Fire** ☎ 150
> - **Police** ☎ 158

Vecar (☎ 224 314 361; www.vecar.cz; Svatovítská 7, Dejvice)
West Car Praha (☎ 235 365 307; www.westcarpraha.cz; Veleslavínská 17, Veleslavín)

Local Transport

City buses and trams operate from around 4.30am to midnight daily. Tickets must be purchased in advance – they're sold at bus and train stations, newsstands and vending machines – and must be validated in the time-stamping machines found on buses and trams and at the entrance to metro stations. Tickets are hard to find at night, at weekends and out in residential areas, so carry a good supply.

Taxis have meters – just make sure they're switched on.

Train

Czech Railways provides efficient train services to almost every part of the country. Fares are based on distance – one-way, 2nd-class fares cost around 64/120/224/424Kč for 50/100/200/400km. For travel within the Czech Republic only, the Czech Flexipass is available (from US$48 to US$78 for three to eight days' travel in a 15-day period).

The sales clerks at ticket counters seldom speak English, so try writing down your destination, with the date and time you wish to travel, on a piece of paper and showing it to them. You can check train timetables on www.vlak.cz.

If you have to purchase a ticket or pay a supplement on the train for any reason, you'll have to pay a fine if you do not tell the conductor *before* you're asked for your ticket.

Some Czech train conductors try to intimidate foreigners by pretending there's a problem with their ticket. Don't pay any 'fine', 'supplement' or 'reservation fee' unless you first get a *doklad* (written receipt).

PRAGUE

pop 1.19 million

Magic, golden, mystical Prague, Queen of Music, City of a Thousand Spires, famed for Kafka, the Velvet Revolution and the world's finest beers. The locals call her *matička Praha*, Little Mother Prague, the cradle of Czech culture and one of Europe's most beautiful and fascinating cities.

The tourist brochures go into overload when describing the Czech capital, but the city lives up to the hype. Luckily, Prague escaped WWII almost unscathed – the city centre is a smorgasbord of stunning architecture, from Gothic, Renaissance and baroque to neoclassical, Art Nouveau and Cubist. There's a maze of medieval lanes to explore, riverside parks for picnics, lively bars and beer gardens, jazz clubs, rock venues, museums and art galleries galore.

Prague is a must-see stop on Europe's backpacker trail. Beware, though – Prague is a city that gets under your skin, and many people stay longer than they planned. As Kafka once wrote, 'this little mother has claws'.

ORIENTATION

Central Prague nestles in a bend of the Vltava River, which separates Hradčany, the medieval castle district, and Malá Strana (Little Quarter) on the west bank from Staré Město (Old Town) and Nové Město (New Town) on the east.

Prague Castle overlooks Malá Strana, while the twin Gothic spires of Týn Church dominate the open space of Staroměstské nám, the Old Town Square. The broad avenue of Václavské nám (Wenceslas Square) stretches southeast from Staré Město towards the National Museum and the main train station.

GETTING INTO TOWN

Prague's Ruzyně airport is 17km west of the city centre. To get into town, buy a ticket from the public transport (DPP) desk in arrivals and take bus No 119 (12Kč, 20 minutes, every 15 minutes) to the end of the line (Dejvická), then continue by metro into the city centre (another 10 minutes; no new ticket needed). Note, you'll need a half-fare (6Kč) ticket for your backpack or suitcase.

INFORMATION
Internet Access

There are lots of Internet cafés in the city centre.

Bohemia Bagel (per min 1.50Kč; ☑ 7am-midnight Mon-Fri, 8am-midnight Sat & Sun) Staré Město (☎ 224 812 560; Masná 2; metro Staroměstská); Malá Strana (☎ 257 310 694; Újezd 16) Good coffee.

net k@fe (Na poříčí 8; Nové Město; metro Nám Republiky; per min 1Kč; ☑ 9am-11pm)

Planeta (☎ 267 311 182; Vinohradská 102, Vinohrady; metro Flora; per min 0.40-0.80Kč; ☑ 8am-11pm) Cheapest before 10am and after 8pm weekdays, all day weekends.

Medical Services

Canadian Medical Care (☎ 235 360 133, after hr ☎ 724 300 301; Veleslavínská 1, Veleslavín; ☑ 8am-6pm Mon, Wed & Fri, 8am-8pm Tue & Thu) Expats centre with English-speaking doctors, 24-hour medical aid, physiotherapist and pharmacy.

Na Homolce Hospital (☎ 257 271 111, after hr ☎ 257 272 527; 5th Flr, Foreign Pavilion, Roentgenova 2, Motol) City's main casualty department; 6km southwest of city centre.

Polyclinic at Národní (☎ 222 075 120; Národní 9, Nové Město; metro Národní třída; ☑ 8.30am-5pm Mon-Fri) With English-, French- and German-speaking staff.

Praha lékárna (☎ 224 946 982; Palackého 5, Nové Město; metro Můstek) One of several 24-hour *lékárna* (pharmacies) in the centre; for emergency service after hours, ring the bell.

Money

The major banks – Komerční banka, ČSOB and Živnostenská banka – are the best places for changing cash, but using a debit card in an ATM gives a better rate of exchange. Avoid private exchange booths (*směnárna*), which advertise misleading rates and make exorbitant charges.

American Express (☎ 222 800 237; Václavské nám 56, Nové Město; metro Můstek; ☑ 9am-7pm)

Travelex (☎ 221 105 276; Národní 28, Nové Město; metro Národní třída; ☑ 9am-1.30pm & 2-6.30pm)

Post & Telephone

Pick up poste restante at the **main post office** (☎ 221 131 111; Jindřišská 14, Nové Město; metro Můstek; ☑ 7am-8pm). There's a 24-hour telephone centre to the left of the right-hand entrance.

Bohemia Bagel Bagel (per min 5Kč; ☑ 7am-midnight Mon-Fri, 8am-midnight Sat & Sun) Staré Město (☎ 224 812 560; Masná 2; metro Staroměstská); Malá Strana (☎ 257 310 694; Újezd 16) has phones for making international calls (see also Internet Access opposite).

Tourist Information

Prague Information Service (Pražská informační služba, or PIS; ☎ 12 444; www.prague-info.cz) Staré Město (Old Town Hall, Staroměstské nám; metro Staroměstská; 9am-7pm Mon-Fri, 9am-6pm Sat & Sun); Nové Město (Na příkopě 20; metro Nám Republiky; 9am-7pm Mon-Fri, 9am-5pm Sat & Sun); Malá Strana (Bridge Tower, Charles Bridge; metro Malostranská; 10am-6pm Apr-Oct) English-speaking staff. Maps, brochures and guides, as well as public transport tickets, concert tickets, accommodation desk, currency exchange etc.

Travel Agencies

CKM Travel Centre (☎ 222 721 595; www.ckm.cz; Mánesova 77, Vinohrady, metro Jiřího z Poděbrad; 10am-6pm Mon-Thu, 10am-4pm Fri) Books air and bus tickets, with discounts for those aged under 26. Sells International Youth Travel Cards (IYTC).

Eurolines-Sodeli CZ (☎ 224 239 318; www.eurolines.cz; Senovážné nám 6, Nové Město; metro Nám Republiky; 8am-6pm Mon-Fri) Agent for Eurolines buses.

GTS International (☎ 222 211 204; www.gtsint.cz; Ve Smečkách 33, Nové Město; metro Muzeum; 8am-6pm Mon-Fri, 11am-3pm Sat) Air, bus and train tickets, sells IYTC.

SIGHTS

All the main sights are in the city centre, and are easily reached on foot – you can take in the castle, Charles Bridge and the Staroměstské nám in a day. The easiest way to get to the castle is on tram No 22 or 23 (from Národní třída on the southern edge of Staré Město, Malostranská nám in Malá Strana, or Malostranská metro station) to the U Prašného mostu stop.

Prague Castle & Hradčany

If you're going to do the touristy thing, head for the city's number one attraction, **Prague Castle** (Map p290; ☎ 224 373 368; www.hrad.cz; metro Hradčanská; 9am-5pm Apr-Oct, 9am-4pm Nov-Mar; grounds 5am-midnight Apr-Oct, 6am-11pm Nov-Mar). Ticket B (adult/concession 220/110Kč) gives access to St Vitus Cathedral (choir, crypt and tower), the Old Royal Palace and Golden Lane; Ticket A (350/175Kč) includes these plus the Basilica of St George, Powder Tower and the Story of Prague Castle exhibit. However, you're free to wander around the castle courtyards and gardens and the cathedral nave, and watch the changing of the guard at noon, without a ticket.

Castle highlights include jewel-studded **St Wenceslas Chapel** in **St Vitus Cathedral**; the view from the **cathedral tower**; the spectacular **Vladislav Hall** in the Old Royal Palace; and the **Basilica of St George**, Prague's finest Romanesque church. **Golden Lane**, a 16th-century tradesmen's quarter of tiny houses built into the castle walls, now lined with souvenir shops, is an overcrowded tourist trap that you can safely miss.

If you're hungry for art rather than spectacle, head for the **Convent of St George** (adult/concession 100/50Kč; 10am-6pm Tue-Sun), next to the basilica, which houses the National Gallery's collection of Czech art from the 16th to 18th centuries. Outside the castle entrance is the 18th-century Šternberg Palace home to the main branch of the **National Gallery** (Map pp286-8; ☎ 220 514 599; adult/concession150/70Kč; 10am-6pm Tue-Sun), the country's principal collection of 14th- to 18th-century European art.

The exuberantly baroque **Sanctuary of Our Lady of Loreta** (Map pp286-8; Loretánské nám 7; adult/concession 90/70Kč; 9.15am-12.15pm & 1-4.30pm), west of the castle, is a place of pilgrimage housing a replica of the Santa Casa (the house of St Anne, mother of the Virgin Mary), and a fabulous treasury of religious artefacts encrusted in diamonds, pearls and gold.

Malá Strana

Heading downhill from the castle takes you through the beautiful baroque backstreets of Malá Strana (Little Quarter), built in the 17th and 18th centuries by Catholic clerics and nobles. Close to the café-crowded main square, Malostranské nám, is **St Nicholas Church** (metro Malostranská; admission 50Kč; 9am-6pm Apr-Oct, 9am-4pm Nov-Mar), one of the greatest baroque buildings in the city – if you only visit one church in Prague, make it this one. Take the stairs up to the gallery to see the 17th-century Passion Cycle paintings and the scratchings of bored 1820s tourists and wannabe Franz Kafkas.

If the old legs need a rest, grab some picnic munchies and head for **Kampa** park, a broad grassy swathe on a low-lying island beside the river, one of the city's favourite chill-out zones. At the north end of Kampa is the famous and elegant **Charles Bridge** (Karlův Most), graced by 30 statues dating from the 18th century, and lined with jewellery stalls, portrait artists and the odd jazz band. In high season the bridge can be

CENTRAL PRAGUE

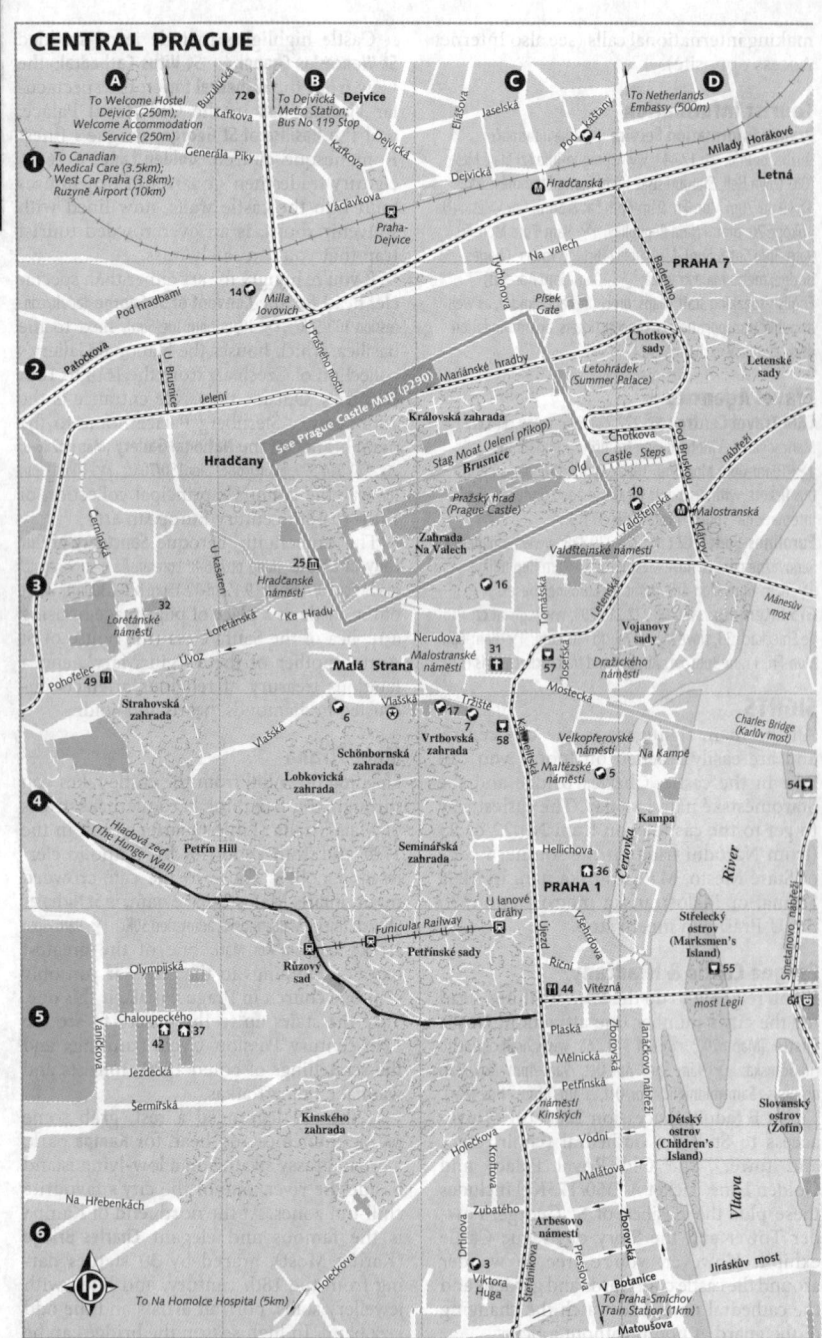

A

To Welcome Hostel
Dejvice (250m);
Welcome Accommodation
Service (250m)

To Canadian
Medical Care (3.5km);
West Car Praha (3.8km);
Ruzyně Airport (10km)

Buzulucká

Kafkova

72

Generála Píky

Václavkova

Pod hradbami

14 Milla
Jovovich

Patočkova

U Brusnice

Jelení

Černínská

U kaštanu

Loretánské
náměstí

32

Pohořelec
49

Strahovská
zahrada

Hladová zeď
(The Hunger Wall)

Petřín Hill

Olympijská

Vaníčkova

Chaloupeckého
42 37

Jezdecká

Šermiřská

Na Hřebenkách

B

To Dejvická
Metro Station;
Bus No 119 Stop

Dejvice

Dejvická

Kafkova

Dejvická

Eliášova

Jaselská

C

Pod kaštany

4

D

To Netherlands
Embassy (500m)

Milady Horákové

Letná

Hradčanská

Na valech

PRAHA 7

Písek
Gate

Tychonova

Mariánské hradby

See Prague Castle Map (p290)

Pražského mostu

Milla
Jovovich

Chotkovy
sady

Letenské
sady

Letohrádek
(Summer Palace)

Královská zahrada

Stag Moat (Jelení příkop)

Brusnice

Chotkova

Castle Steps

Old

Hradčany

Pražský hrad
(Prague Castle)

Zahrada
Na Valech

**Zahrada
Na Valech**

25

Hradčanské
náměstí

16

Valdštejnská

Valdštejnské náměstí

10

Malostranská

Pod Bruskou

Klárov

Mánesův
most

Loretánská

Ke Hradu

Úvoz

Nerudova

Malostranské
náměstí

Malá Strana

31

57

Josefská

Dražického
náměstí

**Vojanovy
sady**

Tomášská

Letenská

Vlašská

Vlašská

6

Schönbornská
zahrada

Lobkovická
zahrada

Vlašská
X

17
7

**Vrtbovská
zahrada**

58

Tržiště

Mostecká

Na Kampě

Maltézské
náměstí

5

Velkopřevorské
náměstí

Charles Bridge
(Karlův most)

54

Kampa

River

Smetanovo nábřeží

Seminářská
zahrada

Hellichova

36

PRAHA 1

U lanové
dráhy

Funicular Railway

Petřínské sady

Růžový
sad

Kinského
zahrada

Holečkova

Krohova

Zubatého

Drtinova

Štefánikova

3

Viktora
Huga

To Na Homolce Hospital (5km)

Úĵezd

Vítězná

Zborovská

Janáčkovo nábřeží

Plaská

Mělnická

Petřínská

náměstí
Kinských

Holečkova

Vodní

Malátova

**Arbesovo
náměstí**

Přeslova

Matoušova

Certovka

Vítězná

Říční

44

**Střelecký
ostrov
(Marksmen's
Island)**

55

most Legií

**Détský
ostrov
(Children's
Island)**

V Botanice

To Praha-Smíchov
Train Station (1km)

**Slovanský
ostrov
(Žofín)**

Vltava

Jiráskův most

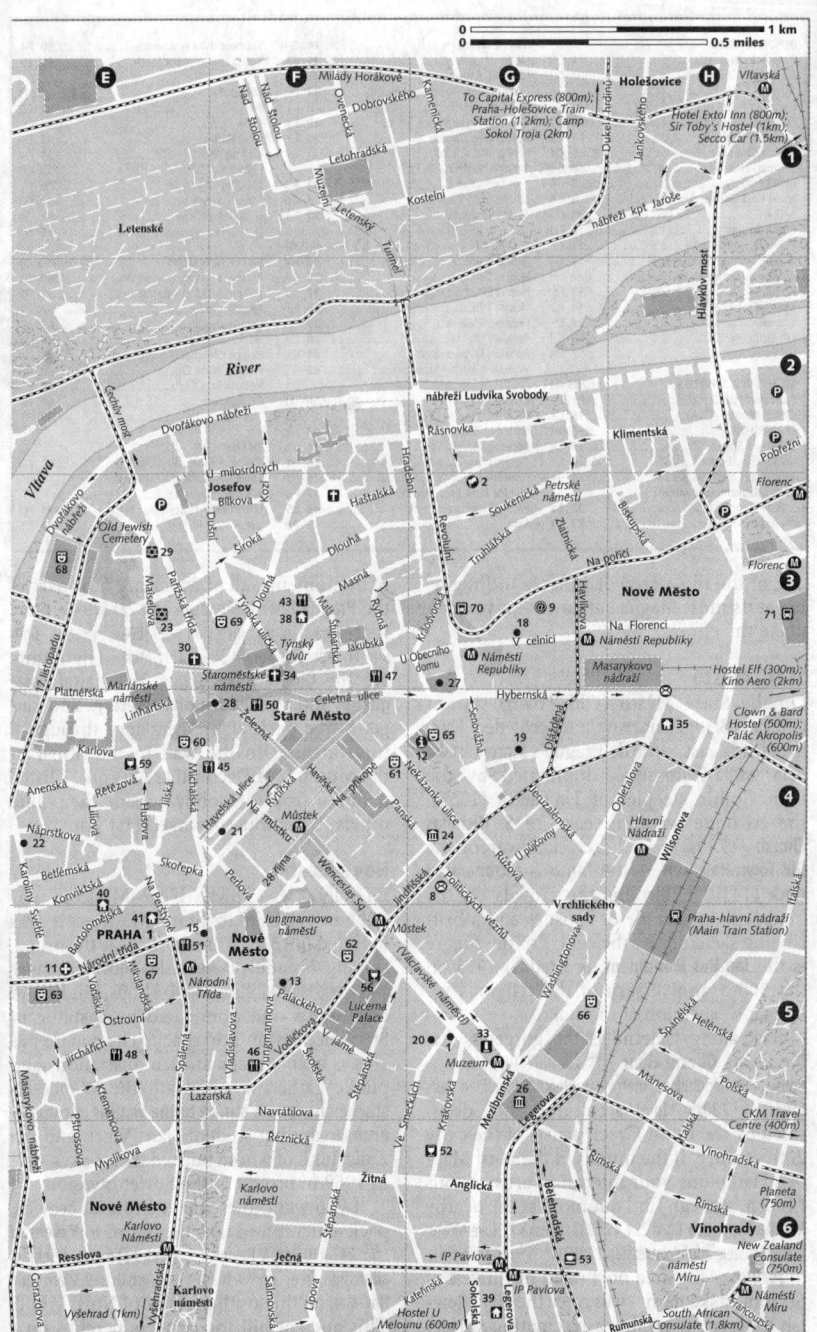

0 — 1 km
0 — 0.5 miles

E F Milady Horákové G H Vltavská M

To Capital Express (800m);
Praha-Holešovice Train
Station (1.2km); Camp
Sokol Troja (2km)

Hotel Extol Inn (800m);
Sir Toby's Hostel (1km);
Secco Car (1.5km)

Overlicová Dobrovského Kamenická Holešovice 1

Nad Štolou Nad Štolou Muzejní Letenský Letenský Tunnel Kostelní Dukelských hrdinů Jankovského

Letenské Letohradská

nábřeží kpt Jaroše

Hlávkův most 2

Vltava River Český most nábřeží Ludvíka Svobody

Čechův most Dvořákovo nábřeží Rásnovka Klimentská Pobřežní P

nábřeží Ludvíka Svobody Florenc M

Dvořákovo nábřeží U milosrdných Josefov Bílkova Kozí Haštalská Hradební 2 Soukenická Petrské náměstí Bakupská P Florenc M 3

Old Jewish Cemetery 68 29 Dušní Široká Dlouhá Masná Revoluční Truhlářská Zlatnická Na poříčí Nové Město 71

Maiselova Pařížská 23 Tynská Dlouhá 43 38 Malá Štupartská Rybná 70 9 18 celnici Na Florenci Náměstí Republiky

Platnéřská 30 Tynský dvůr Jakubská Obecního Náměstí domu 27 Republiky M Masarykovo nádraží Hostel Elf (300m); Kino Aero (2km)

Staroměstské náměstí 34 Kožná 47 Hybernská ⊗ 35 Clown & Bard Hostel (500m); Palác Akropolis (600m)

Mariánské náměstí Platnéřská Linhartská 28 50 Zelezná Celetná ulice

Staré Město 65 19 Dlážděná

Karlova 60 45 Zelezná 12 61 Nekázanka ulice Opletalova

Anenská 59 Michalská Husova Havelská Na příkopě Panská Jeruzalémská Hlavní Nádraží M 4

Řetězová Pštros Na Můstku Můstek 24 U prašný Wilsonova

Náprstkova 22 Karoliny Světlé Betlémská Konviktská Havelská ulice Perlova 28 října Václavské nám Jindřišská Ružová politických vězňů Vrchlického sady Praha-hlavní nádraží (Main Train Station)

40 Na Perštýně 8 Washingtonova

PRAHA 1 41 15 Jungmannovo náměstí Můstek Italská 5

Národní třída 11 67 51 Nové Město 13 62 56 Václavské náměstí 66 Španělská Helénská

63 Národní Třída Palackého Lucerna Palace Polská

Ostrovní 46 V jámě Štěpánská 20 33 Muzeum M 26 CKM Travel Centre (400m)

Jirchářích 48 Jungmannova Vodičkova Mánesova

Vladislavova Spálená Lazarská Navrátilova Ve Smečkách Krakovská Mezibranská Legerova Rimská Vinohradská Planeta (750m) Rimská

Masarykovo nábřeží Pštrossova Myslíkova Řeznická 52 Žitná Anglická Belehradská Vinohrady

Nové Město Karlovo náměstí Štěpánská Lípová Sokolská New Zealand Consulate (750m) náměstí Míru 6

Resslova Karlovo Náměstí M Ječná IP Pavlova 53 náměstí Míru M Náměstí Míru

Gorazdova Vyšehrad (1km) Karlovo náměstí Kateřinská Hostel U Melounu (600m) 39 IP Pavlova M Rumunská South African Consulate (1.8km)

INFORMATION
American Express 1 G5
Australian Consulate 2 G3
Austrian Embassy 3 C6
Bohemia Bagel Internet Café ..... (see 44)
Bohemia Bagel Internet Café ..... (see 43)
Canadian Embassy 4 C1
French Embassy 5 C4
German Embassy 6 B4
Irish Embassy 7 C4
Main Post Office 8 G4
netk@fe 9 G3
Polish Embassy 10 D3
Polyclinic at Národní 11 E5
Prague Information Service 12 G4
Prague Information Service ..... (see 28)
Praha Lékárna 13 F5
Slovak Embassy 14 B2
Travelex 15 E5
UK Embassy 16 C3
US Embassy 17 C4

SIGHTS & ACTIVITIES (pp285–8)
Astronomical Clock ..... (see 28)
Czech Airlines (ČSA) 18 G3
Dvořák Hall ..... (see 68)
Eurolines-Sodeli CZ 19 G4
GTS International 20 G5
Kingscourt Express 21 F4
Klub mladých cestovatelů (KMC) 22 E4
Maisel Synagogue 23 E3
Mucha Museum 24 G4
National Gallery 25 B3
National Museum 26 G5
Obecní dům (Municipal House) 27 G3
Old Town Hall 28 F4
Old-New Synagogue 29 E3
St Nicholas Church 30 E3
St Nicholas Church 31 C3
Sanctuary of Our Lady of Loreta 32 A3
Statue of St Wenceslas 33 G5
Týn Church 34 F3

SLEEPING (pp289–90)
Hostel Jednota 35 H4
Hostel Sokol 36 C4
Hostel SPUS Strahov 37 A5
Hostel Týn 38 F3
Pension Březina 39 G6
Pension Unitas 40 E5
Penzión U Medvídků 41 E5
Welcome Hostel Strahov 42 A5

EATING (pp290–1)
Beas Vegetarian Dhaba ..... (see 38)
Bohemia Bagel 43 F3
Bohemia Bagel 44 C5
Country Life 45 F4
Country Life 46 F5
Pivnice Radegast 47 F3
Pizzeria Kmotra 48 E5
Sate 49 A3
Staroměstská restaurace 50 F4
Tesco Department Store 51 E5

DRINKING (p291)
AghaRTA Jazz Centrum 52 G6
Café FX ..... (see 53)
Club Radost FX 53 G6
Karlovy lázně 54 D4
Letní bar 55 D5
Lucerna Music Bar 56 F5
Malostranská beseda 57 C3
U Malého Glena 58 C4
U Zlatého Tygra 59 E4

ENTERTAINMENT (pp291–2)
Bohemia Ticket International 60 E4
Bohemia Ticket International 61 F4
Kino Světozor 62 F5
Laterna Magika 63 E5
National Theatre 64 D5
Palace Cinemas Slovanský dům 65 G4
Prague State Opera 66 G5
Reduta Jazz Club 67 E5
Rudolfinum 68 E3
Ticketpro 69 F3

TRANSPORT
Cedaz Airport Minibus Stop 70 G3
Eurolines-Bohemia Express International ..... (see 71)
ÚAN Praha Florenc Bus Station 71 H3
Vecar (Car Rental) 72 B1

one of the most crowded places in Prague. It's at its most magical at dawn – if you can make the effort.

Staré Město

On the Staré Město (Old Town) side of Charles Bridge, narrow and crowded Karlova leads east towards Prague's **Staroměstské nám** (metro Staroměstská), dominated by the twin Gothic steeples of **Týn Church** (1365), the baroque wedding cake of **St Nicholas Church** (1730s) and the clock tower of the **Old Town Hall**, where the famous **astronomical clock** (1410) entertains the crowds on the hour with its parade of apostles and a bell-ringing skeleton. At the centre of the square is the **Jan Hus Monument**, erected in 1915 on the 500th anniversary of the religious reformer's execution at the stake.

East along Celetná is the gorgeous Art Nouveau **Obecní dům** (☎ 222 002 100; Municipal House; nám Republiky 5; metro Nám Republiky; guided tours 150Kč; 🕒 7.30am-11pm), a cultural centre decorated by the finest Czech artists of the early 20th century. If the murals in the Lord Mayor's Hall pique your interest in artist Alfons Mucha, you can find out more at the nearby **Mucha Museum** (☎ 221 451 333; Panská 7, Nové Město; metro Můstek; adult/concession 120/60Kč; 🕒 10am-6pm).

Josefov – the area north and northwest of Staroměstské nám – was once the city's Jewish Quarter. It retains a fascinating variety of monuments, all of which are now part of the **Prague Jewish Museum** (☎ 224 819 456; metro Staroměstská; adult/concession 450/300Kč; 🕒 9am-6pm Sun-Fri Apr-Oct, 9am-4.30pm Nov-Mar). Highlights are the **Old-New Synagogue**, the **Maisel Synagogue**, and the **Old Jewish Cemetery**. You can get a free peek at the cemetery through a tiny opening in the wall to the north of the Museum of Decorative Arts on 17.listopadu, or from the lobby outside the public toilets in the museum itself (1st floor).

Nové Město

Literally 'New Town', Nové Město is new only in relation to Staré Město – it was founded in 1348! Its main focus is the broad, sloping avenue of **Wenceslas Square** (Václavské nám; metro Můstek), lined with shops, banks and restaurants and dominated by a statue of St Wenceslas on horseback. The square has always been a focus for demonstrations and public gatherings. Beneath the Wenceslas statue there is a **shrine to the victims of communism**, including students Jan Palach and Jan Zajíc, both of whom burned themselves alive in 1969 in protest at the Soviet invasion.

If you want to escape the tourist crowds, pack a picnic and take the metro to **Vyšehrad** (☎ 241 410 348; V Pevnosti 5, Vyšehrad; metro Vyšehrad; admission free; 🕒 9.30am-6pm Apr-Oct, 9.30am-5pm Nov-Mar) on the southern edge of Nové Město. This ancient hill-top fortress perches on a cliff top above the Vltava – there are great views from the southern battlements.

FESTIVALS & EVENTS

Prague Spring (www.festival.cz; 12 May to 3 June) One of Europe's biggest festivals of classical music

Mystic Skate Cup (www.mysticsk8cup.cz; early July) Major international skateboarding competition, with pro riders from around the world.

Prague International Jazz Festival (http://philipsjazz .ami.cz; late September)

New Year's Eve (31 December) Mad crowds in Staroměstské nám and fireworks over Prague Castle.

SLEEPING

If you're visiting during Christmas, Easter or May to September, book a room. The prices quoted are for high season, generally April to October; however, even these rates can increase by up to 15% on certain dates, notably at Christmas, New Year, Easter, and at weekends in May (during the Prague Spring festival). Some hotels, but not all, have slightly lower rates in July and August. November to March is low season.

The following accommodation agencies are recommended:

AVE (☎ 224 223 226, reservations ☎ 251 551 011; www.avetravel.cz) Convenient offices at Praha-hlavní nádraží and Praha-Holešovice train stations, Ruzyně airport and PIS offices (see p285).

Hostels in Prague (www.hostel.cz) Database of around 60 hostels, with a secure online booking system.

Welcome Accommodation Service (☎ 224 320 202; www.bed.cz; Zikova 13; Dejvice) Offers rooms in student dormitories, hostels and hotels.

Hostels

Hostel Týn (☎ 224 808 333; www.hostel-tyn.web2001 .cz; Týnská 19, Staré Město; metro Staroměstská; dm/d/tr 400/1100/1350Kč; ✕) Spotless two- to six-bed rooms, a superb location only 200m from Staroměstské nám, and a sauna, spa and vegetarian restaurant in the same courtyard – highly recommended.

Sir Toby's Hostel (☎ 283 870 635; www.sirtobys .com; Dělnická 24, Holešovice; dm 290-340Kč, s/d 900/ 1100Kč; ▣ Ⓟ) Friendly staff, a quiet, nicely refurbished apartment building, and only 10 minutes from the city centre – what more could you want?

Hostel U Melounu (☎ 224 918 322; www.hostel umelounu.cz; Ke Karlovu 7, Vinohrady; metro IP Pavlova; dm 380Kč, s/d 550/900Kč; ▣ Ⓟ) An attractive hostel set in a historic building on a quiet back-

street, U Melounu has the added advantage of a peaceful, sunny garden complete with barbecue.

Hostel Elf (☎ 222 540 963; www.hostelelf.com; Husitská 11, Žižkov; metro Florenc; dm/s/d 290/700/840Kč) Readers have recommended this convivial hostel, with its little beer-garden terrace, cosy lounge and cheerful dorms.

Clown & Bard Hostel (☎ 222 716 453; www.clown andbard.com; Bořivojova 102, Žižkov; dm/d 250/900Kč; ▣ Ⓟ) Set in the heart of Žižkov's pub district, the bright and buzzing Clown & Bard is a full-on party place – don't come looking for peace and quiet.

Hostel Jednota (book through Alfa Tourist Service ☎ 224 230 038; www.alfatourist.cz/ejednota.html; Opletalova 38, Nové Město; metro Hlavní Nádraží; dm/s/d with breakfast 350/550/760Kč; ☾ mid-Jul–mid-Sep; ▣) Don't be put off by the glum Soviet-style lobby: the rooms at Jednota are light, airy, and well laid out for maximum privacy.

Hostel Sokol (☎ 257 007 397; post@sokol-cos.cz; Tyršův dům, Nosticova 2, Malá Strana; dm 350Kč; ✕) Sokol may be a bit crowded and lacking in character, but it's cheerful, clean and central.

There's plenty of accommodation at the student dormitory complex opposite the Strahov football stadium, west of the centre. The main providers are **Hostel SPUS Strahov** (☎ 220 513 419; www.spushostels.cz; Block 4, Chaloupeckého, Strahov; dm/s/d 250/480/760Kč; Ⓟ) and **Welcome Hostel Strahov** (☎ 224 320 202; www.bed.cz; Block 3, Vaníčkova, Strahov; dm/s/d 150/400/600Kč; Ⓟ). Both offer a 10% discount to ISIC cardholders.

There's another concentration of student dorms in Dejvice, only five minutes' walk from Dejvická metro station, including **Welcome Hostel Dejvice** (☎ 224 320 202; www.bed.cz; Zikova 13, Dejvice; metro Dejvická; s/d 500/700Kč; ▣).

Pensions & Hotels

Pension Unitas (☎ 224 211 802; www.unitas.cz; Bartolomějská 9, Staré Město; metro Národní třída; dm 270-500Kč, s/d 1100/1400Kč; ✕) This former convent is an interesting place to stay – its cramped rooms were once prison cells (Havel did time here); shared bathrooms and a generous breakfast is included. There's a choice of cramped dorms or more spacious pension rooms.

Pension Březina (☎ 296 188 888; www.brezina.cz; Legerova 41, Vinohrady; metro IP Pavlova; s/d economy 1100/1300Kč, luxury 2000/2200Kč; Ⓟ) Ask for a room at the back of this converted Art Nouveau apartment block with a small garden; those

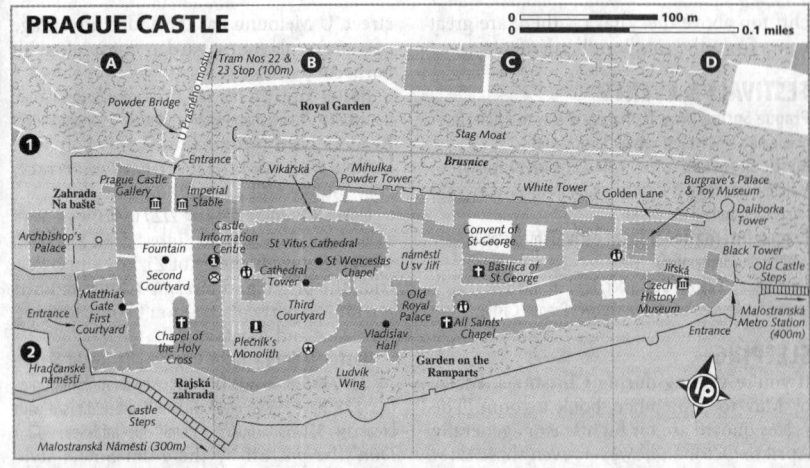

PRAGUE CASTLE

0 ———— 100 m
0 ———— 0.1 miles

facing the street can be pretty noisy. Five minutes south of IP Pavlova metro station.

Penzión U Medvídků (☎ 224 211 916; www.umedvidku.cz; Na Perštýně 7, Staré Město; metro Národní třída; s/d 2150/3300Kč) For a romantic splurge, choose one of the historic rooms with exposed wooden beams in this cosy, centrally located pension. Rates are 25% less in winter.

Hotel Extol Inn (☎ 220 876 541; www.extolinn.cz; Přístavní 2, Holešovice; s/d economy 700/1190Kč, three-star 1290/1990Kč; P) Recently renovated and excellent value, the bright, modern Extol Inn offers hefty discounts on economy rooms for Hostelling International (HI) members. More expensive rooms have a private bathroom, TV, minibar and free use of sauna and whirlpool.

Camping

There's a string of half-a-dozen riverside camping grounds in the suburb of Troja, 15 minutes north of the centre, including **Camp Sokol Troja** (☎ 233 542 908; www.camp-sokol-troja.cz; Trojská 171A; tram Nos 14, 17; per adult 105Kč; ☯ all year; 💻 P), complete with kitchen and laundry.

EATING

Traditional Czech cuisine is strong on meat, dumplings and gravy, and weak on fresh vegetables – the classic Bohemian dish is *knedlo-zelo-vepřo* – bread dumplings, sauerkraut and roast pork. Other tasty home-grown delicacies to look out for include *cesneková* (garlic soup), *svíčková na smetaně* (roast beef with sour cream sauce

and cranberries) and *kapr na kmíní* (fried or baked carp with caraway seed).

Prague has several vegetarian restaurants; elsewhere, *bezmasá* ('without meat') dishes are often limited to pizzas, *smažený sýr* (fried cheese) and *knedlíky s vejci* (scrambled eggs with dumplings).

Prague has a vast selection of restaurants offering all kinds of cuisines and price ranges. Places in Prague's main tourist streets and squares tend to be pricey, but you can find considerably cheaper eats just by walking a block or two away from them.

Sate (☎ 220 514 552; Pohořelec 3, Hradčany; mains 80-110Kč; ☯ 11am-10pm) Just five minutes' walk west of the castle, this place serves tasty Indonesian and Malaysian dishes.

Bohemia Bagel (☎ 224 812 560; mains 50-100Kč; ☯ 7am-midnight Mon-Fri, 8am-midnight Sat & Sun); Malá Strana (Újezd 18); Staré Město (Masná 2; metro Staroměstská) A great informal place to eat, with fresh bagel sandwiches, home-made soups and free coffee refills; one of the few places offering early morning breakfast. Doubles as an Internet café (see p284).

Staroměstská Restaurace (☎ 224 213 015; Staroměstské nám 19, Staré Město; metro Staroměstská; mains 100-300Kč; ☯ 9am-midnight Apr-Oct, 9am-11pm Nov-Mar) The best-value place on the square, with good Czech food and beer – it's cheaper to eat indoors than at the outside tables.

Country Life (☎ 257 044 419; mains 75-150Kč); Staré Město (Melantrichova 15; metro Můstek; ☯ 8.30am-7pm Mon-Thu, 8.30am-4pm Fri, 11am-6pm Sun); Nové Město (Jungmannova 1; metro Národní třída; ☯ 9.30am-6.30pm

Mon-Sat, 10am-4pm Sun) All-vegan cafeteria offering inexpensive salads, sandwiches, pizzas, *guláš* (goulash), soy drinks, sunflower-seed burgers etc.

Beas Vegetarian Dhaba (Týnská 19, Staré Město; metro Staroměstská; meals 78-93Kč; ⊙ 8.30am-8pm Mon-Fri, 10am-6pm Sat & Sun) This stylish and friendly place offers a vegetarian curry (changes daily) served with rice, salad, chutneys and raita; an extra 15Kč gets you a drink and dessert.

Pivnice Radegast (☎ 222 328 237; Templová 2, Staré Město; metro Nám Republiky; mains 60-120Kč; ⊙ 11am-12.30am) This is a classic, old-fashioned beer hall with good cheap Czech food; try the tasty goulash.

Pizzeria Kmotra (☎ 224 934 100; V Jirchářích 12, Nové Město; metro Národní třída; pizza 70-160Kč; ⊙ 11am-midnight) One of Prague's oldest and best pizzerias – 26 varieties cooked in a wood-fired oven.

Tesco (☎ 222 003 111; Národní 26, Nové Město; ⊙ 7am-10pm Mon-Fri, 8am-8pm Sat & 9am-8pm Sun) If self-catering you can stock up at Prague's best-stocked supermarket, in the basement of this four-floor department store.

DRINKING

Prague is a beer drinker's paradise – where else could you get two half-litre glasses of top-quality Pilsner for under a dollar? Bohemian beer is probably the best in the world – the most famous brands are Budvar and Plzeňský Prazdroj (Pilsner Urquell), and Prague's own Staropramen.

As with eating, you can find cheaper drinks by keeping away from the most popular tourist areas; there are plenty of bars selling half-litres for 20Kč or less, compared with 60Kč and up around Malostranské nám and Staroměstské nám.

Trad pubs open from 11am to 11pm daily; more stylish modern bars open from noon to 1am and often stay open till 3am or 4am on Friday and Saturday.

Malostranská beseda (☎ 257 532 092; Malostranské nám 21, Malá Strana) Big, bustling bar popular with students where rock, jazz, folk and country can be heard nightly from 8.30pm.

U malého Glena (☎ 290 003 967; Karmelitská 23, Malá Strana; metro Malostranská) This is a long-established, cosy basement bar that has live jazz most nights.

Letní bar (Summer Bar; Střelecký ostrov, Malá Strana; ⊙ noon-midnight Jun-Sep) Basically a shack serving Budvar in plastic cups (20Kč), this is the place to pick up a beer before hitting the beach at the northern end of the island.

U Zlatého Tygra (☎ 222 221 111; Husova 17, Staré Město; metro Staroměstská; ⊙ 3-11pm) Just about the only truly authentic Czech pub left in Staré Město, this was a favourite haunt of novelist Bohumil Hrabal.

CLUBBING

Karlovy lázně (☎ 222 220 502; Smetanovo nábřeží 198, Staré Město; metro Staroměstská; admission 50-120Kč; ⊙ 9pm-5am) Huge club complex near Charles Bridge, playing anything from 1960s hits to the latest DJ mixes on each of its three floors.

Lucerna Music Bar (☎ 224 217 108; Lucerna pasáž, Vodičkova 36, Nové Město; metro Můstek; ⊙ 8pm-3am) This is a grungy basement bar with a crowded, student-union atmosphere and eclectic programme of live music ranging from rock and blues to classical and even gospel.

Palác Akropolis (☎ 296 330 911; Kubelikova 27, Žižkov; ⊙ 24 hr) A 'cultural complex' comprising pub, café, club, live music stage and theatre, the Akropolis is Prague's coolest venue – expect anything from hip hop, house and reggae to jazz, bhangra and world music.

Club Radost FX (☎ 224 254 776; Bělehradská 120, Vinohrady; metro Nám Míru; admission 100Kč; ⊙ 10pm-5am) Prague's most comfortable, gorgeous and stylish venue for lounge, soul, R&B, Buddha nights, house and alternative.

Mecca (☎ 283 870 522; U Průhonu 3, Holešovice; metro Nádraží Holešovice; admission 150-250Kč; ⊙ 10pm-6am Fri & Sat) Prague's fashionistas, models, film stars, DJs and a legion of clubbers flock to this ultra-trendy, industrial-chic club to dance the night away to house, drum'n'bass and techno.

Jazz

There are dozens of jazz clubs in Prague. Two of the best are the touristy **Reduta Jazz Club** (Národní 20, Nové Město; metro Národní třída; admission 200Kč; ⊙ 9-3am), founded in 1958 and one of the oldest in Europe; and the unpretentious **AghaRTA Jazz Centrum** (Krakovská 5, Nové Město; metro Muzeum; ⊙ 9pm-midnight).

ENTERTAINMENT

For up-to-date listings, check the *Prague Post, Culture in Prague* and the *Do města – Downtown* freesheet, and keep an eye out for posters and bulletin boards.

For classical music, opera, ballet, theatre and some rock concerts – even the most *vyprodáno* (sold-out) events – you can often find a ticket or two on sale at the box office 30 minutes before concert time.

In addition, there are plenty of ticket agencies around Prague that will sell the same tickets at a high commission, including **Ticketpro** (☎ 296 329 999; www.ticketpro.cz; Salvátorská 10, Staré Město; metro Staroměstská; ✆ 9am-12.30pm & 1-5.15pm Mon-Fri), with branches in PIS offices (see p285) and many other places, and **Bohemia Ticket International** (☎ 224 227 832; www.ticketsbti.cz; Staré Město (Malé nám 13; metro Staroměstská; ✆ 9am-5pm Mon-Fri, 9am-2pm Sat) Nové Město (B° Na příkopě 16; metro Nám Republiky; ✆ 10am-7pm Mon-Fri, 10am-5pm Sat, 10am-3pm Sun).

Cinema

Most films are screened in their original language with Czech subtitles (*české titulky*), but Hollywood blockbusters are often dubbed into Czech (*dabing*); look for the labels 'tit.' or 'dab.' on cinema listings. Tickets generally cost from 90Kč to 170Kč.

Kino Aero (☎ 271 771 349; Biskupcova 31, Žižkov) A couple of kilometres east of the centre, this is Prague's best-loved arthouse cinema, with themed weeks, retrospectives and unusual films, often with English subtitles.

Kino Světozor (☎ 224 946 824; Vodičková 41, Nové Město; metro Můstek) Under the same management as Kino Aero but more central – this is your best bet for finding Czech films with English subtitles.

Palace Cinemas Slovanský dům (☎ 257 181 212; Na příkopě 22, Nové Město; metro Nám Republiky) Central Prague's main popcorn palace – modern 10-screen multiplex showing first-run Hollywood films.

Classical Music & Performance Arts

The main concert venues in Prague are the Dvořák Hall in the neo-Renaissance **Rudolfinum** (nám Jana Palacha, Staré Město) and the Smetana Hall in the city's wonderful Art Nouveau **Obecní dům** (Municipal House; nám Republiky 5, Staré Město; metro Nám Republiky) – see p288 for more information. The latter always hosts the opening concert of the Prague Spring festival (p289).

You'll find opera, ballet and classical drama (in Czech) performed at the neo-Renaissance **Prague State Opera** (☎ 224 227 832; Wilsonova; Nové Město) and **National Theatre** (☎ 224 901 448; Národní 2; Nové Město). Next door is the modern **Laterna Magika** (☎ 224 931 482; Národní 4; Nové Město), established in 1983, which offers a combination of theatre, dance and film.

GETTING THERE & AWAY

See p282.

GETTING AROUND
Public Transport

Buy a ticket before you enter a tram, bus or metro – available from metro stations, vending machines, newsstands, tobacco kiosks, hotels and tourist information offices.

Validate your ticket (once only, even if you transfer) by sticking it in the yellow machine in the metro station lobby or on the bus or tram. Once validated, a 12Kč *jízdenka* (ticket) remains valid for 60 minutes from the time of stamping (90 minutes if stamped between 8pm and 5am weekdays, or at any time on weekends); within this period, unlimited transfers between tram, metro and bus are allowed. Note that you also need a half-fare (6Kč) ticket for large backpacks.

The metro operates from 5am to midnight daily; night trams and buses continue to rumble across the city about every 40 minutes all night.

Taxi

The best way to avoid being ripped off is to telephone a reliable taxi company such as **AAA** (☎ 223 11 33 11) or **ProfiTaxi** (☎ 261 31 41 51). If you feel you're being overcharged, ask for an *účet* (bill). Most taxi trips within the city centre should cost around 100Kč to 150Kč.

AROUND PRAGUE

The following places are easy day trips from Prague.

KARLŠTEJN

Fairytale **Karlštejn Castle** (☎ 274 008 154; www.hradkarlstejn.cz; Karlštejn; ✆ 9am-6pm Tue-Sun Jul & Aug; 9am-5pm May, Jun & Sep; 9am-4pm Apr & Oct; 9am-3pm Nov-Mar) perches above the Berounka River, 30km southwest of Prague. The highlight is the **Chapel of the Holy Rood**, with walls covered in 14th-century painted panels and precious stones. The 45-minute guided tours (in English) on Rte I cost 200/100Kč. Rte II, which includes the chapel (July to November only), must be prebooked at 300/100Kč per person.

Trains from Praha-hlavní nádraží and Praha-Smíchov train stations to Beroun stop at Karlštejn (46Kč, 45 minutes, hourly).

KUTNÁ HORA
pop 22,000

In the 14th-century Kutná Hora rivalled Prague as the most important town in Bohemia, having grown rich on the veins of silver ore that laced the rocks beneath it. Today it's an attractive medieval town with several fascinating and unusual historical attractions.

The helpful **information office** (☎ 327 512 378; www.kh.cz; Palackého nám 377; per min 1Kč, 15Kč minimum; ☺ 9am-6pm Apr-Sep; 9am-5pm Mon-Fri, 10am-4pm Sat & Sun Oct-Mar) books accommodation and has Internet access.

A 10-minute walk south from Kutná Hora-hlavní nádraží train station leads to the remarkable **Sedlec Kostnice** (Sedlec Ossuary; ☎ 327 561 143; adult/concession 45/30Kč; ☺ 8am-6pm Apr-Sep, 9am-noon & 1-5pm Oct, 9am-4pm Nov-Mar). This chapel crypt contains the bones of 40,000 people arranged in the form of pyramids, garlands, a chandelier, and even the Schwarzenberg coat of arms – a truly macabre sight. From here it's another 15-minute walk or five-minute bus ride to central Kutná Hora.

In the town centre is the **Czech Silver Museum** (České Muzeum Stříbra; Barborská 28; adult/concession 60/30Kč; ☺ 10am-6pm Jul & Aug; 9am-6pm May, Jun & Sep; 9am-5pm Apr & Oct; closed Mon), a 15th-century palace housing an exhibit on the mines that made Kutná Hora wealthy. You can even don a miner's helmet and lamp and join a 45-minute **guided tour** (adult/concession 110/70Kč) through 500m of **medieval mine shafts** beneath the town.

Kutná Hora's greatest monument is the Gothic **Cathedral of St Barbara** (☎ 776 393 938; Havlíčkovo náměstí 1; adult/concession 30/15Kč; ☺ 9am-5.30pm Tue-Sun May-Sep, 10am-11.30am & 1-4pm Apr & Oct, 10am-11.30am & 2-3.30pm Nov-Mar), which rivals Prague's St Vitus in size and magnificence.

There are direct trains from Prague's main train station to Kutná Hora-hlavní nádraží (62Kč, 55 minutes, seven daily). The train station is 3km northeast of the town centre.

Buses to Kutná Hora from Prague (68Kč, 1¼ hours, hourly) depart from stand No 2 at ÚAN Praha Florenc bus station; services are less frequent at weekends. Kutná Hora's bus station is on the northern edge of the old town centre.

BOHEMIA

KARLOVY VARY
pop 60,000

Karlovy Vary (Karlsbad in German) is the oldest and biggest of Bohemia's fashionable spas. Wealthy hypochondriac wrinklies with oversized sunglasses, yappy dogs and too much jewellery flock here from Germany, Austria and Russia to take the waters and sign up for courses of 'lymphatic drainage' and 'hydrocolonotherapy'.

According to legend, Emperor Charles IV discovered the hot springs in 1350 while hunting a stag. From the 19th century on, celebrities from Beethoven to Yuri Gagarin have come here to indulge in the town's mix of convalescence and culture – music and entertainment were always an important part of the spa cure.

Even if the thought of being slathered in smelly mud and hosed down by a Rosa Kleb lookalike doesn't appeal, there are plenty of more tempting activities: strolling along the riverbanks admiring the elegant colonnades and baroque mansions, sipping beer at riverside cafés and walking in the wooded hills above the town.

Orientation

Karlovy Vary has two train stations – Dolní nádraží (Lower Station), beside the main bus station, and Horní nádraží (Upper Station), across the Ohře River north of the city centre.

Trains from Prague arrive at Horní nádraží. To get into town, take bus No 11, 12 or 13 from the stop across the road to the Tržnice stop; bus No 11 continues to Divadelń nám in the spa district. It's 10 minutes to the centre on foot; cross the road outside the train station and go right, then first left on a footpath that leads downhill under the highway. At its foot, turn right on U Spořitelny, then left at the end of the big building and head for the bridge over the river.

The Tržnice bus stop is three blocks east of Dolní nádraží, in the middle of the town's modern commercial district. Pedestrianised TG Masaryka leads east to the Teplá River; the old spa district stretches upstream from here for 2km.

Information

Infocentrum (☎ 353 224 097; www.karlovyvary.cz; Lázeňská 1; ⊗ 8am-6pm Mon-Fri, 10am-4pm Sat & Sun) Maps, brochures and general tourist info. Branch office at Dolní nádraží.

Main post office (☎ 353 161 111; TG Masaryka 1; ⊗ 7.30am-7pm Mon-Fri, 7am-1pm Sat, 7am-noon Sun) Includes a telephone centre.

VIR Centrum (☎ 603 360 181; TG Masaryka 12; per hr 80Kč; ⊗ 10am-10pm) Internet access.

Sights & Activities

At the heart of the old spa district, on the west bank of the river, is the neoclassical **Mlýnská Kolonáda** (Mill Colonnade; Lázeňská), where bands play in summer. There are several other elegant colonnades and imposing 19th-century spa centres scattered along the Teplá River, though the 1970s concrete monstrosities of the **Hotel Thermal** and the **Vřídelní Kolonáda** (Geyser Colonnade) spoil the effect slightly.

You can pretend to be a spa patient by purchasing a *lázeňské pohár* (spa cup; from 45Kč) and a box of *oplátky* (spa wafers) and sampling the various hot springs (free), which are prominently displayed in shops all over the spa. There are 12 springs in the 'drinking cure', ranging from the **Skalní Pramen** (Rock Spring), which dribbles a measly 1.3L per minute, to the lusty **Vřídlo** (Geyser), which spurts 2000L per minute in a steaming, 14m-high jet. The tourist office hands out a leaflet detailing the 12 springs, all of which lie along the banks of the river.

The sulphurous water carries a whiff of rotten eggs. **Becherovka**, a locally produced herbal liqueur, is famously known as the '13th spring' – a few shots will take away the taste of the spring waters and leave you feeling sprightlier than a week's worth of 'hydrocolonotherapy'.

Rainy day alternatives include the **Karlovy Vary Museum** (Nová Louka 23; adult/concession 30/15Kč; ⊗ 9am-noon & 1-5pm Wed-Sun), which has displays on local and natural history, and the **Jan Becher Museum** (☎ 353 170 156; www.janbecher.cz; TG Masaryka 57; adult/concession 100/25Kč; ⊗ 9am-

5pm), dedicated to the inventor of the local liqueur; the website has some interesting ideas for Becherovka cocktails.

Sleeping

Accommodation is pricey, and can be tight at weekends and during festivals, so book ahead. Agencies **Čedok** (☎ 353 223 335; Dr Bechera 21; ⊗ 9am-6pm Mon-Fri, 9am-noon Sat) and **W-Privat** (☎ 353 227 768; nám Republiky 5; ⊗ 8.30am-5pm Mon-Fri, 9.30am-1pm Sat) can book private rooms from 350Kč per person. **Infocentrum** (☎ 353 224 097; www.karlovyvary.cz; Lázeňská 1; ⊗ 8am-6pm Mon-Fri, 10am-4pm Sat & Sun) can find hostel, pension and hotel rooms.

Buena Vista Hostel (☎ 353 239 002; www.premium-hotels.com/buenavista; Moravská 44; b per person 230-260Kč; ▣ ℗) This is the only place in town that's really geared towards backpackers, offering clean, modern, two- to six-bed rooms with shared kitchen and an outdoor terrace with good views. Breakfast is 80Kč extra. It's a steep walk uphill from the river; alternatively, take bus No 11 or 13 from Horní nádraží or Tržnice to the Na Vyhlídce stop.

Penzión Hestia (☎ 353 225 985; hestiakv@volny.cz; SOU Bldg, Stará Kysibelská 45; b per person 155Kč; ℗) Hestia is a spacious and comfortable student hostel with two- and four-bed rooms. It's a 20-minute walk east of the centre; take bus No 6 from Tržnice to the Blahoslavova stop.

Europension (☎ 353 332 117; www.pension-euro.cz; Studentská 45; s/d with bathroom 650/1100Kč; ℗) On the far western edge of town on the road to Plzeň (take bus No 6 from Tržnice to the U Zámečku stop), this bright and modern 15-room place offers rooms with TV at bargain rates.

Eating

Restaurant prices in the spa district are on a par with central Prague; cheaper places are concentrated in the commercial district.

Restaurant Bernard (☎ 353 221 667; Ondřejská 14; mains 90-110Kč; ⊗ 11.30am-10pm) A cosy, rustic wood-panelled cellar with half-a-dozen convivial booths, the Bernard has a genial, moustachioed host in waistcoat and apron dishing up tasty Czech pub grub washed down with Pilsner. Live jazz every second Friday from 8pm.

Parlament (☎ 353 586 155; Zeyerova 5; mains 70-90Kč; ⊗ 9am-10pm Mon-Sat) A good bet for cheap food, serving salads as well as pork, sauerkraut and dumplings, and other classic Czech dishes. Outdoor tables in summer.

Vg Vegetarian Restaurant (☎ 353 229 021; IP Pavlova 25; mains 60-100Kč; ❍ 11am-10pm) This basic caféteria-style eatery (around the back of the building) offers meat-free soups, salads, sandwiches and hearty hot dishes.

Getting There & Away
Direct buses to Prague (130Kč, 2¼ hours, eight daily) and Plzeň (86Kč, 1½ hours, hourly) depart from the bus station beside Dolní nádraží train station.

There are direct (but slow) trains from Karlovy Vary to Prague (250Kč, four hours, three daily). Heading west to Nuremberg (920Kč, three hours, two daily) and beyond, you'll have to change at Cheb (Eger in German). A slow but scenic alternative is a trundle north through the hills and forests to Leipzig (850Kč, 4½ hours, 10 daily); there are several routes, involving two or three changes of train.

PLZEŇ
pop 175,000

Plzeň (Pilsen in German) is famed among beer-heads worldwide as the motherlode of all lagers, the fountain of eternal froth – Pilsner lager was invented here in 1842. It's the home town of Pilsner Urquell (Plzeňský prazdroj), the world's first and finest lager beer. 'Urquell' (in German; *prazdroj* in Czech) means 'original source' or 'fountainhead', and beer drinkers from around the world flock to worship at the Pilsner Urquell brewery.

Plzeň is a gritty industrial city with an attractive old town, centred on the broad square of nám Republiky and ringed with tree-lined gardens. The central bus station is west of the centre on Husova, opposite the Škoda Engineering Works. The main train station, Plzeň-hlavní nádraží, is on the eastern side of town, 10 minutes' walk from the old town square.

Information
City Information Centre (☎ 378 035 330; www.plzen -city.cz; nám Republiky 41; ❍ 10am-6pm daily Apr-Sep; 10am-5pm Mon-Fri, 10am-3.30pm Sat & Sun Oct-Mar)
Internet Kavárna Aréna (☎ 377 220 402; Františkánská 10; per min 0.90Kč; ❍ 9am-10pm Mon-Fri, 10am-10pm Sat & Sun) On 1st floor; press buzzer for entry.

Sights
In summer people congregate at the outdoor beer bar in nám Republiky, the broad and sunny old town square, beneath the towering, Gothic **Church of St Bartholomew**. You can climb the 102m **church tower** (admission 20Kč; ❍ 10am-6pm), the highest in Bohemia, for a great view of the city.

The **Brewery Museum** (☎ 377 235 574; Veleslavínova 6; adult/concession 60/30Kč, with guide 100/50Kč; ❍ 10am-6pm Apr-Dec, 10am-4pm Jan-Mar) is a block east of the square in an authentic medieval malt house – you can sample the lager in the museum's own bar.

In previous centuries beer was brewed, stored and served in a labyrinth of subterranean tunnels beneath the old town. The earliest were probably dug in the 14th century and the latest date from the 19th century; some 500m of passages are now open to the public, and you can take a 30-minute guided tour at the **Plzeň Historical Underground** (☎ 377 225 214; Perlová 4; adult/concession 45/25Kč; ❍ 9am-5pm Tue-Sun Jun-Sep; 9am-5pm Wed-Sun Apr, May, Oct & Nov). The temperature is a constant 10°C, so take a jacket.

True beer aficionados will make the pilgrimage east across the river to the famous **Pilsner Urquell Brewery** (☎ 377 062 888; www.beer world.cz; tours 120Kč; ❍ 10am-9pm Mon-Sat, 10am-8pm Sun) to prostrate themselves at the famous twin-arched gate and wail 'We're not worthy, we're not worthy!' One-hour guided tours (with beer tasting) in English or German begin at 12.30pm and 2pm daily; no advance booking is needed.

Sleeping
CKM (☎ 377 236 393; info@ckmplzen.cz; Dominikánská 1; b per person from 150Kč; ❍ 9am-6pm Mon-Fri) This travel agency can find you a room in a student hostel in summer.

Ubytovna TJ Lokomotiva (☎ 377 448 041; info@ tjloko-plzen.cz; Úslavská 75; b per person 150Kč) This clean and comfortable sports centre hostel offers two- to four-bed rooms with shared facilities, just 10 minutes' walk south of the train station.

Pension v Solní (☎ 377 236 652; Solní 8; www.volny .cz/pensolni; s/d 600/1020Kč) Set in a pleasant little townhouse close to the main square, this cosy pension has only three rooms, so bookings are essential.

Hotel Slovan (☎ 377 227 256; hotelslovan@iol.cz; Smetanovy sady 1; s/d 500/750Kč) This is a grand old hotel with a magnificent central stairway, dating from the 1890s. The cheaper rooms are a bit tired looking; you can splurge on posh rooms with bathroom & TV for 1450/2100Kč per single/double.

Eating & Drinking

Plzeňská bašta (☎ 377 237 262; Riegrova 5; mains 60-80Kč; ⏱ 10.30am-midnight Mon-Sat, 10.30am-10pm Sun) This local institution, supported by a network of ancient wood beams, has oodles of personality, lashings of beer and big plates of meaty, local grub.

U Mansfeldu (☎ 377 333 844; Dřevěna 9; mains 65-185Kč; ⏱ 11am-11pm Mon-Sat, 11am-9pm Sun) A busy modern pub with lots of gleaming copper and young, efficient staff, Mansfeldu serves up hearty Bohemian fodder washed down with Pilsner Urquell.

Měšťanská Beseda (☎ 378 037 922; Kopeckého sady 13; mains 80-150Kč; ⏱ 9am-10pm) Enjoy a coffee or a light meal in elegant Art Nouveau surroundings in this renovated cultural centre. There's live classical music from 6pm to 9pm on Tuesday.

You can get decent pizzas at **Pizzerie** (☎ 377 237 965; Solní 9; pizza 65Kč; ⏱ 10am-10pm Mon-Thu, 10am-11pm Fri, 11am-11pm Sat, 11.30am-10pm Sun), and healthy baguettes at **Slunečnice** (☎ 377 236 093; Jungmannova 4; sandwiches 35Kč; ⏱ 8am-5pm Mon-Fri, 8am-noon Sat).

You can hear live bands at **Zach's Pub** (☎ 377 223 176; Palackého nám 2; admission 80-150Kč; ⏱ 11am-1am Mon-Thu, 11am-2am Fri, 5pm-2am Sat, 5pm-midnight Sun), which serves draught Guinness as well as local beers.

Getting There & Away

All international trains from Munich and Nuremberg to Prague stop at Plzeň. There are fast trains from Plzeň to Prague (140Kč, 1½ hours, eight daily) and České Budějovice (162Kč, two hours, five daily).

If you're heading for Karlovy Vary, take a bus (86Kč, 1¾ hours, five daily). There are also express buses to Prague (80Kč, 1½ hours, hourly).

ČESKÉ BUDĚJOVICE

pop 100,000

The **City Information Centre** (Městské informační centrum; ☎ 386 801 413; infocb@c-budejovice.cz; nám Přemysla Otakara II 1; ⏱ 8.30am-6pm Mon-Fri, 8.30am-5pm Sat, 10am-4pm Sun) sells maps and can arrange guides, tickets and accommodation.

České Budějovice (Budweis in German) is another stop on the Bohemian beer trail, famous as the home of Budweiser Budvar lager. It's the regional capital of South Bohemia, a charming medieval city with a vast old town square surrounded by 18th-century arcades, one of the largest of its kind in Europe.

Just as beer from Pilsen (see Plzeň p295) is called Pilsner, so beer from Budweis is called **Budweiser**. Indeed, the founders of US brewer Anheuser-Busch chose the brand name Budweiser in 1876 because it was synonymous with good beer. The name has been used by both breweries since the late 19th century, and a century-long legal tussle over the brand name continues. However, there's no contest as to which beer is superior; one taste of Budvar and you'll be an instant convert. True.

The **Budweiser Budvar Brewery** (☎ 387 705 341; www.budvar.cz; cnr Pražská & K Světlé; tours 70Kč Mon-Fri, 100Kč Sat & Sun; ⏱ 9am-5pm) is 3km north of the main square. The 2pm tour (Monday to Friday only) is open to individual travellers; beer tasting costs 22Kč extra. The brewery's **beer hall** is open 10am to 10pm daily.

Sleeping & Eating

The youth travel agency **CKM** (☎ 386 351 270; Lannova třída 63; ⏱ 9am-5pm Mon-Thu, 9am-3.30pm Fri) and the **City Information Centre** (Městské informační centrum; ☎ 386 801 413; infocb@c-budejovice.cz; nám Přemysla Otakara II 1; ⏱ 8.30am-6pm Mon-Fri, 8.30am-5pm Sat, 10am-4pm Sun) can arrange dorm accommodation from 120Kč per person.

Kolej jihočeské univerzity (☎ 387 774 201; Studentská 13-19; d 350Kč; Ⓟ), 2km west of the centre, offers beds from July to September.

Small private pensions are a better deal than hotels. **Penzión Centrum** (☎ 386 352 030; Na Mlýnské stoce 6; d 850Kč), just off Kanovnická, has been recommended by readers, as has its namesake (no relation) **Penzión Centrum** (☎ 387 311 801; penzion_restaurant@centrum.cz; Biskupská 3; s/d 800/1000Kč).

There are lots of good little restaurants and bars in the streets around the main square, including **Pizzeria U Dvou Domů** (☎ 777 696 948; Panská 17; pizzas 75-120Kč; ⏱ 10am-9pm Mon-Fri, 3-9pm Sat) and **Columbia** (☎ 387 315 915; Česká 30; mains 100-200Kč; ⏱ 10am-11pm Mon-Sat, 11am-10pm Sun). The best coffee in town is served up at friendly little **Caffé Bar Piccolo** (Na Mlýnské stoce 9; ⏱ 7.30am-7pm Mon-Thu, 7.30am-10pm Fri & Sat).

Getting There & Away

There are fast trains from České Budějovice to Plzeň (162Kč, two hours, five daily), Prague (204Kč, 2½ hours, hourly). Heading for Vienna (740Kč, four hours, two daily) you'll have to change at Gmünd, or take a direct train to Linz (375Kč, 2¼ hours, one daily) and change there.

The bus to Brno (210Kč, 3½ to 4½ hours, four daily) travels via Telč. Twice a week there's a direct Eurolines bus to Linz (400Kč, 2½ hours) and Salzburg (700Kč, 4½ hours) in Austria.

ČESKÝ KRUMLOV
pop 14,600

Český Krumlov, in Bohemia's deep south, is one of the most picturesque towns in Europe, a little like Prague in miniature. It has a stunning castle above the Vltava River, an old town square and hordes of tourists, but all on a smaller scale – you can walk from one side of town to the other in 10 minutes. In the last five years or so Krumlov has become a huge hit with backpackers, who flock here in summer to enjoy the laid-back hostels, lively bars, cheap beer and riverside picnic spots.

Krumlov's appearance has remained almost unchanged since the 18th century. The old town is almost encircled by a looping bend of the Vltava River, watched over by the chateau sprawling along a ridge above the west bank, its ornately decorated tower looking like a space rocket designed by Hans Christian Andersen.

Arriving by bus from České Budějovice, get off at the Špičák bus stop, the first in town. The train station is 1.5km north of the old town centre; bus Nos 1, 2 and 3 go from the station to the Špičák bus stop.

Information

Infocentrum (☎ 380 704 622; www.ckrumlov.cz; nám Svornosti 2; per 5 min 5Kč; ⏱ 9am-8pm Jul & Aug; 9am-7pm Jun & Sep; 9am-6pm Apr, May & Oct; 9am-5pm Nov-Mar) Official tourism, transport and accommodation information, books and maps.

Unios Tourist Service (☎ 380 712 219; www.unios.cz; Castle Courtyard; per min 1Kč; ⏱ 9am-6pm, Internet café 9am-9pm) Tourist information, accommodation booking and Internet café.

Sights & Activities

You can wander through the courtyards and gardens of fairytale **Český Krumlov Castle** (☎ 380 704 721; adult/concession 150/80Kč; ⏱ 9am-6pm Tue-Sun Jun-Aug; 9am-5pm Apr, May, Sep & Oct) for free; guided tour No 1 takes in the over-the-top Renaissance and baroque apartments that the aristocratic Rožmberk and Schwarzenberg families once called home. The **Castle Tower** (adult/concession 30/20Kč) offers a superb view over the town.

Across the river is Nám Svornosti, the old town square, ringed by pleasant outdoor cafés. Nearby is the **Regional Museum** (Horní 152; adult/concession 60/30Kč; ⏱ 10am-5pm May-Sep; 10am-6pm Jul & Aug; 9am-4pm Tue-Fri, 1-4pm Sat & Sun Apr & Oct-Dec), with a surprisingly interesting collection that includes folk art, archaeology and a model of the town as it was in 1800.

The big attraction on a hot summer day is just messing about on the river. You can rent canoes, rafts and rubber rings from various places, including **Maleček** (☎ 380 712 508; Rooseveltova 28; half-hour canoe rental 300Kč; ⏱ 9am-5pm). **Vltava** (☎ 380 711 988; Kájovská 62; ⏱ 9am-noon & 12.30-5pm) rents bikes (320Kč a day) and organises horse riding (250Kč an hour).

For details on Big Beat, the Five-Petalled Rose Festival and the Český Krumlov International Music Festival, see p301.

Sleeping

Krumlov House (☎ 377 711 935; www.krumlovhostel .com; Rooseveltova 68; dm/d 250/600Kč) An excellent hostel in a peaceful spot overlooking the river with spacious dorms, cooking facilities, a small English library and a laundry.

Hostel 99 (☎ 380 712 812; hostel99@hotmail.com; Věžní 99; dm/d 300/600Kč; 🖵) Laid-back lodgings set in the city walls, with a sunny outdoor terrace, barbecue, laundry and bike hire.

Travellers' Hostel Soukenická (☎ 380 711 345; www.travellers.cz; Soukenická 43; dm/d/apt 270/760/2000Kč) Big, brash party place with a lively bar and occasional live music; rates include breakfast. There's a beautiful four-bed, self-catering attic apartment.

Pension Myší Díra (☎ 380 712 853; www.cesky krumlov-info.cz; Rooseveltova 28; s/d 1290/1390Kč; 🅿) Great location overlooking the river, and bright, attractive rooms with lots of pale wood. Deluxe rooms and weekends (June to August) are 300Kč extra, but rates fall by 40% in winter.

You can camp at the basic riverside **Kemp Nové Spolí** (☎ 380 728 305; per adult 55Kč; ⏱ Jun-Aug; 🅿) about 2.5km south of town; take bus No 3 from the train or bus station.

Eating & Drinking

There are lots of lively restaurants and bars in town.

Cikánská jizba (☎ 380 717 585; Dlouhá 31; mains 70-110Kč; ⏲ 3-11pm Mon-Thu, 3pm-midnight Fri & Sat) Hearty Czech and Roma grub in a crowded, convivial vault, with live gypsy music at weekends.

Krčma v Šatlavské (☎ 380 713 344; Horní 157; mains 100-200Kč; ⏲ 11am-11pm) Pork and beef barbecued at the fireplace and wine served in rustic earthenware beakers are trademarks of this atmospheric, candle-lit cellar.

Self-caterers will find a handy **potraviny** (minimarket; Latrán 55; ⏲ 7am-6pm Mon-Fri, 7am-noon Sat, 9am-3pm Sun) near the castle entrance.

For outdoor boozing sessions with a view, **Krčma Barbakán** (Horní 26; ⏲ noon-11pm Sun-Thu, noon-midnight Fri & Sat) has a splendid terrace perched high above the river. **M-Club** (cnr Rybářská & Plešivecké schody; ⏲ 4pm-2am) offers pounding rock music and a pool table.

Getting There & Away

The bus station is on Tavírna, on the eastern edge of the town centre; the train station is 1.5km north of town. There are buses from Prague to Český Krumlov (140Kč, three hours, seven daily) via České Budějovice. Buses depart from Na Knížecí bus station, near the Anděl metro station in Smíchov, or from ÚAN Praha Florenc bus station.

Local buses (26Kč, 50 minutes, seven daily) and trains (46Kč, one hour, eight daily) run to/from České Budějovice, where you can change for onward travel to Brno, Plzeň or Austria.

MORAVIA

BRNO

pop 387,200

Buzzing, bustling Brno – capital of Moravia, and the Czech Republic's second city – is a good place to experience Czech city living away from the tourist crowds of Prague. It's a modern place, with a largely 18th- and 19th-century old town and 20th-century suburbs; there are some interesting historical sights and many museums and art galleries.

The train station (Brno-hlavní nádraží) is at the southern edge of the old town, which can be easily covered on foot. The main bus station (Brno ÚAN Zvonařka) is 800m south of the train station (Zvonařka).

The **Culture & Information Office** (KIC; ☎ 542 211 090; www.brno.cz; Radnická 8; ⏲ 8am-6pm Mon-Fri, 8am-5pm Sat & Sun) in the old town hall can book accommodation and help out with other information.

Sights & Activities

On a hill above the old town perches the sinister silhouette of **Špilberk Castle** (☎ 542 215 012; www.spilberk.cz; ⏲ 9am-6pm May-Sep, 9am-5pm Oct-Apr, closed Mon Sep-Jun). Founded in the 13th century and converted into a citadel during the 17th century, it served as a prison for opponents of the Habsburgs until 1855. The labyrinthine tunnels of the **Casemates** (adult/concession 30/15Kč) house a creepy prison museum, while the main building is home to the fascinating **Brno City Museum** (adult/concession 70/35Kč).

The old town itself boasts one of the country's most gruesome tourist attractions – the **Capuchin Monastery** (☎ 542 213 232; Kapucínské nám 5; adult/concession 40/20Kč; ⏲ 9am-noon & 2-4.30pm Tue-Sat, 11-11.45am & 2-4.30pm Sun Feb–mid-Dec; open Mon-Sat May-Sep), where the desiccated corpses of 18th-century monks and local aristocrats are displayed in the crypt.

Gregor Mendel (1822–84), the monk whose studies of peas and bees at Brno's Abbey of St Thomas established the modern science of genetics, is commemorated in the excellent **Mendel Museum** (☎ 543 424 043; www.mendel-museum.org; Mendlovo nám 1; adult/concession 80/40Kč; ⏲ 10am-6pm, closed Mon & Tue Nov-Apr). The city has many other museums and art galleries – get details from the Culture & Information Office.

Fans of modern architecture will love Brno, which has many examples of Cubist, Functionalist and Internationalist styles. Finest of all is the Functionalist **Vila Tugendhat** (☎ 545 212 118; Černopolní 45; tours adult/concession 80/40Kč; ⏲ 10am-6pm Wed-Sun), designed by Mies van der Rohe in 1930.

The big event on Brno's sporting calendar is August's **Motorcycle Grand Prix** (www.motograndprix.com; admission 490Kč), when the city packs out with petrol-heads. The race circuit is just off the D1 road to Prague, 10km west of Brno.

Sleeping & Eating

Čedok (☎ 542 321 267; Nádražní 10/12; ⏲ 9am-5pm Mon-Fri, 9am-noon Sat) can arrange accommodation in student dormitories during July and August from 150Kč per person, and private rooms from 550Kč per person a night. Most are far from the centre but can easily be reached on public transport.

Traveller's Hostel (☎ 542 213 573; www.travellers.cz; Jánská 22; dm incl breakfast 270Kč; ✪ Jul & Aug) Set in a grand old building in the heart of the old town, this place provides the most central, cheap beds in the city.

Hotel Interservis (☎ 545 234 232; Lomená 48; b per person 225Kč) South of the centre, this HI-listed student hostel rents beds in double rooms. Take tram No 12 eastbound from the train station to the end of the line, go through the underpass and continue south on the main road, then turn left along Pompova.

There are lots of inexpensive places to eat. **Vinárna U zlatého meče** (☎ 542 211 198, Mečová 3; mains 60-110Kč; ✪ 9am-midnight) is a pleasant place to sample a bottle of local wine with your meal. The Hare Krishna-run **Haribol** (☎ 545 215 636; Lužanecká 4; mains 50-90Kč; ✪ 11am-4pm Mon-Fri) dishes up wholesome vegetarian food.

Getting There & Away
There are frequent buses to Prague (150Kč, 2½ hours, hourly) and Bratislava (125Kč, 2¼ hours, hourly). Buses to Vienna (350Kč, 2½ hours, two daily) depart from stand No 20 at the bus station.

All trains travelling between Berlin and Budapest via Prague stop at Brno (160Kč; three hours; every two hours). If you're travelling on to Vienna, change trains at Břeclav.

TELČ
pop 6000
The **information office** (☎ 567 243 145; www.telc-etc.cz; ✪ 8am-5pm Mon-Fri, 11am-4pm Sat & Sun) is in the town hall; you can check email here (1Kč a minute).

Telč is a quiet and pretty town – a good place to relax with a book and a glass of wine. Its vast and unspoilt old town square, ringed with Gothic arcades and elegant Renaissance façades, is a Unesco World Heritage site. At the square's northwestern end is its greatest monument, the **Water Chateau** (☎ 567 243 821; tours in Czech 70/35Kč, in English 140/70Kč; ✪ 9am-noon & 1-5pm Tue-Sun May-Aug; 9am-4pm Tue-Sun Apr, Sep & Oct), a jewel of Renaissance architecture.

There's no hostel in town but there are several cheap pensions around the main square; **Pavel Drbal** (☎ 567 243 511; nám Zachariáše z Hradce 12; b per person 300Kč) is next to the information office. If you have a sleeping bag, you can crash at the very basic, summer-only sports club **SK Telč** (☎ 567 231 873; krejcib@seznam.cz; Mládkova; b per person 90Kč; ✪ 4-6pm Jun, 11am-noon & 6-7pm Jul & Aug).

Šenk pod věží (☎ 567 243 889; Palackého 116; mains 90-140Kč; ✪ 11am-3pm & 6-9pm Mon-Fri, 11am-10pm Sat, 11am-4pm Sun) has a cosy dining room and summer terrace, and serves good pizzas and a mean garlic soup.

Buses from České Budějovice to Brno stop at Telč (90Kč, two hours, two daily); there are five buses a day to Prague (120Kč, 2½ hours). The bus station is on the eastern side of town.

CZECH REPUBLIC DIRECTORY

ACCOMMODATION
You'll have to show your passport when checking in at accommodation in the Czech Republic – some older places may insist on keeping it for the duration of your stay, but you can demand to get it back as soon as the receptionist has registered your details. If they hang on to it, don't forget to ask for it back before you leave!

Klub Mladých Cestovatelů (KMC: Young Travellers Club; ☎ 222 220 347; www.kmc.cz; Karolíny Světlé 30, Prague 1) is the HI affiliate in Prague, and can book hostel accommodation throughout the country. In July and August many student dormitories become temporary hostels, while a number in Prague have been converted into year-round backpacker hostels. Prague and Český Krumlov are the only places with a solid choice of backpacker-oriented hostels.

Dorm beds costs around 370Kč to 500Kč in Prague, and 250Kč to 350Kč elsewhere; it's best to book ahead. An HI-membership card is not usually needed, although it will often get you a reduced rate. An **ISIC** (International Student Identity Card; www.isic.com), **ITIC** (International Teacher Identity Card; www.isic.com), **IYTC** (International Youth Travel Card; www.isic.com) or **Euro26 card** (www.euro25.org) may also get you a discount.

Another category of hostel accommodation is *turistické ubytovny* (tourist hostels), which provide very basic and cheap (150Kč to 300Kč) dormitory accommodation; rooms can usually be booked through a local tourist office or KMC branch.

You can find private rooms in most tourist towns (look for signs reading *privát* or *Zimmer frei* – like B&Bs without the breakfast), and many tourist offices can book them for you; expect to pay from 250Kč to 500Kč per person outside Prague. Some have a three-night minimum-stay requirement. These are classified as beds per person in reviews.

Penzióny (pensions) are a step up – small, homely and often family-run, but offering rooms with private bathroom, and often breakfast too. Rates range from 1000Kč to 1500kč for a double room (1500Kč to 2500Kč in Prague).

Hotels in central Prague and Brno are expensive, whereas those in smaller towns are usually much cheaper. Two-star hotels usually offer reasonable comfort for about 600Kč to 800Kč for a double, or 800Kč to 1200Kč with private bathroom (about 50% higher in Prague).

There are several hundred camping grounds spread around the Czech Republic; most are open from May to September only and charge around 50Kč to 100Kč per person. Camping on public land is prohibited.

For more information on the seasonal price variations in Prague, see p289. Outside Prague, hotel and pension rates can fall by up to 40% in low season (October to March).

ACTIVITIES

There is good hiking in the Šumava hills south of Český Krumlov, in the forests around Karlovy Vary, and in the Moravian karst area, north of Brno. Canoeing and rafting are popular on the Vltava River around Český Krumlov (p297, and the whole country is ideal for cycling and cycle touring.

BUSINESS HOURS

Outside Prague, almost everything closes on Saturday afternoon and all day Sunday. Most restaurants are open every day. As a general rule, banks are open from 8am to 4.30pm Monday to Friday, bars from 11am to 11pm daily, and post offices from 8am to 6pm Monday to Friday and 8am to noon

Saturday. Shops open from 8.30am to 5pm or 6pm Monday to Friday and 8.30am to noon or 1pm Saturday.

CUSTOMS

Customs officers can be strict about antiques and will confiscate goods that are even slightly suspect. There is no limit to the amount of Czech or foreign currency that can be taken into or out of the country, but amounts exceeding 350,000Kč must be declared.

DANGERS & ANNOYANCES

Pickpocketing can be a problem in Prague's tourist zone, and there are still occasional reports of robberies on overnight international trains. There is intense racism directed at the local Roma population, which sometimes boils over into assaults by gangs of skinheads on darker-skinned people.

DISABLED TRAVELLERS

Ramps for wheelchair users in Prague are becoming more common, but cobbled streets, steep hills and stairways make getting around difficult. Transport is a major problem as most buses, trains and trams have no wheelchair access. **Prague Wheelchair Users Organisation** (Pražská organizace vozíčkářů; ☎ 224 827 210; pov@gts.cz; Benediktská 6, Josefov) publishes a web guide to Barrier-Free Prague (www.pov.cz/cd-rom/startwww.htm) in both English and German.

EMBASSIES & CONSULATES
Embassies & Consulates in the Czech Republic

Most embassies and consulates are open from at least 9am to noon Monday to Friday.

Australia (☎ 296 578 350; fax 296 578 352; Klimentská 10, Prague 1) Honorary consulate for emergency assistance only (eg a stolen passport); nearest Australian embassy is in Vienna.

Austria (☎ 257 090 511; www.austria.cz; Viktora Huga 10, Prague 10)

Canada (☎ 272 101 800; www.canada.cz; Muchova 6, Prague 6)

France (☎ 251 171 711; www.france.cz; Velkopřerovské nám 2, Prague 2)

Germany (☎ 257 113 111; www.deutschland.cz; Vlašská 19, Prague 1)

Ireland (☎ 257 530 061; www.irishembassy.cz; Tržiště 13, Prague 1)

Netherlands (☎ 224 312 190; www.netherlands embassy.cz; Gotthardská 6/27, Prague 6)

New Zealand (☎ 222 514 672; egermayer@nzconsul.cz; Dykova 19, Prague 10) Honorary consulate providing emergency assistance only (eg stolen passport); the nearest NZ embassy is in Berlin.

Poland Embassy (☎ 257 530 388; www.ambpol.cz; Valdštejnská 8, Prague 1) Consular Dept (☎ 224 228 722; konspol@mbox.vol.cz; V úžlabině 14, Prague 10) Go to Consular Department for visas.

Slovakia (☎ 233 113 051; www.slovakemb.cz; Pod hradbami 1, Prague 6)

South Africa (☎ 267 311 114; saprague@terminal.cz; Ruská 65, Prague 10)

UK (☎ 257 402 111; www.britain.cz; Thunovská 14, Prague 1)

USA (☎ 257 530 663; www.usembassy.cz; Tržiště 15, Prague 1)

Czech Embassies & Consulates Abroad

Austria (☎ 01-894 2125; www.mzv.cz/vienna; Penzingerstrasse 11-13, Vienna 1140)

Australia (☎ 02-6290 1386; www.mzv.cz/canberra; 8 Culgoa Circuit, O'Malley, ACT 2606)

Canada (☎ 613-562 3875; www.mzv.cz/ottawa; 251 Cooper St, Ottawa, Ontario K2P 0G2)

France (☎ 01 72 76 13 00; www.mzv.cz/paris; 75 Bld Hausmann, 75008 Paris)

Germany (☎ 030-22 63 80; www.mzv.cz/berlin; Wilhelmstrasse 44, 10117 Berlin)

Ireland (☎ 031-668 1135; www.mzv.cz/dublin; 57 Northumberland Rd, Ballsbridge, Dublin 4)

Netherlands (☎ 070-346 9712; www.mzv.cz/hague; Paleisstraat 4, 2514 JA Den Haag)

New Zealand Honorary Consulate (☎ 09-353 9766; auckland@honorary.mzv.cz; Level 24, Bank of NZ Towers, 125 Queen St, Auckland) Postal address is PO Box 3798, Auckland.

Poland (☎ 22-628 7221; www.mzv.cz/warsaw; Koszykowa 18, Warsaw 00-555)

Slovakia (☎ 259 203 303; www.mzv.cz/bratislava; Hviezdoslavova nám 8, Bratislava 810 00)

South Africa (☎ 012-431 2380; www.mzv.cz/pretoria; 936 Pretorius St, Arcadia, Pretoria 0083)

UK (☎ 020-7243 1115; www.mzv.cz/london; 26 Kensington Palace Gardens, London W8 4QY)

USA (☎ 202-274 9100; www.mzv.cz/washington; 3900 Spring of Freedom St NW, Washington, DC 20008)

FESTIVALS & EVENTS

Festival of Sacred Music (www.mhfb.cz; Easter) Celebration of religious music held in Brno.

Prague Spring (www.festival.cz; 12 May to 3 June) International music festival.

Big Beat (www.musicfest.cz; May) Rock festival held in Český Krumlov.

World Roma Festival Khamoro (www.khamoro.cz; late May) Prague festival celebrating Roma culture.

Five-Petalled Rose Festival (June) Medieval festival held in Český Krumlov.

Karlovy Vary International Film Festival (www.kviff .com; July) Attended by the big names in film industry.

Český Krumlov International Music Festival (www .auviex.cz; mid-July to late August) Six weeks of classical music concerts in and around the castle and its gardens.

Dvořák Autumn (September) Classical music festival held in Karlovy Vary.

Moravian Autumn (www.mhfb.cz; September) International music festival held in Brno.

GAY & LESBIAN TRAVELLERS

The bimonthly magazine **Amigo** (www.amigo.cz) has a few pages in English and an English-language website. **GayGuide.Net Prague** (www .gayguide.net/Europe/Czech/Prague) is another useful source of information.

HOLIDAYS

New Year's Day 1 January
Easter Monday March/April
Labour Day 1 May
Liberation Day 8 May
SS Cyril and Methodius Day 5 July
Jan Hus Day 6 July
Czech Statehood Day 28 September
Republic Day 28 October
Struggle for Freedom and Democracy Day 17 November
Christmas 24 to 26 December

INTERNET RESOURCES

Czech Tourism (www.czechtourism.com) Official tourist information.

IDOS (www.vlak.cz) Train and bus timetables.

Mapy (www.mapy.cz) Online maps.

Prague Information Service (www.prague-info.cz) Official city tourism site.

Prague Post (www.praguepost.cz) News and features.

Prague TV (www.prague.tv) Independent city guide.

MONEY
Currency

The Czech crown (Koruna česká, or Kč) is divided into 100 hellers (*haléřů*, or h). Banknotes come in denominations of 20, 50, 100, 200, 500, 1000, 2000 and 5000Kč; coins are of 10, 20 and 50h and one, two, five, 10, 20 and 50Kč. Keep small change handy for use in public toilets, telephones and tram-ticket machines. For more information on costs and money, see p28.

Exchanging Money

There's a good network of ATMs *(bankomaty)* throughout the country. The main banks – Komerční banka, Česká spořitelna, ČSOB and Živnostenská banka – are the best places to change cash and travellers cheques or get a cash advance on Visa or MasterCard. American Express and Thomas Cook offices change their own-brand cheques without commission.

Beware of the private exchange offices *(směnárna)*, especially in Prague – they advertise misleading rates and often charge exorbitant commissions or 'handling fees'.

Credit cards are widely accepted in petrol stations, mid-range and top-end hotels, restaurants and shops.

Costs

Food, transport and admission fees are fairly cheap, but accommodation in Prague can be expensive. Staying in hostels and buying food in supermarkets, you could survive on US$15 a day in summer. Staying in private rooms or pensions, eating at cheap restaurants and using public transport, you should count on US$25 to US$30 a day. Get out of the capital and your costs will drop dramatically.

Tipping

Tipping in restaurants is optional but increasingly expected in Prague. If there is no service charge you should certainly round up the bill to the next 10Kč or 20Kč (a 5%

to 10% tip is normal in Prague). The same applies to tipping taxi drivers.

POST

General delivery mail can be addressed to Poste Restante, Pošta 1, in most major cities. For Prague, the address is: Poste Restante, Jindřišská 14, 11000 Praha 1, Czech Republic. An aerogram costs 8Kč; letters up to 20g cost 9Kč to European countries, 14Kč to elsewhere.

TELEPHONE

All Czech phone numbers have nine digits – you have to dial all nine for any call, local or long distance. You can make international calls at main post offices or directly from cardphone booths. The international access code is ☎ 00. The Czech Republic's country code is ☎ 420.

VISAS & DOCUMENTS

Everyone requires a valid passport (or ID card for EU citizens) to enter the country. Citizens of EU and EEA countries do not need a visa for any type of visit. Citizens of Australia, Canada, Israel, Japan, New Zealand, Switzerland and the USA can stay for up to 90 days without a visa; other nationalities need a visa. Visas are not available at border crossings or Prague's Ruzyně airport; you'll be refused entry if you arrive without one.

Visa regulations change from time to time, so check one of the Czech embassy websites listed on p300.

Denmark

HIGHLIGHTS

- **Copenhagen** Day and night – its history-packed centre buzzes into the small hours (p307)
- **Århus** Drinking in the art and the history, and then drinking in the pubs and clubs (p320)
- **Skagen** Beneath luminous skies where land ends and two angry seas collide (p325)
- **Bornholm** Explore the forests, empty beaches and smokehouses of this sleepy island (p317)

DENMARK

FAST FACTS

- **Area** 43,075 sq km (the same size as Switzerland)
- **ATMs** Widespread
- **Budget** Dkr300-400 per day
- **Capital** Copenhagen
- **Country codes** ☎ 45; international access code 00
- **Famous for** Hans Christian Andersen, the Little Mermaid, bacon, Carlsberg beer, marauding Vikings
- **Head of State** Queen Margrethe II
- **Language** Danish
- **Money** Danish krona ($A1 = 4.38Dkr, CA$1 = 4.78Dkr, €1 = 7.43Dkr, ¥100 = 5.46Dkr, NZ$1 = 4.08Dkr, UK£1 = 10.77Dkr, US$1 = 6.03Dkr)

- **Phrases** *Jah/nie* (yes/no), *tak* (thanks), *farvel* (goodbye), *skål* (cheers)
- **Population** 5.3 million
- **Time** GMT/UTC +1
- **Visas** None needed for citizens of the EU, USA, Canada, Australia and New Zealand.

TRAVEL HINTS

Takeaway beer and wine are cheap by Scandinavian standards, but hit the happy hours for the best bar deals. Pastries and *smørrebrød* (open sandwiches) are the ways to eat well cheaply.

ROAMING DENMARK

Three days is enough for a taste of Copenhagen, then head west to Odense for a day, and up to Århus before heading north to Aalborg and Skagen.

Denmark may lack the natural grandeur of its larger Scandinavian neighbours but it packs within its modest borders a compelling mix of lively modern cities, historic towns, enchanting villages, rolling farmland, graceful beech woods and sleepy islands. The outwardly sensible Danes like a party and Copenhagen, a compact world-class city with a rich history and a burgeoning bar, café and restaurant scene, is where they do it best; but the regional capitals of Århus and Odense try hard too.

Beyond the cities lies much of the country's natural wealth: kilometres of white sand beaches and numerous islands, including magical Bornholm, stuck out in the middle of the Baltic.

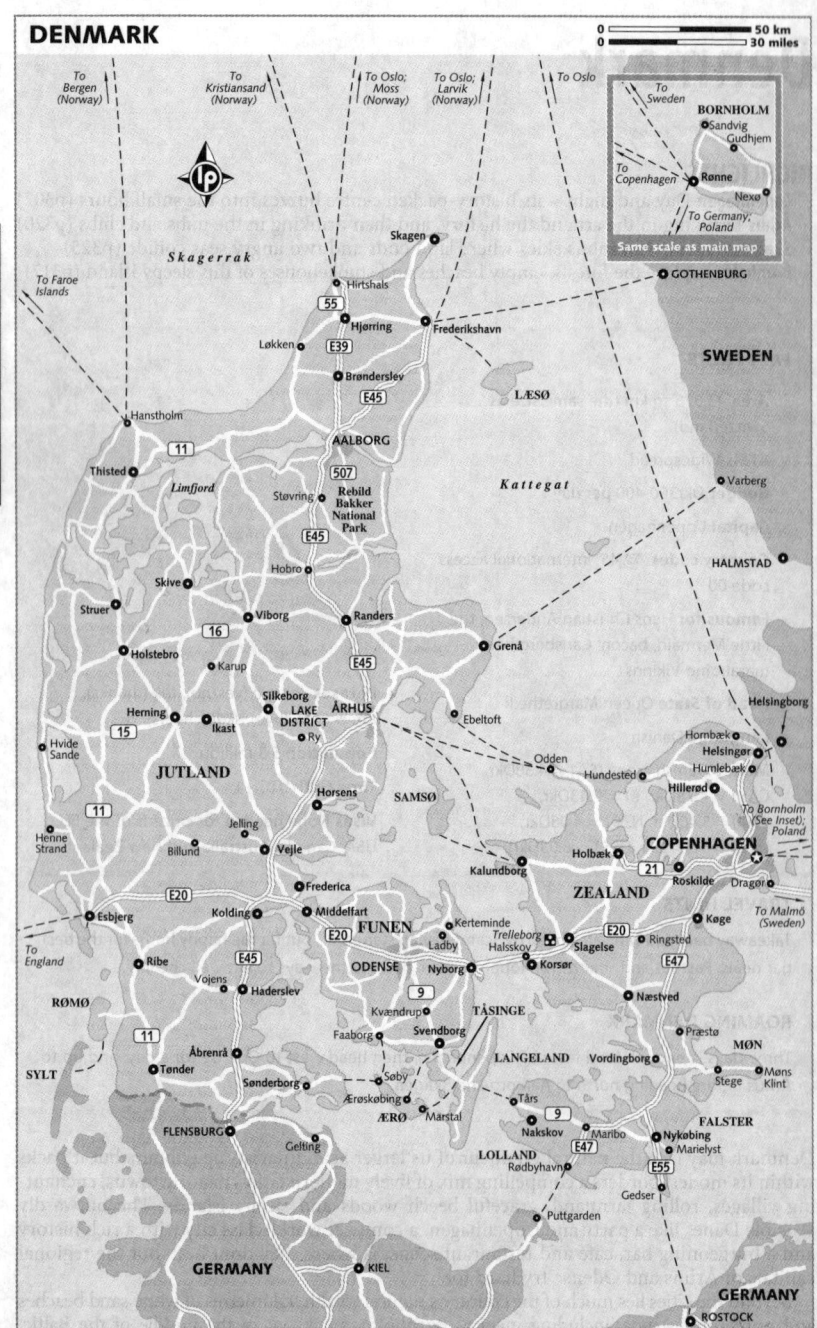

DENMARK

0 ⸻ 50 km
0 ⸻ 30 miles

Inset map (top right):

To Sweden

BORNHOLM
Sandvig
Gudhjem
To Copenhagen
Rønne
Nexø
To Germany; Poland

Same scale as main map

Main map labels:

To Bergen (Norway)
To Kristiansand (Norway)
To Oslo; Moss (Norway)
To Oslo; Larvik (Norway)
To Oslo

Skagerrak

Skagen
Hirtshals
55
Hjørring
Frederikshavn
Løkken
E39
Brønderslev
E45

GOTHENBURG

SWEDEN

LÆSØ

To Faroe Islands

Hanstholm
11
Thisted
Limfjord
AALBORG
507
Støvring
Rebild Bakker National Park
E45
Hobro

Kattegat

Varberg

HALMSTAD

Skive
Struer
16
Viborg
Randers
Karup
E45
Grenå
Holstebro
Herning
15
Silkeborg
LAKE DISTRICT
Ikast
Ry
ÅRHUS
Ebeltoft

Helsingborg

Hornbæk
Helsingør
Humlebæk
Hillerød

Hvide Sande
JUTLAND
Horsens
SAMSØ
Odden
Hundested

To Bornholm (See Inset); Poland

Henne Strand
11
Jelling
Billund
Vejle

COPENHAGEN

Holbæk
21
Roskilde
Dragør

Kalundborg
ZEALAND

E20
Frederica
Kolding
Middelfart
FUNEN
Kerteminde
Ladby
Trelleborg
Halsskov
Slagelse
Ringsted
E20
Køge

To Malmö (Sweden)

Esbjerg
E45
ODENSE
Nyborg
Korsør
E47

To England

Ribe
Vojens
Haderslev
Kvændrup
TÅSINGE
Næstved

RØMØ

Faaborg
Svendborg
Søby
LANGELAND
Vordingborg
Præstø
MØN

Åbenrå
Tønder
SYLT
Sønderborg
Ærøskøbing
ÆRØ
Marstal
Tårs
9
Stege
Møns Klint

FLENSBURG
Gelting
Maribo
E47
Nakskov
9
Rødbyhavn
LOLLAND
FALSTER
Nykøbing
Marielyst

E55
Gedser

Puttgarden

GERMANY
KIEL

GERMANY
ROSTOCK

There are historic treasures aplenty too: castles, haunting Neolithic burial chambers, the bodies of startlingly well-preserved Iron Age people exhumed from peat bogs, medieval churches, Renaissance castles and the preserved hulks of Viking longships, reminders both of the country's proud Viking past and of the command of the seas that for centuries made Denmark Scandinavia's powerful hub.

HISTORY

Present-day Denmark traces its linguistic and cultural roots to the arrival of the Danes, a tribe thought to have migrated south from Sweden around AD 500. In the late 9th century, the Viking chieftain Hardegon conquered the Jutland Peninsula. The Danish monarchy (Europe's oldest) dates back to Hardegon's son, Gorm the Old, who reigned in the early 10th century. Gorm's son, Harald Bluetooth, completed the conquest of Denmark and converted the Danes to Christianity. Successive Danish kings invaded England and conquered most of the Baltic region.

In 1397 Margrethe I of Denmark established a union between Denmark, Norway and Sweden. Sweden withdrew from the union in 1523, and over the next few hundred years Denmark and Sweden had numerous border skirmishes and wars over control of the Baltic Sea.

Denmark's golden age was under Christian IV (1588–1648), with Renaissance cities, castles and fortresses flourishing throughout his kingdom. In 1625 Christian IV, hoping to neutralise Swedish expansion, fought and lost the Thirty Years' War to the Swedes, who won large chunks of Danish territory.

Denmark was neutral throughout WWI. In WWII, baulking from a full-scale invasion by German troops in 1940, the Danes agreed to run the country under Nazi supervision, until August 1943 when the Germans took outright control. The Danish Resistance movement mushroomed and

7000 Jewish Danes were quickly smuggled into neutral Sweden.

Denmark joined NATO in 1949 and the European Community – now the EU – in 1973. The Danes support an expanding EU only tepidly. Many fear losing local control to a European bureaucracy dominated by stronger nations.

In 2004 the already popular and much-loved royal family gave Danes a reason to celebrate its enduring appeal when the country's most eligible bachelor Crown Prince Frederick married Australian Mary Elizabeth Donaldson in a hugely popular and exhaustively covered million-dollar fairy-tale wedding.

PEOPLE & CULTURE

Denmark's often difficult history at the heart of a volatile part of Europe has taught the modern Dane to avoid too much conflict or rivalry and travellers will find Danes to be relaxed, casual, self-effacing, reserved and not given to extremes or to ostentation. They are tolerant of different lifestyles; in 1989 Denmark became the first European nation to legalise same-sex marriages.

About 70% of Denmark's population lives in urban areas, 1.5 million of them in Copenhagen. Foreign nationals account for 7.8% of people.

ARTS

Hans Christian Andersen has long loomed large over Denmark's literary landscape. His fairy tales are the second-most translated work worldwide, surpassed only by the Bible. Religious philosopher Søren Kierkegaard, whose writings were a forerunner of existentialism, and Karen Blixen, who penned Out of Africa and Babette's Feast, are other notable literary Danes.

In cinema, Danish director and maverick Lars von Trier won the Cannes Film Festival's Palme d'Or in 2000 for his film Dancer in the Dark.

Denmark is a leader in industrial design, with a style marked by cool, clean lines applied to everything from architecture

---

READING UP

Denmark: A Modern History, written by W Glyn Jones, gives a comprehensive account of contemporary Danish society.

'Just as Well I'm Leaving' – Around Europe with Hans Christian Andersen, by Michael Booth, is a funny, entertaining travelogue retracing Andersen's footsteps around Denmark and Europe.

to silverware and furniture. Denmark has produced a number of leading 20th-century architects, including Jørn Utzon who designed Australia's Sydney Opera House.

In painting, the 'Skagen School' evolved from the movement towards outdoor painting of scenes from working life, especially of fishing communities on the northern coasts of Jutland and Zealand. Leading exponents were PS Krøyer, Michael Ancher and Anna Ancher.

ENVIRONMENT

The eco-conscious Danes are keen recyclers, users of alternative energy (such as wind turbines or their own pedal power) and increasingly interested in sourcing sustainable, organic and fair-trade food and goods, so it's an easy country in which to be environmentally responsible.

The Danish landmass has been heavily exploited by agriculture and 70% of its land is farmed mainly for barley and root crops. With almost 20% of farmland near sea level, many environmentally sensitive wetlands were made arable by draining. EU quotas now make farming such land less viable, and the Danish government has initiated an ambitious plan to restore these wetlands and re-establish marshes and streams throughout the country.

Still commonly seen in Denmark are wild hare, deer and many species of birds, including magpies, coots, swans and ducks. Restoring the wetlands should help endangered species such as the freshwater otter to make a comeback.

TRANSPORT

GETTING THERE & AWAY
Air

At the time of writing, the European budget airfare war was fiercer than ever, making flights into Denmark from elsewhere on the Continent, Ireland and the UK very affordable. If you're coming from European destinations, flying into an airport other than **Copenhagen** (☎ 32 31 32 31; www.cph.dk), such as **Århus** (☎ 87 75 70 00; www.aar.dk) or **Billund** (☎ 76 50 50 50; www.bll.dk), can be much cheaper, and afford fast access with some great parts of northern and central Jutland. **Scandinavian Airlines** (SAS; airline code SK; ☎ 70 10 30 00;

> **DEPARTURE TAX**
> Departure tax is included in the price of tickets.

www.scandinavian.net) is the largest carrier serving Denmark, connecting it with much of Europe and the rest of the world.

Boat
GERMANY

The frequent Rødbyhavn-Puttgarden ferry takes 45 minutes and is included in train tickets for those travelling by rail; otherwise, the cost per adult is Dkr45 and for a car with up to nine passengers it's Dkr345.

Other ferries run from Rømø to Sylt (Dkr35, one hour), Rønne on Bornholm to Sassnitz (Dkr135, 3½ hours) and Gedser to Rostock (Dkr60, two hours).

NORWAY

A daily overnight ferry operates between Copenhagen and Oslo. Ferries also run from Hirtshals to Oslo, Kristiansand and Moss; from Hanstholm to Bergen; and from Frederikshavn to Oslo and Larvik. More details are provided in the relevant Getting There & Away sections of the cities.

POLAND

Polferries (☎ 33 11 46 45; www.polferries.pl) operates ferries to Świnoujście from both Copenhagen (from Dkr395, 10 hours) and Rønne (from Dkr225, 5½ hours).

SWEDEN

The cheapest and most frequent ferry to Sweden is the shuttle between Helsingør and Helsingborg (Dkr18, 20 minutes); ferries leave opposite the Helsingør train station every 20 minutes during the day and once an hour through the night. Passage for a car with up to nine people costs Dkr270.

Other ferries go from Frederikshavn to Gothenburg and Oslo, and Rønne to Ystad. See the relevant Getting There & Away sections in this chapter.

UK

DFDS Seaways (in UK ☎ 08705 333 000, in Denmark ☎ 33 42 30 00; www.dfdsseaways.co.uk) sails from Esbjerg to Harwich at least three times a week at 6pm year-round. It takes 19 hours.

Bus & Train

Three railway lines link Germany and Denmark; 2nd-class fares from Copenhagen to Frankfurt are Dkr1100. Eurolines operates buses from Copenhagen to Berlin (Dkr290, 6½ hours) and Frankfurt via Hamburg (Dkr720, 15 hours) several times a week.

Trains operate between Copenhagen and Oslo; the 2nd-class fare (via Sweden; 7½ hours, one or two daily) is Dkr604. Eurolines offers a daily bus service between Oslo and Copenhagen (Dkr310, eight hours) via Gothenburg. Trains run many times a day between Denmark and Sweden via a bridge linking Copenhagen with Malmö. The 2nd-class train fare from Copenhagen is Dkr70 to Malmö (40 minutes), Dkr400 to Gothenburg and Dkr580 to Stockholm (five hours). If you're travelling by train, the bridge crossing is included in the fare, but for those travelling by car, there's a Dkr230 toll per vehicle. There are numerous buses between Copenhagen and Sweden, including Eurolines buses to Gothenburg (Dkr160, five hours) and Stockholm (Dkr346, 9½ hours).

GETTING AROUND

Air

Most internal flights cost around Dkr1000 for a standard ticket and can be much cheaper if you book in advance.

Denmark's domestic air routes are operated by the following airlines:

Cimber Air (☎ 74 42 22 77; www.cimber.dk) Services include Copenhagen to Aalborg (55 minutes, five times daily), Rønne (Bornholm, 35 minutes, at least three times daily) and Karup (central Jutland, 50 minutes, 12 times daily weekdays, at least twice on weekends).

SAS (☎ 70 10 30 00; www.scandinavian.net) Links Copenhagen with Aalborg, Århus and Billund about a dozen times a day.

Bicycle

Cycling is a practical way to get around Denmark. There are extensive bike paths linking towns throughout the country and bike lanes through most city centres. You can rent bikes in most towns for around Dkr60 a day, plus a deposit of about Dkr250. Bikes can be taken on ferries and most trains for a modest cost.

Boat

A network of ferries links virtually all of Denmark's populated islands. Where there's not a bridge, there's usually a ferry, most of which take cars.

Bus

All large cities and towns have a local bus system and most places are also served by regional buses, many of which connect with trains. There are also a few long-distance bus routes, including from Copenhagen to Aalborg or Århus. Travelling by bus on long-distance routes costs about 20% less than travel by train, although it's usually a bit slower.

Car & Motorcycle

A home driving licence, rather than an international one, is sufficient to drive and hire cars in Denmark, although a passport is sometimes also required.

Hire rates for the cheapest cars, including VAT, insurance and unlimited kilometres, begin at about Dkr680 a day, or Dkr520 a day for rentals of two days or more.

Train

Danish State Railways (DSB; www.dsb.dk) runs most of Danish train services. There are two types of long-distance trains: sleek inter-city (IC) trains that usually need reservations (Dkr20) and older, slower inter-regional (IR) trains that make more stops and don't need reservations. Both trains charge the same fares, as long as you avoid the cushy InterCity-Lyn.

Overall, train travel in Denmark is not expensive, largely because the distances are short. Scanrail, Eurail and other rail passes are valid on DSB ferries and trains, but not on the private lines.

COPENHAGEN (KØBENHAVN)

pop 1.5 million

Copenhagen (København) has the cultural and social attractions of a major European capital but all in a bite-size portion, making it by far Scandinavia's largest, liveliest and most entertaining city.

Its allure lies in the buzz of its streets, squares and the throngs that spill from endless bars, cafés, eateries and music venues that line them. Central Copenhagen (and many of the adjacent neighbourhoods) has an active nightlife that rolls into the early hours.

DENMARK

DENMARK

COPENHAGEN (KØBENHAVN)

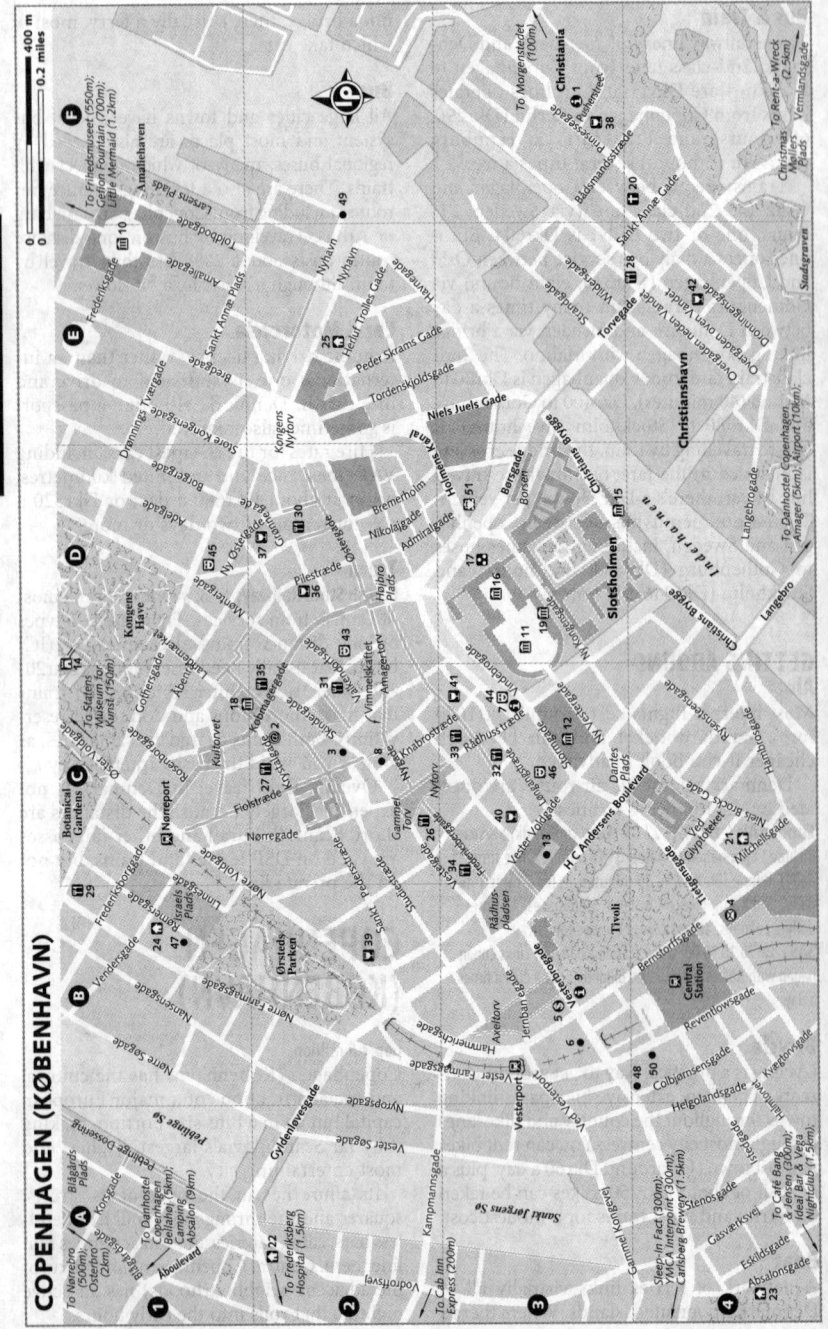

DENMARK

ORIENTATION

The always-bustling train station, Central Station (Hovedbanegården or København H), is flanked on its west by the main hotel zone. To the east of the station's main entrance, across the broad and busy Bernstorffsgade, is the Tivoli amusement park. Outside of traffic-bound HC Andersens Boulevard lies the spacious Rådhuspladsen: the central city square, main bus transit point and gateway to Copenhagen's heart.

From Rådhuspladsen, the narrow opening of Frederiksberggade is the unassuming introduction to Strøget, a linked sequence of lively, crowded streets (made up of Frederiksberggade, Nygade, Vimmelskaftet, Amagertorv and Østergade) running through the city linking Rådhuspladsen and the other great square of Kongens Nytorv and, beyond it, Nyhavn canal.

INFORMATION
Emergency
Frederiksberg Hospital (☎ 38 16 38 16; Nordre Fasanvej 57) West of the city centre, has a 24-hour emergency ward.

GETTING INTO TOWN

Getting into central Copenhagen couldn't be simpler: trains from Sweden, Norway and Germany terminate right in the heart of Copenhagen at Central Station. A train also links the airport with Central Station three times an hour (Dkr19.50, 12 minutes). The airport is 15 minutes and about Dkr170 from the city centre by taxi.

Internet Access
Hovedbiblioteket (☎ 33 73 60 60; Krystalgade 15; ✆ 10am-7pm Mon-Fri, 10am-2pm Sat) A public library offering free Internet access but you must book a slot.
Use It (Rådhusstræde 13) Offers free Internet access, within reasonable time restraints.

Left Luggage
Central Station has lockers in the lower level near the Reventlowsgade exit. Storage costs are Dkr25/35 for a small/large bag per 24 hours, for a maximum of 72 hours.

Medical Services
Private doctor visits usually cost around Dkr350. Phone ☎ 33 93 63 00 for referrals.
Steno Apotek (Vesterbrogade 6c; ✆ 24hr) Opposite Central Station.

Money
You'll find 24-hour ATMs that exchange major foreign currencies for Danish krona, minus a hefty Dkr25 to Dkr30 fee, at:
Den Danske Bank (in Central Station)
Nordea (Axeltorv)

Post
Central Station post office (✆ 8am-9pm Mon-Fri, 9am-4pm Sat, 10am-5pm Sun)
Main post office (Tietgensgade 35-39; ✆ 11am-6pm Mon-Fri, 10am-1pm Sat) Offers poste-restante services.

Tourist Information
Use It (☎ 33 73 06 20; www.useit.dk; Rådhusstræde 13; ✆ 9am-7pm mid-Jun–mid-Sep, 11am-4pm Mon-Wed, 11am-6pm Thu, 11am-2pm Fri mid-Sep–mid-Jun) A first-class information centre aimed at young budget travellers, but open to all. It books rooms for free, stores

luggage (by day only), holds mail, offers free Internet use and provides information on everything, from working in Denmark to cheap sleeps and affordable nightlife. *Playtime* is Use It's free annual guide to the city and around and is packed with information.

Wonderful Copenhagen (☎ 70 22 24 42; www .visitcopenhagen.dk; Vesterbrogade 4a; ☺ 9am-8pm Mon-Sat, 10am-8pm Sun May-Aug, 9am-4.30pm Mon-Fri, 9am-1.30pm Sat Sep-Apr) North of Central Station, distributes the informative *Tourist in Copenhagen* and *Copenhagen This Week*, a free city map, and brochures for all regions of Denmark. In summer the queues can be long and fretful.

Travel Agencies

Kilroy Travels (☎ 33 11 00 44; www.kilroytravels.com; Skindergade 28)

Wasteels (☎ 33 14 46 33; Skoubogade 6; ☺ 9am-5pm Mon-Fri, 10am-noon Sat)

SIGHTS & ACTIVITIES

Slotsholmen

On an island separated from the city centre by a moat-like canal, Slotsholmen is the site of **Christiansborg Palace** (☎ 33 92 64 92) and the seat of Denmark's national government. Of the many sites the grandest is the **Royal Reception Chambers** (admission Dkr40; ☺ guided tours 11am, 1pm & 3pm May-Sep, 11am & 3pm Tue, Thu, Sat & Sun Oct-Apr), the ornate Renaissance hall where the queen entertains heads of state. The tours have commentary in English.

The **Ruins of Absalon's Fortress** (admission Dkr25; ☺ 9.30am-3.30pm May-Sep, 9.30am-3.30pm Tue, Thu, Sat & Sun Oct-Apr) are the excavated foundations of Bishop Absalon's original castle of 1167.

Tøjhusmuseet (☎ 33 11 60 37; admission Dkr50, Wed free; ☺ noon-4pm Tue-Sun), the royal arsenal built in 1600, has an impressive collection of hand weapons and old armour and a huge hall filled with historic cannons.

The **Royal Library** (☎ 33 47 47 47; Søren Kierkegaards Plads; ☺ 10am-7pm Mon-Sat) dates from the 17th century, but the focal point these days is its new ultramodern walkway-connected extension dubbed the 'Black Diamond' for its shiny black granite façade. The sleek, seven-storey building houses 21 million books and other literary items such as Hans Christian Andersen's original manuscripts. There's free Internet access.

Nationalmuseet

Holding the world's most extensive collection of Danish artefacts from the Palaeolithic period to the 19th century is **Nationalmuseet**

(National Museum; ☎ 33 13 44 11; www.natmus.dk; Ny Vestergade 10; admission Dkr25, Wed free; ☺ 10am-5pm Tue-Sun). Highlights include Bronze Age burial remains in oak coffins and *lurs* (musical horns) that were used for ceremony and communication, ancient rune stones, a golden sun chariot, the silver Gundestrip cauldron and Viking weaponry.

Rosenborg Slot

A 17th-century castle built by Christian IV in Dutch Renaissance style, **Rosenborg Slot** (☎ 33 15 32 86; admission Dkr60; ☺ 10am-4pm May & Sep, 10am-5pm Jun-Aug, 11am-3pm Oct, 11am-2pm Tue-Sun Nov-Apr) stands at the edge of the peaceful Kongens Have (King's Gardens). There are glorious marbled and painted ceilings, gilded mirrors, Dutch tapestries, silver lions and gold and enamel ware. The Royal Treasury is in the castle basement and here glow the Danish crown jewels, including Christian IV's crown, the sword of Christian III and Queen Margrethe II's pearls.

Tivoli

Right in the heart of the city, Copenhagen's century-old amusement park **Tivoli** (☎ 33 15 10 01; www.tivoli.dk; admission Dkr65; ☺ 11am-11pm Sat-Thu, 11am-1am Fri mid-Apr–mid-Jun & mid-Aug–mid-Sep, 11am-midnight Sun-Thu, 11am-1am Fri & Sat mid-Jun–mid-Aug) is something of a mishmash of gardens, food pavilions, amusement rides, carnival games and various stage shows. The Demon, a corkscrewing, feet-in-space roller coaster, and the 'dead drop' tower (forming the park's most prominent landmark) are two of the most high-adrenaline and stomach-lurching rides. It's well worth checking out the free (you still have to pay the entrance though) programme of Friday concerts, with mostly Danish bands and occasionally more widely known bands like the Cardigans. Fireworks go off at 11.45pm on Saturdays.

Rundetårn

Providing a fine vantage point to see the old city's red-tiled rooftops and abundant church spires is **Rundetårn** (Round Tower; ☎ 33 73 03 73;

Købmagergade 52; admission Dkr20; ⊙ 10am-8pm Mon-Sat, noon-8pm Sun Jun-Aug, 10am-5pm Mon-Sat, noon-5pm Sun Sep-May). It was built by Christian IV in 1642 as an astronomical observatory. Halfway up the 209m spiral walkway is a hall with changing exhibits. Peter the Great of Russia is said to have ridden his horse up the ramp followed by the Czarina in a horse-drawn carriage; everyone else walks.

Statens Museum for Kunst

Denmark's national gallery, **Statens Museum for Kunst** (☎ 33 74 84 94; www.smk.dk; Sølvgade 48-50; admission Dkr50, Wed free; ⊙ 10am-5pm Tue & Thu-Sun, 10am-8pm Wed) contains an enormous collection of superb paintings. The main collection includes works by 19th-century Danish masters, and 17th-century Dutch and Flemish masters Rembrandt and Rubens. Leading European artists including Matisse, Picasso, Braque, Utrillo and Munch are well represented. The gallery is about 800m north of the city centre.

Christianshavn

Christianshavn was established by King Christian IV in the early 1600s as a commercial centre and military buffer for the expanding city of Copenhagen. Still surrounded by ramparts and cut by canals, it has some good cafés and bars, not to mention Christiania (see the boxed text below).

To reach Christianshavn, walk cross the bridge from the northeastern side of Slotsholmen or take bus No 8 from Rådhuspladsen.

Vor Frelsers Kirke

Close to Christiania is the 17th-century **Vor Frelsers Kirke** (☎ 31 57 27 98; Sankt Annæ Gade 29; admission free, tower Dkr20; ⊙ 11am-4.30pm Apr-Aug, 11am-3.30pm Sep-Mar, no admission during services, tower closed Nov-Mar), which has a big, impressive baroque altar and an elaborately carved pipe organ. For a panoramic city view, climb the 400 steps of the church's 95m spiral tower. The last 160 steps run spectacularly and dizzyingly along the outside rim, narrowing to the point where they disappear at the top.

Carlsberg Brewery

At the Carlsberg Brewery **visitor centre** (☎ 33 27 13 14; Gamle Carlsberg Vej 11; ⊙ 10am-4pm Tue-Sun), free self-guided tours provide the lowdown on the history of Danish beer, capped off

---

THE 'FREETOWN' OF CHRISTIANIA

Things have changed in Christiania, a self-declared 'independent state' and, depending who you talk to, either a worthy social experiment or an anarchic den of iniquity that should be bulldozed to release a valuable piece of Christianshavn real estate.

The story started in the early 1970s when hippies, artists, political activists and other urban escapees, fired with the dream of an alternative 'New Society' run by and for the community (not to mention the lure of no rent or local taxes), broke into an abandoned barracks here and stayed despite violent police confrontations.

A hard drugs problem resulted in police raids, a moral backlash and a community ban on the use of hard drugs in the early 1980s.

The government eventually agreed to let Christiania be as a 'social experiment' and it has emerged as a 1000-strong alternative ghetto with its own commercial life, political structure, education system, radio station and a thriving music, theatre and social scene.

It is famous (or notorious) to most visitors, however, for its hash culture and was, until recently, the place where every type of weed, resin and perception-altering fungus was openly, though illegally, sold from Pusherstreet's stalls.

But no more. The uneasy compromise between state and dealers ended with a massive police raid in 2004, which netted dozens of suspected drug dealers and smashed the hash market. Christianians no longer sell hash openly and fear politicians and developers could use its druggy reputation against Christiania as a pretext to reclaim the site, ending this long social experiment, and perhaps the last vestige of the 1960s hippy 'peace and love' dream.

Pusherstreet may be an emptier, rather deflated place these days but Christiania has many other attractions (inexpensive cafés and restaurants, eccentric shops, clubs and galleries) that make it well worth a visit. The **information office** (☎ 32 95 65 07; www.christiania.org; Nyt Forum, Pusherstreet; ⊙ noon-6pm Mon-Thu, noon-4pm Fri) organises guided tours most days in summer.

DENMARK

with a sampling of the present-day product. Take bus No 26 westbound.

WALKING TOUR

A walk from **Rådhus** (City Hall) to the **Little Mermaid** is a pleasant way of becoming familiar with the city.

From Rådhus, start your stroll down Strøget, a sequence of pedestrianised streets starting at Frederiksberggade which, after a couple of blocks, cuts between the cobbled squares of **Gammel Torv**, where you'll find the elegant **Caritas**, the 'Charity' Fountain.

Strøget now enters Nygade and then becomes Vimmelskaftet before widening again into the lively square of **Amagertorv**. Ahead is the famous **Storkespringvandet** (Stork Fountain), a popular meeting place and venue for street entertainers. To the right is Højbro Plads and the great statue of the city founder, Bishop Absalon, on horseback. Beyond it is the spire of entwined dragons' tails that crowns the **Børsen**, the beautiful Renaissance stock exchange building.

From the lively heart of Amagertorv, Strøget continues along the narrow Østergade. Strøget soon ends at **Kongens Nytorv**, on the eastern side of which is picturesque **Nyhavn** canal, packed with busy pavement cafés on its sunny northern side and once the haunt of sailors, local characters, and writers, such as Hans Christian Andersen, who lived for many years at No 67.

From the northern side of Nyhavn, head north on Toldbodgade, turn right into Sankt Annæ Plads and then turn left along the airy waterfront. When you reach a fountain, turn inland to the great cobbled square of Amalienborg Plads and to **Amalienborg Palace** (admission Dkr40; ☯ 10am-4pm May-Oct, 11am-4pm Nov-Apr), home of the royal family since 1794 and still guarded by sentries, who are relieved at noon by a ceremonial changing of the guard.

Head north along Amaliegade for 500m to **Frihedsmuseet** (admission Dkr25, Wed free; ☯ 10am-4pm Tue-Sat, 10am-5pm Sun May–mid-Sep, 11am-3pm Tue-Sat, 11am-4pm Sun mid-Sep–Apr), which depicts the history of Danish Resistance against Nazi occupation.

Keep heading straight on from Frihedsmuseet and in 150m you pass the spectacular **Gefion Fountain** that features the mythical goddess Gefion, ploughing the island of Zealand with her four sons yoked as oxen.

Continue north along the waterfront for another 400m to the statue of the famed **Little Mermaid** (Den Lille Havfrue), a rather forlorn little bronze statue that tends to disappoint all but the most steadfast Hans Christian Andersen fans.

TOURS
Canal Tours

For a different angle on the city, hop onto one of the hour-long boat tours that wind through Copenhagen's canals April to mid-October. Multilingual guides give a lively commentary in English. The largest company, **DFDS Canal Tours** (adult Dkr50), leaves from the head of Nyhavn. Tours pass by the Little Mermaid, Christianshavn and Christiansborg Slot, and leave a few times an hour between 10am and 5pm. **Netto-Boats** (☎ 32 54 41 02; adult Dkr25) are cheaper, run the same times and depart from Holmens Church and from Nyhavn. Visit www.canaltours.dk for more information.

FESTIVALS & EVENTS

The **Copenhagen Jazz Festival** (☎ 33 93 20 13; http://festival.jazz.dk) is the biggest event of the year, with 10 days of music in early July. The festival presents a wide range of Danish and international jazz, blues and fusion music. It's a cornucopia of some 500 indoor and outdoor concerts, with music wafting out of practically every public square, park, pub and café from Strøget to Tivoli.

SLEEPING
Rooms & Booking Services

The tourist office can book unfilled hotel rooms, often at discounted rates. There's a Dkr60 fee per booking. The airport information booth outside customs offers a similar service.

Use It (Rådhusstræde 13) books private rooms (singles/doubles from Dkr200/300) free of booking fees, keeps tabs on which hostel beds are available, and is a good source of information for subletting student housing and other long-term accommodation.

Hostels

Many of the hostels lie a few kilometres from the city. Those in and near Vesterbro and Nørrebro are good options, not too distant from the centre and close to their own lively little clusters of cafés and bars.

City Public Hostel (☎ 33 31 20 70; www.city-public -hostel.dk; Absalonsgade 8; dm Dkr130; ⊙ early May–mid-Aug, 24hr reception) A good bet but not exactly party central (probably because it's so close to the bar and café action in Vesterbro). Avoid the noisy 72-bed dorm if you can.

Mick & Blodwyn's Backpackers Inn (☎ 33 93 23 00; mickandblodwyns.homepage.dk; Herluf Trolles Gade 9; dm Dkr180; ▯) Tiny, friendly and a stumble from Nyhavn's bars. Serves cheap beer from its own bar and throws in breakfast, bedding and Internet access free. Bathrooms and accommodation in four- or six-bed dorms are a tad cramped.

Copenhagen has two HI hostels, each about 5km from the city centre. They often fill early from May to September so book ahead.

Danhostel Copenhagen Bellahøj (☎ 38 28 97 15; www.danhostel.dk/bellahoej; Herbergvejen 8; dm/d Dkr95/300; ⊙ Mar–mid-Jan, 24hr reception; [P] ▯) Good for (relative) peace and quiet given the suburban neighbourhood location. Take bus No 2-Brønshøj from Rådhuspladsen and get off at Fuglsangs Allé, or night bus 82N.

Danhostel Copenhagen Amager (☎ 32 52 29 08; www.danhostel.dk/copenhagen; Vejlands Allé 200, Amager; dm/d Dkr95/300; ⊙ mid-Jan–Nov; [P] ▯ ⛭) In an isolated part of Amager just off the E20, this hostel is massive but dorms are in five-bed rooms. Take the S-train to Sjælør Station, then change to bus No 100S. Until 5pm Monday to Friday, bus No 46 runs from Central Station directly to the hostel.

Even when the HI hostels are full you can nearly always find a bed at one of the city-sponsored (often summer-only) hostels. The larger ones are central crash pads. Sleeping bags are allowed.

Sleep-In (☎ 35 26 50 59; www.sleep-in.dk; Blegdamsvej 132; dm Dkr110; ⊙ late Jun-31 Aug, 24hr reception; [P] ▯) In the pleasant Østerbro area just north of the city centre, this is busy and popular. It occupies a sports hall that's partitioned off into 'rooms' with four to six beds. There's a group kitchen, a café and free lockers. Take bus No 1 or 14 from Rådhuspladsen to Trianglen and walk 300m south on Blegdamsvej. Night buses are 85N and 95N.

Sleep-In Heaven (☎ 35 35 46 48; www.sleepinheaven .com; Struenseegade 7; dm Dkr130) In the Nørrebro area, this has beds in a basement dorm. There is an age limit of 35 years. Breakfast is included, sheets cost Dkr30. Take bus No 8 to the Kapelvej stop; the night bus is 92N.

Sleep-In Green (☎ 35 37 77 77; www.sleep-in -green.dk; Ravnsborggade 18; dm Dkr100; ⊙ mid-May–mid-Oct; [P] ▯) In the Nørrebro area, close to its buzzing cafés and bars. Take bus No 5a, nightbus 81N or 84N or the S-train to Nørreport Station, then walk northwest on Frederiksberggade over the canal. The organic breakfast costs Dkr30.

YMCA Interpoint (☎ 33 31 15 74; Valdemarsgade 15; dm Dkr85; ⊙ end Jun-early Aug, reception 8.30-11.30am, 3.30-5.30pm & 8pm-12.30am) A small place in the heart of Vesterbro. There are only 28 dorm beds, so book ahead. Bed sheets (Dkr15), breakfast (Dkr25) and a kitchen are available. It's a 15-minute walk from Central Station (take Vesterbrogade west to Valdemarsgade), or you can take bus No 6a or 26.

Sleep-In Fact (☎ 33 79 67 79; www.sleep-in-fact.dk; Valdemarsgade 14; dm Dkr120; ⊙ mid-Jun–end Aug, reception 7am-noon & 3pm-3am; ▯) In a refurbished factory building close to YMCA Interpoint, with 10- to 30-bed dorms and plenty of activities and services including bike rental, a gym, pool and table football.

Hotel Jørgensen (below) also offers dorm accommodation.

Hotels – Around Central Station

Copenhagen's main hotel area lies in Vesterbro on the western side of Central Station. All rates include breakfast unless otherwise specified.

Cab Inn City (☎ 33 46 16 16; www.cabinn.com; Mitchellsgade 14; s/d/tr/q Dkr510/630/750/870; [P] ✖ ▧ ▯ ⛭) You are a number not a name here: rooms are small, uniform and rather clinical, most with sleeper-train–style folding bunk beds, but are modern, spotless and boast good facilities (including kettle and TV) and a central location. There's free lobby Internet access.

Hotels – Elsewhere in Copenhagen

Hotel Jørgensen (☎ 33 13 81 86; hotel@post12.tele.dk; Rømersgade 11; dm Dkr135, s/d Dkr575/700, with shared bathroom Dkr475/575) A great budget hotel near Nørreport Station and the area's cafés and bars. Simple rooms have shared bathrooms. Dorms have either six or 12 beds.

Cab Inn Scandinavia (☎ 35 36 11 11; www.cabinn .com; Vodroffsvej 57; s/d/tr/q Dkr510/630/750/870; [P] ⛭) Has 201 compact rooms in this chain's familiar clinical style. The rooms are comfortable and have TV and private bathroom. The third sister hotel **Cab Inn Express** (☎ 33 21 04 00;

www.cabinn.com; Danasvej 32-34; ⓟ ⓖ) costs the same and is a few blocks away.

Camping
About 9km west of the city centre near Brøndbyøster Station on the S-train's line B is **Camping Absalon** (☎ 36 41 06 00; www.camping-absalon.dk; Korsdalsvej 132; adult/tent Dkr64/20; ⓨ year-round).

EATING
Around Central Station
Ankara (☎ 33 31 14 99; Vesterbrogade 35; buffet noon-4pm Dkr49, 4pm-midnight Dkr79) Extensive Middle Eastern buffet includes dishes such as calamari, chicken, lamb and salads.

Central Station has a **DSB café** (ⓨ 5.30am-12.45am Sun-Thu, 5.30am-1.45am Fri & Sat), a **supermarket** (ⓨ 8am-midnight), the Kringlen bakery with good breads and pastries, a fruit shop and fast-food outlets.

Around Strøget & Latin Quarter
Pasta Basta (☎ 33 11 21 31; Valkendorfsgade 22; mains Dkr79-169, lunch mains Dkr59-69; ⓨ 11.30am-3am Sun-Thu, 11am-5am Fri & Sat) There's a superb selection of hot pasta dishes served with fish and meat mains. Eat as much as you like of cold pasta dishes and salads for Dkr30 to Dkr69.

Riz Raz (☎ 33 15 05 75; Kompagnistræde 20; buffet 11.30am-5pm Mon-Fri, 11.30am-4pm Sat & Sun Dkr59, evening buffet 5-11pm Mon-Fri, 4-11pm Sat & Sun Dkr69) Another excellent-value, high-quality buffet-style place, just south of Strøget, offering a fresh, tasty Mediterranean-style vegetarian buffet including salads, pasta and falafels.

Restaurant Puk (☎ 33 11 14 17; Vandkunsten 8; lunch platter Dkr79-128; ⓨ 11am-late) Serves up a tempting range of inexpensive Danish food inside and out. *Smørrebrød* (open sandwiches) costs Dkr38 to Dkr79.

Studenterhusets (☎ 35 32 38 61; Købmagergade 52; ⓨ noon-midnight Mon-Fri) A relaxed student hangout with drinks and light eats, including vegetarian or meat sandwiches for Dkr20.

Strøget has an abundance of cheap fast-food joints including hole-in-the-wall kebab joints selling falafels and kebabs for under Dkr30. The best is **Shawarma Grill House** (Frederiksberggade 16; sandwiches Dkr30-40, kebabs Dkr44; ⓨ 11am-10pm), a bustling spot two minutes' walk from Rådhuspladsen at the western end of Strøget. There's a 24-hour 7-Eleven minimarket on the corner of Gammel Torv. Netto supermarket, near the eastern end of Strøget, is relatively cheap.

Elsewhere in Central Copenhagen
Govindas (☎ 33 33 74 44; Nørre Farimagsgade 82; buffet Dkr59; ⓨ noon-8.30pm Mon-Sat) You can get good vegetarian food here south of the Botanical Gardens; the Hare Krishna members offer an all-you-can-eat buffet and vegan meals. Students and senior citizens pay Dkr45 for the standard buffet.

Christianshavn & Christiania
Christianshavns Bådudlejning (☎ 32 96 53 53; Overgaden neden Vandet 29; fish & meat mains Dkr115-125) A deservedly popular place on a canalside deck. It has a tasty lunch menu, with sandwiches for Dkr45 and salads for Dkr60 to Dkr70.

Morgenstedet (Langgaden; mains Dkr35; ⓨ noon-9pm; ⓧ) A long-established vegetarian and vegan place with a pretty garden in the heart of Christiania where a main dish and salad costs Dkr50.

DRINKING & CLUBBING
You're spoilt for choice for cafés and bars in Copenhagen. The further-flung districts such as Nørrebro and Vesterbro (especially along the eastern end of Istedgade and Halmtorvet) are well worth exploring.

For a cheap, convivial evening (weather permitting), head to Nyhavn via a bottle shop and suck down a few cold take-out pilsners amid the happy throngs that gather by the canal.

Joe & the Juice (Ny Østergade 11; ⓨ 9am-7pm Mon-Sat) This is one of the few fresh fruit juice bars in town.

Charlie's Bar (☎ 33 32 22 89; Pilestræde 33) Cosy and hugely popular with lager-sated Danes who worship enthusiastically at this temple to the gods of real British cask ale.

Café Bang & Jensen (Istedgade 130) It's small and a fair trek from the centre but it buzzes.

Ideal Bar (☎ 33 25 70 11; Enghavevej 40) Further west, this bar attracts a young, hip crowd, often for preclubbing drinks before heading next door to Vega Nightclub, which stages hugely popular Friday and Saturday night sessions.

The west-side Nørrebro area has a number of good entertainment spots.

Rust (☎ 35 24 52 00; Guldbergsgade 8; admission Dkr30-50) A multilevel dance venue attracting a college-age crowd.

Studenterhusets (☎ 35 32 38 61; Købmagergade 52; admission Dkr60-80) Another popular student venue that has live music (jazz on Thursdays and rock on Fridays) and DJ nights on the other weeknights. There's a very cheap beer happy hour from noon to 7pm.

Sofie Kælderen (☎ 32 57 27 87; Sofiegade 1) In Christianshavn this engaging local bar opens at noon and does lunches until 4pm and there's often live jazz and rock until late.

Loppen (☎ 32 57 84 22; Loppebygningen, Christiania; admission Dkr50-70; ☾ nightclub 2am-5am Fri & Sat) A celebrated venue that has live music from soul to punk on various nights and a late disco.

Gay & Lesbian Venues

Oscar (☎ 33 12 09 99; Rådhuspladsen 77; ☾ noon-2am, kitchen noon-10pm) This popular meeting place for gay men is central, near the Rådhus.

Never Mind (Nørre Voldgade 2; ☾ 10pm-6am) The long-established, late-night Never Mind is a dance bar for mainly gay men, but with a dash of transgendered and lesbians enjoying its kitsch décor.

Kvindehuset (The Women's House; Gothersgade 37) Stages various dance nights for lesbians and has a café and bar.

PAN Club (☎ 33 11 37 84; Knabrostræde 3; admission Dkr50; ☾ 11pm-6am Thu-Sat) The largest gay club in town with five levels, two dance floors and seven bars.

ENTERTAINMENT

Copenhagen is a 24-hour party city. For free entertainment simply stroll along Strøget, especially between Nytorv and Højbro Plads, usually a stage for musicians, magicians, jugglers and other street performers.

Copenhagen has scores of backstreet cafés with live music. Entry is often free on weeknights, while there's usually a cover charge averaging Dkr60 at weekends.

The free publications *Nat & Dag*, *Musik Kalenderen*, *Film Kalenderen* and *Teater Kalenderen* list concerts and entertainment schedules in detail.

Copenhagen Jazz House (☎ 33 15 26 00; Niels Hemmingsensgade 10) This is the city's leading jazz spot and has a terrific ambience. Danish musicians and occasional international names feature.

Mojo (☎ 33 11 64 53; Løngangstræde 21; admission Dkr50; ☾ 8pm-3am) A prime spot for blues, with entertainment nightly.

Huset (☎ 33 15 20 02; Rådhusstræde 13) In the same courtyard as the Use It information centre, Huset houses a cinema, theatre, café and restaurant and live music, sometimes free.

Several cinemas show first-release movies along Vesterbrogade between Central Station and Rådhuspladsen.

GETTING THERE & AWAY
Bus & Train

International buses leave from Central Station; advance reservations on most routes can be made at **Eurolines** (☎ 33 88 70 00; Reventlowsgade 8).

There are three ways of buying a train ticket. *Billetautomats* are coin-operated machines and are the quickest, if you've mastered the zone-system prices. They are best for S-train tickets. If you're not rushed, then **DSB Billetsalg** (☾ 8am-7pm Mon-Fri, 9.30am-4pm Sat) is best for reservations. There's a numbered-ticket queuing system. **DSB Kviksalg** (☾ 5.45am-11.30pm) is for quick ticket buying, although queues can build at busy times.

Car

A fair trek from the centre at Amager Strand, **Rent A Wreck** (☎ 70 25 26 70; Amagerstrandvej 100) hires out battered but usually reliable old wagons from as little as Dkr239 per day.

GETTING AROUND
Bicycle

At Central Station, Københavns Cykler rents bicycles for Dkr75 a day. For cheaper prices (Dkr40 a day) walk a few blocks northwest to **Danwheel** (Colbjørnsensgade 3).

Bus & Train

Copenhagen has an extensive public-transport system consisting of a small but excellent new underground and overground driverless Metro system, an extensive metropolitan rail network called S-train, whose 10 lines pass through Central Station (København H), and a vast bus system, whose main terminus is nearby at Rådhuspladsen.

They use a common fare system based on the number of zones you pass through. The basic fare of Dkr17 for up to two zones covers most city runs and allows transfers between buses, metros and trains on a single ticket as long as they're made within an hour. Pay the driver on the buses. On S-trains buy tickets at the station and then punch them in the yellow time clock on the platform.

Taxi

Taxis with signs saying '*fri*' can be flagged down or you can phone ☎ 35 35 35 35.

DENMARK

DENMARK

ZEALAND

Zealand (Sjælland) has a tempting range of places for day trips from the capital. Northern Zealand has wonderful beaches, likeable fishing villages and some breathtaking castles, most of them easily accessible thanks to the excellent rail network.

NORTH ZEALAND

The northern part of Zealand is a compact region of wheat fields and beech woodlands interspersed with small towns and tiny hamlets. One of the most popular day trips from Copenhagen is a loop tour taking in Frederiksborg Slot in Hillerød and Kronborg Slot in Helsingør.

Frederiksborg Slot

Hillerød, 30km northwest of Copenhagen, is the site of **Frederiksborg Slot** (☎ 48 26 04 39; admission Dkr60; ⊙ 10am-5pm Apr-Oct, 11am-3pm Nov-Mar), an impressive Dutch Renaissance castle that's spread across three islands.

The sprawling castle has a magnificent interior with gilded ceilings, full wall-sized tapestries, royal paintings and antiques. The richly embellished **Riddershalen** (Knights' Hall) and the **coronation chapel**, where Danish monarchs were crowned between 1671 and 1840, are well worth the admission fee.

The S-train (A and E lines) runs every 10 minutes between Copenhagen and Hillerød (Dkr59.50, 40 minutes). From Hillerød Station follow the signs to Torvet, then continue along Slotsgade to the castle, a 15-minute walk in all. Alternatively, take bus No 701 or 702, which can drop you at the gate.

Helsingør (Elsinore)

Helsingør is a busy, attractive port town, with ferries continuously shuttling across the Øresund Strait to and from Sweden to disgorge thirsty Swedes who stock up on booze here. The **tourist office** (☎ 49 21 13 33; www.visithelsingor .dk; Havnepladsen 3; ⊙ 9am-5pm Mon-Thu, 9am-6pm Fri, 10am-3pm Sat mid-Jun–Jul, 9am-4pm Mon-Fri, 10am-1pm Sat Aug–mid-Jun) is opposite the train station.

Helsingør's top sight is **Kronborg Slot** (☎ 33 92 65 33; admission Dkr50; ⊙ 10.30am-5pm May-Sep, 11am-4pm Oct & Apr, 11am-3pm Tue-Sun rest of year), made famous as the Elsinore Castle of Shakespeare's *Hamlet*. Kronborg's primary function was

not as a royal residence, but rather as a grandiose tollhouse, wresting taxes, the infamous and lucrative 'Sound Dues', for more than 400 years from ships passing through the narrow Øresund. You can cross the moat and walk around the courtyard for free.

From the tourist office head up Brostræde and along Sankt Anna Gade. This will take you through the **medieval quarter** and past the old cathedral, **Sankt Olai Kirke** (⊙ 10am-4pm Mon-Sat Apr-Oct, 10am-2pm Mon-Sat Nov-Mar); the **City History Museum** (admission Dkr10; ⊙ noon-4pm); and **Karmeliterklostret** (admission Dkr10; ⊙ 10am-3pm Mon-Fri mid-May–mid-Sep, 10am-2pm mid-Sep–mid-May), one of Scandinavia's best-preserved medieval monasteries.

SLEEPING & EATING

Danhostel Helsingør (☎ 49 21 16 40; www.helsingor hostel.dk; Nordre Strandvej 24; dm Dkr110, r Dkr450; ⊙ Feb-Nov; P &) The hostel is 2km northwest of the centre and right on the Øresund beach.

Café Kringlen (Hovedragtsstræde 2; ⊙ 7am-6pm Mon-Fri, 7am-5pm Sat & Sun) The pastries are mouth-wateringly good and it serves bottomless cups of coffee.

The **China Box** (Stengade 28; ⊙ noon-9pm Mon-Sat, 2-9pm Sun) offers food box takeaways for Dkr28. The nearby **Pakhus Pizzeria** (☎ 49 21 10 50; Stengade 26C; pizzas & pastas Dkr49-60), set back from the street in an attractive courtyard, serves decent Italian fare.

GETTING THERE & AWAY

Trains from Hillerød (Dkr51, 30 minutes) run at least once an hour. Trains from Copenhagen run a few times hourly (Dkr59.50, 55 minutes). For more information on ferries to Helsingborg (Dkr18, 20 minutes) see p306.

ROSKILDE

pop 52,000

Roskilde was Denmark's original capital and was a thriving trading port throughout the Middle Ages. It was also the site of Zealand's first Christian church, built by Viking king Harald Bluetooth in AD 980 and is one of the best places in the country to get a feel for Denmark's Viking heritage at the excellent Viking Ship Museum. It fell into decline after the Reformation and its quietude today is only disturbed during the hugely popular annual Roskilde music festival.

Roskilde has a helpful **tourist office** (☎ 46 31 65 65; www.visitroskilde.com; Gullandsstræde 15; ☽ 9am-5pm Mon-Fri, 10am-1pm Sat Apr-Jun, 10am-6pm Mon-Fri, 10am-2pm Sat Jul & Aug, 9am-5pm Mon-Thu, 9am-4pm Fri, 10am-1pm Sat Sep-Mar).

The cathedral is on Torvet, 10 minutes northwest of the train station; cut diagonally across the old churchyard and go left along Algade. The Viking Ship Museum is north of the cathedral, a pleasant 15-minute stroll through city parks.

Though most of Roskilde's medieval buildings have vanished in fires over the centuries, the imposing **Roskilde Domkirke** (☎ 46 35 27 00; Domkirkepladsen; admission Dkr25; ☽ 9am-4.45pm Mon-Sat, 12.30-4.45pm Sun Apr-Sep, 9am-4pm Mon-Fri, 10am-1pm Sat Oct-Mar) still dominates the city centre. Started by Bishop Absalon in 1170, Roskilde Domkirke has been rebuilt and added to so many times that this mighty brick edifice represents a millennium of Danish church architectural styles. Its **crypts** contain the sarcophagi of 39 Danish kings and queens.

From the northern side of the cathedral, walk across a field where beautiful wild flowers blanket the unexcavated remains of Roskilde's original medieval town, then continue through a green belt all the way to the **Viking Ship Museum** (☎ 46 30 02 00; Vindeboder 12; admission Dkr60, low season Dkr45; ☽ 10am-5pm May-30 Sep, 10am-4pm Oct-30 Apr) which contains five reconstructed Viking ships (c 1000), excavated from the bottom of Roskilde Fjord in 1962 and brought to shore in thousands of fragments. There are excellent audiovisual displays and equally good **waterfront workshops** where Viking ship replicas are being built using Viking-era techniques, showing just what incredible skill and arduous labour went into building these magnificent ships.

The **Roskilde Festival** (www.roskilde-festival.dk), northern Europe's largest music festival, rocks Roskilde each summer on a weekend in late June/early July with some of the best headline acts in the world such as Bob Dylan, U2, Radiohead, Robbie Williams, Beastie Boys and the Chemical Brothers. The festival is a showcase for rising talent and new trends. Camping is free, but tightly packed, and there are subsidiary happenings and events.

Trains from Copenhagen to Roskilde (Dkr59.50, 25 minutes) are frequent.

MØN

Møn is celebrated for its spectacular, and totally un-Danish, sea cliffs of bone-white chalk.

Stege, the main settlement on Møn, is an everyday place, but it is enlivened by its role as the island's gateway town and main commercial centre. Møn **tourist office** (☎ 55 86 04 00; www.moen-touristbureau.dk; Storegade 2; ☽ 9.30am-5pm Mon-Fri, 9am-6pm Sat mid-Jun–Aug, 9.30am-4.30pm Mon-Fri, 9am-noon Sat Sep–mid-Jun) is at the entrance to Stege and has good information on the entire island.

The chalk cliffs at Møns Klint were created during the final Ice Ages when the calcareous deposits from aeons of compressed seashells were lifted from the ocean floor. The woods of Klinteskoven, behind the cliffs, have a network of paths and tracks. From near the cafeteria you can descend the cliffs by a series of wooden stairways. It's quite a long descent and, consequently, a strenuous return up the 500-odd stairs.

Møn has a wealth of prehistoric remains, although many are vestigial burial mounds. The best-preserved sites are the late–Stone Age passage graves of **Kong Asgers Høj** and **Klekkende Høj**. Both are on the west side of the island within a 2km radius of the village of Røddinge.

Danhostel Møns Klint (☎ 55 81 20 30; www .danhostel.dk/moen; dm Dkr105, d/tr/q Dkr300/390/420; ☽ May–mid-Sep; ℗ ✗) occupies an enchanting lakeside spot opposite a camping ground 3km from the cliffs.

From Copenhagen take the train to Vordingborg (Dkr92, 1½ hours), from where it's a 45-minute bus ride (No 52; Dkr36) to Stege. From late June to mid-August, buses make the 45-minute run (Dkr13) from Stege to Møns Klint a few times a day. The bus stops at the hostel and camping ground en route.

BORNHOLM

pop 44,000
Life is satisfyingly slow-paced, but never dull, on Bornholm, a remarkable self-contained little world stuck in the middle of the Baltic 200km east of Copenhagen. A lush swathe of wheat fields and extensive forests covers the centre while the coast is beaded with small fishing villages and stretches of powdery white sand.

The island's main **tourist office** (Bornholms Velkomstcenter; ☎ 56 95 95 00; www.bornholm.info; Nordre Kystvej 3; ☼ 9am-5pm Mon-Sat, 10am-3pm Sun late Jun-Aug, 9am-4pm Mon-Fri, 10am-1pm Sat Mar-May, Sep & Oct, 9am-4pm Mon-Fri Nov-Feb) is a few minutes' walk from Rønne harbour and has masses of information on all of Bornholm.

Unique among Bornholm's attractions are its four 12th-century **round churches**, splendid buildings whose whitewashed walls, 2m thick, are framed by solid buttresses and crowned with black, conical roofs. Each was designed as both a place of worship and a fortress against enemy attacks, with a gun slot–pierced upper storey.

Gudhjem is a compact, attractive seaside village crowned by a squat windmill standing over half-timbered houses and sloping streets that roll down to the pleasant harbour front. The **tourist office** (☎ 56 48 52 10; Åbogade 7; ☼ 10am-4pm Jul & Aug, 1-4pm Mon-Sat Sep & Mar-Jun) is a block inland from the harbour alongside the library.

A bike path leads inland 4km south from Gudhjem to the thick-walled, buttressed **Østerlars Rundkirke**, the most impressive of the island's round churches; bus No 3 goes by the church.

Sandvig is tucked away under Bornholm's rocky northwestern tip of Hammeren and boasts an excellent sandy beach to add to its distinctive appeal. Bornholm's best-known sight, **Hammershus Slot**, is 3km south on the road to Rønne. The impressive, substantial ruins of this 13th-century castle are the largest of their kind in Scandinavia.

Tiny **Christiansø** (about 500m long) is a charmingly preserved, 17th-century fortress-island just an hour's sail northeast of Bornholm and well worth making the time for a day trip. A seasonal fishing hamlet since the Middle Ages, Christiansø fell briefly into Swedish hands in 1658, after which Christian V decided to remake the island into an invincible naval fortress. Bastions and barracks were subsequently built; a church, a school and a prison then followed.

Sleeping & Eating

Danhostel Gudhjem (☎ 56 48 50 35; www.danhostel -gudhjem.dk; dm Dkr118, s/d Dkr325/375) Just up from the harbourside bus stop on an attractive spot right by the harbour with small cosy, bright white six-bed dorms. The staff can book rooms in private homes at Dkr275/375 for singles/doubles.

Gudhjem Rogeri (☎ 56 48 57 08) Has an all-you-can-eat buffet for Dkr92 and some challenging seating, including on the upper floor, which is reached by rope ladder. It has live folk, country and rock music most nights in summer.

You'll find a bakery and a few reasonably priced cafés along Brøddegade, a little inland from the harbour.

Getting There & Around

Bornholmstrafikken (☎ 33 13 18 66; www.bornholm strafikken.dk) operates ferries between Køge and Rønne. While not as fast as the boat/train option, overnight sailing (departing daily at midnight and arriving at 6.30am) on the car ferry from Køge is worth considering. The bunk-style berths (Dkr76 extra one-way) and cabins (from Dkr186 extra one-way) are reasonably inexpensive. A peak return per person costs Dkr325. A car with up to five people costs Dkr1280.

Bornholmstrafikken also operates the ferry service several times daily between Rønne and Ystad (Dkr144 one-way or same-day return, 1½ or 2½ hours) and on a near-daily basis from April to October **Scandlines** (www.scandlines.com) sails from Sassnitz-Mukran in Germany (Dkr135, 3½ hours).

The fastest land option between Bornholm and Copenhagen is the train-ferry combination from Copenhagen to Rønne via Ystad, Sweden with **DSB** (☎ 70 13 14 15; www.dsb.dk). This trip goes a few times a day, takes three hours and costs Dkr230.

A good, inexpensive bus service around the island is operated by Bornholms Amts Trafikselskab (BAT). Fares are based on a zone system and cost Dkr10 per zone, with the maximum fare set at 10 zones.

Cycling is a great way to get around the place. Rønne tourist office sells the 60-page English-language *Bicycle Routes on Bornholm* (Dkr45), which maps out routes and helpfully describes sights along the way. In Rønne, **Bornholms Cykeludlejning** (☎ 56 95 13 59; Nordre Kystvej 5), next to the tourist office, has a large fleet of bikes renting at Dkr60 for a day or Dkr240 a week. Bicycles can usually be rented from hostels and camping grounds around the island for about Dkr55 a day.

FUNEN

pop 471,000

Funen (Fyn) is Denmark's garden island, largely rural with undulating woodlands, picture-postcard pastures and cornfields peppered with old farmhouses and sleepy villages. The railway line from Copenhagen runs straight through Odense, Funen's main city, and westward onto Jutland.

ODENSE

pop 183,000

Denmark's third-largest city takes great pride in being the birthplace of Hans Christian Andersen. It's a friendly university city with busy, central pedestrianised areas, a fairly lively social scene and the worthwhile Andersen museum.

The **tourist office** (☎ 66 12 75 20; www.odense turist.dk; ☼ 9.30am-6pm Mon-Fri, 10am-5pm Sat & Sun mid-Jun–Aug, 9.30am-4.30pm Mon-Fri, 10am-3pm Sat & Sun Sep–mid-Jun), at Rådhus, is a 15-minute walk from the train station. **Odense Central Library** (Odense Banegård Center; ☼ 10am-7pm Mon-Thu, 10am-4pm Fri & Sat) offers free use of the Internet.

The **HC Andersens Hus** (☎ 65 51 46 01; Bangs Boder 29; admission Dkr50; ☼ 9am-7pm mid-Jun–Aug, 10am-4pm Tue-Sun Sep–mid-Jun) tells Andersen's fairy-tale life story.

Odense's 13th-century Gothic cathedral **Sankt Knuds Kirke** (☎ 66 12 03 92; Flakhaven; admission free; ☼ 9am-5pm Mon-Sat, noon-5pm Sun) reflects Odense's medieval wealth and stature. The stark white interior has a handsome rococo pulpit, a dazzling, 16th-century altarpiece and a magnificent gilded wooden triptych crowded with over 300 carved figures.

Sleeping

Danhostel Odense City (☎ 63 11 04 25; www.city hostel.dk; dm Dkr118, s/d Dkr360/450; ✖ 🖳) A bright, modern place with four- and six-bed dorms, a kitchen and laundry facilities next to the train and bus stations.

Det Lille Hotel (☎ 66 12 28 21; Dronningensgade 5; s/d Dkr350/550, with shared bathroom Dkr300/430) A good place to meet fellow travellers, although everyone smokes; this friendly place is a 10-minute walk west of the train station.

Eating

There are numerous places, mainly fast food, along Kongensgade.

China Box (☎ 66 20 62 44; Vestergade; small/large takeaway box Dkr25/38; ☼ 11am-9pm Mon-Sat) Close to the tourist office, it does inexpensive takeaway Chinese food.

Café Biografen (☎ 66 13 16 16; Brandts Klædefabrik; brunch Dkr65; ☼ 11am-midnight) Does a good selection of baguettes for around Dkr40 and salads for about Dkr60, as well as pastries, light meals and beer at reasonable prices.

Restaurant Mamma's (☎ 66 14 55 40; Klaregade 4; lunch pizza or pasta mains Dkr49, dinner mains pizza Dkr72-89, pasta Dkr78-89) A very decent pasta and pizza place with good lunch deals. There's a super little **deli** (☎ 66 13 13 03; ☼ 10am-5.30pm Mon-Fri, 10am-2pm Sat) attached for picnickers and self-caterers.

Drinking

Ryan's (Nørregade) is a friendly Irish-style pub with live music every weekend, a dance bar and cheap pints (Dkr25) for students all day. **Boogies** (Nørregade 21; admission Dkr35; ☼ from midnight), a dance place with bands on weekends downstairs from Birdy's Café, is popular with students.

Jazzhus Dexter (☎ 66 13 68 88; Vindegade 65) has good live (mostly jazz) groups. Just along the road is **Den Smagløse Café** (Vindegade 47; ☼ 1pm-2am Mon-Sat), a buzzing, atmospheric little place where a hip young crowd relaxes on beaten-up but comfortable old sofas.

Getting There & Around

Odense is on the main railway line between Copenhagen (Dkr207, 1½ hours, every 15 minutes), Århus (Dkr181, 1¾ hours, hourly) and Aalborg (Dkr276, three hours, hourly). Buses leave from the rear of the train station.

In Odense you board city buses at the front and pay the driver (Dkr12) when you get off. Rent bicycles at **Rolsted Cykler** (☎ 66 17 77 36; Østre Stationsvej 33; ☼ 10am-5.30pm Mon- Fri, 10am-2pm Sun) for Dkr85 a day, Dkr500 a week.

EGESKOV CASTLE

Egeskov (☎ 62 27 10 16; www.egeskov.com; combined ticket for all sights except castle Dkr85, with castle interior Dkr140; ☼ 10am-5pm May, Jun, Aug & Sep, 10am-7pm Jul) is a magnificent Renaissance castle, complete with moat and drawbridge. You can easily fill a day in the grounds, which contain free-roaming peacocks, aerial woodland walkways and a bamboo-grass labyrinth.

Egeskov is 2km west of Kvændrup on route 8. From Odense take the Svendborg-bound train to Kvændrup Station (Dkr49) and continue on foot or by taxi, or for Dkr40 take bus No 801 to Kvændrup Bibliotek, where you can switch to bus No 920. From June to August bus No 801 may run all the way to the castle.

JUTLAND

Come to Jutland's northern tip and its west coast for endless stretches of windswept sandy beaches and dramatic seas, to its central lake district for excellent cycling and canoeing and to the main cities, Århus and Aalborg, for student-filled party zones.

ÅRHUS

pop 285,000

Århus, the second-largest city in Denmark, is one of Scandinavian Europe's most modern and sophisticated regional capitals with a varied music and entertainment scene, yet this university city (with more than 20,000 students) retains all the friendliness and ease of a small country town.

Information

INTERNET ACCESS

Boomtown (Åboulevarden 21; per hr 25Dkr; ☑ 10am-2am Mon-Thu, 10am-8am Fri & Sat, 11am-midnight Sun)

TOURIST INFORMATION

Tourist Office (☎ 89 40 67 00; www.visitaarhus.com; Park Allé; ☑ 9.30am-6pm Mon-Fri, 9.30am-5pm Sat, 9.30am-1pm Sun mid-Jun–mid-Sep, 9.30am-5pm Mon-Fri, 10am-1pm Sat May–mid-Jun, 9.30am-4.30pm Mon-Fri, 10am-1pm Sat Jan-Apr & mid-Sep–Dec) In Rådhuset, the city hall. It has a very friendly and helpful staff and offers numerous brochures and leaflets on the city and Jutland.

TRAVEL AGENCIES

Kilroy Travels (☎ 86 20 11 44; Fredensgade 40) Specialises in discount and student travel and has friendly, helpful staff.

Sights & Activities

Århus' new showpiece art museum **ARoS** (☎ 87 30 66 00; www.aros.dk; Aros Allé 2; admission Dkr60; ☑ 10am-5pm Thu-Sun & Tue, 10am-10pm Wed), all sweeping curves, soaring spaces and white walls, houses a comprehensive collection of 19th- and 20th-century Danish art and a wide range of arresting and vivid contemporary art, including Ron Mueck's startlingly lifelike giant 'Boy'.

Den Gamle By (The Old Town; ☎ 86 12 31 88; www .dengamleby.dk; Viborgvej 2; admission Dkr70; ☑ 9am-6pm Jun-Aug, 10am-5pm Apr, May, Sep & Oct, 10am-4pm Feb, Mar, Nov & Dec, 11am-3pm Jan) is an engaging open-air museum of 75 half-timbered houses brought here from around Denmark and reconstructed as a provincial town, complete with a functioning bakery, silversmith, bookbinder etc. It's a 20-minute walk from the city centre. After-hours you can walk the old streets for free. Bus Nos 3, 14, 25 and 55 will take you there.

The impressive **Århus Domkirke** (☎ 86 12 38 45; Bispetorvet; admission free; ☑ 9.30am-4pm Mon-Fri May-Sep, 10am-3pm Mon-Fri Oct-Apr) is Denmark's longest cathedral. Parts of it date from the 12th century, while most of the rest of the church is 15th-century Gothic. Many fine frescoes that were covered over post-reformation have now been uncovered and restored. They range from fairy-tale paintings of St George slaying a dragon, to scenes of hellfire.

Visit **Moesgård**, 4.5km south of the city centre, for its glorious beech woods and the trails threading through them towards sandy beaches, for the well-presented exhibits on the Stone Age to the Viking Age at **Moesgård Museum of Prehistory** (admission Dkr45; ☑ 10am-5pm Apr-Sep, 10am-4pm Tue-Sun Oct-May), and for the museum's most dramatic exhibit: the 2000-year-old Grauballe Man (Grauballemanden), whose astonishingly well-preserved body was found in 1952, 35km west of Århus, in Grauballe. Bus No 6 from Århus train station terminates at the museum year-round, while bus No 19 terminates at Moesgård Strand from May to September.

Festivals & Events

The 10-day **Århus Festival** (www.aarhusfestuge.dk) in early September turns the city into a stage for nonstop revelry with jazz, rock, classical music, theatre and dance. The festival has hosted such varied bill-toppers as the Rolling Stones, Philip Glass, Anne-Sophie Mutter, Ravi Shankar, City of Birmingham Symphony Orchestra, New York City Ballet, Günter Grass and many more.

Sleeping

Danhostel Århus (☎ 86 16 72 98; www.hostel-aarhus .dk; Marienlundsvej 10; dm Dkr108, r Dkr472; ☑ late

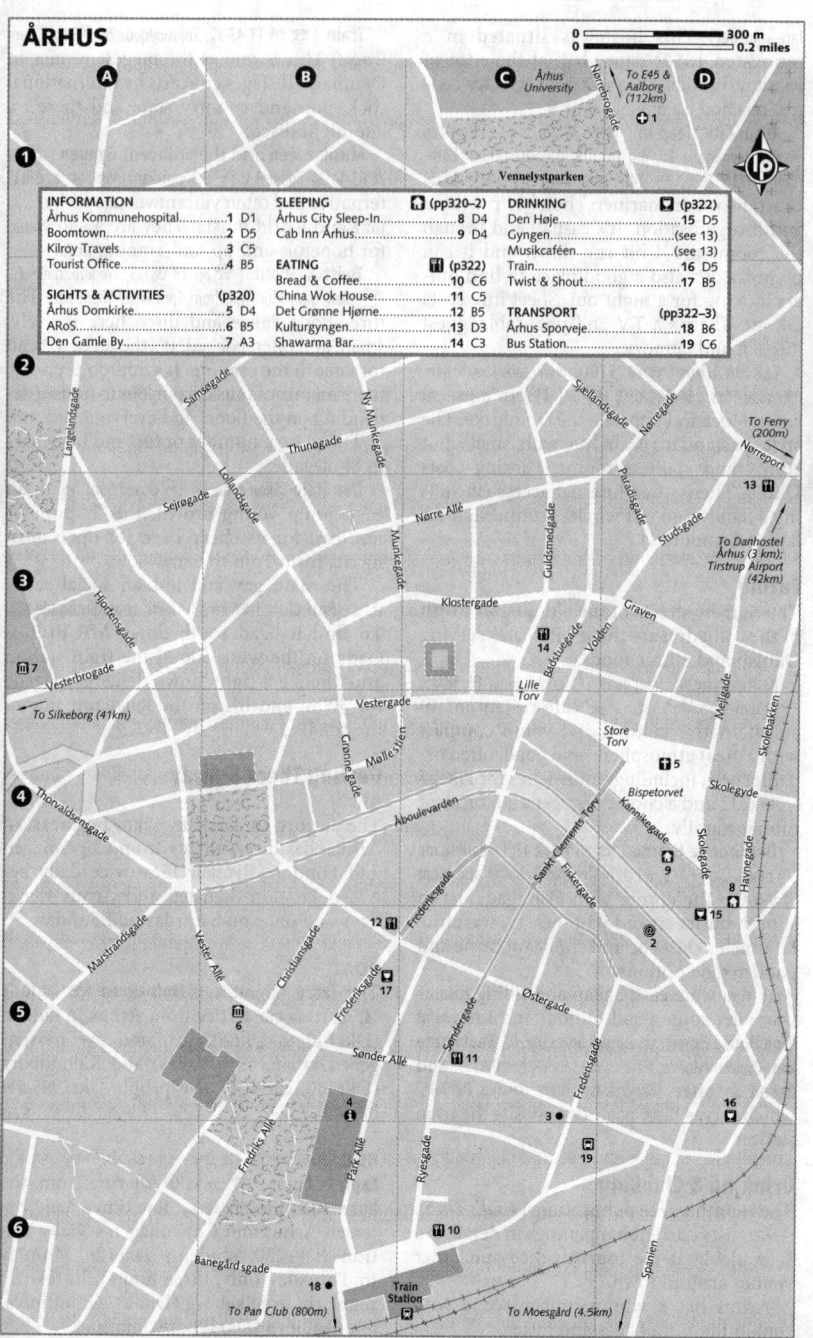

ÅRHUS

| | | 0 | 300 m |
| | | 0 | 0.2 miles |

INFORMATION
Århus Kommunehospital..............1 D1
Boomtown.....................................2 D5
Kilroy Travels...............................3 C5
Tourist Office...............................4 B5

SIGHTS & ACTIVITIES (p320)
Århus Domkirke............................5 D4
ARoS...6 B5
Den Gamle By...............................7 A3

SLEEPING (pp320–2)
Århus City Sleep-In......................8 D4
Cab Inn Århus..............................9 D4

EATING (p322)
Bread & Coffee............................10 C6
China Wok House.........................11 C5
Det Grønne Hjørne.......................12 B5
Kulturgyngen...............................13 D3
Shawarma Bar.............................14 C3

DRINKING (p322)
Den Høje......................................15 D5
Gyngen....................................(see 13)
Musikcaféen.............................(see 13)
Train..16 D5
Twist & Shout...............................17 B5

TRANSPORT (pp322–3)
Århus Sporveje............................18 B6
Bus Station...................................19 C6

DENMARK

Jan–mid-Dec) This hostel is situated in a renovated 1850s dance hall at the edge of Risskov Woods, 4km north of the city centre, reached by bus No 6 or 9.

Århus City Sleep-In (☎ 86 19 20 55; www.citysleep -in.dk; Havnegade 20; dm Dkr105, d with/without bathroom Dkr360/320; ☷ 24hr reception; ☒ ☐) This central former mariners' hotel is run by a youth organisation. It's casual, and though the rooms are a bit run-down and it can be noisy, it's also a good place to find others looking for a night out. Sheet hire costs Dkr40. There's a TV and pool table, guest kitchen and laundry.

Cab Inn Århus (☎ 86 75 70 00; www.cabinn.com; Kannikegade 14; s/d Dkr510/630; ☒ ☒ ☐) In an ideal central location opposite the Domkirke. The style is standard Cab Inn with small, but comfy and spotless rooms. Parking costs Dkr60. There's free Internet access (including a handy and fast wireless connection for laptop computers).

Eating

The narrow streets of the old quarter north of the cathedral are thick with cafés serving Danish and ethnic foods.

Kulturgyngen (Mejlgade 53; lunch/dinner Dkr38/75; ☷ 11am-9pm Mon-Sat) The café-restaurant of an alternative cultural and youth complex with a great atmosphere, and good, often organic food, including sandwiches for Dkr27 to Dkr32 and a choice of vegetarian or meat dinner nightly.

Det Grønne Hjørne (☎ 86 13 52 47; Frederiksgade 60; mains Dkr99-149, lunch buffet Dkr59, buffet after 4pm Dkr99) On the corner with Østergade, has a superb buffet spread with hearty, warming fare such as lasagne and chilli con carne and good veggie options.

If you want fast, cheap and filling takeaway fare, some good options include **China Wok House** (Søndergade; lunch boxes Dkr20), **Shawarma Bar** (Guldsmedgade; pitta-bread sandwiches Dkr25), and **Bread & Coffee** (Banegårdspladsen; pastries Dkr9-15) which serves tasty pastries opposite the train station.

Drinking & Clubbing

The monthly free publication *What's On in Århus* lists current happenings in detail and is available at the tourist office and other venues around town.

Århus has a vibrant music scene with something for all ages and tastes.

Train (☎ 86 13 47 22; Toldbodgade 6; ☷ until 5am Thu-Sat) This is one of the biggest venues in Denmark. It stages concerts by international rock, pop and country stars and there's a late-night disco.

Musikcaféen and the adjacent **Gyngen** (☎ 86 76 03 44; Mejlgade 53; ☷ 8.30pm-2am Mon-Sat) are alternative and often vibrant venues with rock, jazz and world music. They are a showcase for hopefuls and up-and-coming acts.

Twist & Shout (☎ 86 18 08 55; Frederiksgade 29; ☷ 10am-5am Mon-Thu, from 5pm Fri & 10pm Sat) The three-floor dance and disco here is lively, small, and often packed. It's the place to head for later in the evening. It's not too precious, there's a mix of music from '60s to house (depending on the floor) and everyone has fun.

There are a number of fun and busy bars in Skolegade.

Den Høje (Skolegade 28; ☷ closed Sun) With an easy-going young crowd, this is popular not least for its cheap beer. It's open most nights from 7pm to 5am.

The main gay and lesbian social scene is at **Pan Club** (☎ 86 13 43 80; Jægergårdsgade 42). To find it head south down MP Bruuns Gade on the west side of the train station and then go right down Jægergårdsgade for 300m and it's on the left-hand side of the road.

Getting There & Away

AIR

The airport, in Tirstrup 43km northeast of Århus, has direct flights from Copenhagen and London. Ryanair flies twice daily between London Stansted and Århus weekdays and once on Saturday and Sunday.

BOAT

The ferry operator is **Mols-Linien** (☎ 70 10 14 18). It runs car ferries from Århus to Odden (Dkr140 to Dkr205, car and five passengers Dkr545, 65 minutes) and Kalundborg (Dkr140, car with five people Dkr296, 2½ hours).

BUS

Express buses (☎ 98 90 09 00) run from the bus station (Fredensgade) a few times daily between Århus and Copenhagen's Valby Station (Dkr220, students Dkr120 Monday to Thursday only, three hours). Buses run regularly to Silkeborg (Dkr48, 48 minutes) and Aalborg (Dkr120, two hours).

TRAIN

Trains to Århus, via Odense, leave Copenhagen on the hour from early morning to 10pm (Dkr287, 3¼ hours) and there's a night train at 2am. There are regular trains to Aalborg (Dkr145, one hour 25 minutes) and Esbjerg (Dkr199, 2¾ hours). There's a ticket-queuing system at the station, red for internal, green for international. For local journeys, unless you have mastered use of the quicker ticket machines, be prepared for quite long waits at busy times. Friday trains are always very busy and it's advised to reserve a seat for long journeys.

Getting Around

The airport bus to Århus train station costs Dkr60 and takes about 45 minutes. Most in-town buses stop in front of the train station or around the corner on Park Allé. City bus tickets are bought from a machine in the back of the bus for Dkr17 and are good for unlimited rides within the time period stamped on the ticket, which is about two hours.

You can buy tickets and passes at **Århus Sporveje** (☎ 89 40 10 10; Banegårdspladsen 20; 🕑 10am-6pm Mon-Fri, 10am-1pm Sat), the city transport service shop across from the train station.

Taxis wait outside the station and at Store Torv. Expect to pay around Dkr60 for destinations within the city.

THE LAKE DISTRICT

The Danish Lake District is the closest thing to hill country in Denmark. There is excellent canoeing, biking and hiking to be had amid the woods and on the water.

The Lake District's biggest town, **Silkeborg**, is an ideal base for exploring the surrounding forests and waterways. The helpful **tourist office** (☎ 86 82 19 11; www.silkeborg.com; Åhavevej 2A; 🕑 9am-5pm Mon-Fri, 10am-2pm Sat & Sun mid-Jun–Aug, 9am-4pm Mon-Fri, 9am-noon Sat Sep–mid-Jun) is near the harbour and has lots of leaflets including detailed route descriptions of walks and cycle routes. **Internettet** (Ngade 37) is an Internet café charging Dkr25 per hour.

If you're even slightly interested in Denmark's ancient history, a compelling reason to visit is to head to the **Silkeborg Museum** (☎ 86 82 14 99; Hovedgården; admission Dkr40; 🕑 10am-5pm mid-May–Oct, noon-4pm Sat & Sun only Nov–mid-May) to see the Tollund Man, the body of a preserved Iron Age 'bog person' who looks for all the world as if he's merely asleep.

Danhostel Silkeborg (☎ 86 82 36 42; silkeborg@danhostel.dk; Åhavevej 55; dm Dkr115; 🕑 Mar-Dec; P ⊠ 💻 ♿) Has a scenic river-bank location and is a few minutes' walk east of the train station.

Nygade has a number of grill bars and pizza places with quick bites for Dkr20 to Dkr35.

Café Rookie's (☎ 86 81 33 44; Nygade 18; sandwiches Dkr25-48; 🕑 11am-11pm) Does good ciabatta sandwiches, salads, smoothies and shakes and has a vegetarian menu for Dkr28 to Dkr49.

Nygade has several good music bars and discos. **Brews 'n Bongo** (🕑 from 11pm Thu, Fri & Sat) on the corner with Hostrupsgade is a late-night music bar and **Chaplin's** (🕑 until late Thu, Fri & Sat) is behind Café Rookie's. Both bars admit over-18s only.

Hourly trains connect Silkeborg with Århus (Dkr60, 49 minutes) via Ry. There are regular daily buses to Århus (Dkr48, 48 minutes).

AALBORG

pop 155,000

On the face of it, northerly Aalborg is an industrial and trading centre without many great buildings or much medieval quaintness to enliven its commercialism, but it's well worth a visit for the impressive Lindholm Høje, Denmark's largest Viking burial ground, and for its surprisingly vibrant and party-crazed nightlife. The town centre is a 10-minute walk from the train and bus stations, north on Boulevarden. The **tourist office** (☎ 99 30 60 90; www.visitaalborg.com; Østerågade 8; 🕑 9am-5.30pm Mon-Fri, 10am-1pm Sat mid-Jun–Aug, 10am-4pm Mon-Fri, 10am-4pm Sat Jul, 9am-4.30pm Mon-Fri, 10am-1pm Sat Sep–mid-Jun) is friendly and helpful, with masses of information. **Hovedbiblioteket** (City library; Rendsburggade 2; 🕑 10am-8pm Mon-Fri, 10am-3pm Sat) offers free Internet access.

Old Town

The whitewashed **Buldolfi Domkirke** marks the centre of the old town, and has colourful frescoes in the foyer. About 75m east of the cathedral is the **Aalborg Historiske Museum** (Algade 48; admission Dkr20; 🕑 9am-4pm Mon-Fri, 9am-2pm Sat) with interesting artefacts from prehistory to the present and Renaissance furnishings.

Lindholm Høje

On a hill-top pasture overlooking the city and ringed by a wall of tall beech trees,

Lindholm Høje (admission free; ☼ dawn-dusk) is the site of nearly 700 graves from the Iron Age and Viking age. Many of the Viking graves are marked by stones placed in the outline of a Viking ship, with two larger end stones as stem and stern. There is a compelling atmosphere. A **museum** (☎ 96 31 04 28; admission Dkr30; ☼ 10am-5pm Apr-Oct) depicts, in an imaginative way, the site's history, while huge murals behind the exhibits speculate on what the people of Lindholm looked like and how they lived; it is adjacent to the field. Lindholm Høje is 15 minutes from Aalborg centre on bus No 2.

Sleeping

The tourist office books rooms in private homes for Dkr200/300 for singles/doubles plus a Dkr25 booking fee.

Danhostel Aalborg (☎ 98 11 60 44; www.danhostel .dk/aalborg; Skydebanevej 50; dm Dkr118, r Dkr480; P ▯) At the marina 4km west of the centre; there's an adjacent camping ground with cabins.

Prinsens Hotel (☎ 98 13 37 33; www.prinsen-hotel .dk; Prinsensgade 14; s/d from Dkr545/645; P ✕ ▯) An up-market option, but good value, given the free extras available (such as Internet, solarium and tea and coffee). There's also a sauna and Jacuzzi.

Eating & Drinking

A good place for food, drink and diversion is Aalborg's famous Jomfru Ane Gade, a lively pedestrian street jammed solid with restaurants and bars, most with pavement tables and competitive prices. It is the heart of Aalborg's nightlife and most places are open to the early hours.

Sushi & Ko (☎ 98 10 98 40; Ved Stranden 11b; menus Dkr69-159; ☼ 4-10pm Mon-Fri, noon-10pm Sat, 3-9pm Sun) Sit and enjoy or pay and take away terrific, fresh, fresh sushi from this small place round the corner from Jomfru Ane Gade. Tackle the fierce but toothsome wasabi-roasted peas if you dare.

Algade, a pedestrian shopping street a block south of the tourist office, offers inexpensive options, including **Schak Nielsen** (☎ 98 12 35 92; Algade 23), a good fish shop that has takeaway salmon burgers and a range of tasty fish specialities. There's a bakery just opposite. **Café Underground** (Algade 21) offers natural ice cream, crepes and sandwiches.

A good budget drinking and entertainment option (and a surprisingly cosy one,

lined with books on shelves) is the **Studenterhuset** (student union; ☎ 98 11 05 22; Gammeltorv 10). There's inexpensive beer and regular live bands and DJ nights.

Getting There & Around

Trains run at least hourly to Århus (Dkr145, one hour 25 minutes) and every two hours to Frederikshavn (Dkr68, one hour). **Express buses** (☎ 70 21 08 88) run daily to Copenhagen (Dkr220, five hours).

City buses leave from the intersection of Østerågade and Nytorv. The bus fare is Dkr13 to any place in greater Aalborg.

FREDERIKSHAVN

pop 34,000

Frederikshavn is a major ferry town and industrial port with a fairly featureless dockside area; but the town has a pleasant pedestrianised centre with plenty of shops and several attractive bars and restaurants.

The **tourist office** (☎ 98 42 32 66; www.frederik shavn-tourist.dk; Skandiatorv 1; ☼ 8.30am-7pm Mon-Sat, 8.30am-5pm Sun Jul–mid-Aug, until 5pm daily last 2 weeks Jun & Aug, 9am-4pm Mon-Fri, 11am-2pm Sat Sep–mid-Jun) is a 10-minute walk south of the train station and adjacent bus terminal.

Danhostel Frederikshavn (☎ 98 42 14 75; www .danhostel.dk/frederikshavn; Buhlsvej 6; dm Dkr100, s/d Dkr240/300; ☼ Feb–mid-Dec; P ✕ &.) A pleasant, neat place with chalet-style six-bed dorms 2km north of the ferry terminal.

City Hostel (☎ 98 42 14 21; www.city-hostel.dk; s/d/tr/q Dkr200/300/400/500; P) Adjoining Hotel Herman Bang, this is a good, if basic, central budget option.

Damsgaard Supermarked (Havnegade), beside the tourist office, has a cheap cafeteria with a harbour view and a good buffet breakfast (Dkr45), and there are pizzerias on nearby Danmarksgade and Søndergade.

Frederikshavn is the northern terminus of the DSB train line. Trains run about hourly south to Aalborg (Dkr71.50) and on to Copenhagen (Dkr310). **Nordjyllands Trafikselskab** (NT; ☎ 98 11 11 11; www.nordjyllandstrafikselskab.dk) has both a train (40 minutes) and bus service (one hour) north to Skagen (Dkr45).

Stena Line (☎ 96 20 02 00) runs ferries six to 10 times daily (Dkr100 to Dkr160, two to 3¼ hours) from Frederikshavn to Gothenburg, Sweden. It also runs to Oslo once daily (Dkr170 to Dkr350, 8½ hours). Prices depend on season and day of week.

Color Line (☎ 99 56 20 00; www.colorline.com) has daily ferries to Larvik, Norway (Dkr180 to Dkr420, 6¼ hours).

SKAGEN

Artists (who came to be known as the 'Skagen School') discovered Skagen's luminous light and its colourful, heath-and-dune landscape in the mid-19th century and fixed eagerly on the romantic imagery of the area's fishing life that had earned the people of Skagen a hard living for centuries.

Today, Skagen is a major tourist resort, packed in high summer but picturesque even so. The peninsula is lined with fine beaches, including a sandy stretch on the eastern end of Østre Strandvej, a 15-minute walk from the town centre.

Sankt Laurentii Vej, Skagen's main street, runs almost the entire length of this long thin town. The **tourist office** (☎ 98 44 13 77; www .skagen-tourist.dk; Sankt Laurentii Vej 22; ⏰ 9am-6pm Mon-Sat, 10am-4pm Sun late Jun-early Aug, closes rest of Jun & Aug at 5pm, 9am-4pm Mon-Sat, 10am-1pm Sat May & Sep, otherwise earlier closing) is in the train/bus station.

Appropriately for such a neatly kept country, Denmark doesn't end untidily at its most northerly point, but on a neat finger of sand just a few metres wide. You can paddle at its tip, but not too far. Bathing is strictly forbidden here because of the ferocious tidal currents and often-angry seas that collide here.

The tip is the culmination of a long, curving sweep of sand at Grenen, about 3km northeast of Skagen along route 40. Crowds head along the last stretch of beach for the 30-minute walk to the tip.

Sleeping & Eating

Danhostel Skagen (☎ 98 44 22 00; www.danhostel.dk /skagen; Rolighedsvej 2; dm Dkr118, s/d from Dkr250/300; ♿ ℗) A 162-bed place 1km west of the centre.

You'll find a couple of pizzerias, a kebab shop, a burger joint and an ice-cream shop clustered near each other on Havnevej. **Super Brugsen** (Sankt Laurentii Vej 28), a grocery store just west of the tourist office, has a bakery.

Getting There & Around

Either a bus or a train leaves Skagen Station for Frederikshavn (Dkr45) about once an hour. The seasonal Skagerakkeren bus (No 99) runs half a dozen times daily between

Hirtshals and Skagen (Dkr37, 1½ hours) from mid-June to mid-August. The same bus continues on to Hjørring and Løkken.

Cycling is an excellent way of exploring Skagen and the surrounding area. **Skagen Cykeludlejning** (☎ 98 44 10 70; Banegårdspladsen) rents bicycles for Dkr75 a day (Dkr200 deposit) and has a stand on the western side of the train station and at the harbour.

HIRTSHALS
pop 7000

Hirtshals takes its breezy and friendly character from its commercial fishing harbour and ferry terminal. The seaward end of Nørregade opens out into a wide, airy space, Den Grønne Plads, the 'Green Square' that overlooks the fishing harbour and its tiers of blue-hulled boats. There is a **tourist office** (☎ 98 94 22 20; www.visithirtshals.com; Nørregade 40; ⏰ 9am-4pm Mon-Sat mid-Jul–Aug, 9am-4pm Mon-Fri, 9am-noon Sat Aug-Jun).

Hirtshals Hostel (☎ 98 94 12 48; www.danhostel nord.dk/hirtshals; Kystvejen 53; dm Dkr115, s/d Dkr350/400; ⏰ Mar-Nov) A basic place about 1km from the centre.

Staff at the tourist office can book rooms in private homes starting at Dkr150 plus a Dkr25 booking fee.

Hotel Hirtshals (☎ 98 94 20 77; info@hotelhirtshals .dk; Havnegade 2; s/d Dkr645/785), right on the main square above the fishing harbour, has bright, comfortable rooms with high, steepled ceilings and good sea views at the front.

There are cafés and a good bakery at the northern end of Hjørringgade, and a couple of pizza and kebab places on Nørregade.

From May to September there's a **bus** (☎ 70 13 14 15) from Hirtshals Station to Hjørring (Dkr22.50) that stops en route at Tornby Strand six times a day.

Hirtshals' main train station is 500m south of the ferry harbour, but there's also a stop near the Color Line terminal. The railway, which is operated by a private company, connects Hirtshals with Hjørring (Dkr22.50), 20 minutes to the south. Trains run at least hourly, with the last departure from Hjørring to Hirtshals at 10.25pm. From Hjørring you can take a DSB train to Aalborg (Dkr67.50) or Frederikshavn (Dkr45).

Color Line (☎ 99 56 20 00) runs year-round ferries to the Norwegian ports of Oslo (8½ hours, 10 times daily from May to September) and Kristiansand (2½ to five hours, four times daily from May to September). Fares on both routes are from Dkr180 midweek in the low season to Dkr420 on summer weekends for passengers, from Dkr160 to Dkr310 for a motorcycle and from Dkr220 to Dkr600 for a car.

RIBE
The crooked, cobblestone streets and half-timbered, 16th-century houses of Ribe, in southern Denmark, date from 869. It's one of the oldest towns in Scandinavia and was an important medieval trading centre. Almost everything, including the hostel and train station, is within 10 minutes' walk of Torvet, the town square, which is dominated by the huge Romanesque cathedral. The **tourist office** (☎ 75 42 15 00; www.ribetourist.dk; Torvet 3; ⏱ 9.30am-5.30pm Mon-Fri, 10am-5pm Sat, 10am-2pm Sun Jul & Aug, 9am-5pm Mon-Fri Apr-Jun & Sep, 9.30am-4.30pm Mon-Fri, 10am-1pm Oct-Dec), opposite, hands out *Sommer I Ribe*, a good events magazine.

Ribe Domkirke (☎ 75 42 06 19; Torvet; admission Dkr12) dominates the heart of the town and boasts a variety of styles from Romanesque to Gothic. Its monumental presence is literally sunk into the heart of Ribe. The cathedral floor is over 1m below the level of the surrounding streets.

Ribes Vikinger (☎ 76 88 11 22; Odins Plads 1; admission Dkr50; ⏱ 10am-6pm Jul & Aug, 10am-4pm Apr-Jun, Sep & Oct, 10am-4pm Tue-Sun Nov-Mar), a substantial museum opposite the train station, has archaeological displays of Ribe's Viking history, including a reconstructed marketplace and Viking ship, with lots of hands-on features.

Ribe Vikingecenter (☎ 75 41 16 11; Lustrupvej 4; admission Dkr60; ⏱ 11am-5pm Jul & Aug, 10am-3.30pm Tue-Sun May-Jun & Sep), 3km south of the centre, is a re-created Viking village complete with working artisans and interpreters decked out in period costumes. There are hands-on activities such as woodwork and archery to take part in during May to August, and animals such as ponies to pet. Bus No 51 (Dkr15) will take you there from Ribe.

Danhostel Ribe (☎ 75 42 06 20; www.danhostel .dk/ribe; Sankt Pedersgade 16; dm Dkr90, s Dkr270, d Dkr300-440; Ⓟ Ⓖ) The modern, 140-bed hostel has friendly staff and a good, uncrowded location. The new rooms at the top are especially appealing and worth splashing out extra for.

Weis Stue (☎ 75 42 07 00; www.weisstue.dk; Torvet; s/d with shared bathroom Dkr400/500) This weeny, ancient wood-beamed house has rather small, crooked rooms right above its restaurant but they have bags of character.

Jacob's (☎ 75 42 42 30; Nederdammen 36) Turns out good-value light lunches (Dkr35 to Dkr65), brunches (Dkr65), sandwiches (Dkr35 to Dkr42) and salads (Dkr45) in a pleasant setting. There are several fast-food outlets along Nederdammen.

There are trains from Esbjerg to Ribe (Dkr60, 40 minutes, hourly) and from Århus to Ribe (Dkr207, two hours 40 minutes, hourly).

DENMARK DIRECTORY

ACCOMMODATION
Camping & Cabins
Denmark's 516 camping grounds typically charge from Dkr50 to Dkr65 per person to pitch a tent. Many places add about Dkr20 for the tent. A camping pass (available at any camping ground) is required (Dkr80) and covers a family group with children under 18 for the season. If you do not have a seasonal pass you pay an extra Dkr20 a night for a temporary pass.

Camping is restricted to camping grounds, or on private land if you have the owner's permission.

Hostels
Most of Denmark's 100 *vandrerhjem* (hostels) in its Danhostel association have private rooms in addition to dormitory rooms, making hostels an affordable and popular alternative to hotels (so book ahead in summer). Dorm beds cost from about Dkr95 to Dkr118, while private rooms range from Dkr200 to Dkr450 for singles and Dkr300 to Dkr475 for doubles. Blankets and pillows are provided, but not sheets; bring your own or hire them for Dkr40. Sleeping bags are not allowed.

Travellers can buy international hostel cards in Denmark for Dkr160 or pay Dkr30 extra a night. All Danish hostels have an all-you-can-eat breakfast for Dkr45 or less. Nearly all hostels also have guest kitchens with pots and pans where you can cook your own food.

Danhostel (☎ 33 31 36 12; www.danhostel.dk; Vesterbrogade 39, 1620 Copenhagen V) is the national Hostelling International office.

Hotels

Budget hotels start at around Dkr450/600 for singles/doubles. *Kros*, a name that implies country inn but is more often the Danish version of a motel, are generally cheaper than hotels by about a third. Both hotels and *kros* usually include an all-you-can-eat breakfast.

Rates listed in this chapter include all taxes and are for rooms with toilet and shower, unless otherwise specified. Some hotels offer discount schemes from May to September, when business travel is light, and at weekends year-round.

ACTIVITIES

Cycling is a popular holiday activity in Denmark and there are thousands of kilometres of established cycling routes. Those around Bornholm, Funen and Møn, as well as the 440km Old Military Rd (Hærvejen) through central Jutland, are among the most popular.

Dansk Cyklist Forbund (DCF; ☎ 33 32 31 21; www .dcf.dk; Rømersgade 7, 1362 Copenhagen K) publishes *Cykelferiekort*, a cycling map of the entire country, as well as more detailed regional cycling maps.

DCF also publishes *Overnatning i det fri*, which lists hundreds of farmers who provide cyclists with a place to pitch a tent for Dkr15 a night. Cycling maps can be purchased in advance from DCF or from tourist offices and bookshops upon arrival.

Even though Denmark does not have substantial forests, many small tracts of woodland are crisscrossed by pleasant walking trails. **Skov og Naturstyrelsen** (Forest and Nature Bureau) produces brochures with sketch maps that show trails in nearly 100 such areas. The brochures can be picked up free at public libraries and some tourist offices. Denmark's coastline is public domain lined with scenic walking tracks.

Canoeing possibilities on Denmark's inland lakes, such as canoe touring between lakeside camp sites in Jutland's Lake District, are superb. You can hire canoes and equipment at many such camping grounds or in main centres such as Silkeborg. The lakes are generally undemanding as far as water conditions go although some experience is a help.

Denmark's remarkable coastline offers terrific windsurfing and kite-surfing possibilities. Good areas are along the northern coast of Zealand at places such as Smidstrup Strand, and in northwest Jutland.

BUSINESS HOURS

Office hours are generally 9am to 4pm Monday to Friday. Most banks are open 9.30am to 4pm Monday to Friday (to 6pm Thursday). Shops are usually open to 5.30pm Monday to Friday and 2pm on Saturday.

EMBASSIES & CONSULATES

For visa information, see p329.

Embassies & Consulates in Denmark

Australia (☎ 70 26 36 76; www.denmark.embassy.gov.au; Dampfægevej 26, Copenhagen)
Canada (☎ 33 48 32 00; www.canada.dk; Kristen Bernikows Gade1, Copenhagen)
Germany (☎ 35 45 99 00; www.kopenhagen.diplo.de; Stockholmsgade 57, Copenhagen)
Ireland (☎ 35 42 32 33; Østbanegade 21, Copenhagen)
Norway (☎ 33 14 01 24; www.norsk.dk; Amaliegade 39, Copenhagen)
Poland (☎ 39 46 77 00; www.ambpol.dk; Richelius Allé 12, Hellerup)
Sweden (☎ 33 36 03 70; www.sverigesambassad.dk; Sankt Annæ Plads 15A, Copenhagen)
UK (☎ 35 44 52 00; www.britishembassy.dk; Kastelsvej 40, Cope   nhagen)
USA (☎ 35 55 31 44; www.usembassy.dk; Dag Hammarskjölds Allé 24, Copenhagen)

Danish Embassies & Consulates Abroad

Australia (☎ 03-9247 2224; Suite 3, 546 Malvern Rd, Prahran East, VIC 3142)
Canada (☎ 613-562 1811; www.danish-embassy -canada.com; 47 Clarence St, Suite 450, Ottawa, Ontario K1N 9K1)
Finland (☎ 09-684 1050; www.kolumbus.fi/danmark; Centralgatan 1A, 00101 Helsinki)
Germany (☎ 030-5050 2000; www.daenemark.org; Rauchstrasse 1, 10787 Berlin)
Ireland (☎ 01-475 6404; www.denmark.ie; 121 St Stephen's Green, Dublin 2)
Netherlands (☎ 070-302 59 59; www.danishembassy .nl; Koninginnegracht 30, 2514 Den Haag)
New Zealand (☎ 09-537 3099; 273 Bleakhouse Rd, Howick, PO Box 619, 1015 Auckland)
Norway (☎ 22 54 08 00; www.denmark-embassy.no; Olav Kyrres Gate 7, 0244 Oslo)
Sweden (☎ 08-406 75 00; www.danemb.se; Jakobs Torg 1, 11186 Stockholm)
UK (☎ 020-7333 0200; www.amblondon.um.dk/en; 55 Sloane St, London SW1X 9SR)
USA (☎ 202-234 4300; www.denmarkemb.org; 3200 Whitehaven St NW, Washington, DC 20008)

FESTIVALS & EVENTS

Midsummer's Eve Begins with bonfires in late June, and Denmark buzzes with outdoor activity throughout the summer. Main attractions are the 180 music festivals that run almost nonstop throughout the country, covering a broad spectrum of music that includes not only jazz, rock and blues but also gospel, folk, classical, country, Cajun and much more.

Roskilde rock festival (last weekend June) This internationally acclaimed festival presents big international names; a single admission fee includes tent space and entry to all concerts.

Copenhagen Jazz Festival (early July) This acclaimed 10-day festival holds outdoor concerts and numerous performances in clubs around the city.

There are **folk festivals** in Skagen near the end of June and in Tønder in late August.

Århus Festival (early September) A 10-day event featuring an array of music and multicultural events.

GAY & LESBIAN TRAVELLERS

Denmark is a popular destination for gay and lesbian travellers. Copenhagen in particular has an active, open gay community and lots of nightlife options. A good English-language website with links to gay organisations is www.copenhagen-gay-life.dk.

HOLIDAYS

Summer holidays for schoolchildren begin around 20 June and finish around 10 August. Many Danes go on holiday during the first three weeks of July. Public holidays observed in Denmark:

New Year's Day 1 January
Maundy Thursday Thursday before Easter
Good Friday to Easter Monday March/April
Common Prayer Day Fourth Friday after Easter
Ascension Day Fifth Thursday after Easter
Whit Sunday Fifth Sunday after Easter
Whit Monday Fifth Monday after Easter
Constitution Day 5 June
Christmas Eve 24 December (from noon)
Christmas Day 25 December

LEGAL MATTERS

Although marijuana and hashish are available in Denmark, all forms of cannabis, and harder drugs, are illegal. If you are arrested for any offence in Denmark, you can be held up to 24 hours before appearing in court. You have a right to know the charges against you and a right to a lawyer. You are not obliged to answer police questions before speaking to a lawyer.

You can get free legal advice on your rights from the EU legal aid organisation **EURO-JUS** (☎ 33 14 41 40; ☼ 9am-6pm Mon-Thu, 9am-4.30pm Fri). Free legal advice clinics can be found in over 90 places across Denmark. The service is organised by the Danish bar, **Det Danske Advokatsamfund** (☎ 38 38 36 38).

MONEY

ATMs

Major banks have ATMs, the vast majority of them accessible outside normal banking hours, which accept Visa, MasterCard and the Cirrus and Plus bank cards. All major credit and debit cards are widely accepted throughout Denmark, although some shops impose a surcharge of up to 5% if you use them, even in the case of debit cards.

Changing Money

All common travellers cheques are accepted in Denmark. Buy your travellers cheques in higher denominations as bank fees for changing money are a hefty Dkr25 to Dkr30 per cheque, with a Dkr40 minimum for the transaction (so one cheque or two costs Dkr40 regardless). If you're exchanging cash, there's a Dkr25 fee for a transaction. Travellers cheques command a better exchange rate than cash by about 1%.

Post offices will also exchange foreign currency at comparable rates to those at banks.

The Euro

Although Denmark remains outside the euro zone, euros are widely accepted, apart from by government institutions and in more remote areas.

Tipping & Bargaining

Restaurant bills and taxi fares include service charges in the quoted prices and further tipping is unnecessary. Bargaining is not a common practice in Denmark.

VAT

The Danish sales tax is a steep 25%, although non-EU residents can claim back between 14% to 19% of the price of items they are taking home which cost over Dkr300. For further details go to www.globalrefund.com.

POST

Denmark has an efficient postal system. Most post offices are open 9am or 10am to 5pm or

5.30pm Monday to Friday and 9am to noon on Saturday. You can receive mail c/o poste restante at any post office in Denmark.

TELEPHONE
There are no regional country codes. It costs Dkr3 to make a local call at coin phones. You get about twice as much calling time for your money on domestic calls made between 7.30pm and 8am daily and all day on Sunday. Phonecards (Dkr30 to Dkr100) can be bought at post offices and newspaper kiosks.

VISAS
Citizens of the EU, USA, Canada, Australia and New Zealand need a valid passport to enter Denmark, but don't need a visa for stays of less than three months. If you wish to apply for a visa make sure to do so at least three months in advance of your planned arrival.

Estonia

HIGHLIGHTS

▪ **Tallinn's Town Hall Square** A trip to Estonia wouldn't be complete without several hours of blissful hanging out on the city's main square, nursing a beer at one of the cafés (p335)

▪ **Oleviste Kirik (St Olaf's Church)** The city's best viewpoint can be accessed by climbing 60m up one of Tallinn's narrowest staircases; you're forgiven if you get dizzy (p337)

▪ **Pärnu** Estonia's summer party capital, where you can go clubbing, then crash on the beach and be greeted by a sweet sunrise across Pärnu Bay (p343)

▪ **Student Days Festival** Visiting Tartu in late April when it rocks hardest, as the university's students let it all – and everything else – hang out! (p340)

▪ **Best journey** For a day or two, spend time looking for beavers, canoeing or discovering your own slice of deserted coastland, and take a plunge at Lahemaa National Park (p339)

▪ **Off-the-beaten track** Go where some tourists fear to sweat – a furnace-like sauna to release all those toxins! (p337)

FAST FACTS

▪ **Area** 45, 226 sq km (1½ times the size of Belgium)

▪ **ATMS** Available everywhere

▪ **Budget** 260-390EEK per day

▪ **Capital** Tallinn

▪ **Country Code** ☎ 372

▪ **Famous for** Supermodel Carmen Kass; composer Arvo Pärt

▪ **Head of State** President Arnold Rüütel

▪ **Language** Estonian (a Finno-Ugric language)

▪ **Money** Kroon (A$1 = 9.21EEK, CA$1 = 10.07EEK, €1=15.6EEK, ¥100 = 11.48EEK, NZ$1 = 8.58EEK, UK£1 = 23.26EEK, US$1 = 13.04EEK)

▪ **Phrases** Tere! (hi!), äitah (thanks), mis su nimi on? (what's your name?), kui palju sa maksab? (how much does this cost?)

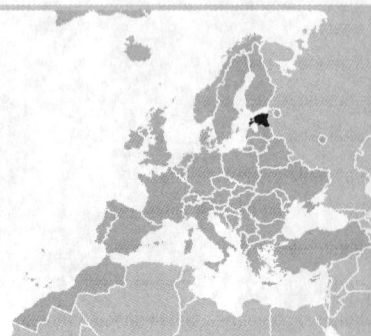

▪ **Population** 1.35 million

▪ **Time** GMT/UTC + 2

▪ **Visas** None required for travellers from the EU, the USA, Canada and Australia. South Africans require visas but can enter on Latvian and Lithuanian visas.

TRAVEL HINTS

You'll get on well with Estonians if you can have fun while not being loud or showy!

ROAMING ESTONIA

Tallinn's Old Town is the main must-see, but try to check out Tartu, Otepää or Pärnu's beaches as well.

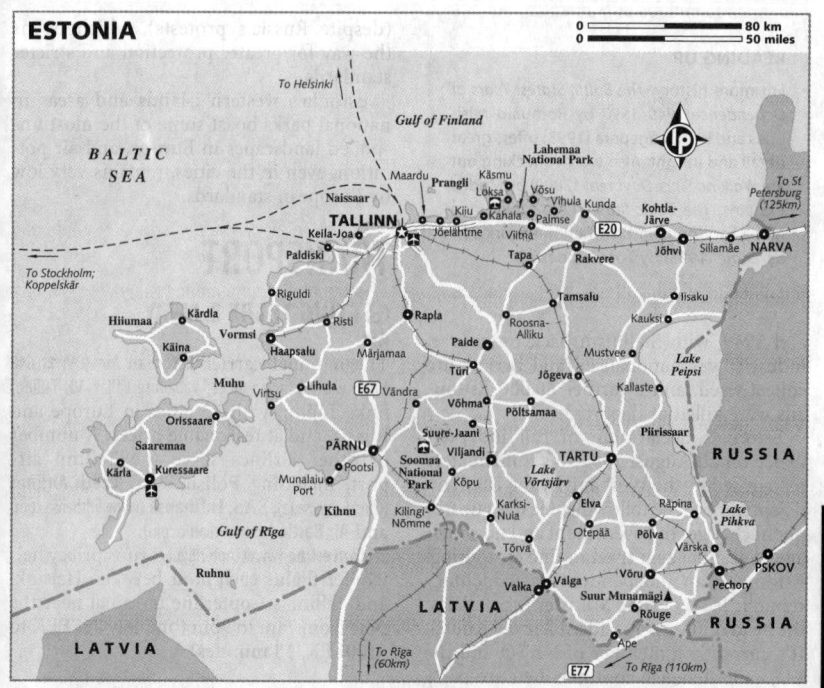

ESTONIA

0 _____ 80 km
0 _____ 50 miles

BALTIC SEA

To Helsinki

Gulf of Finland

To Stockholm;
Koppelskär

To St Petersburg
(125km)

Naissaar · Maardu · Prangli · Käsmu · Lahemaa National Park · Vihula · Kunda
TALLINN · Loksa · Vōsu · Palmse · Kohtla-Järve
Keila-Joa · Jōelähtme · Kiiu · Kahala · Viitna · Tapa · Rakvere · Jōhvi · Sillamäe · NARVA
Paldiski · E20
Riguldi · Risti · Rapla · Tamsalu · Kauksi · Iisaku
Hiiumaa · Kärdla · Vormsi · Haapsalu · Mārjamaa · Paide · Roosna-Alliku · Mustvee · *Lake Peipsi*
Käina · Lihula · E67 · Vändra · Türi · Jōgeva · Kallaste
Muhu · Virtsu · Vōhma · Pōltsamaa
Orissaare · Suure-Jaani · Viljandi · TARTU · Piirissaar · RUSSIA
Saaremaa · PÄRNU · Soomaa National Park · Kōpu · *Lake Vōrtsjärv* · Elva · Rāpina · *Lake Pihkva*
Kārla · Kuressaare · Munalaiu Port · Pootsi · Karksi-Nuia · Otepää · Pōlva · Vārska · PSKOV
Kihnu · Kilingi-Nōmme · Tōrva · Vōru · Pechory
Gulf of Riga · Valka · Valga · Suur Munamägi · Rōuge · RUSSIA
Ruhnu · LATVIA · Ape · E77
To Riga (60km) · To Riga (110km)

LATVIA

ESTONIA

Ten years ago it didn't help to describe Estonia's location as 'in the Baltics' or even 'near Finland' – the first made people think of a war zone; the second brought images of snow drifts and vodka. (Well, at least the vodka part was right!) Now that this bite-sized country has joined the EU, the word is out that Estonia is the pretty little country that could – and did! Its subtle, quiet charm weaves its way into your heart before you're aware of it.

Tallinn, Estonia's capital, is one of the coolest spots in Europe. Visitors trade stories about haunting Gothic spires poking out from the seductive Old Town (northern Europe's best preserved), the tasty local beer, the wild discos, and how mobile phone–addicted and Internet-literate everyone is. Outside the capital, there are interesting and nature-soaked excursions.

Nearly every Estonian speaks fluent English, so communication is not likely to be a problem. While the population is quite homogenous, the significant Russian minority lends a welcome contrast with its reputation for being extroverted and spontaneous where Estonians tend to be quieter and more cautious.

HISTORY

Most of Estonia's history has been one of occupation and domination. Bandied about between European major powers, it has enjoyed only sparse periods of independence, notably in the 20th century between the World Wars and since 1991.

In the 3rd millennium BC Finno-Ugric tribes from the east mixed with the Baltic tribes already there.

The Germanic Teutonic Order took control in 1346, placing Estonians under servi-

tude to a German nobility that would last until the early 20th century despite Danish, Swedish and Russian rulers.

After the Great Northern War (1700–21), Estonia became part of the Russian Empire. During WWI, the Soviet government relinquished Estonia. Until 1940 Estonia was ruled by benevolent dictator Konstantin Päts, who was forced to accept Soviet occupation. After fabricated elections, over 10,000 Estonians were killed or deported before German occupation. Between 1945

READING UP

For more history, *The Baltic States: Years of Dependence 1940–1990* by Romuald Misiunas and Rein Taagepera (1993) offers great detail and insight. Also worth checking out are *Walking Since Daybreak* (2000) by Modris Eksteins, *The Baltic States* (2002) by Signe Maria Landgren and the fictional work *Border State* (1993) by Tõnu Õnnepalu.

---

and 1949, with Stalinism back on course, industry was nationalised and agriculture collectivised, and a further 60,000 Estonians were killed or deported.

Estonia's declaration of full independence on 20 August 1991 was immediately recognised by the West and by the USSR on 6 September. The following decade saw frequent changes of government and no shortage of scandal as it tried to find its footing. Estonia is an independent parliamentary republic led by Prime Minister Juhan Parts; the head of state is President Arnold Rüütel. It's currently a member of NATO and the EU, and intends to continue the Euro party until the wee hours!

PEOPLE & CULTURE

Estonia's population of 1.35 million is 68% Estonian, 26% Russian, and 3% Ukrainian and Belarusian, with a growing number of resident, retired Finns. The Russian speakers are concentrated in Tallinn and in the industrial northeast, forming around 40% and up to 96% of the respective populations.

The Estonians are historically a rural people cautious of outsiders and stereotypically shy and reticent. They are nature lovers who enjoy a sauna with friends by a cool lake. Estonians have a habit of taking flowers whenever they go visiting or attend any kind of celebration. When visiting, always remove your shoes before entering someone's home.

ENVIRONMENT

Since independence, there have been major 'clean-up' attempts to counter the effects of Soviet-era industrialisation. In 2004 the International Marine Organisation designated the heavily polluted Baltic Sea one of the planet's five particularly sensitive areas

(despite Russia's protests), which opens the way for greater protection and stricter standards.

Estonia's western islands and areas in national parks boast some of the most unspoiled landscapes in Europe, and air pollution, even in the cities, remains very low by European standards.

TRANSPORT

GETTING THERE & AWAY

Air

The national carrier **Estonian Air** (OV; ☎ 640 1101; www.estonian-air.ee; Vabaduse väljak 10, Tallinn) links Tallinn with 13 cities in Europe and Russia, and at reasonable prices. A number of other airlines serve the Tallinn airport, including Polish LOT, **Czech Airlines** (ČSA; www.csa.cz), SAS, **Lufthansa** (www.lufthansa.com) and **Air Baltic** (www.airbaltic.com).

Copterline (www.copterline.ee) runs pricey helicopter flights each hour between Helsinki and Tallinn's Copterline terminal near the port from 7am to 9pm (one way 767EEK to 3100EEK, 18 minutes).

Boat

FINLAND

About 25 ferries and hydrofoils (catamarans) cross between Helsinki and Tallinn daily. Ferries make the crossing in 2½ to 3½ hours, hydrofoils in just over an hour. All companies provide concessions and charge higher prices for weekend travel. Expect to pay around the price of an adult ticket extra to take a car.

Tallink (☎ 640 9808; www.tallink.ee) runs up to 12 ferries and hydrofoils daily from terminals A and D. Ferry tickets start from 190EEK, and hydrofoils cost from 315EEK. **Lindaline** (☎ 699 9333) makes up to eight hydrofoil crossings each way daily from the Linnahall Terminal, to the west of the other main port terminals. A one-way trip costs from 345EEK. **Eckerö Line** (☎ 631 8606) operates a daily or twice-daily auto catamaran from terminal B, making the crossing in 3½ hours, with one-way tickets starting from 220EEK. **Nordic Jet Line** (☎ 613 7000) has several auto catamarans departing terminal C, making the trip in around 1½ hours several times a day; one-way/return tickets cost from 300EEK. There are also **Silja Line**

(☎ 611 6661; www.silja.ee) ferries that make the crossing between Tallinn and Helsinki in 1½ hours, with worthwhile day-trip packages available to Helsinki (from 340EEK, departing from terminal D).

SWEDEN

Tallink (☎ 640 9808; www.tallink.ee) runs nightly ferries from Tallinn's terminal D to Stockholm (from 650EEK, 15 hours), as well as daily ferries from Paldiski, 52km west of Tallinn, to Kappelskär near Stockholm (from 450EEK, 12 hours). There are slight reductions for students and children (under 18). Tickets should be booked well in advance in Tallinn or at Stockholm's **Frihamnen** (Free Port; ☎ 08-667 0001).

Bus

Buses are the cheapest but least comfortable way of reaching the Baltics. All long-distance domestic and international buses arrive and depart from the Autobussijaam (central bus station). **Eurolines** (☎ 680 0909; www.eurolines.ee; Lastekodu tänav 46, Tallinn), inside the bus station, runs direct buses daily to Tallinn from several destinations in Germany. Direct services connect Tallinn to Riga in Latvia (200EEK to 275EEK, five to 5½ hours, eight daily) and Vilnius in Lithuania (370EEK, 10½ hours, two daily).

Buses leave Tallinn for St Petersburg, Russia, five times daily (280EEK, eight hours). There is also one bus from Tallinn to Kaliningrad daily (300EEK, 15 hours).

Car & Motorcycle

From Finland, just put your vehicle on a Helsinki–Tallinn ferry.

Train

St Petersburg and Tallinn are serviced by an overnight train on alternate evenings (2nd/3rd class 370/196EEK, 8¾ hours). An overnight train runs every evening between Moscow and Tallinn (2nd/3rd class 690/490EEK, 15½ hours).

GETTING AROUND
Air

Avies Air (☎ 605 8022; www.avies.ee; airport) operates flights from Tallinn to Kuressaare on Saaremaa (385EEK, one to two daily) from Sunday to Friday.

TOP FIVE ESTONIA

- **Festival** Tallinn's Old Town Days (p345) in early June brings the medieval back into full swing.

- **Walk** Explore up and down the narrow cobbled streets of Tallinn's Old Town (p334) and be prepared for a charm attack!

- **Restaurant** Tallinn's Olde Hansa (p338) is a good bet for dropping a wad of cash but being happy you did so!

- **Impressive sight** Yes, these frigid northern shores have great beaches; Pärnu's (p343) wins the contest here.

- **Getaway** Break free from Tallinn for a dayscapade into nature at Lahemaa National Park (p339).

Bicycle

Estonia is predominantly flat, with good roads and light traffic, and distances between urban centres are relatively small. As few locals cycle within main cities, be wary of inconsiderate motorists. A number of travel agencies offer bicycle tours.

Bus

Long-distance buses serve all major Estonian towns. Buses are generally cheaper, more frequent and faster, and they cover many destinations not serviced by trains.

Buses to within about 40km of Tallinn leave from the local bus platform beside the train station. Information and timetables can be had 24 hours via **Harju Linnid** (☎ 644 1801). For detailed bus information and advance tickets for all other country destinations, contact the **Autobussijaam** (central bus station; ☎ 680 0900; www.bussireisid.ee; Lastekodu tänav 46).

EMERGENCY NUMBERS

- **Fire, ambulance or urgent medical advice** ☎ 112
- **First-aid hotline** ☎ 697 1145
- **Info Line** ☎ 626 1111
- **Police** ☎ 110
- **Roadside assistance** ☎ 1188

ESTONIA

Car & Motorcycle

An International Driving Permit (IDP) is necessary, as are your vehicle's registration papers and compulsory accident insurance, which can be bought at border crossings.

Train

Trains are slower and rarer than buses; the most frequent trains service the suburbs of Tallinn. Regional train schedules are listed at www.edel.ee.

TALLINN

pop 400,000

One of Europe's smallest capitals is in the mood to celebrate these days and it's inviting everyone along to the party. To a city that already had a lot going for it (beaches, parks, one of Europe's most enchanting and best-preserved Old Towns, raucous nightclubs and cheap beer!), add a freshly built, new downtown and recent entry into the EU. With every reason to expect a bright future, Tallinn is strutting its stuff and waiting to be admired.

The jewel in Tallinn's crown remains the beautiful two-tiered Old Town, a 14th- and 15th-century jumble of turrets, spires and winding cobbled streets. An old Hanseatic trading town, Tallinn was dominated mainly by German barons, then Russian/Soviet forces until its rebirth as an independent capital in 1991. Despite its small size and easy-going rhythm of life, it boasts a vibrant populace of Estonians and Russians (about 40% of the population), and loads of opportunities for fun and discovery.

GETTING INTO TOWN

From the airport, just 3km from the centre, take bus No 2 for five stops; the taxi mafia outside should not charge more than 50EEK to 60EEK for the same journey. From the Autobussijaam (bus station), walk one block to Tartu maantee, cross the street and hop on any tram into town; the Old Town's but four stops away. The train station is directly across the street, to the northwest, from the Old Town and is served by trams No 1 & 2, which whisk you downtown in three or four stops.

ORIENTATION

The medieval Old Town, just to the south of Tallinn Bay, comprises Toompea (the upper town) and the lower town. The lower town spreads around the eastern foot of Toompea, which is still surrounded by much of its 2.5km defensive wall. Its centre is Raekoja plats (Town Hall Square). Around the Old Town is a belt of green parks that follow the line of the city's original moat defences. Immediately west of the Old Town is the modern city centre, with shopping plazas and the closest Estonia has to skyscrapers.

INFORMATION
Discount Card

Available from the Tallinn tourist office (see opposite), the **Tallinn Card** (60-325EEK) gives free admission to museums, discounts and rides on public transport.

Internet Access

Matrix Club (☎ 641 9442; Tartu Maantee 31; per hr 15EEK; ☯ 24 hr)

Neo Internetcafé (☎ 628 2333; Väike Karja tänav 12; per hr 35EEK; ☯ 24 hr) Full printing services.

Medical Services

Aia Apteek (☎ 627 3607; Aia tänav 10; ☯ 8.30am-midnight) One of the many well-stocked pharmacies around town.

East Tallinn Central Hospital (☎ 620 7015; Ravi tänav 18; ☯ 24 hr) Full range of services, including a polyclinic and a 24-hour emergency room.

Money

Currency exchange is available at all transport terminals, exchange bureaus around the city, the post office and inside all banks and major hotels. ATMs are numerous.

Estravel (☎ 626 6266; www.estravel.ee; Suur-Karja tänav 15) This travel agency is also the official agent for American Express.

Tavid (☎ 627 9900; Aia tänav 5; ☯ 24 hr) Reliably good rates.

Post

Central Post Office (☎ 625 7300; fax receiving service 661 6054; Narva maantee 1; incoming faxes per page 12EEK; ☯ 7.30am-8pm Mon-Fri, 8am-6pm Sat) Full postal services.

Telephone

If you're one of the few not sporting a mobile phone, you can buy 30EEK, 50EEK and

100EEK chip cards from newsstands to use for local and international calls at any of the blue phone boxes scattered around town.

Tourist Information

Visit the **tourist office** (☎ 645 7777; www.visitestonia .com; Niguliste tänav 2; 9am-8pm Mon-Fri, 10am-6pm Sat & Sun May-Aug, 9am-6pm Mon-Fri, 10am-5pm Sat & Sun Sep; 9am-5pm Mon-Fri, 10am-3pm Sat Oct-Apr) to pick up free and paid maps and booklets, get info about travel to all regions of Estonia, buy museum discount cards, and arrange accommodation, guides and excursions.

Travel Agencies

City and country tours, guided trips to provincial Estonia and accommodation in other towns are all part of most travel agencies' stock in trade. Leading ones:
Baltic Tours (☎ 630 0460; www.bt.ee; Pikk tänav 31)
Estonian Holidays (☎ 627 0500; www.holidays.ee; Lai tänav 5)
Estravel (☎ 626 6266; www.estravel.ee; Suur-Karja tänav 15)

SIGHTS
Raekoja Plats & Around

Compact Raekoja plats (Town Hall Square) has been the centre of Tallinn life since the 11th century. It's dominated by northern Europe's only surviving Gothic **town hall** (☎ 645 7900; adult/student 25/15EEK; tower 11am-6pm May-Aug), built 1371–1404. Vana Toomas (Old Thomas), Tallinn's symbol and guardsman, has been keeping watch perched on his weathervane atop the building since 1530. Toomas was a much-beloved 16th-century Town Hall guard. The **Raeapteek** (Town Council Pharmacy), on the north side of the square, is another ancient Tallinn institution; there's been a pharmacy or apothecary's shop here since at least 1422. An arch beside it leads into narrow Saia käik (White Bread Passage), at the far end of which is the lovely 14th-century Gothic **Pühavaimu Kirik** (Holy Spirit Church; ☎ 644 1487; 10am-4pm, free concerts 6pm Mon), with carvings from 1684 and a tower bell cast in 1433.

A medieval merchant's home at Vene tänav 17, on the corner of Pühavaimu tänav, houses Tallinn's most interesting museum – the **Linnamuuseum** (City Museum; ☎ 644 6553; Vene tänav 17; adult/student 25/10EEK; 10.30am-6pm Wed-Mon Mar-Oct, 10.30am-7pm Nov-Feb), which traces Tallinn's development through to 1940 via creative interactive displays, period recreations and old documents. The 20th-century section will satisfy your thirst for Soviet propaganda material.

From Vene an arched doorway leads into a cosy courtyard and the world of the **Dominican Monastery** (☎ 644 4606; kloostri@hot.ee; Vene tänav 16/18; admission 25/15EEK; 9.30am-6pm mid-May–mid-Sep), founded in 1246 as a base for Scandinavian monks. Today the monastery complex houses Estonia's largest collection of very impressive **stone carvings**.

The majestic **Niguliste Kirik** (St Nicholas' Church; ☎ 644 9911; Niguliste tänav 3; adult/student 35/20EEK; 10am-5pm Wed-Sun), a minute's walk south of Raekoja plats, is now used to stage concerts and serves as a museum of medieval church art.

At the foot of the slope below the Niguliste are the exposed foundations of buildings that stood there before the Soviet bombing of Tallinn on the night of 9 March 1944.

Toompea

A regal approach to Toompea is through the red-roofed 1380 **gate tower** at the western end of Pikk tänav in the lower town, and then along Pikk jalg (Long Leg). The 19th-century, still-active Russian Orthodox **Alexander Nevsky Cathedral** (☎ 644 3484; 8am-7pm) dominates Lossi plats at the top of Pikk jalg, sited strategically across from **Toompea Castle**, traditionally Estonia's seat of power. Only a section of the Old Town wall and the **Pikk Herman Bastion**, from which the state flag flies, are left from medieval times. The *riigikogu* (parliament) meets in the pink, baroque-style building in front, an 18th-century addition. To take a cool virtual tour of Toompea, check out www.tallinn.info/toompea.

The Lutheran **Toomkirik** (Dome Church; ☎ 644 4140; Toomkooli tänav 6; 9am-5pm Tue-Sun) is Estonia's oldest church, founded in 1219 (though the exteriors date from the early 14th century). Across the way from Toomkirik, an 18th-century noble's house is now the **Rüütelkonnahoone** (Knighthood House; ☎ 644 9340; Kiriku plats 1; adult/student 20/5EEK; 11am-6pm Wed-Sun), the Art Museum of Estonia's main branch, featuring Estonian artists. There are several **lookouts** nearby, from which to peer across the Old Town roofs and snap those touristy photos to take home; artists and souvenir vendors set up stands here as well.

CENTRAL TALLINN

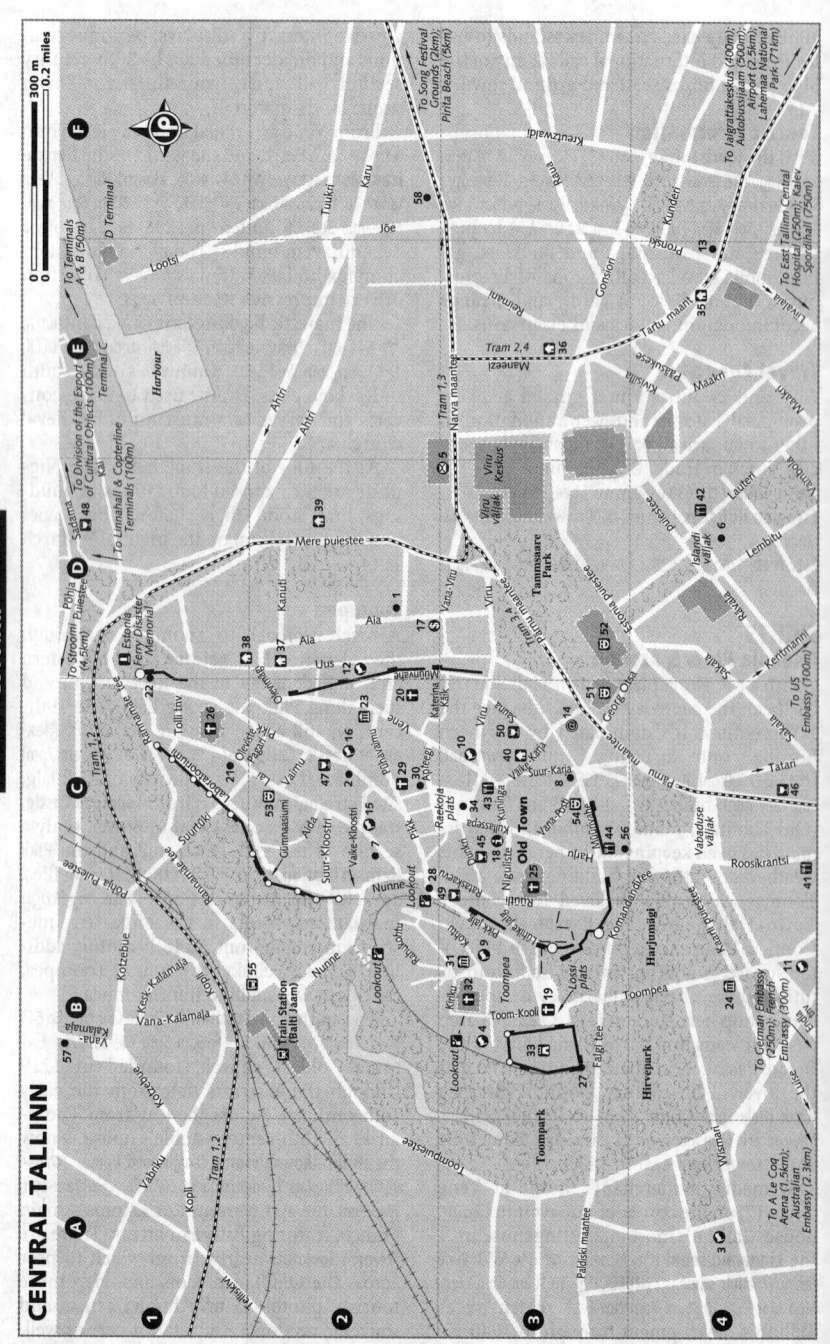

The **Museum of Occupation & Fight for Freedom** (☎ 668 0250; Toompea tänav 8; adult/student 10/5EEK; ☽ 11am-6pm Tue-Sun), just down the hill from Toompea, is a new and worthwhile exhibit on Estonia's history of occupation, focusing on the most recent Soviet one.

Lower Town

Pikk tänav, running north from Raekoja plats to the **Great Coast Gate** and the **Fat Margaret Bastion** (the medieval exit to Tallinn port), is lined with many 15th-century houses of medieval merchants and gentry. Also here are the buildings of several old Tallinn guilds, and some museums.

Near the end of Pikk tänav stands a chief Tallinn landmark, **Oleviste Kirik** (St Olaf's Church). This is a great place to start any Tallinn expedition as there's a superb **observation deck** (☎ 621 4421; adult/student 20/10EEK; ☽ 10am-6pm) halfway up its 124m structure offering the city's best views of the Old Town (it's a long and narrow climb up, though – bring a hanky to wipe off the sweat). First built in the early 13th century, this was once the world's tallest building (it used to be 159m high before a major fire and several reconstructions). Just south of the church is the **former KGB headquarters** (Pikk tänav 46/48); the basement windows were bricked up to conceal the sounds of interrogations from those on the street above.

ACTIVITIES

The sauna is an Estonian institution and is seen as almost a religious experience. **Kalma Saun** (☎ 627 1811; Vana-Kalamaja 9A; admission 65-75EEK Mon-Thu, 90EEK Fri-Sun; ☽ 10am-11pm) is the best of the public saunas.

In Tallinn, the most popular beaches are at Pirita and Stroomi.

TOURS

Raeturist (☎ 668 8400; www.raeturist.ee; Narva maantee 13A) organises accommodation, transport, city tours of all kinds and excellent cross-country bicycle tours.

FESTIVALS & EVENTS

One of Tallinn's hot-ticket events is the mid-April **Jazzkaar** (www.jazzkaar.ee), bringing together jazz greats from around the world in a series of concerts.

Usually lasting four days, the **Old Town Days** festival in early June sees the Old Town come alive with market stalls, concerts, dancing and medieval-themed merry-making.

SLEEPING

In the last 10 years, a sumptuous array of top-end hotels has sprouted across Tallinn's landscape. The city's still focused on luring big spenders, it seems, from the relatively small choice of decent, central budget options. All is not lost, however; there are a few great hostels and, if you don't mind public

ESTONIA

transport, good options outside the centre. To rent a central, modern apartment for up to four people from 1500EEK a night, contact **Cassandra Apartments** (☎ 630 9820; www .cassandra-apartments.com; Tartu maantee 18). **Rasastra Bed & Breakfast** (☎ 661 6291; www.bedbreakfast.ee; Mere puiestee 4) can set you up with a room in a private home from 260EEK per person.

Old House (☎ 641 1464; www.oldhouse.ee; Uus tänav 22 & 26; dm 290EEK, 1-/2-/3-/5-/6-person room 390/ 550/825/900/1080EEK, guesthouse s/d/tr 450/650/975EEK, apt 950-2000EEK) You won't get a better location than at this recently refurbished hostel-guesthouse filling two nearly adjacent houses in the Old Town. Sure, the walls are paper-thin, but it's cosy and spotless, and a hearty breakfast is included. The apartments are a good splurge. Holders of an ISIC get 10% off all rates.

Vana Tom (☎ 631 3252; Väike-Karja tänav 1; dm Hostelling International member/nonmember 220/235EEK, dm from 595EEK) As a place to crash, this is a great option – if, that is, you arrive soused and ready to pass out. It feels crowded (dorm rooms hold nine, 12 and 15 beds) and the noise from the upstairs strip club can be annoying. Otherwise, it has an excellent location and is squeaky clean.

Hotel G9 (☎ 626 7100; www.hotelg9.ee; Gonsiori tänav 9; s/d/tr 500/600/750EEK) Just a two-minute walk from the new city centre, this nondescript but modern and cheerful place is a very good deal.

Stroomi (☎ 630 4200; Randla tänav 11; s 500-550EEK, d 700-950EEK) Some 5km from the centre (a 40EEK to 50EEK taxi ride or 20 minutes on bus No 40 or 3, both from Viru Väljak), this fairly nondescript though perfectly decent place has some advantages: it's a two-minute

---

SPLURGE!

Olde Hansa (☎ 627 9020; Vana turg 1; mains 75-225EEK; 🕓 11am-midnight) If you splurge just once in Tallinn, here's where to do it. This medieval-themed restaurant (more authentic than kitsch!) boasts first and foremost the most ebullient and friendly service in the city, plus exotic meats (elk, wild boar) and homemade delights (such as juniper cheese and honey beer). It's a fun atmosphere inside or out on the terrace, and the food and its creative presentation is always first rate.

---

walk from a beach, and you get to see a different side of Tallinn life in this residential, mainly Russian neighbourhood. Bicycle and inline-skate rental are available.

EATING

Many ethnic restaurants can be found, serving anything from Turkish mezes to Thai Kai Phad – though even on exotic dishes be prepared for an Estonian touch (the sudden appearance of sour cream or cucumbers, for example)! Very reasonable lunch specials (30EEK to 50EEK) abound in the city, so it's economical to fill up in the daytime. There are fast-food options along Viru tánav and inside the **Viru Keskus shopping centre** (Viru väljak). All places listed under Drinking (following) also serve up tasty grub.

Café VS (☎ 626 2627; www.cafevs.ee; Pärnu Maantee 28; mains 55-125EEK; 🕓 10am-1am Mon-Thu, 10am-3am Fri & Sat, 1pm-1am Sun) A trendsetter on the food and club-music scene for years, this fashion-conscious restaurant, bar and, by night, club takes its industrial décor seriously – and so does its very beautiful-people clientele. The expansive menu specialises in Indian food – it's the city's best, hands down. Many vegetarian options.

Eesti Maja (☎ 645 5252; www.eestimaja.ee; Lauteri tänav 1; buffet 75EEK, meals from 125EEK; 🕓 11am-11pm) Here's a good place to sample some traditional Estonian fare in a fun, folksy interior. The small weekday lunch buffet is a good deal and lets you try some of the heavy, exotic fare without a full-plate commitment.

Pizza Americano (☎ 644 8837; Müürivahe tänav 2; pizzas from 85EEK; 🕓 11.30am-10.30pm) Thick, tasty pizzas of every possible permutation and combination are on offer here, including several vegetarian options.

DRINKING

Tallinn without its café and bar culture is simply inconceivable. Even in Soviet times, Tallinn was renowned for its cafés. Due to the charm of the surroundings, the Old Town is the obvious place to head to for cellar bars and absurdly cosy cafés.

Tristan ja Isolde (☎ 644 8749; Town Hall, Raekoja plats 1; 🕓 8am-11pm) You may be turned off Starbucks forever when you step into this tiny café, an essential stop for lovers of fine coffee in intimate medieval surroundings.

Beer House (☎ 627 6520; Dunkri tänav 5; 🕓 9am-midnight Sun-Thu, 9am-4am Fri-Sat) A little piece of Austria in the heart of the Old Town, this multileveled place is great for a night of revelling in the company of many foreigners and a few locals. Tallinn's only microbrewery is located here and whips up a prize-winning array of fresh beers (30EEK to 40EEK). There's also a nightclub, and a sauna for rent by the hour upstairs.

Hell Hunt (☎ 681 8333; Pikk tänav 39; ☺ noon-2am) A trooper on the pub circuit for years, this place boasts an amiable atmosphere and reasonable prices for locally brewed beer and cider (half-litre for 24EEK).

Von Krahli Teater Baar (☎ 626 9096; Rataskaevu tänav 10/12; ☺ noon-1am Sun-Thu, noon-3am Fri & Sat) A good place to relax any time, this is one of the city's best hang-outs. It often has live bands (and sometimes stages fringe plays) and is a good place to meet the interesting locals.

CLUBBING

Club Hollywood (☎ 627 4770; www.club-hollywood.ee; Vana-Posti tänav 8; ☺ 10pm-5am Wed-Sat) A multilevel emporium of mayhem, this is the one to draw the largest crowds. Their Friday hip-hop eves are the most popular.

Terrarium (☎ 661 4721; Sadama tänav 6; ☺ 10pm-5am Wed-Sat) A more down-to-earth club experience is ensured here – prices are lower and there's less attitude than in the posher Old Town clubs. The DJs still kick out the disco, and the 20-something crowd eats it up.

Gay & Lesbian Venues

X-Baar (☎ 692 9266; Sauna tänav 1; ☺ 2pm-1am) The only place in the Old Town flying the rainbow flag is Tallinn's premier gay bar, whose miniscule dance floor comes alive late on weekends.

G-Punkt (Pärnu maantee 23; ☺ 4pm-midnight Sun-Tue & Thu, 4pm-2am Wed, Fri & Sat) The fact that this club is hidden in an alley behind Pärnu maantee and has no sign recalls the secrecy of old Eastern European gay bars. Friendly and cosy. Wednesday night is the big disco night.

ENTERTAINMENT
Theatre

Estonia Theatre & Concert Hall (theatre ☎ 626 0215, concert hall ☎ 614 7760; Estonia puiestee 4) The city's biggest concerts and shows are held here. This is Tallinn's main theatre, also housing the Estonian national opera and ballet.

Estonian Drama Theatre (☎ 680 5555; Pärnu maantee 5) Stages mainly classical plays and tends to avoid modern or alternative fare.

Linnateater (City Theatre; ☎ 665 0800; www.linna teater.ee; Lai tänav 23) This theatre always stages something memorable – watch for their summer plays on an outdoor stage.

Sport

A Le Coq Arena (☎ 627 9940; Asula tänav 4c) This sparkling, newly refurbished arena is home to Tallinn football team Flora, Estonia's toughest, meanest players. Watching a match is great fun.

Kalev Sporhidall (☎ 644 5171; Staadioni tänav 8) Basketball is Estonia's most passionately watched game, and the best national tournaments are usually held in this stadium.

Cinemas

Sõprus (☎ 644 1919; Vana-Posti tänav 8) Housed in a magnificent Stalin-era theatre, this arthouse cinema has an excellent repertoire of European, local and independent productions.

GETTING THERE & AWAY
See p332 for more details.

GETTING AROUND

Tallinn has an excellent network of buses, trolleybuses and trams that run from 6am to midnight. In Estonia, *piletid* (tickets) are sold from street kiosks (adult/student 10/7EEK) or can be purchased from the driver (15EEK). Validate your ticket using the hole-punch inside the vehicle.

There is a glut of taxis in Tallinn – more per capita than in Helsinki. They cost from 4.50EEK to 8EEK per kilometre. In Tallinn, call **Iks Takso** (☎ 638 1381) or **Raadio-takso** (☎ 601 1111).

Jalgrattakeskus (☎ 637 6779; Tartu maantee 73) rents bicycles by the hour, with deals for long-term rentals.

AROUND TALLINN

LAHEMAA NATIONAL PARK
☎ 32

A rocky stretch of the north coast – encompassing 251 sq km of marine area plus 474 sq km of hinterland with 14 lakes, eight rivers and many waterfalls – forms the lovely

ESTONIA

Lahemaa National Park. Roads crisscross the park from the Tallinn–Narva highway, and some places are accessible by bus. This is the perfect Tallinn getaway.

Lahemaa National Park Visitors Centre (☎ 95 555; www.lahemaa.ee; ☒ 9am-7pm May-Aug, 9am-5pm Sep, 9am-5pm Mon-Fri Oct-Apr) is in Palmse, 8km north of Viitna (71km east of Tallinn) in the park's southeast.

There is an unlimited amount of sightseeing, hiking, biking and canoeing/rafting possibilities, as well as remote islands to be explored. The park has several well-signposted nature trails and cycling paths winding through it. The small coastal towns of Võsu, Käsmu and Loksa are popular but always peaceful seaside spots in summer. There are also **prehistoric stone barrows** (tombs) at Kahala, Palmse and Vihula, and a **boulder field** on the Käsmu Peninsula.

The visitors centre arranges accommodation to suit every budget, and it can also advise on the best places for camping. **Ojaärse hostel** (☎ 34 108; sagadi.hotell@rmk.ee; dm 200 EEK; ☒ year-round) is a lushly converted 1855 farmhouse 1.5km southeast of Palmse. **Viitna Holiday Centre** (☎ 93 651; d with/without bathroom 350/200EEK) is in a tranquil wooded area beside a clean lake, about a five-minute walk from the Viitna bus stop.

There are approximately 20 buses daily from Tallinn to Rakvere, which stop at Viitna (30EEK, one hour), and one a day from Tallinn to Käsmu and Võsu. From Viitna, you can hike to the visitors centre, or call a **taxi** (☎ 50 92 326) from Võsu to pick you up. There are also buses from Tallinn to Loksa (25EEK, 1¼ hours, two to three daily).

SOUTHEASTERN ESTONIA

The focus of southeastern Estonia is the historic university town of Tartu, Estonia's second city. Beyond is a pretty region of gentle hills and beautiful lakes – old Livonia.

TARTU

☎ 7 / pop 101,190

Tartu lays claim to being Estonia's spiritual capital, and locals talk about the special Tartu 'vaim', or spirit. Small and provincial, it's also a university town, with students

forming nearly one-fifth of the population; this injects a boisterous vitality into the leafy, serene and extremely pleasant surroundings. During the Student Days festival at the end of April, carnival-like mayhem erupts throughout the city.

The university was founded in 1632. The Estonian nationalist revival in the 19th century had its origins here, and Tartu was the location for the first Estonian Song Festival in 1869. Tartu provides visitors with a true glimpse of the Estonian rhythm of life, boasts great museums and is a convenient gateway to exploring areas south of it.

Orientation & Information

Toomemägi Hill and the area of older buildings between it and the Emajõgi River are the focus of 'old' Tartu. At its heart is Raekoja plats (Town Hall Square). Ülikooli tänav and Rüütli tänav are the main shopping streets; ATMs are scattered throughout the centre. The bus station is located in the centre of town, near the banks of the Emajõgi River. Just cross the street and head to the pedestrianised Küüni tänav and head north for 200m to reach Raekoja plats. From the train station, the centre is a 35EEK taxi ride or approximately 1.2km walk east along Kuperjanovi then Tiigi tänav.

INTERNET ACCESS

Internetikohvik (☎ 423 443; Küüni 2; per hr 25EEK; ☒ 11am-11pm) Basement Internet salon.

POST

Central Post Office (Vanemuise tänav 7; ☒ 8am-7pm Mon-Fri, 9am-4pm Sat)

TOURIST INFORMATION

Tourist Office (☎ /fax 442 111; http://turism/tartumaa.ee; Raekoja plats 14; ☒ 9am-5pm Mon-Fri, 10am-3pm Sat & Sun) Books accommodation and sells maps and guides.

TRAVEL AGENCIES

Estravel (☎ 440 300; tartu1@estravel.ee; Vallikraavi tänav 2) Official American Express agent.

Hermann Travel (☎ 301 444; tartu@hermann.ee; Lossi tänav 3) Specialising in nature tours, but can help arrange pretty much anything.

Sights & Activities

At the town centre on Raekoja plats is the beautifully proportioned **town hall** (1782-89), topped by a tower and weather vane

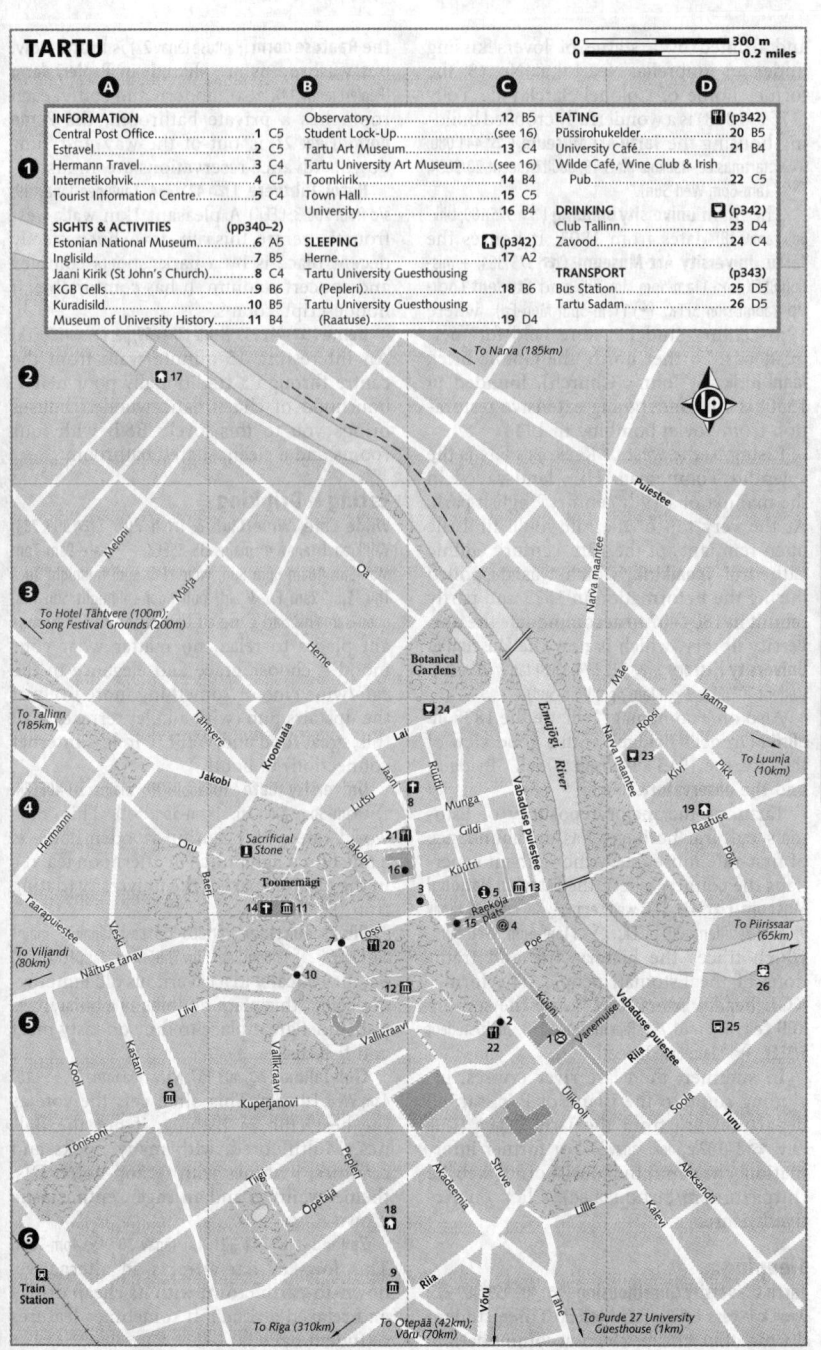

TARTU

0 _____ 300 m
0 _____ 0.2 miles

INFORMATION
Central Post Office..............................1 C5
Estravel...2 C5
Hermann Travel...................................3 C4
Internetikohvik....................................4 C5
Tourist Information Centre.....................5 C4

SIGHTS & ACTIVITIES (pp340–2)
Estonian National Museum.....................6 A5
Inglisild...7 B5
Jaani Kirik (St John's Church)................8 C4
KGB Cells..9 B6
Kuradisild...10 B5
Museum of University History...............11 B4

Observatory.......................................12 B5
Student Lock-Up............................(see 16)
Tartu Art Museum...............................13 C4
Tartu University Art Museum............(see 16)
Toomkirik..14 B4
Town Hall..15 C5
University..16 B4

SLEEPING (p342)
Herne...17 A2
Tartu University Guesthousing
    (Pepleri)..18 B6
Tartu University Guesthousing
    (Raatuse).......................................19 D4

EATING (p342)
Püssirohukelder..................................20 B5
University Café...................................21 B4
Wilde Café, Wine Club & Irish
    Pub..22 C5

DRINKING (p342)
Club Tallinn.......................................23 D4
Zavood...24 C4

TRANSPORT (p343)
Bus Station..25 D5
Tartu Sadam......................................26 D5

ESTONIA

To Narva (185km)

To Hotel Tähtvere (100m);
Song Festival Grounds (200m)

To Tallinn
(185km)

Botanical
Gardens

Emajõgi River

To Luunja
(10km)

To Viljandi
(80km)

Sacrificial
Stone

Toomemägi

To Piirissaar
(65km)

To Rīga (310km)

To Otepää (42km);
Võru (70km)

To Purde 27 University
Guesthouse (1km)

Train
Station

and fronted by a statue of lovers kissing under an umbrella. Nearby at No 18, the former home of Colonel Barclay de Tolly (1761–1818) is a wonderfully crooked building housing the **Tartu Art Museum** (☎ 441 080; www.tartmus.ee; Raekoja plats 18; adult/student 20/5EEK; ☺ 11am-6pm Wed-Sun).

The main **university building** (☎ 375 100; Ülikooli tänav 18) dates from 1803. It houses the **Tartu University Art Museum** (☎ 375 384; admission 8EEK; ☺ 11am-5pm Mon-Fri) and **Student Lock-Up** (admission 5EEK; ☺ 11am-5pm Mon-Fri), where 19th-century students were held for their misdeeds. Further north, the Gothic brick **Jaani Kirik** (St John's Church), founded in 1330, is still undergoing extensive restoration from Soviet bombing in 1944.

Rising to the west of Raekoja plats is the splendid Toomemägi Hill, landscaped in the manner of a 19th-century English park. At the very top of the hill you'll find the open remnants of the 13th-century Gothic cathedral **Toomkirik**, which was despoiled during the Reformation in 1525 and partly rebuilt in 1804–07 to accommodate the university library, which is now the **Museum of University History** (☎ 375 674; Lossi tänav 25; adult/student 20/5EEK; ☺ 11am-5pm Wed-Sun).

Also on Toomemägi Hill are the 1838 **Inglisild** (Angel's Bridge), with a good view of the city; the 1913 **Kuradisild** (Devil's Bridge); and the **observatory**.

Tartu, as the major repository of Estonia's cultural heritage, has an abundance of first-rate museums. Among them is perhaps the country's best: the **Estonian National Museum** (☎ 421 311; www.erm.ee; Kuperjanovi tänav 9; adult/student 20/14EEK; ☺ 11am-6pm Wed-Sun), which traces the history, life and traditions of the Estonian people. The former KGB headquarters now house the sombre **KGB Cells** (☎ 461 717; Riia maantee 15B; adult/student 5/3EEK; ☺ 11am-6pm Tue-Sat).

In summer, there are river cruises, including some from the island of Piirissaar; all departures are from the **Tartu Sadam** (Tartu Port; ☎ 340 026; Soola tänav 5). For further information, check out the tourist office website (http://turism.tartumaa.ee). Click on Active Leisure.

Sleeping

Tartu University Guesthousing (☎ 409 959, 409 955; www.kyla.ee; s 150-250EEK, d 400EEK) Three student dorms offer cheap, clean accommodation:

the **Raatuse dorm** (Raatuse tänav 22) is brand new, but washrooms are shared; in **Pepleri dorm** (Pepleri tänav 14), also modern and spiffy, each room has a private bathroom; the **Purde dorm** (Purde 27) is out-of-the-way and run-down. Advance reservations are a must.

Hotel Tähtvere (☎ 421 364; Laulupeo tänav 19; s/d from 200/350EEK) A pleasant 1km walk west from the centre, this run-down but perfectly decent place is by a park, sports complex and concert stadium. It has comfortable, if nondescript, rooms.

Herne (☎ 441 959; Herne tänav 59; per person 200EEK) An interesting 15-minute walk from the centre through a traditionally poor neighbourhood of charismatic wooden houses brings you to this lovely B&B with four rooms and a clean, shared bathroom.

Eating & Drinking

Wilde Café, Wine Club & Irish Pub (☎ 309 764; Vallikraavi tänav 4; mains 35-85EEK; ☺ café 9am-7pm Mon-Sat, 10am-6pm Sun, wine club 5pm-midnight Tue-Thu, 5pm-2am Fri & Sat, pub noon-midnight Sun-Thu, noon-3am Fri & Sat) One of the city's most pleasant places to relax, no matter what your mood – choose grace and elegance in the café/wine club or something more lively at the upstairs pub (with a killer terrace) – all this, great food and WIFI (wireless Internet connection) to boot!

University Café (Ülikooli 20; mains 30-40EEEK; ☺ 9am-5pm Mon-Fri, 11am-5pm Sat) This old-world café with beautiful wooden floors is a must for a light lunch or afternoon tea. It's in the original part of the university (dating from 1632).

Püssirohukelder (☎ 303 555; Lossi tänav 28; mains 40-100EEK; ☺ noon-2am Sun-Thu, noon-3am Fri & Sat) Set majestically in a cavernous old gunpowder cellar, this place doubles as a boisterous pub and a great place to dine on tasty meat and fish dishes.

Club Tallinn (☎ 403 157; Narva Maantee 27; ☺ 10-4am Wed, Fri & Sat) This often gets the vote as the best club in Estonia, if not the Baltics. Multifloored, with many nooks and crannies, it shines with its top-notch DJs, theme evenings and an eager, enthusiastic crowd.

Zavood (☎ 441 321; Lai tänav 30; ☺ 4pm-2am) This low-key bar attracts an alternative, down-to-earth crowd with its cheap drinks and relaxed attitude. It sometimes features a student band.

Getting There & Away

Some 50 buses a day run to/from Tallinn (50EEK to 80EEK, 2½ to 3½ hours). There are also two trains daily (70EEK to 120EEK, 2½ to 3½ hours).

OTEPÄÄ & AROUND

☎ 76 / pop 2200

The tiny hilltop town of Otepää, 44km south of Tartu, is the centre of a pretty area beloved by Estonians for its hills and lakes – and thus its endless opportunities for sports.

The centre of town is the triangular main 'square', Lipuväljak, with the bus station just off its eastern corner. There you'll find the **tourist office** (☎ 61 200; www.otepaa.ee; Lipuväljak 13; ☻ 9am-6pm Mon-Fri, 10am-5pm Sat & Sun). The post office, bank and main food shop are beside the bus station. Staff at the **Otepää Travel Agency** (☎ 54 060; otepaarb@hot.ee) are efficient and friendly.

Otepää's pretty little 17th-century **church** is on a hilltop about 100m northeast of the bus station. It was in this church in 1884 that the Estonian Students' Society consecrated its new blue, black and white flag, which later became the flag of independent Estonia. The best views are along the shores of the 3.5km-long **Pühajärv** (Holy Lake), on the southwestern edge of the town. The lake was blessed by the Dalai Lama in 1992. Every summer the lake is blessed by thousands of raucous partiers during the **Beach Party Festival** in early June.

Sleeping & Eating

Edgari (☎ 54 275; Lipuväljak 3; s/d 250/350EEK) One of the cheapest places to stay right in town, this is a guesthouse that feels like a hostel, with thin walls, a shared kitchenette and a communal lounge, all in a pleasant but nondescript environment.

Setanta Irish Pub & Hotel (☎ 68 200; www .setanta.ee; Núpli village; mains 70-100EEK, d from 500EEK) Better known for its Irish pub, this lively place just 3km southeast of Otepää has some fabulous rooms boasting great views over Lake Pühajärv.

Getting There & Away

Bus services run between Otepää and Tartu (20EEK to 30EEK, 45 minutes to 1½ hours, 15 daily), Tallinn (100EEK, 3½ hours, three daily) and Võru (50EEK, 1¼ hours, one or two daily).

SOUTHWESTERN ESTONIA

PÄRNU

☎ 44 / pop 45,000

Pärnu is Estonia's leading seaside resort and it's a magnet for party-loving Estonians and spa-seeking Finns. Those looking for relaxation will enjoy the wide leafy streets and white sandy beaches.

Orientation

The town lies on either side of the estuary of the Pärnu River, which empties into Pärnu Bay. The tourist office is on the main commercial street in the heart of the Old Town, around 150m south of the bus station.

Information

Central Post Office (☎ 71 111; Akadeemia 7; ☻ 8am-6pm Mon-Fri, 9am-3pm Sat)

Rütli Internetipunkt (☎ 31 552; Rütli tänav 25; per hr 20EEK; ☻ 10am-9pm Mon-Fri, 10am-6pm Sat & Sun) Internet café.

Tourist Office (☎ 73 000; www.parnu.ee; Rütli tänav 16; ☻ 9am-5pm Mon-Fri) On the main commercial street in the heart of the Old Town, around 150m south of the bus station.

Ühispank (Rütli tänav 40A; ☻ 9am-6pm Mon-Fri, 9am-2pm Sat) Behind the bus station; cashes travellers cheques, gives cash advances on credit cards and has an ATM.

Sights

The **Punane Torn** (Red Tower; Hommiku tänav; adult/student 10/5EEK; ☻ 10am-6pm Mon-Fri, 10am-3pm Sat), the city's oldest building (and despite its name, white), survives from the days of the Knights of the Sword. Parts of the 17th-century Swedish moat and ramparts remain in Vallikaavi Park, including the tunnel-like **Tallinna Värav** (Tallinn Gate) at the western end of Kuninga. Local history features at the revamped **Pärnu Museum** (☎ 33 231; Rüütli 53; adult/student 30/15EEK; ☻ 10am-6pm Wed-Sun).

The **Pärnu New Art Museum** (☎ 30 772; www .chaplin.ee; Esplanaadi tänav 10; adult/student 15/10EEK; ☻ 9am-9pm), southwest of the centre, is among Estonia's cultural highlights, with its café, bookshop, and exhibitions that always push the envelope.

The wide white-sand **beach** south of Ranna puiestee is Pärnu's finest attraction. It's possible to walk west along the coast from here

to the 2km stone breakwater that stretches
out into the mouth of the river.

Sleeping

Camping Konse (☎ 53 435 092; www.konse.ee; Suur-
Jõe 44A; per tent/d/tr from 100/500/650EEK) One of
several camping options near the city, this
one is barely 1km from the centre on a
perfect spot on the river, and offers tent,
rowboat and bike rentals. Most rooms share
bath and shower.

Tanni-Vakoma Majutüsburoo (☎ 31 070; tanni@
online.ee; Hommiku tänav 5; per person 130-300EEK)
Organises B&B accommodation in local
homes.

Lõuna Hostel (☎ 30 943; hostellouna@hot.ee; Lõuna
tänav 2; dm 180-250EEK) Overlooking a park, this
spotless hostel offers quality budget accommodation in two seven-bed rooms. Shared
kitchen, showers and bath.

Eating

Tex Mex (☎ 30 929; Akadeemia tänav 5; mains 50-100EEK;
☉ noon-midnight Sun-Thu, noon-1am Fri & Sat) The
colourful, cheerful interior is reason enough
to chow down here, but the menu boasts a
dizzying array of first-rate Mexican fare.

Georg (☎ 31 110; Rütli tänav 43; mains 20-50EEK;
☉ 7.30am-7.30pm Mon-Fri, 9am-7.30pm Sat & Sun)
This cafeteria-style, smoky café has the
cheapest, though not the best, eats in town.
Soups, salads and daily specials are great for
a quick fill-up.

Steffani Pizzeria (☎ 31 170; Nikolai tänav 24;
☉ 11am-midnight Sun-Thu, 11am-2am Fri & Sat) The
city's best pizza and pasta are doled out
in this very comfy, country kitchen-style
restaurant, which also boasts many large
vegetarian choices.

Entertainment

Sunset Club (☎ 30 670; Ranna puiestee 3; ☉ 10pm-
4am Wed, Thu & Sun, 10pm-6am Fri & Sat) Pärnu's biggest and most famous nightclub is set in
a grandiose seafront building dating from
1939. Imported DJs and bands plus a wild
young crowd keep things moving until the
early hours.

Viies Villem (☎ 27 999; Kuninga tänav 11; ☉ 11am-
midnight Sun-Thu, 11am-2am Fri & Sat) This cellar
pub is a fine place for catching local live
music and is a guaranteed hit any night of
the week.

Jazz Café (☎ 27 546; Ringi tänav 11; ☉ 9am-10pm
Sun-Wed, 9am-midnight Thu-Sat) A classy choice for a

night out or pre-club drink. Jazz music or live
bands complement a dining hall that doubles
as gallery space. Good food is also served.

Getting There & Away

More than 20 buses daily connect Pärnu
with Tallinn (50EEK to 75EEK, two hours).
Details on a multitude of other destinations
are available at the **Pärnu bus station ticket office** (☎ 71 002; ☉ 5am-8.30pm) nearby on Ringi
tänav, across from the bus station. There
are also two daily Tallinn-Pärnu trains
(40EEK, three hours).

ESTONIA DIRECTORY

ACCOMMODATION

Finding a decent place to lay your head in
Estonia is generally not a problem: places,
even budget ones, are usually clean and very
orderly. There are a few *kämpingud* (camping grounds, open from mid-May to September) that allow you to pitch a tent, but
most consist mainly of permanent wooden
cabins, with communal showers and toilets.

There are a number of homestay organisations that will rent you a room in a private
home, which is an excellent way to experience local life. Farms offer more than a choice
of rooms; in many cases meals, sauna and
a wide range of activities are also available.
Your best bet is to contact the regional tourist
offices throughout Estonia. There's an excellent search engine at www.visitestonia.com
for all types of accommodation throughout
the country. On farms or at hostels, expect to
pay at least 200EEK per person, which usually includes breakfast. Bed and breakfasts
cost from 250EEK to 500EEK per person,
depending on the services offered, and hotels are upwards of 250EEK per person. In
Tallinn, apartments for one to four persons
can be rented from 750EEK to 1200EEK.

ACTIVITIES

Many travel agencies arrange a variety of
activity-based tours of Estonia. For more
information on one such agency, Raeturist,
see p337.

Cross-country skiing is extremely popular. The main skiing centre is Otepää in
southeastern Estonia, where there are several ski centres that hire out equipment. See
www.otepaa.ee for more information.

CUSTOMS
In general, travellers aged over 21 years are allowed to bring into, or take out of, the country up to 200 cigarettes, 1L of hard alcohol and 2L of wine.

There are restrictions on taking out antiques and works of art. Permits can be obtained from the **Division of the Export of Cultural Objects** (☎ 644 6578; Sakala tänav 14, Tallinn).

EMBASSIES & CONSULATES
For up-to-date contact details of Estonian diplomatic organisations, and foreign embassies and consulates in Estonia, contact the **Estonian Foreign Ministry** (☎ 631 7600; www .vm.ee; Islandi Väljak 1, Tallinn).

Embassies & Consulates in Estonia
Australia (☎ 650 9308; mati@standard.ee; Marja tänav 9)
Canada (☎ 627 3311; tallinn@canada.ee; Toomkooli tänav 13)
Finland (☎ 610 3200; Kohtu tänav 4)
France (☎ 631 1492; www.ambafrance-ee.org not in English; Toom-Kuninga 20)
Germany (☎ 627 5300; www.germany.ee; Toom-Kuninga tänav 11)
Ireland (☎ 681 1888; Vene tänav 2)
Latvia (☎ 627 7850; fax 627 7855; Tõnismägi tänav 10)
Lithuania (☎ 641 2014; fax 641 2013; Uus tänav 15)
Russia (☎ 646 4146; www.estonia.mid.ru; lai tänav 18)
Sweden (☎ 640 5600; www.sweden.ee; Pikk tänav 28)
UK (☎ 667 4700; www.britishembassy.ee; Wismari tänav 6)
USA (☎ 668 8100; www.usemb.ee; Kentmanni tänav 20)

Estonian Embassies & Consulates Abroad
Australia (☎ 02-9810 7468; estikon@ozemail.com.au; 86 Louisa Rd, Birchgrove, NSW 2041)
Canada (☎ 416-461 0764; estconsu@ca.inter.net; 202-958 Broadview Ave, Toronto, Ontario M4K 2R6)
Finland (☎ 9-622 0260; www.estemb.fi; Itäinen Puistotie 10, 00140 Helsinki, Suomi)
France (☎ 1-5662 2200; 46, rue Pierre Charron, 75008 Paris)
Germany Embassy (☎ 30-25 460 600; www.estemb.de; Hildebrandstrasse 5 10785 Berlin); Consulate (☎ 40-450 40 26; fax 450 40 515; Badestrasse 38, 20143 Hamburg)
Ireland (☎ 1-219 6730; Riversdale House, Ailesbury Rd, Dublin 4)
Latvia (☎ 781 20 20; www.estemb.lv; Skolas iela 13, Rīga, LV 1010)
Lithuania (☎ 5-278 0200; www.estemb.lt; Mickeviciaus gatvė 4A, Vilnius 08119)
Russia Embassy (☎ 095-290 5013; www.estemb.ru; Malo Kislovski 5, 103009 Moscow); Consulate (☎ 812-109 0920; fax 109 0927; Bolsaja Monetnaja 14, St Petersburg 197101)

Sweden (☎ 08-5451 2280; www.estemb.se; Tyrgatan 3, Stockholm 10041)
UK (☎ 020-7589 3428; www.estonia.gov.uk; 16 Hyde Park Gate, London SW7 5DG)
USA Embassy (☎ 202-588 0101; www.estemb.org; 2131 Massachusetts Ave, NW, Washington, DC 20008); Consulate (☎ 212-883 0636; www.nyc.estemb.org; 600 3rd Ave, 26th fl, New York, NY 10016-2001)

FESTIVALS & EVENTS
The biggest occasion is the night of 23 June, which is Jaanipäev (St John's Eve), a celebration of the pagan Midsummer's Night. It's best experienced out in the country where huge bonfires are lit for all-night parties. If you can't get invited to a private party, head to Pirita or any other beach to watch the revellers.

Estonia also has a busy calendar of festivals encompassing all aspects of contemporary and folk culture.

All-Estonian Song Festival (www.laulupidu.ee; early July) This festival convenes every five years and culminates in a 30,000-strong traditional choir. It takes place at the Song Festival Grounds in Tallinn, just outside the centre on the way to Pirita Beach. The next festival will be held in 2009.

Baltika International Folk Festival (usually mid-July) A week of music, dance and displays focusing on Baltic and other folk traditions.

Beer Summer (www.ollesummer.ee) On another level, a hugely popular festival, which takes place at the Song Festival Grounds (see above) in Tallinn in early July.

GAY & LESBIAN TRAVELLERS
While open displays of same-sex affection are discouraged in Estonia, the overall attitude is more of curiosity and openness than antagonism. Most local gays and lesbians live to some degree in the closet. For more information, contact the **Estonian Gay League** (☎ 653 4812; gayliit@hotmail.com).

HOLIDAYS
New Year's Day 1 January
Independence Day 24 February
Good Friday & Easter March–April
Spring Day 1 May
Victory Day (commemorating the Battle of Võnnu, 1919) 23 June
Jaanipäev (St John's Day or Midsummer Day) 24 June
Day of Restoration of Independence (1991) 20 August
Christmas Day 25 December
Boxing Day 26 December

MONEY

The kroon (EEK; pronounced 'krohn') comes in two, five, 10, 25, 50, 100 and 500EEK notes. One kroon is divided into 100 sents, and there are coins of five, 10, 20 and 50 sents, as well as one- and five-kroon coins.

The best currencies to bring into Estonia are euros or US dollars, although all Western currencies are readily exchangeable. Private exchange bureaus offer the most favourable rates.

All major credit cards are widely accepted, although Visa is the most common. Most banks (but not shops and restaurants) accept travellers cheques, but their commissions can be unpleasantly high.

Students, pensioners and groups should ask about concessions on tickets, which are available for most transport services and sights.

The *käibemaks* consumption tax, levied on most goods and services, is 18%. Tipping has become traditional in the last few years, but generally no more than 10% is expected.

For more information on costs and money, see Getting Started p28.

POST

The mail service in and out of Estonia is highly efficient. There is a poste-restante bureau, where mail is kept for up to one month, at Tallinn's **central post office** (Narva maantee 1, Tallinn 10101). To post a letter up to 20g to Scandinavia, Europe or the rest of the world costs 6EEK, 6.50EEK and 8EEK, respectively.

TELEPHONE

Tallinn phone numbers, which all begin with 6, have no city codes; from anywhere outside Tallinn, dial the seven-digit number (preceded by the country code if calling from abroad). To call other cities in Estonia, dial the city code and telephone number (to call Tartu, dial ☎ 7 followed by the six-digit number). All Estonian phone numbers, including their city code, add up to seven digits (save for mobile numbers, which begin with 5 and can be eight digits long). Estonia's country code is ☎ 372.

VISAS

Make sure your passport extends at least two months after the end of your travels. Citizens of EU countries, Australia, Canada, the USA and many other countries can enter Estonia visa-free for a maximum 90-day stay over a six-month period.

Visa regulations are constantly changing, so check with your local Estonian consulate or embassy, or directly with the **Estonian Foreign Ministry** (☎ 631 7600; www.vm.ee; Islandi Väljak 1, Tallinn). Visas cannot be obtained at the border.

Finland

HIGHLIGHTS

- **Helsinki** Finland's dynamic capital, boasting some of Scandinavia's most sophisticated nightlife (p352)
- **Kuopio** Home of the world's biggest smoke sauna (p363)
- **Rovaniemi** The Arctic Circle and Santa's official grotto (p364)
- **Tampere** Lovable, post-industrial city admired by Lenin and Finlayson (p360)
- **Best journey** Overnight sleeper train from Helsinki to Rovaniemi; wake up in snow-covered Arctic Lapland (p364)
- **Off-the-beaten track** Cycle through the unspoilt archipelago of the Åland Islands (p362)

FAST FACTS

- **Area** 338,000 sq km (about four Irelands)
- **ATMs** Available everywhere
- **Budget** €35-50 per day
- **Capital** Helsinki
- **Country Code** ☎ 358, international access code 00
- **Famous for** Saunas, reindeer, Formula One drivers Kimi Raikkonen and Mika Hakkinen
- **Head of State** President Tarja Halonen
- **Languages** Finnish, Swedish, English
- **Money** Euro (A$1 = €0.58, UK£1 = €1.45, US$1 = €0.81,)
- **Phrases** *Kiitos* (thank you), *hei/tervet* (hello), *näkemin* (goodbye), *anteeksi* (sorry)

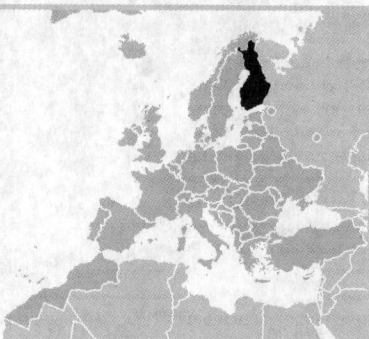

- **Population** 5.2 million
- **Time** GMT/UTC + 2
- **Visas** Not required by Western nationals for stays of up to three months.

FINLAND

TRAVEL HINTS

Fill up on inexpensive (all-you-can-eat) breakfast and lunchtime buffets. Check the *kaupahalli* (market hall) in every town to see what local foods are on offer. Buy alcohol cheaply at Alko shops, supermarkets or R-kiosks (convenience stores). Internet access is free at libraries.

ROAMING FINLAND

For a quick tour of Finland, spend a day in Helsinki, take a train to Turku or Tampere, stay overnight in Rovaniemi to sample Lapland and Santa's pad, then head south to Kuopio's smoke sauna and back to Helsinki.

Finland has always been the surprise package of Scandinavia. Sandwiched between Sweden and Russia (and ruled by both in its history), it's a serenely beautiful country of lakes and forests, a peaceful land where happiness is a ramshackle cottage by a lakeshore and a properly stoked sauna.

FINLAND

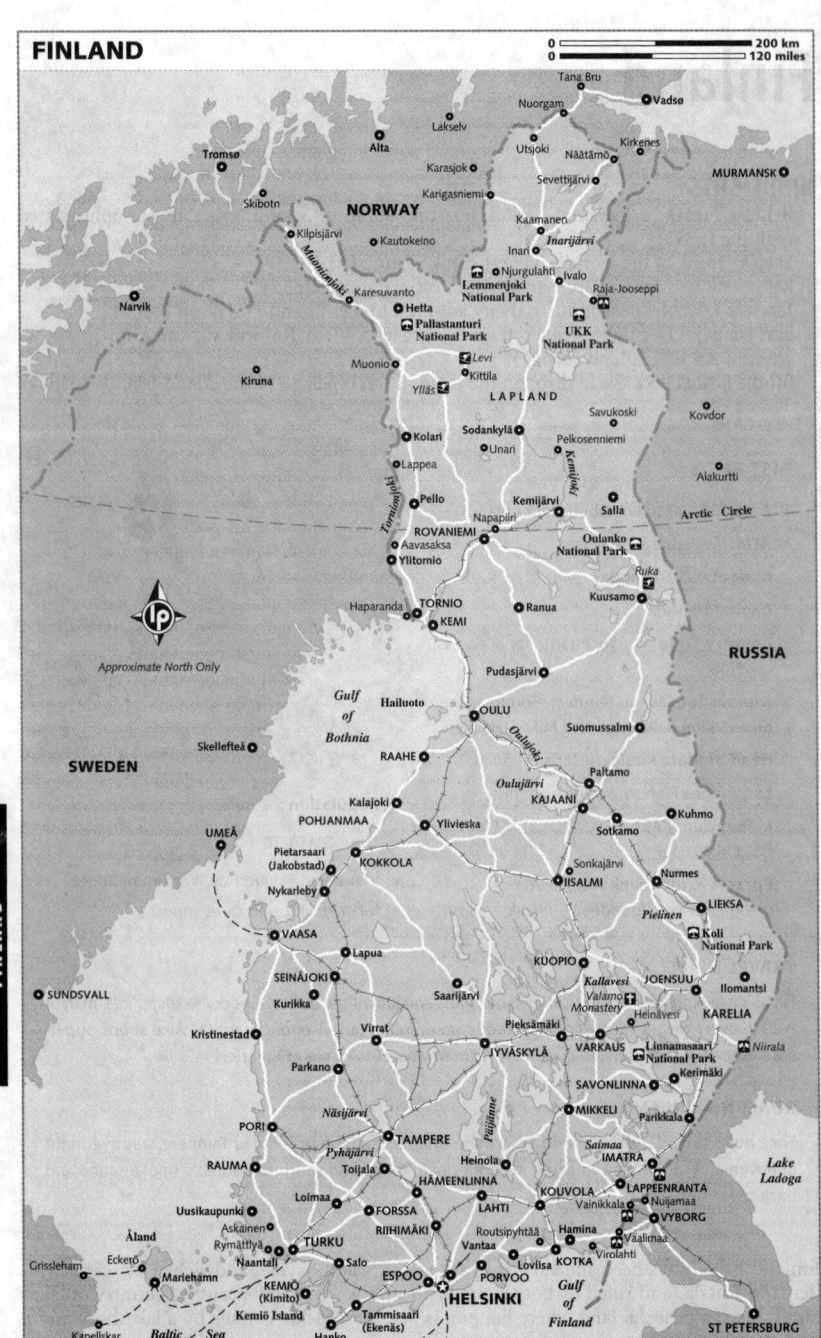

FINLAND

0 _____ 200 km
0 _____ 120 miles

Tana Bru
Nuorgam
Vadsø
Lákselv
Alta
Utsjoki
Kirkenes
Karasjok
Näätämö
MURMANSK
Tromsø
Karigasniemi
Sevettijärvi
Skibotn
Kaamanen
NORWAY
Inarijärvi
Kilpisjärvi
Inari
Kautokeino
Njurgulahti
Ivalo
Raja-Jooseppi
Muonionjoki
Lemmenjoki
National Park
Karesuvanto
Narvik
Hetta
Pallastanturi
National Park
UKK
National Park
Muonio
Levi
Kittila
Yllas
LAPLAND
Kiruna
Savukoski
Kovdor
Kolari
Sodankylä
Pelkosenniemi
Lappea
Unari
Alakurtti
Tornionjoki
Pello
Kemijärvi
Salla
Arctic Circle
Napapiiri
Kemijoki
ROVANIEMI
Oulanko
National Park
Aavasaksa
Ruka
Ylitornio
Kuusamo
Haparanda
TORNIO
Ranua
KEMI

LP
Approximate North Only

Pudasjärvi

Gulf
Hailuoto
of
OULU
Bothnia
Suomussalmi
Skellefteå
RAAHE
Oulujoki
SWEDEN
Paltamo
Oulujärvi
Kalajoki
KAJAANI
Kuhmo
POHJANMAA
Ylivieska
UMEÅ
Sotkamo
Pietarsaari
(Jakobstad)
KOKKOLA
Sonkajärvi
Nurmes
Nykarleby
IISALMI
Pielinen
LIEKSA
VAASA
Koli
National Park
Lapua
Kallavesi
SUNDSVALL
KUOPIO
SEINÄJOKI
Saarijärvi
Valamo
JOENSUU
Ilomantsi
Kurikka
Monastery
Heinävesi
Virrat
KARELIA
Pieksämäki
Kristinestad
VARKAUS
Niirala
JYVÄSKYLÄ
Linnansaari
National Park
Parkano
SAVONLINNA
Kerimäki
Näsijärvi
Päijänne
MIKKELI
PORI
TAMPERE
Parikkala
Pyhäjärvi
Heinola
Saimaa
RAUMA
Toijala
IMATRA
Lake
Uusikaupunki
HÄMEENLINNA
KOUVOLA
LAPPEENRANTA
Ladoga
Loimaa
LAHTI
Vainikkala
Nuijamaa
Askainen
FORSSA
Vantaa
Hamina
VYBORG
Rymättylä
RIIHIMÄKI
Routsipyhtää
Virolahti
Åland
TURKU
Loviisa
Vaalimaa
Eckerö
Salo
ESPOO
KOTKA
Grisslehamn
Naantali
PORVOO
Mariehamn
KEMIÖ
(Kimito)
HELSINKI
Gulf
Tammisaari
of
Kemiö Island
(Ekenäs)
Finland
Kapellskar
Baltic *Sea*
Hanko
ST PETERSBURG

RUSSIA

Although Finland is riding a wave of hi-tech revolution, for travellers nature reigns supreme here, whether it's cruising on lake ferries, hiking in empty forests, cycling on endless bike paths or skating on frozen lakes. Lapland, one of Europe's last great wilderness areas, is an irresistible draw. Reindeer herds wander across fells, and above the Arctic Circle the sun never truly sets in midsummer. Here you'll find the kitsch but fun Santa Claus Village and Santa's official post office, and get to meet the man himself.

Finland really comes into its own in the summer months, with long hours of daylight and some of northern Europe's best music festivals and off-beat events springing to life somewhere virtually every day.

Sophisticated Helsinki is an intimate city with some of Scandinavia's most enviable nightlife. Working-class Tampere is studded with quirky museums, and tranquil Savonlinna lies snuggled marvellously between two lakes. Don't miss the chance to take a sauna with the locals wherever you go.

Finns and Finland have a reputation for being tough, quiet and mysterious, but if you look under the surface, you'll find some of the warmest people you'll ever meet.

HISTORY

Human settlement in Finland dates back almost 10,000 years. After arriving on the Baltic coast from Russia, the Finns' ancestors established themselves in the forests and drove the nomadic Sami people north, where some 6500 still live in a region of north Lapland known as Sápmi.

By 1155 the Swedes had moved in and made Finland a province. The Russians were never far away, though, and in the 16th century Peter the Great attacked and occupied much of Finland. In 1809 Sweden ceded Finland to Russia and the capital was moved to Helsinki, but the communist revolution of October 1917 brought the downfall of the Russian tsar and enabled the Finnish senate to declare independence.

Anticommunist violence broke out during the 1930s. Finland sought neutrality, but Soviet deals with Germany led to demands for Finland's eastern Lakeland (Karelia). In 1939 the Winter War between the Soviet Union and Finland began, in which the massively outnumbered Finns were defeated and Finland was forced to cede territory.

Finland accepted assistance from Germany and in 1941 fought the Soviets in the Continuation War, which cost Finland almost 100,000 lives.

Finland eventually signed a new treaty, which allowed it to take an independent stance during the Cold War, and with this new sense of security came the opportunity for Finland to develop its economy and welfare system. Finland recovered from its worst post-war recession in 1990–94, joined the EU in 1995 and adopted the euro in 1999.

The rise of hi-tech industries such as phone giant Nokia has assured Finland economic prosperity, and in 2001 it was voted one of the least corrupt countries in the world.

PEOPLE & CULTURE

Thinly populated Finland has only 17 people per square kilometre. There are around 300,000 Swedish-speaking Finns on the west and south coasts and the Åland Islands. Russians number around 23,000, mainly in the east, and a small number of Roma live in the south.

The indigenous Sami (Lapp) population of 6500 in the north consists of three distinct groups, with the majority living in Inari, Hetta and Utsjoki and most involved in reindeer husbandry.

A capacity for silence and reflection is the trait that best sums up the Finnish character (get a Finn near a stack of duty-free liquor and see if this remains the case!). The image of a log cabin with a sauna by a lake tells much about Finnish culture: independence, endurance (*sisu*, or 'guts'), and a love of open space and nature.

READING UP

A Brief History of Finland by Matti Klinge, *Finland at Peace and War* by HM Tillotson and *Finland Today* by Raimo Suikkari are good sources of detailed information about Finland's history and politics. Eino Friberg's *Kalevala Epic of the Finnish People,* a synopsis of the national epic (see Arts, following), provides another angle on the Finnish psyche.

FINLAND

SPORT

Ice hockey is Finland's number one national passion, with the season running from late September to March. The best place to see a quality match in the national league is Tampere or Helsinki, but Turku, Oulu and Rovaniemi also have major stadiums. Another popular winter spectator sport is ski-jumping – Lahti, with its vast sports centre, is the best place to see it, but Kuopio also has a jump on Puijo Hill.

In summer, football (soccer) is the national team sport, although it's not as popular here as elsewhere in Europe. Pesäpallo is the Finnish version of baseball and is a popular spectator sport.

ARTS

Tove Jansson, who died in 2001, is internationally famous for her Moominland children's stories. Another high-profile Finn is the late architect Alvar Aalto, whose design work features in many Finnish public buildings, furniture and the Savoy vase.

Jean Sibelius, one of the most famous late Romantics, was at the forefront of the Finnish nationalist movement. His stirring tone-poem *Finlandia* has been raised to the status of a national hymn. Sibelius and the nationalistic painter Akseli Gallen-Kallela fell under the spell of 'Karelianism', a movement that drew its inspiration from the folk songs collected in the 1830s by Elias Lönnrot to form the national epic the *Kalevala*.

The best-known Finnish film maker is Aki Kaurismäki, director of the 1989 *Leningrad Cowboys Go America,* while director Renny Harlin has established himself in Hollywood.

More recent popular music successes from Finland include the Rasmus and trance artist Darude.

ENVIRONMENT

Europe's seventh-biggest country is waterlogged – there are 187,888 lakes in Finland (with 98,050 islands), fed by a network of rivers and rapids. Compared to Sweden and Norway, Finland is a flat country, with a scattering of fells (forested hills) in the northern Lakeland and Lapland area, some of which are cleared and used for downhill skiing.

Finland boasts over 120,000 sq km of publicly owned lands and waters in 32 national parks – some of the last great wilderness

---

TOP FIVE FINLAND

- **Steaming Saunas** Relax in one of Finland's 1.6 million saunas (p363)
- **All that Jazz** A week of international jazz comes to Pori in July (p366)
- **Midnight Sun** Cross the Arctic Circle and visit Santa at Rovaniemi (p364)
- **Best Bar** Ride a tractor at Zetor (p357), then party at Club Helsinki (p358)
- **Step Back in Time** Wander the cobbled streets of Porvoo (p358) or admire Savonlinna's medieval castle (p362)

---

areas in Europe. For more information, contact **Metsähallitus** (☎ 09-270 5221; www.metsa.fi) at Tikankotti, the parks office in Helsinki.

Elk, brown bears and wolves are native to Finland's forests, although sightings are rare. In Lapland, the Sami keep commercial herds of some 22,000 reindeer.

TRANSPORT

GETTING THERE & AWAY
Air

Most major European carriers have flights to/from Helsinki's **Vantaa airport** (☎ 0200-14636; www.helsinki-vantaa.fi). **Finnair** (☎ 0203-140160; www.finnair.com; Asemaaukio 3, Helsinki; ☑ 9am-5pm Mon-Sat) is the national carrier, with direct flights to Helsinki from New York, Toronto, Bangkok, Singapore, Tokyo, Hong Kong and most European capitals. Fly cheaply to Tampere with **Ryanair** (www.ryanair.com) from London or Frankfurt (Internet fares one-way from UK€10 plus taxes), or to Helsinki with Swedish budget carrier **FlyMe** (www.flyme.com) from Stockholm (one-way from €22). **Blue 1** (www.blue1.com) offers cheap Internet fares between Helsinki and Amsterdam, Brussels, Copenhagen, Oslo and Stockholm.

In Finland, contact student-travel agent **Kilroy Travels** (☎ 680 7811; www.kilroytravels.com; Kaivokatu 10C).

Boat

There's no better way to cruise into Helsinki than on board a huge Baltic ferry. The ships are like floating luxury hotels, nightclubs and shopping malls all rolled into one, but fares are kept reasonably low by competition and duty-free shopping. Services between major cities, such as Stockholm–Turku–Helsinki and Tallin–Helsinki, are year-round, and there are two ferry services from Travemünde (Germany) to Finland.

Ferry tickets can be bought at the terminals or from the ferry companies' offices in Helsinki's centre:

Eckerö Line (☎ 228 8544; www.eckerolinjen.fi; Mannerheimintie 10) Boats depart from Länsiterminaali (West Terminal).

Linda Line (☎ 668 9700; www.lindaline.fi) Boats depart from Makasiini Terminal.

Nordic Jet Line (☎ 681 770; www.njl.fi) Boats depart from Kanava Terminal.

Silja Line (☎ 0203-74552; www.siljaline.fi; Mannerheimintie 2) Boats depart from Olympia Terminal.

Tallink (☎ 2282 1222; Erottajankatu 19) Boats depart from Kanava Terminal.

Viking Line (☎ 123 577; www.vikingline.fi; Mannerheimintie 14) Boats depart from Katajanokka Terminal.

ESTONIA

Dozens of boats ply the Gulf of Finland between Helsinki and Tallin.

Eckerö Line has only one departure daily but is the cheapest, with a return fare at €25 (€15 in low season). Tallink, Viking and Silja Line have several daily departures by ferry (three hours) and catamaran (1½ hours) costing €30 to €40 return. Linda Line is the cheapest fast boat at €24/36 one-way/return.

SWEDEN

The Stockholm–Helsinki, Stockholm–Turku and Kapellskär–Mariehamn runs are covered by Silja Line and Viking Line.

On both lines you can buy a passenger-only ticket and sleep in the salons (or stay up all night partying, as many passengers do!). In summer, overnight crossings (passenger ticket only) from Stockholm start at €34 to Turku (11 to 12 hours) and €45 to Helsinki (16 hours). Cabins start at an additional €24 (€40 in summer). Viking Line usually has the cheapest fares.

Eckerö Line also sails from Grisslehamn to Eckerö in Åland (€5.50, €8.90 in summer, three hours).

Bus

Going between Finland and Norway, the main Nordkapp route heads from Rovaniemi to Karigasniemi (via Inari) and across the border to Karasjok and Lakselv (adult/student €101.50/77.10, 11 hours). Bus services run between Ivalo and Karasjok (direct to Nordkapp in summer). The road from the northernmost point of Finland, at Nuorgam, will take you to Tana Bru, with connections to various parts of Finnmark in Norway. Direct buses from Ivalo to Kirkenes (Norway) run in summer only.

Daily express buses run from Turku and Helsinki to St Petersburg (€50.40, nine hours). A Russian visa is required.

Train

The only international railway service from Finland is to Russia – there are three daily trains from Helsinki.

The romantic *Tolstoi* sleeper departs Helsinki daily at 5.42pm and travels via St Petersburg and Vyborg to Moscow (€84.60 one way), arriving at 8.30am. It departs Moscow at 10.50pm daily.

The *Sibelius* and *Repin* have daily services between Helsinki and St Petersburg (5½ hours). The *Sibelius* departs Helsinki at 7.42am (€50.20, seats only). The *Repin* departs at 3.42pm and has 2nd-class seats for €50.20 or 1st-class sleeping berths for €88.20. From St Petersburg departures are at 4.32pm (*Sibelius*) and 7.32am (*Repin*).

Check timetables at www.vr.fi. A Russian visa is needed for all trains.

GETTING AROUND
Bicycle

Finland is wonderfully bicycle-friendly, with miles of flat bike paths, and Finns are avid cyclists. In most cities you can hire bikes from around €10/50 a day/week. Ask at tourist offices, train stations or hostels (see also p358 for information on hiring a bike in Helsinki). Bikes can be taken on most buses, trains and ferries.

In summer, the city of Helsinki provides 300 distinctive green 'City Bikes' at stands within a radius of 2km from the *kauppatori* – although sometimes you'll wonder where they're all hiding. These bikes are free: you deposit a €2 coin into the stand that locks them, then reclaim it when you return the bike to any stand.

Boat

Lake and river ferries operate in summer (June to August). More than mere transport: a cruise is a bona fide Finnish experience.

Some of the best: Savonlinna–Kuopio; Lahti–Jysvaskyla; Tampere–Hämeenlinna; and the coastal ferries from Turku. Many ferries that run between the islands along the coast are free, especially in Åland.

Bus

Buses cover 90% of Finland's roads. There are frequent daily departures between major towns, but fewer services on Sunday and in winter. Most bus stations are closed at weekends and in the evening.

Long-distance and express bus travel is handled by **Oy Matkahuolto Ab** (☎ 09-682 701, 0200-4000 for national timetables; www.matkahuolto.fi). Private lines operate local services but all share the same ticketing and fare system.

Fares are calculated by distance. The adult fare for a 100km trip is €15.20/12.90 express/regular. From Helsinki to Rovaniemi by express bus (13½ hours) costs €86 one way. Return tickets are 10% cheaper than two one-way fares. Discounts of 50% (on journeys over 80km) are available for students, but you must have a Matkahuolto student card.

Train

Finnish trains are efficient, fast and cheap. Rovaniemi is the main northern rail terminus, and there are frequent services from Helsinki to Turku (€24.40), Tampere (€24.40), Kuopio (€48.20) and Oulu (€61.20). On longer routes there are two- and three-bed sleepers that are slightly more expensive than normal tickets – the fare for a seat on the overnight train to Rovaniemi is €70.20, while in a three-bed sleeper it's €82.

VR Ltd Finnish Railways (☎ 0600-41902; www .vr.fi) in Helsinki has a travel bureau at main train stations where staff can advise on tickets. The 50% student discount is only available to Finnish students or foreigners studying in Finland.

The Finnrail Pass is a one-month pass good for unlimited rail travel for three/five/10 days (€118/158/214). There's also a Holiday Pass (valid June to August), which allows three days of travel in one month for €109.

EMERGENCY NUMBERS

- Police, fire & ambulance ☎ 112
- Directory assistance ☎ 020208

HELSINKI

☎ 09 / pop 560,000

Chugging into the heart of Helsinki on a ferry from Sweden or Estonia is an unforgettable experience, and Finland's sophisticated capital – with its Russian and Swedish influences – doesn't disappoint. This is the nerve centre of Finland, where trends begin and things happen.

Although it's Finland's largest and most vibrant city, Helsinki is small and intimate compared to other Scandinavian capitals, and in summer walking or cycling is an easy way to appreciate its cafés, parks, markets and nearby islands. Summer beer terraces, funky bars and chic nightclubs endow the city with some of the best nightlife in Scandinavia, and the locals know how to party.

The area has been settled since 1550. While the Swedes were here in the 1700s they erected a fortress on the nearby island of Suomenlinna. After falling to the tsar in 1808, Helsinki became the seat of the Russian Grand Duchy. The monumental buildings of Senaatintori (Senate Square) were designed and built by German architect Carl Engel from 1818 to 1840 to give the new city an appropriate measure of oomph.

ORIENTATION

Helsinki occupies a peninsula and is linked by bridge and boat to nearby islands. The city centre surrounds the main harbour, Eteläsatama, and the *kauppatori* (market square); huge international ferry terminals lie either side. The main street axes are the twin shopping avenues of Pohjoisesplanadi and Eteläesplanadi, and Mannerheimintie.

INFORMATION
Bookshops

Akateeminen Kirjakauppa (Academic Bookshop; Pohjoisesplanadi 39; ☺ 9am-9pm Mon-Fri, 9am-6pm Sat) Finland's biggest bookshop, with a massive range, including maps.

Discount Cards

The Helsinki Card is worthwhile if you plan to do a lot of sightseeing. The pass gives free urban transport (including island ferries) and free entry to more than 50 attractions in and around Helsinki. A card valid for 24/48/72 hours costs €25/35/45.

Buy the card at the Helsinki tourist office, or at hotels, R-kiosks (convenience stores) and transport terminals.

Internet Access

Internet access at Helsinki's public libraries is free. Several cafés and bars also have free Internet access for customers.

Helsinki University Library (☎ 1912 3196; Unioninkatu 36; ☼ 9am-6pm Mon-Fri, 9am-4pm Sat) Email is discouraged, but the 2nd floor of this superb library is a serene place to surf the Net.

Kirjakaapeli library (Cable Book Library; ☎ 3108 5000; Lasipalatsi Multimedia Ctre, Mannerheimintie 22-24; ☼ 10am-10pm Mon-Thu, noon-6pm Sat & Sun) Upstairs in the Lasipalatsi Multimedia Centre. First-come-first-served terminals or book a half-hour slot. At time of research, it was due to move to the post office building, Mannerheiminaukio 1, in 2005.

Mbar (☎ 6124 5420; Mannerheimintie 22-24; per 20 min/hr €2/5; ☼ 9am-midnight Mon-Tue, 9am-3am Wed-Sat, noon-10pm Sun) Smoky bar and Internet café behind Lasipalatsi.

Netcup (Roberts Coffee, Stockman department store, Aleksanterinkatu 52; ☼ 10am-9pm Mon-Fri, 9am-6pm Sat) Two free terminals for customers.

Left Luggage

There are **lockers** (€2/3 small/large) at the main train station, bus station and ferry terminals. The train station and Viking Line Terminal have **left-luggage counters** (per piece per day €2).

Medical Services

Töölö Hospital (☎ 4711; Töölönkatu 40) Private 24-hour medical clinic.

Yliopiston Apteekki (Mannerheimintie 96) 24-hour pharmacy.

Money

Forex (☼ 8am-9pm) offers good rates and is the best place in Helsinki to change cash or travellers cheques (€2 flat fee). It has branches at Pohjoisesplanadi, Mannerheimintie and the train station. There are currency-exchange counters at the airport and the Katajanokka Terminal.

Post

The **Main Post Office** (☎ 204 511; Mannerheiminaukio 1; ☼ 7am-9pm Mon-Fri, 10am-6pm Sat & Sun) has a **poste restante office** (☼ 8am-6pm Mon-Fri) at the rear.

Tourist Information

Finnish Tourist Board (☎ 4176 9300; www.visitfinland .fi; Eteläesplanadi 4; ☼ 9am-5pm Mon-Fri year-round, 10am-4pm Sat May-Sep) Maps and information for destinations around the country.

Helsinki tourist office (☎ 169 3757; www.hel.fi /tourism; Pohjoisesplanadi 19; ☼ 9am-7pm Mon-Fri, 9am-3pm Sat & Sun May-Sep, 9am-5pm Mon-Fri, 9am-3pm Sat Oct-Apr)

Kompassi (☎ 3108 0080; www.lasipalatsi.fi/kompassi; Mannerheimintie 22-24; ☼ 11am-6pm Tue-Thu, 11am-4pm Fri, 11am-6pm Sun) Youth information centre.

SIGHTS & ACTIVITIES

Kiasma (☎ 1733 6501; www.kiasma.fi; Mannerheiminaukio 2; adult/student under 18 €5.50/4; ☼ 9am-5pm Tue, 10am-8.30pm Wed-Sun) is in the curvaceous and quirky metallic building housing Finland's best exhibitions of contemporary and postmodern art from the 1960s to the 1990s.

The impressive **Kansallismuseo** (National Museum; ☎ 40501; www.nba.fi; Mannerheimintie 34; adult/student €5/4; ☼ 11am-8pm Tue-Wed, 11am-6pm Thu-Sun) covers prehistory and archaeological finds, church relics, Sami history and cultural exhibitions. Check out the *Kalevala* frescoes on the ceiling.

The list of painters at the **Ateneum** (National Gallery; ☎ 173 36401; www.fng.fi/ateneum; Kaivokatu 2; adult/student €5.50/4, admission free 5pm-8pm Wed; ☼ 9am-6pm Tue & Fri, 9am-8pm Wed & Thu, 11am-5pm Sat & Sun) reads like a who's who of Finnish art, and has international works such as Rodin's famous sculpture *The Thinker*.

The fascinating **Mannerheim Museum** (☎ 635 443; Kalliolinnantie 14; admission €7; ☼ 11am-4pm Fri-Sun) in Kaivopuisto Park is the preserved home of CGE Mannerheim, former Finnish president, commander-in-chief of the army, Civil War victor and all-round good guy.

The massive **Cable Factory** (☎ 4763 8300; www.kaapelitehdas.fi; Tallberginkatu 1; metro Ruolahti; ☼ 8am-6pm Mon-Fri) is now home to alternative theatre, art exhibitions and dance performances, many of them free.

FINLAND

HELSINKI

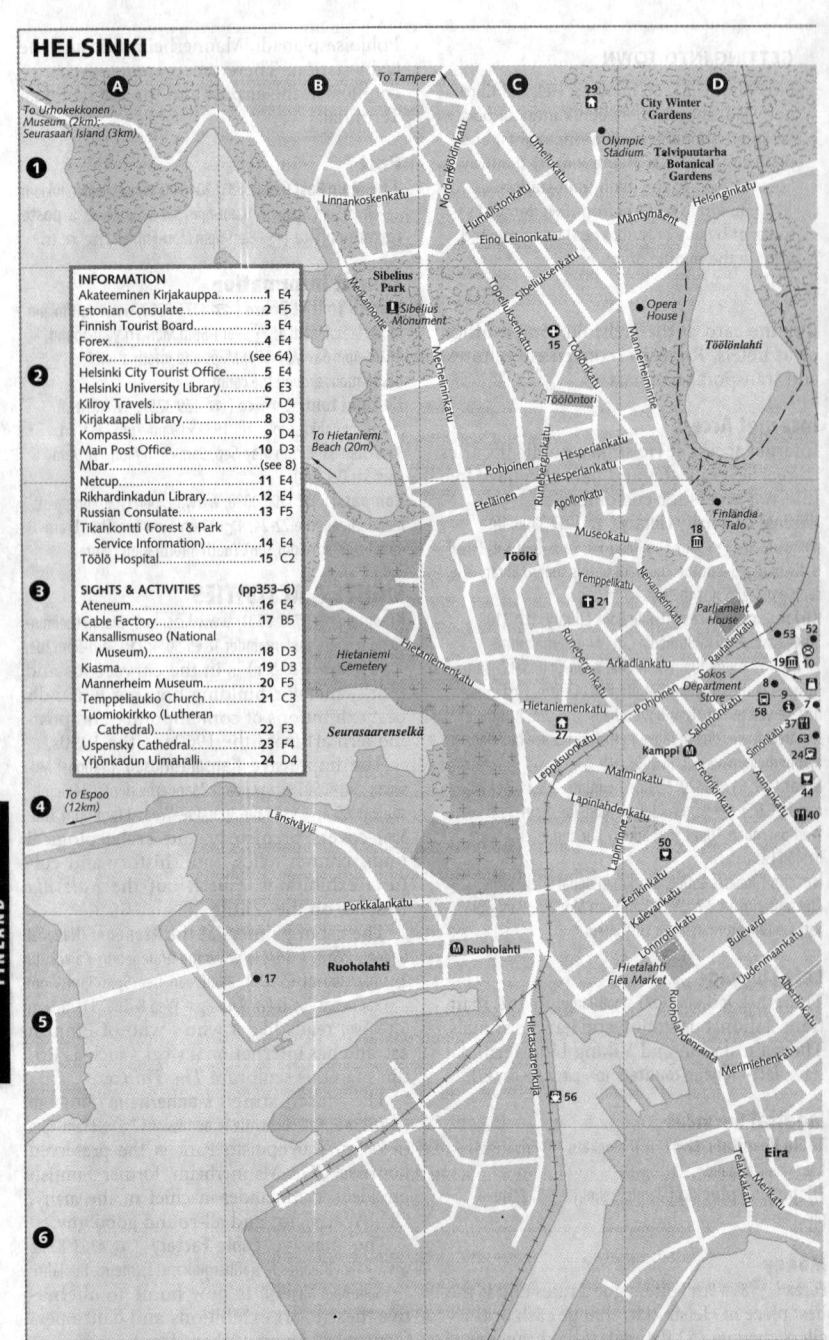

INFORMATION

Akateeminen Kirjakauppa.............1 E4
Estonian Consulate........................2 F5
Finnish Tourist Board....................3 E4
Forex...4 E4
Forex.......................................(see 64)
Helsinki City Tourist Office............5 E4
Helsinki University Library.............6 E3
Kilroy Travels...............................7 D4
Kirjakaapeli Library.......................8 D3
Kompassi......................................9 D4
Main Post Office.........................10 D3
Mbar..(see 8)
Netcup.......................................11 E4
Rikhardinkadun Library................12 E4
Russian Consulate.......................13 F5
Tikankontti (Forest & Park
    Service Information).................14 E4
Töölö Hospital............................15 C2

SIGHTS & ACTIVITIES   (pp353–6)

Ateneum......................................16 E4
Cable Factory..............................17 B5
Kansallismuseo (National
    Museum).................................18 D3
Kiasma..19 D3
Mannerheim Museum...................20 F5
Temppeliaukio Church..................21 C3
Tuomiokirkko (Lutheran
    Cathedral)...............................22 F3
Uspensky Cathedral.....................23 F4
Yrjönkadun Uimahalli..................24 D4

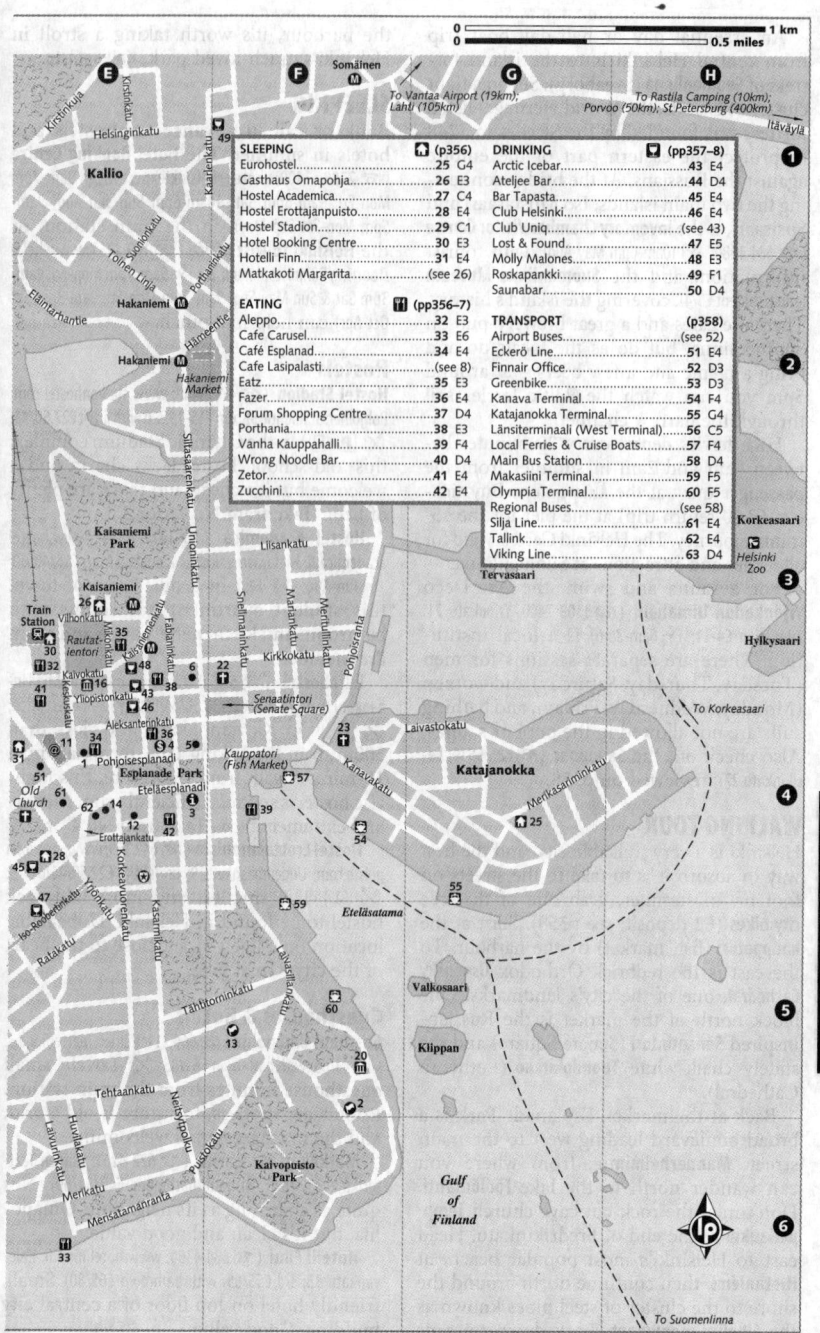

SLEEPING 🏠 (p356)
Eurohostel.....................................25 G4
Gasthaus Omapohja.....................26 E3
Hostel Academica.........................27 C4
Hostel Erottajanpuisto.................28 E4
Hostel Stadion..............................29 C1
Hotel Booking Centre...................30 E3
Hotelli Finn...................................31 E4
Matkakoti Margarita..................(see 26)

EATING 🍴 (pp356–7)
Aleppo..32 E3
Cafe Carusel.................................33 E6
Café Esplanad..............................34 E4
Cafe Lasipalasti........................(see 8)
Eatz..35 E3
Fazer...36 E4
Forum Shopping Centre...............37 D3
Porthania......................................38 E3
Vanha Kauppahalli.......................39 F4
Wrong Noodle Bar.......................40 D4
Zetor..41 E4
Zucchini..42 E4

DRINKING 🍷 (pp357–8)
Arctic Icebar.................................43 E4
Ateljee Bar....................................44 D4
Bar Tapasta..................................45 E4
Club Helsinki................................46 E4
Club Uniq..................................(see 43)
Lost & Found................................47 E5
Molly Malones..............................48 E3
Roskapankki.................................49 F1
Saunabar.......................................50 D4

TRANSPORT (p358)
Airport Buses............................(see 52)
Eckerö Line...................................51 E4
Finnair Office................................52 D3
Greenbike......................................53 D3
Kanava Terminal...........................54 F4
Katajanokka Terminal...................55 G4
Länsiterminaali (West Terminal)...56 C5
Local Ferries & Cruise Boats........57 F4
Main Bus Station..........................58 D4
Makasiini Terminal.......................59 F5
Olympia Terminal.........................60 F5
Regional Buses.........................(see 58)
Silja Line......................................61 E4
Tallink..62 E4
Viking Line....................................63 D4

FINLAND

An essential day or half-day boat trip from central Helsinki is to the island fortress of **Suomenlinna** (Sveaborg). Set on a tight cluster of islands, the World Heritage–listed fortress was founded by the Swedes in 1748 to protect the eastern part of the empire against the Russians. At the bridge connecting the two main islands, Iso Mustasaari and Susisaari, is the **Inventory Chamber Visitor Centre** (☎ 684 1880; ☉ 10am-6pm May-Aug), with tourist information, and the **Suomenlinna Museum** (adult/student €5/4), covering the island's history. There are cafés and a great brewery-pub on Suomenlinna, but do as the locals do and bring a picnic and a few beers – at around 5pm you can watch the Baltic ferries sail through the narrow channel.

HKL ferries depart every 20 minutes between 6am and 2am in summer from the passenger quay at the *kauppatori*. Buy tickets (€3.60 return trip) at the pier for the 15-minute journey. The Helsinki Card is valid for all ferries and attractions at Suomenlinna.

For a sauna and swim, the Art Deco **Yrjönkadun Uimahalli** (☎ 3108 7400; Yrjönkatu 21; admission €4-11; ☉ 6am-8pm) is a local institution. There are separate sessions for men (Tuesday, Thursday, Saturday) and women (Monday, Wednesday, Friday), and bathing suits are not allowed in the pool or saunas. Also check out the **Saunabar** (☎ 685 5550; Eerikinkatu 27), reviewed on p358.

WALKING TOUR

Helsinki is a very walkable city, and the best way to absorb it is to take to the streets on foot or, in summer, grab one of the free **city bikes** (€2 deposit; see p358). Start at the **kauppatori** (fish market) by the harbour. To the east is the redbrick Orthodox **Uspensky Cathedral**, one of the city's landmarks. One block north of the market is the Russian-inspired **Senaatintori** (Senate Square) and the stately chalk-white **Tuomiokirkko** (Lutheran Cathedral).

Back at the market, Esplanade Park is a broad boulevard leading west to the main street, **Mannerheimintie**, from where you can wander north to the lake **Töölönlahti**. Don't miss the rock-cut cave church **Temppeliaukio** at the end of Fredrikinkatu. Head east to Helsinki's most popular beach, at **Hietaniemi**, then continue north around the shore to the cluster of steel pipes known as the **Sibelius monument**. Back down towards the harbour, it's worth taking a stroll in Helsinki's much-loved park, **Kaivopuisto**.

SLEEPING

Book or call in advance for hostels and hotels in summer. The **Hotel Booking Centre** (☎ 2288 1400; hotel@helsinkiexpert.fi; ☉ 9am-7pm Mon-Fri, 9am-6pm Sat, 10am-6pm Sun Jun-Aug, 9am-5pm Mon-Sat Sep-May), in the train station, or the **Helsinki tourist office** (☎ 169 3757; www.hel.fi /tourism; Pohjoisesplanadi 19; ☉ 9am-7pm Mon-Fri, 9am-3pm Sat & Sun May-Sep, 9am-5pm Mon-Fri, 9am-3pm Sat Oct-Apr) can help in a pinch.

Hostels

Hostel Stadion (☎ 477 8480; www.stadionhostel.com; Pohjoinen Stadiontie 3B; dm €15-19, s/d with linen €27.50/41; ☒ ℗ ▢) In the Olympic Stadium complex, this 'old-school' hostel lacks charm and a welcome but it's cheap and there are plenty of beds. Take tram No 7A or 3T.

Hostel Academica (☎ 1311 4334; www.hostel academica.fi; Hietaniemenkatu 14; dm/s/d from €16/40/60; ☉ Jun-Aug; ☒ ▢) In a quiet part of town, this student apartment has rooms with bathroom and kitchenette. Sauna and swim are included.

Eurohostel (☎ 622 0470; www.eurohostel.fi; Linnankatu 9; dm/s/d/tr €22/36.50/44/66; ☉ 24-hr reception; ☒ ▢) On Katajanokka Island, less than 500m from the Viking Line Terminal and a 15-minute walk from the centre, this high-rise hostel is spotless, efficiently run, friendly and extremely busy. Take tram No 4 or 7.

Hostel Erottajanpuisto (☎ 642 169; www.erottajan puisto.com; Uudenmaankatu 9; dm/s/d/tr €22.50/46/60/78; ☒ ▢) The smallest and most laid-back hostel to be found in Helsinki. Unbeatable location on a lively street close to the heart of the city. Great vibe.

Guesthouses & Hotels

Gasthaus Omapohja (☎ 666 211; Itäinen Teatterikuja 3; s/d €44/65, with bathroom €64/85; ☒) Lovely, small guesthouse minutes from the train station. Rooms are spotless, furniture is old world, and the management is welcoming.

Matkakoti Margarita (☎ 622 4261; Itäinen Teatterikuja 3; s/d/tr without bathroom €40/54/69) Not quite as charming as its neighbour Omapohja, but it's clean and good value.

Hotelli Finn (☎ 684 4360; www.hotellifinn.fi; Kalevankatu 3B; s/d €55/65, with bathroom €65/80) Small, friendly hotel on top floor of a central city building. Good value.

FINLAND

Camping

Rastila Camping (☎ 321 6551; rastilacamping@hel.fi; Karavaanikatu 4; metro Rastila; per person/group €11/17, cabins for 2/4 people €43/62; ☯ all year) Although 10km out of town, it's easily reached by metro. Facilities include a lakeside sauna.

EATING

Helsinki has by far Finland's best range of cafés and restaurants. From Finnish and Russian to Asian and Italian, sushi joints to kebab stands and terrace cafés to fine French dining – this is the place for a splurge. As with elsewhere in Finland, seek out the lunchtime specials – many restaurants (even the fancy ones) have buffet lunch deals for under €10.

Self-Catering

If you're self-catering, stock up at **Aleppo**, a budget supermarket in the pedestrian tunnel by the train station.

Cafés

Café Esplanad (☎ 665 496; Pohjoisesplanadi 37; mains €3-10; ☯ 8am-11pm Mon-Fri, 9am-10.30pm Sat, 10am-10pm Sun) Helsinki's most popular café, with Danish pastries and Finnish *pulla* (wheat bun), spectacular salads and a great people-watching terrace.

Café Carusel (☎ 622 4522; Merisatamanranta 10; mains €2-10; ☯ 9am-6pm, longer hr in summer) Busy self-service waterfront café on the edge of Kaivopuisto Park. Great foccaccias and snacks.

Fazer (☎ 6159 2959; Kluuvikatu 3; cakes from €3; ☯ 9am-10pm; ✗) The best place in town for cakes, pastries and mouth-watering sweets.

Zucchini (☎ 622 2907; Fabianinkatu 4; mains €5-12; ☯ 11am-5pm Mon-Fri, closed July; ✗) Trendy little vegetarian café serving quiche, pancakes, soups, salads and juices.

Helsinki University has several student cafeterias around the city, where lunch costs less than €5. They include **Porthania** (☎ 1311 4298; Hallituskatu 11-13; ☯ 10am-4pm Mon-Fri) and the huge **Ylioppilasaukio** (☎ 260 9491; Mannerheimintie 3B; ☯ 11am-5pm Mon-Sat, noon-5pm Sun), tucked away down an alley opposite the train station.

Quick Eats

In summer there are food stalls and fresh produce at the *kauppatori*, but the real gourmet stuff is in the fabulous **Vanha Kauppahalli** (Old Market Hall; Eteläranta 1; ☯ 6.30am-6pm Mon-Fri, 6.30am-4pm Sat all year, 10am-4pm Sun late Jun–early Aug) at the harbour, where you can get filled rolls, cheese, breads, and an array of Finnish snacks and delicacies. It also sports a small Alko, selling alcohol.

For everything from Asian noodles to burgers and kebabs, head to the food court in the basement of the **Forum shopping centre** (Mannerheimintie 20).

Restaurants

Café Lasipalasti (☎ 621 6700; Lasipalatsi Multimedia Centre, Mannerheimintie 22-24; lunch buffet €8; ☯ lunch 11am-3pm Mon-Sat) This place specialises in Finnish food and has a good soup and salad buffet.

Wrong Noodle Bar (☎ 2486 2442; Annankatu 21; mains €6.80-8.20; ☯ 11am-9pm Mon-Sat, 3-9pm Sun) Ultra-modern and trendy place for a fast and filling bowl of ramen noodles, laksa, satay or curry, including vegetarian.

Zetor (☎ 666 966; Mannerheimintie 3-5; mains €7-26; ☯ 3pm-1am Sun & Mon, 3pm-3am Tue, 3pm-4am Wed-Fri, 11-4am Sat) Wacky Finnish restaurant-bar with deeply ironic tractor décor, designed by those crazy guys from the Leningrad Cowboys. Traditional Finnish dishes (reindeer, vendace etc) and steaks and burgers.

Eatz (☎ 687 7240; Mikonkatu 15; mains €10-22; ☯ 10am-late) The versatile and colourful Eatz manages to serve up everything from Thai and Indian to Italian, and even has a sushi bar and Brazilian beach grill! It's also the cornerstone of Helsinki's biggest summer beer terrace.

DRINKING

Helsinki has probably the most lively and sophisticated nightlife scene in Scandinavia. In summer, drinking starts early at the many beer terraces that sprout up all over town. The biggest is along Mikonkatu at the front of Eatz.

For the cheapest beer in Helsinki (from €2 a pint during the seemingly perpetual happy hours), head to the working-class suburb of Kallio (metro Somäinen), north of the centre. There's a string of pubs along Helsinginkatu – start with **Roskapankki** (Trash Bank) and crawl east. The main areas for nightlife in the centre include Uudenmaankatu, Eerikinkatu and Yliopistonkatu.

Ateljee Bar (☎ 43360; Yrjönkatu 26; ☯ 2pm-1am Mon-Thu, 2pm-2am Fri, noon-2am Sat, 2pm-midnight

FINLAND

Sun) Tiny rooftop bar on 14th floor of the Sokos Hotel Torni (Helsinki's tallest building). The views from the toilets are the best in the city!

Bar Tapasta (☎ 640 724; Uudenmaankatu 13; ◉ 11am-midnight Mon-Thu, 11-2am Fri, 2pm-2am Sat) Intimate Spanish bar with a welcoming atmosphere and great tapas – wash it down with a jug of sangria.

Molly Malone's (☎ 5766 7500; Kaisaniemenkatu 1C; ◉ 11-2am Mon & Tue, 11-3am Wed-Sat, noon-2am Sun) Great place to meet travellers, expats and Finns. Live music upstairs most nights.

Saunabar (☎ 685 5550; Eerikinkatu 27; ◉ noon-2am Tue-Sat, noon-11pm Sun & Mon) Popular student bar with occasional live music and two saunas that are available 3pm to midnight Sunday and Monday (€4.50 per person) and at other times for private bookings.

Lost & Found (☎ 680 1010; Annankatu 6; ◉ until 4am) Sophisticated gay & hetero bar and popular late-night hang-out.

Club Helsinki (☎ 4332 6302; Yliopistonkatu 8; ◉ 10pm-4am) is a heaving mainstream dance club. **Arctic Icebar** (☎ 0800-94411; Yliopistonkatu 5; ◉ 5pm-4am), inside the nightclub Club Uniq, is a balmy -5°C. For €10 you get an insulated coat and a vodka shot.

GETTING THERE & AWAY
Air
Finnair flies to 20 Finnish cities generally at least once a day but usually several times daily. Full fares are €165 to Tarku, €118 to Tampere, €254 to Rovaniemi and €258 to Oulu. The **Finnair office** (reservations ☎ 0203-140160; Asemaaukio 3; ◉ 9am-5pm Mon-Sat) is near the train station.

Bus
The **main bus station** (☎ 682 701; Salomonkatu; ◉ 7am-7pm Mon-Fri, 7am-5pm Sat, 9am-6pm Sun) is behind Lasipalatsi off Mannerheimintie. At the time of research, a new underground bus station was being built.

Train
A pedestrian tunnel links the train station to Helsinki's metro system.

Express trains run daily to Turku, Tampere and Lappeenranta, and there's a choice of day and overnight trains to Oulu, Rovaniemi and Joensuu. There are also daily trains to the Russian cities of Vyborg, St Petersburg and Moscow.

GETTING AROUND
A one-hour flat-fare ticket for the bus, tram, metro, Suomenlinna ferry and local trains within Helsinki's **HKL network** (www .hel.fi/HKL) costs €2. It allows unlimited transfers but should be validated in the stamping machine on board when you first use it. Tourist tickets for one/three/five days are €5.40/10.80/16.20. Tram 3T from the *kauppatori* makes a good sightseeing trip.

Greenbike (☎ 8502 2850; rental per day/24 hr €10/24),in the old railway goods sheds, rents quality bikes.

AROUND HELSINKI

PORVOO
☎ 019 / pop 46,000
With its picture-postcard medieval **Old Town**, rust-coloured timber shore houses lining the river, and quaint cafés and bars, Porvoo (Borgå) makes a perfect day or overnight trip from Helsinki, 50km away.

The **tourist office** (☎ 520 2316; www.porvoo.fi; Rihkamakatu 4; ◉ 9am-6pm Mon-Fri, 10am-4pm Sat & Sun Jun-Aug, 9.30am-4.30pm Mon-Fri, 10am-2pm Sat & Sun Sep-May) has plenty of information on local sights, and a free Internet terminal.

Porvoo Hostel (☎ 523 0012; porvoohostel@co.inet.fi; Linnankoskenkatu 1-3; dm/s/d €13/27/32; ⊠ P) is a HI hostel in a lovely old building with spotless rooms and a well-equipped kitchen. It's a 10-minute walk south of the *kauppatori*. Book ahead (reception closed 10am to 4pm).

Frequent buses connect Porvoo and Helsinki (€8.40, one hour), as do ferries in summer. In summer (exact dates vary) the historic steamship **JL Runeberg** (☎ 019-5243331) sails from Helsinki at 10am daily, returning at 4pm (one-way/return trip €20/29).

SOUTHWESTERN FINLAND

TURKU
☎ 02 / pop 175,000
Once the capital under the Swedes, Turku (Åbo) is Finland's oldest town, and it brims with museums, a stunning harbourside castle and a magnificent cathedral. These days Turku is a modern maritime city defined by the Aurojoki River – in summer a high-

light is wandering along the river banks, pausing for a drink in the boat bars and restaurants.

Information

The **tourist office** (☎ 262 7444; www.turkutouring.fi; Aurakatu 4; ❧ 8.30am-6pm Mon-Fri, 9am-4pm Sat & Sun; ▣) hires out bikes (€10 per day) and sells the **Turku Card** (1/2 days €21/28), which gives free admission to most museums and attractions in the region.

Forex (☎ 251 0800; Eerikinkatu 12; ❧ 9am-7pm Mon-Fri, 9am-3pm Sat) is the best place to exchange cash and travellers cheques. The **main post office** (Humalistonkatu 1; ❧ 9am-8pm Mon-Fri) has conveniently long hours.

There are free Internet terminals at the **public library** (☎ 262 3611; Linnankatu 2; ❧ 10am-8pm Mon-Thu, 10am-6pm Fri, 10am-3pm Sat).

Sights & Activities

A great way to soak up Turku's summertime vibe is simply to walk or cycle along the river bank between the cathedral and the castle, crossing on the bridges or the much-loved local pedestrian ferry *Föri* (rides are free, and it runs constantly from early morning till dusk). Pick up a walking tour brochure from the tourist office.

At the western (harbour) end, **Turku Castle** (☎ 262 0300; admission €6.50, guided tours €1.50; ❧ 10am-6pm daily mid-May–mid-Sep, 10am-3pm Tue-Fri mid-Sep–mid-May) is a historical highlight, dating from 1280 and boasting dungeons, banquet halls and a medieval museum.

Forum Marinum (☎ 282 9511; Linnankatu 72; admission €10; ❧ 11am-7pm daily May-Sep, 10am-6pm Tue-Sun Oct-Apr) is a vast maritime museum near the castle. As well as an impressive large-scale exhibition space devoted to Turku's shipping background, it incorporates three **museum ships** moored on the river: the mine layer *Keihässalmi*, the three-masted barque *Sigyn* and the beautiful 1902 sailing ship *Suomen Joutsen* (Swan of Finland).

Turku's 50-odd museums and galleries cover everything from Sibelius to stuffed animals. They are generally open daily in summer and closed Monday in winter, and most are free with the Turku Card.

Archipelago cruises are popular in summer, with daily departures from Martinsilta Bridge. The best option is the 1½-hour cruise out to Naantali aboard the SS *Ukkopekka* **steamship** (☎ 515 3300; www.ukkopekka.fi; one way/return €17/20; ❧ 10am & 2pm Jun-Aug). See the tourist office for information about other cruises.

Sleeping

HI Hostel Turku (☎ 262 7680; hostel@turku.fi; Linnankatu 39; dm/s/d €13.80/33.30/37.60; ❧ reception 6am-10am & 3pm-midnight; ✗ Ⓟ) Well located on the river, close to the town centre, this warren of rooms includes a well-equipped kitchen, laundry (€2), lockers and bike hire.

Interpoint Hostel (☎ 231 4011; Vähä-Hämeenkatu 12A; dm €8.50-10.50; ❧ 15 July–15 Aug; ✗) Open for only one month, this is the cheapest place in Turku, but for good reason – 30 mattresses on the floor and one shower!

Eating & Drinking

Pizzeria Dennis (☎ 469 1191; Linnankatu 17; mains €8-12) A genuine Italian flavour and cosy dining rooms put this above most Finnish pizza-and-pasta places.

Blanko (☎ 233 3966; Aurakatu 1; mains €4-14; ❧ 11am-1am Mon-Thu, 11am-2am Wed-Thu, 11am-3am Fri, noon-3am Sat, noon-midnight Sun) Opposite the tourist office, this ultra-chic café is where Turku's hip young things get down to DJs on weekend nights; great sidewalk terrace and excellent tapas.

Vaakahuoneen Paviljonki (☎ 515 3324; Linnankatu 38; mains €7-15, fish buffet €8; ❧ dusk-dawn May-Sep) In summer this riverfront restaurant situated opposite the youth hostel is *the* place to go for great-value food and live jazz. Angle for the daily 'archipelago fish buffet', served between 11am and 10pm, June to August.

There are plenty of cheap eateries around Turku's *kauppatori* and in the **kauppahalli** (Eerikinkatu 16; ❧ Mon-Sat). Cheap meals are served at the **Turku University Student Café** (☎ university 33351; Hameenkatu).

In summer the decks of Turku's boat bars, which line the river bank on the southeast side of Auransilta Bridge, are crammed with drinkers, but the town also has some charmingly eccentric bars: **Puutorin Vessa** (☎ 233 8123; Puutori; ❧ noon-midnight), near the bus station, is a former public toilet; **Uusi Apteeki** (☎ 250 2595; Kaskenkatu 1; ❧ 10am-3am) is a wonderful bar in a converted old pharmacy; and **Panimo Koulu** (☎ 274 575; Eerikinkatu 18; ❧ 10am-3am) is an enormous brewery-restaurant in an old school.

FINLAND

Getting There & Away

From the main **bus station** (☎ 0200 0400; Aninkaistenkatu 20; ☷ 7am-9pm Mon-Sat, 8am-9pm Sun) there are hourly express buses to Helsinki (€22.30, 2½ hours) and frequent services to Tampere (€18.20, two hours) and Rauma (€11.90, 1½ hours).

Express trains run to and from Helsinki (€22.40, two hours) and Tampere (€16.60, 1¾ hours). There are direct train connections between Turku harbour and Helsinki. Bus No 30 shuttles between the centre and the train station.

Silja Line (☎ 335 255; www.silja.fi) and **Viking Line** (☎ 33 311; www.vikingline.fi) ferries sail between Turku and Stockholm (9½ hours) and Mariehamn (six hours). **Seawind Line** (☎ 210 2800; Linnankatu 84) sails to Stockholm via Långnäs (Åland). All three have offices at the harbour, and Viking Line also has an office in the Hansa shopping arcade on the east side of the *kauppatori*.

TAMPERE

☎ 03 / pop 199,800

Tampere really grows on you. Wedged between two lakes and once known for its powerful textile industry, this 19th-century manufacturing centre bristles with dozens of redbrick chimneys from former factories; most have now been transformed into superb cultural centres, bars or restaurants. Long known as the 'Manchester of Finland', on a grey day Tampere takes on a sort of Dickensian quality, with steam rising in the air like industrial fog. But don't be put off: Tampere works beautifully, combining working-class energy with Finnish sophistication and great nightlife.

Information

The **tourist office** (☎ 3146 6800; www.tampere.fi; Verkatehtaankatu 2; ☷ 8.30am-8pm Mon-Fri, 10am-5pm Sat & Sun Jun-Aug, 9am-4pm Mon-Fri rest of year; ☐), on the river just south of Hämeenkatu, has two free Internet terminals.

There are also free Internet terminals available at the **public library** (☎ 314 614; Pirkankatu 2; ☷ 9.30am-8pm Mon-Fri, 9.30am-3pm Sat, noon-6pm Sun, closed Sun in winter).

Sights & Activities

A walk along the banks of the Tammerkoski Rapids will give you a good feel for Tampere's industrial past – check out the renovated **Finlayson Mill**, which houses restaurants, a cinema and the off-beat **Spy Museum**. The **Vapriikki Centre** (☎ 3146 6966; Veturiaukio 4; admission €8; ☷ 10am-6pm Tue-Sun, 11am-8pm Wed), in the old Tampella mill, is Tampere's premier museum and exhibition space, and includes the **Ice Hockey Museum**.

Don't miss the tiny **Lenin Museum** (☎ 276 8100; Hämeenpuisto 28; admission €4; ☷ 9am-6pm Mon-Fri, 11am-4pm Sat & Sun), which gives a fascinating insight into the life and work of the Russian revolutionary leader. There's a zany gift shop.

Sleeping

Tampere has two HI-affiliated hostels at opposite ends of town.

Hostel Uimahallin Maja (☎ 222 9460; www.hosteltampere.com; Pirkankatu 10-12; dm/s/d €19.50/37/52) Although a bit further from the action, this is a better choice, with a great first-floor café, friendly staff and tidy rooms with linen included.

Hostel Tampere YWCA (☎ 254 4020; fax 254 4022; Tuomiokirkonkatu 12A; dm/s/d €13.50/31/44; ☷ Jun–late Aug; ☒) About 300m north of the train station, this summer hostel is simple and clean, with kitchen and laundry facilities.

Eating & Drinking

Cobbled Hämeenkatu is Tampere's broad main street running east–west from the train station to Hämeenpuisto, and it's along here that you'll find most of the city's restaurants, cafés and bars, and the *kauppatori*, where you can sample Tampere's frightening speciality, *mustamakkara* (blood sausage).

Donatello (☎ 222 0169; Aleksanterinkatu 37; buffet €6; ☷ 10.30am-9pm Mon-Thu, 11.30am-10pm Fri, noon-10pm Sat, 9am-9pm Sun) Lavish all-you-can-eat pizza-and-pasta buffet for lunch and dinner.

Panimoravintola Plevna (☎ 260 1200; Itäinenkatu 8; mains €7.60-23; ☷ 11am-1am Mon-Thu, 11am-2am Fri & Sat, noon-11pm Sun) This German-style brewery-pub-restaurant in the old Finlayson textile mill is one of the most enjoyable places to dine in Tampere. The specialities here are German sausages such as bratwurst and bockwurst (€7.60 to €11.40) – wash them down with a pint of Plevna's strong stout.

Entertainment

Café Europa (☎ 2235526; Aleksanterinkatu 29; ☷ 11am-midnight Mon-Wed, 11am-2am Thu, 11am-3am Fri & Sat, noon-1am Sun) The coolest bar in Tampere, with old-world couches, candlelight and a hip crowd. Upstairs is a small dance club called Attic, which opens at 10pm.

O'Connell's (Rautatienkatu 24; ⊙ 4pm-1am Sun-Thu, 4pm-1am Fri, 4pm-2am Sat) Unpretentious Irish pub – a good place to meet travellers, expats and locals.

Telakka (☎ 225 0720; Tullikamarinaukio 3; mains €8-12; ⊙ 11am-8pm Mon-Fri, noon-8pm Sat, 1-5pm Sun) Bohemian bar-theatre-restaurant with live music, theatre performances and a brilliant summer terrace.

Getting There & Away

Ryanair (☎ 0600 1610; www.ryanair.com) flies between London Stansted and Tampere once daily. The airport is 15km southwest of the centre, but all flights are met by a bus (€6).

The **main bus station** (Hatanpäänvaltatie 7) is a block south of the Koskikeskus shopping centre. Regular express buses make the trip to/from Helsinki (€26.30, 2½ hours) and Turku (€18.20, two hours).

Hourly express trains link Tampere with Helsinki (€22.40, 2½ hours). From Tampere, intercity trains go on to Oulu (€51.40, five hours), and there are direct trains to Turku, Pori, Jyväskylä, Vaasa and Joensuu.

ÅLAND

An easy stop on the ferry between Sweden and Finland, the Åland Islands are a slightly schizophrenic municipality with an archipelago stretching all the way to the mainland. The autonomous, self-governed islands have their own flag, stamps and culture, which leans more towards Sweden than Finland – several Swedish dialects are spoken, but few Ålanders speak Finnish. This situation goes back to a 1921 League of Nations decision after a dispute over sovereignty.

In summer the main reason to visit is for cycling and camping – the flat, picturesque islands are connected by bridges or free ferries, and along the way you'll pass medieval parish churches, ancient ruins and undisturbed fishing villages. Midsummer celebrations here are among the best in Finland.

Getting There & Around

Viking Line (☎ 26011; www.vikingline.fi; Storagatan 2) and **Silja Line** (☎ 16711; www.silja.fi; Torggatan 14) have daily ferries between Mariehamn and Turku (one way from €14, six hours), where they cross to Stockholm – the cruise through the archipelago is stunning.

Eckerö Line (☎ 28000; www.eckerolinjen.fi; Torggatan 2) plies the route between Grisslehamn in Sweden and Eckerö in Åland (€5.50 one way, three hours).

There's an island bus service, but a bike is the way to go. **Ro-No Rent** (☎ 018-12 820) rents bicycles at Mariehamn and Eckerö harbours starting from €7/35 a day/week (€13/65 for a mountain bike).

MARIEHAMN

☎ 018 / pop 11,000

Mariehamn, the 'town of a thousand linden trees', becomes the town of a thousand tourists in summer, but it still manages to retain its small-town flavour. The main ferry terminals are at Västra Hamnen (West Harbour), but the more colourful local marina is at Östra Hamnen (East Harbour).

The **tourist office** (☎ 24000; www.visitaland.com; Storagatan 8; ⊙ 9am-6pm daily Jun-Aug, 9am-4pm Mon-Fri, 10am-3pm Sat Sep-May; 🖳), on the main east–west esplanade, has free Internet access.

Sights

The **Maritime Museum** (☎ 19930; Västra Hamnen; admission €4.50; ⊙ 9am-5pm May-Aug, 9am-7pm Jul, 10am-4pm Sep-Apr) is a wonderfully kitsch museum of fishing and maritime commerce. Outside is the museum ship **Pommern** (admission €4.50), a beautifully preserved four-masted barque built in Glasgow in 1903. A combined ticket to both is €7.

The **Ålands Museum** (☎ 25426; Stadhusparken; admission €2.50; ⊙ 10am-4pm Wed-Mon, 10am-7pm Tue, closed Mon Sep-May) gives an absorbing account of Åland's history and culture from prehistory to the present.

Sleeping & Eating

Gästhem Kronan (☎ 12617; Neptunigatan 52; s/d €17/55; ⊙ Jun-Aug; ✗ P) Basic but clean enough rooms with a shared bathroom; the owners have another guesthouse up the road if Kronan is full.

Gröna Uddens Camping (☎ 21121; Oster-näsvägen; camping €17.50; ⊙ mid-May–Aug) One kilometre south of town, this is the closest camping to Mariehamn.

Café Julius (Torggatan 10; snacks €2-8; ⊙ 8am-6pm) Has plenty of cheap sandwiches, pastries and snacks, and you can sample the local speciality, Åland pancakes, made with semolina and served with fruit and whipped cream.

Dino's Bar & Grill (☎ Strandgatan 12; mains €8-15) Popular meeting spot with enormous hamburgers, pasta and pizza.

THE ISLANDS

☎ 018 / pop 26,300

There are more than 6500 islands in the Åland archipelago, but even on a bicycle you can explore the main ones in a few days. The central group of islands comprises **Jomala** and **Sund**, north of Mariehamn, and **Eckerö** to the west. Pick up a copy of the *Visit Åland* brochure and the camping guide from the Mariehamn tourist office for details of places to stay.

Åland's most striking attraction is the medieval castle **Kastelholm** (admission €5; ☉ 10am-4pm daily Jun-Aug, till 7pm Jul, Mon-Fri only in May) in Sund, 20km northeast of Mariehamn. Catch bus No 4 from Mariehamn or go by bike.

SOUTHEASTERN FINLAND

Eastern Finland is a romantic region of lakes, rivers, locks and canals, encompassing Karelia and the Savo region, of which Savonlinna is the centre. In summer this is a highlight of any trip to Finland.

SAVONLINNA

☎ 015 / pop 27,600

Lorded over by Olavinlinna, the best-preserved medieval castle in Scandinavia, and split by two stunning lakes, Savonlinna is the quintessential Lakeland town and the centre of the Savo region. In July the town erupts in a cultural frenzy during the renowned Savonlinna Opera Festival (see Festivals & Events, following).

The **tourist office** (☎ 517 510; www.savonlinna travel.com; Puistokatu 1; ☉ 9am-5pm Mon-Fri Aug-Jun, 8am-8pm daily Jul) is a good place for opera festival information and accommodation bookings.

Sights & Activities

Take a walk out to the forested island of **Sulosaari** via the footbridges (behind the Casino Spa Hotel) – it's beautiful on sum-

mer evenings, but it's popular with boozing local teens on weekends.

The dramatic medieval castle **Olavinlinna** (☎ 531 164; adult/student €5/3.50; ☉ 10am-5pm Jun-Aug, 10am-3pm Sep-May) was used by both Swedish and Russian overlords but is now famous as the setting for the opera festival. Excellent guided tours are given hourly.

Dozens of 1½-hour **scenic cruises** (tickets €7-10) leave from the harbour at the *kauppatori* daily in summer.

Festivals & Events

The **Savonlinna Opera Festival** (☎ 476 750; www .operafestival.fi; Olavinkatu 27), held throughout July, is perhaps the most famous international festival in Finland. Tickets cost from €30 to €100 but can be picked up for as little as €20 on some nights. Book over the Internet.

Sleeping & Eating

Book accommodation well in advance during the opera festival.

During summer the **SS Heinävesi** (☎ 533 120; upper/lower deck cabins per person €19/17) offers two-person cabin accommodation after its last nightly cruise, which finishes about 6pm.

Vuorilinna (☎ 739 5495; casino.myynti@svlkylpy laitos.fi; Kylpylaitoksentie; dm/s/d from €23/50/65; ☉ Jun–late Aug; ✗ ℗ ✿) HI-affiliated summer hostel with great facilities near to (and run by) the spa hotel on Kasinosaari (Casino Island).

Vuohimäki Camping (☎ 537 353; myyntipalvelu@ lomaliitto.fi; camping €19, cabins €56-82; ☉ Jun-Aug) Seven kilometres west of town, it still fills up quickly in July.

Liekkilohi (Flaming Salmon; mains €7-8.50; ☉ 6pm-2am Jun-Aug) Bright-red, covered pontoon anchored just off the *kauppatori*, serving salmon, vendace and other fishy snacks.

Huvila (☎ 555 0555; www.savonniemi.com; Puistokatu 4; mains €11.50-21; ☉ noon-11pm Mon-Thu, noon-1am Fri & Sat, noon-8pm Sun) This superb lakeside brewery-restaurant is the place for a splurge in Savonlinna. As well as quality Finnish cuisine, the brewery produces fine beers, including some of Finland's best *sahti* (a sweet high-alcohol beer).

On the *kauppatori*, Café Torppa is a popular student-run kiosk for coffee and late-night snacks.

Getting There & Away

Regular and express buses make the journey between Savonlinna and Helsinki (€37.70,

4½ hours), Joensuu (€19.70, two hours), Kuopio (€24.60, two hours) and Kerimäki (€4.40, 30 minutes).

There are trains to Helsinki (€46.80, five hours) via a change at Parikkala. For Kuopio, you need to take a bus to Pieksämäki and a train from there (€23.60, three hours, including bus leg). The main train station is a long walk from the centre; get off at the *kauppatori* platform instead.

In summer the lake ferry MS *Puijo* travels to Kuopio on Monday, Wednesday and Friday at 9.30am (€65, 10½ hours), returning on Tuesday, Thursday and Saturday. Book on ☎ 555 0120.

KUOPIO
☎ 017 / pop 87,800

Home to the world's biggest smoke sauna, Kuopio is a vibrant Lakeland town in a beautiful location, surrounded by forest and lakes. Visit on Tuesday or Thursday in summer, when the sauna is cranked up.

Kuopio Travel Shop (☎ 182 585; www.kuopioinfo .fi; Haapaniemenkatu 17; ☉ 9.30am-4.30pm Mon-Fri year-round & 10am-3pm Sat Jul) is behind the town hall on the north side of the *kauppatori*.

Don't miss the chance to sweat in the world's largest **smoke sauna** (Jätkänkämpällä; ☎ 473 473; admission €10; ☉ 5pm-10pm Tue & Thu Jun-Aug, closed Thu Sep-May), near the Rauhalahti Hotel Spa. This 60-person sauna is mixed, and guests are given wraps to wear. If you really want to feel Finnish, bring a swimsuit for a dip in the lake afterwards.

Kuopio has a handful of museums, which can all be visited with the **museum card** (€11) available from the tourist office.

Sleeping & Eating
Retkeilymaja Virkkula (☎ 263 7839; Asemakatu 3; dm €14; ☉ Jun-Aug; ✗) Right next to the train station, this is a conveniently central and cheap summer hotel with large dorms. Reception is open from 6pm.

Hostelli Rauhalahti (☎ 473 473; Katiskaniementie 8; dm/s/d €34/60/68; ✗ P 🖳 🖳) Next to the Rauhalahti Hotel-Spa, 5km southwest of the centre, this is pricey but close to the smoke sauna and you also get to use the hotel's facilities. Take bus No 7 from the *kauppatori*.

Camping Rauhalahti (☎ 361 2244; Kiviniementie; per person/camp site €4/7, 2-4-person cottages €55; ☉ mid-May–Sep) Adjacent to the Rauhalahti

spa complex, this luxury camping ground has a beautiful lakeside location.

Café-Restaurant Helmi (☎ 261 1110; Kauppakatu 2; mains €4.50-7; ☉ 11am-11pm Mon-Thu, 11am-1pm Fri & Sat, noon-10pm Sun) In Kuopio's oldest stone building (1850), this atmospheric bar and restaurant specialises in great pizzas. There's often live music in the courtyard at the side.

There are indoor and outdoor markets in the main square, where you can try *kalakukko*, fish baked inside a rye loaf (eaten hot or cold). The 2nd-floor **Golden Rax Pizza & Pasta** (Puijonkatu 45; buffet lunch & dinner €7; ☉ 10am-9pm) serves the usual all-you-can-eat fare.

Burts Café (☎ 262 3995; Puijonkatu 15) is the best place in town for coffee and homemade cakes and pastries.

Most of Kuopio's nightlife is along Kauppakatu, running east from the *kauppatori* to the harbour. **Wanha Satama** (☎ 197 304; ☉ 4pm-10pm Mon-Fri, 11am-10pm Sat, noon-5pm Sun), down at the harbour, is a lively pub with a sprawling summer terrace.

Getting There & Away
Kuopio has bus connections to Helsinki (€46.10, five hours), Joesnuu (€21.70, two hours), Kajaani (€24, 2½ hours) and Savonlinna (€24.60, 2½ hours). The express bus station is north of the train station. There are direct trains to Helsinki (€48.20, 5½ hours).

In summer the lake ferry MS *Puijo* departs for Savonlinna (€65, 8½ hours) on Tuesday, Thursday and Saturday, returning Monday, Wednesday and Friday. Call ☎ 266 2466 for more details.

NORTHERN FINLAND

Northern Finland includes the provinces of Oulu, Kainuu and Lapland. This is Finland's true wilderness and a place of extremes: continuous daylight in summer and continuous night in winter. During the Arctic winter, October, February and March are ideal times to see the stunning aurora borealis. September brings exceptional autumn colours, and in the far north *kaamos*, the season of eerie bluish light, begins in late October.

Finnish Lapland is home to some 6500 indigenous Sami people – along with about

200,000 reindeer. The region includes ski resorts, a golf course at Tornio that's half in Finland and half in Sweden, and a winter ice castle at Kemi.

OULU

☎ 08 / pop 124,600

The lively, fast-growing university town of Oulu looks out on the Gulf of Bothnia and a string of interconnected islands. For travellers it's not the sights that make Oulu worth a stop but its summertime energy, superb cycling paths, friendly locals and frenetic nightlife.

The **tourist office** (☎ 5584 1330; www.oulutourism .fi; Torikatu 10; ⏰ 9am-6pm Mon-Fri, 10am-3pm Sat mid-Jun–mid-Aug; 9am-4pm Mon-Fri Sep–mid-Jun) is two blocks southeast of the *kauppatori*.

Sleeping & Eating

Nallikari Camping (☎ 5586 1350; nallikari.camping@ ouka.fi; Hietasaari; camping €15-17, 2-/4-bed summer camping cabins €29, 2-/5-/7-person cottages €53/75/109) Cheap summer cabins are available on the island of Hietasaari, 3km from Oulu by foot or bicycle via the pedestrian bridges.

Kesähotelli Oppimestari (☎ 884 8527; fax 884 8772; Nahkatehtaankatu 3; s/d €37/55; ⏰ Jun–early Aug; ✗ Ⓟ) Across from the Tietomaa Science Centre, this summer hotel has the cheapest rooms in Oulu.

Café Bisketti (☎ 375 768; Kirkkokatu 8; cakes €2.50-5) Excellent rolls, croissants, quiche and cakes, and a terrace facing the pedestrian square.

Rotuaari is the main pedestrian strip between the *kauppatori* and Isokatu, and along here are plenty of bars and cafés.

Cheap snacks and local specialities can be found on the impressive *kauppatori*, which is bordered by timber restaurants and summer beer terraces. The *kauppahalli* is on the south side of the square.

Getting There & Away

Trains and buses connect Oulu with all main centres; eight to 10 direct trains a day go to Helsinki (€59, seven to 10 hours) and Rovaniemi (€26.40, 2½ hours).

ROVANIEMI

☎ 016 / pop 35,400

Rovaniemi is the capital of and gateway to Lapland, though there's not much Lappish about the modern town centre since it was razed by retreating Germans in WWII and rebuilt to a plan by architect Alvar Aalto. Many travellers make a beeline here from Helsinki, either to say they've visited Lapland or to 'cross' the Arctic Circle and meet Santa and his famous post office.

If you've got the euros, there's no better place to organise winter reindeer-sleigh, dog-sledding or snowmobile trips. Ask at the tourist office.

The shamelessly named **Santa Claus Tourist Centre** (☎ 346 270; www.rovaniemi.fi; Koskikatu 1; Internet access per 15 min €3; ⏰ 8am-6pm Mon-Fri, 10am-4pm Sat & Sun Jun–late Aug, 8am-4pm Mon-Fri late Aug–May) is an excellent source of information for all of Lapland.

The Aalto-designed **regional library** (☎ 322 2463; Jorma Eton tie 6; ⏰ 11am-7pm Mon-Fri, 11am-5pm Sat, 11am-3pm Sun) has free Internet access.

Sights & Activities

Arktikum (☎ 317 830; www.arktikum.fi; Pohjoisranta 4; adult/student €11/8.50; ⏰ 9am-7pm mid-Jun–mid-Aug, 10am-6pm early Jun & late Aug, 10am-6pm Tue-Sun Sep-May), with its beautifully designed glass tunnel, is one of Finland's premier museums. Exhibits include Arctic flora and fauna, Sami culture and an aurora borealis show.

The official **Arctic Circle marker** is 8km north of Rovaniemi. This is home to the 'official' **Santa Claus Village** (☎ 356 2096; ⏰ 10am-5pm, 9am-7pm Jun-Aug). The Santa Claus post office receives close to a million letters each year. As tacky as it sounds, it's all good fun. You can send a postcard home with an official Santa stamp (to be delivered at Christmas) and have your picture taken with St Nick (€17!). To get there, take bus No 8 (return trip €5.20) from the Rovaniemi train station.

Sleeping & Eating

Rovaniemi's youth hostel was demolished in 2004.

Matka Borealis (☎ 342 0130; Asemieskatu 1; s/d €45/58; ✗ Ⓟ) Rovaniemi's cosiest guesthouse is opposite the train station. Clean, simple rooms with attached bathroom; breakfast is included.

Matkustajakoti Outa (☎ 312 474; Ukkoherrantie 16; s/d €35/45; ✗) Cheap, no-frills guesthouse with shared bathrooms, right in the town centre.

Ounaskoski Camping (☎ 345 304; Jämerentie 1; camping €5; ⏰ Jun-Aug) Across the river from the town centre, with tent and van sites only.

Mariza (☎ 319 616; Ruokasenkatu 2; lunch buffet €5.90-6.50; ⏰ 10am-3pm Mon-Fri) Casual, working-class diner offering a fabulous lunch buffet of home-cooked Finnish food.

Koskikatu has many inexpensive and mid-range restaurants, including branches of Rosso and Golden Rax Pizza Buffet. You'll also find the world's northernmost McDonald's here.

Rovaniemi has loads of bars and night-clubs in the town centre. In summer, kick back under the midnight sun in the open beer terrace of **Oluthuone** (Koskikatu). **Pub Ylityö** (Overtime Bar; Kosikatu 5), further down, is a tiny, eccentric pub with no seats – it was voted one of the world's best bars by *Newsweek* in 1996!

Getting There & Away

Frequent buses travel south to Oulu (€27.80, 3½ hours), and north to Inari (€42.70, five hours), continuing on to Norway.

The train is the best way to travel between Helsinki and Rovaniemi (€70.20, 10 to 12 hours). It's quicker and cheaper than the bus. There are eight daily trains (via Oulu), including four overnight services.

INARI

From Rovaniemi, Hwy 4 heads north into Lapland and the Sami heartland of Sápmi. The tiny village of Inari is the main Sami community and a centre of Sami Duodji (the official Sami handicrafts label).

It may seem unprepossessing at first, but Inari has a beautiful setting on Lake Inari-järvi and a brilliant museum of Sami culture. **Siida** (☎ 665 212; www.samimuseum.fi; adult/student €7/6; ⏰ 9am-8pm daily Jun-Sep, 10am-5pm Tue-Sun Oct-May) successfully brings to life Sami origins, culture, lifestyle and present-day struggles, with indoor and open-air displays.

Hostel Jokitörmä (☎ 672 725; www.jokitorma.com; camping €13, dm €16.50, s/d cabins €13.50/26; ℗) is a HI hostel 23km north of Inari, with cosy rooms and a separate set of cottages – all buses will stop here on request.

The local **Hotel Inari** (☎ 671 026; s/d/tr €38/45/60) has clean rooms, a restaurant serving cheap pizzas and Lappish dishes, and a pub.

Gold Line (☎ 016-334 5521; www.goldline.fi; Marttiin-intie 10, Rovaniemi) buses run daily between Ivalo and Rovaniemi (€37.70, 4½ hours), Nord-kapp (adult/student €101.50/77.10, 11 hours) in Norway, and Inari (€6, 40 minutes).

FINLAND DIRECTORY

ACCOMMODATION

With a tent and sleeping bag, camping is the cheapest way to travel around Finland. Most sites are open only from June to August, and popular spots are crowded during July and the midsummer weekend, which is called Juhannus (the third weekend in June). Contact the **Finnish Camping Association** (☎ 09-4774 0740; www.camping.fi) for more information.

The **Finnish Youth Hostel Association** (SRM; ☎ 09-64 0377; info@srm.inet.fi; Yrjönkatu 38B, 00100 Helsinki) operates 91 hostels. About half are open all year, and the rest are summer only (June to August) and are usually student accommodation buildings vacated for school holidays. Hostel prices quoted in this chapter are without the €2.50 discount given to holders of a valid HI card.

There's little seasonal variation in the budget range: camping sites cost from €8 to €18 and hostel dorm beds from €12 to €25.

ACTIVITIES

Finland is all about nature and the great outdoors. Hiking or trekking is best from June to September, although in July mosquitoes and other insects can be a problem in Lapland. Wilderness huts line the northern trails (they are free and must be shared), and you're generally allowed to hike in any forested or wilderness area and camp for a night anywhere outside inhabited, privately owned areas.

Canoes and kayaks can be hired in most towns near a lake, often from camping grounds.

Nordic and downhill skiing is popular and the season runs from October to April. Other winter activities include reindeer-sledding, dogsledding and snowmobiling (see p364), but they're expensive.

Most towns have an indoor swimming pool with saunas and spas (see p356 and p363).

BUSINESS HOURS

Shops generally open from 9am to 5pm weekdays and to 1pm on Saturday. Banks are open from 9.15am until 4.15pm weekdays. Many supermarkets and Helsinki department stores stay open until 9pm or 10pm on weeknights and are open all day on Saturday.

Cafés are usually open from 9am or 10am to 6pm – later if they're licensed. Restaurants open from around 11am to 10pm, with lunch from 11am to 3pm. Pubs open from 11am to 10pm (1am or later on Friday and Saturday) and nightclubs stay open as late as 4am.

EMBASSIES & CONSULATES

Embassies & Consulates in Finland

The following embassies are in Helsinki:

Australia (☎ 447 233; Museokatu 25B, Vantaa)
Canada (☎ 228 530; Pohjoisesplanadi 25B)
Denmark (☎ 684 1050; Keskuskatu 1A)
Estonia (☎ 622 0288; Itäinen Puistotie 10)
France (☎ 618 780; Itäinen Puistotie 13)
Germany (☎ 458 580; Krogiuksentie 4)
Ireland (☎ 646 006; Erottajankatu 7)
Japan (☎ 686 0200; Eteläranta 8)
Netherlands (☎ 228 920; Eteläsplanadi 24A)
Norway (☎ 686 0180; Rehbinderintie 17)
Russia (☎ 661 876; Tehtaankatu 1B)
Sweden (☎ 687 7660; Pohjoisesplanadi 7B)
UK (☎ 2286 5100; Itäinen Puistotie 17)
USA (☎ 616 2500; Itäinen Puistotie 14A)

Finnish Embassies Abroad

Finland maintains embassies in the following countries:

Australia (☎ 02-6273 3800; sanomat.can@formin.fi; 12 Darwin Ave, Yarralumla, ACT 2600)
Canada (☎ 613-288 2233; embassy@finland.ca; 55 Metcalfe St, Ste 850, Ottawa K1P 6L5)
Denmark (☎ 3313 4214; sanomat.kob@formin.fi; Sankt Annae Plads 24, 1250 Copenhagen K)
France (☎ 01 44 18 19 20; sanomat.par@ formin.fi; 1 Pl de Finlande, 57007 Paris)
Germany (☎ 030-505030; info.berlin@formin.fi; Rauchstrasse 1, 10787 Berlin)
Ireland (☎ 01-478 1344; sanomat.dub@ formin.fi; Russell House, Stokes Pl, St Stephen's Green, Dublin 2)
Netherlands (☎ 070-346 9754; sanomat.haa@formin.fi; Groot Hertoginnelaan 16, 251r EG Den Haag)
New Zealand (☎ 04-499 4599; Level 24, HSBC Tower, 195 Lambton Quay, Wellington) Or contact the Australian embassy.
Norway (☎ 2212 4900; sanomat.osl@ formin.fi; Thomas Heftyes gate 1, 0244 Oslo)
Russia (☎ 095-787 4174; sanomat.mos@ formin.fi; Kropotkinskij Pereulok 15/17, 119034 Moskva G-34)
Sweden (☎ 08-676 6700; info@finland.se; Gärdesgatan 11, 11527 Stockholm)
UK (☎ 020-7838 6200; sanomat.lon@formin.fi; 38 Chesham Pl, London SW1X 8HW)
USA (☎ 202-298 5800; sanomat.was@formin.fi; 3301 Massachusetts Ave NW, Washington, DC 20008)

FESTIVALS & EVENTS

Finland has a barrage of festivals between mid-June and mid-August – you could easily plan your summer vacation around them. Check www.festivals.fi for more details.

Kaustinen Folk Music Festival (June)
Provinssirock (June) Seinajöki rock festival.
Ruisrock (June) Big rock festival in Turku.
Pori Jazz Festival (July)
Savonlinna Opera Festival (July)
Helsinki Festival (August)

For something a bit more offbeat, check out the action at the Wife-Carrying World Championships at Sonkajärvi in July or Oulu's World Air Guitar Championships in late August (see p366).

FOOD & DRINK

Typical Finnish food is heavy on fish, potatoes, dark rye bread, hearty soups and stews. In Lapland or Lappish restaurants reindeer is commonly served. Most restaurants offer special lunch menus for around €8, which include a buffet of salad, bread, juice, coffee and dessert, plus big helpings of fish or meat. Fill up between 11am and 2pm or 3pm!

Most towns have a covered market called a *kauppahalli* where you can buy cheap sandwiches and snacks. Inexpensive pizzerias are everywhere – Golden Rax Pizza Buffet has all-you-can-eat pizzas, pasta, chicken wings, salad, ice cream, coffee and soft drinks for under €8.

A large beer in a bar costs €4 to €5. To drink cheaply, visit the state-run Alko shops, which sell all kinds of beer, wine and spirits, or any supermarket, R-kiosk or petrol station.

HOLIDAYS

Finland grinds to a halt twice a year – around Christmas and New Year and during the Midsummer weekend. Plan ahead so that you can avoid travelling during those times.

Vappu (30 April to 1 May) is a big day for Finns – students dress in white caps and coloured overalls, people take to the streets and parks, and everyone proceeds to get blind drunk.

New Year's Day 1 January
Epiphany 6 January

Easter (Good Friday to Easter Monday, inclusive) March/April
Vappu Eve (May Day Eve) 30 April
Vappu (May Day) 1 May
Ascension Day 40 days after Easter
Whit Sunday Late May or early June
Juhannus (Midsummer weekend) Third weekend in June
All Saints Day 1 November
Independence Day 6 December
Christmas Eve 24 December
Christmas Day 25 December
Boxing Day 26 December

MONEY

Finland uses the euro. In cities, independent exchangers such as Forex are a better alternative to banks for exchanging cash and travellers cheques (€2 flat fee).

Undoubtedly the best way to get in by in Finland is with the plastic – a debit or credit card, or both. Finnish ATMs, called 'Otto', are everywhere, and all are linked to international networks such as Cirrus, EC, Eurocard, Visa, Plus and MasterCard. Credit cards are widely accepted.

For more information on costs and money, see p28.

POST

Main post offices are generally open from 9am to 7pm weekdays, but in cities they are also open on Saturday. Stamps (€0.65 for letters and postcards) can be bought at bus or train stations and R-kiosks (convenience stores). Address post restante mail to 'Post Restante, Mannerheiminaukio 1, 00100 Helsinki'.

TELEPHONE

Most public telephones only accept Telecards, and international calls are cheapest with a prepaid calling card from any R-kiosk. The off-peak period is between 10pm and 8am on weekdays and all day on weekends. Finland's country code is ☎ 358, and its international code is ☎ 00. For national directory assistance, dial ☎ 020 202; for international help, dial ☎ 020 208.

Finns love mobile phones, and it's easy to get hooked up to the network for a limited period. If you bring your own phone, buy a SIM card (around €15) from an R-kiosk or phone shop and use the Sonera or DNA prepaid network.

VISAS

A valid passport is required to enter Finland. Citizens of EU countries (except Greece), Norway and Iceland can travel with only an identity card. Most Western nationals don't need a tourist visa for stays under three months; South Africans require a Schengen visa. The **Directorate of Immigration** (☎ 09-476 5500; www.uvi.fi; Panimokatu 2A, 00580 Helsinki) handles visas and work permits.

Australian and New Zealand citizens aged between 18 and 30 can apply for a 12-month working-holiday visa to Finland under a reciprocal agreement.

Russian visas can be obtained from the Russian consulate in Helsinki. You need to leave your passport at the consulate and allow a week to 10 days for processing. Travel agencies in Helsinki can expedite the visa process for a fee.

France

HIGHLIGHTS

- **Paris** For grandeur, other cities struggle to match beautiful, elegant Paris, home to shaded boulevard cafés and exceptional museums such as the Louvre, the Musée d'Orsay and the Pompidou Centre (p376)
- **The Côte d'Azur** The French Riviera for vertigo-inducing Corniches (mountain roads) and coastal railway lines hugging the dazzling blue Mediterranean, for chic seaside resorts and for the lively nightlife of Nice (p429)
- **Mont St-Michel** The invisible pull of moon and sun wash the tides around the mysterious fortress and abbey Mont St-Michel in Normandy (p400)
- **Versailles Palace** The largest and most grandiose of the hundreds of chateaux throughout the country, a dazzling marker of royal power, excess and extravagance (p390)
- **Brittany** Remote, wild, wave-pounded Brittany is a stirring mix of Celtic culture and ancient sea ports such as St-Malo, a medieval town of winding streets (p401)

FAST FACTS

- **Area** 551,000 sq km (twice the size of Britain)
- **Budget** €40-50 per day
- **Capital** Paris
- **Country codes** ☎ 33; international code ☎ 01 Paris, ☎ 02 Northwest, ☎ 03 Northeast, ☎ 04 Southeast (& Corsica), ☎ 05 Southwest
- **Famous for** Paris, croissants, wine, cheese
- **Head of State** President Jacques Chirac
- **Languages** French
- **Money** Euro (A$1 = €0.58, CA$1 = €0.64, ¥100 = €0.73, NZ$1 = €0.54, UK£1 = €1.45, US$ = €0.81)
- **Phrases** *Bonjour* (hello), *au revoir* (goodbye), *s'il vous plait* (please) *merci* (thank you)

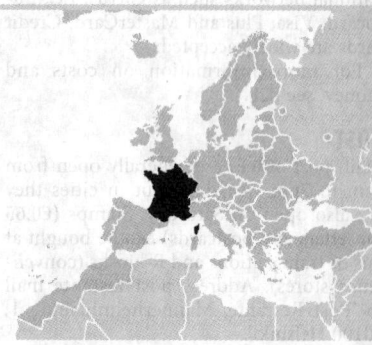

- **Population** 60.2 million
- **Visas** Not for EU citizens, prospective EU member states and citizens of Iceland, Norway, Australia, the USA, Canada, New Zealand, Japan or Israel.

TRAVEL HINT

Fill sticks of delicious French bread with local cheese or *charcuterie* (deli meat) and wash it down with wine for budget picnic feasts.

ROAMING FRANCE

Use Paris as your hub for trips west to Normandy, Brittany and the Atlantic coast before heading south through Burgundy to the Mediterranean.

Is it any wonder France is one of Europe's most-visited countries? And is it a coincidence that so many holidaying French are such stay-at-homes? Surely not, for they have everything they need right on their doorstep: mountains, beaches, countryside, vibrant cities and national parks rich in natural wonders.

The largest country in Western Europe, France stretches from the rolling hills of the north to the seemingly endless beaches of the south; from the wild coastline of Brittany to the icy crags of the Alps. It is liberally strewn with remnants of a rich, often illustrious past from grand Roman ruins and awe-inspiring medieval cathedrals to grand public palaces. It retains a confident culture today with a strong sense of identity and a rich treasure house of arts.

France's food and wine are truly without peer. What other European country is so spoiled for choice by the bounty of farm, forest and vineyard, not to mention two seas (the Atlantic and the Mediterranean)?

Once the western boundary of Europe, today France stands firmly at the crossroads: between England and Italy, Belgium and Spain, North Africa and Scandinavia. Of course, this is exactly how the French have always regarded their country – at the very centre of things.

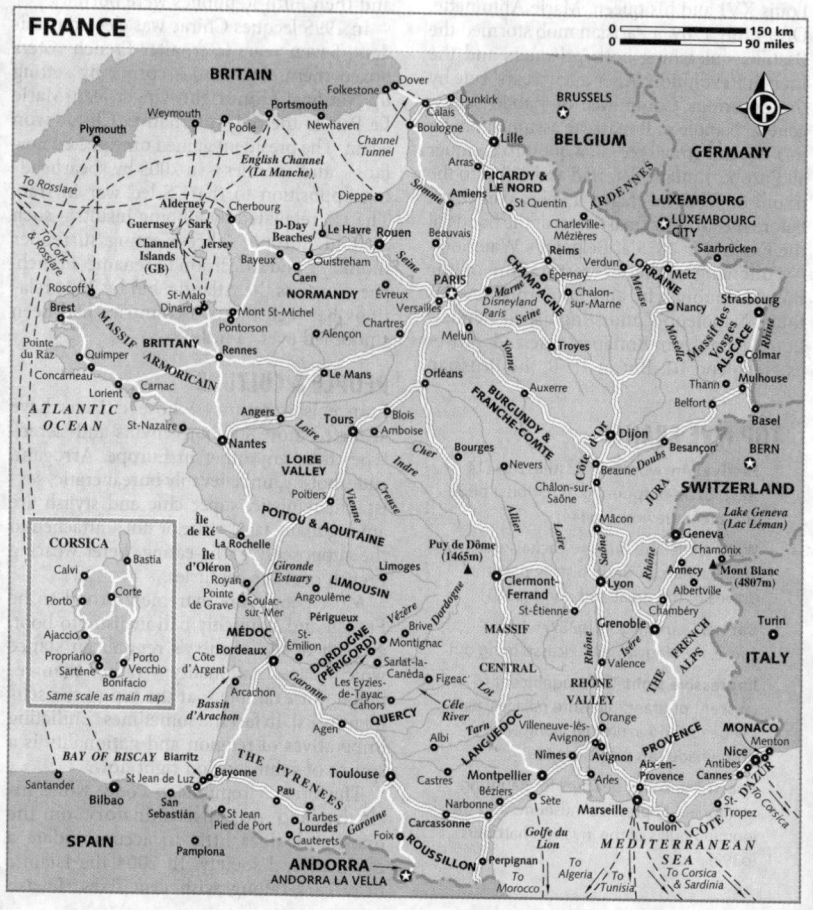

HISTORY

France's early history is humorously encapsulated in the popular *Astérix* comic books: the Celtic Gauls moved in between 1500 and 500 BC, and they bridled under the rule of Roman legions from 52 BC until the 5th century. After the Roman Empire's decline, France was governed by a series of monarchs, including Charlemagne (from 800). William the Conqueror even extended French rule to England in 1066.

As the Reformation took hold in the 16th century, fighting between Catholics and Protestants brought the French state close to disintegration. However, that paled beside the seismic events of the 1780s, when the population rose up against the dissolute Louis XVI and his queen, Marie Antoinette. On 14 July 1789, a Parisian mob stormed the Bastille, unleashing both prisoners and the French Revolution. After a few years' rule by the notorious Committee of Public Safety, general Napoleon Bonaparte assumed power in 1799 and embarked on a quest to conquer all Europe. Initially defeated and exiled to the island of Elba, he staged a short comeback before meeting his final defeat at the hands of the English, in 1815 at Belgium's Waterloo.

Following a chaotic restoration of the Bourbon monarchy and numerous revolutions, Napoleon's undistinguished nephew Louis-Napoleon Bonaparte seized power as Napoleon III. But in 1870, the Prussian prime minister Bismarck goaded Napoleon III into declaring war on Prussia and suffering prompt defeat. The emperor was deposed and the Third Republic proclaimed.

Central to France's entry into WWI was the desire to regain Alsace and Lorraine, lost to Germany in 1871. This was achieved but at immense human cost: 1.3 million killed and almost one million crippled. In WWII, France capitulated to Germany by June 1940, giving rise to the collaborationist Vichy regime.

The liberation of France began with the US, British and Canadian landings in Normandy on D-day (6 June 1944). General Charles de Gaulle, leader of the French government-in-exile, returned to Paris and set up a provisional government. The Fourth and then Fifth Republics were born.

In 1995 Jacques Chirac was elected president. Seven years later, after French voters boxed themselves into a corner by setting up National Front right-winger Jean-Marie Le Pen as the only alternative, Chirac won again. The president gained unexpected new fans – and enemies – in 2003 by spearheading opposition to the US-led war in Iraq. The US retaliated by lobbing insults – such as 'Old Europe', 'cheese-eating surrender monkeys' and a decision to rename 'French' fries – across the Atlantic, but by 2004 relations between the two countries had been smoothed over (a little).

PEOPLE & CULTURE

France is a country whose citizens have attracted more stubborn myths and stereotypes than any other in Europe. Arrogant, rude, bolshy, unbelievably bureaucratic, sexist, chauvinistic, super chic and stylish are among many tags – true or not – attached to the supposedly garlic-eating, beret-wearing French over the centuries.

Most people are extremely proud to be French and staunchly nationalistic to boot, a result of the country's republican stance which places nationality – rather than religion, for example – at the top of the self-identity list. In fact the sometimes conflicting imperatives of religion and nationality is a source of some tension right now.

The French republican code, while inclusive and non-discriminatory on the one hand, does little to accommodate a multicultural society. In 2004 the Islamic headscarf (along with crucifixes, Jewish

TOP FIVE FRANCE

- **Festival** Anywhere on Bastille Day (14 July) for an outpouring of national pride and great fireworks (p444)
- **Walk** Cimetière du Père Lachaise, a verdant walk through history past the graves of the great and good (p381)
- **Bar** Les Deux Magots (p387) where Sartre, Hemingway and Picasso hung out
- **Impressive sight** The magnificent crescent of grand pleasure palaces, pebbly beach and azure sea along Nice's promenade des Anglais (p429)
- **Beach** The D-day beaches for haunting memorials, impressive museums and the looming hulks of the invasion harbours (p399)

skullcaps and other religious symbols) was banned in French schools. The law, intended to protect the secular nature of state education, was cited by many French muslims as evidence that the French state was unwilling or unable to integrate them fully.

Bald statistics certainly strengthen their argument: 90% of France's Muslim community are noncitizens, many are illegal immigrants and most live in depressing poverty-stricken bidonvilles (tinpot towns) surrounding major metropolitan centres.

ARTS
Literature
The philosophical work of Voltaire (1694–1778), and of Swiss-born philosopher Jean-Jacques Rousseau, dominated the 18th century. A century on, the poems and novels of Victor Hugo – Les Misérables and Notre Dame de Paris (The Hunchback of Notre Dame) among them – became landmarks of French Romanticism.

In 1857 two literary landmarks were published: Madame Bovary by Gustave Flaubert (1821–80) and Charles Baudelaire's collection of poems, Les Fleurs du Mal (The Flowers of Evil). Émile Zola (1840–1902) meanwhile strove to convert novel-writing from an art to a science.

The expression of mental states was the aim of symbolists such as Paul Verlaine (1844–96). Verlaine's poems, alongside those of Arthur Rimbaud (1854–91), are seen as French literature's first modern poems.

After WWII, existentialism developed around the lively debates of Jean-Paul Sartre (1905–80), Simone de Beauvoir (1908–86) and Albert Camus (1913–60) in Paris' Left Bank cafés of St-Germain des Prés.

Cinema & TV
The Lumière brothers, shot the world's first-ever motion picture in March 1895 and French cinema has been making an impact on the wider world ever since.

One of its most notable successes was the movement known as the nouvelle vague (new wave), which burst forth in the late 1950s and the 1960s. With small budgets and no extravagant sets or big-name stars, filmmakers produced uniquely personal films using real-life subject matter: Claude Chabrol, Alain Resnais, François Truffaut and perhaps most famously Godard (who directed the classic A Bout de Souffle) were all pioneers of the movement.

Big-name stars, slick production values and a focus on nostalgia were the dominant motifs in the 1980s. Claude Berri's presentation of prewar Provence in Jean de Florette (1986), Jean-Paul Rappeneau's Cyrano de Bergerac (1990) and Bon Voyage (2003) set in 1940s Paris, and Astérix et Obélix: Mission Cléopâtre (2001) – all starring France's best known (and biggest-nosed) actor Gérard Depardieu – found huge audiences in France and abroad.

In 2001 the delightfully uncontroversial Le Fabuleux Destin de Amélie Poulain (Amélie; 2001), a feel-good story of a winsome Parisian do-gooder directed by Jean-Pierre Jeunet of Delicatessen (1991) fame proved an instant hit – everywhere. French film has enjoyed a massive renaissance ever since, French-film cinema-goers outside of France rising from 17 million in 2000 to a current 37.5 million a year.

Music
Jazz hit 1920s Paris, while the chanson française was revived in the 1930s by Édith Piaf and Charles Trenet. In the 1950s the Left Bank cabarets nurtured chansonniers (cabaret singers) such as Léo Ferré, Georges Brassens, Claude Nougaro, Jacques Brel and Serge Gainsbourg.

French pop music has evolved massively since the 1960s yéyé (imitative rock) days of Johnny Halliday. Particularly strong is world music, from Algerian rai and other North African music (such as Natacha Atlas) to Senegalese mbalax (Youssou N'Dour) and West Indian zouk (Zouk Machine). One musician who combines many of these elements is Paris-born Manu Chao.

Another hot musical export is Parisian electronic music from bands such as, Daft Punk and Air. French rap was spearheaded in the 1990s by Senegal-born Paris-reared rapper MC Solaar and is a popular genre today.

Architecture
Southern France is the place to find France's Gallo-Roman legacy: the Pont du Gard (p438) and the amphitheatre in Nîmes (p437).

Impressive 12th-century Gothic structures include Avignon's massive pontifical palace (p426).

Art Nouveau (1850–1910) combined iron, brick, glass and ceramics in new ways. See for

FRANCE

yourself in Paris's noodle-like metro entrances and inside the Musée d'Orsay (p380).

Under Napoleon, many of Paris' best-known sights – including the Arc de Triomphe (p377) and the Arc du Carrousel at the Louvre (p377) – were designed and subsequent political leaders have similarly sought to immortalise themselves by building public edifices. Georges Pompidou commissioned the once-reviled but now much-revered Centre Pompidou (p377) in Paris while François Mitterrand commissioned IM Pei's glass pyramid at the Louvre.

Painting

An extraordinary flowering of artistic talent occurred in 19th- and 20th-century France. The impressionists, who endeavoured to capture the ever-changing aspects of reflected light, included Edouard Manet, Claude Monet, Edgar Degas, Camille Pissarro and Pierre-Auguste Renoir.

They were followed by the likes of Paul Cézanne, Paul Gauguin and Georges Seurat. A little later the Fauves, the most famous of whom was Henri Matisse, became known for their radical use of vibrant colour.

France was also where cubism, a form of art based on abstract and geometric representation, was pioneered by Georges Braque and Spain's Pablo Picasso.

ENVIRONMENT

Hexagon-shaped France, the largest country in Western Europe, is hugged by water or mountains along every side except its northeastern boundary – a relatively flat frontier abutting Germany, Luxembourg and Belgium.

Its 3200km-long coastline encompasses everything from white chalk cliffs (Normandy) and treacherous promontories (Brittany) to fine-sand (Atlantic coast) and pebbly-stroke-rocky (Mediterranean coast) beaches. Inland, five major river systems crisscross the country.

Europe's highest peak, Mt Blanc (4807m), spectacularly tops the French Alps which stagger along France's eastern border from Lake Geneva to the Côte d'Azur. North of Lake Geneva the gentle limestone Jura Range runs along the Swiss frontier to reach heights of 1700m, while the Pyrenees lace France's entire 450km-long border with Spain. The ancient Massif Central covers one-sixth (91,000

> **READING UP**
>
> For solid and superbly illustrated insights into French history and culture seek out the *Cultural Atlas of France* by John Ardagh. For a terrific first-hand narrative of life at the bottom in depression-era France (and Britain) read George Orwell's *Down and Out in Paris and London*. And you thought *you* were doing Paris on a budget.

sq km) of the country and is renowned for its chain of extinct volcanoes.

France has more mammals to see (around 110 species) than other country in Europe. Couple this with its 363 bird species, 30 amphibian types, 36 varieties of reptiles and 72 kinds of fish and wildlife-watchers are in paradise.

TRANSPORT

GETTING THERE & AWAY
Air

Air France and scores of other airlines link Paris with every section of the globe. Other French cities with international air links (mainly to places within Europe) include Bordeaux, Lyon, Marseille, Nice, Strasbourg and Toulouse.

In France, inexpensive flights offered by discount airlines and charter clearing houses can be booked through many regular travel agents. Reliable travel agency chains include the French student travel company **OTU** (☎ 0820 81 78 17; www.otu.fr) and **Nouvelles Frontières** (☎ 0825 00 08 25; www.nouvelles-frontieres.fr).

Budget airlines flying to France include:
Basiqair (HV; www.basiqair.com; hub Amsterdam)
BMI BritishMidland (BD; www.flybmi.com; hub London)
easyJet (EZY; ☎ 023-568 4880; www.easyjet.com; hub London Luton)
Ryanair (FR; www.ryanair.com; hubs London Stansted, Dublin)

British Airways (BA; ☎ 0825 82 54 00; www.britishairways.com; hub London) also has competitive rates and is worth checking out.

Boat

Tickets for ferry travel to/from the UK, Channel Islands and Ireland are available from most travel agencies in France. In some cases, return fares cost less than two one-way tickets.

FROM THE UK

Check out **Ferry Savers** (☎ 0870 990 8492; www .ferrysavers.com), which guarantees the lowest prices on Channel crossings. Ferry companies might try to make it hard for people who use super cheap, one-day return tickets for one-way passage – a huge backpack is a dead giveaway.

The Newhaven–Dieppe route is handled by **Hoverspeed** (☎ 0870 240 8070, in France ☎ 00 800 1211 1211; www.hoverspeed.co.uk) and **Transmanche Ferries** (☎ 0800 917 1201; www.transmancheferries.com). The hovercraft trip (one to three daily) takes 2¼ hours, while the ferry trip (two daily) takes four hours. Pedestrians pay from UK£30 one way, with special deals available.

The fastest way across the English Channel is either between Dover and Calais, served by Hoverspeed's 50-minute SeaCats (catamarans) or between Dover and Boulogne, with **Speed One** (in the UK ☎ 01304 203000; www.speedferries.com) which makes five crossings daily and costs from £60 return for five passengers and a car.

For foot passengers, a one-way trip (or a return completed within five days) costs UK£39. From Calais, there are five daily trains to Le Tréport, the northernmost town in Normandy (€19, five hours).

The Dover–Calais crossing is also handled by car ferries, run by **SeaFrance** (☎ 0870 571 1711, in France ☎ 0804 04 40 45; www.seafrance.com; 1½hr, 15 daily) and **P&O Ferries** (☎ 0870 520 2020; www.posl .com; 1-1¼hr, 29 daily) for about the same price.

Brittany Ferries also has car ferries from Portsmouth to Caen (Ouistreham; six hours, three per day). Tickets cost the same for the 4¼-hour crossing (two or three per day) from Poole to Cherbourg with Brittany Ferries (☎ 0870 366 5333, in France 0825 82 88 28; www .brittany-ferries.com). Foot passengers pay from UK£33 one way.

FROM IRELAND

Eurail pass holders pay 50% of the adult pedestrian fare for crossings between Ireland and France on Irish Ferries (book ahead). **Irish Ferries** (☎ 01-638 3333, in France ☎ 01 43 94 46 94; www.irishferries.com) has overnight runs from Rosslare to either Cherbourg (18 hours) or Roscoff (16 hours) every other day.

Bus & Car

If you are doing a lot of travel around Europe, look for discount bus and train passes, which can be combined with discount air fares. Buses are less comfortable than trains, but they are cheaper, especially for people under 26, over 60, teachers and students.

Eurolines (☎ 0892 69 52 52 or 01 43 54 11 99; www .eurolines.com) groups together 31 bus companies and links points across Europe. You can usually book online. In France, the main hub is Paris.

French coach company **Intercars** (Paris office ☎ 01 42 19 99 35; www.intercars.fr, French only; 139 bis rue de Vaugirard, 15e; metro Falguière) links France with other European cities, notably in Eastern Europe and Russia.

High-speed **Eurotunnel shuttle trains** (in the UK ☎ 0870 535 3535, in France ☎ 03 21 00 61 00; www.euro tunnel.com) carry cars, motorbikes and coaches from Folkestone through the Channel Tunnel to Coquelles, 5km southwest of Calais. Shuttles run 24 hours a day, every day. The one-way fare for a passenger car, including all passengers, costs from UK£150 (in February or March) to UK£250 (in July or August); return passage is double. Return fares valid for fewer than five days are much cheaper.

Train

Rail services link France with every country in Europe; schedules are available from major train stations in France and abroad. You can book tickets and get information from **Rail Europe** (www.raileurope.com) up to two months ahead. In France, ticketing is handled by the **SNCF** (☎ 0892 35 35 35; www.sncf.fr).

The highly civilised **Eurostar** (in France ☎ 0892 35 35 39, in the UK ☎ 08705 186 186; www .eurostar.com) links London to Paris in less than three hours. A full-fare, 2nd-class ticket from London to Paris can be as low as UK£59 or as high as UK£300. Student travel agencies often have youth fares not available directly from Eurostar.

GETTING AROUND
Air

Air France (☎ 0820 820 820; www.airfrance.com) controls the lion's share of France's domestic airline industry although British budget carrier easyJet has flights linking Paris with Marseille, Nice and Toulouse.

Any French travel agency or Air France office can make bookings for domestic flights and supply information on the complicated fare options. Outside France, Air France representatives sell tickets for many domestic flights.

Up to 84% reduction is available if you fly during the week (since normal last minute scheduled flights during weekdays aimed at business travellers are more expensive) if you purchase your ticket three weeks in advance. Significant discounts are available to children, young people, families and seniors. Special last-minute offers are posted on the Air France website every Wednesday.

Bicycle

France is eminently easy to cycle around. On train timetables, a bicycle symbol indicates that bicycles are allowed on particular trains. The SNCF baggage service **Sernam** (☎ 0825 84 58 45) will transport your bicycle (or any other luggage) door-to-door or station-to-station for €44.90.

Bus

Buses are used quite extensively for short-distance travel within *départements*, especially in rural areas with relatively few train lines (eg Brittany and Normandy), but services are often slow and few and far between.

Car & Motorcycle

Having your own wheels brings freedom but it's expensive, and city parking and traffic are frequent headaches. Motorcyclists will find France great for touring. The websites www.viamichelin.com and www.autoroutes.fr both calculate how much you will pay in petrol and tolls for specified journeys.

To hire a car in France you'll generally need to be over 21 years old and hold a valid driver's licence and an international credit card. Your credit card may cover collision damage waiver (CDW) if you use it to pay for the car rental.

If you don't live in the EU and need a car in France (or Europe) for 17 days (or a bit more) to six months, it's *much* cheaper to 'purchase' one from the manufacturer and then 'sell' it back than it is to rent one. The *achat-rachat* (purchase-repurchase) paperwork is not your responsibility. Both Renault's **Eurodrive** (in the US ☎ 800-221-1052; www.eurodrive.renault.com) and Peugeot's **Vacation Plan/Sodexa** (in the US ☎ 212-581-3040; www.peugeot-openeurope.com) offer great deals that include insurance with no deductible (excess).

Deals can be found on the Internet, with travel agencies and through companies like **Auto Europe** (in the US ☎ 1-888 223 5555; www.autoeurope.com) and **Holiday Autos** (in the UK ☎ 0870 5300 400; www.holidayautos.co.uk).

Some competitive rental agencies include:
ADA (☎ 0825 16 91 69; www.ada.fr)
Easycar (☎ 0906 33 33 33 3; www.easycar.com) Cheap rates; offices in Paris and Nice.
OTU Voyages (☎ 01 40 29 12 12; www.otu.fr) For students; office in Paris.

Hitching

Getting out of big cities like Paris, Lyon and Marseille or going around the Côte d'Azur by thumb is nigh impossible. Remote rural areas are your best bet, but few cars are likely to be going further than the next large town. Women should not hitch alone.

It's an excellent idea to hold up a sign with your destination followed by the letters *s.v.p.* (for *s'il vous plaît* or 'please'). Some people have reported good luck hitching with truck drivers from truck stops. It's illegal to hitch on autoroutes, but you can stand near the entrance ramps.

Train

Eurail and Inter-Rail passes are valid in France. France's superb rail network reaches almost every part of the country. Many towns and villages not on the SNCF train and bus network are linked by intra-departmental bus lines.

France's most important train lines radiate from Paris like the spokes of a wheel, making train travel between provincial towns situated on different 'spokes' rather slow. In some cases, you have to transit through Paris.

TGV Atlantique Sud-Ouest & TGV Atlantique Ouest
These link Paris' Gare Montparnasse with western and southwestern France, including Brittany (Rennes, Quimper,

Brest), Nantes, Tours, Poitiers, La Rochelle, Bordeaux, Biarritz and Toulouse.

TGV Nord, Thalys & Eurostar These link Paris' Gare du Nord with Arras, Lille, Calais, Brussels, Amsterdam, Cologne and, via the Channel Tunnel, Ashford and London Waterloo.

TGV Sud-Est & TGV Midi-Méditerranée These link Paris' Gare de Lyon with the southeast, including Dijon, Lyon, Geneva, the Alps, Avignon, Marseille, Nice and Montpellier.

A train that is not a TGV is often referred to as a *corail*, a *classique* or a *train express régional* (TER).

Fantastic deals are available exclusively on www.sncf.com. Last-minute offers, up to 50% off, are published on the website every Tuesday.

Before boarding the train you must validate your ticket by time-stamping it in a *composteur*, one of those orange posts situated at the start of the platform. If you forget, find a conductor on the train so they can punch it for you (otherwise you could be fined). Tickets can be purchased on board the train (straight away from the conductor) with cash, but there is a surcharge.

Reservation fees are optional unless you're travelling by TGV or want a couchette or special reclining seat. On popular trains (eg on holiday weekends) you may have to reserve ahead to get a seat.

EUROPEAN TRAIN PASSES

In France, Eurail and some other international train passes must be validated at a train station ticket window before you begin your first journey, to begin the period of validity. It's best to check if you're not sure. For details of the international passes available see p373.

Purchasing tickets well in advance will also usually get you a discounted fare. The Découverte J30, which must be purchased 30 to 60 days before the date of travel, offers savings of 45% to 55%. The Découverte J8, which you must buy eight days ahead, gets you 20% to 30% off.

The **France Railpass** entitles nonresidents of France to unlimited travel on SNCF trains for four days over a one-month period. In 2nd class, it costs US$218; each additional day US$28. The **France Youthpass** entitles holders to four days of travel over one month. In 2nd class it costs US$164, plus US$21 for an extra day. These two passes can be purchased from travel agents or on www.eurorail.com.

PARIS

pop 2.2 million, metropolitan area 10.6 million

Oft imitated, but never duplicated, Paris stands in a class of its own. France's *bijou extraordinaire* (extraordinary jewel) remains the benchmark for beauty, culture and class the world over. Even the most cynical traveller, sceptical that any city could live up to Paris' reputation, can't help but be charmed by its magnificent avenues and cosy café life, its unparalleled arts scene and energetic but composed pace. Paris is the Paris of the Parisians, the Paris of France, the one and only Paris. Nothing comes close.

ORIENTATION

In central Paris (Intra-Muros – 'within the walls'), the Rive Droite (Right Bank) is north of the Seine, while the Rive Gauche (Left Bank) is south of the river. For administrative purposes, Paris is divided into 20 *arrondissements* (districts) that spiral out from the centre. Addresses include the *arrondissement* number, listed here after the street address using the usual French notation (eg 1er stands for *premier* – 1st, 19e for *dix-neuvième* – 19th etc).

Lonely Planet's *Paris city map* includes central Paris, the Métropolitain, Montmartre, a walking tour and an index of all streets and sights.

GETTING INTO TOWN

Suburban 'RER' trains travel from Roissy Charles de Gaulle airport, in the northeast, and Orly airport, in the south, to main train stations such as Gare du Nord, Gare de Lyon and Gare Montparnasse. From these, you can hop on the metro system to your destination. RER Line B goes from Charles de Gaulle, Line C from Orly. Other options include Air France coaches (you needn't have flown with the airline to use these) and public buses. See p388 for details.

The Eurostar from London arrives centrally at Gare du Nord, as do TGV trains from the north. TGV trains from the south reach Gare de Lyon or Gare Montparnasse (see p373). All three stations are linked to the metro.

INFORMATION
Emergency
The numbers listed below are for emergencies only.

SOS Helpline (in English ☎ 01 47 23 80 80)
SOS Médecins (24hr house calls ☎ 01 47 07 77 77 or 0820 33 24 24)
Urgences Médicales de Paris (Paris Medical Emergencies; 24hr house calls ☎ 01 53 94 94 94 or 01 48 28 40 40)

Internet Access
Some metro and RER stations also offer free Internet access.

Access Academy (Map pp384-5; ☎ 01 43 25 23 80; www.accessacademy.com – French only; 60-61 rue St-André des Arts, 6e; metro Odéon; per hr/day/week/month around €3.50/6.80/14.90/35.70; ☒ 8am-2am) France's largest Internet café is in St-Germain and has 400 screens.
XS Arena Luxembourg branch (Map pp384-5; ☎ 01 43 44 55 55; 17 rue Soufflot, 5e; metro Luxembourg; per 1/2/3/4/5hr €3/6/8/10/12; ☒ 24hr) Les Halles branch (Map pp384-5; ☎ 01 40 13 02 60; 43 rue Sébastopol, 1er; metro Les Halles)

Left Luggage
All the train stations have left-luggage offices or lockers. Most are closed from about 11.15pm to about 6.30am.

Money
All of Paris' six major train stations have exchange bureaux open daily until at least 7pm. Big exchange-bureau chains like Chequepoint and ExactChange offer much poorer rates. Exchange offices at both airports are open until 10.30pm.

ÉTOILE & CHAMPS-ÉLYSÉES
Bureau de Change (Map pp378-9; ☎ 01 42 25 38 14; 25 av des Champs-Élysées, 8e; metro Franklin D Roosevelt; ☒ 9am-8pm)
Thomas Cook (Map pp378-9; ☎ 01 47 20 25 14; 125 av des Champs-Élysées, 8e; metro Charles de Gaulle-Étoile; ☒ 9.15am-8.30pm)

MONTMARTRE & PIGALLE
European Exchange Office (Map pp378-9; ☎ 01 42 52 67 19; 6 rue Yvonne Le Tac, 18e; metro Abbesses; ☒ 10am-6.30pm Mon-Fri, 10.30am-6pm Sat)
Travelex (Map pp378-9; ☎ 01 42 57 05 10; 82-86 blvd de Clichy, 18e; metro Blanche; ☒ 10am-8.30pm Mon-Sat, 9.45am-8.30pm Sun)

Post
Main post office (Map pp384-5; ☎ 01 40 28 76 00; 52 rue du Louvre, 1er; metro Sentier or Les Halles; ☒ 24hr) Open 24 hours for basic services such as sending letters, but during normal business hours for other services, including currency exchange.

Tourist Information
Office de Tourisme et de Congrès de Paris (Paris Convention and Visitors Bureau; Map pp384-5; ☎ 0892 683 3000; www.paris-touristoffice.com; 25-27 rue des Pyramides, 1er; metro Pyramides; ☒ 9am-8pm Apr-Oct, 9am-8pm Mon-Sat, 11am-7pm Sun Nov-Mar, closed 1 May) About 50m northwest of the Louvre.

SIGHTS
Île de la Cité
The site of the first settlement in Paris around the 3rd century BC and later the Roman town of Lutèce (Lutetia), the Île de la Cité stayed the centre of royal and ecclesiastical power even after the city spread to both banks of the Seine during the Middle Ages.

CATHÉDRALE DE NOTRE DAME DE PARIS
The **Cathédrale de Notre Dame de Paris** (Cathedral of Our Lady of Paris; Map pp384-5; ☎ 01 42 34 56 10; place du Parvis Notre Dame, 4e; metro Cité; ☒ 8am-6.45pm Mon-Fri, 8am-7.45pm Sat & Sun) is the true heart of Paris, a French Gothic masterpiece and the focus of Catholic Paris for seven centuries.

Built on a site which had occupied by earlier churches – and, a millennium before that, a Gallo-Roman temple – it was begun in 1163 and largely completed by the middle of the 14th century. Striking features include the three main portals, whose statues were once brightly coloured to make them more effective as a Biblia pauperum – a 'Bible of the poor' to help the illiterate understand the Old Testament stories. Inside look out for the three spectacular rose windows, the most renowned of which is the 10m-wide

AH, LA CARTE!
The **Carte Musées-Monuments** (Museums-Monuments Card; ☎ 01 44 61 96 60; one/three/five days €18/36/54) is valid for entry to three dozen sights in Paris – including the Louvre, the Centre Pompidou and the Musée d'Orsay – and another two dozen 22 in the Île de France, including parts of the chateaux at Versailles. The pass is available from the participating venues as well as tourist offices, Fnac outlets, RATP information desks and major metro stations.

one over the western facade above the 7800-pipe organ, and the window on the northern side of the transept, which has remained virtually unchanged since the 13th century.

One of the best views of Notre Dame is from Square Jean XXIII, the lovely little park behind the cathedral, where you can see the mass of ornate flying buttresses that encircle the chancel and support its walls and roof.

Distances from Paris to every part of metropolitan France are measured from **place du Parvis Notre Dame**, the square in front of Notre Dame.

Right Bank
MUSÉE DU LOUVRE
The vast Palais du Louvre was constructed as a fortress by Philippe-Auguste in the early 13th century and rebuilt in the mid-16th century. In 1793 the Convention turned it into the **Musée du Louvre** (Louvre Museum; Map pp384-5; ☎ 01 40 20 53 17 or 01 40 20 51 51; www .louvre.fr; metro Palais Royal-Musée du Louvre; admission to permanent/all collections €7.50/11.50, after 3pm & all day Sun €5/9.50, 1st Sun of month & for under-18s free; ✆ 9am-6pm Thu-Sun, 9am-9.45pm Mon & Wed).

The most widely celebrated work of art hanging on its walls is da Vinci's *Mona Lisa* but don't just make a beeline for this and leave before exploring some of the rest of the Louvre's fabulously rich collection.

The paintings, sculptures and artefacts on display include works of art and artisanship from all over Europe and important collections of Assyrian, Etruscan, Greek, Coptic and Islamic art and antiquities. Traditionally the Louvre's *raison d'être* is to present Western art from the Middle Ages to about the year 1848 (at which point the Musée d'Orsay takes over – see p380).

ARC DE TRIOMPHE & CHAMPS-ELYSÉES
Commissioned in 1806 by Napoleon to commemorate his imperial victories, the **Arc de Triomphe** (Triumphal Arch; Map pp378-9; ☎ 01 55 37 73 77 or 01 44 95 02 10; www.monum.fr; metro Charles de Gaulle-Étoile; viewing: platform adult/concession €7/4.50, 1st Sun of month & for under-18s free; ✆ 9.30am-11pm Apr-Sep, 10am-10.30pm Oct-Mar) remained unfinished when he started losing battles and then entire wars. It was not completed until 1836. Today this national icon stands several kilometres northwest of the Louvre, in the middle of place Charles de Gaulle or place de l'Étoile, the world's largest traffic roundabout.

A dozen avenues radiate from this roundabout, most famously the av des Champs-Elysées. This broad boulevard, whose name refers to Greek mythology's 'Elysian Fields'(or heaven), links the Arc de Triomphe with place de la Concorde to the southeast. Symbolising the style and *joie de vivre* of Paris since the mid-19th century, the avenue remains a popular tourist destination.

PLACE DE LA CONCORDE
Place de la Concorde (metro Concorde) was laid out between 1755 and 1775. The 3300-year-old pink granite **obelisk** with the gilded top in the middle of the square once stood in the Temple of Ramses at Thebes (today's Luxor) and was given to France in 1831 by Mohammed Ali, viceroy and pasha of Egypt.

CENTRE POMPIDOU
Since it was inaugurated in 1977, the **Centre National d'Art et de Culture Georges Pompidou** (Georges Pompidou National Centre of Art and Culture; Map pp384-5; ☎ 01 44 78 12 33; www.centrepompidou .fr; place Georges Pompidou, 4e; metro Rambuteau) has amazed and delighted visitors, not just for its outstanding collection of modern art, but for its radical architectural statement. It was among the first buildings to have its 'insides' turned outside.

HÔTEL DE VILLE
Gutted during the Paris Commune of 1871, Paris' **Hôtel de Ville** (city hall; Map pp384-5; ☎ 0820 00 75 75; www.paris.fr; place de l'Hôtel de Ville, 4e; metro Hôtel de Ville) was rebuilt in the neo-Renaissance style (1874–82). The Hôtel de Ville faces the majestic **place de l'Hôtel de Ville**, used from the Middle Ages to the 19th century to stage many of Paris' celebrations, rebellions, book burnings and public executions.

MUSÉE PICASSO
The **Musée Picasso** (Picasso Museum; Map pp384-5; ☎ 01 42 71 25 21; 5 rue de Thorigny, 3e; metro St-Paul or Chemin Vert; adult/concession €6.70/5.20, Sun €5.20, 1st Sun of month & for under-18s free; ✆ 9.30am-6pm Wed-Mon Apr-Sep, 9.30am-5.30pm Wed-Mon Oct-Mar), housed in the mid-17th-century Hôtel Salé, is one of Paris' best loved art museums and includes more than 3500 of the *grand maître's* works.

PLACE DE LA BASTILLE
The Bastille, built during the 14th century as a fortified royal residence, is the most famous

FRANCE

PARIS

Île de la Grande Jatte

Pont de Levallois-Bécon
R Anatole France

SAINT-OUEN

Porte de Clignancourt

Blvd Ney

Porte de St Ouen

Cimetière Sud

Cimetière Parisien des Batignolles

Blvd Bessières

Porte de Clichy

Blvd Berthier

Pablo Neruda

Louison Bobet

Parc de la Planchette

Anatole France

Guy Môquet

R Guy Môquet

Jules Joffrin

Lamarck Caulaincourt

R Lamarck

R Caulaincourt

Louise Michel

Porte de Champerret

Av de la Porte de Champerret

Blvd Pereire (Nord)

R Jouffroy d'Abbans

Brochant

La Fourche

Cimetière de Montmartre

MONTMARTRE

Square Willette

Abbesses

Wagram

R de Rome

Maleherbes

Av de Villiers

Place de Clichy

Blvd de Clichy

Pigalle

Blvd des Anvers

Av Bineau

Blvd Victor Hugo

Av de la Porte de Villiers

Porte de Villiers

Gouvion St Cyr

Av des Ternes

Av du Roule

Péreire

Monceau

Parc de Monceau

Villiers

Europe

Blanche

Liège

St Georges

Trinité

Notre Dame de Lorette

R de Châteaudun

Cadet

Le Peletier

Jardin d'Acclimatation

Blvd Maillot

TEP Jean Pierre Wimille

Av de l'Amrl Bruix

Argentine

Av de la Grande Armée

Porte Maillot

Place Charles de Gaulle

Av Mac Mahon

Ternes

Blvd de Courcelles

Courcelles

Charles de Gaulle-Etoile

Av Hoche

Av de Courcelles

St Augustin

Blvd Haussmann

Havre Caumartin

Chaussée d'Antin

Richelieu Drouot

Grands Boulevards

Av de Friedland

Miromesnil

Opéra

Opéra Garnier

Bourse

Réaumur

RIGHT BANK

Av Foch

Victor Hugo

Kléber

St Philippe du Roule

Av George V

Les Champs Elysées

Franklin D Roosevelt

St Georges

Madeleine

Blvd de la Madeleine

Royale

Quatre Septembre

Porte Dauphine

Av Victor Hugo

Av Raymond Poincaré

Av Kléber

Boissière

Iéna

Av d'Iéna

Av Marceau

TRIANGLE D'OR

Av Montaigne

Champs-Elysées Clemenceau

Concorde

Pyramides

Place de la Concorde

Jardin des Tuileries

Tuileries

Jardin du Palais Royal

Jardin du Carrousel

Rue de la Pompe

Av Georges Mandel

Cimetière de Passy

Trocadéro

Av du Pdt Wilson

Av de New York

Pont de l'Alma

Alma-Marceau

Q d'Orsay

Seine

Q des Tuileries

Q du Louvre

La Muette

Av Paul Doumer

Passy

Champ de Mars Tour Eiffel

Port de la Bourdonnais

Pont de l'Alma

Invalides

Assemblée Nationale

Solférino

Anatole France

Q Voltaire

Q de Conti

Île de la Cité

To Camping du Bois de Boulogne (2km)

Av du Président Kennedy

Bir Hakeim

Av de la Bourdonnais

Av de la Motte Picquet

La Tour Maubourg

Varenne

Rue du Bac

FAUBOURG SAINT-GERMAIN

Blvd St Germain

Blvd Raspail

LATIN QUARTER

R Raynouard

Av de Suffren

Ecole Militaire

Parc du Champ de Mars

Jardin Catherine Labouré

LEFT BANK

Dupleix

Blvd de Grenelle

La Motte Picquet Grenelle

Av de la Motte Picquet

Av de Breteuil

St François Xavier

Jardin des Invalides

Sèvres Babylone

Jardin du Luxembourg

Q Louis Blériot

André Citroën

Javel

R de la Fédération

Avenue Emile Zola

Cambronne

Av Emile Zola

Ségur

Av de Saxe

Vaneau

Duroc

Rennes

St Placide

Notre Dame des Champs

See The Latin Quarter & Île De La Cité & Marais Map (pp384–5)

Charles Michels

Commerce

Blvd Garibaldi

Sèvres Lecourbe

Falguière

Montparnasse Bienvenüe

Vavin

Parc André Citroën

Cimetière de Grenelle

Félix Faure

Boucicaut

Lourmel

Volontaires

Pasteur

Edgar Quinet

Raspail

Val de Grâce

Blvd de Port Royal

Balard

Blvd du Général Martial Valin

R de Lourmel

R Balard

Cimetière de Vaugirard

Vaugirard

Convention

Jardin de l'Atlantique

Gaîté

Cimetière du Montparnasse

Denfert Rochereau

Observatoire de Paris

Héliport de Paris

Palais des Sports

Paris Expo

Porte de Versailles

R de Dantzig

Parc Georges Brassens

R de Vouillé

R d'Alésia

Pernety

Plaisance

Denfert Rochereau

St Jacques

Blvd St Jacques

Glacière

Corentin Celton

Blvd Victor

R de Vaugirard

Blvd Lefebvre

Stade de la Porte de la Plaine

Porte de Vanves

Stade Didot

Mouton Duvernet

Alésia

Ste Anne

Parc de Montsouris

R d'Alésia

Mairie d'Issy

Général Leclerc

FRANCE

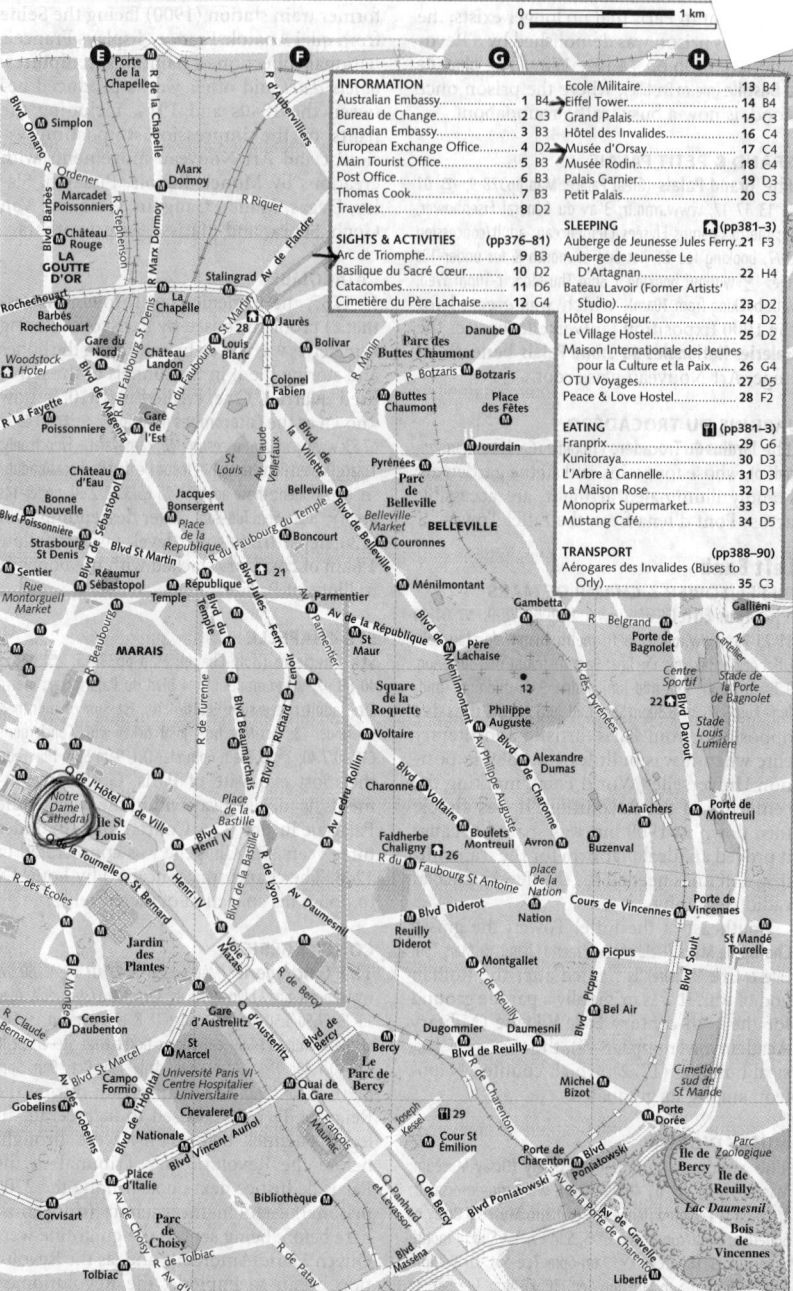

0   1 km

INFORMATION
Australian Embassy....................1 B4
Bureau de Change.......................2 C3
Canadian Embassy......................3 B3
European Exchange Office........4 D2
Main Tourist Office...................5 B3
Post Office..................................6 B3
Thomas Cook.............................7 B3
Travelex.....................................8 D2

SIGHTS & ACTIVITIES   (pp376–81)
Arc de Triomphe.......................9 B3
Basilique du Sacré Cœur.........10 D2
Catacombes..............................11 D6
Cimetière du Père Lachaise....12 G4
Ecole Militaire..........................13 B4
Eiffel Tower..............................14 B4
Grand Palais.............................15 C3
Hôtel des Invalides..................16 C4
Musée d'Orsay.........................17 C4
Musée Rodin............................18 C4
Palais Garnier..........................19 D3
Petit Palais...............................20 C3

SLEEPING   (pp381–3)
Auberge de Jeunesse Jules Ferry.21 F3
Auberge de Jeunesse Le
   D'Artagnan...........................22 H4
Bateau Lavoir (Former Artists'
   Studio).................................23 D2
Hôtel Bonséjour......................24 D2
Le Village Hostel......................25 D2
Maison Internationale des Jeunes
   pour la Culture et la Paix....26 G4
OTU Voyages............................27 D5
Peace & Love Hostel................28 F2

EATING   (pp381–3)
Franprix....................................29 G6
Kunitoraya................................30 D3
L'Arbre à Cannelle...................31 D3
La Maison Rose........................32 D1
Monoprix Supermarket...........33 D3
Mustang Café...........................34 D5

TRANSPORT   (pp388–90)
Aérogares des Invalides (Buses to
   Orly)....................................35 C3

FRANCE

monument in Paris that no longer exists; the notorious prison was demolished by a Revolutionary mob on 14 July 1789. The **place de la Bastille** (metro Bastille), where the prison once stood, is now a busy traffic roundabout.

GRAND & PETIT PALAIS

The **Grand Palais** (Great Palace; Map pp378-9; ☎ 01 44 13 17 17; www.rmn.fr; 3 av du Général Eisenhower, 8e; metro Champs-Élysées Clemenceau; adult/concession €9/7, booking fee €1, 1st Sun of month & for under-18s free; ☺ without booking 1-8pm Thu-Mon, 1-10pm Wed, with booking from 10am), which was erected for the 1900 Exposition Universelle, houses the **Galeries Nationales du Grand Palais** beneath its huge, Art Nouveau glass roof.

JARDINS DU TROCADÉRO

The **Jardins du Trocadéro** (Trocadero Gardens; metro Trocadéro), whose fountains and statue garden are grandly illuminated at night, are accessible across Pont d'Iéna from the Eiffel Tower.

Left Bank
EIFFEL TOWER & CHAMP DE MARS

The **Tour Eiffel** (Eiffel Tower; Map pp378-9; ☎ 01 44 11 23 23; www.tour-eiffel.fr; metro Champ de Mars-Tour Eiffel or Bir Hakeim; ☺ lifts: 9am-midnight mid-Jun–Aug, 9.30am-11pm Sep–mid-Jun, stairs: 9am-midnight mid-Jun–Aug, 9.30am-6.30pm Sep–mid-Jun) faced massive opposition from Paris' artistic and literary elite when it was built for the 1889 Exposition Universelle (World Fair), marking the centenary of the Revolution. It was almost torn down in 1909 but was spared because it proved an ideal platform for the transmitting antennas needed for the new science of radiotelegraphy.

Southeast of the Eiffel Tower, the grassy **Champ de Mars** (Field of Mars; metro Champ de Mars-Tour Eiffel or École Militaire) is named after the Roman god of war. It was originally a parade ground for the 18th-century **École Militaire** (Military Academy; Map pp378–9), the vast, neoclassical building (1772), which counted Napoleon among its graduates.

MUSÉE D'ORSAY

The spectacular **Musée d'Orsay** (Orsay Museum; Map pp378-9; ☎ 01 40 49 48 84; www.musee-orsay.fr; 1 rue de la Légion d'Honneur, 7e; metro Musée d'Orsay or Solférino; adult/concession €7/5, Sun €5, 1st Sun of month & for under-18s free; ☺ 9am-6pm Tue-Sat, to 9.45pm Thu, 9am-6pm Sun late Jun-Sep, 10am-6pm Tue-Sat, to 9.45pm Thu, 9am-6pm Sun Oct-late Jun), housed in a former train station (1900) facing the Seine from quai Anatole France, displays France's national collection of paintings, sculptures, *objets d'art* and other works produced between the 1840s and 1914, including the fruits of the impressionist, postimpressionist and Art Nouveau movements with creations by Monet, Renoir, Pissarro, Sisley, Degas, Manet, Gauguin, Cézanne, Van Gogh, Seurat and Matisse, among others.

CATACOMBES

In 1785, the hygienic (not to mention aesthetic) problems posed by Paris' overflowing cemeteries was solved by exhuming the bones and storing them in the tunnels of three disused quarries. One, created in 1810, is now known as the **Catacombes** (Map pp378-9; ☎ 01 43 22 47 63; www.paris.fr/musees/musee_carnavalet – French only; 1 place Denfert Rochereau, 14e; metro Denfert Rochereau; adult/senior & student/those aged 14-25 €5/3.30/2.60, under-14s free; ☺ 10am-5pm Tue-Sun). After descending 20m (130 steps) from street level, visitors follow 1.6km of corridors stacked with the bones of millions of Parisians.

STE-CHAPELLE

Ste-Chapelle (Holy Chapel; Map pp384-5; ☎ 01 53 40 60 97; www.monum.fr; 4 blvd du Palais, 1er; metro Cité; adult/concession €6.10/4.10, 1st Sun of month & for under-18s Oct-Mar free, joint ticket with Conciergerie €10.40/7.40; ☺ 9.30am-6pm Mar-Oct, 9am-5pm Nov-Feb), the most exquisite of Paris' Gothic monuments, is tucked away within the walls of the Palais de Justice (Law Courts). Built in under three years, Ste-Chapelle was consecrated in 1248. The chapel was conceived by Louis IX to house his collection of sacred relics.

CONCIERGERIE

The **Conciergerie** (Map pp384-5; ☎ 01 53 40 60 97; www.monum.fr; 2 blvd du Palais, 1er; metro Cité; adult/aged 18-25 €7.50/5.50, free for under-18 & everyone on 1st Sun of the month Oct-Mar only, joint ticket with Ste-Chapelle €10.40/7.40; ☺ 9.30am-6pm daily Mar-Oct, 9am-5pm daily Nov-Feb), was the main prison during the Reign of Terror and used to incarcerate alleged enemies before they were brought before the Revolutionary Tribunal in the Palais de Justice next door. Among the 2700 prisoners held in the cachots (dungeons) here before being sent to the guillotine were Queen Marie-Antoinette and, as the Revolution began to implode, the Revolutionary radicals Danton and Robespierre.

MUSÉE NATIONAL DU MOYEN AGE

The **Musée National du Moyen Age** (National Museum of the Middle Ages; Map pp384-5; ☎ 01 53 73 78 16 or 01 53 73 78 00; www.musee-moyenage.fr – French only; Thermes de Cluny, 6 place Paul Painlevé, 5e; metro Cluny-La Sorbonne or St-Michel; adult/concession €5.50/4, 1st Sun of month & for under-18s free; ⏰ 9.15am-5.45pm Wed-Mon), sometimes called the Musée de Cluny, is housed in two structures: the **frigidarium** (cooling room) and other remains of Gallo-Roman baths dating from around AD 200, and the late-15th-century **Hôtel de Cluny**, considered the finest example of medieval civil architecture in Paris. Displays include statuary, illuminated manuscripts, arms, furnishings and objects made of gold, ivory and enamel.

PANTHÉON

The domed landmark now known as the **Panthéon** (Map pp384-5; ☎ 01 44 32 18 00; www .monum.fr; place du Panthéon, 5e; metro Luxembourg; adult/concession €7/4.50, 1st Sun of month & for under-18s Oct-Mar free; ⏰ 9.30am-6.30pm Apr-Sep, 10am-6.15pm Oct-Mar) was commissioned about 1750 as an abbey church dedicated to Ste-Geneviève, but wasn't completed until 1789. Buried in the crypt are Voltaire, Jean-Jacques Rousseau, Victor Hugo, Émile Zola, Jean Moulin and Nobel Prize-winner Marie Curie, among others.

JARDIN DU LUXEMBOURG

In fine weather, Parisians flock to the formal terraces and chestnut groves of the 23-hectare **Jardin du Luxembourg** (Luxembourg Garden; metro Luxembourg; ⏰ 7am-9.30pm Apr-Oct, 8am-sunset Mar-Nov) to read, relax and sunbathe.

MUSÉE RODIN

The **Musée Rodin** (Rodin Museum; Map pp378-9; ☎ 01 44 18 61 10; www.musee-rodin.fr; 77 rue de Varenne, 7e; metro Varenne; adult/concession €5/3, Sun €3, 1st Sun of month & for under-18s free, garden only €1; ⏰ 9.30am-5.45pm Apr-Sep, 9.30am-4.45pm Oct-Mar) is both a sublime museum and one of the most relaxing spots in the city, with a lovely **garden** full of sculptures and shade trees.

HÔTEL DES INVALIDES

The **Hôtel des Invalides** (Map pp378-9; metro Varenne or La Tour Maubourg) was built in the 1670s by Louis XIV to provide housing for 4000 *invalides* (disabled war veterans). On 14 July 1789, a mob forced its way into the building and, after fierce fighting, seized 28,000 rifles

before heading on to the prison at Bastille and revolution.

Other Districts

CIMETIÈRE DU PÈRE LACHAISE

Molière, Oscar Wilde, Balzac, Proust, Gertrude Stein, Édith Piaf and, of course, the Doors' lead singer Jim Morrison, are among the 70,000 who rest in **Cimetière du Père Lachaise** (Père Lachaise Cemetery; Map pp378-9; ☎ 01 55 25 82 10; metro Philippe Auguste, Gambetta or Père Lachaise; ⏰ 8am-6pm Mon-Fri, 8.30am-6pm Sat, 9am-6pm Sun mid-Mar–early Nov, 8am-5.30pm Mon-Fri, 8.30am-5.30pm Sat, 9am-5.30pm Sun early Nov–mid-Mar). So, with such celebrity, it's little wonder this is the world's most visited graveyard. Having opened in 1804, its ornate tombs today form a verdant, open-air sculpture garden. Jim Morrison (1943–71) is buried in division No 6.

MONTMARTRE & PIGALLE

During the late 19th and early 20th centuries the bohemian lifestyle of Montmartre in the 18e attracted many important writers and artists, including Picasso, who lived at the studio called **Bateau Lavoir** (Map pp378-9; 11bis Émile Goudeau) from 1908–12. Montmartre retains an upbeat ambience that all the tourists in the world couldn't spoil.

Only a few blocks southwest of the tranquil, residential streets of Montmartre is lively, neon-lit Pigalle (9e and 18e), a red-light district that also boasts plenty of trendy nightspots, including clubs and cabarets.

BASILIQUE DU SACRÉ CŒUR

Perched at the very top of the Butte de Montmartre (Montmartre Hill), the **Basilique du Sacré Cœur** (Basilica of the Sacred Heart; Map pp378-9; ☎ 01 53 41 89 00; www.sacre-coeur-montmartre.com; place du Parvis du Sacré Cœur, 18e; metro Anvers; ⏰ 6am-11pm) was built from contributions pledged by Parisian Catholics as an act of contrition soon after the humiliating Franco-Prussian War of 1870–71. Some 234 spiral stairs lead you to the basilica's **dome** (admission €5; ⏰ 9am-7pm Apr-Sep, 9am-6pm Oct-Mar), which affords one of Paris' most spectacular panoramas.

SLEEPING

Many hostels impose a three-night maximum stay, especially in summer. Only official *auberges de jeunesse* (youth hostels) require guests to present Hostelling International (HI) cards or equivalent. Curfew – if enforced – tends to be 1am or 2am. Few hostels accept reservations by telephone.

Accommodation Services

The student travel agency **OTU Voyages** (Map pp378-9; ☎ 01 40 29 12 22 or 0825 00 40 24; www.otu .fr – French only; 119 rue St-Martin, 4e; metro Rambuteau; ⏰ 9.30am-6.30pm Mon-Fri, 10am-5pm Sat), directly across the *parvis* (square) from the Centre Pompidou, can *always* find you accommodation. An agency that arranges bed and breakfast accommodation in Paris and gets praise from readers is **Alcôve & Agapes** (☎ 01 44 85 06 05; info@paris-bedandbreakfast.com). Expect to pay between €45 and €100 for a double.

Louvre & Les Halles

Centre International BVJ Paris-Louvre (Map pp384-5; ☎ 01 53 00 90 90; bvj@wanadoo.fr; 20 rue Jean-Jacques Rousseau, 1er; metro Louvre-Rivoli; s €25, d per person €28; ✗) This modern, 200-bed hostel, run by the Bureau des Voyages de la Jeunesse, has bunks in a single-sex room for two to eight people; rates include breakfast. Guests should be aged under 35.

Hôtel de Lille Pélican (Map pp384-5; ☎ 01 42 33 33 42; 8 rue du Pélican, 1er; metro Palais Royal-Musée du Louvre; s/d/tr with washbasin €35/43/65, d with shower €50; ✗) This old-fashioned but clean 13-room hotel down a quiet side street has recently been given a face-lift. Some of its rooms have just washbasin and bidet, with communal showers in the hallway (€4.50), but some have their own shower. The helpful manager speaks good English.

Marais & Bastille

Maison Internationale de la Jeunesse et des Étudiants (☎ 01 42 74 23 45; www.mije.com; s/d/tr per person €42/32/28; ✗ 🖵) The MIJE runs three hostels in attractively renovated 17th- and 18th-century *hôtels particuliers* (private mansions) in the heart of the Marais, and it's difficult to think of a better budget deal in Paris. Costs are the same for all three. A bed in a shower-equipped, single-sex dorm sleeping four to eight people is €27. Rooms are closed from noon to 3pm, and curfew is from 1am to 7am.

The three are listed below:

MIJE Le Fourcy (Map pp384-5; 6 rue de Fourcy, 4e; metro St-Paul) This 207-bed branch is the largest of the three. There's a cheap eatery with a three-course *menu* including a drink for €10.50 and a two-course *formule* plus drink for €8.50.

MIJE Le Fauconnier (Map pp384-5; 11 rue du Fauconnier, 4e; metro St-Paul or Pont Marie) This 125-bed hostel is two blocks south of MIJE Le Fourcy.

MIJE Maubuisson (Map pp384-5; 12 rue des Barres, 4e; metro Hôtel de Ville or Pont Marie) This 103-bed place (and the pick of the three in our opinion) is half a block south of the *mairie* (town hall) of the 4e.

Maison Internationale des Jeunes pour la Culture et la Paix (Map pp378-9; ☎ 01 43 71 99 21; mij.cp@wana doo.fr; 4 rue Titon, 11e; metro Faidherbe Chaligny; dm €20; ✗ 🖵) This hostel with 166 beds is 1.3km east of place de la Bastille. It offers accommodation in comfortable but rather institutional dormitory rooms for up to eight people.

Latin Quarter & Jardin des Plantes

Centre International de Séjour BVJ Paris-Quartier Latin (Map pp384-5; ☎ 01 43 29 34 80; bvj@wanadoo.fr; 44 rue des Bernardins, 5e; metro Maubert Mutualité; per person in 1-/2-/6-bed r €35/28/26; ✗) This 38-bed Left Bank hostel is a branch of the Centre International BVJ Paris-Louvre (left) and has the same rules. All the rooms here have *en suite* showers and telephones.

Grand Hôtel du Progrès (Map pp384-5; ☎ 01 43 54 53 18; fax 01 56 24 87 80; 50 rue Gay Lussac, 5e; metro Luxembourg; basic s/d/tr €35/42/55, s/d with shower & toilet €46/54) This budget, 26-room hotel has been a favourite of students for generations. There are washbasin-equipped singles and large, old-fashioned doubles with views and lots of morning sun. Rates include breakfast. Hall showers are free.

Young & Happy Hostel (Map pp384-5; ☎ 01 47 07 47 07; www.youngandhappy.fr; 80 rue Mouffetard, 5e; metro Place Monge; dm €20-22, d per person €23-25; ✗ 🖵) A friendly though slightly tatty place in the centre of the most happening area of the Latin Quarter. The 2am curfew is strictly enforced. Beds are in smallish rooms for two to four people. In summer, the best way to get a bed is to stop by at about 9am.

Gare du Nord, Gare de l'Est & République

Auberge de Jeunesse Jules Ferry (Map pp378-9; ☎ 01 43 57 55 60; www.fuaj.fr; 8 blvd Jules Ferry, 11e; metro République or Goncourt; dm €19.50, d per person €20; ✗ 🖵) It's somewhat institutional and the rooms could be cleaner, but the atmosphere is relaxed. Beds are in rooms for two to six people. There is no curfew. Those without a HI card or equivalent pay an extra €3 per night.

Auberge de Jeunesse Le D'Artagnan (Map pp378-9; ☎ 01 40 32 34 56; www.fuaj.fr; 80 rue Vitruve, 20e; metro Porte de Bagnolet; dm €20.60; ✗ 🖳) This is the other official hostel in central Paris. It is far from the centre of the action but just one metro stop from the Gare Routière Internationale de Paris-Gallieni (international bus terminal). The largest hostel in France, with 439 beds, the D'Artagnan has rooms with two to eight beds, big lockers, laundry facilities, a bar and cinema.

Peace & Love Hostel (Map pp378-9; ☎ 01 46 07 65 11; www.paris-hostels.com; 245 rue La Fayette, 10e; metro Jaurès or Louis Blanc; dm per person €17-21, d per person €21-26; 🖳) This modern-day hippy hang-out is rather chaotically run with beds in smallish, shower-equipped rooms for two to four people. There's a great kitchen and eating area and a lively bar (open till 2am).

Gare de Lyon, Nation & Bercy

Blue Planet Hostel (Map pp384-5; ☎ 01 43 42 06 18; www.hostelblueplanet.com; 5 rue Hector Malot, 12e; metro Gare de Lyon; dm €18.30-21; 🖳) This 43-room hostel is very close to Gare de Lyon, which is convenient if you're heading south or west. Dorm beds are in rooms for three or four people. No curfew.

Montmartre & Pigalle

Hôtel Bonséjour (Map pp378-9; ☎ 01 42 54 22 53; fax 01 42 54 25 92; 11 rue Burq, 18e; metro Abbesses; s with washbasin €22-25, d €30-32, d with shower €38-40, tr €53) The 'Good Stay' is at the end of a quiet Montmartre street. Some rooms (eg Nos 14, 23, 33, 43 and 53) have little balconies and at least one room (No 55) offers a fleeting glimpse of Sacré Cœur. It's a simple place to stay – no lift, linoleum floors etc – but comfortable and friendly. Hall showers cost €2.

Le Village Hostel (Map pp378-9; ☎ 01 42 64 22 02; www.villagehostel.fr; 20 rue d'Orsel, 18e; metro Anvers; dm/d/tr per person Nov–mid-Mar €20/23/21.50, mid-Mar–Oct €21.50/25/23; 🖳) 'The Village' is a fine 25-room hostel with beam ceilings and Sacré Cœur views. *En suite* dorms accommodate four to six people. Kitchen facilities are available, and there is a lovely terrace. Curfew is 2am.

Woodstock Hostel (☎ 01 48 78 87 76; www.woodstock.fr; 48 rue Rodier, 9e; metro Anvers; dm/d per person Oct-Mar €15/17, Apr-Sep €20/23; 🖳) Woodstock is just down the hill from raucous Pigalle in a quiet, residential quarter. Dorms are for four to six people and there's a kitchen. Curfew is 2am.

Camping

Camping du Bois de Boulogne (☎ 01 45 24 30 81; www.abccamping.com/boulogne.htm; 2 allée du Bord de l'Eau, 16e; sites off/mid/peak season €11/14.20/15.40, d with vehicle €18.50/22.50/24.50, with electricity €22.50/26.50 /31.70, first-time booking fee €12; ⏰ 6am-2am) The only camp site within the city limits lies along the Seine at the far western edge of the Bois de Boulogne. It gets very crowded in summer, but there's always space for a small tent. Fully equipped caravans sleeping four to five cost €50 to €85. Porte Maillot metro station, 4.5km to the northeast through the wood, is linked to the site by RATP bus No 244, which runs from 6am to 8.30pm daily, and from April to October by a privately operated shuttle bus charging about €2.

EATING

Paris has more 'generic French', regional and ethnic restaurants than any other place in France. Over the years ethnic food has become as Parisian as that ubiquitous onion soup; the *nems* and *pâtés impérials* (spring or egg rolls) and *pho* (soup noodles with beef) of Vietnam, the couscous and tajines of North Africa, the *boudin antillais* (West Indian blood pudding) from the Caribbean are all eaten with relish throughout the capital.

Louvre & Les Halles

If you're on the hunt for Asian food, Japanese businesspeople flock to this area for the freshest sushi and soba. There are also some good-value restaurants serving other Asian cuisines around rue Ste-Anne just west of the Jardin du Palais Royal.

Kunitoraya (Map pp378-9; ☎ 01 47 03 33 65; 39 rue Ste-Anne, 1er; metro Pyramides; dishes €8.50-16, lunch menu €12.50; ⏰ 11.30am-10pm) With seating on two floors, this simple place has a wide and excellent range of Japanese noodle dishes and set lunches and dinners.

L'Arbre à Cannelle (Map pp378-9; ☎ 01 45 08 55 87; 57 passage des Panoramas, 2e; metro Grands Boulevards; dishes €6.50-9.50; ⏰ noon-6.30pm Mon-Sat) This lovely tea room has original 19th-century décor, *tartes salées* (savoury pies; €6.50 to €7) and excellent salads (€6.25 to €9.30).

Joe Allen (Map pp384-5; ☎ 01 42 36 70 13; 30 rue Pierre Lescot, 1er; metro Étienne Marcel; lunch menu €12.90, dinner menus €18 & €22.50, brunch €11.90-15; ⏰ noon-midnight) A local institution for three decades, Joe Allen is a little bit of New York in Paris. Excellent brunch from noon to 4pm at the weekend.

THE LATIN QUARTER, ÎLE DE LA CITÉ & MARAIS

A 3 ①
B
C
D

Jardin du Palais Royal

Av de l'Opéra
R des Pyramides
R de Molière
R Montpensier
Banque de France
R de Valois

Pyramides
37
Place des Pyramides
Palais Royal

RIGHT BANK

Jardin du Carrousel
Palais Royal Musée du Louvre
R de Rivoli
Jardin de l'Oratoire

R de Richelieu
Galerie Véro-Dodat
Cour des Petits Champs
R Hérold
R Coquillière
R du Louvre
R Jean Jacques Rousseau
R du Jour
2
Montmartre
R Française
R Tiquetonne

Étienne Marcel
34
R du Cygne
R aux Ours
R de Turbigo
R de Palestro
R St Martin

23
20
Galerie Véro-Dodat
R St Honoré
R de Viarmes

Place René Cassin
Les Halles
R de Rambuteau
31
Châtelet les Halles

Rambuteau
7
Place Georges Pompidou

Jardin de l'Infante
Louvre Rivoli
Bailleul
43
R Perrault
R de l'Amiral de Coligny
R de la Monnaie
Pont Neuf

Cour Carrée
Musée du Louvre
Place M Quentin
R St Honoré
Place M de Navarre
Place Jean du Bellay
53
Place St Michel
R des Lombards
Place Igor Stravinsky

Q des Tuileries
Terrasse des Tuileries

Seine
Pont du Carrousel
Q du Louvre
Q Voltaire
R de Lille
Q Malaquais

Square du Vert Galant
Place de l'Institut
Q de Conti

Pont Neuf
Place du Pont Neuf
Jardin Mazarin
Q de la Mégisserie
Théâtre Musical de Paris
Place du Châtelet
Av Victoria

Théâtre de la Ville
Square de la Tour St Jacques
52
Hôtel de Ville

Q de l'Hôtel de Ville
10
R de l'Ave Maria

R de Lille
R de Verneuil
R Visconti
R Mazarine
Q des Grands Augustins
R Dauphine
Q des Orfèvres
Q de l'Horloge
Place Dauphine
8
18
Île de la Cité
Blvd du Palais
Cité

Notre Dame
Hôtel Dieu
Châtelet
Q des Gesvres
Pont Notre Dame
Pont au Change

41
45
Square F Desruelles
R de Rennes
Mabillon
St Germain des Prés
R Clément
Blvd St Germain
Odéon
R de Buci
R St-André des Arts
1
St André des Arts
Place St André des Arts
R Danton
R de la Huchette
St Michel
St Michel
48
St Séverin
R de la Harpe

St Michel Notre Dame
Place du Parvis Notre Dame
15
14
Square Jean XXIII
Square l'Île de France

Carrefour de l'Odéon
Place H Mondor
R de l'École de Médecine
Cluny la Sorbonne
R Hautefeuille
R du Sommerard
12
51
Square R Viviani
Q de Montebello

Maubert Mutualité
Place Maubert
Blvd St Germain
Square l'Île de France
Q de la Tournelle

R St Sulpice
Place St Sulpice
R Mabillon
de Tournon
R de Condé
R de Vaugirard
R de Seine
R Racine
Square et Place P Painlevé

Place Maubert Market
Square F A Mariette
R des Carmes
21
Square Paul Langevin
R Lagrange
R St Victor
R de Poissy
R de Pontoise
R des Écoles

Place de l'Odéon
Place Paul Claudel
Place de la Sorbonne
R Monsieur le Prince
R de Médicis

LATIN QUARTER
R Cujas
46
Place Ste Geneviève
Jardin Carré
Cardinal Lemoine
28

Place Edmond Rostand
6
Luxembourg
R Soufflot
17
39
40
16
Place du Panthéon
R Clotilde
R Clovis

R Guynemer
R Férou

Jardin du Luxembourg
R Auguste Comte
Jardin R Cavelier-de-la-Salle
Blvd St Michel
R Gay Lussac
R de l'Abbé de l'Épée
R de l'Estrapade
R Thouin
R du Cardinal Lemoine
R Descartes
R Mongé
Square des Arènes de Lutèce

Université Paris V
R d'Assas
Jardin du Marco Polo
de l'Observatoire
R Henri Barbusse
22
R des Ursulines
R des Fossés St Jacques
R Lhomond
R Rataud
R Tournefort
R Mouffetard
27
44
36
Place Monge
R Lacépède
R Gracieuse

FRANCE

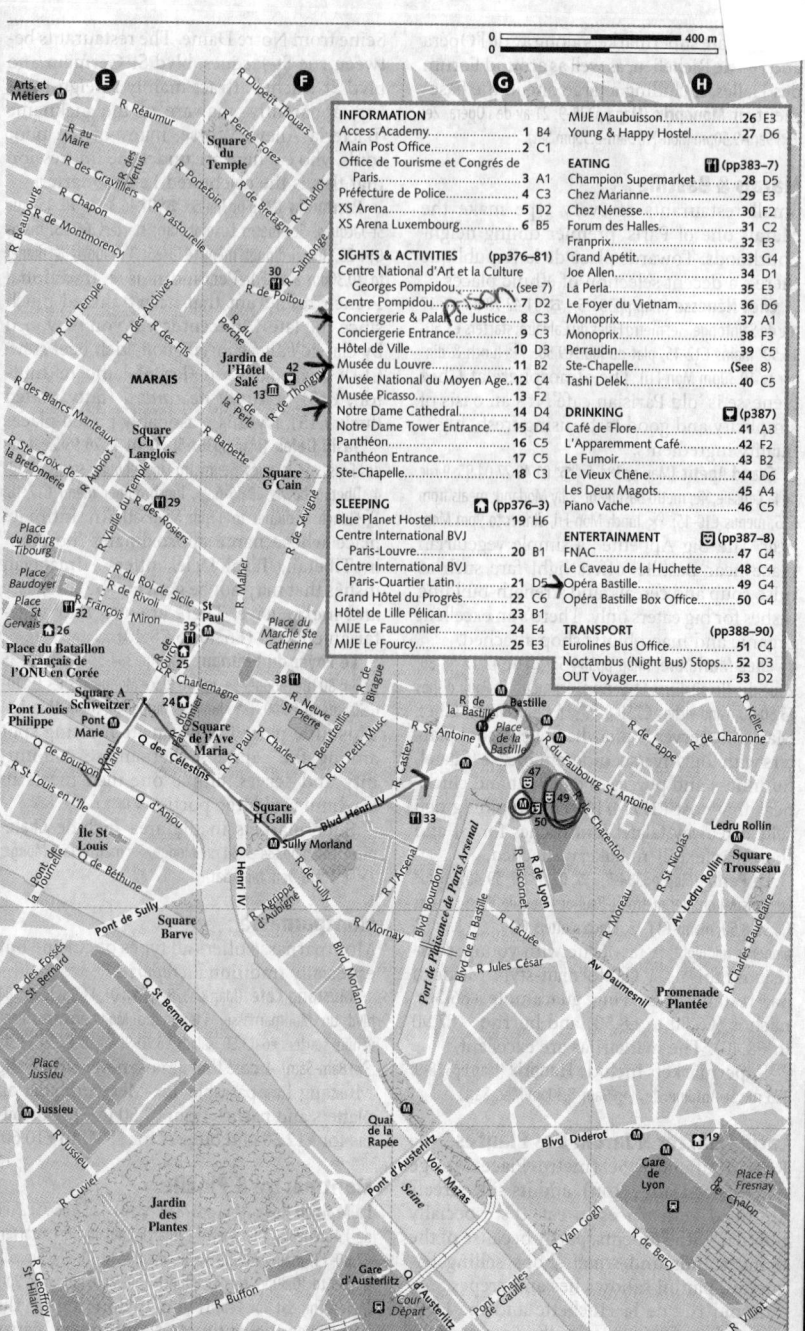

INFORMATION
Access Academy.................................1 B4
Main Post Office.................................2 C1
Office de Tourisme et Congrès de
  Paris..3 A1
Préfecture de Police...........................4 C3
XS Arena...5 D2
XS Arena Luxembourg.......................6 B5

SIGHTS & ACTIVITIES (pp376–81)
Centre National d'Art et la Culture
  Georges Pompidou.....................(see 7)
Centre Pompidou...............................7 D2
Conciergerie & Palais de Justice.........8 C3
Conciergerie Entrance........................9 C3
Hôtel de Ville..................................10 D3
Musée du Louvre.............................11 B2
Musée National du Moyen Age.........12 C4
Musée Picasso.................................13 F2
Notre Dame Cathedral......................14 D4
Notre Dame Tower Entrance............15 D4
Panthéon..16 C5
Panthéon Entrance...........................17 C5
Ste-Chapelle....................................18 C3

SLEEPING (pp376–3)
Blue Planet Hostel............................19 H6
Centre International BVJ
  Paris-Louvre.................................20 B1
Centre International BVJ
  Paris-Quartier Latin.....................21 D5
Grand Hôtel du Progrès....................22 C6
Hôtel de Lille Pélican.......................23 B1
MIJE Le Fauconnier..........................24 E4
MIJE Le Fourcy................................25 E3

MIJE Maubuisson.............................26 E3
Young & Happy Hostel......................27 D6

EATING (pp383–7)
Champion Supermarket.....................28 D5
Chez Marianne.................................29 E3
Chez Nénesse...................................30 F2
Forum des Halles..............................31 C2
Franprix...32 E3
Grand Apétit....................................33 G4
Joe Allen...34 D1
La Perla...35 E3
Le Foyer du Vietnam........................36 D6
Monoprix...37 A1
Monoprix...38 F3
Perraudin..39 C5
Ste-Chapelle................................(See 8)
Tashi Delek......................................40 C5

DRINKING (p387)
Café de Flore...................................41 A3
L'Apparement Café...........................42 F2
Le Fumoir..43 B2
Le Vieux Chêne................................44 D6
Les Deux Magots..............................45 A4
Piano Vache.....................................46 C5

ENTERTAINMENT (pp387–8)
FNAC..47 G4
Le Caveau de la Huchette.................48 C4
Opéra Bastille..................................49 G4
Opéra Bastille Box Office..................50 G4

TRANSPORT (pp388–90)
Eurolines Bus Office.........................51 C4
Noctambus (Night Bus) Stops............52 D3
OUT Voyager....................................53 D2

There are supermarkets along av de l'Opéra and rue de Richelieu, as well as around Forum des Halles, including a large one in the basement of **Monoprix** (Map pp378-9; 21 av de l'Opéra, 2e; 🕑 9am-9.50pm Mon-Fri, 9am-8.50pm Sat).

Marais & Bastille

Small restaurants of every type make the Marais one of Paris' premier dining neighbourhoods. Towards place de la République there's a decent selection of ethnic places.

Chez Nénesse (Map pp384-5; 🕾 01 42 78 46 49; 17 rue de Saintonge, 3e; metro Filles du Calvaire; starters €3.50-14.50, mains €12-15, plat du jour €9.50; 🕑 lunch & dinner to 10.30pm Mon-Fri) The atmosphere at Chez Nénesse is 'old Parisian café'. It's an oasis of simplicity and good taste, using fresh, high-quality ingredients.

Grand Apétit (Map pp384-5; 🕾 01 40 27 04 95; 9 rue de la Cerisaie, 4e; metro Bastille or Sully Morland; meals from €15, menus €10-15; 🕑 lunch Mon-Fri, dinner to 9pm Mon-Wed) 'The Big Appetite', a simple vegetarian place near Bastille, offers light fare such as miso soup and cereals, and strength-building dishes for big eaters only. There's an excellent organic and macrobiotic shop attached.

Chez Marianne (Map pp384-5; 🕾 01 42 72 18 86; 2 rue des Hospitalières St-Gervais, 4e; metro St-Paul; dishes €3.50-20, sandwiches €5.50-8; 🕑 noon-midnight) Chez Marianne serves Sephardic-style kosher platters with four/five/six different mezze (falafel, hummus) and purées of eggplant and chickpeas that cost €12/14/16. The adjoining deli sells takeaway falafel sandwiches for €4 and there's an excellent bakery attached.

La Perla (Map pp384-5; 🕾 01 42 77 59 40; 26 rue François Miron, 4e; metro St-Paul or Hôtel de Ville; starters €6.30-8.50, mains €11-15, lunch platters €6-9; 🕑 lunch & dinner to midnight) A favourite with younger Parisians, this is a Californian-style Mexican bar-restaurant serving guacamole (€6.30), nachos (€5.50 to €8.50) and burritos (€7.90 to €8.40). The margaritas are excellent.

Supermarkets include **Franprix** (Map pp378-9; 135 rue St-Antoine, 4e; 🕑 9am-8.30pm Mon-Sat).

Latin Quarter & Jardin Des Plantes

Rue Mouffetard, 5e (metro Place Monge or Censier Daubenton), and its side streets are filled with places to eat. It's especially popular with students, partly because of the many stands and small shops selling baguettes, panini sandwiches and crepes.

Avoid rue de la Huchette and the labyrinth of narrow streets in the 5e across the Seine from Notre Dame. The restaurants between rue St-Jacques, blvd St-Germain and blvd St-Michel attract mainly foreign tourists, apparently unaware of the nickname 'Bacteria Alley'. Worse, many of the poor souls who eat here are under the impression that this is the celebrated Latin Quarter.

Perraudin (Map pp384-5; 🕾 01 46 33 15 75; 157 rue St-Jacques, 5e; metro Luxembourg; starters €6-15, mains €14-23, lunch/dinner menu €18/26; 🕑 lunch & dinner to 10.30pm Mon-Fri) Perraudin is a traditional French restaurant that hasn't altered much since the late 19th century. If you're wooed by classic *bœuf bourguignon* (rich beef stew; €14), *gigot d'agneau* (leg of lamb or mutton; €15) or *confit de canard* (fatty potted duck; €15), try this reasonably priced place.

Tashi Delek (Map pp384-5; 🕾 01 43 26 55 55; 4 rue des Fossés St-Jacques, 5e; metro Luxembourg; soups €3.50-4, Tibetan bowls €5.35-6.25, lunch/dinner menu €12/18; 🕑 lunch & dinner to 11pm Mon-Sat) An intimate place whose name approximates 'bonjour' in Tibetan, Tashi Delek offers Himalayan dishes that may not be gourmet but are tasty and inexpensive. There are also four vegetarian choices (€6.40 to €8.40).

Le Foyer du Vietnam (Map pp384-5; 🕾 01 45 35 32 54; 80 rue Monge, 5e; metro Place Monge; dishes €3.10-6.50, menu €8.40; 🕑 lunch & dinner to 10pm Mon-Sat) This little place is a favourite meeting spot among the capital's Vietnamese community and serves simple one-dish meals in medium and large portions.

Supermarkets in the area include **Champion** (Map pp384-5; 34 rue Monge, 5e; metro Place Monge; 🕑 8.30am-9pm Mon-Sat).

Montparnasse

Montparnasse offers all types of cuisine but especially traditional *crêperies*.

Mustang Café (Map pp378-9; 🕾 01 43 35 36 12; 84 blvd du Montparnasse, 14e; metro Montparnasse Bienvenüe; starters €6-13.50, salads €6.70-9, mains €7.50-13.30; 🕑 8am-5am) A café that almost never sleeps, the Mustang has passable Tex-Mex combination platters and nachos from €7.50 to €13.30, fajitas for €12.50 and burgers for €8.90 to €10.60.

Montmartre & Pigalle

La Maison Rose (Map pp378-9; 🕾 01 42 57 66 75; 2 rue de l'Abreuvoir, 18e; metro Lamarck Caulaincourt; starters €7.80-13, mains €14.50-16.50, menu €14.50; 🕑 lunch & dinner to 10.30pm Mar-Oct, lunch Thu-Mon, dinner to 9pm Mon & Thu-Sat Nov-Feb) If you are looking for the quintessential intimate Montmartre bistro, head for the tiny 'Pink House' just north of place du Tertre.

Towards place Pigalle there are lots of grocery stores, many of them open until late at night; try the side streets leading off blvd de Clichy (eg rue Lepic). Heading south from blvd de Clichy, rue des Martyrs, 9e is lined with food shops almost all the way to metro Notre-Dame de-Lorette.

DRINKING
Louvre & Les Halles
Le Fumoir (Map pp384-5; ☎ 01 42 92 00 24; 6 rue de l'Amiral Coligny, 1er; metro Louvre-Rivoli; ☾ 11am-2am) 'The Smoking Room' is a huge bar/café just opposite the Louvre with a gentleman's club/library theme. It's a friendly, lively place and quite fun. Happy hour is 6pm to 8pm daily.

Marais & Bastille
L'Apparement Café (Map pp384-5; ☎ 01 48 87 12 22; 18 rue des Coutures St-Gervais, 3e; metro St-Sébastien Froissart; ☾ noon-2am Mon-Fri, 4pm-2am Sat, 12.30pm-midnight Sun) Not so 'Apparently' tucked behind the Musée Picasso, this oasis of peace looks like a private living room.

Latin Quarter & Jardin des Plantes
Piano Vache (Map pp384-5; ☎ 01 46 33 75 03; 8 rue Laplace, 5e; metro Maubert Mutualité; ☾ noon-2am Mon-Fri, 9pm-2am Sat & Sun) Just down the hill from the Panthéon, 'The Mean Piano' plays great music (guest DJs) and attracts a good crowd of very mixed ages. Happy hour is from opening to 9pm Monday to Friday.

Le Vieux Chêne (Map pp384-5; ☎ 01 43 37 71 51; 69 rue Mouffetard, 5e; metro Place Monge; ☾ 4pm-2am Sun-Thu, 4pm-5am Fri & Sat) 'The Old Oak' is popular with students and has jazz at the weekend. Happy hour is from opening until 9pm daily.

St-Germain, Odéon & Luxembourg
Café de Flore (Map pp384-5; ☎ 01 45 48 55 26; 172 blvd St-Germain, 6e; metro St-Germain des Prés; ☾ 7.30am-1.30am) The Flore is an Art Deco café where the red, upholstered benches, mirrors and marble walls haven't changed since the days when Sartre, de Beauvoir, Camus and Picasso bent their elbows here. The terrace is a much sought-after place to sip beer (€7.50 for 400mL), the house Pouilly Fumé (€7.50 a glass or €29 a bottle) or coffee (€4).

Les Deux Magots (Map pp384-5; ☎ 01 45 48 55 25; 170 blvd St-Germain, 6e; metro St-Germain des Prés; ☾ 7am-1am) This erstwhile literary haunt is best known

as the favoured hang-out of Sartre, Hemingway, Picasso and André Breton. Everyone has to sit on the terrace here at least once and have a coffee (€4), beer (€5.50) or the famous hot chocolate served in porcelain jugs (€6).

Montmartre & Pigalle
La Fourmi (☎ 01 42 64 70 35; 74 rue des Martyrs, 18e; metro Pigalle; ☾ 8am-2am Mon-Thu, 10am-4am Fri-Sun) A trendy Pigalle hang-out, the 'Ant' buzzes (marches?) all day and night and is a convenient place to meet before heading off to the clubs.

CLUBBING
Paris is great for music (techno remains very popular) and there are some mighty fine DJs based here. Latino and Cuban salsa music is also huge.

Le Batofar (☎ 01 56 29 10 33; www.batofar.net, French only; opp 11 quai François Mauriac, 13e; metro Quai de la Gare or Bibliothèque; admission free-€12; ☾ 9pm-midnight Mon & Tue, 9pm or 10pm-4am, 5am or 6am Wed-Sun) What looks like an unassuming tugboat moored near the imposing Bibliothèque Nationale de France is a rollicking dancing spot that attracts some top international techno and funk DJ talent.

Le Cithéa (☎ 01 40 21 70 95; www.cithea.com, French only; 114 rue Oberkampf, 11e; metro Parmentier or Ménilmontant; ☾ 5pm-5.30am Tue-Thu, 10pm-6.30am Fri & Sat) This popular concert venue has bands playing soul, Latin and funk but especially world music and jazz, usually from 10.30pm with DJs from 1am.

ENTERTAINMENT
It's virtually impossible to sample the richness of Paris' entertainment scene without first studying *Pariscope* (€0.40) or *Officiel des Spectacles* (€0.35), both of which come out on Wednesday. *Pariscope* includes a six-page insert in English at the back, courtesy of London's *Time Out* magazine.

You can buy tickets for cultural events at many ticket outlets, including **FNAC** (Map pp384-5; ☎ 0892 68 36 22; www.fnac.com, French only) and **Virgin Megastore branches** (www.virginmega.fr, French only), for a small commission.

Cinemas
Expect to pay €6 to €8 for a first-run film. Students and those aged under 18 or over 60 usually get discounts of about 25% except on Friday, Saturday and Sunday nights.

FRANCE

Live Music
OPERA & CLASSICAL
The **Opéra National de Paris** (ONP; ☎ 0892 89 90 90; www.opera-de-paris.fr – French only) splits its performance schedule between the **Palais Garnier** (Garnier Palace; Map pp378-9; place de l'Opéra, 9e; metro Opéra) and the modern Opéra Bastille, which opened in 1989. Both opera houses also stage ballets and classical-music concerts (September to July) performed by the ONP's affiliated orchestra and ballet companies.

Opéra Bastille (Map pp384-5; 2-6 place de la Bastille, 12e; metro Bastille) Tickets are available from the **box office** (Map pp384-5; 130 rue de Lyon, 12e; ⏰ 11am-6.30pm Mon-Sat) some 14 days before the date of the performance, but the only way to ensure a seat is by **post** (120 rue de Lyon, 75576 Paris CEDEX 12) about two months in advance. Operas cost €6 to €114. Ballets cost €13 to €70; seats with limited or no visibility available at the box office only are €6 to €9. Unsold tickets are offered to people aged under 26 or over 65 and students for €20 15 minutes before the curtain goes up.

JAZZ
Paris is very much à la mode for jazz; the city's better clubs attract top international stars.

Le Caveau de la Huchette (Map pp384-5; ☎ 01 43 26 65 05; 5 rue de la Huchette, 5e; metro St-Michel; adult Sun-Thu €10.50, Fri & Sat €13, student €9; ⏰ 9pm-2.30am Sun-Thu, 9pm-3.30am Fri, 9pm-4am Sat) Housed in a medieval *caveau* (cellar) that was used as a courtroom and torture chamber during the Revolution, this club is where virtually all the jazz greats have played since the end of WWII.

GETTING AROUND
To/From the Airports
If you get stuck, a taxi will cost about €25/40 from Orly/Charles de Gaulle. Private shuttle buses (€18 to €25) to your hotel include: **Shuttle Van PariShuttle** (☎ 0800 69 96 99; www.parishuttle.com), **Paris Airports Service** (☎ 01 46 80 14 67; www.parisairportservice.com), **World Shuttle** (☎ 01 46 80 14 67; www.world-shuttles.com) and **Allô Shuttle** (☎ 01 34 29 00 80; www.alloshuttle.com).

AÉROPORT ROISSY CHARLES DE GAULLE
Roissy Charles de Gaulle lies 37km northeast of central Paris. It has two train stations: Aéroport Charles de Gaulle 1 (CDG1) and Aéroport Charles de Gaulle 2 (CDG2), both served by commuter trains on RER line B3.

A free shuttle bus links the terminals with the train stations. Tickets for bus services are sold on board.

RER B3 (☎ 0890 36 10 10; €7.75; ⏰ every 4-15min, 4.56am-11.40pm in each direction, journey time 30min) links CDG1 and CDG2 with Gare du Nord, central metro stations Châtelet des Halles and St-Michel, before continuing southeast to metro Denfert Rochereau, 14e and beyond. To reach the airport take any RER line B train whose four-letter destination code begins with E (eg EIRE) and a shuttle bus (every five to eight minutes) will ferry you to your terminal. Metro ticket offices can't always sell RER tickets as far as the airport so you might have to buy one at the RER station where you board.

Air France bus No 4 (☎ 0892 35 08 20; www.cars-airfrance.com – French only; one-way/return €11.50/19.55; ⏰ every 30min, to Paris 7am-9pm, to Roissy Charles de Gaulle 7am-9.30pm, journey time 45-55min) Links the airport with Gare de Lyon, 12e and Gare Montparnasse, 15e.

Air France bus No 2 (☎ 0892 35 08 20; www.cars-airfrance.com – French only; one-way/return €10/17; ⏰ every 15min, 5.45am-11pm in each direction, journey time 35-50min) links the airport to near the Arc de Triomphe just outside 2 av Carnot, 17e and the Palais des Congrès de Paris on blvd Gouvion St-Cyr, 17e).

Other options include:

RATP Bus Nos 350 or 351 (☎ 0892 68 77 14; €3.90 or 3 metro/bus tickets; ⏰ journey time 1¼hr) Bus 350 links CDG with Gare de l'Est, 10e and Gare du Nord, 10e; bus 351 goes to place de la Nation, 11e.

Roissybus (☎ 0892 68 77 14; €8.20; ⏰ every 15-20min, 5.45am-11pm in each direction, journey time 1hr) Goes to rue Scribe near the metro station Opera.

AÉROPORT D'ORLY
Orly is 24km south of central Paris, with two terminals – Orly-Nord and Orly-Sud. An Aéroports de Paris (ADP) shuttle bus links the airport with **RER C** (☎ 0890 36 10 10; €5.35; ⏰ every 12-20min, 5.45am-11pm in each direction, journey time 50min). From the city, take a C2 train towards Pont de Rungis or Massy-Palaiseau and alight at Pont de Rungis-Aéroport d'Orly RER station. Travelling from Orly to Paris, tickets are valid for onward travel on the metro.

Air France Bus No 1 (☎ 0892 35 08 20; www.cars-airfrance.com – French only; one-way/return €7.50/12.75; ⏰ every 15min, 6am-11.30pm to Paris, 5.45am-11pm to Orly, journey time 30-45min) is a *navette* (shuttle bus) that runs to/from the eastern side of Gare Montparnasse (rue du Commandant René Mouchotte, 15e; metro Montparnasse Bienvenüe) as well as Aérogare des Invalides (metro Invalides) in the 7e. En route, you can ask to get off at metros Porte d'Orléans or Duroc.

Orlyval (☎ 0892 68 77 14; €8.80 to/from Paris, €10.65 to/from La Défense; ⏰ every 4-12min, 6am-11pm in each direction, journey time 33min to Paris, 50min to La Défense) is a driverless shuttle train that runs between the airport and Antony RER station (eight minutes) on line B, from where it's an easy journey into the city; to get to Antony from the city (26 minutes), take line B4 towards St-Rémy-lès-Chevreuse. Orlyval tickets are valid for travel on the RER and for metro travel within the city.

Other options include:

Jetbus (☎ 01 69 01 00 09; €5.15; ⏰ every 15-20min, 6.43am-10.49pm to Paris, 6.15am-10.15pm to Orly, journey time 55min) Runs to/from metro Villejuif Louis Aragon, a bit south of the 13e on the city's southern fringe.

Orlybus (☎ 0892 68 77 14; €5.70; ⏰ every 15-20min, 6am-11.30pm to Paris, 5.35am-11pm to Orly, journey time 30min) This RATP bus runs to/from metro Denfert Rochereau, 14e and makes several stops in the eastern 14e.

RATP Bus No 183 (☎ 0892 68 77 14; €1.30 or 1 metro/bus ticket; ⏰ every 35min, 5.35am-8.35pm in each direction, journey time 1hr) Links Orly-Sud (only) with metro Porte de Choisy, 13e.

Public Transport
BUS
Paris' bus system, also operated by the RATP, runs from 5.45am to 12.30am Monday to Saturday. Services are drastically reduced on Sunday. After the metro lines have finished their last runs at about 1am, the Noctambus network of night buses lines links the place du Châtelet (1er) and av Victoria just west of the Hôtel de Ville in the 4e with most parts of the city. Short bus rides cost one metro/bus ticket; longer rides require two. Whatever kind of single-journey ticket you have, you must *oblitérer* (cancel) it in the *composteur* (cancelling machine) next to the driver.

The cheapest and easiest way to use public transport in Paris is to get a **Carte Orange**, which is a weekly or monthly combined metro, RER and bus pass. The basic ticket, zone 1 and 2, should be sufficient. To buy your first Carte Orange, take a passport-size photograph to any metro or RER ticket window.

The **Mobilis card** and its coupon allow unlimited travel for one day in two to eight zones (€5.20 to €18.30), but you would have to make at least six metro trips in a day (based on the carnet price) in zones 1 and 2 to break even on this pass.

Paris Visite passes provide the holder with discounted entry to certain museums and activities as well as discounts on transport fares. They are valid for one, two, three or five consecutive days of travel in either three, five or eight zones. The version covering up to three zones costs €8.35/13.70/18.25/26.65 for one/two/three/five days.

METRO & RER
Paris' underground network consists of two separate but interlinked systems: the Métropolitain, known as the metro, with 14 lines and 372 stations; and the RER (Réseau Express Régional), a network of suburban lines that passes through the city centre.

Each **metro** train is known by the name of its terminus. Blue-on-white directional signs in metro and RER stations indicate the way to the correct platform for your line. On lines that split into several branches (eg line Nos 3, 7 and 13), the terminus served by each train is indicated on the cars with back-lit panels. The last metro trains run sometime between 12.35am and 1.04am and start again around 5.30am.

The **RER** is faster than the metro, but the stops are much further apart. RER lines are known by an alphanumeric combination: the letter (A to E) refers to the line, the number to the spur it will follow somewhere out in the suburbs. The same RATP tickets are valid on the metro, the RER (for travel within the city limits), buses, the Montmartre funicular and Paris' two tram lines. They cost €1.30 if bought individually and €10 (€5 for children aged four to 11) for a carnet of 10. Always keep your ticket until you exit from your station; you may be stopped by a *contrôleur* (ticket inspector).

Taxi
The *prise en charge* (flag fall) in a Parisian taxi is €2. Within the city limits, it costs €0.62 per kilometre for travel between 7am and 7pm Monday to Saturday and €1.06 per kilometre from 7pm to 7am at night, all day Sunday and on public holidays. Pick-ups from SNCF mainline stations cost another €0.70.

FRANCE

Radio-dispatched taxi companies, on call 24 hours, include the following:

Alpha Taxis ☎ 01 45 85 85 85
Taxis Bleus ☎ 01 49 36 10 10
Taxis Radio 7000 ☎ 01 42 70 00 42

You'll be charged for the distance from the driver's base to your pick-up location.

AROUND PARIS

VERSAILLES
pop 85,300
The prosperous, leafy and very bourgeois suburb of Versailles, 21km southwest of Paris, is the site of the grandest and most famous chateau in France. It served as the kingdom's political capital and the seat of the royal court for more than a century, from 1682 to 1789, the year Revolutionary mobs massacred the palace guard and dragged Louis XVI and Marie-Antoinette back to Paris where they eventually had their heads lopped off.

The **Office de Tourisme de Versailles** (☎ 01 39 24 88 88; www.versailles-tourisme.com; 2bis av de Paris; ☽ 9am-7pm Apr-Oct, 9am-6pm Tue-Sat, 9am-5pm Sun & Mon Nov-Mar) has themed guided tours (adult/child €8/4) of the city and chateau throughout the week year-round.

Sights
CHÂTEAU DE VERSAILLES
The splendid and enormous **Château de Versailles** (Palace of Versailles; ☎ 01 30 83 78 00 or 01 30 83 77 77; www.chateauversailles.fr; passport adult/aged 10-17 €20/6 Apr-Oct, €14.50/4 Nov-Mar; ☽ 9am-5.30pm Tue-Sun Nov-Mar, 9am-6.30pm Tue-Sun Apr-Oct) was built in the mid-17th century during the reign of Louis XIV – the Roi Soleil (Sun King) – to project the absolute power of the French monarchy. The palace, a 580m-long structure with innumerable wings, grand halls and sumptuous bedchambers, has vast **gardens** (admission free Nov-Mar, adult €3, free for under-18s & all after 6pm Apr-Oct; ☽ 8am-5.30pm or 6.30pm Nov-Mar, 9am-sunset Apr-Oct). Tickets are on sale at Entrée A (Entrance A), which is off to the right from the equestrian statue of Louis XIV as you approach the palace.

Getting There & Away
RER line C5 (€2.35) takes you from Paris' Left Bank RER stations to Versailles-Rive Gauche station, which is located roughly 700m southeast of the chateau and close to the tourist office. The last train back to Paris leaves shortly before midnight.

SNCF operates 70 trains a day from Paris' Gare St-Lazare (€3.20) to Versailles-Rive Droite, which is 1.2km from the chateau. The last train to Paris leaves just after midnight.

CHARTRES
pop 40,250
The magnificent 13th-century cathedral of Chartres, crowned by two very different spiresn, one Gothic, the other Romanesque, rises from rich farmland 88km southwest of Paris and dominates the medieval town around its base. With its astonishing blue stained glass and other treasures, the cathedral is a must-see for any visitor to Paris.

For information try the **Office de Tourisme de Chartres** (☎ 02 37 18 26 26; info@otchartres.fr; place de la Cathédrale; ☽ 9am-7pm Mon-Sat, 9.30am-5.30pm Sun Apr-Sep, 10am-6pm Mon-Sat, 10am-1pm & 2.30-4.30pm Sun Oct-Mar).

Sights
CATHÉDRALE NOTRE DAME DE CHARTRES
The 130m-long **Cathédrale Notre Dame de Chartres** (Cathedral of Our Lady of Chartres; ☎ 02 37 21 22 07; www.cathedrale-chartres.com – French only; place de la Cathédrale; ☽ 8.30am-7.30pm), one of the crowning architectural achievements of Western civilisation, was built in the Gothic style during the 13th century. **English-language audioguide tours** (per 25/45/70min €2.90/3.80/5.65) with three different themes can be hired from the cathedral bookshop. The cathedral's 172 extraordinary **stained-glass windows** form one of the most important ensembles of medieval stained glass in the world.

Sleeping & Eating
Auberge de Jeunesse (☎ 02 37 34 27 64; fax 02 37 35 78 85; 23 av Neigre; dm €11; ✗ 🖳) Reception at this hostel, which is about 1.5km east of the train station via blvd Charles Péguy and blvd Jean Jaurès, opens from 2pm to 10pm daily; curfew is 10.30pm in winter and 11.30pm in summer. To get there from the train station, take bus No 5 (direction: Mare aux Moines) to the Rouliers stop.

Le Buisson Ardent (☎ 02 37 34 04 66; 10 rue au Lait; starters €9.50-16, mains €13-22, lunch/dinner menu €18/22; ☽ lunch Thu-Tue, dinner to 10.30pm Mon, Tue & Thu-Sat) 'The Burning Bush' is a charming, old-style place with good-value *menus*.

Covered market (place Billard; ☼ 7am-1pm Sat) This market just off rue des Changes south of the cathedral dates from the early 20th century. There are a lot of **food shops** surrounding it.

Getting There & Away
Some 30 SNCF trains a day (20 on Sunday) link Paris' Gare Montparnasse (€11.80, 55 to 70 minutes) with Chartres, all of which pass through Versailles-Chantiers (€9.90, 45 to 60 minutes).

ALSACE & LORRAINE

Though often spoken of as if they were one, Alsace and Lorraine, neighbouring regions in France's northeastern corner, are linked by little more than a common border through the Massif des Vosges (Vosges Mountains) and the imperial ambitions of late-19th-century Germany. In 1871, after the Franco-Prussian War, the newly created German Reich annexed Alsace and part of Lorraine, making their return to rule from Paris a rallying cry of French nationalism.

STRASBOURG
pop 427,000

Situated just a few kilometres west of the Rhine, prosperous, cosmopolitan Strasbourg (City of the Roads) is France's great northeastern metropolis and the intellectual and cultural capital of Alsace. Strasbourg serves as an important European crossroads thanks to the presence of the European Parliament, the Council of Europe, the European Court of Human Rights and 48,000 students.

Towering above the restaurants, *winstubs* (traditional Alsatian restaurants) and pubs of the lively old city is the cathedral, a medieval marvel in pink sandstone. Nearby you'll find one of the finest ensembles of museums anywhere in France.

Orientation
Strasbourg's train station is about 400m west of the Grande Île (Big Island), the core of ancient and modern Strasbourg. The quaint Petite France area in the Grande Île's southwestern corner is subdivided by canals. Much of the city centre is for pedestrians only. The European Parliament building and Palais de l'Europe are about 2km northeast of the cathedral. The city centre

is about 3.5km west of Pont de l'Europe, the bridge that links the French bank of the Rhine with the German city of Kehl.

Information
Main tourist office (☎ 03 88 52 28 28; www.ot-stras bourg.fr; 17 place de la Cathédrale; ☼ 9am-7pm) The Strasbourg Pass (€10.60), a coupon book valid for three consecutive days, may save you a fair bit of cash.
NeT SuR CouR (☎ 03 88 35 66 76; 18 quai des Pêcheurs; tram stop Gallia; per hr €2; ☼ 9.30am-9.30pm Mon-Fri, 2-8pm Sat & Sun) At the end of a narrow courtyard.

Grande Île
The enchanting Grande Île is a paradise for an aimless amble through bustling public squares, busy pedestrianised areas and up-market shopping. The narrow streets of the **old city**, crisscrossed by narrow lanes, canals and locks, have a fairy-tale feel. The romantic Terrasse Panoramique atop **Barrage Vauban** (admission free; ☼ 9am-7.30pm), a dam built to prevent river-borne attacks on the city, affords views of the Ill River.

Inhabiting a cluster of magnificent 14th- and 16th-century buildings, the renowned **Musée de l'Œuvre Notre-Dame** (☎ 03 88 32 88 17; 3 place du Château; adult/student under 26 & senior/under-18s & disabled incl audioguide €4/2/free; ☼ 10am-6pm Tue-Sun) has one of Europe's premier collections of Romanesque, Gothic and Renaissance sculptures, 15th-century paintings and stained glass.

The outstanding **Musée d'Art Moderne et Contemporain** (☎ 03 88 23 31 31; place Hans Jean Arp; tram stop Musée d'Art Moderne; adult/student/over-60s & under-18s €5/2.50/free; ☼ 11am-7pm Tue, Wed, Fri & Sat, noon-10pm Thu, 10am-6pm Sun) has an exceptionally diverse collection of works representing every major art movement of the past century.

Strasbourg's lacy, fragile-looking Gothic **Cathédrale Notre Dame** (☼ 7am-7pm) is one of the marvels of European architecture. The western façade was completed in 1284, but the 142m spire, the tallest of its time, was not in place until 1439; its southern companion was never built. The 30m-high Gothic and Renaissance contraption just inside the southern entrance is the *horloge astronomique* (astronomical clock), a late-16th-century clock that strikes solar noon every day at 12.30pm. The 66m-high **platform** (☎ 03 88 43 60 40; adult/student & under-18s €3/1.50; ☼ 9am-5pm Mon-Fri, 10am-5pm Sat & Sun Apr-Oct, 9am-4.30pm Mon-Fri, 10am-4.30pm Sat & Sun Nov-Mar) above

STRASBOURG

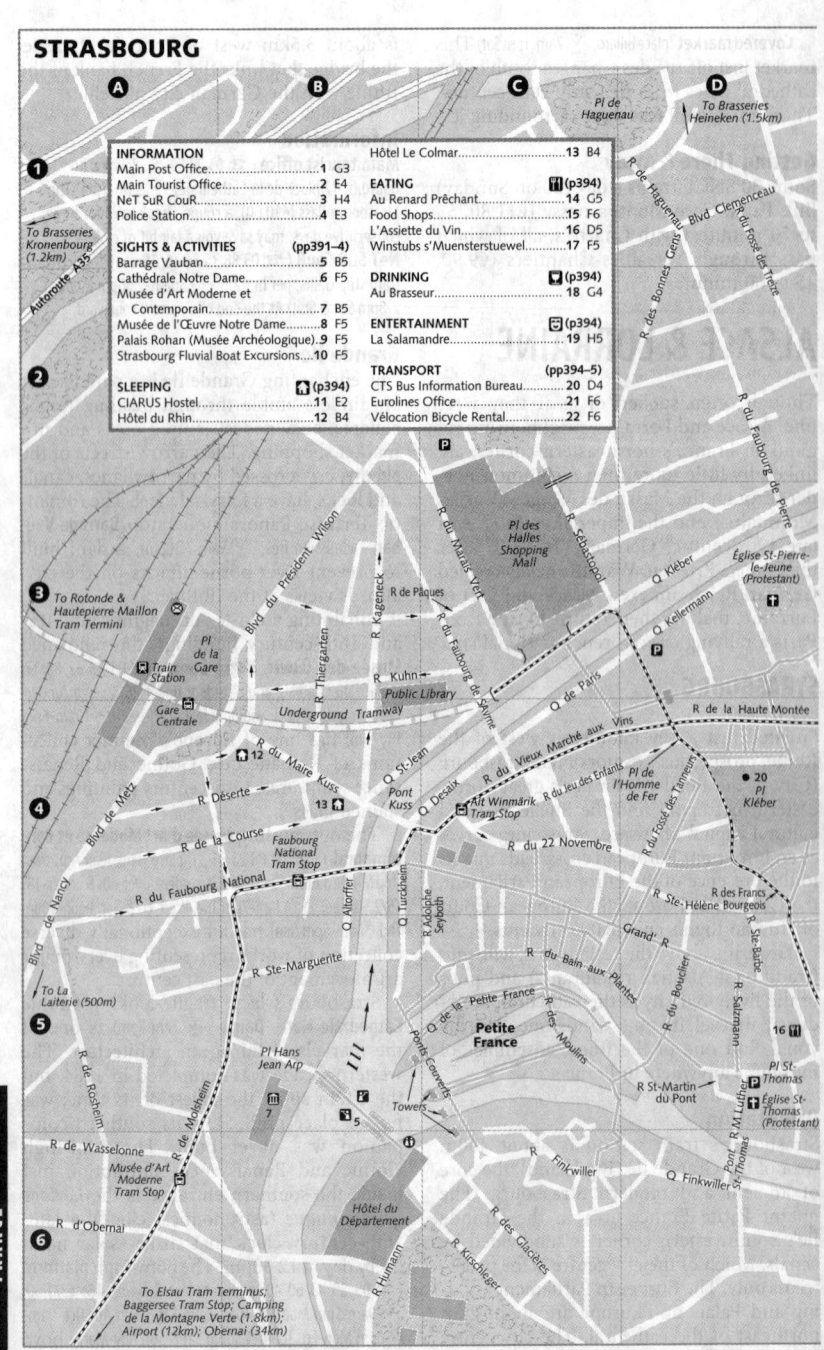

INFORMATION
Main Post Office..............................1 G3
Main Tourist Office.........................2 E4
NeT SuR CouR.................................3 H4
Police Station..................................4 E3

SIGHTS & ACTIVITIES (pp391–4)
Barrage Vauban................................5 B5
Cathédrale Notre Dame....................6 F5
Musée d'Art Moderne et
  Contemporain...............................7 B5
Musée de l'Œuvre Notre Dame........8 F5
Palais Rohan (Musée Archéologique).9 F5
Strasbourg Fluvial Boat Excursions....10 F5

SLEEPING (p394)
CIARUS Hostel................................11 E2
Hôtel du Rhin.................................12 B4

Hôtel Le Colmar.............................13 B4

EATING (p394)
Au Renard Prêchant........................14 G5
Food Shops....................................15 F6
L'Assiette du Vin............................16 D5
Winstubs s'Muensterstuewel...........17 F5

DRINKING (p394)
Au Brasseur....................................18 G4

ENTERTAINMENT (p394)
La Salamandre................................19 H5

TRANSPORT (pp394–5)
CTS Bus Information Bureau............20 D4
Eurolines Office..............................21 F6
Vélocation Bicycle Rental...............22 F6

0 — 300 m
0 — 0.2 mile

E

F

To Hoenheim Gare Tram Terminus

G

H

Blvd Clemenceau

R. Oberlin

Contades Park

1

R. Sellénick

R. Strauss Dürkheim

Synagogue de la Paix

11 R. Finkmatt

Av. des Vosges

Av. de la Paix

R. Turenne

R. du Général Gouraud

Q. Zorn

Église St-Pierre-le-Jeune (Catholic)

R. du Général de Castelnau

R. du Maréchal Foch

2

Q. Zorn

Law Courts

R. du Général de Castelnau

Palais du Rhin

Préfecture

Av. d'Alsace

To European Parliment Building (1.3km)

Q. Jacques Sturm

Pl de la République

Bibliothèque National et Universitaire

Q. Koch

To Parc de l'Orangerie (1km)

Fossé du Faux Rempart

Q. Schoepflin

Théâtre National

Église St-Paul (Protestant)

To Palais de l'Europe (1km); Palais des Droits de l'Homme (1.4km)

R. de la Fonderie

République Tram Stop

Av. de la Liberté

Av. de la Marseillaise

Pont d'Auvergne

3

4 Impasse de l'Ecrevisse

R. de la Nuée Bleue

Broglie Tram Stop

Pl Broglie

P

Hôtel de Ville

R. Brûlée

R. Lezay-Marnésia

Q. du Maire Dietrich

Pl de l'Université

University

R. de la Mésange

Gallia Tram Stop

Blvd de la Victoire

4

Grande Île

R. de l'Outre

Temple Neuf (Protestant)

R. des Juifs

R. du Faisan

Pl St-Étienne

Q. des Pêcheurs

3

To Esplanade Tram Terminus; Jardin des Deux Rives (2.7km); Pont de l'Europe (3km); Rhine & Kehl, Germany (5km)

R. des Orfèvres

R. des Hallebardes

Sengsta

R. du Dôme

R. des Frères

18

Pl du Marché Neuf

R. des Écrivains

R. des Veaux

R. St-Guillaume

2

6

R. de la Râpe

R. des Sœurs

Footbridge

R. de l'Académie

Pl de la Cathédrale

Pl du Château

9

R. de la Manufacture des Tabacs

R. Mercière

R. du Vieil Hôpital

17

8

Pl du Marché aux Cochons de Lait

10

Q. des Bateliers

Krutenau District

R. des Poules

19

R. Paul Janet

5

Pl Gutenberg

R. Gutenberg

R. des Grandes-Arcades

R. des Serruriers

R. des Tonneliers

R. du Vieux Marché aux Poissons

R. des Bateliers

Ste-Catherine

R. de Zurich

R. de la Krutenau

R. du Jeu de Paume

Q. St-Thomas

R. de l'Ail

R. de la Division Leclerc

R. de l'Écurie

Pl du Puits

R. des Couples

Pl de Zurich

R. de Zurich

14

R. du St-Gothard

6

Q. St-Nicolas

R. d'Or

Porte de l'Hôpital

22

R. des Bouchers

R. d'Austerlitz

15

Pl de l'Hôpital

R. de la Toise aux Blés

Pl d'Austerlitz

21

R. des Orphelins

R. de Berne

To Pl de l'Étoile (200m); Étoile Polygone & Illkirch Lixenbuhl Tram Termini; Jardin des Deux Rives (3.7km); Pont de l'Europe (4km); Kehl, Germany (5km)

R. de la Brigade Alsace-Lorraine

R. Sédillot

To Pl de l'Étoile (200m); Eurolines Bus Stops (2.5km)

LP

FRANCE

the façade affords a spectacular stork's-eye view of Strasbourg.

The **Palais Rohan** (☎ 03 88 52 50 00; 2 place du Château; for whole complex: adult/student under 26 & senior/under-18s & disabled €6/3/free, for each museum: €4/2/free; ✆ 10am-6pm Wed-Mon) was built between 1732 and 1742 as a residence for the city's princely bishops. It has several museums including the **Musée Archéologique**, which takes you from the Palaeolithic period to AD 800.

Tours

Boat excursions (70 minutes) that take in Petite France and the European institutions are run by **Strasbourg Fluvial** (☎ 03 88 84 13 13 or 03 88 32 75 25; behind Palais Rohan; adult/student €6.80/3.40, at night €7.20/3.60; ✆ at least 4 times a day).

BREWERIES

Brasseries Kronenbourg (☎ 03 88 27 41 59; siegevisites@kronenbourg-fr.com; 68 route d'Oberhausbergen; tram stop Ducs d'Alsace) has interesting and thirst-quenching tours (adult/12 to 18 years €3/2).

Brasseries Heineken (☎ 03 88 19 57 55; 4 rue St-Charles) has free, two-hour tours.

Sleeping

It is *extremely* difficult to find last-minute accommodation from Monday to Thursday when the European Parliament is in plenary session (usually for one week each month). Contact the tourist office for dates.

The municipal **Camping de la Montagne Verte** (☎ 03 88 30 25 46; 2 rue Robert Forrer; sites/adult €4.50/3.35; ✆ mid-Mar–Oct & late Nov-early Jan) is a grassy place a short walk from the Nid de Cigognes stop on bus line No 2.

Centre International d'Accueil et de Rencontre Unioniste de Strasbourg (Ciarus; ☎ 03 88 15 27 88; www.ciarus.com; 7 rue Finkmatt; dm in r with 8/4/2 beds incl breakfast €16.50/20/22.50; Ⓟ ▯) This welcoming hostel, outfitted with 295 beds, is so stylish it even counts a few European Parliament members among its regular clients.

Two- and three-star hotels line place de la Gare.

Hôtel du Rhin (☎ 03 88 32 35 00; www.hotel-du-rhin.com; 7-8 place de la Gare; tram stop Gare Centrale; d from €34, with shower & toilet €60) This 61-room, two-star establishment has comfortable, soundproofed rooms.

Hôtel Le Colmar (☎ 03 88 32 16 89; hotel.le.colmar@wanadoo.fr; 1 rue du Maire Kuss; tram stop Alt Winmärik; s/d from €24.50/27.50, with shower & toilet €37/40; ✆ reception closed 1.30-5.30pm Sun) A 15-room cheapie that's convenient and good value. Hall showers cost €2.50.

Eating & Drinking

Just south of place Gutenberg, pedestrianised rue des Tonneliers is lined with mid-range restaurants, both ethnic and French. Inexpensive places can be found northeast of the cathedral along rue des Frères.

Au Renard Prêchant (☎ 03 88 35 62 87; 33 place de Zurich; mains €9-16; ✆ closed lunch Sat & lunch Sun) Housed in a 16th-century chapel, this convivial, crowded restaurant offers excellent, reasonably priced French fare. *Gibier* (game) is a seasonal speciality.

L'Assiette du Vin (☎ 03 88 32 00 92; 5 rue de la Chaîne; lunch menu €19.90, 2-/3-course menus €21/26, 4-course menu with 4 wines €45; ✆ closed Sun, lunch Sat & Mon) The cuisine changes with the seasons, inspired by what's available fresh in the marketplace. The wine list is extensive.

Winstub s'Muensterstuewel (☎ 03 88 32 17 63; 8 place du Marché aux Cochons de Lait; lunch menu €23; ✆ Tue-Sat) This *winstub* has an excellent reputation – for mains and desserts – thanks to its English-speaking Paul Bocuse–trained owner, who's happy to whip up vegetarian options on demand.

A few blocks south of the cathedral, pedestrianised rue d'Austerlitz is home to quite a few **food shops**.

Au Brasseur (☎ 03 88 36 12 13; 22 rue des Veaux; ✆ 11am-1am) Four types of beers (*brune, ambrée, blonde* and *blanche*) are brewed in this warm, dimly lit microbrewery, which also has some of the best deals in town on Alsatian treats.

Entertainment

Strasbourg's entertainment options are legion. Details on cultural events appear in the free monthly *Spectacles* (www.spectacles-publications.com), available at the tourist office.

La Salamandre (☎ 03 88 25 79 42; www.lasalamandre-strasbourg.fr – French only; 3 rue Paul Janet; adult/student incl 1 drink €10/6; ✆ 10pm-4am Wed-Sun) Billed as a *bar-club-spectacles*, this discotheque has theme nights each Friday (salsa, disco etc).

Getting There & Away

Eurolines' buses stop 2.5km south of the **Eurolines' office** (☎ 03 90 22 14 60; 6D place d'Austerlitz ✆ 10am-6.30pm Mon-Fri, 10am-noon & 2-5pm Sat) near Stade de la Meinau (the city's main football stadium), on rue du Maréchal Lefèbvre about 200m west of av de Colmar and the Lycée Couffignal tram stop.

Strasbourg city bus No 21 (€1.20) links place Gutenberg with the Stadthalle in Kehl, the German town just across the Rhine.

Train information and tickets are available on the Grande Île at the **SNCF Boutique** (5 rue des France-Bourgeois; ☒ 10am-7pm Mon-Fri, 10am-5pm Sat). The train station is linked to Lyon (€42.30, five hours) and Paris' Gare de l'Est (€40.90, four to 4½ hours); and, internationally, to Basel (Bâle; €17.40, 1¼ hours) and Frankfurt (€35.60, 2½ hours).

Getting Around
Four tram lines form the centrepiece of Strasbourg's public transport network, run by **CTS** (☎ 03 88 77 70 70; information bureau: 31 place Kléber). The main hub is at place de l'Homme de Fer. The city government's Vélocation system can supply you with a well-maintained one-speed bike for €4/7 per half/whole day (plus a €100 deposit). Outlets: **Train station** (☎ 03 88 23 56 75; 4 rue du Maire Kuss; tram stop Alt Winmärik; ☒ 6am-7.30pm Mon-Fri, 9.30am-noon & 2-7pm Sat year-round, 9.30am-noon & 2-7pm Sun & holidays Apr-late Oct); **City centre** (☎ 03 88 24 05 61; 10 rue des Bouchers; tram stop Porte de l'Hôpital; ☒ 9.30am-noon & 2-6.30pm Mon-Fri, to 7pm Sat, Sun & holidays Apr-late Oct, 10am-5pm Mon-Fri late Oct-Mar)

COLMAR
pop 67,000
Colmar makes a good base for exploring the surrounding wine country. The town is a maze of cobbled pedestrian malls and Alsatian-style restored, half-timbered houses dating from the late Middle Ages and Renaissance.

The **tourist office** (☎ 03 89 20 68 92; www .ot-colmar.fr; 4 rue des Unterlinden; ☒ 9am-noon & 2-6pm Mon-Sat, 10am-1pm Sun & holidays, longer hours in some seasons) supplies information about the Route du Vin (Wine Road).

The **Issenheim Altarpiece** (Rétable d'Issenheim), acclaimed as one of the most dramatic and moving works of art ever created, is the pride and joy of the **Musée d'Unterlinden** (☎ 03 89 20 15 50; www.musee-unterlinden.com; adult/student 25 & under incl audioguide €7/5; ☒ 9am-6pm May-Oct, 9am-noon & 2-5pm Wed-Mon Nov-Apr).

Sleeping & Eating
Auberge de Jeunesse Mittelhart (☎ 03 89 80 57 39; fax 03 89 80 76 16; 2 rue Pasteur; dm/d with 2 bunks incl breakfast €11.65/28.30; ☒ reception 8-10am & 5-11pm, to

midnight during daylight saving time, closed mid-Dec–mid-Jan) Situated 1.2km northwest of the tourist office, just around the corner from 76 route d'Ingersheim. Curfew is 11pm (midnight during daylight saving time). By bus take No 4, 5, 6, 12 or 15 to the Pont Rouge stop.

Hôtel Kempf (☎ 03 89 41 21 72; www.chez.com /mawo/kempf.html; 1 av de la République; d from €28, with shower & toilet €40) The mattresses at this family-run two-star place are especially comfortable and the showers squirt torrents of hot water.

La Maison Rouge (☎ 03 89 23 53 22; 9 rue des Écoles; menus €16.90-34.30; ☒ Mon-Sat; ☒) A variety of hearty Alsatian specialities, including mouth-watering *jambon braisé* (spit-roasted ham; €10.90), are on offer at this rustic restaurant.

Self-caterers should head for the **food markets** (place de l'Ancienne Douane & in the covered market on rue des Écoles; ☒ 8am-noon or 12.30pm Thu) at the handsome sandstone *marché couvert*.

Getting There & Away
Buses and bus-train combos (via Breisach) also serve the German city of Freiburg. Hours are posted and available at the tourist office or online at www.l-k.fr.

Colmar has rail links to Basel (Bâle; €10.20, 50 minutes), Paris' Gare de l'Est (€46.20, five to six hours via Strasbourg) and Strasbourg (€9.30, 31 minutes to one hour).

FAR NORTHERN FRANCE

Le Nord de France (www.cdt-nord.fr) is made up of three historical regions: Flanders (Flandre or Flandres), Artois and Picardy (Picardie). Traditionally an industrial area, this is not one of the best-known corners of France. Most travellers will pass through this area on the way from England, via Calais.

LILLE
pop 1 million
Once a grimy industrial centre, Lille has been transformed into a glittering and self-confident arts hub, which was a European Capital of Culture in 2004. Highlights include an attractive old town, renowned art museums and a happening nightlife scene.

Lille is centred around three public squares: place du Général de Gaulle (also called the Grand' Place), place du Théâtre and place Rihour where you'll find the

tourist office (☎ 03 59 57 95 00; www.lilletourism .com; place Rihour; ✿ 9.30am-6.30pm Mon-Sat, 10am-noon & 2-5pm Sun & holidays).

Gare Lille-Flandres is about 400m southeast of place du Général de Gaulle; ultramodern Gare Lille-Europe is 500m further east.

Sights

North of place du Général de Gaulle, **Vieux Lille** gleams with restored 17th- and 18th-century houses. The world-renowned **Palais des Beaux-Arts** (☎ 03 20 06 78 00; place de la République; metro République; adult/12-25 years €4.60/3; ✿ 2-6pm Mon, 10am-6pm Wed, Thu, Sat & Sun, 10am-7pm Fri) possesses a superb collection of 15th- to 20th-century paintings.

Sleeping & Eating

Auberge de Jeunesse (☎ 03 20 57 08 94; lille@fuaj.org; 12 rue Malpart; metro Mairie de Lille; dm incl breakfast €16.25; ✿ closed late Dec-late Jan) The spartan rooms house 165 beds (up to six beds per room).

Hôtel de France (☎ 03 20 57 14 78; fax 03 20 57 06 01; 10 rue de Béthune; s/d from €30/35, with shower & toilet €39/46) Central and great value.

Rue Royale is *the* place for ethnic cuisine. Rue d'Amiens is full of pizzerias.

Aux Moules (☎ 03 20 57 12 46; 34 rue de Béthune; ✿ meals served noon-midnight) A casual, brasserie-style place specialising in Flemish dishes including rabbit in Kriek beer sauce with frites (€9) and mussels (€10 to €11.50).

Carrefour hypermarket (✿ 9am-10pm Mon-Sat) is on the upper level of the Euralille shopping mall.

Drinking

Lille has two main nightlife zones: Vieux Lille, whose bars tend to be small and oriented towards a fairly chic clientele, and, 750m southwest of the tourist office, rue Masséna and rue Solférino, whose inexpensive high-decibel bars draw mainly students.

Getting There & Away

Eurolines (☎ 03 20 78 18 88; 23 parvis St-Maurice; ✿ 9.30am-12.30pm & 1.30-6pm Mon-Fri, to 7pm summer, 1-6pm Sat) destinations include Brussels (€10, 1½ or two hours), Amsterdam (€34, six hours) and London (€39, six hours). Buses depart from the unsignposted bus parking lane on rue de Turin, on the northeast side of Gare Lille-Europe.

Lille's two train stations are one stop apart on metro line No 2. **Gare Lille-Flandres** is used by almost all regional services and most TGVs to Paris' Gare du Nord (€33.70 to €45.80, 62 minutes) while **Gare Lille-Europe** handles Eurostar trains to London, TGVs/ Eurostars to Brussels (weekdays/weekends €22.40/14.40, 38 minutes) and TGVs to Nice (€104.90 or €123.70, 7¼ hours).

CALAIS

pop 75,000

Except for Rodin's *The Burghers of Calais*, there's little to encourage the 22 million people who travel by way of grim, industrial Calais each year to tarry.

Orientation

Gare Calais-Ville is 650m to the south of the main square, place d'Armes, and 700m to the north of Calais' commercial district (around blvd Léon Gambetta and the Place du Théâtre bus hub). The car ferry terminal is 1.5km northeast of place d'Armes; the Hoverport (for SeaCats) is another 1.5km further out. The Channel Tunnel's vehicle loading area is about 6km southwest of the town's centre.

Information

Tourist Office (☎ 03 21 96 62 40; www.calais-cot edopale.com; 12 blvd Georges Clemenceau; ✿ 9am-7pm Mon-Sat, 10am-1pm Sun & holidays Easter-Aug, 10am-1pm & 2-6.30pm Mon-Sat Sep-before Easter)

Sights & Activities

Calais' Flemish Renaissance-style **town hall** (1911–25) contains Rodin's *Les Bourgeois de Calais* (1895).

Original WWII artefacts (uniforms, weapons, proclamations) fill the display cases of the **Musée de la Guerre** (☎ 03 21 34 21 57; adult/ student/family of 4 incl audioguide €6/5/14; ✿ 10am-6pm May-Aug, 11am-5.30pm Apr & Sep, 11am-5pm Wed-Mon mid-Feb–Mar, noon-5pm Wed-Mon Oct–mid-Nov), which is in a concrete bunker built as a German naval headquarters.

Sleeping & Eating

Some two-star hotels can be found along rue Royale.

The modern, well-equipped 162-bed **Auberge de Jeunesse** (Centre Européen de Séjour; ☎ 03 21 34 70 20; www.auberge-jeunesse-calais.com; av Maréchal de Lattre de Tassigny; dm with breakfast €15.20; ✿ 24hr; ℗), just 200m from the beach, is a good source of information on local events.

Hôtel Richelieu (☎ 03 21 34 61 60; www.hotelriche lieu-calais.com; 17 rue Richelieu; d/q from €46/92) At this quiet two-star place the 15 cheery rooms are outfitted with antique furniture redeemed by the owner from local markets.

Camping Municipal (☎ 03 21 97 89 79; av Raymond Poincaré; adult/sites €3.24/2.27; ☺ year-round) Occupies a grassy but soulless site inside Fort Risban. Served by bus No 3.

Rue Royal and place d'Armes are lined with touristy places to eat.

Aux Mouettes (☎ 03 21 34 67 59; 10 rue Jean Pierre Avron; menus €15-32; ☺ closed Sun dinner & Mon) Fishers sell their daily catch across the street at the quay so this unassuming place serves only the very freshest fish.

There's a **food market** (place d'Armes; ☺ Wed & Sat morning) and a **Match supermarket** (place d'Armes; ☺ 9am-7.30pm Mon-Sat).

Getting There & Away
For details on getting across the Channel, see p372.

BOAT
Every day, 45 to 54 car ferries from Dover dock at the busy **car ferry terminal**, about 1.5km northeast of place d'Armes. Company bureaus at the ferry terminal are **P&O Ferries** (☎ 03 21 46 10 10; ☺ 24hr) and **SeaFrance** (☎ 03 21 46 80 05; ☺ 6am-10.45pm). Their offices in town are **P&O Ferries** (☎ 01 55 69 82 28; 41 place d'Armes) and **SeaFrance** (☎ 03 21 19 42 42; 2 place d'Armes). Shuttle buses (€1.50 for P&O) coordinated with departure times link Gare Calais-Ville and each company's office at place d'Armes with the car ferry terminal.

Hoverspeed's car-carrying SeaCats to Dover (operational from mid-March to 22 December) use the **Hoverport** (High Speed Ferry Terminal; ☎ 03 21 46 14 00 or 00 800 12 11 12 11), which is 3km northeast of the town centre.

BUS
Inglard (☎ 03 21 96 49 54), with an office in the car ferry terminal, links Calais' train station with the beautiful Côte d'Opale and Boulogne.

Cariane Littoral (☎ 03 21 34 74 40; 10 rue d'Amsterdam) operates express BCD services from Calais' train station to Boulogne and Dunkirk.

CAR & MOTORCYCLE
To reach the Channel Tunnel's vehicle loading area at Coquelles, follow the road signs on the A16 to the 'Tunnel Sous La Manche' (Tunnel under the Channel) at exit No 13.

TRAIN
Calais has two train stations: Gare Calais-Ville in the city centre; and Gare Calais-Fréthun, a TGV station 10km southwest of town near the Channel Tunnel entrance. They are linked by the free Navette TER, a bus service operated by **Cariane Littoral** (☎ 03 21 34 74 40; 10 rue d'Amsterdam).

Gare Calais-Ville runs routes to Boulogne (€6.60, 27 to 48 minutes, 15 to 19 daily Monday to Saturday, nine daily Sunday), Dunkirk (€7, 50 minutes, four daily Monday to Friday, two on Saturday) and Lille-Flandres (€14, 1¼ hours, 18 daily Monday to Friday, 11 on Saturday, seven on Sunday).

Calais-Fréthun is served by TGVs to Gare du Nord in Paris (€35.50 or €47.90, 1½ hours, five daily Monday to Saturday, two on Sunday) as well as the Eurostar to London.

Getting Around
To reach the car ferry terminal, free shuttles run by SeaFrance Sealink and P&O Stena stop around the corner from Calais-Ville train station (turn left out of the station) and outside each company's office on place d'Armes. Last buses leave around 9pm.

Hoverspeed runs free buses to the hoverport from the train station roughly 45 minutes before each departure.

NORMANDY (NORMANDIE)

Often compared with the countryside of southern England, Normandy (Normandie) is the land of the *bocage*, farmland subdivided by hedges and trees. In 911 the Rouen region became home to the invading Viking Norsemen (or Normans), who gave their name to the region.

ROUEN
The city of Rouen, for centuries the furthest point downriver where you could cross the Seine by bridge, is known for its many spires, church towers and half-timbered houses. Rouen also has a renowned Gothic cathedral and some excellent museums. The city was occupied by the English during the

Hundred Years' War when the young Joan of Arc (Jeanne d'Arc) was tried for heresy and burned at the stake here in 1431.

Orientation & Information

The main train station (Gare Rouen-Rive Droite) is at the northern end of rue Jeanne d'Arc, the main thoroughfare running south to the Seine. The old city is centred around rue du Gros Horloge between place du Vieux Marché and the cathedral.

The **tourist office** (☎ 02 32 08 32 40; www.mairie-rouen.fr; 25 place de la Cathédrale; ☑ 9am-7pm Mon-Sat, 9.30am-12.30pm & 2-6pm Sun May-Sep, 9am-6pm Mon-Sat, 10am-1pm Sun Oct-Apr) faces the western side of the Cathédrale Notre Dame.

Sights

The old city's main street is rue du Gros Horloge, which runs from the cathedral to **place du Vieux Marché**, where 19-year-old Joan of Arc was executed. The striking **Église Jeanne d'Arc** (☑ 10am-12.15pm & 2-6pm, closed Fri & Sun morning) marking the site contains marvellous 16th-century stained-glass windows.

Rouen's **Cathédrale Notre Dame** (☑ 8am-6pm Tue-Sun, 2-6pm Mon) is considered a masterpiece of French Gothic architecture. There are several guided visits each day to the crypt and ambulatory.

The **Tour Jeanne d'Arc** (☎ 02 35 98 16 21; rue du Donjon; adult/student €1.50/free; ☑ 10am-12.30pm & 2-6pm Mon & Wed-Sat, 2-6.30pm Sun Apr-Sep, 10am-12.30pm & 2-5pm Mon & Wed-Sat, 2-5.30pm Sun Oct-Mar) is where Joan of Arc was imprisoned before her execution.

Sleeping & Eating

Ask the tourist office about its 'Bon Weekend' offer of two weekend nights for the price of one in some hotels. You'll have to reserve eight days in advance.

Five kilometres northwest of Gare Rouen-Rive Droite, in Déville-lès-Rouen, is **Camping Municipal** (☎ 02 35 74 07 59; rue Jules Ferry; sites per tent/car/child €4/1.50/1; ☑ year-round).

The pick of the budget options is **Hôtel des Flandres** (☎ /fax 02 35 71 56 88; 5 rue des Bons Enfants; d with shower/shower & toilet €26/29) with comfy, newly renovated doubles.

Hôtel Le Palais (☎ 02 35 71 41 40; 12 rue du Tambour; s or d with washbasin €25, s/d with shower & toilet €32/34) is well situated near the Palais de Justice and the Gros Horloge.

Les Maraîchers (☎ 02 35 71 57 73; 37 place du Vieux Marché; menus €14.95-21) This is the pick of the Vieux Marché's many restaurants. It has a lively pavement terrace and varied *menus*.

Le P'tit Bec (☎ 02 35 07 63 33; 182 rue Eau de Robec; lunch menus €11 & €13.50, mains €7-9; ☑ closed Mon-Thu evening & Sun) On a peaceful square, it offers a delicious array of dishes including some vegetarian specialities.

Dairy products, fish and fresh produce are on sale at the **covered food market** (place du Vieux Marché; ☑ 6am-1.30pm Tue-Sun). There is a **Monoprix supermarket** (65 rue du Gros Horloge; ☑ 8.30am-9pm Mon-Sat).

Getting There & Away

Regional bus information is dispensed by **Espace Métrobus** (☎ 02 35 52 92 00; 9 rue Jeanne d'Arc). Buses leave from quai du Havre and quai de la Bourse. Trains to Paris and far-flung destinations depart from Gare Rouen-Rive Droite. The Gare Rouen-Rive Gauche south of the river has mainly regional services.

BAYEUX

pop 15,000

Bayeux is rejoiced for two trans-Channel invasions: the conquest of England by William the Conqueror in 1066 (an event chronicled in the renowned Bayeux Tapestry) and the Allied D-day landings of 6 June 1944, which launched the liberation of Nazi-occupied France. It was the first town in France to be freed and survived virtually unscathed. Today, Bayeux is a very attractive town with several excellent museums and serves well as a base for visits to the D-day beaches.

Orientation & Information

The Cathédrale Notre Dame, the major landmark in the centre of Bayeux and visible throughout the town, is 1km northwest of the train station.

Just off the northern end of rue Larcher is the **tourist office** (☎ 02 31 51 28 28; www.bayeux-tourism.com; Pont St-Jean; ☑ 9.30am-12.30pm & 2-6pm Mon-Sat, 10am-12.30pm & 2-5.30pm Sun Apr-Jun, 9am-7pm Mon-Sat, 9am-12.30pm & 2-6.30pm Sun Jul-Sep, 9.30am-12.30pm & 2-5.30pm Mon-Sat Jan-Mar & Oct-Dec).

Sights

The world-famous Bayeux Tapestry narrates the dramatic story of the Norman invasion and the events that led up to it (from the Norman perspective). It is housed in the **Musée de la Tapisserie de Bayeux** (☎ 02 31 51 25 50; rue de Nesmond; adult/student €6.40/2.60; ☑ 9am-7pm

May-Aug, 9am-6.30pm mid-Mar–Apr, Sep & Oct, 9.30am-12.30pm & 2-6pm Nov–mid-Mar).

The spectacular **Cathédrale Notre Dame** (☺ 8am-7pm Jul & Aug, 8.30am-6pm Sep-Jun) is a fine example of Norman Gothic architecture, dating from the 13th century.

Bayeux's huge war museum, the **Musée Mémorial 1944 Bataille de Normandie** (☎ 02 31 51 46 90; blvd Fabien Ware; adult/student €5.40/2.50; ☺ 9.30am-6.30pm May–mid-Sep, 10am-12.30pm & 2-6pm mid-Sep–Apr), displays thousands of photos, uniforms, weapons, newspaper clippings and lifelike scenes associated with D-day and the Battle of Normandy.

The peaceful **war cemetery** (☎ 02 21 21 77 00; blvd Fabien Ware), a few hundred metres west of the war museum, is the largest of the 18 Commonwealth military cemeteries in Normandy. It contains 4868 graves of soldiers from the UK and 10 other countries.

Sleeping

Family Home (☎ 02 31 92 15 22; 39 rue du Général de Dais; dm with/without HI card €16/18, s €25) This excellent old hostel is a great place to meet travellers. Dorm rates include breakfast. Multicourse French dinners cost €10, including wine. A few tents can be pitched in the back garden for €5 per person. There's a laundry too.

Centre d'Accueil Municipal (☎ 02 31 92 08 19; fax 02 31 92 12 40; 21 rue des Marettes; s €11.90) In a large, modern building, 1km southwest of the cathedral. The singles (all that's available) are a great deal, and prices include breakfast.

Hôtel de la Gare (☎ 02 31 92 10 70; fax 02 31 51 95 99; 26 place de la Gare; s/d from €22/37, tr €64.50) Old but well maintained, it has recently installed showers and toilets in all the rooms.

Camping Municipal de Bayeux (☎ 02 31 92 08 43; sites per adult/tent & car €2.85/3.50; ☺ mid-Mar–mid-Nov, check-in 7am-9pm Jul & Aug, 8-9am & 5-7pm Sep-Jun) This camp site is about 2km north of the town centre, just south of blvd d'Eindhoven.

Eating

Le Petit Normand (☎ 02 31 22 88 66; 35 rue Larcher; lunch menu €8.85, dinner menus €12.95 & €22.10; ☺ closed Thu Nov-Apr) Traditional Norman food is served here, including dishes such as mussels with apple cider, or ham with camembert sauce.

Le Petit Bordelais (☎ 02 31 92 06 44; 15 rue du Maréchal Foch; plat du jour €7.20; ☺ noon-2pm Tue-Sat) An extension of an old wine shop this place serves good home-cooked meals, local cheeses and home-made pâté for lunch only.

There are lots of takeaway shops along or near rue St-Martin and rue St-Jean, including **Le Petit Glouton** (42 rue St-Martin).

Getting There & Away

A service is offered by **Bus Verts** (☎ 0810 21 42 14; office opp train station; ☺ 10am-noon & 3-6pm Mon-Fri, closed most of Jul) from the train station and place St-Patrice to Caen, the D-day beaches. Train services include Paris' Gare St-Lazare (€28.50, 2½ hours).

D-DAY BEACHES

The D-day landings, codenamed 'Operation Overlord', were the largest military operation in history. Early on the morning of 6 June 1944, swarms of landing craft – part of a flotilla of almost 7000 boats – hit the beaches, and tens of thousands of Allied soldiers poured onto French soil.

Most of the 135,000 Allied troops stormed ashore along 80km of beaches north of Bayeux codenamed Utah, Omaha, Gold, Juno and Sword. The landings were followed by the Battle of Normandy, which led to the liberation of Europe from Nazi occupation.

Maps of the D-day beaches are available at *tabacs* (tobacconists), newsagents and bookshops in Bayeux and elsewhere.

Arromanches

To make it possible to unload the quantities of cargo necessary, the Allies established two prefabricated ports codenamed **Mulberry Harbours**. One of them, Port Winston, can still be viewed at Arromanches, a seaside town 10km northeast of Bayeux. In the three months after D-day, 2.5 million men, four million tonnes of equipment and 500,000 vehicles were unloaded there. At low tide you can walk out to many of the crumbling concrete hulks of the old Mulberry harbours *(caissons)*.

The well-regarded **Musée du Débarquement** (Invasion Museum; ☎ 02 31 22 34 31; place de 6 Juin; adult/student €6/4; ☺ 9.30am-5.30pm Mar-May & Sep, 9am-7pm Jun-Aug, 10am-5pm Feb & Oct-Dec), right in the centre of Arromanches, explains the logistics and importance of Port Winston and makes a good first stop before visiting the beaches.

Omaha & Juno Beaches

The most brutal fighting on D-day took place 15km northwest of Bayeux along 7km of coastline known as Omaha Beach. A memorial marks the site of the first US military

FRANCE

cemetery on French soil, which contained the bodies of soldiers killed on the beach as they ran inland towards German positions on the nearby ridge. Dune-lined Juno Beach, 12km east of Arromanches, was stormed by Canadian troops on D-day.

Military Cemetery

The bodies of the American soldiers who died during the pivotal Battle of Normandy were either sent back to the USA or buried in the **American Military Cemetery** (☎ 02 31 51 62 00; ⏰ 9am-6pm mid-Apr–Sep, 9am-5pm Oct–mid-Apr) at Colleville-sur-Mer. The graves of 9386 American soldiers are here, alongside a memorial to 1557 others whose remains were never found. The huge, immaculately tended expanse of lawn, with white crosses and Stars of David set on a hill overlooking Omaha Beach, testifies to the extent of the killings that took place in 1944.

Tours

An organised tour is an excellent way to see the D-Day beaches. **Normandy Tours** (☎ 02 31 92 10 70; Hôtel de la Gare, Bayeux) has four-hour tours in eight-person minibuses stopping at Longues-sur-Mer, Arromanches, Omaha Beach, the American Military Cemetery and Pointe du Hoc for €31. The tour times and itineraries are flexible.

Getting There & Away

The rather infrequent Line No 70 operated by **Bus Verts** (☎ 0810 21 42 14) from Bayeux goes westwards to the American Military Cemetery at Colleville-sur-Mer and Omaha Beach, and on to Pointe du Hoc and the town of Grandcamp-Maisy.

CAR

For three or more people, renting a car can actually be cheaper than a tour. **Lefebvre Car Rental** (☎ 02 31 92 05 96; blvd d'Eindhoven) in Bayeux charges €65 per day with 200km free.

MONT ST-MICHEL

pop 42

It's difficult not to be impressed by your first view of Mont St-Michel. Its fame derives from the bay's extraordinary tides. The difference between low and high tides can reach 15m. The Mont either looks out onto bare sand stretching many kilometres into the distance or, at high tide only about six

hours later an expanse of water. However, the Mont and its causeway are completely surrounded by the sea only at the highest of tides, which occur at seasonal equinoxes.

The Mont's major attraction is the renowned **Abbaye du Mont St-Michel** (☎ 02 33 89 80 00; adult/student & aged 18-25/under-17s incl guided tour €7/4.50/free; ⏰ 9am-7pm May-Aug, 9.30am-6pm Sep-Apr). To reach it, walk to the top of the Grande Rue and then climb the stairway. From Monday to Saturday between mid-May and September, there are self-paced illuminated night-time visits (adult/under-25s €9/6.50) of Mont St-Michel complete with music from 9pm to midnight.

Pontorson (population 4100), the nearest town to Mont St-Michel, is 9km south and the base for most travellers. Route D976 from Mont St-Michel runs right into Pontorson's main thoroughfare, rue du Couësnon.

Information

Tourist Office (☎ 02 33 60 14 30; www.mont-saint -michel.net; ⏰ 9am-noon & 2-6pm Easter-Jun, Sep & Oct, 9am-7pm Jul & Aug, 9am-noon & 2-5.30pm Mon-Sat, 10am-noon & 2-6pm Sun Nov-Easter) Up the stairs to the left as you enter Porte de l'Avancée.

Sleeping & Eating

Camping Les Portes du Mont St-Michel (☎ 02 33 60 22 10; fax 02 33 60 20 02; sites per adult/tent & car €3/4.65; ⏰ Mar-Oct) This grassy camp site is on the shop-lined D976 to Pontorson, only 2km from the Mont. It also has bungalows with shower and toilet.

About 1km west of the train station, in Pontorson, is **Centre Duguesclin** (☎ /fax 02 33 60 18 65; aj@ville-pontorson.fr; blvd du Général Patton; dm €7.30; ⏰ year-round), in an old three-storey stone building opposite No 26. It's a modern, newly renovated hostel offering accommodation in four- to six-bed rooms and kitchen facilities. The hostel closes from 10am to 6pm, but there's no curfew.

Hôtel Saint-Aubert (☎ 02 33 60 08 74; fax 02 33 60 35 67; d €29-54) is a bland but adequate hotel with private facilities at the beginning of the 2km causeway that leads to Mont St-Michel.

The cheapest hotels are in Pontorson, including **Hôtel Le Rénové** (☎ 02 33 60 00 21; 4 rue de Rennes; s/d with shower €23/35) with basic but adequate rooms.

La Squadra (☎ 02 33 68 31 17; 102 rue Couësnon; meals from €6; ⏰ Mon-Sat), in Pontorson, has decent pizza, salads and pasta for lunch and dinner.

Getting There & Away

The bus company **Courriers Bretons** (☎ 02 33 60 11 43; 2 rue du Docteur Bailleul) runs buses from Pontorson train station to Mont St-Michel (€1.17, 30 minutes). There are 14 buses daily from Monday to Friday and six buses daily at weekends in July and August; this falls to three or four buses daily during the rest of the year. Most buses connect with trains to/from Paris, Rennes and Caen.

Services to/from Pontorson include Rennes (via Dol; €10.50, 50 minutes, two daily) and Cherbourg (€20.70, 2½ hours, two daily). From Paris, take the train to Caen (from Gare St-Lazare), to Rennes (from Gare Montparnasse), or to Pontorson via Folligny (from Gare Montparnasse; €35.60).

BRITTANY (BRETAGNE, BREIZH)

Brittany stands slightly aloof from the rest of France, set apart by its Celtic roots and a stubborn independent streak. Brittany's shoreline possesses some of France's finest coastal scenery, while its festivals of traditional music and culture are among the liveliest and most colourful in Europe. The province has dozens of classic seaside resorts and offers some of the best yachting, windsurfing, sea-kayaking and coastal hiking in France. You might well hear Breton (Breiz), a Celtic language related to Cornish and Welsh, spoken in western Brittany.

QUIMPER

pop 59,400

Quimper (kam-*pair*), lying where the small Rivers Odet and Steïr meet, takes its name from the Breton word *kemper,* meaning 'confluence'. Strongly Breton in character and the administrative capital of the *département* of Finistère, it's very much the cultural and artistic capital too, with its cobbled streets, half-timbered houses, waterways and magnolias imparting a pleasing village feel. The old city clusters around the cathedral on the north bank of the Odet, overlooked by Mont Frugy on the south bank.

Information

Tourist office (☎ 02 98 53 04 05; www.quimper-tourisme.com - French only; place de la Résistance; ☻ 9am-7pm Mon-Sat, 10am-1pm & 3-5.45pm Sun Jul-Aug, 9.30am-12.30pm & 1.30-6pm Mon-Sat Sep-Jun, 10am-12.45pm Sun Jun & 1-15 Sep) Can reserve accommodation. Arranges weekly guided city tour in English, July and August.

Sights & Activities

The twin spires and soaring vertical lines of Quimper's **Cathédrale St-Corentin** dominate the city centre. Begun in 1239, it wasn't fully completed until the 1850s. The inside gives an extraordinary feeling of light and space.

The **Musée Départemental Breton** (☎ 02 98 95 21 60; 1 rue du Roi Gradlon; adult/child €3.80/2.50; ☻ 9am-6pm Jun-Sep, 9am-noon & 2-5pm Tue-Sat, 2-5pm Sun Oct-May) is in what used to be the bishop's palace, beside the cathedral. It has superb exhibits on the history, furniture, costumes, crafts and archaeology of the area. Adjoining the museum is the **Jardin de l'Évêché** (Bishop's Palace Garden; admission free; ☻ 9am-5pm or 6pm).

The **Musée de la Faïence** (☎ 02 98 90 12 72; 14 rue Jean-Baptiste Bousquet; adult/child €4/2.30; ☻ 10am-6pm Mon-Sat mid-Apr–mid-Oct) occupies a one-time ceramics factory and displays over 2000 pieces of choice china.

Sleeping & Eating

Camping Municipal (☎ /fax 02 98 55 61 09; av des Oiseaux; person/tent/car €3.26/0.75/1.55; ☻ year-round) This camp site is 1km west of the old city. Take bus No 1 from the train station to the Chaptal stop.

Auberge de Jeunesse (☎ 02 98 64 97 97; quimper@fuaj.org; 6 av des Oiseaux; dm €8.90) Beside the camp site, on the edge of a wooded park.

Crêperie du Frugy (☎ 02 98 90 32 49; 9 rue Ste-Thérèse; galettes €3.70-6.55; ☻ closed lunch Sun & lunch Mon) This tiny place, in the shadow of Mont Frugy, dishes up excellent inexpensive crepes and galettes.

Crêperie du Sallé (☎ 02 98 95 95 80; 6 rue du Sallé; galettes €3-9; ☻ Tue-Sat) Locals crowd into this bright and breezy *crêperie* during lunchhour so arrive early to guarantee a table. Sample some real Breton specialities such as *saucisse fumée* (smoked sausage; €6.60) and *coquilles St-Jacques* (scallops; €8.60).

La Mie Calîne (14 quai du Steïr) A hugely popular bakery where you can get a whopping filled baguette, pastry and soft drink for only €5.20.

Getting There & Away

Caoudal (☎ 02 98 56 96 72) runs buses to Concarneau (€4.60, 45 minutes, seven to 10 daily).

There are frequent trains to Brest (€13.80, 1¼ hours, up to 10 daily) and Paris (Gare Montparnasse; €63.30, 4¾ hours, eight daily).

ST-MALO
pop 52,700

The port of St-Malo, famed for its walled city, fantastic nearby beaches (and one of the world's highest tidal ranges), is one of Brittany's most popular tourist destinations. It was a key port during the 17th and 18th centuries, serving as a base for both merchant ships and government-sanctioned pirates.

Orientation & Information

St-Malo consists of the harbour towns of St-Malo and St-Servan plus the modern suburbs of Paramé and Rothéneuf to the east. The old walled city of St-Malo is known as Intra-Muros or Ville Close. From the train station, it's a 15-minute walk westwards along av Louis Martin.

Tourist office (☎ 02 99 56 64 48; www.saint-malo -tourisme.com; esplanade St-Vincent; ☺ 9am-7.30pm Mon-Sat, 10am-6pm Sun Jul-Aug, 9am-12.30pm & 1.30-6pm or 6.30pm Mon-Sat Sep-Jun, 10am-12.30pm & 2.30-6pm Sun Easter-Jun & Sep)

Sights

The old walled city, originally an island, became linked to the mainland by the isthmus of Le Sillon in the 13th century. During 1944, the battle to drive German forces out of St-Malo destroyed around 80% of it. The main historical monuments were faithfully reconstructed, while the rest of the area was rebuilt in the style of the 17th and 18th centuries.

Constructed between the 12th and 18th centuries, the town's centrepiece, **Cathédrale St-Vincent** (place J de Châtillon; ☺ 9.30am-6pm), was severely damaged by the 1944 bombing. If the narrow streets become claustrophobic, escape to the ramparts, constructed at the end of the 17th century. You can make a complete circuit (around 2km); there's free access at several places, including all the main city gates. From their northern stretch, you can look across to the remains of **Fort National** (admission free; ☺ Jun-Sep).

You can walk to the rocky islet of **Île du Grand Bé**, where the great 18th-century writer Chateaubriand is buried, via the Porte des Bés. Once the tide rushes in, the causeway

remains impassable for about six hours so check tide times with the tourist office.

The **Musée International du Long Cours Cap-Hornier** (Museum of the Cape Horn Route; ☎ 02 99 40 71 58; adult/child €4.80/2.40; ☺ 10am-noon & 2-6pm daily Apr-Sep, 10am-noon & 2-6pm Tue-Sun Oct-Mar) is in the 14th-century Tour Solidor. Displaying lives of hardy sailors who followed the Cape Horn route, it provides superb views from the tower.

A nice day trip from St-Malo is to **Dinard** where you can stroll along the famous beachfront **promenade du Clair de Lune**. For details, ask the tourist office.

Sleeping

Camping Aleth (☎ 02 99 81 60 91; camping@ ville-saint-malo.fr; allée Gaston Buy, St-Servan; 2 people, tent & car €11.10; ☺ Apr-Sep) Camping Aleth (also spelled Alet) enjoys an exceptional view in all directions. Take bus No 6 year-round.

Auberge de Jeunesse (☎ 02 99 40 29 80; info@ centrevarangot.com; 37 av du Père Umbricht; dm €13.20, s €20.70-22, d €29.40-32, all with breakfast) This place offers a considerably more luxurious stay than the usual hostel. Take bus No 5 from the train station or No 1 (July and August only) from the bus station and tourist office.

Hôtel Le Neptune (☎ 02 99 56 82 15; 21 rue de l'Industrie; basic d €20-27.50, with bathroom €27-42) Close to the Grande Plage, this comfortable, family-run place is above a cheerful bar.

Eating

Le Petit Crêpier (☎ 02 99 40 93 19; 6 rue Ste-Barbe; dishes €5.50-8; ☺ closed Tue & Wed except Jul & Aug) This famous *crêperie* is known for its gourmet specialities such as a galette with plaice in a seaweed and Muscadet sauce or a crepe with a mousse of dates and spices.

La Coquille d'Oeuf (☎ 02 99 40 92 62; 20 rue de la Corne de Cerf; menus €12-23.50) Neat, trim and with a nautical theme, this small restaurant with its tables for two makes for intimate, good-value dining.

Among the food shops along rue de l'Orme is an excellent **cheese shop** (☺ Tue-Sat) at No 9. Just down the street is **Hall au Blé**, a covered market.

Getting There & Away

Brittany Ferries (reservations: in France ☎ 0825 82 88 28, in the UK ☎ 0870 556 1600; www.brittany-ferries.com) sails between St-Malo and Portsmouth and **Condor Ferries** (in France ☎ 0825 16 03 00, in the UK

FRANCE

☎ 0845 345 2000; www.condorferries.co.uk) sails to/from both Poole and Weymouth via Jersey or Guernsey.

Hydrofoils and catamarans depart from the Gare Maritime de la Bourse; car ferries leave from the Gare Maritime du Naye.

From April to September, **Corsaire** (☎ 02 23 18 15 15) runs the **Bus de Mer** (Sea Bus; adult/child return €5.90/3.60; 10 minutes, hourly) shuttle service between St-Malo and Dinard.

Courriers Bretons (☎ 02 99 19 70 80) has services to Cancale (€3.80, 30 minutes), Fougères (€13.90, 1¾ hours, one to three daily), Pontorson (€8.30, one hour) and Mont St-Michel (€9.20, 1½ hours, three to four daily). It also offers all-day tours to Mont St-Michel (return €25) running Tuesday and Saturday June to September.

TIV (☎ 02 99 82 26 26) has buses to Dinard (€3.40, 30 minutes, hourly) and Rennes (€9.90, one to 1½ hours, three to six daily).

CAT (☎ 02 99 82 26 26) bus No 10 goes to Dinan (€5.70, 50 minutes, three to eight daily) via the Barrage de la Rance.

Trains or SNCF buses operate between St-Malo and Rennes (€11.40, one hour, frequent). Change at Rennes for Paris' Gare Montparnasse (€53, 4¼ hours, eight daily).

THE LOIRE

Defensive fortresses thrown up in the 9th century to fend off marauding Vikings were superseded by whimsical pleasure palaces as this area became the playground of nobles who spent fortunes turning it into a neighbourhood of lavish chateaux. The result is a rich concentration of architectural treasures that are great to explore, especially by bicycle. The region is a Unesco World Heritage site.

BLOIS
pop 49,300
From the 15th to the 17th centuries, Blois (pronounced blwah) was a hub of court intrigue, and during the 16th century it served as a second capital of France. Several dramatic events involving some of the most important personages in French history, such as the kings Louis XII, François I and Henri III, took place inside the city's outstanding attraction, Château de Blois.

Orientation & Information
Blois, on the bank of the River Loire, is a compact town – almost everything is within 10 minutes' walk of the train station. The old city is the area south and east of Château de Blois, which towers over place Victor Hugo.

Tourist office (☎ 02 54 90 41 41; www.ville-blois.fr or www.loiredeschateaux.com; 23 place du Château; ☺ 9am-7pm Mon-Sat, 10am-7pm Sun Apr-Sep, 9am-12.30pm & 2-6pm Mon-Sat, 9.30am-12.30pm Sun Oct-Mar) Charges €2.30 to make hotel or B&B reservations.

Sights
The **Château de Blois** (☎ 02 54 90 33 32; adult/student/child €6.50/4.50/2; ☺ 9am-7pm Jul & Aug, 9am-6pm Apr-Jun, Sep & Oct, 9am-12.30pm & 2-5.30pm Nov-Mar) has four wings constructed around a central courtyard, each reflecting the favoured style of the period in which it was built. The distinctive brick-and-stone **Louis XII section**, which includes the hall where entrance tickets are sold, is ornamented with porcupines, the kings' heraldic symbol.

Opposite is the **Maison de la Magie** (House of Magic; ☎ 02 54 55 26 26; 1 place du Château; adult/aged 12-17/aged 6-11 €7.50/6.50/5; ☺ 10am-12.30pm & 2-6.30pm Jul & Aug, 10am-12.30pm & 2-6pm Tue-Sun Apr-Jun, 10am-noon & 2-6pm Wed, Thu, Sat & Sun Sep-Mar) which faces the chateau and has magic shows, interactive exhibits and displays of clocks invented by the Blois-born magician Jean-Eugène Robert-Houdin (1805–71), after whom the great Houdini named himself.

The **Cathédrale St-Louis** (☺ 7.30am-6pm) in the **old city** was rebuilt in a late-Gothic style after the devastating hurricane of 1678. There's a great view of Blois and the River Loire from the lovely **Jardins de l'Évêché** (Gardens of the Bishop's Palace), behind the cathedral.

Across the square from the cathedral, the timbers of the 15th-century **Maison des Acrobates** (House of the Acrobats; 3 bis rue Pierre de Blois) are decorated with characters taken from medieval farces. This was one of the few medieval houses to survive WWII.

Sleeping
Camping des Châteaux (☎ 02 54 78 82 05; sites for 2 adults, tent & car €9; ☺ Jul-Sep) This two-star site is in Vineuil, about 4km south of Blois.

Auberge de Jeunesse Les Grouëts (☎ 02 54 78 27 21; blois@fuaj.org; 18 rue de l'Hôtel Pasquier; dm €7, sheets €2.70, breakfast €3.20; ☺ Mar–mid-Nov) In Les Grouëts, 4.5km southwest of Blois train station. Be sure to call before arriving, as it's often full. Beds are in two 24-bed, single-sex dorms and kitchen facilities are available.

Hôtel du Bellay (☎ 02 54 78 23 62; http://hoteldubellay .free.fr; 12 rue des Minimes; d with washbasin €23-25, d/tr/q with shower & toilet €35/45/55) Some of the rooms here are tiny, but all have charm, lovingly adorned with older-style, mumsy wallpaper.

Eating & Drinking

Popular restaurants line rue Foulerie and several café-brasseries dot place de la Résistance. There are several good bars in the old town.

Le Triboulet (☎ 02 54 74 11 23; Place du Château; menus €16.50-23.50; ☺ closed Sun & Mon) A busy restaurant right by the chateau offering traditional French dining. The tasty *menu du terroir* (€23.50) showcases Loire area specialities. There's a pleasant garden and terrace.

As well as the **Intermarché supermarket** (av Gambetta; ☺ 9am-12.30pm & 3-7.15pm Mon-Sat), in the old city, a **food market** fills rue Anne de Bretagne on Tuesday, Thursday and Saturday until 1pm. There are several **charcuteries** (delicatessen specialising in dried and raw meat) in the area around place Louis XII offering cold meats and prepared dishes.

Le St James (☎ 02 54 74 44 99; 50 rue Foulerie; ☺ 10pm-5am Thu-Sun) This is a lively bar serving 162 different cocktails, with an atmospheric courtyard to enjoy them in.

Getting There & Away

The **TLC bus network** (☎ 02 54 58 55 44) has a very limited service, reduced further during the holidays and on Sunday. TLC buses to destinations around Blois leave from in front of the **Point Bus information office** (☎ 02 54 78 15 66; 2 place Victor Hugo; ☺ 1.30-6pm Mon, 8am-noon & 1.30-6pm Tue-Fri, 1.30-4.30pm Sat) and the bus station – a patch of car park with schedules posted – in front of the train station.

The train station is on ave Dr Jean Laigret at the western end of the street. There are frequent trains to/from Tours (€8.30, 40 minutes, 11 to 17 daily) and the nearest TGV station, St-Pierre des Corps (€8, 25 to 35 minutes, half-hourly).

There are four direct non-TGV trains daily from Blois to Paris' Gare d'Austerlitz (€20.80, 1½ to two hours), plus several more if you change trains in Orléans. There are also direct trains to Nantes (€27.10, two hours, three daily).

AROUND BLOIS
Château de Chambord

The pinprick village of Chambord is dominated by the spectacular **Château de Chambord** (☎ 02 54 50 50 02; www.chambord.org; adult/aged 18-25/ child €7/4.50/free; ☺ 9am-6.15pm Apr-Sep, 9am-5.15pm Oct-Mar), which François I had built from 1519 as a base for hunting game in the Sologne forests. Ironically, the king chose the site for its easy two-day ride by horse and carriage from Paris, but he stayed here a total of only 42 days during his reign (1515–47).

The chateau's famed **double-helix staircase**, attributed by some to Leonardo da Vinci who briefly lived in nearby Amboise (p407), consists of two spiral staircases that wind around a central axis but never meet.

Ticket sales end 30 minutes before the chateau closes. As well as free miniguides in English distributed on arrival, you can rent an audioguide (€4).

GETTING THERE & AROUND

Chambord is 16km east of Blois and 20km northeast of Cheverny. To/from Blois there are TLC buses during the school year and coach tours to Chambord and Cheverny between mid-May and 31 August.

Bicycles, ideal for exploring Forêt de Chambord, can be rented in Chambord from the **Echapée Belle kiosk** (☎ 02 54 33 37 54) beside Pont St-Michel in the castle grounds. They cost €5.50/13/24 per hour/day/weekend.

Château de Cheverny

The elegant, perfectly symmetrical **Château de Cheverny** (☎ 02 54 79 96 29; www.chateau-cheverny .fr; adult/student/child €6.10/4.10/3; ☺ 9.15am-6.45pm Jul & Aug, 9.15am-6.15pm Apr-Jun & Sep, 9.30am-noon & 2.15-5.30pm Oct & Mar, 9.30am-noon & 2.15-5pm Nov-Feb), built in 1625–34, is the region's most magnificently furnished chateau. Sitting like a sparkling white ship amid a sea of beautifully manicured gardens, the chateau is graced with a finely proportioned neoclassical façade. Inside, room after sumptuous room is fitted out with the finest of period appointments. In the 1st-floor dining room, 36 panels illustrate the story of *Don Quixote*. The grounds shelter the 18th-century **Orangerie**, where Leonardo's *Mona Lisa* was hidden during WWII. The chateau was also the inspiration for the mythical Marlinspike Hall, home of French cartoon favourite *Tintin*. It features in many Tintin adventures, and a permanent Tintin exhibition, **Les Secrets de Moulinsart** (The Secrets of Marlinspike Hall; combined ticket for chateau & exhibition adult/student/child €10.50/8.40/6.20; ⏲ same as chateau), has now been created in the grounds.

GETTING THERE & AWAY

Cheverny is 16km southeast of Blois and 20km southwest of Chambord. The TLC bus No 4 from Blois to Villefranche-sur-Cher stops at Cheverny (€2.40, 25 to 35 minutes). Buses leave Blois at 12.25pm Monday to Friday. Returning to Blois, the last bus leaves Cheverny at 6.52pm. Departure times can vary; check with TLC or the **Blois tourist office** (☎ 02 54 58 55 55).

Château de Chaumont

It's a short climb up to **Château de Chaumont** (☎ 02 54 51 26 26; adult/aged 18-25/child €5.50/3.50/ free; ⏲ 9.30am-6pm mid-Mar–mid-Oct, 10am-4.30pm mid-Oct–mid-Mar), set on a bluff overlooking the Loire. The entrance, across a wooden drawbridge between two wide towers, opens onto an inner courtyard from where there are stunning views. The building resembles a feudal castle and is modestly sized for a chateau. Opposite the main entrance are the luxurious **stables**, built in 1877.

GETTING THERE & AROUND

Chaumont-sur-Loire is 17km southwest of Blois and 20km northeast of Amboise, on the Loire's southern bank. The path leading to the park and chateau starts at the intersection of rue du Village Neuf and rue du Maréchal Leclerc (D751).

By public transport, the only way to get to Chaumont-sur-Loire is via local train on the Orléans–Tours line. Get off at Onzain (10 minutes), from where it is about a 20-minute, 2km walk across the river to the chateau. Single rail fares are €2.80/6.60/10.30 to Onzain from Blois/Tours/Orléans.

By bicycle, the quiet back roads on the southern bank of the river are a tranquil option. The Chaumont-sur-Loire **tourist office** (☎ 02 54 20 91 73; 24 rue du Maréchal Leclerc) rents out bicycles for €10 per day.

Château de Beauregard

Built in the early 16th century to serve as a hunting lodge for François I, the most famous feature of **Château de Beauregard** (☎ 02 54 70 36 74; adult/student & child €6.50/4.50; ⏲ 9.30am-7.30pm Jul & Aug, 9.30am-12.30pm & 2-6.30pm Apr-Jun & Sep, 9.30am-12.30pm & 2-5pm Thu-Tue Oct-Dec & mid-Feb–Mar) is its **Galerie des Portraits**, the walls of which are plastered with 327 portraits from the 14th to 17th centuries.

GETTING THERE & AWAY

Beauregard is 6km south of Blois. It can also be reached via a pleasant 15km cycle ride through the forest from Chambord. There is road access to the chateau from the Blois-Cheverny D765 and the D956 (turn left at the village of Cellettes).

The **TLC bus** (☎ 02 54 58 55 44) from Blois to St-Aignan stops at Cellettes (€1.50), 1km southwest of the chateau, Monday to Friday at 7.50am and on Wednesday, Friday and Saturday; the first bus from Blois to Cellettes leaves at 12.25pm. Unfortunately, there's no afternoon bus back except for the Châteauroux-Blois line operated by **Transports Boutet** (☎ 02 54 34 43 95), which passes through Cellettes around 6.15pm Monday to Saturday, and (except during August) at about 6pm on Sunday.

TOURS

pop 270,000

Lively Tours has the cosmopolitan, bourgeois air of a miniature Paris, with wide 18th-century avenues, formal public gardens, café-lined boulevards and a thriving university. The French spoken in Tours is said to be the purest in France.

Twice in its history Tours briefly hosted the French government: in 1870 during the Franco-Prussian war and again in 1940, with the onset of WWII. Since then, it has become better known for its crisp white Vouvray and Montlouis wines.

Orientation & Information

Its focal point is place Jean Jaurès, where the city's major thoroughfares – rue Nationale, blvd Heurteloup, av de Grammont and blvd Béranger – meet. The train station is 300m east of place Jean Jaurès. The old city is centred on place Plumereau, which is about 400m west of rue Nationale. The northern boundary of the city is demarcated by the River Loire, which flows roughly parallel to the River Cher, 3km south.

Office de Tourisme de Tours (☎ 02 47 70 37 37; www .ligeris.com; 78-82 rue Bernard Palissy; ⏲ 8.30am-7pm Mon-Sat, 10am-12.30pm & 2.30-5pm Sun mid-Apr–mid-Oct,

FRANCE

9am-12.30pm & 1.30-6pm Mon-Sat, 10am-1pm Sun mid-Oct–mid-Apr)

Sights

In an exceptional 17th- to 18th-century archbishop's palace, the **Musée des Beaux-Arts** (☎ 02 47 05 68 73; 18 place François Sicard; adult/student/child €4/2/free; ☼ 9am-12.45pm & 2-6pm Wed-Mon) has an excellent collection of paintings, furniture and *objets d'art* from the 14th to the 20th centuries.

Tours' Gothic-style **Cathédrale St-Gatien** (☼ 9am-7pm, closed during services) dates from the 13th to the 16th centuries. The spectacular exterior does not however overshadow the interior, which is renowned for its marvellous 13th- to 15th-century **stained-glass windows**.

The **Musée de l'Hôtel Goüin** (☎ 02 47 66 22 32; 25 rue du Commerce; adult/child €3.50/2.60; ☼ 9.30am-12.30pm & 1.15-6.30pm Apr-Sep, 9.30am-12.30pm & 2-5.30pm Oct-Mar) is housed in a Renaissance residence built around 1510 for a wealthy merchant. Its façade is worth seeing, even if the eclectic prehistoric, Gallo-Roman, medieval, Renaissance and 18th-century artefacts don't appeal.

Sleeping

Camping Municipal des Rives du Cher (☎ 02 47 27 27 60; fax 02 47 25 82 89; 61 rue de Rochpinard, St-Avertin; sites for 2 adults, tent & car €11; ☼ Apr–mid-Oct) This three-star site is 5km south of Tours. To get there, take bus No 5 from place Jean Jaurès to the St-Avertin bus terminal, then follow the signs.

Auberge de Jeunesse du Vieux Tours (☎ 02 47 37 81 58; tours@fuaj.org; 5 rue Bretonneau; dm HI members/nonmembers €12.70/15.60; ☼ 8am-12.30pm & 6-10pm; ▨) Large and friendly, this is a new, well-equipped hostel near the old town.

Hôtel Régina (☎ 02 47 05 25 36; fax 02 47 66 08 72; 2 rue Pimbert; s/d with washbasin €20.50/23.50, s/d/q with shower from €25/29/38) The best of the lower-priced options, this popular and good-value hotel has a range of rooms depending on your budget.

Eating

In the old city, place Plumereau and nearby rue du Grand Marché and rue de la Rôtisserie are loaded with restaurants, cafés, *crêperies* and *boulangeries* (bakeries), many with lovely street terraces. Another tasty cluster graces rue Colbert.

Comme Autre Fouée (☎ 02 47 05 94 78; 11 rue de la Monnaie; lunch/dinner menus from €10/19.50) You can install yourself in this old stone building for a good few hours while they constantly replenish your basket with oven-fresh *fouée*, an age-old regional speciality: a small disc of dough thrown into a wood-fired oven for 45 seconds and served immediately, piping hot. The pitta-like bread is then used to scoop up fouéefuls of *rillettes* (potted pork, duck or goose), *haricots blanc* (white beans) or farmhouse goat's cheese.

Le Petit Patrimoine (☎ 02 47 66 05 81; 58 rue Colbert; lunch menu €9, dinner menus €12-26) This simple but atmospheric place is excellent value for hearty portions of tasty, well-presented French food.

Sandwich stalls sell well-filled baguettes and pastries in the **Grand Passage shopping centre** (18 rue de Bordeaux). There's a large, permanent **covered market** (place Gaston Pailhou) and an **Atac supermarket** (5 place du Général Leclerc; ☼ 8.30am-8pm Mon-Sat, 9.30am-12.30pm Sun).

Drinking & Entertainment

Bars and cafés are easy to find in Tours, especially in place Plumereau. A favourite is the stylish **Le Vieux Mûrier** (☎ 02 47 61 04 71; 11 place Plumereau; ☼ 11am-midnight).

Au Temps des Rois (☎ 02 47 05 04 51; 3 place Plumereau; ☼ 11am-2am) Across the square from Le Vieux Mûrier, there's more of a student vibe here.

There are also lively student bars along rue de la Longue Echelle and the southern strip of rue du Dr Bretonneau.

Entertainment

Live jazz venues include alternative café-theatre **Le Petit Faucheux** (☎ 02 47 64 50 50; 12 rue Leonard de Vinci) and the brilliant **Bistro 64** (☎ 02 47 38 47 40; 64 rue du Grand Marché) – blues in a 16th-century interior.

Getting There & Away

There's a **Eurolines ticket office** (☎ 02 47 66 45 56; 76 rue Bernard Palissy; ☼ 2-6pm Mon, 9am-noon & 1.30-6.30pm Tue-Fri, 9am-noon & 1.30-5.30pm Sat).

Buses operated by **Touraine Fil Vert** (☎ 02 47 47 17 18) serve destinations around Tours and the Indre-et-Loire *département*, including Amboise (€2.10), leaving from the **bus station** (☎ 02 47 05 30 49; place du Général Leclerc). There's an **information desk** (☎ 02 47 05 30 49; ☼ 7am-7pm Mon-Sat), but only drivers sell tickets.

The station, overlooking place du Général Leclerc, has an **information office** (⌚ 8.30am-6.30pm Mon-Sat, closed public holidays). Tours is linked to St-Pierre des Corps (Tours' TGV train station) by shuttle train.

To get from Paris to Tours by rail take a TGV from Gare Montparnasse (€35 to €45, 1¼ hours, 10 to 15 daily) – often requiring a change at St-Pierre des Corps – or a direct non-TGV from Gare d'Austerlitz (€25.80, two to three hours, five to eight daily).

Getting Around

The bus network serving Tours and its suburbs is run by **Fil Bleu** (☎ 02 47 66 70 70), which has an information office at 5 bis rue de la Dolve. Most lines stop around the periphery of place Jean Jaurès.

From May to September, friendly **Amster' Cycles** (☎ 02 47 61 22 23; 5 rue du Rempart) rents out road and mountain bikes (€14/21/55 for one/two/seven days).

TOURS AREA CHATEAUX

Some of the most interesting Loire chateaux can be seen in an easy day trip from Tours. Those accessible by train or SNCF bus from Tours include Chenonceau, Villandry, Azay-le-Rideau, Langeais, Amboise, Chaumont, Chinon and Saumur. The tourist office in Tours has details of *son et lumières* (sound and light shows), medieval re-enactments, and other spectacles performed at the chateaux during summer.

The best chateau is the 16th-century **Château de Chenonceau** (☎ 0820 20 90 90; www.chenonceau.com; adult/student & child €8/6.50; ⌚ 9am-7pm mid-Mar–mid-Sep, to 6.30pm mid-end Sep, to 6pm early Oct & early Mar, to 5.30pm mid-end Oct & mid-end Feb, to 4.30pm Nov-Jan, to 5pm early Feb). With its stylised moat, drawbridge, towers, turrets and vast park it's how a fairy-tale castle should be (but its interior is only moderately interesting).

Built on an island in the River Indre, and adorned with ornate fortifications and turrets, **Château Azay-le-Rideau** (☎ 02 47 45 42 04; adult/aged 18-25/child €6.10/4.10/free; ⌚ 9.30am-6pm Apr-Jun & Sep-Oct, 9.30am-7pm Jul & Aug, 9.30am-12.30pm & 2-5.30pm Nov-Mar) also has an elegant exterior.

Tours

Touring chateaux by public transport can be slow and expensive, so consider taking an organised bus tour. The interesting English-language tours are surprisingly relaxed and informal. Most allow you between 45 minutes and one hour at each chateau. Tour prices don't include entrance fees, but as part of a group you may get discounts. If you can get five to seven people together, you can design your own minibus itinerary. Try **Acco-Dispo** (☎ 06 82 00 64 51; www.accodispo-tours.com), **Quart de Tours** (☎ 06 85 72 16 22; www.quartdetours.com) and **St-Eloi Excursions** (☎ 02 47 37 08 04; www.saint-eloi.com). Typical prices are from €18 to €31 for a half-day trip to various chateaux sharing a minibus for up to eight people. Reservations can be made at the Tours tourist office (p405) or via its website.

Services Touristiques de Touraine (STT; ☎ 02 47 05 46 09; www.stt-millet.fr) operates full-sized coaches for individuals rather than groups from April to mid-October. These have wine tasting in Vouvray or Montlouis-sur-Loire. Afternoon/day tours taking in three chateaux cost €34, including admission fees.

Getting There & Away

Château de Chenonceau, in the town of Chenonceaux, is 34km east of Tours, 10km southeast of Amboise and 40km southwest of Blois. Chenonceaux SNCF train station is in front of the chateau. Between Tours and Chenonceaux there are four to six trains daily (€5.20, 30 minutes).

Château Azay-le-Rideau is 26km southwest of Tours; the D84 and D17, either side of the River Indre, are a delight to cycle along. Azay-le-Rideau is on SNCF's Tours–Chinon line (four or five daily Monday to Saturday and one on Sunday). From Tours, the 30-minute trip (50 minutes by SNCF bus) costs €4.40; the station is 2.5km from the chateau. The last train/bus to Tours leaves Azay at about 6.35pm (8pm Sunday).

AMBOISE

pop 11,000

The picturesque town of Amboise, nestling under its fortified chateau on the southern bank of the Loire, reached its peak around 1500, when the luxury-loving King Charles VIII enlarged it and King François I held raucous parties here. Leonardo da Vinci lived his last years here under the patronage of François I.

Amboise is protected from the river by a dike, whose flower-covered heights are a fine place for a riverside promenade. Tours, 23km downstream, and Blois, 34km upstream, are easy day trips from here. Amboise makes a good base for visiting the chateaux east of Tours.

The **tourist office** (☎ 02 47 57 09 28; www.amboise -valdeloire.com; ☺ 10am-1pm & 2-6pm Mon-Sat, 10am-1pm & 3-6pm Sun Apr-Jun & Sep, 9am-8pm Mon-Sat, 10am-6pm Sun Jul & Aug, 10am-1pm & 2-6pm Mon-Sat, 10am-1pm Sun Oct-Mar) is in a pavilion opposite 7 quai du Général de Gaulle.

The rocky outcrop topped by **Château d'Amboise** (☎ 02 47 57 00 98; place Michel Debré; adult/student/aged 7-14 €7.50/6.50/4.20; ☺ 9am-6.30pm Apr-Jun, Sep & Oct, 9am-7.30pm Jul & Aug, 9am-noon & 2-5pm Nov-May) has been fortified since Roman times. Charles VIII (r 1483–98), who was born and brought up here, enlarged the chateau in 1492 after a visit to Italy, where he was impressed by that country's artistic creativity and luxurious lifestyle.

Today just a few of the 15th- and 16th-century structures survive. These include the Flamboyant Gothic **Chapelle St-Hubert** and the **Salle des États** (Estates Hall). The chateau entrance is at the end of rampe du Château.

Leonardo da Vinci came to Amboise in 1516 at the invitation of François I. Until his death three years later at the age of 67, Leonardo lived and worked in the brick manor house called **Le Clos Lucé** (☎ 02 47 57 62 88; 2 rue du Clos Lucé; adult/student/aged 6-15 €9.50/7.50/5; ☺ 9am-8pm Jul & Aug, 9am-7pm Apr, Jun, Sep & Oct, 9am-6pm Nov, Dec, Feb & Mar, 9am-5pm Jan). It now contains restored rooms and fascinating scale models of Leonardo's inventions, including a proto-automobile, armoured tank, parachute and hydraulic turbine.

Getting There & Away
Buses to/from Amboise stop at the bus shelter opposite the tourist office.

CAT's line No 10 links the town with Tours' bus terminal (€2.10 one-way, 30 to 50 minutes, eight daily Monday to Saturday, six daily summer holidays).

The **train station** (☎ 02 47 23 18 23; blvd Gambetta), across the river from the centre of town, is served by trains from Paris' Gare d'Austerlitz (€24.20, 2¼ to three hours, 11 daily).

About three-quarters of the trains on the Blois–Tours line (11 to 17 daily) stop here. Fares are €5.50 to Blois (20 minutes) and €4.40 to Tours (20 minutes).

SOUTHWESTERN FRANCE

The southwestern part of France consists of diverse regions, ranging from the Bordeaux wine-growing area, near the beach-lined Atlantic seaboard, to the Basque Country and the Pyrenees mountains in the south. The region is linked to Paris, Spain and the Côte d'Azur by convenient rail links.

LA ROCHELLE
pop 120,000
The focal point of La Rochelle, a lively and increasingly chic port city midway down France's Atlantic coast, is the picturesque café- and restaurant-lined old port, which basks in the bright Atlantic sunlight by day and is grandly illuminated by night.

Orientation & Information
The train station is linked to the Vieux Port by the 500m-long av du Général de Gaulle. Place du Marché and place de Verdun are at the northern edge of the old city.
Tourist Office (☎ 05 46 41 14 68; http://larochelle-tour isme.com or www.ville-larochelle.fr; ☺ 9am-8pm Mon-Sat, 11am-5.30pm Sun Jul & Aug, 9am-7pm Mon-Sat, 11am-5pm Sun Jun & Sep, 9am-6pm Mon-Sat, 10am-1pm Sun Oct-May) On the southern side of the Vieux Port in an area of brightly painted wooden buildings known as Le Gabut.

Sights & Activities
To protect the harbour at night and defend it in times of war, an enormous chain used to be stretched between the two 14th-century stone towers at the harbour entrance. **Tour de la Chaîne** affords fine views from the top and has displays on the history of the local Protestant community. Across the harbour you can also climb to the top of the 36m-high, pentagonal **Tour St-Nicolas** if you don't get lost in the maze of stairs and corridors.

The three **towers** (☎ 05 46 34 11 81; admission per tower adult/aged 18-25/child €4.60/3.10/free; ☺ 10am-7pm Apr-Sep, 10am-12.30pm & 2-5.30pm Tue-Sun Oct-May, closed during holidays) can be visited on a combined ticket (€10/6.50).

South of Le Gabut is the impressive **Aquarium** (☎ 05 46 34 00 00; adult/student & child €10/7; ☺ 9am-11pm Jul & Aug, to 8pm Apr-Jun & Sep, 10am-8pm Oct-Mar), a relatively new attraction, thoughtfully laid-out and well stocked with over 10,000 specimens of sea-based flora and fauna.

Sleeping & Eating

Camping du Soleil (☎ 05 46 44 42 53; av Marillac; bus No 10; ☺ mid-May–mid-Sep) Nearest to the city centre, but is often completely full.

Centre International de Séjour-Auberge de Jeunesse (☎ 05 46 44 43 11; fax 05 46 45 41 48; av des Minimes; bus No 10; dm/d with breakfast €13/32) This is 2km southwest of the train station in Les Minimes. Check-in from 8am to midnight.

The best place to pick up your own edibles is at the lively, 19th-century **covered market** (place du Marché; ☺ 7am-1pm). Food shops in the vicinity include two cheap east Asian **takeaway places** (4 & 10 rue Gambetta). In the old city, there's **Monoprix supermarket** (30-36 rue du Palais; ☺ 8.30am-8pm Mon-Sat).

Getting There & Away

The bus station and bus information offices are at place de Verdun. Eurolines ticketing is handled by **Citram Littoral** (☎ 05 46 50 53 57; 30 cours des Dames; ☺ closed Sat afternoon, Mon morning & all day Sun).

The **train station** (☎ 0836 35 35 35) is linked by TGV to Paris' Gare Montparnasse (€53.60, three hours, five or six direct daily). Other places served by direct trains include Bordeaux (€22.60, two hours, five to seven daily).

Getting Around

The innovative local public transport system, **Autoplus** (☎ 05 46 34 02 22), has a bus hub and **information office** (place de Verdun; ☺ 7am-7.30pm Mon-Sat). Tickets are €1.20. Bus No 21 runs from place Verdun to the train station, returning via the Vieux Port. No 10 links place de Verdun with the youth hostel and Les Minimes.

At **Les Vélos Autoplus** (☎ 05 46 34 02 22) you can hire a bike for free for the first two hours; after that the charge is €1 per hour. Child seats, but not bike helmets, are available for no extra charge. Bikes, as well as electric motorcars for €16 per day, are available at the **Electrique Autoplus office** (☎ 05 46 34 84 58; place de Verdun; ☺ 7.30am-7pm Mon-Sat, 1-7pm Sun).

BORDEAUX

pop 735,000

Bordeaux is buzzing thanks, in part, to a massive renovation programme: streets have been pedestrianised, squares repaved, trees planted and a state-of-the-art tram system

installed. Against a backdrop of neoclassical architecture, wide avenues and pretty parks, the city boasts excellent museums, a vibrant nightlife, an ethnically diverse population and a lively university community.

Orientation

The city centre lies between place Gambetta and the tidal, 350m- to 500m-wide Garonne. From place Gambetta, place de Tourny is 500m northeast, and the tourist office is 400m to the east.

The train station, Gare St-Jean, is in a seedy area about 3km southeast of the city centre. Cours de la Marne stretches from the train station to place de la Victoire, which is linked to place de la Comédie by the long and straight pedestrianised shopping street, rue Ste-Catherine.

Information

Banks offering currency exchange can be found near the tourist office on cours de l'Intendance, rue de l'Esprit des Lois and cours du Chapeau Rouge.

Main post office (37 rue du Château d'Eau)

NetZone (☎ 05 57 59 01 25; 209 rue Ste-Catherine; per hr €3; ☺ 9.30am-midnight) Internet access.

Tourist office (☎ 05 56 00 66 00; www.bordeaux -tourisme.com; 12 cours du 30 Juillet; ☺ 9am-7.30pm Mon-Sat Jul & Aug, to 7pm May & Jun, to 7pm Sep & Oct, 9.30am-6.30pm Sun May-Oct, 9am-6.30pm Mon-Sat, 9.45am-4.30pm Sun Nov-Apr) Helpful and well informed, it is right next to the tram stop Comédie.

Sights

The sights mentioned below appear pretty much from north to south.

Entrepôts Lainé was built in 1824 as a warehouse for the rare and exotic products of France's colonies (such as coffee, cocoa, peanuts and vanilla). Its capacious spaces now house the **Musée d'Art Contemporain** (Museum of Contemporary Art; CAPC; ☎ 05 56 00 81 50; Entrepôt 7, rue Ferrère; ☺ 11am-6pm Tue & Thu-Sun, 11am-8pm Wed). Most of the exhibits that the museum hosts are temporary, presenting major artistic movements over the last 30 years.

The beautifully landscaped **Jardin Public** (cours de Verdun), established in 1755 and laid out in the English style a century later, includes the meticulously catalogued **Jardin Botanique** (☎ 05 56 52 18 77; admission free; ☺ 8.30am-6pm), founded in 1629 and at its present site since 1855; and the nearby **Musée d'Histoire Naturelle**

(Natural History Museum; ☎ 05 56 48 29 86; ☼ 11am-6pm Mon & Wed-Fri, 2-6pm Sat & Sun). There's a **children's playground** on the island.

The most prominent feature of **esplanade des Quinconces**, a square laid out in 1820, is the fountain monument to the Girondins, a group of bourgeois National Assembly deputies during the French Revolution, 22 of whom were executed in 1793 after being convicted of counter-Revolutionary activities.

Nowadays, **place Gambetta** is an island of greenery in the midst of the city centre's hustle and bustle, but during the Reign of Terror that followed the Revolution, a guillotine placed here severed the heads of 300 alleged counter-Revolutionaries.

FREE MUSEUMS

Bordeaux's municipal museums, including the Musée d'Art Contemporain (CAPC), Musée d'Histoire Naturelle, Musée des Beaux-Arts and Musée d'Aquitaine, are free to those under 18 and students holding a valid student card. They're free for everyone on the first Sunday of each month.

The **Musée des Beaux-Arts** (☎ 05 56 10 20 56; 20 cours d'Albret; ☼ 11am-6pm Wed-Mon) occupies two wings of the Hôtel de Ville complex (built in the 1770s); between them is a verdant public park, the **Jardin de la Mairie**. Founded in 1801, the museum has a large collection of paintings, including Flemish, Dutch and Italian works from the 17th century and a particularly important work by Delacroix.

In 1137 the future King Louis VII married Eleanor of Aquitaine in **Cathédrale St-André** (☎ 05 56 81 26 25; admission free; ☼ 10-11.30am & 2-6.30pm Mon, 7.30-11.30am & 2-6pm Tue-Fri, 9-11.30am & 2-7pm Sat, 8am-12.30pm Sun, but 2.30-5.30pm 1st Sun of month), now listed as a Unesco World Heritage site. Behind the choir, the 50m-high, 15th-century **Tour Pey-Berland** has a panoramic view at the top of 232 narrow steps.

The outstanding **Musée d'Aquitaine** (Museum of Aquitaine; ☎ 05 56 01 51 00; 20 cours Pasteur; ☼ 11am-6pm Tue-Sun) presents 25,000 years of Bordeaux's history and ethnography. Exceptional artefacts include several stone carvings of women and a collection of Gallo-Roman steles, statues and ceramics. A detailed, English-language catalogue is worth borrowing at the ticket counter (€1.50 deposit).

Sleeping

Auberge de Jeunesse (☎ 05 56 33 00 70; fax 05 56 33 00 71; 22 cours Barbey, annexe at 208 cours de l'Argonne; dm HI member/nonmember incl breakfast €16/17.50; 🖳) Ultramodern, well equipped and available 24 hours, there's a café-bar, kitchen, laundry and facilities for the disabled. All the rooms are dorms, but most are for four people or less. Take bus Nos 7/8 to the Meunier stop.

Hôtel Boulan (☎ 05 56 52 23 62; fax 05 56 44 91 65; 28 rue Boulan; s/d €20.25/23.50, with shower €28.25/28.50) Tucked away in a quiet street, but still handy for many of the sights (and the Connemara bar), this friendly place has rooms of a good standard for this price.

Hôtel de Famille (☎ 05 56 52 11 28; fax 05 56 51 94 43; 76 cours Georges Clemenceau; s & d €18-22, with shower, toilet & TV €29-36) A variety of ordinary but homey rooms. There's no lift, so the higher your room, the cheaper (and smaller) it is. Light sleepers beware – there's no double-glazing.

Eating & Drinking

Cassolette Café (☎ 05 56 92 94 96; www.cassolettecafe .com; 20 place de la Victoire; cassolette (5 choices) €10.50, lunch/dinner menus €8.50/10.50; ☼ noon-midnight) Extremely popular and great value, you order your *menu* or the ingredients of your *cassolette* (casserole cooked on a terracotta plate) using a check-off form.

Le Bistrot d'Édouard (☎ 05 56 81 48 87; 16 place du Parlement; menus €11-20) The great-value three-course *menu* at €11 keeps this *bistrot* packed. Outside tables are in a calming spot by the fountain in place du Parlement.

Marché des Capucins (☼ 6am-1pm Tue-Sun) A few blocks east of place de la Victoire is this one-time wholesale market. Nearby rue Élie Gintrec has super-cheap **fruit and veggie stalls** on weekdays and Saturday until 1pm.

Le Fournil des Capucins (62-64 cours de la Marne) Near place de la Victoire, this bakery never closes.

Bodega Bodega (☎ 05 56 01 24 24; 4 rue des Piliers de Tutelle; ☼ noon-3.15pm & 7pm-2am Mon-Sat, 7pm-2am Sun) Two floors of tapas, tunes and trendy types; this is the biggest and best Spanish bar in town.

Café Brun (☎ 05 56 52 20 49; 45 rue St-Rémi; ☼ 10am-2am) This bar-bistro with a warm atmosphere and cool jazz is great for an apéritif.

Entertainment

Bordeaux has a vibrant nightlife scene; details of events appear in *Bordeaux Plus* and

Clubs & Concerts (French website at www
.clubsetconcerts.com), both free and available at the tourist office.

Subtitled films are screened at two art
cinemas: **Centre Jean Vigo** (☎ 05 56 44 35 17; 6 rue
Franklin) and the popular, five-screen **Cinéma
Utopia** (☎ 05 56 52 00 03; 3 place Camille Jullian).

Getting There & Away
Bordeaux airport (☎ 05 56 34 50 50; www.bordeaux
.aeroport.fr) is in Mérignac, 10km west of the
city centre. Air France and **Ryanair** (www.ryanair
.com) operate regular flights from the UK.

The Gironde is an area and an administrative *département* surrounding the
large Gironde estuary, which is formed by
the confluence of the Garonne and Dordogne rivers near the Bay of Biscay. Buses
to places all over the Gironde leave from
the **Halte Routière** (bus terminal; allées de Chartres),
in the northeast corner of esplanade des
Quinconces; schedules are posted. Citram
Aquitaine runs most buses to destinations
in the Gironde and has an **information kiosk**
(☎ 05 56 43 68 43; ☽ 1-8pm Mon-Fri, 9am-1.30pm &
5-8pm Sat) at the Halte Routière.

Eurolines (☎ 05 56 92 50 42; 32 rue Charles Domercq;
☽ Mon-Sat) faces the train station. The station, **Gare St-Jean**, is about 3km from the city
centre at the southern terminus of cours de
la Marne. Destinations include Paris' Gare
Montparnasse (€58.90, three hours, at least
16 daily), Bayonne (€24.40, 1¾ hours, eight
daily) and La Rochelle (€22.50, two hours,
five to seven daily).

BORDEAUX WINE-GROWING REGION
The 1000-sq-km wine-growing area around
the city of Bordeaux is, along with Burgundy, France's most important producer
of top-quality wines. Bordeaux has over
5000 chateaux (also known as *domaines*,
crus or *clos*), the properties where grapes
are raised, picked, fermented and then ma-
tured as wine. The smaller chateaux often
accept walk-in visitors, but at many places,
especially the better-known ones, you have
to make advance reservations by phone.
Many chateaux are closed during the *ven-
dange* (grape harvest) in October.

ST-ÉMILION
pop 2500
The medieval village of St-Émilion, 39km
east of Bordeaux, is encircled by vineyards

renowned for their full-bodied, deeply coloured red wines.

The **tourist office** (☎ 05 57 55 28 28; www.saint
-emilion-tourisme.com; place des Créneaux; ☽ 9.30am-7pm
mid-Jun–mid-Sep, 9.30am-12.30pm & 1.45-6pm mid-Sep–
mid-Jun) has brochures in English and details
on visiting almost 100 nearby chateaux.

St-Émilion's most interesting historical
sites can only be visited with one of the
tourist office's 45-minute guided tours
(adult/student/child €5.50/3.60/2.90, plus
entry to sites) departing several times daily.
Most are in French. Check ahead for English tour times (usually 1pm).

The tour is the only way to see the astounding **Église Monolithe**, carved out of solid limestone from the 9th to the 12th centuries.

BAYONNE
pop 42,000
The cultural and economic capital of the
French Basque Country, Bayonne, unlike
the up-market seaside resort of Biarritz, retains much of its Basqueness: you'll hear
almost as much Euskara (the Basque language) as French in certain quarters. The
town's premier fiesta is the five-day **Fêtes
de Bayonne**, in early August, like Pamplona's
running of the bulls – only here with cows.

Orientation & Information
The Rivers Adour and Nive split Bayonne
into three: St-Esprit, the area north of the
Adour; Grand Bayonne, the oldest part of
the city, on the western bank of the Nive;
and the very Basque Petit Bayonne quarter
to its east.

Cyber Net Café (☎ 05 59 50 85 10; place de la République;
per hr €4.50; ☽ 7am-11pm Mon-Sat, noon-11pm Sun)
Tourist office (☎ 05 59 46 01 46; www.bayonne
-tourisme.com; place des Basques; ☽ 9am-7pm Mon-Sat,
10am-1pm Sun Jul & Aug, 9am-6.30pm Mon-Fri, 10am-
6pm Sat Sep-Jun) Has useful free brochures including *Fêtes*,
listing French Basque Country cultural and sporting events
and *Tout à Loisir*, for hiking, biking and other activities.

Sights
Construction of Bayonne's Gothic **Cathédrale Ste-Marie** (☽ 7.30-11.45am & 3-5.45pm Mon-Sat,
3.30-5.45pm Sun) began in the 13th century,
when Bayonne was ruled by the Anglo-
Normans, and was completed well after
France assumed control in 1451.

The **Musée Basque et de l'Histoire de Bayonne**
(☎ 05 59 46 61 90; 37 quai des Corsaires; adult/student/

FRANCE

under-18s €5.50/3/free; ☺ 10am-6.30pm Tue-Sun May-Oct, 10am-12.30pm & 2-6pm Tue-Sun Nov-Apr) presents the history and culture of this unique people.

There is a **combined ticket** (adult/student €9/4.50) to both the Musée Basque and **Musée Bonnat** (☎ 05 59 59 08 52; 5 rue Jacques Lafitte; adult/student/child €5.50/3/free; ☺ 10am-6.30pm Wed-Mon May-Oct, 10am-12.30pm & 2-6pm Wed-Mon Nov-Apr), an art gallery featuring canvases by El Greco, Goya, Degas and Rubens.

Sleeping

Auberge de Jeunesse (☎ 05 59 58 70 00; anglet@fuaj.org; 19 route des Vignes, Anglet; B&B 1st night €17, subsequent nights €14.20; ☺ mid-Feb–mid-Nov) In Anglet, it's complete with a Scottish pub, and is lively and popular. Reservations are essential in summer. The hostel has some **camping** (sites per adult incl breakfast €10). From Bayonne station, take STAB bus No 2, direction Anglet. At the Cinq Cantons stop, change to No 72, direction Les Plages, which stops outside the hostel. Alternatively – and in high season when bus No 72 doesn't run. Take No 2 to the Moulin Barbot stop, from where the hostel is a 10-minute signed walk. On Sunday take line C from the town hall.

Hôtel Paris-Madrid (☎ 05 59 55 13 98; sorbois@wanadoo.fr; place de la Gare; s/d from €16/22, r with shower from €25; 🅿) This friendly place is highly recommended, especially for those arriving at the train station opposite. The owners speak English and the rooms, decorated with flair, are good value.

Eating & Drinking

A good selection of medium-priced restaurants surrounds the covered market and all along quai Amiral Jauréguiberry.

Bodega Ibaia (☎ 05 59 59 86 66; 45 quai Amiral Jauréguiberry; mains €8-12; ☺ closed Sun & Mon lunch) Atmospheric Basque restaurant/tapas bar with wooden benches, sawdust on the floor and traditional Spanish tiling.

Restaurant Koskera (☎ 05 59 55 20 79; 2 rue Hugues; menus around €10; ☺ lunch Mon-Sat) A dark, cave-like place serving inexpensive daily specials of hearty Basque fare.

The **covered market** (quai Commandant Roquebert; ☺ 7am-1pm & 3.30-7pm Fri, 8am-1pm Mon-Thu & Sat) occupies an imposing riverside building. There are several tempting **food shops** and **delicatessens** along rue Port Neuf and rue d'Espagne.

The greatest concentration of pubs and bars is in Petit Bayonne, especially along

rue Pannecau, rue des Cordeliers and quai Galuperie.

Entertainment

Each Thursday in July and August, there's traditional **Basque music** (free entry) at 9.30pm in place Charles de Gaulle.

Getting There & Away

Biarritz-Anglet-Bayonne airport (☎ 05 59 43 83 83; www.biarritz.aeroport.fr) is 5km southwest of central Bayonne and 3km southeast of Biarritz. Air France flies to/from Paris Orly about eight times daily and less frequently to Lyon and Geneva. Ryanair flies daily to/from London Stansted.

From place des Basques, **ATCRB buses** (☎ 05 59 26 06 99) follow the coast to the Spanish border. Transportes Pesa buses leave twice a day for Irún and San Sebastián in Spain (€6.20, 1¾ hours). **Eurolines** (☎ 05 59 59 19 33; 3 place Charles de Gaulle) stops opposite the company office.

TGVs run between Bayonne and Paris' Gare Montparnasse (€71.60, five hours, five daily). There are frequent trains to Biarritz (€2.10, 10 minutes), Bordeaux (€24.40, 2¼ hours, at least 10 daily) and Lourdes (€17.80, 1¾ hours, six daily).

BIARRITZ

pop 30,000

The stylish coastal town of Biarritz, 8km west of Bayonne, is known for its fine beaches and some of Europe's best surfing. If you're travelling on a budget, consider staying in Bayonne and visiting Biarritz from there. Many surfers camp or stay at one of the two excellent youth hostels in Biarritz and in Anglet.

Orientation & Information

Place Clemenceau, at the heart of Biarritz, is just south of the main beach (Grande Plage). Pointe St-Martin, topped with a lighthouse, rounds off Plage Miramar, the northern continuation of the Grande Plage. Both the train station and airport are about 3km southeast of the centre.

Génius Informatique (☎ 05 59 24 39 07; 60 av Édouard VII; per hr €5) Internet access.

Tourist office (☎ 05 59 22 37 10; www.biarritz.fr; 1 square d'Ixelles; ☺ 8am-8pm Jul & Aug, 9am-6pm Mon-Sat, 10am-5pm Sun Sep-Jun) Publishes *Biarritzscope*, a free monthly what's-on guide.

Sights

Musée de la Mer (☎ 05 59 22 75 40; www.musee delamer.com; esplanade de la Vierge; adult/child €7.20/4.60; ⌚ 9.30am-12.30pm & 2-6pm Tue-Sat) has an aquarium seething with underwater life from the Bay of Biscay (Golfe de Gascogne) plus exhibits on commercial fishing and Biarritz's whaling past.

Biarritz's fashionable beaches, the **Grande Plage** and **Plage Miramar** to its north, are lined with striped bathing tents and are often packed in summer. Beyond Pointe St-Martin, the superb surfing beaches of **Anglet** stretch northwards for over 4km. Take eastbound bus No 9 from place Clemenceau. The best board rental and instruction bargains are to be had at the Auberge de Jeunesse in Anglet (opposite). The French-language **Swell Line** (☎ 08 36 68 40 64; www.swell-line.com) details surf conditions.

Sleeping

Camping de Parme (☎ 05 59 23 03 00; www.campingde parme.com; route de l'Aviation; sites for 2 people & car €15.50-23) The area's only year-round camp site is in a quiet, leafy spot 1.25km northeast of the train station. It's normally fully booked months in advance for July and August.

Biarritz Camping (☎ 05 59 23 00 12; www.biarritz -camping.fr; 28 rue d'Harcet; sites for 2 people & car €13.50-19.50; ⌚ mid-May–mid-Sep; ⬛) This summer camp site has spacious and shady sites, 3km southwest of the centre. Take westbound bus No 9 to the Biarritz Camping stop.

Auberge de Jeunesse (☎ 05 59 41 76 00; biarritz@fuaj .org; 8 rue Chiquito de Cambo; dm incl breakfast €14.90; ⌚ mid-Jan–mid-Dec) This popular place offers a host of outdoor activities including surfing and sailing. To get here, follow the railway westwards from the train station for 800m.

Eating & Drinking

Bistrot des Halles (☎ 05 59 24 21 22; 1 rue du Centre; mains €13-17) This is one of a cluster of little restaurants that take their produce fresh from the nearby **covered market** (⌚ 7am-1.30pm).

La Table de Don Quichotte (12 av Victor Hugo) Just downhill, this place sells Spanish hams and sausages. There's a tempting array of cheeses, wines and pâtés at nearby **Mille et Un Fromages** (8 av Victor Hugo).

There are several good bars along rue du Port Vieux and the streets radiating from it including **Le Surfing** (☎ 05 59 24 78 72; 9 blvd Prince des Galles), the place to come and discuss

waves and wipe-outs. There's an outside terrace with decent views.

Entertainment

Two discos near the town centre are **Le Caveau** (☎ 05 59 24 16 17; 4 rue Gambetta; ⌚ 11pm-5am) and **Biarritz Latino** (☎ 05 59 22 77 59; ⌚ 11pm-5am Tue-Sat), in the Casino Municipal.

Getting There & Away

Stopping outside the tourist office, nine **ATCRB buses** (☎ 05 59 26 06 99) daily follow the coast southwestwards. For other destinations, it's better to go from Bayonne – not least to ensure a seat in high season. Biarritz-La Négresse train station is about 3km from the town centre. Buses Nos 2 and 9 connect the two. There is a town centre office of **SNCF** (13 av du Maréchal Foch; ⌚ Mon-Fri).

LOURDES

pop 15,000 / elevation 400m

Lourdes, 43km southeast of Pau, was just a sleepy market town until 1858, when Bernadette Soubirous (1844–79), a near-illiterate, 14-year-old peasant girl, saw the Virgin Mary in a series of 18 visions that came to her in a grotto. The Vatican declared her Ste Bernadette in 1933. Five million visitors now flock here annually. Well over half are pilgrims, including many invalids seeking cures.

Orientation & Information

Lourdes' two main east–west streets are rue de la Grotte and blvd de la Grotte, both leading to the Sanctuaires Notre Dame de Lourdes. The principal north–south thoroughfare, called Av Général Baron Maransin where it passes above blvd de la Grotte, connects the train station with place Peyramale.

The huge religious complex that has grown up around the original cave where Bernadette's visions took place is across the River Pau, west of the town centre.

Tourist office (☎ 05 62 42 77 40; www.lourdes-info tourisme.com; place Peyramale; ⌚ 9am-7pm Mon-Sat, 10am-6pm Sun Jul-Aug, 9am-6.30pm Mon-Sat, 10am-12.30pm Sun Apr-Jun & Sep–mid-Oct, 9am-noon & 2-6pm Mon-Sat Jan-Mar & mid-Oct–Dec)

Sights

SANCTUAIRES NOTRE DAME DE LOURDES

The Sanctuaries of Our Lady of Lourdes were developed within a decade of the events of 1858. The most revered site is the **Grotte**

FRANCE

de Massabielle (Massabielle Cave or Grotto) or the Grotte des Apparitions (Cave of the Apparitions), its walls worn smooth by the touch of millions of hands. Nearby are 19 **pools** in which 400,000 pilgrims seeking cures immerse themselves each year.

The main 19th-century section of the sanctuaries includes the neo-Byzantine **Basilique du Rosaire** (Basilica of the Rosary), the **crypt** and above it the spire-topped, neo-Gothic **Basilique Supérieure** (Upper Basilica).

Visitors to the sanctuaries should dress modestly. All four places of worship open 6am to 10pm in summer and 7am to 7pm in winter.

Sleeping & Eating
Camping de la Poste (☎ 05 62 94 40 35; 26 rue de Langelle; 2 people & car €9; ☺ Easter–mid-Oct) Right in the heart of town, it's tiny, friendly – and often full. It also rents eight excellent-value *en suite* rooms (d/tr/q €25/32/40).

Hôtel du Viscos (☎ 05 62 94 08 06; fax 05 62 94 26 74; 6 bis av St-Joseph; basic d €29, with bathroom €34; ☺ Feb–mid-Dec) This friendly, family-run place near the station has a bustling bar for guests and offers great value.

Le Cardinal (☎ 05 62 42 05 87; 11 place Peyramale; salads €5.50-6, menu du jour €8.50; ☺ Mon-Sat) This unpretentious bar/brasserie is where the staff of the tourist office lunch – and they should know what's best. Tuck into steak, chips and salad for only €6.50.

Lourdes' **covered market** occupies most of place du Champ Commun.

Getting There & Away
The **bus station** (place Capdevieille) has services northwards to Pau (€7.20, 1¼ hours, four to six daily). SNCF buses to Cauterets (€6.10, one hour, six daily) leave from the train station.

Lourdes is well connected by train to cities all over France, including Bayonne (€17.80, 1¾ hours, three to four daily). There are four daily TGVs to Paris' Gare Montparnasse (€72.40 to €81.40, six hours).

THE DORDOGNE

Known to the French as Périgord, this region was one of the prehistoric cradles of human civilisation. The remains of Neanderthal and Cro-Magnon people have been discovered throughout the area and several local caves, including the world-famous Lascaux, are decorated with extraordinary works of prehistoric art. During the warmer months, the Dordogne, famed for its rich cuisine (such as truffles and *foie gras*), attracts vast numbers of tourists.

PÉRIGUEUX
pop 33,294
Founded over 2000 years ago on a hill bounded by a curve in the gentle River Isle, Périgueux has one of France's best museums of prehistory. The city is at its liveliest during the Wednesday and Saturday truffle and *foie gras* markets.

The medieval and Renaissance old city, Puy St-Front, is on the hillside between the Isle (to the east) and blvd Michel Montaigne and place Bugeaud (to the west). The train station is about 1km northwest of the old city.

The main **tourist office** (☎ 05 53 53 10 63; tourisme.perigueux@perigord.tm.fr; 26 place Francheville; ☺ 9am-1pm & 2-6pm Mon-Sat year-round, 10am-1pm & 2-6pm Sun mid-Jun–mid-Sep) is next to the medieval Tour Mataguerre.

Musée du Périgord (☎ 05 53 06 40 70; 22 cours Tourny; admission €4; ☺ 11am-6pm Mon & Wed-Fri, 1-6pm Sat & Sun Apr-Sep; 10am-5pm Mon & Wed-Fri, 1-6pm Sat & Sun Oct-Mar) The museum is renowned for its extensive collection of prehistoric tools and implements and for its Gallo-Roman displays.

Hôtel des Voyageurs (☎ 05 53 53 17 44; 26 rue Denis Papin; s/d from €14/16) This is one of half a dozen inexpensive hotels near the train station, along rue Denis Papin and rue des Mobiles de Coulmiers. The rock-bottom prices here mean tiny rooms and flimsy furniture and possibly noise from the rowdy bar next door.

The **bus station** (place Francheville) is on the southern side of the square; hours are posted at the bus stops. One of the carriers, **CFTA** (☎ 05 53 08 43 13; ☺ Mon-Fri), has an office on the storey overlooking the waiting room. The tourist office and the train station information office can supply you with schedules.

The **train station** (rue Denis Papin) is served by local bus Nos 1, 4 and 5. Destinations with direct services include Bordeaux (€16.30, 1¼ hours, nine to 13 daily). Services to Paris' Gare d'Austerlitz (€45.90, three to five hours, 12 to 16 daily) are via Limoges. To get to Sarlat-la-Canéda (€12) change at Brive.

SARLAT-LA-CANÉDA
pop 10,000

The beautiful, well-restored town of Sarlat, administratively twinned with nearby La Canéda, is the capital of Périgord Noir. Its medieval and Renaissance townscape, much of it built of tan sandstone in the 16th and 17th centuries, attracts large numbers of tourists, especially for the year-round Saturday market.

The heart-shaped Medieval Town (Cité Médiévale) is bisected by the ruler-straight rue de la République (La Traverse), which (along with its continuations) stretches for 2km north from the viaduct and nearby train station to the Auberge de Jeunesse. The Medieval Town is centred on place de la Liberté, rue de la Liberté and place du Peyrou.

Sarlat is an excellent base for car trips to the prehistoric sites of the Vézère Valley.

Sarlat's **main tourist office** (☎ 05 53 31 45 45; www.ot-sarlat-perigord.fr; rue Tourny; ⏱ 9am-7pm Mon-Sat, 10am-noon Sun Apr-Oct, 9am-noon & 2-7pm Mon-Sat Nov-Mar) is in a building attached to the cathedral. In summer, it charges €2 for hotel and B&B bookings.

Auberge de Jeunesse (☎ 05 53 59 47 59 or 05 53 30 21 27; 77 av de Selves; beds €10) Cooking facilities are available at the modest but friendly 15-bed hostel; call ahead for a reservation.

Bus services are very limited; schedules are available at the tourist office. Departures are from the train station, place Pasteur or place de la Petite Rigaudie. There are one or two buses daily (fewer in July and August) to Périgueux (€6.80, 1½ hours) via Montignac.

The **train station** (☎ 05 53 59 00 21), 1.3km south of the old city at the southern end of av de la Gare, is poorly linked with the rest of the region. Destinations served include Bordeaux (€19.90, 2½ hours, two to four direct daily) which is on the same line as Bergerac, Périgueux (change at Le Buisson; €12, 1½ hours, two daily). The SNCF bus to Souillac (€4.90, 40 minutes, two to four daily) links up with trains on the Paris (Gare d'Austerlitz)–Limoges–Toulouse line.

PREHISTORIC SITES & THE VÉZÈRE VALLEY

Of the Vézère Valley's 175 known prehistoric sites, the most famous ones, including the world-renowned cave paintings in Lascaux, are found between **Le Bugue** (near where the Vézère conflows with the Dordogne) and, 25km to the northeast, Montignac. Most of the valley's sites are closed in winter.

Les Eyzies-de-Tayac
pop 850

The two museums in the one-street touristy village of Les Eyzies-de-Tayac provide an excellent introduction to the valley's prehistoric legacy. The very interesting **Musée National de Préhistoire** (National Museum of Prehistory; ☎ 05 53 06 45 45; adult/those aged 18-25/under-18s €4.50/3/free, on Sun adults €3; ⏱ 9.30am-6.30pm Jul & Aug, 9.30am-noon & 2-5.30pm Wed-Mon Sep-Jun) is built into the cliff above the tourist office and has a well-presented collection of artefacts.

About 250m north of Musée National de Préhistoire along the cliff face is the **Abri Pataud** (☎ 05 53 06 92 46; adult/those aged 6-12 €5.20/3.20; ⏱ 10am-7pm except Mon, Fri & Sat Sep-Jun), a Cro-Magnon *abri* (shelter) inhabited over a period of 15,000 years starting some 37,000 years ago.

Montignac
pop 3101

The relaxing and picturesque town of Montignac, on the Vézère 25km northeast of Les Eyzies, achieved sudden fame after the discovery of the nearby Grotte de Lascaux.

The **tourist office** (☎ 05 53 51 82 60; www.bienvenue-montignac.com; place Bertrand de Born; ⏱ 9am-7pm Jul-Sep, 9am-noon & 2-6pm Mon-Sat Oct-Jun), 200m west of place Tourny, is next to the 14th-century Église St-Georges le Prieuré. IGN maps and topoguides are sold at the **Maison de la Presse** (closed Sun afternoon except Jul & Aug) located just across the street.

The dramatic **Château de Beynac** (☎ 05 53 29 50 40; adult/aged 5-11 €7/3; ⏱ 10am-6pm) fortress is perched atop a sheer cliff, dominating a strategic bend in the Dordogne.

BURGUNDY & THE RHÔNE

Best known for its cooking and its world-class wine, Burgundy is also one of France's most varied *départements* – an enticing blend of hill-top villages and bustling market towns, grand chateaux and tiny churches, rolling fields and abandoned abbeys.

DIJON

pop 230,000

Dijon is one of France's most appealing provincial cities, with an inviting centre graced by elegant medieval and Renaissance buildings. It served as the capital of the Dukes of Burgundy from the 11th to 15th centuries during which time Dijon was turned into one of the great centres of European art. Modern Dijon is a lively, dynamic city with 24,000 university students and a thriving cultural scene.

Orientation & Information

Dijon's commercial centre stretches from the tourist office eastwards to Église St Michel; the main shopping streets are rue de la Liberté and rue du Bourg. Place Grangier, with its many bus stops, is north of rue de la Liberté, while the train station is at the western end of av Maréchal Foch. The old city is around place François Rude and the surrounding streets.

Main post office (place Grangier; ⏰ 8am-7pm Mon-Fri, 8am-noon Sat)

Multi-Rezo (☎ 03 80 66 33 21; 74 rue Vannerie; per 12min/1hr €1/5; ⏰ 9am-midnight Mon-Sat, 2-10pm Sun) Internet access.

Tourist office (☎ 03 80 44 11 44; www.dijon-tourism .com; place Darcy; ⏰ 9am-7pm May–mid-Oct, 10am-6pm mid-Oct–Apr)

Sights & Activities

Palais des Ducs et des États de Bourgogne, an elaborate palace complex that lies at the heart of old Dijon, was once home to the region's rulers. The eastern wing houses the Musée des Beaux-Arts. The 46m-high, 15th-century **Tour Philippe-le-Bon** (Tower of Philip the Good; adult/concession €2.30/1.20; ⏰ 9am-noon, 1.45-5.30pm Easter-end Nov, ⏰ 9am-11pm & 1.30-3.30pm Wed, Sat & Sun Nov-Easter) affords fantastic views over the city.

Dijon has several outstanding museums. The **Dijon Card** (per 24/48/72hr €8/11/14) gets you into the main ones, and includes a guided city tour and use of public transport. Several museums are free to students and to everyone on Sundays.

Musée des Beaux-Arts (☎ 03 80 74 52 70; adult/ senior/student €3.40/1.60/free, free Sun; ⏰ 9.30am-6pm Wed-Mon May-Oct, 10am-5pm Wed-Mon Nov-Apr) is housed in the eastern wing of the Palais des Ducs. This is one of the most renowned museums in France – considered by many

to be second only to the Louvre. The museum has important collections of French, Flemish and Italian art.

Musée Archéologique (☎ 03 80 30 88 54; 5 rue du Docteur Maret; adult/senior/student €2.20/1.10/free, Sun free; ⏰ 9.30am-12.30pm & 1.30-6pm Wed-Sun Oct-May, 9.30am-6pm Jun-Sep) displays Celtic artefacts and a particularly fine 1st-century bronze of the goddess Sequana standing on a boat.

You couldn't leave Dijon without paying homage to the city's most famous export. Visits to the **Musée de la Moutarde** (48 quai Nicolas Rolin; adult/under-12s €3/free) at the factory of Amora, Dijon's main mustard company, can be arranged at the tourist office.

Sleeping

Centre de Rencontres Internationales et de Séjour de Dijon (CRISD; ☎ 03 80 72 95 20; reservation@auberge -cri-dijon.com; 1 blvd Champollion; s/d/q per person €26/16/13.50) An institutional, 260-bed place 2.5km northeast of the centre. By bus, take No 5 (towards Épirey) from place Grangier; at night take line A to Épirey.

Hôtel le Chambellan (☎ 03 80 67 12 67; hotelcham bellan@aol.com; 92 rue Vannerie; s €34-48, d €42-52) A great deal on one of the city's oldest streets with flower boxes and shuttered windows and a small 17th-century courtyard where breakfast is served in summer.

Hôtel du Palais (☎ 03 80 67 16 26; fax 03 80 65 12 16; 23 rue du Palais; s with shower €30-37, d €34-43, s with bath €40-45, d €48-65, tr €52-70) One of Dijon's best-kept secrets, this place oozes old-world charm. The rooms are spacious and welcoming (the best are on the 1st floor).

Hostellerie du Sauvage (☎ 03 80 41 31 21; hoteldusauvage@free.fr; 64 rue Monge; d from €41; P) On an idyllic cobbled courtyard in a 15th-century relais de poste (relay posthouse), this great-value hotel is off buzzy rue Monge.

Eating & Drinking

Chez Nous (☎ 03 80 50 12 98; 8 impasse Quentin; plat du jour €7; ⏰ Tue-Sat) A tiny neighbourhood bistro down an alleyway off place du Marché. Locals come for the coffee and lunch-time menu; the décor and atmosphere could have been lifted from a café on Paris' Left Bank.

La Petite Marche (☎ 03 80 30 15 10; 27-29 rue Musette; menus €10-15; ⏰ evenings & Sun) Vegetarians sick of Burgundy's meat-heavy menus should head for this popular organic restaurant.

Osteria Enoteca Italiana (☎ 03 80 50 07 36; 32 rue Amiral Roussin; lunch menu €14; ⏰ Tue-Sun) A small

Italian diner with delicious pasta and fish dishes.

For picnic treats, head for the 19th-century **covered market** (Halles du Marché; ⏰ to 1pm Tue & Thu-Sat) and the nearby **fromagerie** (28 rue Musette; ⏰ closed Sun & Mon morning). Supermarkets include **Monoprix** (11-13 rue Piron; ⏰ 9am-9pm Mon-Sat) and **Marché Plus** (rue Bannelier; ⏰ 7am-9pm Mon-Sat, 9am-noon Sun).

Pick-Up Café (☎ 03 80 30 61 44; 9 rue Mably; ⏰ 8am-2am) A typically French idea of an American bar-diner, complete with jukeboxes and pinball machines.

Coco-Loco (☎ 03 80 73 29 44; 18 av Garibaldi; ⏰ 6pm-2am Tue-Sat) A friendly, noisy bar that attracts legions of students.

Entertainment

For the latest on Dijon's cultural scene, pick up *Spectacles*, available free from the tourist office. Dijon's club scene is centred around place de la République.

L'An-Fer (☎ 03 80 70 03 69; 8 rue Marceau; with/without drink Wed & Thu €7/5, Fri €9.50, Sat & Sun €8; ⏰ 11pm-5am Wed-Sun, closed Wed mid-Jul–mid-Sep) This club achieved fame for pioneering techno music (Laurent Garnier worked here for four years); house takes centre stage on Saturday.

Getting There & Away

The bus station is in the train station complex. Details of services are available at the **Transco information counter** (☎ 03 80 42 11 00; ⏰ 5.30am-8.30pm Mon-Fri, 6.45am-12.30pm & 4-8.30pm Sat, 10am-1pm & 4-8.30pm Sun). Timetables are posted on the platforms; tickets are sold on board.

Paris' Gare de Lyon is just 1¾ hours away by TGV (€46.20, nine to 16 daily). Most trains to Lyon (€22.50, two hours, at least 12 daily) go to Gare de la Part-Dieu. Other long-haul destinations include Nice (€76.20, six hours, two daily) and Strasbourg (€34.60, four hours, three or four nondirect daily).

Getting Around

Details on Dijon's bus network, operated by STRD, are available from **L'Espace Bus** (☎ 03 80 30 60 90; place Grangier; ⏰ 7.15am-7.15pm Mon-Fri, 7.15am-12.15pm & 2.15-7.15pm Sat). Single tickets, sold by drivers, cost €0.80 and last for an hour; a Forfait Journée ticket is valid all day and costs €2.70 (available from the tourist office or L'Espace Bus).

CÔTE D'OR VINEYARDS

Burgundy's finest vintages come from the vine-covered Côte d'Or (Golden Hillside), the narrow, eastern slopes of a limestone, flint and clay ridge that runs south from Dijon for about 60km.

BEAUNE

pop 22,000

Beaune (pronounced similarly to 'bone') is the unofficial capital of the Côte d'Or. This thriving town's *raison d'être* is wine – making it, tasting it, selling it, but most of all, drinking it.

Orientation & Information

The old city is partly enclosed by ramparts and encircled by a one-way boulevard. The train station is 1km east of the **tourist office** (☎ 03 80 26 21 30; www.beaune-burgundy.com; 1 rue de l'Hôtel-Dieu; ⏰ 9.30am-8pm Mon-Sat 21 Jun-21 Sep, 9.30am-7pm Mon-Sat Apr-20 Jun, 22 Sep–mid-Nov, 10am-6pm Mon-Sat mid-Nov–Mar, 10am-12.30pm & 2-5pm or 6pm Sun year-round), and most of the town's sights. The main commercial area centres on place Carnot.

Sights & Activities

Hôtel-Dieu des Hospices de Beaune (☎ 03 80 24 45 00; rue de l'Hôtel-Dieu; adult/student/under-18s €5.40/4.50/2.60; ⏰ 9am-6.30pm Easter–mid-Nov, 9-11.30am & 2-5.30pm mid-Nov–Easter), Beaune's celebrated charity hospital, was founded in 1443 by Nicolas Rolin (chancellor to Philip the Good). One highlight is the graphic **Polyptych of the Last Judgement** (1443), an ornate altarpiece by the Flemish painter Roger van der Weyden.

Underneath Beaune, millions of dusty bottles of wine are being aged to perfection in cool, dark, cobweb-lined cellars including **Patriarche Père et Fils** (☎ 03 80 24 53 78; http://patriarche.com; 5 rue du Collège; tastings 9.30-11.30am & 2-5.30pm). There is an audioguided tour and the opportunity to compare 13 wines costs €9. Circuits take 40 minutes.

Sleeping & Eating

Budget deals are tough to find in Beaune.

Hôtel Rousseau (☎ 03 80 22 13 59; 11 place Madeleine; s from €24-40, d from €30-50, tr from €47-55) The best option is the endearingly shabby Hôtel Rousseau. Some of the old-fashioned rooms have shower or toilet.

There's a four-star **camp site** (☎ 03 80 22 03 91; 10 rue Auguste Dubois; adult/tent €3/4; ⏰ mid-Mar–Oct) 700m north of the centre.

FRANCE

The covered market in place de la Halle hosts a **food market** (🕙 to 1pm Sat) and a smaller **marché gourmand** (gourmet market; 🕙 Wed morning).

Shopping

Wine can be purchased *en vrac* (in bulk) for as little as €1.10 per litre at **Cellier de la Vieille Grange** (27 blvd Georges Clemenceau; 🕙 closed Sun afternoon).

Getting There & Away

Beaune has frequent trains to Dijon (€6, 20 minutes, 15 to 20 daily). Other destinations include Paris' Gare de Lyon (from €35.30, two direct TGVs daily) and one or both of Lyon's train stations (€19.20, 1½ to 2¼ hours, seven to nine daily).

LYON

pop 415,000

Lyon boasts outstanding museums, a dynamic cultural life, a hot clubbing and bar scene, a large university, fantastic shopping and a Unesco protected historical centre.

Orientation

The city centre is on the Presqu'île, a 500m-to 800m-wide peninsula bounded by the Rivers Rhône and Saône. Public squares running down the peninsula from north to south include place de la Croix Rousse; place Louis Pradel, north of the opera house; place des Terreaux; place de la République, attached to pedestrianised rue de la République; vast place Bellecour; and place Carnot, just north of Gare de Perrache, one of Lyon's two mainline train stations. On the western bank of the Saône, Vieux Lyon (Old Lyon) is sandwiched between the river and the hill-top area of Fourvière.

Information

The Albion (☎ 04 78 28 33 00; 12 rue Ste-Catherine, 1er; metro Hôtel de Ville; 🕙 7pm-2am Sun-Thu, 7pm-3am Fri & Sat) English pub with free WiFi zone and free Internet access on two terminals.

Tourist office (☎ 04 72 77 69 69; www.lyon-france .com; place Bellecour, 2e; metro Bellecour; 🕙 9am-7pm Mon-Sat, 10am-6pm Sun mid-Apr–mid-Oct, 10am-6pm Mon-Sat, 10am-5.30pm Sun mid-Oct–mid-Apr) Buy your **Lyon City Card** (€15/25/30 for 1/2/3 days) here. It gets you into every museum in Lyon, onto the roof of Basilique Notre Dame de Fourvière, and up Fourvière's Tour de l'Observatoire. It gets you unlimited travel on buses, trams, the funicular and the metro and lets you take one of the

tourist office's guided or audioguided city tours, and – between April and October – to set sail on a river excursion.

Sights

VIEUX LYON

Old Lyon, with its cobbled streets and **medieval and Renaissance houses** below Fourvière hill, is split into three quarters: St-Paul at the northern end, St-Jean in the middle and St-Georges in the south. Facing the river is the **Palais de Justice** (Law Courts; quai Romain Rolland).

The partially Romanesque **Cathédrale St-Jean** (place St-Jean, 5e; metro Vieux Lyon; 🕙 8am-noon & 2-7.30pm Mon-Fri, 8am-noon & 2-5pm Sat & Sun), seat of Lyon's 133rd bishop, was built from the late 11th to the early 16th centuries.

FOURVIÈRE

Over two millennia ago, the Romans built the city of Lugdunum on the slopes of Fourvière. Today, Lyon's 'hill of prayer' – topped by a basilica and the **Tour Métallique**, a grey, Eiffel Tower–like structure erected in 1893 and used as a TV transmitter – affords spectacular views of Lyon and its two rivers. The funicular departing from place Édouard Commette in Vieux Lyon is the easiest way up; use a metro ticket or buy a funicular return ticket (€2.20).

PRESQU'ÎLE

The centrepiece of beautiful **place des Terreaux** (metro Hôtel de Ville), 1er, is a 19th-century fountain made of 21 tonnes of lead and sculpted by Frédéric-Auguste Bartholdi, creator of New York's Statue of Liberty.

Next door, the **Musée des Beaux-Arts** (Museum of Fine Arts; ☎ 04 72 10 17 40; 20 place des Terreaux, 1er; metro Hôtel de Ville; adult/under-18s €6/free; 🕙 10am-6pm Wed-Mon, from 10.30am Fri) showcases France's finest collection of sculptures and paintings – from every period of European art – outside Paris. The free **cloister garden** is a great picnic venue.

Other Attractions

The brick-and-glass **Cité Internationale**, designed by Italian architect Renzo Piano to host the G7 summit in 1996. Inside, the **Musée d'Art Contemporain** (Museum of Contemporary Art; ☎ 04 72 69 17 17; www.moca-lyon.org; 81 quai Charles de Gaulle, 6e; metro; adult/under-18s €3.80/free; 🕙 noon-7pm Wed-Sun) displays works created after 1960.

Cinema's glorious beginnings are featured at the **Institut Lumière** (☎ 04 78 78 18 95;

LYON

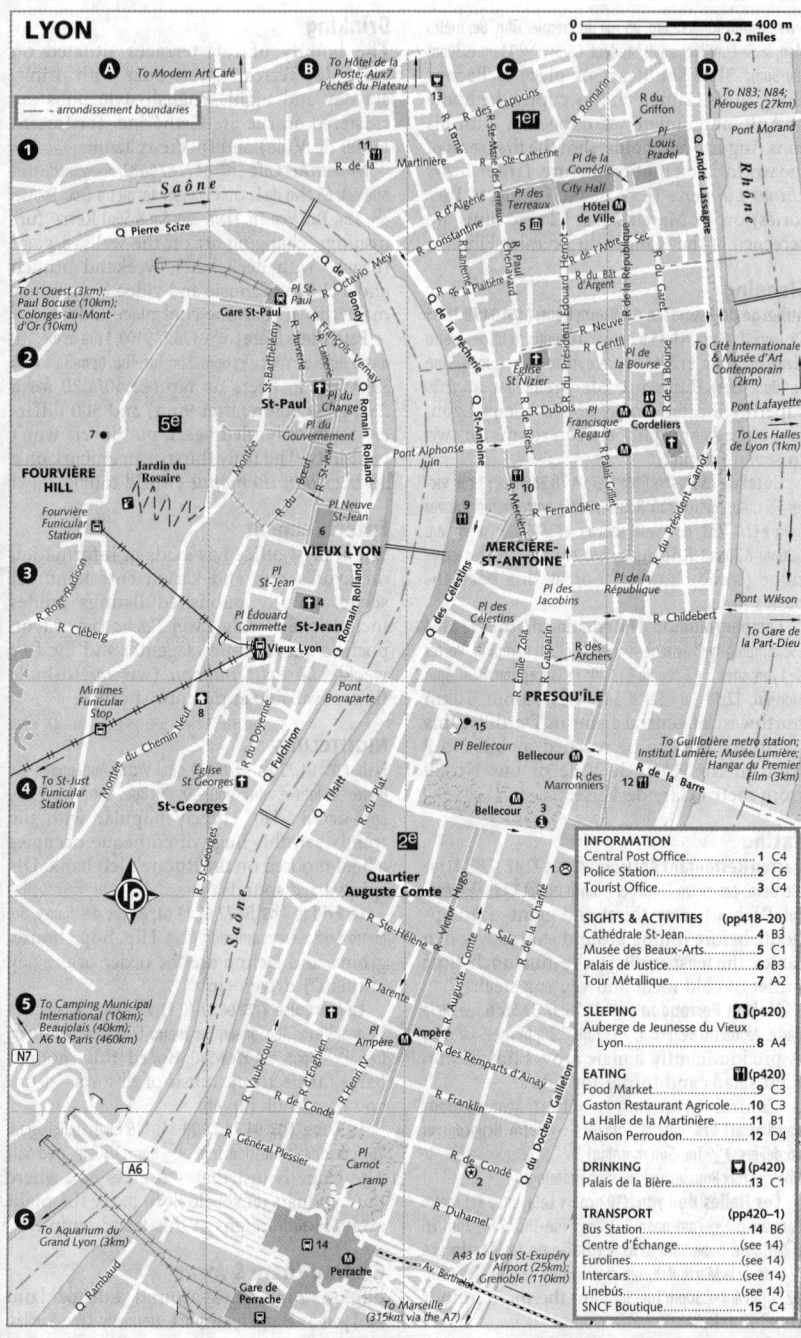

— – arrondissement boundaries

INFORMATION
Central Post Office.................1 C4
Police Station.......................2 C6
Tourist Office.......................3 C4

SIGHTS & ACTIVITIES   (pp418–20)
Cathédrale St-Jean................4 B3
Musée des Beaux-Arts.........5 C1
Palais de Justice...................6 B3
Tour Métallique....................7 A2

SLEEPING   (p420)
Auberge de Jeunesse du Vieux
    Lyon...............................8 A4

EATING   (p420)
Food Market.........................9 C3
Gaston Restaurant Agricole...10 C3
La Halle de la Martinière......11 B1
Maison Perroudon................12 D4

DRINKING   (p420)
Palais de la Bière.................13 C1

TRANSPORT   (pp420–1)
Bus Station.........................14 B6
Centre d'Échange...............(see 14)
Eurolines..........................(see 14)
Intercars...........................(see 14)
Linebús............................(see 14)
SNCF Boutique....................15 C4

FRANCE

www.institut-lumiere.org; 25 rue du Premier Film, 8e; metro Monplaisir-Lumière; adult/student €6/5; 🕙 11am-6.30pm Tue-Sun), 3km southeast of place Bellecour along cours Gambetta. It occupies the home of Antoine Lumière who, together with his sons Auguste and Louis, shot the first reels of the world's first motion picture, *La Sortie des Usines Lumières* (Exit of the Lumières Factories) on 19 March 1895. Classic films are screened at the Hangar du Premier Film.

Sleeping

Auberge de Jeunesse du Vieux Lyon (☎ 04 78 15 05 50; lyon@fuaj.org; 41-45 montée du Chemin Neuf, 5e; metro Vieux Lyon; dm €12.70; 🕙 reception: 7am-1pm & 9pm or 10pm-1am) Rates include breakfast at this superbly located hostel above Vieux Lyon. Its 180 beds are split between rooms for two to seven people.

Hôtel de la Poste (☎ /fax 04 78 28 62 67; 1 rue Victor Fort, 4e; metro Croix Rousse; s/d/q with shared shower from €17/17/33, d/tr with shower €33/46; 🕙 reception: 6.30am-8.30pm) Rooms share toilets on the corridor (some showers too) at this back-to-basics hotel.

Camping Municipal International (☎ 04 78 35 64 55; camping-lyon@marie-lyon.fr; allée du Camping, Portes de Lyon; sites for 2 people €13.70; 🕙 reception: 8am-8pm Mon-Fri, 12.30-8pm Sat & Sun; 🐾) About 10km northwest of central Lyon in Dardilly, this 215-place site can be reached by bus No 3 from metro Hôtel de Ville or bus No 89 from metro Gare de Vaise.

Eating

Gaston Restaurant Agricole (☎ 04 72 41 87 86; 41 rue Mercière, 2e; metro Cordeliers; lunch buffet €12; 🕙 Mon-Sat) Pack a hearty thirst and giant-sized appetite before dining around shared wooden tables: the feast-until-you're-full lunch-time buffet of cold meat and veg is a steal.

Maison Perroudon (☎ 04 78 37 37 56; 6 rue de la Barre, 2e; metro Bellecour; 🕙 7am-7.30pm Tue-Sun; 🚫) A predominantly female crowd lunches on light salads and to-die-for cakes.

Central Lyon has two fantastic **outdoor food markets** quai St-Antoine, 2e (metro Bellecour or Cordeliers; 🕙 Tue-Sun morning) blvd de la Croix Rousse, 4e (metro Croix Rousse; 🕙 Tue-Sun morning).

Les Halles de Lyon (102 cours Lafayette, 3e; metro Part-Dieu; 🕙 7am-noon & 3-7pm Tue-Thu, 7am-7pm Fri & Sat, 7am-noon Sun) and **La Halle de la Martinière** (24 rue de la Martinière, 1er; metro Hôtel de Ville; 🕙 8am-12.30pm & 4-7.30pm Tue-Sun) are the main indoor food markets.

Drinking

The bounty of café-terraces situated on place des Terreaux, 1er, buzz with drinkers day and night. English-style pubs are clustered on rue Ste-Cathérine, 1er (metro Hôtel de Ville) and in Vieux Lyon.

Modern Art Café (☎ 04 72 87 06 82; www.modernart cafe.net; 65 blvd de la Croix Rousse, 4e; metro Croix Rousse; 🕙 5am-1am Mon-Fri, 11am-1am Sat & Sun) Retro furnishings, changing art on the walls, a *plage* (beach) with deckchairs, weekend brunch and a clutch of music and video happenings make this art bar one cool place to lounge.

Palais de la Bière (☎ 04 78 27 94 00; 1 rue Terme, 1er; metro Hôtel de Ville; 🕙 6pm-2am Tue-Thu, 6pm-3am Fri & Sat) With 15 beers on tap (€3.40/4.20 for a 25cl glass before/after 9pm) and 300 different types of bottled beers, pint lovers won't go thirsty. The truly thirsty can embark on a 15-beer *tour du monde* (world tour).

Entertainment

The tourist office has loads of information on Lyon's rich and varied entertainment scene. Locally published listings guides include the weekly *Lyon Poche* (www.lyon poche.com; €1 at newsagents) and the free weekly *Le Petit Bulletin* (www.petit-bulle tin.fr) available at the tourist office.

NIGHTCLUBS

Fish (☎ 04 72 84 98 98; 21 quai Victor Augagneur, 3e; metro Guillotière; admission €10; 🕙 8pm-5am Wed & Thu, 8pm-6am Fri & Sat). Hugely popular with the trendy set, this huge discothèque occupies a boat moored on the Rhône's left bank. DJs spin varied sounds.

Le Fridge (☎ 04 72 61 13 61; 67 rue des Rancy, 3e; metro Guillotière; admission free) Hip hop, house, groove and techno are the order of the day at this DJ-driven club.

La Marquise (☎ 04 37 40 13 93; www.marquise.net; 20 quai Victor Augagneur, 3e; metro Guillotière; admission free; 🕙 10pm-5am Wed-Sat) Board this moored barge for electronic music of all sorts – drum and bass, soul, rap etc.

Le Cube (☎ 04 78 17 29 84; 115 blvd Staliningrad, Villeurbanne; admission free; 🕙 8pm-5.30am Wed-Sat) The Cube is just that – a glass box where the Lyonnais jet set flock to party the night away. House reigns at this trend temple.

Getting There & Away

Flights from cities around Europe land at **Lyon-St Exupéry airport** (formerly Lyon-Satolas;

☎ 0800 826 826; www.lyon.aeroport.fr), 25km east of the city.

In the Perrache complex, **Eurolines** (☎ 04 72 56 95 30), **Intercars** (☎ 04 78 37 20 80) and Spain-oriented **Linebús** (☎ 04 72 41 72 27) have offices on the bus level of the Centre d'Échange (follow the 'Lignes Internationales' signs).

Lyon has two mainline train stations: **Gare de la Part-Dieu** (metro Part-Dieu), 1.5km east of the Rhône, which handles all long-haul trains; and **Gare de Perrache** (metro Perrache), on the Presqu'île, which is increasingly becoming just a regional station. Many long-distance trains stop at both. Just a few local trains stop at **Gare St-Paul** (metro Vieux Lyon) in Vieux Lyon. Tickets are sold at all three stations and in town at the **SNCF Boutique** (2 place Bellecour, 2e; metro Bellecour; ☉ 9am-6.45pm Mon-Fri, 10am-6.30pm Sat).

Destinations accessible by direct TGV include Paris' Gare de Lyon (€55.60, two hours, every 30 to 60 minutes), Dijon (€24.20, 1¾ to two hours, at least 12 daily) and Strasbourg (€42.30, five hours, four or five direct daily).

Getting Around

Public transport – buses, trams, a four-line metro and two funiculars linking Vieux Lyon to Fourvière and St-Just – is run by **TCL** (☎ 0820 42 70 00; www.tcl.fr; 17 bis blvd Vivier Merle, 3e; metro Part-Dieu; ☉ 8.30am-5pm Mon-Fri). It operates from around 5am to midnight.

Tickets cost €1.40/11.50 for one/10 and are available from drivers and from machines at metro entrances. Tickets allowing unlimited travel for two hours/one day (€2/4.20) are also available, as are a couple of *tickets jumelés* which combine a return public transport ticket with admission to the Institut Lumière (adult/child €7/6) or aquarium (€11/7).

THE FRENCH ALPS

The French Alps, where green valleys meet soaring peaks topped with craggy, snow-bound summits, one of the most awesome mountain ranges in the world. Skiing and snowboarding are the region's obvious attractions, but in summer, visitors can explore hundreds of kilometres of hiking trails.

If you're going to ski or snowboard, expect to pay at least €45 a day (including equipment hire, lifts and transport) at low-altitude stations, which operate December to March. Larger, high-altitude stations cost €55 to €65

a day. There are good deals in January between the school holiday periods.

CHAMONIX

pop 10,000 / elevation 1037m

Chamonix is surrounded by the most spectacular scenery in the French Alps. It's almost Himalayan: deeply crevassed glaciers point towards the valley from the icy crown of Mont Blanc, which soars 4.8km above the valley floor.

Information

Le CyBar (☎ 04 50 53 69 70; 80 rue des Moulins; from 10c per 1min; ☉ 10am-1.30am) Has computers spread over two floors.

The Maison de la Montagne (190 place de l'Église) The first port of call for finding out about the Mont Blanc area, winter sports, ski lessons, hiking and guided tours and activities.

Post office (place Balmat; ☉ 8am-noon & 2-6pm Mon-Fri, 8am-noon Sat Sep-Jun, 8am-7pm Mon-Fri, to noon Sat Jul & Aug) Right in the centre of town.

Tourist office (☎ 04 50 53 00 24; www.chamonix.com; 85 place du Triangle de l'Amitié; ☉ 8.30am-12.30pm & 2-7pm Jun-Sep & Dec-Apr, 9am-12.30pm & 2-6.30pm off-season) Weather bulletins are posted here.

Sights

AIGUILLE DU MIDI

A jagged pinnacle of rock rising above glaciers, snowfields and rocky crags, 8km from Mont Blanc's domed summit, the Aiguille du Midi is one of the Chamonix's most famous landmarks. The panoramic views from the summit are absolutely breathtaking.

Return *téléphérique* (cable-car) tickets from Chamonix to the Aiguille du Midi cost €34 for adults, €24 for children. A ride to the *téléphérique*'s halfway point, Plan de l'Aiguille (2317m) – an excellent place to start hikes in summer – costs €12.30/14.40 one-way/return.

The *téléphérique*, which leaves from the end of av de l'Aiguille du Midi, runs year-round from 8am (7am in summer). The last ride up is at 3.30pm (5.30pm in summer). Be prepared for long queues. You can make advance **reservations** (☎ 0892 68 00 67 premium rate number; booking fee €2) 24 hours a day.

From the Aiguille du Midi, between May and September, you can make the 5km ride in the Panoramic Mont Blanc cable car to **Pointe Helbronner** (3466m) on the Italian border, crossing a vista of glaciers, snow plains and shimmering ice-fields en route.

LE BRÉVENT
The highest peak on the western side of the valley, Le Brévent (2525m) has fabulous views of Mont Blanc. It can be reached by **télécabine and téléphérique** (☎ 04 50 53 13 18; adult/child return €15.50/11), from the end of chemin de la Mollard. The lifts are open 8am to 5.45pm in summer, 9am to 5pm in winter.

Several hiking trails can be picked up at Le Brévent or at the *télécabine*'s midway station, **Planpraz** (1999m; single/return €8.50/10.50).

MER DE GLACE
The Mer de Glace (Sea of Ice), the second-largest glacier in the Alps, is about 14km long, 1800m wide and up to 400m deep. The glacier moves 45m a year at the edges, and up to 90m a year in the centre.

With avalanche proofing over parts of the tracks, the train, which leaves from **Gare du Montenvers** (☎ 04 50 53 12 54) in Chamonix and creeps up to Montenvers (1913m), runs year-round. Trains run from 10am to 4pm in winter (longer in summer). The 20-minute trip costs €14 return.

The Mer de Glace can be reached on foot via the Grand Balcon Nord trail from Plan de l'Aiguille. The uphill trail from Chamonix (two hours) begins near the summer luge track. Traversing the glacier and its crevasses requires proper equipment and an experienced guide.

Activities
From about mid-June to October, 310km of spectacular walking trails open up around Chamonix. The most rewarding are the high-altitude trails reached by *téléphérique*. The *téléphériques* shut down in the late afternoon, but in June and July there is enough light to walk until 9pm or later.

The combined map and guide *Carte des Sentiers du Mont Blanc* (€4) is ideal for straightforward day walks, sold at **Photo Alpine Tairraz** (☎ 04 50 53 14 23; 162 ave Michel Croz), a photographic shop which also sells mountaineering books and prints.

The **Grand Balcon Sud** trail along the western side of the valley stays at around 2000m and affords fantastic views of Mont Blanc. By walking, it can be approached from behind Le Brévent's *télécabine* station. For

less uphill walking, take either the Planpraz or La Flégère lifts.

Sleeping
CAMPING
Because of the altitude, it's nearly always chilly at night.

L'Île des Barrats (☎ 04 50 53 51 44; 185 chemin d'Île des Barrats; ⌖ May-Oct) A three-star site in a quiet clearing, near the base of the Aiguille du Midi *téléphérique*.

Les Deux Glaciers (☎ 04 50 53 15 84; glaciers@ clubinternet.fr; 80 route des Tissières; ⌖ closed mid-Nov–mid-Dec) Another three-star place in Les Bossons, 3km south of Chamonix. Take the train to Les Bossons or the Chamonix Bus to the Tremplin-le-Mont stop.

REFUGES
Most mountain *refuges* (€14 to €20 a night) are accessible to hikers, though some can be reached only by mountain climbers. Breakfast and dinner, prepared by the warden, are often available. It's essential to reserve a place – you don't want to hike halfway across Mont Blanc to find the *refuge* full. For information, see Maison de la Montagne (p421).

HOSTELS & GÎTES D'ÉTAPE
Auberge de Jeunesse (☎ 04 50 53 14 52; chamonix@ fuaj.org; 127 montée Jacques Balmat; dm with breakfast in summer €17; ⌖ check-in: 8am-noon & 5-10pm, closed early May & Oct–mid-Dec) The hostel, 2km southwest of Chamonix in Les Pélerins, can be reached by bus. Take the Chamonix-Les Houches line and get off at the Pélerins École stop. In winter, only weekly packages are available, including bed, food, ski pass and ski hire for six days. There's no kitchen.

Gîte (cottage) accommodation can be a good way to cut costs.

Gîte La Montagne (☎ 04 50 53 11 60; levagabond .co.uk; 789 promenade des Crémeries; dm €12; ⌖ closed 11 Nov-20 Dec) An attractive *gîte* in a traditional alpine-style building on a forested site, 1.5km north of the train station (near La Frasse bus stop).

Gîte Vagabond (☎ 04 50 53 15 43; fax 04 50 53 68 21; 365 av Ravanel-le-Rouge; dm €12.50, half-board €25; ▣) A neat hostelry with a kitchen, bar/ restaurant with Internet access, barbecue area, climbing wall and parking. Beds are in four- or six-person dorms.

Eating

Neapolis (☎ 04 50 53 98 41; 79 Gallerie Alpina; pizza & pasta €6.40-9.90; ☻ Mon-Sat) This simple Italian restaurant overlooks the river and has cheap, wholesome cooking – which makes it very popular.

Le Bumble Bee Bistro (☎ 04 50 53 50 03; 65 rue des Moulins) A tiny, welcoming café which serves hot, hearty meals throughout the day. Cod fritters, chargrilled chicken, steak and ale pie and potato wedges are ideal after a hard day on the slopes, but veggies should try the Red Dragon Pie, stuffed full of vegetables, lentils and spicy beans.

Poco Loco (☎ 04 50 53 4303; 47 rue du Docteur Paccard; pizza €5-7, menus from €7) One of several sandwich shops near place Balmat, with hot paninis (from €3.80), sweet crepes (from €1.50) and huge burgers.

There's a **Super U Supermarket** (117 rue Joseph Vallot; ☻ 8.15am-7.30pm Mon-Sat, 8.15am-12.45pm Sun in winter).

Getting There & Away

The bus station is in the train station building. The office of **SAT Autocar** (☎ 04 50 53 01 15; www.satobus-alps.com; ☻ 6.45-10.30am & 1.25-4.45pm Mon-Fri, 6.45-11am & 1.25-4.45pm Sat & Sun in winter, seasonal hours vary) is near the train station entrance. Buses operate to Geneva bus station (€33, 1½ to two hours) and Geneva airport (€33, 2¼ hours). Services to Italy, through the Mont Blanc tunnel, include Courmayeur (€18 return) and Aoste (€22 return).

The Chamonix-Mont Blanc **train station** (☎ 04 50 53 12 98) is at the end of av Michel Croz. There's a **left-luggage counter** (☻ 6am-8pm). Major destinations include Paris' Gare de Lyon (€86.50, six to seven hours, five daily), Lyon (€31.70, 4½ hours via Annecy) and Geneva (€16.60, four hours via Annecy or Chambéry). There's an overnight train to Paris (€98.90, 10 hours) year-round.

Getting Around

Bus transport is handled by **Chamonix Bus** (☎ 04 50 53 05 55; place du Triangle de l'Amitié; ☻ 7am-7pm in winter, 8am-noon & 2-7pm Jun-Aug).

PROVENCE

First-time visitors might be as captivated by this ruggedly lovely chunk of France, as the painter Van Gogh was. 'What intensity of colours, what pure air, what vibrant serenity', he wrote on arrival from a gloomy Paris. 'Nature here is extraordinarily beautiful, everything and everywhere.'

It's a culturally and historically as well as visually rich region too. The Romans were among the earliest to spot its charms, invading it and then sending their favourite legions to retire here. They left many unmissable monuments behind, including theatres and thermal baths (some still in use).

MARSEILLE
pop 807,071

In parts African, in others Middle Eastern but in its entirety unmistakeably French, the cosmopolitan port of Marseille is a brusque, bustling place with bags of character. There's the attractive old port, the gritty (and often stinking) backstreets, lively markets with the atmosphere of a Moroccan *souq* and heavenly harbourside restaurants. Its old (largely exaggerated and outdated) reputation as a place of crime and racial tension dies hard. Visitors who enjoy exploring on foot will be rewarded with more sights, sounds, smells and big-city commotion than almost anywhere else in the country.

Orientation

The city's main thoroughfare, the wide boulevard called La Canebière, stretches eastwards from the Vieux Port (Old Port). The train station is north of La Canebière at the northern end of blvd d'Athènes. The ferry terminal is west of place de la Joliette, a few minutes' walk north of the Nouvelle Cathédrale. Addresses given below include *arrondissements* (1er being the most central).

Information

Info Cafe (☎ 04 91 33 74 98; 1 quai du Rive Neuve, 1e; per 30min/1hr €2/3.60; ☻ 9am-10pm Mon-Sat, 2.30-7.30pm Sun) Internet access.

Tourist annexe (☎ 04 91 50 59 18; main train station; ☻ 10am-1pm & 2-6pm Mon-Sat)

Tourist office (☎ 04 91 13 89 00; www.marseille-tourisme.com; 4 La Canebière, 1er; ☻ 9am-7pm Mon-Sat, 10am-5pm Sun, to 7.30pm mid-Jun—mid-Sep) You can make hotel reservations at this often overwhelmed and understaffed place.

Dangers & Annoyances

Despite its reputation for crime, Marseille is not significantly more dangerous than other

French cities. At night, avoid walking alone in the Belsunce area, a poor neighbourhood southwest of the train station bounded by La Canebière, cours Belsunce and rue d'Aix, rue Bernard du Bois and blvd d'Athènes.

Sights

Unless noted otherwise, the museums open 10am to 5pm Tuesday to Sunday October to May and 11am to 6pm June to September. Admission to each museum's permanent exhibitions costs €2/1 for adults/children.

Centre de la Vieille Charité (Old Charity Cultural Centre; ☎ 04 91 14 58 80; 2 rue de la Charité, 2e) in the mostly North African Panier Quarter is home to **Musée d'Archéologie** (☎ 04 91 14 58 80) with some worthwhile exhibits on ancient Egypt and Greece.

Musée d'Histoire de Marseille (☎ 04 91 90 42 22; ground floor, Centre Bourse shopping centre, 1er; ☼ noon–7pm Mon-Sat), a relatively small place just north of La Canebière, gives a good overview of the cultures that have made their home in Marseille and the crafts they practised over the centuries including the remains of a 3rd-century AD merchant vessel.

Not to be missed for great panoramas and handsome, if overwrought, 19th-century architecture is the **Basilique Notre Dame de la Garde** (☎ 04 91 13 40 80; admission free; ☼ basilica & crypt: 7am-8pm summer, 7am-10pm mid-Jun–mid-Aug, 7am-7pm winter). Dress conservatively when you visit. Bus No 60 links the old port (from cours Jean Ballard) with the basilica.

Château d'If (☎ 04 91 59 02 30; adult/student €4.60/3.10; ☼ 9.30am-6pm Sep-Mar, 9.30am-6.30pm Jun-Aug), the 16th-century fortress-turned-prison made infamous by Alexandre Dumas' classic novel *Le Comte de Monte Cristo* (The Count of Monte Cristo), is on a 30-sq-km island, 3.5km west of the entrance to the Vieux Port. In reality all sorts of political prisoners, hundreds of Protestants, the Revolutionary hero Mirabeau, the rebels of 1848 and the Communards of 1871 were imprisoned here.

GACM (☎ 04 91 55 50 09; www.answeb.net/gacm; 1 quai des Belges, 1er) runs boats to the Château d'If at 9am, 10.30am, noon, 2pm and 3.30pm (€9 return, 20 minutes).

Sleeping

Generally, the better hotels cluster around the old port (where budget options are pretty much non-existent) and as you head east out of the centre along the corniche.

Hôtel d'Athènes (☎ 04 91 90 12 93; fax 04 91 90 7203; 37-39 blvd d'Athènes, 1er; s/d with shower €24/34, s/d/tw with shower & toilet €39/46/56) At the foot of the grand staircase leading from the train station into town you'll find average but well-kept rooms and an elevator. It runs the adjoining one-star **Hôtel Little Palace** (r with shower only €25-34).

Auberge de Jeunesse de Bonneveine (☎ 04 91 17 63 30; fax 04 91 73 97 23; impasse du Docteur Bonfils, 8e; beds €14.55; ☼ Feb-Dec) About 4.5km south of the centre, rates here include breakfast. Take bus No 44 from the Rond Point du Prado metro stop and get off at the place Bonnefons stop.

Eating & Drinking

No trip to Marseille is complete without sampling *bouillabaisse*, a rich red soup full of chunks of Mediterranean fish, the Vieux Port area is a good hunting ground. Get your fresh fruit and veg at the **Marché des Capucins** (place des Capucins; ☼ Mon-Sat), a block south of La Canebière.

Le Resto Provençal (☎ 04 91 48 85 12; 64 cours Julien, 1er; ☼ closed Sat lunch & Sun) A winning combination of an outside dining terrace, a *menu* offering regional fare for €21, a *plat du jour* for around €9 and a good-value lunch-time *menu* for €12.

Pizzeria Chez Mario (☎ 04 91 54 48 54; 8 rue Euthymènes, 1er; mains €8.50-15) Does good fish, grilled meats, pizza and pasta.

Roi du Couscous (☎ 04 91 91 45 46; 63 rue de la République, 2e; couscous €8-12; ☼ Tue-Sun) Serves large and delicious portions of steamed semolina with meats and vegetables.

O'Stop (☎ 04 91 33 85 34; 15 rue Saint-Saëns, 1er; menu €9; ☼ 24hr) Never stops serving sandwiches, pasta and simple, authentic regional specialities.

Le Bar de la Marine (☎ 04 91 54 95 42; 15 quai de Rive Neuve) Chic metropolitan espresso sippers mix it with grizzled *pastis*-gulping sailor types at this gregarious bar right on the water.

L'Heure Verte (☎ 04 91 90 12 73; 108 quai du Port; ☼ 11am-11pm in high season) The place to go to sample many different types of *pastis* and some fierce *absinthe*.

Entertainment

Cultural event listings appear in the monthly *Vox Mag* and weekly *Taktik* and *Sortir*, all distributed free-of-charge at the tourist office. It's also worth consulting the website http://marseillebynight.com.

Le Trolleybus (☎ 04 91 54 30 45; 24 quai de Rive Neuve; ⏰ 11pm-dawn Wed-Sat) Inside the various sections of this tunnel-like club by the harbour there could be techno, funk and indie playing at the same time. The sound system is terrific.

Getting There & Away

The **Marseille-Provence airport** (☎ 04 42 14 14 14), also known as the Marseille-Marignane airport, is 28km northwest of the city in Marignane.

The **bus station** (gare des autocars; ☎ 04 91 08 16 40; 3 place Victor Hugo, 3e) is 150m to the right as you exit the train station. Services include Aix-en-Provence (€4.20, 35 minutes), Avignon (€17, 35 minutes, one daily) and Nice (€22, 2¾ hours).

Eurolines (☎ 04 91 50 57 55) has buses to Spain, Belgium, the Netherlands, Italy, Morocco, the UK and other countries. **Intercars** (☎ 04 91 50 08 66), whose office is next to Eurolines in the bus station, has buses to the UK, Spain, Portugal, Morocco, Poland and Slovakia. Both firms share an office at the bus station and at 3 allées Leon Gambetta (☎ 04 91 50 57 55).

Marseille's passenger train station, served by both metro lines, is called Gare St-Charles. There's a large information and **ticket reservation office** (⏰ 9am-8pm Mon-Sat). Destinations include Paris' Gare de Lyon (€83.90, three hours, 17 daily), Avignon (€19.40, 30 minutes, 27 daily), Lyon (€39.40, 3¼ hours, 16 daily) and Nice (€25, 2½ hours, 21 daily).

There's a **left-luggage office** (per 72hr €3.40; ⏰ 7.15am-10pm) next to platform A.

BOAT

Just 250m south of place de la Joliette, 2e, Marseille's **passenger ferry terminal** (gare maritime; ☎ 04 91 56 38 63; fax 04 91 56 38 70). The **Société Nationale Maritime Corse Méditerranée** (SNCM; ☎ 0836 67 95 00; sncm.fr; 61 blvd des Dames, 2e; ⏰ 8am-6pm Mon-Fri, 8.30am-noon & 2-5.30pm Sat) links Marseille with Corsica, Sardinia and Tunisia.

Getting Around

TO/FROM THE AIRPORT

Navette shuttle buses (Marseille ☎ 04 91 50 59 34; airport ☎ 04 42 14 31 27) link Marseille-Provence airport (€8.50, one hour) with Marseille's train station. Airport-bound buses leave

from the train station's main entrance every 20 minutes.

BUS & METRO

Marseille is served by two fast, well-run metro lines (Métro 1 and Métro 2) and an extensive bus network. The metro and most buses run from about 5am to 9pm. From 9.25pm to 12.30am, metro and tram routes are covered every 15 minutes by buses M1 and M2.

Bus/metro tickets cost €1.50. A pass for one/three days costs €4/9.50.

AIX-EN-PROVENCE

pop 137,067

Aix-en-Provence, or Aix (pronounced like the letter 'x'), is one of France's most graceful, and popular, cities with a lively nightlife (much of it sustained by the presence of 30,000 students) and plenty of charm.

Tourist office (☎ 04 42 16 11 61; www.aixenprovence tourism.com; 2 place du Général de Gaulle; ⏰ 8.30am-7pm Mon-Sat, 10am-1pm & 2-6pm Sun Jul & Aug; 8.30am-7pm Mon-Sat, 10am-1pm & 2-7pm Sun Sep-Jun) A highly efficient place but it can get very busy indeed in summer.

The **Cours Mireabeau**, a graceful plane tree–lined boulevard, is the perfect place to watch the world pass as you nurse a slow espresso on one of the many large cafés lining it. The warren of streets running off it into the old town are full of ethnic restaurants and specialist shops, mingled with handsome old 17th- and 18th- century mansions.

Cathédrale St-Sauveur (rue J de Laroque; ⏰ 8am-noon & 2-6pm) is an interesting ragtag of styles through the ages incorporating architectural features of every major period from the 5th to 18th centuries stuck onto one another.

Sleeping & Eating

Although a student town, Aix is not cheap. Even so, the centre can fill up fast so book ahead.

Camping Arc-en-Ciel (☎ 04 42 26 14 28; route de Nice; camp sites €17.10; ⏰ Apr-Sep) There are peaceful wooded hills out back but a busy motorway out front. It's 2km southeast of town, at Pont des Trois Sautets. Take bus No 3 to Les Trois Sautets stop

Auberge de Jeunesse du Jas de Bouffan (☎ 04 42 20 15 99; fax 04 42 59 36 12; 3 av Marcel Pagnol; beds incl breakfast & sheets €15) A smart, modern place with great views of a distant Mont Ventoux.

It's 2km west of the centre. Rooms are locked between 9am and 5pm. Take bus line No 4 from La Rotonde to the Vasarely stop.

Hôtel Paul (☎ 04 42 23 23 89; hotel.paul@wanadoo .fr; 10 av Pasteur; s/d/tr €35/45/55) Welcoming rooms and a pleasant courtyard garden make this an appealing budget option just north of blvd Jean Jaurès and a 10-minute walk from the tourist office or take minibus No 2 from La Rotonde or the bus station.

Aix's cheapest dining street is rue Van Loo, lined with tiny restaurants offering Italian, Chinese, Thai and other Asian cuisines.

Le Dernier Bistrot (☎ 04 42 21 13 02; 15-19 rue Constantin; lunch menu €10, dinner menus €16/19/23; ☺ Mon-Sat) Mixes traditional bistro recipes with Provençal culinary fodder such as beef *daubes* (a very slowly stewed beef casserole) and *carpaccios* (razor thin slices of raw beef), *soupe au pistou* (soup with pesto) and courgette flan.

Aix is known for its superb markets. A myriad of **fruit and vegetable stands** are set up each morning on place Richelme, just as they have been for centuries.

AVIGNON

pop 88,312

Avignon is synonymous in France today with the annual performing arts festival held here each summer but there's plenty to see in this bustling walled city year-round, including some interesting museums and the massive fortress of the medieval popes, the Palais des Papes.

The city first acquired wealth and power, its mighty ramparts and its reputation as a city of art and culture during the 14th century, when Pope Clement V and his court fled political turmoil in Rome and established themselves near Avignon.

Orientation

The main avenue within the *intra-muros* runs northwards from the train station to place de l'Horloge; it's called cours Jean Jaurès south of the tourist office and rue de la République north of it.

Place de l'Horloge is 300m south of place du Palais, which abuts the Palais des Papes. The city gate nearest the train station is Porte de la République, while the city gate next to Pont Édouard Daladier, which leads to Villeneuve-lès-Avignon, is Porte de l'Oulle.

Information

Tourist office (☎ 04 32 74 32 74; www.ot-avignon.fr; 41 cours Jean Jaurès; ☺ 9am-6pm Mon-Sat, 9am-5pm Sun Apr-Jun & Aug-Oct, 9am-6pm Mon-Fri, 9am-5pm Sat, 10am-noon Sun Nov-Mar, 9am-7pm Mon-Sat, 10am-5pm Sun Jul) 300m north of the train station.

Webzone (☎ 04 32 76 29 47; 3 rue St Jean le Vieux; per hr €4.57; ☺ 11am-10pm Mon-Sat, noon-5pm Sun) Internet access.

Sights

Pont St-Bénézet (Le Pont d'Avignon; ☎ 04 90 27 51 16; full price/pass €3.50/3; ☺ 9am-7pm Apr, May, Oct & Nov, 9am-8pm Jul-Sep, 9.30am-5.45pm Dec-Mar) was built between 1177 and 1185 to link Avignon with the settlement across the Rhône that later became Villeneuve-lès-Avignon. Yes, this is also the Pont d'Avignon mentioned in the French nursery rhyme. Many people find a distant view of the bridge from the Rocher des Doms or Pont Édouard Daladier much more interesting (and it's free).

The huge **Palais des Papes** (☎ 04 90 27 50 00; place du Palais; full price/pass €9.50/7.50; ☺ 9am-7pm Apr, May, Oct & Nov, 9am-8pm Jul-Sep, 9.30am-5.45pm Dec-Mar) was built during the 14th century as a fortified palace for the pontifical court. The cavernous stone halls testify to the enormous wealth amassed by the papacy while it resided here.

The **Musée du Petit Palais** (☎ 04 90 86 44 58; place du Palais; full price/pass €6/3; ☺ 10am-1pm & 2-6pm Wed-Mon Jun-Sep, 9.30am-1pm & 2-5.30pm Wed-Mon Oct-May), a former archbishop's palace, houses an outstanding collection of lavishly coloured 13th- to 16th-century Italian religious paintings.

Just up the hill from the cathedral is **Rocher des Doms**, a delightful bluff-top park that has great views of the Rhône, Pont St-Bénézet, Villeneuve-lès-Avignon and the Alpilles. There's all you could ask for up here: shade, a breeze and benches aplenty. A good spot for a picnic.

Villeneuve-lès-Avignon, across the Rhône from Avignon (and in a different *département*), was founded in the late 13th century. Here you'll find the **Musée Pierre de Luxembourg** (☎ 04 90 27 49 66; rue de la République; full price/pass €3/1.90; ☺ 10am-12.30pm & 2-6.30pm, closed Mon mid-Sep–mid-Jun) If you're remotely interested in religious art it's well worth the visit for Enguerrand Quarton's lavish and dramatic 1453 painting *The Crowning of the Virgin*.

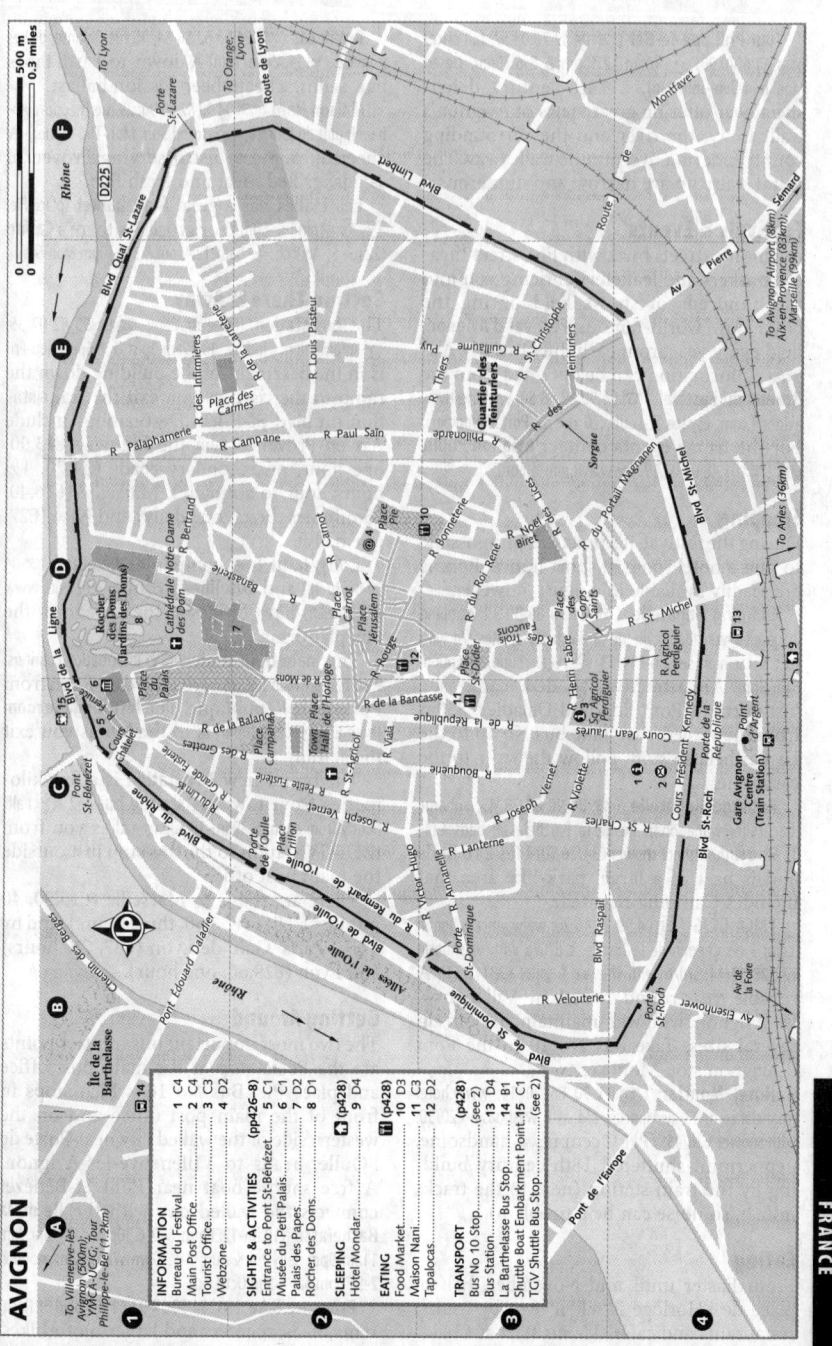

AVIGNON

0   500 m
0   0.3 miles

To Villeneuve-lès-
Avignon (500m);
YMCA-UCJG; Tour
Philippe-le-Bel (1.2km)

To Lyon

To Orange;
Lyon

Rhône (D225)

Route de Lyon

Porte
St-Lazare

Blvd Qual St-Lazare

Porte
St-Benezet

Rhône

R de la Ligne

Rocher
des Doms
(Jardins des Doms)

Pont
St-Bénezet

Blvd du Rhône

Allées de l'Oulle

Blvd de l'Oulle

Pont de l'Europe

Cathédrale Notre Dame
des Dom

Place
du
Palais

R de la Balance

Place
Crillon

Porte
de l'Oulle

R du Limas

R des Grottes

Petite Fusterie

R Joseph Vernet

R Victor Hugo

R Annanelle

Porte
St-Dominique

Blvd de St-Dominique

R Veloutterie

Blvd Raspail

Place
campane

Grande Fusterie

R St-Agricol

R Vidal

R de la Bancasse

R de la République

R Bouquerie

R Lanterne

R St Charles

R Violette

Cours Jean-Jaurès

Porte
St-Roch

Av Eisenhower

Av de
la Foire

Place
Pignotte

Place
Jerusalem

R Carnot

Place
Carnot

Place Pie

R Rouge

Place
St-Didier

R Henri Fabre

R Agricol Perdiguier

R Agricol
Perdiguier

Cours Président Kennedy

Porte de la
République

Point
d'Argent

Blvd St-Roch

Bananerie

R Bertrand

R des Infirmières

Place des
Carmes

R de Carreterie

R Palaphamerie

R Campane

R Paul Sain

R Louis Pasteur

R Thiers

R St-Guillaume

R Puy

R St-Christophe

Quartier des
Teinturiers

R des
Teinturiers

R Philonarde

Sorgue

R Bonneterie

R du Roi René

R Noel Biret

R St-Michel

R du Portail Magnanen

Place
des
Corps
Saints

Place des
Trois
Faucons

Blvd Limbert

Montfavet

Blvd St-Michel

Av (Pierre)

Route de

Gare Avignon
Centre
(Train Station)

To Arles (36km)

To Avignon Airport (8km);
Aix-en-Provence (83km);
Marseille (99km)

Cesmard

Ile de la
Barthelasse

Chemin des Berges

Pont Édouard Delaplier

<table>
<tr><td colspan="2">INFORMATION</td></tr>
<tr><td>Bureau du Festival</td><td>1 C4</td></tr>
<tr><td>Main Post Office</td><td>2 C4</td></tr>
<tr><td>Tourist Office</td><td>3 C3</td></tr>
<tr><td>Webzone</td><td>4 D2</td></tr>
<tr><td colspan="2">SIGHTS & ACTIVITIES   (pp426–8)</td></tr>
<tr><td>Entrance to Pont St-Bénézet</td><td>5 C1</td></tr>
<tr><td>Musée du Petit Palais</td><td>6 C1</td></tr>
<tr><td>Palais des Papes</td><td>7 D2</td></tr>
<tr><td>Rocher des Doms</td><td>8 D1</td></tr>
<tr><td colspan="2">SLEEPING   (p428)</td></tr>
<tr><td>Hôtel Monclar</td><td>9 D4</td></tr>
<tr><td colspan="2">EATING   (p428)</td></tr>
<tr><td>Food Market</td><td>10 D3</td></tr>
<tr><td>Maison Nani</td><td>11 C3</td></tr>
<tr><td>Tapalocas</td><td>12 D2</td></tr>
<tr><td colspan="2">TRANSPORT   (p428)</td></tr>
<tr><td>Bus No 10 Stop</td><td>(see 2)</td></tr>
<tr><td>Bus Station</td><td>13 D4</td></tr>
<tr><td>La Barthelasse Bus Stop</td><td>14 B1</td></tr>
<tr><td>Shuttle Boat Embarkment Point</td><td>15 C1</td></tr>
<tr><td>TGV Shuttle Bus Stop</td><td>(see 2)</td></tr>
</table>

FRANCE

Tour Philippe-le-Bel (☎ 04 32 70 08 57; full price/pass €1.60/0.90; ☻ 10am-12.30pm & 2-6.30pm, closed Mon mid-Sep–mid-Jun), a 14th-century defensive tower offering great views of Avignon's walled city, the river and the surrounding countryside, is a five-minute walk away. The spiral stairs up are narrow and numerous.

Festivals & Events

Avignon's streets buzz with life, street theatre, buskers and leafleters enticing you into the hundreds of shows held during the city's now world-famous **Festival d'Avignon**, held every year from early July to early August. Information can be obtained from the **Bureau du Festival** (☎ 04 90 27 66 50; www.festival-avignon.com; Espace St-Louis, 20 rue du Portail Boquier). For the fringe events contact **Avignon Public Off** (☎ 01 48 05 01 19; www.avignon-off.org).

Sleeping

During the festival, it's practically impossible to find a hotel room at short notice. Rooms are readily available in August, however.

Camping Bagatelle (☎ 04 90 86 30 39; camping .bagatelle@wanadoo.fr; Île de la Barthelasse; sites s/d with tent & car high season €11/13; ☻ year-round, reception: 8am-9pm) An attractive, shaded, camp site just north of Pont Édouard Daladier, 850m from the walled city. Take bus No 10 to the La Barthelasse stop. Follow the river to the camp site.

Auberge Bagatelle (☎ 04 90 85 78 45; auberge .bagatelle@wanadoo.fr; Île de la Barthelasse; beds €11-11.50, d with/without shower €34/26.50) Has 210 beds and is part of a large, park-like area that includes Camping Bagatelle.

YMCA-UCJG (☎ 04 90 25 46 20; www.ymca-avignon .com; 7 bis Chemin de la Justice; s/d/tr/q with washbasin €22/28/33/44, s/d/tr with shower & toilet €33/42/51) A reliable year-round hostel in Villeneuve-lès-Avignon, with well-maintained rooms in several sizes. Take bus No 10 to the Pont d'Avignon stop Monteau.

Hôtel Monclar (☎ 04 90 86 20 14; www.hotel -monclar.com; 13 av Monclar; s/d with washbasin €20/30, with shower €26/45; ☐P☐) Occupies a handsome, peppermint-shuttered 18th-century building by the train station (next to the tracks in fact, so noise can be a problem).

Eating

From Easter until mid-November, half of place de l'Horloge is taken over by tourist restaurants and cafés. *Menus* start at €14.

Tapalocas (☎ 04 90 82 56 84; 15 rue Galante; dishes from €2; ☻ 11.45am-1am) A down-to-earth tapas bar, selling cheap, beer-session ballast.

Maison Nani (☎ 04 90 82 60 90; 29 rue Théodore Aubanel; plat du jour €9; ☻ closed Sun, Mon-Thu dinner) A cheerful, popular bistro serving Provençal salads, grilled meat and fresh fish.

Les Halles has a great **food market** (place Pie; ☻ 7am-1pm Tue-Sun). For groceries there's **Casino** (22 rue St-Agricol; ☻ 8am-12.45pm & 3-7.30pm Mon-Sat).

Getting There & Away

The **bus station** (halte routière; ☎ 04 90 82 07 35; ☻ information window: 10.15am-1pm & 2-6pm Mon-Fri) is in the basement of the building down the ramp to the right as you exit the train station on blvd St-Roch. Destinations include Aix-en-Provence (via the highway €13.90, one hour, on secondary roads €11.70, 1½ hours, four to six daily), Marseille (€16.40, 35 minutes direct, one daily) and Nice (€27, one daily).

Long-haul bus companies **Linebús** (☎ 04 90 85 30 48) and **Eurolines** (☎ 04 90 85 27 60; www .eurolines.fr) have offices at the far end of the bus platforms.

The **main train station** (☻ information counters: 9am-6.15pm Mon-Sat) is across blvd St-Roch from Porte de la République. The **left-luggage room** (from €3; ☻ 6am-10pm) is to the left as you exit the station.

The brand new **TGV station** is a few kilometres from town. A **shuttle bus** (€2; ☻ half-hourly from about 5.30am-10.50pm) takes you from the TGV station to the bus stop just outside the main post office.

There are trains to Marseille (€15.50, 40 minutes), Nice (€38.80, three hours), and by TGV, Paris' Gare de Lyon (€67, 2½ hours) and Lyon (€29.60, one hour).

Getting Around

The two most important bus transfer points are the Poste stop at the main post office and place Pie. Bus No 10, which stops in front of the main post office and on the western side of the walled city near Porte de l'Oulle, heads to Villeneuve-lès-Avignon. A free shuttle boat near Pont St-Bénézet connects the walled city with the **Ile de la Bathelasse** (10am-12.30pm & 2-6.30pm daily Apr-Jun; 11am-9pm daily Jul & Aug; 2-5.30pm Wed, 10am-noon & 2-5.30pm Sat & Sun Oct-Dec).

Provence Bike (☎ 04 90 27 92 61; 52 blvd St Roch) rents bikes, scooters and larger motorbikes.

FRANCE

CÔTE D'AZUR & MONACO

Many towns along the beautiful Côte d'Azur (Azure Coast; also called the French Riviera), Nice, Monaco, Cannes, St-Tropez, are coined the playgrounds of the rich, famous and tanned. There's a lot to attract all sorts: sun, 40km of beach, sea water as warm as 25°C, and cultural events.

NICE
pop 345,892

The capital of the Riviera, Nice makes a great base for exploring the Côte d'Azur. The city has lots of budget places to stay and is only a short train or bus ride from Monaco, Cannes and other Riviera hot spots. It's also blessed with fine museums and a lively nightlife in the old city's warren of narrow streets.

Orientation

Av Jean Médecin runs south from near the train station to place Masséna. The modern city centre, ie the area north and west of place Masséna, includes the up-market pedestrianised streets of rue de France and rue Masséna. The intercity bus station is three blocks east of place Masséna. The famous promenade des Anglais follows the gently curved beachfront from the city centre to the airport, 6km west.

Information

Le Change (☎ 04 93 88 56 80; 17 av Thiers; ☽ 7.30am-8pm) Opposite the Gare Nice Ville (main train station), to the right as you exit the terminal building.
Tourist Office (☎ 04 92 70 74 07; www.nicetourism .com; av Thiers; ☽ 8am-8pm Mon-Sat, 9am-7pm Sun Jun-Sep, 8am-7pm Mon-Sat, 9am-6pm Sun Oct-May) This is the most convenient, next to the Gare Nice Ville. There's also another, less crowded **office** (☎ 0892 70 74 07; fax 04 92 14 48 03; 5 promenade des Anglais; ☽ 8am-8pm Mon-Sat, 9am-7pm Sun Jun-Sep, 9am-6pm Mon-Sat Oct-May).
Worldwide Web Service (☎ 04 93 80 51 12; 32 rue Assalit; ☽ 10am-7pm Mon-Sat) Internet access.

Sights & Activities

The Carte Musées Ville de Nice, which allows entry into all of Nice's museums except the Chagall, costs €6/18.30 for seven/15 days.

The **Musée d'Art Moderne et d'Art Contemporain** (☎ 04 93 62 61 62; av St-Jean Baptiste; adult/student €4/2.50; ☽ 10am-6pm Wed-Mon) focuses in French and American edgy works. Artists include Nice-born Yves Klein (1928–62), Andy Warhol, Christo, Marseille-born sculptor César and sculptor Niki de Saint Phalle.

Musée National Message Biblique Marc Chagall (☎ 04 93 53 87 20; Avenue du Docteur Ménard; adult/student €5.50/4, in summer €5.80/4.25; ☽ 10am-6pm Wed-Mon Jul-Sep, 10am-5pm Wed-Mon Oct-Jun) contains a series of large, impressive and colourful paintings of Old Testament scenes. Take bus No 15 from place Masséna to the front of the museum or walk.

Musée Matisse (☎ 04 93 81 08 08; 164 av des Arènes de Cimiez; adult/student €4/2.50; ☽ 10am-6pm Wed-Mon) houses a fine collection of works by Henri Matisse in the bourgeois district of Cimiez. Well-known pieces in the permanent collection include blue paper cutouts of *Blue Nude IV* and *Woman with Amphora*. Take bus No 15, 17, 20, 22 or 25 from the Station Centrale to the Arènes stop.

Free sections of **public beach** alternate with 15 **plages concédées** (private beaches), for which you have to pay. There are outdoor showers on every beach, and indoor showers and toilets opposite 50 promenade des Anglais.

Sleeping

Nice has a surfeit of reasonably priced places to stay, particularly in the city centre and around the main train station, along rue d'Angleterre, rue d'Alsace-Lorraine and av Durante. In summer budget places can be hard to find after 10am or 11am.

HOSTELS

Villa St Exupery (☎ 04 93 84 42 83; www.villasaint exupery.com; 22 av Gravier; dm/s/d from €18/28/44; P ☐) Out of town, this hostel in a lovely old former monastery has been recommended by readers. There's no curfew, a friendly, party vibe and free Internet access, breakfast and station shuttle.

Backpackers Chez Patrick (☎ 04 93 80 30 72; chezpatrick@voila.fr; 32 rue Pertinax; dm beds €18-21, r with 2 or 3 beds per person €20-25) A popular 24-bed spot; there's no curfew and Patrick, who runs the place, can direct party-mad backpackers to the hot spot of the moment.

Auberge de Jeunesse (☎ 04 93 89 23 64; fax 04 92 04 03 10; route Forestière de Mont Alban; dm beds with breakfast €14; ☽ curfew midnight) This is 4km east of the Gare Nice Ville. Rooms are locked

FRANCE

NICE

0 _____ 300 m
0 _____ 0.2 miles

E **F** **G** **H**

To Cimiez (1.2km); Musée Matisse (1.3km)

Blvd Villebois Mareuil

Montée de Cimiez

Av Raymond

Av George V

Camboul

Av Dr de l'Olivetto

Av e l'Olivetto

Ménard

8

Blvd de Cimiez

R Marceau

Autoroute Urbaine Sud

Blvd Raimbaldi

Av Malausséna

Blvd de Cimiez

Av de Normandie

R Moret

R Assalit

R Pertinax

Av Desambrois

Av Emile Chemin du Bois

9

R de Paris

R de Lépante

Av Notre Dame

R d'Angleterre

Av du Maréchal Foch

R E Thanis

R Lamartine

Av du Maréchal

15

R Biscarra

4

Blvd Carabacel

R Penchienatti

Blvd

Dubouchage

R Pen Delpolin

R Delille

R Tonduti de l'Escarène

R A Mortier

Av St-Jean-Baptiste

Esplanade des Victoires

Av de la République

Av Gallieni

R Barla

Pl Arson

R Auguste Cal

R Arson

Blvd Riquier

3

R Cassini

R Bonaparte

To Auberge de Jeunesse (2.5km)

4

R Pastorelli

R Gioffredo

R de l'Hôtel des Postes

R Alberti

R Chauvain

R Gubernatis

R de la Liberté

Passage Négrin

R Cdt Av Dalpozzo

R Jean Médecin

Pl Masséna

Espace Masséna

Sq Général Leclerc

Av Félix Faure

Promenade du Paillon

Blvd Jean Jaurès

Pl Garibaldi

R Rossetti

16

de Verdun

R Paradis

Jardin Albert 1er

R St-François de Paule

R A Mari

14

25

R de la Préfecture

Pl Pierre Gautier

Cours Saleya

Q des États-Unis

Parc du Château

VIEUX NICE

Pl Robilante

R Fodéré

Pl Île de Beauté

Blvd

R Cassini

See Enlargement

Baie des Anges

Colline du Château

WWI Memorial

Rauba Capeu

Q Lunel

Q Infernet

21

22

Bassin des Amiraux

Q Papacino

Bassin Lympia

Q des Deux Emmanuel

Carrot

5

To Monaco via Corniche Inférieure (N98) (18km)

20

Q du Commerce

Q des Docks

23

Bassin du Commerce

6

MEDITERRANEAN SEA

0 _____ 100 m
0 _____ 0.1 miles

1

12

R Patrolière

Promenade du Paillon

24

Blvd Jean Jaurès

Pl St-François

R du Collet

R de la Boucherie

R Ste Claire

17

R de la Loge

Pl Rossetti

R Ste Réparate

R Centrale

R Benoît Bunico

R Droite

R Rossetti

2

R de la Préfecture

R de la Barillerie

R J Gilly

Cours Saleya

Parc du Château

Colline du Château

Allée Professeur Bésoff

VIEUX NICE

3

FRANCE

from noon to 5pm. Take bus No 14 (last one at 8.20pm) from the Station Centrale bus terminal on place Général Leclerc, which is linked to the Gare Nice Ville by bus Nos 15 and 17, and get off at L'Auberge stop.

HOTELS
The quickest way to get to these hotels is to walk straight down the steps opposite the Gare Nice Ville onto av Durante.

Hôtel Belle Meunière (☎ 04 93 88 66 15; fax 04 93 82 51 76; 21 av Durante; beds with shower & toilet for under-26s €15, d with shower/shower & toilet €47/51) A great and central option. The large four-bed dorm rooms are posh, panelled affairs and the place touts a great tree-studded garden to lounge in. Rates include breakfast.

Hôtel Les Orangers (☎ 04 93 87 51 41; fax 04 93 82 57 82; 10 bis av Durante; 6-bed dm €16, s/d with shower €25/40) Les Orangers is recommended for its large-windowed, sunlit rooms, although this scruffy old place could do with a refit. Rooms come with a fridge (and hotplate on request).

Eating
The cours Saleya and the narrow streets of Vieux Nice are lined with restaurants, cafés and pizzerias. Local specialities to watch out for include *socca* (a thin layer of chickpea flour and olive oil batter fried on a griddle), *salade Niçoise, ratatouille* (vegetable stew) and *farcis* (stuffed vegetables, especially stuffed courgette flowers).

Chez Rene Socca (☎ 04 93 92 05 73; rue Pairoliére; ☺ 9am-10.30pm Jul & Aug, 9am-9pm Sep-Jun, closed Mon) A lively, rough-and-ready place to sample those local specialities for around €2, including good portions of *socca*.

Le Pain Quotidien (cnr rue Louis Gassin & cours Saleya; breakfast from €6) *The* place in town to break fast. Choose your breakfast *formule,* enjoy the excellent hot chocolate, and take in the colour and fragrance of the adjacent flower market.

There's a fantastic **fruit & vegetable market** (☺ 7am-1pm Tue-Sun) in front of the prefecture on cours Saleya. There is a **Monoprix supermarket** (33 av Jean Médecin; ☺ 8.30am-8.30pm Mon-Sat).

Drinking
Almost all nightlife is in Vieux Nice, which throbs with activity on summer nights. The most popular pubs in Nice are run by Anglophones, with happy hours and live music.

Chez Wayne's (☎ 04 93 13 46 99; 15 rue de la Préfecture; ☺ 3pm-late) The best place for liquor-fuelled carousing. Happy 'hour' is until 9pm.

Entertainment
Jonathan's (☎ 04 93 62 57 62; 1 rue de la Loge) This is a live music hot spot every night in summer.

Getting There & Away
AIR
Nice's international airport, **Aéroport International Nice-Côte d'Azur** (☎ 08 20 42 33 33), is about 6km west of the city centre. The free shuttle bus connects both terminals.

BOAT
The fastest and least expensive SNCM ferries from mainland France to Corsica depart from Nice.

The **SNCM office** (☎ 04 93 13 66 66; ferry terminal, quai du Commerce) issues tickets (otherwise try a travel agency in town). From ave Jean Médecin take bus 1 or 2 to the Port stop. You can also try **Corsica Ferries** (☎ 08 25 09 50 95; www.corsicaferries.com; quai Lunel).

BUS
There's a busy information counter at the **intercity bus station** (☎ 04 93 85 61 81; 5 blvd Jean Jaurès). There are slow but frequent services until about 7.30pm daily to Cannes (€5.90, 1½ hours), Menton (€5.10, 1¼ hours) and Monaco (€3.90 return, 45 minutes). **Intercars** (☎ 04 93 80 08 70) runs to various European destinations.

TRAIN
Nice's main train station, **Gare Nice Ville** (or Gare Thiers; av Thiers), is 1.2km north of the beach. There are fast and frequent services (up to 40 trains a day in each direction) to towns along the coast including Cannes (€5.20, 40 minutes), Menton (€3.90, 35 minutes) and Monaco (€3, 20 minutes).

Two or three TGVs link Nice with Paris' Gare de Lyon (€81, 5½ hours), via Lyon (€55.50, 4½ hours).

Getting Around
Sunbus route No 23 (€1.30), which runs to the airport every 20 or 30 minutes from about 6am to 8pm, can be picked up at the Gare Nice Ville or on blvd Gambetta, rue de France or rue de la Californie. The Nice by Bus pass, valid for one/five/seven days costs

€4/12.95/16.75 and includes a return trip to the airport. **ANT airport bus** (☎ 04 92 29 88 88; €3.50), which bears the symbol of an aeroplane shuttles between town and airport every 20 minutes (30 minutes on Sunday).

CANNES
pop 68,214

The harbour, the bay, the hill west of the port called Le Suquet, the beachside promenade, the beaches and the people sunning themselves provide more than enough natural beauty to make at least a day trip here worth the effort. Cannes is famous for its cultural activities and many festivals, the most renowned being the 10-day International Film Festival in mid-May, which sees the population treble overnight.

Information

Cybercafe Webstation (☎ 04 93 68 72 37; 26 rue Hoche; per 30min/1hr €3/6; ☽ 10am-11pm Mon-Sat)
Tourist Office (☎ 04 92 99 84 22; www.cannes.com; ☽ 9am-8pm Jul & Aug, 9am-7pm Mon-Sat Sep-Jun) On the ground floor of the Palais des Festivals.
Tourist Office Annexe (☎ 04 93 99 19 77; ☽ 9am-7pm Mon-Sat) Next to the train station.

Sights

One of the best ways to spend time here is to meander aimlessly east from the **Vieux Port** and its massive yachts along the **Croisette** where you can sit and watch Cannes' human circus pass by in all its costly-but-strangely dressed, perma-tanned, facelifted, small-yappy-type-dog-carrying glory.

Unlike Nice, Cannes is endowed with sandy beaches, most of which are sectioned off for guests of the fancy hotels lining blvd de la Croisette. There's a small strip of public sand near the Palais des Festivals. Free public beaches, **Plages du Midi** and **Plages de la Bocca**, stretch westwards from the Vieux Port along blvd Jean Hibert and blvd du Midi.

Activities

Cannes makes a good base for boat trips up and down the coast. **Trans Côte d'Azur** (☎ 04 92 98 71 30; www.trans-cote-azur.com) runs boats to St-Tropez or Monaco (adult/child €31/16 return), Île de Porquerolles (€46/21) and San Remo (€41/19.50) in Italy. Its office is on quai St-Pierre.

A good trip from Cannes is to nearby **Îles de Lérins**. The eucalyptus- and pine-covered

Île Ste-Marguerite 1km from the mainland is where the enigmatic Man in the Iron Mask – immortalised by Alexandre Dumas in his novel *Le Vicomte de Bragelonne* (The Viscount of Bragelonne) – was held during the late 17th century. The **Musée de la Mer** (☎ 04 93 38 55 26; adult/child €3/2; ☽ museum & cells: 10.30am-1.15pm & 2.15-5.45pm Wed-Mon Apr-Sep, 10.30am-1.15pm & 2.15-4.45pm Wed-Mon Oct-Mar), in the Fort Royal, has interesting exhibits dealing with the fort's history.

The smaller, forested 1.5km-long and 400m-wide **Île St-Honorat** is home to Cistercian monks.

All boats for the isles leave from the same point on the quai des Îles at the far end of the western arm of the harbour. **Compagnie Maritime Cannoise** (CMC; ☎ 04 93 38 66 33) runs ferries to Île Ste-Marguerite (€9 return, 20 minutes) along with **Compagnie Esterel Chanteclair** (☎ 04 93 39 11 82), which runs boats to Île St-Honorat (€10 return, 20 minutes).

Sleeping

Tariffs rise by up to 50% in July and August. During the film festival hotel rooms, many booked months in advance, are virtually impossible to find.

Parc Bellevue (☎ 04 93 47 28 97; fax 04 93 48 66 25; 67 av Maurice Chevalier; camping for 2 adults, tent & car €20; ☽ Apr-Sep), in Cannes-La Bocca, is the nearest place to camp, 5.5km west of the centre. No 9 from the bus station on place Bernard Cornut Gentille stops 400m away.

Le Chalit (☎ 04 93 99 22 11; www.lechalit.com; 27 av du Maréchal Galliéni; dm beds in 4-/6-bed r €16/20; ☽ Jan-Oct, reception: 8.30am-7.30pm) Around 300m northwest of the station, this private hostel is friendly and pleasant. Sheets cost €3. There is no curfew.

Getting There & Away

Buses to Nice (€5.90, 1½ hours, every 20 minutes) leave from place Bernard Cornut Gentille. There is an **information office** (☎ 04 93 39 11 39). From the **train station** (☎ 36 35; rue Jean Jaurès) there are regular services to Nice (€5.20, 40 minutes, two an hour) and Marseille (€22.30, two hours).

ST-TROPEZ
pop 5542

A destination for the jet set, St-Tropez has long since ceased to be the quiet, charming, isolated fishing village that attracted artists, writers and the glitterati here in the 20th century. The year that really changed things for good was 1956, when *Et Dieu Créa la Femme* (And God Created Woman) starring Brigitte Bardot was shot here. Its stunning success brought about St-Tropez's massive popularity.

Information

Tourist Office (☎ 04 94 97 45 21; www.saint-tropez.st; quai Jean Jaurès; ☼ 9.30am-8.30pm Jul & Aug, 9.30am-12.30pm & 2-7pm Apr-Jun, Sep & Oct, 9.30am-12.30pm & 2-6pm Nov-Mar)

Sights

Musée de l'Annonciade (☎ 04 94 97 04 01; place Grammont, Vieux Port; adult/student €4.50/2.50; ☼ 10am-noon & 3-7pm Wed-Mon Jun-Sep, 10am-noon & 2-6pm Wed-Mon Oct-May, closed Nov) contains an impressive collection of modern art, including works by Matisse, Bonnard, Dufy, Derain, Rouault and Signac.

If you're bored with watching the antics of the rich and (maybe not so) famous, the **Citadelle de Saint Tropez** (☎ 04 94 97 59 43; adult/concession €4/2.50; ☼ 10am-12.30pm & 1.30-6.30pm Apr-Sep, 10am-12.30pm & 1.30-5.30pm Oct-Mar) is worth strolling to just for the bay views. Inside the citadel there are displays on the town's maritime history and the Allied landings that took place here in 1944.

About 4km southeast of the town is the start of a magnificent sandy beach, **Plage de Tahiti**, and its continuation, Plage de Pampelonne. It runs for about 9km between Cap du Pinet and the rocky Cap Camarat.

Getting There & Away

St-Tropez **bus station** (av Général de Gaulle) is on the southwest edge of town on the main road out. There's an **information office** (☎ 04 94 54 62 36; ☼ 8am-noon & 2-6pm Mon-Fri, 8am-noon Sat). A day trip by boat from Nice or Cannes can be a good way to avoid St-Tropez's notorious traffic jams and high hotel prices.

MENTON

pop 29,266

Menton, a confection of elegant historic buildings in sugared-almond pastels, is only a few kilometres from the Italian border and reputed to be the warmest spot on the Côte d'Azur. It's big with older holiday-makers, making the town's after-dark entertainment

a tad tranquil compared to other spots along the coast.

The **tourist office** (☎ 04 92 41 76 76; www.menton .fr; 8 av Boyer; ☼ 9am-7pm Mon-Sat, 10am-noon Sun Jul & Aug, 8.30am-12.30pm & 2-6pm Mon-Fri, 9am-noon & 2-6pm Sat low season) is inside the Palais de l'Europe.

The early-17th-century **Église St-Michel** (Church of St Michael; ☼ 10am-noon & 3-5.15pm, closed Sat morning), the grandest and probably prettiest baroque church in this part of France, is perched in the centre of the Vieille Ville.

Two-star **Camping Saint Michel** (☎ 04 93 35 81 23; route des Ciappes de Castellar; ☼ 1 Apr-15 Oct) is 1km northeast of the train station up Plateau St-Michel. Around 500m from Camping Saint Michel is **Auberge de Jeunesse** (☎ 04 93 35 93 14; fax 04 93 35 93 07; Plateau St-Michel; dm with breakfast €14.40; ☼ closed noon-5pm, 10am-5pm winter; **P**) on a lovely spot high on a hill overlooking town and bay. The walk from the train station is quite a hike uphill. Otherwise take a Line 6 bus and get off at the camp site. Curfew is midnight (or 10pm in winter).

Hôtel Le Terminus (☎ 04 92 10 49 80; fax 04 92 10 49 81; place de la Gare; s/d with washbasin €28/31, with shower & toilet €30/40; **P**) Has no stars, but is a welcoming, clean place with a few rooms right next to the station. Hall showers are free.

The **bus station** (☎ 04 93 28 43 27) is next to 12 promenade Maréchal Leclerc, the northern continuation of av Boyer. There's an **information office** (☎ 04 93 35 93 60). There are buses to Monaco (€2.10 return, 30 minutes), Nice (€5.10 return, 1¼ hours). Trains to Ventimiglia in Italy cost €2.10 and take 10 minutes.

MONACO (PRINCIPAUTÉ DE MONACO)

pop 30,000

Tiny, glamorous Monaco covering a mere 1.95 sq km is a fantasy land of perfectly groomed streets, lush gardens, chic boutiques and extravagantly opulent 19th-century pleasure palaces. The Principality of Monaco has been under the rule of the Grimaldi family for most of the period since 1297 and is a sovereign state with close ties to France. It has been ruled since 1949 by Prince Rainier III (b 1923), who updated Monaco and weaned it from its dependence on gambling revenue. His marriage to Princess Grace (remembered from her Hollywood days as the actress Grace Kelly) restored Monaco's glamour.

Information

Direction du Tourisme et des Congrès de la Principauté de Monaco (☎ 92 16 61 16; www. monaco-tourisme.com; 2a blvd des Moulins; ☺ 9am-7pm Mon-Sat, 10am-noon Sun) Across the public gardens from the casino.

Sights

The changing of the guard takes place daily outside the **Palais du Prince** (☎ 93 25 18 31), at the southern end of rue des Remparts in Monaco Ville, at precisely 11.55am. You can also visit the **state apartments** (adult/child €6/3; ☺ 9.30am-6.30pm Jun-Sep, 10am-5pm Oct, closed Nov-May) with commentary through audioguides.

If you're planning to see just one aquarium on your whole trip, the world-renowned **Musée Océanographique de Monaco** (☎ 93 15 36 00; av St-Martin, Monaco Ville; adult/student €11/6; ☺ 9.30am-7pm Jul-Sep, 9.30am-6.30pm Apr-Jun) should be it. It has 90 tanks, and upstairs there are all sorts of exhibits on ocean exploration. Bus Nos 1 and 2 are the alternatives to a relatively long walk up the hill.

Getting There & Away

Intercity buses leave from various stops around the city. There's an **information desk** (av Prince Pierre) at Monaco train station. Taking the train along the coast is highly recommended – the sea and the mountains provide a truly magnificent sight. There are frequent trains eastwards to Menton (€1.70, 10 minutes), Nice (€2.90, 20 minutes) and Ventimiglia (€3, 25 minutes).

LANGUEDOC-ROUSSILLON

pop 2,295,000

Languedoc – land of bullfighting, rugby and robust red wines – is home to some interesting towns, such as Montpellier, the region's vibrant capital, sun-baked Nîmes with its magnificent Roman amphitheatre, and fairy-tale Carcassonne, with its witches' hat turrets, hovering over the hot plain like a medieval mirage. On the coast, good beaches abound.

MONTPELLIER

pop 230,000

The 17th-century philosopher John Locke may have had one glass of Minervois wine too many when he wrote: 'I find it much better to go twise (sic) to Montpellier than once to the other world'. Paradise it ain't, but Montpellier continues to attract visitors with its reputation for innovation and vitality. Students form nearly a quarter of the population.

Orientation

Montpellier's mostly pedestrianised historic centre, girdled by wide boulevards, has place de la Comédie at its heart. To the northeast of this square is esplanade Charles de Gaulle, a tree-lined promenade. Westwards, between rue de la Loge and Grand Rue Jean Moulin, sprawls the city's oldest quarter, a web of narrow alleys and fine *hôtels particuliers* (private mansions).

Information

Main Tourist Office (☎ 04 67 60 60 60; www.ot -montpellier.fr; ☺ 9am-6.30pm or 7.30pm Mon-Fri, 10am-6pm Sat, 10am-1pm & 2-5pm Sun) At the southern end of esplanade Charles de Gaulle.

Point Internet (☎ 04 67 54 57 60; 54 rue de l'Aiguillerie; per hr €1.60; ☺ 9.30am-midnight Mon-Sat, 10.30am-midnight Sun)

Sights

Musée Languedocien (☎ 04 67 52 93 03; 7 rue Jacques Cœur; adult/student €5/3; ☺ 3-6pm Mon-Sat Jul-Aug, 2-5pm Mon-Sat Sep-Jun) displays the area's rich archaeological finds as well as *objets d'art* from the 16th to 19th centuries.

Sleeping

The closest camp sites are around the suburb of Lattes, some 4km south of the city centre.

Oasis Palavasienne (☎ 04 67 15 11 61; www.oasis -palavasienne.com; route de Palavas; 2 people with car according to season €16.70-24.50; ☺ mid-May–Aug) This shady camp site has a large pool. Take bus No 17 from Montpellier bus station.

Auberge de Jeunesse (☎ 04 67 60 32 22; mont pellier@fuaj.org; 2 impasse de la Petite Corraterie; dm €8.90; ☺ mid-Jan–mid-Dec) Montpellier's HI-affiliated youth hostel is just off rue des Écoles Laïques. The dorms are basic but it's a cheap place to crash and there's a friendly bar. Take the tram to the Louis Blanc stop.

FRANCE

Hôtel des Étuves (☎ 04 67 60 78 19; www.hotel desetuves.fr – French only; 24 rue des Étuves; s €20.50-31, d €32-38) This welcoming, 13-room family hotel creeps around a spiral staircase like a vine.

Eating & Drinking
You'll find plenty of cheap and cheerful places on rue de l'Université, rue des Écoles Laïques and the streets interlinking them.

Roule Ma Poule (☎ 04 67 60 36 15; 20 place Candolle; plat du jour €7.50) Like most places in this area, pulls in a mainly student crowd with its decent, cheap fare and a quiet, atmospheric location in a shady old town square.

Tripti Kulai (☎ 04 67 66 30 51; 20 rue Jacques Cœur; salads €8.50, menus €11 & €15; ☉ noon-9.30pm Mon-Sat) Barrel-vaulted and cosy, this popular vegetarian place stands out for the inventiveness of many of its dishes.

The city's food markets include **Halles Castellane** (rue de la Loge), the biggest, and **Halles Laissac** (rue Anatole France).

Place de la Comédie is alive with cafés where you can drink and watch street entertainers strut their stuff. Smaller, more intimate squares include place Jean Jaurès and place St-Ravy. With over 60,000 students, Montpellier has a profusion of places to drink and dance.

Getting There & Away
Montpellier's **airport** (☎ 04 67 20 85 00) is 8km southeast of town. British Airways flies three times per week (daily in summer) to/ from London (Gatwick) and Ryanair operates daily to/from London (Stansted).

The **bus station** (☎ 04 67 92 01 43; rue du Grand St-Jean) is an easy walk from the train station. **Hérault Transport** (☎ 08 25 34 01 34) runs hourly buses to La Grande Motte (No 106; €1.25, 35 minutes) from Odysseum at the end of the tram line.

Eurolines (☎ 04 67 58 57 59; ticketing & information office 8 rue de Verdun) has buses to most European destinations. **Linebús** (☎ 04 67 58 95 00) mainly operates services to destinations in Spain.

Major destinations from Montpellier's two-storey train station include Paris' Gare de Lyon by TGV (€70 to €83, 3½ hours, 12 daily), Carcassonne (€19.50, 1½ hours, six to eight daily) and Nîmes (€7.50, 30 minutes, 20 daily).

CARCASSONNE
pop 46,250
From afar, Carcassonne looks like some fairy-tale medieval city. Bathed in late-afternoon sunshine and highlighted by dark clouds, La Cité, as the old walled city is known, is truly breathtaking. The Ville Basse (Lower Town), established in the 13th century and a more modest stepsister to camp Cinderella up the hill, also merits a browse.

The River Aude separates the Ville Basse from La Cité, up on a hill 500m southeast. Pedestrianised rue Georges Clemenceau leads from the train station and Canal du Midi southwards through the heart of the lower town.

For information go to the **main tourist office** (☎ 04 68 10 24 30; www.carcassonne-tourisme.com; 28 rue Verdun; ☉ 9am-7pm Jul-Aug, 9am-6pm Sep-Jun).

Sights
La Cité, dramatically illuminated at night, is one of Europe's largest city fortifications. Only the lower sections of the walls are original; the rest, including the anachronistic witch's hat roofs (the originals were altogether flatter and weren't covered with slate), were stuck on by Viollet-le-Duc in the 19th century.

The entrance fee to the 12th-century **Château Comtal** (adult/student/under-18s €6.10/4.10/free; ☉ 9.30am-6.30pm Apr-Sep, 9.30am-5pm Oct-Mar) lets you visit the castle itself and also join a 30- to 40-minute **guided tour** of both castle and ramparts.

Sleeping
Camping de la Cité (☎ 04 68 25 11 77; www.campeoles .com; route de St-Hilaire; 2 people with car according to season €13.50-19; ☉ mid-Mar–mid-Oct) A walking and cycling trail leads from the site to both La Cité and the Ville Basse. From mid-June to mid-September, bus No 8 connects the camp site with La Cité and the train station.

Auberge de Jeunesse (☎ 04 68 25 23 16; carcas sonne@fuaj.org; rue Vicomte Trencavel; B&B €15.50; ☉ Feb–mid-Dec; 🖳) Carcassonne's cheery, welcoming, HI-affiliated youth hostel is in the heart of La Cité. It has a members kitchen, snack bar offering light meals and a great outside terrace. Although it has 120 beds, it's smart to reserve year-round.

Hôtel Astoria (☎ 04 68 25 31 38; hotel-astoria@ wanadoo.fr; 18 rue Tourtel; basic d €20, with shower €29, with bathroom €32-36; 🅿) New owners have repainted all rooms and laid fresh tiles or parquet at this hotel and its equally agreeable annexe. Great value.

Eating

Au Bon Pasteur (☎ 04 68 25 49 63; 29 rue Armagnac; menus €13-22; 🕥 closed Sun-Mon Jul-Aug, Sun & Wed Sep-Jun) At this welcoming, intimate family restaurant, you can warm yourself in winter with the yummy *cassoulet* (casserole) or *choucroute* (sauerkraut). Year-round, the *menu classique* (€13) and *formules de midi* (lunch specials; €9.50 to €11) both represent excellent value.

La Divine Comédie (☎ 04 68 72 30 36; 29 blvd Jean Jaurès; pizzas €8-9.50, mains €12.50-14.50; 🕥 Mon-Sat) Beside Hôtel Central, this restaurant serves both pizzas and regional dishes on its pleasant outside terrace.

There's a **covered market** (rue Verdun; 🕥 Mon-Sat) and an **open-air market** (place Carnot; 🕥 Tue, Thu & Sat).

Getting There & Away

Carcassonne-Salvaza airport (☎ 04 68 71 96 46), 5km from town, has two flights daily – **Ryanair** (☎ 04 68 71 96 65) to/from London (Stansted) and to/from Brussels (Charleroi). Carcassonne is on the main line linking Toulouse (€12.10, 50 minutes, frequent) and Montpellier (€18.90, 1½ hours).

NÎMES

pop 134,000

Nîmes is graced by some of France's best-preserved Roman buildings. Founded by Emperor Augustus, the Roman Colonia Nemausensis reached its zenith during the 2nd century AD, receiving its water from a Roman aqueduct system that included the Pont du Gard, a magnificent arched bridge 23km northeast of town. Ransacked by the Vandals in the early 5th century the city began a downward spiral from which it has never quite recovered.

For information try the **tourist office** (☎ 04 66 58 38 00; www.ot-nimes.fr; 6 rue Auguste; 🕥 8am-8pm Mon-Fri, 9am-7pm Sat, 10am-5pm Sun Jul & Aug & 8.30am-7pm Mon-Fri, 9am-7pm Sat, 10am-5pm Sun rest of the year).

Sights

A **combination ticket** (adult/child €5.70/4.65) admits you to both Les Arènes and Tour Magne, dating back to around 15BC and one of the largest of a chain of towers that

once ran along the city's 7km-long Roman ramparts. From here, there's a magnificent view of Nîmes and the surrounding countryside. Alternatively, pick up a **three-day pass** (adult/child €10/5), giving access to all of Nîmes' museums and sites, from the tourist office or the first place you visit.

LES ARÈNES & MAISON CARRÉE

The superb Roman amphitheatre, **Les Arènes** (adult/child €4.65/3.40; 🕥 9am-7pm mid-Mar–mid-Oct, 10am-5pm mid-Oct–mid-Mar) was built around AD 100 to seat 24,000 spectators. It's wonderfully preserved, even retaining its upper storey, unlike its counterpart in Arles. This accompanying rectangular Roman temple, today called the Maison Carrée (Square House), was constructed around AD 5 to honour Emperor Augustus' two adopted sons. It has survived the centuries as a medieval meeting hall, private residence, stable, church and, after the Revolution, archive.

Festivals & Events

Nîmes becomes more Spanish than French during its *férias* (festivals). Each – the three-day Féria Primavera (Spring Festival) in February, the five-day Féria de Pentecôte (Whitsuntide Festival) in June, and the three-day Féria des Vendanges coinciding with the grape harvest on the third weekend in September – is marked by daily *corridas* (bullfights). The **Bureau de Locations des Arènes** (☎ 04 66 02 80 90; 2 rue de la Violette) sells tickets.

Sleeping & Eating

Auberge de Jeunesse (☎ 04 66 68 03 20; nimes@fuaj .org; 257 chemin de l'Auberge de Jeunesse, la Cigale; dm with breakfast €13.25) Comprehensively renovated, this hostel is in a lovely park 3.5km northwest of the train station. Take bus No 2, direction Alès or Villeverte, and get off at the Stade stop.

Hôtel de La Mairie (☎ 04 66 67 65 91; fax 04 66 76 07 92; 11 rue des Greffes; s with washbasin €23, with shower €30, d with bathroom €39-42; 🕥 closed 15-31 Oct) Several rooms in this hyperfriendly two-star, 13-room hotel have separate WC. Ceilings are high and rooms cool, even in high summer.

La Truye qui Filhe (☎ 04 66 21 76 33; 9 rue Fresque; menu €8.70; 🕥 noon-2pm Mon-Sat, closed Aug) Within the vaults of a restored 14th-century inn, this, the ultimate bargain of Nîmes, blends a self-service format with a homely atmosphere and does a superb-value *menu*.

There are colourful Thursday **markets** in the old city in July and August. There is a large **covered food market** (rue Général Perrier).

Getting There & Away

Nîmes' **airport** (☎ 04 66 70 49 49), 10km southeast of the city on the A54, handles one plane daily – the Ryanair flight to/from London Stansted.

The **bus station** (rue Ste-Félicité) is immediately south of the train station. Regional destinations include Pont du Gard (€5.40, 45 minutes, up to seven daily). There are also buses to/from Avignon (€7.30, 1½ hours, seven daily).

Long-haul operator **Eurolines** (☎ 04 66 29 49 02) covers most European destinations together with **Line Bus** (☎ 04 66 29 50 62), which has services to/from Spain.

There's an **SNCF sales office** (11 rue de l'Aspic). Ten TGVs daily run to/from Paris' Gare de Lyon (€68.90 to €82.80, three hours). There are frequent services to/from Avignon (€7.40, 30 minutes), Marseille (€16.20, 1¼ hours) and Montpellier (€7.50, 30 minutes).

AROUND NÎMES
Pont du Gard

The Pont du Gard, a Unesco World Heritage site, is an exceptionally well-preserved, three-tiered Roman aqueduct that was once part of a 50km-long system of canals built about 19 BC by the Romans to bring water from near Uzès to Nîmes. The scale is huge: the 35 arches of the 275m-long upper tier, running 50m above the River Gard, contain a watercourse designed to carry 20,000 cubic metres of water per day and the largest construction blocks weigh over five tonnes. The best view of the Pont du Gard is from upstream, beside the river, where you can swim on hot days.

TOULOUSE
pop 398,423

France's fourth-largest and one of its fastest-growing cities, Toulouse has a vibrant centre with a large student population. It's also known as *la ville rose* (the pink city) because of the profusion of rose-red brick buildings.

Its heart is framed to the east by blvd de Strasbourg and, to the west, by the Garonne River. Its two principal squares are place du Capitole and place Wilson. From the latter, the wide allées Jean Jaurès lead northeastwards to the main bus station and Gare Matabiau, the train station, both just across the Canal du Midi.

The **tourist office** (☎ 05 61 11 02 22; www.ot -toulouse.fr; square Charles de Gaulle; ☉ 9am-7pm Mon-Sat, 10am-1pm & 2-6.15pm Sun Jun-Sep, 9am-6pm Mon-Fri, 9am-12.30pm & 2-6pm Sat, 10am-12.30pm & 2-5pm Sun Oct-May) is in the base of the Donjon du Capitole, a 16th-century tower.

Sights

Bustling, pedestrianised **place du Capitole** is the city's main square and makes a great place to stop for a drink.

The small, 18th-century **Vieux Quartier** is a web of narrow lanes and plazas south of place du Capitole and place Wilson. Typical is place St-Georges with many cafés and restaurants.

A former Benedictine abbey church, **Basilique St-Sernin** (☎ 05 61 21 80 45; place St-Sernin; ☉ 8.30am-5.45pm Mon-Sat, 8.30am-7.30pm Sun Jul-Sep, 8.30am-11.45am & 2-5.45pm Mon-Sat Oct-Jun) is a vast, 115m-long brick basilica, France's largest and most complete Romanesque structure. It was built between 1080 and 1096.

Sleeping & Eating

There's no youth hostel in or near Toulouse. The hotels near the train station are mostly inexpensive but quality varies widely so chose carefully.

Hôtel Splendid (☎ /fax 05 61 62 43 02; 13 rue Caffarelli; r from €17, s/d with shower €23/26, s/d/tr with bathroom €25/29/37) A good, central budget choice.

Six kilometres northwest of the train station, **Camping de Rupé** (☎ 05 61 70 07 35; 21 chemin du Pont de Rupé; sites for 2 people & car €12.50, tents mid-Jun–mid-Sep) is often packed. From place Jeanne d'Arc take bus No 59.

You'll find plenty of places offering excellent-value lunch *menus* for under €16 including the great-value, lunch-time **restaurants** (menus €11-19; ☉ Tue-Sun) serving delicious, generous portions above Les Halles, Toulouse's classy covered market.

Getting There & Away

Northwest of the city centre (8km) is **Toulouse-Blagnac international airport** (☎ 05 61 42 44 00; www.toulouse.aeroport.fr). Air France and easyJet between them have over 30 flights daily to/

from Paris (mainly Orly). British Airways and easyJet each fly from Gatwick daily.

Intercars (☎ 05 61 58 14 53) and **Eurolines** (☎ 05 61 26 40 04) use Toulouse's modern **bus station** (☎ 05 61 61 67 67; blvd Pierre Sémard; ☼ information office: 8am-7pm) just north of the train station.

The train station, **Gare Matabiau** (☎ 36 35; blvd Pierre Sémard), is about 1km northeast of the city centre. Destinations served by multiple daily direct services include Bayonne (€44, 3¾ hours) and Bordeaux (€27.70, 2½ hours).

The fare from Toulouse to Paris is €80 by Corail (6½ hours, to Gare d'Austerlitz) and €77.10 by TGV (5½ hours, to Gare Montparnasse via Bordeaux).

CORSICA (CORSE)

Though Corsica has been governed by mainland France for more than 200 years, the island remains a nation apart, with its own distinctive language, customs, character and a unique landscape: 1000km of seaswept coastline, snowcapped mountain ranges, a world-renowned marine reservation, uninhabited desert and a 'continental divide' running down the island's centre.

AJACCIO (AJACCIU)
pop 60,000
The pastel-shaded port of Ajaccio (pronounced *ja-xio*) is the most cosmopolitan city in Corsica with designer shops, fashionable restaurants and hectic traffic. There are several museums dedicated to Ajaccio's most famous native son, Napoleon Bonaparte.

Orientation & Information
Ajaccio's main street is cours Napoléon, which stretches from place de Gaulle northwards to the train station and beyond. The old city is south of place Foch.
Main tourist office (☎ 04 95 51 53 03; tourisme.fr/ajaccio; 3 blvd du Roi Jérôme; ☼ 8am-7pm Mon-Sat, 9am-1pm Sun)

Sights
You can't walk far in Ajaccio without stumbling across some reference to the Ajaccio-born boy who became Emperor of France, Napoleon Bonaparte.

The saga commences at the **Maison Bonaparte** (☎ 04 95 21 43 89; rue St-Charles; adult/concession €4/2.60; ☼ 9am-noon & 2-6pm Tue-Sun, 2-6pm Mon

Apr-Sep, 10am-noon & 2-5pm Tue-Sat, 2-5pm Mon Oct-Mar), the grand building in the old city where Napoleon was born and spent the first nine years of his childhood.

The impressive **Musée Fesch** (☎ 04 95 21 48 17; 50-52 rue du Cardinal Fesch; adult/student €5.35/3.80; ☼ 1.15-5.15pm Mon, 9.15am-12.15pm & 2.15-5.15pm Tue-Sun Apr-Jun & Sep, 1.30-6pm Mon, 9am-6pm Tue-Fri, 10.30am-6pm Sat & Sun Jul & Aug, 9.15am-12.15pm & 2.15-5.15pm Tue-Sat Oct-Mar), established by Napoleon's uncle, has the finest collection of 14th- to 19th-century Italian art outside the Louvre (mostly looted during Napoleon's foreign campaigns), including works by Titian, Botticelli, Raphael, Poussin and Bellini.

Getting There & Away
Bus companies operate from Terminal Maritime et Routier on quai l'Herminier. Most have ticket kiosks on the right as you enter the station. The **information counter** (☎ 04 95 51 55 45; ☼ 7am-7pm) provides schedules.

Eurocorse (☎ 04 95 21 06 30) and **Autocars Ricci** (☎ 04 95 51 08 19) serve the main destinations, including Bastia (€18, three hours, two daily), Bonifacio (€19.50, four hours, two or three daily), Corte (€10.50, 2¾ hours, two daily) and Porto (€11.45, 2½ hours, two daily). Services run Monday to Saturday.

The **train station** (☎ 04 95 23 11 03; place de la Gare) is staffed until 6.30pm (8pm May to September). Services include Bastia (€20.70, four hours, three to four daily) and Corte (€11, two hours, three to four daily).

The ferry terminal is in the same building as the bus station. The **SNCM ticket office** (☎ 04 95 29 66 99; 3 quai l'Herminier; ☼ 8am-6pm Mon, 8am-8pm Tue-Fri, 8am-1pm Sat) is across the street.

BASTIA
pop 37,800
Bustling Bastia, once the seat of Corsica's Genoese governors and retaining a distinctly Italian atmosphere, is Corsica's main centre of business and commerce. You can easily spend a day exploring, the old port being Bastia's highlight – but most visitors move on pretty quickly.

The focal point of the city is place St-Nicolas. Bastia's main thoroughfares are the busy shopping street of boulevard Paoli and av Maréchal Sébastiani, which links the ferry port with the train station.

There is a **main tourist office** (☎ 04 95 55 96 85; www.bastia-tourisme.com; place St-Nicolas; ☼ 8am-6pm Mon-Sat, 8am-1pm Sun).

Getting There & Away

Buses leave from several locations around town. Call the tourist office. **Eurocorse** (☎ 04 95 31 73 76) goes to Ajaccio (€18, three hours) via Corte (€10, two hours) twice daily except on Sundays.

The **train station** (☎ 04 95 32 80 61; av Maréchal Sébastiani; ☼ 6am-8.40pm Mon-Sat, 8.40am-12.40pm & 4.15-8.40pm Sun) is beside the large roundabout on square Mal-Leclerc. Destinations include Ajaccio (€20.70, four hours).

The southern ferry terminal is at the eastern end of av François Pietri. There's an **SNCM office** (☎ 04 95 54 66 81; sncm.fr; ☼ 8-11.45am & 2-5.45pm Mon-Fri, 8am-noon Sat) in the southern terminal. **Moby Lines** (☎ 04 95 34 84 94; www .mobylines.it; 4 rue du Commandant Luce de Casabianca; ☼ 8am-noon & 2-6pm Mon-Fri, 8am-noon Sat) has a bureau in the ferry terminal, open two hours before each sailing. **Corsica Ferries** (☎ 04 95 32 95 95; www.corsicaferries.com; 15 bis rue Chanoine Leschi; ☼ 8.30am-noon & 2-6pm Mon-Fri, 9am-noon Sat) is across the road from the ferry terminal.

PORTO (PORTU)

pop 460

The seaside village of Porto, nestling among huge outcrops of red granite and fragrant groves of eucalyptus, is renowned for its fiery sunsets. Hotel prices are reasonable, making it a good base for exploring Les Calanques, a spectacular mountain landscape of orange and red granite.

The **main tourist office** (☎ 04 95 26 10 55; ☼ 9am-noon & 2-6pm Mon-Sat Apr-Jun, Sep & Oct, 9am-6pm Jul & Aug) is built into the wall below the marina's upper car park.

A short trail leads up the rocks to a **Genoese tower** (€2.50; ☼ 10am-noon & 2-7pm Apr-Jun, Sep & Oct, 9am-9pm Jul & Aug). Nearby, the marina overlooks the estuary of the Porto river. On the far side, across a footbridge, there's a modest pebbly **beach** and one of Corsica's best-known **eucalyptus groves**.

Le Funtana al' Ora (☎ 04 95 26 11 65; fax 04 95 26 15 48; person/tent/car €5.50/2.20/2.20; ☼ Apr-Oct) This camp site is 2km east of Porto on the road to Évisa. Four-person bungalows cost €300/540 in low/high season.

Le Golfe (☎ 04 95 26 13 33; Marina; r low season €35-50, high season €55-70) This cheap hotel above

a café offers basic rooms, some with little balconies overlooking the bay.

Autocars SAIB (☎ 04 95 22 41 99) has two buses daily, linking Porto and Ota with Ajaccio (€11, two hours, none on Sunday). **Transports Mordiconi** (☎ 04 95 48 00 44) links Porto with Corte (€19, 2½ hours, one daily) via Évisa and Ota.

BONIFACIO (BUNIFAZIU)

pop 2700

The citadel of Bonifacio sits 70m above the Mediterranean on a rock promontory that is sometimes referred to as 'Corsica's Gibraltar'. On all sides, white limestone cliffs drop vertically into the sea, while the tall houses of the old city lean precariously over the water. The northern side of the citadel overlooks Bonifacio Sound (Goulet de Bonifacio) at the southeastern corner of which is the lively marina, while the southern ramparts afford views of Sardinia, 12km away across the Strait of Bonifacio (Bouches de Bonifacio).

The **main tourist office** (☎ 04 95 73 11 88; http: //bonifacio.com; 2 rue Fred Scamaroni; ☼ 9am-8pm Jul & Aug, 9am-noon & 2-6pm Mon-Fri, 9am-noon Sat Sep-Jun) is located in the citadel.

Sights

The steps linking rue St-Érasme with Porte de Gênes are known as Montée Rastello and Montée St-Roch further up. At the top of Montée St-Roch stands the Porte de Gênes. Just inside the gateway, you can visit the **Grand Bastion** (admission €2; ☼ 9am-6pm Mon-Sat Apr & May, Sep & Oct, 9am-6pm daily Jul & Aug) above Porte de Gênes.

Nearby, along the citadel's ramparts, there are great views from **place du Marché** and **place Manichella**.

From the citadel, the **Escalier du Roi d' Aragon** (Staircase of the King of Aragon; €2) leads down the cliff.

Outside the citadel, west along the limestone headland, stands **Église Ste-Dominique**, one of the only Gothic buildings in Corsica. Further west the elaborate tombs of the **Cimetière Marin** stand out against a backdrop of crashing waves and wheeling gulls.

Sleeping & Eating

Noncamping budget options are scarce.

Camping L'Araguina (☎ 04 95 73 02 96; av Sylvére Bohn; person/tent/car €5.50/1.70/1.85; ☼ Mar-Oct)

FRANCE

is near the Hôtel des Étrangers, shaded by olive trees and only a short walk into town.

L'Archivolto (☎ 04 95 73 17 58; rue de l'Archivolto; plats du jour €7-14; ☾ Mon-Sat) A wonderfully quirky restaurant-cum-antique shop in the citadel, serving imaginative food. Try the chicken in beer and the fresh herb tart with *brocciu* (soft white cheese).

Super Marché Simoni (93 quai Jérôme Comparetti; ☾ 8am-12.30pm & 3.30-7.30pm Mon-Sat, 8am-12.30pm Sun) is on the marina. Next door, **Coccinelle** supermarket has a fresh bakery counter.

Getting There & Away

Eurocorse (in Porto Vecchio ☎ 04 95 70 13 83) runs two buses to Ajaccio (€19.50, three to four hours) via Sarténe from Monday to Saturday. For Bastia, change at Porto Vecchio (€6.50, 45 minutes, two to four buses daily). Buses leave near the Eurocorse kiosk on the marina (summer only).

Daily ferries to Santa Teresa in Sardinia are offered by **Saremar** (☎ 04 95 73 00 96) and **Moby Lines** (☎ 04 95 73 00 29) from Bonifacio's ferry port (50 minutes, two to seven daily).

Saremar charges €6.70/8.50 one-way in low/high season, while Moby Lines charges €22/30 return. Cars cost between €21 and €43. Port taxes are €3.

CORTE (CORTI)

pop 5700

When Pasquale Paoli led Corsica to independence in 1755, one of his first acts was to make this fortified town at the centre of the island the country's capital. To this day, Corte remains a potent symbol of Corsican independence and arguably the island's most authentic town. Ringed with mountains and bordered eastwards by the forest region of Castagniccia, it's a perfect base for hiking. Some of the island's highest peaks are just west of town.

For information try the **main tourist office** (☎ 04 95 46 26 70; corte.tourisme@wanadoo.fr; La Citadelle; ☾ 9am-noon & 2-6pm Mon-Sat Apr & May, 9am-1pm & 2-7pm Mon-Sat Jun & Sep, 9am-8pm daily Jul & Aug, 9am-noon & 2-6pm Mon-Fri Oct-Mar).

Citadel

Corte's citadel juts from a rocky outcrop above the Tavignanu and Restonica Rivers and the cobbled alleyways of the Ville Haute. The highest point is the **chateau** (known as the Nid d'Aigle, or Eagle's Nest), built in 1419 by a Corsican nobleman allied with the Aragonese. It was expanded during the 18th and 19th centuries and served as a Foreign Legion base from 1962 until 1983.

Outside the ramparts, a path leads to the **belvédére** (viewing platform), which has views of the city and the Eagle's Nest. Nearby, a precarious staircase leads down to the river.

Sleeping & Eating

Hôtel de la Poste (☎ 04 95 46 01 37; 2 place du Duc de Padoue; r €33.50) This is a typically Corsican no-frills hotel with mismatched décor and run-down charm.

Camping Alivetu (☎ 04 95 46 11 09; fax 04 95 46 12 34; faubourg de St-Antoine; adult/car/tent €5/2/2; ☾ Apr-Oct) Attractive and shaded by olive trees.

Grand Café (☎ 04 95 46 00 33; 22 cours Paoli; ☾ 7am-2am) A cosy student hang-out underneath the Hôtel du Nord where you can leave your backpacks for free.

La Trattoria (☎ 04 95 46 00 76; 6 cours Paoli; menus €9-14; ☾ closed Sun) A family-run restaurant loved by locals and serving up classic Corsican meat dishes and enormous salads.

Corte's top *boulangerie* is **Casanova**, next door to La Trattoria – practically the whole town comes here to buy their cakes. There's also a **Eurospar** (7 av Xavier Luciani) and a **Casino Supermarket** (allée du 9 Septembre).

Getting There & Away

Eurocorse travels through town twice daily from Ajaccio (€9.90, 2¾ hours) towards Bastia (€8.40, 1¼ hours) except Sunday.

The **train station** (☎ 04 95 46 00 97; ☾ 6.30am-8.30pm Mon-Sat, 9.45am-noon & 4.45-8.35pm Sun) is 1km east of the city centre. Destinations include Bastia (€9.70, two hours, three to four daily) and Ajaccio (€11.00, two hours, three to four daily).

FRANCE DIRECTORY

ACCOMMODATION

During periods of peak domestic or foreign tourism popular destinations are packed out. Tourist offices will often reserve rooms (often for a fee).

Camping & Caravan Parks

Camping is immensely popular in France, and many of the thousands of camp sites are near rivers, lakes or oceans. Most close from

FRANCE

October or November to March or April. Hostels sometimes let travellers pitch tents. Gîtes de France coordinates farm camping and publishes an annual guide, *Camping à la Ferme*.

Camping in nondesignated spots, or *camping sauvage* (ie just pitching your tent anywhere) is usually illegal. Camping on the beach is not a good idea in areas with high tidal variations.

Gîtes Ruraux & B&Bs

A *gîte rural* is a self-contained holiday cottage (or part of a house) in a village or on a farm. A *chambre d'hôte*, basically a B&B, is a room in a private house rented by the night. The website www.bbfrance.com is useful for arranging B&Bs and vacation rentals.

Ask about Gîtes de France offices and brochures and guides at local tourist offices, or contact directly the **Fédération Nationale des Gîtes de France** (☎ 01 49 70 75 75; www.gites-de -france.fr; 59 rue St-Lazare, 9e, Paris; metro Trinité).

Hostels & Foyers

Official hostels are known as *auberges de jeunesse*. A hostel bed generally costs around €20 including breakfast in Paris, and €8 to €13 in the provinces.

France's major hostel associations, **Fédération Unie des Auberges de Jeunesse** (FUAJ; ☎ 01 48 04 70 30; www.fuaj.org; 9 rue de Brantome, 3e, Paris; metro Rambuteau) and **Ligue Française pour les Auberges de la Jeunesse** (LFAJ; ☎ 01 44 16 78 78; www.auberges-de-jeunesse.com; 7 rue Vergniaud, 13e, Paris; metro Glaciére) will require you to have or purchase a HI card or a nightly Welcome Stamp. You can bring your own sleeping sheet or rent one for a small fee.

The nonprofit organisation **Union des Centres de Rencontres Internationales de France** (UCRIF; ☎ 01 40 26 57 64; www.ucrif.asso.fr) has 'international holiday centres' with bedrooms, dorm rooms and restaurant facilities.

In university towns, *foyers d'étudiant* (student dormitories) are sometimes converted for use by travellers during summer. Relatively unknown, these places frequently have space when other hostels are full.

Hotels

A double has one double bed, so specify if you prefer *deux lits séparés* (two twin beds). **Logis de France** (☎ 01 45 84 83 84; www.logis-de-france .fr) publishes an annual guide with maps.

ACTIVITIES

France's varied geography and climate make it a superb place for a wide range of outdoor pursuits, and its stunning scenery lends itself to adventure sports and exhilarating outdoor activities of all kinds.

Adventure Sports

France is a top spot for adventurous activities. In big cities and picturesque places, particularly the Côte d'Azur and the Alps, local companies offer all kinds of high-adrenaline pursuits such as canyoning and bungy jumping.

Cycling

Some of the best areas for cycling (with varying grades of difficulty) are in the French Alps, the Jura, and the Pyrenees, the Dordogne, Quercy, Brittany, Normandy and the Atlantic coast. Lonely Planet's *Cycling France* includes essential maps, directions, technical tips and advice.

Skiing

France has more than 400 ski resorts in the Alps, the Jura, the Pyrenees, the Vosges, the Massif Central and even Corsica. The ski season generally lasts from December to March or April. January and February tend to have the best overall conditions.

The Alps have some of Europe's finest (and priciest) ski facilities. Much cheaper and less glitzy, smaller, low-altitude stations are in the Pyrenees and the Massif Central.

One of the cheapest ways to ski in France is to buy a package deal before leaving home. Websites for online bookings include www.ski-europe.com and www.alps week.com.

Walking

France is crisscrossed by a staggering 120,000km of *sentiers balisés* (marked walking paths), which pass through every imaginable kind of terrain (note that there are restrictions on where you can camp, especially in national parks). Probably the best-known trails are the *sentiers de grande randonnée*, long-distance footpaths marked by red-and-white striped track indicators.

The **Club Alpin Français** (☎ 01 53 72 87 00; www .clubalpin.com; 24 av de Laumiére, 19e, Paris; metro Laumiére) has a centre with useful information in Paris – joining is probably worthwhile if you're doing a great deal of hiking.

Lonely Planet's *Walking in France* is packed with essential practical information.

Water Sports

France has lovely beaches. The fine, sandy beaches along the family-oriented Atlantic coast (eg near La Rochelle) are less crowded than their often pebbly counterparts on the Côte d'Azur. Corsica has some magnificent spots. Brittany and the north coast are also popular (though cooler) beach destinations.

The best surfing in France is on the Atlantic coast around Biarritz, where waves can reach heights of 4m. Windsurfing is popular wherever there's water and a breeze, and renting equipment is often possible on lakes.

White-water rafting and kayaking are practised on many French rivers, especially in the Massif Central and the Alps. The **Fédération Française de Canoë-Kayak** (FFCK; ☎ 01 45 11 08 50; www.ffck.org) can supply information on canoeing and kayaking clubs in France.

BUSINESS HOURS

Shop hours are usually 9am or 10am to 6pm or 7pm, often (except in Paris) with a break from noon or 1pm to 2pm or 3pm. Most businesses close on Sunday; exceptions include grocery stores, *boulangeries* (bakeries) and *pâtisseries* (cake and pastry shops). Many also close on Monday.

Restaurants are usually open for lunch between noon and 2pm and for dinner from 7.30pm. Cafés open from early morning until around midnight. Bars usually open early evening and close at 1am or 2am.

Banks usually open from 9am to 1pm and 2pm to 5pm, Monday to Friday or Tuesday to Saturday. Post offices generally open 8.30am or 9am to 5pm or 6pm on weekdays (perhaps with a midday break) and Saturday morning.

Supermarkets open Monday to Saturday usually from about 9.30am to 7pm (plus a midday break in smaller towns); some open on Sunday morning.

EMBASSIES & CONSULATES
French Embassies & Consulates

France's diplomatic and consular representatives abroad are listed on www.france .diplomatie.fr.

Australia embassy (☎ 02-6216 0100; www.ambafrance -au.org; 6 Perth Ave, Yarralumla, ACT 2600) consulate (☎ 02-9261 5779; www.consulfrance-sydney.org; 20th floor, St Martin's Tower, 31 Market St, Sydney, NSW 2000)
Canada embassy (☎ 613-789 1795; www.ambafrance -ca.org; 42 Sussex Dr, Ottawa, Ont K1M 2C9) consulate (☎ 416-925 8041; www.consulfrance-toronto.org; 130 Bloor West, Suite 400, Toronto, Ont M5S 1N5)
Germany embassy (☎ 030-590039 000; www.botschaft -frankreich.de; Parizer Platz 5, Berlin, 10117) consulate (☎ 089-419 4110; Möhlstrasse 5, Munich, 81675)
Italy embassy (☎ 06-686011; www.ambafrance-it.org; Piazza Farnese 67, Rome, 00186)
Netherlands embassy (☎ 070-312 5800; www .ambafrance-nl.org; Smidsplein 1, The Hague, 2514 BT) consulate (☎ 020-530 6969; www.consulfrance -amsterdam.org; Vijzelgracht 2, Amsterdam, 1017 HR)
New Zealand embassy (☎ 04-384 2555; www .ambafrance-nz.org; Rural Bank Building, 34-42 Manners St, Wellington)
UK embassy (☎ 020-7073 1000; www.ambafrance -uk.org; 58 Knightsbridge, London SW1X 7JT) consulate (☎ 020-7073 1200; 21 Cromwell Rd, London SW7 2EN) visa section (☎ 020-7838 2051; 6A Cromwell Place, London SW7 2EW)
USA embassy (☎ 202-944 6000; 4101 Reservoir Rd NW, Washington, DC 20007) consulate (☎ 212-606 3600/89; www.consulfrance-newyork.org; 934 Fifth Ave, New York, NY 10021) consulate (☎ 415-397 4330; www.consulfrance -sanfrancisco.org; 540 Bush St, San Francisco, CA 94108)

Embassies & Consulates in France

All foreign embassies can be found in Paris. Many countries – including the USA, Canada and most European countries – also have consulates in other major cities. To find an embassy or consulate not listed here, look up Ambassades et Consulats in the Yellow Pages (Pages Jaunes; www.pagesjaunes.fr) for Paris.

The countries represented in Paris include the following:
Australia (Map pp378-9; ☎ 01 40 59 33 00; www .austgov.fr; 4 rue Jean Rey, 15e; metro Bir Hakeim)
Canada (Map pp378-9; ☎ 01 44 43 29 00; www.amb -canada.fr; 35 av Montaigne, 8e; metro Franklin D Roosevelt) consulate (☎ 04 9392 93 22; 10 rue Lamartine, Nice)
Ireland (☎ 01 70 20 00 20; 33 rue Miromesnil, 8e; metro Miromesnil)
Netherlands (☎ 01 40 62 33 00; www.amb-pays-bas .fr; 7 rue Eblé, 7e; metro St-François Xavier)
New Zealand (☎ 01 45 01 43 43; www.nzembassy .com; 7 ter rue Léonard de Vinci, 16e; metro Victor Hugo)
UK (☎ 01 44 51 31 00; www.amb-grandebretagne .fr; 35 rue du Faubourg St-Honoré, 8e; metro Concorde) consulate (☎ 01 44 51 3102; 16 bis rue d'Anjou, 8e; metro

Madeleine) consulate (☎ 04 93 62 13 56; 26 av Notre Dame, Nice) consulate (☎ 04 91 15 72 10; 24 av du Prado, Marseille)

USA (☎ 01 43 12 22 22; www.amb-usa.fr; 2 av Gabriel, 8e; metro Concorde) consulate (☎ 01 43 12 47 08; 2 rue St-Florentin, 1er; metro Concorde) consulate (☎ 04 93 88 89 55; 7 av Gustav V, Nice, 06000) consulate (☎ 04 91 5492 00; place Varian Fry, Marseille)

FESTIVALS & EVENTS

Most French cities, towns and villages have at least one major music, dance, theatre, cinema or art festival each year.

MAY & JUNE

May Day (France, 1 May) Workers day is celebrated with trade union parades and diverse protests. People give each other *muguet* (lilies of the valley) for good luck. No-one works (except waiters and *muguet* sellers).

International Film Festival (Cannes, mid-May; www .festival-cannes.com) The stars walk the red carpet at Cannes, the epitome of see-and-be-seen cinema events in Europe.

Fête de la Musique (France, 21 June) Bands, orchestras, crooners, buskers and spectators take to the streets for this national celebration of music.

JULY

National Day (France, 14 July) Fireworks, parades and all-round hoo-ha to commemorate the storming of the Bastille in 1789, symbol of the French Revolution.

Gay Pride (Paris and other cities, July; www.gaypride .fr) Effervescent street parades, performances and parties throughout Paris and other major cities.

AUGUST & SEPTEMBER

Festival Interceltique (Lorient, August; www.festival -interceltique.com) This event pulls hordes of Celts from Brittany and the UK for a huge fiesta of their shared culture.

DECEMBER

Christmas Markets (Alsace, December) Alsace is the place to be for a traditional-style festive season, with world-famous Christmas markets, decorations and celebrations.

HOLIDAYS

The following *jours fériés* (public holidays) are observed in France.

New Year's Day (Jour de l'An) 1 January – parties in larger cities; fireworks tend to be subdued by international standards

Easter Sunday and Monday (Pâques & lundi de Pâques) Late March/April

May Day (Fête du Travail) 1 May – traditional parades

Victoire 1945 8 May – the Allied victory in Europe that ended WWII

Ascension Thursday (L'Ascension) May – celebrated on the 40th day after Easter

Pentecost/Whit Sunday and Whit Monday (Pentecôte & lundi de Pentecôte) Mid-May to mid-June – celebrated on the seventh Sunday after Easter

Bastille Day/National Day (Fête Nationale) 14 July – *the* national holiday

Assumption Day (L'Assomption) 15 August

All Saints' Day (La Toussaint) 1 November

Remembrance Day (L'onze novembre) 11 November – celebrates the WWI armistice

Christmas (Noël) 25 December

MONEY

The official currency of France is the euro. You always get a better exchange rate in-country, though it's a good idea to arrive with enough local currency to take a taxi to a hotel. ATMs, or *distributeurs automatiques de billets* (DAB), are plentiful in all major cities and towns. Visa and MasterCard (Access or Eurocard) are widely accepted. In general cards can be used in shops, supermarkets, for train travel, car rentals, autoroute tolls and cash advances. Don't assume that you can pay for a meal or a budget hotel with a credit card – inquire first.

For lost cards, these numbers operate 24 hours:

Amex (☎ 01 47 77 72 00) Amex offices arrange on-the-spot replacements.

Diners Club (☎ 0810 314 159)

MasterCard, Eurocard & Access (Eurocard France; ☎ 0 800 90 13 87)

Visa (Carte Bleue; ☎ 0 800 90 20 33)

For lost travellers cheques call **Amex** (☎ 0 800 90 86 00) and **Thomas Cook** (☎ 0 800 90 83 30) for replacements.

POST

Each of France's 17,000 post offices is marked with a yellow or brown sign reading 'La Poste'. Since La Poste also has banking, finance and bill-paying functions, queues can be very long, but there are automatic machines for postage.

Postal Rates

Domestic letters of up to 20g cost €0.50. Internationally, there are three different zones: a letter or package under 20g/2kg costs

€0.50/12.50 to Zone A (EU, Switzerland, Iceland, Norway); €0.75/14 to Zone B (the rest of Europe and Africa); and €0.90/20.50 to Zone C (North and South America, Asia, the Middle East and Australasia). Worldwide express mail delivery, called **Chronopost** (☎ 0825 80 18 01), costs a fortune and is not as rapid as advertised.

Receiving Mail

Collecting poste-restante mail costs €0.50; you must show your passport or national ID card. Mail will only be kept for 15 days. Poste-restante mail not addressed to a specific branch will go to the city's main post office.

TELEPHONE
International Dialling

Phonecards offer better international rates than Country Direct services (which allow you to be billed by the long-distance carrier you use at home). To call reverse-charges (collect; *en PCV*) or a person-to-person call (*avec préavis*), dial ☎ 3123 or ☎ 0 800 990011 (for the USA and Canada) and ☎ 0 800 990061 for Australia. Expect about €12 for a three-minute call.

Mobile Phones

France uses GSM 900/1800, which is compatible with the rest of Europe and Australia but not with the North American GSM 1900 (though some North Americans have GSM 1900/900 phones that do work here).

The three major mobile networks are **Bouygues** (☎ 0 810 6301 00; www.bouygtel.com), France Telecom's **Orange** (☎ 0 800 8308 00; www.orange.fr) and **SFR** (0800 10 60 00; www.sfr.com). If you already have a compatible phone, you can by a prepaid phone SIM-card with a mobile phone number. You can purchase a recharge card at most *tabacs*.

National Dialling Areas

France has five telephone dialling areas. You dial the same 10-digit number no matter where you are, but it is cheaper to call locally. The five regional area codes are: ☎ 01 (the Paris region); ☎ 02 (the northwest); ☎ 03 (the northeast); ☎ 04 (the southeast; including Corsica) and ☎ 05 (the southwest).

For France Telecom's *services des renseignements* (directory inquiries), dial ☎ 12 (around €0.45 per minute). Not all operators speak English. Emergency numbers and 0800 numbers can be dialled free from public and private telephones.

Public Phones & Phonecards

Almost all public telephones in France are card-operated. Cards can be purchased for €7.50 or €15 at post offices, *tabacs* (tobacconists) and anywhere that you see a blue sticker reading '*télécarte en vente ici*'. A whole bevy of other cards are available for cheap international calls.

VISAS

EU nationals and citizens of Switzerland, Iceland and Norway need only a passport or national identity card to enter France. Citizens of Australia, the USA, Canada, New Zealand, Japan and Israel do not need visas to visit France as tourists for up to three months.

Those not exempt will need a visa allowing unlimited travel throughout the entire EU zone for 90 days. Apply to the consulate of the country you are entering first, or that will be your main destination. Among other things, you will need medical insurance and proof of sufficient funds to support yourself. See www.eurovisa.com for information.

GERMANY

Germany

HIGHLIGHTS

- **Berlin** The most culture, the most history, the most buzz, the most fun you'll have in a European capital (p451)
- **Dresden** Pomp, circumstance and lecture-loads of students amid Germany's finest baroque architecture (p463)
- **Munich** A heady mix of high culture, beer gardens and laid-back living (p472)
- **Schloss Neuschwanstein** This dreamlike castle at the foot of the Alps will have you believing in fairy tales (p481)
- **Best journey** Hop on a boat and cruise down the Rhine (p493)
- **Off-the-beaten track** Pedal or paddle for the uninterrupted horizon in the lake plains of Mecklenburg (p516)

FAST FACTS

- **Area** 356,866 sq km (about two-thirds the size of France)
- **ATMs** Readily available
- **Budget** €20-50 per day
- **Capital** Berlin
- **Country code** ☎ 49, international access code 00
- **Famous for** beer, BMWs, invading Poland
- **Head of State** President Horst Köhler
- **Language** German
- **Money** euro (A$1 = €0.58, CA$1 = €0.64, ¥100 = €0.73, NZ$1 = 0.54, UK£1 = €1.45, US$1 = 0.81)
- **Phrases** Hallo (hello), tschüss (goodbye), danke (thank you), Entschuldigung (sorry), Igitt! (yuck)
- **Population** 83 million

- **Time** GMT/UTC + 1
- **Visas** None required for passport holders of the EU, the USA, Canada, Australia and New Zealand.

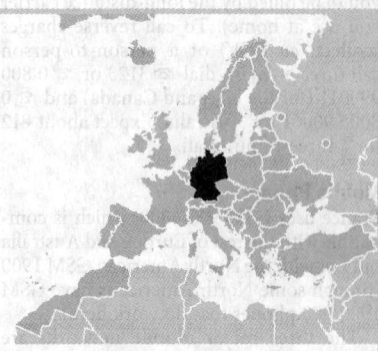

TRAVEL HINTS

Try the end carriages on busy trains – most people head for the middle. Fassbier (draught beer) is cheaper than Flaschenbier (bottled).

ROAMING GERMANY

Try combining major cities (Berlin, Dresden, Munich, Hamburg) with the scenic heartlands (Thuringia, the Rhine Valley, the Black Forest).

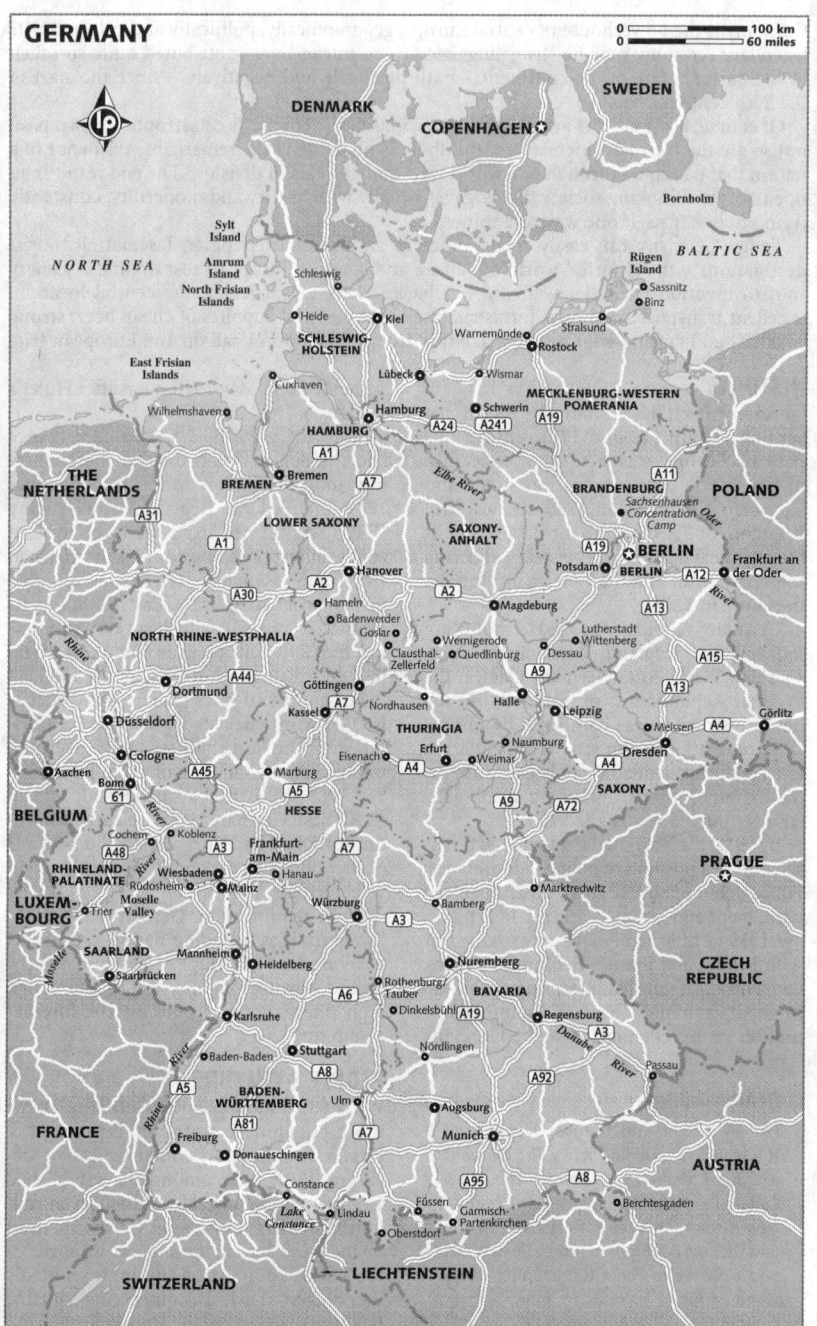

GERMANY

GERMANY

Germany is the powerhouse of central Europe, geographically, politically and culturally. Its legendary economy may be struggling, but few countries have contributed quite so much to the current state of the continent – both positively and negatively – since the start of the 20th century.

Of course, most visitors are still very conscious of the country's catastrophe-strewn past, but so are the Germans themselves, and there is no denying the remarkable resilience of a nation that has come through two world wars and 40 years of division. The end result is an open, forward-looking society that engages equally with history and modernity, constantly trying to better itself one way or another.

Today Germany can easily rival France as an accessible, popular, fascinating tourist destination, with centuries' worth of culture and some of Europe's most dramatic scenery (not to mention friendlier waiters). For backpackers in particular, the central location, excellent transport and hostel infrastructures, and plentiful supplies of cheap beer, strong cocktails and cutting-edge music make this an essential port of call on any European trip.

HISTORY

Germany itself is a relatively recent invention – until the mid-19th century this part of Europe was a motley collection of constantly changing nation-states and sovereign territories. In 1866 the powerful Kingdom of Prussia (present-day Brandenburg) annexed the northern states, allowing the creation of a united Germany for the first time in 1871.

Germany's rapid growth led to mounting tensions with England, Russia and France, sparking WWI. After Germany's defeat the Weimar Republic was proclaimed, but the new government was hampered by impossible reparation payments. Hyperinflation and economic depression bolstered support for extreme groups, including Adolf Hitler's National Socialists (Nazis).

By 1933, the Nazis had manoeuvred themselves into a position of political dominance; Hitler was appointed chancellor, dissolved parliament and assumed control. In September 1939 he attacked Poland, provoking war with Britain and France. Behind the scenes, concentration camps exterminated an estimated six million Jews and another one million more 'enemies of state'. Germany surrendered in May 1945, soon after Hitler's suicide.

After the war, the USA, Britain, France and the Soviet Union divided the country into four occupation zones. In September 1949 the Federal Republic of Germany (FRG) was formed from the three western zones; in response, the communist German Democratic Republic (GDR) was founded in the Soviet zone, with (East) Berlin as its capital. To prevent skilled workers emigrating, the GDR built a wall around West Berlin in 1961, closing its border with the FRG.

For almost 40 years capitalist and socialist Germany coexisted uneasily. In 1989, however, the Peaceful Revolution overtook the reform-shy GDR regime. On 9 November 1989 the Berlin Wall opened, and in 1990 East Germans voted clearly for reunification. The Allies ended the postwar occupation, and the countries were unified on 3 October 1990.

Since reunification, Germany has established itself as a leading nation in Europe; despite soaring unemployment and an economic downturn, it looks set to maintain a high international profile for the foreseeable future.

READING UP

For an insight into German history and the issues surrounding it, try *The Germans* (Gordon A Craig, 1997), *German Thought & Culture* (HJ Hahn, 1995), *The Third Reich: A New History* (Michael Burleigh, 2001), *The East German Dictatorship* (Corey Ross, 2002) and *Goodbye to Berlin* (Christopher Isherwood, 1939).

PEOPLE & CULTURE

With 83 million people, Germany is the most populous country in Europe after Russia. Immigration compensates for declining birth rates among the established German population. More than seven million foreigners now live in Germany, most in the west; by far the biggest minority is the Turkish population (Berlin is reputedly the biggest Turkish community outside Istanbul), followed by immigrants from

Eastern Europe, Russia and the former Soviet states.

Racial problems are relatively rare in Germany, but the international climate since the USA's 'war on terror' has increased tension between local and Muslim communities, often hindering the integration process.

On a personal level Germans are generally open, personable and interested in enjoying life, a far cry from their common strict and humourless reputation. However, in public this is quite a formal culture, and manners remain important. A little politeness goes a long way with officialdom in particular, and you should always introduce yourself by name when making a phone call.

ARTS
Historically Germany has always been strong in the arts, with the legacies of such literary, musical, artistic and architectural greats as Goethe, JS Bach, Karl Friedrich Schinkel and Caspar David Friedrich providing a rich vein of inspiration for modern successors like Günter Grass, Arnold Schönberg, Walter Gropius and Paul Klee.

Today the arts still occupy a key place at the heart of German culture. Tradition is scrupulously preserved around the country, but for the new generation of artists experimentation is the way forward. Germany is a hotbed of exciting new architecture, avant garde art and left-field literature. Above all, the burgeoning popular music scene is much more wide-ranging than radio playlists suggest, particularly where electronic dance music is concerned.

ENVIRONMENT
Germany can be divided from north to south into several geographical regions, including the Northern Lowlands, the Central Uplands (Germany's heartland), the Alpine Foothills and the Alps.

German weather can be variable. The most reliable weather is from May to October. Shoulder periods (late March to May and September to October) can bring fewer tourists and surprisingly pleasant weather. Camping season is May to September.

Environmental issues are taken seriously in Germany, and almost every household will have several separate bins for recycling glass, packaging, paper and organic waste. On a

national level, Germany regularly introduces environmental initiatives to combat problems such as industrial emissions and energy wastage, and actively supports international agreements such as the Kyoto Treaty.

TRANSPORT

GETTING THERE & AWAY
Air
The main arrival and departure points in Germany are Frankfurt, Berlin, Munich and Düsseldorf. **Berlin Schönefeld** (www.berlin-airport.de) is the favoured airport for low-cost airlines, with companies such as Ryanair, Easyjet, Air Berlin and Germanwings serving destinations throughout Europe.

From the US, Lufthansa, United Airlines, Air Canada and Delta Air Lines have the most frequent flights. You can often get better fares by flying with European carriers and changing planes at their home-country hub. Asian carriers offer the cheapest – but often the most indirect – flights from Australia and New Zealand.

Boat
If you're heading to Scandinavia or the UK, the German port options are Hamburg, Lübeck, Rostock, Sassnitz and Kiel. The most common destinations are Trelleborg, Gothenburg and Oslo; other services go as far as Helsinki, Tallinn and St Petersburg.

GERMANY

Bus

It's generally cheaper to get to Germany by bus than by train or plane, but you trade price for speed. **Eurolines** (www.eurolines.com), a consortium of national bus companies, operates throughout the continent.

Sample one-way fares and travel times include London–Frankfurt (€76, 16 hours), Amsterdam–Frankfurt (€39, eight hours), Paris–Hamburg (€62, 11½ hours), Paris–Cologne (€39, 6½ hours), Prague–Berlin (€31, seven hours) and Barcelona–Frankfurt (€81, 20 hours).

Under-26 youth fares save around 10%. Tickets can be bought at most train stations in Germany. Eurolines' German arm is **Deutsche-Touring** (☎ 069-790 350; www.deutsche-touring.com).

Car & Motorcycle

Germany is served by an excellent *autobahn* (motorway) system. If you're coming from the UK, the quickest option is via the Channel Tunnel; ferries take longer but are cheaper. Either way, you can be in Germany three hours after arriving in France.

You must have third-party insurance to enter Germany with a car or motorcycle.

Hitching & Ride Services

Lonely Planet does not recommend hitching, but should you decide to try it you may encounter long delays. The best way to pick up lifts is to head for a service area on the main route you wish to use.

Aside from hitching, the cheapest way to get to Germany is as a paying passenger in a private car. Rides are arranged through *Mitfahrzentrale* (ride-sharing agencies) in many German cities; you pay a reservation fee to the agency and a share of petrol and costs to the driver. Tourist offices can direct you to local agencies, or call ☎ 194 40 in large German cities.

Train

Trains are a lot more comfortable (and expensive) than buses. Long-distance trains

---

DEPARTURE TAX

The international airline departure tax is always included in your ticket price on purchase.

---

between major German cities and other countries are called EuroCity (EC) trains. The main German hubs with the best connections to/from major European cities are Hamburg (Scandinavia); Cologne (France, Belgium and the Netherlands, plus London via Eurostar); Munich (southern and southeastern Europe); and Berlin (Eastern Europe). Frankfurt-am-Main has the widest range of international connections, but not always the quickest.

Generally the longer international routes are served by at least one day train and often a night train as well. Many night trains only carry sleeping cars, which cost more but are considerably more comfortable than a standard compartment.

GETTING AROUND
Bicycle

Radwandern (bicycle touring) is very popular in Germany. Favoured routes include along the Rhine, Moselle, Elbe and Danube Rivers and around the Lake Constance area. Cycling is strictly *verboten* (forbidden) on *autobahns*. There are well-equipped cycling shops in almost every town, and a fairly active market for used touring bikes. Simple three-gear bicycles can be hired from around €8/32 per day/week, and more robust mountain bikes from €10/48. The DB publishes *Bahn&Bike*, an excellent handbook covering shops, routes, maps and other resources.

A separate ticket must be purchased whenever you carry your bike on most trains (€3 to €6). Most trains (excluding ICEs) have at least one bicycle compartment.

The central office for the main cycling organisation in Gemany is the **Allgemeiner Deutscher Fahrrad Club** (ADFC; ☎ 0421-346 290; www.adfc.de in German) in Bremen.

Boat

Boats are most likely to be used for basic transport when travelling to the Frisian Islands, although tours along the Rhine, Elbe and Moselle Rivers are also popular.

Bus

The bus network functions primarily in support of the rail network, cutting corners and going where trains don't. Bus stations or stops are usually near the train station in any town.

Deutsche Bahn (DB) agents have information on certain regional services; otherwise, check with tourist offices. Deutsche-Touring services include the Romantic and Castle Roads buses in southern Germany, as well as organised bus tours of a week or more. See p479 for details.

Car & Motorcycle

Although hiring a vehicle can be a great way to tour the country, it's expensive. For information, contact the Munich-based **Allgemeiner Deutscher Automobil Club** (ADAC; ☎ 089-767 60); it has offices in all major cities and a national breakdown service.

Local Transport

Local transport is excellent within big cities and small towns, generally based on buses, *Strassenbahn* (trams), S-Bahn and/or U-Bahn (underground trains). Fares cover all these and are generally determined by zones or the time travelled. Multiticket strips or day passes are generally better value than single-ride tickets.

Train

Operated almost entirely by the **Deutsche Bahn** (DB; www.bahn.de), the German train system is one of the best in Europe. Schedules are integrated throughout the country so that connections between trains are tight, often only five minutes. Of course, this means that when a train is late, connections are missed. Put some slack in your itinerary so you won't miss a connection and be stranded.

German trains fall into specific classifications; *Zuschläge* (supplements) for faster trains are built into fares. From fastest to slowest, these include InterCityExpress (ICE), InterCity (IC) or EuroCity (EC), InterRegio (IR), RegionalExpress (RE), StadtExpress (SE), RegionalBahn (RB) and S-Bahn (not to be confused with U-Bahn, which are run by local authorities who don't honour rail passes). EN, ICN and D trains are generally night services.

Buy your ticket before boarding, as buying from a conductor carries a surcharge (€1.50 to €4.50). Ticket agents cheerfully accept credit cards, as do most machines. During peak travel periods, a reservation (€2.50) on a long-distance train can mean the difference between squatting in the corridor or relaxing in your own seat.

EMERGENCY NUMBERS

- **Ambulance** (☎ 112)
- **Fire brigade** (☎ 112)
- **Police** (☎ 110)

A host of special train fares offered by DB allow you to cut costs for journeys. Most ticket agents are quite willing to help you find the cheapest options for your intended trip. For schedule and fare information (available in English), you can call ☎ 01805-996 633 from anywhere in Germany (€0.13 per minute).

Travel agents outside Germany sell German Rail Passes valid for unlimited travel on all DB trains for a given number of days within a 30-day period; prices start at US$180 for four days. They're worth it if you're going to do a few long intercity journeys with stops in between. These are only available to visitors from outside Europe.

Eurail and Inter-Rail passes are also valid in Germany.

BERLIN

☎ 030 / pop 3.35 million

Pomp and circumstance, character and history, rags and riches, boozing and cruising – Berlin is a city that thrives on variety and takes great pride in catering for every taste (and budget). Above all, it's a city that has made a virtue out of its past upheavals, constantly reinventing itself like some feckless ageing rock star. As the tourist board proudly proclaimed in a recent campaign, Berlin really is 'different every hour', and exploring the many sides of this shapeshifting metropolis could take a day or the rest of your life.

ORIENTATION

Most travellers endeavour to visit only eight of Berlin's *Bezirken* (districts) – Charlottenburg, Tiergarten, Mitte, Prenzlauer Berg, Friedrichshain, Kreuzberg, Schöneberg and Wilmersdorf.

At the city's centre, Unter den Linden, the fashionable wide avenue of aristocratic old Berlin, extends east from the Brandenburg

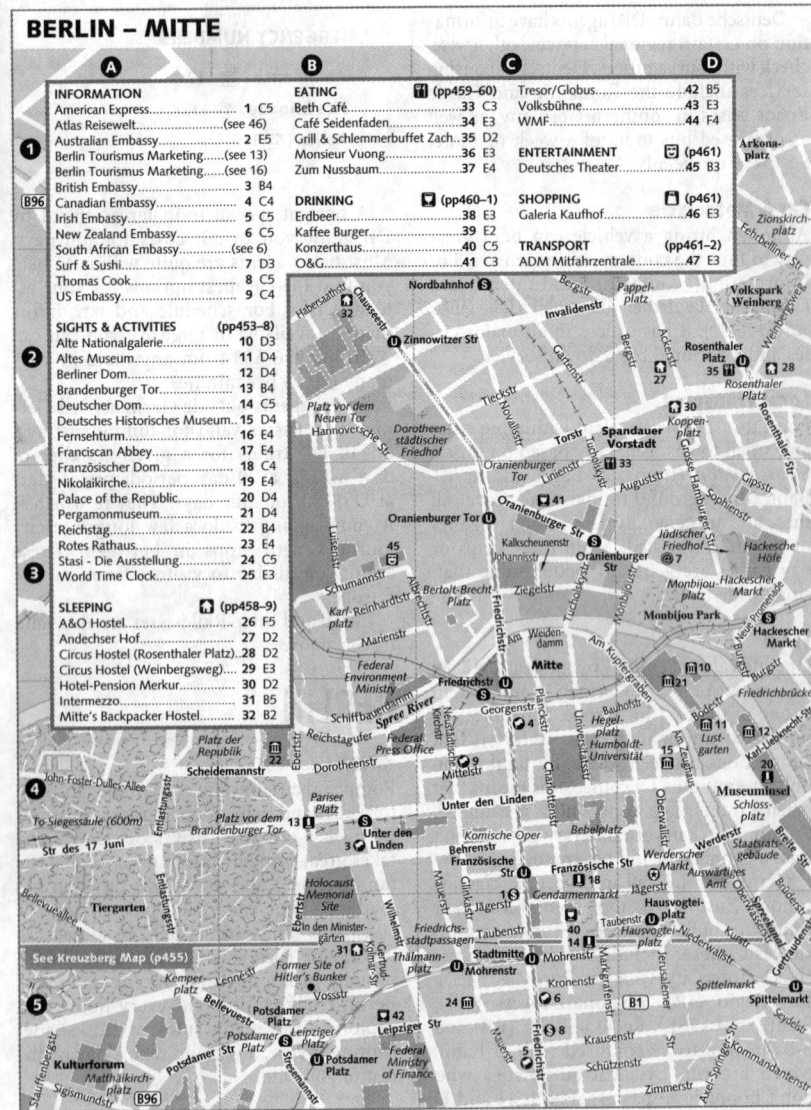

BERLIN – MITTE

INFORMATION	
American Express	1 C5
Atlas Reisewelt	(see 46)
Australian Embassy	2 E5
Berlin Tourismus Marketing	(see 13)
Berlin Tourismus Marketing	(see 16)
British Embassy	3 B4
Canadian Embassy	4 C4
Irish Embassy	5 C5
New Zealand Embassy	6 C5
South African Embassy	(see 6)
Surf & Sushi	7 D3
Thomas Cook	8 C5
US Embassy	9 C4

SIGHTS & ACTIVITIES	(pp453–8)
Alte Nationalgalerie	10 D3
Altes Museum	11 D4
Berliner Dom	12 D4
Brandenburger Tor	13 B4
Deutscher Dom	14 C5
Deutsches Historisches Museum	15 D4
Fernsehturm	16 E4
Franciscan Abbey	17 E4
Französischer Dom	18 C4
Nikolaikirche	19 E4
Palace of the Republic	20 D4
Pergamonmuseum	21 D4
Reichstag	22 B4
Rotes Rathaus	23 E4
Stasi - Die Ausstellung	24 C5
World Time Clock	25 E3

SLEEPING	(pp458–9)
A&O Hostel	26 F5
Andechser Hof	27 D2
Circus Hostel (Rosenthaler Platz)	28 D2
Circus Hostel (Weinbergsweg)	29 E3
Hotel-Pension Merkur	30 D2
Intermezzo	31 B5
Mitte's Backpacker Hostel	32 B2

EATING	(pp459–60)
Beth Café	33 C3
Café Seidenfaden	34 E3
Grill & Schlemmerbuffet Zach	35 D2
Monsieur Vuong	36 E3
Zum Nussbaum	37 E4

DRINKING	(pp460–1)
Erdbeer	38 E3
Kaffee Burger	39 E2
Konzerthaus	40 C5
O&G	41 C3

Tresor/Globus	42 B5
Volksbühne	43 E3
WMF	44 F4

ENTERTAINMENT	(p461)
Deutsches Theater	45 B3

SHOPPING	(p461)
Galeria Kaufhof	46 E3

TRANSPORT	(pp461–2)
ADM Mitfahrzentrale	47 E3

Gate towards Alexanderplatz, once the heart of socialist Germany. En route are some of Berlin's finest museums and the unsightly Fernsehturm (TV tower). The former western centre, around Zoo station, is still busy but is rapidly losing its privileged status as the Mitte district has reasserted its central position.

INFORMATION
Discount Cards
Berlin-Potsdam Welcome Card (72hr €21) Unlimited transport for three days and discounted admission to major museums, shows, attractions, tours and boat cruises.

SchauLust Museen Berlin (72hr €10) Free admission to over 50 museums.

To Pension Amsterdam (600m); STA Travel (700m); Sonntags Club (800m)

To X Bar (300m); Al Hamra (500m); Lette'm Sleep (750m)

To Friedrichshain (500m); Odyssee Globetrotter Hostel & Hotel 26 (1.5km); Nil (1.7km); Dachkammer (1.8km); Plan@t Internettreff & Feuermelder (2km)

To East Side Gallery (1.5km)

Netz Galaxie (Map p457; ☎ 7870 6446; Joachimstaler-strasse 19; per hr €1; ⏰ 11am-2am)

Plan@t Internettreff (☎ 209 488; Niederbarnim-strasse 4; per hr €2; ⏰ from 11am)

Surf & Sushi (Map p452-3; ☎ 2838 4898; Oranien-burger Strasse 17; per 30min €2.50; ⏰ from noon)

Medical Services
Kassenärztliche Bereitschaftsdienst (☎ 310 031) 24-hour medical aid, advice and referrals.

Money
American Express (Map pp452-3; Friedrichstrasse 172)
Reisebank (Map p457; Hardenbergplatz 1)
Thomas Cook (Map pp452-30; Friedrichstrasse 56)

Post
Main post office (Map p4570; Joachimstalerstrasse)

Tourist Information
Berlin Tourismus Marketing (☎ 250 025; www .berlin-tourism.de) Europa-Center (Map p457; Budapester Strasse 45) Mitte (Map pp452-3; Brandenburger Tor) Alexanderplatz (Map pp452-3; Fernsehturm)
EurAide (Map p457; Bahnhof Zoo; ⏰ 8am-noon & 1-4pm Mon-Sat) English-language service.

Travel Agencies
Alternativ Tours (Map p457; ☎ 881 2089; Wilmersdorfer Strasse 94)
Atlas Reisewelt (Map pp452-3; ☎ 247 5760; Galeria Kaufhof, Alexanderplatz 9)
STA Travel Prenzlauer Berg (☎ 2859 8264; Gleimstrasse 28) Charlottenburg (Map p457; ☎ 311 0950; Goethestrasse 73)

SIGHTS & ACTIVITIES
Among Berlin's 170 museums, the state museums (marked 'SMB' here) are reliable highlights. Unless otherwise noted, SMB museums are closed Monday and are free the first Sunday of each month; admission is by day pass (adult/concession €6/3), which generally allows admission to other nearby or related SMB museums.

Central Berlin
BRANDENBURGER TOR & REICHSTAG
At the western end of Unter den Linden is the **Brandenburger Tor** (Brandenburg Gate; Map pp452-3), the symbol of Berlin and once the boundary between east and west. Built in 1791 by Karl Gotthard Langhans, it's crowned by the Quadriga, a winged Goddess of Victory in a four-horse chariot.

Emergency
Police Headquarters (☎ 6995; Platz der Luftbrücke 6) Beside Tempelhof airport.

Internet Access
Al Hamra (☎ 4285 0095; Raumerstrasse 16; per 15min €1; ⏰ from 10am) Surfing goes exotic with waterpipes and cocktails.

GETTING INTO TOWN

Schönefeld airport, Berlin's main hub, is served by Airport Express RE trains to Zoo station every half-hour (€2.40, 33 minutes). The train also stops at Ostbahnhof, Alexanderplatz and Friedrichstrasse. A taxi to Zoo station costs between €25 and €35.

Tegel airport is connected to Zoo station by bus No 109 (€2.10). JetExpress Bus TXL (€3.10) goes via Unter den Linden and Potsdamer Platz.

Just north of the gate is the **Reichstag** (Map pp452-3; ☾ 8am-midnight, last admission 10pm), where at midnight on 2 October 1990 the reunification of Germany was enacted. Again the home of the German parliament, the Reichstag has become Berlin's number one attraction, thanks to Sir Norman Foster's stunning 1999 reconstruction. The lift to the distinctive glass cupola is free and doesn't require reservations; tours of the building's interior can be arranged by writing to Deutscher Bundestag, Besucherdienst, Platz der Republik 1, 11011 Berlin.

ALEXANDERPLATZ

Soaring above the city, the restored 368m **Fernsehturm** (TV tower; Map pp452-3; ☎ 242 3333; Panoramastrasse 1a; adult/concession €6.50/3; ☾ 9-1am Mar-Oct, 10am-midnight Nov-Feb) is Berlin's best-known landmark. Its aesthetic qualities are debatable, but the views are superb. On the opposite side of the elevated train station is **Alexanderplatz** (affectionately known as 'Alex'), the square named after Tsar Alexander I, who visited Berlin in 1805. It was bombed in WWII and rebuilt in the 1960s Soviet style. The **World Time Clock** (1969) is another GDR curiosity.

MUSEUMSINSEL

Berlin's famed **Museum Island** (Map pp452-3) is a scene of heavy construction as its grand buildings are restored. On an island west of the Fernsehturm is the GDR's **Palace of the Republic** (1976), which occupies the site of the bombed, baroque Berliner Schloss. During the communist era, the *Volkskammer* (People's Chamber) used to meet in this monstrosity; intense discussion is currently under way about whether or not the original Schloss should be reconstructed in

its place. North of Marx-Engels-Platz looms the great neo-Renaissance dome of the 1904 **Berliner Dom** (Map pp452-3; ☎ 202 690; Am Lustgarten; adult/concession €5/3; ☾ 9am-7pm Mon-Sat, noon-7pm Sun), the bombastic former court church of the Hohenzollern family.

Of the museums that give the area its name, the 1930 SMB **Pergamonmuseum** (☎ 2090 5555; Am Kupfergraben; adult/concession €8/4; ☾ 10am-6pm Tue-Sun, 10am-10pm Thu) is an archaeologist's dream, crammed with relics of classical Greek, Babylonian, Roman, Oriental and Islamic antiquity. The world-renowned Ishtar Gate from Babylon (580 BC), the reconstructed Pergamon Altar from Asia Minor (160 BC) and the Market Gate from Greek Miletus (Asia Minor, 2nd century AD) are among the artefacts on display. Other good museums include the SMB **Alte Nationalgalerie** (☎ 2090 5801; Bodestrasse 1-3; adult/concession €8/4; ☾ 10am-6pm Tue-Sun, 10am-10pm Thu), with classical sculpture and paintings by European masters, and Karl Friedrich Schinkel's 1829 neoclassical SMB **Altes Museum** (☎ 2090 5201; Am Lustgarten; adult/concession €8/4; ☾ 10am-6pm Tue-Sun), the first museum to be built on the Insel, with its famed rotunda area featuring statues of the Greek divinities.

NIKOLAIVIERTEL

The rebuilt, 13th-century **Nikolaikirche** (Map pp452-3) stands at a jaunty angle amid the forced charms of the **Nikolai quarter**, conceived and executed under the GDR's Berlin restoration programme (which actually involved razing many old streets). The monumental **Rotes Rathaus** (Red Town Hall), a neo-Renaissance structure from 1860, has been proudly restored and is once again the centre of Berlin's municipal government. Across Grunerstrasse, the remains of the bombed-out shell of the late-13th-century **Franciscan Abbey** mark the position of the former Spandauer Tor as well as the earliest town wall.

UNTER DEN LINDEN

A stroll west of Museumsinsel along the Unter den Linden boulevard takes in the greatest surviving monuments of the former Prussian capital. The **Deutsches Historisches Museum** (Map pp452-3; ☎ 203 040; Unter den Linden 2; admission €2; ☾ 10am-6pm Tue-Sun) offers a collection on German history from AD 900 to the present in a former *Zeughaus* (armoury), built in 1706 and renovated in 2004. Special exhibits are housed in a spectacular extension by modernist architect IM Pei.

To the west, **Bebelplatz** was the site of the Nazis' first book-burning on 10 May 1933. Just south lies **Gendarmenmarkt**, an elegant square and cultural fulcrum containing a trio of magnificent buildings: the **Deutscher Dom** (German Cathedral), **Französischer Dom** (French Cathedral) and the statuesque **Konzerthaus** (Concert Hall; see p461). Nearby, **Stasi – Die Ausstellung** (Stasi Exhibition; Map pp452-3; ☎ 2324 7951; Mauerstrasse 38; ⏰ 10am-6pm Mon-Sun) gives a fascinating insight into the practices of the GDR's secret police, the regime's 'sword and shield'.

Tiergarten & Kreuzberg
POTSDAMER PLATZ

Europe's busiest square before WWII, **Potsdamer Platz** was occupied by the Wall and its death strip until reunification. Since then it has been updated at a roaring pace and is now among the city's main tourist attractions, with exceptional buildings by world-famous architects including Renzo Piano, Arata Isozaki, Rafael Moneo and Helmut Jahn.

A major highlight here is the excellent **Filmmuseum** (Map p455; ☎ 300 9030; Sony Center, Potsdamer Strasse 2; adult/concession €6/4; ⏰ 10am-6pm Tue-Sun, 10am-8pm Thu), a multimedia journey through German film history with lots on the big Berlin names and a behind-the-scenes look at special effects.

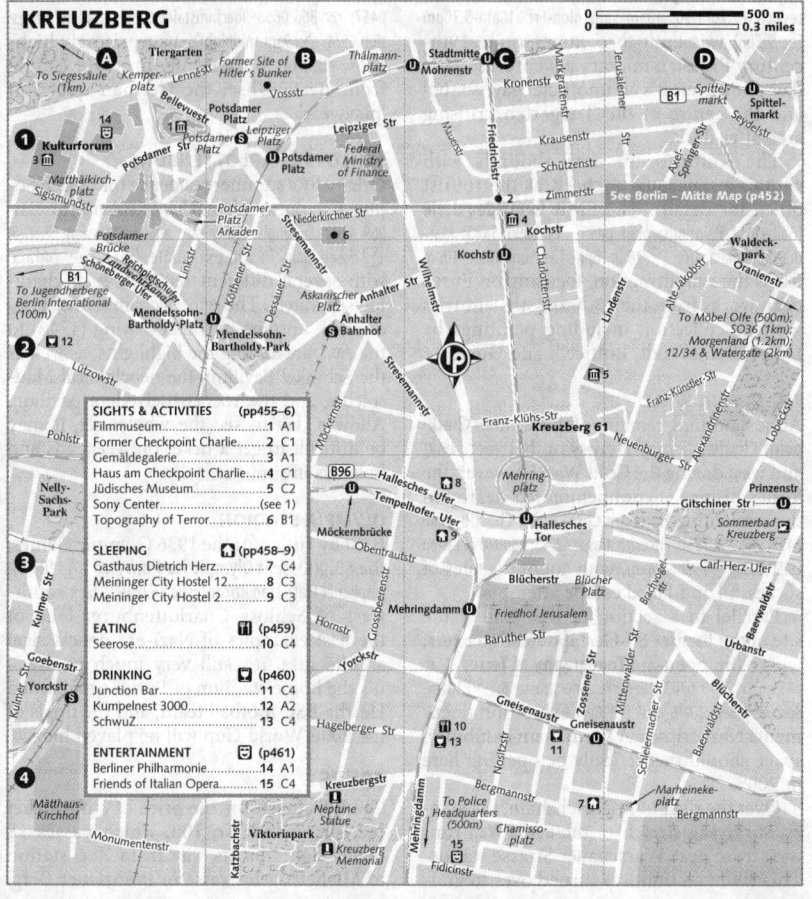

JÜDISCHES MUSEUM

Even before it opened in 2001, the zinc-clad shell of the Daniel Libeskind–designed **Jewish Museum** (Map p455; ☎ 2599 3300; Lindenstrasse 9-14; adult/concession €5.50/2.50; ☼ 10am-10pm Mon, 10am-8pm Tue-Sun) drew thousands of visitors. Now its collection covers 1000 years of Jewish history in Germany in a manner that's both admiring and wistful.

TIERGARTEN PARK & KULTURFORUM

The huge city park, **Tiergarten** (Map p455), stretches west from the Brandenburger Tor towards Zoo station. Strasse des 17 Juni (named after the 1953 workers' uprising in East Berlin) leads from the Brandenburger Tor through the park. In the middle of this street, the **Siegessäule** (Victory Column; adult/concession €2.20/1.50; 10am-5pm Mon-Fri, 10am-5.30pm Sat & Sun) was built to commemorate 19th-century Prussian military adventures; these days, however, it's an unofficial gay symbol and the centre of the Tiergarten cruising area after dark.

The Kulturforum area abounds with stunning museums – check at the tourist office for details. The SMB **Gemäldegalerie** (Gallery of Paintings; Map p455; ☎ 2090 5555; Matthäiskirchplatz 4/6; ☼ 10am-6pm Tue-Sun, 10am-10pm Thu) is the star attraction, focusing on European works from the 13th to 18th centuries with its collection including paintings by Dürer, Rembrandt, Botticelli and Goya.

THE BERLIN WALL

Almost nothing remains of the famous **Checkpoint Charlie**, a major crossing between east and west during the Cold War. However, the Wall's history is commemorated nearby in the fascinating **Haus am Checkpoint Charlie** (Map p455; ☎ 253 7250; Friedrichstrasse 43-45; adult/concession €9.50/5.50; ☼ 9am-10pm), with countless tales of successful and failed escape attempts.

Parallel to a section of the Wall is the site of the former SS-Gestapo headquarters, where the open-air **Topography of Terror** (Map p455; ☎ 2548 6703; Niederkirchnerstrasse 8; ☼ 10am-8pm May-Sep, 10am-dusk Oct-Apr) exhibition documents Nazi crimes. A permanent exhibition space should theoretically be opening here in 2005.

Over the river in Friedrichshain, the longest surviving stretch of the **Berlin Wall** runs west from near Warschauer Strasse station. This 300m section was turned over to graffiti writers and artists who created the **East Side Gallery**, a permanent, open-air art gallery along the side facing Mühlenstrasse. The area can be a bit seedy, although it's improving with gentrification. The gallery also has a showcase in Ostbahnhof.

Kurfürstendamm & Charlottenburg

ZOOLOGISCHER GARTEN

Once the commercial heart of West Berlin, the 'Ku'damm' is now largely an expensive shopping centre, and can become a tourist ghetto in summer. The stark and haunting ruin of the **Kaiser-Wilhelm-Gedächtniskirche** (1895) on Breitscheidplatz, left as a war memorial amid raging consumerism, is a world-famous landmark.

For light 'relief' try the **Erotik-Museum** (Map p457; ☎ 866 0666; Joachimstalerstrasse 4; adult/concession €5/4; ☼ 9am-midnight), a surprisingly highbrow display on sexuality in world culture from Beate Uhse, the German queen of 'playwear'.

SCHLOSS CHARLOTTENBURG

Originally a summer residence for Queen Sophie Charlotte, **Schloss Charlottenburg** (☎ 0331-969 4202; Luisenplatz; day card adult/concession €7.50/5; ☼ closed Mon) is an exquisite baroque palace with several different sections, each charging separately. The winter chambers of Friedrich II, upstairs in the new wing (1746) to the east, are among the highlights, as well as the Schinkel Pavilion, the neoclassical Mausoleum and the rococo Belvedere pavilion. Allow a day to see the whole site; it may be difficult to get a ticket on weekends and holidays in summer.

OLYMPIA STADION

Built by Hitler for the 1936 Olympic Games, the 85,000-seat **Olympic Stadium** (☎ 301 1100; Olympischer Platz 3; adult/concession €2.50/1) lies southwest of Schloss Charlottenburg. One of the best examples of Nazi-era neoclassical architecture, it's still very much in use – it's the home stadium of Berlin's embattled Hertha BSC football team, and the finals of the 2006 World Cup will be played here.

TOURS

Guide yourself for the price of a bus ticket (€2.10) on bus No 100, which passes 18 major sights on its way from Zoo station to Michelangelostrasse in Prenzlauer Berg.

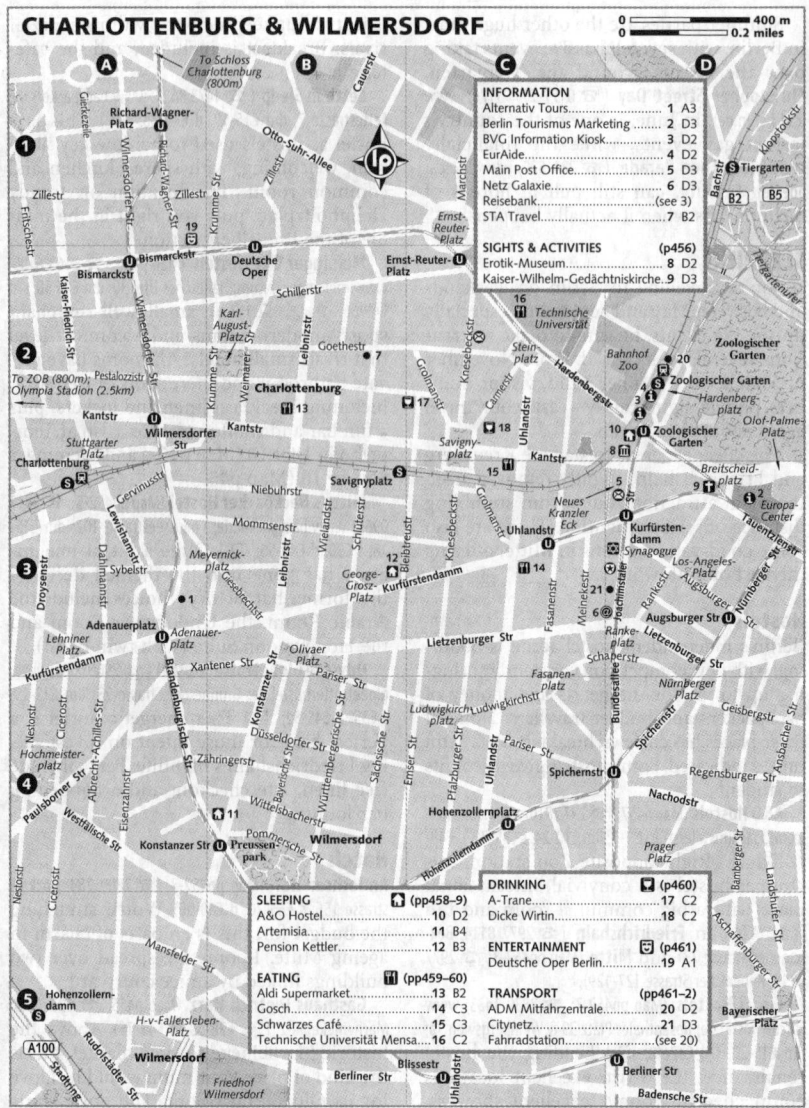

CHARLOTTENBURG & WILMERSDORF

0   400 m
0   0.2 miles

To Schloss Charlottenburg (800m)

INFORMATION
Alternativ Tours................................ 1 A3
Berlin Tourismus Marketing 2 D3
BVG Information Kiosk.................... 3 D2
EurAide... 4 D2
Main Post Office.............................. 5 D3
Netz Galaxie...................................... 6 D3
Reisebank....................................(see 3)
STA Travel.. 7 B2

SIGHTS & ACTIVITIES   (p456)
Erotik-Museum................................. 8 D2
Kaiser-Wilhelm-Gedächtniskirche. 9 D3

SLEEPING   (pp458–9)
A&O Hostel....................................... 10 D2
Artemisia... 11 B4
Pension Kettler................................. 12 B3

EATING   (pp459–60)
Aldi Supermarket............................. 13 B2
Gosch.. 14 C3
Schwarzes Café................................ 15 C3
Technische Universität Mensa....... 16 C2

DRINKING   (p460)
A-Trane... 17 C2
Dicke Wirtin....................................... 18 C2

ENTERTAINMENT   (p461)
Deutsche Oper Berlin....................... 19 A1

TRANSPORT   (pp461–2)
ADM Mitfahrzentrale........................ 20 D2
Citynetz... 21 D3
Fahrradstation............................(see 20)

The public-transport company BVG (see p462) puts out a special brochure describing the route.

Berlin Walks (☎ 301 9194; for over/under 26 €10/7.50)
Brewer's Best of Berlin Walking Tour (☎ 7013 1037; all tours €10)
Insider Tours (☎ 692 3149; walking tour €12/9, bike tour €20/17)

FESTIVALS & EVENTS
As a prominent cultural capital, the Berlin calendar is crammed with parties, festivals and celebrations all year round. The international **Berlinale** (☎ 259 200; www .berlinale.de) film festival in February is the city's highest-profile event, with screenings all over town.

Summer parties are the other huge draw in Berlin, with several massive events taking over the streets around the Tiergarten. **Christopher Street Day** (☎ 0177-277 3176; www .csd-berlin.de), in June, is one of the country's largest gay events, while the financially troubled **Love Parade** (☎ 284 620; www.lovepar ade.de), in July, can still pull in hordes of technoheads when it actually happens.

SLEEPING

If you're travelling to Berlin on weekends and between May and September, especially during big events, be sure to make reservations several weeks ahead. From November to March, on the other hand, visitor numbers plunge significantly – ask your travel agent about cheap deals.

The cheapest areas to stay are Kreuzberg and Friedrichshain, slightly removed from the main attractions but within stumbling distance of serious nightlife. There are also some good-value options in Mitte, offering the best of both worlds.

Hostels

Berlin's independent hostel scene is booming, with new competition constantly springing up to vie for the hearts and money of backpackers and budget travellers. None of these places has curfews; breakfast costs extra unless indicated. Some hostels give discounts to students.

A&O Hostels (Map p457; ☎ 297 7810; www.aohostels .com; Joachimstalerstrasse 1-3; dm €10-24, s €49-70, d €48-72; ☒ ☐) Right opposite Zoo station, this chipper hostel is a convivial, international place with a big communal room and fun bar. Also in **Friedrichshain** (☎ 2977 8114; Boxhagener Strasse 73) and **Mitte** (Map pp452-3; ☎ 2977 8115; Köpenicker Strasse 127-129).

Circus Hostels (Map pp452-3; ☎ 2839 1433; www .circus-hostel.de; Rosenthaler Platz 39 & Weinbergsweg 1a; dm €15-20, s/d €32/48; ☐) Leading the hostel renaissance, these two excellent locations count cheerful rooms, excellent showers, free lockers and competent staff among their many good qualities. The fantastic penthouse apartments (two/four people €75/130) are also amazing value.

Jugendherberge Berlin International (☎ 2579 9808; www.hostel.de; Kluckstrasse 3; dm junior €12-19, senior €16-23, d per person junior/senior €23.50/27.60; ☐ ☐) The only DJH hostel within the city centre, this institutional 364-bed place

is just about keeping pace with its snazzier rivals. Breakfast is included, and the cafeteria is open 24/7.

Lette'm Sleep (☎ 4473 3623; www.backpackers.de; Lettestrasse 7; dm €15-19, d €44-66; ☐) This is a hostel as hostels used to be: low-key, lowtech, welcoming, with shared kitchen and common room. The location on trendy Helmholtzplatz puts you right in the middle of the Prenzlberg action.

Meininger City Hostels (Map p455; ☎ 6663 6100; www.meininger12.com; Hallesches Ufer 30; dm €13.50, s/d €49/66; ☐ ☒ ☐) This small, well-run chain sports modern rooms and a comfort level that rivals small hotels. All rooms have private bathroom and there's lots of free stuff, including breakfast, linen and lockers, plus a fun bar and rooftop terrace. Also at Tempelhofer Ufer 10 (Map p455) and Meininger Strasse 10 (Map p459).

Mitte's Backpacker Hostel (Map pp452-3; ☎ 2839 0965; www.backpacker.de; Chausseestrasse 102; dm €15-18, s €30, d €46-56; ☐) Quite a bit of imagination has gone into the themed décor of this former hat factory; choices include the Arabic Room, the Underwater Room and the Honeymoon Suite (with twin beds!).

Odyssee Globetrotter Hostel (☎ 2900 0081; www. globetrotterhostel.de; Grünberger Strasse 23; dm €13-19, s €35, d €45-52; ☐) This energetic hostel is a perfect base for those intent on investigating Friedrichshain's nightlife. Perks include free linen, late checkout and a happening bar-lounge.

Hotels

Andechser Hof (Map pp452-3; ☎ 2809 7844; Ackerstrasse 155; s €65-70, d €80-90) Worth stretching the budget for, this is an oasis of charm in ageing Mitte. Rooms are spread over two buildings linked by a nice courtyard.

Gasthaus Dietrich Herz (Map p455; ☎ 691 7043; Marheinekeplatz 15; s €28-53, d €45-75) Above the historic Marheineke covered market, this is the kind of place your mum would just love for its Old Berlin colour. The noise starts early but the charm is always there.

Hotel 26 (☎ 297 7780; Grünberger Strasse 26; s €59-69, d €69-79; ☐ ☒) Budget rooms for grownups, with hotel standards at quasi-hostel prices. It has largish, bright rooms with a modern look and good amenities, including a terraced garden café.

Hotel-Pension Merkur (Map pp452-3; ☎ 282 8297; Torstrasse 156; s €40-78, d €60-96) This amazingly central guesthouse has survived since GDR days, and while it's hardly top-end stuff you'll aways get a warm welcome.

Pension Amsterdam (☎ 448 0792; Gleimstrasse 24; s €25-33, d €50-67; 🖳) There's plenty to like about this contemporary *pension*: big apartments, full kitchens, rooms with four-poster beds, and a buzzy downstairs café.

Pension Kettler (Map p457; ☎ 883 4949; Bleibtreustrasse 19; s €50-75, d €60-90) If you want kitsch and true Berlin character, you'll find heaps of it at this nostalgic retreat, strewn with objects best described as 'esoterica'. The place's most memorable feature, though, is its owner!

There are two women-only hotels in Berlin: **Intermezzo** (Map pp452-30; ☎ 2248 9096; Gertrud-Kolmar-Strasse 5; s/d €56/90) and the smaller but smarter **Artemisia** (Map p457; ☎ 873 8905; Brandenburgische Strasse 18; s €64-79, d €89-104; ✗).

EATING

Berliners love eating out, and the culinary community here is happy to oblige. You'll seldom need to travel far to satisfy your cravings, as every neighbourhood has its own clutch of eateries running the gamut of local and international cuisines. The blocks around Savignyplatz, Kollwitzplatz and Winterfeldtplatz are great places to browse.

Restaurants

Gosch (Map p457; ☎ 8868 2800; Kurfürstendamm 212; mains €6-15) A stylish but good-value fish bistro, serving take-out sandwiches (€2 to €3.50) as well as proper 'pick-your-own-fish' meals.

Monsieur Vuong (Map pp452-3; ☎ 3087 2643; Alte Schönhauser Strasse 46; mains €6.40) Even with a limited daily menu, the cooked-to-order Vietnamese fare here is rapidly acquiring cult status – be prepared to queue for a seat.

Nil (☎ 2904 7713; Grünberger Strasse 52; mains €1.80-4) Unique in Berlin (and probably elsewhere), this Sudanese *Imbiss* (snack bar) dishes up *fuul* (mashed beans), falafel and other Arabic titbits.

Seerose (Map p455; ☎ 6981 5927; Mehringdamm 47; mains €3-7) Vegetarians in the know flock to this eatery, which tempts tastebuds with delicious casseroles, soups, salads, pasta and juices.

Zum Nussbaum (Map pp452-3; ☎ 242 3095; Am Nussbaum 3; mains €6-9) For old-time Berlin flair and gut-busting traditional cuisine,

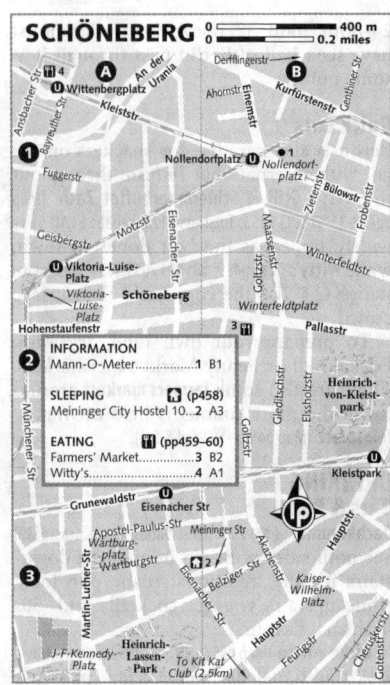

this touristy but no-nonsense pub in the Nikolaiviertel is on the money.

To take advantage of student prices, try the **Technische Universität Mensa** (Map p457; Hardenbergstrasse 34; lunch €3-6, nonstudents €5-8; ⌚ 11am-2.30pm).

Cafés

The number and variety of cafés in Berlin is simply astonishing. They're wonderful places to relax over coffee and cake, and many also honour the great Berlin tradition of serving breakfast all day.

Beth Café (Map pp452-3; ☎ 281 3135; Tucholskystrasse 40; mains €2-9; ✗) This is a good-value kosher café-bistro with a delightful inner courtyard, perfect for enjoying a leisurely lunch.

Café Seidenfaden (Map pp452-3; ☎ 283 2783; Dircksenstrasse 47) Near Hackesche Höfe, this is a pleasant lesbian hang-out.

Morgenland (☎ 611 3183; Skalitzer Strasse 35; mains €5-12) This eastern Kreuzberg café is a top spot for breakfast, especially on Sundays.

Schwarzes Café (Map p457; ☎ 313 8038; Kantstrasse 148; mains €4.50-9) Founded in 1978, this

GERMANY

24-hour food 'n' booze institution must have seen half of Berlin pass through it at some point.

Quick Eats

Berlin is also paradise for snackers on the go, with international *Imbisse* throughout the city. **Grill & Schlemmerbuffet Zach** (Map pp452-3; ☎ 283 2153; Torstrasse 125; kebabs €1.10-5) is widely tipped as the best doner in town; while **Witty's** (Map p459; ☎ 853 7055; Wittenbergplatz; sausages €2-4) has the edge amid the sausage crowd.

To prepare your own food, try Aldi, Edeka, Lidl or Penny Markt supermarkets. There are also some **farmers markets** around town; the most famous is held on **Winterfeldtplatz** (Map p459; ☒ Wed & Sat).

DRINKING
Bars & Pubs

Dachkammer (☎ 296 1673; Simon-Dach-Strasse 39) See both sides of Berlin in one bar: downstairs it's the traditional rustic pub look, while upstairs you get cocktails and '50s flashback flavour.

Dicke Wirtin (Map p457; ☎ 314 4952; Carmerstrasse 9) A traditional Berliner *Kneipe* (pub) par excellence, saved from insularity by its fashionable location and regular influxes of students seeking cheap food and booze.

Erdbeer (Map pp452-3; Max-Beer-Strasse 56) The red colour scheme and €7 pints of daiquiri make drinking here pretty sweet, and the no-frills approach separates it from standard Mitte cocktail joints.

Feuermelder (Krossener Strasse 21) Defiantly not part of Friedrichshain's lounge explosion, punks, rockers and other leather-clad folk seek solace in this loud music bar.

Kumpelnest 3000 (Map p455; ☎ 8891 7960; Lützowstrasse 23) Once a brothel, always an experience – the Kumpelnest has been famed since the '80s for its wild nights. Much of the original whorehouse décor remains intact.

Möbel Olfe (☎ 6165 9612; Reichenberger Strasse 177) Livening up the flagging Kottbusser Tor area, this sparsely furnished beer hall is good for at least a couple of hours after the regular places close.

O&G (Map pp452-3; ☎ 2576 2667; Oranienburger Strasse 48-49) Sporting tasteful retro pastels, this unironically cool bar was one of the first joints to open here after the Wende,

and while the interior's grown up a bit it still pulls in a friendly young crowd.

X Bar (☎ 443 4909; Raumerstrasse 17) Not for the indecisive, this smart cocktail/sushi bar has the biggest drinks menu you'll ever see. Of course, with drinks containing up to eight different spirits it's probably a good idea to take your time.

Live Music

A-Trane (Map p457; ☎ 313 2550; Bleibtreustrasse 1; admission €5-20) Still *the* place in Berlin for jazz. Entry is free most Mondays and Tuesdays when the local boys play.

Junction Bar (Map p455; ☎ 694 6602; Gneisenaustrasse 18; admission €3-6) Live music of all shades, 365 days a year – check your lungs and eardrums at the door before descending into this bastion of Kreuzberg chaos.

Gay & Lesbian Venues

Forget Amsterdam – Berlin is about the gayest city in Europe. Consult gay and lesbian freebie *Siegessäule* or strictly gay *Sergej* magazine, or contact **Mann-O-Meter** (Map p459; ☎ 216 8008; Bülowstrasse 106).

SchwuZ (Map p455; ☎ 693 7025; Mehringdamm 61) On Saturdays the Melitta Sundström café out front turns warm-up bar for this mainstream dance club, with flamboyant drag queens and two dance floors.

Sonntags-Club (☎ 449 7590; Greifenhagener Strasse 28) This friendly, relaxed lesbigay café-bar is open to all and holds frequent events.

CLUBBING

Nightlife is a law unto itself in Berlin, with enough quality, quantity and variety to outdo any city in Europe. The most dynamic scenes are in Prenzlauer Berg and Friedrichshain, where the feel is energetic, experimental and expanding. Western Kreuzberg is alternative with trendy touches, while eastern Oranienstrasse retains a rowdy, grungy feel despite gradually losing favour. In Schöneberg, you'll find dozens of 30-somethings with pointedly alternative lifestyles. Clubs in southern Mitte tend to be overly exclusive, but the looser scene around Oranienburger Strasse and Rosenthaler Platz is still resisting gentrification.

Not much starts before 11pm, except for 'after-work' parties on weekdays and some Sunday sessions. Admission ranges from €3 to €15. Venues are always changing, so check listings and seek out insider tips for the best parties. Once a year Berlin holds a *Clubnacht*, where entry to most major parties is free.

Kaffee Burger (Map pp452-3; ☎ 2804 6495; Torstrasse 60) A cornerstone of Berlin's alternative scene, decked out in original GDR '60s wallpaper. Come here for indie, rock, punk and the legendary *Russendisko* (Russian disco).

SO36 (☎ 6140 1307; Oranienstrasse 190) Kreuzberg's punk heart is still going strong, with thrashy live gigs and a hugely popular range of gay and lesbian nights.

Tresor/Globus (Map pp452-3; ☎ 609 3702; Leipziger Strasse 126a) Berlin is still the home of techno, and this long-term survivor from the early rave days keeps flying the flag, though its location is threatened. New sister club **12/34** (☎ 5207 2301; Stralauer Allee 1) has a housey vibe.

Watergate (☎ 6128 0394; Falckensteinstrasse 49a) Berlin's hottest recent arrival has a fantastic location with a downstairs lounge overlooking the Spree. The music is mainly electro, drum 'n' bass and hip hop, and it seldom closes early.

WMF (Map pp452-3; ☎ 2838 8850; Karl-Marx-Allee 34) This classic electro/downtempo club is now on its sixth location – a great spacious ex-GDR lounge. Regular appearances by remix gods Jazzanova count among the best nights anywhere in Germany; Sunday is GayMF.

Berlin also has a thriving (or throbbing) scene of no-holds-barred sex clubs and parties. The notorious **KitKat Club** (☎ 7889 9704; Bessemerstrasse 2-14) is the original and best.

ENTERTAINMENT

With a long history of subsidising the arts, Berliners take culture almost as seriously as fun, and there's no shortage of edifying options to raise your brow a bit.

Classical Music

Berliner Philharmonie (Map p455; ☎ 2548 8132; Herbert-von-Karajan Strasse 1) The Potsdamer Platz 'circus tent' is famous for its acoustics; current director Sir Simon Rattle has consolidated its supreme musical reputation. All seats are excellent.

Deutsche Oper Berlin (Map p457; ☎ 343 8401; Bismarckstrasse 35) Specialising in Wagner, the staple diet here includes classical works by mostly Italian and French composers, plus contemporary works.

Konzerthaus (Map pp452-3; ☎ 250 025; Gendarmenmarkt) Home to the world-renowned Berlin Symphony Orchestra.

Theatre

Berlin has around 150 theatres, ranging from the stoically traditional to the screamingly experimental. In the former east, they cluster around Friedrichstrasse station; in the west they're concentrated along the Ku'damm.

Deutsches Theater (Map pp452-3; ☎ 250 025; Schumannstrasse 13a) The historic German National Theatre offers classic as well as modern productions.

Friends of Italian Opera (Map p455; ☎ 691 1211; Fidicinstrasse 40) Berlin's only English-language theatre venue.

Volksbühne (Map pp452-3; ☎ 247 6772; Rosa-Luxemburg-Platz) Nonconformist, radical and intense, director Frank Castorf's provocative programming pulls in a sharp young audience, with moments of genius amid the frequent controversy.

GETTING THERE & AWAY

Air

Berlin is a cheap-flight paradise, with local and international companies such as **Air Berlin** (www.airberlin.com), **Germanwings** (www.germanwings.com), **Germania** (www.gexx.de), **Ryanair** (www.ryanair.com), **Easyjet** (www.easyjet.com) and **Volareweb** (www.volareweb.com) operating no-frills services to dozens of European destinations. The inner-city Tegel and Tempelhof airports will be closed down within the next couple of years, leaving Schönefeld (redubbed Berlin-Brandenburg-International) as the airport hub.

Bus

Berlin is well connected to the rest of Europe by long-distance bus. Most utilise the **Zentraler Omnibusbahnhof** (ZOB; ☎ 302 5361; Masurenalee 4-6) in Charlottenburg, opposite the Funkturm radio tower (take the U2 to Kaiserdamm or S45 to Witzleben). Tickets are available from travel agencies in Berlin or at the bus station.

Ride Services

Mitfahrzentralen (ride-share agencies) organise lifts and charge a fixed amount payable to the driver, plus commission from €6 to €10.50. Sample fares (including commission) are Leipzig (€13.50), Hanover (€17),

Frankfurt-am-Main, Munich or Cologne (€28.50).

ADM Mitfahrzentrale Zoo station (Map p457; ☎ 194 40; ☯ 9am-8pm Mon-Fri, 10am-6pm Sat & Sun) Alexanderplatz U-Bahn (Map pp452-3; ☎ 194 40; ☯ 10am-6pm Mon-Fri, 11am-4pm Sat & Sun)

Citynetz (Map p457; ☎ 194 44; Joachimstalerstrasse 17)

Train

ICE and IC trains have hourly services to every major city in Germany. There are night trains to the capitals of most major central European countries. Until the opening of the huge new centralised Lehrter Bahnhof (scheduled for 2007), you should check carefully which station your train leaves from.

Zoo station is the principal station for long-distance travellers going west. It has scores of lockers (from €1) and a large *Reisezentrum* (reservation and information office). Ostbahnhof and Lichtenberg generally handle trains for eastern Germany and countries beyond.

Through trains serving Zoo station also stop at Ostbahnhof and often at Friedrichstrasse and Alexanderplatz. Check schedules carefully and be aware that you may need to switch stations. Conventional train tickets to and from Berlin are also valid for all trains on the S-Bahn network.

GETTING AROUND
Bicycle

Fahrradstation (Map p457; ☎ 2974 9319; Zoo station) is Berlin's largest bicycle-rental agency, with branches all over the city. Bikes cost from €10 a day with a €50 deposit.

Public Transport

Berlin's public transport system offers services jointly provided by **Berliner Verkehrsbetriebe** (BVG; ☎ 194 49), which operates the U-Bahn, buses, trams and ferries; and **Deutsche Bahn** (DB; www.bahn.de), which runs the S-Bahn and regional trains (rail-pass holders can use DB trains for free). The **BVG Information Kiosk** (Map p457; Hardenbergplatz; ☯ 6am-10pm), outside Zoo station, provides free network maps, and also sells tickets.

One type of ticket is valid on all forms of transport. Unless you're venturing to Potsdam or the very outer suburbs, you'll need only the AB zone ticket. Taking a bicycle in specially marked carriages of the S-Bahn or

U-Bahn costs €1.25. On the U-Bahn, bikes are allowed only between 9am and 2pm and from 5.30pm to closing time on weekdays (any time at weekends). Tickets range from *Kurzstrecke* (short trip; €1.20; three stops by U-/S-Bahn, six stops by bus or tram) to *Tageskarte* (day pass; €5.60). U-/S-Bahn tickets must be purchased in advance. Most types of tickets are available from vending machines; they must be validated at the platform entrances, at bus stops before boarding, or as you enter the bus or tram.

U-/S-Bahn services operate from 4am until just after midnight on weekdays; some 70 *Nachtbus* (night bus) lines fill the gap until morning services resume. At weekends, major U-Bahn lines now run every 15 minutes all night, while most S-Bahns continue to operate hourly.

Taxi

Taxi stands are located throughout the city. Flag fall is €2.50 to €3, then €1.53 per kilometre; short trips (under 2km) cost €3. You can call a cab on ☎ 194 10, ☎ 210 101 or ☎ 210 202.

AROUND BERLIN

The state of Brandenburg has a poor reputation among Berliners, but in fact the rundown outer suburbs of the capital see far more social problems than the upstanding, very Prussian towns further afield, where locals take great pride in their communities. The historic town of Potsdam in particular is a must for anyone venturing outside Berlin.

POTSDAM
☎ 0331 / pop 131,000

Only 24km from central Berlin, the capital of Brandenburg state is the number one side trip of choice for tour groups and minibreakers, and is well worth a day out even if you're not one of the above. The town was devastated by British bombers in 1945; fortunately most of the spectacular palaces in Sanssouci Park escaped undamaged.

Information

Potsdam Information (☎ 275 580; www.potsdam tourismus.de in German; Neuer Markt 1; ☯ 9am-7pm Mon-Fri, 10am-6pm Sat & Sun Apr-Oct, 10am-6pm Mon-Fri, 10am-2pm Sat & Sun Nov-Mar)

Sanssouci Besucherzentrum (☎ 969 4202; An der Historischen Windmühle; ☼ 8.30am-5pm Mar-Oct, 9am-4pm Nov-Feb) Provides information on the park palaces.

Sights & Activities

Pride of place in Potsdam goes to **Sanssouci Park** (☼ dawn-dusk), a sprawling pleasure garden strewn with myriad palaces and outbuildings. Various combined tickets offer admission to some or all of the park sites (48 hours €15). Highlights include von Knobelsdorff's **Schloss Sanssouci** (☎ 969 4190; mandatory tour adult/concession €8/5; ☼ 9am-5pm Tue-Sun Apr-Oct, 9am-4pm Tue-Sun Nov-Mar), the celebrated 1747 rococo palace with glorious interiors; the imposing late-baroque 1769 **Neues Palais** (☎ 969 4255; adult/concession €5/4; ☼ 10am-5pm Sat-Thu), the summer residence of the royal family; and the charmingly eccentric **Chinesisches Haus** (Chinese Teahouse; ☎ 969 4222; admission €1; ☼ 10am-5pm Tue-Sun May 15-Oct 15).

Potsdam boasts scores of other architectural and artistic marvels, as well as the odd bit of cinematic history – the tourist office can fill you in on the full scope of its charms.

Sleeping & Eating

Cheap accommodation is thin on the ground in Potsdam – it's just as easy to stay in Berlin and come down for the day.

Pension Alice (☎ 292 304; Lindenstrasse 16; s/d €25/50) This is Potsdam's most central budget option, with a few quirky rooms above a busy café.

Madia (Lindenstrasse 53; meals from €3.50; ☼ noon-7pm; ✗) Veggies, hippies and eco-warriors should try this fair-trade food haven, tucked away in a nice courtyard.

Brandenburger Strasse has plenty of cafés, shops and snack shops.

Getting There & Around

Potsdam Hauptbahnhof is served by S-Bahn and regional trains, as well as ICE and IC services (€7, 15 minutes from Zoo station, up to every two hours) linking Berlin with points west. Both the S-Bahn (45 minutes from Potsdamer Platz, every 10 minutes) and regional trains (20 minutes from Zoo station, twice an hour) to Potsdam are covered by ABC-zone BVG tickets (day pass €6). A comprehensive bus and tram network operates within the town (day pass €3).

SACHSENHAUSEN

In 1936 the Nazis opened a 'model' **concentration camp** (☎ 03301-200 200; ☼ 8.30am-6pm Tue-Sun Apr-Sep, 8.30am-4.30pm Tue-Sun Oct-Mar) near Oranienburg, about 35km north of Berlin. By 1945 about 220,000 men from 22 countries had passed through the gates of Sachsenhausen. About 100,000 died here. After the war, the Soviets and the communist leaders of the GDR used the camp for *their* undesirables.

Plan on spending at least two hours at Sachsenhausen, which is easily reached from Berlin. Among the many museums and monuments are **Barracks 38 and 39**, which contain excellent displays on the camp's history. At the front gate an information office sells maps, brochures and books; you can also rent a chilling audioguide in English (€2.50).

From Berlin take the S1 to Oranienburg (€2.40, 40 minutes, every 10 minutes). The camp is an easy 1.5km walk northeast of the station.

EASTERN GERMANY

Germany's eastern heartland is made up of three states, all with their own distinct character. Saxony is perhaps the most determinedly individual, with an impenetrable dialect and a reputation based on the momentous history of cities such as Leipzig and Dresden. Thuringia, the 'green heart' of Germany, is if anything even more culturally aware, regularly enticing hordes of visitors to the humanist bastions of Weimar and state capital Erfurt. Saxony-Anhalt suffered more from postwar politics than its neighbours, but still boasts some lovely little towns like Wernigerode, in the Harz Mountains, as well as Martin Luther's home base, Wittenberg.

Together with Brandenburg, East Berlin and Mecklenburg-Western Pomerania, these states made up the GDR, and several good museums in the region illustrate the ups and downs of the socialist past.

DRESDEN
☎ 0351 / pop 479,000

In the 18th century Dresden was famous throughout Europe as 'the Florence of the north', as Italian artists, musicians, actors and master craftsmen flocked to the court, bestowing countless masterpieces upon the city. Today, however, it's best known for the carpet-bombing of February 1945, when Allied aircraft levelled much of the city, killing at least 35,000 people at a time when the war was almost over.

Luckily you can't keep a great city down, and many of Dresden's monumental baroque buildings have been restored, putting the Saxon capital firmly back at the forefront of Germany's tourist towns. Floods in 2002 set things back a bit, but with major restoration work going on for its 800th anniversary in 2006 and a bid for European Capital of Culture 2010 in the offing, the next few years should see Dresden garner even more fans.

Information

DISCOUNT CARDS
Dresden City-Card (48hr €18) Includes local public transport and free or discounted admission to many leading museums.
Museums day card (adult/concession €10/6)

INTERNET ACCESS
E@sy Internet (☎ 0172-579 5652; Pfarrgasse 1; per hr €3.60) Unstaffed Internet office.
Media Call Shop (☎ 656 7277; Rothenburger Strasse; per hr €3)

MONEY
Dresdner Bank (☎ 4890; Prager Strasse)
Reisebank (☎ 471 2177; Hauptbahnhof)

TOURIST INFORMATION
Dresden Information Hauptbahnhof (☎ 4919 2100; www.dresden-tourist.de; Prager Strasse 21; ☽ 9.30am-6pm Mon-Fri, 9.30am-4pm Sat) Schinkelwache (☎ 491 1705; Theaterplatz 2; ☽ 10am-6pm Mon-Fri, 10am-4pm Sat & Sun)

Sights & Activities
Dresden straddles the River Elbe, with the attraction-studded Altstadt in the south and the livelier Neustadt to the north. The focal point of the Altstadt is **Neumarkt**, where Dresden's one-time pride and joy, the bombed-out **Frauenkirche** (Church of Our Lady; 1738), is being reconstructed in all its towering former glory. With a lot of sentiment attached to the project, the proposed reopening in 2006 should be a very big event indeed.

Leading northwest from Neumarkt is Augustusstrasse, with the stunning 102m-long **Procession of Princes** porcelain mural covering the outer wall of the old royal stables. Augustusstrasse leads directly to Schlossplatz and the baroque Catholic **Hofkirche** (1755). Just south of the church is the Renaissance **Schloss**, which is being reconstructed (slowly!) as a museum.

THEATERPLATZ
On the western side of the Hofkirche is Theaterplatz, with Dresden's glorious opera house, the neo-Renaissance **Semperoper** (☎ 491 1496; tours adult/concession €5/3) – if you've watched any German TV you'll probably recognise it from a certain beer commercial. The opera tradition goes back 350 years, and many works by Richard Strauss, Carl Maria von Weber and Richard Wagner premiered here.

Next door, the baroque **Zwinger fortress** (Theaterplatz 1; ☽ 10am-6pm Tue-Sun) is another great Dresden heavyweight, with no fewer than six museums within its ornate walls. The most important are the **Old Masters Gallery** (☎ 491 4619), which features masterpieces including Raphael's *Sistine Madonna;* and the **Rüstkammer** (armoury; ☎ 491 4619), with its superb collection of ceremonial weapons. A combined ticket costs €6/3.50 per adult/concession. The dazzling **Porcelain Collection** (☎ 491 4622; adult/concession €5.50/3.50) includes plenty of local Meissen classics.

BRÜHLSCHE TERRASSE
East of the Augustusbrücke, this pleasant elevated promenade looks out over the Elbe, with imposing views in every direction. At the eastern end is the **Albertinum** (☎ 491 4619; combined museum ticket €6; ☽ 10am-6pm Fri-Wed), which houses major collections including the Gemäldegalerie Neue Meister (New Masters' Gallery), with renowned 19th- and 20th-century paintings (particularly from the impressionist school).

Sächsische Dampfschiffahrt (☎ 866 090; tours €10) runs river tours on rebuilt steam ships from the docks below the terrace.

Sleeping
City-Herberge (☎ 485 9900; Lingnerallee 3; s/d €36.50/63; P) Large and very central, this basic tourist hotel is a good bet if you arrive at a busy time.

DJH Jugendgästehaus Dresden (☎ 492 620; jhdresden@djh.de; Maternistrasse 22; s/d €25/42; ☒ ☐) This former Communist Party training centre is now a fantastic hostel, with small dorms and a bistro, plus wheelchair access and a lift. Take tram No 7/10.

Hostel Mondpalast (☎ 804 6061; Louisenstrasse 77; dm €13.50, s €29-39, d €37-50; ☒) Looking even better after a quick move, the Moon Palace has bedrooms decorated by theme (Australia, Greece, space travel etc) and a great bar/café.

Jugendhotel Die Boofe (☎ 801 3361; Hechtstrasse 10; s €29, d €44-48; ☒) Well known locally, rooms here are nicer than your average hostel and the bar is a popular hang-out.

Lollis Homestay (☎ 810 8458; Seitenstrasse 2a; dm €13, s/d €25/34; ☒ ☐) We've had some good feedback about this small, friendly place north of the Neustadt. As the name suggests, you're essentially a house guest.

Mezcalero (☎ 810 770; Königsbrücker Strasse 64; dm €15-23, s €30-45, d €50-60; ℗) How about a Mexican/Aztec B&B, complete with sombreros, red-yellow colour scheme, tiles and tequila bar? *Ay caramba.*

Camping Mockritz (☎ 471 5250; Boderitzerstrasse 30; adult/child €4.50/2, car €1, tent €1.50-3) Next to a nature reserve, this popular camp site is 5km out of town, served by the No 76 bus.

Eating

The Neustadt is Dresden's food and nightlife hub and student central, though there are still a few reasonable options in the tourist-saturated Altstadt.

Café Europa (☎ 389 923; Königsbrücker Strasse 68) A smart and relaxed café, with newspapers, strange décor features, intimate lighting and free Internet.

Italienisches Dörfchen (☎ 498 160; Theaterplatz 3; mains €5-20) This collection of four restaurants offers everything from bargain barbecue on the terrace to swish Italian inside.

Raskolnikoff (☎ 804 5706; Böhmische Strasse 34; mains €5.20-7) This café/gallery/*pension* couldn't be more bohemian if it tried – it's even on Bohemian St! The menu sorts its good-value light meals by compass direction.

Scheunecafé (☎ 802 6619; Alaunstrasse 36-40; mains €6.40-10.10) Devotees of Indian food and alternative rock come together nightly in the beer garden of this unusual venue.

X-fresh (☎ 484 2791; Altmarkt Galerie; mains €6.50-14.90, buffet €7.80) Dresden's only 'Wellness-bistro' provides healthy alternatives to traditional stodge, with salads, shakes and a Sunday prosecco (Italian sparkling white wine) buffet.

Drinking & Clubbing

The Neustadt zone between Alaunstrasse and Kamenzer Strasse is Dresden's 'Barmuda Triangle'; with pubs and clubs lining both sides of just about every street, it's easy to get lost until the early hours!

Neue Tonne (☎ 802 6017; Königstrasse 15; admission free-€15; ☒ varies) Live jazz up to five nights a week.

Reisekneipe (☎ 889 4111; Görlitzer Strasse 15) Run by a travel company, this exotic bar gives a taste of various cultures. It's popular with students, backpackers and the wanderlusty.

Strasse E (☎ 866 600; Werner-Hartmann-Strasse 2; free-€8) A massive 6000 sq metres of clublife, from disco to drum 'n' bass. Take tram No 7 to Industriegelände.

Gay visitors could start at **Roses cocktail bar** (☎ 802 4264; Jordanstrasse 10), the lively **Queens club** (☎ 803 1650; Görlitzer Strasse 3), or **Sappho women's café** (☎ 404 5136; Hechtstrasse 23).

Entertainment

Opera at the **Semperoper** (www.semperoper.de; Theaterplatz) is a quintessential Dresden experience. The two great theatres are the **Staatsschauspiel** (☎ 491 3555; Theaterstrasse 2) and the **Staatsoperette** (☎ 207 9929; Pirnaer Landstrasse 131, Leuben). Tickets can be bought from Dresden Information (see p464). A variety of musical and big-name events are presented in the **Kulturpalast** (☎ 486 60; Schlossstrasse 2).

Sax (€1.30) has comprehensive German-language listings for most forms of entertainment.

Getting There & Away

Dresden is south of Berlin-Ostbahnhof (€30.20, two hours, every two hours); there's also a Leipzig–Riesa–Dresden service (€16.80, 70 minutes, hourly). There's a **Mitfahrzentrale** (☎ 194 40; Dr-Friedrich-Wolfsstrasse 2) near Neustadt station.

AROUND DRESDEN
Meissen

☎ 03521 / pop 29,000

Just 27km northwest of Dresden, Meissen is a perfectly preserved old German town and the centre of a rich wine-growing region. It straddles the Elbe, with the old town on the western bank and the train station on the eastern bank. **Meissen-Information** (☎ 419 40; www.touristinfo-meissen.de in German; Markt 3; ☯ 10am-6pm Mon-Fri, 10am-4pm Sat & Sun Apr-Oct, 9am-5pm Mon-Fri, 10am-3pm Sat Nov-Mar) is on the central Markt.

Head straight up the steeply stepped lanes to the **Albrechtsburg cathedral** (☎ 452 490; Domplatz 7; adult/concession €2/1.50; ☯ 10am-6pm Mar-Oct, 10am-4pm Nov-Feb), Meissen's top attraction. Beside it is the equally remarkable 15th-century **castle** (☎ 470 70; Domplatz 1; adult/concession €3.50/2.50; ☯ 10am-6pm Mar-Oct, 10am-5pm Nov-Feb). Constructed with an ingenious system of internal arches, it was the first palace-style castle built in Germany.

Meissen's other claim to fame is its distinctive chinaware, sporting the trademark blue crossed-swords insignia. The **factory** (☎ 468 700; Talstrasse 9; adult/concession €4.50/4; ☯ 9am-6pm May-Oct, 9am-5pm Nov-Apr) is 1km southwest of town, with some stunning pieces on show.

Most budget accommodation is found outside the Altstadt; the independent **Jugendgästehaus** (☎ 453 065; Wilsdrufferstrasse 28; dm €12) is the cheapest, about 20 minutes' walk south of the Markt. Sidestep the pricey Albrechtsburg restaurants by trying **Gaststätte Winkelkrug** (☎ 453 711; Schlossberg 13; mains €4-7.50; ☯ dinner Wed-Sun), a quaint wine house in a lovely old building.

Half-hourly S-Bahn trains travel to Dresden (€4.50, 30 minutes).

LEIPZIG

☎ 0341 / pop 493,000

Leipzig is the second-largest city in the former Eastern Germany and indisputably the most dynamic, with a booming business community, a thriving cultural scene and contagious nightlife. Mostly unruffled by the disappointing rejection of its 2012 Olympic bid, the city's international profile has never been higher, and its incredibly amenable atmosphere continues to win over visitors from across the globe. Even without the Games, Leipzig is definitely on the up.

Information
DISCOUNT CARDS
Leipzig Card (24/72hr €5.90/11.50) Unlimited local transport and discounts at attractions and some restaurants.

INTERNET ACCESS
Copytel.de (☎ 993 8999; Grimmaisch Strasse 23; per hr €2.50)
Webcafe (☎ 0700-1999 3000; Reichsstrasse 18; per hr €2.60-4)

MONEY
Reisebank (☎ 980 4588; South hall, Hauptbahnhof)

TOURIST INFORMATION
Leipzig Tourist Service (☎ 710 4260; www .leipzig.de; Richard-Wagner-Strasse 1; ☯ 9am-7pm Mon-Fri, 9am-4pm Sat, 9am-2pm Sun)

Sights & Activities
Wandering around Leipzig is a genuine pleasure, particularly if you take the time to investigate the various elaborate shopping passages that crisscross many Altstadt buildings. The focus of the old town is the **Markt**, where the Renaissance 1556 **Altes Rathaus** is one of Germany's most beautiful town halls. East of here, the remarkable **Nikolaikirche** (☎ 960 5270; Nikolaikirchhof 3) was built in 1165 and was a rallying point for the 'Gentle Revolution', which helped overthrow the communist regime in 1989.

The former East German Stasi (secret police) headquarters, diagonally opposite the Schauspielhaus, now houses the **Stasi Museum** (☎ 961 2443; Dittrichring 24; ☯ 10am-6pm), outlining the force's favoured methods of investigation and intimidation. More prosaic facts of everyday GDR life can be found in the **Zeitgeschichtliches Forum** (Forum of Contemporary History; ☎ 222 20; Grimmaische Strasse 6; ☯ 9am-6pm Tue-Fri, 10am-6pm Sat & Sun), a history of East Germany that's both informative and wrenching.

Across the street are the temporary quarters of Leipzig's finest museum, the **Museum der bildenden Künste** (Museum of Fine Arts; ☎ 216 990; Grimmaische Strasse 1-7; adult/concession €2.50/1; ☯ 10am-6pm Tue & Thu-Sun, 1-8pm Wed), with an excellent collection of old masters. If all goes well it should have moved to a new building on Sachsenplatz by 2005.

Just southwest of the Markt is the **Thomaskirche** (☎ 960 2855; Thomaskirchhof 18), built in 1212, with JS Bach's tomb in front of the altar. Bach worked in Leipzig from 1723 until his death in 1750, and the St Thomas Boys' Choir, which he once led, is still going strong. Opposite the church is the **Bach Museum** (☎ 964 110; Thomaskirchhof 16; adult/concession €3/2; ☯ 10am-5pm).

To the southeast of town is Leipzig's most impressive sight, the **Völkerschlachtdenkmal** (Battle of Nations Monument; ☎ 878 0471; Prager Strasse; adult/concession €2.50/1.25; ⏰ 10am-6pm Apr-Oct, 10am-4pm Nov-Mar), a scary-looking 91m-high monument erected in 1913 to commemorate the decisive victory by combined Prussian, Austrian and Russian armies over Napoleon's forces here in 1813.

Sleeping

Hostel Sleepy Lion (☎ 993 9480; www.hostel-leipzig.de; Käthe-Kollwitz-Strasse 3; dm €14-15, s/d €24/36; ✕ 💻) This playful hostel is a really great deal, right by the Gottschedstrasse bars in a nicer location than its newer sister **Globetrotter** (Kurt-Schumacher-Strasse 41). Breakfast costs an extra €3.

Jugendherberge (☎ 245 7011; jhleipzig@djh.de; Volksgartenstrasse 24; dm junior/senior €18/20.70; P 💻) Decent but uncompetitive, you'll find Leipzig's DJH offering about 3km from the city centre. Take tram No 17, 27 or 31 to Löbauer Strasse.

Kosmos-Hotel (☎ 233 4422; www.kosmos-hotel.de in German; Gottschedstrasse 1; s/d €40/75; P) Ever fancied waking up next to Marilyn Monroe? You can in this fantastically different hotel, which puts some genuine inspiration into its highly individual rooms and manages to create luxury on a budget. Baroque, Arabian, cow print – take your pick...

Weisses Ross (☎ 960 5951; Auguste-Schmidt-Strasse 20; s €26-35, d €41-55) The neighbourhood is nothing special but if you don't fancy a dorm this is a good, simple, cheap option close to Augustusplatz.

Most other central accommodation is provided by big-name chain hotels, from the sublimely comfortable to the ridiculously expensive; the **Hotel Ibis** (☎ 218 60; Brühl 69; r €58; P ✕) and **Hotel Mercure** (☎ 214 60; Augustusplatz 5-6; s €61-88, d €71-105; P ✕ 💻) are at the more reasonable end of the scale.

Eating

Auerbachs Keller (☎ 216 100; Mädlerpassage; mains €10.50-20.60) Founded in 1525, Auerbachs is one of Germany's all-time classic restaurants, and even features in Goethe's *Faust*. It's popular with locals and tourists alike, and rightly so.

Barthel's Hof (☎ 141 310; Hainstrasse 1; mains €8-14) This is a sprawling, historic place with some fantastic buffets (€8.30 to €11.99)

and quirky Saxon dishes such as *Heubraten* (lamb roasted on hay).

House of India (☎ 993 9270; Richard-Wagner-Strasse 2; mains €4.40-6.20) Throwing some Indian spice into Leipzig's cross-cultural mix, this is a good-looking curry house with reasonable prices just opposite the station.

Kebab Lounge (☎ 268 9715; Gottschedstrasse 6; mains €2.30-6) If you like your doners but would rather forego the *Imbiss* experience, head for this smart little kebab café, where you can sit at a proper table and eat pide, falafel, shish kebabs and other Turkish delights off a plate.

Zill's Tunnel (☎ 960 2078; Barfussgässchen 9; mains €8.60-13.40) This place offers outstanding Saxon specialities and some fine seasonal dishes, with outside seating in the covered 'tunnel' courtyard. There are also a couple of lovely rooms upstairs (doubles €67).

For snacks, cheap bites and fast food, the Hauptbahnhof is packed with eateries and supermarkets.

Drinking & Clubbing

Leipzig has two main *Kneipenmeilen* (pub miles): Barfussgässchen is densely packed with bars, cafés and restaurants; while Gottschedstrasse has a high concentration of cocktail dens.

Moritz-Bastei (☎ 702 590; Universitätsstrasse 9) One of the best student clubs in Germany, located in a spacious cellar below the old city walls. It has bands or DJs most nights and a great Sunday brunch.

Nachtcafe (☎ 211 4000; Markgrafenstrasse 10) This popular two-level club has a large plastic swimming pool outside, which can be great fun (in summer, anyway).

Entertainment

Dating back to 1743, the **Neues Gewandhaus** (☎ 127 0280; Augustusplatz 8) has Europe's longest established civic orchestra. Leipzig's modern **Opernhaus** (☎ 126 1261; Augustusplatz) is just across the square. The **Schauspielhaus** (☎ 126 8168; Bosestrasse 1), a few blocks to the west of Markt, mixes classic theatre with modern works.

Getting There & Around

Leipzig is linked by fast and frequent trains to all major German cities, including Dresden (€16.80, 1½ hours, every 20 to 30 minutes), Berlin (€33.20, 1¾ hours, hourly) and Munich (€65.20, five hours, every two hours). Ride sharers can visit the **Mitfahrzentrale** (☎ 194 40; Goethestrasse 7-10).

Trams are the main form of public transport in Leipzig. A single ticket costs €1.50 and a day card €4.40; four-journey strips cost €5.40.

ERFURT
☎ 0361 / pop 202,000

The capital of Thuringia escaped with relatively small-scale damage during WWII, and many burgher town houses, churches and monasteries still grace its surprisingly well-preserved medieval quarter. With increasing passenger traffic coming through the small airport, Erfurt is fast becoming an ideal base for exploring central Germany.

Information

DISCOUNT CARDS
ErfurtCard (24/72hr €7/14) Unlimited use of public transport and entry to museums.
Erfurt Family Card (72hr €33) Two adults and all children; includes additional benefits.

INTERNET ACCESS
Lokal-Global (☎ 262 3834; Ratskellerpassage, Fischmarkt 5; per 30min €1.50; ☺ 1-8pm Mon-Sat)

MONEY
Reisebank (Hauptbahnhof; ☺ 8am-7pm Tue-Fri, 8am-4pm Mon & Sat)

TOURIST INFORMATION
Erfurt Tourismus (☎ 664 00; www.erfurt-tourist -info.de; Benediktsplatz 1; ☺ 10am-7pm Mon-Fri, 10am-4pm Sat & Sun)

Sights

The numerous interesting lanes and alleys in Erfurt's surprisingly large Altstadt make this a fascinating place to explore. Whatever you do, though, you shouldn't miss the massive 13th-century Gothic **Dom St Marien** and **Severikirche**, which dominate the central Domplatz square. The stained glass and elaborate portals make the cathedral one of the most richly ornamented medieval churches in Germany. The Severikirche, meanwhile, boasts the sarcophagus of St Severus (surely everyone's favourite saint?).

The eastbound street beside the Rathaus leads to the restored **Krämerbrücke** (1325), a narrow medieval bridge lined with timber-

framed shops – it's the only such structure north of the Alps. Further north, on the same side of the river, is the **Augustinerkloster** (☎ 576 600; www.augustinerkloster.de in German; adult/ concession €3.50/3; ☺ tours hourly 10am-noon & 2-5pm Tue-Sat, 11am-5pm Sun), a late-medieval monastery that was home to Martin Luther in the 16th century and now puts up tourists and conference guests.

Sleeping & Eating

Jugendherberge (☎ 562 6705; jh-erfurt@djh-thuerin gen.de; Hochheimer Strasse 12; dm junior/senior €16.50/19.50; ℗ ☒ 🖳) Erfurt's nicely renovated DJH hostel is in a quiet area southwest of the centre. Take tram No 5 to Steigerstrasse.

Pension am Dom (☎ 5504 8660; Lange Brücke 57; s/d €39/55; ℗ ☒) True to its name, this friendly little central *pension* is good value and has superb views of the cathedral – but only from the breakfast room and terrace.

Pension Reuss (☎ 731 0344; Spittelgartenstrasse 15; s €26, d €42-46; ℗) North of the city centre, the pine-heavy rooms here are a great bargain. You can even demand room service to go with your 'minibar'.

Anger Maier (☎ 566 1058; Schlösserstrasse 8; mains €3.30-9.80) A tunnel-like Erfurt institution, with cheap, quality eats. It's always busy, often smoky, and has its own TV show.

Double B (☎ 642 1671; Marbacher Gasse 10; mains €4.30-8.90) This cosy pub-restaurant is a student favourite for its all-day breakfasts, offering everything from a VIP *Sekt* (sparkling wine) 'n' brie blowout to the 'hangover breakfast': two aspirin and a glass of water.

Entertainment

Besetztes Haus (www.topf.squat.net in German; Rudolstädterstrasse 1) A long-term squat and alternative cultural centre, with strong politics and a variety of concerts, films and talks on the bill.

DasDie (☎ 551 166; Marstallstrasse 12) Two venues offering entertainment from live bands to hypnotists and everything in between.

P33 (☎ 2108714; Pergamentergasse 33) Warehouse-sized pub-theatre with beamed ceilings that presents a mixed bag of variété, cabaret and music at weekends.

Studentenzentrum Engelsburg (☎ 244 770; Allerheiligenstrasse 20-21) This student haunt in historic digs has bands, DJs and all kinds of performances most nights.

Getting There & Away

Erfurt's Hauptbahnhof has direct services to Berlin (€41.20, 3¼ hours, every two hours), Dresden (€39, 2¼ hours, every two hours) and Frankfurt (€41.80, 2¼ hours, every two hours). Trains to Weimar (€4.20, 15 minutes) and Eisenach (€8.40, 50 minutes) run several times hourly.

WEIMAR & AROUND
☎ 03643 / pop 62,000

Weimar is Thuringia's cultural centre of gravity, renowned throughout Germany for the heavyweight humanist traditions that shaped much of its history. Famous residents include Lucas Cranach the Elder, Johann Sebastian Bach, Franz Liszt, Walter Gropius, Wassily Kandinsky, Paul Klee and of course the ultimate Weimar classicists, Friedrich Schiller and Johann Wolfgang von Goethe. The town is also known as the place where the German republican constitution was drafted after WWI, hence the popular name Weimar Republic. As a sinister counterpoint, the ruins of the Buchenwald concentration camp nearby provide a haunting reminder of the Nazi period.

Information

DJH Service Centre (☎ 850 000; www.djh-thueringen. de in German; Carl-August-Allee 13; ⊙ 1-4pm Mon, 9am-noon & 1-5pm Tue & Thu, 9am-noon Fri) Reservations for all DJH hostels.

Stiftung Weimarer Klassik (Weimar Classics Foundation; ☎ 545 401; Frauentorstrasse 4; ⊙ 9am-4pm Mon-Sat) Museum tickets and literature.

Tourist Information (☎ 240 00; www.weimar.de in German; Markt 10; ⊙ 9.30am-6pm Mon-Fri, 9.30am-3pm Sat & Sun)

Weimar Card (72hr €10)

Sights & Activities
CENTRAL WEIMAR

Most attractions are open 9am to 6pm April to October and 9am or 10am to 4pm November to March, and close on either Monday or Tuesday.

Weimar's cultural life is centred on several main squares. On the central Markt you'll find the neo-Gothic **Rathaus** (1841) and the **Cranachhaus**, where Lucas Cranach the Elder died in 1553. West of here is Theaterplatz, dominated by the **German National Theatre** (☎ 755 334), where the Weimar Republic constitution was drafted in

1919. On this same square is the **Bauhaus Museum** (☎ 545 401; adult/concession €4/3; ⊙ closed Mon), which documents the evolution of this influential artistic and architectural movement. Weimar was the original home of the Bauhaus group, and retains a distinct resonance despite the later move to Dessau.

From here, the elegant Schillerstrasse curves around past the **Schiller Haus** (☎ 545 401; Schillerstrasse 12; adult/concession €3.50/2.50; ⊙ closed Tue) to Frauenplan, a smaller square with one corner occupied by the **Goethe Haus** (☎ 545 401; adult/concession €6/4.50; ⊙ closed Mon), where *Faust* was written, and the **Goethe-Nationalmuseum** (☎ 545 401; adult/concession €2.50/2; ⊙ closed Mon), which contains exhibits on Schiller, Goethe and their life and times. The specially commissioned mural in the **Faustina** café here adds a bit of modern controversy to proceedings.

For those who like their history a bit less staid, the **Weimar Haus** (☎ 901 890; Schillerstrasse 16-18; adult/concession €6.50/5.50; ⊙ 10am-7pm Apr-Oct 12, 10am-6pm Oct 13-Mar) offers a half-hour multimedia tour of Weimar's past, with an animatronic Goethe as your guide.

Moving away from the city's biographical exhibits, the **Schlossmuseum** (☎ 5460; Burgplatz; adult/concession €4.50/3.50; ⊙ 10am-6pm Tue-Sun Apr-Oct, 10am-4.30pm Nov-Mar) has a large art collection that occupies three floors of the castle, with masterpieces by Cranach, Dürer and others. Several restored rooms can also be viewed. North of the centre, the **Neues Museum** (☎ 5460; Carl-August-Allee; adult/concession €3/2; ⊙ closed Mon) houses one of Germany's most important private collections of contemporary art.

Weimar boasts three large parks, each replete with monuments, museums and attractions. Most accessible is **Park an der Ilm**, which runs right along the eastern side of Weimar.

BUCHENWALD

Buchenwald museum and concentration camp (☎ 03643-4300; Ettersberg Hill; ⊙ 9.45am-6pm May-Sep, last admission 5.15pm, 8.45am-5pm Oct-Apr, last admission 4.15pm) is 10km north of Weimar (take bus No 6). You first pass the memorial with mass graves of some of the 56,500 WWII victims from 18 nations, including German antifascists, Jews, and Soviet and Polish prisoners of war. The concentration camp and museum are 1km beyond. Many prominent German communists and Social Democrats were murdered here. On 11 April 1945, as US troops approached, the prisoners overcame the SS guards and liberated themselves.

After the war the Soviets turned the tables by establishing Special Camp No 2, in which thousands of (alleged) anticommunists and former Nazis were worked to death.

Sleeping & Eating

At last count Weimar had no fewer than four DJH hostels, catering for backpackers and the many student visitors. **Jugendherberge Germania** (☎ 850 490; jh-germania@djh-thueringen.de; Carl-August-Allee 13; dm junior/senior €17/20; ✗), just south of the station, is the most convenient.

Hababusch (☎ 850 737; Geleitstrasse 4; dm €10, s/d €15/24; ✗) Undercutting even the DJH hostels, this independent establishment is run by student volunteers in an unrestored 19th-century house. Luxury it ain't, but you won't find a cheaper bed anywhere.

Pension Savina (☎ 866 90; Meyerstrasse 60 & Rembrandtweg 13; s €40-45, d €55-75; ✗) On quiet side streets near the Hauptbahnhof, this smart *pension* and its annexe offer excellent value, with sauna, solarium and a shuttle service.

Hotel Am Frauenplan (☎ 494 40; Brauhausgasse 10; s €46-56, d €66-86; **P** ✗) Set in its own courtyard, this is a decent new guesthouse and pub-restaurant facing out onto the square just opposite the Goethe Haus.

ACC (☎ 851 161; Burgplatz 2; mains €6.80-9.80) A long-running student stalwart, the ACC theatre café has imaginative menus on two-week rotations and plenty of lighter options.

Cato (☎ 495 929; Obere Schlossgasse 1; mains €4.90-9.90) It may look off-puttingly smart, but price tags on the Italian/international meals here are surprisingly reasonable, and you certainly can't complain about steak for under €10.

Crêperie du Palais (☎ 401 581; Am Palais 1; mains €3.80-5.40) Why wait for Pancake Day? The tasty savoury *galettes* and sweet crepes in this little corner of France are excellent value.

Drinking & Clubbing

Studentenclub Kasseturm (☎ 851 670; Goetheplatz 10) A Weimar classic, the Kasseturm is a historic round tower with three floors of live music, DJs, cabaret or just games nights.

Studentenclub Schützengasse (☎ 778 996; Schützengasse 2) Pitching to the same crowd as the Kasseturm, this large club has 20 different beers (from €1).

Getting There & Away

There are frequent direct IR trains to Berlin-Zoo (€39.20, three hours, every two hours) via Naumburg and Halle, and to Frankfurt-am-Main (€44.20, 2½ hours, every two hours) via Erfurt and Eisenach. ICE trains go to Dresden (€36.40, two hours) and Leipzig (€22.40, one hour, every two hours).

EISENACH

☎ 03691 / pop 44,000

Eisenach is a small, picturesque city on the edge of the Thuringian Forest. Its main attraction is Wartburg castle, from where the landgraves (German counts) ruled medieval Thuringia. Martin Luther went into hiding here after his excommunication, and the town is also famous as the birthplace of JS Bach.

Information

Eisenach Classic-Card (72hr €14) Free admission to the castle and most museums, and use of public transport.
Tourist-Information (☎ 792 30; www.eisenach.de in German; Markt 9; ☾ 10am-6pm Mon, 9am-6pm Tue-Fri, 10am-2pm Sat & Sun)
Wartburg Information (☎ 2500; Schlossberg; ☾ 9am-12.30pm & 1-5pm Tue-Fri)

Sights

The world-famous **Wartburg** (☎ 2500; tours adult/concession €6/3; ☾ tours 8.30am-5pm) is where an incognito Martin Luther translated the New Testament into German, contributing greatly to the development of the written German language. It also provided the inspiration for Richard Wagner's opera *Tannhäuser*. You can visit the castle's interior with a guided tour, which includes the museum, Luther's study (complete with whale-vertebra footstool) and the amazing Romanesque great hall; arrive early to avoid the crowds.

Sleeping & Eating

Gasthof & Wanderpension Storchenturm (☎ 0700-4040 4050; www.gasthof-am-storchenturm.de in German; Georgenstrasse 43; dm €18, r €35) For cheap stays in the centre of town, try this hostel-like place with guest rooms and monastic dorms, plus a fun restaurant in a former barn.

Jugendherberge Artur Becker (☎ 743 259; jh-eisenach@djh-thueringen.de; Mariental 24; dm junior/senior €15/18; **P** ✗) Eisenach's DJH hostel, in the woods south of town, has been recently renovated.

Pension Mahret (☎ 742 744; Neustadt 30; r per person €22.50-44) East of the centre, on the edge of the Wartburg forest, this is a self-styled 'dolls-house hotel' offering apartment-style rooms of varying sizes.

Brunnenkeller (☎ 212 358; Markt 10; mains €7-9) For good hearty Thuringian dishes in an authentic Weinkeller setting, try the old monastery cellars south of the Georgenkirche.

Getting There & Away

Frequent direct trains run to Erfurt (€8.10, 50 minutes) and Weimar (€10.70, one hour). ICE trains to Frankfurt-am-Main (€35.80, 1¾ hours) and IC trains to Berlin (€47.40, 3¾ hours) also stop here.

WERNIGERODE

☎ 03943 / pop 35,000

Flanked by the foothills of the Harz Mountains, Wernigerode is a charming tourist town full of traditional half-timbered houses and crowned by a romantic ducal castle. It's a perfect base for the many walking trails into the Harz, including the path up to the famous Brocken mountain.

Wernigerode Tourismus (☎ 633 035; www.wernigerode.de in German; Nicolaiplatz 1; ☒ 9am-7pm Mon-Fri, 10am-4pm Sat, 10am-3pm Sun) is near the central Markt.

The stunning **Rathaus** (1277), with its pair of pointed black-slate towers, is a focal point on the Markt itself. From here it's just a short climb to the neo-Gothic **Schloss** (☎ 553 030; adult/concession €4.50/4; ☒ 10am-6pm, closed Mon Nov-Apr). Built in the 12th century, the castle has been renovated and enlarged throughout its history. If the architecture doesn't get your blood pumping, try **hiking** through the beautiful deciduous forest.

Sleeping & Eating

Hotel zur Tanne (☎ 632 554; Breite Strasse 57-59; s €41, d €49-75; ☒) The rooms are small but modern, there's a restaurant downstairs where the boss still cooks personally, and if you're so inclined you can try an infrared sauna.

Jugendgästehaus (☎ 632 061; www.jugendgaestehaus-wernigerode.de; Friedrichstrasse 53; dm junior/senior €16/19.80; ☒) Better located than its newer DJH counterpart on Am Eichberg, this city hostel has a few quirks: junior price is for under-18s, and includes full board.

Krummelsches Haus (☎ 602 626; Breite Strasse 72; mains €8-12) A tourist attraction in its own

right, the house with the great façade also has a popular restaurant, with breakfasts, sandwiches and bistro meals.

Getting There & Away

Frequent trains run to Goslar (€6.60, 50 minutes, every two hours) and Hanover (€16, 1¼ hours, every two hours). Change trains in Halberstadt for Magdeburg (€12.90, 1¼ hours, hourly).

QUEDLINBURG

☎ 03946 / pop 23,600

Unesco-listed and unspoiled, Quedlinburg dates back over 1000 years and still boasts an amazing, almost entirely half-timbered Altstadt. **Quedlinburg-Information** (☎ 905 625; www.quedlinburg.de in German; Markt 2; ☒ 9am-7pm Mon-Fri, 10am-4pm Sat & Sun Apr-Oct, 9.30am-5.30pm Mon-Fri, 9.30am-2pm Sat Nov-Mar) books rooms at no cost.

The focal point for visitors is the hill with the old castle district, known as **Schlossberg**. The area features the 1129 Romanesque **Church of St Servatius** (☎ 709 900; adult/concession €3/2; ☒ 10am-6pm Tue-Fri, 10am-4pm Sat, noon-6pm Sun), with a 10th-century crypt and priceless reliquaries and early Bibles. In 1938 SS meetings were held here.

For accommodation, the basic but comfy private rooms offered by **Familie Klindt** (☎ 702 911; Hohe Strasse 19; s/d €20/32) are a good deal. **Zum Alten Fritz** (☎ 704 880; alter-fritz@quedlinburg.de; Pölkenstrasse 18; s/d €45/55; ☒) is less tradition-steeped than its rival hotels but beats most on price, and also offers some deluxe 'Romantik' rooms for €95/125.

To eat, try the quirky but charming **Zum Roland** (☎ 4532; Breite Strasse 2-6; mains €5.75-14.75), spread over seven different houses, for traditional meals, pasta and international dishes. **Brauhaus Lüdde** (☎ 705 206; Blasiistrasse 14; mains €8.50-13; ☒) is a lively microbrewery which offers hearty lunches and dinners and also houses a lot of coach parties (singles/doubles €80/130).

You can change trains in Magdeburg (€10.70, 1¼ hours, hourly) for long-distance routes. To Wernigerode (€6.60, one hour, every half to one hour), trains connect via Halberstadt.

LUTHERSTADT-WITTENBERG

☎ 03491 / pop 53,000

As you can guess from the name, Wittenberg is a key site for devotees of Martin Luther, who did some of his most famous work here, including launching the Protestant Reformation in 1517. Sadly not much of interest has happened here since, but it's an engaging little town nevertheless.

Wittenberg-Information (☎ 498 610; www.witten berg.de; Schlossplatz 2; ☼ 9am-6pm Mon-Fri, 10am-3pm Sat, 11am-4pm Sun Mar-Oct, 10am-4pm Mon-Fri, 10am-2pm Sat, 11am-3pm Sun Nov-Feb) is very well organised – just as well, as it can get crowded in summer.

The newly revamped **Lutherhaus** (☎ 420 30; Collegienstrasse 54; adult/concession €5/3; ☼ 9am-6pm Apr-Oct, 10am-5pm Tue-Sun Nov-Mar), inside the Lutherhalle (a former monastery), is a full-on interactive Reformation museum. Luther stayed here in 1508 while teaching at Wittenberg University and made it his home after returning in 1511.

The very large altarpiece in **Stadtkirche St Marien** (☎ 404 415; Jüdenstrasse 35; admission free; ☼ 9am-5pm Mon-Sat, 11.30am-5pm Sun May-Oct, 10am-4pm Mon-Sat, 11.30am-4pm Sun Nov-Apr) was created jointly by Renaissance painter Lucas Cranach the Elder and his son in 1547. It shows Luther and other Reformation figures, as well as Cranach himself, in biblical contexts. Luther preached in this church and was married here.

Another major Luther site here is the **Schlosskirche** (Schlossplatz; ☼ 10am-5pm Mon-Sat, 11.30am-5pm Sun), where the Great Reformer and his close friend Philipp Melanchthon are buried. According to legend it was on the door of this church that Luther nailed his 95 theses in 1517; there's no proof it really happened, and the present door only dates back 100 years, but it's still a magnet for visitors.

Once you've had enough of old Martin, check back into the 20th century by visiting the **Haus der Geschichte** (House of History; ☎ 409 004; Schlossstrasse 6; adult/concession €3/2; ☼ 10am-5pm Tue-Fri, 11am-6pm Sat & Sun), a fascinating reconstruction of the everyday trappings of life in the GDR.

Sleeping & Eating

Jugendherberge (☎ 403 255; jugendherberge@witten berg.de; Schloss; dm junior/senior €16.80/19.50; ℗ ☐) Settings don't come much better than this, actually inside the town's historic castle building. The rooms are disappointingly unspectacular, but with the hostel-standard prices who's complaining?

Hotel am Schwanenteich (☎ 402 807; Töpfer strasse 1; s €31-36, d €50-59; ℗) This small *pension* has much nicer rooms than you'd expect for the price, plus a convenient location. That and the charming owners make this Wittenberg's best budget option.

Brauhaus Wittenberg (☎ 433 130; www.brauhaus -wittenberg.de in German; Im Beyerhof, Markt 6; s/d €50/70; ℗) One for night owls and beer lovers, this brewery restaurant has good spacious rooms upstairs to sleep off the local produce, once the pub noise dies down at least.

Café Hundertwasserschule (☎ 410 685; Markt 15; mains €4-14) Named for the famous Wittenberg school designed by out-there Viennese architect Friedensreich Hundertwasser, this is the best spot in town for home-made, healthy, vegetarian food, with plenty of more indulgent treats as well.

Getting There & Away

Wittenberg is on the main train line between Leipzig (€15.80, 30 minutes, every two hours) and Berlin (€23.60, one hour, hourly). Be sure you buy tickets to 'Lutherstadt-Wittenberg' – *not* Wittenberg.

BAVARIA

Although Bavaria (Bayern) fulfils all the stereotypes visitors have of Germany – *Lederhosen*, beer halls, oompah bands and romantic castles – it is in fact unique and more the exception rather than the rule for the rest of the country. It has a long history of conservative politics, Munich being a periodic exception, and a reputation for being culturally closer to Italy than parts of Germany to the north. If you only have time for one part of Germany after Berlin, this is it. Munich, the capital of Bavaria, is its heart and soul. The Bavarian Alps, Nuremberg and the medieval towns on the Romantic Road are other attractions.

MUNICH

☎ 089 / pop 1.2 million

Munich (München) is the Bavarian mother lode. But this beer-quaffing, sausage-eating city can be as cosmopolitan as anywhere in Europe. Munich residents have figured out how to enjoy life – and are perfectly happy to show outsiders, as a visit to a beer hall will confirm. But Munich is more than a beer mecca, as 11 universities, 300 churches and many fine museums attest. Throw in one of the largest parks in Europe and it's easy to understand why it's the number one destination for foreign visitors to Germany.

Munich didn't really achieve prominence until the 19th century, under the guiding hand of King Ludwig I. In the aftermath of WWI, the city became a hotbed of right-wing political ferment. Hitler staged a failed coup attempt here in 1923 but it took another decade for the National Socialists to seize power. WWII brought bombing and more than 6000 civilian deaths. Today it's a centre of the high-tech and publishing industries.

Orientation

The main train station is just west of the centre. From the station, head east along Bayerstrasse, through Karlsplatz, and then along Neuhauser Strasse and Kaufingerstrasse to Marienplatz, the hub of Munich.

North of Marienplatz are the Residenz (the former royal palace), Schwabing (the famous student section) and the parklands of the Englischer Garten. East of Marienplatz is the Platzl quarter for beer houses, restaurants and Maximilianstrasse, a fashionable street ideal for strolling and window-shopping.

Information
DISCOUNT CARD
Munich Welcome Card (72hr €16) Unlimited travel on public transport, plus discounts for many museums, galleries and other attractions. You can buy them from both tourist offices.

EMERGENCY SERVICES
Ambulance (☎ 112)
Police (☎ 110) Police station on Arnulfstrasse right beside the Hauptbahnhof.

INTERNET ACCESS
easyEverything (☎ 5599 9696; Bahnhofplatz 1; per 80min €2; ⊗ 6am-1am Sun-Fri, 24hr Sat) Hundreds of terminals in the post office building.
Internet-Cafe (☎ 2070 2737; Marienplatz 20; ⊗ 24hr) In the subway directly in front of the stairway up to the Viktualienmarkt.

MEDICAL SERVICES
Home Medical Service (☎ 551 771, 724 2001)

MONEY
American Express (☎ 2280 1465; Promenadeplatz 6)
Reisebank (☎ 551 0830; main train station) If you

GETTING INTO TOWN
Munich's Flughafen airport is connected by the S8 and the S1 to Marienplatz and the main train station (€8, 40 minutes, every 20 minutes 4am to 12.30am). The airport bus also runs from Arnulfstrasse on the north side of the main train station (€9, 45 minutes, every 20 minutes 6.50am to 7.50pm). Forget taxis (they're at least €50!).

show an EurAide newsletter, *The Inside Track* (see below), the commission will be 50% cheaper.
Thomas Cook (☎ 235 0920; Petersplatz 10)

POST
Main post office (Bahnhofplatz 1; ⊗ 7.30am-8pm Mon-Fri, 9am-4pm Sat) The poste restante address is: Hauptpostlagernd (Poste Restante), Bahnhofplatz 1, 80074 München.

TOURIST INFORMATION
The excellent *Young People's Guide* (€0.50) is available from information offices. The English-language monthly *Munich Found* (€3) is also useful (find it at English bookshops, cafés and restaurants) as is the annual *Visitors' Guide* (free).
Branch tourist office (Marienplatz; ⊗ 10am-8pm Mon-Fri, 10am-4pm Sat) Beneath the Neues Rathaus.
EurAide (☎ 593 889; www.euraide.com; Hauptbahnhof; ⊗ 7.45am-12.45pm & 2-6pm May-Oct, 8am-noon & 1-4pm Mon-Fri Nov-Mar) Near platform 11 at the main train station, EurAide has well-informed staff giving advice on local and European train travel, and helping to find rooms (€3 per booking).
Jugendinformationszentrum (Youth Information Centre; ☎ 5141 0660; Paul-Heyse-Strasse 22; ⊗ noon-6pm Mon-Fri, to 8pm Thu) Wide range of information for young people, an extensive library of periodicals and cheap Internet access.
Main tourist office (☎ 2333 0300; www.muenchen -tourist.de; Hauptbahnhof, Bahnhofplatz 2; ⊗ 8am-8pm Mon-Sat) To the right as you exit the train station via the eastern entrance. Its room-finding service is free and you must apply in person.

Sights
PALACES
The huge **Residenz** (Max-Joseph-Platz 3) housed Bavarian rulers from 1385 to 1918. Apart from the actual palace itself, the **Residenzmuseum** (☎ 290 671; www.schloesser.bayern.de; Residenzstrasse 1; adult/concession €4/2; ⊗ 9am-6pm Tue-Sun,

CENTRAL MUNICH (MÜNCHEN)

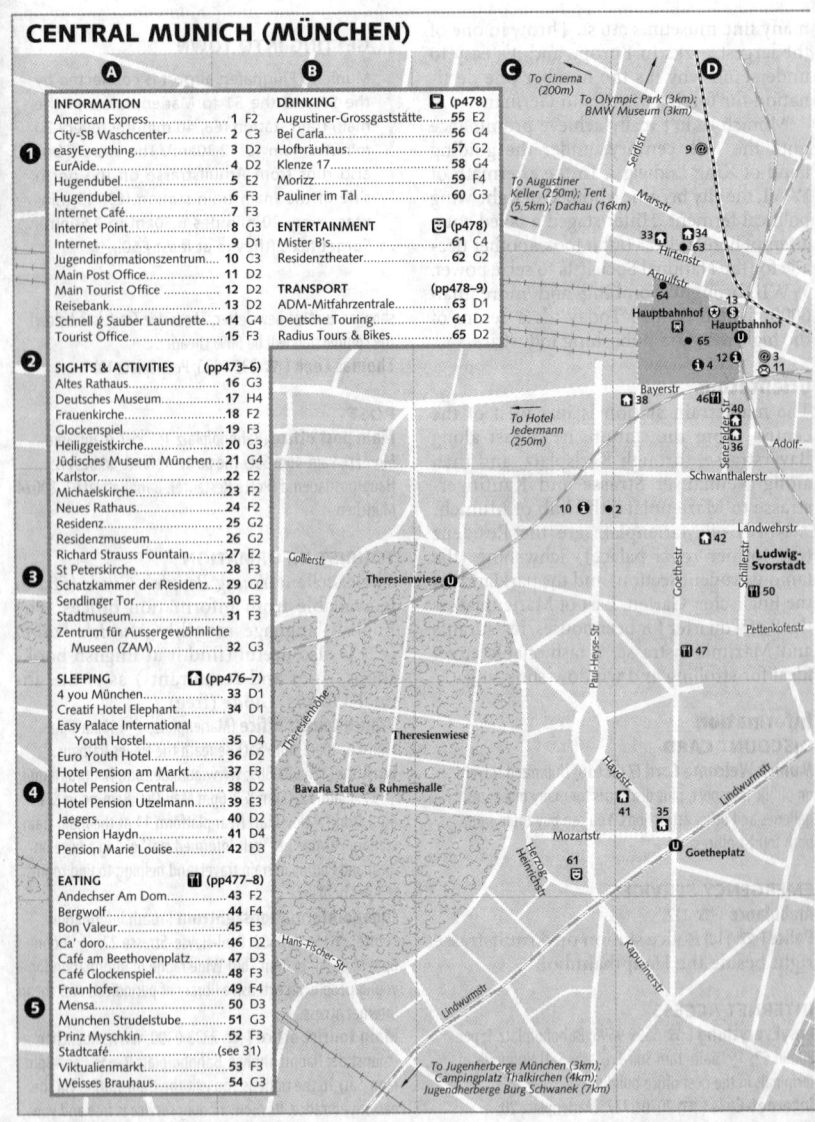

INFORMATION
American Express	1	F2
City-SB Waschcenter	2	C3
easyEverything	3	D2
EurAide	4	D2
Hugendubel	5	E2
Hugendubel	6	F3
Internet Café	7	F3
Internet Point	8	E2
Internet	9	D1
Jugendinformationszentrum	10	C3
Main Post Office	11	D2
Main Tourist Office	12	D2
Reisebank	13	D1
Schnell & Sauber Laundrette	14	G4
Tourist Office	15	F3

SIGHTS & ACTIVITIES (pp473–6)
Altes Rathaus	16	G3
Deutsches Museum	17	H4
Frauenkirche	18	F2
Glockenspiel	19	F3
Heiliggeistkirche	20	G3
Jüdisches Museum München	21	G4
Karlstor	22	E2
Michaelskirche	23	F2
Neues Rathaus	24	F2
Residenz	25	G2
Residenzmuseum	26	G2
Richard Strauss Fountain	27	E2
St Peterskirche	28	F3
Schatzkammer der Residenz	29	G2
Sendlinger Tor	30	E3
Stadtmuseum	31	F3
Zentrum für Aussergewöhnliche Museen (ZAM)	32	G3

SLEEPING (pp476–7)
4 you München	33	D1
Creatif Hotel Elephant	34	D1
Easy Palace International Youth Hostel	35	D4
Euro Youth Hotel	36	D2
Hotel Pension am Markt	37	F3
Hotel Pension Central	38	D2
Hotel Pension Utzelmann	39	E3
Jaegers	40	D2
Pension Haydn	41	D4
Pension Marie Louise	42	D3

EATING (pp477–8)
Andechser Am Dom	43	F2
Bergwolf	44	F4
Bon Valeur	45	E3
Ca' doro	46	D2
Café am Beethovenplatz	47	D3
Café Glockenspiel	48	F3
Fraunhofer	49	F4
Mensa	50	D3
Munchen Strudelstube	51	G3
Prinz Myschkin	52	F3
Stadtcafé	(see 31)	
Viktualienmarkt	53	F3
Weisses Brauhaus	54	G3

DRINKING (p478)
Augustiner-Grossgaststätte	55	E2
Bei Carla	56	G4
Hofbräuhaus	57	G2
Klenze 17	58	G4
Morizz	59	F4
Pauliner im Tal	60	G3

ENTERTAINMENT (p478)
Mister B's	61	C4
Residenztheater	62	G2

TRANSPORT (pp478–9)
ADM-Mitfahrzentrale	63	D1
Deutsche Touring	64	D2
Radius Tours & Bikes	65	D2

To Cinema (200m)
To Olympic Park (3km); BMW Museum (3km)
To Augustiner Keller (250m); Tent (5.5km); Dachau (16km)
To Hotel Jedermann (250m)
To Jugenherberge München (3km); Campingplatz Thalkirchen (4km); Jugendherberge Burg Schwanek (7km)

Theresienwiese
Bavaria Statue & Ruhmeshalle

9am-8pm Thu) has an extraordinary array of 100 rooms containing the Wittelsbach house's belongings. In the same building, the **Schatzkammer** (☎ 290 671; enter from Max-Joseph-Platz 3; adult/concession €4/2; ♥ 9am-6pm Tue-Sun, 9am-8pm Thu) exhibits a ridiculous quantity of beautiful jewels, crowns and ornate gold.

If this doesn't satisfy your passion for palaces, visit **Schloss Nymphenburg** (☎ 179 080; www.schloesser.bayern.de; adult/concession €5/4, museum & gallery €10/8; ♥ 9am-6pm Apr-15 Oct, 10am-4pm 16 Oct-Mar), northwest of the city centre via tram No 17 from the main train station. This was the royal family's equally impressive summer home.

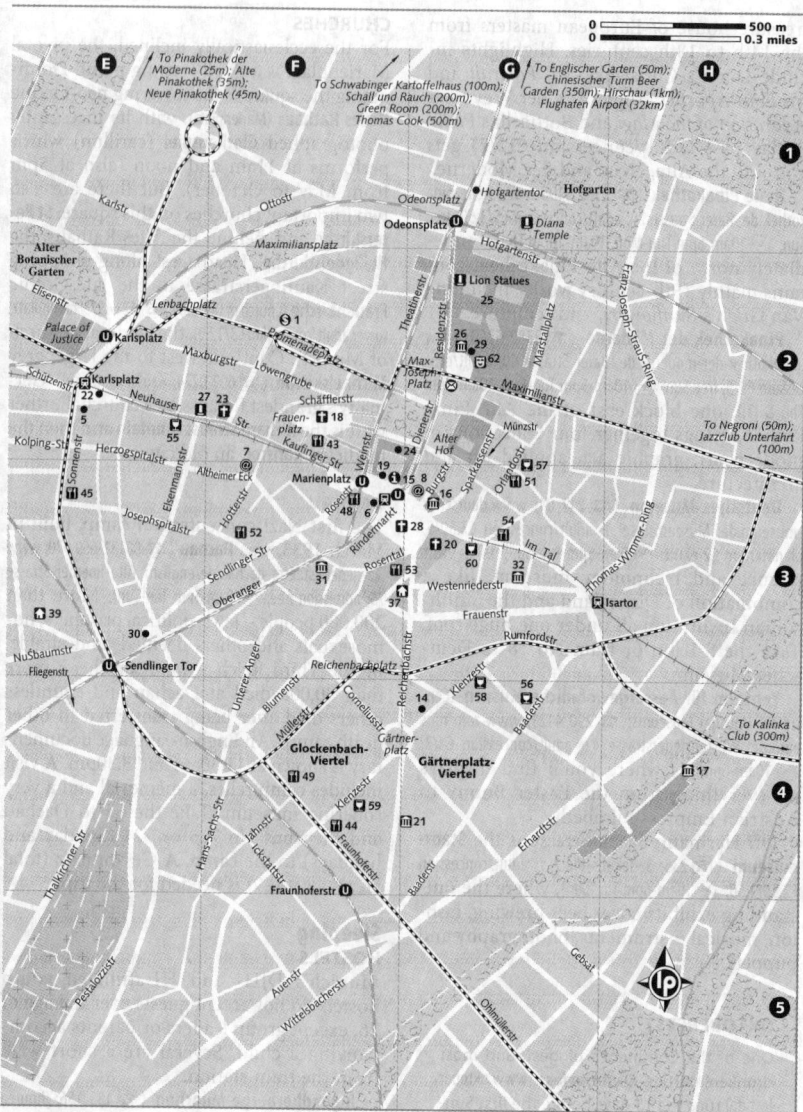

GARDENS

One of the largest city parks in Europe, the **Englischer Garten**, north, is a great place for strolling, especially along the Schwabinger Bach. In summer, nude sunbathing is the rule rather than the exception. If people aren't doing this, they're probably drinking merrily at one of the park's three **beer gardens** (see p478). Check out the surfers riding the waves from the bridge near the Haus der Kunst.

MUSEUMS

The **Alte Pinakothek** (☎ 2380 5216; www.alte-pinako thek.de; Barer Strasse 27; adult/concession €5/3.50, free Sun; ☼ 10am-5pm Tue-Sun, 10am-10pm Thu) is a veritable treasure house of European masters from the 14th to 18th centuries. Highlights include Dürer's Christ-like *Self Portrait* and his *Four Apostles*, Rogier van der Weyden's *Adoration of the Magi* and Botticelli's *Pietà*. A day pass (adult/concession €12/7) gets you into the Alte, Neue and der Moderne.

Neue Pinakothek (☎ 2380 5195; www.neue-pina kothek.de; Barer Strasse 29; adult/concession €5/3.50, free Sun; ☣ 10am-5pm Thu-Mon, 10am-10pm Thu), immediately north of the Alte Pinakothek, contains mainly 19th-century works, including Van Gogh's *Sunflowers*, and sculpture.

Pinakothek der Moderne (☎ 2380 5360; www .pinakothek-der-moderne.de; Barer Strasse 40; adult/concession €9/5, free Sun; ☣ 10am-5pm Tue-Sun, 10am-8pm Thu & Fri), one block east of the Alte Pinakothek, brings together four collections of modern art, graphic art, applied art and architecture.

Deutsches Museum (☎ 217 91; www.deutsches -museum.de; Museumsinsel 1; adult/concession €7.50/5, planetarium €2 extra; ☣ 9am-5pm Tue-Sun) is a vast science and technology museum, like a combination of Disneyland and the Smithsonian Institution all under one huge roof. Take the S-Bahn or tram No 18 to Deutsches Museum.

Zentrum für Aussergewöhnliche Museen (Centre for Unusual Museums; ☎ 290 4121; www.zam-mus eum.de; Westenriederstrasse 41; adult/concession €4/3; ☣ 10am-6pm) is where you'll find displays on everything from the Easter Bunny to Austrian Empress Elisabeth.

Off Hermann-Saack-Strasse is the **Stadt-museum** (☎ 233; St-Jakobs-Platz 1; adult/concession €2.50/1.50; ☣ 10am-6pm Tue-Sun), where the outstanding exhibits cover beer brewing, fashion, musical instruments, photography and puppets.

OKTOBERFEST

One of the Continent's biggest, and most drunken, parties, **Oktoberfest** (www.oktober fest.de) runs the 15 days before the first Sunday in October. Reserve accommodation well ahead and go early in the day so you can grab a seat in one of the hangar-sized beer 'tents'. The action takes place at the Theresienwiese grounds, about a 10-minute walk southwest of the main train station. While there is no entrance fee, those €6 1L steins of beer add up fast.

CHURCHES

For the ecclesiastically inclined, the pivotal Marienplatz is a good starting point. Dominating the square is the towering neo-Gothic **Neues Rathaus** (Marienplatz), with its incessantly photographed **Glockenspiel** (carillon) which performs at 11am and noon (also at 5pm from May to October). But there are also two important churches on this square: **St Pe-terskirche** and, behind the Altes Rathaus, the **Heiliggeistkirche**. Head west along shopping street Kaufingerstrasse to the late-Gothic **Frauenkirche** (Church of Our Lady; ☎ 423 457; Frauenplatz; tower adult/concession €3/1.50), the landmark church of Munich. Continue west to the large, grey **Michaelskirche** (☎ 609 0224; Kaufingerstrasse), Germany's grandest Renaissance church. Further west is the **Richard Strauss Fountain** and then the medieval **Karlstor**, an old city gate.

DACHAU

The first Nazi concentration camp, built in March 1933, was **Dachau** (☎ 08131-669 970; www .kz-gedenkstaette-dachau.de/english; Alte-Roemer-Strasse 75; admission free; ☣ 9am-5pm Tue-Sun). More than 200,000 people – Jews, political prisoners, homosexuals and others deemed 'undesirable' by the Third Reich – were sent here; more than 30,000 died at Dachau and countless others died after being transferred to other death camps. An English-language documentary is shown at 11.30am and 3.30pm. A visit includes camp relics, a memorial and a very sobering museum. Take the S2 to Dachau and then bus No 726 or 724 (Sunday and holidays) to the camp. A Gesamtnetz (total area) ticket (€9) is needed for the trip.

Sleeping
HOSTELS

Munich's DJH- and HI-affiliated youth hostels do not accept guests over the age of 26, except group leaders or parents accompanying a child. Several are a short walk from the train station.

Jugendherberge München (☎ 131 156; jhmuen chen@djh-bayern.de; Wendl-Dietrich-Strasse 20; dm €19.20; ☒) Short on atmosphere, long on beds. Northwest of the centre (U1 to Rotkreuz-platz).

Jugendherberge Burg Schwaneck (☎ 7448 6670; info@jugendherberge-burgschwaneck.de; Burgweg 4-6; dm €15.50; ℗) A castle, a hostel? Which is it? Both. Take the S7 to Pullach, then it's a 10-minute walk.

Euro Youth Hotel (☎ 5990 8811; www.euro-youth -hotel.de; Senefelderstrasse 5; dm €17, s/d without bathroom €35/50; ✗ ⬜) The party never stops here. Euro and non-Euro youths alike work on international relationships in the bar and lounge. Rooms and facilities are well maintained and the staff is a good source of info.

Jaeger's (☎ 555 281; www.jaegershotel.de; Senefelderstrasse 3; dm €15, s/d €45/80) Jaeger's next door is more subdued, less social but it may be possible to actually get some zzz's in the basement dormitory.

Easy Palace International Youth Hostel (☎ 558 7970; www.easypalace.com; Mozartstrasse 4; dm/s/d €17/29/50; Ⓟ ⬜) Noisy when school groups are in; otherwise, it's on a nice quiet block. The attached restaurant cooks up good pizza.

4 you München (☎ 552 1660; www.the4you.de; Hirtenstrasse 18; dm under/over 27s €17/19, s/d with breakfast €44/70; ✗) Eco-friendly and just a short walk from the train station.

HOTELS

There are plenty of relatively inexpensive, if somewhat scruffy, hotels in the area surrounding the train station. During holidays and trade fairs, prices rise significantly.

Hotel Pension Central (☎ 543 9846; pension .central@t-online.de; Bayerstrasse 55; s/d with breakfast €34/52) Not as bad as it looks from the outside; rooms are adequate. Across from the train station.

Hotel Pension Utzelmann (☎ 594 889; info@hotel -utzelmann.de; Pettenkoferstrasse 6; s/d with breakfast €33/53; Ⓟ) In an attractive pastel painted home; call or book to guarantee someone's there when you arrive.

Pension Haydn (☎ 5440 4703; www.pension-haydn .de; Haydnstrasse 9; s/d from €38/52; Ⓟ) Not far from the Goetheplatz U-Bahn station on a quiet residential street, the Haydn's superior rooms are tended with love and care.

Pension Marie Luise (☎ 5525 5660; comfort-hotel -andi@t-online.de; Landwehrstrasse 35; s/d €30/45) Simple rooms at a good price.

Creatif Hotel Elephant (☎ 555 785; www.munich -service.de/elephant.htm; Lämmerstrasse 6; s/d €69/89; ✗) A good, slightly upmarket option near the train station. Does a good breakfast buffet.

CAMPING

Campingplatz Thalkirchen (☎ 7243 0808; fax 724 3177; Zentralländstrasse 49; adult/tent €4.40/3.60, heated cabin per person €10.50; ⊙ mid-Mar–Oct) Take the U3 to Thalkirchen and then bus No 57 (about 20 minutes), southwest of the city centre.

Tent (☎ 141 4300; www.the-tent.com; In den Kirschen 30; b in main tent €9, camp site €5.50; ⊙ Jun–Sep) Roll out of your tent to this camping ground's own beer garden. Take Tram 17 to the Botanic Gardens, then follow the signs.

Eating

RESTAURANTS

Bergwolf (☎ 2325 9858; Fraunhoferstrasse 17; meals €5) Inexpensive *Wurst*, fries and beer are the speciality at this informal hang-out.

Bon Valeur (☎ 5488 3994; Sonnenstrasse 17; mains €7) Try the Bon Valeur for organic food and freshly squeezed juices in a casual setting.

Fraunhofer (☎ 266 460; Fraunhoferstrasse 9; mains €8-13) The highly recommended and always crowded Fraunhofer serves up good Bavarian cuisine.

Schwabinger Kartoffelhaus (☎ 303 677; Hohenzollernplatz 4; mains €5-15) Large potato-oriented portions in Schwabing.

Andechser Am Dom (☎ 298 481; Weinstrasse 7; mains €9-14) Slip behind the Frauenkirche for hearty Bavarian chow at its best.

Prinz Myschkin (☎ 265 596; Hackenstrasse 2; mains €9-14) For the discerning vegetarian, Myschkin provides tasty pizzas and pastas.

Weisses Brauhaus (☎ 290 1380; Tal 7; mains €10-15) One of the oldest breweries in Munich; serves up specials like boiled ox cheeks.

CAFÉS

Most of Munich's café culture centres on Schwabing, the university haunt, where you'll find plenty of snug little spots.

Café Am Beethovenplatz (☎ 5440 4348; Goethenstrasse 51; mains €7-10) A casual hang-out with no airs and graces. Great, affordable food, live music from 7.30pm on.

Schall und Rauch (☎ 288 0957; Schellingstrasse 22; dishes €5) This small unpretentious café has its own CD shop. The menu changes daily but soups are always good.

Café Glockenspiel (☎ 264 256; Marienplatz 28) A window seat at the Glockenspiel is a much-sought-after, if ambitious, goal.

Stadt Café (☎ 266 949; St-Jakobsplatz 1) At the Stadtmuseum, this café has funky décor, an intellectual crowd and nice courtyard.

QUICK EATS

There are plenty of cheap eats in the blocks lying south of the train station. And student card-holders can fill up for around €2 in any of the university **Mensas** (Schillerstrasse 47, Leopoldstrasse 13B, Arcistrasse 17B & Lothstrassa 13D).

Ca'Doro (Bayerstrasse 31; pizza slices €1.90) The food and service are better than you might expect at Ca'Doro, in the middle of the train station traffic.

Munchen Strudelstube (☎ 5386 8710; Orlandostrasse; 3 strudels €6) Eat your fill of greasy fritters and strudels here.

Viktualienmarkt, just south of Marienplatz, is a large open-air market open every day except Saturday afternoon and Sunday, where you can put together a picnic feast to take to the Englischer Garten.

Drinking & Clubbing

Beer drinking is an integral part of Munich's entertainment scene. Germans drink an average of 130L of the amber liquid each per year; Munich residents manage to drink much more than this!

BEER HALLS & GARDENS

Hofbräuhaus (☎ 2901 3610; www.hofbraeuhaus.de; Am Platzl 9) Though tourists come by the busload, it's still a good-time place.

Augustiner Grossgaststätte (☎ 5519 9257; Neuhauser Strasse 27) This is probably what you imagine an old-style Munich beer hall looks like, filled with laughter, smoke and drunkenness.

Augustiner Keller (☎ 594 393; Arnulfstrasse 52) Only five minutes from the Hauptbahnhof, the Keller has a large and leafy beer garden and fine beer.

Pauliner im Tal (☎ 219 9400; Tal 12) If you've had your fill of beer, the Pauliner also has an extensive wine menu.

On a summer day there's nothing better than sitting and sipping among the greenery in the Englischer Garten. The **Chinesischer Turm** (☎ 383 8730) is a classic, although the nearby **Hirschau** (☎ 369 942) beer garden on the banks of Kleinhesseloher See is less crowded.

BARS & NIGHTCLUBS

Munich has no shortage of lively bars and clubs. Thirty to 40 are clustered in industrial buildings in the Kultafabrik (formerly known as Kunstpark Ost) neighbourhood southeast of the Altstadt on the other side of the Isar River. The *Young People's Guide* keeps abreast of the hot spots to party.

Klenze 17 (☎ 228 5795; Klenzestrasse 17) The extensive whisky selection is almost as large as its two small rooms. Popular with students.

Kalinka Club (☎ 4090 7260; Grafingerstrasse 6; ☽ from 10pm Thu-Sat) This Russian bar in the Kultafabrik attracts an eclectic mix.

Green Room (☎ 3306 6352; Leopoldstrasse 13) Funky and unpretentious Asian-themed bar in Schwabing. Prop yourself up on the cushions and enjoy the 150 kinds of cocktails. Well, maybe just a few.

Negroni (☎ 4895 0154; Innere Weinerstrasse 38) This small classically designed cocktail bar serves them up stiff.

GAY & LESBIAN VENUES

Much of Munich's gay and lesbian nightlife is in the area just south of Sendlinger Tor. *Our Munich* is a monthly guide to gay and lesbian life, and is available at **Our Munich Shop** (☎ 2601 8503; Müllerstrasse 36). Resembling a Paris bar, **Morizz** (☎ 201 6776; Klenzestrasse 43) is a popular haunt for gay men; and **Bei Carla** (☎ 227 901; Buttermelcherstrasse 9) is an exclusively lesbian bar-café with lots of regulars.

Entertainment

Munich is one of the cultural capitals of Germany; the publications listed in Information (p473) can guide you to the best events or check out www.munichfound.de, a cultural events website updated monthly.

Residenztheater (☎ 2185 1920; Max-Joseph-Platz 2) Home of the Bavarian State Opera and site of many cultural events.

Cinema (☎ 555 255; www.cinema-muenchen.com; Nymphenburger Strasse 31) Current films in English are screened here.

Jazzclub Unterfahrt (☎ 448 2794; Kirchenstrasse 42-44) Near the Max-Weber-Platz U-Bahn station. It has live music every night and open jam sessions on Sunday night.

Mister B's (☎ 534 901; Herzog-Heinrichstrasse 42) Take the U-Bahn to Goetheplatz to hear live jazz Thursday to Sunday at this tiny club.

Getting There & Away

AIR

Munich International Airport (www.munich-airport .de/en) is second in importance only to Frankfurt for international and national connections. Flights will take you to all major destinations worldwide. Main German cities are serviced by at least half a dozen flights daily.

CAR & MOTORCYCLE

Munich is linked to the Romantic Road by the Deutsche-Touring (also known as the Europabus) Munich–Frankfurt service (see below). Inquire at **Deutsche-Touring** (☎ 545 8700; service@deutsche-touring.com), near platform 26 of the main train station, about its international services to destinations such as Prague and Budapest. Buses stop along the northern side of the train station.

RIDE SERVICES

For arranged rides, the **ADM-Mitfahrzentrale** (☎ 194 40; Lämmerstrasse 6) is near the main train station.

TRAIN

Train services to/from Munich are excellent. There are rapid connections every two hours to all major cities in Germany, as well as frequent EC trains to other European cities such as Zürich (€61, five hours, four daily), Vienna (€59, five hours, hourly), Prague (€60, seven hours, two daily), Paris (€105, nine hours, three daily) and Amsterdam (€143, nine hours, hourly). High-speed ICE services from Munich include Frankfurt (€76, 3½ hours, hourly), Hamburg (€135, six hours, hourly) and Berlin (€142, seven hours, hourly).

Getting Around
PUBLIC TRANSPORT

Most places of interest to tourists (except Dachau and the airport) are within the 'blue' *Innenraum* (inner zone). MVV tickets are valid for the S-Bahn, U-Bahn, trams and buses, but must be validated before use. The U-Bahn stops operating around 12.30am on weekdays and 1.30am at weekends, but there are some later buses and S-Bahns. Rail passes are valid only on the S-Bahn.

Kurzstrecke (short rides) cost €1 and are good for no more than four stops on buses and trams and two stops on the U- and S-Bahns. Longer trips cost €2. It's cheaper to buy a strip card of 10 tickets (*Mehrfahrtenkarte*) for €9 and stamp one strip per adult on short rides, and two strips for longer rides in the inner zone. *Tageskarte* (day passes) for the inner zone cost €4.50, while three-day tickets cost €11, or €15 for two adults.

TAXI & BICYCLE

Taxis are expensive and not much more convenient than public transport. **Radius**

Bike Rental (☎ 596 113; main train station) rents out two-wheelers from €14/43 per day/week.

ROMANTIC ROAD

Even if you are not particularly romantic, this route running from north to south through western Bavaria from Würzburg to Füssen near the Austrian border will pull at your heart strings. Originally conceived as a way of promoting tourism, the popular Romantic Road (Romantische Strasse) links a series of picturesque Bavarian towns and cities. Tourist offices are efficient at finding accommodation in almost any price range you need. Expect to pay around €15 to €25 per person in private homes.

In the north of the route, Würzburg is well served by trains. To start at the southern end, take the RE train from Munich to Füssen (€18.20, two hours, hourly). Rothenburg is linked by train to Würzburg, Nuremberg and Munich via Steinach. To reach Dinkelsbühl, take a train to Ansbach and from there a frequent bus onwards. Nördlingen has train connections to Stuttgart and Munich. There are four daily buses between Füssen and Garmisch-Partenkirchen (€7; all stop at Hohenschwangau and Oberammergau), as well as several connections between Füssen and Oberstdorf (€8.10; via Pfronten).

Deutsche-Touring GmbH (☎ 069-790 350; www.deutsche-touring.com; Am Römerhof 17, 60486 Frankfurt-am-Main) runs a daily 'Castle Road' coach service in each direction between Mannheim and Rothenburg via Heidelberg (€29, 5½ hours).

It is possible to do this route using train connections, local buses or car, but most train pass-holders prefer to take the Deutsche-Touring (also known as Europabus) bus. From April to October Deutsche-Touring runs one coach daily in each direction between Frankfurt and Munich (12 hours), and another in either direction between Dinkelsbühl and Füssen (4½ hours). You can break the journey at any point and continue the next day (reserve a seat for the next day as you disembark). The full fare from Frankfurt to Füssen is €74 (change buses at Rothenburg). Eurail and German Rail passes are valid and Inter-Rail pass-holders receive a 50% discount, while those under 26 save 10%.

Würzburg

☎ 0931 / pop 131,000

More than 1300 years old, surrounded by forests and vineyards – including three of the four largest wine-growing estates in all of Germany – the charming city of Würzburg straddles the upper Main River. Rebuilt after bombings late in the war (it took only 17 minutes to almost completely destroy the city), Würzburg is a centre of art and beautiful architecture.

The **tourist office** (☎ 372 335; www.wuerzburg.de; Oberer Markt; ✆ 10am-6pm Mon-Fri, 10am-2pm Sat) is in the rococo masterpiece, Haus zum Falken. On the 1st floor of the same building, the **Stadtbücherei** (☎ 373 438; per 20min €1) offers Internet access.

The magnificent, sprawling **Residenz** (☎ 355 170; www.schloesser.bayern.de; Residenzplatz 2; adult/concession €4.50/3.50; ✆ 9am-6pm Apr-Oct, 10am-4pm Nov-Mar) took a generation to build and boasts the world's largest ceiling fresco painting. The Hofgarten at the back is a beautiful spot. The **Dom St Kilian** (☎ 3866 5600; www.museum-am-dom.de in German; Kiliansplatz; admission €4; ✆ 10am-7pm Apr-Oct, 10am-5pm Nov-Mar) interior and the adjacent **Neumünster** in the old town continue the baroque themes of the Residenz.

The medieval fortress **Marienberg**, across the river on the hill, is reached by crossing the 15th-century stone **Alte Mainbrücke** (bridge) from the city and walking up Tellstiege, a small alley. It encloses the **Fürstenbau Museum** (☎ 438 38; adult/concession €3/1.50; ✆ 9am-6pm Tue-Sun Apr-Sep, 10am-4pm Tue-Sun Oct-Mar) featuring the episcopal apartments, and the regional **Mainfränkisches Museum** (☎ 430 16; adult/concession €3/1.50; ✆ 10am-6pm Tue-Sun Apr-Sep, 10am-4pm Tue-Sun Oct-Mar). See both on a combined card (€4). For a simple thrill, wander the walls enjoying the panoramic views.

Jugendgästehaus Würzburg (☎ 425 90; www .jugendherberge.de/jh/wuerzburg in German; Burkarderstrasse 44; dm €18; P) looks like a mini version of the fortress that looms above (take tram 3 or 5 from the station). **Hotel-Pension Spehnkuch** (☎ 547 52; www.pension-spehnkuch.de in German; Röntgenring 7; s/d/tr from €29/52/75) is in a nice spot near the river and park. Rooms are spotless.

Kanu-Club (☎ 725 36; Mergentheimer Strasse 13b; tent/person €3.50/3.50) is the place to camp on the west bank of the Main; take tram No 3 or 5 to Jugendbühlweg.

Cafe Klug (Peterstrasse 2; dishes €6) is a student café/bar/restaurant with a rock'n'roll theme.

The atmosphere, food and local wines at **Bürgerspital** (☎ 352 880; Theaterstrasse 19; mains €5-18) are first class in this former medieval hospice.

Frequent RE trains head to Würzburg from Frankfurt (€19.20, two hours) and Nuremberg (€14.40, one hour). It's a major stop-off for the ICE trains on the Hamburg–Munich line. It is also on the Deutsche-Touring Romantic Road bus route (2½ hours to/from Rothenburg by bus).

Rothenburg ob der Tauber

☎ 09861 / pop 12,000

Not a single modern building is within sight in Rothenburg and it's soon obvious why this charmingly preserved medieval town is continually under siege from tourists.

There's a helpful **tourist office** (☎ 404 800; www.rothenburg.de; Marktplatz 2; ✆ 9am-noon & 1-6pm Mon-Fri, 10am-3pm Sat May-Oct, 9am-5pm Mon-Fri, 10am-1pm Sat Nov-Apr).

The **Rathaus on Markt** was commenced in Gothic style in the 14th century but completed in Renaissance style. The **tower** (admission €1) gives a majestic view over the town and the Tauber Valley.

The **Puppen und Spielzeugmuseum** (Doll & Toy Museum; ☎ 7330; Hofbronnengasse 13; adult/concession €4/2.50; ✆ 9.30am-6pm Mar-Dec, 11am-5pm Jan & Feb) is the largest private doll and toy collection in Germany. The **Reichsstadt Museum** (☎ 939 043; www.reichsstadtmuseum.rothenburg.de; Klosterhof 5; adult/concession €3/2; ✆ 10am-5pm Apr-Oct, 1-4pm Nov-Mar), in the former convent, features the superb *Rothenburger Passion*. Get a gruesome glimpse of the past at the **Kriminalmuseum** (☎ 5359; www.kriminalmuseum.rothenburg.de; Burggasse 3-5; adult/concession €3.50/2.30; ✆ 9.30am-6pm Apr-Oct, 2-4pm Nov-Mar), which houses all manner of torture devices.

The **Jugendherberge** (☎ 941 60; www.jugendher berge.de; Mühlacker 1; dm €18; P) is housed in two enormous renovated old buildings in the south of the old town. A good budget option, **Das Lädle** (☎ 6130; www.das-laedle.de; Spitalgasse 18; s/d with breakfast €22/38; P) is casual, with comfortable rooms in a central location. Camping options are a few kilometres north of the town walls at Detwang. **Tauber-Romantik** (☎ 6191; fax 868 99; Detwang 39; adult/tent €3.75/4; ✆ Apr-Nov) is east of the road on the river.

Vine-covered and cosy, the **Altfränkische Weinstube** (☎ 6404; Klosterhof 7; mains €6-13) is justifiably popular, with a varied and well-priced menu and fantastic atmosphere.

There's frequent train service from Würzburg (€9, 1½ hours) but travel to/from Munich (from €36.40, 3½ hours) may require two or three changes. The Europabus stops in the main bus park at the Hauptbahnhof. The A7 autobahn runs right past town.

Nördlingen
☎ 09081 / pop 21,000

Nördlingen is encircled by its original 14th-century walls and lies within the basin of the **Ries**, a huge crater created by a meteor more than 15 million years ago. The crater is one of the largest in existence (25km in diameter) and the **Rieskrater Museum** (☎ 273 8220; Eugene-Shoemaker-Platz 1; adult/concession €3/1.50; 10am-noon & 1.30-4.30pm Tue-Sun) gives details. For a bird's-eye view of the town, climb the tower of **St Georg Kirche**. You'll find the **tourist office** (☎ 841 16; www.noerdlingen.de; Marktplatz 2) very helpful. The **Jugendherberge** (☎ 271 816; Kaiserwiese 1; dm €11.25) is a signposted 10-minute walk from the centre. **Altreuter Garni** (☎ 4319; fax 9797; Markt 11; s/d with bathroom & toilet €38/52) has simple, pleasant rooms. The hostel was closed at the time of writing, but is scheduled to reopen in 2005.

Füssen
☎ 08362 / pop 14,000

If you've ever wondered how the other half lives (that is slightly mad royalty), then the two castles in nearby Schwangau associated with King Ludwig II are not to be missed. Just short of the Austrian border and the foothills of the Alps, Füssen also has a monastery, a castle and splendid baroque architecture.

INFORMATION
Tourist Office (☎ 938 50; www.fuessen.de; Kaiser-Maximillian-Platz 1; 9am-5pm Mon-Fri, 10am-1pm Sat)

SIGHTS
Neuschwanstein and Hohenschwangau Castles provide a fascinating glimpse into what happens when a romantic king with a well-developed ego and questionable grasp of reality has an unlimited interior design budget. More interesting than the comparatively staid Hohenschwangau, where Ludwig lived as a child, is the adjacent **Neuschwanstein** (☎ 810 35; adult/concession €9/8, combination €17/15; 9am-6pm Apr-Sep, 10am-4pm Oct-Mar), which the king himself created. Here there is plenty of evidence of Ludwig's twin

obsessions: swans and Wagnerian operas. The sugary pastiche of architectural styles reputedly inspired Disney's Fantasyland castle. To get to the top from the ticket centre you can walk (30 minutes), take a bus (€2.60) or horse and buggy carriage (€7.50). There's a great view of Neuschwanstein from the Marienbrücke (bridge) over a waterfall and gorge just above the castle. From here you can hike the Tegelberg for even better vistas. Take the bus from Füssen train station (€2.80 return), share a **taxi** (☎ 7700; €8.50) or walk the 5km. The only way to enter the castles is with a 35-minute guided tour, which can be purchased from the **ticket centre** (Alpseestrasse 12, near Hohenschwangau). Go early to avoid the massive crowds.

SLEEPING & EATING
A pavilion near the tourist office has a computerised list of vacant rooms in town; most of the cheapest rooms, at around €12 per person, are located in private homes just a few minutes from the Altstadt.

Jugendherberge (☎ 7754; www.djh.de/jugendherbergen/fuessen; Mariahilferstrasse 5; dm €15; P) It gets a bit loud when there are groups in residence; otherwise it's quiet and only a signposted 10-minute walk from the train station.

Try the **Aquila Restaurant** (Brotmarkt 9; lunch special €5) for top-quality German fare in a dark, wood-panelled dining room.

GETTING THERE & AWAY
If you want to 'do' the royal castles on a day trip from Munich (€18.20, two to 2½ hours) you'll need to start early. The first train leaves Munich at 5.45am, getting to Füssen at 7.54am. Later trains depart at roughly five minutes to the hour but always check schedules before you go.

BAMBERG
☎ 0951 / pop 70,000

Tucked away from the main routes in northern Bavaria, Bamberg is a magnificent, untouched monument to the Holy Roman Emperor Heinrich II, and a town recognised by Unesco as a World Heritage Site.

The **tourist office** (☎ 871 161; www.bamberg.info; Geyerswörthstrasse 3; 9am-6pm Mon-Fri, 9am-3pm Sat year-round, plus 10am-2pm Sun May-Oct) is on an island in the Regnitz River.

Bamberg's main appeal is its fine buildings. Most are spread either side of the Regnitz

River, but the colourful **Altes Rathaus** is actually in it, precariously perched on its own islet. The princely and ecclesiastical district is centred on Domplatz, where the biggest attraction is the Romanesque and Gothic **cathedral**, housing the statue of the chivalric king-knight, the *Bamberger Reiter*. The **Kirche St Michael** is a must-see for its baroque art and the herbal compendium painted on its ceiling.

For the **Jugendherberge Wolfsschlucht** (☎ 560 02; www.djh.de; Oberer Leinritt 70; dm €14.60; 🕑 closed mid-Dec–mid-Jan), which looks something like a gingerbread home tucked into a forest on the river's west bank, take bus No 18 to Rodelbahn, walk northeast to the river bank, then turn left.

The **Petrolthof Fässla** (☎ 265 16; kasparzschultz@ t-online.de; Hallstadter Strasse 174; s/d €34/52; **P**) is a drinker's dream – a bed in a brewery. Rooms are large, clean and comfy.

Hotel Graupner (☎ 980 400; www.hotel-graupner.de; Langestrasse 5; s/d with shared bathroom €35/50; **P**) has individually decorated rooms and an elegant café.

Campingplatz Insel (☎ 563 20; campinginsel@ web.de; Am Campingplatz 1; adult/tent €3.50/6) is the place to camp.

Fränkischer Gästhaus (Obere Sandstrasse 1; mains €5-15) serves hearty mains and excellent *Bratwurst* (spicy sausage) on outdoor tables. **Wirsthaus zum Schlenkerla** (Dominikanerstrasse 6; mains €7-12) has been brewing its extraordinary *Rauchbier* since 1678. Franconian specialities accompany the beer.

There are RE and RB trains to/from both Würzburg (€14, one hour, hourly) and Nuremberg (€9, one hour, hourly). Bamberg is also served by ICE trains running between Munich (€45.20, 2½ hours) and Berlin (€68.80, 4½ hours) every two hours.

NUREMBERG
☎ 0911 / pop 493,000

Nuremberg's (Nürnberg) relatively oversized historical old town – imposing and picturesque – is where tourists flock here, especially during its world-famous Christmas market. The city played a major role during the Nazi years, was reduced to rubble by Allied bombing, and was the scene for the war crimes trials afterwards.

The main artery, the mostly pedestrian Königstrasse, takes you through the old town and its major squares.

Information
Flat-S (☎ 815 7521; 2nd fl, middle hall, main train station; per hr €4; 🕑 24hr) Internet access.
Main Post Office (Bahnhofplatz 1) By the station.
Main Tourist Office (☎ 233 6132; www.tourismus .nuernberg.de; Königstrasse 93; 🕑 9am-7pm Mon-Sat) Across from the train station.
Nuernberg Card (48hr €18) Both tourist offices sell this card, which provides free public transport, and entry to all museums and attractions.
Reisebank (main train station)
Tourist Office (☎ 233 6135; Hauptmarkt 18; 🕑 9am-6pm Mon-Sat year-round, 10am-4pm Sun May-Sep) Smaller branch operating on the city's main square.

Sights
The spectacular **Germanisches Nationalmuseum** (☎ 133 10; www.gnm.de; Kartäusergasse 1; adult/ concession €4/3, free 6-9pm Wed; 🕑 10am-5pm Tue-Sun, 10am-9pm Wed) is the most important general museum of German culture. It displays works by German painters and sculptors, an archaeological collection, arms and armour, musical and scientific instruments and toys. Close by, the sleek **Neues Museum** (☎ 240 200; www.nmn.de; Luitpoldstrasse 5; adult/ concession €3.50/2.50; 🕑 10am-8pm Tue-Fri, 10am-6pm Sat & Sun) contains a superb collection of contemporary art and design.

The scenic **Altstadt** is easily covered on foot. On Lorenzer Platz there's the **St Lorenzkirche**, noted for the 15th-century tabernacle that climbs like a vine up a pillar to the vaulted ceiling.

To the north is the bustling **Hauptmarkt**, where the most famous Christkindlesmarkt in Germany is held from the Friday before Advent to Christmas Eve. Near the Rathaus is **St Sebalduskirche**, Nuremberg's oldest church (dating from the 13th century), with the shrine of St Sebaldus.

Climb up Burgstrasse to the enormous **Kaiserburg complex** (☎ 225 726; Burg 13; adult/ concession €5/4; 🕑 9am-6pm Apr-Sep, 10am-4pm Oct-Mar) for a good view of the city. Nearby is the renovated **Albrecht-Dürer-Haus** (☎ 231 2568; Albrecht-Dürer-Strasse 39; adult/concession €5/2.50; 🕑 10am-5pm Tue-Sun, 10am-8pm Thu), where Germany's renowned Renaissance draughtsman lived from 1509 to 1528.

The Nazis chose Nuremberg as their propaganda centre and for mass rallies, which were held at **Luitpoldhain**, a (never completed) sports complex of megalomaniac proportions. Not to be missed is the

GERMANY

Dokumentationzentrum (☎ 231 5666; www.museen .nuernberg.de; Bayernstrasse 110; adult/concession €5/2.50; ☺ 9am-6pm Mon-Fri, 10am-6pm Sat & Sun), which features mesmerising film and audio footage dealing with the causes, relationships and consequences of the Nazi ideology, and its links with Nuremberg. Take tram No 9 or 6 to Doku-Zentrum.

Sleeping & Eating

Lette'm Sleep (☎ 992 8128; www.backpackers.de; Frauentormauer 42; dm €15, s/d €30/48; ☐) In the Altstadt just a short walk from the train station, this place has a good vibe and quirky, charming private rooms.

Jugendherberge Nürnberg (☎ 230 9360; jhnuern berg@djh-bayern.de; Burg 2; dm with linen €19) More character than most hostels.

Hotel Pension Vater Jahn-Parma (☎ 444 507; fax 431 5236; Jahnstrasse 13; s/d from €20/31; **P**) It's only about 200m southwest of the Hauptbahnhof and offers clean rooms with shared facilities.

Pension Zum Schwänlein (☎ 225 162; www.tis cover.de/schwaenlein; Hintere Sterngasse 11; s/d €26/42) Small, comfy rooms in the Altstadt just a short walk from the train station. There's a pub attached.

Knaus-Campingpark 'Am Dutzendteich' (☎ 981 2717; Hans-Kalb-Strasse 56; camp site incl 1 adult €8, additional person €5; ☺ year-round) Southeast of the centre (U1 to Messezentrum).

Don't leave Nuremberg without trying its famous *Bratwurstl* (small grilled sausages). At **Bratwursthäusle** (☎ 227 695; Rathausplatz 2; 10 for €8.30) they're flame-grilled and scrumptious. For inexpensive Franconian fare, try **Landbierparadies** (☎ 287 8673; Rothenburgerstrasse 26; meal €6), only a 15-minute walk west of the train station.

Getting There & Around

IC trains run to/from Frankfurt (€37.20, 2¼ hours, hourly) and Munich (€38, 1½ hours, hourly). IR trains run to Stuttgart (€28, two hours, every two hours) and ICE trains to Berlin Ostbahnhof (€78.20, five hours, every two hours). Several EC trains travel to Vienna (€94, seven hours, daily) and Prague (€62, 5½ hours, daily). Buses to regional destinations leave from the station just east of the main train station.

Tickets on the bus, tram and U-Bahn system cost €1.35/1.75 for each short/long ride in the central zone. A day pass is €3.50.

REGENSBURG

☎ 0941 / pop 128,000

Regensburg's lively university scene ensures that this delightful spot on the Danube River continues to captivate. The city escaped WWII carpet bombing, and lacks the packaged feel of other towns in the region.

There's a **tourist office** (☎ 507 4410; www.reg ensburg.de; ☺ 9.15am-6pm Mon-Fri, 9.15am-4pm Sat & Sun) in the Altes Rathaus. **City Point** (☎ 0941; Wahlenstrasse; per hr €3.50; ☺ 9am-10.30pm) offers Internet access.

Dominating the skyline are the twin spires of the Gothic **Dom St Peter** (☎ 597 1002; Domplatz; admission free; tours in German adult/concession €2.50/1.50; ☺ tours 10am, 11am & 2pm Mon-Fri, noon & 2pm Sun May-Nov, 11am Mon-Fri, noon Sun low season), built during the 14th and 15th centuries. The **Altes Rathaus** was progressively extended from medieval to baroque times and remained the seat of the Reichstag for almost 150 years. The **Roman wall**, with its **Porta Praetoria** arch, follows Unter den Schwibbögen onto Dr-Martin-Luther-Strasse.

Take bus No 3 to the Eisstadion stop for the **Jugendherberge** (☎ 574 02; jhregensburg@ djh-bayern.de; Wöhrdstrasse 60; dm €16). Across the river is the **Spitalgarten Hotel** (☎ 847 74; www .spitalgarten.de in German; St Katharinenplatz 1; s/d €23/46), with simple rooms and a beer garden. **Hotel Am Peterstor** (☎ 545 45; www.hotel-am-peterstor.de; Fröliche-Türkenstrasse 12; s/d €35/40) is good value, with clean, basic rooms. Bus No 6 from the train station goes to the entrance of **Azur-Camping** (☎ 270 025; fax 299 432; Weinweg 40; camp site/person €5.50/4.50).

Carlitos (Am Wiedfang 2) is a lively Latin bar. Students come to the **Neue Filmbüche** (☎ 570 37; Bismarckplatz 9) for its great terrace. **Historische Wurstküche** (☎ 590 98; Thundorferstrasse 3; snacks €6) is the best spot for a snack of *Bratwurstl* on the banks of the Danube.

Regensburg is on the train line between Nuremberg (€19, one hour) and Austria and there are EC/IC trains in both directions every two hours, as well as RB/RE trains to Munich (€19.20, 1½ hours). Regensburg is a major stop on the Danube bike route.

BAVARIAN ALPS

The Bavarian Alps (Bayerische Alpen) rise so abruptly from the rolling hills of southern Bavaria that their appearance seems as dramatic as their sister summits further south in Austria. The rugged topography means that the picturesque towns are fewer and further apart, a welcome relief from the dense development elsewhere. Stretching westward from Germany's southeastern corner to the Allgäu region near Lake Constance, the Alps take in most of the mountainous country fringing the southern border with Austria.

Outdoor pursuits are extraordinarily well organised in the Bavarian Alps, with skiing, snowboarding and hiking being the most popular. The ski season usually runs from mid-December to April. Ski gear is available for hire in all the resorts. During the warmer months, activities include hiking, canoeing, rafting, biking and paragliding.

While the public transport network is very good, the mountain geography means there are few direct routes between main centres; sometimes a short cut via Austria is quicker (such as between Füssen and Oberstdorf). Regional RVO (Regionalvekehr Oberbayern GmbH) bus passes (☎ 089-551 640) give free travel on the network between Füssen, Garmisch and Mittenwald, and are excellent value.

Berchtesgaden
☎ 08652 / pop 8200
Berchtesgaden is perhaps the most romantically scenic place in the Bavarian Alps. To reach the centre from the train station, cross the footbridge and walk uphill up Bahnhofstrasse.

INFORMATION
Tourist office (☎ 9670; www.berchtesgaden.de; Königseer Strasse 2; ☺ 8am-6pm Mon-Fri, 8am-5pm Sat, 9am-3pm Sun mid-Jun–Sep) Just across the river from the train station. It has helpful staff.

SIGHTS
Tours of the **Salzbergwerk** (☎ 600 20; Bergwerkstrasse 83; adult/concession €12/6.50; ☺ 9am-5pm May–mid-Oct, 12.30-3.30pm Mon-Sat mid-Oct–Apr) combine history with carnival-like rides and games. Visitors descend into the salt mine for a 1½-hour tour.

Nearby **Obersalzberg** is an innocent-looking place with a creepy legacy as the second seat of government for the Third Reich. Hitler, Himmler, Goebbels and the rest of the Nazi hierarchy maintained homes here. The **Dokumentation Obersalzberg museum** (☎ 947 960; www.obersalzberg.de; Salzbergstrasse 41; adult/concession €2.50/1.50; ☺ 9am-5pm Apr-Oct, 10am-3pm Tue-Sun

Nov-Mar) documents their time in the area (don't miss the photo of the fun-loving Führer relaxing in *Lederhosen*), as well as the horrors their policies produced. The admission fee also gets you into the eerie **Hitler's bunker**. Catch bus No 9538 (€3.70 return) from the Nazi-constructed Berchtesgaden train station to Obersalzberg-Hintereck.

Kehlstein (☎ 2969; admission €12; ☺ May-Oct) is a spectacular meeting house built for, but seldom used by, Hitler. Despite its reputation as the 'Eagle's Nest', it's a popular destination because of the stunning views. Entry includes transport on special buses which link the summit with Obersalzberg-Hintereck as well as the 120m lift through solid rock to the peak. Buses run from 7.40am to 4.25pm.

You can forget the horrors of war at the **Königssee**, a beautiful alpine lake situated 5km south of Berchtesgaden (and linked by hourly buses in summer).

The wilds of Berchtesgaden National Park offer some of the best **hiking** in Germany. A good introduction to the area is a 2km path up from St Bartholomä beside the Königssee to the Watzmann-Ostwand, a massive 2000m-high rock face where scores of ambitious mountaineers have died.

Berchtesgaden has five major **skiing resorts**, and you can buy five-day lift passes that cover them all (€98). Rossfeld is the cheapest for day passes (€13), while Götschen, with a permanent half-pipe, is the destination for snowboarders (€20 per day).

SLEEPING & EATING
Jugendherberge (☎ 943 70; www.djh.de; Gebirgsjägerstrasse 52; dm €13; ☺ closed Nov-Dec) Take bus 9539 to this hostel where the spectacular views more than make up for the fact that it's not a particularly attractive building.

Hotel Watzmann (☎ 2055; fax 5174; Franziskanerplatz 2; s/d from €28/50; ☺ closed Nov–mid-Dec; P 🗶) This comfortable hotel is decorated in traditional upper-Bavarian style, and has an excellent outdoor terrace with top food.

Hotel Bavaria (☎ 966 10; Sunklergaesschen 11; s/d €46/80) Just 400m from both the bus and train stations, Hotel Bavaria has a sauna for your aching muscles.

Of the five camping grounds in the Berchtesgaden area, the nicest are at Königssee: **Grafenlehen** (☎ 4140; camp site/person €5.11/4.35) and **Mühleiten** (☎ 4584; camp site/person €5.11/4.35).

Choose from 15 varieties of schnitzel at **Alt Berchtesgaden** (☎ 4519; Bahnhofstrasse 3; schnitzel €4.99).

GETTING THERE & AWAY

Both RB and RE trains run hourly trips to Munich and cost €25.

BADEN-WÜRTTEMBERG

Although Bavaria is more familiar to most foreigners, Baden-Württemberg is deservedly one of Germany's main tourist regions. With recreational centres such as the Black Forest and Lake Constance, medieval towns such as Heidelberg and Freiburg and the very modern Stuttgart, it has as much to offer as any part of Germany.

STUTTGART

☎ 0711 / pop 587,000

Hemmed in by vine-covered hills and full of greenery, Stuttgart is a haven for its residents, who enjoy a high quality of life. Nevertheless it is Baden-Württemberg's state capital and the hub of its industries.

Information

Level One Cyber Bar (☎ 120 4665; Königstrasse 22; per 30min €3; ⌚ noon-midnight)
Main post office (Bolzstrasse 3)
StuttCard plus (72hr €17) Allows free public transport and free entry to some museums.
Tourist office (☎ 222 80; www.stuttgart-tourist.de; Königstrasse 1a; ⌚ 9.30am-8.30pm Mon-Fri, 9.30am-6pm Sat, 10.30am-6pm Sun) Opposite the main train station. Sells StuttCard plus card.

Sights

The **tower** (admission free; ⌚ 10am-10pm Tue-Sun) at the main train station sports the three-pointed star of the Mercedes-Benz. It's also an excellent vantage point for the sprawling city and is reached via a lift.

Stretching southwest from the Neckar River to the city centre is the **Schlossgarten**, an extensive strip of parkland divided into three sections, complete with ponds, swans, street entertainers and modern sculptures. At their southern end the gardens encompass the sprawling baroque **Neues Schloss** and the Renaissance **Altes Schloss**, which houses a **regional museum** (☎ 279 3400; Schillerplatz 6; adult/concession €2.60/1.50; ⌚ 10am-5pm Wed-Sun, 10am-1pm Tue).

Next to the Altes Schloss is the city's oldest square, Schillerplatz and the 12th-century **Stiftskirche**. Adjoining the park you'll find the **Staatsgalerie** (☎ 212 4050; Konrad-Adenauer-Strasse 30; adult/concession €4.50/2.50; ⌚ 10am-6pm Fri-Wed, 10am-9pm Thu) housing an excellent collection from the Middle Ages to the present. Next door there's the **Haus der Geschichte** (House of History; ☎ 212 3950; Urbansplatz 2; admission €3) which covers the past 200 years of the Baden-Württemberg area in film, photography, documents and multimedia.

The motor car was first developed by Gottlieb Daimler and Carl Benz at the end of the 19th century. The impressive **Mercedes-Benz Museum** (☎ 172 2578; Mercedesstrasse 137; admission free; ⌚ 9am-5pm Tue-Sun) is in the suburb of Bad-Cannstatt; take S-Bahn No 1 to Neckarstadion. For even faster cars, cruise over to the **Porsche Museum** (☎ 911 5685; Porscheplatz 1; admission free; ⌚ 9am-4pm Mon-Fri, 9am-5pm Sat & Sun); take S-Bahn No 6 to Neuwirtshaus. Sadly, neither place offers free samples.

Sleeping & Eating

Jugendherberge (☎ 241 583; www.djh.de; Haussmannstrasse 27; dm junior/senior €14.30/19) It's a steep climb up to this hostel, which is a signposted 15-minute walk from the train station.

Museumstube (☎ 296 810; www.museumstube.de; Hospitalstrasse 9; s/d €35/55) No-frills rooms but it's only a short walk to several nearby bars and clubs.

Hotel Espenlaub (☎ 222 8233; Charlottenstrasse 27; s/d €30/40; P) Take S-Bahn No 5, 6 or 7 from the train station to reach this pleasing hotel.

Campingplatz Stuttgart (☎ 556 696; info@campingplatz-stuttgart.de; Mercedesstrasse 40; person/tent/car €5/3.10/2.20) Beside the river and 500m from the Bad-Cannstatt S-Bahn station.

Stuttgart is a great place to sample Swabian specialities such as *Spätzle* (home-made noodles) and *Maultaschen* (similar to ravioli).

Markthalle (Dorotheenstrasse 4; ⌚ 7am-6.30pm Mon-Fri, 7am-4pm Sat) An excellent Art Nouveau–style market that's jam-packed with fresh fare.

Mensa (Holzgartenstrasse 11; mains €2.50) Fill up at the university eatery.

Iden (☎ 235 989; Eberhardtsrasse 1; meals around €5.75) Vegetarians (and those who have overdosed on German sausages) should try Iden, which serves cheap, self-serve salad (€1.50), 100g of vegetarian lasagne (€1.50) and soup (€2.50).

HEIDELBERG

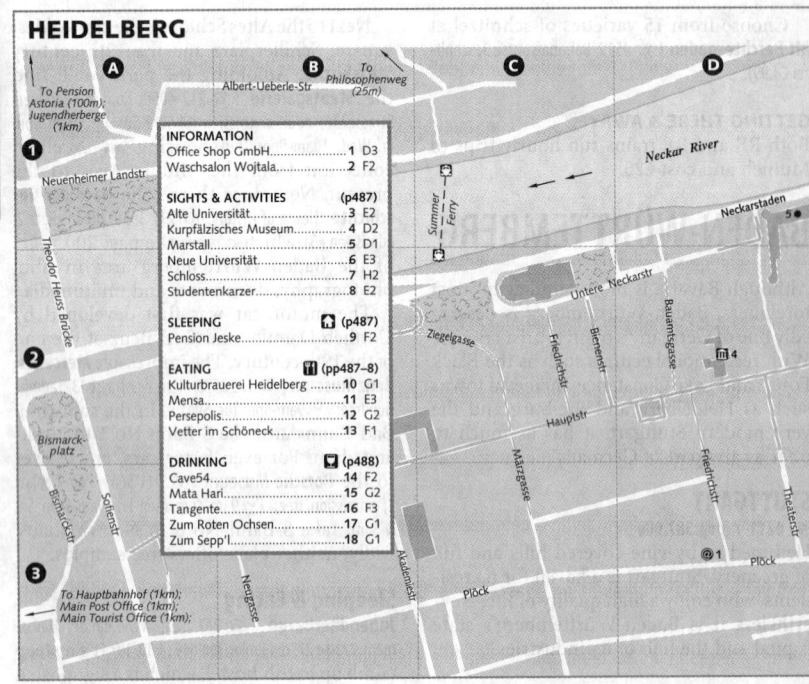

INFORMATION
Office Shop GmbH....................1 D3
Waschsalon Wojtala.................2 F2

SIGHTS & ACTIVITIES (p487)
Alte Universität.......................3 E2
Kurpfälzisches Museum............4 D2
Marstall...................................5 D1
Neue Universität.....................6 E3
Schloss...................................7 H2
Studentenkarzer......................8 E2

SLEEPING (p487)
Pension Jeske..........................9 F2

EATING (pp487–8)
Kulturbrauerei Heidelberg......10 G1
Mensa....................................11 E3
Persepolis...............................12 G2
Vetter im Schöneck................13 F1

DRINKING (p488)
Cave54....................................14 F2
Mata Hari...............................15 G2
Tangente.................................16 F3
Zum Roten Ochsen..................17 G1
Zum Sepp'l.............................18 G1

Alte Kanzlei (☎ 294 457; Schillerplatz 5a; mains €6-17) Excellent for a sunny lunch, with pastas, wraps and salads.

Drinking

Lift Stuttgart (€1) is a comprehensive guide to the local entertainment scene including events. It is available at kiosks around the city and the tourist information office. There are several funky drinking holes around Hans-im-Glück-Platz, a compact square that's often brimming over with party-goers. There is also a beer garden in the Mittlerer Schlossgarten, northeast of the main train station.

Tea Room (Theodor-Heuss- Strasse 4) Good cocktails and a DJ keep a hip crowd at the Tea Room until late.

Bar Code (☎ 887 8104; Theodor-Heuss-Strasse 30) A cool modern bar with a young crowd.

Biddy Early's (☎ 615 9853; Marienstrasse 28) This Irish pub has live music four nights a week and karaoke every Wednesday.

Palast der Republik (☎ 226 4887; Friedrichstrasse 27) A tiny bar that pulls a huge crowd of laid-back drinkers.

Getting There & Around

There are frequent train departures for all major German and many international cities. ICE trains run to Frankfurt (€45, 1½ hours, hourly), Berlin (€127, 5½ hours, hourly) and Munich (€44, two hours, hourly). Regional and long-distance buses leave from the station next to the main train station.

One-way fares on Stuttgart's public transport network are €1.10/5.30 for short/long trips. A four-ride strip ticket costs €5.80 and a central zone day pass is €4.70.

HEIDELBERG

☎ 06221 / pop 141,000

The French destroyed Heidelberg in 1693; they may have been the last visitors to dislike this charming town on the Neckar River. Its magnificent castle and medieval town are irresistible drawcards for most travellers in Germany. Throw in nice weather and lively pubs and you understand why many of Heidelberg's students (attending the oldest university in the country) rarely graduate on time.

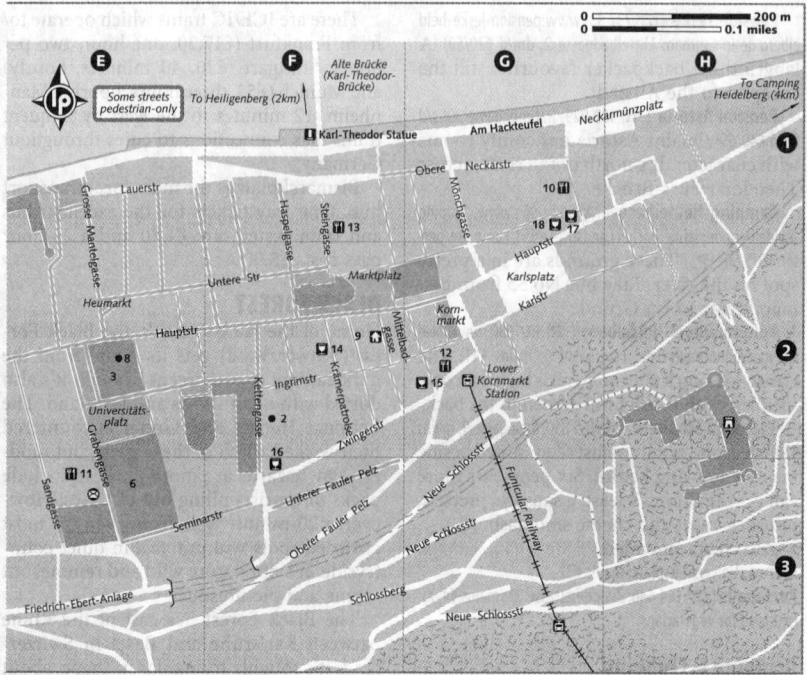

Information

Heidelberg Card (€12) Offers 24 hours of unlimited public transport and free admission to many sights.

Main tourist office (☎ 194 33; www.heidelberg.de; Willy-Brandt-Platz 1; ⏰ 9am-7pm Mon-Sat year-round, plus 10am-6pm Sun Apr-Nov) Outside the train station.

Office Shop GmbH (Plock 85; per 15min €1.30) Internet access.

Post office (Hugo-Stotz-Strasse 14) To the right as you leave the train station.

Sights

Heidelberg's imposing red-sandstone **Schloss** (☎ 538 421; grounds admission free, castle adult/concession €2/1; ⏰ 8am-5.30pm) is one of Germany's finest examples of grand Gothic-Renaissance architecture. The building's half-ruined state actually adds to its romantic appeal. The entry fee includes the **Grosses Fass** (Great Vat), an enormous 18th-century keg capable of holding 221,726L. You can take the funicular railway from lower Kornmarkt station (adult/concession €3/2 return), or enjoy an invigorating 10-minute walk up steep, stone-laid lanes.

Dominating Universitätsplatz are the 18th-century **Alte Universität** and the **Neue Uni-**versität. Nearby there's the **Studentenkarzer** (student jail; ☎ 543 554; Augustinergasse 2; adult/concession €2.50/2; ⏰ 10am-noon & 2-5pm Tue-Sat Apr-Oct, 10am-2pm Tue-Fri Nov-Mar) where from 1778 to 1914 unruly students were incarcerated for infractions such as drinking, singing and womanising. The Marstall is the former arsenal, now a student *mensa* (cafeteria). The **Kurpfälzisches Museum** (Palatinate Museum; ☎ 583 402; Hauptstrasse 97; adult/concession €2.50/1.50; ⏰ 10am-5pm Tue-Sun, 10am-9pm Wed) contains paintings, sculptures and the jawbone of the 600,000-year-old Heidelberg Man.

A stroll along the **Philosophenweg**, north of the Neckar River, is a welcome respite from Heidelberg's tourist hordes.

Sleeping & Eating

Finding any accommodation in Heidelberg's high season can be difficult. Arrive early in the day or book ahead.

Jugendherberge (☎ 651 190; www.djh.de; Tiergartenstrasse 5; dm junior/senior €14.90/17.60; P) Across the river from the train station. From the station or Bismarckplatz, take bus No 33 towards Ziegelhausen.

Pension Jeske (☎ 237 33; www.pension-jeske-heid elberg.de in German; Mittelbadgasse 2; dm/d €20/50) A labyrinthine backpacker favourite, still the cheapest in the Altstadt.

Pension Astoria (☎ 402 929; Rahmengasse 30; s/d from €40/65) Quaint Astoria has comfy rooms with character. It's north of the river, across Theodor-Heuss-Brücke.

Camping Heidelberg (☎ 802 506; www.camping -heidelberg.de; Schlierbacher Landstrasse 151; camp site/per-son €3/5.50; P) These grounds are in a pretty spot on the river. Take bus No 35 from Bis-marckplatz to Im Grund.

Kulturbrauerei Heidelberg (☎ 502 980; www.heid elberger-kulturbrauerei.de; Leyergasse 6; mains €11) The classic-looking Kulturbrauerei is highly recom-mended, with a delightful garden in the back.

Vetter im Schöneck (☎ 165 850; Steingasse 9; mains €10) Meat and potatoes just seem suited beside massive brewing kettles. Six people or more can get the Brewer's feast, a sausage, pretzels, radishes, meat and cheese smorgasbord.

Also recommended:

Mensa (Universitätsplatz; mains €3)

Persepolis (☎ 164 646; Zwingerstrasse 21; mains €4-7) Fast food for vegetarians.

Drinking & Clubbing

You won't have to go far to find a happening backstreet bar in this university town. Lots of the action centres on Unterestrasse.

Mata Hari (☎ 181 808; Oberbadgasse 10; ☽ to 3am Tue-Sun) Mata Hari is a mellow place.

'T Club Tangente (☎ 169 444; Kettengasse 23) For-merly known as Tangente, this small disco in the old part of town is often crowded. Expen-sive drinks attract a relatively posh clientele.

Zum Roten Oschen (☎ 209 77; www.roterochsen.de; Hauptstrasse 213) One of Heidelberg's most fa-mous historic student pubs, now frequented by tourists.

Zum Sepp'l (☎ 230 85; Hauptstrasse 217) Also gets much of the tourist trade, though the graffiti attests to a colourful history.

Cave54 (☎ 278 40; Krämerpetrolse 2; ☽ Thu-Sun) For live jazz and blues, head to this under-ground stone cellar that oozes character.

Getting There & Around

Heidelberg is on the Castle Road route from Mannheim to Nuremberg. From mid-May until the end of September Deutsche-Tour-ing has a daily coach service, with one bus in either direction between Heidelberg and Rothenburg ob der Tauber (€29, five hours).

There are ICE/IC trains which operate to/ from Frankfurt (€17.20, one hour, two per hour), Stuttgart (€20, 40 minutes, hourly) and Munich (€53, three hours, hourly). Man-nheim, 12 minutes to the west by frequent trains, has connections to cities throughout Germany.

Bismarckplatz is the main local transport hub. One-way tickets for the excellent bus and tram system are €1.80 and a 24-hour pass costs €5.90.

BLACK FOREST

Home of the cuckoo clock, the Black For-est (Schwarzwald) gets its name from the dark canopy of evergreens, though it's also dotted with open slopes and farmland. The fictional Hansel and Gretel encountered their wicked witch in these parts, but mod-ern-day hazards are more likely to include packs of tourists piling out of buses. How-ever, a 20-minute walk from even the most crowded spots will put you in quiet coun-tryside. It's not nature wild and remote, but serene and picturesque.

The Black Forest lies east of the Rhine between Karlsruhe and Basel in Switzer-land. It's roughly triangular in shape, about 160km long and 50km wide. Baden-Baden, Freudenstadt, Titisee and Freiburg act as convenient information posts for excur-sions. Even smaller towns in the area gen-erally have tourist offices.

Information

Feldberg tourist office (☎ 07655-8019; tourist -info@feldbergschwarzwald.de; Kirchpetrolse 1, Feldberg; ☽ 8am-5.30pm Mon-Fri year-round, plus 9am-noon Sat, 10am-noon Sun Jun-Oct & Dec-Mar) Can supply ski information.

Freudenstadt tourist office (☎ 07441-8640; touristinfo@freudenstadt.de; Am Markt-platz; ☽ 9am-6pm Mon-Fri, 10am-2pm Sat & Sun Mar-Nov, 10am-5pm Mon-Fri, 10am-1pm Sat & Sun Dec-Feb)

Hinterzarten Breitnau tourist office (☎ 07652-120 60; www.hinterzarten-breitnau.de; Freiburgerstrasse 1) Also covers the southern Black Forest.

Titisee tourist office (☎ 07651-980 40; www.titisee.de; Strandbadstrasse 4; ☽ 8am-noon & 1.30-5.30pm Mon-Fri year-round, 10am-noon Sat & Sun May-Oct) Inside the Kurhaus.

Sights & Activities

Along the Schwarzwald-Hochstrasse (Black Forest Hwy), the first major tourist sight is the **Mummelsee**, south of the Hornisgrinde peak. It's a small, deep lake inhabited, it is said, by an evil sea king. Further south, the town of **Freudenstadt** is mainly used as a base for excursions into the countryside.

The area situated between Freudenstadt and Freiburg is (overpriced) cuckoo-clock country. A few popular stops are Schramberg, Triberg and Furtwangen. In Furtwangen, visit the **Deutsches Uhrenmuseum** (German Clock Museum; ☎ 07723-920 117; Gerwigstrasse 11; adult/concession €3/2.50; ☼ 9am-6pm Apr-Oct, 10am-6pm Nov-Mar) for a look at traditional clock-making.

The southern Black Forest, especially around the 1493m **Feldberg summit**, offers some of the best hiking; small towns such as Todtmoos or Bonndorf serve as bases. The 10km **Wutachschlucht** (Wutach Gorge) outside Bonndorf is justifiably famous. You can also windsurf, go boating or swim at the highland lakes. Titisee boasts several beaches.

The Black Forest ski season runs from late December to March. While there is some good downhill **skiing**, the area is more suited to cross-country skiing. The Titisee area is the main centre for winter sports, with uncrowded downhill runs at Feldberg (day passes €20) and numerous, graded, cross-country trails. In midwinter, **ice skating** is also possible on the Titisee and the Schluchsee.

Sleeping & Eating

Away from the major towns you can find scores of simple, warm, cheap guesthouses. The DJH hostel network is extensive in the southern Black Forest but limited in the north. Some convenient options are the modern hostel about 2.5km from the train station in **Freudenstadt** (☎ 07441-7720; www.djh.de; Eugen-Nägele-Strasse 69), or on the northern shore of the lake at **Titisee** (☎ 07652-238; www.djh.de; Bruderhalde 27) – catch bus No 7300 from the train station. The hostel at **Triberg** (☎ 07722-4110; www.djh.de; Rohrbacher Strasse 3) is perched on a ridge above town and is a long walk from the train station; take a bus to the Markt from where you're left with a steep uphill climb. The **Zuflucht** (☎ 07804-611; www.djh.de; Schwarzwald-hochstrasse) hostel is an attractive whitewashed building surrounded by forest at an altitude of almost 1000m. All of these places charge €14/16 for juniors/seniors in dorms.

Lodges may outnumber cows in the Black Forest. Tourist offices can also direct you to private rooms from about €16 per person. In Freudenstadt, you'll find simple rooms at **Petrolthof Pension Traube** (☎ 07441-917 450; fax 853 28; Markt 41; s/d €30/57). When in Feldberg, try the **Bergpetrolthof Wasmer** (☎ 07676-230; fax 430; An der Wiesenquelle 1; s/d from €23/46) for small, comfortable timber-lined rooms. **Hotel Pfaff** (☎ 07722-4479; hotel-pfaff-triberg@t-online.de; Hauptstrasse 85; s/d with bathroom €38/66) in Triberg offers comfortable lodgings near the waterfall. Regional specialities include *Schwarzwälderschinken* (Black Forest ham). Rivalling the ubiquitous clocks in fame (but not price), *Schwarzwälderkirschtorte* (Black Forest cake) is a chocolate-and-cherry concoction. Restaurants are often expensive, so a picnic in the woods makes sense.

Getting There & Around

The Mannheim–Basel train line has numerous branches that serve the Black Forest. Trains for Freudenstadt and the north leave from Karlsruhe (€13, one hour and 40 minutes, at least hourly). Triberg is on the busy line linking Offenburg and Constance. Titisee has frequent services from Freiburg (€9, 35 minutes, about every half-hour), with some trains continuing to Feldberg and others to Neustadt.

The rail network is extensive, and where trains don't go, buses do. Check schedules at bus stops or consult with the tourist offices.

FREIBURG

☎ 0761 / pop 208,300

Nestled between hills and vineyards and the southern Black Forest, Freiburg im Breisgau is a fun place, thanks to the city's large and thriving university community. The monumental 13th-century cathedral is the city's key landmark but the real attractions are the vibrant cafés, bars and street life, plus the local wines. The best times for tasting are early July during *Weinfest* (Wine Festival), or early August for the nine days of *Weinkost* (loosely 'wine as food').

Information

Alexis (Marienstrasse 10; per hr €2.40; ☼ 10am-1am Mon-Sat, noon-1am Sun) Central Internet café.

Tourist office (☎ 388 1880; www.freiburg.de; Rotteckring 14; ☼ 9.30am-8pm Mon-Fri, 9.30am-5pm Sat, 10am-noon Sun Jun-Sep, 9.30am-6pm Mon-Fri, 9.30am-2pm Sat, 10am-noon Sun Oct-May) Has piles of information on the Black Forest.

Sights

The major sight in Freiburg is the 700-year-old **Münster** (Cathedral; Münsterplatz; steeple adult/child €1.30/0.80; 9.30am-5pm Mon-Sat, 1-5pm Sun Easter-Oct, 10am-4pm Tue-Sat, 1-5pm Sun Nov-Easter), a classic example of both high and late-Gothic architecture which looms over Münsterplatz, Freiburg's market square. The bustling **university quarter** is northwest of the Martinstor (one of the old city gates).

Freiburg's main museum, the **Augustinermuseum** (201 2531; Salzstrasse 32; adult/concession €2/1; 10am-5pm Tue-Sun) has a fine collection of medieval art.

The popular trip by cable car to the 1286m **Schauinsland peak** (one-way/return €6.60/10.20, concession €3.60/5.60; 9am-5pm) is a quick way to reach the Black Forest highlands. Numerous easy and well-marked trails make the Schauinsland area ideal for day walks. From Freiburg take tram No 4 south to Günterstal and then bus No 21 to Talstation.

Sleeping & Eating

Black Forest Hostel (881 7870; www.blackforest-hostel.de; Kartäuserstrasse 33; dm/s/d €12/27/44) Take tram No 1 to Römerhof (direction: Littenweiler), then follow the signs down Fritz-Geigesstrasse for this less than convenient hostel.

Hotel Sonne (403 048; fax 409 8856; Basler Strasse 58; s/d €35/52) A 15-minute walk south of the centre, friendly Sonne has decent, simple rooms and a magnificent breakfast buffet.

Gasthaus Löwen (331 61; fax 362 38; Herrenstrasse 47; s/d €35/80) Has clean, basic rooms in a busy part of the Altstadt.

Camping Möslepark (729 38; campingfreizeit@aol.com; Waldseestrasse 77; tent €2.10-2.60, person €5) Take tram No 1 to Stadthalle (direction: Littenweiler), turn right under the road, go over the train tracks and follow the bike path.

There's a good selection of *Wurst* and other quick eats from stalls set up in the market square during lunch.

UC Uni-Café (383 355; Niemensstrasse 7; mains €3-7) A popular hang-out that serves light bites on its highly visible outdoor terrace.

Laubfrosch (Kaiser Josephstrasse 273; pizzas €3.80) A pizzeria by the river just across the Martinstor. You get a complimentary shot of liquor with your meal.

Warsteiner Keller (329 29; Niemensstrasse 13; mains €7.50) A bar/café that oozes atmosphere, and has an excellent range of cheap chow.

Salatstuben (Löwenstrasse 1; 100g salad €1.20, hot meal €4.10) There's a great range of cheap vegetarian dishes at this self-serve place.

Drinking

Jazzhaus (349 73; Schnewlinstrasse 1; cover from €6) Live jazz every night.

Schlappen (Lowenstrasse 2) This happening student night spot is a large, sprawling bar with a lively vibe, a budget menu and late closing.

Galerie (Milchstrasse 7) An intimate watering hole with a nice courtyard and cheap Spanish eats.

Cohibar (Milchstrasse 9) Mellow and candle-lit, the Cohibar doesn't close until 3am at weekends.

Getting There & Around

Freiburg is situated on the Mannheim–Basel train corridor. Trains to Titisee leave every 30 minutes (€9, 35 minutes). The regional bus station is next to Track 1. For information on ride-sharing contact the **Citynetz Mitfahr-Service** (194 44; Belfortstrasse 55).

LAKE CONSTANCE

Often jokingly called the 'Swabian Ocean', Lake Constance (Bodensee) is an oasis in landlocked southern Germany. Even if you never make contact with the water, this giant bulge in the sinewy course of the Rhine can breathe life into the weary traveller. The many historic towns around its periphery, while inviting in their own right, are enhanced by the breeze and the chance to get wet. The lake's southern side belongs to Switzerland and Austria, where the snow-capped mountain tops provide a perfect backdrop when viewed from the northern (German) shore. The German side features Constance, Meersburg, Friedrichshafen and the island of Lindau.

Information

Tourist office (133 030; www.konstanz.de/tourismus; Bahnhofplatz 13; 9am-6.30pm Mon-Fri, 9am-4pm Sat, 10am-1pm Sun Apr-Oct, 9.30am-12.30pm & 2-6pm Mon-Fri Nov-Mar) Around 150m to the right from the train station exit in Constance. The tourist booklet *Rad Urlaub am Bodensee* lists routes, rental places and a wealth of other information for the region.

Velotours (07531-982 80; Fritz-Arnold-Strasse 2b; bike rental daily/weekly €11/52) In Constance. Rents out bikes and organises cycling tours.

Sights

If you have time while in Constance, head across to **Mainau Island** (☎ 3030; www.mainau.de; adult/concession €10/5, after 4pm €5/2.50; ❂ 7am-8pm mid-Mar–Nov, 9am-6pm Nov–mid-Mar), with its baroque castle set among gorgeous gardens. Five public beaches are open from May to September, including the Strandbad Horn with shrub-enclosed nude bathing. You can get there by boat, or via the bridge that connects the island to the mainland with bus No 4 from the main train station, or car.

Sleeping & Eating

Jugendherberge (☎ 322 60; www.jugendherberge.de; Zur Allmannshöhe 16; dm junior/senior €19/22) Take bus No 1 or 4 from the Constance train station to the Jugendherberge stop to stay in this converted water tower.

Exxtra (☎ 233 94; Hussenstrasse 21; lunch special €5) You can't beat Exxtra for a leisurely meal of tasty *Kässpätzle*.

Hafenalle Biergarten (☎ 211 26; Hafenstrasse 10) In a perfect spot, this beer garden catches the breeze off the lake. Snack on pretzels and *Wurst*.

Charming Meersburg across the lake is a good base for watery pursuits. There is no DJH hostel or handy camping ground but relatively inexpensive accommodation can still be found and the promenade has dozens of cafés and restaurants.

Ins Fischernetz (☎ 5845; Unterstadstrasse 32; sandwiches €4) The best place for cheap eats from the ocean.

Getting There & Away

Constance has train connections every one to two hours to Offenburg (€25.40) and Stuttgart (€34). Meersburg is easily reached by bus No 7395 from Friedrichshafen (€6.40, every 30 minutes), or by **Weisse Flotte** (☎ 07531-281 398; www.bsb-online.com) boats from Constance (€3.40, several times daily in season).

Trains link the towns Lindau, Friedrichshafen and Constance, and buses fill in the gaps. The most enjoyable, albeit slowest, way to get around this area is on the Weisse Flotte boats which, from Easter to late October, call several times a day at the larger towns along both sides of the lake; there are discounts on tickets for rail pass-holders.

WESTERN GERMANY

The western section of Germany comprises the states of Rhineland-Palatinate, Saarland, Hesse and North Rhine-Westphalia. Rhineland-Palatinate (Rheinland-Pflaz) is rugged and beautiful, dotted by wineries and medieval castles. Saarland, western Germany's poorest region, does not lie on most travellers' itineraries. Hesse is home to the architecturally un-German city of Frankfurt, a major transport hub and a good base to explore the region. Finally, North Rhine-Westphalia (Nordrhein-Westfalen) shelters a quarter of Germany's population. Although the area is densely populated and contains its fair share of bleak industrial centres, some of the cities are steeped in history, and are fine examples of how the ancient and modern can coexist and even thrive.

THE MOSELLE VALLEY

For a taste of German culture and people – and, of course, the wonderful wines – you can't beat exploring the vineyards and wineries of the Moselle (Mosel) Valley. Below the steep rocky cliffs planted with vineyards, the Moselle is bursting with historical sites and picturesque towns. Stunning views reward intrepid hikers who brave the hilly trails.

Sights

The most scenic section of the Moselle Valley runs 195km northeast from Trier to Koblenz; it's most practical to begin your Moselle Valley trip from either of these two hubs.

South of Koblenz, at the head of the beautiful Eltz Valley, the medieval castle of **Burg Eltz** (☎ 02672-950 500; adult/concession €5/3; ❂ Apr-Nov) is not to be missed. It's best reached by train to Moselkern, from where it's a 50-minute walk up through the forest.

For a great view of the picture-postcard town of Cochem, head up to the **Pinnerkreuz** with the chairlift (€4) on Endertstrasse.

Sleeping

Many wine-makers have their own small *pensions* but in May, on summer weekends or during the local wine harvest (mid-September to mid-October), accommodation is hard to find. Koblenz's wonderful **Jugendherberge** (☎ 972 870; jh-koblenz@djh-info.de; dm €14.20-17.50) is housed in the old Ehrenbreitstein fortress.

Getting Around

It is not possible to travel the length of the Moselle River via rail. Local and fast trains run every hour between Trier and Koblenz (€16, 1½ hours), but the only riverside stretch of this line is between Cochem and Koblenz. Apart from this run – and the scenic Moselweinbahn line taking tourists between Bullay and Traben-Trarbach (€2.50, 20 minutes) – travellers must use buses, ferries, bicycles, or cars to travel between Moselle towns.

Moselbahn (☎ 0653-196 800; www.moselbahn.de in German) runs eight buses on weekdays (fewer at weekends) between Trier and Bullay (three hours each way), a very scenic route following the river's winding course. Buses leave from outside the train stations in Trier, Traben-Trarbach and Bullay. Frequent buses operate between Kues (Alter Bahnhof) and the Wittlich main train station (€3.60, 30 minutes one-way, at least every half hour), and connect with trains to Koblenz and Trier.

A great way to explore the Moselle in the high season is by boat; getting from Koblenz to Trier using scheduled ferry services takes two days. Between early May and mid-October, **Köln-Düsseldorfer (KD) Line** (☎ 0221-208 8318; www.k-d.com) ferries sail between Koblenz and Cochem (€20.20 one-way, 4½ hours, daily), and the **Gebrüder Kolb Line** (☎ 02673-1515) runs boats upriver from Cochem to Trier and back via Traben-Trarbach and Bernkastel. Various smaller ferry companies also operate on the Moselle. Eurail and German Rail passes are valid for all normal KD Line services, and travel on your birthday is free.

The Moselle is a popular area among cyclists, and for much of the river's course there's a separate 'Moselroute' bike track. **Touren-Rad** (☎ 0261-911 6016; Hohenzollernstrasse 127), six blocks from the main train station in Koblenz, rents quality mountain and touring bicycles for €6 to €10 per day.

TRIER

☎ 0651 / pop 99,700

Vineyards line the Moselle River on the way to Trier, and Luxembourg only a few kilometres away. Trier is touted as Germany's oldest town and you'll find more Roman ruins here than anywhere else north of the Alps. Its proximity to France can be tasted in its cuisine and its large student population ensures that it feels nothing like a relic.

Information

Tourist Office (☎ 978 080; www.trier.de; ☼ 9am-6pm Mon-Sat, 10am-3pm Sun Apr-Oct, 10am-5pm Mon-Sat, 10am-1pm Sun Nov-Mar) From the main train station, head west along Bahnhofstrasse and Theodor-Heuss-Allee to the Porta Nigra, where you'll find the tourist office. Ask about the Saturday guided city walking tours in English (€6).

Sights

The town's chief landmark is the **Porta Nigra** (adult/concession €2.10/1.60; ☼ 9am-6pm Apr-Sep, 9am-5pm Oct-Mar), the imposing city gate on the northern edge of the town centre, which dates back to the 2nd century. From Porta Nigra, walk along Simeonstrasse's pedestrian zone to Hauptmarkt, the heart of the old city. Most of the sights are within this area of roughly one square kilometre.

Trier's massive Romanesque **Dom** shares a 1600-year history with the nearby and equally impressive **Konstantin Basilika**. Also worth visiting are the ancient Amphitheater, Kaiserthermen and Barbarathermen (Roman baths). History buffs and nostalgic socialists can visit the **Karl Marx Haus Museum** (☎ 970 680; Brückenstrasse 10; adult/concession €2/1; ☼ 10am-6pm Tue-Sun, 1-6pm Mon Apr-Oct, 10am-1pm & 2-5pm Tue-Sun, 2-5pm Mon Nov-Mar), the birthplace of the man.

Sleeping & Eating

The tourist office can recommend nice camping spots further afield.

DJH Jugendgästehaus (☎ 146 620; www.djh.de; An der Jugendherberge 4; dm/s/d €16/30/44) Not an especially pretty spot, but this clean, modern hostel is on the river south of town.

Hille's Hostel (☎ 710 2785; www.hilles-hostel-trier.de; Gartenfeldstrasse 7; dm €14) Only a small sign identifies this house on the outskirts of the town centre as Hille's Hostel. The rooms, furnished with Ikea-like bunk beds, are set back from the road and quiet, but the building itself and the facilities feel somewhat neglected.

Warsberger Hof Jugendgästehaus (☎ 975 250; www.warsberger-hof.de in German; Dietrichstrasse 42; dm/s/d €15/25/42; [P]) In a large old mansion in the centre of town. Nice bar attached.

Hotel Weinhaus Haag (☎ 975 750; www.hotel-weinhaus-haag.de; Stockplatz 1; s/d €25/50) The best-value hotel in the Altstadt.

The narrow Judenpetrolse, near Markt, has several bars and cafés, whereas a slicker crowd gravitates towards a cluster of bars on Viehmarktplatz. **Astarix** (☎ 722 39;

Karl-Marx-Strasse 11) is a favourite student hangout that serves large salads and main dishes for under €6.

Getting There & Away

Trier has local and fast trains to Koblenz (€15.60, 1½ hours, hourly), as well as services to Luxembourg (€7.40, 45 minutes, about hourly) and Metz (in France; €18.20, 2½ hours, about hourly). For information on river ferries, see p492.

RHINE VALLEY – KOBLENZ TO MAINZ

A trip along the Rhine is on the itinerary for most travellers. The section between Mainz and Koblenz offers the best scenery, especially the narrow tract downriver from Rüdesheim. Spring and autumn are the best times to visit; in summer it's overrun and in winter most towns go into hibernation.

The Koblenz-to-Mainz section of the Rhine Valley is great for wine tasting, with Bacharach, 45km south of Koblenz, being one of the top choices for sipping. For tastings in other towns, ask for recommendations at the tourist offices.

Getting Around

Though the trails here may be a bit more crowded with day-trippers than those along the Moselle, hiking along the Rhine is also excellent. Koblenz and Mainz are the best starting points. The Rhine Valley is also easily accessible from Frankfurt on a long day trip, but that won't do justice to the region.

The **Köln-Düsseldorfer (KD) Line** (☎ 0221-208 8318; www.k-d.com) runs many slow and fast boats daily between Koblenz and Mainz. The most scenic stretch is between Koblenz and Rüdesheim; the journey takes about four hours downstream and about 5½ hours upstream (€24). Boats stop at many riverside towns along the way. Train services operate on both sides of the Rhine River, but are more convenient on the left bank.

Mainz

☎ 06131 / pop 184,000
A 30-minute train ride from Frankfurt, Mainz has an attractive old town. Though it can't compare to the compact beauty of the nearby towns along the Rhine, Mainz impresses with its massive **Domstrasse** (cathedral; admission free) and the **St Stephanskirche** (Weisspetrolse 12; admission free), with stained-glass windows by Marc Chagall. Mainz's museums include the **Gutenberg Museum** (☎ 2640; Liebfrauenplatz 5; adult/concession €3/1.30; ⊙ Tue-Sun), which contains two precious copies of the first printed Bible.

If you are staying overnight, try the **Jugendgästehaus** (☎ 853 32; www.djh.de; Otto-Brunfels-Schneise 4; dm €16.10-21.20; P); take bus No 62, 63 or 92 towards Weisenau. The **Hotel Stadt Coblenz** (☎ 227 602; fax 223 307; Rheinstrasse 499; s/d with shared bathroom €42/55, with private bathroom €52/68) has hostel-quality rooms. The **Augustiner Keller** (☎ 222 662; Augustinerstrasse 26; mains €6-14) serves tasty Alsatian-style pizzas in a homey, old-fashioned setting.

St Goar/St Goarshausen

☎ 06741 / pop 3250
Where the slopes along the Rhine aren't covered with vines, you can bet they built a castle. One of the most impressive is **Burg Rheinfels** (☎ 383; adult/concession €4/2; ⊙ 9am-5pm Apr-Oct, 10am-4pm Sat & Sun in good weather Nov-Mar) in St Goar. An absolute must-see, the labyrinthine ruins reflect the greed and ambition of Count Dieter V of Katzenelnbogen, who built the castle in 1245 to help levy tolls on passing ships. Across the river, just south of St Goarshausen, is the Rhine's most famous sight, the **Loreley Cliff**. Legend has it that a maiden sang sailors to their deaths against its base. The view's worth a trek to the top.

St Goar's **Jugendherberge** (☎ 388; jh-st-goar@ djh-info.de; Bismarckweg 17; dm €12.70) is right below the castle.

FRANKFURT-AM-MAIN

☎ 069 / pop 650,000
Several skyscrapers punctuate the Frankfurt skyline. While it may seem an exaggeration to refer to the city as 'Mainhattan' – it's on the Main (pronounced 'mine' River) – the nickname of 'Bankfurt' is more appropriate since it is the financial centre of western Germany. Officially referred to as Frankfurt-am-Main, or Frankfurt/Main, since there is another large city called Frankfurt (Frankfurt an der Oder) near the Polish border, it's also the geographical centre of western Germany and Germany's most important transport hub, so you'll probably end up here at some point. Don't be surprised if you find this cosmopolitan melting pot much more interesting than you had expected.

GERMANY

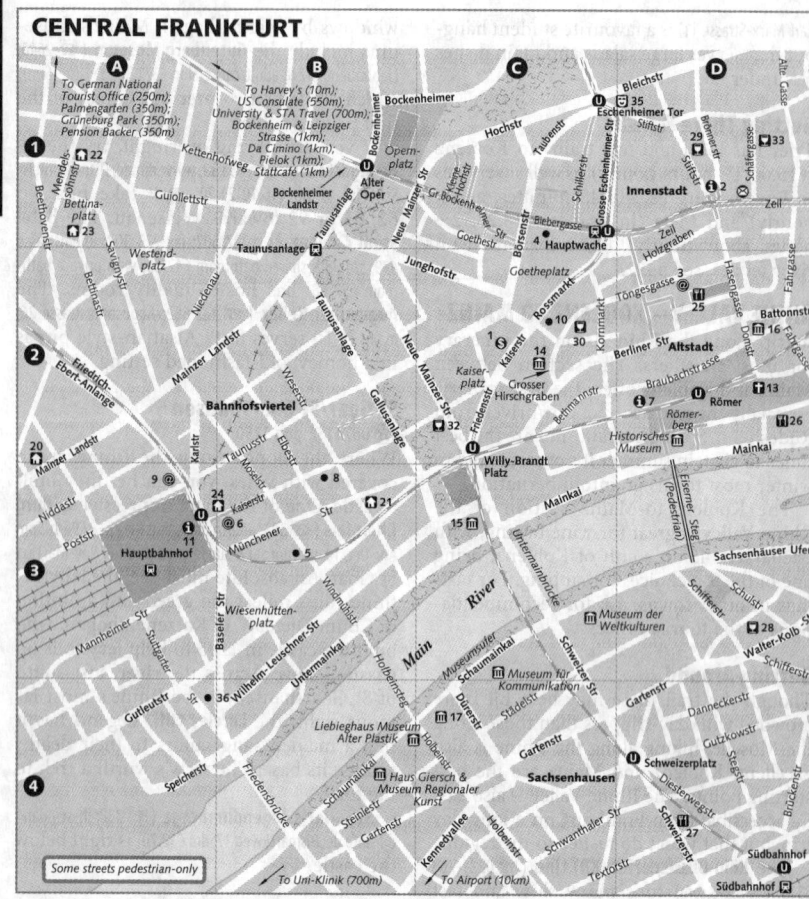

CENTRAL FRANKFURT

Some streets pedestrian-only

To Uni-Klinik (700m) / To Airport (10km)

Orientation

The Main River flows just south of the Altstadt, with several bridges leading the way to one of the city's livelier areas, Sachsenhausen. Its northeastern corner, behind the youth hostel (see p496), is known as Alt-Sachsenhausen and is an interesting area full of quaint old houses and narrow alleyways.

Information

DISCOUNT CARDS

One-/two-day Frankfurt cards (€7.80/11.50) give 50% reductions on admission to all of the city's important museums, the zoo and Palmengarten, as well as unlimited travel on public transport.

INTERNET ACCESS

CyberRyder (☎ 396 754; Töngesgasse 31; per 30min €3.20)

Prepaidmarkt.de (☎ 2424 7939; Kaiserstrasse 81; per hr €3)

Telebistro (☎ 6199 1187; per 30min €2.10; Poststrasse 2) Directly across from the train station.

MEDICAL SERVICES

Medical Queries (☎ 192 92; 🕑 24hr) Doctor service.

Uni-Klinik (☎ 630 10; Theodor Stern Kai, Sachsenhausen; 🕑 24hr)

MONEY

American Express (Kaiserstrasse 10)

Reisebank (Terminal 1, arrival hall B, airport; 🕑 6am-11pm) One of the numerous banks and ATMs at the airport.

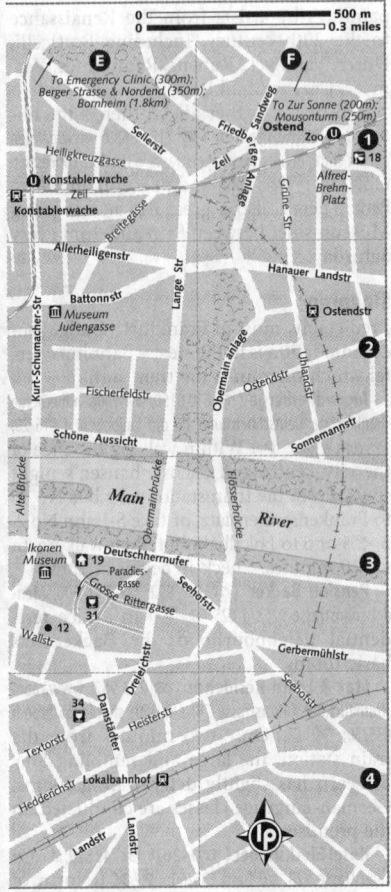

Reisebank (Head of platform No 1, main train station; ☒ 6.30am-10pm)

Thomas Cook (Kaiserstrasse 11)

POST

Main post office (ground fl, Karstadt department store, Zeil 90)

Post office (main train station; ☒ 7am-7.30pm Mon-Fri, 8am-4pm Sat)

Post office (waiting lounge, departure hall B, airport; ☒ 7am-9pm)

TOURIST INFORMATION

CityInfo Zeil (☎ 2123 8800; cnr Zeil & Stiftstrasse; ☒ 10am-6pm Mon-Fri, 10am-4pm Sat & Sun)

German National Tourist Office (☎ 974 64; www.deutschland-tourismus.de; Beethovenstrasse 69)

Good place to contact if you're still planning your trip to Germany; it has brochures on all areas of the country.

Römer tourist office (☎ 2123 8800; Römerberg 27; ☒ 9.30am-5.30pm Mon-Fri, 10am-4pm Sat & Sun) Northwest corner of the Römerberg square.

Tourist office (☎ 2123 8800; www.frankfurt-touris mus.de; main hall, train station; ☒ 8am-9pm Mon-Fri, 9am-6pm Sat, Sun & holidays) Frankfurt's most convenient tourist office. Efficient room-finding service for €3.

Sights

About 80% of the old city was wiped off the map by two Allied bombing raids in March 1944, and postwar reconstruction was subject to the demands of the new age. Rebuilding efforts were more thoughtful, however, in the **Römerberg**, the old central area of Frankfurt west of the cathedral, where restored 14th- and 15th-century buildings provide a glimpse of the beautiful city this once was. The old town hall, or **Römer**, is in the northwestern corner

GETTING INTO TOWN

The S-Bahn's S8/S9 train runs every 15 minutes between the airport and Frankfurt Hauptbahnhof (11 minutes), usually continuing via Hauptwache and Konstablerwache to Offenbach; a fixed fare of €3.25 applies. Taxis (about €25 and taking 30 minutes without traffic jams) or the frequent airport bus No 61 (from Südbahnhof; €3.10) take longer. The Hauptbahnhof is on the western side of the city, but within walking distance of the old city centre.

The safest route to the city centre through the sleazy train station area is along Kaiserstrasse. This leads to Kaiserplatz and then to a large square called An der Hauptwache. The area between the former lockup (Hauptwache), and the Römerberg, in the tiny vestige of Frankfurt's original old city, is the centre of Frankfurt.

of Römerberg and consists of three 15th-century houses topped with Frankfurt's trademark stepped gables.

East of Römerberg is the **Frankfurter Dom**, the coronation site of Holy Roman emperors from 1562 to 1792. It's dominated by the elegant 15th-century Gothic **tower** (completed in the 1860s) – one of the few structures left standing after the 1944 raids.

Anyone with an interest in German literature should visit **Goethe Haus** (☎ 138 800; Grosser Hirschgraben 23-25; adult/concession €5/3; ⏱ 9am-6pm Mon-Fri Apr-Sep, 9am-4pm Mon-Fri Oct-Mar, 10am-4pm Sat & Sun all year), where Johann Wolfgang von Goethe was born in 1749.

Museum für Moderne Kunst (☎ 2123 0447; Domstrasse 10; adult/concession €5/0.50), north of the cathedral, features works of modern art by Joseph Beuys, Claes Oldenburg and many others. Also on the north bank there's the **Jüdisches Museum** (☎ 2123 5000; Untermainkai 14-15; adult/concession €2.60/1.30, free Sat; ⏱ 10am-5pm Tue-Sun), a huge place with exhibits on Jewish life in the city from the Middle Ages to the present.

Numerous museums line the south bank of the Main River along the so-called **Museumsufer** (Museum Embankment). Pick of the crop is the **Städelsches Kunstinstitut** (☎ 605 0980; www.staedelmuseum.de; Schaumainkai 63; adult/concession €6/5; ⏱ 10am-5pm Tue & Fri-Sun, 10am-9pm Wed & Thu), with a world-class collection of paintings by artists from the Renaissance to the 20th century, including Botticelli, Dürer, Van Eyck, Rubens, Rembrandt, Vermeer, Cézanne and Renoir.

A little bit further afield, there's the botanical **Palmengarten** (☎ 2123 6689; www.palmengarten-frankfurt.de; Siesmayerstrasse 63; adult/concession €3.50/1.50; ⏱ 9am-6pm) and peaceful **Grüneburg Park**. There's also a great **flea market** along Museumsufer between 8am and 2pm every Saturday.

Sleeping

Predictably, most of Frankfurt's budget accommodation is in the sleazy Bahnhofsviertel which surrounds the train station.

Jugendherberge (☎ 610 0150; www.jugendherberge-frankfurt.de; Deutschherrnufer 12; dm junior/senior €16/20; ⏱ curfew 2am; P) Within walking distance of the city centre and Sachsenhausen's night spots. From the train station take bus No 46 to Frankensteinerplatz, or take S-Bahn No 2, 3, 4, 5 or 6 to Lokalbahnhof, then walk north for 10 minutes. Check-in begins at 1pm.

Pension Backer (☎ 747 992; fax 747 900; Mendelssohnstrasse 92; s/d €25/40; P) In a nice residential neighbourhood, the Backer has basic rooms.

Stay & Learn Residence (☎ 253 952; www.room-frankfurt.de; Kaiserstrasse 74; s/d with shared bathroom €35/50; ✗ 💻) Only two minutes from the train station, the large and rambling Stay & Learn has slightly deteriorating rooms. German-language classes are conducted on the premises.

Hotel Glockshuber (☎ 742 628; fax 742 629; Mainzer Landstrasse 120; s/d from €35/60; P ✗) North of the main train station, the Glockshuber is another pleasant option.

Hotel-Pension Bruns (☎ 748 896; fax 748 846; Mendelssohnstrasse 42; s/d with shared bathroom €40/50, with private bathroom €50/65) Simple rooms in a spacious house, but the highlight is breakfast in bed.

Hotel Memphis (☎ 242 6099; www.memphis-hotel.de; Münchenerstrasse 15; s/d €60/80; P 💻) The stylish modern rooms are fully equipped and the front desk staff are trained to assist with all your needs, business or otherwise.

Campingplatz Heddernheim (☎ 570 332; An der Sandelmühle 35; camp sites €3.50, plus adult/car €5.20/4.50; ⏱ year-round) In the Heddernheim district northwest of the city centre. It's a 15-minute ride on the U1, U2 or U3 from the Hauptwache U-Bahn station.

Eating

Known to the locals here as Fresspetrols (Munch-Alley), the Kalbächer Petrolse and Grosse Bockenheimer Strasse area, between Opernplatz and Börsenstrasse, has some medium-priced restaurants and fast-food places with outdoor tables in summer.

The area around the main train station has a variety of cuisines. Baseler Strasse in particular has a Middle Eastern tone. Wallstrasse and the surrounding streets in Alt-Sachsenhausen also have lots of mid-priced restaurants selling non-German food.

Another good place for ravenous hunters and gatherers is the cosmopolitan Berger Strasse and Nordend areas north of the Zeil.

Da Cimino (☎ 771 142; Abdelstrasse 28; pizzas €4-8) Customise your pizza at this small neighbourhood spot just north of the centre, which gets especially busy during lunch time.

Zum Gemalten Haus (Schweizer Strasse 67; mains €10-20) A lively place full of paintings of old Frankfurt where you can try apple-wine with your meal.

Zur Sonne (☎ 459 396; Berger Strasse 312; mains €7) A gorgeous yard for summer tippling in Bornheim. Take the U-4 to Bornheim-Mitte.

Pielok (Jordanstrasse 3; mains €7-11) Looks like your grandmother had a hand in the decorations at Pielok, 1km north of the centre. It's cosy and the food is traditional, filling and very popular with students.

Stattcafé (☎ 708 907; Grempstrasse 21; mains from €6) In Bockenheim, Stattcafé offers vegetarian and meat dishes, as well as good coffee and cakes.

Metropol (☎ 288 287; Weckmarkt 13-15; mains €7-13) Serves up well-priced and filling salads, casseroles and the like until late. It's near the Dom and you can sit unharassed for hours with a book.

Kleinmarkthalle (Hasengasse 5-7; ⏰ 7.30am-6pm Mon-Fri, 7.30am-3pm Sat) is a great produce market with loads of fruit, vegetables, meats and hot food. Fresh produce **markets** are held from 8am to 6pm on Thursday and Friday at Bockenheimer Warte and Südbahnhof respectively.

Drinking & Clubbing

Apple-wine taverns are a Frankfurt eating and drinking tradition. They serve *Ebbelwoi* (Frankfurt dialect for Apfelwein), an alcoholic apple cider, along with local specialities like *Handkäse mit Musik* (literally 'hand-cheese

with music'). This is a round cheese soaked in oil and vinegar and topped with onions; your bowel supplies the music. Some good *Ebbelwoi* are situated in Alt-Sachsenhausen – the area directly behind the DJH hostel – which bulges with eateries and pubs.

Bar Oppenheimer (☎ 626 674; Oppenheimerstrasse 41) Minimalist décor, cosmopolitan clientele and worldly drinks.

Zur Germania (☎ 613 336; Textorstrasse 16) An apple-wine place in Sachsenhausen.

Keeper's Lounge (☎ 6060 7210; Schweizerstrasse 78) Another Sachsenhausen joint, the extensive drink menu at Keeper's will keep you occupied for most of the night.

Zum Schwejk (☎ 293 166; Schäfferpetrolse 20) This is a popular gay bar.

Living XXL (☎ 2429 3710; Kaiserstrasse 29) Living large is what it's all about at Frankfurt's largest nightclub located on the ground floor of the Eurotower.

Cave (☎ 283 808; Brönnerstrasse 11) A club that spins Goth and has occasional live concerts.

Cooky's (Am Salzhaus 4) Open until the wee hours, delivering a winning combo of hip hop and house nights and live indie bands.

Entertainment

Journal Frankfurt (€1.50) and *Fritz* have good listings in German of what's on in town.

Turm-Palast (☎ 281 787; Am Eschenheimer Turm) A multiscreen cinema showing films in English.

Mousonturm (☎ 4058 9520; Waldschmidtstrasse 4) Arty rock, dance performances and politically oriented cabaret are on tap at this converted soap factory in Bornheim.

Getting There & Away

Germany's largest airport is **Flughafen Frankfurtam-Main** (☎ 6901). The airport train station has two sections: platforms 1 to 3 (below Terminal 1, hall B) handle regional and S-Bahn connections, whereas IR, IC and ICE connections are in the long-distance train station. Signs point the way. IC or EC trains go to Cologne (€35, two hours, hourly) and Nuremberg (€39, 2½ hours, hourly) and ICEs run to/from Hamburg on weekdays (€90, five hours).

Long-distance buses leave from the southern side of the main train station, where there's a **Deutsche Touring/Eurolines office** (☎ 790 350; Mannheimerstrasse 4) that handles bookings. It handles most European destinations.

The Hauptbahnhof handles more departures and arrivals than any other station in Germany. For rail information, call ☎ 01805-996 633. The **DB Lounge** (◷ 6am-11pm) above the information office is a comfortable retreat for anyone with a valid train ticket.

All main car rental companies have offices in the main hall of the train station and at the airport. The **ADM-Mitfahrzentrale** (☎ 194 40; Baselerplatz) is a three-minute walk south of the train station.

Getting Around

Single or day tickets for Frankfurt's excellent transport network (RMV) can be purchased from automatic machines at almost any stop. Peak period *Kurzstrecken* (short-trip tickets) cost €1.05, single tickets cost €1.60 and a *Tageskarte* (24-hour ticket) is €4.70 without a trip to the airport and €7.20 with an airport trip.

There are numerous taxi ranks throughout the city, or you can book a **taxi** (☎ 230 001, 250 001, 545 011).

COLOGNE

☎ 0221 / pop 1,020,000

The justly famous cathedral dominates the cityscape, but it's also worth visiting this lively city for its interesting museums and vibrant nightlife. Located at a major crossroads of European trade routes, Cologne (Köln) was an important city even in Roman times. In later years it remained one of northern Europe's main cities, and it is still the centre of the German Roman Catholic church. Almost completely destroyed in WWII, it was quickly rebuilt and its old churches and monuments have been meticulously restored.

Information

American Express (Burgmauer 14)

Jetzt Dom Internet Cafe (☎ 277 9932; per hr €2; Komödienstrasse 37)

Post office (main train station; ◷ 6am-10pm Mon-Sat, 7am-10pm Sun) In Ludwig im Bahnhof bookshop, near track 6.

Reisebank (main train station; ◷ 8am-10pm)

Thomas Cook (Burgmauer 4)

Tourist office (☎ 2213 0400; www.koelntourismus.de; Unter Fettenhennen 19; ◷ 8am-9pm Mon-Sat, 9.30am-7pm Sun & holidays May-Oct, 8am-9pm Mon-Sat, 9.30am-7pm Sun & holidays Nov-Apr) Opposite the cathedral's main entrance. The room-finding service (€3) is a bargain when the city is busy with trade fairs.

Sights

The heart and soul of Cologne is the **Kölner Dom** (◷ 7am-7.30pm). The structure's sheer size, with spires rising to 157m, is overwhelming. Building began in 1248 in the French Gothic style. The huge project was stopped in 1560 but started again in 1842, in the style originally planned, as a symbol of Prussia's drive for unification. It was finally finished in 1880. Miraculously, it survived WWII's heavy night bombing intact. The five magnificent **stained-glass windows** along the north aisle depict the lives of the Virgin and St Peter. Behind the high altar you can see the **Magi's Shrine** (c. 1150–1210), believed to contain the remains of the Three Wise Men. Guided tours in English are held at 10.30am and 2.30pm Monday to Saturday (at 2.30pm only on Sunday) and cost €4/2 per adult/concession; meet inside the main portal. Tours in German are more frequent and cost €3/2. For a fitness fix, climb 509 steps up the Dom's south tower to the base of the stupendous **steeples** (adult/concession €2/1; ◷ 9am-5pm Mar-Sep, 9am-4pm Oct-Feb). Look at the 24-tonne **Peter Bell**, the largest working bell in the world. At the end of your climb, the view from the vantage point, 98.25m up, is absolutely stunning.

Next to the cathedral there's the **Römisch-Germanisches Museum** (Roman Germanic Museum; ☎ 2212 2304; Roncalliplatz 4; adult/concession €4.30/2.70; ◷ 10am-5pm Tue-Sun), which displays artefacts from all aspects of the Roman settlement in the Rhine Valley. The **Wallraf-Richartz-Museum** (☎ 2212 1119; Martinstrasse 39; adult/concession €5.80/3.30; ◷ 10am-6pm Wed-Fri, 10am-8pm Tue, 11am-6pm Sat & Sun) has a fantastic collection that includes paintings by Rubens, Rembrandt and Monet. The **Museum Ludwig** (☎ 2212 6165; www.museenkoeln.de; Bischofsgartenstrasse 1; adult/concession €7.50/5.50; ◷ 10am-6pm Wed-Fri, 10am-8pm Tue, 11am-6pm Sat & Sun) displays prime pieces from Kirchner, Kandinsky and Max Ernst, as well as pop-art works by Rauschenberg and Andy Warhol.

The multimedia **Deutsches Sport- und Olympia-Museum** (☎ 336 090; www.sportmuseum-koeln.de in German; Rheinauhafen 1; adult/concession €4/3.50; ◷ 10am-6pm Tue-Fri, 11am-7pm Sat & Sun) is a great place to find out all about the history of sport from ancient times to the present. Learn everything you wanted to know about the history and making of chocolate at the aptly named **Chocolate Museum** (☎ 931

8880; Rheinauhafen; adult/concession €5.50/5; 10am-6pm Tue-Fri, 11am-7pm Sat & Sun). It's on the river in the Rheinauhafen near the Altstadt.

Festivals & Events

Try to visit Cologne during the wild, crazy period of the **Cologne Carnival** (Karneval), rivalled only by Munich's Oktoberfest. People dress in creative costumes, clown suits and whatever else their alcohol-numbed brains may invent. The streets explode with activity on the Thursday before the seventh Sunday before Easter. The party lasts through Monday.

Sleeping

Accommodation prices in Cologne increase by at least 20% when fairs are on. The tourist office has a room-finding service that can help with hotel rooms in the lower price range. A lot of budget and mid-range hotels cluster in the streets just north and east of the main train station.

Jugendgästehaus Köln-Riehl (767 081; jh-koeln -riehl@djh-rheinland.de; An der Schanz 14; r per person €21-34) Around 3km north of the city, this hostel has one- to six-bed rooms. Take the U15 or U16 to Boltensternstrasse.

Jugendherberge Köln-Deutz (814 711; jh-koeln -deutz@djh-rheinland.de; Siegesstrasse 5a; dm junior/senior €17/19.50; P X) This hostel is in Deutz, 500m east from the main train station over the Hohenzollernbrücke.

Station Hostel (912 5301; www.hostel-cologne.de; Marzellenstrasse 44-48; dm/s €15/27; X) Just a short walk from the main train station, this is a good place to meet fellow travellers, and is close to Cologne's pubs.

Station Hostel & Bar (22 123 0247; www.hostel -cologne.de; Rheingasse 34-36; dm/s €16/27;) A 20-minute walk south of the train station on the banks of the Rhine, the rooms at this hostel are somewhat cramped but the bar is busy and social.

Hotel Im Kupferkessel (270 7960; www.im -kupferkessel.de; Probsteigasse 6; s/d from €30/60) The cheaper rooms at the Kupferkessel have shared facilities but all are well kept and it's about 1.5km west of the train station.

Hotel Good Sleep (257 2257; www.goodsleep.de in German; Komödienstrasse 19-21; s/d €35/50) The Dom looms majestically just a block away and the rooms are bright and clean.

Rhein-Hotel St Martin (257 7898; www.koeln-alt stadt.de/rheinhotel; Frankenwerft 31-33; s/d €34/70) One

of the better choices along the Rhine, the St Martin is modern and has a nice restaurant.

Campingplatz der Stadt Köln (831 966; camp sites €4, plus per person €4; Easter–mid-Oct) On Weidenweg in Poll, 5km southeast of the city centre. Take U16 to Marienburg and cross the Rodenkirchener bridge.

Eating

Cologne's beer halls serve cheap and filling meals to go with their home brew (see Drinking, below). The Belgisches Viertel (Belgian Quarter) around and west of Hahnentor is packed with restaurants. To put together a picnic, visit a market; the biggest is held on Tuesday and Friday at the Aposteln-Kloster near Neumarkt.

Gaffel Haus (Alter Markt 20-22; mains €10) Another nice place to eat and sample the local concoction.

Buffet Chang (250 9909; Breitestrasse 80-90; all-you-can-eat buffet €6) Stuff yourself full of Chinese cuisine in the DuMont Carré centre.

4 Cani Della Città (257 4085; Benesisstrasse 61; pizza €6) A busy café with lively street-side seating that attracts a fashionable clientele.

Früh am Dom (258 0394; Am Hof 12-14; breakfast €4-10, mains €5-14) Rightly famous for its own-brew beer.

Drinking

As in Munich, beer in Cologne reigns supreme. The city has more than 20 local breweries, all producing a variety called *Kölsch*, which is relatively light and slightly bitter. The breweries run their own beer halls and serve their wares in skinny glasses holding a mere 200mL, but they add up. Evenings and weekends in the Altstadt are like miniature carnivals, with bustling crowds and lots to do. The *Monatsvorschau* (€1.20), the monthly what's-on booklet, can be purchased at the tourist office.

Peter's Brauhaus (Mühlengasse 1) In the heart of the Altstadt, Peter's serves up its own brew.

Biermuseum (Buttermarkt 39) This beer museum beside Papa Joe's has 18 varieties on tap.

Brauhaus Sion (Unter Taschenmacher 9) A big beer hall, packed most nights and with good reason: a couple of beers and a full meal will only set you back €12.

Papa Joe's Klimperkasten (Alter Markt 50) A lively jazz pub with a wonderful pianola.

Papa Joe's Em Streckstrump (257 7931; Buttermarkt 37) More intimate and more traditional.

GERMANY

COLOGNE (KÖLN)

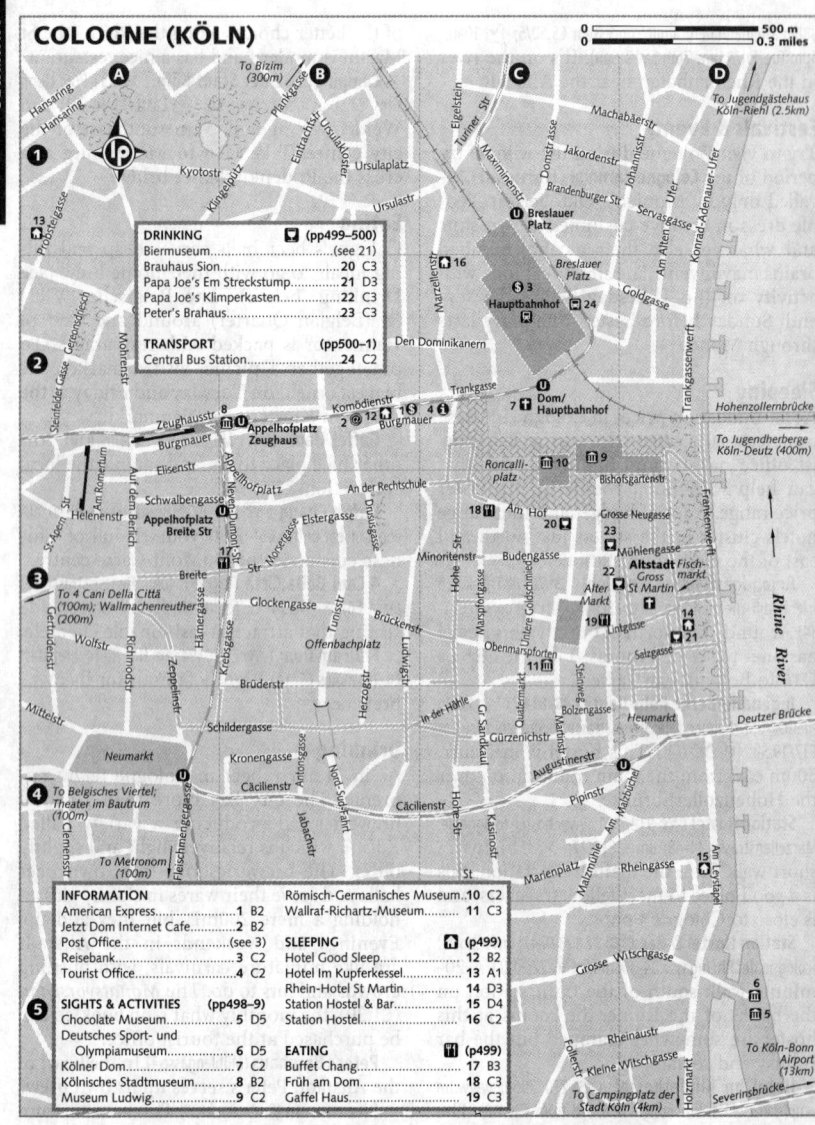

DRINKING   (pp499–500)
Biermuseum.................................(see 21)
Brauhaus Sion..............................**20** C3
Papa Joe's Em Streckstump............**21** D3
Papa Joe's Klimperkasten...............**22** C3
Peter's Brahaus............................**23** C3

TRANSPORT   (pp500–1)
Central Bus Station.......................**24** C2

INFORMATION
American Express.........................**1** B2
Jetzt Dom Internet Cafe.................**2** B2
Post Office................................(see 3)
Reisebank..................................**3** C2
Tourist Office.............................**4** C2

SIGHTS & ACTIVITIES   (pp498–9)
Chocolate Museum.......................**5** D5
Deutsches Sport- und
  Olympiamuseum........................**6** D5
Kölner Dom................................**7** C2
Kölnisches Stadtmuseum................**8** B2
Museum Ludwig...........................**9** C2
Römisch-Germanisches Museum......**10** C2
Wallraf-Richartz-Museum...............**11** C3

SLEEPING   (p499)
Hotel Good Sleep.........................**12** B2
Hotel Im Kupferkessel....................**13** A1
Rhein-Hotel St Martin.....................**14** D3
Station Hostel & Bar......................**15** D4
Station Hostel..............................**16** C2

EATING   (p499)
Buffet Chang..............................**17** B3
Früh am Dom...............................**18** C3
Gaffel Haus................................**19** C3

Metronom (☎ 213 465; Weyerstrasse 59) Near the
Kwartier Latäng (Latin Quarter), the Metronom is Cologne's most respected bar for jazz
enthusiasts; live performances on weekdays.

Wallmachenreuther (Brüsseler Platz 9) An off-
beat bar in the Belgisches Viertel that also
serves food. The gay scene also centres on
the Belgisches Viertel.

Getting There & Around

Deutsche Touring's Eurolines (☎ 135 252; www
.deutsche-touring.de; train station) offers overnight
trips to Paris (€34, 6½ hours, daily).

There are frequent services operating to
both nearby Bonn (€6, 18 minutes, about
every half-hour) and Düsseldorf (€7, 40
minutes, about every half-hour) as well

as to Aachen (€11, one hour, about every half-hour). Frequent direct IC/EC (€47.80, 3¼ hours, hourly) and ICE (€53.40, 2¾ hours, hourly) trains go to Hanover. There are ICE links with Frankfurt-am-Main (€30, 2¼ hours, three per hour) and Berlin (€90, 4½ hours, hourly). The Thalys high-speed train connects Paris and Cologne via Aachen and Brussels (€75/67 weekdays/weekends, four hours, seven times daily), with only a small discount for rail pass-holders. Bus No 170 runs between Cologne/Bonn airport and the main bus station every 15 minutes from 5.30am to 11.20pm daily (€5, 20 minutes).

Cologne offers a convenient and extensive mix of buses, trams and local trains. The best ticket option is the one-day pass: €5.50 if you're staying near the city.

BONN
☎ 0228 / pop 311,000

This pleasant city on the Rhine south of Cologne became West Germany's temporary capital in 1949 but now hosts international associations and large corporations after the seat of government and embassies moved to Berlin. Classical music buffs can pay homage to Bonn's most famous son – Ludwig van Beethoven.

The **tourist office** (☎ 775 000; www.bonn.de; Windeckstrasse 1; ☷ 9am-6.30pm Mon-Fri, 9am-4pm Sat, 10am-2pm Sun) is a three-minute walk along Poststrasse from the Hauptbahnhof.

Bonn is a city that lives and breathes Beethoven. You can visit the **Beethoven-Haus** (☎ 981 7525; www.beethoven-haus-bonn.de; Bonngasse 20; adult/concession €4/3; ☷ 10am-6pm Mon-Sat Apr-Oct, 10am-5pm Mon-Sat Nov-Mar, 11am-4pm Sun year-round), where the composer was born in 1770.

There are several interesting museums to choose from on Museumsmeile. **Pawlow** (☎ 653 603; Heerstrasse 64) is a relaxed place for a beer or late breakfast in the Altstadt.

There are frequent trains to Cologne in the north and to Koblenz (€15.40, 30 minutes, half-hourly) in the south.

DÜSSELDORF
☎ 0211 / pop 567,000

This elegant and wealthy capital of North Rhine-Westphalia is an important centre for fashion and commerce, and a charming example of big-city living along the Rhine River.

Information
Internet Café World (Worringer Platz 21; per 30min €2) Three blocks north of the train station.
Main post office (Immermannstrasse 1; ☷ 8am-8pm Mon-Fri, 9am-2pm Sat) Across the street from Internet Café World.
Tourist office (☎ 172 020; www.duessel dorf.de; ☷ 8am-8pm Mon-Sat, 4-8pm Sun) Opposite the main exit of the train station. Another branch is at the northern end of Marktplatz.

Sights
To catch a glimpse of Düsseldorf's swish lifestyle, head for the famed Königsallee, or 'Kö', with its stylish (and pricey) boutiques and arcades. Stroll north along the Kö to the **Hofgarten**, a large park in the city centre.

City museums include the **Museum Kunst Palast** (☎ 899 2460; Ehrenhof 5; adult/concession €6/3.50; ☷ 10am-6pm Tue-Sun), with a comprehensive European collection and the impressive Glasmuseum Hentrich. The quite expansive modern art collection in the **Kunstsammlung Nordrhein-Westfalen** is displayed in two different galleries: **K20** (☎ 838 1130; Grabbeplatz 5; adult/concession €6.50/4.50; ☷ 10am-6pm Tue-Fri, 11am-6pm Sat & Sun) and **K21** (☎ 838 1600; Ständehausstrasse 1; adult/concession €6.50/4.50). A combined ticket to both costs €10/8. The **Goethe-Museum Düsseldorf** (☎ 899 6262; Jacobistrasse 2; adult/concession €2/1; ☷ 11am-5pm Tue-Fri & Sun, 1-5pm Sat) in Schloss Jägerhof pays tribute to the life and work of one of Europe's great men of letters.

In summer, the town's youth hang out on the steps below the **Schlossturm**. From here the pedestrian-only Rheinuferpromenade provides perfect strolling along the river.

Sleeping & Eating
Düsseldorf's frequent trade shows inflate already high hotel and *pension* prices.

Jugendgästehaus (☎ 557 310; www.djh.de; Düsseldorfer Strasse 1; dm/s/d €21/26/48; Ⓟ ☒ ▯) In posh Oberkassel across the Rhine from the Altstadt. Take U-Bahn No 70, 74, 75, 76 or 77 from the main train station to Luegplatz. From there it's a short walk.

Backpackers-Düsseldorf (☎ 302 0848; www.back packers-duesseldorf.de; Fürstenwall 180; dm/s €20/29; Ⓟ ▯) Rents out bicycles, has free Internet access and is only 1km from the train station. Take bus No 725 to Kirchplatz.

Hotel Komet (☎ 178 790; www.hotelkomet.de; Bismarckstrasse 93; s/d from €33/44) Provides reasonable rooms.

Campingplatz Nord Unterbacher See (☎ 899 2038; camp sites €5.50, plus per person/car €3.25/4; ☒ 4 Apr-27 Sep) At Kleiner Torfbruch in Düsseldorf-Unterbach (take S-Bahn No 7 to Eller, and then bus No 735 to Seeweg).

Anadolou (Mertenspetrolse 10; mains from €4) Serves delicious Anatolian sit-down and takeaway food including vegetarian dishes.

Brauerei zur Uer (Ratinger Strasse 16) A rustic place to fill up for less than €10. Ratinger Strasse is also home to a couple of other pub-style places where you can eat and drink.

Drinking & Clubbing

The Altstadt is affectionately referred to as the 'longest bar in the world'. Favoured streets include Bolkerstrasse, Kurze Strasse and Andreasstrasse, and the surrounding side streets. The beverage of choice is Alt beer, a dark and semisweet brew typical of Düsseldorf.

Zum Uerige (Berger Strasse) The only place where you can buy Uerige Alt beer is (surprise, surprise) Zum Uerige. At €1.40 per 250mL glass, the beer flows quickly.

Et Kabüffke (☎ 133 269; Flingerstrasse 1) Taste *Killepitsch*, a herb liqueur; it's only sold here and in the shop next door.

Night-Live (Bolkerstrasse 22) has live bands and upstairs **dä Spiegel** (Bolkerstrasse 22) is a popular bar.

Getting There & Around

Düsseldorf is part of a dense S-Bahn and train network in the Rhine-Ruhr region and there are regular IC/EC services to/from Hamburg (€63, 3½ hours), ICE services to Hanover (€49, 2¾ hours) and Frankfurt (€44, 2½ hours), and trains to Cologne (€7, 40 minutes) and most other major German cities. The schedules are quite irregular, and range from every half-hour to every two hours, depending on the time of day.

A short-trip ticket on Düsseldorf's public transport system up to 1.5km costs €2. Better value is the 24-hour *TagesTicket* for €12, valid for up to five people in zone A.

AACHEN

☎ 0241 / pop 251,000

Aachen was famous in Roman times for its thermal springs. The great Frankish conqueror Charlemagne was so impressed by their revitalising qualities that he settled here and made it the capital of his kingdom

in AD 794. Now an industrial and commercial centre, its proximity to the Netherlands and Belgium, and the country's largest technical university, give it a dynamic international flare.

Aachen's compact old centre is contained within two ring roads that roughly follow the old city walls.

Information

Main post office (An den Frauenbrüdern 1)

Tourist office (☎ 180 2960/1; www.aachen-tourist.de; Friedrich-Wilhelm-Platz; ☒ 9am-6pm Mon-Fri, 9am-2pm Sat year-round, 10am-2pm Sun Jul-Sep) Efficient tourist office at Atrium Elisenbrunnen.

Web (Kleinmarschierstrasse 74-76; per 30min €2) Internet access.

Sights

Aachen's biggest drawcard is its **Dom** (Kaiserdom or Münster; ☒ 7am-7pm), whose subtle grandeur, historical significance and interior serenity make a visit almost obligatory. No fewer than 30 Holy Roman emperors were crowned here from 936 to 1531. The heart of the cathedral is a Byzantine-inspired octagon, built on Roman foundations. Charlemagne lies buried here in the golden shrine. His white-marble throne is on the upper gallery of the octagon on the western side, where the nobles sat.

North of the cathedral, the 14th-century **Rathaus** (adult/concession €2/1; ☒ 10am-1pm & 2-5pm) overlooks Markt, a lively gathering place in summer, with its fountain statue of Charlemagne.

Foremost among Aachen's worthwhile museums is the **Ludwig Forum for International Art** (☎ 180 70; Jülicherstrasse 97-109; adult/concession €3/1.50; ☒ noon-6pm Tue-Sun) with works by Warhol, Lichtenstein, Baselitz and others.

The 8th-century Franks called the town 'Ahha', which is supposed to mean water. A visit to the city-owned **Carolus Thermen** (☎ 182 740; www.carolus-thermen.de; Passstrasse 79) costs €8 for two hours (€15 with the sauna), or €14 for up to five hours (€24 with sauna). It's in the city garden, northeast of the centre.

Sleeping

To arrange a room in advance, call Aachen's room reservation line from Monday to Friday day on ☎ 180 2950/1.

Jugendgästehaus (☎ 711 010; Maria-Theresia-Allee 260; dm/s/d €20.90/34.20/51.80; Ⓟ ☒) This DJH outpost is 4km southwest of the train station on a hill overlooking the city. Take bus No 2 to Ronheide, or bus No 12 to the closer Colynshof at the foot of the hill.

Hotel Marx (☎ 375 41; www.hotel-marx.de; Hubertusstrasse 33-35; s/d €34/62, with private bathroom from €49/67; P ⊠) Good cheap rooms but the facilities are a little cramped.

Hoeve de Petroltmolen (☎ 0031-43 306 5755; Lemierserberg 23; camp sites with 1 car €7, plus per person €2.50) About 6km outside Aachen in the town of Vaals, in Belgium. Take bus No 15 or 65 and get off at the 'Heuvel' stop.

Eating & Drinking

Being a university town, Aachen is full of spirited cafés, restaurants and pubs, especially along Pontstrasse, referred to by locals as the 'Quartier Latin'.

Café Kittel (Pontstrasse 39; mains around €6) Vegetarians and those seeking lighter options should stop by Café Kittel, a cosy hang-out with a lively garden area.

Petroltstätte Labyrinth (Pontstrasse 156-158; mains €7-11) You may have trouble finding your way back to your table if you drink too much at this labyrinthine beer hall. Good, filling meals should provide sustenance for your journey.

Domkeller (Hof 1) Students have frequented Domkeller since the 1950s. Jazz or blues is usually featured on Mondays.

B9 (Blondelstrasse 9) The style of music changes nightly at B9, but young patrons are a standby.

Entertainment

Concerts and opera are performed almost nightly at the **City Theatre** (☎ 478 4244; Theaterplatz).

Getting There & Around

There are fast trains almost every hour to Cologne (€10, 43 minutes) and Liège (€9.90, 40 minutes). The high-speed Thalys passes through seven times daily on its way to Brussels (€22, 2½ hours) and Paris (€62, three hours and 10 minutes). There's also a frequent bus service to Maastricht (€5, 55 minutes). The bus station is at the northeastern edge of Grabenring.

Aachen's city centre is covered easily on foot. A 24-hour Familienkarte und Gruppenkarte is valid for up to five people and costs €4.85.

BREMEN & LOWER SAXONY

Among the more popular attractions of this beautiful region are the scenic Harz Mountains, the old student town of Göttingen, and the picturesque towns along the so-called Fairy-Tale Road.

BREMEN

☎ 0421 / pop 550,000

Bremen is, after Hamburg, the most important harbour in Germany, even though the open sea lies 113km to the north. Once known as the 'Rome of the North' because it was used as a base for bringing Christianity to Scandinavia, it now enjoys a reputation for liberal politics and a congenial atmosphere. Bremen's vibrant student population ensures the fun continues long after dark.

Information

Internet Café/Callshop (per hr €4) There's also access inside the train station.

Main post office (Domsheide 15) There's another branch near the train station.

Tourist office (☎ 308 000; www.bremen-tourism.de in German; main train station; ◷ 8am-8pm Mon-Thu, 9am-6pm Fri-Sun) There is also a booth at the Rathaus opposite the smaller of the main Altstadt churches.

Sights

Around Am Markt, don't miss the splendid and ornate **Rathaus**, and the **St-Petri-Dom**, which has a tower lookout. There's also the large **statue of Roland**, Bremen's sentimental protector, which was erected in 1404.

Walk down **Böttcherstrasse**, a must-see recreation of a medieval alley, complete with tall brick houses, shops, galleries and restaurants. There are also three **museums** (adult/concession combined ticket €6/3; ◷ 11am-6pm Tue-Sun), including the **Paula Modersohn-Becker Museum** (Böttcherstrasse 8), which has works by its namesake contemporary painter. The **Glockenspiel**, active in summer hourly from noon to 6pm, plays an extended tune between rooftops.

The nearby **Schnoorviertel** area features fishing cottages that are now a tourist attraction, with shops, cafés and tiny lanes. An excellent walk is along the **Wallanlagen**, with peaceful parks stretching along the old city walls and moat. Backing onto the parkland is Bremen's **Kunsthalle** (art gallery; ☎ 329 080; www.kunsthalle-bremen.de; Am Wall 207; adult/concession €5/2.50; ☺ 10am-5pm Wed-Sun, 10am-9pm Tue).

Tours of **Beck's Brewery** (☎ 5094 5555; www .becks.de in German; Am Deich 18-19; tours €3; 10am-5pm Tue-Sat, 10am-3pm Sun) are available (take tram No 1 or 5 from the train station to Westerstrasse).

Sleeping

Jugendgästehaus Bremen (☎ 171 369; www.djh.de; Kalkstrasse 6; dm junior/senior €17/22; P ♨) It's only a short trip across the river to Beck's Brewery. Take tram No 3 or 5 from the train station to Am Brill.

Gastehaus Bremer Backpacker Hostel (☎ 223 8057; www.bremer-backpacker-hostel.de; Emil-Waldmannstrasse 5-6; dm/s/d €16/27/44; P) More convenient is this well-maintained hostel, only a few minutes from the train station.

Hotel-Pension Weidmann (☎ 498 4455; Am Schwarzen Meer 35; s/d €21/42) For homey hospitality, this is great value. Take tram No 2 from Domsheide or No 10 from the station.

Gästehaus Peterswerder (☎ 447 101; www.gaeste hauspeterswerder.de in German; Cellerstrasse 4; s/d €28/50) Another welcoming option, the Peterswerder, not far from the Weidmann, has excellent rooms including an especially small but cosy attic.

Campingplatz Bremen (☎ 212 002; Am Stadtwaldsee 1; camp sites €4, plus per person/car €4/2) Take tram No 6 from the train station to the Klagenfurter Strasse stop.

Eating

A prowl around Ostertorsteinweg (near Am Dobben) will offer all sorts of gastronomic possibilities. The long courtyard of Auf den Höfen, north of Ostertorsteinweg, has several restaurants and bars and serves as one of the centres of Bremen's nightlife.

Casablanca (☎ 326 429; Ostertorsteinweg 59; mains €5-12) Known for its breakfasts; it also has cheap pastas and soups.

Piano (☎ 785 46; Fehrfeld 64) Just east of Am Dobben, Piano serves huge Mediterranean-inspired salads and tasty baked casseroles for around €5.50 to €7.50.

Also recommended: **Captain Sushi** (☎ 256 789; Böttcherstrasse 2; lunch specials €8).

Getting There & Around

There are frequent regional and IC trains servicing Hamburg (€16.80, one hour,

hourly). There are IC trains to Cologne (€46.60, three hours, hourly). A couple of ICE trains run direct to Frankfurt (€88.40, 3½ hours, hourly) and Munich (€124, six hours, hourly) daily. Change trains in Hanover for Berlin (€135, 3½ hours, hourly). For Amsterdam (€54, four hours, hourly), you change in Osnabrück. To get to Am Markt follow the tram route from directly in front of the train station. The tourist office stocks good public transport maps. Short trips on buses and trams cost €1.85, a four-trip transferable ticket is €5.60 and a day pass is €4.50.

HANOVER

☎ 0511 / pop 520,000

Hanover has few architectural gems but plenty of parks and greenery. Savaged by heavy bombing in 1943, Hanover was rebuilt into a prosperous city known throughout Europe for its trade fairs. The **tourist office** (☎ 1223 5555; www.hannover-tourism.de; Ernst-August-Platz 2; ☺ 9am-6pm Mon-Fri, 9am-2pm Sat) is next to the main post office and near the main train station.

Sights

The chief attractions are the glorious and regal parks of the **Herrenhäuser Gärten** (☎ 1684 7743; www.herrenhaeuser-gaerten.de; ☺ 9am-sunset), especially the baroque **Grosser Garten** and the **Berggarten** (admission for both €4; ☺ until 8pm in summer), with its newly installed rainforest exhibit, the **Regenwald Haus** (adult/concession €9/6).

Sprengel Museum (☎ 1684 3875; Kurt-Schwitters-Platz; adult/concession €3.50/1.80; ☺ Tue-Sun) exhibits contemporary works, the highlights being Picasso and Max Beckmann.

At Am Markt in the old town is the 14th-century **Marktkirche**. Apart from its truncated tower, it is characteristic of the northern red-brick Gothic style; the original stained-glass windows are particularly beautiful. The **Altes Rathaus** – across the marketplace – was built in various sections over a century.

Sleeping & Eating

Tourist office staff will find you a private room only during trade fairs, but can arrange a hotel room year-round for €6.50.

Jugendherberge (☎ 131 7674; www.jugendherberge .de/jh/hannover in German; Ferdinand-Wilhelm-Fricke-Weg 1; dm junior/senior €17/20; P ♨) Look for the space-lab–looking structure 3km out of town, near the Maschsee, an artificial lake. Take the U3 or U7 from Hauptbahnhof to Fischerhof, then cross the river on the Lodemannbrücke bridge and turn right.

Backpacker Gästehaus (☎ 131 9919; www.back packerhannover.de; Lenausstrasse 12a; dm €18; P 🖵) This friendly private hostel is more conveniently located than the DJH hostel and reasonably comfortable too. Take U-Bahn No 10 to Goetheplatz, and once on Lenausstrasse (across Goetheplatz), ring the doorbell at No 12 and wait; the hostel itself is located through the courtyard.

Hotel Flora (☎ 383 910; www.hotel-flora-hannover .de; Heinrichstrasse 36; s/d from €33/62, with private bathroom €47/75; P) At the edge of the city forest, the Flora provides pleasant rooms.

Hotel am Thielenplatz (☎ 327 691; hotel.am.thiel enplatz@t-online.de; Thielenplatz 2; s/d from €45/68) This hotel is a good choice if you need to be centrally located.

The Altstadt area behind Marktkirche has plenty of well-priced restaurants offering German cuisine. The **Markthalle** (cnr Karmarschstrasse & Leinestrasse) is a gourmand's paradise – it keeps normal shop hours and has lots of budget food stalls, some vegetarian offerings and fresh produce.

Brauhaus Ernst August (Schmiedestrasse 13a; mains €5-17) A Hanover institution, this *brauhaus* brews its own Hannöversch beer and also serves German dishes.

Sawaddi (☎ 344 367; Königstrasse 7; mains about €11) A Thai restaurant behind the train station; its all-you-can-eat lunch buffet is good value.

Getting There & Around

Hanover's spruced-up train station is a major hub. ICE trains to/from Hamburg (€34.40, 1½ hours), Munich (€110, 4½ hours), Frankfurt (€72, 2½ hours) and Cologne (€53.40, 2¾ hours) leave hourly, and every two hours to Berlin-Zoo (€51.80, 1¾ hours). A web of regional services fills in the gaps locally.

GOSLAR

☎ 05321 / pop 46,000

It's especially peaceful to wander through the cobblestone streets of this 1000-year-old city, with its beautifully preserved half-timbered buildings, at night. The town and the nearby Rammelsberg Mine are listed as World Heritage Sites by Unesco, and Goslar is a centre for Harz Mountain tourism.

Information

Harzer Verkehrsverband (☎ 340 40; www.harz info.de; Marktstrasse 45; ☿ 8am-4pm Mon-Thu, 8am-1pm Fri) For information on the Harz Mountains.

Tourist office (☎ 780 60; www.goslar.de in German; Markt 7; ☿ 9.15am-6pm Mon-Fri, 9.30am-4pm Sat, 9.30am-2pm Sun May-Oct, 9.15am-5pm Mon-Fri, 9.30am-2pm Sat Nov-Apr) Can help when the area's accommodation is packed.

Sights

The **Marktplatz** has several photogenic houses. The one opposite the Gothic **Rathaus** has a chiming clock depicting four scenes from the history of mining in the area.

The **Kaiserpfalz** (Kaiserbleek 6; adult/concession €4.50/ 2.50; ☿ daily) is a reconstructed 11th-century Romanesque palace jammed with visitors. Just below is the restored **Domvorhalle**, which displays the 11th-century 'Kaiserstuhl' throne, used by German emperors.

At the **Rammelsberger Bergbaumuseum** (adult/ concession €8.50/5.50; ☿ 9am-6pm), about 1km south of the town centre on Rammelsberger Strasse, you can delve into the 1000-year mining history of the area.

Sleeping & Eating

Jugendherberge (☎ 222 40; fax 413 76; Rammelsberger Strasse 25; dm junior/senior €19/22) Situated up the hill near the Kaiserpfalz (take bus No 803 to Theresienhof from the train station), the youth hostel is a peaceful refuge when not full of high-school students.

Hotel Zur Börse (☎ 345 10; www.hotel-boerse-go slar.de; Bergstrasse 53; s/d with shared bathroom €25/50; P 🗙) Housed in a traditional Goslar home, just a short walk from the market square.

Gästehaus Schmitz (☎ 234 45; fax 306 039; Kornstrasse 1; s/d €30/40, apt from €30) This centrally located guesthouse offers the best value with bright, cheerful rooms.

Die Tanne (☎ 343 90; www.die-tanne.de in German; Bäringerstrasse 10; s/d €30/60) Another excellent choice. The rooms are modern and there's even a small, private sauna.

Hotel und Campingplatz Sennhütte (☎ 225 02; Clausthaler Strasse 28; camp sites €2.50, plus per person/car €3.30/2, s/d from €20/40; ☿ Fri-Wed) Located 3km south on Route B241. Take bus No 830 from the train station to Sennhütte. There are also several simple rooms and you'll find lots of trails nearby.

Altdeutsches Kartoffelhaus (Breite Strasse; mains €6-13) Can one ever tire of the potato? The owner of this eatery in the Kaiserpassage shopping arcade says no.

Brauhaus Wolpertinger (Marstallstrasse 1; mains €5-15) Whimsical *brauhaus* with a beer garden in summer.

Getting There & Away

Goslar is regularly connected by train to Göttingen (€12.40, 1¼ hours, half-hourly), Hanover (€12.40, one hour, hourly) and Wernigerode (€5.50, 30 minutes, hourly).

GÖTTINGEN

☎ 0551 / pop 134,000

Student life seems fairly idyllic in this leafy university town, an ideal stopover on your way north or south; it's on the direct train line between Munich and Hamburg. Though small, Göttingen is lively, mostly because its large student population appreciates the art and science of hanging out as much as studying. A legion of notables, including Otto von Bismarck and the Brothers Grimm, studied and worked here, and the university has produced more than 40 Nobel Prize winners.

Information

Computerwerk (☎ 4880 5090; per 30min €2; Düsterestrasse 20)

Main tourist office (☎ 499 800; www.goettingen-tourismus.de; Markt 9; 🕑 9.30am-6pm Mon-Fri, 10am-4pm Sat) In the old Rathaus.

Post office (Altstadt, Groner Strasse 15-17)

Sights

At Markt, don't miss the **Great Hall** in the Rathaus where colourful frescoes cover every centimetre of wall space. Just outside, students and a lively assortment of harmless punk rockers mill about the **Gänseliesel** fountain, the town's symbol.

The 15th-century **Junkernschänke** (Barfüsserstrasse 5), with its colourful carved façade, is the most stunning of the town's half-timbered buildings. A walk on top of the old **town wall** along Bürgerstrasse takes you past the pretty **Botanical Gardens** and **Bismarckhäuschen** (admission free; 🕑 10am-1pm Tue, 3-5pm Wed, Thu & Sat), a modest building where the Iron Chancellor lived in 1833 during his wild student days.

Sleeping & Eating

Jugendherberge (☎ 576 22; Habichtsweg 2; jh-goettingen@djh-hannover.de; dm junior/senior €15/18; [P] [🖳]) This hostel is in a quiet residential tree-filled

neighbourhood northeast of the centre. From the train station main entrance take bus No 6 to the Jugendherberge stop.

Hotel Weender Hof (☎ 503 750; www.weender-hof.de in German; Hannoverschestrasse 150; s/d from €35/65; [P] [✕]) Situated on the edge of town, the Weender Hof has simple rooms.

Camping am Hohen Hagen (☎ 05502-2147; camping.lesser@t-online.de; Hoher-Hagen-Strasse; camp sites €3, plus €5 per person; 🕑 year-round) This camp site is about 10km west of town in Dransfeld (bus No 120).

Nikolaistrasse and Goethe Allee offer loads of takeaway options.

Salamanca (Gartenstrasse 21b; mains €5-10) Come to Salamanca for the affordable and tasty food, but stay a long time for the bohemian, politically conscious conversation.

Naturell (Lange-Seismarstrasse 40) Does up inventive vegetarian and wholefood cuisine.

Cron & Lanz (☎ 560 22; Weenderstrasse 25) Has a wonderful roof terrace to enjoy your cake.

Drinking & Clubbing

Göttingen's bars and clubs give this small university town a lively, big-city atmosphere. The salsa, hip hop and funk dance nights at the **Blue Note** (☎ 46907; Wilhelmsplatz 3) are popular with students and nonstudents alike. **Tangent** (☎ 463 76; Goetheallee 8a) draws an older crowd – OK, graduate students. Göttingen's hippest dance club, tiny **Elektroosho** (☎ 531 4970; Weenderstrasse 38) specialises in house music. Things don't get started there until late.

Getting There & Away

Hourly ICE trains pass through on their way to/from Hanover (€26, 30 minutes), Berlin (€62, 2¼ hours), Hamburg (€53, two hours), Frankfurt (€48, two hours) and Munich (€93, 4½ hours). Direct RB trains depart every two hours from Göttingen for Goslar in the Harz Mountains (€12, 1¼ hours).

NORTHERN GERMANY

There's more to the north besides the hip and happening city of Hamburg, although it's certainly a good start if your time is limited. Apart from this town, Germany's far north is home to the states of Schleswig-Holstein and Mecklenburg-Western Pomerania. The former, bordering Denmark at the southern end of the Jutland Peninsula, broke away from Denmark in the mid-17th century. Since then, Germany and Denmark have fought three wars over the region. Travellers will appreciate why the region was so hotly contested after sampling the attractions of the North Frisian Islands and the lovely historical city of Lübeck. Stretching from Schleswig-Holstein to Poland, Mecklenburg-Western Pomerania (Mecklenburg-Vorpommern) is home to some of Germany's most untouched spots, such as Poel Island and resorts like Rügen.

HAMBURG

☎ 040 / pop 1.7 million

One of the few growing cities in Germany, Hamburg has profited since reunification, and still maintains its reputation as one of the most important media and cultural centres in Germany. While this is a sprawling port city with exclusive shopping districts and numerous waterways, casually fashionable neighbourhoods like Schanzenviertel, St Pauli and Altona more accurately express Hamburg's personality and self-image.

Orientation

The Hauptbahnhof is very central, near Aussenalster lake and fairly close to most of the sights. These cluster south of Aussenalster and north of the Elbe River, which runs all the way from the Czech Republic to Hamburg before flowing into the North Sea. The port is west of the city centre, facing the Elbe.

Information

Hamburg Cards Unlimited public transport and free or slightly discounted admission to many attractions, museums and cruises can be obtained via the 'Day Card', valid for 24 hours after purchase; it costs €6.80 (single) or €12.70 (for up to five people). The 'Multiday Card' (€14/22.50) is valid for three days. Even better value is the 'Power Pass', which gives steep discounts to anyone under 30 for a mere €6.70 (extendable for an extra €3 per day).

Main post office (cnr Dammtorstrasse & Stephansplatz) Close to the Stephansplatz U-Bahn stop.

Post office (near Kirchenallee exit, Hauptbahnhof; ☻ 8am-8pm Mon-Fri, 9am-6pm Sat, 10am-6pm Sun)

Spiele Netzwerk (☎ 4503 8210; www.spielenetzwerk.com; Kleiner Schäferkamp 24; per hr €3)

Tourist office (☎ 3005 1300; www.hamburg-tourism.de; Kirchenallee exit, Hauptbahnhof; ☻ 7am-11pm) Offers a room-finding service (€4).

Tourist office (Between piers 4 & 5, St Pauli Harbour; ☻ 10am-5.30pm)

Sights

Much of Hamburg's old city centre is laced with wonderful canals (called 'fleets') running from the Alster lakes to the Elbe.

The Altstadt is centred on Rathausmarkt, which houses the large **Rathaus** (tours adult/concession €1/0.50; ☻ in English hourly 10.15am-3.15pm Mon-Thu, 10.15am-1.15pm Fri-Sun). The building has 647 rooms – six more than Buckingham Palace – and the huge clock tower overlooks the lively square.

It is a transcending experience to visit the remaining tower of the devastated **St-Nikolai-Kirche** (Ost-West-Strasse), currently an anti-war memorial. From there, walk a few blocks west to the baroque **Hauptkirche St Michaelis** and take the lift up the **tower** (adult/concession €2.50/1.25; ☻ 10am-6pm Apr-Oct, 10am-5pm Nov-Mar) for a great view of the city and the port.

The **port cruises** are touristy but still worthwhile. If you're in the port area early on a Sunday, head for **Fischmarkt** (Fish Market; St Pauli; ☻ 5-10am Sun Apr-Sep, 7-10am Sun Oct-Mar), right on the Elbe. Hamburg's oldest market (established 1703) is popular with locals and tourists alike and everything under the sun is sold here. Cap your morning with a visit to the live music session at the **Fischauktionshalle** (Fish Auction Hall; Grosse Elbstrasse 9).

Among Hamburg's biggest tourist attractions is the famous **Reeperbahn** red-light district. It is 600m long and is the heart of the St Pauli entertainment district, which includes shows, bars, cabarets, clubs, theatres and a casino. The Reeperbahn sex establishments have been gradually moving over for popular restaurants and bars, with a dwindling number of peep shows and sex shops. On **Grosse Freiheit**, Safari is one of the more famous clubs. Notorious **Herbertstrasse** is where prostitutes pose in windows offering their wares. It is fenced off at each end, and men under 18 and women are not allowed in.

Hamburg's **Kunsthalle** (☎ 42 813 1200; www.hamburger-kunsthalle.de; Glockengiesserwall; adult/concession €7.50/5; ☻ 10am-6pm Tue-Sun, 10am-9pm Thu) has old masters and a large collection of German paintings from the 19th and 20th centuries. Contemporary art is housed next door in the modern **Galerie der Gegenwart** (adult/concession for both museums €7.50/5; ☻ 10am-6pm Tue-Sun, 10am-9pm Thu).

Harry's Hamburger Hafenbasar (☎ 312 482; Balduinstrasse 18; adult/child €2.50/1.50; ☻ noon-6pm Tue-Sun) is a fascinating 'shop'. It's the life's

GERMANY

HAMBURG

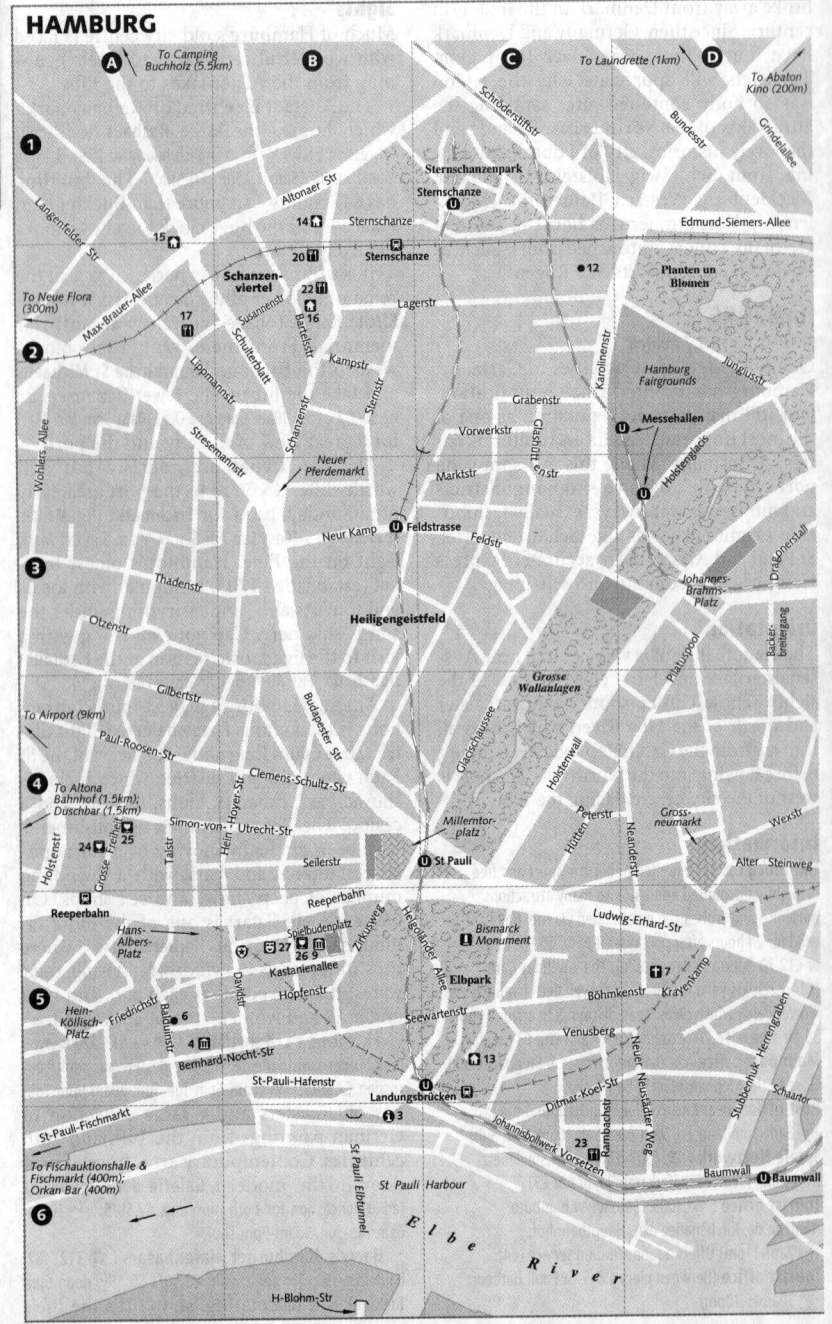

To Camping Buchholz (5.5km)

To Laundrette (1km)

To Abaton Kino (200m)

Schröderstiftstr

Bundesstr

Grindelallee

Sternschanzenpark

Sternschanze

Langenfelder Str

Altonaer Str

Sternschanze

Edmund-Siemers-Allee

15

14

Sternschanze

Sternschanze

Planten un Blomen

12

To Neue Flora (300m)

Max-Brauer-Allee

Schanzen-viertel

20

Lagerstr

Karolinenstr

Hamburg Fairgrounds

Jungiusstr

22

16

17

Susannenstr

Bartelsstr

Kampstr

Sternstr

Grabenstr

Messehallen

Schulterblatt

Lippmannstr

Vorwerkstr

Glashütten str

Holstenglacis

Wöhlers Allee

Stresemannstr

Schanzenstr

Neuer Pferdemarkt

Marktstr

Johannes-Brahms-Platz

Dragonerstall

Neuer Kamp

Feldstrasse

Feldstr

Thadenstr

Heiligengeistfeld

Bäcker-breitergang

Otzenstr

Grosse Wallanlagen

Gilbertstr

Budapester Str

Clausdichhaussee

Holstenwall

Platuspool

To Airport (9km)

Paul-Roosen-Str

Clemens-Schultz-Str

Holstenwall

Peterstr

Gross-neumarkt

Wexstr

To Altona Bahnhof (1.5km); Duschbar (1.5km)

Simon-von-Utrecht-Str

Heln-Hoyer-Str

Millerntor-platz

Hütten

Neanderstr

Alter Steinweg

24

25

Seilerstr

St Pauli

Holstenstr

Grosse Elbstr

Talstr

Reeperbahn

Reeperbahn

Ludwig-Erhard-Str

Reeperbahn

Hans-Albers-Platz

Spielbudenplatz

Zirkusweg

Heiligolander Allee

Bismarck Monument

7

Böhmkenstr

Kraylenkamp

Hein-Köllisch-Platz

Friedrichstr

Davidstr

27

26

9

Elbpark

Stubbenhuk, Herrengraben

Baldinstr

6

Höpfenstr

Venusberg

Neuer Neustädter Weg

Schaartor

4

Bernhard-Nocht-Str

Seewartenstr

13

St-Pauli-Hafenstr

St Pauli-Fischmarkt

Landungsbrücken

Ditmar-Koel-Str

Rambachstr

Baumwall

Baumwall

To Fischauktionshalle & Fischmarkt (400m); Orkan Bar (400m)

3

St Pauli Elbtunnel

St Pauli Harbour

Johannisbollwerk

Vorsetzen

23

H-Blohm-Str

E l b e   R i v e r

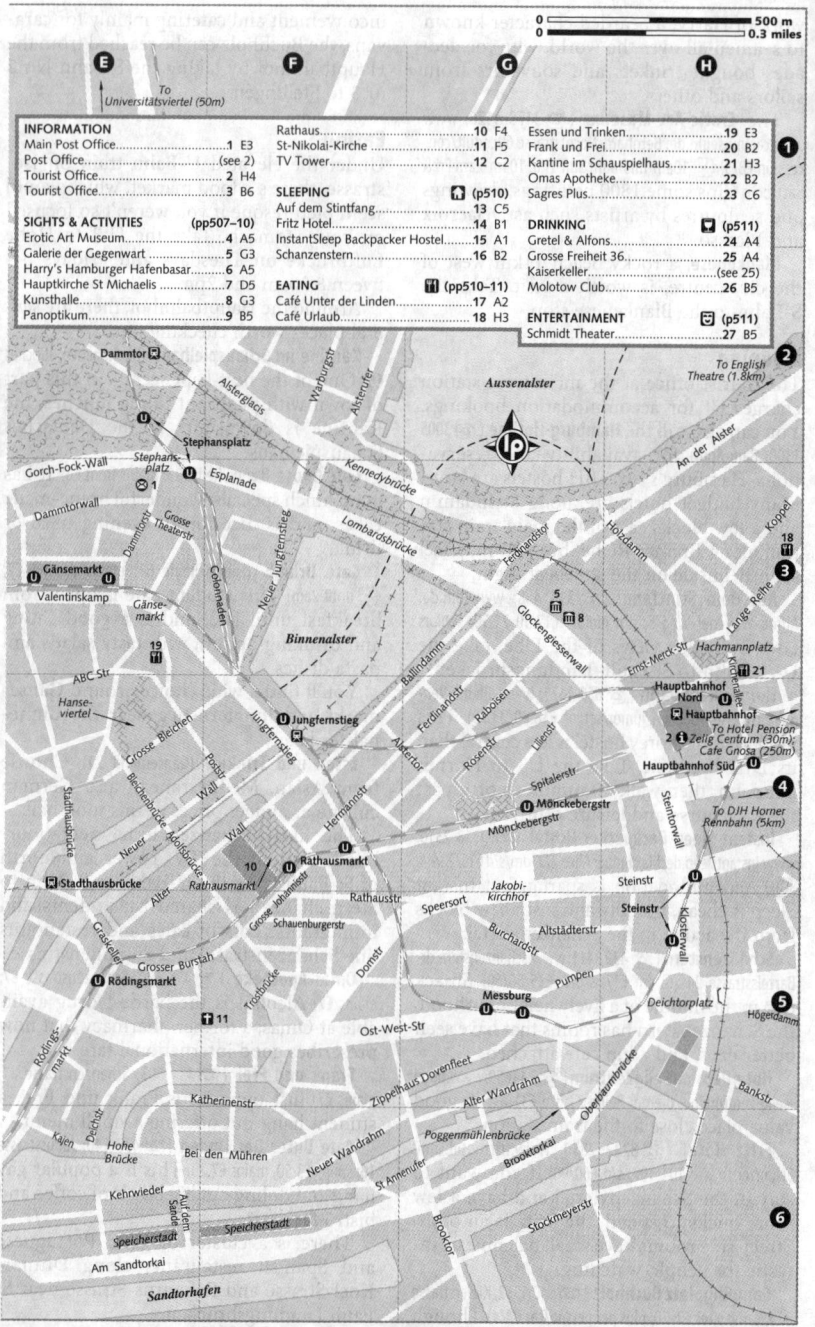

0 ————— 500 m
0 ————— 0.3 miles

INFORMATION
Main Post Office...................................1 E3
Post Office.......................................(see 2)
Tourist Office.......................................2 H4
Tourist Office.......................................3 B6

SIGHTS & ACTIVITIES   (pp507–10)
Erotic Art Museum.................................4 A5
Galerie der Gegenwart..........................5 G3
Harry's Hamburger Hafenbasar........6 A5
Hauptkirche St Michaelis 7 D5
Kunsthalle...8 G3
Panoptikum...9 B5

Rathaus...10 F4
St-Nikolai-Kirche 11 F5
TV Tower..12 C2

SLEEPING   (p510)
Auf dem Stintfang............................13 C5
Fritz Hotel...14 B1
InstantSleep Backpacker Hostel......15 A1
Schanzenstern...................................16 B2

EATING   (pp510–11)
Café Unter den Linden......................17 A2
Café Urlaub..18 H3

Essen und Trinken.............................19 E3
Frank und Frei....................................20 B2
Kantine im Schauspielhaus...............21 H3
Omas Apotheke.................................22 B2
Sagres Plus..23 C6

DRINKING   (p511)
Gretel & Alfons.................................24 A4
Grosse Freiheit 36.............................25 A4
Kaiserkeller....................................(see 25)
Molotow Club.....................................26 B5

ENTERTAINMENT   (p511)
Schmidt Theater.................................27 B5

work of Harry, a bearded character known to seamen all over the world, who for decades bought trinkets and souvenirs from sailors and others.

The **Erotic Art Museum** (☎ 3178 4126; www .eroticartmuseum.de; Bernhard-Nochtstrasse 69; adult/concession €8/5; ⓨ 10am-midnight Sun-Thu, 10am-2am Fri & Sat) contains some 1800 paintings, drawings and sculptures by artists such as Delacroix and Picasso.

Blankenese, a rocky beach 11km west of the city centre, is worth a visit. Take the S-Bahn to the Blankenese stop.

Sleeping

The tourist office at the main train station charges €4 for accommodation bookings. You can also call the **Hamburg-Hotline** (☎ 3005 1300; 8am-8pm) for availability and reservations. Hamburg's two DJH hostels are large. Many budget hotels are along Steindamm and a few blocks east of the main train station along Bremer Reihe, but you may feel slightly unsafe on the streets at night.

Auf dem Stintfang (☎ 313 488; www.djh.de; Alfred-Wegener-Weg 5; dm juniors €17.50-21.50, seniors €19.50-24.20) For views of the Elbe, take the U-/S-Bahn to St Pauli–Landungsbrücken.

Horner Rennbahn (☎ 651 1671; www.djh.de; Rennbahnstrasse 100; dm junior/senior €18.80/23.70) This modern four-storey hostel is less central than its DJH brethren. Take the U3 to Horner Bennahn, then walk 10 minutes north past the racecourse and leisure centre.

Instant Sleep Backpacker Hostel (☎ 4318 2310; www.instantsleep.de; Max Brauer Allee 277; dm/s/d €15/28/44; 🖳) Accommodation is spartan but Instant Sleep is cheap, friendly and just a few blocks from the action in the Schanzenviertel.

Schanzenstern (☎ 439 8441; www.schanzenstern.de; Bartelsstrasse 24-26; dm €17, s/d/tr €35/50/60) Smack dab in the middle of a lively neighbourhood, the Schanzenstern has rooms that have seen better days, and a hip café attached.

Hotel Pension Selig Zentrum (☎ 244689; www.hotel -selig-zentrum.de; Bremer Reihe 23; s/d €31/61) A good value place close to the train station.

Fritz Hotel (☎ 8222 2830; www.fritzhotel.com; Schanzenstrasse 101-103; s/d €60/90) If you want to stay in the Schanzenviertel and have a few more bucks to spend, the Fritz is an oasis. Street-side rooms have small balconies, fantastic for people-watching.

Campingplatz Buchholz (☎ 540 4532; Kielerstrasse 374; camp sites €7-10, plus per person/car €4/4) Though

inconvenient and catering mainly for caravans, the Buchholz can be reached from the Hauptbahnhof by taking the S-Bahn No 2 or 3 to Stellingen.

Eating

Under the elevated U-Bahn train on Isestrasse, there's a food market, which would seem picturesque if you weren't so focused on your stomach. Take the U-3 to Hohe Luftbrücke on Tuesdays and Fridays between 8.30am and 2pm.

Around the Hauptbahnhof, there are several places worth checking out.

Kantine im Schauspielhaus (Kirchenallee; lunches €6) One of the best-kept secrets in this part of town with plain but filling lunches, the Kantine is downstairs in the Deutsches Schauspielhaus.

Café Gnosa (Lange Reihe 93; mains from €6) It has good lunch specials, wonderful home-made cakes, and is nice for an evening meal or drink.

Café Urlaub (Lange Reihe 63; mains around €7; ⓨ until 2am) This student café is open from breakfast until late, and is a good eating and drinking option, with tasty salads and pasta dishes.

You'll find a wide choice around Gänsemarkt and Jungfernstieg near the Binnenalster lake.

Essen und Trinken (Gänsemarkt 21) Choose from Asian, Mediterranean and German cuisine at budget prices at this food hall.

The lively Schanzenviertel neighbourhood, west of the TV Tower and north of St Pauli (take the U-Bahn or S-Bahn to Sternschanze), is shared by students and immigrants. Lots of cafés and restaurants line Schanzenstrasse and Susannenstrasse.

Omas Apotheke (☎ 436 620; Schanzenstrasse 87; mains €7) Alcohol is the hardest drug available at Omas, a former pharmacy that now prescribes good international fare.

Frank und Frei (☎ 434 803; Schanzenstrasse 87; mains €7) Just opposite is Frank und Frei, a student hang-out offering a small menu.

Cafe Unter Der Linden (☎ 438 140; Juliusstrasse 16; soups €3.50, mains €7.20) This is a popular gay hang-out doling out big bowls of coffee and bistro fare.

There is a cluster of good Portuguese and Spanish restaurants along Ditmar-Koel-Strasse and Reimarus-Strasse near St Pauli Landungsbrücken.

Sagres Plus (☎ 371 201; Vorsetzen 52; mains €10) Always packed Sagres specialises in fresh-off-the-boat fish dishes done Portuguese style.

Drinking & Clubbing

For cultural events and lifestyle information, look for the daily magazines *Morgen Post* (€.50), *Szene* (€2.50) and *Prinz* (€1). Not surprisingly, St Pauli is the flash point for nightclubs. Young people meet in Hans Albersplatz, especially during the summer, before heading off to the pubs.

Duschbar (☎ 3990 4006; Bahrenfelderstrasse 168) Washing is the theme at this quirky bohemian hang-out, replete with a shower curtain door, sink tables and shower-head lamps.

Molotow Club (☎ 310 845; Spielbudenplatz 5) An alternative, independent music scene – indie, electro, garage and punk – thrives at Molotow.

Grosse Freiheit 36 (☎ 36 317 7780; Grosse Freiheit 36) Wedged between live sex theatres and peep shows, this is one of the most popular places for live rock and pop. The Beatles played in the **Kaiserkeller**, the disco in the basement.

Gretel & Alfons (☎ 313 491; Grosse Freiheit 29) Across the street, you can have a drink where the Beatles once quaffed.

Also recommended are **Turm Bar** (☎ 444 567; Rothenbaumchausse 2) and **Orkan Bar** (Fischmarkt 5).

Entertainment

Hamburg has a lively jazz scene, as well as an excellent alternative and experimental theatre scene. For central theatre or concert bookings, go to the **Theaterkasse** (☎ 353 555; basement, Alsterhaus shopping complex, Grosse Bleichen).

Abaton Kino (☎ 41320320; Allende-Platz 3) English-language films are screened here.

English Theatre (☎ 227 7089; Lerchenfeld 14) This theatre, 2km northeast of the train station, is good for a language fix.

Schmidt Theater (☎ 3177 8899; Spielbudenplatz 27) The Schmidt Theater's wild variety shows are decidedly adult.

Getting There & Away

AIR

Lufthansa, British Airways, Air France and low-cost carrier Air Berlin all fly from **Hamburg airport** (☎ 507 50; www.ham.airport.de; Fuhlsbüttel). Low-cost carrier Ryanair flies from London-Stansted to Hamburg-Lübeck airport, with coordinated shuttle buses to central Hamburg (€8, 1¼ hours).

BUS

Berlin Linienbus (☎ 030-861 9331; www.berlinlinienbus.de) goes to, you guessed it, Berlin (€37, three hours, every two hours) from the central bus station.

Eurolines (☎ 2090 9997) serves international destinations that aren't served directly by train, such as Amsterdam (€44.50, 6½ hours) and London (€61.50, 17½ hours).

A good option for getting to London is **Rainbow Tours** (☎ 3209 3309; fax 3209 3099; Gänsemarkt 45), offering return trips without an overnight stay from €55 – a cheap way to get to London, even if you don't use the return portion of the ticket. The central bus station is southeast of the main train station on Adenauerallee.

TRAIN

Hamburg's Hauptbahnhof is one of the busiest in Germany. There are frequent RE/RB trains to Lübeck (€9, 45 minutes) and Kiel (€15, 1¼ hours), various services to Hanover (€26, 1½ hours) and Bremen (€16, 1¼ hours), as well as ICE trains to Berlin (€51, 2½ hours) and Frankfurt-am-Main (€98, 3½ hours).

There are overnight services to Munich (€111, six hours, hourly), Vienna (€146, nine hours, every two hours) and Paris (€150, nine hours, every two hours) and Zürich via Basel (€132, 7½ hours, every two hours) as well as trains to Copenhagen. Hamburg-Altona station is quieter but has a monopoly on some services to the north. Carefully read the timetables when booking to/from Hamburg stations.

Scandlines (☎ 01805-722 635 4637; www.scandlines.com) operates a busy car and passenger ferry from the German harbour town of Puttgarden, northeast of Lübeck and Hamburg, to Rodby in Denmark, which leaves every half-hour 24 hours a day and takes 45 minutes. The cost is €60 each way for a car including up to five people. A single passenger pays €3 (€6 mid-June to August) each way. If you're travelling by train, the cost of the ferry is included in your ticket.

Getting Around

Public buses, the U-Bahn and the S-Bahn operate in Hamburg. A day pass for most of Hamburg is €4.25. Single journeys cost €2.20 for the city tariff area. A three-day pass is €12.25. Hamburg's bike tracks are extensive and reach almost to the centre of the city.

GERMANY

LÜBECK

☎ 0451 / pop 213,000

Medieval Lübeck was known as the Queen of the Hanseatic League, as it was the capital of this association of towns that ruled trade on the Baltic Sea from the 12th to the 16th centuries. This beautiful city, with its red-stone buildings, is a highlight of the region and well worth taking the time to explore. Lübeck's old town is set on an island ringed by the canalised Trave River, a 15-minute walk east from the main train station.

Information

Lübeck-Information (☎ 122 5419; www.luebeck -tourismus.de;Breite Strasse 62; ❂ 9.30am-7pm Mon-Fri, 10am-3pm Sat, 10am-2pm Sun Jun-Sep & Dec, 9.30am-6pm Mon-Fri, 10am-3pm Sat Jan-May, Oct & Nov) Near the Rathaus. Runs a room-finding service.

Main post office (Königstrasse 46) Across from the Katarinenkirche.

Private room–finding office (☎ 864 675; fax 863 024; train station; service €3, free if reserved by phone)

Sights

The landmark **Holstentor** (☎ 122 4129; Holstentorplatz;adult/concession €5/3; ❂ 10am-6pm Tue-Sun Apr-Sep, 10am-4pm Tue-Sun Oct-Mar), a fortified gate with huge twin towers, serves as the city's symbol as well as its museum. For a literary kick, visit the **Buddenbrookhaus** (☎ 122 4192; www.buddenbrookhaus.de; Mengstrasse 4; adult/concession €5-4.10; ❂ 10am-6pm Apr-Oct, 10am-5pm Nov-Mar), the family home where Thomas Mann was born and which he made famous in his novel *Buddenbrooks*. The must-see **Marienkirche** (Markt) contains a stark reminder of WWII; a bombing raid brought the church bells crashing to the stone floor and the townspeople have left the bell fragments in place, with a small sign saying: 'A protest against war and violence'. Also on Markt is the imposing **Rathaus** which covers two full sides of the square. Lübeck's **Marionettentheater** (Puppet Theatre; ☎ 700 60; cnr Am Kolk & Kleine Petersgrube; ❂ Tue-Sun) is a must. Usually there is a daily afternoon performance (€4) for children (3pm) and an evening performance (€8 to €11) for adults only on Saturday.

The tower lift at the partly restored **Petrikirche** (adult/concession €2/1.20; ❂ 9am-7pm Mar-Sep, closed Oct-Feb) affords a superb view over the Altstadt.

Sleeping

Jugendgästehaus Lübeck (☎ 702 0399; www.djh.de; Mengstrasse 33; dm junior/senior €17.40/20.10, s/tw €25.60/51.20) Clean, comfortable and well situated in the middle of the old town.

Sleep-Inn (☎ 719 20; fax 789 97; Grosse Petersgrube 11; dm €10, d €30, apt per person €32; ❂ mid-Jan–mid-Dec) This centrally located YMCA charges extra for breakfast and sheets.

Hotel Stadt Lübeck (☎ 838 83; fax 863 221; Am Bahnhof 21; s/d €43/63) Fairly good rooms, just outside the main train station.

Campingplatz Schönböcken (☎ 893 090; Steinrader Damm 12; camp site/person/car €3.50/4.50/1; ❂ Apr-Oct) This camping ground is located in a western suburb of Lübeck. For camping grounds in the nearby coastal resort of Travemünde ask at the tourist office.

DJH Hostel Vor der Burgtor (☎ 334 33; jhluebeck@ djh-nordmark.de; Am Gertrudenkirchhof 4; dm junior/senior €24.40/27.10; P 🖫) Huge and popular with school groups; just outside the Altstadt. Prices drop by €1.30 for three nights or more. To get here, take bus No 1, 3, 11, 12 or 31 to Gustav-Radbruch-Platz.

Sleep-Inn (☎ 719 20; www.cvjm-luebeck.de in German; Grosse Petersgrube 11; dm/d €10/40; ❂ mid-Jan–mid-Dec) Pretty basic, but central and with a nice bar. Breakfast costs an additional €4.

Eating & Drinking

The best eating and drinking options are in the area directly east of the Rathaus. Save room for a dessert or a snack of marzipan, which was invented in Lübeck (local legend has it that the town ran out of flour during a long siege and resorted to grinding almonds to make bread).

Tipasa (Schlumacherstrasse 12-14; mains from €4.40) Whatever your taste, tandoori to tacos, Tipasa is a great place to eat and drink.

Hieronymus (☎ 706 3017; Fleischhauerstrasse 81; mains €4.50-19.40) Spread over three floors of a 15th-century building. The lunch specials are good value.

JG Niederegger (Breite Strasse 89; per kg €29) Directly opposite the Rathaus, JG Niederegger is Lübeck's mecca of marzipan.

Getting There & Around

Ryanair (www.ryanair.com) has cheap flights from London to Lübeck and a shuttle bus to Hamburg.

Lübeck has train services to Hamburg (€9, 45 minutes, at least hourly). There are also frequent services to Kiel (€12, 1¼ hours) and Schwerin (€11, 1¼ hours, hourly). Trains to/from Copenhagen also stop here. The central bus station is next to the main train station. Services to/from Wismar stop here, as well as **Autokraft** (☎ 0431-6660; www.autokraft.de) buses to/from Hamburg, Schwerin, Kiel, Rostock and Berlin.

Frequent double-decker buses run to Travemünde (€3.50, 45 minutes, every 15 minutes) from the central bus station.

NORTH FRISIAN ISLANDS

Sylt ☎ 04651 / pop 21,000
Amrum ☎ 04682 / pop 2100

The Frisian Islands reward those who make the trek with sand dunes, sea, pure air and, every so often, sunshine. Friesland covers an area stretching from the northern Netherlands along the coast up into Denmark. After WWII, the German jet set invaded the islands, and tourists have been travelling here ever since. The most popular of the North Frisian Islands is the glamorous resort of Sylt, which gets very crowded in summer; the neighbouring islands of Föhr and Amrum are far more relaxed and less touristy. Low-budget accommodation is hard to find on the islands, but the tourist offices can help with private rooms from €20 per person.

Nature is the prime attraction on the North Frisian Islands. Beautiful dunes stretch out for kilometres, red and white cliffs border wide beaches, and bird lovers will be amply rewarded. Amazingly, when the tide is out, it's possible to walk from the mainland to the islands. However, several people are killed every year making this trek.

The excellent **tourist office** (☎ 9988; www .sylt.de; ✸ 9am-6pm Mon-Fri, 9am-4.30pm Sat year-round, plus 9am-2pm Sun Jun-Sep) is inside Westerland's train station on Sylt. Visit one of Sylt's **beach saunas** – the tourist office can point you in the right direction. For **cycling** in Westerland, **Fahrrad am Bahnhof** (☎ 5803) is conveniently situated at the train station (€5 per day).

On Amrum, the friendly **tourist office** (☎ 194 33; fax 940 394; ferry landing, Wittdün) is at the harbour car park. Amrum has only a few restaurants and many of them close early or are closed entirely in the low season.

Sylt is connected to the mainland by a scenic train-only causeway right through the Wattenmeer. Around seven trains leave from Hamburg-Hauptbahnhof daily

for Westerland (€33, 3¼ hours). To get to Amrum and the island of Föhr, you must board a ferry in Dagebüll Hafen. Take the Sylt-bound train from Hamburg-Altona and change in Niebüll. A day return from Dagebüll costs €18, which allows you to visit both islands. The trip to Amrum takes around two hours, stopping at Föhr on the way. Sylt's two north–south bus lines run every 20 to 30 minutes, and three other frequent lines cover the rest of the island.

SCHWERIN

☎ 0385 / pop 100,000

Mecklenburg-Vorpommern's capital city Schwerin has to be one of the prettiest in northern Germany. The oldest city in the state, it has so many lakes that locals and officials can't even agree on the number! The centre, an interesting mix of 16th-, 17th- and 19th-century architecture, is small enough to explore on foot, but you can easily take two or three days to get to know the city and its surrounds properly. Schwerin's beauty and charm are infectious, and few people regret spending a bit of extra time here.

Orientation

Down the hill east of the Hauptbahnhof is Pfaffenteich, the rectangular lake whose southern end is at the beginning of Schwerin's main street, Mecklenburgstrasse. Markt is southeast of here. Further southeast, around Alter Garten on the Schweriner See, are the monumental Marstall (the former royal stables), the Schloss (ducal castle), and parks, museums, tour boats and other treats.

Information

In-Ca Internet (☎ 500 7883; Wismarsche Strasse 123; per hr €2.50; ✸ 1pm-midnight)
Schwerin-Information (☎ 592 5212; www.schwerin.de in German; Rathaus, Markt 10; ✸ 9am-7pm Mon-Fri, 10am-6pm Sat & Sun)
Schwerin-Ticket (48hr adult/child €6/4) Includes local transport and discounted admissions.

Sights

Above Markt rises the tall 14th-century Gothic **Dom** (☎ 565 014; Am Dom 4; ✸ 10am-5pm Mon-Fri, noon-5pm Sun), a superb example of north German red and glazed-black brick architecture. To the southeast of Alter Garten, over a causeway, is Schwerin's neo-Gothic

Schloss (☎ 525 2920; www.schloss-schwerin.de in German; adult/concession €4/2.50; ☼ 10am-6pm Tue-Sun 15 Apr-14 Oct, 10am-5pm 15 Oct-14 Apr), with expansive parks, great lake views and superb interiors; look out for the wonderfully graphic 'Death of Niklot' painting.

Staatliches Museum (☎ 595 80; Alter Garten 3; adult/concession €6/4; ☼ 10am-8pm Tue, 10am-6pm Wed-Sun), on the city side of Alter Garten, has a very good collection of works by old Dutch masters and exhibitions of 20th-century art.

Sleeping & Eating

Jugendherberge (☎ 326 0006; jh-schwerin@djh-mv.de; Waldschulweg 3; dm junior/senior €14.50/17.50) This fairly standard hostel is about 4km south of the city centre, just opposite the zoo. Take bus No 14.

Hospiz am Pfaffenteich (☎ 550 7024; Buschstrasse 13; s €35-45, d €60-65) Occupying a prime location in the northern Schelfstadt area of the old town, this stately white building offers welcome extras such as minibars and balconies in some rooms.

Pension am Theater (☎ 593 680; www.pension amtheater.m-vp.de in German; Theaterstrasse 1-2; s €50-60, d €66.50-82; **P**) In the shadow of the huge theatre building and (just) within sight of the castle, you get a friendly welcome and big, comfortable rooms here.

Kleine Mecklenburger Gasthaus (☎ 555 9666; Puschkinstrasse 37; mains €5.40-10.90) The little sister of **Weinhaus Uhle** (☎ 562 956; Schusterstrasse 13-15), Schwerin's longest-standing family wine merchant, is less fancy but equally fine. The food at both places is excellent, and the wine list is practically encyclopaedic.

There are **food courts** in the Schlosspark Center and Der Wurm shopping malls. For decent Chinese with fast-food service, try **Asia Bistro** (Marienplatz; mains €3.50-8.50).

Getting There & Away

Various fast trains serve Rostock (€12.90, 1¼ hours), Stralsund (€21.60, 2½ hours) and Hamburg (€17.60, 1¼ hours). Travel to/from Berlin (€37.20, two hours) often requires a change at Wittenberge or Ludwigslust.

ROSTOCK & WARNEMÜNDE

☎ 0381 / pop 205,000

Rostock is the largest city in lightly populated northeastern Germany, and has long been a major Baltic port and shipbuilding centre. The years after reunification were difficult here – unemployment soared and neo-Nazi attacks dominated the headlines.

Today, however, the city centre along Kröpeliner Strasse and the former dock area on the Warnow River have been redeveloped into pleasant pedestrian zones. Rostock also hosted the International Garden Show (IGA) in 2003, which brought in enough visitors to put the city firmly on the Mecklenburg tourist map. Coupled with the hugely popular annual Hansa Sail regatta and some of the liveliest nightlife east of Hamburg, the transformation has made the city a mandatory stop on the Baltic coast.

Another reason to visit is the town's chief suburb, the beach resort and fishing village of Warnemünde. In winter this popular getaway offers a picturesque accommodation alternative, while on warm days it's jammed with beach nuts and sun-seekers.

Information

DISCOUNT CARDS

Rostock Card (48hr €8) Free walking tour (in German), discounts and free public transport.

INTERNET ACCESS

Das Netz (☎ 490 0270; Grubenstrasse 49; per hr €2; ☼ 2-8pm Tue-Thu & Sun, 2pm-midnight Fri & Sat)
Universitätsbuchhandlung Thalia (☎ 492 2603; Breite Strasse 15-17; per hr €1)

TOURIST INFORMATION

Tourist-Information (☎ 381 2222; www.rostock.de; Neuer Markt 3-8; ☼ 10am-7pm Mon-Fri, 10am-4pm Sat & Sun)
Tourist-Information Warnemünde (☎ 548 000; Am Strom 59; ☼ 10am-7pm Mon-Fri, 10am-4pm Sat & Sun)

Sights & Activities

Rostock's splendid 13th-century **Marienkirche** (☎ 453 325; Am Ziegenmarkt; admission €1; ☼ 10am-5pm Mon-Sat, 11.15am-noon Sun) survived WWII unscathed. This huge brick edifice contains a functioning astronomical clock (1472), a Gothic bronze baptismal font (1290), a Renaissance pulpit (1574) and a baroque organ (1770). For a bird's-eye view of town, visit the **Petrikirche** (☎ 211 01; Alter Markt; tower €2; ☼ 10am-4pm), where you can scale the 196 stairs or just take the lift up the tower.

Kröpeliner Strasse, a broad pedestrian mall lined with 15th- and 16th-century burgher houses, runs west from the **Rathaus** on Neuer Markt up to the 14th-century **Kröpeliner Tor**

(☎ 454 177; Kröpeliner Strasse; adult/concession €3/1.50; ⊙ 10am-6pm Wed-Sun), which contains the city's Regional History Museum, near a stretch of old city wall. Off the southwestern corner of Universitätsplatz is the **Kloster Zum Heiligen Kreuz** (☎ 203 590; Klosterhof; adult/concession €3/1.50; ⊙ 10am-6pm Tue-Sun), a small cultural complex and museum in an old convent (1270).

Rostock's **Schifffahrtsmuseum** (Maritime Museum; ☎ 252 7788; Liegeplatz Schmarl, IGA-Park; adult/concession €3/1.50; ⊙ 10am-6pm Tue-Sun), with displays on all things seafaring, is now on board an old ship at the IGA grounds, halfway to Warnemünde.

In Warnemünde itself, a broad, sandy **beach** stretches west from the **lighthouse** (1898). It's chock-a-block with bathers on hot summer days; the promenade makes for a nice stroll in any weather.

Sleeping & Eating

The tourist office books private rooms from around €15, plus a €3 fee. In summer, however, central rooms are thin on the ground.

City-Pension (☎ 459 0704; Krönkenhagen 3; s €40-55, d €64-88) Central, quiet and homy, this small family *pension* is in a lovely quiet street near the harbour, in the heart of the old-fashioned northern Altstadt.

Jugendgästeschiff (☎ 670 0320; jugendgaesteschiff frostock@t-online.de; Am Stadthafen 72-3; dm junior/senior €17/22, s/d €27.50/50) On board the 1950s Belgian cargo ship MS *Georg Büchner*, this is definitely more exciting than your average hostel. Dorms, spacious standard rooms and an amazing wood-panelled dining room all add to the effect.

Jugendherberge (☎ 548 170; Parkstrasse 47, Warnemünde; dm junior/senior €20/24; (P) (□)) A bit more down to earth, this new DJH block is just two minutes' walk from the beach.

Captain Flint's (☎ 252 4763; www.captain-flint.de in German; Warnowufer 64a; mains €8.90-15.80) The swashbuckling theme at the Captain's tables is so OTT you're almost embarrassed for the staff, but it's fun to look at, and the tiered waterfront terraces are great.

Krahnstöver Likörfabrik (☎ 252 3551; Grosse Wasserstrasse 30 & Grubenstrasse 1; mains €4.80-8.40) Managed by Rostock's oldest family-run wine merchant, you can choose between hearty German pub grub in the *Kneipe* and more sophisticated wine-bar fare around the corner.

Quick bites are available in the **Rostocker Hof shopping centre** (off Universitätsplatz). Fish-lovers: head for Warnemünde and follow your nose along **Alter Strom**, the picturesque fishing harbour, where stallholders sell the daily catch – fresh, smoked or in bread rolls.

Getting There & Around

Frequent trains run from Berlin (€29.60, three hours, every two hours), Stralsund (€11.10, one hour, every two hours), Schwerin (€12.90, 1¼ hours, hourly) and Hamburg (€26, 2¼ hours, every two hours).

Various ferry companies operate from Rostock Seaport. **Scandlines** (☎ 673 1217; www .scandlines.de in German) has services daily to Trelleborg in Sweden (€15 to €20, 5¾ hours) and Gedser in Denmark (€5 to €8, two hours). **TT-Line** (☎ 670 790; www.ttline.de) departs for Trelleborg several times daily (€18 to €30, three to six hours). **Silja Line** (☎ 350 4350; www .silja.com) sails to St Petersburg (€90 to €211, 39 hours) and Helsinki (€67 to €87, 24 hours), both via Tallinn, once or twice a week.

For local transport, a *Tageskarte* (day ticket) costs €3.10. For two zones (covering Rostock and Warnemünde), single rides cost €1.50; for one zone it's €1.20.

STRALSUND

☎ 03831 / pop 60,000

Sparkling like a water-ringed jewel on the Baltic coast, Stralsund is one of the nicest cities in northern Germany, and is worth just as much time as Schwerin or Rostock. It was a Hanseatic city in the Middle Ages and later was under Swedish control. Today it's an attractive, historic town with fine museums and buildings, pleasant walks and a busy waterfront. It's also the access point for the beautiful and popular Rügen Island and the unspoilt island of Hiddensee.

Information

M@trix Internet (☎ 278 80; Wasserstrasse 8-9; per hr €4; ⊙ 2pm-midnight)

Stralsund Tourismuszentrale (☎ 246 90; info@stralsund-tourismus.de; Alter Markt 9; ⊙ 9am-7pm Mon-Fri, 9am-2pm Sat, 10am-2pm Sun May-Sep, 9am-5pm Mon-Fri, 10am-2pm Sat Oct-Apr) Has Internet access.

Sights & Activities

On Alter Markt is the medieval **Rathaus**, where you can stroll through the vaulted and pillared structures and around to the impressive **Nikolaikirche** (☎ 297 199; Alter Markt; ⊙ 10am-5pm Mon-Sat, 11.15am-noon & 2-4pm Sun).

The 14th-century **Marienkirche** (☎ 293 529; Neuer Markt; ☺ 10am-6pm Mon-Fri, 10am-5pm Sat & Sun) is a massive, red-brick edifice typical of northern German Gothic architecture.

There are two excellent museums on Mönchstrasse. The **Deutsches Meeresmuseum** (German Oceanographic Museum; ☎ 265 00; Katharinenberg 14-20; adult/concession €4/2.50; ☺ 9am-6pm Jun-Sep, 10am-5pm Oct-May) is an oceanic complex in a 13th-century convent church. Some tanks contain tropical fish and coral, while others display creatures of the Baltic and North Seas. The **Kulturhistorisches Museum** (Cultural History Museum; ☎ 287 90; Mönchstrasse 25-27; adult/concession €3/1.50; ☺ 10am-5pm Tue-Sun) has a collection housed in the cloister of an old convent.

Many fine buildings have been restored on the showpiece **Mühlenstrasse** near Alter Markt. The old harbour is close by, and you can stroll along the sea wall, then west along the waterfront park for a great view of the skyline of Stralsund.

Sleeping & Eating

Jugendherberge (☎ 292 160; jh-stralsund@t-online.de; Am Kütertor 1; dm junior/senior €14.50/17.50; ✗) The excellent Stralsund DJH hostel is in the 17th-century waterworks at the western edge of the Altstadt, and fills up pretty quickly in high season.

Pension Cobi (☎ 278 288; www.pension-cobi.de in German; Jakobiturmstrasse 15; s €32-42, d €46-62; ℗) In the shadow of the Jakobikirche, this is a great location for exploring the Altstadt, and also offers bike hire. Rooms are smart, clean and some have balconies.

Royal Hotel (☎ 295 268; www.royal-hotel.de in German; Tribseer Damm 4; s/d €65/80, ste from €90; ℗) A regal Art Nouveau building near the train station houses this excellent-value option; 12m-long buffet table and lovely big affordable suites make up for a bit of street noise.

Hansekeller (☎ 703 840; Mönchstrasse 48; mains €7.50-13) In an old guard house, the Hansekeller serves up hearty regional dishes at moderate prices in its vaulted brick cellar.

Tiffany (☎ 309 0088; Am Langenwall; buffet €4.99) This loosely themed breakfast bar is simply fantastic, darling. Try the Audrey Hepburn drink-all-you-can champagne buffet (€28, including fruit bowl).

Getting There & Away

Regional trains run to Rostock (€10.70, 1¼ hours), Berlin-Ostbahnhof (€30.80, 3½ hours) and Hamburg (€33, four hours) at least every two hours. International trains between Berlin and Stockholm or Oslo use the car ferry connecting Sassnitz Mukran harbour on Rügen Island with Trelleborg and Malmö.

RÜGEN ISLAND

Germany's largest island is just northeast of Stralsund, connected by a causeway. Once the summer haunt of Germany's leading thinkers (including Einstein, politicos and businesspeople, it fell on hard times during the war and GDR eras, but since reunification it is being brought back to life.

Sights

The island's highest point is the 117m **Königsstuhl**, reached by car or bus from Sassnitz. The **chalk cliffs** that tower above the sea are the main attraction. Much of Rügen and its surrounding waters are either national park or protected nature reserves. The **Bodden** inlet area is a bird refuge popular with bird-watchers. **Kap Arkona**, on Rügen's north shore, is famous for rugged cliffs and two lighthouses.

The main resort area is in eastern Rügen, around the towns of Binz, Sellin and Göhren. A lovely **hike** from Binz to Sellin skirts the cliffs above the sea through beech and pine forest and offers great coastal views. Another destination is **Jagdschloss Granitz** (1834), which is also surrounded by lush forest. **Prora**, up the coast from Binz, is the site of a 2km-long workers' retreat built by Hitler before the war and now housing several museums.

Information

Along with the following, Rügen has dozens of tourist offices, both municipal and private.

Tourismus Verband Rügen (☎ 03838-807 70; www.ruegen.de; Am Markt 4) In Bergen, the administrative centre, this office publishes a huge list of all accommodation on the island.

Tourismusgesell-schaft Binz (☎ 038393-134 60; touris musAG@binz.de; Hauptstrasse 1, Binz) Especially helpful.

Sleeping & Eating

Rügen has 21 camping grounds; the largest concentration is found at Göhren.

Jugendherberge (☎ 038393-325 97; fax 325 96; ju-gendherberge-binz@t-online.de; Strandpromenade 35; dm junior/senior €18.30/22.30) The island's only hostel is across from the beach in Binz. Binz is the island's top resort, with lodgings known for their distinctive *Bäderarkitektur* (spa architecture) of whitewashed wooden balconies.

Hotel Villa Neander (☎ 038393-4290; glasner@binz .de; Hauptstrasse 16; r per person from €41) Has warm rooms and friendly owners.

Lohme (☎ 038302-9221; Dorfstrasse 35, Lohme) On the island's northern side, you can dine on regional specialities while watching the sun set over Kap Arkona.

Getting There & Away

Local trains run almost hourly from 8am to 9pm between Stralsund and Sassnitz (€8.10, one hour) or Binz via Bergen (€8.10, one hour). A fun narrow-gauge train links Putbus to Göhren via Binz.

Fares for Baltic ferries vary with the season. **Scandlines** (www.scandlines.de) runs five passenger-vehicle ferries daily from Sassnitz Mukran ferry terminal, 5km south of town, to/from Trelleborg, Sweden (€10 to €15 one-way). Scandlines also has at least two services weekly to/from Ronne on Bornholm, Denmark (€12 to €17, daily in summer). To reach the ferries by train, make sure you go to Sassnitz Mukran station. Otherwise, catch a bus or walk from Sassnitz.

GERMANY DIRECTORY

ACCOMMODATION

Germany's accommodation is well organised, though some cities are short on budget hotels; private rooms are a good option in such situations. Accommodation usually includes breakfast. Look for signs saying *Zimmer frei* (rooms available) or *Fremdenzimmer* (tourist rooms). Most tourist offices offer a *Zimmervermittlung* (room-finding service), sometimes at a small charge.

Camping

There are more than 2000 organised camping grounds in Germany. Most are open April to September, but several hundred stay open year-round. Get permission before camping on private property. The best source of information is the **Deutscher Camping Club** (☎ 089-380 1420; www.camping-club.de in German; Mandlstrasse 28, Munich).

Hostels

The **Deutsches Jugendherbergswerk** (DJH; ☎ 05231-740 10; www.djh.de) coordinates all Hostelling International (HI) hostels in Germany. Almost all German hostels are open all year. Guests must be members of an HI-affiliated organisation or join the DJH when checking in. The annual fee is €10/17.50 for juniors/ seniors (above/below 26 years of age). If you don't have a hostel-approved sleeping sheet, it usually costs from €2.50 to €3.50 to hire one. Breakfast is always included.

Prior booking or early arrival determines who gets rooms. In Bavaria, the strict maximum age is 26. Most hostels have a curfew, which may be as early as 10pm in small towns.

DJH *Jugendgästehäuser* (youth guesthouses) offer better facilities, freer hours and smaller dorms at marginally higher prices.

Pensions, Guesthouses & Hotels

Pensions offer the basics of hotel comfort without asking hotel prices. Many are private homes, often a bit out of the centre of town. It's easiest to arrange bookings through tourist offices.

Cheap hotel rooms are hard to find during summer. Average budget prices are €30 for a single and €45 for a double (without bathroom). Rates usually include breakfast.

ACTIVITIES

Germany is ideal for hiking and mountaineering; popular areas include the Black Forest, the Harz Mountains, Saxon Switzerland, the Thuringian Forest and the Bavarian Alps. Good sources of information on hiking and mountaineering are **Verband Deutscher Gebirgs- und Wandervereine** (Federation of German Hiking Clubs; ☎ 0561-938 730; www.wanderverband.de in German; Wilhelmshöher Allee 157-9, Kassel) and **Deutscher Alpenverein** (German Alpine Club; ☎ 089-140 030; www .alpenverein.de in German; Von-Kahr-Strasse 2-4, Munich).

The Bavarian Alps have the most extensive area for winter sports. Cross-country skiing is also good in the Black Forest and Harz Mountains. Local tourist offices are the best sources of information.

Eastern Germany has much to offer cyclists in the way of lightly travelled back roads, especially in the flat and less-populated north. There's also an extensive cycling trail along the Elbe River.

BUSINESS HOURS

Shops are generally open from 8am or 9am to 6pm Monday to Friday and possibly a few hours on Saturdays. Banking hours are generally 8.30am to 1pm and 2.30pm to 4pm Monday to Friday and until 5.30pm on Thursday. Museums are generally closed on Monday or Tuesday. Restaurants open 11am to midnight, often closing from 3pm to 6pm; bars open around 6pm, while most nightclubs kick off at 11pm. Shops and banks are closed on public holidays.

DANGERS & ANNOYANCES

Although the usual precautions should be taken, crimes against travellers are rare in Germany. Africans, Asians and southern Europeans may encounter racial prejudice, especially in eastern Germany. The animosity is directed against immigrants, not tourists.

DISABLED TRAVELLERS

Germany caters reasonably well to the needs of *Behinderte* (disabled) travellers, with access ramps or lifts where necessary in most public buildings. Assistance is usually required when boarding public transport. On Deutsche Bahn distance services, you can arrange this when buying your ticket.

DISCOUNT CARDS

Many tourist offices offer local discount cards, generally including free public transport and free or discounted entry to attractions.

EMBASSIES & CONSULATES
German Embassies & Consulates

German embassies can be found in many countries:

Australia (☎ 02-6270 1911; www.germanembassy .org.au; 119 Empire Circuit, Yarralumla, ACT 2600)
Canada (☎ 613-232 1101; www.ottawa.diplo.de; 1 Waverley St, Ottawa, ON K2P 0T8)
New Zealand (☎ 04-473 6063; www.wellington .diplo.de; 90-92 Hobson St, Wellington)
UK (☎ 020-7824 1300; www.german-embassy.org.uk; 23 Belgrave Sq, London SW1X 8PZ)
USA (☎ 202-298 4000; www.germany-info.org; 4645 Reservoir Rd, NW Washington, DC 20007-1998)

Embassies & Consulates in Germany

All embassies are in Berlin.
Australia (Map pp452-3; ☎ 030-880 0880; Wallstrasse 76-78)

Canada (Map pp452-3; ☎ 030-203 120; Friedrichstrasse 95)
Ireland (Map pp452-3; ☎ 030-220 720; Friedrichstrasse 200)
New Zealand (Map pp452-3; ☎ 030-206 210; Friedrichstrasse 60)
South Africa (Map pp452-3; ☎ 030-825 2711; Friedrichstrasse 60)
UK (Map pp452-3; ☎ 030-204 570; Wilhelmstrasse 70-71)
USA (Map pp452-3; ☎ 030-238 5174; Neustädtische Kirchstrasse 4-5)

FESTIVALS & EVENTS
JANUARY
Carnival season (Shrovetide, known as *Karneval* or *Fasching*) Most notably in Cologne, Munich, Düsseldorf and Mainz.

FEBRUARY
International Toy Fair Held in Nuremberg.
International Film Festival Held in Berlin (p457).

MARCH
Frankfurt Music Fair and Frankfurt Jazz Fair (☎ 069-757 50; http://musik.messefrankfurt.com)
Spring Fairs Held throughout Germany.

APRIL
Stuttgart Jazz Festival
Munich Ballet Days
Walpurgisnacht Festivals Traditional pagan celebrations held the night before May Day in the Harz Mountains.

MAY
Dresden International Dixieland Jazz Festival
Dresden Music Festival (☎ 0351-486 6317; www.musikfestspiele.com) Held in last week of May into first week of June.

JUNE
Munich Film Festival
International Theatre Festival Held in Freiburg.

JULY
Folk festivals Held throughout Germany.
Berlin Love Parade (p458)
Munich Opera Festival
Richard Wagner Festival (☎ 0921- 787 80; www.bayreutherfestspiele.de) Europe's largest festival dedicated to the wild man of opera, held in Bayreuth.

AUGUST
Heidelberg Castle Festival (www.schlossfestspiele -heidelberg.de) Theatre festival held in the famous castle.
Wine festivals Held throughout the Rhineland area.

SEPTEMBER-OCTOBER
Oktoberfest (p476; www.oktoberfest.de) Held in Munich.
Frankfurt Book Fair (www.frankfurt-book-fair.com) The publishing industry's biggest annual event.
Bremen Freimarkt

NOVEMBER
St Martin's Festival Lantern processions and feasting, held throughout Rhineland and Bavaria.

DECEMBER
Christmas fairs Held throughout Germany.

FOOD & DRINK

Germany is a pig-and-potatoes kind of country, although vegetarians shouldn't go hungry. Students can often eat at *mensas* (university cafeterias). Other popular cheap options are the ubiquitous doner kebab or a takeaway *China-Pfanne* (noodle dish). Asian restaurants are generally quite fast food–oriented and will usually do vegetarian dishes on demand. Sunday brunch buffets are an institution at many cafés and restaurants.

Wurst (sausage), in its hundreds of forms, is by far the most universal main dish. Regional favourites include *Bratwurst* (spiced sausage), *Weisswurst* (veal sausage), *Blutwurst* (blood sausage) and of course the Berlin *Currywurst*. Other popular main dishes include *Rippenspeer* (spare ribs), *Sauerbraten* (roast pork) and many forms of *Schnitzel* (breaded pork or veal cutlet).

Potatoes feature prominently in German meals, often as *Bratkartoffeln* (fried), *Kartoffelpüree* (mashed) or Swiss *Rösti* (grated, then fried). Popular desserts include *Schwarzwälder Kirschtorte* (Black Forest cherry cake), as well as endless varieties of *Apfeltasche* (apple pastry).

At the liquid end of things, German beer is a cultural phenomenon that must be adequately explored (well, that's our excuse). *Helles Bier* is light, *Schwarzbier* or *dunkles Bier* is dark, and *Pils* is slightly more bitter than normal lager, while *Alt* is darker and more full-bodied. A speciality is *Weizenbier,* made with wheat instead of barley malt and served either as *Kristall* (filtered) or *Hefe* (with yeast).

German wines are fairly inexpensive and typically white, light and intensely fruity. The Rhine and Moselle Valleys are classic wine-growing regions.

GAY & LESBIAN TRAVELLERS

Germans are generally fairly tolerant of homosexuality, but gays *(Schwule)* and lesbians *(Lesben)* still don't enjoy quite the same social acceptance as in some other northern European countries. Most progressive are the large cities, particularly Berlin and Frankfurt. The age of consent is 18 years. Christopher Street Day (Gay Pride) festivals are held in Berlin, Bielefeld, Bochum, Hamburg, Mannheim and Würzburg in June, and in July in Cologne.

HOLIDAYS

New Year's Day 1 January
Easter March/April – Good Friday to Easter Sunday
Labour Day 1 May
Ascension Day May/June, 40 days after Easter
Pentecost/Whit Monday May/June, 50 days after Easter
Corpus Christi 10 days after Pentecost
Day of German Unity 3 October
All Saints' Day 1 November
Day of Prayer & Repentance 18 November
Christmas 24-26 December

INTERNET ACCESS

If there's no dedicated Internet café around, you'll find terminals at Vobis computer stores as well as in some amusement arcades and libraries.

LANGUAGE

The official language, *Hochdeutsch* (High German), is universally understood. English is widely understood by young or educated Germans, but less so outside big cities, especially in eastern Germany. See the Language chapter (p1275) for pronunciation guidelines and useful words and phrases.

LEGAL MATTERS

Police in Germany are well trained and usually treat tourists with respect. You are required by law to prove your identity if asked by the police, so always carry your passport, or an identity card if you're an EU citizen.

MONEY
Credit Cards

Credit cards are especially useful for emergencies, although they are often not accepted by budget hotels and restaurants outside major cities. Most widely accepted are Eurocard (linked to Access and MasterCard), Visa and American Express.

GERMANY

Exchanging Money

The easiest places to change cash in Germany are banks or foreign-exchange counters at airports and train stations, particularly those of the Reisebank. Main banks in larger cities generally have money-changing machines for after-hours use, though they don't often give good rates. The Reisebank charges a flat €2.50 to change cash. Some local Sparkasse banks have good rates and low charges.

There are ATMs virtually everywhere in Germany; most accept Visa, MasterCard, American Express (American Express), Eurocard, Plus and Cirrus. Typically, withdrawals over the counter against cards at major banks cost a flat €5 per transaction.

For emergencies, the Reisebank (Western Union) and Thomas Cook (MoneyGram) offer fast international cash transfers, but commissions are costly.

Tipping

Restaurant bills include a service charge and tipping is not compulsory. If you're satisfied with the service, add about 5% to 10%. It's customary to tip as you're paying. If you have the exact amount, just say 'Stimmt so' (that's fine).

Travellers Cheques

Travellers cheques can be cashed at any bank; the most widely accepted are American Express, Thomas Cook and Barclays. Most banks charge commission, even on cheques issued in euros. American Express charges no commission on its own cheques.

POST

Standard post office hours are 8am to 6pm Monday to Friday and to noon on Saturday. Many train station post offices stay open later or offer limited services outside these hours. Mail can be sent Postlagernde (poste restante) to the main post office in your city. There's no fee for collection, but German post offices will hold mail for two weeks only. The postage for letters up to 20g within Europe is €0.55, and outside Europe €1.55.

TELEPHONE

Home direct services for reverse-charge (collect) calls are only possible to some countries. The prefix is ☎ 0800 followed by the home number. For the USA dial ☎ 888 225 5388 (AT&T) or ☎ 888 0013 (Sprint); for

Canada ☎ 080 1014; for Australia ☎ 080 0061 (Telstra); for Britain dial ☎ 080 0044.

For directory assistance within Germany call ☎ 118 33 (☎ 118 37 in English); both cost €0.25 plus €0.99 per minute. International information is ☎ 118 34 (€0.55 per 20 seconds).

Phonecards

Most payphones in Germany only accept phonecards, available for €5, €10 and €20 at post offices, kiosks, tourist offices and banks. Prepaid calling cards are good for international calls.

TOURIST INFORMATION

Before your trip you can consult the **German National tourist office** (Deutsche Zentrale für Tourismus, DZT; ☎ 069-974 640; www.visits-to-germany.com; Beethovenstrasse 69, Frankfurt-am-Main). DZT representatives abroad include the following:

Australia & New Zealand (☎ 02-9267 8148; gnto@germany.org.au; PO Box A 980, Sydney, NSW 1235)
Canada (☎ 416-968 1570; gnto@aol.com; 175 Bloor St East, North Tower, 6th fl, Toronto, Ont M4W 3R8)
South Africa (☎ 011-643 1615; c/o Lufthansa Airlines, PO Box 10883, Johannesburg 2000)
UK (☎ 020-7317 0908; PO Box 2695, London W1A 3TN)
USA (☎ 212-661 7200; gntony@aol.com; 122 East 42nd St, 52nd fl, New York, NY 10168-0072)

Other offices are in Amsterdam, Brussels, Copenhagen, Helsinki, Hong Kong, Madrid, Milan, Moscow, Oslo, Paris, Stockholm, Tel Aviv, Tokyo, Vienna and Zürich.

VISAS

Americans, Australians, Britons, Canadians, Israelis, Japanese, New Zealanders and Singaporeans require no visa. Citizens of the EU and some other Western European countries can enter on an official identity card. Germany is part of the Schengen visa scheme. Three months is the usual limit of stay.

WOMEN TRAVELLERS

Women should not encounter particular difficulties, and most large cities have women-only organisations. If you are a victim of harassment or violence, contact **Frauenhaus München** (Munich ☎ 089-354 8311, 24hr service ☎ 089-354 830) or **LARA – Krisen und Beratungszentrum für vergewaltigte Frauen** (Crisis & Counselling Centre for Rape Victims; Berlin ☎ 030-216 8888).

Greece

HIGHLIGHTS

- **Acropolis** In the capital, Athens, the most famous monument of the ancient world literally towers above all else (p528)
- **Santorini** The sheer cliffs of the caldera provide one of the most spectacular sights in Greece (p550)
- **Nafplio** This gorgeous old Venetian town is one of the country's most romantic destinations (p540)
- **Best journey** Starting in Athens, pop over to Mykonos (p546) then visit Naxos (p548) and Santorini (p550) followed by Crete (p551) and then back to Athens via Nafplio (p540)
- **Off-the-beaten track** Off most tourist itineraries, Thessaloniki offers great nightlife and fine Byzantine churches (p543)

GREECE

FAST FACTS

- **Area** 131,900 sq km (two-fifths the size of France)
- **ATMs** Widespread, particularly in tourist areas
- **Budget** €40-50 per day
- **Capital** Athens
- **Country Code** ☎ 30
- **Currency** Euro (A$1 = €0.58, CA$1 = €0.64, ¥100 = €0.73, NZ$1 = €0.54, UK£1 = €1.45, US$1 = €0.81)
- **Famous for** Ancient ruins and beautiful beaches
- **Language** Greek
- **Phrases** *Yasas* (hello), *andio* (goodbye), *parakalo* (please), *efharisto* (thank you), *ne* (yes), *ohi* (no)

- **Population** 10,939,771
- **Time** GMT/UTC + 2
- **Visas** None required for most travellers to visit for up to three months.

TRAVEL HINTS

Don't leave home without sunglasses, sunscreen, swimwear, shorts and sandshoes. Take a couple of paperbacks for those long ferry rides.

ROAMING GREECE

After exploring Athens, travel to Ancient Corinth and then Ancient Olympia. Head to Nafplio for a side trip to Mycenae. After checking out Mystras, catch a boat from Gythio to Crete. After exploring Crete, move on to Santorini and Mykonos before heading back to Athens.

Perennially popular, Greece has been saying *yasas* (hello) to travellers for thousands of years. Indeed it's been almost 2000 years since the Greek geographer and historian Pausanias penned the first travel guide to Greece. Today, visiting the country's magnificent archaeological sites leads travellers on a journey not only through the landscape but also

GREECE

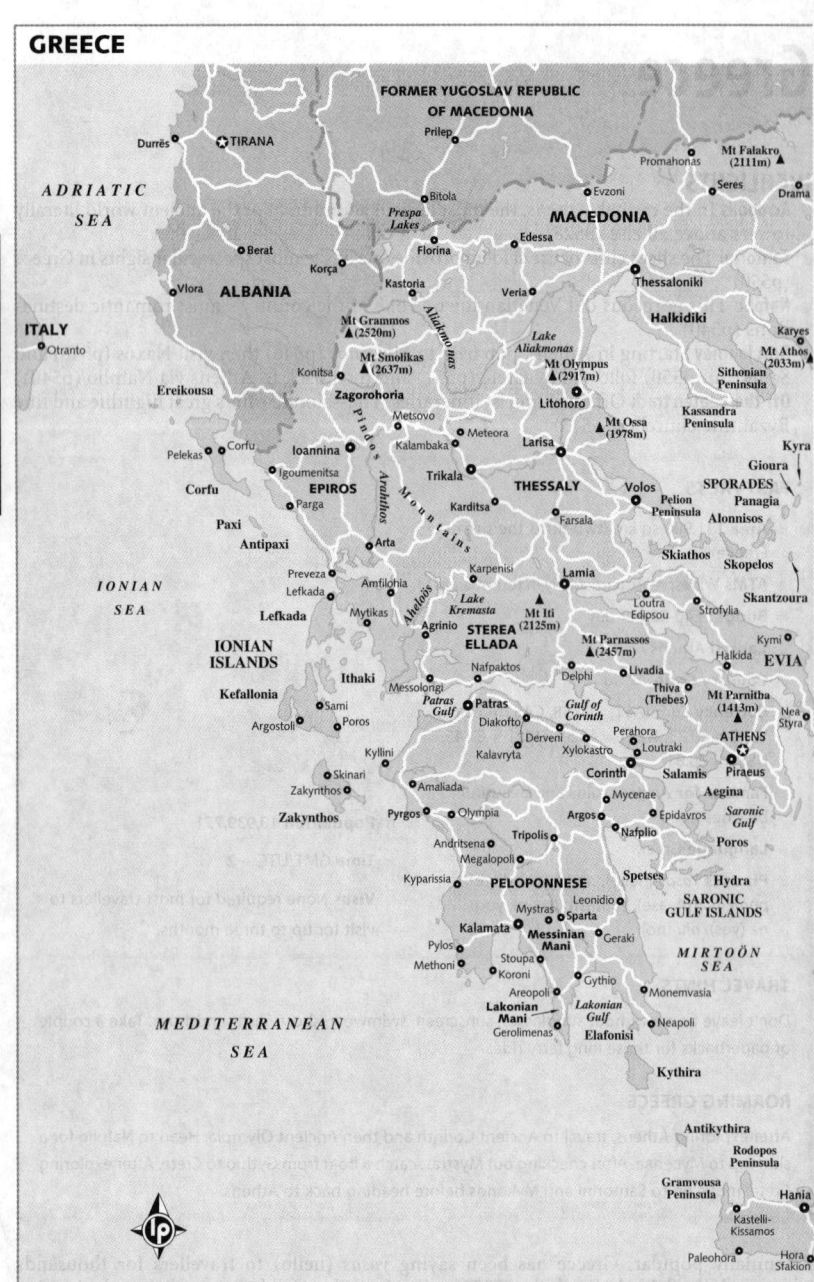

GREECE

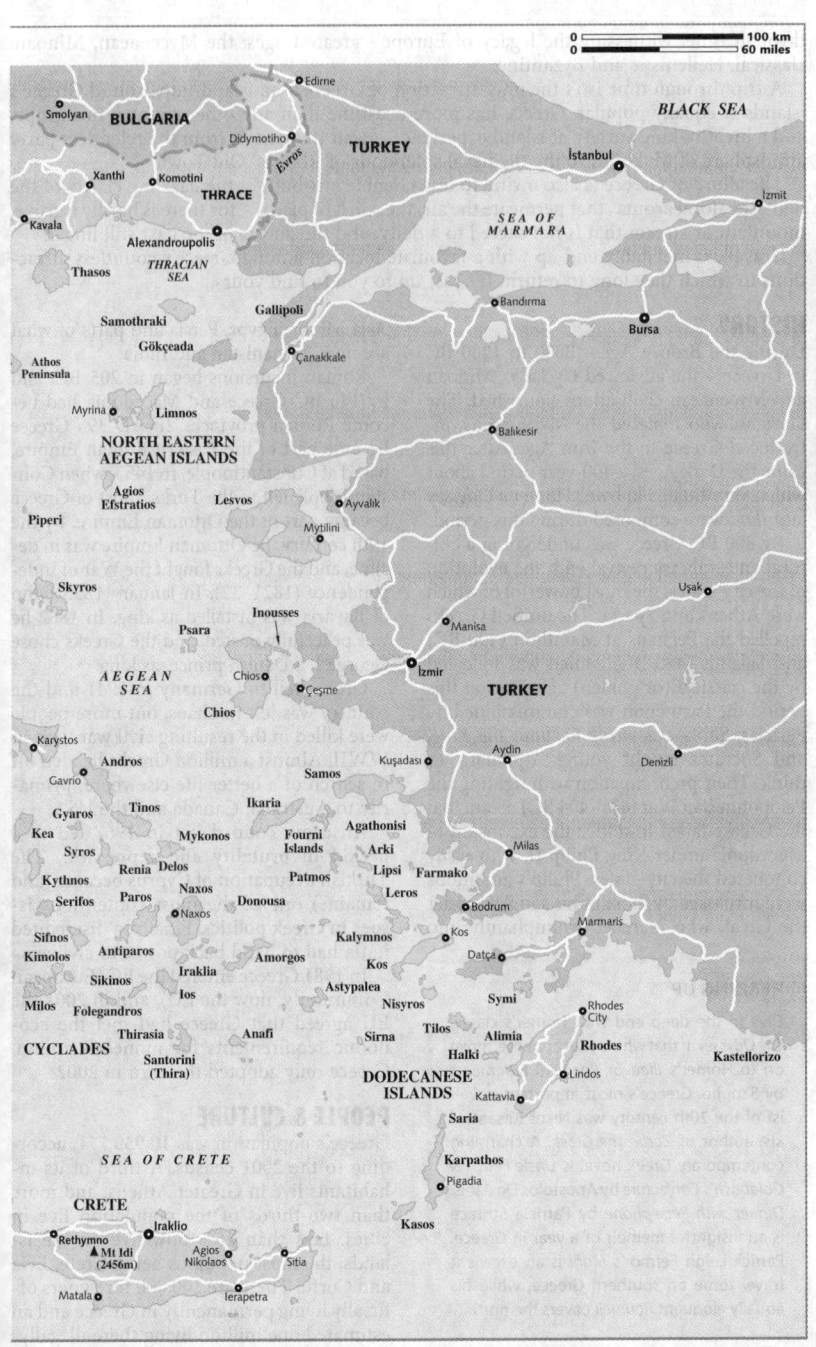

| 0 | | | 100 km |
| 0 | | | 60 miles |

BULGARIA

Smolyan

Didymotiho

Edirne

TURKEY

BLACK SEA

İstanbul

İzmit

Xanthi Komotini

THRACE

Evros

Kavala

Alexandroupolis

SEA OF
MARMARA

Thasos

THRACIAN
SEA

Samothraki

Gökçeada

Gallipoli

Bandırma

Bursa

Athos
Peninsula

Çanakkale

Myrina Limnos

NORTH EASTERN
AEGEAN ISLANDS

Balıkesir

Agios
Efstratios

Lesvos

Ayvalık

Piperi

Mytilini

Skyros

Uşak

Inousses

AEGEAN
SEA

Psara

Chios

Çeşme

İzmir

Manisa

Chios

TURKEY

Karystos

Andros

Samos

Kuşadası

Aydın

Denizli

Gavrio

Gyaros Tinos

Ikaria

Kea

Mykonos

Fourni
Islands

Agathonisi

Milas

Syros

Renia Delos

Arki

Lipsi Farmako

Kythnos Naxos

Patmos

Leros

Serifos Paros

Donousa

Bodrum

Sifnos Naxos

Marmaris

Antiparos

Kalymnos

Kos

Kimolos

Iraklia

Amorgos

Kos

Datça

Milos Sikinos

Ios

Astypalea

Nisyros

Symi

Rhodes
City

Folegandros

Anafi

Sirna Tilos

Alimia

Thirasia

Halki

Rhodes

Kastellorizo

CYCLADES

Santorini
(Thira)

DODECANESE
ISLANDS

Lindos

Kattavia

Saria

SEA OF CRETE

Karpathos

Pigadia

Ecuador

CRETE

Iraklio

Kasos

Rethymno ▲Mt Idi
(2456m)

Agios
Nikolaos

Sitia

Matala Ierapetra

through time, witnessing the legacy of Europe's greatest ages: the Mycenaean, Minoan, classical, Hellenistic and Byzantine.

A trip through time isn't the only attraction of Greece – an island-hop around Greece's islands is equally popular. Greece has more coastline than any other country in Europe, and a breathtaking variety of island experiences await the visitor, from the relentless party atmosphere of Mykonos to the medieval splendour of Rhodes' Old Town.

The allure of Greece is also owing to less tangible attributes – the dazzling clarity of the light, the floral aromas that permeate the air, the spirit of places – for there is hardly a grove, mountain or stream that is not sacred to a deity, and the ghosts of the past still linger.

Travellers inevitably end up with a favourite location among Greece's countless attractions to which they long to return. It's just up to you to find yours.

HISTORY

During the Bronze Age – 3000 to 1200 BC in Greece – the advanced Cycladic, Minoan and Mycenaean civilisations flourished. The Dorians, who replaced the Mycenaeans, introduced Greece to the Iron Age. After this came the Dark Ages, a 400-year period about which very little is known. Homer's *Odyssey* and *Iliad* were composed during this period.

By 800 BC Greece was undergoing a cultural and military revival with the evolution of the city-states, the most powerful of which were Athens and Sparta. The unified Greeks repelled the Persians at Marathon (490 BC) and Salamis (480 BC), which was followed by the classical (or golden) age. During this period the Parthenon was commissioned by Pericles, Sophocles wrote *Oedipus the King*, and Socrates taught young Athenians to think. Their preoccupation with fighting the Peloponnesian War (431–404 BC) meant that the Greeks failed to notice the expansion of Macedonia under King Philip II, who easily conquered the city-states. Philip's ambitions were surpassed by those of his son Alexander the Great, who marched triumphantly into Asia Minor, Egypt, Persia and parts of what are now Afghanistan and India.

Roman incursions began in 205 BC, and by 146 BC Greece and Macedonia had become Roman provinces. In AD 395 Greece became part of the Eastern Roman Empire, based at Constantinople. In 1453, when Constantinople fell to the Turks, most of Greece became part of the Ottoman Empire. By the 19th century the Ottoman Empire was in decline, and the Greeks fought the War of Independence (1821–32). In January 1833 Otho of Bavaria was installed as king. In 1862 he was peacefully ousted, and the Greeks chose George I, a Danish prince, as king.

Greece fell to Germany in 1941 and the country was left in chaos, but more people were killed in the resulting civil war than in WWII. Almost a million Greeks headed off in search of a better life elsewhere, primarily to Australia, Canada and the USA.

An army coup d'état in 1967 led to a period of brutality and repression. The Turkish occupation of Cyprus became (and remains) one of the most contentious issues in Greek politics. Finally, a discredited junta had to hand back power to civilians.

In 1981 Greece entered the EC (European Community, now the EU), and in 2001 the EU agreed that Greece had met the economic requirements for monetary union. Greece duly adopted the euro in 2002.

PEOPLE & CULTURE

Greece's population was 10,939,771, according to the 2001 census. A third of its inhabitants live in Greater Athens, and more than two-thirds of the population live in cities. Less than 15% now live on the islands; the most populous being Crete, Evia and Corfu. There are 100,000 foreigners officially living permanently in Greece and an estimated one million living there illegally.

READING UP

Dive in the deep end with Homer's classic *The Odyssey*. If that whets your appetite, move on to Homer's *Iliad* or *Poems & Fragments* by Sappho. Greece's most important novelist of the 20th century was Nikos Kasantzakis, author of *Zorba the Greek*. A charming contemporary Greek novel is *Uncle Petros & Goldbach's Conjecture* by Apostolos Doxiadis. *Dinner with Persephone* by Patricia Storace is an insightful memoir of a year in Greece. Patrick Leigh Fermor's *Mani* is an excellent travel tome on southern Greece, while his equally eloquent *Roumeli* covers the north.

Immigration is changing the social landscape, yet Greece remains culturally homogeneous, and traditional customs play a huge role in the Greek way of life. This is inexorably tied to the Greek Orthodox Church, its influence extending beyond the life-cycle events such as births, funerals and weddings. Greeks of the younger generation follow tradition, yet they are far more cosmopolitan in their outlook and are in tune with the latest world trends in fashion and music.

SPORT

Football (soccer) is by far the most popular spectator sport in Greece, and the two most popular teams are Olympiakos of Piraeus and Panathinaikos of Athens. The season runs from September to mid-May. The aforementioned clubs are also the main players in Greece's other main sport, basketball. These teams fare well in European competition and achieve more consistent success than their soccer-playing counterparts.

RELIGION

About 98% of the Greek population belongs to the Greek Orthodox Church. The remainder is split between the Roman Catholic, Protestant, Evangelist, Jewish and Muslim faiths. Older Greeks and those in rural areas tend to be deeply religious, yet most young people are decidedly more secular – but will still make a sign of the cross when passing a church.

ARTS

The arts have been integral to Greek life since ancient times. Of all the ancient Greek arts, architecture has had the most profound influence. Today, however, in Greece's major cities cheap concrete apartment blocks built in the 20th century belie this legacy.

Thankfully, the great works of Greek literature are not as easily besmirched. The first and greatest ancient Greek writer was Homer, author of *Iliad* and *Odyssey*.

Pindar (c 518–438BC) is the pre-eminent lyric poet of ancient Greece, and he was commissioned to recite his odes at the Olympic Games. The great writers of the tradition of love poetry were Sappho (6th century BC) and Alcaeus (5th century BC), both of whom lived on Lesvos. Sappho's poetic descriptions of her affections for women gave rise to the term 'lesbian'.

TOP FIVE GREECE

- **Festivities** Milopotas Beach Party (p549)
- **Walk** Samaria Gorge (p554)
- **Bar/Club** (p556)
- **Impressive sight** Meteora (p543)
- **Ancient ruin** The Acropolis (p529)

The Alexandrian, Constantine Cavafy (1863–1933), revolutionised Greek poetry by introducing a personal, conversational style. Nikos Kazantzakis, the author of *Zorba the Greek* and numerous other novels, plays and poems, is the most famous of 20th-century Greek novelists.

Famous painters of the 20th century include Konstantinos, Partenis and later George Bouzianis, whose work can be viewed at the National Art Gallery.

Greeks have always had a love of music. The *bouzouki* (stringed lute-like instrument) is heard everywhere and is one of the main instruments of *rembetika* music – which is in many ways the Greek equivalent of the American blues, and is commonly associated with the underworld of the 1920s. See (p535) for live rembetika venues.

Alongside music, dance is an integral part of Greek life. Whether at a wedding, nightclub or village celebration, traditional dance is still widely practised. Try to catch the Dora Stratou Dance Company (p535) in Athens.

ENVIRONMENT

Greece lies at the southern tip of the Balkan Peninsula, and of its 1400 islands, only 169 are inhabited. The land mass is 131,900 sq km, and Greek territorial waters cover a further 400,000 sq km. Around four-fifths of Greece is mountainous. It lies in one of the most seismically active regions in the world,

EMERGENCY NUMBERS

- **Ambulance** ☎ 166
- **Fire** ☎ 199
- **Police** ☎ 100
- **Roadside Assistance** (ELPA) ☎ 104
- **Tourist Police** ☎ 171

recording more than 20,000 earthquakes in the last 40 years – most of them very minor.

Greece is belatedly becoming environmentally conscious. However, deforestation and soil erosion are problems that go back thousands of years. Olive cultivation and goats have been the main culprits, but firewood gathering, shipbuilding, housing and industry have all taken their toll.

TRANSPORT

GETTING THERE & AWAY

Air

Although there are 16 international airports in Greece, most of them handle only summer charter flights to the islands. Athens handles most international flights, including all intercontinental flights, and has regularly scheduled flights to the European capitals. Thessaloniki is also well served, and Iraklio, Crete's capital, takes scheduled flights.

Athens Eleftherios Venizelos International Airport (ATH; ☎ 2103 530 000; www.aia.gr)

Iraklio Nikos Kazantzakis International Airport (HER; ☎ 2810 228 401)

Thessaloniki Macedonia International Airport (SKG; ☎ 2310 473 700)

Olympic Airways (www.olympic-airways.gr) is the country's national airline. **Aegean Airlines** (www.aegeanair.com) flies direct from Athens to Rome and Venice, and from Thessaloniki to Cologne, Düsseldorf, Frankfurt, Munich and Stuttgart. Aegean has an excellent online 'e-ticket' booking system.

Bus & Train

NORTHERN EUROPE

Overland travel between northern Europe and Greece is uneconomical, as buses and trains are unable to compete with cheap airfares. All bus and train services now go via Italy and take the ferries over to Greece. However, Greece is part of the Eurail network, and passes are valid on the ferries operated by Adriatica di Navigazione and Hellenic Mediterranean Lines from Brindisi to Corfu, Igoumenitsa and Patra.

NEIGHBOURING COUNTRIES

The OSE (Organismos Sidirodromon Ellados; Greek railways organisation) operates buses from Athens to İstanbul (€67.50, 22 hours, daily except Wednesday). There are

daily trains between Athens and İstanbul (€63, 22 hours) via Thessaloniki (€42.50).

The crossing points into Turkey are at Kipi and Kastanies, the crossings into the Former Yugoslav Republic of Macedonia (FYROM) are at Evzoni and Niki, and the Bulgarian crossing is at Promahonas. All are open 24 hours a day. The crossing points to Albania are at Kakavia and Krystallopigi.

GETTING AROUND

Greece is easy to travel around. Buses travel to just about every dot on the map, and trains offer a good alternative where available. Island-hopping in Greece is easy as there are countless ferries criss-crossing the Adriatic and the Aegean.

Air

Most domestic flights are handled by Greece's financially turbulent national carrier, **Olympic Airways** (☎ 8011 144 444; www.olympic -airways.gr). Crete-based **Aegean Airlines** (☎ 8011 120 000; www.aegeanair.com) offers flights to many of the same destinations and has youth discounts as well as occasional discount fares.

Boat

CATAMARAN

High-speed catamarans are as fast as hydrofoils and have roughly the same fare structure, but are much more comfortable. They are also much less prone to cancellation in rough weather. The main players are Hellas Flying Dolphins and Blue Star Ferries.

FERRY

Most islands have ferry services, although in winter these are pared back. Services become more frequent from April, and during July and August Greece's seas are a mass of wake and wash. The hub of the ferry network is Piraeus (p536), Athens' main port. Piraeus has ferries to the Cyclades, Crete, the Dodecanese, the Saronic Gulf Islands and the northeastern Aegean Islands. Patra (p539) is the main port for ferries to the Ionian Islands, and Volos and Agios Konstantinos are the ports for the Sporades islands.

New high-speed ferries are slashing travel times on some of the longer routes. **NEL Lines** (☎ 2251 026 299; www.nel.gr), for example, does Piraeus to Chios in 4½ hours – nearly half the time of a normal ferry – but at twice the price. The newer ferries also have the ad-

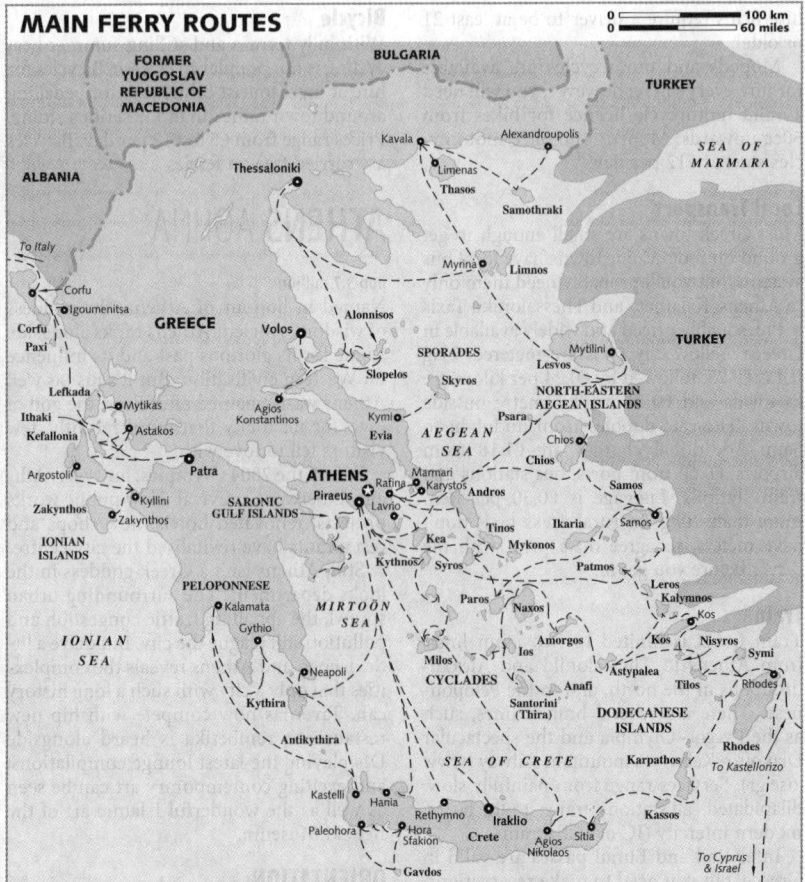

MAIN FERRY ROUTES

vantage of being inherently safer than some of the older tubs plying the routes.

Hydrofoils offer a faster alternative to ferries on some routes, particularly to islands close to the mainland. They take half the time but cost twice as much. Most routes operate only during July and August.

Bus

Greece's comfortable and punctual, long-distance buses are operated by regional collectives known as **KTEL** (Kino Tamio Eispraxeon Leoforion; www.ktel.org). Fares can be fixed by the government, and routes can be found on its website. Journeys cost about €4 per 100km, and tickets should be bought at least an hour in advance to ensure a seat.

Car & Motorcycle

Greece recognises all national driving licences and the International Driving Permit. The automobile club, Automobile and Touring Club of Greece (ELPA), offers reciprocal services to the members of other national motoring associations.

Rental cars are widely available throughout the country. Local companies' rates are about 25% lower than those of the big multinational companies, and best of all, they are more willing to bargain. High-season weekly rates including unlimited mileage start at around €280 for the smallest models, dropping to €200 in winter, that's without taxes and extras such as insurance. The minimum driving age in Greece is 18, but most car hire firms require a driver to be at least 21 or older.

Mopeds and motorcycles are available for hire everywhere; however, you will need a valid motorcycle licence for bikes from 50cc upwards. Mopeds and 50cc motorcycles start at €12 per day.

Local Transport

Most Greek towns are small enough to get around on foot. Major towns have local bus systems, but you'll probably need them only in Athens, Kalamata and Thessaloniki. Taxis are reasonably priced and widely available in Greece. Yellow city taxis are metered. Flag fall is €0.75, followed by €0.24 per kilometre in towns and €0.44 per kilometre outside towns. The rate doubles from midnight to 5am. Additional charges are €1.18 from airports, €0.60 from ports, bus stations and train stations. Luggage is €0.30 per item more than 10kg. In rural areas taxis don't have meters, so agree on a price with the driver before you get in.

Train

Train travel is limited to two main lines: from Athens to Thessaloniki and Alexandroupolis in the north, and to the Peloponnese. There are several branch lines, such as the Pyrgos–Olympia and the spectacular Diakofto–Kalavryta mountain railway (www .ose.gr). Services range from painfully slow, dilapidated, 'all stations' trains, to the faster, modern intercity (IC or ICE) trains.

Inter-Rail and Eurail passes are valid in Greece, but you need to make reservations. In summer you make reservations a couple of days in advance.

Bicycle

With hilly terrain and stifling summer heat cycling is not popular in Greece. Bicycles for hire at most tourist centres are for pedalling around town rather than for serious riding. Prices range from €5 to €12 per day. Bicycles are carried free on ferries.

ATHENS ΑΘΗΝΑ

pop 3.7 million

Named in honour of Athena, the goddess of wisdom, Ancient Athens ranks alongside Rome for its glorious past and its influence on Western civilisation. But it's just as well Athens wasn't named after Eros, the god of love, for it's a city that, until recently, few visitors fell in love with.

Before the 2004 Olympics, however, Athens underwent a revival. New public works projects, renovated hotels, new shops and restaurants have revitalised the city centre.

Still, Athens isn't a Greek goddess in the looks department. The surrounding urban sprawl, the appalling traffic congestion and pollution still plague the city. But delve a little deeper, and Athens reveals the complexities that only a city with such a long history can. Tavernas now compete with hip new restaurants; rembetika is heard alongside DJs playing the latest lounge compilations; and exciting contemporary art can be seen as well as the wonderful Islamic art of the Benaki Museum.

ORIENTATION

Although Athens is a huge, sprawling city, nearly everything of interest to travellers

---

GETTING INTO TOWN

From the airport, **Bus Service E95** (Map p533; 24hr, every 30 minutes, 60 to 90 minutes) operates between the airport and Plateia Syntagmatos. Bus Service E96 (24hr, every 40 minutes, 60 to 90 minutes) operates between the airport and Plateia Karaïskaki in Piraeus. If arriving in Piraeus, you can also take Line 1 to the city centre.

Tickets for these services cost €2.95, which also includes free public transport in Athens for 24 hours.

Linked with the train system, Line 3 of the Metro was scheduled to continue to the airport from May 2004, but at the time of writing remained unfinished. By the time you read this, you should be able to take Line 3 to the city centre in less than 30 minutes.

Taxi fares vary according to the time of day and level of traffic, but you should expect to pay €20 to €30 from the airport to the city centre, and €20 to €25 from the airport to Piraeus. Both trips can take anywhere between an hour and 90 minutes.

is located within a small area bounded by Omonia Square (Plateia Omonias) to the north, Monastiraki Square (Plateia Monastirakiou) to the west, Syntagma Square (Plateia Syntagmatos) to the east and Plaka to the south. The city's two major landmarks, the Acropolis and Lykavittos Hill, can be seen from just about everywhere in this area.

Syntagma is the heart of modern Athens. Flanked by luxury hotels, banks and fast-food restaurants, the square is dominated by the old royal palace – home of the Greek parliament since 1935.

Once a smart address, Omonia is known today for its prostitutes and pickpockets rather than its position as a central *plateia* (square). All the major streets of central Athens meet here. Panepistimiou (El Venizelou) and Stadiou run parallel southeast to Syntagma, while Athinas leads south to the market district of Monastiraki. Monastiraki is in turn linked to Syntagma by Ermou – home to some of the city's smartest shops – and Mitropoleos.

Mitropoleos skirts the northern edge of Plaka, the delightful old quarter of town. Its labyrinthine streets are nestled on the northeastern slope of the Acropolis, and most of the city's ancient sites are close by.

INFORMATION
Emergency
Duty Doctor (☎ 105; ☒ 2pm-7am)
Duty Hospital (☎ 106)
Duty Pharmacy (☎ 107)
First-Aid Service (☎ 166)
Police Emergency (☎ 100)
SOS Doctors (☎ 2103 220 046/015) This 24-hour call-out service employs multilingual doctors.
Tourist Police (☎ 2108 707 000; Tsoha 7, Ambelokipi; h24hr)
Tourist Police Information Service (☎ 171; ☒ 24hr) Offers general tourist information as well as emergency help.

Internet Access
Most Internet cafés charge around €3 per hour.
Arcade Internet Café (Map p533; ☎ 2103 210 701; Stadiou 5, Syntagma; ☒ 10am-10pm Mon-Sat, Sun noon-8pm) has dedicated laptop connections.
C@fe4U Exarhia (Map pp530-1; ☎ 2103 611 981; Ippokratous 44; ☒ 24hr)
Omonia (Map pp530-1; ☎ 2105 201 564; Tritis Septemvriou 24; ☒ 8am-11pm)
Plaka Internet World (Map p533; Pandrosou 29, Monastiraki; ☒ 11am-11pm)

Money
American Express (Map p533; ☎ 2103 223 380; Ermou 7; Syntagma; ☒ 8.30am-4pm Mon-Fri, 8.30am-1.30pm Sat)
Eurochange Syntagma (Map p533; ☎ 2103 220 155; Karageorgi Servias 4; ☒ 8am-8pm Mon Fri, 10am-6pm Sat & Sun) Plaka (Map p533; ☎ 2103 243 997; Filellinon 22; ☒ 8am-8pm Mon-Fri, 9am-7pm Sat, 10am-7pm Sun)

Post
Athens Central Post Office (Map pp530-1; Eolou 100, Omonia; ☒ 7.30am-8pm Mon-Fri, 7.30am-2pm Sat) Unless specified otherwise, all poste restante will be sent here.
Parcel post office (Map p533; Stadiou 4, Syntagma; ☒ 7.30am-2pm Mon-Fri) Parcels more than 2kg going abroad must be taken here and unwrapped for inspection.
Syntagma post office (Map p533; cnr Mitropoleos & Plateia Syntagmatos; ☒ 7.30am-8pm Mon-Fri, 7.30am-2pm Sat, 9am-1pm Sun) Get post restante sent here.

Tourist Offices
EOT (Ellinikos Organismos Tourismou; Greek National Tourist Organisation; www.gnto.gr) Ambelokipi (Map pp530-1; ☎ 2108 707 000; Tsoha 7; ☒ 9am-4pm Mon-Fri) Syntagma (Map pp530-1; ☎ 2103 310 561/562; Amerikis 2; ☒ 9am-4pm Mon-Fri); Eleftherios Venizelos International Airport (☎ 2103 530 445; Arrivals Hall; ☒ 9am-7pm Mon-Fri, 10am-3pm Sat & Sun) The head office is the Ambelokipi branch.

SIGHTS
The Acropolis
The defining feature of Athens is the **Acropolis** (Map p533; ☎ 2103 210 291; adult/concession €12/6 sites & museum; ☒ site 8am-6.30pm, museum noon-6.30pm Mon, 8am-6.30pm Tue-Sun Apr-Oct; site & museum 8am-4.30pm Nov-Mar), arguably the most important ancient monument in the Western world.

The entrance to the Acropolis is through the **Beule Gate**, a Roman arch added in the 3rd century AD. Beyond this is the **Propylaia**, the monumental gate that was the entrance to the city in ancient times. It was damaged in the 17th century when lightning set off a Turkish gunpowder store, but it has since been restored. To the south of the Propylaia

---

CHEAPER BY THE HALF DOZEN

The €12 admission charge at the Acropolis buys a collective ticket that also gives entry to all the other significant ancient sites: the Ancient Agora, the Roman Agora, the Keramikos, the Temple of Olympian Zeus and the Theatre of Dionysos. The ticket is valid for 48 hours.

GREECE

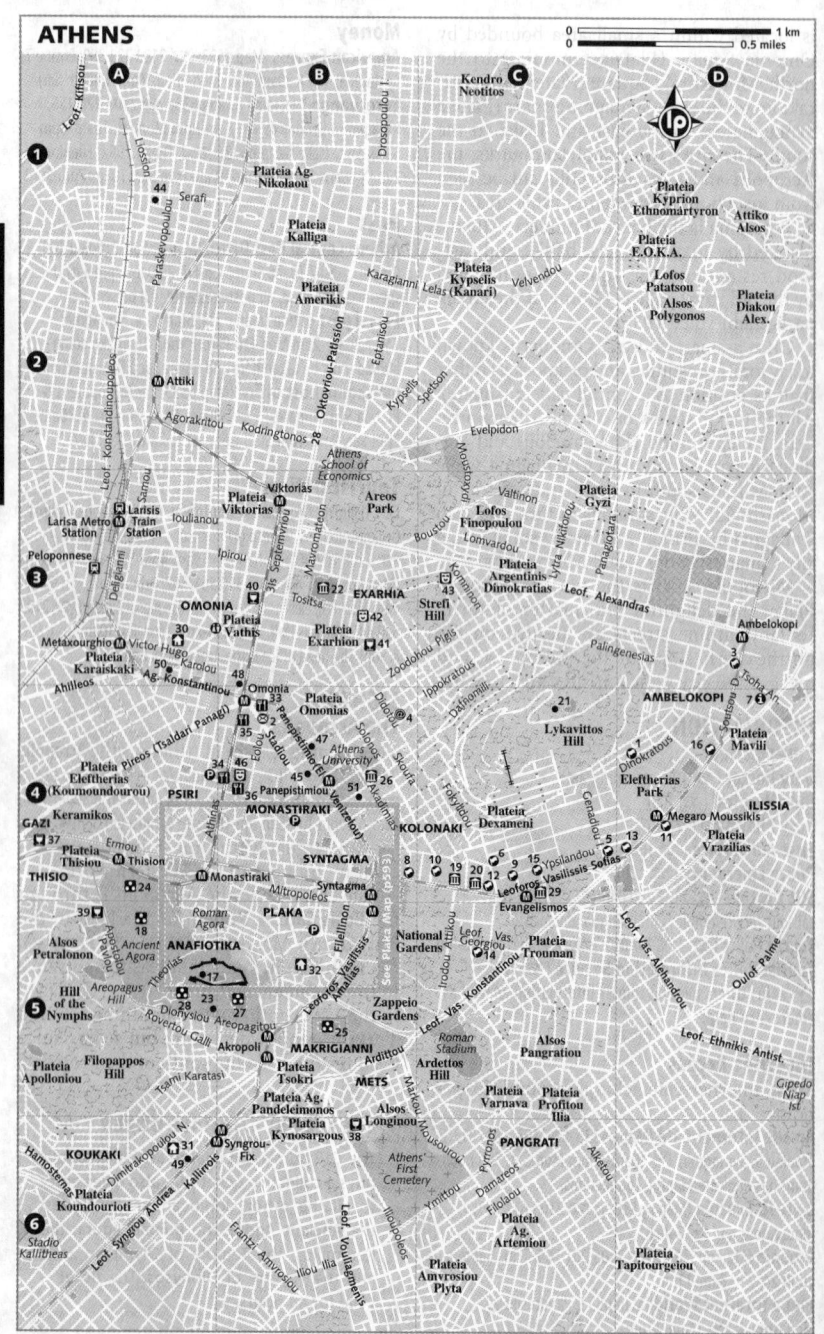

ATHENS

0 _____ 1 km
0 _____ 0.5 miles

A   **B**   Kendro **C**   **D**
Neotitos

Leof. Kifisou
Ilioni

1

Serafi
44

Plateia Ag.
Nikolaou

Plateia Kyprion
Ethnomartyron
Attiko
Alsos

Paraskevopoulou

Plateia
Kalliga

Plateia
E.O.K.A.

Karagianni Lelas (Kanari)

Plateia
Kypselis

Velvendou

Lofos
Patatsou
Alsos
Polygonos

Plateia
Diakou
Alex.

Plateia
Amerikis

Epaminou

Oktovriou-Patision

Kypselis
Spetson

Leof. Konstandinoupoleos

2

M Attiki

Agorakritou

Kodringtonos

28

Athens
School of
Economics

Evelpidon

Mouraouri

Valtinon

Plateia
Gyzi

Viktorias

Plateia
Viktorias

Areos
Park

Lofos
Finopoulou
Lomvardou

Plateia
Argentinis
Dimokratias

Leof. Alexandras

Ioannou

Loukianou

Plateia
Karaiskaki
50

Larisa Metro M
Station

Larisis
Train
Station

Peloponnese

Delfi

Ipirou

3is Septemvriou

Mavromateon

3

40
30

OMONIA

Plateia
Vathis

Tositsa

22 EXARHIA
42

Strefi
Hill
43

Plateia
Exarhion
41

Kountouri

Lykavittos
Hill
21

Ambelokipi
M

3

Plateia
Mavili

16
7

AMBELOKIPI

Metaxourghio M

Victor Hugo

Karolou

Ag. Konstandinou

48

33

M Omonia

Plateia
Omonias

Palingenesias

Dinokratous

Eleftherias
Park

Achilleos

Menandrou

35
2

47

Athens
University

Stournari

Skoufa

Dafnomili

Fokilidou

7

ILISSIA
Megaro Moussikis
M

13
11

Plateia
Vrazilias

Plateia
Pireos (Tsaldari Panagi)

34
46

Plateia
Eleftherias
(Koumoundourou)

36 M
PSIRI

51
26

45 Panepistimiou

KOLONAKI

Plateia
Dexameni

GAZI
37

Keramikos

Ermou

MONASTIRAKI

SYNTAGMA

Ypsilandou
5
29

Leoforos Vasilissis Sofias

Plateia
Thisiou
24

THISIO

39

Thision

M Monastiraki

Mitropoleos

Syntagma
M

8   10
19
20 2

6
15
9

Leof. Vas. Alexandrou

18

Roman
Agora

Filellinon

PLAKA
P

National
Gardens

Evangelismos
M

Leof. Georgiou

14

Vas.
Sofias

Plateia
Trouman

Alsos
Petralonon

Ancient
Agora

ANAFIOTIKA
17

32

Leoforos Vasilissis Amalias

Eleftherios Venizelou (Panepistimiou)

Leof. Vas. Konstandinou

Iroou Attikou

Plateia
Apolloniou

Hill
of the
Nymphs

Areopagus Hill

Apostolou Pavlou

Theorias

29
23
27

Dionysiou Areopagitou

Akropoli

Roverlou Galli

25

Zappeio
Gardens

Roman
Stadium

Alsos
Pangratiou

Oulof Palme

Filopappos
Hill

Tsami Karatasi

MAKRIGIANNI

Plateia
Tsokri

Plateia Ag.
Pandeleimonos

Ardittou

Ardettos
Hill

Plateia
Varnava

Plateia
Profitou
Ilia

Leof. Ethnikis Antist.

Gipedo
Niap

Plateia
Kynosargous

MErs

Alsos
Longinou

38

Athens'
First
Cemetery

PANGRATI

Hamostenas

KOUKAKI

Dimitrakopoulou N
31

49

Kallirois

M Syngrou-
Fix

Pyrronos

Damareos

Filolaou

Alketou

Plateia
Ag.
Artemiou

Plateia
Tapitourgeiou

Plateia
Koundourioti

Leof. Syngrou Andrea

Frantzi Amvrosiou

Iliou Ilia

Leof. Vouliagmenis

Ilioupoleos

Ymittou

Stadio
Kallitheas

Plateia
Amvrosiou
Plyta

4

5

6

INFORMATION				Goulandris Museum of Cycladic &				DRINKING	🖬 (p534)		
Albanian Embassy..............................	1	D4		Ancient Greek Art...........................	20	C4		+ Soda...	37	A4	
Athens Central Post Office................	2	B4		Lykavittos Hill....................................	21	C4		Half Note...	38	B6	
Australian Embassy............................	3	D3		National Archaeological Museum......	22	B3		Kirkis & Lizard..................................	39	A5	
C@fe4U Exarhia..................................	4	B4		Stoa of Eumenes...............................	23	A5		Rodon Club..	40	B3	
Canadian Embassy..............................	5	C4		Temple of Hephaestus......................	24	A4		Wunderbar...	41	B3	
Cypriot Embassy................................	6	C4		Temple of Olympian Zeus.................	25	B5					
EOT Head Office & Tourist Police......	7	D4		Theatre Museum................................	26	B4		ENTERTAINMENT	🖬 (pp534–5)		
French Embassy..................................	8	B4		Theatre of Dionysos..........................	27	B5		Aroma Gynekas................................	42	B3	
German Embassy................................	9	C4		Theatre of Herodes Atticus..............	28	A5		Decadence...	43	C3	
Italian Embassy..................................	10	C4		War Museum......................................	29	C4		Gagarin 205 Club..............................	44	A1	
Japanese Embassy..............................	11	D4						Hellenic Festival Box			
New Zealand Embassy........................	12	C4		SLEEPING	🏠 (pp532–3)			Office..	45	B4	
South African Embassy.......................	13	D4		Athens International Youth Hostel......	30	A3		Rembetika Stoa			
Turkish Embassy................................	14	C5		Marble House Pension.......................	31	A6		Athanaton..	46	B4	
UK Embassy..	15	C4		Student & Travellers' Inn...................	32	B5		Ticket House.....................................	47	B4	
US Embassy..	16	D4									
				EATING	🍴 (pp533–4)			TRANSPORT	(pp535–6)		
SIGHTS & ACTIVITIES	(pp529–32)			Bazaar Discount Supermarket............	33	B4		Olympic Airways................................	48	B3	
Acropolis..	17	A5		Fruit & Vegetable Market...................	34	B4		Olympic Airways Headquarters.........	49	A6	
Ancient Agora....................................	18	A5		Marinopoulos (Supermarket).............	35	B4		OSE Office..	50	A3	
Benaki Museum..................................	19	C4		Taverna Papandreou..........................	36	B4		OSE Office..	51	B4	

is the small, graceful **Temple of Athena Nike**, which is not accessible to visitors.

Standing supreme over the Acropolis is the monument that more than any other epitomises the glory of ancient Greece: the **Parthenon**. Completed in 438 BC, this building is unsurpassed in grace and harmony. To achieve perfect form, its lines were ingeniously curved to counteract optical illusions.

Above the columns are the remains of a Doric frieze. The best surviving pieces are the Parthenon Marbles, carted off to Britain by Lord Elgin in 1801 and controversially kept ever since in London's British Museum. The Parthenon, dedicated to Athena, contained an 11m-tall gold-and-ivory statue of the goddess completed in 438 BC by Phidias of Athens.

Just north is the **Erechtheion** and its much-photographed Caryatids, the six maidens who support its southern portico. These are plaster casts – the originals (except one taken by Lord Elgin) are in the site's **museum**.

South of the Acropolis

The importance of theatre in the life of the Athenian city-state can be gauged from the dimensions of the enormous **Theatre of Dionysos** (Map pp530-1; ☎ 2103 224 625; entrance on Dionysiou Areopagitou; adult/concession €2/1; ⏰ 8am-7pm May-Oct, 8am-sunset Nov-Apr), just south of the Acropolis. Built between 342 and 326 BC on the site of an earlier theatre, in its time it could hold 17,000 people spread over 64 tiers of seats. About 20 tiers survive.

The **Stoa of Eumenes**, a shelter and promenade for theatre audiences, runs west from the Theatre of Dionysos to the **Theatre of Herodes Atticus**, built in Roman times and used for performances during the Hellenic Festival.

Temple of Olympian Zeus

Begun in the 6th century BC, this massive **temple** (Map pp530-1; ☎ 2109 226 330; adult/concession €2/1; ⏰ 8.30am-3pm Tue-Sun) took more than 700 years to complete. Emperor Hadrian eventually finished the job in AD 131. It was the largest temple in Greece and is impressive for the sheer size of its 104 **Corinthian columns** (17m high with a base diameter of 1.7m).

Roman Stadium

The stadium, east of the Temple of Olympian Zeus, hosted the first Olympic Games of modern times in 1896. It was originally built in the 4th century BC as a venue for the Panathenaic athletic contests.

Ancient Agora

The **agora** (Map pp530-1; ☎ 2103 210 185; adult/concession €4/2; ⏰ 8.30am-3pm Tue-Sun) was the marketplace of ancient Athens and the focal point of civic and social life. The main monuments are the well-preserved **Temple of Hephaestus**, the 11th-century **Church of the Holy Apostles** and the reconstructed **Stoa of Attalos**, which houses the site's museum.

Roman Agora

The Romans built their **agora** (Map p533; ☎ 2103 245 220; cnr Pelopida Eolou & Markou Aureliou; adult/concession €2/1; ⏰ 8.30am-3pm Tue-Sun) just west of its ancient counterpart. Its principle monument is the wonderful **Tower of the Winds**, built in the 1st century BC by a Syrian astronomer named Andronicus.

Museums

One of the world's great museums, the **National Archaeological Museum** (Map p533; ☎ 2108

GREECE

FREE MUSEUMS

Athens has nearly 30 museums. The follow-ing free museums are interesting and well worth a visit.

Museum of Greek Popular Instruments (Map p533; ☎ 2103 254 119; Diogenous 1-3, Plaka; ⏱ 10am-2pm Tue-Sun, noon-6pm Wed) This popular museum has displays and re-cordings of traditional instruments.

War Museum (Map pp530-1; ☎ 2107 290 543/544; cnr Leof Vasilissis Sofias & Rizari 2; ⏱ 9am-2pm Tue-Fri, 9.30am-2pm Sat & Sun) An interesting histori-cal record of Greece in war through the ages.

Theatre Museum (Map pp530-1; ☎ 2103 629 430; Akadimias 50, Syntagma; ⏱ 9am-2pm Mon-Fri) Contains memorabilia from Greek theatre in the 19th and 20th centuries.

Centre of Folk Arts & Traditions (Map p533; ☎ 2103 243 987; Hatzimihali Angelikis 6, Plaka; ⏱ 9am-1pm & 5-9pm Tue-Fri, 9am-1pm Sat & Sun) Good displays of costumes, embroideries, musical instruments and pottery.

217 717; 28 Oktovriou-Patission 44; www.culture.gr; adult/concession €6/3; ⏱ 12.30-7pm Mon, 8am-7pm Tue-Sun Apr-Oct, 10.30am-5pm Mon, 8am-5pm Tue-Sun Nov-Mar) contains important finds from all the major archaeological sites around the country. The crowd-pullers are the magnificent, exqui-sitely detailed gold artefacts from Mycenae and spectacular Minoan frescoes from San-torini (Thira).

The sumptuous collection of Antoine Benaki is housed in the **Benaki Museum** (Map pp530-1; ☎ 2103 671 000; cnr Leof Vasilissis Sofias & Koum-bari 1, Kolonaki; adult/concession €6/3; ⏱ 9am-5pm Mon, Wed, Fri & Sat, 9am-midnight Thu, 9am-3pm Sun). The collection includes ancient sculpture, Per-sian, Byzantine and Coptic objects, Chinese ceramics, and two El Greco paintings.

The **Goulandris Museum of Cycladic & Ancient Greek Art** (Map pp530-1; ☎ 2108 015 870; Neofytou Douka 4; adult/concession €3.50/2; ⏱ 10am-4pm Mon & Wed-Fri, 10am-3pm Sat) was custom-built to display a fabulous collection of Cycladic art, with an emphasis on the early Bronze Age. Particu-larly beautiful are the marble figurines.

FESTIVALS & EVENTS

The annual **Hellenic Festival** (www.greekfestival .gr), running from mid-June to late Septem-ber, is the city's most important cultural event. It features a line-up of international music, dance and theatre at the Theatre of Herodes Atticus. Information and tickets (on sale three weeks before the event) are available from the **festival box office** (Map pp530-1; ☎ 2103 221 459; fax 2103 235 172; Stadiou 39, Syntagma; ⏱ 8.30am-4pm Mon-Fri, 9am-2.30pm Sat).

SLEEPING

Athens is a late-night and noisy city, so we've selected accommodation that is close to the action but lets you get some sleep. The Plaka district is the most popular place to stay, as it's well situated and has a good range of budget sleeping options. It fills up quickly in the high season period of July and August, so book well ahead for this time of year.

Athens International Youth Hostel (Map pp530-1; ☎ 2105 234 170; fax 2105 234 015; Victor Hugo 16; dm HI members €8.66, joining fee €15, daily stamp €2.50) Al-though it's long been popular with travellers, the dodgy location is a drawback. As long as you're not bothered by the junkies and pros-titutes who inhabit the district, the rooms are good value.

Tempi Hotel (Map p533; ☎ 2103 213 175; www .travelling.gr/tempihotel; Eolou 29, Monastiraki; s/d with shared bathroom €30/42, s/d/tr with private bathroom €40/48/60) A friendly, family-run hotel on the quiet pedestrian-precinct part of Eolou. Rooms at the front overlook pretty Plateia Agia Irini. With a communal kitchen, re-frigerator and a location close to the mar-kets, it's a good choice for self-caterers.

Student & Travellers' Inn (Map p533; ☎ 2103 244 808; www.studenttravellersinn.com; Kydathineon 16, Plaka; dm €15-22, s/d €45/50, d/tr with private bathroom €60/75; 🖾 💻) Despite a small hike in prices, this place is still a backpacker favourite. It's well run and has rooms that range widely in size. Facilities include a courtyard with big-screen TV, Internet access and a travel service.

Marble House Pension (Map pp530-1; ☎ 2109 234 058; www.marblehouse.gr; Zini 35A, Koukaki; d/tr €37/44, s/d/tr with bathroom €35/43/50) Located on a quiet cul-de-sac off Zini, this long-standing pension is one of Athens' better budget hotels. Rooms have a bar fridge, ceiling fans and safety boxes for valuables and air-con is available.

Also recommended are **Acropolis House Pen-sion** (Map p533; ☎ 2103 222 344; fax 2103 244 143; Ko-drou 6-8, Plaka; s/d €38.90/51.55, s/d/tr with bathroom from €64/80/96; 🖾) and **Hotel Adonis** (Map p533; ☎ 2103 249 737; fax 2103 231 602; Kodrou 3; s/d from €44/59; 🖾).

Athens has no camping ground that's conveniently placed for the city. The closest is **Athens Camping** (☎ 2105 814 114, fax 2105 820 353; Leof Athinon 198; per adult/tent €5/3; ⏰ year-round) located 7km west of the city centre on the road to Corinth. It has reasonable facilities, but little else going for it.

EATING

Although for travellers, eating in Athens is traditionally associated with a taverna meal in Plaka, city eating has become more diversified recently. Athens has plenty of places where you can eat and run. Locals grab a

coffee and a snack from a branch of the ubiquitous Flocafe's and a quick bite from a branch of the Everest sandwich shops.

Savas (Map p533; ☎ 2103 245 048; Mitropoleos 86; gyros €1.30; ⏰ 9am-3am) One of the best places to try a gyros – either pork, beef or chicken – all equally greasy and equally good.

O Platanos (Map p533; ☎ 2103 220 666; Diogenous 4, Plaka; mains €7; ⏰ noon-4.30pm, 7.30pm-midnight Mon-Sat, noon-4.30pm Sun) This unpretentious taverna serves up great home cooking. Try one of the lamb dishes and the barrel retsina that, for

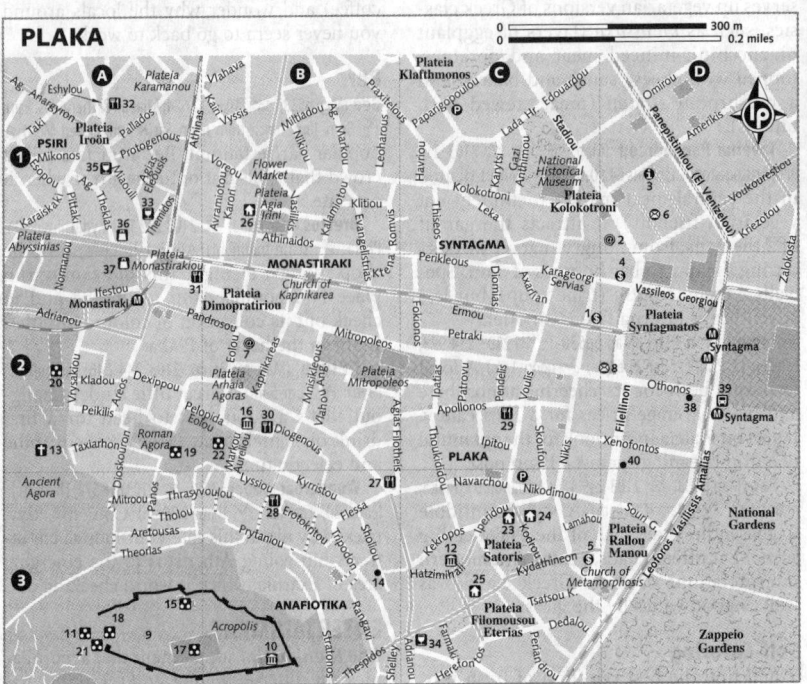

PLAKA

GREECE

once, is more suited for drinking than stripping the paint off a car. No credit cards.

Noodle House (Map p533; ☎ 2103 318 585; Apollonos 11, Plaka; mains €8; ⏰ 11am-midnight Mon-Sat, 5pm-midnight Sun) The pick of several Asian restaurants around Plaka, Noodle House serves up tasty Thai and Singapore noodles and soups at honest prices.

Eden Vegetarian Restaurant (Map p533; ☎ 2103 248 858; Lyssiou 12, Plaka; mains €4.70-8.50; ⏰ 11am-midnight Wed-Mon) The long-standing champion of vegetarian restaurants in Athens, Eden serves up vegetarian versions of Greek classics, such as *moussaka* (layers of eggplant or zucchini, minced meat and potatoes, topped with cheese sauce and baked) and a mushroom *stifado* (meat stewed with onions).

Taverna Papandreou (Map pp530-1; ☎ 2103 214 970; Aristogeitonos 1; mains €4.50-6.80; ⏰ 24hr) Located in the central meat market (definitely not vegetarian friendly), it attracts the gamut of Athenians, from hungry market workers during the day to bar hoppers at 5am. Specialties include *patsa* (tripe soup), but less adventurous taverna fare is on offer.

Taverna tou Psiri (Map pp530-1; ☎ 2103 214 923; Eshylou 12, Psiri; €25 for 2 people; ⏰ noon-1am) A local favourite, both for its cheerful atmosphere and below-average prices for a Psiri eatery. It's set off Plateia Iroön; look for the apt mural of a drunk leaning against a lamp post.

Eat (Map p533; ☎ 2103 249 129; Adrianou 91, Plaka; mains €12; ⏰ 10am-12.30am) A stylish antidote to the endless tavernas of the Plaka eating scene, Eat offers salads, pastas and modern interpretations of some Greek classics as well as good wines by the glass.

Self-Catering

You'll find the best selection of fresh produce at the fruit and vegetable market (map pp530-1) on Athinas, which is opposite the meat market. The main supermarkets in central Athens are **Bazaar Discount Supermarket** (Map pp530-1; Eolou 104, Omonia), **Marinopoulos** (Map pp530-1; Kanari 9, Kolonaki) and **Vasilopoulou** (Map pp530-1; Stadiou 19, Syntagma).

DRINKING

Athens has more than its fair share of drinking establishments. There are casual student hang-outs, and bars where you can flash your cash. During the summer months, however, most of the action heads for the islands. Outside summer, the bars of Kolonaki and Psiri are popular.

Cafés

Athens café society is as strong as ever, despite having some of the highest coffee prices in Europe. For the best experience of the Athens café scene, head for Kolonaki, where a mind-boggling array of cafés run off Plateia Kolonakiou on Skoufa and Tsakalof streets. Grab whatever free seats you can, settle in for drinking some slow frappé (frothy ice coffee) and wonder why the locals around you never seem to go back to work.

Bars

Bee (Map p533; ☎ 2103 212 624; Miaouli & Themidos, Psiri; ⏰ 8pm-1am, lunch from noon Sat & Sun, closed Mon) A popular bar/restaurant, Bee attracts a mixed crowd that spills out onto the street when it gets late.

Brettos (Map p533; ☎ 2103 232 110; Kydathineon 41, Plaka; ⏰ 10am-midnight) A distillery and bottle shop by day, at night this old family-run place is a popular stop to imbibe and to check out its collection of coloured bottles. Right in the heart of Plaka.

I Psyrra (Map p533; ☎ 2103 244 046; Miaouli 19, Psyrri; ⏰ 3pm-5am) A great little student hangout that's a good spot to head for a first drink on a night out. Plays excellent indie and eclectic tunes.

Wunderbar (Map pp530-1; ☎ 2103 818 577; Themistokleous 80, Exarhia; ⏰ 10am-3.30am) Cool by day, packed by night, this café-cum-lounge bar attracts hip young Athenians to the emerging area of Exarhia, which is worth checking out.

ENTERTAINMENT

The *Kathimerini* supplement that accompanies the *International Herald Tribune* has daily event listings, and the weekly *Athens News* carries an entertainment guide.

Gay & Lesbian Venues

Most gay nightlife is found around Makrigiann, south of the Temple of Olympian Zeus. Most places don't get going till midnight.

Aroma Gynekas (Map pp530-1; ☎ 2103 819 615; Tsamadou 15, Exarhia; ⏰ 10.30pm-late) Packed on weekends, this lesbian dance club is one of the busiest in Athens. It plays both mainstream and Greek music.

Kirkis & Lizard (Map pp530-1; ☎ 2103 466 960; Apostolou Pavlou 31, Thisio; ⏰ 10am-3am, Lizard 11pm-late Fri-Sun)

A popular gay and lesbian hang-out, Kirkis café is busy from late afternoon, and Lizard, the upstairs club, gets busy at weekends.

Clubbing

The clubs don't get busy until midnight, as most people stay at bar-restaurants until then. Expect to pay at least €5 for a beer. A cover charge usually applies, especially later in the week and when there's a guest DJ.

+ Soda (Map pp530-1; ☎ 2103 456 187; Ermou 161, Thisio; admission €10-20, including one drink; ☉ midnight-late, closed Jun-Aug) Multilevel superclub that features international guest DJs. Attracts a young group of clubbers who come for progressive and hardcore house and techno. **Decadence** (Map pp530-1; ☎ 2108 823 544; Voulgaroktonou 69, cnr Pouliherias, Lofos Strefi; admission €6-8, including one drink; ☉ 10.30pm-4am) For indie and alternative music lovers, Decadence has two levels of sonic mayhem, with a quieter bar scene on the lower floor and a club upstairs.

Live Music

Tickets for concerts are sold at **Ticket House** (Map pp530-1; ☎ 2103 608 366; Panepistimiou 42).

Rodon Club (Map pp530-1; ☎ 2105 247 427; Marni 24, Omonia; ☉ from 10pm) The city's main rock venue.

Gagarin 205 Club (Map pp530-1; ☎ 2108 547 601; Liossion 205; ☉ from 9.30pm) A newer and more intimate live venue.

Half Note (Map pp530-1; ☎ 2109 213 310; Trivonianou 17, Mets; ☉ from 10.30pm) The principal jazz venue in Athens.

Rembetika Stoa Athanaton (Map pp530-1; ☎ 2103 214 362; Sofokleous 19; ☉ 3-6pm & midnight-6am Mon-Sat, Oct-Apr) Located above the meat market, this is *the* place to experience the Greek version of the blues.

Dora Stratou Dance Company (Map p533; ☎ 2109 216 650; Filopappos Hill; tickets €13; ☉ 9.30pm Tues-Sat, 8.15pm Sun May-Sep) A colourful 90-minute traditional folk dancing show featuring more than 75 dancers and musicians.

SHOPPING

Athens offers excellent shopping opportunities. The most concentrated shopping is on Ermou, from Syntagma to Monastiraki, with clothes and shoes being the major attraction. The boutiques are scattered around Kolonaki; designers and jewellers are on Voukourestiou. Plaka and Monastiraki are full of souvenir and gift shops. You can pick up popular souvenirs such as backgammon sets, olive wood gifts, key rings, worry beads, and silver and gold jewellery.

Sandal wearers head for **Stavros Melissinos' Store** (Map p533; ☎ 2103 219 247; Aghias Theklas 2, Monastiraki) for some custom-made Jesus sandals and some poetry from the sandal maker.

If you're in Athens on a Sunday, it's essential to visit the **Sunday market** (Map p533; ☉ 7am-2pm), which starts at Plateia Monastiraki and goes onto Ermou.

GETTING THERE & AWAY
Air

Athens is served by **Eleftherios Venizelos International Airport** (☎ 2103 530 000; www.aia.gr) at Spata, 27km east of Athens. See Getting into Town (p528).

Most domestic flights are handled by Greece's often financially troubled national carrier, **Olympic Airways** (www.olympic-airways.gr); Head office (Map pp530-1; ☎ 2103 569 111; toll free 8011 144 444, flight information 2109 666 666 Leof Syngrou Andrea 96); Syntagma (Map p533; ☎ 2109 264 444; Filellinon 15) Omonia (Map pp530-1; ☎ 2109 267 218; Kotopouli Merakas 1).

Crete-based competitor **Aegean Airlines** (reservations ☎ 8011 120 000; www.aegeanair.com) offers flights to many of the same destinations as Olympic. It has a city sales office at **Syntagma** (Map p533; ☎ 2103 315 502; Othonos 10).

Bus

Athens has two main intercity bus stations. EOT gives out schedules for both stations that detail fares and departure times.

Terminal A (☎ 2105 298 740; Kifissou 100), northwest of Omonia, has buses to the Peloponnese, Ionian Islands and western Greece. To get to Terminal A, take bus No 015 from the junction of Zinonos and Menandrou, near Plateia Omonia.

Terminal B (☎ 2108 317 096; off Liossion; north of Omonia) has departures to central and northern Greece, plus to Evia. To get to Terminal B, take bus No 024 from outside the main gate of the National Gardens on Amalias. Hop off at Liossion 260, turn right onto Gousiou and the terminal is at the end of the road.

Buses for Attica leave from the Mavromateon bus terminal at the junction of Alexandras and 28 Oktovriou-Patission.

Hitching

Athens is a difficult place to hitchhike from. Ask the truck drivers at the Piraeus cargo wharves. Otherwise, for the Peloponnese, take a bus from Panepistimiou to Dafni, where National Rd 8 begins. For northern Greece, take the metro to Kifissia, then a bus to Nea Kifissia and walk to National Rd 1. In any case, keep in mind that hitching is never entirely safe, and Lonely Planet doesn't recommend it.

Train
When the city's new **Central Station** at Arharnon opens in 2005 all intercity train services will leave from there. Until it opens, trains to central and northern Greece leave from Larsis train station (Map pp530-1) and trains to the Peloponnese leave from the Peloponnese station, which is 200m away from Larsis.

More information on services is available from the **OSE offices** (Omonia Map pp530-1; ☎ 2105 240 647; Karolou 1; ☻ 8am-6pm Mon-Fri, 8am-3pm Sat); Syntagma (Map p533; ☎ 2103 624 402; Sina 6; ☻ 8am-3.30pm Mon-Fri, 8am-3pm Sat).

GETTING AROUND
The new metro system has made getting around central Athens (and to Piraeus) very easy, but Athens' road traffic is still horrendous. A daily travel pass, valid for all forms of public transport, including a trip to/from the airport, costs €2.90.

Bus & Trolleybus
Blue-and-white suburban buses run from 5am to midnight. Route numbers and destinations, but not the actual routes, are listed on the free EOT map. Timetables can be obtained from its website (www.gnto.gr), or from the **Athens Urban Transport Organisation** (OASA; www.oasa.gr).

Special buses operate 24 hours a day to Piraeus (every 20 minutes from 6am to midnight, then hourly until 6am). Bus No 040 leaves from the corner of Syntagma and Filellinon, and No 049 leaves from the Omonia end of Athinas.

Tickets for all these services cost €0.45, and must be purchased before you board – either from a ticket booth or from *periptera* (street kiosks).

Metro
The first phase of the long-awaited new metro system transformed travel around central Athens. For the latest metro information, visit www.ametro.gr. The following

is a brief outline of the three lines that make up the network:

Line 1 (Green) This line is the old Kifissia–Piraeus line. It is indicated in green on maps and signs. Useful stops include Piraeus (for the port), Monastiraki and Omonia (city centre), Plateia Viktorias (National Archaeological Museum) and Irini (Olympic Stadium).

Line 2 (Red) This line runs from Sepolia in the northwest to Dafni in the southeast. It is indicated in red on maps and signs. Useful stops include Larisa (for the train stations), Omonia, Panepistimiou and Syntagma (city centre) and Akropoli (Makrigianni).

Line 3 (Blue) This line runs northeast from Syntagma to Ethniki Amyna. It is indicated in blue on maps and signs. Useful stops are Evangelismos (for the museums on Vasilissis Sofias) and Ethniki Amyna (buses to the airport). Syntagma is the transfer station for Line 2.

Travel on lines 2 and 3 costs €0.75, while Line 1 is split into three sections: Piraeus–Monastiraki, Monastiraki–Attiki and Attiki–Kifissia. Travel within one section costs €0.60, and a journey covering two or more sections costs €0.75. The metro operates from 5am to midnight. Trains run every three minutes during peak periods, and every 10 minutes at other times.

Taxi
Athenian taxis are yellow. The flag fall is €0.75, and there's an additional surcharge of €0.60 from ports and train and bus stations, as well as a €1.18 surcharge from the airport. After that, the day rate (tariff 1 on the meter) is €0.23/km. The rate doubles between midnight and 5am (tariff 2 on the meter). Baggage is charged at the rate of €0.30 per item heavier than 10kg. The minimum fare is €1.50, which covers most journeys in central Athens.

AROUND ATHENS

PIRAEUS ΠΕΙΡΑΙΑΣ
pop 175,697
Greece's main port, and one of the main ports of the Mediterranean, Piraeus is the hub of the Aegean ferry network. The streets that most travellers see going to catch a ferry are every bit as traffic-clogged as in Athens, but a trip to tranquil and picturesque Mikrolimano (Small Harbour), with its cafés and restaurants, reveals another side to Piraeus.

Piraeus consists of a peninsula surrounded by three harbours, the largest being the Great Harbour (Megas Limin), where all the boats depart from. Zea Marina (Limin Zeas) and Mikrolimano, on the eastern side of the peninsula, are for private yachts. An Internet café, **Internet Center** (☎ 2104 111 261; Akti Poseidonos 24; ⏰ 10am-11pm),

is on the main road across from the main harbour.

If you're sightseeing in Athens for more than a few days, **Mikrolimano** makes a great break from the chaos of the inner city. Cafés, seafood restaurants and bars line the harbour, and **Istioploikos** (☎ 2104 134 084; ⏰ 10am-3am), part of the yacht club, is a café

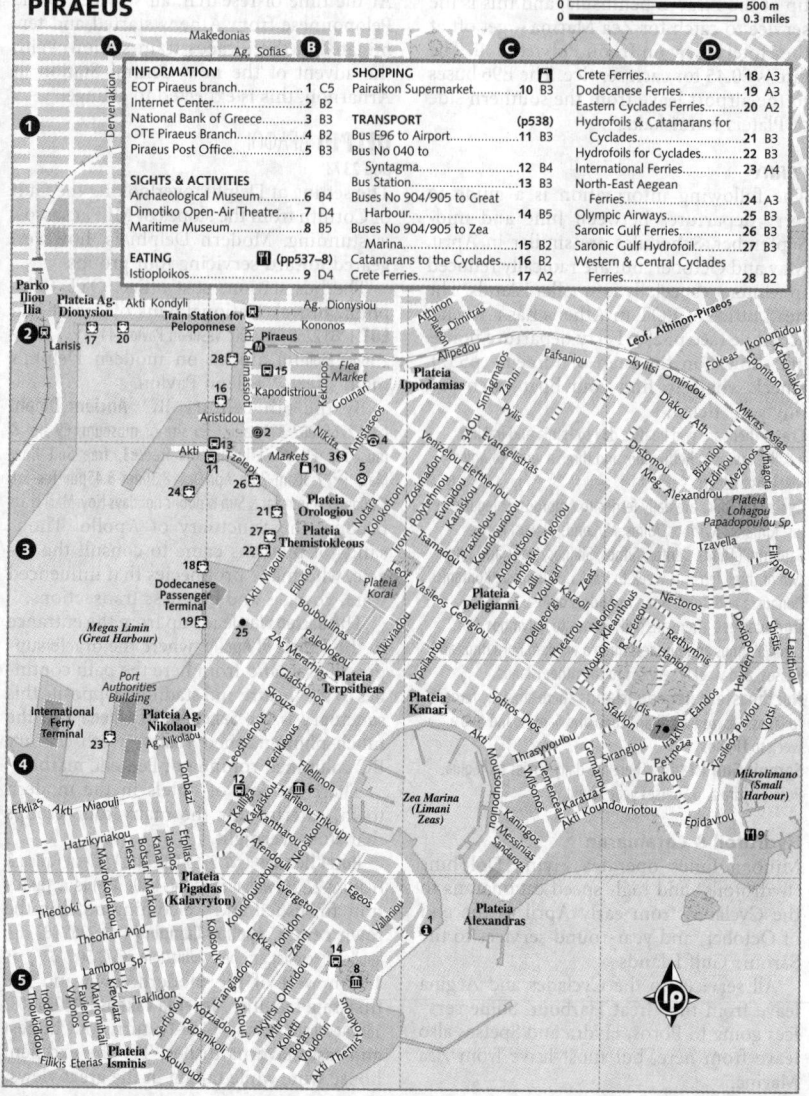

PIRAEUS

0 ———————————————— 500 m
0 ———————————————— 0.3 miles

INFORMATION				SHOPPING			Crete Ferries..........................18 A3
EOT Piraeus branch...............1 C5				Pairaikon Supermarket............10 B3			Dodecanese Ferries................19 A3
Internet Center.....................2 B2							Eastern Cyclades Ferries........20 A2
National Bank of Greece........3 B3				TRANSPORT		(p538)	Hydrofoils & Catamarans for
OTE Piraeus Branch...............4 B2				Bus E96 to Airport..................11 B3			Cyclades............................21 B3
Piraeus Post Office................5 B3				Bus No 040 to			Hydrofoils for Cyclades..........22 B3
				Syntagma..........................12 B4			International Ferries...............23 A4
SIGHTS & ACTIVITIES				Bus Station............................13 B3			North-East Aegean
Archaeological Museum.........6 B4				Buses No 904/905 to Great			Ferries................................24 A3
Dimotiko Open-Air Theatre....7 D4				Harbour..............................14 B5			Olympic Airways....................25 B3
Maritime Museum..................8 B5				Buses No 904/905 to Zea			Saronic Gulf Ferries................26 B3
				Marina................................15 B2			Saronic Gulf Hydrofoil............27 B3
EATING		(pp537–8)		Catamarans to the Cyclades.....16 B2			Western & Central Cyclades
Istioploikos...........................9 D4				Crete Ferries..........................17 A2			Ferries................................28 B2

with a panoramic view by day and a lively and fun bar by night.

Getting There & Away

BUS

Two 24-hour bus services operate between central Athens and Piraeus. Bus No 049 runs from Omonia to the Great Harbour, and bus No 040 runs from Syntagma to the tip of the Piraeus peninsula, and this is the service to catch for Zea Marina – get off at the Hotel Savoy on Iroön Polytehniou. The fare is €0.45 for each service. The E96 buses to the airport leave from the southern side of Plateia Karaïskaki.

FERRY

The following information is a guide to ferry departures between June and mid-September. Schedules are similar in April, May and October, but are radically reduced in winter – especially to smaller islands. The head office of EOT in Athens has a weekly schedule (see p529). Ferry departure points are shown on the map of Piraeus (p537). Check where to find your boat when you buy your ticket.

Crete There are two boats a day to Hania and Iraklio; a daily service to Rethymno; and three a week to Agios Nikolaos and Sitia.

Cyclades There are daily ferries to Amorgos, Folegandros, Ios, Kimolos, Kythnos, Milos, Mykonos, Naxos, Paros, Santorini (Thira), Serifos, Sifnos, Sikinos, Syros and Tinos; two or three ferries a week to Iraklia, Shinoussa, Koufonisi, Donoussa and Anafi; none to Andros or Kea.

Dodecanese There are daily ferries to Kalymnos, Kos, Leros, Patmos and Rhodes; three a week to Karpathos and Kassos; and weekly services to the other islands.

Northeastern Aegean Islands There are daily ferries to Chios, Lesvos (Mytilini), Ikaria and Samos; and two a week to Limnos.

Saronic Gulf Islands There are daily ferries to Aegina, Poros, Hydra and Spetses year-round.

Hydrofoil & Catamaran

Minoan Lines operates Flying Dolphins (hydrofoils) and high-speed catamarans to the Cyclades from early April to the end of October, and year-round services to the Saronic Gulf Islands.

All services to the Cyclades and Aegina leave from the Great Harbour. Some services going to Poros, Hydra and Spetses also leave from here, but most leave from Zea Marina.

METRO

The fastest and most convenient link between the Great Harbour and Athens is the metro. The station is close to the ferries, at the northern end of Akti Kalimassioti. There are metro trains every 10 minutes from 5am to midnight.

TRAIN

At the time of research, all services to the Peloponnese from Athens started and terminated at the Piraeus train station. With the advent of the new Central Station at Arharnon, this is expected to change.

DELPHI ΔΕΛΦΟΙ

pop 2373

The setting at Delphi, overlooking the Gulf of Corinth from the slopes of Mt Parnassos, is stunning. Modern Delphi is, however, geared toward servicing tour groups.

The bus station, post office, OTE (telephone office), National Bank of Greece and **EOT** (☎ 2265 082 900; Vasileon Pavlou 44; ⏱ 7.30am-2.30pm Mon-Fri) are all on modern Delphi's main street, Vasileon Pavlou.

By the 6th century BC, **Ancient Delphi** (☎ 2265 082 312; adult €6 site or museum, €9 site & museum, EU/non-EU students free/€3, free Sun Nov-Mar; ⏱ 7.30am-7pm Apr-Oct, 8.30am-6.45pm Tue-Fri, 8.30am-2.45pm Sat & Sun & public holidays Nov-Mar) had become the Sanctuary of Apollo. Thousands of pilgrims came to consult the oracle, who made prophecies that influenced wars, voyages and business transactions.

The **Sacred Way** leads up from the entrance to the **Temple of Apollo**, where the oracle supposedly sat, and from here the path continues to the theatre and stadium. Opposite this sanctuary is the **Sanctuary of Athena** and the much-photographed **Tholos**, a 4th-century BC columned rotunda of Pentelic marble.

There are lots of hotels in the modern town, catering for the many tour groups that stop overnight.

Hotel Hermes (☎ 2265 082 318; Vasileon Pavlou & Friderikis 27; s/d with breakfast €34/40; ✹) is a tastefully furnished and welcoming hotel in the town centre. **Apollon Camping** (☎ 2265 082 762; apollon4@otenet.gr; per adult/tent €5/3.50; ✹) is 1.5km west of the modern town and has first-rate facilities. **Taverna Vakhos** (☎ 2265 083 186; Apollonos 31; mains €4.50-11) turns out honest and tasty taverna dishes. Try the excellent house wine while taking in the great views.

Buses to Delphi from Athens (€10.90, three hours, six daily) leave from the **bus station** (☎ 2266 082 317).

SARONIC GULF ISLANDS
ΝΗΣΙΆ ΤΟΥ ΣΑΡΩΝΙΚΟΎ

The five Saronic Gulf Islands are the closest island group to Athens. Their proximity to the congested capital makes them a popular escape, so accommodation is scarce during summer and weekends year-round. **Aegina** is the closest island to Athens and a popular destination for day-trippers. **Hydra** is the most stylish destination of the island group and has a fine natural harbour. The main attraction is the tranquillity as there are no motorised vehicles. Pine-covered **Spetses** is perhaps the most beautiful island in the group.

THE PELOPONNESE
ΠΕΛΟΠΌΝΝΗΣΟΣ

The Peloponnese is a region of outstanding beauty situated at the southern extremity of the rugged Balkan Peninsula. It's linked to the rest of Greece by the narrow Isthmus of Corinth, yet it feels like an island destination.

The Peloponnese has played a major role in Greek history, one of the main sites being Olympia, birthplace of the Olympic Games. Other highlights are Mycenae, Epidavros and Corinth in the northeast – all within easy striking distance of the pretty Venetian town of Nafplio. In the south, romantic Monemvasia is a highlight, and the rugged Mani Peninsula is famous for its spectacular wild flowers in spring.

PATRA ΠΆΤΡΑ
pop 160,400

Patra, Greece's third-largest city, is the principal port for ferries to Italy and the Ionian Islands. Despite its long history, stretching back 3000 years, today few travellers hang around any longer than it takes to catch that next connection. The city is laid out on a grid that stretches uphill from the port to the old *kastro* (castle). Most services are along the waterfront, known as Othonos Amalias, in the middle of town, and Iroön Politehniou to the north. The train station is in the middle of town on Othonos Amalias, and the main bus station is close by.

Information
EOT (☎ 2610 620 353; outside the international arrival terminal; ☾ 7am-8pm)
Main post office (cnr Zaïmi & Mezonos; ☾ 7.30am-8pm Mon-Fri, 7.30am-2pm Sat, 9am-1.30pm Sun)
National Bank of Greece (Plateia Trion Symahon; ☾ 8am-2pm Mon-Thu, 8am-1.30pm Fri & 6-8.30pm Mon-Fri)
Netrino Internet Café (☎ 2610 623 344; Karaïskaki 133; ☾ 10am-2am)

Sleeping & Eating
Pension Nicos (☎ 2610 623 757; cnr Patreos & Agiou Andreou 121; d/tr €30/40, s/d/tr with bathroom €20/35/45) The best budget choice in town, it has hot water and clean sheets, and is just up from the waterfront.

Europa Centre (☎ 2610 437 006; Othonos Amalias 10; mains €5.50-7; ☾ 7am-midnight) A convenient cafeteria-style place close to the international ferry dock, Europa serves up decent taverna fare and vegetarian meals.

Getting There & Away
The **KTEL Achaias bus station** (☎ 2610 623 888; Othonos Amalias) has buses to Athens (€12.90, three hours, half-hourly) via Corinth. There are also 10 buses daily to Pyrgos (for Olympia).

Buses to the Ionian islands of Kefallonia and Lefkada leave from the **KTEL Kefallonia bus station** (☎ 2610 277 854; Othonos Amalias). Buses to Zakynthos leave from the **KTEL Zakynthos bus station** (☎ 2610 220 219; Othonos Amalias 58). These services travel via the port of Kyllini.

There are four slow trains to Athens (€5.30, five hours) and five express trains (€10, 3½ hours), as well as trains to Pyrgos and to Kalamata.

There are daily ferries to Kefallonia (€11.50, 2½ hours), Ithaki (€11.70, 3¾ hours) and Corfu (€21, seven hours). Ticket agencies line the waterfront.

CORINTH ΚΟΡΙΝΘΟΣ
pop 29,787

Modern Corinth (ko-rin-thoss), 6km west of the Corinth Canal, is an uninspiring town but a convenient base from which to visit **Ancient Corinth** (☎ 2741 031 207; site & museum €4; ☾ 8am-7pm Apr-Oct, 8am-5pm Nov-Mar), which lies 7km southwest of the modern city. There is little left of the ancient Greek city apart from the imposing **Temple of Apollo**; the other remains are Roman. Towering over the site is Acrocorinth, the ruins of an ancient citadel.

GREECE

Hotel Apollon (☎ 2741 022 587; hotapol@otenet.gr; Pirinis 18; s/d with bathroom €40/50; 🔣), located near the train station, is the best of Corinth's budget hotels. The rooms generally go for €25/30 outside peak season. **Blue Dolphin Campground** (☎ 2741 025 766; skoupos@otenet .gr; per adult/tent €5.50/4; 🚗) is a well-organised site with its own stretch of pebble beach, 4km west of town near the port of Lecheon. Buses from Corinth can drop you here. **Restaurant To 24 Hours** (☎ 2741 083 201; Agiou Nikolaou 19; mains €3.25-7.35) turns out an ever-changing selection of taverna favourites.

Buses to Athens (€6, 1½ hours, half-hourly) leave from the **KTEL Korinthos bus station** (☎ 2741 075 424; Dimocratias 4) opposite the train station. Buses to Ancient Corinth (€0.90, 20 minutes, hourly) and Lecheon leave from here. Buses to Nafplio leave from the **Argolis bus station** (junction of Ethnikis Antistaseos & Aratou).

There are 14 trains a day to Athens, five of which are intercity services. There are also trains to Kalamata, Nafplio and Patra.

NAFPLIO ΝΑΥΠΛΙΟ
pop 13,822

The narrow streets in the old quarter of Nafplio, one of Greece's prettiest towns, are filled with elegant Venetian houses and neoclassical mansions. There's a **municipal tourist office** (☎ 2752 024 444; 25 Martiou; 🕑 9am-1.30pm & 4-8pm). Terrific views of the Old Town and the surrounding coast can be seen from the magnificent hilltop **Palamidi Fortress** (☎ 2752 028 036; €4; 🕑 8am-6.45pm summer, 8am-5pm outside summer).

The Old Town is the place to stay, and the most affordable is **Dimitris Bekas** (☎ 2752 024 594; Efthimiopoulou 26; s/d/tr with shared bathroom €16/22/27), a decent budget pension with agreat location above the church on the slopes of the Akronafplia.

The streets of the Old Town of Nafplio are filled with restaurants. Staïkopoulou, in particular, is a very busy eat street. **Taverna Paleo Arhontiko** (☎ 2752 022 449; cnr Ypsilandou & Sofroni; mains €4.40-7.65), one of the most popular tavernas in town, has excellent food and live music after 10pm in summer.

The **KTEL Argolis bus station** (☎ 2752 027 323; Syngrou 8) has hourly buses to Athens (€9, 2½ hours) via Corinth, as well as services to Argos (for Peloponnese connections), Mycenae and Epidavros.

MYCENAE ΜΥΚΗΝΕΣ

Ancient Mycenae (☎ 2751 076 585; €6; 🕑 8am-7pm Apr-Oct, 8am-5pm Nov-Mar) was the most powerful influence in Greece between 1600 and 1200BC. The rise and fall of Mycenae is shrouded in myth, but it was settled as early as the sixth millennium BC. Mycenae's entrance, the **Lion Gate**, is Europe's oldest monumental sculpture.

Excavations of **Grave Circle A** by Heinrich Schliemann in the 1870s uncovered magnificent gold treasures (such as the **Mask of Agamemnon**) now on display at the National Archaeological Museum (pp530-1).

Most people visit on day trips from Nafplio, and there are buses to Mycenae from Argos and Nafplio.

SPARTA ΣΠΑΡΤΗ
pop 14,817

Modern, neat and relaxed, Sparta (*spar-tee*) is in stark contrast to its ancient image of discipline and deprivation. It makes a convenient base from which to visit Mystras. Sparta's street grid system sees Palaeologou running north–south through the town and Lykourgou running east–west. The **municipal tourist office** (☎ 2731 024 852; Plateia Kentriki; 🕑 8am-2.30pm Mon-Fri) is in the town hall.

Hotel Cecil (☎ 2731 024 980; fax 2731 081 318; Palaeologou 125; s/d €35/45; 🔣) is a family-run place that has clean comfortable rooms with TV. **Camping Paleologou Mystras** (☎ 2731 022 724; fax 2731 025 256; per adult/tent €4/3.50; 🕑 year-round; 🚗), 2km west of Sparta, is friendly and well-organised with good facilities. Buses to Mystras can drop you there. **Restaurant Elysse** (☎ 2731 029 896; Palaeologou 113; mains €4.50-8.90) offers Lakonian specialities such as *bardouniotiko* (chicken cooked with onions and feta cheese).

Sparta's well-organised **KTEL Lakonias bus station** (☎ 2731 026 441; cnr Lykourgou & Thivronos) has buses to Athens (€13.30, 3¼ hours, 10 daily), Monemvasia (three daily) and Kalamata (two daily). There are frequent buses to Mystras (€0.90, 30 minutes).

MYSTRAS ΜΥΣΤΡΑΣ

The magnificent **ruins of Mystras** (☎ 2731 083 377; adult/concession €6/3; 🕑 8am-6pm Apr-Oct, 8am-3.30pm Nov-Mar), 7km from Sparta, were once the shining light of the Byzantine world. The streets of Mystras are lined with palaces, monasteries and churches, most of them dating from between 1271 and 1460.

GEFYRA & MONEMVASIA
ΓΕΦΥΡΑ & ΜΟΝΕΜΒΑΣΙΑ

Monemvasia, 99km southeast from Sparta, might no longer be an undiscovered paradise, but tourism hasn't lessened the impact of this extraordinary town. Separated from mainland Gefyra by an earthquake in AD 375, Monemvasia occupies a great outcrop of rock that rises dramatically from the sea. From the causeway, a road curves around the base of the rock for about 1km until it comes to a narrow tunnel in the massive fortifying wall, from which you emerge, blinking, into magical Monemvasia.

The cobbled main street is flanked by stairways leading to a complex network of stone houses with tiny walled gardens and courtyards. Signposted steps lead to the ruins of the **fortress** built by the Venetians in the 16th century. From here you can explore the Byzantine **Church of Agia Sophia**, perched precariously on the edge of the cliff.

All the tourist facilities are based in Gefyra. Malvasia Travel just up from the causeway acts as the bus stop, and the National Bank of Greece and the **post office** (🕙 7.30am-2pm Mon-Fri) are opposite.

There is no budget accommodation in Monemvasia, but there are *domatia* (rooms to rent) in Gefyra, as well as cheap hotels. However, romantic Monemvasia is certainly worth breaking the budget for. One option is **Hotel Monemvasia** (☎ 2732 061 381; fax 2732 061 707; s/d with bathroom €30/40), a small modern hotel 500m north of Gefyra on the road to Molai. It has large balconies with views. **Malvasia Hotel** (☎ 2732 061 113; fax 2732 061 722; d €45-78, tr €60, 4-person apt €70-150; 🔀) offers a variety of excellent rooms. Prices include breakfast. **Camping Paradise** (☎ 2732 061 123; paradise@otenet.gr; per adult/tent €5/3; 🕙 year-round), 3.5km from Gefyra, is the nearest camping ground, a pleasant, well-shaded place with good facilities.

Taverna O Botsalo (☎ 2732 061 491; Gefyra; mains €5.70-23.50) serves up tasty meals overlooking the port in Gefyra. **Matoula** (☎ 2732 061 660; Monemvasia; mains €6-12), on the main street, is the pick of the bunch in the Old Town. Grab a table on the terrace, and try the tasty local *barbounia* (red mullet).

Buses leave from outside **Malvasia Travel** (☎ 2732 061 752), where you can pick up tickets. There are buses to Athens (€20, 5½ hours, four daily), travelling via Sparta, Tripolis and Corinth.

The Flying Dolphin hydrofoil service to Monemvasia is currently suspended. Visit www.dolphins.gr for updates.

GYTHIO ΓΥΘΕΙΟ
pop 4489

Once the port of ancient Sparta, Gythio (*yee*-thih-o) is a bustling, attractive fishing town at the head of the Lakonian Gulf and the gateway to the rugged Mani Peninsula to the south. Picturesque **Marathonisi Islet** is linked to the mainland by a causeway. According to mythology, this islet is ancient Cranae, where Paris (Prince of Troy) and Helen (the wife of Menelaus of Sparta) consummated their affair, sparking the Trojan War. An 18th-century tower on the islet has been turned into the **Museum of Mani History** (☎ 2733 024 484; admission €1.50; 🕙 9am-7pm).

Xenia Karlaftis Rooms to Rent (☎ 2733 022 719; s/d/tr €25/35/40), opposite the causeway to Marathonisi, is the pick of the budget options. It has clean rooms and a communal kitchen. **Camping Meltemi** (☎ 2733 022 833; www .campingmeltemi.gr; per adult/tent €5/4; 🕙 year-round) is the pick of the camp sites along the coast south of town. It's situated right behind the beach, 3km south of Gythio. Buses to Areopoli stop outside. The waterfront is lined with countless fish *tavernas*.

The **KTEL Lakonias bus station** (☎ 2733 022 228; cnr Vasileos Georgios & Evrikleos) has buses to Athens (€16.30, 4¼ hours, five daily) via Sparta (€2.90, one hour) and south to Areopoli (€1.80, 30 minutes, four daily), Gerolimenas (€4, 1¼ hours, two daily), and one to the Diros Caves (€2.50, one hour).

ANEN Lines (www.anen.gr) runs ferries between June and September to Kissamos on Crete (€19.20, seven hours, five weekly) via Kythira (€8.90, 2½ hours). Check with **Rozakis Travel** (☎ 2733 022 207; rosakigy@otenet.gr) for ferry times.

THE MANI Η ΜΑΝΗ

The Mani covers the central peninsula in the south of the Peloponnese and is divided into two regions, the Lakonian (inner) Mani in the south and the Messinian (outer) Mani in the northwest, below Kalamata.

Lakonian Mani

The wild and remote Lakonian Mani has a landscape dotted with the striking stone-tower houses that are a feature of the region.

In spring, the barren countryside briefly bursts into life with a spectacular display of wild flowers.

The region's principal village is **Areopoli**, 30km southwest of Gythio. There are several fine towers on the narrow, cobbled streets of the Old Town at the lower end of the main street, Kapetan Matepan.

Just south of here are the magnificent **Diros Caves** (☎ 2733 052 222; adult/concession €12/6; 🕑 8am-5.30pm Jun-Sep, 8am-3pm Oct-May), where a subterranean river flows. **Gerolimenas**, 20km further south, is a tranquil fishing village built around a sheltered bay. Most accommodation in the Lakonian Mani is in Areopoli.

Tsimova Rooms (☎ 2733 051 301; Kapetan Matepan; s/d €25/40, apt €45) has cosy rooms tucked away behind the Church of Taxiarhes. **Nicola's Corner Taverna** (☎ 2733 051 366; Plateia Athanaton; mains €4-7) is a popular spot on the central square and has a good choice of tasty taverna staples.

The **bus station** (☎ 2733 051 229; Plateia Athanaton) in Areopoli is the focal point of the local bus network. Buses go to Gythio and Sparta, Gerolimenas and Itilo, and Diros Caves.

Messinian Mani

The Messinian Mani runs north along the coast from Itilo to Kalamata. The region has excellent beaches set against the dramatic backdrop of the Taygetos Mountains. The picturesque coastal village of **Kardamyli**, 37km south of Kalamata, is a favourite destination for trekkers. Many of the walks incorporate the spectacular **Vikos Gorge** (p543).

Olympia Koumounakou rooms (☎ 2721 073 623; s/d €20/28), a favourite with budget travellers, has clean comfortable beds and a communal kitchen. It's signposted opposite the post office. There are several village tavernas, the best being **Lela's Taverna**.

There are buses from Kalamata to Itilo (two daily), stopping at Kardamyli and Stoupa.

OLYMPIA ΟΛΥΜΠΙΑ
pop 1286

The site of ancient Olympia is 500m past the modern town, surrounded by the foothills of Mt Kronion. On the main street there is a well-organised **municipal tourist office** (☎ 2624 023 100; Praxitelous Kondyli; 🕑 9am-9pm Jun-Sep, 8am-2.45pm Mon-Sat Oct-May), which also changes money.

Ancient Olympia was a sacred place of temples, priests' dwellings and public buildings, as well as the venue for the Olympic Games, first staged in 776 BC. The city-states were bound by a sacred truce to stop fighting for three months and compete.

Ancient Olympia (☎ 2624 022 517; museum adult/concession €6/3, site & museum €9/5; 🕑 8am-7pm Apr-Oct, 8am-5pm Mon-Fri, 8.30am-3pm Sat & Sun Nov-Mar) is dominated by the immense ruins of the **Temple of Zeus**, to whom the games were dedicated. In the museum, the statue of **Hermes of Praxiteles** is a classical sculpture masterpiece.

The **Youth Hostel** (☎ 2624 022 580; Praxitelous Kondyli 18; dm €8) has free hot showers. There are more budget options around the corner on Stefanopoulou. **Taverna To Steki tou Vangeli** (☎ Stefanopoulou 13; mains €2.95-6.75) represents better value than most of Olympia's tavernas.

There are buses to Olympia from Athens (€20, 5½ hours, four daily) and regular buses to Pyrgos, 24km away on the coast.

NORTHERN GREECE
ΒΟΡΕΙΑ ΕΛΛΑΔΑ

Northern Greece comprises Epiros, with its stark and rugged mountains, Macedonia, with its rich archaeological sites and shimmering lakes, and Thrace, where rolling plains front forested mountains laced with meandering rivers.

IGOUMENITSA ΗΓΟΥΜΕΝΙΤΣΑ
pop 9104

The west-coast port of Igoumenitsa (ih-goo-meh-*nit*-sah) is a transport hub for ferries to Corfu and Italy.

If you need to stay the night, you'll find signs for domatia around the port. Try the aptly named **Rooms to Let** (☎ 2665 023 612; Xanthou 12; s/d €30/38), where the rooms are decent enough and handy for the ferry.

From the **bus station** (☎ 2665 022 309; Kyprou 29) there are buses to Ioannina (€6.40, two hours, nine daily) and Athens (€29.80, eight hours, five daily).

There are ferries to Corfu (€5.10, 1¾ hours, hourly) and to the Italian ports of Ancona, Bari, Brindisi, Trieste and Venice.

IOANNINA ΙΩΑΝΝΙΝΑ
pop 61,629

Ioannina (ih-o-*ah*-nih-nah), on the western shore of Lake Pamvotis, is the capital and largest town in Epiros. It was a major commercial and intellectual centre during Ottoman rule and still retains these attributes today. The town centre is around Plateia Dimokratias, and all facilities are nearby, such as the **EOT** (☎ 2651 041 142; Dodonis 39; ⏰ 7.30am-2.30pm). **Robinson Expeditions** (☎ 2651 029 402; www.robinson.gr; Mitropoleos 23) is an outfit that specialises in treks in the Zagoria region. For Internet access, try **Web** (☎ 2651 026 813; Pyrsinella 21; ⏰ 24hr; per hr €2.50).

The **Old Town** juts out into the lake on a small peninsula. Inside the fortifications lies a maze of streets flanked by traditional Turkish houses. The serene **Nisi Island** has four monasteries set among its trees. Island ferries (€1) leave from just north of the Old Town.

In Perama (take bus No 8), **Rooms to Rent** (☎ 2651 081 786; Spileou 76, Perama; s/d €22/27) is one of many domatia in the neighbourhood. Rooms are smallish but clean and have private bathrooms. **To Rembetiko** (☎ 2651 075 535; Plataia Georgiou 14; mains €3.50-6.50) might not have live rembetika, but it does serve up delicious *mezedes* (appetizers), mixed platters and grills.

Aegean Airlines (☎ 2651 064 444) and **Olympic Airways** (☎ 2651 026 518) both fly twice a day to Athens, and Olympic has a daily flight to Thessaloniki.

The **main bus station** (☎ 2651 026 404) is 300m north of Plateia Dimokratias on Zossimadon, the northern extension of Markou Botsari. Destinations include Athens (€26, 7½ hours, 10 daily), Igoumenitsa, Thessaloniki and Trikala via Kalambaka.

ZAGORIA VILLAGES & VIKOS GORGE ΤΑ ΖΑΓΟΡΟΧΩΡΙΑ & ΧΑΡΆΔΡΑ ΤΟΥ ΒΊΚΟΥ

The Zagoria region covers a large expanse of the Pindos Mountains north of Ioannina. It's a wilderness of raging rivers, crashing waterfalls and deep gorges, with snowcapped mountains rising out of dense forests.

The fairytale village of **Monodendri** is the starting point for treks through the dramatic **Vikos Gorge**. A strenuous but well-signposted walk is to the twin villages of **Megalo Papingo** and **Mikro Papingo** (7½ hours). Ioannina's EOT office has more information.

There is excellent accommodation but little budget accommodation. One good option in Monodendri is cosy **To Kalderimi** (☎ 2653 071 510; d/tr €35/41). **Haradra tou Vikou** (☎ 2653 071 559) specialises in fabulous *pittes* (pies).

Buses run from Ioannina to Megalo and Mikro Papingo (€3.65, two hours, 5am and 3pm Monday, Wednesday and Friday) and Monodendri (€2.50, one hour, two daily).

METEORA ΜΕΤΕΩΡΑ

The jutting pinnacles of Meteora (meh-*teh*-o-rah) with stunning late 14th-century monasteries perched atop them are one of Greece's most extraordinary sights. Meteora is just north of Kalambaka, on the Ioannina–Trikala road. **Kastraki**, which is 2km from Kalambaka, is a charming village west of the monasteries.

There were once monasteries on each of the 24 pinnacles, but only six are still occupied. They are **Megalou Meteorou** (Grand Meteora; ⏰ 9am-5pm Wed-Mon), **Varlaam** (⏰ 9am-2pm & 3.20-5pm Fri-Wed), **Agiou Stefanou** (⏰ 9am-2pm & 3.30-6pm Tue-Sun), **Agias Triados** (Holy Trinity; ⏰ 9am-12.30pm & 3-5pm Fri-Wed), **Agiou Nikolaou Anapafsa** (⏰ 9am-3.30pm Sat-Thu) and **Agias Varvaras Rousanou** (⏰ 9am-6pm). Admission is €2 per monastery.

Kastraki is the best base for visiting Meteora, and **Dupiani House** (☎ 2432 075 326; dupiani-house@kmp.forthnet.gr; s/d/tr €30/45/55) is a welcoming guesthouse, 500m from the town square. The spotless rooms have balconies and splendid views from the garden. **Vrachos Camping** (☎ 2432 022 293; camping-kastraki@kmp.forthnet.gr; per adult & tent/car €3.50/1; 🏊) is an excellent camping ground on the edge of the village, with good facilities including a supermarket, restaurant and a barbecue. **Taverna Paradisos** (☎ 2432 022 723; mains €4-6.50), a large and lively taverna, serves up excellent traditional dishes.

There are hourly buses to Trikala (€1.50, 30 minutes), the region's major transport hub. There are buses to Ioannina (€8.10, three hours, two daily). Local buses shuttle constantly between Kalambaka and Kastraki; five a day continue to Metamorphosis.

From Trikala, there are buses to Athens (€19.10, 5½ hours, eight daily). From Kalambaka's new station, express trains run to Athens (€19.10, five hours, two daily). There are trains to Thessaloniki (change at Paliofarsalos; €9.50, four hours, two daily) and Volos (change at Paliofarsalos; €5, 1½ hours, two daily).

THESSALONIKI ΘΕΣΣΑΛΟΝΙΚΗ

pop 788,551

Thessaloniki (thess-ah-lo-*nee*-kih), known also as Salonica, was the second city of Byzantium and is the second city of modern Greece. It's a bustling, sophisticated city with good restaurants and a busy nightlife.

GREECE

THESSALONIKI

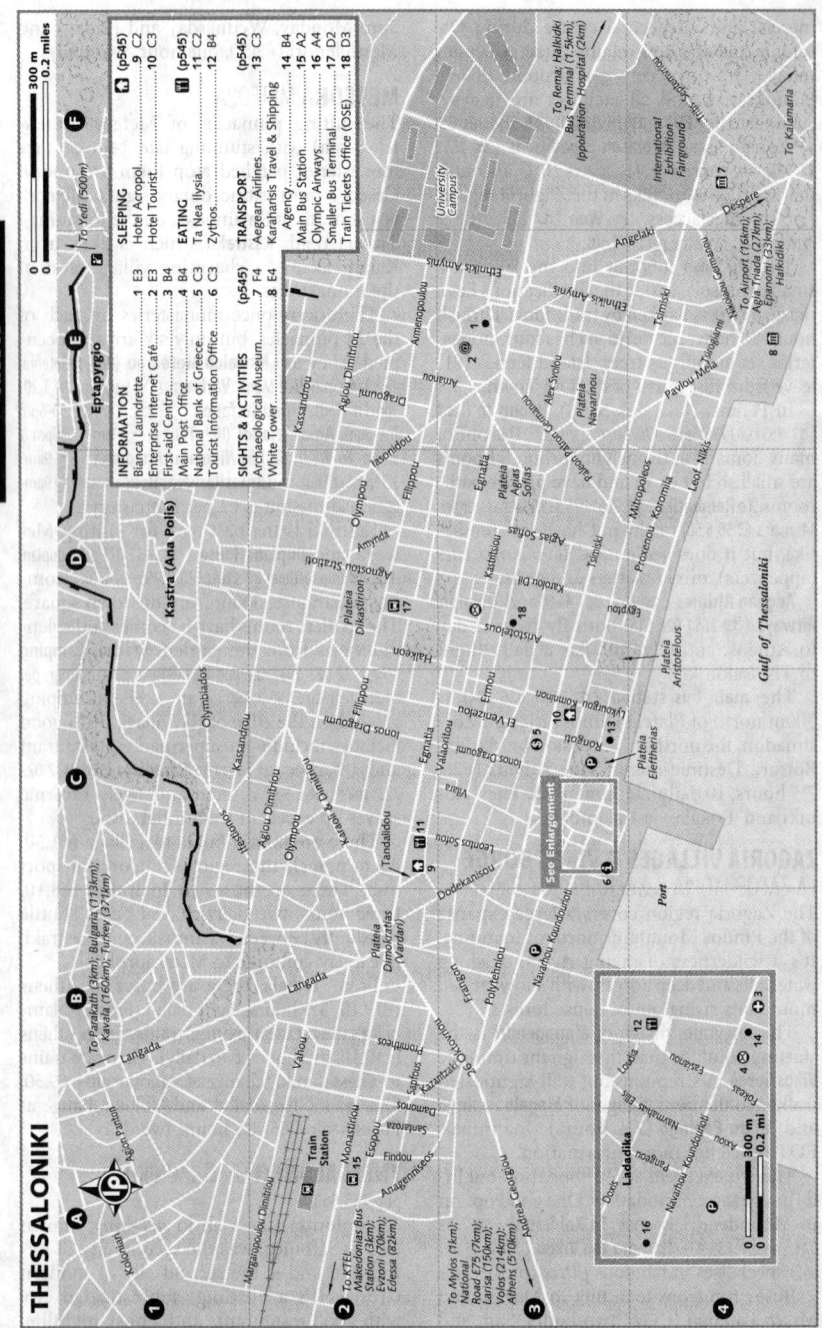

INFORMATION
Bianca Laundrette	1	E3
Enterprise Internet Café	2	E3
First-aid Centre	3	B4
Main Post Office	4	B4
National Bank of Greece	5	C3
Tourist Information Office	6	C3

SIGHTS & ACTIVITIES (p545)
Archaeological Museum	7	F4
White Tower	8	E4

SLEEPING (p545)
Hotel Acropol	9	C2
Hotel Tourist	10	C3

EATING (p545)
Ta Nea Ilysia	11	C2
Zythos	12	B4

TRANSPORT (p545)
Aegean Airlines	13	C3
Karaharisis Travel & Shipping Agency	14	B4
Main Bus Station	15	A2
Olympic Airways	16	A4
Smaller Bus Terminal	17	D2
Train Tickets Office (OSE)	18	D3

To Rema; Halkidiki Bus Terminal (1.5km); (Ippokration Hospital (2km)

To Airport (16km); Agia Triada (27km); Epanomi (33km); Halkidiki

To Kalamaria

International Exhibition Fairground

University Campus

To Perakath (3km); Bulgaria (113km); Kavala (160km); Turkey (371km)

To Yedi (500m)

To KTEL Makedonias Bus Station (3km); Evzoni (100km); Edessa (92km)

To Mylos (1km); National Road E75 (7km); Larisa (150km); Volos (214km); Athens (510km)

Train Station

Gulf of Thessaloniki

Port

Kastra (Ana Polis)

Eptapyrgio

300 m / 0.2 miles

Ladadika
300 m / 0.2 mi

Orientation & Information

Thessaloniki is laid out on a grid pattern. The main thoroughfares – Tsimiski, Egnatia and Agiou Dimitriou – run parallel to Nikis, on the waterfront. Plateias Eleftherias and Aristotelous, both on Nikis, are the main squares.

The train station is on Monastiriou, the westerly continuation of Egnatia beyond Plateia Dimokratias, and the airport is 16km to the southeast and is serviced by bus No 78. A taxi to/from the airport costs about €9 (20 minutes).

Information

Enterprise Internet Café (☎ 2310 211 722; Gounari 52; ☼ 9am-3am; per hr €2)

Main post office (Aristotelous 26; ☼ 7.30am-8pm Mon-Fri, 7.30am-2.15pm Sat, 9am-1.30pm Sun)

National Bank of Greece (Tsimiski 11) Open Saturday and Sunday for currency exchange.

Tourist Information Office (☎ 2310 500 310; passenger terminal, Thessaloniki port; ☼ 7.30am-3pm Mon-Fri, 8am-2pm Sat)

Sights

The **Archaeological Museum** (☎ 2310 830 538; Manoli Andronikou 6; ☼ 10.30am-5pm Mon, 8.30am-3pm Tue-Sun) lost much of its lustre when the treasures of the Vergina tombs were relocated to Vergina. At the time of research, the museum was being renovated.

The 15th-century **White Tower** (☎ 2310 267 832; Lefkos Pyrgos; ☼ 8am-6pm Tue-Sun) is the city's most prominent landmark. It was whitewashed after independence as a symbolic gesture, but the whitewash has been removed.

Sleeping & Eating

Hotel Acropol (☎ 2310 536 170; fax 2310 528 492; Tandalidou 4; s/d with shared bathroom €18/26) The rooms are basic, but it's comfortable and the best budget option in town.

Hotel Tourist (☎ 2310 270 501, fax 2310 226 865; Mitropoleos 21; s/d €53/67.50; ☒) A fine old neoclassical hotel that has comfortable rooms with TV and air-con. Prices include breakfast.

Ta Nea Ilysia (☎ 2310 536 996; Leotos Sofou 17; mains €4-6) A popular place with travellers and locals alike, it serves up a good choice of daily specials.

Zythos (☎ 2310540 284; Katouni 5; mains €8) This pub-restaurant does a roaring trade. It serves excellent pub food and pastas and has an impressive beer and wine list.

Mylos (☎ 2310 525 968; Andreou Georgiou 56; admission free) A huge old mill that has been converted into an entertainment complex with an art gallery, restaurant, bar and live music club.

Getting There & Away

AIR

Olympic Airways and Aegean Airlines have several daily flights to Athens (€96). **Olympic Airways** (☎ 2310 368 666; Navarhou Koundourioti 1-3) also has daily flights to Ioannina, Lesvos and Limnos; three weekly to Corfu, Iraklio and Mykonos; and two weekly to Chios, Hania and Samos. **Aegean Airlines** (☎ 2310 280 050; Venizelou 2) also has flights to Iraklio on Crete, and Lesvos, Rhodes and Santorini.

BUS

Most of Thessaloniki's buses depart from the new **main bus station** (☎ 2310 595 408; Monastiriou 319). Destinations include Athens (€30.80, 13 daily), Ioannina (€21.45, five daily) and Volos (€12.45, seven daily).

Buses to the Halkidiki Peninsula leave from the **smaller bus terminal** (☎ 2310 924 445; Karakasi 68) in the eastern part of the city. To get there, take local bus No 10 from Egnatia to the Botsari stop.

TRAIN

Domestic trains leave from the **train station** (☎ 2310 517 517; Monastiriou). There are several regular daily trains to Athens (€14, 7½ hours) and seven express intercity services (€27.60, six hours). Of the five daily trains to Alexandroupolis, two are express (€16.20, 5½ hours). All international trains from Athens stop at Thessaloniki. Get more information from the **OSE office** (☎ 2310 598 120; Aristotelous 18).

FERRY & HYDROFOIL

There's a Sunday ferry to Lesvos (€30, 13 hours), Limnos (€20, eight hours) and Chios (€30, 18 hours) throughout the year. In summer there are several ferries a week to Iraklio (Crete), stopping in the Sporades and the Cyclades. Daily hydrofoils go to Skiathos, Skopelos and Alonnisos. **Karaharisis Travel & Shipping Agency** (☎ 2310 524 544, fax 2310 532 289; Navarhou Koundourioti 8) handles ticket sales.

MT OLYMPUS ΟΛΥΜΠΟΣ ΟΡΟΣ

Greece's highest mountain, Mt Olympus was chosen by the ancients as the abode of their gods, and they believed it to be the exact centre of the earth. Olympus has eight peaks, the highest being Mytikas (2918m). The area is popular with trekkers, who use **Litohoro** as a base. This village is 5km inland from the Athens–Thessaloniki highway. The **EOS office** (Ellinikos Orivatikos Syndesmos, Greek Alpine Club; ☎ 2352 084 544; Plateia Kentriki; ◷ 9.30am-12.30pm & 6-8pm Mon-Sat) has information on treks.

Hotel Enipeas (☎ 2352 084 328, fax 2352 081 328; Plateia Kentriki; d/tr €35/40) is bright, breezy and clean. The hotel's rooms have balconies with some of the best views of Mt Olympus in town. **Olympios Zeus** (☎ 2352 022 115; Plaka Litohorou; per adult/tent €4.50/3.20), one of several good camping grounds, has a taverna, snack bar and minimarket. **Psistaria Dias** (☎ 2352 082 225; Agiou Nikolaou 36; grills €5-6) attracts hordes of locals, who order the popular grills.

From the **bus station** (☎ 2352 081 271) there are buses to Litohoro from Thessaloniki (€6.20, 1½ hours, 10 daily) and Athens (€25.90, 5½ hours).

CYCLADES ΚΥΚΛΑΔΕΣ

The Cyclades (kih-*klah*-dez), named after the circle (*kyklos*) they form around the island of Delos, are exactly how you imagine Greek Islands to be: rugged outcrops of rock, appealing beaches, azure waters, white cubist buildings and blue-domed Byzantine churches.

For more on these wonderful islands, check out Lonely Planet's *Greek Islands*.

MYKONOS ΜΥΚΟΝΟΣ
pop 9300
The most visited and expensive of the Cyclades, Mykonos survives on tourism but handles it well. The island has marvellous variety with sandy beaches, countless bars, trendy boutiques, and romantic sunsets. Mykonos has long been a mecca for gay travellers.

Orientation
Mykonos has two ferry quays. The old quay, where most of the conventional ferries and some fast ferries dock, is 400m north of the town waterfront. The new quay is 2.5km north of town. Buses and vociferous domatia owners meet arriving ferries. When buying outgoing tickets, check which quay the ferry leaves from.

Information
There is no tourist office. There are countless options for Internet access, most charging around €3 per hour.

Hoteliers Association of Mykonos (☎ 2289 024 540; www.mykonosgreece.com; Old Port; ◷ 9am-11pm)
Island Mykonos Travel (☎ 2289 022 232; www.discovergreece.org; Taxi Sq)

Sights & Activities
Summer crowds consume the island's capital, shuffling through snaking streets of chic boutiques and blinding white walls with balconies of cascading flowers. **Little Venice**, where the sea laps up to the edge of the buildings, and Mykonos' famous hilltop row of **windmills** should be included in a stroll. The most popular beaches are **Platys Gialos**, the often nude **Paradise Beach** and mainly gay **Super Paradise**, **Agrari** and **Elia beaches**.

Sleeping
In town, rooms fill up quickly in high season so it's wise to go with the first domatia owner who accosts you. Outside July and August, rooms are cheap as chips.

Zorzis Hotel (☎ 2289 022 167; www.zorzishotel.com; 30 Kalogera; s/d €92/115; ﹖) Rooms are immaculate in this impressive hotel, which is run by a Greek Australian. If you turn up outside July and August, they are also as cheap as €40 for a double.

Hotel Philippi (☎ 2289 022 294, fax 2289 024 680; 25 Kalogera; s/d €60/75) Spacious rooms and a large garden in a convenient part of town.

Mykonos has two camping areas, both on the south coast. Minibuses meet the ferries, and buses jog regularly into town.

Paradise Beach Resort and Camping (☎ 2289 022 852; www.paradisemykonos.com; per adult/tent €8/4) Skin-to-skin mayhem in summer, a party atmosphere and plenty of facilities.

Mykonos Camping (☎ 2289 024 578; www.mycamp.gr; per adult/tent €8/4) This site near Platys Gialos beach also parties, but is a bit more relaxed.

Eating & Drinking
Madupas (☎ 2289 022 224; dishes €5-12) on the waterfront serves a mean Mykonian sausage, and **Nikos Taverna** (☎ 2289 024 320; Porta; dishes €4-13) dishes out seafood by the kilo. **Antonini's** (☎ 2289 022 319; dishes €3.50-12.50) is a local hang-out in Taxi Square that serves great Greek food.

In Little Venice, **Katerina's Bar** (☎ 2289 023 084; Agion Anargiron) has a huge view.

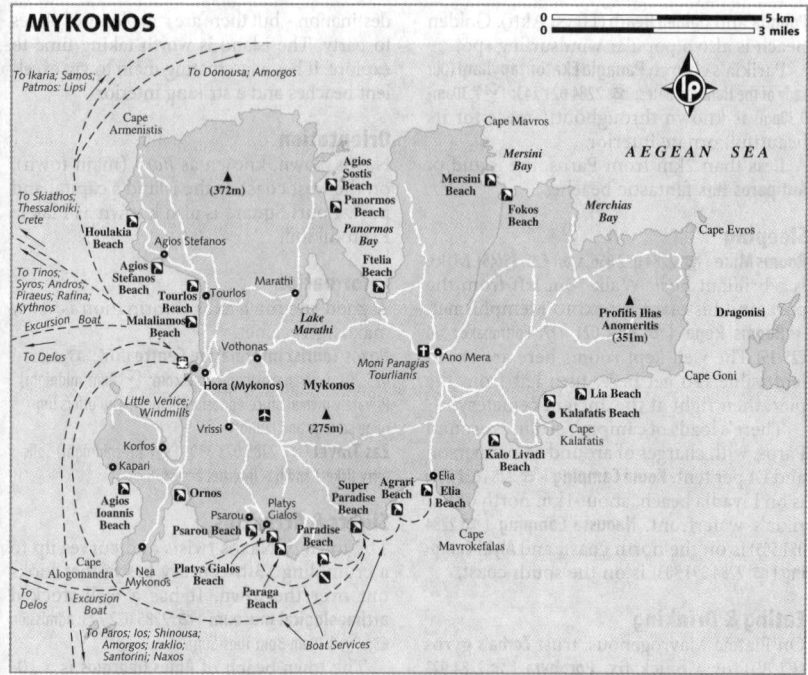

MYKONOS

0 ____ 5 km
0 ____ 3 miles

To Ikaria; Samos;
Patmos: Lipsi

To Donousa; Amorgos

Cape
Armenistis

Cape Mavros

AEGEAN SEA

Agios
Sostis
Beach

*Mersini
Bay*

To Skiathos;
Thessaloniki;
Crete

(372m)

Mersini
Beach

Panormos
Beach

Houlakia
Beach

Agios Stefanos

*Panormos
Bay*

Fokos
Beach

*Merchias
Bay*

Cape Evros

To Tinos;
Syros; Andros;
Piraeus; Rafina;
Kythnos

Agios
Stefanos
Beach

Tourlos
Beach

Tourlos

*Ftelia
Beach*

Marathi

Dragonisi

Excursion Boat

Malaliamos
Beach

*Lake
Marathi*

*Profitis Ilias
Anomeritis
(351m)*

To Delos

Vothonas

Moni Panagias
Tourlianis

Ano Mera

Cape Goni

Hora (Mykonos)

Mykonos

Little Venice;
Windmills

Vrissi

(275m)

Lia Beach

Kalafatis Beach

*Cape
Kalafatis*

Korfos

Kalo Livadi
Beach

Kapari

Agios
Ioannis
Beach

Ornos

Elia

Psarou

Platys
Gialos

Super
Paradise
Beach

Agrari
Beach

Elia
Beach

Psarou Beach

Paradise
Beach

*Cape
Mavrokefalas*

Cape
Alogomandra

Nea
Mykonos

Platys Gialos
Beach

Paraga
Beach

To
Delos

Excursion
Boat

To Paros; Ios; Shinousa;
Amorgos; Iraklio;
Santorini; Naxos

Boat Services

GREECE

Long feted as a gay travel destination, Mykonos has plenty of gaycentric clubs and hang-outs. **Kastro** (☎ 2289 023 072; Agion Anargiron), **Diva** (☎ 2289 027 271) and **Pierro's** (☎ 2289 022 177), just in from Taxi Square, are particularly popular.

Getting There & Away

There are daily flights from Mykonos to Athens (€76). Daily ferries arrive from Piraeus (€18.20). From Mykonos, there are daily ferry connections to most Cycladic islands. The northern bus station is near the old port. It serves Agios Stefanos, Elia, Kalafatis and Ano Mera. The southern bus station, southeast of the windmills, serves Agios Ioannis, Ornos, Psarou, Platys Gialos and Paradise Beach. In summer, *caïques* (small fishing boats) from Mykonos Town and Platys Gialos putter to Paradise, Super Paradise, Agrari and Elia beaches.

PAROS ΠΑΡΟΣ

pop 12,850

Paros is more open and laid-back than Mykonos. It is an attractive island with good swimming beaches and terraced hills that build up to Mt Profitis Ilias (770m). It is famous for its pure white marble from which the *Venus de Milo* was sculpted.

Orientation

The main town and port is Parikia, on the west coast. Agora, also known as Market St, is Parikia's main commercial thoroughfare. It runs from Plateia Mavrogenous, the main square (opposite the ferry terminal).

Information

Rooms Association (☎ 2284 022 861; ⏰ 9am-1am) Accommodation booking service with kiosk on the quay.

Santorineos Travel (☎ 2284 024 245) On the waterfront, it also provides tourist information.

Memphis.net (☎ 2284 022 878; per hr €4; ⏰ 9am-midnight) Opposite the ferry quay, to the left.

Sights & Activities

A great option on Paros is to rent a scooter at one of the many outlets in Parikia. There are sealed roads the whole way round the island. En route, you can visit villages, such as **Naoussa**, **Marpissa** and **Aliki**, or swim at **Logaras**,

Pounda and **Golden Beach** (Hrysi Akti). Golden Beach is also a popular windsurfing spot.

Parikia's church **Panagia Ekatontapyliani** (Our Lady of the Hundred Gates; ☎ 2284 021 243; ☽ 7.30am-9.30pm) is known throughout Greece for its beautiful, ornate interior.

Less than 2km from Paros, the island of **Antiparos** has fantastic beaches.

Sleeping

Rooms Mike (☎ 2284 022 856; s/d/t €25/35/45) Mike is a brilliant host. Walk 50m left from the port, and his place is next to Memphis.net.

Rooms Rena (☎ 2284 021 427; Epitropakis; s/d €25/35) The well-kept rooms here are excellent value. To get here, turn left from the pier, then right at the ancient cemetery.

There's loads of camping grounds around Paros, with charges of around €6 per person and €4 per tent. **Koula Camping** (☎ 2284 022 081) is on Livadia beach, about 1km north of Parikia's waterfront. **Naoussa Camping** (☎ 2284 051 565) is on the north coast, and **Alyki Camping** (☎ 2284 091 303) is on the south coast.

Eating & Drinking

On Plateia Mavrogenous, trust **Zorba's** gyros (€1.80) for a quick fix. **Porphyra** (☎ 2284 023 410; dishes from €5), next to the ancient cemetery, serves excellent fresh seafood. Vegetarians should head to **Happy Green Cows** (☎ 2284 024 691; dishes from €5; ☽ 7pm-midnight), back behind the main square, for a creative menu.

Pirate (☎ 2284 021 114) plays great jazz and blues in Market St, while **Pebbles Bar** (☎ 2284 022 283) is perched above the waterfront and has stunning views. The **Dubliner** (☎ 2284 021 113), at the southern end of town, houses three bars in one and is loud and large.

Getting There & Around

Paros has daily flights to Athens (€72). Parikia is a major ferry hub with daily connections to Piraeus (€19) and frequent ferries and catamarans to Naxos, Ios, Santorini (Thira) and Mykonos.

The bus station, 100m left from the port, has services to the entire island. In summer there are hourly excursion boats to Antiparos from Parikia port.

NAXOS ΝΑΞΟΣ

pop 18,200

Naxos is the biggest and greenest of the Cyclades, and enjoys its reputation as a family

destination – but there are still plenty of places to party. The island is worth taking time to explore. It has a fascinating main town, excellent beaches and a striking interior.

Orientation

Naxos Town, known as *hora* (main town), on the west coast, is the island's capital and port. Court Square is also known as Plateia Protodikiou.

Information

A good site for Naxos information is www.naxos-greece.net.

Naxos Tourist Information Centre (NTIC; ☎ 2285 025 201; www.naxostownhotels.com; ☽ 8am-midnight) Privately owned office opposite the port; also offers luggage storage and laundry.

Zas Travel (☎ 2285 023 330; ☽ 8am-midnight) Sells ferry tickets and has Internet access.

Sights & Activities

The town of Naxos twists and curves up to a crumbling 13th-century **kastro** that looks out over the town. It has a well-stocked **archaeological museum** (☎ 2285 022 725; admission €3; ☽ 8.30am-3pm Tues-Sun).

The town beach of **Agios Georgios** is a 10-minute walk south from the port. Beyond it, wonderful sandy beaches stretch as far south as **Pyrgaki Beach. Agia Anna Beach**, 6km from town, and **Plaka Beach** are lined with accommodation and packed in summer.

A rental car or scooter helps reveal Naxos' dramatic landscape. The **Tragea region** has tranquil villages, churches atop rocky crags and huge olive groves. **Filoti**, the largest inland settlement, perches on the slopes of **Mt Zeus** (1004m). It's a tough three-hour trail to the summit. In Apollonas you'll find the mysterious 10.5m **kouros** (naked male statue), constructed circa 7th century, lying abandoned and unfinished in an ancient marble quarry.

Sleeping

Domatia owners and camping ground staff meet ferries, picking up those who have a booking and competing for those who haven't.

Pension Sofi (☎ 2285 023 077; www.pensionsofi.gr; d €30-60) The friendly Koufopoulos family keep their rooms immaculate, and all have bathroom and kitchen. Rates halve out of the high season, and all guests are greeted with a glass of family-made wine or *ouzo* (a distilled spirit made from grapes and flavoured with aniseed).

Studios Panos (☎ 2285 026 078; www.studiospanos .com; Agios Georgios Beach; d €30-60) The sister establishment of Pension Sofi, with the same friendly vibe, at the southern end of town.

Pension Irene (☎ 2285 023 169; irenepension@ hotmail.com; d/t €30/60) This pension is split into two locations: one old, with OK rooms, and one new, with a pool.

The best camping ground options are **Camping Maragas** (☎ 2285 042 552) on Agia Anna Beach and **Plaka Camping** (☎ 2285 042 700) at Plaka Beach, both south of town and charging €5 per person.

Eating & Drinking

Naxos' waterfront is lined with eating and drinking establishments.

Taverna O Apostolis (☎ 2285 026 777; dishes €1.50-25) Up the road by Zas Travel, this is a good place to try for ouzo and octopus.

Picasso Mexican Bistro (☎ 2285 025 408; dishes €3.50-9) Sensational Tex-Mex is served in this stylish place 20m off Court Square.

Nightlife clusters around the southern end of the waterfront. There's the tropical **Med Bar**, **Caesar's Club** and, if you're up for dancing, **Ocean**, which opens at 11pm and goes wild after midnight.

Getting There & Around

Naxos has daily flights to Athens (€64). There are daily ferries to Piraeus (€21.50) and good ferry and hydrofoil connections to most Cycladic islands.

Buses travel to most villages regularly (including Apollonas and Filoti) and the beaches towards Pyrgaki. The bus terminal is in front of the port.

IOS ΙΟΣ

pop 1850

Ios has a deserved reputation as a party island, with sunbathing all day and drinking all night.

The island has three population centres, all close together on the west coast: the port (Ormos), the capital, Hora (also known as 'the village'), 2km inland and up from the port, and Milopotas, the beach 2km down from the Hora. The village has an intrinsic charm with its labyrinth of white-walled streets, and it's very easy to get lost, even if you haven't had one too many.

The bus stop in Ormos is straight ahead from the ferry quay. The bus trundles regularly up to the village. There is no tourist office, but **Acteon Travel** (☎ 2286 091 343; www .acteon.gr) has four offices in Ormos, the village and Milopotas. Internet access costs around €4 an hour, and is scattered among hotels, cafés, bars and Acteon Travel.

Milopotas Beach has everything a resort beach can ask for, and isolated **Manganari** on the south coast has four sandy crescent beaches.

In the village, **Francesco's** (☎ 2286 091 223; www.francescos.net; dm/d €10/30, doubles with bathroom €50; ⊠) is a lively meeting place with superlative views from its terrace bar. All rooms have television. It's very convenient for clubbing, and the rates halve out of the high season.

Milopotas Beach parties hard from noon until midnight with up to 3000 people. **Far Out Beach Club** (☎ 2286 091 468; www.faroutclub.com; camp site per person €7; 🏊 🖳) has tons of facilities, including bungalows and hotel rooms, and its four pools are open to the public. **Camping Ios** (☎ 2286 092 035; per person €6; 🏊) is in Ormos.

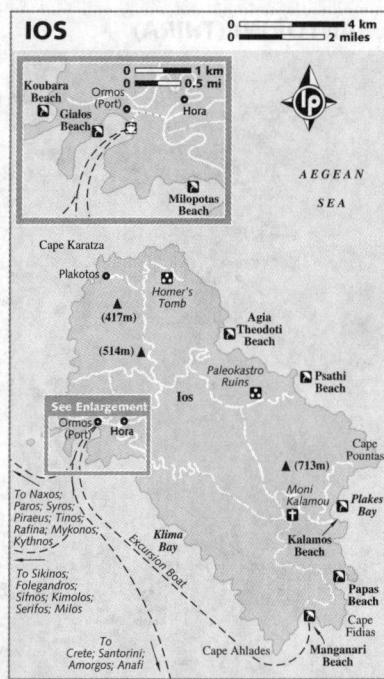

GREECE

In the village, **Porky's**, just off the main square, is a legend for cheap eats. **Ali Baba's** (☎ 2286 091 558; dishes €6.50-9) is popular and parties until late. **Fiesta** (☎ 2286 091 766; dishes from €3) is a short tumble down the hill from Francesco's and has great wood-oven pizzas.

At night, the village erupts with bars to explore. Perennial favourites include **Red Bull** (☎ 2286 091 019), **Slammers** (☎ 2286 092 119) and **Blue Note** (☎ 2286 092 271).

Ios has daily ferry connections to Piraeus (€18.80), and there are frequent hydrofoils and ferries to the major Cycladic islands. There are buses every 20 minutes between the port, the village and Milopotas Beach until early morning, and two to three per day to Manganari Beach.

SANTORINI (THIRA) ΣΑΝΤΟΡΙΝΗ (ΘΗΡΑ)

pop 13,400

Stunning Santorini, officially known as Thira, is surely the most spectacular of the Greek Islands. Around 1450 BC, the volcanic heart of the island exploded and sank, leaving an extraordinary landscape. Visitors cannot help but gaze at the startling sight of the submerged caldera almost encircled by sheer cliffs.

Orientation

The capital, Fira, perches on top of the caldera on the west coast, and the port of Athinios is 10km away by road. The bus station and taxi station are located just south of Fira's main square, Plateia Theotokopoulou.

Information

Dakoutros Travel (☎ 2286 022 958; www.dakoutros travel.gr; ☼ 8:30am-10pm) Opposite the taxi station.

Lava Internet Café (☎ 2286 025 551; €1.50 per 15min) Just up from the square.

Post office One block south of the taxi station.

Santosun Travel (☎ 2286 081 456; santosun@otenet.gr) On the main street of Perissa, on the southeast coast. Also has Internet access.

FIRA

The shameless commercialism of Fira has not quite reduced its dramatic aura. The **Museum of Prehistoric Thira** (☎ 2286 023 217; admission €3; ☼ 8.30am-3pm Tue-Sun) has wonderful displays of artefacts, predominantly from

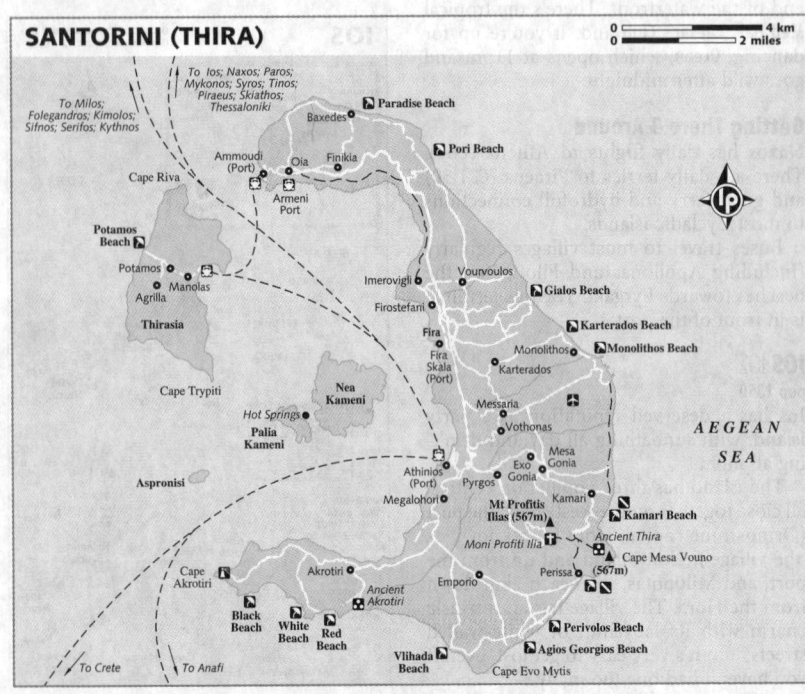

SANTORINI (THIRA)

ancient Akrotiri. It's two blocks south of the main square.

Just behind the Catholic Cathedral, the **Megaron Gyzi Museum** (☎ 2286 022 244; admission €3; ✆ 10.30am-1.30pm & 5pm-8pm Mon-Sat, 10.30am-4.30pm Sun), houses local memorabilia, including photographs of Fira before and after the 1956 earthquake.

AROUND THE ISLAND

Santorini's **beaches** have black volcanic sand, and they sizzle in the sun. It's a strange feeling to walk over black sand then onto smooth lava when going for a dip. **Perissa** and **Kamari** in particular are popular.

At the north of the island, the flawless village of **Oia** (pronounced ee-ah), famed for its postcard sunsets, is less hectic than Fira. It's possible to walk from Fira in about three hours along the top of the caldera.

You can clamber around on volcanic lava on **Nea Kameni**, then swim into warm springs in the sea at **Palia Kameni** as a day excursion.

Sleeping

Decide where you want to stay before aggressive domatia owners who meet the boats try to decide things for you. Fira has spectacular views but is miles from the beaches. Perissa has a great beach but is on the east coast away from the caldera views. Pick one side of the island, so you don't get stuck in the middle.

Maria's Rooms (☎ 2286 025 143; Agiou Mina; d €40-50; 🌐) This pension on the southern edge of Fira has small but immaculate rooms and stunning caldera views from its terrace.

Pension Petros (☎ 2286 022 573; fax 2286 022 615; s/d €55/60) Its central location in Fira, 250m east of the square, makes this place very handy, but it lacks views.

Santorini Camping (☎ 2286 022 944; www.santorinicamping.gr; per adult €7; P 🌐) This site 500m east of the main square is a bit tired, but it does have a restaurant. No views.

Stelio's Place (☎ 2286 081 860; www.steliosplace.com; d from €25; 🌐 P 🌐) An excellent option just back from the beach in Perissa, Stelio's offers port/airport transfers and very friendly service.

Perissa Camping (☎ 2286 081 343; per adult €7; P) Right on the beachfront in Perissa.

Eating & Drinking

Cheap eateries such as **Grill House** are in abundance around the square in Fira. You'll find excellent-value Greek classics at **Naoussa** (☎ 2286 024 869; dishes €3-20) on Erythrou Stavrou, and **Nikolas** (☎ 2286 024 550; dishes €5-10), on the same street, receives rave reviews. In Perissa, **Taverna Lava** (☎ 2286 081 776; dishes €3-8), along the waterfront, is an island-wide favourite where you can go out to the kitchen and pick what looks good.

Most of the popular bars and clubs in Fira are clustered along the same street, Erythrou Stavrou. **Kira Thira** (☎ 2286 022 770) plays smooth jazz. Once things hot up, **Koo Club** (☎ 2286 022 025) and **Enigma** (☎ 2286 022 466) more than meet late-night requirements. In Perissa, the **Full Moon Bar** (☎ 2286 081 177) on the main street goes off from 9pm until late.

Getting There & Around

Santorini's international airport has daily flights to Athens (€85) and less regular ones to Rhodes (€90) and Mykonos (€65).

There are daily ferries to Piraeus (€22.50), daily connections in summer to Mykonos, Ios, Naxos, Paros and Iraklio, and ferries to the smaller islands in the Cyclades. Large ferries use Athinios port, where they are met by buses (€1.20) and taxis. Small boats use Fira Skala port, where the mode of transport up to Fira is by donkey or cable car (€3); otherwise it's a clamber up 600 steps.

Buses go frequently from Fira to Oia, Kamari, Perissa and Akrotiri.

CRETE KPHTH

Greece's largest and southernmost island, Crete hosts a quarter of all visitors to the country. The major towns are on the more hospitable northern coast. Most of the south coast is too precipitous to support large settlements. The mountainous interior offers rigorous trekking and climbing.

Crete was the birthplace of Minoan culture, Europe's first advanced civilisation, which flourished from 2800 to 1450 BC. Very little is known about the Minoan civilisation, which came to an abrupt end, possibly destroyed by Santorini's volcanic eruption.

Snap up a copy of Lonely Planet's *Crete*. Good websites to read include www.in terkriti.org, www.infocrete.com and www .explorecrete.com.

GREECE

CRETE

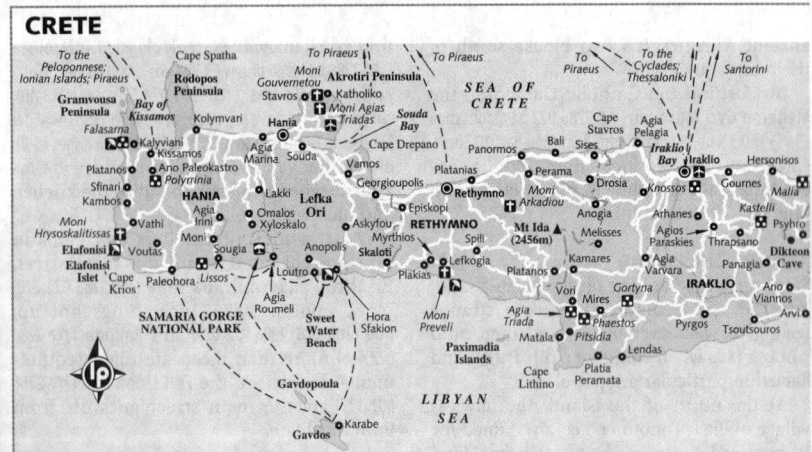

IRAKLIO ΗΡΑΚΛΕΙΟ

pop 133,000

Iraklio, Crete's capital, is a bustling modern city and the fifth largest in Greece. It has a lively city centre about 500m west of the port. There is no official tourist office, but the **tourist police** (☎ 2810 283 190; Dikeosynis 10; ☺ 7am-11pm) have maps and information. **Skoutelis Travel** (☎ 2810 280 808; www.skoutelis .gr; 25 Avgoustou) can make airline and ferry bookings, and it rents cars. Internet access is available next door at **SportC@fé** (25 Avgoustou; per hr €2; ☺ 24hr).

Iraklio's **archaeological museum** (☎ 2810 226 092; Xanthoudidou; adult/student €6/3; ☺ 12.30pm-7pm Mon, 8am-7pm Tue-Sun) has an outstanding Minoan collection, second only to the National Archaeological Museum in Athens. Even a superficial look will take half a day. The **Battle of Crete Museum** (☎ 2810 346 554; cnr Doukos Beaufort & Hatzidaki; free; ☺ 8am-3pm) chronicles the historic WWII battle.

Sleeping & Eating

Rent Rooms Hellas (☎ 2810 288 851; Handakos 24; dm/d €10/25) A popular budget choice, it's clean and has packed dorms, a rooftop bar and a bargain breakfast.

Hotel Kronos (☎ 281 282 240; www.kronoshotel.gr; Sofokli Venizelou 2; s/d with breakfast €35/45; ✄ 🖵) This hotel on the waterfront has large airy rooms.

Hotel Mirabello (☎ 281 028 5052; www.mirabello -hotel.gr; Theotokopoulou 20; s/d €38/50; ✄) A pleasant place in the centre of town.

There's a congregation of cheap eateries in the Plateia Venizelou and El Greco Park area, as well as a bustling, colourful **market** all the way along Plateia 1866.

Giakoumis Taverna (☎ 2810 280 277; Theodosaki 5-8; dishes €2.50-8) In the market area, this taverna offers a full menu of Cretan specialties.

Ippokampos Ouzeri (☎ 2810 280 240; Mitsotaki 2; dishes €3.50-8) On the waterfront, it serves up popular well-priced dishes.

Getting There & Around

There are several flights a day to Athens and, in summer, flights to Thessaloniki and Rhodes. Ferries head to Piraeus (€29.50, daily). Most days boats go to Santorini (Thira) and continue on to other Cycladic islands.

Iraklio has two bus stations. Bus Station A, just inland from the new harbour, serves eastern Crete (Agios Nikolaos, Ierapetra, Sitia and the Lasithi Plateau). The Hania and Rethymno terminal is across the street from Bus Station A. Bus Station B, 50m beyond the Hania Gate, serves the southern route (Phaestos, Matala, Anogia). Check out www. ktel.org for long-distance bus information.

KNOSSOS ΚΝΩΣΟΣ

About 5km southwest of Iraklio, **Knossos** (☎ 2810 231 940; admission €6; ☺ 8am-7pm Apr-Oct, 8am-5pm Nov-Mar) is the most famous of Crete's Minoan sites. The ruins were uncovered by Arthur Evans in 1900. Although archaeologists tend to disparage Evans' reconstruction, the buildings give an idea of what a Minoan palace might have looked like. There's an immense palace, courtyards, private apartments, baths, lively frescoes and more.

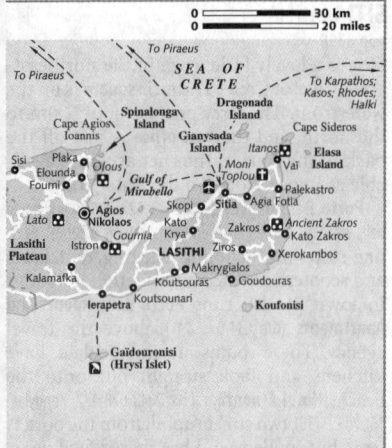

From Iraklio, local bus No 2 goes to Knossos (€0.95, every 10 minutes) from Bus Station A; it also stops on 25 Avgoustou.

RETHYMNO ΡΕΘΥΜΝΟ
pop 29,000

Rethymno's gracious old quarter of crumbling Venetian and Turkish buildings is on a peninsula sticking out into the Sea of Crete. Not quite as gracious are its restaurant touts. El Venizelou is the main strip by the waterfront. Running parallel behind it is Arkadiou, the main commercial street.

The **municipal tourist office** (☎ 2831 029 148; Eleftheriou Venizelou; ⊙ 8.30am-2pm Mon-Fri) is on the beach side of El Venizelou, but is of little help. **Ellotia Tours** (☎ 2831 051 981; www.forthnet .gr/elotia/; Arkadiou 155), however, will answer all transport, accommodation and tour inquiries. **Galero Café** (☎ 2831 054 345; per hr €4), beside the Rimondi fountain with its spouting lion heads, has Internet access.

The impressive **Venetian Fortress** (☎ 2831 028 101; Paleokastro Hill; admission €3; ⊙ 8am-8pm), on the point, affords great views across the town and mountains. **Happy Walker** (☎ 2831 052 920; www.happywalker.com; Tombazi 56) has excellent daily walks in the countryside (€25 per person).

Rethymno Youth Hostel (☎ 2831 022 848; www .yhrethymno.com; Tombazi 41; dm €7) is a well-run place with crowded dorms. **Rent Rooms Sea Front** (☎ 2831 051 981; www.forthnet.gr/elotia/; Arkadiou 159; ⊠), run by Ellotia Tours, has all sorts of options and is ideally positioned with beach views and spacious rooms.

Gounakis Restaurant & Bar (☎ 2831 028 816; Koroneou 6; mains from €5) is the place to go for live Cretan music and reasonably priced food. **Restaurant Symposium** (☎ 2831 050 538; www.symposium-kriti.gr; dishes from €3.50), near the Rimondi fountain, takes its food seriously but has good prices.

Ferries travel from Piraeus to Rethymno (€24, daily). Buses depart regularly to Iraklio (€5.90, 1½ hours) and Hania (€5.30, one hour).

HANIA ΧΑΝΙΑ
pop 53,500

Hania (often spelt Chania) is Crete's second largest city and the former capital. The Venetian quarter that surrounds the Old Harbour lures tourists in droves.

The **tourist office** (☎ 2821 036 155; www.chania .gr; ⊙ 9am-8pm Mon-Fri, 9am-2pm Sat), at Kydonias 29 (near Plateia 1866) is very helpful. There's also a stack of travel agencies on Halidon, the street leading down to the Old Harbour. There is Internet access at **Hotel Manos** (☎ 2821 094 156; www.manoshotel.gr; Zambeliou 24; per hr €4).

The **archaeological museum** (☎ 2821 090 334; Halidon 21; admission €2; ⊙ 8.30am-3pm Tue-Sun) was once the Venetian Church of San Francesco, until the Turks made it into a mosque. Hania's spectacular covered **food market** is worth a visit, even if you aren't self-catering. Part of the city wall had to be demolished in 1911 to make way for the cruciform market.

There is a swathe of sleeping options around the Venetian port. **Pension Fidias** (☎ 2821 052 494; Sarpaki 6; dm/d/t €9/18/27), behind the Orthodox Cathedral, is still the budget choice. **Pension Lena** (☎ 6932 829 788; www.travelling -crete.com/lena; Ritsou 3; s/d €28/50; ⊠) is a friendly place in an old Turkish building near the mouth of the old harbour. **Camping Hania** (☎ 2821 031 138; per adult/tent €5/3.50) is 3km west of town on the beach. Take the Hania-Stalos bus from the southeast corner of Plateia 1866.

Amphora Restaurant (☎ 2821 093 224; Akti Koundourioti 49; mains €4.50-7), on the waterfront under the hotel of the same name, has excellent pasta dishes and a fine reputation. **Café Kriti** (☎ 2821 058 661; Kalergon 22) is the best place to hear live Cretan music while having a drink.

There are several flights a day to Athens (€74) and two flights a week to Thessaloniki (€110). Ferries depart daily to Piraeus (€22) from the port of Souda, 7km east of town. Frequent buses plough daily to Iraklio,

Rethymno and Kastelli-Kissamos; buses run less frequently to Paleohora, Omalos and Hora Sfakion from the main bus station on Kydonias. Buses for Souda (the port) leave frequently from outside the food market.

SAMARIA GORGE
ΦΑΡΑΓΓΙ ΤΗΣ ΣΑΜΑΡΙΑΣ

Samaria Gorge (☎ 2825 067 179; admission €5; ☺ 6am-3pm May-Oct) is one of Europe's most spectacular gorges. Rugged footwear, food, water and sun protection are essential for this strenuous five- to six-hour trek, which is not recommended for inexperienced walkers.

You can do the walk as part of an excursion tour arranged at travel agencies in Crete's main cities, or independently by taking the Omalos bus from the main bus station in Hania (€4.70, one hour, four daily, 6.15am, 7.30am, 8.30am, 1.45pm) to the head of the gorge at Xyloskalo (1230m). It's a 16.7km walk out to Agia Roumeli on the coast, from where you take a boat to Hora Sfakion (€5, 1¼ hrs, three daily) and then a bus back to Hania (€5.65, two hours, four daily).

PALEOHORA ΠΑΛΑΙΟΧΩΡΑ
pop 2550
Paleohora, discovered by hippies back in the 1960s, has a relaxing 'end of the line' feel about it, and you might not want to leave. Isolated and a bit hard to get to, the village is on a peninsula with a beach on each side. There's a welcoming **tourist office** (☎ 2823 041 507), but don't expect it to be up and running before June. **Notos Rentals/Tsiskakis Travel** (☎ 2823 042 110; notosgr@yahoo.gr; Eleftheriou Venizelou), in the main street, handles everything, including tickets, Internet access at €4 per hour, rental cars and scooters, and laundry.

Homestay Anonymous (☎ 2823 041 509; s/d €14/18) is a great place for backpackers with its warm service and a communal kitchen. On the beach, **Poseidon Hotel** (☎ 2823 041 374; www.c-v.net /hotel/paleohora/poseidon; s/d €25/35; ⚇) has rooms with kitchen facilities. About 1.5km northeast of town **Camping Paleohora** (☎ 2823 041 225; per adult/tent €4/2.50) is near the pebble beach. There's a restaurant and nightclub nearby.

Vegetarians rave about the **Third Eye** (☎ 2823 041 234; mains €4-6), while the special omelette at **Coconuts Cafetaria** (☎ 2823 041 523; dishes €3-8) is a winner.

There are at least five buses daily between Hania and Paleohora (€5.65, two hours).

SITIA ΣΗΤΕΙΑ
pop 8750
Sitia is a lovely little town in the northeastern corner of Crete. The **main square** is on the waterfront. The ferry port is about 500m to the north, and the **post office** is just off the back of the square. Internet access is available at Itanos Hotel on the waterfront.

Porto Belis Travel (☎ 2843 022 370; www.porto belis-crete.gr; Karamanli Aven 34; ☺ 9am-8.30pm) is a one-stop shop, handling ticketing, rental cars and scooters, and accommodation bookings in town. It also runs **Porto Belis Rooms and Apartments** (d/q €34/57; ⚇) above the travel agency. These rooms are immaculate, have kitchens and look straight out onto the beach. **Hotel Arhontiko** (☎ 2843 028 172; Kondylaki 16; s/d €25/30), two streets uphill from the port, is basic but spotless, and has shared facilities.

Popular with locals is **Gato Negro** (☎ 2843 025 873; dishes €3-12), near the ferry quay, serving Cretan specialties. **Kali Kardia** (☎ 2843 022 249; Foundalidou 22; mains €4-6), a couple of streets back from the waterfront, is also superb.

Sitia airport has three flights per week to Athens (€75). There are regular ferries from Piraeus to Sitia (€27.50) and ferries to Rhodes via Karpathos (three weekly). There are six buses daily to Ierapetra and five to Iraklio, via Agios Nikolaos. In peak season, there are four buses daily to Vaï Beach, a superb spot 24km away on the east coast.

DODECANESE
ΔΩΔΕΚΑΝΗΣΑ

Closer to Asia Minor than mainland Greece, the 18 islands of the Dodecanese are strung out along the coast of western Turkey. Their strategic position has meant a turbulent past of invasions and occupation, which has endowed them with a fascinating wealth of diverse archaeological remains. The islands themselves are verdant and mountainous with appealing beaches.

RHODES ΡΟΔΟΣ
According to mythology, the sun god Helios chose Rhodes as his bride and bestowed light, warmth and vegetation upon her. The blessing seems to have paid off, for Rhodes produces more flowers and sunny days than most Greek islands.

The ancient sites of Lindos and Kamiros are legacies of Rhodes' importance in antiquity. In 1291 the Knights of St John, having fled Jerusalem, came to Rhodes and established themselves as masters. In 1522 Süleyman I, sultan of the Ottoman Empire, staged a massive attack on the island and took Rhodes City. The island, along with the other Dodecanese islands, then became part of the Ottoman Empire.

In 1912 it was the Italians' turn, and in 1944 the Germans took over. The following year Rhodes was liberated by British and Greek commandos. In 1948 the Dodecanese became part of Greece. These days, tourists rule.

Rhodes City

pop 54,000

Rhodes' capital and port is Rhodes City, on the northern tip of the island. Almost everything of interest lies in the Old Town, enclosed within massive walls. The new town to the north is for package tourists.

ORIENTATION

The main port, Commercial Harbour, is east of the Old Town, and northwest of here is Mandraki Harbour, the supposed site of the Colossus of Rhodes, a giant 32m-high bronze statue of Apollo built over 12 years (294–282 BC). The statue stood for a mere 65 years before being toppled by an earthquake.

INFORMATION

Directorate for the Dodecanese Islands (☎ 2241 044 335; www.ando.gr/eot; cnr Makariou & Papagou; ☼ 7.30am-3pm Mon-Fri)

Mango Café Bar (☎ 2241 024 8770; Plateia Dorieos 3; per hr €5) Internet access in the Old Town.

Municipal tourist office (☎ 2241 035 945; Plateia Rimini; ☼ 8am-8pm daily) Open summer only.

Tourist police (☎ 2241 027 423) Next door to the Directorate for the Dodecanese Islands.

Triton Holidays (☎ 2241 021 690; www.tritondmc.gr; 1st floor, Plastira 9) Handles accommodation bookings, ticketing and rental cars.

SIGHTS & ACTIVITIES

The Old Town is reputedly the world's finest surviving example of medieval fortification. The 12m-thick walls are closed to the public, but you can take a **guided walk** (☎ 2241 023 359; tours €6; ☼ 2.30pm Tue & Sat) along them, starting in the courtyard of the Palace of the Knights.

Odos Ippoton (Avenue of the Knights) is lined with magnificent medieval buildings, the most imposing of which is the **Palace of the Knights** (☎ 2241 023 359; admission €6; ☼ 8.30am-3pm Tue-Sun), restored as a holiday home for Mussolini but never used for the purpose.

The 15th-century Knight's Hospital now houses the **archaeological museum** (☎ 2241 027 657; Plateia Mousiou; admission €3; ☼ 8am-5.40pm Tue-Sun). It's a splendid building, restored by the Italians, with an impressive collection that includes the ethereal marble statue, the *Aphrodite of Rhodes*.

SLEEPING

Domatia owners meet ferries. Negotiate if you arrive out of season. Prices can halve.

Rodos Youth Hostel (☎ 2241 030 491; Ergiou 12; dm/d €8/25) In the Old Town, off Agio Fanouriou, this place has a lovely garden and a couple of excellent-value studios out the back.

Mango Rooms (☎ 2241 024 877; karelas@hotmail.com; Plateia Dorieos 3; s/d €30/45) This place has everything: a restaurant, bar and Internet café down below, and six well-kept rooms above.

Pink Elephant Pension (☎ 2241 022 469; www.pinkelephantpension.com; Irodotou 42; d €32-53; ☒) Compact but clean rooms.

Hotel International (☎ 2241 024 595; diethnes@ote net.gr; Ioannu Kazouli 12; s/d €25/35; ☒) In the New Town, the International is a real bargain with excellent facilities and a friendly owner.

EATING & DRINKING

There is food and drink every way you look in Rhodes. Outside the walls, there are a lot of cheap places to eat in the **New Market**.

Taverna Kostas (☎ 2241 026 217; Pythagora 62; mains €5-10) No wonder this Old Town venue has stood the test of time. It's good value and can't be beaten on quality.

Kasbah (☎ 2241 078 633; Platonos 4-8; ☼ dinner only; mains from €10) Huge Moroccan-influenced meals are dished up in a refined atmosphere.

Kafe Besara (☎ 2241 030 363; Sofokleous 11) is one of the Old Town's liveliest bars, but **Mango Café Bar** (see above) claims to have the cheapest drinks. In the New Town, head to Orfanidou in the city's northwest. The drink-till-you-droppers are there, and there is a bar for every nationality.

ENTERTAINMENT

Rhodes' impressive **Sound & Light Show** (☎ 2241 021 922; www.hellenicfestival.gr; adults/concession €5/3;

(☼ Mon-Sat) is held by the walls of the Old Town off Plateia Rimini. English-language sessions are staggered, but are generally at 9.15pm or 11.15pm.

AROUND THE ISLAND
The **Acropolis of Lindos** (☎ 2244 031 258; admission €6; ☼ 8.30am-6pm Tue-Sun), 47km from Rhodes City, is Rhodes' most important ancient city and is spectacularly perched atop a 116m-high rocky outcrop. Below the site is Lindos town, a tangle of streets with elaborately decorated 17th-century houses. The bus to Lindos (€3.70) departs from Rhodes City's east-side station.

The extensive ruins of **Kamiros** (admission €4; ☼ 8am-5pm Tue-Sun), an ancient Doric city on the west coast, are well preserved and include the remains of houses, baths, a cemetery and a temple.

GETTING THERE & AWAY
There are daily flights from Rhodes to Athens (€90) and Karpathos (€28) and, in summer, regular flights to Iraklio.

Ferries depart daily from Rhodes to Piraeus (€33). Most sail via the Dodecanese north of Rhodes, but at least three times a week there is a service via Karpathos, Crete and the Cyclades.

Excursion boats (€20 return trip) and hydrofoils (€12.50, one-way) run daily to Symi. Ferries travel less often (€8, one-way). Similar services also run to Kos, Kalymnos, Nisyros, Tilos, Patmos, Leros and Samos.

Between April and October, there are boats from Rhodes to Marmaris in Turkey (one-way/return trip €45/60, daily).

GETTING AROUND
Rhodes City has two bus stations. The **west-side bus station**, next to the New Market, has services between the airport (€1.70, frequent) and the west coast (including Kamiros); the **east-side bus station** (Plateia Rimini) serves the east coast and the inland southern villages.

SYMI ΣΥΜΗ
pop 2600
Symi is superb. The island itself is rocky and dry, but the port town of Gialos is a Greek treasure. Pastel-coloured mansions are heaped up the hills surrounding the protective little harbour. The town is divided into Gialos, the harbour, and the tranquil *horio* (village)

above it, accessible by taxi, bus or 360 steps from the harbour.

There is no tourist office or tourist police. The best source of information is the free and widely available monthly English-language *Symi Visitor* (www.symivisitor .com), which includes maps of the town. For Internet access head for **Orange & Lemon Café** (☎ 2246 071 988; per hr €4) on the waterfront.

Kalodoukas Holidays (☎ 2246 071 077; www .symi-greece.com) handles sleeping options, bookings and ticketing. It has a book that details island walking trails.

Budget accommodation is scarce.

Rooms Katerina (☎ 2246 071 813/6945 130 112; d €25-30) You need to get in quick here because, although it's excellent, it has only three rooms. Each has a private bathroom, and there is a communal kitchen with breathtaking views.

Pension Catherinettes (☎ 2246 071 671; marina -epe@rho.forthnet.gr; d €55) Sleep in airy rooms inside the waterfront building where the treaty surrendering the Dodecanese Islands to the Allies was signed in 1945.

Bella Napoli (☎ 2246 072 456; pizzas from €5) In the port area, this place serves exceptional wood-fired pizzas.

Vapori Bar (☎ 2246 072 082) Bella Napoli's neighbour is open all day. Drop by to use the Internet or read the free newspapers by day, for drinks and cruising at night.

There are frequent ferries and hydrofoils between Rhodes and Kos that also call at Symi, as well as less frequent services to Tilos, Nisyros, Kalymno, Leros and Patmos. Excursion boats visit inaccessible east coast beaches including spectacular **Agios Georgious**, which is backed by a 150m sheer cliff, daily in summer.

KOS ΚΩΣ
pop 17,900
Only 5km from the Turkish peninsula of Bodrum, Kos is a long, narrow island with a mountainous spine. Hippocrates, the father of medicine, was born here, but that's as Greek as this place gets. With its ruins and Turkish buildings on a backdrop of pretty palm-lined streets, neon cafés, pulsing clubs and tourist trains, Kos Town exudes the aura of a mini-Las Vegas.

Orientation & Information
Kos Town, on the northeast coast, is the main town and port.

Café Del Mare (☎ 2242 024 244; Megalou Alexandrou 4; per hr €4) Internet café.

Municipal tourist office (☎ 2242 024 460; www .hippocrates.gr; Vasileos Georgiou 1; 8am-8pm Mon-Fri, 8am-3pm Sat, May-Oct), On the waterfront directly south of the port; provides maps and accommodation information.

Pulia Tours (☎ 2242 026 388; 3 Vas Pavlou) Handles schedules, ticketing, money exchange, excursions and rental cars.

Sights & Activities

Sculptures from excavations around the island are the focus of the **archaeological museum** (☎ 2242 028 326; Plateia Eleftherias; adult/student €3/2; ☿ 8am-2.30pm Tue-Sun). The **ancient agora**, with the ruins of the **Shrine of Aphrodite** and **Temple of Hercules**, is just off Plateia Eleftherias. It's free but has zero information. North of the Agora is the **Hippocrates Plane Tree**, under which the man himself is said to have taught his pupils.

On a pine-clad hill, 4km southwest from Kos Town, stand the extensive ruins of the renowned healing centre of **Asklipieion** (☎ 2242 028 763; adult/student €4/3; ☿ 8.30am-6pm Tue-Sun), where Hippocrates practised medicine.

Kos has excellent beaches, particularly at the southern end of the island. **Kamari Beach** and **Paradise Beach** are popular.

Sleeping

Pension Alexis (☎ 2242 028 798, fax 2242 025 797; Irodotou 9; s/d €23/29) A convivial place, this has long been a budget favourite with travellers. It has large rooms and shared facilities, and is highly recommended. Try the legendary feta omelette for breakfast. If you call ahead, they'll pick you up from the port.

Hotel Afendoulis (☎ 2242 025 321; afendoulishotel@ kos.forthnet.gr; Evripilou 1; s/d €29/42) This superior hotel boasts well-kept rooms in a quiet area. Will pick up from the port if you call ahead.

Kos Camping (☎ 2242 023 910; per adult/tent €4.50/2.50) is 3km along the eastern waterfront, with good shade and a minimart. Hop on any of the buses from the harbourfront going to Agios Fokas.

Eating & Drinking

Restaurants line the central waterfront, but you might want to hit the backstreets for value.

Barbas (☎ 2240 027 856; Evripilou 6; mains €4-7) Come here for excellent chicken souvlaki and speciality grills. Opposite Hotel Afendoulis.

Taverna Hirodion (☎ 2242 026 634; Artemisias 27; mains €5-8) You'll find that Hirodion, virtually next door to Barbas, serves good and inexpensive food.

There are a dozen discos and clubs catering to the different music moods of the crowd around the streets of Diakon and Nafklirou, just north of the Agora. **Fashion Club** (☎ 2242 022 592; Kanari 2), off Dolphin Square, is a monster with three bars. **Kalua** (☎ 2242 024 938; Akti Zouroudi 3) is up by the beach to the north of the harbour. There are no shortage of bars around that area, either.

Getting There & Around

There are daily flights to Athens (€82) from Kos' international airport.

Frequent ferries arrive from Rhodes that continue on to Piraeus (€27), via Kalymnos, Leros and Patmos. There are less frequent connections to Nisyros, Tilos, Symi, Samos and Crete. Daily excursion boats visit Nisyros, Kalymnos, Patmos and Rhodes. In summer, ferries depart for Bodrum in Turkey (one-way/return trip €20/34, daily).

Next to the tourist office is a blue minitrain that leaves hourly for Asklipion (€3) and a mini-green train that does city tours (€2). Buses regularly serve all parts of the island.

PATMOS ΠΑΤΜΟΣ
pop 3050
Orthodox and Western Christians have long made pilgrimages to Patmos, for it was here that St John wrote his revelations.

The **tourist office** (☎ 2247 031 666; ☿ 8am-6pm Mon-Fri, summer only), post office and police station are in the white building at the island's port and capital of Skala. Buses leave regularly for the hora, 4.5km inland and above the port.

Apollon Travel (☎ 2247 031 324; apollon@12net.gr) on the waterfront handles schedules and ticketing. The *Patmos Times*, an excellent English-language magazine on the island, is readily available. **Blue Bay Hotel**, 200m left from the port (facing inland), has Internet access for €4 per hour.

The **Cave of the Apocalypse** (☎ 2247 031 234; ☿ 8am-1.30pm daily, 4-6pm Tue, Thu & Sun), where St John wrote the divinely inspired *Book of Revelations*, is halfway between the port and the hora. The **Monastery of St John the Theologian** (☎ 2247 031 223; admission monastery/

treasury free/€5) looks more like a castle than a monastery, and it crowns the island. It is open the same hours as the cave and exhibits monastic treasures.

Lambi Beach, on the north coast, is a pebble-beach lover's dream come true.

Hotel Australis (☎ 2247 031 576; www.patmosweb .gr/australishotel_en.htm; d with breakfast €40-60) Rooms have private facilities and there's an oasis-like garden. It's 500m north of the quay

Villa Knossos (☎ 2247 032 189; fax 2247 032 284; d €25-50; 🔀) Exceptional rooms.

Stefanos Camping (☎ 2247 031 821; per adult/tent €6/3) On Meloï Beach, 2km northeast of Skala.

Grigoris Taverna (☎ 2247 031 515; mains €4-8), opposite the port gate, is popular, or you could head for **Kipos Garden Restaurant** (☎ 2247 031 884; dishes €3-8), which serves home-grown vegetable dishes such as fried aubergines. **Aman** (☎ 2247 032 323) has a tree-shaded patio and relaxing music.

Patmos is well connected by ferry with Piraeus (€22) and Rhodes (€19) via Leros, Kalymnos and Kos. In summer, there are daily hydrofoils to Leros, Kalymnos, Kos, Rhodes, Fourni, Ikaria, Agathonisi and Samos.

NORTHEASTERN AEGEAN ISLANDS

This group consists of seven major islands strewn across the northeastern corner of the Aegean, closer to Turkey than mainland Greece. With wonderful hiking, crowd-free beaches and unique villages on offer, they reward exploration.

LESVOS (MYTILINI) ΛΕΣΒΟΣ (ΜΥΤΙΛΗΝΗ)
The third largest of the Greek islands, fertile Lesvos has always been a centre of philosophy and artistic achievement, and it still attracts creative types on sabbatical.

Mytilini
pop 27,250
The capital and main port, Mytilini, is a large working town. The **tourist office** (☎ 2251 042 511; 6 Aristarhou; 🕙 9am-1pm Mon-Fri) is 50m up Aristarhou by the quay. **Samiotis Tours** (☎ 2251 042 574; samiotistours@hotmail.com; Kountourioti 43), 400m from the ferry on the waterfront, handles flights, boat schedules and ticketing, and runs excursions to Turkey. **Sponda** (☎ 2251 041 007;

Komninaki; per hr €2), a block back from the waterfront in a pool bar, has Internet access.

Mytilini's excellent neoclassical **archaeological museum** (☎ 2251 022 087; adult/senior €3/2; 🕙 8.30am-7pm Tue-Sun) has a fascinating collection that ranges from Neolithic to Roman times. Five kilometres from Mytilini on the Gulf of Yera are the **Therma hot springs** (☎ 2251 024 575; admission €2.50; 🕙 8am-6pm) where you can bathe in a steamy white room while looking at views over the water and mountains.

Salina's Rooms (☎ 2251 024 640; cnr Fokeas & Kinikiou; s/d €25/30) has clean rooms, a garden and a kitchen that guests can use. Virtually next door and run by the same people is **Pension Thalia** (☎ 2251 042 073; Kinikiou 1; s/d €25/30), which has clean bright rooms in a large house. They are about a five-minute walk north of the main square, up Ermou, then right on Adramytiou.

Ocean Eleven Bar (Kountourioti 17) in the corner on the waterfront is an excellent place to start or end the evening. **Restaurant Averof** (☎ 2251 022 180; Ermou 52; mains from €4), just back from the main square, dishes up hearty Greek staples such as *patsas* (tripe soup).

There are daily flights to Athens (€78) and to Thessaloniki (€88). In summer, there are daily boats to Piraeus (€24), some via Chios, Mykonos and Syros, and one boat per week to Thessaloniki (€30). There is also a ferry to Skiathos in the Sporades group (€26, weekly). There are ferries Ayvalik in Turkey (one-way/return trip €30/45, four weekly).

Local buses leave regularly for Therma from the main square on the waterfront. Long-distance buses to Mithymna, Sykaminia, Mantamados and Agia Paraskevi leave from next to Agia Irinis park, a block inland at the southern end of the waterfront.

Mithymna
pop 1500
The gracious, preserved town of Mithymna (known by locals as Molyvos) is 62km north of Mytilini. Cobbled streets canopied by flowering vines wind up the hill below the impressive castle. You'll be tempted never to leave.

The helpful **municipal tourist office** (☎ 2253 071 347; www.mithymna.gr; 🕙 8am-9pm Mon-Fri, 9am-7pm Sat & Sun), 100m towards town from the bus stop, has good maps. Fifty metres on, take the right fork onto 17 Noemvriou, the cobbled main thoroughfare, or continue straight ahead to reach the colourful **fishing port**. There are countless travel agencies and three Internet cafés along the port road.

The noble **Genoese castle** (☎ 2253 071 803; admission €2; ⊙ 8am-7pm Tue-Sun) sits above the town like a crown and affords tremendous views out to Turkey. **Eftalou hot springs** (☎ 2253 071 245; public/private baths per person €3.50/5; ⊙ 10am-2pm & 4-8pm public, 9am-4pm private), 4km from town on the beach, is a superb bathhouse complex with a whitewashed dome and steaming, pebbled pool. There are also new private baths where you don't need a bathing suit. Buses go regularly from Mithymna.

Nassos Guest House (☎ 2253 071 432; nassosguesthouse@hotmail.com; Arionis; d/t €25/30) is an airy, friendly place with shared facilities and a communal kitchen. The views are rapturous. To get there, head up 17 Noemvriou and take the second right (a sharp switchback). **Camping Mithymna** (☎ 2253 071 169; per adult/tent €3.5/3) is in a shady spot 2km from town. It's signposted from the tourist office. **Betty's Restaurant** (☎ 2253 071 421; Agora; mains from €5), in a building that used to be a notorious bordello, has superb views and atmosphere. Head down to the port for few drinks.

Around the Island

East of Mithymna, the traditional picturesque villages surrounding **Mt Lepetymnos** (Sykaminia, Mantamados and Agia Paraskevi) are worth your time.

Southern Lesvos is dominated by **Mt Olympus** (968m) and the very pretty day-trip destination of **Agiasos**, which has good artisan workshops.

SPORADES ΣΠΟΡΑΔΕΣ

In the Sporades group, Skiathos has the best beaches and a throbbing tourist scene; Skopelos is relaxed with a postcard waterfront and lush forest trails; and far-less-visited Alonnisos retains more local character. The main ports for the Sporades are Volos and Agios Konstantinos on the mainland.

SKIATHOS ΣΚΙΑΘΟΣ
pop 6150

Lush and green, Skiathos has a universal beach-resort feel about it. An international airport has brought loads of package tourists, but the island has enough on offer to keep everyone happy.

Orientation & Information

There is a **tourist information booth** (☎ 2427 023 172) to the left as you leave the port, but it opens irregularly. Skiathos Town's main thoroughfare is Papadiamanti, running inland opposite the quay. Here you'll find the **post office** and the helpful **tourist police** (☎ 2427 023 172; ⊙ 8am-9pm).

Travel Agency Skiathos (☎ 2427 022 209; www .skiathosoe.com) on the waterfront corner is flat out with travel schedules and tickets. **Internet Zone Café** (☎ 2427 022 767; per hr €3; ⊙ 10.30am-1am) is 100m up Evangelistrias, off Papadiamanti.

Skiathos has some excellent beaches, particularly on the south coast. **Koukounaries** is popular with families. A short stroll over the headland, **Big Banana Beach** is superb, but for

---

SAPPHO, LESBIANS AND LESVOS

If you saw *My Big Fat Greek Wedding*, you might remember that the main character Toula's father had a passion for showing how virtually every word in common use in English today can be traced back to Greek. He even found a way to show that the word *kimono* has Greek origins. One he didn't come up with at the wedding party, however, was the word *lesbian*. Nevertheless he would undoubtedly be aware of the word's origins.

One of Greece's great ancient poets, Sappho, was born on the island of Lesvos during the 7th century BC, in the town of Eresos. Her poetry quickly became famous for its lyrically evocative style and richly sumptuous imagery. Most of Sappho's work was devoted to love and desire, and the objects of her affection were often female. Owing to this last fact, her name and birthplace have come to be associated with female homosexuality. An excellent statue of Sappho takes pride of place in the main square on the waterfront in Mytilini.

These days, Lesvos is visited by many lesbians paying homage to Sappho. The whole island is very gay-friendly; in particular, the southwestern beach resort of Skala Eresou, which is built over ancient Eresos, Sappho's birthplace.

a full tan, head a tad further on to **Little Banana Beach** where bathing suits are a rarity.

Sleeping

There is a **Rooms to Let** (☎ 2427 022 990) bookings kiosk on the waterfront that opens when ferries and hydrofoils arrive. Domatia owners meet ferries. Negotiate if you arrive out of season.

Pension Pandora (☎ 2427 024 357 / 6979 156 019; www.skiathosinfo.com/accomm/pension-pandora; Paleokastro; s/d/q €30-60; 🍴 🅿) Run by the effervescent Georgina, this is a superb place 10 minutes' walk north of the quay. The 14 rooms have TV, kitchens and balconies. It also has two exceptional apartments just off Papadiamanti.

Apartments Filitsa (☎ 2427 021 185; Metaxa; apartments €30-100; 🍴) These two-bedroom apartments sleep from two to six people, have a fully equipped kitchen, and are perfect for a long stay. They're in the old part of town near Panagia Theotokos church.

Camping Koukounaries (☎ 2427 049 250; per adult/tent €6/3) Thirty minutes away by bus at Koukounaries Beach, this camping ground has a minimart, taverna and good facilities.

Eating & Drinking

There are several places serving cheap eats on Papadiamanti.

Taverna Dionysos (☎ 2427 022 675; Panora; three-course meal from €7) This place knows how to keep its diners happy and presents you with an ouzo before dinner and a Metaxa (brand of Greek brandy) with coffee to finish. In between, you can opt for tasty three-course menus.

Psaradiki Ouzeri (☎ 2427 023 412; Paralia; mains €3.50-10) As it's located by the fish market at the far end of the old port, it's little surprise that this place is the town's seafood winner.

Nightlife sprawls along Politehniou. Check out Skiathos' low-key gay and lesbian scene at **La Skala Bar** (☎ 2427 023 102; Politehniou) above the old port. **Kahlua Bar** (☎ 2427 023 205), on the club strip at the eastern waterfront end of town, is popular and pulses with mainstream DJ sets.

Getting There & Around

In summer, there are daily flights from Athens to Skiathos (€55).

There are frequent ferries to the mainland ports of Volos (€11.60) and Agios Konstantinos (€20.80), and frequent hydrofoils each day to Skopelos (€9.10) and Alonnisos (€13). In summer, there are two boats a week to Thessaloniki (€16.80).

Crowded buses ply the south-coast road between Skiathos Town and Koukounaries every 20 minutes, stopping at all the beaches along the way. The bus stop is at the eastern end of the harbour.

SKOPELOS ΣΚΟΠΕΛΟΣ
pop 4700

Skopelos island, mountainous and forest-covered, is less commercialised than Skiathos. Skopelos Town skirts a semicircular bay and clambers in tiers up a hillside, culminating in a ruined fortress.

There is no tourist office or tourist police, but **Thalpos Leisure & Services** (☎ 2424 022 947; www.holidayislands.com), on the waterfront, is handy for accommodation and tours.

Head 50m up the road opposite the port entrance to find Platanos Square. Along Doulidi, the street to the left, are the post office, **Internet@Café** (☎ 2424 023 093; 🕑 9am-2.30pm, 5pm-midnight) and a stack of popular nightspots. The bus station is next to the port.

Velanio Beach on the south coast is the island's nudie spot. On the west coast, pebbled **Panormos Beach**, with its sheltered emerald bay surrounded by pine forest, is superb. The 2km stretch of **Milia Beach**, a few kilometres further on, is considered the island's best.

Domatia owners meet the boats. **Pension Sotos** (☎ 2424 022 549; www.skopelos.net/sotos; s/d €25/50), in the middle of the waterfront, has big rooms in an enchanting building. There's also a communal kitchen and courtyard. **Pension Soula** (☎ 2424 022 930; d/t €25/55), a 10-minute walk from the port, is a welcoming place with airy rooms; you'll awake in rural bliss to birdsong and donkeys braying.

The top spot in town to chill out is under the huge plane tree at **Platanos Jazz Bar** (☎ 2424 023 661) opposite the excursion boat quay. It's open all day, serves a mean omelette (€3) for breakfast, and plays wicked jazz and blues until the late hours. Fifty metres inland from Platanos Square, **Perivoli Taverna** (☎ 2424 023 758; mains €6-13) serves great vegetarian dishes. There is a clutch of popular bars on Doulidi, including **Dancing Club Kounos** (☎ 2424 023 623).

In summer, there are daily ferries to Volos (€15.10) and Agios Konstantinos (€28.40) that also call at Skiathos. Flying Dolphin hydrofoils dash several times a day to Skiathos, Alonnisos, Volos and Agios Konstantinos. For schedules and tickets, visit the **Skopelos Ferry Office** (☎ 2424 022 767) opposite the port. There are frequent buses to the beaches.

ALONNISOS ΑΛΟΝΝΗΣΟΣ
pop 2700
Green, serene Alonnisos is the least visited of the Sporades. The area surrounding the island has been declared a marine park and reputedly has the cleanest waters in the Aegean.

There are two main thoroughfares in the port village of Patitiri; facing inland from the ferry quay, Pelasgon is to the left and Ikion Dolopon is to the far right. There is no tourist office or tourist police, but the post office, police and Internet access at **Il Mondo Café** (☎ 2424 065 834; per hr €4) are on Ikion Dolopon. On the waterfront itself, **Alonnisos Travel** (☎ 2424 065 188; www .alonnisostravel.gr) handles boat scheduling and ticketing.

The tiny hora, **Old Alonnisos**, is a few kilometres inland. Alonnisos is ideal for walking. *Alonnisos on Foot: A Walking & Swimming Guide* by Bente Keller & Elias Tsoukanas is excellent and available at newsstands.

The **Rooms to Let service** (☎ 2424 066 188; fax 2424 065 577; ⏰ 10am-2pm, 6.30-10.30pm), opposite the quay, books accommodation all over the island. Bright and cheerful **Pension Pleiades** (☎ 2424 065 235; pleiades@internet.gr; s/d €25/45; ❄) looks out over the harbour and is visible from the quay. **Camping Rocks** (☎ 2424 065 410; per adult €5) is a shady, basic camping ground. It's about 1.5km from the port; go up Pelasgon and take the first road on your left.

To Kamaki Ouzeri (☎ 2424 065 245; Ikion Dolopon; mains €4-10) is a traditional island eatery. Check the ready-to-eat dishes out in the kitchen. **Café Flisvos** (☎ 2424 065 307; mains from €5) is the pick of the waterfront restaurants, under the canopy opposite the dock. **Club Enigma** (☎ 2424 065 307; Pelasgon) rocks once the tourist season kicks in.

There are daily ferries from Alonnisos to Volos (€15.70) and Agios Konstantinos (€28.40), via Skiathos and Skopelos. Flying Dolphin hydrofoils travel several times a day to Volos and Agios Konstantinos and between the islands. The local bus runs to the hora every hour.

IONIAN ISLANDS
ΤΑ ΕΠΤΆΝΗΣΑ
The idyllic Ionian group of islands stretch down the western coast of Greece from Corfu in the north to remote Kythira, off the southern tip of the Peloponnese. These mountainous islands, with their soft light and Italian influence, offer a contrasting experience from other island groups in Greece.

CORFU ΚΕΡΚΥΡΑ
pop 109,540
Corfu is the second largest and most important island in the group and is one of Greece's most beautiful islands. The capital, Corfu Town, is built on a promontory, and the Old Town, wedged between two fortresses, offers up a medley of occupying influences. Ferries dock at the new port, just west of the new fortress. The long-distance bus station on Avrami is inland from the port.

Information
National Bank of Greece (cnr Voulgareos & Theotoki)
On Line Internet Café (Kapodistria 28; per hr €4)
Tourist Police (☎ 2661 030 265; 3rd fl, Samartzi 4)

Sights
Housed in the **Archaeological Museum** (☎ 2661 030 680; P Vraili 5; admission €3; ⏰ 8.30am-3pm Tue-Sun) is a collection of finds from Mycenaean to classical times. Corfu's most famous church, the **Church of Agios Spiridon**, has a richly decorated interior.

Most of the coast of northern Corfu is package-tourist saturated, but the view from the summit of **Mt Pantokrator** (906m), Corfu's highest mountain, is spectacular. There's a road to the top from the village of **Strinila**.

The main resort on the west coast is **Paleokastritsa**, built around a series of pretty bays. Further south, there are good beaches around **Agios Gordios**. Between Paleokastritsa and Agios Gordios is the hilltop village of **Pelekas**, a great sunset spot.

Sleeping
Hotel Hermes (☎ 2661 039 268; G Markora 14; s/d €28/33, s/d with bathroom €36/44) It's a tad noisy,

but has a certain shabby charm and is popular with backpackers.

Hotel Konstantinoupolis (☎ 2661 048 716; www .konstantinoupolis.com.gr; K Zavitsianou 11; s/d/tr €55/80/ 96; ❄) This renovated hotel has an unbeatable position overlooking the old harbour (ask for a front room). The rooms are spotless, all come with TV and there are good discounts off-season.

At the southern end of Pelekas Beach is **Sunrock** (☎ 2661 094 637; www.geocities.com/sunrock _corfu; r per person €18, with bathroom, including breakfast & dinner per person €24; ⊠ ⍰), a family-run place with excellent facilities and activities that make it a backpacker favourite. Outside Agios Gordios, the **Pink Palace** (☎ 2661 053 103; www.thepinkpalace.com; A-/B-class room including breakfast & dinner per person €25/32; ⍰), has long been considered an obligatory stop on the European backpacker circuit. You'll either love or hate the summer-camp-without-supervision vibe.

No matter where you eat in Corfu, you can't miss sitting on the Liston nursing a frappé (€3.50) and indulging in some people-watching.

Getting There & Away

Three flights daily to Athens are offered by both **Olympic Airways** (☎ 2661 038 694; Polila 11, Corfu Town) and **Aegean Airlines** (☎ 2661 027 100). Olympic also flies to Thessaloniki three times a week.

There are also buses to Athens (€29.50, 8½ hours, daily) and Thessaloniki (€28.50, eight hours, daily) from the Avrami terminal in Corfu Town.

There are ferries to Igoumenitsa (€5.10, 1½ hours, hourly) and a daily ferry to Paxi. In summer, there are daily services to Patra (€21.50 to €25, six hours) on the international ferries that call at Corfu on their way from Italy.

Getting Around

Buses for villages close to Corfu Town leave from Plateia San Rocco. Services to other destinations leave from the station on Avrami. There's no bus from the airport, and a taxi to the Old Town costs around €9.

ITHAKI ΙΘΑΚΗ

pop 3080

Ithaki, or ancient Ithaca, was Odysseus' long-lost home in Homer's *Odyssey*. Ithaki doesn't attract large crowds, mainly because of its lack of good beaches, but it's perfect for a quiet holiday. From the main town of Vathy you can walk to the **Fountain of Arethousa**, the fabled site of Odysseus' meeting with the swineherd Eumaeus on his return to Ithaki.

Ithaki has daily ferries to the mainland ports of Patra and Astakos, as well as daily services to Kefallonia and Lefkada.

KEFALLONIA ΚΕΦΑΛΛΟΝΙΑ

pop 35,600

Quiet Kefallonia found itself in spotlight following the success of *Captain Corelli's Mandolin*. Unfortunately for visitors to the island's capital, Sami, the old Venetian streets featured in the movie were as fake as Nicholas Cage's accent. There's an **EOT office** (☎ 2671 022 248) on the waterfront in Argostoli.

In Sami, **Hotel Melissani** (☎ 2674 022 464; d €53) is a slightly eccentric and pleasant older-style hotel offering such comforts as TV and fridge. Some rooms have air-con. **Karavomilos Beach Camping** (☎ 2674 022 480; www.camping -karavomilos.gr; per adult/tent €6/3.50; ⍰), located 800m from Sami, is a well-maintained camping ground that offers plenty of shade as well as a minimarket, laundry and restaurant.

Riviera (☎ 2674 022 777; mains €3.50-8.50), located on the waterfront, is a welcoming café-pizzeria that also has simple rooms (available for €45) above the café.

There are daily ferries from Sami to Patra (€11.50, 2½ hours), as well as from Argostoli and the southeastern port of Poros to Kyllini in the Peloponnese. There are also ferry connections to the islands of Ithaki, Lefkada and Zakynthos.

ZAKYNTHOS ΖΑΚΥΝΘΟΣ

pop 39,020

Zakynthos, or Zante, is a beautiful island resplendent with gorgeous beaches – but during summer it's completely overrun with tourists. Its capital and port, Zakynthos Town, is an imposing old Venetian town.

The area around the huge **Bay of Laganas** in the south has some of the best beaches, but endangered loggerhead turtles come ashore here to lay their eggs in August – at the peak of the tourist invasion. The Greek government has declared this area a National Marine Park. There are regular ferries between Zakynthos and Kyllini in the Peloponnese.

GREECE

GREECE DIRECTORY

ACCOMMODATION

There is a good range of budget accommodation in Greece, and it is subject to price controls set by the tourist police. By law, a notice must be displayed in every room, stating the category of the room and also the seasonal price. If you think you've been ripped off, contact the tourist police. Prices quoted in this chapter are for the high season, unless otherwise stated. Prices are about 40% cheaper between October and May.

Greece has around 350 camping grounds, but many are open only between April and October. Standard facilities include hot showers, kitchens, restaurants and minimarkets – and often a swimming pool. Prices vary according to facilities, but expect to pay €4.50 to €6 per adult, €3.50 for a small tent and €6 for a large one. Free camping is illegal in Greece, but rarely enforced.

Greece has 55 mountain refuges, which are listed in the booklet *Greece Mountain Refuges & Ski Centres*, available free of charge at EOT and EOS (Ellinikos Orivatikos Syndesmos; Greek Alpine Club) offices.

You'll find youth hostels in most major towns and on half a dozen islands. The only place affiliated with Hostelling International (HI) is the Athens International Youth Hostel (p532).

Most other youth hostels throughout Greece are run by the **Greek Youth Hostel Organisation** (☎ 2107 519 530; y-hostels@otenet.gr; Damareos 75, Athens 116 33). There are affiliated hostels in Athens, Olympia, Patra and Thessaloniki on the mainland, and on the islands of Crete and Santorini (Thira). Most charge €8 to €10, and you don't have to be a member to stay in any of them.

Domatia, the Greek equivalent of a bed and breakfast (minus the breakfast), can represent good value. Expect to pay about €25 to 35 for a single and €40 to 50 for a double. Owners shouting 'Room!' generally greet ferries and buses. Just make sure that your room isn't half an hour's walk from the action.

ACTIVITIES
Diving & Snorkelling

There is excellent snorkelling in Greece. Corfu, Mykonos and Santorini are popular destinations with diving schools. Diving without certified supervision is forbidden in order to protect the many antiquities in the depths of the Aegean.

Sailing

Sailing facilities are generally found at the same locations recommended for windsurfing. Hrysi Akti on Paros and Mylopotas Beach on Ios are two of the best locations. Hire charges for catamarans range from €20 to €25.

Skiing

Greece's 16 resorts offer some of the cheapest skiing in Europe as they cater mainly to locals and are basic compared to the glitzy resorts of northern Europe. There is a brochure available from EOT offices (p529). Information about snow conditions is available at www.snowreport.gr.

Trekking

Greece has excellent trekking opportunities, but outside the main popular routes trails are generally overgrown and poorly marked. Several companies run organised treks; the biggest is **Trekking Hellas** (Map p533; ☎ 2103 310 323; www.trekking.gr; Filellinon 7, Athens 105 57).

Windsurfing

Windsurfing is the most popular water sport in Greece. Sailboards are widely available for hire, priced at €12 to €15 per hour. The top spots for windsurfing are Golden Beach (Hrysi Akti) on the southeast coast of Paros, and Vasiliki on the southern part of Lefkada, which is a popular place to learn.

BUSINESS HOURS

Banking hours are 8am to 2pm Monday to Thursday, and 8am to 1.30pm Friday (also afternoons and Saturday morning in large cities). Many shops are open from 8am to 1.30pm and from 5.30pm to 8.30pm Tuesday, Thursday and Friday and from 8am to 2.30pm Monday, Wednesday and Saturday. Restaurants are generally open for lunch from 11am to 2pm and for dinner from 8pm to 1am. Bars generally open after 8pm and close after midnight. Clubs open around 11pm but don't really get going until after midnight. If going to an upmarket restaurant, locals generally don't make a booking for earlier than 10pm.

DISABLED TRAVELLERS

If mobility is a problem, the hard fact is that most hotels, museums and ancient sites are not wheelchair-accessible. Although facilities in Athens improved for the 2004 Olympics, elsewhere the uneven terrain is an issue even for able-bodied people.

EMBASSIES & CONSULATES
Embassies in Greece

All foreign embassies in Greece are in Athens and its suburbs:

Australia (Map pp530-1; ☎ 2106 450 404; Dimitriou Soutsou 37, 115 21)

Canada (Map pp530-1; ☎ 2107 273 400; Genadiou 4, 115 21)

France (Map pp530-1; ☎ 2103 611 663; Leof Vasilissis Sofias 7, 106 71)

Germany (Map pp530-1; ☎ 2107 285 111; Dimitriou 3 & Karaoli, Kolonaki 106 75)

Italy (Map pp530-1; ☎ 2103 617 260; Sekeri 2, 106 74)

New Zealand (Map pp530-1; ☎ 2106 874 701; Kifissias 268, Halandri)

South Africa (Map pp530-1; ☎ 2106 806 645; Kifissias 60, Maroussi, 151 25)

UK (Map pp530-1; ☎ 2107 236 211; Ploutarhou 1, 106 75)

USA (Map pp530-1; ☎ 2107 212 951; Leoforos Vasilissis Sofias 91, 115 21)

Greek Embassies Abroad

Australia (☎ 02-6273 3011; 9 Turrana St, Yarralumla, ACT 2600)

Canada (☎ 613-238 6271; 76-80 Maclaren St, Ottawa, Ontario K2P 0K6)

France (☎ 01-47 23 72 28; www.amb-grece.fr/presse; 17 Rue Auguste Vaquerie, 75116 Paris)

Germany (☎ 0228-83010; www.griechische-botschaft .de; Jaegerstrasse 54-55, 10117 Berlin-Mitte)

Italy (☎ 06-854 9630; Via S Mercadante 36, Rome 3906)

Japan (☎ 03-3403 0871/0872; www.greekemb.jp; 3-16-30 Nishi Azabu, Minato-ku, Tokyo 304-5853)

New Zealand (☎ 04-473 7775; 5-7 Willeston St, Wellington)

South Africa (☎ 12-430 7351; 1003 Church St, Hatfield, Pretoria 0028)

Spain (☎ 01-564 4653; Avenida Doctor Arce 24, Madrid 28002)

UK (☎ 020-7229 3850; www.greekembassy.org.uk; 1A Holland Park, London W11 3TP)

USA (☎ 202-939 1300; www.greekembassy.org; 2221 Massachusetts Ave NW, Washington, DC 20008)

FESTIVALS & EVENTS

Funnily enough, in Greece it's easier to list the dates when festivals and events are not on! Some are religious, some are cultural and others are seemingly just an excuse to party. More details can be found at the website www.cultureguide.gr. Easter is a celebratory event right across Greece, and the Hellenic Festival is the most important of the festivals staged throughout Greece during summer. The Theatre of Herodes Atticus, in Athens, and the Theatre of Epidavros, near Nafplio, are venues for traditional events.

GAY & LESBIAN TRAVELLERS

Although there is no legislation against homosexual activity, it's wise to be discreet in Greece. Nevertheless it is a popular destination for gay travellers. Athens has a busy gay scene – but the islands are really the place to head. Mykonos in the Cyclades has long been famous for its bars, beaches and hedonism, and the town of Eresos on Lesvos has become a pilgrimage site for lesbians.

HOLIDAYS

New Year's Day 1 January
Epiphany 6 January
First Sunday in Lent February
Greek Independence Day 25 March
Good Friday/Easter Sunday March/April
Spring Festival/Labour Day 1 May
Feast of the Assumption 15 August
Ohi Day 28 October
Christmas Day 25 December
St Stephen's Day 26 December

INTERNET ACCESS

Internet cafés are springing up everywhere in Greece. Charges are generally between €3 and €5 per hour.

INTERNET RESOURCES

Culture Guide (www.cultureguide.gr) Plenty of information about contemporary culture and the arts.
Greek Ferries (www.greekferries.gr) Get all your ferry information from the source. Covers international and domestic ferries.
Greek National Tourist Organisation (www.gnto.gr) Concise tourist information.
Lonely Planet (www.lonelyplanet.com) Has postcards from other travellers and the Thorn Tree bulletin board, where you can pose those tricky questions or help answer other travellers' questions on your return.
Ministry of Culture (www.culture.gr) Information on ancient sites, art galleries and museums.

MONEY

Banks exchange all major currencies, in either cash or travellers cheques. Post offices charge less commission than banks, but won't cash travellers cheques. Many smaller cafés and tavernas do not accept credit cards. You'll find ATMs everywhere, particularly in tourist areas.

Greece is still a cheap destination by northern European standards. An absolute rock-bottom daily budget would be €40. This would mean hitching, staying in youth hostels or camping, staying away from bars, and occasionally visiting a restaurant or using a ferry. Allow at least €80 per day for your own room, eating out regularly and seeing the sights. Travel outside the summer months is cheaper owing to heavily discounted accommodation prices.

POST

Post offices *(tahydromia)* are easily identified by the yellow sign outside. Regular post boxes are yellow, and red post boxes are for express mail. Postcards and airmail letters within the EU cost €0.60. To other destinations the rate is €0.65. Post within Europe takes five to eight days and to the USA, Australia and New Zealand, nine to 11 days. Some tourist shops also sell stamps, but with a 10% surcharge.

Mail can be sent poste restante to any main post office and is held for up to a month. Your surname should be underlined, and you'll need to show your passport to collect your mail. Parcels are not delivered in Greece – they must be collected from a post office.

TELEPHONE

The international access code is ☎ 00. Area codes are part of the 10-digit number within Greece. The landline prefix is 2, the mobile prefix is 6.

The Greek telephone service is maintained by the public corporation Organismos Ti-lepikoinonion Ellados, always referred to as OTE (pronounced o-*teh*). Public phones are everywhere, and all use OTE phonecards, sold at OTE offices and *periptera* (street kiosks). These cards are sold in €3, €5 and €9 versions, and a local call costs €0.30 for three minutes. There are also discount-card schemes available that give you double time for your money. If you have a GSM phone from a country with a global roaming agreement with Greece, you will be able to use your phone in Greece.

TOURIST INFORMATION

Tourist information is handled by the Greek National Tourist Organisation (GNTO), known as EOT. There is either an EOT office or a local tourist office in almost every town of consequence and on many of the islands. The head office is in Athens (see p533).

VISAS

The list of countries whose nationals can stay in Greece for up to three months includes Australia, Canada, all EU countries, Iceland, Israel, Japan, New Zealand, Norway, Switzerland and the USA. For longer stays, apply at a consulate abroad or at least 20 days in advance to the **Aliens Bureau** (Map p533; ☎ 2107 705 711; Leoforos Alexandras 173, Athens; ◷ 8am-1pm Mon-Fri) at Athens Central Police Station. Elsewhere in Greece, apply to the local police authority.

In the past, evidence of a visit to Turkish-occupied Northern Cyprus has been problematic when entering Greece. If visiting Northern Cyprus, have officials stamp a piece of paper rather than your passport.

WORKING

Your best chance of finding work is at the tourist hotels and bars during the summer season. Despite the long hours and low pay, these jobs are hotly contested. EU nationals don't need a work permit.

Hungary

HIGHLIGHTS

- **Budapest** The Queen of the Danube still reigns: great nightlife, tons of history… how can you go wrong? (p571)
- **Eger** Tasting your way through the wine cellars of Szépasszony völgy (Valley of the Beautiful Women) or exploring the ancient castle in Eger (p585)
- **Kecskemét** Strolling the lovely streets of old town Kecskemét (p584) to admire some dramatic Art Nouveau architecture. Afterwards, you might want to make a day trip to the horse show at Bugac in the nearby Kiskunság National Park
- **Best journey** Taking the train from Budapest around the Danube Bend (towards Slovakia), enjoy great views of the river and the hills. Watch for the remains of Visegrád Citadel (p580) high on one hill and the colossal cathedral at Esztergom (p580) glistening on another

FAST FACTS

- **Area** 93,000 sq km (similar size to Portugal)
- **ATMs** Widespread, even in smaller towns
- **Budget** 5000-10,000Ft per day
- **Capital** Budapest
- **Country Code** ☎ 36
- **Famous for** Paprika, goose-liver pâté and csardas music
- **Heads of State** President Ferenc Mádl, Prime Minister Péter Medgyessy
- **Language** Hungarian (Magyar)
- **Money** Hungarian forint (A$1 = 146Ft, CA$1 = 159Ft, €1 = 246Ft, ¥100 = 183Ft, NZ$1 = 135Ft, UK£1 = 358Ft, US$1 = 200Ft)
- **Phrases** Jo napot kivanok (Good day/hello), szia (hi/bye), köszönöm (thank you)
- **Time** GMT/UTC + 1
- **Visas** Most foreign nationals don't need a visa if staying for less than 90 days.

TRAVEL HINTS

Hungry? Look for the word pék (literally 'baker'); storefront shops with this in their name (Primapék, Pékseg…) sell fresh-daily pastries (110Ft to 230Ft per decigram). Many are sweet, filled with túro (sweet cheese), barack (apricot) and the like. But there are also savouries filled with sajt (cheese), virsli (hot dog) or pizza toppings. You'll often find them at train and metro stations; they're a great snack on the go.

ROAMING HUNGARY

Most of a shoestringer's time will be spent in Budapest, and with good reason. Using the capital as a base, day trips can be taken to the Danube Bend or Keszthely. Then a few days can be pleasurably spent further afield in Pécs, Szeged or Eger. Nothing in Hungary is more than five hours away from Budapest by train.

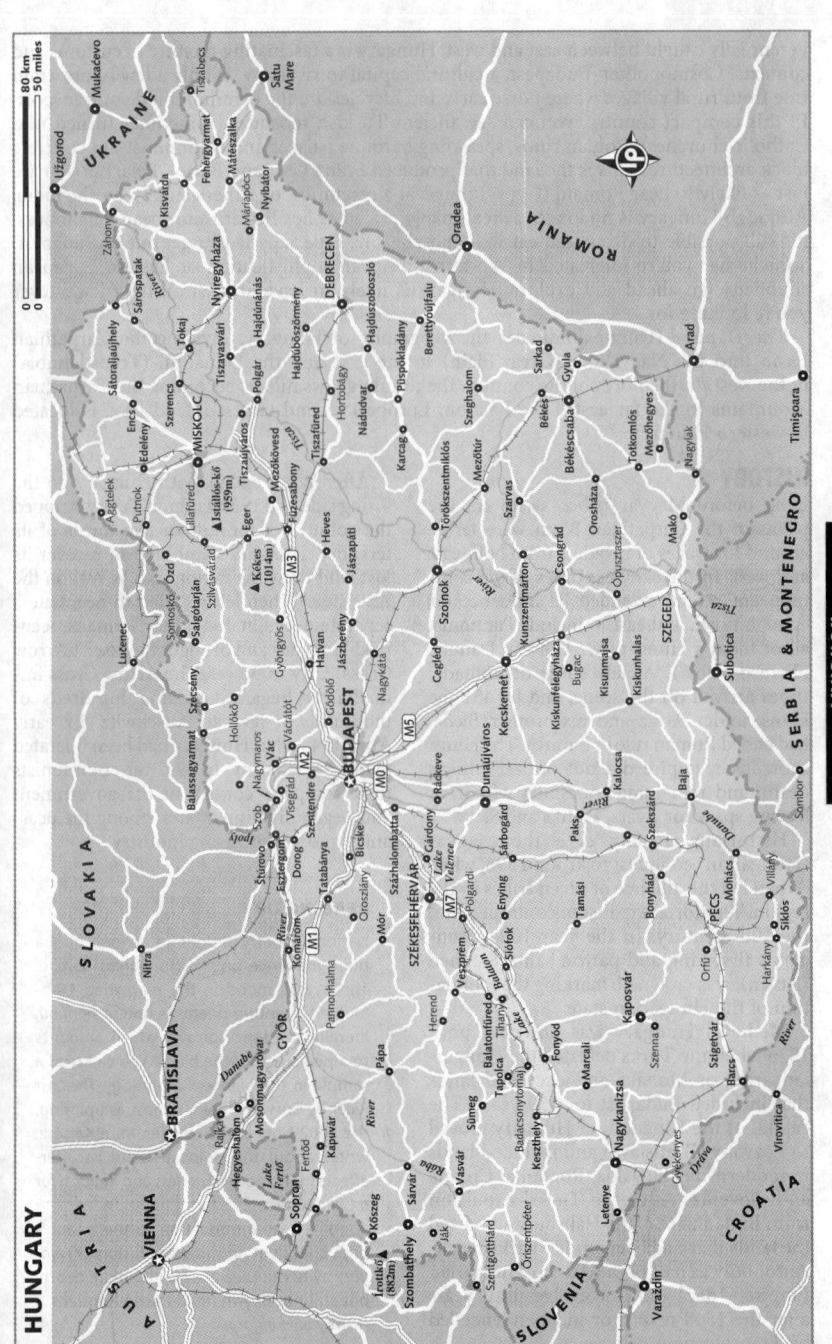

HUNGARY

Perennially caught between east and west, Hungary is a fascinating mixture of customs and contexts. Cosmopolitan Budapest, a cultural capital to rival any, is only a few hours' train ride from rural villages where horse carts and bicycles are the common mode of transport. In this compact country, you can see ancient Turkish mosques (sometimes turned into Catholic churches), Roman ruins, sprawling baroque palaces and communist-era concrete block architecture. This is the land that produced Franz Liszt and Bartók Béla, but you are just as likely to hear Romani (Gypsy) music at a restaurant or American pop on the radio. Although Hungary is no longer as reasonably priced as her Eastern European neighbours, it's still possible to drink and eat well and cheaply, especially if you get out of Budapest. So, whether you're interested in Western European sophistication or Eastern European simplicity, go ahead and explore. Hungary is likely to have at least a little of whatever you're looking for.

The Danube (Duna) dominates the geography of Hungary, dividing the Carpathian Basin into the Nagyalföld (Great Plain) in the east and the Dunántúl (Transdanubia) in the west. In the north of the country, the terrain grows hillier, becoming the Carpathian Mountains in the far east. Lake Balaton, Europe's second-largest inland lake, is located in western Hungary.

HISTORY

Long before Magyar tribes swept in, the plains of the Carpathian Basin were fertile ground for waves of invaders from both east and west. In the early centuries of the common era, Rome extended its influence far enough north and east to include Pannonia, all of today's Hungary west of the Danube (Transdanubia). A new surge of nomadic tribes arrived on the scene, and by 451 the Huns, under Attila and his brother Bleda, had ended Roman rule in the area. The Huns' short-lived empire did not outlast Attila's death, and remaining tribesmen withdrew, leaving space for Avars, Franks and Slavs.

Historians usually date the Magyar (Hungarian) conquest to around 896, when Árpád led the alliance of seven tribes in the region. Territorial expansion continued into the 10th century. In the year 1000, Hungary's first king and patron saint, Stephen (István), was crowned, marking the foundation of the Hungarian state.

Medieval Hungary was powerful until 1526 when the Turks defeated the Hungarian army at Mohács and occupied lands that included Budapest for 150 years. The capital of the Kingdom of Hungary moved to Pozsony (Bratislava) and included lands in modern-day Slovakia, Romania, Croatia and Slovenia. After the Turks' expulsion from Buda in 1686, the Habsburgs annexed the lands that had been under Turkish rule. Autonomy as half of the Austro-Hungarian Empire (1867) did not evolve until years after the 1848 revolt for independence led by Transylvanian princes.

After WWI ended, with Hungary on the losing side, the 1920 Trianon Treaty stripped the country of more than two-thirds of its territory. Hungary's ambition to recover its lost land drew the nation into WWII on the Axis side. When leftists tried to negotiate a separate peace in 1944, the Germans occupied Hungary and brought the fascist Arrow Cross Party to power. The Arrow Cross immediately began deporting hundreds of thousands of Jews to Auschwitz. By early April 1945 all of Hungary had been liberated by the Soviet army. In 1947 the communists took complete control of the government and began dividing estates among the peasantry and nationalising industry.

READING UP

National poetry taught in schools has a huge influence on the Hungarian psyche. The overall mood in the renowned 18th- and 19th-century poems is one of *honfibú*, literally 'patriotic sorrow', which amounts to a penchant for the blues. You can read a sample in the bilingual anthology *The Lost Rider* by Corvina Books. Almost as uplifting, the 2002 Nobel prize-winner, Imre Kertész, writes about the Holocaust and its after-effects in the novels *Fateless* and *Kaddish for a Child Not Born*.

For a easy introduction to the nation's past, check out *An Illustrated History of Hungary* by István Lázár. To go into more depth, but still not drown, read László Kontler's *A History of Hungary*.

On 23 October 1956 student demonstrators demanding the withdrawal of Soviet troops were fired upon. Soviet tanks moved into Budapest, and by the end of the fighting, more than 25,000 people had died. Still, Soviet control was not as tight in Hungary as in its Slavic satellite states, and the ruling system that emerged is often labelled 'Goulash Communism'.

Hungary began moving towards full democracy in 1989. The Republic of Hungary was proclaimed in October, and democratic elections were scheduled for March 1990. The last Soviet troops left the country in June 1991. The painful transition to a market economy resulted in declining living standards for most people, but the late 20th and early 21st centuries have seen astonishing economic growth. Hungary became a full member of NATO in 1999 and joined the European Union on 1 May 2004.

THE CULTURE

Hungarians speak Magyar, which, unlike most tongues you'll hear in Europe, is not an Indo-European language. It is traditionally categorised as Finno-Ugric and is distantly related only to Finnish and Estonian. Many young people speak at least some English, and retirees often understand German.

Although there are 13 officially recognised minorities in Hungary, ethnic Magyars make up about 98% of the population. The number of Roma is estimated to be between 500,000 and a million people. Other minorities include: Rusyns, Slovaks, Germans, Croats, Slovenian and Romanians. Hungary has a parliamentary government headed by the prime minister. The current PM, Péter Medgyessy, took office in May 2002. The majority interest is a coalition of the socialists (former communists) and a liberal party.

FOOD & DRINK

The omnipresent seasoning in traditional Hungarian cooking is paprika; it appears on restaurant tables beside the salt- and pepper-shakers as well as in many recipes. *Pörkölt*, a paprika-infused stew, can be made from different meats, including *borju* (veal), but usually has no vegetables. *Galuska* (small, gnocchi-like dumplings) are a good accompaniment to soak up the sauce. *Töltött kaposzta* (cabbage rolls

---

TOP FIVE BUDAPEST

- **Thermal water** Get into hot water at the Gellért Baths (p574) in Buda or the Széchenyi Baths (p574) in Pest

- **Szobor Park** Walk among the concrete ghosts left over from communist Hungary and buy a Stalin candle or Rákocsi pin

- **Ráday utca** Bars, cafés, restaurants, lunch counters, take-away joints: pedestrian Ráday utca (p577) has it all...grab an outdoor table and enjoy

- **Sziget Music Festival** Camp out on an island in the Danube, listen to bands from around the world, and consume lots of beer: that's what most people do at the week-long Sziget Music Festival (p574)

- **Aquincumi Múzeum** you can explore the excavated ruins of a 2nd-century Roman town at the edge of an empire (p574)

---

stuffed with meat and rice) is cooked in a roux made with paprika and topped with sour cream, as is *székelygulyás* (stewed pork and sour cabbage). Another Hungarian favourite is *halászlé* (fisherman's soup), a rich mix of several kinds of poached freshwater fish, tomatoes, green peppers and...paprika. Although served as a stew outside the country, inside Hungary *gulyás* (goulash) is a beef soup prepared with a paprika roux.

You'll also find turkey, pork and veal cutlets breaded, sometimes stuffed, and fried on menus nationwide. For desert you might try the cold *gyümölcs leves* (fruit soup) or *palincsinta* (crêpes) stuffed with jam, sweet cheese or chocolate sauce. A good foodstand snack is *langos*, fried dough that can be topped with cheese and/or *tejföl* (sour cream).

Two Hungarian wines are known internationally: the sweet, dessert wine Tokaji Aszú and the full-bodied red, Egri Bikavér (Eger Bull's Blood). But the country produces a number of other eminently drinkable wines as well. For the harder stuff, try *pálinka*, a strong, firewater-like brandy distilled from a variety of fruits, most commonly plums or apricots.

NO HUNS HERE

Hungarians have had a reputation for being an aggressive, warlike people ever since Attila the Hun. The only problem is that Attila wasn't a Hungarian. Although they were able warriors, the ancient ancestors of modern-day Magyars (what Hungarians call themselves in their native language) did not arrive in the Carpathian Basin (part of modern Hungary) until at least 400 years after the Huns had dispersed among other populations or fled back over the hills toward the Volga River.

The Indo-European root for what foreigners call the Magyar people (Hungarian, *Ungarn*, *Hongrie*) comes from the Latin word *ungri* (*Onogur* in Turkic). Before the Magyar tribes crossed the Carpathian Mountains, they are thought to have lived for centuries near or among Turkic peoples and were part of the tribal alliance of Onogur (Ten Peoples). The earliest confirmed Western writing (839) refers to the Magyars as *ungri*, or *Onogur*. So not even the European name for the Magyars has anything to do with the Huns.

Not that historical figures haven't tried to make the leap. Medieval chroniclers propagated the myth that heroic twin brothers Hunor and Magor, descendants of Noah, were the progenitors of the Huns and Magyar people. That way, the Magyars had a historical connection with the land they inhabited, and their kings had a link with the greatness of Attila. It's been an enduring legend…

TRANSPORT

GETTING THERE & AWAY
Air
International carriers fly from Budapest's Ferihegy 2 airport to destinations throughout mainland Europe, the UK, Russia and beyond. Low-cost airlines fly out of the older Ferihegy 1, a few kilometres down the road, to destinations such as London Stansted Airport.

Air Berlin (☎ 49-1805 737 800; www.airberlin.com) Low cost to Berlin, Munich, Hamburg, Düsseldorf, London and Mallorca.

Malév Hungarian Airlines (☎ 1-235 3888; www .malev.hu) National carrier; nonstop to Europe, North America and the Middle East, linking Hungary with Asia and Australia via Europe.

Sky Europe (☎ 1-777 7000; www.skyeurope.com) This budget airline flies to London, Paris, Amsterdam, Rome, Venice, Warsaw and Zurich.

Boat
There are international Mahart PassNave hydrofoil services on the Danube daily from April to early November between Budapest and Vienna (5½ hours), stopping in Bratislava (3½ hours). Adult one-way/return fares for Vienna are €75/99, for Bratislava €68/93. Students with ISIC cards pay €59/84. Boats leave from the Nemzetközi hajóállomás (International Ferry Pier), next to the **Mahart PassNave Ticket Office** (☎ 1-484 4010; www.mahartpassnave.hu; Belgrád rakpart, Nemzetközi hajóállomás).

Bus
Most international buses arrive at the Népliget Bus Station in Budapest. **Eurolines** (☎ 1-219 8080; www.eurolines.com), in conjunction with its Hungarian affiliate, **Volánbusz** (☎ 1-485 2162; www.volanbusz.hu), is the international carrier. Two of the closest destinations from Budapest are Vienna (5490Ft, 3½ hours, four daily) and Bratislava (Pozsony; 4400Ft, four hours, one daily).

Eurolines has passes valid for 15/30/60 days that allow unlimited travel between 32 Western and Central European cities, including Budapest. Adults pay €285/345/339, those 25 and younger or 60 and older pay €240/325/329 in high season.

Car & Motorcycle
Border controls between Hungary and Slovakia and Austria were not scheduled to be removed at the time of writing, despite Hungary's joining the EU. Third-party car insurance is compulsory for driving in Hungary. If your car is registered in the EU, it's assumed you have it. Other motorists must show a Green Card or buy insurance at the border.

Train
The Hungarian State Railways, **MÁV** (☎ 1-461 5500 international information; www.elvira.hu), links up with international rail networks in all directions; the schedule is available online. Eurail passes are valid in Hungary. EuroCity (EC) and Intercity (IC) trains require payment of a supplement. Sample destinations from Budapest include Vienna (6600Ft,

3½ hours, five daily); Bratislava (Pozsony; 3100Ft, 2½ hours, eight daily); Arad, Romania (7400Ft, 4½ hours, six daily); and Prague (11,400Ft, nine hours, two daily). Most larger train stations have left luggage rooms open at least 9am to 5pm.

GETTING AROUND
Bus
Volán buses are a good alternative to trains, and might be the only option if you are travelling between cities outside the capital. Bus fares average 1270Ft per 100km. Timetables are posted at stations and stops. Common footnotes you might see are *naponta* (daily) and *munkanapokon* (on work days). A few large bus stations have luggage rooms, but they generally close by 6pm.

Car & Motorcycle
All the big international car-rental firms have offices in Budapest, and there are local companies throughout the country, but don't expect many bargains. Motorways (M1, M3, M7) require toll passes (10-day, 2000Ft) that can be purchased at petrol stations and at some motorway entrances; rental cars usually come with them.

Hitching
In Hungary, hitchhiking is legal except on motorways. **Kenguru** (Map pp576-7; ☎ 1-266 5837; www.kenguru.hu; VIII Kőfaragó utca 15, Budapest; open 8am-6pm Mon-Fri, 10am-4pm Sat) is an agency that matches riders with drivers who want to take a paying passenger. Catch a ride to Amsterdam for 11,000Ft, Munich (5500Ft) or Paris (11,700Ft), among other destinations.

Local Transport
Public transport is efficient and extensive, with city bus and, in many towns, trolleybus services. Budapest and Szeged also have trams, and there's an extensive metro (underground or subway) and a suburban commuter railway in Budapest. Purchase tickets at newsstands before travelling and validate them once aboard.

Train
MÁV (Map pp576-7; ☎ 1-461 5400 domestic information; www.elvira.hu) operates a reliable train service on its 8000km of track, which branches out from Budapest like the spokes on a wheel. Second-class train fares are 824Ft per 100km.

Intercity (IC) trains are the most comfortable and the newest express trains. *Gyorsvonat* (fast trains) take longer and use older cars; *személyvonat* (passenger trains) stop at every village along the way. Seat reservations (*helyjegy*) are required on IC and some fast trains, which is indicated on the timetable by an 'R' in a box or a circle. (Just a plain 'R' means seat reservations are simply available.)

BUDAPEST

☎ 1 / pop 1.8 million

A commerce-rich city, Budapest is Hungary's capital, where about a fifth of the nation's residents reside. Despite its growth, this city retains a strong sense of history. Stroll up Andrássy utca (on the Unesco World Heritage List since 2002) to see ornate 19th-century mansions (turned into offices); admire the leaders of the Hungarian past – tribal chiefs, kings, poets and politicians – at Heroes' Square; climb Castle Hill to discover the few remaining medieval buildings; or seek out the Roman ruins at Aquincum. In today's Budapest glass-encased shopping centres stand beside ancient buildings, and mobile phones are everywhere. So take a soak in a

HUNGARY

GETTING INTO TOWN
The train and bus stations are all quite central, with metro stops attached, so it's easy to navigate. The airport is a bit further afield, 24km outside the city. To get into town, the cheapest way is to take the BKV Ferihegy bus (from outside the baggage claim at Ferihegy 2, or on the main road outside Ferihegy 1) to the end of its run, which is at the blue line metro terminus, the Kobany-Kispest stop. The bus ride takes about 25 minutes, as does the metro ride to the centre (Deák tér). You need a 230Ft ticket, available at newsstands or vending machines, validated on the bus and in the metro. If you want to switch metro lines, you'll need a second ticket.

A simpler way is to take the **Airport Minibus** (☎ 296 8555; one-way/return 2100/3600Ft; ⏱ 5am-1am) directly to the place you're staying (the bus will take you wherever you need to go). Buy tickets at the clearly marked stands near arrivals.

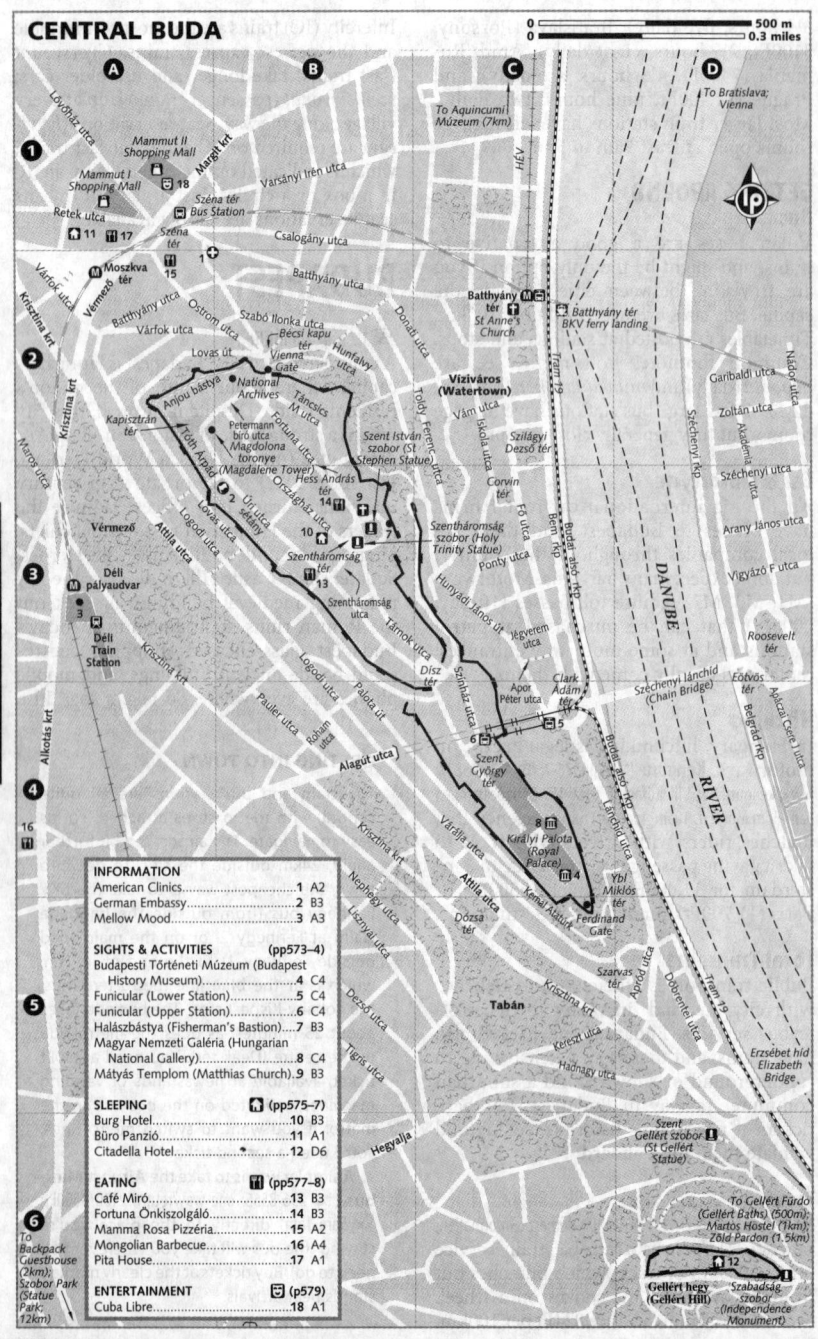

CENTRAL BUDA

0 _____ 500 m
0 _____ 0.3 miles

To Aquincumi Múzeum (7km)

To Bratislava; Vienna

Mammut II Shopping Mall

Mammut I Shopping Mall

Retek utca

Lövőház utca

Margit krt

Varsányi Irén utca

Széna tér Bus Station

Csalogány utca

Moszkva tér

Vérmező út

Várfok utca

Krisztina krt

Batthyány utca

Ostrom utca

Szabó Ilonka utca

Batthyány tér
St Anne's Church

Batthyány tér BKV ferry landing

Vízíváros (Watertown)

Vám utca

Garibaldi utca

Zoltán utca

Akadémia utca

Várfok utca

Vienna Gate

Lovas út

Anjou bástya

Hunfalvy utca

Donáti utca

National Archives

Szent István szobor (St Stephen Statue)

Szilágyi Dezső tér

Corvin tér

Arany János utca

Vigyázó F utca

Petermann bíró utca

Magdolona torony (Magdalene Tower)

Kapisztrán tér

Fortuna utca

Táncsics M utca

Hess András tér

Szentháromság szobor (Holy Trinity Statue)

Ponty utca

Roosevelt tér

Vérmező

Attila utca

Logodi utca

Úri utca

Országház utca

Tóth Árpád sétány

Szentháromság tér

Szentháromság utca

Hunyadi János út

Jégverem utca

Déli pályaudvar

Déli Train Station

Krisztina krt

Logodi utca

Palota út

Tárnok utca

Dísz tér

Szarvas tér

Clark Ádám tér

Apor Péter utca

Szarvas tér

Széchenyi lánchíd (Chain Bridge)

DANUBE

Eötvös tér

Belgrád rkp

DANUBE RIVER

Alkotás krt

Alagút utca

Pauler utca

Krisztina krt

Nőrám utca

Szent György tér

Szín utca

Clark Ádám tér

Budai alsó rkp

Lánchíd utca

16

Váralja utca

Krisztina krt

Naphegy utca

Lisznyai utca

8 Királyi Palota (Royal Palace)

4

Ybl Miklós tér

Ferdinand Gate

Kemál Atatürk

To Backpack Guesthouse (2km); Szobor Park (Statue Park; 12km)

Dózsa tér

Tabán

Dejsző utca

Tigris utca

Szarvas tér

Szendő utca

Hadnagy utca

Kereszt utca

Döbrentei utca

Tram 19

Erzsébet híd (Elizabeth Bridge)

Hegyalja

Szent Gellért szobor (St Gellért Statue)

To Gellért Fürdő (Gellért Baths) (500m); Martos Hostel (1km); Zöld Pardon (1.5km)

12

Gellért hegy (Gellért Hill)

Szabadság szobor (Independence Monument)

HUNGARY

centuries-old bath by day and then party at a swank nightclub rivalling any in Western Europe by night. Budapest is constantly evolving, and that's the best thing about the city – it's exciting and not a museum.

ORIENTATION

Originally three cities, Budapest straddles a gentle curve in the Danube (Duna) River, with hilly, house-filled Buda to the west, suburban Óbuda to the northwest and flat, commercial Pest across the river to the east. The Danube is spanned by nine bridges; two ring roads link three of the bridges across the Danube and essentially define central Pest. The most central square in Pest is Deák tér, the hub where the three metro lines meet. Buda is dominated by Castle and Gellért Hills; the main square is Moszkva tér.

The city is divided into 23 districts; a Roman numeral before or after the street address indicates the district. The Castle Hill district in Buda is district I, and the central pedestrian area of Pest is district V.

INFORMATION

Discount Card

The **Budapest Card** (www.budapestinfo.hu; 48-hour card 4350Ft, 72-hour 5450Ft) gives you free access to many museums and free transport on city trams, buses and metros, as well as discounts on other traveller services. You can buy the card at hotels, travel agencies, large metro kiosks and some tourist offices.

Internet Access

Most year-round hostels (see p575) offer Internet access. Budapest abounds in Internet cafés. Among the most accessible are:
Ami Internet Coffee (Map pp576-7; ☎ 267 1644; V Váci utca 40; per hr 700Ft; ⊗ 9am-2am) Tons of terminals, super central but also super busy.
Privat Link (Map pp576-7; ☎ 334 2057; VIII József körút 52; per hr 800Ft; ⊗ 24hr) To get a password and sign on, buy a card at the desk (an hour's the minimum).

Medical Services

American Clinics (Map pp572; ☎ 224 9090; I Hattyú utca 14, 5th floor; ⊗ 8.30am-7pm Mon-Thu, 8.30am-6pm Fri, 8am-noon Sat, 10am-2pm Sun) On call for emergencies 24/7.

Money

ATMs are quite common, especially on the ring roads and large arteries. Most banks have both an ATM and an exchange service.

EMERGENCY NUMBERS

- **National emergency number** (English spoken) ☎ 112
- **Police** (nationwide) ☎ 107
- **Fire** (nationwide) ☎ 105
- **Ambulance** (nationwide) ☎ 104
- **Budapest crime hotline** (English spoken) ☎ 1-438 8000
- **Car assistance** (24hr; nationwide) ☎ 188

OTP Bank (Map pp576-7; V Nádor utca 6) Good rates.
American Express (Map pp576-7; ☎ 235 4330; V Deák Ferenc utca 10; ⊗ 9am-5.30pm Mon-Fri, 9am-2pm Sat) Will change its own travellers cheques without commission. Rates aren't the best.

Post

Main post office (Map pp576-7; V Városház utca 18)

Tourist Office

Tourinform (Map pp576-7; ☎ 06 80 630 800 24hr; www.hungarytourism.hu; Sütő utca 2; ⊗ 8am-8pm)

Travel Agencies

You can get information, arrange a tour and book private rooms, flats, hostels or other accommodation in the capital city – and often for other towns throughout the country – at travel agencies in Budapest. You can also buy discount cards here.
Ibusz (Map pp576-7; ☎ 485 2716; www.ibusz.hu; V Ferenciek tere 10; ⊗ 9am-5pm Mon-Fri, 9am-1pm Sat Jul-Aug) National agency: exchange office, air and train tickets, private rooms, pensions – the works.
Mellow Mood Ltd (Map pp572; ☎ 413 2065; www .mellowmood.hu; Keleti & Déli train stations; ⊗ 7am-8pm) Staff at the train station stands will help you find hostel, student and other accommodation, as well provide info. Affiliated with Hostelling International.
Vista Visitor Centre (Map pp576-7; ☎ 268 0888; www .vista.hu; VI Paulay Ede utca 2; ⊗ 9am-6pm Mon-Fri, 10am-3pm Sat) Book flats here. Internet access available, café on site.

SIGHTS & ACTIVITIES

Buda

Places mentioned in this section are shown on the Central Buda map (p572) unless otherwise indicated. Most of what remains of medieval Budapest is on **Várhegy** (Castle Hill),

HUNGARY

perched above the Danube. From the red line metro station at Moszkva tér, climb the staircase to street level and continue up Várfok utca, or cross the street and board the Vár bus (a minibus with a picture of a castle on the sign). Walking around the old streets and appreciating the city views is part of the attraction. You can't miss the neo-Gothic **Mátyás Templom** (Matthias Church; ☎ 489 0717; I Szentháromság tér; adult/student 550/270Ft; ◷ 9am-5pm Mon-Sat, 1-5pm Sun), which has a colourful tiled roof and lovely murals inside. Across the square is **Halászbástya** (Fishermen's Bastion; adult/student 300/150Ft; ◷ 8.30am-11pm), a neo-Gothic arcade built in 1905. To the southeast is the entrance for the **Funicular** (uphill/downhill ticket adult 600/500Ft, child 3-14 350Ft; ◷ 7.30am-10pm) in Szent György tér, which can take you back down the hill to Clark Adam tér. The massive **Királyi Palota** (Royal Palace) occupies the far end of Castle Hill; inside are the **Magyar Nemzeti Galéria** (Hungarian National Gallery; ☎ 375 7533; I Szent György tér 6; adult/student 800/400Ft; ◷ 10am-6pm Tue-Sun) and the **Budapesti Történeti Múzeum** (Budapest History Museum; ☎ 375 7533; I Szent György tér 2; adult/student 400/250Ft; ◷ 10am-6pm mid-May–mid-Sep, 10am-4pm Wed-Mon mid-May–mid-Sep).

The city's most famous thermal spa is the **Gellért Fürdő** (Gellért Baths; ☎ 466 6166; XI Kelenhegyi út; thermal baths & swimming pool 2700Ft; ◷ 6am-7pm Mon-Fri, 6am-5pm Sat-Sun May-Sept; baths only Oct-Apr), south of Castle Hill.

Many of the statues that once commemorated Soviet liberators, socialist ideals and Communist leaders are now on display at **Szobor Park** (Statue Park; ☎ 227 7446; www.szoborpark.hu; XXII Szabadkai út; admission 600Ft; ◷ 10am-dusk) in far southwest Buda. Take tram No 19 from Clark Adam tér to the XI Etele tér terminus, then catch a yellow Volán bus to Diósd-Érd. A direct bus goes from Deák tér in Pest at 11am daily (2450Ft return, including admission).

Aquincumi Múzeum (Map p572; ☎ 430 1563; III Szentendre út 139; adult/student 700/300Ft; ◷ 10am-5pm Tue-Sun Apr-Oct, 10am-6pm May-Sep) contains the heart of the most complete 2nd-century Roman civilian town ruins left in Hungary.

Pest

Places mentioned in this section are shown on the Central Pest map (pp576-7). The oldest, yellow metro line, constructed in the 19th century, runs beneath leafy Andrássy út.

Start at **Hősök tere** (Heroes' Square), above the metro station of the same name, to see the monument constructed to honour the millennial anniversary (1896) of the Magyar conquest of the Carpathian Basin. The **Szépmüvészeti Múzeum** (Museum of Fine Arts; ☎ 469 7100; www2.szepmuveszeti.hu; XIV Hősök tere; adult/student 900/500Ft; ◷ 10am-5.30pm Tue-Sun), across the street, houses a collection of foreign art, including that of El Greco. To the north, in **Városliget** (City Park), is the 19th-century **Széchenyi Fürdő** (Széchenyi Baths; ☎ 363 3210; XIV Állatkerti út 11; admission 1700Ft; ◷ 6am-7pm Mon-Fri, 6am-5pm Sat & Sun), which has more than nine indoor and outdoor pools.

If you walk southwest from Heroes' Square on Andrássy út, you'll pass many grand, World Heritage–listed 19th-century buildings along the way to the **Terror Háza** (House of Terror; ☎ 374 2600; www.terrorhaza.hu; Andrássy út 60; foreigner 3000Ft; ◷ 10am-6pm Tue-Fri, 10am-7.30pm Sat & Sun), a museum of spying and atrocities in what was once the headquarters of the dreaded ÁVH, the secret police. The ornate, neo-Renaissance **Magyar Állami Operaház** (Hungarian State Opera House; ☎ 332 8197; www.opera.hu; VI Andrássy út 22; admission 1200Ft; tours 3pm & 4pm), further along, was completed in 1884.

Other sights worth seeing:

Nagy Zsinagóga (Great Synagogue; ☎ 342 8949; VII Dohány utca 2; 10am-5pm Mon-Thu, 10am-2pm Fri & Sun; synagogue & museum adult/child 600/200Ft) Dates from 1859.

Nagycsarnok (Great Market; IX Fővám körút 1-3; ◷ 6am-5pm Mon, 6am-6pm Tue-Fri, 6am-2pm Sat) Vast iron and glass structure: vegetables and other produce on the ground level, souvenirs/snacks upstairs.

Váci utca (District V) Extensive pedestrian shopping street. Tourist Central.

Magyar Nemzeti Múzeum (Hungarian National Museum; ☎ 338 2122; www.museum.hu; VIII Múzeum körút 14-16; adult/student 800/400Ft; ◷ 10am-6pm Tue-Sun) Historic relics.

Parlament (Parliament; ☎ 441 4904; V Kossuth Lajos tér 1-3; adult/student 1700/800Ft; ◷ Hungarian-language tours 8am-6pm Mon-Fri, 8am-4pm Sat, 8am-2pm Sun; English-language tours 10am & 2pm) National icon. Book ahead. Schedules vary when parliament is in session.

FESTIVALS & EVENTS

Classical concerts and performances are scheduled all over town during the **Spring Festival** (March) and **Autumn Festival** (mid-October to early November). The **Sziget Music Festival** (Óbudai hajógyár-sziget, www.sziget.hu), in late July or early August, is a week-long international jam-fest. Consider camping out to get the most out of the experience. The **Hungaroring Formula-1 races** held at Mogyoród, 24km northeast of Budapest (mid-August), attract worldwide attention – hotels fill up and prices skyrocket.

SLEEPING

For a European capital city, Budapest still offers some surprisingly good deals, except in mid-August when the Formula 1 race crowd is in town and every price goes up. Hostels, private rooms, pensions and guesthouses are all good alternatives to a pricey hotel, although you'll occasionally find a more reasonable place billing itself as a 'hotel' because it has satellite TV and minibars. Many places offer triples. The accommodation price usually includes a cold breakfast. Air-conditioning is pretty rare, and the definition of non-smoking rooms varies. Some say the rooms are non-smoking, but ash rays and matches are provided in each; those listed here have stricter policies.

Hostels

Year-round hostels, often occupying middle floors of old apartment buildings in Pest, usually have a communal kitchen, laundry and Internet service available, but not necessarily a lift. Rooms tend to be non-smoking, but there's a lounge or a balcony nearby. Having an HI card is not required, but one might get you a 10% discount. Come summer (July to late August), basic student dormitories at colleges and universities open to all travellers. **Tourinform** (www.youthhostels.hu) publishes a youth hostel brochure. HI-affiliated Mellow Mood Ltd runs a few hotels year-round, and many more summer hostels (see p573).

BUDA

The following places are all shown on the Central Buda map (p572).

Back Pack Guesthouse (☎ 385 8946; www.back packbudapest.hu; XI Takács Menyhért utca 33; dm/r 2200-2800/6600Ft; ☒ 🖳) Zany and laid-back, with an island-time feel in the suburbs. Escape the city's noise and take a snooze in the back garden hammock. Bus No 7 (Erzsébet híd or Keleti Train Station in Pest), tram No 49 from the little ring road in central Pest, and tram No 19 from Batthyány tér in Buda make the 2km trip to the guesthouse.

Additional options:

Martos Hostel (☎ 209 4883; reception@hotel.martos .bme.hu; XI Sztoczek utca 5-7; s/d with shared bathroom €16/20; ☒) Primarily student accommodation, open year round to all. Private bathroom rooms available.

Citadella Hotel (☎ 466 5794; www.citadella.hu; XI Citadella sétány; dm/r €10/51; ☒) Inside the old fortress atop Gellért Hill. Well worn and remote, but with great views. Take bus No 27 from XI Móricz Zsigmond körtér in Buda, then hike 10 minutes up a steep hill.

PEST

The following places are all shown on the Central Pest map (pp576-7).

Red Bus Hostel (266 0136; www.redbusbudapest.hu; V Semmelweiss utca 14, 1st floor; dm/s/d 2900/6500/7500Ft; ☒ 🖳) This spacious, if spartan, hostel has a faithful following because of its congenial owners. Quite central. Downstairs is a store selling English-language used books.

Caterina Hostel (☎ 2695990; www.caterinahostel.hu; VI Teréz körút 30, 3rd floor; dm/s/d 2000/5000/8000Ft; ☒ 🖳) Super clean, bright, modern – but small (no lounge). The clientele is quiet, even if the street noise that seeps in isn't. The owners have young children.

Museum Guest House (☎ 318 9508; www.budapest hostel.com; VIII Mikszáth Kálmán tér 4, 1st floor; dm 2600-3000Ft; ☒ 🖳) Wind your way through the maze of rooms. The eclectic decor includes some bunk lofts with curtains and red log bedsteads.

Also recommended:

Station Guesthouse (☎ 221 8864; www.stationguest house.hu; XIV Mexikói út 36/b; dm/r 1900-2700Ft/6400Ft; ☒ 🖳) Party house: 24-hour bar, pool table, occasional live music. Bus red No 7 from Keleti train station.

Best Hostel (☎ 332 4934; www.besthostel.hu; VI Podmaniczky utca 27, 1st floor; dm/s/d 3000/4200/8400Ft; ☒ 🖳) Closest to Nyugati Train Station, and not too noisy.

Yellow Submarine Hostel (☎ 331 9896; www.yellow submarinehostel.com; VI Teréz körút 56, 3rd floor; dm/s/d 2800/7000/8000Ft; ☒ 🖳) Overlooking busy ring road, near Nyugati.

Private Rooms

Private rooms in Budapest are plentiful, and staying in one can be a great opportunity to experience Hungarian culture. You generally share a bathroom with the family. Landlords are often retired and/or widowed women. Costs range from 4000 to 7500Ft for a single, 9000 to 12,000Ft for a double and 12,000Ft to 14,000Ft for a small flat, with a supplement if you stay fewer than four nights. Ibusz has the

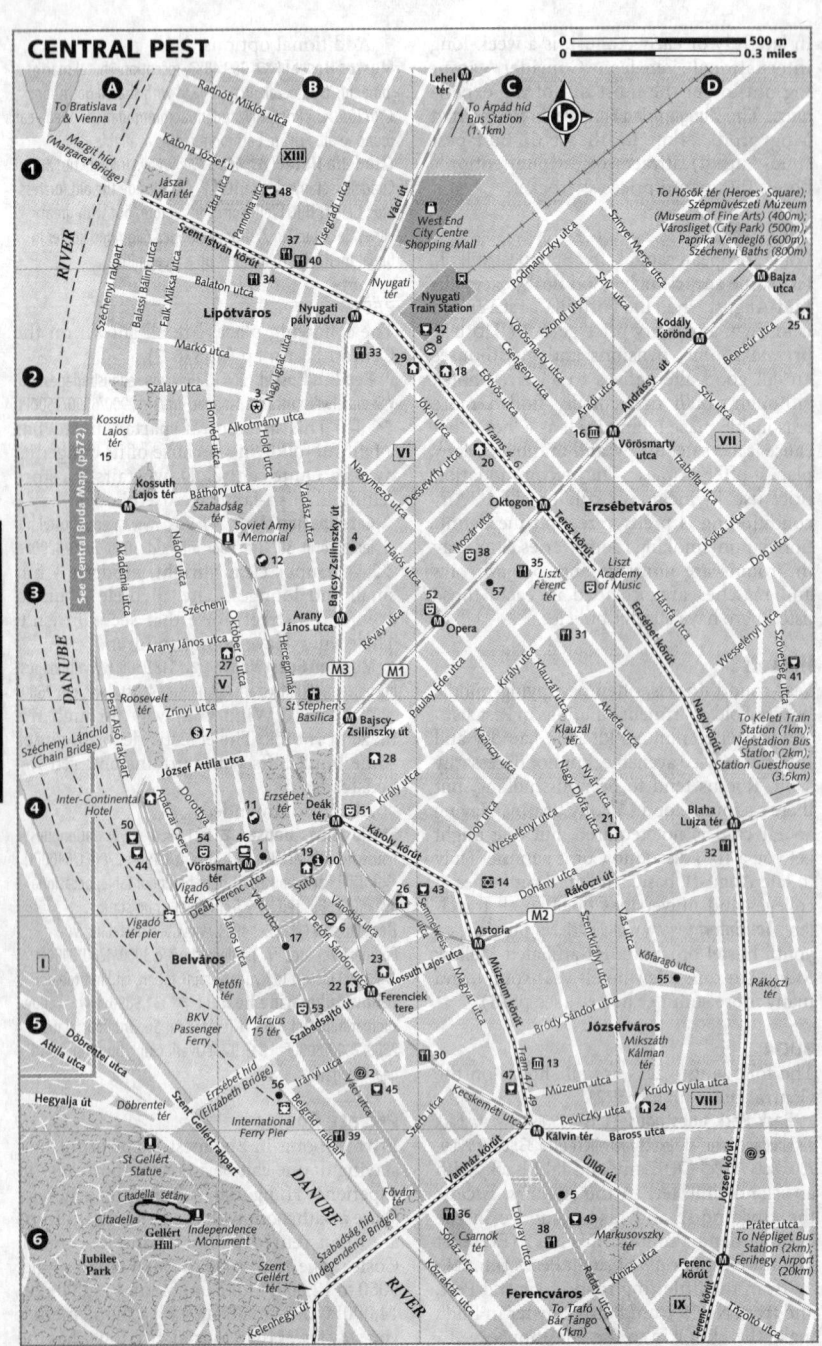

INFORMATION		
American Express	1	B4
Ami Internet Coffee	2	B5
District V Police Station	3	B2
Hungarian Bicycle Touring Association	4	B3
Hungarian Equestrian Tourism Association	5	C6
Main Post Office	6	B5
OTP Bank	7	A4
Post Office	8	C2
Privat Link	9	D6
Tourinform	10	B4
UK Embassy	11	B4
US Embassy	12	B3

SIGHTS & ACTIVITIES	(pp573–4)	
Magyar Nemzeti Múzeum (Hungarian National Museum)	13	C5
Nagy Zsinagóga (Great Synagogue)	14	C4
Parlament (Parliament)	15	A2
Terror Háza (House of Terror)	16	C2
Váci utca	17	B5

SLEEPING	🏠 (pp575–7)	
Best Hostel	18	C2
Best Hotel Service	19	B4
Caterina Hostel	20	C2
Hostel Marco Polo	21	C4
Ibusz	22	B5
Leo Panzió	23	B5
Museum Guest House	24	D5
Radio Inn	25	D2
Red Bus Hostel	26	B4
To-Ma Travel Agency	27	B3
Vista Visitor Centre	28	B4
Yellow Submarine Youth Hostel	29	B2

EATING	🍴 (pp577–8)	
Café Károlyi	30	C5
Frici Papa	31	C3
Kaiser's	32	D4
Kaiser's	33	B2
Kis Italia	34	B2
Menza	35	C3
Nagycsarnok (Great Market)	36	C6
Okay Italia	37	B1
Shiraz	38	C6
Taverna Dionysos	39	B6
Wabisabi	40	B1

DRINKING	🖥🔲 (pp578–9)	
Angyal	41	D3
Bahnhof Music Club	42	C2
Café Eklektika	43	C4
Columbus	44	A4
Fat Mo's	45	B5
Gerbeaud	46	B4
Irish Cat Pub	47	C5
Mosselein	48	B1
Paris, Texas	49	C6
Spoon	50	A4

ENTERTAINMENT	🎭 (p579)	
Gödőr Klub	51	B4
Magyar Állami Operaház (Hungarian State Opera House)	52	C3
Music Mix	53	B5
Vigádó Jegyiroda	54	A4

TRANSPORT	(pp579–80)	
Kenguru	55	D5
Mahart PassNave Ticket Office	56	B5
MÁV Ticket Office	57	C3

most extensive listings in town (some have photos on their website), and Vista Travel Centre is good for flats (see p573).

Other accommodation brokers:

Best Hotel Service (Map see opposite; ☎ 318 4848; www.besthotelservice.hu; V Sűtő utca 2; ☻ 8am-8pm)

To-Ma Travel Agency (Map see opposite; ☎ 353 0819; www.tomatour.hu/beut/; V Október 6 utca 22; ☻ 9am-noon & 1-8pm Mon-Fri, 9am-5pm Sat & Sun)

Pensions & Hotels

BUDA

The following places are shown on the Central Buda map (p572).

Burg Hotel (☎ 212 2928; www.burghotelbudapest .com; I Szentháromság tér 7-8; s/d €79-99/89-109; ☒ ☒ 🔲) Contemporary comfort in the absolute centre of Castle Hill: you can't beat the price-location-value combination.

Büro Panzió (☎ 212 2929; buro-panzio@axelero.hu; II Dékán utca 3; s/d 6000-8000/10,000-12,000Ft; ☒ 🔲) Rooms are basic 1980s style (black, mint green, neon pink), but they're clean enough.

PEST

The following places are shown on the Central Pest map (opposite).

Leo Panzió (☎ 266 9041; www.leopanzio.hu; V Kossuth Lajos utca 2/a, 2nd floor; s/d €45-66/69-82; ☒ ☒) Just steps from Váci utca, in the middle of everything. Rooms have an Art Deco-ish flair with cherry-stained beds inset with blond wood. Small, sparkling bathrooms. Some views of Elisabeth Bridge.

Radio Inn (☎ 342 8347; www.radioinn.hu; VI Benczúr utca 19; s/d without breakfast €45-50/50-70; ☒) All the rooms are flats with full kitchens, sitting areas and one or two bedrooms. On a quiet, tree-lined street among embassies near the Bajza utca metro stop (M1 yellow line).

Hostel Marco Polo (☎ 413 2555; www.marcopolo hostel.com; VII Nyár utca 6; dm/s/d 3800-5800/10,800-12,800/14,200-17,000Ft; ☒ 🔲) With phones and satellite TV in the rooms, and a bar-restaurant in the cellar, this hostel is rather hotel-like. Not the most renovated neighbourhood.

EATING

Fast-food restaurants, 'to go' windows and food stands abound on the ring roads of Pest and in or near train and metro stations. Two pedestrian areas in Pest, Ráday utca and Liszt Ferenc tér, are crammed with cafés, bars and eateries – all with outdoor tables in good weather. To keep prices down, look for: a *grill* (generally serving gyros and other grilled meats at self-service counters), an *étkezde* (literally 'eating place', where workers lunch; can be sit-down service), an *önkiszolgáló* (self-service canteen), a *kinai gyorsbüfé* (a Chinese 'fast' buffet) or a *szendvicsbar* (selling open-face sandwiches to go). Many more expensive places offer discount two- or three-course set lunch menus on weekdays. Always make sure you check your bill; you might just be presented with a handwritten list of prices, or the 'suggested tip' might already be added in and totalled.

Buda

The following places are all shown on the Central Buda map (p572).

Mamma Rosa Pizzéria (☎ 201 3456; I Ostrom utca 31; pizza & pasta 690-1100Ft; ☻ 11am-11pm; ☒) It's hard to resist the smells coming from this cellar Italian restaurant. Relax among murals reminiscent of ancient Rome.

Mongolian Barbecue (☎ 353 6363; XII Márvány utca 19a; before/after 5pm 1990/3690Ft; ☒) Choose your meat and watch as it's grilled in front of you. The all-you-can-eat price includes as much beer and wine as you can sink, too.

Café Miró (☎ 375 5458; I Úri utca 30; mains 690-2190Ft; ☺ 9am-midnight) Most restaurants on Castle Hill have surly service and are full of tourists. This arty café is no exception, but the soups, Greek salad and desserts are good.

For quicker bite to eat near the castle, climb the passageway stairs to **Fortuna Önkiszolgáló** (☎ 375 2401; I Hess András tér 4, 1st floor; ☺ 11.30am-2.30pm Mon-Fri; ☒). Or if you're in Moszkva tér, try **Pita House** (☎ 315 1479; II Margit körút 105; mains 500-800Ft, salad bar 410Ft; ☺ 8am-midnight; ☒).

Pest

The following places are all shown on the Central Pest map (pp576-7).

Frici Papa (☎ 351 0197; Királyi utca 55; mains 400-700Ft; ☺ 11am-8pm Mon-Sat) Basic, no-frills Hungarian. There's a surprising amount of white meat in the chicken soup for the price.

Menza (☎ 413 1482; V Liszt Ferenc tér 2; mains 890-1990Ft; ☺ 11am-11pm; ☒) This place is a parody of communist style (a *menza* was a state-run canteen). Hungarians drag their out-of-town guests here to see what much of 1970s Budapest looked like – until well into the 1990s. Traditional favourites done stylishly.

Café Károlyi (☎ 328 0117; V Károly Mihály utca 16; mains 1200-2700Ft; ☺ 8.30am-midnight Mon-Fri, 9.30am-midnight Sat & Sun; ☒) A trendy, upscale take on local ingredients. Goose liver enveloped in a crêpe pocket with plum sauce, anyone? Breakfast is also served.

Paprika Vendeglö (☎ 06 70 574 6508; Dózsa György utca 72; mains 950-1600Ft; ☺ 11am-11pm) Step inside what looks like a rustic Hungarian farmhouse on the very urban street bordering City Park (M1 yellow line, Hősök tere, or Heroes' Square, metro). Good game dishes.

Wabisabi (☎ 412 0427; XIII Visegrádi utca 2; mains 1080-1480Ft; ☺ 11am-11pm Sun-Thu, 11am-midnight Fri & Sat; ☒) Come here for organic, vegan-friendly food – a rarity in meat-crazy Hungary.

Gerbeaud (☎ 429 9000; V Vörösmarty tér 7; ☺ 9am-9pm) King of the genteel, Old World, coffee-and-cake culture, Gerbeaud has been serving since 1870.

Of the many Italian restaurants in town, **Okay Italia** (☎ 349 2991; XIII Szent István körút 20; pizzas & pasta 1280-1690Ft; ☺ 11am-11.30pm; ☒ ☒) and **Kis Italia** (☎ 269 3145; V Szemere utca 22; pizza & pasta 760-990Ft; ☺ 11am-10pm Mon-Sat; ☒) are reliable choices. Just ignore the cheesy synthesiser player at the latter. For Greek, go to **Taverna Dionysos** (☎ 318 1222; V Belgrád rakpart 16; mains 1250-2750Ft; ☺ noon-midnight; ☒).

Stock up on picnic supplies at Nagycsarnok, Budapest's biggest market (p574). There are food stalls and a pricey cafeteria on the upper level. Large grocery stores are everywhere in Pest, including Kaiser's Supermarket, which has branches across from Nyugati pályaudvar and Blahalujza tér metro stops.

DRINKING

There are plenty of pseudo British-Irish-Belgian pubs, smoky *sörözö* (Hungarian beer bars where drinking is taken very seriously) and nightclubs. However, the most pleasant place to imbibe might be in a *kávéház*. There are cafés all over the city in nice weather, especially along pedestrian-only Ráday utca and Liszt Ferenc tér.

Of the pubs in Pest, **Fat Mo's** (Map pp576-7; ☎ 267 3199; V Nyári Pál utca 11; ☺ noon-2am Mon-Wed, noon-4am Thu-Fri, 6pm-4am Sat, 6pm-2am Sun) is one of the best. It has live music on Sunday through Thursday. **Irish Cat Pub** (Map pp576-7; ☎ 266 4085; V Múzeum körút 41; ☺ 11am-2am) runs a close second. **Mosselein** (Map pp576-7; ☎ 452 0535; XIII Pannónia utca 14; ☺ noon-midnight) has a selection of Belgian brews and sports on TV.

Café-wise, **Paris, Texas** (Map pp576-7; ☎ 281 0570; XI Ráday utca 22; ☺ 10am-2am Mon-Fri, 1pm-2am Sat, 4pm-2am Sun) attempts to recreate an old Wild West saloon with turn-of-the-century pictures on the walls; anyway, expats seem to like it. You can smoke a water pipe filled with fruit tobacco at **Shiraz** (Map pp576-7; ☎ 218 0881; IX Mátyás utca 22, at Ráday utca; ☺ noon-midnight), a take-me-to-the-kasbah kind of place. **Café Eklektika** (Map pp576-7; ☎ 266 3054; V Semmelweiss utca 21; ☺ noon-midnight Mon-Fri, 5pm-midnight Sat & Sun) attracts a mixed, beat-generation-style crowd, and is very lesbian-friendly.

If you want to float on a boat in the Danube while enjoying an adult beverage, **Spoon** (Map pp576-7; ☎ 411 0933; V Vigadó tér 3; ☺ noon-2am; ☒ ☒) is the swank place to do so. Next door, so to speak, **Columbus** (Map pp576-7; ☎ 266 9013; Vigadó tér 4; ☺ noon-midnight; ☒) is more down-to-earth and publike.

In Buda, **Zöld Pardon** (Map p572; Írini József utca at Petőfi híd; ✆ 9am-6am mid-Apr–mid-Sep) is a big beer-garden-cum-disco, popular with college students on a budget.

ENTERTAINMENT

Tickets for classical music concerts, dance performances, folk concerts and operas or operettas are still quite reasonable by Western European standards, and the venues are often stunning. Tourinform (see p573) and ticket offices can help you find out what's playing, or you could look in the free, bimonthly *Programme Magazine*, available at tourist spots. The *Budapest Sun* (www.buda pestsun.com) also has some listings. The free weekly *Pesti Est* (available at restaurants and clubs) lists live music acts and guest DJs for clubs.

Ticket offices:

Music Mix (Map pp576-7; ✆ 266 1655; V Váci utca 33; ✆ 10am-6pm Mon-Fri, 10am-3pm Sat)

Vigádó Jegyiroda (Map pp576-7; ✆ 327 4322; V Vigado tér 6; ✆ 10am-8pm Mon-Fri)

Clubbing

Clubbing in Budapest can mean anything from a floor-thumping techno dance club to a hip place to hang out and listen to jazz. Most are in Pest. Cover charges range from 200Ft to 1000Ft.

Gödör Klub (Map pp576-7; ✆ 06 20 943 5463; V Erzsébet tér; ✆ 2pm-2am) A large underground club (with a glass ceiling revealing the square above) provides the venue for truly eclectic live music – from world beat to the Doors to jazz – played to a local crowd of all ages, shapes and sizes.

Trafó Bár Tangó (Map pp576-7; ✆ 456 2049; IX Lilliom utca 41; ✆ 6pm-1am) An artsy crowd makes the scene beneath a cultural house and exhibit space. Latin, jazz, disco.

Angyal (Map pp576-7; ✆ 351 6490; VII Szövetség utca 33; ✆ 10pm-5am Fri & Sat) Budapest's flagship gay nightclub has three bars and high-energy dance mixes. Men only on Saturday (admission 800Ft).

Also recommended:

Cuba Libre (Map p572; ✆ 345 8367; Lövőház utca 2, Mammut II; ✆ noon-midnight Sun-Wed, noon-5am Thu-Sat) Pretty people pose on the top floor of a shopping mall in Buda. Dance, funk, R&B.

Bahnhof Music Club (Map pp576-7; ✆ 302 4751; VI Teréz körút 55, Nyugati Train Station; ✆ 10pm-4am Thu-Sat) Teenyboppers shake it on two dance floors.

GETTING THERE & AWAY

Air

There is no domestic air service in Hungary. See p570 for more on international destinations.

Boat

In addition to hydrofoils that travel internationally (see p570), **Mahart PassNave ferries** (✆ 484 4005; www.mahartpassnave.hu; Vigádó tér pier) depart for Visegrad and Esztergom in the Danube Bend daily from April to October.

Bus

Volánbusz (✆ 485 2162; www.volanbusz.hu) is the national bus line. All international buses and some buses to/from southern Hungary arrive at and depart from **Népliget Bus Station** (Map pp576-7; ✆ 264 3939; IX Üllői út 131). **Népstadion Bus Station** (Map pp576-7; ✆ 252 4498; XIV Hungária körút 48-52; metro Népstadion) serves most buses to domestic destinations. Most buses to the northern Danube Bend arrive at and leave from the **Árpád híd Bus Station** (Map pp576-7; ✆ 329 1450, off XIII Róbert Károly körút). All three stations are on metro lines, and are in Pest. If the ticket office is closed, you can buy your ticket on the bus.

Car & Motorcycle

Big international car rental chains have branches at the airports. A standard daily rate is €40 per day with unlimited kilometres. Petrol costs about 300 Ft per litre.

Train

The **MÁV Ticket Office** (Map pp576-7; ✆ 461 5400 domestic information, 461 5500 international information; www.elvira.hu; VI Andrássy út 35; ✆ 9am-6pm Mon-Fri Apr-Sep, 9am-5pm Mon-Fri Oct-Mar) provides information and sells domestic and international train tickets and seat reservations. You can also by tickets at the stations.

All three main train stations are on metro lines. **Keleti Train Station** (Map pp576-7; Eastern; ✆ 333 6342; VIII Kerepesi út 2-4) handles international trains from Vienna and many other points east, plus domestic trains to/from the north and northeast. For some Romanian, German and Slovak destinations, as well as domestic ones to/from the northwest and the Danube Bend, head for **Nyugati Train Station** (Western; Map pp576-7; ✆ 349 0115; VI Nyugati tér). For trains bound for Lake Balaton and the south, go to **Déli Train Station** (Southern; Map p572; ✆ 375 6293; I Krisztina körút 37).

HUNGARY

GETTING AROUND
Public transport
Public transport is run by **BKV** (☎ 342 2335; www
.bkv.hu). The three underground metro lines –
M1 yellow, M2 red, M3 blue – meet at Deák
tér in Pest. The HÉV above-ground suburban railway runs north from Batthyány tér
in Buda. There's also an extensive network of
buses, trams and trolleybuses. Public transport runs from 4.30am until 11.30pm. There
are also 18 night buses (marked with an 'É')
that run along main roads. A single ticket for
all forms of transport is 140Ft (60 minutes of
uninterrupted travel, no metro line changes).
The three-day, *turista* ticket (2200Ft) makes
things easier as it allows unlimited travel inside the city. Keep your ticket handy; the fine
for 'riding black' is 2000Ft to 4000Ft.

Taxis
Overcharging is extremely common. Never
get into a taxi that does not have a yellow
licence plate, the logo of a taxi firm and a
posted table of fares. If you have to take a taxi,
it's best to have the place you're staying call
one; this costs less than flagging one down.

AROUND BUDAPEST

Between Vienna and Budapest, the Danube
breaks through the Pilis and Börzsöny Hills
in a sharp bend. Here medieval kings once
ruled Hungary from majestic palaces overlooking the river. Today the historic monuments, rolling green scenery and souvenir
craft shops lure day-trippers from Budapest.

SZENTENDRE
☎ 26 / pop 22,700
A pretty little town of steep narrow streets,
Szentendre (*sen*-ten-dreh) is just 19km north
of Budapest. With its Orthodox churches,
charming old centre, plentiful cafés, art and
craft galleries, and easy accessibility from
the capital, the place swells with crowds
during the summer. Avoid weekends.

The **Tourinform** (☎ 317 965; Dumtsa Jenő utca 22;
🕑 9am-6.30pm Mon-Fri, 10am-2pm Sat & Sun) has information about the many small museums
in town. Outside the town is the humungous
Szabadtéri Néprajzi Múzeum (Open-Air Ethnographic
Museum; ☎ 502 500; adult/student 800/400Ft; 🕑 9am-
5pm Tue-Sun Apr-Oct). Walking through reassem-
bled homes and villages from around the

country in this *skansen* (village museum),
you can see what life was – and sometimes
still is – like in rural Hungary. Take the
Skansen bus from stand No 7 (20 minutes).

To get to Szentendre, take the commuter
HÉV from Buda's Batthyány tér metro station to the end of the line (370Ft, 40 minutes). At least one of the Mahart PassNave
ferries (see p579) that travel daily from
Budapest to Visegrad stops at Szentendre
(950Ft, 1½ hours).

VISEGRÁD
☎ 26 / pop 1540
Visegrád (*vish*-eh-grahd) is superbly situated on the Danube's abrupt loop between
the Pilis and Börzsöny Hills. After the 13th-
century Mongol invasions, Hungarian kings
built mighty **Visegrád Cittadella** (☎ 398 101;
Várhegy; adult/student 750/350Ft; 🕑 9.30am to 5.30pm)
high on the hilltop. It's a climb. The **Királyi Palota** (Royal Palace; ☎ 398 026; Fő utca 29; adult/
student 400/200Ft; 🕑 9am-4.30pm Tue-Sun) stands
on the flood plain at the foot of the hills.

Buses from Budapest's Árpád híd Bus
Station (463Ft, 1¼ hours), the Szentendre HÉV station (405Ft, 45 minutes) and
Esztergom (405Ft, 45 minutes) are very
frequent. Between mid-April and early September, at least one Mahart PassNave (see
p579) ferry daily shuttles between Budapest
and Visegrád (1050Ft, two to three hours).
Some of them continue on to Esztergom.

ESZTERGOM
☎ 33 / pop 28,900
Some of Hungary's most historically important moments have been played out in Esztergom (*es*-ter-gohm). The 2nd-century Roman
emperor-to-be Marcus Aurelius wrote his
famous *Meditations* while he camped here.
Stephen I, founder of the Hungarian state, was
born here and crowned at the cathedral, and
Esztergom was the royal seat from the late
10th to the mid-13th centuries.

Gran Tours (☎ 502 000; Széchenyi tér 25; 🕑 8am-
6pm Mon-Fri) is the best source of information
in town. Built on a hill high above the Danube is **Esztergom Basilica** (☎ 411 895; admission
free; 🕑 7am-6pm), the largest church in Hungary. At the southern end of the hill is the
extensive **Vár Múzeum** (Castle Museum; ☎ 415 986;
adult/student 460/240Ft; 🕑 10am-6pm Tue-Sun Apr-Oct,
10am-4pm Nov-Mar). The earliest excavated remnants date from the 2nd & 3rd century.

On the way to the old town from the bus and train stations, you pass by food stands and the open-air market. Buses run to/from Budapest's Árpád híd Bus Station (579Ft, 1½ hours via the shortest route) and to/from Visegrád (405Ft, 45 minutes) at least hourly. Trains to Esztergom depart from Budapest's Nyugati Train Station (490Ft, 1½ hours) up to 13 times a day. Mahart Pass Nave ferries (see p579) to Esztergom from Visegrad (700Ft, 1½ to two hours) and Budapest (1200Ft, five hours), at least once a day from mid-April to early September.

WESTERN HUNGARY

Beyond the Bakony Hills is an area bounded by the Danube and the Alps. Conquered by the Romans but never fully occupied by the Turks, this enchanting corner of Hungary contains picturesque small towns and cities, like Sopron, which has a decidedly Austro-Hungarian-Empire air.

Lake Balaton, southwest of Budapest, is the largest freshwater lake in Europe outside Scandinavia (it's 77km long). The southeastern shore is shallow, with sandy beaches and high-rise condos; better scenery, more historic sites and deeper water are found on the northwestern side. Keszthely has a view of both shores. Balaton's popularity means that accommodation, restaurants and beaches are packed with Hungarians and Austrians on holiday in summer, especially during July and August. Many towns are deserted from October to April.

SOPRON
☎ 99 / pop 55,400

Sitting right on the Austrian border, only 69km south of Vienna, is Sopron (*shop*-ron). The Mongols and Turks never got this far, so many medieval structures remain intact.

From the main train station, walk north on Mátyás király utca, which becomes Várkerület, part of a loop following the line of the former city walls. **Tourinform** (☎ 338 892; www.sopron.hu; Előkapu 11; ☺ 9am-noon & 1-5pm Mon-Fri, 9am-1pm Sat) is at the northeastern entrance to the old town. Nearby is the 60m-high **Tűztorony** (Fire Tower; ☎ 311 327, Fő tér; adult/student 500/250Ft; ☺ 10am-6pm Tue-Sun), run by Soprini Múzeum. You can climb the 154 steps for views as far as the Alps.

There are several museums, monuments and churches around Fő tér.

Outside Sopron in Fertőd is one of the country's most impressive palaces, the 126-room, Versailles-like baroque **Esterházy Kasthély** (☎ 537 640; Joseph Hayden út 2; adult/student 1000/600Ft; ☺ 10am-6pm Apr-Oct, 10am-4pm Sat & Sun Nov-Mar). Just 27km east of Sopron, it's easily accessible by bus (347Ft, 40 minutes).

Sleeping & Eating

The brand-spankin' new **Vákació Vendégház** (☎ 338 502; www.szallasinfo.hu/vakaciovendeghaz; Ade Endre út 31; per person 2150Ft; ☒) is a student-oriented youth hostel about a 20-minute walk east of the town centre. Rooms have two to 12 beds each; there's no kitchen. **Jégverem Fogadó** (☎ 510 113; www.jegverem.hu; Jégverem utca 1; s/d 5000/8000Ft) is a pension in an 18th-century building, but its furniture is nondescript. The restaurant's menu has multiple variations on the fried meat cutlet theme (mains 850Ft to 1890Ft).

Wooden platters of Wurst and cheese make a good lunch at **Cézár Pince** (☎ 311 337; Hátsókapu 2; mains 480-890Ft; ☺ 11am-11pm). Had enough meat? Stop at the Italian **Capri Étterem** (☎ 311 525; Várkerület 103; ☺ noon-10pm Mon-Sat; mains 550-960Ft; ☒ ☒) for vegetarian pastas and a salad bar that actually has aubergines. Next door is a **Match supermarket** (Várkerület 100) in case you prefer self-catering.

Entertainment

The **Liszt Ferenc Kulturális Központ** (☎ 517 517; Liszt Ferenc tér 1; ☺ ticket office 9am-5pm Tue-Fri, 9am-noon Sat) has the latest on classical music and other cultural events.

If you crave a coffee, or something stronger, there are several cafés around Fő tér to stop at. **Swing** (☎ 06 20 214 8029; Várkerület 15; 5pm-midnight Sun-Fri, 5pm-2am Sat) has live jazz, county, rock or blues nightly. The rustic courtyard at **Papa Joe's Saloon & Steakhouse** (☎ 340 933; Várkerület 108; ☺ 11am-midnight Sun-Fri, 11am-2am Sat; ☒) is an interesting place to nurse a glass of *sör* (beer). Live country-ish music Thursday at 7pm.

Getting There & Away

There are four buses a day to Budapest (2220Ft; four hours). Trains to Vienna's Südbahnhof (€12, 1 hour 20 minutes) depart at least 10 times daily and to Budapest's Keleti Train Station (2564Ft, 2½ to three hours) eight times a day.

HUNGARY

KESZTHELY

☎ 83 / pop 21,800

Keszthely (*kest*-hay) is the only year-round town on Lake Balaton; the large old section is slightly east and north of the lake. Bus and train stations are close to the water. Summer activity centres on paid-admission beaches, waterfront parks, beer gardens and cafés near the ferry pier. **Tourinform** (☎ 314 144; Kossuth Lajos utca 28; ☼ 9am-5pm Mon-Fri & 9am-1pm Sat Sep-Jun, 9am-8pm Mon-Fri & 9am-6pm Sat Jul & Aug) offers excellent information on the whole Balaton area.

At the northern end of pedestrian Kossuth Lajos utca is the sprawling, white, 1745 **Festetics Kastély** (Festetics Palace; ☎ 312 190; Kastély utca 1; museum adult/student 1200/600Ft; ☼ 10am-5pm Tue-Sun). Part of the former residence has been turned into a museum. There's a small café in the courtyard, and roaming the grounds is free.

Private rooms are commonly available from May to August. Tourinform has brochures and lists, or you could look for *szoba kiadó* or *Zimmer frei* signs on Móra Ferenc utca, to the east of the town centre. **János Vajda College** (☎ 311 361; Gagarin utca 4; dm 1600-2000Ft) opens its dorm to all from July to August. The big, basic rooms, with shared kitchens, at **Párizsi Udvar** (☎ 311202; www.hotels.hu /parizsi_udvar; Kastély utca 5; d/tr/q 7900-9900/9600-12,600/13,500-15,600Ft) used to be part of the Festetics Palace complex.

Tons of food and beer stands, with outdoor tables, line the gravel trail between Kazinczky utca and the waterfront (before Erzsébet királyné utca); head east from the train station. Grab breakfast, burgers and marinated salads in town at **Hamburger Saláta Bár** (Erzsébet királyné utca at Jókai utca; breakfast 220-290Ft, burgers 330-450Ft; ☼ 7am-9pm). **Oázis** (☎ 311 023; Rákóczi tér 3; lunches 430-520Ft; ☼ 11am-4pm Mon-Fri) serves changing daily vegetarian dishes. **Margaréta Étterem** (☎ 314 882; Bercsényi út 60; mains 600-1240Ft; ☼ 11am-10pm; ✗) is where locals go for Hungarian specialties. Nice patio, too.

Besides the waterfront, Kossuth Lajos utca is where to look for pubs. **Jancsi Kocsmája** (Kossuth Lajos utca 46; ☼ noon-midnight Mon-Fri, 6pm-midnight Sat & Sun) is the most fun – filled with young people. Tin advertising signs hang on the walls.

Buses run to towns on both the northern and southern shores of Lake Balaton, as well as to Budapest (2780Ft, three hours, six daily), Sopron (1620Ft, 2½ hours, one daily) and Pécs (2430Ft, 3½ hours, two

daily). Keszthely is on a branch rail line that parallels the southern shore on its way to Budapest Déli Train Station (2324Ft, three to four hours, 10 daily). **Mahart PassNave** (www.mahartpassnave.hu) ferries link Keszthely with other towns on the lake from late May to early September.

SOUTH HUNGARY

Southern Hungary is generally flat, with the Mecsek and Villány Hills rising in isolation from the plain. Pécs is the largest city in this region.

PÉCS

☎ 72 / pop 158,900

Near the southern border of Hungary, you can most strongly see the influence of the 150-year Turkish occupation of the country. Pécs (pronounced 'paich') has a distinctly different architectural feel to it from the towns closer to Austria (and to Hapsburg influence). For 400 years in early history, Pécs served as the capital of Roman Lower Pannonia. By the 9th century, the town was known as Quinque Ecclesiae for its five churches, and the first Hungarian university was founded here in the mid-14th century. Ancient churches, mosques and a synagogue, numerous small museums, bustling modern life and the green Mecsek Hills as a backdrop make Pécs an interesting place to spend a couple of days.

Take bus 30 the two long stops from the train station to Kossuth tér, just south of the town's heart, Széchenyi tér. **Tourinform** (☎ 213 315; www.pecs.hu; Széchenyi tér 9; ☼ 8am-5.30pm Mon-Fri, 9am-4pm Sat May-Sep, 8am-4pm Mon-Fri Sep-Mar) has tons of local info, including a list of museums, and has **internet access** (per hr 100Ft). The **main post office** (Jókai Mór utca 10) is in a beautiful Art Nouveau building (1904) with a colourful Zsolnay Porcelain roof.

Sights

Széchenyi tér is dominated on the north by the largest remaining Turkish building in Hungary, today in use as the **Mecset templom** (Mosque church; ☎ 321 976; Széchenyi tér; admission free; ☼ 10am-4pm Mon-Sat, 11.30am-4pm Sun mid-Apr–mid-Oct, 10am-noon Mon-Sat, 11.30am-2pm Sun mid-Oct–mid-Apr). The city's beautifully preserved **Zsinagóga** (Synagogue; ☎ 315 881; Kossuth tér; adult/child 200/100Ft; 10am-5pm Sun-Fri May-Oct) is to the south. To the north, climb Szepessy Ignéc utca and turn west (left) on Káptalan utca, a street lined with museums. Check out the **Zsolnay Porcélan Múzeum** (Zsolnay Porcelain Museum; ☎ 324 822; Káptalan utca 2; adult/student 700/350Ft; 10am-4pm Tue-Sun Apr-Oct), which has examples of the famous ceramics from the local factory's illustrious early days in the mid-19th century to the present.

Continue west to Dóm tér and the walled bishopric complex containing the four-towered **St Peter's Bazilika** (☎ 513 030; Dóm tér; adult/student combined ticket 1000/500Ft; 9am-5pm Mon-Sat, 1-5pm Sun). The oldest part of the building is the 11th-century crypt below. The 1770 **Püspöki Palota** (Bishop's Palace; 2-5pm late Jun-Aug) stands in front of the cathedral, and a 15th-century **barbican**, the only stone bastion to survive from the old city walls.

Other attractions in town include the **Csontváry Múzeum** (☎ 310 544; Janus Pannonius utca 11; adult/student 600/300Ft; 10am-4pm Tue-Sun Apr-Oct), which displays works by the incomparable scenic painter Tivadar Kosztka Csontváry (1853–1919), and the 16th-century **Hassan Jakovali mecset** (Hassan Jakovali Mosque; ☎ 313 853; Rákóczi út 2; adult/student140/80Ft; 10am-1.30pm & 2-6pm Thu-Tue Apr-Sep), complete with minaret and a small museum of Ottoman history.

Sleeping & Eating

In July and August, central **Mátyás Kollégium** (☎ 312 888; Széchenyi tér 11; dm 1400-4000Ft) is good. **Ibusz** (☎ 212 157; Apáca utca 1; per person 2540Ft; 8am-5pm Mon-Fri, 8am-2pm Sat) arranges private rooms. Up in the Mecsek Hills, **Mandulás Camping** (☎ 515 655; Ángyán János utca 2; tent sites 1200Ft, motel room 3200Ft) is open May to October. Catch bus 34.

The small, immaculate **Hotel Diana** (☎ 328 594; www.dianahotel.hu; Tímár utca 4a; s/d 7000/10,000Ft;), near the synagogue, has rustic accents like split-wood chair rails. Rooms with four beds are available (13,600Ft). **Kishotel Centrum** (☎ 311 707; Szepessy Ignác utca 4; s/d/tr 4500/5800/8750Ft) resembles a true Hungarian home with paintings covering every inch of wall space and mix-n-match furniture.

Király utca is lined with pubs, cafés and eateries, including **Oázis** (☎ 215 367; Király utca 17; mains 500-1000Ft; 10am-11pm). Unlike at most of the gyros stands across Hungary, the owner at this take-away actually hails from the Middle East. You can taste the

difference. There's a little counter space if you want to eat inside. The best deal in town is the cafeteria **Aranygaluska Gyorsétterem** (☎ 310 210; Irgalmasok utca 4; mains 430-640Ft; 7.30am-8pm Mon-Fri, 7.30am-5pm Sat & Sun;). The *töltöt paprika* (stuffed peppers) alone makes a filling meal. Ever-popular Italian restaurant **Az Elefánthoz** (☎ 216 055; Jókai tér 6; mains 1100-2000Ft;) serves meal-sized salads, pastas, pizzas and soups. The **Co-op Szupermarket** is at the corner of Irgalmasok and Timár utca.

Entertainment

Pécs has well-established opera and ballet companies as well as a symphony. Ask at Tourinform about performance schedules, or you could check the biweekly freebie *Pécsi Est* for listings.

Los Bongos (☎ 06 20 468 9491; Jókai tér 6; 390-550Ft; 6pm-2am Mon-Sat) nightclub, above Elefánthoz, sizzles. Every Friday is a Latin fiesta. On the ground floor, **Mozik Caffé** (☎ 215 026; Jókai tér 6; 9am-midnight) is a more relaxed place to imbibe your beverage of choice, with outdoor seating.

Getting There & Away

At least four buses a day travel between Pécs and Budapest (2660Ft, 4½ hours), eight go to/from Szeged (2310Ft, four hours) and two to/from Keszthely (1740Ft, three hours). Pécs is on a main rail line to Budapest's Déli Train Station (2610Ft, 2½ hours). One daily train departs Pécs at 8.40pm (1880Ft, two hours) for Osijek in Horvátország (Croatia).

GREAT PLAIN

Where the Tisza River drainage basin meets the wide expanse of level *puszta* (prairie or steppe), so begins the Nagyalföld (Great Plain) of myth and legend. For centuries this area and its horsemen and shepherds have represented the Hungarian ethos in poems, songs, paintings and stories. Much of the *alföld* has been turned into farmland for growing apricots and raising geese, but other parts are little more than grassy, saline deserts sprouting juniper trees. Two national parks, Kiskunság in the Bugac Puszta, near Kecskemét, and Hortobágy in the Hortobágy Puszta (www.hnp.hu) preserve examples of this unique environment.

KECSKEMÉT

☎ 76 / pop 108,250

About halfway between Budapest and Szeged, Kecskemét is a green, pedestrian-friendly city famous for potent *barack pálinka* (apricot brandy), *libamaj* (goose liver), fine architecture and nearby horse farms, as well as a national park.

Tourinform (☎ 481 065; www.kecskemet.hu; Kossuth tér 1; ☉ 8am-5pm Mon-Fri, 9am-1pm Sat Jul & Aug) is on the west side of the terracotta-coloured Town Hall, which dominates the central square. It has a list of colleges offering accommodation and provides information on day trips to the horse show in **Kiskunság Nemzeti Park** (Kiskunság National Park; www.knp.hu), 30km southwest of Kecskemét at Bugacs.

Walk around the adjacent, parklike squares, Kossuth tér and Szabadsag tér, and admire the eclectic building styles, including the Technicolor Art Nouveau at the **Cifrapalota** (Ornamental Palace; Rákóczi út 1). Southwest, the **Magyar Naive Müvészek** (Hungarian Naive Art Museum; ☎ 324 767; Gáspár utca 11; adult/student 150/50Ft; ☉ 10am-5pm Tue-Sat) is strong on folk themes.

Take bus No 1 to get to **Autós Camping** (☎ 329 398; Csabai Géza körút 5; tent site s/d 1350/2100Ft, caravan site 2200Ft, bungalows 5400Ft; ☉ Apr-Oct) southwest of town. Don't be surprised if it's jammed with caravans and Germanic speakers. For a fabulous place to stay – flowery courtyard, homemade sweets with breakfast – choose **Fábián Pension** (☎ 477 677; www.hotels.hu/fabian; Kápolna utca 14; s/d 6900/7000-8900Ft). They'll pull an extra bed into a single to make a cheaper double for you. A basic alternative is the **Palma Hotel** (☎ 321 045; www.holidayhungary.com; Arany János utca 3; s/d/tr 4950-6550/7300-8600/8250-10,050Ft) with shared baths.

Grab a quick bite and a beer at **Boston Grill** (☎ 484 444; Kápolna utca 2; burgers 320-550Ft, ☉ 11am-10pm) or **Gody Papa** (☎ 415 515; Arany János utca 3; pizzas 330-550Ft; ☉ 11am-11pm). For a sit-down Hungarian meal, there's **Öregház Vendéglö** (☎ 496 973; Kólcsey utca 3; mains 600-1000Ft; ☉ 11am-10pm). **Rolling Rock Café** (☎ 06 70 335 3935; Jókai utca 44; ☉ noon-midnight Tue-Thu, noon-5am Fri & Sat), outside the centre, is *the* place for live music weekends, and for a happenin' beer any time.

Twenty buses a day connect Kecskemét with Budapest Népliget (2080Ft, 1½ hours) and 10 a day with Szeged (2430Ft, two hours). Kecskemét is on the rail line that links Budapest's Nyugati Train Station

(1203Ft, 1½ hours) with Szeged (1150Ft, one hour) at least eight times per day.

SZEGED

☎ 62 / pop 162,800

Szeged (*seh*-ged), a college town on the southern Great Plain, straddles the Tisza River just before it enters Yugoslavia. The Maros River from Romania enters the Tisza just east of the centre. All that water makes the town historically prone to flooding. Much of the old town is architecturally quite homogeneous. Its buildings include some Art Nouveau palaces, built after the disastrous 1879 flood. Nationally well-known brands Pick salami and Szegedi paprika are made here.

The train station is south-southwest of town; the bus station is to the northwest. Pedestrian Kárász utca is lined with cafés and stores, leading northwest to the parklike square, Széchenyi tér. **Tourinform** (☎ 488 690; Dugonics tér 2; ☉ 9am-5pm Mon-Fri) is tucked away in a quiet courtyard off the southwest end of Kárász. East, along the Tisza River, is the huge, neoclassical **Ference Mora Múzeum** (☎ 549 040; Várkert; adult/student 400/200Ft; ☉ 10am-5pm Tue-Sun). There are exhibits on the Avar people (5th to 8th centuries) and on archaeological finds unearthed when the route for the M5 motorway was excavated, as well as some on folk life and art.

Two religious sites in homemade are especially worth a visit: the 1778 **Szerb Ortodox Templom** (Serbian Orthodox Church; cnr Béla and Somogyi utca; adult/student 150/100Ft; ☉ 8am-8pm) for its fantastic gold iconostasis; and the **Új Zsinagóga** (New Synagogue; ☎ 423 849; Gutenberg utca 13; adult/student 250/100Ft; ☉ 10am-noon & 1-5pm Sun-Fri Apr-Sep, 10am-2pm Sun-Fri Oct-Mar) for the ornate, painted interior.

Plenty of student accommodation is open to travellers in July and August, including the central **István Apáthy College** (☎ 545 896; Eötvös utca 4; dm 1600-2500Ft). **Ibusz** (☎ 471 177; Oroslán utca 3; per person 4000-5000Ft; ☉ 9am-5pm Mon-Fri, 9am-1pm Sat) travel agency can help with private rooms. The comfortable **Illes Panzió** (☎ 315 640; Maros utca 37; s/d 5900/6900Ft; Ⓟ) is northeast of the centre, not far from the Tisza. Central **Numero Uno** (☎ 424 745, Széchenyi tér 5; mains 360-730Ft; ☉ 11am-11pm Mon-Sat, noon-11pm Sun) sells good pizzas and calzones. The staff at the barrel-ceilinged **Zodia'kus** (☎ 420 914; Oskola utca 13; mains 890-2100Ft; ☉ 8am-1am Mon-Sat, 11am-midnight Sun) is exceptionally accommodating. Innovative entrées include dishes like beef tenderloin cooked to order and topped with red currents and cheddar cheese.

There's a vast array of bars, clubs and other nightspots, especially around Dugonics tér. Nightclub programs are listed in the free *Szegedi Est* magazine. Join the 20-somethings drinking at **John Bull Pub** (☎ 484 217; Oroslán utca 6; 🕑 10am-midnight Sun-Thu, 10am-1am Sat & Sun) – if you can find a free table. **Sing Sing Disco** (cnr Mars tér & Dr Baross József utca; 500Ft; 🕑 10pm-4am Wed-Sat) is a pretty typical party place that holds theme raves.

Buses run to Budapest (2430Ft, three hours, six daily), Kecskemét (2430Ft, two hours, 10 daily) and Pécs (3010Ft, four hours, eight daily). Szeged is on the main rail line to Budapest's Nyugati Train Station (2324Ft, 2½ hours, 11 daily).

NORTHEASTERN HUNGARY

Hills give way to mountains as you approach the Carpathian Mountains, which stretch into modern day Ukraine and Romania. The Tisza River is the dominating water element, and flooding is not uncommon.

EGER
☎ 36 / pop 57,000

A lovely baroque city, Eger is full of churches, schools and palaces dating from the 18th century. Much of the old town centre is pedestrian-only, making it easy to explore but hard to park. Egri Bikavér (Eger Bull's Blood), a full-bodied red wine produced in the surrounding hills, is known the world over. The friendly staff at **Tourinform** (☎ 36-517 715; www.eger.hu; Bajcsy-Zsilinszky utca 9; 9am-5pm Mon-Fri, 9am-1pm Sat, 9am-6pm Mon-Fri Jul & Aug) can supply all the information you need.

Egri Vár (Eger Castle; ☎ 312 744; Vár 1; adult/student combined ticket 800/400Ft; open 8am-8pm Tue-Sun Apr-Aug, 8am-7pm Sep, 8am-6pm Oct & Mar, 8am-5pm Nov-Feb), up the hill off Dósza tér, was erected in the 13th century after the Mongol invasion. Inside the walled complex are several museums, the Bishop's Palace and the older foundations of St John's Cathedral, which was destroyed by the Turks. East of the castle hill is a 40m-high **Minaret** (Knézich Károly utca; 200Ft; 🕑 10am-6pm Mar-Oct), the most northerly of such monuments that the Turks left during their occupation in the 16th century. Don't try to climb the 97 narrow spiral steps to the top if you're claustrophobic.

A 15-minute walk southeast of the town centre, **Szépasszony völgy** (Valley of the Beautiful Women; off Király utca) is home to dozens of small wine cellars that produce Bull's Blood and other regional wines. Walk the horseshoe-shaped street through the valley (between about 10am and 5pm), stop at any cellar door that strikes your fancy and ask to taste their wares (50Ft per decilitre). Bring an empty bottle (Coke, water, anything) and they'll fill it up for about 600Ft per 1.5 litres.

The covered **piac** (market; Katona István tér 1; 🕑 6am-5pm Mon-Fri, 6am-1pm Sat, 6-10am Sun) has produce on the ground floor and food stands upstairs. **Elefanto** (☎ 411 031; Katona István tér 2; pizzas 490-900Ft, mains 1350-2000Ft; 🕑 11am-midnight) serves pizza, international dishes and good, cold beer. The covered balcony is great for al fresco dining.

Tourinform can help you locate student accommodation in the summer. The **Bartók Tér Panzió** (☎ 515 556, fax 515 572; Bartók Béla tér 8; s/d/tr 5000/8000/10,000Ft; 🗶) is a reasonable alternative year round. Rooms with skylights and pastel colours are in an old building organised around a courtyard; one has five beds (14,500Ft). Trains run between Eger and Budapest's Keleti Train Station (1468Ft, two hours) at least four times a day.

AROUND EGER

Another well-known wine destination is the smaller village of Tokaj, 43 km northeast of Eger, which has long been celebrated for its legendary sweet wines. The **Tourinform** (☎ 47-352 258; www.tokaj.hu; Serház utca 1; 🕑 8am-5pm Mon-Fri) is just off Rákóczi út.

HUNGARY DIRECTORY

ACCOMMODATION
Camping

Hungary has more than 400 camping grounds, which are usually challenging to reach without a car. Tourinform's *Camping Hungary* map/brochure (www.camping.hu) lists every camp site in Hungary.

Hostels & Student Dormitories

Despite the places listed by the Budapest-based **Hungarian Youth Hostel Association** (Mellow

Mood Ltd; ☎ 1-413 2065; www.youthhostels.hu; main office, VII Baross tér 15, 3rd floor), from July to August, the cheapest rooms are in vacant student accommodation (dorm beds and sometimes private rooms, too). Local Tourinform offices can help you locate colleges and universities.

Pensions & Hotels
Quaint, often family-run, *panziók* (pensions) are abundant and usually less expensive than hotels. Although they don't always have in-room telephones or restaurants attached, they do usually serve a breakfast buffet. Some hotels *(szállók* or *szállodák)* have less expensive rate options, if you're willing to share the toilet down the hall.

Private Rooms
Private rooms are usually assigned by travel agencies. You're probably better off avoiding individuals at train stations in Budapest offering private rooms. Outside Budapest, you can look for houses with signs that read *'szoba kiadó'* or the German *'Zimmer frei'* (room to let, or free room). A supplement is sometimes required if you stay less than four nights.

ACTIVITIES
More than 100 thermal baths are open to the public. Request the brochure *Water Tours in Hungary* from Tourinform. It's a gold mine of information for planning itineraries and rentals and learning the rules and regulations. A booklet on equestrian tourism is also available, or you could contact the **Hungarian Equestrian Tourism Association** (MLTSZ; ☎ 1-456 0444; www.equi.hu; IX Ráday utca 8, Budapest).

Hungary now counts 2500km of dedicated bicycle lanes around the country, with more on the way. For information and advice, contact the helpful **Hungarian Bicycle Touring Association** (MKTSZ; ☎ 1-311 2467; mktsz@enternet.hu; VI Bajcsy-Zsilinszky út 31, Budapest).

BUSINESS HOURS
Open hours are posted on front doors. *Nyitva* means 'open' and *zárva* 'closed'. The majority of grocery stores are open from 7am to 6pm Monday to Friday, and to 1pm on Saturday. Most towns have a 'nonstop' convenience store, and many have hyper-supermarkets that are open 24 hours. Main post offices open 8am to 6pm weekdays,

to noon or 1pm Saturday. Bank hours are from 8am to 4pm Monday to Thursday and 8am to 1pm on Friday.

CUSTOMS
You can bring and take out the usual personal effects, 200 cigarettes, 1L of wine or champagne and 1L of spirits. You are not supposed to export valuable antiques without a special permit; this should be available from the place of purchase. You must declare the import/export of any amount of cash exceeding the sum of 1,000,000Ft.

DANGERS & ANNOYANCES
Hungary is not a violent or dangerous society, but racially motivated attacks against Roma, Africans and Arabs are not unknown. Beware of pickpockets and taxi louts. In Budapest, especially around Váci utca, guys should avoid gorgeous women offering to take them to a nightclub – that is, unless they want to pay upwards of €80 per drink (for them and the girls).

DISABLED TRAVELLERS
Facilities are virtually nonexistent, although audible traffic signals are becoming more common and there are Braille markings on the higher-denominated forint notes. For more information, contact the **Hungarian Disabled Association** (MEOSZ; ☎ 1-388 5529; meosz@matavnet.hu; III San Marco utca 76, Budapest).

EMBASSIES & CONSULATES
To find out about Hungarian embassies around the world, or foreign ministries in Hungary, contact the **Ministry of Foreign Affairs** (☎ 1-458 1000; www.kum.hu; II Bem rakpart 47, Budapest).

GAY & LESBIAN TRAVELLERS
For up-to-date information, primarily focused on Budapest, contact **GayGuide.Net** (☎ 06 30 932 3334; http://budapest.gayguide.net).

HOLIDAYS
Hungary's public holidays are: New Year's Day (1 January), 1848 Revolution Day (15 March), Easter Monday (March/April), International Labour Day (1 May), Whit Monday (May/June), St Stephen's Day (20 August), 1956 Remembrance Day (23 October), All Saints' Day (1 November) and Christmas and Boxing Days (25 and 26 December).

MONEY

The unit of currency is the Hungarian forint (Ft). Coins come in denominations of one, two, five, 10, 20, 50 and 100Ft, and notes are denominated 200, 500, 1000, 2000, 5000, 10,000 and 20,000Ft. ATMs are quite common throughout the country, including at train stations, and accept most credit and cash cards. Banks usually offer exchange services as well as having ATMs. Branches can be found around the main square in an old town centre, or on the main thoroughfare leading to it. Bank hours are from 8am to 4pm Monday to Thursday and 8am to 1pm on Friday. Visa and MasterCard are the most widely accepted credit cards.

Although Hungary is part of the EU, it will not adopt the euro as the national currency for a number of years. In this chapter, where prices are listed in euros, they are pegged to the euro. Places with prices listed in euros accept either euros or forints; the price in forints will vary according to that day's euro exchange rate. Places with prices listed in forints charge a fixed price, to be paid in forints only.

POST

A *légiposta* (airmail) postcard within Hungary costs 40Ft, to neighbouring countries, 50Ft, within Europe, 110Ft and to the rest of the world, 150Ft. Although you can buy stamps at some youth hostels and hotels, go to a post office to actually send your letter or card. If you put it in a post box on the street, it could languish for weeks. Otherwise, service is pretty speedy – less than a week to Europe, less than two to the USA.

TELEPHONE

Hungary's country code is ☎ 36. To make an out-going international call, dial ☎ 00 first. To dial city-to-city (and all mobile phones) within the country, first dial ☎ 06 (dialling in from out of the country, leave off the 06), then the city code. Mobile phone numbers all use the prefix ☎ 06; no city code is necessary. Budapest numbers have seven digits, most others six digits.

The best place to make international telephone calls is from a phone box with a phone card, which you can buy at news stands in 2000Ft and 5000Ft denominations. Some cards, such as Neophone, get

you an international call for as little 19Ft per minute. Buy a Matáv *telefonkártya* at newsstands (800Ft) to make domestic calls at card-operated machines. Some pay phones still take coins.

TOURIST INFORMATION

The Hungarian National Tourist Office (HNTO) has a chain of 120 **Tourinform** (☎ 30 30 30 600 international hotline; www.tourinform.hu, www.hungary.com) information offices across the country, and these are the best places to ask general questions and pick up brochures. The HNTO operates an international hotline in Hungarian, English and German. Their Hungary.com website has a list of the more than 20 international HNTO representatives located abroad under Representation under Travel Trade Pages.

VISAS

To enter Hungary, everyone needs a valid passport or, for citizens of the European Union, a national identification card. Citizens of virtually all European countries, Australia, Canada, Israel, Japan, New Zealand and the USA do not require visas to visit Hungary for stays of up to 90 days. UK citizens do not need a visa for a stay of up to six months. Check with the **Ministry of Foreign Affairs** (☎ 1-458 1000; www.kum.hu) for an up-to-date list of which country nationals require visas.

Visas are issued at Hungarian consulates or missions, most international highway border crossings, Ferihegy airport and the International Ferry Pier in Budapest. However, visas are never issued on trains and rarely on buses.

WORKING

Working legally in Hungary always involved a Byzantine paper chase to get a permit, and it looks like it will get harder, given EU membership requirements. The government has said it will crack down on illegal workers. No-one thinks they're going to target English teachers, but the work situation for foreigners is in a state of flux. The umbrella Hungarian-government website is www.hungary.hu. English-language newspaper the *Budapest Sun* (www.budapestsun.com) sometimes lists teaching positions or agencies that can help with permits in its classifieds.

Iceland

HIGHLIGHTS

- **Reykjavík runtur** Friday night's wild pub-crawl around the capital's rowdy bars (p597)
- **Þingvellir** Fissure-ridden national park where you can walk from America to Europe without getting your toes wet (p599)
- **Blue Lagoon** Steaming, sapphire water feature that is Iceland's most famous attraction (p599)
- **Off-the-beaten track** Þórsmörk's glacial gorges and mountain flowers (p600)

FAST FACTS

- **Area** 103,000 sq km (89 Icelands would fit into mainland USA)
- **ATMs** Widespread
- **Budget** Minimum Ikr4000 per day
- **Capital** Reykjavík
- **Country codes** ☎ 354; international access code ☎ 00; operator ☎ 533 5310
- **Famous for** Björk!
- **Head of State** President Ólafur Ragnar Grímsson
- **Language** Icelandic
- **Money** Icelandic króna (A$1 =51.26Ikr, CA$1 = 56.17Ikr, €1 = 87.28Ikr, ¥100 = 64.53, NZ$1 = 47.84Ikr, UK£1 = 127.27Ikr, US$1 = 70.66Ikr)
- **Phrases** *Halló* (hello), *gjörðu svo vel* (please), *takk fyrir* (thanks), *skál!* (cheers!)
- **Population** 294,000
- **Time** GMT/UTC (no daylight saving)
- **Visas** Unnecessary for visitors from Scandinavia, EU countries, the USA and the Commonwealth for under three months.

TRAVEL HINTS

Take a sleeping bag for discounted accommodation. Buy booze from the State Alcohol shop and start Friday night at home.

ROAMING ICELAND

Go wild at Reykjavík's Friday-night *runtur*, then sober up in a geothermal pool. Visit the amazing Golden Circle sights and the unearthly Blue Lagoon.

Iceland's scenery is mind-blowing: chuck a lump of lava and you'll hit a glacier, geyser, volcano or bubbling geothermal spring. The high-energy landscape seems to infect the people, too – the average inhabitant is a fisherman, farmer, drinker, thinker, knitter, poet and skier!

Densely populated seabird colonies are found on the coasts, and it's well worth saving some beer money for an Icelandic horse trek or whale-watching trip. Iceland's natural wonders form a backdrop to the bloodthirsty sagas, some of the world's finest medieval stories.

In Reykjavík, the top destination for most travellers, fashionable young things thrive on vast quantities of coffee, music, sex and beer: see for yourself on the infamous *runtur*, the city's weekend pub-crawl.

HISTORY

Irish monks desperate for peace and quiet were Iceland's first inhabitants, arriving around AD 700. Their solitude was shattered by the Age of Settlement (874–930), when a wave of Vikings descended, driven from Norway by political clashes. The settlers decided against Scandinavian-style monarchy in favour of the world's first democratic parliament, the Alþing, established at Þingvellir (Parliament Plains; p599).

In the early 13th century, violent blood feuds among Icelandic chieftains led to periods of first Norwegian (1281) then Danish (1397) rule. For the next six centuries, Iceland was devastated by a Dark Age of famine, disease and disastrous volcanic eruptions.

Despite never-ending catastrophes, a sense of nationalism was slowly growing. By 1874, Iceland had drafted its own constitution. The Republic of Iceland was established on 17 June 1944.

During WWII, first British then US troops occupied the island (the USA still operates a NATO base at Keflavík). The war marked a dramatic change in the country's fortunes, as subsistence farming gave way to frenzied building and prosperity.

PEOPLE & CULTURE

Most Icelanders are descended from early Scandinavian settlers and their Celtic slaves. The current population is just over 290,000, almost half of whom live in Reykjavík. The people are self-reliant but friendly souls, with one of the world's highest life expectancies – 77.5 for men and 82.2 for women. Icelanders do everything to extremes, from working to partying.

Björk is Iceland's most famous musical export. Other bands with world domination in their view include Quarashi, SigurRos, Mínus and Maus. See Icelandic musicians live at venues such as Gaukur á Stöng in Reykjavík (p597).

ENVIRONMENT

Iceland is a young country with an active volcanic zone, running from southwest to northeast and responsible for all those lava flows, geysers, hot springs and volcanoes.

READING UP

Lonely Planet's *Iceland* is the guide for in-depth travel. For a flavour of Viking life, try *Grettis Saga,* translated by Anthony Faulkes. *Independent People,* a dark comedy about early-20th-century Iceland, won its author Halldór Laxness the Nobel Prize.

The only indigenous land mammal is the arctic fox. Iceland compensates for this shortage with huge numbers of birds and 17 species of whale.

Iceland announced its intention in August 2003 to resume scientific whaling. See the International Whaling Commission's website (www.iwcoffice.org) for details.

TRANSPORT

GETTING THERE & AWAY
Air

Keflavík Airport (airport code KEF; ☎ 425 0680; www.keflavikairport.com), located 48km west of Reykjavík, is Iceland's main gateway. Flights to Greenland and the Faroe Islands use **Reykjavík Domestic Airport** (airport code REK) in the city centre.

Icelandair (airline code FI; www.icelandair.net) does direct European flights to Keflavík from Britain, Denmark, France, Germany, Holland and Sweden, and the US. Free stopovers in Iceland are possible when flying from the US to Britain or mainland Europe.

Iceland Express (airline code AEU; www.icelandexpress.com) is the cheapest airline, flying to Keflavík from London and Copenhagen.

In summer, **Flugfélag Íslands** (Air Iceland; airline code NY; ☎ 570 3030; www.airiceland.is) flies from Reykjavík to the Faroe Islands and Kulusuk (Greenland).

DEPARTURE TAX

Departure tax for international flights is included in the price of the plane ticket. There's a Ikr415 tax on every domestic departure.

ICELAND

ICELAND

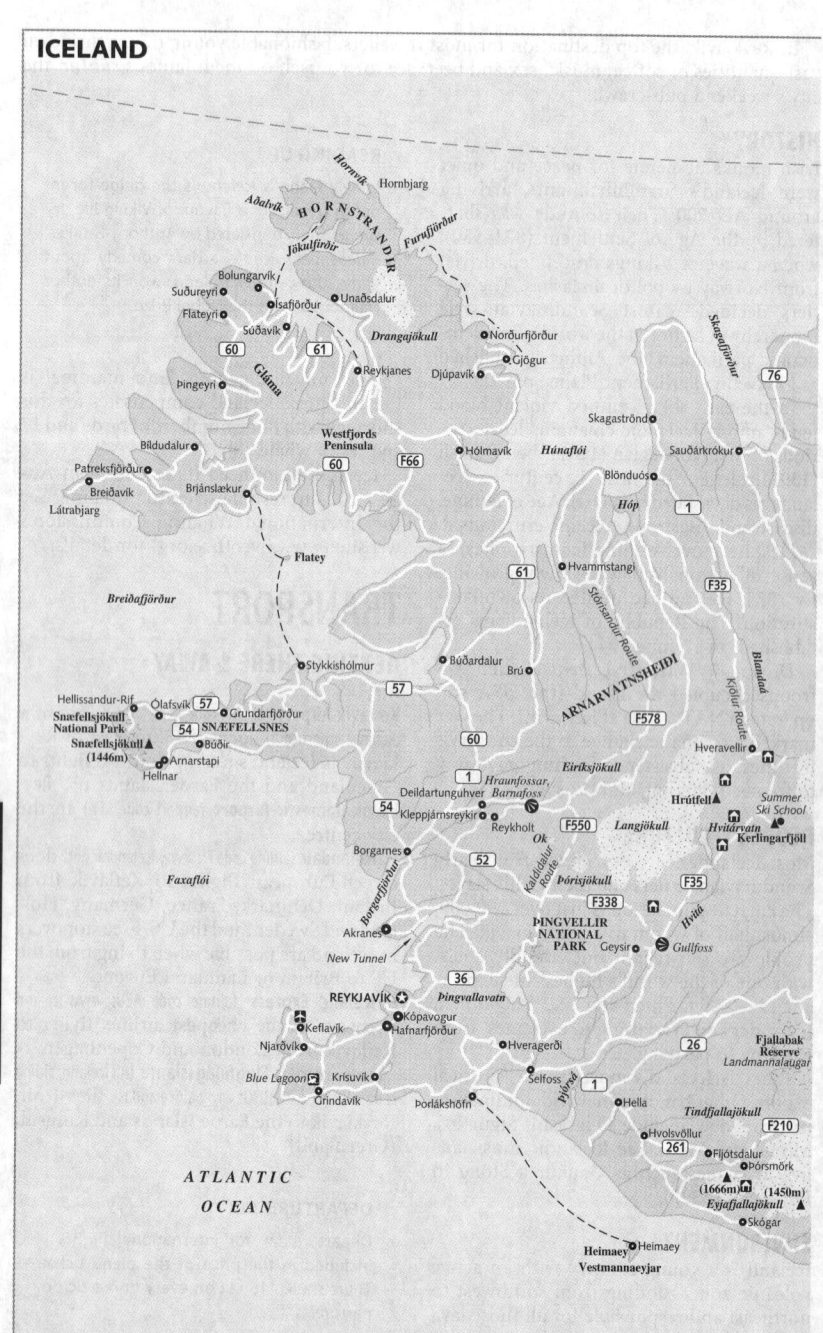

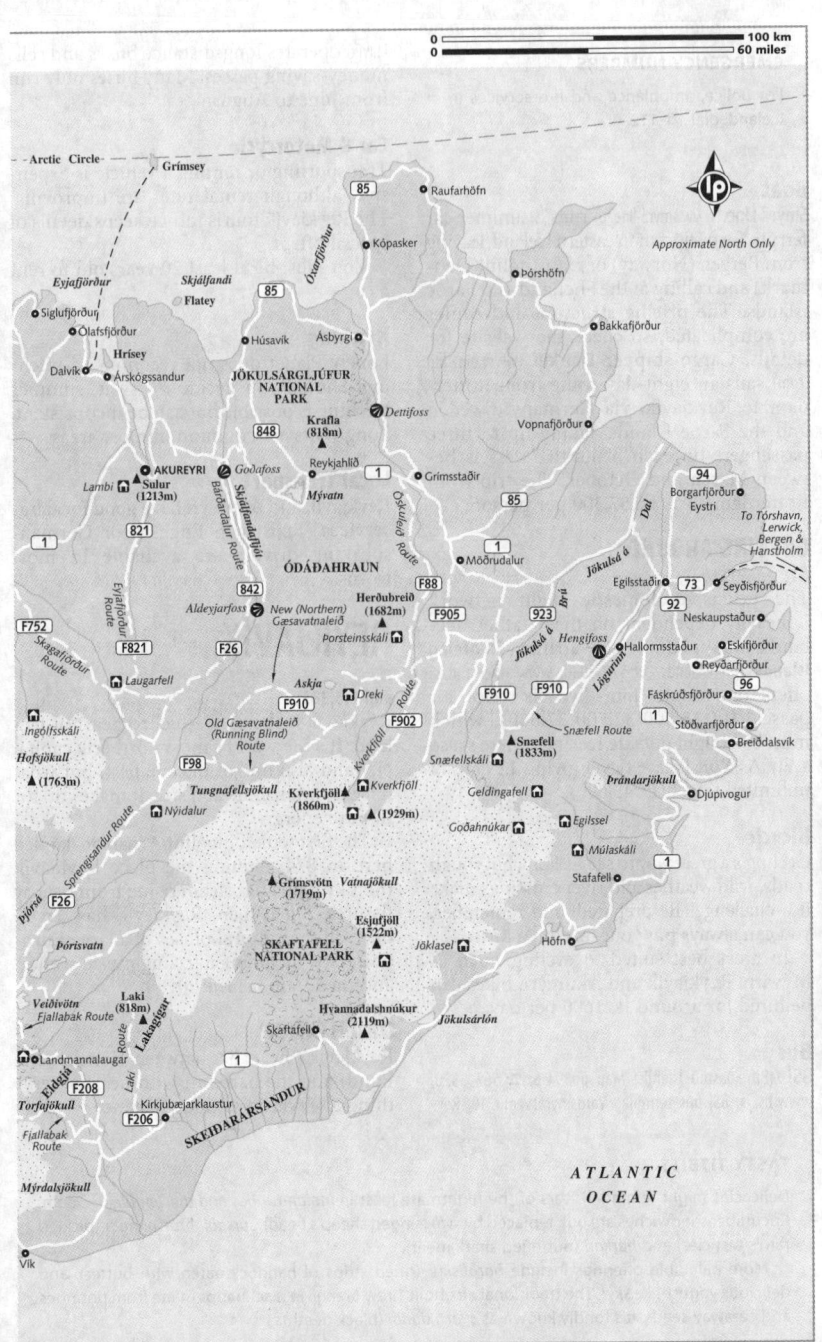

0   100 km
0   60 miles

Arctic Circle — Grímsey

Approximate North Only

ATLANTIC
OCEAN

ICELAND

> **EMERGENCY NUMBERS**
>
> For police, ambulance and fire services in Iceland, dial ☎ 112.

Boat

Smyril Line (www.smyril-line.fo) runs a summer car ferry to Seyðisfjörður in eastern Iceland, leaving from Bergen (Norway) or Hanstholm (Denmark) and calling at the Shetland and Faroe islands. The pricing structure and routes are complicated, so check the website for details. Cargo-shipper **Eimskip** (www.eimskip .com) sails an eight-day route from Rotterdam to Reykjavík, via Germany, Sweden and the Faroe Islands, taking up to three passengers on each of its two vessels between March and October. The trip from Rotterdam costs Ikr57,300 per person.

GETTING AROUND
Air

The extensive domestic flight network is heavily dependent on the weather. Iceland's main domestic airline **Flugfélag Íslands** (Air Iceland; ☎ 570 3030; www.airiceland.is) offers one-month four-/five-/six-sector air passes (Ikr28,800/32,700/37,600) which must be bought outside Iceland. There's also a Fly As You Please ticket giving 12 days of unlimited travel (Ikr45,600).

Bicycle

Cycling's a great way to see Iceland, but rough roads, wild weather and river crossings make it a challenge! Be prepared; and remember, you can always put your bike on a bus.

In areas best suited to cycling, such as Mývatn, Reykjavík and Akureyri, bikes can be hired for around Ikr1600 per day.

Bus

BSÍ (Bifreiðastöð Íslands; Map pp594-5; ☎ 562 3320; www.bsi.is; BSÍ bus terminal, Vatnsmýrarvegur 10, Reykjavík) operates long-distance buses and sells money-saving passes. Many buses only run from June to August.

Car & Motorcycle

Transporting or renting a vehicle is expensive, although rental rates are improving. The Reykjavík tourist office keeps details of special offers.

You must be at least 20 years old to rent a car.

Hitching

Lonely Planet does not recommend hitching. Should you decide to try it, summer hitching is possible but can be inconsistent. Long waits are common in most areas.

Local Transport

Reykjavík and Akureyri have good local bus services. Taxis with English- or German-speaking drivers are available in most towns.

REYKJAVÍK

pop 113,387

Reykjavík is the coffee-fuelled heart of Iceland. It's the world's most northerly capital city and also one of the smallest; but what it lacks in sunshine and size, it makes up for in pure energy.

The first settler, Ingólfur Arnarson, landed here in 874, naming the place Reykjavík (Smoky Bay) after steam rising from nearby fissures. Since then, Reykjavík has developed all the cultural pluses of a large European city, including a fizzing music scene... and the infamous *runtur*.

ORIENTATION

Reykjavík's heart lies between Tjörnin (The Pond) and the harbour, with nearly everything else within walking distance.

> **TASTY TITBITS**
>
> Delicacies might remind visitors of the nightmare feast in *Indiana Jones and the Temple of Doom*. Cucumber sandwiches are out, replaced by *svið* (singed sheep's head), *súrsaðir hrútspungar* (pickled ram's testicles) and *hárkarl* (putrefied shark meat).
>
> More palatable offerings include *harðfiskur* (dried strips of haddock eaten with butter), and delicious yogurt-like *skyr*. The traditional alcoholic brew *brennivín* is schnapps made from potatoes and caraway seeds. It's fondly known as *svarti dauði* (black death).

ICELAND

INFORMATION
Emergency
Landspítali University Hospital (Map pp594-5; ☎ 525 1000; Fossvogur) 24-hour emergency ward.

Internet Access
Libraries have the cheapest Internet access (Ikr200 per hour):
Aðalsafn (Reykjavík City Library; Map p598; ☎ 563 1717; www.borgarbokasafn.is; Tryggvagata 15; ☯ 10am-8pm Mon-Thu, 11am-7pm Fri, 1-5pm Sat & Sun)

Medical Services
Health Centre (Map p589; ☎ 585 2600; Vesturgata 7) Doctor's appointment required (Ikr700).
Lyf og Heilsa – Austurvegi (Map pp594-5; ☎ 581 2101; Háaleitisbraut 68; ☯ until midnight) Late-night pharmacy.

Money
Banks, clustered round Austurstræti and Bankastræti, offer the best exchange rates. **Landsbanki Íslands** (Map p598; Austurstræti) has no commission charges.

Post
Central Post Office (Map p598; Pósthússtræti 5; ☯ 9am-4.30pm Mon-Fri)

Telephone
Public coin/cardphones are found at the main tourist office and the Kringlan shopping centre (Map pp594-5).

Tourist Information
Upplýsingamiðstöð Ferðamála (Map p598; ☎ 562 3045; www.visitreykjavik.is; Aðalstræti 2; ☯ 8.30am-7pm Jun-15 Sep, 9am-6pm Mon-Fri, 10am-2pm Sat & Sun 16 Sep-May)

SIGHTS & ACTIVITIES
The immense concrete church **Hallgrímskirkja** (Map p598; ☎ 510 1000; Skólavörðuholt; ☯ 9am-6pm) was designed to resemble basalt columns, and took a staggering 34 years to build. Heavenly choir music accompanies you up the **75m tower** (Ikr300)!

Eccentric eruption-chaser Villi Knutsen screens his films at the awesome **Volcano Show** (Map p598; ☎ 551 3230; Hellusund 6a; 1hr show adult/student Ikr750/200). English shows begin at 11am, 3pm and 8pm in July and August (less frequently outside high season).

Iceland is a great place for whale-spotting: minkes often swim right up to the

---

boats. **Elding Whale Watching** (Map pp594-5; ☎ 555 3565; www.elding.is; adult Ikr3700) and **Hvalstöðin** (Map pp594-5; ☎ 533 2660; www.whalewatching.is; adult Ikr3500) run three-hour trips from the harbour (Map pp594-5) in summer.

The tourist complex **Perlan** on Öskjuhlíð hill includes the excellent **Saga Museum** (Map pp594-5; ☎ 511 1517; www.sagamuseum.is; adult/student Ikr800/600; ☯ 10am-6pm Jun-Aug, noon-5pm Mon-Fri, 10am-6pm Sat & Sun Sep-May), which brings Iceland's history to life with silicon models and bloodcurdling screams. Two **artificial geysers** blast off every few minutes, and there's a superb **viewing area** upstairs. Take bus No 7 from Lækjartorg bus terminal (Map p598).

One hundred percent cheaper than the Blue Lagoon, **Nautholsvík Geothermal Beach** (Ylströndin; admission free; ☯ 10am-10pm 15 May-15 Sep) is a dinky stretch of golden sand heated by geothermal water (at 18°C to 20°C). A small café nearby sells beer and ice cream. **Laugardalur** (Map pp594-5; ☎ 553 4039; Sundlaugavegur 30; adult Ikr200; ☯ 6.50am-9.30pm Mon-Fri, 8am-8pm

---

GETTING INTO TOWN
From the BSÍ bus terminal: Walk left along Vatnsmýrarvegur, then turn right along Njarðargata. Cross the major ring road, then take the first road on the left, Sóleyjargata, which takes you to the city centre (1km). Alternatively, take a taxi.

From the airport: The **Flybus** (Map pp594-5; ☎ 562 1011; www.re.is) to/from Keflavík Airport (Ikr1100, 50 minutes) meets all incoming flights. Credit cards are accepted.

ICELAND

REYKJAVÍK

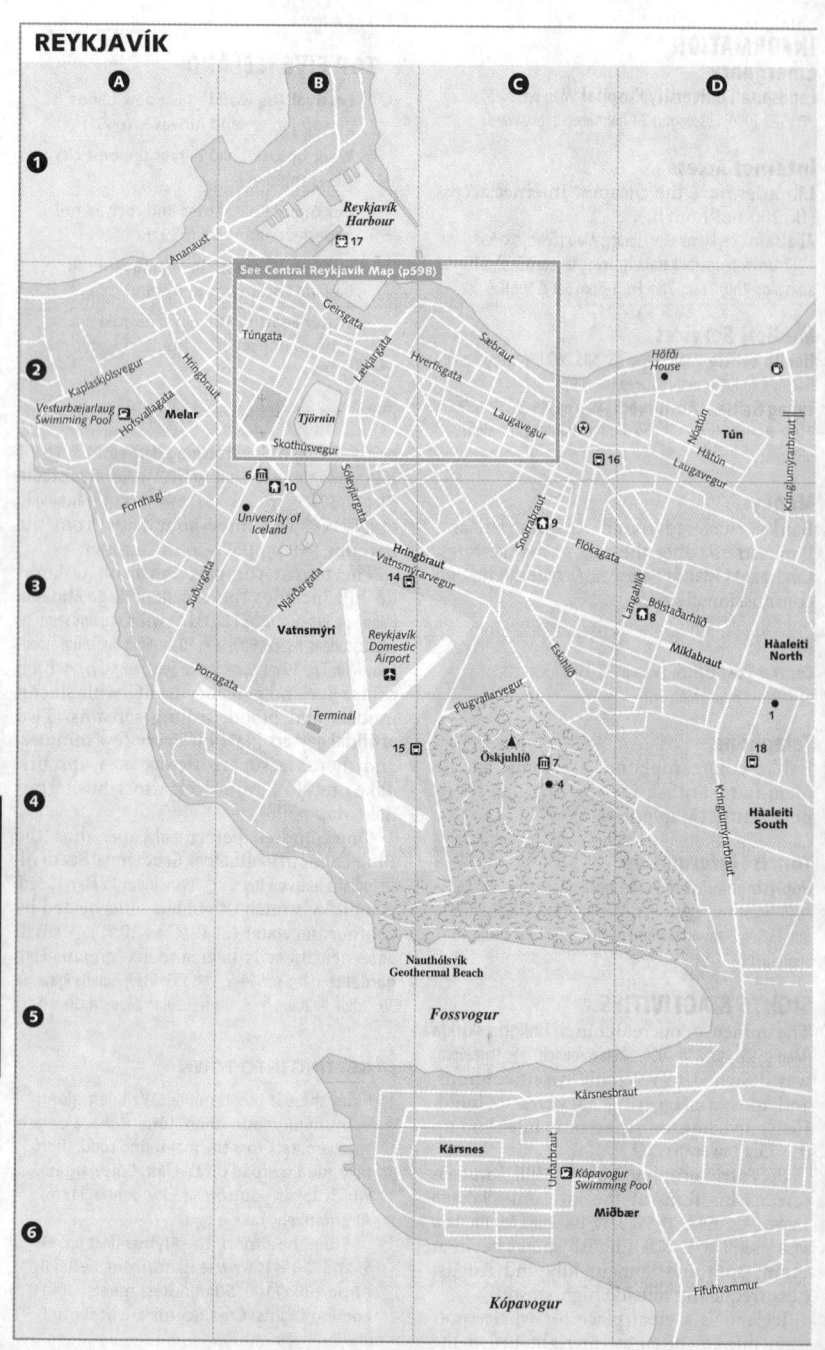

A **B** **C** **D**

1

Reykjavík
Harbour
17

See Central Reykjavík Map (p598)

Geirsgata

Túngata
Lækjargata
Hverfisgata
Sæbraut

Höfði
House

2
Kaplaskjólsvegur
Hringbraut
Nýlún
Tún
Vesturbæjarlaug
Swimming Pool
Holtsvallagata
Melar
Tjörnin
Skothúsvegur
Laugavegur
16
Hátún
Laugavegur
Kringlumýrarbraut

Fornhagi
6 10
Skólavörðustígur
University of
Iceland
Snorrabraut
9
Flókagata
Suðurgata
Njarðargata
Hringbraut
Vatnsmýrarvegur
14
Langahlíð
Bólstaðarhlíð
8
**Háaleiti
North**

3
Vatnsmýri
Reykjavík
Domestic
Airport
Eskihlíð
Miklabraut

Þorragata
Terminal
Flugvallarvegur
1

15
Öskjuhlíð
7
18

4
4
**Háaleiti
South**
Kringlumýrarbraut

Nauthólsvík
Geothermal Beach

5
Fossvogur

Kársnesbraut

6
Kársnes
Urðarbraut
Kópavogur
Swimming Pool
Miðbær

Fífuhvammur

Kópavogur

ICELAND

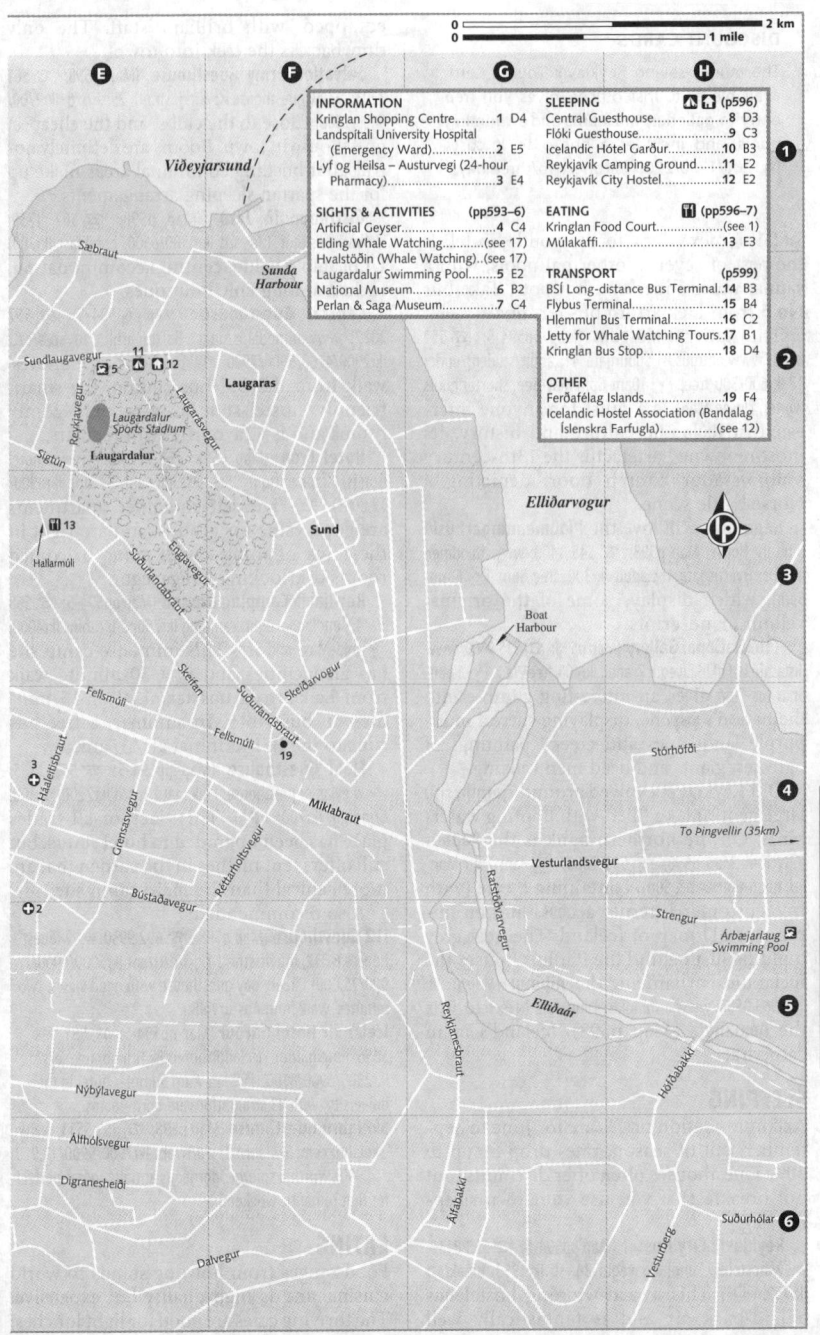

INFORMATION
Kringlan Shopping Centre............**1** D4
Landspítali University Hospital
(Emergency Ward)....................**2** E5
Lyf og Heilsa – Austurvegi (24-hour
Pharmacy)..............................**3** E4

SIGHTS & ACTIVITIES (pp593–6)
Artificial Geyser..........................**4** C4
Elding Whale Watching............(see 17)
Hvalstöðin (Whale Watching)..(see 17)
Laugardalur Swimming Pool.......**5** E2
National Museum.......................**6** B2
Perlan & Saga Museum..............**7** C4

SLEEPING (p596)
Central Guesthouse....................**8** D3
Flóki Guesthouse........................**9** C3
Icelandic Hótel Garður..............**10** B3
Reykjavík Camping Ground.......**11** E2
Reykjavík City Hostel................**12** E2

EATING (pp596–7)
Kringlan Food Court...................(see 1)
Múlakaffi...................................**13** E3

TRANSPORT (p599)
BSÍ Long-distance Bus Terminal.**14** B3
Flybus Terminal..........................**15** B4
Hlemmur Bus Terminal...............**16** C2
Jetty for Whale Watching Tours.**17** B1
Kringlan Bus Stop......................**18** D4

OTHER
Ferðafélag Íslands......................**19** F4
Icelandic Hostel Association (Bandalag
Íslenskra Farfugla)................(see 12)

ICELAND

DISCOUNT CARDS

The money-saving Reykjavík Tourist Card, available at tourist offices, gives you free entry to galleries, museums and swimming pools, and includes a bus pass. It costs Ikr1200/1700/2200 for one/two/three days.

Sat & Sun), next door to the youth hostel, is the best of seven geothermal pools, with a sauna, water slides and hot pots. Take bus No 5 from Lækjartorg bus terminal.

The **National Museum** (Map pp594-5; ☎ 552 8888; www.natmus.is; Suðurgata 41; adult/student/under 18 Ikr600/300/free; ⊙ 10am-6pm May-Sep, shorter hours winter, closed Mon) is a must for anyone interested in Icelandic culture and history. Its most renowned artefact is the 13th-century Valþjófssaður church door, depicting a Norse battle scene.

Saga fans will love the **Þjóðmenningarhúsið** (Culture House; Map p598; ☎ 545 1400; www.thjodmenning.is; Hverfisgata 15; adult Ikr300, free Sun; ⊙ 11am-5pm), which displays some of the original vellum manuscripts.

The **National Gallery** (Map p598; ☎ 515 9600; www.listasafn.is; Fríkirkjuvegur 7; adult Ikr400, free Wed; ⊙ 11am-5pm Tue-Sun) gives an interesting glimpse into the nation's psyche, displaying surreal mud-purple landscapes and creepy paintings of ogresses, giants and dead men walking.

Old Reykjavík evolved around **Tjörnin**, the large central lake filled with hooting waterbirds. On the northern bank is the **Raðhús** (City Hall; Map p598; ☎ 563 2005; ⊙ 8am-7pm Mon-Fri, noon-6pm Sat & Sun), containing a café (with free customer Internet access) and an impressive 3D map of Iceland. The neat grey building just behind the Raðhús houses the Icelandic parliament, the **Alþingi** (Map p598; ☎ 563 0500; www.althingi.is; Túngata). Next to it is the **Dómkirkja** (Map p598), Iceland's main cathedral.

SLEEPING

Accommodation prices are for June to September; out of season, rates drop by up to 30%. Guesthouses often offer discounts (but not breakfast) if you use your own sleeping bag.

Reykjavík City Hostel (Map pp594-5; ☎ 553 8110; www.hostel.is; Sundlaugavegur 34; sb Ikr1950, breakfast Ikr750; ⊡) This award-winning hostel has a laid-back air and is fantastically well equipped, with brilliant staff. The only drawback is the trek into town!

Salvation Army Guesthouse (Map p598; ☎ 561 3203; www.guesthouse.is; Kirkjustræti 2; sb/s/d Ikr2700/5000/7500) Close to the clubs, and the cheapest guesthouse in town. Rooms are definitely no-frills, but bustling communal areas make up for the spartan sleeping arrangements.

Gistiheimilið Jörð (Map p598; ☎ 562 1739; Skólavörðustígur 13a; s/d Ikr4500/6500, breakfast Ikr700) Unbeatable value, central accommodation, tucked among chic boutiques.

Central Guesthouse (Map pp594-5; ☎ 552 2822; www.mmedia.is/gakr; Bólstaðarhlíð 8; sb/s/d/tr Ikr2900/4700/5900/7900; ⊡) About 10 minutes' walk from the BSÍ bus station, the smart, friendly hostel-style Central has comfy rooms and is a favourite with regulars.

Hótel Frón (Map p598; ☎ 511 4666; www.hotelfron.is; Klapparstígur 35a; s/studio apt/2-r apt Ikr8900/12,800/14,900) The self-contained apartments are good value for groups, and are right in the thick of things, with some balconied rooms overlooking Laugavegur.

Reykjavík Camping Ground (Map pp594-5; ☎ 568 6944; Sundlaugavegur; camping Ikr750, 2-b cabins Ikr4000; ⊙ mid-May–mid-Sep) This immense camp site has all facilities and is a 30-minute walk from Lækjartorg bus terminal or 15 minutes on bus No 5. In summer, a free bus runs to the BSÍ terminal at 7.15am.

Flóki Guesthouse (Map pp594-5; ☎ 552 1155; www.eyjar.is/guesthouse; Flókagata 1; s/d Ikr7200/10,300, camping Ikr700; ⓟ) This jack-of-all-trades place has been upgraded to hotel status, but still offers tent pitches in the garden that are more central than the main camp site.

Also recommended:

i12 Guesthouse (Map p598; ☎ 692 9930; www.guesthouses.is/i12; Ingólfsstræti 12; s/d/tr/apt Ikr5000/6000/7000/25,000) Cheery gay guesthouse with good views, two minutes' walk from Austurvöllur.

Icelandic Hotel Garður (Map pp594-5; ☎ 551 5656; hotelgardur@icelandichotels.is; Hringbraut; sb/s/d Ikr2800/6900/8100; ⊙ Jun-Aug) Summer hotel in the university, with 43 straightforward dorm rooms.

Skólabrú Guesthouse (Map p598; ☎ 551 5511; www.skolabru.com; Skólabrú 2; s/d/tr/apt Ikr7900/9900/11,900/14,900) Worth a splurge: gorgeous antique rooms perfect for that romantic weekend.

EATING

Food ranges from hot-dog stands to world cuisine, and is high quality but expensive. The thriving cafés are good for light lunches;

many turn into bars at night. Restaurants are pricey places for dressed-up evening dining. Most eateries, including fast-food stands, mushroom along Laugavegur, Austurstræti and Ingólfstorg.

Restaurants

Hornið (Map p598; ☎ 551 3340; Hafnarstræti 15; mains Ikr890-3340) Big yellow Hornið does Italian and Icelandic grub in a relaxed bistro environment. Service is speedy, so it's great if you're starving.

Á Næstu Grösum (First Vegetarian; Map p598; ☎ 552 8410; Laugavegur 20b; daily special lunch/dinner Ikr990/1190; ✛ closed lunch Sun) The best vegetarian/vegan restaurant, its inventive salad dressings give lettuce a reason to exist.

Si Señor (Map p598; ☎ 552 6030; Lækjargata 10; mains Ikr1290-2190) This comfortable, candlelit restaurant serves sizzling Mexican food to a salsa soundtrack. Wash it down with a tangy strawberry margherita (Ikr890) – *arrrriba*!

Café Victor (Map p598; ☎ 561 9555; Hafnarstræti 1-3; mains Ikr950-2450) Once the king's falcon house, now a favoured spot to people-watch and scoff bar snacks. At weekends, the barnlike interior swells with revellers until 5.30am.

Kína Húsið (Map p598; ☎ 551 1014; Lækjargata 8; mains Ikr1100-2500, lunch specials Ikr750) Authentic Chinese food at low prices.

Cafés

Kaffi Brennslan (Map p598; ☎ 561 3600; Pósthússtræti 9; snacks Ikr390-1790) Usually packed to the gills, this Art Deco place draws a mixed crowd, including families, artists and hangover-sufferers. It's a popular bar at night, selling beer from 19 countries.

Cultura (Map p598; ☎ 530 9314; Hverfisgata 18; snacks Ikr350-990; ✗) This arty intercultural café has round-the-world snacks, Scrabble in six languages, and live music until 3am at weekends. Recommended.

Café 22 (Map p598; ☎ 511 5522; Laugavegur 22) An endearing, bluesy coffee shop. Later, its three floors divide into buzzy bar, thronging dance floor and darkened room for drunken slumping.

Svarta Kaffið (Map p598; ☎ 551 2999; Laugavegur 54; ✗) Filled with African masks, this quirky caff does thick home-made soup in brilliant bread bowls (Ikr850), as well as cheap evening beers.

Vegamót (Map p598; ☎ 511 3040; Vegamótastígur 4; mains Ikr1090-2190) A clubby place to eat, drink,

gossip, see and be seen. At night, it gets packed out with fashion-conscious drinkers.

Quick Eats

Múlakaffi (Map pp594-5; ☎ 533 7737; Hallarmúli; meals Ikr990-1290; ✛ 8am-8pm Mon-Fri) is a basic but decent workers' cafeteria offering meaty canteen meals. The good-value food court in the Kringlan shopping centre (Map pp594-5) contains several fast-food franchises.

Nonnabiti (Map p598; ☎ 551 2312; Hafnarstræti 18; snacks Ikr280-690; ✛ until 2am) serves burgers and chips into the wee hours. When you've overdone fried meat, **Kebabhúsið** (Map p598; ☎ 561 3070; Lækjargata 2) offers falafel (Ikr650) and fish and chips (Ikr770).

For ultra-quick 3am eats, nothing beats the snack kiosks (Map p598) on Hafnarstræti and Austurstræti. Icelanders swear by the hot dogs from **Bæjarins Bestu** (Map p598; Tryggvagata): use the vital sentence *Eina með öllu* ('One with everything'!).

Self-Catering

The cheapest supermarket, with a convenient central branch, is **Bónus** (Map p598; Laugavegur 59; ✛ closed Sun).

DRINKING

Reykjavík is renowned for its weekend *runtur*, when hard-working Icelanders get sozzled at home, then circulate round bars and clubs from midnight onwards. Reykjavík is dressy, but there are places where you won't feel scruffy in jeans.

Grand Rokk (Map p598; ☎ 551 5522; Smiðjustígur 6) This utterly unpretentious bar fits like a favourite T-shirt. Chess enthusiasts play here, and it's great for live music, with up to three bands per session.

Sirkus (Map p598; ☎ 511 8022; Klapparstígur 31) Rated by its regulars for the funky, fairy-lit ambience, Sirkus also has a summer garden where you can partially escape the crush.

Gaukur á Stöng (Map p598; ☎ 551 1556; Tryggvagata 22; after 11pm Ikr1000) Stalwart Gaukurin, which invented vodka-spiked beer, is another fine live music venue.

Also recommended are **Dillon** (Map p598; ☎ 511 2400; Laugavegur 30), good on weeknights when other places can be tumbleweed empty; **Bar 11** (Map p598; ☎ 511 1180; Laugavegur 11), with jukebox, table football and weeknight gigs; **Nelly's Café** (Map p598; ☎ 562 1250; Þinghóltstræti 2), a student favourite for cheap

ICELAND

CENTRAL REYKJAVÍK

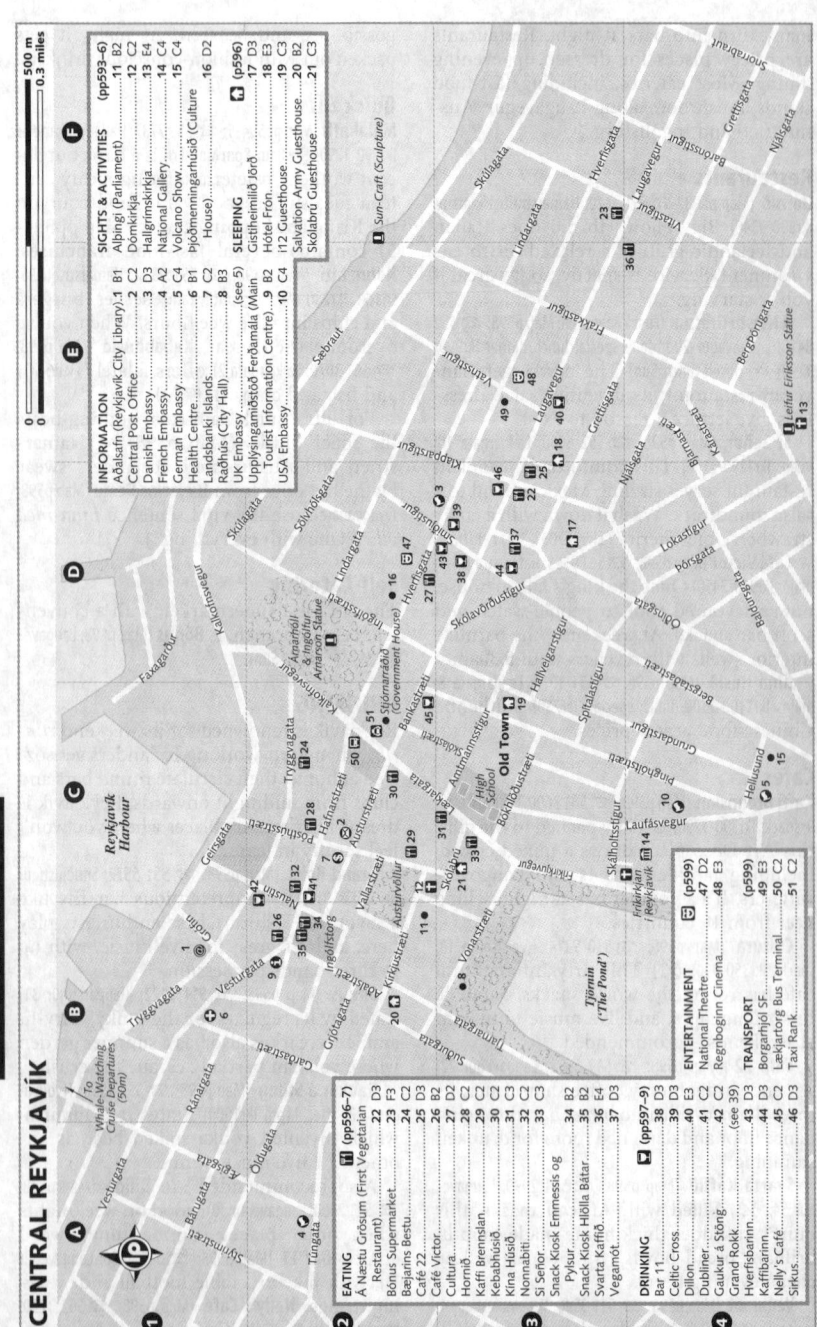

ICELAND

INFORMATION
Aðalsafn (Reykjavík City Library)...1 B1
Central Post Office.....................2 C2
Danish Embassy............................3 D3
French Embassy.............................4 A2
German Embassy..........................5 C4
Health Centre...................................6 B1
Landsbanki Íslands.......................7 C2
Ráðhús (City Hall).........................8 B3
UK Embassy..........................(see 5)
Upplýsingamiðstöð Ferðamála (Main
    Tourist Information Centre)...9 B2
USA Embassy................................10 C4

SIGHTS & ACTIVITIES (pp593–6)
Alþingi (Parliament).....................11 B2
Dómkirkja......................................12 C2
Hallgrímskirkja.............................13 E4
National Gallery............................14 C4
Volcano Show................................15 C4
Þjóðmenningarhúsið (Culture
    House).......................................16 D2

SLEEPING (p596)
Gistiheimilið Jörð........................17 D3
Hótel Frón.....................................18 E3
I12 Guesthouse.............................19 C3
Salvation Army Guesthouse.......20 B2
Skólabrú Guesthouse..................21 C3

EATING (pp596–7)
Á Næstu Grösum (First Vegetarian
    Restaurant)...............................22 D3
Bónus Supermarket......................23 F3
Bæjarins Bestu..............................24 C2
Café 22..25 D3
Café Victor.....................................26 B2
Cultura..27 D2
Hornið...28 C2
Kaffi Brennslan..............................29 C2
Kebabhúsið.....................................30 C2
Kína Húsið.......................................31 C3
Nonnabiti...32 C2
Si Señor...33 C3
Snack Kiosk Emmessís og
    Pylsur..34 B2
Snack Kiosk Hlölla Bátar.............35 B2
Svarta Kaffið..................................36 E4
Vegamót..37 D3

DRINKING (pp597–9)
Bar 11..38 D3
Celtic Cross....................................39 D3
Dillon..40 E3
Dubliner..41 C2
Gaukur á Stöng..............................42 C2
Grand Rokk.......................(see 39)
Hverfisbarinn.................................43 D3
Kaffibarinn......................................44 D3
Nelly's Café....................................45 C2
Sirkus..46 D3

ENTERTAINMENT (p599)
National Theatre.............................47 D2
Regnboginn Cinema......................48 E3

TRANSPORT (p599)
Borgarhjól SF..................................49 E3
Lækjartorg Bus Terminal..............50 C2
Taxi Rank...51 C2

beer and regular DJ sets; and **Celtic Cross** (Map p598; ☎ 511 3240; Hverfisgata 26) and **Dubliner** (Map p598; ☎ 511 3233; Hafnarstræti 4), cosy Irish pubs favoured by travellers.

More glamorous:

Kaffibarinn (Map p598; ☎ 551 1588; Bergstaðastræti 1) Damon Albarn from Blur has a stake in this *über*-trendy bar, popular with celebs. The petite, packed dance floor throbs to funk, hip hop and house.

Hverfisbarinn (Map p598; ☎ 511 6700; Hverfisgata 20) In-vogue club, with the queues to prove it: be young and dress immaculately! The music hardly matters – it's a fashion thing.

ENTERTAINMENT

Reykjavík's **National Theatre** (Map p598; ☎ 585 1200; www.leikhusid.is; Lindargata 7; admission Ikr2500) puts on around 350 performances a year. The most central cinema is **Regnboginn** (Map p598; ☎ 551 9000; Hverfisgata 54; Ikr800). Listings can be found in daily newspapers.

GETTING AROUND
To/From the Airport

The **Flybus** (☎ 562 1011; www.re.is) to/from Keflavík Airport (Ikr1100, 50 minutes) meets incoming flights outside the terminal, and accepts credit cards. Returning, the bus leaves two hours before international departures from Hótel Loftleiðir, the Flybus terminal.

Bicycle

Hire bikes from **Borgarhjól SF** (Map p598; ☎ 551 5653; Hverfisgata 50) or the Reykjavík City Hostel (Map pp594-5) for around Ikr1700 a day.

Bus

Reykjavík's excellent **city bus system** (☎ 551 2700; www.bus.is) runs from 7am to midnight, with night buses at weekends. Bus stops are marked with the letter S, and the two central terminals are at Hlemmur (Map pp594-5) and on Lækjargata (Map p598).

The fare is Ikr220 (no change given), but *skiptimiði* (transfer tickets) are available. The Reykjavík Tourist Card (see p598) includes a bus pass.

Taxi

There are four metered taxi companies in the Reykjavík area: **Hreyfill-Bæjarleiðir** (☎ 588 5522), **BSR** (☎ 561 0000), **Borgarbíll** (☎ 552 2440) and **BSH** (☎ 555 0888). There's a large taxi rank on Lækjargata opposite the Lækjartorg bus terminal.

AROUND REYKJAVÍK

BLUE LAGOON (BLÁA LÓNIÐ)

The **Blue Lagoon** (☎ 420 8800; www.bluelagoon.is; adult Ikr1200, towel/swimsuit/robe hire Ikr300/350/700, spa treatments from Ikr1300; ☼ 9am-9pm 15 May-31 Aug, 10am-8pm 1 Sep-14 May), 50km southwest of Reykjavík, is justifiably Iceland's most famous attraction. Set in a massive black lava field, the milky-blue spa is fed by water (at a perfect 38°C) from the futuristic Svartsengi geothermal plant. Swimmers in silica-mud facepacks drift round steaming silver vents and loll in hot pots. Once you're in, you really won't want to leave. Be careful on the slippery bridges and bring plenty of conditioner to stop your hair going solid.

To get there, the **Þingvallaleið Bus Service** (☎ 511 2600; www.bluelagoonbus.is) leaves from the BSÍ bus station in Reykjavík (Ikr850 one-way, 40 minutes, six buses between 10am and 6pm).

THE GOLDEN CIRCLE

The 'Golden Circle' refers to Gullfoss, Geysir and Þingvellir National Park, the 'big three' destinations for most visitors. At **Gullfoss**, the Hvitá River drops 32m in a rainbow-tinged double cascade, before running away along a vast rift. Ten kilometres down the road is **Geysir**, after which all spouting hot springs are named. The **Great Geysir** was plugged by rubble in the 1960s, thrown in by tourists trying to set it off. Luckily, the world's most reliable geyser, **Strokkur** (Butter Churn), is right next door, spouting up to 35m every six minutes. There's an interesting audiovisual exhibition on volcanoes, geysers and the northern lights at the otherwise tacky **Geysisstofa Geocentre** (☎ 486 8704; www.geysircenter.com; adult/student Ikr500/350; ☼ 10am-7pm May-Sep, noon-5pm Oct-Apr).

Þingvellir is Iceland's most significant historical site: the world's first democratic parliament, the Alþing, was established here in AD 930. In 1928 it became Iceland's first national park, thanks to its weighty history and superb natural setting, on the edge of an immense rift caused by the separating North American and Eurasian tectonic plates.

The popular Reykjavík Excursions and Destination Iceland Golden Circle day tours to Gullfoss, Geysir and Þingvellir cost around Ikr6500, without lunch. They leave

ICELAND

the BSÍ bus terminal in Reykjavík at 8.40am daily, or can collect you from your accommodation on request.

ÞÓRSMÖRK

The stunning glacial valley of Þórsmörk (Woods of Thor) boasts weird rock formations, twisting gorges, a singing cave, mountain flowers and icy streams. Its proximity to Reykjavík (130km southeast) makes it a popular spot in summer, when tents pile up and camp sites become partyville. You don't have to go far, though, to escape the crowds.

Wild camping is prohibited, but there are three Þórsmörk huts – **Skagfjörðsskáli** (Ferðafélag Íslands; ☎ 568 2533; www.fi.is; sb Ikr1700), **Básar** (Útivist; ☎ 562 1000; www.utivist.is; sb Ikr1600) and **Austurleiðarskáli** (Austurleið-SBS; ☎ 545 1717; www .austurleid.is; sb Ikr1600) – which have tent sites (per person Ikr600) around them.

From June to September, buses run between Reykjavík and Húsadalur (over the hill from Þórsmörk) at 8.30am daily and at 5pm Monday to Friday (Ikr3470, four hours).

ICELAND DIRECTORY

ACCOMMODATION
Camping
Apart from private land and national parks and reserves, where camping is forbidden or restricted, you're free to camp anywhere.

Guesthouses
Gistiheimilið (guesthouses) range from private homes to elaborate institutions. Some offer sleeping-bag accommodation – a godsend if you're on a tight budget. Many places only open from mid-May to August.

Hotels
There are 16 **Edda Hotels** (☎ 444 4000; www.hotel edda.is), run by Icelandair Hotels, which open in the summer only and are based in schools. Some offer sleeping-bag accommodation in rooms or classrooms.

Mountain Huts
Ferðafélag Íslands (Icelandic Touring Club; Map pp594-5; ☎ 568 2533; www.fi.is; Mörkin 6, IS-108 Reykjavík) maintains a system of *sæluhús* (mountain huts).

Youth Hostels
Iceland's 25 superb youth hostels are administered by the **Icelandic Hostel Association** (Bandalag Íslenskra Farfugla; Map pp594-5; ☎ 553 8110; www.hostel.is; Sundlaugavegur 34, IS-105 Reykjavík). All hostels have hot showers, cooking facilities, sheet-hire, luggage storage and sleeping-bag accommodation.

ACTIVITIES
July, August and September are the best months for walking. For details on hiking and mountaineering, contact **Ferðafélag Íslands** (☎ 568 2533; www.fi.is; Mörkin 6, IS-108 Reykjavík; ✆ 9am-5pm Mon-Fri summer, noon-5pm Mon-Fri winter).

BUSINESS HOURS
Banking hours are 9.15am to 4pm Monday to Friday. Most post offices open 8.30am or 9am to 4.30pm or 5pm Monday to Friday.

Weekday shopping hours are generally 9am to 6pm. Shops close early on Saturday and most are shut on Sunday. Cafés open until 6pm, although many become bars and remain open until 11pm during the week or 3am on weekends. Restaurants generally close by 10pm.

CUSTOMS
See www.tollur.is for Icelandic customs regulations.

EMBASSIES & CONSULATES
Also see the Visas section (p1242). A full list of Icelandic embassies and consulates is available at www.mfa.is.

Embassies & Consulates in Iceland
Denmark (Map p598; ☎ 575 0300; www4.mmedia .is/rekamb; Hverfisgata 29)
France (Map p598; ☎ 551 7621; www.ambafrance.is; Túngata 22)
Germany (Map p598; ☎ 530 1100; embager@ internet.is; Laufásvegur 31)
UK (Map p598; ☎ 550 5100; britemb@centrum.is; Laufásvegur 31)
USA (Map p598; ☎ 562 9100; www.usa.is; Laufásvegur 21)

Icelandic Embassies & Consulates Abroad
Australia (☎ 02-9365 7345; iceland@bigpond.net.au; 16 Birriga Rd, Bellevue Hill, Sydney, NSW)
Canada (☎ 613-482 1944; www.iceland.org/ca; 360 Albert St, Ste 710, Ottawa ON K1R 7X7)

Denmark (☎ 33 18 10 50; www.iceland.org/dk;
Strandgade 89, DK-1401 Copenhagen K)
France (☎ 01 44 17 32 85; www.iceland.org/fr;
8 av Kléber, F-75116 Paris)
Germany (☎ 030-5050 4000; www.iceland.org/de;
Rauchstrasse 1, DE-10787 Berlin)
New Zealand (☎ 04-385 7345; denis@foot.co.nz;
c/o Foot Law, 18-24 Allen St, Courtenay Pl, Wellington)
UK (☎ 020-7259 3999; www.iceland.org/uk; 2a Hans St,
London SW1X 0JE)
USA (☎ 202-265 6653; www.iceland.org/us; 1156 15th
St NW, Suite 1200, Washington, DC 20005-1704)

FESTIVALS & EVENTS
Sumardagurinn fyrsti (First Day of Summer; April)
Arrives optimistically early on the third Thursday in April,
with Reykjavík holding the biggest carnival-style bash.
Independence Day (17 June) The largest nationwide festival, commemorating the founding of the Republic in 1944.
Midsummer Celebrated around 24 June in Iceland, but
with less fervour than on the Scandinavian mainland.
Iceland Airwaves (end October; www.icelandairwaves
.com) Held in Reykjavík, this youthful event is carving a
reputation as one of the world's most cutting-edge music
festivals.

HOLIDAYS
The following public holidays are observed
in Iceland.
New Year's Day 1 January
Maundy Thursday Thursday before Easter
Good Friday to Easter Monday March/April
First Day of Summer April
Labour Day 1 May
Ascension Day May
Whit Sunday & Whit Monday May
Independence Day 17 June
Shop & Office Workers' Holiday First Monday in August
Christmas Eve 24 December
Christmas Day 25 December
Boxing Day 26 December
New Year's Eve 31 December

MONEY
The unit of currency is the Icelandic króna
(Ikr) and it is divided into 100 aurar. Coins
come in denominations of one, five, 10,
50 and 100 króna, and notes in 500, 1000,
2000 and 5000 króna. The 24.5% Icelandic
söluskattur (VAT) is included in marked
prices. If you spend over Ikr4000 in a shop
with the sign 'Iceland Tax-Free Shopping',
you'll get a tax-refund coupon. Tipping
isn't required.

Cash can be withdrawn from banks using
a MasterCard, Visa or Cirrus ATM card;
exchange rates for ATM cards are usually
good. Maestro, EDC and Electron debit
cards are widely accepted. MasterCard and
Visa can be used at many retail outlets;
Diners Club and Amex are rarely accepted.
Travellers cheques, postal cheques and
banknotes may be exchanged for Icelandic
currency commission-free at Landsbanki
Íslands banks.

POST
Poste restante should be addressed with
your name to Poste Restante, Central Post
Office, Pósthússtræti 5, IS-101 Reykjavík,
Iceland.

TELEPHONE
International direct dialling is available.
The international access code is ☎ 00. Iceland's country code is ☎ 354 and there are
no area codes.

VISAS
Schengen Agreement countries can enter
Iceland with a valid identity card. Citizens
of the European Economic Area (EEA), including Ireland and Great Britain, the USA
and Commonwealth countries can visit on
a valid passport.

ICELAND

Ireland

HIGHLIGHTS

- **Dublin** The optimism will get you as tipsy as the pints among the city's old Georgian architecture, literary ghosts, Guinness and mad *craic* (p608)
- **Aran Islands** Bike riding across one of the windswept and starkly beautiful islands in search of magical Stone-Age forts (p627)
- **Kilkenny** Smelling the roses and sunbathing amid the ghosts of wealthy families past at the Kilkenny Castle park (p617)
- **Best journey** Twisting and turning along the Causeway Coast's dramatic sea cliffs, broad, sweeping beaches, picturesque harbours and the surreal geological centrepiece of the Giant's Causeway (p634)
- **Off-the-beaten track** Rambling through the trippy lunar landscape of the Burren, secretly home to millions of wildflowers and fairy trees, and fighting off vertigo at the dramatic Cliffs of Moher (p624)

FAST FACTS

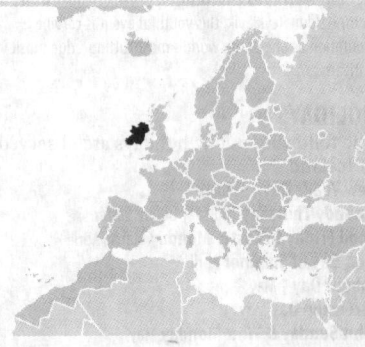

- **Area** 84,421 sq km (slightly smaller than Portugal)
- **ATMs** Available everywhere
- **Budget** €65 per day
- **Capitals** Dublin (Ire), Belfast (NI)
- **Country codes** ☎ 353 (Ire), ☎ 44 28 (NI)
- **Famous for** James Joyce, St Patrick, pub life, rolling green hills
- **Head of State** President Mary McAleese (Ire), Queen Elizabeth II (NI)
- **Languages** English, Irish Gaelic
- **Money** Euro (A$1 = €0.58, CA$1 = €0.65, ¥100 = €0.73, NZ$1 = €0.54, UK£1 = €1.45, US$1 = €0.81)
- **Phrases** *Sláinte!* (cheers!), *dia duit* (hello), *go raibh* (thank you), *slán leat* (goodbye)

- **Populations** 3.9 million (Ire), 1.7 million (NI)
- **Time** GMT/UTC + 0
- **Visas** Not necessary for citizens of the EU, Australia, Canada, New Zealand or the USA.

TRAVEL HINTS

Keep an umbrella with you at all times, dress in layers and always, always stop to chat.

ROAMING IRELAND

Take in Dublin before swinging through Kilkenny and Cork. Hike around a West Coast peninsula or two and then let it all hang out in Galway or Belfast.

IRELAND

0 — 80 km
0 — 50 miles

ATLANTIC OCEAN

ARGYLL

Lochgilphead
Port Askaig
Loch Fyne
SCOTLAND
Lochranza
Sound of Jura
Campbeltown
Kintyre
Giants Causeway
Bushmills
Ballycastle
Carrick-a-Rede Island
Portrush
Portstewart
Cushendun
To Cairnryan; Troon;
Stranraer; Heysham;
Liverpool; Holyhead;
Douglas
Coleraine
Cushendall
Glenariff
Horn Head
Inishowen Peninsula
Buncrana
Muff
Glens of Antrim
North Channel
Bloody Foreland
Portstewart
Letterkenny
Lough Swilly
Derry
Strabane
Ballymena
Larne
NORTHERN IRELAND
Carrickfergus
Island Magee
Loughrea Peninsula
Ardara
Glencolumbcille
Killybegs
Carrick
Donegal
Antrim
Newtownabbey
Bangor
BELFAST
Newtownards
Lough Neagh
Cookstown
Lisburn
Strangford Lough
Donegal Bay
Ballyshannon
Bundoran
Belleek
Omagh
Dungannon
Portadown
Strangford
Portaferry
Lower Lough Erne
Enniskillen
Irvinestown
Armagh
Downpatrick
Dundrum
Newcastle
Mullet Peninsula
Belmullet
Bangor
Killala
Sligo
Ballysadare
Iron Mountains
Belturbet
Monaghan
Newry
Mourne Mountains
IRISH SEA
Achill Island
Keel
Mulrany
Castlebar
Ballina
Boyle
Carrick on Shannon
Cavan
Carrickmacross
Dundalk
Clare Island
Clew Bay
Louisburgh
Westport
Charlestown
Longford
Ardee
Inishbofin Island
Cleggan
Cong
Roscommon
Lanesborough
Kells
Slane
Drogheda
Clifden
Tuam
Lough Ree
Mullingar
Navan
Newgrange
Connemara
Lough Corrib
Athlone
Moate
Trim
To Liverpool; Holyhead; Douglas
Rossaveal
Galway
Clonmacnois
Maynooth
Malahide
Howth
Inishmór
Spiddal
Galway Bay
Kinvarra
IRELAND
Tullamore
DUBLIN
Inishmaan
Doolin
Lisdoonvarna
Kilfenora
Birr
Kildare
Naas
Dun Laoghaire
Enniskerry
Powerscourt
Bray
Greystones
To Holyhead
Inisheer
Aran Islands
Ennistymon
The Burren
Ennis
Nenagh
Roscrea
Port Laoise
Glendalough
Wicklow
Mt Lugnaquilla (924m)
Rathdrum
Loop Head
Kilrush
Shannon
Shannon River
Limerick
Durrow
Carlow
Arklow
Foynes
Thurles
Brittas Bay
Tarbet
Kilmallock
Cashel
Kilkenny
Gorey
Castlegregory
Dingle Peninsula
Dingle
Tralee
Rathluirc (Charleville)
Tipperary
Callan
Thomastown
Enniscorty
Curracloe Beach
Dunquin
Dingle Bay
Killorglin
Killarney
Mitchelstown
Carrick-on-Suir
New Ross
Wellington Bridge
Wexford
Blanket Islands
Glenbeigh
Mt Carrantuohil (1038m)
Mallow
Fermoy
Clonmel
Waterford
Ballyhack
Rosslare Harbour
Valentia Island
Ring of Kerry
Killarney National Park
Dungarvan
Passage East
Iveragh Peninsula
Waterville
Sneem
Glengarriff
Blarney
Cork
Youghal
Ardmore
St George's Channel
To Fishguard; Pembroke (Britain); Cherbourg; Roscoff (France)
Cahirciveen
Kenmare
Ringaskiddy
Cobh
Beara Peninsula
Bantry
Bandon
Kinsale
Cork Harbour
Allihies
Sheep's Head
Schull
Skibbereen
Clonakilty
Mizen Head
Roaringwater Bay
Baltimore
Cape Clear Island
To Swansea (Britain); Roscoff (France)

IRELAND

After centuries of suffering, Ireland has finally started to enjoy its day in the sun. Money has arrived – and it has changed everything. Cities are more cosmopolitan, small towns now do latte, and farmers have built dream homes that don't look like anything the Irish countryside has ever seen.

But no amount of money will ever wipe away Ireland's long and tragic history, whose traces appear at every turn: Stone Age passage tombs and ring forts, medieval monasteries and castles, the stately homes and splendid Georgian architecture of the 18th and 19th centuries as well as the ubiquitous reminders of Ireland's long and difficult relationship with Britain.

And no amount of money can change the Irish. Famously friendly and down-to-earth, they'll draw you into their circle like the nice kid at the new school. You might find yourself feeling oddly at home here rather quickly, like you belong right there in that old pub, among those sheep and green hills, along those moody coastlines of rock and flower, and over that long, chatty cup of tea.

This chapter covers the independent Republic of Ireland plus Northern Ireland, which forms part of the United Kingdom (UK).

HISTORY

Celtic warriors reached Ireland around 300 BC. Christian monks, including St Patrick, arrived around the 5th century AD, and Ireland became the land of saints, scholars and missionaries. From the end of the 8th century, the rich monasteries were targets of raids by Vikings, who then settled in. They in turn were followed by Anglo-Norman forces in 1169.

The British sought to reinforce authority in the 16th century, and under Elizabeth I, oppression of the Catholic Irish got seriously under way. Huge swaths of land were given to Protestant settlers, sowing the seeds of the divided Ireland that exists today.

In 1685 James II (a Scotsman) became king, but angered his English Protestant subjects with his outspoken Catholicism and was forced to flee the country. He sought unsuccessfully to regain his throne, which had been handed over to the Protestant William of Orange (a Dutchman) and his wife, Mary (James' daughter). William's victory over James at the Battle of the Boyne on 12 July, 1690, is commemorated to this day by northern Protestants as a pivotal triumph over 'popes and popery'.

By the early 18th century, Catholics held less than 15% of the land and suffered brutal restrictions in employment, education and religion. Irish movements for civil rights alarmed the Protestant gentry, and in 1800 the Act of Union, joining Ireland with Britain, was passed.

Ireland was moving towards peaceful progress under Catholic political leader Daniel O'Connell when one of Ireland's worst tragedies, the Great Famine, broke out. Successive failures of potato crops between 1845 and 1851 brought about mass starvation, while Britain and the Irish ruling classes, many of whom profited from inflated food prices, enacted shamefully inadequate and ill-conceived relief schemes. About one million people died from disease or starvation, and another million emigrated.

In the early 20th century, a bungled uprising precluded a slow, peaceful path to autonomy. The 1916 Easter Rising was, in fact, heavy on rhetoric, light on planning and lacking in public support. The British response was just as badly conceived – a series of trials and executions (15 in all) turned the ringleaders into martyrs and roused international support for Irish independence.

In the 1918 general election, Irish republicans under the banner of Sinn Féin (We Ourselves or Ourselves Alone) won a majority of Irish seats. Ignoring London's parliament, the newly elected deputies declared Ireland independent and formed the first Dáil Éireann (Irish assembly), led by Eamon de Valera. The resulting Anglo-Irish War (1919–21) pitted Sinn Féin and its military wing, the Irish Republican Army (IRA), against the British. The increasingly brutal responses of Britain's hated Black and Tans infantry further roused anti-British sentiment, and atrocity was met with atrocity. This was the period when Michael Collins came to the fore, a charismatic and ruthless leader who masterminded the IRA's campaign of violence against the British (while serving as finance minister in the new Dáil). After months of negotiations,

Michael Collins and Arthur Griffith led the delegation that signed the Anglo-Irish Treaty in 1921, which gave 26 counties of Ireland independence and allowed six largely Protestant counties in the North the choice to opt out.

Under the Anglo-Irish Treaty, the British monarch remained the (nominal) head of the new Irish Free State. To de Valera and many Irish Catholics, the compromise was considered a betrayal of republican principles, and a brief civil war ensued. A new 1937 constitution abolished the oath of British allegiance and claimed sovereignty over the six counties of Ulster. In 1948 the Irish government declared the country a republic.

In the North, the Protestant majority had systematically excluded Catholics from power. In January 1969 (mostly Catholic) civil rights marchers walking from Belfast to Derry were attacked by a Protestant mob outside Derry. British troops were sent to Derry and Belfast in August to maintain law and order. The peaceful civil rights movement lost ground, and an armed independence struggle under the IRA took flight.

The so-called Troubles rolled throughout the 1970s and the 1980s. Passions reached fever pitch in 1972 when 13 unarmed Catholics were shot dead by British troops in Derry on 'Bloody Sunday' (30 January), then again in 1981 when 10 IRA prisoners fasted to death.

In August 1994 a 'permanent cessation of violence' by the IRA was announced by Sinn Féin, to be matched by a Protestant cease-fire two months later. After some setbacks, the peace process regained momentum with the May 1997 victory of Britain's Labour Party, and in July 1997, the IRA declared another cease-fire.

To worldwide acclaim, all-party talks produced the Good Friday Agreement in April 1998. The agreement allows the people of Northern Ireland to decide their political future by majority vote, and commits its signatories to 'democratic and peaceful means of resolving differences'. In May 1998, the agreement was approved by 71% of voters in the North and 94% in the South in simultaneous referenda. Since the Good Friday Agreement, though, the peace process has stopped and started, largely over wrangles about how and when the IRA should 'decommission' its weapons stockpiles.

TOP FIVE IRELAND

- **Festival** Belfast's Festival at Queens (p631)
- **Walk** A hike through the Burren (p624)
- **Bar** Dublin's Stag's Head (p615)
- **Impressive sight** The Cliffs of Moher (p625)
- **Monastic ruins** Skellig Michael (p624)

The November 2003 elections did not bode well for further negotiations, either. The leaders of the newly elected majority parties – Reverend Ian Paisley of the hardline Democratic Unionist Party and Sinn Féin's Gerry Adams – are widely considered the two figures least likely to collaborate in a new devolved administration, with Paisley essentially refusing to share power with Adams. But a very cautious optimism still seems to prevail, and although it often seems that bickering of one sort or another will continue forever, most agree (with fingers crossed) that the 'war' is over. The question now is how far optimism can take the process, and how long it will last.

PEOPLE & CULTURE

Prior to the 1845–51 Great Famine, Ireland's population was around eight million; death and emigration reduced it to around six million, and emigration continued at a high level for the next 100 years. It wasn't until the 1960s that Ireland's population finally began to recover.

Lately, economic migrants, including relatively wealthy Western European nationals and poorer migrants from elsewhere, have had a minor but palpable impact on the population.

READING UP

For a recap of Ireland's history in 250 pages or less, look for *A Traveller's History of Ireland* by Peter Neville or *Ireland: A Concise History* by Máire and Conor Cruise O'Brien. Roddy Doyle's *Paddy Clarke Ha Ha Ha*, Frank McCourt's *Angela's Ashes* and Seamus Heaney's *The Spirit Level* are good glimpses into Irish culture.

IRELAND

RELIGION

Religion has always played a pivotal role in Irish history. About 92% of residents in the Republic are Roman Catholic, followed by 3% Protestant. In the North the breakdown is about 53% Protestant and 44% Catholic, but this varies widely between towns (Catholics make up 71% of Derry's urban population, for example).

The Catholic Church has always opposed attempts to liberalise laws governing contraception, divorce and abortion. Today, condom machines can be found all over Ireland, and divorce is legal, but abortion remains illegal in the Republic. Though still wielding considerable influence in the South, the Catholic Church has been weakened recently by drastically declining attendance, falling numbers of young men and women entering religious life, and damaging paedophile sex scandals. It's now treated with a curious mixture of respect and derision by various sections of the community.

ARTS
Literature

The Irish have made an enormous impact on world literature. Important writers include Jonathan Swift, Oscar Wilde, WB Yeats, George Bernard Shaw, James Joyce, Sean O'Casey, Samuel Beckett, Roddy Doyle and Ulster-born poet Seamus Heaney, who was awarded the Nobel Prize for Literature in 1995. Frank McCourt became a world favourite in 1996 with his autobiographical *Angela's Ashes*.

Music

You're likely to encounter traditional Irish music – played on the *bodhrán* (a flat goatskin drum), *uilleann* (or 'elbow') pipes, flute and fiddle – on your travels. Almost every town and village in Ireland seems to have a pub renowned for its traditional music. Of Irish music groups, perhaps the best-known are the Chieftains, the Dubliners, Altan, De Danann and the wilder Pogues. Popular Irish musicians who have made it on the international stage include Van Morrison, U2, the Cranberries, the Corrs, Westlife and Zambian-Irish Samantha Mumba.

Theatre

Ireland's late-19th-century literary revival resulted in the establishment of Dublin's Abbey Theatre (see p615), now Ireland's national theatre, which presents works by the greats – WB Yeats, George Bernard Shaw, JM Synge and Sean O'Casey – and promotes modern Irish dramatists. One of the most outstanding playwrights of the last two decades is Frank McGuinness (born 1956), whose plays explore the aftermath of Bloody Sunday.

ENVIRONMENT

Ireland is divided into 32 counties: 26 in the Republic and six in Northern Ireland. The island measures 84,421 sq km and stretches 486km north to south and 275km east to west. The jagged coastline extends for 5631km. The midlands of Ireland are flat, generally rich farmland with huge swaths of brown peat (which is rapidly being depleted for fuel).

Carrantuohill (1038m), on the Iveragh Peninsula in County Kerry, is the highest mountain on the island. The Shannon River, the longest in Ireland, flows for 259km before emptying into the Atlantic west of Limerick.

Ireland's rivers and lakes are well stocked with fish such as salmon and trout, and the island is home to some three dozen mammal species. The Office of Public Works (OPW) maintains five national parks and 76 nature reserves in the Republic; the Department of the Environment owns or leases more than 40 nature reserves in Northern Ireland.

TRANSPORT

GETTING THERE & AWAY
Air

There are scheduled nonstop flights from Britain, continental Europe and North America to **Dublin airport** (www.dublin-airport.com) and **Shannon airport** (www.shannonairport.com), and good nonstop connections from Britain and continental Europe to **Cork airport** (www.cork-airport.com). In Northern Ireland flights from Britain, continental Europe and the USA go to **Belfast International airport** (www.bial.co.uk).

Aer Lingus (☎ 01-886 8844; www.aerlingus.com), the Irish national airline, has direct flights to Britain, the USA and a number of countries in Europe. Budget airline **Ryanair** (☎ 01-609 7800; www.ryanair.com) is the next-largest Irish carrier, with many routes to Britain and continental Europe. **Aer Arann** (☎ 01-814 5240; www.aerarann.ie)

is a small carrier that operates flights within Ireland and to Britain. Ryanair and **easyJet** (☎ 048-9448 4929; www.easyjet.com) sometimes have really cheap advance-purchase fares. Competition is fierce on UK–Ireland routes; you might save money flying to London first.

Other airlines flying to/from the UK:
BMI British Midland (in UK ☎ 01332-854 854; www.flybmi.com)
British Airways (in UK ☎ 0845-773 3377; www.ba.com)
Flybe (in UK ☎ 0870 567 6676; www.flybe.com)

Boat

There's a great variety of ferry services from Britain and France to Ireland. Prices vary drastically, depending on season, time of day, day of the week and length of stay. One-way fares for an adult foot passenger can be as little as £20, but nudge £50 in summer.

Keep an eye out for special deals, discounted return fares and other money savers. And plan ahead – some services are booked up months in advance.

BRITAIN

Ferry services run to ports in the Republic and Northern Ireland from Scotland (Cairnryan–Larne, Stranraer–Belfast, Troon–Belfast and Troon–Larne), England (Heysham–Belfast, Liverpool–Belfast and Liverpool–Dublin), Wales (Fishguard–Rosslare Harbour, Holyhead–Dublin, Holyhead–Dun Laoghaire, Pembroke–Rosslare Harbour and Swansea–Cork) and the Isle of Man (Douglas–Dublin, Douglas–Belfast).

Irish Ferries (☎ 0818 300 400, 01-638 3333, in UK 0870 517 1717; www.irishferries.com) Holyhead to Dublin (two or 3¼ hours) and Pembroke to Rosslare Harbour (3¾ hours).

Isle of Man Steam Packet Company/Sea Cat (☎ 1800 805 055, in UK 0870 552 3523; www.steam -packet.com) Douglas (Isle of Man) to Belfast (2¾ hours, Easter to September) and Dublin (2¾ hours, Easter to September), Liverpool to Dublin (3¾ hours, February to October), and Troon to Belfast (2½ hours).

Norse Merchant Ferries (☎ 028-9077 9090, in UK 0870 600 4321; www.norsemerchant.com) Liverpool to Belfast (8½ hours).

P&O European Ferries (☎ 01-407 3434, in UK 0870 242 4777; www.poirishsea.com) Cairnryan to Larne (one or 1¾ hours), Troon to Larne (two hours, April to September) and Liverpool to Dublin (eight hours).

Stena Line (☎ 01-204 7777, in UK 0870 570 7070; www.stenaline.co.uk) Holyhead to Dublin (three hours) and Holyhead to Dun Laoghaire (1¾ hours), Fishguard to Rosslare Harbour (1¾ or 3½ hours), and Stranraer to Belfast (1¾ or 3¼ hours).

Swansea Cork Ferries (☎ 021-427 6000, in UK 01792-456116; www.swanseacorkferries.com) Swansea to Cork (10 hours).

FRANCE

Ferries run between Roscoff and Cherbourg to Rosslare Harbour and Cork.

Brittany Ferries (☎ 021-427 7801, in France 02-9829 2800; www.brittanyferries.com) Roscoff to Cork (11 hours, April to September).

Irish Ferries (in France ☎ 01-4394 4694) Roscoff and Cherbourg to Rosslare Harbour (17½ and 20½ hours respectively, April to December).

P&O European Ferries (☎ 01-407 3434, in UK 0870 242 4777; www.poirishsea.com) Cherbourg to Rosslare Harbour (19 hours).

Bus

Because of cheap flights, getting to Ireland by land is not very popular. National Express and Bus Éireann's Eurolines operate services direct from London and other UK centres to Dublin, Belfast and other cities. For details in London, contact **National Express** (☎ 0870 514 3219; www.nationalexpress.com); in Dublin, contact **Bus Éireann** (☎ 01-836 6111; www.buseireann.ie). London to Dublin by bus takes about 11 hours and costs £25/39 one way/return. To Belfast it's 13 hours and £40/54.

IRELAND

EMERGENCY NUMBERS

■ **Ambulance, fire & police** ☎ 999

GETTING AROUND

In Ireland, the route from A to B is seldom a straight line, and public transport can be expensive, infrequent or both. For these reasons having your own transport – car or bicycle – can be a major advantage.

Bicycle

Ireland is a great place for cycling, despite bad road surfaces in places and inclement weather. Typical rental costs are €10 to €20 a day or €50 to €100 a week. Raleigh Rent-a-Bike agencies are all over Ireland. Contact them at **Eurotrek Raleigh Group** (☎ 01-465 9659; www.eurotrekraleighgroup.com). Like many local bike shops, some offer one-way rentals for an extra charge.

Bicycles can be transported by bus if there's enough room; it usually costs €10 per trip. By train, costs start at €2.50 for a one-way journey.

Bus

Bus Éireann (☎ 01-836 6111; www.buseireann.ie) operates services all over the Republic and into Northern Ireland. Fares are much cheaper than regular rail fares. Returns are usually only slightly more expensive than one-way fares, and special deals are often available. Most intercity buses in Northern Ireland are operated by **Ulsterbus** (☎ 048-9066 6630; www.translink.co.uk).

Car & Motorcycle

Unless you have an EU licence, which is treated like an Irish one, your driving licence is valid for 12 months from the date of entry to Ireland, but you should have held it for two years prior to that. Your own local licence is usually sufficient to hire a car for up to three months.

Train

Iarnród Éireann (☎ 1850-360 222, 01-836 6222; www.irishrail.ie) has routes fanning out from Dublin. Tickets can be twice as expensive as the bus, but travel times may be dramatically reduced. A mid-week return ticket is sometimes just a bit more than the single fare, but fares may be jacked up on Friday and Sunday. **Northern Ireland Railways** (☎ 048-9066 6630, in Dublin 01-679 1977; www.translink.co.uk) has four routes from Belfast, one of which links up with the Republic's rail system.

DUBLIN (BAILE ÁTHA CLIATH)

☎ 01 / pop 1.1 million

If it seems like Dubliners are all young, cool and international, that's because they are. Ireland's young population (41% of the country is under 25), combined with a manic dual influx of money and immigrants, has created a town full of energy, amnesia and optimism. More foreign languages float through the air than you can identify.

And the buzz is contagious. Visitors swarm to Dublin like moths to a light bulb – for the historic museums, top-class attractions and Georgian architecture, sure. But they also come for the humour and warmth of the people, the legendary kindness and relaxed feel: they come for the *craic*.

ORIENTATION

Dublin is divided by the River Liffey into the more affluent south side and the grittier north side. North of the river, important landmarks are O'Connell St, a major shopping thoroughfare, and Gardiner St, with its many B&Bs and guesthouses. Pedestrianised Henry St, running west off O'Connell St, is another main shopping area.

Immediately south of the river is the bustling, sometimes raucous, Temple Bar district, Dame St, Trinity College and just below it, lovely St Stephen's Green. The pedestrianised Grafton St and its surrounding streets and lanes are crammed with shops.

INFORMATION
Internet Access

Both Talk Shop and Wired have several branches around town, all with cheap international calls and Internet access.

Talk Shop (per hr €3.50); Dame St (Map p614; ☎ 1890-890 200; Dame St); Temple Lane (Map p614; ☎ 672 7212; 20 Temple Lane); O'Connell St (☎ 872 0200; 5 Upper O'Connell St)

Wired (http://mail.wired.ie; per hr €2.50; ☽ 9am-midnight); Aungier St (Map pp610-11; ☎ 405 4814; 15 Aungier St); Dame St (Map p614; ☎ 679 0950; 76 Dame St)

Medical Services

Eastern Regional Health Authority (Map pp610-11; ☎ 679 0700; Dr Steevens's Hospital, 138 Thomas St; ❤ 9am-5pm Mon-Fri) Just opposite Heuston Station; can advise on a suitable doctor.

O'Connell's Pharmacy (Map pp610-11; ☎ 873 0427; 55-56 O'Connell St; ❤ 7.30am-10pm Mon-Fri, 8am-10pm Sat, 10am-10pm Sun)

Money

The Dublin airport and Dublin Tourism Centre have currency-exchange counters. The Central Bank offers the best exchange rates, while the airport and ferry terminal bureaus offer the worst.

Post

General post office (GPO; Map pp610-11; ☎ 705 7000; O'Connell St; ❤ 8am-8pm Mon-Sat)

Post office South (Map pp610-11; Anne St South); Central (Map pp610-11; St Andrew's St)

Tourist Information

Dublin Tourism Centre (Map p614; ☎ 605 7700; www.visitdublin.com; St Andrew's Church, 2 Suffolk St; ❤ 9am-7pm Mon-Sat, 10.30am-3pm Sun Jul & Aug, 9am-5.30pm Mon-Sat Sep-Jun) Accommodation bookings, car rentals, maps, tickets for tours and more. Offices also on O'Connell St and on the waterfront at Dun Laoghaire.

Fáilte Ireland (Baggot St; ❤ 9am-5pm Mon-Fri) Less conveniently situated, but much less crowded.

Information Line (☎ 1850-230 330) Dublin Tourism's toll-free service.

Northern Ireland Tourist Board (NITB; Map p614; ☎ 679 1977; www.discovernorthernireland.com; 16 Nassau St; ❤ 9.15am-5.30pm Mon-Fri, 10am-5pm Sat) Information and free booking services.

Temple Bar Information Centre (Map p614; www.templebar.ie; 12 East Essex St) Provides free maps and information on the many cultural activities in the neighbourhood.

SIGHTS

Trinity College & Book of Kells Map p614✓

Until 1793 Trinity's students were all Protestants, but today most of its 9500 students are Catholic. Women were first admitted to the college in 1903 – earlier than at most British universities.

In summer, **walking tours** (❤ 10.45-3.40pm Mon-Sat, 10.15am-3pm Sun mid-May–Sep) depart every 40 minutes from the main gate on College Green. The €10 fee includes admission to the *Book of Kells*, an elaborately illuminated manuscript dating from around AD 800. It's on display in the **East Pavilion of the Colonnades**

(adult/concession €7.50/6.50; ❤ 9.30am-5pm Mon-Sat year-round, 9.30am-4.30pm Sun Jun-Sep, noon-4.30pm Sun Oct-May) together with the 9th-century *Book of Armagh*, the even older *Book of Durrow* (AD 675) and the harp of Brian Ború, who led the Irish against the Vikings in the Battle of Clontarf.

Museums

Among the highlights of the exhibits at the impressive **National Museum** (Map pp610-11; ☎ 667 7444; www.museum.ie; Kildare St; admission by donation; ❤ 10am-5pm Tue-Sat, 2-5pm Sun) are the superb collection of Bronze Age, Iron Age and medieval gold objects in the treasury, the skeleton of a once tall, mighty Viking and the slighter but incredibly well-preserved 'Bog Body'.

The **Chester Beatty Library** (Map p614; ☎ 407 0750; www.cbl.ie; Dublin Castle; admission free; ❤ 10am-5pm Mon-Fri, 11am-5pm Sat, 1-5pm Sun, closed Mon Oct-Apr) houses a breathtaking collection of more than 20,000 manuscripts, rare books, miniature paintings, clay tablets, costumes and other objects spread across two floors. The 270 illuminated Qur'ans are just one draw.

Dublin Writers Museum (Map pp610-11; ☎ 872 2077; 18-19 Parnell Sq; adult/student €6.25/5.25; ❤ 10am-5pm Mon-Sat, 11am-5pm Sun), north of the river, celebrates the city's long and continuing role as a literary centre, with displays on Joyce, Swift, Yeats, Wilde, Beckett and others.

Galleries

The **National Gallery** (Map pp610-11; ☎ 661 5133; www.nationalgallery.ie; Merrion Sq West; admission free; ❤ 9.30am-5.30pm Mon-Wed & Fri & Sat, 9.30am-8.30pm

IRELAND

DUBLIN

Ⓐ

INFORMATION
Dublin Tourism.................................1 F3
Eastern Regional Health Authority......2 A5
General Post Office...........................3 F3
Post office..4 F6
Talk Shop...5 F3
Wired...6 E6

SIGHTS & ACTIVITIES (pp609-13)
Dublin City Gallery, The Hugh Lane...7 E2
Dublin Writers Museum......................8 F2
Guinness Storehouse.........................9 B6
Marsh's Library................................10 E6
Monument of Light..........................11 F3
National Gallery...............................12 H6
National Museum.............................13 G6
St Patrick's Cathedral.......................14 D6

SLEEPING ⌂ (p613)
Avalon House...................................15 E6
Fatima House...................................16 F1

Ⓑ

Isaac's Hostel...................................17 H3
Jacob's Inn......................................18 H3
Marian Guesthouse..........................19 F1
Mount Eccles Court..........................20 F2

EATING 🍴 (pp613-15)
Ailang...21 G2
Cobalt Café & Gallery......................22 F2
Govinda's..23 F6

DRINKING 🍷 (p615)
Dice Bar..24 C4
Forum Bar.......................................25 F2
Voodoo Lounge...............................26 C4

ENTERTAINMENT 🎭 (p615)
Gaiety Theatre.................................27 F6

TRANSPORT (p616)
Busáras...28 H3
Dublin Bus Office.............................29 F3

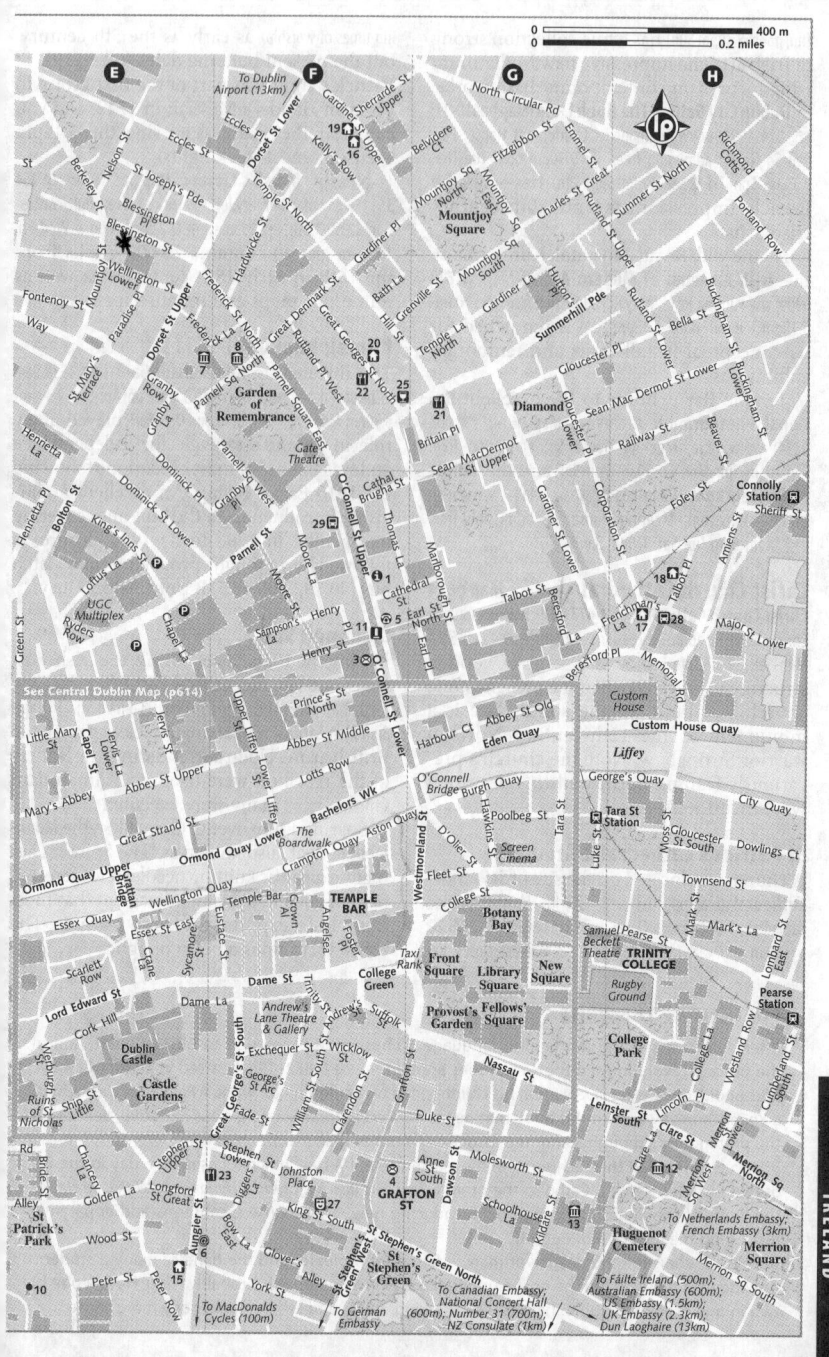

Thu, noon-5.30pm Sun) has a fine collection strong in Irish art. The impressive new Millennium wing focuses on contemporary Irish works.

Dublin City Gallery The Hugh Lane (Map pp610-11; ☎ 874 1903; www.hughlane.ie; Charlemont House, Parnell Sq North; admission free; ☀ 9.30am-6pm Tue-Thu, 9.30am-5pm Fri & Sat, 11am-5pm Sun) has work by French Impressionists and 20th-century Irish artists.

At the old Royal Hospital Kilmainham, the **Irish Museum of Modern Art** (IMMA; ☎ 612 9900; www.imma.ie; Military Rd; admission free; ☀ 10am-5.15pm Tue-Sat, noon-5.15pm Sun) is renowned for its conceptual installations and temporary exhibitions.

Temple Bar is home to the excellent **National Photographic Archives** (Map p614; ☎ 603 0374; www.nli.ie; Meeting House Sq; admission free; ☀ 10am-5pm Mon-Fri, 10am-2pm Sat) and the **Gallery of Photography** (Map p614; ☎ 671 4654; www.irish-photography.com; Meeting House Sq; admission free; ☀ 11am-6pm Tue-Sat, 1-6pm Sun).

Christ Church Cathedral   Map p614

Christ Church Cathedral (☎ 677 8099; www.cccdub.ie; Christ Church Pl; adult/concession €5/2.50; ☀ 9.45am-5pm Mon-Sat, 12.30-3pm Sun) was a simple wooden structure until 1169, when the present stone church was built. In the south aisle is a monument to the 12th-century Norman warrior Strongbow. Note the church's precariously leaning north wall (it's been that way since 1562).

St Patrick's Cathedral & Around

A church was located on the site of **St Patrick's Cathedral** (Map pp610-11; ☎ 475 4817; www.stpatrickscathedral.ie; St Patrick's Close; adult/concession €4.20/3.20; ☀ 9am-5pm year-round, 9am-6pm Sat Mar-Oct, closed during times of worship) as early as the 5th century, but the present building dates from 1191. St Patrick's choir was part of the first group to perform Handel's Messiah in 1742, and you can hear their successors sing the 5.45pm evensong most weeknights.

Nearby **Marsh's Library** (Map pp610-11; ☎ 454 3511; www.marshlibrary.ie; St Patrick's Close; adult/concession €2.50/1.50; ☀ 10am-1pm & 2-5pm Mon & Wed-Fri, 10.30am-1pm Sat) contains 25,000 books from the 16th to early 18th centuries as well as numerous maps and manuscripts.

Kilmainham Gaol

The threatening **Kilmainham Gaol** (☎ 453 5984; Inchicore Rd; admission €5; ☀ 9.30am-6pm Apr-Sep, 9.30am-5.30pm Mon-Fri, 10am-6pm Sun Oct-Mar) played a key role in Ireland's struggle for independence and was the site of mass executions following the 1916 Easter Rising. An excellent audiovisual introduction to the building, covering its opening in 1796 to its 1924 closure, is followed by a thought-provoking tour. Catch bus No 79, 78A or 51B from Aston Quay.

O'Connell St

During the 1916 Easter Rising, the Irish Volunteers used the **General Post Office building** (GPO; Map pp610-11; ☎ 705 7000; O'Connell St; ☀ 8am-8pm Mon-Sat) as a base for attacks against the British army. Upon surrendering, the leaders of the rebellion were taken to Kilmainham Gaol, where many were executed.

Soaring 120m over O'Connell St, the **Monument of Light**, also known as 'The Spire', is actually a gigantic knitting needle. It was erected here in 2003 in a flashy homage to that most humble of exports, the Aran sweater. The teeny 15cm tip is a beam of light.

PORTRAIT OF THE WRITER

After quickly mastering the English language, James Joyce proceeded to blow it apart, and in the process revolutionised the way stories are told. Joyce (1882–1941), raised in a strict Catholic household, drew extensively upon his childhood in his earliest major work, *A Portrait of the Artist as a Young Man*. It was with this book that he introduced a stream-of-conscious narrative, describing the protagonist's thoughts and free associations rather than simply chronicling events.

Joyce developed this technique in his masterpiece, *Ulysses*, which focuses on a day in the life of two Irishmen – one a Catholic, the other a Jew. His last major work, *Finnegans Wake*, stretches the limits of the English language by introducing new, often nonsensical terms and apparently discarding the idea of plot entirely.

Joyce's works are the delight of many a literature professor and the bane of many a student. Anyone who tells you that he or she understands *Finnegans Wake* is probably lying. Have a pint or two in one of Joyce's Dublin haunts (see Drinking, p615) and see if it makes any more sense.

IRELAND

Guinness Storehouse ✓

The **Guinness Storehouse** (Map pp610-11; ☎ 408 4800; www.guinness-storehouse.com; Market St; admission €13.50; ⏰ 9.30am-5pm Sep-Jun, 9.30am-9pm Jul & Aug) sits in the malty fug of the mighty Guinness brewery southeast of the centre. The tour is uninspired, but the building is impressive, and you won't get a better Guinness than the free pint served at the end of the tour. Take bus No 51B or 78A from Aston Quay or No 123 from O'Connell St.

SLEEPING

At weekends and other unexpected times Dublin beds fill up fast, so reserve in advance, even for hostels. Don't forget that Dublin Tourism offices can find and book accommodation for €4 plus a 10% deposit for the first night's stay.

North of the Liffey

Globetrotters Tourist Hostel (Map p614; ☎ 878 8088; gtrotter@indigo.ie; 46-48 Lower Gardiner St; dm €21.50-24) The décor is funky at this friendly, city-centre place with 94 beds in a variety of *en-suite* dorms. There's a little patio garden to the rear for the elusive sunny day, and a full Irish breakfast is included.

Mount Eccles Court (Map pp610-11; ☎ 873 0826; info@ ecclescourt.com; 42 Great George's St North; dm €11-27.50, d €34-37; 🖳) In a renovated Georgian town house on one of the north side's most beautiful streets, Mount Eccles is a pristine place with *en-suite* dorms and doubles.

Modest B&B options on Upper Gardiner St (north of the city centre) include the friendly **Fatima House** (Map pp610-11; ☎ 874 5410; 17 Upper Gardiner St; s/d €48/84; 🅿) and **Marian Guesthouse** (Map pp610-11; ☎ 874 4129; 21 Upper Gardiner St; s/d from €35/60; 🅿).

Other recommended hostels:

Isaac's Hostel (Map pp610-11; ☎ 855 6215; www .isaacs.ie; 2-5 Frenchman's Lane; dm/d from €16.50/52.50; 🖳) Busy and grungy, with loads of character.

Jacob's Inn (Map pp610-11; ☎ 855 5660; www.isaacs .ie; 21-28 Talbot Pl; dm/d from €16.50/72; 🖳) Just behind Busáras, with some wheelchair-accessible rooms.

South of the Liffey

Barnacles Temple Bar House (Map p614; ☎ 671 6277; www.barnacles.ie; 19 Temple Lane; dm/d from €17.50/78; 🖳) Bright and spacious, in the heart of Temple Bar, Barnacles is immaculately clean and has nicely laid out *en-suite* dorms and doubles with in-room storage. Rooms

> **SPLURGE!**
>
> **Number 31** (☎ 676 5011; www.number31.ie; 31 Leeson Close; s/d/tr from €105/150/210) The coach house and former home of modernist architect Sam Stephenson (of Central Bank fame) still feels like a real 1960s home, complete with sunken sitting room, leather sofas, mirrored bar, Perspex lamps and ceiling-to-floor windows. It's a hidden oasis of calm, a five-minute walk from St Stephen's Green.

are quieter in the back. Probably the best hostel south of the river.

Ashfield House (Map p614; ☎ 679 7734; ashfield@ indigo.ie; 19-20 D'Olier St; dm/d from €15/80; 🖳) A stone's throw from Temple Bar and O'Connell Bridge, this relatively new hostel has only one 14-bed *en-suite* dorm, but its 25 other rooms include four-bed family rooms as well as doubles. It feels more like a small hotel, without the price tag.

Grafton Guesthouse (Map p614; ☎ 679 2041; graftonguesthouse@eircom.net; 26-27 South Great George's St; s/d €60/100) In a Gothic-style building over the George's St Arcade market, this friendly guesthouse has 16 bright rooms and is a good choice if you don't mind the old-school chintz and brocade.

Other recommendations:

Avalon House (Map pp610-11; ☎ 475 0001; www .avalon-house.ie; 55 Aungier St; dm/d from €17/64; 🖳) Busy, fun megahostel near St Stephen's Green with several lounges and a pool room.

Kinlay House (Map p614; ☎ 679 6644; www.kinlay house.ie; 2-12 Lord Edward St; dm/d from €16/62; 🖳) Massive, mixed 24-bed dorms and smaller rooms. Not for the faint-hearted.

EATING

Dubliners' increased spending power, combined with the city's influx of immigrants, has spawned an explosion of new restaurants. You'll find a spate of international spots around Parnell St, while Temple Bar is awash with eateries of mixed quality. Dublin has a reputation for being an expensive place to eat, but you'll find plenty of cheap eats, too.

North of the Liffey

Epicurean Food Hall (Map p614; Lower Liffey St; lunch €3-12; ⏰ 9.30am-5.30pm Mon-Sat) You'll be spoilt for choice in this newly refurbished arcade that has almost every imaginable type of

IRELAND

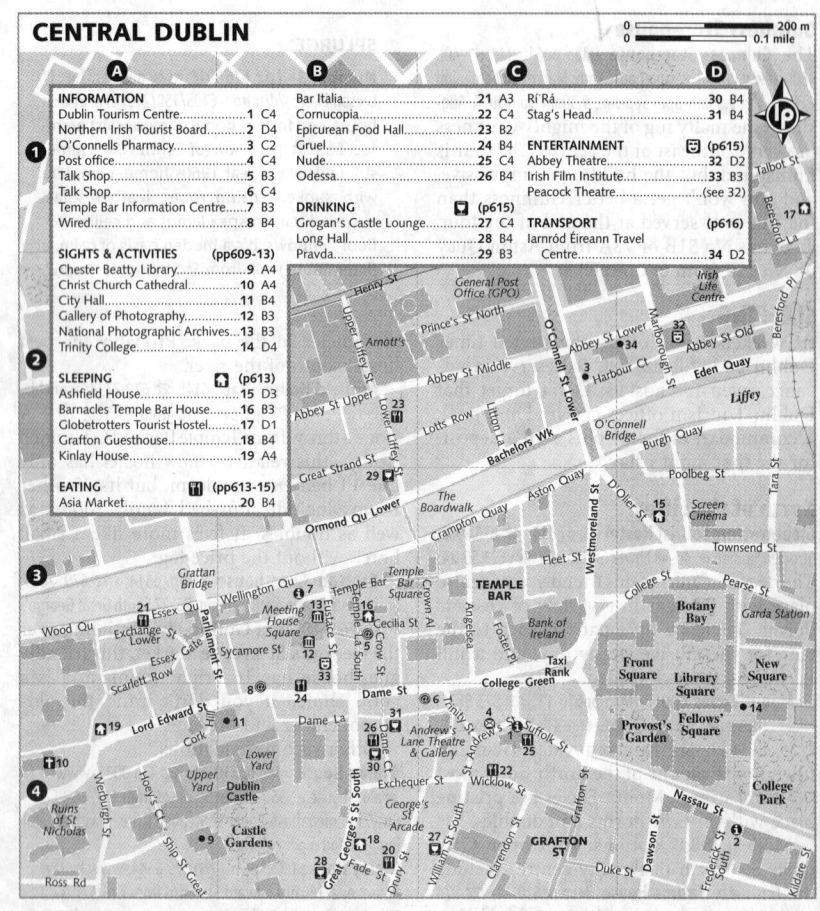

CENTRAL DUBLIN

0 -------- 200 m
0 -------- 0.1 mile

INFORMATION
Dublin Tourism Centre.....................1 C4
Northern Irish Tourist Board...............2 D4
O'Connells Pharmacy.......................3 C2
Post office...............................4 C4
Talk Shop.................................5 B3
Talk Shop.................................6 C4
Temple Bar Information Centre.............7 B3
Wired....................................8 B4

SIGHTS & ACTIVITIES (pp609-13)
Chester Beatty Library....................9 A4
Christ Church Cathedral..................10 A4
City Hall................................11 B4
Gallery of Photography...................12 B3
National Photographic Archives...........13 B3
Trinity College..........................14 D4

SLEEPING (p613)
Ashfield House...........................15 D3
Barnacles Temple Bar House...............16 B3
Globetrotters Tourist Hostel.............17 D1
Grafton Guesthouse.......................18 B4
Kinlay House.............................19 A4

EATING (pp613-15)
Asia Market..............................20 B4

Bar Italia...............................21 A3
Cornucopia...............................22 C4
Epicurean Food Hall......................23 B2
Gruel....................................24 B4
Nude.....................................25 C4
Odessa...................................26 B4

DRINKING (p615)
Grogan's Castle Lounge...................27 C4
Long Hall................................28 B4
Pravda...................................29 B3

Rí Rá....................................30 B4
Stag's Head..............................31 B4

ENTERTAINMENT (p615)
Abbey Theatre............................32 D2
Irish Film Institute.....................33 B3
Peacock Theatre.....................(see 32)

TRANSPORT (p616)
Iarnród Éireann Travel
   Centre................................34 D2

---

food stall. The quality varies, but good choices include Itsabagel, Taco Taco and Istanbul House.

Cobalt Café & Gallery (Map pp610-11; ☎ 873 0313; 16 Great George's St North; mains €4-7; ⏱ 10.30am-4.30pm Mon-Fri) This elegant café in a bright and airy Georgian drawing room is a must if you're in the 'hood. You'll be welcomed with hearty soups by a roaring fire in winter or fresh sandwiches in the garden on warmer days.

Alilang (Map pp610-11; ☎ 874 6766; 102 Parnell St; mains €6-15; ⏱ noon-3pm daily & 5-11.30pm Sun-Thu, 5pm-12.30am Fri & Sat) With elements of Chinese, Japanese and Thai cuisine, this new Korean restaurant has plenty to whet Western appetites – *padun* (a seafood pancake), cod and tofu hotpot, or barbecued meats brought to

your table with gas burner, skillet and spicy marinade.

South of the Liffey

Gruel (Map p614; ☎ 670 7119; 68½ Dame St; mains €3.50-10; ⏱ 10am-9.30pm Sun-Wed, 10am-10.30pm Thu-Sat) Gruel, which wouldn't look amiss in downtown New York, sells good food that bursts with flavour: sandwiches to die for (slow-roasted organic meats or vegetables in a bap), zinging salads, or its trademark bangers and mash in the evening.

Govinda's (☎ 475 0309; 4 Aungier St; mains €5-9; ⏱ noon-9pm Mon-Sat) The soup at this branch of the Hare Krishna chain is so subtle and flavoursome you'll think Krishna himself cooked it. The place is totally vegetarian,

IRELAND

with a cheap, wholesome mix of salads and Indian-influenced hot daily specials.

Cornucopia (Map p614; ☎ 677 7583; 19 Wicklow St; mains €9.75; ❤ 9am-8pm Mon-Sat, 9am-9pm Thu, noon-7pm Sun) For those escaping the Irish cholesterol habit, Cornucopia is a popular wholefood café turning out scrumptious healthy goodies. There's even a hot vegetarian breakfast as an alternative to muesli.

Odessa (Map p614; ☎ 670 7634; 13 Dame Ct; brunch €9-12, mains €15-20; ❤ 6-10pm Mon-Wed, 6-11pm Thu-Fri, 11.30am-4.30pm & 6-11pm Sat & Sun) Odessa's loungy atmosphere attracts Dublin's hipsters, who flock in for its home-made burgers and daily fish specials. Try a few of Odessa's renowned cocktails, quaffed to a game of backgammon.

Other recommendations:

Asia Market (Map p614; ☎ 677 9764; 18 Drury St; ❤ 10am-7pm) Aisles of fresh produce, mysterious dried things and stir-fry sauces for self-caterers.

Bar Italia (Map p614; ☎ 679 5128; 4 Essex Quay; mains €7.50-9; ❤ 8am-6pm Mon-Fri, 9am-6pm Sat) A little Italian café serving proper risotto, pasta dishes and paninis.

Nude (Map p614; ☎ 677 4804; 21 Suffolk St; light meals €5-8; ❤ 8am-9pm Mon-Sat, 11am-7pm Sun) Wraps with all kinds of Asian fillings.

Stag's Head (Map p614; ☎ 679 3701; 1 Dame Ct; mains from €7) The best pub lunch in town.

DRINKING & CLUBBING

Dublin's 'party district' is undoubtedly Temple Bar, which can devolve into debauchery after sundown. If that's not your style, don't despair: there's plenty to do beyond Temple Bar. In fact, most of the best old-fashioned pubs are outside the district.

Pubs close at midnight Monday to Wednesday, 1am Thursday to Saturday and 11.30pm on Sunday. However, many also have late licences, which means they can still serve up to around 2.30am Monday to Saturday and 1am Sunday. Note that smoke-filled pubs are a thing of the past, with smoking banned in all public places in the Irish Republic from March 2004.

Dice Bar (Map pp610-11; ☎ 674 6710; 79 Queen St) The Dice Bar looks like something you'd find on New York's Lower East Side. Its black and red interior, dripping candles and inspired DJs most nights make it a magnet for Dublin's beautiful beatnik crowds.

Long Hall (Map p614; ☎ 475 1590; 51 Great George's St South) Luxuriating in full Victorian splendour, this is one of the city's most beautiful

and best-loved pubs. Check out the ornate carvings in the woodwork behind the bar and the elegant chandeliers.

Stag's Head (Map p614; ☎ 679 3701; 1 Dame Ct) Built in 1770, remodelled in 1895 and unbeatable in 2005, the Stag's Head is the best pub in Dublin (and therefore the world). You may find yourself philosophising in the ecclesiastical atmosphere, as James Joyce did.

Gaiety Theatre (Map pp610-11; ☎ 677 1717; www .gaietytheatre.com; King St South; ❤ to 4am) The Gaiety is a sort of amusement park on Fridays and Saturdays, with a nightclub, live bands and bad movies all on at the same time in its many halls.

Rí Rá (Map p614; ☎ 677 4835; Dame Ct; ❤ closed Sun) Rí Rá is one of the friendlier clubs in the city centre. Full nearly every night, it attracts a diverse crowd that comes for the mostly funk music downstairs or more laidback lounge tunes and movies upstairs.

Other good spots include the decadent **Voodoo Lounge** (Map pp610-11; ☎ 873 6013; 37 Arran Quay), the hip-hop **Forum Bar** (Map pp610-11; ☎ 878 7084; 144 Parnell St), laid-back **Grogan's Castle Lounge** (Map p614; ☎ 677 9320; 15 William St South) and the northside's USSR-style **Pravda** (Map p614; ☎ 874 0076; 35 Lower Liffey St).

ENTERTAINMENT

For events and reviews, pick up a copy of the bimonthly freebie *Event Guide* (www .eventguide.ie) or the weekly *In Dublin*, available at cafés and hostels. Thursday's *Irish Times* has a great pull-out section called the *Ticket*.

Cinema

Irish Film Institute (IFI; Map p614; ☎ 679 3477; www .irishfilm.ie; 6 Eustace St) The fantastic IFI has two screens showing classic and art-house films. It also has a decent bar, a café and a bookshop.

Theatre & Classical Music

The famous **Abbey Theatre** (Map p614; ☎ 878 7222; www.abbeytheatre.ie; Lower Abbey St) is Ireland's national theatre. The smaller and less expensive **Peacock Theatre** (Map p614; ☎ 878 7222; Lower Abbey St) is part of the same complex.

Gaiety Theatre (Map pp610-11; ☎ 677 1717; www. gaietytheatre.com; King St South) and the **National Concert Hall** (☎ 417 0000; www.nch.ie; Earlsfort Tce) host a variety of performances. Demystify opera with the Gaiety's pre-opera lectures.

GETTING THERE & AWAY
Air
Dublin airport (☎ 814 1111; www.dublin-airport.com), about 13km north of the city centre, is Ireland's major international gateway airport, with direct flights from Europe, North America and Asia. See p606 for more details.

Boat
There are two direct services from Holyhead on the northwestern tip of Wales – one to Dublin Port and the other to Dun Laoghaire at the southern end of Dublin Bay. Boats also sail direct to Dublin Port from Liverpool and from Douglas, on the Isle of Man. See p607 for more details.

Bus
Busáras station (☎ 836 6111; www.buseireann.ie) is just north of the Liffey on Store St. Standard one-way fares from Dublin include Belfast (€19, three hours, five to seven daily), Cork (€20.50, 3½ hours, six daily), Galway (€13, 3¾ hours, 15 daily), and Rosslare Harbour (€14.50, three hours, 12 daily).

The private company **City Link** (☎ 626 6888) has slightly cheaper daily services to Galway; see p626.

Train
Just north of the Liffey is **Connolly station** (☎ 703 2358), the station for Belfast, Derry, Sligo, other points north and Wexford. **Heuston station** (☎ 703 2131), south of the Liffey and well west of the centre, is the station for Cork, Galway, Killarney and most other points to the south and west. For travel information and tickets, contact the **Iarnród Éireann Travel Centre** (☎ 836 6222, 703 4070; www.irishrail.ie; 35 Abbey St Lower). Trains from Dublin include Belfast (€31, two hours, up to eight daily), Cork (€50, three hours, up to nine daily) and Galway (€25, three hours, five daily).

GETTING AROUND
Bicycle
Most rental places open during high season only, and daily rental costs can reach €25 per day. Try **MacDonalds Cycles** (☎ 475 2586; 38 Wexford St).

Public Transport
Dublin Bus (Bus Átha Cliath; ☎ 873 4222; www.dublinbus.ie; 59 O'Connell St) local services cost €0.85 for one to three stages, up to a maximum of €1.75.

One-day passes cost €5 for bus (including Airlink), or €7.70 for bus and DART.

Late-night Nitelink buses (fare €4) operate until 4.30am on Thursday, Friday and Saturday nights from the College St/Westmoreland St/D'Olier St triangle, south of the Liffey.

DART provides quick rail access to the coast as far north as Howth (€1.80) and south to Bray (€2.60). Pearse station is handy for central Dublin.

LUAS (www.luas.ie) – the name comes from the Irish word for 'light' – is a new light rail system that is currently running on two (unconnected) lines; the green line runs from the east side of St Stephen's Green southeast to Sandyford, and the red line runs from Tallaght to Connolly Station, with stops at Heuston Station, the National Museum and Busáras.

Taxis
Taxis in Dublin are expensive; flag-fall is €2.75. Call **National Radio Cabs** (☎ 677 2222).

AROUND DUBLIN
Dun Laoghaire √
☎ 01
Dun Laoghaire (pronounced 'dun leary') is a popular resort and a busy harbour with ferry connections to Britain. On the southern side of the harbour is the **Martello Tower**, where James Joyce's epic novel *Ulysses* opens; it's now the **James Joyce Museum** (☎ 280 9265; admission €6.50; ⏲ 10am-1pm & 2-5pm Mon-Sat, 2-6pm Sun Apr-Oct).

Bus No 7, 7A or 46A, or the DART rail service (€1.70, 20 minutes), will take you from Dublin to Dun Laoghaire. For information on Dun Laoghaire ferries, see p607.

THE SOUTHEAST

WEXFORD
☎ 053 / pop 9443
Viking Waesfjord, the 'Ford of Mud Flats', has long been a popular spot for invaders, thanks to its handy location at the mouth of the River Slaney. But only Wexford's name, narrow streets and West Gate have survived the town's glorious Viking and Norman past. Cromwell, on his bloody 1649–50 Irish tour, destroyed the town's churches and slaughtered three-quarters of

its 2000 inhabitants. Today, Wexford is a pleasant town and a convenient stopover for those travelling to France or Wales via the Rosslare Harbour ferry port.

Orientation & Information

The train and bus stations are at the northern end of town, on Redmond Pl. Follow the River Slaney 700m south along the waterfront quays to reach the **tourist office** (☎ 23111; www.southeastireland.com; The Crescent; ☼ 9am-6pm Mon-Sat May-Sep, 9am-5pm Oct-Apr). The curiously tight North Main and South Main Sts are a block inland and parallel to the quays. The **main post office** (Anne St) is northwest of the tourist office. Internet access is available at the **Westgate Computer Centre** (☎ 46291; Westgate; per hr €5; ☼ 9am-1pm & 2-5pm Mon-Fri).

Sights

Of the six original town gates, only the 14th-century **West Gate** (Slaney St) survives. Nearby **Selskar Abbey** is in a ruined state as a result of Cromwell's 1649 visit. The **Bullring** (cnr Cornmarket & North Main St) was the site of one of Cromwell's massacres.

Sleeping & Eating

Kirwan House (☎ 21208; kirwanhostel@eircom.net; 3 Mary St; dm/s/d €15/25/40; **P**) A lovely old Georgian building houses this IHH hostel. Comfortable rooms and a tranquil garden add extra class.

Ferrybank Camping & Caravan Park (☎ 42611; info@wexfordcorp.ie; tent & 2 people €12; ☼ Easter-Oct; ☒) Location and luxury, right across the river from the town centre. Ferrybank has a pool and laundry.

Cappuccino's (☎ 23669; 25 North Main St; mains €4-12; ☼ 8am-6pm Mon-Fri, 8am-6.30pm Sat, 10am-6.30pm Sun) From heartstopper to healthy, this little eatery is perfect for bagel breakfasts or lasagne lunches.

North and South Main Sts have something for most tastes, including a delicious range of picnic supplies at **Greenacres Food Hall** (☎ 22975; 54 North Main St; ☼ 9am-6pm Mon-Sat).

Drinking

Many of Wexford's pubs are strung along North and South Main Sts.

Sky & the Ground (☎ 21273; 112-113 South Main St) A great place to eat and one of the most popular pubs in town, this family establishment has traditional sessions almost every night.

Thomas Moore Tavern (☎ 24348; Cornmarket) Locals would call this an 'old man's pub', meaning it's good for a quiet drink and a chat.

Entertainment

Theatre and dance productions go on at the **Wexford Arts Centre** (☎ 23764; www.wexfordarts centre.ie; Cornmarket).

Getting There & Away

Rosslare Harbour, 21km southeast of Wexford, has frequent ferry services to France and Wales (see p607). There's no reason to linger in town, so catch the first bus or train to Wexford or beyond from the Europort station at the ferry terminal.

O'Hanrahan train station (☎ 22522; www.irish rail.ie), on the Dublin–Rosslare line, is served by three trains daily in each direction. The three-hour trip to Dublin costs €16.50 (more on weekends); to Rosslare Harbour (30 minutes) it's €4.50. **Bus Éireann** (☎ 23939, 051-879 000) runs from the train station to Rosslare Harbour (€3.80, 30 minutes, every 45 minutes Monday to Saturday, 10 on Sunday), Dublin (€11.50, 2¼ hours, 10 Monday to Saturday, eight on Sunday) and beyond.

KILKENNY (CILL CHAINNIGH)

☎ 056 / pop 8594

Kilkenny is renowned throughout Ireland for its devotion to the arts and its world-class festivals. It's also perhaps the most attractive city in the country, retaining some of its medieval ground plan (in spite of destruction wreaked by Cromwell), and has an excellent selection of eating, drinking and accommodation options. The magnificent Kilkenny Castle overlooks a bend of the river and is nestled in lush, expansive grounds.

Most places of interest lie close to Parliament St and its continuation (High St), which runs parallel to the River Nore; or along Rose Inn St, which changes its name to John St and leads away from the river to the northeast. Trains and buses both operate out of McDonagh train station.

Information

Kilkenny e.centre (☎ 776 0093; 26 Rose St; per hr €5; ☼ 10am-9pm Mon-Sat, 11am-8pm Sun) Internet access, comfy and central.
Tourist office (☎ 775 1500; www.southeastireland.com; Rose Inn St; ☼ 9am-6pm Mon-Sat May-Sep, 9am-1pm & 2-5pm Mon-Sat Oct-Apr) Near the castle.

Sights

Stronghold of the powerful Butler family, **Kilkenny Castle** (☎ 772 1450; admission incl tour €5; ⏲ 9.30am-7pm Jun-Aug, 10am-6.30pm Sep, 10.30am-5pm Oct-May) has a history dating back to 1172, when the legendary Anglo-Norman Strongbow erected a wooden tower on the site. The Long Gallery, with its vividly painted ceiling and extensive portrait collection of Butler family members over the centuries, is quite remarkable.

The approach on foot to **St Canice's Cathedral** (☎ 776 4971; www.cashel.anglican.org; adult/concession €3/2; ⏲ 9am-6pm Mon-Sat, 2-6pm Sun Apr-Sep; 10am-1pm & 2-4pm Mon-Sat, 2-4pm Sun Oct-Mar) from Parliament St leads over Irishtown Bridge and up St Canice's Steps, which date from 1614. Although the present cathedral dates from 1251, it has a much longer history and contains some remarkable tombs and monuments.

Sleeping

Foulksrath Castle (☎ 776 7674; foulksrath@eircom.net; dm €14; ⏲ closed 10am-5pm) An Óige's out-of-the-way hostel is beautifully situated in a 16th-century Norman castle 13km north of Kilkenny in Jenkinstown, near Ballyragget. **Buggy's Coaches** (☎ 774 1264) has a bus service into town (€3, 20 minutes) twice daily.

Kilkenny Tourist Hostel (☎ 776 3541; kilkenny hostel@eircom.net; 35 Parliament St; dm/tw €15/38) This IHH hostel is friendly, clean and central. Check the excellent information board for happenings.

Rose Inn (☎ 777 0061; 9 Rose Inn St; dm/d €15/50) Little Rose Inn, opposite the tourist office, is a serviceable cheapie. It's central and cheerful, and rooms in the back are quiet.

Tree Grove Caravan & Camping Park (☎ 777 0302; www.camping-ireland.ie; tent & 2 people €12.50; ⏲ Mar–mid-Nov) You can walk into town along the riverfront from the Tree Grove. By car, it's 1.5km south of Kilkenny on the New Ross (R700) road.

Eating & Drinking

ML Dore (☎ 776 3374; 65 High St; mains €8-17; ⏲ 8am-9pm Nov-Apr, 8am-10pm May-Oct) A funny place, with its over-the-top kitsch décor with price stickers. It's an old standby for traditional Irish grub, with a smattering of veggie dishes.

Marble City Bar (☎ 776 1143; 66 High St; lunch €8-13, dinner €10-14; ⏲ 10am-9pm) Sleek meets cosy at this bar that looks more expensive than it is. You may not be able to get the deep-fried brie in filo pastry with mixed wild berries out of your mind. It has jazz and blues on Fridays.

Gourmet Store (☎ 777 1727; 56 High St; ⏲ 9am-6pm Mon-Sat) Foodstuffs for classy hostellers.

Entertainment

Maggie's (☎ 776 2273; St Keiran St) Little Maggie's is the best pub in town for traditional Irish music.

John Cleere's (☎ 776 2573; 22 Parliament St) Cleere's often has good alternative bands, and the occasional poetry reading, at its theatre out the back.

Watergate Theatre (☎ 776 1674; www.watergate kilkenny.com; Parliament St) The Watergate hosts musical and theatrical productions throughout the year.

Getting There & Around

Several trains a day link Kilkenny's **McDonagh train station** (☎ 772 2024; Dublin Rd) with Dublin's Heuston station (€18.50, four to six daily).

Bus Éireann (☎ 776 4933, 051-879 000) runs buses to Dublin (€11, 2¼ hours, eight daily, five on Sunday), Cork (€17, three hours, four daily, one on Sunday), and one or two to Wexford (€14) and Rosslare Harbour (€15).

JJ Wall (☎ 772 1236; 86 Maudlin St) rents out bikes for €15 per day with photo identification.

AROUND KILKENNY
Cashel

☎ 062 / pop 2403

The **Rock of Cashel** (☎ 61437; www.heritageireland.ie; adult/student €5/2; ⏲ 9am-7pm Jun–mid-Sep, 9am-4.30pm mid-Sep–mid-Mar, 9am-5.30am mid-Mar–May) is one of Ireland's most striking archaeological sites. On the outskirts of town rises a huge lump of limestone bristling with ancient fortifications. Mighty stone walls encircle a complete round tower, a roofless abbey and the country's finest 12th-century **Romanesque chapel**.

Six buses on line 8 (Dublin to Cork) pass through Cashel daily.

THE SOUTHWEST

CORK (CORCAIGH)

☎ 021 / pop 123,338

Cork, the Irish Republic's second-largest city, buzzes with the energy and promise of a city on the rise. The 2005 European Capital of Culture prides itself on a great mix of pubs, cafés and restaurants, and its university and burgeoning arts and music scene keep things interesting. It rivals Dublin as a place to party, but lacks the capital's edgy feel.

Cork has long been an important city in Ireland, not least during the Anglo-Irish War and the civil war that followed independence. Irish leader Michael Collins was ambushed and killed nearby in 1922.

Orientation

Oliver Plunkett St and the curve of St Patrick's St are the main shopping/eating/drinking areas. The train station and several hostels are north of the river.

Information

Internet Exchange (☎ 425 4666; Paul St; per hr €3; ☷ 9am-10pm Mon-Sat, from 10am Sun)

Main Post Office (Oliver Plunkett St)

Tourist Office (☎ 425 5100; www.corkkerry.ie; Grand Pde; ☷ 9.15am-5.15pm Mon-Fri, 9.30am-4.30pm Sat, to 6pm Sat Jun-Aug)

Sights

The architecturally striking **Crawford Municipal Art Gallery** (☎ 427 3377; www.crawfordartgallery .com; Emmet Pl; admission free; ☷ 10am-5pm Mon-Sat) puts on contemporary shows and retrospectives. Its permanent collection includes works by Jack Yeats, among others.

Cork's notable churches include the 1879 Protestant **St Fin Barre's Cathedral** (☎ 496 3387; www.cathedral.cork.anglican.org; Bishop St; admission €3; ☷ 10am-5.30pm Mon-Fri Apr-Sep, 10am-12.45pm & 2-5pm Mon-Fri Oct-Mar), with its fairytale riot of spires and buttresses, and the 18th-century **St Anne's Church** (☎ 450 5906; www.shandonbells.org; John Redmond St, Shandon; adult/student €6/5; ☷ 9am-5pm Mon-Sat). Admission lets you climb the tower, ring the Shandon Bells and see an audiovisual presentation about the Shandon area.

The **Cork Public Museum** (☎ 427 0679; Fitzgerald Park; museum@corkcity.ie; admission free Mon-Fri, €1.50 Sun; ☷ 11am-1pm & 2.15-5pm Mon-Fri, 3-5pm Sun Sep-May; to 6pm Sun-Fri Jun-Aug) recently underwent a major renovation and expansion, and has a fine collection of artefacts that trace Cork's history from prehistory to the present.

Cork City Gaol (☎ 430 5022; www.corkcitygaol.com; Convent Ave; adult/concession €6/5; ☷ 9.30am-5pm) received its first prisoners in 1824 and its last in 1923, including many prominent independence fighters. The 35-minute taped tour around the restored cells is very moving.

GETTING INTO TOWN

To get to the centre from the bus station, walk west along the water or south to Oliver Plunkett St. The train station, about 1.5km northeast of town, is further, but you can walk it via MacCurtain St if you're staying on Wellington Rd. Frequent buses head from the airport (€3.50, 25 minutes) and ferry terminal (€5, 40 minutes) to the bus station.

Sleeping

Kinlay House Shandon (☎ 450 8966; www.kinlayhouse.ie; Bob & Joan's Walk; dm €14-16, s/d €30/45, d with private bathroom €50; ☐) A light breakfast is included in the price at this excellent hostel where smart décor and a fun but sensible atmosphere are pluses.

Sheila's Hostel (☎ 450 5562; www.sheilashostel.ie; 4 Belgrave Pl, Wellington Rd; dm €14-16.50, s €28-30, d €44-50; ☐) Sheila's is a big and busy place with a sauna (!), currency exchange and bike hire (€14 per day).

Cork International Hostel (☎ 454 3289; 1-2 Western Rd; dm €18-20, tw €44; ☐) The cheerful staff at this bright and busy An Óige hostel do a great job coping with the flow of young travellers and lively groups. Bus No 8 stops outside the hostel.

Close to the train station on the northeast end of town there's a handful of basic but perfectly fine B&Bs, including **Auburn House** (☎ 450 8555; auburnhouse@eircom.net; Wellington Rd; s/d €42/66, with private bathroom €52/75; P).

Eating

Gingerbread House (☎ 427 6411; Paul St; light meals €3-6; ☷ 8am-10.30pm Mon-Tue, 8am-12:30am Wed-Thu, 8am-5am Fri-Sat, 9am-12.30am Sun) Good coffee, pastries and pizza are served up in this huge but comfy cafeteria that never seems to close. It's set among several narrow lanes packed with restaurants.

Quay Co-op Café (☎ 431 7026; 24 Sullivan's Quay; mains €7.50-9; ☷ 9am-9pm Mon-Sat) This long-established favourite rattles out delectable veggie options in a chic and homey environment, with art on the walls depicting the universal life force. The shop next door has plenty for green self-caterers.

The **English Market** has everything you need to do your own cooking.

Farmgate Restaurant (☎ 427 8134; English Market; mains €8.50-12; ☷ 8.30am-5pm Mon-Sat) This place

IRELAND

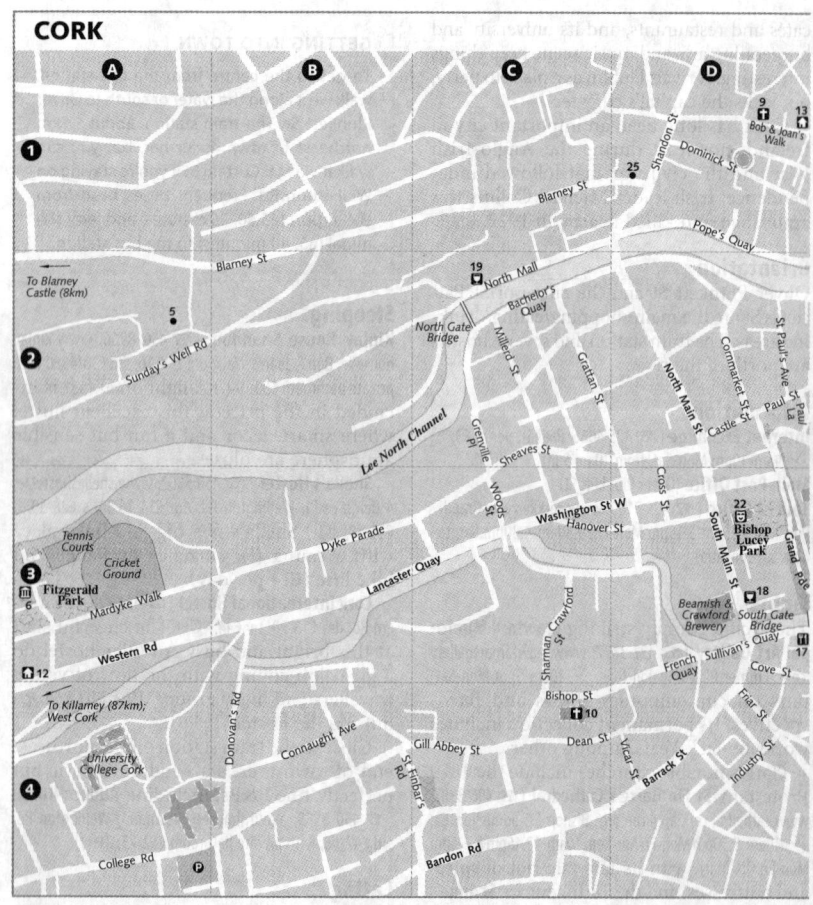

CORK

serves filling breakfasts and lunches on a balcony overlooking the market.

Drinking

Cork's pub life is brimming. Locally brewed Murphy's is the stout of choice here, not Guinness.

An Spailpín Fánach (☎ 427 7949; 28 South Main St) The 'wandering labourer' hosts traditional sessions almost every night.

Lobby (☎ 431 9307; 1 Union Quay) The Lobby gets traditional on weekends and has an upstairs space (€5 to €15 cover) that hosts a range of performers. Tuesday is jazz night.

Franciscan Well Brewery (☎ 421 0130; North Mall) Serves its own ales brewed in the gleaming copper vats behind the bar.

Entertainment

WhazOn, a free monthly publication available around town, lists all Cork's goings-on. The Cork International Jazz Festival and the International Film Festival both take place in October.

Cork Opera House (☎ 427 0022; www.corkopera house.ie; Emmet Pl) The Opera House has put on shows as varied as *Carmen*, Malian singer Oumou Sangaré, and the *Vagina Monologues*. The **Half Moon Theatre** (☎ 427 0022), behind the Opera House, hosts live bands and DJs.

Triskel Arts Centre (☎ 427 2022; www.triskelarts centre.com; Tobin St) An important venue for contemporary art, film, music and media arts.

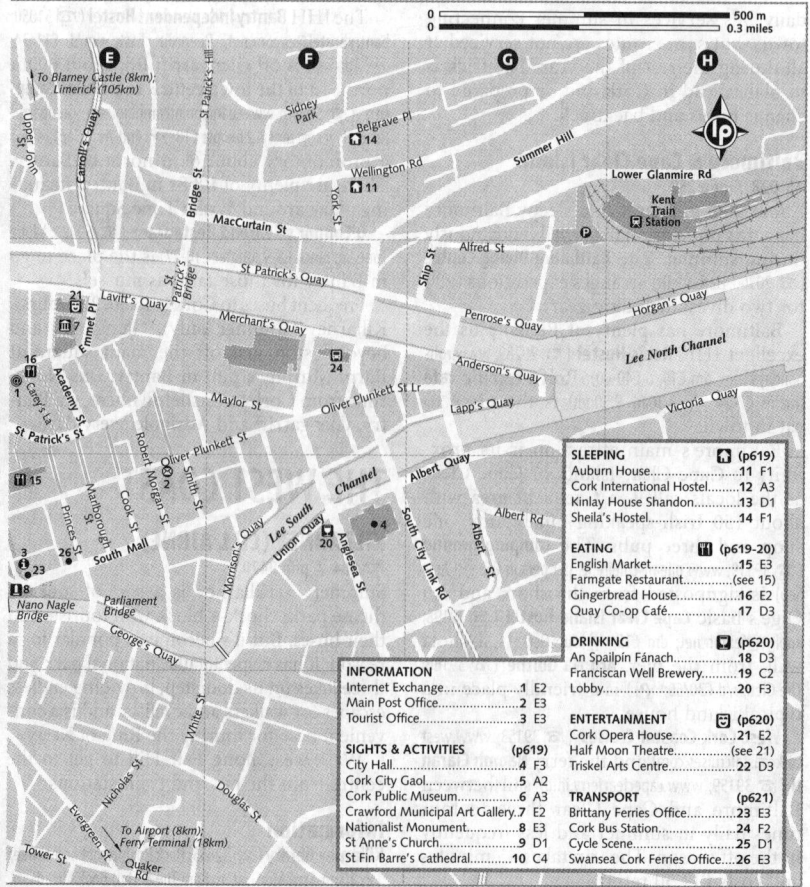

Getting There & Around

Buses connect Cork's **station** (☎ 450 8188; cnr Merchants Quay & Parnell Pl) with Dublin (€20.50, 4¼ hours, six daily), Killarney (€13.50, two hours, 12 daily), Wexford (€17.50, four hours, two to three daily) and more.

Trains go to Dublin (€50, three hours, nine daily) and Killarney (€20, 1½ hours, five daily) from **Kent train station** (☎ 450 4777; Lower Glanmire Rd).

Cork's ferry terminal is at Ringaskiddy; **Swansea Cork Ferries** (☎ 427 6000; 52 South Mall) and **Brittany Ferries** (☎ 427 7801; 42 Grand Pde) have offices in town. See p607 for more details.

Hire a bike for €15 per day from **Cycle Scene** (☎ 430 1183; 396 Blarney St).

AROUND CORK
Blarney (An Bhlarna)

Blarney is a village with one reason to visit: the imposing walls of 15th-century **Blarney Castle** (☎ 438 5252; www.blarneycastle.ie; adult/concession €7/5; ☉ 9am-7pm Mon-Sat, 9.30am-5.30pm Sun Jun-Aug, shorter hr rest of year). If you don't mind putting your lips where millions have also been, you can kiss the castle's legendary **Blarney Stone** on the high battlements. Legend has it, you'll be blessed with the gift of the gab.

Buses run regularly from the Cork bus station (€4.70 return, 30 minutes).

WEST COUNTY CORK

Travelling west by public transport from Cork can be tough. There are at least two

IRELAND

daily bus services in summer connecting towns, but some routes are not serviced at all during the rest of the year. The trick is to plan ahead in Cork and be prepared to change buses and backtrack.

Baltimore & Cape Clear Island

☎ 028 / pop 250

About 100km from Cork, sleepy Baltimore has a tiny population that swells enormously during summer. The **Baltimore Diving Centre** (☎ 20300; Harbour Dr) arranges expeditions (€80 for two dives, including gear).

Baltimore has plenty of B&Bs, plus the excellent IHH **Rolf's Hostel** (☎ 20289; www.rolfs holidays.com; dm €15, d €40-60). Rolf's terrific **café** (mains €7-24; ☽ 8.30am-9.30pm) is the place to eat in town.

Baltimore's main attraction is its proximity to Cape Clear Island, or Cape Clear as the locals call it, a Gaeltacht area with about 150 Irish-speaking inhabitants, one shop and three pubs. The **camping ground** (☎ 39119; www.oilean-chleire.ie; per person €6; ☽ Jun-Sep) is signposted from the shop; and An Óige's basic **Cape Clear Island Hostel** (☎ 39198; anoige@fenlon.net; dm €15; ☽ Jun-Oct) is a short walk from the pier. **Ard Na Goithe** (☎ 39160; The Glen; s/d €30/60; [P]) is a friendly place in a typical island house.

West Cork Coastal Cruises (☎ 39153; www.west corkcoastalcruises.com) and the ferry **Naomh Ciarán II** (☎ 39159; www.capeclearferry.info) sail between Baltimore and Cape Clear three to four times daily in summer and less frequently in the off season. The trip takes 45 minutes and costs €11.50 return.

Bantry & the Beara Peninsula

☎ 027 / pop 2936

Wedged between hills and the waters of Bantry Bay, Bantry is a good base for coastal explorations. The **tourist office** (☎ 63084; www.cork kerry.ie; 9am-6pm Mon-Sat, 10am-5pm Sun Jun-Aug, 9.15am-5.15pm Mon-Sat Apr-May & Sep-Oct, closed Mar-Nov) is on the east end of Wolfe Tone Square.

The Beara Peninsula, far less on the tourist trail than the Ring of Kerry or the Dingle, is a wild, handsome, rocky landscape ideal for exploring by foot or bike. If you're driving or cycling don't miss the beautiful Healy Pass. Walkers might like to tackle the ruggedly beautiful Hungry Hill, made famous by Daphne DuMaurier's book of the same name.

The IHH **Bantry Independent Hostel** (☎ 51050; bantryhostel@eircom.net; Reenrour East; dm/d €11/24; ☽ Apr-Sep) is off Glengarriff Rd, about 600m northeast of the town centre. **Eagle Point Camping** (☎ 50630; www.eaglepointcamping.com; Glengarriff Rd, Ballylickey; tent & 2 people €18; ☽ end-Apr–Sep) is on a promontory about 6km north of Bantry. There are plenty of B&Bs in Bantry, including a few around Wolfe Tone Square.

O'Connor's Seafood Restaurant (☎ 50221; Wolfe Tone Sq; lunch €8-9, dinner €18-27) is the place to go in Bantry for those famous mussels.

Frequent buses to Cork (€13.50, 2½ hours), Killarney (summer only), Glengarriff and beyond stop just off the main square at Barry Murphy's pub in Bantry. Bus No 46 runs from Cork to Castletownbere, via Bantry, Glengarriff and Adrigole every day.

THE WEST COAST

KILLARNEY (CILL AIRNE)

☎ 064 / pop 9470

Summer in Killarney is a sort of tourism theme park, chock-a-block with tourists and their buses. But it's become so popular for a reason: it has a spectacular national park and three lakes on its doorstep, providing endless escapes for walkers and cyclists, and is a convenient base for touring the Ring of Kerry.

Walk west along Fair Hill to get to the centre from the bus and train stations.

Information

Killarney library (☎ 32655; Rock Rd; Internet access free; ☽ 10am-5pm Mon-Sat, to 8pm Tue & Thu) Book ahead.

Main post office (New St)

Tourist office (☎ 31633; www.corkkerry.ie; Beech Rd; ☽ 9am-8pm Mon-Sat, 10am-6pm Sun Jul & Aug, shorter hr rest of year) Huge and helpful.

Sights & Activities

Most of Killarney's attractions are just outside town, but the 1855 **St Mary's Cathedral** (☎ 31014; Port Rd) is worth a look.

The picture-perfect backdrop of mountains beyond town is, in fact, part of the 10,236-hectare **Killarney National Park**. Within the park are beautiful Lough Leane, Muckross Lake and the Upper Lake. As well as boasting ruins and ex-gentry housing, the park is excellent for exploring by foot, bicycle or boat. The *Killarney Area Guide* (€1.90 at the tourist office) has some advice.

In summer the **Gap of Dunloe**, a heather-clad valley at the foot of Purple Mountain (832m), is Killarney tourism at its worst. Forgo the horse and trap and instead cycle to **Ross Castle**. From here take a boat across to **Lord Brandon's Cottage** and bike down through the Gap and back into town via the N72 and a path through the golf course. Including bicycle hire, this should cost you about €25. The 90-minute boat ride alone justifies the trip.

Sleeping

Wherever you plan to stay, book ahead from June to August. The tourist office books rooms for a €4 fee.

Killarney International Hostel (☎ 31240; anoige@ killarney.iol.net; dm €14-16; ☽ Easter-Sep; P ☐) Occupying a splendid 18th-century manor house on 28 hectares of lakes and woods, this An Óige hostel is 5km west of the centre off the N72 to Killorglin. A shuttle service runs to/from the bus and train stations in summer.

Súgán (☎ 33104; www.killarneysuganhostel.com; Lewis Rd; dm €15) A hostel with a big heart and a trail's-end atmosphere, the very down-to-earth Súgán has a rack of guitars, a cosy dining room with a fireplace, and showers in the back garden.

Rathmore House (☎ 32829; rathmorehousekly@ iol.ie; Rock Rd; s/d €42/70; P) There's a real Irish welcome at this long-established family-run B&B at the entrance to town.

Other recommendations:

Flesk Muckross Caravan Park (☎ 31704; www.camp ingkillarney.com; Muckross Rd; tent & 2 people €17; ☽ mid-Apr–Sep) Great views of the mountains, 1.5km out on the N71.

Killarney Railway Hostel (☎ 35299; railwayhostel@ eircom.net; dms/s/d €13.50/25/36; P) Well equipped, cheerful and conveniently located near the train station.

Eating

Jam (☎ 31441; High St; light meals €2.50-7.50; ☽ 8am-5pm Mon-Sat) The cutest coffee shop in town has bottomless cups and high-calibre sandwiches and quiches.

Busy B's Bistro (☎ 31972; 15 New St; mains €3-10; ☽ 11am-9pm) This all-purpose diner has veggie burgers, spaghetti and baked potatoes.

Stonechat (☎ 34295; Flemings Lane; lunch €7-9, dinner €10-15; ☽ noon-10pm) In a little stone house, Stonechat has a range of veggie options that includes tagliatelle in a creamy mushroom and bean sauce.

Entertainment

Killarney Grand (☎ 31159; Main St) Has interesting takes on the traditional thing from 9pm and modern bands from 11pm (€6 cover).

O'Connor's (☎ 30200; 7 High St) Reliable O'Connor's puts on an interesting mix of traditional stand-up comedy and pub theatre.

Poets Café (☎ 31954; Bishop's Lane; ☽ 9am-10pm, noon-10pm Sun) A good pub alternative is the tiny Poets Café, where great organic coffees go with open-mike poetry readings and prose and film nights.

Getting There & Around

Bus Éireann (☎ 30011) operates from the **train station** (☎ 31067), with regular services to Cork (€13.50, two hours, four daily), Galway (via Limerick; €19, five hours, six daily) and Dublin (€20.50, six hours, five daily). Travelling by train to Cork (€20, 2¼ hours, three daily) or Dublin (€52.50, six hours, three daily) usually involves changing at Mallow.

O'Sullivan's (☎ 22389), near Poets Café, rents out bikes for €12/70 per day/week.

→THE RING OF KERRY ←
☎ 066

The Ring of Kerry, a 179km circuit around the Iveragh Peninsula, is one of Ireland's best attractions. Most travellers tackle the Ring by bus on a day trip from Killarney, but the stunning region deserves much more time.

Sights

The **Ballaghbeama Pass** cuts across the peninsula's central highlands and has spectacular views with remarkably little traffic. The shorter **Ring of Skellig**, at the end of the peninsula, has fine views of the Skellig Rocks and is less touristy. You can forgo roads completely by walking along some of the 214km **Kerry Way**, which winds through the Macgillycuddy's Reeks mountains past Carrantuohill (1038m), Ireland's highest mountain.

The pretty pastel-coloured town of Kenmare is an excellent alternative base for exploring the Ring of Kerry.

Catholic political leader Daniel O'Connell was born near **Cahirciveen**, one of the Ring's larger towns. The excellent **Barracks Heritage Centre** (☎ 947 2777; adult/student €4/3; ☽ 10am-5pm Mon-Sat, 2-5pm Sun Jun-Sep, 10am-5pm Mon-Fri Apr, May & Oct), off Bridge St, has exhibits on O'Connell and moving material on the local impact of the Great Famine.

IRELAND

South of Cahirciveen, the R565 branches west to the 11km-long **Valentia Island**, a jumping-off point for one of Ireland's most unforgettable experiences: the **Skellig Rocks**, two tiny islands 12km off the coast. The vertiginous climb up uninhabited Skellig Michael inspires a mild terror and an awe that monks could have clung to life in the beehive-shaped stone huts that stand on the only flat strip of land on top. On a clear day the views from the summit are astounding.

Calm seas permitting, boats run from spring to late summer from Portmagee, just before the bridge to Valentia, to Skellig Michael. The standard fare is €35 return. Booking is essential; contact **Joe Roddy & Sons** (☎ 947 4268; www.skelligtrips.com) or **Des Lavelle** (☎ 947 6124; lavelles@indigo.ie).

Sleeping

Book your next night as you make your way around the Ring; some places are closed out of season and others fill up quickly. Hostels typically charge €12 to €15 for dorm beds.

Cycling around the Ring, there's the IHH **Laune Valley Farm** (☎ 976 1488), 2km east of Killorglin; the IHO **Cáitín Hostel** (☎ 947 7614; patscraftshop@eircom.net) in Kells; IHO's **Ring Lyne Hostel** (☎ 947 6103) in Chapeltown; the large **Royal Pier Hostel** (☎ 947 6144; www.royalpiervalentia .com) in Knightstown on Valentia Island; An Óige's **Baile an Sceilg** (☎ 947 9229; ☾ Jun-Sep) in Ballinskelligs; and the **Travellers' Rest Hostel** (☎ 947 5175; www.caherdanielhostel.com).

An Óige's **Black Valley Hostel** (☎ 064-34712; ☾ Apr-Oct), in the Macgillycuddy's Reeks mountains, is a good starting point for walking the Kerry Way.

Getting There & Around

If you're not up to cycling, **Bus Éireann** (☎ 064-30011) has a Ring of Kerry bus service daily from late May to mid-September. In June, buses leave Killarney at 8.30am, 1.30pm and 3.45pm (Sunday at 9.40am and noon), stopping at Killorglin, Glenbeigh, Kells, Cahirciveen, Waterville, Caherdaniel and Sneem before returning to Killarney (the 3.45pm service terminates at Waterville).

Travel agencies in Killarney, including **Destination Killarney Tours** (☎ 064-32638; Scott's Gardens), offer daily tours of the Ring for about €20. Hostels in Killarney arrange tours for around €18.

THE DINGLE PENINSULA
☎ 066

The Dingle Peninsula, with its awesome mountains, picturesque lakes and wild terrain splashed with flowers, is just as beautiful as the Ring of Kerry. Narrow roads that discourage bus traffic mean it's also less crowded. The region's main hub, Dingle Town (An Daingean), is a workaday fishing village, while the western tip of the peninsula, predominantly Irish speaking, has an extraordinary number of ring forts, beehive dwellings and high crosses.

From Tralee the N86 heads west along the coast. The 'quick' route to Dingle Town is southwest from Camp via Anascaul and the N86. The scenic route follows the R560 northwest and crosses the wildly scenic **Connor Pass** (456m). Heading west from Dingle Town, follow signs for the 'Slea Head Drive', a scenic coastal stretch of the R559. To the southwest, **Slea Head** offers some of the peninsula's best views.

In Dingle Town, the inviting **Grapevine Hostel** (☎ 915 1434; Dykegate St; dm €14-16) has a faint smell of beer and a cosy lounge where guests bond before the fireplace. For a more rural setting, try the popular IHH **Ballintaggart Hostel** (☎ 915 1454; www.dingleaccommodation .com; tent & 2 people €12, dm €14-18, d €54; ☾ Apr-Oct), in an old 18th-century hunting lodge about 1.5km east of Dingle on the Tralee road.

Other hostels east of Dingle include IHH's **Fuchsia Lodge** (☎ 915 7150; fuchsia@eircom .net; camping per person €6, dm/s/d €14/25/35) in Anascaul; and the IHH **Connor Pass Hostel** (☎ 713 9179; dm €13; ☾ Apr-Oct) in Stradbally.

West of Dingle, look for the fantastic **Ballybeag Hostel** (☎ 915 9876; dm/d €15/42) in Ventry, with bike hire, cheap laundry and a swing amid the bluebells in the garden.

Buses stop outside the car park at the back of the Super Valu store in Dingle Town. Killarney–Tralee–Dingle buses run four times daily from Monday to Saturday (€13, 2½ hours).

Dingle has several bike-rental places. **Paddy Walsh** (☎ 915 2311; Dykegate St), near the Grapevine Hostel, has bikes for €10/50 per day/week.

THE BURREN

County Clare's greatest attraction is the haunting Burren (from the Irish *Boireann* – 'Rocky Country'), a bleakly beautiful and harsh stretch of country. Unwelcoming from the surface, the Burren transforms as you enter it into a complex landscape littered with ancient dolmens (Neolithic stone formations), ring forts, round towers, high crosses and a surprisingly diverse range of flora. Rocky foreshores, occasional beaches and splendid limestone cliffs also line its coast. Oh, and among the stunning scenery are some of the best music pubs in Ireland.

A number of companies, including **O'Neachtain Tours** (☎ 091-553188; www.oneachtain tours.com), run day trips to the Burren and Cliffs of Moher from Galway for €25. **Burren Hill Walks** (☎ 065-707 7168; Ballyvaughan) and **Burren Wild** (☎ 087-877 9565; www.burrenwalks.com; Kinvara) both give half-day guided walks for €20 per person.

Doolin

☎ 065 / pop 200

Tiny Doolin's reputation for top-notch traditional Irish music has spread like wildfire, and with it has spread its popularity among holidaymakers from around the world. Doolin's also a convenient base for exploring the Burren and the awesome Cliffs of Moher, and it's a gateway for boats to Inisheer, the easternmost and smallest of the Aran Islands. In summer it can be difficult to get a bed in Doolin, so book ahead.

In a converted 17th-century farmhouse by the river in the upper village, **Aille River Hostel** (☎ 707 4260; www.esatclear.ie/~ailleriver; dm/d €12/28; ℗ 🖳) is the best budget choice. It has turf fires, hot showers, free laundry and good company. Almost as good, the **Rainbow Hostel** (☎ 707 4415; www.rainbowhostel.com; dm/s/d €12/45/60; ℗) has *en-suite* rooms with lots of exposed wood and bright colours. **O'Connors Riverside Camping & Caravan Park** (☎ 707 4314; www.oconnorsdoolin.com; tent & 2 people €12; ☼ May-Sep; ℗) is a friendly camp site with immaculate facilities.

Doolin's three pubs serve basic, cheap pub grub, and **Doolin Café** (☎ 707 4795; lunch €3.50-9.50, dinner €17-22.50; ☼ 10am-3pm & 6-10pm Fri-Wed, closed Feb) has a laid-back atmosphere and fantastic food.

There are direct buses to Doolin from Limerick (€13, 2¼ hours, twice daily) and Galway (€12, 1½ hours, two to five daily); the main Bus Éireann stop is across from Paddy Moloney's Doolin Hostel. See the Aran Islands (p627) for details on ferries

to and from the islands. Some of the hostels rent out bikes for around €8 a day plus deposit.

Cliffs of Moher

About 8km south of Doolin are the towering Cliffs of Moher, one of Ireland's most famous natural features. In summer, the cliffs are overrun by day-trippers, so consider staying in Doolin and hiking or biking along the Burren's quiet country lanes, where the views are just as good and crowds are never a problem. Either way, be careful walking along these sheer cliffs, especially in wet or windy weather.

Near the **Cliffs of Moher visitors centre** (☎ 065-708 1171; ☼ 9.30am-5.30pm May-Sep) is **O'Brien's Tower**, which you can climb for €1. From here walk south or north and the crowds soon disappear.

GALWAY (GAILLIMH)

☎ 091 / pop 65,774

Galway, with its narrow, cobbled streets, fast-flowing river, ramshackle shop-fronts, and great restaurants, pubs and clubs, is the preferred city of buskers, fishermen and bohemians. Weekend nightlife attracts folk from as far as Dublin, and various festivals draw international crowds that cram the streets. Galway is also a departure point for the rugged Aran Islands and enchanting Connemara.

The town's tightly packed town centre is spread evenly on both sides of the Corrib River. The bus and train stations are within a stone's throw of Eyre Square.

Information

iSupply (☎ 585770; 10-12 Sea Rd; per hr €2; ☼ 9am-6pm Mon-Fri, 10am-4pm Sat) Internet access.

Main post office (Eglinton St)

Tourist office (☎ 537700; www.irelandwest.ie; Forster St; ☼ 9am-5.45pm Jul-Sep; 9am-5.45pm Mon-Fri, 9am-12.45pm Sat Oct-May) Just off Eyre Square.

Sights

Eyre Square is the focal point of the eastern part of the city centre. In the square is **Kennedy Park**, honouring a visit by John F Kennedy in 1963. To the north of the square is a controversial statue to the Galway-born writer and hell-raiser Pádraic O'Conaire (1883–1928). Southwest of the square, the **Collegiate Church of St Nicholas of Myra** (Shop St) dates from 1320 and has several interesting tombs.

IRELAND

Also on Shop St, parts of **Lynch Castle**, now a bank, date back to the 14th century. Lynch was a mayor of Galway in the 15th century; the story goes that when his son was condemned for murder, he personally acted as hangman. The stone façade that is the **Lynch Memorial Window** (Market St) marks the spot of the sorrowful deed.

The **Nora Barnacle House Museum** (☎ 564743; www.norabarnacle.com; 8 Bowling Green; admission €2.50; 🕒 10am-1pm & 2-5pm Tue-Sat mid-May–mid-Sep or by appointment) is in the former home of James Joyce's wife and lifelong muse.

Little remains of Galway's old city walls apart from the **Spanish Arch**, found by the river mouth.

Festivals

The **Galway Arts Festival** (www.galwayartsfestival.com) in July is huge (see p638), but maybe not as big as the **Galway Oyster Festival** (www.galwayoysterfest.com; see p638), held every autumn.

Sleeping

Be sure to book ahead during summer, during festivals and at weekends.

Barnacle's Quay Street House (☎ 568644; www.barnacles.ie; 10 Quay St; dm €15.50-22, d €53) Barnacle's is in a great position at the heart of the action on the pedestrian mall, surrounded by all the pubs, restaurants and cafés you came to Galway for.

Kinlay House (☎ 565244; www.kinlayhouse.ie; Merchant's Rd; dm €16-21, d €49-52; 💻) Modern, spacious and slightly sterile Kinlay House, just off Eyre Sq, is a convenient base. You can book discounted bus tours (€20) and Aran Islands ferries (€12) at reception.

St Martin's B&B (☎ 568286; 2 Nun's Island Rd; s/d €35/65) St Martin's is in an ideal spot, with views of the William O'Brien Bridge and a simple garden along the banks of the Corrib. The home cooking, comfortable rooms, friendliness of the owners and central location make it extremely popular.

Salthill Caravan Park (☎ 523972; www.salthillcaravanpark.com; tent & 2 people €15, 🕒 Apr-Sep; P) Just west of Salthill, off Salthill Rd, is this scenic spot right on the water. A bus runs the 4km into town every half-hour.

Other recommended hostels:

Galway Hostel (☎ 566959; www.galwayhostel.com; Frenchville Lane; dm €15-20, d €40)

Sleepzone (☎ 566999; www.sleepzone.ie; Bóthar na mBan, Wood Quay; dm €15-18, s/d €35/50; P 💻)

Eating & Drinking

Java's (☎ 567400; Upper Abbeygate St; sandwiches €4-7; 🕒 11-3am Mon-Sat, 2pm-3am Sun) A small room with an open fire going on cold days, this is a good spot to head for an afternoon coffee or to revive yourself with a sweet snack long past midnight.

Massimo (☎ 582239; 10 West William St; lunch €3.50-8; 🕒 noon-3pm) The décor is pub nouveau, the menu hearty and chic. Try a sandwich of char-grilled veggies with pesto.

Café du Journal (☎ 568426; Quay St; mains €4-8; 🕒 9am-6pm winter, 10am-10pm summer) Among old books and library lighting, Café du Journal serves light but filling meals and good espresso.

Conlons (☎ 562268; Eglington St; mains €8-17; 🕒 11am-midnight Mon-Sat, 4-10pm Sun) Nobody does fish and chips better.

Crane Bar (☎ 587419; 2 Sea Rd) The Crane is an atmospheric old pub that's good for a laid-back pint, and a top-notch *ceilidh* (traditional music session) is usually on.

Róisín Dubh (☎ 586540; Upper Dominick St) Appearing like a reliable local boozer, Róisín Dubh is better known as *the* place to see new rock and roll talents before they get too big for such intimate venues.

Séhán Ua Neáchtain (☎ 568820; 17 Upper Cross St) Known simply as Neáchtains, this dusty old pub has a truly fabulous atmosphere and attracts an eccentric, mixed crowd.

Entertainment

The free *Galway Advertiser* includes listings of what's on in the city. It's available Thursday at the tourist office and newsstands around town.

cuba (☎ 565991; www.cuba.ie; Eyre Sq) Exuding Latin swank and attracting exuberant crowds, cuba has three cavernous floors with soulful DJs and live bands, often going simultaneously.

Druid Theatre (☎ 568660; Chapel Lane) The long-established Druid is famed for its experimental works by young Irish playwrights.

Getting There & Around

The **bus station** (☎ 562000) is just behind the Great Southern Hotel, next to the **Ceannt train station** (☎ 561444). Bus Éireann operates services to Doolin (€12, 1½ hours, five daily Monday to Saturday in summer), Dublin (€13, 3¾ hours, 15 daily), Killarney (€19, 4¾ hours, three daily), Sligo and beyond.

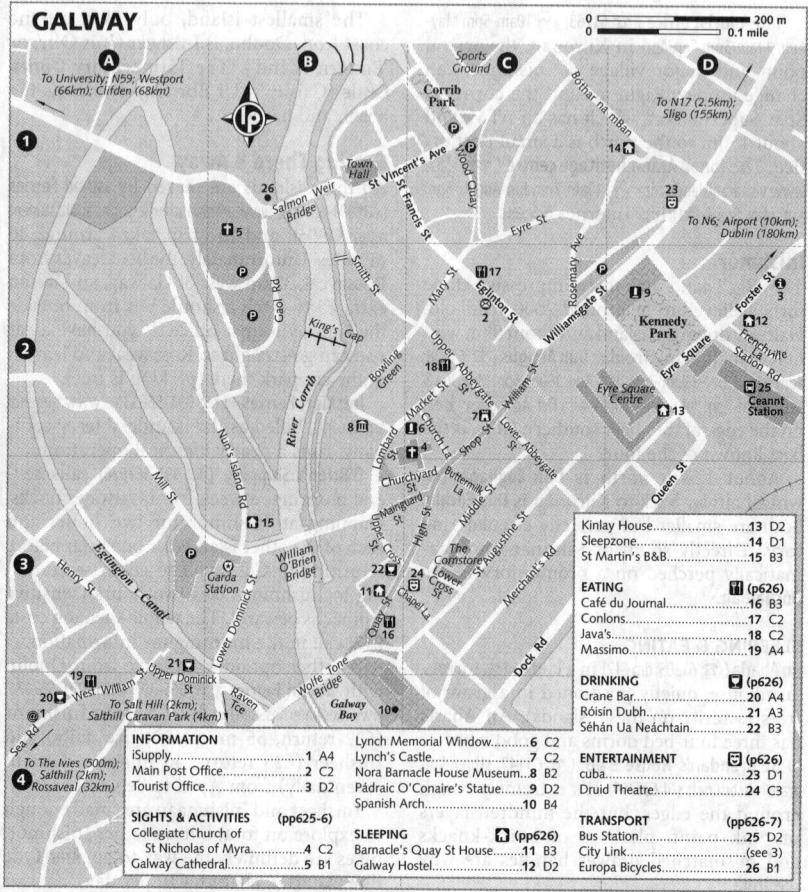

GALWAY

0 ─────── 200 m
0 ─────── 0.1 mile

INFORMATION	
iSupply.......................................1 A4
Main Post Office.........................2 C2
Tourist Office.............................3 D2

SIGHTS & ACTIVITIES	(pp625-6)
Collegiate Church of	
St Nicholas of Myra..............4 C2
Galway Cathedral......................5 B1
Lynch Memorial Window..........6 C2
Lynch's Castle............................7 C2
Nora Barnacle House Museum..8 B2
Pádraic O'Conaire's Statue.......9 D2
Spanish Arch.............................10 B4

SLEEPING	(pp626)
Barnacle's Quay St House........11 B3
Galway Hostel.........................12 D2
Kinlay House...........................13 D2
Sleepzone................................14 D1
St Martin's B&B.......................15 B3

EATING	(p626)
Café du Journal.......................16 B3
Conlons..................................17 C2
Java's......................................18 C2
Massimo..................................19 A4

DRINKING	(p626)
Crane Bar................................20 A4
Róisín Dubh............................21 A3
Séhán Ua Neáchtain...............22 B3

ENTERTAINMENT	(p626)
cuba.......................................23 D1
Druid Theatre..........................24 C3

TRANSPORT	(pp626-7)
Bus Station..............................25 D2
City Link.............................(see 3)
Europa Bicycles.......................26 B1

Private bus companies, generally a bit cheaper than Bus Éireann, also operate from Galway. **Citylink** (☎ 564163; www.citylink.ie) runs 13 buses a day to Dublin airport (€16) via the city centre (€11).

Six trains a day run to and from Dublin (€25, 2¾ hours). Connections with other train routes can be made at Athlone.

Europa Bicycles (☎ 563355; Earl's Island), opposite Galway Cathedral, charges €10/50 per day/week.

ARAN ISLANDS
☎ 099 / pop 1781

The windswept, stark Aran Islands seem to exist in another time and another tempo, with their ancient forts looking out silently over the sea. Part of the Gaeltacht, the three islands are also in another language, and you'll hear Irish alone spoken among locals. In addition to stunning natural beauty, the islands have some of the country's oldest Christian and pre-Christian ruins.

The abundance of stone walls on the islands, particularly on tiny **Inisheer**, is dramatic, with countless kilometres of stone separating every little patch of rocky land. Most visitors head for long and narrow **Inishmór** (or Inishmore), which is 14.5km by a maximum 4km. **Inishmaan** and **Inisheer** are much smaller and receive far fewer visitors. All the islands can get crowded at holiday times and in summer, when advance reservations are advised.

The **tourist office** (☎ 61263; ☺ 10am-5pm May-Aug, 11am-5pm Sep-Apr) in Kilronan, the arrival point and major village of Inishmór, can change money. Right around the corner is Spar Supermarket, which has an ATM, and about 150m to the north is a small post office. The **Ionad Árann heritage centre** (☎ 61355; www.visitaranislands.com; ☺ 10am-7pm Jun-Aug, to 5pm Apr, May, Sep & Oct) has Internet access.

Inishmór

The 'Big Island' has three impressive stone forts, believed to be around 2000 years old. Halfway down the island and about 8km west of Kilronan, semicircular **Dún Aengus** (☎ 61008; admission €2; ☺ 9am-7pm Jul & Aug, 10am-6pm May, Jun & Sep, 10am-7pm Jul & Aug, 10am-4pm Oct-Apr), perched on the edge of the sheer southern cliffs, is the best known of the four.

About 1.5km north is **Dún Eoghanachta**, while halfway back to Kilronan is **Dún Eochla**; both are smaller but perfectly circular ring forts. Directly south of Kilronan and dramatically perched on a promontory is **Dún Dúchathair**.

SLEEPING & EATING

An Aharla (☎ 61305; dm €12) In a laid-back former farmhouse, quietly positioned in a grove of trees (a rarity on these islands), An Aharla has three four-bed dorms and good vibes.

St Brendan's House B&B (☎ 61149; stbrendans aran@eircom.net; s/d €25/50) It's extremely rough around the edges, but the hundred layers of pink paint, plethora of knick-knacks and mismatched drawer handles are why we love it.

Mainistir House (☎ 61169; www.mainistirhouse aran.com; buffet €12; ☺ 8pm-close summer, 7pm-close winter) Book ahead for the great-value organic, largely vegetarian buffet dinners at Mainistir, which also has colourful rooms (dorm beds/singles/doubles €15/30/45) and Internet access.

Lios Aengus (☎ 61030; light meals €5-8; ☺ 9.30am-5pm) A simple coffee shop with OK soups and sandwiches.

Inishmaan & Inisheer

The least visited of the three islands is Inishmaan (Inis Meáin, or 'Middle Island'). High stone walls border its fields, and it's a delight to wander along the lanes. The main archaeological site is **Dún Chonchúir**, a massive oval-shaped stone fort built on a high point.

The smallest island, only 8km off the coast from Doolin, is Inisheer (Inis Oírr, or 'Eastern Island'). The 15th-century **O'Brien Castle** (Caislea'n Uí Bhriain) overlooks the beach and harbour.

Getting There & Away

All three islands are served by **Island Ferries** (☎ 091-568903; www.aranislandferries.com; adult/student return €19/15), and the trip takes around 40 minutes. Unfortunately, the boat leaves from Rossaveal, 37km west of Galway, and it's an extra €5 to catch a shuttle bus from outside the Galway tourist office. If you have a car you can go straight to Rossaveal and leave it in the car park there (parking is free).

InisMór Ferries (☎ 091-566535; www.queenof aran2.com), billed as the islanders' ferry company, runs a nearly identical operation.

O'Brien's Shipping (☎ 091-567676) sails several mornings a week from Galway's docks, stopping at Inishmór for two hours and each of the other islands for one hour before returning to Galway. The 46km sea crossing to Inishmór takes two hours (sensitive stomachs beware). The whole shebang costs €12; call in the morning for information.

Another option is to leave from Doolin with **Doolin Ferries** (☎ 065-707 4455, 091-567676; www.doolinferries.com), which runs to Inishmór (€32 return, 55 minutes, twice daily) and Inisheer (€25 return, 40 minutes, four to seven daily) from April to September.

Inisheer and Inishmaan are small enough to explore on foot, but on larger Inishmór, bikes are definitely the way to go. **Aran Cycle Hire** (☎ 61132) charges €10 per day.

CONNEMARA

☎ 095

The northwest corner of County Galway is the wild and barren region known as Connemara. It's a stunning patchwork of bogs, lonely valleys, pale-grey mountains and small lakes that shimmer when the sun shines. Connemara's isolation has allowed Irish Gaelic to thrive, and it is widely spoken here.

By car or bicycle the most scenic routes through Connemara are Oughterard–Recess (via the N59), Recess–Kylemore Abbey (via the R344) and Leenane–Louisburgh (via the R335). From Galway, **Lally Tours** (☎ 091-562905; www.lallytours.com) and **O'Neachtain Tours** (☎ 091-553188; www.oneachtaintours.com) run day-long bus trips through Connemara for around €25.

Sights

Aughanure Castle (☎ 091-552214; admission €2.75; ⏰ 9.15am-6pm May-Sep), 3km east of Oughterard, is a 16th-century tower house on a rocky outcrop overlooking Lough Corrib.

Just west of **Recess** (Straith Salach) on the N59, the turn north at the R334 takes you through the stunning Lough Inagh Valley. At the end of the R334 is the equally scenic **Kylemore Abbey** (☎ 41146; www.kylemore abbey.com; admission €10; ⏰ 9.30am-5.30pm mid-Mar–Nov, 10.30am-4pm Nov–mid-Mar) and its adjacent lake. The neo-Gothic 19th-century abbey is run by nuns.

From Kylemore, take the N59 east to Leenane (An Líonán), then detour north on the R335 to Louisburgh and onwards to Westport; or travel 17km southwest along the N59 to **Clifden** (An Clochán), Connemara's largest town. Clifden is quiet and pleasant and has a few good pubs and restaurants. The **Connemara Walking Centre** (☎ 21379; www.walkingireland.com; Island House, Market St) runs guided walking trips from €20.

Sleeping

Canrawer House Hostel (☎ 091-552388; www.oughter ardhostel.com; dm/d €13/34; ⏰ Feb-Oct) An attractive place at the Clifden end of town, just over 1km down a signposted turning. It rents out bikes for €15 per day.

Jolly Lodger (☎ 091-552682; jollylodger@eircom .net; s/d €30/54; P) In town, the Jolly Lodger serves up excellent breakfast pancakes.

Ben Lettery Hostel (☎ 51136; dm/tw €15/32; ⏰ Mar-Nov; P 🖳) An Óige's super-friendly Ben Lettery Hostel is on the N59 halfway between Recess and Clifden.

In Clifden, the IHH **Clifden Town Hostel** (☎ 21076; Market St; dm/d €13/34; P) is in the centre of town; the IHH/IHO **Brookside Hostel** (☎ 21812; Hulk St; dm/d from €11.50/30; ⏰ Mar-Oct; P) is down by the Owen Glin River.

Mallmore House (☎ 21460; http://indigo.ie/~mall more/index.html; d €64; ⏰ Mar-Oct) Two kilometres out of town on 14 hectares of woodland, Mallmore is a lovingly restored Georgian manor house.

Getting There & Away

Galway–Westport buses stop in Clifden, as well as Oughterard, Maam Cross and Recess; a few lines also stop in Cong and Leenane. There are three express buses a day between Clifden and Galway (one on Sunday).

THE NORTHWEST

The Northwest is Irish tourism's last frontier. The hordes haven't yet hit Counties Sligo and Donegal, so you can still get good and lost here. Sligo is somewhat known to travellers from the evocative poetry of WB Yeats, but it's still a well-kept secret. Donegal, with its magnificent coastline, has an especially wild feel to it, and no other county in Ireland can boast such unspoilt splendour.

SLIGO (SLIGHEACH)
☎ 071 / pop 18,429

William Butler Yeats (1865–1939) was born and educated elsewhere, but his poetry is infused with the landscapes, bitter history and rich folklore of his mother's native Sligo.

The train and bus station is a short walk west of the centre on Lord Edward St. The **North-West Regional Tourism Office** (☎ 916 1201; www.irelandnorthwest.ie; Temple St; 9am-5pm mid-Jun–Aug, 9am-5pm Mon-Fri Sep–mid-Jun) is just south of the centre. The **main post office** (Wine St) is east of the train and bus station. **Café Online** (☎ 914 4892; Stephen St; per hr €5; ⏰ 10am-10pm Mon-Sat, noon-8pm Sun), across from the library, has Internet access.

Sligo's two major attractions are outside town. **Carrowmore**, 5km to the southwest, is the site of a **megalithic cemetery** (☎ 916 1534; carrowmoretomb@duchas.ie; admission €2; ⏰ 10am-5.15pm Easter-Oct), with more than 60 stone rings, passage tombs and other Stone Age remains. It's the largest Stone Age necropolis in Europe.

If it's a fine day, don't miss the hilltop cairn-grave **Knocknarea**, a few kilometres northwest of Carrowmore. About 1000 years younger than Carrowmore, the huge cairn is said to be the grave of the legendary Maeve, 1st-century AD Queen of Connaught.

The very popular IHH **White House Hostel** (☎ 914 5160; Markievicz Rd; dm €12.50; P) is just north of the town centre. About 1km northeast of the centre, IHH's comfortable **Harbour House** (☎ 917 1547; www.harbourhousehostel.com; Finisklin Rd; dm/s/d €18/25/40; P) is modern and well equipped.

Café Bar Deli (☎ 914 0101; 15-16 Rear Stephen St; mains €8-20; ⏰ 6-10pm daily, noon-3pm Sun), a popular pasta-and-pizza place, is upstairs from the equally popular **Garavogue Bar** (mains €4-9; food served noon-6pm), which has superior bar food – outside on the river, if the weather agrees.

IRELAND

Bus Éireann (☎ 916 0066) has services to/from Dublin (€15, four hours, six daily). The Galway–Sligo–Donegal–Derry service runs five times daily; it's €12.50 and 2½ hours to Galway, and €15 and 2½ hours to Derry. Buses operate from below the **train station** (☎ 916 9888), where you can also get a train to Dublin (€22, three hours, three daily).

DONEGAL & AROUND (DÚN NA NGALL)
☎ 074 / pop 3723

Donegal Town is not the major centre in County Donegal, but it's a pleasant and laid-back place and well worth a visit. The triangular Diamond is the centre of Donegal; the bus stop is also here, outside the Abbey Hotel. A few steps south along the River Eske is the **tourist office** (☎ 972 1148; www.irelandnorthwest.ie; Quay St; ☾ 9am-6pm Mon-Sat, 10am-4pm Sun Jun-Aug, 10am-5.30pm Mon-Fri Sep-May).

Donegal Castle (☎ 972 2405; donegalcastle@duchas.ie; admission €3.50; ☾ 10am-6pm mid-Mar–Oct, 9.30am-4.30pm Sat & Sun Nov-Dec), on a rocky outcrop over the River Eske, stands in ruins but is impressive all the same.

The awe-inspiring cliffs at **Slieve League**, dropping 300m into the Atlantic Ocean, are a recommended side trip from Donegal. To drive to the cliff edge, take the Killybegs–Glencolumbcille road (R263) and, at Carrick, take the turn-off signposted 'Bunglas'. Continue beyond the track signposted for Slieve League (this trail is good for hikers) to the signpost for Bunglas. Daily Bus Éireann coaches stop in Kilcar and Carrick on the Donegal–Glencolumbcille line.

The comfortable IHH/IHO **Donegal Town Independent Hostel** (☎ 972 2805; camping per person €6, dm/d €12/28; **P**) is 1km northwest of town on the Killybegs road (N56).

Blueberry Tearoom (☎ 972 2933; the Diamond; mains €5-8; ☾ 9am-7pm) has substantial sandwiches and baked goods. The **Famous Donegal Chipper** (☎ 972 1428; Upper Main St; fish & chips from €5; ☾ 4.30-11pm Mon-Tue, 4.30-11.30pm Thu-Sun) really is famous for its fish and chips.

Bus Éireann (☎ 972 1101) goes to Derry (€11.50, 1½ hours, six daily), Sligo (€11, one hour, five daily), Galway (€20.50, four hours, four daily) and Dublin (€15, 4¼ hours, five daily). **McGeehan Coaches** (☎ 954 6150; www.mcgeehancoaches.com) does a quicker Donegal–Dublin return once or twice a day, departing from the police station opposite the tourist office. It's €16.50 and the trip takes 3½ hours.

NORTHERN IRELAND

☎ 028

First of all, Northern Ireland is part of the United Kingdom. The accent here is distinctly different, the currency is pounds sterling and people smoke *inside* bars and not on the footpath; otherwise, cross-border differences are minimal.

Travellers have been slowly rediscovering the North since the 1998 ratification of the Good Friday Agreement, and there's plenty to rediscover. The scenery of the Causeway Coast ranks among the most beautiful in Ireland – dramatic sea cliffs, picturesque harbours and the surreal Giant's Causeway – while the urban centres of Derry and Belfast are good bets for a good time. Even the few signs of the Troubles that remain – the powerful street murals in Belfast and Derry, for example – are strong draws, reminders that peace is fragile and hope priceless.

BELFAST (BÉAL FEIRSTE)
pop 277,390

Imposing architecture, foot-stomping music in packed-out pubs and the UK's second-biggest arts festival – Belfast is a city that confounds expectations. Massive investment, combined with the optimism engendered by the peace process, has transformed Belfast into something of a boom town, and today there's little sign of the daily tension of bomb threats and army check points.

The city is easy to get around, with most points of interest within easy walking distance of one another. Nightlife is vibrant and inspired, and a colourful new wave of stylish bars and restaurants has emerged to complement the splendid old Victorian pubs.

Belfast has not shaken its past altogether, however, and the passions that have torn Northern Ireland apart over the decades still run deep. But despite occasional setbacks, the prevailing atmosphere of determined optimism seems to be propelling Belfast towards a peaceful future.

Orientation

The city centre is a compact area with the imposing City Hall as the central landmark. To the south lies the Golden Mile, a restaurant- and pub-filled stretch of Dublin Rd, Shaftesbury Square, Bradbury Pl and Botanic Ave.

Information
INTERNET ACCESS
Internet café (☎ 9043 4058; Belfast Welcome Centre, 47 Donegall Pl; per hr £3)

POST
Main post office (Castle Pl)
Post office (Botanic Ave, by Shaftesbury Sq)

TOURIST INFORMATION
Belfast Welcome Centre (☎ 9024 6609; www.goto belfast.com; 47 Donegall Pl; ☺ 9am-5.30pm Mon-Sat Sep-May, 9am-7pm Mon-Sat, noon-5 pm Sun Jun-Aug)
Fáilte Ireland (☎ 9032 7888; www.ireland.ie; 53 Castle St; ☺ 9am-5pm Mon-Fri year-round, 9am-12.30pm Sat Jun-Sep) Information on the Republic.
Hostelling International Northern Ireland (HINI; ☎ 9032 4733; www.hini.org.uk; Belfast International Youth Hostel, 22-32 Donegall Rd)

Sights
ULSTER FOLK & TRANSPORT MUSEUM
Belfast's biggest tourist attraction is also one of Northern Ireland's best museums, the **Ulster Folk & Transport Museum** (☎ 9042 8428; www .magni.org.uk; adult/concession combined ticket for both museums £6.50/3.50; ☺ 10am-6pm Mon-Sat, 11am-6pm Sun Jul-Sep, 10am-5pm Mon-Fri Mar-Jun, less hrs Oct-Feb), 11km northeast of the centre beside the Bangor road (A2) near Holywood. The 30 buildings on the 60-hectare site range from urban terraced houses to thatched farm-cottages. A bridge crosses the A2 to the Transport Museum, a sort of automotive zoo of various Ulster-related vehicles. From Belfast, take Ulsterbus No 1 or any Bangor-bound train that stops at Cultra station.

AROUND THE CITY
At the northeastern corner of the 1906 **City Hall** (☎ 9027 0456; Donegall Sq; admission free) is a statue of Sir Edward Harland, who founded Belfast's Harland & Wolff shipyards, where the ill-fated *Titanic* was built. His yellow twin cranes **Samson and Goliath** tower above the city.

The famed **Crown Liquor Saloon** (☎ 9027 9901; 46 Great Victoria St; ☺ 11.30am-midnight Mon-Sat, 12.30-10pm Sun) was built in 1885 and displays Victorian architecture at its most extravagant. The Crown was lucky to survive a 1993 bomb that devastated the (now fully restored) **Grand Opera House** (☎ 9024 1919; www.goh.co.uk) nearby (see Entertainment, p634).

Ulster Museum (☎ 9038 3000; www.magni.org.uk; admission free; ☺ 10am-5pm Mon-Fri, 1-5pm Sat, 2-5pm

GETTING INTO TOWN

Belfast's two bus stations, Laganside Bus Centre, near the river, and the bigger Europa Bus Centre, next to Great Victoria St train station, are both central. Centrelink buses (travel free with your bus or train ticket) ply a circular route linking Belfast Central, Great Victoria St Station and Europa and Laganside stations to Donegall Square in the city centre; they run every 10 minutes. Local trains also connect Belfast Central with Great Victoria St Station via Botanic Station. Most local bus services depart from Donegall Sq, near the City Hall, where there's a ticket kiosk.

AirBus buses link Belfast international airport with the Europa Bus Centre every 30 minutes (£6, 30 minutes). A taxi costs about £25. See p634 for details on getting into town from ferry ports.

Sun) in the **Botanic Gardens** (☎ 9032 4902; admission free; ☺ 8am-sunset) has excellent exhibits on Irish art, wildlife, dinosaurs and more. The gardens are well worth a wander, and the glass Palm House contains a luxuriant riot of greenery.

FALLS & SHANKILL ROADS
The Catholic Falls Rd and the Protestant Shankill Rd have been battlefronts since the 1970s. Even so, these areas are quite safe and worth venturing into, if only to see the large **murals** expressing local political and religious passions.

The best way to visit the sectarian zones of the Falls and Shankill Rds is by 'people's taxi'. These former black London cabs run a bus-like service up and down their respective roads from terminuses in the city. **Black Taxi Tours** (☎ 9064 2264; www.belfasttours.com) and **Original Belfast Black Taxi Tours** (☎ 0800 032 2003) run organised people-taxi tours, giving even-sided accounts of the Troubles in a refreshingly down-to-earth way. Prices are £8 per person, based on four sharing, and pick-up can be arranged.

Festivals & Events
For three weeks in late October and early November, Belfast hosts the UK's second-largest arts festival, the **Festival at Queen's** (☎ 9066 7687; www.belfastfestival.com), in and around Queen's

IRELAND

BELFAST

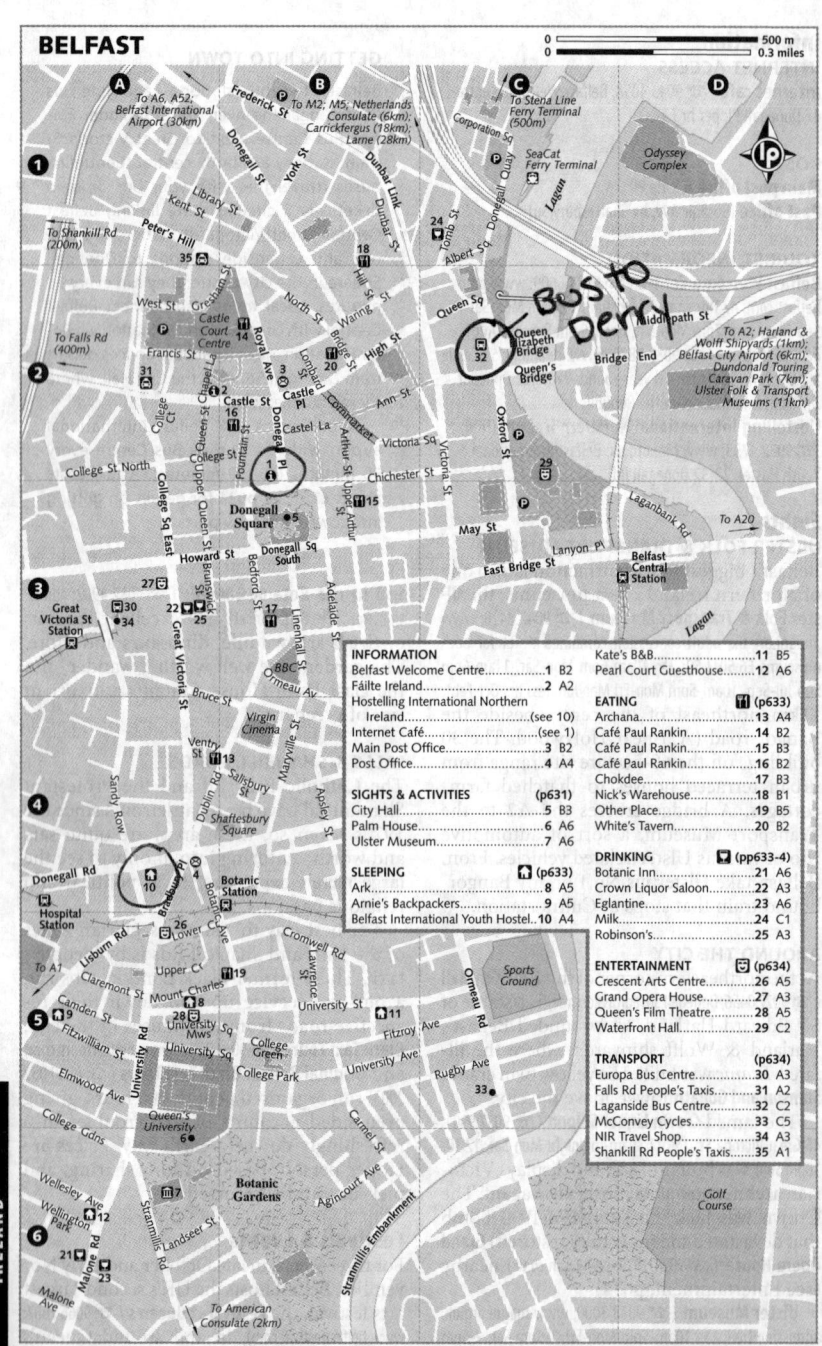

0 — 500 m
0 — 0.3 miles

Handwritten on map: Bus to Derry

INFORMATION

Belfast Welcome Centre	1 B2
Fáilte Ireland	2 A2
Hostelling International Northern Ireland	(see 10)
Internet Café	(see 1)
Main Post Office	3 B2
Post Office	4 A4

SIGHTS & ACTIVITIES (p631)

City Hall	5 B3
Palm House	6 A6
Ulster Museum	7 A6

SLEEPING (p633)

Ark	8 A5
Arnie's Backpackers	9 A5
Belfast International Youth Hostel	10 A4
Kate's B&B	11 B5
Pearl Court Guesthouse	12 A6

EATING (p633)

Archana	13 A4
Café Paul Rankin	14 B2
Café Paul Rankin	15 B3
Café Paul Rankin	16 B2
Chokdee	17 B3
Nick's Warehouse	18 B1
Other Place	19 B5
White's Tavern	20 B2

DRINKING (pp633-4)

Botanic Inn	21 A6
Crown Liquor Saloon	22 A3
Eglantine	23 A6
Milk	24 C1
Robinson's	25 A3

ENTERTAINMENT (p634)

Crescent Arts Centre	26 A5
Grand Opera House	27 A3
Queen's Film Theatre	28 A5
Waterfront Hall	29 C2

TRANSPORT (p634)

Europa Bus Centre	30 A3
Falls Rd People's Taxis	31 A2
Laganside Bus Centre	32 C2
McConvey Cycles	33 C5
NIR Travel Shop	34 A3
Shankill Rd People's Taxis	35 A1

University. Also worth checking out is the fantastic **Cathedral Quarter Arts Festival** (☎ 9023 2403 www.cqaf.com) in early May, which attracts a range of pioneering writers, comedians, musicians and artists, and theatre productions.

Sleeping

Arnie's Backpackers (☎ 9024 2867; www.arniesback packers.co.uk; 63 Fitzwilliam St; dm £7-9.50; ✗) This long-established, exceedingly friendly hostel is set in a quiet terraced house in the university area with plenty of lively bars and restaurants nearby. It's a bit on the cramped side, but lots of fun.

Ark (☎ 9032 9626; www.arkhostel.com; 18 University St; dm/s/d £9.50/20/32; ✗ 🖥) The Ark is a cosy, compact hostel in a pleasant terraced house in a quiet street. It's a good place to look for temporary work, and long-term accommodation is available.

Belfast International Youth Hostel (☎ 9032 4733, 9031 5435; www.hini.org.uk/hostels/belfast.cfm; 22-32 Donegall Rd; dm/s/d £9.50/17/26; **P** ✗ 🖥) HINI's 112-bed Belfast International is conveniently situated on the Golden Mile, but it can be a bit noisy at night when the pubs and clubs empty.

Camping options include **Dundonald Touring Caravan Park** (☎ 9080 9100; www.theicebowl.com; 111 Old Dundonald Rd; sites £7-13; ✆ Apr-Sep), in a park next to the Dundonald Icebowl, 7km east of the centre (bus No 21 from the Laganside Bus Centre).

Many B&Bs are in the university area, which is close to the centre, safe and well stocked with restaurants and pubs. Botanic Ave, Malone Rd, Wellington Park and Eglantine Ave are good hunting grounds.

Kate's B&B (☎ 9028 2091; katesbb127@hotmail .com; 127 University St; s/d £25/50) Friendly Kate's, in a lovingly restored 1860 town house, will make you feel right at home. Kate advertises her fried breakfast with 'go on – kill yourself!' Discounted weekly rates are available.

Pearl Court Guesthouse (☎ 9066 6145; pearlcourt gh@hotmail.com; 11 Malone Rd; s £25-35, d £52) Expect big bedrooms and bigger breakfasts at this elegantly old-fashioned B&B in a 200-year-old terraced house south of Queen's University. Six of the 10 rooms have *en suites*.

Eating

Café Paul Rankin (☎ 9031 5090; 27-29 Fountain St; snacks £2-5.25; ✆ 7.30am-5.30pm Mon-Sat, 7.30am-7.30pm Thu; ✗) Owned by Northern Ireland's top celebrity chef, this café serves quality coffee, focaccia, soups, pastas and salads, and has comfy benches and sofas for lounging on. Other locations are at 12 Upper Arthur St and Castle Court Centre.

White's Tavern (☎ 9024 3080; 1-4 Wine Cellar Entry; mains £6-7; ✆ food served noon-6pm Mon-Sat) Historic White's is a popular lunchtime meeting spot, serving down-to-earth pub food – fish dishes, Irish stew, and sausage and champ.

Other Place (☎ 9020 7200; 79 Botanic Ave; mains £7-10; ✆ 8am-10pm) Another student favourite, where you can linger over the Sunday paper amid red brick, orange pine and antiques, or get full on big plates of lasagne, Cajun pita or home-made hamburger.

Archana (☎ 9032 3713; 53 Dublin Rd; lunch £5-6, dinner £9-11; ✆ noon-2pm & 5.30-11pm Mon-Sat) A cosy Indian restaurant, Archana has a good lunch *thali* – a platter of two curries with rice and salad at £2.50/6 for the veggie/meat version.

Chokdee (☎ 9032 3211; 44 Bedford St; mains £6-12; ✆ 11am-11pm Mon-Sat, 4-10pm Sun) Cute little Chokdee (it means 'good luck' in Thai) serves up a variety of Asian-ish food in a stylish setting saturated with colour. It has plenty for vegetarians.

Nick's Warehouse (☎ 9043 9690; 34-39 Hill St; lunch £6-9, dinner £9-15; ✆ noon-3pm Mon-Fri, 6-9.30pm Tue-Sat) Nick's is a huge wine bar and restaurant buzzing with happy diners. The menu's full of inventive seafood and veggie dishes.

Drinking & Clubbing

Pubs are generally open until 11pm Monday to Saturday, though pubs with an entertainment licence stay open until 1am or 1.30am and to 11pm Sunday.

Eglantine (☎ 9038 1994; 32 Malone Rd) The 'Eg' is a local institution and widely reckoned to be the best of Belfast's student pubs. It serves good beer and food, and DJs spin most nights except Tuesday, which is quiz night.

Botanic Inn (☎ 9050 9740; 23-27 Malone Rd) The 'Bot' is the second pillar of Malone Rd's student pubs. It's a wild place, with dancing in the upstairs Record Club Wednesday to Saturday, live music downstairs Monday to Wednesday, and big-screen sport when there's a match on.

Milk (☎ 9027 8876; www.clubmilk.com; 10-14 Tomb St; cover £2-10) Milk, in a converted warehouse, is one of Belfast's hottest and most sophisticated clubs. Monday is gay night, with cabaret acts hosted by Baroness Titty Von Tramp.

Also recommended:

Crown Liquor Saloon (☎ 9024 9476; 46 Great Victoria St) Belfast's most famous bar, with a wonderfully ornate Victorian interior.

Robinsons (☎ 9024 7447; 38-40 Great Victoria St) A theme pub spread over four floors with music most nights.

Entertainment

The Belfast Welcome Centre issues *Whatabout?*, a free monthly guide to Belfast events. The website www.wheretotonight.com is another useful guide.

Queen's Film Theatre (☎ 0800 328 2811; www .qftbelfast.info; 20 University Sq) The QFT is a two-screen art-house cinema and a major venue for March's Belfast Film Festival.

Crescent Arts Centre (☎ 9024 2338; www.crescent arts.org; 2 University Rd) The Crescent puts on excellent concerts, New York jazz to top-rate Irish music. It also stages a literary festival each March, and a dance festival in June.

Other venues:

Grand Opera House (☎ 9024 1919; www.goh.co.uk; 2-4 Great Victoria St) Opera, ballet and comedy, among other things.

Waterfront Hall (☎ 9033 4400; www.waterfront.co.uk; Lanyon Pl) Belfast's enormous flagship concert venue.

Getting There & Away

For all Ulsterbus, Northern Ireland Railways (NIR) and local bus information, call **Translink** (☎ 9066 6630; www.translink.co.uk). The **NIR Travel Shop** (☎ 9023 0671, 9024 2420; Great Victoria St Station; ☽ 9am-5pm Mon-Fri, 9am-12.30pm Sat) can make bookings and provide information on trains, buses and ferries.

AIR

There are flights from some regional airports in Britain to the convenient **Belfast city airport** (☎ 9093 9093; www.belfastcityairport.com; Airport Rd), but everything else goes to **Belfast international airport** (☎ 9448 4848, 9442 2888; www.bial.co.uk), 30km north of the city in Aldergrove, by the M2.

BOAT

Three main ferry routes connect Belfast to Stranraer, Liverpool and the Isle of Man. See p607 for more details on ferries to/from Northern Ireland.

Steam Packet/SeaCat (☎ 0870 552 3523; www.sea cat.co.uk) catamaran car ferries dock at Donegall Quay, a short walk north of the city centre. **Norse Merchant Ferries** (☎ 9077 9090, 0870

600 4321; www.norsemerchant.com) to Liverpool leave from Victoria terminal, 5km north of central Belfast; take a bus from Europa Bus Centre or catch a taxi (£4). **Stena Line** (☎ 0870 570 7070; www.stenaline.co.uk) services to Stranraer leave from nearby Corry Rd.

BUS

The smaller of Belfast's two bus stations is the **Laganside Bus Centre** (Oxford St), with connections to counties Antrim, Down and Derry. Buses to everywhere else in Ireland and the Larne ferries leave from **Europa Bus Centre** (Glengall St).

Ulsterbus has buses to Dublin (£13, three hours, seven daily, six on Sunday) and Derry (£9, 1¾ hours, at least seven daily).

For general transport information in Northern Ireland, contact **Translink** (☎ 9066 6630; www.translink.co.uk).

TRAIN

Destinations served from **Belfast Central** (East Bridge St), east of the centre, include Derry and Dublin. Belfast–Dublin trains (£22/32 one way/return, two hours) run up to eight times a day (five on Sunday).

Great Victoria St Station has services to Derry (£8.20, 2¼ hours, every two hours) and Larne Harbour (£4.10, one hour, hourly).

Getting Around

A short trip on a bus costs £0.70 to £1.20. If you're driving, be fastidious about where you park; car theft is a problem here. The tourist office has a free leaflet showing all the multistorey car parks.

McConvey Cycles (☎ 9033 0322; www.mcconvey cycles.com; 182 Ormeau Rd) rents out bikes for £10/40 a day/week. A £50 deposit is required.

THE BELFAST–DERRY COASTAL ROAD

Ireland isn't short of fine stretches of coastline, but the Causeway Coast from Portstewart in County Derry to Ballycastle in County Antrim, and the Antrim Coast from Belfast to Ballycastle are as magnificent as they come.

From late May to late September, Ulsterbus's Antrim Coaster bus No 252 operates twice daily (except Sunday) between Belfast and Coleraine (four hours), stopping at all the main tourist sights. An open-topped Bushmills Bus (No 177) travels from the Giant's Causeway to Coleraine five times daily in July and August. It takes just over an hour. Bus No 172 runs year-round along the coast between Ballycastle and Portrush.

Carrickfergus

Only 13km northeast of Belfast is Carrickfergus and its impressive Norman **castle** (☎ 9335 1273; adult/concession £3/1.50; ☜ 10am-6pm Mon-Sat, 2-6pm Sun Apr-Sep, 10am-4pm Mon-Sat, 2-4pm Sun Oct-Mar), built in 1180 by John de Courcy and overlooking the harbour where William III landed in 1690.

Glens of Antrim

Between Larne and Ballycastle, the nine Glens of Antrim are extremely picturesque stretches of woodland and downland where streams cascade into the sea. **Glenariff** is 'Queen of the Glens', while the port of **Cushendall** has been dubbed the 'Capital of the Glens'. Between Cushendun and Ballycastle, eschew the main A2 road for the narrower and more picturesque B92, and take the turn-off down to sweeping Murlough Bay.

Good for a budget bed, and possibly a bedtime story, is the modern **Ballyeamon Camping Barn** (☎ 2175 8699; www.taleteam.demon.co.uk; dm £8-12; P ⊠ ☐) near Cushendall on the B14. The proprietor is a professional storyteller.

Carrick-a-Rede Island

A 20m **rope bridge** (☎ 2076 9839; admission £2; ☜ 10am-6pm Mar-Sep, closed in strong winds) connects Carrick-a-Rede Island to the mainland, swaying some 25m above pounding waves. The island is the site of a salmon fishery, and it's a nesting ground for gulls and fulmars.

Giant's Causeway (Clochán an Aifir)

It's easy to see why photographers love Northern Ireland's main tourist attraction. The hexagonal basalt columns, all 38,000 of them (counting the ones underwater) are amazingly uniform. Legend has it that the giant in question, Finn McCool, built the Causeway to get to Scottish rival giant Benandonner on the Scottish island of Staffa (which has similar rock formations). The more prosaic explanation is that lava erupted from an underground fissure and crystallised some 60 million years ago.

Bus No 172 runs about four times a day between Portrush and Ballycastle, passing by the Giant's Causeway.

A recommended walk is from the Giant's Causeway 16km east along the coast (not the highway), past Dunseverick Castle to the beach at Whitepark Bay. Be careful walking this route: the windy clifftop conditions have been known to send walkers over the edge. A great place to crash at the end is the terrific, modern HINI **Whitepark Bay Hostel** (☎ 2073 1745; dm/d £13/30; ☜ closed Dec-Feb; P ⊠).

Portstewart, Portrush & Downhill

These seaside resorts are only kilometres apart. The pleasant Portstewart has a slightly decayed, early-20th-century feel, while Downhill has a lovely long stretch of beach.

Portstewart's friendly **Causeway Coast Hostel** (☎ 7083 3789; 4 Victoria Tce; dm/s £8/12, d £20-24; ⊠) is at the eastern end of town. The Belfast–Portrush bus, No 218, stops 100m away.

Harder to get to, but well worth the effort, is the **Downhill Hostel** (☎ 7084 9077; www.downhillhostel.com; 12 Mussenden Rd; dm/d £8/25; P ⊠), a lovely converted period house on the beach with open fires. Pick-ups can be arranged from Castlerock train station. The No 134 Coleraine–Limavady bus also passes nearby.

DERRY (DOIRE)
pop 83,100

Derry or Londonderry? In practice, it's better known as Derry, whatever your politics. Doire means 'oak grove' in Irish, and the 'London' was added after settlers were granted much of the land in the area by James I.

In the 1960s, resentment at Protestant domination of the city council boiled over in the civil rights marches of 1968. The UK government sent British troops into Derry a year later, following fighting between police and local youths in the poor Catholic Bogside district. This tension came to a head in January 1972, when the British army killed 13 unarmed Catholic civil rights marchers in Derry, and 'Bloody Sunday' marked the beginning of the Troubles in earnest.

Today Derry is as safe to visit as anywhere in Northern Ireland. Its dramatic history is still palpable – in the 17th-century city walls, in the captivating Bogside murals – but it's also a laid-back place with a reputation for musical excellence and a lively arts scene.

Orientation

The old centre of Derry is the small, walled city on the west bank of the Foyle River. The heart of the walled city is the Diamond, intersected by Shipquay St, Ferryquay St, Bishop

---

GETTING INTO TOWN

A free Linkline shuttle bus connects Derry's Waterside train station, across the Foyle River from the centre, with the bus station. From there, follow Foyle St towards the Guildhall and edge along the outside of the town walls towards pedestrianised Waterloo Pl. Continue down Strand Rd; the hostels and B&Bs all have their check-in points on Great James St, off Strand Rd.

St Within and Butcher St. The Catholic Bogside area is below the walls to the northwest. To the south is a Protestant estate called the Fountain. The Waterside district across the river is mostly Protestant.

Information

Bean-there.com (☎ 7128 1303; 20 the Diamond; per hr £3.50; ☒ 8.30am-5.30pm Mon-Fri, 10am-5.30pm Sat) Internet access, plus snacks and coffee.

Derry Visitor & Convention Bureau (☎ 7126 7284; www.derryvisitor.com; ☒ 9am-7pm Mon-Fri, 10am-6pm Sat, 10am-5pm Sun, shorter hr rest of year) Handles all of Northern Ireland and the Republic as well as Derry.

Main post office (Custom House St) Just north of the Tower Museum.

Sights & Activities

Derry's magnificent **city walls**, built between 1613 and 1618, encircle the old city for 1.5km and make for a fantastic walk; the gates give an excellent view of Bogside (itself worth a closer look on foot) and its defiant **murals**, one notably proclaiming 'You Are Now Entering Free Derry'.

Just inside Coward's Bastion to the north, O'Doherty's Tower is home to the excellent **Tower Museum** (☎ 7137 2411; tower.museum@derrycity .gov.uk; admission £4.20; ☒ 10am-5pm Mon-Sat, 2-5pm Sun Jul & Aug, 10am-5pm Tue-Sat Sep-Jun), which traces the story of Derry from the days of St Columbcille to the present. At the time of writing, the museum was being expanded to include an interactive Spanish Armada exhibition; and a modified Story of Derry exhibition was up at the **Harbour Museum** (☎ 7137 7331; Harbour Sq; admission free; ☒ 10am-1pm & 2-4.30pm Mon-Fri).

The fine redbrick **Guildhall** (☎ 7137 7335; admission free; ☒ 9am-5pm Mon-Fri) was originally built in 1890, just outside the city walls, and is noted for its stained-glass windows. Austere **St Columb's Cathedral** (☎ 7126 7313; requested donation £1; ☒ 9am-5pm Mon-Sat Apr-Oct, 9am-4pm Nov-Mar) dates from 1628 and stands at the southern end of the walled city.

Sleeping

Derry City Independent Hostel (Steve's Backpackers; ☎ 7137 7989; www.derryhostel.com; 44 Great James St; dm/d £10/28; ☒ 🖳) It's a little cramped but funky and fun, with an eating nook covered in Indian paintings and pillows. There's no checkout time, and a light breakfast and free Internet access are included in rates. Steve also runs **Derry Backpackers** (Steve's Backpackers; ☎ 7137 7989; www.derryhostel.com; 4 Asylum Rd, check in at 44 Great James St; dm/d £10/28; ☒ 🖳), a smaller place in a quieter spot a little further from the walled city. Be sure to book ahead.

Saddler's House (☎ 7126 9691; www.thesaddlers house.com; 36 Great James St; s/d £27.50/45; 🅿 ☒) Centrally located a few minutes' from the walled city, this friendly place is set in a lovely Victorian town house. Its sister B&B, **Merchant's House** (16 Queen St; s £20-27.50, d £40-45) is in a Georgian-style town house around the corner. Both are extremely comfortable and artfully decorated with antiques and *objets*.

Eating

An Bácús (☎ 7126 4678; 37 Great James St; soups & sandwiches £1.50-2.50; ☒ 7.30am-5pm Mon-Fri, 9am-5pm Sat) The bilingual menu at this little Irish-language café is a little confusing, but you'll learn the Irish word for egg (ubh).

Ramsey's (William St; mains £1-3; ☒ 8-12am) Greasy Ramsey's is doing it old-school diner style, dishing out cheap burgers and fish and chips in a setting that probably hasn't changed in 25 years.

Lloyd's No 1 Bar/Ice Wharf (☎ 7127 6610; 22 Strand St; mains £5-7; ☒ 10am-10pm Mon-Sat) Big, bustling Lloyd's serves a meat or veggie fried breakfast, tasty bar snacks, hearty meals like steaks and pastas, and a range of veggie dishes.

Entertainment

Mullan's Bar (☎ 7126 5300; 13 Little James St) Has jazz, blues and traditional music on Wednesday and Thursday nights.

Peadar O'Donnell's (☎ 7126 2318; 63 Waterloo St) Puts on traditional sessions every night around 11pm.

Sandino's (☎ 7130 9297; 1 Water St) The alternative Latin American–themed venue Sandino's is popular with up-and-coming bands and visiting musicians.

Derry has several theatres. The newest and spiffiest is the **Millennium Forum** (☎ 7126 4455; www.millenniumforum.co.uk; New Market St), with several performance spaces for theatre, dance, comedy and concerts.

Getting There & Away

From the **bus station** (☎ 7126 2261; Foyle St) just outside the city walls, Ulsterbus's No 212, the *Maiden City Flyer*, is the fastest service to Belfast (£8.60, 1¾ hours, every 30 minutes, six daily on Sundays). Bus No 234 runs to Portrush and Portstewart in July and August (£6.50, 1½ hours, four daily). At least four buses a day head to Dublin (£12.80, 4¼ hours). **Lough Swilly Bus Service** (☎ 7126 2017), with an office at the Ulsterbus station, serves County Donegal.

Air Porter Buses (☎ 7126 9996; www.airporter .co.uk) runs eight daily services (four at weekends) between Belfast airport and Derry's Quayside Shopping Centre for £15.

Linkline buses head to **Waterside train station** (☎ 7134 2228) 15 minutes before each train departure. Trains run daily to Belfast (£8.20, three hours, nine Monday to Saturday, four on Sunday) via Portrush.

IRELAND DIRECTORY

ACCOMMODATION

Booking ahead is essential in peak season. **Fáilte Ireland** (Irish Tourist Board; www.ireland.ie) will book accommodation for a 10% room deposit and a fee of €4. The **Northern Ireland Tourist Board** (NITB; www.discovernorthernireland.com) books accommodation at no cost with a 10% room deposit. Accommodation for the Republic and the North may also be booked online, via the **Gulliver booking service** (www.gulliver.ie). A deposit of 10% and a €4 fee is payable.

All accommodation prices in this chapter are high-season rates (generally June to August); at other times of year, subtract 15% to 25% from the listed prices.

For disabled travellers, Fáilte Ireland's various accommodation guides indicate which places are wheelchair accessible, and the NITB publishes *Accessible Accommodation in Northern Ireland*.

Camping & Hostels

Fáilte Ireland's caravan and camping guide costs €4; the NITB has a similar publication.

Commercial camping grounds charge €12 to €18 for a tent and two people, and some hostels also have space for tents.

Hostels in Ireland can be heavily booked in summer. **An Óige** (☎ 01-830 4555; www.anoige .ie; 61 Mountjoy St, Dublin 7), meaning 'youth', and **Hostelling International Northern Ireland** (HINI; ☎ 028-9032 4733; www.hini.org.uk; 22-32 Donegall Rd, Belfast BT12 5JN) are branches of Hostelling International (HI); An Óige has 33 hostels in the Republic, while HINI administers another seven in the North. Other hostel associations include **Independent Holiday Hostels** (IHH; ☎ 01-836 4700; www.hostels-ireland.com; 57 Lower Gardiner St, Dublin 1), a cooperative group with about 120 hostels, and the **Independent Hostels Owners in Ireland** (IHO; ☎ 074-973 0130; www.holidayhound.com/ihi; Dooey Hostel, Glencolumbcille, County Donegal) association, which has more than 100 members around Ireland.

From June to September, nightly costs at most hostels are €15-20, except for the more expensive hostels in Dublin, Belfast and a few other places.

B&Bs

The bed and breakfast is as Irish a form of accommodation as there is. It sometimes seems that every other house is a B&B, and you'll stumble upon them in the most unusual and remote locations. Typical costs are around €35 per person a night, though more luxurious B&Bs can cost from €55 or more per person. Most B&Bs are small, so in summer they can quickly fill up.

ACTIVITIES

Ireland is a great place for outdoor activities, and the tourist boards put out a wide selection of information sheets covering bird-watching (County Donegal), surfing (great along the west coast), scuba diving (West Cork), climbing, fishing, ancestor tracing, horse riding, canoeing and many other activities.

Walking is particularly popular, but you must come prepared for wet weather. There are now well over 20 way-marked trails, varying in length from the 26km Cavan Way to the 900km Ulster Way.

EMBASSIES & CONSULATES
Embassies & Consulates in Ireland

Countries with diplomatic offices in Dublin: **Australia** (☎ 01-676 1517; www.australianembassy.ie; 2nd fl, Fitzwilton House, Wilton Tce)

Canada (☎ 01-478 1988; www.canada.ie; 4th fl, 65-68 St Stephen's Green)

France (☎ 01-277 5000; www.ambafrance.ie; 36 Ailesbury Rd)

Germany (☎ 01-269 3011; www.germanembassy.ie; 31 Trimleston Ave, Booterstown)

Netherlands (☎ 01-269 3444; www.netherlands embassy.ie; 160 Merrion Rd)

New Zealand (☎ 01-660 4233; 37 Leeson Park)

UK (☎ 01-205 3700; www.britishembassy.ie; 29 Merrion Rd, Ballsbridge)

USA (☎ 01-668 7122; http://dublin.usembassy.gov; 42 Elgin Rd, Ballsbridge)

In Northern Ireland, nationals of most countries should contact their embassy in London (see p220). Consulates in the North:

Netherlands (☎ 028-9038 0223; fax 028-9037 1104; 14-16 West Bank Rd, Belfast, BT3 9JL)

USA (☎ 028-9038 6100; www.americanembassy.org.uk; Danesfort House, 223 Stranmillis Rd, Belfast BT9 5GR)

Irish Embassies & Consulates Abroad

Australia (☎ 02-6273 3022; irishemb@cyberone .com.au; 20 Arkana St, Yarralumla, ACT 2600) There is also a consulate in Sydney.

Canada (☎ 613-233 6281; embassyofireland@ rogers.com; 130 Albert St, Suite 1105, Ottawa, Ontario K1P 5G4)

France (☎ 01 44 17 67 00; paris@iveagh.irlgov.ie; 4 rue de Paris, 75116 Paris)

Germany (☎ 030-220 720; Friedrichstrasse 200, D-10117 Berlin)

Netherlands (☎ 070-363 09 93; www.irishembassy.nl; Dr Kuyperstraat 9, 2514 BA Den Haag)

New Zealand (☎ 09-977 2252; consul@ireland.co.nz; 6th fl, 18 Shortland St, 1001 Auckland)

UK (☎ 020-7235 2171; 17 Grosvenor Pl, London SW1X 7HR) There are also consulates in Edinburgh and Cardiff.

USA (☎ 202-462 3939; 2234 Massachusetts Ave NW, Washington DC 20008-2849) Boston, Chicago, New York and San Francisco have consulates.

FESTIVALS & EVENTS

St Patrick's Day (17 March) Celebrations of the national saint's day include parades in Dublin, Cork and Belfast (see p44).

Dublin International Film Festival (www.dubliniff .com) April.

Bloomsday (16 June) In Dublin, Leopold Bloom's Joycean journey around the city is marked by various events.

Marching season (Northern Ireland only; July) Orange-men (Unionists) march through the streets to celebrate historic victories, especially the Battle of the Boyne in 1690, on the 'glorious 12th'.

Galway Arts Festival (www.galwayartsfestival.com) Two-week extravaganza of theatre, comedy, music, arts and partying every July (see p626).

Kilkenny Arts Festival (www.kilkennyarts.ie) Theatre, music, literature, visual arts and outdoor activities for 10 days in August.

The All-Ireland hurling and football finals (September) In Dublin.

Galway Oyster Festival (www.galwayoysterfest.com) Thousands come every autumn for the oysters and the shucking competitions.

Belfast Festival (www.belfastfestival.com) The UK's second-largest arts festival held in and around Queen's University each November.

FOOD & DRINK

Irish B&B breakfasts almost inevitably include 'a fry', that heart attack on a plate that consists of fried eggs, bacon, sausages, the ubiquitous black pudding (a blood sausage) and tomatoes as well as toast and butter. A bowl of the day's soup with brown bread can be an inexpensive lunch. Traditional meals (like Irish stew, often found in pubs) are also cheap and hearty.

In Ireland a drink means a beer, either lager or stout. Stout is usually Guinness, the famous black beer of Dublin, although in Cork it can mean a Murphy's or a Beamish. Simply asking for a Guinness will get you a pint (570ml); if you want a half-pint, ask for a 'glass' or a 'half'.

Listening to music in a pub while nursing a Guinness is a popular form of entertainment in Ireland. If someone suggests visiting a pub for its good *craic*, it means a good time, convivial company, sparkling conversation and scintillating music. In the Republic, cigarettes are *not* part of the mix: smoking in all public places was banned in March 2004.

HOLIDAYS

Public holidays in the Irish Republic, Northern Ireland or both:

New Year's Day 1 January

St Patrick's Day 17 March

Easter (Good Friday to Easter Monday, inclusive) March/April

May Holiday 1 May

Christmas Day 25 December

St Stephen's Day (Boxing Day) 26 December

NORTHERN IRELAND

Spring Bank Holiday Last Monday in May

Orangemen's Day 12 July

August Bank Holiday 1st Monday in August

IRISH REPUBLIC
June Holiday 1st Monday in June
August Holiday 1st Monday in August
October Holiday Last Monday in October

MONEY

The Irish Republic is part of the euro zone, while Northern Ireland uses the British pound sterling (£). Banks offer the best exchange rates; exchange bureaus, open longer, have worse rates and commissions. Post offices generally have exchange facilities and open on Saturday morning. In Northern Ireland several banks issue their own Northern Irish pound notes, which are equivalent to sterling but not readily accepted in Britain.

Costs

Ireland is an expensive place, marginally more costly than Britain, but prices vary. Entry prices to sights and museums are usually 20% to 50% lower for children, students and senior citizens (OAPs).

For the budget traveller, €65 per day should cover hostel accommodation, getting around and a meal in a restaurant, leaving just enough for a pint at the end of the day.

Tipping

Fancy hotels and restaurants add a 10% or 15% service charge onto the bill. Simpler places usually don't add service; if you decide to tip, just round up the bill (or add 10% at most). Taxi drivers do not have to be tipped, but if you're feeling flush, 10% is generous.

POST

The post offices (An Post) throughout the Republic are open from 9am to 5.30pm Monday to Friday, and from 9am to 1pm Saturday; smaller offices close for lunch.

Letters weighing less than 50g cost €0.60 to Britain and €0.65 to continental Europe and the rest of the world.

Post offices in Northern Ireland are open 9am to 5pm Monday to Friday and till noon on Saturday. First-class mail is quicker and more expensive (28p per letter) than 2nd-class mail (21p). Postcards sent overseas cost 40p (Europe) or 43p (outside Europe).

Mail can be addressed to poste restante at post offices, but is officially held for only two weeks. Writing 'hold for collection' on the envelope may help.

TELEPHONE

Local telephone calls from a public phone in the Republic cost €0.25 for around three minutes (around €0.50 to a mobile). In Northern Ireland a local call costs a minimum of £0.20. Some payphones in the North take euros. Pre-paid phonecards by Eircom or private operators, available in newsagencies and post offices, work from all payphones and dispense with the need for coins.

The mobile (cell) phone network in Ireland runs on the GSM 900/1800 system, compatible with the rest of Europe and Australia, but not the USA.

To call Northern Ireland from the Republic, you do not use ☎ 0044 as for the rest of the UK. Instead, you dial ☎ 048 and then the local number.

TOURIST INFORMATION

The Irish tourist board, **Fáilte Ireland** (www .ireland.ie), and the **Northern Ireland Tourist Board** (NITB; www.discovernorthernireland.com) operate separate offices. Both are well organised and helpful, though Fáilte Ireland won't provide any information on places (such as B&Bs and camping grounds) that it hasn't approved. Every town big enough to have a few pubs will certainly have a tourist office, although smaller ones may close in winter. Most will find you a place to stay for a fee of €2 to €4.

Tourism Ireland (www.tourismireland.com) handles tourist information for both tourist boards overseas.

Tourist Offices Abroad

Australia (☎ 02-9299 6177; 5th fl, 36 Carrington St, Sydney, NSW 2000)
Canada (☎ 1 800 223 6470; 2 Bloor St W, Suite 3403, Toronto M4W 3E2)
New Zealand (☎ 09-977 2255; Level 6, 18 Shortland St, Private Bag, 92136 Auckland)
UK (☎ 0800 039 7000; Nations House, 103 Wigmore St, London W1U 1QS)
USA (☎ 1 800 223 6470; 345 Park Ave, New York, NY 10154)

VISAS

Citizens of the EU and other Western countries don't need a visa to visit either the Republic or Northern Ireland. EU nationals are allowed to stay indefinitely, while other visitors can remain for three to six months.

UK nationals born in Britain or Northern Ireland do not need a passport, but should carry some form of identification.

IRELAND

ITALY

Italy

HIGHLIGHTS

- **Naples** This edgy city and its sparkling bay is sure to elicit strong emotions (p699)
- **Aeolian Islands** Aquamarine coves and a steaming volcano create a traveller's idyll (p710)
- **Venice** Little matches the beauty, and teeth-grinding frustration, of stunning Venice where boats jostle chintzy gondolas, and the pigeons are outnumbered by the tourists (p671)
- **Ancient Rome** More than 2500 years of visible archaeological and anthropological history will leave you awestruck (p647)
- **Best journey** Italy has some of the word's best cycling. Tuscany and Umbria have classic, vineyard-laced routes: take a one-day trip with www.bicycletuscany.com (p685)
- **Off-the-beaten track** Proud Puglia has crowd-free coastline, delicious cuisine and baroque treasures in delightful Lecce (p707)

FAST FACTS

- **Area** 301,230 sq km (around half the size of Ukraine)
- **ATMs** Readily available throughout the country
- **Budget** €60-100 per day
- **Capital** Rome
- **Country code** ☎ 39, international code ☎ 00
- **Famous for** emperors, gladiators, gelato, pasta, wine, Renaissance art, racing cars
- **Head of State** President Carlo Azeglio
- **Language** Italian
- **Money** euro (A$1 = €0.58, C$1 = €0.64, ¥100 = €0.73, NZ$1 = €0.54, UK£1 = €1.45, US$ = €0.81)
- **Phrases** *buongiorno* (hello), *grazie* (thanks), *mi scusi* (excuse me), *come si chiama?* (what's your name?), *prego* (that's fine), *sogni d'oro* (dreams of gold)

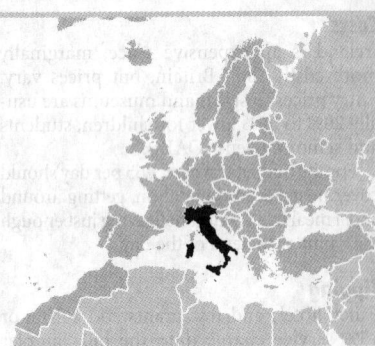

- **Population** 57.8 million
- **Time** GMT/UTC + 1
- **Visas** Citizens from many countries, including the USA, Australia, Canada and New Zealand, don't need visas to enter Italy as tourists; a *permesso di soggiorno* is necessary if you plan to study, work or live in Italy. EU citizens with a passport or national identity card can stay as long as they like.

TRAVEL HINTS

Dress the part by wearing modest dress in churches and a sassy pair of shades on the street. You can snack for free by ordering a drink, and often receiving a complimentary bowls of olives, chips and nuts. For discount fares try www.volareweb.com, Italy's no-frills, multilanguage travel site.

ROAMING ITALY

Start at Rome, before heading to Florence. Make a Tuscan detour to Siena, San Gimignano and Pienza. With more time, visit Naples and make forays to the Amalfi Coast.

ITALY

0 — 100 km
0 — 60 miles

GERMANY
Munich
VIENNA

FRANCE
Basel
Zurich
Lucerne
BERN
SWITZERLAND
VADUZ
LIECHTENSTEIN
Innsbruck
AUSTRIA
BUDAPEST
HUNGARY

Mont Blanc (4807m)
Courmayeur
Aosta
VALLE D'AOSTA
Verbania
Sondrio
Bolzano
TRENTINO-ALTOADIGE
Trent
Belluno
FRIULI-VENEZIA GIULIA
SLOVENIA
LJUBLJANA
Trieste
ZAGREB
SERBIA & MONTENEGRO

FRANCE
Monviso (3841m)
Turin
PIEDMONT
Alessandria
Cuneo
LOMBARDY
Brescia
Milan
Vicenza
Verona
VENETO
Padua
Venice
Gulf of Venezia
Rijeka
Karlovac
CROATIA
BanjaLuka
BOSNIA HERZEGOVINA
SARAJEVO

Nice
LIGURIA
Imperia
Savona
Genoa
Piacenza
Parma
Mantua
Modena
EMILIA-ROMAGNA
Bologna
Ferrara
Ravenna
Zadar
Split

Ligurian Sea
Gulf of Genova
La Spezia
Lucca
Pisa
Pistoia
Florence
Forlì
Cesena
Rimini
SAN MARINO
Pesaro
Urbino
Ancona
ADRIATIC SEA

MONACO
Livorno
TUSCANY
Siena
Arezzo
Gubbio
LE MARCHE
Assisi
Perugia
UMBRIA
Dubrovnik
To Greece, Turkey & Albania

Capraia
Piombino
Grosseto
Spoleto
L'Aquila
Pescara
Chieti

Elba
Viterbo
LAZIO
ABRUZZO
Promontorio del Gargano

CORSICA
Civitavecchia
Fiumicino
Lido di Ostia
ROME
Frosinone
MOLISE
Campobasso
Foggia

Latina
Gulf of Gaeta
CAMPANIA
Vesuvio (1277m)
Benevento
Avellino
Andria
Bari
To Greece
APULIA

Asinara
Porto Torres
Olbia
Golfo Aranci
Naples
Ischia
Pompeii
Salerno
Potenza
Matera
Taranto
Brindisi

Sassari
Alghero
Bosa
Nuoro
Dorgali
Capri
Gulf of Salerno
Paestum
BASILICATA
Lecce

Oristano
SARDINIA
Arbatax
Gulf of Taranto
Otranto
Gallipoli

Cagliari
Sant'Antioco
Tyrrhenian Sea
Cosenza
CALABRIA
Catanzaro
Crotone
Capo Rizzuto

AEOLIAN ISLANDS
Salina
Stromboli
Gulf of Squillace
Ionic Sea

Filicudi
Alicudi
Panarea
Lipari
Vulcano
Milazzo
Messina
Reggio di Calabria

Trapani
Palermo
Mt Etna (3350m)
Taormina

Marsala
Cefalù
Catania

SICILY
Agrigento
Syracuse

ALGERIA
TUNIS
Ragusa
MEDITERRANEAN SEA

Pantelleria

TUNISIA
MALTA
Valletta

ITALY

Rare is the traveller who isn't smitten by Italy. Everyone loves the Italians – their quirky, outspoken zest for life, and their gorgeous country and rich culture. Teeming with ancient history, artistic splendour, divine food and wine, and a romantic olive-grove dappled landscape, Italy hits the heart and soul fast. It's an intoxicating place, with raw beauty and simple *passione*, but also rough around the edges, frustrating at times and exceptionally humorous.

From dazzling Renaissance and baroque masterpieces, to stunning natural beauty, Italy offers tangible pleasures to all. Whether you're cycling through Tuscany, ancient ruins–hopping through Rome, sunning on the Amalfi coast, or trekking in the Dolomites, the cities and landscapes will undoubtedly enrapture you, and a first visit soon grows into an unquenchable thirst for more. Natural and historic beauties aside, modern Italy is exceptionally vibrant and simmers with a hedonistic passion – for food and wine, football (soccer) and women, the everyday happenings of *la dolce vita*. But if you come looking for efficient systems, fast-paced living and a low-carb menu, best leave your expectations and diets at the border. It's a moveable feast – prepare to indulge yourself.

HISTORY

According to ancient mythology, Romulus (who was reared by a she-wolf along with his brother Remus) founded Rome in 753 BC. In fact, the country had already been inhabited by Italic tribes since around 2000 BC. From 900 BC the Etruscan civilisation developed; the Romans overwhelmed the last Etruscan city at the end of the 3rd century BC.

The new Roman republic expanded into southern Italy and claimed Sicily after the Second Punic War in 241 BC. Rome defeated Carthage in 202 BC and claimed Spain as well as Greece. Under Julius Caesar, Rome conquered Gaul and Egypt. After Caesar's assassination, Caesar's adopted son Octavius defeated rivals Mark Antony and Cleopatra, establishing the Roman Empire in 27 BC and adopting the title of Augustus Caesar. Emperor Constantine heralded in Christianity, and in AD 330 moved the Empire to Byzantium (Constantinople), soon to be sacked by the Goths and Vandals. Over the next few centuries, Huns and Arabs moved into the region from the south.

Italy's Middle Ages were marked by the development of powerful city-states in the north. In the 15th century, the Renaissance fostered artistic geniuses like Donatello, Botticelli, Leonardo da Vinci, Raphael and Michelangelo. By the early 16th century much of Italy was under Austrian Habsburg rule. After Napoleon's invasion in 1796, a degree of unity was introduced for the first time in centuries. In the 1860s the unification movement (The Risorgimento) gained momentum, thanks in part to patriots Giuseppe Mazzini and Giuseppe Garibaldi. In 1861 the Kingdom of Italy was declared under the rule of King Vittorio Emanuele.

In 1921, Benito Mussolini's Fascist Party took control. Mussolini was a German ally in WWII; he was killed by Italian partisans in April 1945.

Italy was a founding member of the European Economic Community in 1957. The country enjoyed economic growth for a while, but the 1990s heralded a period of crisis, both economically and politically. National bribery scandals rocked the nation. A programme of fiscal austerity was needed to usher in Italy's entry into the EMU. Italy also moved decisively against the Sicilian Mafia, prompted by the 1992 assassinations of prominent anti-Mafia judges.

Since 2001, media magnate Silvio Berlusconi has been prime minister, with his right-wing Forza Italia party. His tenure thus far has disappointed many and been marred by continued allegations of corruption.

READING UP

For historical background, scoop up the *Concise History of Italy* by Vincent Cronin, and Giuseppe Tomasi di Lampudesa's modern classic, *The Leopard*.

Charles Richards' *The New Italians* offers a fascinating look at modern Italian life. EM Forster's *A Room with a View* gorgeously portrays Florence's romantic appeal, while George Negus' *The World from Italy: Football, Food and Politics*, is a light-hearted look at the country's charm.

PEOPLE & CULTURE

Despite the legendary reputation of Italians as impassioned, fiery individuals who drive with abandon, ooze charm, wear their hearts on their sleeve and feast daily on sinfully good food and wine – they are vigorously proud and sensitive. Scratch the stylish veneer and get to know Italy's remarkably diverse and welcoming inhabitants. Italians are fiercely protective of their home towns, of regional dialects and cuisine. Yet when faced with a foreigner, they exude more of a national pride, making those strong regional distinctions harder to discern.

Italians are supremely family oriented, and *nonne* (grandmothers) are downright revered – there's even a 'coolest granny' title doled out annually (the most recent winner beat the competition by dancing a barefoot *tarantella*).

ARTS

Italy has often been called a living museum. Art is everywhere as you walk through Italian cities. The 15th and early 16th centuries saw one of the most remarkable explosions of artistic and literary achievement in recorded history – il Rinascimento (the Renaissance).

LITERATURE

Before Dante wrote his *Divina Commedia* (Divine Comedy), Latin was the language of writers. Among ancient Rome's greatest writers were Cicero, Virgil, Ovid and Petronius. Petrarch (1304–74) was a contemporary of Dante's. Giovanni Boccaccio (1313–75), author of the *Decameron*, is considered the first Italian novelist. Machiavelli's (1469–1527) *The Prince*, a dark study of political power, has proved a lasting volume.

Italy's richest contribution to modern literature has been in the novel and short story. Umberto Eco's (b. 1932) best-known work, *The Name of the Rose*, is a highbrow murder mystery. Both Italo Calvino (1923–85), who penned *If on a Winter's Night a Traveller*, and Primo Levi (1919–87), whose works include *Se Questo é un Uomo* (If This is a Man), are brilliant Italian authors.

MUSIC

Italian artists have had a dominant place in the realms of opera and instrumental music. Antonio Vivaldi (1675–1741) created the concerto in its present form. Verdi, Puccini, Bellini, Donizetti and Rossini, composers from the 19th and early 20th centuries, are all stars of the modern operatic era. Tenor Luciano Pavarotti (b. 1935) has recently had his crown as 'King of Mother's Day CD Sales' taken by Andrea Bocelli (b. 1958).

ARCHITECTURE, PAINTING & SCULPTURE

Patronised by the Medici family in Florence and the popes in Rome, painters, sculptors, architects and writers flourished during the Renaissance. The High Renaissance (about 1490–1520) was dominated by three men – Leonardo da Vinci (1452–1519), Michelangelo Buonarrotti (1475–1564) and Raphael (1483–1520). The baroque period (17th century) was characterised by sumptuous architecture and richly decorative painting and sculpture. In Rome there are innumerable works by the great baroque sculptor and architect Gianlorenzo Bernini (1598–1680) and many by Michelangelo Merisi da Caravaggio (1573–1610). Neoclassicism produced the sculptor Canova (1757–1822).

Of Italy's modern artists, Amedeo Modigliani (1884–1920) is most famous. The early 20th century also produced the futurists, who rejected the sentimental art of the past and were infatuated by new technology, including modern warfare. Fascism produced its own style of architecture, characterised by the EUR satellite city and the work of Marcello Piacentini (1881–1960).

SPORT

Football (soccer) is a national passion, and Italy's club teams traditionally do well in European tournaments. Check newspapers for details of who's playing where. In May, the *Gazzetta dello Sport* sponsors the Giro d'Italia, held annually since 1909. This multistage bicycle race covers a great swathe of the countryside and draws legions of fans. Italy hosts two major motor races each year: the Italian Formula 1 Grand Prix in September at Monza, and the San Marino Grand Prix in May at Imola. Local luxury car manufacturer Ferrari bankrolls the long-time favourite team.

RELIGION

To most foreigners, Italy is synonymous with Catholicism. Just under 85% of Italians profess to be Catholic. While millions of people still flock to Rome to catch a glimpse of the Pope each year, the role of religion has lessened in recent years, with more attention on the formalities than actual faith. Still, first communions, church weddings and

TOP FIVE ITALY

- **Festival** Join in the excitement of Siena's Il Palio (p718), the famous horse race around the town's main piazza

- **Walk** Explore the five tiny villages clustered along some eye-popping Unesco-protected coastline in the Cinque Terre (p663)

- **Bar** Have a cocktail at Vineria (p659) in Rome's Campo de'Fiori

- **Impressive sight** Visit a volcano in the Aeolian Islands (p710)

- **Alpine views** Check out the stunning scenery of the Dolomites (p683)

regular feast days are an integral part of daily life, and pilgrimages continue to be big business.

There are also about 700,000 Muslims, 400,000 evangelical Protestants, 350,000 Jehovah's Witnesses, and smaller numbers of Jews and Buddhists.

ENVIRONMENT

Boot-shaped Italy incorporates Sicily and Sardinia and is bound by the Adriatic, Ligurian, Tyrrhenian, Ionian and Mediterranean Seas. Around 75% of the peninsula is mountainous, with the Alps dividing the country from France, Switzerland and Austria, and the Apennines forming a backbone that extends from the Alps into Sicily. Italy has 20 national parks, with several more planned.

Not known for environmental awareness, Italy's major cities, and much of the industrialised north, suffer from air pollution, attributed to high car usage. Aesthetically, the result of industrious humankind is not always displeasing – much of Tuscany's beauty lies in the mazing of olive groves with vineyards. But centuries of tree clearing, combined with illegal building, have led to severe land degradation and erosion woes. New laws are extending environmental protection.

Italy also has its share of natural hazards, including flood-induced landslides, mud-flows, earthquakes and volcanic eruptions.

FOOD & DRINK

Italian cuisine features distinct regional and seasonal variations. While Tuscan cooking is simple with fresh flavours, dishes in the south tend to be more complex and spicier. Vegetarians won't have a problem in Italy.

A full meal consists of an antipasto, such as *bruschetta* (grilled bread with toppings), followed by the *primo piatto*, a pasta dish, and the *secondo piatto*, meat or fish. Next comes an *insalata* (salad) or *contorni* (vegetable) before finishing with *dolci* (sweets) and *caffé* (coffee).

Italian wine is delicious and a drinkable bottle costs as little as €7. In Tuscany, sample Chianti, *sangiovese* and *brunello* for reds, *vernaccia* for white; Piedmont produces excellent Barolo, Sicily terrific *nero di avola*, and crisp *vermentino* hails from Sardinia and Liguria. Peroni is the national *birra;* for a draught, order it *alla spinna.*

TRANSPORT

GETTING THERE & AWAY
Air

The national airline is **Alitalia** (www.alitalia.it), with **Meridiana** (www.meridiana.it) and **Air One** (www.flyairone.it) offering additional domestic service. There's been an increase in low-cost carriers servicing Italy, particularly for European travellers, including **Ryanair** (www.ryanair.com) and **easyJet** (www.easyjet.com). Also check out Italy's travel portal on www .volareweb.com for good deals. Italy's main intercontinental gateway is the **Leonardo da Vinci Airport** (Fiumicino; ☎ 06 659 51; www.adr.it) in Rome, but regular intercontinental flights also serve Milan's **Linate Airport** (☎ 02 748 52 200; www.sea-aeroportimilano.it).

Boat

Ferries connect Italy to Spain, Croatia, Greece, Turkey, Tunisia and Malta. There are also services to Corsica (from Livorno) and Albania (from Bari and Ancona). See Brindisi on p707 for ferries to/from Greece), Ancona on p698 (to/from Greece, Albania and Croatia), Venice on p680 (to/from Greece) and Sicily on p708 (to/from Malta and Tunisia).

Bus

Eurolines (www.eurolines.com) has offices in all major European cities. The multilingual website gives details of prices, passes and travel agencies where you can book tickets. In

Italy, the main represented bus company is **Lazzi** (Florence Map pp686-7; ☎ 055 35 10 61; Piazza Adua 1 Rome ☎ 06 884 08 40; Via Tagliamento 27b). Buses leave from Rome, Florence, Milan, Turin, Venice and Naples, as well as other Italian towns, for major cities throughout Europe.

Eurojet (Map p654; ☎ 06 474 28 01; Piazza della Repubblica 54) runs services from Rome to Bari, Brindisi, Sorrento, the Amalfi Coast and Pompeii, as well as to Matera.

Car & Motorcycle

To rent a car or motorcycle, you'll need a valid EU driving licence, an International Driving Permit, or your driving licence from your own country. If you're driving your own car, you'll need an international insurance certificate, known as a Carta Verde (Green Card), which can be obtained from your insurer.

Train

Eurostar (ES; ☎ 0870 518 6186; www.eurostar.com) trains run from major destinations throughout Europe direct to major Italian cities. On overnight hauls, you can book a couchette for around €25. Travellers aged under 26 can take advantage of the Inter-Rail pass, Eurail Pass Youth and Europass Youth. For price and purchasing details, visit www.eurail.com. You can book tickets at train stations and most travel agencies. For the latest fare information on journeys to Italy, contact the **Rail Europe Travel Centre** (☎ 0870 848 848; www.raileurope.co.uk).

GETTING AROUND
Bicycle

Bikes are available for rent in quite a few Italian towns (from about €10 a day) and can travel in the baggage compartment of some Italian trains (but not on Eurostar or Intercity trains); bikes travel free on ferries.

Boat

Navi (large ferries) service Sicily and Sardinia, and *traghetti* (smaller ferries) and *aliscafi* (hydrofoils) service the smaller islands, including Elba, the Aeolian Islands, Capri and Ischia. The main embarkation points for Sicily and Sardinia are at Livorno, Genoa, La Spezia, Civitavecchia, Fiumicino and Naples. **Tirrenia Navigazione** (www.gruppotirrenia.it) services nearly all the Italian ports and has offices throughout the country.

Bus

Numerous bus companies operate within Italy. Generally it's only necessary to make reservations for long trips, such as Rome–Palermo. Buses can be a cheaper and faster way to get around if your destination is not on major rail lines, such as from Umbria to Rome. Major companies that run long-haul services include **Marozzi** (☎ 071 280 23 98) for Rome to Brindisi; **Interbus** (☎ 0931 667 10) for Rome to Sicily; and **Lazzi** (☎ 055 35 10 61 or ☎ 06 884 08 40) from Lazio, Tuscany and other regions to the Alps.

Car & Motorcycle

Roads are generally good and there's an excellent system of *autostrade* (freeways). Despite what you see, helmets are required for every motorcycle and moped rider and passenger. Petrol prices are very high.

Some Italian cities, including Rome and Florence, have introduced restricted access to both private and rental cars in their historical centres. The restrictions, however, do not apply to vehicles with foreign registration nor do they apply to mopeds and scooters.

Train

Trenitalia (☎ 848 88 80 88 in Italian; www.trenitalia.com) is the partially privatised state train system that runs most of the services in Italy. There are several types of trains. Some stop at all the stations, like *regionale* or *interregionale*, while faster trains, such as the Intercity (IC) and the fastest Eurostar Italia (ES), stop only at major cities. It is cheaper to buy all local train tickets in the country.

There are 1st and 2nd classes on all Italian trains, with the former costing almost double the latter. Intercity and Eurostar trains require a supplement (usually €4 to €16) determined by the distance of travel. Check up-to-date prices of routes on www.fs-on-line.com.

All tickets must be validated (in the yellow machines at the entrance to all train platforms) before you board.

Trenitalia offers its own discount passes for travel within Italy, available at major train stations. These include the Carta Verde, with a 20% discount for people aged from 12 to 26 years, valid for one year. The Trenitalia Pass allows for four to 10 days of travel within a two-month period. At the time of writing, passes for 10 travel days for 1st/2nd class cost €349/282.

ROME (ROMA)

pop 2.65 million

If you had time for just one city in life, Rome's your spot – gloriously artistic, romantically beautiful and endearingly *pazzo* (crazy). No other city so stylishly meshes its significant, visible history with its hip, contemporary, fun-loving self. Whether you have a weekend or a month, beguiling Rome will swallow you whole, charm you to pieces, then leave you craving more.

Rome's 2500-plus years of history have produced a veritable archive of Western culture, from the remnants of ancient Rome to the artistic splendours of the Renaissance and baroque periods. Historic beauties aside, modern Rome is exceptionally vibrant and simmers with passion. Take a big breath, dive in and prepare for sensory overload.

ORIENTATION

Despite Rome's vastness, most major sights are within the relatively small *centro storico* (historic centre), just west of and walkable from Stazione Termini, the central train station. The main bus terminus is in Piazza del Cinquecento, directly in front of the train station. Many intercity buses arrive and depart from the Piazzale Tiburtina, in front of Stazione Tiburtina, accessible from Termini on the Metro Linea B.

GETTING INTO TOWN

If arriving by train, the centre of town is a 15-minute walk from Stazione Termini to the northwest; if arriving by intercity bus, hop on Metro Linea B to Termini. The airport is 30km southwest of the city – catch the half-hourly Leonardo Express train to Termini.

INFORMATION
Emergency
Foreigners' Bureau (Map p654; ☎ 06 468 62 977; Via Genova 2) You can report thefts here.
Police Headquarters (Map p654; ☎ 06 468 61; Via San Vitale 11; ☉ 24hr)

Internet Access
There are Internet cafés scattered all over town.

EMERGENCY NUMBERS

- **Ambulance** ☎ 118
- **Automobile Club d'Italia** (ACI) ☎ 116
- **Carabinieri** (police with military and civil duties) ☎ 112
- **Police** ☎ 113
- **Fire** ☎ 115

East Internet Café (Map pp650-1; Via Barberini 2; per 30min €1; ☉ 24hr) Has plenty of terminals.

Medical Services
A list of all-night pharmacies in the city centre is posted on www.romaturismo.it and in all pharmacy windows.
24-hour Pharmacy (Map p654; ☎ 06 488 00 19; Piazza dei Cinquecento 51) Opposite Termini.
Bambino Gesú (Map pp648-9; ☎ 06 685 92 351; Piazza di Sant'Onofrio 4) Rome's paediatric hospital.
Ospedale San Gallicano (Map pp656-7; ☎ 06 588 23 90; Via di San Gallicano 25a, Trastevere)
Ospedale San Giacomo (Map pp650-1; ☎ 06 362 61; Via Canova 29) South of Piazza del Popolo.
Policlinico Umberto I (Map p654; ☎ 06 499 71; Viale del Policlinico 155) Near Termini.

Money
Banks are open 8.45am to 1.30pm and from 2.45pm to 4pm Monday to Friday. There's a bank and exchange booths at Stazione Termini, and an exchange booth and ATMs at Fiumicino airport.

There are numerous Bancomats (ATMs) and exchange booths dotted throughout the city.
American Express (Map pp650-1; ☎ 06 676 41; Piazza di Spagna 38)
Thomas Cook (Map pp650-1; ☎ 06 482 81 82; Piazza Barberini 21)

Post & Telephone
There are Telecom offices at Termini.
Main post office (Map pp650-1; Piazza di San Silvestro 20; ☉ 9am-6.30pm Mon-Fri, 9am-1pm Sat)
Vatican post office (Map pp650-1; ☎ 06 698 83 406; Piazza di San Pietro; ☉ 8.30am-6pm Mon-Fri, 8.30am-1pm Sat) Purportedly with faster and more reliable service.

Tourist Information
Enjoy Rome (Map p654; ☎ 06 445 18 43; www.enjoyrome.com; Via Marghera 8a; ☉ 8.30am-7pm

Mon-Sat, 8.30am-2pm Sun) Privately run office five minutes' walk northeast of Stazione Termini.

APT Branch Tourist Office (Map p654; ☎ 06 489 06 300; ☺ 8am-9pm) At Stazione Termini, in the central causeway and with a multilingual staff.

APT Tourist Office (Map p654; ☎ 06 360 04 399; Via Parigi 5; ☺ 9am-7pm Mon-Sat)

SIGHTS & ACTIVITIES

When it comes to seeing the sights, that old adage – *Roma, non basta una vita* (Rome, a lifetime is not enough) – couldn't be more true. It would take 900 days just to visit all of Rome's churches, one a day. Fortunately, you can briskly cover many of the important sights in three days. Entry to various attractions is free for EU citizens aged under 18 and over 65, and half-price for EU citizens aged between 18 and 25, those from countries with reciprocal arrangements, and many students. Cumulative tickets represent good value with discounts for multiple main attractions; ask at primary sites or call ☎ 06 399 67 700.

Roman Forum & Palatine Hill

The ancient Roman commercial, political and religious centre, the **Roman Forum** (Map pp656-7; ☎ 06 399 67 700; admission to Forum free, to Palatine Hill with Colosseum €8; ☺ 9am-1hr before sunset Mon-Sat), stands in a valley between the Capitoline and Palatine Hills. Originally marshland, the area was drained during the early republican era and began as a typical public piazza (square). Its importance declined along with the empire after the 4th century AD, and the temples, monuments and buildings constructed by emperors, consuls and senators over a period of 900 years fell into ruin until eventually the site was used as pasture land.

As you enter, to your left is the **Tempio di Antonino e Faustina**, erected by the senate in AD 141 and transformed into a church in the 8th century. To your right are the remains of the **Basilica Aemilia**, built in 179 BC and plundered for marble during the Renaissance. The Via Sacra, which traverses the Forum from northwest to southeast, runs in front of the basilica. Towards the Campidoglio is the **Curia**, once the meeting place of the Roman senate and converted into a church. In front of the Curia is the **Lapis Niger**, a large piece of black marble that purportedly covered Romulus' grave.

The **Arco di Settimo Severo** was erected in AD 203 in honour of this emperor and his sons, and is considered one of Italy's major triumphal arches. A circular base stone beside the arch marks the *umbilicus urbis*, the symbolic centre of ancient Rome.

To the southwest of the arch is the **Tempio di Saturno**, one of the most important ancient Roman temples, used as the state treasury. The **Basilica Giulia**, in front of the temple, was the seat of justice, and nearby is the **Tempio di Giulio Cesare**, erected by Augustus in 29 BC on the site where Caesar's body was burned and Mark Antony read his famous speech.

Southeast of the temple is the **Chiesa di Santa Maria Antiqua**, the oldest Christian church in the Forum, now closed to the public. Back on the Via Sacra is the **Case delle Vestali**, home of the virgins who tended the sacred flame in the adjoining **Tempio di Vesta**. The **Arco di Tito**, at the Colosseum end of the Forum, was built in AD 81 in honour of the victories of Titus and Vespasian against Jerusalem.

From this point, climb the **Palatine**, where wealthy Romans built their homes and Romulus supposedly founded the city. Worth a look is the impressive **Domus Augustana**, the private residence of the emperors; the **Domus Flavia**, the residence of Domitian; the **Tempio della Magna Mater**, built in 204 BC; and the fresco-adorned **Casa di Livia**, thought to belong to the wife of Emperor Augustus.

Piazza del Campidoglio

Perched atop Capitoline Hill, elegant **Piazza del Campidoglio** (Map pp656-7) was designed by Michelangelo in 1538. Formerly the seat of the ancient Roman government, it is now the seat of the city's municipal government. Michelangelo also designed the façades of the three palaces bordering the piazza. A modern copy of the bronze equestrian statue of Emperor Marcus Aurelius is at its centre; the original is on display in the ground-floor portico of the **Palazzo Nuovo** (also called Palazzo del Museo Capitolino). This forms part of the **Musei Capitolini** (Map pp656-7; ☎ 06 671 02 071; admission €6.20; ☺ 9am-8pm Tue-Sun), well worth visiting for their collections of ancient Roman sculpture.

Vatican City   Map pp650-1

In 1929, Mussolini, under the Lateran Treaty, gave the pope full sovereignty over what is now the world's smallest country.

The **tourist office** (☎ 06 698 81 662; Piazza di San Pietro; ☺ 8.30am-7pm Mon-Sat) is to the left of the

ITALY

ROME (ROMA)

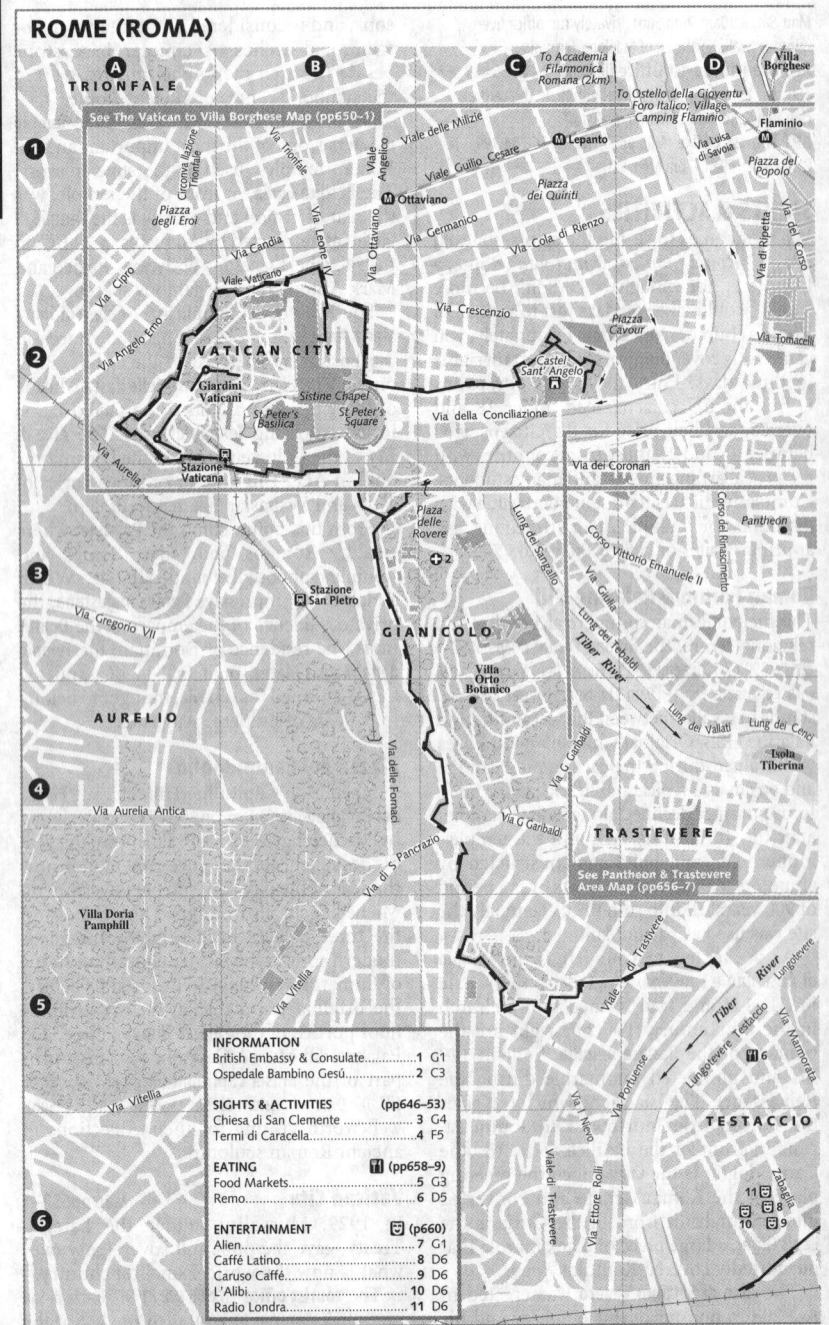

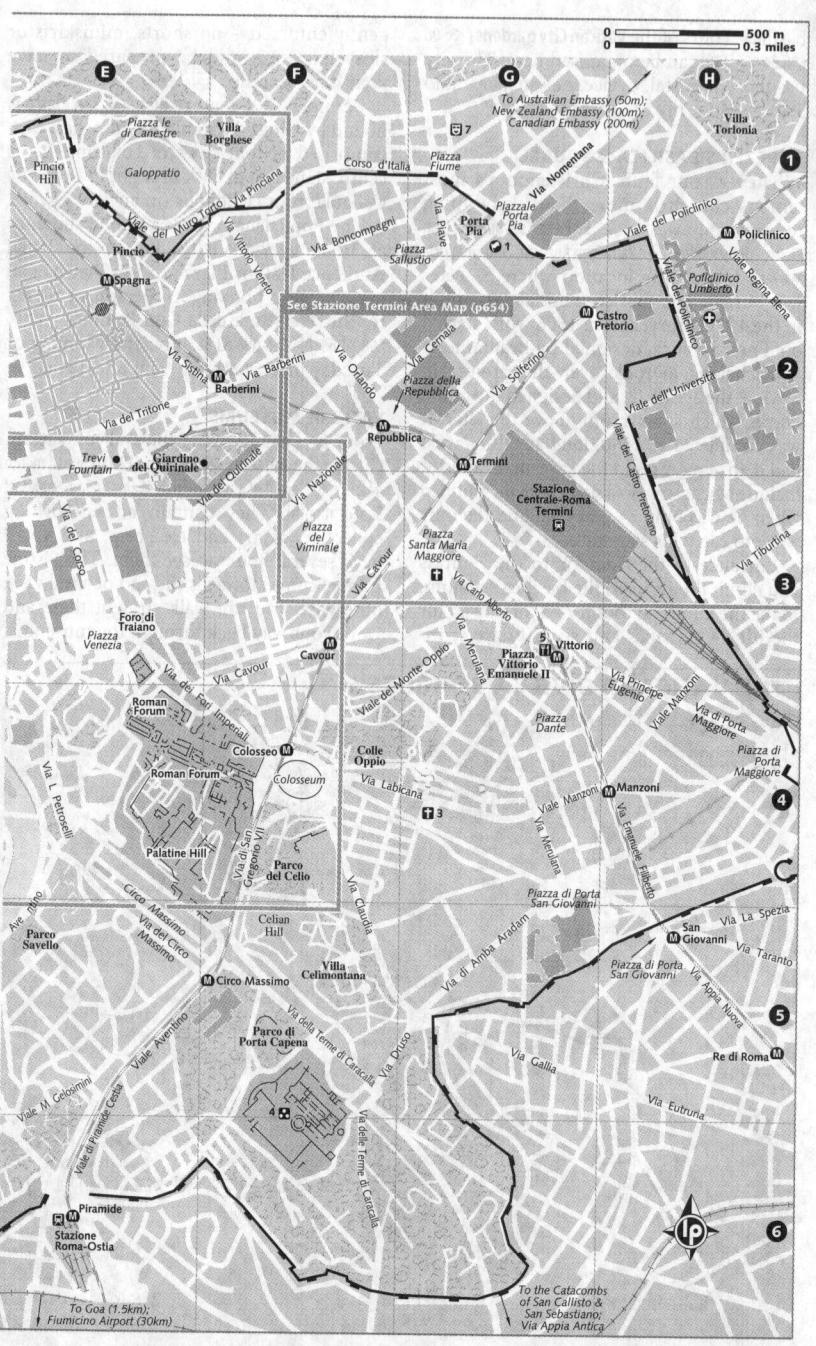

0   500 m
0   0.3 miles

E   **F**   **G**   **H**

Piazza le
di Canestre

Villa
Borghese

Galoppatio

Pincio
Hill

To Australian Embassy (50m);
New Zealand Embassy (100m);
Canadian Embassy (200m)

Villa
Torlonia

1

Corso d'Italia

Piazza
Fiume

Via Nomentana

7

Via Pinciana

Viale del Muro Torto

Via Vittorio Veneto

Via Boncompagni

Piazzale
Porta
Pia

Porta
Pia

Via del Policlinico

Policlinico M

Pincio

Piazza
Sallustio

1

Viale del Policlinico

Spagna M

Via Plave

Viale Regina Elena

Policlinico
Umberto I

See Stazione Termini Area Map (p654)

Castro M
Pretorio

2

Via Sistina

Via Barberini

Via Orlando

Via Cernaia

Via Solferino

Viale dell'Università

Barberini M

Via del Tritone

Piazza della
Repubblica

Viale del Castro Pretorio

Trevi
Fountain

Giardino
del Quirinale

Repubblica M

Via del Quirinale

Termini M

Via Nazionale

Stazione
Centrale-Roma
Termini

Via Tiburtina

3

Via del Corso

Piazza
del
Viminale

Piazza
Santa Maria
Maggiore

Via Cavour

Via Carlo Alberto

Foro di
Traiano

Piazza
Venezia

Via dei Fori Imperiali

Via Cavour

Cavour M

Viale del Monte Oppio

Via Merulana

5 Vittorio
Piazza
Vittorio
Emanuele II

M

Via Principe
Eugenio

Via di Porta
Maggiore

Roman
Forum

Colosseo M

Roman Forum

Colosseum

Colle
Oppio

Via Labicana

3

Piazza
Dante

Via Merulana

Manzoni M

Viale Manzoni

Via Emanuele Filiberto

Piazza di
Porta
Maggiore

4

Via L. Petroselli

Palatine Hill

Via di San Gregorio VII

Parco
del Celio

Via Claudia

Piazza di Porta
San Giovanni

San M
Giovanni

Via La Spezia

5

Parco
Savello

Circo Massimo

Celian
Hill

Via del Circo Massimo

Villa
Celimontana

Via di Amba Aradam

Piazza di Porta
San Giovanni

Via Appia Nuova

Via Taranto

Re di Roma M

Ave nino

Circo Massimo M

Viale M Gelsomini

Viale Aventino

Parco di
Porta Capena

Via delle Terme di Caracalla

Via Druso

Via Gallia

Via Eutruna

Piramide

Via di Piramide Cestia

4

Via delle Terme di Caracalla

6

Stazione
Roma-Ostia

To Goa (1.5km);
Fiumicino Airport (30km)

To the Catacombs
of San Callisto &
San Sebastiano;
Via Appia Antica

basilica. Tours of the **Vatican City gardens** (☎ 06 698 84 466; €10) can be organised here. The city has its own postal service, newspaper, radio station and army of Swiss Guards.

ST PETER'S BASILICA & SQUARE

Whatever your faith, Christendom's most famous church is more than likely going to leave you awestruck. **St Peter's Basilica** (San Pietro; admission free; ☒ 7am-7pm Apr-Sep, 7am-6pm Oct-Mar) stands on the location where St Peter was buried. The first church here was built in the 4th century, and in 1506 work started on a new basilica, designed by Bramante.

Michelangelo took over the project in 1547, at the age of 72, and designed the grand dome, which soars 120m above the altar. It was completed in 1590, long after the artist had died. Treasures in the cavernous interior include Michelangelo's superb *Pietá*, sculpted when he was only 24 years old and the only work to carry his signature.

Entrance to the dome is to the right as you climb the stairs to the basilica's atrium. Make the climb on foot for €4, or pay €5 for the lift. Dress rules and security are strin-gently enforced – no shorts, miniskirts or sleeveless tops, and be prepared to have your bags searched.

Bernini's 17th-century **Piazza di San Pietro** is bound by two semicircular colonnades, each comprised of four rows of columns. In its centre stands an obelisk brought to Rome by Caligula from Heliopolis (in ancient Egypt).

The Pope usually gives a public audience at 10am every Wednesday in the Papal Audience Hall or Piazza di San Pietro. You must make a booking, in person or by fax to the **Prefettura della Casa Pontifica** (☎ 06 698 84 631; fax 06 698 83 865), on the Monday or Tuesday prior, between 9am and 1pm.

VATICAN MUSEUMS

From St Peter's follow the wall of Vatican City to the **museums** (admission €12, last Sun of month free; ☒ 8.45am-4.45pm Mon-Fri, 8.45am-1.45pm Sat & last Sun of month). They contain an astonishing collection of art and treasures, and you'll need several hours to see them. The Sistine Chapel comes towards the end of a full visit; otherwise, you can walk straight there and work your way back through the museums.

THE VATICAN TO VILLA BORGHESE

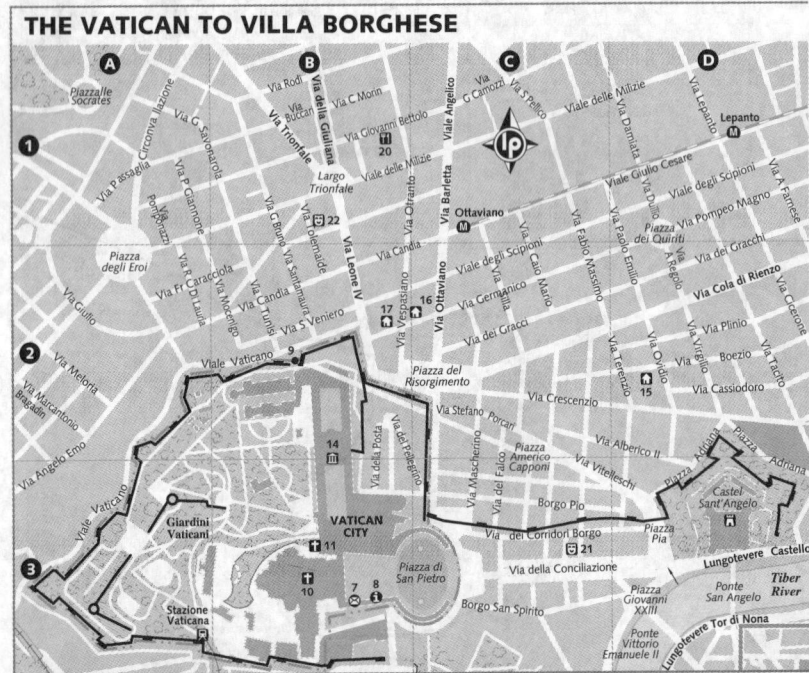

ITALY

The **Museo Pio-Clementino**, containing Greek and Roman antiquities, is on the ground floor near the entrance. Past the superb **Galleria delle Carte Geografiche** (Map Gallery) and the **Galleria degli Arazzi** (Tapestry Gallery) are the magnificent **Stanze di Rafaello**, once the private apartments of Pope Julius II, decorated with frescoes by Raphael. Of particular interest is the magnificent **Stanza della Segnatura**, which features **Raphael's masterpieces**, *The School of Athens* and *Disputation on the Sacrament*.

From Raphael's rooms, go down the stairs to the sumptuous **Appartamento Borgia**, decorated with frescoes by Pinturicchio, and then down another flight of stairs to the **Sistine Chapel**, the private papal chapel built in 1473 for Pope Sixtus IV. Michelangelo's frescoes of the *Creation* and *Last Judgement* have been superbly restored to their original brilliance. It took Michelangelo four years, at the height of the Renaissance, to paint the *Creation*; 24 years later he painted the extraordinary *Last Judgement*. The other walls of the chapel were painted by artists including Botticelli and Signorelli.

Pantheon

The **Pantheon** (Map pp656-7; Piazza della Rotonda; admission free; 8.30am-7.30pm Mon-Sat, 9am-6pm Sun) is the best-preserved building of ancient Rome. The original temple was built in 27 BC by Marcus Agrippa, son-in-law of Emperor Augustus, and dedicated to the planetary gods. Agrippa's name remains inscribed over the entrance.

Over the centuries the Pantheon was consistently plundered and damaged. The gilded-bronze roof tiles were removed by an emperor of the eastern empire, and Pope Urban VIII had the bronze ceiling of the portico melted down to make the canopy over the main altar of St Peter's and 80 cannons for Castel Sant' Angelo. The Pantheon's extraordinary dome is considered the most important achievement of ancient Roman architecture. The Italian kings Vittorio Emanuele II and Umberto I, and the painter Raphael are buried here.

Piazza Navona

This vast and beautiful square, lined with baroque palaces, was laid out on the

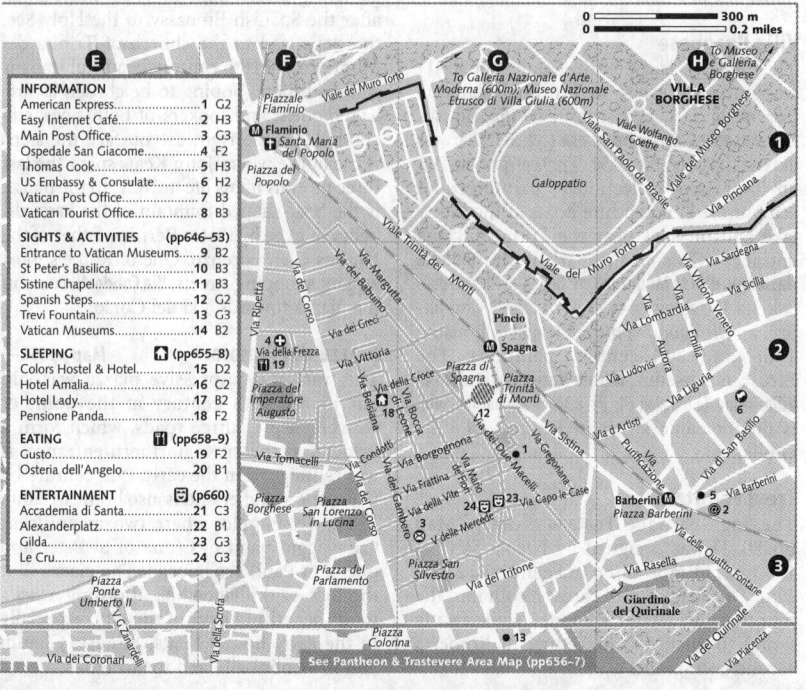

```
INFORMATION
American Express.....................1  G2
Easy Internet Café.....................2  H3
Main Post Office.......................3  G3
Ospedale San Giacome................4  F2
Thomas Cook...........................5  H3
US Embassy & Consulate.............6  H2
Vatican Post Office....................7  B3
Vatican Tourist Office................8  B3

SIGHTS & ACTIVITIES        (pp646-53)
Entrance to Vatican Museums.......9  B2
St Peter's Basilica....................10  B3
Sistine Chapel........................11  B3
Spanish Steps.........................12  G2
Trevi Fountain........................13  G3
Vatican Museums.....................14  B2

SLEEPING              (pp655-8)
Colors Hostel & Hotel...............15  D2
Hotel Amalia..........................16  C2
Hotel Lady............................17  B2
Pensione Panda......................18  F2

EATING                (pp658-9)
Gusto..................................19  F2
Osteria dell'Angelo..................20  B1

ENTERTAINMENT        (p660)
Accademia di Santa..................21  C3
Alexanderplatz.......................22  B1
Gilda..................................23  G3
Le Cru.................................24  G3
```

0   300 m
0   0.2 miles

To Museo e Galleria Borghese

Piazzale Flaminio
Viale del Muro Torto
To Galleria Nazionale d'Arte Moderna (600m); Museo Nazionale Etrusco di Villa Giulia (600m)
VILLA BORGHESE

Flaminio
Santa Maria del Popolo
Piazza del Popolo
Galoppatio
Viale San Paolo de Brasile
Viale Wolfango Goethe
Via Pinciana
Viale del Museo Borghese

Viale Trinità dei Monti
Viale del Muro Torto
Via Sardegna
Via Sicilia
Via Vittorio Veneto
Via Lombardia
Via Emilia

Pincio
Spagna
Piazza di Spagna
Piazza Trinità ai Monti
Via Ludovisi
Via Lombardia
Via Liguria
Via di San Basilio

Via della Frezza
Via Vittoria
Via della Croce
Via della Vite
Via Frattina
Via Borgognona
Via Condotti
Piazza del Imperatore Augusto
Via delle Carrozze
Via Due Macelli
Via Gregoriana
Via Sistina
Via d'Artisti
Via Purificazione

Via Tomacelli
Piazza Borghese
Piazza San Lorenzo in Lucina
Via del Corso
Via Capo le Case
Barberini
Piazza Barberini
Via Barberini

Piazza del Parlamento
Piazza San Silvestro
Via delle Mercede
Via del Tritone
Via Rasella
Via delle Quattro Fontane

Piazza Ponte Umberto II
V. di Campo Marzio
Via della Scrofa
Piazza Colonna
Giardino del Quirinale
Via Piacenza
Via del Quirinale

Via dei Coronari
See Pantheon & Trastevere Area Map (pp656-7)

ITALY

ruins of Domitian's stadium and features three fountains. In its centre is Bernini's masterpiece, **Fontana dei Quattro Fiumi** (Fountain of the Four Rivers; Map pp656–7). Relax on one of the stone benches or at the expensive cafés and watch the artists who gather in the piazza to work.

Campo de'Fiori

'Il Campo' (Map pp656–7) was a place of execution during the Inquisition, and Caravaggio went on the run after killing a man who beat him in tennis on this piazza. Nowadays a flower and vegetable market is held here Monday to Saturday, and revellers fill the many bars at night.

The **Palazzo Farnese**, within the piazza of the same name, is just off the Campo. A magnificent Renaissance building, it was started in 1514 by Antonio da Sangallo, carried on by Michelangelo and finally completed by Giacomo della Porta. Built for Cardinal Alessandro Farnese (later Pope Paul III), the palace is now the French embassy. The piazza has two fountains, enormous granite baths taken from the Baths of Caracalla.

Villa Borghese

This lovely, leafy park (Map pp650–1) was once the estate of Cardinal Scipione Borghese. His 17th-century villa houses the **Museo e Galleria Borghese** (☎ 06 328 10; www .ticketeria.it; admission €8.50; ☺ 9am-7pm Tue-Sat), an impressive collection of paintings and sculptures. You can hire boats at the lovely lake and bicycles near the Porta Pinciana entrance. Outside the park is the **Galleria Nazionale d'Arte Moderna** (☎ 06 323 40 00; Viale delle Belle Arti 131; admission €6.50; ☺ 8.30am-7.30pm Tue-Sun), a *belle époque palazzo* (palace) housing 19th- and 20th-century paintings. The Etruscan museum, **Museo Nazionale Etrusco di Villa Giulia** (admission €4; ☺ 8.30am-7.30pm Tue-Sun), is on the same street in Piazzale di Villa Giulia.

Trevi Fountain

The high-baroque **Fontana di Trevi** (Map pp650–1) was designed by Nicola Salvi in 1732 and immortalised in Fellini's *La Dolce Vita*. The custom is to throw a coin into the fountain (over your shoulder while facing away) to ensure your return to Rome; a second coin grants a wish.

Colosseum & Arch of Constantine

Originally known as the Flavian Amphitheatre, Rome's best-known monument, the **Colosseum** (Map pp656-7; ☎ 06 399 67 700; admission with Palatine Hill €8; ☺ 9am-1hr before sunset) was begun by Emperor Vespasian in AD 72. The massive structure could seat 80,000 and featured gory and profusely deadly gladiatorial combat and wild beast shows.

During the Middle Ages the Colosseum became a fortress then later a quarry for travertine and marble to build Palazzo Venezia and other buildings. Restoration works have been under way since 1992. Skip paying the admission to see the barren interior.

On the west side of the Colosseum is the **triumphal arch** built to honour Constantine following his victory over his rival Maxentius at the battle of Milvian Bridge in 312. Its decorative reliefs were taken from earlier structures.

Piazza di Spagna & Spanish Steps

This exquisite piazza, church and famous staircase (Scalinata della Trinitá dei Monti; Map pp650–1) have long provided a major gathering place. Built in 1725 and named after the Spanish Embassy to the Holy See, the steps lead to the church of Trinitá dei Monti. In the 18th century beautiful Italians gathered there, hoping to be chosen as artists' models, and lookers of both sexes still abound. To the right as you face the steps is the house where John Keats spent the last three months of his life in 1821. In the piazza is the boat-shaped fountain of the **Barcaccia**, believed to be by Pietro Bernini, father of the famous Gian Lorenzo. One of Rome's most elegant shopping streets, **Via Condotti**, runs off the piazza towards Via del Corso.

Piazza del Popolo   Map pp650–1

This vast and impressive piazza was laid out in the 16th century at the point of convergence of three roads, which form a 'trident' at the city's northern entrance. It was redesigned in the early 19th century by Giuseppe Valadier and is also home to Santa Maria del Popolo, where two magnificent Caravaggio paintings (one of St Peter and one of St Paul) are housed. The piazza is at the foot of the **Pincio Hill**, affording a *bella vista* (beautiful view) of the city, especially in the early hours; Keats, Strauss, Ghandi and Mussolini all liked to stroll here.

Trastevere
Map pp650–1

Wander through Trastevere's narrow medieval streets, which retain a sense of bonhomie and the air of a typical Roman neighbourhood despite the influx of foreigners. Especially beautiful at night, this is a great area for eating and bar-hopping (see p659).

Go to the **Basilica di Santa Maria in Trastevere**, in the lovely piazza of the same name, believed to be the oldest church dedicated to the Virgin in Rome. Its interior was redecorated during the baroque period, but the vibrant mosaics in the apse and on the triumphal arch date from the 12th century. Also worth a look is the **Basilica di Santa Cecilia in Trastevere**, with its magnificent 13th-century fresco.

Via Giulia

Bramante designed this elegant street (Map pp656–7) for Pope Julius II as a new approach to St Peter's. It is lined with Renaissance palaces, antique shops and art galleries, and spanning the southern end is Michelangelo's ivy-draped **Arco Farnese.**

Terme di Caracalla

The huge **Terme di Caracalla complex** (Map pp648-9; ☎ 06 399 67 70; Via della Terme di Caracalla 52; admission €5; ☼ 9am-1hr before sunset Tue-Sun, 9am-2pm Mon), covering 10 hectares, could hold 1600 people and included shops, gardens, libraries and entertainment. Begun by Antonius Caracalla and inaugurated in AD 217, the baths were used until the 6th century.

Churches

Down Via Cavour from Stazione Termini is massive **Basilica di Santa Maria Maggiore** (Map p654), built in the 5th century. Its baroque façade was added in the 18th century, preserving the 13th-century mosaics of the earlier façade. There are 5th-century mosaics decorating the triumphal arch and nave.

Basilica di San Pietro in Vincoli (Map pp656–7), just off Via Cavour, houses Michelangelo's *Moses* and his unfinished statues of Leah and Rachel, as well as the *vincoli* (chains) worn by St Peter during his imprisonment before he was crucified.

Chiesa di San Clemente (Map pp648-9; Via San Giovanni in Laterano), near the Colosseum, defines how history in Rome exists on many levels. The 12th-century church at street level was built over a 4th-century church that was, in turn, built over a 1st-century Roman house containing a temple dedicated to the god Mithras.

Santa Maria in Cosmedin (Map pp656–7), northwest of Circus Maximus, is regarded as one of the finest medieval churches in Rome. It has a seven-storey bell tower and its interior is decorated with Cosmatesque inlaid marble, including the beautiful floor. The main attraction for tourists is, however, the **Bocca della Veritá** (Mouth of Truth). Legend has it that if you put your right hand into the mouth and tell a lie, it will snap shut.

Baths of Diocletian & Basilica di Santa Maria degli Angeli

Just across the piazza from Termini, the **Baths of Diocletian** (Map p654; ☎ 06 488 05 30; Viale E de Nicola 79; admission €5; ☼ 9am-7.45pm Tue-Sun) were created at the turn of the 3rd century. Rome's largest baths, they could accommodate 3000 people; the 13-hectare complex also included libraries, concert halls and gardens. In 536, invaders destroyed the aqueduct that fed the baths and the complex fell into decay.

Parts of the ruins are incorporated into the **Basilica di Santa Maria degli Angeli** (☼ 7.30am-6.30pm). Designed by Michelangelo, this church incorporates what was the great central hall and *tepidarium* (lukewarm room) of the original baths. Over the centuries his original work was drastically changed and little evidence of his design, apart from the great vaulted ceiling of the church, remains. An interesting feature of the church is a double meridian in the transept, one tracing the polar star and the other telling the precise time of the sun's zenith.

Catacombs

There are several catacombs in Rome, consisting of miles of tunnels carved out of volcanic rock, which were the meeting and burial places of early Christians. The largest are along the **Via Appia Antica** (the Appian Way), just outside the city and accessible on Metro Linea A to Colli Albani, then bus No 660. The **Catacombs of San Callisto** (admission €5; ☼ 8.30am-noon & 2.30-5pm Thu-Tue Mar-Jan) and **Catacombs of San Sebastiano** (admission €5; ☼ 8.30am-noon & 2.30-5pm Mon-Sat 10 Dec-10 Nov) are almost next to each other. Admission to each is with a guide only.

ITALY

STAZIONE TERMINI AREA

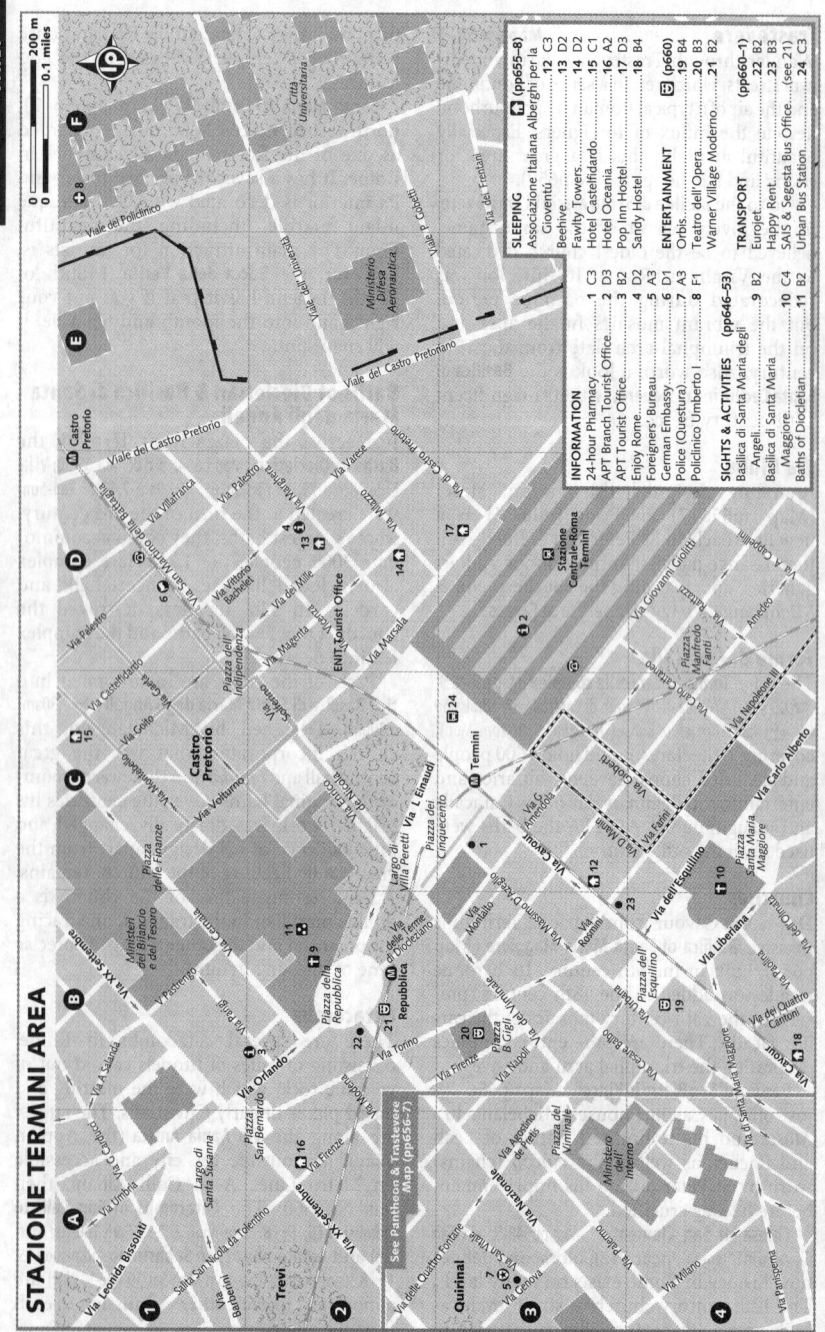

0   200 m
0   0.1 miles

INFORMATION
24-hour Pharmacy............................1 C3
APT Branch Tourist Office..............2 D3
APT Tourist Office.............................3 B2
Enjoy Rome...4 D2
Foreigners' Bureau.............................5 A3
German Embassy..................................6 D1
Police (Questura)................................7 A3
Policlinico Umberto I.........................8 F1

SIGHTS & ACTIVITIES (pp646–53)
Basilica di Santa Maria degli
    Angeli...9 B2
Basilica di Santa Maria
    Maggiore.......................................10 C4
Baths of Diocletian...........................11 B2

SLEEPING (pp655–8)
Associazione Italiana Alberghi per la
    Gioventù.......................................12 C3
Beehive..13 D2
Fawlty Towers...................................14 D2
Hotel Castelfidardo..........................15 C1
Hotel Oceania...................................16 A2
Pop Inn Hostel...................................17 D3
Sandy Hostel.....................................18 B4

ENTERTAINMENT (p660)
Orbis...19 B4
Teatro dell'Opera..............................20 B3
Warner Village Moderno..................21 B2

TRANSPORT (pp660–1)
Eurojet...22 B2
Happy Rent..23 B3
SAIS & Segesta Bus Office..........(see 21)
Urban Bus Station............................24 C3

See Pantheon & Trastevere
Map (pp656–7)

SLEEPING

Rome's municipal government keeps a full list of accommodation options on its excellent website www.romaturismo.it.

Hostels & B&Bs

Associazione Italiana Alberghi per la Gioventú (Map opposite; ☎ 06 487 11 52; www.ostellionline.org; Via Cavour 44; 🕙 9am-5pm Mon-Fri) This head office has information about all the hostels in Italy and will assist with bookings to stay at universities during summer. You can join HI here.

Ostello della Gioventu Foro Italico (☎ 06 323 62 67; aig.sedenazionale@uni.net; Viale delle Olimpiadi 61; dm €15) Rome's main hostel has over 300 beds and opens from 7am to midnight. It ain't glamorous, but it's cheap and you're bound to meet new friends. Take Metro Linea A to Ottaviano, then bus No 32 to Foro Italico.

The tourist office has a list of private B&B operators, as does **Bed & Breakfast Italia** (☎ 06 688 01 513; www.bbitalia.it; Corso Vittorio Emanuele II 282; s/d from €37/28, with bathroom €50/40).

Hotels & Pensioni

AROUND STAZIONE TERMINI MAP P654

Most of the less-expensive options near the station are along Via Castro Pretorio, to the right as you leave the train platforms. The area can be seedy but improves closer to the Colosseum.

Fawlty Towers (☎ 06 445 03 74; www.fawltytowers .org; Via Magenta 39; dm €20, with bathroom €23, s/d €47/65, with bathroom €55/70; 🖳) This ever-popular spot is a great choice. It offers hostel-style accommodation, cheap Internet access and a lively common room with satellite TV – the flower-filled terrace and lack of curfew are icing on the cake.

The Beehive (☎ 06 447 04 553; www.the-beehive .com; Via Marghera 8; dm €20, d per person with/without bathroom €40/35) This clean, cheery spot with a friendly American couple at the helm has a nice garden and communal kitchen. Walk-ins are not accepted, and party animals will be happier elsewhere.

Sandy Hostel (☎ 06 488 45 85; www.sandyhostel .com; Via Cavour 136; dm €18, with bathroom €20) Rome's version of a backpackers' crash pad is on the 5th floor (no lift), has no curfew, not-great bathrooms, metal lockers without keys, and a party atmosphere for the young and tolerant crowd. Only cash is accepted.

Pop Inn Hostel (☎ 06 495 98 87; www.popinnhostel .com; Via Marsala 80; dm €17-25, s €35-95, d €20-49; 🖳)

Comfortable and squeaky clean, this notch-above hostel has exceptionally helpful, friendly and multilingual staff; other *simpatico* features include no curfew, free breakfast, free luggage storage and laundry.

Hotel Castelfidardo (☎ 06 446 46 38; castelfidardo@ italmarke.it; Via Castelfidardo 31; s/d €46/65, with bathroom €55/74) Just off Piazza dell'Indipendenza, this well-run spot is one of Rome's better one-star hotels. The English-speaking staff is friendly and helpful.

Hotel Oceania (☎ 06 482 46 96; www.hoteloceania .it; Via Firenze 38; s €52-104, d €62-135) You'll be greeted with a warm welcome at this small hotel, with outstanding hospitality, smart rooms, wonderful owners, and thoughtful extras like English newspapers in the morning.

CITY CENTRE MAP

Truly budget rooms don't exist once you foray from the noisy Termini area. But what you lose in euros, you more than make up for in convenience and the unbeatable pleasure of staying in the heart of historic Rome.

Pensione Panda (Map pp650-1; ☎ 06 678 01 79; www .pensionepanda.com; Via della Croce 35; s/d €48/68, with bathroom €65/98) Close to the Spanish Steps, this 2nd-floor *pensione* has comfortable rooms with arched ceilings and a helpful, English-speaking staff.

Albergo del Sole (Map pp656-7; ☎ 06 687 94 46; www.solealbiscione.it; Via del Biscione 76; s/d €65/95, with bathroom €83/125) A short walk from Campo de'Fiori, this sunny spot dates from 1462. Cheery rooms, some with antiques, lots of communal space, a pretty patio and rooftop terrace make this hotel a standout.

NEAR THE VATICAN   Map pp650–1

Bargains are rare here, but it is comparatively quiet and reasonably close to the main sights. Bookings are a must. Take Metro Linea A to Ottaviano, or bus No 64 from Termini, which stops at St Peter's.

Colors Hostel (☎ 06 687 40 30; www.colorshotel .com; Via Boezio 31; dm €22, d/tr €75/85, with shower €85/90) Run by the people at Enjoy Rome (p646), Colors offers tidy rooms, a mini-gym and cooking facilities; the owners are supposed to be opening a new mid-range hotel next door.

Hotel Lady (☎ 06 324 21 12; 4th fl, Via Germanico 198; d with/without shower €125/90) A quiet, old-world *pensione* with pleasant rooms and rustic antiques. The friendly owners don't speak

ITALY

PANTHEON & TRASTEVERE AREA

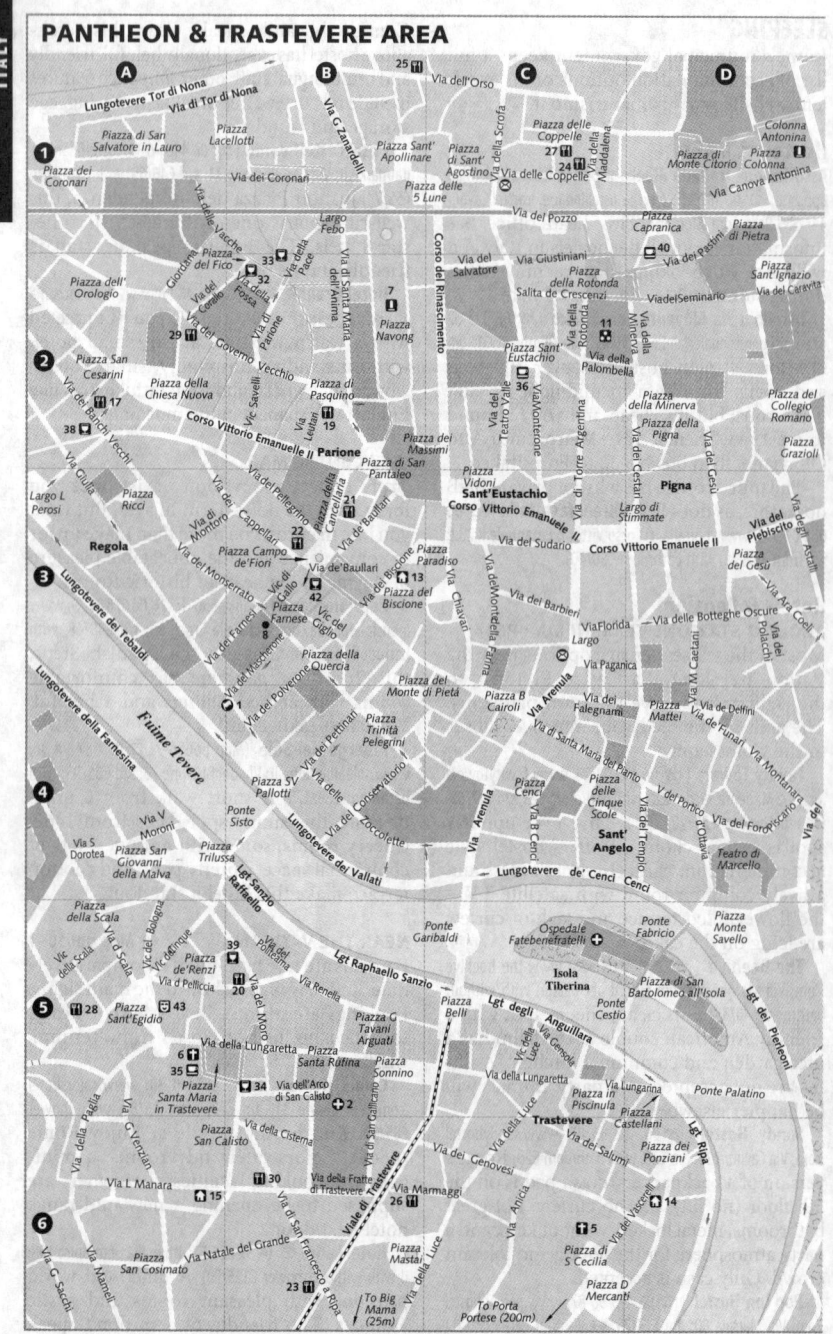

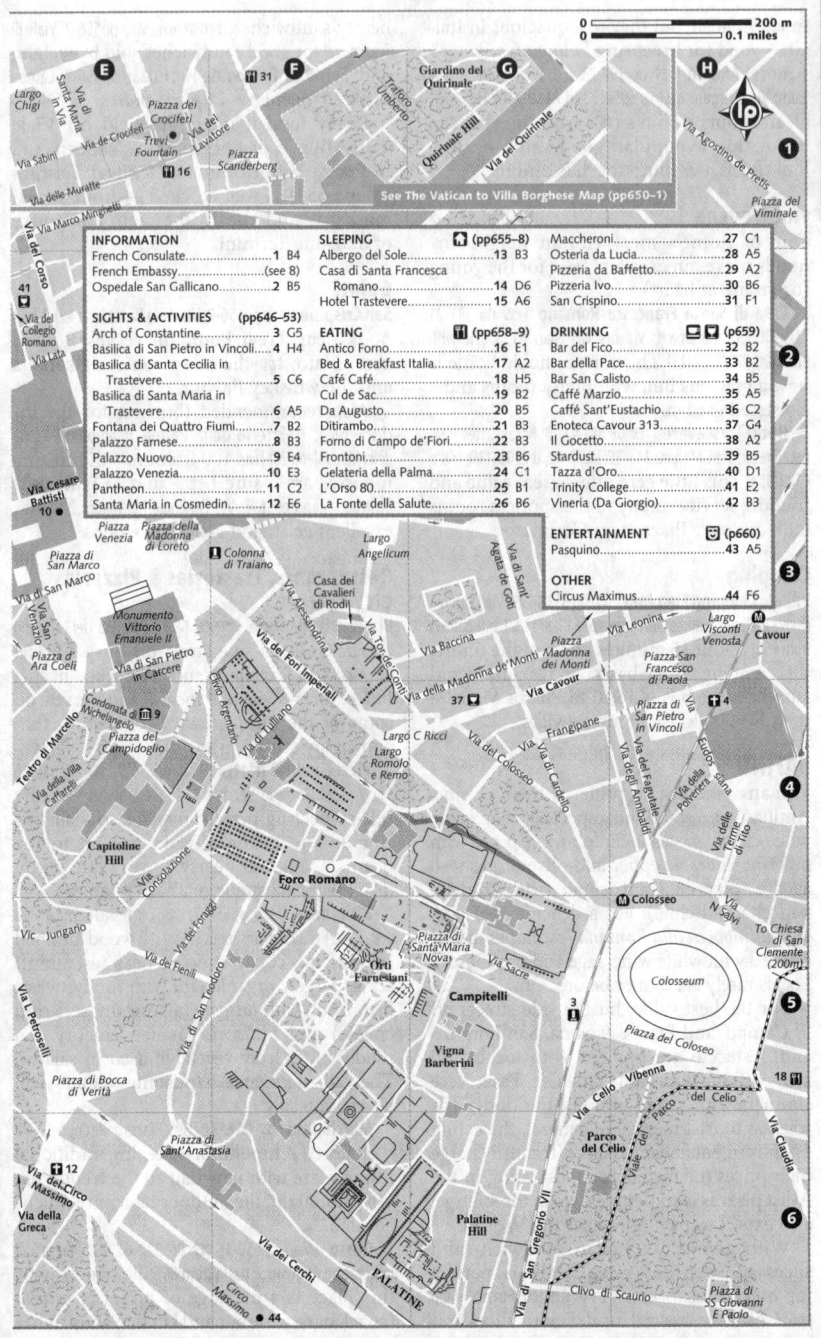

INFORMATION
French Consulate.............................1 B4
French Embassy.........................(see 8)
Ospedale San Gallicano...................2 B5

SIGHTS & ACTIVITIES   (pp646–53)
Arch of Constantine........................3 G5
Basilica di San Pietro in Vincoli.....4 H4
Basilica di Santa Cecilia in
    Trastevere..................................5 C6
Basilica di Santa Maria in
    Trastevere..................................6 A5
Fontana dei Quattro Fiumi.............7 B2
Palazzo Farnese.............................8 B3
Palazzo Nuovo...............................9 E4
Palazzo Venezia...........................10 E3
Pantheon.....................................11 C2
Santa Maria in Cosmedin.............12 E6

SLEEPING   (pp655–8)
Albergo del Sole..........................13 B3
Casa di Santa Francesca
    Romano...................................14 D6
Hotel Trastevere...........................15 A6

EATING   (pp658–9)
Antico Forno................................16 E1
Bed & Breakfast Italia..................17 A2
Café Café....................................18 H5
Cul de Sac..................................19 B2
Da Augusto.................................20 B5
Ditirambo....................................21 B3
Forno di Campo de'Fiori..............22 B3
Frontoni......................................23 B6
Gelateria della Palma..................24 C1
L'Orso 80....................................25 B1
La Fonte della Salute...................26 B6

Maccheroni.................................27 C1
Osteria da Lucia..........................28 A5
Pizzeria da Baffetto......................29 A2
Pizzeria Ivo.................................30 B6
San Crispino................................31 F1

DRINKING   (p659)
Bar del Fico................................32 B2
Bar della Pace.............................33 B2
Bar San Calisto............................34 B5
Caffé Marzio...............................35 A5
Caffé Sant'Eustachio....................36 C2
Enoteca Cavour 313....................37 G4
Il Gocetto...................................38 A2
Stardust......................................39 B5
Tazza d'Oro................................40 D1
Trinity College.............................41 E2
Vineria (Da Giorgio).....................42 B3

ENTERTAINMENT   (p660)
Pasquino.....................................43 A5

OTHER
Circus Maximus...........................44 F6

much English, but they're loquacious in Italian – good for practising *la lingua*.

Hotel Amalia (☎ 06 397 23 356; www.hotelamalia .com; Via Germanico 66; s €95-130, d €150-210) Bright, clean rooms a coin's toss from the Vatican make this a popular good-value option; look for last-minute specials online.

TRASTEVERE   Map pp656–7
One of Rome's most vibrant neighbourhoods makes an excellent base for the young (or young at heart).

Casa di Santa Francesca Romano (☎ 06 581 21 21; istituto@sfromana.it; Via dei Vascellari 61; s/d/tr with breakfast €70/100/123) This former noble home is now a gracious inn, with pretty rooms and a cloistered garden.

Hotel Trastevere (☎ 06 581 47 13; hoteltrastevere@ tiscalinet.it; Via L Manara 24a-25; s €77-83, d €103-119, tr & q €129-154) This little gem offers great value and friendly service; many of the spotless rooms look out over Piazza San Cosimato.

Camping
Village Camping Flaminio (☎ 06 333 14 29; Via Flaminia Nuova 821; per adult/child/camp site €11/8/12.50, bungalows from €56) About 15 minutes north of the centre, this camping village has a bar, restaurant and laundry; take bus No 910 to Piazza Mancini then No 200 to the camping village.

EATING
Romans take visible pride in their cuisine. Antipasto is a stand out, especially *bruschetta*, while classic pastas include *cacio e pepe* (with *pecorino* cheese, pepper and olive oil) as well as the spicy *all'Amatriciana* (with tomato, pancetta and chilli). For a delicious *secondo*, try *saltimbocca alla Romana* (escalopes of veal sautéed with white wine, sage and prosciutto). Locals rarely eat dinner before 9pm.

For the best value, hit the side streets off 'Il Campo' and Piazza Navona. San Lorenzo and Testaccio are popular with locals and also offer good-value meals. Trastevere simmers with eating options, but dodge the soulless tourist menus. In general, the eating establishments near Stazione Termini charge high prices for mediocre food. Eating in the A-list piazzas is sometimes worth the splurge; also expect to pay more near the Vatican.

With *panini* (an Italian sandwich) and slices of oven-hot pizza, Italy is perfect for quick, cheap eats. Try **Antico Forno** (Map pp656-7; Via delle Muratte 8) for delicious slices and

hearty sandwiches; **Frontoni** (Map pp656-7; Viale di Trastevere) for good sandwiches sold by weight; and **Forno di Campo de'Fiori** (Map pp656-7; Campo de'Fiori 22) for metres of *pizza bianca*.

Lively food markets are held off Viale delle Millizie, just north of the Vatican, and in Piazza Vittorio Emanuele, near Termini (Map p654). A well-stocked 24-hour supermarket is underneath the main concourse of Stazione Termini.

Gelati
San Crispino (Map pp656-7; Via della Panetteria 42) This nook near Trevi Fountain serves Rome's best gelato; try the in-season fruit sorbets and the whiskey flavour.

Also recommended (but not for the indecisive), **Gelateria della Palma** (Map pp656-7; Via della Maddalena 20) has 100 flavours – the creamy mousses are a sure bet – and **La Fonte della Salute** (Map pp656-7; Via Cardinale Marmaggi 2-6) has excellent gelati and generous scoops.

Restaurants, Trattorias & Pizzerias
CITY CENTRE
Pizzeria il Leoncino (☎ 06 687 63 06; Via del Leoncino 28; pizza €5) On a side street off busy Via del Corso, this excellent spot is cheap, hectic, full of beer-swigging locals, and serves up some of the finest pizza *alla romana* (thin and crispy crusts) in town.

Pizzeria da Baffetto (Map pp656-7; ☎ 06 686 16 17; Via del Governo Vecchio 114; pizza about €7) Any self-respecting pizza fan will also visit this Roman institution, always packed to the beams. Come very early or very late if you don't want to queue or share a table.

Ditirambo (Map pp656-7; ☎ 06 687 16 26; Piazza della Cancelleria 72; mains about €9) With wood-beamed ceilings, this cosy *trattoria* (cheap restaurant) serves largely organic fare with funky twists, like ravioli with *taleggio* (a pungent, soft-rind cheese) and *radicchio* (Italian chicory – a mildly bitter leafy vegetable used in salads). The tall, dark and handsome waiters will charm you silly.

Maccheroni (☎ 06 683 07 895; Piazza delle Coppelle 44; mains from €9) A hip *trattoria* serving traditional Roman fare with new flair to the trendy set. On a hot night, the outdoor tables are much-coveted.

Gusto (Map pp650-1; ☎ 06 322 62 73; Piazza del Imperatore Augusto 9; pasta from €6) Slick and savvy, this place is a melange of pizzeria, *osteria* (snack bar), wine bar and kitchen shop. It has an excellent wine list, an enormous cheese selection and good people-watching.

L'Orso 80 (Map pp656-7; ☎ 06 686 49 04; Via dell' Orso 33; from €15) Delicious and plentiful anti-pastos are the stars at this popular spot, and the friendly waiters are happy to keep bringing small plates until you yell *basta* (enough); a good option for vegetarians.

Cul de Sac (Map pp656-7; ☎ 06 688 01 094; Piazza Pasquino 73; pasta from €7) Tucked into a nook off Piazza Navona, this favourite local wine bar has communal wood benches out the front, a social vibe inside, and serves up solid meals and excellent wines.

WEST OF THE TIBER

Café Café (☎ 06 700 87 43; Via dei Santi Quattro 44; salads from €4) A low-key, neighbourhood joint not far from the Colosseum, it offers excel-lent salads, light meals and sandwiches – not to mention international newspapers, cups of brew, and wines by the glass. So com-fortable you may have trouble leaving.

Remo (Map pp648-9; ☎ 06 574 62 70; Piazza Santa Maria Liberatice 44; pizza from €4.50) This is loud and rowdy – it fills with party types at weekends – but the cheap prices, pizza and *bruschette al pomodoro* (bruschettas with tomato) make the chaos and obligatory queues worth it.

Osteria dell'Angelo (Map pp650-1; ☎ 06 372 94 70; Via G Bettolo 24; mains from €12) Offering the best value near the Vatican, this popular spot serves delicious authentic Roman fare, like *salsicce al cinghiale* (wild boar sausage).

Pizzeria Ivo (Map pp656-7; ☎ 06 581 70 82; Via di San Francesco a Ripa 158; pizza €4.75) Nice outdoor tables, excellent *bruschetta,* and a spirited local crowd who gather to watch soccer games, make up for the too-small-but-tasty pizzas and long queues.

Da Augusto (Map pp656-7; ☎ 06 580 37 98; Piazza de'Renzi 15; mains from €8) This bare-bones-but-beloved mamma's kitchen serves Roman classics with an occasionally surly attitude.

Osteria da Lucia (Map pp656-7; ☎ 06 580 36 01; Via del Mattinato 2; mains from €8) Dine under the stars with laundry flapping on the line at this terrific neighbourhood *trattoria* serving a *trippa alla romano* (Roman tripe) that may well make you a convert.

DRINKING

Much of the activity is in the centre, where Campo de'Fiori fills with young revellers, and there are nifty late-night spots fringing Piazza Navona. Trastevere is packed with friendly bars and co-mingling tourists and locals; the Monti, Esquilino and Testaccio districts also have lots of watering holes, including some gay venues. Romans love their *enotecas* (wine bars), and these cool places can offer a good-value way to sample *vini* and meet locals over a glass.

Tazza d'Oro (Map pp656-7; Via degli Orfani) Head here for positively outstanding coffee, just off Piazza della Rotonda.

Caffè Sant'Eustachio (Map pp656-7; Piazza Sant' Eustachio 82) Serves sublime creamy coffee, served extra sweet.

Caffè Marzio (Map pp656-7; Piazza Santa Maria) In Trastevere, this café has terrific coffee and a gorgeous view onto one of Rome's prettiest piazzas; perfection with a price though.

Bar della Pace (Map pp656-7; Via della Pace 3-7) With its gilded ambience and dashing in-crowd, this is an atmospheric drinking spot.

Vineria (Map pp656-7; ☎ 06 688 03 268; Campo de'Fiori 15) Cosy Vineria, on Il Campo, was once the gathering place of the Roman literati.

Bar del Fico (Map pp656-7; Piazza del Fico 24) This pretty bar is popular with artists, has tables beneath its namesake fig tree and a snug interior with tasteful music and local art.

Bar San Calisto (Map pp656-7; Piazza dell'Arco San Calisto) The slacker Trastevere set hangs at unglamorous San Calisto; besides the cheap drinks and arty crowd, it has memorable chocolate offerings.

Stardust (Map pp656-7; Viccolo dei Renzi 4) Also in the hood is this tiny local's haunt that purrs with sultry jazz and doesn't close until the last customers tumble out the door.

Try **Il Gocetto** (Map pp656-7; Via dei Banchi Vecchi 14), one of the city's best wine bars and like a club for locals, and **Enoteca Cavour 313** (Map pp656-7; Via Cavour 313), with wine-packed shelves, wood benches, good antipastos and a convivial staff.

Trinity College (Map pp656-7; Via del Collegio Romano 6) If you're hankering for pub night, try Trinity College, with a good selection of import brews, great food and an easy-going ambience; it gets packed at weekends.

CLUBBING

At Roman discos, expect to pay upward of €20 to get in, which might or might not include one drink. Popular stayers include **Alien** (Map pp648-9; ☎ 06 841 22 12; Via Velletri 13), for sci-fi décor, dancers on raised platforms, and hip-hop rhythms, and the far-flung **Goa** (☎ 06 574 82 77; Via Libetta 13; ☾ Oct-May), with a groovy ethnic décor and glam crowd but a distant location near metro stop Garbatella.

Newcomer **Le Cru** (Map pp650-1; ☎ 06 678 48 38; Via della Mercede 10/d), next door to older-crowd **Gilda** (Map pp650-1), oozes smoke and is bedecked with tapestries, candlelit tables and kissing couples; no cover, but the cocktails, served in voluptuous glasses, are steep.

L'Alibi (Map pp648-9; ☎ 06 574 34 48; Via di Monte Testaccio 44) is considered Rome's premier gay venue.

ENTERTAINMENT

The best entertainment guide is the Thursday-published *Roma C'è* (www.romace.it), with an English-language section; *Wanted in Rome* (www.wantedinrome.it), published on alternate Wednesdays, is also good; *La Repubblica* and *Il Messagero* daily newspapers have cinema, theatre and concert listings. All are available at newsstands. Rome's entertainment schedule is particularly heady in summer, with numerous alfresco performances; be sure to catch one if possible.

For theatre, opera and sporting events, you can book ahead via **Hello** (Stazione Termini) or **Orbis** (Map p654; Piazza dell'Esquilino 37).

Cinema

Cinemas screening films in English include **Pasquino** (Map pp656-7; ☎ 06 580 36 22; Piazza Sant'Egidio), just off Piazza Santa Maria, and **Warner Village Moderno** (Map p654; ☎ 06 588 00 99; Via Merry del Val 14), a megaplex showing Hollywood blockbusters and Italian films. Expect to pay €7, with discounts on Wednesdays.

Live Music

Decked out like an air-raid shelter, the popular **Radio Londra** (Map pp648-9; ☎ 06 575 00 44; Via di Monte Testaccio 65b), has live music four nights a week. Just down the street are the more sedate Caruso Caffè (Map pp648-9) at No 36, with live music twice weekly and good DJs otherwise, and Caffè Latino (Map pp648-9) at No 96, with live Latin American music and a disco of Latin and funk.

For jazz and blues, head to **Alexanderplatz** (Map pp650-1; ☎ 06 397 42 171; Via Ostia 9), showing top international musicians, and **Big Mama** (☎ 06 581 24 51; Via San Francesco a Ripa 18) in Trastevere.

Opera & Classical Music

Teatro dell'Opera (Map p654; ☎ 06 481 60 28 706; www.operaroma.it; Piazza Beniamino Gigli) This has Rome's finest offerings from December to June; ticket prices are steep.

For a full season of concerts, there's the **Accademia di Santa Cecilia** (Map pp650-1; ☎ 06 361 10 64; Via della Conciliazione 4) and the **Accademia Filarmonica Romana** (☎ 06 323 48 90; Teatro Olimpico, Piazza Gentile da Fabriano 17).

GETTING AROUND
To/From the Airport

Rome's main airport, Leonardo da Vinci (Fiumicino), is 30km southwest of the city centre. The cheapest transport to town is via the Leonardo Express train service (follow the signs to the station from the airport arrivals hall), which costs €8.80, arrives at and leaves from platform Nos 25 to 29 at Termini and takes 35 minutes. The first direct train leaves the airport at 6.37am, and then trains run half-hourly until the last one at 11.37pm. From Termini to the airport, trains start at 5.51am and run half-hourly until the last train at 10.51pm. Another train from Fiumicino (with destination Orte or Fara Sabina) stops at Trastevere, Ostiense and Tiburtina stations (€4.70), but not at Termini, with service from the airport every 20 minutes from 5.57am to 11.27pm and from Tiburtina from 5.06am until 10.36pm. From midnight to 5am, an hourly bus runs from Stazione Tiburtina to the airport. Taxis to the city centre cost about €47. The **Airport Shuttle** (☎ 06 420 14 507; www.airportshuttle.it) offers transfers to/from Fiumicino for €28.50 for one or two passengers, €35 for three and €46.50 for four.

Rome's other airport is Ciampino, used for most domestic and international charters.

Bus & Metro

Rome has an integrated public transport system, so the same **Metrebus** (www.metrebus.it) ticket is valid for all modes of transport. You can buy tickets at all *tabacchi* (tobacconists' shops), newsstands and vending machines at main bus stops. Single tickets cost €0.75 for 75 minutes, daily tickets cost €3.10 and weekly tickets cost €12.40. Tickets must be purchased before you get on and validated in the orange machine as you board. Ticketless riders risk a hefty €53 fine – there's zero tolerance for tourists being or acting dumb.

ATAC (☎ 800 43 17 84; www.atac.roma.it) is the city's public transport company. Free transport maps and details on bus routes are available at the ATAC information booth in the centre of Piazza dei Cinquecento, where many bus routes terminate. Largo di Torre Argentina, Piazza Venezia and Piazza San Silvestro are other hubs. Buses generally run from about 6am to midnight, with limited services throughout the night on some routes. A fast tram service, the No 8, connects Largo di Torre Argentina with Trastevere, Porta Portese and Monteverde Nuovo.

The Metropolitana has two lines, A and B. Both pass through Stazione Termini. Take Linea A for Piazza di Spagna, the Vatican (Ottaviano) and Villa Borghese (Flaminio), and Linea B for the Colosseum, Circus Maximus and Piramide (Testaccio and Stazione Ostiense). Trains run approximately every five minutes between 5.30am and 11.30pm (12.30am on Saturday).

Car & Motorcycle

Negotiating Roman traffic by car is hard enough, but you're in for high stress if you ride a motorcycle or Vespa in the city. If your car goes missing after being parked illegally, check with the **traffic police** (☎ 06 676 91).

Happy Rent (Map p654; ☎ 06 481 81 85; www .happyrent.com; Via Farini 3) hires scooters (from €31 per day), motorcycles (around €104 and up) as well as bicycles (from €62 per week).

Taxi

Cooperativa Radio Taxi Romana (☎ 06 35 70) oversees many operators. Major taxi ranks are at the airports, Stazione Termini and Largo di Torre Argentina in the historical centre (look for the orange-and-black taxi signs). There are surcharges from €1 to €3 for luggage, night service, Sunday and public holidays; travel to/from Fiumicino airport has a surcharge of €7.45/6.10. The flag fall is €2.75 (for the first 3km), then €0.75 for every kilometre.

AROUND ROME

OSTIA ANTICA

The Romans founded this port city at the mouth of the Tiber in the 4th century BC and its ruins provide a fascinating contrast to the ruins at Pompeii (p703), which was a resort town for the wealthy.

Information about the town and ruins is available from the Rome tourist office (see p646) or Enjoy Rome (p646).

Of particular note in the **excavated city** (☎ 06 563 58 099; admission €4.20; ⏰ 9am-5pm Tue-Sun winter, to 7pm summer) are the mosaics of the **Terme di Nettuno** (Baths of Neptune); a **Roman theatre** built by Agrippa; the **forum** and **Capitolium** temple, dedicated to Jupiter, Juno and Min erva; and the **Piazzale delle Corporazioni**, offices of Ostia's 70 merchant guilds, distinguished by mosaics depicting their different trades.

To get to Ostia Antica from Rome, take the Metro Linea B to Piramide or Magliana, then the Ostia Lido train (getting off at Ostia Antica). By car, take the Via del Mare or the parallel-running Via Ostiense.

TIVOLI
pop 53,000

Set on a hill by the Aniene River, Tivoli was an ancient Roman resort town that became popular as a summer playground for the wealthy during the Renaissance. The main draws are the terraced gardens and fountains of the Renaissance **Villa d'Este** (admission €6.50; ⏰ 9am-1hr before sunset Tue-Sun), which was built in the 16th century for Cardinal Ippolito d'Este on the site of a Franciscan monastery. However, the ruins of **Villa Adriana** (☎ 07 745 302 03; admission €6.50; ⏰ 9am-1hr before sunset) are more evocative and interesting. They were built in the 2nd century by the Roman emperor Hadrian as a summer villa. The **tourist office** (☎ 07 743 11 249; Largo Garibaldi; ⏰ 8.30am-2.30pm Tue-Sat & 3-6pm Tue-Thu) is near the Cotral bus stop.

Tivoli is 30km east of Rome and accessible by Cotral bus from outside the Ponte Mammolo station on Metro Linea B. Buses depart every 20 minutes, stopping at Villa Adriana, about 1km from Tivoli, along the way; the trip takes about one hour. Local bus No 4 goes to Villa Adriana from Tivoli's Piazza Garibaldi.

TARQUINIA
pop 15,300

Believed to have been founded in the 12th century BC, and home of the Tarquin kings who ruled Rome before the creation of the republic, beautiful Tarquinia was an important economic and political centre of the Etruscan League, which was comprised of the most powerful city-states. One major attraction is the **necropolis** (burial grounds; ☎ 07 668 56 308; admission incl Museo Nazionale Tarquiniense €6.20; ⏰ 8.30am-6.30pm Tue-Sun) and its painted tombs. The other is the **Museo Nazionale**

Tarquiniense (☎ 07 668 56 036; 🕑 9am-7pm Tue-Sun), whose significant collection of Etruscan treasures includes frescoes from the tombs. Keep an eye out for a few red-and-black plates featuring acrobatic sex acts.

The **tourist office** (☎ 07 668 56 384; Piazza Cavour 1; 🕑 8am-2pm Mon-Sat) is just past the medieval ramparts. Ask here for directions to the necropolis, which is a 15- to 20-minute walk.

Tarquinia is an easy day trip from Rome. Cotral buses leave approximately every hour for Tarquinia from outside the Lepanto stop on Metro Linea A, arriving at Barriera San Giusto, a short distance from the tourist office.

NORTHERN ITALY

Italy's 'well-heeled' north isn't short of finery. From the Alps to Liguria's beaches and the fairy-tale beauty of La Serenissima (Venice), its physical riches are matched only by its cultural treasures. The only danger is lingering in bigger cities, when there are delights throughout Piedmont, Lombardy, Emilia-Romagna and the Veneto.

GENOA (GENOVA)

pop 628,800

Liguria's capital, busy Genoa is simultaneously aristocratic, grandiose and dingy. But the mighty maritime republic once lauded as 'La Superba' somehow retains a salty exuberance that her favourite son, Christopher Columbus (1451–1506), would salute. Genoa was a European City of Culture in 2004.

Orientation

Most trains stop at the main stations, Principe and Brignole. Brignole is closer to Genoa's centre and convenient for slightly better accommodation. Principe, nearer to the port, has many cheaper, 'challenging' options nearby; it's an area best avoided at night by women travelling alone. From Brignole take Via Fiume toward Via XX Settembre and the historical centre. Local ATM buses service both stations.

Information

In-Centro IT (Via XX Settembre 17-21; per hr €4; 🕑 10am-1pm & 2.30-7.30pm Mon-Fri, 10am-1pm & 3.30-7.30pm Sat & Sun) A tourism 'shop' with Internet access upstairs.

Main post office (☎ 531 87 08; Via Dante 4a; 🕑 8am-6.30pm Mon-Sat) Off Piazza de Ferrari.
Ospedale San Martino (☎ 010 55 51; www .hsanmartino.liguria.it; largo Rosanna Benzi 10) A hospital east of the centre.
Telecom office (Piazza Verdi; 🕑 8am-9pm) To the left of Stazione Brignole.
Tourist office (www.apt.genova.it) Stazione Principe (☎ 01 024 62 633; 🕑 9.30am-1pm & 2.30-6pm Mon-Sat) Stazione Marittima (☎ 01 024 63 686; 🕑 based on ship arrivals/departures) airport (☎ 01 060 15 247; 🕑 9.30am-12.30pm & 1.30-5.30pm Mon-Sat) Offers helpful information about the region.

Sights & Activities

Any tour of Genoa should include the backstreets around the port. Newer parts of the harbour also attract at night, when the hill-top lights form an appealing backdrop for the popular *passegiata* (stroll).

Search out the gorgeous 12th-century, black-and-white marble **Cattedrale di San Lorenzo** and the huge **Palazzo Ducale** (☎ 010 557 40 00; www.palazzoducale.genova.it; Piazza Matteotti 9; admission cost varies; 🕑 9am-9pm, ticket office to 8pm Tue-Sun) which doubles as the region's major exhibition space/arts hub.

Via Garibaldi is lined with palaces, many housing galleries, including the 16th-century **Palazzo Bianco** (☎ 010 557 20 13; www.museopalazzo bianco.it; Via Garibaldi 11; 1-/3-day card €8/12, bus surcharge €1/3; 🕑 9am-8pm Tue-Sun) and the 17th-century **Palazzo Rosso** (☎ 010 247 63 51; www.palazzorosso .it; Via Garibaldi 18; admission €3.10; 🕑 9am-7pm Tue-Fri, 10am-7pm Sat & Sun). **Galleria Nazionale di Palazzo Spinola** (☎ 010 247 70 61; Piazza Pellicceria 1; admission €4; 🕑 8.30am-7.30pm Tue-Sat, 1-8pm Sun) displays major Italian and Flemish Renaissance works, including Caravaggio's *Ecce Homo*.

Acquario Di Genova (☎ 010 234 52 67; www.acquario .ge.it; Ponte Spinola; adult/child €12.50/7.50; 🕑 9.30am-7.30pm Mon-Wed & Fri, 9.30am-10pm Thu, 9.30am-8.30pm Sat & Sun) is a highlight. The eye-catching Renzo Piano–designed aquarium jutting into the harbour is Europe's biggest; though pricey, it's an interesting example of the genre.

Sleeping

Ostello Genova (☎ 010 242 24 57; hostelge@iol.it; Via Costanzi 120; B&B €13-18, dinner €8; 🕑 closed Jan) In Righi, the nearest AIG (HI) hostel is outside Genoa. Typically clean, but a little soulless (11.30pm curfew). There's a terrace with spectacular views of Genoa, though. Bus No 40 from Brignole.

Carola (☎ 010 839 13 40; Via Gropallo 4; s/d/tr without bathroom €30/45/60, d/tr with bathroom €55/70) In a gracious old *palazzo* near Brignole, Carola offers simple rooms and a warm welcome. On a pleasant street north off Piazza Brignole, 1km from the old port.

Hotel Bel Soggiorno (☎ 010 54 28 80; www.bel soggiornohotel.com; Via XX Settembre 19; s/d with bathroom €73/93; 🖭 🖵) This is worth a splurge for its bright, airy, slightly chintzy rooms. The charming owner works hard to ensure a pleasant stay, and will negotiate discounts for multiple nights. Superbly located.

Eating & Drinking

Genoa offers many Ligurian specialities, including the eponymous local 'dish', *pesto Genovese*. There's also delicious *pansoti* (ravioli in ground walnut sauce) and focaccia.

Check out the **oriental market** (Via XX Settembre) for fantastic produce. Head to the Via Sottoripo arcades on the waterfront for fresh seafood (€2 to €5 per bag of fried calamari). There's a slew of places along Via Balbi, near Principe, frequented by local students and offering good-value pasta (€5 to €6).

Bar Ristoro (☎ 010 58 82 60; Piazza Colombo 10/12; courses €3-5; 🕑 lunch & dinner) A lively little bar-*ristorante* near Brignole that hums at lunch time with local workers stopping in for the excellent, filling two-course meals – the perfect Italian quick lunch.

Il Barbarossa (☎ 010 246 50 97; Piano di Sant Andrea 21-3r; meals €12-18; 🕑 7.30am-3.30am Mon, 7.30am-2.30am Tue-Fri, 12.30pm-2.30am Sat & Sun) Metres from Columbus' house, dark Barbarossa is cosy and atmospheric. A great place for a quick *panini* and a beer.

Good bars are clustered around Piazza Raibetta and Piazza delle Erbe. A perfect example is **Threegaio** (☎ 010 246 57 93; www .threegaio.it; Piazza delle Erbe 17/19r; light meals €5-10; 🕑 lunch & dinner Mon-Sat), hip but unpretentious with a laid-back vibe, noticeably lifting at *aperitivo* (cocktail hour) time.

Entertainment

Genoa's nightlife is subdued; try the three floors at **Dueseiuno** (☎ 010 251 15 58; Mura della Marina 21r; 🕑 noon-2am). Live music fans should seek out **Cosa Zapata** (Via Sampierdarena 36; 🕑 9pm-3am Fri & Sat) where 'Bohemian' types mosh to rowdier music within medieval walls. There are cinemas and abundant shops in the **Magazin del Cotone complex** (Porto Antico).

Getting There & Away

There are regular domestic and international flights from **Cristoforo Colombo airport** (☎ 010 601 54 10; Sestri Ponente), 6km west of the centre. Buses for Rome, Florence, Milan and Perugia leave from Piazza della Vittoria, south of Stazione Brignole, where Eurolines coaches also depart for European destinations. Book at **Geotravels** (☎ 010 58 71 81) in the piazza. Genoa has rail links to major cities; phone ☎ 848 88 80 88 for information.

Genoa is a major embarkation point for ferries to Sicily, Sardinia and Corsica. Companies are **Corsica Ferries** (☎ 019 21 55 11; www .corsicaferries.com) in Savona; **Moby Lines** (☎ 010 254 15 13; www.moby.it) at Ponte Asserato for Corsica; **Tirrenia** (☎ 199 12 31 99, 800 82 40 79; www.gruppo tirrenia.it) at the Stazione Marittima, Ponte Colombo for Sicily and Sardinia; and **Grandi Navi Veloci** (www.gnv.it) and **Grandi Traghetti** (☎ 01058 93 31; Via Fieschi 17) for Sardinia, Sicily and Malta.

RIVIERA DI LEVANTE

The Ligurian coast from Genoa south to La Spezia is spectacular, rivalling the Amalfi Coast in beauty. Summer here is congested; try going in spring and autumn when the smaller crowds make sightseeing easier and the heat is less stifling. A good option is using either Santa Margherita Ligure in the north or La Spezia in the south as a base.

The **tourist office** (☎ 0185 28 74 85; Via XXV Aprile 4) in Santa Margherita is central; in La Spezia the **tourist office** (☎ 0187 77 09 00; Via Mazzini 45) is close to the waterfront. Both have information on the Cinque Terre and the surrounding coastal towns.

Sights & Activities

From Santa Margherita Ligure you can explore **Portofino**, a haunt of the glamour set, and **Camogli**, a gorgeous fishing village turned resort town. The Benedictine monastery of **San Fruttuoso** is a 2½-hour hilly walk from Camogli or Portofino, with sensational views.

Don't miss the **Cinque Terre** – Riomaggiore, Manarola, Corniglia, Vernazza and Monterosso, five tiny villages clustered along some eye-popping Unesco-protected coastline, among the most beautiful regions in Italy. Linked by a 12km path, the **Via dell'Amore** (Lovers' Lane; toll €3) makes perfect (occasionally challenging) walking.

In summer, **swimming** is allowed in some bays and coves (check first) – bring snorkelling gear for an all-too often-overlooked treat (that's free).

Sleeping & Eating
Between April and September, book ahead.

Ostello 5 Terre (☎ 0187 92 02 15; www.cinqueterre.net /ostello; Via B Riccobaldi 21; dm €17-22, breakfast/dinner €3.50/14) This orderly, well-run hostel in Manorola is always crowded, so book ahead. Manorola is a 15-minute walk from Riomaggiore.

La Dolce Vita (☎ 0187 76 00 44; fax 0187 92 09 35; Via Colombo 120; bed from €20) The Natale family's booking service in Riomaggiore is worth dropping a few extra euro for; rooms are excellent (many with views) and Giacomo will do his utmost to accommodate you.

A Pie De Ma (☎ 338 222 00 88; Via dell'Amore; snack/ light meals €5-8; ☺ breakfast, lunch & dinner) Perched on a cliff-side above the perfect teal of a tiny Riomaggiore bay, this offers one of Italy's most stunning backdrops for a snack, coffee or wine – or just whiling away the hours.

Bar Centrale (☎ 0187 92 02 08; barcentr@tin.it; Via Colombo 144; Internet per hr €6; ☺ rarely closed) This is the hub of Riomaggiore hijinks and the most raucous carousing option in the Cinque Terre. Owner/barman Ivo serves the drinks (and jokes) with practised ease.

Getting There & Around
All towns are accessible by train from Genoa. Buses leave from Santa Margherita's Piazza Martiri della Libertà for Portofino. **Servizio Marittimo del Tigullio** (☎ 0185 28 46 70; www.traghettiportofino.it; ☺ summer) runs ferries from Santa Margherita to Portofino, San Fruttuoso and the Cinque Terre. Ferry routes service the coast from La Spezia. The *biglietto giornaliero Cinque Terre* (24-hour Cinque Terre rail pass; €5.80) allows unlimited travel between Monterosso and La Spezia.

TURIN (TORINO)
pop 898,400

An imminent Winter Olympics host-city (2006), Turin smacks of faded grandeur. The former capital of Italy (until 1945) and seat of the Savoys feels like a once-regal place coasting on reputation. The Agnelli family's FIAT automobile empire and Italy's most notorious footballers, Juventus, keep Turin in the headlines. Curiously, many famous edibles come from Turin: Ferrero Rocher chocolates, Nutella and Tic Tacs.

Turin's other famous icon is *Il Sindone*, or 'The Shroud of Turin', believed to have been Christ's burial cassock.

Orientation & Information
Porta Nuova train station is the usual arrival point. For the centre, cross Corso Vittorio Emanuele II and walk through the grand Carlo Felice and San Carlo piazzas towards Piazza Castello.

Torino Card (☎ 011 53 51 81; www.turismotorino.org; 48/72hr card €15/17) Museum enthusiasts should consider this card, valid for all public transport and discounts/entry to 120 sights.

Tourist offices Piazza Castello (☎ 011 53 51 81; www .turismotorino.org; Piazza Castello 161; ☺ 9.30am-7pm Mon-Sat, 9.30am-3pm Sun) Porta Nuova train station (☎ 011 53 13 27) airport (☎ 011 567 81 24)

Sights & Activities
Start at Piazza San Carlo ('Turin's drawing room'), capped by the baroque churches of San Carlo and Santa Cristina. Nearby Piazza Castello features the sumptuous Palazzo Madama, home to the Museo Civico d'Arte Antica and the 17th-century **Palazzo Reale** (Royal Palace), where the gardens were designed in 1697 by Louis le Nôtre, noted for his Versailles work.

True film buffs shouldn't miss the impressive **Museo Nazionale del Cinema** (☎ 011 812 56 58; www.museonazionaledelcinema.it; Via Montebello 20; full/concession €5.20/4.20; ☺ 9am-8pm Tue-Fri & Sun, 9am-11pm Sat), Italy's broadest archive of imaging history. Exhibits range from original Charlie Chaplin storyboards to HR Giger–designed *Aliens* props.

The Cattedrale di San Giovanni Battista houses the **Turin Shroud** (*Il Sindone*), a linen cloth purportedly used to wrap Christ's body. Radiocarbon dating challenges this, measuring the cloth's age at around 800 years, and, in 2004, Italian scientists discovered a 'secondary image' on its reverse side. Rarely shown (check at the museum), a copy is displayed in the cathedral. The **Museo della Sindone** (Museum of the Shroud; Via San Domenico 28; admission €5.50; ☺ 9am-noon & 3-7pm) answers most questions.

Turin's **Museo Egizio** (Egyptian Museum; ☎ 011 561 77 76; www.museoegizio.org; Via Accademia delle Scienze 6; admission €6.50; ☺ 8.30am-7.30pm Tue-Sun) is considered among the best museums of Egyptian artefacts after those in London and Cairo.

Outside town is the chichi **Palazzina di Caccia di Stupinigi** (Savoy Hunting Lodge; ☎ 011 358 12 20; www.mauriziano.com; Piazza Principe Amedeo 7; ☒ 10am-5pm Tue-Sun, to 6pm summer), the gaudiest example of Turin's French-baroque architecture.

Sleeping & Eating
Turin thinks highly of itself, so prices can be disproportionate.

Ostello Torino (☎ 011 660 29 39; www.ostellionline .org; Via Alby 1; dm B&B/d €12/17; dinner €8.50; ☒ closed 9.30am-2pm; ☒) To get to the quiet HI hostel, catch bus No 52 from Porta Nuova (No 64 on Sunday). Don't believe the signs near the station; it's a 2km walk up a steep hill. Book ahead to snag a double room.

Campeggio Villa Rey (☎ 011 819 01 17; Strada Superiore Val San Martino 27; per adult/camp site €3.65/6; ☒ Mar-Oct) This camping ground in the hills east of the Po has access and bathrooms for travellers with disabilities. Take bus No 52, as for the HI hostel.

Bologna (☎ 011 562 02 90; www.hotelbolognasrl.it; Corso Vittorio Emanuele II 60; s/d/tr with bathroom €57/88/100) Near the station, and deservedly popular. Looking grim at first, rooms are clean and comfortable, if a little exposed to noise.

Al Pigaron (☎ 011 812 50 18; Via Accademia Albertina 27; 3-course lunch incl wine €8; ☒ lunch & dinner) This place serves the cheapest three-course lunch in Turin. There's a pasta course followed by a meat course, plus one vegetable dish of choice; and a *quartino* (250mL) of house wine and dessert – a killer bargain! Décor is '70s shabby-tacky, but the simple Piemontese dishes are delicious and large.

La Stua (☎ 011 817 83 39; Via Giuseppe Mazzini 46; pizza €7-9; ☒ noon-2pm & 6.45pm-midnight Tue-Sun) This wonderful pizzeria offers a fantastic range of the trademark dish, as well as excellent pasta and main meals. It has a warm atmosphere, great prices and friendly staff.

Gelati and chocolate choices abound; try **Caffè Fiorio** (Via Po 8) – good enough for Italian unification hero Camillo Cavour.

Getting There & Around
Turin is serviced by **Caselle international airport** (☎ 011 567 63 61), for domestic and European flights. **Sadem buses** (☎ 011 300 01 66; ☒ every 45min) service the airport from the corner between Via Sacchi and Corso Vittorio Emanuele II. National and international buses use the terminal on Corso Castelfidardo. Regular trains connect

with Milan, Aosta, Venice, Genoa and Rome. The centre is well serviced by buses and trams.

MILAN (MILANO)
pop 1.3 million

Milan is a glitzy city, obsessed with money, looks and glamour. Not traditionally a huge draw for budget travellers, it's worth a look to see how those in the top tax brackets live. Offering the best in Italian theatre, nightlife and clothes, you almost need to be among its worshipped modelling or football elite to afford all Milan offers.

Originally believed to have been Celtic, Milan was conquered by the Romans (222 BC) and soon became a major trading and transport centre. Today, it's at the cutting-edge of Italian manufacturing, media and design.

Milan practically closes down in August, when most of the city's populace take their holidays.

Orientation
From Milan's central train station (Stazione Centrale), approach the centre on the underground (the Metropolitana Milanese, or MM). Use the Duomo (cathedral) and the Castello Sforzesco as your landmarks; the main shopping areas and sights are around these two.

Information
BOOKSHOPS
Feltrinelli International (☎ 02 659 56 44; www .lafeltrinelli.it; Piazza Cavour 1) The foreign-language arm of Italy's best book chain.

EMERGENCY
Milan City Council (☎ 02 546 68 118; Via Friuli 30) Call for lost property.
Police Headquarters (☎ 02 622 61; Via Fatebenefratelli 11)
Ufficio Stranieri (Foreigners' Office; ☎ 02 622 61; Via Montebello 26) English is spoken.

INTERNET ACCESS
Grazia Internet (☎ 02 670 05 43; Piazza Duca D'Aosta 40; per hr €4; ☒ 8am-2am) One of Milan's cheapest Internet places, it's beside Stazione Centrale.

LAUNDRY
Lavanderia Self-Service (Via Tadino 4; per small/large load €3.10/6.10; ☒ 7.30am-9.30pm)

ITALY

CENTRAL MILAN

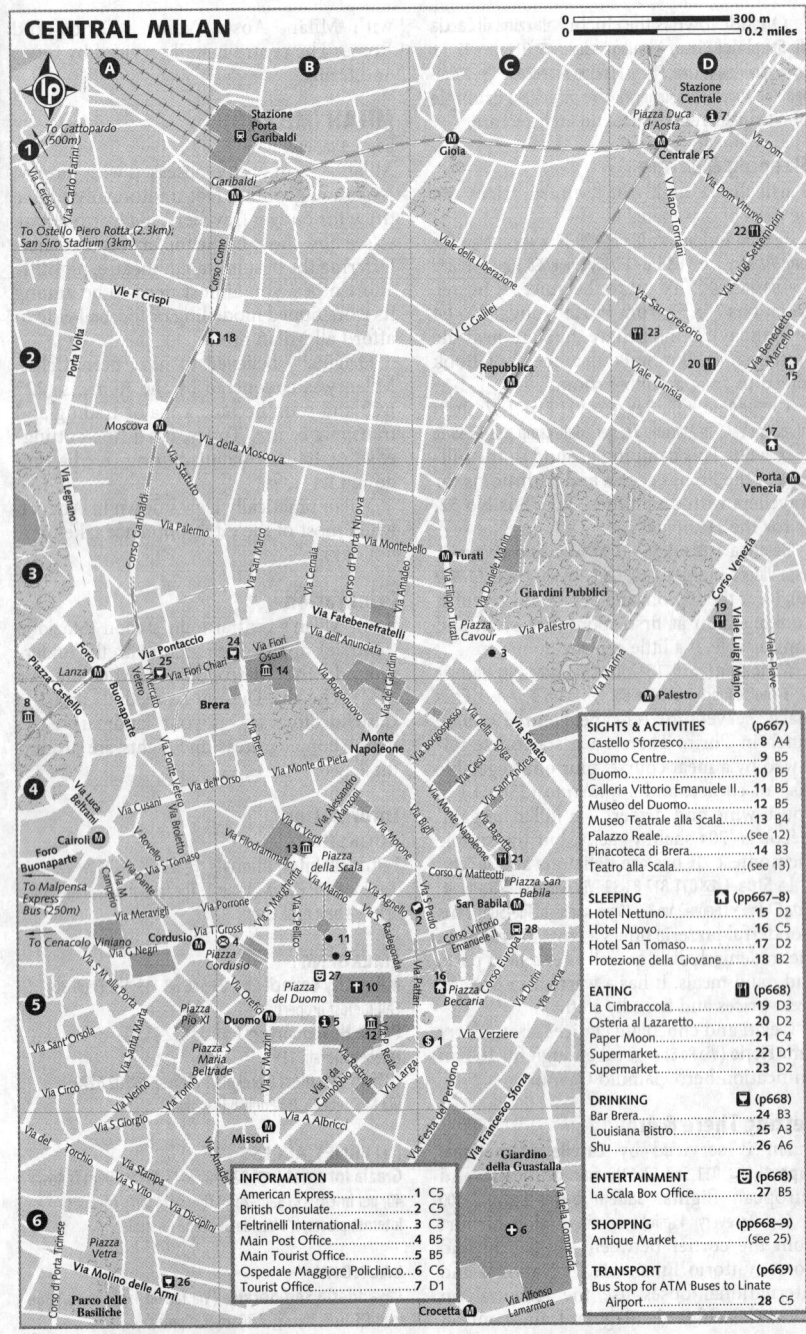

| 0 | 300 m |
| 0 | 0.2 miles |

To Gattopardo (500m)

To Ostello Piero Rotta (2.3km);
San Siro Stadium (3km)

To Malpensa
Express
Bus (250m)

To Cenacolo Vinciano

SIGHTS & ACTIVITIES (p667)
Castello Sforzesco............8 A4
Duomo Centre..................9 B5
Duomo............................10 B5
Galleria Vittorio Emanuele II...11 B5
Museo del Duomo............12 B5
Museo Teatrale alla Scala...13 B4
Palazzo Reale.................(see 12)
Pinacoteca di Brera..........14 B3
Teatro alla Scala.............(see 13)

SLEEPING (pp667–8)
Hotel Nettuno.................15 D2
Hotel Nuovo....................16 D2
Hotel San Tomaso............17 D2
Protezione della Giovane...18 B2

EATING (p668)
La Cimbraccola................19 D3
Osteria al Lazzaretto........20 D2
Paper Moon.....................21 C4
Supermarket....................22 D1
Supermarket....................23 D2

DRINKING (p668)
Bar Brera........................24 B3
Louisiana Bistro...............25 A3
Shu...............................26 A6

ENTERTAINMENT (p668)
La Scala Box Office..........27 B5

SHOPPING (pp668–9)
Antique Market...............(see 25)

TRANSPORT (p669)
Bus Stop for ATM Buses to Linate
Airport..........................28 C5

INFORMATION
American Express...............1 C5
British Consulate................2 C5
Feltrinelli International.........3 C3
Main Post Office................4 B5
Main Tourist Office............5 B5
Ospedale Maggiore Policlinico...6 C6
Tourist Office...................7 D1

MEDICAL SERVICES

For an ambulance phone ☎ 118.

Ospedale Maggiore Policlinico (☎ 02 550 31; Via Francesco Sforza 35) The public hospital is central.

Pharmacy (☎ 02 669 07 35; Stazione Centrale; 🕒 24hr)

MONEY

Bank hours (8.30am to 1.30pm and 2.45pm to 3.45pm Monday to Friday) are regulated. Most major banks have ATMs near the Duomo. There are exchange offices at Stazione Centrale.

American Express office (Via Larga 4; 🕒 9am-5.30pm Mon-Fri)

POST & TELEPHONE

Main post office (Via Cordusio 4; 🕒 8am-7pm Mon-Fri, 8.30am-noon Sat) Off Via Dante, near Piazza del Duomo. Additional offices are at the station and Linate airport.

Telecom office (upper level Stazione Centrale; 🕒 8am-9.30pm) Has various directories. The office in Galleria Vittorio Emanuele II (🕒 8am-9.30pm) also has fax services and phonecards.

TOURIST INFORMATION

Main tourist office (☎ 02 725 24 301; www.milanoinfotourist.com; Via Marconi 1; 🕒 8.45am-1pm & 2-6pm Mon-Sat, 9am-1pm & 2-5pm Sun) In Piazza del Duomo; pick up the free *Hello Milano* and *Milano Mese* here, and a *Milan is Milano* map. Other branches are at Stazione Centrale (☎ 02 725 24 360; 🕒 9am-6.30pm Mon-Sat, 9am-12.30pm & 1.30-5pm Sun) and both airports.

Dangers & Annoyances

Milan's main shopping areas are haunts for thieves, some employing diversionary tactics. Be alert, particularly around Stazione Centrale, to people 'crowding' you around the platforms.

Sights & Activities

Milan is grimily pretty, with a distinctly French influence. Despite the high cost of the city's most favoured activities, there's plenty to see that's free.

The city's landmark **Duomo** looks like a back drop for an animated story. Commissioned in 1386 to a florid French-Gothic design and finished nearly 600 years later, the façade is an unforgettable marble mass of statues, spires and pillars. The view from the **roof** (stairs/lift €3.50/5; 🕒 9am-5.30pm) is wonderful.

Join the throngs for a *passegiata* through the magnificent **Galleria Vittorio Emanuele II** towards **La Scala** (see also p668), the world's most famous opera house, recently reopened after (appropriately, for Milan) a 'face-lift'.

The immense **Castello Sforzesco** (☎ 02 80 14 10; www.milanocastello.it; Piazza Castello 3; admission free; 🕒 9.30am-5.30pm Tue-Sun), once a fortress, now houses collections of furniture, artefacts and sculpture, notably Michelangelo's unfinished *Pietà Rondanini*. Nearby, on Via Brera is the 17th-century Palazzo di Brera, home to the **Pinacoteca di Brera** (☎ 02 86 07 96; www.amicidibrera.milano.it; Via Brera 28; admission €5; 🕒 8.30am-7.30pm Tue-Sun) whose collection includes Mantegna's masterpiece, the *Dead Christ*.

Leonardo's *Last Supper* is in the **Cenacolo Vinciano** (☎ 02 894 21 146; Piazza Santa Maria delle Grazie 2; admission €6.50; 🕒 8am-7.30pm Tue-Sun). Phone ahead to book.

Festivals & Events

St Ambrose's Day (7 December) is Milan's major festival, with celebrations at the Fiera di Milano (MM1 – red line: stop Amendola Fiera).

Sleeping

Milan's hotels are probably the most heavily booked in Italy. There are few hostel-type options, but many budget hotels, concentrated around Stazione Centrale. Short of Venice, it's Italy's most expensive city.

Ostello Piero Rotta (☎ 02 392 67 095; Viale Salmoiraghi 1; dm €16; 🕒 lockout 9am-3.30pm, curfew 12.30am) This large HI hostel is northwest of the centre near San Siro. It has friendly, multilingual staff and a sedate ambience. Take the MM1 (red line, direction: Molino Dorino) to stop QT8.

Protezione della Giovane (☎ 02 290 00 164; Corso Garibaldi 123; dm €22) This accommodation is run by nuns for single women aged 16 to 25 years, handy if after-hours action isn't a priority. Bookings required.

Hotel Nettuno (☎ 02 294 04 481; Via Tadino 27; s/d/tr €45/68/87, with bathroom €50/95/125; ❄ ⊠) This modest outfit is much nicer than its spartan foyer might suggest. The gracious multilingual staff ensure a pleasant stay. Small groups should ask about the (one) quad room (€165).

Hotel San Tomaso (☎ 02 295 14 747; hotelsantomaso@tin.it; Viale Tunisia 6; s/d without bathroom from €30/45, d with bathroom from €65; ❄ 💻) Just off Corso Buenos Aires, this super-friendly place is well located for shopping, and as cosy as can be. Room prices vary because some have views, but all have TV and phone. Renovated in 2004.

Hotel Verona (☎ 02 669 83 091; hotel-verona@ tiscali.it; Via Carlo Tenca 12; s €40-70, d €60-100; ✖) Basic but comfy, Verona is perfectly situated between Stazione Centrale and the Duomo. Good breakfast is included, and the air-conditioned rooms have TV, phone and understated charm.

Hotel Nuovo (☎ 02 864 60 542; fax 02 720 01 752; Piazza Beccaria 6; s/d without bathroom €31/51, d/tr with bathroom €93/124) Off Corso Vittorio Emanuele II and the Duomo, the Nuovo is a perennial budget favourite in a city that doesn't care much for 'cheap'. A good deal at great rates for the simple rooms. Call ahead.

Eating

The Milanese are busy-bees, eating on the go, so quick-eat places abound. If you're seeking a traditional *trattoria,* try south of the station and along Corso Buenos Aires. *Risotto Milanese* is the local rice dish, flavoured with saffron and stewing bones. *Aperitivo* and happy hours are often augmented by large buffets. The 'all you can eat' philosophy is understood! A drink costs about €6, but you'll eat plenty before any Italian would bat an eyelid.

Osteria del Lazzaretto (☎ /fax 02 669 62 34; Via Lazzaretto 15; 2-course lunch €9; ⏰ lunch & dinner) The fantastic, understated restaurant whose daily lunch special is a truly gobsmacking bargain. Heaped portions, gracious service and all in a rustic dining room on a quiet street off Viale Tunisia. Try the authentic eggy *carbonara* – it's a myth that the dish contains cream.

Fabbrica (☎ 02 655 27 71; Via Pasubio 2; pizza €10; ✖) Around the corner from clubbing nexus Corso Como this slick, super-cool pizzeria serves fab slices (and more) in industrio-chic settings. Way cool.

Ristorante La Cimbraccola (☎ 02 869 22 50; Via San Tommaso 8; fixed menu choice of 3 €15; ⏰ lunch & dinner Tue-Sun) A student favourite for its cheap set menu, La Cimbraccola serves up excellent pizzas and pasta and is a skip from Via Dante. Service can be iffy, but the food is good.

Paper Moon (☎ 02 79 60 83; Via Bagutta 1; courses €10-15; ⏰ Mon-Sat) It may be 'only' a paper moon, but one worth seeking for its understated dishes, many vegetarian. Great seasonal ingredients and simple flavours highlight the produces' inherent qualities to full effect.

The Italian Brek, Ciao and Spizzico chains offer good-value pizza/pasta options (around €4 to €5). All have numerous Milan outlets. There are abundant supermarkets, including two at Stazione Centrale. Others are at Via D Vitruvio 32 and Via Casati 30.

Drinking

Nightlife is centred on chilled Brera and pumping Navigli. Clubs are expensive and exclusive (by 'door selection') so dress up. Hot tip: many Italian bartenders eschew spirit measures, preferring the showy 'skilfulness' of free-pouring – cocktails can be 'potent' value!

Bar Brera (☎ 02 87 70 91; Via Brera 23; cocktails €6; ⏰ to 2-3am) Brera is a relaxed rendezvous nook before a big night in the artsy precinct. It's low-key and friendly, and a great *aperitivo* option.

Gattopardo (☎ 02 345 37 699; www.gattopardocafe .com; Via Piero della Francesca 47; happy hr buffet €6; ⏰ 8-10pm) Looking H-O-T-T *hott!* is the only admission price to one of Milan's hippest nightspots; if you've got 'it', bring it!

Louisiana Bistro (☎ 02 864 65 315; www.louisian abistro.it; Via Fiori Chiari 17; ⏰ until late) An American-owned expat and student-oriented place with enormous, nuclear-strength cocktails for around €6. Use caution.

Shu (☎ 02 583 15 720; Via della Chiusa) A wesomely hipper-than-thou-but-bearably-so place with cool art on the walls and foxy cocktails.

Entertainment

Music, theatre and cinema dominate Milan's entertainment calendar. The opera season at **Teatro all Scala** (☎ 02 86 07 75; www.teatroalla cala.org) runs from 7 December until July.

Football fans must visit the San Siro Stadium (Stadio Olympico Meazza), home to both AC Milan (the *rossoneri*, 'red and blacks') and Inter (the *ner'azzuri*, 'black and blues'). Local rivalry is savage; confusing the two will offend. Match tickets are expensive (€15), but it's free to stroll by the ground.

Shopping

Looking good is religion; shopping is nearly blood-sport in Milan, and expensive. Hit the streets behind the Duomo around Corso Vittorio Emanuele II for clothing, footwear and accessories, or dream on and window-shop along Via Monte Napoleone, Via della Spiga and Via Borgospesso.

Markets are held around the canals, on Viale Papiniano on Tuesday and Saturday morning. A **flea market** (Viale Gabriele d'Annunzio) is held on Saturday and there's an **antique market** (Via Fiori Chiari) in Brera every third Saturday.

Getting There & Away

AIR

Most international flights use Malpensa airport, about 50km northwest of Milan. Domestic and some European flights use Linate airport, 7km east of the city – for flight information for both call ☎ 02 748 52 200.

CAR & MOTORCYCLE

Milan is the major junction of Italy's motorways, including the A1 (Rome), A4 (Milan–Turin), A7 (Milan–Genoa), the Serenissima (Verona and Venice) and the A8/A9 north to the lakes and Swiss border. All these join the Milan ring road – the Tangenziale Est and Tangenziale Ovest (east and west bypasses). The A4 is particularly busy; accidents delay traffic interminably. In winter roads can become hazardous.

TRAIN

Trains depart Stazione Centrale for Venice, Florence, Bologna, Genoa, Turin and Rome, and major European cities. Call for **timetable information** (☎ 848 88 80 88; ◷ 7am-9pm) or visit the office in Stazione Centrale (English spoken).

Getting Around

TO/FROM THE AIRPORT

STAM buses leave for Linate airport (€1.80, every 30 minutes 5.40am to 9.35pm) from Piazza Luigi di Savoia, on the east side of Stazione Centrale, or use local bus No 73 from Piazza San Babila (€1, 20 minutes). For Malpensa airport, the Malpensa Shuttle and Malpensa Bus Express depart from Piazza Luigi di Savoia (€4 to €5, one hour, every 20 minutes 4.30am to 12.15am). Buses also link the airports (hourly, 8am to 9.30pm).

The *Malpensa Express* train connects Malpensa airport with Cadorna underground station (5.50am to 8.20pm from Cadorna; buses €9.30, every 40 minutes 8.20am to 11.10pm).

BUS & METRO

Milan's public transport is excellent, with underground (MM), tram and bus services (tickets €1/one ride and/or 75 minutes on buses and trams). You can buy tickets at MM stations, and most tobacconists and newsstands.

CAR & MOTORCYCLE

If your car is clamped or towed, call the **Polizia Municipale** (☎ 02 772 72 59).

TAXI

Don't hail passing taxis; they won't stop. Head for the taxi ranks.

MANTUA (MANTOVA)

pop 48,000

Poised quietly beside Lake Superior, Mantua is associated with the Gonzaga family, who ruled from 1328 until 1707. These days, Mantua is considered a stronghold of Umberto Bossi's separatist Lega Nord party, though you'd barely notice except for some mild graffiti. The sumptuous Gonzaga palaces might justify a detour.

The **tourist office** (☎ 0376 32 82 53; www.apt mantova.it; Piazza Andrea Mantegna 6; ◷ 8.30am-12.30pm & 3-6pm Mon-Sat, 9.30am-12.30pm Sun) is a short walk from the station on Corso Vittorio Emanuele, which becomes Corso Umberto 1.

Piazza Sordello is surrounded by impressive buildings, including the eclectic **cattedrale**, but the main focal point is the **Palazzo Ducale** (adult/concession €6.50/3.25; ◷ 8.45am-7.15pm Tue-Sun), the former seat of the Gonzaga family. With a massive 500 rooms and 15 courtyards, its showpieces include the Gonzagas' private apartments and impressive art collection, and the **Camera degli Sposi** (Bridal Chamber), with frescoes by Mantegna. The Gonzagas' lavish lakeside summer palace, **Palazzo del Tè** (admission €8; ◷ 9am-6pm Tue-Sun) was completed in 1534. The weekend **market** encompasses several piazzas, and it beats similar fare in cities twice Mantua's size, with cheap snack options and good clothes in particular.

Albergo ABC (☎ 0376 32 23 29; www.hotelabcmantova .it; Piazza Don Leoni 25; s €44-77, d €66-110) Opposite the train station, Albergo ABC is sufficient in the unlikely event of an overnight stay. Breakfast is included, and rooms have TV, telephone and bathroom. There are also *agriturismo* (farm stay) options nearby, including **Agricampeggio Corte Chiara** (☎ 0376 39 08 04; per adult/camp site €6/6), near to town and in a quiet spot.

Osteria Vecchia Mantova (Piazza Sordello 26; 2-course meal €13-20; ◷ lunch & dinner Tue-Sun) This small, elegant *osteria* has rustic specialities, such as the sensational pumpkin tortellini (€6.50) at unbeatable prices.

Mantua is accessible by train and bus from Verona (40 minutes), and by train from Milan and Bologna (change at Modena).

VERONA
pop 256,100

Among Italy's prettiest cities, Verona is perpetually associated with Romeo and Juliet. But the city was an important Roman centre long before the Della Scala (aka the Scaligeri) family took the reins around the mid-13th century, a period noted for the savage, clannish feuding that inspired Shakespeare's tragedy. In centuries past, Verona was even referred to as *piccola Roma* (little Rome). Leave your preconceptions aside and you might fall for Verona's real stars; its charming centre and amazing amphitheatre.

Orientation & Information

Buses to the centre leave from the train station; otherwise, it's a 2km walk. Turn right to leave the station, cross the river and follow Corso Porta Nuova to Piazza Brà.

APT Tourist Office (☎ 045 806 86 80; info@tourism .verona.it; Via degli Alpini 9; ✹ 9am-6pm Mon-Sat, 9am-2pm Sun) Faces Piazza Brà. Other branches are at the train station (☎ 045 800 08 61; ✹ 9am-6pm Mon-Sat) and airport (☎ 045 861 91 63; ✹ 11am-5pm Mon-Sat). Ask about the **Verona card** (1/3 days €8/12) for cramming lots into a short time.

Post office (Piazza Viviani)

Internet Fast (☎ 045 803 32 12; Via Oberdan 16/b; per hr €4; ✹ 10am-10pm Mon-Fri, 10am-8pm Sat, 2-8pm Sun)

Sights & Activities

Piazza Brà's 1st-century Roman **amphitheatre** (known as 'the Arena') is the third largest in the world. Smaller than Rome's, but better preserved, it is now Verona's opera house (see right), also hosting popular artists such as Bjork and Pearl Jam.

On Via Cappello is **Casa di Giulietta** (Juliet's House), whose balcony overlooks a graffiti-covered courtyard and statue of Juliet. Romantic superstition suggests rubbing Juliet's 'heart' brings a new lover. It's the right-side (read: wrong) breast with the gleaming shine, suggesting 'the loveless might perhaps be less so if they had a better grasp of anatomy...

Further along the street is **Porta Leoni**, one of the gates to the old Roman Verona; the other, **Porta Borsari**, is north of the Arena.

Piazza delle Erbe is all palaces and market stalls. Nearby is charming **Piazza dei Signori**, flanked by the medieval town hall, and the Della Scala (Scaligeri) residence, partly decorated by Giotto and nowadays the **Governor's Palace**.

Sleeping & Eating

Ostello Villa Francescatti (☎ 045 59 03 60; fax 045 800 91 27; Salita Fontana del Ferro 15; B&B €14; dinner €8.50) Possibly the best HI hostel in Italy, this 500-year-old former church has vaulted roofs and remnants of original frescoes on some walls – wonderfully evocative. It also serves a fantastic two-course dinner. Take bus No 73 from the station, then follow the signs.

Boiled meats are a Veronese speciality, as is Soave white wine.

Hosteria All'Orso (☎ 045 59 72 14; Via Sottoriva 3/c; mains €14-20; ✹ lunch & dinner Tue-Sat, dinner Mon) This friendly restaurant nestled under the Sottoriva porticoes serves hearty northern Italian and Veronese dishes. In the heart of Verona's nightlife 'district', it's the perfect place to kick off with a substantial meal and drinks.

Pizza Doge (Via Roma 21b; slice €3.50) For tasty pizza-to-go, you won't find any better than this pizzeria.

Trattoria All'Isolo (☎ 045 59 42 91; Piazza dell' Isolo 5a; menu €12) Adventurous diners can saddle up here across the river, where a local Veronese clientele tuck into some equestrian gastronomy: try the horse-meat pie, or donkey stew. Giddyup!

Drinking

For bar/late-night action, head for Via Sottoriva.

square (☎ 045 59 71 20; Via Sottoriva 15; ✹ 6.30pm-2am Mon-Fri, 3.30pm-2am Sat & Sun) This place is a bizarrely cool 'lifestyle-bar', where DJ-assisted shtick includes shiatsu massage, sampling elegant homewares, swanky cocktails, fusion snacks and free Internet.

Sottoriva 23 (☎ 045 800 99 04; Via Sottoriva 23; ✹ 10am-2am) More traditional is this cosy, low-lit cavern for drinks and chatter, usually crammed with friendly locals.

Entertainment

Verona hosts shows throughout the year, culminating in an excellent opera/drama season at the **Arena** (☎ 800 28 80; www.arena.it; Via dei Mutilati 4; tickets from €21.50; ✹ Jul-Sep). For other events, check the website or **box office** (☎ 045 800 51 51; Via Dietro Anfiteatro 6b).

Getting There & Around
Verona-Villafranca airport (☎ 045 809 56 66) is 16km away, accessible by bus and train. The APT airport bus (€4.20, every 20 minutes) departs from the train station. Bus Nos 11, 12, 13 and 14 (Nos 91, 92 and 98 on Sunday) connect the station (bus stop A) with Piazza Brà, and Nos 72 and 73 go to Piazza delle Erbe. The main **bus station** is in the piazza in front of Porta Nuova train station. Buses service surrounding towns including Mantua, Ferrara and Brescia.

Verona is on the Brenner Pass train line to Austria/Germany, and directly linked by rail to Milan, Venice, Florence and Rome.

PADUA (PADOVA)
postcode 35100 / pop 211,500

In millennia past, a pilgrimage to Padua was usually to see Saint Anthony's tomb. These days, it's Giotto's restored frescoes in the Cappella degli Scrovegni (Scrovegni Chapel), among the world's greatest works of figurative art. Masterpieces aside, Padua is a pleasant city, and – partly thanks to the many students – lively and engaging.

Orientation & Information
The centre is a 15-minute walk from the train station, or take bus No 3 or 8 along Corso del Popolo (which becomes Corso Garibaldi). Padua's centre is easily covered on foot.
Tourist office (☎ 049 875 20 77; ⏱ 9.15am-6.30pm Mon-Sat, 9am-12.30pm Sun) At the station, with another office in the centre (☎ 049 876 79 27; Galleria Pedrocchi; ⏱ 9am-12.30pm & 3-7pm Mon-Sat). The *padovacard* (1 adult & 1 child €13; valid 48hr) provides discounts on many sights and all public transport.
Post office (Corso Garibaldi 33)

Sights & Activities
Cappella degli Scrovegni (☎ 049 201 00 20; www .cappelladegliscrovegni.it; Piazza Eremitani 8; €12, free 25 Mar; ⏱ 9am-7pm, visit 30min) is Padua's highlight, housing Giotto's transcendent frescoes (1303–05). The 38 glorious panels movingly depict Christ's life. Booking ahead is mandatory, as is arriving at the chapel 10 minutes before your allotted time. The ticket accesses the neighbouring **Musei Civici agli Eremitani** (☎ 049 829 45 50; www.padovanet.it/museicivici; ⏱ 9am-6pm Tue-Sun winter, to 7pm spring-autumn).

Thousands of pilgrims annually seek out Padua's **Basilica di Sant'Antonio** (St Anthony's Basilica) in the hope that St Anthony, patron saint of lost things (and Padua), will help them find whatever they're looking for. The saint's gaudy **tomb** is in the basilica, along with 14th-century frescoes, and sculptures by Donatello adorning the high altar. Just outside the basilica is a statue, the *Gattamelata* (Honeyed Cat), also by Donatello.

Sleeping & Eating
Ostello della Città di Padova (☎ /fax 049 65 42 10; www.ctgveneto.it/ostello; Via A Aleardi 30; dm B&B €15.50) The HI hostel is a five-minute bus ride from the station. Take bus No 3, 8 or 12 to Prato della Valle and then ask.

Koko Nor Association (☎ 049 864 33 94; www .bandb-veneto.it/kokonor; Via Selva 5; s/d from around €35/60) This is a good organisation to consult if you're after the privacy of *affittacamere* (rented rooms in private family homes). The tourist office keeps similar lists.

Dalla Zita (Via Gorizia 16; panini from €2.30) You won't find cheaper eats than at this great sandwich bar, popular with local workers and skint students. Value and quality are matched only by variety; the details of 100-plus types of *panini* cover the place more like wallpaper than a menu.

Godenda (☎ 049 877 41 92; www.godenda.it; Via Squarcini 4/6; meal of 2-3 dishes €10-15; ⏱ lunch & dinner) This is a great place to grab a bite in a hurry. It's a combination restaurant, wine bar and takeaway *provedore*, with dozens of delicious prepared dishes (sold by weight).

Pe Pen (☎ 049 875 94 83; www.pepen.it; Piazza Cavour 15; pizza & pasta €10-12; ⏱ lunch & dinner) The place for a splurge. Try the Umbrian speciality *tagliolini* (hand-cut pasta) with *con ostriche e porri* (fresh oysters and sautéed leeks).

Getting There & Away
Padua has direct rail links to Milan, Venice and Bologna, and is accessible from other major cities. Buses serve Venice, Milan, Trieste and surrounding towns. The **bus terminal** (Piazzale Boschetti) is off Via Trieste, near the train station. There is a car park in Prato della Valle, near the Basilica del Santo.

VENICE (VENEZIA)
pop 272,100

No single reason can account for the 'floating' city's 15 million annual visitors, but the Grand

Dame of northern Italy remains arguably the nation's biggest draw. Little matches the pulse-quickening beauty – and teeth-grinding frustration – of stunning Venice.

Countless travellers, dreamers, legendary lovers and dictators have fallen for La Serenissima. Writers from Byron to contemporary best-seller Jeanette Winterson have all used Venice to bewitching effect. Even Napoleon pronounced Piazza San Marco 'the finest drawing room in Europe'. The lagoon's islands were settled during barbarian invasions around 1500 years ago, when the Veneto's inhabitants sought refuge in the area, building the city on pole foundations pounded into the marshy subsoil. Following centuries of Byzantine rule, Venice morphed into a republic ruled by a succession of doges (chief magistrates), enjoying one thousand years of independence.

Expansion of trade links followed in the wake of rapid evolution in maritime expertise – Marco Polo ultimately left from here on his epic China expedition in 1271, just one of many seafarers who stimulated cultural cross-pollination at this strategic nexus. Venice eventually dominated half the Mediterranean, the Adriatic and trade routes to the Levant.

Today, delivery boats jostle chintzy gondolas, and the pigeons are only outnumbered by the swarms of tourists. Regular flooding (*acqua alte* – 'high waters') and sky-high prices make it difficult to actually live here: most 'locals' commute from Mestre, across the lagoon.

Walking is the key to discovering Venice. Dorsoduro and Castello rarely see tourists; you can wander for hours in the streets between the Accademia and the train station. Another tactic is choosing your hours strategically; even San Marco is basically empty from midnight to dawn. At this moonlit moment, you'll be suddenly and irrevocably seduced by the Queen of the Seas.

Orientation

Venice is built on 117 islands with 150-odd canals and 400 bridges. Only three bridges cross the Canal Grande (Grand Canal): the Rialto, the Accademia and the Scalzi near the railway.

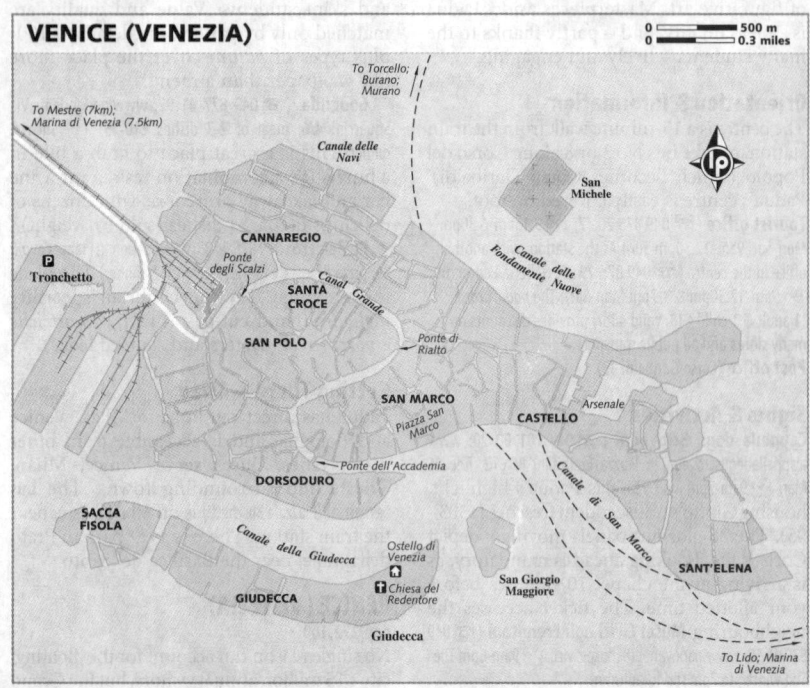

The city is divided into six *sestieri* (quarters): Cannaregio, Castello, San Marco, Dorsoduro, San Polo and Santa Croce. A street can be a *calle, ruga* or *salizzada;* beside a canal it's a *fondamenta,* a canal is a *rio*, a filled canal-turned-street is a *rio terra*. The only square in Venice called a piazza is San Marco; the others are called *campo*. Venice's street numbering is unique, too. Instead of a system based on individual streets, each *sestiere* has a series of numbers; addresses are virtually meaningless unless you are a Venetian postie. Getting lost is inevitable, so enjoy!

There are no cars. All public transport is via the canals, on *vaporetti* (water buses) or with 'Shanks' Pony' (your feet). Walking from the train station to San Marco along the main drag, Lista di Spagna (whose name changes often), takes about 30 minutes – follow the signs to San Marco. From San Marco the Rialto, the Accademia and the train station are well signposted but sometimes confusingly, particularly in Dorsoduro and San Polo.

Information

INTERNET ACCESS

There are tonnes of Internet cafés but none of them are cheap. The airport is a Wi-Fi hotspot.

Casanova (☎ 041 524 06 64; Rio Tera Lista di Spagna, Cannaregio 158/a; per hr €7; 🕑 9am-11.30pm) A cheesy club and a combined webcafé in one, close to the station.

Netgate (☎ 041 244 02 13; Calle dei Preti Crosera 3812, Dorsoduro; per hr €6; 🕑 10.15am-8pm Mon-Fri, 10.15am-10pm Sat, 2.15-10pm Sun)

Nethouse (☎ 041 277 11 90; Campo Santo Stefano, San Marco 2967; per 20min/1hr €3/9; 🕑 24hr) Nethouse has tonnes of screens, plus printing and fax services.

Planet Internet (☎ 041 524 41 88; Rio Terrà San Leonardo, Cannaregio 1520; per hr €7; 🕑 8am-11pm) Good central location; the perfect place to surf while doing laundry.

LAUNDRY

Speedy Wash (Rio Terrà San Leonardo, Cannaregio 1520; 8kg wash/dry €4.50/3; 🕑 9am-10pm)

MEDICAL & EMERGENCY SERVICES

For emergency services responses in foreign languages, call ☎ 112.

Ospedale Civile (☎ 041 529 41 11; Campo SS Giovanni e Paolo)

Police Headquarters (☎ 041 271 55 11; Fondamenta di San Lorenzo, Castello 5053) Handles thefts etc.

MONEY

Ouch. Venice is Italy's expensive city. Prepare yourself for paying nearly double here for things of similar standard elsewhere in Italy.

American Express (☎ 041 520 08 44; Salizzada San Moisè 1471; 🕑 9am-5.30pm Mon-Fri, 9.30am-12.30pm Sat & Sun)

Change office (🕑 7am- 9pm) At the train station.

Travelex (Thomas Cook; ☎ 041 522 47 51; Piazza San Marco 141; 🕑 9am-7pm Mon-Sat, 9.30am-5pm Sun)

POST

Post office (Salizzada del Fontego dei Tedeschi; 🕑 8.10am-7pm Mon-Sat) In an atmospheric former trading house near the Rialto.

TOURIST INFORMATION

Central Venice has three **tourist offices** (☎ 041 529 87 11) train station (🕑 8am-8pm) Piazza San Marco 71f (🕑 9.45am-3.15pm Mon-Sat) Venice Pavilion (🕑 10am-6pm), the latter on the waterfront. Further offices are at **Piazzale Roma** (🕑 8am-8pm), the Lido and the airport.

Visitors aged 14 to 29 can buy a **Rolling Venice card** (☎ 041 241 39 08; €3), offering discounts on food, accommodation, shopping, transport and museums. Available from various outlets, you'll need your passport and a colour photograph. The excellent **Chorus Pass** (adult/child/student €8/5/5) gets you into 15 of Venice's most beautiful churches, many boasting a masterpiece or two. For both passes, ask at the tourist offices.

The **Venice Card** (☎ 041 24 24; www.venicecard.it; blue card under 29 years 1/3/7 days €9/22/49, over 29 years €14/29/51, orange card under 29 years €18/35/61, over 29 years €28/47/68) isn't always a saving, but could be, depending on your itinerary; check its coverage before spending.

Sights & Activities

Before you visit Venice's churches, museums and monuments, take *vaporetto* (water bus) No 1 along the **Grand Canal**, lined with rococo, Gothic, Moorish and Renaissance palaces. Then, stretch your legs with a decent walk: start at **San Marco** and either delve into the tiny lanes of tranquil **Castello** or head for the **Ponte dell'Accademia** to reach the narrow streets and squares of **Dorsoduro** and **San Polo**. Most museums are closed Monday.

PIAZZA & BASILICA DI SAN MARCO

San Marco's dreamy quality stuns, first time or fiftieth. The piazza is enclosed by

SAN MARCO, SAN POLO & SANTA CROCE

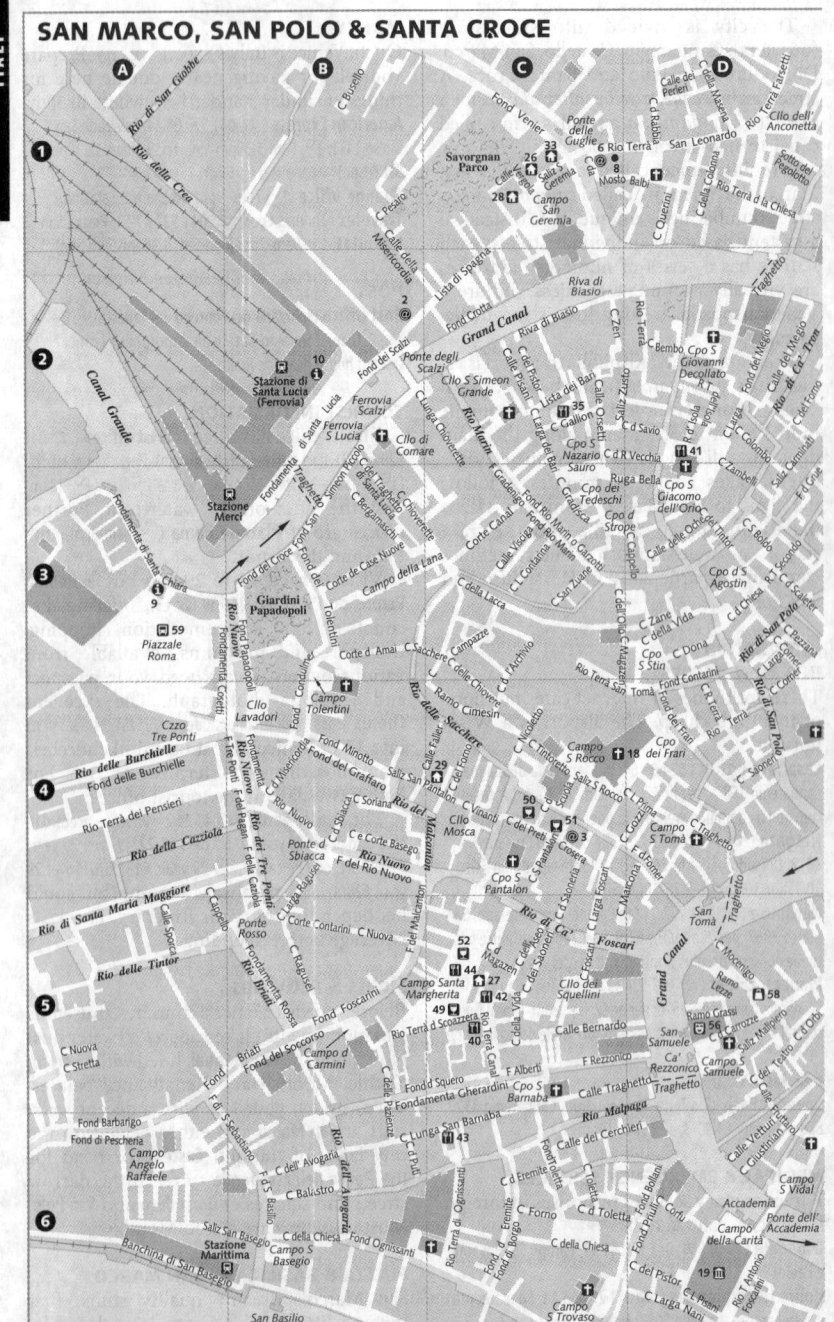

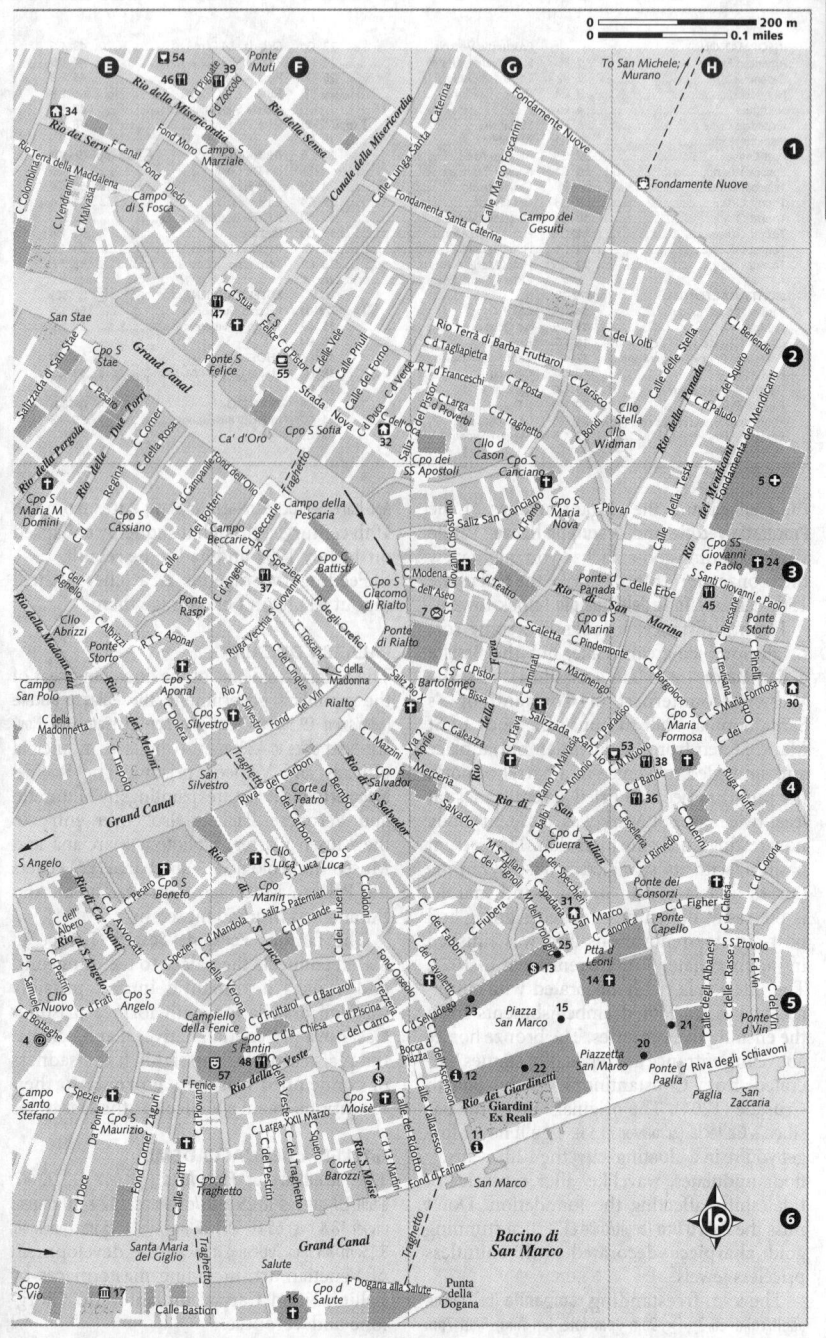

the basilica and the elegant arcades of the **Procuratie Vecchie** and **Procuratie Nuove**. While you're standing gob-smacked you might view the bronze *mori* (Moors) strike the bell of the 15th-century **Torre dell'Orologio** (clock tower).

From a distance, it looks like some sort of glorious ice-cream cake, but the **Basilica di San Marco** (St Mark's Basilica) was the Western counterpart of Constantinople's Santa Sophia, built to house the body of St Mark. Stolen from his Egyptian burial place and smuggled to Venice in a barrel of pork, the saint has been reburied several times (at least twice poor St Mark was 'lost'), his body now resting under the high altar. The present basilica, with its spangled spires, Byzantine domes and façade of mosaics and marble, is the result of centuries of redesigning and post-disaster renovations and was finished in (approximately) its current form in 1071. The interior is richly decorated with mosaics, as well as looted embellishments from the ensuing five centuries. The bronze horses above the entrance are replicas of statues 'liberated' from Constantinople in the Fourth Crusade (1204). The originals are in the basilica's **Galleria** (admission €1.55). You'll never forget you're in a 'floating' city; the 12th-century floor undulates, wavelike, after centuries of tidal shifts affecting the foundation. Don't miss the **Pala d'Oro** (adult/child €1.50/1), a stunning gold altarpiece decorated with countless priceless jewels.

The 99m freestanding **campanile** (bell tower; adult/child €6/3; ☼ 9am-9pm late Jun-Aug, 9am-7pm

Apr-Jun & Sep-Oct, 9am-4pm Nov-Mar) dates from the 10th century, although it suddenly collapsed on 14 July 1902 and had to be rebuilt.

Feeding the pigeons is a 'cheep' thrill (about €1). Don't encourage them.

PALAZZO DUCALE
The official residence of the doges and seat of the republic's government, the **Palazzo Ducale** (admission €9.50; ☼ 9am-7pm Apr-Oct, 9am-5pm Nov-Mar, ticket office to 4.30pm) also housed municipal officials and Venice's prisons. The **Sala del Maggior Consiglio** features paintings by Tintoretto and Veronese. Tickets also cover entry to the Museo Correr, Biblioteca Marciana and Museo Archeologico. A surcharge (€6) covers the Palazzo Mocenigo (San Stae area), and Burano and Murano museums.

The famous **Ponte dei Sospiri** (Bridge of Sighs) connects the palace to the dungeons, and evokes a romantic image, possibly through association with former prisoner Casanova (a Venetian native). Far bleaker is the real reason for the sighing; the sadness of condemned prisoners en route to their executions, seeing Venice for the last time.

GALLERIA DELL'ACCADEMIA
The **Academy of Fine Arts** (☎ 041 522 22 47; adult/EU citizens 18-25 years/child under 12 & EU citizens under 18 & over 65 €6.50/3.25/free; ☼ 8.15am-2pm Mon, 8.15am-7.15pm Tue-Sun) traces the development of Venetian art, including masterpieces by Bellini, Titian, Carpaccio, Tintoretto, Giorgione and Veronese.

Don't miss the **Collezione Peggy Guggenheim** (☎ 041 240 54 11; www.Guggenheim-venice.it; Palazzo Venier dei Leoni, Dorsoduro 701; adult/student & child €8/5; ☾ 10am-6pm Wed-Fri & Sun-Mon, 10am-10pm Sat) displayed in the American heiress' former home. The brilliant, anachronistic collection runs the gamut of modern art (Bacon, Pollock, Picasso, Dalí, Magritte and more) and the palace is in a sculpture garden where Peggy and her dogs are buried. Aww.

CHURCHES
Venice has hundreds of churches but don't investigate them without a Chorus Pass (p673). The **Chiesa del Redentore** (Church of the Redeemer) on Giudecca was built by Palladio to commemorate the end of the Great Plague (1576) and is the scene of the annual Festa del Redentore (right). Longhena's **Chiesa di Santa Maria della Salute** 'guards' the Grand Canal's entrance and contains works by Tintoretto and Titian. Definitely visit the great Gothic churches **SS Giovanni e Paolo**, with its glorious stained-glass windows, and the **Frari**, home to Titian's tomb and his uplifting *Assumption*.

THE LIDO
This thin strip of land separating Venice from the Adriatic is easily accessible by *vaporetto* Nos 1, 6, 14, 61 and 82. Once *the* most fashionable resort – still very popular – it's near impossible to find space in summer.

ISLANDS
The island of **Murano** is the home of Venetian glass. Tour a factory for a behind-the-scenes look at production. **Burano**, still a relatively sleepy fishing village, is renowned for its lace and colourful houses. **Torcello**, the republic's original island settlement, was abandoned due to malaria. Little remains on the hauntingly deserted island, besides the Byzantine cathedral, with its mosaics intact. *Vaporetto* No 12 services all three.

GONDOLAS
Ring-tones have supplanted serenades, but if you must, you must... And it'll cost you – before/after 8pm €62/78, for 50 minutes. These fixed/official rates are per-gondola (licensed for six people).

Festivals & Events
Venice knows how to party. **Carnevale** (translated as 'truth in/of flesh) is the city's famed last-knees-up-before-Lent (late February, early March). Everyone dons spectacular masks and costumes for a 10-day street party. At its 18th-century peak, the drinking, dancing and debauchery lasted six months!

At **Feste del' Laure**, students lampoon their graduating comrades (getting their PhDs) by putting up caricatured posters all over town, and singing many verses of a decidedly anatomical ditty while parading drunkenly through the streets. It's held mainly in March and November.

Held on the third weekend in July, **Festa del Redentore** (Festival of the Redeemer) celebrates the Great Plague's end; it features a spectacular fireworks display.

The **Regata Storica** is a wildly colourful gondola race held on the Grand Canal the first Sunday in September.

Venice Biennale is the major, year-long exhibition of international visual arts held every even-numbered year, while the **Venice International Film Festival** is Italy's take on Cannes; programmed by the Biennale organisers, it's held every September.

Sleeping
Prices are extremely high in peak times (Christmas, Carnevale, Easter etc), but drop somewhat in others. Always book ahead.

HOSTELS
Ostello di Venezia (☎ 041 523 82 11; fax 041 523 56 89; Fondamenta delle Zitelle 86; dm €16; dinner €8; ☾ curfew 11.30pm) On the island of Giudecca, the HI hostel is members only, or buy membership there. Take *vaporetto* No 41, 42 or 82 from the train station, alighting at Zitelle. It's bland, and necessitates *vaporetto* use, but it's cheap.

Foresteria Valdese (☎ 041 528 67 97; fax 041 241 62 38; Castello 5170; dm €20, d €55, with bathroom €75) Behave yourself at this popular option run by nuns (both sexes welcome) in the former Palazzo Cavagnis. It is tidy and wonderfully located.

Ostello Santa Fosca (☎ 041 71 57 75; cpu@iuav .unive.it; Cannaregio 2372; dm €18, s/d without bathroom €21; ☾ check-in 5-8pm) Students and travellers on the cheap will feel at home in these basic but clean university dorms beside a pleasant canal less than 15 minutes' walk from the station.

HOTELS
Hotel Marte & Biasin (☎ 041 522 72 57; www.hotel martebiasin.com; Fondamenta di Cannaregio 338; s/d

€35/45, d with bathroom €65; ⚅ ⊠) A pair of friendly one-star hotels in a great location near the Ponte delle Guglie in Cannaregio. Beds are slightly limp and the appointments spartan, but rooms are clean and quiet and the bilingual staff lovely.

Hotel Bernardi Semenzato (☎ 041 522 72 57; www.hotelbernardi.com; SS Apostoli, Cannaregio 4366; s/d €28-33/€58-68, s/d with bathroom €45-50/€78-88) This sweet place is great value for Venice, on a quiet street near a lovely square. Ask about the popular annexe, which sleeps three to four. All rooms are beautifully tended.

Albergo Antico Capon (☎ 041 528 52 92; Campo Santa Margherita, Dorsoduro 3004b; s with bathroom €25-90, d €45-90) In the coolest square in Venice, 'the old (fat) cockerel' provides airy, colourful rooms – many with *campo* views – to roost in. Opposite some of Venice's best cafés and cheap eateries, it's central, yet off the tourist trail.

Casa Gerotto & Alloggi Calderan (☎ 041 71 55 62; www.casagerottocalderan.com; Campo San Geremia, Cannaregio 283; dm €21, s/d €36/65, s/d/tr with bathroom €46/90/108). A popular choice for the prices and location on a buzzing *campo* near a morning produce market. Pleasantly ramshackle atmosphere suited to travellers used to the delightful chaos of hostelling.

Al Gobbo (☎ 041 71 50 01; www.albergoalgobbo.it; Campo San Geremia, Cannaregio 312; s/d €45/67, with bathroom €65/83) It looks a little grim at first, and it's called 'The Hunchback', but the enthusiastic owner is more a jolly pixie. Friendly service and good rooms will allay fears. Prices are subject to fluctuation; call ahead or check the website for deals.

Casa Peron (☎ 041 71 10 21; www.casaperon.com; Salizzada San Pantalon, San Polo 84; s/d/tr with bathroom €48/75/105) You get some idea of the relaxed atmosphere at Casa Peron after being greeted by Pierino, the owner's enormous parrot, presiding calmly over the reception. The place is no menagerie, though. Neat as a pin and in a lovely area close to happenin' Campo Santa Margherita.

Hotel ai Do Mori (☎ 041 520 48 17; www.hotel aidomori.com; Calle Larga, San Marco 658; d €60-90, s/d with bathroom €50-100/€80-135; ⚅ summer; ⊠) If you're lashing out a little, here's your hotel. Up some steep stairs, rooms have views of San Marco, plus there's a breakfast terrace practically in the shadow of the Campanile! Simple, unaffected rooms and friendly staff make this sensational for the price.

CAMPING
Litorale del Cavallino, northeast of the city on the Adriatic coast, has numerous camping grounds, many with bungalows. Try **Marina di Venezia** (☎ 041 530 09 55; camping@ marinadivenezia.it; Via Montello 6, Punta Sabbioni; per adult/camp site €7.50/19; ☽ mid-Apr–end Aug).

Eating
Eating in Venice is generally expensive. Value lies lurking away from big landmarks though, and affordable self-catering/snack options abound. Staples of Venetian cuisine are rice, beans and seafood. Try *risotto con piselli* (risotto with peas) followed by a glass of *fragolino*, a fragrant strawberry wine. Around 4pm you'll notice everyone drinking *sprizze* – an apéritif of *prosecco* (Venetian sparkling white), soda and a bitter mixer, usually Aperol, giving the drink its trademark colour. Delicious!

CAFÉS & BARS
Venetian café culture isn't limited to *de rigueur* string sections and extortionate dollars in San Marco's.

Torrefazione Costarica (☎ 041 71 63 71; Strada Nuovo, Cannaregio 1337; ☽ 8am-6.30pm) serves Venice's best (and cheapest) coffee. Unassuming purveyors, Camillo Marchi and family, make wonderful espresso for €0.65 (cappuccinos €1.05). You can even watch him roasting tomorrow's beans, comforted in the knowledge he's supplying the cafés across town charging 10 times as much.

Barbanera (☎ 041 541 07 17; Calle de le Bande, Castello 5356; ☽ 11am-midnight) A *birreria/enoteca* (wine and beer bar) which does good food. The fish soup is cheap (€5) and authentic, the deep-fried olives (€3) pure salty deliciousness.

GELATI & PASTRIES
There's no shortage of great pastries and gelato in Venice.

Il Doge (☎ 041 523 46 07; Campo Santa Margherita, Dorsoduro 3058/a; small/large gelato €1.50/3; ☽ 10am-2am Feb-Nov) The finest gelato on the sweetest piazza.

Rosa Salva (☎ 041 522 79 49; rsalva@doge.it; Campo SS Giovanni e Paolo, Castello 6779; ☽ 7.30am-8.30pm Thu-Tue) One hundred years after launching as a 'travelling kitchen', delivering hot meals by gondola, Rosa Salva's reputation is lofty. Enjoy some of the best coffee and pastries in Venice while perusing local art exhibits.

RESTAURANTS

Sahara (☎ 041 72 10 77; Fondamenta della Misericordia, Cannaregio 2519; mains €10, set menu without drinks €20; ✆ lunch & dinner Tue-Sun) In what passes for a nightlife district in Cannaregio, Sahara is an excellent Arabic alternative to Italian food. The Syrian cooking is delicious, and there's belly dancing every Saturday night.

Iguana (☎ 041 71 35 61; Fondamenta della Misericordia, Cannaregio 2521; meals €9-11, happy hr sprizze €1; ✆ 6pm-1am Tue-Sun, happy hr 6.30-8pm) If Tex-Mex is your thing, hit Iguana for Americano flavours, or simply swing by at happy hour for 1½ hours of cheap sprizzing!

Vino Vino (☎ 0415237027; www.vinovino.co.it; Ponte delle Veste, 2007/a, San Marco; mains €10; ✆ 10.30am-midnight Wed-Mon) At Ponte Veste near Teatro La Fenice, this fantastic wine bar also does excellent food. Typical Venetian specialities abound; a moodily evocative place to try some polenta or *pasta con nero di seppia* (pasta in shellfish ink). There is a choice of 350 wines by the bottle/glass.

Cip Ciap (☎ 041 523 66 21; Calle del Mondo Nuovo, Castello, 5799; pizza slice €2.30) Cip Ciap is cheap and cheerful, just right for a simple snack. Near buzzy Campo Santa Maria Formosa.

Ae Oche (Three Geese; ☎ 041 524 11 61; Calle del Tintor, Santa Croce 1552a/b; pizza €7; ✆ lunch & dinner) Venice's best pizzeria is worth the extra cost. Choose from 90 (!) pizzas or excellent pastas in the inviting, saloon-style dining room, then chase it all with *sgroppino*. This cool, creamy, alcoholic lemon sorbet is heavenly after a meal, a little-known Venetian treat.

La Zucca (The Pumpkin; ☎ 041 524 15 70; San Giacomo dell'Orio, Santa Croce 1762; mains €10-16; ✆ lunch & dinner Mon-Sat) This is a smashing, tiny *osteria* purveying innovative dishes using seasonal vegetables. The vegetarian lasagne is stunning, the fennel in spicy olive sauce transcendent. Rabbit, wild fowl and horse are also offered. Rustic ambience and magnificent service. Book ahead.

Osteria ai 4 Ferri (☎ 041 520 69 78; Calle Lunga San Barnaba, Dorsoduro 2754/a; mains €12-17; ✆ lunch & dinner) Splash out at this briny *osteria* off Campo San Barnaba, respected for its seafood delights (especially shellfish). The combination of young owners and traditional outlook is working; booking is required.

Cantina do Mori (☎ 041 522 54 01; Sottoportego dei do Mori, San Polo 429; light meals €4-8; ✆ 8.30am-8.30pm Mon-Sat) A small, very popular wine bar also serving great sandwiches and *cicchetti*

(Venetian 'tapas', or light snacks). Two centuries of superb snacks mean it's usually packed with dedicated locals. Great for a light meal or *aperitivo*.

Pizza Al Volo (☎ 041 522 54 30; Campo Santa Margherita, Dorsoduro 2944; slice €1.50, whole pizzas €4-6; ✆ lunch & dinner) Venice's favourite cheapie pizza takeaway serves tasty slices the size of sheets. Don't miss this bargain beauty.

SELF-CATERING

For fruit, vegetables, and deli items, head for the **markets** in the streets on the San Polo side of the Rialto, or the Rio Terrà San Leonardo in Cannaregio. There are also supermarkets: **Mega 1**, just off Campo Santa Margherita, and **Standa** (Strada Nova).

Drinking

The holy trinity for late drinks are the three 'coloured' cafés: Blue, Noir and Rosso.

Il Caffè (☎ 041 528 79 98; Campo San Margherita, Dorsoduro 2963; ✆ until late) Better known as Café Rosso for its big red sign, this fantastic hub is heavingly popular. The cool staff make the best *sprizze* in Venice, and might even let you assault their piano – student-fuelled jams aren't uncommon. A slice of Venetian heaven.

Café Blue (☎ 041 71 02 27; cafébluevenezia@hotmail.com; Calle San Pantalon, Dorsoduro 3778; ✆ until late Mon-Sat; 🖳) A pub-like den not far from Santa Margherita, Café Blue usually figures in any Dorsoduro *giro d'ombra* (Venetian-style low-key pub crawl). Dark and atmospheric, it's a slightly shabby option, but still warm and inviting. Free Internet access.

Café Noir (☎ 041 71 09 25; Calle San Pantalon 3805; ✆ 7am-2am Mon-Sat, 9am-2am Sun) A laid-back, more studenty hang-out, occupied night and day with locals catching up on gossip, flirting, drinking, eating and enjoying the casual atmosphere.

Paradiso Perduto (Paradise Lost; ☎ 041720581; Fondamenta della Misericordia, Cannaregio 2540; ✆ 7pm-late, happy hr 6.30-7.30pm Thu-Mon, lunch Sat & Sun) Popular, dim, faux-Bohemian bar/eatery/club with live and DJ-fuelled music. It's queer-friendly, self-consciously outré and does an awesome quasi-buffet lunch at weekends.

Inishark (☎ 041 523 53 00; Calle Mondo Nuovo, Castello 5787; ✆ 5.30pm-2am Tue-Sun, closed Aug) A fun Irish bar so low-lit you'll need the light from the TV screens showing football games to even *see* your Guinness.

ITALY

Bar Du Champ (☎ 041 528 62 55; Campo Santa Margherita, Dorsoduro 3019; ☽ 10am-2am) Hip bar considered studenty because of the location, but really pulling a mixed crowd. It has *panini* for €1 to €2 and Tetley's on tap. It's more swish than it sounds, and a real Venetian hot spot.

Entertainment

Teatro La Fenice (☎ 041 78 65 11; www.teatrolafenice .it, Campo San Fantin, San Marco 1970; admission varies; ☽ varies) Fire damage in 1996 saw the city's grandest theatre closed for repairs for seven years, only to re-emerge from the ashes, like the phoenix it's named after. The nexus of high (performance) art in Venice.

Palazzo Grassi (www.palazzograssi.it; San Samuele, San Marco 3231; tickets adult/concession €9/6.50; ☽ 10am-7pm) Backed by the financial clout of automotive giant FIAT, Palazzo Grassi is *the* schmick venue for major art exhibitions, from ancient to modern.

Shopping

Venice is synonymous with elaborate decorative work and craftworks, primarily Murano's glassware and Burano's lace. Marbled paper and luscious velvet fabrics are other famous items. There are several workshops and showrooms in Venice, but the quality is inconsistent – there are many knockoffs.

Getting There & Away

Some 12km from Venice is **Marco Polo airport** (☎ 041 260 61 11, flight info: ☎ 041 260 92 60), servicing domestic and European flights.

From Piazzale Roma use **ATVO buses** (☎ 041 520 55 30; €2.70) or ACTV bus No 5 (€0.80).

ACTV buses (☎ 899 90 90 90; Piazzale Roma) service surrounding areas (including Mestre and fishing port Chioggia) and also Padua and Treviso.

The train station, **Stazione di Santa Lucia** (☎ 848 88 80 88), is directly linked to Padua, Verona, Trieste, Milan and Bologna, and easily accessible for Florence and Rome. You can also reach points in France, Germany, Austria, Switzerland, Slovenia and Croatia. The Venice Simplon **Orient Express** (London office: ☎ 020-7805 5100; www.orient-express.com) runs twice-weekly between Venice and London, via Innsbruck, Zürich and Paris.

Minoan Lines (☎ 041 240 71 01; Porto Venezia, Zona Santa Marta) at the Venice Port run ferries to Greece (€72 one-way summer, daily summer, four times weekly winter).

Getting Around

Cars must be parked on Tronchetto or at Piazzale Roma (Lido allows cars – take car ferry No 17 from Tronchetto). The car parks aren't cheap (€18 per day); an option is leaving the car at Fusina, near Mestre, taking *vaporetto* No 16 to Zattere, and then No 82 to Piazza San Marco or the train station.

As Venice is carless, *vaporetti* (single/return €3.10/5.20, 24-/72-hour unlimited use ticket €19/31) are the city's mode of public transport. Full timetables are available at ticket offices (€0.50). The most useful vaporetti are:

No 1 – From Piazzale Roma, the No 1 zigzags along the Grand Canal to San Marco, then to the Lido.

No 12 – Departs from Fondamenta Nuove for the islands of Murano, Burano and Torcello.

No 82 – Faster than the No 1 if you're anxious to get to San Marco. Also services Giudecca.

Traghetti (the public gondolas used for crossing the Grand Canal; per crossing €0.50) get you a less romanticised 'gondola' experience. Use them; they're quick, cheap, fun and authentically Venetian.

FERRARA
pop 131,600

Lovely Ferrara outshines some of its bigger-named neighbours. The colourful medieval centre retains the dynamism of its heyday as a seat of the Este family (1260–1598). Castello Estense is the central identifiable landmark in this charming town, though its friendly people are reason enough to visit this place.

The **tourist office** (☎ 0532 29 93 03; www.ferrara terraeacqua.it; ⊗ 9am-1pm & 2-6pm Mon-Sat, 9.30am-1pm & 2-5.30pm Sun) is inside Castello Estense.

Sights & Activities

The small historical centre encompassing medieval Ferrara lies south of the **Castello Estense** (info/tickets ☎ 0532 29 93 03/0243 35 35 22; www.castelloestense.it; Viale Cavour; full/under 18/over 65 €10/8.50/8.50, reservations €1; ⊗ 9am-8pm Mon-Thu, 9am-10pm Fri-Sun). Complete with moat and drawbridges, it was begun by Nicolò II d'Este in 1385. The foreboding atmosphere of its interior isn't mirrored outside, where there's a bubbly marketplace.

The pretty pink-and-white striped **Duomo** dates from the 12th century, with Gothic and Renaissance additions. Its **museum** (☎ 0532 76 12 99; Via San Romano 1-9; admission €4.20; ⊗ 9am-1pm & 3-8pm Tue-Sun) is worth seeing, with some Renaissance works. The **Palazzo Schifanoia** (☎ 0532 20 99 88; Via Scandiana 23; admission €4.20; ⊗ 9am-6pm Tue-Sun) is one of the city's major Renaissance buildings and another Este palace. Head for the 'Room of the Months' for Ferrara's finest frescoes.

Sleeping & Eating

You won't need to stay overnight to see Ferrara's sights, though it's a viable base for visiting Venice. It's small, so tourist information can help you find *affittacamere*.

Pensione Artisti (☎ 0532 76 10 38; Via Vittoria 66; s/d without bathroom €22/40, d with bathroom €57) A fabulously friendly place on a medieval street, with attentive hosts ensuring the warmest welcome. Clean, bright rooms are secure and comfy, and there's a good guest kitchen available.

Woodpecker (☎ 0532 20 94 63; Via Saraceno 14; pizza €7, pasta €8-10; ⊗ dinner) This popular pizzeria/*ristorante* has a buoyant ambience and crisp Italian décor. Try the local speciality *cappellacci di zucca* (a hat-shaped pasta filled with pumpkin) that is superb simply with butter, sage and *grana* (parmesan).

Drinking

Fusion (☎ 0532 20 14 73; www.viascienze8.it; Via Delle Scienze 8/a; ⊗ 7.30am-3.30pm Mon, 7.30am-1.30am Tue-Sat, 6pm-1.30am Sun) This super-slick wine bar is an arena for personal-grooming for Ferrara's

foxiest. Warm colours, comfy décor, chilled DJ-ing (and occasional live jazz) provide entertainment, but ogling's the real action.

Messisbugo (☎ 0532 76 40 60; www.messisbugo .com; Via Carlo Mayr; ⊗ late Tue-Sun) Ferrara's finest bar provides a cooler counterpoint to Fusion. Boisterously casual without being raucous, sophisticated friendly staff keep everything flowing.

Getting There & Around

Ferrara is on the Bologna–Venice train line, with regular trains to both (40 minutes from Bologna, 1½ hours from Venice) plus nearby Ravenna. Buses run from the train station to Modena (in the Emilia-Romagna region).

BOLOGNA

postcode 40100 / pop 381,000

Bologna is vibrant, beautiful and *red* – and it's often joked that its politics are reflected in the colour of its buildings. Traditionally well to the left, Bologna's reputation for socialist sympathies seems exaggerated these days, possibly reflecting stereotypes more easily pinned to the thousands of students who come to attend Europe's oldest university. Founded here in 1088, it was churning out graduates while Oxford and La Sorbonne were still wearing short pants.

Emilia-Romagna's capital is, tellingly, lauded as one of Italy's greatest culinary cities. Bologna's traditional nickname was La Grassa ('the fat one') for the richness of the food; besides spaghetti bolognese (known as *spaghetti al ragù*) Bologna also gave the world tortellini and lasagne. Wonderful displays fill many a restaurant window.

Orientation & Information

Via dell'Indipendenza, the main north–south artery, leads from the train and bus stations into Piazza del Nettuno and Piazza Maggiore, the heart of the city.

Easy Internet (☎ 051 23 10 74; www.easyInternetcafe .it; Via Rizzoli 9; ⊗ 9am-11pm)
Main Post Office (☎ 051 23 06 99; Piazza Minghetti 1; ⊗ 8am-6pm Mon-Fri, 8am-noon Sat)
Ospedale Maggiore (☎ 051 647 81 11)
Police Headquarters (☎ 051 640 11 11; Piazza Galileo 7)
Tourist Information call centre (☎ 051 24 65 41; ⊗ 9am-7pm Mon-Sat) tourist office (Piazza Maggiore 1; ⊗ 9am-8pm) train station (⊗ 8.30am-7.30pm Mon-Sat) airport (⊗ 8am-8pm Mon-Sat, 9am-3pm Sun)

ITALY

Sights & Activities

Simply strolling Bologna's 40km of porticoes is lovely. There's abundant atmosphere to be absorbed in the architecture. Start in the pedestrianised centre formed by **Piazza Maggiore**, the adjoining **Piazza del Nettuno** and **Fontana del Nettuno** (Neptune's Fountain – note the sirens' 'functional' nipples), sculpted in bronze by Giambologna. The **Basilica di San Petronio** (☎ 051 22 54 22; ⏱ 7.30am-1pm & 2-6pm, free tours 11.30am Tue, Thu & Sat) in Piazza Maggiore is dedicated to Bologna's patron saint, Petronius. Its partially complete state, most detectable in the cracked façade, doesn't diminish its status as the fifth-largest basilica in the world. The chapels contain many notable artworks. The adjacent **Palazzo Comunale** (town hall; admission free) combines disparate architectural styles harmoniously. **Basilica di San Domenico** (☎ 051 640 04 11; admission free; ⏱ 8am-1.30pm & 2.30-7.30pm) is a 16th-century Nicoló Pisano–designed chapel housing the sarcophagus of St Dominic, namesake of the Dominican order: its shrine features carvings by a young Michelangelo, and Mozart once played the church's organ.

Arriving at **Piazza di Porta Ravegnana**, climb the 97m **Torre Asinelli** (climb €3; ⏱ to 6pm), the larger of Bologna's leaning towers, for wonderful views.

Sleeping

Budget hotels are in perpetual demand (conventions/conferences are often held here) and not as cheap as you'd expect in a student city.

Ostello Due Torri/San Sisto (☎/fax 051 50 18 10; Via Viadagola 5; dm/d €13.50/15, sheets €1.50; ⏱ curfew 11pm) These two adjacent HI hostels are painfully located. Take bus No 93 (or No 301 Sunday, and No 21b daily after 8.30pm) from Via Irnerio to the San Sisto stop (6km). There's nothing notable nearby; bring everything with you, or plan your return from the centre before journeying in/out.

Albergo Garisenda (☎ 051 22 43 69; fax 051 22 10 07; Via Rizzoli 9, Galleria del Leone 1; s/d/tr without bathroom incl breakfast €45/65/90) In the shadow of the towers, Garisenda has some rooms with views (of the aforementioned, and buzzing Via Rizzoli). It's conveniently located and good value.

Pensione Marconi (☎ 051 26 28 32; fax 051 23 50 41; Via G Marconi 22; d €55, s/d with bathroom €50/75) Marconi's functional but plain rooms are a good option for couples or trios splitting

room costs. No frills, but fine for a short stay. Rear rooms are quieter.

Hotel Accademia (☎ 051 23 23 18; www.hotelaccademia.it; Via delle Belle Arti 6; s/d €45-70/€65-100, s/d with bathroom €70-90/€80-125) Good rooms with satellite TV, phone and decent breakfast (included) make the Accademia good value. There is also uncommonly good disabled access. In the thick of the university quarter, it's close to excellent eateries.

Eating & Drinking

Bologna's eating and drinking scenes are lively.

Trattoria da Danio (☎ 051 55 52 02; Via San Felice 50a; menu €11.50; ⏱ lunch & dinner) The quintessential Bolognese *trattoria;* atmospheric, unpretentious, with quality food that would cost double in other cities. The three-course lunch special includes a half-litre of mineral water or a *quartino* of house wine. Perfect for authentic tagliatelle *al ragù.*

Rosa Rose Bistro (☎ 051 22 50 71; www.rosarose.it; Via Clavature 18; lge salad €7; ⏱ lunch & dinner) Surprisingly, the stars of Rosa Rose's menu are the lush, enormous salads. Maybe it's something to do with the floral décor. A great café with a gorgeous terrace for alfresco dining.

Trattoria Caminetto D'Oro (☎ 051 26 34 94; www.caminettodoro.it; Via Falegnami 4; mains €14-18; ⏱ lunch Thu-Tue, dinner Thu-Mon) This award-winning *trattoria* is cosily ensconced under a portico in a nice part of town. In winter, the earthy smell of grilling fills the intimate dining rooms. The food's tops.

Cantina Bentivoglio (☎ 051 26 54 16; Via Mascarella 4b; meals €12-15; ⏱ 8pm-2am) A liberal sauce of live jazz (nightly) and 500-plus wines can accompany your excellent meal at this mid-range marvel. Indulgently, brilliantly Bolognese.

Clorofilla (☎ 051 235 53 43; Strada Maggiore 64/c) An uncommon thing in Italy: a specialist vegetarian restaurant! Lots of great dishes made with locally grown ingredients and all manner of fab cheeses.

Cluricaune (☎ 051 26 34 19; www.cluricaune.com; Via Zamboni 18/b; ⏱ until late) Deep in student territory is an Irish pub to embarrass Temple Bar. Heavily popular, and rightly so.

SELF-CATERING

Self-caterers should hit **Mercato delle Erbe** (Via Ugo Bassi 27; ⏱ Mon-Sat), a covered market offering all sorts of local fare. Try supermarket **Pam** (Via Marconi 28a) for staple items, or the extravagant **La Baita** (Via Pescheria Vecchie) for deluxe ingredients.

Clubbing

Corto Maltese (☎ 051 22 97 46; Via Borgo San Pietro 9/2; ☺ until late) Fantastic bar/pub/dancing spot with pool tables, free pasta and an inclusive vibe.

Kinki (☎ 051 587 51 78; www.kinkidisco.com; Via Zamboni 1; ☺ until late) It's hot! It's vinyl! Gays, lesbians and uber-cool straights are welcome to work it 'til all hours at Kinki's themed nights. Wicked fun.

Getting There & Around

Bologna's **Guglielmo Marconi airport** (☎ 051 647 96 15) is northwest of the city. On land, Bologna is a major transport hub. Trains from around Italy stop here. National and international coaches depart from the **bus terminal** (Piazza XX Settembre) around the corner from the train station in Piazza delle Medaglie d'Oro.

The city is linked to Milan, Florence and Rome via the A1. The A13 services Venice and Padua, the A14 handles Rimini and Ravenna. Traffic is restricted in Bologna's centre; park cars outside city walls.

Bologna's local buses are efficient. To get to the centre from the station take bus No 25 or 27, or enjoy a 10-minute walk.

RAVENNA

pop 139,800

Unless you're *really* into tilework, Ravenna's a sleepy town best for a day trip. Its genuinely amazing mosaics, relics from its days as capital of the Western Roman Empire and western seat of the Byzantines, are the only real drawcard. Dante (Alighieri) arrived in 1302 after being exiled from Florence, writing most of *The Divine Comedy* – and ultimately dying – here (1321).

The **IAT tourist office** (☎ 0544 354 04; Via Salara 12; ☺ 8.30am-7pm Mon-Sat Apr-Sep, 8.30am-7pm Mon-Sat Oct-Mar, 10am-4pm Sun) is near Via Cavour. For medical assistance, see **Ospedale Santa Maria delle Croci** (☎ 0544 40 91 11; Via Missiroli 10).

There are two ticket types (costing €8.50 or €6.50) for seeing Ravenna's famed **mosaics**, but only the first is useful for the central ones, in: the **Basilica di Sant'Apollinare Nuovo** (Via di Roma; ☺ 9am-7pm); the **Basilica di San Vitale** (☺ 9am-7pm); the oldest of them all in **Mausoleo di Galla**

Placidia (☺ 9am-7pm); the **Battistero Neoniano** (Via Battistero; ☺ 9am-7pm) and the **Museo Arcivescovile**.

Dante's Tomb (Via Dante Alighieri 9; admission free; ☺ 9am-7pm) itself is unremarkable. Worth noting, however, is the 'perpetual' lamp kept permanently alight in tribute – a belated admission from Florence that they'd fumbled in exiling the 'father of modern Italian [language]'.

Cheapest beds are at **Ostello Dante** (☎ 0544 42 11 64; Via Aurelio Nicolodi 12; B&B €12.50, per person €14) This HI hostel is as neat as a pin, with friendlier than normal staff and good evening meals. It's 1km out of town; take bus No 1 from Viale Pallavacini, by the train station (a taxi costs €6).

Albergo Al Giaciglio (☎ /fax 0544 394 03; Via Rocca Brancaleone 42; s/d/tr €30/42/55, with bathroom €36/51/65) This family-run hotel near the station has bright blue rooms and a good restaurant (set menu €13).

Cá de Vén (☎ 0544 301 63; Via Corrado Ricci 24; pasta €6-8, mains €9-14; ☺ Tue-Sun; ✗) The best all-round eating option in Ravenna offers affordable regional dishes and wicked wines in monastic surroundings, with a big nonsmoking section. Pasta courses are ample for a small meal.

Ravenna is accessible by train from Bologna (1½ hours), sometimes involving a change at Castel Bolognese. Cycling is a popular way to get around, as Ravenna is fairly flat. Rental is available from **COOP San Vitale** (Piazza Farini XX; per hr/day €1.20/8) outside the station, or the **tourist office** (free; available spring & summer).

THE DOLOMITES

The limestone Dolomites stretch across Trentino-Alto Adige and into the Veneto. Eastern sections were a coral reef around 100 million years ago; when the planet warmed, seas receded and the rest of the ranges formed seismically around it, the seabed elevating by up to 3000m. Glacial flows in the interceding Ice Age and a few millennia of erosion shaped their present stunning formations, snapping at the sky like jagged teeth. This spectacular Alpine region is a favoured area for skiing and trekking.

Information

Information about Trentino-Alto Adige can be obtained in Trent (Trento) at the

APT del Trentino (☎ 0461 83 90 00; www.trentino .to; Via Romagnosi 11); in **Rome** (☎ 06 360 95 842; Via del Babuino 20); and in **Milan** (☎ 02 864 61 251; apt. milano@trentino.to; Piazza Diaz 5). Bolzano's **tourist office** (☎ 0471 30 70 00; www.bolzano-bozen.it; Piazza Walther 8) also has information on the region. The **APT Dolomiti** (☎ 0436 32 31/2/3; fax 0436 32 35) at Cortina can provide details on trekking and skiing in the Veneto.

Skiing

The Dolomites' many resorts range from beautiful-millionaires-only Cortina d'Ampezzo in the Veneto to family-oriented resorts in the Val Gardena (Trentino-Alto Adige). Most of the ski resorts have helpful tourist offices.

High season (Christmas to early January and early February to April) costs. Buy a *settimana bianca* (literally, 'white week') – a package deal including seven days of accommodation, food and ski passes, available throughout Italy.

Most resort areas also offer their own passes for unlimited use of lifts at several resorts within nominated periods. Prices vary with resort (from €130 to €160 for six days). Average cost of ski-plus-boot hire (downhill/cross-country €15/10) in the Alps is bearable. The **Superski Dolomiti pass** (www .dolomitisuperski.com; 3/6 days high season €100/175) accesses 464 lifts and 1220km of runs in 12 valleys.

Trekking

Without doubt, the Dolomites provide the most breathtaking opportunities for walking in the Italian Alps (season June to September), from basic half-day strolls with the kids to hardcore trekking and mountaineering. Alpine *rifugi* (refuges) usually close around 20 September. Trails are well marked with numbers on red-and-white bands on trees and rocks, or by numbers inside coloured triangles for the four Alte Vie (High Routes) through the Dolomites linking a chain of *rifugi* that can take two weeks to walk. The best maps are the Tabacco 1:25,000 series, widely available at bookshops throughout the region. Lonely Planet's *Walking in Italy* outlines several treks in detail; as does the *Italy* guide.

Recommended trekking areas include:
Alpe di Siusi – A vast plateau above the Val Gardena, at the foot of the spectacular Sciliar.

Cortina area – Featuring the magnificent Parco Naturale di Fanes-Sennes-Braies.
Pale di San Martino – Accessible from San Martino di Castrozza.

WARNING

The weather is extremely changeable in the Alps; even if it's sweltering when you set off, be prepared for very cold/wet weather on even the shortest walks. Essentials include good-quality, worn-in walking boots, an anorak or pile/wind jacket, lightweight backpack, warm hat and gloves, waterproof poncho, light food and plenty of water.

Getting There & Away

The region has excellent public transport. The two principal bus companies are **SAD** (☎ 800 846 04 09) in Alto Adige and the Veneto, and **Atesina** (www.atesina.it) in Trentino. A network of long-distance buses operated by various companies (eg Lazzi, SITA, Sena, STAT and ATVO) connects major towns and resorts with big cities such as Rome, Florence, Venice, Bologna, Milan as well as Genoa. Information is available from tourist offices and regional bus stations. For long-distance travel information, try **Lazzi Express** Rome (☎ 06 884 08 40; Via Tagliamento 27b) Florence (☎ 055 28 71 18; Piazza Stazione 47r). There is a **SITA office** (☎ 055 29 49 55; Via Santa Caterina da Siena 15) in Florence.

Getting Around

If you're planning an Alpine trek during warmer months, you'll find that hitching is no problem; normal caution should still apply. Areas near major resorts are well serviced by local buses, and tourist offices have information on routes. During winter, most resorts have 'ski bus' shuttle services to the main facilities.

CANAZEI

pop 1780

Set in the Fassa Dolomites, Canazei has over 100km of trails and is linked to a challenging network of runs, the **Sella Ronda**. Canazei also offers cross-country and summer skiing on Marmolada, the highest peak in the Dolomites (3342m).

Spend a cheap night at the Marmolada **camping ground** (☎ 0462 60 16 60; per adult/camp site €8/8; ☉ year-round), or contact the **APT tourist office** (☎ 0462 60 11 13; Via Roma 34) for further details on accommodation. The resort is accessible by bus with **Atesina** (☎ 0461 98 36 27; www.atesina.it) from Trent and SAD bus from Bolzano.

VAL GARDENA

This is a popular area in the Alps, with good prices and top facilities. There are superb walking trails in the Sella Group and the Alpe di Siusi. The Vallunga, behind Selva, is great for family walks and cross-country skiing.

The valley's main towns are Ortisei, Santa Cristina and Selva, all offering plenty of accommodation and easy access to runs. Each town has a **tourist office** Ortisei (☎ 0471 79 63 28) Santa Cristina (☎ 0471 79 30 46) Selva (☎ 0471 79 51 22), with extensive information on local facilities. Staff speak English and will send details on request. The Val Gardena is accessible from Bolzano by SAD bus, and connected to major Italian cities by coach (Lazzi, SITA and STAT).

SAN MARTINO DI CASTROZZA
pop 700

In a sheltered position beneath the Pale di San Martino, this resort is popular, offering good skiing and a toboggan run. The **APT office** (☎ 0439 76 88 67) provides lists of accommodation. **Hotel Suisse** (☎ 0439 680 87; Via Dolomiti 1; B&B from €33) is a pleasant hotel. Buses travel often from Trent, Venice and Padua.

CENTRAL ITALY

Though you'll be cheek-by-jowl with hordes of culture-vultures in hubs like Florence – and even some of the smaller locales nearby – it's still possible to lose yourself down a medieval side street in Umbria and Le Marche (the Marches) only to turn a corner and find some of Italy's sweetest vistas. *La dolce vita* lies here in Italy's heartland, and it needn't cost the earth.

FLORENCE (FIRENZE)
postcode 50100 / pop 375,000

Italy has been successfully selling itself on Florence's appeal for centuries – it's a beautiful city with an almost unparalleled artistic heritage – but it can also be disheartening. For most of the year, you'll overhear more conversations in English than Italian, and in summer the heat, pollution and crowds are stifling. Home of Dante, Machiavelli, Michelangelo, the Medici and Carlo Collodi (who created Pinocchio), the wealth of history, art and culture can overwhelm. It's not so much money you'll feel short of, as time.

Florence was founded as a colony of the Etruscan city Fiesole around 200 BC, later becoming the Roman settlement of Florentia. In the Middle Ages the city developed a flourishing mercantile economy, sparking a period of growth previously unequalled in Italy. Reaching full bloom under the Medicis (1469–1737), its cultural, artistic and political fecundity culminated in the Renaissance.

Following unification, Florence was the capital of the new kingdom of Italy (1865–1871). During WWII parts of the city were destroyed by bombs, including all Florence's bridges except the Ponte Vecchio, and in 1966 a devastating flood destroyed or severely damaged many important artworks.

Florence is perhaps the most enticing city in Italy, with a keen, almost youthful dynamism offsetting the heavy-browed focus on its history and the culture 'industries'.

Orientation

The main train station Santa Maria Novella, is a useful landmark. The main thoroughfare to the centre is Via de' Panzani and then Via de' Cerretani. You'll know you've arrived when you see the Duomo.

Once at Piazza del Duomo, Florence is easy to negotiate, with most major sights within comfortable walking distance. Many museums close on Monday, but you won't waste your time just strolling. Take the city ATAF buses to Piazzale Michelangelo, or to the suburb of Fiesole northeast of the centre, both offering panoramic views.

A good map of the city, on sale at newsstands, is *Firenze: Pianta della Città*.

Information
BOOKSHOPS

Feltrinelli International (Map p689; ☎ 055 21 95 24; Via Cavour 12r) Italy's best foreign-language bookstore has a huge outlet here.

Paperback Exchange (Map pp686-7; ☎ 055 247 81 54; Via Fiesolana 31r) Has a huge range of new and second-hand books.

INTERNET ACCESS

Internet Train (www.Internettrain.it; per hr around €4) Via dell'Oriuolo (Map p689; ☎ 055 263 89 68) Borgo San Jacopo 30r (Map p689; ☎ 055 265 79 35) beneath Stazione

ITALY

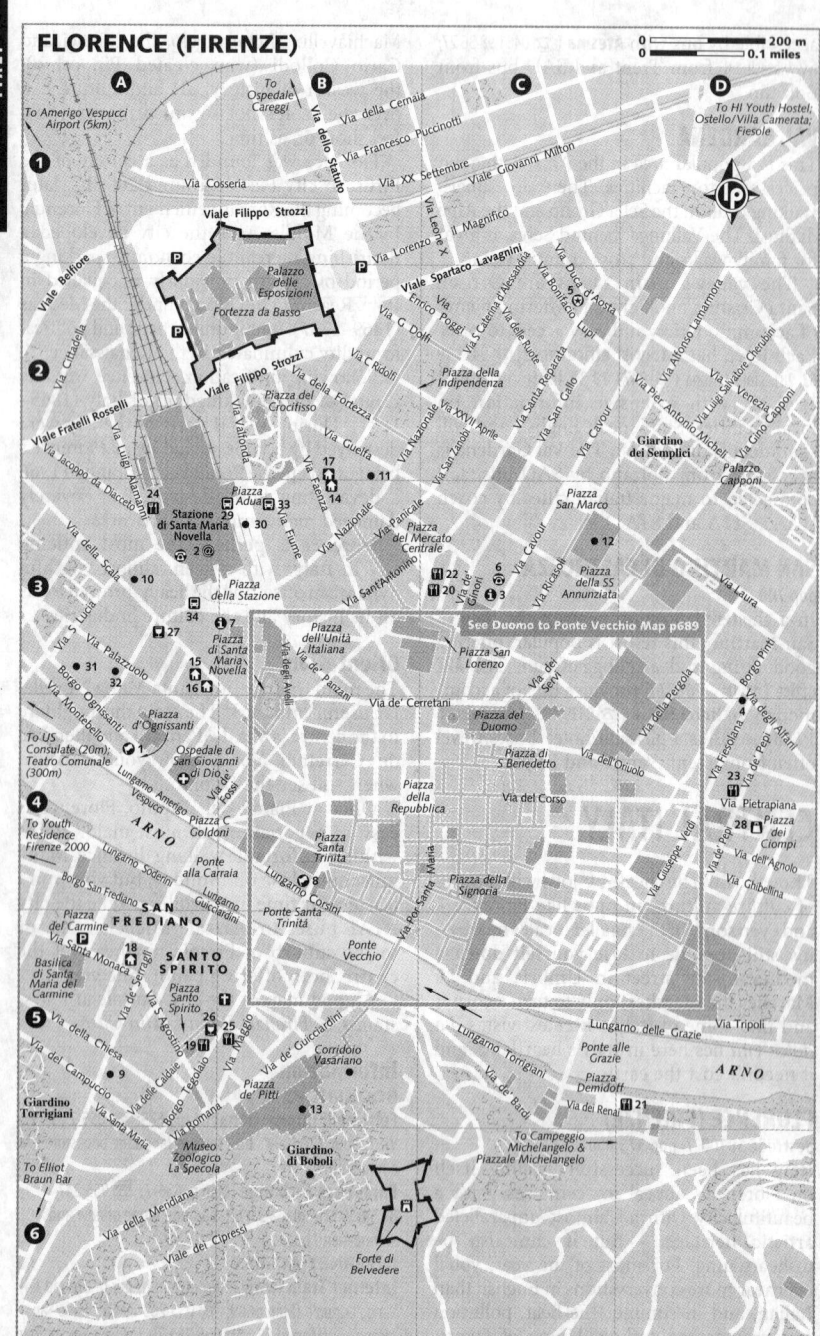

FLORENCE (FIRENZE)

| 0 | 200 m |
| 0 | 0.1 miles |

To Amerigo Vespucci
Airport (5km)

To
Ospedale
Careggi

To HI Youth Hostel;
Ostello/Villa Camerata;
Fiesole

Via della Cernaia
Via della Scala
Via Francesco Puccinotti
Via XX Settembre
Viale Giovanni Milton

Via Cosseria

Viale Filippo Strozzi

Via Leone X il Magnifico

Via dello Statuto

Via Belfiore

Palazzo
delle
Esposizioni

Fortezza da Basso

Viale Spartaco Lavagnini

Via
Enrico
Poggi

Via Catena d'Alessandria

Via delle Ruote

Via Duca d'Aosta

Via Bonifacio Lupi

Via Pier Antonio Micheli

Via Alfonso Lamarmora

Via Gino Capponi

Via Venezia

Via Salvatore Cherubini

Via Luigi Salvatore Cherubini

Viale Filippo Strozzi

Via della Fortezza

Via G. Dolfi

Via C Ridolfi

Piazza della
Indipendenza

Via XXVII Aprile

Via Santa Reparata

Via San Gallo

Via Cavour

Giardino
dei Semplici

Palazzo
Capponi

Via Cittadella

Via Fratelli Rosselli

Via Iacopo da Diacceto

Via Luigi Alamanni

Via della Scala

Via S. Lucia

Via Valfonda

Via Faenza

Piazza del
Crocifisso

Via Guelfa

Via Nazionale

Via San Zanobi

Piazza
San Marco

● 12

Via Laura

Piazza Adua

33

30

Stazione
di Santa Maria
Novella

17
14

● 11

Via Panicale

Piazza
del Mercato
Centrale

6
5
3

Via Cavour

Via Ricasoli

Piazza
della SS
Annunziata

● 10

Piazza
della Stazione

Via Fiume

Via Sant'Antonino

22
20

Via de'
Ginori

See Duomo to Ponte Vecchio Map p689

Borgo Pinti

Via Fiesolana

Via de' Pepi

34

27

7

Piazza
di Santa
Maria
Novella

15
16

● 31

32

Via Palazzuolo

Via degli Avelli

Via de' Panzani

Piazza
dell'Unità
Italiana

Piazza San
Lorenzo

Via de' Servi

Via dell'Oriuolo

Via della Pergola

4

23

Via Pietrapiana

Borgo Ognissanti

Via Montebello

Piazza
d'Ognissanti

1

Ospedale di
San Giovanni
di Dio

Via del Moro

Via de' Cerretani

Piazza del
Duomo

Piazza di
S Benedetto

Via del Corso

Via del Proconsolo

28

Piazza
dei
Ciompi

Via dell'Agnolo

Via Ghibellina

To US
Consulate (20m);
Teatro Comunale
(300m)

Lungarno Amerigo Vespucci

Piazza C
Goldoni

ARNO

Piazza
della
Repubblica

Piazza
Santa
Trinita

Via Por Santa Maria

Via Giuseppe Verdi

To Youth
Residence
Firenze 2000

Lungarno Soderini

Borgo San Frediano

SAN
FREDIANO

Lungarno
Guicciardini

Ponte
alla Carraia

Lungarno Corsini

8

Ponte Santa
Trinità

Piazza della
Signoria

Piazza
del Carmine

18

Basilica
di Santa
Maria del
Carmine

Via Santa Monaca

Via de' Serragli

Via S. Agostino

Piazza
Santo
Spirito

SANTO
SPIRITO

25
19

Via Maggio

Via de' Guicciardini

Ponte
Vecchio

Corridoio
Vasariano

Lungarno Torrigiani

Via de' Bardi

Lungarno delle Grazie

Ponte alle
Grazie

Piazza
Demidoff

Via Tripoli

ARNO

Via della Chiesa

9

Via del Campuccio

Via delle Caldaie

Borgo Tegolaio

Piazza
de' Pitti

● 13

Via dei Renai

21

Giardino
Torrigiani

Via Santa Maria

Via Romana

Museo
Zoologico
La Specola

Giardino
di Boboli

To Campeggio
Michelangelo &
Piazzale Michelangelo

To Elliot
Braun Bar

Via della Meridiana

Via dei Cipressi

Forte di
Belvedere

Santa Maria Novella (Map opposite; ☎ 055 239 97 20) Has 15 branches.

Netgate (Map p689; ☎ 055 658 02 07; www .thenetgate.it; Via Sant' Egidio 10-20r; ⏰ 10am-10.30pm, happy hr free access 10.30-11am & 2-2.30pm Sat)

LAUNDRY

Wash & Dry (☎ 800 23 11 72; ⏰ 8am-10pm) Via del Sole 29r (Map p689) Via della Scala 52-54r (Map opposite) Via de' Seragli 87r (Map opposite)

MEDICAL SERVICES

For an ambulance call ☎ 118.

Farmacia Comunale (☎ 055 28 94 35) Inside the train station, its open late.

Misericordia di Firenze (Map p689; ☎ 055 21 22 22; Vicolo degli Adimari 1; ⏰ 1.30-5pm Mon-Fri) A medical service for tourists, just off Piazza Duomo.

Molteni (Map p689; ☎ 055 28 94 90; Via dei Calzaiuoli 7r; ⏰ 24hr) A late-night city centre pharmacy.

Police station (Map opposite; general: ☎ 055 497 71, lost property: ☎ 055 328 39 42, towed vehicles: ☎ 055 41 57 81; Via Zara 2) Has a foreigners' office.

MONEY

American Express (Map p689; ☎ 055 509 81; Via Dante Alighieri 22r; ⏰ 9am-5.30pm Mon-Fri, 9.30am-12.30pm Sat)

Travelex (Map p689; ☎ 055 28 97 81; Lungarno degli Acciaiuoli 6r)

POST & TELEPHONE

Main post office (Map p689; Via Pellicceria 3; ⏰ 8.15am-7pm Mon-Fri, 8.15am-12.30pm Sat).

Telecom office (Map opposite; Via Cavour 21r; ⏰ 7am-11pm) Has fax services.

TOURIST INFORMATION

Amerigo Vespucci Airport (☎ 055 31 58 74; ⏰ 7.30am-11.30pm)

Tourist office (Map opposite; ☎ 055 29 08 32; www .firenzeturismo.it; Via Cavour 1r; ⏰ 8.30am-6.30pm

Mon-Sat, 8.30am-1.30pm Sun) There is another **office** (Map opposite; ☎ 055 21 22 45; Piazza della Stazione 4; ⏰ 8.30am-7pm Mon-Sat, 8.30am-2pm Sun).

Sights & Activities

Enjoying Florence's sights can be taxing, as lengthy queues stretch patience. But don't despair, call **Firenze Musei** (☎ 055 29 48 83; www.firenzemusei.it; fee per museum €3; ⏰ phone lines: 8.30am-6.30pm Mon-Fri, 8.30am-12.30pm Sat) which advance-books tickets for all state museums, including the Uffizi, Palazzo Pitti, Galleria dell'Accademia and Cappelle Medicee.

DUOMO

The terracotta-orange roof contrasts dramatically with the red, green and white marble façade of the skyline-dominating cathedral, the **Duomo** (Map p689; ☎ 055 230 28 85; ⏰ 10am-5pm Mon-Sat) – among Italy's most beloved monuments. Officially the Cattedrale di Santa Maria del Fiore, the breathtaking structure was begun in 1294 by Sienese architect Arnolfo di Cambio, taking almost 150 years to complete.

Brunelleschi won a competition (1420) to design the enormous octagonal dome, the first of its kind since antiquity. The interior is decorated with frescoes by Vasari and Zuccari, and stained-glass windows by Donatello, Paolo Uccello and Lorenzo Ghiberti. The façade is a 19th-century replacement of the unfinished 16th-century original. For a bird's-eye view of Florence, climb to the top of the **cupola** (admission €6; ⏰ 8.30am-6.20pm Mon-Fri, 8.30am-5pm Sat).

Giotto designed and began building the graceful 82m **campanile** (bell tower; Map p689; climb €6; ⏰ 8.30am-6.50pm) in 1334, but died before it was completed. The climb yields gorgeous views.

ITALY

The Romanesque **battistero** (baptistry; Map opposite; admission €3, ☽ noon-6.30pm Mon-Sat, 8.30am-1.30pm Sun & holidays), believed to have been built between the 5th and 11th centuries on the site of a Roman temple, is the oldest building in Florence. Dante was baptised here, and it's famous for its gilded-bronze doors. The celebrated *Gates of Paradise* by Lorenzo Ghiberti face the Duomo to the east. The south door (1336), by Andrea Pisano, is the oldest.

PALAZZO DEGLI UFFIZI

Ignore killjoys citing the two- to four-hour wait to enter the **Palazzo degli Uffizi** (Map opposite; ☎ 055 238 86 51; reservations 055 294 883, €1.55; www .uffizi.firenze.it; admission €8; ☽ 8.15am-6.50pm Tue-Sun, ticket office closes 6.05pm) for the Galleria degli Uffizi – it's worthwhile. Begun by Vasari in 1560 and ultimately bequeathed to the city by the Medicis in 1743, the *palazzo* houses the greatest collection of Italian and Florentine art anywhere, including many of the world's most-recognisable Renaissance paintings.

The gallery's masterpieces include gems by Giotto and Cimabue; Botticelli's *Birth of Venus* (Room 10 to 14); plus works by Filippo Lippi and Fra Angelico. *The Annunciation* by Leonardo da Vinci is here (Room 15), along with Michelangelo's *Holy Family* (Room 25), Titian's *Venus of Urbino* (Room 28) and renowned works by Raphael, Andrea del Sarto, Tintoretto and Caravaggio.

PIAZZA DELLA SIGNORIA & PALAZZO VECCHIO

Designed by Arnolfo di Cambio and built between 1298 and 1340, **Palazzo Vecchio** (Map opposite; adult/child €5.70/4.30; ☽ 9am-7pm Fri-Wed, 9am-2pm Thu) is the traditional seat of the Florentine government. In the 16th century it became the ducal palace of the Medici (before they occupied the Palazzo Pitti), and was given an interior face-lift by Vasari. Visit the Michelozzo courtyard just inside the entrance and the lavish apartments upstairs.

The **Loggia della Signoria** stands at right angles to the Palazzo Vecchio, displaying sculptures. The statue of *David* is a fine copy of Michelangelo's masterpiece; the original (1504) was once here, but now 'lives' indoors at the Galleria dell'Accademia (below).

PONTE VECCHIO

This 14th-century bridge (Map opposite), lined with gold and silversmiths' shops, was the only one to survive Nazi bombing in WWII. Originally, the shops housed butchers, but when a corridor along the 1st floor was built by the Medici to link the Palazzo Pitti and Palazzo Vecchio, they ordered that goldsmiths rather than noisome butchers should trade there. The engaging area south of the river is 'the Oltrarno' (literally, 'beyond the Arno').

PALAZZO PITTI

The immense **Palazzo Pitti** (Map pp686-7; ☎ 055 238 86 14) was built for the Pitti family, great rivals of the Medici, who moved in a century later. The **Galleria Palatina** (Palatine Gallery; admission before/after 4pm €8.50/4; ☽ 8.15am-6.50pm Tue-Sun) has works by Raphael, Filippo Lippi, Titian and Rubens hung in lavishly decorated rooms. The gallery and (almost hysterically) luxuriant decoration of the **royal apartments** are not to be missed. The palace also houses the **Museo degli Argenti** (Silver Museum; ☽ 8.15am-4.20pm Tue-Sun, 2nd & 3rd Mon each month), the **Galleria d'Arte Moderna** (Modern Art Gallery; ☽ 8.15am-1.50pm Tue-Sat) and the **Galleria del Costume** (Costume Gallery; ☽ 8.15am-1.50pm Tue-Sat), all of which are worth a visit.

While you're here, don't miss the Renaissance **Giardino di Boboli** (Boboli Gardens; admission €4; ☽ 8.15am-7.30pm Jun-Aug, 8.15am-6.30pm Apr-May & Sep, 8.15am-5.30pm Mar & Oct, 8.15am-4.30pm Nov-Feb), with secluded grottoes, leafy walkways and panoramic views.

GALLERIA DELL'ACCADEMIA

Beating even Rodin's *The Thinker* and *The Kiss* for the title of 'Most Famous Sculpture in the Western World', Michelangelo's **David** is housed in the **Galleria dell'Accademia** (Map pp686-7; ☎ 055 238 86 09; Via Ricasoli 60; admission €6.50; ☽ 8.15am-6.50pm Tue-Sun). *David* truly *is* an amazing work close-up, being much bigger and more intricately detailed than many imagine, and recently cleaned (2004). A 90-minute wait is typical.

BASILICA DI SAN LORENZO & CAPPELLE MEDICEE (MEDICI CHAPELS)

The **Basilica di San Lorenzo** (Map below) was built by Brunelleschi in the 15th century for the Medici and includes his **Sagrestia Vecchia** (Old Sacristy), with sculptural decoration by Donatello. The cloister leads to the **Biblioteca Laurenziana**, the library built to house the Medici collection of some 10,000 manuscripts. Enter via Michelangelo's flowing mannerist stairway.

The **Cappelle Medicee** (Map below; ☎ 055 238 86 02; admission €6; ⏱ 8.15am-5pm Mon-Sat, 1st, 3rd & 5th Sun of the month, 2nd & 4th Mon of the month) are around the corner in Piazza Madonna degli Aldobrandini. The **Cappella dei Principi**

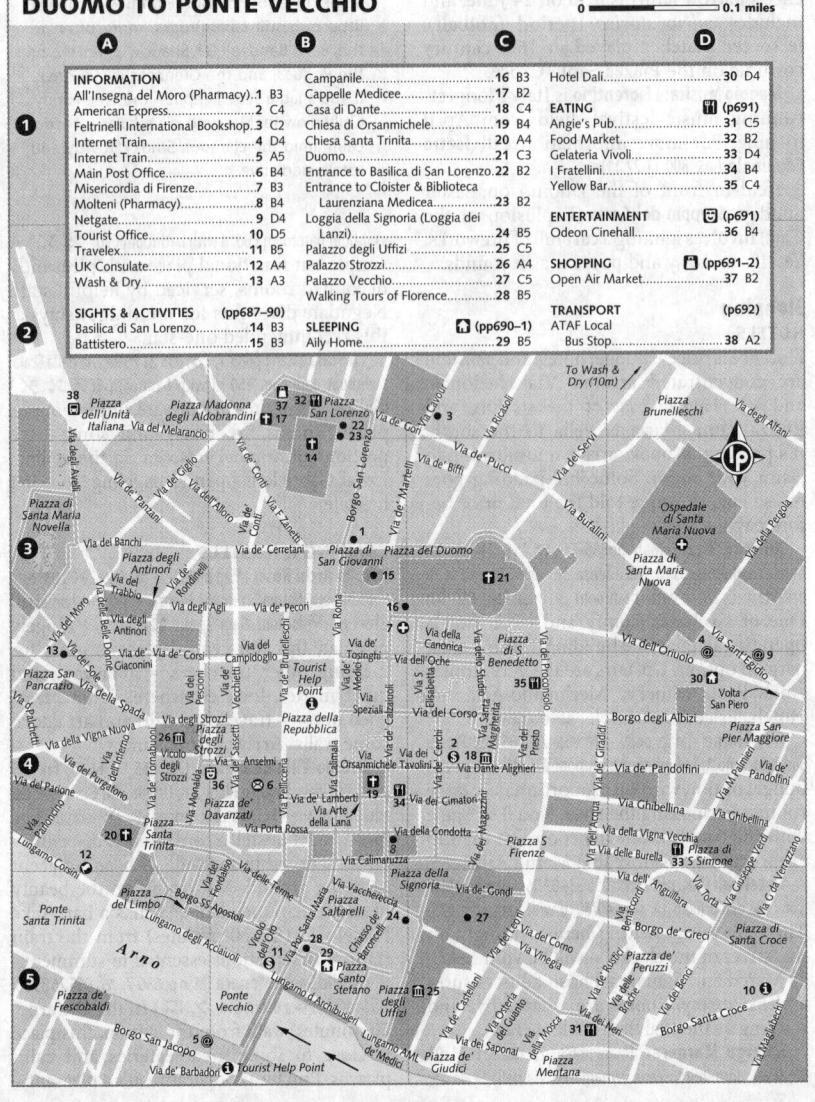

DUOMO TO PONTE VECCHIO

0 ————— 200 m
0 ————— 0.1 miles

INFORMATION
All'Insegna del Moro (Pharmacy)..1 B3
American Express......................2 C4
Feltrinelli International Bookshop.3 C2
Internet Train...........................4 D4
Internet Train...........................5 A5
Main Post Office.......................6 B4
Misericordia di Firenze...............7 B3
Molteni (Pharmacy)...................8 B4
Netgate...................................9 D4
Tourist Office..........................10 D5
Travelex................................11 B5
UK Consulate..........................12 A4
Wash & Dry............................13 A3

SIGHTS & ACTIVITIES   (pp687–90)
Basilica di San Lorenzo...........14 B3
Battistero..............................15 B3

Campanile..............................16 B3
Cappelle Medicee....................17 B2
Casa di Dante.........................18 C4
Chiesa di Orsanmichele............19 B4
Chiesa Santa Trinita.................20 A4
Duomo...................................21 C3
Entrance to Basilica di San Lorenzo.22 B2
Entrance to Cloister & Biblioteca
   Laurenziana Medicea...........23 B2
Loggia della Signoria (Loggia dei
   Lanzi)...............................24 B5
Palazzo degli Uffizi..................25 C5
Palazzo Strozzi.......................26 A4
Palazzo Vecchio......................27 C5
Walking Tours of Florence........28 B5

SLEEPING   (pp690–1)
Aily Home..............................29 B5

Hotel Dali..............................30 D4

EATING   (p691)
Angie's Pub............................31 C5
Food Market...........................32 B2
Gelateria Vivoli......................33 D4
I Fratellini.............................34 B4
Yellow Bar.............................35 C4

ENTERTAINMENT   (p691)
Odeon Cinehall.......................36 B4

SHOPPING   (pp691–2)
Open Air Market......................37 B2

TRANSPORT   (p692)
ATAF Local
   Bus Stop............................38 A2

was the burial place of the Medici dukes. The incomplete **Sagrestia Nuova** represents Michelangelo's first effort at architecture, and contains his *Medici Madonna, Night & Day* and *Dawn & Dusk* sculptures, adorning the Medici tombs.

Festivals & Events

Festa di San Giovanni (Feast of St John, Florence's patron saint) is held on 24 June, and includes *calcio storico* (period football), ie soccer matches played in 16th-century costume on the Piazza Santa Croce.

Maggio Musicale Fiorentino is Italy's longest-running music festival, held from April to June. For more information call **Teatro Comunale** (☎ 800 11 22 11).

Held in front of the Duomo on Easter Sunday, **Scoppio del Carro** (Explosion of the Cart) involves igniting a cart full of fireworks. Yes, it's as noisy and popular as it sounds.

Sleeping

HOTELS

Florence is pricey. Budget hotels and *pensioni* are concentrated around Via Nazionale and Via Faenza east of the station, and Piazza Santa Maria Novella to the south. It's prudent to book; arrive midmorning to claim your room. Some bill-padding goes on, so ensure you're told the total price before paying.

Albergo Azzi (Map pp686–7; ☎ 055 21 38 06; hotelazzi@hotmail.com; Via Faenza 56; dm €30, s/d with breakfast €42/67, with bathroom & breakfast €60/90) One of six basic, comfy and clean hotels operating in the same building, this is a great bargain option. Upstairs are the very similar Anna, Paola, Minerva, Merlin and Armonia Hotels. Prices are flexible, so bargain.

Aily Home (Map p689; ☎ 055 239 65 05; Piazza Santo Stefano 1; s/d without bathroom €35/45) A great budget option with disproportionately large rooms overlooking the river. You'll struggle with the tiny lift, but the rooms at the top are worth it, as is loveable Mama Aily.

Hotel Dalí (Map p689; ☎ 055 234 07 06; www.hoteldali.com; Via dell'Oriuolo 17; s/d €40/60, d with bathroom €75) The only thing melting here – fittingly on the 'street of the clocks' – will be your heart, as Marco and Samanta's hospitality ensures a pleasant stay. Rooms are as attractive and relaxing as the (Salv)adorable owners.

Albergo Margaret (Map pp686–7; ☎ 055 21 01 38; www.dormireintoscana.it/margaret; Via della Scala 25;

s without bathroom €60, d with bathroom €90; 🛇 🗶) A simple but functional place with pleasantly decorated rooms, serviced by helpful staff. Negotiate discounts for multinight stays at this recommended one-star.

La Scala (Map pp686–7; ☎ 055 21 26 29; Via della Scala; s without bathroom €60, d with bathroom €85; 🛇 🗶) Gabriele Bini runs this private, unpretentious place. Rooms are lovely and some have portions of original frescoes on the ceiling. Jovial Gabriele is open to haggling, so don't hesitate.

CAMPING & HOSTELS

Ostello Archi Rossi (Map pp686–7; ☎ 055 29 08 04; ostelloarchirossi@hotmail.com; Via Faenza 94r; dm incl breakfast €16–19; ⊙ lockout 9am–2pm; 🛇 💻 🗶) Hugely popular, this fun central place is great for meeting other travellers – if privacy and quiet matter, look elsewhere. Bright, frescoed décor – traveller graffiti and art adorn some walls. Arrive before 9am.

Ostello/Villa Camerata (☎ 055 60 14 51; fax 055 61 03 00; Viale Augusto Righi 2–4; Ostello: dm €15, Villa: per adult/camp site €6/5; Ostello: dinner €8; ⊙ lockout 9am–2pm) The HI hostel, a converted 17th-century villa, is superbly located, with an adjacent camping ground. Not drunk on the beauty of your surrounds alone? It has a bar! Take bus No 17 (€1, 30 minutes) from the train station. Reservations essential in summer.

Ostello Santa Monaca (Map pp686–7; ☎ 055 26 83 38; Via Santa Monaca 6; dm €16; 🗶 💻) In the Oltrarno, 20 minutes' walk from the station, this place is close to some great eateries and calm piazzas. Run by a cooperative, it's a pleasant –

if spartan – alternative to the central hostels, and is great value, despite no breakfast.

Campeggio Michelangelo (☎ 055 681 19 77; Viale Michelangelo 80; per adult/camp site €8/5) The camping ground closest to town is near Piazzale Michelangelo. Bus No 13 goes here from the station. It's in a beautiful location, but there's a steep trek coming back from town.

Eating

Tuscan cuisine is about simplicity and quality. It's also surprisingly good value. A local delight that must be sampled at least once is *ribollita*, a heavy soup of vegetables and *canellini* (white beans).

Angie's Pub (Map p689; ☎ 055 28 37 64; Via dei Neri 35r; snacks €3-5; ☀ noon-1am Mon-Sat, 6pm-1am Sun) One of Florence's better pubs, it does great cheap lunches, with a huge *panini* list.

Yellow Bar (Map p689; ☎ 055 21 17 66; Via del Proconsolo 39r; pizza meals €7-10; ☀ lunch & dinner) A rambunctious restaurant whose atmosphere is as infectious as it is lively, the ambience as good and simple as the food. Plenty of seating doesn't see it being regularly full.

Mario's (Map pp686-7; Via Rosina 2r; pasta €5, mains €5; ☀ lunch Mon-Sat) Two generations of expertise fuel this much-loved diner perpetually heaving with hungry locals. Delicious authentic pastas can be had for a song. Budgeting or not, Mario's offers a glimpse of the quintessential Italian eatery in all its glory – the value is a welcome bonus.

da Garibardi (Map pp686-7; ☎ 055 21 22 67; www .garibardi.it; Piazza del Mercato Centrale 38r; meals €15-20; ☀ noon-11pm) Leave nearby Za Za to the other tourists (ignore the impressive queue – that's English they're speaking) and indulge at this wonderful *trattoria*. Highly recommended is the *pasta al cinghiale* (with wild boar in a sauce of olives, bay leaves, mushrooms and peppercorns).

Trattoria Casalinga (Map pp686-7; ☎ 055 21 86 24; Via dei Michelozzi 9r; meals about €16) The pick of the Piazza Santa Spirito tratts is crammed with locals young and old, lunch and dinner. There's a 'hurry-up!' feel, but you won't mind being nudged along for food this good at these prices. Homey, tasty, fantastic – the real *ribollita* is superb.

I Tarocchi (Map pp686-7; ☎ 055 234 39 12; Via dei Renai 16r; pizza/course €5/7; ☀ Tue-Fri & dinner Sat & Sun) Serving good pizza and huge pasta portions has kept this humble place among the most popular in the Oltrarno. Students with shallow pockets abound at lunch time.

Borgo Antico (Map pp686-7; ☎ 055 21 04 37; Piazza Santo Spirito 6r; mains €7-10; ☀ lunch & dinner) Heaped portions are part of the draw at this great eatery, popular with a hip crowd. It could also be the excellent Tuscan dishes, prime terrace space on a lovely piazza, or the amazing prices.

Gelateria Vivoli (Map p689; ☎ 055 29 23 34; Via dell'Isola delle Stinche 7) South of Via Ghibellina, this is widely considered Florence's best for gelato.

I Fratellini (Map p689; ☎ 055 239 60 96; Via dei Cimatori 38r; panini €2-3) This Florentine institution has been dishing up fresh, quick takeaway *panini* for nearly 130 years.

Stock up on basics at the **food market** (☀ 7am-2pm Mon-Sat) in San Lorenzo or at the **supermarket** on the western side of the train station (Map pp686–7), or east of Piazza Duomo at Via Pietrapiana 94.

Drinking

Stick to cocktails or the *aperitivo*/happy hours at the following places. Also, see left for details of **Angie's Pub** and **Yellow Bar**.

Cabiria (Map pp686-7; ☎ 055 21 53 72; Piazza Santa Spirito 4/r; ☀ until late Wed-Mon) This blissful bar has a happy vibe and is perfect for hours of languid people-watching.

Elliot Braun Bar (☎ 055 35 23 52; Via Ponte alle Mosse 117r; ☀ 10am-4pm Mon-Fri & 6pm-2am Mon-Sat, aperitivo 6-8pm) An alt-cool mish-mash that's a unique treat: art exhibits, cocktails, food and live music, renowned for its *aperitivo*; buy a drink and gorge on the monster buffet. Anywhere else it would be 'freeloading' – in Italy, it's called 'timing'.

Entertainment

Firenze Spettacolo (€1.75), the definitive monthly entertainment guide, is sold at newsstands.

Teatro Comunale (☎ 800 11 22 11; Corso Italia 16) Concerts, opera and dance are performed here year-round.

Odeon Cinehall (Map p689; ☎ 055 21 40 68; www .cinehall.it; Piazza degli Strozzi; tickets €7.20; ☀ Mon, Tue & Thu, other days Italian only) Screens original-language films.

Shopping

Shopping is concentrated between the Duomo and the Arno. The **open-air market** (Map p689;

Mon-Sat) in the San Lorenzo district offers leather goods, clothing and jewellery, sometimes of dubious quality. The **flea market** (Map pp686–7; Piazza dei Ciompi; daily), off Borgo Allegri and north of Santa Croce, is better for finding genuine bargains.

Getting There & Away

Florence is served by two airports. **Amerigo Vespucci** (055 306 15, flight information: 055 306 13 00/02), 5km northwest of the city centre, serves domestic and European flights. **Galileo Galilei** (050 84 92 02) is 50 minutes away, near Pisa, and is one of northern Italy's main air transport hubs.

The **SITA bus station** (Map pp686–7; 800 37 37 60; Via Santa Caterina da Siena 17) is just west of the train station. Buses leave for Siena, San Gimignano and Volterra. **Lazzi** (055 35 10 61; Piazza Adua 1), next to the station, runs services to Rome, Pistoia and Lucca.

Florence is conveniently located on the main Rome–Milan train line; phone 848 88 80 88 for information.

Florence is connected by the A1 motorway to Bologna and Milan in the north and Rome and Naples to the south. The A11 links Florence with Prato, Pistoia, Lucca, Pisa and the Versilia coast, and a *superstrada* (dual carriageway) joins the city to Siena.

Getting Around

TO/FROM THE AIRPORT

Regular trains to Galileo Galilei depart platform five at Santa Maria Novella station (1½ hours, 6.45am to 5pm). Leave your bags at the **air terminal** (21 60 73; platform 5) at least 15 minutes before train departure. You can get to Amerigo Vespucci with the Vola in Bus shuttle from the SITA depot in Via Santa Caterina da Siena (€4, 25 minutes, every 30 minutes, 6am to 11.30pm). Purchase tickets on board.

BIKES & SCOOTERS

Alinari (Map pp686–7; 055 28 05 00; www.alina rirental.com; Via Guelfa 85/r; bike per 1hr/5hr/day/week from €3/12/16/70, scooter from €8/22/28/140) hires bikes and scooters – prices vary with the model. Compulsory helmet is supplied.

BUS

ATAF buses service the centre and Fiesole. The best terminal is in a small piazza to the left as you exit the station onto Via Valfonda. Bus No 7 leaves for Fiesole, stopping at the Duomo. Tickets (one/three/24 hours €1/1.80/4) must be bought before boarding and are sold at tobacconists and newsstands.

CAR & MOTORCYCLE

There are car parks dotted around the centre. A good choice is Fortezza da Basso (€1.10 for one hour). Further details are available from **Firenze Parcheggi** (055 500 19 94). To rent a car, try **Hertz** (Map pp686–7; 055 239 82 05; Via M Finiguerra 33r), or **Avis** (Map pp686–7; 055 21 36 29; Borgo Ognissanti 128r).

PISA

pop 92,000

Pisa's iconic tower is among Italy's most recognisable sights. Whether or not the construction snafu is enough to sway you, it's certainly among the most exploited of the country's drawcards.

Today an otherwise quiet university town, Pisa was once a maritime power rivalling Genoa and Venice, and the home of Galileo Galilei (1564–1642). Levelled by the Genoese in the 13th century, its history eventually merged with that of Florence, its neighbour along the River Arno. You'd be pressed to find reasons for an extended stay, but the city has a certain charm.

Orientation & Information

The Campo dei Miracoli is a 1.5km walk from the train station across the Arno. Bus No 3 will save time. The medieval town centre around Borgo Stretto is 1km or so from the station.

Internet Planet (050 83 07 02; Piazza Cavallotti 3-4; per hr €3.10; 10am-midnight Mon-Sat, 2pm-midnight Sun)

Onda Blu (800 86 13 46; Via San Francesco 8a; per 7kg wash/dry €5/5; 8am-10pm)

Tourist office (050 56 04 64; www.pisaturismo .toscana.it; Piazza del Duomo; 9am-6pm Mon-Sat, 10.30am-4.30pm Sun) There is also a train station **office** (050 422 91; Piazza della Stazione; 9am-7pm Mon-Sat, 9.30am-3.30pm Sun).

Sights & Activities

Pisans claim their **Campo dei Miracoli** (Field of Miracles) is among the world's most beautiful squares. It's tricky: while the manicured lawns provide a gorgeous backdrop for the cathedral, baptistry and bell tower – *all* leaning – you do have to negotiate throngs of souvenir hawkers to approach them. It's underwhelming precisely because the square is so spartan – there's not much going on apart from slanting.

And enchanting. The buildings *are* gorgeous. The candy-striped **cathedral** (admission €2; ☼ 10am-7.40pm Mon-Sat, 1-7.40pm Sun summer, 10am-12.45pm & 3-4.45pm Mon-Sat, 3-4.45pm Sun winter), begun in 1063, has a graceful façade and cavernous interior. The transept's bronze doors, facing the tower, are by Bonanno Pisano, while the 16th-century bronze entrance doors are by Giambologna. The cathedral's **battistero** (admission €5; ☼ 8am-7.40pm summer, 9am-4.40pm winter), begun in 1153 (completed 1260), contains a pulpit by Nicola Pisano.

The irony is, Bonanno's biggest cock-up ended up being his signature work. The *campanile*, better known as the **Leaning Tower** (Torre Pendente; www.opapisa.it; admission €15; 8am-8pm summer, 9am-7pm winter), was wonky immediately; just three of the tower's seven tiers were completed before it started tilting, continuing at a rate of about 1mm per year.

Currently 4.1m from the perpendicular (despite 11 years of ground-levelling), British engineer John Burland was given the task of saving the tower in the early 1990s. By 2001, 'the old lady of Pisa' was restored to her (secure) 1838 angle by base-weighting and soil drilling, making her sink back towards stability.

Visits are limited to groups of 30; entry times are staggered and waiting inevitable. There are many combination-tickets, but admission to the Leaning Tower is *always* separate. It's free to soak up the *campo*'s atmosphere, though.

Sleeping & Eating
Book ahead if Pisa appeals enough to stay.

Ostello per la Gioventù (☎ /fax 050 89 06 22; Via Pietrasantina 15; dm €22; ☼ closed 9am-6pm) The non-HI youth hostel is basic but friendly, clean and usually full. Take bus No 3 from the station. It's a 10-minute walk from Campo dei Miracoli.

Albergo Helvetia (☎ 050 55 30 84; Via Don Gaetano Boschi 31; s/d €35/45, d with bathroom €62) This is a reasonable option a few cuts above the hostel, best tackled by a couple or friends sharing costs. It's a little rough around the edges, but the rooms are nicer than the general upkeep suggests.

Hotel di Stefano (☎ 050 55 35 59; www.hoteldistefano.pisa.it; Via Sant'Apollonia 35-37; s/d without bathroom €45/60, s/d/tr/q with bathroom €70/85/110/120) Decorated rooms and a lovely breakfast terrace are just two features of this good hotel, walking distance from all sights in a calm street behind Piazza dei Cavalieri. Affordable for cost-sharers planning one night or so.

La Tana (☎ 050 58 05 40; Vicolo San Frediano 6; 1st-course €4, meals €10-14; ☼ Sat-Thu) Studenty hot spot dishing up voluminous pizza and pasta options. Atmospheric, friendly, with tasty food and fab service. It'll be hard to stay vewy qwiet after sampling *spaghetti al coniglio* (pasta with rabbit).

Trattoria La Buca (☎ 050 56 06 60; Via Galli Tussi 6; mains €6-10, pizza €6; ☼ Sat-Thu) Highly recommended *trattoria* doing hearty Tuscan fare at fair prices. Cheap pizzas are a budget winner, but the whole menu's great. Subdued ambience, and a garden terrace for fine weather dining.

Getting There & Away
The airport, with domestic and European flights, is minutes away by train, or bus No 3 from the station. **Lazzi** (☎ 050 462 88) buses run to Florence via Lucca. Pisa is linked by train to Florence, Rome and Genoa.

SIENA
pop 54,350
Surrounded by more-glamorous neighbours, Siena is a surprisingly captivating preserved medieval town. Its partly intact ramparts, corkscrew-coiled streets and labyrinthine centre are jam-packed with majestic Gothic buildings in various shades of 'burnt sienna'. It's also usually teeming with visitors.

According to legend, Siena was founded by the sons of Remus. In the Middle Ages the city became a free republic, its dramatic rise – through banking expertise – causing friction with Florence. Painters of the Sienese School produced significant works of art, and the city was home to St Catherine and St Benedict.

Siena is divided into 17 *contrade* (districts) and 10 are chosen annually to contest the Palio, a tumultuous horse race (and pageant) held in the Piazza del Campo on 2 July and 16 August. Heavily touristed anyway, securing accommodation during the Palio will require foresight or luck.

Orientation & Information

Leaving the train station, cross the concourse to the bus stop for bus No 3, 9 or 10 to central Piazza Gramsci, then walk along Via dei Termini (10 min to reach Piazza del Campo). Visitors' cars aren't permitted in the centre.

Internet Train (Via di Città 121 & Via di Pantaneto 57; per hr €5)

Libreria Senese (☎ 0577 28 08 45; libreria_senese@libero.it; Via di Città 62/66) Fantastic bookshop with English books, and a professional-standard ESL section.

Police Headquarters (☎ 0577 20 11 11; Via del Castoro 23)

Post office (Piazza Matteotti 1) North of the centre.

Tourist office (☎ 0577 28 05 51; www.terresiena.it; Piazza del Campo 56; 🕑 9am-7pm) Can explain the myriad tickets for combinations of Siena's sights.

Sights & Activities

Siena's uniquely scalloped **Piazza del Campo** (simply, Il Campo) has been the city's focus for 700 years. The piazza's base is formed by the nobly proportioned **Palazzo Pubblico** (town hall; admission/tower/both €5.50/6.50/9.50; 🕑 10am-7pm mid-Mar–end Oct, 10am-5.30pm end Nov–mid-Feb, to 6.30pm otherwise), also known as Palazzo Communale, counted among Italy's most graceful Gothic buildings. Climb the 102m-high **Torre del Mangia** for a pigeon's-eye view of proceedings, and those pretty red roofs.

The spectacular **Duomo** (admission free) is another Gothic masterpiece. Begun in 1196, extravagant expansion plans were stymied by the niggling arrival of the Black Death (1348), which claimed nearly 70,000 of Siena's

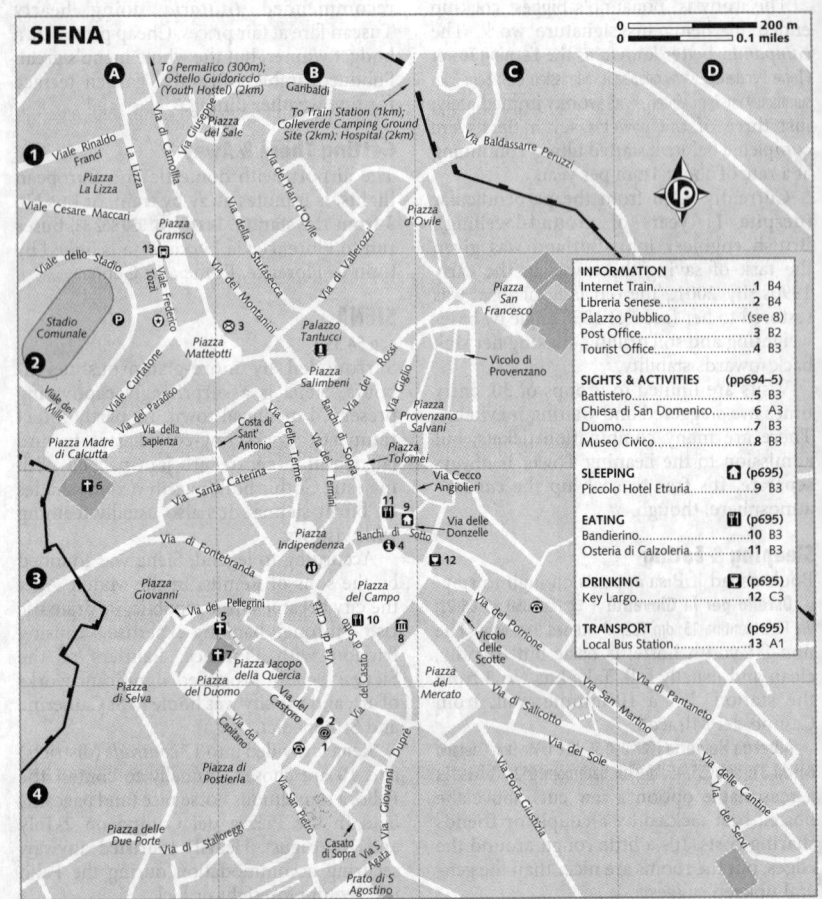

SIENA

0 ——— 200 m
0 ——— 0.1 miles

INFORMATION	
Internet Train..................	1 B4
Libreria Senese...............	2 B4
Palazzo Pubblico.............	(see 8)
Post Office.....................	3 B2
Tourist Office.................	4 B3

SIGHTS & ACTIVITIES	(pp694–5)
Battistero......................	5 B3
Chiesa di San Domenico.......	6 A3
Duomo.........................	7 B3
Museo Civico..................	8 B3

SLEEPING	(p695)
Piccolo Hotel Etruria.........	9 B3

EATING	(p695)
Bandierino....................	10 B3
Osteria di Calzoleria.........	11 B3

DRINKING	(p695)
Key Largo.....................	12 C3

TRANSPORT	(p695)
Local Bus Station.............	13 A1

100,000 people. Venice aside, Siena has the most striking cathedral interior in northern Italy. The striped marble of the exterior is, incredibly, maintained throughout – a noteworthy distinction from comparable cathedrals; Florence's Duomo, despite dramatic external decoration, is bland inside.

The Romanesque lower section has carvings by Giovanni Pisano, and the inlaid-marble floor features 56 biblical panels. The **battistero** (admission €2.50; ◷9am-7.30pm mid-Mar–Sep, 9am-6pm Oct, 10am-1pm & 2.30-5pm Nov–mid-Mar) behind the cathedral has a Gothic façade and 15th-century frescoes.

Want to see the preserved head of a saint? Head for the **Chiesa di San Domenico** and the **Santuario di Santa Caterina** (shop: ☎ 0577 28 68 48; Piazza San Domenico; admission free; ◷7.30am-1pm & 3-6.30pm) inside, where St Catherine's is displayed. The church itself is tranquil and airy, and friendly Federico Muzzi in the souvenir shop sells some funky Christian kitsch.

Sleeping

It's always advisable to book in advance, but for August/Palio, it's essential.

Colleverde Camping Ground (☎ 0577 28 00 44; Strada di Scacciapensieri 47; per adult/camp site €8/8; ◷late Mar-early Nov) Siena's handiest camping ground is 2km north of the historic centre (take bus No 3 from Piazza Gramsci). Tell the driver you're headed for the *'campeggio'* (cam-*peh*-gee-oh).

Ostello Guidoriccio (☎ 0577 522 12; Via Fiorentina; B&B €16.50) The HI hostel is an inconvenient 3km haul from the centre, up a hill in Stellino, but it's clean and affordable. Take bus No 3 from Piazza Gramsci, and tell the driver you're after the 'ostello' (hostel). Rooms are quiet, and shutters afford pitch-blackness, at least ensuring sound sleep.

Piccolo Hotel Etruria (☎ 0577 28 80 88; fax 0577 28 84 61; Via delle Donzelle 3; s €39, s/d/tr/q with bathroom €44/73/96/119) Siena's best all-round value (despite breakfast not being included); you practically exit onto the Piazza del Campo. Basic, large rooms are passable, and the 12.30am curfew won't hinder, as Siena's no night-owl town.

Eating & Drinking

The ubiquitous Ciao and Spizzico have outlets on Il Campo. Also try:

Permalico (☎ 0577 411 05; www.permalico.net; Via di Camollia 193; light meals €5-8; ◷lunch & dinner

Mon-Sat) A great little medieval cavern/tavern, complete with vaulted ceilings, serving simple Tuscan grub. A fine place to grab a tasty *panini* and a cold beer.

Bandierino (☎ 0577 28 22 17; Piazza del Campo 66; pizza/pasta €8/10; ◷lunch & dinner) The best if you *must* eat on Il Campo. The pastas and risotti are excellent – particularly variations *ai funghi porcini* (with rich, musty mushrooms); worth opting for over the popular (and cheaper) pizzas. Staff are brisk, but amenable.

Osteria di Calzoleria (☎ 0577 28 90 10; Via di Calzoleria 12; meals €15-20; ◷dinner) Fantastic hole-in-the-wall on a winding street off Il Campo with evocative Tuscan fare, particularly its *contorni* (vegetable side dishes); they make a great vegetarian meal. Splurge here, slurping some *ribollita* or twirling *pici* (the traditional Sienese 'thick' pasta) round yer fork.

Getting There & Away

Regular Tra-In buses run from Florence to Siena, arriving at Piazza Gramsci. Buses also go to San Gimignano, Volterra and other points in Tuscany, plus there are daily buses to Rome. For Perugia, buses leave from the train station. Siena is not on a main train line; from Rome, change at Chiusi (from Florence at Empoli).

SAN GIMIGNANO
pop 7100

In a region famed for its beauty, this tiny hill-top town in deepest Tuscany is still gaspworthy. It's not really the town itself that appeals – these days custom-built for tourists – but some of the incredible vistas available from its steep walkways or remaining medieval towers; of 72 originally built as fortresses for the town's feuding families, 13 remain.

The **tourist office** (☎ 0577 94 00 08; Piazza del Duomo 1; ☼ 9am-1pm & 3-7pm, to 6pm winter) is in the town centre. Climb San Gimignano's tallest tower, **Torre Grossa** off Piazza del Duomo, for stunning views. Entrance is via the **Palazzo del Popolo**, which houses the **Museo Civico** (☎ 0577 94 00 08; adult/child €5/4; ☼ 9.30am-7.20pm Mar-Oct, 10am-5.50pm Nov-Feb). The **Duomo** has a Romanesque interior, frescoes by Ghirlandaio in the **Cappella di Santa Fina** and a gruesome *Last Judgment* by Taddeo di Bartolo.

San Gimignano is generally visited from Florence or Siena. Hotels are expensive but there are private rooms for rent and *agriturismo* is well organised locally. See the tourist office.

Foresteria Monastero di San Girolamo (☎ 0577 94 05 73; Via Folgore 26-32; dm B&B €23) If budget's the priority and you don't mind moderating your behaviour, the sweet nuns at Girolamo run the best cheap option. Mind your Ps & Qs, now.

For good pasta and decent local wines, stop at **Il Castello** (☎ 0577 94 08 78; Via del Castello 20; pastas €5-6), while **Gelateria di Piazza** (☎ 0577 94 22 44; Piazza della Cisterna 4; ☼ Mar–mid-Nov) provides great gelato.

Regular buses link San Gimignano with Florence and Siena, arriving at Porta San Giovanni.

PERUGIA

pop 158,300

Perugia is a well-preserved hill town offering sweeping panoramas at every turn. Best known for its University for Foreigners (established 1925), the city is also noted for the Umbria Jazz Festival (July) and another excessive indulgence: chocolate.

Highlights (or lowlights) of Perugia's gory history include the vicious internal feuding of the Baglioni and Oddi families and the odd papal death. Art and culture, however, have thrived; the painter Perugino, and Raphael, his student, both worked here.

Orientation & Information

Perugia's hub is Corso Vannucci, running from Piazza Italia, through Piazza della Repubblica, to Piazza IV Novembre. From the train station catch any bus to Piazza Italia, then get a **scala mobila** (public escalator; free; ☼ 6.45am-1.45am) up to the medieval heart.

Internet Train (Via Ulisse Rocchi 30; per hr €4)
IAT tourist office (☎ 075 572 33 27; Palazzo Dei Priori, Piazza IV Novembre 3; ☼ 8.30am-1.30pm & 3.30-6.30pm Mon-Sat, 9am-1pm Sun) Opposite the Duomo.
Post office (Piazza Matteotti; ☼ 8.10am-6pm Mon-Sat)

Sights & Activities

Perugia's austere **Duomo** (☎ 075 572 38 32; Piazza IV Novembre; admission free; ☼ 8am-noon & 4pm-sunset) has an unfinished façade. Inside are 300 years' worth of artworks, and the Virgin Mary's wedding ring, unveiled every 30 July. The **Palazzo dei Priori** is a rambling 13th-century palace housing the impressively frescoed **Sala dei Notari** (☎ 075 573 03 66; Corso Vannucci 15; admission free; ☼ 9am-1pm & 3-7pm Tue-Sun, plus Mon Jun-Sep) and the **Galleria Nazionale dell'Umbria** (☎ 075 572 10 09; www.gallerianazionaledellumbria.it; Corso Vannucci 19; adults/18-25 year olds/EU citizens btwn 18 & 65 €6.50/3.25/free; ☼ 8.30am-7.30pm), with works by Perugino and Fra Angelico. The fountain in Piazza IV Novembre is the **Fontana Maggiore**, designed by Fra Bevignate (1278) and carved by Nicola and Giovanni Pisano.

At the other end of Corso Vannucci is the **Rocca Paolina** (Paolina Fortress), the ruins of a 16th-century citadel. A series of escalators traverse the underground innards, sometimes used to host exhibitions. Etruscan remains in Perugia include the **Arco Etrusco** (Etruscan Arch), near the university, and the **Pozzo Etrusco** (Etruscan Well), near the Duomo.

Sleeping

Centro Internazionale per la Gioventù (☎ 075 572 28 80; www.ostello.perugia.it; Via Bontempi 13; dm €11.50, sheets €1.50; ☼ from 4pm, midnight curfew, closed Dec-Jan) This is among Italy's best hostels for sheer value. The TV room's frescoed ceiling beats anything on the screen, the terrace view is fabulous, and there's a guest kitchen. Just don't arrive before 4pm.

Albergo Anna (☎ 075 573 63 04; www.albergoanna .it; Via dei Priori 48; s/d €30/48, with bathroom €40/58) Charming place with delightful rooms off Corso Vannucci, full of character and antiques, and a super-friendly owner (Signora Emma Citti). Great value for this comfort.

Hotel Eden (☎ 075 572 81 02; www.hoteleden.191 .it; Via Cesare Caporali 9; s/d/tr/q with bathroom €36/57/77/103; P ✿ ✕) If brightness appeals the white rooms in this 700-year-old building are perfect for 'tired starlings' to nest in. They're also tended by friendly staff. There are modem points for tech-toting travellers, too. A great cost-sharing option.

Eating

Caffe Morlacchi (☎ 075 572 17 60; Piazza Morlacchi 8; light meals €7-12; ☯ 8am-1am Mon-Sat) *The* meeting place in Perugia and kick-off place for many a *festa dell' laurea* (graduation celebration) is also a great place to grab a light meal. Absolutely packed at peak times, with good reason.

Pizzeria Mediterranea (☎ 075 572 63 12; Piazza Piccinino 11/12; pizza €4-6; ☯ Wed-Mon) Popular pizzeria serving pizzas *al fondo* (wood-fired). Deservingly popular, time your arrival, otherwise there'll be some queuing. Lovely atmosphere.

Ristorante dal Mi'Cocco (☎ 075 573 25 11; Corso Giuseppe Garibaldi 12; mains €6-7, set menu €13; ☯ Tue-Sun) Super place near the university with communal tables and an 'antica taverna' vibe. The set-menu (in local dialect) means you eat what's served, and it changes weekly, but it's always 'dal'cocco' – from the 'coconut' (head) of the creative cook. Luckily, it's always tasty. Book ahead.

Perugina (Corso Vannucci 101; ☯ 9.30am-7.45pm, closed Mon morning) A visit here will address sublimated desires… Sample the legendary *Baci* (kisses), wrapped in 'romantic' quotes.

Sandri (☎ 075 449 41; Corso Vannucci 32; ☯ 8am-11pm Tue-Sun) Another Perugian institution, with the best cakes around and free chocolate nibbles at the bar.

Getting There & Away

Perugia is not on the Rome–Florence railway line, but there are direct trains from both cities. Most services require a change, either at Foligno (from Rome) or Terontola (from Florence). Intercity buses leave from Piazza dei Partigiani (by the Rocca Paolina escalators) for Rome, Fiumicino airport, Florence, Siena and towns throughout Umbria, including Assisi, Gubbio and nearby Lake Trasimeno.

Getting Around

The train station is way downhill from the centre. Catch any bus heading for Piazza Italia. Tickets (€0.80) are available from the ticket office as you leave the station. There's a supervised car park at Piazza dei Partigiani, from where you can catch the Rocca Paolina escalator to Piazza Italia, and

two more car parks beside the Via dei Priori escalator.

ASSISI

pop 25,500

Birthplace and spiritual home of animal-loving St Francis, picturesque Assisi is a major destination for millions of pilgrims wishing to retrace his holy footsteps. Somehow this hamlet halfway up Mt Subasio maintains a tranquil air, particularly in the lanes off the central streets.

The **APT tourist office** (☎ 075 81 25 34; info@iat .assisi.pg.it; Via S Croce; ☯ 8am-6.30pm Mon-Sat, 10am-1pm & 2-5pm Sun summer, 8am-2pm & 3-6pm Mon-Sat, 9am-1pm Sun winter) has information.

Sights & Activities

If you're intending to visit religious sites, look the part, as dress rules are strict – absolutely no shorts, miniskirts, low-cut dresses or tops allowed. Assisi's greatest charm lies in simply wandering its soothingly quiet and pretty paths.

The **Basilica di San Francesco** (☎ 075 81 90 01; Piazza di San Francesco; admission free; ☯ 7am-7pm Apr-Sep, to 5pm Oct-Mar) comprises two churches, one above the other. The lower church is decorated with frescoes, and contains the crypt where St Francis is buried. The Italian Gothic upper church has a stone-vaulted roof, and decoration by Giotto and Cimabue. The frescoes in the apse and entrance were damaged in a 1997 earthquake.

The frescoed 13th-century **Basilica di Santa Chiara** (St Clare's Basilica; ☎ 075 81 22 82; Piazza Santa Chiara; admission free; ☯ 7am-noon & 2-7pm) contains the remains of St Clare, friend of St Francis and founder of the Order of Poor Clares. For spectacular views, the massive 14th-century fortress **Rocca Maggiore** (☎ 075 81 52 92; Via della Rocca; admission €2.60; ☯ 10am-sunset) is perfect.

Sleeping & Eating

Assisi is used to tourists. Peak periods are Easter, August and September, and the Feast of St Francis (3–4 October). The tourist office has extensive *affittacamere* listings.

Fontemaggio (☎ 075 81 36 36; Via Eremo delle Carceri 8; dm €18.50) The non-HI hostel also has camping facilities. From Piazza Matteotti, at the far end of town from the basilica, it's a 30-minute uphill walk.

Pensione La Rocca (☎ /fax 075 81 22 84; Via Porta Perlici 27; s/d with bathroom €38/45; ✖ ▣ ✖ ℗)

Tucked away in a quiet corner this *pensione* has sunny *en suite* rooms, some with awesome valley views.

Pizzeria Flipper (Via San Francesco 2/d; slice €2; ☼ 9am-7.30pm Thu-Tue) Does cheap, convenient *pizze al taglio* and *calzoni* (folded pizza pockets) for mobile munching.

Cantine Di Oddo (Via San Francesco; mains €7-8; ☼ Thu-Tue) This place affords saintly eating; it's mostly vegetarian with mouth-watering spinach and ricotta ravioli, presented simply with butter and sage.

Getting There & Away

Buses connect Assisi with Perugia, Foligno and nearby towns, leaving from Piazza Matteotti. Buses for Rome and Florence leave from Piazzale dell'Unità d'Italia. Assisi's train station is in the valley (Santa Maria degli Angeli on the Perugia line); shuttle buses run between Piazza Matteotti and there.

ANCONA
pop 100,100

Ancona, a grimly industrial port city and capital of Le Marche, is worth mentioning mostly because you may be catching ferries to Croatia, Greece or Turkey from here.

Take bus No 1 from the train station to the port. The main **APT tourist office** (☎ 071 35 89 91; www.comune.ancona.it; Via Thaon de Revel 4; ☼ 9am-2pm & 3-6pm Mon-Fri, 9am-1pm & 3-6pm Sat, 9am-1pm Sun, fewer in winter) is out of the way. Stazione Marittima has a **tourist office** (☎ 071 20 11 83; ☼ 8am-8pm Tue-Sat & 2-8pm Sun & Mon summer). There's a **post office** (Largo XXIV Maggio; ☼ 8.15am-7pm Mon-Sat).

Many backpackers sleep at the ferry terminal, but Ancona does have cheap hotels. **Ostello della Gioventú** (☎ /fax 071 422 57; Via Lamaticci 7; dm €12) is 400m from the station, clean quiet and cheap, with a lift and bathrooms big enough for wheelchairs.

Buses depart from Piazza Cavour for towns throughout Le Marche. Rome is served by **Marozzi** (☎ 071 280 23 98). Ancona is on the Bologna–Lecce train line and easily accessible from major towns. Connect to Rome via Foligno.

Ferry operators have booths at the terminal, off Piazza Kennedy. Companies include **Superfast** (☎ 071 207 02 40) to Patras in Greece (€78), **Minoan Lines** (☎ 071 20 17 08) to Igoumenitsa and Patras (€68) and **Adriatica** (☎ 071 20 49 15) to Durrës in Albania (€86)

and Split in Croatia (€47). These prices are one-way, deck class in high season.

URBINO
pop 6000

This beautiful medieval town can be tricky to reach, but the 'pride of the Marches' rewards the effort. Birthplace of Raphael and Bramante, university town Urbino remains a bustling centre of culture and learning. It's small, steep and the streets meander snakily around a gorgeous cobbled core that's been World Heritage–listed by Unesco.

The **IAT tourist office** (☎ 0722 26 13; Via Puccinoti 3; ☼ 9am-1pm Mon-Sat, also 3-6pm & 9am-1pm Sun & holidays May-Sep) is central. There's a **post office** (☎ 0722 37 79 17; Via Bramante 18; 8.30am-6.30pm Mon-Sat).

Urbino's centrepiece is the **Palazzo Ducale** (☎ 0722 32 90 57; Piazza Duca Federico; adult/child incl Galleria Nazionale €4.15/free; ☼ 8.30am-7.15pm Tue-Sun, 8.30am-2pm Mon), designed by Laurana and completed in 1482. Enter from Piazza Duca Federico and visit the **Galleria Nazionale delle Marche**, with works by Raphael, Paolo Uccello and Verrocchio. The **Casa di Raffaello** (☎ 0722 32 01 05; Via Rafaello 57; admission €2.60; ☼ 9am-1pm & 3-7pm Mon-Sat, 10am-1pm Sun spring & summer, morning only Nov-early Mar) is where Raphael was born.

The tourist office has an *affittacamere* list. There's also:

Albergo Italia (☎ 0722 27 01; www.albergo-italia-urbino.it; Corso Garibaldi 32; s/d with bathroom €41/62; buffet breakfast €8; P ☒ ☒) Good mid-range hotel covering a range of needs from cheap singles to deluxe doubles. Rooms are comfy.

Across the road are some great dining options, notably **Gula** (☎ 0722 26 94; Corso Garibaldi 23; meals €6-10; ☼ lunch & dinner), a sprawling *birreria/osteria* serving cheap but excellent meals, attracting many local students.

Trains don't run to Urbino. Buses (Monday to Friday) connect to Ancona, Pesaro and Arezzo. There's a bus link to the train station at Fossato di Vico, on the Rome–Ancona line, or to Pesaro on the Bologna–Lecce line.

SOUTHERN ITALY

While not as wealthy as the north in the traditional sense, you'll be well rewarded by the south's abundant riches. The land of the *mezzogiorno* (midday sun) sizzles with palpable passion – the food is magnificent, the landscape resplendent, and the locals friendly. Campania, Puglia and Basilicata are still under the tourist radar in parts, and Naples is as unforgettable as your first love.

NAPLES (NAPOLI)

pop 1,000,470

Stunningly situated on the Bay of Naples, and lorded over by Vesuvio (Mt Vesuvius), Naples is gorgeous, edgy, raucous, overwhelming, and above all fun. Expect to be blown away by the disarming energy this city exudes. And yes, the drivers aren't the best, and petty thieves are rampant, so look both ways and watch your back.

Orientation

If arriving by bus or train, the train station and Piazza Garibaldi are a 10-minute walk from the centre; follow Via Mezzaconnone. From Molo Beverello and the ferry terminals, hop on bus No R2 to the station, and from the airport, 7km from town, take bus No 3S.

Information

INTERNET ACCESS

Internetbar (☎ 081 29 52 37; Piazza Bellini 74; per hr €3; 9am-2am Mon-Sat, 8pm-2am Sun)

MEDICAL SERVICES

Ambulance (☎ 081 752 06 96 or 112)
Guardia Medica After-hours medical service; phone numbers are listed in *Qui Napoli*.
Ospedale Loreto-Mare (☎ 081 254 27 01; Via A Vespucci)
Pharmacy (⏱ 8am-8pm) In Stazione Centrale.
Police station (☎ 081 794 11 11; Via Medina 75) Off Via Armando Diaz, with an office for foreigners where you can report thefts. To report a stolen car, call ☎ 081 794 14 35.

MONEY

There are plenty of ATMs throughout the city, as well as foreign-exchange booths.
Every Tour (☎ 081 551 85 64; Piazza Municipio 5-6) Represents American Express, changes money and is a Western Union agent.

POST & TELEPHONE

Main post office (Piazza G Matteotti; ⏱ 8.15am-7pm Mon-Sat) Off Via Armando Diaz.
Telecom office (Via A Depretis 40; ⏱ 9am-1pm & 2-5.30pm Mon-Fri)

TOURIST INFORMATION

Ask for *Qui Napoli* (Here Naples), published monthly in English and Italian, which lists events in the city, as well as information about transport and other services. The **Campania artecard** (☎ 800 60 06 01; www.campaniartecard.com; €13) gives access to six museums at reduced rates and to public transport. Buy it at the airport, train and metro stations and selected museums.

AAST tourist office (☎ 081 552 33 28; Piazza del Gesú Nuovo; ⏱ 9am-8pm Mon-Sat, 9am-3pm Sun)
CTS (☎ 081 552 79 60; Via Mezzocannone 25) Student travel centre.
Main tourist office (☎ 081 20 66 66; ⏱ 9am-7.30pm Mon-Sat, 9am-1.30pm Sun) At the train station, the helpful staff will make hotel bookings for you.

Dangers & Annoyances

Although the city's home-grown mafia is still a pervasive local force, you're more likely to encounter a thief. The petty crime rate is high, and pickpockets, moped bandits and bag-snatchers abound. Car theft is also a major problem. Pay attention at night near the station, Piazza Dante, the area west of Via Toledo and as far north as Piazza Carità.

Sights

Start your sightseeing at **Spaccanapoli**, the historic centre of Naples. From the station and Corso Umberto I turn right onto Via Mezzocannone, which takes you to Via Benedetto Croce, the bustling main street of the quarter. To the left is spacious Piazza del Gesú Nuovo, with the 15th-century rusticated façade of **Chiesa di Gesú Nuovo** and the 14th-century **Chiesa di Santa Chiara**, restored to its original Gothic-Provençal style after being severely damaged in WWII. The beautifully tiled **Chiostro delle Clarisse** (Nuns' Cloisters; admission €4; ⏱ 9.30am-1pm daily & 2.30-5.30pm Mon-Sat) behind the church is also worth visiting.

The **Duomo** (☎ 081 44 90 97; Via Duomo; ⏱ 8am-12.30pm & 4.30-7.30pm Mon-Sat, 8.30am-1pm & 5-8pm Sun) has a 19th-century façade but was built by the Angevin kings at the end of the 13th century, on the site of an earlier basilica. Inside is the **Cappella di San Gennaro**, containing the head of St Januarius (the city's patron saint) and two vials of his congealed blood. The saint is said to have saved the city from disasters like plague and volcanic eruptions.

Turn off Via Duomo onto the very characteristic **Via Tribunali** and head for Piazza Dante, through the 17th-century **Port' Alba**, one of the city's gates. Via Roma, the most fashionable street in old Naples, heads south

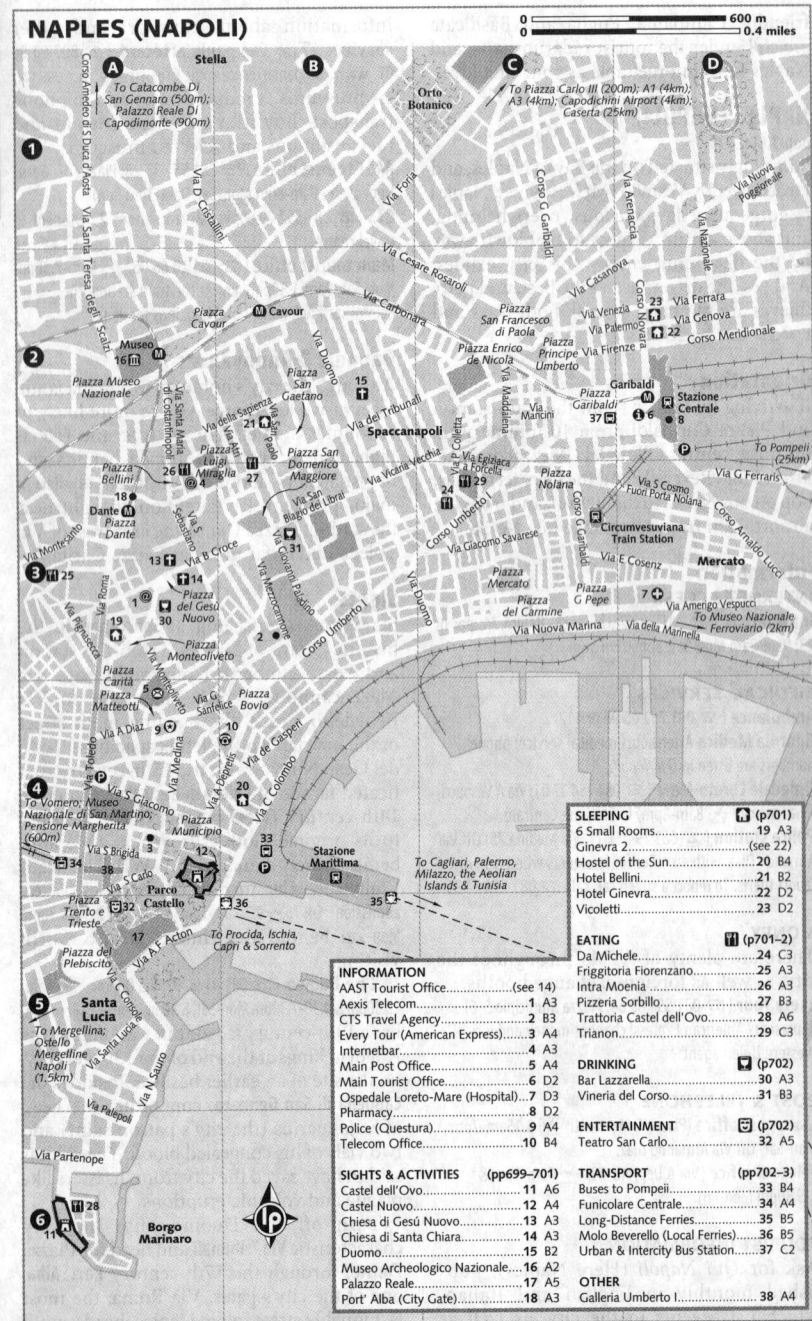

NAPLES (NAPOLI)

0 ————————— 600 m
0 ————————— 0.4 miles

(becoming Via Toledo) and ends at Piazza Trento e Trieste and Piazza del Plebiscito.

In the piazza is **Palazzo Reale** (☎ 081 794 40 21; admission €4.50; ♥ 9am-8pm Thu-Tue), the former official residence of the Bourbon and Savoy kings, now a museum. Just off the piazza is the world-renowned **Teatro San Carlo** (Via San Carlo 98), famed for its perfect acoustics and lavish interior (see also p702).

The 13th-century **Castel Nuovo** overlooks Naples' ferry port. The early Renaissance triumphal arch commemorates the entry of Alfonso I of Aragon into Naples in 1443. Situated southwest along the waterfront at Santa Lucia is the **Castel dell'Ovo**, originally a Norman castle, surrounded by **Borgo Marinaro**, a tiny fishing village.

Museo Archeologico Nazionale (☎ 081 44 01 66; Piazza Museo Nazionale 17; admission €6.50; ♥ 9am-7.30pm Wed-Mon), north of Piazza Dante, contains one of the most important collections of Greco-Roman artefacts in the world, mainly the rich collection of the Farnese family, and the art treasures discovered at Pompeii and Herculaneum (see p703). Book a (free) tour to see the **Gabinetto Segreto** (Secret Cabinet), reopened to the public in 2000. The ancient smut is heady stuff!

Catch the Funicolare Centrale (funicular), on Via Toledo, to **Vomero** and the Certosa di San Martino, a 14th-century Carthusian monastery, rebuilt in the 17th century in Neapolitan-baroque style. It houses the **Museo Nazionale di San Martino** (☎ 081 578 17 69; Via Tito Angelini; admission €6; ♥ 8.30am-7.30pm Tue-Sun). Worth a visit, the monastery's church has exquisite marble work and frescoes and magnificent views from the terraced gardens.

Festivals & Events
Festa di San Gennaro honours the city's patron saint and is held three times a year (on the first Sunday in May, 19 September and 16 December). Thousands swarm the Duomo to witness the saint's blood liquefy, a miracle said to save the city from potential disasters. If you're in town, don't miss it.

Sleeping
While accommodation is cheapest near the station and Piazza Garibaldi, there's a vast range in quality in this unsavoury area. Stick to our listings – clean, safe and reliable – or ask the tourist office to recommend and book you a room. Staying in Spaccanapoli is the best way to experience the festive vibe of the historic centre, while Vomero and Mergellina are more tranquil neighbourhoods.

STAZIONE CENTRALE AREA
Hotel Ginevra (☎ 081 28 32 10; www.hotelginevra .it; Via Genova 116; s/d/tr €30/50/70, d/tr with bathroom €60/100) This long-time favourite is tidy and lovingly kept by the exuberant owners; the same holds true for the same-floor sister hotel, **Ginevra 2**, with plusher rooms.

Vicoletti (☎ 081 564 11 56; Via S Domenico Soriano 46; s/d/tr €42/62/90, with bathroom €55/78/100) This cheery spot has a colourful décor, a pretty terrace, spacious rooms and friendly owners.

AROUND SPACCANAPOLI
6 Small Rooms (☎ 081 790 13 78; www.at6smallrooms .com; Via Diodato Lioy 18; dm/d incl breakfast €18/25) This friendly and sociable hostel has sun-lit rooms, a spacious kitchen, and an excellent reputation with travellers.

Hotel Bellini (☎ 081 45 69 96; Via San Paolo 44; s/d with bathroom €51/70) Tucked away in the heart of the old centre, this snug hotel oozes Neapolitan charm.

OTHER AREAS
Hostel of the Sun (☎ /fax 081 420 63 93; www.hostel napoli.com; Via Melisurgo 15; dm/s/d €18/40/50, d with bathroom €70; ▯) Handy for ferry travellers, this popular 7th-floor spot has a ready-to-please young staff, kitchen and laundry.

Pensione Margherita (☎ 081 556 70 44; Via D Cimarosa 29; s/d/tr €35/62/87) Just near the Piazza Fuga funicular station, this is a no-frills place in a pretty part of town; ask for a room with a bay view, and have a coin handy for the lift.

Ostello Mergellina Napoli (☎ 081 761 23 46; Salita della Grotta 23; dm €13.50) This HI hostel is modern, safe and soulless, but even with 200 beds, it fills up during busy periods; take the Metro to Mergellina and follow the sign to the hostel.

Eating
It'd be hard to not eat well in Naples, and the centre is packed with good options. Pizza was created here during the 18th century, and once you sample a classic *margherita* (with fresh mozzarella, tomato sauce, olive oil and sea salt) you'll want one every meal. Save room for *calzone* (puffed-up dough stuffed with toppings), *misto di frittura* (deep-fried vegetables) and the excellent local seafood.

Da Michele (☎ 081 55 39 204; Via Cesare Sersale 1; pizzas €5-7) A contender for world's best pizza, this unpretentious place draws legions of fans who queue patiently for the master pies.

Trianon (☎ 081 553 94 26; Via P Colletta 46; pizzas €5-10) This local institution, with marble-topped tables and a warm welcome, has been tossing very good pizzas since 1923.

Intra Moenia (☎ 081 29 07 20; Piazza Bellini 70; salads from €5) Tucked onto a pretty piazza, this café/bookshop is arty, literary, left-leaning, with excellent salads to boot.

Pizzeria Sorbillo (☎ 081 44 66 43; Via dei Tribunali; pizza from €5) A long line of talented *pizzaioli* have secured this always-packed place as a shoe-in vying for Naples' No 1 pizza place.

Trattoria Castel dell'Ovo (☎ 081 764 63 52; Via Luculliana 28; secondi from €8) This unpretentious spot serves well-priced delicious seafood at harbourside tables with lovely views of Borgo Marinaro.

Naples has many good *alimentari* (grocery shops) and food stalls – try **Friggitoria Fiorenzano** (Piazza Montesanto 6) and gorge yourself silly on heavenly fried veggies at bargain prices.

Drinking

There are a handful of lively bars in Piazza Gesú Nuovo, including **Bar Lazzarella** (Calata Trinita Maggiore 7-8), a popular watering hole, and the snug **Vineria del Centro** (Via Paladino 8a) with a good wine list, welcoming lighting, charming décor and low-key electronica played at a polite volume.

Entertainment

The monthly *Qui Napoli* and local newspapers are the best guides to what's on when. In May the city organises Maggio dei Monumenti, a month of mostly free concerts and cultural events. Ask at the tourist offices for details.

Teatro San Carlo (☎ 081 797 21 11; www.teatrosancarlo.it; tickets from €20) Has year-round concerts and performances of opera and ballet.

Getting There & Away

Capodichino airport (☎ 081 789 62 59) is about 6km northeast of the city centre and links Naples with most Italian and several European cities. Take **ANM** (☎ 800 63 95 25) city bus No 3S (€0.77, 30 minutes, every 15 minutes) from Piazza Garibaldi or the Alibus airport bus (€3, 20 minutes, at least hourly) from Piazza Municipio. A taxi costs about €30.

Naples is the rail hub for the south, and regular trains for most major Italian cities arrive and depart from the Stazione Centrale. There are up to 30 trains daily to/from Rome.

Buses leave from Piazza Garibaldi, in front of the station, for destinations including Salerno, the Amalfi Coast, Caserta, Bari, Lecce and Brindisi. Signage is sparse, so check destinations carefully or ask at the information kiosk.

Traghetti (ferries), *aliscafi* (hydrofoils) and *navi veloci* (fast ships) leave for Sorrento and the islands of Capri, Ischia and Procida from Molo Beverello, in front of Castel Nuovo. Some hydrofoils leave for the bay islands from Mergellina, and ferries for Ischia and Procida also leave from Pozzuoli. All operators have offices at the various ports from which they leave. Hydrofoils cost around double the price of ferries but take half the time. **Tirrenia** (☎ 199 12 31 99) operates ferries to Palermo (daily) and Cagliari (weekly), while **Siremar** (☎ 081 580 03 40) services the Aeolian Islands and Milazzo. **SNAV** (☎ 081 428 51 11) runs hydrofoils to Capri, Procida and Ischia, and the daily *Sicilia Jet* to Palermo from mid-April to September. **Caremar** (☎ 081 551 38 82) services Capri, Ischia and Procia by ferry and hydrofoil.

Getting Around

You can make your way around Naples by bus, tram, metro and funicular. **ANM** (☎ 800 63 95 25) buses leave from Piazza Garibaldi for the centre of Naples and Mergellina. You can buy 'Giranapoli' tickets at stations, ANM booths and tobacconists. A ticket costs €0.77 and is valid for 1½ hours of public transit. A daily ticket is good value at €2.32. Useful buses include No 3S to the airport; the R1 to Piazza Dante; the R3 from Mergellina; and No 110 from Piazza Garibaldi to Piazza Cavour and Museo Archeologico Nazionale. Tram No 1 leaves from east of Stazione Centrale for the centre. To get to Molo Beverello and the ferry terminal, take bus No R2 or the M1.

The metro station is downstairs at the train station. Line one runs north from Piazza Dante, with stops at Piazza Cavour, Salvator Rosa, Cilea, Piazza Vanvitelli, Piazza Medaglie d'Oro and seven stops beyond. Line two heads west to Mergellina, with stops at Piazza Cavour, Piazza Amedeo and the funicular to Vomero, and on to the Campi Flegrei and Pozzuoli.

The main funicular, **Funicolare Centrale**, connecting the city centre with Vomero is in Piazza Duca d'Aosta, next to Galleria Umberto I, on Via Toledo.

The Ferrovia Circumvesuviana runs trains for Herculaneum, Pompeii and Sorrento. The station is about 400m southwest of Stazione Centrale, in Corso Garibaldi (take the underpass from Stazione Centrale). The Ferrovia Cumana and the Circumflegrea, based at Stazione Cumana in Piazza Montesanto, operate services to Pozzuoli, Baia and Cumae every 20 minutes.

AROUND NAPLES
Pompeii & Herculaneum

In AD 79 Vesuvio blew its top and buried Pompeii under layers of *lapilli* (burning fragments of pumice stone), killing 2000 in the deluge. The world's most famous volcano disaster left behind fascinating **ruins** (☎ 081 857 53 47; www.pompeiisites.org; admission €10, combined ticket incl Herculaneum & 3 minor sites €18; ☼ 8.30am-7.30pm Apr-Oct, 8.30am-5pm Nov-Mar) that provide insight into the daily life of ancient Romans. Once a resort town for the wealthy, the vast ruins include impressive temples, a forum, an amphitheatre, and streets lined with shops and luxurious homes. Most of the site's original mosaics and frescoes are on view at Naples' Museo Archeologico Nazionale (p701), but those adorning Villa dei Misteri are still intact. Many ruins are open to the public; allow four hours to visit and bring a hat or umbrella, depending on the weather.

There are two tourist offices, one in **Pompeii town** (☎ 081 850 72 55; Via Sacra 1; ☼ 8am-3.30pm Mon-Sat Oct-Mar, 8am-7pm Mon-Sat Apr-Sep), and another just outside the excavations at **Porta Marina** (☎ 800 01 33 50; Piazza Porta Marina Inferiore 12; ☼ 8am-3.30pm Mon-Sat).

Catch the Ferrovia Circumvesuviana train from Naples and get off at the Pompeii Scavi-Villa dei Misteri stop; the Porta Marina entrance is nearby.

Nearby **Herculaneum**, once a peaceful fishing town and resort, had a parallel fate. It's closer to Naples and doubles as a base for visiting Vesuvio. The **ruins** (☎ 081 739 09 63; admission €10, combined ticket incl Pompeii & 3 minor sites €18; ☼ 8.30am-7.30pm Apr-Oct, 8.30am-5pm Nov-Mar) here are smaller but the buildings, particularly the private houses, are remarkably well preserved, with better examples of frescoes, mosaics and furniture.

Herculaneum is easily accessible on the Circumvesuviana train from Naples (get off at Ercolano Scavi; €1.70 one-way). If you want to peer into the crater of Vesuvio, **Trasporti Vesuviani** (☎ 081 559 31 73) buses run from the Ercolano train station (€3.10 return, five daily), to Vesuvius car park. From there, it's a 1.5km walk to the summit area (admission €6). All services leave Pompeii's Piazza Anfiteatro (€5.16 return) 30 minutes earlier. Pack a sweater for the windy top.

CAPRI
pop 7250

Gorgeous Capri (*ca*-pri) has been charming holiday-seekers since Emperors Augustus and Tiberius made the island their summer play pad around AD 27. Come summer, hordes of day-trippers and jet-setters pack onto the island, less than an hour by boat from Naples and heavily geared towards tourism. Nonetheless, the place never loses its appeal and remains fetchingly beautiful. Famed for its grottoes, Capri also has fantastic walking.

There are several **tourist offices** (☼ 8.30am-8.30pm) Marina Grande (☎ 081 837 06 34) town centre (☎ 081 837 06 86; Piazza Umberto I) Anacapri (☎ 081 837 15 24; Piazza Vittoria 4). Online information can be found at www.capri.it and www.capritourism.com. In spring or autumn you'll find good off-season rates.

Sights & Activities

There are plenty of boat trips along Capri's craggy coast and to the famous **Grotta Azzurra** (Blue Grotto; admission €4; ☼ visits 9am-1hr before sunset). Boats leave to visit the cave from the Marina Grande and a return trip costs €15.30, including the motor to/from the grotto, rowing boat in, admission fee, and singing captains; allow an hour for the trip.

You can walk to most of the interesting points on the island. Close to Capri's centre are the commanding **Giardini d'Augusto**. One hour uphill along Via Tiberio is **Villa Jovis** (admission €2; ☼ 9am-1hr before sunset), the ruins of one of Tiberius' villas. It's a gorgeous walk along Via Matrimonia to the **Arco Naturale** – follow the spur trail, marked by splashes of paint, winding up the hillside. Near Anacapri, the resplendent **Villa San Michele** (☎ 081 837 14 01; Viale Axel Munthe; admission €5; ☼ 9am-6pm May-Sep, 10.30am-4.30pm Oct-Apr) was the home of Swedish writer and dog-lover Dr Axel Munthe.

ITALY

Sleeping & Eating

Albergo Stella Maris (☎ 081 837 04 52; Via Roma 27; s/d with bathroom €45/80) Right in the noisy heart of town and just off Piazza Umberto I, this place is convenient with functional but small rooms.

Loreley (☎ 081 837 14 40; fax 081 837 13 99; Via G Orlandi 16; s/d with bathroom & breakfast high season €75/115; ☒ Mar-Nov) In Anacapri, this above-average hotel has decent rooms, some with pretty views.

Pulalli Wine Bar (☎ 081 837 41 08; Piazza Umberto I; dishes from €4) Perched in the clock tower overlooking Capri's main piazza, this great spot serves light meals and good wine.

La Grottelle (☎ 081 837 57 19; Via Arco Naturale 13; pasta from €8) Tucked inside a couple of small caves near Arco Naturale, this popular spot has simple and tasty dishes.

Il Saraceno (☎ 081 837 20 99; Via Trieste e Trento 18; pasta from €7) A homey Anacapri spot with tasty ravioli *caprese* (mozzarella, tomato and basil) and the proprietor's own wine and *limoncello* (a local lemon-infused liquor sipped ice cold).

Getting There & Around

There are hydrofoils and ferries virtually every hour from Naples' Molo Beverello and Mergellina, especially in summer. In Naples, pick up the daily *Il Mattino* for sailing times. Several companies make the trip; see p702. Hydrofoils cost about €12 each way and take about 30 minutes; ferries cost €6 each way and take about 1½ hours.

From Marina Grande, a funicular takes you to the town of Capri, at the top of a steep hill some 3km from the port up a winding road. Local buses connect the port with Capri, Anacapri and other points around the island, and run between the two main towns until past midnight. Tickets for the funicular and buses cost €1.30 each trip or €6.71 per daily ticket.

SORRENTO

pop 17,450

A shameless resort town, pretty Sorrento gazes out over the Bay of Naples and lures throngs of holiday-seekers to its sunny, crowded streets. Still, southern Italian charm hits hard – come in the off-season for its most pleasant side, or use it as a handy pause before heading to Capri and the Amalfi Coast.

The centre of town is Piazza Tasso, a short walk from the train station along Corso Italia. If you arrive by boat at Marina Piccola, walk south along Via Marina Piccola then climb the 200 steps to reach the piazza.

There's an excellent **tourist office** (☎ 081 807 40 33; www.sorrentotourism.it; Via Luigi de Maio 35; ☒ 8.45am-6.15pm Mon-Sat) inside the Circolo dei Forestieri complex; a **post office** (Corso Italia 210) and a **Telecom office** (Piazza Tasso 37). The **Deutsche Bank** (Piazza Angelina Laura) has an ATM.

Near the station, **Sorrento Info** (Via Tasso 19; per hr €6) has Internet access.

For emergencies contact the **Ospedale Civile** (☎ 081 533 11 11; Corso Italia 1) or **police station** (☎ 081 807 44 33; Corso Italia 236).

Villa Elisa (☎ 081 878 27 92; Piazza S Antonino 2; s/d high season €70/90) Five pretty rooms surround a courtyard at this convenient homey spot with a sweet rooftop terrace and in-room kitchen facilities.

Pensione Linda (☎ 081 878 29 16; Via degli Aranci 125; s/d with bathroom high season €35/70) This modest hotel has good-value, old-fashioned courtesy, spacious rooms and eclectic but attractive furnishings.

Nube d'Argento (☎ 081 878 13 44; www.nube dargento.com; Via del Capo 21; per adult/camp site high season €9/9.50) This camping ground is tucked into a sea of olive trees and 200m from the beach; head south along Corso Italia, then follow Via del Capo.

Self-Service Angelina Lauro (☎ 081 807 47 08; Piazza Angelina Lauro 39; pasta from €4) A cheap snack venue with a nice selection for vegetarians.

Pizzeria Gastronomia (☎ 081 807 40 97; Via degli Aranci; pizza from €3) A tasty and cheery spot opposite Pensione Linda.

Bollicine (☎ 081 878 46 16; Via dell'Accademia 9; glass of wine from €2) This snug wine bar serves good local varietals and light meals.

Circumvesuviana trains run every half-hour between Sorrento and Naples via Pompeii and Ercolano. At least 12 SITA buses a day leave from outside the train station for the Amalfi Coast. Hydrofoils and ferries leave for Capri, Napoli and Ischia from the port at Marina Piccola; the tourist office has timetables.

AMALFI COAST

This 50km of cliff-hugging coast is some of Europe's most dazzling, luring wealthy holiday-seekers paying skyrocket-high prices in summer. The lemon-terraced land

and aquamarine coves aren't to be missed – save money and patience by visiting in spring or autumn.

There are tourist offices in the individual towns, including in **Positano** (☎ 089 87 50 67; Via del Saracino 4; ❧ 8am-2pm & 3.30-8pm Mon-Sat year-round, 3.30-8pm Jul & Aug) and **Amalfi** (☎ 089 87 11 07; Corso Roma 19; ❧ 8.30am-1.30pm & 3-5.30pm Mon-Fri, 8.30am-12.30pm Sat). For itinerary planning, www.amalficoast.com is useful.

GETTING THERE & AWAY
SITA buses head to Sorrento (€2.30, more than 10 daily; accessible from Naples on the Circumvesuviana train line), via Positano (€1.30), and hourly to Salerno (€1.80), a 40-minute train trip from Naples. Buses stop in Amalfi at Piazza Flavio Gioia, from where you can catch a bus to Ravello.

Hydrofoils and ferries also service the coast between April and mid-September daily, leaving from Salerno and stopping at Amalfi and Positano. There are also boats between Positano and Capri.

Positano & Around
postcode 84017 / pop 3900
Because of its Moorish flair and colourful houses, Positano is the most photographed, fashionable and expensive town on the coast. The hills behind town offer some great walks; pick up a walking map in the town.

Visit **Nocelle**, a tiny village above Positano, accessible by trail from the end of the road in Positano. Have lunch at **Trattoria Santa Croce** (☎ 089 81 12 60; pasta from €6; ❧ lunch & dinner Mar-Nov), and enjoy panoramic views. Nocelle is accessible by local bus from Positano, via Montepertuso.

Ostello Brikette (☎ 089 87 58 57; www.brikette .com; Via G Marconi 358; dm €22) Close to the trek-king trails and Bar Internazionale, this characterful spot offers the least expensive and perhaps most social lodging in town.

Villa Nettuno (☎ 089 87 54 01; www.villanettuno positano.it; Via Pasitea 208; s/d with bathroom high season €70/80) This cheery hotel is tucked into a pretty garden and most rooms have balconies.

Il Saraceno d'Oro (pizza about €6) Close to Villa Nettuno this popular eatery has decent pizzas and exceptional profiteroles.

On the way from Positano to Amalfi is the town of **Praiano**, not as scenic but with the Amalfi Coast's only camping ground, **La Tranquillità** (☎ 089 87 40 84; Via Roma 21; 2 people & tent €39, bungalows €90), which has many sleeping options; the SITA bus stops outside.

Amalfi & Around
postcode 84011 / pop 5528
A maritime superpower during the 11th century, Amalfi is now a legendary tourist resort. It has an impressive **Duomo**, and nearby is the **Grotta dello Smeraldo**, a rival to Capri's Grotta Azzurra.

In the hills behind Amalfi is delightful and breezy **Ravello**, accessible by bus and walking paths, with the magnificent 11th-century **Villa Rufolo** (admission €4; ❧ 9am-6pm), once the home of popes and later of the German composer Richard Wagner. The 20th-century **Villa Cimbrone**, a Greta Garbo hideaway, is also set in pretty gardens, which end at a terrace offering a spectacular view of the Gulf of Salerno.

Locanda Costa d'Amalfi (☎ 089 83 19 50; Via G Augustariccio 50; s/d with breakfast €55/60) This well-priced newcomer, a few kilometres before town, has six well-appointed rooms and a sunny air.

Hotel Lidomare (☎ 089 87 13 32; www.lidomare .it; Largo Duchi Piccolomini 9; s/d with bathroom & breakfast €50/90) This lovely family-run hotel is excellent value – romantic rooms, elegant furnishings and kind service.

Ostello Beato Solitudo (☎ /fax 089 82 50 48; Piazza G Avitabile 4; dm €9.50) The HI hostel is in Agerola San Lazzaro, a village just 16km west of Amalfi. Regular buses leave from Amalfi throughout the day, the last at 8.45pm.

Pizzeria al Teatro (Via E Marini 19; pizza about €7) This pizzeria has tasty local fare and a welcoming ambience.

Cantina S Nicola (Salita Marino Sebaste 8) This new wine bar serves excellent light meals.

The best pastries are at **Pasticceria Andrea Pansa** (Piazza Duomo 40), with luxe charm, and **Casbahr** (Piazza Umberto 1) gets the local vote for friendliest coffee spot.

PAESTUM
One of southern Italy's most lasting impressions is that of three stark white Greek temples towering in an open field of brilliant red poppies. This majestic trio, just south of Salerno, are among the best-preserved **temples** (❧ 9am-1hr before sunset) of the ancient Greek world. At the site, there's a **tourist office** (☎ 0828 81 10 16; ❧ 9am-4pm) and an evocative **museum** (❧ 9am-7pm). Buy a

combined entrance ticket (€6.50), covering the temples and museum; separate admissions are €4 each.

Paestum is accessible by **CSTP** (☎ 800 01 66 59) and **SCAT** (☎ 0974 834 15) buses, departing hourly from Salerno's Piazza della Concordia, and by train.

MATERA
pop 57,315
The filming location for Mel Gibson's controversial *The Passion of the Christ*, Matera was famous beforehand for its unique *sassi* – stone houses carved into the two ravines that slice through town. As recently as the 1950s, these houses were occupied, before the town's peasant class was relocated to new government housing just outside of town. Now a Unesco World Heritage site, the cave homes still evoke a powerful image of a poverty that's difficult to imagine in a developed European country.

There's a **tourist office** (☎ 0835 33 19 83; Via De Viti De Marco 9; 🕑 9am-1pm Mon-Sat & 4-6.30pm Mon & Thu), off the main Via Romas. It's easy enough to navigate yourself through the *sassi*, particularly with the helpful map *Matera: Percorsi Turistici* (€1.30), with four easy-to-follow itineraries.

Buses arrive in Piazza Matteotti, a short walk down Via Roma to the town centre.

SIGHTS
The two *sassi* areas, **Barisano** and **Caveoso**, had no electricity, running water or sewerage system until well into the 20th century. The oldest *sassi* (dating from medieval times or earlier) are at the top of the ravines, while the dwellings in the lower sections that appear to be the oldest were created in the 1920s – as space ran out, the population began moving into hand-hewn or natural caves. The *sassi* zones are accessible from Piazza Vittorio Veneto and Piazza del Duomo in the centre of Matera. Caveoso is the more picturesque and highlights include the rock churches of **Santa Maria d'Idris** and **Santa Lucia alla Malve**, both with well-preserved Byzantine frescoes. The 13th-century Apulian-Romanesque **cathedral**, overlooking Sasso Barisano, also warrants a stop. A couple of *sassi* have been refurnished as they were when the last peasant inhabitants occupied them; of these **Casa-Grotta di Vico Solitario** (admission €1.50) is worth a visit.

SLEEPING & EATING
Albergo Roma (☎ /fax 0835 33 39 12; Via Roma 62; s/d €22/32) This very central hotel has basic rooms at unbeatable prices.

Locanda Di San Martino (☎ /fax 0835 25 66 00; www.locandadisanmartino.it; Via San Martino 22; s/d with breakfast €60/80) This new *sassi* hotel elegantly meshes the past and present, with pretty rooms, balconies and a cave bar.

Le Botteghe (☎ 0835 34 40 72; Piazza San Pietro Barisano 22; pasta from €6) Has tasty local dishes and good wines.

There's a **fresh produce market** (Via A Persio), near Piazza V Veneto.

GETTING THERE & AWAY
SITA buses connect Matera with Taranto and Metaponto. The town is on the private Ferrovie Apulo-Lucane train line, which connects with Bari, Altamura and Potenza. There are also three Marozzi buses a day between Rome and Matera (€30). Buy tickets at **Biglietteria Manicone** (☎ 0835 332 86 21; Piazza Matteotti 3).

PUGLIA
The province of Puglia comprises the heel of Italy's boot, bound by the Adriatic and Ionian Seas. In the past, this coastline was fought over by nearly every major colonial power, from the Greeks to the Spanish, all intent on establishing a strategic foothold in the Mediterranean. Today, there's a strong regional pride and the area remains relatively untouristed. A helpful source for planning is www.pugliaturismo.com.

Brindisi
pop 90,020
Despite its shady reputation, Brindisi is more boring than dangerous. The major embarkation point for ferries to Greece, the city swarms with people in transit – and there's little to do but wait for your boat. Most backpackers gather at the station, ferry terminal or in pedestrianised Piazza Cairoli or Piazza del Popolo. The old port is a 10-minute walk from the station, along Corso Umberto I, which leads into Corso Garibaldi; the new port (Costa Morena) is east of town, 7km from the station, with free bus connections linking the two. Be exceedingly mindful of your possessions at all times.

Carpe Diem (☎ 0831 59 79 54; Via N Brandi 2; dm €14) is a cheery private hostel 2km from town, with laundry and an evening meal (€7); call for a pick-up or take bus No 3. For port convenience, **Hotel Altair** (☎ 0831 56 22 89; Via Giudea 4; s/d €20/37, with bathroom €30/50) has airy, high-ceilinged rooms.

For boat supplies, hit the **supermarket** (Corso Garibaldi 106) or the **morning market** (Piazza Mercato).

GETTING THERE & AWAY

Marozzi (☎ 071 280 23 98) runs four buses daily to Rome's Stazione Tiburtina (€32.55, nine hours) leaving from Viale Arno. **Appia Travel** (☎ 0831 52 16 84; Viale Regina Margherita 8-9) sells tickets. There are rail connections to major cities in northern Italy, as well as to Bari, Lecce, Ancona, Naples and Rome.

Ferries leave Brindisi for Greek destinations such as Corfu, Igoumenitsa, Patras and the Ionian Islands. Major ferry companies are **Hellenic Mediterranean Lines** (HML; ☎ 0831 52 85 31; www.hml.gr; Corso Garibaldi 8); **Blue Star Ferries** (☎ 0831 56 22 00; www.bluestarferries.com; Corso Garibaldi 65); **Italian Ferries** (☎ 0831 59 08 40; www.italianferries.it; Corso Garibaldi 96); and **Med Link Lines** (☎ 0831 52 76 67; www.ferries.gr/medlink; Corso Garibaldi 49).

The largest, most expensive and most reliable of the lines, HML also officially accepts Eurail and Inter-Rail passes, entitling you to travel free in deck class (paying a €15 supplement in July and August). If you intend to use your pass, it is best to reserve in advance in summer.

Discounts are available for travellers under 26 years of age and holders of some Italian rail passes. Fares generally increase by up to 40% on peak travel days in July and August, and you might save 20% on a round-trip ticket. At the time of writing, HML's low-/high-season fares for one-way deck-class service to Greece were €30/49; for a car €29/55; for a motorcycle €12/20.

Look up details of fares and timetables on www.ferries.gr. Be wary of any too-good-to-be-true offers from fly-by-night operators claiming your Eurail and Inter-Rail pass is accepted by them or invalid with anyone else.

The port tax is €6, payable when you buy your ticket. Check in at least two hours before departure or risk losing your reservation. To get to the new port of Costa Morena from the train station take the free Portabagagli bus, departing a handy two hours before boat departures.

Lecce
pop 97,462

This sparkling little city hosts an astonishing array of baroque architecture. Unabashedly opulent, the local style is known to Italians as *barocco leccese* (Lecce baroque), and Lecce is often referred to as the 'Florence of the South'. A university town, Lecce exudes a sassy charm and sports a vibrant bar scene.

To get to the centre from the train station, take bus No 1, 2 or 4 to Viale Marconi, or it's a 10-minute walk. There is a sleepy **tourist office** (☎ 0832 24 80 92; Corso Vittorio Emanuele 24) near Piazza Duomo.

Lecce's baroque style is most famously on display at the **Basilica della Santa Croce** (☎ 0832 24 19 57; Via Umberto I; admission free; ☩ 8am-1pm & 4-7.30pm). A team of artists worked throughout the 16th and 17th centuries to decorate the building and its extraordinarily ornate façade. In Piazza del Duomo are the 12th-century **cathedral** (☩ 6.30am-noon & 5-7.30pm), completely restored in baroque style by Giuseppe Zimbalo, and its 70m-high **bell tower**; the 15th-century **Palazzo Vescovile** (Bishop's Palace); and the **Seminario**, with its elegant façade and baroque well in the courtyard. The piazza is particularly beautiful at night, when it's floodlit. In **Piazza Sant'Oronzo** are the remains of a 2nd-century AD **Roman amphitheatre**.

Centro Storico Prestige (☎ 0832 24 33 53; www.bbprestige-lecce.it; Via S Maria del Paradiso; per person with breakfast €40) On the 3rd floor of a 16th-century *palazzo*, this gem has elegantly furnished and balconied rooms, a roof garden, and a hip owner (next door is **Al di Vino Bicchiere**, a terrific little wine bar).

Hotel Cappello (☎ 0832 30 88 81; Via Montegrappa 4; s/d with bathrooms €30/45) For station convenience, this welcoming spot has simple-but-clean rooms.

Trattoria Casereccia (☎ 0832 24 51 78; Via Colonnello Costadura 19; pasta from €6) This family-run favourite serves good-value home cooking.

Ristorante Da Guido e Figli (☎ 0832 30 58 68; Via XXV Luglio 14; antipastos from €2) Hit the adjoining self-service area for a delicious antipasto buffet, where you can feast for a pittance.

Seemingly sedate Lecce comes alive at weekend nights, and there are some great bars in its historic centre. Try **Caffé Letterario** (Via Paladini 46), where you can enjoy wine by the glass in colourful surrounds; **I Merli** (Via Federico D'Aragona), where locals crowd nightly; and funky **B Lounge**, just across the street.

ITALY

STP buses connect Lecce with towns throughout the Salentine peninsula, leaving from Via Adua. There are frequent trains to Brindisi, Bari, Rome, Naples and Bologna, as well as points throughout Puglia.

SICILY (SICILIA)

Sun-baked Sicily shines with visible layers of its rich and often turbulent history. Afloat in the Mediterranean Sea, Italy's largest island coddles Greek temples, Arab domes, Byzantine mosaics, Norman churches and baroque architecture. Its magnificent landscape is equally varied, dominated by Mt Etna (3350m) on the east coast, terraced with citrus groves, fringed with dazzling coastline, and with a vast plateau at its heart.

With a population just over five million, Sicily has a mild climate in winter and a relentlessly hot summer. The best times to visit are spring and autumn.

Most ferries from Italy arrive at Sicily's capital, Palermo, which is convenient as a jumping-off point. If you're short on time, spend a day in Palermo and then hit Taormina, Syracuse or Agrigento.

Getting There & Away
BOAT
Sicily is accessible by ferry from Genoa, Livorno, Naples, Reggio di Calabria and Cagliari, and also from Malta and Tunisia. The main companies servicing the Mediterranean are **Tirrenia** (☎ 199 12 31 99; www.gruppo tirrenia.it) and **Grimaldi** (☎ 091 58 74 04; www .grimaldi.it), which runs Grandi Navi Veloci. **SNAV** (Palermo ☎ 091 58 60 66, Naples ☎ 081 761 23 48; www.snav.com) runs a summer ferry between Naples and Palermo. Prices vary by season and are highest July to September. Timetables can change each year, and it's best to check at a travel agency that takes ferry bookings. Book well in advance during summer, particularly if with a car.

At the time of writing, the high-season fares for a *poltrona* (airline-type seat) were: Genoa–Palermo (€75, 18 hours) and Livorno–Palermo (€80, 19 hours) with Grimaldi's Grandi Navi Veloci, and Naples–Palermo (€45, 9¾ hours) and Cagliari–Palermo (€39, 13½ hours) with Tirrenia.

Virtu Ferries (www.virtuferries.com) serves the route between Sicily and Malta.

ZBUS & TRAIN
Direct bus services between Rome and Sicily are operated by **SAIS** (☎ 091 616 60 28; www .saistrasporti.it; Via P Balsamo 20, Palermo) and **Segesta** (☎ 091 616 90 39; Via P Balsamo 16, Palermo), which depart from Rome's Piazza Tiburtina. Buses service Messina (€27, 9¼ hours), Catania (€30, 11 hours) Palermo (€35, 12 hours) and Syracuse (€32.50, 11½ hours).

For train information, call ☎ 147 88 80 88 (7am to 9pm) or go to the information office at any station; ticket cost includes the 3km ferry crossing from Villa San Giovanni (Calabria) to Messina.

Getting Around
Bus is the most common, and convenient, mode of public transport in Sicily. There are numerous services between Syracuse, Catania and Palermo, as well as to Agrigento and towns in the interior. The coastal train service between Messina and Palermo, and Messina and Syracuse varies from being efficient and reliable to delayed and unpredictable, as does the run between Palermo and Agrigento.

PALERMO
pop 750,000
Once regarded as Europe's grandest city, Palermo on first glance is more decrepit than dazzling, due to heavy WWII bombing and years of neglect. But look closer and this dignified city's gilded 3000-year history – with stints as an Arab emirate and the seat of a Norman kingdom – shines forth. It's a truly fascinating city, where you'll eat like royalty.

Orientation
Palermo is a large but easily manageable city. The main streets of the historical centre are Via Roma and Via Magueda, which extend from the central station to Piazza Castelnuovo, a vast square in the modern part of town.

To get to the historical centre from the train station and nearby bus station, take bus No 101 or walk along Via Roma; from the port, take bus No 139 to the station.

Information
MEDICAL SERVICES
For an ambulance call ☎ 091 30 66 44.
Lo Cascio (☎ 091 616 21 17; Via Roma 1) A late-night pharmacy near the train station.

ITALY

Ospedale Civico (☎ 091 666 11 11; Via Carmelo Lazzaro) Main hospital.

Police Station (theft & lost documents: ☎ 091 21 01 11, foreigners office: ☎ 091 651 43 30; Piazza della Vittoria; ⏱ 24hr)

MONEY

ATMs are scattered throughout the city.

Exchange offices Stazione Centrale (8am-8pm) airport (8am-7pm)

Ruggieri & Figli (☎ 091 58 71 44; Via Enrico Amari 40; ⏱ 9am-1pm & 4-7pm Mon-Fri, 9am-1pm Sat) Represents American Express and will cash travellers cheques for card-holders only.

POST & TELEPHONE

Aexis Telecom (Via Maqueda 347; Internet per hr €5) Has fax, phone and Internet services.

Palazzo delle Poste (Via Roma 322; ⏱ 8.30am-6.30pm Mon-Fri, 8.30am-12.30pm Sat)

TOURIST INFORMATION

Main tourist office (☎ 091 605 81 11; Piazza Castelnuovo 35; ⏱ 8.30am-2pm & 2.30-6pm Mon-Fri, 8.30am-2pm Sat) Has brochures and the helpful bimonthly *Agenda*. There are branch offices at **Stazione Centrale** (☎ 091 616 59 14), with the same opening hours, and the **airport** (☎ 091 59 16 98; ⏱ 8am-noon).

Sights

The intersection of Corso Vittorio Emanuele and Via Maqueda marks the **Quattro Canti**, the ideal and actual centre of historic Palermo. Called *il teatro*, it's marked by four 17th-century Spanish baroque façades each decorated with a statue. Nearby Piazza Pretoria houses the ornate **Fontana Pretoria**, created by Florentine sculptors in the 16th century and dubbed the Fountain of Shame because of the cavorting nude statues; despite restoration work, you can still sneak a peek. Also in the piazza are the baroque **Chiesa di Santa Caterina** and the **Palazzo del Municipio** (town hall). Around the corner in Piazza Bellini is Palermo's top wedding spot, the famous **La Martorana** church (☎ 091 616 16 92; admission free; ⏱ 8am-1pm & 3.30-5.30pm Mon-Sat, 8.30am-1pm Sun), with a striking Arab-Norman bell tower and stunning Byzantine mosaic interior. It stands next to the red-domed **Chiesa di San Cataldo**, meshing Arab and Norman styles.

The huge **cathedral** (☎ 091 33 43 76; Corso Vittorio Emanuele; admission free; ⏱ 7am-7pm Mon-Sat, 8am-1.30pm & 4-7pm Sun & holidays), modified many times over the centuries, is a good example of Sicily's unique Arab-Norman style. At Piazza Indipendenza is **Palazzo Reale**, also known as the Palazzo dei Normanni, now the seat of the Sicilian parliament. Step inside and downstairs to see the **Cappella Palatina** (☎ 091 705 48 79; admission free; ⏱ 9-11.45am & 3-4.45pm Mon-Fri, 9-11.45am Sat, 9-10am & noon-1pm Sun), a truly jaw-dropping example of Arab-Norman architecture, designed by Roger II in 1130 and lavishly decorated with exquisite mosaics. King Roger's former bedroom, **Sala di Ruggero** (☎ 091 705 43 17; admission free; ⏱ 9am-noon Mon, Fri & Sat), is adorned with 12th-century mosaics; you can only visit the room with a guide (free).

Take bus No 389 from Piazza Indipendenza to the nearby town of **Monreale**, 8km southwest of Palermo, to see the gorgeous mosaics in the world-famous 12th-century **Duomo** (☎ 091 640 44 13; admission free; ⏱ 8am-6pm), plus its **cloisters** (admission €4.50; ⏱ 9am-7pm Mon-Sat, 9am-1.30pm Sun).

Sleeping

Albergo Ariston (☎ 091 33 24 34; Via Marino Stabile; s/d €40/55) Tucked into an unattractive apartment block is Palermo's best lower-priced hotel, this has a great location, sparkling-clean rooms and an exceedingly polite (non-English-speaking) staff.

Hotel Letizia (☎ 091 58 91 10; www.hotelletizia .com; Via dei Bottai 30; s/d €78/110) This lovely little hotel off the quaint Piazza Marina has pretty rooms with wood floors, an airy ambience, a cheery reading nook and breakfast terrace.

Albergo Verdi (☎ 091 612 03 86; Via Maqueda 417; s/d €80/120, cash only) This welcoming hotel has bright rooms with dark wood furnishings, a tiny bar and an Art Deco look; excellent value for the location.

Trinacria (☎ /fax 091 53 05 90; Via Barcarello 25; per adult/camp site €4.10/7.50) The area's best camping is at Sferracavallo by the sea. Catch bus No 628 from Piazzale Alcide de Gasperi, or bus No 101 or 107 from the station.

Eating

Traditional dishes featuring both sweet and spicy flavours reflect the area's Arab past. A popular Palermitan dish is *pasta con le sarde* (with sardines, fennel, peppers, capers and pine nuts). Locals dine late and restaurants rarely open for dinner before 8.30pm.

Antica Focacceria di San Francesco (☎ 091 32 02 64; Via A Paternostro 58; mains €7) A local institution that's popular with workers and families alike, this fast-food spot has a bustling atmosphere and serves delicious *calzone,* pizza slices and some Palermitan speciality snacks, like *panini* stuffed with ricotta and steaming veal innards.

Trattoria Stella (Via Alloro 104) In the La Kalsa quarter, this bright eatery serves a smashing *pesce spada* (swordfish) and you'll be serenaded by the lilting Arabic-influenced songs coming from the kitchen.

Palermo's best open-air markets are the Vuccíria, held daily except Sunday in the narrow streets around Piazza San Domenico, and Il Ballaro, held in the Albergheria quarter off Via Maqueda; both have excellent offerings and unbeatable local colour.

Getting There & Away

The main intercity bus station is around Via P Balsamo, to the right as you leave the train station. Offices for the various companies are all in this area, including **SAIS Trasporti** (☎ 091 617 11 41; www.saistrasporti.it; Via Balsamo 20), **SAIS Autolinee** (☎ 091 616 60 28; www.saisautolinee.it; Via Balsamo 18) and **Segesta** (☎ 091 616 90 39; www.segesta.it; Via Balsamo 26). Regular trains leave from the Stazione Centrale for Milazzo, Messina, Agrigento, Trapani, Syracuse and Catania as well as for nearby towns such as Cefalú. Direct trains go to Reggio di Calabria, Naples and Rome.

Boats leave from the port (Molo Vittorio Veneto) for Sardinia and the mainland (see p708). The **Tirrenia office** (☎ 091 602 11 11) is at the port.

Getting Around

Most of Palermo's city buses stop near the train station. Bus Nos 101 and 107 run along Via Roma from the train station to Piazza Castelnuovo in a loop. Bus No 139 goes from the station past the port. Purchase tickets before you board; they cost €0.80 and are valid for two hours or €2.60 for a day pass.

AEOLIAN ISLANDS

These seven breezy islands – volcanic spurs strewn north of Milazzo – are stunning. Also known as the *Liparis,* they display an extraordinary range of landscapes: lush Lipari, a well-honed resort; tiny and exclusive Panarea; rugged Vulcano; the gorgeous scenery of Stromboli (with its fiercely active volcano); the fertile vineyards of Salina; and

tranquil Alicudi and Filicudi. The islands have been inhabited since the Neolithic era, when migrants sought the valuable volcanic glass, obsidian. The Isole Eolie are so named because the ancient Greeks believed they were home to Aeolus, the god of wind; Homer wrote of their natural beauties in the *Odyssey.* Best come in spring or autumn or compete with the hordes of summer hedonists.

The **tourist office** (☎ 090 988 00 95; www.netnet.it/aasteolie; Via Vittorio Emanuele 202; ♥ 8am-2pm Mon-Sat & 4.30-7.30pm Mon-Fri) for the islands is on Lipari. Other offices are open on Vulcano, Salina and Stromboli during summer.

Sights & Activities

On **Lipari** visit the **citadel** (♥ 9am-7pm), with its fabulous **Museo Archeologico Eoliano** (☎ 090 988 01 74; admission €4.50; ♥ 9am-1.30pm & 3-7pm Mon-Sat). There are excellent walks on the island, as well as good snorkelling and scuba diving. The tourist office has information on trails, beaches and excursions.

Vulcano, with its pungent sulphurous odour, is a short boat trip from Lipari. The main volcano, Vulcano Fossa, is still active, although the last recorded period of eruption was 1888–90. You trek for one hour to the crater, or take a bath in the therapeutic hot mud.

Stromboli is the most spectacular of the islands. Climb the volcano (924m) at night to see the Sciara del Fuoco (Trail of Fire) – lava streaming down the side of the volcano. Many people make the trip (four hours) alone during the day, but at night go with a guide. Contact **Magmatrek** (☎ 090 986 57 68; www.magmatrek.it) for guided treks to the crater (they only depart if groups are large enough).

Sleeping & Eating

Camping facilities are available on Salina and Vulcano. Most summer accommodation is booked out well in advance on the smaller islands, particularly on Stromboli, and many places close during winter.

LIPARI

Lipari provides the best accommodation options. Don't dismiss outright offers for *affittacamere* by touts when you arrive at the port – they're often genuine.

Diana Brown (☎ 090 981 25 84; dbrown@netnet.it; Vico Himera 3; s/d with bathroom €62/68) These comfortable, homey rooms are centrally located and Diana is a fount of local expertise; she and her husband also run **Gruppo di Navigazione** (www.navigazioniregina.com), featuring boat tours of all the islands.

Baia Unci (☎ 090 981 19 09; baiaunci@tin.it; per adult/camp site high season €7.75/14) The island's only camping ground is at Canneto, about 3km out of Lipari town; take the bus from the Esso service station at Marina Lunga.

La Cambusa (☎ 349 476 60 61; Via Garibaldi 72; mains from €12) This tiny, locals-filled gem serves delicious pastas and fish.

STROMBOLI & VULCANO

Casa del Sole (☎ 090 98 60 17; Via Soldato Cincotta; s/d €21/42) This popular joint, on the road to the volcano, has decent rooms and a good kitchen.

Hotel Torre (☎ /fax 090 985 23 42; Via Favaloro 1; d low/high season €38/75) On Vulcano. Good-value large rooms with kitchen and terrace, and beach access.

ALICUDI & FILICUDI

If you want seclusion and still-wild beauty, head for Alicudi or Filicudi. The former offers the simple but nice **Ericusa** (☎ 090 988 99 02; fax 090 988 96 71; Via Regina Elena; d €62, half-board per person €60), while Filicudi has the truly delightful **La Canna** (☎ 090 988 99 56; vianast@tin.it; Via Rosa 43; s/d €40/80). There are good restaurants at both places.

Getting There & Around

Ferries and hydrofoils leave for the islands from Milazzo (reached by train from Palermo and Messina) and all ticket offices are along Corso dei Mille at the port. SNAV and Siremar run hydrofoils (€10.10 one-way), and the latter also has ferries (€7.50 one-way). If arriving at Milazzo by train, catch a Giunta bus to the port. SNAV also runs hydrofoils between the islands and Palermo in summer.

You can also travel directly to the islands from the mainland. Siremar runs regular ferries from Naples, and SNAV runs hydrofoils from Naples, Messina and Reggio di Calabria. Occasionally rough seas cancel sailings.

TAORMINA
pop 10,700

Spectacularly located on a mountain terrace, with resplendent views of the glistening sea and Mt Etna, beautiful Taormina has been charming mortals for centuries. Sicily's glitziest resort was long ago discovered by the European jet set, and the chic town is expensive and touristy. But nothing can hamper the allure, and its magnificent setting, Greek theatre, medieval centre and great beaches are as seductive now as they were for Goethe and DH Lawrence.

If arriving by train, the station is on the coast and regular buses will take you to Via Pirandello, near the centre. The **tourist office** (☎ 0942 232 43; www.gate2taormina.com; ☼ 8.30am-2pm & 4-7pm) in Palazzo Corvaja has extensive information on the town and its sights.

Sights & Activities

The **Teatro Greco** (☎ 0942 232 20; admission €4.50; ☼ 9am-7pm Mon-Sat, 9am-1pm Sun), a perfect horseshoe theatre, was built in the 3rd century BC and later expanded and remodelled by the Romans. Concerts, theatre and festivals are staged here in summer and wonderful views of Mt Etna abound. From **Villa Comunale** (☎ 9am-7pm), colourful and well-tended gardens, there's a panoramic view of the sea. Along Corso Umberto I is **Piazza del Duomo**, with a baroque fountain and Norman-Gothic cathedral. The postcard-perfect local beach is **Isola Bella**, accessible by cable car (€2.70 return, 8am to 1am).

Mt Etna trips (€27) can be organised via **CST** (☎ 0942 62 60 88; Corso Umberto I 101).

Sleeping & Eating

Odyssey Youth Hostel B&B (☎ 0942 245 33; www .taorminaodyssey.it; Via G Martino 2; dm with breakfast €15.50) A 10-minute walk from town, this friendly place has very pleasant rooms and a nice terrace.

Pensione Svizzera (☎ 0942 237 90; svizzera@tao.it; Via Pirandello 26; s/d €70/90; ☼ Feb-Nov) Teetering on the edge of the cliff, this cheery *pensione* is convenient and comfortable; the views and breakfast served in a pretty garden terrace are bonuses.

Campeggio San Leo (☎ 0942 246 58; Via Nazionale; per adult/camp site per night €4.20/14.50) This barebones camping spot is accessible from the train station by the bus to Taormina – ask the driver to drop you off.

Granduca (☎ 0942 249 83; Corso Umberto 172; pizza from €5) Excellent pizza and a spectacular terrace make this a consistently good choice.

Arco Rosso (Via Naumachie 7) is a good spot for a stiff drink any time, as is newcomer

DiVino Wine Bar (Piazza Raggia 4) with local wines, terrific owners and nice plates of cheese.

There are *alimentari* throughout town and a **Standa supermarket** (Via Apollo Arcagetta 19) near Porta Catania.

Getting There & Away

Bus is the easiest way to get to and from Taormina. Interbus services leave for Messina (€2.50 one-way, 1½ hours, 12 daily) and Catania (€3.80, 1½ hours, hourly). Taormina is on the main train line between Messina and Catania.

ETNA

Dominating the landscape in eastern Sicily between Taormina and Catania, Mt Etna (3350m) is Europe's largest live volcano and one of the world's most active. Eruptions occur frequently, both from the four live craters at the summit and on the volcano's slopes, which are littered with fissures and extinct cones.

Recent activity has meant disruption to services and visitors should be aware that excursions are at the mercy of volcanic activity. Due to the volcano's unpredictability, you can no longer climb to the craters, although it is still possible to climb one of the peaks in front of the Rifugio Sapienza to get a small taste of the real thing. **Gruppo Guide Alpine Etna Sud** (☎ 095 791 47 55) or **Natura e Turismo** (☎ 095 33 35 43) organise excursions involving trekking and 4WD vehicles led by a vulcanologist or alpine guide.

Mt Etna is best approached from Catania by **AST bus** (☎ 095 746 10 96), departing from in front of the main train station at 8.30am, and leaving from Rifugio Sapienza at about 4.45pm (€4.65 return). The private **Ferrovia Circumetnea train line** (☎ 095 54 12 50; www .circumetnea.it) circles Mt Etna from Catania to Riposto, a 3½-hour trip. You can also reach Riposto from Taormina by train or bus.

Agora Hostel (☎ 095 723 30 10; agorahostel@hotmail .com; Piazza Curro 6; dm/d €15.50/40) is known for its live music, cheap eats and good bar; proximity to La Pescheria market is an added boon.

SYRACUSE

pop 126,000

Once rivalling Athens in power and prestige, Syracuse is a highlight of a visit to Sicily. Founded in 734 BC by Corinthian settlers, the city became a sultry and dominant Mediterranean power, prompting Athens to attack in 413 BC. Syracuse was the birthplace of Archimedes, Cicero frequented town and Plato attended the court of the tyrant Dionysius, who ruled from 405 to 367 BC.

The main sights are on the island of Ortygia and the archaeological park 2km across town. The **tourist office** (☎ 0931 48 12 00; www.apt-siracusa.it; Via San Sebastiano 45; ☼ 8.30am-1.30pm & 3.30-6.30pm) has English-speaking staff and a useful city map; there is also an **Ortigia Tourist Office** (☎ 0931 46 42 55; Via Maestranza 33; ☼ 8.30am-2pm & 2.30-5pm Mon-Fri, morning only Sat).

Sights

ORTYGIA

The island of Ortygia is the spiritual and physical heart of Syracuse. Despite eye-catching baroque palaces and churches, its Greek essence is everywhere. The **cathedral** was built in the 7th century on top of the Temple of Athena, incorporating most of the original columns in its three-aisled structure; the splendid **Piazza del Duomo** is lined with baroque palaces. Just down the winding street from the cathedral is the **Fontana Aretusa**, a natural freshwater spring. Greek legend has it that the goddess Artemis transformed her handmaiden Aretusa into the spring to protect her from the unwelcome attention of the river-god Alpheus. Undeterred, Alpheus turned himself into the river that feeds the spring.

NEAPOLIS-PARCO ARCHEOLOGICO

To get to this **archaeological zone** (☎ 0931 662 06; Viale Paradisa; admission €4.50; ☼ 9am-2hr before sunset), catch bus No 1 or 2 from Riva della Posta on Ortygia. The main attraction here is the sparkling white 5th-century BC **Greek theatre**, entirely hewn out of solid rock and gazing seaward over the city. Nearby is the **Orecchio di Dionisio**, an ear-shaped artificial grotto used by Dionysius to eavesdrop on his prisoners. The impressive 2nd-century **Roman amphitheatre** is well preserved.

The excellent **Museo Archeologico Paolo Orsi** (☎ 0931 46 40 22; admission €4.50; ☼ 9am-1pm Tue-Sat), about 500m east of the archaeological zone, contains Sicily's best-organised and most interesting archaeological collection.

Sleeping & Eating

B&B Casa Mia (☎ 0931 46 33 49; Corso Umberto 112; s/d €45/75) You'll feel at home in this comfy old mansion with a breakfast area designed for lingering.

Fontane Bianche (☎ 0931 79 03 33; Via dei Lidi 476; per adult/camp site €6/4.50; ☼ May–Sep) About 15km southwest of town, this camp site is near a beach that teems with active bars come summer; catch bus No 21 or 22 from Corso Umberto.

Ortygia has the best food and prices.

Trattoria Archimede (Via Gemellaro 8; mains from €8) Smart service and a changing menu with a seafood bent and excellent pastas.

Pizzeria Nonna Margherita (Via Cavour 12; pizza from €4) Casual and popular, with a wide range of pizzas.

Fermento (Via Crocifisso 44/46) This atmospheric wine bar has a nice buzz and good cheese as well as meat plates.

Pasticceria Tipica Catanese (Corso Umberto 46) The place for decadent Sicilian sweets.

Getting There & Away

Interbus (☎ 0931 667 10) services leave from Via Trieste for Catania, Palermo, Enna and surrounding towns. The service for Rome also leaves from here, connecting with the Rome bus at Catania. **AST** (☎ 0931 46 48 20) buses service the town and the surrounding area from Riva della Posta. Syracuse is easy to reach by train from Messina and Catania.

AGRIGENTO

pop 55,500

Founded around 582 BC, Agrigento is today a pleasant (if a little brutish) medieval town, but the Greek temples strewn in the valley below are the reason to visit. There's a so-so **tourist office** (☎ 0922 204 54; Via Cesare Battisti 15; ☼ 8.30am–1.30pm Mon–Fri). To get to the temples from the town, catch bus No 1, 2 or 3 from the train station.

Agrigento's **Valley of the Temples** (☎ 0922 261 91; admission €2, with museum €6; ☼ 8.30am–1hr before sunset) is one of the major Greek archaeological sights in the world. Despite its name, the five main Doric temples stand along a highly visible ridge. In varying states of ruin, the 5th-century BC temples offer a tantalising glimpse of one of the most luxurious cities in Magna Graecia. The only temple to survive relatively intact was **Tempio della Concordia**, transformed into a church. **Tempio di Giunone**, a short walk uphill to the east, has an impressive sacrificial altar. **Tempio di Ercole** is the oldest of the structures. Across the main

road that divides the valley is the imposing **Tempio di Giove**, which used to cover an area measuring 112m by 56m, with columns 18m high. *Telamoni*, colossal statues of men, were used in the structure, and the remains of one are in the **Museo Archeologico** (☎ 0922 40 15 65; admission €4.50, with temples €6; ☼ 9am–1.30pm & 2–7.30pm Tue–Sat, 9am–1.30pm Sun & Mon), just north of the temples on Via dei Templi. Nearby is **Tempio di Castore e Polluce**, partly reconstructed in the 19th century.

Bella Napoli (☎ 0922 204 35; Piazza Lena 6; s/d/tr €22/54/75) is a friendly hotel with clean, comfortable if unremarkable rooms; the owners also run **Antica Foresteria Catalana** (☎ 0922 204 35; s/d €45/75), next door, with newer rooms not necessarily worth the price jump.

La Corte degli Sfizzi (☎ 0922 59 55 20; Via Atenea 4; pizza from €5) is a popular, good-value pizzeria with a garden setting; just down the road is **Café Girasole**, a great little wine bar.

Intercity buses leave from Piazza Rosselli, off Piazza Vittorio Emanuele, for Palermo, Catania and surrounding towns.

SARDINIA (SARDEGNA)

The Mediterranean's second-largest island feels like a minicontinent all to itself. Sardinia was colonised by the Phoenicians and Romans, the Pisans and Genoese, and finally the Spaniards. Despite constant domination, the proud *Sardi* have retained a strong sense of identity, far removed from mainland influences. The striking landscape ranges from a wild interior pocked with gorges and valleys, to stunning stretches of unspoiled coastline. The gorgeous island gets overrun with sun-seekers in August.

Getting There & Away

Sardinia is accessible by ferry from Genoa, Livorno, Fiumicino, Civitavecchia, Naples, Palermo, Trapani, Bonifacio and Porto Vecchio (both Corsica) and Tunis. Departure points in Sardinia are Olbia, Golfo Aranci, Palau, Santa Teresa di Gallura and Porto Torres in the north, Arbatax on the east coast and Cagliari in the south.

The main company, **Tirrenia** (www.tirrenia .com) runs a service between Civitavecchia and Olbia, Arbatax or Cagliari, and between Genoa and Porto Torres, Olbia, Arbatax or Cagliari. There are fast ferries between

ITALY

Fiumicino and Golfo Aranci/Arbatax and Civitavecchia and Olbia (both summer only). The national railway, Ferrovie dello Stato (FS), also runs a service between Civitavecchia and Golfo Aranci. **Moby Lines** (www.mobylines.it) and **Sardinia Ferries** (www .sardiniaferries.com), also known as Elba and Corsica Ferries, both operate services from the mainland to Sardinia, as well as to Corsica and Elba. They depart from Genoa, Livorno, Civitavecchia and arrive at Olbia, Cagliari or Golfo Aranci. **Grandi Navi Veloci** (www.gnv.it) runs a service between Genoa and Olbia (June to September) or Porto Torres (year-round). Most Italian travel agencies have brochures on the different services.

Timetables change and prices fluctuate with the season. Prices for a *poltrona* on Tirrenia ferries in the 2004 high season were: Genoa to Porto Torres or Olbia (€46, 13 hours); Naples to Cagliari (€41, 16¼ hours); Palermo to Cagliari (€39, 13½ hours); Civitavecchia to Olbia (€25, eight hours); and Civitavecchia to Cagliari (€41, 14½ hours).

Getting Around

The two main bus companies are the state-run **ARST** (☎ 0800 86 50 42; www.arst.sardegna .it), with extensive service throughout the island, and the privately owned **PANI** (☎ 070 65 23 26), linking the main towns.

The main **Trenitalia** (www.trenitalia.it) train lines link Cagliari with Oristano, Sassari and Olbia, and are generally reliable but can be slow. The private railways that link smaller towns throughout the island can be *very* slow. However, the *Trenino Verde* (little green train), running a scenic route from Cagliari to Arbatax through the Barbagia, is a relaxing and lovely way to see part of the interior.

The best way to explore Sardinia properly is by road; for rental agencies, see opposite.

CAGLIARI

pop 176,000

Sardinia's capital and largest city is an attractive, friendly and cosmopolitan enclave, with a beautifully preserved medieval section, the delightful beach of Poetto, and salt lakes that are home to pink flamingos.

Orientation

If you arrive by bus, train or boat, you will find yourself near the port area, beside Piazza Matteotti, and a good tourist office.

The main street along the harbour is Via Roma, and the old city stretches up the hill behind it to the castle. The area around the marina, perfectly safe and pleasant, is good for accommodation and good *trattorias*.

Information

Guardia Medica (☎ 070 50 29 31) For medical emergencies.

Information office (☎ 070 66 92 55; Piazza Matteotti 9; ☺ Mon-Sat) Additional offices are at the airport and in the Stazione Marrittima.

Main post office (☎ 070 603 11; Piazza del Carmine 27; ☺ 8.15am-6.40pm Mon-Fri, 8.15am-1.20pm Sat)

Ospedale San Giovanni di Dio (☎ 070 66 32 37; Via Ospedale)

Police station (☎ 070 49 21 69; Via Amat 9) The main office is tucked behind the imposing law courts.

Web Travel Point (☎ 070 65 93 07; Via Maddalena 34; per 30min €2.60) Offers Internet service.

Sights

The **Museo Archeologico Nazionale** (☎ 070 68 40 00; Piazza Arsenale; admission €4; ☺ 9am-8pm Tue-Sun), in the Citadella dei Musei, has a fascinating collection of Nuraghic bronzes, objects found in stone constructions all over Sardinia.

It's enjoyable to wander through the medieval quarter. The Pisan-Romanesque **Duomo** (☎ 070 66 38 37; Piazza Palazzo) was built in the 13th century and has an interesting pulpit.

There are good views from **Bastione di San Remy** in Piazza Costituzione, in the town's centre.

The **Torre di San Pancrazio** (Piazza Indipendenza; ☺ 9am-5pm Tue-Sun) is also worth a look. The **Roman amphitheatre** (Viale Buon Cammino; ☺ 9am-5pm Tue-Sun) is considered the most important Roman monument in Sardinia. During summer, opera is performed here.

Sleeping

Hotel A&R Bundes Jack (☎ /fax 070 66 79 70; Via Roma 75; s/d €40/60, with bathroom €47/72) This choice spot has a warm welcome and spotless, high-ceilinged rooms.

Hotel Aurora (☎ 070 65 86 25; Salita Santa Chiara 19; s/d €27/42, with bathroom €39/52) Just off busy Piazza Yenne, this cheery place has nice enough rooms, some with views.

Eating & Drinking

Lillicu (☎ 070 65 29 70; Via Sardegna 78; mains from €9) An authentic *trattoria* that's often packed with happy locals downing good seafood dishes at large communal marble tables.

Trattoria GennarGentu (☎ 070 67 20 21; Via Sardegna 60; pasta from €8) At this welcoming spot, try the Sardinian specialities like *spaghetti bottarga* (with dried tuna roe).

Brasserie Vecchia Bruxelles (Via Sulcis 4) Impressive stone vaults and long comfy sofas make this an excellent stop for a beer, snack or nip of whisky.

Getting There & Away

Departing from Piazza Matteotti are **ARST buses** (☎ 070 409 83 24) servicing nearby towns, the Costa del Sud and the Costa Rei. **PANI buses** (☎ 070 65 23 26) leave from Stazione Marittima for towns including Sassari, Oristano and Nuoro. The main train station is also in Piazza Matteotti, with regular service to Oristano, Sassari, Porto Torres and Olbia. The private **Ferrovie della Sardegna** (FdS; ☎ 070 49 13 04) train station is in Piazza Repubblica.

Ferries arrive at the port adjacent to Via Roma. Bookings for **Tirrenia** (☎ 070 66 60 65) can be made at the Stazione Marittima in the port area.

For rental cars try **Hertz** (☎ 070 66 81 05; Piazza Matteotti 1); **Autonoleggio Cara** (☎ 070 66 34 71) can deliver a scooter or bike to your hotel.

CALA GONONE

postcode 08022 / pop 1010

This attractive seaside resort makes a good base for exploring the coves along the coastline, as well as the Nuraghic sites and rugged terrain inland. Major points are accessible by bus and boat, but you'll need a car to really explore.

The **tourist office** (☎ 0784 936 96; Viale Bue Marino 1a; ⏰ 9am-6pm Apr-Oct, 9am-11pm Jul & Aug) has maps, a list of hotels and plenty of local information. There is another **tourist office** (☎ 0784 962 43; Via Lamarmora 181; ⏰ 9am-1pm & 3.30-7pm Mon-Fri) in nearby Dorgali. Also in Dorgali, **Coop Ghivine** (☎ /fax 0784 967 21; www.ghivine.com; Via Montebello 5) organises excellent guided treks and farm stays from €30 per person.

Sights & Activities

From Cala Gonone's tiny port, catch a boat to the **Grotta del Bue Marino** (admission €5.50), where a guide will take you on a 1km walk to see vast caves with stalagmites and stalactites. Sardinia's last colony of monk seals once lived here but have not been

seen for some time. Boats also leave for **Cala Luna**, an isolated beach where you can walk along **Codula di Luna**, a fabulous gorge. The beach is packed with day-tripping tourists in summer. The boat trip to visit the grotto and beach costs around €20.

A **walking track** along the coast links Cala Fuili, about 3.5km south of Cala Gonone, and Cala Luna (about 1½ hours one-way). There's also some good mountain biking and diving in the area; ask at the tourist office for information on outfitters and rentals.

If you want to descend the impressive **Gorropu Gorge**, ask for information from the team of expert guides based in Urzulei – **Società Gorropu** (☎ 0782 64 92 82, 0347 775 27 06; francescomurru@virgilio.it) – which also offers a wide range of guided walks in the area. It is necessary to use ropes and harnesses to traverse the Gorropu Gorge.

Sleeping & Eating

Pop Hotel (☎ 0784 931 85; lfancel@box1.tin.it; s/d €59/93) Despite the ugly sign, this terracotta-hued hotel near the port has clean, pleasant rooms and a decent restaurant.

Camping Gala Gonone (☎ 0784 931 65; www .campingcalagonone.it; per person €16, 4-bed bungalows up to €135; ⏰ Apr-Oct; 🐾) Along the main road from Dorgali, this camp site has good-quality, shady sites, pool and restaurant, but gets overrun in August.

Getting There & Away

Catch a PANI bus to Nuoro from Cagliari, Sassari or Oristano and then take an ARST bus to Cala Gonone (via Dorgali). If you are travelling by car, you will need a proper road map of the area.

ALGHERO

pop 40,600

With a distinctive Spanish flair, this colourful resort town is on the west coast, known as the Coral Riviera. The town makes a good base for exploring the magnificent coastline to the south, and the famed Grotte di Nettuno on the Capocaccia to the north. The medieval centre, with its sea walls intact, is one of Sardinia's most charming towns. Visit in the off season to see it at its peaceful best.

Orientation & Information

The train station, on Via Don Minzoni, is about 1km north of town and is connected to the centre by a regular bus service. Intercity buses arrive in Via Catalogna, just outside the historic centre.

The exceedingly helpful **tourist office** (☎ 079 97 90 54; www.infoalghero.it; Piazza Porta Terra 9; ☺ 8am-8pm Mon-Sat) is near the port and just across the gardens from the bus station; the old city and most hotels and restaurants are just west of here.

Nearby is the **main post office** (Via Carducci 35). In an emergency, call the police on ☎ 113; for medical attention dial ☎ 079 98 71 61, or go to **Ospedale Civile** (☎ 079 99 62 33; Via Don Minzoni).

Sights & Activities

The narrow streets of the old city and around the port are lovely. The most striking church is the **Chiesa di San Francesco** (Via Carlo Alberto; ☺ 7.30am-noon & 5-8.30pm). Although constant changes have ruined the cathedral, the **bell tower** (admission €1.50; ☺ 7-9.30pm Jun-Sep) is still a fine example of Gothic-Catalan architecture.

Near Alghero at the beautiful **Capocaccia** are the **Grotte di Nettuno** (☎ 079 94 65 40; admission adult/child €8/4; ☺ 9am-7pm Apr-Sep, 10am-5pm Oct, 9am-2pm Nov-Mar), an underground fairyland accessible by boat (€10, not including grotto admission, 2½ hours, hourly 8am to 7pm June to September) from the port, or by the FdS bus from Via Catalogna (€3.25 return, 50 minutes, three daily trips June to September).

If with a car, don't miss the **Nuraghe di Palmavera** (☎ 079 95 32 00; admission €2.10; ☺ 9am-7pm), a ruined settlement 10km out of Alghero on the road to Porto Conte.

The coastline to Bosa is picturesque, with rugged cliffs and solitary beaches. If you want to rent a bicycle (from €9 a day) or motorcycle (from €70) to explore, try **Cicloexpress** (☎ 079 98 69 50; Via Garibaldi) at the port.

Festivals & Events

In summer Alghero stages a summer music festival in the cloisters of the church of San Francesco. A festival, complete with fireworks display, is held on 15 August for the Feast of the Assumption.

Sleeping & Eating

It is almost impossible to find a room in August unless you book ahead; other times are fine.

Ostello dei Giuliani (☎ /fax 079 93 03 53; ostello deigiuliani@ticalinet.it; Via Zara 1; dm incl breakfast €12)

This decent HI hostel serves meals (€8) and is located in Fertilia – take the hourly bus 'AF' from Via Catalogna to Fertilia.

Hotel San Francesco (☎ /fax 079 98 03 30; Via Ambrogio Machin 2; s/d €47/85; ℗) In the old town, this hotel housed in a former convent exudes charm; the rooms are simple but comfortable, and there's a cloistered courtyard shared with the church of the same name.

Camping La Mariposa (☎ 079 95 03 60; Via Lido 22; per adult/camp site €10.50/5, bungalows up to €72; ☺ Apr-Oct) About 2km north of the centre, this low-key camp site is on the beach.

Trattoria Maristella (☎ 079 97 81 72; Via Fratelli Kennedy 9; mains from €10) This popular spot, with Mediterranean-splashed décor, offers good value, reliable grub and alfresco dining.

For coffee, wine or snacks, head to **Caffe Costantino** (Piazza Civica 30) or **Focacce Sarde Ripiene** (Via Garibaldi 11).

Getting There & Away

Alghero is accessible from Sassari by train or bus. The main bus station is on Via Catalogna, next to the public park. **ARST** (☎ 079 95 01 79) buses leave for Sassari and Porto Torres. **FdS buses** (☎ 079 95 04 58) also service Sassari, Macomer and Bosa. **PANI buses** (☎ 079 23 69 83) serve Cagliari, Nuoro and Macomer from Sassari.

ITALY DIRECTORY

ACCOMMODATION

Hotels and *pensioni* make up the bulk of accommodation, with a growing range of B&Bs, hostels and *agriturismo* (farm stay) options. Prices fluctuate throughout the country, and depending on the season, with Easter, the summer and Christmas holidays being peak tourist times. During the low season, prices can be 20% cheaper. Tourist offices have listings for all local accommodation.

Agriturismo & B&Bs

Farm stays are increasingly popular, particularly in Tuscany and on the islands. For a countrywide directory, contact **Agriturist** (☎ 06 685 23 42; www.agriturist.it; Corso Vittorio Emanuele II 89, 00186 Rome).

Bed and breakfast options range from city *palazzi* (palaces) to seaside bungalows. Prices are typically between €70 and €150.

For information contact **Bed & Breakfast Italia** (☎ 06 687 86 18; www.bbitalia.it; Palazzo Sforza Cesarini, Corso Vittorio Emanuele II 282, 00186 Rome).

Camping

Most camp sites in Italy have a swimming pool, tennis court and restaurant, and are graded according to a star system. Prices range from €4 to €10 per person and €5 to €12 or more for a site. Lists of sites are available from local tourist offices or through **Touring Club Italiano** (TCI; www.touringclub.it).

Hostels

Hostels in Italy are called *ostelli per la gioventú* and are run by the Associazione Italiana Alberghi per la Gioventú (AIG; Italian Youth Hostels Association), affiliated with Hostelling International (HI; www.iyhf .org). A valid HI card is required, which you can get in your home country, at the youth hostel in Rome, from CTS offices and from AIG offices throughout Italy. The national head office of **AIG** (☎ 06 487 11 52; www.ostellion line.org; Via Cavour 44, Rome; ☼ 9am-5pm Mon-Fri) has a booklet detailing all Italian hostels.

Accommodation is in segregated dormitories, although some hostels offer higher-priced doubles. Nightly rates, often including breakfast, range from €10 to €20. Lockout times are usually from 9am to 5pm. Check-in is 6pm to 10.30pm, and curfew is around midnight.

Hotels & Pensioni

There is often little difference between a *pensione* and an *albergo*. However, the former will generally be of one- to three-star quality, while the latter can be awarded up to five stars. *Locande* (inns) and *affittacamere* (rooms for rent) are cheaper and not included in the star classification system, although the standard can be very high (particularly in the Aeolian Islands and the Alps).

Always check on prices before committing to stay in a place. Proprietors have been known to pad bills, so make a complaint to the local tourist office if you believe you've been overcharged.

Prices are higher in northern Italy and in major tourist destinations. Rates soar in the high season. A *camera singola* (single room) costs from €40; a double room with *camera doppie* (twin beds) or *camera matrimoniale* (double bed) will cost from €55.

Mountain Refuges

Before trekking in the Alps, Apennines or other mountains in Italy, obtain information about Italy's wonderful network of *rifugi* (refuges) from local tourist offices. Refuges are generally open from July to September, and dorm-style accommodation prevails, though some larger ones have double rooms. The price per person for an overnight stay with breakfast is around €20, with dinner another €15.

The locations of *rifugi* are marked on good trekking maps. **Club Alpino Italiano** (CAI; www.cai.it in Italian) owns and runs many of the refuges. CAI offers discounts to members of associated foreign alpine clubs.

ACTIVITIES
Cycling

Cycling is an excellent way to see Italy's gorgeous countryside. Classic areas include Tuscany and Umbria. Lonely Planet's *Cycling in Italy* is a terrific reference with detailed itineraries.

There is good mountain biking in Sardinia, Sicily and around Maratea. Tourist offices offer information on trails, guided rides and rentals.

Skiing

The numerous excellent ski resorts in the Alps and the Apennines offer dramatic scenery and usually good conditions from December to April.

Trekking & Walking

Italy is a walker's paradise with thousands of kilometres of *sentieri* (marked trails). The **CAI** (www.cai.it in Italian) is a useful resource. There are plenty of organised trekking trips, but solo trekkers will find easy-to-follow trails and refuges; the magnificent Dolomites are the most popular area. On Sardinia, head for the coastal gorges between Dorgali and Baunei, and on Sicily for Mt Etna. Coastal walkers will enjoy Liguria and the Amalfi Coast. Check out Lonely Planet's *Walking in Italy* for detailed descriptions of more than 50 walks.

BUSINESS HOURS

Hours can vary, but generally businesses are open 9am to 1pm and 3.30pm to 7.30pm Monday to Saturday, with some also open on Sunday morning. They may close on Saturday afternoon and on Thursday or

718 ITALY DIRECTORY •• Customs

Monday afternoon. Banks tend to open 8.30am to 1.30pm and from 3.30pm to 4.30pm Monday to Friday. Major post offices open 8.30am to 6pm Monday to Friday, and until 1pm on Saturday. Most museums are now opening from 9.30am to 7pm, later in summer; many close on Monday.

CUSTOMS

There is no limit on the amount of euros brought into the country, and duty-free sales within the EU no longer exist. Travellers coming from outside the EU can import, duty-free: 200 cigarettes, 1L of spirits, 2L of wine and other goods up to a total value of €175.

EMBASSIES & CONSULATES

For visa requirements, see opposite.

Embassies & Consulates in Italy

The headquarters of most foreign embassies are in Rome, although there are generally British and US consulates in other major cities. Following are the embassies in Rome:

Australia (☎ 06 85 27 21; Via Alessandria 215, 00198)
Canada (☎ 06 44 59 81; Via G B de Rossi 27, 00161)
France embassy (Map pp656-7; ☎ 06 68 60 11; Piazza Farnese 67, 00186) consulate (Map pp686-7; ☎ 055 230 25 56; Piazza Ognissanti 2)
Germany (Map p654; ☎ 06 49 21 31; Via San Martino della Battaglia 4, 00185)
New Zealand (☎ 06 441 71 71; Via Zara 28, 00198)
UK embassy (Map pp648-9; ☎ 06 422 00 001; Via XX Settembre 80a, 00187) consulate (Map p689; ☎ 055 28 41 33; Lungarno Corsini 2)
USA (Map pp650-1; ☎ 06 467 41; www.usis.it; Via Vittorio Veneto 119a, 00187)

For a complete list of embassies in Rome and other major Italian cities, look in the local telephone book under *ambasciate* or *consolati*, or ask for a list at the tourist office.

Italian Embassies & Consulates Abroad

Italian diplomatic missions abroad include:
Australia Canberra (☎ 02-6273 3333; www.ambitalia .org.au; 12 Grey St, Deakin ACT 2600) Melbourne (☎ 03-9867 5744; itconmel@netlink.com.au; 509 St Kilda Rd, Vic 3004) Sydney (☎ 02-9392 7900; itconsyd@armadillo.com .au; Level 43, The Gateway, 1 Macquarie Place, NSW 2000)
Canada Ottawa (☎ 613-232 2401; www.italyincanada .com; 21st fl, 275 Slater St, Ontario, K1P 5H9) Vancouver (☎ 604-684 7288; consolato@italianconsulate.bc.ca; Standard Bldg 1100-510 West Hastings St, BC V6B IL8)

Toronto (☎ 416-977 1566; consolato.it@toronto .italconsulate.org; 136 Beverley St, Ontario M5T 1Y5)
Montreal (☎ 514-849 8351; cgi@italconsul.montreal.qc.ca; 3489 Drummond St, Quebec H3G 1X6)
France Paris (☎ 01 49 54 03 00; ambasciata@amb -italie.fr; 7 rue de Varenne 75007) 5 Blvd Emile Augier 75116 (☎ 01 44 30 47 00; italconsulparigi@mailcity.com)
New Zealand Wellington (☎ 04-473 5339; www.italy -embassy.org.nz; 34 Grant Rd, Thorndon)
UK London (☎ 020-7312 2200; www.embitaly.org.uk; 14 Three Kings Yard, W1Y 4EH) Eaton Place (☎ 020-7235 9371; 38 Eaton Place, SW1X 8AN)
USA Washington (☎ 202-328 5500; www.italyemb.org; 1601 Fuller St, NW Washington, DC 20009) New York (☎ 212-737 9100; www.italconsulnyc.org; 690 Park Ave, 10021) Los Angeles (☎ 310-820 0727; www.conlang.com; Suite 300, 12400 Wilshire Blvd, 90025)

FESTIVALS & EVENTS

Italy's calendar teems with cultural events ranging from colourful traditional celebrations, with a religious and/or historical flavour, to festivals of the performing arts, including opera, music and theatre. Annual events worth catching include:

Carnevale During the 10 days before Ash Wednesday, many towns stage carnivals. Venice's is the best known, but there are others, including at Viareggio in Tuscany and Ivrea near Turin.

Holy Week There are important festivals during the week before Easter countrywide; of note are Sicily's colourful and sombre traditional festivals, and Assisi's rituals, attracting thousands of pilgrims.

Scoppio del Carro Literally 'Explosion of the Cart', this event held in Florence on Easter Sunday features the explosion of a cart full of fireworks and dates back to the Crusades. If all goes well, it is seen as a good omen for the city.

Corso dei Ceri One of Italy's strangest festivals is held in Gubbio on 15 May and features a race run by men carrying enormous wooden constructions called *ceri*, in honour of the town's patron saint, Sant'Ubaldo.

Il Palio On 2 July and 16 August, Siena stages this extraordinary horse race in the town's main piazza.

Natale (Christmas) During the weeks preceding Christmas, there are numerous processions and religious events. Many churches set up elaborate cribs or nativity scenes – Naples is famous for these.

HOLIDAYS

Epiphany 6 January
Easter Monday March or April
Liberation Day 25 April
Feast of St Mark Venice only; 25 April
Labour Day 1 May

Feast of St John the Baptist Florence, Genoa and Turin; 24 June
Feast of St Peter & St Paul Rome; 29 June
Feast of St Rosalia Palermo only; 15 July
Ferragosto (Feast of the Assumption) 15 August
Feast of St Januarius Naples only; 19 September
All Saints' Day 1 November
Feast of St Ambrose Milan only; 7 December
Feast of the Immaculate Conception 8 December
Christmas Day 25 December
Feast of St Stephen 26 December

MONEY

Italy's currency since 2002 is the euro. There is little advantage in bringing foreign cash into Italy. A combination of travellers cheques and credit cards is the best way to take your money. If you buy travellers cheques in euro there should be no commission charged for cashing them. There are exchange offices at all major airports and train stations.

Major credit cards, including Visa, Master-Card and American Express, are widely accepted. They can also be used to get money from ATMs or, if you don't have a PIN, over the counter in major banks.

Bargaining & Tipping

You are not expected to tip in restaurants, but it is common to leave around 10% if you'd like to show your appreciation. In bars leave small change. Bargaining is common in flea markets, but not in shops.

POST

Italy's postal system is notoriously unreliable. The most efficient service to use is *posta prioritaria* (priority mail). Registered mail is known as *raccomandato,* insured mail as *assicurato* and express post as *postacelere.* *Francobolli* (stamps) are available at post offices and *tabacchi* (tobacconists). Information about postal services and rates can be obtained on ☎ 800 22 26 66 or at www .poste.it (Italian only).

TELEPHONE

Italy's country code is ☎ 39. Area codes are an integral part of the telephone number, even if you're dialling a local number.

Italy's rates, particularly long-distance, are among the highest in Europe. Most public phones accept only *carte/schede telefoniche* (phonecards), sold at tobacconists and news-stands. Off-peak hours for domestic calls are from 10pm to 8am, and for international calls from 11pm to 8am and Sunday.

To make a reverse-charge (collect) inter-national call from a public phone, dial ☎ 170. For European countries call ☎ 15. All operators speak English. For international directory inquiries call ☎ 176.

Mobile Phones

Italy has one of the highest levels of mobile phone penetration in Europe, and there are several companies, including Telecom Italia Mobile, through which you can get a temporary or prepaid account if you already own a GSM, dual- or tri-band cellular phone. You will usually need your passport to open an account.

VISAS

EU citizens with a national identity card or passport can stay in Italy for as long as they like. Citizens of many other countries including the USA, Australia, Canada and New Zealand don't need visas if they are entering as tourists. Visitors are technically obliged to report to a police station if they plan to stay at the same address for more than one week. Tourists staying in hotels or hostels are not required to do this since proprietors register guests with the police.

A *permesso di soggiorno* is necessary (for non-EU citizens) if you plan to study, work (legally) or live in Italy. Non-EU citizens who want to study at a university or language school in Italy must have a study visa.

Latvia

HIGHLIGHTS

- **Rīga** Check out the cobbled medieval streets and Art Nouveau flourishes and watch the sun rise over the skyline of spires and turrets atop Bastion Hill (p728)
- **Jūrmala** Chill out, sunbathe or hike westwards on deserted beaches (p730)
- **Sigulda** Get your adrenalin pumping by bungee jumping off a cable car, bobsleighing or skiing in this exquisite landscape (p730)
- **Best journey** Taste freshly caught fish, breathe in the fresh air and get off the beaten track en route from Rīga to windswept, solitary Cape Kolka (p732)
- **Off-the-beaten track** Go wolf-spotting or bog walking in Ķemeri National Park (p730) or hike through unspoilt country in Gauja National Park (p730)

FAST FACTS

- **Area** 64,600 sq km (twice the size of Belgium)
- **ATMs** Springing up like mushrooms in towns and cities, take cash for rural zones
- **Budget** 20-25Ls per day
- **Capital** Rīga
- **Country code** ☎ 371
- **Famous for** Winning the Eurovision Song Contest 2002
- **Head of State** President Vaira Vike-Freiberga
- **Languages** Latvian, Russian, English
- **Money** Latvian Lat (A$1 = 0.39Ls, CA$1 = 0.42Ls, €1 = 0.67Ls, ¥100 = 0.49, NZ$1 = 0.37Ls, UK£1 = 0.96Ls, US$1 = 0.53Ls)
- **Population** 2.4 million

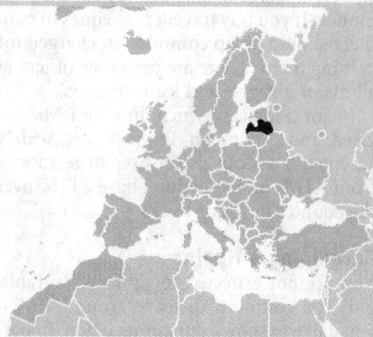

- **Time** GMT/UTC + 2
- **Visas** None required for up to 90 days for EU countries, Australian and New Zealand citizens.

TRAVEL HINTS

Look out for shops and bakeries selling Pelmeņi, Latvia's answer to fast food in the form of very cheap, very filling dumplings (0.6Ls each). Buy fresh food from markets as it's cheaper still.

ROAMING LATVIA

Gaze at Rīga's Art Nouveau, hang out on Jūrmala beach, then canoe down the Gauja River near Sigulda for a perfect Latvian week.

There's no need to sex-up this Baltic beauty. Latvia (Latvija) has a magical charm guaranteed to lure any unwary backpacker into its clutches.

You'll want to head straight to Rīga which combines the elegant charm of its Art Nouveau architecture with a raucous bar and club life that pulls in young, lively crowds year-round. Then chill out on crystal clean beaches with ice blue seas and white sands, or experience the stunning wilderness of Gauja National Park.

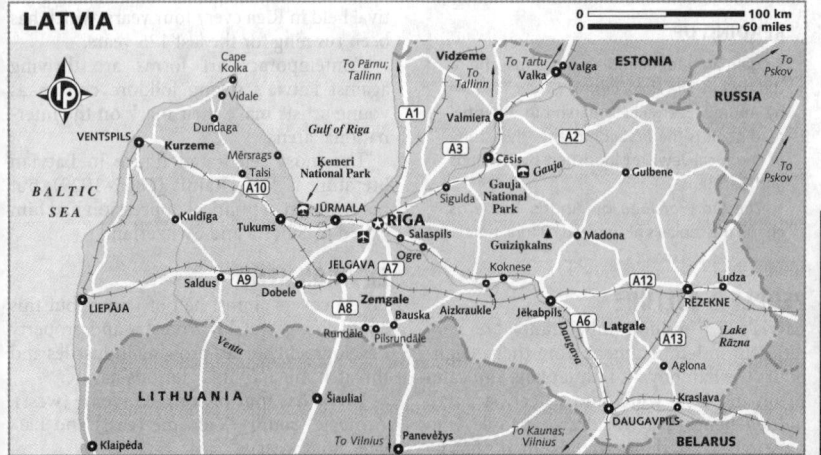

Despite this newfound popularity, Latvia has the strange, undiscovered feel of a land on the brink of fame and fortune. It's one of those places where you'll still feel like you're an explorer, especially off the beaten track on the western coastline and eastern reaches.

This tiny, vibrant nation grew out of the intense suffering of its people under the occupations of the Soviets and Nazis. You'll never believe it shed its Russian stranglehold less than two decades ago as it has a serenity and charm rarely found elsewhere in Europe.

Go before everybody else does and see Latvia's treasures for yourself.

HISTORY

The history of Latvia is best described as a troubled whirlwind of fierce struggle and downright rebellion.

The Latvians descended from tribes that settled on the Baltic coast in 2000 BC. They carried on their pagan shenanigans until 1190 when the first Christian missionaries tried to convert them – only for the Livs (inhabitants of Livonia, as Latvia was then known) to jump into the nearest river to wash off their baptism.

Twenty years later the German Knights of the Sword charged in and conquered Latvia; they dominated for another 700 years.

Latvia was conquered by Poland in 1561 and Catholicism was firmly rooted. Sweden colonised Latvia in 1629 and occupied the country until the Great Northern War (1700–21), after which it became part of Russia.

Soviet occupation began in 1939 with the Molotov-Ribbentrop Pact, nationalisation, mass killings and about 35,000 deportations. Latvia was then occupied by Nazi Germany from 1941 to 1945, when an estimated 175,000 Latvians were killed or deported, before being reclaimed by the Soviets.

The first public protest was on 14 June 1987 when 5000 people rallied at Rīga's Freedom Monument to commemorate the 1941 Siberia deportations. On 23 August 1989 two million Latvians, Lithanians and Estonians formed a 650km human chain from Vilnius, through Rīga, to Tallinn, to mark the 50th anniversary of the Molotov-Ribbentrop Pact.

The Latvian Popular Front won a big majority in the March 1990 elections but Russia barged back in on 20 January 1991. Soviet troops stormed the Interior Ministry building in Rīga, killing four people.

Latvia declared full independence on 21 August 1991 and the first democratic elections were held in June 1993.

Rīga celebrated its 800th birthday in 2001, the same year the Dalai Lama visited. The commercial development enveloping the historic centre prompted a warning from Unesco that the city could lose its World Heritage status – bestowed in 1997.

On 1 May 2004 the EU opened its doors to 10 new members, including Latvia, amid huge expectations of securing of its border with Russia and better times to come.

READING UP

To gain an understanding of the psyche of the nation *The Holocaust in Latvia 1941-44* by Andrew Ezergailis is harsh but essential reading. It is the first comprehensive study of the local Jewish bloodshed by Latvians and Germans.

The Story of Rīga by Andris Kolbergs charts the capital's history and cultural trends.

PEOPLE & CULTURE

Latvia's 2.3 million inhabitants are very different in temperament from their neighbours the flamboyant Lithuanians and calm Estonians. Here you'll find a steely strength hidden beneath a withdrawn people who have to be coaxed into friendship. It's hardly surprising, considering their history of oppression – and the fact that Latvians are still a minority group in each of their main cities.

In Latvia only 58% are ethnic Latvians; Russians account for 30% of the populace, and minority groups include Belarusians (4%), Ukrainians (2.5%), Poles (2.5%) and a tiny Jewish population.

Many Latvians live in expat communities around the world – up to as many as 200,000 are living in the US, Australia, Canada and Britain.

Latvians generally adore nature – their traditions and customs reach back to their pagan past. In many rural households it's counted as lucky to have a green snake (nonvenomous grass snake) living in the home. To impress a Latvian, it's always wise to present them with an odd number of flowers (even numbers are for funerals).

RELIGION

More than 60% of Latvians are Lutheran, but that's no barrier to the wealth of denominations in this tolerant nation. Around 30% of the population is Russian Orthodox and there is quite a significant Roman Catholic minority.

ARTS

The traditional importance of song as Latvia's greatest art form is shown in the 1.4 million *dainas* (folk songs), identified and collected by Krišjānis Barons (1835–1923). In tribute to its rich oral history Latvia has a song fes-

tival held in Rīga every four years, which has been running for the last 125 years.

Contemporary art forms are thriving against Latvia's strong folklore culture as young artists make their mark on the international arena.

The most celebrated figure in Latvian literature is Jānis Rainis (1865–1929), but his criticism of political oppression had him exiled to Siberia and Switzerland.

ENVIRONMENT

Forest covers almost half of Latvia, but this could change quickly. Forestry and property development are fast growing industries and threaten much of this glorious nature.

Latvia has four regions: Kurzeme (west), Zemgale (south), Vidzeme (east) and Latgale (southeast).

Creatures such as wild boar, wolves and deer roam the woodlands of Latvia along with one of the world's rarest bovine species, the Latvian Blue Cow. Legend has it that a mermaid brought these cows from the sea. Always remember we are the odd ones out so never feed any animals you meet and respect their environment by not leaving rubbish of any sort. Hunting is strictly forbidden.

More than a million hectares of land, forest and lakes are protected national parks, including **Slītere** (www.slitere.gov.lv), **Ķemeri** (www.kemeri.vdc.lv), **Gauja** (www.gnp.lv in Latvian) and the **North Vidzeme Biosphere Reserve** (www.biosfera.lv). Protecting these lands is vital so only camp in designated areas.

TRANSPORT

GETTING THERE & AWAY
Air

Rīga Airport (☎ 720 7009; www.riga-airport.com) is served by direct flights from Amsterdam, Berlin, Brussels, Copenhagen, Frankfurt, Helsinki, Kyiv, London Heathrow, Moscow, Prague, Stockholm, Tallinn, Vilnius and Warsaw.

There are several carriers at the airport:
AirBaltic (☎ 720 7777; www.airbaltic.lv; ⊙ 5am-8pm Mon-Thu, 5am-7pm Fri, 5am-6.30pm Sat, 5am-9pm Sun) National carrier that now does cheap no-frills deals.
British Airways (☎ 720 7097; www.britishairways.com; ⊙ 9am-5pm Mon-Fri, 9am-1pm Sat & Sun)
Lufthansa (☎ 750 7711; www.lufthansa.com; ⊙ 9am-6pm Mon-Fri, 11am-3pm Sat & Sun)

Boat

Ferries depart from the **Passenger Terminal** (☎ 720 5460; Eksporta iela 1), 1.5km downstream of Akmens Bridge in Rīga. Tickets for Rīga–Stockholm trips can be bought at travel agents, and prices start as low as 20Ls for a single.

Bus

Rīga's **Bus Station** (☎ 900 0009; Prāgas iela 1; ☾ 5am–midnight) has the international bus companies, **Eurolines** (☎ 721 4080; www.eurolines.lv; ☾ 8am–11pm) and **Ecolines** (☎ 721 4512; www.ecolines.lv; ☾ 7am-9.30pm).

Eurolines has daily services to Vilnius (7Ls, four daily), Moscow (12Ls), Hamburg (50Ls), Tallinn (8.50Ls, five daily), St Petersburg (11Ls) and Berlin (44Ls). Ecolines has daily buses to Kyiv (24Ls), Odessa (31Ls), Paris (69Ls), Amsterdam (59Ls), London (77Ls), Oslo (25Ls) and Kristianstade (17Ls).

International buses leave from platforms 1, 1a and 2.

Car & Motorcycle

Insurance is compulsory and can be purchased at the border points.

Train

Rīga's **Central Station** (Centrālā Stacija; ☎ 583 2134; Stacijas Laukams) has international ticket booth 1-6 for trains to/from Latvia.

International services include Moscow (Latvijas Ekspresis, seat/couchette/first class 24/38/45Ls, 17½ hours, two daily) and St Petersburg (Baltija, seat/couchette/first class 21/33/48Ls, 14 hours, daily).

Vilnius can only be reached by bus.

GETTING AROUND

Air

There are no internal flights in Latvia.

Bicycle

Cyclists can get advice from the **Latvian Bicycle Tourism Information Centre** (www.velokurjers.lv). Latvia is nice and flat so cycling is easy, but roads in rural areas leave much to be desired so take all necessary repair equipment.

Bus

The best way to get around Latvia is by bus, as it's quicker and cheaper. See p729 for information about services to/from Rīga.

Car & Motorcycle

Driving across Latvia can be a surreal experience – an hour can pass and the only traffic you'll see will be a horse and cart or dishevelled tractor.

The A2 Sigulda road, A6 Ogre road, A8 Jelgava and A10 Jūrmala routes are Western standard highways, but expect potholes, gravel roads and ancient traffic on rural routes. Your home driving licence is normally acceptable with car hire firms and at the borders. Driving is on the right side of the road, and speed limits are generally 50km/hr within towns and between 70km/hr and 110km/hr on highways. Keep strictly to speed limits as police can fine between 5Ls and 50Ls on the spot. Headlights must be on at all times while driving. Using a mobile when driving is illegal. There's zero tolerance on drinking and driving (and a hefty fine of 450Ls if caught).

There are an abundance of garages for fuel, parts and repairs in Latvia and surrounding Baltic countries. Cars can be hired but daily costs can be as much as 100Ls.

Hitching

Lone women: don't even think about it. However, in rural areas hitching may be the only bet due to sporadic public transport, so keep to daylight hours and travel in pairs.

Local Transport

Trams, buses and trolleybuses (buses run by electricity from overhead wires) provide public transport around towns and cities, from 5.30am to midnight. Tickets cost a flat rate of 0.20Ls and must be punched in a machine on board the tram, bus or trolleybus. Check all this on the Tram & Trolleybus authority's website (www.ttp.lv).

Taxis officially cost 0.30Ls per kilometre in the daytime and 0.4Ls after 10pm. Expect to have to haggle your fare as you're a tourist and these tariffs may be deemed an irrelevance to some local cabbies – you're rich right?

Train

Timetables are posted on the Internet by **Latvian Railways** (www.ldz.lv). Local trains are generally dirty, not known for their safety and basic in the extreme. Sole women travellers may prefer to travel by a different method.

LATVIA

RĪGA

pop 790,000

Intriguing Rīga will blow you away – it's a real-life medieval city with a stunning Art Nouveau heritage, and extremely funky bars and music scene set against a skyline of steeples and turrets.

OK, so the stag-night crew might be noticing this gem, but there's good reason. You won't want to leave once you're settled into candle-lit bars after getting lost in winding, sun-dappled or snow-covered cobbled streets.

The Old Town may be a Unesco World Heritage Site but this fairytale city, once dubbed the 'Paris of the East', is also a major metropolis. It's careering into the 21st century with a queue of eager backers pouring much-needed money into its infrastructure. So much so that Unesco has warned Rīga that it may withdraw its special protected status due to the number of glittering glass hotels and business centres springing up like mushrooms after rain.

Lavish beauty, timeless elegance and a restless fusion of old and new has created a potent charm – you have been warned!

ORIENTATION

The Daugava River arches through Rīga. On the eastern bank is Old Rīga (Vecrīga), the city's historic heart with a skyline dominated by three steeples: St Peter's, Dome Cathedral and St Jacob's.

INFORMATION

Bookshops

Jāna sēta (☎ 724 0892; Elizabetes iela 83-85; ☼ 10am-7pm Mon-Fri, 11am-5pm Sat) Superb collection of travel titles and maps including Lonely Planet guides to the region and the world!

Globuss (☎ 722 6957; Vaļņu iela 26; ☼ 8am-10pm) Get your mag fix with international titles downstairs and a small but excellent range of English language novels upstairs.

EMERGENCY NUMBERS

- Ambulance ☎ 03
- Fire ☎ 01
- Police ☎ 02

GETTING INTO TOWN

The train and bus stations are five minutes' walk apart on the southeastern edge of Old Rīga. It's a short 10-minute walk northwest to Rātslaukams. The ferry terminal is 1.5km north of Akmens Bridge in Old Rīga and the airport is 8km west of the city; bus No 22 runs to the central train station from the airport.

Discount Card

Rīga Card (8/12/16Ls for 24/48/72hr, half price for under-16s) Free sightseeing tour of the city, free rides on trolleybuses and trams and free entry to some museums. Available at the City of Rīga Information Centre (below).

Internet Access

Dualnet (☎ 781 4440; Peldu iela 17; per hr 1Ls; ☼ 24hr) Have a beer and settle back to read your emails, day or night.

Internet Kafe (☎ 722 0030; Vaļņu iela 41; per hr 0.45Ls; ☼ 24hr) Rīga's cheapest option for surf lovers.

Left Luggage

Baggage store (luggage 1Ls; ☼ 5.30am-11pm) In the bus station.

Left-luggage room (luggage 1Ls; ☼ 4.30am-midnight) In the basement of the train station.

Medical Services

ARS Clinic (☎ 720 1001/3; Skolas iela 5; ☼ 24hr) English-speaking service and an **emergency home service** (☎ 720 10 03).

Vecpilsētas aptieka (☎ 721 3340; Audēju iela 20; ☼ 24hr) Excellent pharmacy.

Money

Chequepoint Exchange (☎ 722 1219; Kaļķu iela 28; ☼ 8am-10pm)

Parex Banka (☎ 701 0873; Smilšu iela 3; ☼ 9am-8.30pm Mon-Fri) Offers currency exchange, ATM and money transfer.

Unibanka (☎ 721 5502; Pils iela 23; ☼ 9am-5pm Mon-Fri) Offers currency exchange, ATM and money transfer.

Post

Central Post Office (☎ 701 8804; Stacijas laukams 1; ☼ 8am-8pm Mon-Fri, 8am-6pm Sat, 8am-4pm Sun) Located by the train station.

Tourist Information

City of Rīga Information Centre Rātslaukams (☎ 704 4377; Rātslaukams 6; www.rigatourism.com; ☼ 10am-7pm); Main Bus Station (☎ 722 0555; ☼ 10am-6pm) Books tours and offers free city maps and info on regional tourism inside the House of Blackheads. English-speaking staff.

Riga Sightseeing (☎ 727 1915; adult/child 9/5Ls) Daily walking, bus and boat tours of Rīga. Can be booked at the information centre.

Travel Agencies

Latvia Worldwide (☎ 732 6006; Torņu iela 4; ◷ 9am-7pm Mon-Fri) Excellent service and friendly multilingual staff.

Student & Youth Travel Bureau (SJCB; ☎ 728 4818; sjcb@sjcb.lv; Lāčplēša iela 29; ◷ 9am-5pm Mon-Fri)

SIGHTS & ACTIVITIES

The World Heritage-listed Old Town is a joyous cacophony of 17th-century architecture, crumbling streets and church spires, ideal for Rīga's main activity – strolling.

Start at the **Dome Cathedral** (☎ 721 3498; admission 0.5Ls; ◷ 1-5pm Tue-Fri, 10am-2pm Sat, closed Sun & Mon). It's the largest church in the Baltics, boasts the world's fourth largest organ (1880) and is the heart of the city, with concerts held inside its majestic belly (see the cathedral board for details). The foundations were laid in 1211.

The **Museum of the History of Rīga & Navigation** (☎ 735 6676; admission 1Ls; ◷ 11am-5pm Wed-Sun) is in a cloister next to the cathedral. There's a mummified hand of a criminal on display and the 16th-century executioner's sword. Allow a good hour to wander round.

It's a short walk east to Rīga's skyline centrepiece; **St Peter's** (☎ 722 9426; Skārņu iela 19; tower admission 1.5Ls; ◷ 10am-5pm, closed Mon). Take the lift up to the excellent viewing tower 72m skyward (the spire reaches 123.3m). The church was built in 1209 and the wooden tower was destroyed several times by fire.

The church overlooks the **House of Blackheads** (☎ 704 4300; Rātslaukams 7; admission 1Ls; ◷ 10am-5pm, closed Mon), Rīga's architectural gem. Built in 1344 for the Blackheads' guild of unmarried merchants, it was damaged in 1941, flattened by the Soviets seven years later and rebuilt from scratch in 2000.

The **town hall** opposite was also raised from the ashes in 2002. A statue of Rīga's patron saint **St Roland** (Rātslaukams) stands in the town hall square between the two buildings. He's a replica of the original, erected in 1897, but moved to St Peter's during WWII for protection.

Both the Soviet and Nazi occupations of Latvia are chronicled in the chilling yet spirited **Museum of the Occupation of Latvia** (☎ 721 2715; www.occupationmuseum.lv; Strēlnieku Laukams 1; admission free; ◷ 11am-5pm, closed Mon). An anonymous inscription inside reads: 'They took it all – our native land, our honour and our name. They punished us for being human beings'. Allow two hours to absorb the detail.

The 14th-century **Great Guild** (Amatu iela 5) and **Small Guild** (Amatu iela 6) were once the seat of wealthy German power brokers, and now house the Philharmonic Orchestra. Snoop around or pay 0.5Ls to see the exquisite stained glass windows.

Show off some nifty Torville and Dean moves on the city's **outdoor ice rink** (Līvu laukams; admission 1Ls; ◷ 11am-midnight Mon-Thu, 11-1am Fri, 10-1am Sat, 10am-midnight Sun in winter), overlooked by the Small Guild.

To the north is the 14th-century **Powder Tower** (Torņa iela), which has nine Russian cannonballs still embedded in its walls. From here go under the **Swedish Gate** (cnr Torņa & Aldaru ielas), which was built into the city walls in 1698 to celebrate Swedish occupation.

Along Mazā Pils iela are Rīga's oldest stone houses, Nos 17, 19 and 21, which have been dubbed the **Three Brothers**. Nearby is Latvia's **Parliament** (Saeima; Jēkaba iela 11). Medieval **Rīga Castle** (Pils laukams 3), built in 1330, now houses the president and a dusty museum of foreign art.

Dividing the old and new towns is the **Freedom Monument** (Brīvības bulvāris), topped by a bronze statue of Liberty (affectionately known to locals as Milda) holding three stars, representing the historic regions of Kurzeme, Latgale and Vidzeme. During the Soviet years placing flowers at Milda's base was a crime for which people were deported to Siberia. The **Laima Clock** stands

LATVIA

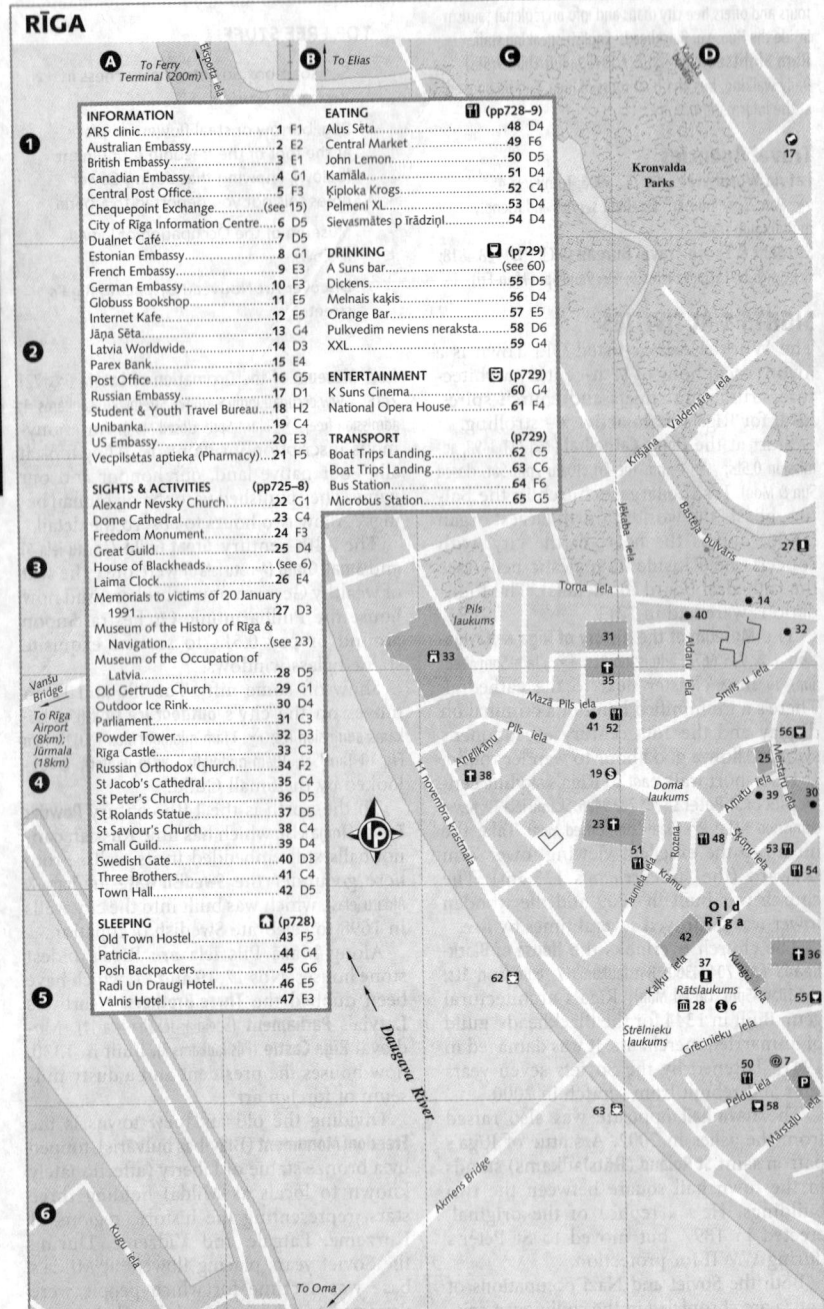

RĪGA

A To Ferry Terminal (200m) **B** To Elias **C** **D**

INFORMATION
ARS clinic	1 F1
Australian Embassy	2 E2
British Embassy	3 E1
Canadian Embassy	4 G1
Central Post Office	5 F3
Chequepoint Exchange	(see 15)
City of Rīga Information Centre	6 D5
Dualnet Café	7 D5
Estonian Embassy	8 G1
French Embassy	9 E3
German Embassy	10 F3
Globuss Bookshop	11 E5
Internet Kafe	12 E5
Jāņa Sēta	13 G4
Latvia Worldwide	14 D3
Parex Bank	15 E4
Post Office	16 G5
Russian Embassy	17 D1
Student & Youth Travel Bureau	18 H2
Unibanka	19 C4
US Embassy	20 E3
Vecpilsētas aptieka (Pharmacy)	21 F5

SIGHTS & ACTIVITIES (pp725–8)
Alexandr Nevsky Church	22 G1
Dome Cathedral	23 C4
Freedom Monument	24 F3
Great Guild	25 D4
House of Blackheads	(see 6)
Laima Clock	26 E4
Memorials to victims of 20 January 1991	27 D3
Museum of the History of Rīga & Navigation	(see 23)
Museum of the Occupation of Latvia	28 D5
Old Gertrude Church	29 G1
Outdoor Ice Rink	30 D4
Parliament	31 C3
Powder Tower	32 D3
Riga Castle	33 C3
Russian Orthodox Church	34 G2
St Jacob's Cathedral	35 C4
St Peter's Church	36 D5
St Rolands Statue	37 D5
St Saviour's Church	38 C4
Small Guild	39 D4
Swedish Gate	40 D3
Three Brothers	41 C4
Town Hall	42 D5

SLEEPING (p728)
Old Town Hostel	43 F5
Patricia	44 G4
Posh Backpackers	45 G6
Radi Un Draugi Hotel	46 D5
Valnis Hotel	47 E3

EATING (pp728–9)
Alus Sēta	48 D4
Central Market	49 F6
John Lemon	50 D5
Kamāla	51 D4
Ķiploka Krogs	52 C4
Pelmeni XL	53 D4
Sievasmātes p īrādziņl	54 D4

DRINKING (p729)
A Suns bar	(see 60)
Dickens	55 D5
Melnais kaķis	56 D4
Orange Bar	57 E5
Pulkvedim neviens neraksta	58 D6
XXL	59 G4

ENTERTAINMENT (p729)
K Suns Cinema	60 G4
National Opera House	61 F4

TRANSPORT (p729)
Boat Trips Landing	62 C5
Boat Trips Landing	63 C6
Bus Station	64 F6
Microbus Station	65 G5

Eksporta iela

Kronvalda Parks

Kr̄išjāņa Valdemāra iela

Bastejā bulvāris

Hanzas iela

Jēkaba iela

Torņa iela

Pils laukums

Mazā Pils iela

Pils iela

Aldaru iela

Smilšu iela

Mēstaru iela

Amatu iela

Jauņiela iela

Rozena iela

Kramu iela

Krāmu iela

Domā laukums

Skārņu iela

Old Rīga

Kaļķu iela

Kungu iela

Rātslaukums

Strēlnieku laukums

Grēcinieku iela

Peldu iela

Mārstaļu iela

11 novembra krastmala

Vanšu Bridge

To Rīga Airport (8km); Jūrmala (18km)

Daugava River

Akmens Bridge

Kuģu iela

To Oma

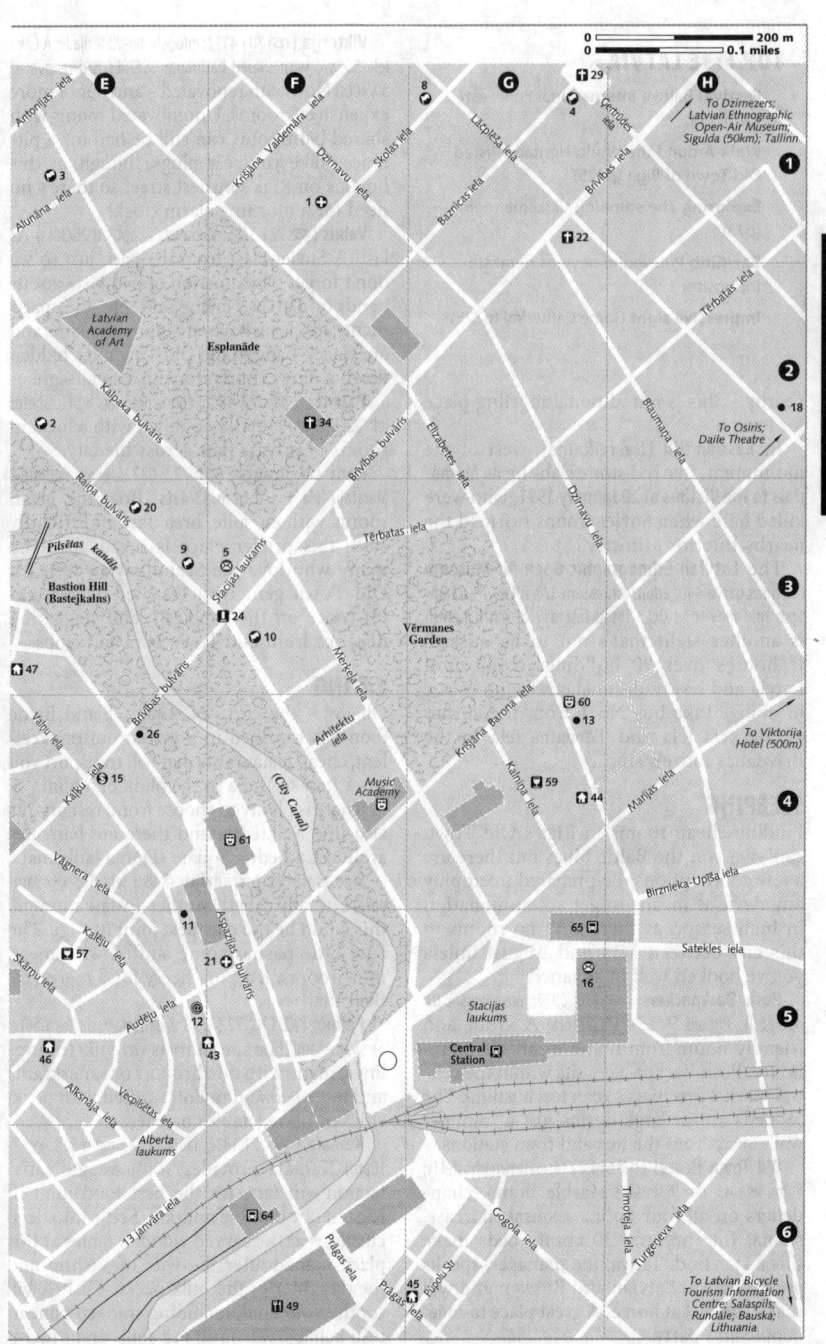

LATVIA

LATVIA

TOP FIVE LATVIA

- **Festival** Baltika International Folk Festival (p733)
- **Walk** Around the World Heritage–listed Old Town of Rīga (p725)
- **Exploring** The stunning Vidzeme region (p730)
- **Bar/Club** Pulkvedim neviens neraksta (opposite)
- **Impressive sight** Dome Cathedral (p725)

nearby – this is a traditional meeting place for lovers.

In **Bastion Hill** (Bastejkalns), west of the monument, five red stone slabs lie as **Memorials to the Victims of 20 January 1991**, who were killed here when Soviet troops stormed the nearby Interior Ministry.

The **Latvian Ethnographic Open-Air Museum** (Brīvības gatve 440; adult/concession 1/0.50Ls; ☼ 11am-5pm mid-May–mid-Oct, closed last day of each month) is another sight that's not to be missed. It houses over 90 buildings from rural Latvia and has traditional crafts and music to enjoy. Take bus No 1 from the corner of Merķeļa iela and Tērbatas iela to the Brīvdabas muzejs stop.

SLEEPING

Finding cheap rooms in Rīga's Old Town can give you the Baltic blues but there are a few good options. Be prepared to employ any devious means to get accommodation in high season as there ain't no rooms in this city between May and August unless you've booked well in advance.

Posh Backpackers (☎ 721 0917; posh@poshback packers.lv; Pūpolu Str 5; dm/d 8/16Ls) A clean and friendly home-from-home in an old warehouse, Posh Backpackers sits within the central market precincts so can feel bustling. The 59 beds are in large dorms just a minute's walk away from the bus and train stations.

Old Town Hostel (☎ 614 7214; oldtown@hostel.lv; Vaļņu iela 43; dm 9Ls; 🖳) Marble floors, chandeliers on all four floors, a spiral staircase, sauna, Internet and 30 comfy beds make this a star find. Tanya, the manager, speaks good English, Latvian and Russian and will make you feel at home. A great place to meet people and party.

Viktorija (☎ 701 4111; info@.hotel-viktorija.lv; A Čaka iela 55; s/d with shared bathroom 15/20Ls, s/d renovated 30/40Ls) Now with renovated – and hence more expensive – rooms. Unrenovated rooms with shared bathrooms can still be had for a pittance. Take your ear plugs, though, as this hotel is on Rīga's busiest street so there's no need for a morning alarm clock!

Valnis (☎ 721 3785; Vaļņu iela 2; apt s/d 20/30Ls) At last! A Soviet blast from the past, just so we don't forget which nation of bad taste got its hands on Latvia. Having said that, the apartments are clean, have en-suite bathrooms and are smack-bang in the Old Town. It's hidden down a dingy courtyard with a small sign.

Patricia (☎ 728 4868; tourism@parks.lv; Elizabetes iela 22; B&B s/d 16/26Ls) Bed down with a local in rooms in private flats across the city.

Radi un Draugi (☎ 722 0372; www.draugi.lv; Mārstaļu iela 1; s/d from 33/42Ls) Boasting clean rooms with en-suite, breakfast and friendly staff, this pricier place is raved about by many who love the Scandinavian feel. An Old Town gem with disabled access and lift (once off the cobbles!), and staggering distance from Old Town bars and clubs.

EATING

Oh joy – the curse of stodgy, bland Baltic food has vanished in a maelstrom of excellent, cheap restaurants that will transport you from Italy to India in the blink of a blini.

There is plenty to choose from; restaurants also line Kaļķu iela and there are bar/cafés around Cathedral Square (Doma laukams).

Sievasmātes p īrādziņi (Kaļķu iela 10; ☼ 9am-9pm) Literally called 'mother-in-law's *pīrāgi*', this could be the cheapest joint in Rīga. The cute little pasties come stuffed with meat, mushrooms, fruit or cheese for a mere 1Ls. Beat that!

Pelmeni XL (☎ 722 2728; Kaļķu iela 7; dishes 1.50Ls; ☼ 9am-4am) The speciality is *vareņiki* (dumplings, made with mushrooms or sauerkraut) and huge *pelmeņi* ravioli, stuffed with pork, chicken or vegetables or cheese.

Kamāla (☎ 721 1332; Jauniela 14; mains 3Ls; ☼ 7-10pm) Kamāla provides 100% veggie satisfaction –in fact, it's the best food joint in Rīga in our humble opinion. Settle into deep cushions at the carved wooden tables at this place named after the wife of Vishnu and the daughter of the milk ocean. Dishes will soothe your soul, including spinach paneer, tofu kebabs, warming veg soup and salads.

Alus Sēta (☎ 722 2431; Tirgoņu iela 6; mains 4Ls; ☺ 10-1am) Alus Sēta entices with good, solid Latvian cooking and a homely feel. Wash down traditional favourites like shashlik, salads and potatoes with plenty of home-brewed Lido beer.

Ķiploka krogs (☎ 721 1451; Jēkaba iela 3; mains 3Ls; ☺ 11am-11pm) Garlic addicts rejoice – if you fancy garlic soup, garlic roasted chicken, garlic salad and garlic ice cream for dessert then you've found paradise. If you're on a date there's a parsley sprig apéritif!

John Lemon (☎ 722 6647; Peldu iela 21; mains 2Ls; ☺ 10am-midnight Mon-Fri, 10am-5am Sat, noon-midnight Sun) So good it should be illegal. Slinky green '60s space station sofas with orange walls, a pink bar and excellent cheap menu make this a funky favourite, especially with women travellers. Meals include pasta, jacket potatoes and breakfasts.

You can also stock up at Rīga's bustling **central market** (Prāgas iela; ☺ 7am-4pm).

DRINKING & CLUBBING

Rīga's pub/bar/club scene doesn't disappoint. Once you've settled in with your party posse from Posh or Old Town hostels, get out and show the locals how it's done. Most places are open from 11am until 1am on weeknights and until dawn breaks on Friday and Saturday nights. Backpackers head to the following haunts:

A Suns (Elizabetes iela 83/85) Ex-pat favourite. The neon signs around the walls must give off a strange allure because it's always packed at weekends. Bar grub can be had but the emphasis is on sinking beers in this friendly, laid-back bar.

Dickens (Grēcinieku iela 9/1) Dream of your homeland with a pint surrounded by Latvians pretending they're in Blighty. Weird but pretty authentic pub which screens English Premiership matches.

Pulkvedim neviens neraksta (No-one Writes to the Colonel; Peldu iela 26-28) An off-beat dance bar with two floors of alternative music. Very trendy crowd so ditch your smelly combats for something a bit more glam.

Orange Bar (Jāņa sēta 5) Small bar filled to the brim at weekends. DJs on Friday/Saturday nights play alternative sounds.

Melnais kaķis (Black Cat; Meistaru iela 10-12) See where the bikers go to play. This is an institution because it's open until 7am for food, drinks, and lots of heavy rock.

XXL (Kalniņa iela 4) This gay club IS Rīga's gay scene – with hard techno DJs and a dark room.

ENTERTAINMENT

Rīga has independent and mainstream cinemas, a glorious opera house and theatres to keep you amused. Listings for films, ballet and any cultural events are found in city guides *Rīga This Week* and *InYourPocket*, or check www.rigathisweek.lv.

K Suns (☎ 728 5411; Elizabetes iela 83/85; tickets before/after 5pm 1.50/2.50Ls) Independent cinema with English-language and foreign films.

National Opera House (☎ 707 3777; www.opera .lv; Aspazijas bulvāris 3; ☺ 10am-7pm) Known as 'The White House' by locals, this awesome building is home to the Latvian National Opera, and the Rīga Ballet where Mikhail Baryshnikov made his name.

Daile Theatre (☎ 727 9566; Brīvības iela 75) The Daile stages national and international productions. Check the theatre's box office for ticket prices/productions.

GETTING THERE & AWAY
Bus

Timetables are to the right inside the bus station, as is an information centre (see p724).

Daily routes to/from Rīga include Kolka (3Ls, 5¾ hours, 160km, one daily), Kuldīga (2.30Ls, three hours, 150km, six daily), Liepāja (3.20Ls, four hours, 220km, hourly), Sigulda (0.90Ls, one hour, 50km, hourly), Valmiera (1.30Ls, 2½ hours, 120km, about 12 daily) and Ventspils (2.70Ls, 2½ to four hours, 200km, about 12 daily).

Car & Motorcycle

There are several firms based at Rīga airport, including **Budget** (☎ 720 7327; www.budget .lv; ☺ 10am-6pm) and **National Car Rental** (☎ 720 7710; ☺ 9am-8.30pm Mon-Fri, 11am-6pm Sat, 11am-8.30pm Sun).

Train

Train tickets are sold in the main departures hall of Rīga's Central Station: windows 1 to 6 sell tickets for international trains; Nos 7 to 9 sell tickets for mainline services; and Nos 10 to 13 sell tickets for slower suburban trains. Mainline services include Valmiera (1.37Ls, 3½ hours, 168km, four daily), Sigulda (0.71Ls, three hours, 13 daily) and Majori (0.51Ls, 25 minutes, every 20 minutes).

LATVIA

AROUND RĪGA

JŪRMALA
pop 56,000

Life's definitely a beach on this 32km stretch of white sands, ice-blue seas, bracing breezes and pale sand dunes.

Jūrmala (Seashore), dubbed the 'pearl of Latvia', is the largest resort in the Baltics and definitely an up-and-coming seaside resort in Eastern Europe.

There are hotels, guesthouses, bars and shops along the 4km stretch between Bulduri and Dubulti. Majori's Jomas iela is the main pedestrian hub.

Information

Tourist Office (☎ 776 4676; www.jurmala.lv; Jomas iela 42; ⏰ 9am-6pm Mon-Fri, plus 10am-4pm Sat summer only) Based in Majori, the centre has maps, leaflets and the guide *Jūrmala This Week*.

Sights

See the incredible **wooden architecture** at Bulduri and Dzintari, soak up rays on the best **beaches** of Bulduri, Dubulti and Majori, climb the highest **dunes** at Lielupe, get away from it all by heading westwards onto deserted sands or make a splash in Vaivari at the **Nemo Water Park** (☎ 773 6392; nemo@apollo.lv; Atbalss iela 1). Or simply go for a paddle.

And within a whisper is **Ķemeri National Park**, a natural wonder of protected land established in 1997 and stretching across 42 hectares of marshland and forest. The **Ķemeri National Park Visitor Centre** (☎ 776 5387; nacionalparks@kemeri.apollo.lv; Meža māja, Jūrmala; ⏰ 10am-4pm May–mid-Oct) gives information on forest trails, flora and fauna, and spa resorts.

Sleeping & Eating

Kempings Nemo (☎ 773 6392; nemo@apollo.lv; Atbalss iela 1; chalet b per person 13Ls, tents 3Ls) Camp or wake up in a chalet at this popular family spot at the water park.

Elina Guesthouse (☎ 776 1665; Lienes iela 43; d Sep-May 15Ls, Jun-Aug 25Ls) Elina is a beautiful wooden house with elegant, understated rooms.

Jomas iela in Majori is lined with bars and restaurants.

Veranda (☎ 776 3127; Jomas iela 58; mains 5Ls; ⏰ 11am-11pm) Veranda is an old-fashioned bar/restaurant with rough edges but good Latvian staples such as shashlik and salads.

Getting There & Away

Microbuses run from Rīga central station. Take either the Dubulti or Jaunķemeri bus to Majori (1Ls, 25 minutes).

Trains go to Dubulti on the Tukums, Sloka or Ķemeri (0.5Ls, 35 minutes, every 20 minutes). Most go to Majori but not all.

EASTERN LATVIA

When the hangover really kicks in, city living gets too much and you need that scent of oxygen and pine that Latvia is so famous for, head east and explore the stunning Vidzeme region.

Its ancient forests, deep ravines and historic castles will lure unsuspecting urban travellers into a blissful commune with nature.

Be warned though: the heady scent of pine forest in the exquisite Gauja National Park, which covers 49,000 hectares in the valleys of the Gauja River, could make you dizzy. The sight of castle turrets peeping through dense woodland in Sigulda may seduce you into extending your stay.

The area is home to the medieval town of Cēsis and the Latgale Upland lake district. On Ascension Day (15 August) thousands of people flock to Lake Egles to worship at Latvia's leading Roman Catholic shrine.

SIGULDA
pop 10,855

You'll swoon at the 'Switzerland of Latvia' as this gorgeous town is known. This enchanted place lies 53km east of Rīga, boasts a string of medieval castles and legendary caves, and is the gateway to Gauja National Park.

It is also a minor health resort and winter sports centre with an Olympic bobsled run.

Information

Gauja National Park Visitor Centre (☎ 797 1345; www.gnp.gov.lv in Latvian; Baznīcas iela 3; ⏰ 9.30am-7pm Apr-Oct, 10am-4pm Nov-Mar)

Makars Tourism Bureau (☎ 797 3724; www.makars.lv; Peldu iela 2) Organises boat trips along the Gauja River.

Sigulda Tourism Information Centre (☎ 797 1335; info@sigulda.lv; Pils iela 6; ⏰ 10am-7pm May-Oct, 10am-5pm Nov-Apr)

Sights & Activities

Sigulda's main attraction is the **Turaida Museum Reserve** (Turaidas muzejrezervats; www.turaida

-muzejs.lv; adult/concession 1/0.5Ls; 🕙 10am-5pm Nov-Apr, 10am-6pm May-Oct), which houses **Turaida Castle** (Turaidas pils; ☎ 797 1402; 🕙 10am-5pm Nov-Apr, 10am-6pm May-Oct). The site was a Liv stronghold and the red-brick archbishop's castle was founded in 1214. There's an interesting museum inside the 15th-century granary charting the region from 1319 to 1561.

The **Dainu Hill Song Garden** boasts 25 beautiful stone sculptures of Latvian folklore characters made by artist Indulis Ranka, scattered among the grounds.

Between the castle and road, near the small wooden-spired **Turaida Church**, two lime trees shade the grave of the 'Turaida Rose' – a beautiful maiden called Maija who was murdered by a Polish soldier whose advances she spurned. She died in the early 17th century in Gutmaņa Cave, where she had often met with her true love, gardener Viktors.

Viktors' Cave, a little further along the valley, was supposedly dug out by Viktors for Maija to sit and watch the castle gardens where he worked.

There's little left of **Sigulda Castle**, which was built between 1207 and 1226. Its ruins are more a memory of the Knights' stronghold.

On the way to the ruins you pass the 1225 **Sigulda Church**, rebuilt in the 18th century, and the 19th-century **New Sigulda Castle**, the former residence of Prince Kropotkin.

A **cable car**, recently renovated, runs every 30 minutes between 7.30am and 6.30pm across to Krimulda Castle (0.75/1Ls one way/

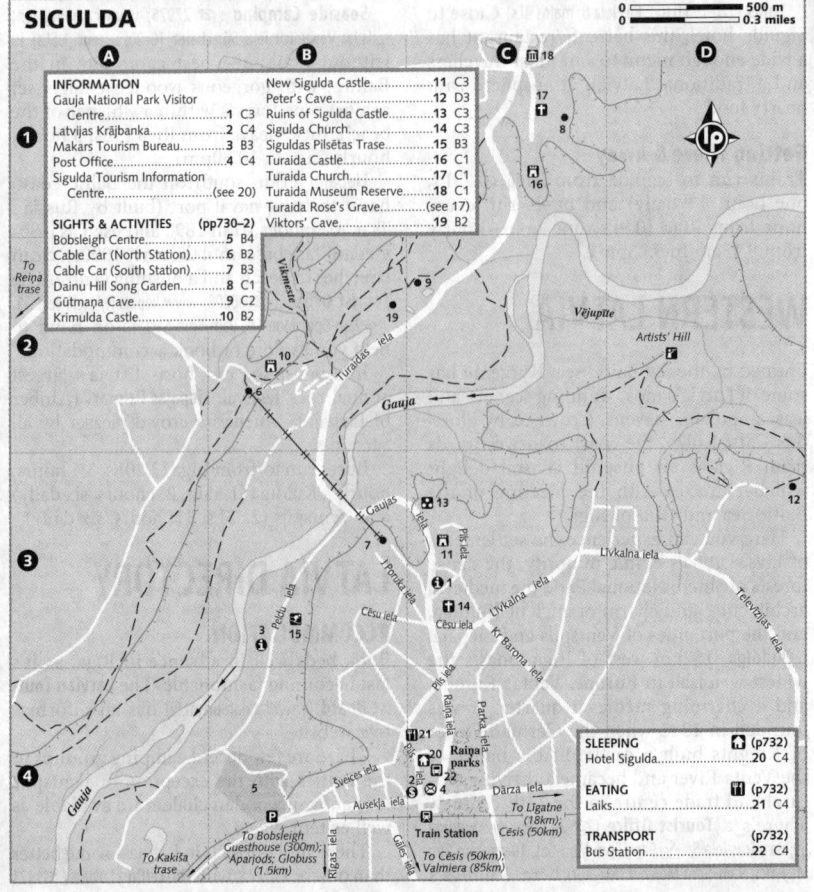

SIGULDA

INFORMATION
Gauja National Park Visitor Centre............................1	C3
Latvijas Krājbanka...................2	C4
Makars Tourism Bureau...........3	B3
Post Office................................4	C4
Sigulda Tourism Information Centre...........................(see 20)	

SIGHTS & ACTIVITIES (pp730–2)
Bobsleigh Centre.......................5	B4
Cable Car (North Station).........6	B2
Cable Car (South Station).........7	B3
Dainu Hill Song Garden...........8	C1
Gūtmaņa Cave..........................9	C2
Krimulda Castle.......................10	B2

New Sigulda Castle..................11	C3
Peter's Cave...........................12	D3
Ruins of Sigulda Castle...........13	C3
Sigulda Church........................14	C3
Siguldas Pilsētas Trase............15	B3
Turaida Castle.........................16	C1
Turaida Church........................17	C1
Turaida Museum Reserve.........18	C1
Turaida Rose's Grave...........(see 17)	
Viktors' Cave...........................19	B2

SLEEPING	(p732)
Hotel Sigulda............................20	C4

EATING	(p732)
Laiks.......................................21	C4

TRANSPORT	(p732)
Bus Station..............................22	C4

0 ___ 500 m
0 ___ 0.3 miles

LATVIA

return). You can **bungee jump** (☎ 797 2531; Poruka iela 14; jump 13Ls; ☺ 6.30pm onwards Sat & Sun May–Sep) from the cable car over the Gauja River.

Thrill-seekers can also fly down Sigulda's **bobsled track** (☎ 797 3813; Šveices iela 13; admission per person 2Ls; ☺ Oct–Mar) in groups of five people.

Skiers and snowboarders can speed down the steepest track Latvia at **Kaķīšu Trase** (☎ 657 9939; run 0.25Ls; ☺ 2–10pm Thu & Fri, noon–10pm Sat, 9am–midnight Sun).

Sleeping & Eating

There's a distinct lack of budget options.

Hotel Sigulda (☎ 797 2263; www.hotelsigulda.lv; Pils iela 6; s/d 24/30Ls; ☒) This slick, modern hotel in the centre of Sigulda boasts a steam room, sauna and pool, and a charming restaurant with an excellent Latvian menu.

Laiks (☎ 795 0104; Pils iela 8; mains 4Ls) Close to Sigulda hotel, this bar/café/restaurant has a wide enough menu to suit most travellers and a traditional Latvian atmosphere with hearty food.

Getting There & Away

Trains run to Sigulda from Rīga (0.71Ls, one hour, 13 daily) and buses run every hour from Rīga (0.9Ls, one hour, hourly from 8.15am to 5.25pm).

WESTERN LATVIA

Framed by the icy Baltic sea, Kurzeme has some of Latvia's most stunning scenery and least populated havens. Crowned by glorious Cape Kolka, the coast road westwards from Rīga is an unspoilt coastal delight which climaxes with the meeting of the Baltic Sea and Gulf of Rīga.

Here you can experience the settlements of Livs, Latvia's ethnic minority, the dense forests of Slītere National Park, the medieval architecture and charm of ancient Kuldīga, and the port cities of Ventspils and Liepāja.

Kuldīga, 152km west of Rīga, boasts the widest waterfall in Europe, Ventas Rumba, and a charming medieval quarter. It was founded in 1242 when the German Order of Knights built a castle on the banks of the Venta River and became a thriving cultural and trade centre in the 14th century. There's a **Tourist Office** (☎ 22259; www.kuldiga .lv; Baznīcas iela 5; ☺ 9am–5pm Mon–Sat, 10am–2pm Sun May–Oct; 9am–5pm Mon–Fri Nov–Apr) here. Kuldīga's

best hotel is **Jāņa Nams** (☎ 23456; Liepājas iela 36; s/d 11/20Ls) with clean, comfy rooms and a funky restaurant and bar. Six buses run daily from Rīga (2.30Ls, 2½ hours).

Ventspils is one of the largest ports on the Baltic Sea, and is the wealthy Dallas of Latvia. The city, 60km north of Kuldīga, is a major gateway for oil and chemical exports to Russia. For information, head to **Ventspils Tourist Office** (☎ 22263; www.tourism.ventspils.lv; Tirgus iela 7; ☺ 8am–7pm Mon–Fri, 8am–5pm Sat, 10am–5pm Sun May–Oct; 9am–5pm Mon–Fri, 10am–3pm Sat Nov–Apr). The 13th-century **Livonian Order Castle** (☎ 22031; Jana iela 17; admission 1Ls; ☺ 9am–6pm May–Oct, 10am–5pm Nov–Apr) has a permanent digital exhibition called Living History which is worth visiting. There's also an **Aqua-Park** (☎ 65853; Medņu iela 19; adult/child 3/1.5Ls per day; ☺ 10am–10pm May–Sep).

Seaside Camping (☎ 27925; www.camping.vent spils.lv; Vasamīcu iela 56; chalet 10–20Ls, tent 1.5Ls) is without doubt the best camp site in the Baltics, with gorgeous wooden chalets set against pine forests within a whisper of the beach. Buses leave from Rīga (3Ls, 3 hours, hourly 7am to 10.30pm).

Liepāja, 11km south on the Baltic coast, has a thriving naval port (built by Russian Tsar Alexander III in 1890 and used as a Soviet military base until the early 1990s), clean stretches of beach and a bustling centre. The **Tourist Office** (☎ 80808; www.liepaja.lv; Lielā iela 11; ☺ 9am–6pm Mon–Fri, 9am–5pm Sat) is on hand to help you explore or book accommodation.

In August the city hosts Latvia's largest annual rock festival, **Liepājas Dzintars** (Amber of Liepāja), which is a crowd-pleaser by all accounts.

Buses run to/from Rīga (3.20Ls, 3½ hours, hourly), Kuldīga (1.55Ls, 2¼ hours, six daily) and Ventspils (2.55Ls, 3¾ hours, six daily).

LATVIA DIRECTORY

ACCOMMODATION

Book beds well in advance in Rīga, as it's fast becoming fashionable. The **Latvian Tourist Board** (www.latviatourism.lv) has an informative website.

There are few decent camping grounds in the Baltics with the exception of Ventspils (see above); wooden chalets are available as well as tent places.

There are 11 hostels in Latvia – some better than others. Check with **Hostelling Latvia** (☎ 921

8560; www.hostellinglatvia.com; Siguldas Pr 17-2, Rīga) and book accommodation on the Internet. Prices range from 5Ls to 15Ls per night.

The cheapest hotels in the country cost between 8Ls and 20Ls for a room in a budget/mid range place.

ACTIVITIES

Latvia's abundance of unspoilt nature lends itself to outdoor pursuits. Whether canoeing or kayaking down the Gauja River (p730), hiking on nature trails and bird watching in Ķemeri National Park (p730), bungee jumping over the Gauja Valley (p730), or skiing in Sigulda (p730), there's plenty to keep thrill-seekers happy.

National park offices have hiking maps and information about the area's activities.

BUSINESS HOURS

Most shops open between 10am and 6pm in the larger towns/cities on weekdays and Saturdays. Banks are generally open between 9am and 5pm and shut at weekends. Bars and restaurants vary, but generally they open between 10am and 11am and stay open until 11pm Monday to Thursday nights, 2am Friday nights and 4am Saturday nights.

Main post offices open 9am to 6pm on weekdays with shorter opening hours on Saturday and Sundays of 9am to 1pm. The main branches in Rīga open until 10pm.

CUSTOMS

People over 18 can bring 2L of alcohol, 5L of beer and 200 cigarettes to Latvia without paying duty tax. You can bring any amount of hard currency. Customs rules are posted on www.latviatourism.lv or check with the **Ministry of Culture** (☎ 721 4100; Pils iela 22, Rīga; ⏲ 8:30am-5pm Mon-Fri only).

EMBASSIES & CONSULATES
Embassies & Consulates in Latvia

The following diplomatic offices are in Rīga:

Australia (☎ 722 2383; Raiņa bulvāris 3)
Canada (☎ 722 6315; Baznīcas iela 20/22)
Estonia (☎ 781 2020; Skolas iela 13)
France (☎ 703 6600; Raiņa bulvāris 9)
Germany (☎ 722 9096; Raiņa bulvāris 13)
Lithuania (☎ 732 1519; Rūpniecības iela 24)
Russia (☎ 733 2151; Antonijas iela 2)
UK (☎ 777 4700; Alunāna iela 5)
USA (☎ 703 6200; Raiņa bulvāris 7)

Latvian Embassies & Consulates Abroad

Australia (☎ 02-9744 5981; 32 Parnell St, Strathfield 2135, Sydney)
Canada (☎ 613-238 6014; latvia-embassy@magma.ca; Suite 300, 208 Albert St, Ottawa, K1P 5G8 Ontario)
Estonia (☎ 646 13 13; ilze@latvia.lv; Tõnismägi 10, EE10119 Tallinn)
France (☎ 01 53 64 58 10; ambleton@wanadoo.fr; 6 Villa Said, F-75116 Paris)
Germany (☎ 030-826 00 222; latembger@mfa.gov.lv; Reinerzstrasse 40-41, D-14193 Berlin)
Lithuania (☎ 2231 220; lietuva@latvia.balt.net; Čiurlionio 76, LT-2009 Vilnius)
Russia (☎ 095 9252707; latemb@co.ru; Chapligina 3; RUS-103062 Moscow)
UK (☎ 020-731 20 040; embassy@embassyoflatvia.co.uk; 45 Nottingham Place, London W1U 5LR)
USA (☎ 202-726 82 13; latvia@ambergateway.com; 4325 17th St NW, Washington, DC 20011)

FESTIVALS & EVENTS

Latvia is awash with festivals marking seasonal changes or as an excuse to have fun. The key events are the **Baltika International Folk Festival**, which Latvia hosts every three years, and the **All-Latvian Song & Dance Festival**, held every five years. Both fell in 2003.

In April Latvia is consumed with **Easter** celebrations and there's the annual Baltic Ballet Festival in Rīga (from 22 to 24 April). In June the **Gadatirgus folklore festival** is held during the first weekend at Rīga's Ethnographic Open-Air Museum. On 25 July, Rīga hosts the **Summer Singing Fair** across squares and market places. The **Arsēnals Cinema Forum**, an international film festival, is held from 17 to 19 September.

FOOD & DRINK

Traditional Latvian cuisine is not for the faint-hearted (or vegetarians). Pork is what these Baltic brothers love – and they'll wash half a side of pig down with *alus* (beer).

The hearty food is half Russian, half Germanic; expect to find food designed to keep the cold out such as potato-based dishes, *zupa* (soups), *siļe* (herring) and *lasis* (salmon). One thing that will warm your cockles is Rīga Black Balsam, a treaclelike alcoholic beverage with potent medicinal qualities – apparently!

Restorans (restaurants), normally open from 10am to 11pm, all have menus outside so you can peruse what's on offer before going in. Choose anywhere that doesn't have an English menu for authenticity and resort to gesticulating wildly before getting a plate of pig's trotters and a balsam by mistake!

Vegetarian options are limited outside Rīga – even the most harmless of potato pancakes comes smothered in bacon bits so we've highlighted veggie options in this chapter.

HOLIDAYS

Latvia's national holidays include:
New Year's Day 1 January
Good Friday March/April
Labour Day 1 May
Mother's Day Second Sunday in May
Ligo Midsummer Festival; 23 June
Jāni Summer solstice; 24 June
Day of Proclamation of the 18 November Latvian Republic, 1918 18 November
Christmas Eve & Day 24 & 25 December
Boxing Day 26 December
New Year's Eve 31 December

MONEY

The national currency is the Lat (Ls). 1Ls equals 100 santīmi. Latvia could theoretically adopt the euro after 2006. Banks, ATMs and exchange offices will convert currency. Rīga has plenty of ATMs and most hotels and restaurants accept the major credit cards. Tattered notes are still refused at exchange booths so keep all banknotes pristine.

National bank **Latvijas Bankas** (Latvian Bank; www.bank.lv) posts daily exchange rates on its website.

POST

Mail generally takes between five and seven days to reach Europe and 10 to 14 days for the US and Australia. It costs 0.20Ls to send a postcard and 0.30Ls for a standard letter to Europe, 0.4Ls to the USA.

Telegrams can be sent by phone (☎ 900 2178; � 24hr). The **poste-restante desk** (☎ 701 8804; Stacijas laukums 1) at the train station post office keeps mail for one month. Address letters to Poste Restante, Rīga 50, LV-1050, Latvia.

There's an express mail service at Rīga Airport: **DHL Freight Express Latvia** (☎ 707 0400).

TELEPHONE

To make an international phone call to Latvia, dial your international dialling code, followed by the country code (371) and the seven-digit number. Local Rīga numbers start with a '7' and all country-wide numbers have seven digits including the area code.

Most public phones use phonecards which can be bought in denominations of 2Ls, 3Ls or 5Ls from kiosks. **Telenets** (www.telenets.lv) does international cards, as does **lattelecom** (www.lattelekom.lv/ltk).

VISAS

Holders of most EU passports don't need a visa to enter Latvia, nor do Australian and New Zealand citizens; check with the **Department of Citizenship & Immigration** (☎ 721 9639; pmlp@pmlp.gov.lv).

Liechtenstein

HIGHLIGHTS

- **Vaduz** The tiny village masquerading as a capital; make sure to snap a picture of the royal castle with its stunning mountain backdrop (p737)
- **Malbun** Just to say you did, write a postcard home from this ski resort. How many people really can say they were skiing in Liechtenstein? (p739)
- **Hiking trails** Check out the country's 400km of trails through stunning alpine scenery – this can be accomplished anywhere in the tiny principality (p739)

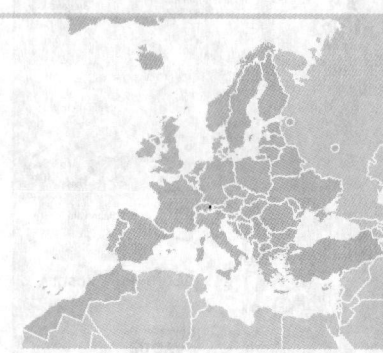

FAST FACTS

- **Area** 150 sq km (2½ Liechtensteins would fit into Andorra!)
- **ATMS** Found throughout Vaduz
- **Budget** Sfr50-120 per day
- **Capital** Vaduz
- **Country codes** ☎ 423, international access code 00
- **Famous for** sending postcards home stamped by the country's postal service, dentures
- **Head of State** Prince Hans-Adam II
- **Language** German
- **Money** Swiss franc (A$1 = Sfr0.90, CA$1 = Sfr0.98, €1 = Sfr1.54, ¥100 = Sfr1.13, NZ$1 = Sfr0.85, UK£1 = Sfr2.22, US$1 = Sfr1.23)
- **Phrases** *Guten tag* (good day), *danke* (thanks), *auf wiedersehen* (goodbye), *sprechen sie Englisch?* (do you speak English?)
- **Population** 32,860
- **Time** GMT/UTC + 1
- **Visas** None required for passport holders of the UK, Ireland, the USA, Canada, Australia, New Zealand and South Africa.

TRAVEL HINTS

The compact size of this principality means that you can stay outside Vaduz and still access all of the attractions.

ROAMING LIECHTENSTEIN

You can tour the entire country in a day if you want to, but better to spend a night in Vaduz and another in Malbun to really appreciate all it has to offer.

Blink and you might miss Liechtenstein: the pocket-sized principality is so small (it measures just 25km from north to south and about 6km from west to east) that a cross-country run really means across the whole country.

Lose concentration and you might think you're still in Switzerland: the Swiss franc is the currency, travel documents are the same for both countries and the only border regulations are on the Austrian side. Switzerland even represents Liechtenstein abroad.

But don't let the locals know you think you never left Heidi's home turf. They'd never forgive you. Generally eager to underscore its independent status, Liechtenstein often takes a different route from its big sister – seemingly just to be difficult. And although the countries share the Swiss postal system, Liechtenstein issues its own stamps.

There's not much for the budget traveller in this prosperous country other than a museum, some hiking and skiing, and bragging rights. Many tourists come to Liechtenstein for the stamps – in the passport for you and on a postcard for the folks back home. But it's also worth heading to the hills. There's some 400km of hiking trails through alpine scenery on offer.

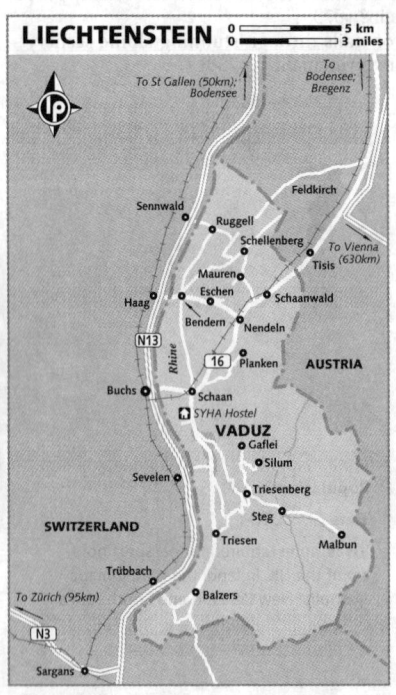

HISTORY

A merger of the domain of Schellenberg and the county of Vaduz in 1712 by the powerful Liechtenstein family created the country. A principality under the Holy Roman Empire from 1719 to 1806, it achieved full sovereign independence in 1866. A modern constitution was drawn up in 1921, but even today the prince retains the power to dissolve parliament and must approve every act before it becomes law. Prince Franz Josef II was the first ruler to live in the castle above the capital city of Vaduz. He died in 1989 and was succeeded by his son, Prince Hans-Adam II, who has

since clashed with the government over his proposed constitutional reforms that would limit government power.

Liechtenstein has no military service and its minuscule army (80 men!) was disbanded in 1868.

Known for its status as a tax haven, in 2000 Liechtenstein's financial and political institutions were rocked by allegations that money laundering was rife in the country. In response to international outrage, banks agreed to stop allowing customers to bank money anonymously.

Liechtenstein has two political regions (upper and lower) and three distinct geographical areas: the Rhine Valley in the west, the edge of the Tirolean Alps in the southeast, and the northern lowlands.

TRANSPORT

GETTING THERE & AWAY

Liechtenstein has no airport (the nearest is in Zürich); instead get there by postbus. There are usually three buses an hour from the Swiss border towns of Buchs (Sfr2.40) and Sargans (Sfr3.60) that stop in Vaduz. There are trains from Zürich to Sargans (Sfr27, one hour, hourly).

Buses run every 30 minutes from the Austrian border town of Feldkirch; you sometimes have to change at Schaan to reach Vaduz (the Sfr3.60 ticket is valid for both buses).

By road, route 16 from Switzerland passes through Liechtenstein via Schaan and terminates at Feldkirch. The N13 follows the Rhine along the Swiss/Liechtenstein border.

GETTING AROUND

Postbus travel within Liechtenstein is cheap and reliable; all fares cost Sfr2.40 or Sfr3.60, with the higher rate for journeys exceeding 13km (such as Vaduz to Malbun). A weekly/

monthly pass is only Sfr10/20 (half-price for students and seniors).

The only drawback is some services finish early; the last of the hourly buses from Vaduz to Malbun, for example, leaves at 6.20pm. Grab a timetable from the Vaduz tourist office.

VADUZ

pop 4930

Despite being a capital, Vaduz does a really good impersonation of a village. You can jog end-to-end in five minutes, although you'll want to walk slowly to appreciate its points of interest.

Two adjoining streets beneath the castle, Äulestrasse and pedestrian-only Städtle, enclose the town centre. Everything of importance is within this small area. The postal bus stops in the centre of town.

Liechtenstein Tourism (☎ 239 63 00; www.tourismus.li; Städtle 37; ☼ 9am-noon & 1.30-5pm May-Oct, closed Sat & Sun Nov-Apr) Has plenty of useful information; for Sfr2, staff will stamp your passport with a souvenir entry stamp.

Main Post Office (Äulestrasse 38; ☼ 7.45am-6pm Mon-Fri, 8-11am Sat)

Telecom FL Shop (☎ 237 74 74; Aurstrasse 77; ☼ 9am-noon & 1.30-6.30pm Mon-Fri, 9am-1pm Sat) About 1km south of Vaduz, provides free Internet access.

Vaduz Hospital (☎ 235 44 11; Heiligkreuz 25)

SIGHTS & ACTIVITIES

Although the **Schloss Vaduz** (Vaduz Castle) is not open to the public, the exterior graces many a photograph. It is worth climbing the hill for a closer look. At the top, there's a magnificent vista of Vaduz with a spectacular backdrop of the mountains. There's also a network of marked walking trails along the ridge.

Philatelists will lick their lips in anticipation of the **Briefmarkenmuseum** (Postage Stamp Museum; ☎ 236 61 05; Städtle 37; admission free; ☼ 10am-noon & 1-5pm), which exhibits 300 frames of national stamps issued since 1912.

The national art collection is housed in a sleek modern building at the **Kunstmuseum Liechtenstein** (☎ 235 030 00; Städtle 32; www.kunstmuseum.li in German; adult/student Sfr8/5; ☼ 1-8pm Tue & Thu, 1-5pm Wed & Fri, 11am-5pm Sat & Sun). Highlights include 16th- to 18th-century works from the prince's private collection.

LIECHTENSTEIN DIRECTORY

Liechtenstein and Switzerland share almost everything – a postal system, a currency, an airport – so for more information about Liechtenstein basics check out the Switzerland Directory on p1182.

The **Ski Museum** (National Museum; ☎ 232 15 02; www.skimuseum.li in German; Bangarten 10; admission Sfr6; ☼ 2-6pm Mon-Fri) showcases more than 100 years of skiing history in Europe – everything from old bindings to Toni Sailer's 1958 world cup skis and Hanni Wenzel's 1980 Olympic gear.

Look out for processions and fireworks on 15 August, Liechtenstein's national holiday. The **Little Big One** (www.littlebigone.com) open-air music festival draws bands from all over when it sweeps into town on the third weekend in June.

It is possible to sample the wines from the prince's own vineyard, but only with a group of 10 or more. Advance reservations are essential. If you get a group together, contact the **Hofkellerei** (☎ 232 10 18; www.hofkellerei.li; Feldstrasse 4).

SLEEPING

You can base yourself anywhere and still be within easy cycling or postbus distance of the centre. Ask at the tourist office for a list of private rooms and chalets outside Vaduz.

Camping Mittagspitz (☎ 392 26 86; per adult/tent/car Sfr8.50/5/4, dm Sfr22; ☼ year-round) Located on a hillside terrace overlooking the Rhine valley, this is Liechtenstein's only camping area. Check out the comfortable dorms. It's south of Triesen, so not exactly in Vaduz.

IT'S LIECHTENSTEIN TRIVIA TIME

▪ If you ever meet the prince in the pub make sure he buys a round. The royal family is estimated to be worth UK£3.3 billion.

▪ The number of companies registered in the principality is more than double the population of Liechtenstein.

▪ Liechtenstein bites into a large chunk of the false teeth market – it is the world's largest exporter of the product.

LIECHTENSTEIN

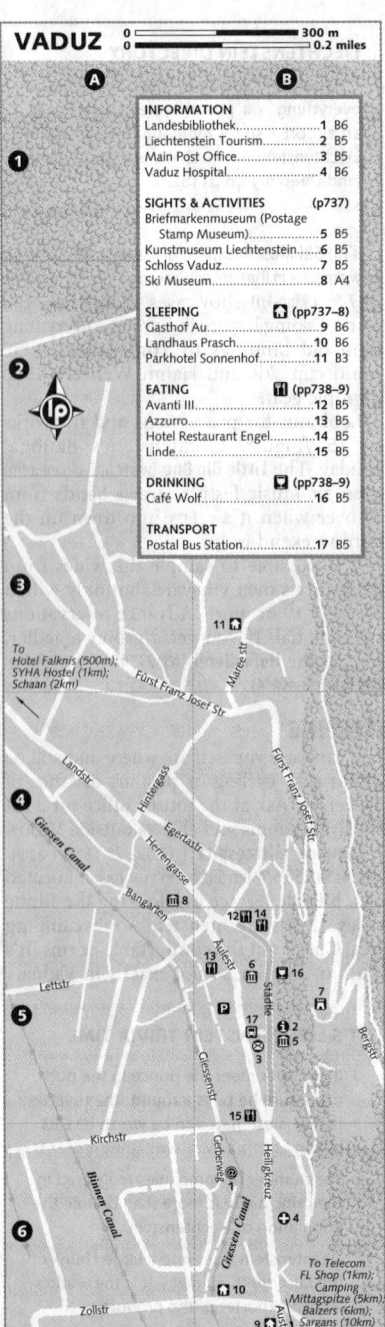

VADUZ

0	300 m
0	0.2 miles

INFORMATION
Landesbibliothek.....................1 B6
Liechtenstein Tourism.............2 B5
Main Post Office......................3 B5
Vaduz Hospital.......................4 B6

SIGHTS & ACTIVITIES (p737)
Briefmarkenmuseum (Postage
 Stamp Museum)...................5 B5
Kunstmuseum Liechtenstein......6 B5
Schloss Vaduz.......................7 B5
Ski Museum...........................8 A4

SLEEPING (pp737–8)
Gasthof Au.............................9 B6
Landhaus Prasch...................10 B6
Parkhotel Sonnenhof..............11 B3

EATING (pp738–9)
Avanti III..............................12 B5
Azzurro................................13 B5
Hotel Restaurant Engel..........14 B5
Linde...................................15 B5

DRINKING (pp738–9)
Café Wolf.............................16 B5

TRANSPORT
Postal Bus Station.................17 B5

To
Hotel Falknis (500m);
SYHA Hostel (1km);
Schaan (2km)

To Telecom
FL Shop (1km);
Camping
Mittagsspitze (5km);
Balzers (6km);
Sargans (10km)

SYHA hostel (☎ 232 50 22; schaan@youthhostel.ch; Untere Rütigasse 6; dm from Sfr29, d with shared/private bathroom Sfr75/87; ✆ mid-Mar–Nov) The hostel is in a quiet rural setting between Vaduz and nearby Schaan. Take the postbus to the Muhleholz stop; it's a five-minute walk (signposted) from there.

Hotel Falknis (☎ 232 63 77; Landstrasse 92; s/d with shared bathroom Sfr55/110) With a pub and smart, if rather basic, rooms, this is a cheapish option just outside Vaduz. It's a 15-minute walk north from the centre (or take the postbus).

Gasthof Au (☎ 232 11 17; fax 232 11 68; Austrasse 2; s/d with shared bathroom Sfr65/70, with private bathroom Sfr90/130) Intimate and warmly decorated rooms, some with balcony, are featured at this hotel south of the centre. There is an attached garden restaurant.

Landhaus Prasch (☎ 232 46 63; www.news.li/touri /prasch in German; Zollstrasse 16; s/d Sfr95/130; ✆ Apr-Oct; ☀) This is a quaint place with a sauna as well as a indoor swimming pool. When it's quiet, ask about cheaper rates.

EATING & DRINKING

The pedestrian-only Städtle has a clutch of pavement restaurants and cafés to choose from.

Azzurro (☎ 232 48 18; cnr Äulestrasse & Badwegli; mains Sfr8; ✆ 9am-7pm) This little stand delivers quick sandwiches, kebabs, small pizzas and salads.

Avanti III (Städtle 5; mains Sfr5-14; ✆ 9am-9pm) Serving cheap, but filling, snacks and meals, this place doubles as a souvenir shop. Sit at the outside tables.

Linde (☎ 233 10 05; Kirchstrasse 2; mains Sfr16-32; ✆ 8.30am-11pm Mon-Sat) A trendy bar popular with locals, it has a great '70s retro vibe. The bamboo décor is slightly kitschy, but grows on you. Mexican and Asian dishes are served in heaping portions.

Hotel Restaurant Engel (☎ 236 17 17; Städtle 13; mains from Sfr17; ✆ daily) A popular option inside the hotel, it serves Swiss meals that prove to

LIECHTENSTEIN

be just as tasty as those across the border. There also is a range of Chinese food.

Café Wolf (1st fl, Städtle 29; mains from Sfr24; daily) Head here for live music in the evenings, when the place fills quickly. There is also a range of dishes if you are hungry.

AROUND VADUZ

Northern Liechtenstein is punctuated with small, tranquil communities with pleasant village churches. **Schellenberg** has a Russian monument, commemorating the night in 1945 when a band of 500 heavily armed Russian soldiers crossed the border.

Triesenberg, located on a terrace above Vaduz, commands excellent views over the Rhine valley. It has a pretty onion-domed church and the **Heimatmuseum** (262 19 26; adult/student Sfr2/1; 1.30-5.30pm Tue-Sat), which is devoted to the Walser community, whose members came from Switzerland's Valais to settle in the 13th century.

Dominated by the soaring sides of the Gutenberg Castle is **Balzers**, in the extreme south of the country.

MALBUN
pop 100

Nestled amid the mountains in the southeast is tiny Malbun, Liechtenstein's ski resort.

The road from Vaduz terminates at Malbun. The **tourist office** (263 65 77; 9am-noon & 1.30-5pm Mon-Fri, 1-4pm Sat, closed mid-Apr–May & Nov-Dec) is by the first bus stop. Malbun has no bank, but the sports shop changes

> **SPLURGE!**
>
> **Parkhotel Sonnenhof** (232 11 92; www .sonnenhof.li; Mareestrasse 29; s/d Sfr220/330;) Liechtenstein's contribution to luxury accommodation is where to splash out in this country. Rooms are painted bright colours and offer excellent views. Pamper yourself in the large indoor swimming pool or top-class sauna.

money. The ATM by the tourist office doesn't accept Visa cards.

Although rather limited in scope – the runs are mostly novice and intermediate – Malbun's skiing is rather inexpensive, and really, how many people can say they rode the slopes in Liechtenstein?

The resort has ski and snowboard schools. A ski pass per day/week costs Sfr36/164 for adults and just Sfr30/136 for students under 28. Equipment rental costs Sfr44 per day, and can be hired from the **sports shop** (263 37 55) in town.

In summer, skis give way to mountain boots as the hiking fraternity hits town. Worthwhile treks in the area include the **Panorama** and **Furstin-Gina** paths, which start and finish in Malbun. One of the resort chairlifts operates in the summer (one-way/return Sfr8/12), so you can ride up and hike down.

The village has eight hotels, each with a restaurant. Try the **Alpenhotel Malbun** (263 11 81; fax 263 96 46; s/d with shared bathroom from Sfr45/90;), by the bus stop, for cosy, wooden rooms.

Lithuania

HIGHLIGHTS

- **Vilnius** Beautiful cobbled streets, baroque architecture and skyline pinpricked with church spires (p743)
- **Šiauliai** Hearing the wind blow between the thousands of crosses at the eerie Hill of Crosses (p750)
- **Curonian Spit** Breathing in pure oxygen and pine-scented forests (p752) **Hill of Crosses** An awe-inspiring sight, representing the amazing spirit, soulfulness and quietly rebellious nature of the Lithuanian people (p750)

FAST FACTS

- **Area** 65,200 sq km
- **ATMs** Plenty in major cities, take cash for rural areas
- **Budget** 70-100Lt per day
- **Capital** Vilnius
- **Country code** ☎ 370, international access code ☎ 00
- **Famous for** world's only Frank Zappa statue
- **Head of State** President Valdas Adamkus
- **Languages** Lithuanian, Russian, English
- **Money** litas (A$1 = 2.02Lt, CA$1 = 2.20Lt, €1 = 3.45Lt, ¥100 = 2.53Lt, NZ$1 = 1.90Lt, UK£1= 4.99Lt, US$1=2.77Lt)
- **Phrases** *Labas* (hello), *ačiū* (thanks), *prašau* (please), *taip* (yes), *ne* (no), *viso gero* (goodbye)

- **Population** 3.6 million
- **Time** GMT/UTC + 2
- **Visas** None required for citizens of the EU, Canada, the USA, Australia and New Zealand

TRAVEL HINTS

Be adventurous: wander into courtyards, investigate back streets and you'll get the most from this country.

ROAMING LITHUANIA

Discover the nooks and crannies of Vilnius, head west to Šiauliai and Kaunas before paddling in the Baltic Sea at the Curonian Spit.

Possibly the Baltic States' finest weapon of mass attraction, lovely Lithuania is a treasure trove of unspoiled natural beauty, magical coastline and cobbled baroque cities.

This tiny nation is a bastion of eccentricity and spirit. It threw off the might of the Soviet Union less than two decades ago and is careering into the future with an optimism rarely seen.

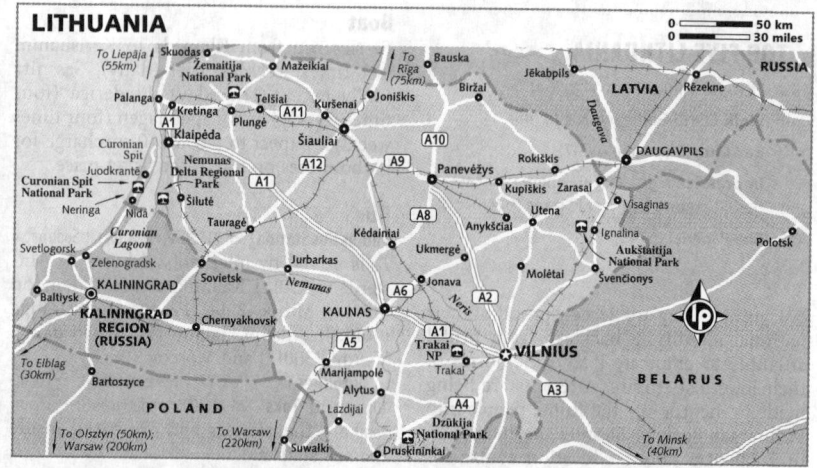

You'll love the sense of the bizarre here – there's the unofficial break-away state of artists in the capital, Vilnius, which also boasts a statue of Frank Zappa. There's also the strange Hill of Crosses at Šiauliai, the breathtaking natural wonder of the Curonian Spit and former capital Kaunas to entertain and transfix.

HISTORY

It's the classic riches to rags story – Lithuania once had an empire stretching all the way from the Baltic to the Black Sea. A powerful state from the 14th to 16th centuries, Lithuania disappeared off the maps of Europe when it was colonised by Poland and Russia.

In 1940, Lithuania was forced to become part of the USSR. Within a year 40,000 Lithuanians were killed or deported. Up to 300,000 more people, mostly Jews, died in concentration camps and ghettos during the 1941–44 Nazi occupation. The USSR returned with a vengeance in 1945, and an estimated 200,000 people were murdered or deported to Siberia.

In the late 1980s Lithuania was the first Soviet state to legalise non-communist parties, and on 11 March 1990 the new majority party declared independence. Moscow responded by marching troops into Vilnius and in January 1991 Soviet troops stormed key buildings in Vilnius, killing 14 people. The Soviets recognised Lithuanian independence on 6 September 1991, and the first ex-USSR republic was born.

Lithuania replaced the rouble with the litas in March 1993, joined NATO in April 2004 and was accepted as a full member of the EU on 1 May 2004. But Lithuania's ride into Europe has not been without controversy. In April 2004 the constitutional court ruled that President Rolandas Paksas violated the country's constitution by arranging citizenship for Yuri Borisov, a businessman with alleged links to organised crime. The President was impeached and ousted days later.

PEOPLE & CULTURE

With a population of 3.6 million, Lithuanians themselves form a massive 81.8% of the populace – unusual for the Baltics. After them, you'll find 8.1% Russians, 6.9% Poles, 1.4% Belarusians, 1% Ukranians and 0.1% Jews.

Regularly described as the 'Spanish of the Baltics', Lithuanians are a lively, friendly bunch with a tendency to overdramatise

> **READING UP**
>
> *Of Gods & Holidays: The Baltic Heritage* (1999), edited by Jonas Trinkūnas, discusses Lithuania's pagan roots.
>
> *Lithuanian Traditional Foods*, edited by Birutė Imbrasierie, covers traditional foods, costumes and the ancient way of life.

LITHUANIA

everything. They are fiercely proud of their national identity, a backlash from brutal attempts to eradicate it and memories of their long-lost empire. Attempts are being made to incorporate the Roma people into Lithuanian society. Despite the formation in 2000 of a public education centre for Roma in Vilnius as part of a government-funded project, much prejudice still exists – on both sides.

ENVIRONMENT

Lush forests and more than 4000 lakes mark the landscape of Lithuania – a country which is largely flat with a 100km-wide lowland centre. Retreating glaciers left higher areas in the northwest (the Žemaičiu Upland), across the southeast (the Baltic highlands) and in the east (stretches of the Lithuanian-Belarusian uplands including the country's highest hill, 294m Juozapinė). Forest covers a third of the country.

Lithuania's forests contain wild boar, wolves, deer and elk. The dunes and wooded areas of Neringa are home to 37 different mammal species, 470 types of butterfly and 200 bird species.

Lithuania has five national parks, and many more acres of protected land. Its natural highlight is the **Curonian Spit** (Kuršiu Nerija; www.nerija.lt).

TRANSPORT

GETTING THERE & AWAY
Air

Vilnius Airport (☎ 230 6666; www.vilnius-airport.lt; Rodūnios gatvė 2) is served by direct flights from Amsterdam, Berlin, Brussels, Copenhagen, Frankfurt, Helsinki, Kyiv, London, Moscow, Prague, Rīga, Stockholm, Tallinn and Warsaw.

Boat

Ferries run from Klaipėda to Karlshamm (six times weekly), Kiel (daily), Sassnitz (daily except Thursday), Frederica (four times weekly) and Copenhagen (four times weekly). Expect to pay a €10 surcharge for harbour fees on top of the ticket price.

Bus

Vilnius Bus Station (☎ 216 2977; www.toks.lt; Sodu gatvė 22) is served by international buses to Amsterdam (350Lt), Kaliningrad (48Lt), London (495Lt), Minsk (22Lt), Prague (160Lt), Rīga (40Lt, five daily), Tallinn (90Lt, two daily), Vienna (300Lt) and Moscow (96Lt).

Eurolines (☎ 215 1377; www.eurolines.lt; ☼ 6am-10pm) and **Toks** (☎ 216 0054; info@toks.lt; ☼ 6am-9pm) are the carriers and are based inside the bus station.

Car & Motorcycle

Insurance is compulsory and can be purchased at the border crossings.

Train

Vilnius Train Station (☎ 233 0088; www.litrail.lt; Geležinkelio gatvė 16) is served by international trains to/from Moscow (couchette/four berth 270/139Lt, 13 hours, one daily), St Petersburg (215/129Lt, 14 hours, even-numbered days) and Kaliningrad (165/93Lt, seven hours, one daily). The Warsaw-bound train runs to Šeštokai (18.80Lt, three hours, 198km, even-numbered days).

GETTING AROUND
Bicycle

Get information, help and advice about cycling in Lithuania from the **BaltiCCycle** (www.bicycle.lt). They offer organised tours of the region, bicycle rental, specific travel guides and maps.

Bus

Timetables for local and international buses are displayed on a large board in the main hall of the Vilnius Bus Station or check www.autobusai.lt (in Lithuanian). There are daily domestic buses to Kaunas (13Lt, two hours, 100km, every 20 minutes), Klaipėda (41Lt, five to seven hours, 310km, eight daily), Šiauliai (27Lt, 4½ hours, 220km, two daily) and Trakai (3.5Lt, 45 minutes, 28km, 30 daily). There are also regular microbuses to Kaunas.

Car & Motorcycle

Numerous 24-hour petrol stations selling Western-grade fuel and offering repairs/parts are dotted at strategic points in Vilnius and on the main highways.

Litinterp (www.litinterp.lt) rents chauffeured or self-drive cars and minibuses in Vilnius, Kaunas and Klaipėda from 210Lt a day. Another hire company based in Vilnius is **Rimas** (☎ 277 6213; rimas.cars@is.lt), which has the cheapest self-drive cars to rent – from about 80Lt to 100Lt a day.

Local Transport

Trolleybuses and buses start running at 4am in Vilnius and finish at midnight. A single ticket for a journey on either costs 0.80Lt from a press kiosk (or 1Lt from the driver). See www.vilniustransport.lt for details of local transport. A monthly pass costs 35Lt.

Microbuses zoom around most cities and offer a quicker and slightly more expensive way of getting from A to B at 1Lt to 2Lt per journey.

Train

There are daily domestic services to Kaunas (9.80Lt, 1¼ to two hours, nine daily), Klaipėda (30Lt, five hours, three daily), Šiauliai (24Lt, four hours, three daily) and Trakai (2.50Lt, 40 minutes, five daily).

VILNIUS

☎ 5 / pop 600,000

Collect your backpacker points here. You won't find a stranger city than this to hang out in. Within hours you could be mixing with the artists and dreamers of an unofficial breakaway republic, complete with its own borders and Independence Day. Or you could be standing before the world's only statue of weirdo rocker Frank Zappa.

Aside from its quirkiness, the Unesco world heritage–listed Old Town offers candle-lit bars, cobbled streets and a skyline of baroque church steeples to inspire and bewitch.

ORIENTATION

The heart of Vilnius is Cathedral Square (Katedros aikštė), with Gediminas Hill rising behind it. Southwards are the streets of the Old Town; to the west Gedimino

prospektas is the axis of the newer part of the city. The train and bus stations are 1.5km south of Katedros aikštė.

INFORMATION
Internet Access

Collegium (☎ 261 8334; Pilies gatvė 22; per hr 8Lt; 🕑 8am-10pm)

VOO2 (☎ 279 1866; ianplinka@post.5ci.lt; Ašmenos gatvė 8; 🕑 24hr) Boasts a resident iguana and coffee bar. Different rates for day/night usage.

Medical Services

Baltic-American Medical & Surgical Clinic (☎ 234 2020; Antakalnio gatvė 124; 🕑 24hr) Professional, Western-standard health care at Vilnius University Antakalnis hospital.

Pharmacy (Gedimino Vaistinė; ☎ 261 0135; Gedimino prospektas 27; 🕑 24hr).

Money

Vilnius is littered with ATMs and banks, most offering the usual exchange, money transfer, travellers cheques and cash advance services.

Currency Exchange (Parex Bankas; ☎ 213 5454; Geležinkelio gatvė 6; 🕑 24hr) This exchange, on your left as you exit the train station, has an ATM and generally the best exchange rates in town.

Vilniaus Bankas (☎ 262 7869; Vokiečių gatvė 9; 🕑 8am-6pm Mon-Fri) Takes Thomas Cook and AmEx travellers cheques and has ATMs.

Hansabank (☎ 212 7861; Vokiečių gatvė 26; 🕑 9am-5pm Mon-Fri)

EMERGENCY NUMBERS

- **Ambulance** ☎ 03
- **Fire** ☎ 01
- **Police** ☎ 02

GETTING INTO TOWN

From the adjacent train and bus stations it's a 10-minute walk into the heart of the Old Town northeastwards. Hop on trolleybus No 1, 2, 5 or 7, which run through the city centre (1Lt).

From the airport it's a 5km taxi ride (15Lt) into town. Alternatively, get on bus No 2 which heads to Lukiškių aikštė on Gedimino Prospektas, or bus No 1 to the train station.

LITHUANIA

CENTRAL VILNIUS

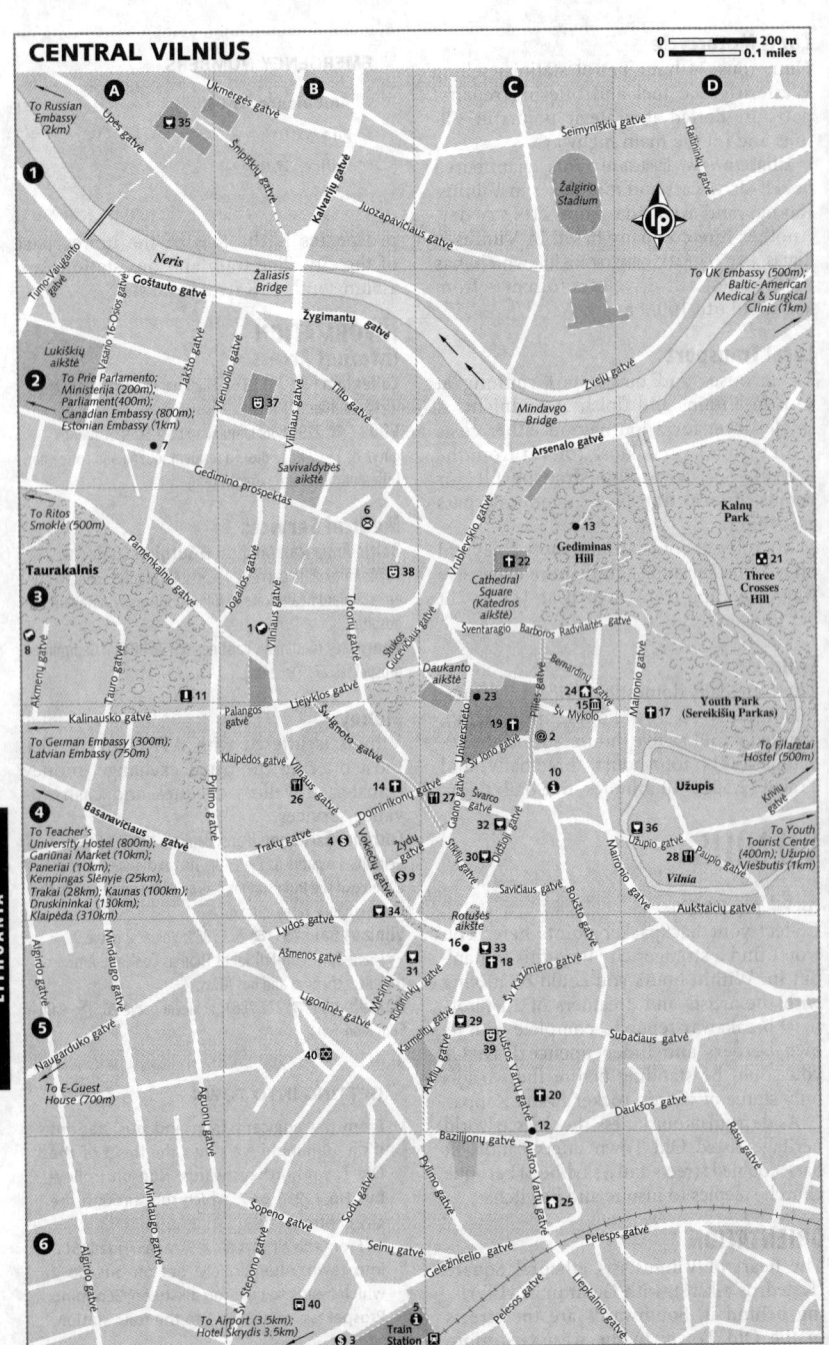

0 — 200 m
0 — 0.1 miles

Ukmergės gatvė

A **B** **C** **D**

1

To Russian
Embassy
(2km)

Upės gatvė

Kalvarijų gatvė

Juozapavičiaus gatvė

Šeimyniškių gatvė

Rotinių gatvė

Žalgirio
Stadium

Šnipiškių gatvė

Neris

Tumo-Vaižganto gatvė

Goštauto gatvė

Žaliasis
Bridge

To UK Embassy (500m);
Baltic-American
Medical & Surgical
Clinic (1km)

2

Lukiškių
aikštė

To Prie Parlamento;
Ministerija (200m);
Parliament (400m);
Canadian Embassy (800m);
Estonian Embassy (1km)

Žygimantų gatvė

Žvejų gatvė

Vasario 16-Osios gatvė

Jakšto gatvė

Vienuolio gatvė

Vilniaus gatvė

Tilto gatvė

Mindaugo
Bridge

35

37

7

Gedimino prospektas

Savivaldybės
aikštė

Arsenalo gatvė

3

To Ritos
Smoklė (500m)

Taurakalnis

Pamėnkalnio gatvė

Jogailos gatvė

Vilniaus gatvė

Totorių gatvė

Vrublevskio gatvė

Cathedral
Square
(Katedros
aikštė)

13

Gediminas
Hill

Kalnų
Park

21

Three
Crosses
Hill

6

38

22

8

Algirdo gatvė

Tauro gatvė

Kalinausko gatvė

11

Palangos
gatvė

Liejyklos gatvė

Šv Ignoto gatvė

Stuokos Gucevičiaus gatvė

Universiteto

Daukanto
aikštė

Šventaragio

Barboros Radvilaitės gatvė

Bernardinų gatvė

Pilies gatvė

Maironio gatvė

1

23

24

15

Šv Mykolo

Šv Jono gatvė

19

2

17

Youth Park
(Sereikiškių Parkas)

To Filaretai
Hostel (500m)

To German Embassy (300m);
Latvian Embassy (750m)

4

To Teacher's
University Hostel (800m);
Ganiūnai Market (10km);
Paneriai (10km);
Kempingas Slėnyje (25km);
Trakai (28km); Kaunas (100km);
Druskininkai (130km);
Klaipėda (310km)

Basanavičiaus gatvė

Pylimo gatvė

Klaipėdos gatvė

Vilniaus gatvė

Trakų gatvė

Dominikonų gatvė

Vokiečių gatvė

Žydų gatvė

Gaono gatvė

Švarco

Stiklių gatvė

Dobelio

Šv Jono gatvė

10

Savičiaus gatvė

Bokšto gatvė

Maironio gatvė

Užupis

Užupio gatvė

Paupio gatvė

Vilnia

Krivių gatvė

To Youth
Tourist Centre
(400m); Užupio
Viešbutis (1km)

14

26

27

9

32

30

34

36

28

Aukštaičių gatvė

5

To E-Guest
House (700m)

Naugarduko gatvė

Mindaugo gatvė

Algirdo gatvė

Lydos gatvė

Ašmenos gatvė

Mėsinių

Rūdninkų gatvė

Ligoninės gatvė

Arklių gatvė

Karmelitų gatvė

Šv Kazimiero gatvė

Aušros Vartų gatvė

Rotušės
aikštė

16

33

18

29

39

31

40

20

12

Subačiaus gatvė

Daukšos gatvė

Rasų gatvė

6

Mindaugo gatvė

Algirdo gatvė

Šopeno gatvė

Stepono gatvė

Šodų gatvė

Pylimo gatvė

Bazilijonų gatvė

Aušros Vartų gatvė

25

Pelesps gatvė

Pelesos gatvė

Liepkalnio gatvė

40

Seinų gatvė

Geležinkelio gatvė

To Airport (3.5km);
Hotel Skrydis 3.5km)

5

3

Train
Station

INFORMATION		Mickiewicz Memorial Apartment &		DRINKING & CLUBBING	(p747)
Australian Consulate.............1 B3		Museum...............15 C4		Bix.................29 C5	
Collegium Internet.............2 C4		Old Town Hall...........16 C5		Bix.................30 C4	
Currency Exchange.............3 B6		St Anne's Church.........17 D4		Brodvėjus...............31 B5	
Hansabank.................4 B4		St Casimir's Church........18 C5		Café de Paris.............32 C4	
Kelvita Tourist Information......5 B6		St John's Church..........19 C4		G-Lounge.............(see 30)	
Main Post Office.............6 B3		St Teresa's Church........20 C5		Helios Club.............33 C5	
Pharmacy.................7 A2		Three Crosses...........21 D3		Savas Kampas...........34 B4	
US Consulate...............8 A3		Vilnius Cathedral.........22 C3		Sky Bar...............35 A1	
Vilniaus Bankas.............9 B4		Vilnius University.........23 C3		Užupio Kavinė...........36 D4	
Vilnius Tourist Information Centre......10 C4					
		SLEEPING	(pp746–7)	ENTERTAINMENT	(p747)
SIGHTS & ACTIVITIES	(pp745–6)	Litinterp..............24 C3		Lithuanian Opera & Ballet	
Frank Zappa Memorial.........11 A3		Old Town Hostel.........25 C6		Theatre...............37 B2	
Gates of Dawn..............12 C5				National Drama Theatre......38 B3	
Gedimino Tower.............13 C3		EATING	(p747)	National Philharmonic.......39 C5	
Higher Castle Museum.........(see 13)		Balti Dramblai...........26 B4			
Holy Spirit Church............14 B4		PUB.................27 C4		TRANSPORT	(pp747–8)
Lower Castle Museum.........(see 13)		Užupio Picerija..........28 D4		Bus Station.............40 B6	

Post

EMS (☎ 261 6759; inside post office, Gedimino prospektas 7; ☷ 7am-7pm Mon-Fri, 9am-4pm Sat) For express post.

Main Post Office (☎ 262 5468; www.post.lt; Gedimino prospektas 7; ☷ 7am-7pm Mon-Fri, 9am-4pm Sat)

Tourist Information

Kelvita tourist office (☎ 231 0229; Geležinkelio gatvė 16; ☷ 8am-6pm Mon-Fri) In the international hall of the train station, these guys sell visas for Belarus, Russia and Ukraine, and can sort out accommodation and car rental too.

Vilnius tourist offices (www.vilnius.lt) Vilniaus gatvė (☎ 262 9660; Vilniaus gatvė 22; ☷ 9am-7pm Mon-Fri); Old Town Hall (☎ 262 6470; Didžioji gatvė 31; ☷ 9am-7pm Mon-Fri); inside Train Station (☎ 269 2091; Geležinkelio iela 16; ☷ 9am-6pm Mon-Fri, 10am-4pm Sat & Sun) English-, Polish- and German-speaking staff have a wealth of glossy brochures, tour guides, hotel booking and general information at these friendly centres. There's a room reservation fee of 6Lt.

Travel Agencies

Lithuanian Student & Youth Travel Bureau (☎ 239 7397; www.jaunimas.lt in Lithuanian; Basanavičiaus gatvė 30/13; ☷ 9am-6pm Mon-Fri, 10am-2pm Sat) Cheap fares for ISIC cardholders, employment in Europe opportunities and discount flights.

SIGHTS & ACTIVITIES
Cathedral Square

Start any trip to Vilnius at its heart – in **Cathedral Square** (Katedros aikštė). **Vilnius Cathedral** (☎ 261 1127; katedros aikšte 1), which was reconsecrated in 1989 after being used as a gallery during the Soviet period, dominates the square with its classic, 18th-century white façade. Amuse yourself by hunting for the secret *Stebuklas* (miracle) tile, which if found can grant a wish (you need to spin

around it three times). It marks the spot where the Tallinn-Vilnius human chain ended in 1989.

Behind the cathedral is **Gedimino Tower** at the top of the 48m **Gedimino Hill** (Gedimino Kalnas) with the Higher Castle Museum on top. A **funicular** (single/return 1/2Lt; ☷ 10am-6pm Tue-Sun) runs from the barracks up to the tower.

Spot the white **Three Crosses** atop Three Crosses Hill. They're said to have stood here since the 17th century in memory of three monks who were crucified at this spot. The crosses, erected in 1989, are replicas of three knocked down and buried by the Soviet authorities.

Old Town

The largest Old Town in Europe stretches for 1.5km south of Katedros aikštė. **Vilnius University** occupies the block between Pilies gatvė and Universiteto gatvė. Founded in 1579, it was one of the greatest centres of Polish learning in the 17th and early 19th centuries. The southern gate on Šv Jono gatvė brings you into the Didysis or Skarga Courtyard and to **St John's Church** (Šv Jono bažnyčia), which features an outstanding 18th-century baroque façade. The arch through the 16th-century building opposite St John's leads to a two-domed **observatory**, its late 18th-century façade adorned with zodiac reliefs.

Across Maironio gatvė is the fine 1581 brick façade of **St Anne's Church** (Šv Onos bažnyčia), a Gothic architectural masterpiece.

Southern Didžioji gatvė widens into a plaza that was the centre of Vilnius life from the 15th century. **St Casimir's Church** (Šv Kazimiero bažnyčia) is Vilnius' oldest baroque church. It was built by Jesuits (1604–15) and was a museum of atheism under Soviet rule.

LITHUANIA

TOP FREE STUFF

■ Make a wish once you've discovered the elusive *Stebuklas* tile in Cathedral Square (p745)

■ Wish for a miracle to happen by praying to the black Virgin Mary at the Gates of Dawn (below

■ Get lost in Vilnius University's maze of courtyards (p745)

■ Watch sunset/sunrise over the Three Crosses Hill (p745)

■ Go abroad – visit the republic of Užupis, read the constitution, watch the drunks and see the angel (below)

Aušros Vartų gatvė was once the start of the Moscow road. On the eastern side of the street is the big, pink 17th-century **Holy Spirit Church** (Šv Dvasios bažnyčia), Lithuania's chief Russian Orthodox church. The preserved bodies of three 14th-century martyrs lie in a chamber in front of the altar. The Catholic **St Teresa's Church** (Šv Teresės bažnyčia) is early baroque outside and more elaborate late baroque inside.

At the southern end of Aušros Vartų gatvė are the **Gates of Dawn** (Aušros Vartai), the only one of the town wall's original nine gate towers still intact. The stairs lead to an 18th-century chapel directly over the gate arch. Here is a 'miracle-working' **icon of the Virgin**, souvenired from the Crimea by Grand Duke Algirdas in 1363. The chapel is one of Eastern Europe's leading pilgrimage destinations.

New Town

Sandwiched between the cathedral's dramatic skyline and the silver-domed **Church of the St Virgin's Apparition** is the main street of modern Vilnius, Gedimino prospektas, dotted with shops, restaurants and banks.

A statue of Lenin once towered over Vilnius from Lukiškių aikštė. At Kalinuasko gatvė 1 is the world's only memorial to American rock and roll legend **Frank Zappa**, who died in 1993.

Independent Republic of Užupis

When you cross little Vilnia River (or Užupis seaside by those in the know), you enter an unofficial breakaway republic of artists, squatters and drunks who have declared themselves a separate state from Lithuania. The 41 points of the constitution are inlaid on metal sheets in English and Lithuanian, including 'Everyone has the right to love and take care of the cat, everyone has the right to be happy, everyone has the right to be unhappy…' etc. See the glorious Angel of Užupis statue, unveiled on 1 April 2002.

Museums

The names of those who were murdered in the former KGB prison are carved into the stone walls outside the **Museum of Genocide Victims** (Genocido Aukų Muziejus; ☎ 249 6264; admission 4Lt; ⊙ 10am-6pm Tue-Sun) Inside there's a museum guide (Russian-speaking) who was a former inmate in the prison where thousands were tortured before being sent to Siberia.

The **Lower Castle Museum** (☎ 262 9988; Katedros aikštė 3a) is on the site of the Royal Palace and an important Lithuanian archaeological dig. The palace was built in the 16th century and was the home of grand dukes of Lithuania for 300 years. Ring ahead for opening times.

The **Mickiewicz museum** (☎ 261 8836; Bernardinų gatvė 11; ⊙ 10am-5pm Tue-Fri, 10am-2pm Sat & Sun) celebrates romantic Lithuanian poet Mickiewicz, who grew up near Vilnius and studied at its university (1815–19) before he was exiled for anti-Russian activities.

TOURS

Bright yellow buses do **city tours** (☎ 273 8625; tours 10Lt) from the town hall square which run up to five times a day (except Monday and Tuesday) and last one hour.

SLEEPING

This gorgeous treasure of a city is getting very popular indeed, so try to book cheap rooms in advance or you'll be left fighting over the last beds in high season.

Filaretai Hostel (☎ 215 4627; www.filaretaihostel.lt; Filaretų gatvė 17; dm 24-29Lt, tr 28-32Lt, d 45Lt, plus 5Lt extra 1st night) A lovely, friendly quieter hostel with six- to eight-bed dorms. There's a clean kitchen, washing machine and satellite TV in a cosy shared lounge.

Youth Tourist Centre (Jaunųjų turistų centras; ☎ 261 1547; Polocko gatvė 7; b in tr or q 24Lt) This cheap, clean, relatively cheerful place is not much to shout about, but it'll mean you get your head down. And it's close to Filaretai if they're full.

Old Town Hostel (☎ 262 5357; www.balticback packers.com; Aušros Vartų gatvė 20/10; dm 32Lt) Take your ear plugs or enjoy this party hostel. It's the place to meet other travellers, swap tales and get drunk. Not for the faint-hearted, nor for the choosy. It's also a two-minute walk from the train and bus stations.

Užupio Viešbutis (Užupis Hotel; ☎ 264 3113; Paupio gatvė 31a; b per person 30-170Lt; ℗) Huge imposing manor house with an entrance around the back and front garden. It's a crumbling but good-value place with friendly young staff and lots of travellers eager to stay in Užupis and soak up the bohemian atmosphere.

Litinterp (☎ 212 3850; www.litinterp.lt; Bernardinų gatvė 7-2; s 80-100Lt; d 140-160Lt) Litinterp has some of the best-value rooms in Vilnius and excellent service. Stay in the gorgeous clean guesthouse or be placed with a local family.

EATING

From curry to *kepta duona, cepelinai* to haute-cuisine, Vilnius is bursting with international eateries. Head to Gedimino Prospektas for contemporary eats or stay in the Old Town around Vokiečių, Gatvė for Lithuanian and international haunts.

Savas Kampas (☎ 212 3203; Vokiečių gatvė 4; lunch 10Lt) Set lunch is an institution – a pot of the day cooked in an open fire. It's excellent value for filling, tasty nourishment.

Užupio Picerija (☎ 215 3666; Paupio gatvė 3; mains 15Lt; ☽ 8am-11pm) The only restaurant in Užupis – and a strange place to sit among plush surroundings eating pizza while watching the drunks hang out.

PUB (☎ 261 8393; Dominikonų gatvė 9; mains 15-20Lt; ☽ 11-2am Mon-Fri, 10-5am Fri & Sat) From shepherd's pie to fish and chips and the occasional platter of pigs' trotters this cosy split-level restaurant/bar is a backpacker favourite.

Balti Drambliai (☎ 262 0875; Vilniaus gatvė 41; mains 15Lt) Veggie heaven – the menu veers from Indian to Mexican to Italian favourites but there's no meat in sight.

Prie Parlamento (☎ 249 6606; Gedimino prospektas 46; mains 20-25Lt; ☽ 10-3am Mon-Thu, 10-5am Fri & Sat, 10-2am Sun) Upmarket haunt with seafood menu being chomped by the local expat posse.

DRINKING & CLUBBING

Get a grip on the local music/clubbing scene by checking party website www.ore.lt (in Lithuanian). Hanging around Vokiečių gatvė in the summer is a safe bet for nightlife.

G-Lounge (☎ 260 9430; Didžioji gatvė 11) The trendiest restaurant/bar in Vilnius boasts superb fusion/Asian cooking, divinely stylish white décor and fab DJs.

Bix (Etmonų gatvė 6) A favourite among backpackers and the city's studenty crowd.

Užupio kavinė (Užupio gatvė 2) A haven for artists, musicians and various bohemian, long-haired, drunk people, this Vilnius institution has a riverside terrace.

Café de Paris (Didžioji gatvė 1) Joined to the French Cultural Centre this is one of the best bars in Vilnius with an eclectic crowd, no banging techno and good tunes.

Sky Bar (Konstitucijos gatvė 20, Royal Lietuva Hotel) Twenty-two floors up, it has the best views in the city, a requisite amount of beautiful people and heavenly (but pricey) cocktails.

There are a few clubs worth checking:

Brodvėjus (Mėsinių 4) Two bars, local DJs and live music for a relaxed, traveller crowd.

Helios (Didžioji gatvė 28) Serious house music played loud and dirty for a hot young crowd.

Men's Factory (www.gayclub.lt) Centre of Vilnius' gay scene, changing its position as we went to press. Check the website for its new location.

ENTERTAINMENT

Vilnius has cinemas, an opera house, theatres and concert halls to delight any cultured visitor. The tourist offices post event listings.

Vilnius also has a €10 million Akropolis shopping complex with ice-skating rink and multi-screen **cinema** (☎ 248 4848; Ozo 25).

Cinema

Coca-Cola Plaza (☎ 265 2525; Savanorių gatvė 7) Multiplex with 12 screens and disabled seats.

Classical Music

National Philharmonic (☎ 266 5216; Aušros Vartų gatvė 5; box office ☽ 11am-7pm Tue-Sat, 11am-1pm Sun)

Lithuanian Opera & Ballet Theatre (☎ 262 0727; www.opera.lt; Vienuolio gatvė 1; ☽ 10am-7pm Mon-Fri, 10am-6pm Sat, 10am-3pm Sun)

Theatre

National Drama Theatre (☎ 262 9771; www.teatras.lt; Gedimino Prospektas 4; ☽ 10am-6pm Mon-Fri, 11am-6pm Sat & Sun) Stages national and international productions.

GETTING AROUND

Trolleybuses and buses run daily from 4am to midnight. A single ticket for any mode of

LITHUANIA

public transport costs 0.80Lt when bought from a press kiosk or 1Lt when bought from the driver. Validate your ticket by punching it in a machine on the bus or trolleybus.

Minibuses shadow most routes; expect to pay 2Lt per journey. Check the website www.vilniustransport.lt.

Taxis officially charge 1Lt to 1.30Lt per kilometre but it's cheaper and safer to call ahead. Recommended numbers for cab companies are ☎ 1445, 1422, 1313, 1818, 1446 and 1411 – no code is required.

There are ranks outside the train station, the Radisson SAS Astorija hotel and in front of the Old Town Hall on Didžioji gatvė.

AROUND VILNIUS

PANERIAI

Lithuania's brutal history is starkly portrayed at this site of Jewish mass murder. Between July 1941 and July 1944 100,000 people were killed in the Nazi death camp at Paneriai, 10km southwest of central Vilnius.

The entrance path leads to the small **Paneriai Museum** (☎ 260 2001; Agrastų gatvė 17; ☼ 11am-6pm Wed-Sun, call to check winter opening times).

There are about 20 suburban trains daily from Vilnius to Paneriai station (0.90Lt, 20 minutes). From the station, it is a 1km walk southwest along Agrastų gatvė to the site.

TRAKAI

☎ 528

The ancient capital of Lithuania is a dreamy day trip away. Two castles sit among five scenic lakes just 28km west of Vilnius.

It was Gediminas who made this charming complex his capital in 1321. Trakai is famous for the presence of the Karaites, or Karaimai people. They're a mixed Judaic and Hebrew sect originating in Baghdad, who adhere to the Torah (rejecting the rabbinic Talmud).

Some Karaites were brought to Trakai from the Crimea by Vytautas around 1400 to serve as bodyguards. Of the 10,000 Karaites left in the world, 360 live in Lithuania (mostly in Trakai).

The **Tourist Office** (☎ 51934; trakaitic@is.lt; Vytauto gatvė 69; ☼ 8.30am-4.15pm Mon, 8.30am-5.30pm Tue-Fri, 9am-5pm Sat) sells maps, and books accommodation.

Trakai Castle & Museum (☎ 58246; Pilies island; adult/child 8/4Lt; ☼ 10am-6pm Tue-Sun) dates from

the 14th century. The **Karaite Ethnographic Exhibition** (☎ 55286; Karaimų gatvė 22; ☼ 10am-6pm Wed-Sun) offers an incredible look at a fast-disappearing culture and religion. Among the wooden cottages along Karaimų gatvė is an early-19th-century **Kenessa** (prayer house; Karaimų gatvė 30) belonging to the Karaites.

Kempingas Slėnyje (☎ 53880; www.camptrakai.lt in Lithuanian; Slėnio 1; b per person 25-120Lt) is an excellent camping complex and hostel 5km out of Trakai on the northern side of Lake Galvė. You can pitch your tent by the lake or stay in wooden cabins or the hostel, which has a sauna, a diving club, boat rental and hot air balloon rides.

Apvalaus Stalo Klubas (☎ 55595; Karaimų, gatvė 53; mains 10-20Lt) is a lovely waterside French restaurant with separate pizzeria and stunning sunset views.

Daily buses run between Vilnius bus station and Trakai (3Lt, 45 minutes, at least 30 daily from 6.47am to 8.45pm). There are also several daily trains (2.80Lt, 40 minutes, eight daily plus more at weekends).

DRUSKININKAI

☎ 313 / pop 20,000

Spa town Druskininkai, 130km south of Vilnius, is the most famous health resort in Lithuania.

The **tourist office** (☎ 51777; Gardino gatvė 1; ☼ 9am-5pm Mon-Fri) can book accommodation.

Around 7km from Druskininkai, the quasi-controversial **Grūto Parkas** (☎ 55511; hesona@druskininkai.omnitel.net; adult/child 5/2Lt; ☼ 9am-sunset) attracts visitors to its idiosyncratic collection of Lenins and Stalins. Open since 2000, this Soviet sculpture theme park is filled with those communist monstrosities formerly based in parks and squares across Lithuania.

There are direct buses (14.50Lt, two hours, 125km, four daily) between Vilnius and Druskininkai. You can ask to be let off at the village and walk the 1km to the park, which is well signposted.

CENTRAL LITHUANIA

KAUNAS

☎ 37 / pop 378,900

Founded in the 13th century, Lithuania's second largest city boasts a historic Old Town, a strong cultural and arts scene and a pretty boulevard forming the main artery of the city – oh yeah, and excellent bars!

The historic heart is Rotušės aikštė (City Hall Square), between the two rivers at the western end of the city centre. The new town is focused on the pedestrianised Laisvės alėja, which is further east.

The bus and train stations are about 1km south of the eastern end of Laisvės alėja, down Vytauto prospektas.

Information

Bendroji Medicinos Praktika (☎ 313 665; Savanorių prospektas 423; ⏰ 9am-7pm Mon-Fri, 9am-2pm Sat) Offers dental, medical and general health services.

Hansabank (☎ 322 454; Laisvės alėja 79; ⏰ 8am-6pm Mon-Fri, 8am-3pm Sat)

Kaunas Tourist Office (☎ 323 436; www.kaunas.lt; Laisvės alėja 36; ⏰ 9am-6pm Mon-Fri & 9am-3pm Sat Apr-Sep, 9am-6pm Mon-Thu & 9am-5pm Fri Oct-Mar) This swanky new tourist office can book accommodation, tours and sell you maps and brochures.

Kavinė Internetas (☎ 225 364; Vilniaus gatvė 26; per hr 7Lt; ⏰ 10am-10pm)

Main Post Office (☎ 401 368; Laisvės alėja 102; ⏰ 7.30am-6.30pm Mon-Fri, 7.30am-4.30pm Sat)

Sights

Start any trip to Kaunas wandering through the charming Old Town streets. The 18th-century white, baroque former city hall is now the Palace of Weddings and the **Ceramics Museum** (☎ 203 572; Rotušės aikštė; admission 2Lt; ⏰ 11am-5pm Tue-Sun).

A **statue of Maironis** stands in the square; he was the priest and poet considered radical by the Soviets.

Kaunas Cathedral, which is on the square's northeastern corner, reflects baroque reconstruction, but the early-15th-century Gothic shape of its windows remain. **Maironis' tomb** is outside the south wall of the cathedral. A reconstructed tower is all that remains of the 13th-century **Kaunas Castle**.

The transformation of Kaunas is resplendent in the form of Laisvės alėja (Freedom Ave), which resembles a European boulevard more than an old communist thoroughfare.

At its western end stands a **statue of Vytautas the Great**. In 1972, in the park opposite, student Romas Kalanta burnt himself to death as a protest against Soviet occupation.

The blue, neo-Byzantine 1893 **St Michael the Archangel Church** (Nepriklausomybės aikštė) dominates the eastern end of Laisvės alėja

alongside the infamous **Man statue**. You can't miss him – and his nakedness.

He stands in front of the **Mykolas Žilinskas Art Museum** (☎ 222 853; Nepriklausomybės aikštė 12; ⏰ 11am-5pm). Inside there's the only Rubens in Lithuania and a wide collection of Lithuanian and international artworks.

The **Military Museum of Vytautas the Great** (☎ 320 939; Donelaičio gatvė 64; ⏰ 11am-5.30pm Tue-Sun, closed Mon) recounts Lithuania's history from prehistoric times to the present day. Next door is the **M-K Čiurlionis Museum** (☎ 229 475; Putvinskio gatvė 55; ⏰ 11am-5pm, closed Mon), with an extensive collection of the romantic symbolic paintings of Čiurlionis (1875–1911).

Prepare yourself to come face to face with Beelzebub in his hundreds at the bizarre and fantastic **Devil Museum** (Velnių Muziejus; ☎ 221 587; Putvinskio gatvė 64; ⏰ 11am-5pm, closed Mon).

Admission to museums is between 2Lt and 5Lt.

Built in the late 19th century, the **Ninth Fort** (☎ 377 750; Žemaičių Plentas 73; admission 4Lt; ⏰ 10am-4pm Wed-Sun), 7km from Kaunas, was used by the Nazis during WWII as a death camp. Take bus No 35 or 23 from the bus station; they run at least every half-hour between 1.50am and 9.15pm.

Sleeping

Kaunas isn't well-endowed with cheap hotels. There are no hostels, so book in advance.

Litinterp (☎ 228 718; kaunas@litinterp.lt; Gedimino prospektas 28; s/d/tr 80/140/180Lt) Offers excellent B&B choices. These ever-brilliant people will find you a nice cosy room somewhere for a fraction of the cost of staying in a hotel.

Metropolis (☎ 205 992; Daukanto gatvė 21; s/d with breakfast 100/140Lt) A Soviet dream of a hotel with some of the cheapest rooms in Kaunas. And for good reason – it's seen better days.

Eating & Drinking

Simply wander down Laisvės alėja and choose a restaurant. There are plenty here, most with English menus and none that will break the bank.

Arbatinė (☎ 323 732; Laisvės alėja 100; mains 15Lt; ⏰ 9am-6pm Mon-Fri, 10am-6pm Sat) This café sets vegan pulses racing with its dairy-free/meat-free policy. Serves sandwiches, salads and smoothies, so is perfect for lunch.

Jums (☎ 203 705; Laisvės alėja 61; mains 15Lt) Jums is the nicest café/restaurant in Kaunas. Aside from staring at the grass on the ceiling

LITHUANIA

or art on the walls, you can peer at an excellent fusion menu with such wonders as beef teriyaki and chicken in champagne.

Miesto Sodas (☎ 424 424; Laisvės alėja 93; mains 20-30Lt; 11am-midnight) Very trendy eatery with funky orange décor and an excellent international menu. The steaks are the biz and there's live music sometimes too.

There are cool hang-outs aplenty in funky Kaunas. **BO** (Muitinės gatvė 9) is where students and bohemian types hang out. **Los Petrankos nightclub** (Savanorių prospektas 124) has a state-of-the-art sound system for 1500 clubbers.

Entertainment

Check out what's on in the *Kaunas & Klaipėda InYourPocket* guide or ask at the tourist office.

Kaunas State Drama Theatre (☎ 224 064; Laisvės alėja 71; box office 10am-7pm)

Planeta Cinema (☎ 338 330; Vytauto prospektas 6)

Getting There & Away

AIR

Kaunas International Airport (☎ 399 307; Savanorių prospektas) is 10km north of the Old Town. Minibuses run from the bottom of Savanorių (1Lt).

International flights are operated by **Air Lithuania** (☎ 228 176; Kęstučio 69; 8am-6pm Mon-Fri, 9am-3pm Sat) to Hamburg, Oslo and Billund via Palanga.

BUS

From **Kaunas' long-distance bus station** (☎ 409 060; Vytauto prospektas 24), **Kautra bus Lines** (☎ 342 440; www.kautra.lt) runs buses to St Petersburg, Kaliningrad, Rīga and Tallinn.

TRAIN

From **Kaunas train station** (☎ 372 260; Čiurlionio gatvė 16) there are 12 daily trains going to/from Vilnius (9.80Lt, two hours). Kaunas–Šeštokai trains connect with the Šeštokai–Suwałki train into Poland. There's also one Moscow train, and trains to/from Klaipėda (23.40Lt, six hours, eight daily), Rīga (22Lt, five hours, one daily) and Šiauliai (14.10Lt, three hours, three daily).

ŠIAULIAI

☎ 41 / pop 147,000

Lithuania's fourth-largest city is a stone's throw from the legendary Hill of Crosses and 140km north of Kaunas.

The **Tourist Office** (☎ 523 110; www.siauliai.lt; Vilniaus gatvė 213; 9am-6pm Mon-Fri, 10am-3pm Sat) arranges trips to the Hill of Crosses, and has maps and brochures on the city.

There's a **post office** (Aušros alėja 42) and **Vilniaus Bankas** (Tilžės gatvė) offers currency exchange.

Sleep at the basic **Youth Hostel** (☎ 523 992; romaspp@takas.lt; Rygos gatvė 36; dm 15Lt).

Buses run to Kaunas (17.50Lt, three hours, about 20 daily), Klaipėda, (20Lt, 2½ hours, six daily) and Vilnius (24Lt to 27Lt, four hours, about 12 daily). There are frequent trains to Vilnius (24.10Lt, four hours), Klaipėda (14.50Lt, four hours) and Kaunas (14.10Lt, four hours).

HILL OF CROSSES

Lithuania's most incredible, awe-inspiring sight is the legendary Hill of Crosses (Kryžių kalnas), a two-hump hillock blanketed by thousands of crosses. Each and every cross represents the amazing spirit, soulfulness and quietly rebellious nature of these people, who have been planting these crosses in the hillside since the 14th century. Some are devotional, others are memorials (many for people deported to Siberia) and some are finely carved folk-art masterpieces. Even when the crosses were bulldozed by the Soviets in more recent times, people crept past soldiers and barbed wire to plant more. Today this strange place, 10km north of Šiauliai and 2km east off the road to Joniškis and Rīga, is still a place of national pilgrimage.

Buses run from 5am to 11pm daily from Šiauliai bus station (0.80Lt) or you can pay 1Lt and grab a microbus. They run from 6am to 11pm and are quicker. Get off at the Domantai stop and walk the 2km track to the hill. Look for the sign 'Kryžių kalnas 2'. A one-way taxi costs between 25Lt and 30Lt.

WESTERN LITHUANIA

KLAIPĖDA

☎ 46 / pop 194,000

Sea port Klaipėda is the oldest city in Lithuania (1252), formerly the German town of Memel and gateway to the lush natural beauty of the Curonian Spit.

Orientation

The Danės River flows west across the city centre to the Curonian (Kuršių) Lagoon,

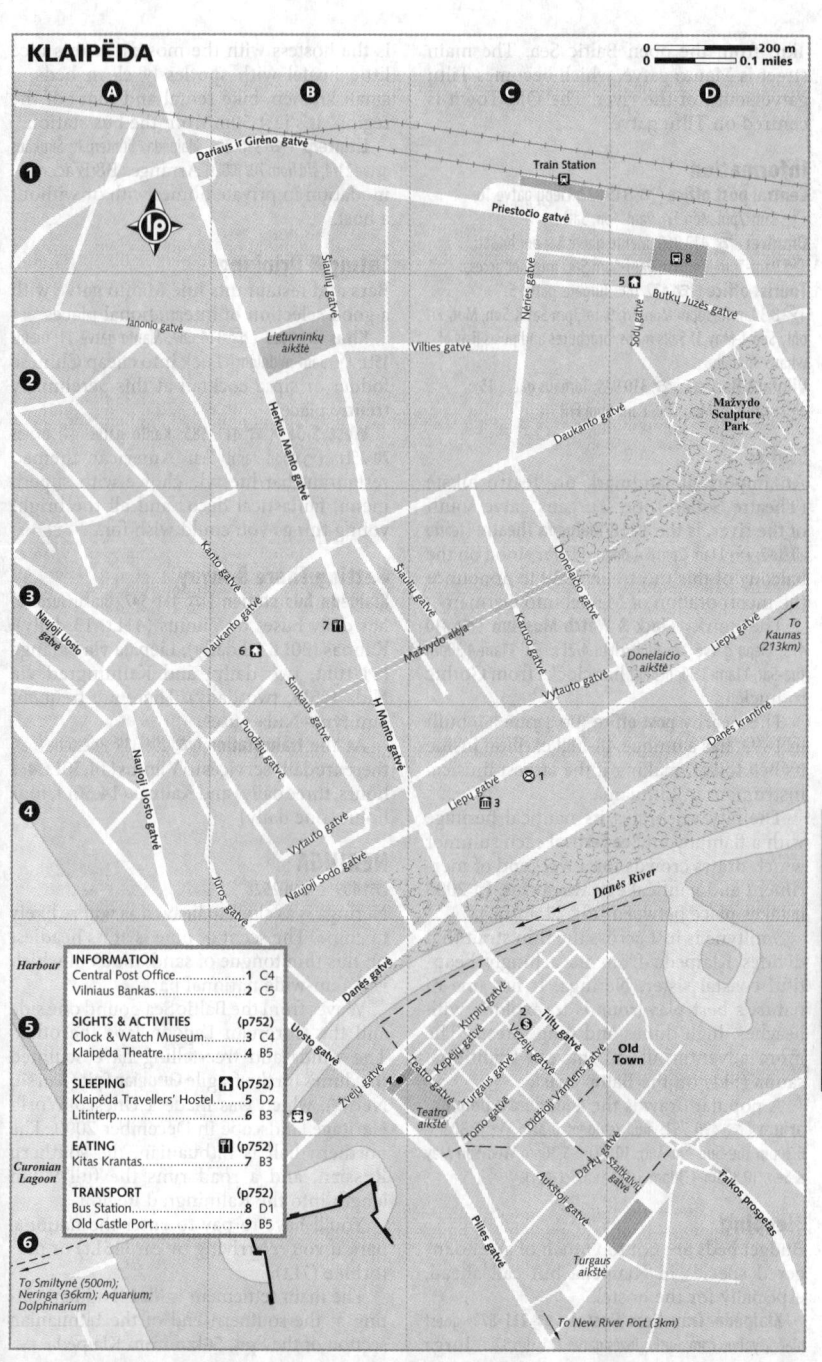

KLAIPĖDA

0 — 200 m
0 — 0.1 miles

A   **B**   **C**   **D**

Dariaus ir Girėno gatvė

Train Station

Priestočio gatvė

Šiaulių gatvė

Neries gatvė

5   Butkų Juzės gatvė

Sodų gatvė

8

Janonio gatvė

Lietuvninkų aikštė

Vilties gatvė

Daukanto gatvė

Mažvydo Sculpture Park

Herkus Manto gatvė

Kanto gatvė

Daukanto gatvė

Šiaulių gatvė

Donelaičio gatvė

To Kaunas (213km)

Naujoji Uosto gatvė

6

Mažvydo alėja

Kanto gatvė

Donelaičio aikštė

Liepų gatvė

Šimkaus gatvė

7

Vytauto gatvė

Danės krantinė

Naujoji Uosto gatvė

Puodžių gatvė

H. Manto gatvė

Liepų gatvė

1

3

Vytauto gatvė

Naujojų Sodo gatvė

Jūros gatvė

Danės River

LITHUANIA

Harbour

Danės gatvė

Uosto gatvė

Kurpių gatvė

Tiltų gatvė

2

Kepėjų gatvė

Vėžėlių gatvė

Old Town

Teatro gatvė

Žvejų gatvė

4

Turgaus gatvė

Tomo gatvė

Didžioji Vandens gatvė

Teatro aikštė

Curonian Lagoon

9

Daržų gatvė

Šaltkalvių gatvė

Taikos prospektas

Aukštoji gatvė

Piliės gatvė

Turgaus aikštė

To Smiltynė (500m);
Neringa (36km); Aquarium;
Dolphinarium

To New River Port (3km)

INFORMATION

Central Post Office........................**1** C4
Vilniaus Bankas............................**2** C5

SIGHTS & ACTIVITIES (p752)

Clock & Watch Museum.................**3** C4
Klaipėda Theatre..........................**4** B5

SLEEPING (p752)

Klaipėda Travellers' Hostel............**5** D2
Litinterp....................................**6** B3

EATING (p752)

Kitas Krantas...............................**7** B3

TRANSPORT (p752)

Bus Station..................................**8** D1
Old Castle Port............................**9** B5

4km from the open Baltic Sea. The main street is Manto gatvė, which becomes Tiltų gatvė south of the river. The Old Town is centred on Tiltų gatvė.

Information

Central post office (☎ 315 022; Liepų gatvė 16; 🕙 8am-7pm Mon-Fri, 9am-4pm Sat)

Omnitel (☎ 412 360; Manto gatvė 18; per hr 3Lt; 🕙 9am-7pm Mon-Fri, 9am-5pm Sat) Internet access.

Tourist office (☎ 412 186; Turgaus gatvė 5; 🕙 8.30am-6.30pm Mon-Fri, 9am-3pm Sat & Sun, Mon-Fri only Sep 1-May 1) Sells maps, brochures and posts lists of what's on daily.

Vilniaus Bankas (☎ 310 925; Turgaus gatvė 15; 🕙 8am-6pm Mon-Thu, 8am-5pm Fri)

Sights

An important landmark on Teatro aikštė (Theatre Square), off Turgaus gatvė south of the river, is the 1818 **Klaipėda Theatre** (Teatro aikštė 2; 🕙 11am-2pm & 4-6pm). Hitler stood on the balcony of this theatre in 1939 to announce the incorporation of Memel into Germany.

The quirky **Clock & Watch Museum** (☎ 410 413; Liepų gatvė 12; adult/child 4/2Lt; 🕙 11am-4.30pm Tue-Sat, 11am-3.30pm Sun) has clocks from Gothic to nuclear.

The nearby **post office** (Liepų gatvė 16), built in 1893, has a unique 48-bell carillon inside its bell tower, making it the largest musical instrument in Lithuania.

The city celebrates its nautical heritage with a flamboyant **Sea Festival** each summer which draws crowds for a weekend of merriment and nautical extravaganzas. In 2005 it takes place between July 22 and 24.

Smiltynė is just across the thin strait that divides Klaipėda from its achingly beautiful coastal sister, Neringa. It has one of nature's best playgrounds to explore, with beaches, high dunes and pine forests. The more adventurous can have a traditional sauna (5Lt) on the Baltic coast.

A popular draw is the **Aquarium & Dolphinarium** (☎ 490 751; adult/student 6/3Lt; 🕙 10.30am-6.30pm Tue-Sun Jun-Aug, 10.30am-5.30pm Wed-Sun May & Sep, 10.30am-4.30pm Sat & Sun Oct-Apr).

Sleeping

Budget beds are not too much of an endangered species in Klaipėda but call ahead, especially for the hostel.

Klaipėda Travellers Hostel (☎ 211 879; guest place@yahoo.com; Butkų Juzės gatvė 7/4; dm 32Lt) Jurga is the hostess with the mostest at this nice little hostel with spotlessly clean beds, a small kitchen, bike rental and tours of the region. It's just 50m from the bus station.

Litinterp (☎ 310 296; klaipeda@litinterp.lt; Šimkaus gatvė 21/4; s/d from 70/100Lt) Arranges B&B accommodation in private homes with or without a host.

Eating & Drinking

Bars and restaurants line Manto gatvė with a good selection of international places.

Kitas Krantas (☎ 314 687; Manto gatvė 11; mains 15Lt; 🕙 9am-midnight) Tuck into cheap Chinese fodder or sip a cocktail at this perennially trendy place.

West Side (☎ 411 585; Kanto gatvė 44; mains 20-25Lt; 🕙 noon-2am) An American-themed restaurant/bar/lifestyle choice with superb menu, fantastical décor and all the bright young things you could wish for.

Getting There & Away

Klaipėda bus station (☎ 411 547; Butkų Juzės 9) has daily buses to Vilnius (41Lt, 13 daily), Kaunas (30Lt, 18 daily), Liepaja via Palanga (11.10Lt, two daily) and Kaliningrad via Nida (25Lt, two daily). There are frequent Smiltynė-Nida buses.

At the **train station** (☎ 296 385; Priestoties 5a), there are daily services to Vilnius (14.50Lt, 4½ hours, three daily) and Kaunas (14.50Lt, four hours, one daily).

NERINGA

☎ 469 / pop 2528

Neringa is as close to heaven as you're likely to come. The scent of pine is at its headiest on this thin tongue of sand, much of which is a 4km-wide national park.

Waves from the Baltic Sea pound one side and the Curonian Lagoon laps the other. The winds and tree-felling have sculpted the dunes on the fragile **Curonian Spit** (Kuršių Nerija), which was made a Unesco World Heritage landscape in December 2000. The northern half is Lithuanian, the southern Russian, and a road runs the full 97km length into the Kaliningrad Region.

You'll have to pay to enter the national park if you're arriving by car (15Lt) or motorbike (7Lt).

The main settlement is **Nida** (Nidden), sitting at the southern end of the Lithuanian section of the Spit, 50km from Klaipėda.

Nida Tourist Office (☎ 52345; Taikos gatvė 4; ⏰ 10am-8pm) has a wealth of information from boat trips to accommodation booking.

Get a great view of the spit by climbing up designated paths on **Parnidis Dune** (52m) to the sundial. The 'Lithuanian Sahara' is a breathtaking sight.

Summer really hots up on the bed front so book in advance. **Litinterp** in Klaipėda (see opposite) can arrange rooms.

Getting There & Away

A passenger ferry departs every half hour from the Old Castle Port in Klaipėda for the northern tip of Neringa. Pedestrians are free. Motorists use the vehicle ferry at the **New River Port** (Nemuno gatvė 8), 3km south.

From Smiltynė, buses and microbuses run throughout the day to/from Nida (7Lt, one hour), stopping at Juodkrantė on the way.

LITHUANIA DIRECTORY

ACCOMMODATION

Book beds well in advance for trips to Vilnius; like the rest of the Baltics, it's fast becoming the number-one choice for stag nights and hen parties as well as fashionable on the travelling circuit. The **Lithuanian State Tourism Department** (www.tourism.lt) has a good website for forward planning, listing rural farm stays, health resorts and hotels.

There are few camping grounds to recommend in Lithuania. They are generally basic, dirt cheap (5Lt to 20Lt to pitch a tent, 15Lt to 30Lt for a wooden cabin) and rundown.

The **Lithuanian Hostels Association** (see Filaretai Hostel, p746) is based at the largest hostel it runs. The association runs a second hostel in Vilnius Old Town, and has an affiliated hostel in Klaipėda. A bed in a shared room costs per night 24Lt to 32Lt.

Alternatively, budget travellers can look to **Litinterp** (www.litinterp.lt) which offers B&Bs and self-catering facilities in Vilnius, Klaipėda, Kaunas and Nida. In Vilnius prices start at 80Lt for a single, while outside the capital city the rates are from 70Lt.

Tourist offices can book countryside home stays from 100Lt a double. As an alternative, check the tourism website listed above.

Hotels are aplenty in Vilnius, most offering decent rates for Europe, between 80Lt and 200Lt for a night, with mid-range coming in at 140Lt and above. In rural places hotel choice can be limited and the standard poor with accompanying price downsizing.

Useful websites for booking accommodation or pre-trip planning include www.visitlithuania.lt, www.vilniushotels.lt and www.lithuanianhotels.com.

BUSINESS HOURS

Most shops open between 10am and 6pm in the larger towns and cities on weekdays and Saturdays. Expect rural places to have their own code of conduct. Banks are open between 8am and 5pm on weekdays only. Restaurants tend to open at 10am and shut at 11pm; those that are attached to bars/clubs may not shut until dawn!

Main post offices open between 7am and 7pm Monday to Friday and between 9am and 4pm on Saturday. In smaller towns/villages, opening times can differ greatly.

EMBASSIES & CONSULATES
Embassies & Consulates in Lithuania

The following embassies and consulates are in Vilnius:

Australia (☎ 2123369; aust.con.vilnius@post.omnitel.net, Vilniaus gatvė 23)

Canada (☎ 249 0950; vilnius@canada.lt; Gedimino prospektas 64)

Estonia (☎ 278 0200; sekretar@estemb.l; A Mickevičiaus gatvė 4a)

Germany (☎ 210 6400; germ.emb@takas.lt; Sierakausko gatvė 24)

Latvia (☎ 213 1260; lietuva@latvia.balt.net; MK Čiurlionio gatvė 76)

Russia (☎ 272 1763; rusemb@rusemb.lt; Latvių gatvė 53/54)

UK (☎ 212 2070/1; be-vilnius@britain.lt; Antakalnio gatvė 2)

USA (☎ 266 5500; mail@usembassy; Akmenų gatvė 6)

Lithuanian Embassies & Consulates Abroad

Lithuania has representatives in the following countries:

Australia (☎ 02-9498 2571; 40B Fiddens Wharf Rd, Killara, NSW 2071)

Canada (☎ 613-567 5458; 130 Albert St, Suite 204, Ottawa, Ontario K1P 5G4)

Estonia (☎ 2-631 4030; amb.ee@urm.lt; Uus tn 15, Tallinn)

France (☎ 0140 54 50 50; 22 bvd de Courcelles, Paris)

Germany (☎ 030-890 6810; Charitestrasse 9, 10711 Berlin)

LITHUANIA

Latvia (☎ 2-732 1519; Rūpniecības iela 22, 1010 Rīga)
Russia Moscow (☎ 095-785 8605; Borisoglebsky per
10, Moscow 121069); Kaliningrad (☎ 0112-551 444; ul
Proletarskaya 133, Kaliningrad)
UK (☎ 020-7486 6401; 84 Gloucester Place, London
W1H 3HN)
USA (☎ 202-234 5860; 2622 16th St NW, Washington,
DC 20009)

FESTIVALS & EVENTS
Lithuania hosts many cultural, spiritual and
nonsensical events each year with the addition of the Vilnius Carnival – they're hoping to rival Rio by 2005!

APRIL
Kaunas Jazz Festival (www.kaunasjazz.com) An international crowd flocks to the city for a month of jazz events.

MAY
Vilnius Carnival (www.saldogrupe.lt) The first carnival
in the Baltics kicked off between 28 May and 6 June 2004.

JUNE
Vilnius Festival Month-long classical music festival
organised by the Lithuanian National Philharmonic Society.

HOLIDAYS
There are several national holidays:
New Year's Day 1 January
Independence Day (anniversary of 1918 independence
declaration) 16 February
The Restoration of Lithuania's Independence 11
March
Good Friday & Easter Monday April
Labour Day 1 May
**Commemoration of Grand Duke Mindaugas'
coronation** 6 July
All Saints' Day 1 November
Christmas Day 25 December
Boxing Day 26 December

MONEY
Lithuania's currency is the litas (plural: litų;
Lt). The litas comes in 10, 20, 50, 100, 200
and 500Lt notes and one, two and five litų
coins. One litas is 100 centų (ct).

Lithuania's main cities and towns have
banks and exchange offices that convert
currency. Vilnius, Klaipėda, Kaunas and
Šiauliai all have major bank chains that have
ATMs, transfer money facilities, cash travellers cheques and give cash advances. The
euro is accepted in hotels as legal tender;
some prices are only quoted in euros, but
across the rest of your trip all costs are in
litų. Smaller places may have only one bank
and/or one ATM so forward planning may
prove necessary.

POST
To post a letter it will cost you 1.7Lt to send
anywhere abroad via airmail, or 1.2Lt if it's
a postcard. Mail generally takes up to seven
days to reach Europe and up to 14 days to
get to the USA.

TELEPHONE
To call other cities within Lithuania, dial
☎ 8, wait for the tone, then dial the area
code and telephone number.

To make an international call, dial ☎ 00
before the country code. To call Lithuania
from abroad, dial your international dialling access code, ☎ 370, then the area code
and the telephone number.

To call a mobile you need nine digits – if
in doubt, take the number and count back
nine digits from the last number. Then always precede that with an 8. If taking your
own mobile to Lithuania it's worth getting a
local SIM card. Omnitel or Bitė offer cards
in denominations of 20Lt, 40Lt and 100Lt.

There are card-only blue booths dotted
around the cities. Cards are sold at press
booths and are in units of 50/100/200 costing
9/16/30Lt. Dial ☎ 8-191 for the operator.

VISAS
A valid passport is the only entry requirement for Lithuania's European neighbours
for a stay up to 90 days within a single year.

Australian, UK, Canadian, American and
New Zealand nationals don't need a visa
either. Having said that, it's always worth
checking visa status before making a trip.
Citizens from nations not included in the
visa-free gang must apply for one. A single-entry tourist visa costs €20 and must be
arranged before travel (they can't be bought
on Lithuania's borders). Contact the **Consular Department of Ministry of Foreign Affairs**
(☎ 262 0147; www.urm.lt) for all visa-related
information.

Luxembourg

HIGHLIGHTS

- **Luxembourg City** The capital's great for idly wandering, and don't miss the Chemin de la Corniche, a pedestrian promenade hailed as 'Europe's most beautiful balcony' (p758)
- **Echternach** Fab base for hiking the Müllerthal forests (762)
- **Best journey** Flanked by forest on one side and the Sûre River on the other, the road from Echternach (p762) to Vianden (p761) is one of Luxembourg's most scenic trips
- **Off-the-beaten-track** Lofty Château de Bourscheid (p762) offers superb views in an out-of-the-way location

---

FAST FACTS

- **Area** 2586 sq km (slightly smaller than Rhode Island, USA)
- **ATMs** Widespread in the capital; limited elsewhere
- **Budget** €35-40 per day
- **Capital** Luxembourg City
- **Country Code** ☎ 352
- **Famous for** Banking
- **Head of State** Grand Duke Henri
- **Languages** Lëtzebuergesch, French, German
- **Money** Euro (A$1 = €0.58, CA$1 = 0.64, ¥100 = €0.73, NZ$1 = 0.54, UK£1 = €1.45, US$1 = €0.81)
- **Phrases** *Moien/bonjour* (Lëtzebuergesch/French) hello, *äddi/au revoir* (goodbye)

- **Population** 440,000
- **Time** GMT/UTC+ 1
- **Visas** None required for most travellers to visit for up to three months.

TRAVEL HINTS

Alcohol, tobacco, perfume and petrol are cheap in Luxembourg compared with neighbouring countries – stock up here.

ROAMING LUXEMBOURG

Explore the ancient core of Luxembourg City, then head to Echternach, Vianden, Diekirch and Remich – in that order.

Let your attention slip on the E25 Brussels–Metz highway, and chances are you'll miss the Grand Duchy of Luxembourg (Luxemburg, Lëtzebuerg). Just 57km wide and 82km long, Luxembourg is Europe's third-smallest country. Not that size is an issue. With one of Europe's healthiest economies and a generally high standard of living, Luxembourgers are proud to live in a seriously diminutive country – and a beautiful one to boot. The countryside is dotted with feudal castles, deep river valleys and quaint wine-making towns, while Luxembourg City, the capital, is often described as the most dramatically situated in Europe.

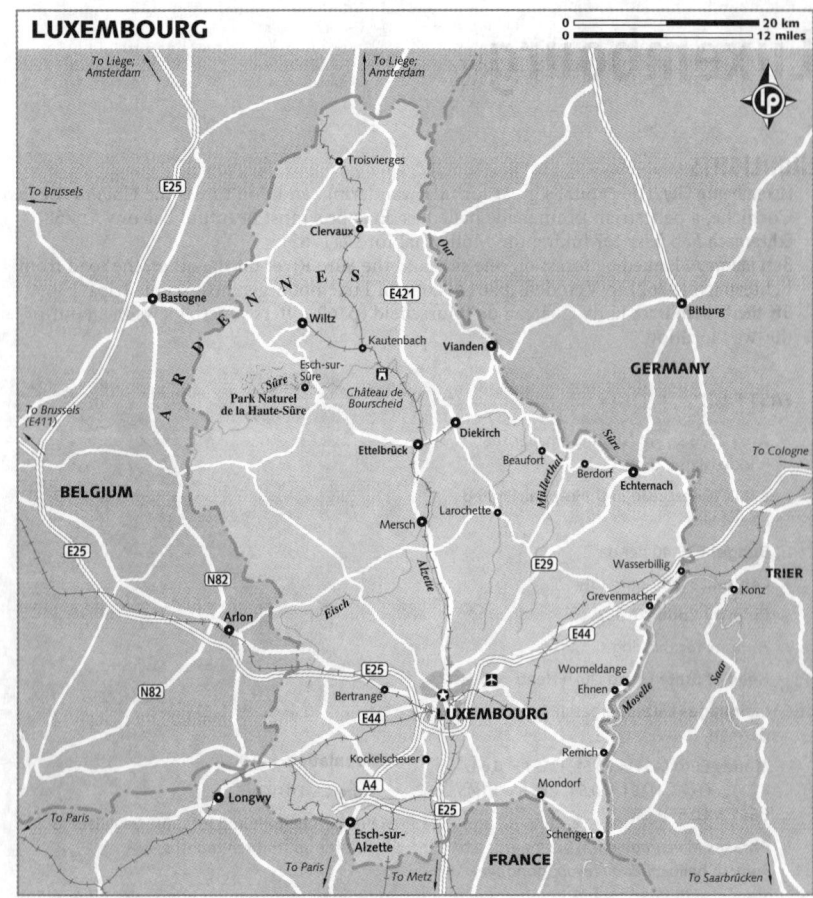

LUXEMBOURG

HISTORY

Luxembourg's history reads like the fairy tale its name evokes. More than 1000 years ago, in 963, a count called Sigefroi (or Siegfried, Count of Ardennes) built a castle high on a promontory, laying the foundations for both the present-day capital and a dynasty that spawned rulers throughout Europe.

By the end of the Middle Ages the fortified city was much sought after. Besieged, devastated and rebuilt more than 20 times in 400 years, it became the strongest fortress in Europe after Gibraltar, hence its nickname, 'Gibraltar of the north'.

The Duchy's current borders were set in 1839. Its delicate position between France and Germany led to the major European

powers declaring the Duchy neutral in 1867. As a result, much of its historic fortifications were dismantled, though the damp galleries known as the Bock Casemates (p760) can still be visited.

When Germany invaded in 1914, Luxembourg's neutrality was quashed. It was occupied for the whole of WWI and again in WWII – for insight into the 1944 Battle of the Ardennes, visit the Musée National d'Histoire Militaire in Diekirch (p763).

Luxembourg rode out the depression in the iron and steel industries in the 1970s to become a noted financial centre and tax haven. Now home to key EU institutions, it entered this century with one of Europe's healthiest economies.

PEOPLE & CULTURE

Luxembourgers are a confident lot. A motto occasionally seen carved in stone walls sums up the people's character: *'Mir wëlle bleiwe wat mir sin'* (We want to remain what we are).

More than a third of Luxembourgers are immigrants, predominantly Italians who came a century ago to work the iron-ore mines in the country's southwest corner, and Portuguese who arrived in the 1970s when iron and steel boomed. These communities are well integrated and cultural clashes are few.

ENVIRONMENT

Forests, home to wild boar, fox and deer, cover about a third of Luxembourg. There are no national parks. The main environmental concerns are air and water pollution in urban areas.

TRANSPORT

GETTING THERE & AWAY
Air

Luxembourg's only international airport is **Aérogare Findel** (☎ 47 98 50 50; www.luxair.lu), 6km east of the capital.

The national carrier, Luxair, flies to a number of European destinations, including London, Paris and Frankfurt. In 2002, a Luxair plane landing at Findel crashed killing 15 people and bringing to an end four decades of accident-free flight.

Airlines flying into Luxembourg include:
British Airways (BA; ☎ 34 20 80-83 23, www.british airways.com)
Lufthansa (LH; ☎ 47 98 50 50; www.lufthansa.com)
Luxair (LG; ☎ 47 98 1, ☎ 47 98 50 50 for flight arrival and departure information; www.luxair.lu)
VLM Airlines (VG; ☎ 49 33 95; www.vlmairlines.com)

Boat

From Easter to September it's possible to take a boat from various points along the Moselle to destinations in Germany (for example, Remich to Bernkastel costs €16 and takes four hours). For more details contact **Navitours** (☎ 75 84 89).

Land

Into Luxembourg, the main routes are the E411 from Brussels, the A4 from Paris, the

TOP FIVE LUXEMBOURG

- **Festival** Luxembourg National Day (p764)
- **Impressive sight** Vianden Castle (p761)
- **Walk** Gorge du Loup in the Müllerthal region (p762)
- **Pubs** Clausen quarter in Luxembourg City (p761)
- **Cycling** Diekirch to Echternach (p762)

E25 from Metz in France and the E44 from Trier in Germany.

Note that Eurolines buses do not pass through Luxembourg.

International train services include: Brussels (€26 for a one-way 2nd-class ticket, 2¾ hours, hourly), Amsterdam (€46.40, 5½ hours, hourly), Paris (€43, four hours, six daily) and Trier (€8.40, 40 minutes, 11 daily). For all international rail inquiries, contact the Luxembourg City **station office** (☎ 49 90 49 90; ☽ 24hr).

GETTING AROUND
Bus & Train

Luxembourg does not have an extensive rail system, so once you leave the main north–south train line, getting around by bus takes time. The main bus stations are Place Hamilius in the Old Town and Gare Centrale.

Both buses and trains are operated by **Société Nationale des Chemins de Fer Luxembourgeois** (CFL; ☎ 49 90 55 44; www.cfl.lu). The fare system is simple: €1.40 for a 'short' trip of about 10km or less (valid for one hour) or €4.60 for a 2nd-class unlimited day ticket (known as a *Billet Réseau*). The latter is good for travelling on buses and trains anywhere in the country and is valid from the first time you use it until 8am the next day.

The Luxembourg Card gives free bus and train travel plus discounted admissions – see p763.

DEPARTURE TAX

Departure tax for airline passengers leaving Luxembourg is included in the plane ticket.

Car & Motorcycle

Road rules are easy to understand and standard international signs are in use. The blood-alcohol limit for drivers is 0.08%. The speed limit on motorways is 120km. Fuel prices are among the cheapest in Western Europe: lead-free costs €0.88 per litre and diesel is €0.64.

The country's only motoring club is **Club Automobile de Luxembourg** (☎ 45 00 45 1; 54 Route de Longwy, L-8007 Bertrange).

LUXEMBOURG CITY

pop 80,176

Turrets and spires pierce the skyline, while deep valleys plunge to rivers below. There's no denying the striking composition of the Grand Duchy's 1000-year-old capital. Situated high on a promontory overlooking the Pétrusse and Alzette Rivers, Luxembourg City is still defined by the gorges that hampered invading armies for centuries. One of Europe's financial leaders, it radiates a composed air of old and modern, the latter evident by state-of-the-art museums and a gleaming new gallery devoted to contemporary art that's expected to open in 2005.

A ROYAL AFFAIR

Luxembourgers love their royalty. In 1919, the Grand Ducal family was put up for referendum and after a resounding 'yes', their existence has never again been questioned. In fact, unlike Britain where slagging off the royals is a public pastime, the relationship here is stronger than ever. Grand Duke Henri and Grand Duchess Maria Teresa can take the credit for this popularity pull. On coming to the throne in 2000, they appeared as a couple for their televised Christmas message, and shocked and pleased their audience by *both* addressing the nation. Welcome to the 21st century, Luxembourg!

ORIENTATION

Luxembourg City's pedestrianised Old Town is based around two squares – Place d'Armes and Place Guillaume II. To the south is the train station quarter, an area of little appeal. Below the Old Town are the river valley neighbourhoods of Grund, Clausen and Pfaffenthal. Easy access to the Grund is provided by an elevator on Plateau du St Esprit.

INFORMATION
Internet Access

Centre Information Jeunes (CIJ; ☎ 26 29 32 00; www.youth.lu; Galerie Kons, 26 Place de la Gare; ☾ 10am-6pm Mon-Fri) Youth information centre providing free Internet access (bookings necessary).

Sparkey's (☎ 26 20 12 23; 11a Ave Monterey; ☾ 7am-1am Mon-Sat) Bar with two terminals.

Medical Services

Clinique Ste Thérèse (☎ 49 77 61; 36 Rue Ste Zithe) Central hospital providing emergency service.

Money

ATMs Inside Gare Centrale; outside main post office; inside Findel airport terminal.

Kredietbank Luxembourg (Place de la Gare; ☾ 8.30am-4.30pm Mon-Fri)

Post & Telephone

Main post office (☎ 47 65 44 51; 25 Rue Aldringen; ☾ 7am-7pm Mon-Fri, 7am-5pm Sat)

Tourist Information

Luxembourg City Tourist Office (☎ 22 28 09; www.lcto.lu; Place d'Armes; ☾ 9am-6pm Mon-Sat, 10am-6pm Sun) Free city maps, walking tour pamphlets and events guides.

Luxembourg National Tourist Office (☎ 42 82 82 20; www.ont.lu; Place de la Gare; ☾ 8.30am-6.30pm Mon-Sat, 9am-12.30pm & 2-6pm Sun Jun-Sep, 9.15am-2.30pm & 1.45-6pm daily Oct-May) National information.

SIGHTS

Start at **Place d'Armes**, Luxembourg's central pedestrianised square, from where it's an easy walk to the **Musée National d'Histoire et d'Art** (☎ 47 93 30-1; www.mnha.lu; Marché-aux-Poissons; admission €5; ☾ 10am-5pm Tue-Sun). The country's principal museum, it has permanent collections of Roman and medieval relics, fortification models, and art dating from the 13th century.

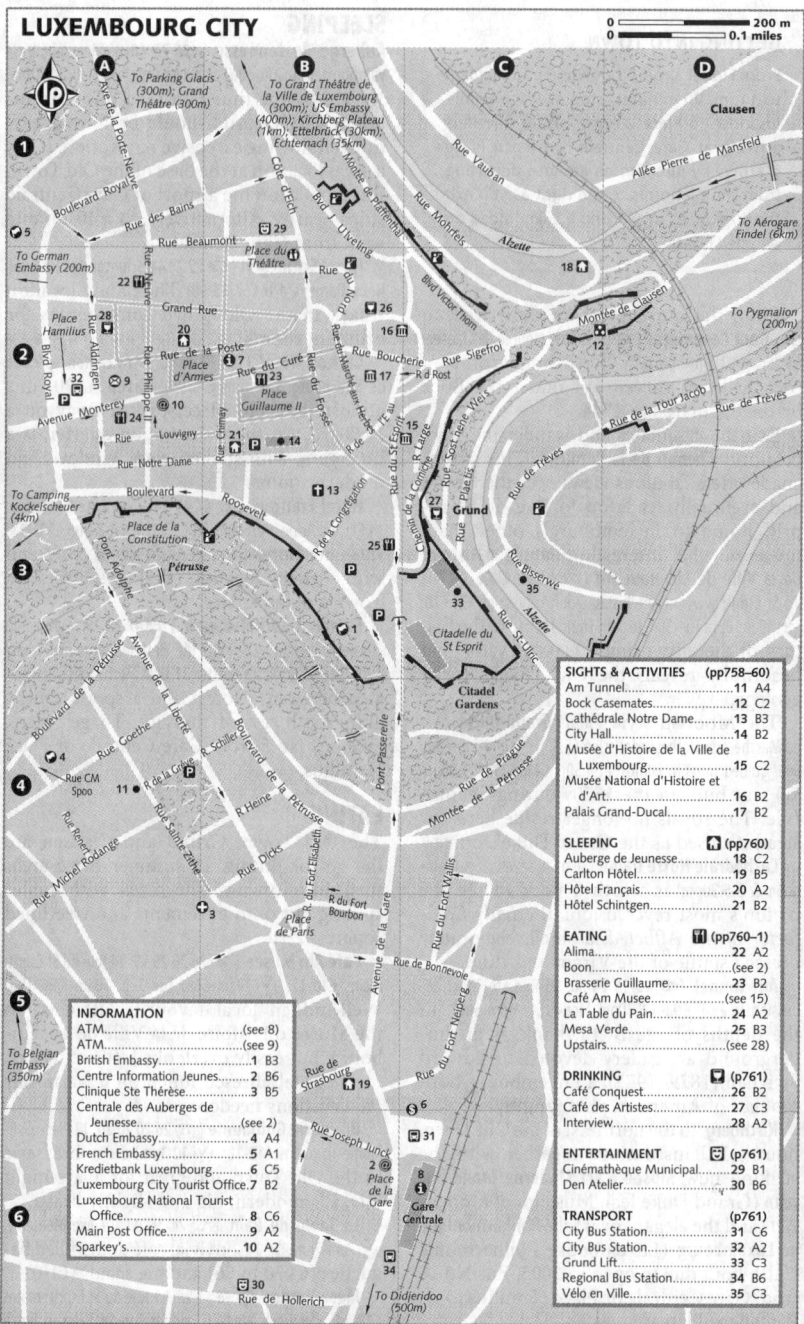

LUXEMBOURG CITY

SIGHTS & ACTIVITIES	(pp758–60)
Am Tunnel	11 A4
Bock Casemates	12 C2
Cathédrale Notre Dame	13 B3
City Hall	14 B2
Musée d'Histoire de la Ville de Luxembourg	15 C2
Musée National d'Histoire et d'Art	16 B2
Palais Grand-Ducal	17 B2

SLEEPING	(pp760)
Auberge de Jeunesse	18 C2
Carlton Hôtel	19 B5
Hôtel Français	20 A2
Hôtel Schintgen	21 B2

EATING	(pp760–1)
Alima	22 A2
Boon	(see 2)
Brasserie Guillaume	23 B2
Café Am Musee	(see 15)
La Table du Pain	24 A2
Mesa Verde	25 B3
Upstairs	(see 28)

DRINKING	(p761)
Café Conquest	26 B2
Café des Artistes	27 C3
Interview	28 A2

ENTERTAINMENT	(p761)
Cinémathèque Municipal	29 B1
Den Atelier	30 B6

TRANSPORT	(p761)
City Bus Station	31 C6
City Bus Station	32 A2
Grund Lift	33 C3
Regional Bus Station	34 B6
Vélo en Ville	35 C3

INFORMATION	
ATM	(see 8)
ATM	(see 9)
British Embassy	1 B3
Centre Information Jeunes	2 B6
Clinique Ste Thérèse	3 B5
Centrale des Auberges de Jeunesse	(see 2)
Dutch Embassy	4 A4
French Embassy	5 A1
Kreditbank Luxembourg	6 C5
Luxembourg City Tourist Office	7 B2
Luxembourg National Tourist Office	8 C6
Main Post Office	9 A2
Sparkey's	10 A2

LUXEMBOURG

GETTING INTO TOWN

From Findel airport, bus Nos 9 and 16 (5am to 11pm, 20 minutes) stop at Place Hamilius close to Place d'Armes. Train travellers arriving at Gare Centrale can reach Place d'Armes by jumping on any bus departing from the platforms to the right as you exit the station, or by walking 1.25km (head up Ave de la Gare).

From the museum, it's a short walk to the **Bock Casemates** (☎ 22 28 09; Montée de Clausen; €1.75; ◔ 10am-5pm Mar-Oct), a honeycomb of rock galleries carved out under the Bock by the Spaniards in 1744.

Exit the casemates and wander the city's beautiful **Chemin de la Corniche**. This promenade offers fabulous views over the Grund and eventually leads up to Rue du St Esprit, home to Luxembourg's other main museum, the interesting **Musée d'Histoire de la Ville de Luxembourg** (☎ 47 96 45 00; 14 Rue du St Esprit; www.musee-hist.lu; adult/concession €5/3.70; ◔ 10am-6pm Tue-Sun, to 8pm Thu). Explore the history of the city, using a glass elevator that beautifully reveals the Old Town's rocky geology.

The Moorish-style **Palais Grand-Ducal** (Rue du Marché-aux-Herbes; admission €5.50; ◔ mid-Jul–early Sep, guided tours in English at 4.30pm Mon-Fri & 1.30pm Sat) was built in the 1570s during Spanish rule. The royals no longer reside here; instead it's used as the Grand Duke's office.

Cathédrale Notre Dame (Blvd Roosevelt; ◔ 10am-noon & 2-5.30pm) is worth a peek to see the nation's most revered idol, the *Lady Comforter of the Afflicted*, a small, elaborately dressed statue of the Virgin and child.

Am Tunnel (☎ 40 15 24 50; 16 Rue Ste Zithe; admission free; ◔ 9am-5.30pm Mon-Fri, 2-6pm Sun), in the depths of the BCEE bank, is an underground art gallery devoted to Edward Steichen (1879–1973), a Luxembourg-born pioneer of American photography.

Kirchberg, to the northeast of the Old Town, houses EU institutions together with the striking new **Musée d'Art Moderne Grand-Duc Jean** (Grand Duke Jean Museum of Modern Art) and the elegant oval **Salle Philharmonique de Luxembourg** (Luxembourg Philharmonic Hall), both due to open in 2005. Bus No 18 from Gare Centrale or Place Hamilius tours Kirchberg Plateau.

SLEEPING

Auberge de Jeunesse (☎ 22 68 89; luxembourg@youthhostels.lu; 2 Rue du Fort Olizy; dm/s/d €16.50/24.50/45; ℗ ✗) By the time you read this, Luxembourg City's hostel should be fully operational following extensive renovation. It has a great location at the base of the Old Town. Bus No 9 from the airport or Gare Centrale stops nearby. Alternatively it's a 40-minute walk from Gare Centrale.

Hôtel Schintgen (☎ 22 28 44; schintgn@pt.lu; 6 Rue Notre Dame; s/d/tr €67/85/90) The handy location smack in the Old Town compensates for ordinary rooms.

Carlton Hôtel (☎ 29 96 60; www.carlton.lu; 9 Rue de Strasbourg; s/d from €75/90) Circa 1920, this atmospheric old place, tucked away on a backstreet in the train station quarter, is a little gem, with stained-glass windows and modern rooms.

Hôtel Français (☎ 47 45 34; www.hotelfrancais.lu; 14 Place d'Armes; s/d Mon-Fri €97/125, Sat & Sun €90/118) Intimate hotel dotted with *objet d'art* and with a prized location overlooking the Old Town's main square.

Camping Kockelscheuer (☎ 47 18 15; www.camp-kockelscheuer.lu; 22 Route de Bettembourg; per adult/camp site €3.50/4; ◔ Easter-31 Oct) Pleasantly situated between a forest and a sports centre, 4km southwest of the city. To get there, take bus No 5 from Gare Centrale or Place Hamilius.

EATING

The Old Town, Grund and Clausen are the go for dining. In summer these areas turn into open-air terraces with tables spilling out onto pavements and tree-lined squares.

Café Am Musee (☎ 26 20 25 95; 14 Rue du St Esprit; mains €10-12; ◔ 10am-6pm Tue-Sun, 10am-8pm Thu) Well-hidden local favourite, attached to the Musée d'Histoire de la Ville de Luxembourg, but easily overlooked. It's at its best for a casual alfresco lunch on a warm day (reservations needed).

Brasserie Guillaume (☎ 26 20 20 20; 12 Place Guillaume II; mains €12-18; ◔ 10-1am) Best brasserie in the Old Town and great for a late-night bite. It's modern, big and slightly brash.

La Table du Pain (☎ 24 16 08; 19 Ave Monterey; ◔ 7am-7pm; ✗) Convivial café doing filled baguettes (€4.50 to €6) and big salads (€10).

Mesa Verde (☎ 46 41 26; 11 Rue du St Esprit; mains €18-24; ◔ lunch Wed-Fri, dinner Tue-Sat, closed lunch

Aug; ⊠) Imaginative vegetarian and sea-food dishes are the mainstay of this exotic restaurant.

Upstairs (☎ 26 27 01 12; 21 Rue Aldringen; mains €20; ☾ lunch Tue-Sat, dinner Tue-Fri) Great Vietnamese and Japanese dishes in no-fuss surroundings are on offer.

Recommended supermarkets are **Boon** (Place de la Gare), opposite Gare Centrale, and **Alima** (Rue Neuve) in the Old Town.

DRINKING & CLUBBING

The Old Town, Grund, Clausen and Hollerich are the most popular spots for a night out.

Café des Artistes (☎ 46 13 27; 22 Montée du Grund; ☾ evenings Tue-Sun) Nostalgic Grund café that has been around since 1968 and has candles to prove it.

Pygmalion (☎ 42 08 60; 19 Rue de la Tour Jacob; ☾ 4pm-1am, to 3am Fri-Sat) This moody little Irish haunt is one of several good pubs in Clausen, an area favoured by late-night revellers. Take bus No 9 or night bus CN1.

Didjeridoo (☎ 44 00 49; 41 Rue de Bouillon; ☾ Fri & Sat) Funky Hollerich nightclub into techno and house.

Interview (☎ 47 36 65; 19 Rue Aldringen) Raw café close to Place Hamilius and a great place to hang with a drink.

Café Conquest (☎ 22 21 41; 7 Rue du Palais de Justice) A popular gay pub in the heart of the city.

ENTERTAINMENT

The informative entertainment guide, *Luxembourg Weekly*, is available free from the tourist office.

Cinémathèque Municipal (☎ 47 96 26 44; 17 Place du Théâtre; adult/concession €3.80/2.50) Closest thing in Luxembourg to an arthouse cinema and cheap to boot.

Den Atelier (☎ 49 54 66; www.atelier.lu; 56 Rue de Hollerich) The main venue for live music, placed 500m west of Gare Centrale in Hollerich, an off-the-beaten-track nightlife area.

Grand Théâtre de la Ville de Luxembourg (☎ 47 08 95 1; www.luxembourgticket.lu; 1 Rond Point Schuman) The nation's biggest performing arts complex, renovated in 2003 and offering state-of-the-art facilities.

GETTING AROUND

For bike rental there's **Vélo en Ville** (☎ 47 96 23 83; 8 Bisserwée; half-/full-day €12.50/20; ☾ 10am-noon & 1-8pm Apr-Oct).

AROUND LUXEMBOURG CITY

The rest of Luxembourg is easily accessible from the capital. The Ardennes' verdant forests stretch over the country's northern tip and hide beguiling towns such as Vianden and Clervaux, and ruined castles including Château de Bourscheid.

East is the enchanting Müllerthal region and its ancient base, Echternach. This is a fabulous area for hikers, distinguished by an almost primeval landscape of deep gorges scoured by ancient streams through sandstone plateaux.

Immediately north of Luxembourg City is the heavily farmed region of Central Luxembourg; the best base here is Diekirch. Wine-producing Moselle Valley with its waterfront playground, Remich, is southeast of the capital.

VIANDEN

pop 1600

Vianden is Luxembourg's most dramatically sited countryside town, nestled in the valley of the Our River and framed by wooded hills. To get there from Luxembourg City, take the train to Ettelbrück (30 minutes) and then a bus (30 minutes, 10 daily).

The **tourist office** (☎ 83 42 57-1; www.vianden.lu; 1a Rue du Vieux Marché; ☾ 8am-6pm Mon-Fri, 10am-2pm Sat & Sun Apr-Aug, 9am-noon & 1-5pm Mon-Fri Sep-Mar) is down by the river.

Looming over the town is the **château** (☎ 83 41 08-1; Grand Rue; ☾ 10am-4pm Jan-Feb & Nov-Dec, 10am-5pm Mar & Oct, 10am-6pm Apr-Sep). The oldest part of the castle dates to the 11th century, but it has all been impeccably restored.

Vianden's picturesque position can be photographed from the **télésiège** (chairlift; ☎ 83 43 23; 39 Rue du Sanatorium; admission €4.50; ☾ 10am-6pm daily Jun-Sep, closed Mon Easter-May & Oct).

The **Maison de Victor Hugo** (☎ 26 87 40 88; www.victor-hugo.lu; 37 Rue de la Gare; admission €4; ☾ 11am-5pm Tue-Sun Easter–mid-Oct) was home to author Victor Hugo for three months during his 19-year exile from France.

The pleasant **Auberge des Jeunesse** (☎ 83 41 77; vianden@youthhostels.lu; 3 Montée du Château; dm/s/d €14.50/22.50/41; ☾ closed Dec-Mar; ⊠) is in the shadow of the château – it's a 1km uphill walk from the bus station.

LUXEMBOURG

The rambling **Hôtel/Restaurant Petry** (☎ 83 41 22; www.hotel-petry.com; 15 Rue de la Gare; s/d from €35/50; mains €12-20; **P**) has a new wing with modern rooms and castle views. The restaurant does good French cuisine, and there are also cheaper pizzas.

Draped along the river bank to the south of town is **Camping de l'Our** (☎ 83 45 05; www .camping-our-vianden.lu; 3 Route de Bettel; per adult/camp site €4/3.50; ☺ closed Nov-Easter).

CLERVAUX
pop 1800

Hidden deep in the valley of the Clierf River in Luxembourg's northern tip, Clervaux is best associated with a permanent photographic exhibition that draws visitors from far afield. Clervaux is easily reached from Luxembourg City by train (one hour, every two hours).

The **tourist office** (☎ 92 00 72; ☺ 2-5pm Mon-Fri Easter-Jun, 9.45-11.45am & 2-6pm daily Jul-Aug, 9.45-11.45am & 1-5pm Sep-Oct) is housed in a side turret of Clervaux's castle.

The castle, damaged in 1944, is visited mostly for the famous **'Family of Man' exhibition** (☎ 92 96 57; admission €4.50; ☺ 10am-6pm daily Apr-Sep, Tue-Sun Mar & Oct-Dec) collated by Edward Steichen. Steichen compiled the 500 B&W photos in 1955 at the age of 76 and they travelled the world for years before coming to rest here.

Hôtel/Restaurant du Parc (☎ 92 06 50; www.hotel duparc.lu; 2 Rue du Parc; s/d €44/70; ☺ Feb-Dec; **P**) is the town's most atmospheric option for eating and sleeping. It's an old whitewashed mansion fitted with a mix of modern and old.

WILTZ
pop 4600

Wiltz is the so-called capital of the Luxembourg Ardennes. It's a relatively quiet place that bursts into life in July for the Grand Duchy's biggest theatrical and musical event, the **Festival de Théâtre et de Musique** (www.festivalwiltz.online.lu). Wiltz is easily accessible by train from Luxembourg City (1½ hours) – take the train (direction Clervaux) to Kautenbach, and catch another train from there.

The town's **Auberge de Jeunesse** (☎ 95 80 39; wiltz@youthhostels.lu; 6 Rue de la Montagne; dm/s/d €14.30/22.30/41; ☺ closed Jan-Mar & mid-Nov–Dec; ✗) is a 1km climb from the train station.

CHÂTEAU DE BOURSCHEID

Roughly halfway between Wiltz and Ettelbrück, a road winds up to the magnificent **Château de Bourscheid** (☎ 99 05 70; 1 Schlasswee; adult/child €3/1.50; ☺ 11am-5pm Apr, 10am-6pm May-Jun & Sep, 10am-7pm Jul-Aug, 11am-4pm Oct, 11am-4pm Sat & Sun Nov-Mar). This 1000-year-old castle is one of the most beautiful in the Grand Duchy and, indeed, affords the best views. However, you'll need wheels to get here.

ECHTERNACH
pop 5100

The ancient town of Echternach flanks the western bank of the Sûre River and makes a superb base for exploring the Müllerthal region. Only buses connect Echternach with Luxembourg City – the trip takes 40 minutes.

The **tourist office** (☎ 72 02 30; Parvis de la Basilique; ☺ 9am-noon & 2-5pm Mon-Fri, also Sat & Sun Jul-Aug) is in a courtyard next to the town's huge basilica.

The **basilica** (☺ 9.30am-6.30pm), the country's most important religious building, is the town's main sight. Here lies St Willibrord, an Anglo-Saxon monk who founded Echternach's abbey in the 7th century.

Marked **hiking trails** start from near the town's bus station. The best is path 'B', which winds up via Troosknepchen and Wolfsschlucht to the **Gorge du Loup**, a sheer-sided canyon flanked by dramatic sandstone formations; it takes 2½ hours return.

The **Auberge de Jeunesse** (☎ 72 01 58; echternach@youthhostels.lu; 9 Rue André Duchscher; dm/s/d €14.50/22.50/41; ☺ Feb-Oct; ✗) is a wonderfully sited hostel in the centre of town.

Hôtel Le Pavillon (☎ 72 98 09; www.lepavillon.lu; 2 Rue de la Gare; s/d €62/72; **P** €7) is a corner hotel with just 10 well-equipped rooms.

Camping Officiel (☎ 72 02 72; www.camping-echternach.lu; 5 Route de Diekirch; per adult/camp site €4/4; ☺ Easter-Oct; ☎) sits about 200m from the bus station, draped along the hillside.

DIEKIRCH
pop 6000

This pleasant little town on the banks of the gushing Sûre River in Central Luxembourg is home to the country's main wartime museum. From Luxembourg City, there are hourly trains to Diekirch (40 minutes).

The **tourist office** (☎ 80 30 23; www.diekirch.lu; 3 Place de la Libération; ☺ 9am-noon & 2-5pm Mon-Fri,

2-4pm Sat Sep-Jun, 9am-5pm Mon-Fri, 10am-4pm Sat & Sun Jul-Aug) is a 10-minute walk from the train station.

An excellent collection of memorabilia detailing the WWII Battle of the Bulge and the liberation of Luxembourg by US troops is presented at Diekirch's **Musée National d'Histoire Militaire** (☎ 80 89 08; 10 Rue Barnertal; admission €5; ☯ 10am-6pm Apr-Nov, 2-6pm Dec-Mar). It is well worth a visit.

Good **cycling** paths follow the river all the way from Diekirch to Echternach (27km). Bikes are available from one of Luxembourg's few rental outfits, **Speicher Sport** (☎ 80 84 38; 56 Rue Clairefontaine; half-/full-day €10/15; ☯ 8.30am-noon & 1.30-6pm Tue-Sat).

The region's only **Auberge des Jeunesse** (☎ 81 22 69; ettelbruck@youthhostels.lu; Rue Josephine-Charlotte; dm/s/d €14.50/22.50/41; ☒) is at Ettelbrück, a 5km train ride west of Diekirch.

Back in Diekirch, **Hôtel/Restaurant Hiertz** (☎ 80 35 62; fax 80 88 69; 1 Rue Clairefontaine; s/d €60/75; mains €25-30; ☯ hotel closed late Dec–early Jan, restaurant closed lunch Sat, dinner Sun & all Mon) is a delight. The whole place oozes understatement and the restaurant does the region's best French food.

By the river and within a few minutes' walk from central Diekirch is **Camping de la Sûre** (☎ 80 94 25; fax 80 27 86; 34 Route de Gilsdorf; per adult/camp site €4.50/4.50; ☯ Apr-Sep).

REMICH

Less than half an hour's drive east of the capital, the Luxembourg section of the Moselle Valley is one of Europe's smallest wine regions. More than a dozen towns and hamlets are draped along the **Route du Vin** (Wine Road); the nicest is Remich. From Luxembourg City, there are twice-daily buses to Remich.

Wine tasting is the premier attraction here and several *caves* (cellars) give tours. The best of these is at **St Martin** (☎ 23 69 97 74; 53 Route de Stadtbredimus; admission €2.50; ☯ 10am-noon & 1.30-6pm Apr-Oct), about 1.5km north of Remich. Here tours lead through damp tunnels hewn in the cliff. Bus No 450 from Remich to Grevenmacher stops in front of the winery.

Remich is lined with waterfront hotels. **Auberge des Cygnes** (☎ 23 69 88 52; hpcygnes@pt.lu; 11 Esplanade; s/d/tr €48/65/83; ☯ closed mid-Jan–mid-Feb; **P**) has calm, pastel-toned rooms and a restaurant doing good woodfire-baked pizzas.

LUXEMBOURG DIRECTORY

ACCOMMODATION

A dozen hostels are operated by **Centrale des Auberges de Jeunesse Luxembourgeoises** (☎ 26 29 35 00; www.youthhostels.lu; Galerie Kons, 24-26 Place de la Gare, L-1616 Luxembourg City), which is affiliated with Hostelling International (HI). Most close irregularly throughout the year, so ring ahead.

B&Bs and cheap hotels are very light on the ground – most hotels are in the mid-range and top-end brackets. Camping grounds are abundant.

ACTIVITIES

With a huge 5000km network of marked walking paths, the Grand Duchy is a hiking haven. Tracks, marked by white triangles, connect the HI hostels. Local tourist offices stock regional walking maps. The Müllerthal region offers amazing hiking tracks (see p762).

Cycling is a popular pastime but rental outfits are few – see Vélo en Ville (p761) or Speicher Sport (p763). Bikes can be taken on trains for €1.10.

BOOKS

How to Remain What You Are, by Luxembourg psychologist George Müller, is a humorous look at local ways. *182 x Luxembourg* describes 182 hiking trails, while *40 Cycle Routes* is the cyclist's equivalent.

BUSINESS HOURS

Trading hours are 9am to 5.30pm weekdays (except Monday when some shops open about noon), and a half or full day on Saturday. Many shops close for lunch. Banks have shorter hours: 8.30am to 4.30pm Monday to Friday (in Luxembourg City banks also open on Saturday morning); country branches close for lunch.

DISCOUNT CARDS

Offering great value for the traveller, the **Luxembourg Card** (one/two/three days €9/16/22) gives free admission to many attractions plus unlimited use of public transport. It's valid from Easter to 31 October, and is available from tourist offices.

LUXEMBOURG

EMBASSIES & CONSULATES
Embassies & Consulates in Luxembourg
The nearest Australian, Canadian and New Zealand embassies are in Belgium (see p129). The following foreign embassies are in Luxembourg City:

Belgium (☎ 44 27 46 1; 4 Rue des Girondins, L-1626)
France (☎ 45 72 71 1; 8 Blvd Joseph II, L-1840)
Germany (☎ 45 34 45 1; 20-22 Ave Émile Reuter, L-2420)
Ireland (☎ 45 06 10; 28 Route d'Arlon, L-1140)
Netherlands (☎ 22 75 70; 5 Rue CM Spoo, L-2546)
UK (☎ 22 98 64; 14 Blvd Roosevelt, L-2450)
USA (☎ 46 01 23; 22 Blvd Emmanuel Servais, L-2535)

Luxembourg Embassies & Consulates Abroad
France (☎ 01 45 55 13 37; fax 01 45 51 72 29; 33 Ave Rapp, F-75005 Paris)
Germany (☎ 228-21 40 08; fax 228-22 29 20; Adenauerallee 108, D-53113 Bonn)
Netherlands (☎ 070-360 75 16; fax 070-356 33 03; Nassaulaan 8, NL-2514 JS Den Haag)
UK (☎ 020-7235 6961; fax 020-7235 9734; 27 Wilton Crescent, London SW1X 8SD)
USA (☎ 202-265 41 71; fax 202-328 82 70; 2200 Massachusetts Ave NW, Washington, DC 20008)

In countries where there is no representative, contact the nearest Belgian or Dutch diplomatic missions.

FESTIVALS & EVENTS
Luxembourg National Day Festivities begin on 22 June with fireworks in Luxembourg City; cafés and bars are open all night. On 23 June, a military parade winds through the capital.
Summer in the City Summer-long series of concerts and street animation in Luxembourg City including **Rock um Knuedler** (early July), a one-day open-air rock festival, and **Blues'n Jazzrallye** (mid-July).

FOOD & DRINK
Luxembourg is a carnivore's capital – game, pork and freshwater fish dominate. While French and Germanic-style foods are most common, there's modest culinary diversity in Luxembourg City.

The national dish is *judd mat gaardebounen* (smoked pork served in a cream-based sauce with chunks of potato and broadbeans). Other specialities include *ferkelsrippchen* (grilled spareribs), *liewekniddelen mat sauerkraut* (liver meatballs with sauerkraut),

traipen (black pudding), *kuddelfleck* (boiled tripe) and *kachkeis* (a cooked cheese).

Luxembourg's wine industry is known for fruity whites and sparkling wines at affordable prices. Try those made by St Martin at Remich (p763).

HOLIDAYS
New Year's Day 1 January
Easter Monday March/April
May Day 1 May
Ascension Day 40th day after Easter
Whit Monday 7th Monday after Easter
National Day 23 June
Assumption 15 August
All Saints' Day 1 November
Christmas Day 25 December

LANGUAGE
Luxembourg has three official languages – French, German and Lëtzebuergesch. The latter is most closely related to German and it was proclaimed as the national tongue in 1984. Luxembourgers speak Lëtzebuergesch to each other but generally switch to French or English when talking to foreigners.

MONEY
Banks are the best place to change money – you'll have no trouble finding one in Luxembourg. Tipping is not obligatory as service and VAT are included in hotel and restaurant prices.

POST
Letters (under 20g) costs €0.60 to EU countries, and €0.80 to non-EU countries. The most useful poste restante address is: Poste Restante, Luxembourg-Centre Bureau de Post, L-1118 Luxembourg 2.

TELEPHONE
Luxembourg's international country code is ☎ 352. To telephone abroad, the international access code is ☎ 00. To get an international operator, call ☎ 12410. Numbers prefixed with 0800 are toll-free numbers. Collect calls can be made by dialling ☎ 8002 00 first.

VISAS
Visa requirements are the same as for Belgium (see p131).

Macedonia Македонија

HIGHLIGHTS

- **Ohrid** The smooth mirror of Ohrid Lake where swans glide at dusk; small streets of the town running between seven spectacular churches (p772)
- **Skopje** Urban vibe meets colourful traditional Turkish bazaar; up-and-coming art and music scene; a great riverside promenade (p768)
- **Off-the-beaten track** A magnificent hike up the mountain to the mystical Treskavec monastery (p767) with colourful ancient icons, bare rock and views to die for

FAST FACTS

- **Area** 25,713 sq km (slightly bigger than Wales)
- **ATMS** Skopje has a handful of ATMs
- **Budget** US$25-30 per day
- **Capital** Skopje
- **Country code** ☎ 389
- **Head of State** President Branko Crvenkovski
- **Famous for** Mother Teresa (ethnically Albanian, born in Skopje)
- **Languages** Macedonian, Albanian
- **Money** Macedonian denar (A$1 = 36.28MKD, CA$1 = 39.87MKD, €1 = 62.53MKD, ¥100 = 45.85MKD, NZ$1 = 34.25MKD, £1 = 90.04MKD, US$1=50.16MKD)
- **Phrases** Zdravo (hello), prijatno (goodbye)
- **Population** 2,022,547

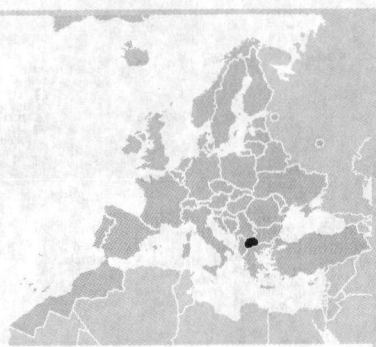

- **Time** GMT/UTC + 1
- **Visas** EU and New Zealand citizens need no visa; US and Australia citizens can receive a visa issued free at the port of entry; Canada and South Africa citizens pay US$12, either from an embassy or at the border.

TRAVEL HINTS

Book ahead for Skopje's one youth hostel, as accommodation is pricey. The Cyrillic alphabet is used almost exclusively, so it's worth trying to learn it before you go.

ROAMING MACEDONIA

Start at Skopje roaming the Turkish bazaar and viewing the luxurious architecture of its old baths-cum-art galleries, then head south to culturally opulent Ohrid, with its magnificent monasteries and churches.

The Former Yugoslav Republic of Macedonia (FYROM) is a real treat for travellers, especially those who like open spaces, majestic mountains, fantastic lakes and soaring waterfalls, spiced up with outdoor activities such as trekking, skiing or swimming, and stirred with a rich helping of culture along the way. There are remote Orthodox monasteries to be discovered,

MACEDONIA

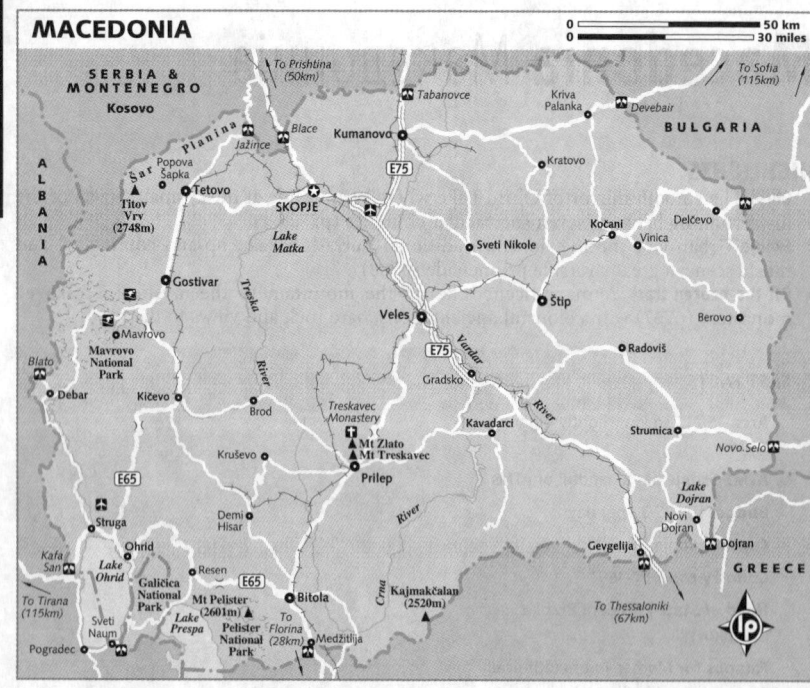

MACEDONIA

ancient mosques to be seen, and you can roam around rich Oriental bazaars. Ohrid town is a worthwhile destination, with the magnificent lake and charming churches. Along with that, Macedonia's up-and-coming capital Skopje is a kicking little city with a good nightlife – there's a buzzing youth scene for crazy nights out if you overdose on the healthy life.

HISTORY

Historical Macedonia (the birthplace of Alexander the Great) is today contained mostly in present-day Greece. The Romans subjugated the region, which subsequently became part of the Byzantine Empire. Slav tribes settled in the 7th century, and in the 9th century the region was conquered by Bulgaria. Next came a long period in which Macedonia passed back and forth between Byzantine, Bulgarian and Serbian rule. Most of the Balkans were conquered by the Ottomans in 1389.

Five centuries later, in 1893, Macedonian nationalists formed the Internal Macedo-

READING UP

For a collection of informative essays and articles on Macedonia, read James Pettifer's *The New Macedonian Question* (2001).

nian Revolutionary Organisation (IMRO) to fight for independence. When royalist Serbia took over from the Ottomans in 1913, IMRO continued its struggle. Macedonia finally gained full republic status as part of Yugoslavia in 1943.

Over the next 40 years Yugoslavia prospered in comparison with the other Eastern European states and the country was relatively open as a tourist destination.

In January 1992, following Yugoslavia's break-up, the country declared full independence. Belgrade cooperated by ordering all Federal troops to withdraw, and, because the split was peaceful, road and rail links were never broken.

Initially, Greece refused to recognise the new country, worried that the name 'Macedonia' might imply territorial claims on northern Greece, so in 1993 Macedonia gained admission to the UN under the 'temporary' title of FYROM. When the USA formally recognised FYROM in 1994, Greece declared an economic embargo and closed the port of Thessaloniki. The embargo was lifted in November 1995 after Macedonia changed its flag and agreed to discuss its name with Greece. To date, there has been no resolution of this thorny issue.

In August 2001, fighting broke out between Macedonian forces and Albanian would-be separatists. The hostilities ended when both sides agreed to talks that would allow a greater participation by minority groups in the political life of the country. Steps were implemented in May 2002 and tensions have since eased.

After the death of the Macedonian president Boris Trajkovski in a plane accident in Bosnia and Hercegovina in February 2004, the presidential seat was taken by the former prime minister, Branko Crvenkovski, in elections held in April of the same year.

PEOPLE & CULTURE

The republic's two million-plus population comprises Macedonians of Slav ethnicity (66.6%), Albanians (22.7%), Turks (4%), Roma (2.2%) and Serbs (2.1%). The Macedonians are a hospitable people who are extremely proud of their country. If you can help it, don't discuss politics, or at least discuss with caution.

Although men and women in larger towns and cities wear tight, colourful and revealing apparel, do dress modestly when visiting a church, monastery or mosque or

you might not be allowed entry. Take care to dress with respect when walking around predominantly Muslim areas, too, no matter how hot it may be.

TRANSPORT

GETTING THERE & AWAY
Air

A host of international airlines service Skopje's **Petrovac Airport** (☎ 02-235 156). Travel agencies in Skopje or Ohrid can book flights. For daily flights in and out of Macedonia, check www.airports.com.mk. Tickets are pricey, starting from around US$550 for departures from London, so check flights to Thessaloniki, from where you can take a train to Skopje for €10.

Bus

Skopje has two international bus stations (see p772). Buses travel to Sofia (640MKD, six hours, three daily), Istanbul (1860MKD, 14 hours, three to four daily), Belgrade (800MKD, six hours, three daily), Frankfurt (6100MKD, 24 hours, one weekly) and Zagreb (2560MKD, 15 hours, four weekly). Buses also travel to Budapest, Vienna and Sarajevo.

Buses between Skopje and Prishtina, the capital of Kosovo, are fairly frequent. To/from Albania you can travel from Tetovo or Struga to Tirana by bus (six to seven hours, two daily), or walk across the border at Sveti Naum (see p774) or Kafa San.

TRESKAVEC MONASTERY

Dramatically situated atop Mount Zlato, 10km above the town of Prilep, this monastery is the most magnificent place in the country. Even if you're not religious, the few hours of heavy walking here might make you understand the ecstasy experienced by pilgrims upon reaching a church or holy site. The exertion makes you light-headed and adds to your sense of awe.

If that weren't enough, you will be struck by the views of the valley stretching on all sides beneath you, and by the thick rolling clouds moving lightly above your head. The mountain itself is bare and the rock formations are like dinosaurs turned to stone mid-step, with barren trees grazed by the sweeping winds.

The monastery itself was rebuilt in the early 1990s, after it was destroyed by a fire, and forms a sort of pentagon with a courtyard and church in the middle. Inside the monastery, you will be welcomed by the lovely Naumovski couple, who will cook you dinner and let you sleep in the rooms for free. Leave some money at the icons.

Prepare to be amazed at the most colourful and intricate frescoes found in Macedonia at the 14th-century church of the Holy Mother of God, the monastery's spiritual heart. Incisions on the bare walls reveal more frescoes to be uncovered, like small windows into history.

EMERGENCY NUMBERS

- Ambulance ☎ 94
- Police ☎ 92
- Roadside assistance ☎ 987

Car & Motorcycle

There are several main highway border crossings into Macedonia from neighbouring countries. You will need a green card endorsed for Macedonia to bring a car into the country.

Taxi

A cheap and easy way to reach Thessaloniki if you are in a group is by taxi (€120, up to four persons). To Sofia by taxi is €85 (up to four persons) from Skopje or the Kosovo border – contact **Sašo Trajkovski** (☎ 070-279 449; saso_taxi@yahoo.com). The Thessaloniki service is a through-run, while the Sofia service involves a prearranged change of taxi at the border.

Train

Frequent trains shoot out of Skopje's *Blade Runner*-style station, including Skopje–Belgrade via Niš (1209MKD, eight to nine hours, two daily). Sleepers are available. One train goes to Ljubljana, Slovenia (2690MKD, 12 hours, daily). Trains run daily between Skopje and Thessaloniki (700MKD, six hours, two daily, 7.15am and 5.18pm). Note that Thessaloniki in Macedonian is 'Solun'.

You will have to understand Cyrillic to make any sense of the timetables. Staff at the information desk will be of limited use so come prepared with a phrasebook.

GETTING AROUND
Bus

Bus travel is well developed in Macedonia with frequent services from Skopje to Ohrid. The domestic bus fleet is getting old and creaky, but it is still serviceable.

DEPARTURE TAX

The airport departure tax at Skopje and Ohrid is about US$18 and is normally included in your ticket.

Car

Skopje is awash with car-rental agencies, from the large ones (Hertz and Avis) to the smaller local companies. The tourist office has a complete listing.

Taxi

A quick way of getting around the country if buses are not convenient is by taxi, especially if there are two or more to share the cost. A half-hour trip should cost around 350MKD.

Train

Rail destinations include Bitola; Kičevo, in western Macedonia; Veles, south of Skopje; Tabanovce, on the border with Serbia and Montenegro; and Gevgelija, on the Greek border north of Thessaloniki. As an indication of price, the most expensive ticket in Macedonia is 370MKD for a return trip to Bitola.

SKOPJE СКОПЈЕ

☎ 02 / pop 600,000

The up-and-coming city of Skopje is a buzzing capital with plenty of bars, restaurants and outdoor clubs filled with a fun young crowd. During the day you can climb up to Tvrdina Kale (the city fort) overlooking the town from a hill top, wander around the old bazaar and eat delicious *kebapci* (barbecued meat rolls). Check out the small shops full of animal skins, copper coffeepots and jewellery, and step into the beautiful old Turkish baths (now art galleries), where the domed ceilings let in natural light through carved star-shaped holes. Skopje also has several beautiful old mosques and churches where you can spend a quiet moment to two.

The city is divided into the old and new towns by the Vardar River and connected by the 15th-century Kamen Most (Stone Bridge). A leafy riverside promenade has been built in the last year and you can take an afternoon stroll in Skopje's lovely city park (which, conveniently, is where outdoor summer nightclubs are found).

Skopje could swallow up a great portion of your budget with its expensive accommodation. On the bright side, food, drinks and entertainment are relatively cheap.

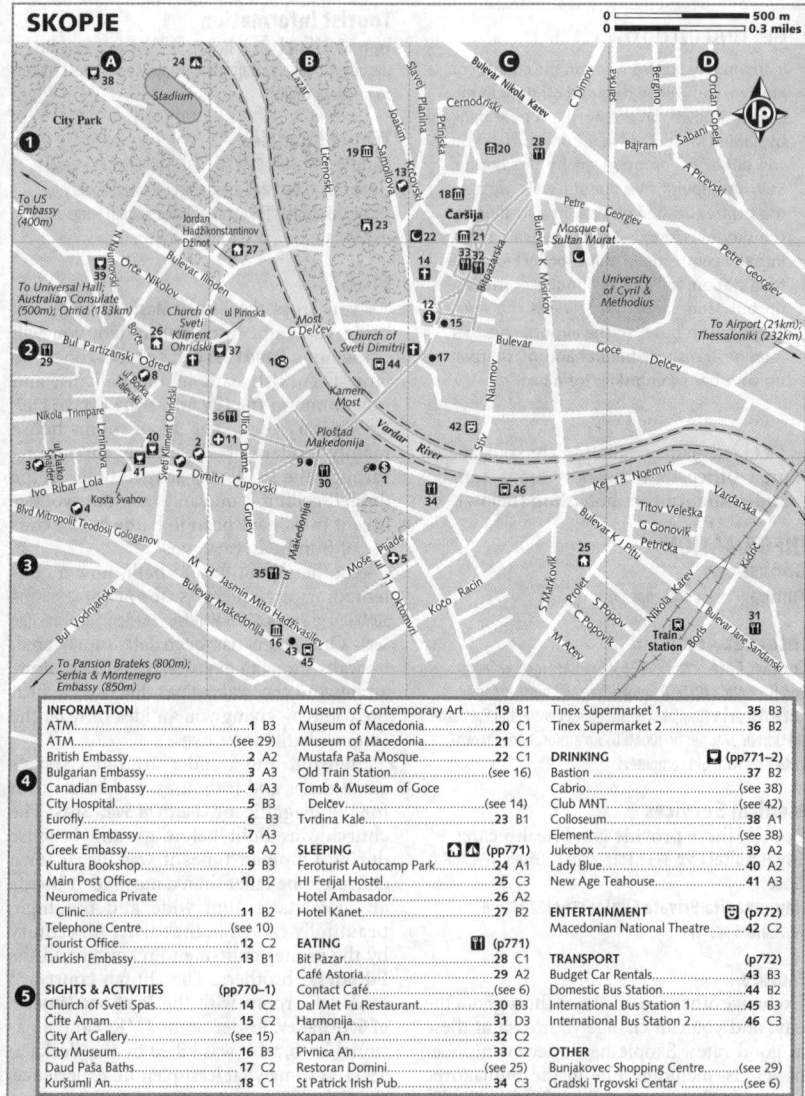

SKOPJE

0 _____ 500 m
0 _____ 0.3 miles

INFORMATION		
ATM	**1**	B3
ATM	(see 29)	
British Embassy	**2**	A2
Bulgarian Embassy	**3**	A3
Canadian Embassy	**4**	A3
City Hospital	**5**	B3
Euroflly	**6**	B3
German Embassy	**7**	A3
Greek Embassy	**8**	A2
Kultura Bookshop	**9**	B3
Main Post Office	**10**	B2
Neuromedica Private Clinic	**11**	A2
Telephone Centre	(see 10)	
Tourist Office	**12**	C2
Turkish Embassy	**13**	B1

SIGHTS & ACTIVITIES	(pp770–1)	
Church of Sveti Spas	**14**	C2
Čifte Amam	**15**	C2
City Art Gallery	(see 15)	
City Museum	**16**	B3
Daud Paša Baths	**17**	C2
Kuršumli An	**18**	C1

Museum of Contemporary Art	**19**	B1
Museum of Macedonia	**20**	C1
Museum of Macedonia	**21**	C1
Mustafa Paša Mosque	**22**	C1
Old Train Station	(see 16)	
Tomb & Museum of Goce Delčev	(see 14)	
Tvrdina Kale	**23**	C1

SLEEPING		
Feroturist Autocamp Park	**24**	A1
HI Ferijal Hostel	**25**	C3
Hotel Ambasador	**26**	A2
Hotel Kanet	**27**	B2

EATING	(pp771)	
Bit Pazar	**28**	C1
Café Astoria	**29**	A2
Contact Café	(see 6)	
Dal Met Fu Restaurant	**30**	B3
Harmonija	**31**	D3
Kapan An	**32**	C2
Pivnica An	**33**	C2
Restoran Domini	(see 25)	
St Patrick Irish Pub	**34**	C3

Tinex Supermarket 1	**35**	B3
Tinex Supermarket 2	**36**	B2

DRINKING	(pp771–2)	
Bastion	**37**	B2
Cabrio	(see 38)	
Club MNT	(see 42)	
Colloseum	**38**	A1
Element	(see 38)	
Jukebox	**39**	A2
Lady Blue	**40**	A2
New Age Teahouse	**41**	A3

ENTERTAINMENT	(p772)	
Macedonian National Theatre	**42**	C2

TRANSPORT	(p772)	
Budget Car Rentals	**43**	B3
Domestic Bus Station	**44**	B2
International Bus Station 1	**45**	B3
International Bus Station 2	**46**	C3

OTHER		
Bunjakovec Shopping Centre	(see 29)	
Gradski Trgovski Centar	(see 6)	

ORIENTATION

Most of central Skopje is a pedestrian zone, and it is best to use Kamen Most as your main point of orientation. South of the bridge is the newly paved Ploštad Makedonija (Macedonia Square), which leads into ul Makedonija running south, and a variety of bars and restaurants. Čaršija (Old Town),

the fantastic Turkish bazaar, and the majority of the sights are on the northern side.

You will notice 'bb' next to some addresses. It means 'without number' and is mainly used by official institutions and businesses. Although inconvenient, it's very common throughout the country, so just make good use of a map or ask for directions.

MACEDONIA

GETTING INTO TOWN

If arriving by bus from within the country or Kosovo, you will be dropped off right in the centre of town, on the northern river bank by Kamen Most. If arriving from abroad, you will either be dropped off by the bridge, Stiv Naumov, a five-minute walk west to the centre (upstream), or a little further, by the City Museum, a 10-minute walk north into the centre, up ul Makedonija. From the train station, walk for 15 minutes northwest up bul Jane Sandanski towards the river. There are no buses to the airport, so either arrange transport beforehand or sharpen up your bargaining skills for a taxi.

Detailed maps of Skopje are sold at the tourist office, but the best maps can be found at the Kultura bookshop (below).

INFORMATION
Bookshops
Kultura (Ploštad Makedonija)

Internet Access
Contact Café (☎ 3296 365; Gradski Trgovski Centar, 2nd fl; per hr 120MKD) Smoke-free and most expensive.
Café Astoria (Bunjakovec Shopping Centre, bul Partizanski Odredi 27a; per hr 100MKD) An atmospheric French-style café with old computers.

Medical Services
Both of these provide good health care:
City Hospital (☎ 3130 111; cnr ul 11 Oktomvri & Moše Pijade)
Neuromedica Private Clinic (☎ 3222 170; ul Partizanski 3-1-4)

Money
Exchange offices are scattered throughout the city, and you can change your cash at these at good rates. Skopje has a decent number of ATMs, including one in the Bunjakovec Shopping Centre, two in the Gradski Trgovski Centar off Ploštad Makedonija and one at the Stopanska Banka on ul Makedonija.

Post & Telephone
Main Post Office (☎ 3141 141; ul Orce Nikolov 1; ⏰ 7am-7.30pm Mon-Sat, 7.30am-2.30pm Sun) Some 75m north of Ploštad Makedonija, along the river.
Telephone Centre (⏰ 24hr) In the same building as the post office.

Tourist Information
Tourist Office (☎ 3116 854; ⏰ Mon-Sat) Opposite the City Art Gallery. Staff will unhappily be at your service. Some speak English.

Travel Agencies
Eurofly (☎ 3136 619; fax 3136 320; Gradski Trgovski Centar, 1st fl) Best and most practical travel agency for airline tickets. Has ticket prices listed in both euros and US dollars.

SIGHTS
As you cross the **Kamen Most**, its arch will bring you right into **Čaršija**. Here you will come upon **Daud Paša Baths** (1466), once the largest Turkish bath in the Balkans, and now home to the **City Art Gallery** (☎ 3133 102; ⏰ 9am-3pm Tue-Sun). The seven rooms house mainly modern art, lit by the sun coming through the small star-shaped holes in the domed ceiling. You can't help but wonder how it must have been to bathe here a couple of hundred years ago.

Another beautiful old bath, now a contemporary art gallery, is **Čifte Amam** (admission 50MKD; ⏰ 9am-4.45pm Mon-Fri, 9am-3pm Sat, 9am-1pm Sun). One room has been left unplastered, its walls showing exposed brickwork, stone arches and clay waterpipes that used to heat the rooms – giving you an idea of what the original baths were like.

Step out and wander around Čaršija's small shops and teahouses, and head north for the magnificent **Church of Sveti Spas**. The church was built below ground because during Ottoman times it was illegal for a church to be taller than a mosque. It boasts an iconostasis 10m wide and 6m high, beautifully carved in the early 19th century by the master-craftsmen Frčkovski and the Filipovski brothers. The church courtyard leads to a room with the **Tomb and Museum of Goce Delčev**, leader of the IMRO and a national hero, who was killed by the Turks in 1903. A somewhat less splendid experience, the ticket gives you access to both.

The 1492 **Mustafa Paša Mosque**, beyond the church, has an earthquake-cracked dome and a shady garden with a fountain. Climb up to the **Tvrdina Kale** ruins across the street for panoramic views of Skopje from the 11th-century Cyclopean wall. If you want more art, the **Museum of Contemporary Art** (☎ 3117 735; Samoilova bb; admission 100MKD; ⏰ 9am-3pm Tue-Sun) is higher up the hill.

Back in Čaršija, beyond the mosque is the white **Museum of Macedonia** (☎ 3116 044; Čurčiska 86; admission 100MKD; ☻ 9am-3pm Tue-Sun), which traces the region's civilisations over the centuries, but unfortunately only in Macedonian. Part of the museum is in **Kuršumli An** (1550), an impressive old caravanserai or inn, where traders would stop off and rest during the Ottoman times, and which was later used as a prison. The building now also houses a small **art gallery** in one of the cells.

On the other side of the city, in the new town, the sights are less obvious, but pay attention to the bizarre architecture of the **post office** beside Kamen Most: it's a futuristic, insect-like structure that's apparently an abstract take on church architecture. Further down, check out the **old train station** and its **clock** frozen at 5.17 on the morning of the great, tragic Skopje earthquake of 27 July 1963. Inside the old station is the **City Museum** (☎ 3114 742; Mito Hadživasilev bb; admission free; ☻ 9am-3pm Tue-Sun) and behind it some cafés sit between old train carriages. On the wall behind them, is a large socialist mural of Yugoslavia's President Tito's message of moral support to the shattered Skopjans after the earthquake.

SLEEPING

Prices are high in Skopje, but some bargains exist. In theory, the tourist office can arrange rooms in **private homes** starting at 1150MKD per person, but in practice they are not too helpful. Insist on something near the centre.

HI Ferijal Hostel (☎ 3114 849; fax 165 029; ul Prolet 25; s members/nonmembers 1280/1590MKD, d 935/1280MKD; ☻ 24hr Apr–mid-Oct; ✸) The best budget beds in town, near the train station and the centre, with clean, basic, individual rooms, and a cheerful atmosphere. Breakfast is included.

Pansion Brateks (☎ 3176 606, 070 243 232; ul Aco Karamanov 3; s/d 1920/3200MKD) This place feels a bit more upmarket with tidy, airy rooms, and is often full, despite being a 20-minute walk from the centre. It's set in a classy neighbourhood at the foot of Mount Vodno.

Hotel Kanet (☎ 3238 353; Jordan Hadžikonstantinov Džinot 20; s/d 2500/3700MKD) Sitting on the edge of the city park, this is a small wooden hotel, with comfortable rooms and intricate showers, TVs and telephones, and a buffet breakfast. Frogs croak in harmony from the park.

Hotel Ambasador (☎ 3215 510; fax 3121 383; ul Pirinska 36; s/d 2800/4340MKD) Pleasant, simple rooms with breakfast, and a 'Statue of Liberty' wielding its torch on the hotel's rooftop. Next to the Russian embassy.

Feroturist Autocamp Park (☎ 228 246; fax 162 677; per adult & camp site around 200MKD; ☻ Apr–mid-Oct) An urban camping option and just a 15-minute walk upstream from Kamen Most along the river's south bank. Bring plenty of mosquito repellent.

EATING

Restoran Domini (☎ 3115 519; ul Prolet 5; snacks 120MKD) Smart and budget-priced, in the basement of the HI Ferijal Hostel, this is an excellent choice.

Kapan An Behind Čifte Amam, features delicious *kebapci* with mouth-watering warm bread that can be enjoyed al fresco here or in any of the many restaurants in Čaršija.

St Patrick Irish Pub (☎ 3220 431; Kej 13 Noemvri; mains 280MKD) The place for the expat community, resembling Irish pubs around the world. Sip your Guinness while you munch on Irish breakfasts from 7.30am onwards and meals such as beef in Guinness or Gaelic steak.

Dal Met Fu Restaurant (☎ 3112 482; Ploštad Makedonija) This popular glass-fronted restaurant with tables outside facing the main square has good thin-base pizza and almost *al-dente* pasta.

Pivnica An (☎ 3212 111; Čaršija; mains 270-300MKD) Traditional and excellent food and beer, with a wide range of Macedonian dishes and a relaxing atmosphere.

Harmonija (☎ 246 0985; Skopjanka Shopping Centre 27; mains 250MKD; ☻ 9am-11pm Mon-Sat) About 500m southeast of the train station, it has a choice of fantastic vegetarian and macrobiotic meals in a cosy atmosphere.

Bit Pazar open market, next to the Čaršija, is the best place for fruit, veg, spices, herbs and nuts, and has plenty of market hubbub for those who want to cook their own grub.

The **Tinex Supermarkets** (ul Dame Gruev B & ul Makedonija 3) are well stocked.

DRINKING

There are more bars in Skopje than you can shake a stick at.

Bastion (☎ 322 3636; Pirinska 43; ☻ 9am-1am) This bar attracts a hip cocktail-and-beer crowd.

Jukebox (Orče Nikolov 99; 9am-1pm) A buzzing place, this is the spot to come for jazz on Thursdays.

New Age Teahouse (3117 559; Kosta Šahov 9; 9am-midnight) Plush floor cushions indoors, chaise-lounges and peacocks in the garden, teas, beers or cocktails, the choice is yours in this bohemian hang-out.

St Patrick Irish Pub This is the king of expat bars (see Eating p771).

ENTERTAINMENT

Universal Hall (3224 158; Partizanski Odredi bb) Just east of the centre, classical and other music performances, as well as Skopje's jazz festival, take place here in October every year.

Colloseum, **Cabrio**, **Element** (www.element.com .mk) In the city park, these are *the* places for summer outdoor clubbers and international DJs.

Macedonian National Theatre (3114 060; Kej Dimitar Vlahov) Stages opera and ballet; its other branch, the **Theatre Centre** (3164 667; Kliment Ohridski) is host to drama and plays, generally in Macedonian.

Club MNT (3220 767; Kej Dimitar Vlahov) Downstairs below the Macedonian National Theatre, this club gets grooving after 10pm.

Lady Blue (cnr Ivo Ribar Lola & Sveti Kliment Ohridski; 9pm-3am) Live jazz, blues and rock music.

GETTING THERE & AWAY

Skopje has two international bus stations: one next to the City Museum, and the other by the river on Kej 13 Noemvri. There are two bus routes from Skopje to Ohrid: the 167km route through Tetovo (300MKD, three hours) is much faster and more direct than the 261km route that goes via Veles and Bitola (four hours). Book a seat to Ohrid the day before if you're travelling in the high season (May to August).

GETTING AROUND

There are no buses to the airport, so you'll be at the mercy of the airport 'taxi mafia', which charges 1290MKD to 2200MKD for a ride into town. Do not get into a taxi that has no official taxi sign. It's better to request your accommodation to help arrange pick-up in advance. Taxis to the airport from the centre cost about 660MKD. Once you get beyond the airport area, Skopje's taxi system is brilliant – the first few kilometres are a flat 50MKD, then it's 15MKD per kilometre.

Inter-suburban city buses in Skopje cost 15MKD to 30MKD per trip, depending on the kind of bus and whether you buy your ticket on board or in advance.

SOUTHERN MACEDONIA

OHRID ОХРИД

☎ 046 / pop 50,000

Ohrid is the most magnificent town in Macedonia and the most popular. It rests on the banks of tranquil Ohrid Lake, a natural tectonic lake shared with Albania that is one of the oldest in the world and the deepest in the Balkans (294m). The town has stunning Byzantine churches, small cobbled streets, art galleries, good budget accommodation, and picturesque pebbly beaches you can relax on. During summer, it is packed with people and there are numerous festivals to entertain you. For quieter moments, the Galičica National Park is nearby, on the way to Sveti Naum monastery 20km south.

Under Byzantium, Ohrid became the episcopal centre of Macedonia. The archbishopric of Ohrid's independence from the Serbian Orthodox Church in 1967 was an important step on the road to nationhood.

Orientation

The Old Town of Ohrid is easy to get around on foot. The lake is to the south, and the picturesque Old Town rises from ul Sveti Kliment Ohridski, the main pedestrian mall.

Information

Asteroida (ul Dimitar Vlahov bb; per hour 60MKD) Internet café.

Cybercity (231 620; www.cybercity.com.mk; 3rd fl, ul Sveti Kliment Ohridski; per hour 60MKD) Also offers cheap overseas calls at 15MKD per minute.

Generalturist (261 071; fax 260 415; ul Partizanska 6) Travel agency providing tourist information, private room accommodation and assorted guided tours.

Jana Poposka (263 875) Voluble and knowledgeable personal guide who speaks good English. She is usually found at the church of Sveti Kliment.

Ohridska Banka (ul Sveti Kliment Ohridski) Has an ATM, changes money and offers Visa advances, minus the commission.

Post Office (Makedonski prosvetiteli) Also changes money.

Telephone Centre (7am-8pm Mon-Sat, 9am-noon & 6-8pm Sun) Just around the corner from the post office.

SIGHTS

Most of Ohrid's churches charge an entry fee of around 100MKD and if not, it is customary to leave some money at the icons. Most of this money goes towards preserving these historical sites.

Start your **walk** from the lower gate of the town wall and the small, 14th-century churches (originally hospital churches) of **Sveta Bogorodica Bolnička** and **Sveti Nikola Bolnički**. These two gems have delicate frescoes and a sweet old granny, Slavica, who'll show you around. A great example of 19th-century Macedonian architecture is the 1827 **National Museum** (☎ 267 173; ul Car Samoil 62; adult/student 100/50MKD; ☒ 10am-3pm Tue-Sun).

Further up is the 11th-century **Church of Sveta Sofija**, originally built as a cathedral. The frescoes are extremely well preserved thanks to having been whitewashed during the church's days as a mosque. An English-speaking guide is usually on hand.

Follow the signs for **Sveti Jovan Kaneo** through the winding streets and this amazing little 13th-century church will appear before you on the cliffs above the lake. As well as being one of the most popular churches in Ohrid, its stunning location has made it into the movies (*Before the Rain* by Milčo Mančevski).

Go up through the park towards the newly built **Sveti Klement i Pantelejmon**, standing next to the remains of Ohrid's oldest church of the same name. The foundations of the 5th-century basilica with their intricate mosaics are on display in front of the new church.

Continue towards the **Upper Gate** (Gorna Porta) to the gorgeous 13th-century **Church of Sveti Kliment** (☒ 9am-5pm), patterned inside with vividly restored frescoes of biblical scenes. Opposite this church is an **icon gallery** (☒ 9am-3pm). The restored walls of the 10th-century **citadel** to the west offer splendid views.

A gnarled 900-year-old **plane tree**, which apparently used to house a café and a barber shop at different points of its long life, stands at the northern end. The medieval town wall isolates the Old Town from the surrounding valley.

FESTIVALS & EVENTS

The five-day **Balkan Festival of Folk Dances & Songs**, held in early July, draws folkloric groups from around the Balkans, and the **Ohrid Summer Festival** has a variety of music and theatre performances.

SLEEPING

Private rooms or apartments are your best bet in Ohrid. They can be organised either through Generalturist or other local agencies and should cost around 400MKD to 600MKD per person. Rooms in the Old Town are more expensive.

Stefan Kanevče (☎ 070-212 352, 234 813; per person €10) Rooms in a 19th-century house with carved wooden ceilings, generous hospitality and home cooking.

Lucija's (☎ 265 608; Kosta Abraš 29; s/d €15/25) A fantastic place in the centre of the Old Town and near all the bars, the rooms are white, clean and spacious, balconies overlook the lake, and the patio is right on the water for a swim. Book early though, as this place is popular.

Mimi Apartments (☎ 250 103; mimioh@mail.com .mk; ul Strašo Pinđur 2; r 800MKD) Friendly Mimi Apostolov owns eight comfortable, heated rooms all with a fridge and satellite TV. Rates include breakfast.

Apartments Čekređi (☎ 261 733, 070-570 717; Kej Maršal Tito 27; d/tr 1500/2700MKD) Roomy, immaculate and spacious quarters close to the lake are good for a stay of a few days as you can self-cater.

EATING & DRINKING

Restaurants, quick eats, cafés and bars are dotted all around Ohrid.

Žito Leb (ul Kliment Ohridski bb) This small kiosk by the old plane tree is the best place for breakfast snacks. Munch on a fresh croissant or warm bread for 10MKD.

Restoran Neim (☎ 254 504; Goce Delčev 71) A local working man's hang-out about 100m west of the old plane tree serves some delicious *musaka* (baked layers of potato slices or aubergines and minced lamb) or *polneti piperki* (stuffed peppers).

Pizzeria Leonardo (☎ 260 359; Car Samoil 31) For a pizza and half a litre of draft wine at around 250MKD, this cosy little spot is the place to be.

Restaurant Dalga (☎ 31 948; Kosta Abraš bb) Here you can enjoy glorious lake views along with some Californian trout at 800MKD per kilo (the famous Ohrid Lake trout is now almost extinct (see p775).

The popular **market** just north of the old plane tree is great for picnic-minded travellers.

Jazz Inn (Kosta Abrašev 27; ☺ 10.30pm-1am) A vibrant atmosphere, with live music on Thursday and the weekend, this must be the most popular place in town.

GETTING THERE & AWAY

Buses travel between Ohrid and Skopje, via Kičevo (300MKD, three hours, ten daily). Another three go via Bitola. The first route is shorter, faster, more scenic and cheaper. During the summer rush, it pays to book a seat the day before.

There is a bus to Sofia from Ohrid (900MKD, 10 to 12 hours, daily, 7am). Buses to Belgrade travel via Bitola (1220MKD, 14 hours, daily, 5am 3.30pm). For Tirana, buses leave from Struga (€10, six hours, daily, noon and 9.30pm), in front of Restaurant Trofta on the main road coming into Struga from Ohrid.

Buses or boats travel to Sveti Naum monastery (80MKD, 29km, six daily in summer, three daily in winter).

There are no direct transport links between Ohrid and Greece. You need to take a bus to Bitola and a taxi from there to the Greek border at Medžitlija/Niki.

MACEDONIA DIRECTORY

ACCOMMODATION

Skopje's hotels are expensive, but camping grounds and private-room agencies in Ohrid and Skopje make budgeting possible. The HI hostel in Skopje is open all year and beds are available at student dormitories in summer. The best budget accommodation is in monastery dorms if travelling around the country, particularly at the Sveti Jovan Bigorski monastery near Mavrovo and Treskavec monastery above Prilep (see the boxed text, p767).

ACTIVITIES

Skiing is great in Macedonia's top resort, Popova Šapka (1845m), on the southern slopes of Šar Planina west of Tetovo near the border with Kosovo. Mavrovo in western Macedonia comes a close second. Hiking is spectacular in any of the three national parks (Galičica and Pelister in the south, and Mavrovo) or at Lake Matka near Skopje, as are rock climbing and sailing.

BOOKS

The Lonely Planet *Mediterranean Europe phrasebook* will help with the language.

BUSINESS HOURS

Businesses are generally open 8am to 8pm weekdays and 8am to 2pm Saturday.

DANGERS & ANNOYANCES

Travellers should be on the lookout for pickpockets in bus and train stations.

EMBASSIES & CONSULATES

Macedonian Embassies & Consulates

Albania (☎ 042-330 36; fax 042 325 14; Rruga Lek Dukagjini, Vila 2, Tirana)

Australia (☎ 02-6249 8000; fax 02-6249 8088; Perpetual Building, Suite 2:05, 10 Rudd St, Canberra, ACT 2600)

Canada (☎ 613-234 3882; fax 613-233 1852; 130 Albert St, Suite 1006, Ottawa ON, K1P 5G4)

Serbia and Montenegro (☎ 011-633 348; fax 011 182 287; Gospodar Jevremova 34, 11000 Belgrade)

Turkey (☎ 012-446 9204; fax 012-446 9206; Filistin sokak 30-2/3, Gaziosman Paşa, Ankara)

UK (☎ 020-7499 5152; fax 020-7499 2864; 19a Cavendish Sq, London, W1M 9AD)

USA (☎ 202-337 3063; fax 202-337 3093; 3050 K St NW, Washington, DC 20007)

Embassies & Consulates in Macedonia

The following countries have diplomatic representation in Skopje:

Albania (☎ 2614 636; fax 2614 200; ul H T Karpoš 94a)

Australia (☎ 2361 114; fax 2361 834; ul Londonska 11b)

Bulgaria (☎ 3116 320; fax 3116 139; ul Zlatko Šnajder 3)

Canada (☎ 3125 228; fax 3122 681; ul Mitropolit Teodosie Gologanov 104)

Germany (☎ 3110 507; fax 3117 713; ul Dimitri Čupovski 26)

Greece (☎ 3130 198; fax 3115 718; ul Borka Talevski 6)

Serbia and Montenegro (☎ 3129 298; fax 3129 427; Pitu Guli 8)

Turkey (☎ 3113 270; fax 3117 024; ul Slavej Planina bb)

UK (☎ 3116 772; fax 3117 005; ul Veljko Vlahovič 26)

USA (☎ 3116 180; fax 3117 103; bul Ilinden bb)

GAY & LESBIAN TRAVELLERS

Given the Balkans traditional culture, Macedonia does not generally endorse homosexuality, so it's best for gay and lesbian visitors to maintain a low profile.

MONEY

Macedonian *denar* (MKD) notes come in denominations of 10, 50, 100, 500, 1000 and 5000, and there are coins of one, two and five denar. The denar is nonconvertible outside Macedonia. Restaurants, hotels and some shops will usually accept payment in euros and sometimes in US dollars; prices are often quoted in these currencies.

Small, private exchange offices throughout central Skopje and Ohrid exchange cash for a rate that is only slightly better than at the banks, but banks cash travellers cheques as well. A handful of ATMs can be found in central Skopje, and offer the best exchange rates.

Costs

Except for accommodation in Skopje, Macedonia is not an expensive country. If you stay in a private room in Skopje, you might keep costs to 1800MKD to 2100MKD a day; outside Skopje, frugal travellers might spend 1200MKD to 1500MKD per day.

Tipping

It is common practice in Macedonia to round up restaurant bills and taxi fares to the nearest convenient figure.

POST & TELEPHONE

Mail services to and from Macedonia are efficient. Poste-restante services are available at the major post offices.

Macedonia's country code is ☎ 389. Long-distance phone calls cost less at main post offices than in hotels. Drop the initial zero in city codes when calling Macedonia from abroad. For outgoing calls the international access code in Macedonia is 99. You can purchase phonecards from post offices. Internet cafés, which abound in Skopje and Ohrid, often offer cheap international phone calls.

RESPONSIBLE TRAVEL

Ohrid Lake trout is almost extinct and in 2004 the government issued a ban on fishing it for seven years. Despite this, many restaurants continue to serve it and are therefore providing opportunities for illegal trout fishing. Do try to resist ordering one and opt for Californian trout, which is just as tasty.

VISAS

Citizens of EU countries and New Zealand do not need visas to enter Macedonia, but visas are required of citizens of most other countries. For US and Australian citizens, the visa is issued free at your port of entry, but this may change frequently, so check with the Macedonian embassy. Canadians and South Africans must buy visas for approximately US$12; these are obtainable either before you go or at the border. Again, please check with the Macedonian embassy.

Malta

HIGHLIGHTS

- **Valletta** Malta's capital, a magnificent fortified city built in the 16th century (p779)
- **Blue Lagoon** Taking a trip to tiny Comino and swimming in exquisitely clear water (p786)
- **Mdina** Wandering the silent streets of the elegant old capital and soaking up the history (p784)
- **Festa Fever** A festa with the locals, accompanied by music, food and fireworks (p787)
- **Off-the-beaten track** Chilling out on Gozo, smaller, greener and quieter that Malta (p785)

MALTA

FAST FACTS

- **Area** 316 sq km (double the size of Liechtenstein)
- **ATMs** Widespread
- **Budget** Lm10-15 per day
- **Capital** Valletta
- **Country code** ☎ 356
- **Head of State** President Guido de Marco
- **Famous for** Prehistoric temples, Knights of St John, old yellow buses, unique language
- **Languages** Malti, English
- **Money** Maltese lira (A$1 = Lm0.25, CA$1 = Lm0.27, €1 = Lm0.43, ¥100 = Lm0.32, NZ$1 = Lm0.23, £1 = Lm0.62, US$1 = Lm0.34)
- **Phrases** Merħba (hello), saħħa (goodbye), grazzi (thanks)

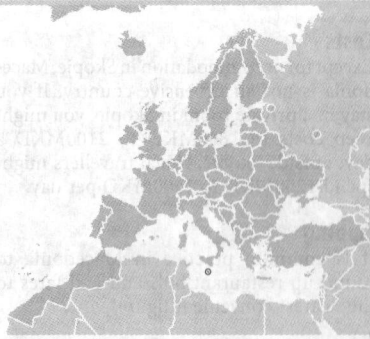

- **Population** 400,000
- **Time** GMT/UTC + 1
- **Visas** Not needed for most visitors for stays of up to three months.

TRAVEL HINTS

Get around on the big old rattling buses, and sate your hunger with cheap *pastizzi* (pastries filled with ricotta cheese or mushy peas).

ROAMING MALTA

Soak up the history of Valletta and Mdina, check out the ancient temples, go diving, chill out on Gozo.

On a map, Malta looks like a tiny speck south of Sicily, but you'll be amazed by how much it has to offer. Strategically placed in the Mediterranean, the islands of Malta have proven a tempting target for explorers and invaders, and have been left with a unique legacy of different dollops of European, North African and British influences.

Its warm climate, scenic coastline and reasonable prices have earned Malta a package-holiday reputation, but look beyond the beaches and there's 5000 years of history to explore.

MALTA

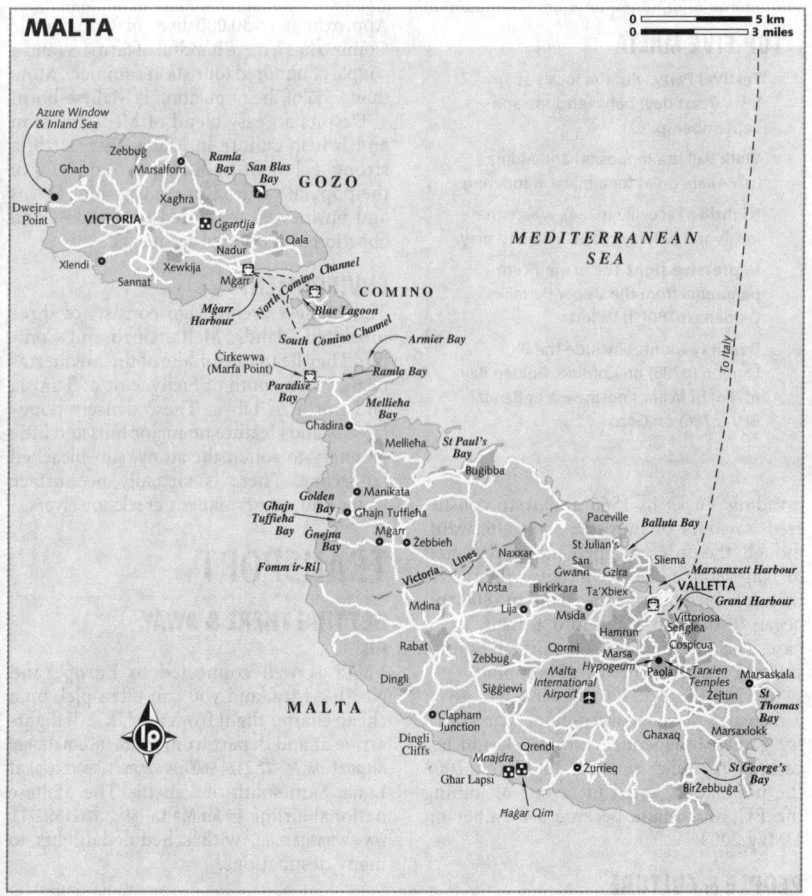

MALTA

0 ___ 5 km
0 ___ 3 miles

MEDITERRANEAN
SEA

To Italy

With attractions ranging from prehistoric temples to baroque architecture, you're never short of things to catch your eye or pique your interest.

Get caught up in the hustle and bustle of the modern-day Mediterranean lifestyle, delve into fascinating history, chill out on a beach, party at a local festa, enjoy some of Europe's best diving or escape to the quiet recesses of rural life on Gozo. Malta proves that good things come in small packages!

HISTORY

Malta's oldest monuments are the mysterious megalithic temples at Ġgantija near Xagħra, and Ħaġar Qim and Mnajdra on the southwest coast, built between 3800 and 2500 BC – the world's oldest surviving freestanding structures. From around 800 to 218 BC, Malta was colonised by the Phoenicians and Carthaginians, and then became part of the Roman Empire. In AD 60, St Paul was shipwrecked on the island, where (according to folklore) he converted the islanders to Christianity. Arabs arrived in 870 and had a considerable influence on agriculture and language. Afterwards came a succession of Normans, Angevins (French), Aragonese and Castilians (Spanish).

In 1530 the islands were given to the Knights of the Order of St John, a religious crusader organisation. The Knights expelled

TOP FIVE MALTA

■ **Festival** Party with the locals at any festa (feast day) between June and September (p787).

■ **Walk** Valletta (opposite) and Mdina (p784) are great for aimless wandering

■ **Nightlife** Paceville (p784), where the locals and holidaymakers come to play

■ **Impressive sight** The magnificent panorama from the Upper Barrakka Gardens (p780) in Valletta

■ **Beach** Favourites include the Blue Lagoon (p786) on Comino, Golden Bay (p786) in Malta's northwest or Ramla Bay (p786) on Gozo

invading Turks in 1565 and were considered 'saviours of Europe'. Soon afterward, though, the order declined and surrendered to Napoleon in 1798 without a fight. The British helped liberate the island in 1800 and began to develop Malta into a major naval base. The new member of the British Empire suffered greatly from WWII bombing.

In 1947 the devastated island was given a measure of self-government. The country gained independence in 1964, and became a republic in 1974. In March 2003 the population voted in favour of joining the EU, and Malta became a member on 1 May 2004.

PEOPLE & CULTURE

Malta's population is around 400,000, with most living in the satellite towns around Valletta, Sliema and the Grand Harbour.

READING UP

Ernle Bradford writes well about Malta in crisis. *The Great Siege* is a page-turning account of the epic 1565 battle between the Ottoman Turks and the Knights of St John. In Bradford's *Siege: Malta 1940-1943*, the role of the bad guys is played by the bomb-dropping Italians and Germans.

The Kappillan of Malta written by Nicolas Monsarrat tells the story of a priest's experience during WWII, interspersed with a potted history of Malta – perfect beach reading.

Approximately 30,000 live on Gozo, while Comino has a mere handful of farmers (and a couple of hundred tourists in summer). More than 95% of the population is Maltese-born.

Despite an easy blend of Mediterranean and British culture in Malta, there's still a strong feeling of tradition. Around 98% of the population are Roman Catholic. Shops and businesses are closed on Sunday, and abortion and divorce are illegal.

ENVIRONMENT

The Maltese archipelago consists of three inhabited islands: Malta, Gozo and Comino. They lie in the middle of the Mediterranean, 93km south of Sicily, east of Tunisia and north of Libya. These densely populated islands feature no major hills and little greenery to soften the stony, sun-bleached landscape. There is virtually no surface water and no permanent creeks or rivers.

TRANSPORT

GETTING THERE & AWAY

Air

Malta is well connected to Europe and North Africa, and you can often pick up a cheap charter flight from the UK. All flights arrive at and depart from **Malta International Airport** (MLA; ☎ 2124 9600; www.maltairport.com) at Luqa, 8km south of Valletta. The Maltese national airline is **Air Malta** (KM; ☎ 2166 2211; www.airmalta.com), with scheduled flights to many destinations.

Boat

Malta has regular sea links with Italy, but schedules change frequently so it's best to confirm information with a travel agent, such as **SMS Travel & Tourism** (☎ 2123 2211; www .smstravel.net; 311 Triq ir-Repubblika, Valletta).

Virtu Ferries (Malta ☎ 2131 8854; Catania ☎ 095-535 711; Pozzallo ☎ 0932-954 062; www.virtuferries.com) runs fast catamaran services to Sicily (Catania and Pozzallo). The Pozzallo–Malta crossing operates year-round (€70/86 one-way/return trip from Pozzallo, Lm24/36 one-way/return trip from Malta, 90 minutes).

Ma.Re.Si Shipping (☎ 2123 3129; www.sms.com.mt /maresi.htm) operates between Catania and Malta (Lm20/35 one-way/return trip, 12 hours, weekly) and also between Malta and Reggio di Calabria (Lm25/45 one-way/return trip,

15 hours, weekly). **Grimaldi Ferries** (☎ 2122 6873; www.grimaldi-ferries.com) operates a service between Malta and Salerno, south of Naples (cabin berth from €93, 19 hours, weekly). **Grandi Navi Veloci** (☎ 2133 4023; www.gnv .it/tunisia.asp) has a twice-weekly service between Genoa and Tunis that calls in at Malta on its return leg. You can sail from Tunis direct to Malta, but from Malta to Tunis you must sail via Genoa. Ticket prices start at €104. The Tunis–Malta journey takes about 13 hours; Malta–Genoa is 27 hours.

GETTING AROUND
Boat
Gozo Channel Company (☎ 2158 0435; www.gozo channel.com) runs regular car ferry services between Ċirkewwa (Malta) and Mġarr (Gozo), with crossings every 45 to 60 minutes from 6am to around 11pm (extended in high season). The journey takes 25 minutes (Lm1.75/4/0.50 per person/car/bike return trip).

The **Marsamxetto ferry service** (☎ 2133 8981) is a frequent daily ferry between Valletta and Sliema (35c, five minutes). Arrival and departure points are at the Strand in Sliema and at the end of Triq San Marku in northwest Valletta.

Bus
Malta and Gozo are served by buses run by the **Public Transport Authority** (ATP; ☎ 2125 0007/8/9; www.atp.com.mt). Most of Malta's services originate from the chaotic City Gate terminus, just outside Valletta's fortifications. Fares are cheap – from 15c to 50c (be sure to have small change for the driver when you board). Services are regular and the more popular routes run till 11pm. Ask at an ATP kiosk (there's one near the bus terminus) or the tourist office for a free timetable.

Bus No 45 runs regularly from Valletta to Ċirkewwa to connect with the ferry to Gozo. On Gozo, the bus terminus is in Victoria, just south of Triq ir-Reppublika. All services depart from here and cost 15c. Bus No 25 runs between Victoria and the ferry port of Mġarr.

Car & Motorcycle
With low rental rates it might make economic sense to hire a car, but unless you're a confident driver it might not be worth the aggravation. Road rules are often ignored,

roads are confusingly signposted and parking can be difficult.

All the major international car-hire companies are at the airport, and there are dozens of local agencies. Shop around – daily rates for the smallest vehicles start from Lm6 to Lm8 a day.

Hitchhiking is not common and is often frowned upon. In any case, Lonely Planet doesn't recommend it.

Taxi
Taxis are expensive; establish a price in advance. From Valletta to St Julian's it's around Lm5. **Wembley Motors** (☎ 2137 4141) offers a 24-hour service.

VALLETTA

Compact Valletta, city of the Knights of the Order of St John, is steeped in history and renowned for its architecture. Commercial activity bustles around Triq ir-Repubblika (Republic St) but the quiet back streets are where you'll get a feel for everyday life. The city overlooks the impressive Grand Harbour to the southeast and Marsamxett Harbour to the northwest. Vittoriosa, Senglea and Cospicua, collectively known as the Three Cities, lie to the southeast.

INFORMATION
Emergencies
Police Station (☎ 2122 5495; Triq Nofs in-Nhar)

Internet Access
MelitaNet (28 Triq Melita; per hr Lm1)
Ziffa (194 Triq id-Dejqa; per 2hr Lm1.80) Also good rates for international phone calls.

Medical services
Royal Pharmacy (☎ 2123 4321; 271 Triq ir-Repubblika) Centraly located open during shopping hours.
St Luke's Hospital (☎ 2124 1251; Gwardamanġa Hill, Gwardamanġa) About 3km southwest of Valletta (take bus No 75).

EMERGENCY NUMBERS

■ Ambulance (☎ 196)
■ Police (☎ 191)

Money
Bank of Valletta (cnr Triq ir-Repubblika & Triq San Ġwann)
Travelex (20 Triq ir-Repubblika)

Post
Post office (Pjazza Kastilja)

Tourist Information
Tourist office Valletta (☎ 2123 7747 or 2125 5844; Misrah il-Helsien; 9am-5.30pm Mon-Sat, 9am-12.30pm Sun, closed public holidays) In the City Arcade on the right as you enter through City Gate; Malta International Airport (☎ 2369 6073/4; ☾ 10am-10pm)

SIGHTS
A walk around the city walls features spectacular views. Be sure to stop at the **Upper Barrakka Gardens** in the southwest to take in the view that puts the grand in Grand Harbour.

Check out the breathtaking baroque interior of **St John's Co-Cathedral** (☎ 2122 5639; entrance on Triq ir-Repubblika; admission Lm1; ☾ 9.30am-12.30pm & 1.30-4.15pm Mon-Fri, 9.30am-12.30pm Sat, closed Sun, public holidays & during services), built in the 1570s. Inside is the **Cathedral Museum** (☎ 2122 0536), which houses two magnificent works by the Italian painter, Caravaggio.

The 16th-century **Grand Master's Palace** (Pjazza San Ġorġ) is now the seat of the Maltese

GETTING INTO TOWN

The airport is 8km south of Valletta. Bus No 8 runs between the City Gate bus terminus and the airport (15c, every half-hour). The bus leaves from outside the departures hall at the airport.

Ferries via Italy dock in the Grand Harbour at Pinto Wharf, near Valletta. Ferries do not have exchange facilities, and there are none at the port. Nor is there any public transport from the ferry terminal up to Valletta – you can either catch a taxi or make the steep 15-minute climb. If you decide to walk it's best to follow the waterfront northeast, under the Lascaris Bastion, then veer left and climb the steps up at Victoria Gate.

parliament. From the public entrance on Triq il-Merkanti, it's possible to visit the **State Apartments** (☎ 2122 1221; admission Lm1; ☾ 7.45am-2pm mid-Jun–Sep, 8.15am-5pm Mon-Sat & 8.15am-4pm Sun Oct–mid-Jun), full of works of art. The apartments are closed when official state visits take place.

At the very interesting **National Museum of Archaeology** (☎ 2122 1623; Triq ir-Repubblika; admission Lm1; ☾ 7.45am-2pm mid-Jun–Sep, 8.15am-5pm Mon-Sat & 8.15am-4pm Sun Oct–mid-Jun) you can admire beautiful objects that have been found at Malta's prehistoric sites – check out the female figurines (the so-called 'fat ladies').

At the furthest point of Valletta is **Fort St Elmo**, built in 1552 by the Knights of St John and generally closed to the public. Next to the fort, the informative **National War Museum** (☎ 2122 2430; Triq il-Fontana; admission Lm1; ☾ 7.45am-2pm mid-Jun–Sep, 8.15am-5pm Mon-Sat & 8.15am-4pm Sun Oct–mid-Jun) commemorates Malta's involvement in WWII.

Built in 1731, the beautiful **Manoel Theatre** (☎ 2124 6389; www.teatrumanoel.com; 115 Triq it-Teatru l-Antik; tours Lm1.65; tours ☾ 10.30am, 11.30am & 5.15pm Mon-Fri, 11.30am & 12.30pm Sat) is one of the oldest in Europe. There's a varied programme of events October to May, or you can take a guided tour to see the baroque auditorium.

SLEEPING
Asti Guesthouse (☎ 2123 9506; http://mol.net.mt/asti; 18 Triq Sant'Orsla; b person Lm5.50) This classy guesthouse offers the best-value accommodation in Valletta, with simple, spacious rooms and spotless shared bathrooms. Breakfast is included and is served in a vaulted dining room complete with huge chandelier.

British Hotel (☎ 2122 4730; www.britishhotel.com; 267 Triq Sant'Orsla, main entrance at 40 Triq il-Batterija; s/d Lm12/18, with sea view Lm16/22) Enjoy excellent views over Grand Harbour with your breakfast. It's a bit of a rabbit warren and though clean, the rooms are basic. It's worth paying extra for a balcony and view.

EATING
Caffe Cordina (☎ 2123 4385; 244 Triq ir-Repubblika; snacks & light meals Lm0.70-3.60) The prime people-watching spot in Valletta is Misrah ir-Repubblika, and the best option here is Caffe Cordina, established in 1837 and perfect for savoury pastries and decadent sweets.

Café Jubilee (☎ 2125 2332; 125 Triq Santa Luċija; snacks & meals Lm0.90-3; ☾ 8-1am) Low lighting,

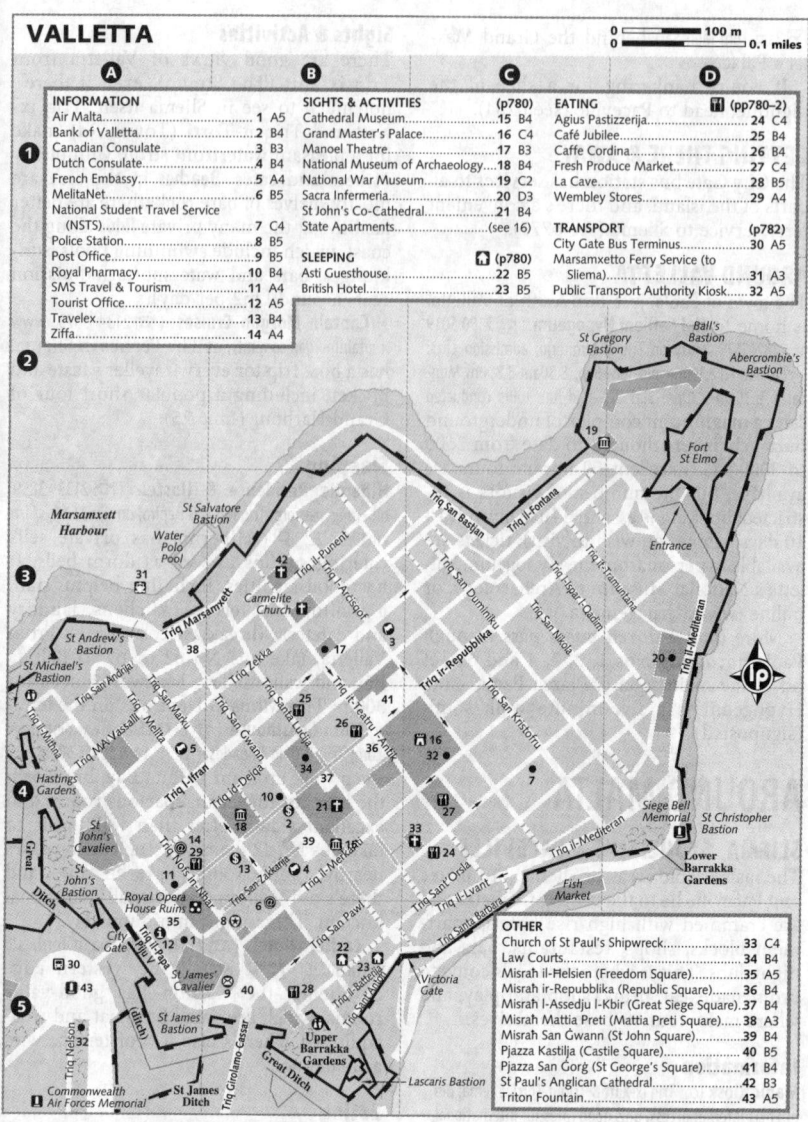

VALLETTA

0 ————— 100 m
0 ————— 0.1 miles

INFORMATION
Air Malta **1** A5
Bank of Valletta **2** B5
Canadian Consulate **3** B3
Dutch Consulate **4** B4
French Embassy **5** A4
MelitaNet **6** B5
National Student Travel Service
(NSTS) **7** C4
Police Station **8** B5
Post Office **9** B5
Royal Pharmacy **10** B4
SMS Travel & Tourism **11** A4
Tourist Office **12** A5
Travelex **13** B4
Ziffa **14** A4

SIGHTS & ACTIVITIES (p780)
Cathedral Museum **15** B4
Grand Master's Palace **16** C4
Manoel Theatre **17** B3
National Museum of Archaeology .. **18** B4
National War Museum **19** C2
Sacra Infermeria **20** D3
St John's Co-Cathedral **21** B4
State Apartments .... (see 16)

SLEEPING (p780)
Asti Guesthouse **22** B5
British Hotel **23** B5

EATING (pp780–2)
Agius Pastizzerija **24** C4
Café Jubilee **25** B4
Caffe Cordina **26** B4
Fresh Produce Market **27** C4
La Cave **28** B5
Wembley Stores **29** A4

TRANSPORT (p782)
City Gate Bus Terminus **30** A5
Marsamxetto Ferry Service (to
Sliema) **31** A3
Public Transport Authority Kiosk ... **32** A5

OTHER
Church of St Paul's Shipwreck **33** C4
Law Courts **34** B4
Misrah il-Helsien (Freedom Square) **35** A5
Misrah ir-Repubblika (Republic Square) **36** B4
Misrah l-Assedju l-Kbir (Great Siege Square) **37** B4
Misrah Mattia Preti (Mattia Preti Square) **38** A3
Misrah San Gwann (St John Square) **39** B4
Pjazza Kastilja (Castile Square) **40** B5
Pjazza San Ġorġ (St George's Square) **41** B4
St Paul's Anglican Cathedral **42** B3
Triton Fountain **43** A5

MALTA

cosy nooks and poster-plastered walls feature at Jubilee. Drop in any time, for coffee and a pastizzi, a lunchtime baguette, dinner of pasta or risotto, or a late-night vino.

La Cave (☎ 2124 3677; Pjazza Kastilja; meals Lm1.80-3.75; ☽ lunch Mon-Fri, dinner nightly) In an atmospheric 400-year-old cellar, this busy restaurant churns out crunchy pizzas big enough for two. There's also an assortment of pasta and salads.

Agius Pastizzerija (273 Triq San Pawl; pastries from 7c) Search out this hole-in-the-wall place for traditional snacks at bargain prices.

Wembley Stores (305 Triq ir-Repubblika; ☽ 7.15am-7pm Mon-Sat) has a wide selection of groceries, and there's a **fresh produce market** (Triq il-Merkanti;

⏰ 7am-1pm Mon-Sat) behind the Grand Master's Palace.

If you're hankering for a slice of the nightlife, head to Paceville (see p784).

GETTING THERE & AWAY

The City Gate bus station has services to all parts of the island, and there's a convenient ferry service to Sliema (see p779).

AROUND VALLETTA

The town of Paola, just 4km south of Valletta, is home to **Hal Saflieni Hypogeum** (☎ 2180 5019 or 2182 5579; entry on Triq iċ-Ċimiterju; admission Lm3; ⏰ 8.30am-12.30pm mid-Jun–Sep, 8.30am-3.30pm Mon-Sat & 8.30am-2.30pm Sun Oct–mid-Jun, tours conducted daily), a magnificent complex of underground burial chambers thought to date from 3600 to 3000 BC. Excellent 50-minute tours are available, but the number of visitors is restricted; booking is essential (usually at least 10 days before you wish to visit); tickets are available in person from the Hypogeum, Valletta's National Museum of Archaeology, or online (www.heritagemalta.org).

More than a dozen buses pass through Paola, including Nos 1, 2, 3, 4 and 6. Get off at the main square, Pjazza Paola – the Hypogeum is a five-minute walk south (signposted).

AROUND MALTA

SLIEMA, ST JULIAN'S & PACEVILLE

The fashionable areas of Sliema, St Julian's and Paceville lie to the north of Valletta and are crammed with high-rise hotels, apartment blocks, shops, restaurants, bars and nightclubs. This is where the locals come to promenade, eat, drink, shop and play, and where many tourists base themselves.

Information

Magic Kiosk (cnr Triq ix-Xatt & Triq it-Torri, Sliema; per hr Lm1) Internet access, plus good rates for international calls.

MelitaNet (Triq Ball, Paceville; per hr Lm1; ⏰ 24hr) Large Internet café inside Tropicana Hotel.

Police station (☎ 2133 0502; cnr Triq Manwel Dimech & Triq Rudolfu, Sliema)

Post office (Triq Manwel Dimech, Sliema)

Tourist office (☎ 2138 1392; Palazzo Spinola, enter from Triq Ross; generally ⏰ 8am-12.30pm & 1.30-5pm Mon-Fri)

Sights & Activities

There are good views of Valletta from Triq ix-Xatt (The Strand), even if there's not much to see in Sliema itself. Triq ix-Xatt and Triq it-Torri (Tower Rd) make for a pleasant waterfront stroll, with plenty of bars and cafés. **Beaches** in the area are mostly shelves of bare rock; there are better facilities at the many private **lidos** along the coast, which include swimming pools, sunlounges, bars and watersports (admission costs around Lm2 per day).

Captain Morgan Cruises (☎ 2134 3373; www .captainmorgan.com.mt), at The Ferries in Sliema, has a boat trip for every traveller's taste and pocket, including a popular short tour of Grand Harbour (Lm6.25).

Sleeping

Hibernia Residence & Hostel (☎ 2133 3859; hibernia@nsts.org; Triq Mons G Depiro; dm Lm23.45, s/d/tr Lm19/18/22; 🖳) Hibernia has private self-catering studios as well as dorm beds. It has good facilities, including helpful staff, a rooftop sun terrace, kitchens, laundry and cafeteria (breakfast costs Lm1). From Valletta, take bus No 62 or 67 to Balluta Bay and walk up Triq Manwel Dimech for 300m; Triq Mons G Depiro is on the left.

Pinto Guesthouse (☎ 2131 3897; www.pintohotel .com; Triq il-Qalb Imqaddsa; s/d/tr Lm8.50/13.50/15) A steep walk up from Balluta Bay, but worth the hike for the clean, spacious rooms and excellent view (better than walking is to take bus No 42 from Valletta, which passes nearby). Some rooms have en suite, and there's a TV lounge and small communal kitchen. Three-night minimum stay.

Carlton Hotel (☎ 2131 5764; Triq it-Torri; s/d Lm18.50/26; 🛇 🖳 🏊) At the western edge of Sliema, the Carlton has good-value rooms, which are small but neat and well-equipped. There's also a roof terrace with a small pool.

Eating

Paparazzi (☎ 2137 4966; Triq San Ġorġ; mains Lm2.50-7) The terrace at Paparazzi is a prime people-watching spot, with a fine view of Spinola Bay. Fight your way through the huge portions on the crowd-pleasing menu.

The Avenue (☎ 2131 1753; Triq Gort; mains Lm1-5; ⏰ lunch Mon-Sat, dinner nightly) The Avenue is cheap, cheerful and always bustling. It's a long-standing favourite among locals, with

MALTA

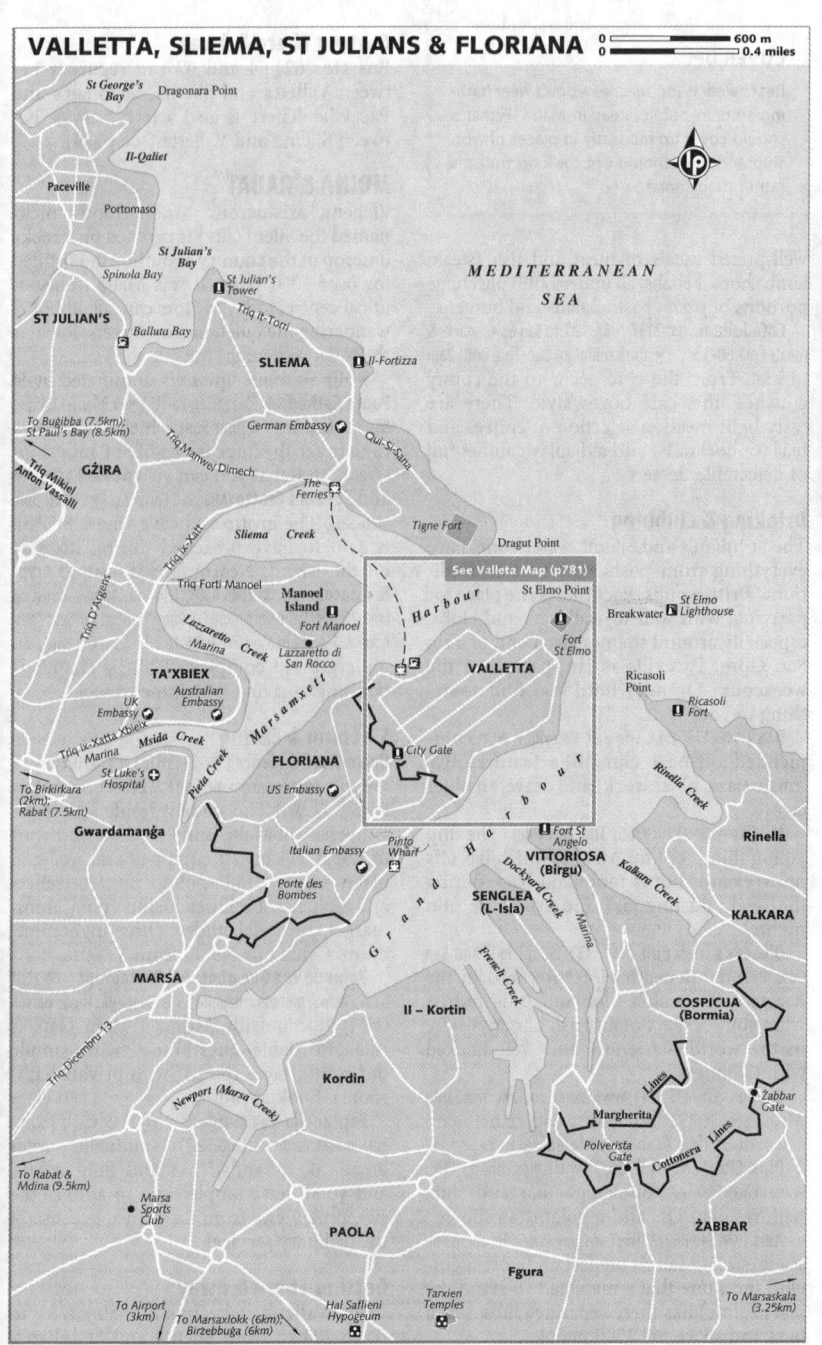

VALLETTA, SLIEMA, ST JULIANS & FLORIANA

0 — 600 m
0 — 0.4 miles

MEDITERRANEAN SEA

St George's Bay
Dragonara Point
Il-Qaliet
Paceville
Portomaso
St Julian's Bay
Spinola Bay
St Julian's Tower
ST JULIAN'S
Balluta Bay
Triq it-Torri
SLIEMA
Il-Fortizza
To Bugibba (7.5km);
St Paul's Bay (8.5km)
GŻIRA
Triq Manwel Dimech
German Embassy
Qui-Si-Sana
Triq Mikiel Anton Vassalli
The Ferries
Tigne Fort
Dragut Point
Triq ix-Xatt
Sliema Creek
Triq Forti Manoel
Manoel Island
Fort Manoel
Lazzaretto di San Rocco
Harbour
St Elmo Point
St Elmo Lighthouse
Breakwater
Triq D'Argens
Lazzaretto Creek
Marina
TA'XBIEX
Australian Embassy
UK Embassy
Marsamxett
See Valleta Map (p781)
VALLETTA
Fort St Elmo
Ricasoli Point
Ricasoli Fort
Triq ix-Xatt ix-Xbiex
Marina
Msida Creek
St Luke's Hospital
To Birkirkara (2km);
Rabat (7.5km)
FLORIANA
US Embassy
City Gate
Rinella Creek
Gwardamanga
Pieta Creek
Italian Embassy
Pinto Wharf
Fort St Angelo
VITTORIOSA (Birgu)
Rinella
Porte des Bombes
Grand Harbour
SENGLEA (L-Isla)
Dockyard Creek
Marina
Kalkara Creek
KALKARA
MARSA
Il – Kortin
French Creek
COSPICUA (Bormla)
Triq Diċembru 13
Kordin
Żabbar Gate
Newport (Marsa Creek)
Margherita
Lines
Lines
To Rabat & Mdina (9.5km)
Marsa Sports Club
Polverista Gate
Cottonera
ŻABBAR
PAOLA
Fgura
Tarxien Temples
To Marsaskala (3.25km)
To Airport (3km)
To Marsaxlokk (6km); Birżebbuġa (6km)
Hal Saflieni Hypogeum

MALTA

COVER UP!

Beachwear is for beaches – don't wear bathing suits in public areas in Malta. Females should cover up modestly in places of worship and men should opt for long trousers rather than shorts.

---

well-priced meals of meat and fish (steak, lamb chops, kebabs, all under Lm5) plus huge portions of pizza, pasta, salads and burgers.

Café Juliani (☎ 2137 7888; 12 Triq San Ġorġ; snacks & meals Lm1.60-3.50; ☽ until midnight Sun-Thu, until 2am Fri & Sat) From the chic décor to the comfy couches, this café oozes style. There are tasty light meals, a selection of coffees and teas (or cocktails) and a display cabinet full of delectable desserts.

Drinking & Clubbing

The St Julian's and Sliema waterfronts have everything from posh wine bars to traditional British pubs. Paceville is the place for partying, with wall-to-wall bars and clubs, especially around the northern end of Triq San Ġorġ. Paceville is jam-packed on the weekends – wander until you find something to your taste.

BJ's (☎ 2133 7642; Triq Ball, Paceville) A recommended off-beat club, BJ's features live music (jazz, blues, rock) and draws an older crowd.

Misfits (☎ 2136 1766; Triq Paceville) The hip young things opt for Misfits, which has DJs on weekends but is more laid-back during the week, hosting jazz and art-house film nights.

O'Casey's Irish Pub (☎ 2137 3900; Triq ix-Xatt San Ġorġ, Paceville) Beneath Hotel Bernard in the heart of Paceville's clubland, this pub is what you'd expect of an Irish bar anywhere in the world – friendly and well-stocked with Guinness.

Fuego (☎ 2137 3211; www.fuego.com.mt; Triq Santu Wistin, Paceville) Get hot and sweaty dancing up a storm at this fashionable salsa bar.

Pips Club (☎ 2137 3957; www.pips.com.mt; Triq Wilga, Paceville) A popular gay bar and club, with resident DJs and regular drag shows.

Axis (☎ 2131 8078; Triq San Ġorġ, Paceville; admission around Lm2.50) Malta's biggest and best nightclub (and one that's managed to stand the test of time) has three separate clubs, seven bars and space for 3500 people.

Getting There & Away

Bus Nos 62, 64 and 67 run regularly between Valletta and Sliema, St Julian's and Paceville. There is also a ferry service between Sliema and Valletta (see p779).

MDINA & RABAT

Elegant, aristocratic Mdina (aptly nicknamed the Silent City) is perched on a rocky outcrop in the country's southwest. Fortified for over 3000 years, it was Malta's old political centre; today visitors can spend hours wandering the quiet, narrow streets. Rabat is the town settlement outside the walls.

Mdina's main square is dominated by **St Paul's Cathedral** (Pjazza San Pawl; ☽ 9.30am-11.45am & 2-5pm Mon-Sat, 3-4.30pm Sun), which is worth visiting to see the huge fresco of St Paul's shipwreck. In Rabat you can visit **St Paul's Church** and **St Paul's Grotto** (Misraħ il-Parroċċa; ☽ 10am-5pm Mon-Sat). The grotto is a cave where St Paul is said to have preached during his stay on the island. Nearby are **St Agatha's Crypt & Catacombs** (☎ 2145 4503; Triq Sant'Agata; admission Lm0.75; ☽ 9am-5pm Mon-Fri, 9am-1pm Sat Jul-Sep; 9am-noon & 1-4.30pm Mon-Fri, 9am-12.30pm Sat Oct-Jun), an underground complex of burial chambers boasting amazing Byzantine frescoes.

Sleeping & Eating

University Residence (☎ 2143 6168 or 2143 0360; www .university-residence.com.mt; Triq R M Bonnici, Lija; dm from Lm5.50; 🖳 🖳) The student residence for the University of Malta is in Lija, 5km northeast of Rabat. It's a well-equipped and well-run place, and a good spot to meet travellers and students. Facilities include pool, minimarket, café and laundry. Three-night minimum. Catch bus No 40 from Valletta.

Point de Vue Guesthouse & Restaurant (☎ 2145 4117; http://mol.net.mt/point; 5 Is-Saqqajja; b per person Lm7-8) Just outside Mdina's Main Gate is this affordable guesthouse, with simple but comfortable rooms (with private bathroom). Book ahead.

Fontanella Tea Gardens (☎ 2145 4264; Triq is-Sur; snacks & meals Lm0.50-3) Fontanella serves great cakes, sandwiches and light meals, and you'll have ample time to admire the sweeping views from its terrace because of the ordinary service!

Getting There & Away

From Valletta, take bus No 80 or 81 to reach Rabat; from Sliema and St Julian's, take No 65. The bus terminus in Rabat is on Is-Saqqajja, 150m south of Mdina's Main Gate.

SOUTHWEST COAST

The views are fantastic from the top of **Dingli Cliffs**, south of Rabat. To the southeast are the prehistoric temples of **Ħaġar Qim** (☎ 2142 4231; admission Lm1; ☺ 7.45am-2pm mid-Jun-Sep, 8.15am-5pm Mon-Sat & d 8.15am-4pm Sun Oct–mid-Jun) and **Mnajdra** (admission Lm1; ☺ as above). Built between 3600 and 3000 BC, these are perhaps the best preserved and most evocative of Malta's prehistoric sites. Bus Nos 38 and 138 run from Valletta to the temples (40c).

GOZO

The island of Gozo is much more tranquil than its big sister Malta. Fewer tourists venture over and, if they do, it's often on a day trip. The sights can be packed into one day but we recommend spending a bit more time – visit the beaches, learn to dive, take a boat trip, or simply relax.

VICTORIA (RABAT)

Victoria, also known as Rabat, is the chief town of Gozo and sits in the centre of the island, 6km from the ferry terminal at Mġarr. The **tourist office** (☎ 2156 1419; Tigrija Palazz, cnr Triq ir-Reppublika & Triq Putirjal; ☺ 9am-12.30pm & 1-5pm Mon-Sat, 9am-12.30pm Sun & public holidays), on the ground floor of a shopping arcade not far from the bus station, can provide information. All bus routes originate and terminate at the station on Triq Putirjal, about 10 minutes' walk from the Citadel.

Pjazza Indipendenza, the main square of Victoria, is a hive of activity with open-air cafés, craft shops and traders peddling fresh produce.

Victoria is crowned by the **Citadel** (also known as Il-Kastell, or Citadella), a miniature version of Malta's Mdina. A stroll around the Citadel offers breathtaking views across the island. The **Cathedral of the Assumption** (Misrah il-Katidral; admission Lm0.25; ☺ 9am-4.30pm Mon-Sat) was built between 1697 and 1711.

Call into nearby **Ta'Ricardo** (4 Triq il-Fossos; ☺ 10am-6pm) for flavoursome local produce. Order a platter (Lm3 for two people), and wash it down with some Gozitan wine.

Gozo is a better option than Malta for cyclists as it is much smaller and quieter. You can rent a bike for the day from **Victoria Garage** (☎ 2155 6414; Triq Putirjal, Victoria, Gozo; per day from Lm1.50).

MARSALFORN

Marsalforn is built around a cove and is the favoured choice for tourists in summer, so it has good facilities but there is nothing to see in the town itself. You can hike eastward a couple of kilometres over the hill to Ramla Bay in about 45 minutes.

The small **Maria-Giovanna Hostel** (☎ 2155 3630; www.gozohostels.com; Triq ir-Rabat; b per person Lm7), just back from the waterfront, is the pick of the budget accommodation on Gozo. There are five rooms (two with en suite) with pretty décor, plus a living room and guest kitchen. Breakfast is included; advance bookings are recommended.

Il-Kartell (☎ 2155 6918; Triq il-Port; mains Lm4-5.50; ☺ lunch & dinner Thu-Tue) is housed in a couple of old boathouses. The menu includes pasta dishes around the Lm2 mark, along with fresh fish, traditional dishes and daily specials.

The Ritz (☎ 2155 8392; Triq il-Wied) is a cheap and cheerful café-bar selling snacks and sandwiches to quickly settle a rumbling tum. Fashionable **Caffino** (☎ 21 562 000; Triq il-Port), at the Calypso Hotel, is a far ritzier option.

Marsalforn is a 4km walk from Victoria, or catch bus No 21.

CALYPSO'S ISLE

Gozo is one of the half-dozen or so contenders for the title of Calypso's Isle – the mythical island of Ogygia described in Homer's *Odyssey* where the nymph Calypso seduced the hero Odysseus and kept him captive for seven years. But she could not overcome his longing for his home in Ithaca, and Zeus eventually sent Hermes to command her to release him.

If the cave above Ramla Bay on Gozo was really Calypso's hideaway, then it is no wonder that Odysseus was keen to get home. Despite the pretty view and delightful island, it's a long, hot and scratchy climb up from the beach, and the cramped living quarters leave a lot to be desired.

XAGĦRA

The tree-lined village square of Xagħra is where old men sit and chat in the shade of the oleanders. Close by are the megalithic temples of **Ġgantija** (☎ 2155 3194; access from Triq L-Imqades; admission Lm1; ☼ 8.30am-4.30pm Mon-Sat, 8.30am-3pm Sun, closed public holidays), dating from 3600 BC. Along with the Ħaġar Qim and Mnajdra temples on Malta's southwest coast (p785), these temples are the oldest freestanding stone structures in the world, predating the pyramids of Egypt by more than 500 years. The purpose of these structures is the subject of much debate, and sadly there's little visitor information at the sites (the best place to learn about them is at Valletta's National Musuem of Archaeology). The Ġgantija temples are the largest in Malta - the walls stand over 6m high.

It's not far from here to one of the best beaches on Gozo. **Ramla Bay** has a beautiful sandy beach perfect for sunbathing. Follow the signposts from town.

Xagħra Lodge (☎ 2156 2362; www.gozo.com/xagħra lodge; Triq Dun Ġorġ Preċa; s/d low season Lm15.75/21, high season Lm18.75/25; ❊ ⊠) is run by a friendly English couple and has excellent facilities including air-con, en suite, balcony and cable TV in all rooms, plus a pool, terrace and an adjacent Chinese restaurant. It's a five-minute walk east of the town square.

Bus Nos 64 and 65 run between Victoria and Xagħra.

COMINO

Tiny Comino, once reportedly the hideout of pirates, now plays host to boatloads of bikini-clad invaders. The island's biggest attraction is the photogenic **Blue Lagoon**, a sheltered cove with a white-sand sea-bed and clear turquoise waters. You can take a day trip to the Blue Lagoon from many resort areas in Malta and Gozo.

The **Comino Hotel** (☎ 2152 9821; www.comino hotels.com; half board per person Lm17-28) provides the only accommodation on the island, but its prices don't exactly fit a shoestring budget. The hotel runs a ferry service from Ċirkewwa in Malta and Mġarr in Gozo (Lm3.50 return trip, seven daily). Note that the boats don't run from November to March when the hotel is closed.

MALTA DIRECTORY

ACCOMMODATION

Accommodation in Malta is plentiful and the **Malta Tourism Authority** (www.visitmalta.com) can provide listings. The prices apply to visits in high season. Camping is not permitted but cheap beds abound in hostels and guesthouses. Most places offer significantly reduced rates during off-peak periods and for stays of multiple nights.

The **National Student Travel Service** (NSTS; ☎ 2124 4983; www.nsts.org; 220 Triq San Pawl, Valletta) manages a few hostels in Malta and has agreements with certain guesthouses to provide cheap accommodation to hostellers. An HI-membership card is required. The NSTS offers a special week-long hostelling package, which includes airport transfers, seven overnight dorm stays (with breakfast) and a week's bus pass, for €140 (approximately Lm60) from October to June, and €170 (approximately Lm72) from July to September.

ACTIVITIES

The website of the **Malta Tourism Authority** (www.visitmalta.com) has loads of information on the different types of activities possible in Malta. Click onto the 'What to Do' pages.

Water-babies are well catered for. Conditions for diving are excellent: visibility often exceeds 30m and there's a huge variety of marine life. The warm temperatures of the Mediterranean mean that diving is possible year-round. There are more than 30 diving schools; the majority are members of the **Professional Diving Schools Association** (PDSA; www.digi gate.net/divers; 1 Msida Court, 61 ix-Xatt Ta-Msida, Msida). See also www.visitmalta.com/en/diving for details of sites, regulations and operators.

Swimming & Sunbathing

The best sandy beaches on Malta are Ġnejna Bay, Għajn Tuffieħa Bay and Golden Bay, all in Malta's northwest (bus No 47 from Valletta, No 652 from Sliema); and Mellieħa Bay in the north (bus Nos 44, 45 and 48). The best sandy beaches on Gozo are Ramla Bay (bus No 42) and Xlendi Bay (bus No 87).

There are some excellent rocky swimming spots on Comino (the Blue Lagoon) and in Malta's south (Għar Lapsi). Gozo has some good rocky sites too, including Dwejra in the west and San Blas Bay in the northeast.

BUSINESS HOURS

From 1 October to 15 June, **Government Museums in Malta** open from 8.15am to 5pm Monday to Saturday, and from 8.15am to 4.15pm Sundays. From 16 June to 30 September the museums are open from 8.15am to 5pm Monday to Saturday and from 7.45am to 2pm Sundays, closed public holidays. The **Government Museums in Gozo** are open from 8.30am to 4.30pm Monday to Saturday, 8.30am to 3pm Sunday, and are closed on public holidays year round.

Banks are generally open from 8.30am to 12.30pm Monday to Friday, and 8.30am to 11.30am Saturdays. **Restaurants** are open from noon to 3pm and 7 to 11pm. **Shops** sometimes open all day during summer, especially in tourist areas, but are otherwise open from 9am to 1pm, and 4pm to 7pm Monday to Saturday, but closed on Sundays and public holidays.

CUSTOMS

Items for personal use are not subject to duty. The duty free allowance per person is 1L of spirits, 1L of wine and 200 cigarettes. Duty will be charged on any gifts over Lm50 intended for local residents.

EMBASSIES & CONSULATES
Maltese Embassies & Consulates

Australia (☎ 02-6290 1724; maltahc@bigpond.com; 38 Culgoa Circuit, O'Malley ACT 2606)
France (☎ 01 56 59 75 90; fax 01 45 62 00 36; 92 Avenue des Champs Elysées, 75008 Paris)
Germany (☎ 030-26 39 110; maltaembgrm@ndh.net; Tiergarten Dreieck, Block 4, Klingelhöferstrasse 7, 10785 Berlin)
Italy (☎ 06-687 99 90; maltaembassy.rome@gov.mt; 12 Lungotevere Marzio, 00186 Rome)
Netherlands (☎ 070-356 1252; malta.embassy@ planet.nl; 2 Scheveningensweg, 2517 KT, Den Haag)
Tunisia (☎ 071-847 048; ambassade.malte@planet.tn; 5 Rue Achart, Nord Hilton, 1082 Tunis)
UK (☎ 020-7292 4800; maltahighcommission. london@gov.mt; Malta House, 36-38 Piccadilly, London W1J OLE)
USA (☎ 202-462 3611/2; malta_embassy@compuserve .com; 2017 Connecticut Avenue NW, Washington DC 20008)

Embassies & Consulates in Malta

Australia (☎ 2133 8201; Villa Fiorentina, Rampa Ta'Xbiex, Ta'Xbiex)
Canada (☎ 2123 3121; 103 Triq I-Arċisqof, Valletta)
France (☎ 2123 3430; 130 Triq Melita, Valletta)

Germany (☎ 2133 6531; Il-Piazzetta, Entrance B, 1st fl, Triq it-Torri, Sliema)
Italy (☎ 2123 3157/8/9; 1 Triq Vilhena, Floriana)
Netherlands (☎ 2569 1790; 19 Triq San Zakkarija, Valletta)
Tunisia (☎ 2141 7171; Valletta Rd, Attard)
UK (☎ 2323 0000; Whitehall Mansions, Xatt Ta'Xbiex, Ta'Xbiex)
USA (☎ 2123 5960; 3rd fl, Development House, Triq Sant'Anna, Floriana)

FESTIVALS & EVENTS

Each village has a *festa* (feast day) honouring its patron saint. You can't avoid getting caught up in the excitement, as the whole community gets involved. Festivities start days before the event. Festa season runs from June to September; the tourist offices will be able to tell you when and where festas are being held, or a good idea is to download info before you travel – go to www.maltachurch .org.mt (in Malti), then click on Feast Days.

Festas aren't the only excuse to throw a party in Malta – the website of the **Malta Tourism Authority** (www.visitmalta.com/en/whats_on) has a comprehensive list of what's on, where and when.

HOLIDAYS

New Year's Day 1 January
St Paul's Shipwreck 10 February
St Joseph's Day 19 March
Good Friday March/April
Freedom Day 31 March
Labour Day 1 May
Commemoration of 1919 Independence Riots 7 June
Feast of Sts Peter and Paul (L-Imnarja Festival) 29 June
Feast of the Assumption 15 August
Victory Day 8 September
Independence Day 21 September
Feast of the Immaculate Conception 8 December
Republic Day 13 December
Christmas Day 25 December

MONEY

The Maltese lira, plural liri (Lm) is divided into 100 cents. The currency is often referred to as the pound.

Banks usually offer better rates of exchange than hotels. There is a 24-hour exchange bureau at the airport. Note that there are no exchange facilities (or ATMs) at the ferry port near Valletta.

Restaurants and taxis expect a 10% tip. Shops have fixed prices, but hotels and car-hire agencies offer reduced rates in the low season (November to May).

TELEPHONE

Public telephones are widely available, and most are card-operated. You can buy phonecards at many kiosks, post offices and souvenir shops. Local calls cost 10c. For local telephone enquiries, call ☎ 1182; for overseas enquiries, call ☎ 1152.

The international direct dialling code is ☎ 00. To call Malta from abroad, dial the international access code, ☎ 356 (Malta's country code) and the eight-digit number (there are no area codes).

VISAS

Visas for Malta are not needed for visits of up to three months by nationals of most Commonwealth countries (excluding South Africa, India and Pakistan). The same is true for most European countries, the USA and Japan. Other nationalities must apply for a visa; the details are on the website of Malta's **Ministry of Foreign Affairs** (www.foreign.gov.mt /service/visa).

Acropolis (p529), Athens, Greece

Black Forest (p488), Germany

Folk dancers in Old Market Square (p909), Krakow, Poland

Museo del Prado (p1063), Madrid, Spain

JON DAVISON

Adriatic Coast, Dubrovnik (p262), Croatia

JEAN-BERNARD CARILLET

Beer is a way of life in Brussels (p116), Belgium

Coffee shop, Amsterdam (p851), The Netherlands

CHRISTIAN ASLUND

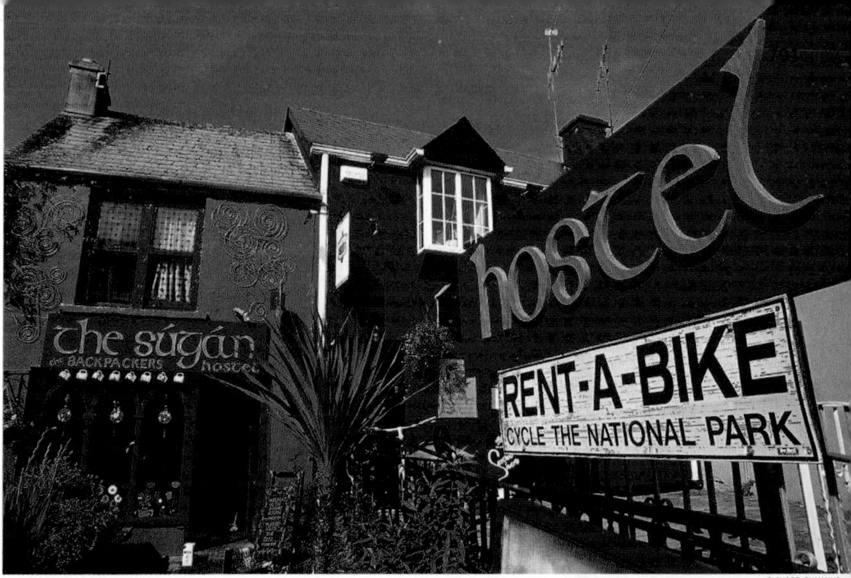

RICHARD CUMMINS

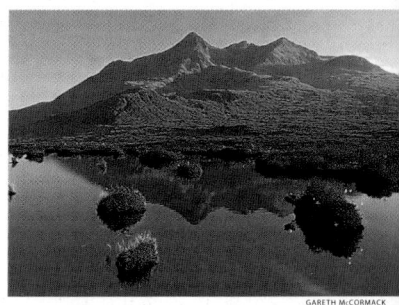

Súgán Hostel (p623), Killarney, Ireland

RICHARD I'ANSON

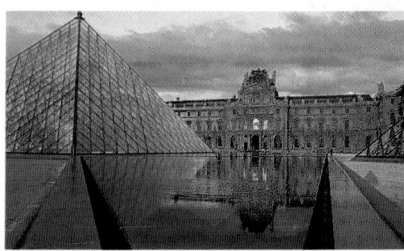

The Louvre (p377), Paris, France

Nationalmuseum (p1136), Stockholm, Sweden

JONATHAN SMITH

GARETH McCORMACK

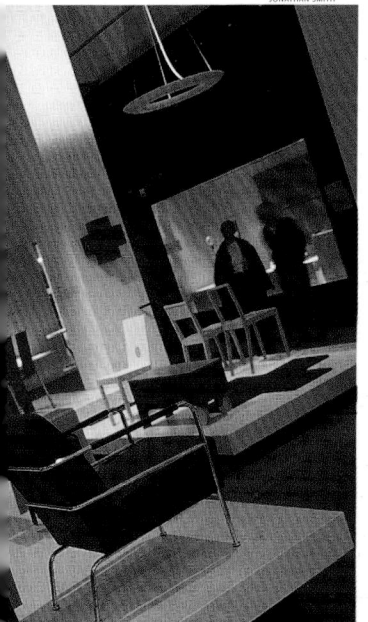

Isle of Skye (p213), Scotland, Britain

NEIL SETCHFIELD

The Cross (p169), London, England

DOUG McKINLAY

Ferris wheel and Eiffel Tower (p380), Paris, France

Grand Canal (p673), Venice, Italy

NEIL SETCH

CATHERINE HANGER

Djemaa el-Fna (p825), Marrakesh, Morocco

St Basil's Cathedral (p968),
Moscow, Russia

MARK NEWMAN

GRANT DIXON

Eiger, Jungfrau region (p1179), Switzerland

Tallinn (p335), Estonia

STEVE KOKKER

JOHN BORTHWICK

Nyhavn Canal (p312), Copenhagen, Denmark

Mont Blanc (p421), Chamonix, France

RICHARD NEBESKY

SARA-JANE C

Ibiza (p1091), Balearic Islands, Spain

RICHARD NEBESKY

Clubbing (p460), Berlin, Germany

CHRISTOPHER WOOD

Fjord near Flåm (p886), Norway

Brest Fortress (p105), Brest, Belarus

JONATHAN SMITH

RUSSELL MOUNTFORD

Duomo (p687), Florence, Italy

Blejski Otok (p1048), Bled, Slovenia

GRANT DIXON

CARLOS COSTA

Lagos (p493), the Algarve, Portugal

Blue Mosque (p1192),
Istanbul, Turkey

ANDERS BLOMQVIST

RICK GERHARTER

Parliament Building (p71), Vienna, Austria

Old Town Square (p285), Prague, Czech Republic

RICHARD NEBESKÝ

Moldova

HIGHLIGHTS

- **Chişinău** Stroll its tree-studded avenues and experience its kick-ass nightlife (p800)
- **Orheiul Vechi** Visit the fantastic cave monasteries of 13th-century monks (p804)
- **Transdniestr** Visit the self-styled republic, a surreal, living museum of the Soviet Union (p804)
- **Off-the-beaten-track** Hike and canoe during the day and indulge in homemade wine in the evenings in the Lower Dniestr National Park (p804)

FAST FACTS

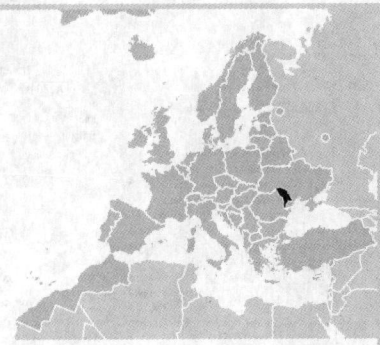

- **Area** 33,843 sq km (twice the size of Denmark)
- **ATMs** In major cities
- **Budget** US$30 per day
- **Capital** Chişinău
- **Country code** ☎ 373
- **Famous for** Wine; folk art
- **Head of State** President Vladimir Voronin
- **Languages** Moldovan, Russian
- **Money** Moldovan lei (A$1 = 8.95lei, CA$1 = 9.82lei, €1=15.41lei, ¥100 = 11.30lei, NZ$1 = 8.44lei, UK£1= 22.17lei, US$1=12.37lei) Prices quoted in this chapter are in US dollars
- **Population** 4.4 million
- **Phrases** *bună* (hello), *mulţumesc/merci* (thank you), *cum vă numiţi?* (what's your name?)

- **Time** GMT/UTC + 2
- **Visa** Required for all EU, US, Canadian, Australian and New Zealand passport-holders.

TRAVEL HINTS

It is far simpler to enter Moldova via Romania, from where connections are frequent and easy, and then either return to Romania or continue eastward, which means you avoid the requirement of a double-entry visa..

ROAMING MOLDOVA

Party in Chişinău, go to Orheiul Vechi, hike in Lower Dniestr National Park, then head to Transdniestr.

OK, so it's had a bad press – Moldova's image is more closely linked to poverty, civil war and communism than as a travel destination.

But actually the accepted image is inaccurate. Instead think sunflower fields, enormous watermelons, bucolic pastoral lands, amazingly friendly people and rivers of delicious wine, as well as a party-crazy capital city. Here you're certainly well off the beaten backpacker track.

MOLDOVA

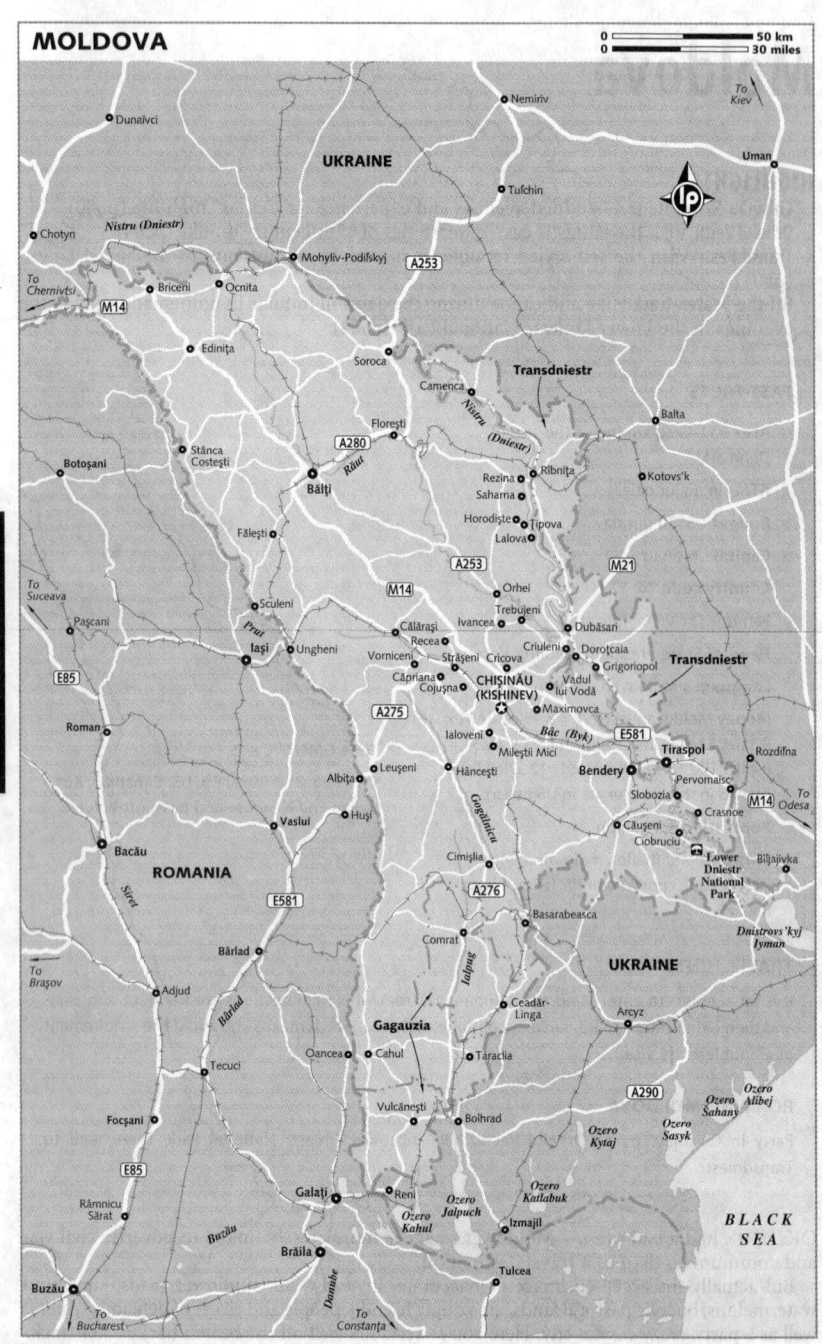

0 ————————— 50 km
0 ————————— 30 miles

UKRAINE

Dunaĭvci

To Kiev

Nemiriv

Tulchin

Uman

Chotyn

Nistru (Dniestr)

Mohyliv-Podilskyj

A253

To Chernivtsi

M14

Briceni

Ocnita

Edinita

Soroca

Transdniestr

Camenca

Floreşti

A280

Balta

Botoşani

Stânca Costeşti

Răut

Nistru (Dniestr)

Rezina

Râbniţa

Kotovs'k

Bălţi

Saharna

Fâleşti

Horodişte

Tipova

Lalova

Sculeni

A253

M14

Orhei

M21

Paşcani

Prut

Iaşi

Ungheni

Recea

Călăraşi

Trebujeni

Ivancea

Dubăsari

To Suceava

E85

Vorniceni

Străşeni

Cricova

Criuleni

Dorotçaia

Transdniestr

Căpriana

Cojuşna

CHIŞINĂU (KISHINEV)

Vadul lui Vodă

Grigoriopol

Roman

A275

Maximovca

Bâc (Byk)

Ialoveni

E581

Tiraspol

Rozdilna

Albiţa

Leuşeni

Hânceşti

Mileşti Mici

Bendery

Pervomaisc

To Odesa

Vaslui

Huşi

Slobozia

Crasnoe

M14

Bacău

Clăuşeni

Ciobruciu

Biljajivka

ROMANIA

Siret

Cimişlia

Gagăuzlâcu

A276

Basarabeasca

Lower Dniestr National Park

Dnistrovs'kyj Łyman

Bârlad

Comrat

UKRAINE

E581

Ialpug

To Braşov

Adjud

Ceadâr-Linga

Arcyz

Gagauzia

Oancea

Cahul

Taraclia

Tecuci

A290

Ozero Alibej

Focşani

Vulcăneşti

Boihrad

Ozero Kytaj

Ozero Sasyk

Ozero Sahany

E85

Râmnicu Sărat

Galaţi

Reni

Ozero Jalpuch

Ozero Katlabuk

Izmajil

BLACK SEA

Buzău

Ozero Kahul

Brăila

Buzău

To Bucharest

Danube

To Constanţa

Tulcea

HISTORY

Moldova today straddles two historic regions divided by the Nistru River. Historic Romanian Bessarabia incorporated the region west of the Nistru, while tsarist Russia governed the territory east of the river (Transdniestr).

Bessarabia, part of the Romanian principality of Moldavia, was annexed in 1812 by the Russian empire. In 1918, after the October Revolution, Bessarabia declared its independence. Two months later the newly formed Democratic Moldavian Republic united with Romania. Russia never recognised this union.

Then in 1924 the Soviet Union created the Moldavian Autonomous Oblast on the eastern banks of the Nistru River, and incorporated Transdniestr into the Ukrainian Soviet Socialist Republic (SSR). A few months later the Soviet government renamed the oblast the Moldavian Autonomous Soviet Socialist Republic (Moldavian ASSR). During 1929 the capital was moved to Tiraspol from Balta (in present-day Ukraine).

In June 1940 the Molotov-Ribbentrop Pact meant Soviet troops occupied Romanian Bessarabia and joined it with the southern part, naming it the Moldavian Soviet Socialist Republic.

During 1941 allied Romanian and German troops attacked the Soviet Union. Bessarabia and Transdniestr fell into Romanian hands. Consequently, thousands of Bessarabian Jews were sent to labour camps and then deported to Auschwitz.

In August 1944 the Soviet army reoccupied Transdniestr and Bessarabia. In July 1949, 25,000 ethnic Moldovans (Romanians) were deported to Siberia, followed by another quarter of a million from 1950 to 1952.

It wasn't until February 1990 that the first democratic elections to the Supreme Soviet (parliament) were won by the Popular Front. Then in April 1990 the Moldovan national flag was reinstated – except in Transdniestr.

In August 1991, Moldova declared its full independence. Today, Vladimir Voronin is president of the republic, and also the president of the parliamentary Communist Party. He has strong Russian sympathies and has taken steps to dissociate Moldova from its Romanian roots, focusing instead on the separateness of the Moldovan identity and language, but ones fashioned very much under its Soviet and Russian history of dominance. Elections were due in 2004, and at the time of writing a major change in government is expected.

PEOPLE & CULTURE

With 4.43 million inhabitants Moldova is the most densely populated region in the former Soviet Union. Moldovans make up 64.5% of the total population, Ukrainians constitute 13.8%, Russians 13%, Gagauz 3.5%, Bulgarians 2%, Jews 1.5%, and other nationalities such as Belarusians, Poles and Roma compose 1.7%.

Most Gagauz and Bulgarians inhabit southern Moldova. In Transdniestr, Ukrainians and Russians make up 53% of the region's population; Moldovans make up 40%. It is one of the least urbanised countries in Europe.

ARTS

There is a wealth of traditional folk art in Moldova; carpet-making, pottery, weaving and carving predominate. The country also has prolific modern composers, painters and sculptors.

Dimitrie Gagauz is the leading composer of songs which reflects the folklore of the Turkic-influenced Gagauz population of southern Moldova.

ENVIRONMENT

Moldova is tiny and landlocked. It's a flat country of gently rolling steppes, gradually sloping towards the Black Sea. Moldova is home to some 16,500 species of animals (only 460 of which are vertebrates).

Moldova has one nascent national park: the Lower Dniestr National Park (p804), southeast of Chişinău.

There are also five scientific reserves (totalling 19,378 hectares) and 30 protected natural sites (covering 22,278 hectares). The reserves protect areas of bird migration, old beech and oak forests, and important waterways.

Never heavily industrial, Moldova faces more issues of protection and conservation than pollution. Most of its 3600 rivers and rivulets were drained, diverted or dammed, threatening ecosystems.

MOLDOVA

TRANSPORT

GETTING THERE & AWAY

All prices that are quoted in this chapter are in US dollars.

Air

Moldova's only main airport is the **Chişinău International** (☎ 22-526 060).

Air Moldova (☎ 21-312 1258; Chişinău KIV) and **Tarom** (☎ 0992 541 254; www.tarom.ro; Bucharest OTP) operate daily flights between Chişinău and Bucharest.

Chişinău is connected by regular flights to/from Amsterdam, Athens, Budapest, Minsk, Moscow, Prague, Rome, Sofia and Vienna. Expect to pay about $250 to $430 for a return flight between any of these capitals.

Bus

Eurolines (www.eurolines.ro, www.eurolines.md) has regular routes to Italy, Spain and Germany (usually around $140 return) as well as to Moscow, St Petersburg and Minsk.

Öz Gülen Turizm (☎ 273 748) runs a daily bus between Chişinău and Istanbul ($34, 6pm). There are also services to Kyiv or Odesa that run through Transdniestr and Tiraspol.

Car & Motorcycle

The Green Card (a routine extension of domestic motor insurance to cover most European countries) is valid in Moldova. Extra insurance can be bought at the borders. For more information, see right.

Train

International routes include Moscow ($36, 27 to 33 hours, three daily), Odesa ($3, five hours, 11 daily), St Petersburg ($42, 37 hours, one daily), Bucharest ($26, 14 hours, one daily), Lviv ($7, eight hours, one daily) and Minsk ($29, 25 hours, two weekly). There's an overnight service between Bucharest and Chişinău.

EMERGENCY NUMBERS

- Ambulance ☎ 903
- Fire ☎ 901
- Gas leaks ☎ 904
- Police ☎ 902

BORDER CROSSINGS

Moldovan visas are available at border crossings with Romania: Albiţa (65km southeast of Iaşi) and Sculeni (24km north of Ungheni).

GETTING AROUND

Bicycle

Being flat as a board, Moldova should be perfect for cycling. But it isn't, really, because of the bad condition of most roads and a lack of infrastructure.

Bus & Microbus

Moldova has a good network of buses running to most towns and villages. Microbuses, which follow the same routes as the buses, are quicker and more reliable.

Car & Motorcycle

In Chişinău, travel agencies can arrange car rental but the roads are in poor condition. EC driving licences are accepted here.

The inter-city speed limit is 90km per hour and in built-up areas 60km per hour. For road rescue, dial ☎ 901. The **Automobile Club Moldova** (ACM; ☎ 22-292 703; www.acm.md) can inform you of all regulations and offer emergency assistance.

Local Transport

In Moldova, buses cost about $0.10, trolleybuses $0.05 and city maxi-taxis $0.20.

Taxi

There are official and unofficial taxis. You'll need to agree upon a price before driving off; a drive to anywhere inside Chişinău is unlikely to cost more than $3. The going rate is about $0.10 to $0.15 per kilometre.

CHIŞINĂU

☎ 22 / pop 709,900

This may be the capital of one of Europe's poorest countries, but you'd never know it walking its streets. In Chişinău, Mercedes and Jaguars line up outside one fancy restaurant after another, and fashionably-dressed youth strut down boutique-lined avenues. The jagged contrast between rich and poor certainly does not please the

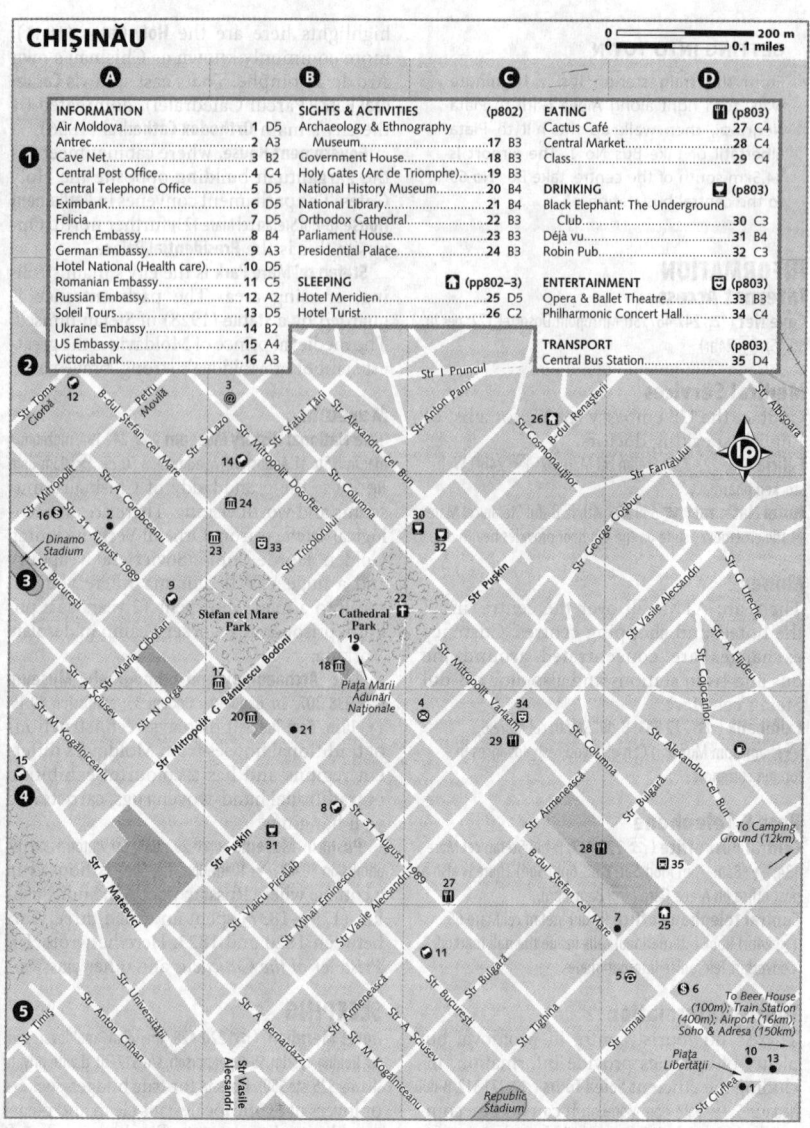

CHIŞINĂU

0 — 200 m
0 — 0.1 miles

INFORMATION		
Air Moldova	1	D5
Antrec	2	A3
Cave Net	3	B2
Central Post Office	4	C4
Central Telephone Office	5	D5
Eximbank	6	D5
Felicia	7	D5
French Embassy	8	B4
German Embassy	9	A3
Hotel National (Health care)	10	D5
Romanian Embassy	11	C5
Russian Embassy	12	A2
Soleil Tours	13	D5
Ukraine Embassy	14	B2
US Embassy	15	A4
Victoriabank	16	A3

SIGHTS & ACTIVITIES		(p802)
Archaeology & Ethnography		
Museum	17	B3
Government House	18	B4
Holy Gates (Arc de Triomphe)	19	B3
National History Museum	20	B4
National Library	21	B4
Orthodox Cathedral	22	B3
Parliament House	23	B3
Presidential Palace	24	B3

SLEEPING		(pp802–3)
Hotel Meridien	25	D5
Hotel Turist	26	C2

EATING		(p803)
Cactus Café	27	C4
Central Market	28	C4
Class	29	C4

DRINKING		(p803)
Black Elephant: The Underground		
Club	30	C3
Déjà vu	31	B4
Robin Pub	32	C3

ENTERTAINMENT		(p803)
Opera & Ballet Theatre	33	B3
Philharmonic Concert Hall	34	C4

TRANSPORT		(p803)
Central Bus Station	35	D4

MOLDOVA

have-nots, but this vibrant, good-natured city is so full of *joie de vivre* that it doesn't get in the way of what's most important here: having a good time.

Yet the city has a brutal history. It was a hotbed of anti-Semitism in the early 20th century; in 1903 the murder of 49 Jews sparked protests from Jewish communities

worldwide, and in 1941 during WWII the notorious Chişinău pogrom was executed.

ORIENTATION

Chişinău's street layout is a typically Soviet grid system of straight streets. The main street, B-dul Ştefan cel Mare, crosses the town from southeast to northwest.

GETTING INTO TOWN

From the train station it's a 10-minute walk; turn right along Aleea Gării to Piaţa Negruzzi, then walk up the hill to Piaţa Libertăţii or take Bus No 1. The airport is 14.5km south of the centre, take Bus No 65 to the central bus station.

INFORMATION
Internet Access
Cave Net (☎ 247 467; Str Mitropolit Dosoftei 122; per hr $0.45; ⏰ 24hr)

Medical Services
Contact the US embassy (p807) for a list of English-speaking doctors.
Felicia (☎ 223 725; Ştefan cel Mare 62; ⏰ 24hr) Well-stocked pharmacy.
Hotel National (☎ 540 305; 4th fl, B-dul Ştefan cel Mare 4) The emergency suite on the 4th floor provides health care.

Money
There are ATMs all over the centre, in all the hotels and shopping centres. Currency exchanges are concentrated around the bus and train stations and also along B-dul Ştefan cel Mare.
Eximbank (☎ 272 583; B-dul Ştefan cel Mare 6; ⏰ 9am-5pm Mon-Fri) Can give you cash advances in foreign currency.

Post & Telephone
Central post office (☎ 227 737; B-dul Ştefan cel Mare 134; ⏰ 8am-7pm Mon-Sat, 8am-6pm Sun) There is also a post office on Aleea Gării (⏰ 8am-8pm).
Central telephone office (B-dul Ştefan cel Mare 65; ⏰ 24hr) Book international calls inside the hall marked 'Convorbiri Telefonice Internaţionale'.

Tourist Information
There's no tourist centre in Moldova, but plenty of agencies provide information, including the efficient **Soleil Tours** (☎ 271 312; B-dul Negruzzi 5; ⏰ 9am-6pm Mon-Fri). It can book accommodation and tickets, but is best known for multi-day excursions into remote Moldova.

SIGHTS
City Centre
A good place to begin is smack in the centre, where Chişinău's best-known parks sit diagonally opposite each other, which form two diamonds at the city's core. The highlights here are the **Holy Gates** (1841), more commonly known as Chişinău's own Arc de Triomphe. To its east sprawls **Cathedral Park** (Parcul Catedralei), dominated by the city's main **Orthodox Cathedral** (1836).

Government House, where cabinet meets, is the gargantuan building opposite the Holy Gates. The parliament convenes in **Parliament House** (B-dul Ştefan cel Mare 123) further north. Opposite this is the **Presidential Palace**.

Ştefan cel Mare Park is the city's main strolling, cruising area. The park entrance is guarded by a **statue** (1928) of Ştefan himself. The medieval prince of Moldavia is the greatest symbol of Moldova's strong, brave past.

Museums
The **National History Museum** (☎ 242 194; muzeum@mac.md; Str 31 August 121A; admission $0.25; ⏰ 9am-6pm Tue-Sat) is the granddaddy of Chişinău's museums and worth visiting. There are archaeological artefacts from Orheiul Vechi including Golden Horde coins, Soviet-era weaponry and a huge WWII diorama where you can speak to a man who spent 12 years as a political prisoner at a worker's camp in desolate Vorkuta.

The **Archaeology and Ethnography Museum** (☎ 238 307; Str Bănulescu Bodoni 35; admission $0.15; ⏰ 10am-6pm Tue-Sat) displays reconstructions of traditional houses from Moldova's different regions and has a colourful exhibition of traditional hand-woven rugs, carpets and wall hangings.

Pushkin Museum (☎ 292 685; Str Anton Pann 19; admission $0.40; ⏰ 10am-6pm Tue-Sun) is housed in a cottage where Russian poet Alexandr Pushkin (1799–1837) spent an exiled three years between 1820 and 1823. Here he wrote *The Prisoner of the Caucacus* and other classics.

SLEEPING
Hotel Meridian (☎ 220 428; meridian@moldovacc.md; Str Tighina 42; dm $5-8 per person, s/d $17/30, d with private shower $25, ste $50) This is for true budget-seekers or lovers of exotic locales; it's clean and pleasant, dorms have two to five beds, and staff are lovely. They'll even pick you up from the train station ($5) or airport ($10).

Hotel Turist (☎ 220 637; B-dul Renaşterii 13; s $20-26, d $25, ste $40-130) For a cool blast of the Soviet past, try this friendly place. It overlooks a giant Soviet memorial to communist youth and sports a snazzy mural on its façade. Rooms are comfortable, if slightly kitsch.

Adresa (☎ 544 392; adresa@mdi.net; B-dul Negruzzi 1; apt from $20; ☯ 24hr) This reliable agency offers great alternatives to hotels, renting out one- to three-room apartments in the city.

EATING

For the cheapest eats, there are some kiosks and small cafés around the bus station and central market, where a dish of mystery meat or meat-filled pastries is less than $1.

Class (☎ 227 774; Str V Alecsandri 121; mains $3-6; ☯ 11am-midnight) One of the country's rare Lebanese restaurants with excellent starters, falafel and eggplant dishes. There are water- pipes ($2.50), and on Fridays there's exotic dancing and a $10 all-you-can-eat buffet.

Cactus Café (☎ 504 094; www.cactus.md; Str Arme- nească 41; mains $1.50-4; ☯ 9am-10pm) This is a true winner. The eclectic interior décor (it's the Wild West meets urban bohemian, but with grace and humour) is matched with the city's most creative menu. There are incred- ible breakfasts, lots of vegetarian meals and wild plates like turkey with bananas.

Beer House (☎ 756 127; B-dul Negruzzi 6/2; mains $3-6; ☯ 11am-11pm) Of all Chişinau's hot din- ing places, you'll be returning to this brew- ery-cum-restaurant again and again – its excellent menu ranges from chicken wings and soups to rabbit grilled in cognac.

The **central market** (Piaţa Centrală; ☯ 7am-5pm) is well worth a visit for a choice of fresh food.

DRINKING & CLUBBING

Déja Vu (☎ 227 693; Str Bucureşti 67; ☯ 11am-2am) This cocktail bar has a tantalising menu of drinks on offer. Come here to lounge about and look gorgeous.

Robin Pub (Str Alexandru cel Bun 83; ☯ 11am-1am) A friendly local pub atmosphere reigns su- preme in this relaxed, tasteful hangout.

Black Elephant: The Underground Club (☎ 234 715; Str 31 August 78a; ☯ 3pm-6am) A highlight of the club scene, this place mainly hosts jazz evenings, but something different goes on here every night.

Soho (☎ 275 800; B-dul Negruzzi 2/4; ☯ 10pm-4am Tue-Sun) The best disco in town has lots of theme nights, special DJs and the occa- sional gay night.

ENTERTAINMENT

Opera & Ballet Theatre (☎ 244 163; B-dul Ştefan cel Mare 152; box office ☯ 10am-2pm & 5-7pm) Home to the esteemed national opera and ballet.

Philharmonic Concert Hall (☎ 224 505; Str Mitro- polit Varlaam 78) Moldova's National Philhar- monic is based here.

National Centre of Culture and Circus Art (☎ 496 803; B-dul Renaşterii 33; box office ☯ 9am-6pm) Circus performances are held at 6.30pm Friday, and noon, 3pm and 6.30pm Saturday and Sunday. Bus No 27 from B-dul Ştefan cel Mare goes there.

GETTING THERE & AWAY

Chişinău has two bus stations. Most buses within Moldova depart from the **central bus station** (Autogară Centrală; ☎ 542 185) on Str Mit- ropolit Varlaam. Buses and maxi-taxis go to Tiraspol and Bendery every 20 to 35 min- utes from 6.30am to 6.30pm. Bus services to/from Comrat and other southern des- tinations use the less crowded **southwestern bus station** (Autogară Sud-vest; ☎ 723 983; cnr Şoseaua Hânceşti & Str Spicului), 2km from the city centre. Local services include five buses daily to Comrat ($2.95) in Gagauzia.

Within Moldova, both Odesa-bound and some of the Moscow-bound trains stop at Bendery ($1, two hours) and Tiraspol ($1.50, 2½ hours). There are 11 extra trains to Bend- ery and 25 to Tiraspol. There are five trains daily to Comrat and four to Ungheni.

GETTING AROUND
To/From the Airport

Bus No 65 departs every 30 minutes between 5am and 10pm from the central bus sta- tion to the airport. Microbus No 65 departs every 20 minutes from Str Ismail, near the corner of B-dul Ştefan cel Mare ($0.25).

Bus & Trolleybus

Bus No 45 (and microbus No 45a) runs from the central bus station (Autogară Centrală) to the southwestern bus station (Autogară Sud-vest). Bus No 1 goes from the train station to B-dul Ştefan cel Mare.

Trolleybus Nos 1, 4, 5, 8, 18 and 22 go to the train station from the city centre. Bus Nos 2, 10 and 16 go to Autogară Sud-vest. Tickets costing $0.15 for buses and $0.10 for trolleybuses are sold at kiosks or direct from the driver.

Taxi

Calling a **taxi** (☎ 746 565, ☎ 705, 706 or 707) is cheaper than hailing one on the street. The official rate is $0.25 per kilometre.

MOLDOVA

AROUND CHIŞINĂU

CRICOVA

Underneath a village of the same name, 15km north of Chişinău, lies a winery called **Cricova** (☎ 22-441 204; info@cricovawine.md; Str Ungureanu 1; ☺ 8am-4pm). Tunnels have existed here at Moldova's leading wine kingdom since the 15th century and the extent of the network makes it one of Europe's biggest, too. You must be in private transport and have advance reservations to get into Cricova. It's most easily done through travel agencies in Chişinău, but you can call the winery yourself and book a time.

COJUŞNA

Cricova's competitor operates 12km northwest of Chişinău in the village of Cojuşna.

Cojuşna (☎ 22-744 820, 22-715 329; Str Lomtadze 4; 2-3hr tour per person $17; ☺ 8am-6pm Mon-Fri) will open its wine cellars and wine-tasting rooms for you at any hour. Bus No 2 runs every 15 minutes from Str Vasile Alecsandri in Chişinău towards Cricova. Get off at the Cojuşna stop. Ignore the turning on the left marked Cojuşna and walk the remaining 2km along the main road to the winery entrance, marked by a tall, totem pole–style pillar.

ORHEIUL VECHI

Ten kilometres southeast of Orhei lies Orheiul Vechi ('Old Orhei'; marked on maps as the village of Trebujeni), with the **Orheiul Vechi Monastery complex** (Complexul Muzeistic Orheiul Vechi; ☎ 23-534 242; admission $0.40; ☺ 9am-5pm Tue-Sun) carved into a massive limestone cliff.

The **Cave Monastery** (Mănăstire în Peşteră), inside a cliff, was dug by Orthodox monks in the 13th century.

On the main road to the complex you'll find the headquarters where you purchase your entrance tickets and can also arrange guides and get general information. Shorts are forbidden and women must cover their heads inside the monastery.

Daily buses depart every half-hour from Chişinău's central train station to Orhei ($1.20). From Orhei, a bus departs daily for Trebujeni at 6am. Ask to be dropped off by the signposted entrance to the complex. There is a daily afternoon bus (3pm) back to Orhei from Orheiul Vechi. A taxi from Orhei to Orheiul Vechi costs around $6.

LOWER DNIESTR NATIONAL PARK

The Parcul Naţional Nistrul Inferior was set up in recent years by the nonprofit **NGO Biotica** (☎ 22-498 837; www.biotica-moldova.org). Comprising more than 50,000 hectares of wetlands, forest and agricultural land, it encompasses some 40 sites of archaeological importance, observation points, many villages and some of Moldova's best vineyards (at Purcari and Tudora for example). Canoeing, hiking, wine-tasting and camping are all possible in this lovely area.

TRANSDNIESTR

pop 633,600
The self-declared republic of Transdniestr (Pridnestrovskaya Moldavskaya Respublika, or PMR in Russian), which stretches along the eastern side of the country, is one of the world's last surviving communist bastions.

It was the scene of a bloody civil war in the early 1990s, when the area declared independence from Moldova. It has its own currency, police force, army and borders, which are controlled by Transdniestran border guards. Transdniestrians boycott the Moldovan independence day and celebrate their own independence day on 2 September.

See http://geo.ya.com/travelimages/transdniestr.html for some excellent photos of the region, and www.cbpmr.net for the 'official' account of Transdniestr.

INFORMATION
Language

The official state languages in Transdniestr are Russian, Moldovan and Ukrainian.

Money

The only legal tender is the Transdniestran rouble (NH). Officially introduced in 1994, it quickly dissolved into a maelstrom of zeros.

Post

Transdniestran stamps featuring local hero General Suvorov can only be used for letters sent within the Transdniestran republic and are not recognised anywhere else. For letters to Moldova, Romania and the West, you have to use Moldovan stamps (available here but less conveniently than in Moldova).

TIRASPOL

☎ 284 / pop 194,000

Tiraspol ('town on the Nistru' river in Greek), 70km east of Chişinău, is the world's largest open-air museum of Soviet-style communism. The city was founded in 1792 following Russian domination of the area.

Orientation

The train and bus stations are next to each other at the end of ulitsa Lenina.

Information

Beltsy (ulitsa 25 Oktober 74; ☻ 9am-10pm) Well-stocked supermarket and department store, which has an exchange office as well.

Bunker (pereulok Naberezhnyi 1; per hr $0.40; ☻ 9am-11pm) Modern Internet club.

Central telephone office (cnr ulitsa 25 Oktober & ulitsa Kommunisticheskaya; ☻ 7-8.45pm) You can buy telephone cards ($2.15 or $7.75) to use in the modern pay telephones.

Prisbank (☻ 8.30am-4.30pm Mon-Sat) Next door to the telephone office. Change money here.

Sights

At the western end of ulitsa 25 Oktober stands a Soviet armoured tank from which the Transdniestran flag flies. Behind is the Heroes' Cemetery with its **Tomb of the Unknown Soldier**, flanked by an eternal flame in memory of those who died on 3 March 1992 during the first outbreak of fighting.

The **Tiraspol National United Museum** (ulitsa 25 Oktober 42; admission $0.30; ☎ 9am-5pm Sun-Fri) is the closest the city has to a local history museum, with an exhibit on poet Nikolai Dimitriovich Zelinskogo who founded the first Soviet school of chemistry. Opposite is the **Presidential Palace**, from where Igor Smirnov rules his mini empire.

The **House of Soviets** (Dom Sovetov), towering over the eastern end of ulitsa 25 Oktober, has Lenin's angry-looking bust peering out from its prime location. Inside is a **memorial** to those who died in the 1992 conflict.

The **Kvint factory** (☎ 37 333; ulitsa Lenina 38) is one of Transdniestr's pride and joys. Since 1897 it's been making some of Moldova's finest brandies.

Sleeping & Eating

Hotel Drushba (☎ 34 266; ulitsa 25 Oktober 116; r $9-32) Basic rooms are on offer at this massive place. Others have hot water, TV, fridge, larger beds and a private bathroom or shower.

Kafe 7 (☎ 32 311; ulitsa 25 Oktober 77; mains $0.35-1.50; ☻ 9-11pm) A great selection of salads, tasty Russian fast food like bliny (stuffed pancakes) and Western imports like pizza, are on offer at this modern, pleasant café.

Getting There & Away

BUS

From Tiraspol five buses go daily to Bălţi, 13 to Odesa, one to Kyiv, and one a week to Berlin. Buses go to Chişinău nearly every half hour from 5.50am to 8.50pm, and maxi-taxis run regularly from 6.30am to 6.10pm.

TRAIN

Most eastbound trains from Chişinău to Ukraine and Russia stop in Tiraspol. Trains go to Chişinău ($0.90, seven daily), Odesa ($2, three daily), Moscow (two daily), Minsk (two daily) and St Petersburg (one daily).

BENDERY

☎ 282 / pop 133,000

Bendery (sometimes called Bender, and previously known as Tighina), sits on the western banks of the Dniestr River.

The bloodiest fighting in the 1992 military conflict was in Bendery; walls in the centre remain pocked-marked from bullets.

Information

Currency Exchange (ulitsa Sovetskaya) Change money at this exchange next to the Central Market. Local maxi-taxis leave from here.

Pharmacy (cnr ulitsa Suvorova & S Liazo; ☻ 8am-8pm Mon-Sat, 8am-4pm Sun).

Telephone office (cnr ulitsa Liazo & ulitsa Suvorova; ☻ 8am-6pm Mon-Fri, 8am-4pm Sat) International telephone calls can be booked here.

Vlasana (☎ 29 477; ulitsa Lenina 29; per hr $0.25; ☻ 9am-9pm) Internet access.

Sights

Bendery's main sight is impossible to see up close. The great Turkish fortress, built in the 1530s to replace a 12th-century fortress built by the Genovese, is now used by Transdniestrian military as a training ground and is off-limits. The best view of it is from the bridge going towards Tiraspol.

At the entrance to the city, close to the famous **Bendery-Tiraspol bridge**, is a **memorial park** dedicated to local 1992 war victims. An eternal flame burns in front of an armoured tank, from which flies the Transdniestran flag.

MOLDOVA

Sleeping

A three-tier pricing system is intact here, with prices for locals, Moldovans, Ukrainians and Belorusians, and all other foreigners.

Hotel Dniestr (☎ 29 478; ulitsa Katachenka 10; s/d $9/23) Pricier doubles with hot water, TV and fridge. There's an adjacent restaurant and terrace café.

Getting There & Around

The train station is at Privokzalnaya ploschad. There are at least 15 trains daily to Chişinău, including ones coming from Moscow and Odesa. There are buses and maxi-taxis every half-hour or so to Chişinău, and two daily to Comrat.

Trolleybus No 19 for Tiraspol ($0.10) departs from the bus stop next to the main roundabout at the entrance to Bendery. Microbuses also regularly make the 20-minute trip ($0.15). There are two buses daily to Odesa and one to Kyiv.

GAGAUZIA

pop 169,300

Gagauzia (Gagauz Yeri) is a self-governing republic covering 3000 sq km in southern Moldova.

The republic has its own flag, police force, weekly journals and university, partly funded by the Turkish government. Students are taught in Gagauzi, Moldovan and Russian – the official languages of the republic. Autonomy was officially recognised by the Moldovan government in December 1994.

COMRAT

☎ 298 / pop 32,000

Gagauzia's capital, 92km south of Chişinău, is no more than a dusty, provincial town.

From the bus station, walk south along the main street, Str Pobedy, past the market to ploshchad Pobedy (Victory Square). St John's Church stands on the western side of the square, and behind it is the central park. Prospekt Lenina runs parallel to Str Pobedy.

Change money at the **Moldovan Agrobank** (Str Pobedy 52; ☺ 8am-2pm Mon-Fri). A small currency exchange is inside the entrance to the market. You can make international calls at the **post office** (Str Pobedy 55; ☺ 8am-6pm Mon-Fri, 8am-5pm Sat). Surf the Web at **IATP** (☎ 25 875; Str Lenina 160; per hr $0.40; ☺ 9am-6pm Mon-Fri).

The regional **başkani** (assembly) is on prospekt Lenina. The Gagauzi and Moldovan flags fly from the roof.

Next to the assembly is the **Gagauz Culture House**; in front stands a statue of Lenin. West of prospekt Lenina is the **Gagauz University** (Komrat Devlet Üniversitesi; Str Galatsăna 17), founded in 1990. Four faculties (national culture, agronomy, economics and law) serve 1500 students who learn in Russian and Gagauz.

Hotel Aina (☎ 22 572; Str Pobedy 127A; s/d $11/16), on the eastern side of ploshchad Pobedy, is a fairly modern hotel. Its bar serves light meals, including delicious şaşlik and salads.

There are five return buses daily from Chişinău to Comrat ($2.95). From Comrat there are two buses daily via Bendery to Tiraspol, and one only as far as Bendery.

MOLDOVA DIRECTORY

ACCOMMODATION

Chişinău has a good range of hotels. Most other towns have small hotels that have survived from communist days. Basic singles and doubles with a shared bathroom cost $30 to $50 per room but outside the capitals, rooms will usually be $20 to $25.

Campgrounds (popas turistic) in Moldova are practically nonexistent. The good news is that wild camping is possible in Moldova unless explicitly prohibited.

In Moldova, the nascent branch of apartment rental agency **Antrec** (☎ 22-237 823; antrec_ong@yahoo.com; Str Serghei Lazo 13, Chişinău) is most helpful, but their choices of places to stay is, so far, small. There are no hostels.

CUSTOMS

See www.turism.md for the latest changes in customs regulations.

You might be asked to prove that you have at least $30 for each day of your stay. You're also allowed to cross the border either way with 1L of alcohol, 2L of beer and up to 200 cigarettes. The **customs office** (☎ 22-569 460; Str Columna 65) is in Chişinău.

EMBASSIES & CONSULATES
Embassies & Consulates in Moldova

Countries with embassies or consulates in Chişinău (phone code ☎ 22):

France (☎ 228 204; www.ambafrance.md in French; Str 31 August 1989, 101A)

Germany (☎ 234 607; www.ambasada-germana
.org.md in German; Str Maria Cibotari 35)
Romania (☎ 228 126; ambrom@ch.moldpac.md; Str
Bucureşti 66/1)
Russia (☎ 234 941; www.moldova.mid.ru in Russian;
B-dul Ştefan cel Mare 153)
Ukraine (☎ 582 124; www.mfa.gov.ua in Ukrainian;
Str V Lupu 17)
UK (☎ 238 991; www.britishembassy.md; Str
Banulescu-Bodoni 57/1)
USA (☎ 233 772; www.usembassy.md; Str A
Mateevici 103A)

Moldovan Embassies & Consulates Abroad

Moldova has embassies worldwide.
France (☎ 01 40 67 11 20; ambassade.moldavie@free.fr;
1 rue Sfax, Paris)
Germany (☎ 069-52 78 08; mongenmold@aol.com;
Adelheidstrasse nr. 8, Frankfurt)
Romania (☎ 01-230 0474; moldova@customers
.digiro.net; Aleea Alexandru 40, Bucharest)
Russia (☎ 095-924 5353; moldemb@online.ru;
18 Kuznetskii most, Moscow)
Ukraine (☎ 044-290 7721; moldovak@sovam.com;
ulitsa Kutuzov 8, Kyiv)
USA (☎ 202-667 1130; moldova@dgs.dgsys.com;
2101 S Street NW, Washington, DC)

FESTIVALS & EVENTS

The major festival is the Wine Festival on
the second Sunday in October (and for
several wine-drenched days preceding and
following it). The government has even in-
stituted a visa-free regime for this period.
Chişinău's City Day is 14 October.

HOLIDAYS

National holidays celebrated in Moldova:
New Year's Day 1 January
Orthodox Christmas 7 January
International Women's Day 8 March
Orthodox Easter March/April/May
Victory (1945) Day 9 May
Independence Day 27 August
National Language Day 31 August

MONEY

Moldovan lei come in denominations of 1,
5, 10, 20, 50, 100, 200 and 500 lei. There are
coins for 1, 5, 10, 25 and 50 bani (there are
100 bani in a leu).

The breakaway Transdniestran republic in
Moldova has its own currency, which is use-
less anywhere else in the world (see p804).

It's easy to find ATMs in Chişinău, but
not in other towns in Moldova. It's near impossible to use travellers cheques in shops
or restaurants. While credit cards won't get
you anywhere in rural areas, they are widely
accepted in larger department stores, hotels
and most restaurants in cities and towns.

POST

From Moldova, it costs $0.35 to send a
postcard or letter under 20g to Western
Europe, Australia and the USA.

DHL (www.dhl.com) is the most popular international courier service in the region. They
have offices in Chişinău, Balţi and Tiraspol.

TELEPHONE

Moldtelecom, the state-run telephone company, sells pay cards that can be used to dial
any number within Moldova for $2.25 or $3.
These are sold at any telephone centre in the
country. To make an international call using
a prepaid card, you need to use a private
company like Treitelecom. Cards are sold at
any Moldpressa newspaper stand.

Cellular phone service in Moldova is
provided by Chişinău-based Moldcell (run
by Moldtelecom) and **Voxtel** (☎ 22-575 757;
www.voxtel.md in Moldovan; Str Alba Iulia 75).

VISAS

All Western travellers need a visa to enter
Moldova. The price of a single/double-entry
tourist visa valid for one month is $60/75.
Single/double-entry transit visas valid for
72 hours are $30/60.

Citizens of the EU, Canada, the USA
and Israel need only present their passports (valid for six months after the visa's
expiration date) and one photo to the
nearest Moldovan consulate. All others
require either a tourist voucher from an accredited travel agency or an invitation from
a company, organisation or individual.

Citizens of the EU, Japan, the USA or
Canada can buy visas on arrival at Chişinău
airport or, if arriving by bus or car from Romania, the three border points Sculeni (north
of Iaşi), Leuşeni (main Bucharest-Chişinău
border) and Cahul. Citizens of countries normally requiring an invitation must present
one at the border if buying a visa there.

See www.moldovavisa.com, or www.tur
ism.md/eng/content/66 to check for the latest changes in the visa regime.

MOLDOVA

Morocco

- **Djemaa el-Fna** Marrakesh's great open-air spectacle, featuring storytellers and snake charmers, musicians and acrobats, not to mention tables piled high with grilled brochettes, fresh salads, steaming hot stews, and roasted sheeps' heads (p825)
- **Fès el-Bali** Getting lost amidst the winding alleys and hidden souks of one of the world's largest living medinas (p831)
- **Hassan II Mosque** Being awestruck by the enormity and craftsmanship of Casablanca's marvel of modern religious architecture (p818)
- **Best journey** Rowing across the river (and back a few centuries) from contemporary Rabat to old-fashioned Salé (p823)
- **Off-the-beaten track** Packing a picnic of fresh-from-the-oven bread and fresh-from-the-goat cheese and heading into the Rif Mountains (p817)

FAST FACTS

- **Area** 446,550 sq km (about one quarter of Russia)
- **ATMs** Widespread
- **Capital** Rabat
- **Country code** ☎ 212
- **Famous for** The film Casablanca; hashish
- **Head of State** King Mohammed VI
- **Languages** Arabic, French, Berber
- **Money** Dirham ($A1 = Dh6.45, CA$1 = Dh7.03, €1 = Dh11.07, ¥100 = Dh8.16, NZ$1 = Dh6.07, UK£1 = Dh15.95, US$1 = Dh8.85)
- **Phrases** Ssalamu'lekum (hello, 'peace upon you'); shukran, (thanks); ensh'allah (God willing)
- **Population** 30.6 million
- **Time** GMT/UTC
- **Visas** Usually not required for visits of 90 days or less, except nationals of Israel, South Africa and Zimbabwe.

TRAVEL HINTS

When you arrive in Morocco, hit the bank and load up on small change for the seemingly incessant payment of taxis, tips, guides and beggars.

ROAMING MOROCCO

Ferry to Tangier, catch the overnight train to Marrakesh and continue on to Essaouira. Make your way back up the coast, stopping at Casablanca, Rabat or Asilah on the way.

Red baked-mud kasbahs beneath the towering High Atlas mountains. Seething souqs (markets) in dusty towns. Breezy beach haunts under massive skies. Morocco is a country full of contrasting images, colourful sights, strange smells and exotic experiences.

Morocco is a destination where you can swelter in the heat of the market place or ramble through Roman ruins, and in the space of a day find yourself trekking through a cool Berber village

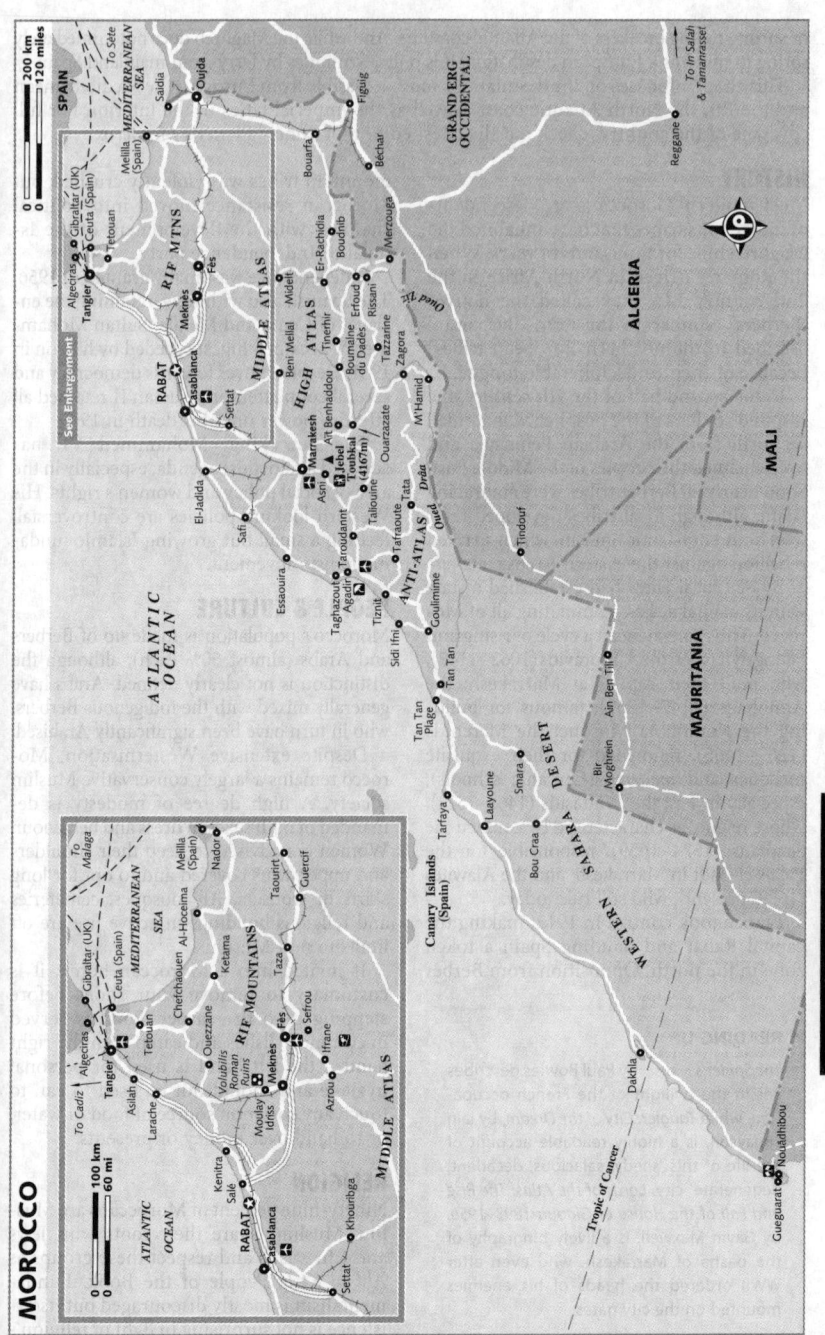

MOROCCO

or surfing rolling breakers of the Atlantic coastline. And while the Maghreb does not immediately spring to mind as a European destination, it is only 35 minutes by ferry from mainland Spain.

This chapter focuses on the destinations most accessible from Europe – the Mediterranean and the Rif, the North Atlantic coast as well as the imperial cities in the interior. For full coverage of the country, check out the latest edition of Lonely Planet's *Morocco*.

HISTORY

Most modern Moroccans are descendents of indigenous tribes that have inhabited the Maghreb hills for thousands of years. When the Romans arrived in North Africa in the 2nd century BC, they called the natives 'Berbers' (similar to the term 'Barbarian' ascribed to the northern European tribes) because of their undecipherable tongue.

In the second half of the 7th century, the inspired soldiers of the prophet Mohammed set forth from the Arabian Peninsula and overwhelmed the peoples of the Middle East. Soon nearly all Berber tribes were embracing Islam, although local tribes developed their own brand of Islamic Shi'ism, which sparked rebellion against the eastern Arabs.

By 829 local elites had established a state with its capital at Fès, dominating all of Morocco. Thus commenced a cycle of rising and falling dynasties: the Almoravids (1062–1147), who built their capital at Marrakesh; the Almohads (1147–1269), famous for building the Koutoubia Mosque; the Merenids (1269–1465), renowned for their exquisite mosques and *medersa* (Qur'anic schools), especially in Fès; the Wattasids (1465–1524), whose reign was characterised by conflict; the Saadians (1524–1659), responsible for the Palais el-Badi in Marrakesh; and the Alawites (1659–present), who still rule today.

France took control in 1912, making the capital Rabat and handing Spain a token zone in the north. Opposition from Berber mountain tribes was violently crushed, but Moroccan resistance moved into political channels with the development of the Istiqlal or Independence party.

Independence was finally granted in 1956. The Spanish also withdrew, retaining the enclaves of Ceuta and Melilla. Sultan Mohammed V became king, succeeded by his son in 1961. Despite moves towards democracy and several coup attempts, Hassan II retained all effective power until his death in 1999.

The new king, Mohammed VI, has adopted a reformist agenda, especially in the area of social policy and women's rights. His Western-looking policies are controversial, feeding a small but growing Islamic fundamentalist movement.

PEOPLE & CULTURE

Morocco's population is made up of Berbers and Arabs (almost 50% each), although the distinction is not clearly defined. Arabs have generally mixed with the indigenous Berbers, who in turn have been significantly Arabised.

Despite extensive Westernisation, Morocco remains a largely conservative Muslim society. A high degree of modesty is demanded of both sexes in dress and behaviour. Women are advised to keep their shoulders and upper arms covered and to opt for long skirts or trousers. All mosques, cemeteries and religious buildings in active use are off limits to non-Muslims.

If invited into a Moroccan home, it is customary to remove your shoes before stepping onto the carpet. Food is served in common dishes and eaten with the right hand – the left hand is used for personal hygiene and should not be used to eat, to touch any common source of food or water, or to hand over money or presents.

RELIGION

Ninety-nine percent of Moroccans are Muslim. Muslims share their roots with Jews and Christians and respect these groups as *Ahl al-Kteb*, People of the Book. Fundamentalism is mostly discouraged but its existence is not surprising in light of religion's

MOROCCO

READING UP

The Spider's House, by Paul Bowles describes Fès in the twilight of the French occupation, while *Tangier: City of the Dream*, by Iain Finlayson, is a highly readable account of the life of this 'seedy, salacious, decadent, degenerate' city. *Lords of the Atlas: The Rise and Fall of the House of Glaoua 1893–1956*, by Gavin Maxwell, is a lively biography of the pasha of Marrakesh, who even after WWII ordered the heads of his enemies mounted on the city gates.

role in Muslim countries: Islam cannot be separated from daily life and politics; it governs both secular and spiritual life.

ENVIRONMENT

Morocco's awesome fusion of rock, sand, and sea presents the most varied topography in North Africa. In the north, the Rif Mountains form an arc of impenetrable limestone and sandstone, which shoots steeply back from the Mediterranean. The Middle Atlas mountains run northeast to southwest from the Rif. The low hills east of Agadir rise to form the High Atlas mountains. Towering over the villages of Marrakesh at 4167m is Jebel Toubkal, North Africa's highest summit. Further south, the low and calloused Anti Atlas drop into the arid wastes of the Sahara. Morocco's coastline stretches across the Mediterranean and down the Atlantic.

Pollution, desertification, overgrazing, deforestation; put them together and you have a glimpse of Morocco's urgent environmental troubles. To combat these problems, a few initiatives are underway, including plantation programmes and public education on rubbish disposal and water pollution. Yet the situation remains grave.

Worried about the increasing loss of habitat and the resulting disappearance of plant and animal species, Morocco has distinguished certain areas for protection. So far, a mere 0.01% of Morocco's land is protected territory; other parks in the Atlas mountains and the Moroccan Sahara are expected in the next few years – particularly to combat threats to argan and thuya trees.

TRANSPORT

GETTING THERE & AWAY
Air
Morocco's main international entry point is **Mohammed V International Airport** (☎ 022 539040), 30km southeast of Casablanca. Other international airports are in Fès, Marrakesh, Rabat and Tangier. For more details on all Morocco's airports, their facilities and customs log on to the website of **Office National des Aéroports** (www.onda.org.ma in French and Arabic).

Sea
There are regular ferries running to Europe from several ports along the Moroccan

TOP FIVE MOROCCO

- **Festival** Gnawa & World Music Festival in Essaouira (p824)
- **Bar/Club** La Bodéga in Casablanca (p820)
- **Walk** Through the winding alleys of Fès el-Bali (p831)
- **Impressive sight** The wide selection of teeth for sale on Djemaa el-Fna in Marrakesh (p825)
- **Beach** Paradise Beach, Asilah (p823)

Mediterranean coast. The most heavily trafficked is Tangier, from where there are boats to Algeciras, Spain (€22-25, 60-70 minutes, hourly); Tarifa, Spain (€21, 35 minutes, five daily); and Sete, France (€53, 36 hours, twice weekly). Ferries also run from Ceuta to Algeciras (€18, 35 minutes, hourly). Less frequent ferries go from Al-Hoceima, Melilla and Nador to Almería and Malaga in Spain. Bringing a bicycle is an additional €8 to €15, while a car is €50 to €80. Tickets are available at the port of departure or from any travel agent in town.

Bus
The Moroccan bus company, **Compagnie de Transports Marocains** (CTM; Casablanca ☎ 022 458080; www.ctm.co.ma) operates daily buses from Casablanca and most other main cities to France, Belgium, Spain, Germany and Italy. Another Moroccan bus service with particularly good links to Spanish networks is **Tramesa** (☎ 022 245274; www.tramesa.ma in French). UK-based companies with services to Morocco include **Eurolines** (www.eurolines.co.uk) and **Busabout** (☎ 020 7950 1661; www.busabout.com).

GETTING AROUND
Air
Royal Air Maroc (RAM; Map p819; ☎ 09000 0800; www.royalairmaroc.com; 44 Ave des FAR) dominates the Moroccan air industry, with paltry competition from one other domestic airline, **Regional Air Lines** (☎ 022 538080). Both airlines use Casablanca as a hub and many internal flights are routed through Mohammed V airport. Student and under-26 youth discounts of 25% are available on all RAM domestic flights but only if the ticket is bought in advance from one of their offices.

MOROCCO

Bus

A dense network of buses operates throughout Morocco, with many private companies competing for business alongside the main national carrier, **CTM** (☎ 022 753677; www.ctm .co.ma; Autoroute de Rabat, kilometre 13.5, Casablanca).

The **Office National des Chemins de Fer** (ONCF; www.oncf.org.ma in French) rail company runs buses through Supratours to widen its train network. Morocco's other bus companies are all privately owned and only operate regionally. It's best to book ahead for CTM and Supratours buses.

Car & Motorcycle

Taking your own vehicle to Morocco is comparatively straightforward. In addition to your vehicle registration document and an International Driving Permit (although many foreign licences, including US and EU, are acceptable), a Green Card is required from the car's insurer (see p1251). Not all insurers cover Morocco.

Renting a car in Morocco isn't cheap, starting from Dh3500 per week or Dh500 per day for a basic car with unlimited mileage. Most companies demand a returnable cash deposit (Dh3000 to Dh5000), unless you pay by credit card.

In Morocco you drive on the right. On a roundabout, give way to traffic entering from the right.

Local Transport

Cities and bigger towns have local *petits taxis*, which are a different colour in every city. They are not permitted to go beyond the city limits. They are licensed to carry up to three passengers and are usually metered.

The old Mercedes vehicles you'll see belting along roads and gathered in great flocks near bus stations are *grands taxis* (shared taxis). They link towns to their nearest neighbours. Grands taxis take six extremely cramped passengers and leave when full.

Train

Morocco's train network is run by the **ONCF** (www.oncf.org.ma in French). There are basically two lines which carry passengers: from Tangier in the north down to Marrakesh; and from Oujda in the northeast, also to Marrakesh, joining with the Tangier line at Sidi Kacem.

The Belgian-made trains are comfortable, fast and preferable to buses. There

---

EMERGENCY NUMBERS

■ **Ambulance** ☎ 15

■ **Fire** ☎ 16

■ **Gendarmerie (countryside police)** ☎ 177

■ **Police** ☎ 19

■ **French-speaking police (Casablanca, Rabat, Tangier)** ☎ 172

---

are different 1st- and 2nd-class fares on all these trains, though there's not much difference in comfort. Second-class is more than adequate on any journey. Couchettes are available on the overnight trains between Marrakesh and Tangier. The compartments fold up into six bunks and they're well worth the extra Dh90.

Two variations of rail discount cards are available in Morocco. For those aged over 26, the Carte Fidelité (Dh149) gives 50% reductions on eight return trips or 16 one-way journeys in a 12-month period. The Carte Jeune (Dh99) gives the same discounts to those under 26 years. To apply you need one passport-sized photo and a photocopy of your passport.

THE MEDITERRANEAN COAST & THE RIF

TANGIER

In the days author William Burroughs called 'Interzone' (when Tangier was officially an 'international zone'), every kind of questionable activity took place here. As such, it was a haven for artists and writers in search of cheap drugs and artistic inspiration, and one of the Mediterranean's most trendy resorts, renowned for its high-profile gay scene. Although it's not quite so hedonistic nowadays, the legend of notoriety lingers on.

The *brigade touristique* (tourist police) has cracked down on Tangier's legendary hustlers, but the city is not altogether hassle-free. If you take it head on and learn to handle the hustlers, you'll find it a likable, lively place. The nightlife is vibrant; the population is cosmopolitan; and the cultural karma – which has attracted artists from Henri Matisse to Paul Bowles to the Rolling Stones – is infamous.

Orientation

Tangier is divided between the tangled web of the old medina and the wide, ordered boulevards of the Ville Nouvelle (New Town). The large square known as the Grand Socco marks the meeting point of new and old.

Information

Plenty of banks with ATMs are along Blvd Pasteur and Blvd Mohammed V in the Ville Nouvelle.

Banque Marocaine du Commerce Extérieur (BMCE; Blvd Pasteur; 🕑 9am-1pm & 3-7pm Mon-Fri, 10am-1pm & 4-7pm Sat & Sun)

Brigade Touristique (Tourist Police; Ave des FAR, Tangier Port; 🕑 24hr)

Consigne (cnr Rue DarDbagh & Rue du Portugal) Left luggage

Cyber Café Adam (☎ 039 948397; Rue ibn Rochd; per hr Dh10; 🕑 9.30-3.30am)

Espace Net (16 Ave Mexique; per hr Dh10; 🕑 9.30am-midnight)

Post office (Blvd Mohammed V)

Tourist office (☎ 039 948050, fax 039 948661; 29 Blvd Pasteur; 🕑 8.30am-noon & 2.30-6.30pm Mon-Fri)

Sights

Heading 500m north from the Petit Socco, Rue des Almohades leads to the **Kasbah**, overlooking the Straits of Gibraltar. Enter from Bab el-Assa into a large courtyard leading to the 17th-century **Dar el-Makhzen** (☎ 039 932097; admission Dh10; 🕑 9am-12.30pm & 3-5.30pm Wed-Mon, closed Fri afternoon), the former sultan's palace. It's now a museum devoted to Moroccan arts.

In the southwest corner of the medina, the **American Legation Museum** (☎ 039 935317; 8 Rue d'Amerique; admission by donation; 🕑 10am-1pm & 3-5pm Mon-Fri) houses a fascinating collection of antique maps, furniture, paintings, prints and drawings by various artists who passed through Tangier.

Housed in a former synagogue, the **Musée de la Fondation Lorin** (☎ 039 930306; 44 Rue Touahine; admission by donation; 🕑 11am-1pm & 3.30-7.30pm Sun-Fri) contains an engaging collection of photographs, posters and prints of Tangier from the Interzone years.

Sleeping

Tangier has no shortage of budget accommodation, mostly clustered in the medina and outside the port gate. Many budget places are inhabited by long-term residents – mostly West Africans awaiting their passage to Europe.

MEDINA

Pension Victoria (☎ 039 931299; 22 Ave Mokhtar Ahardan; r per person Dh30, hot shower Dh10) This straightforward, peaceful place is one of the better cheap options in the medina. Its rooms are set around a cool interior courtyard or overlook the port. All facilities are shared.

Pension Mauritania (☎ 039 934677; Rue des Almohades; r per person Dh45) This place offers rooms with small balconies that have prime views overlooking the Petit Socco.

Pension Agadir (☎ 039 938084; 16 Rue de Palmier; r per person Dh30, hot shower Dh5) Don't expect this accommodation to be particularly clean, although it's friendly and busy.

Pension Becerra (☎ 039 932369; 8 Petit Socco; r per person Dh40, hot shower Dh5) The rooms are clean enough and management is friendly.

Fun fact: the historic **Hôtel Continental** (☎ 039 931024; hcontinental@iam.net.ma; 36 Rue Dar el-Baroud; s Dh275-335, d325-385) was used for scenes in the film of Paul Bowles' *The Sheltering Sky*.

VILLE NOUVELLE

Most of the unrated hotels and pensions along Rue Salah Eddine el-Ayoubi and Ave d'Espagne are little better than the cheapies in the medina. This area is sketchy at night; women especially should beware.

Youth Hostel (☎ 039 946127; 8 Rue al-Antaki; dm with/without HI card Dh30/40, hot shower Dh5; 🕑 8-10am, noon-3pm & 6pm-11pm) Tangier's youth hostel is just off Ave d'Espagne in a rough-and-tumble part of town.

Pension Hollanda (☎ 039 937838; 139 Rue de Hollande; s/d Dh80/150; **P**) A step up from the budget hotels near the port, this friendly pension is clean and quiet. Double rooms have private showers, and even shared facilities have Western toilets.

Hôtel el-Muniria (☎ 039 935337; 1 Rue Magellan; s/d Dh130/150) A nostalgic air hangs from the 1950s, when Jack Kerouac and Allen Ginsberg stayed here. William Burroughs supposedly wrote *The Naked Lunch* in room No 9. Rooms are large, clean and slightly shabby.

Hôtel ibn Batouta (☎ 039 939311; fax 039 939368; 8 Rue Magellan; s/d Dh150/250) Another classic place remaining from the Interzone days. The terrace rooms boast great views, but they tend to be noisy and hot in summer.

MOROCCO

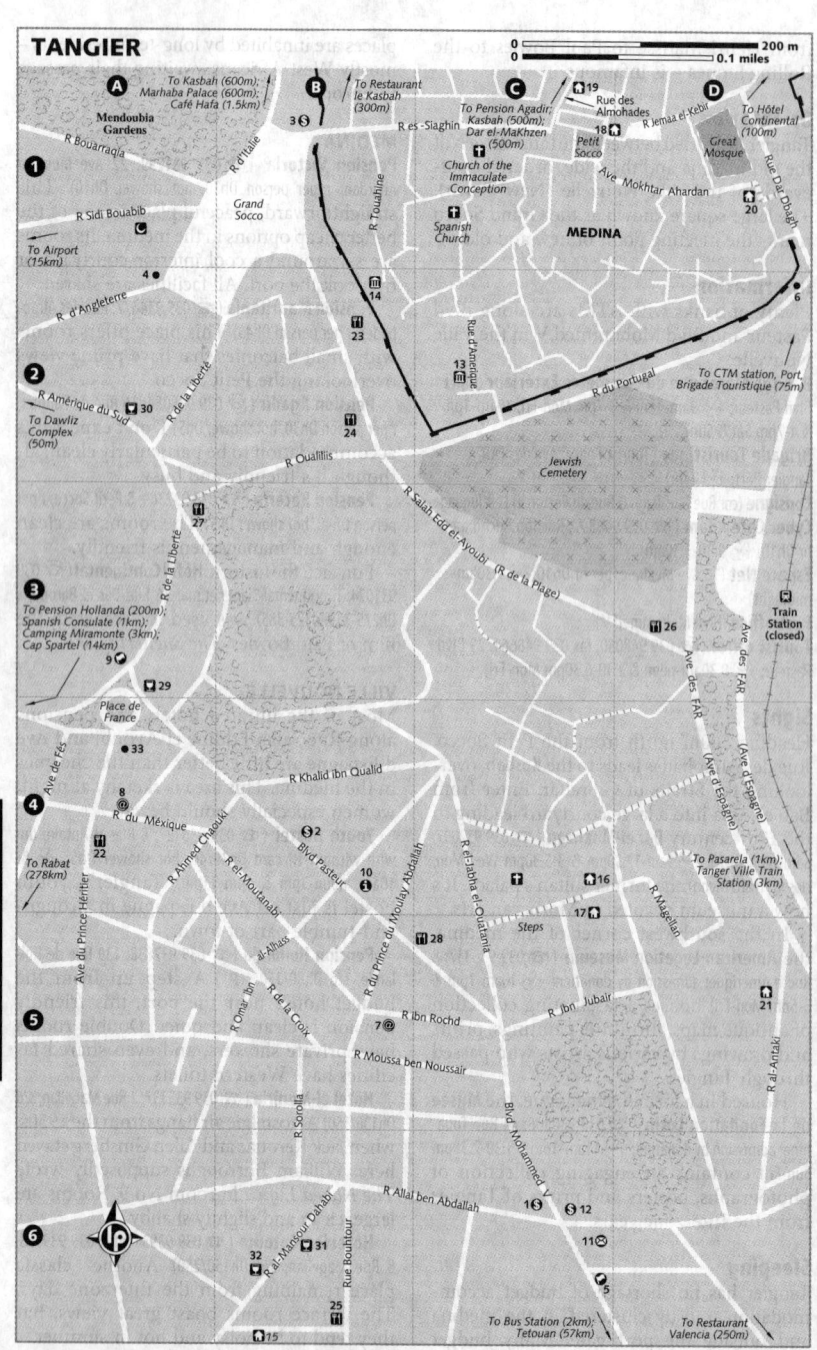

TANGIER

0   200 m
0   0.1 miles

MOROCCO

Hotel Andalucia (☎ 039 941334; 14-16 Rue Vermeer; s Dh190-225 d Dh230/250; P) Possibly the friendliest place in town. Simple, clean rooms – all with private bathroom – are excellent value.

CAMPING

Camping Miramonte (☎ 039 937133; per adult/tent/car Dh20/20/15, hot shower Dh10, electricity Dh10; P ⚡) The most convenient campsite is on a hillside in lush gardens 3km from the city centre.

Eating
MEDINA

For really cheap food, head to the covered markets close to the Grand Socco. Numerous small restaurants around the Petit Socco also offer cheap traditional fare.

Restaurant Le Kasbah (☎ 067 118847; 7 Rue Gzenaya; set menus Dh40-80; ⏰ 11am-10pm) This hole-in-the-wall is one of the more pleasant cheapies in the medina. The simple tiled dining room is perfectly placed for a midday or evening snack – choose from the typical Moroccan fare.

Restaurant Africa (83 Rue Salah Eddine el-Ayoubi; mains from Dh35, set menus Dh50; ⏰ 10am-11pm) One of several places down near the port dishing up straightforward fare.

La Casa della Pizza (☎ 039 324817; 3 Rue Quevada, cnr of Rue Bouhtouri; pizzas from Dh40; ⏰ noon-1am) This friendly and fast pizzeria is unbeatable for tasty, filling pizza and pasta.

Agadir (☎ 068 827696; 21 Ave du Prince Héritier; mains Dh32-40, set menus Dh48) It may not look like much, but this tiny, family-run place offers top-value local fare with a French twist.

Restaurant Populaire Saveur (☎ 039 336326; 2 Escalier Oualilis; set menus Dh100-150; ⏰ closed Fri) This welcoming little fish restaurant serves excellent, filling set menus. Four courses might include steaming fish soup, spicy shrimp pil-pil and grilled fish.

The streets immediately south of Place de France are good for sandwich bars such as **Fast Food Brahim Abdelmalik** (☎ 039 931796; 16 Ave Mexique; sandwiches Dh15-18).

Drinking

As you'd expect from its colourful past, Tangier has its fair share of drinking establishments. Most are typically male oriented.

Café Hafa (Ave Mohammed Tazi; ⏰ 10am-8pm) Set in shaded, terraced gardens, this is a simple but delightful place. It used to be a favourite of artists and writers – including Paul Bowles and the Rolling Stones – who reportedly came here to smoke hashish and watch the sun set over the Straits.

London's Pub (☎ 039 942094; 15 Rue al-Mansour Dahabi; draught beer from Dh20; ⏰ 6.30pm-1am) Tangier's interpretation of an English pub is a civilised place for a drink – suitable for women and men alike.

Classic pubs that remain from the Interzone years include **Dean's Bar** (☎ 039 931671; 2 Rue Amérique du Sud; ⏰ 9am-11pm) and **Tanger Inn** (☎ 039 935337; 1 Rue Magellan, Hôtel el-Muniria; bottle of beer Dh10; ⏰ 10.30pm-1am, 10.30pm-3am Sat & Sun), although the latter can be dodgy after dark. Of the many coffee-drinking establishments along Blvd Pasteur, **Café de Paris** (☎ 039 938444; Place de France; ⏰ 6am-11pm) is the most famous.

Clubbing

Tangier by night rocks, especially in summer, when Europeans descend on the city and party all night. Entry for most nightclubs is around Dh100, although it's not always applied to tourists; drinks usually cost Dh40 to Dh50. Popular clubs include **Regine's** (☎ 039 340238; 8 Rue al-Mansour Dahabi; ⏰ 11.30pm-3am Mon-Sat) and **Pasarela** (☎ 039 945246; Ave des FAR; ⏰ 8pm-3am Mon-Sat, happy hour 8pm-11pm Sep-Jun).

MOROCCO

Getting There & Away

AIR

All flights operated by **Royal Air Maroc** (RAM; ☎ 039 379503; www.royalairmaroc.com; 1 Place de France) from Tangier go via Casablanca (Dh1089 return trip, 50 minutes, five daily).

BUS

The **CTM station** (☎ 039 931172) is beside the port gate, serving Casablanca (Dh115, six hours, four daily), Rabat (Dh78, 4½ hours, four daily), Marrakesh (Dh170, 10 hours, one daily), Fès (Dh85, six hours, four daily), Asilah (Dh15, one hour, four daily), Meknès (Dh70, five hours, four daily) and Chefchaouen (Dh33, three hours, one daily). Cheaper bus companies operate from the **main bus station** (gare routière; ☎ 039 946928; Place Jamia el-Arabia), 2km south of the city centre.

TRAIN

Four trains depart daily from Tanger Ville, the new station 3km southeast of the centre. Two services go to Casa-Voyageurs in Casablanca (Dh117, 5½ hours, two daily); one travels via Meknès (Dh80, four hours, one daily) to Fès (Dh96, five hours, one daily); and a night service (with couchettes) goes all the way to Marrakesh.

TAXI

You can get grands taxis to places outside Tangier next to the main bus station. The most common destinations are Asilah (Dh12) and Fnideq (Dh25) on the Ceuta border.

CEUTA (SEBTA)

Jutting out east into the Mediterranean, the 20 sq km peninsula that is Ceuta has been a Spanish enclave since 1640. As soon as you cross the border, there's no question that Ceuta is a small corner of Mediterranean Europe in Africa. The place has an Andalucían atmosphere, and it remains officially part of that Spanish province.

Information

To phone Ceuta from outside Spain, dial ☎ 0034. Also remember that Ceuta is on Spanish time and uses the euro.

Correos y Telégrafos (Main Post Office; Plaza de España; ☒ 8.30am-8.30pm Mon-Fri, 9.30am-2pm Sat)
Indy Net Café (6 Isabel Cabral; per hr €3; ☒ 10am-10pm)
Tourist Office (www.turiceuta.com in Spanish); Avenida Muelle Cañonero Dato (☎ 956 501401; fax 956 507746; ☒ 9am-3pm Mon-Fri); Ferry Terminal (☎ 956 506275; ☒ 9am-9pm); Plaza de Africa (☎ 956 528146; ☒ 9am-9pm Mon-Fri, 10am-2pm & 5-7pm Sat & Sun)

Sights

The impressive remnants of the **city walls** (☎ 95 511770; Avenida González Tablas; admission free; ☒ 10am-2pm & 5-8pm) and the walled **moat of Foso de San Felipe** remain from the 16th-century Hispano-Portuguese period. They have been restored for visitors to explore.

The most intriguing museum is the **Museo de la Legión** (☎ 606 733566; Paseo de Colón; admission by donation; ☒ 10am-1.30pm & 4-6pm Mon-Fri, 4-6pm Sat & Sun). It is dedicated to and run by the Spanish Legion, an army unit set up in 1920 that played a pivotal role in Franco's republican army at the beginning of the Spanish Civil War.

The **Parque Marítimo del Mediterráneo** (Maritime Park; ☎ 956 517742; admission €6; ☒ 11am-8pm & 9pm-1am) is a huge complex on the seafront, complete with manufactured beach, landscaped pools and waterfalls. Keep in mind that this is a popular spot for children.

Sleeping & Eating

Budget accommodation is limited so reserve in advance if possible. The prices below are subject to 3% tax.

Pensión Charito (☎ 956 513982; pcharito@terra.es; 1st fl, 5 Calle Arrabal; s/d €15/20) The cheapest option in town is a 2km walk east along the waterfront. Don't be put off by the exterior: inside it's clean and cosy.

Pensión La Bohemia (☎ 956 510615; 16 Paseo de Revellín; r €25) One of the best deals in town is on the 1st floor above the shopping arcade.

Two well-priced, two-star sister hotels are **Hostal Central** (☎ 956 516716; Paseo del Revellín; s/d €30/40) and **Hostal Plaza Ruiz** (☎ 956 516733; 3 Plaza Ruiz; s/d €30/40). Spotless rooms have TVs and bathrooms; prices go up by 20% in summer.

For a bite to eat, try **La Mar Chica** (☎ 956 517240; 8 Plaza Rafael Gilbert; mains €3-4; ☒ 8am-7pm Mon-Fri, 8am-5pm Sat) or **La Tasca de Pedro** (☎ 956 510473; 3 Avenida Alcalde Sánchez Prados; mains €5-10).

Getting There & Away

MOROCCO

Bus No 7 runs to the border from Plaza de la Constitución (€0.60, every 10 minutes). Once in Morocco, the most frequent destination for grands taxis is Tetouan (Dh15 per place), although there are occasional departures for Chefchaouen (Dh70) and Tangier (Dh25).

MAINLAND SPAIN
The **estación marítima** (ferry terminal; Calle Muelle Cañonero Dato) is west of the town centre. There are frequent high-speed ferries to Algeciras. You can purchase train tickets to European destinations at the **Renfe office** (☎ 956 511317; 17 Plaza Rafael Gilbert; ☺ 9am-2pm, 4-8pm).

CHEFCHAOUEN (CHAOUEN, XAOUEN)
Set on a wide valley in the Rif Mountains, charming Chefchaouen has long been a favourite with travellers. The air's cool and clear; the medina manageable; and there's more kif (dope) than you can poke a pipe at.

The main square of the charming medina is the shady, cobbled **Plaza Uta el-Hammam**, dominated by the red-hued walls of the kasbah and the striking Great Mosque. Inside the kasbah is a peaceful, garden and a modest **ethnographic museum** (☎ 039 986343; admission Dh10; ☺ 9am-1pm & 3pm-6.30pm Wed-Mon).

For information on excellent trekking opportunities in the Rif, contact Abdeslam Mouden, the president of the **Association des Guides du Tourisme** (☎ 062 113917; guide5@caramail .com) for information.

Sleeping
Loads of budget options dot the medina. Facilities are mostly shared, but toilets are generally Western-style and hot showers are usually included in the price.

Youth Hostel (☎ 039 986979; dm Dh20) Renovations are ongoing at this rough-and-tumble hostel on the hillside north of town. New toilets have been installed, but the place still has no hot water.

Pensión Mauritania (☎ 039 986184; 15 Rue Qadi Alami; r per person Dh30, hot shower Dh5) Among Chefchaouen's cheapest accommodation, this place is popular for its comfortable, communal lounge area and its fantastic breakfasts (Dh10).

Pensión La Castellana (☎ 039 986295; 4 Sidi el-Bouhali; r per person Dh40) This travellers' hangout has a welcoming atmosphere, a fantastic roof terrace and a convenient kitchen.

Hotel Andaluz (☎ 039 986034; 1 Rue Sidi Salem; r per person Dh40) Similar to La Castellana, this hostel is equally inviting and equally popular. Rooms on the upper floors are light and airy.

Below the city walls on Ave Hassan II are a few slightly pricier and more comfortable options, the best of which is **Hotel Madrid** (☎ 039 987496; Ave Hassan II; s/d/tr Dh184/264/368).

Eating
For self-caterers, the market off Ave Hassan II is the place to stock up on fresh produce, plus fresh goat's cheese, a local speciality. The cluster of cafés on Plaza Uta el-Hammam all feature Moroccan and Spanish dishes for Dh25-40.

Restaurant Assada (Calle Abi Jancha; tajines Dh20, set menus Dh40) This friendly, family-run place draws a mostly local crowd, which is always a good sign.

Restaurant Les Raisins (☎ 039 988641; 7 Rue Sidi Sifri; tajines Dh20, set menus from Dh40; ☺ 7am-9pm) Although it's a bit out of the way in the Ville Nouvelle, this simple restaurant has been pleasing the palates of locals and tourists alike for 25 years.

Getting There & Away
One kilometre southwest of the town centre, the new bus station is down the slope on Ave Mohammed V. At the time of research, a temporary bus terminal in the open lot on Rue Mohammed Abdou was in use.

CTM (☎ 039 988769) has services passing through Chefchaouen to Fès (Dh60, five hours, two daily) and to Tangier (Dh36, three hours, one daily) via Tetouan (Dh18, 1½ hours). Other companies run a few cheaper services, to Fnideq (Dh20, 2½ hours, two daily), Tangier (Dh27, three hours, one daily), Casablanca (Dh65, six hours, one daily), Rabat (Dh50, five hours, one daily) and Meknès (Dh45, five hours, one daily).

NORTH ATLANTIC COAST

CASABLANCA
Casablanca, popularly known as Casa, is a massive, modern city that was developed by the French in the early days of the protectorate. Amid the striking, colonial architecture – and there are some Art Deco and modernist jewels – it is Casablanca's residents that leave the greatest impression.

Women wearing the veil are less common than those wearing natty suits and heels. Men and women mix easily here; on the beaches and in the clubs, the bright young things strut their stuff much like the youth of any European country. But elements of traditional Morocco remain: the marvel of modern religious architecture – the enormous Hassan II Mosque – is an undeniable reminder.

Orientation

The relatively small medina sits in the north of the city just south of the port. The heart of the city is south of the medina at the Place des Nations Unies. West of the centre lies the beachfront Blvd de la Corniche, home to several top-end hotels and nightclubs.

Information

EMERGENCY

Service d'Aide Médicale Urgente (SAMU; ☎ 022 252525) Private ambulance service.

SOS Médecins (☎ 022 444444; house call Dh300; ☼ 24hr) Private doctors who make house calls.

INTERNET ACCESS

EuroNet (☎ 022 265921; 51 Rue Tata; per hr Dh10; ☼ 8am-11pm)

Gig@net (☎ 022 484810; 140 Blvd Mohammed Zerktouni; per hr Dh10; ☼ 24hr) A flash new cyber club with two floors of super-fast computers.

MONEY

There are banks with ATMS and foreign exchange offices on every street corner.

Banque Marocain du Commerce Extérieur (BMCE; Hyatt Regency Hotel; ☼ 9am-9pm) Good for after-hours and weekend services.

Crédit du Maroc (48 Blvd Mohammed V) Separate foreign exchange office, which is very central; you can cash American Express travellers cheques for free here.

Wafa Cash (☎ 022 208080; 15 Rue Idriss Lahrizi; ☼ 8am-8pm Mon-Sat) Another convenient bank, which is open longer hours, has an ATM and cashes travellers cheques.

POST

Main post office (cnr Blvd de Paris & Ave Hassan II)

TOURIST INFORMATION

Office National Marocain du Tourisme (ONMT; ☎ 022 271177; 55 Rue Omar Slaoui; ☼ open 8.30am-noon & 2.30pm-6.30pm Mon-Fri)

Syndicat d'Initiative (☎ 022 221524; 98 Blvd Mohammed V; ☼ open 8.30am-noon & 3pm-6.30pm Mon-Fri, til 5pm Sat, 9am-noon Sun)

Sights

Rising above the Atlantic northwest of the medina, the **Hassan II Mosque** is the world's third-largest mosque, built to commemorate the former king's 60th birthday. To see the interior of the mosque you must take a **guided tour** (☎ 022 440448; adults/students Dh100/50; ☼ 9am, 10am, 11am & 2pm Sat-Thu).

The clean, modern **Hammam Ziani** (☎ 022 319695; www.hammamziani.ma; 59 Rue Abou Rakrak; weekdays/weekends Dh30/40; ☼ 7am-10pm) offers all of the normal Turkish bath services – steam room and gommage (moisturising massage) – as well as massage, jacuzzi and juice bar (for an additional cost).

A more traditional but certainly satisfactory hammam is **Ancienne Medina Hammam** (Place Ahmed El Bidaoui; admission Dh7.50; ☼ 6am-noon for men & 1-10pm for women), located near the youth hostel in the old medina.

About 1km southeast of town is the **Quartier Habous**, or 'District of Holy Men'. It is an idealised but attractive French version of a Moroccan medina, sometimes called the 'nouvelle medina'. Take bus No 4 or 40 from Blvd de Paris, across from the post office.

In the trendy suburb of 'Ain Diab, the beachside **Blvd de la Corniche** is lined with beach clubs, hotels, restaurants, bars, coffee shops, nightclubs and a new multiplex cinema. Take bus No 9 from Place Oued al-Makhazine, just west of Place des Nations Unies.

Sleeping

All of the hotels are located in the Ville Nouvelle, mostly in the central pedestrian zone.

Youth Hostel (☎ 022 220551; fax 022 227677; 6 Place Ahmed el-Bidaoui; dm/d/tr with breakfast Dh45/120/180, sheets Dh5; ☼ 8-10am & noon-11pm; ℗) Facing a small square just inside the medina, the youth hostel is comfortable and clean with good facilities. However, readers have complained about poor service.

Hôtel Rialto (☎ 022 275122; 9 Rue Salah ben Bouchaib; s/d Dh100/140, s/d with bathroom Dh120/160) Small, bright and well run, this budget option has a touch (just a touch) of style.

Hôtel Oued-Dahab (☎ 022 223866; 1 Rue Mohamed Belloul; s/d Dh100/140, s/d with shower Dh120/180) This place is pretty basic, but it's clean, friendly and very safe.

Hôtel du Palais (☎ 022 276191; 68 Rue Farhat Hachad; s/d Dh70/100, s/d with bathroom Dh140/200) Features clean, spacious, recently upgraded rooms. The cheaper rooms remaining on the top floor share Asian-style toilets.

Hôtel Gallia (☎ 022 481694; 19 Rue Ibn Batouta; s/d/tr Dh150/220/300) Fresh, clean rooms and

CASABLANCA

0 _____ 600 m
0 _____ 0.4 miles

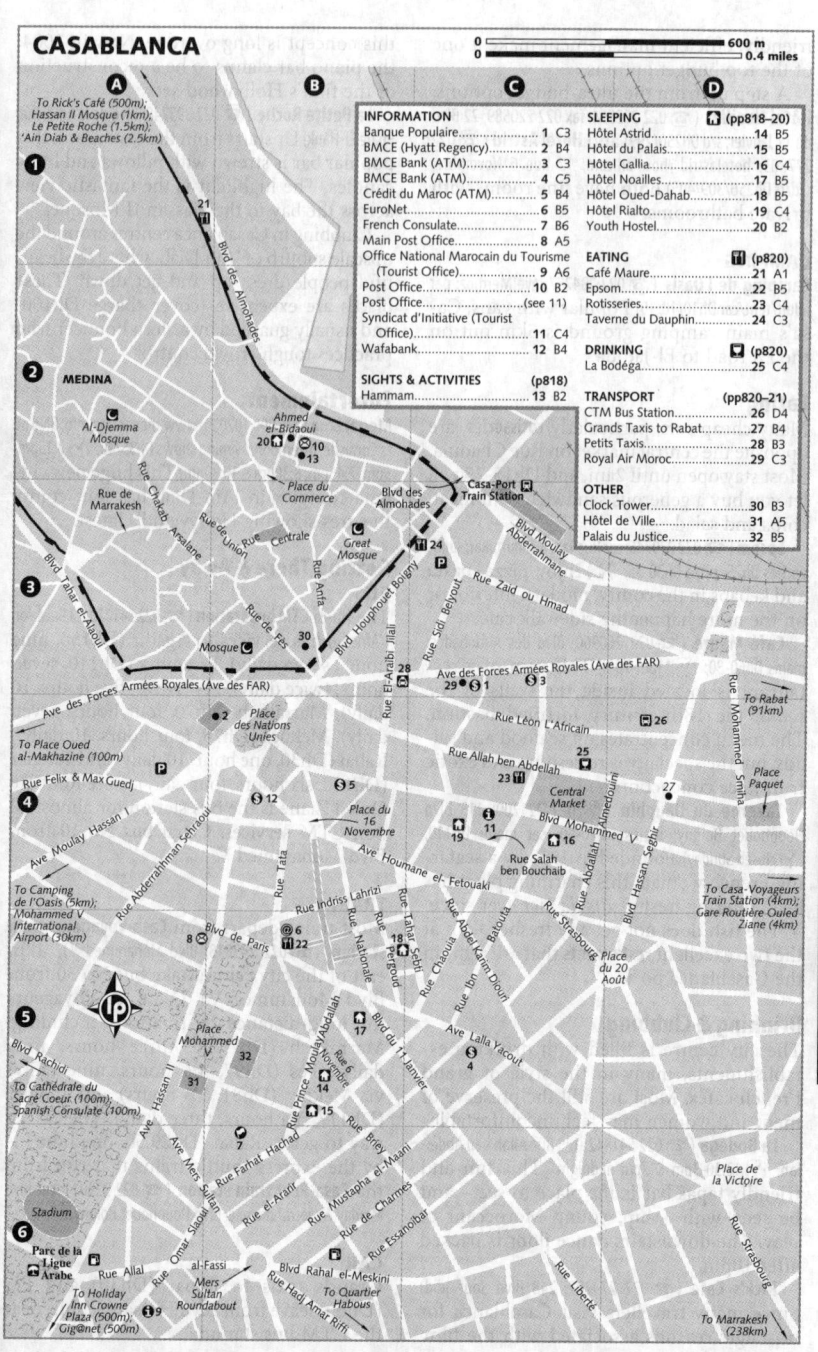

INFORMATION
Banque Populaire.....................1 C3
BMCE (Hyatt Regency).............2 B4
BMCE Bank (ATM)....................3 C3
BMCE Bank (ATM)....................4 C5
Crédit du Maroc (ATM)............5 B4
EuroNet...................................6 B5
French Consulate.....................7 B6
Main Post Office......................8 A5
Office National Marocain du Tourisme
 (Tourist Office)......................9 A6
Post Office.............................10 B2
Post Office.........................(see 11)
Syndicat d'Initiative (Tourist
 Office)................................11 C4
Wafabank..............................12 B4

SIGHTS & ACTIVITIES   (p818)
Hammam................................13 B2

SLEEPING   (pp818–20)
Hôtel Astrid...........................14 B5
Hôtel du Palais......................15 B5
Hôtel Gallia...........................16 C4
Hôtel Noailles.......................17 B5
Hôtel Oued-Dahab.................18 B5
Hôtel Rialto...........................19 C4
Youth Hostel.........................20 B2

EATING   (p820)
Café Maure............................21 A1
Epsom...................................22 B5
Rotisseries.............................23 C4
Taverne du Dauphin..............24 C3

DRINKING   (p820)
La Bodéga.............................25 C4

TRANSPORT   (pp820–21)
CTM Bus Station....................26 D4
Grands Taxis to Rabat............27 B4
Petits Taxis............................28 B3
Royal Air Maroc....................29 C3

OTHER
Clock Tower...........................30 B3
Hôtel de Ville........................31 A5
Palais du Justice....................32 B5

MEDINA

To Rick's Café (500m);
Hassan II Mosque (1km);
Le Petite Roche (1.5km);
'Ain Diab & Beaches (2.5km)

Al-Djemma Mosque

Rue de Marrakesh

Blvd des Almohades

Ahmed el-Bidaoui

Place du Commerce

Rue Chakib Arsalane

Rue de l'Union

Rue Centrale

Blvd des Almohades

Casa-Port Train Station

Blvd Moulay Abderrahmane

Great Mosque

Blvd Tahar el-Aaloui

Rue Anfa

Rue de Fes

Blvd Houphouet Boigny

Rue Zaid ou Hmad

Rue Sidi Belyout

Mosque

Ave des Forces Armées Royales (Ave des FAR)

Ave des Forces Armées Royales (Ave des FAR)

Rue El-Arabi Jilali

To Rabat (91km)

Rue Mohammed Smiha

Place Paquet

To Place Oued al-Makhazine (100m)

Place des Nations Unies

Rue Léon L'Africain

Rue Felix & Max Guedj

Ave Moulay Hassan I

Rue Abderrahman Sehraoui

Rue Tata

Place du 16 Novembre

Rue Allah ben Abdellah

Central Market

Blvd Mohammed V

To Camping de l'Oasis (5km);
Mohammed V International Airport (30km)

Ave Houmane el-Fetouaki

Rue Salah ben Bouchaib

Blvd de Paris

Rue Indriss Lahrizi

Rue Talar Sebti

Rue Perroud

Rue Chaouia

Rue Nationale

Rue Abdel Karim Diouri

Rue Ibn Batouta

Blvd Hassan Seghir

Place du 20 Août

To Casa-Voyageurs Train Station (4km);
Gare Routière Ouled Ziane (4km)

Place Mohammed V

Blvd Rachidi

To Cathédrale du Sacré Coeur (100m);
Spanish Consulate (100m)

Ave Hassan II

Ave Mers Sultan

Rue Prince Moulay Abdallah

Rue de 11 Novembre

Blvd du 11 Janvier

Ave Lalla Yacout

Rue Briey

Rue Farhat Hachad

Rue el-Arani

Rue Mustapha el-Maani

Rue de Charmes

Place de la Victoire

Rue Strasbourg

Stadium

Parc de la Ligue Arabe

To Holiday Inn Crowne Plaza (500m);
Gig@net (500m)

Rue Allal al-Fassi

Rue Omar Slaoui

Mers Sultan Roundabout

Blvd Rahal el-Meskini

Rue Hadj Amar Rifii

To Quartier Habous

Rue Essanobar

Rue Liberté

To Marrakesh (238km)

MOROCCO

friendly, efficient management make it one of the top budget options.

A step up from the ultra-budget options, **Hôtel Noailles** (☎ 022 202554; fax 022 220589; 22 Blvd du 11 Janvier; s/d Dh250/299) and **Hôtel Astrid** (☎ 022 277803; hotelastrid@hotmail.com; 12 Rue 6 Novembre; s/d/tr Dh256/309/405) both have fine rooms with private bathrooms.

CAMPING
Camping de l'Oasis (☎ 022 234257; Ave Mermoz; per adult/tent/car Dh10/10/10) Popular with vans, Casa's main camping ground is 5km out on the P8 road to El-Jadida.

Eating
Many cheap eats, particularly **rotisseries**, are opposite the central market on Rue Chaouia. Most stay open until 2am, and Dh15-25 will let you buy a generous sandwich with meat, chips and salad.

Epsom (☎ 022 220746; cnr Rue Tata & Mouftakar; sandwiches Dh25, pizza Dh30-35; 🕃) Enjoy pizza, pasta and kebabs in the comfy, modern interior or on the more happening sidewalk café.

Café Maure (☎ 022 260960; Blvd des Almohades; mains Dh60-80; 🕭 11am-7pm) This gem of a restaurant is located inside the walls of the *sqala*, the 18th-century fortified bastion. The menu concentrates on seafood and salads, but the specialty is refreshing and exotic fruit juice concoctions.

Taverne du Dauphin (☎ 022 221200; 115 Blvd Houphouet Boigny; mains Dh70-90, set menu Dh110; 🕭 closed Sunday) Founded in 1958 by a seafaring French woman, this charming place has been offering fresh *fruits de mer* ever since.

The fish does not get any fresher than at the two excellent **restaurants** that are right in the Casablanca port.

Drinking & Clubbing
The city centre is filled with drinking establishments, many in the style of grand French cafés. Most are still the preserve of men, and women may feel uncomfortable.

La Bodéga (☎ 022 541842; 129 Rue Allah ben Abdellah; 🕭 12.30-3pm & 7pm-midnight) This fun and friendly tapas bar is *the* place to see – and be seen with – hip, young Moroccans at play. The downstairs dance floor is packed after 10pm.

Rick's Cafe (☎ 022 274207; 248 Blvd Sour Jdid) Since many travellers visit Casablanca for nostalgic reasons associated with the film,

this concept is long overdue. New in 2004, the piano bar claims to be a reconstruction of the film's Hollywood set.

La Petite Roche (☎ 022 395748; Blvd de la Corniche, Phare El-Hank) Upstairs from the restaurant, this popular bar is strewn with pillows and lit by candles. The highlight is the fantastic view across the bay to the Hassan II Mosque.

Clubbing in Casablanca centres around the upscale suburb of 'Ain Diab, where the beautiful people dress up and get down. These places are expensive (cover charge Dh100) and usually guarded by a stern bouncer who practices tough crowd control.

Entertainment
Megarama (☎ 090 102020; www.megarama.info; Blvd de la Corniche; afternoon/evening shows Dh35/40; 🕭 2:15pm, 5pm, 7:45pm, 8:30pm & 10:30pm) This huge new cinema complex in 'Ain Diab has four comfy theatres showing Hollywood's latest.

Getting There & Away
BUS
The flash **CTM bus station** (☎ 022 541010; 23 Rue Léon L'Africain) has services to Agadir (Dh150, nine hours, seven daily), Essaouira (Dh110, seven hours, twice daily), Fès (Dh90, five hours, 10 daily), Marrakesh (Dh70, four hours, seven daily), Meknès (Dh75, four hours, 10 daily), Rabat (Dh30, one hour, 10 daily) and Tangier (Dh130, six hours, four daily). Gare Routière Ouled Ziane is the bus station for almost all non-CTM services. Catch bus No 10 from Blvd Mohammed V.

TRAIN
Most trains depart from **Casa-Voyageurs train station** (☎ 022 243818; Blvd Mohammed V), 4km east of the city centre (take bus No 30 from Blvd Mohammed V). Use Casa-Voyageurs for long-distance destinations including: Marrakesh (Dh75.50, three hours, nine daily), Fès (Dh97, 4½ hours, nine daily) via Meknès (Dh81, 3½ hours) and Tangier (Dh117, 5¾ hours, three daily). The easiest way to get to Rabat (Dh29.50, one hour) is by the express shuttle trains that run from the **Casa-Port train station** (☎ 022 223011; cnr Blvd Moulay Abderrahmane & Blvd Houphouet Boigny).

CAR
Grands taxis to Rabat (Dh30) and Fès (Dh60) leave from Blvd Hassan Seghir, near the CTM bus station.

Getting Around

You can get from Mohammed V International Airport to Casablanca by trains (Dh30, 2nd class, 30 minutes; hourly), which leave from Casa Voyageurs, 4km east of the city centre. A **shuttle bus** (☎ 022 448376) runs from the CTM bus terminal 12 times a day (Dh40, one hour).

There's no shortage of petits taxis in Casablanca; many wait at the taxi stand at the corner of Ave des FAR and Rue El-Araibi Jilali. Expect to pay Dh5 for a ride within the city centre with the meter on.

RABAT

The great walls of Rabat enclose a largely modern city with wide boulevards and bureaucratic-looking buildings. Several quarters, however, recall Rabat's rich past, including the ancient Kasbah des Oudaias and whitewashed Salé, home to the colourful corsairs. Besides being historically rich, Rabat is the modern capital, and thus houses important national monuments and museums.

Orientation

The main administrative buildings and many of the hotels lie just off the city's main thoroughfare, the wide, palm-lined Ave Mohammed V. The entrance to the medina is at the northern end of the avenue, while the train station Rabat Ville is at the southern end.

Information

Menara (Rue Soékarno; per hr Dh12; ◷ 9am-8pm Mon-Sat) Internet access.

Office National Marocain du Tourisme (ONMT; ☎ 037 673756; visitmorocco@onmt.org.ma; cnr Rue Oued El Makhazine & Rue Zalaka, Agdal; ◷ 8.30am-noon & 3-6.30pm Mon-Fri) Take bus No 3 from the train station or take a taxi; the office is opposite the Belle Vue swimming pool.

Post office (cnr Rue Soékarno & Ave Mohammed V)

Sights & Activities

MEDINA

Dating from the 17th century, the walled medina is slightly sanitised compared to the older medinas in the interior – which is not to say that it will not pique the senses with its fresh foodstuffs and souvenir stalls. Head north along the Rue des Consuls to the **Kasbah des Oudaias**, high up on the bluff overlooking the Oued Bou Regreg.

The southern corner of the kasbah houses the **Andalucían Gardens** (◷ sunrise-sun-set), laid out by the French during the colonial period. The centrepiece is the stately 17th-century palace containing the **Musée des Oudaia** (☎ 037 731537; admission Dh10; ◷ 9am-noon & 3-5pm, till 6pm in summer).

TOUR HASSAN & MAUSOLEUM

The Almohad sultan Yacoub al-Mansour in 1195 began constructing an enormous minaret, intending to make it the tallest in the Muslim world, but he died before the project was completed. What remains is Rabat's most famous landmark, **Le Tour Hassan** (Hassan Tower); the adjacent mosque was all but destroyed by an earthquake in 1755. On the same site is the cool marble **Mausoleum of Mohammed V** (admission free; ◷ sunrise-sunset), where the present king's grandfather and father (the late Hassan II) are laid to rest.

ARCHAEOLOGICAL SITES

One of Rabat's most peaceful corners is the site of the ancient Roman city of **Sala Colonia** and the Merenid necropolis of **Chellah** (cnr Ave Yacoub al-Mansour & Blvd ad-Douster; admission Dh10; ◷ 9am-5.30pm) south of the centre.

Many of the relics from Sala Colonia and other highlights of Morocco's ancient history are on display at the **Archaeology Museum** (☎ 037 701919; 23 Rue al-Brihi Parent; admission Dh10; ◷ 9-11.30am & 2.30-5.30pm Wed-Mon).

SURFING

Above the breakers of the Atlantic coast, the modern building between the kasbah and the lighthouse is the **Oudayas Surf Club** (☎ 037 260683, fax 037 260684; 3 Plage des Oudayas; 90-min lesson Dh90, insurance Dh50), a school for surfing and body boarding.

Sleeping

MEDINA

Most of the budget hotels in the medina are barely tolerable, lacking any creature comforts such as, say, showers. A few exceptions are listed.

Hôtel Dorhmi (☎ 037 723898; 313 Ave Mohammed V; s/d Dh80/120, hot shower Dh10) This small, family-run hotel above the Banque Populaire has spotless rooms and a homely atmosphere.

Hôtel al-Maghrib al-Jadid (☎ 037 732207; 2 Rue Sebbahi; s/d Dh60/90, hot shower Dh7.50) Tiny windows and shocking pink walls brighten the otherwise cell-like rooms in this small hotel. The shared Asian-style toilets are clean.

Hôtel Darna (☎ 037 736787; 24 Blvd al-Alou; s/d with bathroom Dh90/130) Its location north of the medina is not too convenient, but rooms are spacious and generally clean.

VILLE NOUVELLE
Youth Hostel (☎ 037 725769; 43 Rue Marassa; dm HI members/nonmembers Dh30/35, hot shower Dh7.50; ☼ 8am-10.30pm, closed 10am-noon & 3-6pm Oct-April) Opposite the walls of the medina, the youth hostel is a pleasant place with a verdant courtyard.

Hôtel Splendid (☎ 037 723283; 8 Rue Ghazza; s/d Dh102/124, s/d with bathroom Dh160/185) Modern bathrooms, wood furniture and linoleum floors outfit the cheery rooms.

Hôtel d'Orsay (☎ 037 202277; fax 037 708208; 11 Ave Moulay Youssef; s/d with bathroom Dh211/264) A friendly hotel opposite Rabat Ville train station. All of the rooms are equipped with televisions and telephones.

Hôtel Royal (☎ 037 721171; fax 037 725491; royal hotel@mtds.com; 1 Rue Jeddah Ammane; s/d with bathroom Dh230/270) Newly renovated in 2004, the Royal provides spacious, comfortable rooms, all equipped with polished-wooden furniture and modern, marble bathrooms.

Hôtel Majestic (☎ 037 722997; www.hotelmajestic.ma; 121 Ave Hassan II; s/d Dh240/280) Modern furniture and clean lines make for an attractive setting. The shady terrace is a nice touch, as is the professional service.

Camping
Camping de la Plage (per adult/small tent/large tent/car Dh15/15/22/12, power & water Dh15, hot shower Dh10) The nearest camping ground is in from the beach at Salé.

Eating
In the southwest corner of the medina, the indoor **fruit and vegetable market** will easily fill your picnic basket with fresh produce, dried fruits and nuts and prepared salads.

City VIPS (☎ 037 202840; 47 Ave Allal ben Abdallah; mains Dh20-40; ☼ 11am-11pm) Everyone from VIPs to LIPs (less-important-people) eats at this popular fast-food joint. Vegetarians will find a decent selection.

Café Weimar (☎ 037 732650; 7 Rue Sana'a; pizza Dh55) The café-restaurant in the Goethe Institut is among the hottest spots for hip, young Moroccans and expats. The menu is mostly Mediterranean.

Le Petit Beur – Dar Tajine (☎ 037 731322; 8 Rue Damas; mains Dh65-85; ☼ closed Sun) This pleasant eatery offers tasty food and traditional atmosphere without the fuss (and financial burden) of the more elaborate places in the medina.

La Mamma (☎ 037 707329; 6 Rue Tanta; mains Dh80-100) Rue Tanta might be Rabat's 'Little Italy', thanks to the Benenatis family's culinary exploits. Besides an ice cream parlour and pizza delivery service, they operate this romantic restaurant serving pizza and pasta.

Drinking
Cafétéria du 7éme Art (☎ 037 733887; Ave Allal ben Abdallah; ☼ 11am-11pm) All genders and ages flock to this trendy outdoor café, set on the grounds of a cinema house.

Pachanga (☎ 037 262931; 10 Place des Alaouites; mains Dh60, bottle of beer Dh40-50; ☼ 11.30am-midnight) The most popular pub at the time of research, Pachanga has a hip, European flare.

Clubbing
Nightclubs in Rabat – some of which are attached to the upscale hotels – normally charge at least Dh60 for entry (which includes the first drink). Most clubs are open from around 11pm and go on until 3am or later. Don't forget to dress the part or you won't get past the front door.

Popular clubs include **Amnesia** (Rue de Monastir; admission Mon-Fri Dh60, Sat & Sun Dh100, women free; ☼ 11pm-3am), which was expected to reopen in 2004, and **5th Avenue** (☎ 037 775254; 4 Rue Bin Alaouidan, Agdal; cover Dh100; ☼ weekends until 5am).

Getting There & Away
BUS
Local bus No 30 makes the 5km trip to the inter-city bus station. **CTM** (☎ 037 795124; Route de Casablanca) has buses to Agadir (Dh166, 12 hours), Casablanca (Dh30, 1½ hours), Essaouira (Dh130, 8 hours), Fès (Dh50, 3½ hours), Marrakesh (Dh90, 5 hours) and Tangier (Dh76, 4½ hours). Other bus lines offer cheaper fares to these destinations.

TRAIN
From **Rabat Ville train station** (☎ 037 736060; Place des Alaouites), trains run to Casa-Port (Dh27.50, one hour, twice hourly). Other second-class express fares include: Fès (Dh72, 3½ hours, eight daily) via Meknès (Dh56, 2½ hours, eight daily), Tangier (Dh90, 4½ hours, three daily) and Marrakesh (Dh101, 4½ hours, eight daily).

GRANDS TAXIS

Grands taxis leave for Casablanca (Dh27) from just outside the intercity bus station. Others leave for Fès (Dh55), Meknès (Dh40) and Salé (Dh3) from Ave Hassan II (between the city's main local bus station and Hôtel Bou Regreg).

AROUND RABAT

Salé

Although just across the estuary, the white-washed city of Salé has a character distinct from Rabat. Little within the city walls seems to have changed over the centuries. The medina's main point of access is **Bab Bou Haja**, on the southwestern wall, which opens onto Place Bab Khebaz. From here it's a short walk to the souqs on the northwest side of the square. The **Grand Mosqué** and the beautiful 14th-century **Medersa** (Qur'anic school; admission Dh10; ☼ 9am-noon & 2.30-6pm) are 500m further northwest along Rue Ras ash-Shajara. Grands taxis and bus No 16 to Rabat leave from Bab Mrisa, the gate in the southeastern corner of the old walled city; you can catch small **boats** across the river below Bab Bou Haja.

ASILAH

The port of Asilah, 46km south of Tangier, has found its niche as a bijou resort town. Affluent Moroccans and Europeans – as well as the Moroccan government – have poured money into gentrifying houses within the whitewashed and mural-painted city walls. Galleries line the narrow streets, which host the sophisticated annual **International Cultural Festival** in July/August.

The impressive 15th-century Portuguese ramparts are largely intact. The southwestern prong offers a peak into the nearby **Koubba of Sidi Mamsur** (which is otherwise closed to non-Muslims) and the **Mujaheddin Graveyard**.

A revolving exhibition of international art is housed in the **Centre de Hassan II** (☎ 039 417065; fax 039 418396; admission free; ☼ 8.30am-12.30pm & 2.30-7pm) and in the **El-Kamra Tower**, a renovated Portuguese fortification on Place Abdellah Guennoun.

Sun worshippers and bathing beauties are advised to head 3km south of Asilah to **Paradise Beach**, a gorgeous, pristine spot that really does live up to its name. A few snack shacks cater to the beach-goers, but otherwise it is simply sand and surf. Paradise Beach is a pleasant walk along the coast

from Asilah. Alternatively, hop on one of the horse-drawn carriages that ply this route.

Sleeping

HOTELS

The budget hotels – all outside the medina walls – offer small, clean rooms and shared facilities.

Hôtel Sahara (☎ 039 417185; 9 Rue Tarfaya; s Dh70-100, d Dh100-128, hot shower Dh5)

Hôtel Belle Vue (☎ 039 417747; Rue Hassan ben Tabit; d Dh200)

Hôtel Las Palmas (☎ 039 418757; 9 Rue Imam al-Assili; s/d Dh150/200)

CAMPING

Various well-equipped camping grounds are along the beach north of town.

Camping as-Saada (☎ 039 417317; per adult/tent/car Dh12/10/10, electricity Dh15, r Dh120)

Camping Echrigui (☎ 039 417182; r Dh200) Facilities include a café and market.

Eating

The cheapest eating option is the string of restaurants and cafés by the medina wall on Ave Hassan II. For finer dining, head to the strip of restaurants opposite Bab Kasbah.

Getting There & Away

Your best bet for getting to and from Asilah is the bus. Services run to Tangier (Dh10 to Dh15, one hour, every 30 minutes), Fès (Dh55, 4½ hours, two to three daily) via Meknès, Casablanca (Dh70, 4½ hours, three to four daily) via Rabat (Dh50, 3½ hours, three to four daily) and Agadir (Dh237, 13 hours, one daily).

ESSAOUIRA

With its picture-postcard ramparts and turrets and its mazelike medina, Essaouira is the most popular of the Atlantic coastal towns. Inside the town walls, it's all light and charm, a labyrinth of narrow lanes, whitewashed houses, tranquil squares and artisan workshops. The snug, fortified harbour is a hive of activity, with nets laid out on the quayside, fishing boats unloading their catch, traditional wooden boats being built and seafood sizzling on grills.

The impressive sea bastion built along the cliffs is known as the **Skala de la Ville**. Down by the harbour, the **Skala du Port** (adult Dh10; ☼ 8.30am-noon & 2.30-6pm) offers more cannons and fantastic views over the fishing port and

MOROCCO

Île de Mogador. The beach stretches some 10km down the coast to the sand dunes of **Cap Sim**. The strong coastal wind has made Essaouira Morocco's best-known **windsurfing** centre, increasingly promoting itself as 'Windy City, Afrika'.

The **Gnawa and World Music Festival** (third weekend in June) is a four-day musical extravaganza with concerts on Place Moulay Hassan. It features international, national and local performers and there are simultaneous art exhibitions.

Sleeping

Most of the budget hotels are clustered on the western side of the medina.

Hôtel Smara (☎ 044 475655; 26 Rue de la Skala; s/d Dh66/96, d with sea view Dh156) This place offers not only some of the cheapest beds in town but also a terrace with unbeatable sea views.

Hôtel Souiri (☎ /fax 044 475339; 37 Rue al-Attarine; B&B s/d Dh95/150, s/d with bathroom from Dh180/250, apt for 4 Dh450) A range of spotless rooms, from tiny singles with pine furniture to rooms decked out with wrought-iron sofas and cheerful fabrics.

Riad Nakhla (☎ 044 474940; riad-nakhla@essaouir anet.com; 2 Rue Agadir; s/d Dh200/300) An excellent choice buried away in the medina. From the fountain in the courtyard to the roof-terrace, it's packed with local atmosphere.

Camping des Oliviers (☎ 044 475500; fax 044 474574; per camp site Dh41, 2-adult Berber tent Dh100, bungalow from Dh250, hot shower Dh5; P ≋) This big, well-maintained four-star site, about 25km out of town on the Marrakesh road, has a restaurant, and the option of neat little bungalows or Berber tents.

Eating

The best cheap eats are en route to the port, at several outdoor **fish grills** offering a fabulous selection of the day's catch for just Dh25.

Riad Al-Baraka (☎ 044 473561; 113 Rue Mohammed el-Qory; mains Dh35, meals with wine Dh90; ☻ noon-3pm & 6.30pm-late Tue-Sun) A funky, new-age *riad* (house located in the old town) with a wonderful courtyard shaded by a huge fig tree. The decor is unpretentiously cool and the food is a combination of Middle Eastern and Moroccan flavours.

Restaurant Ferdaous (☎ 044 473655; 27 Rue Abdesslam Lebadi; mains Dh50, set menus Dh75) The best local restaurant does inventive takes on tajines and other local dishes.

Getting There & Away

The **bus station** (☎ 044 784764) is about 400m northeast of the medina across an open car park. CTM has buses to Marrakesh (Dh45, 2½ hours, one daily), Casablanca (express Dh105, six hours, one daily) and Agadir (Dh40, three hours, one daily).

Supratours (☎ 044 475317) runs buses from outside Bab Marrakech to Marrakesh (Dh55, 2½ hours) to connect with trains to Casablanca. Book in advance.

IMPERIAL CITIES

MARRAKESH

Nomad camp and capital of the south, Marrakesh is the lodestone of the interior, once drawing vast camel caravans from the south, for whom the oasis was the finest city they had seen. Nowadays, Marrakesh draws countless travellers under its mesmerising spell, luring them with medieval myths and mystery.

The heat, the dust, the mudbrick ramparts are features that make Marrakesh a uniquely African, Moroccan city. Even local legend is full of rude and vigorous blood and thunder: stories tell of the city's ochre-red walls being bathed in blood as the soaring minaret of the Koutoubia was planted in the city's heart.

Orientation

It takes about 30 minutes to walk from the centre of the Ville Nouvelle to Djemaa el-Fna, the main square in the the old city's heart. The main area of the Ville Nouvelle is Guéliz, where the bulk of offices, restaurants, cafés and shops, plus a few hotels, are clustered near the main thoroughfare, Ave Mohammed V.

Information

EMERGENCY
Ambulance (☎ 044 443724)
Police (☎ 19; Hôtel de Police; Rue Ouadi el-Makhazine)

INTERNET ACCESS
Askmy Café (☎ 044 430602; 6 Blvd Mohammed Zerktouni; per hr Dh10; ☻ 24hr daily)
Cyber Club (Ave Mohammed V; per hr Dh10; ☻ 9.30am-1pm & 3pm-10.30pm)

MEDICAL SERVICES
All-Night Pharmacy (☎ 044 389564; Rue Khalid ben el-Oualid)

Polyclinique du Sud (☎ 044 447999; 2 Rue de Yougoslavie, Guéliz; ⏰ 24hr emergency service) A private clinic used by nearly all resident expats

MONEY

Most banks will change cash or travellers cheques and there's no shortage of ATMs.
Crédit du Maroc (⏰ 8.45am-1pm & 3-6.45pm Mon-Sat) Ville Nouvelle (215 Ave Mohammed V); Medina (Rue de Bab Agnaou). After-hours exchange facilities available.

POST

Main post office (Place du 16 Novembre; ⏰ 8.30am-2pm Mon-Sat)
Post office (Djemaa el-Fna; ⏰ 8am-noon & 3-6pm) A convenient branch on the medina's main square.

TOURIST INFORMATION

Office National Marocain du Tourisme (ONMT; ☎ 044 436131, fax 044 436057; Place Abdel Moumen ben Ali, Guéliz; ⏰ 8.30am-noon & 2.30-6.30pm Mon-Fri, 9am-noon & 3-6pm Sat)
Syndicat d'Initiative (☎ 044 430886; 170 Ave Mohammed V; ⏰ 8.30am-12.30pm & 2.30-6.30pm Mon-Fri, 9am-noon Sat)

Sights
MEDINA

The focal point of Marrakesh is **Djemaa el-Fna**, the main square in the medina and the backdrop for one of the world's greatest spectacles. See the boxed text 'Street Eats & Street Sights' p829.

Southwest of the Djemaa el-Fna, is that most famous monument, the **Koutoubia Mosque**. At 70-metres tall, its minaret is visible for miles in any direction. Built by the Almohad, Yakoub el-Mansour (1184–1199), on the site of a previous 11th-century Almoravid mosque, this is the oldest and best preserved of their three most famous minarets – the others being the Tour Hassan in Rabat and the Giralda in Seville (Spain). The name (from *koutoub* or *kutub*, Arabic for books) is all that's left of a booksellers' market that once existed here.

The great labyrinth of souqs extends from the north side of the Djemaa el-Fna and ends at the Ali ben Youssef Mosque, making the main area of interest comparatively compact and suitable for strolling. The **Ali ben Youssef Mosque** (Place ben Youssef; closed to non-Muslims) and **Medersa** (Qur'anic school; ☎ 044 390911; Place ben Youssef; Dh20; ⏰ 9am-6pm daily) mark the intellectual and religious heart of the medina.

Nearby, the **Musée de Marrakesh** (☎ 044390911; Place ben Youssef; admission Dh30; ⏰ 9.30am-6pm) is in a restored 19th-century *riad*, Dar Mnebbi. Changing exhibitions cover the full range of arts and crafts.

KASBAH (ROYAL QUARTER)

The most famous of the city's palaces, the **Palais el-Badi** (Place des Ferblantiers, Mellah; admission Dh10; ⏰ 8.30-11.45am & 2.30-5.45pm) is inside the kasbah in the south of the medina. At the time of its construction (1578–1602) it was reputed to be one of the most beautiful palaces in the world. Sadly, the luxury of the palace did not escape the plundering hand of sultan Moulay Ismail, who stripped it bare.

Long hidden from intrusive eyes, the area of the **Saadian Tombs** (Rue de la Kasbah; Dh10; ⏰ 8.30-11.45am & 2.30-5.45pm), alongside the **Kasbah Mosque** (Rue de la Kasbah), was the privileged cemetery for descendents of the Prophet Mohammed. However, the ornate tombs seen today are the resting place of the Saadian princes, most notably Ahmed al-Mansour.

OTHER PALACES

The exquisite **Palais de la Bahia** (☎ 044 389221; Riad Zitoun el-Jedid; admission Dh10; ⏰ 8.30-11.15am & 2.30-5.45pm Sat-Thu, 8.30-11.30am & 3-5.45pm Fri) was built towards the end of the 19th century as the residence of the Grand Vizier of Sultan Moulay al-Hassan I.

Further north, the **Dar Si Said** (☎ 044 389564; Riad Zitoun el-Jedid; admission Dh10; ⏰ 9-11.45am & 2.30-5.45pm Mon, Wed, Thu, Sat & Sun, 9-11.30am & 3-5.45pm Fri, closed Tue), houses the **Museum of Moroccan Arts**.

GARDENS

Now owned by Yves Saint-Laurent, the subtropical **Jardin Majorelle & Museum of Islamic Art** (gardens/museum Dh20/15; ⏰ 8am-noon & 3-7pm May-Aug, 8am-noon & 2-5pm daily Sep-Apr) provides a wonderful haven. In among the cacti, bamboo and cascades of bougainvillaea is a deep-blue villa, which houses the museum.

About a 2km walk south from the Koutoubia Mosque, is the **Jardin Ménara** (Ave de la Ménara; admission free, pavilion Dh15; ⏰ 5am-6.30pm) laid out in the 12th-century by the Almohads. The centrepiece of the olive grove is a large, still pool backed by a pavillion built in 1869.

Festivals & Events

For 40 years, the annual **Festival of Folklore** (☎ 044 446114; www.maghrebarts.ma/festivals) is a

MOROCCO

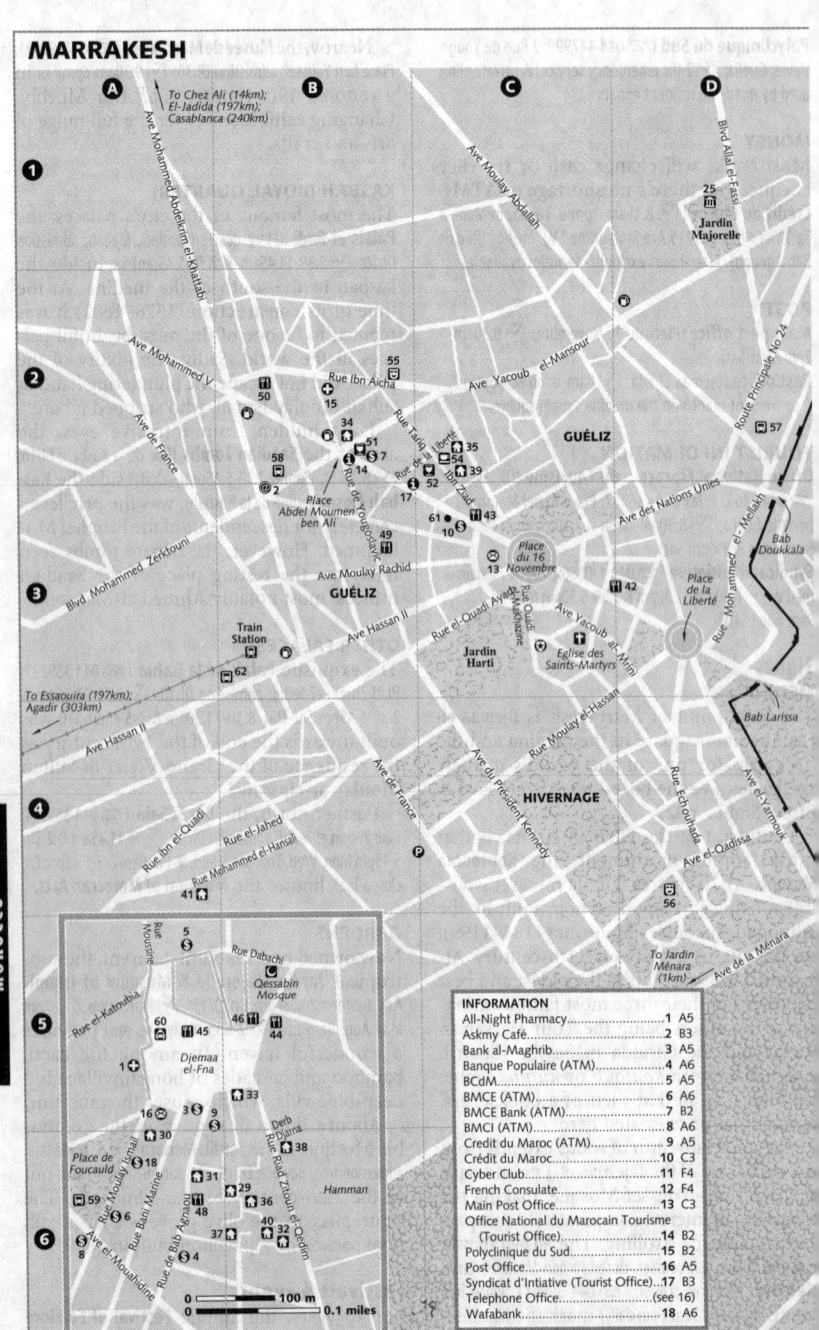

MARRAKESH

To Chez Ali (14km);
El-Jadida (197km);
Casablanca (240km)

To Essaouira (197km);
Agadir (303km)

To Jardin
Ménara
(1km)

GUÉLIZ

GUÉLIZ

HIVERNAGE

Train
Station

Jardin
Harti

Eglise des
Saints-Martyrs

Place
du 16
Novembre

Place
de la
Liberté

Jardin
Majorelle

Bab
Doukkala

Bab Larissa

Place
Abdel Moumen
ben Ali

Djemaa
el-Fna

Qessabin
Mosque

Place de
Foucauld

Hamman

Rue Mohammed Abdelkrim el-Khattabi

Ave Mohammed V

Ave de France

Blvd Mohammed Zerktouni

Rue Ibn Aicha

Ave Moulay Abdallah

Ave Yacoub el-Mansour

Ave des Nations Unies

Blvd Allal el-Fassi

Route Principale No 24

Route Principale No 24

Rue Mohammed el-Mellah

Ave Hassan II

Ave Hassan II

Ave Moulay Rachid

Ave el-Quadi Ayada

Rue el-Quadi Ayada

Ave Yacoub al-Mini

Rue Moulay el-Hassan

Rue el-Jahed

Rue Mohammed el-Hamali

Rue Ibn el-Quadi

Ave de France

Ave du Président Kennedy

Rue Echouhada

Ave el-Yarmouk

Ave el-Qadissa

Ave de la Ménara

Rue Dabachi

Rue el-Katoubia

Rue Mousine

Rue Moulay Ismail

Rue Bani Marine

Rue de Bab Agnaou

Derb Djama

Rue Riad Zitoun el-Qedim

Ave el-Mouahidine

0   100 m
0   0.1 miles

INFORMATION

All-Night Pharmacy	1 A5
Askmy Café	2 B3
Bank al-Maghrih	3 A5
Banque Populaire (ATM)	4 A6
BCdM	5 A5
BMCE (ATM)	6 A6
BMCE Bank (ATM)	7 B2
BMCI (ATM)	8 A6
Credit du Maroc (ATM)	9 A5
Crédit du Maroc	10 C3
Cyber Club	11 F4
French Consulate	12 F4
Main Post Office	13 C3
Office National du Marocain Tourisme (Tourist Office)	14 B2
Polyclinique du Sud	15 B2
Post Office	16 A5
Syndicat d'Intiative (Tourist Office)	17 B3
Telephone Office	(see 16)
Wafabank	18 A6

MOROCCO

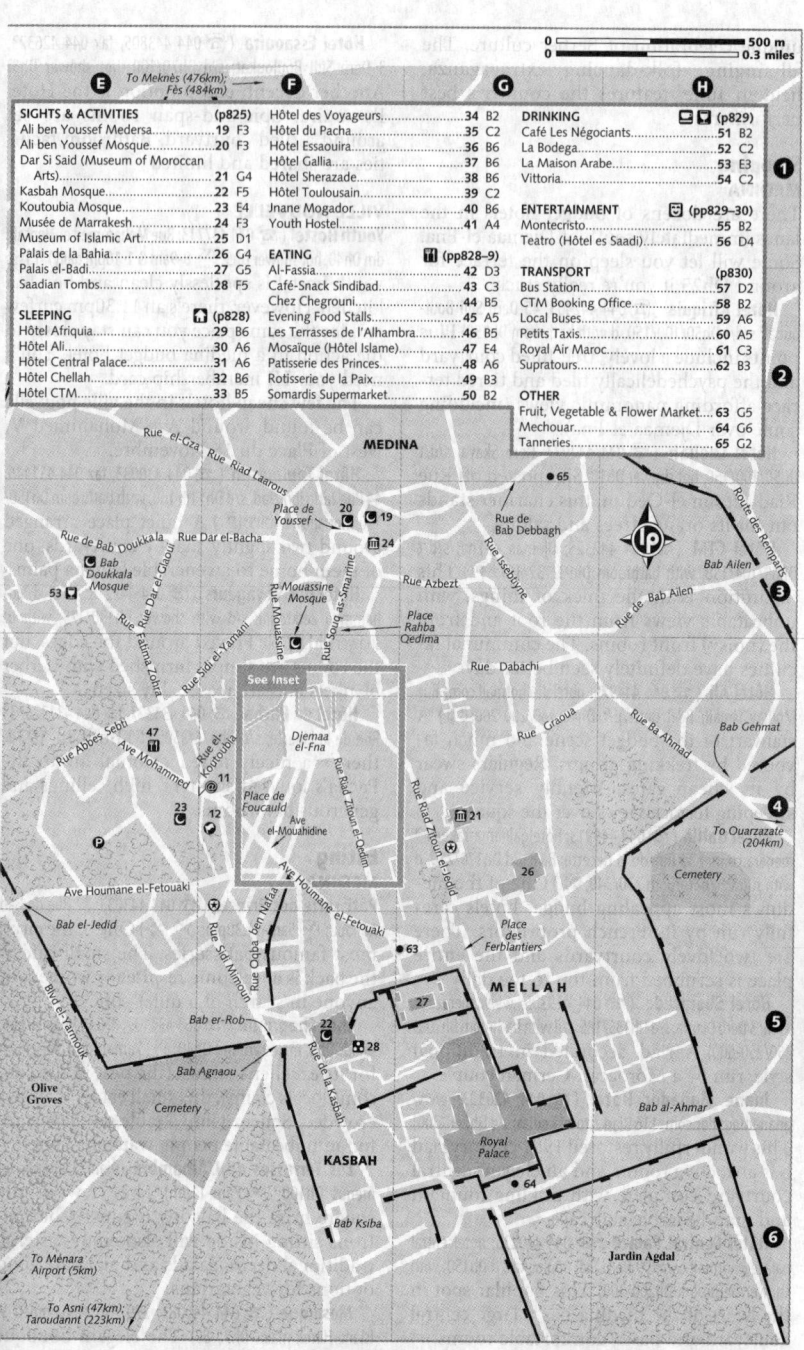

To Meknès (476km);
Fès (484km)

SIGHTS & ACTIVITIES	(p825)
Ali ben Youssef Medersa	19 F3
Ali ben Youssef Mosque	20 F3
Dar Si Said (Museum of Moroccan Arts)	21 G4
Kasbah Mosque	22 F5
Koutoubia Mosque	23 E4
Musée de Marrakesh	24 F3
Museum of Islamic Art	25 D1
Palais de la Bahia	26 G4
Palais el-Badi	27 G5
Saadian Tombs	28 F5

SLEEPING	(p828)
Hôtel Afriquia	29 B6
Hôtel Ali	30 A6
Hôtel Central Palace	31 A6
Hôtel Chellah	32 B6
Hôtel CTM	33 B5

Hôtel des Voyageurs	34 B2
Hôtel du Pacha	35 C2
Hôtel Essaouira	36 B6
Hôtel Gallia	37 B6
Hôtel Sherazade	38 B6
Hôtel Toulousain	39 C2
Jnane Mogador	40 B6
Youth Hostel	41 A4

EATING	(pp828–9)
Al-Fassia	42 D3
Café-Snack Sindibad	43 C3
Chez Chegrouni	44 B5
Evening Food Stalls	45 A5
Les Terrasses de l'Alhambra	46 B5
Mosaïque (Hôtel Islame)	47 E4
Patisserie des Princes	48 A6
Rotisserie de la Paix	49 B3
Somardis Supermarket	50 B2

DRINKING	(p829)
Café Les Négociants	51 B2
La Bodega	52 C2
La Maison Arabe	53 E3
Vittoria	54 C2

ENTERTAINMENT	(pp829–30)
Montecristo	55 B2
Teatro (Hôtel es Saadi)	56 D4

TRANSPORT	(p830)
Bus Station	57 D2
CTM Booking Office	58 B2
Local Buses	59 A6
Petits Taxis	60 A5
Royal Air Maroc	61 C3
Supratours	62 B3

OTHER	
Fruit, Vegetable & Flower Market	63 G5
Mechouar	64 G6
Tanneries	65 G2

MOROCCO

unique celebration of Berber culture. The all-singing, folk-dancing extravaganza, held in June, features the country's best performers.

Sleeping
MEDINA
There are dozens of budget hotels in the lanes immediately south of Djemaa el-Fna. Some will let you sleep on the terrace for around Dh25 if you're really stuck.

Hôtel Afriquia (☎ 044 442403; 45 Derb Sidi Bouloukat; s/d/t Dh50/100/150, d with bathroom Dh150) Plus points include a lovely, tree-filled courtyard and the psychedelically tiled and tiered terrace affording panoramic views (including some over Djemaa el-Fna).

Hôtel Chellah (☎ 044 442977; Derb Skaya; s/d/t Dh50/100/150, hot shower Dh10) Signposted off Rue Riad Zitoun el-Qedim, this charmer stands out for its orange trees and salons.

Hôtel CTM (☎ 044 442325; Djemaa el-Fna; s/d/t Dh68/104/158, with bathroom Dh93/132/187; P) This institution is in the thick of things, with unbeatable views from the roof and from the (noisy) front rooms. The communal facilities have definitely seen better days.

Hôtel Ali (☎ 044 444979; hotelali@hotmail.com; Rue Moulay Ismail; B&B dm/s/d/t Dh40/140/200/260; ✲) A stalwart of the budget scene and much favoured by trekking groups. Regulars swear by its cheap rates, friendly service and sweeping terrace views over the square.

Hôtel Gallia (☎ 044 445913; hotelgalliamarrakech@ menara.co.ma; 30 Rue de la Recette; B&B s/d Dh170/210, d with shower/bathroom 230/340; ✲) One of the medina's most appealing budget hotels carefully run by its French proprietors. There are two lovely courtyards and the entire place is scrubbed from top to toe daily.

Hôtel Sherazade (☎ 044 429305; www.sherazade .com; 3 Derb Djama; s/d Dh135/185, s/d with bathroom Dh200-450/250-500) A riad decorated in traditional style, run by a Moroccan-German couple.

Jnane Mogador Hôtel (☎ 044 426323; www .jnanemogador.com; 116 Riad Zitoun Kedim; s/d Dh260/300) This wonderfully restored 19th-century riad has attractive rooms and an elegant central courtyard complete with tinkling fountain and grand marble staircase.

Hôtel Central Palace (☎ 044 440235; hotelcentral palace@hotmail.com; 59 Derb Sidi Bouloukat; d Dh150, with shower/bathroom Dh200/300) This popular spot in the heart of the medina has a large central courtyard and basic, comfortable rooms.

Hôtel Essaouira (☎ 044 443805, fax 044 426323; 3 Derb Sidi Bouloukat; s/d Dh70/100, hot shower Dh5) Another decent, cheap option is the Hôtel Essaouira. Spic-and-span rooms are set around a tiled courtyard. Bathroom facilities are shared and limited.

VILLE NOUVELLE
Youth Hostel (☎ 044 447713; Rue Mohammed el-Hansali; dm Dh40, hot shower Dh5; ✲ 8-9am & 1-10pm daily) This youth hostel is spotlessly clean and boasts a kitchen. However, there's an 11.30pm curfew and for the same price you can stay closer to the action in a medina budget hotel. You'll need your HI membership card.

The few cheap hotels in the ville nouvelle can be found around Ave Mohammed V, west of Place du 16 Novembre.

Hôtel Toulousain (☎ 044 430033, fax 044 431446; 44 Rue Tariq ibn Ziad; s/d Dh110/160, with bathroom Dh150/ 190, hot shower Dh5; P) A quiet place arranged around two slightly shabby courtyards, one of them home to a venerable banana palm.

Hôtel des Voyageurs (☎ 044 447218; 40 Blvd Mohammed Zerktouni; s/d with shower Dh130/175, without shower Dh110/160) Frayed around the edges, but the rooms are simply furnished with Berber blankets and are reasonably sized.

Hôtel du Pacha (☎ 044 431327, fax 044 431326; 33 Rue de la Liberté; s/d Dh275/350; ✲) Built in 1934, there's a nicely faded colonial air to the Pacha's louvred shutters, high ceilings and generous bathrooms.

Eating
MEDINA
Pâtisserie des Princes (☎ 044 443033; 32 Rue de Bab Agnaou; ✲ 5am-11.30pm; ✖ ✲) One of the city's most famous patisseries. The small café at the back is a welcome respite for women, or anyone in search of a quiet coffee.

Chez Chegrouni (☎ 063 434132; 4-6 Djemaa el-Fna; salads Dh5, mains around Dh40; ✲ 7am-11pm) Known for its excellent tajines (the best in the city, some locals claim), this small eatery is always crowded. Squeeze into a table on the terrace for an unbeatable people-watching spot.

Les Terrasses de L'Alhambra (Djemaa el-Fna; set menus Dh100; ✲ 7am-11pm) The view of the square from the balcony is superb, but patrons sitting inside will also enjoy tasteful traditional decor. Salads and pizza are good options for vegetarians.

Mosaïque (☎ 044 440081; 279 Ave Mohammed V, Islane Hotel; mains Dh75-85) The elegant boutique

---

STREET EATS & STREET SIGHTS

By the time the sun sets, much of Djemaa el-Fna is occupied by food stalls, one piled high with kebabs and salads, and the next serving steamed snails. As you peruse the tables, friendly chefs will woo you with promises of fresh produce and free mint tea. Don't be afraid to talk back: the banter is part of the fun. Almost as soon as you've ordered, your food is in front of you with a range of accompaniments such as chips, salad, eggplant and fried chillies.

You can be sure there won't be a tourist in sight near the stalls selling sheeps' heads, though. Except, perhaps, to gawk. The hair is singed off in a fire, then the head is cleaned in hot water and stewed with chickpeas. It is quite a delicacy – everything but the eyes is eaten.

The large copper urns contain *hunja*, a reddish-brown cinnamon tea, which is especially satisfying in winter. It's traditionally accompanied by a spicy-sweet chocolate-brown dessert known as *tkaout*, somewhat akin to gingerbread.

The activity at the food stalls is entertaining. Meanwhile, on the fringes of the square, another show is unfolding, as musicians, acrobats, storytellers, fortune tellers and snake charmers take the stage.

---

restaurant in the Islane Hotel is filled with artisanal furniture and interesting artwork. Upstairs, the rooftop offers views of the Koutoubia Mosque and international cuisine.

VILLE NOUVELLE

Café-Snack Sindibad (3 Ave Mohammed V; mains Dh25-35; ☻ 6am-11pm) This popular snack shop may look down-at-heel, but the food is tasty and cheap. Try the *tanzhiyya* – a Marrakesh speciality stew – with either lemons or prunes.

Rotisserie de la Paix (☎ 044 433118; 68 Rue de Yougoslavie; mains Dh80-120) The peaceful summer garden never fails to draw a small crowd on a pleasant day in Marrakesh. The staid menu focuses on grills, seafood and big salads.

Al-Fassia (☎ 044 434060; 232 Ave Mohammed V; mains around Dh100, lunch set menus Dh160) A reminder that the Ville Nouvelle is Morocco, Al-Fassia serves some of the best local cuisine in town.

Drinking

The number one spot for a cheap and delicious drink is right on Djemaa el-Fna, where a fresh-squeezed orange juice is only Dh2.50 from the various stalls found there.

CAFÉS

Café Les Négociants (☎ 044 435762; 110 Ave Mohammed V; ☻ 6am-11pm) The wide Parisian-style terrace is a wonderful place for men to sit and watch the world go by. Women may not feel so welcome.

Vittoria (☎ 044 431529; 21 Rue de la Liberté; ☻ 8am-10pm) Run by women for women. While away an afternoon over a coffee on comfy couches in the salon or in the sunny courtyard.

BARS

As elsewhere in Morocco, the bars in Marrakesh are mostly dire, male-oriented places. A few of the up-market places are patronised by women, most of whom are either tourists or prostitutes.

La Bodega (☎ 044 433141; 23 Rue de la Liberté; ☻ 6pm-2am daily) This new, wildly popular spot is unique in Marrakesh for its raucous crowd and unassuming atmosphere.

La Maison Arabe (☎ 044 387010; 1 Derb Assehbe, Bab Doukkala) The only proper bar in the medina.

CLUBBING

Most of the hottest clubs are attached to up-scale hotels in the Ville Nouvelle. Admissions range from Dh100 to Dh150 including the first drink. Dress smartly and remember most places don't get going till after midnight.

Montecristo (☎ 044 439031; 20 Rue Ibn Aicha; ☻ 11pm-3am) This Latin club/salsa bar should be the first stop. If you can't beat the heat on the dance floor, head up to the gorgeous roof terrace.

Teatro (☎ 044 448811; Hôtel es Saadi, Ave el-Quadissia; admission Dh150; ☻ 11pm-5am) Converted from an old theatre, this high-end club pulses to a techno beat. The dance floor is on the former stage – very appropriate for the ladies who now strut their stuff there.

Entertainment

Chez Ali (☎ 044 307730; dinner & show Dh400; ☻ 8pm) Out on the Safi road, 14km from the city centre, this folkloric show offers a sampler of traditional singing and dancing. Buy tickets (including transport and dinner) through hotels or tour agents.

MOROCCO

Al Menara Reflets & Merveilles (☎ 044 439580; admission Dh250-400; ⌚ 9pm Wed-Mon) Each night the Jardin Ménara (p825) becomes the stage for a fantastical sound-and-light show, complete with 50 singers, dancers and acrobats. Tickets are available through travel agents or hotels.

Getting There & Away

AIR

Five kilometres southwest of town is **Ménara airport** (☎ 044 447865 flight information). **RAM** (☎ 044 425500; www.royalairmaroc.com; 197 Blvd Mohammed V, Guéliz; ⌚ 8.30am-noon & 2.30-7pm) has six flights daily to and from Casablanca (Dh935, 40 minutes). There are also international flights to Geneva, London, Madrid and Paris.

BUS

Just outside the city walls, the main **bus station** (☎ 044 433933; Bab Doukkala), where the majority of buses arrive and depart, is a 20-minute walk or roughly Dh5 to Dh10 taxi ride from Djemaa el-Fna.

Window No 10 is the **CTM** (☎ 044 434402) booking desk. CTM operates daily buses to Fès (Dh145, 8½ hours, one daily), Agadir (Dh75, four hours, nine daily), Casablanca (Dh70, fours hours, three daily) and Essaouira (Dh55, 3 hours, one daily).

You can also buy tickets for any of the above services at the **CTM Office** (☎ 044 448328; Blvd Mohammed Zerktouni, Guéliz). This is the arrival and departure point for international buses, including Paris (Dh800 to Dh1100, 48 hours, three weekly) and Madrid (Dh800 to Dh1100, 36 hours, three weekly).

The office of **Supratours** (☎ 044 435525; Ave Hassan II) is west of the train station. Services go to Rabat (Dh80, six hours, half-hourly) via Casablanca (Dh50, five hours), Tangier (Dh150, 11 hours, once daily) and Essaouira (Dh35, three hours, nine daily).

TRAIN

The **train station** (☎ 090 203040 information only; Ave Hassan II) lies on the western side of Guéliz. Catch a taxi or city bus (Nos 3, 8, 10 and 14; Dh3) into the centre.

There are quite a few trains to Rabat (Dh101, four hours, nine daily) via Casablanca (Dh76, three hours, nine daily); and Fès (Dh171, eight hours, eight daily) via Meknès (Dh154, seven hours, eight daily). Overnight trains to Tangier (Dh150-188) leave

once daily. A couchette requires a supplement of Dh90; book it two days in advance.

Getting Around

A petits taxi to Marrakesh from the airport (6km) should be no more than Dh60, but good luck convincing the driver. Alternatively, bus No 11 runs irregularly to Djemaa el-Fna.

The creamy-beige petits taxis around town cost between Dh5 and Dh10 per journey. They're all supposed to use their meters, but you may need to insist, especially coming from the train station or airport.

AROUND MARRAKESH

The highest mountain range in North Africa, the High Atlas runs diagonally across Morocco, from the Atlantic coast northeast of Agadir all the way to northern Algeria, a distance of almost 1000km. In Berber it's called Idraren Draren (Mountains of Mountains). There are several summits higher than 4000m and more than 400 above 3000m. The Toubkal region contains all the highest peaks, and is the most frequently visited area of the High Atlas. It's only two hours from Marrakesh and is easily accessible by public transport.

Although wild and harsh, the area has long been inhabited by the Atlas Berbers. Their flat-roofed, earthen villages cling tenaciously to the mountainsides, while irrigated terraced gardens and walnut groves flourish below. The entire area is crisscrossed by well-used mule trails – some of which once undoubtedly carried trade caravans and pilgrims between the Sahara and the northern plains.

There are now numerous foreign and Moroccan operators offering trekking tours in the High Atlas.

Atlas Sahara Trek (☎ 044 313901; www.atlas-sahara -trek.com; 6 Bis Rue Houdoud, Quartier Majorelle, Marrakesh) Experienced Bernard Fabry organises great trips into the High Atlas. Treks include a 12-day hike through the M'Goun Valley (Dh545 per person based on a group of eight).

Sahara Expeditions (☎ 044 427977; www.sahara expe.ma; cnr Ave el-Mouahidine & Rue Bani Marine, Marrakesh) This outfit is associated with the trekkers' haunt Hotel Ali in Marrakesh.

Nature Trekking Maroc (☎ 044 360149, 061 241643; www.maroctrekking.com; Imm Nakhil, 19 Rue Oum Rabiaa, Marrakesh) Very well organised treks offered by a team of professional mountain guides.

Menara Tours (☎ 044 446654; www.menara-tours.ma; 41 rue Yougoslavie, Marrakesh) is also recommended.

MOROCCO

FÈS

The oldest of the imperial cities, Fès is arguably the symbolic heart of Morocco. Founded shortly after the Arabs swept across North Africa and Spain, it became the country's religious and cultural centre.

The medina of Fès el-Bali (Old Fès) is one of the largest living medieval cities in the world. Its narrow winding alleys and covered bazaars are crammed with every conceivable sort of workshop, restaurant and market, as well as mosques, medersa (Qur'anic schools), dye pits and tanneries – a veritable assault on the senses. It can be totally bewildering, and the constant attention of unofficial guides, touts and shopkeepers does not help.

Fès is a veiled, self-contained city that doesn't easily bare its soul. With time, visitors can glimpse behind the anonymous walls and appreciate the rich culture and spirituality that is Fès.

Orientation

Fès is neatly divided into three parts: Fès el-Bali (the core of the medina) in the east; Fès el-Jdid (containing the *mellah*, or Jewish quarter, and Royal Palace) in the centre; and the Ville Nouvelle, the administrative area constructed by the French, to the southwest.

Information

INTERNET ACCESS

Cyber Club (Map p834; ☎ 055 626286; Rue Abdelkarim el-Ekattabi; per hr Dh10; ⏲ 9am-midnight)

London Cyber (Map p832; Ave de la Liberté; per hr Dh10; ⏲ 10am-10pm)

MEDICAL SERVICES

Clinique Ryad (☎ 055 960000; 2 Rue Benzakour, Place Hussein de Jordainie) South of the ville nouvelle.

Night Pharmacy (Map p834; ☎ 055 623493; Blvd Moulay Youssef; ⏲ 9pm-6am) Staffed by a doctor and pharmacist.

MONEY

The majority of banks (and ATMs) are in the Ville Nouvelle along Ave Hassan II and Blvd Mohammed V.

Société Générale (Ave des Français; ⏲ 8.45am-noon & 2.45-6pm Mon-Thur, 8.45-11am Fri, 8.45am-noon Sat) Immediately outside Bab Bou Jeloud, changes cash and travellers cheques.

POST

Main post office (Map p834; cnr Ave Hassan II & Blvd Mohammed V)

TOURIST INFORMATION

Syndicat d'Initiative (Map p834; ☎ 055 623460, fax 055 654370; Place Mohammed V; ⏲ 8.30am-noon & 2.30-6.30pm Mon-Thu, 8.30-11.30am & 3-6.30pm Fri, 8.30am-noon Sat)

Tourist office (Map p834; ☎ 055 623460, fax 055 654370; Place de la Résistance; ⏲ 8.30am-noon & 2.30-6.30pm Mon-Thu, 8.30-11.30am & 3-6.30pm Fri)

Sights

FÈS EL-BALI

Within the walls of the old medina lies an incredible maze of approximately 9400 twisting alleys, blind turns and hidden souqs. Navigation is confusing, but getting lost and found is a delightful way to explore the old city.

Take a peek into the **Kairaouine Mosque**, one of the largest mosques in Morocco. Founded between AD 859 and 862 for Tunisian refugees, it has one of the finest libraries in the Muslim world. Non-Muslims are forbidden to enter, but you can explore the **Medersa el-Attarine** (Map p832; admission Dh10; ⏲ 8.30am-1pm & 2.30-5pm), the associated Qur'anic school.

The unmistakeable odour of animal excrement and body parts wafts through the streets northeast of Place as-Seffarine. Fork left after about 50m and follow your nose. This is the leather district, the home of the infamous Fès **tanneries.**

Opened in 1998, the **Nejjarine Museum of Wooden Arts & Crafts** (Map p832; ☎ 055 740580; Place an-Nejjarine; admission Dh20; ⏲ 10am-5pm) is in a beautifully panelled and restored *funduq*, or caravanserai. Another excellent collection of traditional arts and crafts is housed in the **Dar Batha Museum** (Museum of Moroccan Arts & Crafts; Map p832; ☎ 055 634116; Place de l'Istiqlal; admission Dh10; ⏲ 8.30am-noon & 2.30-6pm Wed-Mon).

FÈS EL-JDID

In the 14th century, Fès el-Jdid became a refuge for Jews, thus creating a Jewish quarter. The quarter's southwest corner contains the **Jewish Cemetery & Habarim Synagogue** (Map p832; admission free, donations welcome; ⏲ 7am-7pm), where the sea of blindingly white tombs stretches down the hill. The gatekeeper can direct you to the nearby **Ibn Danan Synagogue** (Map p832; admission free, donations welcome), which was restored with the aid of Unesco in 1999.

BORJ NORD FORTRESS & MERENID TOMBS

For a spectacular view of Fès, walk up to the Borj Nord fortress, where all of Fès is

FÈS

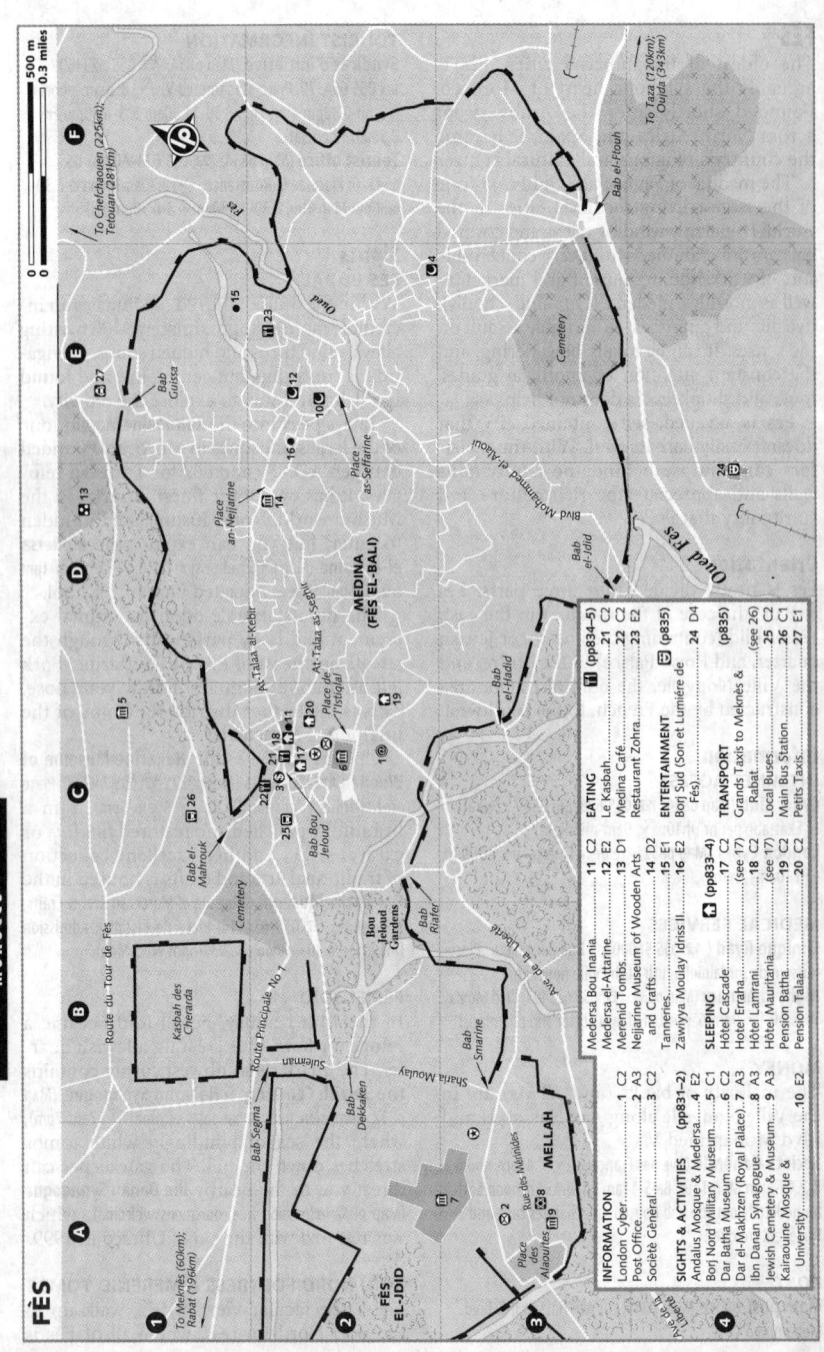

INFORMATION
London Cyber....................................1	C2
Post Office..2	A3
Société Général...............................3	C2

SIGHTS & ACTIVITIES (pp831–2)
Andalus Mosque & Medersa...........4	E2
Borj Nord Military Museum..............5	C1
Dar Batha Museum............................6	C2
Dar el-Makhzen (Royal Palace)........7	A3
Ibn Danan Synagogue......................8	A3
Jewish Cemetery & Museum.............9	A3
Kairaouine Mosque &	
University...................................10	E2
Medersa Bou Inania........................11	C2
Medersa el-Attarine........................12	E2
Merenid Tombs...............................13	D1
Nejjarine Museum of Wooden Arts	
and Crafts..................................14	D2
Tanneries..15	E1
Zawiyya Moulay Idriss II.................16	E2

SLEEPING (pp833–4)
Hôtel Cascade.................................17	C2
Hôtel Erraha.............................(see 17)	
Hôtel Lamrani................................18	C2
Hôtel Mauritania.....................(see 17)	
Pension Batha................................19	C2
Pension Talaa................................20	E2

EATING (pp834–5)
Le Kasbah......................................21	C2
Medina Café...................................22	E2
Restaurant Zohra...........................23	E2

ENTERTAINMENT (p835)
Borj Sud (Son et Lumière de	
Fès)..24	D4

TRANSPORT (p835)
Grands Taxis to Meknès &	
Rabat..................................(see 26)	
Local Buses....................................25	C2
Main Bus Station............................26	C1
Petits Taxis....................................27	E1

sprawled at your feet. The 16th-century Borj Nord houses a **military museum** (Map p832; ☎ 055 645241; admission Dh10; ☼ 8.30am-noon & 2.30-6.30pm Wed-Mon). The Merenid Tombs, mostly ruins, are dramatic against the city backdrop; sunrise and sunset are spectacular but don't come alone, the tombs, on the outskirts of town, can be desolate and dangerous.

Tours

Both tourist offices can make arrangements for an official guide (Dh250 per day), who will enable you to see and experience much more in the medina. The guides *do* know places to shop, but they will also point out incredible architecture and clandestine corners. Be sure to communicate clearly with your guide so he/she can tailor the tour to your needs.

Festivals & Events

Each summer the **Fès Festival of World Sacred Music** (☎ 055 740535, fax 055 740692; www.fesfestival .com) brings together music groups from all corners of the globe.

Sleeping
MEDINA

The most colourful places to stay are the cheapies clustered around Bab Bou Jeloud in Fès el-Bali. Be prepared for a fair amount of hassle when you arrive. Prices tend to increase in summer.

Pension Talaa (Map p832; ☎ 055 633359; pacohicham@ hotmail.com; 14 Talaa Seghira; r per person Dh75) This tiny place is the best deal in the medina. Sadly, it has only four, boxy rooms; but they are spotless, as are the shared toilets (Western) and showers (hot). The English-speaking manager is friendly and efficient.

Pension Batha (Map p832; ☎ 055 741150, fax 055 748827; 8 Sidi Lkhayat; s/d with breakfast Dh100/180) Not to be confused with its three-star neighbour by nearly the same name, this smaller pension offers more intimate but less luxurious accommodation.

Hôtel Lamrani (Map p832; ☎ 055 634411; Talaa Seghira; d/tr Dh150/200) The advantage of this place is its location – in the heart of the medina, but out of the heat of Bab Bou Jeloud.

Hôtel Cascade (Map p832; ☎ 055 638442; 26 Rue Serrajine; r per person Dh50, d Dh120) Ever the travellers' favourite, the Cascade is famous for its roof terraces with unbeatable views, though readers have complained of aggressive touts and even more aggressive cockroaches.

Other cheapies in the same area:

Hôtel Erraha (Map p832; ☎ 055 633226; Place Bou Jeloud; s/d Dh50/80, hot shower Dh10) This has cell-like rooms, but there is a nice roof terrace overlooking Bab Bou Jeloud.

Hôtel Mouritania (Map p832; ☎ 055 633518; 20 Rue Serrajine; r per person Dh70, hot shower Dh10) This place has boxy rooms around a central courtyard.

VILLE NOUVELLE

Budget options in the Ville Nouvelle are generally better value than their counterparts in the medina. The modern bathhouse, **Douche el-Kairouan** (Map p834; 84 Rue du Soudan; admission Dh7; ☼ 7.30am-8.30pm), next to the hotel of the same name, is for men only, but foreign women are also allowed to use it.

Youth Hostel (Map p834; ☎ 055 624085; 18 Rue Abdeslam Serghini; dm/tw HI members Dh45/55, dm/tw nonmembers Dh50/60; ☼ 8-10am, noon-3pm & 6-10pm) One of the best youth hostels in all of Morocco, with a central location.

Hôtel du Maghreb (Map p834; ☎ 055 621567; 25 Ave Mohammed es-Slaoui; s/d/tr Dh80/120/150) This friendly hotel has just one corridor of large, bright rooms with brass bedsteads and balconies.

Hôtel Royal (Map p834; ☎ 055 624656; 36 Rue du Soudan; s/d with shower Dh90/130, s/d with shower & toilet Dh110/140) A reliable choice convenient to the train station. Despite its age, it is well maintained and deservedly popular.

Hôtel Kairouan (Map p834; ☎ 055 623590; 84 Rue du Soudan; s/d Dh120/140) The welcome is warm, while spacious rooms have clean beds and hot showers. The downside is the smelly communal toilets.

Modern, comfortable three-star options, all equipped with telephone, TV and private bathrooms, include **Hôtel de la Paix** (Map p834; ☎ 055 625072; hoteldelapaix@iam.net.ma; 44 Ave Hassan II; s Dh250-289 d Dh290-351 t Dh360-438; ☼), **Hôtel Splendid** (Map p834; ☎ 055 622148; splendid@iam.net.ma; 9 Rue Abdelkarim el-Khattabi; s/d Dh280/340; ℗ ☼ ☼), and **Hôtel Olympic** (Map p834; ☎ 055 932682, fax 055 932665; cnr Blvd Mohammed V & Rue 3; s/d with breakfast Dh269/351).

Camping

Camping International (Map p834; ☎ 055 731439, fax 055 731554; per adult/tent/car Dh40/30/30; ☼) The newer and nicer of Fès' two camp sites is about 4km south of the centre on the Sefrou road. Take bus No 38 from Place Atlas.

Camping Diamant Vert (Map p834; ☎ 055 608369; per adult/tent/car Dh20/15/15; ☼) The second is at

MOROCCO

Aïn Chkef, 28km from the city centre off the Ifrane road. Bus No 17 from Place Florence in the Ville Nouvelle will get you close.

Eating

MEDINA

The snack stands just inside Bab Bou Jeloud are among the most popular places to eat in the medina, especially as they provide prime seats to watch the passing cavalcade.

Médina Café (Map p832; ☎ 055 633430; 6 Derb Mernissi Bab Bou Jeloud; set menus Dh95-105; ⓨ 8am-10pm) The tiny size is part of the charm at this new restaurant/café. It is outside the main medina gate, so has an air of serenity that other nearby places lack.

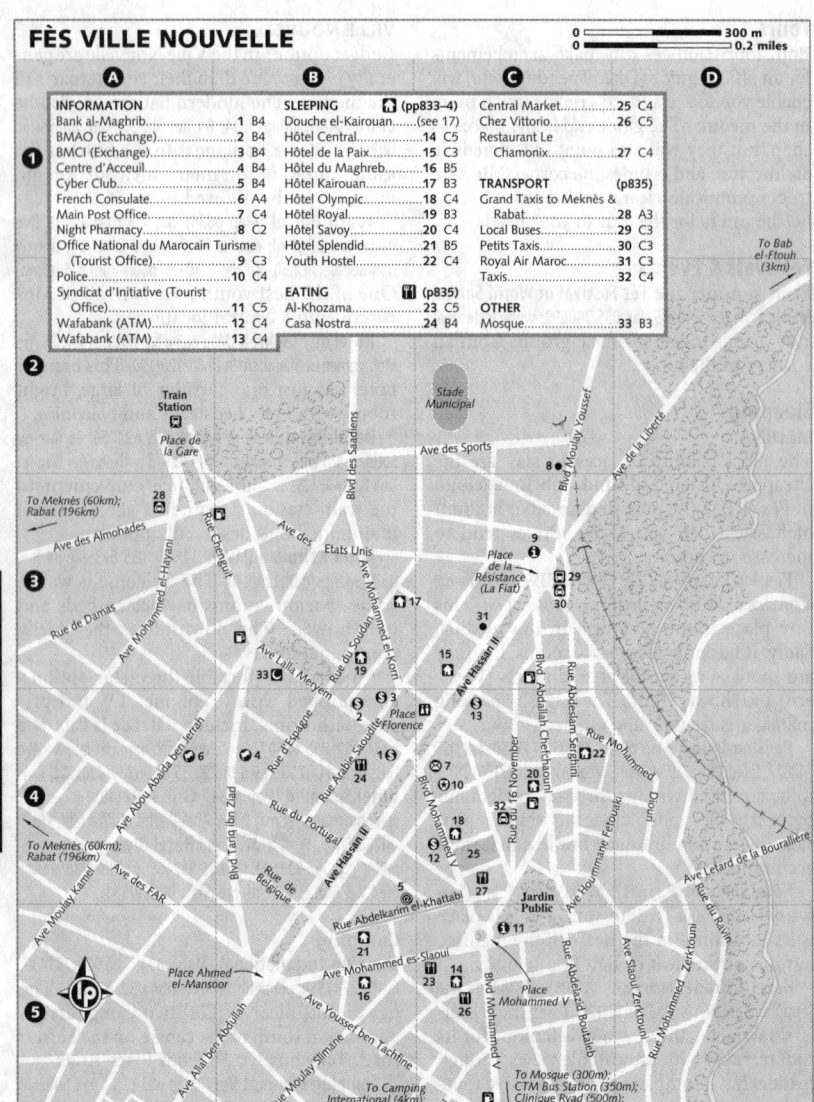

FÈS VILLE NOUVELLE

| | 0 ⸻ 300 m |
| | 0 ⸻ 0.2 miles |

INFORMATION
Bank al-Maghrib.....................1 B4
BMAO (Exchange)....................2 B4
BMCI (Exchange).....................3 B4
Centre d'Acceuil.....................4 B4
Cyber Club...........................5 B4
French Consulate....................6 A4
Main Post Office.....................7 C4
Night Pharmacy......................8 C2
Office National du Marocain Turisme
  (Tourist Office)......................9 C3
Police...............................10 C4
Syndicat d'Initiative (Tourist
  Office)..............................11 C5
Wafabank (ATM)....................12 C4
Wafabank (ATM)....................13 C4

SLEEPING 🛏 (pp833–4)
Douche el-Kairouan.............(see 17)
Hôtel Central.......................14 C5
Hôtel de la Paix....................15 C3
Hôtel du Maghreb..................16 B5
Hôtel Kairouan.....................17 B3
Hôtel Olympic......................18 C4
Hôtel Royal.........................19 B3
Hôtel Savoy........................20 C4
Hôtel Splendid......................21 B5
Youth Hostel........................22 C4

EATING 🍴 (p835)
Al-Khozama.........................23 C5
Casa Nostra........................24 B4

Central Market.....................25 C4
Chez Vittorio.......................26 C5
Restaurant Le
  Chamonix.........................27 C4

TRANSPORT (p835)
Grand Taxis to Meknès &
  Rabat.............................28 A3
Local Buses.........................29 C3
Petits Taxis........................30 C3
Royal Air Maroc....................31 C3
Taxis...............................32 C4

OTHER
Mosque............................33 B3

To Bab
el-Ftouh
(3km)

Train Station

Place de
la Gare

Stade Municipal

Ave des Sports

Blvd des Saadiens

Ave Moulay Youssef

Ave de la Liberté

To Meknès (60km);
Rabat (196km)

28

Ave des Almohades

Rue Chenguit

Ave des Etats Unis

Place
de la
Résistance
(La Fiat)

8

9

29

30

Rue de Damas

Ave Mohammed el-Hayani

Ave Mohammed el-Korri

17

31

15

Ave Hassan II

Blvd Abdallah Chefchaouni

Rue Mohammed Diouri

Ave Lalla Meryem

33

19

2

Place
Florence

13

22

Rue d'Espagne

Rue Arabie Saoudite

To Meknès (60km);
Rabat (196km)

6

4

1

24

7

10

32

Blvd du 16 November

Rue du Portugal

18

12

25

Blvd Mohammed V

Ave Abou Abaida ben Jerrah

Blvd Tariq Ibn Ziad

Rue de Belgique

5

27

Jardin
Public

Ave Letard de la Bouraillière

Ave Moulay Kamel

Ave des FAR

Rue Abdelkarim el-Khattabi

@

21

11

Rue du Ravin

Ave Slaoui Zerktouni

Place Ahmed
el-Mansoor

Ave Mohammed es-Slaoui

14

23

16

26

Place
Mohammed V

Blvd Mohammed V

Ave Abdelaziz Boutaleb

Rue Abdelaziz Zerktouni

Ave Moulay Slimane

Ave Youssef ben Tachfine

Ave Allal ben Abdullah

Rue Moulay Slimane

To Camping
International (4km);
Sefrou (28km)

To Mosque (300m);
CTM Bus Station (350m);
Clinique Ryad (500m);
Airport (14km)

Ave Hourmane Fetouaki

MOROCCO

Le Kasbah (Map p832; Rue Serrajine; mains Dh40, set menus Dh70) Head for the roof to get fantastic views of the surrounding medina.

Restaurant Zohra (Map p832; ☎ 055 637699; 3 Derb Ain Nass Blida; menus Dh70-90) Buried in the medina's backstreets north of the Kairaouine Mosque, this little place is known for its family atmosphere and home cooking. Phone ahead in the evening to make sure it's open.

VILLE NOUVELLE

Al-Khozama (Map p834; ☎ 063 374033; 23 Ave Mohammed es-Slaoui; sandwiches Dh15-20, set menus Dh60; ☺ 7am-11pm) The draw to this eaterie near Place Mohammed V is the indoor terrace – a comfortable, quiet place for women.

Restaurant Le Chamonix (Map p834; ☎ 055 626638; 5 Rue Moukhtar Soussi; set menus Dh52; ☺ 10am-10pm) Service is super friendly at this restaurant south of the central market. It's one of the few cheap places in this area with a large, welcoming seating area.

Casa Nostra (Map p834; ☎ 055 932841; 16 Rue Arabie Saoudite; mains around Dh80, pizza or pasta Dh30-65) This Spanish-Italian restaurant is much frequented by Fès' young, hip crowd. It is fun and upbeat, especially in the evenings.

Entertainment

Son et Lumière de Fès (Sound & Lights of Fes; Map p832; ☎ 055 763652; fax 055 763654; Borj Sud; admission Dh100; ☺ 9.30pm May-Aug; 7.15pm Mar-Apr & Sep-Nov) This laser show recounts 12 centuries of history in 45 minutes.

Getting There & Away

AIR

Fès airport (Map p834; ☎ 055 674712) is 15km south of the city at Saïss. **RAM** (Map p834; ☎ 055 625516; 54 Ave Hassan II) operates flights to Casablanca (Dh864 one-way, 45 minutes, daily) and flights to Paris (Dh5073, three hours) a few times a week.

BUS

The **CTM bus station** (☎ 055 732992) is near Place Atlas, but some buses depart from the main bus station. Buses go to Casablanca (Dh85, five hours, seven daily) via Rabat (Dh55, 3½ hours); to Meknès (Dh15, one hour, six daily); and to Marrakesh (Dh130, nine hours, twice daily). Heading north and east, there are buses for Tangier (Dh80, six hours, three daily); Tetouan (Dh70, five hours, twice daily); and Al-Hoceima (Dh82, six hours, one daily). International services to Spain and France also depart from the CTM bus station.

Non-CTM buses depart from the **main bus station** (Map p832; ☎ 055 636032) outside Bab el-Mahrouk and travel the same routes for slightly cheaper.

TRAIN

The **train station** (Map p832; ☎ 055 930333) is in the Ville Nouvelle, a 10-minute walk northwest of Place Florence. Trains depart every two hours to Casablanca (Dh97, 4¼ hours), via Rabat (Dh72, 3½ hours) and Meknès (Dh17, one hour). *Direct rapide* trains go to Marrakesh (Dh71, eight hours, five daily) and to Tangier (Dh96, five hours, one daily).

TAXI

Taxis for Meknès (Dh16, one hour) and Rabat (Dh55, three hours) leave from in front of the main bus station (outside Bab el-Mahrouk) and from near the train station.

Getting Around

There is a regular bus service (No 16) between the airport and the train station (Dh3, 25 minutes, every 30 minutes). Bus No 47 travels between the train station and Bab Bou Jeloud.

Red petits taxis are metered: expect to pay about Dh10 from the train station to Bab Bou Jeloud. Only grands taxis go out to the airport (Dh80).

MEKNÈS

From the winding, narrow streets of the medina to the grand buildings of the imperial city, Meknès reflects its heritage as the one-time centre of the Moroccan sultanate. Tour programmes may rank Meknès third behind Marrakesh and Fès because it is quieter and smaller; but it is also more laid-back and less hassle. And Morocco's history and its mystery are no less vibrant in this – the third imperial city.

Information

Cyber de Paris (Zankat Accra; per hr Dh6; ☺ 9-2am)
Main post office (Place de l'Istiqlal) The parcel office is around the corner on Rue Tetouan.
Quick Net (28 Ave Emir Abdelkader; per hr Dh8; ☺ 9am-11pm)
Tourist office (☎ 055 524426; fax 055 516046; Place de l'Istiqlal; ☺ 8.30am-noon & 2.30-6.30pm Mon-Thu, 8-11.30am & 3-6.30pm Fri)

MOROCCO

Sights

The heart of Meknès medina lies to the north of the main square, Place el-Hedim, with the Jewish quarter to the west. To the south, Moulay Ismail's imperial city opens up through one of the most impressive monumental gateways in all Morocco, **Bab el-Mansour.** Around to the right, you'll find the **Mausoleum of Moulay Ismail** (admission by donation; ☺ 8.30am-noon & 2-6pm Sat-Thu), the sultan who made Meknès his capital in the 17th century.

Overlooking Place el-Hedim on the north is a palace, built in 1882, that houses the **Dar Jamaï Museum** (☎ 055 530863; Place el-Hedim; admission Dh10; ☺ 9am-noon & 3-6.30pm Wed-Mon). Deeper in the medina, opposite the Grand Mosque, the **Medersa Bou Inania** (Rue Najjarine; admission Dh10; ☺ 9am-noon & 3-6pm), Qur'anic school, is typical of the exquisite interior design that distinguishes Merenid monuments.

Sleeping

Most of the budget accommodation is located in the Ville Nouvelle around Ave Mohammed V.

Hôtel Majestic (☎ 055 522035, fax 055 527427; 19 Ave Mohammed V; s/d Dh112/150, s/d with shower Dh150/180, s/d with bathroom Dh189/225) The best budget option is this 1930s hotel close to the train station.

Hôtel Excelsior (☎ 055 521900; 57 Ave des FAR; s/d/tr Dh65/90, s/d/tr with shower Dh124/147/170) Nobody can complain that this hotel does not have character, with its splashy floral fabrics and coloured bathroom fixtures. The place is clean – even the shared toilet – but some readers have complained of a seedy atmosphere.

Hôtel Toubkal (☎ 055 522218; 49 Ave Mohammed V; s/d/tr Dh70/120/200, hot shower Dh10). This is a friendly, busy place and the management is willing to negotiate during the low season.

Hôtel Maroc (☎ 055 530075; 7 Rue Rouamzine; s/d Dh60/120) This is the best of the ultra budget options clustered along Rue Rouamzine in the medina. It doesn't look much, but it's quiet, friendly and quite well maintained. Toilets are Asian-style and showers are hot.

Youth Hostel (☎ /fax 055 524698; dm with breakfast Dh45, d with breakfast per person Dh60, hot shower Dh5; ☺ 8am-10pm Sep-Jun, 8am-midnight Jul & Aug) The youth hostel is in a quiet residential area 1km northwest of the train station (Dh7 or so by petits taxi). Readers have not been thrilled with the service here, but the setting is pleasant and quiet.

Camping

Camping International d'Agdal (☎ 055 551828; per adult/tent/car/caravan Dh17/10/17/17, hot shower Dh7, electricity Dh15) The camp site, located southwest of the imperial city, is an attractive, shady spot with a bar, restaurant and café and reasonably clean facilities.

Eating

Meknès is famous for its traditional sweetmeats and you won't find a better choice than in the **covered market** on Place el-Hadim.

La Grotte (11 Rue de la Votte) This hideaway near the station is an attractive, quiet spot to wait for your train. It attracts people for the coffee or simple meals like tajine or couscous.

Restaurant Oumnia (☎ 055 533938; 8 Ain Fouki Rouamzine; set menus Dh65; ☺ 7am-10pm) This informal restaurant is inside a family home, just off the main drag of the Meknès medina. The Moroccan salon is warm and welcoming, with Mama Oumnia ready to dish up a delicious, homemade tajine of the day.

Pizzeria Le Four (☎ 055 520857; 1 Rue Atlas; pizzas Dh38-49, mains Dh65-85) The dark timber and whitewashed walls lend a suitably Italian atmosphere to this popular pizzeria.

Sandwich Rossignol (☎ 064 321652; Rue Dar Smen; sandwiches Dh10-20, mains Dh30; ☺ noon-midnight) Filling sandwiches and friendly chatter are the draw to this snackshop next to the Banque Populaire. It also whips up a mean tajine.

Mo Di Niro (☎ 055 517676; 14 Rue Antserapé; pizzas Dh30-70, burgers Dh15-20; ☺ noon-3pm & 5-10.30pm Tue-Sun; ✕) With exposed brick and low lighting, this is as trendy as it gets in Meknès. Decent Western-style fast food includes salads, pizzas, and burgers and chips.

Getting There & Away

BUS

Take Bus No 7 to the new **CTM station** (☎ 055 522585; Ave des FAR), 300m east of the junction with Ave Mohammed V. The main bus station lies outside Bab el-Khemis, west of the medina. Bus routes include Casablanca (Dh65, four hours, six daily), Rabat (D h35, 2½ hours, seven daily), Fès (Dh15, one hour, six daily), Tangier (Dh75, five hours, three daily) and Marrakesh (Dh140, eight hours, one daily).

TRAIN

From **El-Amir Abdelkader train station** (☎ 055 522763), trains go to Fès (2nd-class rapide Dh17, one hour, nine daily) and Casablanca

(Dh81, 3½ hours, eight daily) via Rabat (Dh56, 2¼ hours). There are services to Marrakesh (Dh154, seven hours, five daily) and Tangier (Dh80, four hours, one daily).

TAXI

The main grands taxis rank is a dirt lot beside the bus station, west of the medina. There are regular departures to Fès (Dh16), Rabat (Dh40) and Chefchaouen (Dh100). Grands taxis for Moulay Idriss (Dh7) leave from opposite the Institut Français.

AROUND MEKNÈS

In the midst of a fertile plain about 33km north of Meknès, **Volubilis** (Ouailili; admission Dh20, guided tour Dh120; ☺ 8am-sunset) is the largest and best-preserved Roman ruins in Morocco. One of the country's most important pilgrimage sites, **Moulay Idriss**, is only about 4.5km from Volubilis. The simplest and quickest way to get here from Meknès is to hire a shared taxi for the return trip. A half-day outing will cost around Dh300.

MOROCCO DIRECTORY

ACCOMMODATION

Camping facilities are available around or near most Moroccan cities, while youth hostels (*auberges de jeunesses*) operate in Casablanca, Chefchaouen, Fès, Marrakesh, Meknès, Rabat and Tangier. Hostels are usually safer and more comfortable than the unclassified medina hotels that rival them for price. The prices listed in this chapter are for high season.

ACTIVITIES
Surfing & Windsurfing

With thousands of kilometres of Atlantic coastline, Morocco has some great surfing spots. Highlights are the beaches in Essaouira (see p823) for windsurfing and around Rabat (see p821) for surfing.

Trekking

Morocco's many mountain ranges offer a wide array of trekking opportunities. Most travellers head straight for the highest peaks of the High Atlas – treks can be organised from Marrakesh (p830) or from the nearby village of Imlil. Chefchaouen is the place to start treks through the Rif Mountains. Spring and autumn are the best times for trekking.

BUSINESS HOURS

Information (☎ 8.30am-12.30pm & 2.30-6.30pm Mon-Thu) Often closed longer at midday on Friday
Eating (☎ noon-3pm & 7-11pm daily
Drinking Cafés (☎ 7am-11pm)
Shopping (☎ 9am-12.30pm & 2.30-8pm Mon-Sat) Often closed longer at midday on Friday

DANGERS & ANNOYANCES

Morocco's era as a hippy paradise is long past. Plenty of fine kif is grown in the Rif Mountains, but drug busts are common and Morocco is not a good place to investigate prison conditions.

A few years ago the brigade touristique (tourist police) was set up in the principal tourist centres to clamp down on Morocco's notorious *faux guides* (false guides) and hustlers. Anyone convicted of operating as an unofficial guide faces jailtime or a huge fine or both. This has reduced – but not eliminated – the problem of the faux guides. Plenty of these touts still hang around the entrances to medinas and outside train stations, especially at the Tangier port and near Bab Bou Jeloud in Fès. Most would-be guides will go away if you ignore them, but some can be persistent and even unpleasant. Stay calm and polite, and go about your business. If you end up with one of these people remember their main interest is the commission gained from certain hotels or on articles sold to you in the souqs.

EMBASSIES & CONSULATES
Moroccan Embassies

Australia (☎ 02-9922 4999; Suite 2, 11 West St, North Sydney, NSW 2060)
Canada (☎ 613-236 7391; 38 Range Rd, Ottawa, Ont K1N 8J4)
France (☎ 01 45 20 69 35; affgeneral@amb-maroc.fr; 5 Rue Le Tasse, 75016 Paris)
Germany (☎ 030-206 1240; Niederwallstr 39, 1011 Berlin)
Netherlands (☎ 070-346 9617; Oranjestraat 9, 2514 JB, Den Haag)
Spain (☎ 91 563 1090; www.maec.gov.ma/madrid in Spanish; Calle Serrano 179, 28002 Madrid)
UK (☎ 020-7581 5001; mail@sifamaldn.org; 49 Queen's Gate Gardens, London SW7 5NE)
USA (☎ 202-462 7979; embassy@embassyofmorocco.us; 1601 21st St NW, Washington, DC 20009)

Embassies & Consulates in Morocco

Unless otherwise noted, most embassies are open Monday to Friday, from 9am until noon.

MOROCCO

Australia The Australian embassy in Paris has full consular responsibility for Morocco. Consular services to Australian citizens in Morocco are provided by the Canadian embassy.

Canada (☎ 037 687400, fax 037 687430; 13 Rue Jaafar as-Sadiq, Agdal, Rabat; ◷ 8am-noon & 1.30-5.30pm Mon-Thu, 8am-1.30pm Fri)

France (☎ 037 689700, www.ambafrance-ma.org in French; 3 Rue Sahnoun, Agdal, Rabat); consulate-general (☎ 037 268181; Rue Alla Ben Abdallah, Rabat; ◷ for visa applications 8.30-11.30am and for pick-ups 1.30-3pm Mon-Fri). Consulates also in Agadir, Casablanca, Tangier, Marrakesh and Fès.

Germany (☎ 037 709662; www.amballemagne-rabat .ma in French & German; 7 Rue Madnine, Rabat; ◷ 9am-noon Mon-Fri)

New Zealand The closest embassy is in Madrid, Spain. The UK embassy provides consular support in Morocco.

Netherlands (☎ 037 733512; nlgovrab@mtds.com; 40 Rue de Tunis, Rabat); consulate in Casablanca (☎ 022 221820; 26 Rue Nationale)

Spain (☎ 037 268080, fax 037 707387; 3-5 Rue Madnine, Rabat); consulate in Agadir (☎ 048 845710, fax 048 845643; 49 Rue ibn Batouta); consulate in Casablanca (☎ 022 220752, fax 022 205049; 31 Rue d'Alger); consulate in Tangier (☎ 039 937000, fax 039 932770; 85 Ave Président Habib Bourghiba); consulate in Tetouan (☎ 039 703984, fax 039 704485; Place Moulay al-Mehdi)

UK (☎ 037 729696; www.britain.org.ma; 17 Blvd de la Tour Hassan, Rabat; ◷ 8am-4.30pm Mon-Thurs & 8am-1pm Fri, visa applications 8am-noon Mon-Fri). Staff will help citizens of the Republic of Ireland and some Commonwealth countries without representation in Morocco. consulate-general in Casablanca (☎ 022 364355; british.consulate@casanet.net.ma; 3rd fl, 43 Blvd d'Anfa, Casablanca); consulate in Tangier (☎ 039 941557; uktanger@mtds.com;Trafalgar House, 9 Rue Amerique du Sud, Tangier)

USA (☎ 037 762265; http://rabat.usembassy.gov; 2 Ave de Marrakesh, Rabat; ◷ 8.30am-12.30pm & 2.30-6.30pm Mon-Fri) Consulate in Casablanca (☎ 022 264550, fax 022 204127; 8 Blvd Moulay Youssef; ◷ 8am-6pm Mon-Fri)

FESTIVALS & EVENTS

Religious festivals are of more significance to Moroccans but local *moussems* (saints days) are held all over the country throughout the year and some draw big crowds.

National Folklore Festival (www.maghrebarts .ma/festivals) Held in Marrakesh in May/June.

Gnawa and World Music Festival Held in Essaouira in June (see p823).

Festival of World Sacred Music (www.fesfestival.com) Held in Fès in June/July (see p833).

International Cultural Festival Held in Asilah in July/August.

HOLIDAYS

All banks, post offices and most shops are shut on the main public holidays, including:

New Year's Day 1 January
Independence Manifesto 11 January
Labour Day 1 May
Feast of the Throne 30 July
Allegiance of Wadi-Eddahab 14 August
Anniversary of the King's and People's Revolution 20 August
Anniversary of the Green March 6 November
Independence Day 18 November

In addition to secular holidays there are many national and local Islamic holidays and festivals, all tied to the lunar calendar. The most important include:

Aïd al-Fitr Held at the end of the month-long Ramadan fast, which is fairly strictly observed by most Muslims. The festivities generally last four or five days, during which just about everything grinds to a halt.

Aïd al-Adha Marks the end of the Islamic year. Again, most things shut down for four or five days.

Mawlid an-Nabi (Mouloud) Celebrates the birthday of the Prophet Mohammed.

MONEY

The Moroccan currency is the dirham (Dh), which is divided into 100 centimes. There's not much of a black market and little reason to use it. The Spanish enclaves of Ceuta and Melilla now use the euro.

ATMs *(guichets automatiques)* are now a common sight and many accept Visa, MasterCard, Electron, Cirrus, Maestro and Inter-Bank systems. Major credit cards are widely accepted in the main tourist centres, although their use often attracts a surcharge of around 5% from Moroccan businesses. American Express (AmEx), Visa and Thomas Cook travellers cheques are also widely accepted for exchange by banks. Australian, Canadian and New Zealand dollars are not quoted in banks and are not usually accepted.

POST

Post offices are distinguished by the 'PTT' sign or the 'La Poste' logo. You can sometimes buy stamps at *tabacs*, the small tobacco and newspaper kiosks you see scattered about the main city centres.

The postal system is fairly reliable, but not terribly fast. It takes about a week for letters to get to their European destinations, and two weeks or so to get to Australia and

North America. Sending post from Rabat or Casablanca is quicker.

Postal Rates

A postcard to Europe costs between Dh6 and Dh6.50, Dh7.50 to North America and Dh8.50 to Australia. A 1kg parcel costs Dh102 to Europe, Dh137 to North America and Dh177 to Australia.

The parcel office, indicated by the sign 'colis postaux', is generally in a separate part of the post office building. Take your parcel unwrapped for customs inspection. Boxes are sometimes available for purchase at the parcel office.

TELEPHONE

A few cities and towns still have public phone offices, often next to the post office, but more common are privately run *téléboutiques*, which can be found in every town and village on almost every corner.

Mobile Phones

Morocco has two GSM mobile (cell) phone networks, Méditel and Maroc Telecom, which now cover 85% of the population (compared to land lines which only 6% of the population has access to). Moroccan mobile numbers start with the codes ☎ 061 to ☎ 068.

Phone Codes

All domestic phone calls in Morocco require a nine-digit number, which includes the three-digit area code (or GSM code). When calling overseas from Morocco, first dial the international access code ☎ 00. To call Morocco from overseas, Morocco's country code is ☎ 212.

TOILETS

Outside the major cities, public toilets are rare and you will usually need to bring your own paper (*papier hygiénique*), a tip for the attendant (Dh2 to Dh3), stout-soled shoes and very often a nose clip. Toilets are mostly of the Asian-style 'squat' variety (referred to as 'Turkish toilets') with a tap, hose or container of water for sluicing.

TOURIST INFORMATION
Local Tourist Offices

The national tourism body, **Office National Marocain du Tourisme** (ONMT; www.visitmorocco .com), has offices in the major cities. Regional

offices, called Syndicat d'Initiative are to be found in smaller towns. The majority of tourist offices, national and regional, offer only the standard ONMT brochures and the simplest of tourist maps.

Tourist Offices Abroad

Australia (☎ 02-922 4999, fax 9923 1053; c/o Moroccan Consulate; 11 West St, North Sydney, NSW 2060)
Canada (☎ 514-842 8111; onmt@qc.aira.com; Place Montréal Trust, 1800 Rue MacGill, Suite 2450, Montreal, Quebec H3A 3J6)
France (☎ 01 42 60 63 50; tourisme.marocain@ wanadoo.fr; 161 Rue Saint Honoré, Place du Théâtre Français, 75001 Paris)
Germany (☎ 0211-370551; marokkofva@aol.com; 59 Graf Adolf Strasse 4000, Düsseldorf)
Spain (☎ 91-542 7431; informacion@turismomarruecos .com; Calle Ventura Rodriguez No 24, 1 izq 28008 Madrid)
UK (☎ 020-7437 0073, fax 7734 8172; 205 Regent St, London W1R 7DE)
USA (☎ 212-557 2520; mntonyonmt@aol.com; Suite 1201, 20 East 46th St, New York, NY 10017); Florida (☎ 407-827 5337; inanmrini@aol.com; PO Box 22663, Lake Buena Vista, Orlando, Florida 32830)

VISAS

Most visitors to Morocco do not require visas and are allowed to remain in the country for 90 days on entry. Exceptions to this include nationals of Israel, South Africa and Zimbabwe. Moroccan embassies have been known to insist that you get a visa from your country of origin. Should the standard 90-day stay be insufficient, it is possible to apply at the nearest police headquarters (Préfecture de Police). The Spanish enclaves Ceuta and Melilla have the same visa requirements as mainland Spain.

WOMEN TRAVELLERS

A certain level of sexual harassment is the norm in Morocco. It comes in the form of non-stop greetings, leering and other unwanted attention, but it is rarely dangerous. It is best to avoid overreacting and to ignore this attention. In the case where a would-be suitor is particularly persistent, threatening to go to the police or the brigade touristique is amazingly effective. Women will save themselves a great deal of grief by avoiding eye contact, dressing modestly and refraining from walking around alone at night. It is generally necessary to go to the brigade touristique office if you wish to file a complaint.

MOROCCO

The Netherlands

HIGHLIGHTS

- **Amsterdam** Hash, hedonism and culture; you know the score (p845)
- **Rotterdam** Kooky architecture, crackling urban street life and a nightlife that is totally unique (p857)
- **Maastricht** At the gateway to Belgium and Germany, with stylish (yet accessible) bars, clubs and pubs (p862)
- **Best journey** Catching a train to Den Helder, bus to ferry, then sailing to the lush island of Texel (p861)
- **Off-the-beaten track** Do as the Dutch do: get knee-deep in mud with a spot of *wadlopen*, or mud-flat walking (p860)

FAST FACTS

- **Area** 41,526 sq km
- **ATMs** Widespread
- **Budget** €30-60 per day
- **Capital** Amsterdam
- **Country Code** ☎ 31
- **Famous for** Extraordinary paintings, volatile footballers, cheese, liberal attitudes
- **Head of State** Queen Beatrix; Prime Minister Jan Peter Balkenende
- **Languages** Dutch, Frisian
- **Money** Euro (A$1 = €0.58, CA$1 = €0.64, ¥100 = €0.73, NZ$1 = €0.54, £ = €1.45, US$ = €0.81)
- **Population** 16.2 million
- **Phrases** *Hallo* (hello), *dag* (goodbye), *bedankt* (thanks), *sorry/excuses* (sorry)

- **Time** GMT/UTC +1
- **Visas** None required for passport holders of Australia, Canada, Israel, Japan, South Korea, New Zealand, Singapore, USA and most of Europe.

TRAVEL HINTS

- If you hire a bike, always lock it (80,000 bicycles are stolen here annually).
- Consider buying a Voordeel-Urenkaart pass (p1255) for heavily discounted train travel, up to 65% cheaper in some cases.
- Stay away from canal edges if you've 'had a few'.

ROAMING NETHERLANDS

Try the Randstad belt – including Amsterdam, Den Haag, Delft and Rotterdam – for a diverse slice of Dutch life.

840

THE NETHERLANDS

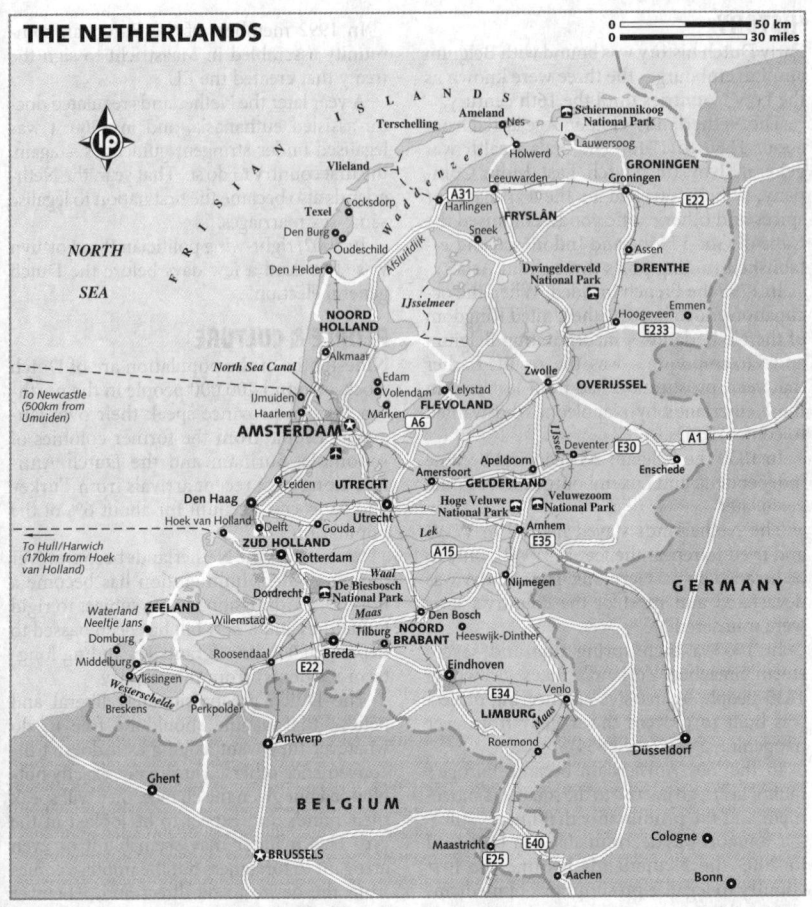

THE NETHERLANDS

'God created the world but the Dutch created the Netherlands' – it's an old saying but it can still tell you a lot about this country. It's a metaphor for the uniqueness of the culture, but it's also literal: the Dutch reclaimed much of their land from the sea, forging one of the most distinctive of all European states.

Amsterdam hogs the headlines, but don't let it be your predominant focus. Leiden, Haarlem and Delft are well-preserved historical cities. Classy Maastricht is a European interzone, hemmed in by Germany and Belgium. Rotterdam, which was heavily bombed during WWII, has rebuilt itself with inimitable architecture and a gutsy attitude. Groningen swarms with university students and a spirited lifestyle, while Den Haag is home to the royals, the government and classy museums. The northern islands boast an exclusive language and lifestyle.

The Netherlands isn't the most budget-conscious option, but there's still an immense concentration of sidewalk cafés and pubs everywhere, where you can nurse a coffee or beer (which is cheap and bountiful) and watch the world. Best of all, transport is efficient and well priced (allowing you to hop from city to city with ease), the nightlife is pumping and the Dutch are most hospitable.

THE NETHERLANDS

HISTORY

Early Dutch history was bound with Belgium and Luxembourg – the three were known as the Low Countries until the 16th century.

The Netherlands' Golden Age lasted from about 1580 to 1740. The era's wealth was generated by the Dutch East India Company, which travelled to the Far East for spices and other exotic goods, colonised the Cape of Good Hope and Indonesia, and established trading posts throughout Asia.

In 1795 the French invaded. When the occupation ended in 1815, the United Kingdom of the Netherlands – incorporating Belgium and Luxembourg – was the result. Earlier that year, prostitution had been legalised in the Netherlands by Napoleon, who wanted to control STDs.

In 1830 the Belgians rebelled and became independent, and Luxembourg followed nine years later.

The Netherlands stayed neutral in WWI and tried to repeat the feat in WWII, only to be invaded by the Germans. The country was devastated and most of the country's Jews were murdered.

In 1953 a high spring tide and severe storm breached Zeeland's dikes, drowning 1835 people. A massive engineering project was built to prevent the tragedy from ever happening again (see p854).

In the '60s Amsterdam became Europe's radical heart, giving rise to the squatter's movement and the promiscuity that lingers still.

Cannabis was decriminalised in 1976, and in 2003 the Netherlands became the first country to legalise prescriptions of medicinal cannabis.

In 1992 members of the European community assembled in Maastricht to sign the treaty that created the EU.

A year later the Netherlands regulated doctor-assisted euthanasia, and in 2000 it was legalised under stringent guidelines – again, the first country to do so. That year, the Netherlands also became the first nation to legalise same-sex marriages.

In 2002, right-wing politician Pim Fortuyn was shot dead a few days before the Dutch general election.

PEOPLE & CULTURE

Nine-tenths of the population are of Dutch stock. Around 400,000 people in the northern Fryslân province speak their own language. People from the former colonies of Indonesia, Surinam and the Dutch Antilles, along with recent arrivals from Turkey and Morocco, account for about 6% of the population.

Recently, as the Netherlands becomes ever more crowded, immigration has become a hot topic. Admission is now subject to rigid guidelines and a new bill has been passed to deport 26,000 immigrants (including long-term residents) from the country.

The Dutch are passionately liberal and believe that people should be free to do whatever they want as long as it doesn't inconvenience others. They're not exactly hot-blooded but given the chance, they will speak their minds and expect to be looked in the eye. This manner may seem blunt or even arrogant to foreigners but the impulse comes from the desire to be direct and, wherever possible, honest.

READING UP

Diary of Anne Frank by Anne Frank is a moving account of a Jewish girl's thoughts while hiding from the occupying Germans. In recent years Frank's words have inspired an entire subculture that re-examines and debates her life and work.

The classic 1972 novel, *The Happy Hooker* by Xaviera Hollander, based on a true story, is an unapologetic, upbeat look at the world of a Dutch sex worker.

The Two Hearts of Kwasi Boachi by Arthur Japin, outlines the true story of two West African princes sent to study in Holland in the 1830s, where they excel but fail to fit in.

Amsterdam: A Traveler's Literary Companion, edited by Manfred Wolf, contains 20 stories arranged by neighbourhood from Amsterdam writers including Harry Mulisch, Cees Nooteboom, Marga Minco and Bas Heijne.

The Rider by Tim Krabbé is about a 150km cycling race, with the four major characters overcoming personal demons to get to the end. Krabbé, Dutch master of the macabre, instils this bare bones outline with his unmistakable gallows humour and psychological precision.

INVENTING WORLDS

Many people are surprised to learn that the reality-TV franchise *Big Brother* is a Dutch invention, when it seems quintessentially American. But if you delve into the undercurrents of the Dutch social order, the concept of peering into the lives of a group of strangers makes sense. At only 41,526 sq km, the Netherlands is Europe's most densely populated country, and while this adds immeasurably to its vibrancy, it can often seem like your neighbour is looking right over your shoulder. Maybe that's why many Dutch leave their curtains open at night for all to see in: in a nation of 16.2 million inhabitants, with space at a premium, there's nowhere to hide. No doubt, the admirable Dutch trait of tolerance stems from this fact, too: when you're standing cheek-by-jowl, 'love thy neighbour' is a sensible motto.

Perhaps because their country is so small, and therefore so familiar, the Dutch find it irresistible to recreate it – Big Brother, with its contestants from different walks of life, can certainly be seen as a miniaturised cross-section of Dutch society (the 'mini-Netherlands', Madurodam, is another example; see p854). But coming from a nation that recovered much of its land from the sea, none of this should surprise: the Dutch were inventing worlds many centuries ago.

ARTS

The Netherlands' most famous artistic legacy is in the visual arts: the country has spawned a realm of celebrated painters including Bosch, Rembrandt, Vermeer and Van Gogh.

These days the Dutch are world leaders in modern dance and the country takes great pride in its world-class museums; many orchestras are based in cities throughout the Netherlands. Their film industry is humble, though, producing about 20 feature films annually. Even so, the Dutch have won four Best Foreign Language Film Academy Awards – the third-best tally in Oscar history.

ENVIRONMENT

Acid, nitrate and phosphate levels in the Dutch biosphere are Europe's highest. Water in the great European rivers Rijn (Rhine), Maas and Schelde (Scheldt) distribute pollutants through the Netherlands and into the North Sea, while the coastal situation of low-lying lands means that soil salination is a persistent problem.

In the late 20th century, Dutch awareness of the environment grew by leaps and bounds. Citizens now sort their rubbish, support pro-bicycle schemes and protest over projects of potential detriment. Congestion has been eased by cutting city parking spaces and erecting speed bumps. Country roads tend to favour bike lanes at the cost of cars.

Billions spent on sewage treatment means that Amsterdam's canals are now fairly clean, and agriculture and industry have been presented with mandatory goals to reduce run-off and pollution.

TRANSPORT

GETTING THERE & AWAY

Air

Schiphol Airport (www.schiphol.nl in Dutch) is the Netherlands' main international airport. **Rotterdam Airport** (www.rotterdam-airport.nl) is smaller. **Eindhoven** (www.eindhovenairport.nl), **Groningen** (www.gae.nl in Dutch) and **Maastricht** (www.maastricht airport.nl) act as feeder airports to Schiphol.

DEPARTURE TAX

Departure tax is included in the price of your airline ticket.

Boat

Stenaline (☎ 08705-70 70 70; www.stenaline.com) sails between the UK and the Netherlands. Train-boat-train combos are cheaper but take two to three hours longer. There are return fares from London to Amsterdam and train links go via Harwich in the UK and Hoek van Holland (eight hours).

Bus

The most extensive European bus network is maintained by **Eurolines** (☎ 020 560 87 88; www.eurolines.com). It offers a range of passes with prices that vary by time of year.

Busabout (☎ +44-20-7950 1661; www.busabout .com) is a UK-based budget alternative to Eurolines. It runs coaches on circuits in Continental Europe including one through Amsterdam; a two-week pass costs €359/329 (over/under 26); passes are available for three weeks to three months. Services to/from Amsterdam run from April to October.

Gullivers Reisen (☎ +49-30-31 10 21 10; www.gul livers.de in German) links Berlin to Amsterdam (€49/89 for single/round-trip, nine hours, once daily).

Car & Motorcycle

You'll need the vehicle's registration papers, third-party insurance and an international drivers' permit (if you're from outside the EU) in addition to your domestic licence. The ANWB (see p1251) provides a wide range of information and services if you can show a letter of introduction from your own automobile association.

Train

The Netherlands has good train links to Germany, Belgium and France. All Eurail, Inter-Rail, Europass and Flexipass tickets are valid on the Dutch national train service, **Nederlandse Spoorwegen** (Netherlands Railway, NS; international inquiries ☎ 0900-9296; www.ns.nl).

Major Dutch train stations have international ticket offices and in peak periods it's wise to reserve seats in advance. You can buy tickets on local trains to Belgium and Germany at the normal ticket counters.

GETTING AROUND
Bicycle

The Netherlands has 20,000km of cycling paths and the ANWB (p1251) publishes cycling maps for each province. Tourist offices have numerous routes and suggestions.

More than 100 train stations throughout the country have bicycle facilities for rental, protected parking, repair and sales. To hire, you'll need to show your passport, and/or leave an imprint of your credit card or a deposit (€25 to €100). Private operators charge €5 to €7 per day, and €25 to €30 per week. Train station hire shops may be slightly cheaper.

Boat

Ferries connect the mainland with the Frisian Islands and Texel and are operated by the following companies:

Rederij Doeksen (www.rederij-doeksen.nl in Dutch)
Wagenborg (www.wpd.nl)

See p861 for Texel information.

Other ferries span the Westerschelde in the south of Zeeland, providing links to

---

> **EMERGENCY NUMBERS**
>
> ■ Police, fire, ambulance (☎ 112)

Belgium and the small region of the Netherlands south of Westerschelde. These are popular with people using the Zeebrugge ferry terminal and run frequently year-round. There is also a frequent ferry service on the IJsselmeer linking Enkhuizen with Stavoren and Urk. You'll also find a few small river ferries providing crossings for remote stretches of the IJssel and other rivers.

Bus

Buses are used for regional transport rather than for long distances. Buses and trams operate in most cities, and Amsterdam and Rotterdam also have metro networks.

Purchase a *strippenkaart* (strip card), valid throughout the country, and stamp off strips depending on how many zones you plan to cross. In the central areas of cities and towns, you usually will only need to stamp two strips – the minimum fee.

Reservations aren't possible on either regional or municipal lines, most of which run quite frequently.

Car & Motorcycle

Petrol and car hire tends to be expensive. Contact the **ANWB** (Royal Dutch Touring Association; ☎ 070-314 71 47; www.anwb.nl in Dutch; Wassenaarseweg 220, Den Haag). You'll need to show a valid driving licence when hiring a car in the Netherlands. Visitors from outside the EU should also consider an international driving permit (IDP). Car rental firms will rarely ask for one but the police might if they pull you up.

Hitching

Lonely Planet does not recommend hitching, but should you decide to try it, expect a very long wait – hitching is not common in the Netherlands.

Train

Trains are frequent and serve domestic destinations at regular intervals. Contact **Nederlandse Spoorwegen** (Netherlands Railways, NS; national inquiries ☎ 0900-9292; www.ns.nl). Tickets can be bought at the window or ticketing machines. Buying a ticket on board means

TOP FIVE NETHERLANDS

- **Festival** The North Sea Jazz Festival in summer (p1235)

- **Walk** Take in some of Europe's most beautiful architecture as you get lost among the concentric canals of Amsterdam's old town (see below)

- **Bars/Clubs** It's hard to pick just one: follow your nose in Amsterdam (pp850-1) for a rocking good time

- **Impressive sight** Maastricht (p862): spread out on both sides of the river Maas, with wide cobblestone streets, it has an airiness and spaciousness unique to the compact Netherlands

- **Classic Tour** Island-hopping from Texel to the Frisian chain (p861)

you'll pay almost double the normal fare, and there's an additional charge when buying tickets at windows: €0.50 for one ticket, €1 for two or more.

If you plan to travel around the country, consider investing €49 in a Voordeel-Urenkaart pass, valid for one year, which gives 40% discount on train travel weekdays after 9am, as well as weekends, public holidays and in July and August. The discount applies to up to three people travelling with you on the same trip and the card also gives access to evening returns valid from 6pm (except Fridays) that are up to 65% cheaper than normal returns.

AMSTERDAM

☎ 020 / pop 731,000

Amsterdam has glowed since the Golden Age, when it led the vanguard of European art and trade. Centuries later, in the 1960s, it again led the way – this time in the principles of tolerance, with broad-minded views on drugs and same-sex relationships. Amsterdam was known as Europe's 'Magic Centre', the heart of a utopian dream where people believed anything could happen. Although the days of excess have been somewhat neutered, much of that famous swagger is still evident (and in some cases, institutionalised and parodied, like in the Red Light district).

Amsterdam is perfect for travellers, with enough sensory delights to keep even the shortest attention spans occupied: take your pick from handsome 17th-century architecture, canals, galleries, museums – and notorious sleaze. Away from that, the endless cafés and bars provide welcoming havens from the rampant crowds. Thrillingly, Amsterdam is compact and user-friendly – walk or ride a bike around the canal grid and bask in the many worlds-within-worlds that make this city so addictive.

ORIENTATION

Amsterdam's old town is so compact you'll be able to get to all the major sights on foot or by bike. Centraal Station is the axis, from where the streets radiate outward across a network of *grachten* (concentric canals).

Dam Square is Amsterdam's heart, five minutes' walk down Damrak from Centraal Station. Leidseplein is the hub of Amsterdam nightlife, and Nieuwmarkt is a vast cobblestone square with open-air markets and popular pubs. The Red Light District is a law unto itself.

Lush 17th-century homes occupy the western canals Prinsengracht, Keizersgracht and Herengracht. The Jordaan is filled with quirky shops, bohemian bars and art galleries. Outside the canal belt is ethnic-influenced De Pijp; posh and residential Oud Zuid, east of the Damrak-Rokin axis; and Nieuw Zuid, to the west of that axis, with its 20th-century housing projects. The Eastern Docklands is a showcase of modern Dutch architecture.

GETTING INTO TOWN

A taxi into Amsterdam from Schiphol airport takes around 45 minutes and costs about €40. Trains to Amsterdam Centraal Station leave every 15 minutes, take 15 to 20 minutes and cost €3.10/5.60 per single/return.

INFORMATION
Discount Card

The Amsterdam Pass (1/2/3 days €26/36/46; available from tourist offices and some hotels) contains 32 vouchers for free public transport, free entry to most museums and 25% discount on some attractions and restaurants (see p1235 for country-wide passes).

THE NETHERLANDS

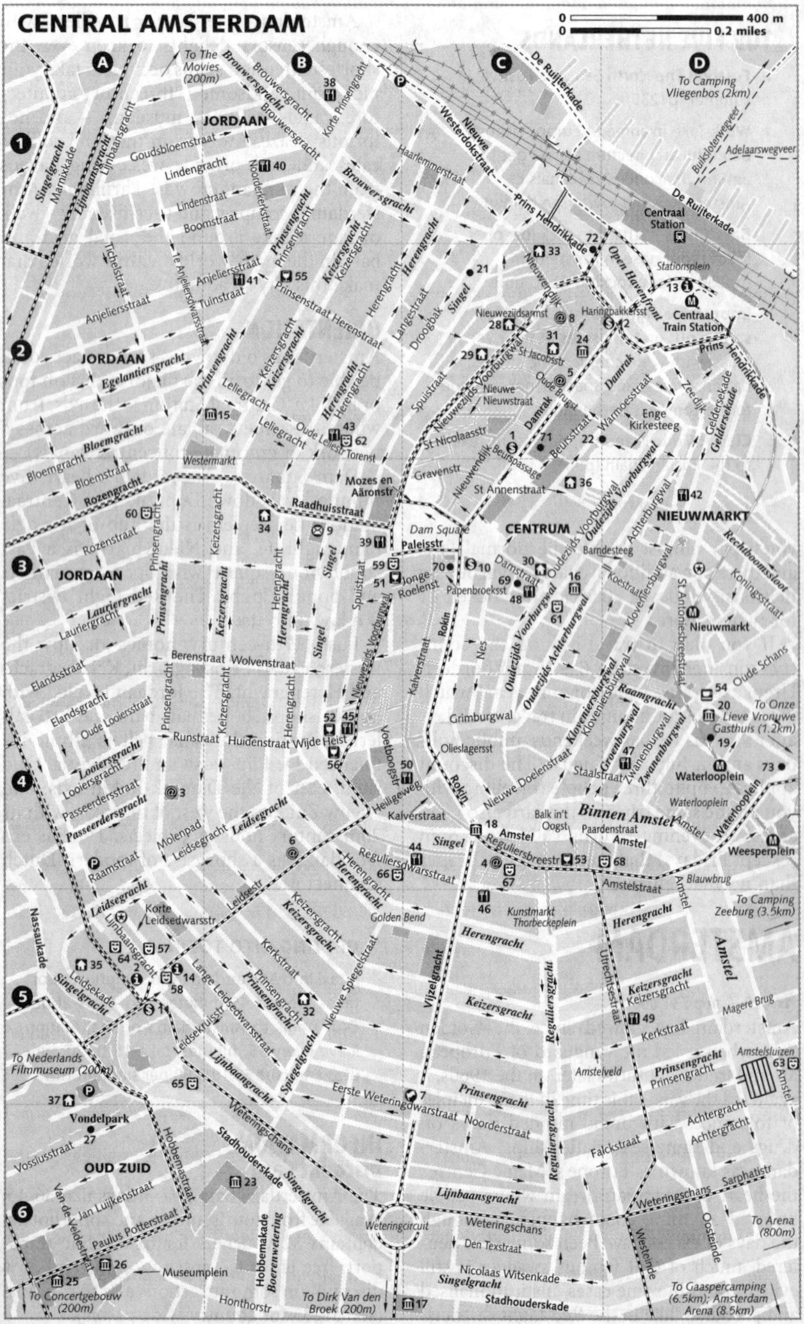

CENTRAL AMSTERDAM
0 400 m
0 0.2 miles
A
B
C
D
1
2
3
4
5
6
To The Movies (200m)
To Camping Vliegenbos (2km)
To Onze Lieve Vrouwe Gasthuis (1.2km)
To Camping Zeeburg (3.5km)
To Arena (800m)
To Gaaspercamping (6.5km); Amsterdam Arena (8.5km)
To Dirk Van den Broek (200m)
To Concertgebouw (200m)
To Nederlands Filmmuseum (200m)
JORDAAN
CENTRUM
NIEUWMARKT
OUD ZUID
Vondelpark
Centraal Station
Centraal Train Station
Stationsplein
Nieuwmarkt
Waterlooplein
Weesperplein
Dam Square
Golden Bend
Kunstmarkt Thorbeckeplein
Amstelsluizen
Museumplein
Weteringcircuit
Balk in't Oogst
Mozes en Aäronstr
Westermarkt
Brouwersgracht
Korte Prinsengracht
Haarlemmerstraat
Nieuwe Westerdokstraat
De Ruijterkade
Prins Hendrikkade
Open Havenfront
Buiksloterwegveer
Adelaarswegveer
Singelgracht
Marnixkade
Lijnbaansgracht
Goudsbloemstraat
Lindengracht
Lindenstraat
Boomstraat
Noorderkerkstraat
Prinsengracht
Keizersgracht
Herengracht
Singel
Tichelstraat
1e Anjeliersdwarsstraat
Anjeliersstraat
Tuinstraat
Egelantiersgracht
Prinsenstraat
Herenstraat
Langestraat
Droogbak
Nieuwendijk
Nieuwezijdsarmst
Haringpakkerssteeg
St Jacobsstr
Nieuwezijds Voorburgwal
Nieuwe Nieuwstraat
Oude Brugst
Damrak
Warmoesstraat
Zeedijk
Geldersekade
Enge Kirkesteeg
Spuistraat
Leliegracht
Oude Leliestr
Torenst
St Nicolaasstr
Gravenstr
Beursstraat
Beurspassage
St Annenstraat
Oudezijds Voorburgwal
Achterburgwal
Bloemgracht
Bloemstraat
Rozengracht
Raadhuisstraat
Rozenstraat
Paleisstr
Jonge Roelenst
Papenbroeksst
Damstraat
Barndesteeg
Koestraat
Kloveniersburgwal
St Antoniesbreestraat
Rechtboomssloot
Koningsstraat
Oudezijds Achterburgwal
Lauriergracht
Laurierstraat
Elandsstraat
Elandsgracht
Berenstraat
Wolvenstraat
Rokin
Kalverstraat
Nes
Grimburgwal
Raamgracht
Oude Schans
Oude Looiersstraat
Runstraat
Huidenstraat
Wijde Heist
Looiersgracht
Passeerdersstraat
Passeerdersgracht
Voetboogstr
Olieslagersst
Nieuwe Doelenstraat
Staalstraat
Groenburgwal
Zwanenburgwal
Heiligeweg
Binnen Amstel
Amstel
Paardenstraat
Molenpad
Leidsegracht
Raamstraat
Reguliersdwarsstraat
Reguliersbreestr
Amstelstraat
Blauwbrug
Nassaukade
Korte Leidsedwarsstr
Leidsestr
Kerkstraat
Leidsekade
Lange Leidsedwarsstraat
Nieuwe Spiegelstraat
Vijzelgracht
Reguliersgracht
Utrechtsestraat
Magere Brug
Leidsekruisstr
Spiegelgracht
Eerste Weteringdwarstraat
Noorderstraat
Amstelveld
Achtergracht
Falckstraat
Sarphatistr
Weteringschans
Stadhouderskade
Hobbemastraat
Vossiusstraat
Jan Luijkenstraat
Van de Veldestraat
Paulus Potterstraat
Hobbemakade
Boerenwetering
Honthorstr
Den Texstraat
Nicolaas Witsenkade
Westeinde
Oosteinde

INFORMATION		SLEEPING	🏠 (pp848–9)	Café De Kroon	53 C4
American Express	1 C2	Anna Youth Hostel	28 C2	Café de Sluyswacht	54 D4
Amsterdam Uitburo	2 A5	Bob's Youth Hostel	29 C2	Café de Vergulde Gaper	55 B2
Centrale Bibliotheek	3 A4	Bulldog Hotel	30 C3	Hoppe	56 B4
easyInternetcafé	4 C3	Flying Pig Downtown Hostel	31 C2	Proeflokaal Wijnand	
easyInternetcafé	5 C2	Hans Brinker Budget Hotel	32 B5	Fockinck	(see 30)
easyInternetcafé	6 B4	Hotel Groenendael	33 C2		
French Consulate	7 C5	Hotel Pax	34 B3	ENTERTAINMENT	🎬 (pp851–2)
Internet City	8 C2	Hotel Quentin	35 A5	Boom Chicago	57 A5
Main Post Office	9 B3	Hotel Winston	36 C3	Bulldog	58 A5
Thomas Cook	10 C3	Stayokay Vondelpark	37 A5	Club Zyon	59 B3
Thomas Cook	11 A5			COC Café	60 A3
Thomas Cook	12 D2	EATING	🍴 (pp849–50)	Greenhouse	61 C3
Tourist Office	13 D2	Albert Heijn	38 B1	Grey Area	62 B2
Tourist Office	14 A5	Albert Heijn	39 B3	Koninklijk Theater	
		Casa Juan	40 B1	Carré	63 D5
SIGHTS & ACTIVITIES	(pp847–8)	De Bolhoed	41 B2	Melkweg	64 A5
Anne Frankhuis	15 B2	Eat Mode	42 D3	Paradiso	65 A5
Hash, Marihuana & Hemp Museum	16 C3	Foodism	43 B2	Soho	66 B4
Heineken Experience	17 C6	Gary's Muffins	44 C4	Tuschinskitheater	67 C4
Het Oranje Voetbal Museum	18 C4	Kantjil to Go	45 B4	Viva la Vie	68 D4
Holland Experience 3D	19 D4	Memories of India	46 C5	Winston International	(see 36)
Museum Het Rembrandthuis	20 D4	Puccini	47 D4		
Poezenboot	21 C2	Sukasari	48 C3	TRANSPORT	(p852)
Prostitution Information Centre	22 C2	Tempo Doeloe	49 D5	Damstraat Rent-a-Bike	69 C3
Rijksmuseum	23 B6	Vlaams Friteshuis	50 C4	Eurolines	70 C3
Sexmuseum Amsterdam	24 C2			GVB	(see 13)
Stedelijk Museum	25 A6	DRINKING	🍷🍺 (p850)	Holland Rent-a-Bike	71 C2
Van Gogh Museum	26 A6	Absinthe	51 B3	Lovers Museum Boat	72 C2
Vondelpark	27 A6	Café Dante	52 B4	MacBike	73 D4

Emergency

De Eerste Lijn (The First Line; ☎ 613 02 45) Sexual violence hotline.

Police (☎ 0900-8844)

Internet Access

Centrale Bibliotheek (Main Library; ☎ 523 09 00; Prinsengracht 587; 🕒 1-9pm Mon, 10am-9pm Tue-Thu, 10am-5pm Fri & Sat, 1-5pm Sun) Free Internet.

EasyInternetcafé (www.easyeverything.com/map/ams; web access per hr from €1) Reguliersbreestraat (Reguliersbreestraat 22; 🕒 9am-10pm); Damrak (Damrak 33; 🕒 9am-10pm); Leidsestraat (Leidsestraat 24; 🕒 11am-7pm Mon, 9.30am-7pm Tue-Sat, 11am-6pm Sun)

Internet City (☎ 620 12 92; Nieuwendijk 76; web access per hr €1.50; 🕒 10am-midnight)

Medical Services

Centrale Doktersdienst (Central Doctors' Service; ☎ 592 34 34) 24-hour service and referrals to a doctor, dentist or pharmacy.

Onze Lieve Vrouwe Gasthuis (☎ 599 91 11; Oosterpark 9) 24-hour public hospital.

Money

American Express (☎ 504 87 77; Damrak 66; 🕒 9am-5pm Mon-Fri, 9am-noon Sat)

GWK (☎ 627 27 31; Centraal Station; 🕒 7am-10.45pm) Converts travellers cheques and books hotel reservations (also at Schiphol).

Thomas Cook Dam (☎ 625 09 22; Dam 23-25; 🕒 9am-7pm); Damrak (☎ 620 32 36; Damrak 1-5, opposite Centraal Station; 🕒 8am-8pm daily); Leidseplein (☎ 626

70 00; Leidseplein 31A; 🕒 9am-7.30pm Mon-Sat; 10am-7.30pm Sun)

Post

Main post office (☎ 556 33 11; Singel 250; 🕒 9am-7pm Mon-Fri, 9am-noon Sat)

Tourist Information

Amsterdam Tourist Board (☎ 0900-400 40 40; 🕒 9am-5pm Mon-Fri) Information line for hotel reservations and general queries.

Amsterdam Uitburo (☎ 0900-0191; www.aub.nl in Dutch; Leidseplein 26; 🕒 10am-6pm Mon-Fri, 10am-9pm Thu, information & ticket line 9am-9pm) For cultural events, with free magazines and tickets at small mark-ups.

Tourist office (☎ 0900-400 40 40; www.vvvamsterdam .nl) Stationsplein (Stationsplein 10; 🕒 9am-5pm); Centraal Track (Centraal Track 2; 🕒 8am-7.45pm Mon-Sat, 9am-5pm Sun); Leidseplein (Leidseplein 1; 🕒 9am-7pm Mon-Fri, 9am-5pm Sat & Sun); Stadionplein (Stadionplein; 🕒 9am-5pm)

SIGHTS & ACTIVITIES
Museums

The **Museum Het Rembrandthuis** (Rembrandt House Museum; ☎ 520 04 00; www.rembrandthuis.nl; Jodenbreestraat 4; adult/child €7/1.50; 🕒 10am-5pm Mon-Sat, 1-5pm Sun) is where Rembrandt ran the Netherlands' largest painting studio, only to lose it all when bankruptcy beckoned. Today, the museum has almost every etching he's known to have made.

Each year, 1.2 million people visit the **Rijksmuseum** (☎ 674 70 47; www.rijksmuseum.nl;

THE NETHERLANDS

Stadhouderskade 42; adult/under 19 €9/free; 10am-5pm), with its collection valued in the billions. Until renovations finish in 2008, there'll only be 200 masterpieces displayed, including the museum's crowning glory – Rembrandt's *Nightwatch* (1650).

The **Stedelijk Museum** (573 27 37; www.stedelijk .nl; Oosterdoksdijk 5; adult/child €7/3.50; 11am-5pm) is in a temporary home; the original building is undergoing renovation until 2007. The collection holds around 100,000 pieces, including impressionist works from Monet, Cézanne, Matisse, Picasso and Chagall; sculptures from Rodin, Renoir and Moore; De Stijl landmarks by Piet Mondriaan; abstract works by Appel and the CoBrA movement; and pop art from Andy Warhol and Roy Liechtenstein.

The **Van Gogh Museum** (570 52 00; www.van goghmuseum.nl; Paulus Potterstraat 7; adult/child €9/2.50; Sun-Thu 10am-6pm, 10am-10pm Fri) houses the world's largest Van Gogh collection: around 200 paintings and 500 drawings by the artist and his contemporaries, including Gauguin, Toulouse-Lautrec, Monet and Bernard.

Anne Frankhuis (Anne Frank House; 556 71 00; www.annefrank.nl in Dutch; Prinsengracht 267; adult/child €7.50/3.50; 9am-7pm Jan-Mar, 9am-9pm Apr-Aug, 9am-7pm Sep-Dec) is where Anne wrote her famous diary. A compelling reminder of Nazi horrors, the house lures 900,000 visitors each year, so consider going in the early evening when crowds are lightest.

There are some interesting artefacts from the history of sexual entertainment at the **Sexmuseum Amsterdam** (622 83 76; Damrak 18; admission €2.50; 10am-11.30pm) – Pompeiian erotica, for example. But with wall-mounted plastic derrieres passing wind at passers-by and an animatronic flasher accosting all-comers, it's more like a tribute to Benny Hill.

For many Dutch football isn't a life or death matter: it's more essential than that. **Het Oranje Voetbal Museum** (Orange Football Museum; 589 89 89; www.supportersclub-oranje.nl in Dutch; Kalverstraat 236; 11am-5pm Sat & Sun) tells the story of orange heroes Cruyff, Van Basten and Gullit, and the revolution that was Total Football.

The zealous, though informative, **Hash, Marihuana & Hemp Museum** (623 59 61; www .hashmuseum.com; Oudezijds Achterburgwal 130; admission €5.70; 11am-10pm) has many exhibits on the uses and history of cannabis (Queen Victoria used marijuana for menstrual cramps, it says here), as well as a seed shop, a greenhouse and a large selection of bongs.

At the **Heineken Experience** (523 94 36; www .heinekenexperience.com; Stadhouderskade 78; admission €7.50; 10am-6pm Tue-Sat), you can peer inside the malt silos and at memorabilia, although the brewery itself is long gone. Tickets include three glasses of Heineken.

Other Attractions

The **Red Light District** is bound by Warmoesstraat in the west, Zeedijk/Nieuwmarkt/Kloveniersburgwal in the east and Damstraat/Oude Doelenstraat/Oude Hoogstraat in the south. It's bewildering, even if near-naked prostitutes propositioning passers-by from black-lit windows is the oldest Amsterdam cliché. Among the usual oddball mix, you'll find tourists of all stripes gawping at the blatant displays of sexual currency.

At the **Prostitution Information Centre** (420 73 28; www.pic-amsterdam.com; Enge Kerksteeg 3; noon-7pm Tue, Wed, Fri & Sat), there's a re-creation of a working girl's place of employment. The centre also organises evening Red Light walks and sells a handy map of the District.

The **Poezenboot** (Cat Boat; 625 87 94; www .poezenboot.nl; Singel 40; 1-3pm) is one of Amsterdam's more unusual 'flea markets'. This barge began life as a shelter for hundreds of homeless cats in the 1960s. It's now a registered charity – pat and pet the current feline inhabitants for a small donation.

Vondelpark (www.vondelpark.nl in Dutch), an English-style park, has free concerts, ponds, lawns, thickets, winding footpaths and three outdoor cafés. It was named after the poet and playwright Joost van den Vondel, the 'Dutch Shakespeare', and is popular with joggers, skaters, buskers and lovers.

Holland Experience 3D (422 22 33; www.hol land-experience.nl; Waterlooplein 17; adult/child €8.50/7.25; 10am-6pm) screens a decidedly odd 30-minute film about Dutch life, presented in the third dimension: when tulips appear, you get sprayed with perfume; when dikes burst, you get sprayed with water. It's all part of that curious Dutch tendency to put the nation under a microscope, see p843.

FESTIVALS & EVENTS
For information on Amsterdam-based and national festivals and events, see p1235.

SLEEPING
Accommodation should be booked ahead anywhere in the Netherlands, especially

during high season; note that many visitors stay in Amsterdam even if travelling elsewhere. The tourist offices and Amsterdam Centraal Station's GWK exchange office have hotel-booking services.

Hostels

Bob's Youth Hostel (☎ 623 00 63; www.bobsyouth hostel.nl; Nieuwezijds Voorburgwal; dm from €17; 🖳) A long-standing favourite with backpackers. It's clean and functional, has a lively bar and lounge, and is right near Centraal station.

Bulldog Hotel (☎ 620 38 22; www.bulldog.nl; Oudezijds Voorburgwal 220; dm from €22) An offshoot of the Bulldog chain of cannabis coffee shops (see p851), this one's located in the heart of the Red Light district. The rooms aren't too bad, with more attention paid to decor and detail than your average spartan hostel.

Flying Pig Downtown Hostel (☎ 420 68 22; www.flyingpig.nl; Nieuwendijk 100; dm €19.70-25.70; 🖳) Very popular with unhurried stoners, who lounge around the throbbing lobby and bar. The Pig's website has a message board featuring lively debate on the virtues (or otherwise) of the facilities.

Anna Youth Hostel (☎ 620 11 55; Spuistraat 6; dm €20, d/tr €80/100 with private bathroom; 🖳) Anna's has a caring proprietor, an inviting, respectful vibe and a cheery Middle Eastern–style interior. Rates include linen, towels and a safe.

Stayokay Vondelpark (☎ 589 89 96; www.stay okay.com/vondelpark; Zandpad 5; dm from €20.50; 🖳) What a top location, right on the perimeter of the lush Vondelpark (see p846). There are the usual Stayokay amenities, like TV lounge, brasserie and laundry.

Hans Brinker Budget Hotel (☎ 622 06 87; www .hans-brinker.com; Kerkstraat 136; dm €21-24) There's a hyperactive 'frat house' feel to the Brinker, with its bouncy bar and disco. They don't take things too seriously here – visit their unflattering (quite deliberately so) website for a lesson in the art of self-mockery, taken to very Dutch extremes.

Hotels

Hotel Groenendael (☎ 624 48 22; www.hotelgroenen dael.com; Nieuwendijk 15; s/d/tr with shared bathroom €29/45/68, incl breakfast) A bargain: central location, neat (though small) rooms, charming owners. As always in this part of town, the quietest rooms are in the back.

Hotel Pax (☎ 624 97 35; Raadhuisstraat 37; s €25-45, d €45-95) Run by a pair of affable brothers, the Pax features eight brightly decorated rooms with a TV in each. There's a trade-off with the larger rooms: they face the busy street and noisy trams.

Hotel Quentin (☎ 626 21 87; www.quentinhotels.com; Leidsekade 89; s with shared bathroom €45, d/tr with private bathroom from €90/125, incl breakfast) This one goes down well with the gay and lesbian community, as well as thespians and musos swinging through town. It's done up in bright murals and handmade furniture. Some rooms have balconies, canal views and TVs.

Hotel Winston (☎ 623 13 80; www.winston.nl; Warmoesstraat 129; s with shared bathroom €60-62, d €75-83; s with private bathroom €62-65, d €83-89, tr €110-118) How to make a lot out of a little: take some functional rooms and get local artists to imaginatively theme them with motifs including Arabian typography, jigsaw puzzles and, fittingly for the Red Light location, bizarre sex. There's a jolly bar and the Winston's own club (p851) next door.

Camping

Gaaspercamping (☎ 696 73 26; www.gaaspercamping .nl; Loosdrechtdreef 7, Gaasperdam; per adult/extra adult/car/caravan €5-6/€4.25/3.75/5-6; 🕑 mid-Mar–Dec) This large park/recreation area, originally built to host 1982's International Horticultural Exhibition, has a café, restaurant, bar, barbecues, a supermarket, lake and beach. Take metro No 53 from Centraal to Gaasperplas.

Camping Zeeburg (☎ 694 4430; www.campingzee burg.nl; Zuider IJdijk 20; per camp site/car €4.50/€2.50) Cabins are available and it has a restaurant and bikes for hire. Take bus No 22 or tram No 14.

Camping Vliegenbos (☎ 636 8855; www.vliegenbos .com; Meeuwenlaan 138; per camp site/car €7.60/€4; 🕑 Apr-Sep) Features a bar and restaurant. It's 10 minutes by bus (No 32 or 36) from Centraal Station.

EATING

Amsterdam has a sizzling culinary scene with hundreds of restaurants and *eetcafés* catering to all tastes. The Dutch colonial legacy has introduced Indonesian and Surinamese cooking and the cuisines of many other nations are also well represented, notably Chinese, Japanese and Greek.

Self-Catering

Albert Heijn (Nieuwezijds Voorburgwal 226) This supermarket chain also has branches at Koningsplein 6 and Museumplein.

THE NETHERLANDS

Dirk van den Broek (Eerste van der Helststraat 25) Cut-rate groceries.

Quick Eats

Kantjil To Go (☎ 620 09 94; Nieuwezijds Voorburgwal 342; dishes small/large €3.50/4.50; ☺ lunch & dinner) Offers excellent, filling takeaway Indonesian (including Nasi Goreng and Gado Gado) with rice or noodles.

Eat Mode (☎ 330 08 06; Zeedijk 107; mains €4.50-12; ☺ lunch & dinner) Billed as an 'Asian Fusion Kitchen: First in Chinatown', it's small and bright, with casual ambience, but the Thai, Chinese, Vietnamese and Japanese meals are filling and tasty. There's a good vegetarian selection, including seaweed salad, and a sushi happy hour.

Puccini (☎ 626 54 74; Staalstraat 21; mains €5.30-12.50; ☺ lunch & dinner Tue-Sun) Refuel on panini rolls and salads with sun-dried ingredients. Puccini also runs the chocolate and cake shop next door, where handmade sweets (like chocs blended with tamarind or lemongrass) induce rapture.

Foodism (☎ 427 51 03; Oude Leliestraat 8; mains €6-8; ☺ lunch & dinner) This groovy little lounge, bathed in garish colours, dishes out all-day breakfasts, healthy sandwiches, salads and various pasta dishes.

Gary's Muffins (☎ 421 59 30; Jodenbreestraat 15; ☺ 9am-5.30pm) Gary used to be a professional ballet dancer; now he gets the nod for delectable fresh bagels, warm chocolate brownies and sweet and savoury muffins. There has to be a connection.

Vlaams Friteshuis (Voetboogstraat 31) This hole in the wall is Amsterdam's best-loved fries joint, an institution since 1887. The default topping is mayonnaise, but there's an arsenal of alternatives – peanut, say, or green peppercorn.

Restaurants

Sukasari (☎ 624 00 92; Damstraat 26-28; mains €4.75-18.50; ☺ lunch & dinner) Decorated with Indonesian artefacts and suffused in golden lighting, Sukasari is a quiet, contemplative oasis just off the manic Dam. The excellent menu serves fragrant, authentic Indonesian, such as coconut chicken with rice.

De Bolhoed (☎ 626 18 03; Prinsengracht 60-62; mains €6-14; ☺ lunch & dinner) Amsterdam's best-known vegetarian restaurant, with a prime canalside location. The food is fresh, organic, and often Mexican- and Italian-inspired.

Dip into pancakes, salads, burritos, homemade breads, biological wines, organic beers and cakes.

Casa Juan (☎ 623 78 38; Lindengracht 59; tapas €3-8, mains €12-17; ☺ dinner) The signature dish is the paella, and it's deservedly popular. *Very* popular. Be sure to book.

Memories of India (☎ 623 57 10; Reguliersdwarsstraat 88; mains €11.50-22.75; ☺ dinner). Stylish, friendly, relaxed. That's the winning combination, especially when combined with reasonable prices and dishes from all over India, including Paneerwala Murg: chicken pieces tossed with homemade cottage cheese, spring onion and ginger.

Tempo Doeloe (☎ 625 67 18; Utrechtsestraat 75; mains €18-22; ☺ dinner) The name means 'The Old Days' (ring a bell to gain entry) and the spice levels at this Indonesian restaurant range from mild to *very* hot. Reservations are essential.

DRINKING

Drinkers rejoice. Amsterdam really is your magic centre: throw a stick in the air and chances are it'll land on a drinking house of some repute. Bear in mind that when locals say café they mean a pub (also known as a *kroeg*) and that Amsterdam has more than 1000 of them.

Absinthe (☎ 320 6780; Nieuwezijds Voorburgwal 171) Devoted to the once-banned, brain-numbing liquor of the same name (reputed to have triggered Van Gogh's self-mutilation). The staff can teach you all about their signature drink, although the jury's out on whether it's as potent as the old days.

Café de Sluyswacht (☎ 625 76 11; Jodenbreestraat 1) A pretty drinking spot, built on foundations that lean dramatically, with secluded tables overlooking a broad canal.

Café Dante (☎ 638 88 39; Spuistraat 320) A large, Art Deco–style space with an art gallery upstairs (where Dutch art-rocker Herman Brood kept a studio). Peaceful during the day, in the evening it's filled with a boisterous, chic clientele.

Café De Kroon (☎ 625 20 11; Rembrandtplein 17-1) This neocolonial gem has a covered terrace, sumptuous velvet armchairs, high ceilings and wall-mounted, taxidermied specimens.

Café de Vergulde Gaper (☎ 624 89 75; Prinsenstraat 30) Decorated with old chemist bottles and vintage posters, this ex-pharmacy has a pleasant terrace that fills for afternoon drinks.

Hoppe (☎ 420 44 20; Spui 18) This gritty brown café, with one of Amsterdam's highest beer turnovers, has been tempting drinkers for more than 300 years. In summer the energetic crowd spills onto the streets.

Proeflokaal Wijnand Fockinck (☎ 639 26 95; www.wynand-fockink.nl; Pijlsteeg 31) This small tasting house (dating from 1679) serves scores of *jenevers* and liqueurs and has an appealing courtyard for lunch and snacks.

CLUBBING

Winston International (www.winston.nl; Warmoesstraat 125) Next to the Hotel Winston (p849), it has a promiscuous programming policy: electronica, spoken word, punk, graffiti art. On Sundays, it hosts Club Vegas, where the dress code is 'jet set' (sequins, suits, stilletos, bow ties, tiaras) and the music is lounge.

Paradiso (☎ 626 45 21; www.paradiso.nl; Weteringschans 6) This converted church is legendary. Saturday's Paradisco draws smart dressers for a sharp line-up of international DJs, while the monthly Kindred Spirits is hip-hop to the max.

Arena (☎ 694 74 44; www.hotelarena.nl; 's-Gravesandestraat 51) Everything from dance classics to salsa. It's worth visiting for the interior – the chapel of this one-time orphanage has been given a lush redo.

Club Zyon (www.clubzyon.nl; Nieuwezijds Voorburgwal 161) With silver walls and queasy pink lighting, the decor is '70s sci fi. The music policy is accessible (Latin, R&B, commercial house) and Monday is Backpackers Night.

ENTERTAINMENT
Live Music

Paradiso (☎ 626 45 21; www.paradiso.nl; Weteringschans 6) The home of rock since the '60s, the Paradiso has hosted big names like Sonic Youth, David Bowie and the Rolling Stones. Also see Clubbing, above.

Melkweg (Milky Way; ☎ 624 17 77; www.melkweg.nl; Lijnbaansgracht 234A) A former milk factory and a top cultural venue since the 1970s, Melkweg is an all-in-one entertainment complex with an art gallery, a café, a multimedia centre and top live music most nights. On Saturdays there are two dance floors with a huge variety of beats.

Loungeroom Concerts (www.liveinthelivingroom .com in Dutch) It's true: staying in is the new going out. On Sunday evenings, local musicians stage intimate concerts in private homes – although they're open to the public.

Hosts provide food and drink and three performers play for 30 minutes each to a maximum of 50 people. Book well ahead.

Coffee Shops

They're not 'cafés' (opposite); coffee shops deal strictly in the cannabis trade.

Grey Area (☎ 420 43 01; www.greyarea.nl; Oude Leliestraat 2) Owned by a couple of laid-back American guys, this tiny shop introduced the extra-sticky, flavourful 'Double Bubble Gum' weed to the city. The relaxed staff will advise on the lengthy menu.

Greenhouse (☎ 627 17 39; Oudezijds Voorburgwal 191) Winner of many awards at the annual High Times festival, it charms smokers with its undersea mosaics, psychedelic stained-glass windows and high-quality weed and hash.

Bulldog (☎ 627 19 08; www.bulldog.nl; Leidseplein 13-17) Amsterdam's most famous coffee shop chain has five branches. This is the largest, with Internet facilities, two bars, pool tables, fluorescent décor and a café.

Cinemas

Find out what's on in Thursday's papers.

The Movies (☎ 638 60 16; www.themovies.nl in Dutch; Haarlemmerdijk 161) Art-house films mixed with independent American and British at a beautiful Art-Deco cinema.

Tuschinskitheater (☎ 626 26 33; Reguliersbreestraat 26) Features mainstream blockbusters. Worth visiting for its sumptuous Art-Deco interior, especially in its main auditorium No 1.

Nederlands Filmmuseum (☎ 589 14 00; www .filmmuseum.nl; Vondelpark 3) Maintains a priceless archive of films, sometimes screening with live music (a recent programme included a retrospective of Dutch silent film). In summer, films are shown on the outdoor terrace at the museum's café.

Gay & Lesbian Venues

COC (☎ 626 30 87; www.cocamsterdam.nl; Rozenstraat 14) Amsterdam's gay and lesbian social centre, with a café and a nightclub.

Soho (☎ 626 15 73; www.reguliersdwars.nl/soho; Reguliersdwarsstraat 36) This giant two-storey bar hums with a young, gay clientele and an increasing number of straights.

Vive la Vie (☎ 624 01 14; Amstelstraat 7) This popular 'lipstick lesbian' café has loud music, large windows and flirty girls, though men are also welcome. In summer, patrons pack the outdoor terrace.

Sport

FOOTBALL

Ajax is the Netherlands' most famous team: it has won the European Cup four times and launched Johan Cruyff to stellar heights in the '70s. Ajax plays in the **Amsterdam ArenA** (☎ 311 13 33; www.amsterdamarena.nl; Arena Blvd 11, Bijlmermeer), usually on Saturday evenings and Sunday afternoons during season (August to May).

Theatre

Boom Chicago (☎ 423 01 01; www.boomchicago.nl; Leidseplein 12) English-language stand-up and improv comedy is performed here year-round; the best way to see it is over dinner and a few drinks at their decent café, boom-Bar.

Koninklijk Theater Carré (☎ 622 52 25; www .theatercarre.nl; Amstel 115-125; ticket office 🕙 10am-7pm Mon-Sat, 1-7pm Sun) The largest theatre in town, with mainstream international shows, musicals, cabaret, opera, operetta, ballet and circuses. Backstage tours are at 3pm on Saturday and Wednesday.

GETTING AROUND

To/From the Airport

A taxi into Amsterdam from Schiphol airport takes 20 to 45 minutes and costs about €40. Trains to Centraal Station leave every 15 minutes, take 15 to 20 minutes and cost €3.10/5.50 per single/return.

Bicycle

These companies require passport/ID and a credit-card imprint or cash deposit.
MacBike (☎ 624 83 91; www.macbike.nl; Stationsplein 12; per day/week €6.50/29.75) Bikes have massive logos; you'll stand out.
Bike City (☎ 626 37 21; www.bikecity.nl; Bloemgracht 68-70; per day/week €7.50/40) Discreet bikes.
Holland Rent-a-Bike (☎ 622 32 07; Damrak 247; per day/week €6.25/32.50)
Damstraat Rent-a-Bike (☎ 625 50 29; www.bikes.nl; Damstraat 20; per day/week €7/31)

Boat

FERRIES

Two free ferries to Amsterdam North leave every six to 10 minutes from the piers directly behind Centraal Station.

CANAL BOAT, BUS & BIKE

Canal Bikes (2/4-seaters per person per hour €8/7) These paddleboats can be hired from kiosks at Leidseplein,

the corner of Keizersgracht and Leidsestraat, the Anne Frankhuis and the Rijksmuseum.
Canal Bus (☎ 623 98 86; day pass adult/child €15/10.50; 🕙 9.50am-8pm) Several circuits between Centraal Station and the Rijksmuseum.
Lovers Museum Boat (☎ 622 21 81; www.lovers.nl in Dutch; day pass adult/child €14.25/9.50) Stops at the Scheepvaartmuseum, Rembrandthuis, Bloemenmarkt, Leidseplein, Rijksmuseum and Anne Frankhuis.

Public Transport

The **GVB** (Amsterdam Transport Authority; ☎ 460 59 59; www.gvb.nl; Stationsplein; 🕙 7am-9pm Mon-Fri, 8am-9pm Sat & Sun) runs the network and there's an information office in front of Centraal Station.

The best ticketing deal is the *strippenkaart*: a multi-fare 'strip ticket' valid on all buses, trams and metros (see p1255). The GVB office also sells a one-week pass valid in all zones for €16.

Night buses take over shortly after midnight when the trams and regular buses stop running. Drivers sell single tickets for €2.50, or you can stamp three strips off your strip card and pay a €1.50 surcharge (which is marginally more expensive).

Taxi

Amsterdam taxis are very expensive, even over short journeys. Try **Taxicentrale Amsterdam** (☎ 677 77 77).

THE RANDSTAD

The Randstad (literally 'Rim City') is the name given to the Netherlands' heavily developed western region, containing two-thirds of the 16 million population.

HAARLEM

☎ 023 / pop 148,000

Haarlem, only 15 minutes by train from Amsterdam, is an appealing, refined town. With its reasonably priced accommodation, it is a fine stopover if the capital's hotels are over-run. Haarlem should be thought of as an attraction in its own right, though, with an intriguing restaurant scene and a 17th-century layout that's better preserved than many Randstad cities.

Information

Library (☎ 515 76 00; Doelenplein 1; 🕙 10am-6pm Mon-Fri, noon-5pm Sat) Free Internet.

Tourist office (☎ 0900-616 16 00; www.vvvzk.nl; Stationsplein 1; ⏰ 9.30am-5.30pm Mon-Fri, 10am-2pm Sat)

Sights

Frans Hals Museum (☎ 511 57 75; www.franshals museum.nl; Groot Heiligland 62; adult/child €5.40/free; ⏰ 11am-5pm Mon-Sat, noon-5pm Sun) has a superb collection, kept in an almshouse where Hals spent his final, impoverished years. Treasures include his two paintings known collectively as the *Regents & the Regentesses of the Old Men's Alms House* (1664) and ceiling-high illustrations of the human anatomy with biblical and mythological allusions.

Teylers Museum (☎ 531 90 10; www.teylersmu seum.nl; Spaarne 16; adult/child €5.50/1; ⏰ 10am-5pm Tue-Sat, noon-5pm Sun), the oldest museum in the country (1778), has an array of kooky inventions, like the 18th-century electrostatic machine that ran on batteries the size of a milk wagon. It also has works from Michelangelo and Raphael.

Sleeping

Stayokay Haarlem (☎ 537 37 93; www.stayokay.com /haarlem; Jan Gijzenpad 3; d €21-24 incl breakfast; 🖳) Take bus No 2 (direction Haarlem Noord) from the train station (10 minutes).

Hotel Carillon (☎ 531 05 91; www.hotelcarillon.com; Grote Markt 27; s private/shared bathroom €55/33, d with private bathroom €76, incl breakfast) The single beds may be the narrowest in all the Netherlands, but the atmosphere is fine, friendly and fun. There's a bar/sidewalk café downstairs and your grand neighbour, the Grote Kerk (a fine historical church), next door.

Campsite De Liede (☎ 533 23 60; fax 535 86 66; Lieoever 68; per adult €2.85) A leafy site 2.5km east of the old centre with a lakeside location and canoes and paddleboats for hire. Take bus No 2 from the train station.

Eating

Eko Eetkafé (☎ 532 65 66; Ziljstraat 39; mains €7-15.50; ⏰ lunch & dinner) This organic restaurant attracts a diverse crowd: singletons, suits, grannies, groovers. The menu is also eclectic (and tasty): fried trout, yakitori, Singapore noodles and more.

Pieck Jacobus (☎ 532 61 44; Warmoesstraat 18; mains €12-17; ⏰ lunch & dinner, Mon-Sat) A chic, intimate *eetcafé* down a picturesque side street. There is a superb lunchtime sandwich menu and appealing mains, such as kebab sausages.

Clubbing

Patronaat (☎ 532 60 10; www.patronaat.nl in Dutch; Oostvest 54) Tasteful club/live venue with an eclectic range of performers that might include industrial noise merchants, Berlin electro DJs or US roots/blues practitioners.

Getting There & Away

Sample train fares include Amsterdam (€3.10, 15), Den Haag (€6.40, 35 minutes) and Rotterdam (€9, 55 minutes).

LEIDEN

☎ 071 / pop 118,000

Leiden, Rembrandt's birthplace, is home to the Netherlands's oldest university – and 20,000 students. The university was a gift from Willem the Silent for withstanding two Spanish sieges in 1574. Defeated, the Spanish legged it so quickly (so the story goes), they abandoned a kettle of *hutspot* (hotchpotch); it's been a Dutch culinary mainstay ever since. The university culture gives Leiden a refreshing, vibrant atmosphere; there's loads of energy in the air. Look for the literary quotes painted on the walls in everything from Russian to Hebrew to Spanish.

Information

Centrale Bibliotheek (Central Library; ☎ 514 99 43; Nieuwstraat 4; web access per hr €2; ⏰ 11am-5pm Oct-Apr, closed Sun Jun-Sep)

Tourist office (☎ 0900-222 23 33; www.leidenpromotie .nl; Stationsweg 2D; ⏰ 11am-5.30pm Mon, 9.30am-5.30pm Tue-Fri, 10am-4.30pm Sat)

Sights & Activities

The 17th-century **Lakenhal** (Cloth Hall; ☎ 516 53 60; www.lakenhal.nl in Dutch; Oude Singel 28-32; adult/child €2/1; ⏰ 10am-5pm Tue-Fri, noon-5pm Sat & Sun) houses the Municipal Museum, with an assortment of works by old masters, as well as period rooms and temporary exhibits.

The **Rijksmuseum van Oudheden** (National Museum of Antiquities; ☎ 516 31 63; www.rmo.nl; Rapenburg 28; adult/child under 18 €6/5.50; ⏰ 10am-5pm Tue-Fri, noon-5pm Sat & Sun) has a class collection of hieroglyphs and 94 mummies.

The windmill called **De Valk** (The Falcon; ☎ 516 53 53; http://home.wanadoo.nl/molenmuseum; 2e Binnenvestgracht 1; adult/child €2.50/1.50; ⏰ 10am-5pm Tue-Sat, 1-5pm Sun) has been carefully restored; its construction and operation laid bare highlights the wonders of pre-industrial engineering.

The upper levels afford a cracking view of the old town.

Rent a canoe from **Botenverhuur 't Galgewater** (☎ 514 97 90; per hr €3.50; 🕙 11am-6pm Oct-May, 11am-10pm Jun-Sep) and explore the canals.

Sleeping

Stayokay Noordwijk (☎ 0252-37 29 20; www.stayokay .com/noordwijk; Langevelderlaan 45; dm from €22) The hostel is 45 minutes away, next to a popular beach. Take bus No 57 or 90 (last bus at 11pm) to the hospital and walk for 10 minutes.

Pension Witte Singel (☎ 512 45 92; www.pension -ws.demon.nl; Witte Singel 80; s/d €36/66, incl breakfast) Warm and welcoming, with fresh, spacious rooms and large windows overlooking most agreeable scenery: this pension has the perfectly peaceful Singel canal in front and a typically Dutch garden in the back. Outstanding value.

De Zuidduinen (☎ 401 47 50; info-zuidduinen@ tours.nl; Zuidduinseweg 1; site €14; 🕙 Apr-Oct) and **De Noordduinen** (☎ 402 52 95; info-noordduinen@tours.nl; Campingweg 1; per camp site €14; 🕙 Apr-Oct) are the closest campgrounds, 8km to the west. Take bus No 31 or 41.

Eating & Drinking

Soup Factory (cnr Steenstraat & Narmstraat; small/large soups €3/3.90; 🕙 noon-10pm) This small corner shop is unfussy in its decor, instead reserving its creative energy for healthy, delicious soups in imaginative variations.

Splinter Eethuis (☎ 514 95 19; Noordeinde 30; €9.95-13.25; 🕙 Thu-Sun) A popular student haunt, with generous two-course meals featuring rotating ethnic cuisines. Good veggie options.

In den Doofpot (☎ 512 24 34; Turfmarkt 9; mains €10.50-43.50; 🕙 dinner) The interior is regal and airy, a sensuous setting for the menu's filling, French-tinged twists on Dutch cooking.

De Burcht (☎ 514 23 89; Burgsteeg 14) This bar/café is in a picturesque spot, next to the Burcht fortification. It's popular with arty subcults and has live music some nights.

COC (☎ 522 06 40; Langegracht 65) Run by the national gay and lesbian organisation, this bar is a focal point of the local scene.

Jazzcafé The Duke (☎ 566 15 85; www.jazzcafethe duke.nl; Oude Singel 2) No windows, but loads of yellowing, vintage jazz posters on the walls. Their motto is, "If we don't have it, you don't need it". It's true: you don't need windows to enjoy this atmospheric den, with its fine live jazz every night and appreciative crowds.

Getting There & Away

Sample train fares include Amsterdam (€5.80, 34 minutes) and Den Haag (€2.80, 10 minutes). Regional and local buses leave from the bus station directly in front of Centraal Station.

DEN HAAG

☎ 070 / pop 464,000

Officially known as 's-Gravenhage (the Count's Domain), Den Haag is the Dutch seat of government and residence of the royal family; the stately mansions and palatial embassies lining its green boulevards are suitably regal. Den Haag has a reputable culinary scene, a clutch of tasty museums and plays host to the world's biggest jazz festival, the North Sea Jazz Festival, held annually near the seaside suburb of Scheveningen (itself worth a visit for its lively kitsch).

Information

Connexion Plazza (cnr Stationsweg & Stationsplein; web access per hr €1)

Tourist office (☎ 0900-3403505; www.denhaag.com; Koningin Julianaplein 30; 🕙 8.30am-5.30pm Mon-Sat year-round, 10am-2pm Sun Jul & Aug)

Sights

The **Mauritshuis** (☎ 302 34 56; www.mauritshuis.nl; Korte Vijverberg 8; adult/under 18 €7.50/free; 🕙 10am-5pm Tue-Sat, 11am-5pm Sun) houses Dutch and Flemish works (and Andy Warhol's Queen Beatrix). Highlights include Vermeer's *Girl with a Pearl Earring* and Rembrandt self-portraits at age 20 and 63.

Escher in Het Paleis Museum (☎ 338 11 20; Lange Voorhout; www.escherinhetpaleis.nl; adult/child €7.50/5; 🕙 11am-5pm Tue-Sun) is a permanent exhibition devoted to Dutch graphic artist MC Escher, from his early realism to later phantasmagoria. Imaginative displays include a virtual reality reconstruction of Escher's impossible buildings and 4D spatial dynamics.

The **Panorama Mesdag** (☎ 364 45 44; www.pano rama-mesdag.nl; Zeestraat 65; adult/child €4/2; 🕙 Mon-Sat 10am-5pm, Sun & holidays noon-5pm) contains the *Panorama* (1881), a gigantic, 360-degree painting of Scheveningen, painted by Hendrik Willem Mesdag. The artist's command of perspective and minute detail was masterful: viewed from a constructed dune, with real sand and beach chairs scattered about and beachy sounds piped through, the panorama is a fully immersive experience.

Madurodam (☎ 355 39 00; www.madurodam.nl; George Maduroplein 1; adult/child under 11 €12/8.75; ⏰ 9am-8pm), 3km out of town, is a miniaturised Netherlands, complete with 1:25 scale versions of Schiphol, Amsterdam, windmills and tulips, Rotterdam harbour, the Delta dikes, and so on. It's an enlightening example of the Dutch tendency to put their world under a microscope, see p843. To get there by public transport, take tram No 9 or bus No 22 from Centraal Station, or tram No 9 from Hollands Spoor Station.

The long beach at **Scheveningen** (www.scheveningen.nl), 4km from the centre, attracts nine million visitors annually. Crowds can get up close and personal when the weather gets warm and the shopping strip gets crassly commercial, but the attraction of sea and sand ensures a palpable frisson of frivolity.

Sleeping

Stayokay Den Haag (☎ 315 78 88; www.stayokay.com/denhaag; Scheepmakerstraat 27; dm from €22.85) Around 15 minutes' walk from Hollands Spoor station.

Strandhotel (☎ 354 01 93; www.strandhotel.demon.nl; Zeekant 111 & Gevers Deynootweg 1344 Scheveningen; s/d €37.50/62.50; ℗ 🅿 🅧) It's on the beach and the rooms have an unreconstructed 1950s motif. Book ahead and keep an eye on the weather – prices soar in summer.

Hotel Astoria (☎ 384 04 01; Stationsweg 139; s/d €35.50/56.70) The rooms are small and a touch bleak (although they do have private facilities,

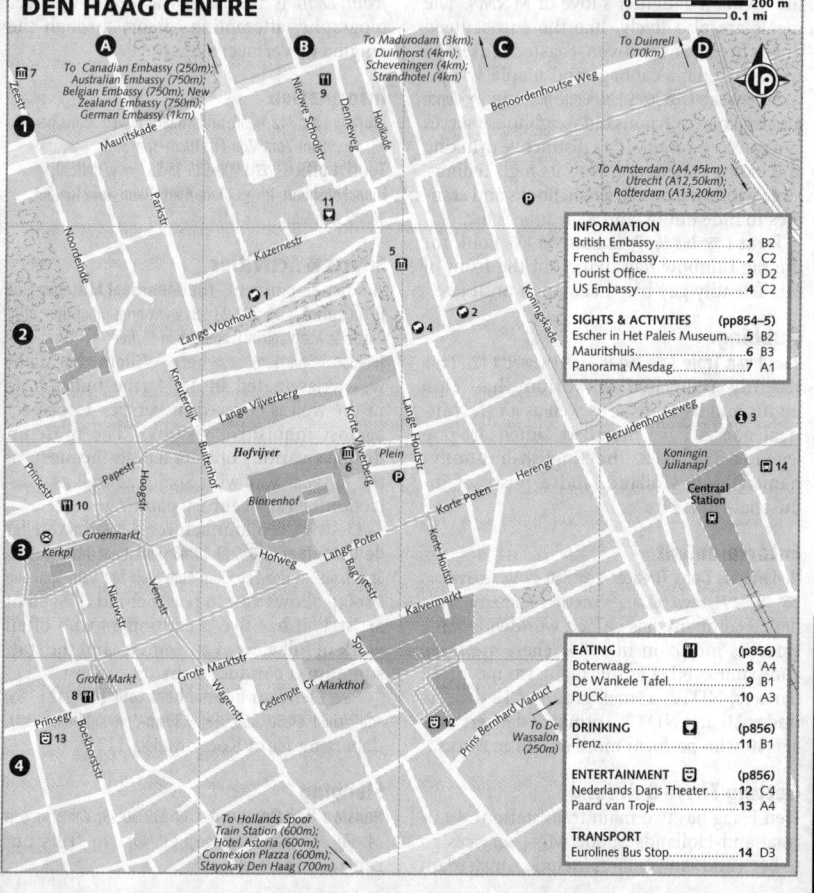

DEN HAAG CENTRE

0 — 200 m
0 — 0.1 mi

To Madurodam (3km);
Duinhorst (4km);
Scheveningen (4km);
Strandhotel (4km)

To Duinrell (10km)

To Canadian Embassy (250m);
Australian Embassy (750m);
Belgian Embassy (750m); New
Zealand Embassy (750m);
German Embassy (1km)

To Amsterdam (A4,45km);
Utrecht (A12,50km);
Rotterdam (A13,20km)

INFORMATION
British Embassy...................................1 B2
French Embassy...................................2 C2
Tourist Office.....................................3 D2
US Embassy.......................................4 C2

SIGHTS & ACTIVITIES   (pp854–5)
Escher in Het Paleis Museum.....5 B2
Mauritshuis.......................................6 B3
Panorama Mesdag..............................7 A1

EATING   (p856)
Boterwaag..8 A4
De Wankele Tafel...............................9 B1
PUCK..10 A3

DRINKING   (p856)
Frenz..11 B1

ENTERTAINMENT   (p856)
Nederlands Dans Theater.......12 C4
Paard van Troje..............................13 A4

TRANSPORT
Eurolines Bus Stop....................14 D3

To Hollands Spoor
Train Station (600m);
Hotel Astoria (600m);
Connexion Plazza (600m);
Stayokay Den Haag (700m)

To De
Wassalon
(250m)

Koningin
Julianapl

Centraal
Station

THE NETHERLANDS

sweetening the deal), but it's one of Den Haag's few budget options.

Duinhorst (☎ 324 22 70; www.duinhorst.nl; Buurtweg 135; person/tent €3.75/2.75; ☯ Apr-Sep) Camping grounds set among the dunes east of Scheveningen. Take bus No 28 from Hollands Spoor station or No 29 from Centraal Station to the end of the line, from where it's about 1km west.

Eating & Drinking

De Wankele Tafel (The Wobbly Table; ☎ 364 32 67; Mauritskade 79; 3-course menu €8-10; ☯ dinner Mon-Sat) A homely little vegetarian haunt with filling three-course meals.

PUCK (☎ 427 76 49; Prinsestraat 33; mains €17.50-23.50; ☯ lunch & dinner Tue-Sat) The restaurant's vibrant paint job is apparently a tribute to the owner's daughter's love of M&Ms. The meals are also lively, like the pan-sautéed duck breast over oven-roasted rosenval fries, with napa cabbage and maple syrup.

Boterwaag (☎ 365 96 86; Grote Markt 8a; ☯ lunch & dinner) This cavernous old weighhouse serves as a café/restaurant. It's a distinctive drinking and eating experience, with its high ceilings, large windows, candle fetish, nooks and crannies to hide out in, and a great beer list.

Frenz (☎ 363 66 57; Kazernestraat 106) Look for the big rainbow flag flying out the front of this friendly gay bar that's open until late.

Clubbing

Paard van Troje (☎ 360 18 38; Prinsegracht 12) This recently renovated emporium has club nights and live music, as well as a café. Musical guests have included Dutch art-pop legends The Nits, the English-but-aptly-named Jools Holland, and a posse of industrial-funk DJs.

Entertainment

Nederlands Dans Theater (☎ 360 49 30, reservations ☎ 360 38 73; www.ndt.nl; ☯ box office 10am-6pm) This dance company has gained worldwide fame since its inception in 1959. There are three companies: NDT1, the main troupe of 32 dancers; NDT2, a small group of 12 dancers under 21; and NDT3, a group of dancers over age 40 who perform more dramatic works.

Getting There & Around

Den Haag has two main train stations: Centraal and Hollands Spoor. Most services go to both and sample fares include Amsterdam

(€8.50, 50 minutes), Leiden €2.50, 13 minutes), Rotterdam (€3.50, 22 minutes) and Utrecht €8.50, 40 minutes). Tram Nos 1, 8 and 9 link Scheveningen with Den Haag.

DELFT

☎ 015 / pop 96,000

Delft, founded around 1100, is compact and charming: a very popular tourist destination. With its narrow, canal-lined streets and remarkable old buildings, it's a gentle and relaxed stopover (except when the crowds peak). The town is famous for its 'delftware', distinctive blue-and-white pottery, and for its status as the home of Golden Age painter Jan Vermeer. *View of Delft* is the title of one of Vermeer's best-loved works, an enigmatic, non-realist vision of the town; *A Clear View from Delft* is the title of a recent Vermeer biography, attempting to sort through the enigma of Vermeer's life.

Information

Library (☎ 212 34 50; Kruisstraat 71; web access per hr €2; ☯ 10am-7pm Mon-Fri, 10am-3pm Sat)

Tourist office (☎ 0900-515 15 55; www.delft.nl; Hippolytusbuurt 4; ☯ 11am-4pm, 10am-4pm Tue-Sat, 10am-3pm Sun)

Sights & Activities

A former convent, the **Municipal Museum Het Prinsenhof** (☎ 260 23 58; www.prinsenhof-delft.nl in Dutch; St Agathaplein 1; adult/child €5/free; ☯ 10am-5pm Tue-Sat, 1-5pm Sun) is where Willem the Silent was assassinated in 1584 (the bullet hole in the wall is covered in Perspex to protect against inquisitive visitors). The museum displays various objects telling the story of the 80-year war with Spain, as well as a selection of 17th-century paintings.

Delftware manufacturer **Aardewerkatelier de Candelaer** (☎ 213 18 48; Kerkstraat 14; ☯ 9am-5pm Mon-Sat Nov-Feb; 9am-6pm Mon-Sat, 9am-5pm Sun Mar-Oct) allows you to peer behind the veil of artistry: it has five practitioners who often work in full view of customers, and the staff sometimes conduct tours on request.

See Delft on a **canal boat tour** (☎ 212 63 85; adult/child €4.50/2.50; ☯ 9.30am-6pm mid-Mar–Oct), departing from Koornmarkt 113

Sleeping

Pension Van Domburg (☎ 212 30 29; Voldersgracht 24; s/d with shared bathroom €35/40) No frills but centrally located.

Hotel de Kok (☎ 212 21 25; www.hoteldekok.nl; Houttuinen 15; s/d from €66/80, incl breakfast; [P]) Managed by an affable family, it has sizeable, elegant rooms and a lovely garden terrace.

Delftse Hout (☎ 213 00 40; Korftlaan 5; sites €20) This camping ground is just northeast of town. Take bus No 64 from the station.

Eating & Drinking

Stads Pannekoeckhuys (☎ 213 01 93; Oude Delft 113; mains €3-10; ☽ lunch & dinner) A typical pancake kitchen with 90 kinds of pancakes at good prices, plus dishes such as the old Dutch favourite, pea soup.

Eetcafe De Ruif (☎ 214 22 06; Kerkstraat 22; mains €11.80-15.80; ☽ lunch & dinner) Rustic, with a wonderful, low ceiling, canal scenery outside and tasty lunches, including lamb soup and innovative sandwich combinations. It gets busy at night, when it takes on the appearance of an exceedingly popular carousing option.

Puur (☎ 213 70 15; Vrouw Juttenland 17; mains €17; ☽ dinner, closed Mon) Choice food in a cheery place with a long vegetarian menu.

Locus Publicus (☎ 213 46 32; Brabantse Turfmarkt 67) A friendly place with good music, lashings of conviviality and an outsized beer list.

Entertainment

Jazzcafé Bebop (☎ 213 52 10; Kromstraat 33) Dark, small and a bit exclusive – maybe how a jazz café should be. Many different beers, swinging music and laid-back staff.

Filmhuis Lumen (☎ 214 02 26; www.filmhuis -lumen.nl in Dutch; Doelenplein 5; screenings around €5) Screens alternative films.

Getting There & Away

Train fares include Den Haag (€2, eight minutes), Rotterdam (€2.80, 13 minutes) and Amsterdam (€8.50, 50 minutes).

ROTTERDAM

☎ 010 / pop 600,000

Rotterdam, the Netherlands' second-largest city, has a long history as a major shipping hub, stretching back to the 14th century. It's had dark times, too. In 1940, the invading Germans issued an ultimatum to the Dutch: surrender, or Rotterdam (among other cities) would be destroyed. The government capitulated, but the raid was carried out anyway and the historic centre was razed.

Rotterdam spent the following decades rebuilding and the result is an architectural aesthetic that's unique in Europe (the city is home to perhaps the best-known modern Dutch architect, Rem Koolhaas). Today, Rotterdam has a crackling energy, with superb nightlife, a diverse, multiethnic community and top-class museums.

It also has a long-standing rivalry with Amsterdam, reflected in most aspects of culture. When Rotterdam unleashed its extreme form of techno, gabber, on the world in the early '90s, one of its most enduring targets was Amsterdam: an early gabber single was memorably titled, 'Amsterdam, Waar Lech Dat Dan?' ('Amsterdam, Where the F*** is That?').

Information

Rotterdam Card (www.rotterdamcard.nl) Available from the tourist office and Use-It. Offers discounts for museums, public transport, tours and restaurants (see p1235 for nationwide discount cards).

EasyInternetcafé (www.easyeverything.com/map/rot; Stadhuisplein 16-18; web access per hr from €1; ☽ noon-8pm Mon & Sun, 9.30am-8pm Tue-Thu & Sat, 9.30am-9pm Fri, noon-8pm Sun)

Tourist Office (☎ 0900-4034065; www.rotterdam.nl; Coolsingel 67; ☽ 9am-6pm Mon-Fri, 9am-5pm Sat & Sun)

Use-It (☎ 240 91 58; www.use-it.nl; Conradstraat 2; ☽ 9am-6pm Tue-Sun mid-May–mid-Sep, 9am-5pm Tue-Sat mid-Sep–mid-May) Aimed at young travellers.

Sights

Museum Boijmans van Beuningen (☎ 441 94 00; www.boijmans.rotterdam.nl; Museumpark 18-20; adult/child under 18 €7/free; ☽ 10am-5pm Tue-Sat, 11am-5pm Sun & holidays) is probably the finest museum in the country (some say Europe). Its permanent collection takes in classic Dutch and European art and there's an utterly absorbing Surrealist wing, featuring ephemera, paraphernalia and famous works from Duchamp, Magritte, Man Ray, and more. Salvador Dali has a dedicated room.

The 185m-high **Euromast** (☎ 436 48 11; www .euromast.com; Parkhaven 20; adult/child €7.75/5; ☽ 9.30am-11pm Apr-Sep, 10am-11pm Oct-Mar) offers unparalleled 360° views of Rotterdam, with its rotating, glass-walled 'Euroscope' contraption ascending to near the summit (scored to the tune of Bowie's *Space Oddity*).

Rotterdam's distinctive architecture is well illustrated by the **Overblaak development** (1978–84), designed by Piet Blom. This postmodern extravaganza – with its its pencil-shaped tower and upended, cube-shaped

THE NETHERLANDS

apartments – seems plucked straight from the novels of JG Ballard. One apartment, the **Show Cube** (☎ 414 22 85; www.cubehouse.nl; adult/child under 12 €1.80/1.35; ⏱ 11am-5pm, closed Mon-Thu Jan & Feb), is open to the public.

Learn more at the **Nederlands Architectuur Instituut** (☎ 440 12 00; www.nai.nl; Museumpark 25; ⏱ 10am-5pm Tue-Sat, 11am-5pm Sun & holidays).

Sleeping

The tourist office and Use-It (p857) make reservations for a small fee.

Sleep-in De Mafkees (☎ 2409158; www.sleep-in.nl; Schaatsbaan 41-45; dm €10) A friendly, cheap winner just two minutes from Rotterdam Centraal Station. There's an atmospheric bar and a free movie every night.

Stayokay Rotterdam (☎ 436 57 63; www.stayokay.com/rotterdam; Rochussenstraat 107-109; dm from €20.25; reception ⏱ until 1am; 🖥) Well placed for the museums, with a low-key bar.

Hotel Boat De Clipper (☎ 331 42 44; Scheepmakershaven; bed €22.50, incl breakfast) This 'botel', docked in Rotterdam's old harbour, has quarters that are, inevitably, a little cramped.

Hotel Amar (☎ 425 57 95; fax 477 73 21; www.amarhotel.nl; Mathenesserlaan 316; s/d €30/50) This friendly, small place is close to the Museumplein and to good shopping and nightlife. The rooms are simple but comfy, and guests can use bikes for free.

Hotel Bazar (☎ 206 51 51; www.hotelbazar.nl; Witte de Withstraat 16; s/d/tr €60/75/120, incl breakfast) Deservedly popular for its Middle Eastern–themed rooms, with lush, brocaded curtains, exotically tiled bathrooms and comfy beds. Breakfast is spectacular, too: Turkish breads, international cheeses, cold cuts, coffee, fruit and yoghurt.

City Camping of Rotterdam (☎ 415 34 40; Kanaalweg 84; per adult/tent/2-adult cabins €4.70/3.70/€27.70) A 20-minute walk northwest from Centraal Station, or take bus No 33.

Eating & Drinking

Happy Sushi (☎ 433 47 30; Kruisplein 42; sushi from €3.50; ⏱ lunch & dinner) Select colour-coded plates (representing different price scales) carrying multiple sushi varieties as they snake past you on a conveyor belt. The endless delicacies are irresistible, so beware: you'll end up paying a little or a lot.

Café Gallery Abrikoos (☎ 477 41 40; Aelbrechtskolk 51; tapas from €4.50; ⏱ lunch & dinner Tue-Sun) This bright, cheery tapas place has a variety of soups, salads, mains and Mediterranean mini-meals.

Bazar (☎ 206 51 51; www.hotelbazar.nl; Witte de Withstraat 16; mains €8-13.90) On the ground floor of the inventive Hotel Bazar (p858), this eatery has similarly stylised Middle Eastern decor and a menu to match: dolmades, falafel, mussels, sardines, couscous and kebabs served up in tangy, attention-grabbing combinations.

Rotown (☎ 436 26 69; Nieuwe Binnenweg 19; mains €10-13.50) Part of the Rotown bar (p858), the restaurant is in a rustic, wood-panelled extension. The menu alternates between hearty (red apple steak) and arty (herbal green tuna), and is delicious at each extreme.

Kip (Chicken; ☎ 436 99 23; Van Vollenhovenstraat 25; mains €15-25; ⏱ dinner Tue-Sun) An elegant dining establishment with a large fireplace and a broad menu featuring immaculately prepared meat, poultry and vegetable dishes.

Stalles (☎ 436 16 55; Nieuwe Binnenweg 11a) This classic brown café is on a great stretch of road near plenty of good shops, cafés and bars. It has an extensive range of single malt whiskeys and some reasonable food, including pizza and lasagne.

Locus Publicus (☎ 433 17 61; Oostzeedijk 364) With more than 200 beers on its menu, it's an outstanding specialist beer café.

Entertainment

Jazzcafé Dizzy (☎ 477 30 14; www.dizzy.nl; 's-Gravendijkwal 129) Live music Tuesday nights and Sunday afternoons. The evening performances are scorching: everything from hot jazz to fast and funky Brazilian and salsa, and a lively, heaving crowd jumping out of their skins.

Rotown (☎ 436 26 69; www.rotown.nl in Dutch; Nieuwe Binnenweg 19) A smooth bar, a dependable live rock venue, an agreeable restaurant (see p858) – a popular meeting place. The musical programme features new local talent, established international acts and crossover experiments.

Off-Corso (☎ 411 38 97; www.off-corso.nl in Dutch; Kruiskade 22) This is where it's at, with bleeding-edge local and international DJs mashing up a high-fibre diet of techno, house, trance and hip hop.

Desire (Nieuwe Binnenweg 148; ⏱ 7-4am) One of Rotterdam's many coffee shops.

Luxor Theater (☎ 413 83 26; www.luxortheater.nl; Posthumalaan 1) A major new performance venue

(2001), the Luxor features diverse theatrical entertainment.

Getting There & Away

BUS

Rotterdam is a hub for Eurolines bus services to the rest of Europe (see p1244). The long-distance bus stops are immediately west of Centraal Station.

TRAIN

Sample fares include Amsterdam (€11.20, 62 minutes), Den Haag (€3.50, 15 minutes), Middelburg (€7.50, 90 minutes) and Utrecht (€8.10, 40 minutes).

THE DELTA REGION

The province of Zeeland (Sea Land) makes up most of the Delta region. Zeeland's three fingers of land are really just islands set in the middle of a vast delta through which many of Europe's rivers drain, including the Rijn (Rhine), Schelde and Maas.

For centuries Zeelanders have been battling the North Sea waters. The St Elizabeth's Day flood of 1421 killed more than 100,000 people and forever altered the landscape (and some would even argue the disposition) of the Netherlands and its population. More recently, in the huge flood of 31 January 1953 almost 2000 people were killed, leaving 500,000 homeless and destroying 800km of dikes.

This last calamity gave rise to the Delta Project, an enormous engineering feat spanning decades to ensure the security of these lands.

MIDDELBURG

☎ 0118 / pop 45,000

Middelburg, Zeeland's capital, is a pleasant and prosperous town and makes a good stopover before exploring the countryside. Its popular Thursday market attracts locals wearing traditional garb.

Information

Tourist Shop (☎ 67 43 00; www.visitmiddelburg.nl in Dutch; Markt 65c; ☼ 9.30am-5.30pm Mon-Fri, 10.30am-5pm Sat)

Zeeland Regional Library (☎ 64 40 00; Kousteensedijk 7; web access per hr €3; ☼ 5-9pm Mon, 10am-9pm Tue-Fri, 10am-1pm Sat)

Sights

Abdij (☎ 61 35 96), on Onderdentoren, is a sizable abbey complex dating from the 12th century. It houses the regional government as well as three churches and two museums. Climb **Lange Jan** (€1.50), a 91m-high tower dating from the 14th century, or visit the **Zeeuws Museum** (☎ 62 66 55; www.zeeuwsmuseum.nl) housed in the former monks' dormitories; it has some of the best first-hand accounts and archival information on the 1953 disaster (closed until 2005 for refurbishment).

The area around **Damplein** (east of the Abdij) preserves many 18th-century houses, some of which have recently been turned into interesting shops and cafés.

Sleeping & Eating

De Kaepstander (☎ 64 28 48; www.kaepstander.nl; Koorkerkhof 10; s/d with shared bathroom €35/60) This amiable place has four rooms with B&B-style accommodation.

Stayokay Domburg (☎ 58 12 54; www.stayokay .com/domburg; Duinvlietweg 8; dm from €20; ☼ Apr-Oct) A hostel notable for its location in a real castle with moat, although it's 10km from Middleburg. Take bus No 53.

Camping Middelburg (☎ 62 53 95; Koninginnelaan 55; per 2 adults & tent €14) Three kilometres from the train station. Take bus No 56 or 58.

De Mug (The Mosquito; ☎ 61 48 51; Vlasmarkt 54; mains €17; ☼ dinner Tue-Sat) Famous for its menu of dishes prepared with unusual beers. Fittingly, the beer list is long and boasts many rare Trappist brews.

De Tuin Van Broeder Ludovicus (☎ 62 60 11; Lange Delft 2a) Excellent for picnickers, with pre-made dishes, cooked meats and salads sold by weight.

Getting There & Away

Sample train fares include Amsterdam (€11, 2½ hours), Roosendaal (€4.60, 45 minutes) and Rotterdam (7.50, 1½ hours).

AROUND MIDDELBURG

Delta Project

The disastrous 1953 flood was the impetus for the Delta Project, which blocked the southwest river deltas with a network of dams, dikes and a remarkable 3.2km storm-surge barrier. It was finished in 1986.

The **Delta Expo** (☎ 0187-49 99 13; www.expo haringvliet.nl; Haringvlietplein 3; adult/child under 12 €4.30/3.30; ☼ 10am-5pm) is an excellent museum

THE NETHERLANDS

and visitors' centre explaining the project. Several floors deal with the effects of the floods and construction of the project. It's also possible to visit the storm surge barrier and see how the huge movable gate works.

Bus No 104 stops at the Expo on its run between Rotterdam's Spijkenisse metro station (25 minutes from Rotterdam Centraal Station) and Vlissingen. The buses take about an hour from Rotterdam and 30 minutes from Middelburg.

THE NORTH & EAST

The Netherlands' northern and eastern regions are made up of several provinces, including Fryslân and Groningen. The north is capped by the Frisian (or Wadden) Islands, a group of five islands which are popular escapes for stressed southerners.

Frisians are fiercely independent: their territory was once part of a Frisian state that included regions of Germany and Denmark, until it became part of the united Netherlands. There have been radio broadcasts in Frisian since 1945 and a Frisian television network since 1994; road signs are in Dutch and Frisian; the province's name was officially changed from Friesland to Fryslân (the Frisian spelling) in 1996; and the national anthem cheekily proclaims Fryslân to be *'it beste lan fan d'ierde'* (the best land on earth).

LEEUWARDEN
☎ 058 / pop 90,500
Leeuwarden is a pleasant place reflecting the serenity of the surrounding farmland. The city's old streets are good for wandering, but even in the middle of holiday season it can seem a little quiet. Leeuwarden's most famous daughter is WWI spy Mata Hari.

Information
Library (☎ 234 77 77; Wirdumerdijk 34; web access per hr €2; 🕐 12.30-5.30pm Mon & Thu, 10am-1pm & 7-9pm Tue & Fri, 10am-1pm Wed & Sat)
Tourist office (☎ 0900-2024060; www.vvvleeuwarden.nl in Dutch; Sophialaan 4; 🕐 9am-5.30pm Mon-Fri, 10am-2pm Sat)

Sights
The **Fries Museum** (☎ 255 55 00; www.friesmuseum.nl; Turfmarkt 11; adult/child under 18 €5/2.50; 🕐 11am-5pm, closed Mon) traces Frisian culture. The huge collection of silver items – long a local speciality – is spectacular, and there's a section on the life of Mata Hari.

The **Princessehof Museum** (☎ 294 89 58; www.princessehof.nl in Dutch; Grote Kerkstraat 11; adult/child €3.50/2; 🕐 11am-5pm Tue-Sun) is the official museum for ceramics and has an impressive selection of Delftware and works from around the globe.

Sleeping
Hotel 't Anker (☎ 212 52 16; www.hotelhetanker.nl; Eewal 73; s/d from €26/47) In a fun and pretty part of town, close to the nightlife district.

De Kleine Wielen (☎ 0511-43 16 60; fax 43 25 84; De Groene Ster 14; per 2-adults camp site €16) This camp site is about 6km east. Bus Nos 10, 13, 50, 51 and 62 all pass close by.

Getting There & Away
Train fares include Amsterdam (€23.50, 140 minutes), Groningen (€7.30, 55 minutes) and Utrecht (€21.30, two hours).

GRONINGEN
☎ 050 / pop 177,000
Groningen was founded around 1000 and has been a crucial centre for trade since the 13th century. The Netherlands' second university was built here in 1614 and like all of the country's large university towns, the student culture gives the place an upbeat, irreverent air.

Information
Tourist Office (☎ 0900-2023050; www.vvvgroningen.nl; Gedempte Kattendiep 6)
The Call Shop (☎ 589 3663; Herestraat 94; Nieuwe Ebbingestraat 80; web access per hr €2)

Sights & Activities
Groninger Museum (☎ 366 65 55; www.groninger-museum.nl in Dutch; adult/child €7/3.50; 🕐 10am-5pm Tue-Sun year-round, 1-5pm Mon Jul-Aug) hosts contemporary design and photography exhibitions alongside classic Golden Age Dutch paintings.

The curious Dutch activity of **wadlopen** (mud-walking) takes place on mud flats stretching all the way to the Frisian Islands. Treks of up to 12km are enthusiastically undertaken by many Dutch, with the 7km walk to Schiermonnikoog the most popular.

Never embark without a skilled guide. Contact Groningen-based **Wadloopcentrum** (☎ 0595-52 83 00; www.waarnaartoe.nl in Dutch; Hoofdstraat

105) and **Dijkstra's Wadlooptochten** (☎ 0595-52 83 45; www.wadloop-dijkstra.nl in Dutch; Hoofdstraat 118) for assistance.

Sleeping & Eating
Simplon Jongerenhotel (☎ 313 52 21; www.simplon jongerenhotel.nl; Boterdiep 72-3; dm from €12) Clean and affordable. Take bus No 1 or 11 from the station to the Boteringestraat stop.

Hotel Friesland (☎ 312 13 07; www.hotelfriesland.nl; Kleine Pelsterstraat 4; s/d €28/48) The rooms are sparse, but the price can't be beat and the location is central.

Stadspark Camping (☎ 525 16 24; www.stadscamp ings.nl; Campinglaan 4; 2 adults & tent €10; ☺ mid-Mar–mid-Oct) Features a shop, restaurant, laundry and playground. From the train station, take bus No 4 about 3km west to the Stadspark stop.

Ugly Duck (☎ 312 31 92; Zwanestraat 28; mains €10.30-14.20; ☺ lunch & dinner) Provençal beef stew and grilled monkfish share the stage with good veggie options, like spanakopita, at this appealing sidewalk café/restaurant.

De 7e Hemel (7th Heaven; ☎ 314 51 41; Zuiderkerkstraat 7; 2-course meal €14-15.50; ☺ dinner Tue-Sat) Serves fantastic vegetarian food and organically farmed meat dishes.

Getting There & Away
Some train fares include: Amsterdam (€24.50, 140 minutes), Leeuwarden (€7.30, 50 minutes), Rotterdam (€27.30, 160 minutes) and Utrecht (€22.30, two hours).

TEXEL
☎ 0222 / pop 13,500
The island of Texel (pronounced *tes*-sel) makes a superb getaway from the mainland rush, with beauty and isolation in abundance: broad beaches, lush nature reserves, forests and picture-book villages. In mid-June, spectators line the beaches for the largest catamaran race in the world, the Cisco Trophy.

Information
Tourist office (☎ 31 47 41; www.vvv-texel.nl in Dutch; Emmalaan 66, Den Burg; ☺ 9am-6pm Mon-Fri, 9am-5pm Sat, 10.30am-1.30pm Sun)
Library (Drijverstraat 7, Den Burg; web access per hr €2; ☺ 2-5pm Tue-Fri, 10.30am-12.30pm Sat & Mon)

Sights
Ecomare (☎ 31 77 41; Ruyslaan 92, De Koog; adult/child €7/3.50; ☺ 9am-5pm) is chiefly a refuge for sick seals retrieved from the Waddenzee wetlands;

rescued birds are the other main tenants. At the aquariums you can sidle up to sharks and even pat a seaskate, and there are seal feedings at 11am and 3pm.

Duinen van Texel national park has salt fens, heath and grass-covered dunes. Much of the area is bird sanctuary and accessible only on foot.

Texel's 30kms of wonderful **beaches** are pristinely white and clean and include two nudist areas.

Sleeping & Eating
Stayokay Texel (31 54 41; www.stayokay.nl/texel; Schansweg 7, Den Burg; dm from €17.50; ☐) Take bus 29 and get off at De Keet stop.

Hotel De Merel (☎ 31 31 32; www.hoteldemerel.nl in Dutch; Warmoesstraat 22, Den Burg; s/d €41/73; ☐) In a quiet street off the marketplace, with a grand piano, a solarium and a truly cosy bar. There's a lawn-side patio for breakfast.

De Bremakker (☎ 31 28 63; www.bremakker.nl in Dutch; Templierweg 40; per 2-adult camp site €25; ☺ Apr-Oct) A calm, leafy campground at the forest's edge, about 1km from the beach. Take bus No 26 to Templierweg.

Getting There & Away
Trains from Amsterdam to Den Helder (€10.90, one hour) are met by a bus that connects with the **car ferry** (☎ 36 96 00; adult/child/car return €4/2/38; ☺ 6.35am-9.35pm), which then makes the crossing in 20 minutes.

AMELAND
☎ 0519 / pop 3600
The 85-sq-km island of Ameland has two distinct centres: picturesque Nes, near the ferry dock, and Hollum, at the west end. Of Ameland's four villages, the 18th-century former whaling port of Nes is the most carefully preserved, its streets lined with tidy little brick houses.

Information
Tourist Office (☎ 54 65 46; www.ameland.nl; Rixt van Doniastraat, Nes; ☺ 9am-12.30pm & 1.30-6pm Mon-Fri, 10am-3pm Sat)

Sleeping & Eating
Stayokay Ameland (☎ 55 53 53; www.stayokay.com /ameland; Oranjeweg 59; dm from €18.10) Near the lighthouse outside Hollum.

Hotel Restaurant de Jong (☎ 54 20 16; fax 54 20 24; http://hoteldejong.vvv-ameland.nl in Dutch; Reeweg 29;

s/d from €45/60) Has decent rooms and a swish café-dining room.

Camping Duinoord (☎ 54 20 70; Jan van Eijckweg 4; per 2-adults & tent €13) This camp site, 2km from Nes, is by the beach. It's lovely but windy.

Herberg De Zwaan (☎ 55 40 02; Zwaneplein 6) A popular restaurant in Hollum.

Getting There & Away

Wagenborg (☎ 54 61 11; www.wpd.nl; adult/child return from €9.10/4.84) operates ferries between Nes and Holwerd. To reach the Holwerd ferry terminal from Leeuwarden, take bus Nos 60 or 66 (40 minutes, hourly). From Groningen, take bus No 34 (80 minutes, four or five daily).

HOGE VELUWE NATIONAL PARK

The **Hoge Veluwe** (☎ 0318-59 16 27; www.hoge veluwe.nl; adult/child €6/3, park & museum €12/6, car €6; ☺ 9am-5.30pm Nov-Mar, 8am-8pm Apr, 8am-9pm May & Aug, 8am-10pm Jun & Jul, 9am-8pm Sep, 9am-7pm Oct) is the Netherlands' largest national park. It was purchased in 1914 by a wealthy German-Dutch couple, Anton and Helene Kröller-Müller, and given to the state in 1930. It's best explored on foot or by one of the park's famous white bicycles, available free at the park entrances or from the visitors centre inside.

The park is a mix of forests and woods, shifting sands and heathery moors, red deer, wild boar and moufflons (a Mediterranean goat). It also features the **Kröller-Müller Museum** (☎ 0318-59 12 41; www.kmm.nl; Houtkampweg 6; adult/child under 12 €5/2.50; ☺ 10am-5pm Tue-Sun & public holidays), with its world-class collection of Van Gogh paintings and works by Picasso, Renoir and Manet.

To get there, take a train to Arnhem then a bus to the park. Contact the **Arnhem tourist office** (☎ 0900-202-4075; www.vvvarnhem.nl; Willemsplein 8) for accommodation advice.

THE SOUTHEAST

DEN BOSCH

☎ 073 / pop 132,500

The official name of Noord Brabant's capital is 's-Hertogenbosch, but it's commonly shortened to Den Bosch (*den boss*). There's a remarkable church, a good museum, some fine cafés and ancient streets. Den Bosch was the birthplace of 15th-century painter Hieronymus Bosch (who took the name of the

town), and the proto-Surrealist is honoured with a statue in front of the town hall.

Information

Tourist Office (☎ 0900-1122334; www.vvvs-hertogen bosch.nl; Markt 77; ☺ 11am-5.30pm Mon, 9am-5.30pm Tue-Fri, 9am-4pm Sat)

Sights & Activities

St Janskathedraal (€3.50; ☺ Mon-Sat 10am-4.30pm, Sun 1-4.30pm), a few minutes' walk from the Markt at the end of Kerkstraat, is one of the finest Gothic churches in the Netherlands; it took from 1336 to 1550 to be completed.

The **Noordbrabants Museum** (☎ 687 78 77; www .noordbrabantsmuseum.nl in Dutch; Verwersstraat 41; adult/child €5.70/3; ☺ 10am-5pm Tue-Fri, noon-5pm Sat) features exhibits about Brabant life and art, and works by Bosch.

Boat tours (☺ Apr-Oct) leave from the canal by Sint Janssingel. Check the pier for times.

Sleeping & Eating

Hotel Terminus (☎ 613 06 66; fax 613 07 26; Boschveldweg 15; r from €27) Decent rooms, an appealing bar and regular live folk music.

All Inn (☎ /fax 613 40 57; Gasselstraat 1; s/d €30/45; ☺ closed Aug) On the lovably shabby but still clean side.

Camping De Wildhorst (☎ 0413-29 14 66; Meerstraat 30; site €10) It's about 12km to the southeast. Take bus No 158 to the church at Heeswijk, from where it's 2km.

Café September (☎ 613 03 08; Verwersstraat 55-57; mains €4-8; lunch & dinner) In a little white building, serving simple meals.

Samtosa (☎ 612 51 22; Vughterstraat 161; mains €28; ☺ dinner) A fantastic vegetarian restaurant on a lovely street, with an extensive menu featuring Mediterranean and Indian influences.

Getting There & Away

Train fares include Amsterdam (€11, one hour), Maastricht (€16, 1½ hours) and Utrecht (€6.50, 30 minutes).

MAASTRICHT

☎ 043 / pop 122,000

Maastricht is completely addictive, with its brace of pavement cafés and wonderful old cobblestone streets, sparkling nightlife, chic dining and elegant atmosphere. Possibly the Netherlands' oldest city (Nijmegen is the other contender), it exists as a hybrid of pan-European influences, hemmed in by Belgium and Germany right near the southernmost point of the Dutch border. Appropriately enough, the city hosted a decisive moment in the history of the European Union: in 1992, the 12 members of the then European Community signed the Maastricht Treaty, thereby creating the European Union.

Information

easyInternetcafé (www.easyeverything.com/map/mas .html; Wolfstraat 8; web access per hr from €1 🕑 9am-6pm Mon-Wed & Fri, 9am-9pm Thu, 9am-5pm Sat)

Tourist Office (☎ 325 21 21; www.vvvmaastricht.nl; Kleine Staat 1; 🕑 9am-6pm Mon-Fri, 9am-5pm Sat, 11am-3pm Sun)

Sights & Activities

The **Bonnefantenmuseum** (☎ 329 01 90; www .bonnefanten.nl in Dutch; Ave Céramique 250; adult/child under 12 €7/3.50; 🕑 11am-5pm Tue-Sun) features a 28m tower that's now a local landmark. The museum is well laid-out with collections divided into departments, each on its own floor: Old Masters and medieval sculpture on one floor, contemporary art by Limburg artists on the next.

Much of Maastricht is riddled with defensive tunnels dug into the soft sandstone over the centuries. The best place to see the tunnels is **Sint Pietersberg**, 2km south of Helpoort. The large fort has tunnels throughout the hill. The tourist office leads **cave tours** (☎ 321 78 78; adult/child €3/1.75; 🕑 3.30pm Jul-Aug & school holidays). Bus No 29 goes past the fort from the Vrijthof, Maastricht's main square. Thirteen species of bats have been found living below the surface.

Stiphout Cruises (☎ 351 53 00; Maaspromenade 27; adult/child €5/3; 🕑 daily Apr-Oct, Sat & Sun Nov-Dec) runs boat cruises on the Maas.

Sleeping

Stayokay Maastricht (☎ 346 67 77; www.stayokay .com/maastricht; Dousbergweg 4; dm €23.75; 🖳) This hostel is on the perimeter of a nature reserve, which is a point in its favour; however, it's a 40-minute walk from the town centre. Take bus 11 (Monday to Friday) or 8 or 18 (Saturday and Sunday) from Maastricht station to the Dousberg stop.

Hotel Randwyck (☎ 361 68 35; www.hotelrand wyck.nl in Dutch; Endepolsdomein 30; s/d €57.50/67.50; 🖳) This is great value: all rooms have TV and bathroom and there's a communal laundry. It's a 20-minute walk from Centraal station, or take the train for one stop to Randwyck station.

De Dousberg (☎ 343 21 71; Dousbergweg 102; 🕑 Feb-Oct) These campgrounds are 10 minutes from the station by bus: Nos 11 and 28 (in the evening) will get you there.

Eating & Drinking

Take Five (☎ 321 09 71; Bredestraat 14; lunch €6; 🕑 lunch & dinner) Combines fusion cooking with a stark interior, soothing music and engaging staff. There's often live jazz.

Pasta & Zo (☎ 325 41 54; Rechtstraat 38; mains from €7; 🕑 lunch & dinner Mon-Sat) Pastas topped with fresh, flavoursome and fulsome homemade sauces. Will do takeaway, too.

Gadjah Mas (☎ 321 15 68; Rechtstraat 42; mains from €12.10-15; 🕑 lunch & dinner) This fabulous restaurant has many vegetarian options among its menu of authentic Indonesian food (as carefully presented as the artistic interior).

Take One (☎ 321 64 23; Rechtstraat 28) This place, though looking cramped and narrow from the outside, is actually expansive on the inside: the extensive beer list covers obscure parts of Europe. The owner encourages clientele to leave their peanut shells on the floor and gleefully refers to customers as 'victims'. Relax: he'll willingly help you select the beer appropriate to your taste.

Matuchi (☎ 354 06 92; Kleine Gracht 34) This is a jaw-achingly hip place to stop for a drink, it's billed as an 'Orient Style Lab'. There's a dash of *Clockwork Orange* in the interior design, mixed with *de rigueur* Arabian themes.

Clubbing

Night Live (☎ 0900-2020158; www.nightlive.nl in Dutch; Kesselskade 43) 'If dance is your religion': that's the motto at this disco in an old church. Everything from hard house to R&B to trance gets an airing.

Entertainment

Derlon Theater (☎ 350 71 71; Plein 1992) Showcases drama and music. The café has fine river views from the terrace.

Getting There & Away

Sample train fares include Amsterdam (€24.50, 155 minutes), Rotterdam (€23.50, 140 minutes) and Utrecht (€21, two hours).

NETHERLANDS DIRECTORY

ACCOMMODATION
Accommodation should always be booked ahead anywhere in the Netherlands, especially during high season; note that many visitors stay in Amsterdam even if travelling elsewhere. The tourist offices have hotel-booking services and keep a list of B&Bs on file.

Be advised that many Dutch hotels have steep stairs but no lifts.

Lists of camp sites are available from the ANWB (p1251) and tourist offices.

Stayokay (☎ 020-501 31 33; www.stayokay.com) is the Dutch hostelling association. A youth hostel card costs €14.50 at the hostels; nonmembers pay an extra €2.50 per night and after six nights you're a member. The usual HI discounts apply.

ACTIVITIES
Cycling, ice-skating, windsurfing, sailing, boating and hanging out at the beach are popular Dutch pastimes. Check the tourist offices for further information.

BUSINESS HOURS
The working week for shop owners starts around lunchtime on Monday. For the rest of the week, most shops open at 8.30am or 9am and close at 5.30pm or 6pm, except Thursday when many close at 9pm, and on Saturday at 5pm. In Amsterdam and tourist centres you will find many shops open on Sunday. Supermarkets often have extended trading hours.

Banks are generally open from 9am to 4pm or 5pm Monday to Friday. Many museums close on Monday.

Restaurants are usually open from 11am to 2.30pm or 3pm for lunch and 5.30pm to 10pm or 11pm for dinner. Most bars open by 11am and close between midnight and 2am. Nightclubs tend to open at 9pm or 10pm and close at 3am or 4am.

DISCOUNT CARDS
These are available from the museums themselves, a *Museumkaart* gives access to 400 museums across the country for €30 (€17 for under 26s).

The **Cultureel Jongeren Paspoort** (Cultural Youth Passport, CJP; €11), available from tourist offices, gives under 27s discounts to nationwide museums and cultural events.

Tourist offices and some large Amsterdam hotels sell the Amsterdam Pass (see p845). A Rotterdam Card is also available (see p857) with similar discounts.

EMBASSIES & CONSULATES
Dutch Embassies & Consulates
Australia (☎ 06-220 9400; www.netherlands.org.au/index.html; 120 Empire Circuit, Canberra, ACT 2600)
Belgium (☎ 02-679 17 11; www.nederlandseambassade.be in Dutch; ave Herrmann-Debroux 48, 1160 Brussels)
Canada (☎ 613-237 50 30; www.netherlandsembassy.ca; Suite 2020, 350 Albert St, Ottawa, Ont K1R 1A4)
Germany (☎ 030-20 95 60; www.dutchembassy.de in Dutch; Friedrichstrasse 95, 10117 Berlin)
New Zealand (☎ 04-471 6390; www.netherlandsembassy.co.nz; Investment House, cnr Ballance & Featherston Sts, Wellington)
UK (☎ 020-7590 3200; www.netherlands-embassy.org.uk; 38 Hyde Park Gate, London SW7 5DP)
USA (☎ 202-244 5300; www.netherlands-embassy.org; 4200 Linnean Ave NW, Washington, DC 20008)

Embassies & Consulates in the Netherlands
EMBASSIES IN DEN HAAG
Australia (☎ 070-310 82 00; www.australian-embassy.nl; Carnegielaan 4)
Belgium (☎ 070-312 34 56; www.diplomatie.be/thehague; Alexanderveld 97)
Canada (☎ 070-311 16 00; www.dfait-maeci.gc.ca/canadaeuropa/netherlands; Sophialaan 7)
France (☎ 070-312 58 00; www.ambafrance-nl.org; Smidsplein 1)
Germany (☎ 070-346 9754; www.duitse-ambassade.nl in Dutch; Groot Hertoginnelaan 18-20)
New Zealand (☎ 070-346 93 24; www.nzembassy.com; Carnegielaan10-IV 6A)
United Kingdom (☎ 070-427 04 27; www.britain.nl; Lange Voorhout 10)
USA (☎ 070-310 92 09; www.usemb.nl; Lange Voorhout 102)

CONSULATES IN AMSTERDAM
Germany (☎ 020-673 62 45; Honthorststraat 36-38)
United Kingdom (☎ 020-676 43 43; Koningslaan 44)
USA (☎ 020-575 53 09; Museumplein 19)

FESTIVALS & EVENTS
February/March
Carnaval Weekend before Shrove Tuesday.
Commemoration of the February Strike (25 February)

Maastricht Art Show (☎ 041-164 50 90; www.tefaf .com) Early March.

April
Amsterdam Fantastic Film Festival (☎ 020-679 48 5; www.afff.nl) Mid-April.
Koninginnedag (Queen's Day, 30 April)

May
Herdenkingsdag & Bevrijdingsdag (Remembrance Day & Liberation Day) 4 & 5 May.
Nationale Molendag (National Mill Day) Second Saturday in May. Nearly every working windmill in the country opens its doors to visitors.

June
Holland Festival (www.hollandfestival.nl) Virtually all month.
Vondelpark Open-Air Theatre (www.openlucht theater.nl in Dutch) Until late August.
Roots Music Festival (Last week of June)

July
North Sea Jazz Festival (www.northseajazz.nl in Dutch) Early July.
Robeco Zomerconcerten (www.robecozomerco certen.nl) Early July-late August. Themed classical concerts at Amsterdam's Concertgebouw.

August
Gay Pride Canal Parade First Saturday (see p41).
FFWD Dance Parade (☎ 010-433 13 00; www.ffwd einekendanceparade.nl in Dutch) Mid-August.
Grachtenfestival (Canal Festival) Late August.
Uitmarkt (www.uitmarkt.nl in Dutch) The re-opening of Amsterdam's cultural season for three days in late August.

September
Bloemencorso (Flower Parade) First Saturday.

November
Sinterklaas Intocht (Mid-November) The Dutch Santa Claus arrives 'from Spain' with his staff.
Cannabis Cup Amsterdam (www.cannabiscup.com) Third week of November.

December
Sinterklaas (5 December) Families exchange small gifts ahead of Christmas religious celebrations.

HOLIDAYS
Public Holidays
Nieuwjaarsdag New Year's Day
Goede Vrijdag Good Friday
Eerste Paasdag Easter Sunday

Tweede Paasdag Easter Monday
Koninginnedag 30 April. Queen's Day
Bevrijdingsdag 5 May. Liberation Day
Hemelvaartsdag Ascension Day
Eerste Pinksterdag Whit Sunday (Pentecost)
Tweede Pinksterdag Whit Monday
Eerste Kerstdag 25 December. Christmas Day
Tweede Kerstdag 26 December. Boxing Day

School Holidays
Spring Holiday Two weeks in mid-February.
May Holiday First week of the month.
Summer Holiday July, August and sometimes the first few days of September.
Autumn Holiday Second half of October.
Christmas Holiday Two weeks through the first full week of January.

LEGAL MATTERS
Dutch police are helpful, with a sense of humour most of the time. One of their pamphlets urges foreigners to seek help if they find themselves in trouble, like falling into a canal stoned: 'Don't be embarrassed,' it says, 'we've seen it all before'. But don't push it: they can hold you for six hours for questioning if you break the law.

Possession of soft drugs up to 5g is tolerated but larger amounts can get you jailed. Hard drugs are treated very seriously. Never buy drugs on the street: you'll get ripped off or mugged. And don't light up just anywhere without checking that it's OK to do so.

MONEY
ATMs
Automatic teller machines can be found outside most banks, at airports and most train stations. Credit cards like Visa and MasterCard/Eurocard are widely accepted, as well as Cirrus cash cards.

Credit Cards
Report lost or stolen cards to the following 24-hour numbers:
American Express (☎ 020-504 80 00, 9am-6pm Mon-Fri; ☎ 020-504 86 66 other times)
Diners Club (☎ 020-654 5511)
Eurocard and MasterCard (☎ 030-283 55 55)
Visa (☎ 020-660 06 11)

Moneychangers
Avoid private exchange booths in tourist areas. Banks and the Postbank (at post offices) stick to official exchange rates and

charge sensible commissions, as does the **GWK** (Grenswisselkantoor; ☎ 0900-0566; www.gwk.nl in Dutch).

Travellers Cheques

Banks charge a commission to cash travellers cheques (with ID such as a passport). American Express and Thomas Cook don't charge commission on their own cheques but their rates might be less favourable. Shops, restaurants and hotels always prefer cash; a few might accept travellers cheques but their rates will be anybody's guess.

POST

Post offices are generally open 9am to 6pm Monday to Friday and 10am to 1pm Saturday. Poste restante is best handled in Amsterdam. Letters up to 20g within Europe cost €0.59 (air mail, known as 'priority') or €0.55 (standard); beyond Europe they are €0.75 (priority) or €0.70 (standard). Postcards cost €0.59 to anywhere outside the country. A *priorityblad* (aerogramme) is €0.50. Within the country, letters up to 20g or postcards cost €0.39.

TELEPHONE

Most public phones accept credit cards as well as various phonecards. Official KPN-Telecom public phoneboxes charge €0.30 per minute for all national calls. Th minimum charge from a public phone €0.20. Calling from private phones is con siderably cheaper.

For mobile phones, the Netherlands use GSM 900/1800, compatible with Europ and Australia but not the North America GSM 1900.

To ring abroad, dial ☎ 00 followed b the country code for your target countr the area code (drop the leading 0) and th subscriber number. The Netherlands cou try code is ☎ 31.

Numbers beginning with ☎ 06 are mo bile or pager numbers.

VISAS

Travellers from Australia, Canada, Israe Japan, New Zealand, the USA and mar other countries need only a valid passpo (no visa) for a stay of up to three month EU nationals can enter for three montl with a national identity card or passpo expired for no more than five years. Natio als of most other countries need a so-calle Schengen Visa, valid for 90 days.

After three months, extensions can b sought through the **Vreemdelingenpolitie** (Alie. Police; ☎ 020-559 63 00; Johan Huizingalaan 757, Amste dam; ☯ 8am-5pm Mon-Fri), but you'll need a goc reason for an extension to be granted.

Norway

HIGHLIGHTS

- **Oslo** Norway's capital, come here for Viking ships, cafés and a subway that drops you off near a bobsled run (p873).
- **Tromsø** Experiencing either the Aurora Borealis or the Midnight Sun in this lively college town far north of the Arctic Circle (p891).
- **Hurtigurten** Sleeping (for free) on the deck of the famous coastal steamer as it wends its way past fjords and islands en route to picture-perfect towns such as Ålesund, Bergen and Trondheim (p891).
- **Best journey** All subsequent rides will be ruined after this seven-hour race on the Oslo–Bergen train past snowy plateaus, spectacular fjords and spotless wilderness (p882).

FAST FACTS

- **Area** 306,800 sq km (4.45 Irelands)
- **ATMs** Widespread, even in arctic towns
- **Budget** Nkr350 per day
- **Capital** Oslo
- **Country Code** ☎ 47
- **Famous for** Cod, off-shore oil-rigs, Vikings, whale consumption
- **Languages** Norwegian, English and Sami
- **Money** Norwegian krone (A$1 = Nkr4.81, CA$1 = Nkr5.25, €1 = Nkr8.23) ¥100 = Nkr6.07, NZ$1 = Nkr4.52, UK£1 = Nkr11.93, US$1 = Nkr6.52)
- **Phrases** *Hei* (hello), *takk* (thanks), *ya* (yes), *nei* (no), *stengt* (closed)
- **Population** 4.5 million

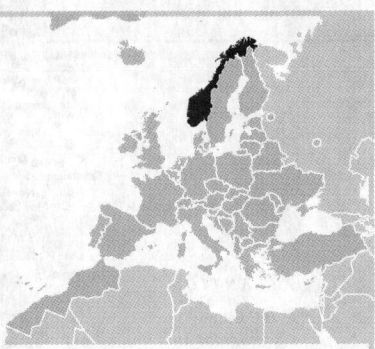

- **Time** GMT/UTC + 1
- **Visas** Unnecessary for visitors from Scandinavia, EU countries, the USA and the Commonwealth for under three months.

TRAVEL HINTS

Bring booze and smokes from other countries. Check legal limits of course. If possible, purchase 'minipris' tickets (p1255) when travelling by rail.

ROAMING NORWAY

Catch the train from Oslo to Bergen via Flåm. Take the Hurtigurten to the Lofoten Islands. Eat cod, go to Trondheim and return to Oslo.

Ruggedly beautiful, Norway (Norge) is a country of high mountains, stunning fjords and blue glaciers. The mainland stretches 2000km from southern beach towns to treeless Arctic tundra in the north; 1000km further north, there's Svalbard, Norway's Arctic archipelago. The country offers incredible wilderness hiking, year-round skiing and some of the most

NORWAY

NORWAY

0 — 200 km
0 — 120 miles

Approximate North Only
UP

SVALBARD

Svalbard
Jan Mayen
NORWAY

0 — 100 km
0 — 60 miles

Nordaustlandet

Ny Ålesund

Spitsbergen

Barentsøya

Longyearbyen
Barentsburg
Sveagruva

Edgeøya

To Jan Mayen

To Norway mainland

ARCTIC OCEAN

BARENTS SEA

Nordkapp
Honningsvåg

Hammerfest

Tana Bru
Vardø
Vadsø
Kirkenes
Storskog

Alta E6
Finnmark
Karasjok

Finnmarksvidda
Kautokeino

RUSSIA

NORWEGIAN SEA

Fjordgard; Husøy
Mefjordvær
Skaland
Gryllefjord
Andenes

Tromsø
Finnsnes
Troms

Setlu

Vesterålen
Stø
Nyksund
Sortland
Stokmarknes
Melbu
Svolvær
Stamsund
Å
Lofoten
Vestfjorden
Kjerringøy
BODØ
Sattstraumen
Fauske

Harstad
E6

Narvik
Storjord
Skutvik

Nordland
Svartisen Icecap

FINLAND

Arctic Circle

Mo i Rana

Mosjøen

ATLANTIC OCEAN

SWEDEN

Nord Trøndelag E6

Steinkjer

TRONDHEIM E14
Hell
Sør Trøndelag

ÅLESUND
Åndalsnes
Røros

Måløy
Nordfjord
Stryn
Geiranger
Dombås
E136
Rondane

Galdhøpiggen ▲ (2469m)
Balestrand
Lærdal **Jotunheimen**
Sognefjorden
Voss
Flåm
Finse
Gello
E16
Lillehammer
Hamar

BERGEN
Odda
Hardangervidda

Haukeligrend
Haugesund
E134
Rjukan
Notodden
Bø
Kongsberg
Telemark
SKIEN
Tau
STAVANGER
Kragerø
E39
Sørlandet
Risør
Lillesand
Arendal
Grimstad
Mandal
KRISTIANSAND

OSLO
Moss
E18
FREDRIKSTAD
Halden
Larvik
E6
Skagerrak

Bottenhavet

HELSINKI

STOCKHOLM

TALLINN
ESTONIA

BALTIC SEA

scenic ferry, and train rides imaginable. Summer days are delightfully long, and in the northernmost parts the sun doesn't set for weeks on end.

In addition to the lure of the spectacular western fjords, Norway boasts several picturesque cities combining urban sophistication with dramatic setting. Otherwise, take your pick from unspoiled fishing villages, Viking ships and medieval stave churches.

HISTORY

Norway's greatest impact on history was in the Viking Age, usually dated from the plundering of England's Lindisfarne monastery by Nordic pirates in 793. Over the next century, the Vikings made raids throughout Europe. The Viking leader Harald Hårfagre (Fairhair) unified Norway in 872. Norwegian naval power was finished off when Alexander III, King of Scots, defeated a Viking force at the Battle of Largs in 1263.

In 1397 Norway was absorbed into a union with Denmark that lasted over 400 years. Denmark's defeat in the Napoleonic Wars resulted in its ceding of Norway to Sweden in January 1814. Tired of forced unions, on 17 May 1814 a defiant Norway adopted its own constitution. In 1884 a parliamentary government was introduced and a growing nationalist movement eventually led to peaceful secession from Sweden in 1905.

Norway stayed neutral during WWI. It was attacked by the Nazis on 9 April 1940. King Håkon established a government in exile in England and placed most of Norway's merchant fleet under the command of the Allies. Although Norway remained occupied until the end of the war, it had an active resistance movement. The royal family returned in June 1945.

Norway joined the European Free Trade Association (EFTA) in 1960, but has been reluctant to forge closer bonds with other European nations. In 1972 Norwegians voted against joining the European Community (EC) amidst a divisive national debate.

Sentiments continue to favour staying outside the EU, though this has wavered recently.

PEOPLE & CULTURE

With only 4,546,000 people, one of the lowest population densities in Europe, Norway is considered to have the world's best standard of living. The largest cities are Oslo with 500,000 residents, then Bergen, Trondheim and Stavanger.

Most Norwegians are of Nordic origin, thought to have descended from central and northern European tribes who migrated northwards around 8000 years ago. In addition, there are about 40,000 Sami (formerly known as Lapps), the indigenous people of Norway's far north who make up the country's largest ethnic minority. Many still live a traditional nomadic life, herding reindeer in Finnmark.

SPORT

'Ski' is a Norwegian word and Norway makes a credible claim to having invented the sport. Norway has thousands of kilometres of maintained cross-country ski trails and many resorts with excellent downhill runs. The Holmenkollen area near Oslo, Geilo, and the Gudbrandsdalen region near Lillehammer are just a few of the more popular spots. Den Norske Turistforening (Norwegian Mountain Touring Association; DNT) is a good source for information about skiing.

Norway has stellar hiking, ranging from easy trails in the forests to long mountain treks. Deep winter snows make many areas seasonal; in the highlands, it's often limited to the period of late June to September. Popular wilderness hiking areas are Jotunheimen, Rondane and Hardangervidda, but many others are equally attractive. For more information, contact DNT.

Norway's wild and scenic rivers are ideal for rafting, with trips ranging from short Class II doddles to Class III and IV adventures and rollicking Class V punishment. **Norges Padleforbund** (☎ 21 02 98 35; www.padling.no; Service boks 1, Ullevål stadion, N-0840 Oslo) provide a comprehensive list of rafting operators.

READING UP

Norwegian Mountains on Foot, by Den Norske Turistforening (Norwegian Mountain Touring Association; DNT) details hiking, with information on trails and huts. James Graham-Campbell's *The Viking World* traces Viking history by detailing excavated sites and artefacts. Norse mythology buffs should peruse *Gods & Myths of Northern Europe* by HR Ellis Davidson.

NORWAY

BLACK METAL

Bored of fjords and peace prizes? Perhaps it's time to check out Norway's highly regarded Black Metal scene, whose notorious, sensational exploits in the mid-90s raised eyebrows across the globe. At that time, the members of a few big name bands (Mayhem and Emperor being the most notable) not only committed suicide, but murdered each other, burned stave churches, allegedly made trinkets out of fragments of their mate's skulls and beat up bouncers and concert-goers alike. In addition to these and other violent acts, a lot of music was created along the way. Depending on your taste, the goods might sound like a dying Cookie Monster singing through a distortion pedal or liberation from what you perceive to be a Christian dominated music industry.

While things have calmed down a bit since the gory days, Black Metal remains popular in Norway. A few bands to look for include Mayhem (much of the previous line-up is dead or jailed), Satyricon, Gorgoroth and Dark Throne, and a few of the clubs to view them are Garage (p879), Hulen (p885), Rockefeller Music Hall (p880) and Blæst (p889). If you're lucky enough to spend April in Oslo, you must attend the Inferno Metal Festival (p877). Don't forget your leather pants!

Favourite spectator sports include skiing, speed skating and football. Empathetic winter visitors will experience displaced vertigo as they witness ski jumping at, amongst other places, Holmenkollen (p877).

ARTS

Norway's best-known artists include Edvard Munch, landscape painter JC Dahl, classical composer Edvard Grieg, sculptor Gustav Vigeland and playwright Henrik Ibsen.

Norway's stave churches are some of the oldest wooden buildings on Earth. Named for their vertical supporting posts, these structures are often distinguished by dragon-headed gables resembling ornately carved prows of Viking ships. Other significant architectural features in the country include the romantic 'dragon style', found in some historic hotels, and occurrences of the Art Nouveau style, best observed in Ålesund.

Norwegians Sigrid Undset and Knud Hamsun (a Nazi collaborator) won the Nobel Prize for Literature in 1928 and 1920, respectively. Undset is best known for *Kristin Lavransdottir*, a trilogy portraying the struggles and earthy lifestyle of a 14th-century Norwegian family, while Hamsun won the Nobel Prize for his novel *The Growth of the Soil*.

Not traditionally a cinematic powerhouse, Norway has recently produced several excellent films including *Elling* (2001), *Buddy* (2003) and *Beautiful Country* (2004). For a Norwegian classic, check out *Ni Liv* (1957).

Norway's rock scene thrives, with Bergen producing most of the bands. Some of the Bergen Wave's most popular artists include Ralph Myerz and the Jack Herrend Band, Sondre Lerche, and Röyksopp.

ENVIRONMENT

Norway's coastline is deeply cut by fjords – long, narrow inlets of the sea bordered by high, steep cliffs. Mountains, some capped with Europe's largest glaciers, cover more than half of the landmass. Only 3% of the country is arable.

The typically rainy climate of the mainland is surprisingly mild for its latitude and, thanks to the Gulf Stream, the coastal ports remain ice-free all year, even though much of Norway lies above the Arctic Circle.

TRANSPORT

GETTING THERE & AWAY
Air

Oslo's **Gardermoen Airport** (OSL; ☎ 81 55 02 50; www.osl.no) is Norway's principle connection to international cities. Other airports with limited connections to international destinations are:

Bergen (BGO; ☎ 55 99 80 00; www.avinor.no)
Stavanger (SVG; ☎ 51 65 80 00; www.avinor.no)
Tromsø (TOS; ☎ 77 64 84 00; www.avinor.no)
Trondheim (TDR; ☎ 74 84 30 00; www.avinor.no)

EMERGENCY NUMBERS

■ Ambulance ☎ 113

■ Fire ☎ 110

■ Police ☎ 112

Airlines Flying to and from Norway:
Air France (AF; ☎ 23 50 20 01; www.airfrance.no)
Braathens (BU; ☎ 81 52 00 00; www.braathens.no)
British Airways (BA; ☎ 80 03 31 42; www.british airways.com)
Finnair (AY; ☎ 81 00 11 00; www.finnair.com)
Icelandair (FI; ☎ 22 03 40 50; www.icelandair.com)
KLM (WA; ☎ 22 64 37 52; www.klm.com)
Lufthansa (LH; ☎ 81 52 04 00; www.lufthansa.com)
Norwegian Air (DY; ☎ 81 52 18 15; www.norwegian.no)
SAS (SK; ☎ 81 52 04 00; www.scandinavian.net)

Boat
DENMARK
DFDS Seaways (☎ 22 41 90 90; www.dfdsseaways.com; Nkr221-915) runs overnight ferries between Copenhagen and Oslo. Fares vary depending on season and kind of cabin selected.

Color Line (☎ 81 00 08 11; www.colorline.com) runs ferries between Hirtshals and Kristiansand (from 4½ hours, two to five daily). Color Line also operates between Frederikshavn and Larvik (from 6¼ hours, one to two daily) and between Hirtshals and Oslo (eight hours, one daily). Fares are the same for all routes – depending on the day of the week and the season, they range from €24 to €58 for passengers and €89 to €225 for cars.

Fjord Line (☎ 55 54 88 00; www.fjordline.com) sails from Hanstholm to Bergen (Nkr340 to Nkr920, 17hrs, one daily most of year). Cabins, cars and folding deck chairs cost extra.

Stena Line (☎ 23 17 91 00, 02010; www.stenaline.com) operates daily ferries between Frederikshavn and Oslo (passenger/car & driver Nkr160-390/Nkr240-1390, 12 hours), except Monday from early September to mid-June.

ICELAND & THE FAROE ISLANDS
Smyril Line (☎ 55 32 09 70; www.smyril-line.com) runs from May to early September between Bergen and Seyðisfjörður in Iceland (25 hrs, one weekly), via Lerwick and the Faroe Islands. One-way low/high season fares to Bergen begin at Dkr630/870 from Tórshavn in the Faroes and Ikr15,990/22,790 from Seyðisfjörður. High season is mid-June to early August.

SWEDEN
DFDS Seaways (☎ 22 41 90 90; www.dfdsseaways.com) operates overnight ferries between Helsingborg and Oslo (from Skr442, 14 hours, one daily).

DFDS Seaways connects Gothenburg and Kristiansand (fares start at Skr118, seven hours, three weekly).

Bus
DENMARK
The **Säfflebussen** (☎ 771-15 15 15; www.safflebussen .se) from Copenhagen to Oslo (Nkr150/220, nine hours, three daily) runs via Malmö in Sweden; the lower fare is valid Monday to Thursday. There's a student discount.

FINLAND
Finnish company **Eskelisen Lapin Linjat** (in Finland ☎ 016-342 2160; www.eskelisen-lapinlinjat.com) runs buses from Rovaniemi (Finland) to Nordkapp (June to August) and Tromsø (June to mid-September).

SWEDEN
Nor-Way Bussekspress (☎ 81 54 44 44; www.nor-way .no) runs between Oslo and Gothenburg (Skr200/160 adult/student, 4¼ hours, four daily) and between Skellefteå and Bodø (Skr480, 8¾ hours, once daily Sunday to Friday).

Train
DENMARK
Trains from Copenhagen to Oslo (nine hours, two daily) require changing in Gothenburg, Sweden; book cheap tickets at least seven days in advance.

SWEDEN
Daily trains operate from Stockholm (seven hours, three daily), Gothenburg (from Skr190, four hours) and Malmö (from Skr450, 8¼ hours) to Oslo; book cheap tickets at least seven days in advance.

GETTING AROUND
Public transport in Norway is efficient, with trains, buses and ferries timed to link effectively. The *NSB Togruter*, available at train stations, has rail schedules and information on connecting buses. Boat and bus departures vary daily and are seasonal, so pick up the latest *ruteplan* (timetables) from regional tourist offices.

NORWAY

Air

Norway has 50 airports. Air travel is worth considering due to the great distances involved in overland travel.

Norway's domestic airlines are **SAS** (☎ 81 52 04 00; www.scandinavian.net), **Braathens** (☎ 81 52 00 00; www.braathens.no), **Widerøe** (☎ 81 00 12 00; www.wideroe.no) and the discount airline **Norwegian Air** (☎ 81 52 18 15; www.norwegian.no). Check for student fares.

Widerøe often has deals, including 'Explore Norway' tickets (around Nkr4000), where you'll have unlimited travel between Norway's airports for two weeks.

Bicycle

Given its geography, Norway is not ideally suited for extensive touring by bicycle. The *Sykkelguide* series of booklets (Nkr120), available at larger tourist offices, have maps and English text.

Boat

An comprehensive network of ferries and express boats links Norway's islands, coastal towns and fjord districts. See specific destinations for details.

HURTIGRUTEN COASTAL STEAMER

For more than a century Norway's **Hurtigruten** (☎ 81 03 00 00; www.hurtigruten.no) has been the lifeline for villages scattered along the remote coast.

One ship heads north from Bergen each night, pulling into 34 ports on its six-day journey to Kirkenes and returns south. With good weather, expect spectacular scenery.

The ships accommodate deck-class travellers, offering free sleeping areas (not so comfortable), baggage rooms, shower rooms, 24-hour cafeterias and coin laundry. Passengers can rent cabins (Nkr200 to Nkr3000). Sample deck-class fares from Bergen are Nkr1533 to Trondheim and Nkr3145 to Tromsø. Accompanying spouses, children, students, and seniors over 67 all receive 50% discount.

From September to April, passengers get 40% off fares on any day except Tuesday, with return journeys at a further 50% reduction on the return portion of the ticket.

Bus

Norway has an extensive bus network. Fares average Nkr150 for the first 100km.

Many bus companies offer child, student senior, group and family discounts of 25% to 50% – always ask.

Nor-Way Bussekspress (☎ 82 02 13 00; www.nor-way.no) has routes connecting every main town. It offers passes valid for 21 consecutive days (Nkr2300).

In Nordland, several routes offer half-price fares to Eurail, InterRail and ScanRail pass holders. These run between Tromsø and Bodø, making stops in towns on the way. InterRail and ScanRail passes get half-price bus tickets to/from the western fjords and various other routes in southern Norway.

Car & Motorcycle

The **Road User Information Centre** (☎ 175) tells you the latest road conditions throughout Norway.

For a full list of ferry schedules, fares and reservation phone numbers, grab the latest copy of *Rutebok for Norge* (Nkr210), available in larger bookshops. For more motoring information, contact the national automobile club, **Norges Automobil-Forbund** (NAF; ☎ 22 34 14 00; www.naf.no; Storgata 2, N-0105 Oslo).

Major car-rental companies have offices at airports and in city centres. The daily rate for a compact car with 200km free is about Nkr1000, including MVA and insurance.

Hitching

Hitching isn't common. One approach is to ask for rides from truck drivers at ferry terminals and petrol stations.

Train

Norway has an excellent, though limited, national rail system. **NSB** (Norges Statsbaner or Norwegian State Railways; ☎ 81 50 08 88; www.nsb.no) operates most lines.

Second-class travel is comfortable. Komfort-class travel, which costs Nkr75 more, isn't worth the extra tariff, unless you really dig free coffee.

Discounted *minipris* tickets are sometimes available. Extremely cheap, you could travel from Oslo to Bergen for just Nkr150, depending on the offering. These tickets may only be purchased online, at least a day in advance. Buy early – these sell out.

NSB sells *Euro Domino* tickets at Nkr1 309/1540/1791/2002/2333/2464 for three/four/five/six/seven/eight days travel on the Norwegian rail network within one month.

Regular fares from Oslo are Nkr670 to Bergen, Nkr644 to Åndalsnes, Nkr783 to Stavanger and Nkr758 to Trondheim. On many long-distance trains reservations (Nkr50) are mandatory.

Second-class sleepers provide cheap sleeps (3-bed/2-bed/private cabins Nrk125/270/580). 'Sleeperettes' (halfway between a chair and a bed) are available on the Trondheim–Bodø line (Nkr70).

OSLO

pop 520,000

Norway's capital city, Oslo offers a rare combination: a diverse web of urbanity – featuring nifty cafés, museums and nightlife – and easy access to nature. A short ride on the metro drops you off at the Nordmarka (North Woods), where you'll find a network of cross country ski trails, small downhill slopes, hiking routes and a bobsled run. In summer, take ferries to the Islands of the Oslofjord for beaches and barbeques. Or lounge around Oslo's hipster district (Grünerløkka) with a beer, street-cred and easy access to some of the city's better restaurants. All visitors are required to stroll through Frognerparken.

ORIENTATION

Oslo's central train station (Oslo Sentralstasjon, or 'Oslo S') is at the eastern end of the city centre. From there the main street, Karl Johans gate, runs through the heart of the city. The neighbourhood of Grünerløkka is reached by taking Storgata across the Akerselva river, while the Grønland immigrant district is just east of Oslo S.

Most central city sights, including the harbour front and Akershus Fortress, are within a 15-minute walk of Karl Johans gate, as are most hotels and pensions.

INFORMATION
Bookshops
Nomaden (☎ 22 56 25 40; Uranienborgveien 4; ⏱ from 10am Mon-Sat) Sells travel guides and maps.

Emergency
Jernbanetorget Apotek (opposite Oslo S) A 24-hour pharmacy.

Oslo Kommunale Legevakten (☎ 22 11 80 80; Storgata 40) This medical clinic provides 24-hour emergency services.

GETTING INTO TOWN

Those arriving by bus or train are dumped off directly in Oslo's centre. The airport is 50km north of the city. High-speed trains run to Oslo S (Nkr150, 24 minutes, every 20 minutes). Alternatively, you can take a local train (Nkr80, 26 to 40 minutes, hourly but fewer on Saturday) or an express airport bus (Nkr90, 40 minutes, three hourly).

Internet Access
You can check your mail for free at the **library** but expect a wait and half-hour time limit.
Studenten (☎ 22 42 56 80; Karl Johans gate 45; per 30 mins/hr Nkr 30/55; ⏱ from noon)

Laundry
Selvebetjent (Ullevålsveien 15; ⏱ 8am-9pm) Charges Nkr40/30 to wash/dry, including soap.

Libraries
Deichmanske Bibliotek (Henrik Ibsens gate 1; ⏱ from 10am Mon-Fri, from 9am Sat)

Money
Change money at the **airport bank** (Gardermoen airport departure hall; ⏱ from 5.30am Sat, 6.30am-8pm Sun), the **post office** and at **Nordea bank** (Oslo S; ⏱ 7am-7pm Mon-Fri, 8am-5pm Sat & Sun). ATMs are everywhere, including Oslo S and the airport.

American Express (☎ 22 98 37 35; Fridtjof Nansens plass 6; ⏱ 9am-4.30pm Mon-Fri, 10am-3pm Sat) exchanges cash and traveller's cheques without transaction fees, though its rates may be somewhat lower.

Post
Main post office (Dronningens gate 15; ⏱ 9am-5pm Mon-Fri)
Branch post office (Oslo S; ⏱ 8.30am-8pm Mon-Fri, 9am-6pm Sat).

Tourist Information
Oslo Promotion (☎ 24 14 77 00; www.visitoslo.com; Fridtjof Nansens Plass; ⏱ 9am-7pm Jun-Aug, shorter hrs otherwise) Provides tourist information for Oslo.
Tourist information window (Oslo S; ⏱ 8am-11pm May-Sep, 8am-5pm Mon-Sat Oct-Apr).
Use-It (☎ 22 41 51 32; www.unginfo.oslo.no; Møllergata 3; ⏱ 9am-6pm Mon-Fri July & Aug, 11am-5pm Mon-Fri Sep-Jun) This youth information office gives honest advice and info about Oslo's goings-on.

NORWAY

OSLO

INFORMATION			
American Express	1 D4	Post Office	13 D4	Museet for Samtidskunst	25 E5
Australian Consulate	2 F4	Studenten	14 D4	Nasjonalgalleriet	26 D3
Canadian Embassy	3 C3	Tourist Information Window	15 F4	Norges Hjemmefront Museet	27 D6
Deichmanske Bibliotek	4 E3	Trafikanten	16 F4	
DNT Office	5 E4	US Embassy	17 B4	**SLEEPING** (pp877–8)
German Embassy	6 A3	Use It	18 E4	Anker Hostel	28 F3
Irish Embassy	7 C4			City Hotel	29 E5
Main Post Office	8 E5	**SIGHTS & ACTIVITIES** (pp876–7)		Cochs Pensjonat	30 B3
Netherlands Embassy	9 B3	Akershus Festning Entrance	19 D5	Ellingsen's Pensjonat	31 A2
Nomaden	10 B3	Akershus Slott	20 D6	Fønix Hotel	32 E4
Oslo Kommunale Legevakten		Det Kongelige Slott	21 B4	MS Innvik	33 F5
(Medical Clinic)	11 F2	Historisk Museet	22 C3	Oslo Vandrerhjem IMI	34 C3
Oslo Promotion	12 D4	Jernbanetorget Apotek	23 E4	Perminalen	35 D5
		Munchmuseet	24 H2	YMCA Sleep-In	36 E4

To Krishna's Cuisine (400m);
Lofotstua (700m);
Skiforeningen (7km);
Tomm Murstad Skiservice (9km);
Nordmarka (10km);
Frognerparken (12km)

Vår Frelsers Gravlund

National Hospital

Slottsparken

Nationaltheatret T-bane Station

University of Oslo

Eidsvolls-plass

Karl Johans gate

Stortinget T-bane Station

Wesselsplass

Fridtjof Nansens plass

Rådhusplassen

Rådhusgata

Rådhusbrygge

To French Embassy (300m);
Russian Embassy (300m);
Finnish Embassy (500m);
Danish Embassy (1.5km);
English Embassy (2km);
New Zealand Embassy (4km)

E18

Pipervika

Akershus Festning

To Bygdøy
Peninsula (3.6km);
Oslo Vandrerhjem
Holtekilen (8km)

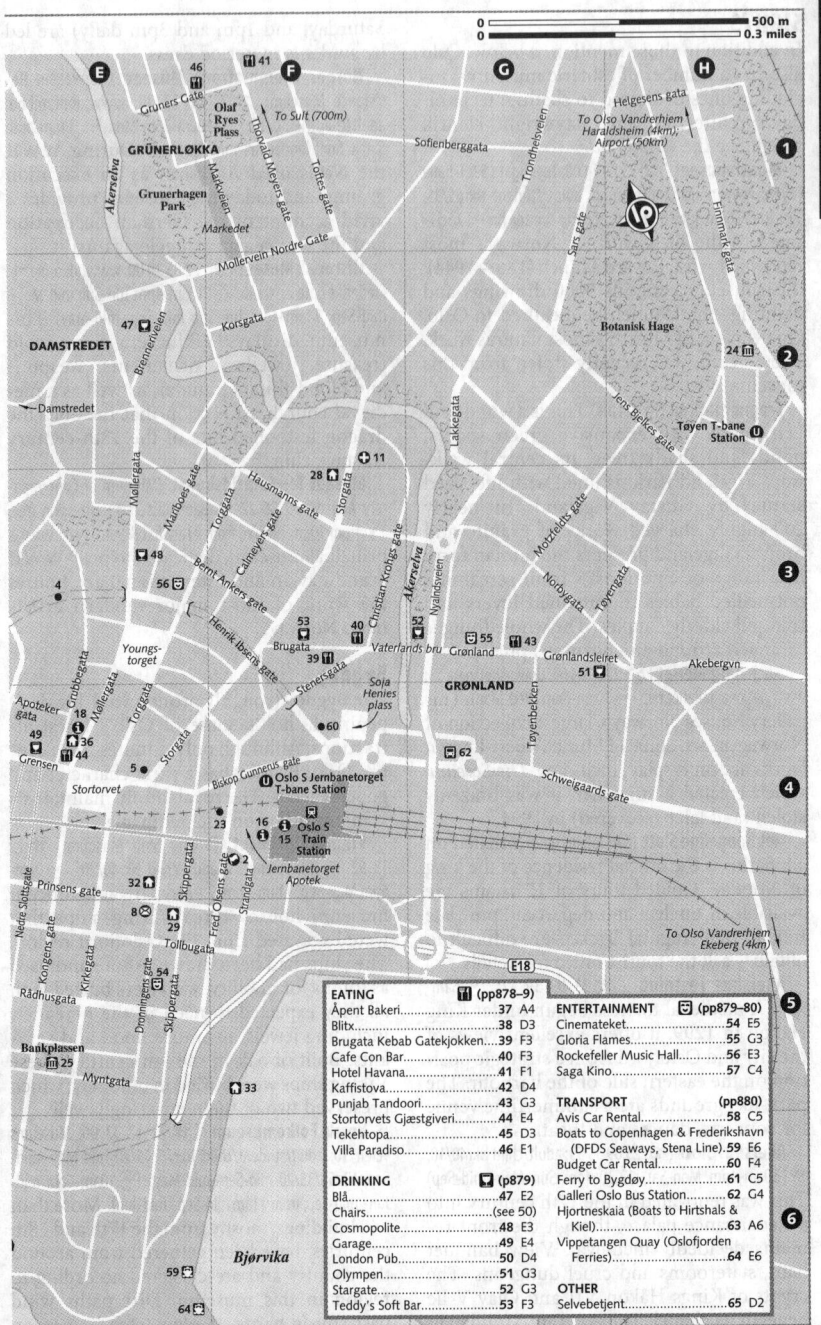

EATING 🍴 (pp878–9)
Åpent Bakeri	37 A4
Blitx	38 D3
Brugata Kebab Gatekjøkken	39 F3
Cafe Con Bar	40 F3
Hotel Havana	41 F1
Kaffistova	42 D4
Punjab Tandoori	43 G3
Stortorvets Gjæstgiveri	44 E4
Tekehtopa	45 D3
Villa Paradiso	46 E1

DRINKING 🍷 (p879)
Blå	47 E2
Chairs	(see 50)
Cosmopolite	48 E3
Garage	49 E4
London Pub	50 D4
Olympen	51 G3
Stargate	52 G3
Teddy's Soft Bar	53 F3

ENTERTAINMENT 🎭 (pp879–80)
Cinemateket	54 E5
Gloria Flames	55 G3
Rockefeller Music Hall	56 E3
Saga Kino	57 C4

TRANSPORT (pp880)
Avis Car Rental	58 C5
Boats to Copenhagen & Frederikshavn (DFDS Seaways, Stena Line)	59 E6
Budget Car Rental	60 F4
Ferry to Bygdøy	61 C5
Galleri Oslo Bus Station	62 G4
Hjortneskaia (Boats to Hirtshals & Kiel)	63 A6
Vippetangen Quay (Oslofjorden Ferries)	64 E6

OTHER
Selvebetjent	65 D2

SIGHTS

In addition to those mentioned below, Oslo also has a number of esoteric museums, including ones dedicated to skating, technology, architecture and playwright Henrik Ibsen. See the *Oslo Guide*.

Munchmuseet (☎ 23 24 14 00; Tøyengata 53; T-bane Tøyen; www.munch.museum.no; adult/student Nkr65/35; ⏰ 10am-6pm Jun–mid-Sep, shorter winter hrs) Dedicated to the life's work of Norway's most renowned artist, Edvard Munch (1863–1944), this museum contains 5000 drawings and paintings that Munch bequeathed to Oslo. One version of Munch's most famous work, *The Scream*, was recently stolen from this museum.

Frognerparken (⏰ 24 hrs) This is a wonderful city park with expansive green spaces, ponds and shady trees. Its central walkway, Vigeland Park, is lined with life-sized statues by Gustav Vigeland. In nearly 200 highly charged works of granite and bronze, Vigeland presents the human form in a range of emotions – from screaming pot-bellied babies to entwined lovers and tranquil elderly couples. The whole thing is arranged around an enormous phallus.

Nasjonalgalleriet (☎ 22 20 04 04; Universitetsgata 13; www.nasjonalgalleriet.no; ⏰ 10am-6pm Wed-Mon) This gallery houses Norway's largest collection of Norwegian art. Some of Munch's best-known works are on display, including *The Scream*, which created a stir when it was brazenly stolen (and later recovered) in 1994.

Det Kongelige Slott (Karl Johans gate) Situated on a hill, this is the official residence of the king of Norway. Guided tours of 15 rooms are available in English and depart at 2pm (late June to mid-August). Tickets are difficult to obtain – ask the tourist office for details.

Akershus Festning (☎ 23 09 39 17; ⏰ 6am-9pm) A medieval fortress begun under King Håkon in 1299, it offers excellent views of the city and Oslofjord from a strategic position on the eastern side of the harbour. The park-like grounds are a summertime venue for concerts, dances and theatre.

Akershus Slott (☎ 23 09 35 53; adult/child Nkr40/10; ⏰ 10am-4pm Mon-Sat, 12.30-4pm Sun May–mid-Sep) This was renovated in the 17th century into a Renaissance palace, though the front remains decidedly medieval. View banquet halls, staterooms and cruel dungeons. The crypts of Kings Håkon VII and Olav V lie beneath its chapel. Tours (11am Monday to Saturday, and 1pm and 3pm daily) are led by students in period dress.

Norges Hjemmefront Museet (Norwegian Resistance Museum; ☎ 23 09 31 38; www.nhm.mil.no; adult/child Nkr30/15; ⏰ 10am-3pm Mon-Fri, 11am-4pm Sat & Sun, longer hrs mid-Apr–Sep) During WWII the Nazis used Akershus as an execution ground and today the museum provides a vivid account of the German occupation and the Norwegian struggle against it.

Historisk Museet (☎ 22 85 19 00; www.ukm.uio.no; Frederiks gate 2; Nkr40; ⏰ 10am-4pm Tue-Sun mid-May–mid-Sep, 11am-4pm Tue-Sun mid-Sep–mid-May) This museum displays Viking-era coins, gold treasure, jewellery, ornaments, weapons and blood-thirsty plunder, as well as a medieval church art section that includes the dragon-festooned bits of the 13th-century Ål stave church.

Museet for Samtidskunst (Museum of Contemporary Art; ☎ 22 86 22 10; Bankplassen 4; admission free; ⏰ from 10am Tue-Fri, from 11am Sat & Sun) Norway's principal museum, dedicated to post-WWII Scandinavian and international art, houses the work of most major modern artists from Norway.

Bygdøy

The Bygdøy (roughly pronounced 'big day') peninsula holds some of Oslo's finest attractions. Although only minutes from central Oslo, Bygdøy has a rural character and good beaches. The royal family maintains a summer home on the peninsula.

Vikingskipshuset (Viking Ship Museum; ☎ 22 13 52 80; Huk Aveny 35; adult/child Nkr40/20; ⏰ 9am-6pm May-Sep, 11am-4pm Oct-Apr) This magnificent museum houses three Viking ships that were excavated from the Oslofjord region. The ships had been drawn ashore and used as tombs for nobility, who were buried with all they expected to need in the hereafter, including jewels, furniture, food and servants. Built of oak in the 9th century, these Viking ships were buried in blue clay, which preserved two of them amazingly well.

Norsk Folkemuseum (☎ 22 12 37 00; Museums veien 10; adult/student/child Nkr75/45/20 mid-May–mid-Sep, Nkr55/35/20 mid-Sep–mid-May; ⏰ 10am-6pm mid-Jun–mid-Sep, from 11am mid-Sep–mid-Jun). More than 140 buildings, mostly from the 17th and 18th centuries, have been gathered from around the country and are clustered according to region in this museum. Dirt paths wind past sturdy barns, *stabbur* (storehouses on stilts) and sod-roofed farmhouses sprouting wildflowers. On Sunday, there's usually folk music and dancing at 2pm (summer only).

GETTING THERE & AWAY
From 12 April to 6 October, ferries make the run to Bygdøy (Nkr22, 15 minutes, every 20 to 40 minutes). The ferries leave from Rådhusbrygge 3 (opposite Rådhus) and stop first at Dronningen, from where it's a 10-minute walk up to the folk museum. The ferry continues to Bygdøynes, where the *Kon-Tiki*, *Fram* and maritime museums are clustered. You can also take bus No 20 to Bygdøy's sights from the National Theatre.

Islands & Beaches
Ferries to half a dozen islands in the Oslofjord leave from Vippetangen quay. **Hovedøya**, the closest island, has a rocky coastline, but its southwestern side is a popular sunbathing area. Boats to Hovedøya leave from Vippetangen once or twice hourly between 6.17am and midnight from late May to mid-August, with fewer runs the rest of the year.

Further south, the undeveloped island of **Langøyene** offers far better swimming. Boats to Langøyene depart daily late May to mid-August.

Bygdøy has two popular beaches, **Huk** and **Paradisbukta**, which can be reached by taking bus No 30 from Jernbanetorget to its last stop.

ACTIVITIES
A network of hiking trails leads into Nordmarka from Frognerseteren, northwest of the city at the end of T-bane line 1. One fairly strenuous walk is from Frognerseteren over to Lake Sognsvann, where you can take T-bane line 5 back to the city. If you're interested in wilderness hiking, contact the **DNT office** (☎ 22 82 28 22; Storgata 3).

Oslo's ski season is roughly December to March. **Tomm Murstad Skiservice** (☎ 22 13 95 00; www.skiservice.no; Tryvannsveien 2), at Voksenkollen T-bane station, one T-bane stop before Frognerseteren, hires out snowboards and skis (from Nkr140). **Skiforeningen** (Ski Society; ☎ 22 92 32 00; Kongeveien 5) can provide more information, or visit www.holmenkollen.com.

FESTIVALS & EVENTS
Oslo's most festive annual event is the 17 May Constitution Day celebration, when

city residents descend on the Royal Palace in traditional garb.

In March, the **Holmenkollen Ski Festival** (☎ 22 92 32 00; www.skiforeningen.no) attracts Nordic skiers and ski jumpers from around the world. August sees the **Oslo International Jazz Festival** (☎ 22 42 91 20; www.oslojazz.no), October brings **Films from the South** (☎ 22 82 24 80; www .filmfrasor.no) and April the **Inferno Metal Festival** (www.infernofestival.net). For details of these and other events, contact the tourist office.

SLEEPING
Hostels
YMCA Sleep-In (☎ 22 42 10 66; Grubbegata 4; dm Nkr130; ☺ July-mid–Aug) This great positioned hostel, only 10 minutes' walk from Oslo S, fills up quickly. There's no bedding so you'll need a sleeping bag; basic shower and kitchen facilities are available. Breakfast costs extra.

Anker Hostel (☎ 22 99 72 10; www.anker.oslo.no; Storgata 55; 4-bed dm Nkr145/170, rm for 1 or 2 people Nkr430) Anker is the only central and cheap hostel in Oslo open year round. When we visited, the drab tower had an unfortunate cockroach problem. Breakfast costs Nkr60 extra. Rooms are with en suite.

Oslo Vandrerhjem Ekeberg (☎ 22 74 18 90; delf .vandre@frikirken.no; Kongsveien 82; dm/d 200/305/465; ☺ Jun–mid-Aug; Ⓟ) Set 4km southeast of Oslo, this place offers 68 beds in an atmospheric old house. Take tram No 18 or 19 towards Ljabru and get off at Holtet; from there, it's about 100m along Kongsveien.

Oslo Vandrerhjem Haraldsheim (☎ 22 22 29 65; www.haraldsheim.oslo.no; Haraldsheimveien 4; dm with/without bath Nkr220/200, s Nkr380/320, d Nkr515/435; Ⓟ) Sitting on a green lawn 4km from the centre, this is the city's prettiest hostel. There's a kitchen, laundry facilities and 270 beds. Take tram No 17 to the Sinsenkrysset stop.

Oslo Vandrerhjem Holtekilen (☎ 67 51 80 40; oslo.holtekilen.hostel@vandrerhjem.no; Michelets vei 55, Stabekk; bus Nos 151, 153, 161, 162, 252, 261; dm/s/d Nkr205/305/445; Ⓟ) This hostel has 195 beds and sits 8km southwest of Oslo. An ugly, modern exterior masks servicable, sunlit rooms.

Oslo Vandrerhjem IMI (☎ 22 98 62 00; oslo.imi .hostel@vandrerhjem.no; Staffelsgata 4, enter from Linstowsgata; dm/s/d 215/320/495; ☺ early Jun–mid-Aug), a summer hostel, enjoys a central position in a boarding school just north of Det Kongelige Slott. There's a kitchen.

Perminalen (☎ 23 09 30 81; perminalen@statenska ntiner.no; Øvre Slottsgate 2; bunks in 4-bed rooms Nkr280, s/d Nkr495/650) is a central 55-room pension that caters to military personnel, but it's open to everyone. Rooms have TV and private bath.

Hotels, Pensions & Private Rooms

MS Innvik (☎ 22 41 95 00; www.msinnvik.no; Langkaia; s/d Nkr350/600) Once a car ferry used as a travelling theatre, this place has been reincarnated as a B&B docked in the harbour. It's still a cultural centre, so don't flush your toilet when puppet shows or theatrical events are occurring below deck.

Fønix Hotel (☎ 23 14 63 00; www.foenix.com; Dronninges gate 19; s/d Nkr395-515/595-865) This place offers plain furniture, white walls and light hardwood floors in this pleasant budget hotel with 60 rooms.

City Hotel (☎ 22 41 36 10; www.cityhotel.no; Skippergata 19; s/d Nkr395-550/750-850) With slight historical ambience in the stairwells, the rooms are regular fare with shared bath. Those sensitive to traffic noise should request a courtyard room.

Ellingsen's Pensjonat (☎ 22 60 03 59; ep@tiscal.no; Holtegata 25; s/d Nkr300-420/490-590) In a neighbourhood of older homes five blocks north of the Royal Palace, this is a good-value pension with 20 small rooms.

Cochs Pensjonat (☎ 23 33 24 00; fax 23 33 24 10; Parkveien 25; s/d from Nkr350/500) Newly remodelled, this place contains fresh hardwood floors and simple modern furniture. Some of the 65 rooms contain a kitchen. It's just north of the royal palace.

Use-It (☎ 22 41 51 32; Møllergata 3). Offering help getting a double room in a private home talk to these people. Rooms range from Nkr300 to Nkr500 (excluding breakfast) and there's no minimum stay or booking fee. If you'll be arriving on a weekend, call ahead and they'll give you phone numbers and/or addresses of places you can call on your own.

Tourist office window at the Oslo S books rooms in private homes for a Nkr35 booking fee. Also worth checking out www.bbnorway.com, which lists around a dozen B&Bs in the city.

Camping

The two main camping grounds in Oslo have full facilities, including kitchens (without cooking implements). Rates below are for one or two people with tent and no car.

Ekeberg Camping (☎ 22 19 85 68; www.ekeberg camping.no; Ekebergveien 65; bus No 34 from Oslo S; Nkr125;

☺ 24 May-2 Sep; **P**) Set on a hill 10 minutes by bus southeast of (and overlooking) the city, this ground gets very crowded. The 40 acres of **Bogstad Camping** (☎ 22 51 08 00; www.bogstad camping.no; Ankerveien 117; bus No 32 from Oslo S; Nkr135; **P**) can get noisy.

EATING

Eating can be an expensive proposition in Oslo. One way to save money is to frequent bakeries, many of which sell reasonably priced sandwiches as well as pastries and hearty wholegrain breads. Otherwise, visit grocery stores – **Kiwi** and **Rema 1000** have branches throughout the city. You can find immigrant-run fruit stands (some open Sunday) on Storgata and Grønland. Good value meals can often be had at hipster cafés, where filling dishes usually cost between Nkr80 and Nkr120 – a price you might be glad to pay after one too many **7-Eleven** hot dogs.

Cafés

Blitx (Pilestredet 30c; sandwiches Nkr8-15; ☺ 11am-5pm Mon-Fri) Inside a barricaded, graffitied building, is this activist institution with 25 years of squatting history. Volunteers run a café serving unbelievably cheap vegetarian and vegan food. Coffee costs Nkr5.

Tekehtopa (☎ 22 20 33 52; St Olav Plas 2; mains Nkr89-139; ☺ from 10am Mon-Sat, noon-1am Sun) A former pharmacy, this café serves espresso and chevre salads (Nkr89) under a beautifully moulded and painted ceiling.

Cafe Con Bar (☎ 22 05 02 00; Brugata 11; mains Nkr93-135; ☺ from 11am) Dominated by fancy shoes, velvet couches and a voyeuristic unisex bathroom is this place over-looking a giant fist erupting from the pavement. Always crowded, enjoy booze, caffeine and salads.

Quick Eats

Åpent Bakeri (Colbjørnsens gate 8; ☺ 7.30am-5pm Mon-Fri, 9am-3pm Sat) This bakery serves giant, grainy rolls that you can pile with berry jam and butter (Nkr8).

Brugata Kebab Gatekjokken (Brugata 10; falafel & kebab Nkr29-35; ☺ 10am-midnight Sun-Thu, 10am-5am Fri & Sat) In a city swarming with unimpressive Middle Eastern food stands, this place turns out some tasty falafel sandwiches.

Punjab Tandoori (Grønland 24; mains Nkr55-65; ☺ 11am-11pm) This Indian restaurant serves chicken tandoori, curries, rice and naan bread in a decidedly no-frills room.

Hotel Havana (☎ 23 23 03 23; Thorvald Meyers gate 36; dishes Nkr49-89 🕑 10am-6pm Mon-Sat) A Grünnerløkka delicatessen, it serves fab takeaway food. Substantial fish burgers (Nkr49) come with homemade aioli. Try Brie sandwiches (Nkr49) and fish and chips (Nkr74).

There are numerous cheap pizza, burger and kebab joints along Grøland and Storgata. Fast food abounds in Oslo S.

Restaurants

Kaffistova (☎ 23 21 42 10; Rosenkrantz gate 8; mains Nkr82-98; 🕑 10am-8pm Mon-Fri, 11am-5pm Sat & Sun) This cafétéria serves traditional Norwegian food, including reindeer or elk carbonades (locally defined as meat cakes) and fish cakes; salad is always included.

Krishna's Cuisine (Kirkeveien 59B; all-you-can-eat Nkr90; 🕑 noon-8pm Mon-Fri) Located near the Majorstuen T-bane station, this place serves up soup, salad, and a hot dish. It's exclusively vegetarian.

Villa Paradiso (☎ 22 35 40 60; Olav Ryes Plass 8; mains Nkr119-139; 🕑 11am-midnight) Easily Norway's finest pizza is prepared here (not difficult in the land of soggy pies). Make reservations weeks in advance for a weekend dinner. Patrons eat the delicious goods surrounded by big windows and wainscotting.

Sult (☎ 22 87 04 67; Thorvald Meyers gate 26; mains Nkr89-169; 🕑 4pm-12.30am Tue-Fri, from 1pm Sat & Sun) This restaurant prepares a changing menu of continental fare for patrons who sit at small tables and listen to Elvis Presley. Cod encrusted with pistachios equals excellent.

Stortorvets Gjæstgiveri's (☎ 23 35 63 60; Grubbegata 3; mains Nkr140-235; 🕑 from 10am) The oldest restaurant in Norway, sagging yellow, wooden walls and a pretty interior court provides an excellent backdrop for traditional meals. Don't try for a table on May 17th or Christmas.

Lofotstua (☎ 22 46 93 96; Kirkeveien 40; mains Nkr170-220; 🕑 3-10pm Mon-Fri) Run by a family from the Lofoten Islands, this place turns out a changing menu of fantastic fish dishes, including whale (in season) in a room that looks sort of like a brown bar.

DRINKING & CLUBBING

While many thrifty backpackers just drink the bottle they brought from home, Oslo has many spots to enjoy hooch. In the summer, you can enjoy a beer in one of Vigeland park's outdoor cafés.

Olympen (☎ 22 17 28 08; Grølandsleiret 15; 🕑 11-2am) A freakish, century-old worker's beer hall, populated by old dudes with red noses and hipsters, Olympen features cheesy cover bands (Bob Jovi) and cheap beer (Nkr33) in a cavernous space full of elaborate wooden booths and oil paintings of faded cityscapes.

Teddy's Soft Bar (☎ 22 17 36 50; Brugata 3a 🕑 from 11am) This place provides a view into the past via its thoroughly unchanged interior. An ancient Wurlitzer sets the tone. While good burgers are served, most come for the suds.

London Pub (☎ 22 70 87 00; CJ Hambros plass 5; 🕑 3pm-3am) Oslo's oldest gay hangout, where you can shoot stick and feed jukeboxes. If you feel like serious dancing, head upstairs to the more youthful **Chairs** (🕑 8pm-3am), where DJs spin every night of the week.

Stargate (Grønland 2; 🕑 11-3.30am) If you prefer a down-to-earth drinking-den atmosphere try here, serving beer for around Nkr33.

Blå (☎ 22 20 91 81; Brenneriveien 9), a cultural centre inside an old industrial building, is where you will meet people that will actually still look sexy the next morning.

King of the Grønland nightclub scene, the DJs and bartenders at **Gloria Flames** (☎ 22 17 16 00; Grønland 18; 🕑 to 3am Thu-Sat) play a heavy mix of rock and indie rock. Why not rub your rear against a banister to something by the White Stripes?

ENTERTAINMENT

The tourist office's monthly *What's On in Oslo* brochure lists concerts, theatre and special events. A good publication for night owls is the free *Streetwise*, published annually by **Use It** (see opposite).

Cinemas

Cinemateket (☎ 22 47 45 00; Dronningens gate 16; tickets Nkr60) screens an art house fare. **Saga Kino** (☎ 41 51 90 00; Stortingsgata 28; tickets Nkr60) shows first-run movies in their original languages.

Live Music

Cosmopolite (☎ 22 11 33 09; www.cosmopolite.no; Møllergata 26) focuses on jazz, folk, rock, and, lately, French electro-pop. Air, St Germain and the Gotan Project have all played here.

Garage (☎ 22 17 16 00; Grønland 18; 🕑 to 3.30am) consistently injects rock into the needy veins of Oslo. In addition to Norwegian bands, expect international acts like Death Cab for Cutie and The Beautiful People.

The **Rockefeller Music Hall** (☎ 22 20 32 32; www .rockefeller.no; Torggata 16) attracts big-name international contemporary musicians, such as Patti Smith and Queensrÿche.

GETTING THERE & AWAY

Air
Most flights land at Gardermoen, 50km north of the city.

SAS (☎ 81 52 04 00) and **Braathens** (☎ 81 52 00 00) airlines have ticket offices in Oslo S. **Ryanair** (☎ 82 06 11 00) flies from London Stansted and Glasgow Prestwick to Oslo Torp, 112km south of the city.

Boat
Boats to and from Copenhagen, operated by **DFDS Seaways** (☎ 22 41 90 90), and from Frederikshavn (Denmark), operated by **Stena Line** (☎ 23 17 91 00), use the docks off Skippergata.

Boats from Hirtshals (Denmark) and Kiel (Germany), run by **Color Line** (☎ 22 94 44 00), dock at Hjortneskaia.

Bus
Long-distance buses use a terminal at Galleri Oslo, just east of Oslo S.

Car & Motorcycle
Unless on a motorcycle you'll have to pay a Nkr15 toll each time you enter Oslo.

All major car-rental companies have booths at Gardermoen airport. The following also have offices in the city centre:

Avis (☎ 81 56 90 44; Munkedamsveien 27)

Budget (☎ 23 16 32 40; Oslo Spektrum)

Train
All trains arrive and depart from Oslo S in the city centre. The reservation desks open 6.30am to 11pm daily. There's an **information desk** (☎ 81 50 08 88).

GETTING AROUND
Oslo has an efficient public-transport system. A one-way ticket on any service costs Nkr20 if you buy it from a station agent or curbside machines. You can also buy your ticket from drivers, but that will add a Nkr10 surcharge. An unlimited *dagskort* (day ticket) costs Nkr60, but can't be used between 1am and 4am.

Trafikanten (☎ 81 50 01 76; ☻ 7am-8pm Mon-Fri, 8am-6pm Sat & Sun) provides schedules and a handy public-transport map.

Boat
Ferries to Bygdøy leave from Rådhusbrygge every 20 to 40 minutes, while ferries to the islands in the Oslofjord leave from Vippetangen.

Bus & Tram
Bus and tram lines extend to the suburbs. Most buses and trams converge at Jernbanetorget in front of Oslo S. Most westbound buses, including those to Bygdøy and Vigeland Park, also stop on the southern side of the National Theatre.

Service frequency drops dramatically at night but, on weekends only, *Nattlinjer* night buses No 200 to 218 follow the tram routes until 4am (tickets Nkr50; passes not valid).

Taxi
Flag fall is up to Nkr91.50 and from Nkr10 to Nkr16 per kilometre thereafter. Any taxi with a lit sign is available for hire. If you must, phone **Taxi2** (☎ 02202), **Norgestaxi** (☎ 08000) or **Oslo Taxi** (☎ 02323) – but be aware that meters start running at the point of dispatch. Fares are ludicrously high.

T-Bane
Oslo's five-line metro train network, underground in the city centre, is faster and goes further outside the centre than most bus lines. All lines pass through the Nationaltheatret, Stortinget and Jernbanetorget stations.

SOUTHERN NORWAY

Sørlandet, the curving south coast, is magnetic for Norwegians when the weather turns warm. The attraction is generally not as great for foreign travellers, the majority of whom have just arrived from places with warmer water and better beaches.

The Sørland train line, which runs 586km from Stavanger to Oslo via Kristiansand, stays inland most of the way, but buses meet the trains and link the rail line with most south-coast towns.

STAVANGER & AROUND
pop 106,000

Don't be misled by Stavanger's title 'Oil Capital of Norway,' this is a small, picturesque city (Norway's 4th largest!), with narrow cobbled streets and small white houses comprising the bulk of the centre: very unlike Houston or Rotterdam. The centre is lively, containing a fine stock of bars, cafés and places to stroll. It's also an excellent point from which to begin exploring the Lysefjord, with boat tours leaving daily in summer.

The adjacent bus and train stations are a 10-minute walk from the harbour. Ask the **tourist office** (☎ 51 85 92 00; www.visitstavanger.com; Rosenkildetorget 1; 9am-8pm Jun-Aug, shorter weekly hrs & closed Sun Sep-May) for details about annual festivals.

Sights & Activities

The area's most popular outing is the two-hour hike to the top of the incredible **Preikestolen** (Pulpit Rock), 25km east of Stavanger. You can inch up to the edge of its flat top and peer 600m straight down to the Lysefjord. The tourist board details public transit to the beginning of the trail.

Piloted by old salts, the **Fjord Tours** (☎ 51 53 73 40; www.fjordpanorama.no) sightseeing boat departs from 18 May to 31 August, cruising the lovely steep-walled Lysefjord. Purchase tickets (adult/child Nkr270/135) at the tourist office.

A fun quarter for strolling about is **Gamle Stavanger** where cobblestone walkways lead through rows of very well-preserved 18th-century whitewashed wooden houses.

The **Norsk Oljemuseum** (☎ 51 93 93 00; www.norskolje.museum.no; Kjeringholmen; adult/child Nkr75/35; 10am-7pm Jun-Aug, shorter hrs otherwise) traces the history of oil formation and exploration in the North Sea.

Also check out the fishy **Canning Museum** and **Stavanger Domkirke**, an impressive medieval cathedral.

Sleeping

Lakeside, utilitarian and painted red, **Stavanger Vandrerhjem Mosvangen** (☎ 51 54 36 36; stavanger.mosvangen.hostel@vandrerhjem.no; Henrik Ibsens gate 19; dm/d Nkr180/345; Jun-Aug; P), is a hostel 3km from the city centre (catch bus No 78 or 79).

At **Rogalandsheimen Gjestgiberi** (☎ 51 52 01 88; Muségata 18; s/d 350-450/500-550; P), paintings cover every surface. The 19th century guesthouse has 13 homey rooms.

Contact the tourist office to book **B&Bs**, with singles/doubles around Nkr300/450 (plus Nkr30 booking fee).

Eating

India Tandoori Restaurant (☎ 51 89 39 35; Valberggata 14; dishes Nkr89-209; 4-11pm Mon-Sat, 2-11pm Sun) serves good korma. The hip bar/café **Resept** (☎ 51 55 39 80; Østervåg 43; mains Nkr49-99; to 2am) serves vegetarian pasta in a room that recalls the supergraphics of the '70s.

Hill-top and pretty, **Café Sting** (☎ 51 89 38 78; Valberget 3; smaller dishes Nkr75-129; from 11am-Midnight Mon-Sat, 2pm-midnight Sun) prepares Cajun fishburgers. It doubles as a nightclub.

There's a **Rema 1000** supermarket at the bus station and a **fish market** at the harbour. **Våland Dampbakeri & Conditori** (☎ 51 86 19 23; Nygaten 24; 10am-4pm Mon-Sat) turns out flaky pastry.

Drinking

Bars and discos cram into the centre like the sardines once canned in town.

Cementen's (☎ 51 56 78 00; Nedre Strandgate 2; 7pm-2am) bartenders play kick-ass tunes and sometimes host bands. Pick up a used book (Nkr5) and an occasional beer special (Nkr31). Dark **Checkpoint Charlie** (☎ 51 53 22 45; www.checkpoint.no; Lars Hertervigs Gate 5; to 2am) often presents live music on a small stage. Happy hour beer is Nkr36.

Getting There & Away

Nor-Way Bussekspress goes all the way to Oslo (Nkr730,10¼ hours, one to six times daily). Buses to Bergen (Nkr400, 5¾ hours) run roughly every two hours. Stavanger's train line runs to Oslo (Nkr783, 7¾ hours, one to three daily) via Kristiansand (Nkr379, three hours, four to seven daily). Save cash by sleeping on the overnight service.

The **HSD Flaggruten** (☎ 51 86 87 80) express passenger catamaran to Bergen (Nkr590/300 adult/student, 4¼ hours) and Haugesund, leaves two or three times daily; Eurail, Norway Rail and ScanRail pass-holders get 50% discounts.

KRISTIANSAND

pop 75,000

Busy Kristiansand, the capital of Sørlandet and the fifth largest city in Norway, is Norway's closest port to Denmark and offers the first glimpse of the country for many ferry travellers from the south. Kristiansand has a grid pattern, or *kvadraturen*, of wide streets laid out by King Christian IV, who founded the city in 1641. It's a busy seaside holiday resort for Norwegians, but foreign visitors generally pile off the ferries and onto the first train.

The train, bus and ferry terminals are together on the west side of the city centre. The **tourist office** (☎ 38 12 13 14; destinasjon@sorlandet.com; Vestre Strandgate 32) is nearby.

The modern hostel **Kristiansand Vandrerhjem Tangen** (☎ 38 02 83 10; kristiansand.hostel@vandrerhjem .no; Skansen 8; dm/s/d Nkr205/315-395/415-450; Ⓨ mid-Jan–mid-Dec; Ⓟ) sits in a quiet, industrialized part of town a short walk from a beach.

Centrum Motel (☎ 38 02 79 69; Vestre Strandsate 49; s/d 350-450/450-580; Ⓟ) wins points for cleanliness and short walk to the train station, but it's ugly.

Express buses head north once or twice daily to Haukeligrend, with connections to Bergen (Nkr590, 12 hours). Trains run to Stavanger (Nkr379, 3 hours, four to seven daily) and Oslo (Nkr531, 4¾ hours, three to six daily), as well as express buses.

Regional buses depart hourly for towns along the south coast, including Arendal (Nkr100, 1½ hours) and Mandal (Nkr64, 45 minutes).

BERGEN & THE WESTERN FJORDS

The formidable, sea-drowned glacial valleys of the western fjords, flanked by almost impossibly rugged terrain, haven't deterred Norwegians from settling and farming their slopes and heights for thousands of years. The much-visited region presents some of the most breathtaking scenery in all of Europe. Information on the entire region is available from **Fjord Norge** (☎ 55 30 26 40; www .fjordnorway.com; Postboks 4108 Dreggen, N-5835 Bergen).

OSLO TO BERGEN

The Oslo–Bergen railway line is Norway's most scenic, a seven-hour journey past forests and alpine villages, and across the starkly beautiful **Hardangervidda** plateau.

Midway between Oslo and Bergen is **Geilo**, a ski centre where you can practically walk off the train and onto a lift. There's good summer **hiking** in the mountains around Geilo, which has a **Hostel** (☎ 32 08 70 60; www .oenturist.no; Lienvegen 137; dm/d Nkr185/345).

From Geilo the train climbs 600m through a tundra-like landscape of high lakes and snow-capped mountains to the tiny village of **Finse**, near the **Hardangerjøkulen** icecap. Finse has year-round **skiing** and is in the midst of a network of summer **hiking trails**. One of Norway's most frequently trodden trails winds from the Finse station down to the fjord town of **Aurland**, a four-day trek. There's breathtaking mountain scenery along the way as well as a series of DNT and private mountain huts a day's walk apart – the nearest is Finsehytta, 200m from Finse station.

Myrdal, further west along the railway line, is the connecting point for the spectacularly steep **Flåm** railway, which twists and turns its way down 20 splendid kilometres to **Flåm** (p886).

BERGEN

pop 230,830

Lovely Bergen contends for the honour of being Norway's most beautiful city. Set on a peninsula surrounded by mountains and the sea, the neatly contained centre offers a tangle of crooked streets and hilltop views. Norway's city second largest city, Bergen provides ample opportunity to linger in cafés and bars, while a large university population helps to secure Bergen's claim as Western Norway's cultural capital, supporting theatres, museums, a philharmonic orchestra and a noted rock music scene. Though big by Norwegian standards, the city retains a charming, almost village-like culture. Here, the picturesque wins over the urbane. Drawback: expect rain at least 275 days of the year.

Orientation & Information

The bus and train stations lie a block apart on Strømgaten, a 10-minute walk from the Express Boats (ferry terminals). Most of the restaurants, hotels, museums, tourist sites and picturesque streets cluster around Vågen, which is the inner harbour.

The **tourist office** (☎ 55 55 20 00; www.visitbergen .com; Vågsallmenningen 1; Ⓨ 8.30am-10pm Jun-Aug, shorter hrs otherwise) is helpful. The **main post office** (Starvhusgaten at Chrisites Gate; Ⓨ 8am-8pm Mon-Fri, 9am-6pm Sat) issues stamps. View the Internet at **Byens Gtørste Spillehall** (Håkons Gaten 15; Nkr0.50 per min; Ⓨ from noon) or the **public library** (Strøm-gaten 6). **Jarlens Vaskoteque** (☎ 55 32 55 04; Lille Øvre-gate 17; Ⓨ from 10am Mon-Sat) does laundry.

There's a **medical clinic** (☎ 55 32 11 20; Vestre Strømkaien 19; Ⓨ emergencies 24 hrs), and a **pharmacy** (Ⓨ to midnight) at the bus station.

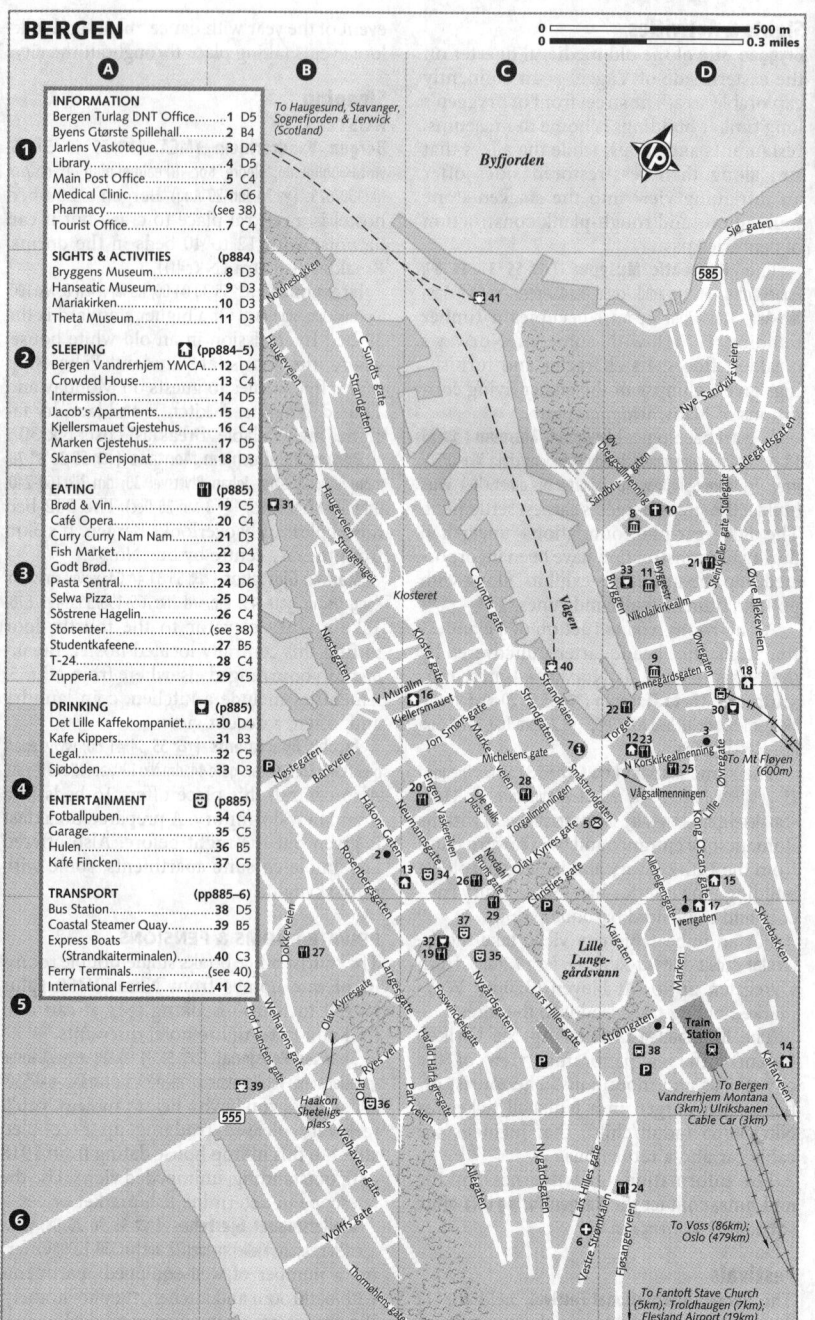

BERGEN

0 ————————— 500 m
0 ————————— 0.3 miles

INFORMATION
Bergen Turlag DNT Office..........1 D5
Byens Gtørste Spillehall..............2 B4
Jarlens Vaskoteque.....................3 D4
Library.......................................4 D5
Main Post Office........................5 C4
Medical Clinic...........................6 C6
Pharmacy............................(see 38)
Tourist Office............................7 C4

SIGHTS & ACTIVITIES (p884)
Bryggens Museum.......................8 D3
Hanseatic Museum......................9 D3
Mariakirken..............................10 D3
Theta Museum..........................11 D3

SLEEPING (pp884–5)
Bergen Vandrerhjem YMCA....12 D4
Crowded House.........................13 C4
Intermission..............................14 D4
Jacob's Apartments...................15 D4
Kjellersmauet Gjestehus............16 C4
Marken Gjestehus......................17 D5
Skansen Pensjonat....................18 D3

EATING (p885)
Brød & Vin...............................19 C5
Café Opera...............................20 C4
Curry Curry Nam Nam..............21 D3
Fish Market...............................22 D4
Godt Brød.................................23 D4
Pasta Sentral............................24 D6
Selwa Pizza..............................25 D4
Søstrene Hagelin.......................26 C4
Storsenter..........................(see 38)
Studentkafeene.........................27 B5
T-24..28 C4
Zupperia...................................29 C5

DRINKING (p885)
Det Lille Kaffekompaniet...........30 D4
Kafe Kippers.............................31 B3
Legal..32 C5
Sjøboden..................................33 D3

ENTERTAINMENT (p885)
Fotballpuben............................34 C5
Garage.....................................35 C5
Hulen.......................................36 B5
Kafé Fincken............................37 C5

TRANSPORT (pp885–6)
Bus Station...............................38 D5
Coastal Steamer Quay..............39 B5
Express Boats
   (Strandkaiterminalen).............40 C3
Ferry Terminals..................(see 40)
International Ferries...................41 C2

To Haugesund, Stavanger,
Sognefjorden & Lerwick
(Scotland)

Byfjorden

Sjø gaten

Vågen

Klosteret

*Lille
Lunge-
gårdsvann*

Train
Station

To Mt Fløyen
(600m)

To Bergen
Vandrerhjem Montana
(3km); Ulriksbanen
Cable Car (3km)

To Voss (86km);
Oslo (479km)

To Fantoft Stave Church
(5km); Troldhaugen (7km);
Flesland Airport (19km)

Haakon
Sheteligs
plass

Sights & Activities

Bryggen, site of the old medieval quarter on the eastern side of Vågen, is an eminently explorable area. The street front of Bryggen's long timber buildings is home to museums, restaurants and shops, while the alleys that run along their less-restored sides offer an intriguing view into the stacked-stone foundations and rough-plank construction of centuries past.

The **Hanseatic Museum** (☎ 55 31 41 89; Finnegårdsgaten 1A; adult/child Nkr45/free; ☿ 9am-5pm Jun-Aug, 11am-2pm Sep-May) occupies a timber building (1704) with some of Norway's creakiest floors. Its character and furnishings give a glimpse of the auster living conditions of Hanseatic merchants.

The archaeological **Bryggens Museum** (☎ 55 58 80 10; Dregsalmenning 3; adult/student/child Nkr40/20/ free; ☿ 10am-5pm May-Aug, shorter hrs otherwise) was built at the site of Bergen's earliest settlement. The 800-year-old foundations unearthed during the construction have been incorporated into the museum's exhibits, along with pottery, human skulls and runes.

A one-room reconstruction of a clandestine Resistance headquarters, uncovered by the Nazis in 1942, is Norway's tiniest museum: the **Theta Museum** (☎ 55 55 20 80; Enhjørningsgården; adult/child Nkr20/5; ☿ 2-4pm Tue, Sat & Sun mid-May–mid-Sep).

The stone **Mariakirken** (☎ 55 31 59 60; Dreggen 15; adult/child Nkr10/free, mid-May–Aug only; ☿ 11am-4pm Mon-Fri mid-May–Aug, shorter hrs otherwise) with its Romanesque entrance and twin towers, dates from the 12th century and is Bergen's oldest building. The interior has 15th-century frescoes and a splendid baroque pulpit.

For an unbeatable city view, take the **funicular** (adult/child Nkr 30/15; ☿ from 7.30am) from Øvregaten up to Mt Fløyen (320m). Well-marked hiking trails lead into the forest.

The **Ulriksbanen cable car** up Mt Ulriken (642m) offers a panoramic view of the city, fjords and mountains. The tourist office sells a Bergen in a Nutshell ticket for Nkr130/65 (adult/child) that includes the cable car and a return bus.

For information on wilderness hiking and huts, contact the **Bergen Turlag DNT office** (☎ 55 32 22 30; Tverrgaten 4).

Festivals

The **Bergen International Festival**, held for 12 days at the end of May, is the big cultural event of the year with dance, music and folklore events taking place throughout the city.

Sleeping
HOSTELS

Bergen Vandrerhjem YMCA (☎ 55 60 60 55; ymca@online.no; Nedre Korskirkealmenning 4; dm/rm Nkr150/625; ☿ 20 Jun-20 Aug) Bergen's 200-bed hostel is a central place to crash but it can be noisy with 12 to 40 beds in the dorms. Breakfast is extra (Nkr40).

Intermission (☎ 55 30 04 00; Kalfarveien 8; Nkr100; ☿ mid-Jun–mid-Aug) Of a higher standard is the 37-bed Intermission in an old white house, where the Christian Student Fellowship serves free waffles to guests on Monday and Thursday nights. A kitchen and laundry facilities are available. Breakfast costs Nkr30.

Bergen Vandrerhjem Montana (☎ 55 20 80 70; montvh@online.no; Johan Blyttsvei 30; dm Nkr160-240, s/d from Nkr425/595; ☿ 3 Jan-20 Dec) The 332-bed hostel pleasantly overlooks Bergen. It's 5km from the city centre by bus No 31.

Marken Gjestehus (☎ 55 31 44 04; www.smisi.no; Kong Oscars gate 45; dm/s/d Nkr165-190/355-495/610) Take a scary elevator to the fourth floor to find this centrally located hostel. Breakfast can be arranged elsewhere from Nkr55. Amenities include a kitchen, coin laundry and, often, a decent view.

Jacob's Apartments (☎ 55 54 41 60; www.apartments.no; Kong Oscars gate 44; dm Nkr180, apt Nkr490-790) Also central, this place offers 16 beds in a brand new dormitory. A prepared breakfast is given out the night before. Also offered are simple en suite apartments, some with nifty skylights.

PRIVATE ROOMS & PENSIONS

The tourist office books single/double rooms in private homes from Nkr250/450 (plus Nkr30 to Nkr50 booking fee); it can also find you last-minute hotel discounts.

Skansen Pensjonat (☎ 55 31 90 80; www.skansen-pensjonat.no; Vetrlidsalmenningen 29; s/d Nkr350-400/550-650). Unless you have a heart problem, you'll feel very pleased trudging up a cobbled street to this hilltop house dating from 1918 with outstanding, unimpeded views. Use the telescope to determine fish market prices.

Kjellersmauet Gjestehus (☎ 55 96 26 08; www.gjestehuset.com; Kjellersmauet 22; apt Nkr350-1200) Offering a number of well-equipped apartments with bathroom and kitchen, they are homely. Big groups are often given good deals.

Crowded House (☎ 55 90 92 00; www.crowded
-house.com; Håkonsgaten 27; s/d Nkr390/590) The 82
rooms at this place come with Ikea furniture and free use of laundry facilities.
No breakfast is included but it has a nice
kitchen. The first floor holds a lively bar.

Eating

Studentkafeene (☎ 55 54 50 50; mains Nkr19-45;
🕙 9.30am-5pm Mon-Thu, 9.30am-4pm Fri late Aug-early
Jun), the university's student caféteria, might
look ugly, but you can grab pasta with fish
(Nkr39), asparagus soup (Nkr19) or a big
sandwich with juice (Nkr30) at low prices.

Popular with university students, **Brød &
Vin** (☎ 55 32 67 04; Christies gate 13; mains Nkr35-65;
🕙 10am-11pm Mon-Wed, 10am-midnight Thu & Fri, 1pm-
midnight Sat, 1-10pm Sun) slings piles of Asian
noodle dishes. Vegetable chop suey runs
Nkr53. A beer costs Nkr35.

From fish to gazpacho, **Zupperia** (☎ 55 55
81 44; Nordahl Bruns gate; soup Nkr49-96; 🕙 11am-mid-
night) serves 11 kinds of soup with sides of
bread. We like the Husenottsuppe (oxtail
boiled with vegetables).

Bergen's night-spot, **T-24** (☎ 98 29 83 28; New-
manns gate 25; mains Nkr50-100; 🕙 noon-1am Sun-Thu,
noon-6am Fri & Sat) serves cheap lasagne, baked
potatoes and fajitas on counters that can become increasingly dirty as nights grow long.

The unassuming **Pasta Sentral** (Vestre Strømkaien 6; dishes Nkr59-84; 🕙 11am-11pm Mon-Sat, 1-11pm
Sun), which isn't all that central, has decent
pizza and pasta. Expect cheesy murals and
chequered table cloths.

Rich curries and vegetarian items come
steaming and delicious at **Curry Curry Nam Nam**
(☎ 55 96 40 76; Steinkjeller Gate 8; mains Nkr49-99; 🕙 from
2pm Tue-Sun), a tiny restaurant at the convergence of several cobbled alleys. Outdoors,
smoke a post-meal water pipe for Nkr50.

Hip **Café Opera** (☎ 55 23 08 15; light meals Nkr44-
78 mains Nkr75-118; 🕙 from 11am Mon-Sat, noon-10.30pm
Sun) begins the day with newspaper readers,
but finishes with sweaty DJs.

Bustling **Godt Brød** (☎ 55 32 80 00; Nedre Kor-
skirkealmenningen 12; 🕙 from 7am Mon-Sat) offers delicious organic breads, pastries, café tables and
pizza bolle (Nkr35). Across the street, pick
up good falafel and shwarma at **Selwa Pizza**
(Nedre Korskirkeallmennigen 5; stuff Nkr35-79; 🕙 11-1am),
a spare room overlooking an old church.

Go to **Söstrene Hagelin** (☎ 55 32 69 49; Olav Kyrres
gate 33; stuff Nkr35-89; 🕙 9am-6pm Mon-Fri, 10am-3pm
Sat) for delicious fish pudding, fish casserole

and other delicacies. Filling take-away fish
balls (Nkr35) come with potatoes.

Storsenter, at the bus station, has fast food
outlets, a Vinmonopolet, and **Rimi** and **Spar**
supermarkets. Torget's **fish market** provides
fresh fruit and seafood snacks, including
salmon rolls for Nkr15; or boiled crab legs
or shrimp for Nkr35 to Nkr75.

Entertainment

For details and schedules of entertainment
events, including classical concerts, contact
the tourist office. Atop Mt Fløyen, classical
concerts are held nightly at 8pm from mid-
June to mid-August (Nkr160).

Fotballpuben (☎ 55 90 05 79; Vestre Torggate
9; 🕙 from 9am Mon-Sat, noon-1am Sun) provides
plenty of scarfs, televisions and fans.

Bergen's top rock music venue, **Garage**
(☎ 55 32 19 80; www.garage.no; Christies gate 14;
🕙 from 6pm), attracts students, as does **Hulen**
(☎ 55 33 38 38; www.hulen.no; Olaf Ryes vei 47), a
former bomb-shelter. **Kafé Fincken** (☎ 55 32 13
16; Nygårdsgaten 2A; from 7pm Wed-Sun) is the main
gay and lesbian venue in town.

Drinking

At **Sjøboden** (☎ 55 31 67 77; Bryggen 29; 🕙 from 6pm),
sing along to bad covers of Bryan Adams
with a drunk, dancing crowd.

Det Lille Kaffekompaniet (☎ 55 32 92 72; Nedre
Fjellsmug 2; 🕙 from 10am) is an intimate coffee
house, hidden on a pedestrian street behind
the Funicular station.

Part of a cultural centre and former sar-
dine cannery, **Kafe Kippers** (☎ 55 31 00 60; Georger-
nes Verft 3; 🕙 to 1am) has harbourside tables that
fill with beer drinkers on warm days.

Legal (Christies gate at Nygårdsgaten; bar menu Nkr45-
72; 🕙 from 2pm) takes its design from 1960s
English rock. Find red lighting, retro flooring and period lamps.

Getting There & Away

BOAT

Sognefjorden express boats go to Balestrand
and Flåm each day, plus northbound express
boats to Måløy and southbound express
boats to Stavanger, leave from Strandkaiterminalen (ferry terminal).

The coastal steamer *Hurtigruten* (p1250)
departs daily.

International ferries to Newcastle, Lerwick (Shetland) and Denmark dock north
of Rosenkrantz Tower.

BUS

Daily express buses run to Odda in Hardanger (Nkr251, 3½ hours) and to the western fjord region. From Bergen it costs Nkr395 (6½ hours) to Stryn, Nkr550 (9½ to 10 hours) to Ålesund and Nkr755 (14½ hours) to Trondheim. A bus runs to Stavanger (Nkr390, 5¾ hours) roughly every two hours.

TRAIN

Trains to Oslo (Nkr670, 6½ to 7¾ hours) depart four or five times daily. Local trains run between Bergen and Voss (Nkr142, 1¼ hours) every hour or two.

Getting Around

City buses cost Nkr17, while fares beyond the centre are based on the distance travelled. Route information is available on ☎ 177.

SOGNEFJORDEN

Sognefjorden, Norway's longest (204km) and deepest (1308m) fjord, cuts a deep slash across western Norway. In some places sheer lofty walls rise more than 1000m above the water, while in others there is a gentler shoreline with farms, orchards and small towns.

The broad main waterway is impressive, but by cruising into the fjord's narrower arms, such as the lovely Nærøyfjorden to Gudvangen, you'll have idyllic views of sheer cliff faces and cascading waterfalls.

Tourist information is available at **Sognefjorden** (☎ 57 67 30 83; www.sognefjorden.no; Postboks 222, N-6852 Sogndal).

Getting There & Away

Fylkesbaatane (☎ 55 90 70 70; www.fylkesbaatane.no) operates a year-round express boat between Bergen and Sogndal, stopping at 10 small towns along the way. Students and InterRail pass holders get a 50% discount. From mid-May to mid-September, Fylkesbaatane runs a second express boat along the same route, terminating in Flåm instead of Sogndal.

There are numerous local ferries linking the fjord towns and an extensive (though not always frequent) network of buses.

Flåm

pop 400

A village of orchards and buildings scenically set at the head of Aurlandsfjorden, Flåm sees 500,000 visitors every summer. It's a jumping-off spot for travellers taking the Gudvangen

or Sognefjorden boats, a turnaround point for the 'Norway in a Nutshell' tour and the base station for the dramatic Flåm railway. Adventurous visitors arrive from Finse by mountain bike. It's five or six hours downhill – obscenely picturesque – and you can return your rental in Flåm's centre. The **tourist office** (☎ 57 63 21 06; www.visitflam.com) has details.

Friendly **Flåm Camping & Hostel** (☎ 57 63 21 21; flaam.hostel@vandrerhjem.no; dm/s/d Nkr135/225/345-395; ⏱ May-Sep; 🅿) has 31 beds – book early. **Heimly Pensjonat** (☎ 57 63 23 00; www.heimly.no; s/d Nkr550-695/695-895; 🅿) has rooms with great fjord views.

The Flåm railway runs between Myrdal and Flåm (Nkr150) numerous times daily, in sync with the Oslo–Bergen service. At Flåm, buses and boats head out to towns around the Sognefjord.

Balestrand

pop 800

This genteel farming community enjoys a mountain backdrop, fjord views and eerie summer light. Due to its lovely surroundings, Balestrand has been a Sognefjorden resort destination for 150 years. The **tourist office** (☎ 57 69 12 55; www.sognefjord.no) rents out bikes.

The road that runs south along the fjord has little traffic and is a pleasant place to stroll. It's lined with orchards, gardens, a 19th-century English church and Viking burial mounds. One mound is topped by a statue of the legendary King Bele, erected by Germany's Kaiser Wilhelm II who spent his holidays here regularly until WWI.

Balestrand HI Hostel (☎ 57 69 13 03; balestrand .hostel@vandrerhjem.no; dm/d Nkr215/585; ⏱ late Jun–mid-Aug; 🅿) is a pleasant lodge-style place. **Midtnes Pensjonat** (☎ 57 69 11 33; www.midtnes.no; s/d Nkr575/680; 🅿), next to the English church, occupies a charming white house. Many rooms have balconies.

There's a supermarket and café near the dock. The hostel restaurant serves dinner for Nkr110.

In addition to the Sognefjorden express boat, local boats run to Hella (from Dragsvik, 10km by road north from Balestrand) and Fjærland. Buses go to Sogndal (Nkr90, 1¼ hours) and Bergen (Nkr237, 3½ hours). The latter departs from Vik, reached by boat (Nkr51, 15 minutes), departing Balestrand 7.55am Monday to Friday. This is cheaper than the express boat, and more scenic.

Sogndal & Around
pop 6600

Sogndal, a modern regional centre, is a starting point for day trips in the area. While it has more amenities than many of the area's smaller towns, it is also far less beautiful. Of most interest is the **Nigardsbreen glacier** 70km to the north, followed by Norway's oldest **stave church** (c. 1150) in Urnes across the Lustrafjord, and the **Sogn Folkmuseum** near Kaupanger, 11km east of Sogndal. The **tourist office** (☎ 57 67 30 83; Kulturhus, Gravensteinsgaten; ☒ to 8pm late Jun-Aug, shorter hrs otherwise) is 500m east of Sogndal bus station.

The tourist office books rooms in private homes from Nkr150 per person. There's a **Hostel** (☎ 57 67 20 33; dm/s/d Nkr100/250/400; ☒ mid-Jun–mid-Aug) 15 minutes east of the bus station.

Buses run from Sogndal to Kaupanger (Nkr25, 10 minutes, hourly) and Balestrand (Nkr90, 1¼ hours, six to nine daily). Twice daily buses (17 June to 26 August) head northeast past Jotunheimen National Park to Lom (Nkr200, 3½ hours) and on to Otta (Nkr275, 4½ hours).

ÅNDALSNES
pop 3500

Åndalsnes, by the Romsdalsfjord, is the northern gateway to the western fjords. Most arrive by train from Dombås, a scenic route descending through a deeply cut valley with dramatic waterfalls. Just before Åndalsnes, the train passes **Trollveggen**, a sheer 1500m-high rock face whose jagged and often cloud-shrouded summit is considered the ultimate challenge among Norwegian climbers.

The town itself is nondescript, but the scenery is top notch. The **tourist office** (☎ 71 22 16 22) is at the train station. The mountains and valleys surrounding Åndalsnes offer excellent **hiking**.

The turf-roofed **Åndalsnes Vandrerhjem Setnes** (☎ 71 22 13 82; aandalsnes.hostel@vandrerhjem.no; dm/s/d Nkr190/350/490; ☒ 20 May-10 Sep; P) offers rustic accommodation with fabulous views and breakfasts. It's 2km from the train station on highway E136 towards Ålesund.

The town centre contains a **grocery store**, **bakery** and several inexpensive **caféterias**.

The train from Dombås runs to Åndalsnes three or four times daily (Nkr171, 1¼ hours), in sync with Oslo–Trondheim trains. Buses to Ålesund (Nkr179, 2¼ hours) meet

the trains. Buses to Geiranger (Nkr145, three hours), via the Trollstigen road, operate from mid-June to late August.

ÅLESUND
pop 24,320

Lucky for you, this pretty coastal town burned to the ground in 1904. The amazing rebuilding created a fantastical downtown unlike anything else in Norway – a harmonious collection of pastel buildings almost entirely designed in the Art Nouveau tradition, well-staged on the end of a hilly peninsula. Many feel it beats Bergen's picturesqueness.

The **tourist office** (☎ 70 15 76 00; www.visit alesund.com; ☒ from 9am-7pm Mon-Sat, 11am-5pm Sun Jun-Aug, otherwise shorter hrs) is near the *Hurtig-urten* quay.

The most popular thing to do is to walk the 418 steps up **Aksla** for a splendid view of Ålesund and the surrounding islands.

The brilliant **Art Nouveau Centre** (☎ 70 10 49 70; www.jugendstilsenteret.no; Apotekergata 16; adult/student Nkr50/40; ☒ 10am-7pm Mon-Fri, 10am-5pm Sat, noon-5pm Sun Jun-Aug, shorter hrs otherwise), occupying a former pharmacy, explains the town's rebuilding with a weirdo time machine and presents the work of well-known continental Art Nouveau masters alongside their Norwegian counterparts.

The tourist office keeps lists of **private rooms** that start at around Nkr250 per person.

Ålesund Hostel (☎ 70 11 58 30; aalesund.hostel@vandrerhjem.no; Parkgata 14; dm/s/d Nkr225/415/535) is tidy and central.

There are several cafés, bakeries and fast food joints about. If you feel like a drink with the hip crowd, stop by **Lille Løvenvold** (☎ 70 12 54 00; Løvenvoldgata 2; ☒ from 11am Mon-Sat, 1pm-1am Sun), which feels like a red light district.

Buses run to Stryn (Nkr220, 3½ hours, one to four daily) via Hellesylt and to other major coastal and fjord towns. The bus to Åndalsnes (Nkr172) is timed to meet arriving and departing trains.

The *Hurtigruten* docks at Skansekaia Terminal.

NORTHERN NORWAY

The counties of Sør Trøndelag, Nord Trøndelag, Nordland, Troms and Finnmark comprise a vast and varied area stretching over 1500km, mostly north of the Arctic

Circle. The terrain ranges from majestic coastal mountains, which rise above tiny fishing villages and scattered farms, to the barren, treeless, Arctic plateau.

Trains run as far north as Bodø; for destinations further north, there are buses and boats (services can be infrequent). Bus travel costs can pile up, though Inter-Rail and ScanRail pass-holders can obtain a 50% discount. An alternative to land travel is the *Hurtigruten* (p1250).

RØROS
pop 2592

Røros is an old copper-mining town with a well-preserved historic district. The first mine opened in 1644, but in 1977, after 333 years of operation, the company went bankrupt. The town makes for some delightful strolling. The **tourist office** (☎ 72 41 11 65; Peder Hiortsgata 2; ☼ 9am-3.30pm Mon-Fri, 10.30am-12.30pm Sat) advises on canoeing, fishing and hiking.

Røros' main attractions are turf-roofed **miners' cottages** as well as other centuries-old timber buildings, a prominent 1784 **church** (Kjerkgata; tours Nkr25; ☼ 10am-5pm Mon-Sat, 2-4pm Sun, mid-Jun–mid-Aug; tours 2pm) with an excellent baroque interior, **slag heaps**, and the old smelting works, part of the **Rørosmuseet** (☎ 72 40 61 70; Malmplassen; adult/student/child Nkr60/50/30; ☼ 10am-7pm mid-Jun–mid-Aug, shorter hrs otherwise).

Idrettsparken HI Hostel (☎ 72 41 10 89; Øra 25; tent sites Nkr60, dm/s/d Nkr225/375/445, cabins Nkr380-600; P) is surrounded by soccer pitches. Many of the inviting rooms of **Vertshuset Røros** (☎ 72 41 93 50; www.vertshusetroros.no; Kjerkgata 34; s/d from Nkr695/880, 2-person apt from Nkr790; P) have floors painted in a folk style common in the Røros area. The informal **Kafestuggu caféteria** (☎ 72 41 10 33; Bergmannsgata 18; light meals Nkr60-85, mains Nkr100-120; ☼ to 8pm) looks like a ski lodge or a Victorian parlour depending on where you sit. Head to **Thomasgården Kafe-Galleri** (☎ 72 41 24 70; Kjerkgata 48; snacks Nkr35-50; ☼ from 10am Mon-Sat, from noon Sun) for a nice read in a rustic room filled with ceramics. Enhance your experience with apple cake.

Røros is 46km west of the Swedish border, via highway Rv31. Trains, some overnight (cheap sleep), run to it from Oslo (Nkr582, five hours) and Trondheim (Nkr246, 2½ hours). Overnight buses run daily except Saturday to Trondheim (Nkr210, three hours) and Oslo (Nkr460, six hours).

TRONDHEIM
pop 138,000

Trondheim, Norway's third-largest city and its original capital, is a lively university town with a rich medieval history. It was founded at the estuary of the winding Nidelva River in 997 by the Viking king Olav Tryggvason. After a fire razed most of the city in 1681, Trondheim was redesigned, with wide streets and a Renaissance flair, by General Caspar de Cicignon. The steeple of the medieval Nidaros Cathedral is still the highest point in the city centre.

The train station and coastal steamer quay are across the canal, a few minutes' north of the centre. The **tourist office** (☎ 73 80 76 60; www.visit-trondheim.com; Torvet; ☼ 8.30am-10pm Mon-Fri, 10am-8pm Sat & Sun, late Jun-early Aug, otherwise shorter hrs) helps with inquiries. Enjoy the **main post office** (Dronningens gate 10). Use the Internet at the **library** (Kongens gate; ☼ 9am-4pm Mon-Fri year-round, 10am-3pm Sat Jul–mid-Aug) or at late night **Space Bar** (☎ 73 51 55 50; Kongens Gate 19; Nkr40 per hour; ☼ 10-2am Sun-Thu, 24hrs Fri & Sat).

Sights

Nidaros Domkirke (☎ 73 53 91 60; Kongsgårdsgata; admission Nkr40; ☼ from 9am Mon-Sat, 1-4pm Sun May–mid-Sep; noon-2.30pm Mon-Fri, 11.30am-2pm Sat, 1-3pm Sun mid-Sep–Apr) is the city's most dominant landmark and Scandinavia's largest medieval building. The first church on this site was built in 1070 over the grave of St Olav, the Viking king who replaced the worship of Nordic gods with Christianity. It's the site of Norwegian coronations.

Completed in 1778, Scandinavia's largest wooden palace, the late baroque **Stiftsgården** (☎ 73 84 28 80; Munkegata; adult Nkr50; ☼ 10am-5pm Mon-Sat, noon-5pm Sun, Jul–mid-Aug, shorter hrs Jun) is now the official royal residence in Trondheim. Admission is by tour only.

The **Ringve Museum** (☎ 73 92 24 11; www.ringve .com; Lade Allé 60; bus Nos 3, 4 from Munkegaten; adult/student Nkr70/40; ☼ 11am-4pm Sun mid-Sep–mid-Apr, 11am-3pm Mon-Fri 11am-4pm Sun mid-Apr–mid-May, 11am-3pm mid-May–mid-Jun, 11am-5pm mid-Jun–mid-Aug, 11am-3pm mid-Aug–mid-Sep), 3km northeast of the city centre, is a fascinating music-history museum in an 18th-century estate. Music students give tours, demonstrating the antique instruments on display.

The superb **Trøndelag Folk Museum** (☎ 73 89 01 00; Sverresborg Allé; adult/child Nkr75/25; ☼ 11am-6pm Jun-Aug, shorter hrs otherwise) has good hill-top views of the city and over 60 period buildings including a small, 12th-century stave church. It's a 10-minute ride on bus No 8 or 9 from Dronningens gate.

Sleeping

Finding a room in mid-August is problematic, with an annual convention filling up every possible spot. Plan ahead if you wish to visit during this time. The tourist office books **rooms** in private homes, mostly on the city outskirts, averaging Nkr300/400 for singles/doubles plus a Nkr20 booking fee.

During summer, university students operate an informal crash pad called **Trondheim InterRail Centre** (☎ 73 89 95 38; www.stud.ntnu.no /groups/tirc; Elgesetergate 1; dm Nkr115; ☉ mid-Jun–mid-Aug). Military surplus cots fill up rooms used as discos the rest of the year. The friendly place provides free Internet.

Trondheim HI Hostel (☎ 73 87 44 50; trondheim .hostel@vandrerhjem.no; Weidemannsvei 41; dm/s/d Nkr235/445/575; ℗), 2km east of the train station, is a plain, modern building with concrete walls and small windows. Halls designed to amplify noise.

Though barren and utilitarian, the rooms at **Pensionat Jarlen** (☎ 73 51 32 18; p-jarlen@frisurf .no; Kongens Gate 40; s/d Nkr400/500) are clean, with showers and kitchens.

A renovated old hotel, **P-Hotel** (☎ 73 80 23 50; www.p-hotels.no; Nordregata 24; s/d Nkr495/595) contains crisp rooms of Scandinavian design. The best deal of the conventional hotels, its comparatively low prices exist in part because you're supposed to book using the Internet.

Eating

Full of students and run by volunteers, **Cafe Edgar** (☎ 73 89 95 00; Elgesetergate 1; dinner Nkr40; ☉ from 5pm Sun-Fri, 3pm Sat) prepares a filling daily meal. Its one of many enterprises inside of the Studentersamfundet (see right).

Mormor's Stue (☎ 73 52 20 22; N Enkelts Killingsveile ; mains Nkr89-97; ☉ 10am-11.30pm Mon-Sat, 1-11.30pm Sun), full of lace, parlours and dusty pictures of grandma, serves sandwiches (Nkr51), pasta and salads. The best and most dangerous time to visit is Sunday, when a calorically evil cake and coffee buffet (Nkr54) fills every seat.

The sunlit rooms of **Café Ni Muser** (☎ 73 63 63 11; Bispegata; dishes Nkr58-90; ☉ 11am-midnight Mon-Fri, noon-midnight Sat & Sun) peer onto a small plaza. It serves fantastic tuna fish sandwiches. Also try the quiche and cake.

Set on a charming street, **Baklandet Skydsstation's** (☎ 73 92 10 44; Øvre Bakklandet 33; meals Nkr58-169; ☉ 4pm-1.30am Mon-Fri, noon-1.30am Sat & Sun) wood burning stove and fish soup keep people warm in the winter. On Sunday, a bottle of wine costs Nkr120.

Overlooking a massive concrete Nazi bunker, **Ramp** (Strandveien at Gregus Gate; meals Nkr35-110; ☉ from 10am Mon-Fri, from noon Sat & Sun) attracts bohemians. Dinners are 'ecological', meaning organic or vegetarian. Breakfast equals bacon and eggs or muesli with yoghurt (Nkr35). Experimental bands sometimes play.

Helios Trondheim (Prinsens gate 53; ☉ 10am-5pm Mon-Fri, Sat 10am-3pm) is a health-food store with a small selection. There's a **Rema 1000** (Torvet) for groceries and baked goodies. The **Ravnkloa fish market** (☉ from 10am Mon-Sat) provides waterside fishcakes (Nkr75) and fisherman (free). For top-notch baguette sandwiches and pastries, try **Godt Brøt** (Thomas Angells Gate 16; ☉ 6am-6pm Mon-Sat).

Entertainment

Den Gode Nabo (☎ 73 87 42 40; Øvre Bakklandet; ☉ 4pm-1.30am) occupies the lower level of an ancient warehouse. Admire several centuries of patchwork carpentry.

Bruk Bar's (☎ 73 50 37 08; Kongens Gate; ☉ from noon) Friday and Saturday night DJs play some serious house and jungle. At other times, volumes decrease.

Studentersamfundet (☎ 73 89 95 00; Elgesetergate 1; ☉ from 5pm), an ideal student centre, features a maze of bars and an excellent calendar of film screenings, DJs and bands – thousands attend. During summer recess it's quiet.

An English pub, **King's Cross** (Nordre gate) features imported draught beer, live widescreen football and bar meals.

Uffa (☎ 72 52 48 50; www.uffahus.org; Innherredsveien 69c; ☉ food from 4pm Mon-Fri) organizes monthly punk and experimental shows in a squat white house with innards covered in graffiti. Uffa hosts informal political meetings. You can often pick up a vegetarian dinner (Nkr20 to Nkr35) around 5pm. To find it, go east on E6. It's opposite a green-steepled church.

Getting There & Away

From the airport in Værnes, 32km east of Trondheim, SAS and Braathens fly to major Norwegian cities.

Nor-Way Bussekspress services run to/ from Ålesund (Nkr502, 7¼ hours, one to three times daily), Bergen (Nkr805, 14½ hours, twice daily) and Oslo (Nkr615, 9½ hours, four days per week).

There are four or five trains to Oslo daily (Nkr745, 6½ hours) and two or three to Bodø (Nkr861, 10 hours). If you're in a hurry to get north, consider taking the overnight train from Oslo, tossing your gear into a locker at the station and spending the day exploring Trondheim before continuing on an overnight train to Bodø (which, incidentally, goes through Hell just after 10.50pm).

Trondheim is a port for the *Hurtigruten*.

Getting Around

Airport buses (Nkr54) leave from the train station, the Britannia Hotel and the Radisson SAS Royal Garden Hotel (Kjøpmannsgata 73).

The central transit point for all city buses is the intersection of Munkegata and Dronningens gate. The bus fare is Nkr22, or you can buy a 24-hour ticket for from Nkr55 to Nkr70, paid to the driver, exact change only.

About 30 stands around the centre have free bicycles borrowed by inserting a Nkr20 coin in their lock.

BODØ

pop 42,000

In addition to being the terminus for the northern railway line, Bodø is Nordland's largest town and is mostly visited as a jumping-off point for Lofoten. Because the town was flattened during WWII air raids and completely rebuilt in the 1950s, Bodø is really quite ordinary in appearance – but it does have a lovely mountain backdrop.

The **tourist office** (☎ 75 54 80 00; www.visitbodo .com; Sjøgata 3; ⏰ to 8pm Jun-Aug, shorter hrs otherwise) is near the waterfront.

The combo **Bodø HI Hostel & Bodø Gjestegård** (☎ 75 52 04 02/75 52 11 22 guesthouse/hostel; bodo .hostel@vandrerhjem.no; Storgata 90; dm/s/d Nkr150/ 250/350) uses two buildings. The hostel is newly remodelled and clean, while the simple, cute guesthouse provides homey rooms with separate bath. The tourist office books **private rooms** from Nkr200 per person.

Above a fisherman's outfitter, **Løvold's** (☎ 75 52 02 61; Tollbugata 9; dishes Nkr35-115; ⏰ 9am-6pm Mon-Fri, 9am-3pm Sat) bustles at lunchtime, offering daily specials of traditional Norwegian food and good views. **Kafé Kafka** (☎ 75 52 35 50; Sandgata 5b; sandwiches Nkr68-89; ⏰ from 11am Mon-Sat, 3pm-midnight Sun), a cool-kid café/ bar, serves marinated vegetable sandwiches. Bands play some weekends. Head to the **docks** for shrimp. **Glasshuset** has a supermarket and several quick-service choices.

Bodø is the northern terminus of the Norwegian rail network. Connect to Trondheim (Nkr861, 10 hours, three times). If you're continuing north by bus, be sure to get off 40 minutes before Bodø at Fauske, where the two daily express buses to Narvik (Nkr467, five hours) meet the train.

The *Hurtigruten* travels to/from Lofoten. There are also car-ferries and express boats that travel to Lofoton. See the tourist office for schedules.

LOFOTEN

The spectacular glacier-carved mountains of Lofoten, separated from the mainland by Vestfjorden, soar straight out of the sea. From a distance they appear as an unbroken line known as the Lofoten Wall.

Lofoten is Norway's prime winter-fishing ground. The warming effects of the Gulf Stream draw spawning Arctic cod from the Barents Sea south to the Lofoten waters each winter, followed by migrating north-coast farmer-fishermen.

Lofoten's islands are all wonderously beautiful. Artists are drawn, moth-like, to Austvågøy's light; art galleries proliferate in Svolvær, Kabelvåg and the busy fishing village of Henningsvær.

The four main islands are all linked by bridge or tunnel. **Nordtraffik Buss Lofoten** (☎ 76 06 40 40) is the regional transport company. Tourist information is available at www.lofoten-info.no.

Svolvær

pop 4100

By Lofoten standards, the main port town of Svolvær on the island of Austvågøy is busy and modern. On the square facing the harbour, you'll find banks, a taxi stand and the helpful regional tourist office, **Destination Lofoten** (☎ 76 06 98 00; Torget; ⏰ to 9.30pm Sun-Fri, to 8pm Sat mid-Jun–mid-Aug, shorter hrs otherwise).

Daredevil mountaineers like to scale **Svolværgeita** (Svolvær Goat), a distinctive two-pronged peak visible from the harbour and jump from one horn to the other. A graveyard at the bottom awaits those who miss. There's also a rough route from the

Goat over to the extraordinary **Devil's Gate**. A fun excursion from Svolvær is a boat trip (Nkr300) into the **Trollfjord**, a spectacularly steep and narrow fjord.

A rustic red beach house, **Svolvær Sjøhuscamping** (☎ 76 07 03 36; www.svolver-sjohuscamp.no; Parkgata 12; d per person Nkr390) has a dockside location: turn right on the first road past the library, and it's a five-minute walk east of the harbour. A **bakery** inhabits the square, a **Rimi supermarket** (Torggata) lives a block inland, and **Bacalao**, a café/bar is behind the tourist office.

Buses to Leknes (Nkr88, two hours) with connections to Å (Nkr163, 3½ hours), depart from Svolvær at least four times per day. The Narvik–Lofoten Ekspressen travels between Svolvær and Narvik (Nkr436, eight to 9¼ hours).

Express boats link Svolvær and Bodø (Nkr246, 3½ hours) and Narvik (Nkr350, 3½ hours), daily except Saturday (but there's no Monday sailing from Svolvær to Narvik).

The *Hurtigruten* stops at Svolvær.

Stamsund

The traditional fishing village of Stamsund makes a fine destination largely because of its dockside hostel, a magnet for travellers, who sometimes stay for weeks. The wonderful old beach house in question is **Justad HI Hostel/Rorbuer** (☎ 76 08 93 34, fax 76 08 97 39; dm/s/d Nkr115/250/300, cabins Nkr600-800; ⊙ mid-Dec–mid-Oct; ℗), where rowboat rental is free – catch and cook your own dinner! Bicycle rental and laundry facilities are available.

The *Hurtigruten* stops en route between Bodø (Nkr325) and Svolvær (Nkr116). Between 20 August to 24 June, buses from Leknes to Stamsund (Nkr29, 25 minutes) run up to eight times daily (less on weekends).

Å

A preserved fishing village, Å's shoreline is lined with red-painted *rorbu*, many sticking out into the sea, perched on forbidding rocks connected by wooden footbridges. Racks of drying cod are placed nearly everywhere and picture-postcard scenes occur at every turn.

The **Tørrefiskmuseum (Stockfish Museum)** (☎ 76 09 12 11; adult/student Nkr40/25 ⊙ 10am-5pm mid-Jun–mid-Aug, 11am-5pm Mon-Fri rest of Jun & Aug), inside a cod plant from 1920, details the history of the stockfish industry. Many of Å's 19th-century buildings are set aside as the

Norwegian Fishing Village Museum (☎ 76 09 14 88; admission Nkr40; ⊙ 10am-5pm late Jun-late Aug, 11am-3pm Mon-Fri late Aug-late Jun), complete with old boats and boat-houses, a bakery from 1844 and Europe's oldest cod liver oil factory.

The **camping ground** (☎ 76 09 13 44; tent sites from Nkr60, huts Nkr300-500; ℗) at the end of the village has a good hillside view of Værøy island, which lies on the other side of **Moskenesstraumen**, the swirling maelstrom that inspired the fictional tales of, amongst others, Jules Verne and Edgar Allen Poe.

Å-Hamna Rorbuer (☎ 76 09 12 11; aa-hamna@lofoten-info.no; dm/d Nkr100/350, rorbuer Nkr500-950; ℗), also at the museum, has pleasant dorms and a pretty communal space in a restored 1860s home and cosy *rorbu*, usually with magnificent views, containing four to eight beds each. Off-season you can get the best *rorbuer* for around Nkr350, firewood included.

You can buy fresh fish from local fishers and pick up other supplies at the **food shop** behind the hostel office.

Nordtrafikk runs one to three daily buses from Å to Leknes (1¾ hours), Svolvær (3¼ hrs) and Sortland (5¼ hrs).

Ofotens og Vesteraalens Dampskibsselskab (OVDS; ☎ 76 96 76 00; www.ovds.no) runs ferries from Bodø to Moskenes (Nkr132/477 passenger/car, four hours) 5km north of Å up to five times daily from 28 June to 11 August (otherwise, once or twice daily except Saturday). Some of these ferries operate via Værøy.

TROMSØ

pop 47,100

Tromsø, at latitude 69°40'N, is the world's northernmost university town. In contrast to some of the more sober communities dotting the north coast of Norway, it's a spirited place with street music, cultural happenings and more pubs per capita than any other Norwegian town. A backdrop of snow-topped peaks provides spectacular scenery, excellent hiking in summer and great skiing and dogsledding December to April.

The **tourist office** (☎ 77 61 00 00; www.destinasjon tromso.no; Storgata 61; open Mon-Fri, daily Jun–mid-Aug) can help with information.

Tromsø's most striking church is the **Arctic Cathedral** (☎ 77 64 76 11; Hans Nilsensvei 41; adult/child Nkr22/free; ⊙ 10am-8pm Jun-Aug, otherwise shorter hrs), on the mainland just over the bridge. It's a freaky building from the '60s that looks like a bunch of triangles stuck together.

Take a midnight sun stroll through the 4-acre **botanical garden** (☎ 77 64 50 78; Breivika; bus No 20; free; ☺ 24 hrs), which blooms brightly despite its northern locale.

Sleeping

Tidy **Tromsø HI Hostel** (☎ 77 65 76 28; tromso.hostel@ vandrerhjem.no; Åsgårdveien 9; dm/s/d Nkr175/275/405; ☺ mid-Jun–mid-Aug; P) is 1.5km west of the city centre. Phone for directions.

The tourist office books rooms in private homes for Nkr250/450 single/double.

Two fine guesthouses, **Hotell Nord** (☎ 77 68 31 59; www.hotellnord.no; Parkgata 4; s/d Nkr450-540/590-695; P) and **Ami Hotel** (☎ 77 68 22 08; www.ami hotel.no; Skolegata 24; s/d Nkr450-500/580-660; P), are a few blocks west of the centre.

Eating & Drinking

Pub-like and student-friendly, **Amtmandens Datter** (☎ 77 68 49 06; Grønnegata 81; mains Nkr88-135; ☺ noon-2.30am Mon-Sat, 3pm-3am Sun) serves beer, salads and a vegetarian sandwich. Patrons may use its newspapers, board games and Internet.

A 1869 relic, **Aunegården** (☎ 77 65 12 34; Sjøgata 29; dishes Nkr69-248; ☺ 10.30am-midnight, 1pm-mindnight Sun) serves amazing cakes (Nkr56) from tables that peer through lacy curtains onto a cobbled street. Also try the sandwiches, nachos, Norwegian fare and wine.

Tromsø's fast-food scene is led by various **kebab carts**. You can buy fresh boiled shrimp from **fishing boats** at Stortorget harbour.

Tromsø enjoys a thriving nightlife. **Blå Rock Café** (Strandgata 14) features theme evenings, 75 types of beer, and live bands and DJs.

The three floors of **Strøket** (☎ 77 68 44 00; Storgata 46; ☺ 4pm-1.30am Tue-Thu, 4pm-3am Fri, noon-3am Sat, 7pm-midnight Sun) pull in the hip crowd like bees to honey. There's a restaurant, bar, and disco.

You can try Tromsø's own Mack beer at pubs or at **Ølhallen** (Storgata 4; ☺ 9am-5pm Mon-Wed, 9am-6pm Fri, Sat 9am-3pm) next to the brewery. It makes up for pathetic hours with old brick walls and stuffed polar bears.

Getting There & Away

Tromsø is the main airport hub for northern Norway, with direct flights to Oslo, Bergen, Bodø, Trondheim, Alta, Hammerfest, Kirkenes and Longyearbyen. Airport buses (Nkr40) depart from the Radisson SAS Hotel Tromsø. A taxi costs Nkr100 to Nkr200.

There two or three daily express buses between Tromsø and Narvik (Nkr315, four to five hours). Buses to/from Alta (Nkr355, 6¾ hours) run once daily.

Tromsø is a port for the *Hurtigruten*. Summer trips to Bodø are Nkr946.

NORDKAPP

Nordkapp (North Cape), a high rugged coastal plateau at 71°10′21″N, claims to be the northernmost point in Europe and is the main destination for most visitors to the far north. The sun never drops below the horizon from mid-May to the end of July. To many visitors, Nordkapp, with its steep cliffs and stark scenery, emanates a certain spiritual aura – long before other Europeans took an interest in the area, Nordkapp was considered a power centre by the Sami people.

Nowadays, there's a rip-off Nkr175 entrance fee and a touristy complex with eateries and souvenirs. If you want to really appreciate Nordkapp, take a walk out along the cliffs.

The continent's real northernmost point, **Knivskjelodden** (latitude 71°11′08$ $) can't be reached by vehicles, but you can hike 18km return (five hours) to this promontory from a car park, 9km south of Nordkapp.

From mid-May to the end of August, local buses run at least twice daily between Honningsvåg and Nordkapp (Nkr72, one hour). Between 2 June and 9 August, the last bus departs Nordkapp at 1.10am, allowing views of the midnight sun.

NORWAY DIRECTORY

ACCOMMODATION

During summer, it's wise to reserve all accommodation, particularly at hostels.

Camping & Cabins

Tent space costs from Nkr50 at the most basic sites to Nkr180 in Oslo. Many camping grounds rent simple cabins from about Nkr250 a day, usually with cooking facilities. Since bedding is rarely provided, bring a sleeping bag.

Norway has an *allemannsretten* (Right of Common Access) dating back around 1000 years. This lets you pitch a tent anywhere in the wilderness for two nights, at least 150m from the nearest house or cottage and leave no trace of your stay. From 15 April to 15 September, lighting a fire in the proximity of woodlands is forbidden.

DNT maintains an extensive network of staffed and unstaffed huts, a day's hike apart, in much of Norway's mountain country. At unstaffed huts, keys must be picked up in advance at DNT offices in nearby towns (you must be a member and pay a Nkr100 deposit to do this); at staffed huts hikers simply show up – no-one is turned away, even if there's only floor space left. Nightly fees in a room with one to three beds are around Nkr150. Basic membership for one calendar year costs Nkr425/250 adult/student.

Hostels

Norway has 72 *vandrerhjem* (hostels) affiliated with Hostelling International (HI). Some are open year-round, while others operate in summer only. Most hostels have private rooms at higher prices. Guests must bring their own sleeping sheet and pillowcase, although most hostels hire linens for around Nkr50. Nearly all hostels have kitchens that guests can use. The Norwegian Hostelling Association is **Norske Vandrerhjem** (☎ 23 13 93 00; www.vandrerhjem.no; Torggata 1, N-0181 Oslo). You can book hostels via the website.

Hotels

Although normal hotel prices are high, many substantially reduce their rates on Saturday and Sunday and in the summer season. Nationwide chains like Rainbow Hotels and Rica offer particularly good summer and weekend deals. With Rainbow, you'll get the lowest rates by buying a Scan+ Hotel Pass (sold at hotels for Nkr90) – usually paying for itself on the first night. Breakfast is usually included.

Pensions & Private Rooms

Private rooms, usually bookable through tourist offices, average Nkr300/400 for singles/doubles. Breakfast isn't normally included. Along highways, you may see *Rom* signs, indicating informal accommodation for around Nkr100 to Nkr250 (without breakfast).

ACTIVITIES
Fishing

No licence is required for saltwater fishing. In fresh water, a national licence (available from post offices for Nkr90 to Nkr180) is mandatory and often a local licence (available from tourist offices, hotels and camping grounds for Nkr50 to Nkr300 per day) is required.

Hiking

Norway has some of Europe's best hiking, ranging from easy trails in the forests around the cities to long treks through the mountains. Due to deep winter snows, hiking in many areas is seasonal; in the highlands, it's often limited to the period of late June to September. The most popular wilderness hiking areas are Jotunheimen, Rondane and Hardangervidda, but many other areas are just as attractive. For more information on hiking and climbing, contact the Norwegian Mountain Touring Association, **Den Norske Turistforening** (DNT; ☎ 22 82 28 22; www.turistforeningen.no; Postboks 7 Sentrum, N-0101 Oslo).

Rafting

Norway's wild rivers are ideal for rafting. Trips range from short, Class II doodles to rollicking Class V punishment. **Norges Padleforbund** (☎ 21 02 98 35; www.padling.no; Service boks 1, Ullevål stadion, N-0840 Oslo) provides a comprehensive list of operators.

Skiing

'Ski' is a Norwegian word, and Norwegians make a credible claim to having invented the sport. Norway has thousands of kilometres of maintained cross-country ski trails and scores of resorts with excellent downhill runs. The Holmenkollen area near Oslo, Geilo on the Oslo-Bergen railway line, and Lillehammer and the surrounding Gudbrandsdalen region are some of the more popular spots.

CLIMATE

The typically rainy climate of mainland Norway is surprisingly mild for its latitude – thanks to the Gulf Stream, all coastal ports remain ice-free throughout the year.

Average July temperatures are 16°C in the Oslo area and 11°C in the north, though temperature extremes are always possible. In January, the average maximum temperature is 1°C in the south and -3°C in the north. However, it can get much colder, especially in areas away from the coast.

For climate charts see p1232.

EMBASSIES & CONSULATES
Embassies & Consulates in Norway

Australia (☎ 22 47 91 70; Jernbanetorget 2, N-0106 Oslo)

Canada (☎ 22 99 53 00; Wergelandsveien 7, N-0244 Oslo)

Denmark (☎ 22 54 08 00; Olav Kyrres gate 7, N-0244 Oslo)

Finland (☎ 22 43 04 00; Thomas Heftyes gate 1, N-0244 Oslo)

France (☎ 22 28 46 00; Drammensveien 69, N-0244 Oslo)

Germany (☎ 22 27 54 00; Oscars gate 45, N-0244 Oslo)

Ireland (☎ 22 12 20 00; Haakon VII's gate 1, N-0212 Oslo)

New Zealand (☎ 66 77 53 30; Billingstadsletta 19B, Postboks 113, N-1376 Billingstad)

Netherlands (☎ 22 19 71 90; Oscars gate 29, N-0244 Oslo)

Russia (☎ 22 55 32 78; Drammensveien 74, N-0271 Oslo)

Sweden (☎ 22 44 35 11; Nobelsgata 16, N-0244 Oslo)

UK (☎ 23 13 27 00; Thomas Heftyes gate 8, N-0244 Oslo)

USA (☎ 22 44 85 50; Drammensveien 18, N-0255 Oslo)

Norwegian Embassies & Consulates Abroad

Find listings of Norwegian embassies and consulates at www.embassies.mfa.no.

Australia & New Zealand (☎ 6273 3444; emb .canberra@mfa.no; 17 Hunter St, Yarralumla, ACT 2600)

Canada (☎ 613-238 6571; emb.ottawa@mfa.no; Royal Bank Centre, 90 Sparks St, Suite 532, Ottawa, Ontario K1P 5B4)

Denmark (☎ 33 14 01 24; emb.copenhagen@mfa.no; Amaliegade 39, DK-1256 Copenhagen K)

Finland (☎ 09 686 0180; emb.helsinki@mfa.no; Rehbinderintie 17, FIN-00150 Helsinki)

France (☎ 01 53 67 04 00; emb.paris@mfa.no; 28 Rue Bayard, F-75008 Paris)

Germany (☎ 030-505050; emb.berlin@mfa.no; Rauchstrasse 1, D-10787 Berlin)

Ireland (☎ 01-662 1800; emb.dublin@mfa.no; 34 Molesworth St, Dublin 2)

Netherlands (☎ 70 311 7611; emb.hague@mfa.no; Lange Vijverberg 11, NL-2513 AC Den Haag)

Sweden (☎ 08-665 6340; emb.stockholm@mfa.no; Skarpögatan 4, SE-11593 Stockholm)

UK (☎ 020-7591 5500; emb.london@mfa.no; 25 Belgrave Square, London, SW1X 8QD)

USA (☎ 212-333 6000; www.norway.org; 2720 34th St NW, Washington DC 20008)

FESTIVALS & EVENTS

Norway is chock-a-block with special festivals, which take place in every city, town and village. Most of these take place during the summer, and a few of the most popular are outlined on the right. For information about the country's biggest festivals, check out www.norwayfestivals.com.

HOLIDAYS

Constitution Day, 17 May, is Norway's biggest holiday, with events throughout the country and many Norwegians taking to the street in traditional folk costumes. The biggest celebration is in Oslo, where marching bands and thousands of schoolchildren parade down Karl Johans gate to Det Kongelige Slott to be greeted by the royal family.

Midsummer's Eve, celebrated by bonfires on the beach, is generally observed on 23 June, St Hans day.

On 13 December, Christian children celebrate the feast of Santa Lucia by dressing in white and holding a candlelit procession.

Norway practically shuts down during Christmas and Easter weeks, when you'll be fortunate to find an open bar or grocery store.

New Year's Day 1 January
Maundy Thursday Thursday before Easter
Good Friday March/April
Easter Monday March/April
Labour Day 1 May
Constitution Day 17 May
Ascension Day The 40th day after Easter
Whit Monday The eighth Monday after Easter
Christmas Day 25 December
Boxing Day 26 December

LEGAL MATTERS

The legal drinking age is 18 years to drink beer and wine, 20 years for spirits. See p872 for requirements to operate a car. Penalties for possessing drugs and controlled substances are severe. The age of consent is 16 years. It is illegal to smoke in public spaces including bars, restaurants and clubs.

MONEY

The Norwegian krone is most often written NOK in international money markets, Nkr in northern Europe and kr within Norway.

One Norwegian krone equals 100 øre. Coins come in denominations of 50 øre and one, five, 10 and 20 kroner, and bills in denominations of 50, 100, 200, 500 and 1000 kroner.

ATMs are available in every town mentioned in this book.

Some post offices and all banks will exchange major foreign currencies and accept all travellers cheques, which command a better exchange rate than cash (by about 2%). Banks open Monday to Friday and close around 3pm, while post offices open later (see below). You can change money in kiosks and hotels, but the rate won't be as good.

POST

In most towns, post offices open from 9am to 4pm (or 5pm) Monday to Friday and 10am to 2pm Saturday. Cards and letters weighing up to 20g cost Nkr5.5 within Norway, Nkr7.5 to other Nordic countries, Nkr9.5 to elsewhere in Europe and Nkr10.5 to the rest of the world. Mail can be received c/o poste restante at almost all post offices in Norway.

TELEPHONE & FAX

Norway has no telephone area codes; domestic numbers consist of eight digits.

Most pay phones accept Nkr1, Nkr5, Nkr10 and Nkr20 coins and will return unused coins but won't give change. The minimum charge for domestic and international calls is Nkr5. Domestic calls get 33% discount between 5pm and 8am weekdays, and on weekends (from 5pm Friday to 8am

Monday). Directory assistance (☎ 180) costs Nkr8 per minute. So-called 'free' calls, with ☎ 800 prefixes, are still charged with cardphones and in hotels. Using a hotel room's phone carries prohibitive charges.

Telekort (phone cards) are sold in Nkr40, Nkr90, Nkr140 and Nkr210 denominations and work out cheaper than coins. Cards can be purchased at post offices, 7-Eleven, and MIX kiosks.

The country code for calling Norway from abroad is ☎ 47. To make an international call from Norway, dial ☎ 00, then the appropriate country code, area code and number you're calling.

VISAS

Citizens of the USA, Canada, the UK, Ireland, Australia and New Zealand need a valid passport to visit Norway, but do not need a visa for stays of less than three months. The same is true for EU and European Economic Area (EEA – essentially EU and Scandinavia) countries, most of Latin America and most Commonwealth countries.

Poland

POLAND

HIGHLIGHTS

▪ **Wawel Hill** Kraków's magnificent castle, with its opulent interiors, is unmissable, and the cathedral where generations of Polish kings were crowned and buried is an icon of the Polish nation (p909)

▪ **Warsaw's Old Town** Exploring the historic heart of Warsaw, left in rubble at the end of WWII and subsequently completely and faithfully restored (p903)

▪ **Wrocław's Ostrów Tumski** Taking time out for a stroll around Wrocław's charming ecclesiastical quarter and whiling away the afternoon in the Botanical Gardens (p916)

▪ **Teatr Wielki, Warsaw** Indulging your cultural side and taking in a top-class opera or ballet at very reasonable prices (p906)

▪ **Off-the-beaten track** Hiking in the hills around the Tatra Mountains and enjoying some of Poland's most spectacular scenery (p913)

FAST FACTS

▪ **Area** 312,685 sq km (roughly the size of France)

▪ **ATMS** Widespread

▪ **Budget** From around 70zł per day in Warsaw

▪ **Capital** Warsaw

▪ **Country Code** ☎ 048

▪ **Famous for** Frederic Chopin, Solidarity, vodka

▪ **Head of State** President Aleksander Kwasniewski

▪ **Language** Polish

▪ **Money** (A1$=2.55zł, CA$1 = 2.80zł, €1=4.38zł, ¥100 = 3.20zł, NZ$1 = 2.40zł, UK£1=6.30zł, US1$=3.42zł)

▪ **Phrases** Dzień dobry (good morning), Ile to kosztuje? (how much is it?), dziękuję (thank you)

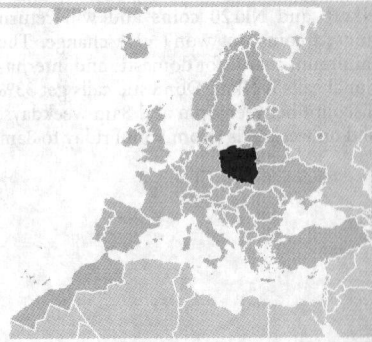

▪ **Population** 39 Million

▪ **Time** GMT/UTC + 1

▪ **Visas** not required for EU citizens; US, Canadian, New Zealand and Australian citizens do not need visas for stays of less than 90 days.

TRAVEL HINTS

Ask about weekend rates in hotels, as discounts are often available. Use private minibuses, which are usually quicker and cheaper than the regular bus service.

ROAMING POLAND

To see the best that Poland has to offer, start with the bustling capital, Warsaw, and from there hop on a train to Kraków, home to the magnificent Wawel Castle. You could also take a day trip to Zakopane from Kraków , before continuing by rail to Wrocław and on up to the city of Gdańsk on the Baltic Sea.

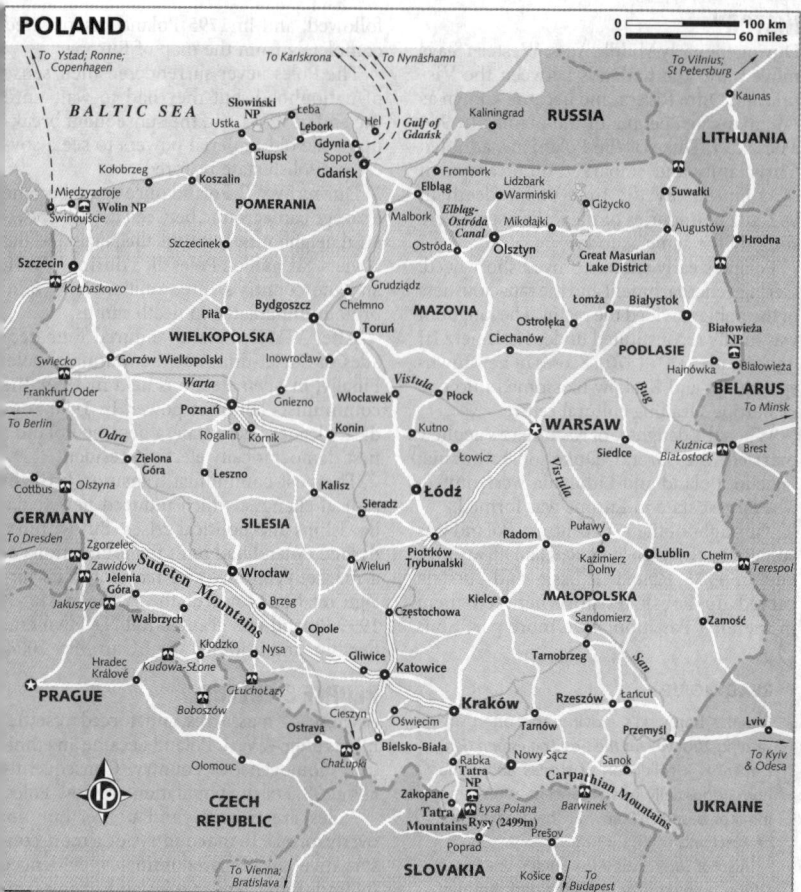

POLAND

Stretching from the Baltic Sea to the Carpathian Mountains, Poland is a big country with a wide variety of landscapes and an ever-present sense of history. Centuries of war, foreign occupation and oppression have failed to dampen the Poles' strong sense of nationhood. The ancient royal capital of Kraków, with its peerless castle, and the painstakingly restored Old Town in Warsaw, which had been bombed to dust and rubble by the end of WWII, are perhaps the best examples of the Poles' pride in their nation and its history. Since the demise of communism, Poland has quickly modernised, reacquainting itself with capitalism. Its bustling cities, such as cosmopolitan Gdańsk and cultured Wrocław, are the antithesis of the old image of Eastern Bloc greyness.

Poland's relatively undeveloped coastline, with its attractive, sandy beaches, and the rugged mountains of the south are sure to delight visitors. There are lots of off-the-beaten-track destinations to discover, from picturesque mountain villages lost in time to big towns where foreigners are still a rare sight.

Poland is still cheap by Western European standards, and it represents excellent value for budget travellers. Prices are rising, however, a trend that is sure to continue apace now that Poland has joined the EU. On the upside, travelling here is easier than ever, and is now visa-free for many nationalities. Now is the perfect time to visit.

POLAND

HISTORY

During the early Middle Ages, Western Slavs moved into the flatlands between the Vistula and Odra Rivers, and became known as Polanians, or 'people of the plains'. In 966 Mieszko I, Duke of the Polanians, adopted Christianity and embarked on a campaign of conquest. By the time of his death in 992, the boundaries of the Polish state were roughly the same as today.

Poland's early success proved short-lived. German encroachment and the rapaciousness of the nobles divided the realm. The kingdom was finally reconstituted under Kazimierz III 'the Great' (1333–1370). Scores of new towns sprang up, and Kraków blossomed into one of Europe's leading cultural centres.

When the daughter of Kazimierz's nephew married the Grand Duke of Lithuania, Jagiełło, Poland and Lithuania were united. The largest state in Europe was formed.

Throughout the 17th century, Poland was subject to Swedish and Russian invasions, and in 1773 Russia, Prussia and Austria carved up Polish territory between them in the First Partition. Two more partitions followed, and in 1795 Poland disappeared completely from the map of Europe.

The Poles never surrendered their sense of nationhood, but they had to wait until the end of WWI and the subsequent breakup of the old imperial powers to see a sovereign Polish state restored.

During WWII Poland once again became a savage battleground between its more powerful neighbours, this time the Nazis and the Soviets. Six million Poles died during WWII and the country's three million Jews were brutally annihilated in death camps.

After WWII, Poland endured four decades of Soviet-dominated communist rule. Finally, in open elections held in 1989, the communists fell from power. In 1990 Solidarity leader Lech Wałęsa became Poland's first democratically elected president.

The post-communist transition brought radical changes, which induced new social hardships and political crises. But within a decade Poland had built the foundations of a market economy and reoriented its foreign relations towards the West. In March 1999 Poland was granted full NATO membership, and it joined the EU in May 2004.

READING UP

Tadeusz Borowski's moving and often unsettling *This way for the Gas, Ladies and Gentlemen*, is a collection of stories about the horrendous daily lives of concentration camp inmates, based on Borowski's own experience of Auschwitz.

Also of interest is Alan Furst's the *Polish Officer*, a spy thriller set in the dark world of wartime Warsaw.

Perhaps Poland's best known and most successful modern writer is Ryszard Kapuscinski, the highly regarded foreign correspondent and journalist. His works include *Another Day of Life*, about the civil war in Angola, *Imperium*, his account of his travels across the collapsing former Soviet Union in 1989, and the *Shadow of the Sun*, a collection of essays based on his wide travels across the continent of Africa.

Jews in Poland by Iwo Cyprian Pogonowski provides a comprehensive record of half a millennium of Polish-Jewish relations in Poland. *God's Playground: A History of Poland* by Norman Davies offers an in-depth analysis of Polish history.

PEOPLE & CULTURE

Because of massacres and forced resettlements after WWII, Poland became an ethnically homogeneous country. Consequently about 98% of the population are now Poles.

Poles are friendly and polite, but not overly formal. In the countryside a more conservative culture predominates, evidenced by traditional gender roles and strong family ties. In both urban and rural settings Poles are devoutly religious, and packed out churches are not uncommon.

When greeting, Polish men are passionate about shaking hands. Polish women too, often shake hands with men, but the man should always wait for the woman to extend her hand first.

Many older Poles, especially in the west, speak German as their second language, but younger people are more likely to speak English. Outside the big towns, knowledge of foreign languages is limited. To polish up your Polish, see the Language chapter (p1264).

ARTS

Poland boasts a rich literary and artistic heritage going back to the Middle Ages.

At the turn of the 20th century, the avant-garde 'Young Poland' movement in art and literature began in Kraków, the most notable representative perhaps being the writer Stanisław Wyspiański (1869–1907).

Without doubt Poland's most famous musician was Frederic Chopin (1810–49), whose melancholy piano compositions have come to symbolise the Polish national style.

Poland's best-known painter is Jan Matejko (1838–93), whose grand historical paintings can be seen in galleries up and down the land.

In more recent times, Poland has produced several world-renowned film directors, including Roman Polanski, who directed international hits such as *Rosemary's Baby* and *Chinatown*, and Krzysztof Kieślowski, best remembered for his trilogy *Three Colours: Blue/White/Red*.

TRANSPORT

GETTING THERE & AWAY
Air
The national carrier, **LOT** (www.lot.com), flies to most major European cities. Warsaw is also serviced by major European carriers, such as Air France, Alitalia, British Airways, KLM and Lufthansa. Other regional airlines with flights to/from Warsaw include Aeroflot, Czech Airlines, Malév, Scandinavian Airlines and Turkish Airlines.

From North America, LOT offers frequent direct flights to Warsaw from Chicago and New York, and a weekly service from Toronto.

Boat
Three companies operate passenger and car ferries year-round.

Polferries (www.polferries.pl) Offers services between Gdańsk and Nynäshamn (18 hours) in Sweden every other day in summer (less frequently in off season). It also has services from Świnoujście to Ystad (9½ hours, daily) in Sweden, to Rønne (six hours, Saturday) in Denmark, and Copenhagen (10½–11 hours, five weekly).

Stena Line (www.stenaline.com) Operates between Gdynia and Karlskrona (11 hours) in Sweden.

Unity Line (www.unityline.pl) Runs ferries between Świnoujście and Ystad (eight hours).

Any travel agency in Scandinavia will sell tickets for these services. In Poland, inquire at the **Orbis Travel Office** (☎ 022 827 72 65; ul Bracka 16) in Warsaw or at its branch at the airport. In summer, passenger boats ply the Baltic coast from Świnoujście to Ahlbeck, Heringsdorf, Bansin and Sassnitz in Germany.

Bus
Bus services throughout Western and Eastern Europe are offered by dozens of Polish and international companies. Tickets are generally cheaper than train tickets, but you will undoubtedly find it more comfortable, and probably quicker, to travel to/from Poland by train.

One of the major bus operators is Eurolines, a consortium of affiliated European bus companies that includes the Polish national bus company **PKS** (☎ 022 652 2321; www.pekaesbus .com.pl; Warsaw central bus station). PKS runs dozens of buses each week to all major cities in Germany from the Dworzec Zachodnia (Western Bus Station) in Warsaw.

Eurolines (☎ 032-351 20 20; www.eurolinespolska.pl) has services three or four days a week (and daily in summer), from London (Victoria) to Zamość, via Poznań, Łódź, Warsaw (Zachodnia) and Lublin, and from London to Kraków, via Wrocław.

Eurolines has three weekly services from Paris to Białystok, via Poznań and Warsaw; from Paris to Kraków, via Wrocław and Częstochowa; and from Paris to Gdynia, via Poznań, Toruń and Gdańsk.

Eurolines also offers regular services from major European cities, including from Stuttgart to Warsaw, Munich to Kraków via Wrocław, Prague to Warsaw via Kraków, from Rome to Gdańsk and from Madrid to Warsaw.

Heading east, Eurolines also run links to Minsk, St Petersburg, Vilnius, Lviv and Riga. Check the website for times and prices.

Train
Domestic trains are significantly cheaper than international services, so you'll save money if you buy a ticket to the first Polish city you arrive at and then take a local train. You can obtain information and buy tickets

---

DEPARTURE TAX

This is included in the price of your airline ticket.

WARNING

Some international trains to/from Poland have recently become notorious for theft. Stay alert and keep a grip on your bags, particularly on the Berlin–Warsaw, Prague–Warsaw and Prague–Kraków overnight trains, and on *any* train travelling to/from Gdańsk. Night trains are best avoided, particularly if travelling alone. Several readers reportedly have been gassed while in their compartments and have had everything stolen while they 'slept'. If possible, sleep in a compartment with others.

for some services from the Polish railways website www.wars.pl.

Several trains serve the Warsaw to Berlin route daily (via Frankfurt/Oder and Poznań), including EuroCity express services (6½ hours, three daily). There are also a number of connections between Warsaw and Cologne, Dresden, Frankfurt-am-Main and Leipzig; between Kraków and Berlin, via Wrocław; and between Gdańsk and Berlin, via Szczecin. To/from Prague trains serve Warsaw (10 to 12 hours, four daily), Wrocław (seven hours, four daily) and Kraków (nine hours, one daily). To/from Vienna, trains serve Warsaw (about 10 hours, two daily) and Kraków (seven hours, one daily).

Trains travel between Budapest and Warsaw (12 hours, two daily), via Bratislava. The train between Budapest and Kraków (11 hours, daily) follows a different route through Košice in eastern Slovakia.

Warsaw has direct train links with Kyiv (Ukraine), Minsk (Belarus), Vilnius (Lithuania), and Moscow and St Petersburg (these trains have only sleeping cars). There are also trains between Gdańsk and Kaliningrad (five hours, daily) in Russia.

EMERGENCY NUMBERS

- **Ambulance** ☎ 999
- **Fire** ☎ 998
- **Pharmacy** (24 hour) ☎ 911
- **Police** ☎ 997
- **Police** (from a mobile/cell phone) ☎ 112
- **Roadside assistance** ☎ 981

Remember that you might need to get transit visas for the countries you'll be passing through.

GETTING AROUND
Bus

Most buses are operated by the state bus company **PKS** (☎ 022 652 2321; www.pekaesbus.com.pl; Warsaw central bus station, or Dworzec Centralny PKS station), which has bus terminals *(dworzec autobusowy PKS)* in all cities and towns. PKS offers two kinds of services: ordinary buses, which cover mostly regional routes, and fast buses, which cover mainly long-distance routes. The largest private bus operator is Polski Express.

Tickets for PKS buses must be bought at the terminal. Tickets for Polski Express buses can be bought up to 14 days in advance at the terminals or stops.

For shorter trips, private minibuses usually provide a better option to PKS buses. They always travel faster than buses, usually leave more frequently and stop *far* less often. They're generally cheaper, too.

Car & Motorcycle

To drive a car into Poland you will need your driving licence from home. Also required are vehicle registration papers and liability insurance. Most major international car-rental companies, such as **Avis** (www.avis.pl) and **Europcar** (www.europcar.com.pl), are represented in larger cities and have smaller offices at the airports. Prices are comparable to full-price rental in Western Europe. An increasing number of local operators, such as **Payless Car Rental** (www.paylesscarrental.pl), provide a reliable and more affordable alternative.

Car theft is a problem in Poland.

Border Crossings

Below is a list of major border crossings by road that accept foreigners. These crossings are open 24 hours.

Belarus (south to north) Terespol and Kuźnica Białostocka.

Czech Republic (west to east) Porajów, Zawidów, Jakuszyce, Lubawka, Golińsk, Kudowa-Słone, Boboszów, Głuchołazy, Pietraszyn and Chałupki.

Germany (north to south) Lubieszyn, Kołbaskowo, Krajnik Dolny, Osinów Dolny, Kostrzyn, Słubice, Ścwiecko, Gubin, Olszyna, Łęknica, Zgorzelec and Sieniawka.

Lithuania (east to west) Ogrodniki and Budzisko.

Russia (Kaliningrad region; east to west) Bezledy and Gronowo.

Slovakia (west to east) Chyżne, Chochołów, Łysa Polana, Piwniczna, Konieczna and Barwinek.
Ukraine (south to north) Medyka, Hrebenne and Dorohusk

Train

Trains will be your main means of transport, especially for long distances. They are cheap, fairly reliable and rarely overcrowded.

Express trains (*pociąg ekspresowy*) are a faster but more expensive way to travel, whereas fast trains (*pociąg pospieszny*) are a bit slower and may be more crowded. Slow passenger trains (*pociąg osobowy*) should be used only for short trips.

InterCity trains operate on some major routes out of Warsaw, including Gdańsk, Kraków, Poznań and Szczecin. They stop only at major cities and are faster than express trains.

Almost all trains offer two classes: 2nd class (*druga klasa*) and 1st class (*pierwsza klasa*), which is 50% more expensive.

WARSAW (WARSZAWA)

☎ 022 / pop 1.71 million

Warsaw is the political and economic heart of Poland, and the country's largest and most cosmopolitan city. Devastated during WWII, when more than half its population perished and 85% of its buildings were reduced to rubble, Warsaw was rebuilt over the following decades. The Old Town was completely reconstructed and is an astounding monument to Polish national pride. There's also a wealth of less appealing Stalinist concrete, and recent years have witnessed a building boom in the city centre.

Warsaw's many museums and galleries, and the ever-increasing roll-call of good quality restaurants and bars, mean there's plenty to keep you occupied for several days. The capital's position at the centre of Poland's transport network makes it an ideal base for exploring the surrounding countryside.

ORIENTATION

The city is divided by the Vistula River into two very different parts. The western left-bank sector is much larger and features the city centre, including the Old Town, the historic nucleus of Warsaw. Almost all tourist attractions, as well as the lion's share of tourist facilities, are on this side of the river.

GETTING INTO TOWN

The cheapest way of getting from the airport to the city centre (and vice versa) is on bus No 175 (every 10 to 15 minutes), which runs to the Old Town, via ul Nowy Świat and the Warszawa Centralna (Warsaw Central) train station. If you arrive in the wee hours, night bus No 611 (every 30 minutes) links the airport with Warszawa Centralna.

The taxi fare between the airport and the city centre should be around 25zł to 30zł. Illicit 'Mafia' cabs operate at the airport and charge astronomical rates; check that fares are displayed in the window and that a meter is running.

If arriving by train, Warszawa Centralna station is within walking distance of the city centre and main attractions. If you arrive by bus at Dworzec Centralny PKS station, hop on a train from the adjoining Warszawa Zachodnia station into the centre. From the Dworzec PKS Stadion, you can again catch a train to Warszawa Centralna from the Stadion train station.

INFORMATION
Discount Cards

Available from all tourist offices, the **Warsaw Tourist Card** (45/85zł for a one-/three-day card) offers free or discounted access to most of the main museums, free public transport and discounts at some theatres, sports centres and restaurants.

Internet Access

Several convenient but dingy Internet centres are also located along the underground mezzanine level of the Warszawa Centralna train station. All charge around 3zł to 4zł per hour.

Casablanca (☎ 828 14 47; ul Krakowskie Przedmieście 4/6; 🕑 9am-1am)

Internet Café (☎ 826 60 62; ul Nowy Świat 18/20; 🕑 9am-11pm Mon-Fri, 10am-10pm Sat & Sun)

Verso Internet (☎ 831 28 54; ul Freta 17; 🕑 8am-8pm Mon-Fri, 9am-5pm Sat, 10am-4pm Sun)

Medical Services

Apteka Grabowskiego (☎ 825 69 86; Warszawa Centralna train station) Pharmacy; open 24 hours.

Hospital of the Ministry of Internal Affairs & Administration (☎ 602 15 78; ul Wołoska 137) Private hospital preferred by government officials and diplomats.

POLAND

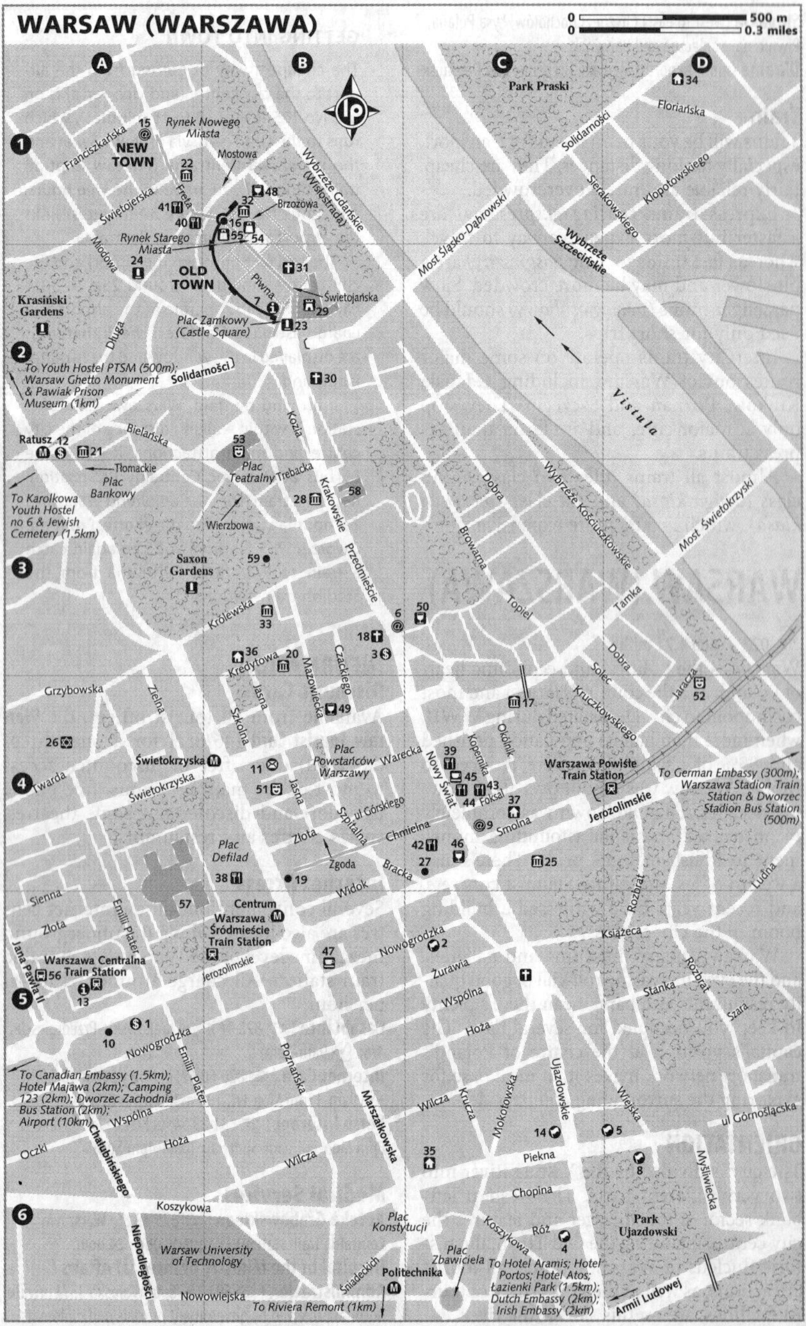
WARSAW (WARSZAWA)
0 500 m
0 0.3 miles
A
B
C
D
1
2
3
4
5
6
Park Praski
34
Floriańska
Solidarności
Sierakowskiego
Kłopotowskiego
Wybrzeże Szczecińskie
Most Śląsko-Dąbrowski
Wybrzeże Gdańskie (Wisłostrada)
Rynek Nowego Miasta
15
Franciszkańska
NEW TOWN
22
Mostowa
Freta
Świętojerska
41
40
48
32
Brzozowa
16
55
54
Rynek Starego Miasta
Miodowa
24
OLD TOWN
31
Piwna
Świętojańska
7
29
Plac Zamkowy (Castle Square)
23
Krasiński Gardens
Długa
To Youth Hostel PTSM (500m); Warsaw Ghetto Monument & Pawiak Prison Museum (1km)
Solidarności
30
Vistula
Ratusz 12
21
Bielańska
Tłomackie
Plac Bankowy
53
Plac Teatralny
Trębacka
Kozla
To Karolkowa Youth Hostel no 6 & Jewish Cemetery (1.5km)
28
58
Wierzbowa
Krakowskie Przedmieście
Dobra
Wybrzeże Kościuszkowskie
Most Świętokrzyski
Browarna
Saxon Gardens
59
Królewska
33
6
50
18
3
Topiel
Tamka
36
Kredytowa
20
Mazowiecka
Czackiego
Dobra
Solec
Jaracza
52
Grzybowska
Zielna
Jasna
Szkolna
49
17
Kruczkowskiego
26
Świętokrzyska
Twarda
Świętokrzyska
11
51
Plac Powstańców Warszawy
Warecka
Nowy Świat
39
45
Kopernika
Okólnik
43
44
Foksal
Warszawa Powiśle Train Station
To German Embassy (300m); Warszawa Stadion Train Station & Dworzec Stadion Bus Station (500m)
Jerozolimskie
37
ul Górskiego
Szpitalna
Chmielna
9
Smolna
Plac Defilad
Złota
42
46
Zgoda
27
Bracka
25
38
19
Widok
Sienna
57
Emilii Plater
Centrum
Warszawa Śródmieście Train Station
Rozbrat
Ludna
Złota
Jana Pawła II
Warszawa Centralna Train Station
56
13
47
Nowogrodzka
2
Książęca
Jerozolimskie
Żurawia
Wspólna
Stanka
Rozbrat
Szara
1
10
Nowogrodzka
Hoża
To Canadian Embassy (1.5km); Hotel Majawa (2km); Camping 123 (2km); Dworzec Zachodnia Bus Station (2km); Airport (10km)
Emilii Plater
Poznańska
Marszałkowska
Krucza
Mokotowska
Ujazdowskie
Wiejska
ul Górnośląska
Wspólna
Wilcza
Chałubińskiego
Hoża
14
5
Oczki
Wilcza
35
Piękna
8
Myśliwiecka
Chopina
Koszykowa
Plac Konstytucji
Róż
Park Ujazdowski
Niepodległości
Warsaw University of Technology
Koszykowa
4
Śniadeckich
Plac Zbawiciela
To Hotel Aramis; Hotel Portos; Hotel Atos; Łazienki Park (1.5km); Dutch Embassy (2km); Irish Embassy (2km)
Politechnika
Nowowiejska
To Riviera Remont (1km)
Armii Ludowej

POLAND

Money

Foreign-exchange offices (kantors) and ATMs are plentiful in the city centre.

American Express (Marriott Hotel, Al Jerozolimskie 65/79) Good for cashing major travellers cheques.

Bank Pekao (ul Krakowskie Przedmieście) This branch is next to the Church of the Holy Cross, but there are dozens of others throughout the city.

PBK Bank (ground fl, Palace of Culture & Science bldg)

PKO Bank (Plac Bankowy 2)

Post

Main post office (ul Świętokrzyska 31/33; ⏰ 24hr)

Telephone

There are numerous public telephone booths all around the city, including inside the main post office. Phonecards are available from street kiosks and post offices.

Tourist Information

Each provides free city maps and booklets (look out for *Warsaw in Short* and *The Visitor: Warsaw*), sells maps of other Polish cities and helps book hotel rooms.

Central tourist office (☎ 9431; www.warsawtour.pl) ul Krakowskie Przedmieście 89 (⏰ 9am-8pm May-Sep, to 6pm Oct-Apr); Warszawa Centralna train station (Main hall; ⏰ 8am-8pm May-Sep, to 6pm Oct-Apr); Dworzec Zachodnia (⏰ 9am-5pm); airport arrivals hall (⏰ 8am-8pm May-Sep, to 6pm Oct-Apr)

SIGHTS & ACTIVITIES
Old Town

The main gateway to the Old Town is **Plac Zamkowy** (Castle Square). Amazingly, all of the historic buildings around this square were completely rebuilt after WWII. In the centre of the square stands the **Monument to Sigismund III Vasa**, who moved the capital from Kraków to Warsaw.

The square is dominated by the massive **Royal Castle** (☎ 657 21 70; pl Zamkowy 4; adult 15zł, free Sun; ⏰ 10am-4pm Mon-Sat, 11am-4pm Sun). The castle was begun in the 13th century and grew as successive Polish kings added wings and redecorated. Reduced to rubble in 1945, it was reconstructed between 1971 and 1984. The most interesting of the sumptuously decorated rooms is the Senators' Antechamber, where 23 landscapes of 18th-century Warsaw by Bernardo Bellotto are on show.

From the castle head down ul Świętojańska to the 15th-century Gothic **St John's Cathedral** (ul Świętojańska 8; crypt 1zł; ⏰ 10am-1pm & 3-5.30pm Mon-Sat), the oldest church in Warsaw. The small crypt houses the tombs of past pastors. This road continues to the magnificent **Rynek Starego Miasta** (Old Town Square).

Alongside this square is the **Warsaw Historical Museum** (☎ 635 16 25; Rynek Starego Miasta 42; adult 5zł, free Sun; ⏰ 11am-5.30pm Tue & Thu, 10am-3.30pm Wed & Fri, 10.30am-4.30pm Sat & Sun). At noon it shows an English-language film (included in the admission fee) that unforgettably depicts the wartime destruction of the city.

One block west is the **Barbican**, part of a medieval wall that encircled Warsaw.

Royal Way (Szlak Królewski)

This 4km route connetcs the Royal Castle with Łazienki Park via ul Krakowskie

Przedmieście, ul Nowy Świat and Al Ujazdowskie. If you want to save time and energy, jump on and off bus No 180, which stops at most places along this route.

Just south of the Royal Castle is the 15th-century **St Anne's Church** (ul Krakowskie Przedmieście 68; ☽ daylight hr), one of the most ornate churches in the city. You can climb up the **tower** (admission 3.50zł; ☽ 10am-6pm Tue-Sun) for views of Plac Zamkowy. About 300m further south is **Radziwił Palace** (not open to the public), the official residence of the Polish president.

To the west of the neoclassical Hotel Europejski are the **Saxon Gardens**. At the entrance is the poignant **Tomb of the Unknown Soldier**, which occupies a fragment of an 18th-century royal palace destroyed in WWII. It's under permanent guard, and there's no access for the public. Be here at noon on Sunday to see the **Changing of the Guard**.

South of the tomb, the **Zachęta Contemporary Art Gallery** (☎ 827 58 54; pl MaLVachowskiego 3; adult 10zł, free Thu; ☽ noon-8pm Tue-Sun) features excellent exhibitions of contemporary painting, sculpture and photography. Some 200m further south is the **Ethnographic Museum** (☎ 827 76 41; ul Kredytowa 1; adult 8zł; ☽ 9am-4pm Tue, Thu & Fri, 11am-6pm Wed, 10am-5pm Sat & Sun). This large building displays Polish folk costumes from across the country and regional arts and crafts.

A CURIE FOR CANCER

Many Polish streets are named after the legendary scientist Marie Curie, but here she has been given the Polish–French name of Marie Skǧodowska-Curie. The modest **Marie Skǧodowska-Curie Museum** (☎ 631 80 92; ul Freta 16; adult 5zł; ☽ 10am-4pm Tue-Sat, 10am-2pm Sun) features displays in the house where she was born.

Marie Curie laid the foundations for radiography, nuclear physics and cancer therapy. She was born in Warsaw in 1867, and lived in Poland for 24 years before leaving to further her studies abroad.

In Paris, she and her French husband Pierre Curie discovered two new radioactive chemical elements: radium and polonium (named after her homeland). She won numerous awards and distinctions, including two Nobel Prizes. She died at the age of 67 from leukaemia caused by prolonged exposure to radiation.

Back along the Royal Way is the 17th-century **Church of the Holy Cross** (ul Krakowskie Przedmieście 3), which has erratic opening hours. Chopin's heart is preserved in the second pillar on the left-hand side of the main nave. It was brought from Paris, where he died of tuberculosis aged only 39. If you want to know more, head along ul Tamka towards the river to the small **Chopin Museum** (☎ 827 54 71; ul Okólnik 1; adult 8zł, free Wed; ☽ 10am-2pm Mon-Wed & Fri & Sat, noon-6pm Thu) It features, among other things, the great man's last piano and a collection of his letters and handwritten musical scores.

Return to the Royal Way and head south along ul Nowy Świat to the roundabout at the junction of Al Jerozolimskie. On the way to the river is the enormous **National Museum** (☎ 621 10 31; Al Jerozolimskie 3; museum admission 11zł, museum & temporary exhibitions admission 15zł, museum-only free Sat; ☽ 10am-4pm Tue, Wed & Fri-Sun, 10am-6pm Thu). It houses a varied and magnificent collection of Greek and Egyptian antiquities, Coptic frescoes, medieval woodcarvings and Polish paintings; look out for the surrealistic fantasies of Jacek Malczewski.

Jewish Warsaw

The vast suburbs northwest of the Palace of Culture & Science were once home to Warsaw's Jews. During WWII the Nazis established a Jewish ghetto in the area, but razed it after crushing the Warsaw Ghetto Uprising in April 1943. This tragic event is immortalised by the **Monument to the Warsaw Uprising** (pl Krasińskich), erected in 1989. In recent years, two powerful films, Roman Polanski's *The Pianist* and Steven Spielberg's *Schindler's List*, were both set in Warsaw's Jewish Ghetto.

The **Warsaw Ghetto Monument** (cnr ul Anielewicza & ul Zamenhofa) uses pictorial plaques to commemorate victims. The nearby **Pawiak Prison Museum** (☎ 831 13 17; ul Dzielna 24/26; admission free; ☽ 9am-5pm Wed, 9am-4pm Thu & Sat, 10am-5pm Fri, 10am-4pm Sun) occupies the former building used as a Gestapo prison during the Nazi occupation. Moving exhibits include letters and other personal items.

Arguably the most dramatic remnant of the Jewish legacy is the vast **Jewish Cemetery** (ul Okopowa 49/51; admission free; ☽ 10am-4pm Mon-Thu, 9am-1pm Fri, 9am-4pm Sun). Founded in 1806, it has more than 100,000 gravestones, the largest assemblage of its kind in Europe. Visitors must wear a head covering to enter the cemetery, which is accessible from the Old Town on tram Nos 22, 27 and 29.

The **Jewish Historical Institute** (☎ 827 92 21; ul Tłomackie 3/5; adult 10zł; 🕑 9am-4pm Mon-Wed & Fri, 11am-6pm Thu) has permanent exhibits about the Warsaw Ghetto, as well as local Jewish artworks. Tucked behind the **Jewish Theatre** is the neo-Romanesque **Nożyk Synagogue** (☎ 620 43 24; ul Twarda 6; admission 3.50zł; 🕑 10am-8pm Sun-Thu, 10am-4pm Fri), Warsaw's only synagogue to survive WWII, open for worship again.

FESTIVALS & EVENTS

Warsaw's major annual events include:
International Book Fair (May)
Warsaw Summer Jazz Days (late June/early July)
Mozart Festival (June/July)
'Art of the Street' International Festival (July)
'Warsaw Autumn' Festival of Contemporary Music (September)

SLEEPING

Warsaw is the most expensive city in Poland for accommodation, and rates at many central hotels are hugely inflated compared with other Polish cities. There's a small but increasing number of modern and reasonably priced hostels around town, but you'll have to head further out to find more affordable hotels. The tourist offices will help.

Hostels

Nathan's Villa Hostel (☎ 622 29 46; www.nathansvilla .com; ul Piękna 24/26; dm/s/d 45/120/140zł; 🖳) A very new, spotless hostel offering the same high standards as its sister establishment in Kraków. There's free laundry and no curfew.

Oki Doki (☎ 826 51 12; www.okidoki.pl; pl Dąbrowskiego 3; dm/s/d 40/120/160zł) Another new, stylish place in a conveniently central location. Rooms are a decent size, and the décor is fresh and cheerful.

Smolna Youth Hostel No 2 (☎ /fax 827 89 52; ul Smolna 30; dm/s/d 35/62/114zł) Very central and very popular; advance bookings are essential, especially in summer. Rooms are maintained to a high standard, but there's an 11pm curfew and a strict no-alcohol rule.

Karolkowa Youth Hostel No 6 (☎ 632 88 29; ssmnr6@ptsm.com.pl; ul Karolkowa 53a; dm/s/d/tr from 30/80/90/150zł; 🖳 🅿) This well established and friendly place has a range of rooms and is a popular choice. It's located in the suburb of Wola and is accessible by tram No 12, 22 or 24 from Warszawa Centralna train station.

Hotels

Hotel Praski (☎ 818 49 89; www.praski.pl; Al Solidarności 61; s 160-180zł, d 240-270zł; 🅿) On the other side of the river, but little more than 1km from the Old Town, Praski has been recently renovated and is one of the best two-star places in the capital.

Hotel Majawa (☎ 822 91 21; fax 823 37 48; ul Warszawskiej 1920r 15/17; d 109zł, double bungalows from 84zł) Southwest of the centre, Majawa offers good value. The bungalows at this camping ground have shared bathrooms but are private and clean, and the hotel rooms are quiet, spotless and bright.

Three near-identical one-star hotels under the same management on ul Mangalia offer good value: **Hotel Aramis** (☎ 842 09 74; www.felix .com.pl; aramis@felix.com.pl; ul Mangalia 3b; s/d 120/150zł; 🅿) is the largest and best set up; **Hotel Atos** (☎ 841 43 95; www.felix.com.pl; atos@felix.com.pl; ul Mangalia 1; s/d 120/150zł; 🅿) is smaller, but equally comfortable; and **Hotel Portos** (☎ 842 09 74; www .felix.com.pl; ul Mangalia 3a; s/d 120/150zł; 🅿) is clean and simple. To get there, catch bus No 118, 403, 503 or 513 along ul Sobieskiego.

Camping

Camping 123 (☎ 823 37 48; ul Warszawskiej 1920r 15/17; camping 10zł; 🚿 🅿) This site is set in extensive grounds near the Dworzec Zachodnia bus station. Hotel rooms are also available, and there's a tennis court on site.

EATING

Warsaw has undergone a gastronomic revolution in recent years, and everything from the cheapest snack-bars to international-standard gourmet restaurants now clamours for business all around town. A good choice can be found along ul Nowy Świat and around.

Restaurant Polska (☎ 826 38 77; ul Nowy Świat 21; mains from 25zł; 🕑 noon-midnight) is a popular spot serving up good-quality Polish cuisine, including game and the ubiquitous *pierogi* (dumplings).

Tam Tam (☎ 828 26 22; ul Foksal 18; soups from 5zł, mains from 19zł; 🕑 noon-midnight) A subterranean 'African-style' place with a varied menu, including pasta, goulash and kebabs, and a big list of teas and coffees. There's occasional live music in the evenings.

Melon (☎ 828 64 28; ul Nowy Świat 52; soups 8zł, mains 14-20zł; 🕑 noon-8pm Mon-Sat) Offers cheap and delicious vegetarian food.

POLAND

Zielony Świat (☎ 826 46 77; ul Nowy Świat 42; mains 10-25zł; ⏱ 10am-9.30pm) Tucked away in a courtyard a few doors down, Zielony is an enticing place offering healthy, meat-free food.

Restauracja Pod Samsonem (☎ 831 17 88; ul Freta 3/5; mains 15-50zł; ⏱ 10am-11pm) In the New Town, this is popular with locals looking for inexpensive and tasty meals with a Jewish flavour. It's always busy, and you might have to wait for a table.

Restauracja Barbakan (☎ 831 45 20; ul Freta 1; mains 14-40zł; ⏱ 10am-11pm) Has a huge menu of meat, fish and vegie dishes, and three-course set-menus starting at 22zł.

The most convenient places to shop for groceries are the MarcPol Supermarket, in front of the Palace of Culture and Science building, and the downstairs Albert Supermarket, close by under Galeria Centrum.

DRINKING

If it's caffeine you're after, **Green Coffee** (☎ 629 83 73; ul Marszałkowska 84/92; ⏱ 7am-11pm) and **Coffee Heaven** (☎ 828 20 57; Nowy Świat 46; ⏱ 7.30am-10pm Mon-Thu, 7.30am-10.30pm Fri, 8am-10pm Sat & Sun) are comfy places to enjoy a latte and a muffin. And there's certainly no shortage of places to try the odd beer or two.

Paparazzi (☎ 828 42 19; ul Mazowiecka 12; ⏱ noon-1am Mon-Fri, 4pm-1am Sat & Sun) One of Warsaw's trendiest venues; sip a bewildering array of (pricey) cocktails under blown-up photos of Hollywood stars.

Morgan's Irish Pub (☎ 826 81 38; ul Okólnik 1; ⏱ 9am-2am) Under the Chopin Museum, this is a popular expat haunt with a more down-to-earth atmosphere than Paparazzi. It offers live music from Thursday to Saturday (7zł).

Pub Harenda (☎ 826 29 00; ul Krakowskie Przedmieście 4/6; ⏱ 9am-3am) At the back of Hotel Harenda, it's often crowded. Jazz performances take place during the week, and there's dance music at weekends.

CLUBBING

Riviera Remont (☎ 660 91 11; ul Waryńskiego 12; ⏱ Jun-Sep) South of the city, this popular, cheap student club offers regular live music.

Kokon (☎ 831 95 39; ul Brzozowa 37; ⏱ 4pm-3am; admission 9zł) A fashionable four-level gay club featuring '70s and '80s hits, 'gay house' music and a weekly drag-show.

EMPiK Club (☎ 625 10 86; ul Nowy Świat 15/17; ⏱ 9am-2am Mon-Wed, 9am-5am Thu-Sat, 11am-midnight Sun; admission 7zł) In the basement of the book

and music store, this club becomes lively, loud and crowded. Bands play regularly.

ENTERTAINMENT

For more information about what to do, check out *The Visitor: Warsaw* and the comprehensive *Warsaw in Your Pocket*, available from tourist offices.

Teatr Ateneum (☎ 625 73 30; ul Jaracza 2) leans towards contemporary Polish-language productions. **Teatr Wielki** (☎ 692 02 00; www.teatrwielki .pl; Grand Theatre; Plac Teatralny 1; tickets 17-110zł) is the main venue for opera and ballet. **Filharmonia Narodowa** (☎ 826 72 81; ul Jasna 5) holds regular classical music concerts.

In **Łazienki Park**, piano recitals are held every Sunday from May to September, and chamber concerts are staged in summer at the **Old Orangery**.

GETTING THERE & AWAY
Air

Frederic Chopin Airport is more commonly called Okęcie airport, after the suburb, 10km southwest of the city centre, where it's based. Domestic and international flights on LOT can be booked at the **LOT head office** (☎ 95 72; www.lot.com; Al Jerozolimskie 65/79) in the Marriott Hotel complex or from any travel agency.

Bus

Warsaw has two major bus terminals for PKS buses. **Dworzec Zachodnia** (Al Jerozolimskie 144), southwest of the city, handles all buses heading south, north and west of the capital, including regular services to Częstochowa (31zł), Gdańsk (50zł), Kazimierz Dolny (22zł), Kraków (39zł), Olsztyn (32zł), Toruń (35zł), Wrocław (45zł) and Zakopane (53zł). The terminal adjoins Warszawa Zachodnia train station. Take the commuter train from Warszawa Śródmieście station.

Dworzec Stadion (Stadium Bus Station; ul Sokola 1), east of the city, adjoins Warszawa Stadion train station. It is also easily accessible by commuter train from Warszawa Śródmieście. Dworzec Stadion handles a few domestic buses to the east and southeast, such as Lublin (25zł), Białystok (23zł) and Zamość (37zł).

Polski Express (☎ 844 55 55) operates coaches from the airport, but passengers can get on or off. Tickets are available at the kiosk along Al Jana Pawła II, next to the Warszawa

Centralna train station. Polski Express buses travel to Białystok (34zł, four daily), Częstochowa (50zł, two daily), Gdynia via Gdańsk (72zł, two daily), Kraków (67zł, two daily), Lublin (34zł, eight daily), Szczecin (80zł, two daily), Toruń (48zł, 15 daily) and Wrocław (67zł, three daily).

International buses depart from/arrive at Dworzec Zachodnia or, occasionally, outside Warszawa Centralna. Tickets for international buses are available from the bus offices at Dworzec Zachodnia, from agencies at Warszawa Centralna or from major travel agencies.

Train

Warsaw has several train stations, but the one that most travellers will use almost exclusively is **Warszawa Centralna** (Warsaw Central; Al Jerozolimskie 54). It handles the overwhelming majority of domestic trains and all international services.

Warszawa Centralna is often not where domestic and international trains start or finish, so make sure you get on or off the train at this station in the few minutes allotted. And watch your belongings closely at all times, because pickpocketing and theft is an increasing problem.

Some domestic trains also stop at Warszawa Śródmieście station, 300m east of Warszawa Centralna, and at Warszawa Zachodnia, next to the Dworzec Zachodnia bus station.

GETTING AROUND
Public Transport

Warsaw's public transport is frequent and cheap; it operates from 5am to 11pm daily. The 2.40zł fare is a flat rate for a bus, tram, trolleybus or metro train travelling anywhere in the city, ie one 2.40zł fare is valid for one ride on one form of transport. Warsaw is the only place in Poland where ISIC cards get a public-transport discount (50%).

Tickets (valid on all forms of public transport) for 60/90 minutes cost 3.60/4.50zł and passes (for all public transport) are available for one-/three-days 7.20/12zł and one week/ one month 24/66zł. Buy tickets from kiosks (including those marked RUCH) before boarding, and validate them on board.

One useful bus is the 'sightseeing route' No 180, which links Powązki Cemetery with Wilanów Park.

Taxi

A quick and easy way to get around is by taxi – as long as you use official taxis and the drivers use their meters. Beware of 'Mafia' taxis parked in front of top-end hotels, at the airport, outside Warszawa Centralna and in the vicinity of most tourist sights.

MAŁOPOLSKA

Małopolska (literally 'little Poland') encompasses the whole of southeastern Poland, from the Lublin Uplands down to the Carpathian Mountains along the borders with Slovakia and Ukraine. The main draw is undoubtedly the former royal capital, Kraków, while the rugged beauty of the Tatra Mountains always attracts a steady stream of visitors.

KRAKÓW
☎ 012 / pop 770,000

Kraków is Poland's third-largest city and one of its oldest, dating from the 7th century. The city was founded by Prince Krak, who, according to legend, secured its prime location overlooking the Vistula River after outwitting the resident dragon.

Kraków flourished as the medieval capital of Poland and, miraculously, it was the only large Polish city to emerge from WWII unscathed. The Old Town with its Gothic churches, and the splendid Wawel Castle are increasingly popular with foreign tourists.

Information

Two free magazines, *Welcome to Cracow & Małopolska* and *The Visitor: Kraków & Zakopane*, are available at tourist offices. The *Kraków in Your Pocket* booklet is also very useful. Foreign-exchange offices and ATMs are common. Most foreign-exchange offices close on Sunday, and areas near Rynek Główny and the main train station offer poor exchange rates.

Bank Pekao (Rynek Główny 31) Travellers cheques and cash advances on MasterCard and Visa.

Cultural Information Centre (☎ 421 77 87; www .karnet.krakow2000.pl; ul Św Jana 2; ☼ 10am-6pm Mon-Fri, 11am-4pm Sat) Good for tickets and information on cultural events.

Cyber Café U Luisa (☎ 421 90 92; Rynek Główny 13; per hr 5zł; ☼ 11am-11pm)

Klub Garinet (☎ 423 22 33; ul Floriańska 18; per hr 5zł; ☼ 10am-midnight) Internet access.

POLAND

POLAND

KRAKÓW – OLD TOWN & WAWEL

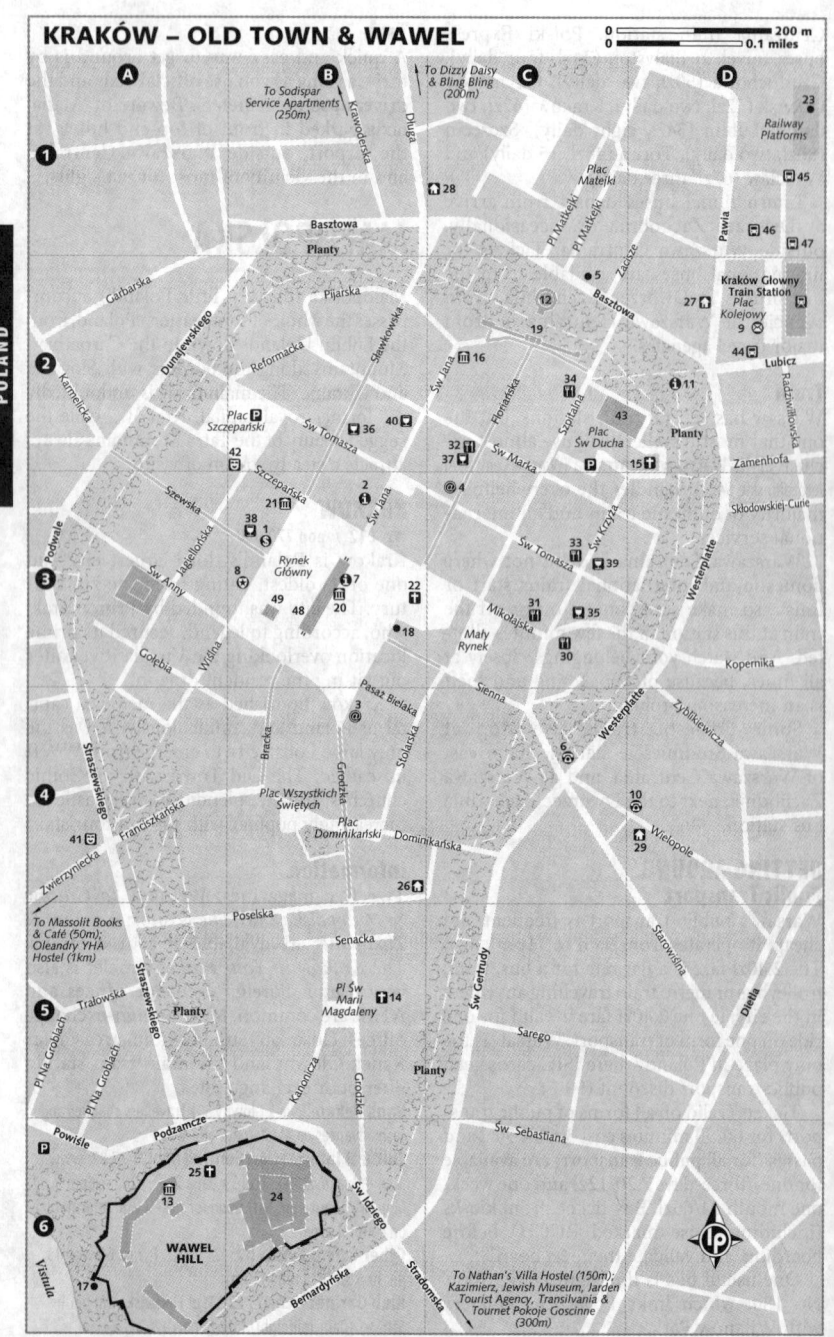

0 — 200 m
0 — 0.1 miles

To Dizzy Daisy & Bling Bling (200m)

To Sodispar Service Apartments (250m)

Railway Platforms

Plac Matejki

Kraków Glowny Train Station
Plac Kolejowy

Basztowa

Planty

Garbarska

Dunajewskiego

Pijarska

Reformacka

Karmelicka

Św Jana

Floriańska

Szpitalna

Plac Szczepański

Św Tomasza

Św Marka

Plac Św Ducha

Szczepańska

Św Jana

Szewska

Jagiellońska

Podwale

Św Anny

Rynek Głowny

Św Tomasza

Św Krzyża

Planty

Zamenhofa

Skłodowskiej-Curie

Westerplatte

Wiślna

Gołębia

Mały Rynek

Mikołajska

Kopernika

Pasaż Bielaka

Sienna

Westerplatte

Zyblikiewicza

Bracka

Grodzka

Stolarska

Plac Wszystkich Świętych

Plac Dominikański

Dominikańska

Wielopole

Starowiślna

Franciszkańska

Straszewskiego

Zwierzyniecka

To Massolit Books & Café (50m); Oleandry YHA Hostel (1km)

Poselska

Senacka

Pl Św Marii Magdaleny

Św Gertrudy

Sarego

Tralowska

Pl Na Grobłach

Pl Na Grobłach

Planty

Kanonicza

Grodzka

Planty

Dietla

Św Sebastiana

Powiśle

Podzamcze

Św Idziego

WAWEL HILL

Bernardyńska

Stradomska

Vistula

To Nathan's Villa Hostel (150m); Kazimierz, Jewish Museum, Jarden Tourist Agency, Transilvania & Tournet Pokoje Goscinne (300m)

Krakowska

Długa

Pl Matejki

Pl Matejki

Zacisze

Pawia

Lubicz

Radziwiłłowska

INFORMATION		Gallery of 19th-Century Polish		DRINKING	⬜ (p911)
Bank Pekao.................................1 B3		Painting...................................20 B3		Black Gallery...............................35 C3	
Cultural Information Centre.................2 B3		Historical Museum of Kraków...........21 B3		Climatic Students' Club..................36 B2	
Cyber Café U Luisa..........................3 B4		St Mary's Church..........................22 B3		Indigo Jazz Club............................37 C2	
Klub Garinet.................................4 C3		Underground Passage to Buses		Klub Pasja....................................38 B3	
LOT Office...................................5 C2		to Oświecim (Auschwitz &		Nic Nowego..................................39 C3	
Main Post Office.............................6 C4		Birkenau)................................23 D1		Pod Papugami...............................40 B2	
Małopolska Tourism Information		Wawel Castle................................24 B6			
Centre.....................................7 B3		Wawel Cathedral............................25 A6		ENTERTAINMENT	🎭 (p911)
Police Station................................8 B3				Filharmonia Krakówska...................41 A4	
Post & Telephone Office....................9 D2		SLEEPING	🏠 (p910)	Stary Teatr...................................42 B2	
Telephone Centre.........................10 D4		Hotel Wawel Tourist.......................26 B4		Teatr im Słowackiego.....................43 C2	
Tourist Office...............................11 D2		Jordan Tourist Information &			
		Accommodation Center...............27 D2		TRANSPORT	(p911)
SIGHTS & ACTIVITIES	(pp909–10)	Pokoje Gościnne Jordan...................28 C1		Bus B to Airport............................44 D2	
Barbican....................................12 C2		Wielopole Guest Rooms...................29 D4		Bus No 208 to Airport.....................45 D1	
Cathedral Museum........................13 A6				Bus Terminal................................46 D1	
Church of SS Peter & Paul................14 B5		EATING	🍴 (p911)	Private Buses to Zakopane................47 D1	
Church of the Holy Cross.................15 D2		Bombaj Tandoori...........................30 C3			
Czartoryski Museum.......................16 C2		Green Way...................................31 C3		OTHER	
Dragon's Cave..............................17 A6		Gruzińskie Chaczapuri.....................32 C2		Cloth Hall....................................48 B3	
EMPiK Megastore..........................18 B3		Ipanema.....................................33 C3		Souvenir Market...........................(see 48)	
Florian Gate................................19 C2		Smaki Świata................................34 C2		Town Hall Tower...........................49 B3	

Main post office (ul Westerplatte 20; ☻ 7.30am-8.30pm Mon-Fri, 8am-2pm Sat, 9am-11am Sun)

Małopolska Tourism Information Centre (☎ 421 77 06; www.mcit.pl; Rynek Główny 1/3; ☻ 9am-7pm Mon-Fri, 9am-4pm Sat & Sun Apr-Sep, 9am-5pm Mon-Fri, 9am-2pm Sat Oct-Mar)

Tourist office (☎ 432 01 10; ul Szpitalna 25; ☻ 8am-8pm Mon-Fri, 9am-5pm Sat & Sun)

Tourist office (☎ 432 08 40; ul Józefa 7, Kazimierz) Closed for renovation at the time of research. Provides information about local Jewish history.

Sights & Activities
OLD TOWN

The magnificent **Rynek Główny** is the largest medieval town square in Europe. Dominating the square is the 16th-century Renaissance **Cloth Hall** (Sukiennice). On the ground floor is a large souvenir market, and upstairs is the **Gallery of 19th-Century Polish Painting** (☎ 422 11 66; adult 5zł, free Sun; ☻ 10am-3pm Tue, Wed & Fri-Sun, 10am-5.30pm Thu), which includes several famous works by Jan Matejko.

The florid 14th-century **St Mary's Church** (Rynek Główny 4; adult 4zł; ☻ 11.30am-6pm Mon-Sat, 2-6pm Sun) fills the northeastern corner of the square. The huge main altarpiece by Wit Stwosz (Veit Stoss) of Nuremberg is the finest Gothic sculpture in Poland.

The **Historical Museum of Kraków** (☎ 422 99 22; Rynek Główny 35; adult 4zł; ☻ 9am-3.30pm Tue, Wed & Fri, 11am-6pm Thu) has paintings, documents and oddments relating to the city.

From St Mary's Church, you can walk northeast up ul Floriańska to the 14th-century **Florian Gate**, the only one remaining of the original eight gates. Nearby, the

Czartoryski Museum (☎ 422 55 66; ul Św Jana 19; adult 7zł; ☻ 10am-3.30pm Tue-Thu, Sat & Sun, 10am-6pm Fri) features an impressive collection of European art, including Leonardo da Vinci's masterpiece, *Lady with an Ermine*.

South of Rynek Główny, along ul Grodzka, is the early 17th-century Jesuit **Church of SS Peter & Paul** (ul Grodzka 64; ☻ dawn-dusk), the first baroque church in Poland.

WAWEL HILL

South of the Old Town is the dominant **Wawel Hill** (grounds free; ☻ 6am-8pm May-Sep, 6am-5pm Oct-Apr). It's crowned with a castle and cathedral, both iconic symbols of Poland.

There are several sections to the castle, each requiring a separate ticket, valid for a specific time. There's a limited daily quota of tickets for some parts, so arrive early if you want to see everything, or phone ahead to reserve a ticket.

Inside the magnificent **Wawel Castle** (☎ 422 16 97), the largest and most popular sections are the **State Rooms** (adult 12zł; free Mon; ☻ 9.30am-noon Mon, 9.30am-4pm Tue & Fri, 9.30am-3pm Wed-Thu & Sat, 10am-3pm Sun) and the **Royal Private Apartments** (adult 15zł; ☻ 9.30am-4pm Tue & Fri, 9.30am-3pm Wed-Thu & Sat, 10am-3pm Sun). Entry to the latter is allowed only on a guided tour (included in the admission fee). If you want a guide who speaks English, French or German, contact the **guides office** (☎ 429 33 36) within the castle compound.

For four centuries, the 14th-century **Wawel Cathedral** (royal tombs & bell tower 8zł; ☻ 9am-3.45pm Mon-Sat, 12.15-3.45pm Sun) was the coronation and burial place of Polish royalty. This is evidenced by the **Royal Tombs**, including that of Kazimierz Wielki. The golden-domed **Sigismund Chapel** (1539), on the southern side of the cathedral, is considered to be the finest Renaissance structure in Poland, and the **bell tower** houses the country's largest bell (11 tonnes).

KAZIMIERZ

Founded by King Kazimierz the Great in 1335, Kazimierz was an independent town with its own municipal charter and laws until the 1820s. In the 15th century, Jews were expelled from Kraków and forced to resettle in a small area in Kazimierz, walled off from the larger Christian quarter. The Jewish quarter later became home to Jews fleeing persecution from all corners of Europe.

By the outbreak of WWII 65,000 Jews lived in Kraków, mostly in Kazimierz. During the war, the Nazis relocated Jews to a walled ghetto in Podgórze, just south of the Vistula River. They were exterminated in the nearby **Płaszów Concentration Camp**, as portrayed in Steven Spielberg's film *Schindler's List*. If you want to learn more, **Jarden Tourist Agency** (☎ 429 13 74; www.jarden.pl; ul Szeroka 2; tours 35-65zł) runs various tours.

Many of the synagogues here miraculously survived the war, including the 15th-century **Old Synagogue**, which is the oldest Jewish religious building in Poland. It now houses the **Jewish Museum** (☎ 422 09 62; ul Szeroka 24; 6zł; ⏲ 10am-2pm Mon, 10am-5pm Tue-Sun), which has exhibitions on Jewish holidays and rituals.

Festivals & Events

Kraków boasts one of the richest cycles of annual events in Poland. Contact the Cultural Information Centre (p907) for programme details and bookings.

Organ Music Festival (March/April)
Jewish Culture Festival (June/July)
International Festival of Street Theatre (July)
Summer Jazz Festival (July)
Corpus Christi Pageant Seven days after Corpus Christi (a Thursday in May or June), Kraków hosts a colourful pageant headed by Lajkonik, a legendary figure disguised as a Tatar riding a hobbyhorse.

Sleeping

Kraków is unquestionably Poland's premier tourist destination. Although there's plenty of accommodation on offer, booking ahead in the busy summer months is recommended.

Nathan's Villa Hostel (☎ 422 35 45; www.nathans villa.com; ul Św Agnieszki 1; dm from 45zł; 🖳) The best budget place in town, it's conveniently located half-way between the Old Town and Kazimierz. Comfy rooms, sparkling bathrooms, free laundry and a friendly atmosphere make this place a big hit with backpackers.

Dizzy Daisy (☎ 292 01 71; www.hostel.pl; ul Pędzichów 9; dm/d/tr 35/100/135zł; 🖳) Another recently refurbished modern chain-hostel with great facilities, frequented by an international crowd of party people. Located north of town.

Bling Bling (☎ 634 05 32; www.blingbling.pl; ul Pędzichów 7; dm 45zł) A couple of doors down from Dizzy Daisy, and offering a similarly shining standard of accommodation.

Oleandry YHA Hostel (☎ 633 88 22; fax 633 89 20; ul Oleandry 4; dm 28zł) Around 1km west of the Old Town is this very big (and often very noisy) place. It has basic dorms in need of updating and is a last resort. Take tram No 15 from outside the main train station building and get off just past Hotel Cracovia.

Wielopole Guest Rooms (☎ 422 14 75; www .wielopole.pl; ul Wielopole 3; s/d from 150/225zł; ☒ Ⓟ) Has smart and simple modern rooms in a renovated block on the eastern edge of the Old Town, all with spotless bathrooms. Breakfast is extra. Great value.

Tournet Pokoje Gościnne (☎ 292 00 88; www .accommodation.krakow.pl; ul Miodowa 7; r from 100zł, tr from 220zł) A neat pension in Kazimierz, offering simple but comfortable and quiet rooms.

Hotel Wawel-Tourist (☎ 424 13 00; ul Poselska 22; s 190-280zł, d 270-360zł; ☒) Back in town, this hotel is ideally located just off busy ul Grodzka. It's reasonably good value, and the pricier, newly renovated rooms are large and comfortable.

PRIVATE ROOMS

The tourist office in Kazimierz can also help to arrange private rooms in that area.

Sodispar Service Apartments (☎ 0602 247 438; www.sodispar.pl; ul Lubelska 12; apt 100-480zł) Several comfortable, modern apartments, north of the Old Town are available, which sleep up to four people. There's a two-night minimum stay with cheaper rates for longer stays. Rooms all have free Internet connections, and computers can be rented for a small charge.

Jordan Tourist Information & Accommodation Centre (☎ 429 17 68; www.jordan.krakow.pl; ul Pawia 8; ⏲ 8am-6pm Mon-Fri, 9am-2pm Sat & Sun; s/d around 90/110zł) offers decent rooms around town.

Eating

By Polish standards, Kraków is a foodies paradise, with a huge variety of international cuisines available. The Old Town is packed with gastronomic venues, and there are lots of cheap takeaway places on ul Grodzka.

Bombaj Tandoori (☎ 422 37 97; ul Mikołajska 11; mains 13-30zł; ☺ noon-11pm) is the best curry house in Kraków, and it has a lengthy menu of Indian standards. The 13zł lunch specials are excellent value, and diners receive a 20% discount off their next evening meal.

Ipanema (☎ 422 53 23; ul Św Tomasza 28; mains from 15zł; ☺ noon-11pm), a smart Brazilian restaurant, features steaks, grills and a range of interesting 'Afro-Brazilian' dishes on the menu.

Smaki Świata (☎ 428 27 70; ul Szpitalna 38; mains 10.50-16.80zł; ☺ 9am-9pm) offers hearty vegetarian dishes, including moussaka, pasta and samosas, plus snacks and a big list of teas.

Gruzińskie Chaczapuri (☎ 604 508 380; cnr ul Floriańska & ul Św Marka; mains 8-20zł; ☺ 9am-midnight) is a cheap and cheerful place that serves up tasty Georgian dishes. Cheese pie is the house speciality. Grills, salads and steaks fill out the menu, and the wine's not bad, either.

Green Way (☎ 431 10 27; ul Mikołajska 14; mains 8-11zł; ☺ 10am-10pm Mon-Sat, 11am-9pm Sun) offers good-value vegetarian fare, such as enchiladas and salads.

Drinking & Clubbing

There are more than 100 pubs and bars in the Old Town alone. Some of the best, although priciest, places for a relaxing drink are to be found around Rynek Główny.

Pod Papugami (☎ 422 82 99; ul Św Jana 18; ☺ 1pm-2am) is a vaguely 'Irish' cellar pub decorated with old motorcycles and other assorted junk.

Transilvania (☎ 431 14 09; ul Szeroka 9; ☺ 10am-2am) is a convivial place in Kazimierz, with a rather more original vampire theme.

Nic Nowego (☎ 421 61 88; ul Św Krzyża 15; ☺ 7am-3am Mon-Fri, 10am-3am Sat & Sun) is a very popular, authentic Irish pub, which also serves food.

For foot-tapping jazz head to the **Indigo Jazz Club** (☎ 429 17 43; ul Floriańska 26), which often has top international acts performing.

Climatic Students' Club (☎ 421 17 71; ul Sławkowska 13-15; ☺ 5pm-late Tue-Sun) is a vast cellar club with techno and dance music that attracts a young crowd at weekends.

Black Gallery (☎ no phone; ul Mikołajska 24; ☺ noon-4am Mon-Sat, 2pm-2am Sun) is a sweaty, crowded underground pub-cum-nightclub

that gets going only after midnight. It also has a more civilised courtyard.

Klub Pasja (☎ 423 04 83; ul Szewska 5) occupies vast brick cellars. It's trendy and popular with foreigners.

Entertainment

The comprehensive monthly Polish–English booklet, *Karnet* (3zł), published by the Cultural Information Centre, lists almost every event in the city.

The best-known venue, **Stary Teatr** (☎ 422 85 66; ul Jagiellońska 5), consistently offers quality productions. **Teatr im Słowackiego** (☎ 422 45 75; Plac Św Ducha 1), built in 1893, focuses on Polish classics and large-scale productions. **Filharmonia Krakówska** (☎ 422 94 77; ul Zwierzyniecka 1) boasts one of the best orchestras in the country. Concerts are usually held on Friday and Saturday.

Getting There & Away

The main **bus terminal** (Plac Kolejowy) is conveniently opposite the main train station building and only minutes on foot from the Old Town. Polski Express buses to Warsaw depart from a spot opposite the bus terminal.

Kraków Główny train station, on the northeastern outskirts of the Old Town, handles all international trains and almost all domestic rail services. From Kraków, Intercity services speed to Warsaw (2¾ hours, five daily), as well as around four express and five fast trains. From Kraków there are also trains to Wrocław (three daily), Poznań (two daily), Lublin (two daily) and Gdynia via Gdańsk (six daily).

OŚWIĘCIM (AUSCHWITZ) & BIRKENAU

☎ 033 / pop 48,000

The Polish name Oświęcim (osh-FYEN-cheem) might be unknown to outsiders, but the German name, Auschwitz, is not. About 60km west of Kraków, this was the scene of the most extensive experiment in genocide in human history. The area makes for a moving day trip from Kraków.

The Auschwitz camp was established in April 1940 on the outskirts of Oświęcim. Originally intended to hold Polish political prisoners, the camp eventually developed into the largest centre for the murder of European Jews. Towards this end, two additional camps were established: the much larger Birkenau (Brzezinka) and Monowitz

POLAND

(Monowice). These death factories killed from 1.5 to two million people of 27 nationalities – about 90% of whom were Jews.

Auschwitz was only partially destroyed by the fleeing Nazis, so some original buildings remain. A dozen of the 30 surviving prison blocks house the **State Museum Auschwitz-Birkenau** (☎ 844 81 00; admission free; ❧ 8am-7pm Jun-Aug, 8am-6pm May & Sep, 8am-5pm Apr & Oct, 8am-4pm March & Nov–mid-Dec, 8am-3pm mid-Dec–Mar).

English-language tours (25zł per person, 3½ hours) of Auschwitz and Birkenau leave daily at 11.30am. Another starts at 1pm if there's enough demand.

About every half hour, the cinema in the **visitors' centre** at the entrance to the camp shows a 15-minute documentary film (2zł) about the liberation of the camp by Soviet troops on 27 January 1945.

Some basic explanations in Polish, English and Hebrew are provided onsite, but you'll understand more if you buy the *Auschwitz Birkenau Guide Book* (translated into about 15 languages) from the Visitors' Centre.

At **Birkenau** (admission free; ❧ same as Auschwitz) the extermination of even greater numbers of Jews took place. This vast (175 hectares), efficient camp had more than 300 prison barracks and four huge gas chambers complete with crematoria. Although much of the camp was destroyed by retreating Nazis, the size of the place, fenced off with barbed wire stretching almost as far as the eye can see, provides some idea of the scale of this heinous crime.

Getting There & Away

From Kraków, most convenient are the approximately hourly buses to Oświęcim (10zł, 90 minutes, daily) that depart from the small bus stop on ul Bosacka. The stop is at the end of the underpass below the railway platforms. Get off at the final stop (outside the PKS bus maintenance building), only 200m from the entrance to Auschwitz.

Every hour on the hour from 11am to 4pm (inclusive) between 15 April and 31 October free buses shuttle passengers between the visitors' centres at Auschwitz and Birkenau. Otherwise, follow the signs for an easy walk (3km) between both places.

CZĘSTOCHOWA

☎ 034 / pop 260,000

Częstochowa (chen-sto-HO-vah), 114km northwest of Kraków, is the spiritual heart of Poland. This likeable town owes its fame to the miraculous Black Madonna kept in the Jasna Góra monastery, founded in 1382 by the Paulites of Hungary. In 1430 the icon was stolen by the Hussites, who slashed the Madonna's face. The wounds began to bleed, so the thieves abandoned the icon. The monks who found the panel wanted to clean it, and a spring miraculously bubbled from the ground. The spring exists to this day, and St Barbara's Church was founded on the site.

From the train station and adjacent bus terminal, turn north up Al Wolności to the main street, Al Najświętszej Marii Panny (Al NMP). At the western end of this broad avenue is the monastery, and at the eastern end is Plac Daszyńskiego. Between both is the **tourist office** (☎ 368 22 60; Al NMP 65; ❧ 9am-5pm Mon-Fri, 9am-2pm Sat) and several banks, foreign-exchange offices and travel agencies.

The **Paulite Monastery on Jasna Góra** (admission free; ❧ dawn-dusk) retains the appearance of a hill-top fortress. The 106m-high **tower** (❧ 8am-4pm Apr-Nov) is the tallest historic church tower in Poland. The baroque church is beautifully decorated. The image of the **Black Madonna** on the high altar of the adjacent chapel is hard to see, so a copy is on display in the **Knights' Hall** (Sala Rycerska) in the monastery. The major **Marian feasts** at Jasna Góra are 3 May, 16 July, 15 August, 26 August, 8 September, 12 September and 8 December. On these days the monastery is thronged with pilgrims.

The **youth hostel** (☎ 324 31 21; ul Jasnogórska 84/90; dm 20zł; ❧ Jul-Aug), two blocks north of the tourist office, has modest facilities. **Dom Pielgrzyma** (☎ 324 70 11; ul Wyszyńskiego 1/31; dm/s/d from 20/60/90zł) is a huge place behind the monastery. Offering quiet and comfortable rooms, it's remarkably good value. Plenty of **eateries** can be found near Dom Pielgrzyma.

From the **bus terminal** (Al Wolności 45) there are services to Kraków (three daily), Wrocław (three daily), Zakopane (one daily) and Warsaw (three daily). From the **train station** (Al Wolności 21) services run to Warsaw (11 daily), Gdynia via Gdańsk (four to five daily), and several go to Kraków and Wrocław.

ZAKOPANE

☎ 018 / pop 30,000

Nestled at the foot of the Tatra Mountains, Zakopane is the most famous resort in Poland and the major winter sports centre. A base for skiing and hiking, Zakopane itself has an enjoyable, laid-back atmosphere, even if it is overpriced.

The **tourist office** (☎ 201 22 11; ul Kościuszki 17; ⏰ 8am-8pm) is helpful. Dozens of foreign-exchange offices and banks line the main streets. The combined **main post office and telephone centre** (ul Krupówki) is centrally located. **GraNet Internet Café** (ul Krupówki 2; per hr 6zł) is a convenient place to surf the Internet.

Centrum Przewodnictwa Tatrzańskiego (Tatra Guide Centre; ☎ 206 37 99; ul Chałubińskiego 42/44; ⏰ 9am-3pm) is able to arrange English- and German-speaking mountain guides.

Mt Gubałówka (1120m) has great views over the Tatras and is a favourite destination for tourists who just want to relax. The **funicular railway** (8/14zł one way/return trip; ski pass half-/full-day 50/70zł) covers the 1388m-long route in less than five minutes. It climbs 300m from the funicular station just north of ul Krupówki. It operates from 9am to 9pm from 1 May to 30 September, but at other times runs only at weekends.

Sleeping

As with all seasonal resorts, accommodation prices fluctuate between the low season (December to February) and the high season (and July to August). Book in advance during peak times. Rates for the high seasons are quoted here.

Few travellers stay in hotels. Most travel agencies in Zakopane can arrange private rooms, but in the high season there's usually a minimum stay of three nights; expect a double room (singles are rarely offered) to cost about 70zł in the town centre. Locals offering private rooms might also approach you at the stations; or you could just look for signs posted outside private homes. Another place to look is the tourist office, which knows of great bargains for guesthouses.

Youth Hostel Szarotka (☎ 201 36 18; ul Nowotarska 45; dm/d 35/50zł) Along a noisy road about a 10-minute walk from the town centre, this friendly and homely place becomes packed (and untidy) in the high season; rates are negotiable at other times.

Api II (☎ 206 29 31; ul Kamieniec 13; d/tr 70/105zł; ✗) A central place that offers good value for money and has big, well-maintained rooms.

Eating

The main street, ul Krupówki, is lined with all sorts of eateries.

Czarny Staw (☎ 201 38 56; ul Krupówki 2; mains 10-25zł; ⏰ 10am-1am) Offers a tasty range of Polish dishes including fish dishes, and there's live music nightly.

Restaurant Sabała (☎ 201 50 92; ul Krupówki 11; mains 15-25zł; ⏰ 11am-midnight) A lively, friendly place serving traditional local specialities, again with live music.

Getting There & Away

From the **bus terminal** (ul Chramcówki), fast PKS buses run to Kraków (9zł, 2½ hours, every 20 to 50 minutes). Two private companies – Trans Frej and Szwagropol – operate less frequent services (10zł). The private buses leave from a stop on ul Kościuszki in Zakopane, and opposite the bus terminal in Kraków.

The **train station** (ul Chramcówki) has services to Kraków (45zł, 3½ hours, every two hours) and Warsaw (five daily). Between one and three daily trains travel to Częstochowa, Gdynia via Gdańsk, Lublin and Poznań.

TATRA MOUNTAINS
☎ 018

The Tatras, 100km south of Kraków, are the highest range of the Carpathian Mountains. Approximately 60km long and 15km wide, this mountain range stretches across the Polish–Slovak border. A quarter is in Poland and is now mostly part of the Tatra National Park (about 212 sq km).

Almost every Polish tourist has made the **Mt Kasprowy Wierch cable-car trip** (29zł return trip; ⏰ 7.30am-8pm in summer, 7.30am-3.30pm in winter) from Kuźnice (3km south of central Zakopane) to the summit of Mt Kasprowy Wierch (1985m). At the end of the trip, you can get off and stand with one foot in Poland and the other in Slovakia. Another incredibly popular park destination is the emerald-green **Lake Morskie Oko** (Eye of the Sea), among the loveliest in the Tatras.

If you're doing any hiking in the Tatras, get a copy of the *Tatrzański Park Narodowy* map (1:25,000), which shows all hiking trails in the area.

Zakopane boasts four major ski areas (and several smaller ones) with more than 50 ski lifts. **Mt Kasprowy Wierch** and **Mt Gubałówka** offer the best conditions and most challenging slopes in the area. The ski season extends until early May.

Tourists are not allowed to take their own cars into the park; you must walk in, take the cable car or use an official vehicle owned by the park or a hotel/hostel.

Camping isn't allowed, but eight PTTK (Polish Tourists Association) mountain refuges/hostels provide simple accommodation. Check availability at the **Dom Turysty PTTK** (☎ 206 32 81; ul Zaruskiego 5) in Zakopane.

LUBLIN

☎ 081 / pop 360,000

For much of its history, Lublin was a strategically important border town – the Lublin Union, which united Poland and Lithuania, was signed here in 1569. The town also experienced centuries of repeated invasions by bellicose neighbours. Today, Lublin's small but well-preserved Old Town, with its elegant mix of Gothic, Renaissance and baroque architecture, is a pleasant place to wander.

Information

Bank Pekao (ul Królewska 1B ul Kra kowskie Przedmieście 64)

LOIT tourist office (☎ 532 44 12; www.lublin.pl; ul Jezuicka 1/3; 10am-6pm Mon-Sat May-Sep, 9am-5pm Mon-Sat Oct-Apr) Helpful English-speaking staff, and lots of free brochures and maps.

Main post office (ul Krakowskie Przedmieście 50)

www.café (☎ 442 35 80; Rynek 9, 3rd fl; 10am-10pm) Internet café.

Sights

The compact historic quarter is centred on the **Rynek**, the irregularly shaped main square surrounding the neoclassical **old town hall** (1781). The **Historical Museum of Lublin** (☎ 532 60 01; Plac Łokietka 3; adult 3zł; 9am-4pm Wed-Sat, 9am-5pm Sun), with displays of documents and photos, is inside the 14th-century **Kraków Gate**, the only significant remnant of the medieval fortifications.

For an expansive **view** of the Old Town, climb to the top of the **Trinitarian Tower** (1819), which houses the **Religious Art Museum** (☎ 743 73 92; Plac Kathedralny; adult 7zł; 10am-5pm Apr-Oct). Next to the tower is the 16th-century **cathedral** (Plac Kathedralny; dawn-dusk), which has impressive baroque frescoes.

The imposing **castle**, which started life in the 14th century, stands on a hill northeast of the Old Town. What remains was actually rebuilt as a prison in the 1820s and remained as such until 1944. During the Nazi occupation, more than 100,000 people passed through this prison before being deported to the death

camps. Most of the edifice is now occupied by the **Lublin Museum** (☎ 532 50 01; www.zamek -lublin.pl; ul Zamkowa 9; adult 10zł, free Sat; 9am-4pm Wed-Sat, 9am-5pm Sun). On show are paintings, silverware, porcelain and weaponry, mostly labelled only in Polish. Check out the 'devil's paw-print' on the foyer's 17th-century table.

At the eastern end of the castle – but accessible only through the museum – is the exquisite 14th-century **Chapel of the Holy Trinity** (joint ticket with museum or 6zł if separate; 9am-3.45pm Mon-Sat, 9am-4.45pm Sun). Its interior is entirely covered with polychrome Russo-Byzantine frescoes painted in 1418 – possibly the finest medieval wall paintings in Poland.

MAJDANEK

About 4km southeast of the Old Town is the **State Museum of Majdanek** (☎ 744 19 55; free; 8am-6pm May-Sep, 8am-3pm Oct-Apr). It commemorates one of the largest death camps in Europe, where 235,000 people, including more than 100,000 Jews, were massacred during WWII. Barracks, guard towers and barbed wire fences remain as they were during the war; even more chilling are the crematorium and gas chambers.

Trolleybus No 156 from near the Bank Pekao on ul Królewska goes to the entrance of Majdanek.

Sleeping

PTSM Youth Hostel (☎ /fax 533 06 28; ul Długosza 6; dm/t 24/28zł) Modest but well run, it's 50m up a lane off ul Długosza and in the heart of the university district. Bedding is 6zł extra.

Wojewódzki Ośrodek Metodyczny (☎ 532 92 41; www.wodn.lublin.pl; ul Dominikańska 5; b per person 45zł) It's good value and often busy, so book ahead. Rooms have between two and five beds. Look for the sign 'Wojewódzki Ośrodek Doskonalenia Nauczycieli' outside.

Dom Studenta Zaocznego (☎ 525 10 81; ul Sowińskiego 17; s/d 70/80zł) Zaocznego is a little out of the way, but it offers clean, simple accommodation at a good price. Bathrooms are communal.

Hotel Piast (☎ 532 16 46; ul Pocztowa 2; s/d/tr 46/62/81zł) Opposite the train station, Piast is ideal for a late-night arrival or early morning departure. However, it's a long way from anywhere else and in a rough part of town.

Lubelski Dom Nauczyciela (☎ 533 82 85, fax 533 03 66; ul Akademicka 4; s/d/tr 90/94/189zł) This is a teachers' hostel. Most of the rooms are tiny but clean and perfectly acceptable, and the renovated rooms have a bathroom.

Camping Marina (☎ 744 10 70; ul Krężnicka 6; camping 8zł, cabins from 55zł; ☺ May-Sep) Lublin's only camping ground is in a peaceful spot around 8km south of the Old Town. Catch bus No 17, 20 or 21 from the train station to Stadion Sygnał, then bus No 25 the rest of the way.

Eating & Drinking

Pizzeria Acerna (☎ 532 45 31, Rynek 2; pizzas from 11zł; ☺ Mon-Thu & Sun 11am-10pm, Fri & Sat 11am-midnight) A popular subterranean place on the square that serves up cheap pizzas and pasta.

Restauracja Pub Alternatywa (☎ 532 48 46; ul Chopina 11; mains 10-20zł; ☺ 11am-midnight Mon-Sat, 2pm-midnight Sun) A busy cellar pub offering regular live music and the ubiquitous pizzas.

Chawerim Klezmer (☎ 534 73 05; ul Złota 2; mains 12-19zł; ☺ 1-11pm Mon-Thu, 1pm-1am Fri & Sat, 1-10pm Sun) This cellar restaurant is off the main square, and has a mix of Polish and Jewish dishes on the menu.

Espresso Bar (☎ 534 49 43; Rynek 9; ☺ noon-midnight) A cosy spot for a cappuccino or something stronger, and it also serves snacks. Amazingly, it's not in a cellar.

There's a supermarket close to the bus terminal.

Getting There & Away

From the **bus terminal** (Al Tysiąclecia), opposite the castle, services head to Białystok (18.50zł, daily), Kraków (25zł, daily) and Zamość (10zł, 12 daily). From the same terminal, Polski Express goes to Warsaw (34zł, eight daily).

Private minibuses to a variety of destinations, including Warsaw (25zł), leave from bus stops north and west of the bus terminal.

Lublin Główny train station (Plac Dworcowy) is 1.2km south of the Old Town and accessible by trolleybus No 160. Services go to Warsaw (32zł, 2½ hours, at least six daily) and fast trains travel to Kraków (55zł, four hours, two daily).

ZAMOŚĆ

☎ 084 / pop 65,000

Zamość (ZAH-moshch) was founded in 1580 by Jan Zamoyski, chancellor and commander-in-chief of Renaissance-era Poland, who intended to create an impregnable barrier against Cossack and Tartar raids. The Old Town is tiny, but the stunningly colourful main square is one of Poland's finest.

Information

Bank Pekao (ul Grodzka 2) ATM, cashes travellers cheques, advances on Visa and MasterCard.

K@fejka Internetowa (☎ 639 29 32; Rynek Wielki10; per hr 3zł)

Library (cnr ul Zamenhofa & ul Bazyliańska; ☺ 8.30am-6.30pm Mon-Fri, to 3pm Sat; per hr 3zł) Internet access.

Main post office (ul Kościuszki) Near the cathedral.

Tourist office (☎ 639 22 93; Town Hall, Rynek Wielki 13; ☺ 8am-6pm Mon-Fri, 10am-4pm Sat, 10am-3pm Sun May-Sep, 8am-4pm Mon-Fri Oct-Apr)

Sights

Rynek Wielki is an impressive Italianate Renaissance square (exactly 100m by 100m) dominated by the lofty pink **town hall** and surrounded by brightly painted, arcaded burghers' houses. The **Museum of Zamość** (☎ 638 64 94; Rynek Wielki 24; adult 4zł; ☺ 9am-4pm Tue-Sun) has intriguing displays on town history, plus folk costumes and woodcarvings.

Southwest of the square is the mighty 16th-century **cathedral** (ul Kolegiacka; ☺ dawn-dusk, except during services), which holds the tomb of Zamoyski.

Before WWII, Jews accounted for 45% of the town's population (of 12,000), and most lived in the area north and east of the palace. The most significant Jewish architectural relic is the Renaissance **synagogue** (cnr ul Zamenhofa & ul Bazyliańska), built in the early 17th century. It's now the town library.

On the eastern edge of the Old Town is the antiquated **Hala Targowa** (Market Hall; ul Lukasinskiego 2; ☺ 8am-5pm Mon-Fri, 9am-3pm Sat & Sun), which houses a foreign-exchange office as well as numerous little shops. Behind it is the best surviving **bastion** from the original wall that encircled Zamość.

Sleeping & Eating

Youth Hostel (☎ 627 91 25; ul Zamoyskiego 4; dm 12-16zł; ☺ Jul & Aug) The hostel is in a school about 1.5km east of the Old Town and not far from the bus terminal. It's pretty basic but functional, and very cheap.

Dom Turysty (☎ 639 26 39; ul Zamenhofa 11; s & d 45zł) Simple rooms with shared facilities are on offer, but it's in a very central location and the price is hard to beat.

Hotel Zamojski (☎ 639 25 16; zamojski@orbis.pl; ul Kollataja 2/4/6; s/d 192/272zł, Sat & Sun 154/218zł; ✕ P)

POLAND

The best place in town, it's in a row of artfully renovated 17th-century burghers' houses leading off the Square. Worth the extra cash if you're looking for a bit of comfort.

Hotel Jubilat (☎ 638 64 01; ul Kardynała Wyszyńskiego 52; s/d 126/166zł, Sat & Sun 104/138zł; **P**) A reasonable, if slightly drab place right beside the bus station. Handy for late arrivals or early departures, but a long way from anywhere else.

Bar Asia (☎ 639 23 04; ul Staszica 10; mains from 8zł; ☼ 8am-5pm Mon-Fri, 8am-3.30pm Sat) Cheap and tasty Polish food is available at this popular cafeteria-style place.

Restauracja Muzealna (☎ 638 64 94; Ul Ormianska 30; mains 10-25zł; ☼ 11am-11pm) Set in an atmospheric cellar decorated with murals, this place serves a better class of Polish cuisine.

There are also a few cheap fast-food joints in the old Hala Targowa.

Getting There & Away

Buses are more convenient and quicker than trains. The **bus terminal** (ul Hrubieszowska) is 2km east of the Old Town and linked by frequent city buses. Fast buses go to Kraków (48zł, four hours, daily), Warsaw (52zł, five hours, four or five daily) and Lublin (10zł, two hours, 12 daily).

Far quicker and cheaper are the minibuses that travel between Lublin and Zamość (9zł, half hourly). They leave from the minibus stand across the road from the bus terminal in Zamość. Several minibus operators also run to Warsaw, Kraków and many other destinations from here. Check the giant timetable for details.

From the **train station**, about 1km southwest of the Old Town, several slow trains head to Lublin (4 to 5 hours, daily) and to Warsaw (six hours, three daily).

SILESIA

Silesia, in southwestern Poland, includes Upper Silesia, the industrial heart of the country; Lower Silesia, a fertile farming region with a cultural and economic centre in Wrocław; and the Sudeten Mountains, which is a forested range running for more than 250km along the Czech border. Silesia has spent much of its history under Austrian and Prussian rule, and the region retains a strong Germanic influence.

WROCŁAW
☎ 071 / pop 675,000

Wrocław (VROTS-wahf) was originally founded on the island of Ostrów Tumski on the Odra River. In the year 1000 Wrocław was chosen as one of the Piast dynasty's three bishoprics, and it subsequently developed into a prosperous trading and cultural centre. The town passed to Bohemia in 1336 and, under the name of Breslau, was absorbed by Prussia in the 18th century.

Wrocław returned to Poland in a sorry state. During the final phase of WWII, 70% of the city was destroyed. However, the old market square and many churches and other fine buildings have been beautifully restored, and today Wrocław is one of Poland's most attractive cities.

Information

Bank Pekao (ul Oławska 2)
Cyber & Tea Tavern (ul Kuźnicza 29) Internet café.
Main post office (Rynek 28) Overlooks the main square.
Tourist office (☎ 344 11 11; www.wroclaw.pl; Rynek 14; ☼ 10am-7pm May-Sep, 10am-5pm Oct-Apr)

Sights

The **Rynek** is Poland's second-largest old market square (after Kraków) and one of the largest in Europe at 3.7 hectares. The ornate **town hall** (built 1327–1504) on the southern side is certainly one of the most beautiful in Poland. Inside, the **Historical Museum** (☎ 347 16 90; adult 10zł; ☼ 10am-5pm Wed & Fri, 11am-5pm Thu & Sat, 10am-6pm Sun) has a few stately rooms on show, although it's disappointingly sparse given the price.

In the northwestern corner of the Rynek are two small houses called **Jaś i Małgosia** (ul Św Mikołaja; not open to the public) linked by a baroque gate. Just behind them is the monumental 14th-century **St Elizabeth's Church** (ul Elżbiety 1; ☼ 9am-4pm Mon-Sat, 1-4pm Sun) with its 83m-high tower, which you can climb for city views.

East of the Rynek, the **Panorama of Racławicka** (☎ 344 22 44; ul Purkyniego 11; adult 20zł; ☼ 9am-4pm Tue-Sun) is a massive 360-degree painting of the 1794 Battle of Racławice, in which the Polish peasant army, led by Tadeusz Kościuszko, defeated Russian forces intent on partitioning Poland. Created by Jan Styka and Wojciech Kossak for the centenary of the battle in 1894, the painting is an overwhelming 114m long and 15m high. Obligatory tours (with English, French or German audio) run every 30 minutes (9.30am to 3.30pm). The ticket also allows free entry to the National Museum on the same day.

The **National Museum** (☎ 343 88 39; Plac Powstańców Warszawy 5; adult 15zł, free Sat; ☺ 10am-4pm Wed-Sat, 10am-6pm Sun) contains exhibits of Silesian medieval art and one of the country's finest collections of modern Polish painting. Entry is free with a ticket to the Panorama.

North of the river is Ostrów Tumski, a quiet, picturesque area full of churches, where you'll find the Gothic **Cathedral** (pl Katedralny; ☺ 10am-6pm except during services). Uniquely, there's a lift to the top of the **tower** (admission 4zł; ☺ 10am-5.30pm Mon-Sat, 2-4pm Sun) for superb views. Nearby are the charming **Botanical Gardens** (☎ 322 51 40; ul Sienkiewicza 23; adult 5zł; ☺ 8am-6pm) where you can chill out among the chestnut trees and tulips.

Festivals & Events

Wrocław's major annual events include:

Musica Polonica Nova Festival (February)

Jazz on the Odra International Festival (March)

Wrocław Marathon (April) Poland's biggest running event.

Castle Party (www.castleparty.com) is a two- to three-day celebration of 'dark independent music', held in July or August at the moody 16th-century Bolkow Castle, around 60km west of Wrocław. It attracts bands, and crowds, from across Europe. Expect lots of black clothes and piercings. Bolkow can be reached by bus from Wrocław. See p41 for more details.

Wratislavia Cantans Oratorio and Cantata Festival (September)

Sleeping

Hotel Tumski Youth Hostel (☎ 322 60 99; www.hotel-tumski.com.pl; ul Słodowy 10; dm 30zł) In a quiet, pleasant area, and part of the hotel of the same name, it's good value, but some rooms are cramped. There's a 10pm curfew.

MDK Youth Hostel (☎ 343 88 56; ul Kołątaja 20; dm/d from 16/30zł) A basic place not far from the train station, in a grand (but poorly sign-posted) mustard-coloured building. It's almost always full, so book ahead.

Bursa Nauczycielska (☎ 344 37 81; ul Kotlarska 42; s/d/q 50/90/104zł) Another basic but spotless hostel with shared bathrooms, ideally located a block northeast of the Rynek.

Hotel Monopol (☎ 343 70 41; monopol@orbis.pl; ul Modrzejewskiej 2; s 115-150zł, d 170-240zł; ☒) Mr Hitler was once a frequent visitor, and although it might not be up to international tyrant standards these days, it's clean and does offer good value. Discounted rates are available at weekends. It's beside the Opera House.

Hotel Europejski (☎ 343 10 71; europejski@odra tourist.pl; ul Piłsudskiego 88; s 99-129 zł, d 188-198zł, incl breakfast & lunch; ☒) This hotel is very handy for the train station. The pricier 'renovated' rooms are large and comfortable, although still a tad dated and very brown. Weekend discounts are available.

Camping Nr 267 Ślęza (☎ 343 44 42; ul Na Grobi 16/18; per adult/tent 14/3zł, d/tr bungalows 60/90zł; P) On the bank of the Odra River, 2km east of the Old Town, this camping ground is neat and well priced. Take tram No 4 to Plac Wróblewskiego from the train station, and walk about 1km east.

Eating

Dwór Polski (☎ 372 48 96; Rynek 5; mains 15-50zł; ☺ 10am-midnight) This is a classy place to sample good Polish cuisine on the main square.

Bar Mleczny Miś (☎ 343 49 63; ul Kuźnicza 45-47; mains 5-12zł; ☺ 7am-6pm Mon-Fri, 8am-5pm Sat) In the university area, Miś is basic but popular with frugal university students.

Bar Wegetariański Vega (☎ 344 39 34; Rynek 1/2; mains 10-20zł; ☺ 8am-7pm Mon-Fri, 8am-5pm Sat, 9am-5pm Sun) A cheap cafeteria in the centre of the Rynek; offers good value vegie dishes.

Drinking

Kalogródek (☎ 0501 778 346; ul Kuźnicza 29; ☺ 10am-midnight) A laid-back, ever-busy beer garden popular with local students and backpackers. The surrounding streets are packed with other cheap and friendly haunts.

Queen (☎ 343 55 29; ul Purkyniego 1; ☺ noon-3am) A moody club housed in an old church, Queen is an OK place for a late-night drink. There's occasional live music.

Entertainment

Wrocław is an important cultural centre, so there's always something going. Check out the free *Wrocław Calendar of Events*, available from the tourist office. The website www.doors2.wroclaw.pl has useful 'youth-oriented' information.

Teatr Polski (☎ 343 86 53; ul Zapolskiej 3) This is Wrocław's main theatrical venue and stages classic Polish and foreign drama.

Filharmonia (☎ 342 20 01; www.filharmonia.wroclaw.pl; ul Piłsudskiego 19) Hosts concerts of classical music, mostly on Friday and Saturday night.

POLAND

POLAND

Getting There & Away

If you're travelling to/from Wrocław on Friday, Saturday or Sunday, book your bus or train ticket as early as possible because of the number of students coming and going over weekends.

The **bus terminal** (ul Sucha 11) is just south of the main train station. Several daily PKS buses go to Poznań, Białystok, Częstochowa and Warsaw (seven hours). Polski Express also runs to Warsaw (67zł, three daily).

The **Wrocław Główny train station** (ul Piłsudskiego 105) was built in 1856 and is a historical monument in itself. Fast trains to Kraków depart daily, every hour or two, and several InterCity and express trains (65zł, six hours) go to Warsaw. Wrocław is also regularly linked by train to Poznań, Częstochowa, Szczecin and Lublin.

WIELKOPOLSKA

Wielkopolska (Great Poland) is the cradle of the Polish nation. It was here, in the 10th century, that Duke Mieszko I unified the local Slavic tribes into a nation-state. Despite the royal seat's move to Kraków in 1038, Wielkopolska remained Poland's most important province until the second partition in 1793, when it was annexed to Prussia. Poznań, which returned to Poland after WWI, is the region's industrial and economic powerhouse, known worldwide for its trade fairs.

POZNAŃ

☎ 061 / pop 610,000

Poznań, midway between Berlin and Warsaw, is the focal point of early Polish history, and was the de facto capital of Poland from 968 to 1038. By the 15th century Poznań was already famous for its trade fairs, which were reinstituted in 1925, and continue to draw vast crowds of international businesspeople.

Information

Bank Pekao (ul Św Marcin 52/56)
City Information Centre (☎ 851 96 45; ul Ratajczaka 44; ☉ 10am-7pm Mon-Fri, 10am-5pm Sat) Handles bookings for cultural events.
Internet Café Bajt (ul Zamkowa 5; per hr 3zł) Off the main square.
Main post office (ul Kościuszki 77) West of the Old Town.
Tourist office (☎ 852 61 56; Stary Rynek 59; ☉ 9am-5pm Mon-Fri, 10am-2pm Sat)

Sights

Stary Rynek (Old Market Square) has been beautifully restored, and the focal point is the Renaissance **Town Hall** (built 1550–60). Inside the building, the **Poznań Historical Museum** (☎ 856 80 00; adult 5.50zł; ☉ 10am-4pm Mon-Tue & Fri, noon-6pm Wed, 10am-3pm Sun) reveals the city's past through splendid period interiors.

The square features the unique **Museum of Musical Instruments** (☎ 852 08 57; Stary Rynek 45/47; adult 5.50zł, free Sat; ☉ 11am-5pm Tue-Sat, 11am-3pm Sun). The **Archaeological Museum** (☎ 852 82 51; ul Wodna 27; adult 3zł, free Sat; ☉ 10am-4pm Tue-Fri, 10am-6pm Sat, 10am-3pm Sun) contains displays on the prehistory of western Poland, as well as some Egyptian mummies.

The 17th-century **Franciscan Church** (ul Franciszkańska 2; ☉ 8am-8pm), one block west of the Rynek, has an ornate baroque interior complete with wall paintings and rich stucco work. Nearby, the **National Museum** (☎ 856 80 00; Al Marcinkowskiego 9; adult 10zł, free Sat; ☉ 10am-6pm Tue, 9am-5pm Wed, 10am-4pm Thu & Sun, 10am-5pm Fri & Sat) holds an excellent collection of mainly 19th- and 20th-century Polish paintings.

The massive 1956 strike by the city's industrial workers was the first major popular upheaval in communist Poland. The strike was cruelly crushed by tanks, leaving 76 dead and more than 600 wounded. In a park in the new city centre, the moving **Monument to the Victims of June 1956** commemorates the event.

Festivals & Events

Poznań's trade fairs are its pride. The largest take place in January, June, September and October. A dozen additional smaller fairs also occur throughout the year. Major cultural events include **St John's Fair** (June) and the **Malta International Theatre Festival** (late June).

Sleeping

During trade fairs, the rates of Poznań's hotels and private rooms tend to increase (and in some cases double). The hard part is knowing when a fair is taking place. The tourist office can help you find a room.

Glob-Tour (☎ 866 06 67), in the main hall of the train station, is an accommodation agency offering cheap rooms from 40zł to 50zł per person. The agency is open 24 hours, but private rooms can be arranged only between 7am and 10pm daily.

Dizzy Daisy (☎ 506 075 306; www.hostel.pl; al Niepodległości 26; dm/s/d 30/50/100zł; ☐) One of the newest and most comfortable hostels in town, Dizzy offers free Internet and laundry and has no curfew.

Youth Hostel No 1 (☎ 866 40 40; ul Berwińskiego 2/4; dm 22zł) This youth hostel is a 15-minute walk southwest of the train station along ul Głogowska and is adjacent to Park Wilsona. It's a pretty basic 'no frills' option, but fills up fast with students and school groups.

Dom Turysty (☎ /fax 852 88 93; Stary Rynek 91; dm/s/d/tr 50/150/250/300zł) Set in an 18th-century former palace that's a bit musty and old-fashioned, but it boasts the best location in Poznań.

Hotel Rzymski (☎ 852 81 21; www.rzymskihotel .com.pl; al Marcinkowskiego 22; s/d 193/247zł) Overlooking Plac Wolności, Rzymski offers three-star comfort, although rooms aren't quite as grand as the elegant façade suggests.

Biuro Zakwaterowania Przemysław (☎ 866 35 60; www.przemyslaw.com.pl; ul Głogowska 16; ☒ 8am-6pm Mon-Fri, 10am-2pm Sat; s/d/apt from 40/60/120zł) Not far from the train station, its rates for weekends and stays of more than three nights are cheaper.

Eating

Bar Caritas (☎ 852 51 30; Plac Wolności 1; mains 8-15zł; ☒ 8am-7pm Mon-Fri, 10am-5pm Sat, noon-5pm Sun) A cheap and convenient milk bar, where you can point at what you want.

Sioux (☎ 851 62 86; Stary Rynek 93; mains from 16zł; ☒ noon-11pm) A 'Western' themed place, complete with waiters dressed as cowboys. Steaks, grills, ribs and enchiladas feature on the colourful menu.

Pod Aniołem (☎ 852 98 54; ul Wrocławska 4; mains from 14zł; ☒ 11am-midnight Mon-Sat, 1pm-midnight Sun) A pleasant pub serving up the usual range of cheap and filling Polish fare such as dumplings, salads and grilled meats.

Klio (☎ 855 75 52; ul Wrocławska 16; mains 15-30zł; ☒ 10am-midnight) A more upmarket place, offering pasta, fish and steaks.

Drinking

Pod Aniołem (☎ 852 98 54; ul Wrocławska 4; ☒ 11am-midnight Mon-Sat, 1pm-midnight Sun) Pod is a convivial place for a beer or two, and it hosts the occasional jazz concert.

Room 55 (☎ 855 32 24; Stary Rynek 80/82; ☒ 9am-midnight Mon-Sat, noon-midnight Sun) One of several trendy places on the main square to enjoy a drink.

Czarna Owca (☎ 853 07 92; ul Jaskółcza 13; ☒ noon-2am Mon-Fri, 5pm-2am Sat) This popular club has

different DJs each night playing a mix of rhythm and blues and hip-hop.

Galaxy Klub (☎ 851 60 22; Stary Rynek 85; ☒ 9pm-3am) A well-frequented place with a tacky sci-fi theme.

Entertainment

Teatr Wielki (☎ 852 82 91; ul Fredry 9) is the venue for opera and ballet, while **Filharmonia** (☎ 852 47 08; ul Św Marcin 81) offers classical concerts at least every Friday night.

Getting There & Away

The **bus terminal** (ul Towarowa 17) is about 600m east of the train station. From the busy **train station** (ul Dworcowa 1) services go to Kraków (6½ hours, nine to 10 daily), Szczecin (12 daily), Gdańsk (seven daily) and Wrocław (seven daily). Trains also head to Warsaw (five hours, 15 daily), including several InterCity services (three hours).

POMERANIA (POMORZE)

Pomerania stretches along the Baltic coast from the German frontier to the lower Vistula valley in the east. The region rests on two large urban pillars: Szczecin at its western end and Gdańsk to the east. Between them stretches the sandy coastline dotted with resorts. Inland is a wide belt of rugged, forested lakeland sprinkled with medieval castles and towns and the charming city of Toruń.

TORUŃ

☎ 056 / pop 208,000

Toruń is a historic city characterised by its narrow streets, burgher mansions and mighty Gothic churches. The compact Old Town was built on the slopes of the wide Vistula River, and is one of the most appealing in central Poland. Toruń is famous as the birthplace of astronomer Nicolaus Copernicus.

Information

ATMs can be found along ul Różana and ul Szeroka. To cash travellers cheques or get cash advances on Visa and MasterCard, go to the banks listed below.

Bank Pekao (ul Wielkie Garbary 11)

Klub Internetowy Jeremi (☎ 663 51 00; Rynek Staromiejski 33) Internet access.

Main post office (Rynek Staromiejski)

PKO Bank (ul Szeroka)

POLAND

POLAND

Tourist office (☎ 621 09 31; www.it.torun.pl; Rynek Staromiejski 25; ☷ 9am-4pm Mon & Sat, to 6pm Tue-Fri, to 1pm Sun)
Tourist office counter (Main train station; ☷ variable)

Sights

Rynek Staromiejski is the focal point of the Old Town. The massive 14th-century brick **old town hall** now shelters the **Regional Museum** (☎ 622 70 38; www.muzeum.torun.pl, Rynek Staromiejski 1; adult 7zł; ☷ noon-6pm Tue & Thu, 10am-4pm Wed & Fri-Sun). Displays recall the town's once numerous guilds, and there's a fine collection of 19th- and 20th-century Polish art. You can also climb the 40m-high **tower** (admission 6zł; ☷ 10am-6pm Tue-Sun, May-Sep) for great views.

Just off the northwestern corner of the square is the late 13th-century **St Mary's Church** (ul Panny Marii; ☷ dawn-dusk), a Gothic building with magnificent 15th-century stalls.

In 1473 Copernicus was born in the brick Gothic house that now contains the dry **Museum of Copernicus** (☎ 622 70 38; ul Kopernika 15/17; adult 7zł; ☷ 10am-4pm Tue, Thu & Sun, noon-6pm Wed, Fri & Sat May-Aug, 10am-4pm Tue-Sun Sep-Apr). It has replicas of the great astronomer's instruments.

One block east of the museum is the **Cathedral of SS John the Baptist & John the Evangelist** (ul Żeglarska; adult 2zł; ☷ 9am-5.30pm Mon-Sat, 2pm-5.30pm Sun), founded in 1233 but not completed until more than 200 years later. Its massive tower houses Poland's second-largest bell (after the Wawel Cathedral in Kraków).

Festivals & Events

Toruń breaks out of its comparative slumber during festival times.
Probaltica Music and Art Festival of Baltic States (May)
Contact International Theatre Festival (May/June)
Music and Architecture International Summer Festival (July and August)

Sleeping

Schronisko Turystyczne Fort IV (☎ 655 82 36; www .fort.torun.pl; ul Chrobrego 86; dm 22zł) Atmospherically located in an old Prussian fort, it has simple, barrack-like dorms. Although inconvenient for town, it's easy to reach on bus No 14 from the bus terminal and main train station.

Youth Hostel (☎ 659 61 84; ul Św Józefa 22/24; dm 13-19zł) The youth hostel is 3.5km northwest of the centre, and offers standard facilities. It's accessible on bus No 11 from the main train station and Old Town.

Hotel Polonia (☎ 657 18 00; www.polonia.torun.pl; Plac Teatralny 5; s/d 130/160zł) Smart, attractively furnished rooms in a restored 19th-century building are on offer, and it's a short walk from the main square. The hotel also has its own foreign-exchange office.

Hotel Gotyk (☎ 658 40 00; www.hotel-gotyk.com.pl; ul Piekary 20; s/d 150/250zł) This hotel is housed in a modernised 14th-century building just off the main square. Rooms are very neat, and all come with sparkling new bathrooms.

Hotel Pod Orłem (☎ 622 50 24; www.hotel.torun.pl; ul Mostowa 17; s/d/apt 110/140/200zł; **P**) Rooms here are relatively small with squeaky wooden floors, and some rooms have poky bathrooms, but the service is good and the location is central. Overall it's good value.

Eating & Drinking

Gospoda Pod Modrym Fartuchem (☎ 622 26 26; Rynek Nowomiejski 8; mains from 14.50zł; ☷ 10am-10pm) A very pleasant, folksy 15th-century pub on the New Town square, which serves the usual meat-and-cabbage Polish dishes at good prices.

Bar Muzyczny Misz-Masz (☎ 652 23 24, ul Św Katarzyny 6; mains 5-10zł; ☷ 10am-9pm) Serves a huge range of cheap and filling fare, including dumplings, pasta, fish and chips, and kebabs, plus lots of teas and stronger drinks.

Pizzeria Verona (☎ 622 04 80; ul Chełmińska 11; pizzas 6.50-27zł; ☷ 11am-late) Offers a big menu of pizzas, plus a few pasta and salad options.

Restauracja Pod Arsenałem (☎ 658 34 40; ul Dominikańska 9; mains 15-60zł) A classier subterranean place serving excellent Polish cuisine, including pheasant dumplings and roasts.

Piwnica Artystyczna Pod Aniołem (☎ 622 70 39; Rynek Staromiejski 1), set in a splendid spacious cellar in the old town hall, offers live music on some nights. Other great places for a drink include **Gospoda Pod Modrym Fartuchem** (☎ 622 26 26; Rynek Nowomiejski 8; ☷ 10am-10pm) and **Piwnica Ratusz** (☎ 621 02 92; Rynek Staromiejski 1), which offers a few outdoor tables in the square and a huge cavernous area downstairs.

Entertainment

Teatr im Horzycy (☎ 622 50 21; Plac Teatralny 1) is the main stage for theatre performances, and **Dwór Artusa** (☎ 655 49 29; Artus Court; Rynek Staromiejski 6) often presents classical music.

Getting There & Away

The **bus terminal** (ul Dąbrowskiego) is about 1km north of the Old Town. **Polski Express** (Al

Solidarności) offers services to Warsaw (48zł, four hours, hourly) and Szczecin (two daily).

The main **Toruń Główny train station** (Al Podgórska) is on the opposite side of the Vistula River and linked to the Old Town by bus Nos 22 and 27. Some trains stop and finish at the more convenient Toruń Miasto train station, about 500m east of the New Town.

From Toruń Główny station there are services to Poznań (three daily), Gdańsk (six daily), Kraków (three daily), Łódź (seven daily), Olsztyn (nine daily), Szczecin (one daily) and Wrocław (two daily) and Warsaw (five daily).

GDAŃSK

☎ 058 / pop 475,000

Gdańsk was already a thriving trading centre when the Teutonic Knights seized it in 1308. After joining the Hanseatic League in 1361, the city, then known as Danzig, became one of the wealthiest ports on the Baltic. After a popular uprising against the Knights in 1454, Gdańsk came under the nominal rule of the Polish monarch. It was annexed by Prussia in 1793 and returned to Poland only after WWII.

Today Gdańsk is best known as the birthplace in 1980 of the Solidarity trade union, which was the catalyst for the fall of communism in Europe. Today it's a bustling, cosmopolitan place that makes an ideal base for exploring the coast.

Information

Almatur (☎ 301 24 24; Długi Targ 11) Travel agency.
Bank Pekao (ul Garncarska 23)
Jazz 'n' Java (☎ 305 36 16; ul Tkacka 17/18; per hr 5zł; ☽ 10am-10pm) Internet access.
Main post office (ul Długa 22)
Orbis Travel (☎ 301 45 44; ul Podwale Staromiejskie 96/97) Travel agency.
PTTK office (☎ 301 13 43; www.pttk-gdansk.pl; ul Długa 45; ☽ 9am-5pm) This tourist office is opposite the main town hall.
Rudy Kot (☎ 301 39 86; ul Garncarska 18/20; per hr 5zł; ☽ 10am-midnight) Internet access.
Telephone centre (ul Długa 26)

Sights
MAIN TOWN

The richest architecture and most thorough restoration are in this historic quarter. Ul Długa (Long Street) and Długi Targ (Long Market) form its main thoroughfare, and are both now pedestrian malls. They are known collectively as the **Royal Way**, along which Polish kings traditionally paraded during their periodic visits. They would enter the Main Town through the **Upland Gate** (built in the 1770s on a 15th-century gate), pass through the **Golden Gate** (1614) and proceed east to the Renaissance **Green Gate** (1568).

The **Central Maritime Museum** (☎ 301 86 11; ul Ołowianka 9-13; 6zł for one section, 14zł for all four sections; ☽ 10am-5pm Tue-Sun), which has branches on both sides of the river, offers a fascinating insight into Gdańsk's seafaring past. It includes the museum-ship *Sołdek*, built here just after WWII.

Outside the Gothic town hall is **Neptune's Fountain** (1633). Nearby, the **Golden House** (1618) may have the richest façade in town.

Two blocks north of Green Gate along the waterfront is the 14th-century **St Mary's Gate**. Through this gate, the most picturesque street in Gdańsk – **ul Mariacka** (St Mary's St)– is lined with 17th-century burgher houses.

At the end of ul Mariacka is the gigantic 14th-century **St Mary's Church** (admission 2zł; ☽ 8am-8pm, except during services), possibly the largest old brick church in the world. Inside the 14m-high astronomical clock, adorned with zodiacal signs, is an amazing example of 15th-century craftsmanship. Watch the little figures troop out at noon. If you're feeling fit, you can climb the 405 steps of the **tower** (admission 3zł) for a giddy view over the town. The tiny viewing platform can quickly get crowded at busy times.

OLD TOWN

The Old Town, almost totally destroyed in 1945, has not been completely rebuilt apart from a handful of churches. The largest and most remarkable is **St Catherine's Church** (ul Wielkie Młyny; ☽ 8am-6pm Mon-Sat), Gdańsk's oldest church, which was begun in the 1220s. Opposite, the **Great Mill** (ul Wielkie Młyny) was built by the Teutonic Knights in around 1350. It used to produce 200 tonnes of flour per day and operated until 1945. It's now occupied by shops.

OLD SUBURB

This section of Gdańsk was also reduced to rubble in 1945. Little of the urban fabric has been reconstructed, except for the former Franciscan monastery, which houses the **National Museum** (☎ 301 68 04; ul Toruńska 1; adult

POLAND

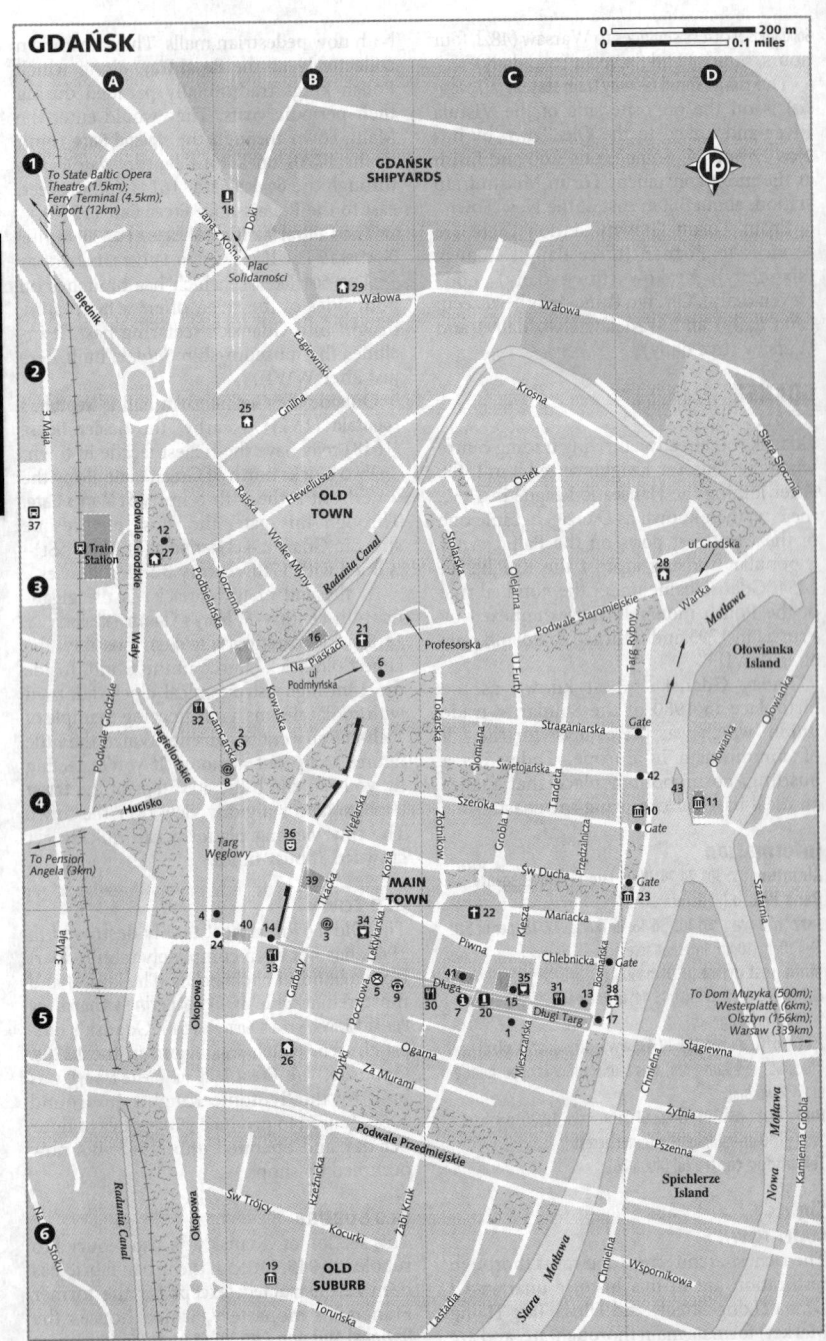

GDAŃSK

0 — 200 m
0 — 0.1 miles

A   **B**   **C**   **D**

1

To State Baltic Opera Theatre (1.5km); Ferry Terminal (4.5km); Airport (12km)

Błędnik

GDAŃSK SHIPYARDS

18

Jana z Kolna

Doki

Plac Solidarności

29 Wałowa

Wałowa

2

3 Maja

Łagiewniki

Gnilna

25

Krosna

Stara Stocznia

37

3

Train Station

Podwale Grodzkie

Wały

Rybacka

Wielkie Młyny

Korzenna

Podbielańska

12
27

Hewaliusza

OLD TOWN

Radunia Canal

Stolarska

Olejarna

Osiek

28

ul Grodska

Wartka

Mołtawa

4

Podwale Grodzkie

Jagiellońska

Hucisko

Na Piaskach
ul Podmłyńska

16

21

6

Profesorska

U Furty

Podwale Staromiejskie

Targ Rybny

Ołowianka Island

Ołowianka

Karmelicka

32

2
8

Kowalska

Tokarska

Straganiarska

Słomiana

Świętojańska

Szeroka

Tandeta

Gate

42

43

10

Gate

11

5

To Pension Angela (3km)

3 Maja

Okopowa

Targ Węglowy

36

39

Tkacka

Kołodziejska

Węglarska

Zlotników

Grobla I

Św Ducha

Przędzalnica

Gate

23

4
40
24
14

33

Garbary

Pocztowa

Lektykarska

34

3

5
9

30

Długa

41

7

15

20

Piwna

Mariacka

Kleszta

22

Chlebnicka

35

31

13

38

17

Bogusławskiego

Gate

Długi Targ

1

To Dom Muzyka (500m); Westerplatte (6km); Olsztyn (156km); Warsaw (339km)

6

26

Zbytki

Za Murami

Ogarna

Mieszczańska

Stągiewna

Chmielna

Żytnia

Mołtawa

Nowa

Kamienna Grobla

Podwale Przedmiejskie

Rzeźnicka

Żabi Kruk

Pszenna

Spichlerze Island

Radunia Canal

Na Stoku

Około

Sw Trójcy

Kocurki

19

OLD SUBURB

Toruńska

Łasztownia

Stara Mołtawa

Chmielna

Wspornikowa

POLAND

8zł, free Sat; 9am-4pm Tue-Fri, 10am-4pm Sat). The museum is famous for its Dutch and Flemish paintings, especially Hans Memling's 15th-century *Last Judgement*.

Festivals & Events

International Organ Music Festival (mid-June to late August) Organ recitals are held at Oliwa Cathedral, St Nicholas' and St Bridget's churches.

International Street and Open-Air Theatre Festival (July)

International Organ, Choir and Chamber Music Festival (every Friday in July and August) Held at St Mary's Church.

Dominican Fair (first two weeks in August) An annual shopping fair dating back to 1260.

Sleeping

Grand Tourist (301 26 34; www.gt.com.pl; ul Podwale Grodzkie 8; 8am-7pm Mon-Fri, 8am-2pm Sat), below the street level and opposite the main train station, is an accommodation agency offering private singles/doubles in the city centre for 60/100zł and rooms in the suburbs from 55/75zł.

Targ Rybny (301 56 27; ul Grodzka 21; dm/d/t from 40/120/180zł;) This popular modern hostel is in a great central location overlooking the quay. It's a little cramped, but clean and sociable, and there's free Internet access.

Dizzy Daisy (301 39 19; ul Gnilna 3; dm/d/t 35/100/135zł; Jul-Aug; P) This is a summer-only party hostel with spotless facilities, free Internet and knowledgeable staff.

Youth Hostel (/fax 301 23 13; ul Wałowa 21; dm/s/d from 12/25/50zł;) This main youth hostel is in a quiet, old building set back from the road. It's generally full, so book ahead.

Smoking and drinking are strictly forbidden, and there's a midnight curfew.

Dom Muzyka (300 92 60; www.dom-muzyka.pl; ul Łąkowa 1/2; s/d 120/180zł; P) Located inside the Music Academy, a high standard is on offer here; the rooms are modern and spotless. It's about 300m east of the city centre, and there's no hotel sign anywhere. Head for the door on the right-hand end of the big yellow-brick building.

Dom Harcerza (3013621; www.domharcerza.prv.pl; ul Za Murami 2/10; d/tr from 96/106zł) Offers good value for its location. The rooms are small but cosy, and the bathrooms are clean.

Pension Angela (/fax 302 23 15, ul Beethowena 12; s & d from 100zł; P) A cosy, family-run pension west of the centre that offers comfortable rooms. It's accessible by bus No 130 or 184 from the main train station.

Eating & Drinking

Bar Mleczny Neptun (301 49 88; ul Długa 33/34; mains 5-10zł; 7.30am-6pm Mon-Fri, 9am-5pm Sat) A cut above your run-of-the-mill milk bar.

Złoty Kur (301 61 63; ul Długa 4; mains 10-20zł; noon-7pm) A cheap and cheerful place, which offers soups, salads and fuller meals.

Grand Café Rotterdam (305 45 80; Długi Targ 33/34; mains 12-20zł; 10am-2am) Serves especially good savoury pancakes, plus other Dutch and Polish specialities.

Green Way (301 41 21; ul Garncarska 4/6; mains 7-10zł; 10am-10pm) Popular with local vegetarians for sandwiches, crepes and salads.

Jazz Club (301 54 33; Długi Targ 39/40; live music charge 7zł; 2pm-1am Sun-Thu, to 4am Fri & Sat) Live music is performed at weekends, although not necessarily jazz.

Grand Café Rotterdam (☎ 305 45 80; Długi Targ 33/34; ☻ 10am-2am) A pleasant spot for an alfresco beer, and there's also a well-stocked cellar wine-bar.

Celtic Pub (☎ 320 29 99; ul Lektykarska 3; ☻ 5pm-1am Sun-Thu, 5pm-3am Fri & Sat) This is a popular and lively place, scattered with the usual pseudo-Irish junk.

Entertainment

State Baltic Opera Theatre (☎ 763 49 12; www.opera baltycka.pl; Al Zwycięstwa 15) In the suburb of Wrzeszcz, not far from the train station at Gdańsk Politechnika.

Teatr Wybrzeże (☎ 301 70 21; Targ Węglowy 1) Next to the Arsenal, this is the main city theatre. Both Polish and foreign classics (all in Polish) are part of the repertoire.

Getting There & Away

BUS

The **bus terminal** (ul 3 Maja 12) handles all domestic and international services. It's behind (west of) the main train station and connected to ul Podwale Grodzkie by an underground passageway. Buses leave for Olsztyn (four daily), Toruń (four daily), Warsaw (six daily), Białystok (one to two daily) and Świnoujście (one to two daily). Polski Express offers buses to Warsaw (72zł, two daily) from this terminal.

TRAIN

The main train station, **Gdańsk Główny** (ul Podwale Grodzkie 1), is conveniently located on the western outskirts of the Old Town. Most long-distance trains actually start or finish at Gdynia, so make sure you get on/off quickly at the Gdańsk Główny station.

About 18 trains head daily to Warsaw, including 10 express trains (59zł/2nd class, five hours) and five InterCity services (3½ hours). Other destinations include Olsztyn (six daily), Kraków (10 daily), Wrocław via Poznań (five daily), Toruń (seven daily) and Szczecin (four daily). Trains also head to Białystok and Lublin once or twice daily.

Getting Around

The local commuter train, known as the SKM, runs every 15 minutes almost all day and night between the Gdańsk Główny and Gdynia Główna Osobowa train stations (4zł), via Sopot (2zł) as well as Gdańsk Oliwa (2.80zł) stations. (The line to Gdańsk Nowy Port, via Gdańsk Brzeżno, is a separate branch line that leaves less regularly from Gdańsk Główny.) Buy tickets at any station, and validate them at the platform entrance.

WARMIA & MASURIA

GREAT MASURIAN LAKES

The Great Masurian Lakes district east of Olsztyn is a verdant land of rolling hills interspersed with glacial lakes, peaceful farms and dense forests. The district has more than 2000 lakes, including **Lake Śniardwy** (110 sq km), Poland's largest lake. Around 200km of canals connect these lakes, so the area is a prime destination for yachties and canoeists, as well as those who prefer to hike, fish and mountain-bike.

The detailed *Wielkie Jeziora Mazurskie* map (1:100,000) is essential for exploring the region by boat, canoe, bike, car or foot. The *Warmia i Mazury* map (1:300,000), published by Vicon and available at regional tourist offices, is perfect for those using private or public transport, and it has explanations in English.

Mikołajki, a picturesque village, is perhaps the best base for exploring the lakes. The **tourist office** (☎ 421 68 50; Plac Wolności 3; ☻ 9am-5pm Mon-Fri, 9am-2pm Sat) is in the town centre. There are several foreign-exchange offices, but nowhere to cash travellers cheques or get cash advances.

The bus terminal and train station are on the southern edge of the town near the lake. Buses go to Olsztyn (four daily) each morning. Some buses also go daily to Giżycko, and two or three depart in summer for Warsaw. From the sleepy train station, a few slow trains shuttle along daily to Olsztyn and two fast trains head for Gdańsk and Białystok.

Hitler's wartime headquarters, called the **Wolf's Lair** ('Wolfsschanze' in German), was about 30km west of Giżycko. This was Hitler's main base between 1941 and 1944, and it was here, in July 1944, that an audacious assassination attempt came within a whisker of claiming his life. The leader of the plot, Claus von Stauffenberg, placed a bomb beneath a table in a meeting room. Hitler was only slightly injured in the blast, which killed two members of his staff. Von Stauffenberg and some 5000 others involved in the plot to varying degrees were executed.

POLAND DIRECTORY

ACCOMMODATION

Camping & Mountain Refuges

Poland has hundreds of camping grounds, many offering good-value cabins and bungalows. Most grounds are open from May to September, but some only bother opening their gates only between June and August.

PTTK (Polish Tourists Association) runs a chain of mountain refuges (schroniska górskie) for trekkers. They are usually simple but very cheap, and serve meals. In the high season even a space on the floor can be hard to find. Refuges are normally open all year, but confirm this with the nearest PTTK office.

Private Rooms, Hostels and Hotels

Some tourist-oriented towns have agencies (called a biuro zakwaterowania or biuro kwater prywatnych) that arrange accommodation in homes. Prices vary according to amenities and distance from the city centre. During the high season, home owners directly approach tourists at train and bus stations. Prices are often lower than through an agency (and open to bargaining), but you're more likely to be offered somewhere out in the sticks. Private homes in smaller towns often have signs outside their gates or doors offering a pokoje (room) or noclegi (lodging).

Youth hostels (schroniska młodzieżowe) in Poland are operated by Polskie Towarzystwo Schronisk Młodzieżowych (PTSM), a member of Hostelling International. Most open only in July and August, and are often very busy with school groups and Polish students. The year-round hostels are more reliable and have more facilities. Curfews are common.

An increasing number of privately operated hostels are springing up in the main cities. They are geared more towards international backpackers and offer more modern facilities than the old youth hostels, although prices are higher. A dorm bed can cost from about 20zł to 45zł per person per night. Single/double rooms, if available, cost from about 50/70zł. In most major cities, a few student dorms open as hostels in summer.

Hotel prices often vary according to the season and are usually posted at hotel reception desks. Top-end hotel sometimes quote prices in euros or US dollars. Discounted weekend rates are often available.

Two reliable companies can arrange accommodation (sometimes with substantial discounts) over the Internet: www.poland4u .com and www.hotelspoland.com.

ACTIVITIES

Hikers can enjoy any of the thousands of kilometres of marked trails across the Tatra and Sudeten mountains and the Great Masurian Lakes district. Hiking trails are easy to follow, and detailed maps are available from most larger bookshops. Poland is fairly flat and ideal for cyclists. Zakopane will delight skiers between December and March.

BUSINESS HOURS

Most shops are open from 9am to 6pm Monday to Friday, and until 2pm on Saturday. Supermarkets and larger stores often have longer hours. Banks in larger cities are open from 8am to 5pm weekdays (sometimes until 2pm on Saturday), but have shorter hours in smaller towns. Foreign exchange offices generally operate from 9am to 6pm on weekdays and until about 2pm on Saturday.

The opening hours of museums and other tourist attractions vary greatly. They tend to open any time between 9am and 11am and close sometime between 3pm to 6pm. Most museums are open at weekends, but many close on Monday and also stay closed on the day following a public holiday.

DANGERS & ANNOYANCES

Poland is a relatively safe country, although crime has increased steadily since the fall of communism. Be particularly alert at any time in the Warszawa Centralna train station, the favourite spot for thieves and pickpockets. Robberies have become increasingly common on night trains, especially on international routes. Try to share a compartment with other people if possible. Watch out, too, for bogus ticket-inspectors on public transport – ask to see ID if they try to fine you.

Smoking is very common in all public places, especially in pubs and restaurants.

DISABLED TRAVELLERS

Poland is not well set up for people with disabilities, although there have been significant improvements over recent years. Wheelchair ramps or lifts are available only at some upmarket hotels and major public buildings, and public transport will be a real challenge for anyone with mobility problems. **Intergracja** (☎ 635 13 30) has information for wheelchair-users, but unfortunately only in Polish.

EMBASSIES & CONSULATES
Embassies & Consulates in Poland

All embassies listed are in Warsaw.
Australia (☎ 521 34 44; www.australia.pl; ul Nowogrodzka 11)
Canada (☎ 584 31 31; www.canada.pl; ul Matejki 1/5)
France (☎ 529 30 00; www.ambafrance.org.pl; ul Puławska 17)
Germany (☎ 584 17 00; www.ambasadaniemiec.pl; ul Dąbrowiecka 30)
Ireland (☎ 849 66 33; www.irlandia.pl; ul Humańska 10)
Netherlands (☎ 559 12 00; fax 840 26 38; ul Kawelerii 10)
UK (☎ 628 10 01; www.britishembassy.pl; Al Róż 1)
USA (☎ 504 20 00; www.usinfo.pl; al Ujazdowskie 29/31)

Polish Embassies & Consulates Abroad

Australia (☎ 02-6273 1208; 7 Turrana St, Yarralumla, ACT 2600)
Canada (☎ 613-789 0468; 443 Daly Ave, Ottawa 2, Ontario K1N 6H3)
France (☎ 01 43 17 34 00; 1 Rue de Talleyrand, 75007 Paris)
Germany (☎ 030-22 31 30; Lassenstrasse 19-21, 14193 Berlin)
Ireland (☎ 01-2830855; www.polishembassy.ie; 5 Ailesbury Rd, Ballsbridge, Dublin)
The Netherlands (☎ 070-799 01 00; Alexanderstraat 25, 2514 JM Den Haag)
UK (☎ 0870-774 27 00; 47 Portland Place, London W1B 1JH)
USA (☎ 202-234 3800; 2640 16th St NW, Washington, DC 20009)

GAY & LESBIAN TRAVELLERS

The Polish gay and lesbian scene is fairly discreet. Warsaw and Kraków are the best places to find bars and clubs.

The best source of information in Warsaw is the **Pride Society** (☎ 0504 299 065; pride society@yahoo.com). Tourist offices in Warsaw might sporadically stock copies of *QC* (www.queercity.pl), a gay listings magazine. Otherwise, check out www.gej.net.

HOLIDAYS

Poland's official public holidays are:
New Year's Day 1 January
Easter Monday March or April
Labour Day 1 May
Constitution Day 3 May
Corpus Christi Thursday in May or June
Assumption Day 15 August

All Saints' Day 1 November
Independence Day 11 November
Christmas 25 and 26 December.

INTERNET RESOURCES

www.insidepoland.com Current affairs and links.
www.poland.pl An excellent place to start surfing.
www.polishworld.com Directories and travel bookings.

MONEY

The official Polish currency is the złoty (pronounced zwo-ti), abbreviated to zł. The złoty is divided into 100 groszy, abbreviated as gr.

Exchanging Money

Cash is easy to change and convenient, and private foreign-exchange offices – called *kantors* – are everywhere. The most widely accepted currencies are the US dollar, the euro and the pound sterling (in that order).

Foreign-exchange offices very rarely cash travellers cheques. Not all banks do either, and most also charge a commission.

ATMs *(bankomats)* are a common sight in all sizeable towns. Banks without an ATM might give cash advances over the counter on credit cards, which are widely accepted.

POST

Most cities have several post offices. The *poczta główna* (main post office) has the widest range of facilities.

TELEPHONE

Major telecommunications facilities are provided by Telekomunikacja Polska (TP), which often provides a telephone centre near the main post office. Most public telephones now use phonecards, which are widely available at post offices and kiosks. All numbers throughout Poland have seven digits.

When calling a number from another telephone district within Poland you must add a prefix of 0, then the area code.

TOURIST INFORMATION

Almost everywhere of interest in Poland has a regional tourist office, which can provide maps, brochures and other information. In some places, PTTK (Polish Tourists Association) offices act as de facto tourist offices, though in essence they are organisations of private travel agencies offering tours, guides, car hire and accommodation booking. Staff usually speak English, or, in some areas, German.

Portugal

HIGHLIGHTS

- **Sintra** A friend of this author proposed marriage here. It's that sort of place. Gorgeous palaces, faded, fabulous manor houses, lush gardens. In short, a must (p940)
- **Porto** Dramatic, Dickensian and thoroughly addictive, Porto has plenty of sights and street life (p949)
- **Best journey** The Algarve rail line is a thong's throw from the coast for most of the way between Lagos and Vila Real de Santo António, with magnificent seagulls-and-sand-style scenery (p942)
- **Off-the-beaten-track** Buçaco Forest (p948) is a haven of peace with lakes, waterfalls and a sumptuous palace/hotel where you can stop for a worth-every-euro cold drink

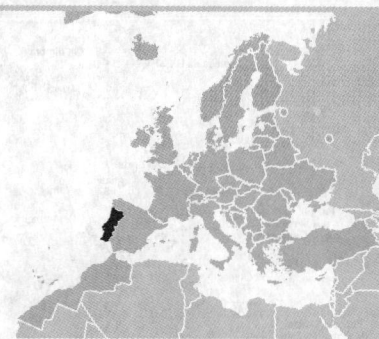

FAST FACTS

- **Area** 92,389 sq km (twice the size of Switzerland)
- **ATMs** Plentiful
- **Budget** €25-30 per day
- **Capital** Lisbon
- **Country codes** ☎ 351 (code for Portugal), ☎ 00 (international access code), ☎ 171 (reverse-charge call)
- **Famous for** *Fado*, death-trap drivers, port wine
- **Head of State** President Jorge Sampaio
- **Language** Portuguese
- **Money** Euro (A$1 = €0.58, CA$1 = €0.64, ¥100 = €0.73, NZ$1 = €0.54, UK1£ = €1.45, US$ = €0.81)
- **Phrases** *Bom dia* (hello), *obrigado/a* (thank you), *por favor* (please), *desculpe* (excuse me, sorry)

- **Population** 10 million
- **Time** GMT/UTC. Daylight savings from March to October.
- **Visas** EU nationals don't need a visa. Most others can stay for up to 90 days in any half-year without a visa.

TRAVEL HINTS

Travel out of season and save up to half on accommodation. Decline breakfast if an added extra at *pensãos* (guesthouses); it's generally better value – and tastier – to eat out.

ROAMING PORTUGAL

Visit Porto then Lisbon. Side-step to Sintra then Óbidos and Nazaré. Move on to sumptuous Évora before heading south and to the Algarve.

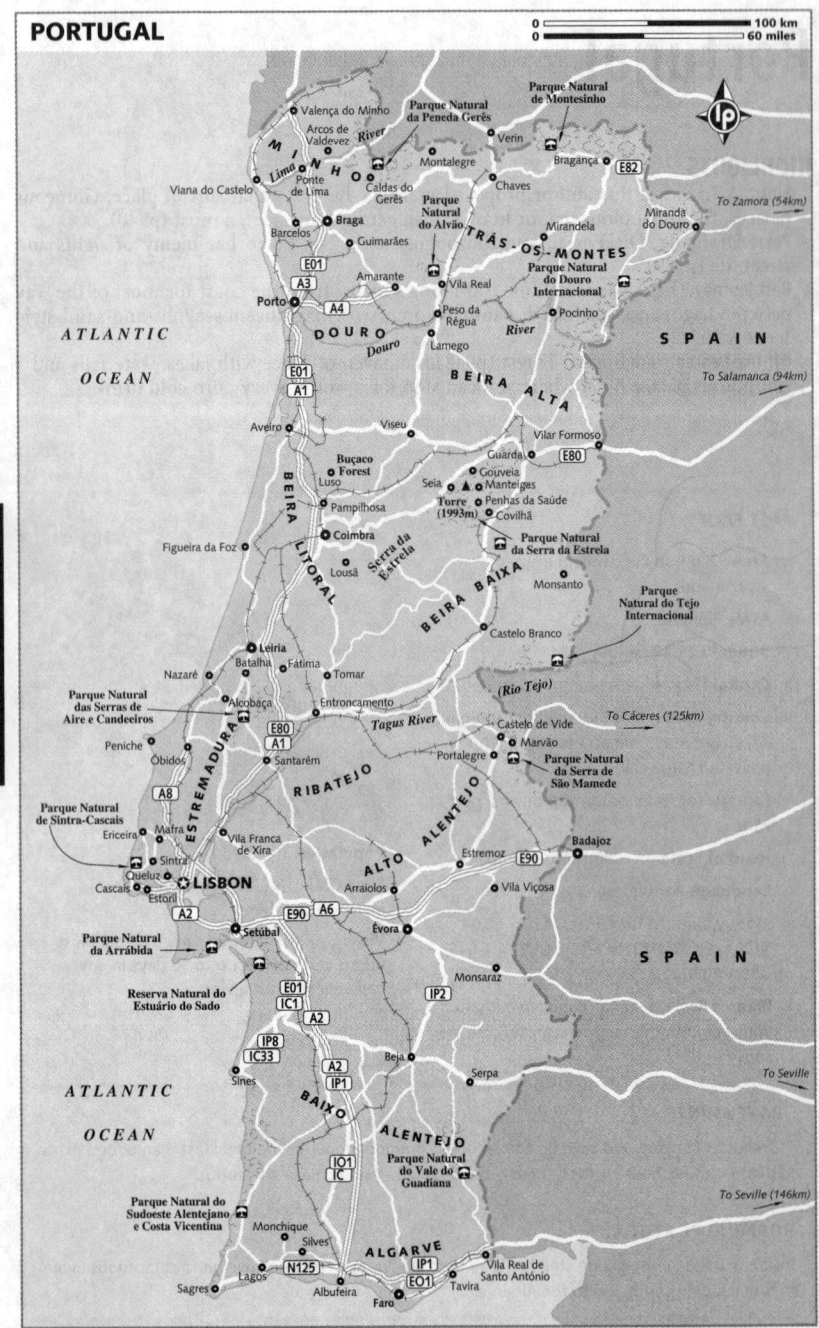

PORTUGAL

0 — 100 km
0 — 60 miles

ATLANTIC OCEAN

SPAIN

Valença do Minho
Arcos de Valdevez
Viana do Castelo
Ponte de Lima
Caldas do Gerês
Parque Natural da Peneda Gerês
Parque Natural de Montesinho
Verín
Montalegre
Bragança
E82
To Zamora (54km)
Barcelos
Braga
Guimarães
Parque Natural do Alvão
Chaves
Mirandela
Miranda do Douro
E01
A3
Amarante
Vila Real
TRÁS-OS-MONTES
Porto
A4
Parque Natural do Douro Internacional
DOURO
Peso da Régua
Pocinho
Lamego
Douro River
BEIRA ALTA
To Salamanca (94km)
E01
A1
Aveiro
Viseu
Vilar Formoso
Buçaco Forest
Luso
Guarda
E80
Seia
Gouveia
Manteigas
Pampilhosa
Torre (1993m)
Penhas da Saúde
Covilhã
Parque Natural da Serra da Estrela
BEIRA LITORAL
Coimbra
Serra da Estrela
Figueira da Foz
Lousã
BEIRA BAIXA
Monsanto
Parque Natural do Tejo Internacional
Leiria
Nazaré
Batalha
Fátima
Tomar
Castelo Branco
Parque Natural das Serras de Aire e Candeeiros
Alcobaça
Entroncamento
(Rio Tejo)
To Cáceres (125km)
E80
A1
Tagus River
Castelo de Vide
Peniche
Óbidos
Santarém
Marvão
Portalegre
Parque Natural da Serra de São Mamede
A8
ESTREMADURA
RIBATEJO
Parque Natural de Sintra-Cascais
Mafra
Ericeira
Vila Franca de Xira
ALTO ALENTEJO
Estremoz
E90
Badajoz
Queluz
Sintra
LISBON
Arraiolos
Vila Viçosa
Cascais
Estoril
A2
E90
A6
Évora
SPAIN
Parque Natural da Arrábida
Setúbal
Monsaraz
Reserva Natural do Estuário do Sado
E01
IC1
IP2
A2
IP8
IC33
A2
Beja
Serpa
Sines
IP1
To Seville
ATLANTIC OCEAN
BAIXO
IO1
IC
ALENTEJO
Parque Natural do Vale do Guadiana
To Seville (146km)
Parque Natural do Sudoeste Alentejano e Costa Vicentina
Monchique
Silves
ALGARVE
IP1
Vila Real de Santo António
Lagos
N125
Albufeira
EO1
Tavira
Sagres
Faro

Portugal is a country full of surprises and small enough to explore with ease. The far north is wonderfully remote with forested mountains dappled by tumbled-down stone hamlets while, a short jaunt southwards, Porto attempts the swagger of a big city, yet remains emphatically and indelibly medieval. In comparison, Lisbon is a hussy of a capital: easy on the eye with an upbeat atmosphere, which is appealingly rough around the edges. Nearby, smaller towns like Coimbra, Sintra and Tomar are headily historic while, to the far south, the Algarve has virtual year-round sunbed appeal with a rural flip side where you still need a phrasebook to order a beer.

Things are pretty good for Portugal right now: EU funding has brought the infrastructure up to speed and several recent big-time international events, like the European Football Championships, have led to a well-deserved showing off.

HISTORY

Early settlers of the Iberian Peninsula included the Celts, Phoenicians, Greeks, Romans and Visigoths. In the 8th century, the Moors conquered Portugal and their influence lingers in the culture, architecture and dark looks of the people, particularly in the Algarve where the Moors established their capital in Silves. After the 12th-century Christian conquest, new trade routes were discovered, creating an empire that extended to four continents and launched Lisbon as the wealthiest city in Europe. In 1580 Spain occupied Portugal's throne and, although the Portuguese regained it within 90 years, their imperial momentum had been lost forever.

In 1755 a massive earthquake tragically destroyed most of Lisbon; this was followed, around 50 years later, by Napoleon's thwarted invasion, and a period of civil war, culminating in the abolition of the monarchy in 1910.

In 1926 a military coup led to the dictatorship of António de Oliveira Salazar. General dissatisfaction with his regime and a ruinous colonial war in Africa led to a peaceful military coup on 25 April 1974. The subsequent granting of independence to Portugal's African colonies produced a flood of nearly one million refugees into the country.

The 1970s and early 1980s saw extreme swings between the political right and left, but Portugal's entry into the EU in 1986 secured a measure of stability. Expo '98 gave the country an essential boost, triggering vast transport and communications projects. This was furthered by Porto's status as a European Capital of Culture in 2001 followed, in 2004, by Portugal's playing host to the European Football Championships. This contributed to a vast injection of funds into the country's infrastructure, including a Porto metro, 10 new/refurbished stadia and plans for a second international airline terminal to be built northwest of Lisbon in 2010.

PEOPLE & CULTURE

Portugal's population of 10.3 million excludes the estimated three million Portuguese living abroad, but includes the considerable number of African and Brazilian immigrants. An influx of new immigrants is anticipated post-May 2004 when the European community embraced 10 new member countries.

Portugal has a strong Catholic influence and remains a conservative country. In general, the Portuguese are congenial, with an unhurried approach to life that can translate into lack of efficiency and tardiness. Speaking Portuguese, however clumsily, will earn you lots of points. In traditionally minded rural areas, particularly in the north, outlandish dress may cause offence and, while beachwear is acceptable in coastal resorts, shorts and skimpy tops in towns and, especially, in church, is frowned upon.

READING UP

Marion Kaplan's classic *The Portuguese, the Land and its People* (1991) is an entertaining account of Portuguese history and culture. More poetic is Paul Hyland's *Backwards out of the Big World: A Voyage into Portugal* (1996); it's a journey of discovery. If you intend striding out, read Bethan Davies and Ben Cole's peerless *Walking in Portugal* (2000) featuring routes in most of the national parks. *The Last Kabbalist of Lisbon* (2000) by Richard Zimler is a thriller based on the harrowing life of secret Jews during Portugal's Inquisition.

ARTS
Music
The best-known Portuguese music is the melancholy, nostalgic songs called *fado* (fate). The late Amália Rodrigues was the Edif Piaf of *fado*. Today it is the heart-wrenching voice of Mariza with her passionate recordings and blonde cornrows of hair that holds sway. Lisbon's Alfama district has plenty of *fado* houses, ranging from grandiose and tourist-conscious to small family affairs (see p939).

Architecture
Unique to Portugal is Manueline architecture, named after its patron King Manuel I (1495–1521). It symbolises the zest for discovery of that era and is hugely flamboyant, characterised by spiralling columns and elaborate ornamentation. An excellent example of Manueline architecture is Lisbon's Mosteiro dos Jerónimos (see p935).

Visual Arts
The most striking Portuguese visual art is the pottery with superb editions of the decorative blue and white *azulejo* tiles based on traditional Moorish designs of the 15th century. Lisbon has its own *azulejo* museum (p935).

SPORT
There's plenty of choice for sporty types. Football (soccer) is a national obsession. Lisbon's teams are Benfica, Belenenses and Sporting. In the Algarve, all that sunshine equals a spoilt-for-choice number of golf courses; click on www.portugalgolf.pt for a list. Tourist offices also have lists of tennis clubs and riding centres. Water-sports enthusiasts can catch the waves at one of Portugal's many surfing beaches – check out the national federation's website at www.fps.pt for more details. For the best wind- and

kite-surfing head for Praia do Guincho, west of Sintra or dramatic windy Sagras at the southwest tip of the country.

Bullfighting remains popular despite opposition from animal-welfare organisations. The season runs from late April to October.

ENVIRONMENT
National Parks
Portugal has one international-standard national park (70,290-hectare Peneda-Gerês), 12 *parques naturais* (natural parks), nine nature reserves and several other protected areas. There are 12 World Heritage sites, including Sintra and the historic centre of Évora. For a complete list check http://whc.unesco.org.

Environmental Issues
Portugal's most heated environmental issue concerns the Alqueva dam that opened in February 2002 as Europe's largest artificial lake. Over one million trees were cut down to create the dam, and some 160 rocks covered

---

INSIDE INFO: FOODIE FACTS

Don't be too tempted to dig into those tasty nibbles that are plonked on your table at the beginning of a meal. They can cost. This unwitting author was once charged €8 for a measly plate of paper-thin slices of cheese and some ham. Find out the cost and if you don't fancy what's on offer send the plate back immediately – nobody will be offended.

---

with Stone Age drawings were submerged. Environmentalists also voiced concern at the inevitable destruction of rare species, including wild boars and the Iberian lynx.

TRANSPORT

GETTING THERE & AWAY
Air
There are scheduled year-round flights from the UK to Lisbon, Porto and Faro with British Airways (BA), Portugalia Airlines (PGA) and TAP Air Portugal (TAP) and from Frankfurt, Germany with Lufthansa.

TAP and Continental Airlines both have a daily flight from New York to Lisbon with connections to Faro and Porto. Air France has multiple daily nonstop Paris–Lisbon and Paris–Porto connections while PGA has a daily flight from Paris to Porto.

TAP, Iberia and Spanair have daily Madrid–Lisbon flights. Elsewhere in Europe, KLM and TAP fly to Lisbon and Porto daily from Amsterdam while PGA has regular direct flights to Lisbon from Berlin, Stuttgart, Cologne and Hamburg.

Among the cheaper options using the UK as a base or transfer point is no-frills easyJet with flights starting as low as UK£100 return. British Midland's bmibaby and Monarch Airlines also have inexpensive flights from various UK airports.

Boat
There are no ferries from the UK to Portugal, but you can travel to northern Spain with the following operators and then hit the road to Portugal.

P&O Ferries (☎ 0870-520 2020; www.poferries.com; from UK£125 per adult one-way) operates the Portsmouth–Bilbao route (30 hours) with crossings twice weekly throughout the year except for January.

Brittany Ferries (☎ 0870-366 5333; www.brittanyferries.com; from UK£110 per adult one-way) operates between Plymouth and Santander twice weekly. The 24-hour crossing can be rough.

Bus
Eurolines (☎ 08705-143 219; www.eurolines.com) offers weekly departures from the UK with several stops including Lisbon (42 hours) and Porto (40 hours). Buses leave Victoria coach station via the Channel ferry, with a 7½-hour stopover in Paris. The current London–Lisbon return fare is UK£145. The company also runs service to Madrid–Lisbon (€38, eight hours), Madrid–Porto (€38, seven hours), Seville–Lisbon (€35, four hours) and Barcelona–Lisbon (€74, 16 hours), all going at least three times weekly.

Busabout (☎ 020-7950 1661; www.busabout.com) is a Europe-wide hop-on-hop-off coach network with unlimited travel passes within a set period. Stops in Portugal are Lisbon and Lagos. An eight-day under-26 Flexipass costs UK£249.

IASA (Paris ☎ 01 43 53 90 82; fax 01 43 53 49 57) has various routes departing from Paris and offers student discounts. Current return fare Paris–Lisbon is €135.

Damas (Huelva ☎ 959 256 900) runs twice daily Monday to Saturday from Seville to Faro and Lagos via Huelva, jointly with the Algarve line EVA.

Car & Motorcycle
There is no border control in Portugal. The quickest routes from the UK are by ferry (see left). For more information about driving in Portugal see p932.

Train
It's only cost-effective to take the train from the UK if you have an under-26 rail pass, such as Inter-Rail.

All services from London to Portugal go via Paris, where you change trains (and stations) for the TGV *Atlantique* to Irún in Spain (change trains again). From Irún there are two standard routes: the *Sud-Expresso* across Spain to Coimbra in Portugal, where you can reach to Lisbon or change for Porto; and an express service to Madrid, changing there to the overnight *Lusitânia* to Lisbon. Change at Lisbon for the south of Portugal.

Buying a one-way, 2nd-class, adult/youth London–Lisbon ticket (seat only) for the cheapest route, via the channel ferry, costs around UK£120; allow at least 24 hours. Tickets for this route are available from bigger train stations or from **Trains Europe** (☎ 01354-660 222; www.trainseurope.co.uk). The Eurostar service to Paris via the Channel Tunnel cuts several hours off the trip but bumps up the cost. Contact **Rail Europe** (☎ 08705-848 848; www.raileurope.co.uk) for details.

GETTING AROUND
Bicycle
Mountain biking is a great way to explore the country although, given the Portuguese penchant for overtaking on blind corners, it can be dangerous on lesser roads. Most towns have bike-rental outfits (around €10 a day). Bicycles can no longer be taken with you on trains, although most bus lines will accept them as accompanied baggage, subject to space and sometimes for an extra fee.

Bus
A baffling number of privatised bus companies operate across the country. However, unless you're a local or speak fluent Portuguese, the only national company worth checking out is **Rede Expressos** (☎ 969 502 050; www.rede-expressos.pt) which has a fleet of 100 buses, a comprehensive website and provides connections to 300 locations throughout the country. Portugal's main Eurolines agents are **Internorte** (Porto ☎ 226 052 420), **Intercentro** (Lisbon ☎ 213 571 745) and **Intersul** (Faro ☎ 289 899 770), serving north, central and southern Portugal, respectively.

There are three classes of bus service: *expressos* are comfortable, fast, direct buses between major cities; *rápidas* are fast regional buses and *carreiras* stop at every crossroad. *Expressos* are generally the cheapest. An under-26 card gets you a discount of around 20%, at least on the long-distance services.

Car & Motorcycle
ACP (Automóvel Clube de Portugal; Map p934; ☎ 213 180 100; www.acp.pt; Rua Rosa Araújo 24, Lisbon; emergency help numbers: southern Portugal ☎ 219 429 103, northern Portugal ☎ 228 340 001) has a reciprocal arrangement with many foreign automobile clubs, including AA and RAC. **ACP Insurance** (☎ 217 991 200; www.acp.pt) can advise members on car and motorcycle insurance and provides medical, legal and breakdown assistance.

To hire a car in Portugal you must be at least 25 and have held your home licence for longer than a year (some companies allow younger drivers at higher rates). To hire a scooter of up to 50cc you must be over 18 years old and have a valid driving licence. For more powerful scooters and motorbikes you must have a valid driving licence covering these vehicles from your home country.

Drive defensively: Portuguese drivers have invented an invisible – and disconcerting – middle lane. Drivers and front passengers in cars must wear seat belts. Motorcyclists and passengers must wear helmets, and motorcycles must have headlights on day and night. Using a mobile phone while driving could result in a fine.

Drink-driving laws are strict with a maximum legal blood-alcohol level of 0.05%.

Hitching
You rarely see any Portuguese hitching, and it is not recommended unless absolutely necessary.

Local Transport
Outside Lisbon or Porto there's little reason to take a municipal bus. Lisbon's underground system is handy for getting around the city centre and out to Parque das Nações, the former Expo site (see p935 for details). Porto is well under way with its own metro.

Taxis are plentiful and cheap. Fares increase by around 20% at night, at weekends and outside the city limits.

Don't miss the trams, an endangered species, in Lisbon and Porto and the funiculars and lifts of Lisbon, Braga and Nazaré.

Train
Caminhos de Ferro Portugueses (CP) operates *rápido* or *intercidade* (IC on timetables), *interregional* (IR) and regional (R) services. *Intercidade* and *interregional* tickets cost at least twice the price of regional

services, with reservations either mandatory or recommended. A special fast IC service called Alfa links Lisbon, Coimbra and Porto. Regional services are slower and cheaper than buses. Youth-card holders get 30% off R and IR services (except at weekends). One-/two-/three-week *bilhetes turísticos* (tourist tickets) are good for 1st-class travel, but worthwhile only if you're practically living on trains.

LISBON

pop 720,000

One of Europe's smallest, cheapest and most beguiling capitals, Lisbon is a life-affirming, lung-busting city of hills offering views over the sparkling Tagus River (Rio Tejo). The narrow streets and alleys of this once-great port city exude a sense of history, with traditional shops and cafés and ancient street trams that rattle up the steep gradients. Away from the centre are great stroll-around districts like Moorish Alfama, with its crumbling pastel-coloured houses packed into a steep shoulder of the city between the river and the castle.

ORIENTATION

North of Rossio train station in Central Lisbon is Praça dos Restauradores, at the bottom of Av da Liberdade. West of the Rossio it's a steep climb to the Bairro Alto district, good for bars and clubs. East of the Rossio, it's more climbing to Castelo de São Jorge and the Alfama district with its moody maze of ancient lanes. Several kilometres west of Rossio is Belém with its not-to-be missed attractions. Parque das Nações, the former Expo '98 site with its Oceanarium, lies on the groovy revamped waterfront, northeast of the centre.

GETTING INTO TOWN

The AeroBus runs every 20 minutes between the airport and Cais do Sodré train station. There should be a metro stop at Santa Apolónia train station by mid-2005. Alternatively, catch bus No 9, 39, 46 or 90 for Rossio. There are several bus terminals; most international services arrive at Oriente. A taxi into town is about €10.

INFORMATION
Bookshops
The English Bookshop (213 428 472; Rua do S. Marcál 83) Has a vast choice of English books ranging from blockbusters to the classics.
Livraria Buchholz (Rua Duque de Palmela 4) Has multilingual literature, including English, French and German.

Emergency
A tourist-oriented multilingual **police office** (Map p936; ☎ 213 466 802; Praça dos Restauradores) is near the ICEP tourist office.

Internet Access
Great Western (Map p936; ☎ 213 431 004; Rua das Portas de Santo Antão 54; ☼ 9am-10pm Mon-Fri, 10am-7pm Sat & Sun)
Lisboa Welcome Center (Map p936; ☎ 210 312 810; 2nd fl, Praça do Comércio; ☼ 9am-8pm)
Web Café (Map p936; ☎ 213 421 181; Rua do Diário de Notícias 126; ☼ 4pm-2am)

Medical Services
British Hospital (Map p934; ☎ 213 955 067; Rua Saraiva de Carvalho 49) English-speaking staff.

Money
Cota Câmbios (Map p936; Rossio 41; ☎ 213 220 470; ☼ 8am-10pm) One of the best exchange rates in town.
Top Atlântico (Map p934; ☎ 213 108 800; Av Duque de Loulé 108; ☼ 9am-8pm Mon-Fri) Commission-free currency exchange for AmEx cardholders and help with lost cards or cheques.

Post
Main post office (Map p936; Praça do Comércio; ☼ 8.30am-6.30pm Mon-Fri, 9am-noon Sat) Handles poste-restante collection.
Post office (Map p936; Praça dos Restauradores; ☼ 8am-8pm Mon-Fri, 9am-noon Sat) Opposite the ICEP tourist office.

Telephone
Portugal Telecom (Map p936; Rossio 68; ☼ 8am-11pm) Telephone booths and phonecards.

Tourist Information
Ask Me Lisboa Kiosks (☼ 6am-midnight) Rua Augusta (Map p936; ☎ 213 259 131) Palácio Foz (☎ 213 463 314) Santa Apolónia train station (Map p934; ☎ 218 821 606) Belém (Map p934; ☎ 213 658 435) airport (☎ 218 450 660) All have free maps, the bimonthly guide *Follow Me Lisboa* and sell the Lisboa Card, a cost-saving pass that covers public transport, museums and various sights.

PORTUGAL

PORTUGAL

LISBON

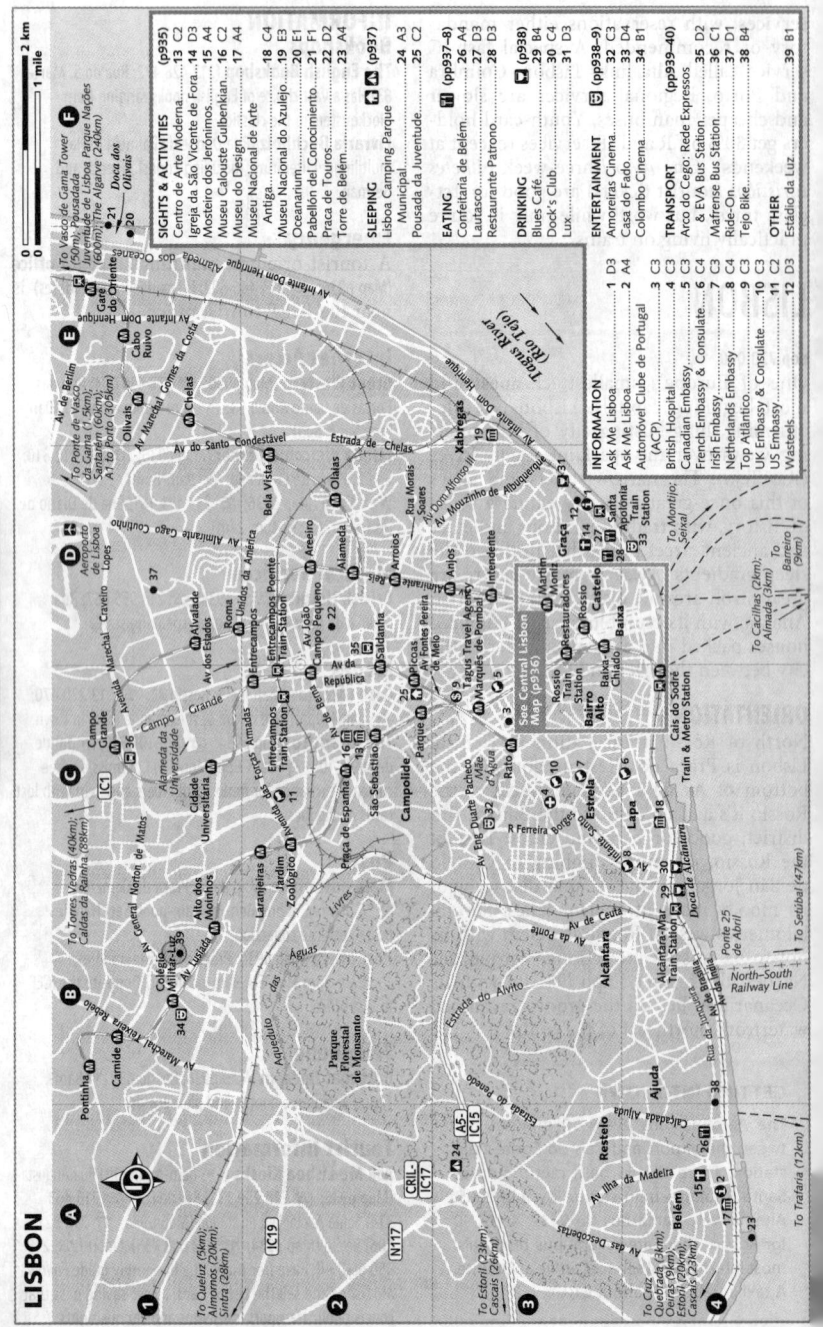

See Central Lisbon Map (p936)

SIGHTS & ACTIVITIES (pp935)
Centro de Arte Moderna.................13	C2
Igreja da São Vicente de Fora......14	D3
Mosteiro dos Jerónimos................15	A4
Museu Calouste Gulbenkian.........16	C2
Museu do Design...............................17	A4
Museu Nacional de Arte	
Antiga..18	C4
Museu Nacional do Azulejo.........19	E3
Oceanarium..20	F1
Pabellón del Conocimiento.........21	F1
Praça de Touros.................................22	D2
Torre de Belém..................................23	A4

SLEEPING 🛏 🏠 (p937)
Lisboa Camping Parque	
Municipal..24	A3
Pousada da Juventude...................25	C2

EATING 🍴 (pp937–8)
Confeitaria de Belém......................26	A4
Lautasco..27	D3
Restaurante Patronn........................28	D3

DRINKING 🍷 (p938)
Blues Café..29	B4
Dock's Club..30	C4
Lux..31	D3

ENTERTAINMENT 🎭 (pp938–9)
Amoreiras Cinema.............................32	C3
Casa de Fado......................................33	D4
Colombo Cinema...............................34	B1

TRANSPORT (pp939–40)
Arco do Cego: Rede Expressos	
& EVA Bus Station..........................35	D2
Mafrense Bus Station......................36	C1
Ride-On...37	D1
Tejo Bike..38	B4

OTHER
Estádio da Luz....................................39	B1

INFORMATION
Ask Me Lisboa......................................1	D3
Ask Me Lisboa......................................2	A4
Automóvel Clube de Portugal	
(ACP)...3	C3
British Hospital....................................4	C3
Canadian Embassy..............................5	C3
French Embassy & Consulate.........6	C4
Irish Embassy..7	C3
Netherlands Embassy.........................8	C4
Top Atlántico.......................................9	C3
US Embassy & Consulate.................10	C2
US Embassy..11	C2
Wasteels...12	D3

ICEP Tourist Office (Map p936; ☎ 213 463 314; www
.askmelisboa.com; Palácio Foz, Praça dos Restauradores;
🕑 9am-8pm) Deals with national inquiries.
Lisboa Welcome Center (Map p936; ☎ 210 312 810;
www.visitlisboa.com; Praça do Comércio; 🕑 9am-8pm)
Concentrates on Lisbon.

Travel Agencies

Tagus (☎ 213 525 986; fax 213 532 715; Rua Camilo
Castelo Branco 20) Youth-orientated agency.
Wasteels (Map p934; ☎ 218 869 793/7; Rua dos
Caminhos do Ferro 90) By Santa Apkónia train station;
offers budget travel options.

SIGHTS & ACTIVITIES

If you have a pair of sturdy walking shoes
and don't baulk at hills, most of Lisbon's
grand-slam sights can be explored by foot.
Alternatively, hop on the funicular, tram or
metro. Admission is usually half-price for
students and free for everyone on Sundays.

Alfama   Map p936

Despite the discouraging multilingual restaurant menus, this ancient district still
looks like a set for a medieval blockbuster
with its moody maze of twisted alleys and
ancient houses strung with washing. The
terrace at **Largo das Portas do Sol** provides *the*
souvenir snapshot of the city.

The **Casa do Fado** (☎ 218 823 470; Largo do Chafariz
de Dentro 1; €2.50; 🕑 10am-1pm & 2-5.30pm) is set in
a former Alfama bathhouse and provides a
spirited audiovisual look at *fado*'s history.

Dating from Visigothic times, **Castelo de
São Jorge** (☎ 218 800 620; admission free; 🕑 9am-
6pm) sits high above the city like a cherry
on a cake. If you don't feel like trekking up,
take bus No 37 from Praça da Figueira or
tram No 28 from Largo Martim Moniz.

Belém   Map p934

This quarter 6km west of the Rossio has
loads of charm, chairs on squares and reputedly the best *pasteis de nata* (custard tarts)
in the country. On a loftier note, Belém
(Bethlehem in English) is also home to Lisbon's most emblematic religious building.

The **Mosteiro dos Jerónimos** (☎ 213 620 034;
Praça do Império; €3, free Sun; 🕑 10am-5pm Tue-Sun)
dates from 1496 and is a soaring extravaganza of Manueline architecture with rich
carvings and stunning *azulejos*. There's a
funky craft market outside here on the first
Sunday of each month.

The **Museu do Design** (☎ 213 612 934; Praça do
Império; €3; 🕑 11am-8pm Mon-Fri, 10am-7pm Sat &
Sun) is a thoroughly groovy museum with
its cutting-edge collection dating from the
1930s that includes jewellery and furniture
from ultimate design gurus.

Saldanha   Map p934

Beret-and-smock types will love the astounding private collection at **Museu Calouste
Gulbenkian** (☎ 217 823 461; Av de Berna 45; €3, free
Sun; 🕑 10am-6pm Tue-Sun). There are Egyptian,
Asian, Greek and Islamic artefacts and contemplative paintings by Renoir, Rembrandt
and Monet. There's a free childcare centre
for restless kiddies.

Lisbon's **Centro de Arte Moderna** (Modern Art
Museum; ☎ 217 823 474; Rua Dr Nicaulau de Bettencourt;
€3, free Sun; 🕑 10am-6pm Tue-Sun) is a showplace
for Portugal's modern painters, including
London-based Paula Rego whose childhood in Portugal is strongly reflected in
her dreamlike and theatrical themes.

Outskirts of Town   Map p934

The following two museums are away from
the centre, but well worth the detour time.

Museu Nacional do Azulejo (☎ 218 100 340; Rua
Madre de Deus 4; €2.50, free 10am-2pm Sun; 🕑 10am-6pm
Wed-Sun, 2-6pm Tue) has an evocative 17th-century
convent setting, plus a magnificent display of
tiles, including a 36m panel of Lisbon.

Museu Nacional de Arte Antiga (Ancient Art Museum; ☎ 213 962 825; Rua das Janelas Verdes; €3, free
10am-2pm Sun; 🕑 10am-5pm Wed-Sun, 2-6pm Tue)
houses a beautifully displayed collection of
works by Portuguese painters.

Parque das Nações   Map p934

The former Expo '98 site, a revitalised 2km-
long waterfront area in the northeast, has a
range of attractions, plus Europe's biggest
Oceanarium (☎ 218 917 002; adult/child €9/4.50;
🕑 10am-7pm) and the **Pabellón del Conocimiento**
(Living Science Centre; ☎ 218 917 100; €5/2.50; 🕑 10am-
7pm) with over 300 interactive exhibits for kids
of all ages. Take the metro to Oriente station,
itself an equally impressive Expo project.

Alcântara   Map p934

The old wharves have been slickly revamped
into a swanky strip of bars and restaurants
with tables sprawling out onto the promenade. After your blowout brunch, enjoy
the half-hour waterfront stroll to Belém.

PORTUGAL

PORTUGAL

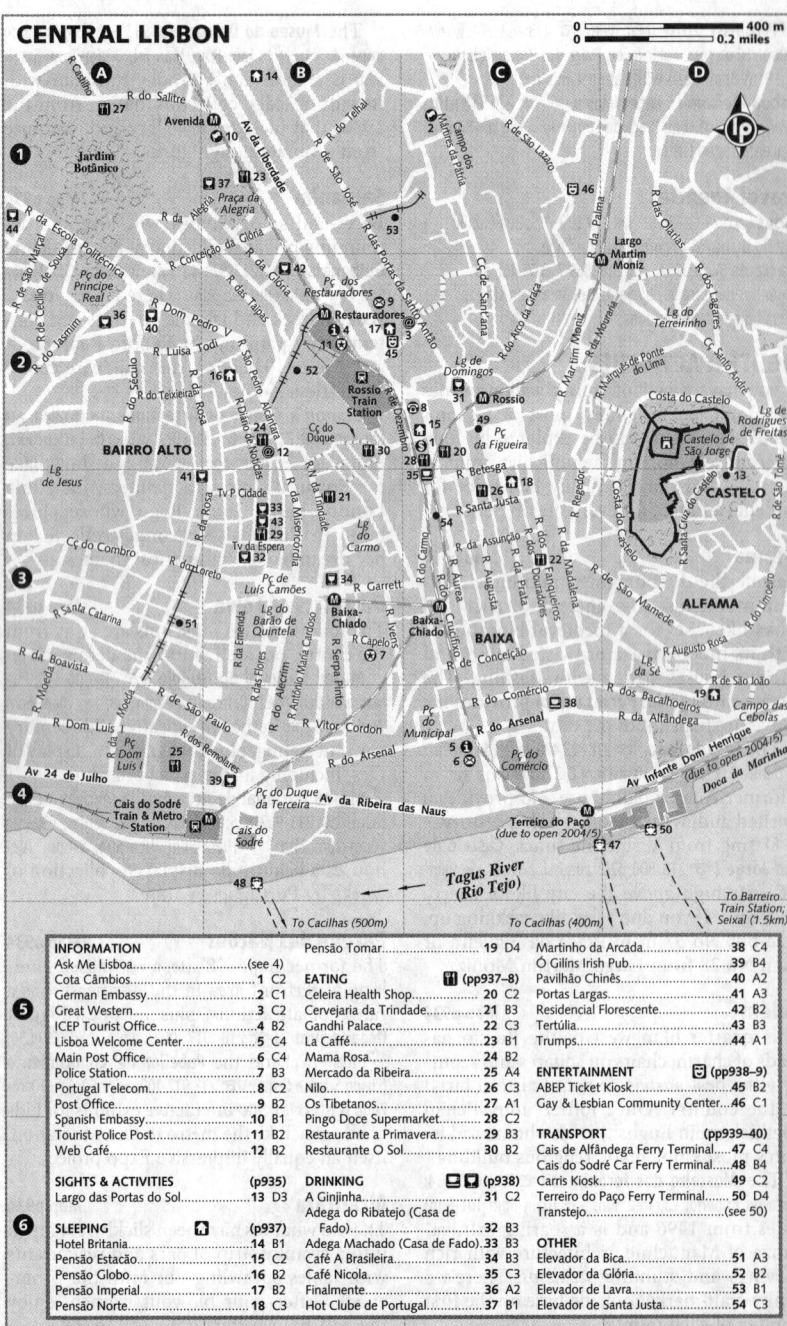

CENTRAL LISBON

0 _____ 400 m
0 _____ 0.2 miles

FESTIVALS & EVENTS

The following list is just a sampling. For a comprehensive list, check out www.rede-almanaque.pt/feiras.

Festas dos Santos Populares These are Christianised versions of traditional summer solstice celebrations and include the Festa de São João (St John; 23–24 June) and the Festa de São Pedro (St Peter; 28–29 June).

Festa de Santo António (12–13 June) St Anthony is Lisbon's patron saint and this festa is the climax of three weeks of partying known as the **Festas de Lisboa**. It's celebrated with particular gusto in the historical quarters of Alfama and Madragoa with dusk-to-dawn parties, music and dancing.

Festival dos Oceanos (15–30 August) Has a nautical theme with regattas and water-sport contests.

Festival do Vinho (1–15 November) Wine fair plus folk dancing and crafts fair.

Festival de Cinema Gay e Lésbico A gay and lesbian film festival, held in late September.

SLEEPING

Lisbon has plenty of small, inexpensive *pensãos* (guesthouses) throughout the centre. If you want to be within stumbling distance of the nightlife, check out the places in the Bairro Alta. Be warned that many places are several flights up, so call first if you're carrying lots of kit.

Pensão Imperial (Map p936; ☎ 213 420 166; 4th fl, Praça dos Restauradores 78; d €35) Charismatic owner and spotless comfortably worn rooms overlooking the city's main square.

Pousada da Juventude de Lisboa Parque Nações (☎ 218 920 890; dm/d €13.50/38) Just north of Gare do Oriente, this is the pick of the hostels, with a welcoming vibe and well-maintained rooms, plus restaurant, kitchen and laundry.

Pousada da Juventude (Map p934; ☎ 213 532 696; Rua Andrade Corvo 46; dm/d €17/43) This a tidy place but there are no cooking facilities. Catch bus No 46 or 90 from Rossio, or take the AeroBus.

Pensão Tomar (Map p936; ☎ 218 888 4849; Poço do Borraté; s/d €20/30) High ceilings, large rooms and chandeliers equal swish surrounds for a bargain-basement price.

Pensão Globo (Map p936; ☎ 213 462 279; www.pglobo.com; Rua do Teixeira 37; d from €30) No-frills with this price range, but you may need a mountaineering degree to reach the best rooms at the top. Close to the nightlife.

Pensão Estação (Map p936; ☎ 213 423 308; 2nd fl, Calçada do Carmo 17; s/d €15/30) Old-fashioned and careworn with a po-faced owner. The main perk is the location, right off Rossio.

Pensão Norte (Map p936; ☎ 218 878 941; 2nd fl, Rua dos Douradores 161; d €35) A quiet option with clean rooms, if a tad pokey as well as old-fashioned. And there's a lift.

Hotel Britania (Map p936; ☎ 213 155 016; www.heritage.pt; Rua Rodrigues Sampaio 17; s/d €146/156; ✷ 🖳 🅿) Classic Art Deco touches and massive luxury rooms are appealing in this go-for-the-splurge hotel a short, high-heeled strut from the centre.

Lisboa Camping Parque Municipal (Map p934; ☎ 217 623 100; Parque Florestal de Monsanto; per adult/camp site €5.30/5.50; bus 43 from Cais do Sodré) This well-treed spot is 6km northwest of town.

EATING

All ages and incomes socialise over food in Lisbon. Watch out for tourist rip-offs like some of the energetic stretch of restaurants on Baixa's Rua dos Correeiros. Bairro Alto has some good-value eateries while Alfama places often have great views. The main **Mercado da Ribeira** (Map p936) is near Cais do Sodré station. A good central supermarket is **Pingo Doce** (Map p936; Rua de Dezembro 73). **Celeira Health Shop** is right next door selling wholesome grub to go.

Baixa & Alfama

Restaurante O Sol (Map p936; ☎ 213 471 944; Calçada do Duque 23; mains €4; ☼ closed Sun) A rare fast-food vegetarian restaurant with outside seating, heady views and takeaways like soy burgers, pasties and seaweed cannelloni.

Gandhi Palace (Map p936; ☎ 218 873 839; Rua dos Douradores 214-216; mains €7-9) Popular and a good central choice for those suffering from curry-house withdrawal.

Restaurante Patrono (Map p934; ☎ 218 868 887; Largo Chafariz de Dentro 20; mains €7) Ideally situated for a spot of refuelling, this is one of the cheapest restaurants in the winding back-streets of Alfama. Try the hearty *aroz detamboril* (stew of monkfish and rice).

Lautasco (Map p934; ☎ Beco do Azinhal 7-7A; mains €9; ☼ closed Sun; ✷) Full points for this atmospheric terrace in the shade of a magnificent rubber tree. All the usual suspects are on the menu, including the *bacalhau* (cod).

Nilo (Map p936; ☎ 213 467 014; Rua dos Correeiros 217; mains €6) No-frills Nilo is one of the better-priced eateries on this restaurant strip. The pork with spicy *piri-piri* (a spicy condiment based on tomatoes and chilli peppers) is recommended.

Avenida de Liberdade

Os Tibetanos (Map p936; ☎ 213 142 038; Rua do Salitre 117; mains from €6; ☖ closed Sat & Sun; ☒ ☒) Doubles as a Tibetan Buddhist school with Zen-style surroundings and diverse, meatless menu; try the Japanese mushrooms with seaweed and tofu.

La Caffé (Map p936; ☎ 213 256 736; Av de Liberdade 129B; mains €6-8; ☖ 12.30-3.30pm daily, 8-11pm Tue-Sun; ☒ ☐) Upbeat minimalist décor and a creative twist on Med cuisine, like parsnip soup with green apple and walnuts and black spaghetti with smoked salmon.

Bairro Alto & Saldanha

Mamma Rosa (Map p936; ☎ 213 465 350; Rua do Grémio Lusitano 14; mains €5-7; ☒) Cosy Italiano atmosphere with red-check tablecloths and exceptional pizzas flamboyantly prepared in the open-plan kitchen.

Restaurante a Primavera (Map p936; ☎ 213 420 477; Travessa da Espera 34; mains from €6; ☒) Hugely popular with a homy informality. Try the clams in garlic and coriander followed by a girth-expanding dessert.

Cervejaria da Trindade (Map p936; ☎ 213 423 506; Rua Nova da Trindade 20-C; mains €7) This vaulted restaurant in a former convent has a nothing-fancy menu, but the sumptuously tiled setting provides serious food for thought.

Belém

Confeitaria de Belém (Map p934; ☎ 213 637 423; Rua de Belém 86-88) A classic tiled warren with the reputedly best *pasteis de nata* in Portugal.

DRINKING

Lisbon is great if you suffer a perpetual sugar low with fabulous Art Deco cafés particularly around Bairro Alto and Rossio. The city also has a thriving bar scene, an important part of its cultural landscape. Alcântara and Oriente area bars attract a well-heeled set while Alfama has plenty of choice including moody low-lit places for locked-eyes-over-cocktail types. You'll have no problem locating a watering hole in Bairro Alto and Chiado. Gay and lesbian bars are mainly concentrated around the Príncipe Real area.

Cafés & Bars

Café Nicola (Map p936; ☎ 213 460 579; Rossio 24; ☖ closed Sat afternoon & Sun) This sumptuous Art Deco café is past winner of the Café of the Year award.

Martinho da Arcada (Map p936; ☎ 218 879 259; Praça do Comércio 3; ☖ closed Sun) Former haunt of writer Pessoa; grab a coffee and head for an outdoor table under the arches.

Café A Brasileira (Map p936; ☎ 213 469 547; Rua Garrett 120) Another historic watering hole for Lisbon's 19th-century greats with warm wooden innards and a busy counter serving daytime coffees and pints at night.

A Ginjinha (Map p936; Largo de Domingos) Titchy, crusty local specialising in powerful *ginjinha* (cherry brandy).

Pavilhão Chinês (Map p936; ☎ 213 424 729; Rua Dom Pedro V 89) A global mishmash of bizarre ornaments, including a roomful of war helmets, and legendary cocktails.

Hot Clube de Portugal (Map p936; ☎ 213 467 369; Praça da Alegria 39; ☖ 10pm-2am Tue-Sat) Hot, sweaty and packed with nightly gigs and raw new jazz sounds.

Ó Gilíns Irish Pub (Map p936; ☎ 213 421 899; Rua dos Remolares 8-10; ☖ 11am-2am) Predictable blarney atmosphere with live music Friday and Saturday evenings.

Tertúlia (Map p936; ☎ 213 346 2704; Rua Diário de Notícias 60; ☖ 8pm-2am) Low-lit bar with newspapers, live jazz, exhibitions and – for those who can't resist a tinkle – a piano for customer use.

CLUBBING

Lux (Map p934; ☎ 218 820 890; Armazém A, Cais da Pedra; ☖ midnight-5am) Part-owned by John Malkovich and achingly trendy, with towering ceilings, riverside terraces and runway-size dance floors.

Dock's Club (Map p934; ☎ 213 950 856; Rua da Cintura do Porto de Lisboa 226; ☖ 11pm-6am Tue-Sat) Another riverside dance temple attracting a voguish clientele.

Blues Café (Map p936; ☎ 213 957 085; Rua da Cintura do Porto de Lisboa; ☖ 11pm-6am Tue-Sat) Jazz, blues and club nights, plus dockside drinking in a cool warehouse development.

Ritz Club (Map p936; ☎ 213 425 140; Rua da Glória 57; ☖ 9pm-3am) This is the city's largest African club; it's an atmospheric place with pulsating music and a friendly vibe.

ENTERTAINMENT

Pick up the free monthly *Follow me Lisboa*, *Agenda Cultural Lisboa* or quarterly *Lisboa Step By Step* from the tourist office for what's on listings. Also, investigate www.visit lisboa.com, www.lisboacultural.pt (cultural events) and www.ticketline.pt (concert information and reservations).

Cinemas

Lisbon has dozens of cinemas, including the multiscreen **Amoreiras** (Map p934; ☎ 213 878 752) and **Colombo** (Map p934; ☎ 217 113 222), both located within shopping centres.

Fado

Adega Machado (Map p936; ☎ 213 224 640; Rua do Norte 91; ◷ 8pm-3am, closed Mon) Earthy and authentic, run by Rita, goddaughter of the legendary Amália Rodrigues; the walls are papered with signed photos of *fado* enthusiasts, including Kirk Douglas.

Adega do Ribatejo (Map p936; ☎ 213 468 343; Rua Diário de Notícias 23; ◷ 8pm-2am) High on atmosphere with nightly *fado*.

Sport

Lisbon's football teams are Benfica, Belenenses and Sporting. See a game at the Estádio da Luz in the northwestern Benfica district. Bullfights are staged at the Praça de Touros near the Campo Pequeno metro station. Tickets are available at the **ABEP ticket kiosk** (Map p936; Praça dos Restauradores).

Gay & Lesbian Venues

Lisbon has a relaxed yet flourishing gay scene; check the **Gay & Lesbian Community Centre** (Comunitário Gay e Lésbico de Lisboa; Map p936; Centro ☎ 218 873 918; Rua de São Lazaro 88; ◷ 5-9pm) or the website www.portugalgay.pt for venues and events.

Portas Largas (Map p936; ☎ 218 461 379; Rua da Atalaia 105) A tiled bar with barn-size doors and infamous giant carafes of sangria.

Trumps (Map p936; Rua da Imprensa Nacional 104B) Not much elbow space in these two bars; one has a dance floor to get jiggy.

Finalmente (Map p936; Rua da Palmeira 38) A heaving dance floor and nightly drag shows.

GETTING THERE & AWAY
Air

Lisbon is connected by daily flights to Porto, Faro and many European centres. For arrival and departure information call ☎ 218 413 700.

Bus

A dozen different companies, including Renex (☎ 222 003 395), operate from Gare do Oriente. The Arco do Cego terminal is the base for **Rede Expressos** (☎ 707 223 344) and **EVA** (☎ 213 147 710), whose networks cover the whole country. There are several regional companies with destinations in the north, including Mafrense (for Ericeira and Mafra).

Train

Santa Apolónia station (Map p934; ☎ 218 816 121) is the terminus for northern and central Portugal, and for all international services (trains also stop en route at the better connected Gare do Oriente). Cais do Sodré station is for Belém, Cascais and Estoril. Rossio station serves Sintra. Barreiro station, which is across the river, is the terminus for southern Portugal; connecting ferries leave frequently from the pier at Terréiro do Paço.

GETTING AROUND
Car & Motorcycle

Car-rental companies at Lisbon airport include the international chains or go for the nearby (and cheaper) **Ride-On** (Map p934; ☎ 218 452 811; ride_on@netcabo.pt; Rua Reinaldo Ferreira 29). **Tejo Bike** (Map p934; ☎ 218 871 976), 300m east of Belém, rents bicycles for €5 an hour to ride along the waterfront.

There are cheap (or free) car parks near Parque das Nações or Belém, from where you can catch a bus or tram to the centre.

Public Transport
BUS & TRAM

Discounted two-journey bus and tram tickets can be bought from Carris kiosks for €0.93 – there's a kiosk at Praça da Figueira. A one/four/seven-day Passe Turístico, valid for trams, buses and the metro, costs €2.55/9.25/13.10. The *Lisboa Card* (see p933) is good for unlimited travel on nearly all city transport.

Buses and trams run from 6am to 1am, with some night services. To reach Belém take bus No 43, from Cais do Sodré, or tram No 15 from Praça da Figueira.

FERRY

Cais da Alfândega is the terminal for several ferries, including to Cacilhas (€0.60), a transfer point for some buses to Setúbal. A car (and bike) ferry runs from Cais do Sodré terminal.

PORTUGAL

METRO

The metro is useful for hops across town and to the Parque das Nações. Individual tickets cost €0.65; a *caderneta* of 10 tickets is €6. An *allé et retour* (return ticket) is €1.20. The metro operates from 6.30am to 1am.

AROUND LISBON

SINTRA
pop 20,000

This hill-top town, less than an hour west of Lisbon, has traditionally been the holiday home for royalty, the rich and the famous. With stunning palaces and manors surrounding by lush countryside it is a captivating camera-clicking place. Visit out of season if you can.

Orientation & Information

The Estefânia train station is 1.5km northeast of the centre, to which it's a 15-minute walk. Sintra's bus station, and another train station, are a further 1km east in the newtown district of Portela de Sintra. Frequent shuttle buses run to the historic centre from the bus and train stations.

The **tourist office** (☎ 219 231 157; www.cm -sintra.pt; Praça da República 23; ☼ 9am-7pm) has an accommodation list. The **Internet Lounge** (☎ 219 109 078; Rua Dr Alfredo da Costa 76; ☼ 10.30am-midnight Mon-Fri, 11.30am-11pm Sat, 12.30-10pm Sun) is near the centre.

Sights & Activities

Although the whole town resembles a historical theme park, there are several compulsory sights. Most are free or discounted with the *Lisboa Card* (p933); pensioners, students and children pay half-price.

Palácio Nacional de Sintra (☎ 219 106 840; €3; ☼ 10am-5.30pm Thu-Tue) is a dizzy mix of Moorish and Gothic architecture incorporating twin chimneys that dominate the town.

Museu do Brinquedo (☎ 219 242 172; Rua Visconde de Monserrate; €3; ☼ 10am-6pm Tue-Sun) is a serious playtime paradise with 20,000 toys from around the world.

An energetic 3km greenery-flanked trek from the centre will bring you to **Castelo dos Mouros** (☎ 219 237 300; €3; ☼ 9am-7pm), with fine views from the 8th-century ramparts.

Palácio da Pena (☎ 219 105 340; €6; ☼ 10am-5.30pm Tue-Sun), an exuberantly kitsch palace,

is a further 20 minutes' walk. Alternatively take bus No 434 (€3.20) from the station, via the tourist office.

Monserrate Gardens (☎ 219 237 116; €3; ☼ 9am-7pm) are lush botanical gardens 4km from town. The **Quinta da Regaleira** (☎ 219 106 650; €10; ☼ 10am-6pm, to 3.30pm winter) World Heritage site is en route to the gardens. Visits to this extraordinary mansion must be prearranged.

Cabra Montêz (☎ 917 446 668; www.cabramontez .com) caters for activities for anorak types, including trekking, mountain biking and canoeing.

Sleeping & Eating

Residencial Adelaide (☎ 219 230 873; Rua Guilherme Gomes Fernandes 11; d from €25) A lick of paint would do wonders for this great-value accommodation with its pretty garden and large well-worn rooms.

Camping Praia Grande (☎ 219 290 581; per adult/ camp site €2.50/4) A pebble's throw from the beach, this camping ground 11km from Sintra with frequent buses.

Xentra (☎ 219 240 759; Rua Consiglieri Pedroso 2-A; mains €6) A beamed cavernous bar and restaurant, with rock music on Sunday nights.

Tulhas (☎ 219 232 378; Rua Gil Vicente 4-6; mains €7) Typically full of happily chomping locals, Tulhas dishes up comfort food like *bacalhau* with cream, plus a vegetarian option.

Taverna Bar (☎ 219 233 587; Escadinhas do Teixeira 3; mains €7) Homy place serving traditional dishes with salutary (and salivary) attention to detail. Try the roast pork.

Getting There & Around

Trains run every 15 minutes from Lisbon's Rossio station (€1.30, 45 minutes). Buses run hourly from Sintra to Estoril (€2.50, 40 minutes) and Cascais (€2.50, 45 minutes).

A taxi to Pena or Monserrate costs around €10 return. Horse-drawn carriages to Monserrate and back cost €55. Old trams run from Ribeira de Sintra (1.5km from the centre) to Praia das Maças, 12km to the west.

CASCAIS
pop 30,000

Cascais has grown from a fishing village into a sunbed-and-sandcastle resort which is packed in summer.

From the train and adjacent bus station it's a short walk south on Rua Frederico Arouca to the centre of town and tourist

office. The **tourist office** (☎ 214 868 204; www
.estorilcoast-tourism.com; Rua Visconde de Luz 14; 🕙 9am-
7pm Mon-Fri Sep-Jun, 9am-8pm Mon-Fri Jul-Aug, 10am-
6pm Sat & Sun year-round) has accommodation
lists and bus timetables; there's also a **tourist
police post** (☎ 214 863 929). You can slurp a
soda while checking your emails at **Golfinho**
(☎ 214 840 150; Sebastião Carvalho e Melo 17; 🕙 10am-
midnight Mon-Sat May-Sep, to 8pm Sat Oct-Apr).

Sights & Activities

Estoril is an old-fashioned resort 2km east
of Cascais with a superb sandy beach and
Europe's largest **casino** (☎ 214 667 700; www
.casino-estoril.pt; 🕙 3pm-3am, nightly floorshow 11pm).

Praia Tamariz beach has an ocean swimming pool. The sea roars into the coast at
Boca do Inferno (Hell's Mouth) 2km west of
Cascais. Spectacular **Cabo da Roca**, Europe's
westernmost point, is 16km from Cascais
and Sintra (served by buses from both
towns). Wild **Guincho** beach, 3km from Cascais, is a popular surfing venue.

Transrent (☎ 214 864 566; www.transrent.pt; Centro
Commercial Cisne, Av Marginal) rents cars, bicycles
and motorcycles.

Sleeping & Eating

Residencial Avenida (☎ 214 864 417; Rua da Palmeira 14; d €30) Sparkling-clean well-placed
accommodation efficiently run by English-
speaking owners.

Camping Orbitur do Guincho (☎ 214 871 014;
Areia; per adult/camp site €4.50/5) A thousand sites
1km from Guincho beach with playground,
tennis courts and grocery.

Dom Grelhas, Casa da Guia (☎ 214 839 963; Rua
Sebastião JC Melo 35; mains €8) En route to Guincho, Casa da Guia is a fashionable, small
complex of edgy boutiques, art galleries,
bars and restaurants – including this one –
with its healthy salad and seafood choice
accompanied by seamless sea views.

Getting There & Away

Trains run frequently to Cascais, via Estoril
(€1.30, 30 minutes) from Cais do Sodré station in Lisbon.

SETÚBAL

pop 110,000

Portugal's third-largest port has a stunning
church, a spectacular castle and a largely
pedestrianised centre packed with good-
looking shops and cafés. Pity about the

in-your-face piped music over the city
sound system.

Orientation & Information

The municipal **tourist office** (☎ /fax 265 534 402;
Praça do Quebedo; 🕙 9am-7pm) is a five-minute
walk east from the **bus station** (Av 5 de Outubro).
There's also a **regional tourist office** (☎ 265
539 130; www.mun-setubal.pt; Travessa Frei Gaspar 10)
with the oddity of a Roman fish-preserv-
ing factory under its glass floor. The **Instituto
Português da Juventude** (IPJ; ☎ 265 534 431; Largo
José Afonso) has free Internet access for limited
periods on weekdays.

Sights & Activities

Portugal's first Manueline building, **Igreja
de Jesus** (Praça Miguel Bombarda), has twisted pillars that resemble coiled ropes. The nearby
Galeria da Pintura Quinhentista (admission free;
🕙 9am-noon & 2-5pm Tue-Sat) has a renowned
collection of 16th-century paintings.

Good **beaches** west of town include Praia
da Figueirinha (accessible by bus in summer).
Across the estuary at Tróia is a more developed beach, plus a ruined Roman settlement.
On the ferry trip you may see some of the
estuary's 30 or so bottlenose dolphins.

SAL (☎ 265 227 685; www.sal.pt; 🕙 Sat only) organises walks from €5 per person. For jeep
safaris, trekking and biking in the Serra
da Arrábida, or canoe trips through the
Reserva Natural do Estuário do Sado, con-
tact **Planeta Terra** (☎ 919 471 871; Praça General Luís
Domingues 9). **Vertigem Azul** (☎ 265 238 000; www
.vertigemazul.com; Av Luísa Todi 375) offers canoe
and dolphin-spotting excursions.

Sleeping & Eating

Pousada da Juventude (☎ 265 534 431; setubal@
movijovem.pt; Largo José Afonso; dm/d €11/35) This
well-equipped tidy hostel has a buzzy vibe.

Municipal Camping (☎ 265 522 475; per adult/
camp site €3.50/4) About 1.5km west of town is
this well-tended and well-equipped site.

Pensão Bom Regresso (☎ 265 229 812; Praça de
Bocage 48; d €40) Monastically basic overlooking
the main square; about as close to church as
you can get without attending confession.

Residencial Bocage (☎ 265 543 080; fax 265 543
089; Rua São Cristovão 14; s/d €27/45) Fairly forgetta-
ble rooms in a newish building; satellite TV
and nearby parking are major perks.

O Beco (☎ 265 524 617; Largo da Misericórdia 24;
mains €8-10) Locals rate this as the city's best

dining option. Go for the cockles for that special seafood moment.

Peregrina (☎ 265 230 602; Rua dos Almocreves 74; mains €8) One of three vegetarian restaurants in town (unfortunately all close at an unsociable 6pm). Quiche, *seitan* (wheat gluten), nut rissoles and more salads than you can shake a carrot stick at.

Getting There & Away
Buses leave every half-hour from Lisbon's Praça de Espanha (€3.10, 60 minutes). Ferries shuttle across the estuary to Tróia roughly every 45 minutes (€1.10, 15 minutes).

THE ALGARVE

The Algarve is popular, not only as a seaside holiday resort, but also for an increasing number of permanent residents, particularly from Germany and the UK. While this may sound depressing, away from the coastal strip (and the golf courses) you are back in Portugal again with attractions that include the forested slopes of Monchique, the fortified village of Silves and windswept, historic Sagres. Faro is the regional capital.

You can travel the Algarve via the rail line running from Lagos to the Spanish border; local tourist offices have timetables.

FARO
pop 45,000
Aside from midsummer when there's no towel-space on the beach, Faro is pleasantly low-key. It's also the main transport hub and commercial centre.

Orientation & Information
From the airport, catch bus No 14 or 16 for the 6km trip to the centre. A taxi costs about €12. The bus and train terminals are on Av da República a few minutes' walk north of town. The **tourist office** (☎ 289 803 604; wwwrt algarve.pt; Rua da Misericórdia) has informative leaflets. **Self-Service Internet** (☎ 289 873 731; Largo Pé da Cruz 1; ☾ closed Sun) is central.

Sights & Activities
The palm-clad **waterfront** has pleasant kickback cafés. Faro's beach, **Praia de Faro** (Ilha de Faro) is 6km southwest of town; take bus No 16 from the bus station. Less crowded

is unspoilt **Ilha Desserta** in the **Parque Natural da Ria Formosa** (☎ 917 811 856; lagoon tours €10). Access is by ferry June to mid-September from Cais da Porta Nova.

Sleeping & Eating
Avoid midsummer when many hotels are block-booked by tours.

Pousada da Juventude (☎ 289 826 521; Rua da Polícia de Segurança Pública 1; dm/d €10/22) Welcoming low-key accommodation that is often filled with groups.

Pensão Residencial Central (☎ 289 807 291; Largo Terreiro do Bispo 10; s/d €30/40) Clean, if characterless. The main drawcard here is its position, overlooking a jacaranda-fringed square.

Residencial Adelaide (☎ 289 802 383; fax 289 826 870; Rua Cruz dos Mestres 7; s/d €35/45) Lots of clinical white with large rooms, balconies, a rooftop terrace and a chatty owner. It has a unit suitable for disabled people.

Sol e Jardim (☎ 289 820 030; Praça Ferreira de Almeida 22; mains €9) This atmospheric seafood restaurant is decorated with nets, jolly murals and aquariums. Try the seafood spaghetti.

Velha Casa (☎ 289 824 719; Rua do Pé da Cruz 33; mains €7) Solid traditional grub is served, including kebabs, pork with pineapple and rib-sticking rice pud.

Getting There & Away
Faro airport handles domestic and international flights.

There are six daily express coaches to Lisbon (€14, four hours) and frequent buses to other coastal towns. Four trains run daily to Lisbon (€10, five hours).

TAVIRA
pop 12,000
Lovely Tavira is more touristy these days, but still oozes old-world charm. The **tourist office** (☎ 281 322 511; Rua da Galeria 9; ☾ 9.30am-12.30pm, 2-5.30pm Mon-Fri Oct-Apr) can help with accommodation. The **Praça da República** (town hall; ☾ closed Sun) provides free Internet access.

One of the town's 30-plus churches, striking **Igreja da Misericórdia** is a concert venue during the **Algarve International Classical Music Festival** (☾ May-Jul). Tavira's ruined **castle** (Rua da Liberdade; admission free; ☾ 8am-4.30pm Mon-Fri, 10am-5.30pm Sat & Sun) dominates the town.

Ilha da Tavira is an island beach accessible by a ferry from Quatro Águas, 2km from the centre. There's a (summer only) bus.

Enjoy pedal power with a rented bike from **Casa Abilio** (☎ 281 323 467). For walking or biking trips call **Exploratio** (☎ 919 338 226). To sail, contact **Clube Náutico** (☎ 281 326 858). José Salvador Rocha organises **diving trips** (☎ 939 017 329).

Pensão Residencial Lagoas (☎ 281 322 252; Almirante Cândido dos Reis 24; s/d €30/40) is handy for self-catering, being across the road from a supermarket. Rooms are dingy but clean. **Residencial Imperial** (☎ 281 322 234; José Pires Padinha 24; s/d €25/40) is a no-nonsense *pensão* with lovely sun-drenched balconies and a classy restaurant. The **Municipal Campsite** (☎ 281 324 455; Ilha da Tavira; per adult/camp site €5/5.50) is a summer-only camping option on the Ilha da Tavira.

For a good meal try **Restaurante Bica** (☎ 281 332 483; below Residencial Lagoas; mains €7; 😃), serving succulent sole with orange followed by home-made almond cake.

Some 15 trains and at least six express buses run daily between Faro and Tavira (€1.80, 45 minutes).

LAGOS
pop 20,000

A busy fishing port with beaches, Lagos has a laid-back vibe. From the train station, cross the river, turn right along Av dos Descobrimentos, and it's a 15-minute walk to the centre. The bus station is a block back from Av dos Descobrimentos: turn right and the centre is an easy 10-minute stroll.

The municipal **tourist office** (☎ 282 764 111; www.lagosdigital.com; Largo Marquês de Pombal; 😃 10am-6pm Mon-Sat) is convenient; the other is a 1km trek from the centre. Surf through a cappuccino and emails at voguish **Bora Café** (☎ 282 083 438; Conselheiro Joaquim Machado 17).

The **municipal museum** houses archaeological finds and ecclesiastical treasures. The best beach scene is at **Meia Praia** to the east, and **Praia da Luz** and reclusive **Praia do Pinhão** to the west.

Blue Ocean (☎ 282 782 718; www.blue-ocean-divers .de) organises diving, kayaking and snorkelling safaris. On the seaside promenade, fishermen run motorboat jaunts to nearby grottoes. For horse riding, ring **Tiffany's** (☎ 282 697 395). Bikes, including motorbikes and mopeds, are available from **Motoride** (☎ 289 761 720; Rua José Afonso 23; per day from €5).

Pousada da Juventude (☎ 282 761 970; Rua Lançarote de Freitas 50; dm/d €16/44) is up there with the best; rooms are light and airy and there's a cosy kitchen and garden. **Pensão Caravaela** (☎ 289 763 361; 25 de Abril 16; d from €32) has plain comfy rooms on a busy pedestrian street; you may need earplugs on a Saturday night. **Campismo da Trindade** (☎ 282 763 893; per adult/camp site €3/3.50) doesn't have much tent-peg space in summer; it's 200m south of the town walls.

Maharaja de Lagos (☎ 282 761 507; Dr Jose Formozinho; mains €7) is high above the old town with spicy stand-bys like baltis, biryanis and bhunas. At **Taberna de Lagos** (☎ 282 084 250; 25 de Abril; mains €7) a former warehouse equals an arty grand space with beams and arches. The menu includes pizzas, pastas and vegetarian dishes. **Lounge www.Cocktail** (☎ 963 821 067; Sr da Graç 2; snacks €3) is a Brit-run bar with chicken tikka, quiche and piled-high nachos. There are DJs on weekend nights.

Bus and train services depart frequently for other Algarve towns and around six times daily to Lisbon (€14, four hours).

SILVES
pop 10,500

This genteel small town is the former capital of Moorish Algarve. Get fortified and trek to the fairy-tale **castle** on the hill.

Silves train station is 2km from town with a connecting bus. If arriving by bus you'll be dropped at the foot of the town. The **tourist office** (☎ 289 442 255; Rua 25 de Abril; 😃 Mon-Fri & Sat morning) is central. The **post office** (Rua do Correio) has a Netpost (Internet) kiosk.

Residencial Sousa (☎ 282 442 502; Rua Samoura Barros 17; s/d €15/30) has no-frills rooms in the centre of town, and **Residencial Ponte Romana** (☎ 282 443 275; d €30) has an excellent location beside a Roman bridge with castle views, Sky TV and a cavernous bar-restaurant full of crusty locals.

Café Ingles (☎ 282 442 585; mains €8), below the castle, is an English-owned, funky place that serves up vegetarian dishes, home-made soups and wood-fired pizza, plus sultry Brazilian café music on Sunday summer afternoons. Push the boat out at **Restaurante Rui** (☎ 282 442 682; Rua C Vilarinho 27; mains from €9), a superb fish restaurant with everything from spider crab to cockles.

Nine trains run daily from Lagos (€1.50, 35 minutes), met by local buses. Six buses run daily to Silves from Albufeira (€2.75, 40 minutes).

PORTUGAL

SAGRES
pop 2500

Sagres is all drama and history with its position in Portugal's southwest corner and its evocative fort perched above the thundering surf. There is a central **tourist office** (☎ 282 624 873; Rua Comandante Matoso; ☺ 10am-1.30pm & 2.30-6pm Mon-Fri, 10am-1.30pm Sat). **Turinfo** (☎ 282 620 003; Praça da República) rents cars and bikes, books hotels and arranges jeep and fishing trips.

The **fort** (€3; ☺ 10am-6.30pm Mon-Sat, 10am-8.30pm Sun) has a 12-minute slide show on the history of Sagres; Henry the Navigator established his navigation school here and primed the explorers who later founded the Portuguese empire.

You can hire windsurfers at sand-dune flanked **Praia do Martinhal**. **Surfcamp** (Mestre António Galhardo; from €30) organises canoeing trips plus surfing and bodyboard classes.

Visit Europe's southwesternmost point, **Cabo de São Vicente** (Cape St Vincent), 6km to the west. A solitary lighthouse stands on this barren cape.

Parque de Campismo Sagres (☎ 282 624 351) is 2km from town, off the Vila do Bispo road. **Mar à Vista** (☎ 282 624 247; Praia da Mareta; mains €8) has sea-and-surf views from the terrace. Med cuisine includes pasta with lobster and an eight-salad choice.

Frequent daily buses run from Lagos (€2.50, 50 minutes). Three of them continue to Cabo de São Vicente on weekdays.

CENTRAL PORTUGAL

The central slice of Portugal has a raw, rugged beauty with tumbling rivers, dense forests and stone villages, and local women still carry their shopping on their head. The coast has more sunbed space than further south, while the more energetic can enjoy trekking and skiing in the dramatic Beiras region. There's good sightseeing with castles, fortresses and Roman temples.

ÉVORA
pop 50,000

A Unesco World Heritage site, medieval-era Évora is walled, with cobblestones, narrow alleys and arches, plus blockbuster mansions and palaces. It is hugely atmospheric and well worth a stroll around, despite the mild overdose of souvenir shops.

Orientation & Information

The train station is 1km southeast of the centre; follow Rua da República. Arriving by bus will land you about 1km out; there are regular shuttle buses. The **tourist office** (☎ 266 702 671; www.cm-evora.pt; Praça do Giraldo 73; ☺ 9am-7pm Mon-Sat) has an excellent city map. Log on at the **Cyber Center** (☎ 266 746 923; Rua dos Mercadores 42; ☺ 9am-2am).

Sights & Activities

Évora's **Sé** (Largo do Marquês de Marialva; €2.25; ☺ 9am-noon & 2-5pm) has fabulous cloisters and a museum jam-packed with ecclesiastical treasures.

A little north of the cathedral, the **Temple of Diana** is the best-preserved Roman temple in Iberia. Enough said. The museum opposite is closed for renovation until early 2005.

Capela dos Ossos (☎ 266 744 307; Largo Conde de Vila Flor; €2; ☺ 9am-1pm & 2.30-6pm) was discovered in 1958. This ghoulish Chapel of Bones is constructed with the bones and skulls of several thousand people; not for the faint-hearted.

Turaventur (☎ 266 743 134; www.evora.net/turaventur; Qta Serrado, Sr Aflitos) runs various adrenaline-fuelled activities, including **canoeing** (half-day/€60) and **mountain biking** (€35 per 4 hr).

Policarpo (☎ 266 746 970; www.policarpo-viagens.pt; Rua 5 de Outubro 63) organises jaunts to megaliths and other nearby attractions. **Bike Lab** (☎ 266 735 500; Centro Comercial da Vista Alegre, Lote 14; ☺ summer only) rents bicycles.

Sleeping & Eating

Pousada da Juventude (☎ 266 744 848; Rua Miguel Bombarda 40; dm/d €14/35) Recently renovated, this youth hostel has a bright and imaginative interior.

Residencial O Alentejo (☎ 266 702 903; Rua Serpa Pinto 74; s/d €30/35) Nothing fancy but with a certain charm thanks to folksy-painted furniture and a courtyard with cats.

Pensão Policarpo (☎ 266 702 424; www.localnet.pt/residencialpolicarpo; Rua da Freiria de Baixo 16; s/d €30/40; ✷) Hats off for the setting: 17th-century manor house with Roman columns and part of the original city wall in the foyer. It has large pleasant rooms with views.

Orbitur Camping Ground (☎ 266 705 190; per adult/camp site €3/3.75) This rudimentary, green camping ground is open year-round. It's 2km southwest of town on the N380.

Sopas da Terra (☎ 266 744 703; Rua da Moeda 5; snacks €3) Expect to queue at this young-vibe

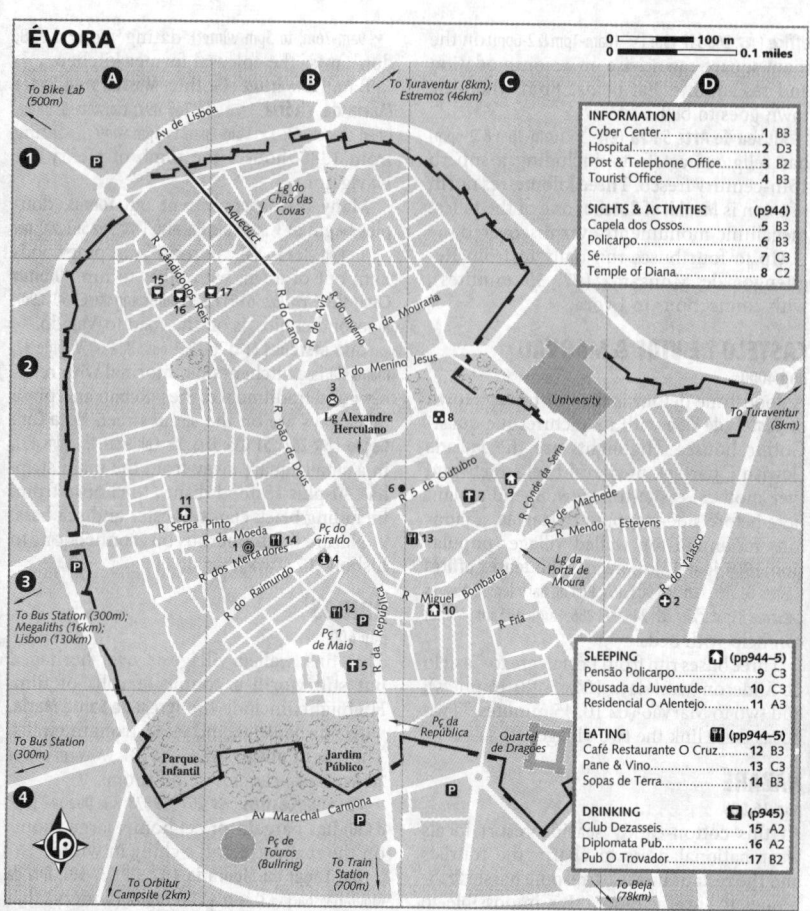

ÉVORA

0 — 100 m
0 — 0.1 miles

café-restaurant serving belly-warming soups, doorstop sandwiches and *salgados* (savoury pasties).

Café Restaurant O Cruz (☎ 266 747 228; Praça 1 de Maio 20; mains €6) Earthy and inexpensive for a spot of refuelling with plain, filling fare such as *acorda com bacalhau e ovo escalfado* (bread soup with codfish and egg).

Pane & Vino (☎ 266 746 960; Páteo do Salema 22; mains €7; ⓒ closed Mon) Sunny colours, cheery staff and a vast menu including an upper-class of pizza, swanky salads and creamy tiramisu.

Drinking
Club Dezasseis (☎ 266 706 559; Rua do Escrivão da Cá-mara 16) Attracts a mix of suits and scruffs.

Diplomata Pub (☎ 266 705 675; Rua do Apóstolo 4) Live music and a frazzled bar staff.

Pub O Trovador (☎ 266 707 370; Rua da Mostar-deira 4) A chilled-out setting for a smarter crowd.

Getting There & Away
Six weekday buses to Lisbon (€9.50, 1½ hours) and two to Faro (€11.50, four hours) run from the main station. Three trains run daily from Lisbon (€7.10, 2½ hours).

MONSARAZ
pop 100
With an exceptional setting, high above the plain, this walled village has a medieval at-mosphere and magnificent views. The **tourist**

PORTUGAL

office (☎ 266 557 136; ☾ 10am-1pm & 2-6pm) on the main square can advise on accommodation and restaurants. Eat before 8pm when the town goes to bed.

Museu de Arte Sacra (€1; ☾ 10am-1pm & 2-6pm) has religious artefacts, including a superb 15th-century fresco. Three kilometres north of town is **Menhir of Outeiro**, one of the tallest megalithic monuments ever discovered.

Up to four buses run daily to/from Reguengos de Monsaraz (€2, 35 minutes), with connections to Évora.

CASTELO DE VIDE & MARVÃO
pop 4000

A good-time detour is the hill-top spa town of **Castelo de Vide** with its picturesque quasi-Gothic houses. Highlights are the **Judiaria** (Jewish Quarter), medieval backstreets and (yet another) castle-top view. Spend a night here before side-stepping to **Marvão**, a fabulous mountain-top walled village (population 190) just 12km away. The **tourist offices** (Castelo de Vide ☎ 245 901 361; Rua de Bartolomeu Álvares da Santa 81; Marvão ☎ 245 993 886; Largo de Santa Maria) can help with beds.

Three buses run from Portalegre to Castelo de Vide on weekdays (€4.65, 20 minutes), and two to Marvão (€2.10, 45 minutes). Two buses daily link the two villages.

NAZARÉ
pop 16,000

At this cotton-candy seaside resort locals wear national dress to charm the tourists and the restaurants use tiresome hassle techniques to lure in diners. It's impossible to park here in summer. On the plus side, the beach is sweeping and sandy and the catch-of-the-day seafood is superb.

The nearest train station, 6km away at Valado, is connected to Nazaré by frequent buses. The bus station is central to town. The **tourist office** (☎ 262 561 194; ☾ 10am-8pm May-Sep, 10am-1pm & 3-7pm Oct-Apr) is on the seafront.

Beaches are the main attraction here. Swimmers should beware of dangerous currents. Climb or take the funicular to cliff-top **Sítio** with its cluster of fisherman's cottages and technicolour views.

Two of Portugal's big-time architectural masterpieces are close by. Follow the signs to **Alcobaça** where, right in the centre of town, is the immense **Mosteiro de Santa Maria de Alcobaça** (☎ 262 505 120; €3, church admission free;

☾ 9am-7pm, to 5pm winter) dating from 1178; don't miss the colossal former kitchen.

Batalha's huge Gothic **Mosteiro de Santa Maria de Vitória** (☎ 244 765 497; cloisters & unfinished chapels €3; ☾ 9am-6pm, to 5pm winter), dating from 1388, houses the tomb of Henry the Navigator.

Many townspeople rent out **rooms**; doubles begin at €35. **Vale Paraíso** (☎ 262 561 800; per adult/camp site €3.50/4) camp site is in pinewoods 2km out of town, with bikes to hire. **Orbitur Campsite** (☎ 262 561 111; per adult/camp site €3.50/3.90), a second choice, is on the road to Valado.

Casa Marques (☎ 262 551 680; Rua Gil Vicente 37; mains €5) is a kitchen-sink informal with reliably good traditional dishes. Kebab and pizza takeaways are on the same street. **Nova Casa Caçao** (☎ 262 551 035; Rua das Caldeiras 1; mains €7), in a small square away from the main strip, has 40-plus seafood dishes to choose from, including black clams, lobster and sea bass.

Nazaré has numerous bus connections to Lisbon (€7, two hours).

ÓBIDOS
pop 600

This tiny walled village is over-heritaged but still worth a couple of rolls of film. Highlights include the **Igreja de Santa Maria**, with fine *azulejos*, and views from the walls. The **tourist office** (☎ 262 959 231; www.cm-obidos .pt; Rua Direita) can advise on rooms.

Casa dos Castros (☎ 262 959 328; Rua Direita 83-85; d €30) has bargain-price, homy, large rooms on the main street. It's chilly in winter.

Bar Lagar da Mouraria (☎ 919 937 601; Rua da Mouraria; snacks €3) is a 1770 *lagar* (winery) that creates a moody setting for a multilevel bar-restaurant dishing up tasty stacked sandwiches such as avocado, peppers and cheese. **Café-Restaurante 1 de Dezembro** (☎ 262 959 298; Largo de São Pedro) is just a swallow's swoop from lovely **Igreja de São Pedro** with a terrace to kick back with a coffee or beer.

There's a weekday direct bus from Lisbon (€7.10, two hours) or via Caldas da Rainha, 10 minutes away.

TOMAR
pop 17,000

This is a town with history, charm – and a rare vegetarian restaurant. Tomar reached dizzy historical heights as the headquarters of the Knights Templar and is home to the outstanding Unesco-listed **Convento de Cristo**.

Cradling the monastery's southern walls is the awesome 17th-century **Aqueduto de Pegões** (aqueduct), beyond which extends the dense greenery of the **Mata Nacional dos Sete Montes** (Seven Hills National Forest). Tomar's **tourist office** (☎ 249 329 000; www.rttemplarios.pt; Rua Serpa Pinto) can provide town and forest maps.

Pensão Residencial União (☎ 249 323 161; Rua Serpa Pinto 94; d €35) is within a reasonable baggage lug from a car park, this gracious older home has dark wood furnishing and creaky floorboards. **Camping Redondo** (☎ 249 376 421; per adult/camp site €4/4.50; 🏊) is run by English-speaking owners, with a pool and a leafy setting 10km south of town.

Gaia (☎ 249 311 109; Rua dos Moínhos 75; mains €6; 🕙 9am-8pm Mon-Fri, 9am-2pm Sat) has just a few tables and daily dishes like *seitan* stew, tofu burgers or meatless *feijada* (Brazilian bean stew). **Casinha d'Avó Bia** (☎ 249 323 828; Rua Dr Joaquim Jacinto 16; mains €8), despite its disquieting multilingual menu, has good-quality meals. Try the seafood *açorda* (fish and bread stew). Also recommended is **Estalagem de Santa Iria** (☎ 249 313 326; Mouchão Parque; s/d €65/85; **P** 🏊).

There are at least four express buses daily to Lisbon (€6.20, two hours) and even more frequent trains (€5.60, two hours).

COIMBRA

pop 150,000

Coimbra has a lively young vibe thanks to the student life centred around the magnificent 13th-century university. It's a handsome, eclectic city with elegant shopping streets and ancient stone walls. Coimbra was the birth and burial place of Portugal's first king, Afonso Henriques.

Coimbra's annual highlight is **Queima das Fitas**, a boozy week of *fado* and revelry that begins on the first Thursday in May.

Orientation & Information

There are three train stations – Coimbra A, Coimbra B and Coimbra Parque. Most trains arrive at Coimbra A, a short walk from the centre. The main bus station is about 15 minutes' walk northwest of the centre.

Esp@ço Internet (Praça 8 de Maio; 🕙 10am-8pm Mon-Fri, to 10pm Sat & Sun) has free Internet access for 30 minutes. The **regional tourist office** (☎ 239 855 930; www.turismo-centro.pt; Largo da Portagem) is not as useful as the **municipal tourist office** (☎ 239 832 591; Praça Dom Dinis) which has a second **branch** (☎ 239 833 202; Praça da República).

Sight & Activities

Mosteiro de Santa Cruz (☎ 239 822 941; Rua Visconde da Luz; €1; 🕙 9am-noon & 2-5pm) has a fabulous ornate pulpit and medieval royal tombs. Get here via the **lift** (single €1, tickets from booth or kiosks) by the market.

On the same street as the monastery is the grand **University Velha** (☎ 239 822 941; www.uc.pt/sri; €3; 🕙 10am-noon & 2-5pm). Visit the library with its gorgeous book-lined hallways and 1517 Manueline chapel.

Machado de Castro Museum (☎ 239 823 727; Largo Dr José Rodrigues; €3; 🕙 9.30am-12.30pm & 2-5.30pm) holds a diverse collection of sculpture and paintings in a 12th-century building, itself a work of art.

Conimbriga, 16km south of Coimbra, is the site of the well-preserved ruins of a **Roman town** (🕙 9am-8pm summer, 10am-6pm winter), including mosaic floors, baths and fountains. There's a good site **museum** (€3; 🕙 same hours) with a restaurant. Frequent buses run to Condeixa, 2km from the site; direct buses depart at 9.05am or 9.35am (only 9.35am at weekends) from Coimbra's **AVIC terminal** (Rua João de Ruão 18) returning at 1pm and 6pm (only 6pm at weekends).

Odabarca (☎ 966 040 695; Parque Dr Manuel Braga; from €18) rents canoes and kayaks for paddling the Mondego River. A free minibus takes you to Penacova for the 25km river journey.

Sleeping

Pousada da Juventude (☎ 239 822 955; coimbra@movijovem.pt; Rua António Henriques Seco 12-14; dm/d €12/29) This is a solid, efficiently run hostel; take bus No 7 from the Astoria hotel on Av Emíilio Navarro 50m south of Coimbra A train station.

Pensão Santa Cruz (☎ 239 826 197; Praça 8 de Maio; d €32) Threadbare large rooms in an old building overlook one of the city's most dynamic squares.

Pensão Flôr de Coimbra (☎ 239 823 865; fax 239 821 545; Rua do Poço 5; d from €35) There's loads of atmosphere in this renovated family home run by the sons; the restaurant has a small daily vegetarian menu.

Casa Pombal Guesthouse (☎ 239 835 175; www.casa.pombal@oninet.pt; Rua das Flores 18; d from €38) Has pretty rooms painted in pastel colours with rooftop views. The Dutch owner includes a blow-out breakfast in the price.

Pensão Residencial Larbelo (☎ 239 829 092; fax 239 829 094; Largo da Portagem 33; d €45) This place lacks charm, but the rooms are standard and large.

Also recommended is **Residência Coimbra** (☎ 239 837 996; fax 239 838 124; Rua das Azeiteiras 55; s/d €35/45).

Eating

Head west of Praça do Comércio, around Rua das Azeiteiras, for cheap eats.

O Cantinho das Escadas (☎ 239 820 578; Rua dos Gato 29; mains €4) The house wine at this brightly lit café would be better for pickling onions, but the stews (fish, pork and veal) are excellent value.

Restaurante Democrática (☎ 239 823 784; Travessa da Rua Nova; mains €6) This barrel-lined restaurant dishes up stoking chow such as *caldo verde* (potato soup with cabbage and sausage) in a low-key, chummy atmosphere.

Restaurante Jardim da Manga (☎ 239 829 156; Rua Olímpio Nicolau Rui Fernanda; mains €7; ☯ closed Sat) A better breed of self-service restaurant at the back of the Mosteiro de Santa Cruz. Vegetarian dishes are available.

Zé Manel (☎ 239 823 790; Beco do Forno 12; mains €5; ☯ Mon-Fri, lunch only Sat) Great food, huge servings and a zany atmosphere with walls papered with diners' comments, cartoons and poems. Vegetarian choices.

Café Santa Cruz (☎ 239 833 617; Praça 8 de Maio) A former chapel has been resurrected into one of Portugal's most atmospheric casual-vibe cafés.

Clubbing

Vinyl (☎ 239 404 047; Av Afonso Henriques 43) and **Via Latina** (☎ 239 833 034; Rua Almeida Garrett 1) are a couple of popular discos for the bump and grinders.

Entertainment

Coimbra-style *fado* is more cerebral than the Lisbon variety, and its adherents staunchly protective. **Bar Diligência** (☎ 239 827 667; Rua Nova 30) and **Boémia Bar** (☎ 239 834 547; Rua do Cabido 6) are popular *casas de fado*.

Á Capella (☎ 239 833 985; Capela de Nossa Senhora de Victoría, Rua Corpo de Deus, Largo da Victoría; ☯ 10.30pm Thu-Sat) is a fabulous new *fado* place attracting a groovy young crowd with nightly shows in a former chapel.

Getting There & Away

At least a dozen buses and as many trains run daily from Lisbon (€9.20, 2½ hours) and Porto (€8.50, 1½ hours), plus there are frequent express buses from Faro and Évora, via Lisbon. Other useful connections are to Figueira da Foz and eight buses daily to Luso/Buçaco (from Coimbra A).

LUSO & THE BUÇACO FOREST
pop 2000

This area has other-worldly appeal with a dense forest of century-old trees surrounded by an impressionist-style landscape dappled with heather, wild flowers and leafy ferns. Buçaco was chosen as a retreat by 16th-century monks and surrounds the pretty spa town of Luso.

The **tourist office** (☎ /fax 231 939 133; Av Emídio Navarro; ☯ 9.30am-12.30pm & 2-6pm) has leaflets about the forest and trails, as well as free **Internet** access. The **Termas** (thermal baths; ☎ 231 937 910; Av Emídio Navarro; ☯ May-Oct) offer various treatments.

Astória (☎ 231 939 182; Av Emídio Navarro; s/d €20/30) has dark wood and beams to create cosy surroundings at this *pensão* near the baths. **Palace Hotel do Buçaco** (☎ 231 930 101; www.almeida hotels.com; s/d from €145/185) is a special-occasion place; a sumptuous pile with gargoyles, Manueline extravagance, ornamental garden and Edwardian-style gracious rooms. The equally elegant **restaurant** has a €40 *menu*.

Restaurante O Cesteiro (☎ 231 939 360; EN 234; mains €7) has a large dining room with an extensive menu of traditional dishes. The grilled chicken is a winner.

There are three buses on weekdays, two on Saturday and one on Sunday from Coimbra (€2.50, 50 minutes). One daily train departs around 10.30am from Coimbra B (€1.30, 30 minutes).

SERRA DA ESTRELA

Forested Serra da Estrela has a raw natural beauty plus some of the country's best trekking. This is Portugal's highest mainland mountain range (1993m), and it's the source of its two great rivers: the Mondego River and the Zêzere River. The **main park office** (☎ 275 980 060; fax 275 980 069), in Manteigas, has loads of information on the park; there are additional offices at Gouveia and Guarda (these are claimed to be the highest city in Europe). Other good sources of information about the region are the local **tourist offices** (Guarda ☎ 271 205 530; www .domdigital.pt/cm-guarda; Covilhã ☎ 275 319 560).

À Descoberta da Estrela is a walking guide with maps and narratives. Park offices and some tourist offices sell an English edition (€4.25), plus a detailed topographic map of the park (€6).

Sleeping

Pousada da Juventude (☎ /fax 275 335 375; penhas@ movijem.pt; Penhas da Saúde; dm/d from €10/25) Located 10km above Covilhã, this excellent hostel and good excursion base provides meals or kitchen facilities. Buses come from Covilhã (twice daily, July to September only), or you can walk or taxi it (about €10).

There's another **Pousada da Juventude** (☎ /fax 271 224 482; guarda@movijovem.pt; dm/d from €9/22) at Guarda; and Seia, Gouveia, Guarda and Covilhã also have an array of modestly priced **guesthouses**.

Getting There & Around

Several buses run daily from Coimbra, along the park's perimeter to Seia, Gouveia, Guarda or Covilhã, plus others via Covilhã (€4, 45 minutes) to Castel Branco (€7.50, 1¾ hours) and Lisbon, and several times daily to Viseu (€6.20, 1½ hours), Porto and Coimbra.

The twice-daily IC Line 110 train links Lisbon and Coimbra to Guarda (€12.80, 4¼ hours).

No buses cross the park, although you can go around it: Seia–Covilhã takes two hours via Guarda. At least two buses link Seia, Gouveia and Guarda daily, and considerably more run between Guarda and Covilhã.

NORTHERN PORTUGAL

Portugal's northern Minho region is a colourful patchwork of rolling country, dense forests and dramatic mountains. It's *vinho verde* country (that wholly addictive young green wine), but its capital Porto is named after another tipple and is a fascinating mix of the medieval and modern. Also here are two more heady historical cities: Braga, the country's religious heart and the finely situated Viana do Castelo.

PORTO

pop 300,000

Portugal's second-largest city, Porto, has definite charm. The combination of its slick commercial hub with the appealingly dilapidated river-frontage district, a well-deserved World Heritage site. Across the water is Vila Nova de Gaia, the headquarters of a thriving port trade since a 1703 agreement with England. More recently, Porto's role as one of the prime venues for the European 2004 Football Championships has meant a healthy boost to the economy and infrastructure.

Orientation

Porto centre is small enough to cover mainly by foot. The city clings to the north bank of the Douro River, spanned by five bridges across from Vila Nova de Gaia, home to the port-wine lodges. The picturesque Ribeira district lies along the waterfront.

Av dos Aliados runs straight through Porto's centre. The major shopping areas are eastward around the Bolhão Market and Rua Santa Catarina, and westward along Rua dos Clérigos. At the southern end of Av dos Aliados, Praça da Liberdade and São Bento train station are major local bus hubs. Another is Jardim da Cordoaria (called Jardim de João Chagas on some maps), about 400m westward.

GETTING INTO TOWN

The **AeroBus** (☎ 808 200 166; www.stcp.pt; €2.60; ☒ every half-hour 7.30am-7pm) runs between Av dos Aliados and the airport via Boavista. If you arrive by train or bus, there are several different terminals, however they are all fairly central to town – see Orientation, above.

Information

INTERNET ACCESS

Portoweb (☎ 222 005 922; Praça General Humberto Delgado 291; ☒ 10am-2am Mon-Sat, 3pm-2am Sun)

MEDICAL SERVICES

Santo António Hospital (☎ 222 077 500; Largo Prof Abel Salazar) Has English-speaking staff.

MONEY

Intercontinental (Rua de Ramalho Ortigão 8) Has exchange facilities.
Portocâmbios (Rua Rodrigues Sampaio 193)
Top Atlântico (☎ 222 074 020; trinidade@topatlantico .com; Rua Alferes Malheiro 96) Doubles as an AmEx representative.

PORTO

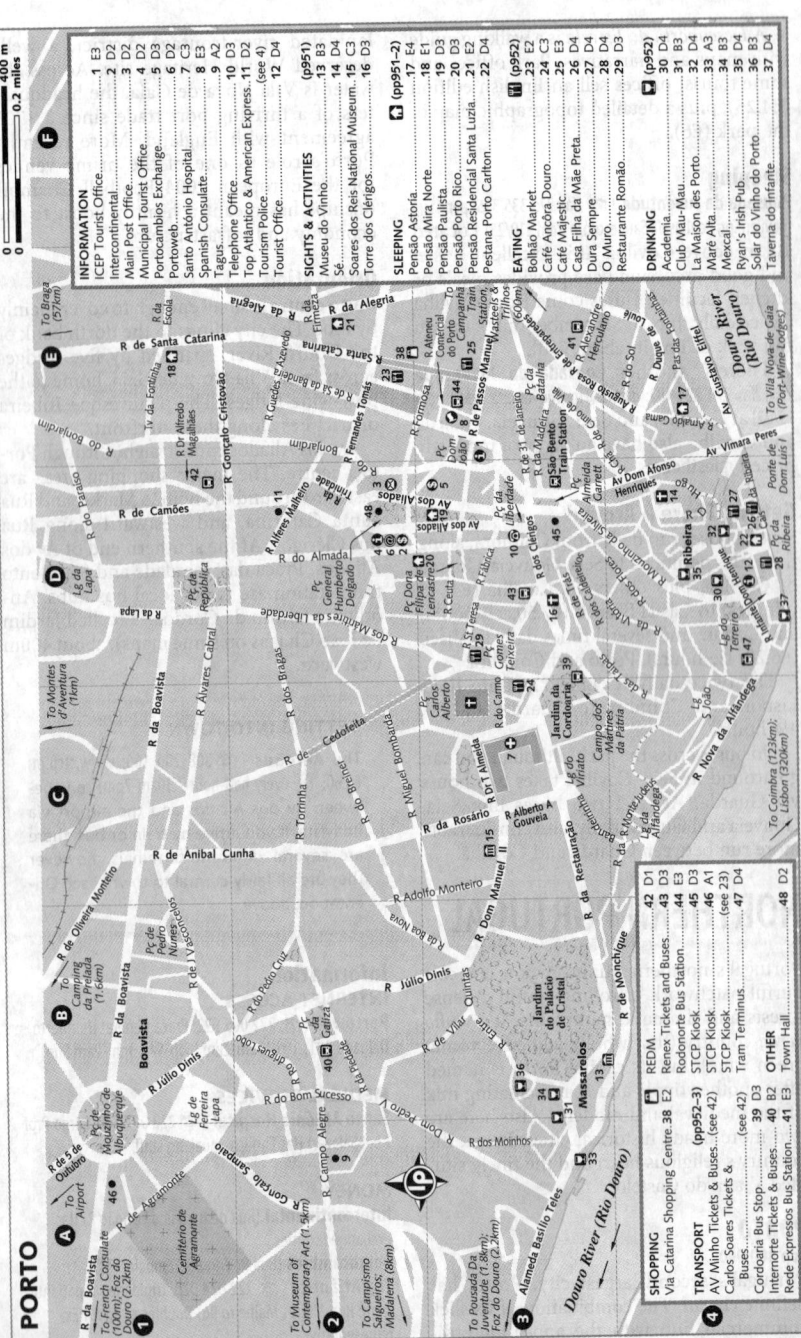

0   400 m
0   0.2 miles

POST

Main post office (Praça General Humberto Delgado) Across from the main tourist office.

TELEPHONE

Telephone office (Praça da Liberdade 62; ☺ 10am-10pm) With fax service.

TOURIST INFORMATION

ICEP Tourist office (☎ 222 057 514; fax 222 053 212; Praça Dom João I 43; ☺ 9am-7pm Mon-Fri, 9.30am-3.30pm Sat & Sun) This is the national tourist office.

Montes d'Aventura (☎ 228 305 157; Alameda Dr Antonio Macedo 19) Organises walking, cycling and canoeing trips.

Municipal tourist office (☎ 223 393 472; www .portoturismo.pt; Rua Clube dos Fenianos 25; ☺ 9am-5.30pm Mon-Fri, 9.30am-4.30pm Sat & Sun Oct-Jun, 9am-7pm Jul-Sep) Next door to the tourist police office.

Tourist office (☎ 222 009 770; Rua Infante Dom Henrique 63; ☺ 9am-5.30pm Mon-Fri)

Trilhos (☎ /fax 225 020 740; www.trilhos.pt; Rua de Belém 94) Another option for canoe and hydro speed excursions.

TRAVEL AGENCIES

Tagus (☎ 226 094 146; fax 226 094 141; Rua Campo Alegre 261) and **Wasteels** (☎ 225 194 230; fax 225 194 239; Rua Pinto Bessa 27/29), near Campanhã station, are youth-oriented agencies. See also **Top Atlântico** (p949).

Sights & Activities

Head for the riverfront **Ribeira** district for an atmospheric stroll around, checking out the gritty local bars, superb restaurants and river cruises. Note that for most museums and attractions, admission is half-price for children, students and seniors, and free for everyone on Sundays.

For a fine view head to **Torre dos Clérigos** (Rua dos Clérigos; €1; ☺ 10am-noon & 2-5pm). After 225 steep steps, you're rewarded with the best panorama of the city.

The **Sé** (☎ 222 059 028; Terreiro da Sé; cloisters €2; ☺ 9am-12.30pm & 2.30-7pm Apr-Oct, to 6pm rest of the year, closed Sun morning) dominates Porto and is worth a visit for its architecture and vast ornate interior.

The **Museum of Contemporary Art** (☎ 226 156 571; www.serralves.pt; Rua Dom João de Castro 210; €5; ☺ 10am-7pm Tue-Fri, 10am-8pm Sat & Sun Apr-Sep, to 7pm Oct-Mar) is enclosed by pretty gardens and has works by contemporary Portuguese artists.

Museu do Vinho (Wine Museum; ☎ 222 076 300; museuvinhoporto@cm-porto.pt; Rua de Monchique 45-52; admission free; ☺ 11am-7pm Tue-Sun) is Porto's newest museum and traces the history of wine and port with informative film and exhibits, and tastings.

Soares dos Reis National Museum (☎ 223 393 770; Rua Dom Manuel II 44; €3; ☺ 10am-6pm Wed-Sun) presents masterpieces of 19th- and 20th-century Portuguese painting and sculpture. Take bus 78 from Praça da Liberdade.

Port-Wine Lodges (Vila Nova de Gaia) offer daily tours and tastings, including **Osborne** (☎ 223 757 517; www.osborne.es; admission free).

Festivals & Events

Porto's big festivals are the **Festa de São João** (St John's Festival) in June and the international film festival **Fantasporto** in February. Also worth catching are the Celtic music festival in April–May, and the rock festival in August.

Sleeping

Pousada da Juventude (☎ 226 177 257; porto@movijovem.pt; Rua Paulo da Gama 551; dm/d €18/35) This tastefully spruced up hostel is 4km west of the centre. Reservations are essential. Take bus No 35 from Praça da Liberdade or No 1 from São Bento station.

Pensão Porto Rico (☎ 223 394 690; Rua do Almada 237; s/d €25/30; ✿) The small neat rooms have balconies, breakfast is provided and there's a homy, small bar.

Pensão Mira Norte (☎ 222 001 118; Rua de Santa Catarina 969; d €30) Basic rooms, well placed for shopaholics, but not so good at siesta time.

Pensão Astória (☎ 222 008 175; Rua Arnaldo Gama 56; d €35) Next to a handy car park or approach via the steep steps from the riverfront. Elegant old doubles, some with river views.

Pensão Residencial Santa Luzia (☎ 222 001 119; Rua da Alegria; d €35; ✿) Very pleasant, spotless rooms run by an elderly *senhora* who is still charging pre-euro rates.

Pensão Paulista (☎ 222 054 692; Av dos Aliados 214; s/d €40/50; ✿) Small shiny-wood rooms with balconies overlooking a tree-lined avenue crowned by the majestic city hall.

Pestana Porto Carlton (☎ 223 402 300; www .pestana.com; s/d €118/140; ⓟ ✕ ✿ ▣) High on atmosphere, this former 16th-century palace has seductive rooms and heady Douro and city views.

Campismo Salgueiros (☎ 227 810 500; fax 227 718 239; Praia de Salgueiros; per adult/camp site €2/2.50) This is one of three sites near the sea; all get packed in summer. Note that the coast here is too rocky and polluted for swimming.

PORTUGAL

Camping da Prelada (☎ 228 312 616; Rua Monte dos Burgos; per adult/camp site €3/3.50) Basic and big. Open all year, this site is 4km northwest of the centre. Take bus No 6 from Praça de Liberdade or 54 from Jardim da Cordoaria.

Also recommended is **Camping Madalena** (☎ 227 122 520; Praia da Madalena).

Eating

O Muro (☎ 222 083 426; Muro dos Bacalhoeiros 88; mains €7; ☽ noon-2am) The charismatic owner here is an ex-professional soccer player and tasty dishes include vegetarian choices. Delightful wacky décor ranges from dried *bacalhau* to Che Guevara; ask to see the guestbook.

Restaurante Romão (☎ 222 005 639; Praça Carlos Alberto 100; mains €7) This agreeable little restaurant has northern specialities such as tripe and roast kid. Leave room for the *torta de noz* (walnut tart).

Dura Sempre (☎ 222 008 488; Rua da Lada; mains €4.50) Fluorescent lighting, cramped tables but sound belly-filling fare such as steak or breaded veal with piles of rice and chips.

Casa Filha da Mãe Preta (☎ 222 055 515; Cais da Ribeira 40; mains €8-10; ☽ closed Sun) Head upstairs for Douro views from the *azulejo*-lined dining room. Simple fish and meat dishes served with veg, rice and boiled potatoes.

Café Majestic (☎ 222 003 887; Rua Santa Catarina 112; ☽ closed Sun) This café is an extravagant Art Nouveau relic where powdered ladies enjoy afternoon tea.

Café Ancôra Douro (☎ 222 003 749; Praça de Parada Leitão 49; snacks €3) Heaving with peckish students; the extensive menu includes veggie-burgers, hot dogs and crepes.

Bolhão market (Rua Formosa; ☽ closed Sun) Sells fruit and veg in season, plus cheese and deli goodies.

Drinking & Clubbing

Solar do Vinho do Porto (☎ 226 094 749; Rua Entre Quintas 220; ☽ 11am-midnight Mon-Sat) Laid-back yet elegant setting for tasting the port made just across the river.

La Maison des Porto (☎ 936 057 340; Rua São Joã 46; ☽ closed Sun) French-owned vinotheque where you can taste and be educated about port by the entertaining multilingual owner.

Ryan's Irish Pub (☎ 222 005 366; Rua Infante Dom Henrique 18) Has the usual range of gluggable beer in Irish-style surroundings.

Academia (☎ 222 005 737; Rua São João 80) Stylishly hip and smoky disco-bar.

Taverna do Infante (☎ 205 49 86; Rua da Alfândega 13) Atmospheric macho den with Brazilian dancers.

Mexcal (☎ 226 009 188; Rua da Restauração 39) Great Latino music for a little bit of late-night hip swinging.

Club Mau-Mau (☎ 226 076 660; Rua do Outeiro 4) A dodging-elbows disco with live music on Thursday nights.

Maré Alta (☎ 226 162 540; Rua do Ouro) Nailbitingly trendy disco with live gigs at times .

Getting There & Away

AIR

There are daily flights from Porto to Lisbon and London, and almost-daily direct links to other European centres. For flight information call ☎ 229 413 260.

BUS

Porto has a baffling number of private bus companies; the main tourist office has a designated department for transport which can assist with information. For Lisbon and the Algarve, **Renex** (☎ 222 003 395; Rua das Carmelitas 32) or **Rede Expressos** (☎ 222 052 459). Three companies operate from or near Praceto Régulo Magauanha, off Rua Dr Alfredo Magalhães: **REDM** (☎ 222 003 152) goes to Braga, **AV Minho** (☎ 222 006 121) goes to Viana do Castelo, and **Carlos Soares** (☎ 222 051 383) goes to Guimarães. **Rodonorte** (☎ 222 004 398; Rua Ateneu Comércial do Porto 19) departs from its own terminal, mainly to Vila Real and Bragança. Northern Portugal's main international carrier is **Internorte** (☎ 226 093 220; www.internorte .com in Portuguese; Praça da Galiza 96), whose coaches depart from its booking office.

TRAIN

Porto is a northern Portugal rail hub, with three stations. Most international trains, and all intercity links, start at Campanhã, 2km east of the centre. Interregional and regional services depart from either Campanhã or the central **São Bento station** (☎ 225 364 141; ☽ 8am-11pm).

Getting Around

Central hubs of Porto's extensive bus system include Jardim da Cordoaria, Praça da Liberdade and São Bento station (Praça Almeida Garrett). Tickets are cheapest from STCP kiosks, newsagents and tobacconists: €0.70 for a short hop, €0.90 to outlying areas. Tickets bought on the bus cost €1.20. A €2.10 day pass is available.

Porto has one remaining tram, the No 1E, trundling daily from the Ribeira to the coast at Foz do Douro.

Work is well under way on Porto's metro (1-2 zones €0.80, 3 zones €1), a combination of upgraded and new track that will reach Campanhã, Vila Nova de Gaia and several coastal resorts. The Blue Line is opening mid-2005 (from Trindade to Gondomar) and already runs to/from Trindade to Sr Matosinhos in the northwest.

ALONG THE DOURO

Portugal's rural heartland of the Douro Valley stretches 200km to the Spanish border. In the upper reaches, port-wine vineyards wrap around every hillside punctuated by wonderfully remote stone villages and, in spring, splashes of dazzling almond blossom.

The Douro River, tamed by eight dams and locks, is navigable right across Portugal. Highly recommended is the train journey from Porto to Peso da Régua (about a dozen trains daily, 2½ hours), the last 50km clinging to the river's edge; four trains continue daily to Pocinho (4½ hours). **Douro Azul** (☎ 223 393 950; www.douroazul.com) and some other companies run one- and two-day river cruises, mostly from March to October. Cyclists and drivers can choose river-hugging roads along either bank, although they're crowded at weekends.

The elegant, detailed colour map *Rio Douro* (€3) is available from Porto bookshops.

VIANA DO CASTELO
pop 18,000
This gracious historic port town, with striking 16th-century buildings, is regarded as the region's folk capital and specialises in (and sells) the traditional embroidered costumes.

Orientation & Information
Arriving by bus, it's a 20-minute walk southwest via Rua da Bandeira to the town centre. The train station is closer, located at the north end of the main Av Combatentes da Grande Guerra which runs right through town. The **tourist office** (☎ 258 822 620; www.rtam.pt; Rua Hospital Velho; ☺ 9am-12.30pm & 2.30-5pm Mon-Fri, 9am-1pm Sat) is helpful. In August Viana hosts the **Festas da Nossa Senhora da Agonia** (see p956).

Sights & Activities
The stately heart of the town is Praça da República, with its delicate fountain and elegant buildings, including the 16th-century **Misericórdia**.

Atop Santa Luzia Hill, the **Templo do Sagrado Coração de Jesus** offers a grand panorama across the river. The funicular railway was temporarily closed at time of research. Check at the tourist office or prepare for a 5km uphill climb.

Sleeping & Eating
Pousada da Juventude (☎ 258 800 260; viana castelo@movijovem.pt; Rua da Argaçosa; dm/d €13/35) Friendly, clean place about 1km east of the town centre.

Residencial Viana Mar (☎ 258 828 962; Av Combatentes da Grande Guerra 215; s/d €30/35) Well-positioned with comfortable chintzy rooms and a sunken bar that dates from the '60s (and looks it) when it was Viana's first nightclub.

Residencial Magalhães (☎ 258 823 293; Rua Manuel Espregueira 62; s/d €30/38) One of the best of a handful of inexpensive *pensãos* on this street. Good-size rooms with freshly dusted plastic flowers and lacy curtains.

Dolce Vita (☎ 258 820 214; Rua do Poço 44; mains €6) Wood-fired pizza and innovative pasta sauces make this *the* obligatory fuelling spot in town.

A Gruta Snack Bar (☎ 258 820 214; Rua Grande 87; mains €5) Canteen-style surrounds with light lunches including a good salad choice.

O Grelhador (☎ 258 825 219; Rua do Anjinho 17; mains €7) There's not much elbowroom at this small bar-restaurant but its delicious crepes make a change if you're suffering from *bacalhau* burn out.

Getting There & Away
Half a dozen express coaches go to Porto (€6.20, two hours) and Lisbon (€14, 5½ hours) on weekdays, fewer at weekends.

BRAGA
pop 80,000
Pity about the brash new McDonald's stuck in the middle of Braga's most beautiful square; otherwise the religious capital of Portugal is monolithic in its ecclesiastical architecture, and contrasted with contemporary pedestrian streets flanked with classy cafés, shops and boutiques.

Orientation & Information

Arriving at the train station, it's a 15-minute walk to the old town via Rua Andrado Corvo. The main bus station is 10 minutes' walk from the old town; turn right along Av General Norton de Matos, cross the Praça Alexandre Herculano and continue to Praça a da República. The **tourist office** (☎ 253 262 550; Praça da República; ✆ 9am-7pm Mon-Fri, 9am-12.30pm & 2-5.30pm Sat) has a good map.

Sights & Activities

In Braga's centre is the **Sé** (museum & chapels €2; ✆ 8.30am-5.30pm), an elegant cathedral complex with an interesting treasury museum.

At Bom Jesus do Monte, a hill-top pilgrimage site 5km from Braga, is a striking stairway, the **Escadaria do Bom Jesus**, with allegorical fountains, chapels and a superb view. Buses run frequently from Braga to the site where you can climb the steps (pilgrims climb them on their knees) or ascend by funicular railway (€1). Braga is home to the Holy Week Festival every Easter.

It's an easy day trip to **Guimarães**, considered the cradle of the Portuguese nation, with a medieval town centre and a palace of the dukes of Bragança.

Sleeping

Pousada da Juventude (☎ 253 616 163; braga@movijovem.pt; Rua de Santa Margarida 6; dm/d €10/26) This bright and cheerful hostel is a 10-minute walk from the centre.

Hotel Francfort (☎ 253 262 648; Av Central 7; d €35) Large rooms, lofty ceilings, antiques and an extremely elderly owner equal – and explain – the mildly threadbare state of the place.

Grande Residência Avenida (☎ 253 609 020; fax 253 609 028; Av da Liberdade 738; d €50; ✆) Has had a glossy makeover with shiny-white bathrooms and good-size carpeted rooms.

Eating & Drinking

Ruby (☎ 253 263 030; Av da Liberdade 74; mains €3.50) About as atmospheric as a railway waiting room, but good for burgers, pizza, sandwiches and all kinds of sugary treats.

Restaurante Pópulo (☎ 253 215 147; Praça Conde de Agrolongo 116; mains €11) The menu is heavy on regional classics including duck, veal and pork dishes. Ask for the daily specials.

Café Vianna (☎ 253 262 336; Praça a da República) Elegant 19th-century café for a classy caffeine hit.

A Brazileira (☎ 253 262 104; Largo do Barã de S Martinho) Mildly decadent corner bar attracting effortlessly stylish regulars.

Getting There & Away

Intercidade trains arrive twice daily from Lisbon (€15, five hours), Coimbra (€10, three hours) and Porto (€2, 1¾ hours), and there are daily connections north to Viana do Castelo. Daily bus services link Braga to Porto (€3.80, 1½ hours) and Lisbon (€14.20, five hours).

PARQUE NATURAL DA PENEDA-GERÊS

This national park with stunning scenery is a popular spot for Portugal's happy campers and has trekking appeal with its wilder northern region around Serra de Peneda. It's also fascinating historically with its dolmens, stone circles and standing stones; most are marked on tourist maps of the area.

The park's main centre is at **Gerês**, a sleepy, hot-spring village.

Information

Gerês' **tourist office** (☎ 253 391 133; fax 253 391 282) has leaflets on activities. Other park offices are at Arcos de Valdevez and Montalegre. All have a map of the park (€3) with some roads and tracks marked but no trails, and a free English-language booklet on the park's features. A more detailed topographical map can be bought in Lisbon or Porto or ordered online at www.igeoe.pt.

Activities

CYCLING

Incentivos Outdoors (☎ 914 863 353) or the German-run **Pensão Carvalho Araújo** (☎ 253 391 185; ✆ May-Sep) hire out mountain bikes.

TREKKING

There are trails and footpaths through the park, some between villages with accommodation. Leaflets detailing these are available from the park offices.

Day treks around Gerês are popular. The Miradouro walk at **Parque do Merendas** is crowded at weekends and in summer. A more adventurous option is the old Roman road from Mata do Albergaria (10km upvalley from Gerês by taxi or hitching), past the **Vilarinho das Furnas** reservoir to Campo do Gerês. More distant destinations include **Ermida** and **Cabril**, both with simple cafés and accommodation.

For guided walks check out **Incentivos Outdoors** (☎ 914 863 353) at Gerês or **Trote-Gerês** (☎ /fax 253 659 860) at Cabril.

HORSE RIDING
The national park organises **horse riding** (☎ 253 390 110) from beside its Vidoeiro camping ground, near Gerês. Incentivos Outdoors (see Trekking, opposite) also has horses for hire.

WATER SPORTS
The Caldo River, 8km south of Gerês, is the base for water sports on the Caniçada reservoir. **Agua Montanha Lazer** (☎ 253 391 779; www .aguamontanha.com) rents canoes and boats. For paddling the Salamonde reservoir, Trote-Gerês (see opposite) rents canoes from its camp site at Cabril.

Gerês' **Parque das Termas** (€1; ✆ daily May-Oct, Sat & Sun Apr) has a **swimming pool** (weekdays/weekends €3.50/5).

Sleeping & Eating
Gerês has plenty of *pensãos*, though many are block-booked by spa patients in summer.

Pousada da Juventude (Campo do Gerês; ☎ /fax 253 351 339; dm/d €10/24) This is a former dam workers' camp and has comfy, sprawling accommodation.

Pensão Adelaide (☎ 253 390 020; fax 253 390 029; d €40; ✆) It's a bit of a trek from the centre but the views are suitable reward. Clean, bright rooms.

Pensão Casa da Ponte (☎ 253 391 125; s/d €20/45; ✆) One of the longest established and could do with a makeover, but the rooms are good-sized and airy and the riverside location is excellent.

Cerdeira Campsite (Campo do Gerês; ☎ 253 351 005; fax 253 353 315) Has shady camp sites, a laundry and minisupermarket.

Vidoeiro Campsite (☎ 253 391 289) Open year-round, just out of Gerês on the river.

Most of Gerês' *pensãos* serve hearty meals, to guests and nonguests. There are several **restaurants**, plus shops in the main street for picnic provisions. The **Cerdeira Campsite** has a cheap OK-standard restaurant.

Getting There & Away
From Braga, at least six coaches daily run to the Caldo River and Gerês, and seven to Campo do Gerês (fewer at weekends). Coming from Lisbon or Porto, change at Braga.

PORTUGAL DIRECTORY

ACCOMMODATION
Most tourist offices have lists of accommodation to suit a range of budgets, and can help with reservations. Although the government uses stars to grade some types of accommodation, criteria seems erratic.

Camping
If you're euro-economising, camping is cheapest, although some camp sites close out of season. The multilingual, annually updated *Roteiro Campista* (€5), sold in larger bookshops, contains details of nearly all Portugal's camping grounds. The price for a camp site and two people is approximately €12 to €15.

Guesthouses
The most common types of guesthouse are the *residencial* and *pensão*. Both are graded from one to three stars, and the best are often cheaper and better run than some hotels. High-season *pensão* rates for a double with bathroom start from around €35; a *residencial*, where breakfast is normally included, is a bit more.

Hostels
Portugal has 41 *pousadas da juventude* (youth hostels), all part of the Hostelling International (HI) system. You can reserve in advance for a €1.50 fee by contacting the **central reservations office** (☎ 213 524 072; reservas@movijovem.pt).

If you haven't obtained a card from your national hostel association, you pay a €2 supplement per night (and have a one- or six-night, or year-long 'guest card').

Another cheaper option is a *quarto particular* (private room). Watch for 'quartos' signs or ask at tourist offices. Rooms are in private homes and usually clean and cheap.

Hotels
The government grades hotels with one to five stars. For a high-season double expect to pay at least €60, and up to as much as €250.

Pousadas
Pousadas are government-run former castles, monasteries or palaces, often in spectacular locations. For details about these

PORTUGAL

and private rural accommodation, contact tourist offices, or **Pousadas de Portugal** (☎ 218 442 001; www.pousadasjuventude.pt).

ACTIVITIES

Off-road cycling (BTT; *bicyclete tudo terrano*, all-terrain bicycle) is booming in Portugal, with bike trips on offer at many tourist destinations – see Tavira (p942), Setúbal (p941), Évora (p944) and Parque Natural da Peneda-Gerês (p954).

Despite some fine rambling country, walking is not a Portuguese passion. Some parks are establishing trails, though, and various agencies offer walking tours – see Serra da Estrela (p948), Setúbal (p941) and Parque Natural da Peneda-Gerês (p954).

Water sports include surfing, windsurfing, canoeing, white-water rafting and water-skiing. For details see Lagos (p943), Sagres (p944), Évora (p944), Tavira (p943), Coimbra (p947) and Parque Natural da Peneda-Gerês (p955).

BUSINESS HOURS

Banks are open 8.30am to 3pm weekdays. Museums and tourist attractions are open 10am to 5pm weekdays but are often closed at lunch time and all day Monday. Shopping hours generally extend from 9am to 7pm on weekdays, and 9am to 1pm on Saturday. Lunch is given lingering attention between noon and 3pm.

EMBASSIES & CONSULATES

For information on visas, see opposite.

Embassies & Consulates in Portugal

Foreign embassies in Portugal include:
Canada (Map p934; ☎ 213 164 600; Ave da Liberdade 200, Lisbon)
France Lisbon (Map p934; ☎ 226 939 292 ; Calçada a Marques de Abrantes 123) Porto (☎ 226 094 805; Rua Eugénio de Castro 352)
Germany (Map p936; ☎ 213 810 210; Campo dos Mártires da Pátria 38, Lisbon)
Ireland (Map p934; ☎ 213 929 440 ; Rua da Imprensa à Estrela 1, Lisbon)
Netherlands (Map p934; ☎ 213 914 900; Avenida Infante Santo 43, Lisbon)
Spain Lisbon (Map p936; ☎ 213 472 792; Rua do Salitre 1); Porto (☎ 225 101 685; Rua de Dom João IV 341)
UK Lisbon (Map p934; ☎ 213 924 000; Rua de São Bernardo 33); Porto (☎ 226 184 789; Av da Boavista 3072); Portimão (☎ 282 417 800; Largo Francisco a Maurício 7).

The UK consulate also oversees consular matters for New Zealand.
USA (Map p934; ☎ 217 273 300; Av das Forças Armadas, Lisbon)

Portuguese Embassies & Consulates Abroad

Portuguese embassies abroad include:
Australia (☎ 02-2901 733; 23 Culgoa Circuit, O'Malley, ACT 2606)
Canada (☎ 613-7290 883; 645 Island Park Dr, Ottawa, Ont K1Y 0B8)
France (☎ 01 47 27 35 29; 3 Rue de Noisiel, 75116 Paris)
Germany (☎ 030-590 063 500; Zimmerstrasse 56, 10117 Berlin)
Ireland (☎ 012-894 46; Knocksinna House, Foxrock, Dublin 18)
Netherlands (☎ 070-363 0217; Bazarstraat 21, 2518 Den Haag)
New Zealand (☎ 09-309 1454; PO Box 305, 33 Garfield St, Parnell, Auckland)
Spain (☎ 915-617 800; Calle Castello 128, 28006 Madrid)
UK (☎ 020-7235 5331; 11 Belgrave Square, London SW1X 8PP)
USA (☎ 202-328 8610; 2125 Kalorama Rd NW, Washington, DC 20008)

FESTIVALS & EVENTS

Holy Week Festival Easter week in Braga features colourful processions, including Ecce Homo, with barefoot penitents carrying torches.
Festas das Cruzes Held in Barcelos in May, the Festival of the Crosses is known for processions, folk music and dance, and regional handicrafts.
Feira Nacional da Agricultura In June Santarém hosts the National Agricultural Fair, with bullfighting, folk singing and dancing.
Festa do Santo António The Festival of St Anthony fills the streets of Lisbon on 13 June.
Festas de São João Porto's big street bash is the St John's Festival, from 16 to 24 June.
Festas da Nossa Senhora da Agonia Viana do Castelo's Our Lady of Suffering Festival runs for three days, including the weekend nearest to 20 August, and is famed for folk arts, parades and fireworks.

HOLIDAYS

New Year's Day 1 January
Carnival Shrove Tuesday February/March
Good Friday and the following Saturday March/April
Liberty Day 25 April (commemorating the 1975 revolution)
Labour Day 1 May

Corpus Christi May/June (the ninth Thursday after Easter)
National Day 10 June
Feast of the Assumption 15 August
Republic Day 5 October
All Saints' Day 1 November
Independence Day 1 December (celebrating independence from Spain in 1640)
Immaculate Conception 8 December

MONEY
ATMs
There are dozens of banks with ATMs throughout Portugal. However some only accept credit, rather than debit cards.

Credit Cards
Credit cards are increasingly accepted in hotels, restaurants and shops, however you will normally be asked to produce photo ID.

Exchanging Money
Exchange bureaux are common throughout Portugal, often located near to or even within the same building as the tourist offices. Unusually, they often offer a better rate of exchange for cash and travellers cheques than the banks.

POST
Portuguese *correios* (post offices) are open Monday to Friday 8.30am to 6pm. In Lisbon and Porto they also open Saturday mornings. Stamps can also be purchased from an *Correio de Portugal – Selos* (automatic dispensing machine). A letter within Europe costs €0.56, €0.72 to elsewhere. An increasing number of post offices also have a Netpost Internet kiosk (€5.50 per three hours).

TELEPHONE
Mobile Phones
Mobile phone numbers within Portugal have nine digits and begin with 9.

Phonecards
Phonecards are the most reliable and cheapest way of calling from a telephone booth. They can be purchased at post offices, newsagents and tobacconists in denominations of €5 and €10.

Phone Codes
All Portuguese phone numbers have nine digits, the first two being the area code in or around Lisbon and Porto, the first three anywhere else in the country. For general information dial ☎ 118, for international inquiries dial ☎ 179, for collect calls dial ☎ 120.

VISAS
EU nationals need only a valid passport or identity card for entry to Portugal, and may stay indefinitely. Citizens of Australia, Canada, New Zealand and the USA can stay for up to 90 days in any half-year without a visa. Check out the following websites for more visa information: www.travel.state .gov/visa_services.html, www.travisa.com.

Romania

HIGHLIGHTS

- **Bucharest** The monstrous Palace of Parliament, cocktails in a trendy bar and some great museums are just some attractions of the capital (p962)
- **Bran castle** This fairy-tale castle, even without a 'real' Dracula, is impressive (p971)
- **Braşov** Cheap, delicious beer is a bonus for many visitors to the Bohemian paradise of this medieval town (p969)
- **Off-the-beaten track** The majestic Carpathian Mountains are a delight for skiers, hikers or those who just want to take in the vista (p968)

FAST FACTS

- **Area** 237,500 sq km (about the size of Britain)
- **ATMs** Widespread
- **Budget** €10-14 per day
- **Capital** Bucharest
- **Country codes** ☎ 40; international access code ☎ 00
- **Famous For** Dracula, beautiful scenery
- **Head of State** President Ion Iliescu
- **Language** Romanian
- **Money** Leu (A$1 = 24,000 lei, CA$1 = 26,170 lei, €1 = 42,345 lei, ¥100 = 30,257 lei, NZ$1 = 22,553 lei, UK£1 = 59,536 lei, US$1 = 32,546 lei)

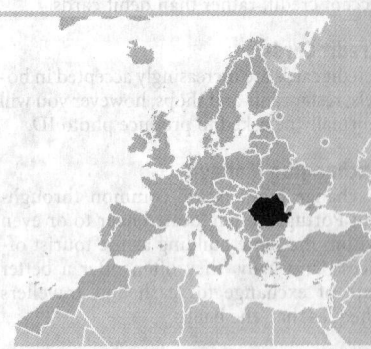

- **Population** 22.4 million
- **Time** GMT/UTC + 2
- **Visa** None required for EU, US, Canadian or UK citizens for stays of up to 30 or 90 days.

ROAMING ROMANIA

Bucharest then Transylvania, stopping at Braşov and Sinaia. See the painted monasteries of Bucovina, then get down to Bran and Sighişoara.

TRAVEL HINTS

Take some brightly coloured stickers or similarly inexpensive gifts as a way of communicating with the children you'll see begging at most train and bus stations.

This is the wild east of Europe. You'll feel like you're the only traveller ever to have stepped on this alien and unpredictable turf.

Time travel is possible here – you'll step back a century in time in its fabled countryside, yet be made brutally aware of its painfully recent history in the form of numerous battle scars from the Ceauşescu era.

This 'final-frontier' country may be a living museum to Europe's lost ways, but it's also defiantly contemporary and boldly strutting into the future. The nightlife in Bucharest and Cluj-Napoca can hold their own against Western contemporaries.

ROMANIA

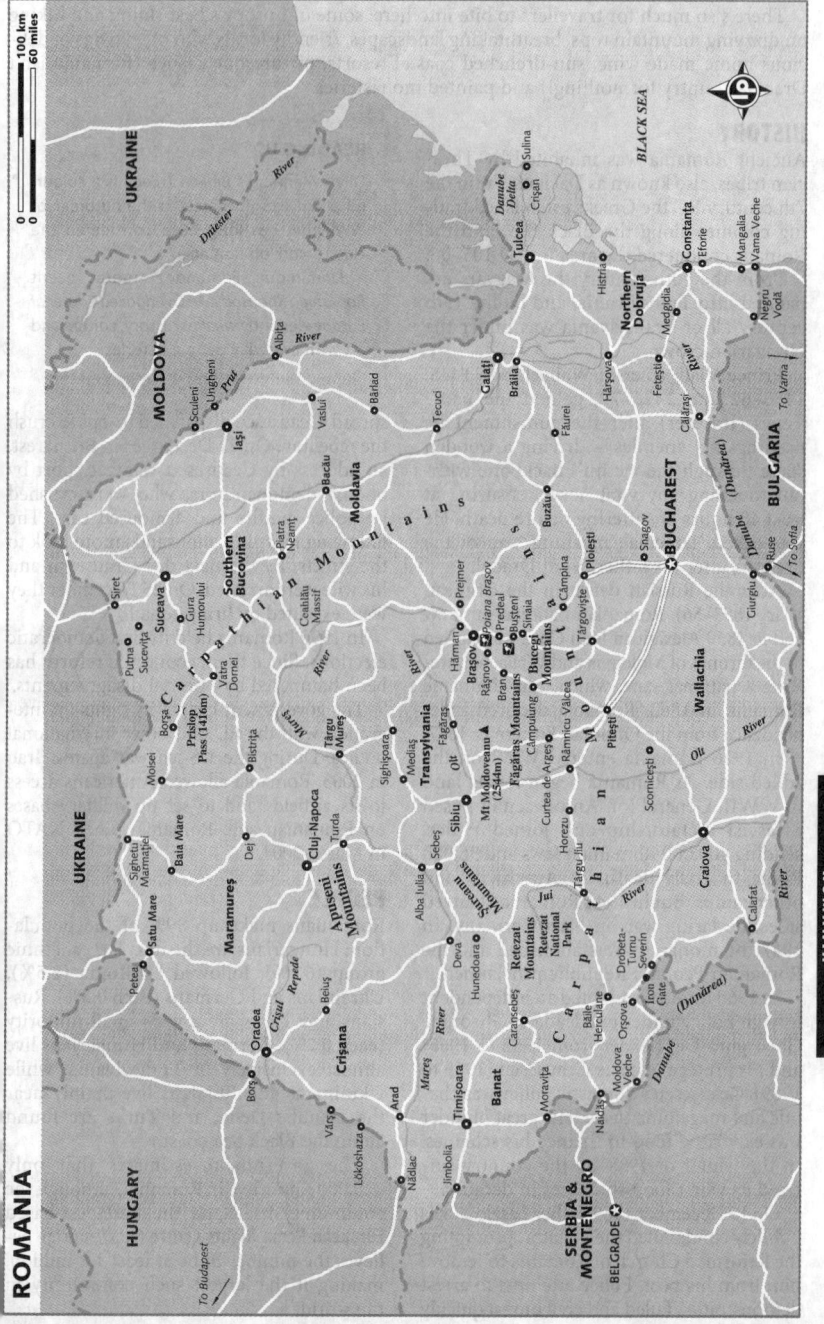

ROMANIA

There's so much for travellers to bite into here: some of Europe's best skiing and hiking on dizzying mountain tops, breathtaking landscapes, friendly locals who offer swigs of delicious home-made wine, sun-drenched coastal resorts, picturesque castles (Romania isn't Dracula country for nothing!) and painted monasteries.

HISTORY

Ancient Romania was inhabited by Thracian tribes, also known as Dacians. From the 7th century BC the Greeks established trading colonies along the Black Sea, and the Romans conquered the area in AD 105–06.

From the 10th century the Magyars expanded into Transylvania, and by the 13th century all of Transylvania was under the Hungarian crown.

Prince Vlad, ruler of Wallachia in 1448, 1456–62 and 1476–77, gained the name Ţepeş (Impaler) after the punishment he used against enemies – driving a wooden stake through the victim's backbone without touching any vital nerve, ensuring at least 48 hours of suffering before death. He was called 'Dracula', meaning 'son of the dragon', after his father, Vlad Dracul.

After the Russian defeat in the Crimean War (1853–56), Romanian nationalism grew and in 1859 Alexandru Ioan Cuza was elected to the thrones of Moldavia and Wallachia, creating a national state, which took the name Romania in 1862. Romania declared independence from the Ottoman Empire in 1877.

In 1916 Romania entered WWI on the Allied side. As Romania began losing land in WWII, General Ion Antonescu imposed a fascist dictatorship and joined Hitler, sending 400,000 Romanian Jews and 36,000 Roma to grisly deaths at Auschwitz and other camps. But in 1944 Romania changed sides, declaring war on Nazi Germany. In 1947 the monarchy was abolished and the Romanian People's Republic proclaimed.

In 1960 Romania adopted an independent foreign policy under two leaders, Gheorghe Gheorghiu-Dej (leader from 1952 to 1965) and his protégé Nicolae Ceauşescu (1965 to 1989). Ceauşescu's domestic policy was chaotic and megalomaniacal. His great blunder was exporting food to finance his schemes. In the winter of 1988–89 the country suffered its worst food shortages in decades.

On 15 December 1989 Father László Tökés publicly condemned the dictator, prompting the Reformed Church of Romania to remove him from his post. Police attempts to arrest demonstrators failed and civil unrest quickly

> **READING UP**
>
> Olivia Manning's *Balkan Trilogy* is a colourful portrait of Bucharest at the outbreak of WWII that has long been considered the classic work on Romania.
>
> Dominique Fernandez' more recent *Romanian Rhapsody: An Overlooked Corner of Europe* elegantly weaves history, culture and art with everyday people's stories.

spread. Ceauşescu dispatched troops to crush the rebellion. On 21 December in Bucharest, an address by Ceauşescu was cut short by booing demonstrators, who were crushed by police gunfire and armoured cars. The following morning, thousands more took to the streets. By the next day Ceauşescu and his wife were arrested. On 25 December they were executed by firing squad.

In 1990 Romania held its first democratic elections. Since then, economic reform has been hampered by internal disagreements.

The government has set its sights on integration with the EU and other international bodies. During the US-led war against Iraq in 2003, Romania allowed Americans access to its airfields and to set up military bases on Romanian soil. Romania joined NATO in March 2004.

PEOPLE

Romanians make up 89% of the population; Hungarians are the next largest ethnic group (6.6%), followed by Roma (2.5%), Ukrainians and Germans (each 0.3%). Russians and Turks are a very small minority (each 0.2%). Germans and Hungarians live almost exclusively in Transylvania, while Ukrainians and Russians live mainly near the Danube Delta, and Turks are found along the Black Sea coast.

The government estimates that only 420,000 Roma live in Romania, although the community itself and the Budapest-based **European Roma Rights Centre** (http://errc.org) believes the number to be at least 1.8 million, making it the largest such community in the world.

ARTS

Romania has a strong tradition of traditional rural crafts, music and dance. Religious icon painting was widely practised, particularly between the 17th and 19th centuries.

Artist Nicolae Grigorescu (1838–1907) is known for adapting impressionism to Romanian peasant themes. However, the Romanian artist most foreigners will have heard of is the sculptor Constantin Brancusi (1876–1957), a central figure of the modernist movement and one of the early pioneers of abstractionism.

ENVIRONMENT

Oval-shaped Romania is made up of three main geographical regions. The mighty Carpathian Mountains form the shape of a scythe sweeping down through the country's centre from Ukraine and then curling northwards.

East of the mountains are low-lying plains that end at the Black Sea and Europe's second-largest delta region, where the Danube spills into the Black Sea.

Rural Romania has thriving animal populations in it's parks and mountains, including chamois, lynxes, foxes, deer, wolves, bears and badgers. Birdlife in the Danube Delta is exceptional.

Romania has more than 500 protected areas, including 12 national parks, three biosphere reserves and one World Natural Heritage Site (the Danube Delta), totalling over 1.2 million hectares. Most of these areas are in the Carpathian Mountains.

TRANSPORT

GETTING THERE & AWAY

Air

Tarom (☎ 21-337 2037; www.tarom.ro) is Romania's state airline. Nearly all international flights to Romania arrive at Bucharest's **Otopeni International Airport** (☎ 21-201 4050; www.otp-airport.ro).

There are regular flights between Bucharest and Prague, Budapest, Warsaw, Sofia and Moscow. See www.otp-airport.ro for the latest schedules. There are daily flights between Bucharest and Chişinău, and daily flights to Timişoara.

Tarom also flies from Arad to Verona, from Timişoara to Milan, from Sibiu to Munich and Stuttgart, and from Cluj-Napoca to Vienna, Frankfurt and Munich.

TOP FIVE ROMANIA

- **Square** Piaţa Sfatului is lined with baroque façades and Bohemian outdoor cafés (p969)
- **Skiing** Sinaia, the pearl of the Carpathians (p968)
- **Hotel & Bar** Lăptăria Enache/La Motor (p967)
- **Impressive sight** Palace of Parliament (p964)
- **Mountains** The magnificent Carpathians (p968)

Carpatair (☎ 416 016; www.carpatair.com) has flights to Italy from Cluj-Napoca.

Bus

Romania is well connected by bus services to Central Europe and Turkey. **Eurolines** (www.eurolines.ro) buses link numerous Romanian cities with destinations in Western Europe.

From Bucharest, several private bus companies operate from near Piaţa Gară de Nord. **Ortadoğu Tur** (☎ 312 24 23, 637 67 78; Piaţa Gară de Nord 1) has daily buses to Istanbul (US$27/51 one-way/round trip). **Autotrans** (☎ 312 22 11, 335 32 90), next door, travels to Chişinău (US$10/20 one-way/return trip) in Moldova. Tickets for daily buses to Germany are sold by **Double T** (☎ 313 36 42; doublet@fx.ro; Calea Victoriei 2).

Car & Motorcycle

Make sure all your documents (personal ID, insurance, registration, and visas if required) are in order before crossing into Romania. The Green Card (a routine extension of domestic motor insurance to cover most European countries) is valid. Extra insurance can be bought at the borders.

Expect long queues at Romanian checkpoints, particularly on weekends. Carry food and water for the wait.

Train

Those travelling on an Inter-Rail pass still need to make seat reservations (€2 to €3) on express trains within Romania.

From Arad it is a mere 28km to the Hungarian border town of Lököshaza, from where it is a further 225km (4½ hours) to

ROMANIA

> ### WHICH CURRENCY?
>
> The only legal tender in Romania is the leu (plural: lei). However, you will see prices quoted in euros or, in the case of national airline Tarom, US dollars.

Budapest. There are five daily trains between Bucharest and Budapest (around €40 one way). A one-way ticket from Arad or Oradea to Budapest costs about €30. It's also possible to pick up the Budapest-bound train from other Romanian cities, including Constanţa, Braşov and Cluj-Napoca.

Between Sofia and Bucharest (11 hours) there are two daily trains, both stop in Ruse.

There's an overnight connection from Bucharest to Istanbul (803km, 17 to 19 hours) on the *Bosfor*. There's also an overnight service between Bucharest and Chişinău. To reach Ukraine, take the daily Bucharest–Moscow train, which goes via Kyiv.

GETTING AROUND
Air
State-owned carrier **Tarom** (www.tarom.ro) is Romania's main carrier and in 2003 invested in new 747s and improved its already excellent on-board service. Smaller airlines like **Angel Airlines** (www.angelairlines.ro) and **Carpatair** (www.carpatair.com) run domestic flights.

Bicycle
Cyclists are becoming a more frequent sight in Romania, particularly in Transylvania and Moldavia. Most major towns rent out bikes and have bike repair shops.

Boat
By boat is the only way to get around much of the Danube Delta. **Navrom** (☎ 0240-511 553) operates passenger ferries along the three main Danube channels from Tulcea.

Bus
Regular buses travel to most corners of the country. Fares are cheap and calculated per kilometre. A 10km trip will cost €0.40, a 100km trip €2.40.

Car & Motorcycle
Romania has only a few short stretches of motorway. Many main roads remain in poor, potholed condition.

EU driving licences are accepted here; or bring your home-country driver's licence and an International Driving Permit (IDP).

There's a 0% blood alcohol tolerance limit, seat belts are compulsory in the front and back (if fitted) seats, and children under 12 are forbidden to sit in the front seat. Speed limits are usually 90km/h on major roads, 100km/h to 110km/h on motorways and 50km/h inside cities.

Local Transport
Buses, trams and trolleybuses run from about 5am to midnight, although services can get thin on the ground after 7pm in more remote areas. Purchase tickets at street kiosks marked *bilete* or *casă de bilete* before boarding, and validate them once aboard.

In many rural parts the humble horse and cart is the most popular form of transport. Bucharest is the only city to sport a metro.

Train
The national train timetable (*mersul trenurilor*) is sold for €2 from **Căile Ferate Române** (CFR; Romanian State Railways; www.cfr.ro) offices (it's a little red book.). It's also available on the CFR website.

The cheapest trains are local *persoane* trains. *Accelerat* trains are faster, hence a tad more expensive and less crowded. Seat reservations are obligatory and automatic when you buy your ticket. There's little difference between *rapid* and *express* trains. Pricier intercity trains are the most comfortable but are not faster than express trains.

Sleepers (*vagon de dormit*) are available between Bucharest and Arad, Cluj-Napoca, Oradea and Timişoara.

Travelling 100km 1st class costs €2 on a *persoane* train, €5 on a *rapid* or *express* and €5.40 on an intercity train.

BUCHAREST

☎ 021 / pop 2million

Forget Prague, forget Budapest: Bucharest (Bucureşti) is where explorers are heading. This is Eastern Europe's secret.

Bucharest presents a fascinating mix of architecture that maps Romania's chequered history. The ugly face of communism sits alongside the incredible beauty of Romania's elegant past and its Parisian pretensions.

GREATER BUCHAREST

0 — 500 m
0 — 0.3 miles

INFORMATION
Australian Consulate..............1 D6
Banca Comercială Română.....2 B3
Branch Post Office..................3 B4
Branch Post Office..................4 A4
British Embassy.......................5 C4
Canadian Embassy..................6 B4
Emergency Clinic Hospital.......7 C3
French Embassy.......................8 B4
French Institute.......................9 C4
German Embassy....................10 B2
Moldovan Embassy................11 B2

SIGHTS & ACTIVITIES (pp964-6)
Arcul de Triumf.....................12 A2
Catedrala Patriahală..............13 B6
Mănăstirea Antim..................14 B6
Muzeul Satului......................15 A1
Muzeul Țăranului Român
 (Museum of the
 Romanian Peasant)..............16 A3
Palace of Parliament.............17 B5

SLEEPING (p966)
Elvis Villa..............................18 D5
Youth Hostel Villa Helga.......19 C4

EATING (p966)
Piața Amzei market...............20 B4
Piața Gemeni market.............21 C4
Piața Unirii market................22 C5

ENTERTAINMENT (p967)
Hollywood Multiplex.............23 D6
Opera Română......................24 A5
Queen's................................25 A1

TRANSPORT (pp967-8)
Autotrans (buses to Chișinău)....(see 26)
Central Bus Station...............26 A4
Ortadoğu Tur (buses to
 Istanbul)............................(see 26)

ROMANIA

GETTING INTO TOWN

From Otopeni airport catch bus No 783 outside the main terminal (€1 from any RATB bus-ticket booth), which takes you to Piaţa Unirii and Piaţa Victoriei. It departs every 15 minutes between 5.37am and 11.23pm (every half-hour at weekends).

From the train station, Gară de Nord, take the metro to the centre of town at Piaţa Victoriei on the northern side or to Piaţa Unirii to the south. Bus Nos 79, 86 and 133 will take you mid-centre to Piaţa Română.

Down dingy side streets flanked by Soviet-style high rises are exquisite 18th-century monasteries, pretty gardens and ornate Orthodox churches.

ORIENTATION

The main boulevard of Bucharest runs between Piaţa Victoriei, Piaţa Română, Piaţa Universităţii and Piaţa Unirii. The main train station, Gară de Nord, is a few kilometres northwest of central Bucharest.

INFORMATION
Internet Access

Internet cafés have sprung up like mushrooms. Rates vary from €0.30 to €1 per hour.
CNET (Map p965; ☎ 311 2682; Calea Victoriei 25; ☑ 9am-7pm Mon-Sat, 9am-1pm Sun)

Medical Services

Emergency Clinic Hospital (Map p963; ☎ 230 0106; Calea Floreasca 8; ☑ 24hr) Bucharest's 'showcase' hospital.
Sensi-Blu Calea Victoriei 12A (Map p965; ☎ 315 3160); B-dul Nicolae Bălescu 7 (Map p965; ☎ 212 4923) Excellent chain of 24-hour pharmacies.

Money

Currency exchanges and ATMs are widespread. For the latter, try the Unirea Shopping Centre inside the main **Agenţie de Voiaj CFR office** (Map p965; Str Domniţa Anastasia 10-14) and at **Teatrul Excelsior** (Str Academei 28).

EMERGENCY NUMBERS

- Ambulance ☎ 961
- Fire ☎ 981
- Police ☎ 955

Alliance Exchange (Map p965; B-dul Nicolae Bălescu 30; ☑ 24hr)
Banca Comercială Română B-dul Regina Elisabeta 5 (Map p965; ☑ 9am-4pm Mon-Fri); Calea Victoriei 155 (☑ 9am-1pm Mon-Fri) For cash transfers, travellers cheques and banking services.

Post

Main post office (Poştă Română Oficiul Bucureşti 1; Map p965; ☎ 315 9030; www.posta-romana.ro; Str Matei Millo 10; ☑ 7.30am-8pm Mon-Fri, 8am-2pm Sat) Collect poste-restante mail here.

Telephone

RomTelecom cards can be bought from kiosks in denominations of €4 to €6 and used for both national and international calls.

Tourist Information

Incredibly, Bucharest still has no official tourist office, so independent ventures fill the gap.
Elvis Villa Tourist Information (Map p963; ☎ 312 1653; Platform 2, Gară de Nord; ☑ 7am-10pm) Friendly staff speak English, French, Italian and Japanese. They also organise city tours, Dracula tours and hand out free maps.

SIGHTS & ACTIVITIES

Most of Bucharest's major attractions lie in a north–south axis through the heart of the city and inner suburbs. The attractions centre round each of the plazas: Piaţa Unirii in the south, Piaţa Universităţii and Piaţa Revoluţiei in the centre, and Piaţa Română and Piaţa Victoriei in the north.

Bucharest's (indeed Romania's) infamous star attraction, the **Palace of Parliament** (Map p963; ☎ 311 3611; cic@camera.ro; Calea 13 Septembrie 1; adult/student €3/1.50; ☑ 10am-4pm), is the big mama of monstrous buildings. Conceived at the height of Ceauşescu's communist fervour, it was called, ironically, the House of the People (Casa Poporului) before 1989. This enormous, 12-floor showcase of Romanian craftsmanship now houses the chamber of deputies. The 45-minute tour (in English, French or Romanian) is a staggering insight into Ceauşescu's ego-driven vision.

The urban wasteland that is **B-dul Unirii** (Map p963) was intended as the Champs Élysées–style axis for the criminal civic project that saw Ceauşescu destroy an entire suburb to build the parliament and **Piaţa Unirii** (Map p963).

Walk southwest across B-dul Unirii and up B-dul Regina Maria to the **Catedrala**

Patriahală (Patriarchal Cathedral; Map p963; Str Dealul Mitropoliei), built in 1658.

Bucharest's historic heart arose around the **Curtea Veche** (Old Princely Court), where the ruins of Vlad Ţepeş (Dracula) lie. To the northwest is **Biserica Stavropoleos** (Stavropoleos Church; Map p965; Str Poştei), a Unesco-protected building erected by a monk in 1724.

North on Calea Victoriei is Piaţa Revoluţiei and **Biserica Creţulescu** (Creţulescu Church; Map p965), a red-brick structure built in 1722 but badly damaged in the 1989 revolution. To its north, dominating the entire western side of the square, is the massive **Royal Palace** (Map p965) an official royal residence from 1834.

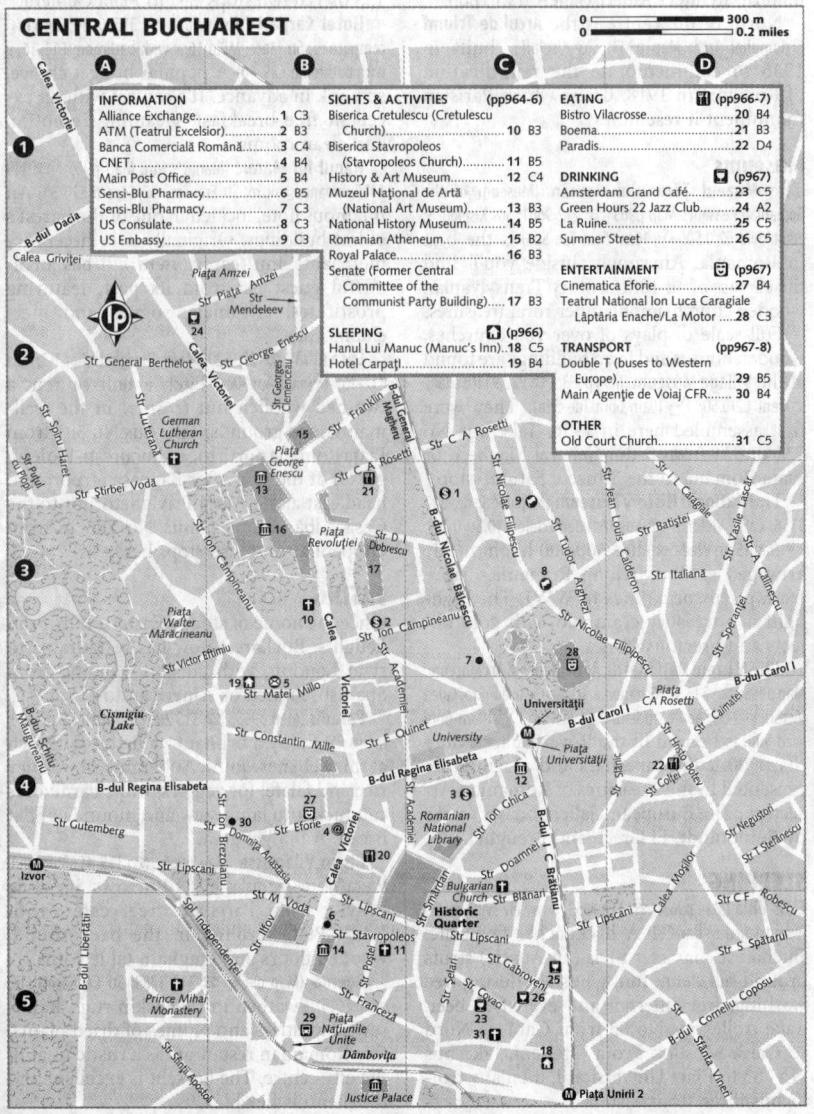

CENTRAL BUCHAREST

INFORMATION	
Alliance Exchange	1 C3
ATM (Teatrul Excelsior)	2 B3
Banca Comercială Română	3 C4
CNET	4 B4
Main Post Office	5 B4
Sensi-Blu Pharmacy	6 B5
Sensi-Blu Pharmacy	7 C3
US Consulate	8 C3
US Embassy	9 C3

SIGHTS & ACTIVITIES	(pp964–6)
Biserica Cretulescu (Cretulescu Church)	10 B3
Biserica Stavropoleos (Stavropoleos Church)	11 B5
History & Art Museum	12 C4
Muzeul Naţional de Artă (National Art Museum)	13 B3
National History Museum	14 B5
Romanian Atheneum	15 B2
Royal Palace	16 B3
Senate (Former Central Committee of the Communist Party Building)	17 B3

SLEEPING	(p966)
Hanul Lui Manuc (Manuc's Inn)	18 C5
Hotel Carpaţi	19 B4

EATING	(pp966–7)
Bistro Vilacrosse	20 B4
Boema	21 B3
Paradis	22 D4

DRINKING	(p967)
Amsterdam Grand Café	23 C5
Green Hours 22 Jazz Club	24 A2
La Ruine	25 C5
Summer Street	26 C5

ENTERTAINMENT	(p967)
Cinematica Eforie	27 B4
Teatrul National Ion Luca Caragiale Lâptăria Enache/La Motor	28 C3

TRANSPORT	(pp967–8)
Double T (buses to Western Europe)	29 B5
Main Agenţie de Voiaj CFR	30 B4

OTHER	
Old Court Church	31 C5

ROMANIA

Ceauşescu made his last speech from the balcony of what is now the **senate building** (Map p965) but was then the Central Committee of the Communist Party building, a white-stone edifice opposite Biserica Creţulescu. Just north is the magnificent neo-classical **Romanian Athenaeum** (Map p965; ☎ 315 87 98; Str Franklin 1), the city's main concert hall, built by architect Albert Galleron in 1888.

North of the centre is the **Arcul de Triumf** (Triumphal Arch; Map p963; Şos Kiseleff), built in 1936 to commemorate the reunification of Romania in 1918. Guess which Parisian monument it resembles.

Museums

The **Muzeul Ţăranului Român** (Museum of the Romanian Peasant; Map p963 ☎ 212 9661; Şos Kiseleff 3; adult/child €2/0.50; ⏰ 10am-6pm Tue-Sun) is the best in Romania. Amazingly, inside you'll find the carcass of an 18th-century Transylvanian wooden church among other rural treasures.

Full-scale displays of over 100 churches, wooden houses and farm buildings are found at the **Village Museum** (Map p963; ☎ 222 9110; adult/student €2/0.50; ⏰ 10am-6pm Tue-Sun). They were first assembled here in 1936. Take bus No 131 or 331 from B-dul General Magheru or Piaţa Română to the 'Muzeul Satului' stop.

The **National History Museum** (Map p965; ☎ 311 3356; Calea Victoriei 12; adult/student/child €10.50/0.30/; ⏰ 9am-5pm Wed-Sun) has 600,000 haphazardly arranged exhibits telling Romania's story from prehistoric times to WWI. The highlight is a treasury crammed with gold objects and precious stones.

The **Muzeul Naţional de Artă** (National Art Museum; Map p965; ☎ 313 3030; national.art@art.museum.ro; Calea Victoriei 49-53; adult/student/child €2/1/1; ⏰ 10am-6pm Wed-Sun) is housed in the Royal Palace. More than 700 icons, tapestries and carvings are presented in the Treasures of Romanian Art section. The European Gallery boasts works by Rembrandt, El Greco and Breughel.

SLEEPING

Elvis Villa (Map p963; ☎ 312 1653; www.elvisvilla.ro; Str Avram Iancu 5; dm €12) A backpacker favourite. Bucharest character Elvis (an Aussie) struts around his clean, funky hostel offering free washing, free Internet and even free beer. Take trolleybus No 85 from Gară de Nord to Calea Moşilor. From Otopeni, take bus No 783 to Piaţa Universităţii, then any trolleybus three stops east.

Youth Hostel Villa Helga (Map p963; ☎ 610 2214; Str Salcâmilor 2; dm €12) Centrally located, this offers peace and quiet in a friendly atmosphere with breakfast, free laundry and Internet to guests. Take bus No 79 or 133 from Gară de Nord for six stops to Piaţa Gemeni. Alternatively, take bus No 783 from Otopeni to Piaţa Română, then walk or take bus No 79, 86, 133 or 126 two stops east to Piaţa Gemeni.

Hotel Carpaţi (Map p965; ☎ 315 0140; carpati@compace.ro; Str Matei Millo 16; s with bathroom €11-16, d with bathroom €29-40) A popular budget choice, so book in advance. It's central with an excellent free breakfast, gleaming reception and clean rooms.

Hanul lui Manuc (Manuc's Inn; Map p965; ☎ 313 1415; hmanuc@rnc.ro; Str Franceză 62-64; s/d €20/35) An infamous hotel located in one of Bucharest's oldest buildings. Originally a 19th-century merchants' inn (caravanserai), it has a colourful guest list from its past, featuring prostitutes, criminals, rogues and merchants alike.

Casa Albă (☎ 230 5203; Aleea Privighetorilor 1-3; huts €12-15; ⏰ mid-Apr–Oct) Pitch a tent or rent a two-bed wooden hut (căsuţe) in the well-maintained grounds. Take bus No 301 from Piaţa Română north to Şos Bucureşti-Ploieşti; get off at the stop after Băneasa airport and head east along Aleea Privighetorilor to the Casa Albă complex. Bus No 783 to/from Otopeni airport also stops here.

EATING

Once the home of stodgy Eastern European delights, Bucharest now has restaurants to rival London, with cuisines ranging from Spanish, French or American to Lebanese.

Paradis (Map p965; ☎ 315 2601; Str Hristo Botev 10; mains €5) Enjoy a brilliant-value buffet lunch at this Lebanese joint. Aubergine stew, spicy rice and falafel for veggies, while carnivores can tuck into lamb stew and mounds of flat bread. A budget gem.

Bistro Vilacrosse (Map p965; ☎ 315 4562; Pasajul Macca/Vilacrosse; mains €5-10) Borrows its style heavily from Parisian street cafés, with Edith Piaf warbling in the background, wooden floors and gingham tablecloths.

Boema (Map p965; ☎ 313 3783; Str CA Rosetti 10; mains €15) Swathed in sheepskin rugs, hand-sewn tapestries and plumes of dried plants, this Romanian restaurant is a rustic treat in the city centre. The borscht is excellent and the menu is flexible.

ROMANIA

Three open-air markets have fresh fruit and veggies: one at Piaţa Amzei between Calea Victoriei and B-dul General Magheru; another on Piaţa Gemeni; and a third east of Piaţa Unirii.

DRINKING

Bucharest's budding bar scene is liveliest in the Lipscani area, which now has a dedicated pedestrianised road called **Summer Street** lined with trendy pubs and outside tables.

Amsterdam Grand Café (Map p965; ☎ 313 7580; Str Covaci 6; ☑ 10am-2am) It's like being at home, yet much nicer, funkier and with better-looking bar staff and better cooking. Get here early and feast on massive portions of excellent European food.

La Ruine (Map p965; ☎ 312 3943; Str Lipscani 88; ☑ 11am-6am) This outdoor, bamboo-clad bar is brilliantly set up in the space left by a demolished building, hence the name.

Lăptăria Enache/La Motor (Map p965; B-dul Nicolae Bălcescu 2) Trendy, rooftop joint on the 4th floor of the National Theatre. With one long bar, it has a lively student crowd, huge metal sculptures and a new wooden seating area.

Green Hours 22 Jazz Club (Map p965; ☎ 314 5751; Calea Victoriei 120; ☑ 24hr) Hip cellar bar with live jazz, a weekend disco and even short theatre performances. The programme is posted inside.

Gay & Lesbian Venues

Bucharest's fledgling gay scene remains stilted by lingering homophobic attitudes across both the city and country as a whole. But there is some action. **Casablanca** (☎ 330 1206; Sala Polivalentă) is a gay-friendly club south of the city centre, and there's also **Queen's** (Str Culmea Veche 2; ☑ noon-3am), with restricted entry (see www.bucharestonline.ro/enclubs.html for details).

ENTERTAINMENT

Şapte Seri (Seven Evenings) is a free, weekly entertainment listings mag.

Cinemas

Most films are shown in their original language with Romanian subtitles and cost around €1 to €3. **Hollywood Multiplex** (Map p963; ☎ 327 7020; Bucureşti Mall, Calea Vitan 55-59) is Bucharest's only multiscreen cinema, while **Cinematica Eforie** (Map p965; ☎ 313 0483; Str Eforie 2) shows art-house and world films.

Opera & Theatre

Opera Română (Opera House; Map p963; ☎ 314 6980; onr@kappa.ro; B-dul Mihail Kogălniceanu 70; tickets €1-4; box office ☑ 10am-1pm & 2-7.30pm Tue-Sun) Enjoy a full-scale opera for a fraction of Western European prices.

Teatrul Naţional Ion Luca Caragiale (Ion Luca Caragiale National Theatre; Map p965; ☎ 614 7171, 615 4746; B-dul Nicolae Bălcescu 2) The **box office** (☑ 10am-7pm) is on the southern side of the building.

GETTING THERE & AWAY
Air

International flights use **Otopeni airport** (☎ 201 4050, 204 1423; Şos Bucureşti-Ploieşti), 16km north of Bucharest on the road to Ploieşti. The airport has a new lower-level floor for domestic flight arrivals and departures.

Arrivals use terminal A and departures leave from the newer terminal B. The Otopeni airport **information desk** (☎ 204 1000; www.otp-airport.ro) in terminal B is open 24 hours.

Romania's national airline, with its head office at Otopeni, is **Tarom** (Transporturile Aeriene Române; www.tarom.ro; ☎ 201 400, 201 1355, 204 1220). The airline also has an **agency** (☎ 337 0220; Splaiul Independentei 17) in central Bucharest. **Air Moldova** (☎ 312 1258; Str Batiştei 5) also serves Otopeni.

Băneasa airport (☎ 232 0020; Şos Bucureşti-Ploieşti 40), 8km north of the centre, is used for internal flights and charter flights for package holidays. New domestic airline **Angel Airlines** (☎ 211 1701) operates flights from here.

Bus

Bucharest's **central bus station** (Calea Griviţei) – more a bus stop, really – is outside Hotel Ibis. Domestic services are poor and timetables are stuck on lampposts.

Train

Most express trains and many local trains use **Gară de Nord** (☎ 223 0880; B-dul Gării de Nord 2).

Wasteels (☎ 222 7844; www.wasteelstravel.ro) sells discounted tickets to Western Europe for under-26s; it's on the right as you enter the main building. Advance ticket purchases can be made from the **Agenţie de Voiaj CFR main office** (Map p965; ☎ 313 7844; Str Domniţa Anastasia 10-14).

GETTING AROUND
Public Transport

For buses, trams and trolleybuses buy tickets (€0.20) at any RATB street kiosk, marked *casa de bilete* or simply *bilete*. Make sure you punch your ticket on board or else you risk a €10 on-the-spot fine.

Public transport runs from 5am to approximately 11pm (services are reduced on Sunday). Bucharest's metro has four lines and 45 stations. Line M4 is brand new. Trains run between 5.30am and 11.30pm, going every five to seven minutes during peak periods and about every 20 minutes off peak.

Tickets valid for either two or 10 journeys cost €0.20 or €1.50 respectively. A one-month unlimited travel ticket costs €4.50.

Taxi
Opt for a cab with a meter. Reputable companies include **CrisTaxi** (☎ 9461), **Meridian** (☎ 9444) and **Prof Taxi** (☎ 9422).

TRANSYLVANIA

To most people, the name 'Transylvania' conjures up images of haunted castles, werewolves and vampires. Certainly the 14th-century castles at Râşnov and Bran appear readymade for a Dracula movie.

However, the charms of Transylvania are far more diverse: mountain scenery, some of Romania's best hiking and skiing, and rural villages that haven't changed much since the 18th century.

SINAIA
☎ 0244 / pop 14,240
It's not dubbed the Pearl of the Carpathians for nothing. It boasts not only Romania's hottest skiing but also the country's most fabulous palace. Floating at an altitude of 800m to 930m, Sinaia is in the narrow Prahova Valley and lies at the foot of the fir-clad Bucegi Mountains.

Orientation
The train station is directly below the centre of town. From the station climb up the stairway across the street to busy B-dul Carol I. Hotel Montana and the cable car are to the left; the monastery and palace are uphill to the right.

Information
Banca Comercială Română (B-dul Carol I; ☺ 8am-5.30pm Mon-Fri, 8.30am-12.30pm Sat) Next to the

primărie (town hall), cashes travellers cheques, gives cash advances on Visa and MasterCard and has an ATM.
Central post office (☎ 311 591; B-dul Carol I, 33; ☺ 7am-8pm Mon-Fri, 8am-noon Sat)
Central telephone office (B-dul Carol I, 33; ☺ 10am-6pm Mon-Fri, 10am-2pm Sat)
Dracula's Land (☎ 311 441; mihneasutu@hotmail .com; B-dul Carol I, 14; ☺ 9am-6pm) One of the country's most active, enthusiastic travel agencies, it doubles as a tourist office.
Internet Room (lobby of the Hotel International; per hr €0.50; ☺ 10am-10pm)
Luxor Agenţie de Turism (☺ 8am-8pm) Currency exchange here offers good rates.
Salvamont (☎ 313 131; Primărie, B-dul Carol I) Also at Cota 2000 at top of chairlift. If you run into problems in the mountains or need to check weather conditions.

Sights & Activities
Sinaia Monastery, named after Mt Sinai, has a large Orthodox church, dating from 1846, and an older church (1695) with its original frescoes in the compound to the left. Beside the newer church is a small **Muzeul de Istorie** (History Museum; adult/child €0.80/0.40; ☺ 10am-6pm).

Just past the monastery begins the road to **Peleş Castle** (☎ 310 918; compulsory tours adult/child €2.50/1.25; ☺ 11am-5pm Wed, 9am-5pm Thu-Sun), the former royal palace, dating from 1883.

A few hundred metres uphill from the main palace is the smaller **Pelişor Palace** (☎ 312 184; compulsory tours adult/child €2/0.65; ☺ 11am-5pm Wed, 9am-5pm Thu-Sun) in mock-medieval style. Pelişor was built for Carol I's son, Ferdinand, and was decorated in the Art Nouveau style by Queen Marie.

Sinaia is a great base for **hiking** in the Bucegi Mountains. Nonhikers should take the **cable car** (☎ 311 674; Str Telecabinei; round trip €2.75; ☺ 8am-4pm Tue-Sun) from Hotel Montana to Cota 1400 and continue on the cable car or ski lift up to Cota 2000.

Sinaia's big attraction is **skiing**. It has 10 downhill tracts, three cross-country trails, three sleigh slopes and a bobsled slope. The **Snow ski school and gear shop** (☎ 311 198; Str Cuza Vodă 2A), at the foot of the cable-car station behind Hotel Montana, rents snowboards and ski equipment.

Sleeping
Cabana Schiorilor (☎ 313 655; Str Drumul Cotei 7; d €22, 5-bed r €20) Pretty fancy as far as cabanas go, it has an on-site, elegant restaurant. It's an easily walkable distance from the centre.

Hotel Economat (☎ 311 151; fax 311 150; Aleea Peleşului 2; s/d €20/24) Just a few minutes' walk from the Peleş Castle, the hotel also runs a series of other one- to three-star villas in the area and so can offer a wide range of accommodation starting from €10 per person.

Eating

There are numerous kebab and fast-food stands to be found along B-dul Carol I and inside the Perla Bucegi shopping complex.

Ferdinand (☎ 0722-526 110; Str Furnica 63; mains €2.50-4; ☿ 11am-midnight) One of the best bets in town, this has a high, arched ceiling topping a rustic dining room.

Snow (☎ 311 198; Str Cuza Vodă; mains €2-4; ☿ 8am-midnight) Offers one of the most pleasant dining experiences in the region, either on its airy double-decker terrace or in its bright yellow-green dining room. Vegetarians will rejoice at having found a respite from cheese and potatoes.

Getting There & Away

Sinaia is on the Bucharest–Braşov train local trains to Braşov are frequent. Approaching Sinaia from the south, don't get off at the 'Halta Sinaia Sud' – a small stop 2km south of Sinaia centre.

Buses run every 45 minutes between 6.20am and 10.45pm from the central bus stop on B-dul Carol I to Azuga and Buşteni. From here you can catch all minibuses linking Braşov with points south, such as Bucharest, Brăila and Constanţa.

BRAŞOV

☎ 0268 / pop 319,908

Dubbed the new Prague, Braşov (Brassó in Hungarian) is one of the most visited cities in Romania. Piaţa Sfatului, the central square, is the finest in the country, and is lined with baroque façades and Bohemian outdoor cafés.

Orientation

The train station (gară) is a long way from the city centre. Take bus No 4 (buy your ticket at a kiosk) to Central Park or Str Mureşenilor.

Braşov has two main bus stations: Autogară 1, next to the train station; and Autogară 2, west of the train station near the Stadion Tineretului stop (local bus No 12 or 22 goes to/from the centre).

Information

There is a 24-hour exchange bureau inside the train station, and many others (along with numerous ATMs) along B-dul Eroilor, along Str Republicii and throughout the centre. There are no tourist offices in Braşov.

Aurofarm (☎ 443 560; Str Republicii 27; ☿ 24hr) Medical clinic.

Banca Comercială Română (Piaţa Sfatului 14; ☿ 8.30am-5pm Mon-Fri, 8.30am-noon Sat) Changes travellers cheques and gives cash advances on Visa and MasterCard.

Blue Net Club (☎ 0740-839 449; Str Michael Weiss 26; per hr €0.40; ☿ 24hr) Internet access.

Central post office (☎ 411 609; Str Iorga Nicolae 1; ☿ 7am-8pm Mon-Fri, 8am-1pm Sat) Opposite the Heroes' Cemetery.

Central Telephone Centre (B-dul Eroilor; ☿ 7am-7pm) Between the Capitol and Aro Palace Hotels.

Roving România (☎ 0744-212 065; www.roving -romania.co.uk) Travel agency with local information.

Sights

In the middle of Piaţa Sfatului is the **Braşov Historical Museum** (☎ 472 363; Piaţa Sfatului; adult/child €0.50/0.25; ☿ 10am-6pm Tue-Sun), where the history of the Saxon guilds is recounted. The 58m Trumpeter's Tower above the building dates from 1582.

Built between 1384 and 1477, the Gothic **Biserica Neagră** (Black Church; adult/child €1/0.50; ☿ 10am-5pm Mon-Sat, mass 10am Sun) looms just south of the square.

Go south a little to the neoclassical **Schei Gate** (1828), then walk 500m up Str Prundului to Piaţa Unirii.

On Piaţa Unirii you'll find the black-spired 1595 **St Nicolae din Schei** (St Nicholas' Cathedral; Piaţa Unirii; ☿ 6am-9pm). Beside the church is the **First Romanian School Museum** (☎ 443 879; adult/child €0.40/0.20; ☿ 9am-5pm Tue-Sun), which dates from 1495 and houses a collection of icons, paintings on glass and old manuscripts.

Go back the way you came and turn right just before the Schei Gate to reach the 16th-century **Muzeul Bastionul Ţesătorilor** (Weavers' Bastion Museum; ☎ 472 368; adult/child €0.40/0.20; ☿ 10am-4pm Tue-Sun). In a corner fort on the old city walls, the museum has a fascinating scale model of Braşov in the 17th century.

The **Tâmpa cable car** (Telecabina Tâmpa; ☎ 443 732; round trip adult/child €0.80/0.40; ☿ 10am-6pm Tue-Fri, 10am-7pm Sat & Sun) rises from 640m to 960m and offers stunning views. The walk to the top, following a series of zigzagging trails, takes 45 minutes and is worth the effort.

ROMANIA

BRAŞOV

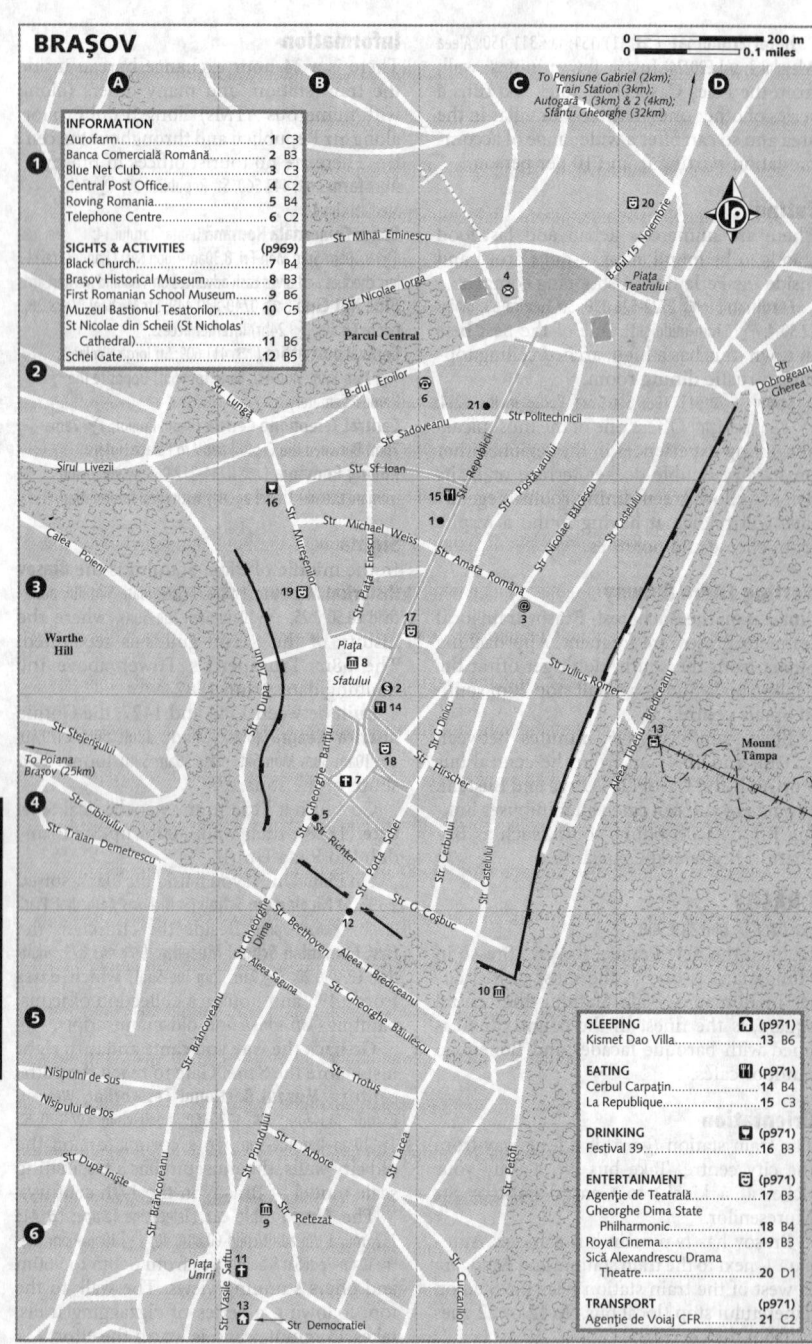

0 ——————— 200 m
0 ——————— 0.1 miles

To Pensiune Gabriel (2km);
Train Station (3km);
Autogară 1 (3km) & 2 (4km);
Sfântu Gheorghe (32km)

INFORMATION
Aurofarm	1 C3
Banca Comercială Română	2 B3
Blue Net Club	3 C3
Central Post Office	4 C2
Roving Romania	5 B4
Telephone Centre	6 C2

SIGHTS & ACTIVITIES (p969)
Black Church	7 B4
Braşov Historical Museum	8 B3
First Romanian School Museum	9 B6
Muzeul Bastionul Tesatorilor	10 C5
St Nicolae din Scheii (St Nicholas' Cathedral)	11 B6
Schei Gate	12 B5

Str Mihai Eminescu

Str Nicolae Iorga

Parcul Central

Piaţa Teatrului

Str Dobrogeanu Gherea

Str Lungă

B-dul Eroilor

Str Sadoveanu

Str Politechnicii

Str Sf Ioan

Str Republicii

Str Poştavarului

Str Nicolae Bălcescu

Str Castelui

Şirul Livezii

Str Michael Weiss

Str Mureşenilor

Piaţa Enescu

Str Amata Română

Calea Poienii

Str După Ziduri

Str Julius Romer

Warthe Hill

Piaţa Sfatului

Str Gheorghe Bariţiu

Str C Diaconu

Mount Tâmpa

Str Hirscher

Aleea Tiberiu Brediceanu

To Poiana Braşov (25km)

Str Stejerişului

Str Cibinului

Str Richter

Str Poarta Schei

Str Cerbului

Str Castelui

Str Traian Demetrescu

Str G Cosbuc

Str Gheorghe Beethoven

Str Dima

Aleea Sălcina

Str Gheorghe Băiulescu

Nisipului de Sus

Str Brâncoveanu

Str Trotuş

Nisipului de Jos

Str Prundului

Str L Arbore

Str Laca

Str După Işte

Str Brâncoveanu

Str Retezat

Str Vasile Saftu

Piaţa Unirii

Str Democraţiei

Str Petôfi

Str Curcanilor

SLEEPING (p971)
Kismet Dao Villa	13 B6

EATING (p971)
Cerbul Carpaţin	14 B4
La Republique	15 C3

DRINKING (p971)
Festival 39	16 B3

ENTERTAINMENT (p971)
Agenţie de Teatrală	17 B3
Gheorghe Dima State Philharmonic	18 B4
Royal Cinema	19 B3
Sica Alexandrescu Drama Theatre	20 D1

TRANSPORT (p971)
Agenţie de Voiaj CFR	21 C2

ROMANIA

Sleeping

Kismet Dao Villa (☎ 514 296; www.elvisvilla.com /brasov; Str Democratiei 2B; dm €10-11, d €26) This is one of the country's finest hostels: well organised, spotless, modern and well located (behind Piața Unirii). Rooms have from five to nine beds. Take Bus No 4 from the train station to the last stop.

Maria & Grig Bolea (☎ 311 962) This pair is hard to miss at the train station, even if you try; they meet almost every train. Maria places tourists in private homes (€10 per person), some of which can be winners, others not so great.

Pensiune Gabriel (☎ 0744-844 223; Str Toamnei 4, B11 Sc et1 ap1; per person €13) This comes recommended by several readers. A 10-minute walk northeast of the centre, the place is clean and friendly and the owner super helpful (often willing to drive guests to Bran and other places).

Eating & Drinking

La Republique (☎ 0744-351 668; Str Republicii 33; mains €0.50-3; ⏰ 9am-midnight) Being a creperie already makes it all the more unique (both meat-filled and dessert crepes are delicious).

Cerbul Carpatin (Carpathian Stag; ☎ 443 981; Piața Sfatului 12; mains €3-6; ⏰ 10am-midnight) Brașov's most famous restaurant is in the elegant Hirscher House (1545).

Festival 39 (☎ 478 664; Str Mureșenilor 23; ⏰ 10am-1am) By far, this is the best bar in town for a relaxed drink. It somehow manages to pull off the feat of having both a lively and subdued atmosphere at the same time.

Entertainment

Brașov has several cinemas, the most central of which is the **Royal** (☎ 419 965; Str Mureșenilor 7).

Gheorghe Dima State Philharmonic (☎ 441 378; Str Apollania Hirscher 10) A good reputation and performs mainly between September and May. Tickets for theatrical and classical music and ballet performances can be purchased at the **Agenție de Teatrală** (☎ 471 889; Str Republicii 4), just off Piața Sfatului.

Sică Alexandrescu Drama Theatre (☎ 418 850; Piața Teatrului 1) Has plays, recitals, and opera year-round.

Getting There & Away

Most minibuses leave from **Autogară 1** (☎ 426 882), next to the train station. There are minibuses to Bucharest every half-hour from 6am to 7.30pm, plus hourly minibuses on a Târgu Mureș–Sighișoara–Brașov–Bușteni–Bucharest route.

Autogară 2 (☎ 426 332; Str Avram Iancu 114), west of the train station, has buses to Râșnov, Bran and Moieciu, marked 'Moieciu–Bran', leaving every half-hour. Other major bus connections include one daily to Făgăraș Câmpulung and Curtea de Argeș two to Pitești; and 11 to Zărnești.

Brașov's connected to Mangalia/Constanța (four daily), Sighișoara (four daily), Cluj-Napoca (four daily) and Oradea (daily). There are 18 trains to/from Bucharest (three to four hours), one to Prague (10½ hours) and Budapest (11 hours) and Vienna (15 hours).

Advance train tickets are sold at the **Agenție de Voiaj CFR office** (470 696; Str Republicii 53; ⏰ 8am-6pm Mon-Fri, 9am-1pm Sat).

BRAN & RÂȘNOV

☎ 0268 / pop 5300

No visit to Romania is complete without seeing **Bran Castle** (adult/child €1.60/0.50; ⏰ 9am-5.30pm Tue-Sun), dating from 1378. Though this fairytale castle is impressive in itself – it's unlikely the real Vlad Țepeș (Dracula) was ever here.

Beside the entrance to the castle is a **Muzeul Satului** (Village Museum; admission incl in castle entry fee; ⏰ 9am-4pm Tue-Sun) with a collection of Transylvanian farm buildings.

Râșnov offers the dual attraction of a convenient camping ground and the ruins of the 13th-century **Cetatea Râșnov** (Râșnov Fortress; ☎ 230 255; adult/child €1.20/0.80 plus parking €0.25; ⏰ 8am-5pm Tue-Sun).

Sleeping

Wild camping is not permitted around Bran Castle.

Antrec (☎ 236 884; Str Aureli Stoian 340; ⏰ 9am-8pm) Arranges accommodation in private homes in and around Bran.

Cabana Bran Castel (☎ 236 404; dm with shared bathroom €5) Just 600m from the castle, Bran Castel serves meals and is open year-round.

Getting There & Away

Buses marked 'Bran–Moieciu' (€0.50, one hour) depart every half-hour from Brașov's Autogară 2. Return buses to Brașov leave Bran every half-hour between 5.30am and 7.30pm Monday to Friday and between 6.40am and 5.40pm Saturday and Sunday. All buses to Brașov stop at Râșnov.

ROMANIA

SIGHIŞOARA

☎ 0265 / pop 36,180

Sighişoara (Schässburg in German, Seges-vár in Hungarian) has an enchantingly pre-served medieval citadel as its core, and is surrounded by beautiful hilly countryside. It tends to win visitors' hearts more than any other city in Transylvania.

Sighişoara was also the birthplace of Vlad Ţepeş.

Orientation

Follow Str Gării south from the train station to the Soviet war memorial, where you turn left to the large Orthodox church. Cross the Târnava Mare River on the footbridge here and take Str Morii to the left, then keep going all the way up to Piaţa Hermann Oberth and the old town.

Information

There are numerous exchange bureaus lining the city's main street, Str 1 Decembrie 1918. Sighişoara has no official tourist office.

Banca Comercială Română (Str Justiţiei 12; ☑ 8.30am-4pm Mon-Fri)

Central Post Office (☎ 771 055; Str 1 Decembrie 1918, 17; ☑ 7am-8pm Mon-Fri)

Internet Café (☎ 771 269; Str Libertăţii 44; per hr €0.60; ☑ 9am-11pm)

Steaua Agenţie de Turism (☎ 772 499; fax 771 932; Str 1 Decembrie 1918, 12; ☑ 9am-5pm Mon-Fri, 9am-1pm Sat) Sells city guides or maps and arranges private accommodation.

Telephone Centre (☎ 771 055; Str 1 Decembrie 1918, 17; ☑ 7am-9pm Mon-Fri, 8am-8pm Sat) Inside post office.

Sights

All Sighişoara's sights are in the old town – a medieval **citadel** with a 14th-century wall, to which 14 towers and five artillery bas-tions were later added. It's on the Unesco World Heritage list and retains just nine of its original towers and two of its bastions.

Entering the citadel, you pass under the **Turnul cu Ceas** (Clock Tower) – the 1648 clock still keeps time – with the **History Museum** (☎ 771 108; Piaţa Muzeului 1; adult/child €0.80/0.40; ☑ 10am-3pm Mon, 9am-6.30pm Tue-Fri, 9am-3.30pm Sat & Sun). Under the tower on the left as you enter the citadel is the **Torture Room Museum** (admission €0.25; ☑ same as museum).

Immediately inside the citadel is the 15th-century **Biserica Mănăstirii** (Church of the Dominican Monastery; ☑ 9am-7pm Mon-Sat, 10am-2pm Sun).

Across Piaţa Muzeului is **Casa Vlad Dracul** (☎ 771 596; Str Cositorarilor 5; ☑ 10am-midnight), the house where Vlad (the Impaler) Ţepeş was born in 1431; it's now a restaurant (see below). The quiet, miniscule **Piaţa Cetăţii** is the heart of old Sighişoara. It was here that markets, craft fairs, public executions, im-palings and witch trials were held.

Sleeping

Elvis Villa (☎ 772 546; www.elvisvilla.com/sighisoara; Str Libertăţii 10; dm €10; ☑) Just 250m west of the train station, it boasts free beer and In-ternet access.

Burg Hostel (☎ 778 489; www.ibz.ro; Str Bastionu-lui 4-6; dm/d €7/24) German-run hostel in the citadel, with a restaurant terrace and smoky basement lounge bar.

Eating & Drinking

Café International & Family Centre (☎ 777 844; Piaţa Cetăţii 8; mains €1-2) This is a double-whammy oasis for vegetarians and homesick Ameri-cans (where else in Romania can you find a peanut butter and jam sandwich, brownies, grilled cheese, and lemon pie?).

Casa Dracula (☎ 771 596; Str Cositorarilor 5; mains €2-6; ☑ 10am-midnight) 'Tourist trap' springs to mind. However, despite being located in the house where little Vlad Ţepeş took his first steps, the menu is varied and there are vegetarian dishes.

Insomnia (☎ 0744-172 498; Str Turnului; ☑ 10am-2am) Sighişoara's best club, a funky mix of bar, lounge, disco and performance/cinema space.

Getting There & Away

The **bus station** (☎ 771 260; Str Libertăţii) is next to the train station. Buses or minibus serv-ices run hourly (from 6.15am to 8.15pm) to Bucharest via Braşov.

The **Agenţie de Voiaj CFR** (☎ 771 820; Str Goga 6A; ☑ 8am-4pm Mon-Fri) sells train tickets. Sighişoara is linked to Bucharest with nine services a day. There are eight services to or from Cluj-Napoca, Satu Mare, Arad, Oradea, Budapest, Prague and Vienna.

CLUJ-NAPOCA

☎ 0264 / pop 331,990

There's a sassy, savvy feel to the univer-sity town of Cluj-Napoca and its residents. There are trendy bars galore and cool places with cool people.

The history of Cluj-Napoca goes back to Thracian (Dacian) times. German merchants arrived in the 12th century. From 1791 to 1848 and again after the union with Hungary in 1867, Cluj-Napoca served as the capital of Transylvania.

Orientation

The train station (gară) is 1.5km north of the city centre. Walk left out of the station and catch tram No 101 or a trolleybus south down Str Horea. Get off the trolleybus immediately after crossing the river; on tram No 101 go two stops, then walk south until you cross the river.

All major bus services arrive at and depart from the bus station (autogară), which is north of town.

Information

The city is full of ATMs and exchange bureaus. See www.cjnet.ro for general information on the city.

Banca Comercială Română (☎ 591 227; Str Gheorghe Barițiu 10-12; ☼ 8am-3pm Mon-Fri) Gives cash advances and changes travellers cheques.

Clematis (Piața Unirii 11; ☼ 8am-10pm) Well-stocked central pharmacy.

Internet Café (Str 1 Decembrie 20; per hr €0.35; ☼ 8-2am)

Post Office (Str Regele Ferdinand 33; ☼ 7am-8pm Mon-Fri, 8am-2pm Sat)

Telephone Centre (Str Regele Ferdinand 33; ☼ 7.30am-8pm Mon-Fri, 8am-1pm Sat) Inside post office.

Youth Hostels România (YHR; ☎ 586 616; www .hihostels-romania.ro; Piața Lucian Blaga; ☼ 9am-5pm Mon-Fri) Inside the imposing Student's Culture House; has local information.

Sights

The vast 14th-century **St Michael's Church** dominates Piața Unirii. The neo-Gothic tower (1859) topping the Gothic hall church is a great landmark.

On the eastern side of the square is the excellent **National Art Museum** (☎ 496 952; Piața Unirii 30; adult/child €0.80/0.40; ☼ noon-7pm Wed-Sun), inside the baroque Banffy Palace (1791).

To the west on Piața Muzeului is the interesting **National History Museum of Transylvania** (☎ 495 677; Str Constantin Daicoviciu 1; adult/child €0.50/0.25; ☼ 10am-4pm Tue-Sun). This museum presents one of the most comprehensive accounts of Transylvanian history.

There's also the **Muzeul Etnografic al Transilvaniei** (Ethnographic Museum; ☎ 592 344; Str Memoran-

dumului 21; adult/child €0.80/0.40; ☼ 9am-5pm Tue-Sun), with a fine collection of folk costumes and beautiful woven carpets.

Activities

For details on caves and walking routes in the Apuseni Mountains to the southwest, contact **Green Mountain Holidays** (☎ 257 142; www.greenmountainholidays.ro; Str Principală 305). Based in the village of Izvoru Crișului, 43km west of Cluj-Napoca on the road to Huedin, the company's website gives accommodation options (from €150 per week) plus walking, caving, rock-climbing and horse-riding trips that can be organised.

Clubul de Cicloturism Napoca (☎ 450 013; office@ccn.ro; Apt 8, Str Sindicatelor 3) are lovers of the outdoors who can help with all your two-wheeler questions.

Sleeping

Retro Hostel (☎ 450 452; www.retro.ro; Str Potaissa 13; dm €10-13; 🖳) Here you can buy maps and CD-ROMs, join fun tours, order a therapeutic massage and follow it with a bottle of țiuca (home-made plum brandy).

Hotel Comfort (☎ 598 410; Calea Turzii 48; s/d/ste €24/37/48; 🖳) This is a modern, clean and friendly place. Beds are low, ceilings are high and soft pastels envelop you everywhere.

Eating & Drinking

Pizza Y (☎ 0722-218 210; Piața Unirii 1; mains €1-3; ☼ 9am-midnight) In a courtyard just off the southern end of the square, Pizza Y serves pastas and fresh salads and an amazing 34 types of pizza.

Restaurant Privighetoarea (☎ 593 480; Str Regele Ferdinand 16; mains €1-3; ☼ 9am-7pm) Serves up hearty portions of meat, potatoes and more traditional soups, spicy meatballs and hot breaded cheese.

Diesel Bar (☎ 598 441; Piața Unirii 17; ☼ 9am-3am) Generally the most happening disco come the weekend. It spins mainly pop-dance and retro hits in its cavernous space.

Entertainment

Șapte Seri (www.sapteseri.ro) is a free biweekly booklet listing all the latest goings on (in Romanian).

Cinema Favorit (Str Horea 6) One of several cinemas in the centre of town.

National Theatre Lucian Blaga (☎ 591 799; Piața Ștefan cel Mare 24) Designed by well-known

ROMANIA

Viennese architects Fellner and Hellmer, a performance here is well attended.

The **opera** (☎ 597 175) is in the same building as the theatre. Tickets can be bought in advance from the **Agenţie de Teatrală** (☎ 595 363; Piaţa Ştefan cel Mare 14; ⏰ 11am-5pm Tue-Fri). Tickets for classical concerts hosted by the **State Philharmonic** (Filarmonica de Stat; ☎ 430 063; Str Mihail Kogălniceanu) are also sold here.

Getting There & Away
AIR
Tarom (☎ 432 524; Piaţa Mihai Viteazul 11; ⏰ 8am-7pm Mon-Fri, 9am-1pm Sat) flies direct to Bucharest (for international flights, see Transport p961). **Carpatair** (☎ 416 016; cluj-napoca@carpatair.ro), with an office at the airport, has flights to Italy.

BUS
From **Autogară 2** (there is no No 1) one daily bus or minibus travels to Braşov, 10 buses per week go to Budapest and three weekly to Chişinau.

Agenţie de Voiaj CFR (☎ 432 001; Piaţa Mihai Viteazul 20; ⏰ 7am-7pm Mon-Fri) has services to Sibiu (four hours, daily), Mangalia (13 hours, daily), Timişoara (seven hours, three daily), Bucharest (7½ hrs, six daily) and Oradea (2¼ to 4½ hours, 10 daily).

TRAIN
Two trains go to Budapest (five hours) daily.

CRIŞANA & BANAT

The areas of Crişana (north of the Mureş River) and Banat (to the south) have a spirited independence found nowhere else in Romania. It was in Timişoara that the 1989 revolution took hold, a fact these charming, tenacious people are mightily proud of.

Crişana and Banat once merged imperceptibly into Yugoslavia's Vojvodina and Hungary's Great Plain.

ORADEA
☎ 0259 / pop 223,700
Elegant Oradea lies a few kilometres east of the Hungarian border in the centre of the Crişana region, at the edge of the Carpathian Mountains.

Of all the cities of the Austro-Hungarian Empire, Oradea best retains its 19th-century romantic style.

Orientation
The train station is a couple of kilometres north of the centre; tram Nos 1 and 4 run south from Piaţa Bucureşti (outside the train station) to Piaţa Unirii, Oradea's main square. Tram No 4 also stops at the northern end of Str Republicii, with a five-minute walk south to the centre.

The main square north of the river is Piaţa Republicii (also called Piaţa Regele Ferdinand I).

Information
There's no official tourist office.
Game Star Internet Café (Str Mihai Eminescu 4; per hr €0.50; ⏰ 24hr)
HVB Bank (☎ 406 700; Piaţa Unirii 24; ⏰ 9am-4pm Mon-Fri) Cash transfers, ATMs and currency-exchange facilities.
Panda Tours (☎ 477 222; Str Iosif Vulcan 6; ⏰ 9am-7pm Mon-Fri, 9am-1pm Sat) This travel agency has English-speaking staff.
Pharmacy (☎ 418 242; junction Str Libertăţii & Piaţa Ferdinand; ⏰ 24hr)
Post Office (☎ 136 420; Str Roman Ciorogariu 12; ⏰ 7am-7.30pm Mon-Fri)
Telephone Office (☎ 418 242; junction Str Libertăţii & Piaţa Ferdinand; ⏰ 8am-8pm) Inside post office.

Sights
Oradea's most imposing sights are on its two central squares, Piaţa Unirii and Piaţa Republicii.

A **statue of Mihai Viteazul**, the prince of Wallachia, who, during his reign (1593–1601), is said to have resided in Oradea in 1600. West of the statue, overlooking the River Crişul Repede, is the magnificent **Vulturul Negru** (Black Vulture) hotel and shopping centre, built in 1908.

The magnificent neoclassical **Teatrul de Stat** (State Theatre; Piaţa Republicii), designed by Viennese architects Fellner and Hellmer in 1900, dominates Piaţa Republicii (see opposite for performance details).

Oradea's other worthy buildings are in a park southwest of the train station. Across the road is **Canon's Corridor**, a series of archways that date to the 18th century. The **Catholic cathedral** (1780) is the largest in Romania.

The **Episcopal Palace** (1770), with 100 fresco-adorned rooms and 365 windows, was modelled after Belvedere Palace in Vienna. Now it's the **Muzeul Ţării Crişului** (Museum of the Land of the Criş Rivers; ☎ 412 725; B-dul Dacia 1-3; admission €1; ⏰ 10am-5pm Tue-Sun).

Sleeping

Pension Gobe (☎ 414 845; Str Dobrogeanu Gherea 26; dm €12) A member of Youth Hostels Romania, it is the city's best budget option with three- to four-bed rooms, a small restaurant and bar.

Hotel Parc (☎ 418 410; Str Republicii 5-7; s/d €20/25) Best of the budget bunch. Ignore the crumbling façade as inside it's clean and gleaming white.

At **Strandul cu Voluti** (cabins/camping per adult €6/2) you can camp from May to mid-September in Băile 1 Mai, 9km southeast of Oradea.

Eating

Calea Republicii is lined with cheap and cheerful eateries and cafés. Oradeans enjoy a spot of evening strolling and this is the street to do it in.

Paninoteca Faustos (Str Republicii 3; mains €5) Watch the world go by while munching €2 pizzas, salads and tiramisu.

Casa Iulia Restaurant (☎ 413 438; Str Republicii 5; mains €7-10) Smart, minimalist joint with trendy bar and massive outdoor terrace, with live music on Thursday evenings and nice wooden bar.

Entertainment

Cinema Libertăţii (☎ 434 097; Str Independenţei 1), in the Vulturul Negru building, shows films in their original language with Romanian subtitles.

Tickets for performances at the **Filarmonica de Stat** (State Philharmonic; ☎ 430 853; Str Moscovei 5) can be purchased from its **ticket office** (☒ 10am-6pm Mon-Fri). The ticket office is inside the **Teatrul de Stat** (State Theatre; ☎ 130 885; Piaţa Ferdinand 4-6; tickets €3-12; ☒ 10-11am & 5-7pm).

Getting There & Away

Tarom (☎ 131 918; Piaţa Ferdinand 2; ☒ 6.30am-8pm Mon-Fri, 10am-1pm Sat) operates flights to Baia Mare, Bucharest and Satu Mare from **Oradea airport** (☎ 416 082; Calea Aradului km6). Prices are US$75/112 one-way/round trip (plus taxes). The **Agenţie de Voiaj CFR** (☎ 130 578; Str Republicii 2; ☒ 7am-7pm Mon-Fri) sells advance tickets.

Daily fast trains from Oradea include three to Budapest (€28), two to Bucharest (€16), five to Băile Felix, three to Cluj-Napoca (€8), one to Braşov and three to Timişoara (€5).

A daily bus runs to Budapest (€12, 10 hours) from outside the train station.

Maxitaxis run daily to Budapest, also from outside the train station (one-way €16).

TIMIŞOARA

☎ 0256 / pop 332,277

Tenacious Timişoara stunned the world as the birthplace of the 1989 revolution. Romania's fourth-largest city is known by residents as 'Primul Oraş Liber' (First Free Town). With a charming Mediterranean air and regal Habsburg buildings, it's a city that residents and tourists alike love.

Orientation

Confusingly, Gară Timişoara-Nord (northern train station) is west of the city centre. Walk east along B-dul Republicii to the Opera House and Piaţa Victoriei. Further north is Piaţa Libertăţii. Piaţa Unirii, the old town square, is two blocks further north. Timişoara's bus station is beside the Idsefin Market, three blocks from the train station.

Information

Central Post Office (☎ 491 999; B-dul Revoluţiei 2; ☒ 8am-7pm Mon-Fri, 8am-noon Sat)

Java Coffee House (☎ 432 495; Str Pacha 6; per hr €0.75; ☒ 24hr) Internet access inside the Java Coffee House (see p976)

Sensi Blu Pharmacy (☎ 406 153; Piaţa Victoriei 7; ☒ 8am-8pm Mon-Fri, 9am-8pm Sat & Sun)

Telephone Office (B-dul Mihai Eminescu; ☒ 7am-9pm)

Tourist Office (☎ 437 973; Str Proclamatia de la Timişoara 1; ☒ 10am-8pm Tue-Sat, 10am-2pm Sun) This new official centre books canoe trips, wildlife tours or just hotels.

Volksbank (☎ 406 101; Str Piatra Craiului 2) Cashes travellers cheques and arranges transfers.

Sights

The centre of town is **Piaţa Victoriei**, a beautifully landscaped pedestrian mall lined with shops, cinemas and cafés, with the **Teatrul Naţional şi Opera Română** (National Theatre & Opera House; ☎ 201 284; Str Mărăşeşti 2) at its head (see p976 for performance details).

Towering over the mall's southwestern end is the Romanian Orthodox **Metropolitan Cathedral** (1946). Next to the cathedral is **Central Park**, and just south of it the **Bega Canal** runs along tree-lined banks.

The 1989 revolution began on 15 December 1989 at the **Biserica Reformată Tökés** (Tökés Reformed Church; ☎ 492 992; Str Timotei Cipariu 1), where Father Lászlo Tökés spoke out against the dictator.

Piaţa Libertăţii and the **primăria veche** (old town hall), built in 1734, lie to the north. **Piaţa Unirii** is Timişoara's most picturesque

ROMANIA

SOUTHERN BUCOVINA

The painted churches of Southern Bucovina are among the greatest artistic monuments of Europe – in 1993 they were collectively designated a World Heritage–listed site by Unesco. Erected at a time when northern Moldavia was threatened by Turkish invaders, the monasteries were surrounded by strong defensive walls. Great popular armies would gather inside these fortifications, waiting to do battle. To educate the illiterate peasants who were unable to understand the liturgy, biblical stories were portrayed on the church walls in colourful pictures. The exteriors of many of the churches are covered with these magnificent 16th-century frescoes. Remarkably, most of the intense colours have been preserved despite five centuries of rain and wind.

Bucovina's monasteries are generally open 9am to 5pm or 6pm daily. The monasteries of Voroneţ, Humor and Moldoviţa, all accessible by bus and train, provide a representative sample of what Bucovina has to offer. The gateway to the painted churches is **Suceava**, erstwhile capital of Moldavia. **Gura Humorului**, a small logging town 37km west of Suceava, is an ideal base from which to visit the monasteries.

---

square, featuring a baroque **Roman Catholic cathedral** (1754) and the **Serbian Orthodox cathedral** (1754).

Sleeping & Eating
Hostel Timişoara (☎ 491 170; Str Arieş 19; dm €9) Large, supermodern building 2km from the centre. Take tram no 8 from Gară Timişoara-Nord.

Hotel Cina Banatul (☎ 491 903; B-dul Republicii 3-5; s/d €25/30) Here you'll find best-value accommodation with clean, ultramodern rooms and a good restaurant.

Camping International (☎ 208 925; camping international@yahoo.com; Aleea Pădurea Verde 6; camping €2.50, 4-bed chalets with central heating €54) The main entrance of this excellent camping ground is on Calea Dorobanţilor. From the train station, catch trolleybus No 11 to the end of the line. The bus stops less than 50m from the camping ground. The site has a restaurant.

Java Coffee House (☎ 432 495; Str Pacha 6; ⏰ 24hr) Go online or just chill out with a frothy caffeine hit.

Entertainment
Movies are screened in their original language at **Cinema Timis** (☎ 491 290; Piaţa Victoriei 7; tickets €1-3).

The **Teatrul Naţional şi Opera Română** (National Theatre & Opera House; ☎ 201 284; Str Mărăşeşti 2; tickets from €1) is highly regarded. Buy tickets in its **Agenţia Teatrală** (☎ 499 908; ⏰ 10am-1pm & 5-7pm Tue-Sun).

Classical concerts are held most evenings at the **Filharmonia de Stat Banatul** (State Philharmonic Theatre; ☎ 492 521; B-dul CD Loga 2; tickets from €1). You can buy tickets at the box office inside the Filharmonia or from the Agenţia Teatrală.

Getting There & Away
Tarom (☎ 490 150, 200 003; B-dul Revoluţiei 3-5; ⏰ 7am-7pm Mon-Fri, 7am-1pm Sat) has four daily flights to Bucharest (US$80 including tax) from Timişoara.

Angel Airlines (ticketing@angelairlines.ro; Str Eugeniu de Savoya 7) has three flights each week going to Bucharest.

Buses run daily to Budapest (€10, leaving at 2pm) and Istanbul. A weekly bus runs to Szeged in Hungary, leaving at 3pm from platform 1 (*linea 1*). Maxitaxis run daily to Oradea, Arad and Brad.

All major train services depart from the **Gară Timişoara-Nord** (☎ 491 696; Str Gării 2). Purchase tickets in advance from the **Agenţie de Voiaj CFR** (☎ 491 889; Piaţa Victoriei 2; ⏰ 8am-8pm Mon-Fri, international tickets 9am-7pm).

Daily fast trains include eight to Bucharest (€16), one to Cluj-Napoca (€8), five to Baile Herculane (€6), one to Baia Mare via Arad (€9), three to Budapest (€38) and one to Belgrade (€14).

ROMANIA DIRECTORY

ACCOMMODATION
Camping grounds in Romania are grubby and generally not recommended. They usually comprise wooden huts (*căsuţe*), which fit two to four people. The good news is that wild camping is legal anywhere in Romania unless specifically prohibited.

Staying in a private home is the best way to get to the roots of Romanian home life. Check out agrotourism (B&B in the countryside) on www.ruraltourism.ro. Local travel agents can also usually help find a private home. The largest agrotourism organisation in Romania is **Antrec** (National Association of Rural, Ecological & Cultural Tourism; www.antrec.iiruc.ro).

Not much separates one- and two-star hotels. Hot water *(apă caldă)* is common but not a given. In rural towns it can be restricted to a few hours in the morning and evening. In Bucharest you'll pay €25 to €40 per room, but outside the capital singles will usually be €15 to €25, doubles €20 to €30.

The headquarters of **Youth Hostels România** (www.hihostels-romania.ro) is in Cluj-Napoca (p973).

In most mountain areas there's a network of cabins or chalets *(cabana)* with restaurants and dormitories.

A particularly helpful website is www .rotravel.com.

ACTIVITIES

Romania's diverse landscape lends itself perfectly to active vacationing. Ski and snowboard centres in the Carpathian Mountains are becoming popular. Sinaia (p968) offers the best downhill skiing.

The ski season runs from December to mid-March. You can hire gear for about €10 per day from all the major hotels in the resorts. Five- to seven-day ski courses usually cost €60 to €80 for adults (€40 to €60 for children).

The Carpathians also offer endless opportunities for walkers, the most popular areas being the Bucegi and Făgăraş Mountains, south and west of Braşov.

Trails are generally well marked, and a system of *cabanas*, huts and occasionally hotels along the trails on the mountain tops and plateaus make even a several-day trek more than comfortable. You can find guides and information at www.alpineguide.ro.

Mountain biking has also taken off. The most active biking clubs are in Cluj-Napoca, Sibiu and Oradea. **Clubul de Ciclotur- ism Napoca** (☎ 0264-450 013; office@ccn.ro; Apt 8, Str Sindicatelor 3, Cluj-Napoca) can offer the best advice for cycling in the region and organises summer tours. **Transylvania Adventure** (☎ 722-289 608; www.adventuretransylvania.com; Petofi 24, Satu Mare 440026) also offers good biking tours.

CUSTOMS

Officially, you're allowed to import hard currency up to a maximum of US$10,000. Valuable goods and foreign currency over US$1000 should be declared upon arrival. For foreigners, duty-free allowances are 4L of wine, 1L of spirits and 200 cigarettes.

EMBASSIES & CONSULATES
Embassies & Consulates in Romania

Unless stated otherwise, the following foreign embassies are in Bucharest (area code 021).

Australia Bucharest (☎ 320 9802; don.cairns@ austrade.gov.au; B-dul Unirii 74)

Canada Bucharest (☎ 307 5000; bucst-im@ dfait-maeci.gc.ca; Str Nicolae Iorga 36)

France Bucharest (☎ 021-312 0217; www .ambafrance-ro.org, in French; Str Biserica Amzei 13–15)

Germany Bucharest (☎ 202 9853; Str Rabat 21)

Ireland Bucharest (☎ 211 3967; Str Vasile Lascăr 42-44)

Moldova Bucharest (☎ 021-230 0474; moldova@customers.dirigo.net; Aleea Alexandru 40)

UK Bucharest (☎ 201 7200; www.britain.ro; Str Jules Michelet 24)

USA Bucharest (☎ 021-210 4042; www.us embassy.ro; Str Tudor Arghezi 7–9); Bucharest (☎ 021-210 4042; Str Nicolae Filipescu 26); Cluj-Napoca (☎ 0264-594 315; Str Universităţii 7-9, Cluj-Napoca)

Romanian Embassies & Consulates Abroad

Romanian embassies and consulates abroad include the following:

Australia (☎ 02-6286 2343; www.roembau.org; 4 Dalman Cres, O'Malley, ACT 2606)

Canada (☎ 613-789 5345; www.cyberus.ca/~romania; 655 Rideau St, Ottawa, Ontario K1N 6A3)

France (☎ 01 47 05 10 46; www.amb-roumanie.fr in French; 5 rue de l'Exposition, F-75007 Paris)

Germany (☎ 030-803 30 18; ro-amb.berlin@t-online .de; Matterhornstrasse 79, D14129 Berlin)

Ireland (☎ 031-269 2852; ambrom@eircom.net; 47 Ailesbury Rd, Ballsbridge, Dublin)

Moldova (☎ 22-228 126; ambrom@ch.moldpac.md; Str Bucureşti 66/1, Chişinău)

UK (☎ 020-7937 9666; www.roemb.co.uk; 4 Palace Green, Kensington Gardens, London)

USA (☎ 202-232 3694; www.roembus.org; 1607 23rd St NW, Washington, DC 20008); New York (☎ 212-682 9120; www.romconsny.org; 200 East 38th St, New York)

FESTIVALS & EVENTS

Most festivals take place in summer although every part of Romania has some kind of festival going on throughout the year, from international film festivals to country get-togethers where shepherds meet and locals sell their wares.

ROMANIA

April
Snow Festival Păltiniş
Juni Pageant Braşov

May/June
Tânjaua de pe Mara Folk Festival Hoteni
Bucharest Carnival Late May/early June in Bucharest

July
Medieval Festival of the Arts Sighişoara

August
International Folk Music and Dance Festival of Ethnic Minorities in Europe Cluj-Napoca
Mountain Festival Fundata

September
Sâmbra Oilor Bran

December
De la Colind la Stea Braşov

HOLIDAYS

Public holidays in Romania:
New Year 1 & 2 January
Easter Monday (Both Catholic and Orthodox celebrations) March/April
Labour Day 1 May
Romanian (National Day) 1 December
Christmas Day 25 December
Boxing Day 26 December

MONEY

Romanian lei come in denominations of 2000, 10,000, 50,000, 100,000 and 500,000. There are (heavy) coins for one, five, 10, 20, 50, 100, 500 and 1000 lei. Prices are regularly quoted in euros.

To change money, you'll need to present your passport. Exchange bureaus are easy to find in any city or town; in villages you'll be out of luck. Dollars and euros are the easiest currencies to exchange.

All branches of the Banca Comercială Română, among others, will cash travellers cheques. Credit cards won't get you anywhere in the rural areas of Romania, but they are widely accepted in cities and large towns.

For more information on costs and money, see p28.

POST

A postcard or letter under 20g to Europe costs €0.15 and takes seven to 10 days; to the rest of the world it costs €0.40 and takes 10 to 14 days. The postal system is reliable, if slow. Recommended mail *(postală recomandată)* can be sent from any post office.

Poste restante is held for one month (address mail to 'c/o Poste Restante, Poştă Română Oficiul Bucureşti 1, Str Matei Millo 10, RO-70700 Bucureşti, Romania') at Bucharest's main post office.

TELEPHONE

Romania's international operator can be reached by dialling ☎ 971. For an English-speaking operator abroad, call **British Telecom** (☎ 01-800 4444), **AT&T USA Direct** (☎ 01-800 4288), **MCI Worldwide** (☎ 01-800 1800) or **Sprint** (☎ 01-800 0877). Any European mobile (cell) phone with roaming will work inside Romania.

Phonecards costing €2.15 or €4 can be bought at any telephone centre and at many newspaper kiosks. International calls can also be made with these.

Romania's country code is ☎ 40; the international access code is ☎ 00.

VISAS

To obtain a visa, your passport must be valid for at least six months after you enter (or plan to enter) the country.

Citizens of Canada, Japan, the USA and most EU countries may travel visa-free for 90 days in Romania. Those from many Eastern European countries can travel visa-free for 30 days. All other foreign visitors require a visa. As visa requirements change frequently, check with the **Ministry of Foreign Affairs** (www.mae.ro) before departure.

Romania issues two types of visas to tourists: transit or single-entry. Transit visas (if you need one) are for stays of up to three days, and cannot be bought at the border.

Check your visa requirements for Yugoslavia, Hungary, Bulgaria and Ukraine if you plan on crossing those borders. Contact the respective embassy in Bucharest for details. If you are taking the Bucharest–St Petersburg train you need Ukrainian and Belarusian transit visas on top of the Russian visa.

Russia Россия

HIGHLIGHTS

- **The Hermitage and Palace Square** One of Europe's greatest piazzas lined by the stunning Winter Palace, containing one of the world's greatest art galleries (p991)
- **The Kremlin and Red Square** There's power in the air at the nerve centre of the world's largest country and Lenin is on daily display on fabulous Red Square (p986)
- **Svetlogorsk** Old Prussia is the place some good beach action (p998)
- **Best journey** The exciting overnight Midnight Express train journey between Moscow and St Petersburg – meet strangers and drink the night away in time-honoured Russian fashion (p983)
- **Off-the-beaten track** The fabulous and remote spit of Kurshkaya Kosa (p999) holds Europe's second-highest dunes and pieces of amber are washed up along the beaches

FAST FACTS

- **Area** 16,995,800 sq km (twice the size of the continental USA)

- **ATMs** Common in Moscow, St Petersburg and Kaliningrad

- **Budget** R1300-1700 per day

- **Country codes** ☎ 7; international access code ☎ 8 (wait for second tone) 10

- **Famous for** Vodka, communism, tATu, Chelsea Football Club–owning billionaires

- **Head of State** Vladimir Putin

- **Language** Russian

- **Money** Russian roubles ($A1 = R21.49, CA$1 = R23.43, €1 = R36.74, ¥100 = R27.1, NZ$1 = R20.19, UK£1 = R53.23, US$1 = R29.12)

- **Phrases** *Privyet* (hi), *do svidaniya* (goodbye), *spasiba* (thanks), *izvinite* (excuse me)

- **Population** 147 million

- **Time** GMT/UTC +3 (Moscow & St Petersburg) GMT +2 (Kaliningrad)

- **Visas** Everyone needs one and they need to be obtained well in advance of travel (€40-55).

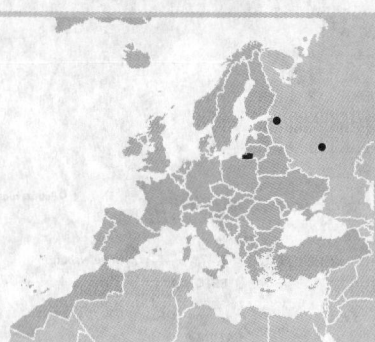

ROAMING RUSSIA

Beginning in Moscow for a couple of days, head north on the overnight train to St Petersburg for a taste of tsarist splendour.

TRAVEL HINTS

Don't lose your immigration card. Keep a photocopy of your visa and passport on you at all times.

Located where Europe begins to slip away into Asia, Russia is an essential and fascinating destination for anyone wanting to see another side to the European continent in all its awkward, mysterious glory. Moscow and St Petersburg are two of Europe's biggest cities, and yet are as unlike each other as it is possible to imagine.

EUROPEAN RUSSIA

0 — 500 km
0 — 300 miles

Novaya Zemlya

KARA SEA

BARENTS SEA

Arctic Circle

NORWAY

SWEDEN

FINLAND

Murmansk

Vorkuta

Salekhard

Pechora

Ob

U R A L   M O U N T A I N S

Arkhangelsk

Petrozavodsk

Syktyvkar

STOCKHOLM

HELSINKI

Vyborg

TALLINN

St Petersburg

Vologda

Vyatka

Perm

Yekaterinburg

BALTIC SEA

ESTONIA

Novgorod

Pskov

Yaroslavl

Kostroma

Izhevsk

Volga

RĪGA

LATVIA

Tver

Ivanovo

Yoshkar-Ola

Kazan

LITHUANIA

MOSCOW

Vladimir

Nizhny Novgorod

Ufa

Kaliningrad

VILNIUS

Vitsebsk

Cheboksary

Ryazan

Ulyanovsk

WARSAW

Smolensk

Kaluga

Tula

Saransk

Tolyatti

MINSK

Bryansk

Penza

Samara

BELARUS

Oryol

Tambov

Orenburg

Orsk

Homel

Kursk

Oral (Uralsk)

POLAND

Voronezh

Saratov

Aqtöbe (Aktyubinsk)

KYIV

Belgorod

KAZAKHSTAN

UKRAINE

Kharkiv

Don

Volga

MOLDOVA

Donetsk

Don

Volgograd

Atyrau (Gurev)

CHIŞINĂU

Rostov-on-Don

Astrakhan

ROMANIA

Odesa

Elista

BUCHAREST

Simferopol

Krasnodar

Stavropol

Mineralnye Vody

CASPIAN SEA

UZBEKISTAN

Novorossiysk

Caucasus

Grozny

Makhachkala

BULGARIA

Sochi

Mts

Vladikavkaz

BLACK SEA

Mt Elbrus (5642m)

GEORGIA

TBILISI

TURKMENISTAN

TURKEY

ARMENIA

AZERBAIJAN

BAKU

RUSSIA

Stately, relaxed and oh-so-cultured, the old Russian capital of St Petersburg is quite simply one of the most beautiful cities in Europe, overflowing with 18th-century palaces and brightly painted Italianate mansions divided by graceful canals. Brash, vulgar and stupendously hedonistic, Moscow is one of the most dynamic and fast-paced cities on earth, demanding your attention. While the Cold War still hangs in the air around the Kremlin and Red Square, elsewhere there's palpable excitement as the Las Vegas of the East continues its frenetic pace of change.

Given the vast size of European Russia, this book only covers Moscow, St Petersburg and the fascinating Russian enclave of Kaliningrad, wedged between Poland and Lithuania on the Baltic Sea. Ignore what you have heard about Russia in the past. Come with an open mind and any trip here will be a hugely rewarding – if a sometimes exhausting – experience.

CURRENT EVENTS

Since Yeltsin's dramatic resignation on New Year's Eve 1999, Vladimir Putin has been the public face of the new Russia. A former KGB officer, Putin is as controversial in the West as he is popular at home among those who argue that Russia needs 'a firm hand'. While tackling the power of the oligarchs whose vast wealth was acquired dubiously during the 1990s and slowly progressing in economic and social reform, Putin has increasingly centralised the Russian government, silenced media critics and brutally fought a dirty war in Chechnya against the independence movement. As a result, Russia has been a target of some huge terrorist attacks, including the 2002 Dubrovka Theatre Siege in Moscow and the 2004 Beslan School Siege in North Ossetia. Despite these brutal acts of killing, Russia is still a safe place to visit and travellers need not worry too much about the actions of insurgents impacting on them personally.

HISTORY

Russia has its cultural origins in Kyivan Rus, the kingdom located in what is today Ukraine and Belarus. From here the Slavs expanded into modern European Russia. The birth of the Russian state is usually identified with the founding of Novgorod in AD 862, although until 1480 Russia was overrun by the Mongols.

It was not until the Romanov dynasty (1613–1917) that Russia became the vast nation it is today – territorial expansion from the 17th to 19th centuries saw the country increase in size exponentially to include Siberia, the Arctic, the Russian Far East, Central Asia and the Caucasus. Peter the Great dragged the country kicking and screaming out of the Dark Ages, setting up a navy and building a new capital, St Petersburg, in 1703. Catherine the Great continued Peter's progressive policies to create a world power by the mid-18th century.

The 19th century saw feverish capitalist development undermined by successively autocratic and backwards tsars. The most prominent example was Nicholas II, whose refusal to countenance serious change precipitated the 1917 revolution. What began as a liberal revolution was hijacked later the same year in a coup led by the Bolsheviks under Lenin, which resulted in the setting up of the world's first communist state.

The Communist Party held power from 1917 until 1991, during which time Russia became a superpower, having created the Union of Soviet Socialist Republics (USSR) and absorbing some 14 neighbouring states between 1922 and 1945. The terror of Stalin, the reforms of Khrushchev and the stagnation during the Brezhnev era finally led to Mikhail Gorbachev's period of reform known as *perestroika* in 1985. Within six years, the USSR had collapsed alongside communism and reformer Boris Yeltsin led Russia into a new world of cut-throat capitalism.

READING UP

Try *Moscow Stations* by Venedikt Yerofeev for a headlong, vodka-fuelled plunge into the Russian soul. *Crime and Punishment* by Fyodor Dostoyevsky is an existentialist masterpiece, but it's also superbly atmospheric of 19th-century St Petersburg.

One of the most popular writers of the 20th century is Mikhail Bulgakov, whose fantastical satirical masterpiece *The Master and Margarita* makes a brilliant companion to any trip to Russia.

TOP FIVE RUSSIA

- **Festival** White Nights in St Petersburg (late June) (p995)
- **Walk** Along the battlements of the Peter & Paul Fortress, St Petersburg (p995)
- **Bar/Club** Tsynik, St Petersburg (p996)
- **Impressive sight** Red Square, Moscow (p986)
- **Experience** A traditional Russian *banya* (wet sauna; p999)

PEOPLE & CULTURE

Russians are a fiercely proud people, who are conscious of their country's numerous problems, but also rejoice in its not inconsiderable achievements. Although they sometimes appear dour and even rude at first, once you get to know a Russian, you have a friend for life.

ARTS

Russian literature is one of the world's greatest – Alexander Pushkin is the national bard, whose most accessible writing in English can be found in his short stories. Other 19th-century greats include Mikhail Lermontov, Leo Tolstoy, Anton Chekhov and Fyodor Dostoyevsky. Second only to its contribution to literature comes Russia's musical heritage; Tchaikovsky, Prokofiev and Shostakovich have all had huge influence on the development of modern classical music.

TRANSPORT

GETTING THERE & AWAY

Air

Moscow is connected to many world cities, particularly throughout Europe. Arrival in Moscow is usually at depressing Sheremetyevo-2, 30km from the city centre, although more and more airlines are defecting to the far better terminal at Domodedovo. St Petersburg is not as well connected, but its

DEPARTURE TAX

There is no departure tax payable when leaving Russia.

Pulkovo airport has daily links to a large number of European capitals. There are also daily connections between Kaliningrad and both Moscow and St Petersburg.

Boat

You can take ferries to St Petersburg from Helsinki, Tallinn and Rostok (Germany). There are also weekly connections between St Petersburg and Kaliningrad. You can buy tickets direct from the ferry companies at the sea port (Morskoy Vokzal) or, more easily, at the centrally located **Paromny Tsentr** (☎ 812-279 6670; www.paromy.ru; ul Vosstaniya 19; Ⓜ Pl Vosstaniya).

Since 2004 **Tallink** (☎ 09 228 311 (in Helsinki); www.tallink.fi) has run a Helsinki–St Petersburg service (€55, 17 hours). The drag is that it sails via Tallinn on the outbound route, although from St Petersburg, the journey is direct. Boats leave Helsinki every other day at 4pm, arriving the same evening in Tallinn, docking in St Petersburg at 9am the next day.

Every three to four days the Finnjet run by **Silja Line** (www.silja.fi) connects Rostok (Germany) with Tallinn (€96, 25 hours) and travels on to St Petersburg (€117, a further 11 hours from Tallinn).

Bus

From Baltiiskaya (Baltic Station) in St Petersburg **Eurolines** (☎ 168 2740; ul Shkapina 10; Ⓜ Baltiiskaya) runs buses to Tallinn (R390, five per day), Riga (R500, daily) and Tartu in Estonia (R360, daily).

From Moscow – considering distances – it's far better to take the train to neighbouring countries.

Car & Motorcycle

We do not recommend driving in Russia. Public transport is very good and Russian driving is aggressive and road rules complex in both Moscow and St Petersburg. However, if you do drive in Russia, you must have a valid international driving permit, your passport and insurance documentation for your vehicle.

Train

Moscow is connected very regularly with Helsinki, Tallinn, Rīga, Vilnius, Warsaw, Berlin, Prague, Minsk, Kyiv, Chişinău and Budapest. It is the centre of the Russian rail network, and trains also serve the Caucasus, Central Asia, Mongolia and China from here. The overnight trains between St Petersburg and Moscow run every day and tickets start at around R500.

From St Petersburg trains go to Tallinn (R800, 8½ hours, odd dates of the month at 11.16pm); Riga (R1100, 12¾ hours, daily at 9.49pm); Vilnius (R1296, 15¼ hours, odd dates of the month at 7.44pm); Kaliningrad (R1047, 27 hours, on even dates of the month at 6.13pm); Kyiv (R1054, 24 hours, daily at 8.03pm); Minsk (R915, 15¼ hours, daily at 7pm); Berlin (R4650, 37 hours, departures Tuesday, Friday and Sunday); Warsaw (R2200, 30 hours, departures Tuesday, Friday and Sunday); Prague (R3758, 41 hours, departures Monday, Wednesday, Thursday and Saturday) and Budapest (R5352, 45 hours, once a week on Tuesday).

GETTING AROUND
Bus
The cheapest way to get around Russia is by bus. The enormous size of the country makes it rather unappealing, but for short trips from major cities it can be faster than the train and there are more regular connections. Some sample costs are R480 (Moscow–St Petersburg) and R145 (St Petersburg–Novgorod). There's almost no need to reserve a seat and, in most places, it's impossible anyway. Just arrive a good 30 minutes to one hour before the departure is scheduled and buy a ticket.

Train
Russia is crisscrossed with an extensive train network. Suburban or short-distance trains are called *elektrichkas*. Tickets can be bought at the *prigorodny poezd kassa* (suburban-train ticket offices) at stations. Long-distance services need to be booked in advance. *Platskartny* compartments, while cheaper, have open bunk accommodation and are not great for those who value privacy. *Obshchiy* (general) class simply has bench- or aeroplane-style seating. Prices between Moscow and St Petersburg in 2nd class begin at R500, going up to R1500 for the fast day trains.

You are advised to reserve at least 24 hours in advance. Bring your passport (or a photocopy), as without it you'll be unable to buy tickets. The queues can be very long and move with interminable slowness. If you're in a hurry go to the service centres that exist in most big stations. Here you pay a R100 surcharge; thus, there are no queues.

MOSCOW МОСКВА

☎ 095 / pop 10 million

With the biggest city population in Europe, Moscow's sheer size is matched only by its brazen right-here-right-now hedonism, its lust for life, its shocking wealth and pitiful poverty. An ancient and brutal city, whose architectural richness encompasses everything from medieval churches to Stalin's fabulously Gothic 'Seven Sisters', Moscow is impressive, contradictory and immensely fun. From the Kremlin to clubbing, it's all here for the taking.

ORIENTATION
The medieval centre of the city, the Kremlin, is a triangle on the northern bank of the Moscow River. The modern city centre radiates around it – the main streets being Tverskaya ul and ul Novy Arbat.

INFORMATION
Internet Access
NetCity (☎ 969 2125; www.netcitycafé.ru in Russian; Kamergersky per 6; Ⓜ Okhotny Ryad; per hr R60; ☾ 24hr)

Phlegmatic Dog (☎ 995 9545; www.phlegmaticdog. ru; 2nd Level, Okhotny Ryad Mall, Alexandrovsky Gdns entrance; Ⓜ Okhotny Ryad; per hr R60; ☾ 11-1am Sun-Thu, 12pm-5am Fri & Sat) 'Internet pub' where Web access is free to anyone drinking.

Time Online (☎ 363 0060; www.timeonline.ru in Russian; Okhotny Ryad Mall; Ⓜ Okhotny Ryad; per hr R60; ☾ 24hr)

Medical Services
American Medical Centre (☎ 933 7700; fax 933 7701; Grokholsky per 1; Ⓜ Prospekt Mira; ☾ 24hr) Expensive, foreign-run health service that features a English-speaking pharmacy.

Botkin Hospital (☎ 945 0045; 2-y Botkinsky proezd 5; Ⓜ Dinamo; ☾ 24hr) The best Russian facility.

Money
ATMs and reliable money-changing facilities are on every corner in Moscow. Russian banks include Alfa Bank, Bank Moskvy and Sberbank (core opening hours are 8am to 7pm Monday to Friday). Most big hotels have a 24-hour bank or money-changing facility.

American Express (☎ 933-6636; fax 9336635; ul Usacheva 33; Ⓜ Sportivnaya; ☾ 9am-6pm Mon-Fri) Can cash AmEx travellers cheques.

MOSCOW

To CityAir Terminal (1.5km);
Dinamo (2km); Star Travel
(4km); Rechnoy
Vokzal (12km);
Sheremetevo 1
& 2 Airports
(30km)

To Hostel
Sherstone (10km)

Novoslobodskaya

Borkinsky
proezd

Hippodrome

Begovaya

Belorusskaya

Belorusskaya

Tverskaya
zastava pl

Belorussky Vokzal
(Belarus Station)

Myusskaya
pl

Aleksandra Nevskogo

41

Aleksandra
Nevskogo per

Gruzinsky val

Gruzinsky per

Bol Gruzinskaya ul

Vasilevskaya ul

Oruzheyny

Mayakovskaya

Khodynskaya ul

Sredny Tishinsky per

Tishinskaya pl

Yuliusa Fuchika

ul Yaroslava Gasheka

Triumfalnaya pl

Triumfalnaya per

Mayakovskaya

Bol Tishinsky per

ul Klimashkina

12

Rastorguevsky per

Mal Gruzinskaya ul

Zoologichesky per

Krasina

Bolshaya Sadovaya ul

Bol Bronnaya ul

Pushkinskaya
Tverskaya

11

Zvenigorodskoe sh

Ulitsa 1905
Goda

ul 1905 goda

ul Sergia Makeeva

Bol Dekabrskaya ul

Zoologicheskaya ul

Sadovaya-Kudrinskaya

Sytinsky per

Mal Bronnaya ul

Tverskoy bul

ul Krasnaya Presnya

Barrikadnaya

Leontyevsky per

Tryokhgorny val

ul 1905 goda

Krasnopresnenskaya

ul Zamorenova

Barrikadnaya ul

Bol Sadovaya-Kudrinskaya

Vspolny per

Spiridonovka

Bol Trekhgorny per

Bol Nikitskaya ul

Rochdelskaya ul

ul Nikolaeva

Gluboky per

Druzhinnikovskaya ul

Komsomolsky per

Kudrinskaya pl

Mal Nikitskaya ul

Povarskaya ul

Skaterny per

Nozh Khlebny per

Nikitsky bul

pl Nikitskie
Vorota

Bol Nikitsky per

Sredny Kislovsky
per

29

ul Mantulinskaya

Park
Krasnaya
Presnya

Krasnopresnenskaya nab

Moscow River

Bol Devyatinsky per

14

Novy Arbat ul

Novy Arbat ul

Arbatskaya pl

ul Vozdvizhenka

7

Arbatskaya

nab Tarasa Shevchenko

Kalininsky
most

13

Pryamoy per

Novinsky bul

Spasopeskovsky
per

Spasopeskovskaya pl

ul Arbat

Gogolevsky bul

Znamensky Bol

Mal Znamenka

Znamenka

30

28

Kutuzovsky prosp

Mal
Novopeskovsky
per

4-y Nikoloshchepovsky per

Karmanitsky per

Smolenskaya

25

Arbatskaya pl

Afanasevsky

Filippovsky per

per Sivtsev Vrazhek

Starokonyushenny per

18

Bryanskaya ul

Bol Dorogomilovskaya ul

nab Tarasa Shevchenko

Ukrainsky bul

Borodinsky
most

smolenskaya ul

Denezhny per

Plotnikov per

Kropotkinskaya

Bryansky per

pl Kievskogo
Vokzala

Smolenskaya-
Sennaya pl

Smolensky bul

Gagarinsky per

Staropansky per

Ostozhenka ul

Soymonovsky proezd

16

Mozhaysky val

Kievskaya

Kievskaya

Kievsky Vokzal
(Kiev Station)

37

Rostovskaya nab

Bol Lyovshinsky

ul Plyushchikha

Pomerantsev per

Bol Vlasevsky per

Kropotkinsky per

Lopukhinsky per

Chisty per

Kievskaya ul

Berezhkovskaya nab

Savvinskaya nab

proezd Devichego Polya

Bol Pirogovskaya ul

Zubovsky bul

Zubovskaya pl

Zubovsky per

To Infinity Travel
(500m)

Park Kultury

To Mama
Zoya (200m)

To American Express; KLM;
Royal Dutch Airlines;
Novodevichy Convent (1.5km)

Park Kultury

2

RUSSIA

0 ⟋⟍ 300 m
0 ⟋⟍ 0.2 miles

E pl Kommuny

Frunze Central Army Park

F 9

To Tramp (4km); All-Russia Exhibition Centre (5km)

G Prospekt Mira

To Travellers Guest House (1km)

H

Bezbozhny per

prosp Mira

Samotechny per

ul Durova

Botanical Gardens

Bol Perejaslavskaja

Kalanchevskaya

Yaroslavsky Vokzal (Yaroslav Station)

Leningradsky Vokzal (Leningrad Station)

ul Samotechnaya

Olimpysky prosp

Grokholsky per

Kalanchevskaya (Station)

Kalanchevskaya ul

To Shchyolkovsky Avtovokzal Bus Station (30km)

Delegatskaya

Troitskaya ul

Komsomolskaya pl

Komsomolskaya

Krasnoprudnaya

ul Karetny Ryad

ul Samotechnaya

ul Sadovaya-Samotechnaya

ul Sadovaya-Sukharevskaya

Bol Spasskaya

Sadovaya-Spasskaya

prosp Akademika Sakharova

Kazansky Vokzal (Kazan Station)

1

2

Mal Likhov per

Tsvetnoy Bulvar

Tsvetnoy bul

Trubnaya ul

Kalanchevskaya ul

Sadovaya-Chornogryazskaya

Park im Baumana

Hermitage Gardens

Krasnye Vorota

Lermontovskaya pl

ul Myasnitskaya

Petrovsky bul

Rozhdestvensky bul

Turgenevskaya

Chistye Prudy

prosp Akademika Sakharova

Kharitonevsky per

Putinkovsky Bol per

Strastnoy bul

Chekhovskaya

Bol Dmitrovka ul

Petrovka

Trubnaya pl

Milyutinsky per

Myasnitskaya ul

Ogorodnoy slobody per

Bol Zhukovskogo

Pokrovka

Zemlyanoy val

3

Glinishchevsky per

32

Stoleshnikov per

Petrovskie linii ul

Zvonarsky per

ul Rozhdestvenka

24

Bol Lubyanka

Chistoprudny bul

21

Pushechnaya ul

Kuznetsky Most

Lubyanka

Lubyanka

Lubyanskaya pl

Potapovsky per

Pokrovsky bul

Kurskaya

27

Kamergersky per

10

38

26

Petrovka

Kuznetsky most

Yauzsky bul

15

Kursky Vokzal (Kursk Station)

6

Gazetny per

Nikitsky per

Tverskaya ul

Bol Cherkassky per

Novaya pl

Staraya pl

34

Teatralnaya

Okhotny Ryad ul

Teatralny proezd

Maroseyka ul

4

Teatralnaya pl

Okhotny Ryad

ul Nikolskaya

ul Ilyinka

Kitay-Gorod

35

31

Pl Revolyutsii

ul Varvarka

Kitay-Gorod

33

KITAY-GOROD

19

Rybny per

Nikolsky per

ul Solyanka

Yauzsky bul

Alexandrovsky Garden

39

5

Borovitskaya

17

Kremlin

Alexandrovsky Sad; Borovitskaya; Biblioteka imeni Lenina

ul Vorontsovo Pole

Mokhovaya ul

8

Biblioteka im Lenina; Borovitskaya

Kremlevskaya nab

Bol Moskvoretsky most

Moskvoretskaya nab

Serebryanicheskaya nab

Yauza

River

Volkhonka

Bol Kamenny most

Sofiyskaya nab

Moscow River

Rauzhskaya nab

Ustinsky most

Bernikovskaya nab

Nikoloyamskaya ul

5

Prechistenskaya nab

Fischbautova nab

Serafimovicha

pl Repina

Bolotnaya pl

Mal Moskvoretsky most

Chugunny most

Ovchinnikovsky nab

Canal

Bol Ustinsky most

Bol Ustinsky most

Kotelnicheskaya nab

Kosmodemyanskaya nab

To Izmaylovsky Park (6km)

Teterinsky per

Bersenevskaya nab

Bolotnaya ul

Vodootvodny Canal

Kadashovsky nab

Lavrushinsky per

Pyatnitskaya ul

Sadovnicheskaya nab

Verkhnyaya Radishchevskaya ul

ul Goncharnaya

Taganskaya

To G&R Hostel Asia (10km)

Mal Kamenny most

Bol Polyanka

20

Novokuznetskaya

Klimentovsky per

Osteenkovskaya nab

Taganskaya pl

Marksistskaya

Taganskaya

Narodnaya ul

6

To French Embassy (500m)

Bol Yakimanka ul

Polyanka

Bol Ordynka ul

Tretyakovskaya

To German Embassy (11.5km)

To Air France (1km); Domodedovo Airport (40km)

36

Pyatnitskaya ul

Bol Kamenshchiki ul

RUSSIA

Post & Telephone

Payphones in Moscow operate with cards, which are widely available in shops, kiosks and metro stations.

Central Telegraph (Tsentralny Telegraf; Tverskaya ul 7; Ⓜ Okhotny Ryad; postal counters ⏲ 8am-10pm, telephone office ⏲ 24hr) Offers postal, telephone; fax and Internet facilities.

Toilets

As a rule, the more you pay for a toilet, the worse it will be. Toilets are in all museums, GUM and around metro stations. Free toilets in smart hotels, cafés and restaurants remain the best choice.

Tourist Information

An entrenched lack of interest in promoting tourism means that there is no tourist office in Moscow, but useful information can be obtained through travel agencies and at hostels.

GETTING INTO TOWN

From Sheremetyevo Airport: Minibuses (48 and 49) and bus 851 go from outside both terminals to the nearest metro station, Rechnoy Vokzal.

From Domodedovo Airport: There is an express train service to the Paveletsky Station. The train runs from the airport to the city hourly on the hour from 8am to 10pm and take 40 minutes. All of Moscow's many train stations are in the centre of the city and have their own metro stations with direct access from the concourse.

Travel Agencies

Capital Tours (☎ 232 2442; www.capitaltours.ru; ul Ilyinka 4; Ⓜ Pl Revolyustii) Offers a city tour (R580, 11am and 2.30pm daily), plus a Kremlin Cathedrals and Armoury tour (R1050, 10.30am and 3pm Friday to Wednesday) departing from its offices off Red Square.

STAR Travel (☎ 797 9555; www.startravel.ru in Russian; 3rd fl, ul Baltiiskaya 9; Ⓜ Sokol) STA Travel's Moscow representative, with other offices throughout the city.

SIGHTS
Red Square

Palpably the centre of Moscow, and of Russia as a whole, Red Square is a massively impressive sight that brings back the full force of the Cold War, even two decades after *perestroika*. Something of a misnomer for this grey and rectangular strip to the side of the Kremlin, Red Square is surrounded by Lenin's Mausoleum to the west, the Russian History Museum to the north, the GUM shopping centre to the east, and fabulous St Basil's to the south. Begin your visit to Moscow by coming here – there's nowhere else like it.

Approaching Red Square through the Voskressensky Gates, you'll emerge with a superb view of the magnificently flamboyant **St Basil's Cathedral** (Sobor Vasilia Blazhennogo; ☎ 298 3304; Ⓜ Okhotny Ryad; admission R100; ⏲ 11am-5pm Wed-Mon). Ivan the Terrible was so keen to immortalise his victory over the Tatars at Kazan that he took the measure of blinding the architects after they completed the dazzlingly bright onion domes in 1561, to ensure that nothing of comparable beauty could ever be built. Its design is the culmination of a wholly Russian style that had been developed through the building of wooden churches. The cathedral owes its name to the barefoot holy fool Vasily (Basil) the Blessed, who predicted Ivan's damnation (as yet unconfirmed) and (correctly) that Ivan would murder his son. It's really worth going inside to see the stark medieval wall paintings.

Lenin's Mausoleum (Mavzoley VI Lenina; ☎ 923 5527; Ⓜ Okhotny Ryad; admission free; ⏰ 10am-1pm Tue-Thu, Sat & Sun) is the first port of call for nostalgic communists. Before joining the queue at the northwestern corner of Red Square, drop your camera and bag at the **left-luggage office** (beneath Kutafya Tower; R60 per bag; ⏰ 9am-6.30pm), as you will not be allowed to take it with you. The visit takes you into the dark crypt under Red Square where Lenin lies swathed in red velvet and the sombre tone is quite hilarious. Any talking will provoke angry shushing from the soldiers who line the route. Bear in mind that Stalin had Lenin's brain removed in a rather fanciful attempt to duplicate the 'pure communist' mind and much of what remains appears to be wax anyway. Following the trip underground, you'll emerge and walk the route along the Kremlin wall, where other greats such as Stalin, Gagarin and Brezhnev are buried. Official plans to rebury Lenin in St Petersburg (where he apparently wished to spend eternity next to his mother) have faltered, and it appears that Vladimir Ilyich isn't going anywhere in a hurry.

The **State History Museum** (Gosudarstvenny Istorichesky Muzey; ☎ 292 4019; www.shm.ru in Russian; Ⓜ Okhotny Ryad; adult/student R150/75; ⏰ 10am-6pm Mon & Wed-Sat, 11am-7pm Sun) is the stunningly ornate red building at the northern end of the square. It has an enormous collection covering the whole of Russian history from the Stone Age onwards.

Finally, drop in to **GUM** (Ⓜ Okhotny Ryad; ⏰ 10am-10pm) to see the showpiece Soviet shopping centre turned designer mall for the new rich with its vast glass roof and centrepiece fountains.

The Kremlin

The nerve centre of Russian politics, the ultimate goal of Cold War espionage, a symbol of power and intrigue recognised the world over – for most first-time visitors what's most unexpected about the Kremlin is that at its heart are several huge cathedrals.

Kremlin simply means 'citadel' in Russian and any medieval Russian town has one. The Moscow one is huge – in effect a walled city –

---

first built in the 1150s. The Kremlin grew with the importance of Moscow's princes and in the 1320s became the headquarters of the Russian Orthodox Church. Between 1475 and 1516 Ivan the Great brought master builders from Pskov and Italy to supervise the construction of new walls and towers, three great cathedrals and more.

Before entering the **Kremlin** (☎ 203 0349; www.kremlin.museum.ru; adult/student R300/150, photography R50; ⏰ 10am-5pm Fri-Wed), deposit your bags at the **left-luggage office** (beneath Kutafya Tower; R60 per bag; ⏰ 9am-6.30pm) just north of the main ticket office. The ticket office, in the Aleksandrovsky Garden, closes at 4.30pm. The ticket covers admission to all buildings except the Armoury and Diamond Fund Exhibition (see p988).

NORTHERN & WESTERN BUILDINGS

From the Kutafya Tower, which forms the main visitors entrance, walk up the ramp and pass through the Kremlin walls beneath the **Troitskaya Bashnya** (Trinity Gate Tower). The lane to the right (south) passes the 17th-century **Poteshny Dvorets** (Poteshny Palace) where Stalin lived. The horribly out of place glass and concrete **Kremlyovksy Dvorets Syezdov** (Kremlin Palace of Congresses) houses a concert and ballet auditorium, where incongruously enough lots of Western pop stars play when they are in town.

SOBORNAYA PLOSHCHAD

On the northern side of Sobornaya pl is the 15th-century **Uspensky Sobor** (Assumption Cathedral), the focal church of pre-evolutionary Russia. It's the burial place of most of the heads of the Russian Orthodox Church from the 1320s to 1700. The tombs are against the north, west and south walls.

The iconostasis dates from 1652, but its lowest level contains some older icons, including the *Vladimirskaya Bogomater* (Virgin of Vladimir), an early-15th-century Rublev School copy of Russia's most revered image.

The 12th-century original, now in the State Tretyakov Gallery, stood in the Assumption Cathedral from the 1480s to 1930. The oldest icon on display is the 12th-century, red-clothed *Svyatoy Georgy* (St George) from Novgorod, positioned by the north wall.

With its two golden domes rising above the eastern side of Sobornaya pl, the 16th-century **Kolokolnya Ivana Velikogo** (Ivan the Great Bell Tower) is the Kremlin's tallest structure. Beside the bell tower stands the world's biggest **Tsar-kolokol** (Tsar bell), a 202-tonne monster that cracked before it ever rang. North of the bell tower is the mammoth **Tsar-pushka** (Tsar cannon), cast in 1586, but never shot.

Back on Sobornaya p, the 1508 **Arkhangelsky Sobor** (Archangel Cathedral), at the square's southeastern corner, was for centuries the coronation, wedding and burial church of tsars. The tombs of Russia's rulers from the 1320s to the 1690s are here bar one (Boris Godunov was buried at Sergiev Posad).

Dating from 1489, the **Blagoveshchensky Sobor** (Annunciation Cathedral), at the southwest corner of Sobornaya pl, contains the celebrated icons of master painter Theophanes the Greek. He probably painted the six icons at the right-hand end of the deesis row, the biggest of the six tiers of the iconostasis. *Archangel Michael* (the third icon from the left on the deesis row) and the adjacent *St Peter* are ascribed to Russian master Andrei Rublev.

ARMOURY & DIAMOND FUND

In the southwestern corner of the Kremlin, the **Oruzheynaya Palata** (Armoury; adult/student R350/175) is a numbingly opulent collection of treasures accumulated over centuries by the Russian State and Church. Your ticket will specify a time of entry. Highlights include the Fabergé eggs in room 2 and the reams of royal regalia in rooms 6 and 9.

If the Armoury hasn't sated your diamond lust, there are more in the separate **Vystavka Almaznogo Fonda** (Diamond Fund Exhibition; adult/student R350/175; closed for lunch 1-2pm) in the same building.

Around Red Square

Manezhnaya pl, at the northern end of Red Square, has been transformed into the vast underground **Okhotny Ryad Shopping Mall**, worth a look simply to shatter images of Russians queuing in the snow for bread. The **Manezh Central Exhibition Hall**, the long, low building on the southwestern side of the square, was home to some of Moscow's most popular art exhibitions until it was burnt to a shell in a mysterious fire in 2003. On the northwestern side of the square is the fine edifice of **Moscow State University**, built in 1793. The 1930s **Hotel Moskva**, once fronting the northeastern side of the square, was being demolished at the time of writing, soon to be replaced by another of Mayor Yuri Luzhkov's idiosyncratic projects.

Teatralnaya pl opens out on both sides of Okhotny Ryad, 200m from Manezhnaya pl. The northern half of the square is dominated by the **Bolshoi Theatre**, where Tchaikovsky's *Swan Lake* was premiered (unsuccessfully) in 1877. Look out too for the stunning artnouveau **Metropole Hotel**, one of Moscow's finest, on Teatralny proezd.

Pushkin Fine Arts Museum & Around

Moscow's premier foreign art museum is close to the southwestern corner of the Kremlin. The **Pushkin Fine Arts Museum** (Muzey Izobrazitelnykh Iskusstv Imeni As Pushkina; ☎ 203 7412; ul Volkhonka 12; adult/student R260/60, audio guide R200; ☼ 10am-6pm Tue-Sun; Ⓜ Kropotkinskaya) is famous for its impressionist and post-impressionist paintings, but also has a broad selection of European works from the Renaissance onward, mostly appropriated from private collections after the revolution. There are also interesting temporary exhibits on regular display.

Nearby is the gigantic **Khram Khrista Spasitelya** (Church of Christ the Saviour; ☎ 201 3847; Ⓜ Kropotkinskaya; ☼ 10am-5pm), rebuilt at an estimated cost of €290 million by Mayor Luzhkov on the site of the original destroyed by Stalin, and in place of what was once the world's largest swimming pool. It's massively impressive with its vast golden dome, although the interior wouldn't look out of place in the equally gauche Okhotny Ryad Shopping Centre.

State Tretyakov Gallery

This fine **gallery** (Gosudarstvennaya Tretyakovskaya Galereya; ☎ 951 1362; www.tretyakov.ru; Lavrushinsky per 10; Ⓜ Tretyakovskaya; adult/student R225/130, audio tour R120; ☼ 10am-6.30pm Tue-Sun) has the world's best collection of Russian icons and an outstanding collection of other pre-revolutionary Russian art, particularly the 19th-century *peredvizhniki* – the group of painters who renounced the St Petersburg Academy of Art's formalism and travelled around Russia depicting provincial scenes in the style of realism.

Novodevichy Convent

A cluster of sparkling domes behind turreted walls on the Moscow River, **Novodevichy Monastyr** (☎ 246 8526; Luzhnetsky proezd 2; **M** Sportivnaya; admission R30; ◷ 10am-5pm Wed-Mon) is resplendent with history and treasures. Founded in 1524 to celebrate the retaking of Smolensk from Lithuania, it is notorious as the place where Peter the Great imprisoned his half-sister Sofia for her part in the Streltsy Rebellion.

You enter the convent under the red-and-white, Moscow-baroque **Preobrazhenskaya Nadvratnaya** (Transfiguration Gate-Church). The oldest and dominant building in the grounds is the white **Smolensky Sobor** (Smolensk Cathedral; 1524–25). **Sofia's tomb** lies in the south nave. The **bell tower** against the convent's east wall, completed in 1690, is generally regarded as Moscow's finest. The adjacent **Novodevichy Kladbishche** (Novodevichy Cemetery) contains the tombs of Khrushchev, Chekhov, Gogol, Mayakovsky, Stanislavsky, Prokofiev, Eisenstein, Raisa Gorbachev and other Russian and Soviet notables.

SLEEPING

Moscow is pricey, and nothing more so than its hotels. Mayor Luzhkov has already demolished the Intourist, Moskva and Minsk Hotels, and rumours are rife that the Rossiya will be next. Sadly, there are few budget places opening to bridge the gap. Near the Belarus Station, **Art Hostel** (☎ 251 2837; www.art hostel.net) was a great option but it was shut for renovations at the time of research, although it might well reopen during the lifetime of this book.

All sleeping prices in this chapter are in euros as this is how most hotels in Russia advertise the cost of their rooms. Hotels and hostels accept both the euro and the rouble.

G&R Hostel Asia (☎ 378 0001; www.hostels.ru; ul Zelenodolskaya 2/3; dm/s/d €18/35/40; **M** Ryazansky Pr) In the old Soviet Hotel Asia a good 10km southeast of the centre, this is nevertheless one of the best budget options. Bathrooms are shared between two rooms, but ensuite rooms are available. Leave Ryazansky Pr

metro from the end of the train and look for the tallest building around.

Galina's Flat (☎ 921 6038; galinas.flat@mtu-net.ru; flat 35, ul Chaplygina 8; dm/s/d €8/15/21; **M** Chistiye Prudi) Galina is a perennial favourite. Her central apartment doubles as a homestay and is great value. There's Internet access and a kitchen that guests can use, as well as breakfast for an extra €2.

Hostel Sherstone (☎ 797 8075; www.sherstone.ru; Gostinichny proezd 8/1; dm/s/d €18/25/€40; **M** Vladykino) This branch of the G&R has more than 100 beds and is a well-run and clean outfit, although rather far-flung, north of the city.

Travellers Guest House (☎ 631 4059; www.tgh.ru; 10th fl, ul Bolshaya Pereyaslavskaya 50; dm/s/d €19/50/50; **M** Pr Mira) The original Moscow hostel – the TGH is still the main hub for backpackers. Unfortunately it's not been touched since it opened in 1993, and is already looking rather shabby. Despite that, it's a safe and fun place to stay, a 10-minute walk from the metro.

Tramp (☎ 551-2876; www.hostelling.ru; Bldg 7, ul Selskohozayistvennaya 17/2; s/d €30/43; **M** Botanichesky Sad) Between the Botanical Gardens and the Vserossiysky Vystavochny Tsentr (VVT or VDNKh; All-Russia Exhibition Centre), Tramp is a great place, although it does not take people without advance reservations.

Hotel Tsentralnaya (☎ 229 8957; fax 292 1221; ul Tverskaya 10; s €30, d €43-50; **M** Chekhovskaya) One of the city's best bargains – the Tsentralnaya is on Moscow's main street and offers great value. Rooms are very basic and Soviet, but clean and safe. All facilities are shared.

Hotel Rossiya (☎ 232 6046; fax 232 6248; ul Vavarka 6; s/d €70/90; **M** Kitay Gorod) Few places cause more controversy than this humungous eyesore next to Red Square. While its rude staff, mediocre rooms and ugliness are indeed reasons to sneer, mid-level accommodation in Moscow is rarely this cheap or well located. However, it may well be demolished in the next few years.

EATING

Check out ultra-cool Kamergersky per for a huge range of cafés and restaurants. For snacks on the run, there are plenty of street stands selling hot dogs, *chebureki* (Caucasian meat pasties) and blini around metro stations and on many central avenues.

Prime (☎ 737 5545; sandwiches R75-95; ◷ 8.30am-11pm) Arbat (ul Arbat 9; **M** Arbatskaya); Kamergersky (Kamergersky per 5/7; **M** Okhotny Ryad) Finally, a place

RUSSIA

to pick up a decent sandwich on the run. Prime is an unnerving copy of London's Prêt à Manger chain – but this is no grounds for complaint, as fresh sandwiches, salads and drinks are available in two central outlets.

Zhiguli (☎ 291 4144; ul Novy Arbat 11; Ⓜ Arbatskaya; mains R100; Ⓥ noon-2am) Smart self-service canteen with a Brezhnevian theme. Good Russian food, such as borsch, pelmeni or meat stew, and very low prices just off the Arbat.

Moo-Moo (☎ 241 1364; ul Arbat 45/24; Ⓜ Arbatskaya; mains R100; Ⓥ 10am-11pm) Always busy due to its large range of tasty and cheap Russian dishes, such as stuffed peppers, blini and a large range of salads, Moo Moo is a self-service place. There's extra seating downstairs.

Pelmeshka (☎ 292 8392; ul Kuznetsky Most 4/3; Ⓜ Teatralnaya; mains from R40; Ⓥ 11am-midnight) Acid casualties should avoid looking at the giant psychotic *pelmeshka* (Russian ravioli) that marks this Russian fast-food stand on the street. However, once past it, you get a big choice of pelmeni and other Russian staples.

Jagannath (☎ 928 3580; ul Kuznetsky Most 11; Ⓜ Kuznetsky; mains R50-250; Ⓥ 8am-11pm) A saviour for vegetarians, this excellent health-food place with a strong Indian theme has both a self-service buffet and a sit-down restaurant. The vegetable curries, samosas and salads are superb, although perhaps the lack of alcohol takes the concept of health food a little far.

Sindibad's (☎ 291 7115; Nikitsky bul 14; Ⓜ Arbatskaya; mains R350; Ⓥ noon-11pm) Lebanese and Arabian cooking at its best – Sindibad's is hugely popular (booking advisable at weekends) with its unpretentious, delicious food and friendly staff. The big plate of mixed *mezze* (R350) – a large selection of dishes served either as a starter or main course depending on their numbers – is fantastic.

DRINKING & CLUBBING

Head to the **Hermitage Gardens** (Ⓜ Pushkinskaya) or **Alexandrovsky Garden** (Manezhnaya ul; Ⓜ Okhotny Ryad) in the summer months for relaxed beer drinking amid the greenery. Other recommended bars include the following, all of which are open until the early hours:

Boar House (☎ 917 9986; Zemlyanoy val 26; admission R60-100; Ⓥ noon-6am; Ⓜ Kurskaya) Run by the creator of the legendary Hungry Duck (once the wildest bar in Europe due to its famously hedonistic ladies night), the Boar House is busy throughout the week and attracts an expat crowd devoted to serious debauchery.

Gogol (☎ 514 0944; Stoleshnikov per 11; Ⓜ Teatralnaya; admission free; Ⓥ 24hr; Ⓜ Chekhovskaya) This is a brilliant, sprawling bar-cum-concert venue with a fantastic summer garden where groups often play in the evenings.

Kitaysky Lyotchik (☎ 924 5611; Lyublyansky proezd; Ⓜ Kitay Gorod; admission R150; Ⓥ 10am-8am) The 'Chinese Pilot' is a long-time favourite with the boho crowd who come here for the live music and lack of aggressive door policy.

Proekt OGI (☎ 229 5489; www.proektogi.ru in Russian; Potapovsky per 8/12; Ⓜ Chistiye Prudi; admission R50-100; Ⓥ 10am-6am) OGI is the acronym of a publishing house that delved into bars and cafés. It's become a phenomenon – the OGI bars/cafés (all with their own in-house bookshop) can be found all over central Moscow.

Negotiating Moscow's clubland is a challenge. 'Face control' (the term for haphazard door policy operated by spiteful thugs) rules the night. The *Exile* (www.exile.ru) has an up-to-date and thoroughly un-PC club guide. While many clubs disappear overnight, some enduringly hip venues include **Propaganda** (☎ 924 5732; Bol Zlatoustinsky per 7; Ⓜ Kitay Gorod; admission R50-200; Ⓥ noon-7am) and **Art Garbage** (☎ 928-8745; Starosadsky per 5/6; Ⓜ Kitay Gorod).

The most fun and accessible gay venue is perhaps **Three Monkeys** (☎ 951 1563 Sadovnicheskaya nab 71; Ⓜ Paveletskaya; admission free to R250; Ⓥ 9pm-9am), where the atmosphere is friendly. Check www.gay.ru/english for listings.

ENTERTAINMENT

Check *The Moscow Times* on Friday for an excellent guide to gigs, clubs, theatre, films and other events.

A night at the Bolshoi Ballet (www.bolshoi.ru) is a treat – tickets are available online and through travel agencies at a premium, although generally the ticket kiosks (*teatralnaya kassa*) around the city will offer some good bargains. Be aware that foreigners are charged extra for tickets – so if you buy one at the Russian price, you may be refused entry unless you stump up for a 400% mark-up.

The **American House of Cinema** (☎ 941 8747; pl Evropy 2, www.americanmovie.ru; Ⓜ Kievskaya), in the SAS Radisson Slavyanskaya Hotel, shows films in English.

GETTING AROUND
Metro

The Moscow metro is probably the best in the world. More than 150 stations in al

parts of the city, and a train every two minutes makes it the best way to get around.
The flat fare is R10, although buying in bulk
saves a lot of money (10 rides cost R50).

Taxi

The standard way to hail a 'taxi' is simply
to hold out your hand, when a car stops,
state your destination, wait for the driver
to give you a price, and then either shut the
door, negotiate or get in. The system seems
perfectly safe, the standard rate for very
short trips is R50, while longer ones will
cost from R100 to R150. Official taxis are
yellow, have taxi written on them and cost
more. You can book through the central
Taxi Reservation Office (☎ 927 0000; ☽ 24hr).

ST PETERSBURG
САНКТ ПЕТЕРБУРГ

☎ 812 / pop 5 million

Simply one of the most enchanting and impressive cities on earth, St Petersburg gives little indication that its incredible architectural
wealth is built on a mosquito-infested swamp
on the Gulf of Finland. Peter the Great, who
wanted to create a modern capital for a country still stuck in the Dark Ages, founded St
Petersburg in 1703. Since then it has grown
to be Europe's fourth-largest city and easily
one of its most culturally significant. A 'window on Europe,' the city of Dostoyevsky and
Shostakovich, cradle of the Russian Revolution – St Petersburg has more to offer than
perhaps anywhere else in Russia.

ORIENTATION

St Petersburg is spread across many different
islands, some real and some created through
the construction of canals. The central street
is Nevsky pr, which extends for 4km from
the Lavra Alexandra Nevskogo (Alexandr
Nevsky Monastery) to the Hermitage.

INFORMATION
Internet Access

Nevsky pr boasts two large, excellent In-
ternet cafés:
Café Max (☎ 273 6655; Nevsky pr 90/92 ; per hr R60;
Ⓜ Mayakovskaya; ☽ 24hr)
Quo Vadis (☎ 311 8011; Nevsky pr 24; per hr R60;
Ⓜ Nevsky Pr; ☽ 24hr)

Medical Services
Apteka Petrofarm (Nevsky pr 22; ☽ 24hr) Pharmacy.
International Clinic (☎ 320 3870; www.icspb.com; ul
Dostoevskogo 19/21; ☽ 24hr) Pricey emergency care and
direct billing to insurance companies.
Poliklinika No 2 (☎ 316 6272; Moskovsky pr 22;
☽ 24hr) Another good clinic, much cheaper than the
International.

Money

There are currency-exchange offices throughout the city. ATMs are inside every metro
station, in hotels and department stores, in
main post offices and along major streets.
Travellers cheques can be exchanged at
most Russian banks (with commission, of
course).

Post & Telephone

You can call direct from any of the card-
operated phone booths all over the city;
cards can be purchased from metro stations
and telephone offices.
Central post office (Glavpochtamt; ☎ 312 8302;
Pochtamtskaya ul 9; ☽ 9am-7.45pm Mon-Sat, 10am-
5.45pm Sun)

Toilets

There are public toilets – in varying states –
all over St Petersburg . Very good ones are
between the Kazansky Sobor (Kazan Cathedral) and Kanal Griboyedova (R10). There
are also toilets around most metro stations,
although not those on Nevsky Pr.

Tourist Information
tourist office (Palace Sq, next to the Hermitage) Russia's
only tourist office offers information, plus guides in many
languages.

Travel Agencies
American Express (☎ 326 4500; fax 326 4501; Malaya
Morskaya ul 23; Ⓜ Nevsky Pr; ☽ 9am-5pm Mon-Fri) No
money-changing facilities; travel services only.
Ost-West Kontaktservice (☎ 327 3416; www.
ostwest.com; 105 Nevsky pr; Ⓜ Pl Vosstaniya) This place
will register visas (R875) for those not staying in hotels.
Sinbad Travel International (☎ 327 8384; 3-aya
Sovetskaya ul 28; Ⓜ Pl Vosstaniya) At the HI St Peters-
burg Hostel; this place can organise discounted travel.

SIGHTS
The Historic Heart

Unquestionably your first stop should be
Dvortsovaya ploshchad (Palace Square), where

ST PETERSBURG

A B C D

Petrovsky Park

ul Krasnogo Kursanta

Sytninskaya ul
Vvedenskaya ul
Monchegorskaya ul

Gorkovskaya

To Troitsky
Most (50m)

Zhdanovskaya

Ofitsersky per

Maly pr

Bolshoy pr

Bol Pushkarskaya ul

Kronverksky pr

Kamennoostrovsky pr

Alexandrovsky
Park

Petrovskaya ul

Malaya

Sezzhinskaya ul

Zverinskaya ul

Tatarsky
per

Sportivnaya

ul Blokhina

Petrovsky
Stadium

Bolshoy pr

Pr Dobrolyubova

ul Yablochkova

ul Blokhina

Yubileyny
Sports
Palace

pr Dobrolyubova

Mytninskaya nab

Kronverksky proliv

Peter & Paul
Fortress

18

Tuchkov
most

KRONVERKSKY

ZAYACHY

Troitsky
most

nab Makarova

River

Birzhevoy
most

Suvorovskaya pl

Dvortsovaya nab

Mars Field

Tuchkov per

Maly pr

2-ya i 3-ya linii

8-9 linii

6-7 linii

nab Makarova

Vasilevsky

Birzhevaya pl

Ermitazhny
most

Millionnaya ul

nab r Moyki

48

Vasileostrovskaya

10-11 linii

12-13 linii

Sredny pr

ul Repina

2-ya i 3-ya linii

University
Botanical
Gardens

St Petersburg
State
University

Birzhevoy
proezd

Dvortsovy
most

Mikhailovsky
Gardens

19

6-7 linii

Bolshoy pr

10-11 linii

12-13 linii

ul Repina

4-ya i 5-ya linii

Universitetskaya nab

31

nab r Moyki

23

28

Admiralteyskaya nab

pl
Dekabristov

Chernomorsky proezd

16

Admiralteysky pr

21

13

Nevsky pr

22

36

44

2

@ 12

Nevsky pr

27

17

River

14-15 linii

Angliyskaya nab

Admiralty
Gardens

Admiralteysky pr

Gostiny
Dvor

most Leytenanta
Shmidta

16-17 linii

18-19 linii

56

nab Leytenanta Shmidta

Galernaya ul

24

Admiralteysky

25

ul Kazanska

33

Bolshaya

Admiralteysky canal

Galernaya ul

Konnogvardeyskiy bul

ul Yakubovicha

pl
Truda

5

Pochtamtsky per

nab r Moyki

Siniy
most

Isaakievskaya pl

Gorokhovaya ul

per Grivtsova

nab r Moyki

Gribedova

Sadovaya ul

Spassky

NOVOADMIRATELSKY

Novaya
Gollandiya

nab r Moyki

Truda

Bol Morskaya

Fonarny per

Pirogova per

canal

Apraksin per

Torgovy per

River

Gorokhovaya

MATISOV

Kolomensky

ul Pisarova

pr Maklina

32

Potseluev
most

Kazansky

nab kanala Griboedova

Sadovaya

Sennaya pl

Semyonovsky
most

Semyonovskaya p

Pokrovsky

ul Dekabristov

ul Soyuza Pechatnikov

55

Teatralnaya
pl

Nikolsky
Gardens

nab kanala Griboedova

Rimskogo-Korsakova

Kokushkin
most

Sadovaya ul

45

Moskovsky pr

Pryazhki

nab r Pryazhki

Drovyanoy per

nab r Fontanka

Lermontovsky pr

Kryukova canala

Kryukova kanala

per Makarenko

35

Sadovaya ul

Yusupovsky
Gardens

Obukhovskaya
pl

Obukhovsky
most

11

Pushkinskaya

ul A Bloka

nab r Pskovskaya ul

ul Vitebskaya

Rimskogo-Korsakova

nab kanala Griboedova

Kanonersky ul

pl Turgeneva

ul Labutina

Fontanka

Izmailovsky
Gardens

Vitebsky pl

Vitebsky Vokzal
(Vitebsk Station)

Lotsmanskaya ul

Staropetergofsky pr

Derptsky per

Sadovaya ul

nab r Fontanki

nab r Fontanki

Voznesensky pr

Bol Podyacheskaya

Derbinskaya ul

Polsky
Gardens

pr Moskvinov

1 Krasnoarmeyskaya ul

Tehnologichesky
Institut

Serpukhovskaya

Klimsky pr

Ruzovskaya ul

Bronnitskaya ul

Podolskaya ul

Olimpia
Gardens

Verejskaya ul

Moskovsky pr

Vvedensky kanala

Vvedensky pr

Zagorodny pr

Rizhsky pr

13 Krasnoarmeyskaya ul
8 Krasnoarmeyskaya ul
9 Krasnoarmeyskaya ul
10 Krasnoarmeyskaya ul
11 Krasnoarmeyskaya ul
12 Krasnoarmeyskaya ul

2 Krasnoarmeyskaya ul
3 Krasnoarmeyskaya ul
4 Krasnoarmeyskaya ul
5 Krasnoarmeyskaya ul
6 Krasnoarmeyskaya ul
7 Krasnoarmeyskaya ul

ul Egorova

Malodetskoselsky pr

4

Kurlyandskaya ul

Troitskogo

nab Obvodnogo kanala

nab Obvodnogo kanala

Flotanka River

nab Obvodnogo kanala

Moskovsky pr

nab r Rozenshteyna

Baltiysky Vokzal
(Baltic Station)

Baltiyskaya

Varshavsky Vokzal
(Warsaw Station)

Fruzhenskaya

RUSSIA

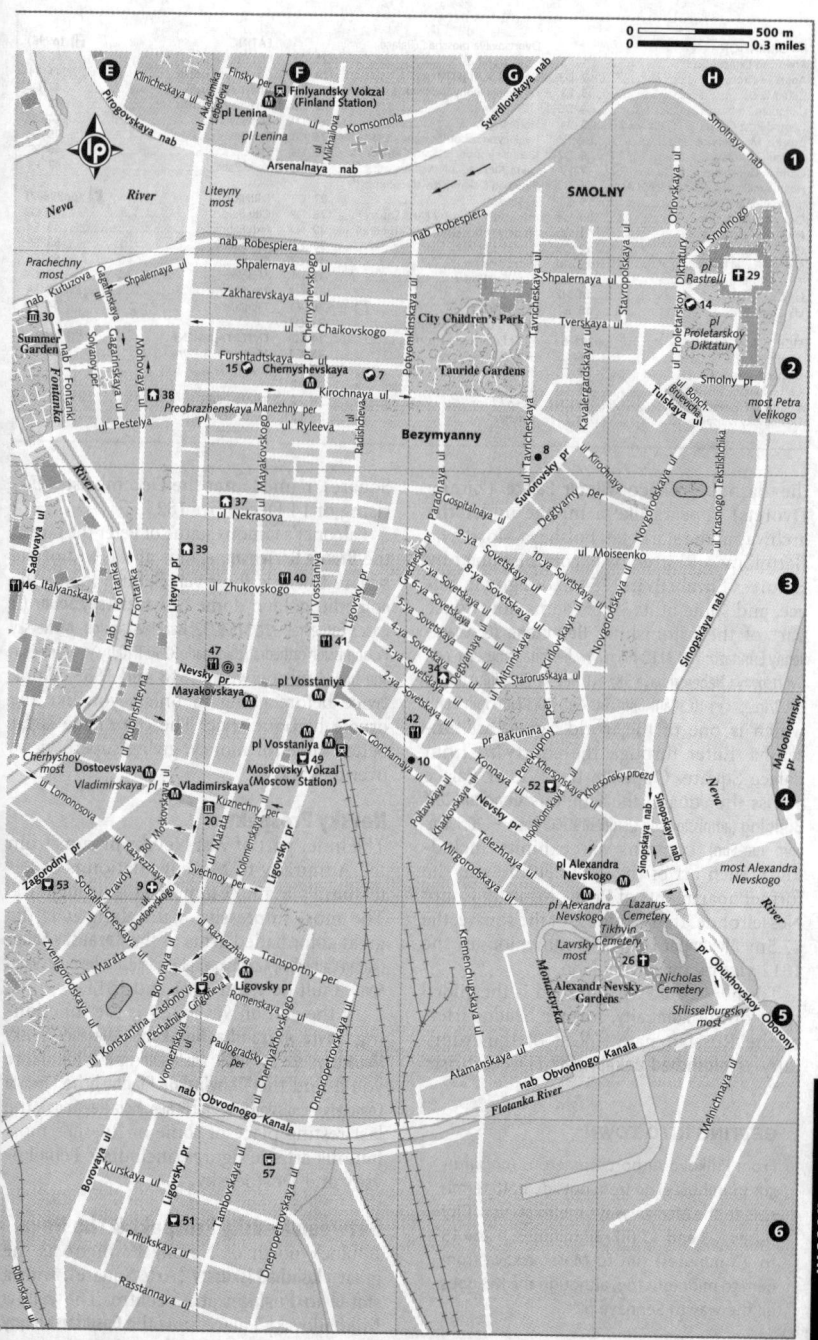

RUSSIA

the baroque/rococo **Winter Palace** (Zimny Dvorets) appears like a mirage under the archway at the start of ul Bolshaya Morskaya. Bartolomeo Rastrelli was commissioned by Empress Elizabeth in 1754 to design the palace, and some of its 1057 rooms now house part of the astonishing **Hermitage** (Gosudarstvenny Ermitazh; ☎ 311 3465; www.hermitagemuseum.org; Dvortsovaya Naberezhnaya 38; Ⓜ Nevsky Pr; adult/student R300/free; ⏱ 10.30am-6pm Tue-Sat, 10.30am-5pm Sun), which is one of the world's great art museums. Enter through the courtyard from Palace Square. Opposite the Winter Palace across the square, the fabulous **General Staff Building** (admission adult/student R160/free; ⏱ 10.30am-6pm Tue-Sun) contains six exhibits including French art of the 20th century and the former apartments of Prime Minister Count Nesselrohde. In the middle of the square, the 47.5m **Alexander Column** commemorates the 1812 victory over Napoleon.

To the west across the road is the gilded spire of the **Admiralty**, former headquarters of the Russian navy. West of the Admiralty is **ploshchad Dekabristov** (Decembrists'

Square), named after the Decembrists' Uprising of 14 December 1825.

Falconet's famous statue of Peter the Great, the **Bronze Horseman**, stands at the end of the square towards the river. Behind looms the splendid golden dome of **Isaakievsky Sobor** (St Isaac's Cathedral; ☎ 315 9732; Isaakievskaya pl; Ⓜ Nevsky Pr; admission cathedral/colonnade R250/R100; ⏱ 11am-6pm Thu-Tue), built between 1818 and 1858. Think twice before going in unless you like the ornate baroque style. The colonnade is far better value for money, giving superb views over the city.

Nevsky Prospekt

The inner part of vast Nevsky pr runs from the Admiralty to Moscow Station is St Petersburg's main commercial thoroughfare. The most impressive sight along it is the great colonnaded arms of the **Kazansky Sobor** (Kazan Cathedral; Kazanskaya pl 2; admission free; ⏱ 9am-6pm), built between 1801 and 1811.

At the end of Nevsky pr is the functioning **Lavra Alexandra Nevskogo** (Alexandr Nevsky Monastery; ☎ 274 0409, adult/student R50/30). Here you'll find the **Tikhvinskoe Kladbishche** (Tikhvin Cemetery; admission R50; Ⓜ Pl Alexandra Nevskogo), the last resting place of some of Russia's most famous artistic figures, including Tchaikovsky and Dostoevsky.

Between Nevsky Prospekt & the Neva

A block north of Nevsky Pr metro is the great **ploshchad Iskusstv** (Arts Square), with a statue to Pushkin at its centre. The yellow Mikhailovsky Palace, now the **Gosudarstvenny**

GETTING INTO TOWN

From Pulkovo Airport, numerous *marshrutkas* (minibuses) go from outside both terminals to the Moskovskaya metro station. City buses K-3 and 13 (R7, 30 minutes, every 15 to 20 minutes) run to Moskovskaya from 6am to midnight too, although the K-3 goes all the way to Sennaya pl.

Russky Muzej (Russian Museum; ☎ 311 1465; M Gostiny Dvor; admission R240; ☼ 10am-5pm Wed-Mon), housing one of the country's finest collections of Russian art, makes up the far side of the square. Behind it are the pleasant **Mikhailovsky Gardens**.

The polychromatic domes of the **Church on Spilled Blood** (☎ 315 1636; Konyushennaya pl; M Gostiny Dvor; adult/student R250/125; ☼ 11am-6pm Thu-Tue) are close by. Also known as the Church of the Resurrection of Christ, it was built from 1887 to 1907 on the spot where Alexander II was assassinated in 1881. The interior is incredible and somewhat overwhelming – having been restored from Soviet times when the church was used as a potato warehouse.

The lovely **Letny Sad** (Summer Garden; admission R10; ☼ 9am-10pm, May-Oct; 10am-6pm, Oct—mid-Apr; closed mid-Apr—end-Apr) is between the open space of Mars Field (Marsovo Pole) and the Fontanka River. Laid out for Peter the Great with fountains and pavilions and his tiny **Summer Palace** (Letny Dvorets) along a geometrical plan, it's a great place in which to relax.

The greatest thing about the unmistakable Rastrelli-designed **Smolny Sobor** (Smolny Cathedral; ☎ 278 5596; pl Rastrelli; M Chernyshevskaya; admission R100; ☼ 11am-5pm Fri-Wed), 3km east of Letny Sad, is the sweeping view from atop one of its 63m-high belfries.

South & West of Nevsky Prospekt

A short walk down the Moyka River is the fascinating **Yusupov Palace** (☎ 314 9883; nab reki Moyki 94; M Sadovaya; adult/student R300/250; ☼ 11am-5pm). Notorious as the scene of Rasputin's grisly murder in 1916, the palace has some of the most magnificent interiors in the city.

Across the meandering Griboedov Canal and the Fontanka River, east of the palace, is Sennaya pl, the heart of Dostoevskyville. The author lived in several flats around here, and many of the locations turn up in *Crime and Punishment*. To find out more head to the small but interesting **Dostoevsky Museum** (☎ 164 6950; Kuznechny per 5/2; M Vladimirskaya; adult/student R60/30, audio tour in English R70; ☼ 11am-5pm Tue-Sun) in the house where the writer died in 1881.

Petrograd Side

This area refers to the group of delta islands between the Malaya Neva and Bolshaya Nevka channels. The principal attraction here is the **Peter & Paul Fortress** (Petropavlovskaya krepost; ☎ 238 4550; admission to grounds free, admission to all buildings adult/student R120/60; ☼ 10am-5pm Thu-Mon, 10am-4pm Tue). Founded in 1703 as the original military fortress for the new city, its principal use up to 1917 was as a political prison: famous residents include Peter's own son Alexei, as well as Dostoevsky, Gorky and Trotsky. At noon every day a cannon is fired from the **Naryshkin Bastion**, scaring the daylights out of tourists. It's fun to walk along the **battlements** (adult/student R50/30; ☼ 10am-10pm). Most spectacular of all is the **Cathedral of Sts Peter & Paul**, with its landmark needle-thin spire and magnificent baroque interior. All Russia's tsars since Peter the Great have been buried here. The latest addition was Nicholas II and his family, finally laid to rest by Yeltsin in 1998.

FESTIVALS & EVENTS

City Day (27 May) celebrates the founding of St Petersburg with mass festivities. The White Nights (around the summer solstice in late June) are truly unique. The city comes alive and parties all night as the sun only barely sinks below the horizon, leaving the sky a magical grey-white throughout the night.

SLEEPING

Prices for accommodation are in euros. Hotels and hostels in Russia usually accept both the euro and the rouble.

Old ladies often offer rooms for rent at the Moscow Station. These are the cheapest options, but be careful of your valuables if you choose this option. Agencies such as **Host Families Association** (HOFA; ☎ 275 1992; Tavricheskaya ul 5/25) and **Russian Room** (☎ 900 9928; www.russianroom.50g.com) can organise reliable homestays in the city centre.

HI St Petersburg Hostel (☎ 329 8018; www.ryh.ru; 3-ya Sovetskaya ul 28; M Pl Vosstaniya; dm/d €18/44) Only five minutes' walk from Moscow Station, this place is popular and prices include breakfast. Spotless dorms have three to six beds and there's one double; all are slightly cheaper in the winter and for holders of ISIC and HI cards (see p1235).

Herzen University Hostel (☎ 314 7472; fax 314 7659; ul Kazanskaya 6; M Gostiny Dvor; s/d €16/40) This place is in a brilliant location and is a well-run hostel used to foreigners. However it does not register visas, so you'll need to have had your visa registered elsewhere to stay here (it does not allow people with unregistered visas to spend more than 3 nights).

Hotel Na Sadovoy (☎ 314 4510; www.nasadovy.sp.ru in Russian; Sadovaya ul 53; Ⓜ Sadovaya; s/d/tr €30/39/43) Very Soviet, but great value, particularly for the triple rooms. The staff speak no English, but are proficient in sign language. Rooms are comfy, all have a TV, sink and fridge and there are clean shared facilities.

Nord Hostel (☎ 117 0342; www.nordhostel.com; Bolshaya Morskaya ul 10; Ⓜ Nevsky Pr; dm/d €24/48) This fantastic addition to the hostel scene has perhaps the single most superb location, just metres from Palace Square. Book ahead, as its location and friendly management make it justly popular. Dorms have eight beds and are very clean; there's also one double room and there are plans to expand into a neighbouring apartment.

Sleep Cheap (☎ 115 1304; www.sleepcheap.spb.ru; Mokhovaya ul 18/32; Ⓜ Chernyshevskaya; dm €19) An excellently appointed small new hostel, which is a 10-minute walk from Nevsky pr, Sleep Cheap has brand new facilities and (like most hostels) plans to expand. Go through into the courtyard of No 18 and the hostel is on the left.

St Petersburg Puppet Hostel (☎ 272 5401; www .hostelling-russia.ru; ul Nekrasova 12; Ⓜ Mayakovskaya; dm/s/d €16/40/40) This is a great option – central, friendly, cosy and clean. Rates include breakfast and tickets to the Puppet Theatre!

Zimmer Frei (☎ 973 3757/273 0867; www.zimmer.ru; flat 23, Liteyny pr 46; Ⓜ Mayakovskaya; s/d €18) This Russian flat is a minihostel with just seven rooms, sharing a kitchen and washing facilities. The downstairs concierge speaks excellent English and is a great source of local information. Enter direct from the street by ringing the unmarked bell at the black door.

EATING

Look out for blini kiosks throughout the city. Their delicious blinis, or Russian pancakes, are superb value (R20 to R30) and a great place to snack. As in Moscow, street food is sold around metro stations.

Subway (☎ 928 3400; Nevsky pr 20; Ⓜ Nevsky Pr; sandwiches from R40; Ⓥ 10am-10pm) Very handily located for picking up their huge, world-famous sandwiches between the Hermitage and Russian Museum.

Blin Donalt's (☎ 277 5902; ul Zhukovskogo 18; Ⓜ Pl Vosstaniya; Ⓥ 10am-10pm) This Russian take on the hamburger giant offers chicken

Kiev (R34), *borsch* (R12) and other Russian standards, disfigured into fast-food form.

Chaynaya Lozhka (mains R100; Ⓥ 9am-10pm) Nesky (Nevsky pr 44; Ⓜ Gostiny Dvor); Nevsky (Nevsky pr 136; Ⓜ Pl Vosstaniya); Vosstaniya (ul Vosstaniya 13; Ⓜ Pl Vosstaniya) This excellent chain serves delicious blinis and a wide range of salads. Orange-clad staff members are extremely helpful and the fare is very cheap. Bear in mind that it's extremely busy at lunchtime.

Tri (☎ 595 4183; Italyanskaya ul 17; Ⓜ Gostiny Dvor; sandwiches R70; Ⓥ 24hr) A coffee, decent sandwich and, oddly enough, wine shop – Tri is good for a light lunch on the run.

Troitsky Most (mains R100-200) Kamenostrovsky (☎ 232 6693; Kamenostrovsky pr 9/2; Ⓜ Gorkovskaya); Zagorodny (☎ 115-1998; Zagorodny pr 38; Ⓜ Dostoyevskaya) Superb vegetarian chain operating in four locations across the city. The mushroom lasagne is legendary.

Sumeto (☎ 310 2411; ul Yefimova 5; R150; Ⓜ Sadovaya; Ⓥ noon-11pm) A brilliant find – this quiet little restaurant off Sennaya pl serves delicious Dagestani food at rock-bottom prices. Dishes include shashlik and *chudu* – a large savoury pancake with pumpkin filling.

Yolki Palki (☎ 273 1594; Nevsky pr 88; Ⓜ Gostiny Dvor; mains R100-200; Ⓥ 11am-11pm) The Moscow chain now has an outlet on Nevsky pr – as kitsch as ever (you dine in a Russian forest attended by waiters in folk costume) but there's a good buffet of Russian food served here.

DRINKING

City Bar (☎ 314 1037; ul Millionnaya 10; Ⓜ Nevsky Pr; Ⓥ 10am-last client) Run by the inimitable local celebrity Elaine, the City Bar has moved to smarter premises on millionaires' row, a short walk from the Hermitage. This is the hub of the expat community and it's full of foreigners most nights of the week.

Tsynik (☎ 312 9526; per Antonenko 4; Ⓜ Sennaya Pl; Ⓥ 1pm-3am, Mon-Fri, to 7am Sat & Sun) Far more authentic is the grungy cool of Tsynik. Famous for its rowdy crowd and *grenki* (fried garlic black bread), this is the place to misbehave.

Fish Fabrik (☎ 164 4857; Ligovsky pr 53; Ⓜ Pl Vosstaniya; Ⓥ 3pm-6am) One of the city's longest-running boho joints – Fish Fabrik is a dive bar for drunken artists and student slackers. You'll inevitably end up playing table football with a stranger if you come.

Moloko (☎ 274 9467; Perekupnoy per 2; Ⓜ Pl Alexandra Nevskogo; Ⓥ 7pm-midnight Tue-Sun) The ultimate Bohemian performance venue, Moloko is a local institution. It's very cheap, though it can be extremely crowded when there are gigs.

ENTERTAINMENT

St Petersburg is Russia's cultural capital and there is a huge range of theatre, ballet, opera and classical concerts from which to choose. A visit to the **Mariinsky Theatre** (☎ 326 4141; www .mariinsky.ru; Teatralnaya pl 1; **M** Sennaya Pl) should not be missed. However, it's not all about high culture – hedonism is engrained in St Petersburg and consequently clubbing and gigs are two much-loved pastimes. Check the *St Petersburg Times* on Fridays for listings.

Some of the best clubs include alternative **Griboyedov** (☎ 164 4355; www.griboedovclub.ru in Russian; Voronezhskaya ul 2a; **M** Ligovsky Pr), classy **Ostrov** (☎ 328 4649; nab Leitenanta Shmita 37; **M** Vasileostrovskaya) and student superclub **Metro** (☎ 166 0204; www.metroclub.ru; Ligovsky pr 174; **M** Ligovsky Pr).

St Petersburg has three gay clubs and Russia's first lesbian club: check out www .xs.gay.ru/English for the latest city-specific information.

GETTING AROUND

The metro (R8 flat fare) is best for covering large distances across the city. The four lines cross over in the city centre and go out to the suburbs. Around the centre, *marshrutkas* (minibuses) are a very quick alternative to the slow trolleybuses. Costs vary on each route, but the average fare is R14, and is displayed prominently inside each van. To stop a *marshrutka*, simply hold out your hand and it will stop, jump in, sit down, pass cash to the driver (a human chain operates if you are not seated nearby) and then call out '*ostanovityes pozhalusta!*' when you want to get out and the driver will pull over.

KALININGRAD REGION
КАЛИНИНГРАДСКАЯ ОБЛАСТЬ

pop 946,700

If you think that travelling through Russia is already an adventure, wait until you get to Kaliningrad! Not only is it the country's newest and most westerly province, it also has a history that differs in all ways from that of the rest of Mother Russia, from which it's cut off by Lithuania and Belarus. It's also now the only bit of Russia completely surrounded by EU-member states. Closer to Berlin, Stockholm and Warsaw than Moscow, locals are in some ways more western-oriented than their fellow Russians, but in other ways the enclave is backwards and its politics a tad on the paranoid side.

Aside from the lively, leafy capital (leafy in the surviving bits of old Königsberg that is; the rest is a smart assembly of cracked concrete), the region boasts ruined Prussian castles, the world's largest amber-producing mine (some 90% of the world's amber comes from here!), long stretches of pristine beach and some of Europe's highest sand dunes.

ORIENTATION & INFORMATION

In Kaliningrad city, Leninsky pr, a broad north–south avenue, is the main artery, running over 3km from the bus and main train station, the Yuzhny Vokzal (South Station), to the Severny Vokzal (North Station).

At newspaper kiosks you'll find several (Russian-language) guides to the region. See www.inyourpocket.com for up-to-date listings. The best travel agency is **Baltma Tours** (☎ 21 18 80; www.baltma.ru; pr Mira 49; 9am-6pm Mon-Fri, 10am-5pm Sat). They can help with visas, accommodation and provide a surprising array of local excursions, including to Yantarny, the village with the world's largest amber mine.

Use chip cards to make long-distance calls or order them at the **telephone and fax centre** (☎ 53 84 64; Teatralnaya ul 13/19; ☼ 24hr). The main **post office** (ul Kosmonavta Leonova 22; ☼ 8.30am-7pm Mon-Fri, 9am-4pm Sat) is about 600m north of pr Mira, and for Internet access, head to **E-Type** (☎ 44 72 42; Sovietsky pr 1; per hr R30; ☼ 9am-9pm Mon-Fri, 9am-7pm Sat).

SIGHTS & ACTIVITIES
Kaliningrad City Калининград

☎ 22/0112 (inside/outside region) / pop 426,000
The outstanding German remnant is the red-brick, Gothic cathedral, **Kafedralny Sobor** (☎ 27 25 83; adult/student R60/20; ☼ 9am-5pm daily). Founded in 1333, it was severely damaged during WWII and, since 1992, has been undergoing total reconstruction. On the top floor is the death mask of Emanuel Kant, whose rose-marble **tomb** lies outside on the outer north side. The 18th-century philosopher was born, studied and taught in Königsberg.

RUSSIA

KALININGRAD REGION

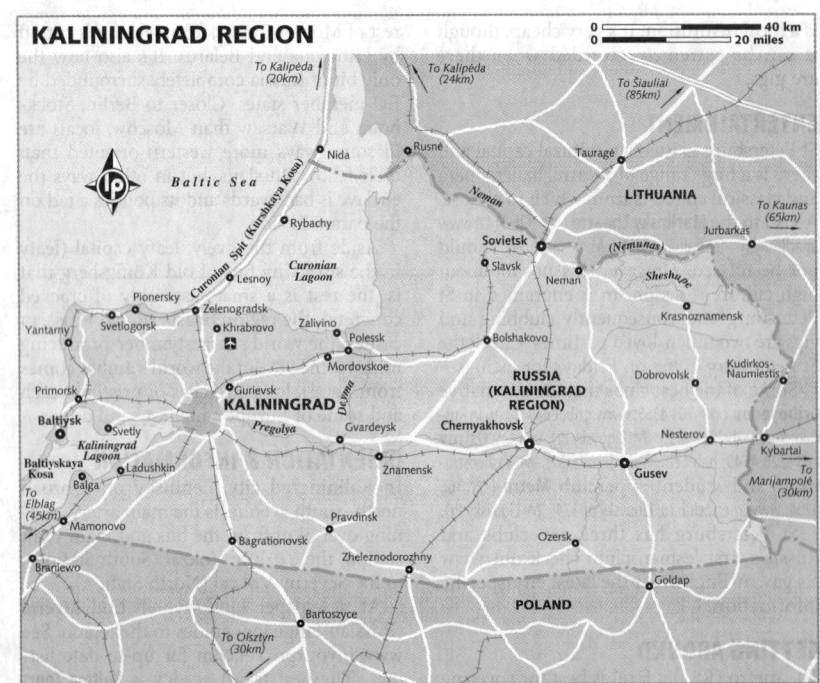

West of the cathedral, along the Petra Velikogo embankment is the **Muzey Mirovogo Okeana** (Museum of the World Ocean; ☎ 34 02 44; nab Petra Velikogo 1; per section adult/student R30/20; ☉ 10am-5pm Wed-Sun). Different displays highlight Soviet sea and space exploration, plus you can visit a submarine and see the skeleton of a 16.8m-long sperm whale.

North of the cathedral is **Tsentralnaya ploshchad** (Central Square) on which sits one of the ugliest of Soviet creations, the H-shaped **Dom Sovietov** (House of Soviets). On this site stood a magnificent 1255 castle, damaged during WWII but dynamited out of existence by narrow-minded Soviet planners in 1967–68. In its place this eyesore was built (over 10 long years), but it has never even been used.

Nearby is the popular **Blindazh Lyasha** (Bunker Museum; ☎ 53 65 93; Universitetskaya ul 2; admission R30; ☉ 10am-6pm), the German command post in 1945 from where the German capitulation to the Soviets was signed. Also worth visiting are the **Muzey Yantarya** (History & Art Museum; ☎ 45 38 44; ul Klinicheskaya 21; adult/student R30/20; ☉ 10am-6pm Tue-Sun) and the impressive

Muzey Yantarya (Amber Museum; ☎ 46 15 63; pl Vasilievskogo 1; adult/student R50/30; ☉ 10am-5pm Tue-Sun). The latter is housed in the attractive **Dohna Tower**, a bastion of the city's old defensive ring sitting at the lower end of **Prud Verkhny** (Upper Pond), a small lake surrounded by parkland. Inside the museum are some 6000 examples of amber artworks.

Svetlogorsk Светлогорск

☎ 253/01153 (inside/outside region) / pop 13,000
Hardly damaged by WWII bombing, Svetlogorsk (formerly Rauschen, founded in 1228), a pleasant, green coastal town 35km northwest of Kaliningrad, is a great place to see old Prussia – and get some beach action.

On Oktyabrskaya ul are the 25m **water tower** and the curious red-tile-domed Jugendstil (Art Nouveau) **bathhouse**. About 200m east of the main beach promenade is an impressive, colourful **sundial**, believed to be the largest in Europe.

Nine trains and over 20 buses and minibuses make the trip from the bus station and the northern train station in Kaliningrad. Minibuses (R30) make the trip in 45 minutes, while buses and trains can take up to 70 minutes. Svetlogorsk's bus station is 500m west of the train station, at the corner of ul Lenina and Kaliningradsky pr.

Kurshkaya Kosa Куршкая Коса
☎ 250/01150 (inside/outside region)

The Kurshkaya Kosa is the Russian half of the thin, 98km-long Curonian Spit, which divides the Curonian Lagoon from the Baltic Sea. The area is a Unesco World Heritage Site. Its dramatic landscapes – high sand dunes, pine forests, an exposed western coast and a calm lagoon – makes it one of Europe's natural highlights.

The **Kurshkaya Kosa National Park** (☎ 213 46; Lesnaya ul 7, Rybachy) is headquartered in Rybachy, but runs a fascinating bird-ringing centre 7km north of Lesnoy, on the site of what was the world's first ornithological station. The **Ecotourism Information Centre** (☎ 282 75; Tsentralnaya ul) in Lesnoy works in collaboration with the national park and organises excursions, transport and accommodation and rents bicycles.

Four buses a day from Kaliningrad (via Zelenogradsk, R25) take the road to Smiltynė (R114) in Lithuania at the northern tip of the peninsula.

SLEEPING

Prices for accommodation are in euros. Hotels and hostels in Russia usually accept both the euro and the rouble.

Komnati Otdykha (☎ 58 64 47; pl Kalinina; s/d €7/11) You might expect this place to be the city's dregs, considering it's inside the south train station, but it is surprisingly clean, relatively quiet, and the shared facilities are better than the ones inside the station!

Hotel Moskva (☎ 27 20 89; pr Mira 19; s/d with shared bathroom €12/17, with private bathroom €50/56) There's one unrenovated floor left: creaky floors, stern attendants and shared toilets, but huge rooms and a great location make this a great deal.

EATING & DRINKING

Razgulyai Bistro (☎ 214 897; pl Pobedy 1; mains from R55; ☼ 10am-10pm) This place is a dream come true: there is a huge selection of delicious meat, fish and vegetarian meals, plus salads galore, served buffet-style in a cosy, folky interior. Try the fresh-juice bar for a quick carrot or kiwi juice fix.

Planeta (☎ 46 52 35; ul Chernyakhovskogo 26; mains R25-75; ☼ noon-6am) This youth hang-out is an uneasy cross between a mall food court, an American diner and a casino, but the creatively designed pizzas (R50 to R165) are great. Even cheaper grub is also served, cafeteria-style.

Reduit (☎ 461951; Litovsky val 27; ☼ noon-midnight) There's lots of food on the menu, but the main reason to come here is for the fresh beer, brewed on the premises – unfiltered is the best! There's a relaxed cellar, an excellent hangout.

ENTERTAINMENT

Vagonka (☎ 55 66 77; Stanochnaya ul 12; ☼ 11pm-4am Fri & Sat) Kaliningrad's liveliest and most down-to-earth nightclub, this attracts a young, slightly alternative crowd for the excellent DJs and elaborate dance shows. Best to take a taxi there the first time – it's not easy to find.

RUSSIA DIRECTORY

ACCOMMODATION

Both Moscow and St Petersburg have a number of well-established (if underwhelming) youth hostels. Though prices are often announced in US dollars or euros, payment is usually in roubles. They are significantly more expensive than in most countries (budget €25 per night). Hotels start from about €35 to €50, although these are mainly pretty shabby Intourist relics. Private rooms are a fairly alien concept, although growing in popularity slowly in Moscow and St Petersburg. The cheapest possible accommodation will be that offered by old ladies at train stations. Be careful of your valuables if you are staying in a private room however. During the White Nights in St Petersburg in late June, booking early is essential.

ACTIVITIES

Checking out a traditional Russian *banya* is a must. These wet saunas are a social hub and a fantastic experience for any visitor to Russia. Leave your inhibitions at home and be prepared for a beating with birch twigs (far more pleasant than it sounds). Russians swear there's no better way of getting clean – ask at your hostel or hotel for the nearest public banya.

RUSSIA

BUSINESS HOURS

Most banks and offices are open for business from 8am or 9am to 5pm or 6pm Monday to Friday. Restaurants usually open from noon until at least 11am – many are in fact virtually 24-hour establishments.

DANGERS & ANNOYANCES

Travellers need to be very careful of pickpockets. Most foreigners stand out a mile in Russia and there's an increased chance you'll be targeted. Bear in mind that, while things have improved slowly, many police officers and other uniformed officials are on the take – some of them are not much better than the people they are employed to protect the public from. Never allow them to go through your wallet or pockets.

Never drink tap water in St Petersburg as it contains *Giardia lamblia*, a parasite that can cause horrific stomach cramps and nausea. Bottled water is available to purchase everywhere.

EMBASSIES & CONSULATES
Embassies in Moscow

Australia (☎ 956 6070; fax 956 6170; Kropotkinsky per 2; Ⓜ Kropotkinskaya)

Canada (☎ 105 6000; fax 105 6025; Starokonyushenny per 23; Ⓜ Kropotkinskaya)

France (☎ 937 1500; fax 937 1577; ul Bolshaya Yakimanka 45; Ⓜ Oktyabrskaya)

Germany (☎ 937 9500; fax 938 2354; ul Mosfilmovskaya 56); Consular Section (☎ 936 2401; Leninsky pr 95A; Ⓜ Pr Verdanskogo/Noviye Chermushki)

Netherlands (☎ 797 2900; fax 797 2904; Kalashny per 6; Ⓜ Arbatskaya)

New Zealand (☎ 956 3579; www.nzembassy.msk.ru; Povarskaya ul 44; Ⓜ Barrikadnaya)

Poland (☎ 255 0017, visa section ☎ 254 3621; ul Klimashkina 4; Ⓜ Ulitsa 1905 Goda)

UK (☎ 956 7200; fax 956 7201; Smolenskaya nab 10; Ⓜ Ulitsa 1905 Goda)

USA (☎ 728 5000; fax 728 5090, Novinsky bul 19/23; Ⓜ Smolenskaya)

Consulates in St Petersburg

Australia (☎ /fax 325 7333; Italyanskaya ul 1; Ⓜ Nevsky Pr)

Canada (☎ 325 8448; fax 325 8393; Malodetskoselsky pr 32B; Ⓜ Tekhnologichesky Institut)

France (☎ 312 1130; fax 311 7283; nab reki Moyki 15; Ⓜ Nevsky Pr)

Germany (☎ 327 2400; fax 327 3117; Furshtadtskaya ul 39; Ⓜ Chernyshevskaya)

UK (☎ 320 3200; fax 325 3111; pl Proletarskoy Diktatury 5; Ⓜ Chernyshevskaya)

USA (☎ 275 1701; fax 110 7022; Furshtadtskaya ul 15; Ⓜ Chernyshevskaya)

Russian Embassies & Consulates Abroad

Check www.russianembassy.net for more listings of Russian embassies abroad.

Australia Embassy (☎ 02-6295 9033/9474; fax 6295 1847; 78 Canberra Ave, Griffith, Canberra ACT 2603); Consulate (☎ 02-9326 1188; fax 9327 5065; 7 Fullerton St, Woollahra, Sydney NSW 2025)

Canada Embassy (☎ 613-235 4341; fax 236 6342; 285 Charlotte St, Ottawa, Ontario KIN 8L5); Visa Section (☎ 613-336 7220; fax 238 6158; 285 Charlotte St, Ottawa, Ontario KIN 8L5); Consulate (☎ 514-843 5901/5343; fax 842 2012; 3685 Ave du Musée, Montreal, Quebec H3G 2EI)

Finland Embassy (☎ 09-66 14 49; fax 66 18 12; Tehtaankatu 1B, Helsinki FIN-00140)

Germany Embassy (☎ 030-220 2821, 226 6320; fax 229 9397; Unter den Linden 63-65, Berlin 10117); Consulate (☎ 0228-312 085; fax 312 164; Waldstrasse 42, 53177, Bonn)

UK Embassy (☎ 020-7229 3628; fax 7727 8625) 13 Kensington Palace Gardens, London W8 4QX); Consular Section (☎ 020-7229 8027, visa information message ☎ 0891-171 271; fax 020-7229 3215; 5 Kensington Palace Gardens, London W8 4QS)

USA Embassy (☎ 202-939 8907; fax 483 7579; 2641 Tunlaw Rd NW, 20007); Visa Department (☎ 202-939 8907; fax 939 8909; 1825 Phelps Place NW, Washington DC 20008)

HOLIDAYS

Main public holidays:

New Year's Day (1 January)
Russian Orthodox Christmas Day (7 January)
International Women's Day (8 March)
International Labour Day/Spring Festival (1 & 2 May)
Victory Day (9 May) Commemorating 1945.
Russian Independence Day (12 June)
Day of Reconciliation and Accord (the rebranded Revolution Day (7 November).

Other days that are widely celebrated are **Defenders of the Motherland Day** (23 February), **Easter Monday** and **Constitution Day** (12 December). Much of Russia shuts down during the first half of May.

MONEY

You are able to use major credit and debit cards (including Cirrus and Maestro) in ATMs and in good restaurants and hotels.

Travellers cheques are possible to exchange, although at a price. Euro or US dollars are the best currencies to bring, and in general should be in pristine condition – crumpled or old notes are often refused.

POST

The Russian postal service gets an unfair rap. Postcards, letters and parcels sent abroad usually arrive within a couple of weeks. A postcard to anywhere in the world costs R10 and a letter R14.

VISAS

Everyone needs a visa to visit Russia, and it's likely to be your biggest single headache. Your visa is an exit permit too, so if you lose it (or overstay), leaving the country can be harder than getting in. Your visa process has three stages – invitation, application and registration.

To obtain a visa, you need an invitation. For a small fee (usually €24) most hotels and hostels will issue an invitation (or 'visa support') to anyone staying with them. The invitation then allows you to apply for a visa at any Russian Embassy. Costs can vary enormously, from €16 to €160 for same day service, so try to plan as far ahead as possible. If you are not staying in a hotel or hostel, you will need to buy an invitation. This can be done through almost any travel agency. Some hostels will issue invites for the same cost of one night's accommodation. Although a commercial website, www

.waytorussia.net is a very reliable source of information.

On arrival you must fill out an immigration card. This is very important – you surrender the first half on entering the country, and the second on leaving. If you lose your immigration card, expect a hefty fine on leaving the country.

Finally, once arriving in Russia, you are – officially at least – obliged to register your visa within three working days. This can nearly always be done by your hotel or hostel, but if you are not staying in one, you will need to pay a travel agency (usually €24) to register it for you. Many people have had no problems leaving the country without registration, but others have been detained and levied very big fines. In the light of the recent tightening of security, it's safest to play by the rules.

Since February 2002, Russia has been running a trial scheme whereby tourists from Schengen countries, Britain, Switzerland or Japan who wish to visit St Petersburg and Moscow for less than 72 hours can obtain visas on arrival. Travellers must apply at an authorised tour operator in their home country 48 hours before departure. Check with your local Russian consulate for details.

Anyone visiting Kaliningrad from Russia proper will require a double-entry visa unless they fly into the enclave. Leaving Russia proper by boat, bus or train entails getting an exit stamp, thus you won't be able to enter Kaliningrad without a double- or multi-entry visa.

Serbia & Montenegro
Србија и Црна Гора

HIGHLIGHTS

- **Belgrade** Massive citadel, cobbled Skadarska restaurant street with wandering Roma musicians, throbbing nightclubs on the river (p1006)
- **Subotica** Art Nouveau architecture with curlicues and crazy-patterned tiling, and laze-about café streets (p1011)
- **Novi Sad** Mighty Petrovaradin Citadel, artists' galleries and 'the' European music festival EXIT (p1011)
- **Kotor** Dramatic fjord and walled city (p1015)
- **Best journey** Zigzag up the road from Kotor fjord to the former mountain capital Cetinje (p1015)
- **Off-the-beaten track** Lake Skadar panorama at Rijeka Crnojevića, Montenegro (p1016)

FAST FACTS

- **Area** 102,350 sq km (about one Iceland)
- **ATMs** Widespread in major towns
- **Budget** €50 per day
- **Capital** Union and Serbian capital – Belgrade; Montenegrin capital – Podgorica
- **Country code** ☎ 381; international access code ☎ 99
- **Famous for** basketball
- **Head of State** Boris Tadic
- **Language** Serbian for Serbia and Montenegro, Albanian for Kosovo
- **Money** Dinar in Serbia, euro in Kosovo; 70.5DIN = €1 (A$1 = €0.58/40.9DIN, CA$1 = €0.64/45.1DIN, ¥100 = €0.73/50.5DIN, NZ$1 = €0.54/38.1DIN, UK£1 = €1.45/102.2DIN, US$1 = €0.81/57.1DIN)
- **Phrases** Serbian *zdravo* (hello), *do viđenja* (goodbye), *hvala* (thanks);

Kosovar Albanian *allo* (hello), *lamturmirë* (goodbye), *ju falem nderit* (thanks)
- **Population** 10,826,000
- **Time** GMT/UTC + 1
- **Visas** Not required for most visitors (see p1018).

TRAVEL HINTS

Feed at 'hole in the wall' stands for pizza, sandwich rolls and *čevapčići* (spiced kebabs). Stay in private rooms on the coast. May, June and September are the best months to go; the weather's dry and warm and the coast's clear of crowds.

ROAMING SERBIA & MONTENEGRO

Fly into Belgrade, then visit Subotica and Novi Sad (maybe on day trips). Then head back through Belgrade to the Montenegrin coast and mountains.

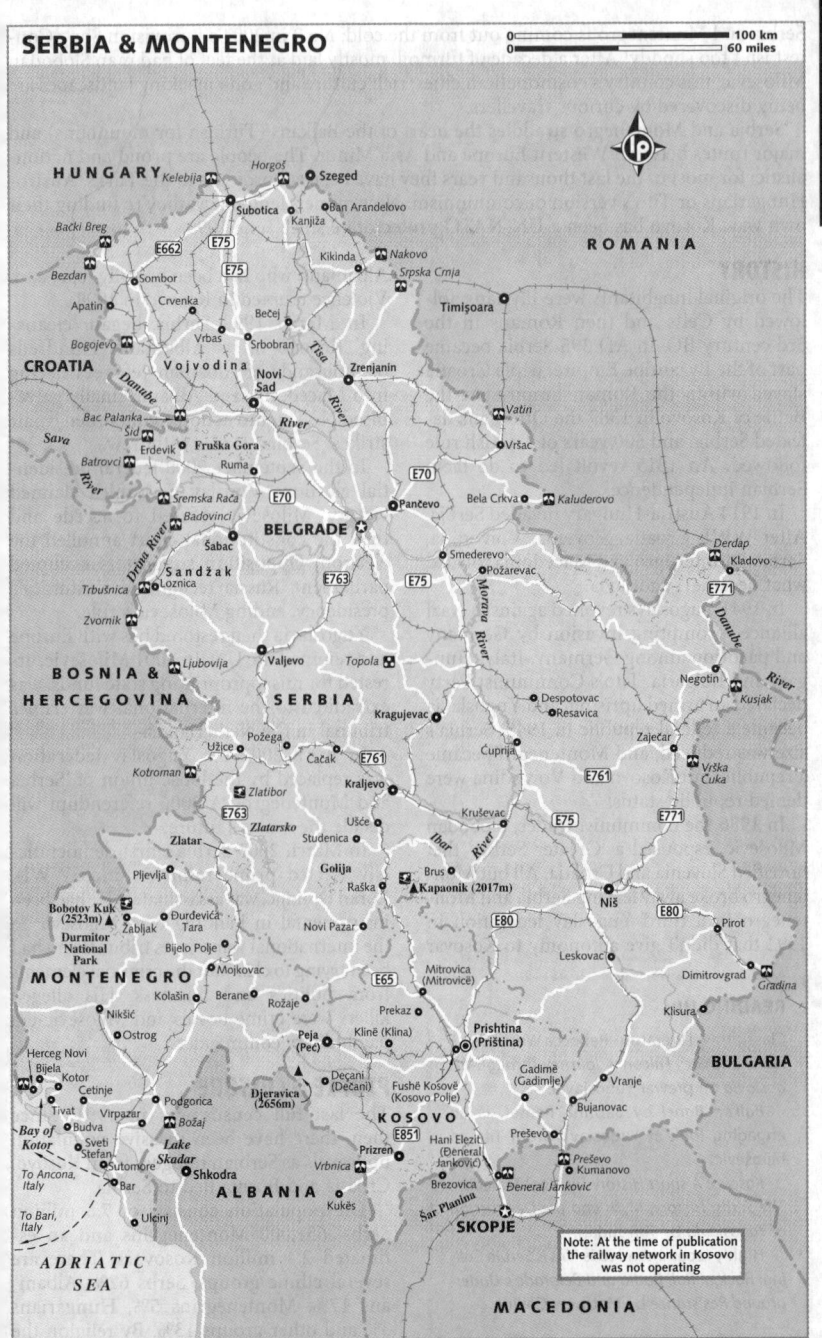

SERBIA & MONTENEGRO

0 — 100 km
0 — 60 miles

HUNGARY

Kelebija · Horgoš · Szeged
Bački Breg · Subotica · Kanjiža
Bezdan · Ban Arandelovo
Sombor · Kikinda · Nakovo
Apatin · Crvenka · Srpska Crnja
Bogojevo · Vrbas · Bečej · **ROMANIA**
Bac Palanka · Srbobran · Timişoara
CROATIA · **Vojvodina** · Novi Sad · Zrenjanin
Šid · Erdevik · **Fruška Gora** · Vatin
Batrovci · Ruma · Vršac
Sremska Rača · Badovinci · Bela Crkva · Kaluderovo
Šabac · **BELGRADE** · Pančevo
Sandžak · Smederevo · Derdap
Trbušnica · Loznica · Požarevac · Kladovo
Zvornik · Topola · Despotovac · Negotin
Ljubovija · Valjevo · **SERBIA** · Resavica · Kusjak
BOSNIA & · Užice · Požega · Kragujevac · Zaječar
HERCEGOVINA · Čačak · Ćuprija · Viška Čuka
Kotroman · Zlatibor · Kraljevo · Kruševac
Zlatarsko · Ušće · Niš · Pirot
Zlatar · Studenica · Brus · Kapaonik (2017m)
Pljevlja · **Golija** · Raška
Bobotov Kuk · Žabljak · Đurđevića · Novi Pazar · Leskovac · Dimitrovgrad
(2523m) · Tara · Mitrovica · Gradina
Durmitor · Bijelo Polje · (Mitrovicë) · Klisura
National · Mojkovac · **KOSOVO**
Park · Kolašin · Berane · Rožaje · Prekaz · Prishtina · **BULGARIA**
MONTENEGRO · Peja · Klinë (Klina) · (Priština) · Vranje
Nikšić · (Peć) · Gadimë · Bujanovac
Herceg Novi · Ostrog · Dečani · (Gadimlje)
Bijela · Kotor · Cetinje · Djeravica · (Dečani) · Fushë Kosovë · Preševo
Tivat · Virpazar · Podgorica · (2656m) · (Kosovo Polje) · Preševo
Bay of · Budva · Božaj · **KOSOVO** · Kumanovo
Kotor · Sveti · Lake · Prizren · Hani Elezit
Stefan · Skadar · Vrbnica · (Ðeneral · Ðeneral Jankovič
To Ancona, · Sutomore · Shkodra · Jankovič)
Italy · Bar · Brezovica
· Ulcinj · **ALBANIA** · Kukës · Šar Planina
To Bari, · **SKOPJE**
Italy
ADRIATIC
SEA · Note: At the time of publication
the railway network in Kosovo
was not operating
MACEDONIA

E662 · E75 · E70 · E763 · E761 · E65 · E80 · E771 · E851 · Danube · Tisa River · Sava River · Drina River · Morava River · Ibar River

Serbia and Montenegro is coming out from the cold; No 2 in 2004's Eurovision Song Contest isn't too shoddy! After a decade of turmoil, mostly laid at the feet of bad man Slobodan Milošević, this country's cosmopolitan cities, rich culture and gob-smacking landscapes are being discovered by curious travellers.

Serbia and Montenegro straddles the heart of the Balkans (Turkish for mountains) and major routes between Western Europe and Asia Minor. The people are proud and nationalistic; for most of the last thousand years they have been subordinate to the Turks, Austro-Hungarians or Tito's version of communism. Now, under democracy, they're finding their own way. Kosovo has been a UN-NATO protectorate since June 1999.

HISTORY

The original inhabitants were Illyrians, followed by Celts and then Romans in the 3rd century BC. In AD 395 Serbia became part of the Byzantine Empire, while Croatia stayed within the Roman Empire. At the Battle of Kosovo in 1389 the Ottomans defeated Serbia, and 500 years of Turkish rule followed. An 1815 revolt led to de facto Serbian independence.

In 1914 Austria-Hungary invaded Serbia. After WWI, Croatia, Slovenia, Vojvodina, Serbia, Montenegro and Macedonia formed what became Yugoslavia.

In 1941 Yugoslavs revolted against a Nazi alliance, prompting invasion by Germany and partition among Germany, Italy, Hungary and Bulgaria. Tito's Communist Party declared an armed uprising, and Yugoslavia became a federal republic in 1945. Serbia's size was reduced, and Montenegro became a republic, but Kosovo and Vojvodina were denied republic status.

In 1986 the communist leader, Slobodan Milošević, espoused a 'Greater Serbia' that horrified Slovenia and Croatia. All but Montenegro broke away leaving Serbia and Montenegro in a third Yugoslav federation in 1992 that didn't give autonomy to Kosovar

Albanians, who had been brutally repressed. Violence erupted in Kosovo in 1998.

In March 1999 Serbia began 'cleansing' Kosovo of its Albanians. Hundreds of thousands of Albanian refugees fleeing into Macedonia and Albania finally galvanised NATO into action. Bombarded by air strikes, Serbian forces withdrew.

In the September 2000 federal presidential elections Vojislav Koštunica claimed victory. Milošević refused to accede and then the constitutional court annulled the election. Opposition supporters occupied parliament. Russia recognised Koštunica's presidency, ending Milošević's rule.

Yugoslavia then restored ties with Europe and rejoined the UN. In 2001 Milošević, arrested for misappropriating state funds, was extradited to the international war crimes tribunal in the Netherlands.

In April 2002 the Yugoslav federation was replaced by the loose union of 'Serbia and Montenegro'. A 2006 referendum will decide the union's future.

In March 2003 Serbia's first democratically elected prime minister since WWII, Zoran Djindjic, was assassinated. He had been instrumental in handing over Milošević to the international war crimes tribunal and had been trying to clear out the criminal elements from politics and business. His alleged killers were crime bosses and Milošević-era paramilitary commanders.

PEOPLE & CULTURE

The last full census was in 1991. Since then, there have been massive population upheavals as Serbian refugees from Kosovo, Croatia and Bosnia fled to Serbia.

The population consists of 7.5 million Serbs, 651,000 Montenegrins and an estimated 2.4 million Kosovars. There are several ethnic groups: Serbs 62%, Albanians 17%, Montenegrins 5%, Hungarians 3% and other groups 13%. By religion the

---

READING UP

Classic travel literature, Rebecca West's *Black Lamb and Grey Falcon: A Journey Through Yugoslavia* on prewar Yugoslavia.

Balkan Babel by Sabrina Ramet, is an engaging look at Yugoslavia from Tito to Milošević.

Kosovo: A short History by Noel Malcolm. *The Serbs: History, Myth and the Destruction of Yugoslavia* by Tim Judah.

Highly recommended is *This is Serbia Calling: Rock n' Roll Radio and Belgrade's Underground Resistance* by Matthew Collin.

people are Orthodox 65%, Muslim 19%, Roman Catholic 4% and others 12%.

The northern region of Vojvodina is more multicultural with perhaps 28 ethnic groups and sizeable populations of Hungarians (25%), Ukrainians and Romanians.

There are large Slavic Muslim and Albanian minorities in Montenegro and southern Serbia; Belgrade has about 10,000 Muslims.

SPORT

Serbia and Montenegro is the regular European and world champion in basketball, volleyball and water polo.

ENVIRONMENT

Vojvodina is pancake-flat agricultural land, but south of the Danube River the landscape rises through rolling green hills, meeting the Dinaric Alps which slice through the country. Within these mountains is Kosovo, a lowland vale.

Djeravica (2656m) in western Kosovo is the highest mountain; Montenegro's is Bobotov Kuk (2523m) in the Durmitor Range. Zlatibor and Kopaonik in Serbia, and Durmitor in Montenegro are winter snow playgrounds.

Montenegro's mountains are mainly limestone, with craggy grey-white outcrops and sparse vegetation with caves beneath. The mountains drop into the Adriatic Sea, leaving just enough foreshore for a string of coastal towns. To the east the vast Lake Skadar straddles the Montenegrin-Albanian border.

The north has a continental climate with cold winters and hot, humid summers. The coastal region has hot, dry summers and relatively cold winters with heavy snowfall inland.

Some environmental issues include marine pollution from sewage, air pollution around Belgrade and rubbish dumping in the countryside.

TRANSPORT

GETTING THERE & AWAY

A currency declaration form is needed for more than €2000. There are no immigration facilities on Kosovo's boundary with Serbia or Montenegro. From Kosovo you can only enter Serbia from Macedonia, or Montenegro from Albania.

EMERGENCY NUMBERS

- Ambulance ☎ 94
- Fire ☎ 93
- Motor vehicle assistance ☎ 987 (Belgrade), 011 9800 (outside Belgrade)
- Police ☎ 92

Air

JAT Airways (the Serbian airline) and Montenegro Airlines have regional services.

Aeroflot, Air France, Austrian Airlines, British Airways, Lufthansa and others fly to Belgrade.

Austrian Airlines, Adria Airlines, British Airways, Malev and Turkish Airlines fly into Prishtina.

Boat

Ferries link Bar (Montenegro) with Bari and Ancona in Italy (p698).

Bus

There's a well-developed bus service to Western Europe and Turkey.

Car & Motorcycle

You'll need an international driving licence and a Green Card for your vehicle. For details contact **Auto-Moto Savez Serbia and Montenegro** (Serbia & Montenegro Automotive Association; ☎ 011 9800; www.amsj.co.yu; Ruzveltova 18, Belgrade).

Train

International trains from Belgrade go to neighbouring countries and beyond. No trains run in Kosovo, and Montenegro has no international services. A Balkans Flexipass (www.raileurope.com) and student cards allow cheap train travel. Daily services from Belgrade go to Budapest (sleeper 980DIN/€37, seven hours), Istanbul (sleeper 360DIN/€44, 26 hours), Sofia (sleeper 360DIN/€12, 11 hours), Vienna (sleeper 980DIN/€65, 11 hours) as well as Zagreb (sleeper 870DIN/€18, seven hours). Note that because these are

---

DEPARTURE TAX

Unless it's included in your ticket you'll get slugged 500DIN for an internal flight and 1000DIN for an international one.

international trains, the tickets are paid for in euros, sleeper supplements however, are paid for in Dinar.

GETTING AROUND
Bus
The bus service is reliable even if some buses verge on the decrepit. Luggage stowed below costs 50DIN/€0.50 per piece; on longer journeys there are restaurant stops every few hours; got to give the smokers puff time!

Car & Motorcycle
VIP, Hertz, Europcar and Net Rent a Car have offices at Belgrade's airport with small cars from €45 a day. Your best bet in Montenegro is Meridian Rent a Car with small cars from €27 a day.

Train
Jugoslovenske Železnice (JŽ; www.yurail.co.yu in Serbian) provide adequate train services from Belgrade to Novi Sad, Subotica and down the highly scenic line to Bar.

SERBIA СРБИЈА

Serbia (Srbija) consists of its more European northern province, Vojvodina, craggy and proud central Serbia, and the hapless province of Kosovo. Administered as a UN/NATO protectorate, Kosovo has a majority Albanian population. While it demands independence, it's the cradle of Serbia's national soul.

Cultural buffs have a wide range of museums (30 in Belgrade alone), art galleries, medieval monasteries with eerie frescoes and several mosques in Kosovo.

BELGRADE БЕОГРАД
☎ 011 / pop 1.58 million
A lumpy hill flanked by the Sava and Danube Rivers was ideal for a fortified settlement. The trouble was that it attracted enemies, and Belgrade has been destroyed and rebuilt 40 times in its 2300-year history. Those fortifications, the Kalemegdan Citadel, were changed by succeeding conquerors and defenders and are now no more than fortified parkland.

Behind the citadel lies older Belgrade with a mishmash of architecture of the last two centuries. These buildings house comprehensive museums, boutiques, cafés,

bars and restaurants; this society goes out, drinks coffee, shops and socialises.

The rivers host strings of floating bars and clubs, belting out music from traditional Serbian folk to the latest in house and techno, allowing Belgraders to party through the night. Belgrade is Europe's new party town.

Orientation
The train and bus stations are on Savski Trg on the city's south. A few blocks northeast is Terazije which, with its northern square, Trg Republike, forms the heart of Belgrade.

From there Kneza Mihailova, Belgrade's lively pedestrian boulevard, runs northwest where the Kalemegdan Citadel lords over the confluence of the Sava and Danube Rivers.

Information
BOOKSHOPS
International Press Service Bookshop (IPS; ☎ 328 1859; Trg Republike 5; ☯ 9am-10pm Mon-Fri, 9am-3pm Sat) Foreign magazines, videos and CDs.
Plato Bookshop (☎ 625 834; Kneza Mihailova 48; ☯ 9am-midnight Mon-Sat, noon-midnight Sun) Books in English, maps and books on Serbia.

INTERNET ACCESS
IPS (☎ 323 3344; off Makedonska 4; per hr 90DIN; ☯ 24hr)
Plato Cyber Club (☎ 635 363; Vase Čarapića 19; per hr 65DIN; ☯ 24hr)

INTERNET RESOURCES
Tourist Organisation of Belgrade (www.belgrade tourism.org.yu)
Belgrade City site (www.beograd.org.yu)
Serbian news in English (www.b92.net/english)

MEDICAL SERVICES
Boris Kidrič Hospital Diplomatic Section (☎ 643 839; Miloša Pocerza Pasterova 1; ☯ 7am-7pm Mon-Fri)
Klinički Centar (☎ 361 8444; Miloša Pocerza Pasterova 2; ☯ 24hr) Medical clinic.
Prima 1 (☎ 361 0999; Nemanjina 2; ☯ 24hr) Pharmacy.
Prvi Maj (☎ 323 7060; Kneza Miloša 9; ☯ 24hr) Pharmacy.

MONEY
There are more ATMs in central Belgrade than your bank balance could manage.
Atlas Bank (☎ 302 4000; Emilijana Joksimovića 4; ☯ 8am-5pm Mon-Fri, 8am-1pm Sat) Cashes travellers cheques.
Delta Bank (☎ 302 2624; Kneza Mihailova 30; ☯ 6.30am-10pm) ATM and cashes travellers cheques.

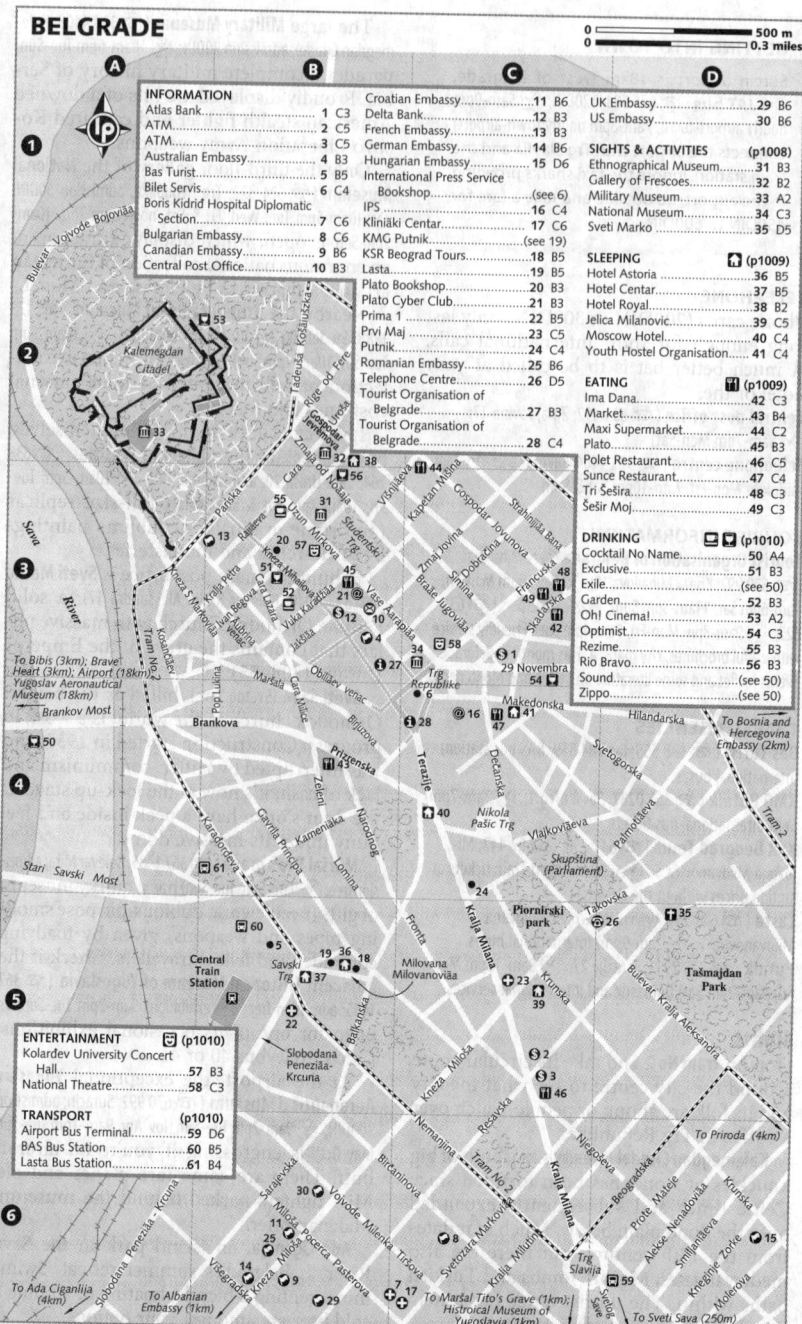

BELGRADE

| 0 | 500 m |
| 0 | 0.3 miles |

INFORMATION
Atlas Bank.................................... 1 C3
ATM... 2 C5
ATM... 3 C5
Australian Embassy....................... 4 B3
Bas Turist.................................... 5 B5
Bilet Servis................................... 6 C4
Boris Kidrič Hospital Diplomatic
Section..................................... 7 C6
Bulgarian Embassy........................ 8 C6
Canadian Embassy......................... 9 B6
Central Post Office........................ 10 B3
Croatian Embassy......................... 11 B6
Delta Bank................................... 12 B3
French Embassy............................ 13 B3
German Embassy........................... 14 B6
Hungarian Embassy....................... 15 D6
International Press Service
Bookshop................................(see 6)
IPS.. 16 C4
Kliniāki Centar............................. 17 C6
KMG Putnik................................(see 19)
KSR Beograd Tours........................ 18 B5
Lasta... 19 B5
Plato Bookshop............................. 20 B3
Plato Cyber Club........................... 21 B3
Prima 1.. 22 B5
Prvi Maj...................................... 23 C5
Putnik... 24 C4
Romanian Embassy........................ 25 B6
Telephone Centre......................... 26 D5
Tourist Organisation of
Belgrade.................................. 27 B3
Tourist Organisation of
Belgrade.................................. 28 C4

UK Embassy.................................. 29 B6
US Embassy................................... 30 B6

SIGHTS & ACTIVITIES (p1008)
Ethnographical Museum................. 31 B3
Gallery of Frescoes........................ 32 B2
Military Museum........................... 33 A2
National Museum.......................... 34 C3
Sveti Marko.................................. 35 D5

SLEEPING (p1009)
Hotel Astoria................................ 36 B5
Hotel Centar................................. 37 B5
Hotel Royal.................................. 38 B2
Jelica Milanovic............................ 39 C5
Moscow Hotel............................... 40 C4
Youth Hostel Organisation............. 41 C4

EATING (p1009)
Ima Dana...................................... 42 C3
Market... 43 B4
Maxi Supermarket......................... 44 C2
Plato... 45 B3
Polet Restaurant........................... 46 C5
Sunce Restaurant.......................... 47 C4
Tri Šešira...................................... 48 C3
Šešir Moj...................................... 49 C3

DRINKING (p1010)
Cocktail No Name.......................... 50 A4
Exclusive...................................... 51 B3
Exile..(see 50)
Garden... 52 B3
Oh! Cinema!................................. 53 A2
Optimist....................................... 54 C3
Rezime... 55 B3
Rio Bravo..................................... 56 B3
Sound..(see 50)
Zippo...(see 50)

ENTERTAINMENT (p1010)
Kolardev University Concert
Hall... 57 B3
National Theatre........................... 58 C3

TRANSPORT (p1010)
Airport Bus Terminal..................... 59 D6
BAS Bus Station............................ 60 B5
Lasta Bus Station.......................... 61 B4

Kalemegdan
Citadel

Sava
River

To Bibis (3km); Brave
Heart (3km); Airport (18km);
Yugoslav Aeronautical
Museum (18km)
Brankov Most

Stari Savski Most

Central
Train
Station

To Ada Ciganlija
(4km)
To Albanian
Embassy (1km)
To Maršal Tito's Grave (1km);
Historical Museum of
Yugoslavia (1km)

To Bosnia and
Hercegovina
Embassy (2km)

To Priroda (4km)

Tašmajdan
Park

Pionirski
park

Nikola
Pašic Trg

Skupština
(Parliament)

Trg
Republike

29 Novembra

Makedonska

Trg
Slavija

To Sveti Sava (250m)

SERBIA & MONTENEGRO

TELEPHONE

Phone cards (200DIN or 300DIN) only last long enough for short international calls. A much better bet is to be called at your hotel or the:

Central post office (☎ 633 492; Zmaj Jovina 17; 🕙 8am-7pm Mon-Sat)

Telephone centre (☎ 323 4484; Takovska 2; 🕙 7am-midnight Mon-Fri, 7am-10pm Sat & Sun)

TOURIST INFORMATION

Tourist Organisation of Belgrade Kneza Mihailova (☎ 629 992; Kneza Mihailova 18; 🕙 9am-8pm Mon-Fri, 9am-6pm Sat, 11am-5pm Sun); Terazije Underpass (☎ 635 622; 🕙 9am-8pm Mon-Fri, 9am-4pm Sat). Friendly service with useful brochures, city maps, a 'This month in Belgrade' events leaflet and some literature on Serbia and Montenegro.

TRAVEL AGENCIES

Bas Turist (☎ 638 555; fax 784 859; BAS bus station) International buses.

KMG Putnik (☎ 361 0287; Savski Trg 1; 🕙 7am-7pm) Sells international bus tickets.

KSR Beograd Tours (☎ 641 258; fax 687 447; Milovana Milovanovića 5; 🕙 6.30am-8pm) Train tickets at station prices without the crowds.

Lasta (☎ 641 251; www.lasta.co.yu; Milovana Milovanovića 1; 🕙 7am-9pm) International buses.

Putnik (☎ 323 2911; Terazije 27; 🕙 8am-10pm Mon-Fri, 8am-2pm Sat) Domestic and international services.

Sights

Hop on **tram No 2** and take its circular route around the city centre to see what the city and its folk are about; or people-watch over a coffee in Trg Republike.

Kalemegdan Citadel (free admission), built of big knuckles of stone, has been fortified since Celtic times and subsequently expanded onto the flood plain below. Much of it dates from the 17th century, but there are also medieval gates, Muslim tombs and Turkish baths within. The tourist office has a map on what to see. Take tram 1, 2 or 13.

The large **Military Museum** (☎ 334 4408; Kalemegdan Citadel; admission 20DIN; 🕙 10am-5pm Tue-Sun) parades a complete military history of Serbia. Proudly displayed are bits of a downed American stealth fighter and captured Kosovo Liberation Army weapons.

Only the third-floor gallery of the **National Museum** (☎ 624 322; Trg Republike; admission 50DIN; 🕙 10am-5pm Tue, Wed, Fri & Sat, noon-8pm Thu, 10am-2pm Sun) is open, which displays a fraction of an enormous national collection of European art, including works by Picasso and Monet.

Nearby the **Ethnographical Museum** (☎ 328 1888; Studentski Trg 13; admission 40DIN; 🕙 10am-5pm Tue-Sat, 10am-1pm Sun) has a comprehensive collection of well-presented Serbian national costumes and folk art.

If you can't get to monasteries themselves, have a peek at the **Gallery of Frescoes** (☎ 638 264; Cara Uroša 20; admission 50DIN; 🕙 10am-5pm Tue-Fri, 10am-4pm Sat & Sun) with full-size replicas (and some originals) of sublime paintings from churches and monasteries.

Behind the main post office is **Sveti Marko** (☎ 323 1940; Bulevar Kralja Aleksandra 17), a solid Serbian Orthodox Church with massive pillars that contains the grave of the Emperor Dušan (1308–55).

Sveti Sava (Svetog Save), billed as the biggest Orthodox church in the world, is a work in progress. Construction started in 1935, and was interrupted by Hitler, communism and lack of cash; it's now at the lock-up stage. If the door's open have a peek inside and feel puny under its massive dome.

Maršal Tito's grave (☎ 367 1485; Bulevar Mira; admission free; 🕙 9am-5pm Tue-Sun) has a quirky museum of gifts (needlework, dubious-purpose smoking pipes and weapons) given by toadying comrades and fellow travellers. Check if the adjacent **Historical Museum of Yugoslavia** (☎ 367 1485; admission free; 🕙 exhibitions 9am-2pm Tue-Sun) is open for one of its occasional exhibitions. Catch trolleybus 40 or 41.

At the airport, the exceptional **Yugoslav Aeronautical Museum** (☎ 670 992; Suracin; admission 300DIN; 🕙 9am-2pm Tue-Sun Nov-Apr, 9am-7pm Tue-Sun May-Oct) is engrossing if you're an aircraft buff. There are some rare planes and old MiG fighters parked behind the museum. Make an offer.

Ada Ciganlija, an island park in the Sava River, is Belgrade's summer retreat. Swimming, renting a bicycle, boating or sipping a cold beer are amongst your options.

Tours

Contact the Tourist Organisation of Belgrade (p1008) for details of city and river tours and KSR Beograd for the steam-hauled railway excursion to Sremski Karlovci.

Festivals & Events

FEST film festival February
Beer festival (www.belgradebeerfest.com) August
Jazz festival August
BITEF international theatre festival September
Classical music festival October

Sleeping

Cheap accommodation is limited; plenty of backpackers are needed to create a demand – simple economics! The **Youth Hostel organisation** (Ferijalni Savez Beograd; ☎ 324 8550; www.hostels .org.yu; Makedonska 22, 2nd fl; ☺ 9am-5pm) does deals with local hotels for discounts. You need Hostelling International membership (300DIN) or an international student card. It also books the **Jelica Milanovic** (☎ 323 1268; Krunska 8; r per person from €7.50; ☺ Jul & Aug) which offers college accommodation during holidays.

Hotel Royal (☎ 634 222; www.hotelroyal.co.yu; Kralja Petra 56; s/d from 910/1470DIN; 🖳) A central, cheap hotel likely to become a travellers' legend. An always-open lobby bar is the matey hang-out of 'local businessmen', backpackers and early morning revellers. The action never stops. Rooms are basic and tidy, and the staff cheerful and friendly.

Hotel Centar (☎ 264 4055; fax 657 838; Savski Trg 7; s/d 910/1380DIN; Ⓟ) In the cream building opposite the train station and next to the raunchy sex shop. It's adequate for the price although the accommodation is spartan and bathrooms are shared.

Hotel Astoria (☎ 264 5422; www.astoria.co.yu; Milovana Milovanovića 1a; s/d 1060/1600DIN shared bathroom, s/d 1360/2260DIN private bathroom) A rattly old socialist hotel, becoming a museum piece but still good enough to make the mark. There's a cosy café/bar.

Moscow Hotel (Moskva; ☎ 268 6255; hotelmoskva@ absolutok.net; Balkanaska; s/d €33/102) It's more of an upmarket central hotel with character, although the 1906 Secessionist-period exterior promises more. The cheaper single rooms make this an attractive stay. The downstairs café/bar has huge windows looking onto Terazije; locals and visitors throng here to take coffee, gorge on delicious cakes and people-watch through the glass.

Eating

Belgraders like to graze on the hop. Plenty of kiosks and cafés offer *burek* (a greasy pie made with cheese, meat, potato or mushrooms), *ćevapčići* (spiced kebabs), sandwich rolls and inventive pizzas. Many establishments around Trg Republike are open 24 hours and offer stomach-fillers for less than 100DIN.

Belgrade's fruit and veg **market** (cnr Brankova Prizrenska & Narodnog Fronta; ☺ 6am-1pm) is a scrounging ground for DIY food and there are many supermarkets like **Maxi supermarket** (cnr Strahinića Bana & Višnjićeva; ☺ 7.30am-8pm).

Plato (pronounced Plarto; ☎ 658 863; Akademski Plato 1; dishes 250-400DIN; ☺ 9am-2am Mon-Thu, 9am-3am Fri, 10am-3am Sat, noon-2am Sun) A multiple personality café, bar, bookshop, live music venue and restaurant with good, mostly Italian food. Eat and drink to jazz or Cuban rhythms in a relaxed ambience.

Polet Restaurant (☎ 323 2454; Kneza Mihaila 31; dishes 200-500DIN; ☺ 11am-11pm) Shiny brass railings and blue and white décor make you feel as if you're at sea. Too many *lozas* (fruit brandies) and you'll be rolling as well. Eat low or eat high here; tasty fish soup (90DIN) or scampi (1150DIN). Chargrilled to perfection and misted with lemon, the calamari (390DIN) is succulent.

Priroda (☎ 411 890; Batutova 11; ☺ 9am-9.30pm, food 12.30-9pm) Battling in the face of adversity, this is an excellent vegetarian restaurant in a land of carnivores. Rediscover delicate flavours of vegetables and pulses absent from traditional Serbian cuisine.

Sunce Restaurant (☎ 324 8474; Dečanska 1; buffet 350DIN; ☺ 9am-9pm Mon-Sat) This place does grills and vegetarian dishes.

Šešir Moj (My Hat; ☎ 322 8750; Skadarska 21; dishes 300-500DIN; ☺ 9am-1am) This ia an intimate restaurant with warmly lit rooms and walls covered with lovely paintings. It's like eating in a film set, especially when a Roma band swirls in playing hauntingly romantic music. The menu presents what the Serbs do best: meat. Try the *punjena belavešanica* (pork fillet stuffed with cream cheese). Finish off with Serbian coffee and some delicious *orasnica* (walnut cake). Also in this street, **Ima Dana** (☎ 323 4422; Skadarska 38; meals 250-500DIN; ☺ 11am-5pm, 7pm-1am) and **Tri Šešira** (Three Hats; ☎ 324 7501; Skadarska 29; dishes 300-500DIN; ☺ lunch & dinner) offer similar menus and entertainment.

Drinking & Clubbing

CAFÉS

Coffee and booze are Belgrade's social lubricants. Top-class cafés offer damn-good coffee straight from the bean. Some also serve drinks and cocktails. Most open from early morning to midnight, with a later start on Sundays. They don't offer food.

Many pavements and pedestrian areas, such as Trg Republike, sprout café terraces when the weather is warm enough.

Garden (Vuka Karadžića 7a) Frothy cappuccinos come no better than from this narrow room off a Kneza Mihailova side street. A smooth, laid-back atmosphere with background jazz.

Rezime (☎ 3284 276; Kralja Petra 41) This classy but non-elitist café is in a magnificently ornate Art Nouveau building. Inside, the décor matches the elegant exterior with polished wood and leather armchairs. The owners are into fashion – hence the magazines.

BARS & CLUBS
City Bars & Clubs

Exclusive (☎ 328 2288; Kneza Mihailova 41-45; snacks 70DIN, 🕒 9am-2am Mon-Sat, noon-1am Sun) A basement beer joint, this is Belgrade's answer to a Munich beer hall. There's plenty of knees-up music and big snacks, sausages, bread, chips and serious drinking.

Rio Bravo (☎ 328 5050; Kralja Petra 54; 🕒 11am-2am Mon-Sat, 5pm-2am Sun) Hitch yer horse, mosey on in and shoot down some hard liquor in this bar kitted out with old Western film sets.

Oh! Cinema! (☎ 328 4000; Kalemegdan Citadel; 9pm-5am) A 'rock into dawn' café/bar on the eastern bulwarks of the citadel overlooking the Danube and zoo. Popular with the in-crowd but not with the insomniac tigers below.

Optimist (☎ 323 8303: 29 Novembra 22; 🕒 10am-late) A big-boozing warehouse near the top of Skadarska.

Also try Strahinića Bana for clubs.

River Bars & Clubs

Adjacent to Hotel Jugoslavija, New Belgrade is a kilometre-long strip of some 20 barges and is famous as the site where warlord and Milošević ally Arkan was shot dead.

Brave Heart (Hrabo Scre; ☎ 851 1480; 🕒 10pm-4am) Appeals to the warrior clan with cartoon-style chunky wooden furniture. A place for young men to show off their female companions and chill out to DJ music until midnight, then live music.

Bibis (☎ 319 2150; 🕒 10am-2am) A quieter place that's a useful starter to a night out; sit over a drink and plan where to go later. It's popular in winter when other barges close.

The Sava River west bank has another strip of floating bars and discos that open for summer. Here you'll find **Cocktail No Name** playing pop and 1980s music, **Zippo** for Serbian folk music, **Exile** pounding out techno and nearby **Sound** playing your traditional house and disco.

Entertainment

The ticketing agency **Bilet Servis** (☎ 628 342; Trg Republike 5; 🕒 9am-8pm Mon-Fri, 9am-3pm Sat) sells tickets for concerts and theatre.

In winter, there's opera at the elegant **National Theatre** (☎ 620 946; Trg Republike; 🕒 box office 10am-2pm Tue-Sun). Belgrade Philharmonia often performs at the **Kolarčev University Concert Hall** (☎ 630 550; Studentski Trg 5; 🕒 box office 10am-noon & 6-8pm). **Sava Centar** (☎ 213 9840; www.savacentar.com; Milentija Popovića 9, New Belgrade) hosts major concerts.

Getting There & Away

Belgrade's bus stations are **BAS** (Bus; ☎ 636 299; Železnička 4) serving distance locations and **Lasta** (☎ 625 740; Železnička bb) for local destinations. Sample services are Budva (1160DIN, 12 hours) and Novi Pazar (580DIN, three hours) for Kosovo.

The **train station** (☎ 629 400; Savski Trg 2) has a very helpful **information office** (☎ 361 8487; platform 1; 🕒 7am-7pm).

Overnight trains run from Belgrade to Bar (1000DIN, sleeper supplement 564DIN, 11½ hours). Frequent trains go to Novi Sad (185DIN, 1½ hours) and Subotica (350DIN, three hours).

Getting Around

Bus, tram and trolleybus tickets cost 12DIN from street kiosks or 20DIN from the driver; make sure you validate the ticket in the machine on board.

Belgrade's taxis are plentiful. Flag fall is 25DIN. Check that the meter's running and avoid the taxi sharks around the airport and stations.

VOJVODINA ВОЈВОДИНА

North of the Danube, this flat fertile plain provides much of the food that fills the nation's larders.

Ruling the region were Hungarians, Turks and Austro-Hungarians until 1918 when it became part of Serbia. After WWII it became an autonomous province until it was absorbed into Serbia in 1990.

Novi Sad Нови Сад
☎ 021 / pop 299,000

Like Belgrade on Valium, Novi Sad has much of what the capital has to offer but at a quieter pace. Some interesting cafés, bars, museums and pedestrian streets merit a visit or a day jaunt from Belgrade.

The original Mrs Einstein came from Novi Sad.

ORIENTATION & INFORMATION
The town can thank a large volcanic plug of rock on a Danube bend for its existence. On that was built the citadel around which the town grew.

In July the town hosts the vastly popular EXIT Festival (www.exitfest.org) involving live music over six stages, film and theatre presentations.

Tourist office (☎ 421 811; www.novisadtourism.org.yu; Mihajla Pupinavi Sad 9; ☼ 9am-8pm Mon-Fri, 9am-2pm Sat) On-the-button office with plenty of info.

SIGHTS
The comprehensive collection of the **Muzej Vojvodine** (☎ 26 555; Dunavska 35 & 37; admission 20DIN; ☼ 9am-7pm Tue-Fri, 9am-2pm Sat & Sun) is spread over two buildings. No 35 covers Vojvodina's history from Palaeolithic times to the late 19th century, and No 37 takes the story to 1945 with an emphasis on WWI and WWII.

Across the river stands the majestic **Petrovaradin Citadel** (free admission; ☼ 24hr), the 'Gibraltar of the Danube', designed by French architect Vauban and completed in 1780. Stairs beside the large church below lead to the fortress. The clock tower's hour hand is the longer one, rendering it easy to read from the river. Within the citadel are artists' studios and a **museum** (☎ 433 145; admission 70DIN; ☼ 9am-5pm) with an exhibition of city history.

SLEEPING & EATING
Branko Kolo (☎ 622 160; fax 422 784; Episkopa Visariona 3; d/t/q per person €8/7/6) Student accommodation only available in July, August and 30 December to 20 January. Contact the tourist office for details.

Hotel Fontana (☎ 621 779; fax 621 779; Nikole Pašića 27; s/d 1500/2000DIN; Ⓟ) Above a restaurant in the back streets behind the cathedral, the Fontana, with basic rooms, is a good cheap find in a town stretched for cheap accommodation.

Atina (☎ 28 863; Njegoševa 2; dishes 50DIN; ☼ 6am-10pm Mon-Sat, 9am-5pm Sun) Cheap and quick, with a basic buffet, the stainless steel tables say you're not going to linger long.

Plava Frajle (☎ 613 675; Sutjeska 2; dishes 300-400DIN; ☼ 9am-midnight) A popular knees-up restaurant. Traditional bands play their hearts out on Thursday and weekends. Diners join in with gusto and the party rolls on until dawn. The menu excels with 55 choices (but only four for vegetarians).

Red Cow (Dunavska 2; ☼ 8am-1am) More green cow than red, given the paint job. The Cow is a look-alike Irish pub with a warm, woody, beery atmosphere. Halt here for a refreshing Guinness or draught Nikšić.

Subotica Суботица
☎ 024 / pop 148,400

Subotica is a useful transit point to Hungary (it's 10km from the border) with some astounding Art Nouveau architecture. The **train station** (☎ 555 606; Miličević) with a left-luggage office and bureau de change, is an amble from the town centre.

The helpful folk at the **tourist office** (☎ 554 809; ticsu@yunord.net; Korzo 15 ☼ 8am-8pm Mon-Sat, 8am-noon Sun) have plenty of information and advice.

The imposing Art Nouveau town hall (1910) contains a worthwhile **historical museum** (☎ 554 700; Trg Republike; ☼ 9am-2pm Tue-Sat) and some expensively decorated council chambers.

The amazing Art Nouveau **Modern Art Gallery** (☎ 553 725; Trg Lenina 5; ☼ 7am-1pm Mon, Wed & Fri, 7am-6pm Tue & Thu, 9am-noon Sat) is one of the most beautiful buildings in Eastern Europe; its swirling colourful lines employ ceramic tiles, mosaics and stained-glass windows. If you like this, check out the interior of the **Ravel café** (Nušićeva 2, near the Town Hall).

Two youth hostels were being developed at the time of research so check with the tourist office.

Hotel Patria (☎ 554 500; www.patria-su.com in Serbian; Đure Đakovica; s/d 1851/2902DIN) Cheeky prices for barrack-room style furniture, but there are very few hotels in the area.

The train station has a decent café and a small supermarket in the basement for your chocolate needs.

Lipa (Đure Đakovica 13; burek 70DIN; ⏱ 24hr) A *burek* shop with the ultimate cheese-and-mushroom *burek* and yogurt for breakfast.

YUFEST (552 292; Trg Republike; Internet per hr 100DIN; ⏱ 9am-midnight Sun-Thu, 9am-2am Fri & Sat) A busy café buzzing with life that flows through the ground floor of this former town hall, past the massive columns and into the street.

Eight kilometres west of Subotica is the resort of Palić, edging onto a 5.5 sq km lake. Activities include boating, swimming, sailing, fishing and sailing. There are two local trains a day to/from Szeged, Hungary (200DIN, 1¾ hours).

KOSOVO

Although Kosovo is populated mainly by Kosovar Muslims, the area holds a special place in the Serbian national soul as the site of fateful battles against the Turks. Since June 1999, Kosovo has been a UN-NATO protectorate. Before Serb-instigated 'ethnic cleansing', some two million people occupied Kosovo's 10,887 sq km.

A reliable bus service links all the main towns and villages. Buses link Prishtina, Prizren and Peja (€3 to €4, about two hours) and run from Prishtina to Novi Pazar (Serbia) and Podgorica (Montenegro) via Peja.

Prishtina

☎ 038 / pop 160,000

Prishtina is a bustling capital engorged with the activity and personnel of foreign agencies. Some post-war reconstruction has occurred but a lot is still to happen. Apart from a few sights it's more a hangout place and base for day trips to the rest of Kosovo.

ORIENTATION & INFORMATION

The main streets, Bulevard Nëna Terezë and Agim Ramadani, run from the south to converge near the National Theatre in the north. The UN Interim Administration Mission in Kosovo (UNMIK) headquarters are off Nëna Terezë. Most of the places in this section are around this area.

Euro-s@-net (☎ 227 225; Luan Haradinaj; per hr €1; ⏱ 9am-11pm Mon-Sat) Internet; you can also phone worldwide for €0.30 per minute.

Pro Credit Bank (☎ 240 248; Skënderbeu; ⏱ 9am-4pm Mon-Fri) Cashes travellers cheques and has a MasterCard ATM.

PTK (Post Telephone Kosova; ☎ 245 339; Nëna Terezë; ⏱ 8am-9pm) Post and telephone.

Raiffeisen Bank (☎ 226 400; Migjeni 1; ⏱ 8.30am-4.30pm Mon-Fri, 9am-12pm Sat) Cashes travellers cheques and has a Visa ATM.

SIGHTS

Kosovo Museum (☎ 249 964; Marte e Driele; foreigners/citizens €5/1.50; ⏱ 10.30am-7pm Tue-Sun) has an interesting and well-captioned exhibition on pre-medieval Kosovo. Behind the museum are two well-decorated mosques and a restored Balkans house.

A number of houses of the old Turkish quarter remain in the market area.

SLEEPING & EATING

Velania Guest House (Pansion Profesor; ☎ 531 742, 044 167 455; Velania 4, 34; s/d €13/18) At last, a Prishtina cheapie! A professor's house welcoming budget travellers; 10 rooms with shared bathrooms over three floors, each floor with a small kitchen. Free tea/coffee ingredients and laundry.

Iliria (☎ 224 275; fax 548 117; Nëna Terezë; s/d €30/60; P) A large former Serbian state hotel, right in the thick of things, this is a central, safe haven for the party animal, with very helpful staff.

Cafés abound in the centre selling *burek* and hamburgers for €1 to €2; pasta and pizza cafés charge up to €2.50.

Ardi Supermarket (Luan Haradinaj; ⏱ 8am-8pm Mon-Sat) A self-catering option; there's also a fruit and veg section in the **market** (off Fehmi Agani; ⏱ 8am-2pm Mon-Fri).

Boom Boom Room (Kosta Novakoviq; ⏱ 10am until the last guest buys) Behind and west of UNMIK, a grungy barn with a considerable range of drinks that's popular with the locals. There's live music on Wednesday night when the room does go boom boom.

Phoenix Bar (opposite UNMIK; snacks €2.50-4; ⏱ 7am-midnight) A lads-away-from-home bar popular with expats and decorated with football team strips as tribal symbols rather than flags. High-cholesterol breakfasts, coffee and snacks are available all day. There's live music some weekends.

AROUND PRISHTINA
Gadimë Cave

The only show cave in Kosovo, **Gadimë Cave** (Marble Cave; admission €2.50; ⏱ 9am-6pm; 30-min tour) 35km south of Prishtina, is worth a plunge underground. It's renowned for its helictites (thin stalactites growing at strange angles). Please don't touch the formations.

Enough buses from Prishtina make this a part-day trip, or a taxi costs €30.

Gračanica

Some 13km southeast of Prishtina is the superbly decorated **Gračanica Monastery**, built by Serbian king Milutin in the early 14th century. Most of the frescoes covering the walls date from then. Entry is no problem, once you've identified yourself to KFOR (Kosovo Force) at the entrance. Catch one of the frequent buses to Gjilan that pass outside.

Memorial Prekaz

This **memorial** (⊙ 8am-8pm) to the 1998 slaughter of the Jeshari clan by the Serbs consists of the shelled remains of their two houses and the cemetery where all 53 are buried. Catch a bus to Skënderaj (€4, two hours), get off at the lurid green mosque and walk 500m uphill, or a taxi from Prishtina costs €50.

Prizren

☎ 029

Although Prizren was the medieval capital of 'Old Serbia', the architectural influence is Turkish. People throng the bars and cafés along the river and in Shadrvan.

It's delightful wandering through small cobbled streets soaking in the age and atmosphere. Unfortunately, the Albanian Kosovar vandalism of March 2004 has added to the ugly scar of houses up the hillside that were burnt out by the Serbs in 1999.

ORIENTATION

The town is centred around the river and Shadrvan, a cobblestone plaza with a fountain. Crossing the river just west of the main bridge is a 'new' medieval bridge built to replace one destroyed by 1979 floods. The bus station is on the Peja road about 2km from the centre.

INFORMATION

Dina Net (Remzi Ademi 31a; per hr €0.60; ⊙ 9am-midnight) Internet.

Gold Tours (☎ /fax 23 491; goldtours2@hotmail.com; Remzi Ademi 31; ⊙ 8.30am-5pm Mon-Fri) Books international buses.

PTK (Post Telephone Kosova; Adem Jashari; ⊙ 8am-10pm Mon-Sat) Post and telephone.

SIGHTS

A slow plod up from Shadrvan brings you to the **castle** (admission free; ⊙ 24hr) that's passed clumsily through Roman, Turkish, Serbian and KFOR army hands. When the Imams call for prayers you'll hear a succession of chants sweep across the town.

The Orthodox churches were mostly destroyed in the March 2004 violence, with little left except collapsed and burnt-out interiors.

Sinan Pasha Mosque (1561) on the riverside dominates the town centre and can be visited (as long as there is staff present) for its fine, decorated high-domed ceiling.

Near the Theranda Hotel, the newly restored **Gazi Mehmed Pasha Baths** (Adem Jashari; admission free; ⊙ only during exhibitions), from 1563, have become an occasional exhibition space. The internal upper floor was destroyed during WWII; maybe it couldn't cope with being a bordello for its Italian occupiers.

Opposite the post office is a solitary **minaret** with a Star of David believed to be the remnants of a synagogue.

Some 200m upriver from the Theranda Hotel is a small **museum complex** (☎ 44 487; adult/child €1/0.20; ⊙ 10am-10pm Sun-Tue) celebrating the Albanian League of Prizren, an independence movement in Turkish times. The museum illustrates the League and historical Prizren.

MONTENEGRO ЦРНА ГОРА

From an interior of Alpine scenery with giddy-deep canyons, to a sparsely vegetated and highly folded limestone mountain range plummeting to an azure Adriatic Sea with fjords, this 13,812-sq-km republic has got the works.

Only tiny Montenegro (Crna Gora) kept above the Turkish tide that engulfed the Balkans. The republic has been a stalwart of several Yugoslav federations and is now in a 'suck it and see' union with Serbia that may last no longer than the 2006 referendum.

Montenegro is a very popular holiday spot. The best times to visit are May, June and September.

A main rail line runs from Belgrade to Bar, where ferries connect with Italy. The country lends itself to a spot of motoring, with easy distances and interesting wayside discoveries.

Visitors with time or transport can choose accommodation from the 'sobe', 'Zimmer' or 'private room' signs all along the coast.

In season a frequent bus service (€2 to €4) links the coastal towns of Podgorica and Cetinje.

BAR БАР

☎ 085 / pop 37,000

With a backdrop of precipitous mountains, modern Bar is a doorway to the coast. Stari Bar (Old Bar), some 4km northeast of the modern town, comprises some 240 ruins dating back 1000 years.

Montenegro Express (☎ /fax 312 589; Obala 13 Jula bb; ☼ 8am-8pm Mon-Sat Jul-Aug, 8am-2pm Mon-Sat Sep-Jun) Opposite the ferry terminal, it books accommodation along the coast. Private rooms are available for €7 to €20, hotels for €30 to €100.

Komercijalna Bank (☎ 311 827; Obala Kralja Nikole bb; ☼ 8am-4pm Mon-Fri, 8am-noon Sat) Cashes travellers cheques. There are several ATMs around town.

Barska Plovidba (☎ 312 336; mlinesagency@cg.yu; Obala 13 Jula bb; ☼ 8am-10pm) The agents for Montenegro Lines sailing between Bar and Bari in Italy. For times and prices check www.montenegrolines.net.

Mecur (☎ 313 617; www.mercuradriatica.com; Obala 13 Jula bb; ☼ 8am-8pm Mon-Fri, 9am-2pm Sat) Book Adriatica ferries to Ancona (€51/61/82 for passage only/deck seat/cabin bed, 16 hours, Thursday 5.30pm).

Four trains travel to/from Belgrade, with the overnight train providing inexpensive accommodation.

ULCINJ УЛЦИЊ

☎ 085 / pop 24,000

The town heads a series of fine beaches from Mala Plaža (Small Beach) below the old town to Velika Plaža (Great Beach), a famous 12km beach stretching east towards Albania. In July and August, Ulcinj bulges with tens of thousands of holidaymakers.

Ulcinj gained notoriety as a North African pirate base and slave market between 1571 and 1878. The Turks ruled here for over 300 years, and today the town shelters many Muslim Albanians.

Real Estate Tourist Agency (☎ 421 612; 26 Novembra bb; ☼ 8am-9pm) This place books accommodation in private rooms (from €10, no meals), hotels (doubles from €16, half board)

and apartments (€27/36/43 two/three/four-person, half board). **Tomi camping ground** (☼ May-Sep) is east of Milena, adjacent to Velika Plaža. Further on is **HTP Velika Plaža** (☎ 413 145; www .velikaplaza.cg.yu; Ada Rd) with a variety of accommodation from €19 to €23 per person or €35 to €100 for an apartment, full board.

Bazar (☎ 421 639; 26 Novembar bb; mains €5-8; ☼ 8am-late) An upstairs restaurant that's an ideal place to escape summer crowds and guzzle a plate of fried lignje na žaru (calamari), the restaurant's speciality.

Bella Vista (☎ 067 315 266; 26 Novembar bb; mains €4-8; ☼ 7am-late) Good for an early breakfast or late-night drink; it also has accommodation (from €25, half board).

The Rock (26 Novembar; ☼ 8am-late) A wannabe Irish pub. Guinness is an occasional visitor but there are enough alternatives to cool the heat of summer.

Many minibuses and buses ply the road to Ada (and Velika Plaža) from the market place or main post office.

BUDVA БУДВА

☎ 086 / pop 11,700

Budva is Serbia and Montenegro's top beach resort. A series of fine beaches punctuate the coastline all the way to Sveti Stefan, with high barren coastal mountains forming a magnificent backdrop.

Budva's big tourist-puller is its old **walled town**. Levelled by earthquakes in 1979, it's been completely rebuilt as a tourist attraction, so picturesque it seems almost contrived. The better beaches are either side of the town.

If you have a tent, try **Autocamp Avala** (☎ 451 205; ☼ Jun-Sep) at Boreti, or check with JAMB travel for the Budva Autocamp.

JAMB travel (☎ 452 992; www.jamb-travel.com; Mediteranska 23; private rooms €5.90-13.50, 2-5 person apt €16-€80; ☼ 8am-3pm Mon-Fri Nov-May, ☼ 8am-8pm Jun-Oct) Books accommodation and organises day tours within Montenegro. Half board/full board is available for €9/13 extra.

The Old Town has plenty of cafés, restaurants and bars to entice visitors edging through the narrow streets.

A good, cheap eatery is the bus station **buffet** (Ivana Milutinovića; meals €2-3; ☼ 7am-9pm).

Restaurant Jadran (☎ 451 028; Slovenska Obala 10; dishes €5-10; ☼ 8am-late) Probably Budva's best restaurant, where you can eat like lords with lobster at €60 per kg or eat low with a substantial soup or *čevapčići* for €2; the choice is your wallet's.

Eight buses run to Belgrade (€15, 12 hours) and one to Žabljak (€8, seven hours). A 2.20pm bus (€10) runs to the Croatian border via Kotor.

KOTOR КОТОР
☎ 082 / pop 22,500

Picturesque Kotor, with its walled town nestled at the head of southern Europe's deepest fjord, has Montenegro's most dramatic setting. Cobbled laneways form a labyrinth connecting small squares with ancient churches and former aristocratic mansions. The fun is simply wandering this atmospheric town.

Significant within the four kilometres of walls are six 12th- and 13th-century Romanesque churches, St Tripun's Cathedral (1166) and a 6th-century clock tower. The **Maritime Museum** (☎ 325 646; admission €2; 🕑 9am-5pm Mon-Fri, 9am-noon Sat) traces Kotor's significant maritime history from when the city had its own navy.

Slog up the steep path to the fortifications on the mountainside above Kotor, where you'll be rewarded with stunning views of Kotor fjord. Vistas are especially spectacular on the road which zigzags up to Cetinje in a series of 'spaghetti' loops. As you dart through pine forests you'll get aerial glimpses of Kotor fjord below and the stark craggy grey mountains above that form the core of central Montenegro.

The **information booth** (☎ 325 950; Jadranski Put; 🕑 9am-1pm & 5-8pm Mon-Sat) at the western gateway to the Old Town has some information on the town and on private accommodation.

Meridian Travel Agency (☎ 322 968; travel@cg.yu; private accommodation €8-15, apts €30-55, hotels s/d 25-44/41-63; 🕑 9am-2pm & 6-7pm Mon-Fri, 9am-2pm Sat) This ever-helpful agency is in a lane behind the clock tower. It books private and hotel accommodation in and around the city.

Hotel Vardar (☎ 325 084; Stari Grad; s/d from €25/41) Overlooking the clock tower, the Vardar is a good-value central hotel with large rooms, some overlooking the square.

Hotel Rendezvous (☎ 322 447; Trg od Mlijeka; s/d from €15/30) Another good bet.

The lanes house several bakeries. Munch on *burek*, pizza or cherry-filled strudel, a speciality of the region.

Pizzeria Giardino (☎ 323 324; Stari Grad; meals €4-5; 🕑 9am-late) Probably the best-value restaurant within the old town. It's pizza marinara is among Montenegro's best.

Kotor's cafés and bars, quiet places by day, turn werewolf on weekend nights when they throb to techno and other rhythms. Try the Portabello or Karampana bars.

CETINJE ЦЕТИЊЕ
☎ 086 / pop 20,000

Nestled in an upland green plateau encircled by grey, craggy mountains, Cetinje is an unusual mix of village and capital, cottages and mansions.

Princes once ruled from here, regal mansions are now museums and Cetinje Monastery remains the town's spiritual home.

Frequent bus services from Kotor and Budva make Cetinje an easy day trip.

The most imposing former parliament building is the **National Museum of Montenegro** (☎ 231 477; Novice Cerovića; admission €5; 🕑 9am-5pm) housing art and history sections. Admission also covers entry to the Biljarda Hall and State Museum.

The art gallery celebrates 19th- and 20th-century Montenegrin and regional art. The prime exhibit is the mysterious 5th-century Icon of Phillarmos, Madonna and child. The history section explores tiny Montenegro's tumultuous history from the year dot to communist times.

The **Biljarda Hall** (Billiard Hall; ☎ 231 050; 🕑 9am-5pm Apr-Oct, 9am-3pm Mon-Fri Nov-Mar) was the 1832 residence of prince-bishop Njegoš and is now a museum dedicated to him. The hall housed the nation's first billiard table (hence the name) and possesses a fascinating scale relief map of Montenegro created by the Austrians in 1917.

The **State Museum** (☎ 230 555; King Nikola Square; 🕑 9am-5pm Apr-Oct, 9am-5pm Mon-Fri Nov-Mar) was the residence (1871) of Nicola Petrović I, the last king of Montenegro. Although looted during WWII, sufficient furnishings, many stern portraits and period weapons remain to give a picture of the times.

Cetinje Monastery (☎ 231 021; 🕑 8am-7pm May-Oct) dates from 1484 but was rebuilt in 1785. A museum, only open to groups or through your persuasive abilities, contains an intriguing collection of portraits, vestments, ancient hand-written texts and gifts from Russian churches. For the curious or devout, the monastery chapel, open to all, has a portion of the true cross and part of the mummified right hand of St John the Baptist.

Further afield is some astounding scenery. Five kilometres off the Podgorica road is a panoramic view of Lake Skadar from Pavlova Strana and further on the old bridge at Rijeka Crnojevića.

Mount Lovcen (1749m) is 20km west. Steps to the top lead to the mausoleum of Njegoš, revered poet ruler. The mausoleum has a sweeping view of the Bay of Kotor, coast, mountains and, on a clear morning, Italy.

DURMITOR NATIONAL PARK ДУРМИТОР
☎ 089 / pop 4,900 / 1450m

Magnificent scenery ratchets up to the awesome in this national park with its dramatic mountain landscape. Some 18 lakes dot the Durmitor Range. You can walk around the largest, **Crno jezero** (Black Lake), 3km from Žabljak, in two hours. Dominating all is the rounded mass of Međed (2287m) flanked by other peaks, including Savin Kuk (2313m).

Scoring deeply into the earth for about 80km, the **Tara Canyon**, 1.3km-deep, is best seen from Curevac.

In winter the park is Montenegro's ski resort; in summer it's an outdoor activity hub centred on the small town of Žabljak.

Orientation & Information
The taxi stand and bus stop are in the town centre; adjacent is Hotel Žabljak with Ski Centar Durmitor. The **bus station** (☎ 61 318) is at the southern end of town.

The snow season runs from December to March; the summer season generally runs from May to September.

There are no ATMs or banks for cashing travellers cheques; come prepared.

Durmitor National Park office (☎ 61 474; fax 61 346; by Hotel Durmitor; 7am-2pm Mon-Fri) Provides park maps and runs rafting, horse riding and walking tours.

Ski Centar Durmitor (☎ 61 144; www.durmitorcg.com; Hotel Žabljak; 8am-6pm Mon-Sat) Ski lessons, passes and equipment rental.

Sveti Đorđije (☎ /fax 61 367; tasaint@cg.yu; Njegoševa bb; 8am-8pm) Fount of information, (English spoken); organises accommodation & activities.

Sights & Activities
Winter activities include skiing, snowboarding and sledding. In summer rafting is possible through the deep Tara Gorge

plus there's horse riding, hiking, mountain biking, mountaineering and paragliding. The National Park office, or Sveti Đorđije, can point you in the right direction.

Sleeping & Eating
Autocamp Ivan-do is just a fenced-off field with no facilities past the National Park office.

Sveti Đorđije (☎ /fax 61 367; tasaint@cg.yu; Njegoševa bb; s/d €10/16, 2-/3-/4-person apts €26/30/39, breakfast/half board €3/9; 8am-8pm) This agency arranges private accommodation in the area.

National Restaurant (☎ 261 337; behind city council offices; dishes €3-8; 8am-late) A pearl of a place! A small, but not crowded, happy restaurant offering the best food around – broths and hot appetisers with slugs of domestic brandy to defeat the winter chill or grilled trout and salad in summer.

Durmitor (☎ 069 637 316; Božidara Žugića bb; dishes €4-8; 7am-11pm) Also recommended.

Getting There & Away
There's one bus to Belgrade (€18, 10 hours, 4.30pm), several to Nikšić (€3.50, two hours) and four to Podgorica (€6, 3½ hours).

SERBIA & MONTENEGRO DIRECTORY

ACCOMMODATION
With a number of hostel closures, cheap accommodation has become scarce. Contact the Youth Hostel organisation (p1009) for current hotel deals. Backpacker accommodation has yet to develop.

Belgrade hotels are reasonably priced for a capital city; Montenegrin hotels outside the coast and Žabljak are unjustly expensive; in Kosovo accommodation is scarce and pricey. The cheapest options are private rooms (along the coast, seldom inland and not in Belgrade) organised through travel agencies. The Montenegrin coast has some summer camping grounds.

ACTIVITIES
Serbia's main skiing resorts are Zlatibor and Kopaonik, while Montenegro's is Žabljak. Ski season is from December to March; in summer, these resorts become popular hiking areas. The Tara River in Montenegro's Durmitor National Park provides great rafting.

BUSINESS HOURS

Banks usually open from 8am to 6pm on weekdays and 8am to noon on Saturday. On weekdays shops open from 8am to 5pm or later. On Saturday, government offices close and many shops close early.

DANGERS & ANNOYANCES

Travel is generally safe except in southeastern Serbia and northern Kosovo where there are Serb-Albanian tensions. Your government travel advice will warn against travel in Kosovo.

Kosovo is believed clear of mines, but if you're going off the beaten track check with UNMIK or KFOR.

Generally, smokers strike up anywhere, regardless of non-smokers.

Check with police before taking photographs of any official building they're guarding.

EMBASSIES & CONSULATES
Embassies & Consulates in Serbia & Montenegro

Albania (☎ 306 6642; Bulevar Mira 25A)
Australia (☎ 330 3400; Čika Ljubina 13)
Bosnia-Hercegovina (☎ 329 1277; Milana Tankosića 8)
Bulgaria (☎ 361 3980; Birčaninova 26)
Canada (☎ 306 3000; Kneza Miloša 75)
Croatia (☎ 361 0535; Kneza Miloša 62)
France (☎ 302 3500; Pariska 11)
Germany (☎ 306 4300; Kneza Miloša 74-6)
Hungary (☎ 244 0472; Krunska 72)
Netherlands (☎ 328 2332; Simina 29)
Romania (☎ 361 8327; Kneza Miloša 70)
UK (☎ 264 5055; Resavska 46)
USA (☎ 361 9344; Kneza Miloša 50)

Serbian & Montenegrin Embassies & Consulates Abroad

Australia (☎ 02-6290 2630, yuembau@ozemail.com.au; 4 Bulwarra Close, O'Malley, Canberra, ACT 2606)
Canada (☎ 613-233 6289, www.embscg.ca; 17 Blackburn Ave, Ottawa, Ontario, K1A 8A2)
France (☎ 01 40 72 24 24, ambasadapariz@wanadoo.fr; 54 rue Faisanderie, 75116 Paris)
UK (☎ 207-235 9049, www.yugoslavembassy.org.uk; 28 Belgrave Square, London, SW1X 8QB)
USA (☎ 202-332 0333, www.yuembusa.org; 2134 Kalorama Rd NW, Washington DC, 20008)

FESTIVALS & EVENTS

Apart from those mentioned in city/town sections, there's an annual festival of brass band music at Guča near Čačak in the last week of August.

FOOD & DRINK

The region is a delight for meat-eaters but a trial for vegetarians. The cheapest snack is *burek*. A good midday meal of soup or kebabs should cost about 120DIN/€2.

Serbia is famous for grilled meats such as *čevapčići*, *pljeskavica* (hamburger steak) and *ražnjići* (pork or veal kebab with onions and peppers). *Duveć* is delicious, consisting of grilled pork cutlets with spiced peppers, zucchini and tomatoes in rice cooked in an oven. Other popular dishes are *musaka* (aubergine and potato layered with minced meat), *sarma* (cabbage stuffed with minced meat and rice), *kapama* (stewed lamb, onions and spinach with yogurt) and *punjena tikvica* (zucchini stuffed with minced meat and rice).

For vegetarians there's pizza or a Serbian salad (*Srpska salata*) of raw peppers, onions and tomatoes seasoned with oil, vinegar and maybe chilli. *Šopska salata* is chopped tomatoes, cucumber and onion, topped with grated soft white cheese. Also ask for *gibanica* (cheese pie), *zeljanica* (cheese pie with spinach) or *pasulj prebranac*, a dish of cooked spiced beans.

Pivo (beer) is universally available. *Nikšićko pivo*, brewed at Nikšic, is transcendent. *Vinjak* (cognac), *loza* and red wine provide good tipples.

Coffee is usually served Turkish-style – 'black as hell, strong as death and sweet as love'. Superb espresso and cappuccino are available in cafés.

HOLIDAYS

Public holidays in Serbia and Montenegro include:
New Year's Day 1 January
Orthodox Christmas 7 January
Nation Day 27 April
International Labour Days 1 & 2 May
Victory Day 9 May
Uprising Day (Montenegro only) 13 July
Flag Day (Kosovo only) 28 November
Republic Day 29 November

Orthodox churches celebrate Easter between one and five weeks later than other churches. Easter Monday is a public holiday in Kosovo.

INTERNET RESOURCES

Montenegro Tourist Organisation (www.visit-monte negro.cg.yu)

Serbian Tourist Organisation (www.serbia-tourism.org)

LANGUAGE

Serbian is the common language but only Albanian is spoken in Kosovo. Many people know some English and German.

Montenegrins and Serbians use both Latin and Cyrillic script. See the language section (p1266) for useful phrases and the Cyrillic alphabet.

MONEY

Montenegro and Kosovo use the euro while Serbia retains the dinar, which is used for most transactions (although euro notes can be accepted).

ATMs are widespread in major towns and Visa, MasterCard and Diners Club are widely accepted.

It's common to round up restaurant and taxi charges to a convenient figure.

POST

Parcels should be taken unsealed to a main post office for inspection. Allow time to complete the transaction. You can receive *poste restante* mail in all towns for a small charge.

TELEPHONE & FAX

Phone cards don't give enough time for an international call, so use the telephone centre at post offices. Faxes can be sent from post offices, but take a photocopy as they will keep the original.

VISAS

Citizens of European countries, Britain, Australia, New Zealand, Canada and USA don't need visas for stays of less than 90 days.

The website of the **Ministry of Foreign Affairs** (www.mfa.gov.yu) has details.

Slovakia

HIGHLIGHTS

- **Vysoké Tatry** Hiking around the dizzy peaks of the High Tatras (p1029)
- **Castles** From picturesque Devin Castle to ghostly Spišský hrad, indulging in Slovakia's grandiose Stone Age (Bratislava p1023; Spišské Podhradie p1032)
- **Levoča** High-tailing it out of the 21st century and soaking up old Slovakia (p1031)
- **Ice Hockey** The thrills, the spills, the punch-ups – spend an evening indulging in Slovakia's national obsession (p1027)

FAST FACTS

- **Area** 49,035 sq km (two-thirds the size of England)
- **ATMs** Widespread
- **Budget** 650-970Sk per day
- **Capital** Bratislava
- **Country code** ☎ 421, international access code ☎ 00
- **Famous for** Ice hockey (Slovakia makes more ice hockey pucks than any other country)
- **Head of State** President Ivan Gasparovic
- **Languages** Slovak, plus German and English in larger towns
- **Money** Slovenská koruna (A$ = 23.34Sk, CA$1 = 25.44Sk, €1 = 40Sk, ¥100 = 29.41Sk, NZ$1 = 21.93Sk, UK£1 = 57.91Sk, US$1 = 31.63Sk)
- **Phrases** *Ahoj* (hello), *dovidenia* (goodbye), *d'akujem* (thank you), *Nevyznám sa tu* (I'm lost)

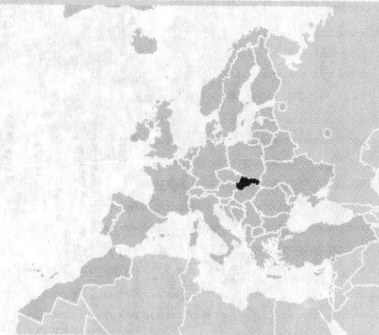

- **Population** 5.4 million
- **Time** GMT/UTC + 1
- **Visas** Citizens of most EU countries, Australia, Canada and New Zealand can enter without a visa for up to 90 days. UK citizens can stay for 180 days; U.S. and Italian citizens for 30 days. South Africans require a visa. If you do require a visa, it must be bought in advance.

TRAVEL HINTS

Follow locals to the super cheap markets – fresh veggies offer welcome reprieve from a surfeit of dumplings. And don't forget to sample the beer – it's cheaper than bottled water.

ROAMING SLOVAKIA

Head east from **Bratislava** (p1023) to **Trenčín Castle** (p1028), before unwinding among the beautiful **Malá Fatra** (p1029), living the high life in the **Vysoké Tatry** (p1029) and drinking up lovely **Levoča** (p1031). End in old **Košice** (p1032).

Whimsical folk music and rickety horse-drawn carts, snow-clad summits and Stalinist suburbs – the clichéd images of this quiet corner of Central Europe cast Slovakia as a bizarre blend of rural idyll and Soviet Moscow.

And at the beginning of the 21st century, Slovakia's personality appears to be splitting still further. Joining the EU club in May 2004, and with a calorific slice of boom-time economic

SLOVAKIA

SLOVAKIA

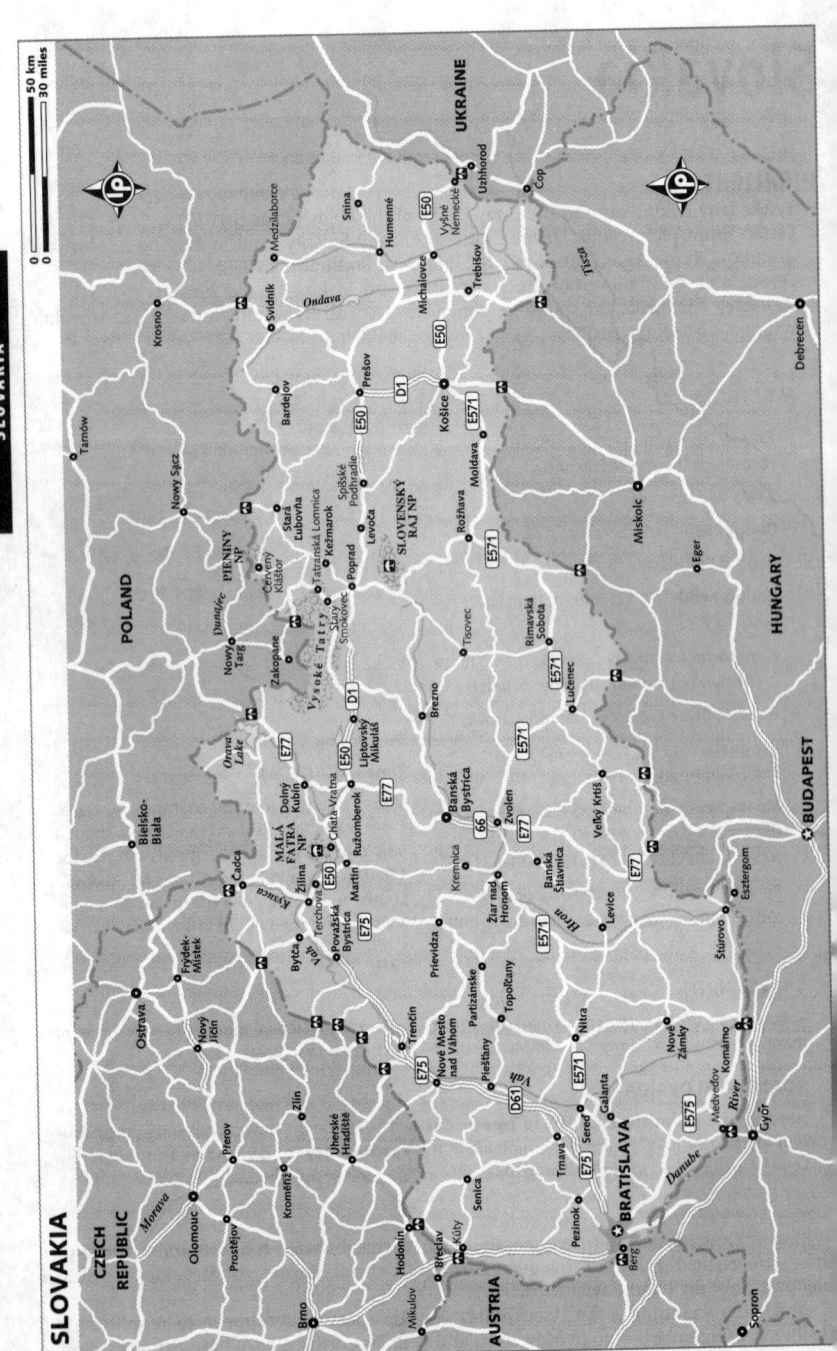

pie now within grasp, Bratislava, at least, is emerging from its frumpy, Communist-era chrysalis to take on the trappings of a flourishing free market. Cappuccino bars and fast cars are only the beginning. Yet Slovakia remains a nation of two halves. While the free market beams some Slovakians into a world of fickle fashion and status symbols, many others, most notably the Roma, continue to live a life that has remained unchanged for decades, keeping alive the vibrant folk traditions that might otherwise have vanished.

And therein lies Slovakia's appeal. Beyond the high life and nightlife of the big cities, this is a country of towering mountains and thick forests, where history is lived rather than just remembered.

HISTORY

In many ways, Slovakia starts the 21st century full of confidence. After centuries in the closet, it now has its name on the registers of many of the world's major clubs, joining NATO in March 2004 and the EU two months later.

It has been a long journey. First occupied by Slavic tribes in the 5th century, Slovakia was soon caught up in centuries of European power play. In the early 16th century, the Hungarians transferred their capital to Bratislava and instigated a policy of 'Magyarisation' (Hungarian assimilation). To counter this, Slovak intellectuals cultivated ties with the Czechs and after WWI took their nation into the united Czechoslovakia.

But Slovaks wearied of Czech political domination and the day before Hitler's troops invaded Czech territory in March 1939, a fascist puppet state was set up. It was not a popular move and in August 1944 Slovak partisans instigated the Slovak National Uprising (*Slovenské Národné Povstanie*, or SNP), a source of national pride even today.

After the communist takeover in 1948, power was again centralised in Prague and resistance was ruthlessly eliminated.

In 1989, however, the Velvet Revolution brought down the curtains on the communist regime. The 1992 elections brought to power the nationalist Movement for a Democratic Slovakia (HZDS), headed by Vladimír Mečiar. In July the Slovak parliament voted to declare sovereignty, and the federation dissolved peacefully on 1 January 1993.

Mečiar's reign, however, was characterised by antidemocratic laws and discrimination, a period that only came to an end in 1998, when Mečiar was ousted.

Reforms have brought Slovakia back into the international fold, but opinion remains starkly divided and two weeks before the country took its place at the EU table, former Mečiar lackey Ivan Gasparovic was elected president. Gasparovic has since distanced himself from Mečiar, but the country's political future still hangs in the balance.

PEOPLE & CULTURE

Religious (84% see themselves as religiously affiliated), conservative and proud, most Slovakians have a strong sense of identity and an insatiable appetite for folk culture. Among the older generation, this occasionally translates into a certain standoffishness, but the country is fast shedding its reputation for surliness and most Slovaks are hospitable. The minority Roma, however, are still viewed with an uncompromising suspicion.

For many Slovaks, weekends are best spent in the great outdoors, soaking up the country's fabulous scenery. Wherever you go, you will doubtless run into a backpack-toting Slovak wandering through the wilderness.

Slovakia's population is 86% Slovak, 10% Hungarian and 1% Czech. There are as many as 400,000 Roma in Slovakia.

SPORT

Three things dominate Slovakian sport: ice hockey, ice hockey and ice hockey. Wander into any bar during puck-pushing season (September to April) and 12 large men and an ice rink will never be far from the TV screen. And it is no surprise that the Slovaks indulge their obsession so passionately. The national team scooped second place in the 2000 world championships, stole the title in 2002 and brought home bronze in 2003.

READING UP

Stanislav Kirschbaum's *A History of Slovakia – The Struggle for Survival* is a very readable history. Lonely Planet's *Czech & Slovak Republics* provides the nuts and bolts of Slovak travel.

Football fills the summer months, and while the Slovaks have yet to attain the dizzy heights the Czechs sometimes aspire to, their club game is a reliable source of red-blooded, terrace bravado. SK Slovan Bratislava is the nation's most successful team – just be careful where you sport their colours.

ARTS

Thankfully, 21st-century Slovakia is as passionate about folk culture as it ever was. Some city dwellers may have been put off by the clichéd image of the communist-era 'happy peasant', but get out into the countryside and traditional arts are an integral part of community life, pervading everything from music to architecture.

Slovakia also has more grandiose art forms. Magnificent religious frescoes decorate St James' Church in Levoča (p1031) and the Cathedral of St Elizabeth in Košice (p1032), while the brutalist architecture of the communist epoch, as evocative as it is ugly, still holds sway over many of Slovakia's towns and cities.

ENVIRONMENT

Culminating in the forested valleys and icy peaks of the Vysoké Tatry (High Tatras), Slovakia is a country punctuated by pockets of weepy natural beauty. Little wonder then that the Slovaks should be so keen to up sticks and head into the countryside.

It is ironic that a nation so pathologically outdoorsy should also boast some of Europe's grimiest industrial landscapes. Soviet-era factories, burping plumes of smoke, provide a stark flipside to Slovakia's environmental coin. But things are on the up. National parks and protected areas now cover 20% of Slovakia and brown bears, wolves and lynxes still stalk its wilder corners.

For more on Slovakia's environmental issues, check out the website (www.sazp.sk).

TRANSPORT

GETTING THERE & AWAY
Air

Bratislava's **MR Štefánika Airport** (BTS; ☎ 02-48 57 33 53; www.airportbratislava.sk) receives limited flights from Continental Europe. Vienna's **Schwechat Airport** (VIE; ☎ 0043-1-70 070; www.vienna airport.com) is 60km from Bratislava, and is served by a range of international flights.

Boat

An appealing way to enter or leave Slovakia is via the hydrofoils that ply the Danube, linking Bratislava with Vienna and Budapest daily from April to September (p1027).

Bus

Eurolines (☎ 02-55 57 13 12; www.eurolines.sk) offers an extremely comprehensive service linking Bratislava with the rest of Europe (see p1027). You can even get to London (3800Sk one-way) in about 24 hours.

Car & Motorcycle

All foreign driving licences with photo ID are valid in Slovakia. As well as your vehicle's registration papers, you need a 'green card' (which proves drivers travelling through Europe have insurance that complies with the minimum insurance requirements of the places that they drive through). Your vehicle must display a nationality sticker and carry a first-aid kit and warning triangle.

Train

Bratislava is linked by train to destinations across Europe, including Budapest (520Sk, 2¾ hours), Prague (700Sk, 4½ hours) and Moscow (2100Sk, 33 hours) – see Bratislava (p1027) and Košice (p1033) for details of some of the direct services.

GETTING AROUND
Bicycle

Roads are often narrow and potholed, and in towns, cobblestones and tram tracks can be a dangerous combination. Theft is a problem, so a lock is a must. You can hire bikes, especially in popular biking areas like the Vysoké Tatry.

The cost of transporting a bicycle by rail is usually 10% of the train ticket.

Bus

Intercity buses, operated by **Slovenská autobusová doprava** (SAD; www.sad-kds.sk in Slovak), are generally slower and less comfortable than the train. One-way bus tickets cost around 110Sk per 100km.

When trying to decipher bus schedules beware of departure times bearing footnotes you don't completely understand. It is helpful to know that *premáva* means 'it operates' and *nepremáva* means 'it doesn't operate'.

For times and prices, check www.vlaky.sk.

Car & Motorcycle

You can drive in Slovakia using your licence. However, to use Slovakia's motorways (denoted by green signs) all vehicles must have a motorway sticker *(nálepka)*, which should be displayed in the windscreen. You can buy stickers at border crossings, petrol stations or Satur offices (100Sk for 15 days, 600Sk for a year; for vehicles up to 1.5 tonnes).

Avis has offices in Bratislava and Košice, but there are also much cheaper local hire car companies (see p1028).

Parking restrictions are draconian and eagerly enforced – always buy a ticket.

Hitching

Slovaks are enthusiastic hitchhikers and it can be an easy way to get between smaller villages. If you do hitch, it is safer to travel in pairs.

Local Transport

City buses and trams operate from around 4.30am to 11.30pm daily. Tickets are sold at public transport offices, at newsstands and from ticket machines, and must be validated once you're aboard.

Train

Slovak Republic Railways (Železnice Slovenskej republiky or ŽSR; www.zsr.sk) provides a cheap and efficient service – charges run at approximately 120Sk per 100km. Most of the places covered in this chapter are on or near the main railway line between Bratislava and Košice.

For times and prices, check www.vlaky.sk.

BRATISLAVA

☎ 02 / pop 452,288

Slovakia has had a roller coaster ride through history and its capital is still reverberating from the highs and lows. Bratislava's small old town harks back to stately days of imperial grandeur, while gigantic suburban housing projects stand like tombstones to the days of communist-era oppression. Yet the centre fizzes with the Eurochic trimmings that

---

have come in the wake of EU accession and a growing sense of economic confidence.

First impressions, however, can be misleading. On a rainy day, new arrivals are confronted with a grey, imposing city, where functionality is foremost and Slovakia's vibrant, traditional culture appears to be on the back foot.

But focused on a meagre, but beautiful, historic centre, Bratislava is at the same time a youthful city, bursting with big ideas and fresh optimism. Bars and restaurants are popping up across town and the city plays host to most of the country's best museums and galleries. For travellers tired of ogling the sights of Budapest and Prague, down-to-earth Bratislava, roughly halfway between the two and largely devoid of tourists, offers an ideal – and cheapish – reality check.

ORIENTATION

All of the attractions are on the north bank of the Danube. Hviezdoslavovo nám (square) is a convenient reference point, with the old town to the north, the Danube to the south and Bratislava Castle to the west.

INFORMATION
Bookshops

Svet Knihy (☎ 54 64 88 37; Obchodná 4; ☼ 9am-7pm Mon-Fri, until 5pm Sat) Has English-language titles on the 1st floor.

GETTING INTO TOWN

Bratislava's airport (Letisko MR Štefánika) is 7km northeast of the centre. Take bus 61 to the train station.

Bratislava's main train station, Hlavná stanica, is located about 700m north of the centre. Tram 1 runs from the station to nám L Štúra, just south of Hviezdoslavovo nám.

The main bus station *(autobusová stanica)* is on Mlynské nivy, 1.5km east of the old town. Bus 210 shuttles between the main bus station and the main train station.

Taxis from the main transport hubs tend to be very expensive unless they use their meter.

SLOVAKIA

Emergency

Main police station (Polícia; ☎ 0961-01 11 11; Sasinkova 23) Located about 600 metres northeast of city centre.

Internet Access

Internet Centrum (☎ 0905-95 72 07; cnr Michalská & Sedlárska; per min 2Sk; ☾ 9am-midnight) Has discounted rates (per min 1Sk) from 9-10am and 9pm-midnight.
Megalnet (☎ 54 43 55 67; Klariská 4; per min 1Sk; ☾ 9am-10pm Mon-Fri, from 2pm Sat & Sun)

Medical Services

Poliklinika (☎ 52 96 24 61; Bezručova 8) Hospital.

Money

There are banks with ATMs and exchange facilities throughout town.
Agentura Alex (☎ 54 41 40 20; Kuzmányho 8; ☾ 8.30am-5pm Mon-Fri) The local Amex agent.
Istrobanka (cnr Laurinská & Rybárska; ☾ 8.30am-4.30pm Mon-Fri)

Post

Mail addressed c/o poste restante, 81000 Bratislava 1, can be collected at the **main post office** (nám SNP 34; ☾ 7am-8pm Mon-Fri, until 2pm Sat).

Tourist Information

Bratislava Information Service (☎ 54 43 37 15; www.bratislava.sk; Klobučnícka 2; ☾ 8.30am-7pm Mon-Fri, 10am-5pm Sat & Sun Jun-Sep, 8.30am-6pm Mon-Fri, 9am-2pm Sat Oct-May) The main tourist office.
Bratislava Information Service (☎ 52 49 59 06; Hlavná stanica; ☾ 7.30am-7pm Mon-Fri, 7.30am-2.30pm Sat & Sun Jun-Sep, 8am-6pm Mon-Fri, 9am-2pm Sat Oct-May) A smaller outlet at the main train station.

Travel Agencies

Tatratour (☎ 52 92 78 88; www.tatratour.sk; Mickiewiczova 2; ☾ 8am-6pm Mon-Fri) Arranges international air, bus and train tickets, accommodation and tours.

SIGHTS & ACTIVITIES

Perched on a hill overlooking the old town, boxy **Bratislava Castle** (Bratislavský hrad; ☾ 9am-8pm Apr-Sep, until 6pm Oct-Mar) is typically (for Bratislava) unostentatious. It offers sweeping views from its ramparts and houses the interesting **Historical Museum** (Historické Múzeum; ☎ 59 34 16 26; adult/concession 60/30Sk; ☾ 9am-5pm Tue-Sun), incorporating the vital ice hockey hall of fame, as well as a plethora of fine art, furniture and historical exhibits. Music junkies should then head to the quirky **Museum of Folk Music** (Hudobné Múzeum; ☎ 54 41 33 49; adult/concession

---

TOP FIVE SLOVAKIA

▪ **Festival** The Východná Folklore Festival, 32km west of Poprad, gathers folk dancers from across the country (p1035)

▪ **Walk** Anywhere in the Vysoké Tatry mountains. Steep valleys and snow-capped peaks provide some of central Europe's most sensational vistas (p1029)

▪ **Bar/Club** It's cheap as chips, but Bratislava's Downtown Backpackers is a great option (p1026). Backus, in Košice, serves hearty fare (p1033) and lashings of atmosphere.

▪ **Impressive sight** Spišský Hrad is the country's biggest castle and an impressive monument to Slovakia's medieval stone age (p1032)

▪ **Skiing** Slovakia has some of the cheapest skiing in Europe. Both Vysoké Tatry (p1029) and Malá Fatra (p1029) have some worthwhile slopes

---

20/10Sk; ☎ 9am-5pm Tue-Sun), at the north end of the castle complex. Running along the base of the castle, Židovská houses excellent museums, including the **Museum of Arts & Crafts** (Expozícia Umeleckých Remesiel; ☎ 54 41 27 84; Beblavého 1; adult/concession 50/20Sk; ☾ 10am-5pm Tue-Sun).

Hardcore castle aficionados should don their daypack and head to **Devin Castle** (☎ 65 73 01 05; Muranská; adult/concession 40/10Sk; ☾ 10am-5pm Tue-Fri, until 6pm Sat & Sun May-Oct), 9km west of Bratislava. Once the military plaything of 9th-century warlord Prince Ratislav, Devin is packed with historical intrigue. No 29 bus links Devin with Nový Most bus terminal.

Back in town, on the riverfront, the **Slovak National Gallery** (Slovenská Národná Galéria; ☎ 54 43 20 81; Rázusovo nábrežie 2; adult/concession 80/40Sk; ☾ 10am-5.30pm Tue-Sun) incorporates an 18th-century palace into its unusual 'Stalinist chic' design. It houses the nation's eclectic art collection and is well worth a visit.

The nearby **Slovak National Museum** (Slovenské Národné Múzeum; ☎ 59 34 91 22; Vajanského nábrežie 2; adult/concession 20/10Sk; admission free last Sun of each month; ☾ 9am-5pm Tue-Sun) is a bit dowdy, but headlines as Slovakia's natural history showcase and features plenty of dusty exhibits.

On nám L Štúra you'll find the neobaroque **Reduta Palace** (see p1027), now Bratislava's

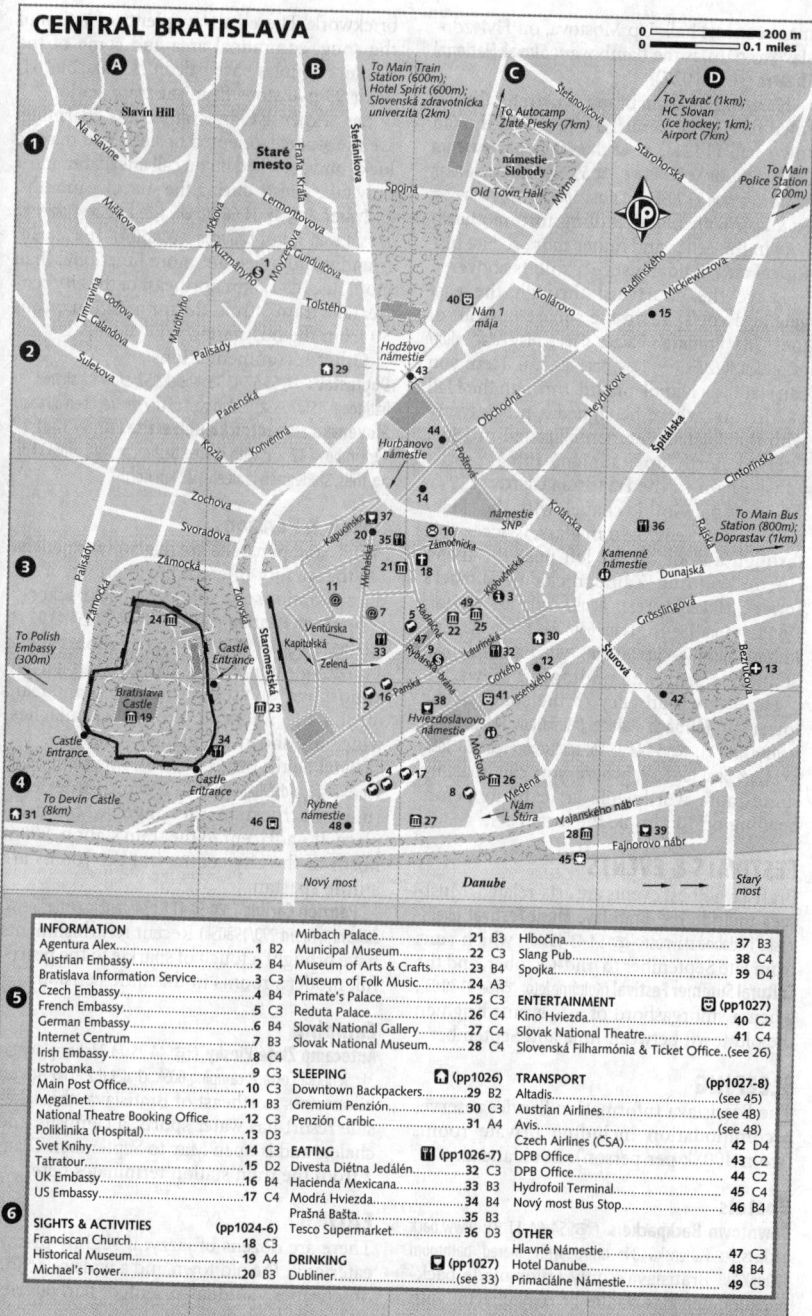

CENTRAL BRATISLAVA

SLOVAKIA

INFORMATION	
Agentura Alex	1 B2
Austrian Embassy	2 B4
Bratislava Information Service	3 C3
Czech Embassy	4 B4
French Embassy	5 C3
German Embassy	6 B4
Internet Centrum	7 B3
Irish Embassy	8 C4
Istrobanka	9 C3
Main Post Office	10 C3
Megalnet	11 B3
National Theatre Booking Office	12 C3
Poliklinika (Hospital)	13 D3
Svet Knihy	14 C3
Tatratour	15 D2
UK Embassy	16 B4
US Embassy	17 C4

SIGHTS & ACTIVITIES	(pp1024–6)
Franciscan Church	18 C3
Historical Museum	19 A4
Michael's Tower	20 B3
Mirbach Palace	21 B3
Municipal Museum	22 C3
Museum of Arts & Crafts	23 B4
Museum of Folk Music	24 A3
Primate's Palace	25 C3
Reduta Palace	26 C4
Slovak National Gallery	27 C4
Slovak National Museum	28 C4

SLEEPING	(pp1026)
Downtown Backpackers	29 B2
Gremium Penzión	30 C3
Penzión Caribic	31 A4

EATING	(pp1026–7)
Divesta Diétna Jedáleň	32 C3
Hacienda Mexicana	33 B3
Modrá Hviezda	34 B4
Prašná Bašta	35 B3
Tesco Supermarket	36 D3

DRINKING	(pp1027)
Dubliner	(see 33)

Hlbočina	37 B3
Slang Pub	38 C4
Spojka	39 D4

ENTERTAINMENT	(pp1027)
Kino Hviezda	40 C2
Slovak National Theatre	41 C4
Slovenská Filharmónia & Ticket Office	(see 26)

TRANSPORT	(pp1027–8)
Altadis	(see 45)
Austrian Airlines	(see 48)
Avis	(see 48)
Czech Airlines (ČSA)	42 D4
DPB Office	43 C2
DPB Office	44 C2
Hydrofoil Terminal	45 C4
Nový most Bus Stop	46 B4

OTHER	
Hlavné Námestie	47 C3
Hotel Danube	48 B4
Primaciálne Námestie	49 C3

main concert hall. Up Mostová, on Hviezdo-slavovo nám, is the flamboyant **Slovak National Theatre** (see p1027).

Narrow Rybárska brána penetrates the old town to Hlavné nám. To one side is the old town hall (1421), now the **Municipal Museum** (Mestské Múzeum v Bratislave; ☎ 59 20 51 30; Hlavné nám; adult/concession 50/20Sk; ☺ 10am-5pm Tue-Fri, 11am-6pm Sat & Sun), with bloodcurdling torture chambers in the cellar and rather more sedate historical and 'feudal justice' exhibits above.

Leave the courtyard through the east gate and you'll be on the square in front of the 1781 **Primate's Palace** (Primaciálny Palác; adult/concession 40/20Sk; ☺ 10am-5pm Tue-Sun). Here you can stroll, as Napoleon did, through the Hall of Mirrors, where he signed a peace treaty with the Austrian emperor Franz I in 1805.

Head north up Radničná into Františ-kánske nám to the **Franciscan Church** (1297). The original Gothic chapel, with the skeleton of a saint enclosed in glass, is accessible through a door on the left near the front. Go on winding Zámočnícka to **Michael's Tower** (Michalská Veža; adult/concession 40/20Sk; ☺ 10am-5pm Tue-Fri, 11am-6pm Sat & Sun May-Sep, 9.30am-4.30pm Tue-Sun Oct-Apr), with a collection of antique arms and photogenic views.

Head down an alley to the south of the tower to **Mirbach Palace** (Mirbachov Palác; Františ-kánske nám 11; ☎ 54 43 15 56; adult/concession 60/30Sk; ☺ 11am-6pm Tue-Sun), where you can soak up some more worthwhile art exhibits before heading off to sample the local beer.

FESTIVALS & EVENTS

Bratislava's best events are arts-related. Must-sees include the **Bratislava Music Festival** (Bratis-lavské hudobné slávnosti; ☎ 54 43 45 46), which runs from late September to mid-October, and the **Cultural Summer Festival** (Kultúrne leto; ☎ 54 41 30 63), when a smorgasbord of arts events brighten the old town between June and September.

SLEEPING

The Bratislava Information Service reserves accommodation including private rooms (from 400Sk per person). Book ahead.

Hostels

Downtown Backpackers (☎ 54 64 11 91; www.back packers.sk; Panenská 31; dm/d with shared bathroom 500/800Sk) Bratislava's only tailor-made back-packers' den has oodles of cosy charm, with blood-red décor and plenty of trendy exposed

brickwork. There's always plenty of action in the snug, communal area and some of the upstairs doubles have balconies. Take bus 81, 91 or 93 two stops from the train station.

Less expensive, but rather less charming, are the student-oriented hostels. You may be lucky and get a bed if you call ahead, but most only take guests during the summer months.

Zvárač (☎ 49 24 66 00; ubyt@cert.vuz.sk; Pionierska 17; s/d with shared bathroom 600/850Sk) It's clean, friendly and quiet, but more functional than fabulous. It's 1.5km northeast of the city centre: take tram 3 from the train station or bus 50 from the bus station.

Other recommendations:

Dopravstav (☎ 55 57 43 13; Košická 52; s/d with shared bathroom 456/798Sk) 1.5km east of city centre, open all year.

Slovenská zdravotnícka univerzita (☎ 59 37 01 11; Limbová 12; s/d with shared bathroom 380/760Sk) For no-frills, student-style sleeps. 2.5km north.

Hotels & Pensions

Hotels and pensions are relatively expensive for the quality offered, but there are a few decent options for splurging backpackers.

Gremium Penzión (☎ 54 13 10 26; fax 54 43 06 53; Gorkého 11; s/d 920/1350Sk) With five rooms above a buzzing eatery/sports bar, this has a lively atmosphere and rocks with cheers and tears during the weekend ice hockey matches, which are shown on giant TV screens.

Hotel Spirit (☎ 54 77 75 61; www.hotelspirit.sk; Vančurova 1; s/d 990/1430Sk; ☐) Avant-garde décor rules the roost in this angular, colourful place. It's adjacent to the train station, 800m north of the city centre, but the rooms are a little spartan.

Penzión Caribic (☎ 54 41 83 34; caribics@stonline.sk; Žižkova 1/A; s/d 990/1980Sk) Recent refurbishments have brought a touch of sparkle to the peaceful, modern rooms in this little pension.

Camping

Autocamp Zlaté Piesky (☎ 44 25 73 73; kempi@netax .sk; Senecká Cesta 2; camping 60Sk, chalet d 250Sk) Seven kilometres northeast of Bratislava, this lakeside resort has water sports, a campsite and chalets and is open May to September. Tram 2 from the train station terminates here.

EATING

There are dozens of jazzy, if slightly pricey, eateries in the old town and a wide selection of cheaper, student-oriented bar/eateries along Obchodná.

Prašná Bašta (☎ 54 43 49 57; Zámočnícka 11; mains 100-185Sk; 🕑 11am-11pm) This dark, atmospheric hideaway oozes old Bratislava charm and whips up a range of hearty, filling fare.

Hacienda Mexicana (☎ 0904-556 886; Sedlárska 6; mains 100-200Sk; 🕑 9am-3am) Harley Davidson memorabilia, saloon-style décor and fiery hot fajitas set the scene in this bustling bar/eatery. It could be the setting for an *El Mariachi*–style shoot-out.

Divesta diétna jedáleň (Laurinská 8; mains 58-68Sk; 🕑 11am-3pm Mon-Fri) The big queues speak volumes about the excellent-value veggie tucker at this central buffet.

Modrá hviezda (☎ 54 43 27 47; Beblavého 14; mains 80-150Sk; 🕑 11.30am-11pm Mon-Sat) On the way up to the castle – follow the mouth-watering smells – this cosy place features Slovak music, exposed timber and a vibrant atmosphere.

Tesco (Kamenné nám; 🕑 8am-10pm Mon-Fri, until 7pm Sat & Sun) A well-stocked supermarket.

DRINKING & CLUBBING

Dubliner (☎ 54 41 07 06; Sedlárska 6; 🕑 11am-3am Mon-Sat, until 1am Sun) This snug Irish bar has log fires, draught Guinness and lashings of late night *craic*.

Slang Pub (☎ 0908-798 061; Hviezdoslavovo nám 23; 🕑 11am-1am Mon-Sat, until midnight Sun) Big-screen MTV and a lively, young crowd bring this basement place plenty of character. They also do huge plates of scrumptious snacks.

Clubs include:

Hlbočina (Kapucínska; 120Sk) More dance music, with a ground floor chill-out space.

Spojka (☎ 52 73 33 76; Prešernova 4; 100Sk) For trance, drum 'n' bass and more progressive dance sounds.

ENTERTAINMENT

Opera and ballet are performed at the **Slovak National Theatre** (Slovenské Národné Divadlo; Hviezdoslavovo nám). Book tickets at the **booking office** (pokladňa; ☎ 54 43 37 64; www.snd.sk; cnr Jesenského & Komenského; 🕑 8am-5.30pm Mon-Fri, 9am-1pm Sat) behind the theatre.

The **Slovenská filharmónia** (cnr nám L Štúra & Medená)is based in the Reduta Palace. The **ticket office** (☎ 54 43 33 51; filharmonia@filharmonia.sk; 🕑 1-7pm Mon, Tue, Thu & Fri, 8am-2pm Wed) is inside the building.

HC Slovan (☎ 44 45 65 00; Odbojárov 3), Bratislava's hallowed ice hockey team, plays at a stadium northeast of the old town.

You can catch a flick at **Kino Hviezda** (☎ 54 43 50 49; nám 1 mája 11).

GETTING THERE & AWAY
Air

The no-frills **Sky Europe Airlines** (www.skyeurope .com) offers budget online fares to Amsterdam, Barcelona, London, Paris and Split from €25 one-way.

Austrian Airlines (☎ 54 41 16 10; www.aua.com; Rybné nám 1; 🕑 9am-5pm Mon-Fri) flies daily to Paris (4755Sk return), London (4602Sk return) and Brussels (4739Sk return; except Sat).

Czech Airlines (ČSA; ☎ 52 96 13 25; Štúrova 13; 🕑 9am-5pm Mon-Fri) has four flights daily to Prague (3462Sk return).

Boat

Boats to Vienna (€22 one-way) and Budapest (€68 one-way) leave daily from the **hydrofoil terminal** (Fajnorovo nábrežie 2) between April and September. Tickets can be bought from **Altadis** (☎ 52 96 35 18; www.lod.sk; 🕑 9am-5pm Mon-Fri, until noon Sat), inside the terminal.

Bus

Bratislava's **main bus station** (SAD information line ☎ 55 56 73 49; www.sad-kds.sk in Slovak; Mlynské nivy) is east of the city centre.

National buses leaving Bratislava daily include nine to Košice (512Sk, seven hours), seven to Bardejov (560Sk, nine hours), six to Žilina (260Sk, 3½ hours) and 14 to Poprad (428Sk, six hours). For all times and prices, visit www.vlaky.sk.

Eurolines (International information ☎ 55 57 13 12, reservations ☎ 55 56 73 49; www.eurolines.sk) buses operate from Bratislava's main bus station to destinations across Europe. Destinations with one-way fares include: Vienna (210Sk, 1½ hours, daily), Prague (410Sk, 4½ hours, daily), Paris (3500Sk, 20 hours, Wednesday, Thursday, Friday, Sunday), London (3800Sk, 22 hours, Tuesday, Wednesday, Friday, Saturday, Sunday), Venice (1700Sk, 12 hours, Friday), Hamburg (2500Sk, 18½ hours, Thursday, Friday) and Győr, in Hungary (240Sk, 2½ hours, Wednesday).

Train

Five trains a day between Budapest (520Sk, 2¾ hours) and Prague (700Sk, 4½ hours) – via Brno (250Sk, 1½ hours) – call at Bratislava. Frequent trains run from Bratislava to Košice (590Sk, six hours), via Žilina (242Sk, 2¾ hours) and Poprad (384Sk, 4¾ hours).

There are two trains daily to Warsaw (1400Sk, 7¾ hours), one to Moscow (2100Sk,

33 hours) and seven to Vienna (376Sk, 1¼ hours).

Train times and prices can be found at www.zsr.sk or www.vlaky.sk.

GETTING AROUND
Bus & Tram

Dopravný podnik Bratislava (DPB; ☎ 59 50 59 50; www .dpb.sk) offers an extensive tram network complemented by bus and trolleybus. You can buy tickets (14/18/22Sk for 10/30/60 minutes) at DPB offices and from machines at main tram and bus stops; validate the ticket in the little red machines when you board.

Tourist tickets (turistické cestovné lístky) for one/two/three/seven days (90/170/210/ 310Sk) are sold at DPB offices and train and bus stations.

Car

Avis (☎ 53 41 61 11; www.avis.sk; Rybné nám 1) has a desk in the Hotel Danube, but prices are high.

Cheaper, local companies offer older cars from 699Sk per day – most deliver to your hotel. Try **Favorit** (☎ 44 88 41 52) or **Auto Danubius** (☎ 44 37 25 02).

Taxi

Bratislava's taxis have meters – make sure they use them. Call **BP** (☎ 16 333) or **VIP** (☎ 16 000).

WEST SLOVAKIA

TRENČÍN
☎ 032 / pop 57,000

Roman legionnaires were the first tourists to arrive here, establishing the outpost of Laugaricio. A rock inscription, which can be viewed from inside Hotel Tatra, is dated AD 179 and mentions the Roman 2nd Legion's victory over the Germanic Kvad tribes.

From the bus and train stations walk west through the city park and under the highway to the Tatra Hotel, where a street bears left uphill to Mierové nám, the main square. The **AiCES information centre** (☎ 16 186; www .trencin.sk; Štúrovo nám 10; ⏰ 8am-6pm Mon-Fri, until 1pm Sat May-Sep, 8am-5pm Mon-Fri Oct-Apr) is helpful.

ČSOB (Vajanského 3; ⏰ 7.30am-5pm Mon-Thu, until 4pm Fri) has an ATM and change facilities. The **main post office** (Mierové nám 21; ⏰ 7.30am-7pm Mon-Fri, 7.30-11am Sat) also houses the telephone centre. Check email at **Internet Klub Modra Linka** (Štúrovo nám; per min 1Sk; ⏰ 10am-10pm).

A stairway from the corner of Mierové nám leads up to **Trenčín Castle** (Trenčiansky hrad; ☎ 743 56 57; adult/concession 100/50Sk; ⏰ 9.15am-4.45pm). The highlight of the compulsory tour (in Slovak only) is the view from the tower.

Penzión Svorad (☎ 743 03 22; www.svorad-trencin .sk; Palackého 4; s/d 400/700Sk) has a whiff of Colditz, but it's the best budget option. Camp or take a cabin at **Autocamping Na Ostrove** (☎ 743 40 13; autocamping.tn@mail.pvt.sk; camping 130Sk, s/d 200/400Sk), on an island north of the centre.

Pizzeria Da Giuseppe (1st fl, Štúrovo nám 5; pizza 80-100Sk; ⏰ 10am-11pm Mon-Thu, until 1am Sat, 1-11pm Sun) whips up a mean Margherita. There is a cheap beer tent in the square below. **Steps Pub** (☎ 744 62 52; Sládkovičova 4; ⏰ 10.30am-1am, until 4am Fri & Sat) has live jazz on Thursdays.

Trains from Bratislava (162Sk, 1¾ hours) to Košice via Žilina stop here. There are six buses a day to Bratislava (142Sk, two hours), Žilina (106Sk, 1½ hours) and Košice (375Sk, five hours).

CENTRAL SLOVAKIA

ŽILINA
☎ 041 / pop 84,000

Founded in the 13th century, Žilina left an indelible mark on the map as a major transport hub. Few tourists pass through on the railways these days, though, making Žilina a distinctly Slovakian city with few tacky tourist trappings.

The adjacent bus and train stations are near the Váh River on the northeastern side of town, a 10-minute walk along Národná from Mariánské nám, Žilina's old town square.

CK Selinan (☎ 562 14 78; www.selinan.sk in Slovak; Burianova medzierka 4; ⏰ 8am-4.30pm Mon-Fri), in a lane off the western side of Mariánské nám, has regional info. **Net Bar** (☎ 0903-328 475; per min 1Sk; ⏰ 10am-midnight), at the south end of Šturová nám, offers Internet access.

Across the Váh River, flaky **Budatín Castle** (Budatín zámok; ☎ 562 00 33; Topoľová 1; adult/concession 30/15Sk; ⏰ 8am-4pm Tue-Sun) houses the **Považské Museum**, showing a collection of naive, tinker-style figures sculpted from metal and wire.

CK Selinan can help with private rooms from 300Sk per person. **Penzión GMK Centrum** (☎ 562 21 36; Mariánské nám 3; s/d 800/1200Sk) has a tip-top location, but smallish rooms. **China Restaurant** (☎ 562 66 74; Štúrovánám 5; mains 60-180Sk; ⏰ 8am-9.30pm Mon-Sat) knocks the socks off many Eastern European Oriental offerings. Bizarrely, they also do pizza.

Žilina is on the main railway line from Bratislava to Košice. Regular express trains head to Trenčín (104Sk, one hour), Bratislava (242Sk, 2¾ hours), Poprad (180Sk, two hours) and Košice (286Sk, three hours).

MALÁ FATRA
☎ 041

A knot of jagged peaks, topped with eerie, sentinel-like formations, the Malá Fatra National Park (Národný park Malá Fatra) incorporates a chocolate box–pretty, 200-sq-km swathe of the Malá Fatra (Little Fatra) mountain range and offers plentiful skiing and hiking. At the heart of the park is the Vrátna dolina, a beautiful mountain valley with forested slopes on all sides. The town of Terchová is the best base to access the park.

Združenie Turizmu Terchová (☎ 599 31 00; www
.terchovaregion.sk; Hurbanova 4; ⏰ 9am-5pm Mon-Fri, 10am-
5pm Sat, 10am-2pm Sun), in Terchová, has information and Internet access (100Sk per hour).

About 1km up the Štefanová road is the **Mountain Rescue Service** (Horská služba; ☎ 569 52 32), an excellent source of trail information.

A **ski lift** (☎ 569 5642; www.vratna.sk in Slovak; 160Sk return) runs from Starý Dvor, opposite the Starý Majer restaurant, to Grúň (1000m).

There are lots of *privaty* (private rooms) in Terchová from 200Sk per person. **Chata Vrátna** (☎ 569 57 39; chata_vratna@vratna.sk; dm/d with shared bathroom 180/500Sk), a cosy place at the far end of the Vrátna dolina, and **Chata Pod Lampášom** (☎ 569 53 92; s/d with shared bathroom 350/700Sk), often filled with muddy hikers and the smell of wood smoke, offer comfy sleeps. **Starý Majer Restaurant** (☎ 569 54 19; mains 60-180Sk; ⏰ 10am-9pm), opposite the ski lift, cooks up a mean spread of hearty tucker.

Buses link Žilina with Terchová (38Sk, 45 minutes) and Chata Vrátna (50Sk, one hour) at least every two hours.

EAST SLOVAKIA

East Slovakia is one of the most attractive touring areas in Central Europe.

VYSOKÉ TATRY
☎ 052

The roof of Slovakia, the Vysoké Tatry (High Tatra) mountains loom over most of Central Europe, culminating in the vertiginous 2654m peak of Gerlachovský štít, the loftiest mountain in the entire Carpathian range. The massif measures just 25km across, but in terms of natural beauty, the peaks are truly monumental, offering the kind of photo opportunities that will get you fantasising about a career at *National Geographic*. Pristine snowfields, ultramarine mountain lakes, crashing waterfalls – as well as the slightly less welcome crowds – come as standard.

The region offers hiking (600km of trails link the valleys and peaks), climbing and skiing possibilities galore – check at the information centres listed for details.

The higher trails are officially closed from November to mid-June, to protect the delicate environment. There's snow from November until May or even June. July and August are the warmest (and most crowded) months, while August and September are the best for high-altitude hiking. For the latest weather and advice contact the **Mountain Rescue Service** (Horská služba; ☎ 18 300; www.hzs.sk in Slovak).

Starý Smokovec, an easily accessible, early-20th-century resort, makes a pleasant base camp.

Information
AiCES Tatra information centre (☎ 442 34 40; www.tatry.sk; ⏰ 8am-8pm Mon-Fri, until 1pm Sat) In the Dom služieb shopping centre, northwest of Starý Smokovec train station.
Mountain Guides Society Office (☎ 442 20 66; www
.tatraguide.sk; ⏰ 10am-6pm Mon-Fri, noon-6pm Sat & Sun Jun-Sep, 10am-6pm Mon-Fri Oct-May) In front of the station at Starý Smokovec, offers advice, plus guides for hikes, climbing excursions and mountain bike tours (from 2000Sk).
Satur (☎ 442 24 97; www.satur.sk; ⏰ 8am-4pm Mon-Fri) Just above the train station at Starý Smokovec, can provide accommodation, transport and activities advice.
Tatrasport (☎ 442 52 41; www.tatry.net/tatrasport; ⏰ 8am-noon, 1-6pm daily) In Starý Smokovec, offers ski (299Sk per day) and mountain-bike (299Sk per day) hire.

Sleeping
Excellent mountain chalets (*chaty*) pepper the upper trails. Many close for maintenance in November and May. Food is available, but you should bring some of your own supplies.

Satur, in Starý Smokovec, can reserve chalet beds. High-season prices are 300Sk to 500Sk per person.

The following are the main chalets, from west to east:

SLOVAKIA

Chata pod Soliskom (☎ 0905-652 036; 1800m) Small, busy chalet above Štrbské Pleso.

Chata Popradské pleso (☎ 449 21 77; 1500m) Large, hotel-like *chata* with restaurant.

Sliezský dom (☎ 442 52 61; 1670m) Large mountain hotel with restaurant and cafeteria.

Zbojnícka chata (☎ 0903-638 000; 1960m) Alpine bunks and restaurant.

Téryho chata (☎ 442 52 45; 2015m) Alpine bunks and restaurant.

Zamkovského chata (☎ 442 26 36; 1475m) Alpine bunks and restaurant.

Bilíkova chata (☎ 442 24 39; 1220m) Attractive wooden chalet with double rooms.

Chata pri Zelenom plese (☎ 446 74 20; 1540m) Dorm accommodation and restaurant.

Satur can help with private rooms (250Sk to 500Sk per person). You can also check www.tanap.sk/homes.html.

Hotel prices almost double in the high seasons (mid-December to February and mid-June to September). Prices quoted here are mid-season.

Eurocamp FICC (☎ 466 77 41; www.eurocamp-ficc .sk; per adult/camp site/d/t 90/120/1000/1500Sk; 🔊) is the area's largest campsite. It's a five-minute stroll from Lomnica-Eurocamp train station.

STARÝ SMOKOVEC & AROUND

Pension Vesna (☎ 442 27 74; vesna@sinet.sk; per person from 500Sk) Daubed in sparkling white paint, this immaculate place offers spotless apartments and excellent service – they even organise 'fireplace parties'. It's behind the sanatorium below Nový Smokovec train station.

Hotel Smokovec (☎ 442 51 91; www.hotelsmokovec .sk; r 800Sk; 🔊) Smelling of fresh varnish, this renovated place mixes mountain charm with slick service and all mod-cons. It is immediately above Starý Smokovec train station.

Hotel Sport (☎ 442 23 61; fax 442 27 19; s/d 310/550Sk) On the eastern edge of Starý Smokovec, this is cheap, but rough.

TATRANSKÁ LOMNICA

Penzión Bělín (☎ 446 77 78; www.belin.sk; s/d with shared bathroom 260/520Sk) This tumbling, hostel-style place is a wee bit crumbly, but warm welcomes come as standard and the price is right.

Penzión Encian (☎ 446 75 20; penzion.encian@sinet .sk; s/d 450/900Sk) All dressed up like a Christmas tree, with fairy lights and decorative

pine branches aplenty, this is on the main road through town.

ŠTRBSKÉ PLESO

Hotel Panoráma (☎ 4492111; www.hotelpanorama.sk; s/d 830/1400Sk) Beamed from a whole different universe of architectural taste, this bizarre pyramid is one of Slovakia's more dramatic eyesores. The rooms are good though, and the view is much nicer looking out. It's above Štrbské Pleso train station.

You'll find some cheaper options down the hill in Tatranská Štrba, including **Hotel Junior Rysy** (☎ 448 48 45; hotel.rysy@ke.telecom.sk; s/d 700/900Sk).

Eating

Most hotels and chalets have their own restaurants. The bistro in Hotel Smokovec is good.

Tatry Pub (☎ 442 24 48; mains 60-160Sk; 🕒 1-11pm Mon-Thu, 11am-midnight Fri-Sun) This Starý Smokovec institution is the official watering hole of the Mountain Guide Club. Expect hearty food, plenty of beer and lots of mountain man machismo. It is on the main street, by the car park.

Getting There & Away

BUS

Daily, early morning buses link Bratislava and Starý Smokovec (428Sk, 6½ hours) and Tatranská Lomnica (435Sk, seven hours).

From Starý Smokovec, there are five buses a day going to Lysá Poľana (53Sk, one hour), six to Levoča (53Sk, one hour), four to Žilina (188Sk, 3¼ hours) and one to Trenčín (296Sk, five hours).

TRAIN

To reach Vysoké Tatry, catch one of the express trains running between Prague, Bratislava and Košice, and change at Poprad (see opposite). There are frequent narrow-gauge electric trains between Poprad and Starý Smokovec (see p1030).

WALKING INTO POLAND

For anyone interested in walking into Poland, there's a highway border crossing at Lysá Poľana near Tatranská Javorina, 30km from Tatranská Lomnica, via Ždiar, by bus (40Sk, 45 minutes).

Also ask Satur about its excursion buses to Zakopane and Kraków.

Getting Around

Electric trains (*električka*) run from Poprad to Starý Smokovec (16Sk, 30 minutes) and Štrbské Pleso (26Sk, one hour) every hour, and from Starý Smokovec to Tatranská Lomnica (11Sk, 15 minutes) every 30 to 60 minutes. A three-/seven-day ticket on the *električka* costs 119/229Sk.

A rack-railway connects Tatranská Štrba (on the main Žilina–Poprad railway line) with Štrbské Pleso (28Sk, 15 minutes).

Local buses run between the resorts every 20 minutes and tend to be quicker than the train – they have fewer stops though.

You can hire mountain bikes from Tatrasport in Starý Smokovec (see p1029).

POPRAD

☎ 052 / pop 53,000

Poprad is an important transport hub. Express trains are the easiest way of getting in and out of Poprad and run to Bratislava (384Sk, 4¼ hours), Žilina (155Sk, two hours) and Košice (138Sk, 1½ hours) every couple of hours. Electric trains climb 13km to Starý Smokovec, the main Vysoké Tatry resort, every hour or so.

There are buses to destinations across Slovakia from the bus station next to the train station, including Bratislava (355Sk, four hours) and Košice (130Sk, two hours).

LEVOČA

☎ 053 / pop 13,000

Few towns evoke images of the old Slovakia as readily as historic Levoča. Largely untouched by modern development, the walled old town is apparently cut off from the 21st century and life goes on around the main square's stunning Renaissance buildings at a distinctly measured pace.

The train and bus stations are 1km south of town.

Information

The **AiCES information centre** (☎ 451 37 63; www.levoca.sk; nám Majstra Pavla 58; 🕙 9am-5pm Mon-Sat, 10am-2pm Sun May-Oct, 9am-4.30pm Mon-Fri Nov-Apr) is at the top of the main square. **Slovenská sporiteľňa** (nám Majstra Pavla 56; 🕙 8am-3pm Mon-Fri, until 4pm Wed) changes travellers cheques and has an ATM.

The telephone centre is in the **post office** (nám Majstra Pavla 42; 🕙 8am-noon & 1-5pm Mon-Fri, 8-10.30am Sat). You can check email at **Levonet Internet Café** (nám Majstra Pavla 38; per min 1.50Sk; 🕙 10am-10pm), at the southern end of the square.

Sights

Nám Majstra Pavla, Levoča's central square, is chock-a-block with superb Gothic and Renaissance buildings. The 15th-century **St James' Church** (chrám sv.Jakuba; ☎ 442 45 00; adult/concession 50/30Sk; 🕙 tours 8.30am, 9.30am, 10.30am, 11.30am, 1pm, 2pm, 3pm, 4pm Tue-Sat) contains a towering Gothic altar (1517) by Majster Pavol of Levoča. Buy tickets in the Municipal Weights House opposite the north door.

Next to St James' is the Gothic **town hall**, enlivened by Renaissance arcades and murals of the civic virtues and containing the so-so **Spiš Museum** (Spišske Múzeum; ☎ 451 24 49; adult/concession 30/15Sk; 🕙 9am-5pm). Beside the town hall is a 16th-century **cage of shame**, where prisoners were once exhibited.

Sleeping & Eating

AiCES can book accommodation, including private rooms from 250Sk per person. You can camp at **Levočská Dolina Autocamp** (☎ 451 27 05; camping 80Sk; 🕙 mid-Jun–Aug), 5km northwest of the centre.

Hotel Faix (☎ 451 11 11; Probstnerova cesta 22; s/d 250/500Sk) Glamorous it is not, but this no-frills place is within easy reach of the train station and old town, and the beds are cheap.

Hotel Barbakan (☎ 451 43 10; recepcia.hot@barbakan.sk; Košická 15; s/d incl breakfast 1150/1450Sk) Carrying a decent dose of old Levoča charm right into the cosy bedrooms, this pleasant place is well worth a splurge.

Reštaurácia Slovenská (☎ 451 23 29; nám Majstra Pavla 62; mains 60-140Sk; 🕙 10am-10pm) Slovak meat feasts, a homely atmosphere and an extremely affordable menu make this a top tip for hungry budget travellers.

Vegetarián (☎ 451 45 76; Uhoľná 137; mains 30-70Sk; 🕙 10am-3.15pm Mon-Fri) Wholesome smells and a no-fuss menu make this basic veggie haunt a hit with locals. It is off the northwest corner of the main square.

Getting There & Away

Hourly trains run to Spišská Nová Ves (17Sk, 15 minutes), on the main Bratislava to Košice line. Bus travel is more practical as there are frequent services to Poprad (38Sk, 30 minutes) and Spišské Podhradie (22Sk, 20 minutes) and eight daily to Košice (120Sk, two hours). All buses stop at nám Š

SLOVAKIA

Kluberta and some local buses also stop at the train station.

SPIŠSKÉ PODHRADIE
☎ 053

Spišské Podhradie is a dusty, bedraggled little town, but sits between two of Eastern Slovakia's hottest tourist trail tickets: Spišský hrad (Spiš castle) and Spišská Kapitula.

Arriving by bus from Levoča, ask the driver to drop you at **Spišská Kapitula**, on a ridge 1km west of Spišské Podhradie. This 13th-century ecclesiastical settlement is encircled by a 16th-century wall and peppered with Gothic houses. At the upper end is the magnificent 1273 **St Martin's Cathedral** (adult/concession 20/10Sk; ☼ 11.15am-2.45pm). Inside are three beautiful, folding Gothic altars (1499). Buy tickets from the nearby **information office** (☎ 0907-388 411; ☼ 11.15am-2.45pm).

On the far side of Spišské Podhradie, ghostly **Spišský hrad** (☎ 454 13 36; adult/concession 60/30Sk; ☼ 8.30am-5.15pm May-Oct, by appointment Nov-Apr) is Slovakia's largest castle and dates back to 1209. Cross the tracks near the train station and follow the yellow markers up the hill. The highest castle enclosure contains a round Gothic tower, a cistern, a chapel and a rectangular Romanesque palace perched over the abyss. Weapons and instruments of torture are exhibited in the dungeon.

Basic **Penzión Podzámok** (☎ 454 17 55; www.penzionpodzamok.sk; Podzámková 28; s/d with shared bathroom 250/500Sk) is the best option in town. To get there, turn left after the bridge just south of Mariánské nám. The **Kolping House** (☎ 450 21 11; www.hotelkolping.sk; s/d 1100/1600Sk) makes an excellent treat and is actually inside the walls of Spišská Kapitula.

A railway line connects Spišské Podhradie to Spišské Vlachy (12Sk, 15 minutes), a station on the main line from Poprad to Košice. Relatively frequent buses run to Levoča (22Sk, 20 minutes) and Poprad (55Sk, 50 minutes).

KOŠICE
☎ 055 / pop 236,500

Steel manufacturing forms Košice's economic backbone, but Slovakia's second city has a heart of gold, with a beautifully restored old town square rivalling anything in Bratislava, and a vibrant, youthful buzz. Stalinist tower blocks today jostle for hegemony over the historic monuments, but Eastern Slovakia's urban hub retains a strong sense of identity and offers a fascinating insight into the country's wilder half.

Orientation & Information

The adjacent bus and train stations are just east of the old town. A five-minute walk along Mlynská brings you into Hlavná.

The **Municipal Information Centre** (☎ 625 88 88; www.kosice.sk/icmk in Slovak; Hlavná 59; ☼ 9am-6pm Mon-Fri, 9am-1pm Sat), in the town hall, has maps, accommodation information and **Internet access** (per hr 30Sk).

The **police station** (☎ 159; cnr Štúrova & Fejova) is just south of the centre, en route to the **hospital** (Fakultná nemocnica L.Pasteura; ☎ 615 31 11; Rastislavova 45).

ČSOB (Hlavná 23; ☼ 8am-5pm Mon-Thu, until 4pm Fri) has an ATM and change facilities.

There's a telephone centre in the **main post office** (Poštová 2; ☼ 7am-7pm Mon-Fri, 7am-2pm Sat).

You can buy international train and bus tickets at **Satur** (☎ 622 31 23; www.satur.sk; Hlavná 1; ☼ 9am-5pm Mon-Fri), next to Hotel Slovan.

Sights & Activities

Košice's magnificent 1345 **Cathedral of St Elizabeth** (Dóm sv Alžbety; ☎ 0908-667 093; guided tours adult/concession 35/20Sk, crypt & tower 30/15Sk; ☼ 9.30am-4.30pm Mon-Fri, 9am-1.30pm Sat; cathedral nave 8am-8pm daily), Europe's easternmost Gothic cathedral, dominates the old town square and is the sight most likely to grace your Košice postcard home. In a crypt on the left side of the nave is the tomb of Duke Ferenc Rákóczi, who was exiled to Turkey after the failed 18th-century Hungarian revolt against Austria. On the south side of the cathedral is the 14th-century **St Michael's Chapel** (closed for renovations at time of writing), and to the north is the **Urban Tower** (closed to the public).

Most of Košice's other historic sites are north along Hlavná. In square's heart is the ornate 1899 **State Theatre** (see opposite). Facing it at Hlavná 59 is the rococo former **town hall** (1780).

The **East Slovak Museum** (Východoslovenské Múzeum; ☎ 622 03 09; Hviezdoslavova 3; adult/concession 30/10Sk; ☼ 9am-5pm Tue-Sat, 9am-1pm Sun), at the northern end of Hlavná, is dedicated to regional culture, history and archaeology. Don't miss the Košice Gold Treasure in the basement, a hoard of 2920 gold coins dating from the 15th to 18th centuries and discovered by chance in 1935.

Walk back along Hlavná towards the State Theatre and turn left on narrow Univerzitná to the **Mikluš Prison** (Miklušova Väznici; ☎ 622 28 56; Pri Miklušovej Väznici; adult/concession 30/10Sk; ⏰ 9am-5pm, until 1pm Sun). This pair of 16th-century houses once served as a prison equipped with medieval torture chambers and cells. You have to buy tickets from an office hidden behind the house at nearby Hrnčiarska 7.

Art lovers should poke their nose into the **East Slovak Gallery** (Východoslovenská galéria; ☎ 622 11 87; Hlavná 27; adult/concession 20/10Sk; ⏰ 10am-6pm Tue-Fri, 1-5.30pm Sat, 2-5.30pm Sun).

Sleeping

The Municipal Information Centre can help with private rooms from 300Sk per person.

K2 (☎ 625 59 48; Štúrova 32; s/d with shared bathroom 330/660Sk) This reasonably central sports complex is the city's cheap sleeps champion, with chirpy staff and a restaurant, fitness centre and sauna.

Ubytovňa Mestský Park (☎ 633 39 04; fax 671 07 66; Mestský Park 13; s/d with shared bathroom 220/440Sk) In the town park, east of the centre, this no-frills hostel is a little rougher and a little cheaper.

Autocamping Salaš Barca (☎ 623 33 97; Alejová 24; camping 70Sk) There's not a whole lot here, but this place, south of the city, remains the best bet for Košice's campers. Call ahead for directions.

For a little more cash, Košice has some decent pensions. Recommendations:

Penzión Krmanová (☎ 623 05 65; krmanova@elvs.sk; Krmanová 14; s/d 1300/1800Sk) For a slick, comforts-packed splurge.

Penzionň Nad Bankou (☎ 683 82 21; vaskoj@isternet sk; Kováčska 63; s/d 900/1200Sk) For spotless, simple, modern sleeps.

Eating & Drinking

Bakchus (☎ 622 18 14; Hlavná 80; mains 55-90Sk; ⏰ 10am-11pm) On the main square, this bustling place has a cosy pub out the back, a nipper restaurant up front and a beer terrace for raucous summer tipples. Hearty Slovakian food is the staple.

Cukráreň Aida (cnr Hlavná 81; snacks 30-100Sk; ⏰ 8am-10pm) Despite the pigeon poo–spattered awnings, this is one of Košice's busiest cafés, notorious for its heavenly ice cream.

Reštaurácia Ajvega (Orlia 10; mains 90-135Sk; ⏰ 10am-10pm) Mountains of vegetarian and Mexican food steal the show here. You can get cheap baguette sandwiches at **Bagetéria** (Hlavná 74).

Diesel Pub (☎ 622 21 86; Hlavná 92; ⏰ noon-midnight Mon-Thu, until 1am Fri-Sun) Down an alley filled with 'music clubs', this Celtic-inspired haunt promises oodles of good cheer and rivers of (slightly overpriced) booze.

Entertainment

The renovated **State Theatre** (Štá Divadlo Košice; ☎ 622 12 31; www.sdke.sk; Hlavná 58; ⏰ box office 9am-5.30pm Mon-Fri, 10am-1pm Sat) stages regular performances.

The **State Philharmonic** (Štátna Filharmónia Košice; ☎ 622 45 14; Moyzesova 66) is the city's principal orchestra and performs throughout town.

Getting There & Away

BUS

Several buses run daily to Levoča (120Sk, two hours), Poprad (130Sk, two hours) and Bratislava (512Sk, seven hours). Buses also travel to Uzhhorod, Ukraine (140Sk, 2½ hours) three times daily, to Nowy Targ, Poland (180Sk, four hours) every Thursday and Saturday, and to Krosno, Poland (170Sk, 3½ hours) every Wednesday, Friday and Saturday.

There's a bus from Košice to Miskolc (120Sk, two hours), in Hungary, on Monday, Thursday, Friday and Saturday.

For further times and prices, check www .vlaky.sk.

TRAIN

There are regular domestic trains that run to Poprad (138Sk, 1½ hours), Žilina (286Sk, three hours), Trenčín (375Sk, five hours) and Bratislava (590Sk, six hours).

A sleeper train leaves Košice every morning for Kiev (Kyiv), in Ukraine (1600Sk, 22½ hours). Overnight trains also run to Prague (1200Sk, 11 hours) and Brno (830Sk, nine hours), in the Czech Republic.

Three daily trains run to Kraków, Poland (930Sk, 6½ hours) and four travel to Miskolc, Hungary (330Sk, two hours), with three of these carrying on to Budapest (900Sk, four hours).

For further times and prices, visit www .zsr.sk or www.vlaky.sk.

SLOVAKIA DIRECTORY

ACCOMMODATION

Prices fluctuate according to season with high season running from May to September, plus the Christmas/New Year and Easter holidays. We quote average prices. High season prices may increase by as much as 20 per cent on prices listed.

If you want to check options before you leave, two useful websites are www .travelguide.sk and www.ubytujsa.sk.

Camping

Most grounds open May to September and are often accessible on public transport. Most have a snack bar, and small cabins that are cheaper than a hotel. Camping wild in national parks is prohibited.

Hostels

There are very backpacker-style hostels in Slovakia, but there's no shortage of cheap places to sleep. The Hostelling International (HI) handbook lists an impressive network of student-style hostels, but they're mostly open in July and August only. Apply for your HI card before you leave home, as it will net you great discounts. Satur and tourist information offices have information on hostels.

Turistické ubytovňy (tourist hostels) that provide very basic and cheap dormitory accommodation are not connected to the HI network. You can ask about them at information offices.

Hotels, Pensions & Private Rooms

Hotels in Bratislava are considerably more expensive than in the rest of the country. Two-star rooms are typically s/d 800/1200Sk.

Many small pensions offer more personalised service and cheaper rates than hotels.

Private rooms (look for signs reading privát or Zimmer frei) are usually available in tourist areas (from 250Sk per person). Tourist information offices can book them.

ACTIVITIES

Slovakia is one of Eastern Europe's best areas for hiking. There is also excellent rock climbing and mountaineering in the Vysoké Tatry. Contact the **Mountain Guides Society Office** (☎ 052-442 20 60/6; www.tatraguide.sk) in Starý Smokovec for more information.

Slovakia, especially in the east, also offers some of the best cycling terrain in Central Europe. Mountain biking in the Vysoké Tatry is excellent. **Tatrasport** (☎ 052-442 52 41; www.tatry .net/tatrasport) has a branch in Starý Smokovec and rents mountain bikes for 299Sk a day.

The country has some of Europe's cheapest ski resorts, but the skiable areas are small. The season runs from December to April in the Vysoké Tatry and Malá Fatra. Ski hire starts at 299Sk per day.

BUSINESS HOURS

On weekdays, shops open around 8am or 9am and close at 5pm or 6pm. Many small shops, particularly those in country areas, close for lunch between noon and 2pm, and almost everything closes on Saturday afternoon and all day Sunday.

Most museums and castles are closed on Monday and the day following a public holiday. Many tourist attractions are closed from November to March and open on weekends only in April and October. Major museums stay open all year.

DANGERS & ANNOYANCES

Crime is low compared with the West. Some taxi drivers and waiters have been known to overcharge foreigners. Robberies on international trains have been increasing.

DISABLED TRAVELLERS

Slovakia is behind many EU countries in terms of facilities for the disabled. For more information contact the **Slovak Union for the Disabled** (Slovenský zväz telesně postihnutých; ☎ 02-50 22 87 08; Trnavské mýto 1, Bratislava).

EMBASSIES & CONSULATES
Embassies & Consulates in Slovakia

Australia and New Zealand do not have embassies in Slovakia; the nearest are in Vienna and Berlin respectively. The following are all in Bratislava (area code ☎ 02).

Austria (☎ 54 43 29 85; Ventúrska 10)
Czech Republic (☎ 59 20 33 01; Hviezdoslavovo nám 8)
France (☎ 59 34 71 11; Hlavné nám 7)
Germany (☎ 54 41 96 40; Hviezdoslavovo nám 10)
Ireland (☎ 54 43 57 15; Carlton Savoy Building, Mostová 2)
Poland (☎ 54 43 27 44; Zelená 6)
UK (☎ 59 98 20 00; Panská 16)
USA (☎ 54 43 08 61; Hviezdoslavovo nám 4)

Slovak Embassies & Consulates Abroad

For a comprehensive list, check www.foreign.gov.sk.

Australia (☎ 02-6290 1516; 47 Culgoa Circuit, O'Malley, ACT 2606)

Austria (☎ 01-318 905 5200; Armbrustergasse 24, 1-1190 Wien)

Canada (☎ 613-749 4442; 50 Rideau Terrace, Ottawa, Ontario K1M 2A1)

Czech Republic (☎ 233 113 051; Pod Hradbami 1, 160 00 Praha 6)

France (☎ 01 44 14 56 00; 125 rue de Ranelagh, 75016 Paris)

Germany (☎ 030-889 2620; Pariser Strasse 44, Berlin 107 07)

Hungary (☎ 01-460 9010; Stefania ut 22-24, H-1143 Budapest XIV)

Ireland (☎ 01-660 0012; 20 Clyde Rd, Ballsbridge, Dublin 4)

UK (☎ 020-7313 6470; 25 Kensington Palace Gardens, London W8 4QY)

USA (☎ 202-237 1054; 3523 International Court NW, Washington DC 20008)

FESTIVALS & EVENTS

During late June or early July, folk dancers from all over Slovakia meet at the Východná Folklore Festival, 32km west of Poprad. There are folk festivals in June in East Slovakia's Červený Kláštor and Kežmarok, and in many other towns from June to August. The two-week Bratislava Music Festival is held in late September to early October, and the Bratislava Jazz Days weekend is in late October.

HOLIDAYS

New Year's & Independence Day 1 January
Three Kings Day 6 January
Good Friday and Easter Monday March/April
Labour Day 1 May
Cyril and Methodius Day 5 July
SNP Day 29 August
Constitution Day 1 September
Our Lady of Sorrows Day 15 September
All Saints' Day 1 November
Christmas 24 to 26 December

INTERNET RESOURCES

The Slovakia Document Store (http://slovakia.eunet.sk) contains links to a wealth of information. The Slovak Tourism Board (www.slovakiatourism.sk) is also worth visiting.

MONEY

Slovakia's currency is the Slovak crown, or slovenská koruna (Sk), containing 100 halier

(hellers). There are coins of 10, 20 and 50 hellers, and one, two, five and 10 crowns (Sk). Banknotes come in denominations of 20, 50, 100, 200, 500, 1000 and 5000 crowns.

The easiest place to change cash and travellers cheques is at a branch of the Všeobecná úver-ová banka (VÚB; General Credit Bank), Slovenská sporiteľňa (Slovak Savings Bank) or the Investičná banka (Investment Bank), where you'll be charged a standard 1% commission.

Credit cards are widely accepted. Some of the larger branches of major banks give cash advances on credit cards. ATMs (bankomat) are widespread.

POST

Poste restante mail can be sent to major post offices in larger cities and will be kept for one month; take your passport for identification.

TELEPHONE

Slovakia's country code is ☎ 421. When dialling from abroad drop the initial 0 of the area code.

To dial internationally from inside Slovakia, dial ☎ 00, the country code and the number. Phonecards are the easiest, and cheapest, way to phone home. Telecards (www.telecard.sk in Slovak), available in most newsagents, come in denominations of 200Sk and 400Sk and can be used from any phone.

TOURIST INFORMATION

There is an extensive network of **municipal information centres** (Mestské informačné centrum; ☎ 16 186) belonging to the Association of Information Centres of Slovakia (AiCES). The staff speak English, can organise sightseeing tours and guides, and can assist with accommodation. Branches of Satur can also help with accommodation.

VISAS

At time of writing, citizens of most EU countries, Australia, Canada and New Zealand could enter without a visa for up to 90 days. UK citizens could stay for 180 days; US and Italian citizens for 30 days. South Africans require a visa. Slovakia joined the EU in May 2004 and restrictions may become more relaxed – check with your embassy before departure. If you do require a visa, it *must* be bought in advance.

Slovenia

HIGHLIGHTS

- **Piran** Strolling through the romantic Venetian minicity or scuba diving on nearby WWII wrecks (p1052)
- **Bled** Watching the sunset across a bewitching lake from a bar-restaurant perched on the castle ramparts (p1048)
- **Bovec** A raft ride on the surreally blue Soča River or paragliding off Mt Kanin (p1051)
- **Karst caving** Postojna's speleological Disney World with the silent awe of Škocjan's gaping underground gorge (p1051)
- **Best journey** Crossing the magnificent Vršič Pass (p1051) by bus
- **Off-the-beaten track** Metelkova's street-art subculture behind Ljubljana's fairy-tale façade (p1045)

FAST FACTS

- **Area** 20,256 sq km (smaller than Wales)
- **ATMs** Remarkably widespread, even in villages
- **Budget** €25-45 per day
- **Capital** Ljubljana
- **Country code** ☎ 386, international access code 00
- **Famous for** Mountain sports, Lippizaner Horses, plonky Ljutomer Riesling
- **Head of State** Anthon Rop
- **Language** Slovene
- **Money** Tolar (SIT); €1 = 238SIT, UK£1 = 367SIT, US$1 = 196SIT, A$1 = 144SIT
- **Phrases** *Živijo* (hello), *dober dan* (good day), *nasvidenje* (goodbye), *hvala* (thanks),

oprostite (sorry), *lakho poskusim vino?* (may I taste the wine?)
- **Population** 1.9 million
- **Time** GMT/UTC + 1, + 2 in summer
- **Visas** Not required by most visitors. South Africans need one in advance.

TRAVEL HINTS

Excellent tourist information centres have great free maps, savings vouchers, accommodation listings and superb websites – notably www.slovenia-tourism.si. Avoid public transport on Sunday.

ROAMING SLOVENIA

Slovenia's so small you could visit everything from Ljubljana, but it's cost efficient and nicer to add bases in the Julian Alps (Bled, Bohinj Valley, Bovec or Kobarid) and on the coast (Koper or Piran).

Slovenia (Slovenija) is the EU's underappreciated scenic gem. Patchworks of lush emerald meadows are crisscrossed by idyllic yet well-paved rural lanes. Church-crowned villages are reminiscent of picture-book Austria. Soaring grey peaks are hemmed with forests and wild valleys offering an unparalleled choice of affordable, adrenaline-rush sports. Lowland hills are covered with vines and riddled with breathtaking caves. The short, developed coastline offers WWII wreck-diving from the wonderfully preserved Venetian microcity of Piran. Many towns have picturesque Habsburg cores: Ljubljana's is a 'mini-Prague' of stylishly atmospheric street cafés contrasting with an idiosyncratic counterculture centre (Metelkova).

Slovenia isn't cheap but it's fabulously good value. It's safe, compact, friendly and multilingual, with fully up-to-date infrastructure and many more attractions than can possibly be squeezed into this book. Just don't call the country 'Eastern European': geographically, emotionally and spiritually Slovenia is right at the heart of the continent.

HISTORY

Slovenes like to claim they had Europe's first democracy. In the 7th-century Slavic state of Carantania (now Carinthia in Austria), ruling dukes were elected by noblemen and land-holders and invested before the people. It's a model that Thomas Jefferson, via French political theorist Bodin, reputedly used as a reference when writing the American Declaration of Independence.

Unfortunately early Slovene independence didn't last. From the 14th century almost uninterrupted until 1918, Austria controlled Slovenia. After ferocious battles in WWI, the Soča Valley was handed to Italy as Austro-Hungarian postwar reparations. The rest of Slovenia joined fellow *yugo* (southern) Slavs in the Kingdom of Serbs, Croats and Slovenes, later Yugoslavia.

Nazi occupation in WWII was courageously resisted by Slovenian partisans, who ended the war regaining Italian-held areas from Piran to Bovec, though Trst (Trieste) and most of divided Gorica (Gorizia) eventually remained in Italy.

Slovenia was the economic powerhouse of Tito's postwar Yugoslavia. By the 1980s the federation was becoming increasingly Serb-dominated and Slovenes feared losing their political autonomy. After free elections

and careful planning that contrasted markedly with Croatia's haste, Slovenia broke away on 25 June 1991. A 10-day war followed but Milošević's rump Yugoslavia swiftly signed a truce and concentrated on bashing Croatia. Slovenia was admitted to the UN in May 1992, and joined the EU on 1 May 2004.

PEOPLE & CULTURE

The population is relatively homogeneous (88% ethnic Slovene), with Croat, Serbian and Bosnian minorities and small, long-term enclaves of Italians and Hungarians. The majority are at least nominally Roman Catholic. Generally, there's little of the interethnic tension which has plagued other former Yugoslav republics, although some reports estimate that there are 130,000 'erased' long-term residents who controversially lost all passport rights by failing to register after independence.

Slovenes are ethnically Slavic, typically multilingual, and friendly without being pushy, and they miraculously manage to combine a Germanic work ethic with a Mediterranean, easy-going *joie de vivre*.

ARTS

Slovenia's best-loved writer is the Romantic poet France Prešeren (1800–49). The writer's lyric poetry helped to raise national consciousness.

You'll notice Ljubljana's recurring pyramid motifs and many other idiosyncratic touches; these were added by celebrated Slovenian architect Jože Plečnik (1872–1957), who learnt his trade working on Prague's Hradčany castle.

Slovenia's vibrant music scene embraces rave, techno, jazz, punk, thrash-metal and *chanson* (eg Vita Mavrič). There's also a folk-music revival: listen out for Katice and Ljoba Jenče (http://users.volja.net/folkslo /people.htm). The controversial contemporary art collective Neue Slowenische Kunst

READING UP

Backgrounders to the present-day country are often out of print, but you should be able to find *Independent Slovenia*, edited by Jill Benderley and Evan Kraft, and *Making a New Nation: The Formation of Slovenia*, by Danica Fink-Hafner and John R Robbins. Laura Silber and Allan Little's superlative *The Death of Yugoslavia* is an essential reference for the region's recent history. In one essay in *Balkan Express*, Slavenka Drakulić gives a rather telling account of her time as a Croatian refugee in Ljubljana.

SLOVENIA

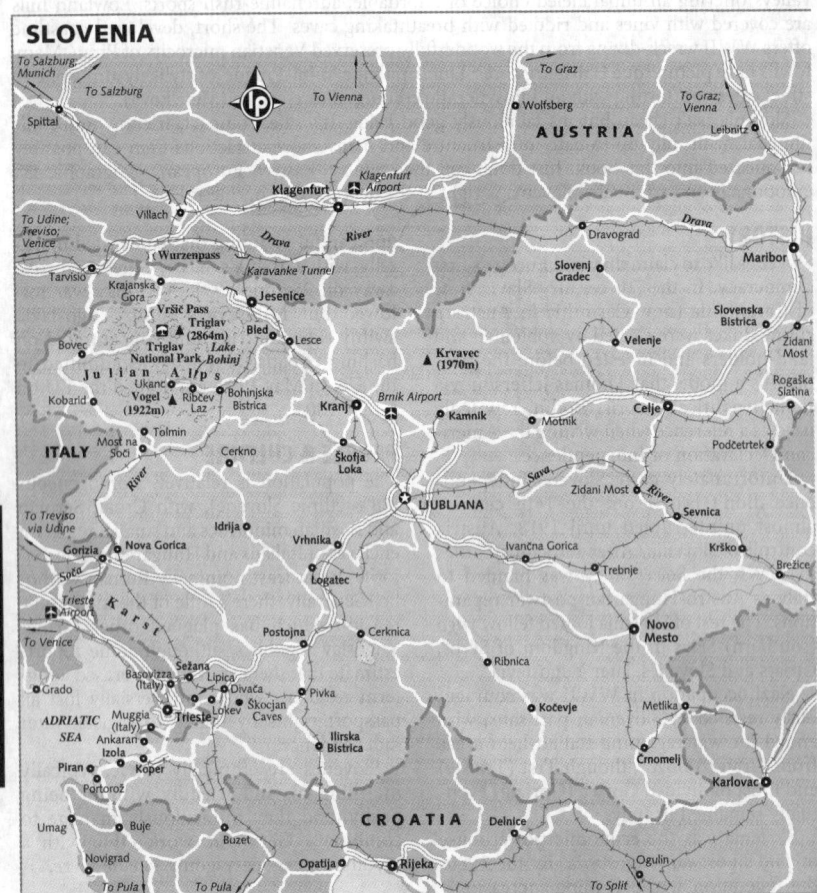

SLOVENIA

(NSK) embraces politically edged painting and physical theatre and spawned the industrial 'music' group Laibach (www.laibach .nsk.si).

Damjan Kozole's 2004 film *Spare Parts* was a pan-European cinematic hit. However, its artistically depressing imagery is part of the movie's message. Don't be discouraged from scenic Slovenia by Krško, the nuclear-power-station town from which the main characters hail!

ENVIRONMENT
Slovenia is amazingly green. It is home to 2900 plant species, and in April patches of the widespread, variegated forests burst gloriously into blossom. Triglav National Park

is particularly rich in indigenous mountain flowers. Living deep in the Karst caves, endemic 'living fossils' *Proteus anguinus* are cute, blind, four-legged salamanders that can survive for years without eating. See some at Postojna (p1051).

TRANSPORT

GETTING THERE & AWAY
Air
Slovenia's national airline, **Adria Airways** (☎ 01-231 3312; www.adria.si; Kuzmičeva 7, Ljubljana), flies to Ljubljana from more than 20 European cities, some code-sharing with Lufthansa, Air France and Austrian. **Czech Airlines** (ČSA

☎ 04-206 1750; www.csa.cz), with an office at the airport , has good-value flights via Prague, but the cheapest direct option is usually low-cost carrier **easyJet** (www.easyjet.com) from London Stansted (from £16.99) and Berlin Shönefeld (from €4.99).

For Piran and the Soča Valley it's handier to use northeast Italian airports. **Trieste airport** (www.aeroporto.fvg.it) has direct if infrequent buses (€2.20, 15 minutes) to Gorizia/Novo Gorica. From **Treviso airport** (www.trevisoairport.it) take bus No 6 (€0.80) to Treviso Centrale,

then a train (€6.90, two hours, generally every two hours) to Gorizia. Both are served by low-cost **Ryanair** (www.ryanair.com), with Internet fares starting at €3.99, which also flies to Graz and Klagenfurt, just across the Slovenian border in Austria. Klagenfurt has cheap flights to several German cities on **Hapag-Lloyd Express** (www.hlx.com).

Boat

Venezialines (☎ 041 24 24 000; www.venezialines.com) catamarans link Venice to Piran (one-way/return €42/65, 2¼ hours) from mid-April until late September, while the **Prince of Venice** (☎ 05 617 8000; portoroz@kompas.si; Obala 41, Portorož) travels from Venice to Izola from March until October (10,800SIT to 14,000SIT). Both operate between one and four times a week. The **Marina** (www.jadroagent .hr) sails from Koper to Zadar in Croatia (5500SIT, 14 hours, weekly mid-June to early September).

Bus

The international bus destinations from Ljubljana include Frankfurt (18,400SIT, 12 hours, 7.30pm) via Munich (8300SIT, 6¾ hours), Sarajevo (8250SIT, 10 hours, 7.15pm Monday, Wednesday and Friday), Split (6550SIT, 10½ hours, 7.40pm) via Rijeka (2280SIT, 2½ hours), and Zagreb (3070SIT, three hours, 2.30am, 7.30am and 8.40am) via attractive Novo Mesto.

As well as one direct Ljubljana–Trieste service (2360SIT, 6.25am Monday to Saturday), there are regular Koper–Trieste buses (610SIT/€3, one hour, nine daily) from Monday to Saturday.

From Koper, buses also serve destinations in Croatia, including Rijeka (2000SIT, 10.10am Monday to Friday), Rovinj (3.55pm daily June to September), Pula (2700SIT, 2pm daily) via Poreč (1700SIT) and Poreč only (notably at 7.30am Monday to Friday).

Train

The daily trains from Ljubljana to Vienna (12,979SIT, 6¼ hours) via Graz (6761SIT) are expensive. Save money by going first to Maribor (1660SIT). Buy a Maribor–Graz ticket (2665SIT, 1¼ hours, six daily) then continue on domestic tickets from Graz to Vienna (€13.50, 2¾ hours). Similar savings also apply via Jesenice and Villach and/or Klagenfurt.

TOP FIVE SLOVENIA

- **Festival** Carnival at Ptuj (p1055)

- **Clubbing area** Start on Ljubljana's old town waterfront, drink your way up Stari trg, and finish in Metelkova (p1047)

- **Impressive sight** The flimsy bridge across the gaping chasm within the Škocjan Caves (p1051)

- **Walk** Strolling around Bled Castle terrace with the view across the picture-perfect lake at sunset (p1048)

- **Heart-attack inducement** Canyoning around Bovec (p1051)

Three trains daily depart Ljubljana for Munich (from 15,199SIT, 6¾ hours). The 11.30pm departure has sleeping carriages available.

Ljubljana–Trieste–Venice trains leave at 2.50am (7945SIT, 6½ hours) or at 10.25am (more expensive, 3¾ hours). It is vastly cheaper to go first to Novo Gorica (1570SIT), walk to Gorizia, then take an Italian train to Venice (€7.90, 2¼ hours).

To get to Zagreb (Croatia) there are two direct trains each day from both Maribor (3331SIT, 2¾ hours) and Ljubljana (2739SIT, 2½ hours). Several trains serve Rijeka (Croatian coast) from Ljubljana (2665SIT, 2½ hours) via Postojna. Ljubljana–Budapest trains (three daily) go via Ptuj and Hodoš (14,854SIT, 8¾ hours) or via Maribor and Graz (17,124SIT, 9½ hours, 2am). The 9.05pm train to Thessaloniki in Greece (19,912SIT, 25 hours) goes via Belgrade (9450SIT, nine hours).

Seat reservations cost 800SIT. The website of **Slovenske Železnice** (Slovenian Railways; www.slo-zeleznice.si) is the best source of detailed railway information, although for most

EMERGENCY NUMBERS

- **Ambulance, fire brigade** ☎ 112

- **Automobile assistance or information (AMZS)** ☎ 530 5300

- **Police** ☎ 113

- **Road emergency or towing** ☎ 1987

international services it redirects you to a German site. At the time of research, online bookings weren't available.

GETTING AROUND

Trains are usually cheaper but less frequent than buses. Beware, however, that frequency on both drops off very significantly on weekends and in school holidays.

Bus

For the very useful **online bus timetable** (www.ap-ljubljana.si), enter destination and *then* departure point. It's worth booking longer-distance buses ahead, especially for Friday afternoon travel. Many buses charge 360SIT per bag for luggage.

Car & Bicycle

Renting a car is recommended and can even save you money as you can access cheaper out-of-centre hotels and farm/village" homestays. Daily rates usually start at €45, with unlimited mileage, collision-damage waiver and theft protection. However, **Hertz** (☎ 01-234 4646; www.hertz.si), beside the Ljubljana bus station, currently offers a tiny Smart at €22, and some Ljubljana hostels advertise Skoda Favourites from €19. Unleaded 95-octane petrol *(bencin)* costs only 193SIT to 196SIT per litre. Keep sidelights on even in daylight.

Bicycles are available for hire at a few train stations, tourist information centres, agencies and hotels.

Hitching

Hitchhiking is fairly common and perfectly legal in Slovenia except on motorways and a few major highways. Even young women do it, but it is never completely safe, of course, and Lonely Planet doesn't recommend that people hitchhike.

Train

Slovenske Železnice (☎ 01-291 3332; www.slo-zeleznice.si; ☯ 5am-10pm) has a useful online timetable that's in Slovene but is easy to use. A useful, scenic railway line from Bled Jezero train station via Bohinjska Bistrica (Bohinj Valley) cuts under roadless mountains to Most na Soči (for Kobarid) then down the Soča Valley to Nova Gorica. Buy tickets before boarding or you'll incur a 200SIT supplement.

LJUBLJANA

☎ 01 / pop 269,800

Inspiring Ljubljana has a small but charming old core, a vibrant street-café culture, a buzzing student community and an alternative-lifestyle centre at Metelkova. Viewed from Ljubljana Castle, the less exciting skirt of concrete suburbs is overshadowed by a magnificent alpine horizon that seems almost leaping distance from the ramparts.

The city was allegedly founded by Golden Fleece–stealing Argonauts, but if so, they left no proof of their sojourn. The later Roman city of Emona was wrecked by the Huns, rebuilt by Slavs and took its present form (as Laibach) under the Austrian Habsburgs, with a brief spell as Napoleon's Illyrian capital. Some fine Art Nouveau buildings filled up the holes left by an 1895 earthquake. Although the city may lack big-name attractions, the great galleries, atmospheric bars and varied, accessible nightlife make it tempting to while away the weeks here.

ORIENTATION

Ljubljana radiates out from the compact old city area that is focused on the Triple Bridge at the base of the castle hill. Most attractions as well as the train and bus stations are within easy walking distance, but much of the cheaper accommodation is a bus ride away, and the airport is 23km north of town at Brnik.

GETTING INTO TOWN

Prešernov trg, the old-city centre, is an easy 10-minute stroll south down Miklošičeva cesta from the joint train and bus stations on Trg Osvobodilne Fronte. Walk a similar distance east to reach the Celica Hostel. See p1047 for information on buses from the airport.

INFORMATION
Bookshops
Geonavtik (www.geonavtik.com in Slovene; Slovenska c 6; ☼ 8.30am-8.30pm Mon-Fri, 8.30am-4pm Sat) Stocks Lonely Planet guides.

Kod-&-Kam (Trg francoske revolucije 7; ☼ 9am-7pm Mon-Fri, 8am-1pm Sat) Map specialist.

Discount Card
The three-day **Ljubljana Card** (3000SIT), available from the Ljubljana tourist information centre, gives free city transport and various discounts but only big museum fans will recoup the cost.

Discount Tokens
Although they are mainly aimed at rural tourism, tokens from the *Guide to Slovenia's Byways* booklet (available free on request from tourist information centres) provide several Ljubljana discounts.

Internet Access
Kotiček (Bus Station, Trg Osvobodilne Fronte; per 10 min 100SIT; ☼ 7am-8.30pm)

Napotnice.com (Trg Ajdovščina 1; per 15 min 200SIT; ☼ 8am-11pm) Small café in the City Centre minimall above Pelican Pub.

Xplorer (Petkovškovo nab 23; per 5 min 110SIT, per hr 800SIT; ☼ 10am-10pm Mon-Fri, noon-10pm Sat & Sun) Good connection, discounts 20% before noon, 10% for students.

Left Luggage
Bus station (Trg Osvobodilne Fronte; per day 320SIT; ☼ 5am-8.30pm)

Train station (Trg Osvobodilne Fronte ; 400SIT or €2; ☼ 24hr) Coin lockers on platform No 1.

Medical Services
Klinični Center (☎ 232 3060; Bohoričeva ul 9; ☼ 24hr) Emergency clinic.

Money
There are ATMs at every turn, including in both train and bus stations, where you'll also find **currency-exchange booths** (☼ 6am-10pm). Dozens of banks change money and travellers cheques.

Gorenska Banka (Dalmatinova ul; ☼ 9-11.30am & 2-5pm Mon-Fri, 8-11am Sat)

Post
Post office (☎ 426 4668; Slovenska cesta 32; ☼ 7am-8pm Mon-Fri, 7am-1pm Sat) Holds poste restante for 30 days.

Tourist Information
Ljubljana Tourist Information Centre (www.ljubljana-tourism.si) Stritarjeva ul (☎ 306 1215; Stritarjeva ul 2; ☼ 8am-9pm Jun-Sep, 8am-7pm Oct-May); Train Station (☎ 433 9475; Trg Osvobodilne Fronte; ☼ 8am-10pm Jun-Sep, 10am-7pm Oct-May) The main office is at Stritarjeva ul.

SLOVENIA

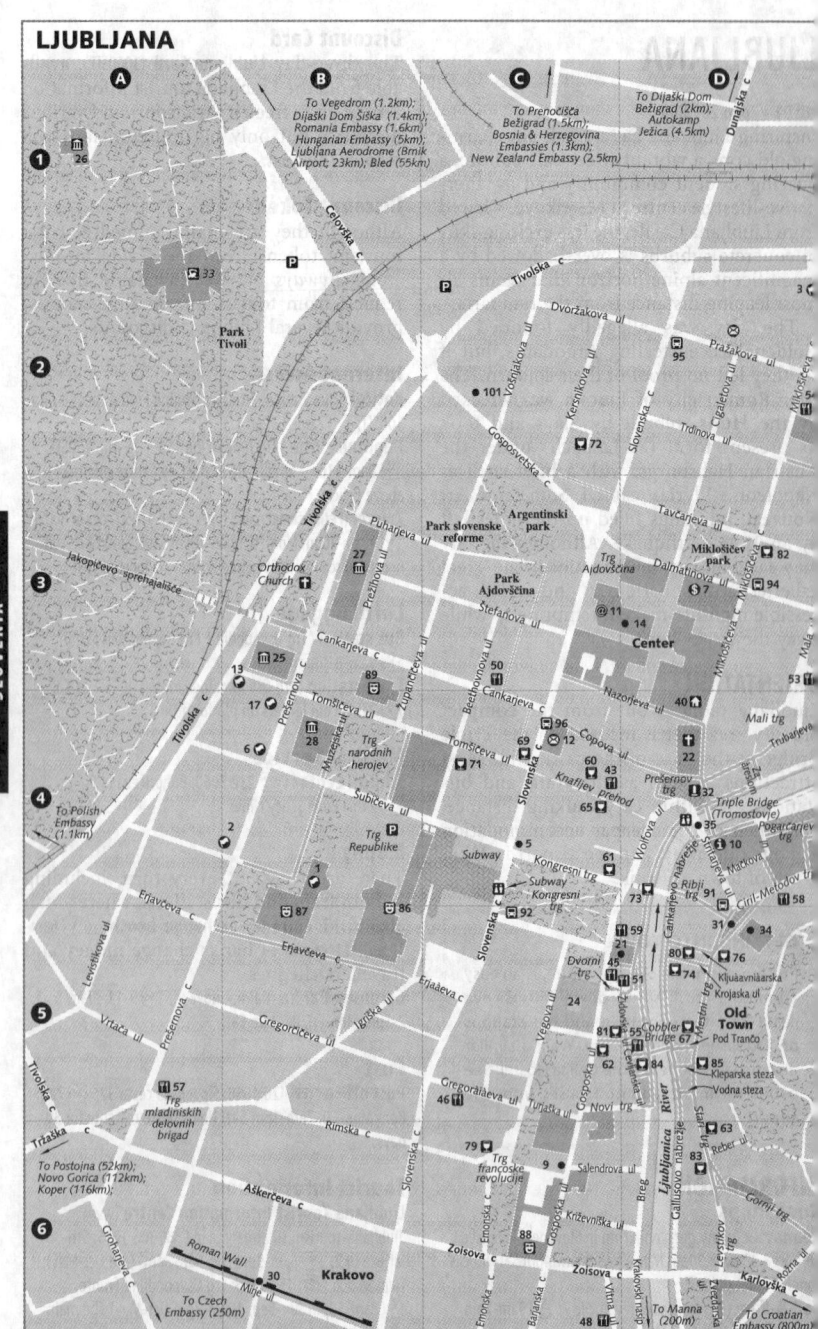

LJUBLJANA

A   **B**   **C**   **D**

To Vegedrom (1.2km);
Dijaški Dom Šiška (1.4km);
Romania Embassy (1.6km);
Hungarian Embassy (5km);
Ljubljana Aerodrome (Brnik
Airport; 23km); Bled (55km)

To Prenočišča
Bežigrad (1.5km);
Bosnia & Herzegovina
Embassies (1.3km);
New Zealand Embassy (2.5km)

To Dijaški Dom
Bežigrad (2km);
Autokamp
Ježica (4.5km)

Park
Tivoli

Orthodox
Church

Park slovenske
reforme

Argentinski
park

Park
Ajdovščina

Miklošičev
park

Center

Trg
Ajdovščina

Trg narodnih
heroji

Trg
Republike

Subway

Subway
Kongresni
trg

Kongresni trg

Triple Bridge
(Tromostovje)

Prešernov
trg

Dvorni
trg

Old
Town

Cobbler's
Bridge

Pod Tranča

Kleparska steza
Vodna steza

Trg
francoske
revolucije

Trg
mladinskih
delovnih
brigad

To Polish
Embassy
(1.1km)

To Postojna (52km);
Novo Gorica (112km);
Koper (116km);

Krakovo

Roman Wall

To Czech
Embassy (250km)

To Manna
(200m)

To Croatian
Embassy (800m)

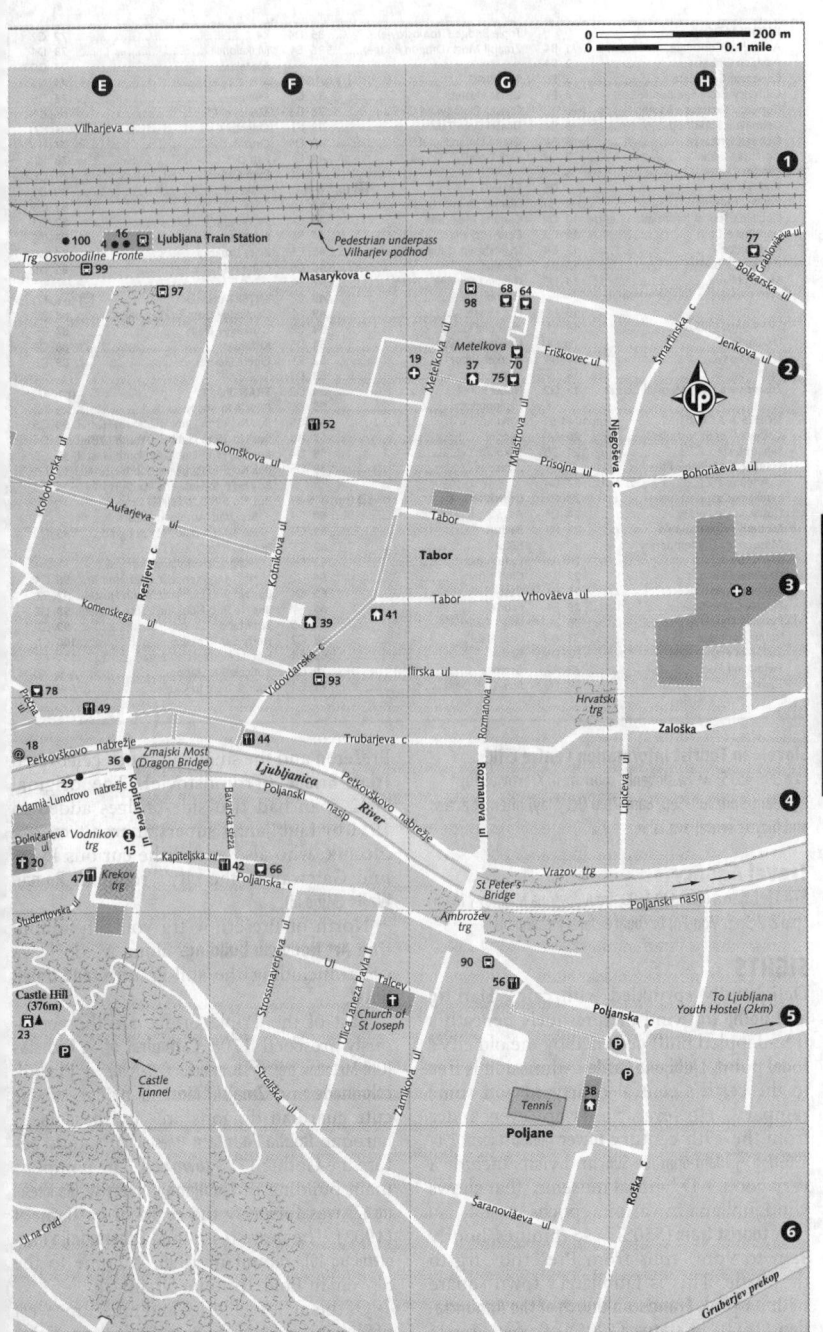

SLOVENIA

Slovenian Tourist Information Centre (STIC; ☎ 306 4575; www.slovenia-tourism.si; Krekov ul 10; ⏲ 8am-9pm Jun-Sep, 8am-7pm Oct-May) Internet access and bicycle rental available.

Travel Agency

STA Ljubljana (☎ 439 1690; Trg Ajdovščina Mall; ⏲ 10am-1pm & 2-5pm Mon-Fri) Discount airfares for students.

SIGHTS

Delightfully sprinkled with cafes, **Stari trg** and **Gornji trg** wind picturesquely beneath a tree-dappled bluff crowned by the old city's focal point, **Ljubljana Castle**. Admission is free to the castle's central courtyard and some ramparts. However, views are even better from the 19th-century **tower** (adult/student 790/490SIT; ⏲ 10am-6pm Tue-Sun) and visits include a very good 3-D 'virtual museum' that shows you Ljubljana in various epochs.

A **tourist tram** (550SIT, 15 minutes, hourly 9am to 9pm) runs from Prešernov trg to the castle. This is Ljubljana's town square with its pink **Franciscan church of the Annunciation** (1660), a **statue** (1905) of poet France

Prešeren and the small but much celebrated **Triple Bridge** (Tromostovje). The original 1842 span had two side-bridges added in 1931 by Ljubljana's superstar architect Jože Plečnik, who also added the curious Pyramid Gateway to the city's remnant **Roman Walls** (Mirje ul).

North of Prešernov trg you can admire fine **Art Nouveau buildings** along Miklošičeva cesta, including the still-grand **Grand Union Hotel**.

East of the Triple Bridge are the generously frescoed 1708 **Cathedral of St Nicholas** (Ciril-Metodov trg; ⏲ 8am-noon & 3-7pm), a Plečnik **colonnade** and **Zmajski Most**, a bridge whose cute guardian dragons are city mascots. A baroque **Robba Fountain** (Mestni trg) stands before the Gothic 1718 **town hall**. The pompous main building of **Ljubljana University** (Kongresni trg 12) was formerly the regional parliament (1902). The more restrained **Filharmonija** (Kongresni trg 10), rebuilt in 1898, is home to the Slovenian Philharmonic Orchestra.

Of the major galleries and museums west of Slovenska cesta, the best are the impressive

National Gallery (☎ 241 5434; www.ng-slo.si; Prešernova cesta 24; adult/student 800/600SIT, admission free Sat afternoon; ⊙ 10am-6pm Tue-Sun), the vibrant though outwardly dowdy **Modern Art Museum** (☎ 251 4106; www.mg-lj.si; Cankarjeva 15; adult/student 1000/700SIT; ⊙ 10am-6pm Tue-Sat, 10am-1pm Sun) and the quiet **Museum of Contemporary History** (☎ 300 9610; www .muzej-nz.si; Park Tivoli; adult/student 500/300SIT; ⊙ 10am-6pm Tue-Sat) with its imaginative economic glance at 20th-century Slovenia.

The **National Museum** (Muzejska ul 1; adult/student 1000/700SIT; ⊙ 10am-6pm Fri-Wed, 10am-8pm Thu) occupies an elegant 1888 building but is partially closed for long-term renovation.

Metelkova, an ex-army garrison taken over by squatters after independence, is now a somewhat daunting, free-living commune – a miniature version of Copenhagen's Christiania. To get the real 'feel' of Metelkova, about 500m east of the train and bus stations, visit after midnight Thursday to Saturday (see p1046). A tour of Metelkova's ultrahip **Celica Hostel** (☎ /fax 430 1890; www .souhostel.com; Metelkova 8; admission free; ⊙ 2pm) is intriguing even if you're staying there.

SLEEPING

Celica Hostel (☎ /fax 430 1890; www.souhostel.com; Metelkova 8; dm/s/d 3500/7000/9500SIT; ▣) This stylishly revamped former prison has designer 'cells' complete with original bars and a packed-full, popular dorm. Check-in starts at 3pm but advance bookings (advisable) are usually only held till 5pm. Discounts (5%) come with Ljubljana Cards, tourist information centre tokens from the *Byways* booklet, or VIP Backpackers membership, but not International Youth Hostel Association (IYHA) membership. Surcharges include 500SIT for one-night stays and another 500SIT for being unfashionably over 35 years old. Laundry costs 1200SIT per load. Free Internet access is available.

Ljubljana Youth Hostel (BIT Center Hotel; ☎ 548 0055; www.bit-center.net; Litijska 57; dm/s/tr 2990/6790/ 9590SIT, breakfast 800SIT; Ⓟ) Smart new IYHA dorms and functionally modern rooms with bathroom are adjacent to the large BIT sports centre, 3km east of centre. Take bus No 5, 9 or 13 to Emona; the entrance is off Pesarska cesta.

Prenočišča Bežigrad (☎ 231 1559; www.preno cisca-bezigrad.com; Podmilščakova ul 51; s/d/tr 7000/ 10,000/13,000SIT without breakfast) Bright, new well-equipped rooms off hospital-style corridors

are good value, despite the road noise and semi-industrial location. It is roughly 3km north of the old city centre, accessible on bus No 14.

Park Hotel (☎ 433 1306; www.hotelpark.si; Tabor 9; s €45-49, d €58-63) This tower block has pleasant, recently renovated rooms in a handily central if rather uninviting area. Cheaper rooms have a toilet but share showers.

Autokamp Ježica (☎ 568 3913; Dunjask 270; camping Jun-Aug/off season 2262/1892SIT; ⚑) This attractively tree-shaded camping ground is 4.5km north of the train and bus stations but easily reached on bus No 8 to the terminus or the more frequent No 6 (both stop across the road from the camp-site gates).

Several fairly spartan student hostels with shared bathrooms accept guests in summer. Breakfast isn't included. The most central are **Dijaški Dom Tabor** (☎ 234 8840; ssljddta1s@guest.arnes .si; b per person €17-20; ⊙ Jul & Aug), entered from Kotnikova ul, and **Dijaški Dom Ivana Cankarja** (☎ 474 8600; dd.lj-ic@guest.arnes.si; Poljanska cesta 26B; s/d/tr 3960/6520/8580SIT; ⊙ Jul), with 10% student discounts. North of the centre are the less convenient **Dijaški Dom Bežigrad** (☎ 534 2867; dd.lj-bezigrad@guest.arnes.si; Kardeljeva 28; b per person from €12, ⊙ Jul & Aug), reached on bus No 6 or 8, and **Dijaški Dom Šiška** (☎ 500 7804; www.ddsiska .com; Aljaževa 32; beds adult/student €11/9; ⊙ Jun-Aug), near pointy-towered Sv Frančišek Church.

EATING
Self-Catering

The handy minimarkets **Živila** (Kongresni Trg 9; ⊙ 7am-9pm) and **Market Tabor** (Kotnikova 12; ⊙ 7.30am-10pm) open even on Sunday.

Quick Eats

Pinki (☎ 544 1111; Poljanska cesta 22; mains 700-800SIT; ⊙ 6.30am-10pm Mon-Sat) Serving lasagnes, tortillas and pizzas, this cheap and cheerful student-oriented diner also does a 240SIT coffee and doughnut breakfast.

Delikatesen Ljubljana Dvor (Gosposka ul; pizza slices 250-350SIT; ⊙ 9am-midnight Mon-Sat) Big, bargain pizza slices, salads and by-weight braised vegies to take away or stand and eat.

Nobel Burek (Miklošičeva 30; burek 450SIT) Local fast food available 24 hours.

Paninoteka (Jurčičev trg; sandwiches 450-650SIT; ⊙ 8am-1am Mon-Sat, 9am-11pm Sun) Healthy sandwich creations on olive ciabatta that you eat outside on a lovely little square with castle views.

SLOVENIA

Hot Horse (Trubarjeva 31; snacks 350-800SIT) Fill up with giant 'horse burgers' (700SIT), veggie burgers (400SIT) or sandwiches.

Restaurants

Great restaurants and cafés fill the old town. For cheaper options try Poljanska cesta or snack bars near the train and bus stations.

Sokol (☎ 439 6855; www.gostilna-sokol.com; Ciril-Metodov Trg 18; mains 900-2500SIT; ☻ 6am-11pm) Traditional Slovene food is served on heavy tables in a vaulted old house by costumed waiters who stop just shy of Disneyesque self-parody. Pizzas and vegetarian options are available if sausage and groats don't appeal.

Gostilna Vodnikov Hram (☎ 234 5260; Vodnikov trg 2; mains 1000-1700SIT; ☻ food till 4pm Mon-Sat) Vegetarian and carnivorous lunch specials at 780SIT to 1100SIT are a bargain in this inviting vaulted pub.

Harambaša (☎ 041 675 155; Vlrtna ul 8; mains 850-1000SIT; ☻ 10am-10pm Mon-Fri, noon-10pm Sat, noon-6pm Sun) Bosnian cuisine served at low tables in a charming modern-cottage atmosphere with quiet Balkan music.

Alamut Orient House (☎ 031 545 595; Poljanska cesta 7; mains 850-1500SIT; ☻ 8am-10pm Mon-Sat) Decorated with Persian rugs and Lurish swords, this modest Iranian restaurant is popular with intellectuals and vegetarians.

Puccini (☎ 426 9136; Trg Mladiniskih Delovnih Brigad; mains 1040-1720SIT; ☻ 11am-10pm Mon-Sat, noon-5pm Sun) Great pastas and salad bar in an old house with sepia photos and curious door-ceilings.

Pre-eminent pizzerias include riverfront **Ljubljanski Dvor** (☎ 251 6555; Dvorni trg 1), warmly vaulted **Foculus** (☎ 251 5643; www.foculus.com; Gregorčičeva ul 3), good-value **Napoli** (☎ 231 2949; Prečna ul 7) and trusty **Čerin** (☎ 232 0990; Trubarjeva 52), which has bargain lunch menus before 3pm.

Joe Pena's (☎ 251 0868; Cankarjeva 6; mains 1800-2800SIT) is Ljubljana's best, mood-lit Mexican restaurant, though luridly colourful **Cantina Mexicana** (☎ 426 9325; Knafljev prehod) has a fabulous sofa-and-lantern terrace ideal for a prandial margarita.

DRINKING

Few cities have Ljubljana's concentration of fabulously inviting cafés, bars and street terraces. Unless noted, those listed below open daily till late and charge 160SIT to 200SIT for an espresso, 300SIT to 350SIT for small

beers, and 900SIT to 1000SIT for cocktails. Just choose the ambience that appeals.

Classics on the willow-banked riverside include **Maček** (Cankarjevo nab 19; ☻ happy hour 4-7pm) and **Zlata Ladjica** (Jurčičev trg) with DJs at weekends. Quaint olde-style places include **Café Antico** (Stari trg), wood-panelled **Roza** (Židovska 6) and patisseries like **Čajna Hisa** (Stari trg 3; ☻ 9am-11pm Mon-Sat) and **Slaščičarna Privodnjaku** (Stari trg 30).

For *Clockwork Orange* designer cool, try **Fraga Gallery-Bar** (Mestni trg 15) or audacious, white-on-white **Minimal** (Mestni trg 4; small beers 450SIT). Anglo-Irish pubs include **Patrick's** (Prečna ul 6), **Sir William's** (Tavčarjeva 8A; ☻ closed Sun) or ever-popular **Cutty Sark** (Knafljev prehod).

BiKoFe (Gosposka 7) has a soft jazz cool attracting both straight and gay clientele. At **Pr'skelet** (Ključavničarska 5; ☻ 10am-1am), skeletons enjoy all-day two-for-one cocktails in an amusing 'Rocky Horror' basement. **Makalonca** (Hribarjevo nab) is an unpretentious cult bar on a glassed-in jetty down easy-to-miss steps. The wonderful **Petit Café** (Trg francoske revolucije 4) transports you to Montmartre.

For something less polished, try the bars of traffic-blighted Poljanska cesta, where **Fabrika** (Poljanska 9; cocktails from 500SIT) is a joyously grungy club/bar popular with students. Many backpackers are so enchanted by the Celica Hostel's **Oriental Café** (☎ /fax 430 1890; www.souhostel.com; Metelkova 8) they forget to explore Metelkova.

CLUBBING

Global (☎ 426 9020; Tomšičeva 2; admission 1000SIT after midnight; ☻ 8am-4am Tue-Sat) After 11pm this retro cocktail bar with Ljubljana's best city views becomes a popular dance venue. Take the bouncer-guarded lift on Slovenska cesta to the top.

K4 (☎ 438 0261; www.klubk4.org in Slovene; Kersnikova ul 4; ☻ 10pm-4am) Two stark cellar-room dance floors beneath the student organisation (enter from rear) feature rave electronic music Friday and Saturday (admission 1000SIT to 1500SIT), with other styles weeknights and a popular gay and lesbian night on Sunday (admission 500SIT after 11pm).

Bachus (☎ 241 8244; www.bachus-center.com) This weekend disco cavern is part of a smart-trendy, bar-restaurant complex.

As (☎ 425 8822; www.gostilnaas.si; Knafljev prehod ☻ 9am-3am) From Thursday to Saturday DJs metamorphose a candle-lit basement bar beneath this incongruously upmarket restaurant into a pumping, crowd-pulling nightclub.

Jazz Club Gajo (☎ 425 3206; www.jazzclubgajo.com; Beethovnova ul 8; admission free; ☺ 11am-2am Mon-Fri, 7pm-midnight Sat & Sun, closed mid-Jul–mid-Aug) For Monday night student jams, midweek concerts or just a convivial drink, the Gajo is always inviting.

Metelkova (www.metelkova.org) Half-a-dozen wonderfully idiosyncratic venues hide behind unmarked doors, coming to life after midnight from Thursday to Saturday. You might well feel uncomfortable amid the street art, graffiti and shadow-lurking youth gangs but don't be scared. Entering from Masarykova cesta, to the right is **Gala Hala** (www.ljudmila.org/kapa /program), with live bands and club nights. Easy to miss on the left are Club Tiffany (gay café-club) and Monokel Club (for lesbians). Beyond the first courtyard, well-hidden Gromka (folk, improv comedy theatre – anything possible) is beneath the bodyless heads. Close by, a purloined blue-arrow road sign marks marvellously grungy Mariĉo (psycho-blues). Cover charges are rare.

Orto Bar (☎ 232 1674; Grabloviĉeva ul 1) Popular for late-night drinking and dancing. With occasional live music, the Orto has red padded walls, whirring steel-propeller fans and a taste for Joy Division.

ENTERTAINMENT

Pamphlets *Ljubljana Calling* (www.ljubljana -calling.com) and Where to? In Ljubljana list cultural events, sports and nightlife options. Glossy *Ljubljana Life* (www.ljubljanalife .com) has some refreshingly frank reviews. All are free from tourist information centres, hotels and certain restaurants.

The most active venue is the multipurpose **Cankarjev Dom** (www.cd-cc.si; Trg Republike), whose basement **ticket office** (☎ 241 7100) lurks within Maximarket Mall. Also check for concerts at the beautiful **Filharmonija** (Kongresni trg) and for ballets at the **Opera House** (☎ 425 4840; Županĉiĉeva ul). **Kriĵanke** (☎ 252 6544; Trg francoske revolucije) stages part of the **Ljubljana Summer Festival** (www.festival-lj.si) in a former ruined monastery.

GETTING THERE & AWAY

Bus

The shedlike **bus station** (Avtobusna postaja; ☎ 234 1600; www.ap-ljubljana.si; Trg Osvobodilne Fronte 4;

☺ 5.30am-9pm) has bilingual info-phones and its web timetable (enter destination first) is very useful. Hourly buses serve Bohinj Valley (1940SIT, two hours) through Bled (1400SIT, 1¼ hours). Most buses to Piran (2670SIT, three hours, up to eight daily) go via Koper (2460SIT, 2½ hours, 10 daily) and Postojna (1320SIT, 1¼ hours, 20 daily). Most Maribor buses (2760SIT, three hours, seven daily) leave in the afternoon. All services are much less frequent at weekends.

Train

Ljubljana train station (☎ 291 3332; www.slo-zeleznice .si; Trg Osvobodilne Fronte) has four daily trains to Koper (2½ hours). These cost 1980SIT at 9.30am and 4.45pm (with InterCity surcharge – see following) but only 1660SIT at 8.50am and 3.25pm. There are up to 19 daily services to Maribor (1660SIT to 2790SIT, 1¾ to 2¾ hours) but for Bled and Novo Gorica the bus is more convenient. A 320SIT surcharge is added for domestic InterCity services. Check the website for more details.

GETTING AROUND

The cheapest way to **Brnik airport** (☎ 04-206 1000; www.lju-airport.si) is by city bus from bus-station lane No 28 (740SIT, 45 minutes). These run hourly from 5.10am till 8.10pm Monday to Friday but only seven times daily at weekends. Another seven Marun/Adria coaches (1000SIT, 30 minutes) run daily. Big hotels offer an **airport shuttle** (per person/car 2500/8800SIT).

If you're staying out of the centre, Ljubljana has excellent city buses, with most lines operating every 10 to 20 minutes from 3.15am to midnight. Buy tokens in advance (180SIT) from newsstands or pay 250SIT once aboard.

In summer you can rent bicycles at the train station, at the **Hotel Lev** (Vošnjakova 1), at a kiosk near **Maĉek café** (Cankarjevo nab) and for free from the **STIC** (☎ 306 4575; www.slovenia-tourism.si; Krekov ul 10; ☺ 8am-9pm Jun-Sep, 8am-7pm Oct-May).

JULIAN ALPS

Dramatic rocky mountain spires straddle the Italian border. Within Slovenia these 'Julian Alps' (named for Julius Caesar) climax at tripeaked Mt Triglav (2864m), the country's highest summit. Along with neighbouring mountains, forests and breathtakingly beautiful valleys, the area forms the Triglav National Park. At weekends half of Ljubljana's population decamps here to ski, cycle, fish, climb or hike between mountain huts. There are adventure sports to suit every level of insanity, especially from Bovec, and few places in Europe offer better rafting, paragliding or canyoning at such affordable prices.

BLED

☎ 04 / pop 5467

Genteel, millennium-old Bled is the gateway to the mountains. Idyllically set on a 2km-long subalpine lake, it's a delightful place to stroll and gaze, but in midsummer the beauty is a bit diluted by ever-expanding crowds and prices.

Information

Several banks have ATMs.

Kompas (Bled Shopping Centre; ☻ 9am-7pm) Sells maps, rents bicycles, offers tours and changes money.

Tourist information centre (☎ 574 1122; www .bled.si; ☻ 9am-7pm Mon-Sat, 11am-4pm Sun) On the lakefront near the Hotel Park.

Union 99 (www.union-bled.com; Ljubljanska cesta 9; per 15 min 270SIT; ☻ 8am-midnight) Internet access.

Sights

On its own romantically tiny island (Blejski Otok), the baroque **Church of the Assumption** (admission free) is Bled's photogenic trademark. Getting there by piloted 'gondola' (*plenta*; per person €10, 1½ hours return) is the archetypal tourist experience. Gondola prices are standard from any jetty and you stay long enough to ring the 'lucky' bell. Ordinary row-yourself boats cost 3000SIT per hour.

Topping a sheer 100m cliff, **Bled Castle** (Blejski Grad; adult/student 1000/600SIT; ☻ 9am-8pm May-Sep, 9am-6pm Oct-Apr) is the perfect backdrop to lake views. A footpath leads up from Bledec Hostel. Admission includes a historical museum section and fabulous views. After official closing time you can get those views for free by having a meal or sunset beer at the superbly situated rampart terrace of the Castle Restaurant (see below).

Activities

Allow around two hours to stroll around the lake and climb to the **Osojnica viewpoints** for perfect photos. Another popular walk is to and through the **Vintgar Gorge** (500SIT May-Oct) crisscrossing the fizzing Radovna River on century-old wooden walkways. The tourist office can suggest tougher multiday mountain **hikes** (hut accommodation available) or help you arrange **gliding** (flights from €30) from nearby Lesce aerodrome. What a view!

Sleeping

Bledec Hostel (☎ 574 5250; www.mlino.si; Grajska cesta 17; dm/d €17/42, peak season €19/46, IYHA discount €2; ☐) On the surface a typical *penzion* (smaller, family-style house-hotel), this well-organised youth hostel has new four-bed dorms with attached bathrooms. It's quiet yet very central.

Penzion Zaka (☎ 574 1709; www.bled-zaka.com; Župančičeva 9; s/d Sep-Jun €28/42, Jul & Aug €33/52, breakfast €3) Seven spacious, if unsophisticated, rooms with balconies and kitchenette above the good-value Regatni Center restaurant. Four have lake views.

Penzion Mlino (☎ 574 1404; www.mlino.si; Cesta Svobode 45; s/d Nov-Apr €32/50, May-Oct €37/60) Facing the lake, this is on the Bohinj road 900m southwest of town. Great views of the castle and water counter slightly cramped rooms and *Fawlty Towers*–style breakfast service.

Hotel Jelovica (☎ 579 6000; www.hotel-jelovica.si; Cesta Svobode 8; s/d €39/54, 1 May-15 Sep & 20 Dec-3 Jan €49/74) Centrally located, this decently renovated communist-era resort charges €5 extra for rooms with a glimpse of the lake.

Camping Bled (☎ 575 2000; www.camping.bled.si; per adult Oct-May 1580SIT, Jun & Sep 2080SIT, Jul-25 Aug 2320SIT; ☻ Apr–mid-Oct) This well-kept, popular site fills a rural valley behind a waterside restaurant at the western end of the lake. Mountain bikes (per day 2300SIT) can be hired and management can arrange ballooning, rafting, parachuting and more.

Sobe (private rooms) are offered by dozens of homes. Agencies **Kompas** (☎ 574 1515; Bled Shopping Centre; s/d for 1 night from 4322/6044SIT, 3 nights from 9762/13,524SIT) and similarly priced **Globtour Bled** (☎ 574 1821; www.globtour-bled.com, Hotel Krim, Ljubljanska cesta 7) have extensive lists.

Eating

Castle Restaurant (Restavracija Blejski Grad; ☎ 574 1607; mains 2000-3200SIT; ☻ 9am-10pm) Typical local food is pricey, but the view from the terrace is utterly unbeatable. If you request a table for after the castle's official closing time, you get into the site for free.

BLED

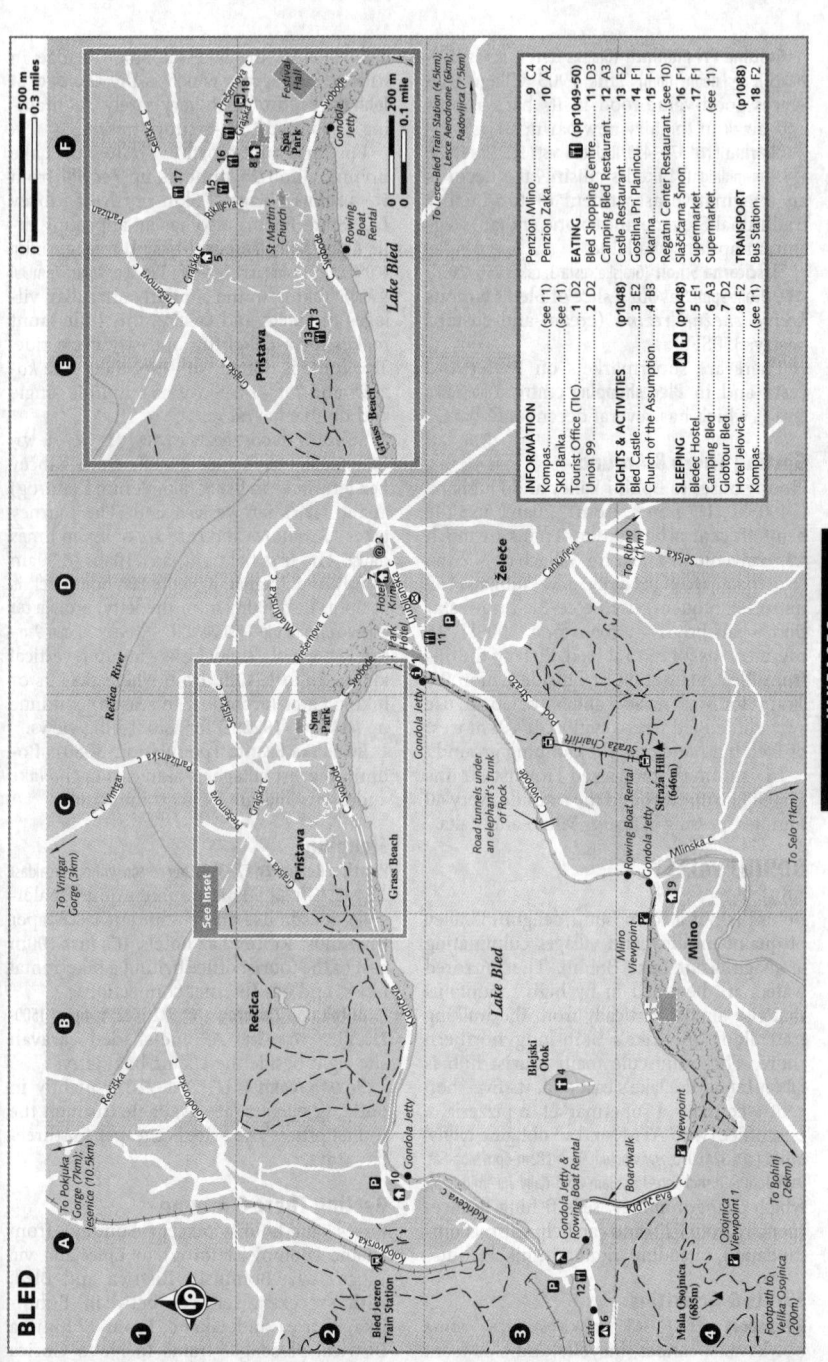

SLOVENIA

Gostilna Pri Planincu (Grajska cesta 8; mains 1200-2000SIT; ☻ noon-10pm) This 1903 village pub serves good-value food in its back rooms and pizza in the airy new bar upstairs.

Okarina (☎ 574 1458; Riklijeva cesta 9; mains €7-20; ☻ 6pm-midnight) Like its cuisine, the décor is an imaginative assortment of top-quality traditional Slovene and exotic Indian. Vegetarian options available.

Slaščičarna Šmon (Grajska cesta 3; cakes 250-400SIT; ☎ 7.30am-9pm) Savour a slice of Bled's famous *krema snežna rezina* (cream-and-custard pastry; 350SIT).

There are supermarkets on Prešernova cesta and in **Bled shopping centre** (Ljubljanska cesta 4), which has several decent café-bars.

Getting There & Around

Hourly buses to Bohinj Valley and Ljubljana (1400SIT, 1½ hours, from 7.20am) use the helpfully central bus station. Trains are much less convenient. Those for Villach or Vienna (Austria, up to eight daily) and Ljubljana (55 minutes, frequent) use Lesce-Bled train station, a half-hourly 4km bus ride (300SIT, 15 minutes) east of central Bled. Pick up the bus from Bled bus station or outside Union 99. Trains for Most na Soči and Nova Gorica use sweet little Bled Jezero station. It's 2km west of Bled but handy for the camping ground.

In summer pint-sized tourist trains (550SIT) trundle round the lakeside every 40 minutes, passing *penzions* Mlino and Zaka.

BOHINJ VALLEY

☎ 04

Bohinj is not a town but a delightful valley of quaint meadowland villages culminating at magnificent Lake Bohinj. The mirrored waters are hemmed in by high mountains that rise almost vertically from the walking trail along the lake's 3km-long northern shore. The minuscule main tourist hub is **Ribčev Laz**, at the lake's east end. Its five-shop centre contains a supermarket, a pizzeria, a post office (with ATM) and an obliging **tourist office** (☎ 574 6010; www.bohinj.si; ☻ 8am-6pm Mon-Sat, 9am-3pm Sun mid-Sep–Jun, 8am-8pm daily Jul–mid-Sep), which changes money, sells fishing licences (per day from €20) and can help with accommodation, including mountain-hikers' huts.

Sights & Activities

Alpinsport (☎ 572 3486; www.alpinsport.si) rents out kayaks, canoes, bicycles and skis from

a kiosk near the lakeside stone bridge in Ribčev Laz, across which is the **Church of St John the Baptist** (open very rarely), containing celebrated 15th-century frescoes.

For brochure-worthy photos of Lake Bohinj, climb 25 minutes up **Peč Hill** from **Stara Fužina** village, 1.5km north of Ribčev Laz. Stara Fužina also has an appealing little **Alpine Dairy Museum** (Planšarski Musej; admission 400SIT; ☻ 10am-noon & 4-6pm Tue-Sun, 11am-7pm Jul & Aug). Taking in the similarly attractive villages of **Studor** and **Češnica**, this little jaunt makes for a delightful but easy cycle ride. The route is dotted with especially fine *kozolci* and *toplarji*, Slovenia's unique single and double hayracks.

Summer **tourist boats** (☎ 041 434 986; one way 1300-1500SIT, return trip 1600-1900SIT) from Ribčev Laz terminate in **Ukanc** (aka Bohinj Zlatorog) at the lake's far western end. The journey takes 15 minutes and runs six or seven times daily. The first boat out is at 10am (8.30am in July and August) and the last boat back is at 6pm. Just 300m from the jetty, a **cable car** (one-way/return trip 1400/2000SIT; ☻ every 30 min 9am-6pm, 8am-8pm Jul & Aug) whisks you up a vertical kilometre to 1540m, from where ski lifts or hiking paths (according to season) continue up **Mt Vogel** (1922m) for astonishing views.

Bohinjska Bistrica (population 3080), Bohinj's biggest village, is 6km east of the lake and useful mainly for its train station.

Sleeping

Penzion Rožic (☎ 572 3393; per person without breakfast 3954-4654SIT; ☐) This unpretentious chalet-style guesthouse and restaurant is cheaper than most Ribčev Laz hotels. It's just 100m east of the tourist office behind a bike-rental kiosk, and has Internet connection.

Autokamp Zlatorog (☎ 572 3482; camping 1500-2200SIT; ☻ May-Sep) A pine-shaded caravan site right beside the Ukanc boat jetty.

Private rooms (s €13-19, d €22-32), mainly in outlying villages, are available through the tourist office. The price is cheaper for three-day stays.

Getting There & Around

Buses run hourly (except Sunday) from Ukanc (Bohinj Zlatorog) to Ljubljana via Ribčev Laz, Bohinjska Bistrica and Bled, with six extra services between Bohinjska Bistrica and Ukanc. From Bohinjska Bistrica, passenger trains to Novo Gorica

(1010SIT, 1½ hours) plus six daily Avtovlak trains to Most na Soči (910SIT, 50 minutes) use a long tunnel that offers the only direct option for reaching the Soča Valley. Avtovlak trains carry cars (2600SIT).

UPPER SOČA VALLEY
☎ 05

The surreal, bluer-than-blue waters of the beautiful Soča River have carved out one of the loveliest valleys in the Julian Alps.

Bovec
pop 1610

For Alpine drama the views are best around Bovec, above which towers Mt Kanin, Slovenia's highest ski area. Bovec's village square (trg Golobarskih Žrtev) has everything you need, including a very helpful **tourist office** (☎ 384 1919; www.bovec.si) and several adrenaline-rush extreme-sports companies: **Planet Sport** (☎ 040 639 433; www.drustvo-planet.si), **Sportmix** (☎ 389 6160; www.sportmix.traftbovec.si), **Top Rafting** (☎ 041 620 636; www.top.si) and the experienced, well-organised **Soča Rafting** (☎ 389 6200; www .socarafting.si). Activities include guided **canyoning** (2-hr tours at Sušec 7900-8700SIT), **hydrospeed** (8km for 6700-7400SIT), **kayaking** (10km with guide from 6500SIT, 2-day training course from €55) and **caving** (with guide from €25). Save 10% to 15% with student cards, the tourist office's *Byways* booklet or just avoid the midsummer and weekends. **Avantura** (☎ 041 718 317) offers awesome tandem-jump paragliding (22,000SIT).

Chalet villages throughout the valley have private-rooms from €12 per person. Contacts are extensively listed on www.bovec .net but finding anything can be very tough in midsummer. **Avrigo Tour agency** (☎ 388 6022; avrigotours.bovec@avrigo.si; Trg Golobarskih Žrtev 47) can often assist. The central **Alp Hotel** (☎ 388 6370; www.bovec.net/hotelalp; s Sep-Jul €36.80-39.80, Aug €45.80; d Sep-Jul €57.20-63.20, Aug €75.20) is smart and good value. Facilities are better in Kobarid but camping ground **Polovnik** (☎ 041 641 898; camping from 1431SIT, showers 120SIT) is handily central.

Kobarid
pop 1240

Nearby **Kobarbid** village (Caporetto in Italian) is quainter than Bovec, albeit set in somewhat tamer woodland scenery. On its main square is extreme-sports agency **XPoint** (☎ 388 5308; www.xpoint.si), Internet-equipped **Bar Cinca Marinca** (Trg Svobode 10; per 30 min 250SIT;

8am-11pm) and renowned **Restaurant Kotlar** (www.kotlar-sp.si; mains 1500-3000SIT; noon-11pm Thu-Mon). The tourist office is within Kobarid's **museum** (adult/student 800/600SIT; 9am-6pm), otherwise mainly devoted to the region's WWI battles. These killed more than 200,000 people and formed the backdrop to Ernest Hemingway's *Farewell to Arms*. The daring Austro-German breakthrough at Kobarid in October 1917 invented 'blitzkrieg'. Remnant WWI troop emplacements as well as Roman and 6th-century archaeological sites can be seen by following a half-day walking loop to impressive **Slap Kozjak** (waterfalls).

Close to the church, **Apartmaji-Sobe Ivančič** (☎ 389 1007; apartma-ra@siol.net; Gregorčičeva 6C; s €18-30SIT, d €30-50SIT) is a popular central homestay that's neat and clean with bathrooms shared between pairs of cheaper rooms.

Lazar Kamp (☎ 388 5333; per adult €6.50-9; Apr-Oct) is probably Slovenia's finest, most welcoming camping ground. Perched idyllically above the Soča, it's 1.7km southeast of Kobarid, halfway to Slap Kozjak. The splendid Wild West–style saloon-café serves delicious *palačinka* (crepes). Try the 'bear's blood'!

Getting There & Away

Public transport is poor. Weekday buses from Bovec via Kobarid run five times daily to Novo Gorica (1670SIT, two hours) and thrice to Ljubljana (3030SIT, 3¾ hours) passing Most na Soči train station (for Bled or Bohinj). In July and August only, six daily buses cross the spectacular Vršič Pass to Kranjska Gora, from where hourly buses continue to Ljubljana.

KARST & COAST

Slovenia's 45km sliver of coastline has no beach worth the name, although that didn't stop Portorož becoming a major resort. The coast's real appeal lies in its charming old Venetian ports, Koper and picture-perfect Piran. En route from Ljubljana you'll cross via Karst (Kras), Slovenia's west-central region, which is synonymous with eccentrically eroded limestone landscapes and riddled with magnificent caves.

POSTOJNA & ŠKOCJAN CAVES
☎ 05

Slovenia's two most famous caves couldn't be more different. An obvious 2km stroll from

SLOVENIA

Postojna town (population 8500), **Postojna Cave** (www.postojnska-jama.si; adult/student 3290/2190SIT) is home to endemic *Proteus anguinus*, cute, eyeless salamanders coined 'human fish'. The cave is filled with endless stalagmites, impressive stalactites and almost as many tourists. One-and-a-half-hour visits (from two to 10 times daily) involve two underground train rides as well as a 1.7km walk with gradients but no steps. Dress up warm or rent a coat (700SIT): inside it's 8°C year-round and train seats may be wet.

The quieter, harder-to-reach **Škocjan Caves** (www.park-skocjanske-jame.si; adult/student 2000/1300SIT) form a Unesco World Heritage site. They're 4km southeast of Divača train station – ask for a free walking map. With few stalactites, the attraction here is an absolutely awesome underground chasm crossed by a dizzying little bridge. Shepherded two-hour visits (10am and 1pm; many more in summer) are on foot, involving hundreds of steps. There's great hiking nearby, signposted from the caves' visitors centre, including an easy, attractive, 20-minute stroll to a viewpoint of the cave mouth.

Sleeping & Eating

Dozens of Postojna houses rent **rooms** (s/d from 4500/7500SIT). Central **Kompas** (☎ 726 4281; info@kompas-postojna.si; Titov trg; ☀ 8am-6pm Mon-Fri, 9am-3pm Sat) or the caveside **tourist office** (www .postojna.si) can help. In rural Predjama village 9km away, the simple **Gostilna Požar** (☎ 751 5252; tw with shared bathroom 7600SIT) faces a unique cave-mouth castle.

In Divača, the modest **Gostilna Risnik** (☎ 763 0008; Kraška 24; s/tw 3500/6000SIT) is 200m northeast of the train station above a smoky bar. The quieter, better **Gostilna Malovec** (☎ 763 1225; Kraška 30A; s/d €20/40) is 300m beyond. Both have restaurants.

Getting There & Around

Ljubljana–Koper buses stop in Postojna (1320SIT, 1¼ hours from Ljubljana) and Divača (1740SIT, 1¾ hours from Ljubljana; 1030SIT, 45 minutes from Koper; up to eight daily) and could drop you off at a junction 1.6km from the signposted Škocjan Caves, though timetables rarely mesh with cave-visit times. Trains (five daily to Divača) are less convenient for Postojna, as the station is over a kilometre east of the centre. At the time of research, a summer-only shuttle between

Postojna Caves and Predjama was planned for 2005. Otherwise, local buses run Monday to Friday (390SIT, school days) from Postojna to Bukovje, 1.3km short of Predjama, from where it's a delightful, well-signed walk.

PIRAN (PIRANO)
☎ 05 / pop 4400

Little Piran is as picturesque a port as you can imagine, especially when viewed from its sawtoothed city walls. Despite summer crowds it's hard to resist waterfront seafood dinners, scuba-diving trips to WWII wrecks or wanderings in the Venetian-Gothic alleyways.

From the bus station stroll five minutes north along the harbourside (Cankarjevo nab), past the appealing **Maritime Museum** (☎ 674 6826; Cankarjevo nab 3; adult/student 600/500SIT; ☀ 9am-noon & 3-6pm Tue-Sun), to reach Tartinijev trg. In this lovely, central square the fine **town hall** hosts a helpful **tourist office** (☎ 673 0220; www .piran.si; ☀ 9am-4pm Mon-Fri, 10am-2pm Sat Sep-Jun, 9am-1.30pm & 3-9.30pm daily Jul & Aug), which can give you maps and dozens of excursion ideas. On the same square ATM-equipped **Banka Koper** (☀ 8.30am-noon & 3-5pm Mon-Fri, 8.30am-noon Sat) changes money, and in the old courthouse the **library** (membership fee 500SIT; ☀ 10am-6pm Mon-Fri, 8am-1pm Sat) has one Internet computer.

Piran is dominated by **St George's Church** (Adamičeva ul 2), whose soaring **bell tower** was visibly modelled on the San Marco Campanile in Venice. Its octagonal 1650 **baptistry** (*krstilnica*) contains a 2nd-century Roman sarcophagus. **St Francis monastery** (ul Bolniška 20), just west of Tartinijev trg, has a delightful cloister.

Subnet (☎ 041-590 746; www.sub-net.si; Prešernovo nab 24; PADI open-water courses from 35,000SIT, boat dives from 7000SIT) on the north shore is a well-equipped dive shop.

Sleeping

Piran's accommodation options are limited. For more choice but less style, try Portorož, which starts 2km southwest of Piran as Korotan and sweeps a further five hotel-crowded kilometres to the Julija area.

Val Hostel (☎ 673 2555; yhostel.val@siol.net; Gregor-čičeva ul 38A; b per person with shared bathroom IYHA member €18-20, nonmember €23-24) Book well ahead for this superbly central hostel-*penzion*.

Max (☎ 041 692 928; ul IX Korpusa 26; www.max hotel-piran.com; s/d without breakfast €55/60) Piran's most romantic accommodation has only six rooms.

Barbara Hotel (☎ 617 9000; hotel.barbarafiesa@rlv.si; s €8500-11,100, d €13,000-18,200; ☒) This good-value holiday hotel is one of two at Fiesa pebble beach, a 10-minute shorefront walk along the north coast from St George's church.

Within 3km of Piran in Portorož are two summer-only hostels. **DIŠ Hostel** (Dijaški in Študentski Dom Portorož; ☎ 674 6340; Sočna Pot 20; b per person from 3500SIT; ☼ Jul & Aug) is fairly basic. **Prenočišča Korotan** (☎ 674 5400; http://prenocisca -korotan.vsk-sdp.si; Obala 11, Korotan; s/d/tr €35/53/66; ☼ Jul & Aug) is contrastingly upmarket, with rooms mostly equipped with bathrooms and Internet access. It is easy to reach as shuttle bus No 1 from Piran passes right outside.

Behind a grotty caravan park, an inse-cure handkerchief of grass known as **Auto-kamp Fiesa** (☎ 674 6230; per adult low/high season 1577/1877SIT; ☼ Apr-Oct) is nonetheless packed full in summer, being just 10 minutes' walk from Piran, near the Barbara Hotel.

There are private rooms available through **Maona travel agency** (☎ 673 4519; www .maona.si; Cankarjevo nab 7; s/d/tr €26-42/38-44/55-63, 3 nights s/d/tr €52-78/72-80/105; add 20% Jul & Aug; ☼ 9am-7pm Mon-Sat, 10am-2pm some Sun). **Turist Biro** (☎ 673 2509; www.turistbiro-ag.si; Tomažičeva trg; ☼ 10am-1pm & 4-9pm or according to custom) offers similarly priced rooms but they ask for a €14 reservation fee.

Eating & Drinking

Pavel 2 (Prešernovo nab; ☼ 11am-11pm) is perhaps the suavest in a tempting row of south-facing seafront fish restaurants west of Tartinijev trg. Several more lie just inland. All charge around 1500SIT for grilled squid, and from 3000SIT per kilogram for fish. Many like **Riva** (Prešernovo nab) serve richly gooey, garlicky pizzas for 1100SIT to 1500SIT. Multimenu dining is marginally cheaper at **Pirat** (Cankar-evo nab) and **Surf** (Grudnov ul), towards the bus station. **Santeé Caffe** (Cankarjevo nab; ☼ 7am-mid-ight) has ice cream, sandwiches (300SIT to 500SIT), salads and walls painted primary colours. There are two Mercator supermar-kets but minimart **Noč in Dan** (Cankarjevo nab; ☼ 6am-midnight) is open for longer.

Behind the Aquarium, atmospheric but expensive **Cafe Teater** (Kidričeva nab) is Piran's top pub, with a lively terrace. **Zizola Kantina** (☼ 9am-midnight) is an appealing, nautically themed bar with tables right on Tartinijev trg.

Getting There & Away

From the bus station buses run every 20 to 40 minutes to Koper (590SIT) via Izola, with five per day to Trieste (1200SIT, 1¾ hours, Monday to Saturday) and up to eight to Ljubljana (2670SIT, 2½ to three hours) via Divača and Postojna.

From Tartinijev trg, minibuses shuttle to Portorož-Lucija (No 1, 220SIT) and Portorož via Strunjan (No 3). **Aquamarine** (☎ 641 8301) runs summer ferries to Koper (one-way /return 1400/1900SIT) up to four times daily via Izola. Piran and Izola have weekly-plus catamarans to Venice (see p1039).

KOPER (CAPODISTRIA)
☎ 05 / pop 24,000

Slovenia's industrial port town camouflages a quaint, quiet old centre that's cheaper and much less touristy than Piran's. From the joint bus and train station (bicycle hire available), central Titov trg is a 1.4km walk northwest: head for the cathedral's Moroc-can-style bell tower.

Close by, the **tourist office** (☎ /fax 627 3791; tic@koper.si; ☼ 9am-5pm Mon-Fri, 9am-1pm Sat Jun-Sep, 9am-9pm Mon-Sat, 9am-noon Sun Jul & Aug) is within the renovated 15th-century **Praetorian Palace** (Titov trg 3; admission free; ☼ 9am-5pm Mon-Fri, 9am-1pm Sat Jun-Sep, 9am-9pm Mon-Sat, 9am-noon Sun Jul & Aug). Opposite, the splendid 1463 **Loggia** (Titov trg; wine per glass from 200SIT; ☼ 7am-10pm) is now an elegant yet affordable café. Part-medieval Kidričeva ul leads west past a *burek* (lay-ered meat pie) shop, Internet café, bank and ATM to the **Koper Regional Museum** (Kidričeva ul 19; adult/student 350/250SIT; ☼ 8am-3pm Mon-Fri, 8am-1pm Sat year-round & 6-8pm Mon-Fri Jun-Aug). It's within the Belgramoni-Tacco mansion and features an Italianate sculpture garden.

Sleeping & Eating

Vila Milka (☎ 040 835 155; Brkinska Ul 6; b per person €15) Multilingual Diorje Ivovanovic's tiny, eccentric homestay is a cult backpacker bolt hole on the eastern edge of the old town.

Dijaški Dom Koper (☎ 627 3252; www.d-dom .kp.edus.si; Cankarjeva ul 5; dm 3500SIT) In July and August this brilliantly central student dorm becomes a hostel.

Capris Time (☎ 631 1555; www.capristime-sp.si; s/d Sep-Jun from 4290/7150SIT, Jul & Aug 5000/8580SIT; ☼ 8am-4pm Mon-Fri) This station-based agency arranges private rooms and gives discounts for three-day stays.

Motel Port (☎ 639-3260; Ankaranska 7; s/d/tr 5162/9124/13,686SIT; ☒) With a mainly male, truck driver clientele, these excellent-value new rooms atop a Mondrianesque shopping centre suffer from truck noise. Air-conditioning costs 1000SIT extra.

Istrska Klet (Župančičeva ul 39; mains around 1200SIT; ☉ 7am-9pm) This downmarket but atmospheric wine cellar serves authentic meals and typical Teran wine from the cask.

Getting There & Away

To Piran (590SIT, 30 minutes) buses run frequently on weekdays from 5am to 10.15pm, and every 40 minutes at weekends. Up to 10 buses daily run to Ljubljana (2460SIT, two to 2½ hours). The train (1700SIT, 2¼ hours, four daily) is more comfortable.

For information on buses to Trieste and destinations in Croatia, see p1039. There are also summer ferries to Zadar (Croatia) p1039.

SLOVENIA DIRECTORY

ACCOMMODATION

Slovenia's small but growing handful of youth hostels includes Ljubljana's unbelievably trendy Celica. However, many hostels are college dormitories which only accept travellers in July and August.

Guesthouses (penzion, gostišče or prenočišča) are often cosy and better value than full-blown hotels, some of which are ugly if well-renovated communist-era Frankensteins. Hotel and guesthouse rates soar in midsummer, when rooms are scarce at any price. Beware that locally listed rates are usually quoted per person. The 150SIT to 200SIT per adult tourist tax and a hefty single-occupancy supplement often lurk in the footnotes. This book quotes the total you'll pay. Unless otherwise indicated, room rates include en-suite toilet, shower with towels and soap, and a ham-and-cheese breakfast.

Tourist offices can help you access extensive networks of private rooms, apartments and 'tourist farms' or can recommend private agencies who will. Such accommodation appears misleadingly cheap if you overlook the 30% to 50% surcharge levied on one- or two-night stays. Also beware that many such properties are in outlying villages with minimal public transport and

that there are relatively few of the cheapest one-star category rooms (with a shared bathroom). You might save a little going directly to any house with a sign reading sobe (rooms).

Camping grounds generally include hot showers in their per-person charges. Almost all close from November to April. Camping 'rough' is illegal.

ACTIVITIES

Slovenia is an outdoor-activities paradise.

Skiing is a national passion, and slopes are particularly crowded at New Year. Check out www.slovenia-tourism.si/skiing for much more information, and www.smucisca.7-s.si/ (in Slovene) for piste web cams and snow reports.

Hiking is extremely popular, with around 7000km of marked trails and 165 summer-only mountain huts (book via tourist offices). Several shorter trails are helpfully outlined in the Sunflower Guide's Slovenia (www.sunflowerbooks.co.uk).

Bovec (p1051) is a magnet for fans of extreme sports, notably paragliding, hydrospeed (like boogie-boarding down a river) and canyoning. The Soča River nearby offers Slovenia's best white-water rafting. Kobarid (p1051) is a great base for fly-fishing, as is the Sava River at Bohinj (p1050). Gliding costs are remarkably reasonable from Lesce aerodrome near Bled (p1048). Scuba diving from Piran (p1052) is good value.

Mountain bikes are rented at Bovec, Bled and Bohinj travel agencies. However, the rental 'season' is usually only from May to October.

Spa cures are also very popular – see www.terme-giz.si.

BUSINESS HOURS

Virtually all businesses post their opening times (delovni čas) on the door. Many shops close on Saturday afternoon. On 'holy' Sunday a handful of grocery stores open including some branches of the ubiquitous Mercator chain, but most shopping areas are as lively as Chernobyl. Museums often close on Monday. Banks often take lengthy lunch breaks; some open on Saturday morning.

The closer winter approaches, the earlier many attractions close and the fewer visits they allow. This leads to complex tables of opening times that are beyond the scope of this book to accurately reproduce. Fortunately most have websites and leaflets displaying complete schedules in all their glory.

EMBASSIES & CONSULATES

Slovenian representations abroad are fully listed on www.gov.si/mzz/eng and include the following:

Austria (☎ 01-586 1309; Nibelungengasse 13, Vienna; ☿ 9-11am Mon-Fri)

Croatia (☎ 01-631 1000; Savska cesta 41, Zagreb; ☿ 9am-noon Mon-Fri)

Czech Republic (☎ 02-3308 1211; Pod Hradbami 15, Prague; ☿ 9am-noon Mon, Wed, Fri)

Hungary (☎ 01-438 5600; Cseppkő ut 68, Budapest; ☿ 9am-noon Mon-Fri)

UK (☎ 020-7222 5400; 10 Little College St, London SW1; ☿ 9am-2pm Mon-Fri)

Embassies and consulates in Ljubljana include the following:

Australia (Map pp1042-4; ☎ 01-425 4252; Trg Republike 3/XII)

Austria (Map pp1042-4; ☎ 01-479 0700; Prešernova 23)

Bosnia and Hercegovina (☎ 01-432 4042; Kolarjeva 26)

Canada (Map pp1042-4; ☎ 01-430 3570; Miklošičeva cesta 19)

Croatia (☎ 01-425 6220; Gruberjevo nab 6)

Czech Republic (☎ 01-420 2450; Riharjeva 1)

Hungary (☎ 01-512 1882; ul Konrada Babnika 5)

Romania (☎ 01-505 8294; Podlimbarskega 43)

UK (Map pp1042-4; ☎ 01-200 3910; Trg Republike 3/IV)

USA (Map pp1042-4; ☎ 01-200 5500; Prešernova cesta 31)

FESTIVALS & EVENTS

Shaggy *kurent* (straw men) make Ptuj carnival the place to be at Mardi Gras, though the Julian Alpine villages have lesser-known equivalents. On 30 April villages hold bonfires and 'tree-raising' nights. Maribor's 'Lent' street-theatre festival is not pre-Easter but held during the last week of June, and throughout the summer there are dozens of musical and cultural events, notably in Ljubljana, Piran and Koper.

FOOD & DRINK

Archetypal Slovene foods like *žlikrofi* (potato-filled ravioli in lamb sauce), *mlinci* (corn-pasta sheets in gravy) and *ajdovi žganci* (buckwheat groats) are relatively hard to find. Inns (*gostilna* or *gostišče)* more frequently serve pizzas, *rižota* (risotto), *klobasa* (sausage), *zrezek* (cutlet/steak), *golaž* (goulash) and *paprikaš* ('stew'). *Postrv* (trout) is

generally half the price of other fish meals. *Lignji na žaru* (grilled squid) with garlic butter (1200SIT to 1500SIT) is a ubiquitous bargain, along with Balkan favourites *cevapčiči* (ground-meat 'fingers'), *pleskavica* (burger patties) and *raznjiči* (shish kebabs). Add 350SIT to 500SIT for the *krompir* (potatoes). Some restaurants add 100SIT to 200SIT for the bread or cover charge.

Snack cheaply on takeaway pizza slices or slabs of *burek* (300SIT to 450SIT), lasagneesque pasta layered with cheese, meat or apple. Alternatives include *štruklji* (cheese dumplings) and *palačinke* (sweet or savoury pancakes).

Some restaurants have 1000SIT to 1600SIT *kosilo* lunch menus, including *juha* (soup) and *solata* (salad) for less than the price of a cheap main course. One choice is frequently vegetarian.

Tap water is safe. Distinctively Slovenian *vino* (wines) include hearty red Teran made from Refošk grapes and the light-red Cviček with a plummy sourness. Slovenians are justly proud of their top vintages; however, cheaper bar-standard 'open wines' (90SIT to 200SIT per 100mL glass) are often pure gut-rot. Some fascinating *suho* (dry) whites are made from sweet grapes like Tokaj and Muskat but *sladko/polsladko* (sweet/semi-sweet) can be very sugary indeed.

Piva (beer), whether *svetlo* (lager) or *temno* (dark), is best on draught *(točeno)*.

There are dozens of hard-hitting *žganje* fruit brandies. *Na zdravje!* (Cheers!).

GAY & LESBIAN TRAVELLERS

On the whole, Slovenia is tolerant. **Roza Klub** (☎ 01-430 4740; Kersnikova ul 4, Ljubljana) is composed of gay and lesbian branches of the ŠKUC (Student Cultural Centre).

The **GALfon** (☎ 01-432 4089; ☿ 7-10pm) is a hotline and source of general information for gays and lesbians. The websites of **Slovenian Queer Resources Directory** (www.ljudmila.org /siqrd) and **Out In Slovenia** (www.outinslovenija.com) are both extensive and partially in English.

HOLIDAYS

New Year's Day 1 and 2 January
Prešern Day of Culture 8 February
Easter (including Monday) March/April
Insurrection Day (against WWII Nazi occupation) 27 April
Labour Days 1 and 2 May
National Day 25 June

Assumption Day 15 August
Reformation Day 31 October
All Saints' Day 1 November
Christmas 25 December
Independence Day 26 December

INTERNET ACCESS

There is Internet access in most towns but so-called Internet cafés rarely have more than one or two terminals. In some places you may have to resort to the local library, school or university. Note: Slovene keyboards reverse Y and Z.

INTERNET RESOURCES

Most Slovenian towns have very good sites, often accessed by typing www.townname.si or www.townname-tourism.si. Examples are www.ljubljana-tourism.si and www.maribor-tourism.si. Other recommended sites:

www.slovenia-tourism.si Fantastically useful.

www.burger.si For city views.

www.matkurja.com/eng Partly in English, with very wide-ranging links.

www.prah.net/slovenia Political links and news, some slightly dated.

www.niagara.com/~jezovnik Explores historical Carantha/Caranntania, the greater Slovenia of which the modern country is only a part.

LANGUAGE

Closely related to Croatian and Serbian, Slovene *(slovensko)* sounds like Russian saturated in honey. It's written in the Latin alphabet. On toilets, *Moški* = Men, *Ženske* = Women. Slovenian 'No Smoking' signs mean 'No Farting' in Slovak. Almost everyone speaks at least one other language; restaurant menus and ATMs are commonly in Slovene, Italian, German and English.

MONEY

Until 2007 Slovenia's legal currency remains the tolar (SIT), but euros are already very widely accepted. Exchanging cash is simple at banks, major post offices, travel agencies and *menjalnica* (exchange bureaus). Travellers cheques are less convenient. Major credit and debit cards are accepted almost everywhere and ATMs are astonishingly ubiquitous. Slovenian and Italian prices are similar, and you'll find Slovenia considerably more expensive than Hungary or the

Czech Republic. For more information on costs, see p28.

POST

An international airmail stamp costs 107SIT. Poste restante is free: address it to Slovenska cesta 32, 1101 Ljubljana.

TELEPHONE

Public telephones require a phonecard *(telefonska kartica)*, available at post offices and most newsstands. The cheapest (700SIT) 25-unit card gives about four minutes' calling time to other European countries.

Mobile phones generally have the prefix 030, 031, 040 or 041.

TOILETS

Toilets are generally free in restaurants but occasionally incur a 50SIT charge at bus stations.

TOURIST INFORMATION

The super-helpful **Slovenian Tourist Board** (www.slovenia-tourism.si) has lots of information centres in Slovenia and branches in nine cities abroad. Request the free *Guide to Slovenia's Byways*, containing tokens for 5% to 15% savings on various hotels, activities and sights, including the Škocjan caves.

VISAS

Passport holders from Australia, Canada, Iceland, Israel, Japan, Norway, New Zealand, Switzerland, the USA and EU countries can stay 90 days without visas. South Koreans get 15 days. Most other citizens including South Africans, must apply for a visa (multiple entry €35) at a Slovenian embassy or consulate (none in South Africa). You'll need travel insurance, passport photocopies and hotel bookings, plus one photo. Same-day processing is possible in Zagreb (Croatia) but elsewhere allow up to a week. EU and Swiss citizens can enter using a national identity card for 30-day stays.

WOMEN TRAVELLERS

Crime is low and harassment rare, but in emergencies contact the **women's crisis help line** (☎ 080 1155). Normally someone on line will speak English.

Spain

HIGHLIGHTS

- **La Sagrada Família** It doesn't get any more jaw-dropping than Barcelona's brazenly weird church (p1082)
- **Ibiza Old Town** Kick back with a large glass of sangria and eye the town's colourful characters (p1091)
- **Costa de la Luz** You can fly high with kite-surfing (p1111)
- **Best journey** The lush countryside and gorgeous coast between La Coruña to Santiago de Compostela (p1119)

FAST FACTS

- **Area** 505,000 sq km (twice the size of Sweden)
- **ATMs** Widespread and a wide variety of cards are accepted
- **Budget** At least €40 per day
- **Capital** Madrid
- **Country code** ☎ 34
- **Famous for** Sunshine, late nights, Don Quixote, Pedro Almodóvar films
- **Head of State** King Juan Carlos, President José Lluís Zapatero
- **Languages** Spanish (Castilian or Castellano), Catalan, Basque, Gallego
- **Money** Euro (A$1 = €0.58, CA$1 = €0.64, ¥100 = €0.73, NZ$1 = €0.54, UK£1 = €1.45, US$ = €0.81)
- **Phrases** *Hola* (hello), *gracias* (thanks), *adios* (goodbye)

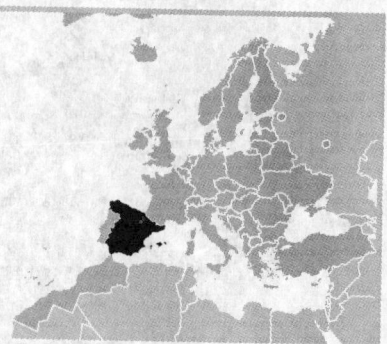

- **Population** 40 million
- **Time** GMT/UTC + 1 in winter, + 2 from last Sunday in March to last Sunday in September
- **Visas** None required for most visitors for stays up to 90 days.

TRAVEL HINTS

Spanish *menú* (fixed-price lunches) are a godsend for the hungry. Also try getting food at local markets. Buy train tickets a day in advance to assure a spot.

ROAMING SPAIN

From Madrid, take day trips to Toledo and Segovia before heading further afield. For longer trips, your best bets are a journey east to Barcelona, stopping in Zaragoza, or a trip south to Sevilla, Córdoba and the Costa de la Luz.

This is the land of flamenco, fiestas and fun in the sun, but go past Spain's tourist-brochure image and you'll find a fascinating country rich in history and culture. A mammoth peninsula jutting out from southern Europe, Spain is home to just about every landscape imaginable, from the beaches of the Costa de la Luz to the rugged peaks of the Pyrenees,

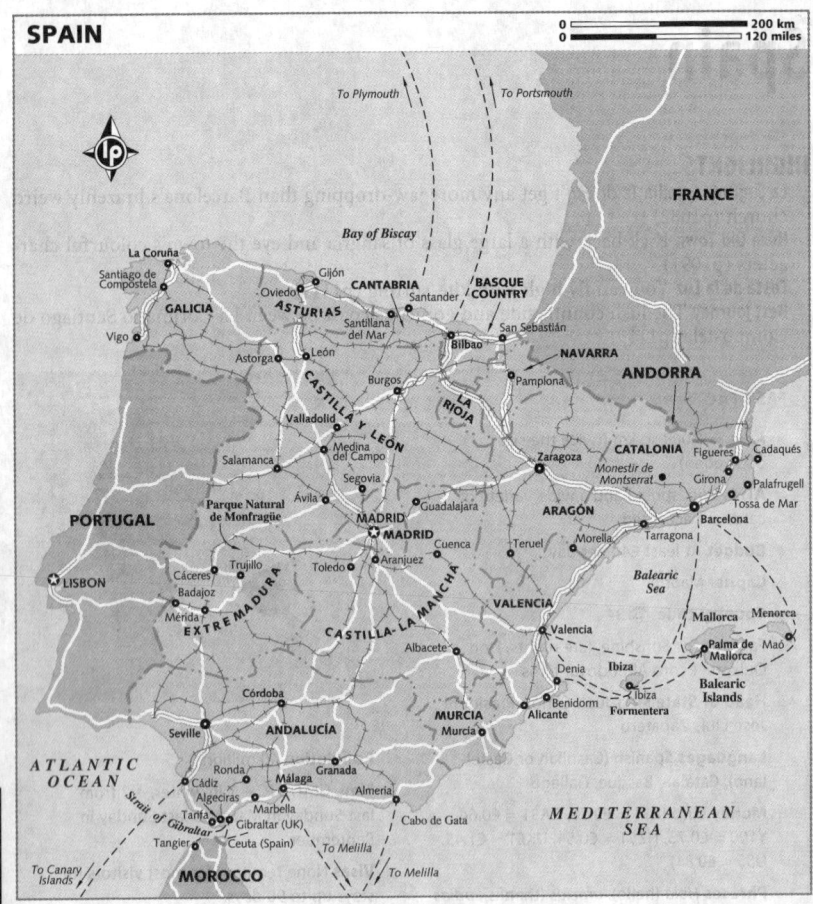

from the damp green of Galicia to the sunburnt plains of Castile. This varied landscape was the backdrop of a long and turbulent history that reveals its presence at every turn.

Mudéjar (a style of architecture originated by the Spanish Moors) buildings in Andalucía and medieval Jewish temples in Toledo are relics of an era when these cultures lived peacefully in Spain. Move on to the breathtakingly beautiful Catholic cathedrals of Burgos, León and Santiago de Compostela for a glimpse of the Church's tremendous power in this historically Catholic country.

Yet not all of Spain's glory lies in the past. The vibrant nightlife in cities such as Madrid and Barcelona are proof of the country's boundless energy, and international success in art, design and cuisine show that Spain's creative juices are flowing.

HISTORY

From around 8000 to 3000 BC, North African pioneers known as the Iberians crossed the Strait of Gibraltar. They were followed by Celts, Phoenicians, Greeks, Carthaginians and Romans. In AD 409 Roman Hispania

was overrun by Germanic tribes; 300 years later, the Moors – Muslim Berbers and Arabs from North Africa – took over the region.

The 8th century is when the Christian Reconquista began. By the mid-13th century, the Christians had taken most of the peninsula. In 1469 the kingdoms of Castile and Aragón were united by Isabel, princess of Castile, marrying Fernando, heir to Aragón's throne. Known as the Catholic Monarchs, they united Spain and laid the path for the Spanish golden age. They also expelled and executed thousands of Jews and other non-Christians under the dark cloud of the Inquisition. In 1492 the last Muslim ruler of Granada surrendered to them, thus marking the end of the Reconquista.

Also in 1492, Columbus stumbled on the Bahamas and claimed the Americas for Spain. This sparked a period of exploration and exploitation that yielded Spain enormous wealth while destroying the ancient American empires. Spain's downfall began soon after, culminating with the disastrous Spanish-American War of 1898, which marked the end of the Spanish empire.

During the Spanish Civil War (1936–39), the Nationalists, led by General Francisco Franco, received heavy military support from Nazi Germany and fascist Italy, while the elected Republican government received support only from Russia and, to a lesser degree, from the International Brigades, made up of foreign leftists. By 1939 Franco had won and an estimated 350,000 Spaniards had died. Franco's 35-year dictatorship began with Spain isolated and crippled by recession. It wasn't until the 1950s and '60s that the country began to recover. By the 1970s Spain had the fastest-growing economy in Europe.

Franco died in 1975, having named King Juan Carlos his successor. Juan Carlos is widely credited with having overseen Spain's transition from dictatorship to democracy. The first elections were held in 1977 and a new constitution drafted in 1978. Spain joined the European Community in 1986. In 1997, it became fully integrated into NATO, and in 1999 met the criteria for launching the euro. Now Spain has one of the world's fastest-growing economies.

In March 2004 Spain was the centre of international attention and sympathy when Al Qaeda attacked four commuter trains in Madrid, killing 200 people. Days after the bombings Spain's ruling Partido Popular was voted out of power in favour of a Socialist government, lead by President José Lluís Zapatero, which stood staunchly against any war not led by the United Nations, including the US-led war with Iraq.

TOP FIVE SPAIN

- **Festival** Las Fallas de San José, mid-March, Valencia (p1096) is a pyromaniac's idea of heaven with fireworks, bonfires and burning effigies.

- **Walk** Pull on your boots and set forth on some, or all, of the Camino de Santiago (p1119), a 750km epic adventure through Northern Spain on an old pilgrimage route.

- **Clubbing area** You've heard the rumours, you've bought the soundtrack, now get over to Ibiza (p1092) and shake your booty.

- **Impressive sight** Sun soak on the perfectly kept, shell-shaped Playa de la Concha in San Sebastián (p1116), one of the world's best urban beaches.

- **History** You'll feel like you've travelled back in time when you explore perfect, medieval towns like Toledo (p1076), Segovia (p1073) and Ávila (p1071)

PEOPLE & CULTURE

Spain has a population of 40 million, descended from all the many peoples who have settled here over the millennia, among them Iberians, Celts, Romans, Jews, Visigoths, Berbers, Arabs and 20th-century immigrants from across the globe. The biggest cities are Madrid (three million), Barcelona (1.5 million), Valencia (750,000) and Seville (700,000).

Most Spaniards are economical with etiquette, but they're on the whole very tolerant and easy-going towards foreigners. It's not easy to give offence. However, obviously disrespectful behaviour won't go down well.

Only about 20% of Spaniards are regular church-goers, but Catholicism is deeply ingrained in the culture. As the writer Unamuno said, 'Here in Spain we are all Catholics, even the atheists'.

ARTS

The giants of Spain's golden age (1550–1650) were Toledo-based El Greco (originally from Crete) and Diego Velázquez, perhaps Spain's most revered painter. Both excelled with insightful portraits. The genius of the

18th and 19th centuries was Francisco Goya, whose versatility ranged from unflattering royal portraits and anguished war scenes to bullfight etchings.

Catalonia was the powerhouse of early 20th-century Spanish art, claiming the hugely prolific Pablo Picasso (born in Andalucía), the colourful symbolist Joan Miró, and the surrealist Salvador Dalí. Important artists working today include Catalan abstract artist Antoni Tàpies and Basque sculptor Eduardo Chillida.

SPORT

Spain's national sport is football (soccer). While every city has at least one team with its loyal band of followers, the greatest rivalry is between Real Madrid and Barça, Spain's top two teams.

Bullfighting is also popular, particularly around Madrid and in southern Spain, where it is present at all important festivals. The ethical debate about bullfighting is still raging. Animal rights' groups emphasise that the slaughter is a cruel 30 minutes that results in the bull being exhausted and defeated. Yet supporters of this 'art' say that *toros bravos* (wild bulls) are treated like kings until the day of the slaughter. Whether or not you want to see this often disturbing tradition must be a personal decision.

READING UP

For more on Spanish history and current events, pick up *A Traveller's History: Spain* by Juan Lalaguna or *The New Spaniards* by John Hooper. Good travel literature includes James A Michener's classic *Iberia* and the excellent book of essays *Travellers' Tales Guide: Spain*, edited by Lucy McCauley. Delve into the culture surrounding the Spanish Civil War with Hemingway's classics like *For Whom the Bell Tolls* and George Orwell's *Homage to Catalonia*. Get a feel for modern Spanish literature with popular mystery novels by authors like Pérez Reverte and Manuel Vazquez Montalban, or with the fantastic anthology *A Traveller's Literary Companion: Spain*, edited by Peter Bush and Lisa Dillman. Of course, the ultimate Spanish novel is *Don Quijote*, by the great Miguel de Cervantes.

ENVIRONMENT

Spain covers 84% of the Iberian Peninsula and spreads over 505,000 sq km, more than half of which is the *meseta* (high tableland). This is supported and divided by some mountain chains, making Spain Europe's second-most mountainous country after Switzerland. The main mountains are the Pyrenees, along the border with France; the Cordillera Cantábrica, backing the northern coast; the Sistema Ibérico, from the central north towards the middle Mediterranean coast; the Cordillera Central, from north of Madrid towards the Portuguese border; and three east–west chains across Andalucía, one being the highest range of all, the Sierra Nevada.

The major rivers are the Ebro, Duero, Tajo (Tagus), Guadiana and Guadalquivir, all entering the Atlantic Ocean (except the Ebro, which reaches the Mediterranean Sea).

TRANSPORT

GETTING THERE & AWAY
Air

Spain has many international airports but the cheapest destinations tend to be Alicante, Almería, Bilbao, Barcelona, Ibiza, Jerez, Girona, Madrid, Málaga, Murcia, Palma de Mallorca, Valencia, Valladolid and Zaragoza. Low-cost airlines offering the best deals to Spain from the UK include **Ryanair** (www.ryanair.com), **easyJet** (www.easyjet.com) and **bmibaby** (www.bmibaby.com).

Boat
MOROCCO

Ferry services between Spain and Morocco include Algeciras–Tangier, Algeciras–Ceuta, Gibraltar–Tangier, Tarifa–Tangier, Málaga–Melilla, Almería–Melilla and Almería–Nador. Those ferries to and from Algeciras are the fastest and cheapest, with over 20 a day to Ceuta (€22, 1½ hours) and 14 to Tangier (€28, 2½ hours). Hydrofoils make the same trip in half the time for about 75% more. Taking a car to Ceuta/Tangier costs €62/73.

You can buy tickets at Algeciras harbour, but it's more convenient to go to one of the many agencies on the waterfront.

THE UK
Brittany Ferries (☎ 942 360 611 in Spain; ☎ 0870-5360360 in UK; www.brittany-ferries.com) operates

Plymouth–Santander ferries from about mid-March to mid-November (24 hours, twice weekly), and usually once a week in other months. One-way passenger fares range from about UK£61 to UK£100; a two-berth cabin is an extra UK£67; a car and driver costs from UK£245 to UK£473.

P&O European Ferries (☎ 902 02 04 61 in Spain; ☎ 0870-2424999 in UK; www.poportsmouth.com) operates Portsmouth–Bilbao ferries virtually year-round (35 hours, Tuesday and Saturday). One-way/return trip prices with a (compulsory) berth start at UK£114/214 in winter and £166/262 in summer.

Bus

There are regular bus services to Spain from all major centres in Europe, including Lisbon, London and Paris. In London, **Eurolines** (☎ 0870-5143219; www.eurolines.com) has services at least three times a week to Barcelona (UK£65/95 one-way/return trip, 26 hours), Madrid (UK£92/122, at least 27 hours) and Málaga (UK£96/128, 35 hours). Tickets are sold by major travel agencies and if you book in advance you can get good discounts of up to a third off. People aged under 26 qualify for a 10% discount.

Car & Motorcycle

If you're driving to Spain from England, you can go through France (check visa requirements) or take a direct ferry. It's cheapest to take a ferry to France, then drive down to Spain.

Train

Return train fares from London to Madrid (via Paris) can be had for as little as UK£137 provided you book well in advance. For more details, contact the **Rail Europe Travel Centre** (☎ 08705-848848; www.raileurope.co.uk) in London or a travel agent. See the Directory (p1256) for more on rail passes and train travel through Europe.

GETTING AROUND

Students are eligible for discounts of 30% to 50% on almost all types of transport within Spain. **TIVE** (Map pp1064-5; ☎ 915 43 74 12; ve.juventud@madrid.org; Calle de Fernando El Católico 88, Madrid) has offices in major cities throughout Spain. It specialises in discounted tickets and travel arrangements for students and young people aged under 26.

Air

Spain's three main domestic airlines, **Iberia** (☎ 902 40 05 00; www.iberia.com), **Air Europa** (☎ 902 40 15 01; www.aireuropa.com) and **SpanAir** (☎ 902 13 14 15; www.spanair.com), compete to produce fares that can make flying worthwhile if you're in a hurry. It may be worth your while investing in the **SpanAir Pass**, which gives you 20 flight coupons valid for 12 months on domestic flights within Spain.

Bicycle

Locating rental bicycles in Spain is a hit-and-miss affair, so it's best to bring your own. The Spanish, however, do enjoy recreational cycling so getting hold of spare parts isn't a problem.

Spain's high-speed AVE and *Talgo* trains will not let bicycles on board unless boxed but slower regional trains will. Buses often take bikes in their lower luggage hold (you'll probably have to remove the front wheel).

Boat

For information on ferries to/from the Balearic Islands, see p1091. In bad weather or rough seas services are restricted.

Bus

Spain's extensive bus network is operated by dozens of independent companies serving remote towns and villages as well as the major routes. Many towns and cities have one main bus station where most buses arrive and depart, and these usually have a desk giving information on all services. The best known national service is run by **ALSA** (☎ 902 42 22 42; www.alsa.es)

Buses to/from Madrid are often cheaper than, or rarely differ from, cross-country routes.

Car & Motorcycle

The Spanish automobile club, **Real Automóvil Club de España** (RACE; Map pp1064-5; ☎ 914 34 11 22; inforace@race.es; Av Ciudad de Barcelona 132, Madrid), has a 24-hour nationwide on-road emergency service (☎ 900 11 22 22).

SPAIN

Car hire rates vary, though the best deals tend to be in major tourist areas. At Málaga airport you can rent a small car for under €110 a week. More generally, you're looking at about €50 a day including unlimited kilometres, insurance, damage waiver and taxes. Hiring for several days can bring the average daily cost down a lot. Local companies often have better rates than the big firms.

Hitching

Lonely Planet does not recommend hitching, but should you decide to try it, please be aware that women should avoid hitching alone. Hitching is illegal on *autopistas* (multilane freeways) and difficult on major highways. Your chances are better on minor roads, although the going can still be painfully slow.

Local Transport

Most towns have an effective local bus system. Tourist offices can provide bus information. Barcelona and Madrid both have efficient metro systems that are faster and easier to use than the buses.

Taxis are pretty cheap. Rates vary slightly from city to city: in Barcelona it's €1.15 flag fall, plus about €0.69 per kilometre; in Madrid it's €1.55 flag fall.

Train

Trains are modern, comfortable and punctual. **Renfe** (☎ 902 24 02 02; www.renfe.es) is the national railway company and its website is a great resource for schedule and fare information. Travel times and fares can vary a lot on the same route depending not just on the type of train but also the time of day.

Regionales are all-stops trains (think cheap and slow). *Cercanías* provide regular services from major cities to the surrounding suburbs and hinterland. Among long-distance trains, the *Talgo* is fastest and dearest. Best of all is the AVE high-speed service that links Madrid and Seville in just 2½ hours. The *Talgo 200* uses part of this line to speed down to Málaga from Madrid. The *Euromed* is an AVE-style train that speeds south from Barcelona to Valencia and Alicante.

The cheapest sleeper option is usually a *litera*, a bunk in a six-berth, 2nd-class compartment. You can buy tickets and make reservations at stations, Renfe offices in many city centres, and travel agencies that display the Renfe logo.

TRAIN PASSES

Rail passes are valid for all Renfe trains, but Inter-Rail users are required to pay €9.50 supplement fees on *Talgo*, InterCity and AVE services. All pass-holders making reservations for long-distance trains pay a fee of about €5.

Renfe's Tarjeta Turística (also known as the Spain Flexipass) rail pass is valid for three to 10 days' travel in a two-month period. In 2nd class, three days costs US$155, and 10 days is US$365. It can be purchased from agents outside Europe, or at a few main train stations in Spain.

MADRID

This might be the capital of Spain, but it doesn't take itself too seriously. Anyone who's been in a 4am traffic jam here or a Thursday night knows that few cities le[t] down their hair like Madrid. Plan to live i[t] up on the anything-goes nightlife scene, bu[t] save energy for visits to the city's amazing art museums and busy historic centre.

ORIENTATION

In Spain's case, all roads lead to Madri[d] and, more specifically, to the Puerta del So[l] kilometre zero, the physical and emotiona[l] heart of the city. Radiating out from thi[s] harried plaza are arms – Calle Mayor, Call[e] del Arenal, Calle de Preciados, Calle de l[a] Montera and Calle de Alcalá – that stretc[h] into the city.

South of the Puerta del Sol is the old[e]st part of the city, with the Plaza Mayo[r] to the southwest and the busy streets o[f] the Huertas district to the southeast. Nort[h] of the plaza is a modern shopping distric[t] and beyond that, the east–west thorough[-]fare Gran Via and the bohemian *barri[o]* (neighbourhood), Chueca. To the west i[s] the stately Palacio Real, while east lies the city's green lung, El Retiro park. All these areas are easily reached by metro.

INFORMATION
Emergency
Medical & Fire Emergencies ☎ 112
Police ☎ 091

Internet Access
Nets (Map pp1064-5; ☎ 915 22 20 17; Calle Palma 24; Ⓜ Tribunal; per hr €1.50; ☻ noon-1am Mon-Sat, noon-midnight Sun) To just skim email, you can log on for up to five minutes for free.
Work Center (Map pp1068; ☎ 913 60 13 95; Calle del Príncipe 1; per hr €2; ☻ 24hr)

Laundry
Lavandería Cervantes (Map pp1068; ☎ 914 29 92 16; Calle de León 6; Ⓜ Antón Martín; per load €2; ☻ 9am-9pm)

Medical Services
Anglo-American Medical Unit (Map pp1064-5; ☎ 914 35 18 23; Calle Conde de Aranda 1; Ⓜ Retiro) For help in English.
Farmacia del Globo (Map pp1064-5; ☎ 913 69 20 00; Plaza Antón Martín 46; Ⓜ Antón Martín) For help with minor medical problems, ask a pharmacist. This is one of several 24-hour pharmacies.

Money
Using your ATM card will give you low banks exchange rates, though some banks charge an extra fee for ATM use. If you're desperate, there are plenty of *bureaux de change* around Puerta del Sol that have rip-off rates but which are open late.

Post
Main post office (Map pp1064-5; ☎ 913 96 24 43; Plaza Cibeles; Ⓜ Banco de España; ☻ 8.30am-9.30pm Mon-Sat) In the gigantic Palacio de Comunicaciones.

Tourist Information
Municipal tourist office (Map pp1068; ☎ 913 66 54 77; www.munimadrid.es; Plaza Mayor 3; Ⓜ Sol; ☻ 10am-8pm Mon-Sat, 10am-3pm Sun)
Regional tourist office (Map pp1068; ☎ 914 29 49 51 or 902 10 00 07; www.madrid.org; Calle del Duque Medinaceli 2; Ⓜ Sevilla; ☻ 9am-7pm Mon-Sat, 9am-3pm Sun)

SIGHTS
Madrid's 'Big Three' – the outstanding Prado, Reina Sofía and Thyssen-Bornemisza

museums – should be the first things on your to-do list.

Museo del Prado
The **Prado** (Map p1068; ☎ 913 30 28 00; http://museoprado.mcu.es; Paseo del Prado s/n; Ⓜ Banco de España; adult €3, free Sun; ☻ 9am-7pm Tue-Sun) is not just the best-known museum in Madrid, it's one of the world's most elite art collections. The main focus is on Spanish, Flemish and Italian art from the 15th to 19th centuries, with great coverage of Goya, Velázquez and El Greco. Velázquez's masterpiece *Las Meninas* is one of the museum's prized works. In it, maids of honour attend the daughter of King Felipe IV, and Velázquez himself paints portraits of the queen and king (through whose eyes the scene is witnessed).

Almost the whole southern wing of the 1st floor presents Goya's works. Others featured include the Flemish masters Hieronymus Bosch and Peter Paul Rubens, and the Italians Tintoretto, Titian and Raphael.

Guided visits are available; ask for details at the ticket booth.

Centro de Arte Reina Sofía
With a fantastic collection of modern, predominately Spanish art, the **Centro de Arte Reina Sofía** (Map pp1064-5; ☎ 914 67 50 62; http://museoreinasofia.mcu.es; Calle Santa Isabel 52; Ⓜ Atocha; admission €3, free 2.30-9pm Sat & Sun; ☻ 10am-9pm Mon-Sat, 10am-2.30pm Sun) showcases Spanish contemporary culture. The exhibition includes Picasso's legendary *Guernica*, his protest of the German bombing of the Basque town during the Spanish Civil War in 1937.

The museum also contains further works by Picasso, as well as works by Dalí and the remarkably simple paintings of Miró.

GETTING INTO TOWN

Madrid has two principal train stations; Chamartín sits far north of the centre, while Atocha is just south. Both have good metro connections and can get you to the Puerta del Sol in minutes. The main bus station, Estación Sur, is a long hike south from the centre, but the Méndez Álvaro metro line is nearby. From the airport, take the metro (€1.15) to Nuevos Ministerios, a transport hub 12 minutes away. From here you can change lines and reach the centre.

SPAIN

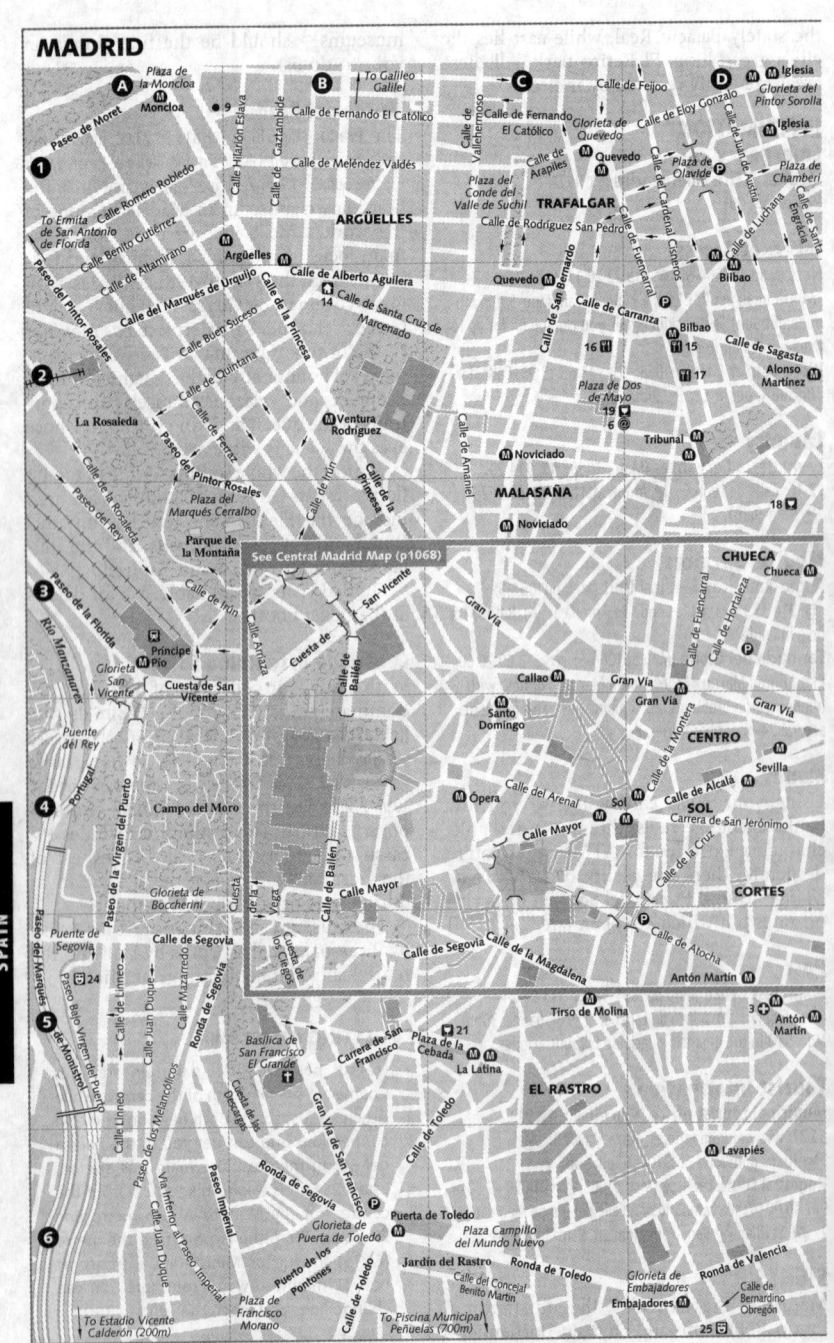

MADRID

See Central Madrid Map (p1068)

SPAIN

INFORMATION

Anglo-American Medical Unit	1 F3
Canadian Embassy	2 G3
Farmacia del Globo	3 D5
Irish Embassy	4 F1
Main Post Office	5 E4
Nets	6 C2
New Zealand Embassy	7 E4
Palacio de Comunicaciones	(see 5)
Red Española de Albergues Juveniles	8 H2
TIVE	9 A1
UK Embassy	10 E2
US Embassy	11 F1

SIGHTS & ACTIVITIES (pp1063–6)

Centro de Arte Reina Sofía	12 E6
Museo del Prado	13 E5

SLEEPING 🏠 (pp1066–7)

Albergue Santa Cruz de Marcenado	14 B2

EATING 🍴 (pp1067–9)

Café Comercial	15 D2
Café de Ruiz	16 C2
Patatus	17 D2

DRINKING 🍷 (pp1069–70)

Areia	18 D3
Café Pepe Botella	19 D2
El Son	20 E2
El Viajero	21 C5
Finnegan's	22 E3
Kapital	23 E5

ENTERTAINMENT 🎭 (p1070)

La Riviera	24 A5
Sala Caracol	25 D6

TRANSPORT

Airport Bus Terminal	26 F3
Real Automóvil Club de España	27 G6

Museo Thyssen-Bornemisza

Sitting just opposite the Prado, the **Thyssen-Bornemisza** (Map p1068; ☎ 913 69 01 51; Paseo del Prado 8; Ⓜ Banco de España; adult €4.80; ☺ 10am-7pm Tue-Sun) is a themeless collection of priceless works offering one of the most comprehensive art history lessons you'll ever have. Starting with medieval religious art, it moves right through to contemporary works. Formerly a private collection, it was purchased by Spain in 1993 for US$300 million.

El Rastro

The city's main market is **El Rastro** (Map pp1064-5; Ⓜ La Latina; ☺ 8am-3pm Sun), a throbbing mass of vendors, browsers, buyers and pickpockets. The madness begins at the Plaza de Cascorro, near La Latina metro stop, and worms its way downhill along the Calle de la Ribera de Curtidores and the streets branching off it.

Palacio Real & Around

Madrid's 18th-century **Palacio Real** (Map p1068; ☎ 915 42 00 59; Calle de Bailén s/n; Ⓜ Ópera; adult €9; ☺ 9.30am-5pm Mon-Sat, 9am-2pm Sun Oct-Mar, 9am-6pm Mon-Sat, 9am-3pm Sun Apr-Sep) is a lesson in what can happen if you give your interior decorators a free hand. You'll see some of the most elaborately decorated walls and ceilings imaginable, including the sublime Throne Room. This over-the-top palace hasn't been used as a royal residence for some time and today is used only for official receptions.

The big white building next door is the cavernous **Catedral de Nuestra Señora de la Almudena** (Map p1068; ☺ 9am-9pm), completed in 1992. Behind it is the sprawling **Campo del Moro** (Map pp1064–5), a pretty park.

Monasterio de las Descalzas Reales

This ornate **monastery** (Convent of the Barefoot Royals; Map p1068; ☎ 915 42 00 59; www.patrimonio nacional.es; Plaza de las Descalzas; Ⓜ Sol; adult €5; ☺ 10.30am-12.45pm & 4-5.45pm Tue-Thu & Sat, 10.30am-12.45pm Fri, 11am-1.45pm Sun) was founded in 1559 by Juana of Austria, daughter of the Spanish King Carlos I, and became one of Spain's richest religious houses thanks to gifts from noblewomen.

Ermita de San Antonio de la Florida

Home to Goya's *panteón* (tomb), the **Ermita de San Antonio de la Florida** (☎ 915 42 07 22; Glorieta de San Antonio de la Florida 5; Ⓜ Príncipe Pío; admission free; ☺ 10am-2pm & 4-8pm Tue-Fri, 10am-2pm Sat & Sun) is also one of the artist's greatest works the entire ceiling and dome are beautifull painted with religious scenes. The images or the dome depict the miracle of St Anthony

Parque del Retiro

A Sunday stroll in **El Retiro** (Map pp1064- Ⓜ Retiro; ☺ 7am-midnight summer, 7am-10pm winte is as much a Madrid tradition as tapas (ligh snacks) and terrace cafés. Time it right an you may even catch a puppet show durin the summer. There are rowing boats fo rent at the small pond.

FESTIVALS & EVENTS

Madrid takes its partying seriously, and fes tive events are generously sprinkled ove the year's calendar. Look out for:

Día de los Reyes (Three Kings' Day; 6 Jan) The three kings bring gifts to children and a mammoth parade takes over the city centre.

Fiesta de San Isidro (Festival of St Isidro; 15 May) Madrid's patron saint is honoured with nonstop processions, parties and bullfights.

Fiesta de Otoño (Autumn Festival; mid-Oct through mid-Nov) Music, dance and theatre take over Madrid during the fantastically cultural weeks of the festival.

SLEEPING

Madrid has a great selection of budget ac commodation, but booking ahead is alway a good idea and may be necessary in sum mer or during holidays.

Most *hostales* (one- to two-star hotels listed here have private bathrooms; hostel have shared bathrooms.

Los Austrias & Centro   Map p106

Los Amigos Backpackers' Hostel (☎ 915 47 17 0 www.losamigoshostel.com; Calle Campomanes 6, 4th Ⓜ Ópera; dm €15; 💻) Polka-dotted curtain and bright walls set the tone at this Eng lish-speaking hostel. Rooms have four 10 bunks and free lockers.

United World International Youth Hostel (☎ 9 48 00 48; www.unitedworldinternational.com; Gran Vía 7 Ⓜ Plaza España; dm incl breakfast & linen €15) Anothe great deal, it offers kitchen access and cosy feeling rooms with bunk beds.

Hostal Orly (☎ 915 31 30 12; Calle de la Monte 47, 7th fl; Ⓜ Gran Vía; s/d/tr €29/39/51) Housed in grand old 19th-century building, this plac feels high-class, with soaring ceilings an wood floors.

Also try **Hostal Triana** (☎ 915326812; www.hostal triana.com; Calle de la Salud 13, 1st fl; Ⓜ Gran Via; s/d €35/47), which has tidy rooms with bathroom and **Hostal Cruz Sol** (☎ 915 32 71 97; www.hostalcruz sol.com; Plaza Santa Cruz 6, 3rd fl; Ⓜ Sol; s/d €38/48), a cheery place with a great location.

Sol, Huertas & Atocha   Map p1068

Hostal Internacional La Posada de Huertas (☎ 914 29 35 26; www.posadadehuertas.com; Calle de las Huertas 21; Ⓜ Antón Martín; dm from €16) Though this youth hostel is clean, with warm blankets and decent (if tiny) bathrooms, it rates a zero on the charm scale. Dorm-style rooms have metal beds and lockers.

Hostal Aguilar (☎ 914 29 59 26; www.hostalaguilar .com; Carrera de San Jerónimo 32, 2nd fl; Ⓜ Sol; s/d/tr €40/47/63; 🖳)) Tacky décor but pluses like the double-glazed, noise-blocking windows and a computer offering Internet access for €3 per hour.

Hostal Dulcinea (☎ 914 29 93 09; www.hostal dulcinea.com; Calle Cervantes 19; s/d €38/42) Also worth trying is this place with friendly owners and well-kept rooms.

Malasaña & Chueca   Map p1068

Hostal Don Juan (☎ 915 22 77 46; Plaza de Vázquez de Mella 1; Ⓜ Gran Via; s/d €34/48) This elegant *hostal* is filled with art (each room has original works) and antique furniture.

Hostal La Zona (☎ 915 21 99 04; www.hostallazona .com; Calle de Valverde 7, 1st fl; Ⓜ Gran Via; d €45-65) Catering to gay clientele, rooms here are simple but stylish. Spacious room 203 is one of the best.

Also recommended are **Hostal El Catalan** (☎ 915 32 30 17; Calle de Hortaleza 17, 2nd fl; Ⓜ Gran Via; s €27-30, d/tr €42/54), which is clean, quiet and good value, and **Hostal María Cristina** (☎ 915 31 63 00; www.iespana.es/hostalmariacristina; Calle de Fuencarral 20; Ⓜ Gran Via; s/d/tr €32/44/62) a friendly option, with lots of light.

Beyond the Centre

Albergue Santa Cruz de Marcenado (Map pp1064-5; ☎ 915 47 45 32; Calle de Santa Cruz de Marcenado 28; Ⓜ Argüelles; dm under/over 26 incl tax, breakfast €7.80/11.26) This place offers rooms for four, six and eight people, this HI hostel is a handy choice if you want to be close to the city's universities.

High Tech Madrid Aeropuerto (☎ 915 64 59 06; www.hthoteles.com; Calle Galeón 25; Ⓜ Aeropuerto; s €100-135, d €120-150; Ⓟ 🍴 🖳 🏊) Within

shouting distance of the airport (they provide free airport transport), the High Tech has stylish rooms and free Internet access.

EATING

Meat lovers prepare your stomachs: Madrid's specialities include *cochinillo asado* (roast suckling pig) and *cocido madrileño*, a hearty stew made of beans and various animals' innards (it's tasty, honest). Vegetarians may be wondering about what local cuisine has to offer them, which is not much. Look out for pastas, salads and *bocadillos vegetales* (vegetable sandwiches), which usually have cheese.

Lunch hour runs from about 1.30pm until 3.30pm, and dinner starts at 9pm and lasts until late. Before mealtimes, many Madrileños head out for a *caña* (small beer) and a tapa or two.

Tapas   Map p1068

Oodles of tapas bars fill the barrios of Huertas, Chueca and La Latina. If the place is crowded, that's a good sign. Sure to be packed, **La Casa del Abuelo** (☎ 915 21 23 19; Calle Victoria 12; Ⓜ Sol) is famous for its garlicky prawns (€4.35). Cafeteria-style **Las Bravas** (☎ 915 32 26 20; Calle Espoz y Mina 13; Ⓜ Sol) is known for its patented version of its spicy *salsa brava* (a creamy sauce made with mayo and hot pepper); slather it over fried potatoes or Spanish tortillas.

Sierra Ángel (☎ 915 31 01 26; Calle Gravina 11; Ⓜ Chueca) Munchers at this classic tapas bar spill onto Plaza de Chueca with their tapas and drinks.

La Chata (☎ 913 66 14 58; Calle Cava Baja 24; Ⓜ La Latina) It has a great cheese plate (€11) and bullfighter-themed décor.

Cafés

Café Comercial (Map pp1064-5; ☎ 915 21 65 55; Glorieta de Bilbao 7; Ⓜ Bilbao) You can get a mean coffee and plenty of ambience at this café, a city classic. **Café de Ruiz** (Map pp1064-5; ☎ 914 46 12 32; Calle Ruiz 11; Ⓜ Bilbao) This cosy café looks like it was lifted out of a 1930s movie, with marble tables, velvet-covered seats and a welcoming attitude.

Mamá Inés (Map p1068; ☎ 915 23 23 33; www .mamaines.com; Calle de Hortaleza 22; Ⓜ Chueca) Popular with gay men – by day get delicious pastries and all the gossip on where that night's hot spot will be.

SPAIN

CENTRAL MADRID

SPAIN

500 m
0.3 miles

Jardines de Ferraz
Calle de Ferraz
Calle del Cadarso
Calle Arriaza

Plaza de España
Calle de San Vicente
Calle del Río
Calle de Ferraz

Jardines de Sabatini
Jardines Cabo Noval
Plaza de Oriente
Jardines de Lepanto

Calle de Bailén

Plaza de la Armería

To Iglesia de San Andrés

Parque del Emir Mohamed I
Jardines de las Vistillas

Calle de la Luna
Calle de la Estrella
Plaza de Santa María Soledad
Calle de San Roque
Calle de Tudescos
Calle Miguel Moya
Calle de Jacometrezo

Gran Vía
Calle del Barco
Calle de la Ballesta
Calle de Valverde
Calle de Fuencarral
Calle San Onofre
Calle Muñoz Tomás

Calle de San Bernardo

Plaza de Mostenses
Plaza de España

Calle de Isabel la Católica
Calle de Leganitos
Calle del Fomento
Calle del Reloj
Calle de Torija

Plaza de la Marina Española
Plaza de la Encarnación
Calle de Cañón III
Plaza de Isabel II
Opera
Plaza de Escalinata
Plaza de Ramales

Calle de Arrieta
Calle de Requena

Calle del Factor
Calle Mayor
Plaza de la Cruz Verde
Plaza del Biombo
Calle del Sacramento
Calle de Segovia
Plaza del Conde de Barajas
Plaza del Cordón
Plaza de San Miguel
Plaza del Comandante las Morenas
Plaza Mayor
Calle de Toledo
Cava de San Miguel
Calle de los Cuchilleros
Calle del Conde de Miranda
Plaza del Conde de Barajas
Calle del Almendro
Travesía del Nuncio
Costanilla de San Pedro

Calle de Hernán Cortés
Calle de Augusto Figueroa
Calle de San Bartolomé
Costanilla de Capuchinos
Calle de Hortaleza
Calle de Barbieri
Plaza de Chueca
Chueca
Calle de la Libertad
Calle de San Marcos
Calle de las Infantas
Calle del Marqués de Valdeiglesias

Calle de San Gregorio
Calle Piamonte
Calle de Prim
Calle del Almirante
Calle de Gravina
Calle de Barquillo

CHUECA

Ministerio del Ejército
Plaza del Rey
Ministerio de Cultura
Banco de España
Plaza de Cibeles
Paseo del Prado
Plaza de la Lealtad (Canovas del Castillo)
Plaza de Neptuno (Canovas del Castillo)

Banco de España
Calle de Alcalá

Calle del Duque de Medinaceli
Calle de Cervantes
Plaza de Jesús
Calle de Jesús
Calle de Lope de Vega
Calle de las Huertas

CORTES
Calle de León
Calle del Infante
Calle de Manuel Fernández y González
Calle del Prado
Calle de Santa Ana
Calle de Núñez de Arce
Calle de San Sebastián
Calle de Atocha
Antón Martín
Calle de Cañizares
Calle del Doctor Cortezo
Calle de la Colegiata
Calle del Conde de Romanones
Calle de Echegaray
Calle del Príncipe
Plaza del Ángel
Plaza de Santa Ana
Calle de la Cruz
Calle de Espoz y Mina
Calle de Carretas
Calle de la Bolsa
Plaza de Benavente
Plaza de Jacinto Benavente
Calle de Zaragoza
Calle Mayor
Calle de la Colegiata
Calle de San Tomás
Calle de Bordadores
Calle de las Hileras

SOL
Puerta del Sol
Sol
Calle del Correo
Calle del Arenal
Plaza de Celenque
Calle de Preciados
Callao
Plaza del Callao
Calle de San Martín
Calle de la Misericordia
Plaza de San Martín
Travesía Trujillos
Calle del Carmen
Plaza del Carmen
Calle de Tetuán
Calle de la Salud
Calle de Chinchilla
Calle de la Abada
Calle de Jardines

Gran Vía
Calle de la Montera
Calle de la Reina
Calle del Clavel
Calle de Caballero de Gracia
Calle de la Virgen de los Peligros
Sevilla
Sevilla
Calle de Sevilla
Calle de Aduana
Calle de Barcelona
Calle de Álvarez Gato

Carrera de San Jerónimo
Calle de San Jerónimo
Calle de los Madrazo
Calle del Duque de Medinaceli

Banco de España
Paseo del Prado

Santo Domingo
Plaza de Santo Domingo
Calle de Campomanes
Calle Señores de Luzón

Plaza de la Red de San Luis
Calle de la Virgen de los Peligros
Calle de Valverde
CENTRO

Calle de Preciados
Calle Concha

CALLE DE GRAN VÍA

Restaurants

La Mallorquina (Map p1068; ☎ 915 21 12 01; Puerta del Sol 8; M Sol; pastries around €1.50) Start the day sweet with a throng of white-jacketed waiters serving up pastries, truffles and candies.

La Gloria de Montera (Map p1068; ☎ 915 23 44 07; Calle de Caballero de Gracia 10; M Gran Via; menú, or fixed price lunch €6.60) For sit-down fare, there's no defeating La Gloria. It's oh-so-stylish, oh-so-cheap, and oh-so-popular.

Cuevas El Secreto (Map p1068; ☎ 915 31 82 91; Calle de Barcelona 2; M Sol; ✆ 6.30pm-2am; mains €4-8) This tavern-styled place serves tasty grilled meat and a few basic tapas.

La Finca de Susana (Map p1068; ☎ 913 69 35 57; Calle de Arlaban 4; M Sevilla; menú €7) Swish Susana serves a mix of Spanish and international fare to a professional-looking crowd.

La Trucha (Map p1068; ☎ 914 29 58 33; Calle de Manuel Fernández y González 3; mains €6-11) Head to this classic restaurant for fish, traditional dishes and tasty tapas.

Patatus (Map pp1064-5; ☎ 915 32 61 29; Calle Fuencarral 98; M Bilbao; to share €9-16) Open late, this is the place for post-partying gorge on junk food.

Bazaar (Map p1068; ☎ 915 23 39 05; Calle de la Libertad 21; M Chueca; menú €7) For real food, the funky, fusion Bazaar is unbeatable.

Omertá (Map p1068; ☎ 917 01 02 42; Calle de Gravina 7; M Chueca; menú €7.50) Bare brick walls and a tall ceiling give this pizzeria the feel of an old warehouse.

DRINKING

For tiled bars and bullfighter motifs, walk the Huertas barrio's streets, mainly around Plaza de Santa Ana. For gay-friendly locales, see the streets around Plaza de Chueca. Malasaña caters to a grungy crowd, while La Latina has chirpy, no-frills bars that have atmosphere each night of the week. In summer, go to the outdoor cafés in the city's plazas.

Bars

Straggling down a stairway passage to Calle de Segovia the **Café del Nuncio** (Map p1068; ☎ 913 66 09 06; Calle Segovia 9; M La Latina) has several cosy levels inside and an outdoor *terraza*. Nearby is the mythic **Chocolatería de San Ginés** (Map p1068; ☎ 913 65 65 46; Pasadizo San Ginés 5; M Sol or Ópera) where you can end the night (it's open until 7am!) with an eye-opening dose of syrupy hot chocolate.

Wander down and around the Calle de la Cava Baja for tonnes of options, including **El Viajero** (Map pp1064-5; ☎ 913 66 90 64; Plaza de la Cebada 11; M La Latina; tapas €3.50-8), where you can get dinner downstairs, or a great view from the rooftop terrace upstairs.

Cervecería Alemana (Map p1068; ☎ 914 29 70 33; Plaza de Santa Ana 6; M Antón Martín or Sol; ✆ closed Aug) This classic is famous for its cold, frothy beers and tasty tapas.

Viva Madrid (Map p1068; ☎ 914 29 36 40; www.bar vivamadrid.com; Calle de Manuel Fernandez y González 7; M Sol) Tapas and beer are the staples at this landmark with a beautifully tiled bar.

Areia (Map pp1064-5; ☎ 913 10 03 07; www.areia chillout.com; Calle de Hortaleza 92; M Chueca) The place to chill amidst its Arabian-style décor.

Finnegan's (Map pp1064-5; ☎ 913 10 05 21; Plaza de las Salesas 9; M Chueca; ✆ 1pm-2am) This is a friendly pub full of regulars.

Café Pepe Botella (Map pp1064-5; ☎ 915 22 43 09; Calle San Andrés 12; M Bilbao or Tribunal) Funky, it has velvet benches and marble-topped tables.

SPAIN

Museo Chicote (Map p1068; ☎ 915 32 67 37; Gran Via 12; Ⓜ Gran Via) This city classic has a lounge atmosphere late at night and a stream of small-time famous faces all day.

CLUBBING

The most popular dance spots are along and around Gran Via. For intimate dancing, head to Chueca or Malasaña, especially Calle de la Palma, which is lined with quirky clubs.

Club entry prices vary wildly, but most charge from €8 to €12, but you can get discounts for arriving early or if you're a girl (sorry guys). Watch out for discount tickets given out in bars or on the street. At most places, dancing starts at around 1am and lasts until daybreak. Come Thursday through Saturday for the best atmosphere.

Around Gran Via there are a number of places to check out.

El Sol (Map p1068; ☎ 915 32 64 90; Calle Jardines 3; Ⓜ Gran Via) Head here for guaranteed great dancing on weekends.

Palacio Gaviria (Map p1068; ☎ 915 26 60 69; Calle del Arenal 9; Ⓜ Sol or Ópera) This is transformed palace to club that's more costly than most. Thursday is international student night.

Teatro Joy Eslava (Map p1068; ☎ 913 66 37 33; www.joy-eslava.com; Calle del Arenal 11; Ⓜ Sol or Ópera) Next to Palacio Gaviria, this is great fun.

El Son (Map pp1064–5; ☎ 915 32 32 83; Calle de Victoria 6; Ⓜ Sol) This one has the Latino grooves. Live shows are on from Monday to Thursday.

Kapital (Map pp1064–5; ☎ 914 20 29 06; Calle de Atocha 125; Ⓜ Atocha) If you can't make up your mind about dance styles, the seven-storey Kapital does the trick. Every floor offers a different mood.

Gay & Lesbian Venues   Map p1068

Chueca is Madrid's lively, gay-friendly neighbourhood, and you'll find gay and lesbian bars and clubs on nearly every street, though some of the bigger-name gay dance clubs are along Gran Via.

Ohm (☎ 915 41 35 00; Plaza del Callao 4; Ⓜ Callao) The weekend party hosted by Sala Bash is a hit on the gay and straight scenes.

Cool (☎ 915 42 34 39; Calle de Isabel la Católica 6; Ⓜ Santo Domingo) Nearby, Cool guarantees a sexy night for a well-heeled crowd.

ENTERTAINMENT

The entertainment bible is the *Guía del Ocio*, a weekly magazine sold at newsstands for €1.

Highlights are given in English at the back. The best gay guide is *Shanguide*, which you can pick up for free in bars around town.

Live Music
FLAMENCO

Madrid is a good place to see professional interpretations of this Andalucían art. Most shows are set up like a dinner theatre and are squarely aimed at tourists, but the quality is generally top-notch. One of the cheapest shows is **Las Tablas** (Map p1068; ☎ 915 42 05 20; Plaza de España 9; Ⓜ España; admission €12-15; ☽ 7pm-late, nightly show 10.30pm).

JAZZ

Café Central (Map p1068; ☎ 913 694 143; www.cafecentralmadrid.com; Plaza del Angel 10; Ⓜ Antón Martín; admission €10-12) and **Café Populart** (Map p1068; ☎ 914 29 84 07; www.populart.es; Calle de la Huertas 22; Ⓜ Antón Martín; admission free) are two of the best locales for live jazz. Smoky, crowded cafés, that are the apt mood for soulful melodies.

ROCK

Sala Caracol (Map pp1064–5; ☎ 915 27 35 94; Calle Bernardino Obregón 18; Ⓜ Embajadores) This temple to variety hosts a different style every night of the week.

Galileo Galilei (☎ 915 34 75 57; Calle Galileo 100; Ⓜ Islas Filipinas) It has been known to stage all from comedy acts to magic shows, though its strength is up-and-coming bands.

La Riviera (Map pp1064–5; ☎ 913 65 24 15; Paseo Bajo de la Virgen del Puerto; Ⓜ Puerta de Angel) A club and concert venue, it has a pretty Art Deco interior and open-air concerts in summer.

Theatre & Opera   Map p1068

Teatro Real (☎ 915 16 06 06; www.teatro-real.com; Plaza de Oriente; Ⓜ Ópera) Madrid's sumptuous opera house is the city's grandest stage.

Teatro de la Zarzuela (☎ 915 24 54 00; Calle de Jovellanos 4; Ⓜ Banco de España) Not as fancy as Teatro Real but well worth a visit, this is the best place to see *zarzuela*, a very Spanish mixture of dance, music and theatre.

GETTING THERE & AWAY

Madrid's international **Barajas Airport** (☎ 90 35 35 70), 16km northeast of the city, is a busy place, with flights coming in from all over Europe and beyond. Most national flight are run by **Iberia** (Map pp1064–5; ☎ 902 40 05 0 www.iberia.com; Calle Velázquez 130); find the bes deals on its website. You can also contact Iberia at the company's airport offices.

Though there are several bus stations dotted around the city, most out-of-town buses use the **Estación Sur** (☎ 914 68 42 00; Calle de Méndez Álvaro; Ⓜ Méndez Álvaro). The largest bus company here is **Alsa** (☎ 902 42 22 42; www.alsa.es).

Renfe trains link Madrid to almost every other point in Spain. For ticket details, visit the Renfe offices inside the stations.

GETTING AROUND

Madrid's huge **metro** (www.madrid.es) can reach almost any city spot. It's quick, clean, relatively safe, and runs from 6am until 2am.

The bus system is also good, but working out the maze of bus lines can be a challenge. Contact **EMT** (☎ 914 06 88 10; www.emtmadrid.es) for more information.

CASTILLA Y LEÓN

The huge area of Castilla y León is splashed across Spain's heartland. Here are the fabled Spanish castles, knights and strong stone bridges, a hilly landscape that's has some of the country's most historic, pretty towns.

ÁVILA

Its old town huddled behind pristine medieval walls, Ávila is a remarkable, romantic city perfect for simply strolling and soaking up history. The city is most proud of its claim as the birthplace of Santa Teresa, a mystical writer and reformer of the Carmelite order.

Both the train and bus stations are about 500m from the centre. The 20-minute walk is mostly uphill.

Information

Cybernet (☎ 920 35 23 52; Av de Madrid 25; per hr €2.50; Ⓨ 11.30am-2.30pm & 4.30pm-1am)

Post office (☎ 920 31 35 06; Plaza de la Catedral 2; Ⓨ 8.30am-8.30pm Mon-Fri, 9.30am-2pm Sat) In a handy location.

Tourist office (☎ 920 21 13 87; www.avilaturismo.com; Plaza de la Catedral 4; Ⓨ 9am-2pm & 5-8pm 15 Sep-Jun, 9am-8pm Sun-Thu, 9am-9pm Fri-Sat Jul-15 Sep) Or try the information kiosks set up in summer at the Renfe train station and just outside the Puerta de San Vincente.

Sights

A stroll on the top of Ávila's splendid **12th-century walls** (Murallas; ☎ 920 21 13 87; admission €3.50;

Ⓨ 11am-5.15pm winter, 10am-7.15pm summer) should be your top priority. More than 1km is open to the public, but it's split into two sections broken up by the cathedral. Made of 2500 turrets and 88 towers, Ávila's walls are some of the best preserved in Spain.

Embedded into the eastern city walls, the **cathedral** (☎ 920 21 16 41; Plaza de la Catedral; admission €3; Ⓨ 10am-5pm Mon-Fri, noon-5pm Sat & Sun Nov-Mar, to 7pm Apr-Oct) is the first Gothic church in Spain. It boasts rich walnut choir stalls and a long, narrow central nave that makes the soaring ceilings seem all the more majestic.

Even more loved by locals is the **Convento de Santa Teresa** (☎ 920 21 10 30; Plaza de la Santa; admission museum €2; Ⓨ museum 10am-2pm & 4-7pm, relic room 9.30am-1.30pm & 3.30-7pm, church 8.30am-1.30pm & 3.30-8.30pm), built in 1636; birthplace of the 16th-century mystic and ascetic. It has a bare interior and a gold-adorned chapel that sits atop Teresa's former bedroom, but the relics have more appeal (plus a bit of the saint's ring finger) and the museum about her life.

Sleeping & Eating

Pensión Continental (☎ 920 21 15 02; Plaza de la Catedral 6; s €15, d €26-33, tr €39) Modest, but offers unbeatable vistas of the cathedral and charming (if aged) décor.

Hostal Don Diego (☎ 920 25 54 75; fax 920 25 45 49; Calle Marqués de Canales y Chozas 5; s €26-28, d €34-48) Here you will find newish bathrooms and sparkling-clean rooms.

Hostal El Rincón (☎ 920 35 10 44; www.plaza-zurraquin.com; Plaza de Zurraquín 3; s €30, d €45-54) One of the town's top *hostales*, squeaky clean, with tiled floors, all-wood furniture and fluffy towels.

Mercado Municipal (☎ 920 21 10 29; Calle Comuneros de Castilla; Ⓨ 9am-2pm & 4.30-7.30pm Mon-Thu, 9am-7.30pm Fri, 9am-2pm Sat) Self-caterers can head here for sandwiches.

Siglo Doce (☎ 920 25 28 85; Plaza de la Catedral 6; sandwiches about €3.50, mains €5.50-7.50; Ⓨ noon-5pm & 8pm-midnight) Right inside the old city walls, this place has a friendly bar atmosphere.

El Portalón (☎ 920 21 43 29; Plaza del Mercado Chico 4; mains €5-14, menú €8; Ⓨ 1-4pm & 8.30-11pm) Sit-down fare like tasty grilled meats, fresh fish and gazpacho (a soup made from tomatoes and peppers and served cold) are offered at fair prices at this unpretentious restaurant.

Drinking

The Puerta del Peso de la Harina is a hot spot after dark, with several bars along Calle

SPAIN

1072 CASTILLA Y LEÓN •• Salamanca

de San Segundo. Try **Bodeguito de San Segundo** (☎ 920 21 42 47; San Segundo 19; ☺ 11am-1am) for a great selection of Spanish wines and tapas.

Getting There & Away

Renfe trains come and go from Madrid (€5.60 to €7.15, up to two hours, at least 24 daily), León (€15.75 to €23.50, about three hours, seven daily) and other cities.

Buses connect Madrid's Estación Sur and Ávila daily (€6.26, 1½ hours, at least 4 daily). Contact the **bus station** (☎ 920 22 01 54; Av de Madrid 2) for more information.

SALAMANCA

A quinessential university town, fun, fairytale Salamanca is a historic city that's still very happening. Salamanca's destiny was changed in 1218, when King Alfonso XI founded what was to become Spain's greatest university. The old city is a showcase of Spanish building styles, with some of the country's best examples of Plateresque, Churrigueresque and Spanish Gothic buildings.

The bus station is 1km west of town; you can walk to the centre. The main train station is further, but you can take a bus No 1 from Gran Via. Reaching town is easier, as the train does a drop-off-only 'pause' to leave folk at the Plaza de España in the centre.

Information

Cyberplace (☎ 923 26 42 81; Plaza Mayor 10; per hr €1.20; ☺ 10.30am-2pm)
Municipal tourist office (☎ 923 21 83 42; www .aytosalamanca.es; Plaza Mayor 32; ☺ 9am-2pm & 4-6.30pm Mon-Fri, 9am-6.30pm Sat, 9am-2pm Sun, open later in summer)

Sights

Salamanca's spirit isn't found inside museums or churches, moreso in the streets and plazas. International students walk busily and café tables spill onto the footpaths.

FIND THE FROG

The university's façade is an ornate mass of sculptures and carvings, and hidden among this 16th-century Plateresqe creation is a tiny stone frog. Legend says that those who find the frog will have good luck in studies, life and love. A hint: look on the right-hand side of the façade.

Start with a stroll in the harmonious **Plaza Mayor**, designed in 1755 by José Churriguera, founder of the architectural style that carries his name. From here head up busy Rúa Mayor to marvel at the **Casa de las Conchas** (House of Shells), a city symbol since it was built in the 15th century and now home to a tourist office and the library.

The **university** (☎ 923 29 44 00; Calle Libreros; adult €4; ☺ 9.30am-1.30pm & 4-7pm Mon-Fri, 9.30am-1.30pm & 4-6.30pm Sat, 10am-1pm Sun), with its ubiquitous presence, is worth a visit. You can peek into the old classrooms, chapel, library and small museum.

Salamanca is curiously home to two cathedrals; the new, larger cathedral was built beside the old Romanesque one instead of on top of it, as was the norm. The **Catedral Nueva** (New Cathedral; ☎ 923 21 74 76; Plaza Anaya; ☺ 9am-1pm & 4-6pm Oct-Mar, 9am-2pm & 4-8pm Apr-Sep), completed in 1733, is a Gothic masterpiece that took 220 years to build. From inside, you can head to the **Catedral Vieja** (Old Cathedral; adult €3; ☺ 10am-12.30pm & 4-5.30pm Oct-Mar, 10am-1.30pm & 4-7.30pm Apr-Sep), a 12th-century temple with a stunning altar and several noteworthy chapels.

Sleeping & Eating

Pensión Feli (☎ 923 21 60 10; Calle de los Libreros 58; r per person €12) Fantastic value, Feli has cheery rooms, though the cramped, shared bathrooms are 1960s relics.

Camping La Capea (☎ 923 25 10 66; Carretera N-630, km 384; per adult €2.95; ☒ Ⓟ) Just 4km from the city, this large, shady camping ground is safe and comfortable and has extras like a supermarket and cafeteria. Hourly buses connect it with Salamanca's Gran Via.

There are several good budget *hostales* on Calle Meléndez, including **Hostal Las Vegas** (☎ 923 21 87 49; Calle Meléndez 13; s €20, d €24-36, tr/q €45/60), a homely place with plants peeking out of every corner. You'll feel like you're at Aunt Edna's.

Hostal Catedral (☎ 923 21 14 27; fax 923 27 06 14; Rúa Mayor 46; s/d €30/45) We can't gush enough over this immaculate, adorable *hostal*, where quiet rooms have sparkling bathrooms and some have cathedral views.

Café El Ave (☎ 923 26 45 11; Calle de los Libreros 24; menú €9.90) This bright café is good for a quick lunch or afternoon coffee. The midday *menú* offers plenty of variety.

El Patio Chico (☎ 923 26 51 03; Calle Meléndez 13; mains €5.90-11) For rustic ambience, try this

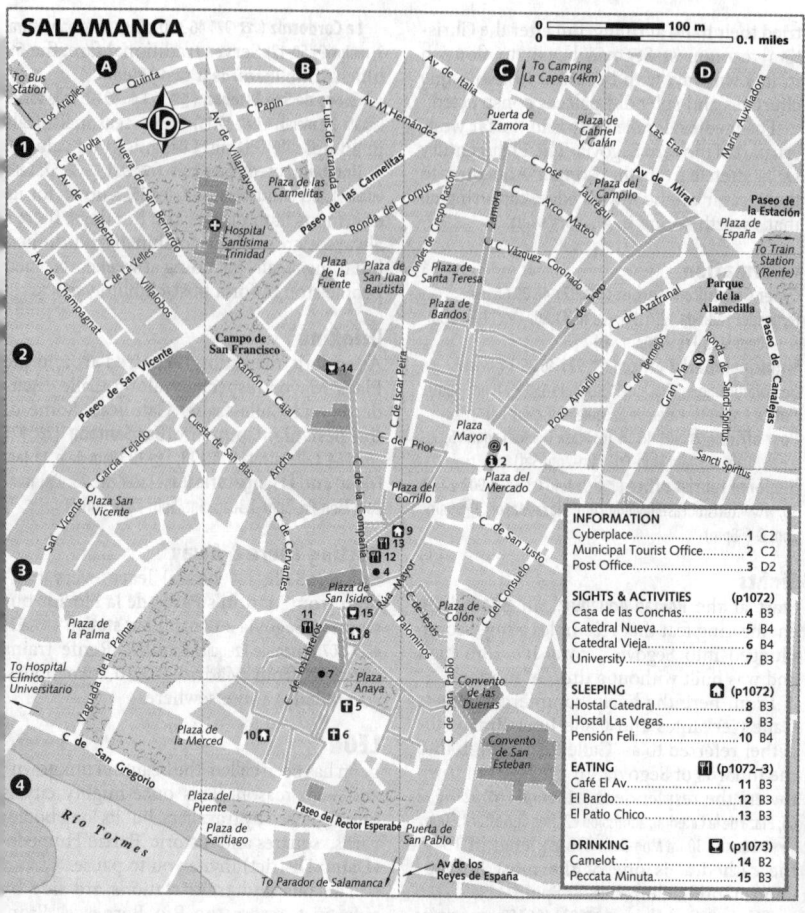

SALAMANCA

INFORMATION
Cyberplace.................................1 C2
Municipal Tourist Office..........2 C2
Post Office..................................3 D2

SIGHTS & ACTIVITIES   (p1072)
Casa de las Conchas..................4 B3
Catedral Nueva.........................5 B4
Catedral Vieja...........................6 B4
University...................................7 B3

SLEEPING   (p1072)
Hostal Catedral..........................8 B3
Hostal Las Vegas.......................9 B3
Pensión Feli.............................10 B4

EATING   (p1072-3)
Café El Av................................11 B3
El Bardo....................................12 B3
El Patio Chico..........................13 B3

DRINKING   (p1073)
Camelot.....................................14 B2
Peccata Minuta.......................15 B3

restaurant offering everything from international standards such as T-bone steaks to local dishes such as 'stewed tongue'.

El Bardo (☎ 923 25 92 65; Av Portugal 88; mains €8.40-13) Has hearty Castilian fare.

Drinking

Salamanca's student population makes sure that there is always something happening after the classrooms are emptied. Wander around the university and Plaza Mayor for low-key bars; **Peccata Minuta** (☎ 923 12 84 47; Calle Francisco Vitoria 3) is a good option for drinks and special coffees. Later on head to the popular disco **Camelot** (☎ 923 21 21 84; Calle Bordadores 3), which is housed in a former convent.

Getting There & Away

Renfe trains trickle in from Madrid (€14.15, 2½ hours, six daily), Valladolid (€5.60, one hour, one daily), Bilbao (€24.50, 5½ hours, one daily) and Ávila (€7.15, 1½ hours, seven daily). There are frequent bus services to Madrid (€10 to €15, 2½ to three hours, eight daily). Other destinations served regularly include Santiago de Compostela, Ávila, Segovia and León.

SEGOVIA

With its towering Roman aqueduct, compact historic centre and setting amid the undulating hills of Castile, Segovia is without doubt one of Spain's most enchanting cities. The Romans, Visigoths and Muslims all tried their hand at ruling, but after the Christian reconquest Segovia began to flourish in its own way, with beautiful Romanesque churches and splendid palaces constructed.

The medieval walled city is in the far western part of modern Segovia. The 11th-century walls stretch from the Roman Aqueduct to the Alcázar on the town's edge, capturing all that's worth seeing in a short visit.

Information

Cyber Graphika Internet (☎ 921 46 09 66; Av Fernández Ladreda 12, 1st fl; per hr €1.80; ⏱ 11am-2pm & 3-10pm Mon-Fri, 4-10pm Sat)

Municipal tourist office (☎ 921 46 29 14; www .segoviaturismo.es; Plaza del Axoguejo 1; ⏱ 10am-8pm)

Police (☎ 091; Paseo de Ezequiel González 22)

Post office (☎ 921 46 16 16; Plaza Doctor Laguna 5; ⏱ 8.30am-8.30pm Mon-Fri, 9am-2pm Sat)

Regional tourist office (☎ 921 46 03 34 or 902 20 30 30; www.turismocastillayleon.com; Plaza Mayor; ⏱ 9am-2pm & 5-8pm)

Sights

Start at the **Roman Aqueduct**, an 894m-long engineering feat that resembles a huge comb plunged into Segovia's core. It's 28m high and was built without a drop of mortar.

From here the lively commercial streets Calle Cervantes and Calle Juan Bravo (together referred to as 'Calle Real') climb into the innards of Segovia. In the heart of town towers the resplendent **cathedral** (☎ 921 46 22 05; Plaza de la Catedral; admission €2, free Sun after 1.30pm; ⏱ 9.30am-5.30pm Mon-Sat). Completed in 1577, the cathedral is one of the most homogenous Gothic churches in Spain.

The fortified **Alcázar** (☎ 921 46 07 59; www.alcazar desegovia.com; Plaza de la Reina Victoria Eugenia; admission €3.50; ⏱ 10am-6pm Oct-Mar, 10am-7pm Apr-Sep) is a fairy-tale castle perched dramatically on the edge of Segovia. Roman foundations are buried somewhere underneath this splendour. What we see today is a late-1800s copy of the 13th-century original, which burned down.

Sleeping & Eating

Hostal Fornos (☎ 921 46 01 98; Calle Infanta Isabel 13; s €32-38, d €45-51) Hand-painted headboards and wall decorations provide a cheerful air.

Hostal Juan Bravo (☎ 921 46 34 13; Calle Juan Bravo 12, 2nd fl; r without/with bathroom €31/36) Up two flights of shaky stairs is this spotless *hostal*. Rooms have parquet floors and new linen. Those with bathrooms are worth the extra €5.

La Codorniz (☎ 921 46 38 07; Calle Hermanos Barral 3; mains €9.50-12) Serves traditional fare; the €9 lunch-time *menú* is a tasty deal.

Cueva de San Esteban (☎ 921 46 09 82; Calle Valdelaguila 15; menús €7.70-12.15) Enjoy seasonal meals in an upscale setting. Lunch is good value.

Hamburguesería San Luís (☎ 921 46 35 57; Calle Infanta Isabel 12; hamburgers €2.40-4.35) Known for its enormous hamburgers and hot dogs, there's always a crowd here for lunch and dinner, but things really get going at weekends when people stop in for a post-clubbing snack.

Drinking

After dark, the action is centred around the Plaza Mayor (especially along Calle Escuderos and Calle Isabel Católica). Some of the best nightspots are **Bar Santana** (☎ 921 46 35 64; Calle Infanta Isabel 18; ⏱ 10.30am-3am, to 4am Fri-Sat) and **El Purgatorio** (Calle Escuderos 26; ⏱ 1pm-2am Mon-Fri, 5pm-3.30am Sat, 5pm-2am Sun).

Getting There & Away

Buses (€5.68, 1¼ hours) leave every half-hour from Madrid's Paseo de la Florida bus stop for Segovia's central **bus station** (☎ 921 42 77 07; Paseo de Ezequiel González). Renfe trains come in from Madrid (€5.10, two hours, seven daily) and elsewhere.

LEÓN

León has been called 'the beautiful unknown' and with reason. This once-mighty city is often ignored by travellers, but its long boulevards, squares and historic 'Barrio Húmedo' (Damp District) invite you to pause.

The bus and train stations are side by side, just across the Río Bernesga. From here, walk 15 minutes straight up Av de Ordoño II to reach the centre.

Information

Cafeteria Santo Domingo (☎ 987 26 13 84; Ordoño II 3; per hr €1; ⏱ 8am-11pm Mon-Fri, 9am-11pm Sun) Has a well-run Internet centre at the back.

Tourist office (☎ 987 23 70 82; www.aytoleon.com; Plaza de la Regla 3; ⏱ 9am-2pm & 5-7pm Mon-Fri, 10am-2pm & 5-8pm Sat & Sun).

Sights

León's best and best-known monument is its breathtaking 13th-century **cathedral** (☎ 987 87 57 70; www.catedraldeleon.org; museum €3.50; ⏱ cathedral: 8.30am-1.30pm & 4-7pm Mon-Sat, 8.30am-2.30pm & 5-7pm Sun Oct-Jun, 8.30am-8pm

Mon-Sat, 8.30am-2.30pm & 5-8pm Sun Jul-Sep, museum: 9.30am-1.30pm & 4-6.30pm Mon-Fri, Sat morning only Oct-May, to 7pm Jun, to 7.30pm Mon-Fri Jul-Sep). A marvel of Gothic architecture, its most outstanding features are the 128 radiant stained-glass windows (with a surface of 1800 sq metres), which give the place an ethereal quality.

Nearby is the **Real Basílica de San Isidoro** (☎ 987 87 61 61; www.sanisidorodeleon.org; admission €3, free Thu afternoon; ☾ 10am-1.30pm & 4-6.30pm Mon-Sat, 10am-1.30pm Sun Sep-Jun, 9am-8pm Mon-Sat, 9am-2pm Sun Jul-Aug), a simple Romanesque church that houses the interesting **Panteón Real**, where Leonese royalty lie buried beneath a canopy of some of the finest frescoes in all of Spain.

Across town is the **Hostal de San Marcos**, a former pilgrim's hospital that now has a luxury Parador hotel. The rich interior is accessed by free **tours** (☾ 1pm & 8.30pm Mon-Thu, 1pm Fri-Sat, 9.30am & 5pm Sun) but the **Museo de León** (☎ 987 24 50 61; adult €1.20, free Sun; ☾ 10am-2pm & 4-7pm Tue-Sat, 10am-2pm Sun Sep-Jun, 10am-2pm & 5-8pm Tue-Sat, 10am-2pm Sun Jul-Aug), also here, exposes some parts of the building. Don't miss the façade, 100m of golden-hued carvings.

Sleeping & Eating

Don Suero (☎ 987 23 06 00; Suero de Quiñones 15; s €17.70-21.10, d €40) a clean, attractive place that could easily pass for a one- or two-star hotel, this is good value in the heart of town.

The Plaza de San Martín is packed with bars and restaurants, many with terraces.

Café Gótico (☎ 987 08 49 56; Calle Varillas 5; menú €8) This is another good option, where you can get tasty but no-frills, inexpensive fare, including an all-vegetarian daily lunch *menú*.

Palomo (☎ 987 25 42 25; Calle Escalerilla 8; mains €5.50-14, menú €9-15) Tuck into traditional Castilian dishes at this cosy establishment.

Getting There & Away

The Renfe train station has trains often running to/from Madrid (€19.20 to €29, four hours, seven daily), Ávila (€15.75 to €23.50, at least 2½ hours, nine daily), Burgos (€15.50 to €21, two hours, four daily) and Santiago de Compostela (€24.50, six hours, one daily).

The **bus station** (☎ 987 21 10 00; Av Ingeniero Saenz de Miera) links with many Spanish cities, among them Madrid (€18.31 to €31, at least 3½ hours, up to 12 daily), Burgos (€11.75, two to four hours, three daily) and Ávila (€14.18, 3½ hours, one daily). For more details, contact **Alsa** (☎ 947 26 63 70; www.alsa.es).

BURGOS

With its grand riverside promenades and outstanding collection of churches and monasteries, Burgos is one of Spain's hidden gems. Marvel at the gleaming white cathedral (one of Christendom's most splendid) and while away the day strolling the characterful boulevards of the centre.

The train station is connected to town by bus Nos 3, 5 and 7. The bus station is just across the river from the cathedral.

Information

Locutorio Capitanía (☎ 947 26 42 28; Plaza Alonso Martínez 3; per hr €1) Internet access.

Municipal tourist office (☎ 947 28 88 74; www.ayto burgos.es; Teatro Principal, Paseo de Espolón 1; ☾ 10am-2pm & 4.30-7.30pm Mon-Sat, 10am-2pm Sun Oct-Jun, 10am-2pm & 5-8pm Mon-Sat, 10am-2pm Sun Jul-Sep)

Police (☎ 947 28 88 39 or ☎ 091)

Sights

Burgos' claim to fame is its commanding 1261 Gothic **cathedral** (☎ 947 20 47 12; adult €3; ☾ 10am-1.15pm & 4-6.45pm Sep-Jun, 9.30am-1.15pm & 4-7.15pm Jul-Aug). Guided visits (in Spanish) are offered for €1.50 from Monday to Friday at 5pm and Sunday at 11am.

A modest Romanesque church once stood here, but today we see ornate spires (each 84m tall) piercing the skyline. Inside, the highlight is the Escalera Dorada (Gilded Staircase) by Diego de Siloé. The warrior El Cid lies buried beneath the central dome.

If you have time, visit the **Monasterio de las Huelgas** (☎ 947 20 16 30; adult €5; ☾ 10am-1.15pm & 4-5.45pm Tue-Sat, 10.30am-2.15pm Sun), still home to 35 nuns of a Cistercian order founded here in 1187 by Eleanor of Aquitaine. You can get here by walking a half-hour west along the southern bank of the Río Arlanzón.

Sleeping & Eating

Pensión Peña (☎ 947 20 63 23; Calle de la Puebla 18; s €15-17, d €22-24) Here you'll pay amazingly low prices for well-kept, cheerful rooms. All have pretty décor and shared bathrooms.

Pensión Victoria (☎ 947 20 15 42; Calle de San Juan 3; s €17-20, d €28-35, tr €39-45) Rooms here are big and bright, and some have TV and washbasins.

Restaurante La Riojana (☎ 947 20 61 32; Calle Avellanos 10; menú €6) A no-frills spot with a solid selection of Spanish dishes, such as paella and Rioja-style codfish, and home to the cheapest midday *menú* in town.

SPAIN

Prego (☎ 947 26 04 47; Huerto del Rey 4; salads & pasta €5-7, pizza €10) One of the few good options for vegetarians. It's an elegant Italian restaurant with impressive prices and tasty dishes.

Getting There & Away

Trains come and go from cities including Salamanca (€17.50, about three hours, four daily) and Madrid (€19.90 to €23, five hours or more, nine daily). The bus station is home to several companies. **Alsa** (☎ 947 26 63 70; www.alsa.es) makes runs to Salamanca (€13 to €16, four hours, three daily), Valladolid (€7 to €9, two to three hours, three to four daily) and other destinations.

CASTILLA-LA MANCHA

Known as the home of Don Quixote, the vast province of Castilla-La Mancha is still off-the-beaten-track. Lonely windmills and bleak treeless plains give way to pretty villages and medieval castles. It has two of Spain's most fascinating cities: Toledo and Cuenca.

TOLEDO

pop 72,549

A jumble of narrow, winding streets, perched on a small hill above the Río Tajo, Toledo is crammed with museums, churches and other monumental reminders of its splendid and turbulent past. It's also quite expensive and terribly touristy. If you can, try to stay overnight so you can really appreciate the spark and soul of this remarkable city.

Information

Main tourist office (☎ 925 22 08 43; www.jccm.es; Puerta de Bisagra; ☯ 9am-6pm Mon-Sat, 9am-3pm Sun) At the northern end of town.

Tourist office (☎ 925 25 40 30; ☯ 10.30am-2.30pm & 4.30-7pm Tue-Sun, 10.30am-2.30pm Mon) A more helpful office, opposite the cathedral.

Scorpions (☎ 925 21 25 56; Calle Matías Moreno 10; per hr €2; ☯ 12.30pm-2am) Internet access.

Sights & Activities

It's not just the many historical sights; even the tourist shops in Toledo are fun – many reflecting the city's swashbuckling past with suits of armour and swords for sale.

You could happily spend an afternoon in Toledo's **cathedral** (☎ 925 22 22 41; Cardenal Cisneros; ☯ 10.30am-6.30pm Mon-Sat, 2-6pm Sun), admiring the glorious stone architecture, stained-glass windows, tombs of kings and art by El Greco, Velázquez and Goya. You have to buy a ticket (€5.50) to enter the Coro, Sacristía, Capilla de la Torre and Sala Capitular, which contain some of the finest art and artisanship.

The **Museo de Santa Cruz** (☎ 925 22 10 36; Calle Cervantes 3; admission free; ☯ 10am-6.30pm Mon-Sat, 10am-2pm Sun) contains a large collection of furniture, faded tapestries, paintings and other paraphernalia. Upstairs is an impressive collection of El Grecos.

The lines from the **Iglesia de Santo Tomé** (☎ 925 25 60 98; Plaza del Conde; admission €1.50; ☯ 10am-6pm Oct-Jun, 10am-7pm Jul-Sep) declares the El Greco's masterpiece *El Entierro del Conde de Orgaz* inside. It shows the Count of Orgaz's burial in 1322 by St Stephen and St Augustine, viewed by a heavenly entourage.

The **Casa-Museo de El Greco** (☎ 925 22 40 46; Calle Samuel Leví; admission €2.40; ☯ 10am-2pm & 4-9pm Tue-Sat, 10am-2pm Sun), in the former Jewish area, has the artist's famed *Vista y Plano de Toledo*. El Greco lived in Toledo from 1577 to 1614, but it is unlikely he lived in this former house.

The **Museo Sefardí** (☎ 925 22 36 65; www.museo sefardi.net; Calle Samuel Leví s/n; admission €4.50; ☯ 10am-6pm Tue-Sat, 10am-2pm Sun) is housed in the beautiful 14th-century **Sinagoga del Tránsito**. Toledo's other synagogue, **Santa María La Blanca** (☎ 925 22 72 57; Calle de los Reyes Católicos 4; admission €1.50; ☯ 10am-6pm), a short way north, dates from the 13th century.

Slightly further north is one of the city's obvious sights, **San Juan de los Reyes** (☎ 925 22 38 02; admission €1.50; ☯ 10am-6pm Oct-Jun, 10am-7pm Jul-Sep), the Franciscan monastery and church founded by Fernando and Isabel. The late Flemish-Gothic style is chinzed with lavish Isabelline ornamentation and *Mudéjar* decoration. Outside hang the chains of Christian prisoners freed after Granada's fall in 1492.

Sleeping

Cheap accommodation is not easy to come by and is often full.

Residencia Juvenil de San Servando (☎ 925 22 45 54; fax 925 21 39 54; dm under/over 26 €8.70/11.30) Toledo's HI hostel is beautifully located in the Castillo de San Servando, a castle that started life as a Visigothic monastery.

Pensión Castilla (☎ 925 25 63 18; Calle Recoletos 6; s/d €15/25) With its wooden floors, ceiling fans and bright rooms, this is one of Toledo's best budget options.

TOLEDO

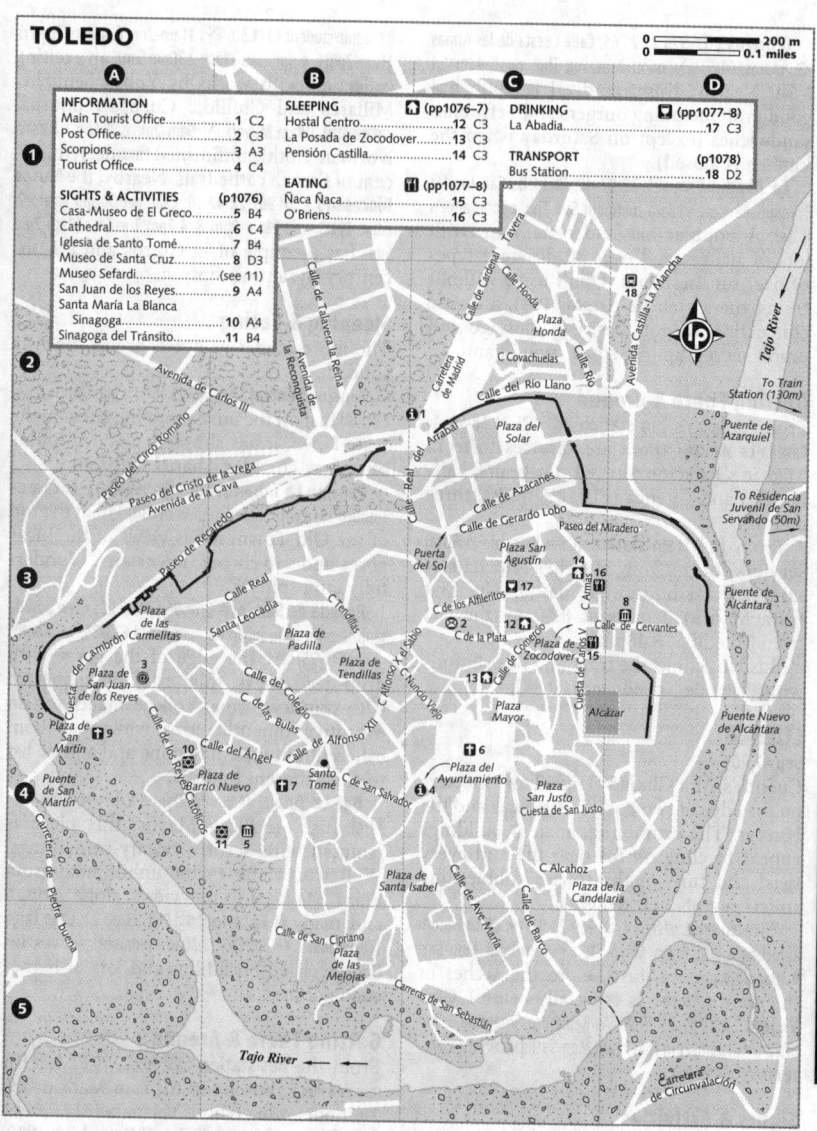

Hostal Centro (☎ 925 25 70 91; www.hostalcentro.com; Calle Nueva 13; s/d/tr €30/45/60; ❄) Just off the social hang-out that is Plaza de Zocodover, the *hostal* has wonderful spacious rooms, some with balconies, and a fabulous rooftop terrace.

La Posada de Zocodover (☎ 925 25 58 14; Calle Condonerias 6; d with bathroom €37.30; ❄) In an old, narrow building, with timbered ceilings,

pretty brass beds and tiled floors, the hotel's seven exquisite rooms get snapped up fast.

Eating & Drinking

Ñaca Ñaca (☎ 925 25 35 59; Plaza de Zocodover 7; bocadillos €2-3; ⏰ 9am-11pm Mon-Thu, 9am-4am Fri, 9am-11pm Sat & Sun) Late-night eats or day snacks? This place does chunky filled rolls to take away.

1078 CASTILLA-LA MANCHA •• Cuenca

O'Briens (☎ 925 21 26 65; Calle Cuesta de las Armas 12; mains €4-5; ☺ noon-2am Sun-Thu, noon-4am Fri & Sat) Nearby, this friendly Irish pub has good grub including burgers and hefty club sandwiches (except on Saturday when the kitchen is closed).

La Abadia (☎ 925 25 07 46; Plaza de San Nicolás 3; mains €6-12; ☺ 8am-midnight Sun-Thu, noon-1am Fri & Sat) A popular bar and restaurant, with lots of alcoves and over 30 different types of beer on the menu. Don't leave without trying the *sartén de patatas* (€4), a divine concoction of potatoes, egg, sausage and onion served up in a small frying pan.

Getting There & Around

From Toledo's **bus station** (☎ 925 21 58 50; Av Castilla-La Mancha) there are services to/from Madrid's Estación Sur (€4, 1¼ hours, half-hourly) and Cuenca (€10, 2½ hours, three daily).

From the **train station** (Calle Paseo de la Rosa) services run to/from Madrid's Atocha station (€5, 1½ hours, five daily). The first from Madrid departs at 8.30am, the last from Toledo at 6.48pm.

Bus No 5 links the train and bus stations with Plaza de Zocodover (€0.80).

CUENCA
pop 47,201

Cuenca's Alta Ciudad (High Town) teeters on the edge of two gorges: the Júcar and the Huécar. The crumbling, ancient buildings appear to cling on for dear life and every twist and turn of the town's cobblestone streets reveals new delights.

The **tourist office** (☎ 969 23 21 19; ofi.turismo@ aytocuenca.org; Plaza Mayor 1; ☺ 9am-9pm Mon-Sat, 9.30am-2.30pm Sun), just before the arches of the main square, is especially helpful. **Ciber Viajero** (☎ 969 23 66 96; Av República Argentina 3; per hr €2 ☺ 10am-2pm & 5-11pm Mon-Sat) provides Internet access.

Sights & Activities

Cuenca's **Casas Colgadas** (Hanging Houses), built in the 15th century, are precariously positioned on a cliff top, their balconies projecting over the gorge. The **Puente de San Pablo** (1902), an iron footbridge that crosses the ravine, provides access to spectacular views of these buildings (and the rest of the old town). Within one of the Casas Colgadas is the **Museo de Arte Abstracto Español** (☎ 969 21 29

83; adult/student €3/1.50; ☺ 11am-2pm & 4-6pm Tue-Fri, 11am-2pm & 4-8pm Sat, 11am-2.30pm Sun), an exciting collection with works by Zobel, Sempere, Millares and Chillida. Cuenca's unusual **cathedral** (Plaza Mayor; ☺ 9am-2pm & 4-6pm) has a Norman-Gothic unfinished façade, reminiscent of French cathedrals. Nearby, the **Museo Diocesano** (☎ 969 22 42 10; Calle del Obispo Valero 2; adult €1.80; ☺ 11am-2pm & 4-7pm Tue-Sat, 11am-2pm Sun) has a couple of El Grecos and a 14th-century Byzantine diptych.

Sleeping & Eating

The more attractive hotels are in the Alta Ciudad.

Pensión Central (☎ 969 21 15 11; Calle Chirino 7; s/d €12/20) Just off the busy shopping street in the New Town, it has simple but warm rooms off a dark corridor. Shared bathroom.

Pensión La Tabanqueta (☎ 969 21 12 90; Calle de Trabuco 13; d with shared bathroom €30) Up at the top of the Old Town, it has views of the Júcar gorge and a lively bar downstairs. Wonderfully atmospheric.

Posada de San José (☎ 969 21 13 00; www.posada sanjose.com; Calle Julián Romero 4; s/d €23/34, with bathroom €47/75) At the edge of the gorge with drop-dead views, this tastefully converted 17th-century former college makes for an evocative romantic retreat with every room different but tastefully done and a price list to suit different budgets.

Bar La Tinaja (Calle del Obispo Valero 4; ☺ noon-1am) Just off Plaza Mayor, this place is jammed with scruffy twenty-somethings. Well worth the 600m uphill hike from Plaza Mayor for the views alone, rough and ready **El Caserío** (☎ 969 23 00 21; Calle Larga 17; bocadillos €3.30; ☺ 11.30am-midnight) serves up Scooby-sized bocadillos and lots of barbecued goodies.

Getting There & Around

From the **bus station** (☎ 969 22 70 87; Calle Fermin Caballero), buses run to/from Madrid (€9, 2½ hours, nine daily), Valencia (€12, 2½ hours to four hours, three daily) and Barcelona (€30, 9½ hours, twice daily).

Cuenca's **train station** (Paseo del Ferrocarril) has direct services to Madrid Atocha (€9.15, 2½ hours, five daily) and Valencia (€10, three hours, four daily).

Bus No 1 or 2 from near the bus and train stations will save you the crippling uphill climb to Plaza Mayor in the old town.

CATALONIA

Forget the Spain of flamenco and bullfights; Catalonia is a proud region that likes to see itself as somewhat independent from the rest of the country. A smallish triangle in the northeastern corner of the peninsula, Catalonia is a varied land with both soaring mountain peaks and long, sandy coasts. Its capital, Barcelona is one of Spain's most beautiful cities, but excursions to the Costa Brava, the Pyrenees, or down to Tarragona are memorable too.

BARCELONA

Sitting right on the Mediterranean, vibrant Barcelona is one of Europe's most exciting cities. With medieval palaces and plazas in the old quarters, fantastical modernist architecture sprinkled throughout L'Eixample district, and an innovative contemporary art and design scene, Barcelona won't disappoint. It also boasts great shopping, a lively nightlife and some of the best cuisine in Spain.

Orientation

Plaça Catalunya is Barcelona's heart and the marker between the historic city and the modern one. From here, the long pedestrian Ramblas shoots southeast down to the sea, with the busy Gothic quarter and El Raval district placed on either side. To the northwest of the plaza is L'Eixample, the grid-like district where you'll find shops and the bulk of the city's offices and residences.

Information
EMERGENCY
General Emergencies (☎ 112)
Guardia Urbana (City Police; Map p1086; ☎ 092; La Rambla 43)

INTERNET ACCESS
Bigg (Map p1086; ☎ 933 01 40 20; Calle Comtal 9; per hr €2; ☺ 9am-11pm Mon-Sat, 10am-11pm Sun; Ⓜ Plaça Catalunya)
Cybermundo (Map p1086; ☎ 933 17 71 42; Calle Bergara 3; per hr €1.20-2.90; ☺ 9am-midnight Mon-Fri, 10am-midnight Sat, 11am-midnight Sun; Ⓜ Plaça Catalunya)

MEDICAL SERVICES
You can get help with minor medical issues at the 24-hour pharmacies scattered around town. There's one at Passeig de Gràcia 26

(Map pp1080–1) and another at Las Ramblas 98 (Map pp1080–1).
Hospital Clinic (Map pp1080-1; ☎ 932 27 54 00; Carrer Villarroel 170; Ⓜ Hospital Clinic) Modern hospital with good services for travellers.

MONEY
It's best to change money at the main tourist office. Also, head to banks like La Caixa or Caixa Catalunya, which give fair rates. Avoid the *casas de cambio* (exchange houses) on Las Ramblas; the rates are too high.

POST
Main post office (Map p1086; ☎ 934 86 80 50; Plaça d'Antoni López; Ⓜ Barceloneta; ☺ 8.30am-9.30pm Mon-Sat, 9am-2pm Sun)

TOURIST INFORMATION
Main tourist office (Map p1086; ☎ 807 11 72 22; Plaça de Catalunya 17; Ⓜ Plaça Catalunya; ☺ 9am-9pm)

Sights
LAS RAMBLAS
You can't leave Barcelona without strolling down **Las Ramblas**, a pedestrian boulevard exploding with life. Stretching from the **Plaça de Catalunya** down to the waterfront, Las Ramblas is lined with street artists, news kiosks and vendors selling everything from live chickens to blue roses.

HUMAN CASTLES

An element in nearly every Catalan festival is *castellers,* or human castle builders. The tradition – unique to Catalonia – is simple: competing teams try to build the biggest pyramid possible, and whoever collapses first loses.

Big, burly men standing with their arms entwined form the castle's base, and up to 10 levels rise above them. Each tier is made by three or four people placed on the shoulders of those below them. It's a terrific display of balance and teamwork.

You can see castellers at most major festivals throughout Catalonia. The best teams are usually from the towns of Vilafranca del Penedès and Valls, both southwest of Barcelona. Bi-annually a huge casteller contest is held in early October in Tarragona's bullring. If you're in town then, it's definitely worth a day trip.

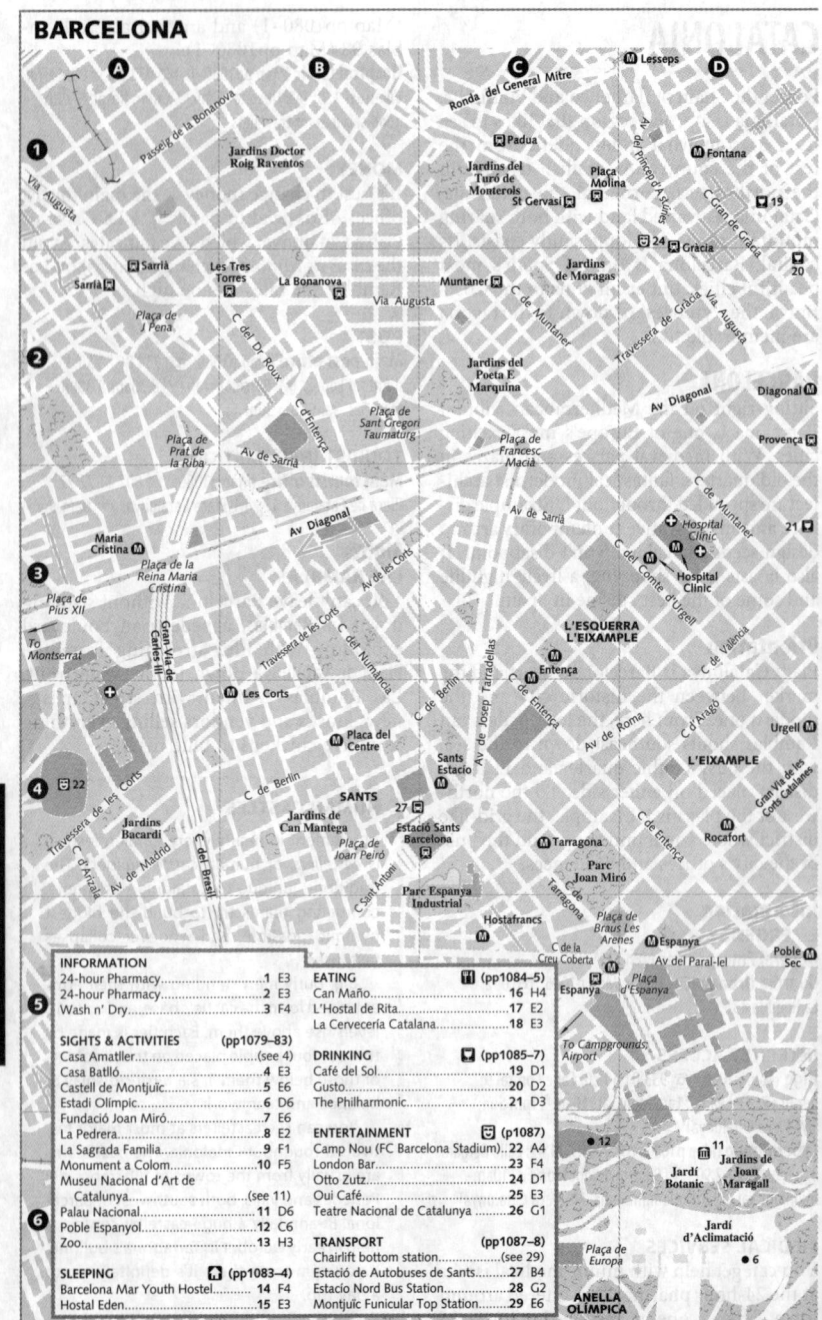

BARCELONA

SPAIN

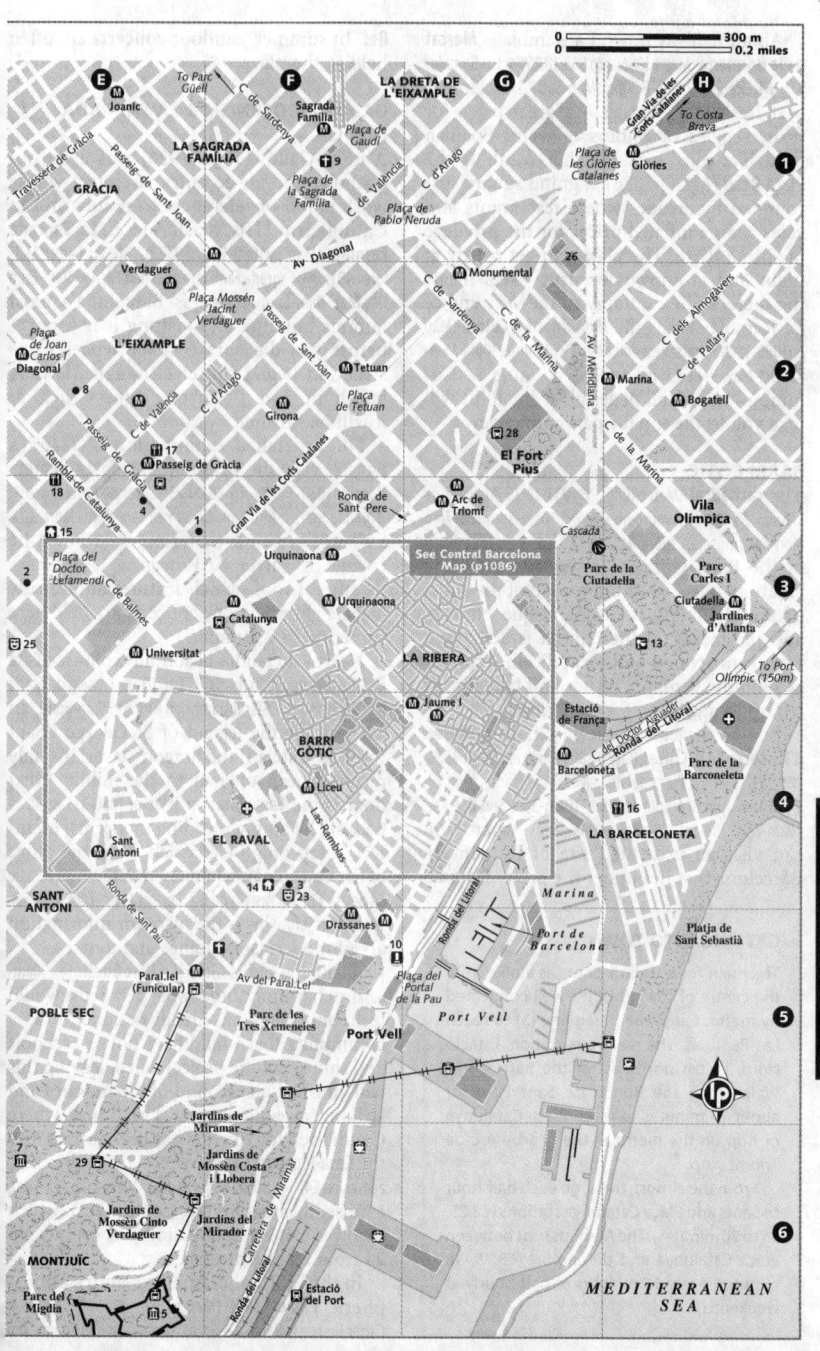

SPAIN

About halfway down La Rambla is **Mercat de la Boquería** (Map p1086; ☎ 933 18 25 84; Las Ramblas 91; Ⓜ Liceu; ⏰ 8am-8.30pm Mon-Sat), Barcelona's best fresh-food market – a great place for fruit, veggies or photos of weird Spanish food like pigs' ears. Further south is the **Plaça Reial** (Map p1086), a grand square surrounded by arcades where restaurants and cafés charge inflated prices for the privilege of sitting there. The plaza can get rowdy at night and is known for drug users meeting there, so be cautious. At the very end of La Rambla stands the **Monument a Colom** (Map pp1080-1; Ⓜ Drassanes; adult €2; ⏰ 10am-6.30pm Mon-Sat Oct-May, 9am-8.30pm Jun-Sep), a statue of Columbus atop a tall pedestal. A small lift will take you to the top for panoramic views.

BARRI GÒTIC

The **cathedral** (Map p1086; ☎ 933 10 25 80; Plaça de la Seu; Ⓜ Jaume I; museum €1; ⏰ 10am-1pm & 5-7pm Mon-Sat, museum morning only), the centrepiece of the Barri Gòtic, is essentially a Gothic creation, but it was built on top of the ruins of an 11th-century Romanesque church, and the façade of the church is actually a 19th-century neo-Gothic addition. Wander around the verdant cloister and take the **lift** (€1) up to a rooftop for nice views.

Just to the east is the fascinating **Museu d'Història de la Ciutat** (City History Museum; Map p1086; ☎ 933 15 11 11; Plaça del Rei; Ⓜ Jaume I; admission €4; ⏰ 10am-2pm & 4-8pm Tue-Sat, 10am-3pm Sun Oct-Apr, 10am-8pm Tue-Sat, 10am-3pm May-Sep), where you can visit an excavated site of Roman-era Barcelona that lies under the pretty **Plaça del Rei**. In summer, outdoor concerts are often held in the plaza.

GAUDÍ, MODERNISM & LA SAGRADA FAMÍLIA

Antoni Gaudí (1852–1926) was a devout Catholic and an eccentric architect whose work is full of references to nature and to Catholicism. His masterpiece, **La Sagrada Família** (Map pp1080-1; ☎ 932 07 30 31; Carrer Mallorca 401; Ⓜ Sagrada Familia; admission €8; ⏰ 9am-6pm Oct-Mar, 9am-8pm Apr-Sep) is Barcelona's most famous building and visiting it is a once-before-you-die sort of experience. Construction began in 1882 though it's only half-built, and it's anyone's guess whether it will be finished by 2082.

For a detailed examination of Gaudí's works, visit the museum inside **La Pedrera** (Map pp1080-1; ☎ 902 40 09 73; Carrer de Provença 261; Ⓜ Diagonal; admission €7; ⏰ 10am-8pm Mon-Sat), a Gaudí creation that ripples around the corner of Carrer de Provença. Don't miss its surreal roof, which features some truly bizarre chimneypots; concerts are held here sometimes in summer.

Nearby is Gaudí's beautifully coloured **Casa Batlló** (Map pp1080-1; ☎ 932 16 03 06; Passeig de Gràcia 43; Ⓜ Passeig de Gràcia; admission €10; ⏰ 9am-8pm), an allegory for the legend of St George ('Sant Jordi' in Catalan) the dragon-slayer. It's only recently been opened to the public. Next door is the **Casa Amatller** (Map pp1080-1; Passeig de Gràcia 41), by another leading modernist architect, Josep Puig i Cadafalch. Now the office of the **Centre de Modernisme** (☎ 934 88 01 39; Passeig de Gràcia 41; Ⓜ Passeig de Gràcia; ⏰ 10am-7pm Mon-Sat, 10am-2pm Sun), this is the place for information about modernist buildings and tours.

Further afield is Gaudí's **Parc Güell** (⏰ 10am-dusk), a charming outdoor park Dr Seuss would feel comfortable in. Gaudí designed it as a community that would have houses, schools and shops, but the project failed, leaving this half-finished playground of tile mosaics and striking organic shapes. The house where Gaudí lived for 20 years has been turned into the **Casa-Museum Gaudí** (☎ 932 19 38 11; Ⓜ Lesseps; admission €4; ⏰ 10am-6pm Oct-Mar, 10am-8pm Apr-Sep), a museum about his life. Go by metro (which involves a steep uphill climb) or on bus No 24 from Plaça Universitat.

In the El Raval district is Gaudí's atmospheric **Palau Güell** (Map p1086; ☎ 933 17 39 74; Carrer Nou de la Rambla 3-5; Ⓜ Drassanes; ⏰ 10am-6pm

---

GETTING INTO TOWN

The main train station, Sants, is a hike from the centre of town, but it's well connected by metro. Catch the green line (3) to reach Las Ramblas. The main bus station, Estació Nord, is just northeast of the Barri Gòtic. Walk along the Ronda de Sant Pere for about 15 minutes to reach Plaça Catalunya or hop on the metro at the nearby Arc de Triomf stop.

From the airport, trains go each half-hour to Sants and Plaça Catalunya stations (€2.25, 15 to 20 minutes). The Aerobus runs between Plaça Catalunya and the airport (€3.75, 40 minutes, every 15 minutes or half-hourly at weekends).

Mon-Sat Mar-Oct, 10am-4pm Nov-Feb), a house built by Gaudí in the late 1880s for his patron, the industrialist Eusebi Güell.

EL RAVAL
To the west of Las Ramblas is the El Raval district, a once-seedy, now-funky area overflowing with cool bars and shops. Here the **Museu d'Art Contemporani de Barcelona** (Macba; Map p1086; ☎ 934 12 08 10; Plaça del Àngels 1; Ⓜ Plaça Catalunya; admission €3; Ⓨ 11am-7.30pm Tue-Sat, 10am-3pm Sun), near Plaça Catalunya, has an impressive collection of international contemporary art.

LA RIBERA   Map p1086
East of the Barri Gòtic, La Ribera is a medieval barrio with some fascinating museums and architecture. You'll immediately see the throngs surrounding the **Museu Picasso** (☎ 933 19 63 10; Carrer de Montcada 15-21; Ⓜ Jaume I; admission €5; Ⓨ 10am-8pm Tue-Sat, 10am-3pm Sun), home of the most important collection of Picasso's work in Spain – more than 3000 pieces. Most represent Picasso's Barcelona periods (1895–1900 and 1901–04) early in his career.

At the end of Carrer de Montcada is the effortlessly elegant **Basílica de Santa Maria del Mar** (Ⓜ Jaume I; Ⓨ 9.30am-1.30pm & 4.30-8pm), a stunning example of Catalan Gothic. All around here you'll find quirky shops and bars; this is a great area for strolling.

Don't miss the **Palau de la Música Catalana** (☎ 932 95 72 00; www.palaumusica.org; Carrer Sant Francesc de Paula 2; Ⓜ Urquinaona; admission €7; Ⓨ 10am-3.30pm Sep-Jul, 10am-6pm Aug), an unabashedly ornate modernist masterpiece designed by Lluís Domènech i Montaner in 1905. Concerts are held here regularly.

WATERFRONT
From the bottom of La Rambla you can cross the Rambla de Mar footbridge to the **Moll d'Espanya** (Map p1086), a former wharf in the old harbour, Port Vell. Stroll around the restaurants and shops here. Northeast of Port Vell, on the far side of the fishing-oriented La Barceloneta area, the city **beaches** begin. Along the beachfront, after 1.3km you'll reach **Vila Olímpica**, site of the 1992 Olympic village, which is fronted by impressive **Port Olímpic**, a large marina with dozens of bars and restaurants. There are some fun nightspots and good restaurants, but locals are few and far between.

Not far off the water is the **Parc de la Ciutadella** (Map pp1080-1; Ⓜ Barceloneta; Ⓨ 8am-9pm), a large park ideal for strolling or picnics. The small city **zoo** (Map pp1080-1; ☎ 932 25 67 80; adult €12.90; Ⓨ 10am-dusk) is inside the park.

MONTJUÏC   Map pp1080–1
The Central Park of Barcelona, this hill is the southwestern boundary of the city and is a perfect place to jog or stroll around. There are amazing panoramic views of the city from the top. Public transport in the area is limited; to get here walk up from Plaça Espanya or wait for bus No 61. A more entertaining option is take the **funicular railway** (€3.20) from Parallel metro station or ride the **cable car** (Transbordador Aeri; €7.50) over from La Barceloneta.

Interesting attractions to see on Montjuïc include:
Museu Nacional d'Art de Catalunya (☎ 936 22 03 75; Palau Nacional; admission €4.80; Ⓨ 10am-7pm Tue-Sat, 10am-2.30pm Sun) Catalan religious art.
Poble Espanyol (Spanish Village; ☎ 935 08 63 30; Avinguda Marquès de Comillas; admission €7; Ⓨ 9am-8pm Mon, 9am-late Tue-Sun) Craft and souvenir shops by day, nightclubs and restaurants by night.
Fundació Joan Miró (☎ 934 43 94 70; Parc de Montjuïc; admission €7.20; Ⓨ 10am-7pm Tue-Sat, 10am-2.30pm Sun) Fantastic temple to modern art, with many Miró works.
Castell de Montjuïc (☎ 933 29 86 13; admission €2.50; Ⓨ 9.30am-5.30pm Nov-Mar, 9.30am-8pm Apr-Oct) A small military museum and great views.

Festivals & Events
Barcelona's biggest festival is the **La Mercè**, a week-long, city-wide party on the days around 24 September. Another red-letter date is the festival of **Sant Joan** (St John's Day; 23 July), when days of endless firecrackers welcome summer. In June and July the arts festival **El Grec** fills Barcelona with theatre, dance and music.

Sleeping
Cheaper *pensiones* and *hostales* are in the Barri Gòtic and El Raval. You'll pay up to €65 for a double (expensive for Spain), and few have much charm to speak of. In summer, you need to book ahead.

YOUTH HOSTELS   Map p1086
In most *albergues juveniles* (youth hostels), you'll pay extra to use the sheets and towels.

SPAIN

Alberg Palau (☎ 934 12 50 80; albergpalau@champ inet.com; Carrer del Palau 6; Ⓜ Liceu; dm €15-20; 🖳) Friendly, English-speaking staff runs this modest hostel, where dorm-style rooms are cramped but clean. There's a kitchen for your use.

Alberg J New York (☎ 933 15 03 04; fax 933 19 53 25; Carrer d'En Cignas 6; Ⓜ Liceu; dm €15-20; 🖳) Nearby with the same style but more rooms.

Gaudí Youth Hostel (☎ 933 17 65 55; www.gaudi hostel.com; Plaça Urquinaona 5; Ⓜ Urquinaona; dm €15-22; ✂) Super staff, and a perfect location for nightlife.

Barcelona Mar Youth Hostel (☎ 933 24 85 30; www.youthostel-barcelona.com; Carrer Sant Pau 80; Ⓜ Drassanes; dm incl breakfast €18-23) Beds have curtains for privacy.

Gothic Point Youth Hostel (☎ 932 68 78 08; www .gothicpoint.com; Carrer Vigatans 5; Ⓜ Jaume I; dm €21; ✂) A great place to meet people, it has sunny terrace and bike rentals.

HOSTALES & PENSIÓNES

Pensión Avinyò (Map p1086; ☎ 933 187 9 45; www.hostal avinyo.com; Carrer d'Avinyò 42; Ⓜ Liceu; s without bathroom €16-26, d €26-42, d with bathroom €38-56) Homey rooms all have ceiling fans.

Pensión Calella (Map p1086; ☎ 933 17 68 41; Carrer Calella 1; Ⓜ Liceu; s €21-26, d €40-46) Calella has just renovated its rooms; now most are comfy and have bathrooms, a feat for this price.

Hostal Morató (Map p1086; ☎ 934 42 36 69; www .hostalmorato.com; Nou de la Rambla 50; Ⓜ Drassanes; s €25-35, d €50-70) This modern *hostal* is excellent value, with spotless rooms that try hard to be stylish. Some have private bathrooms.

Hotel Barcelona House (Map p1086; ☎ 933 01 82 95; www.hotelbarcelonahouse.com; Carrer del Escudellers 19; Ⓜ Liceu; s €29-39, d €55-72, tr €85-101) This hotel is two in one, with both a bare-boned, *hostal*-ish area and a newly renovated wing, where rooms cost a little more. All have bathrooms and the basic comforts, and the price includes breakfast.

Gat Raval (Map p1086; ☎ 934 81 66 70; www.gat accommodation.com; Carrer Joaquim Costa 44; Ⓜ Sant Antoni; s/d €39/54, d with bathroom €71; 🖳) This is by far the coolest *hostal* in town, with well-equipped rooms, neon-green walls and Internet. A second branch, **Gat Xino** (Carrer Hospital 149-155), was about to open at the time of writing.

Pensión Lausanne (Map p1086; ☎ 933 02 11 39; Portal de l'Angel 24; Ⓜ Plaça Catalunya; s/d €40/60, with bathroom €57/87) Housed in appealing,

old modernist-style building, rooms boast soaring ceilings and tile floors.

Hostal Eden (Map pp1080-1; ☎ 934 52 66 20; www .hostaleden.net; Ⓜ Passeig de Gràcia; s/d without bathroom €30/47, s with bathroom €47, d €67-72, tr/q €77/87) In L'Eixample, Eden offers charming but simple rooms; No 11 has a huge jacuzzi!

Pensión Alamar (Map p1086; ☎ 933 02 50 12; Carrer de la Comtessa de Sobradiel 1; Ⓜ Liceu; s/d €25/45) Great value and a sociable atmosphere.

Hostal Benidorm (Map p1086; ☎ 933 02 20 54; www.barcelona-on-line.es/benidorm; Las Ramblas 37; s/d €29/45; Ⓜ Liceu) Has private bathrooms and a superb location.

Hostal Fontanella (☎ 933 17 59 43; Via Laietana 71; Ⓜ Urquinaona; s with bathroom €38 d with bathroom €55-65 s/d without €38/48) Cosy and well kept.

Pensión Mari-Luz (☎ 933 17 34 63; Carrer del Palau 4; Ⓜ Liceu; d €46-52) Bright and friendly.

APARTMENTS

Several private apartment-rental companies operate in Barcelona. These can often be a better deal than staying in a *hostal*, especially if you're travelling in a group. Try www.go2barcelona.com, www.inside-bcn .com or www.selfcateringhols.com.

CAMPING

Around the beachy town of Castelldefels south of Barcelona, the C-31 highway is lined with camping grounds. A sprawling place close to the beach and with its own terrace and bar, **Tres Estrellas** (☎ 936 33 06 37; www.camping3estrellas.com; Autovía de Castelldefels km. 186.2; per camp site for 2 adults with car & tent €25.76; 🕑 15 Mar-15 Oct) is a good option. Catch the L95 bus from Barcelona's Plaça del Catalunya or Plaça Espanya to get there.

Eating

Typical dishes range from rice and shellfish paella, ubiquitous in the restaurants by the port, to hearty Catalan fare like pigs' trotters, rabbit with snails and *butifarra*, a tasty local sausage. Lunch is served from 2pm to until 3.30pm, and dinner begins at 9pm.

The cheapest eats are always found at Chinese restaurants, which are known for their huge portions, and at the Middle Eastern kebab restaurants, selling cheap but tasty pitas stuffed with lamb or falafel. You'll find plenty of both scattered around the centre, especially on roads branching off Las Ramblas like Carrer Ferrán.

AROUND LAS RAMBLAS — Map p1086

A classic breakfast or coffee spot is **Café de l'Òpera** (☎ 933 17 75 85; Las Ramblas 74; M Liceu), a once high-class café that's a bit bruised but still atmospheric. At **Buenas Migas** (☎ 933 18 37 08; Plaça de Bonsuccés 6; M Plaça Catalunya; mains €2.20-5) eat focaccias and awesome desserts in the breezy sidewalk café. For American-style bagel sandwiches and desserts, head to the **Bagel Shop** (☎ 933 02 41 61; Carrer de la Canuda 25; M Liceu; mains €3.50-7). Vegetarians will love the salad choices at grungy-chic **Venus** (☎ 933 01 15 85; Carrer de Avinyó 25; M Liceu; menú €8.50).

Mercat de al Boquería (p1079) Self-caterers can make a beeline to this wildly colourful market for fresh food.

Bar-Bodega Fortuny (☎ 933 17 98 92; Carrer del Pintor Fortuny 31; M Liceu; mains €4.50-9) The quirky Fortuny serves salads, couscous and hummus to a largely bohemian group of regulars. At night this is a popular lesbian hang-out.

Bar Ra (☎ 933 01 41 63; Plaça de Gardunya; M Liceu; mains €6-9) Head here for same offerings as Fortuny, but dine al fresco. It's just behind La Boquería market.

La Fonda (☎ 933 01 75 15; Carrer del Escudellers 10; M Liceu; mains €7-12) Mediterranean and traditional dishes are served here with style.

Els Quatre Gats (☎ 933 02 41 40; Carrer de Montsió 3; M Urquinaona; menú €10) The legendary modernist café where Picasso had his initial exhibit. Now it serves Catalan fare and great seafood dishes, though it's pricey at night.

LA RIBERA & LA BARCELONETA

Comme-Bio (Map p1086; ☎ 933 19 89 68; Vía Laietana 28; menú €8.45) It's not just vegetarian, it's organic at this casual restaurant with a shop attached.

Origins 99.9% (☎ 933 10 75 31; Carrer de Vidrieria 6-8; M Jaume I; menú €12) Another shop-eaterie combo, Origins boasts that 99.9% of everything sold is from Catalonia. The ever-changing daily *menú* features local specialities such as *escalivada* (roasted veggies on bread) and Catalan sausages.

Comerç 24 (☎ 933 19 21 02; Carrer de Comerç 24; M Jaume I; mains €14-20) Head here for a splurge and a real gastronomic treat; this modern one-off is one of the city's most talked-about restaurants.

This is the city to eat seafood. Stroll along the waterfront and around the ports for a wide array of fishy favourites. One of the best priced is **Can Maño** (Map pp1080-1; ☎ 933 19 30 82; Carrer Baluard 12; M Barceloneta; mains €6-12; closed Sun), where décor isn't a priority but lip-smackingly good fresh seafood is.

L'EIXAMPLE

Laie Librería Café (Map p1086; ☎ 933 02 73 10; Carrer de Pau Claris 85; M Passeig de Gràcia; mains €5-12) The delicious buffet and lunch *menú* is packed with healthy food, local specialities and vegetarian options.

La Cervecería Catalana (Map pp1080-1; ☎ 932 16 03 68; Carrer Mallorca 236; M Passeig de Gràcia) Arrive early to try the tapas and delicious long, skinny sandwiches. The same owners run **La Flauta** (Map pp1080-1; ☎ 933 23 70 38; Carrer de Aribau 23; M Universitat) a few blocks away.

L'Hostal de Rita (Map pp1080-1; ☎ 934 87 23 76; Carrer Aragó 279; M Passeig de Gràcia) For a bit of style, this place does the trick. Be prepared to wait in line for samples of its pastas, seafood and traditional dishes.

Drinking & Clubbing
BARS

On weekends bars stay hopping until 2am, but most of the places listed here are open for quiet drinks as early as 8pm.

Head to the Passeig del Born for a great selection of laid-back bars like **Miramelindo** (Map p1086; ☎ 933 19 53 76; Passeig del Born 15; M Jaume I), a Barcelona favourite, and **La Vinya del Senyor** (Map p1086; ☎ 933 10 33 97; Plaça de la Santa María 5; M Jaume I), a romantic wine bar sitting under the shadow of the basilica.

Muebles Navarro (Map p1086; ☎ 607 18 80 96; Carrer de la Riera Alta 4; M Liceu) In El Raval you'll find this funky place decorated like a furniture flea market. Kick back with a cold one and a cheese plate.

Lletraferit (Map p1086; ☎ 933 01 19 61; Carrer de Joaquim Costa 43; M Sant Antoni) Just as chill but a bit more sophisticated is Lletraferit, a book-lovers' café by day and a cocktail bar by night.

Rita Blue (Map p1086; ☎ 933 42 40 86; Plaça de Sant Agustí 3; M Liceu) More upbeat, everyone at this restaurant and bar orders the house speciality, a blue margarita.

The Philharmonic (Map pp1080-1; ☎ 934 51 11 53; Carrer de Mallorca 204; M Provença) In L'Eixample, this is one of Barcelona's most popular pubs. Stop in for all the football matches, some English conversation and a mouth-watering English breakfast.

The Gràcia district, with its intimate plazas and narrow streets, is the perfect spot for

SPAIN

CENTRAL BARCELONA

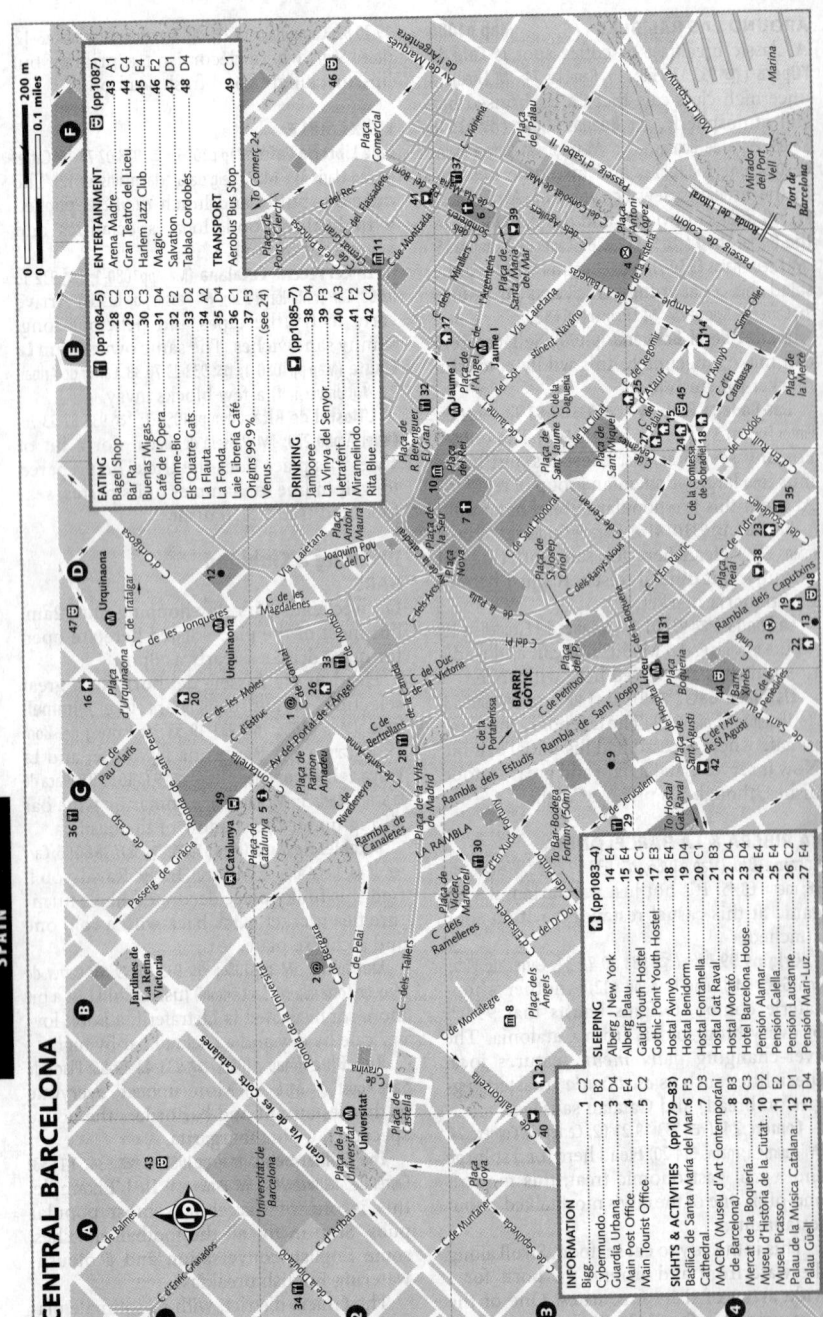

a quiet drink. **Café del Sol** (Map pp1080-1; ☎ 934 15 56 63; Plaça del Sol; Ⓜ Fontana) has a fantastic terrace for sipping outdoors. **Gusto** (Map p1086; Carrer Francisco Giner 24; Ⓜ Fontana) offers a friendly atmosphere and some of the city's best DJs.

CLUBS

For discos of every shape, size and variety, head to the Port Olímpic; in summer, it's a nonstop party, and winter weekends are fun too. One of the biggest clubs here is **Baja Beach Club** (☎ 932 25 91 00; Passeig Marítim de la Barceloneta 34; Ⓜ Ciutadella-Vila Olímpica), where being tan, beautiful and nearly topless seem to be requirements for entry.

Jamboree (Map p1086; ☎ 933 19 17 89; Plaça Reial 17; Ⓜ Liceu) Jumping with hip-hop music every night of the week, this is a magnet for foreign students.

Magic (☎ 933 10 72 67; Passeig Picasso 40; Ⓜ Arc de Triomf) With fantastic live music running the gamut between techno and classic rock, it's one of the city's top clubs.

GAY & LESBIAN VENUES

The gay and lesbian scene is mainly in the blocks near Carrers Muntaner and Consell de Cent (dubbed 'Gay-xample' by the locals). Each night you'll find ambience of the week in the bars, discos and drag clubs.

Oui Café (Map p1086; Consell de Cent 247; Ⓜ Universitat) A sophisticated style and all-white décor reigns here, with a spiffy clientele dropping in for low-key drinks.

Party hard at classic gay discos like **Arena Madre** (Map p1086; ☎ 934 87 83 42; Carrer de Balmes 32; Ⓜ Universitat; Ⓨ closed Mon) and **Salvation** (Map p1086; ☎ 933 18 06 86; Ronda de Sant Pere 19-21; Ⓜ Urquinaona; Ⓨ Fri-Sun).

Bar-Bodega Fortuny Low-key Fortuny is a popular lesbian hang-out – see p1085.

Entertainment

LIVE MUSIC

London Bar (Map pp1080-1; ☎ 933 18 52 61; Carrer Nou de la Rambla 34; Ⓜ Drassanes) This popular expat hang-out hosts concerts almost every night. Groups range from jazz to rock to flamenco.

Harlem Jazz Club (☎ 933 10 07 55; Carrer de la Comtessa de Sobradiel 8; Ⓜ Liceu) Head here for a guaranteed dose of quality jazz and enough smoke to cook a sausage.

Otto Zutz (Map pp1080-1; ☎ 932 38 07 22; Carrer Lincoln 15; Ⓜ Fontana) Frontliners often play here.

Though Barcelona is not the best place to see flamenco, you can catch a reasonably authentic show at **Tablao Cordobés** (Map p1086; ☎ 933 17 57 11; Las Ramblas 35; Ⓜ Liceu).

SPORT

Football fans can see the Fútbol Club Barcelona play at **Camp Nou** (Map pp1080-1; ☎ 934 96 36 00; www.fcbarcelona.com; Arístides Maillol; Ⓜ Collblanc). If you can't score tickets, nose around the **museum** (☎ 934 96 36 08; gates 7 & 9; admission €5, tour €9; Ⓨ 10am-6.30pm Mon-Sat, 10am-2pm Sun).

THEATRE & OPERA

Most theatre in the city is in Catalan, but there are quite a few that stage vanguard drama.

Teatre Nacional de Catalunya (☎ 933 06 57 00; Plaça de les Arts 1; Ⓜ Glòries) If you're up for a language lesson, check out the performances at this classy theatre.

Anything put on anywhere by the wild troupe **La Fura Dels Baus** (www.lafura.com) is bound to be funny and energetic. They manage to communicate without words, so language isn't a problem.

Gran Teatro del Liceu (Map pp1080-1; ☎ 934 85 99 00; www.liceubarcelona.com; Las Ramblas 51-59) Barcelona's glitziest stage is the sumptuous opera house.

Getting There & Away

AIR

Barcelona's airport is 14km southwest of the city centre. Airlines include **Iberia** (☎ 902 40 05 00; www.iberia.com), **Air Europa** (☎ 902 40 15 01; www.aireuropa.com), **SpanAir** (☎ 902 13 14 15; www.spanair.com) and **EasyJet** (www.easyjet.com).

BUS

The terminal for virtually all domestic and international buses is the **Estació Nord** (Map pp1080-1; ☎ 932 65 65 08; Carrer d'Alí Bei 80; Ⓜ Arc de Triomf). Several buses a day go to most main Spanish cities, including Madrid, Zaragoza, Valencia and Granada.

TRAIN

Virtually all trains travelling to and from destinations within Spain stop at **Estació Sants** (metro Sants-Estació). Daily trains run to most major cities in Spain, including Madrid (€33.50 to €59, six to nine hours, seven daily), San Sebastián (€33.50 to €42.50, eight to 10 hours, two daily), Valencia (€28.50 to €34.50, three hours or more, 10 daily) and Granada

SPAIN

(€50, eight hours, two daily). Tickets and information are available at the stations.

Getting Around

Barcelona's metro system spreads its tentacles around the city in such a way that most places of interest are within a 10-minute walk of a station. Buses and suburban trains are needed only for a few destinations. A single metro, bus or suburban train ride costs €1.10, but a T-1 ticket, valid for 10 rides, costs only €6.

MONESTIR DE MONTSERRAT

The prime attraction of Montserrat, 50km northwest of Barcelona, is its incredible setting. The Benedictine Monastery of Montserrat sits high on the side of a 1236m-high mountain of weird bulbous peaks. The monastery was founded in 1025 after a statue of the Virgin Mary was found here. Pilgrims still come from all over Christendom to pay homage to the Black Virgin (La Moreneta), a 12th-century wooden sculpture of Mary, regarded as Catalonia's patroness. The statue stands in the basilica's altar, where the faithful line up to kiss it.

Mass is held several times daily; at the 1pm Mass from Monday to Saturday the monastery boys' choir sings.

Montserrat's **tourist office** (☎ 938 77 77 77; ☒ 10am-6pm) is to the left along the road from the top cable-car station. It has a couple of good free leaflets and maps on the mountain and monastery as well as information about the **Museu de Montserrat** (admission €5.50; ☒ 10am-7pm Mon-Fri, 9.30am-7.30pm Sat & Sun).

Sleeping & Eating

There are several **accommodation options** (☎ 938 77 77 01; www.abadiamontserrat.net) at the monastery. The cheapest rooms are in the **Cel.les Abat Oliba** (d from €25), blocks of simple apartments, with showers, for up to 10 people.

Cafeteria food here is decent but overpriced; you're better off bringing a picnic from Barcelona.

Getting There & Away

The FGC R5 train runs from Barcelona's Plaça Espanya to both Aeri de Montserrat (one hour, 19 daily), where you can catch a cable car up the mountain, and to Monistrol-Vila, where you can alight a cog-wheel railway to head up. The combined return ticket is €11.40.

GIRONA & LA COSTA BRAVA

The rocky, rugged scenery of La Costa Brava has made this once-sleepy, now-sizzling area one of Spain's most popular holiday spots. The main jumping-off points for the Costa Brava are the inland towns of Girona ('Gerona' in Castilian) and Figueres. Along the coast, the most appealing resorts are (from north to south) Cadaqués, L'Escala (La Escala), Tamariu, Llafranc, Calella de Palafrugell and Tossa de Mar.

Information

Tourist offices (☒ 10am-1pm & 4-7pm Mon-Sat, 10am-1pm Sun Sep-Jun, 9am-9pm daily Jul-Aug) Girona (☎ 972 20 84 01; www.costabrava.org; Carrer Emili Grahit 13-15) Figueres (☎ 972 50 31 55; www.figueresciutat .com; Plaça del Sol) Palafrugell (☎ 972 61 18 20; www.palafrugell.net; Plaça de l'Església)

Coastal Resorts & Islands

The Costa Brava (Rugged Coast) is all about picturesque inlets and coves. Beaches tend to be small and scattered. Some longer beaches at places like L'Estartit and Empúries are worth visiting off-season, but there has been a tendency to erect tall buildings wherever engineers think it can be done. Fortunately, in many places it just can't.

Cadaqués, one hour's drive east of Figueres at the end of an ongoing series of hairpin bends, is perhaps the most picturesque of all Spanish resorts. The memory of former resident Salvador Dalí, whose house is nearby, echoes here. Beaches are pebbly, so people spend time sitting at waterfront cafés or wandering along the beautiful coast. Some 10km northeast of Cadaqués is **Cap de Creus**, a rocky mountain park where you can hike and visit a **monastery**.

Further down the coast, past L'Escala and L'Estartit, is **Palafrugell**. Though the town has little to offer, it's near three gorgeous beach towns that have to be seen to be believed. The most northerly of these, **Tamariu**, is also the smallest, least crowded and most exclusive. **Llafranc** is the biggest and busiest, and has the longest beach. **Calella de Palafrugell**, with its truly picture-postcard setting, is rarely overcrowded and always relaxed.

Among the most exciting attractions on the Costa Brava are the **Illes Medes**, off the coast from the package resort of **L'Estartit**. These seven islets and their surrounding coral reefs have been declared a natural park to protect their extraordinarily diverse flora and fauna. Diving is popular here.

Sights

When you have had enough beach for a while, make sure you put the **Teatre-Museu Dalí** (☎ 972 52 28 00; Plaça Gala I Salvador Dalí 5; admission €9, incl admission to other Dalí sites; ☼ 10.30am-5.45pm Oct-Jun, 9am-7.45pm Jul-Sep), in Figueres, at the top of your list. This 19th-century theatre was converted by Dalí himself and houses a huge and fascinating collection of his strange creations. You can also visit Dalí's home, now a **museum** (☎ 972 25 10 15; Portlligat; admission €8; ☼ 10.30am-6pm Oct-May, 10.30am-9pm Jun-Sep) near Cadaqués.

Girona sports a lovely though tiny medieval quarter centred on a Gothic cathedral. For a stroll through antiquity, check out the ruins of the Greek and Roman town of **Empúries**, 2km from L'Escala.

Sleeping & Eating

Visitors to the Costa Brava usually rent apartments. If you're keen on renting your own pad for a week, contact local tourist offices in advance. Many food stalls and cafés cluster in all three towns. Seaside restaurants offer dramatic settings but often at high prices.

FIGUERES

Pensión Mallol (☎ 972 50 22 83; Carrer Pep Ventura 9; s/d €16/28) Has simple, no-frills rooms.

Pensión Isabel II (☎ 972 50 47 35; Carrer Isabel II 16; s/d €22/28) More comfortable and with private bathrooms.

Restaurant Versalles (☎ 972 50 00 02; Carrer Jonquera 18; mains €5-15) Local fare is served away from the cost and noise of the main plaza.

GIRONA

Alberg de Joventut (☎ 972 21 80 03; www.tujuca.com; Carrer de Ciutadans 9; dm €14-19) Basic, offering standard HI accommodation.

Pensión Viladomat (☎ 972 20 31 76; Carrer de Ciutadans 5; d €35) Has comfortable rooms.

Dine on Girona's Rambla for people-watching. **Arts Café** (La Rambla 23) offers a low-key atmosphere and cheap snacky fare.

CADAQUÉS

Hostal Marina (☎ 972 25 81 99; Carrer Riera 3; s/d €35/50) Has sunny, cheerful rooms.

Camping Cadaqués (☎ 972 25 81 26; www.campings online.com; Carretera Port-Lligat 17; per camp site for 2 adults with car & tent €22; ☼ Apr-Sep) Offers all basic services plus soul-satisfying mountain views and easy shore access.

AROUND PALAFRUGELL

Hotel and *pensión* rooms are relatively thin on the ground here, as many people come on package deals. In Calella de Palafrugell, the friendly **Hostería del Plancton** (☎ 972 61 50 81; r from €18; ☼ Jun-Sep) is one of the best deals on the Costa Brava.

Getting There & Away

A few buses run daily from Barcelona to Tossa del Mar, L'Estartit and Cadaqués for a couple of euros, but for the small resorts near Palafrugell you need to get to Girona first. Girona and Figueres are both on the railway connecting Barcelona to France. The dozen or so trains daily from Barcelona to Portbou at the border all stop in Girona (€5.10, 1¼ hours), and most stop in Figueres (€7.30 to €8.40, one hour 40 minutes).

TARRAGONA

Founded in 218 BC as Tarraco, the city is a fascinating place to visit. It was an important Roman centre and the capital of Hispania, and Roman structures figure among its attractions. Good beaches, a nearby theme park and a large student population keep the city from dwelling too much on its past.

Orientation

Tarragona's main street is Rambla Nova, which runs northwest from a cliff top overlooking the Mediterranean. To reach the Roman monuments, from the train station turn right and follow the road, which runs parallel to the sea, until you see the amphitheatre (a 10-minute walk).

Information

Café Cantonada (☎ 977 21 35 24; Carrer de Fortuny 23; ☼ 10am-2pm; per hr €4, minimum 10 min) Internet access.

Main tourist office (☎ 977 25 07 95; Carrer Major 39; ☼ 10am-2pm & 4-7pm Mon-Sat, 10am-2pm Sun) Has maps and accommodation information.

Sights

Start at the fascinating **Museu Arqueològic** (☎ 977 23 62 09; Plaça del Rei 5; admission €2.40; all

SPAIN

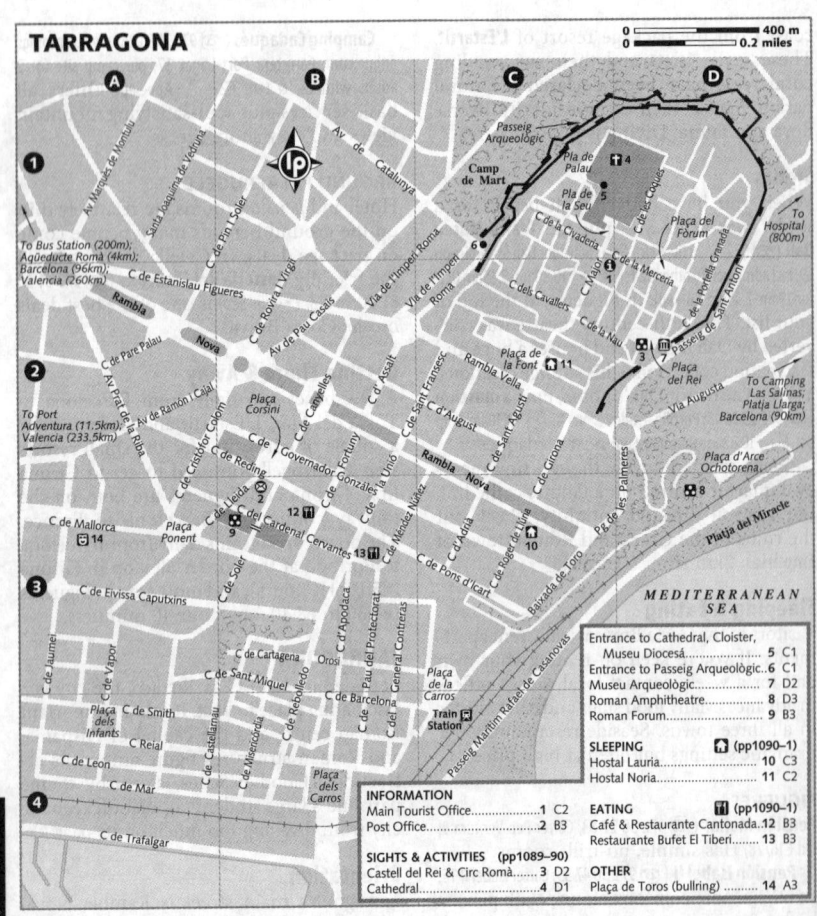

TARRAGONA

INFORMATION	
Main Tourist Office	1 C2
Post Office	2 B3

SIGHTS & ACTIVITIES	(pp1089–90)
Castell del Rei & Circ Romà	3 D2
Cathedral	4 D1
Entrance to Cathedral, Cloister, Museu Diocesà	5 C1
Entrance to Passeig Arqueològic	6 C1
Museu Arqueològic	7 D2
Roman Amphitheatre	8 D3
Roman Forum	9 B3

SLEEPING	(pp1090–1)
Hostal Lauria	10 C3
Hostal Noria	11 C2

EATING	(pp1090–1)
Café & Restaurante Cantonada	12 B3
Restaurante Bufet El Tiberi	13 B3

OTHER	
Plaça de Toros (bullring)	14 A3

Roman sites ⏰ 10am-1.30pm & 4-7pm Tue-Sat, Sun 10am-2pm Oct-May, 10am-8pm Tue-Sat, Sun 10am-2pm Jun-Sep), where you'll gain an excellent understanding of Roman Spain.

Nearby, the **Castell del Rei** (☎ 977 24 19 52) once formed part of the city walls. You can head to the top for views and then see the ruins of the **Roman circus**, where chariot races were held.

Nearby and close to the beach is the preserved **Roman amphitheatre**, where the gladiators fought each other (or unlucky souls were thrown to wild animals) to the death. North of here, the **Passeig Arqueològic** is a peaceful walkway along the old city walls, which are a combination of Roman, Iberian and 17th-century British efforts.

The **cathedral** sits at Tarragona's highest point, overlooking the old town. Some parts of the building date back to the 12th century AD. Entrance is through the beautiful cloister with the excellent Museu Diocesá.

Clean **Platja del Miracle** is the main city beach; south of the Roman amphitheatre.

Sleeping & Eating

If you intend to stay in Tarragona in summer, call ahead to book a room.

Hostal Noria (☎ 977 23 87 17; Plaça de la Font 53; s/d €20/32) This is good value but often full.

Hotel Lauria (☎ 977 23 67 12; Rambla Nova 20; s/d €37/55; 🏊) This three-star is a worthwhile splurge with a wonderful location, a pool and airy rooms.

Camping Las Salinas (☎ 977 20 76 28; Carretera N-340, Platja Llarga; per camp site for 2 adults with tent & car €15.25; 🕒 15 May-Sep) Close to the centre and basic, it's a friendly but no-frills place. Buses Nos 1 and 9 leave Tarragona from Rambla Vieja every 20 minutes, and the ride out takes under 10 minutes.

Rambla Nova has several good places, either for a snack or a meal.

Restaurant Bufet El Tiberi (☎ 977 23 54 03; Carrer de Martí d'Ardenya 5; buffet €9-10; 🕒 morning Tue-Sun) For solid Catalan food, simply head to this stylish restaurant, which provides an all-you-can-eat buffet.

Café Cantonada (☎ 977 21 35 24; Carrer de Fortuny 23; 🕒 10am-2pm) A popular place for tapas.

Restaurante Cantonada (mains from €5) Next door to the café, it has pizza and pasta.

Getting There & Away

More than 20 regional trains a day run from Barcelona to Tarragona. There are about 12 trains daily from Tarragona to Valencia and to Madrid.

The bus station is on Avinguda Roma, off Plaça Imperial Tarraco. Buses reach regional cities, such as Barcelona, and beyond.

BALEARIC ISLANDS

pop 916,968

From the outrageous antics of Ibiza's club scene to the forgotten hill-top villages of Mallorca's Serra de Tramuntana, the Balearic Islands of Mallorca, Ibiza, Menorca and Formentera all have such distinct personalities that there's something here for everyone. Add to this a heady combination of blissed-out beaches, roaring nightlife and dazzling climate and it's easy to see why these Mediterranean playgrounds attract so many millions of visitors a year. It's not all just sun, sea and sangria though – you'll also discover Gothic cathedrals, Stone Age ruins and Moorish remains, as well as simple fishing villages and endless olive groves. High-season prices are quoted here but out of season, you will usually find things are much cheaper.

TRANSPORT
Getting There & Away
AIR

Low cost airlines fly to both Ibiza (airport information ☎ 97 180 90 00) and Palma de Mallorca (airport information ☎ 97 178 90 00). easyJet flies from London Stansted and London Gatwick to Ibiza, it also flies to Palma from London Luton, London Stansted, London Gatwick and Newcastle. bmibaby has regular flights to Ibiza and Palma from UK cities including Manchester and Nottingham.

BOAT

The major ferry company for the islands is **Trasmediterránea** (☎ 902 45 46 45; www.trasmediterranea.es). The travel time of the services varies, depending on the type of ferry (maximum times are given here). Routes run back and forth from: Barcelona–Palma (seven hours, 12 weekly); Valencia–Palma (seven hours, two daily); Barcelona–Ibiza (nine hours, four weekly); Palma–Ibiza (four hours, eight weekly) as well as Palma–Maó (5½ hours, once a week on Sunday).

One-way fares from the mainland to any of the islands are €49.55 for a Butaca Turista (a seat) and €68.90 for the same class on a catamaran. Taking a small car costs €126. Interisland services between Palma–Ibiza City cost €44.20 and Palma–Maó cost €26.70 for a Butaca Turista. A small car is another €74.26.

Balearia (☎ 902 16 01 80; www.balearia.com) operates fast ferries from Dénia (on the coast between Valencia and Alicante) to Palma (€48, five hours, two daily) via Ibiza (from €48, two hours) as well as services between Valencia and Palma (€48, six hours, two daily), Valencia and Ibiza (€48, 3¾ hours, two daily) and Ibiza and Palma (€32, four hours, two daily). There are also services between Ibiza and Formentera (€10, one hour, 12 daily) and Port d'Alcúdia on Mallorca and Cituadella on Menorca (€32, one hour, two daily).

Iscomar (☎ 902 11 91 28; www.iscomarferrys.com) has one to four daily car ferries between Ciutadella and Port d'Alcúdia. **Cape Balear** (☎ 902 10 04 44) operates fast ferries to Ciutadella from Cala Ratjada on Mallorca (€45, one hour, three daily).

IBIZA

From the bohemian atmosphere of Ibiza's Old Town to the hedonistic, foam-soaked fun of its world-famous clubs, Ibiza ('Eivissa' in Catalan) has a unique spirit, which can't fail to captivate.

SPAIN

Away from the remarkable clubbing scene, particularly in the rural villages, you'll discover an island where women wear long black skirts and wide straw hats. Here, you can forget the nudist beaches – the only traffic stoppers are the goatherds.

Orientation

The capital, Ibiza City, is on the southeastern side of the island. This is where most travellers arrive (by ferry or air; the airport is to the south) and it's also the best base. Sant Antoni de Portmany, on the west coast, is for those seriously into clubs and drinking. Other big resorts are scattered around the island.

Information

Tourist office (☎ 971 30 19 00; oitport@cief.es; Carrer Antoni Riquer 2; ☼ 9.30am-1.30pm & 5-7.30pm Mon-Fri, 10.30am-1pm Sat) In Ibiza City, it's opposite Estación Marítima.

Wash and Dry.Com (☎ 971 39 48 22; Avinguda Espanya 53; ☼ 10am-8.30pm Mon-Sat) You can do a load of washing as well as access the Internet cheaply.

Sights & Activities

Shopping is a major pastime in Ibiza City. The port area of **Sa Penya** is crammed with funky and trashy clothes boutiques and hippy market stalls. From here you can wander up into **D'Alt Vila**, the atmospheric old walled town. There are fine views from the walls and from the **cathedral** (Plaça de la Catedral; ☼ 10am-1pm Tue-Sat) at the top.

The heavily developed **Platja de ses Figueretes** beach is a 20-minute walk south of Sa Penya – but better to catch the half-hour ride on the No 11 bus (€1.50) south to the beaches at **Ses Salines**.

Ibiza has numerous unspoiled beaches. On the northeast coast, **Cala de Boix** is the only black-sand beach on the islands, while further north are the lovely beaches of **S'Aigua Blanca**. On the north coast near Portinatx is **Cala Xarraca**, in a picturesque, secluded bay and, near Port de Sant Miquel, is the attractive **Cala Benirras**. On the southwest coast, **Cala d'Hort** has a spectacular setting overlooking two rugged rock-islets.

Sleeping

IBIZA CITY

There are several *hostales* in the streets around the port, although in midsummer cheap beds are scarce.

Casa de Huéspedes Navarro (☎ 971 31 07 71; Carrer de sa Creu 20; d/tr €38/50; ☼ Apr-Oct) With 10 rooms at the top of a long flight of stairs, this place is in a central location with a sunny rooftop terrace.

Casa de Huéspedes Vara de Rey (☎ 971 30 13 76; hibiza@wanadoo.es; Passeig Vara de Rey 7; s/d €36/72; ☼ Mar-Dec) Friendly and eclectic, it has 11 rooms with washbasins and old-fashioned ceiling fans.

Hostal-Restaurante La Marina (☎ 971 31 01 72; reserves@hostal-lamarina.com; Carrer Barcelona 7; s/d €62/77; 🖁) On the waterfront, La Marina has immaculate rooms in cool colours and lots of wrought-iron furniture.

OTHER AREAS

Hostal Cala Boix (☎ 971 33 52 24; s/d incl breakfast €24.50/49; 🖁) By the black-sand beach at Cala de Boix, with a cliff-top location.

Pensión Sa Plana (☎ 971 33 50 73; d incl breakfast €58; 🖁 🖳) Near the S'Aigua Blanca beaches, Sa Plana has a poolside bar and barbecue.

Camping Cala Nova (☎ 971 33 17 74; per person/tent/car €5.40/4.60/4.60) Close to a good beach near the resort town of Cala Nova, this is one of Ibiza's best camping grounds.

Eating & Drinking

Kick off the evening with a drink and some people-watching at one of the bars lining the lively Plaça del Parque including **Herry's Bar** (☎ 971 39 11 52; Plaça del Parque 2; ☼ 11.30am-midnight), with the best *mojitos* (a popular Cuban-based rum concoction) this side of the Atlantic.

Croissant Show (☎ 971 31 76 65; Plaça de la Constitució; ☼ 7am-3pm) Everyone comes here for post-clubbing munchies.

Comidas-Bar San Juan (☎ 971 31 16 03; Carrer de Guillem de Montgri 8; mains €4-7; ☼ 1-3.30pm & 8.30-11pm) A popular, noisy place where diners share tables. The food is hearty and extremely good value for the money.

Teatro Pereyra (☎ 971 19 14 68; Carrer Conde Rosselló 3; ☼ 8am-4am) In an old theatre, this is the place for jazz, blues and soul. Expect lots of atmosphere and live music every night. Entrance is free but the price of drinks shoots up once the music starts.

Clubbing

Ibiza's summer nightlife is renowned. At night, go to the fashion-catwalk of cobblestone streets, dodging the outrageous PR performers hired by the discos to attract dusk-to-dawn clubbers. Lots of bars keep Ibiza City's port area jumping until the wee hours – mostly on Carrer de Barcelona and Carrer de Garijo Cipriano. After they wind down, you can go on to one of the island's famous discos (if you can afford the €40 entry). The big names are **Pacha** (www.pacha.net), on the northern side of Ibiza City's port; **Privilege** (www.privilege.es) and **Amnesia** (www.amnesia -ibiza.com), both 6km out on the road to Sant Antoni; **El Divino** (www.eldivino-ibiza.com), across the water from the town centre (hop on one of its boats); and **Space** (www.space-ibiza.com), south of Ibiza City in Platja d'En Bossa.

Getting Around

Buses to other parts of the island leave from the series of bus stops along Av d'Isidoro Macabich. Pick up a copy of the timetable from the tourist office.

If you want to get to some of the more secluded beaches you will need to rent wheels. In Ibiza City, **Autos Isla Blanca** (☎ 971 31 54 07; Carrer de Felipe II) will hire out a Renault Twingo for €103 for three days all-inclusive.

MALLORCA

Mallorca's capital city of Palma, with its tangle of narrow backstreets and towering Gothic cathedral, is a joy to explore. Inland, you can happily lose yourself in the mountains before stumbling across hill-top villages seemingly unchanged for centuries. And then there are the beaches … Hardly surprising then that so many artists and writers decided to make this beguiling Mediterranean island their home.

Orientation

Palma de Mallorca is on the southern side of the island, on a bay famous for its brilliant sunsets. The Serra de Tramuntana mountain range in the northwest is trekker heaven. Mallorca's best beaches are along the north and east coasts, along with most of the big tourist resorts.

Information

All of the major resorts have at least one tourist office. Palma has four, including the one below.

Big Byte (☎ 971 71 17 54; Carrer Apuntadores 6; per hr €2.75; ☻ 10am-10pm Mon-Thu, 10am-6pm Fri, 11am-7pm Sat & Sun) Internet access.

Main tourist office (☎ 971 71 22 16; www.a-palma.es; Plaça de la Reina 2; ☻ 9am-8pm Mon-Fri, 9am-2.30pm Sat)

Sights & Activities

An awesome mass of sandstone walls and flying buttresses, Palma's magnificent **cathedral** (☎ 971 72 31 30; Plaça Almoina; admission €3.50; ☻ 10am-3.15pm Nov-Mar, 10am-6pm Apr-Oct, closed Sat afternoon & Sun) overlooks the city and its port.

Es Baluard (☎ 971 90 82 00; www.esbaluard.org; Plaça Porta de Santa Catalina; adult/student €6/4.50; ☻ 10am-8pm Tue-Sun Oct-May, 10am-midnight daily Jun-Sep), Palma's striking museum of modern and contemporary art, is a visual feast of works from 20th-century greats.

The atmospheric **Banys Àrabs** (Arab Baths; ☎ 971 72 15 49; Carrer Can Sera 7; admission €1.50; ☻ 9am-9pm Apr-Nov, 9am-7pm Dec-Mar) are the only remaining monument to the Muslim domination of the island. The baths are for sightseeing, not swimming. Mallorca's rugged and rocky northwestern coast is a world away from the high-rise tourism on the other side of the island. Dominated by the Serra de Tramuntana, it's a beautiful region of olive groves, pine forests and small villages with stone buildings. Highlights for drivers include the hair-raising road down to the small port of **Sa Calobra** and the amazing trip along the peninsula to **Cap Formentor**.

One of the most popular and spectacular excursions on the island is the **Palma to Sóller train** (p1094). Sóller is the best place to base yourself for **trekking** and the nearby village of **Fornalutx** is said to be the prettiest on Mallorca.

From Sóller, it's a 10km walk to the beautiful hill-top village of **Deià**, where the poet and author Robert Graves lived most of his life. Scramble downhill to the small shingle beach of **Cala de Deià**, a laid-back haven of naked swimming and weekend-long beach parties.

Most of Mallorca's best beaches have been consumed by tourist developments but the lovely **Cala Mondragó**, on the southeastern coast, is backed by a couple of *hostales*. A little further south, the attractive port town of **Cala Figuera** and nearby **Cala Santanyi** beach have both escaped many of the ravages of mass tourism. There are also some good quiet beaches near the popular German resort of **Colonia San Jordi**, particularly **Ses Arenes** and **Es Trenc**, both a few kilometres back up the coast towards Palma.

SPAIN

Sleeping

PALMA

It's definitely a good idea to make a reservation as accommodation can get quite booked up.

Hostal Ritzi (☎ 971 71 46 10; s/d without bathroom €25/38, d with bathroom €50) This little place is friendly and charming in a cluttered sort of way with satellite TV in the communal sitting room.

Hostal Brondo (☎ 971 71 90 43; www.hostalbrondo .net; Carrer C'an Brondo 1; s/d/tr without bathroom €30/45/55, d with bathroom €60) With a welcoming English owner and pretty communal areas, rooms in this *hostal* are spacious with high ceilings. Some have balconies.

Hostal Terramar (☎ 971 73 99 31; www.palma -hostales.com; Plaza Mediterraneo 8; dm/s/d €17/27/34) Handily located near the port, this is Palma's only *hostal* with cooking and laundry facilities.

OTHER AREAS

Hostal Miramar (☎ 971 63 90 84; www.pension miramar.com; Can Oliver s/n; s/d/tr incl breakfast €31/60/82; Ⓟ) In Deià, this friendly place has old-fashioned rooms with a bird's-eye view of the village and sea.

Hostal Nadal (☎ 971 63 11 80; Carrer Romaguera 29; s/d/tr €18/26/35, with bathroom €22/34/44) In Sóller, with basic, airy rooms and a small patio and bar downstairs.

Hostal Cán Jordi (☎ 971 64 50 35; Carrer de la Virgen del Carmen 58, Cala Figuera; s/d €28/41) On the southeast coast, it's justifiably popular with wonderful views over the inlet.

Hostal Playa Mondragó (☎ 971 65 77 52; Cala Mondragó; s/d €32/64; Ⓨ May-Oct; ☒ ☒) Also on the southeast coast, this five-storey building overlooks one of the island's best (and least developed) sandy beaches.

You can also sleep cheaply at several quirky old monasteries around the island with prices about €20 per person. The tourist office has a list.

Eating & Drinking

For Palma's best range of eateries, wander through the maze of streets between Plaça de la Reina and the port. Carrer Apuntadores is lined with bars and restaurants, including the inexpensive takeaway **Bar Dia** at No 18.

Yate Rizz (Passeig des Born 2; menú with wine €5.30; Ⓨ 1-3.30pm Mon-Sat) Dishes up the cheapest three-course meals in town to a happy mix of locals and tourists crammed shoulder-to-shoulder over red-checked tablecloths.

Restaurant Celler Sa Premsa (☎ 971 72 35 29; www.cellersapremsa.com; Plaça del Bisbe Berenguer de Palou 8; mains €7-8; Ⓨ noon-4pm & 7.30-11.30pm Mon-Sat) This local institution, the size of a warehouse, serves up enormous portions of classic Mallorcan fare.

Bon Lloc (☎ 971 71 86 17; Carrer de San Feliu 7; menú €11; Ⓨ 1-4pm Mon-Sat; ☒) Popular with Palma's young professionals, it serves up tasty vegetarian dishes.

Good late-night drinking dens include **Atlantico** (Carrer de Sant Feliu 12; Ⓨ 8pm-4am), with a unique combination of knockout cocktails and grunge, and **La Bodeguita de Medio** (Carrer Vallseca 18; Ⓨ 8pm-1am Mon-Thu, 8pm-3am Fri-Sat), which blares out salsa to a mojito-fuelled crowd.

Getting Around

Buses to most of the island usually leave from or near Palma's bus station at Plaça Espanya: the tourist office has details. Mallorca's two train lines start from Plaça Espanya. One reaches the inland town of Inca; the other goes to Sóller (€2.50, one hour, five daily).

The best way to get around the island is by car. There are about 30 rental agencies in Palma, and many have harbourside offices along Passeig Marítim.

FORMENTERA

A short boat ride south of Ibiza, Formentera is the smallest and least developed of the Balearic Islands and most of the time it is still possible to spread a towel out on the beach without kicking sand over your neighbour. The island is also famously flat and has some excellent cycling trails – see p1095 for bike rentals.

Ferries arrive at La Savina on the northwest coast; the **tourist office** (☎ 971 32 20 57; www.formentera.es; Ⓨ 10am-2pm & 5-7pm Mon-Fri, 10am-2pm Sat) is at the port. Three kilometres south, the island's pretty capital, Sant Francesc Xavier, has banks and a super-market. Es Pujols, 3km east of La Savina, is the main tourist resort where most of the *hostales* are located (and the only place with any nightlife to speak of).

Sights & Activities

Some of the island's best beaches are the stunning sandy white strips along the narrow promontory reaching north towards Ibiza. A 2km walking trail leads from the La Savina–Es Pujols road to the promontory's end, from where you can wade (carefully) across a fine strait to **S'Espalmador**, a privately owned uninhabited islet with enchanting, quiet beaches. Formentera's south coast, **Platja de Migjorn** is dotted with many coves and beaches. On the west coast is the lovely **Cala Saona** beach.

The tourist office's *Green Tours* brochure, in five languages, outlines 19 excellent walking and cycling trails that take you through some of the island's most scenic areas.

Sleeping & Eating

Camping is not allowed on Formentera. Sadly, the coastal accommodation places mainly cater to German and British package-tour agencies and are overpriced and/or booked out in summer.

Hostal Capri (☎ 971 32 83 52; s/d incl breakfast €46/60; ☑ May-Sep) In Es Pujols, this *hostal* has whitewashed rooms with ceiling fans and balconies. Downstairs, the shaded terrace restaurant specialises in paella.

Hostal Bellavista (☎ 971 32 22 55; s/d €80/120; ☒) In La Savina, it has port views, a terrace bar, clean rooms and parrots in the lobby.

Casa de Huéspedes Miramar (☎ 971 32 70 60; s/d with shared bathroom €30/40; ☑ Apr-Oct) In Es Caló, this family-run place has small rooms.

Hostal Pepe (☎ 971 32 80 33; s/d with bathroom & breakfast €28/46) In Sant Ferrán de ses Roques, this viby place is run by the Med's chattiest landlady. The restaurant has a fine reputation. From here, Es Pujols is an easy cycle or walk along a 1.5km dusty but pretty track.

Thanks to a particularly large Argentine community, there are some excellent places to get grilled meat on the island and in summer fresh seafood bars open up on many of the island's beaches.

Getting There & Around

Ferries run between Ibiza City and Formentera (€10, 30 minutes, 20 daily). A regular bus service connects all the main towns.

A string of bike-rental agencies lines the harbour in La Savina. Bikes start at €5 a day (€7 for a mountain bike) and scooters start at €20.

MENORCA

Quiet, laid-back Menorca is often overshadowed by its noisier neighbours to the south but what it lacks in pizzazz it certainly makes up for with its miles of undeveloped beaches, archaeological sites and environmental areas, such as the Albufera d'es Grau wetlands. Unesco declared the island a Biosphere Reserve in 1993.

Orientation

The capital, Maó (Mahón in Castilian), is at the eastern end of the island. Its busy port is the arrival point for most ferries. The main road runs down the middle of the island to Ciutadella, Menorca's second-largest town, with secondary roads leading north and south to the resorts and beaches.

Information

Main tourist office (☎ 971 36 37 90; infomenorcamao@cime.es; Carrer Sa Rovellada de Dalt 24, Maó; ☑ 9.30am-3pm & 5-7pm Mon-Fri, 9am-1pm Sat)
Tourist office (☎ 971 38 26 93; Plaça la Catedral 5, Ciutadella; ☑ 9.30am-1.30pm & 5-7pm Mon-Fri, 9am-1pm Sat)

Sights & Activities

From Maó and Ciutadella you'll have to commute to the beaches. Maó absorbs most of the tourist traffic but Ciutadella, with its smaller harbour and historic buildings, has a more distinctively Spanish feel. Follow the shopping baskets to the colourful **market** on Plaça Llibertat, surrounded by lively tapas bars.

In the centre, 357m-high **Monte Toro** has great views of the whole island – on a clear day, you can see as far as Mallorca. North of Maó, a drive across a lunarlike landscape leads to the lighthouse at **Cap de Favàritx**. Park just before the gate to the lighthouse, scramble up the rocks behind you and you'll see a couple of the eight secluded beaches just waiting for you.

On the north coast, picturesque **Fornells** is on a large bay popular with windsurfers. Further west, at the beach of Binimella, you can continue to unspoilt **Cala Pregonda**, a good 20-minute walk from the nearest parking spot.

North of Ciutadella is **La Vall** (parking per car €5, admission free; ☑ 10am-7pm), another stretch of untouched beach backed by a private nature reserve. On the south coast, either side of the Santa Galdana resort, are the two good beaches of **Cala Mitjana** and **Macarella**. The interior of the island is liberally sprinkled with reminders of its rich and ancient heritage. Pick up a copy of *Archaeological Guide to Menorca* from the tourist office.

Sleeping & Eating

Posada Orsi (☎ 971 36 47 51; posadaorsi@hotmail.com; Carrer de la Infanta 19, Maó; s/d €23/38) A riot of acid colours and stripy sofas, Orsi is bright, clean and well located. Tent-like mosquito nets add to the exotic air.

Camping Son Bou (☎ 971 37 26 05; www.campingsonbou.com; per person/tent/car €6.20/3.45/4.15; 🏊) Menorca's best camp site is just south of the resort town of Alaior.

Both Maó and Ciutadella's ports are lined with restaurants and you won't have any trouble finding somewhere to eat.

La Bombilla (☎ 971 36 45 76; Plaça Bastión; bocadillos €2.70; 🕙 10.30am-11.30pm Tue-Sun) In Maó, noisy La Bombilla is a great no-nonsense choice for cheap snacks.

Es Fosquet (☎ 971 35 00 58; Moll de Llevant 256; mains €9-12; 🕙 1-4pm & 8-11.30pm Thu-Sun) Down at the port, this tiny but chic hole-in-the-wall serves up freshly caught fish and shellfish.

Latitud 40 (☎ 971 36 41 76; Moll de Llevant 265; 🕙 7pm-1am) Popular with yachties, it's a hip little bar-restaurant – good if you're looking for a job scrubbing decks.

La Guitarra (☎ 971 38 13 55; Carrer Dolores 1; mains €12; 🕙 12.30-3.30pm & 7.30-11.30pm Mon-Sat) A classy place for a local meal in Ciutadella, it has stone vaulted ceilings and specialises in *pato a la menorquina* (Menorcan duck).

There are lots of good drinking holes near Ciutadella's port.

Getting Around

TMSA (☎ 971 36 04 75) runs buses between Maó and Ciutadella (€3.75, six daily), with connections to the major resorts on the southern coast. In summer there are also daily bus services to most of the coastal towns from both Maó and Ciutadella.

Car-hire rates vary seasonally from around €28 to €48 a day.

VALENCIA & MURCIA

Best known for the package resorts of the Costa Blanca, this region also includes the dynamic cities of Valencia and Alicante and the lush fertile plains of Murcia, bounded by some of the Mediterranean's warmest waters.

VALENCIA (VALÈNCIA)

pop 746,610

Exuberant, friendly and appealingly chaotic, Valencia is Spain's third-largest city. Its Old Quarter brims with gracious baroque-fronted houses and its streets buzz with life until the early hours.

There is a **main tourist office** (☎ 963 98 64 22; www.turisvalencia.es; Calle Paz 48; 🕙 10am-6.30pm Mon-Fri, 10am-2pm Sat) in the centre and a handy **tourist information point** (☎ 963 52 54 78 ext 1739; Plaza de la Reina; 🕙 9am-7pm Mon-Sat, 10am-2pm Sun). For Internet, try **Ono** (☎ 963 28 19 02; San Vicente 22; per hr €2; 🕙 9am-1am).

Sights & Activities

One of Spain's prettiest markets, the **Mercado Central** (Plaza de Mercado; 🕙 8am-2.30pm Mon-Sat) is a feast of colours and smells with nearly 1000 stallholders crammed under *Modernista* (Catalan modernism) glass domes.

Valencia's **cathedral** (🕙 7.30am-1pm & 5-8.30pm) boasts three magnificent portals, the only Holy Grail recognised (albeit tentatively) by the Vatican, a fantastic Goya and the withered left arm of St Vincent. Climb the **Miguelete bell tower** (admission €1.50; 🕙 10.30am-12.30pm & 4.30-6.30pm Tue-Fri, 10.30am-1pm Sat-Mon) for sweeping views of the city

Among the city's art galleries, the two unmissables are **Museo de Bellas Artes** (☎ 963 60 57 93; Calle San Pio V 9; admission free; 🕙 10am-2.15pm & 4-7.30pm Tue-Sat, 10am-7.30pm Sun) and **Instituto Valenciano de Arte Moderno** (☎ 963 86 30 00; Guillem de Castro 118; adult/student/Sunday €2/1/free). Don't miss the sculpted rococo façade of the fabulous **Palacio del Marqués de Dos Aguas** (Calle del Poeta Querol).

Festivals & Events

In mid-March, Valencia hosts what has become one of Europe's wildest street parties, **Las Fallas de San José**. For one week the city is engulfed by an anarchic swirl of fireworks, music, festive bonfires and all-night partying. On the final night, giant sculptures of huge *niñots* (effigies), many of political and social identities, are torched in the main plaza.

Sleeping

There are some great budget options in the heart of the old city.

Hôme Youth Hostel (☎ 963 91 62 29; www.likeathome.net; Calle Lonja 4; dm/s/d €14/21/32; 🖳) Every backpacker's fantasy, with brightly painted rooms and a big kitchen. The same owners also run **Hôme Backpackers** (☎ 963 91 37 97; www.likeathome.net; Plaza Vicente Iborra; dm €12-14, d/tr/q €32/48/64; 🖳) with 100 beds (some bunks) and **Hôme Budget Hotel** (☎ 963 92 40 63; www.likeathome.net; Calle Cadirers 11; d incl breakfast €40) with striking individually designed rooms.

Hostal Antigua Morellana (☎ 963 91 57 73; info@hostalam.com; Calle En Bou 2; s/d €33/48; ❄) In an elegant, renovated 18th-century building, this hotel is excellent value for money. Satellite TV and balconies.

Eating

Lots of cheap fishy eats can be found near the market. For authentic paella, head for Las Arenas, just north of the port, where a strip of restaurants serves up the real stuff from €6.60 per person.

Bar Pilar (Calle Moro Zeit 13; tapas €1.50; ❄ noon-midnight). This Valencian classic is where everyone comes to eat mussels, chucking the shells into plastic buckets on the floor.

La Tastaolletes (☎ 963 92 18 62; Calle Salvador Giner 6; mains €7; ❄ 2-4pm & 8pm-midnight Tue-Sat, 2-4pm Sun) An excellent, colourful vegetarian restaurant, especially good at salads and vegetable lasagne to-die-for.

El Rall (☎ 963 92 20 90; Tundidores 2; mains €8; ❄ 2-4.30pm & 9pm-midnight) A firm favourite, El Rall serves up paella and great desserts in a funky setting. Grab a table on the terrace.

Drinking

The freebie mag *24/7 Valencia* is a fantastic guide (in English) to Valencia's bars, clubs and restaurants.

Much of the action centres on Barrio del Carmen, which caters for every taste from grunge to glam. **Café San Jaume** (Calle Caballeros 51; ❄ noon-1am) has a particularly fine terrace for eyeing up the characters on Calle Caballeros.

Café de las Horas (Calle Conde de Almodóvar 1; ❄ 4pm-1am Mon-Thu, 4pm-3.30am Fri & Sat) With red walls, theatrical drapes and frescoes, this bar-café has the feel of an 18th-century boudoir. Serves the best *agua de Valencia* (a mix of orange juice and sparkling wine) in town.

The Lounge Café-Bar (☎ 963 91 80 94; Calle Estamiñería Vieja 2; ❄ 11am-1am) This popular international hang-out has comfy sofas and free Internet. It's a good place to meet other travellers.

Clubbing

Radio City (☎ 963 91 41 51; Santa Teresa 19; ❄ 11pm-late) This is the mecca for post-bar dancing to salsa, house and cheesy pop. There's live flamenco on Tuesdays at 11pm.

Bolsería Café (☎ 963 91 89 03; Calle Bolsería 41; ❄ 11pm-4am) Fashionable, plays house music and has bizarre toilets with see-through walls.

The Black Note (☎ 963 93 36 63; Polo y Peyrolón 15; ❄ from 11.30pm) Jazz cats should try this joint.

Younger groovers head for the university 2km east (€3.50 by taxi from the centre). Along Av Blasco Ibáñez and particularly around Plaza de Xuquer there are scores of dusk-to-dawn bars and discos.

Getting There & Around

From Valencia's **airport** (☎ 96 159 85 15), 10km west of the city centre, Easyjet has daily low-cost flights to/from London Stansted.

From the **bus station** (☎ 963 49 72 22; Av Menéndez Pidal) services go to/from Madrid (€21, four hours, 10 daily), Barcelona (€22, five hours, 12 daily) and Alicante (€15, 2¼ hours, 11 daily).

From Valencia's **Estación del Norte** (Calle Jativa) trains go to/from Madrid (€37, 3½ hours, 10 daily), Barcelona (€29, 3½ hours, 14 daily) and Alicante (€20.50, two hours, 10 daily).

Regular **ferries** go to the Balearic Islands (see p1091).

EMT (☎ 963 52 83 99) buses run until about 10pm, with night services continuing on seven routes until around 1am. Bus No 8 connects the bus station with Plaza de Ayuntamiento. The smart high-speed tram is a pleasant way to get to the beach and the port (€1).

ALICANTE (ALACANT)

pop 299,977

There's an endearing faded grandeur to Alicante, particularly in the Old Quarter, overlooked by the majestic limestone cathedral. The nightlife is also equal to that of any self-respecting Valencian city. There are five tourist offices but the most central is the **main tourist office** (☎ 965 20 00 00; www.landofvalencia.com; Rambla de Méndez Núñez 23; ❄ 10am-7.30pm Mon-Fri, 10am-2pm Sat). Connect to the Internet at **Up Internet** (Angel Lozano 10; per hr €2.95; ❄ 10am-2am).

SPAIN

Sights & Activities

Castillo de Santa Bárbara (☎ 965 26 31 31; Monte Benacantil; admission free; ☷ 10am-8pm), a 16th-century fortress, overlooks the city. You can walk up or take the lift (€2.40 return trip), reached by a footbridge opposite Playa del Postiguet.

Museo de la Asegurada (☎ 965 14 07 68; Plaza de Santa María 3; admission free; ☷ 10am-2pm & 4-8pm Tue-Sat, 10.30am-2.30pm Sun) has exhibitions by contemporary artists. On the same square, the 14th-century **Iglesia de Santa María** (☷ 10.30am-1pm & 6-7.30pm) incorporates a variety of styles from the stunning baroque façade to the Gothic nave.

The closest beach is **Playa del Postiguet**. Less crowded is **Playa de San Juan**, easily reached by bus Nos 21 and 22. Most days, **Kontiki** (☎ 965 21 63 96) runs boat trips (€15 return trip) to the popular **Isla de Tabarca**, where there is excellent snorkelling and scuba diving from quiet beaches.

Sleeping

You shouldn't have too much trouble finding somewhere to kip.

Pensión La Milagrosa (☎ 965 21 69 18; Calle de Villavieja 8; s/d €15/30) Rooms at this large *pensión* are basic, there's a small guest kitchen, lots of religious paintings on the walls and a sunny rooftop terrace with views to the castle.

Hostal Les Monges Palace (☎ 965 21 50 46; www .lesmonges.net; Calle San Agustín 4; s/d €25/37; **P** ☒) Rooms in this fabulous old building have tiled floors, gorgeous bathrooms and lots of theatrical flourishes.

Pensión Portugal (☎ 965 92 92 44; Calle Portugal 26; s/d €21/30) A characterless building overlooking the bus station, this is a good safe place to crash if you get in late. Brutal lighting, though.

Eating & Drinking

Alicante is filled with bars and cafés, including the old-fashioned **Café-Cervecería Ramblas** (Rambla de Méndez Núñez 7; ☷ 8am-2am).

Restaurante Mixto Vegetariano (Plaza de Santa María 2; menú €7.50) This simple place has vegetarian and meat *menús*. Service is an elderly one-man show, but worth it. Best *flan casero* (home-made crème caramel) in Spain.

Cantina Villahelmy (☎ 965 21 25 29; Calle Mayor 37; mains €4-8; ☷ 10am-4pm & 8pm-midnight Tue-Sat, noon-4pm Sun) Intimate, funky and popular, it has lots of snacks, excellent salads and a menu ranging from couscous to octopus.

Popular watering holes cluster around the cathedral, where there is a good choice of early evening bars. Later on, look out for **Celestial Copas** (Calle San Pascual 1; ☷ 10.30pm-4am) and **Desafinado** (Santo Tomas 6; ☷ 10.30pm-4.30am) dance bars. In summer, the disco scene at Playa de San Juan is thumping.

Getting There & Away

From Alicante's **airport** (☎ 96 691 90 00), BMI Baby has low-cost flights to/from UK cities including Manchester, Birmingham and Cardiff. Easyjet has cheap flights between Alicante and London Luton, London Gatwick, Liverpool and Newcastle.

From the **bus station** (☎ 965 13 07 00; Calle Portugal 17) there are services to Almería (€18, five hours, five daily), Valencia (€15, 2¼ hours, 11 daily), Barcelona (€34, eight hours, 10 daily), Madrid (€23, 4½ hours, seven daily) and towns along the Costa Blanca.

From the **train station** (Av de Salamanca), services run to Madrid (€36, four hours, seven daily), Valencia (€20.50, two hours, 10 daily) and Barcelona (€39.50 to €44, five hours, eight daily).

From the **Ferrocarriles de la Generalitat Valenciana (FGV) station** (☎ 965 26 27 31) at the Playa del Postiguet's northeast, a narrow-gauge line follows a pretty coastal route northwards as far as Dénia (€7, 2¼ hours, six daily) via Benidorm and Calpe.

COSTA BLANCA

The Costa Blanca has its share of concrete jungle, but if you're looking for a rollicking nightlife, good beaches and a suntan, you won't be disappointed.

Over two-thirds of annual visitors to **Xàbia** (Jávea) are foreigners, so it's not the greatest place to brush up on your Spanish. This laid-back resort is in three parts: the Old Town (3km inland), the port and the beach zone of El Arenal, lined with pleasant bar-restaurants. In the Old Town, **Hostal Levante** (☎ 965 79 15 91; Calle Maestro Alonso 5; s/d €25/34, d with shower/bathroom €40/43) has basic rooms.

Calpe is dominated by the Gibraltaresque **Peñon de Ilfach** (332m), a giant molar protruding from the sea. The climb towards the summit is popular – while you're up there, decide which of the two long sandy beaches you want to laze on. **Pensión Céntrica** (☎ 965 83 55 28; Plaza de Ilfach; s/d with washbasin €12/24) just off Av Gabriel Miró is squeaky clean.

Benidorm succumbed to cheap package tourism several decades ago, but there are 5km of (crowded) white beaches and a high-spirited nightlife with more karaoke bars per square metre than anywhere else in Spain. There's no truly budget accommodation.

MURCIA

Murcia is one of the most conservative of Spain's provinces. The capital, also called Murcia, has a traditional Spanish appeal, liberally sprinkled with plazas and some gorgeous architecture. The **municipal tourist office** (☎ 968 35 87 49; www.murciaciudad.com; Plaza Cardinal Belluga; ☺ 10am-2pm & 5-9pm Mon-Sat, 10am-2pm Sun) and **regional tourist office** (☎ 902 10 10 70; Plaza Romea 4; ☺ 9.30am-1.30pm & 5-7pm Mon-Fri) are helpful.

Inside Murcia's opulent **cathedral** (Plaza Cardinal Belluga; ☺ 10am-1pm & 5-7pm), the 23 chapels and a 92m-high tower cover a dizzying range of styles but it's the façade, dripping in cherubs, that is the real jaw-dropper. The city's sumptuous 19th-century **casino** (☎ 968 21 22 55; admission €1.20; ☺ 10am-9pm) features an Arabic patio and a magnificent ballroom.

Family-run **Pensión Murcia** (☎ 968 21 99 63; Calle Vinadel 6; s/d €18/38) has cosy rooms with ceiling fans. Something of a local institution, **La Barra del Rincón de Pepe** (☎ 968 21 22 39; Calle Apóstoles 34; menú €12; ☺ 1.30-4pm & 8pm-midnight) serves up delicious Murcian fare.

Murcia's Costa Cálida's (Warm Coast) drawcard is the **Mar Menor**, a salt-water lagoon separated from the sea by a 22km land sliver known as **La Manga**. The water is so warm you can swim here all year round. **Camping Mar Menor** (☎ 968 57 01 33; per person/tent/car €3.30/3/3.30) is on the beach, 4km south of La Ribera.

Ryanair has low-cost flights to Murcia from London Luton, London Stansted and Dublin.

Buses serve Madrid (€21, five hours, nine daily), Alicante (€5, one hour, every two hours), Almería (€11, three hours, five daily) and towns on the Costa Cálida. Trains go to Alicante (€13.50, 75 minutes, five daily) and Madrid (€35.50, five hours, five daily).

ANDALUCÍA

Whether you are soaking up the rays on a beach, strolling the alleyways of some historic barrio or sipping a glass of chilled gazpacho in a leafy plaza, life is sweet in Andalucía.

The stronghold of the Muslims in Spain for nearly eight centuries, the region is peppered with Moorish reminders, including the magnificent Alhambra in Granada and the timeless elegance of Córdoba's Mezquita (Mosque). The regional capital, Seville, is one of the country's most enticing cities.

The region's scenery covers semideserts and lush river valleys and gorge-ridden mountains. Its long coastline stretches from the remote beaches of Cabo de Gata, past the crowds of the Costa del Sol, to come within 14km of Africa at Tarifa before opening up to the Atlantic Ocean with the long sandy beaches of the Costa de la Luz.

SEVILLE
pop 709,975

An impossibly sexy and intoxicating city, Seville seduces all the senses. From the spontaneous bursts of flamenco in the bars to the passion of its festivals, this is the most *andaluz* (Andalucian) of Spain's cities. Even after you've left, the city's memory lingers on.

Seville is an expensive place, so it's worth planning your visit carefully. The best time to come is during the unforgettable Easter week and April *feria* (fairs) although rooms then (if you can get one) cost close to double the regular rates.

Orientation

The Río Guadalquivir intersects Seville, with most interesting places on the river's eastern side. The centre is a confusion of small plazas and winding streets apart from the broad Avenida Consitución. Most of the city's monuments, including the cathedral, the Giralda and the Alcázar are east of Avenida Constitución. Further east, the Barrio de Santa Cruz is an appealing web of streets with most of Seville's budget accommodation.

Information
Internet Multimedia Center (☎ 954 50 25 43; Calle Adriano 7; per hr €2; ☺ 10am-10pm Mon-Fri, 5-10pm Sat & Sun)
Main tourist office (☎ 954 22 14 04; otsevilla@andalucia.org; Av de la Constitución 21; ☺ 9am-7pm Mon-Fri, 10am-2pm & 3-7pm Sat, 10am-2pm Sun) Always extremely busy.
Other tourist offices Paseo de las Delicias 9 (☎ 954 23 44 65; ☺ 8.30am-2.45pm Mon-Fri) Calle de Arjona 28 (☎ 954 50 56 00; ☺ 8am-8.45pm Mon-Fri, 8.30am-2.30pm Sat & Sun)

Sights & Activities

CATHEDRAL & GIRALDA

The city's towering **cathedral** (☎ 954 21 49 71; Calle Alemanes; adult/student/Sunday €7/1.50/free; ☾ 11am-5pm Mon-Sat, 2.30-6pm Sun), one of the biggest in the world, was built on the site of Muslim Seville's main mosque between 1401 and 1507. The adjoining tower, La Giralda, was the mosque's minaret and dates from the 12th century. One highlight of the cathedral's lavish interior is Christopher Columbus' supposed tomb inside the south door.

ALCÁZAR

A residence of Muslim and Christian royalty for many centuries, Seville's **Alcázar** (Fortress; ☎ 954 50 23 23; adult/student €5/free; ☾ 9.30am-7pm Tue-Sat, 9.30am-5pm Sun) was founded in 913 as a Muslim fortress. A fascinating mishmash of styles, it has been adapted by Seville's rulers in almost every century since. Highlights are the **Palacio de Don Pedro**, exquisitely decorated by Muslim artisans in the 1360s, and the large, immaculate **gardens**, the perfect place to ease body and mind.

WALKS & PARKS

To fully appreciate **Barrio de Santa Cruz**, the old Jewish quarter immediately east of the cathedral, you need to head for the tangle of narrow streets and plazas east of Calle Mateus Gago. There's no better place to get lost. Seville's famous bullring, the **Plaza de Toros de la Real Maestranza** (☎ 954 22 45 77; guided tours €4, ☾ 9.30am-7pm, 9.30am-3pm bullfight days), is one of the oldest in Spain. The tour (the only way to see the place) is in English and Spanish.

South of the centre is **Parque de María Luisa**, a maze of paths, tall trees, flowers, fountains and shaded lawns. Seek out the magnificent **Plaza de España** with its fountains, canal and a dazzling semicircle of buildings clad in *azulejo* (ceramic tiles).

MUSEUMS

The **Archivo de las Indias** (☎ 954 21 12 34) has been exhaustively renovated for some years and was still closed at the time of writing. When it does open (ecpected by summer 2005), be blown away by a fascinating array of maps and papers dating from 1492 and documenting the conquest of the Americas and life in the Spanish colonies.

The **Museo de Bellas Artes** (☎ 954 22 07 90 Plaza del Museo 9; non EU/EU citizens €1.50/free; ☾ 2.30-8.15pm Tue, 9am-8.15pm Wed-Sat, 9am-2.15pm Sun) has an outstanding collection of Spanish art, focusing on Seville artists such as Bartolemé Esteban Murillo and Francisco Zurbarán.

Festivals & Events

Semana Santa During the week leading up to Easter Sunday, long processions of religious brotherhoods, dressed in strange penitents' garb with tall, pointed hoods, accompany sacred images through the city.
Feria de Abril Held in late April, it involves six days of music, dancing, horse riding and traditional dress, plus daily bullfights and a general citywide party.

Sleeping

Summer prices given here can come down substantially from October to March but will shoot up in April.

Albergue Juvenil Sevilla (☎ 955 05 65 00; Calle Isaac Peral 2; dm incl breakfast under/over 26 €13/17.50) Seville's youth hostel has 277 beds in modern twins or triples. It's 10 minutes' south by bus No 34 from opposite the main tourist office.

Pensión Vergara (☎ 954 21 56 68; pensionvergarasevilla@yahoo.es; Calle Ximenez de Enciso 11; s/d tr/q €18/36/54/72; 🖳) Far and away the best budget option, this enchanting *pensión* has 12 pretty rooms around an inviting courtyard in a former 15th-century convent.

FLAMENCO FUSION

Flamenco has become much more than the traditional signature music of southern Spain. Once exclusively the music of the Gitanos (Roma), in recent years flamenco has also morphed into a modern fusion of different rhythms and styles. Since the 1970s, bands have experimented with blues, rock, latin, jazz and even punk to create cool new sounds as well as a new fan base of young Spaniards. So much so that these days you are as likely to hear flamenco hip-hop blasting out of a souped-up car on a Friday night as to catch it in a tourist show.

Bands that first erupted in this new flamenco style include the bluesy Pata Negra, Ketama (African, Cuban and Brazilian rhythms) and Radio Tarifa (North African and medieval mix). In recent years Chambao have hit the mark with their flamenco chill and Mala Rodriguez has put flamenco hip into hip-hop.

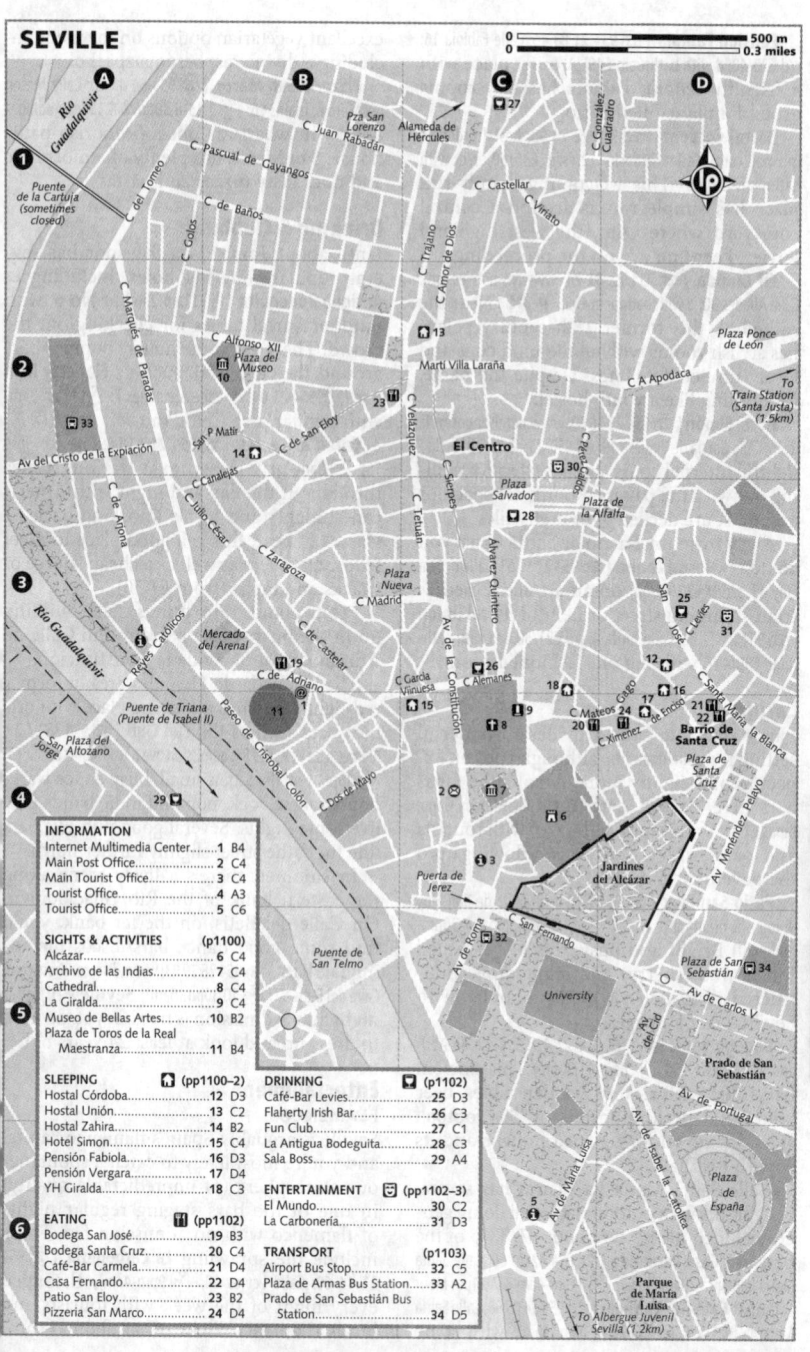

SEVILLE

0 — 500 m
0 — 0.3 miles

SPAIN

Pensión Fabiola (☎ 954 21 83 46; Calle Fabiola 16; s/d €20/40, d with bathroom €46) A quiet place with a friendly *señora*, Fabiola has airy rooms around a plant-filled patio.

Hostal Córdoba (☎ 954 22 74 98; hostalcordoba@ mixmail.com; Calle Farnesio 12; s/d €35/50, s/d with bathroom €40/60) This welcoming, family-run place has simple rooms around a central courtyard where Otto, the west highland terrier, keeps an eye on the proceedings.

YH Giralda (☎ 954 22 83 24; www.yh-hoteles.com; Calle Abades 30; d with bathroom €55; P 🐾) Near the cathedral, this former 18th-century palace has stylish rooms with all the mod cons and lovely timbered ceilings. Despite the name, it's nothing like a youth hostel.

Hotel Simon (☎ 954 22 66 60; www.hotelsimonsevilla .com; Calle Garcia de Vinuesa 19; s/d €50/75; 🐾) The delightful internal courtyard is perfect for chilling out with the papers. Rooms are spacious and most are decked with pretty tiles.

Away from the Barrio de Santa Cruz, you could try **Hostal Zahira** (☎ 954 22 10 61; Calle de San Eloy 43; s/d/tr €30/45/60) on an attractive pedestrian shopping street or helpful **Hostal Unión** (☎ 954 21 17 90; Calle Tarifa 4; s/d €21/30, s/d with bathroom €30/42), with big old-fashioned rooms.

Eating

Barrio de Santa Cruz provides a wonderful setting for restaurants, although you can expect to pay slightly more. Among the tapas bars here, **Bodega Santa Cruz** (Calle Mateos Gago; tapas €1.40; 🐾 8am-midnight) buzzes with tourists and locals, with the crowd overflowing onto the pavement outside.

Patio San Eloy (☎ 954 22 11 48; Calle de San Eloy 9; tapas & montaditos €1.50; 🐾 11.30am-5pm & 7.30pm-midnight) Bright and busy, this bar is famed for its *fino* (sherry) and *montaditos* (multitiered sandwiches); madly popular with Sevillianos of all ages.

Bodega San José (☎ 954 22 41 05; Calle de Adriano 10; tapas €1.50; 🐾 8am-11.30pm) This ancient bar, filled with rickety wooden tables, beer crates and peeling posters of '50s football stars, is known for its fried prawns and its superb tortilla.

Calle Santa María La Blanca has several restaurants with outdoor tables all doing generous lunch *menús* for about €7. Two of the best are **Casa Fernando** (☎ 954 42 26 60; Calle Santa María la Blanca 10; menú €7; 🐾 11am-4pm & 7-11pm Mon-Sat) and **Café-Bar Carmela** (☎ 954 54 05 90; Calle Santa María la Blanca 6; menú €7; 🐾 9am-1am), with some

excellent vegetarian options on the menu including a divine raspberry gazpacho.

Pizzeria San Marco (☎ 954 56 43 90; Calle Mesón del Moro 6; mains €6; 🐾 1.15-4.30pm & 8.15pm-midnight Tue-Sun) In what was once a Moorish bathhouse, San Marco has plenty of atmosphere and does tasty pizzas and pastas.

Drinking & Clubbing

Until about 1am, Plaza Salvador has several popular watering holes, including **La Antigua Bodeguita** (🐾 11am-2am) at No 6, with outdoor barrel tables for checking out the crowd. There are some hugely popular bars around the cathedral, such as **Flaherty Irish Bar** (☎ 954 21 04 51; Calle Alemanes 7; 🐾 11am-3am) with regular, live Celtic music.

Café-Bar Levies (☎ 954 21 53 08; Calle San José 15; 🐾 8am-3am) Heaving at various times throughout the day and night with American students and locals knocking back €1 glasses of beer, this is a good place to meet fellow travellers as well as a cheap source of snacks and tapas (from €1.50).

From about 1am things start building up in the busy music bars around Calle de Adriano, west of Av de la Constitución.

The Alameda de Hércules area, a former red-light district, is a buzzing place with off-beat bars such as the **Fun Club** (☎ 954 38 93 29; Alameda de Hércules 86; admission live music nights about €5; 🐾 10pm-6am Thu-Sat), a small, busy dance warehouse where rock, pop and indie bands play live some nights. Several good pub-like bars line the same street slightly further north.

In summer, there's a lively scene along the eastern bank of the Río Guadalquivir. On Calle del Betis, on the far bank, you'll find some good dance bars/discos including **Sala Boss** (☎ 954 28 19 93; www.discotecaboss.com; Calle del Betis 67; 🐾 10.30pm-6am), Seville's biggest nightclub. Admission is free but you do have to dress up and look at least 24 years old.

Entertainment

FLAMENCO

Seville is arguably Spain's flamenco capital and you're most likely to catch a spontaneous atmosphere (of unpredictable quality) in one of the bars staging regular nights of flamenco with no admission fee. These include the sprawling **La Carbonería** (☎ 954 21 44 60; Calle Levíes 18; 🐾 9pm-4am), thronged every night of the week with tourists and locals (flamenco kicks off at about 11pm) and **El Mundo** (www.elmundotrobar.com; Calle Siete Revueltas 5; 🕙 11pm-late), which has flamenco most Tuesday nights at 11pm.

SPECTATOR SPORTS
The bullfight season runs from Easter to October, with fights most Sundays at about 6.30pm, and each day during the Feria de Abril and the preceding week. The bullring is on Paseo de Cristóbal Colón. Tickets start at €10 or €20, depending on who's fighting.

Getting There & Away
BUS
Buses from **Plaza de Armas bus station** (🕿 954 90 80 40) run to/from Madrid (€16, six hours, hourly), Lisbon (€25, 6¼ hours, three weekly) and Andalucían towns west of Seville and to Extremadura.

Buses to other parts of Andalucía and eastern Spain depart from **Prado de San Sebastián bus station** (🕿 954 41 71 11), with services to/from Córdoba (€9, 1¾ hours, 10 daily), Granada (€16, three hours, 10 daily) and Málaga (€12, 2½ hours, seven daily).

TRAIN
From Seville's **Santa Justa train station** (Av Kansas City), 1.5km northeast of the centre, there are both superfast AVE and regular trains to/from Madrid (€51.50 to €65, 2½ hours to 3¼ hours, hourly) and Córdoba (€7 to €20, 45 minutes to 1¼ hours). Other trains travel to/from Cádiz (€8.40, 1¾ hours, 10 daily), Granada (€17.65, 3¼ hours, four daily), Málaga (€14, 2½ hours, five daily) and Mérida (€11, 4¾ hours, one daily).

Getting Around
Bus No C1, in front of Santa Justa train station, takes a clockwise circuit via Av de Carlos V, close to Prado de San Sebastián bus station and the city centre; No C2 does the same route anticlockwise. No C4, south down Calle de Arjona from Plaza de Armas bus station, goes to Puerta de Jerez; take No C3 on your return.

CÓRDOBA
pop 318,628

There can't be many more enjoyable ways to explore the soul of Andalucía than to lose yourself in Córdoba's old quarter, a maze of winding cobblestone alleyways, pretty plazas and lovely flower-filled patios.

The city is a testament to its Moorish past, when Córdoba became the effective Islamic capital on the peninsula following the Muslim invasion in 711, a position it held for nearly 300 years. Muslim Córdoba at its peak was the most splendid city in Europe and its Mezquita (Mosque) is one of the most magnificent of all Islamic buildings.

Information
Municipal tourist office kiosks (🕙 10am-2pm & 4.30-7.30pm) At Plaza de las Tendillas, Campo Santos Mártires, Plaza Posada del Potro and the train station.
Navegaweb (Plaza de Judá Leví s/n; per hr €1.50; 🕙 10am-10pm) Internet access.
Regional tourist office (🕿 957 47 12 35; Calle de Torrijos 10; 🕙 9.30am-6pm Mon-Fri, 10am-7pm Sat, 10am-2pm Sun) Faces the Mezquita; slightly officious staff.

Sights & Activities
Inside the famous **Mezquita** (🕿 957 47 05 12; adult €6.50; 🕙 10am-7pm Mon-Sat Mar-Oct, 10am-5.30pm Mon-Sat, 2-6.30pm Sun Nov-Feb), dating from 785, is a mesmerising sequence of two-tiered arches and a thicket of columns. From 1236 the mosque was used as a church; in the 16th century a cathedral was built in its centre.

The Judería, Córdoba's medieval Jewish quarter, is an intriguing maze of narrow streets and small plazas. Don't miss the beautiful little medieval **Sinagoga** (🕿 957 20 29 28; Calle Judíos; EU citizens/non-EU citizens free/€0.30; 🕙 10am-7pm Tue-Sun). The **Museo Taurino** (Bullfighting Museum; 🕿 957 20 10 56; Plaza de Maimónides; admission €3; 🕙 10am-2pm & 5.30-7.30pm Tue-Sat, 9.30am-2.30pm Sun) celebrates Córdoba's legendary matadors.

Southwest of the Mezquita, the **Alcázar de los Reyes Cristianos** (Fortress of the Christian Monarchs; 🕿 957 42 01 51; admission €2; 🕙 10am-2pm & 5.30-7.30pm Tue-Sat, 9.30am-2.30pm Sun) has large and lovely gardens.

On the southern side of the river, across the **Puente Romano**, is the **Torre de la Calahorra** (🕿 957 29 39 29; adult/student €4/2.50; 🕙 10am-2pm & 4.30-8.30pm) with a museum highlighting the intellectual achievements of Islamic Córdoba.

It is well worth the 8km trip west of Córdoba to the intriguing **Medina Azahara** (🕿 957 32 91 30; Carretera Palma del Río, km 5.5; EU/non-EU citizens free/€1.50; 🕙 10am-6.30pm Tue-Sat, 10am-2pm Sun), a once-mighty Muslim city-palace in the 10th century. Catch the tourist bus there from Av Alcázar at 11am. Tickets (€5) can be bought from the tourist office.

SPAIN

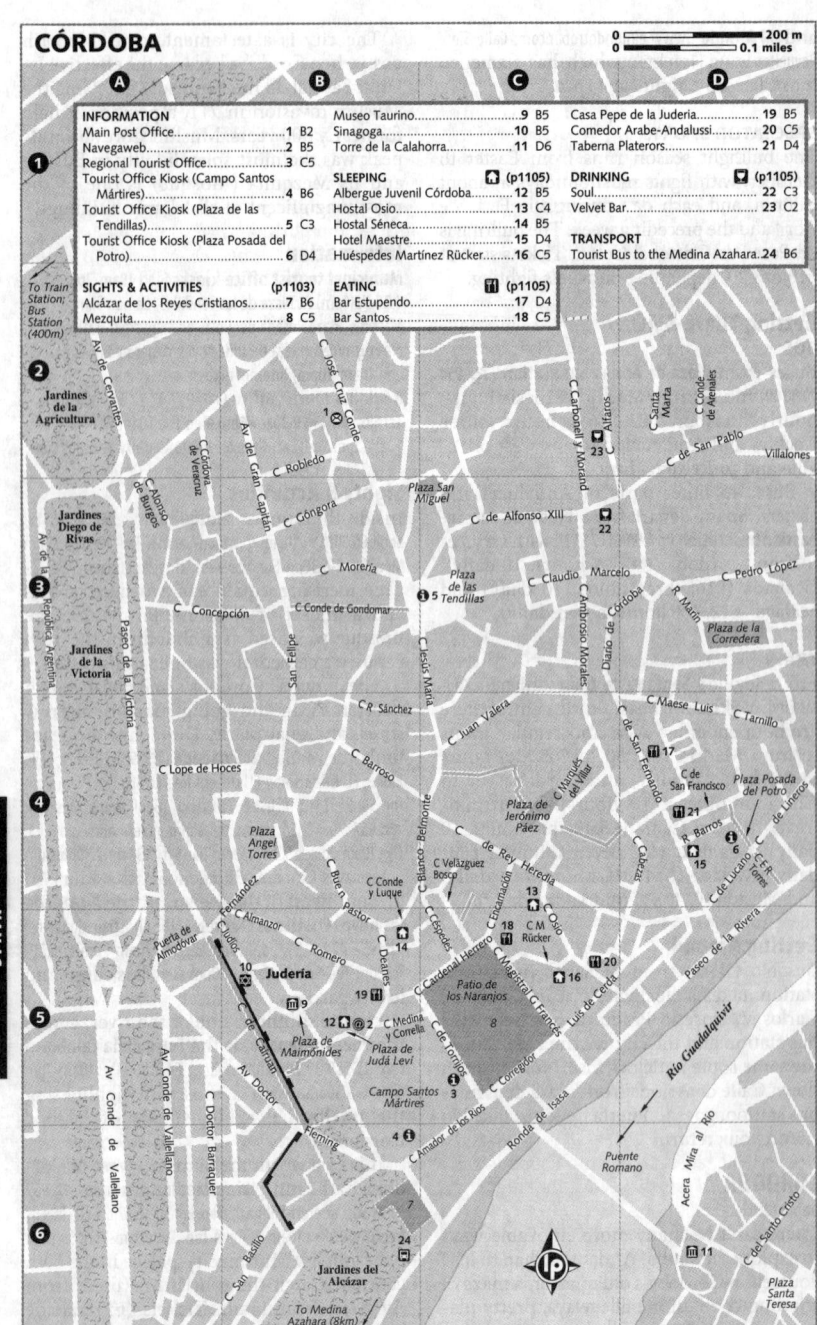

CÓRDOBA

INFORMATION	
Main Post Office.................................	1 B2
Navegaweb.......................................	2 B5
Regional Tourist Office.....................	3 C5
Tourist Office Kiosk (Campo Santos Mártires)....................................	4 B6
Tourist Office Kiosk (Plaza de las Tendillas).....................................	5 C3
Tourist Office Kiosk (Plaza Posada del Potro)..	6 D4

SIGHTS & ACTIVITIES	(p1103)
Alcázar de los Reyes Cristianos........	7 B6
Mezquita...	8 C5

Museo Taurino.................................	9 B5
Sinagoga...	10 B5
Torre de la Calahorra.......................	11 D6

SLEEPING	(p1105)
Albergue Juvenil Córdoba.............	12 B5
Hostal Osio.....................................	13 C4
Hostal Séneca..................................	14 B5
Hotel Maestre..................................	15 D4
Huéspedes Martínez Rücker............	16 C5

EATING	(p1105)
Bar Estupendo.................................	17 D4
Bar Santos.......................................	18 C5

Casa Pepe de la Judería...................	19 B5
Comedor Arabe-Andalussi................	20 C5
Taberna Platerors.............................	21 D4

DRINKING	(p1105)
Soul..	22 C3
Velvet Bar.......................................	23 C2

TRANSPORT	
Tourist Bus to the Medina Azahara.24 B6	

0 — 200 m
0 — 0.1 miles

Sleeping

Most lodgings are close to the Mezquita and nearly all are built around lovely cool patios.

Albergue Juvenil Córdoba (☎ 957 29 01 66; Plaza de Judá Leví; dm under/over 26 incl breakfast €13.35/18.35) Córdoba's excellent youth hostel is perfectly positioned on a pretty and central plaza. It has no curfew.

Huéspedes Martínez Rücker (☎ 957 47 67 97; Calle Martínez Rücker 14; s/d/tr €12.50/25/37.50) Some rooms in this chaotic, leafy haven have gorgeous old beds and are dotted with antiques. All are fairly basic, though, and it can get nippy in winter.

Hostal Osio (☎ 957 48 51 65; Calle Osio 6; s/d €25/40; P 🖳) One of Córdoba's prettiest *hostales*, the Osio has pine furnishings, two patios and good views – try for room No 10 overlooking the adjacent convent.

Hostal Séneca (☎ 957 47 32 34; hostalseneca@ resmas.com; Calle Conde y Luque 7; s/d incl breakfast 22/39, with bathroom €34/46) This welcoming place has rooms around an enchanting patio and a little bar. Phone ahead.

Hotel Maestre (☎ 957 47 24 10; www.hotelmaestre om; Calle Romero Barros 4; s/d €29/47; P 🅿) This small bright hotel has a dash of Spanish chic in a good location northeast of the Mezquita.

Eating & Drinking

There is no shortage of places to eat within striking distance of the Mezquita. Quell hunger pangs with a hefty slice of tortilla from **Bar Santos** (Calle Magistral González Francés 3; tapas €1.20; 🕑 12.30-4pm & 7pm-midnight).

Bar Estupendo (☎ 957 47 04 94; Calle de San Fernando 9; mains €4-5; 🕑 1-4pm & 8-11pm Tue-Sat, 1-4pm Sun) It may not be much to look at with its plastic furniture and gloomy interior, but this bar does a roaring trade serving up hearty three-course *menús* for €7.50 (including drinks).

Comedor Arabe-Andalussi (☎ 957 47 51 62; Plaza bades 4; mains €3.50-5; 🕑 noon-4pm & 7-11pm Tue-un) On a pretty plaza, this Arabian-style eatery is filled with Oriental carpets and ow candlelit tables. The lamb kebab is superb and vegetarians will love the fantastic salads and falafel.

Taberna Platerors (☎ 957 47 00 42; Calle de San Francisco 6; raciónes €4-6; 🕑 1-4pm & 8pm-midnight) This large and noisy tavern may be peeling around the edges but the solid *raciónes* (large tapas servings) are fabulous. Try the

berenjenas fritas, a large plate of aubergines fried in batter – better than French fries.

Casa Pepe de la Juderia (☎ 957 20 07 44; Calle Romero Barros 1; mains €10-15; 🕑 1-4pm & 8.30-11.30pm) This local stalwart is always hopping, and even though it's a bit pricey, it's Córdoban food at its best.

Córdoba's livelier bars are scattered around the north and west of town.

Velvet Bar (Calle Alfaros 29; 🕑 5pm-4am) With flower-power décor over two floors, it pulls in a gay and mixed crowd.

Soul (☎ 957 49 15 80; Calle Alfonso XIII 3; 10am-3am Mon-Fri, 5pm-4am Sat & Sun) Attracts the student/arty type and has regular live music.

Getting There & Away

From the **bus station** (☎ 957 40 40 40; Plaza de las Tres Culturas), 1km northwest of Plaza de las Tendillas, buses run to/from Seville (€9, 1¾ hours, 10 daily), Granada (€13, 2½ hours, eight daily), Madrid (€11, 4¾ hours, seven daily) and Málaga (€11, three hours, five daily).

From the **train station** (Av de América) services run to/from Seville (€7 to €20, 45 minutes to 1¼ hours, 20 daily) and Madrid (€48, 1¾ to 2¼ hours, half-hourly). There are also trains to/from Málaga (€16, 2¼ hours, nine daily) and Algeciras (€26.50, four hours, two daily).

GRANADA

pop 237,663

You can't help falling in love with Granada. This engaging city, popular with travellers, students and street artists, enjoys one of Europe's finest settings beneath the snowy peaks of Andalucía's Sierra Nevada.

From the 13th to 15th centuries, Granada was capital of the last Muslim kingdom in Spain. Today it has the greatest Muslim legacy in the country and one of the most magnificent buildings on the continent – the Alhambra.

Information

Main tourist office (☎ 958 24 71 28; www.turimo granada.org; Plaza de Mariana Pineda 10; 🕑 9am-8pm Mon-Fri, 10am-7pm Sat, 10am-3pm Sun) East of the cathedral.

Navegaweb (Calle Reyes Católicos 55; per hr €1; 🕑 10am-11pm) Internet access.

Tourist office (☎ 958 22 59 90; Plaza Santa Ana; 🕑 9am-8pm Mon-Fri, 9am-6pm Sat, 9am-2pm Sun) More central than the main office.

SPAIN

Sights & Activities

ALHAMBRA

One of the greatest accomplishments of Islamic art and architecture, the **Alhambra** (☎ 902 441 221; admission €10; ☾ 8.30am-8pm Apr-Oct, 8.30am-6pm Nov-Mar) is simply breathtaking. Much has been written about its fortress, palace, patios and gardens, but nothing can really prepare you for what you will see.

The **Alcazaba** is the Alhambra's fortress, dating from the 11th to the 13th centuries. There are spectacular views from the tops of the towers. The **Palacio Nazaries** (Nasrid Palace), built for Granada's Muslim rulers in their 13th- to 15th-century heyday, is the centrepiece of the Alhambra. The beauty of its patios and intricacy of its stucco and woodwork are stunning. Don't miss the **Generalife**, the soul-soothing palace gardens.

OTHER ATTRACTIONS

Explore the narrow, hilly streets of the **Albaicín**, the old Moorish quarter across the river from the Alhambra and head uphill for the **Mirador de San Nicolás** – a viewpoint with stunning vistas and a relaxed, hippy scene. On your way down, stop by the **Museo Arqueológico** (☎ 958 22 56 40; Carrera del Darro; EU/non-EU citizens free/€1.50; ☾ 9am-8pm Wed-Sat, 3-8pm Tue, 9am-2.30pm Sun). Another enjoyable area for strolling is around **Plaza Bib-Rambla**, looking in at the **Capilla Real** (Royal Chapel; ☎ 958 22 92 39; Calle Oficios; admission €3; ☾ 10.30am-1pm & 4.30-7pm), in which Fernando and Isabel are buried. Next door is Granada's **cathedral** (☎ 958 22 29 59; admission €3; ☾ 10.45am-1.30pm & 4-8pm Mon-Sat, 4-8pm Sun) that dates in part from the early 16th century.

Sleeping

Good, budget options can be found around the social hub of Plaza Nueva such as the fabulous, if matchbox-sized, **Hostal Venecia** (☎ 958 22 39 87; Cuesta de Gomérez 2; s/d/tr €15/28/41), whose friendly owners bring you herbal tea in the morning. If this is full, try **Hostal Britz** (☎ 958 22 36 52; Cuesta de Gomérez 1; s/d €19/29), with saggy beds and big, old-fashioned rooms.

Albergue de Juventud (☎ 958 27 26 38 or 958 00 29 00; Calle Ramón y Cajal 2; dm under/over 26 €12/18.50) Granada's modern youth hostel is 1.7km west of the centre and a 600m walk southwest of the train station.

Hostal La Ninfa (☎ 958 22 26 61; Campo del Príncipe s/n; s/d €45/52; ⌘) This charming place is covered

in ceramic designs. The eclectic rooms have pretty beamed ceilings and tiled floors.

Hostal Zacatín (☎ 958 22 11 55; hostalzacatin@hotmail.com; Calle Ermita 11; s/d €17/28, d with bathroom €38) In the Plaza Bib Rambla area, off a hidden alleyway, this *hostal* is a little gem.

Hotel Los Tilos (☎ 958 26 67 12; Plaza Bib-Rambla s/d from €41/55) Has comfortable rooms and overlooks a daily flower market.

Eating

Plaza Nueva and the surrounding streets are the best places for good eats.

Al-Andalus (☎ 958 22 67 30; Calle de Elvira; filled pitas €2; ☾ 11am-3am) Great for those 2am munchies, this place has a divine asortment Arabic food to take away. Vegetarians will adore the felafel-filled pitas.

Bar Casa Julio (Calle Hermosa s/n; ☾ 10.30am-4.30pm & 8.30pm-midnight) This wildly popular no-nonsense bar is renowned for its tapas especially the *boquerones fritos* (fried fresh anchovies).

Mirador de Morayma (☎ 958 22 82 90; Calle Pianista Garcia Carrillo 2; mains €10-15; ☾ 1.30-3.30pm & 8.30-11.30pm) In the Albaicín, this restaurant has fabulous views of the Alhambra, a very pretty terrace and excellent *granadino* dishes such as *remojón* (orange and codfish, €6.40) Live flamenco on Tuesdays at 11pm.

Taberna Salinas (☎ 958 22 14 11; Calle de Elvira 13 mains €7-15; ☾ 1.30-4pm & 8pm-midnight) A busy place, with great grilled seafood and meat.

Boabdil (☎ 958 22 81 36; Hospital de Peregrines 2 mains €4-5; ☾ 1.30-4pm & 8-11.30pm, closed Mon) A kitchen-sink-informal restaurant.

La Gran Taberna (☎ 958 22 88 46; Plaza Nueva 12 tapas €1.50) A traditional-style *bodega* (wine cellar) with inexpensive tapas that is also good for breakfast.

For fresh fruit and veggies, there is the large covered **mercado** (Calle San Agustín).

Drinking

Granada's Moorish legacy lives on in the city's fabulous *teterías* (Arabic-style teahouses). One of the best is **Kasbah** (☎ 958 22 79 36; Calle Calderería Nueva 4; teas €2; ☾ 12.30pm-12.30am), serving up 100 different types of tea in a candlelit den filled with Persian rugs and secret alcoves.

Nightlife in the Albaicín centres or Carrera del Darro, with several bars and clubs within a few doors of each other, including **Rincón de San Pedro** (Carrera del Darro 12

GRANADA

INFORMATION

Main Tourist Office.........................	1 D4
Navegaweb......................................	2 C3
Policía Nacional..............................	3 A2
Post Office.....................................	4 C4
Tourist Office.................................	5 D2

SIGHTS & ACTIVITIES (p1106)

Banco BBV......................................	6 C3
Capilla Real....................................	7 C3
Cathedral.......................................	8 C3
Museo Arqueológico......................	9 D1

SLEEPING (p1106)

Hostal Britz....................................	10 D2
Hostal La Ninfa..............................	11 E3
Hostal Venecia...............................	12 C2
Hostal Zacatín...............................	13 C3
Hotel Los Tilos..............................	14 B3

EATING (p1106)

Al-Andalus.....................................	15 C2
Bar-Casa Julio................................	16 C3
Boabdil..	17 C2
La Gran Taberna............................	18 C2
Mercado..	19 B2
Taberna Salinas..............................	20 C2

DRINKING (pp1106–8)

BMC...	21 D3
Granada 10....................................	22 B2
Kasbah...	23 C2
Rincón de San Pedro......................	24 D1
Sala Príncipe..................................	25 E3
Upsetter...	26 D2
Zoo..	27 C4

ENTERTAINMENT (p1108)

Eshavira..	28 B1

ALHAMBRA TICKETS

It is becoming increasingly essential to book tickets to the Alhambra in advance. You can do this at any branch of the Banco Bilbao Viscaya (BBV) or by calling ☎ 902 22 44 60 (outside Spain call ☎ 0034 915 37 91 78) and paying by credit card or through the website www.alhambratickets.com.

 from 11pm) and the late-night reggae bar **Upsetter** (Carrera del Darro 7; from 11pm).

Further east, the Realejo barrio is an up-and-coming scene stacked with bars such as **BMC** (Calle Escolástica 15; 10pm-3am) pumping out dance music to a young crowd.

Granada 10 (Calle Cárcel Baja; admission €6; midnight-dawn) A disco with Sunday-night salsa.

Sala Principe (Campo del Principe 7; admission €6; 11pm-8am Thu-Sun) Plays house music in an old cinema (dress up).

Zoo (Plaza del Campillo; admission €6; 2am-8am Thu-Sun) Is a good gay/mixed dance club.

Entertainment

Spontaneous flamenco can be found in the bars around Plaza Larga Albaic in Gitanos, or head to **Eshavira** (Postigo de la Cuna 2; 8.30pm-3am) for live jazz and flamenco.

Getting There & Away

Granada's **bus station** (☎ 958 18 54 80; Carretera de Jáen s/n) is 3km northwest of the centre. Catch bus No 3 or 33 to reach the city centre. Buses serve Madrid (€13, five hours, 10 daily), Málaga (€8, two hours, hourly), Seville (€16, three hours, 10 daily) and Córdoba (€10, 2¾ hours, 11 daily).

The **train station** (☎ 958 27 12 72; Av de Andaluces), 1.5km west of the centre, has services to Madrid (€28.50, six hours, two daily) and Seville (€18, three hours, four daily). An overnight train goes to Valencia (€41, 7½ hours) and Barcelona (€50, 11½ hours).

COSTA DE ALMERÍA

Hot, dusty and dry, the coast east of Almería city is perhaps the last section of Spain's Mediterranean coast where you can have a beach to yourself. The main allure of the region is the wonderful coastline and semidesert scenery of the Cabo de Gata promontory, where beautiful, empty beaches alternate with precipitous cliffs and scattered villages.

There are several useful **tourist offices** (Almería ☎ 950 62 11 17 San José ☎ 950 38 02 99 Mojácar ☎ 950 47 51 62).

Sights & Activities

The **Alcazaba** (☎ 950 27 16 17; Calle Almanzor; non-EU/EU citizens €1.50/free; 9am-8.30pm Tue-Sun Apr-Sep, 9am-6.30pm Tue-Sun Nov-Mar), a 10th-century Muslim fortress, is Almería city's highlight.

North of Almería, the rocky landscape looks like something straight out America's Wild West. In the 1960s and '70s, Western moviemakers shot dozens of films here, including parts of *The Magnificent Seven* and *A Fistful of Dollars*. The industry left behind three Wild West town sets that can be visited. The best is **Mini Hollywood** (☎ 950 36 52 36; Ctra Nacional 340-km 364; adult €17; 10am-11pm daily Apr-Oct, 10am-7pm Sat & Sun Nov-Mar).

The **Cabo de Gata** promontory (a protected area) is a trekker's and sun worshipper's heaven. The main village here is laid-back **San José**, with excellent beaches such as **Playa de los Genoveses** and **Playa de Mónsul** less than 7km southwest.

Mojácar Pueblo, 30km north of Agua Amarga, is a white hill town, originally Muslim, 2km from the coast. The long resort strip of Mojácar Playa is soon to be overrun but it's fun and has a lively summer beach scene.

Sleeping & Eating

ALMERÍA CITY

Hostal Americano (☎ 950 28 10 15; Av de la Estación 6; s/d from €18.50/32) This friendly *hostal* is popular with backpackers and well located near the bus station.

Taberna Torreluz (☎ 950 23 43 99; Plaza Flores 3; raciónes €8; noon-4pm & 7.30pm-12.30am) Everyone goes for the fabulous *raciónes* at this cosy wood-panelled bar.

SAN JOSÉ

Albergue Juvenil de San José (☎ 950 38 03 53; Calle Montemar; dm €10; Apr-Sep) A good bet for backpackers is this friendly non-HI hostel.

Hostal Bahía (☎ 950 38 03 07; Calle Correo; s/d €32/45) Attractive, with whitewashed rooms with bathrooms.

Camping Tau (☎ 950380166;tau@parquenatural.com; per person/tent/car €4/4/4; Apr-Oct) Just 250m from San José beach.

Restaurante Azulón (Calle Correo 2; mains €5-8; noon-4.30pm & 8pm-midnight) does an excellent *menú* for €9 as well as fish and pizzas.

MOJÁCAR

Hostal La Esquinica (☎ 950 47 50 09; Calle Cano 1; s/d €20/25) This small place is covered in climbing plants; rooms are simple and sweet with wooden beds, and there's a small bar.

Getting There & Away

From Almería's **airport** (☎ 95 021 37 15), 9km east of the city, Easyjet has daily low-cost flights to/from London Stansted.

From the **bus station** (☎ 950 26 20 98; Plaza de Barcelona), buses go to/from Madrid, Granada, Seville, Málaga, Valencia and Barcelona and also to San José and Mojácar.

From the **train station** (Plaza de la Estación) there are services to/from Madrid (€31, seven hours, two daily), Granada (€11.80, 2½ hours, four daily) as well as Seville (€28.25, 5¾ hours, four daily).

MÁLAGA

pop 547,105

From Moorish monuments and a rollicking nightlife to arguably the best fried fish in Spain, the exuberant port city of Málaga has andaluz charm in spades.

The **main tourist office** (☎ 952 21 34 45; www.malagaturismo.com; Pasaje Chinitas 4; ☺ 8.30am-8pm Mon-Fri, 10am-2pm Sat & Sun) is in the city's historic centre. **Internet Meeting Point** (Plaza de la Merced 20; per hr from €1; ☺ 10am-12.30am) offers Internet access.

Sights & Activities

The historic core of the city is located around the cathedral: an abundant tangle of narrow cobblestone streets lined with faded ochre-coloured buildings, tapas bars, old-fashioned shops and cafés.

The fabulous **Museo Picasso Málaga** (☎ 952 60 27 31; www.museopicassomalaga.org; Calle San Agustín; adult/student €6/3; ☺ 10am-8pm Tue-Sun), in the contemplative setting of the 16th-century Palacio de Buenavista, is stacked with more than 200 of Picasso's works, covering the length and breadth of his brilliant career.

Málaga's **Alcazaba and palace** (☎ 952 22 72 30; Calle Alcazabilla; admission €1.80; ☺ 8.30am-7pm Tue-Sun) dates from the 8th century. A **Roman amphitheatre**, now under restoration, can be viewed near the Alcazaba's main entrance.

The hill-top **Castillo Gibralfaro** (admission €1.80; ☺ 9am-6pm), a Moorish castle, commands spectacular views across the city and sea. The city's **cathedral** (☎ 952 21 59 17; Calle Molina Larios; admission €3; ☺ 10am-6.45pm Mon-Sat) has a peculiar lopsided look (the south tower was never completed) and a magnificent 18th-century baroque façade.

Sleeping

Málaga is short on accommodation, so book ahead.

Albergue Juvenil Málaga (☎ 952 30 85 00; Plaza Pío XII 6; dm under/over 26 €11.65/17.20) The city's HI youth hostel is 1.5km west of the city centre. Take bus No 14 or 31 from the Alameda Principal to get there.

Pensión Rosa (☎ 952 21 27 16; Calle Martinez 10; s/d €25/35) The pretty courtyard entrance is filled with colourful potted plants and rooms are simple but bright.

Hostal Mundial (☎ 952 21 06 18; Calle Hoyo de Esparteros 1; s/d €18/34) Mundial has plenty of spartan, dog-eared rooms.

Hostel Victoria (☎ 952 22 42 24; Calle Sancha de Lara 3; s/d with bathroom €25/50 ⊠) In a good central location, the Victoria has comfortable rooms.

Eating & Drinking

For affordable eats, head for the tapas bars including the wonderful **Bar Logueno** (☎ 952 22 30 48; Marín García 9; tapas from €1.50; ☺ 1-4.30pm & 8pm-midnight), a local institution with 75-plus varieties of tapas to choose from.

La Dehesa (☎ 952 21 21 32; Calle La Bolsa 3; mains €6-7; ☺ 12.30pm-midnight Mon-Sat) Cosy and rustic, La Dehesa is a great place for stews, salads and paellas. All tasty home-cooked fare.

La Vegetariano de la Alcazabilla (☎ 952 21 48 58; Calle Pozo del Rey 5; mains €6-8; ☺ 1.30-4pm & 9-11.30pm Mon-Sat) The décor may be basic but the vegetarian portions are generous. It does a particularly good cheese fondue.

Serious party time kicks off at about midnight around Calle Granada and Plaza de la Merced.

ZZ Pub (Calle Tejón y Rodriguez 6) The grungy ZZ has live music on Monday and Thursday.

Doctor Funk (Calle José Denis Belgrano 19) Just off Calle Granada, this is a heaving reggae/funk club shoe-horned into a small smoky space.

O'Neills Irish Pub (Luis de Velazquez 3) This has huge appeal for young Malagueños.

Liceo (Calle Beatas 21) A bar/disco popular with students and travellers.

Getting There & Away

From the **airport** (☎ 95 204 84 84), 11km southwest of Málaga, Ryanair has low-cost flights to/from Dublin, while Easyjet flies to/from Belfast, Bristol, London Gatwick, London Luton, London Stansted and Newcastle.

From the **bus station** (☎ 952 35 00 61; Paseo de los Tilos), buses go to Madrid (€17, six hours, seven daily), Granada (€8, two hours, hourly), Marbella (€4, one hour, hourly), Ronda (€7.50, two hours, 10 daily) and Algeciras (€10, 2½ hours, 12 daily).

From the **train station** (Esplanada de la Estación), services run to/from Madrid (€54, 4¼ hours, eight daily), Seville (€14.15, 2½ hours, five daily) as well as Córdoba (€16, 2¼ hours, nine daily).

RONDA
pop 35,137

One of Andalucía's prettiest towns, Ronda is split in two by the savagely deep El Tajo gorge, at the heart of some lovely hill country. The **municipal tourist office** (☎ 952 18 71 19; www .turismoderonda.es; Paseo Blas Infante; ☼ 9.30am-7pm Mon-Fri, 10am-2pm & 3.30-6.30pm Sat & Sun) is helpful.

Ronda is a pleasure to wander around, but during the day you'll have to contend with busloads of day-trippers from the coast. The **Plaza de Toros** (1785) is considered the home of bullfighting; inside is the small but fascinating **Museo Taurino** (☎ 952 87 41 32; adult/student €5/3; ☼ 10am-7pm). Vertiginous cliff-top views open out from the nearby **Alameda del Tajo park**.

Sights

The 18th-century **Puente Nuevo** (New Bridge), an amazing feat of engineering, crosses the 100m-deep gorge to the originally Muslim Old Town (La Ciudad), littered with ancient churches, monuments and palaces. At the **Casa del Rey Moro** (☎ 952 18 72 00; Calle Santo Domingo 17; adult €4; ☼ 10am-8pm), you can climb down La Mina, a Muslim-era stairway cut inside the rock, to the bottom of the gorge. Try not to miss the **Iglesia de Santa María la Mayor** (Plaza Duquesa de Parcent; admission €2; ☼ 10am-7pm), whose tower was once the minaret of a mosque, or the beautiful 13th-century **Baños Arabes** (Arab Baths; Barrio de Padre Jesus; adult €2; ☼ 10am-7pm Mon-Fri, 10am-3pm Sat & Sun).

Sleeping & Eating

There are a couple of budget *pensiónes* on Calle Almendre including the dark, old-fashioned **Hostal Biarritz** (☎ 952 87 29 10; s/d €11/17) at No 7.

Hotel Morales (☎ 952 87 15 38; Calle Sevilla 51; s/d with bathroom €21/45; 🖳) Friendly, with decorative rooms.

Camping El Sur (☎ 952 87 59 39; www.campingelsur .com; per person/tent/car €3.85/3.30/3.30; 🖳) Just 1.5km southwest of town on the Algeciras road.

Relax Vegetariano Café-Bar (☎ 952 87 72 07; Calle Los Remedios 27; mains €5; ☼ noon-4pm & 7-11pm) British-owned, it has rustic wooden tables and fabulous vegetarian food. It does big mugs of English tea and curries on Sunday.

Marisquería Paco (Plaza del Socorro 9; mains €10; ☼ 10am-10pm) A tiny, popular seafood place.

Getting There & Away

From the **bus station** (☎ 952 87 26 57; Plaza Concepción García Redondo), services run to/from Seville (€9, 2½ hours, five daily), Málaga (€7.50, two hours, 10 daily) and Cádiz (€7.50, three hours, four daily).

From the **train station** (Av de Andalucía), trains run to/from Granada (€11, three hours, three daily), Algeciras (€6, 1½ hours, four daily) and Madrid (€32, 4½ hours, two daily).

ALGECIRAS
pop 105,070

An industrial and fishing town, Algeciras is the major port linking Spain with Morocco. Keep your wits about you, and ignore offers from the legions of moneychangers, drug-dealers and ticket-hawkers. If you need a room, there's loads of budget accommodation in the streets behind Av de la Marina.

Comes (☎ 956 65 34 56; Calle San Bernardo) runs frequent buses to/from La Línea, and several daily to/from Tarifa, Cádiz and Seville. **Portillo** (Av Virgen del Carmen 15) runs buses to/from Málaga, the Costa del Sol and Granada. **Bacoma**, inside the port, runs to/from Valencia, Barcelona, France, Germany and Holland.

From the **train station** (Calle Agustín Bálsamo 12), direct services run to/from Madrid (€35 to €52, two daily, six hours), Córdoba (€26.50, four hours, two daily), Ronda (€6, 1½ hours, four daily) and Granada (€15.75, 4¾ hours, three daily).

Frequent ferries to/from Tangier, in Morocco, and Ceuta, the Spanish enclave on the Moroccan coast, are operated by **Trasmediterránea** (☎ 902 45 46 45), **EuroFerrys** (☎ 956 65 11 78) and other companies. At least 20 daily go to Tangier (€28, 2½ hours) and more to Ceuta (€22, 1½ hours). From late June to September there are ferries almost around the clock.

Buy your ticket in the port or at agencies on Av de la Marina – prices are the same.

CÁDIZ
pop 134,989

The historic port of Cádiz is beautiful with an aged atmosphere, winding streets and magnificent, if dishevelled, 18th-century buildings. The best visiting time is during the February **carnaval**, which is close to Rio's in terms of exuberance. The **municipal tourist office** (☎ 956 24 10 01; Plaza de San Juan de Dios 11; ✆ 9.30am-1.30pm & 4-7pm Mon-Fri) has helpful staff.

Sights & Activities

Cadiz's soaring 18th-century **cathedral** (Plaza de la Catedral; adult €4; ✆ 10am-1.30pm & 4.30-8pm Tue-Fri, 10am-2pm Sat, 11am-1pm Sun) is the city's most striking landmark.

Get your bearings by climbing up the baroque **Torre Tavira** (☎ 956 21 29 10; Calle Marqués del Real Tesoro; admission €3.50; ✆ 10am-6pm), the most soaring of city's watchtowers, with a camera obscura and sweeping views of the city.

The **Museo de Cádiz** (☎ 956 21 22 81; Plaza de Mina; EU/non-EU citizens free/€1.50; ✆ 2.30-8pm Tue, 9am-8pm Wed-Sat, 9.30am-2.30pm Sun) has an excellent range of archaeological remains and fine art.

Sleeping & Eating

Accommodation can get quite booked up at weekends so it's worth phoning ahead.

Quo Qádis (☎ /fax 956 22 19 39; Calle Diego Arias 1; dm/d €9/36, d with shower €42) Cádiz's excellent independent hostel is colourful and quirky. You can rent bikes here for €6 a day, or tuck into a vegetarian supper for just €2. Prices drop significantly from October to June.

Hostal Bahía (☎ 956 25 90 61; Calle Plocia 5; s/d €47/64) Just off the bustling main square, this one is a winner.

It's a pleasure to graze your way through Cadiz's superb *marisquerías* (seafood bars).

Cervecería Aurelio (☎ 956 22 10 31; Calle Zorrilla 1; tapas/raciónes €1.50/5; ✆ 12.30-5pm & 8.30pm-1am) Kick off here with a fishy tapa.

Restaurante Parissien (☎ 956 22 36 77; Plaza de San Francisco 1; mains €6-8; ✆ 9am-11.30pm) With lots of tables on a pretty cobblestone plaza, it does excellent fried fish.

Cádiz's streets and plazas throng until the early hours.

Woodstock Bar (☎ 956 21 21 63; Calle Canovas del Castillo 25; ✆ 4pm-2am Sun-Thu, 4pm-4am Fri & Sat) A fashionable late-night hang-out.

Getting There & Away

From the **bus station** (☎ 956 80 70 59; Plaza de la Hispanidad), there are buses to/from Algeciras (€9, 2¾ hours, 10 daily), Seville (€9.50, 1½ hours, hourly), Córdoba (€18, 4½ hours, two daily), Málaga (€18, five hours, six daily) and Tarifa (€7, 1¼ hours, five daily).

From the **train station** (Plaza de Sevilla) services go to/from Seville (€8.40, 1¾ hours, 10 daily), Córdoba (€31, three hours, four daily) and Madrid (€56, five hours, twice daily).

TARIFA & THE COSTA DE LA LUZ

Windy, laid-back Tarifa, perched at continental Europe's most southerly point, is so close to Africa you can see the sunlight flashing on Morocco's minarets. The town, a bohemian haven of cafés and crumbling Moorish ruins, has a lively windsurfing and kite-surfing scene.

Stretching west from Tarifa are the long, sandy (and largely deserted) beaches of the Costa de la Luz, backed by cool pine forests, green hills and windmills.

Tarifa's **tourist office** (☎ 956 68 09 93; www.tarifaweb.com; Plaza de Alameda; ✆ 9am-9pm Jun-Sep, 9am-3pm Oct-May) has lots of information on the area. Internet access is fairly pricey; your best bet is **Planet** (www.planet-up.com; per hr €3; ✆ 10.30am-2.30pm & 6-10pm).

Sights & Activities

Enjoy exploring Tarifa's winding old streets and breezy plazas and visit the castle, **Castillo de Guzmán** (☎ 956 68 46 89; Calle Guzmán El Bueno; adult €1.80; ✆ 11am-2pm & 5-7pm), dating from the 10th century.

The waters of Algeciras Bay are prime whale- and dolphin-watching territory. **Whale Watch España** (☎ 956 62 70 13; www.whalewatchtarifa.org; Av de la Constitución 6) runs daily boat excursions (€27 per person, 1½ to two hours).

Playa de los Lances, the 10km-long beach beloved of windsurfers and kite-surfers, stretches northwest from Tarifa. For **windsurfing and kite-surfing rental and classes** you can try places up the coast including **Club Mistral** (☎ 956 68 49 19) at the Hurricane Hotel and **Spin Out Surf Base** (☎ 956 68 08 44; www.tarifaspinout.com) at Valdevaqueros beach; or places along Calle Batalla de Salado in Tarifa town such as **Big Fish** (☎ 956 68 02 19; El Recreo III, Local 16, Batalla de Salado) which rents out surfboards for €20 a day and can arrange three-day kite-surfing and windsurfing courses for €180.

SPAIN

If you have your own wheels, head west to the Costa de la Luz. Don't miss out on the spectacular Roman ruins of **Baelo Claudia** (EU/non-EU citizens free/€1.50; ☺ 10am-6pm Tue-Sat, 10am-2pm Sun) at Bolonia and the magical villages of **Zahara de los Atunes** and **Los Caños de Meca**.

Sleeping & Eating

Pensión Correo (☎ 956 68 02 06; Calle Coronel Moscardó 8; r €25-35, with bathroom €40-50) Italian-run; it has fabulous, if fairly basic, rooms with high-beamed ceilings and a ramshackle air.

Hostal Facundo (☎ 956 68 42 98; h.facundo@terra.es; Batalla de Salado 47; s/d €15/22, d with bathroom €36, dm in Aug €12) Popular with windsurfers.

There are a few good camp sites heading west along the coast. **Camping Tarifa** (☎ 956 68 47 78; www.camping-tarifa.com; per person/tent/car €5.60/3/3) has plenty of shade and sea views.

Tarifa has no shortage of places to hang out and wait for the *poniente* (westerly) wind to pick up. The legendary **Café Central** (☎ 956 68 05 90; Calle Sancho IV el Bravo; ☺ 9am-1am) is at the heart of it all, with a daily wind report posted on its walls and the best cooked breakfasts in town.

La Vaca Loca (Calle de Alcantarillo s/n; mains €8-12; ☺ 6pm-1am) Has surf videos on the TV and amazing barbecued food.

Getting There & Away

Comes (☎ 956 68 40 38; Batalla de Salado) runs buses to/from Algeciras (€1.50, 30 minutes, 17 daily), La Línea (€3, one hour, seven daily), Cádiz (€7, 1¼ hours, seven daily) and Seville (€14, three hours, four daily).

FRS (☎ 956 68 18 30; Estación Marítima) runs ferries between Tarifa and Tangier (adult/car €24.50/73, 1½ hours, five daily).

GIBRALTAR

pop 27,776

The British colony of Gibraltar is 1960s Britain on a sunny day. It's old-fashioned and safe, drawing coach-loads of visitors from the Costa del Sol who come here to be reassured by the helmet-wearing policemen, the double-decker buses and Marks & Spencer.

Information

EU, US, Canada, Australia, New Zealand, Israel, South Africa and Singapore passport-holders are among those who don't need

visitor's visas for Gibraltar; but, anyone who needs a visa for Spain should have at least a double-entry Spanish visa if they want to return to Spain from Gibraltar (see p1124).

There is a **main tourist office** (☎ 45000; www.gibraltar.gov.gi; Duke of Kent House, Cathedral Sq; ☺ 9am-5.30pm Mon-Fri) in the centre, and a second **tourist office** (☎ 74982; Casemates Sq; ☺ 9am-5.30pm Mon-Fri, 10am-3pm Sat, 10am-1pm Sun).

The currency is the Gibraltar pound or pound sterling but you can always use euros. At the time of writing, the exchange rate was €1 to £0.70.

To phone Gibraltar from Spain, the telephone code is ☎ 9567; from other countries dial the international access code, then 350 and the local number.

Sights & Activities

Central Gibraltar can get crowded and claustrophobic but the **Gibraltar Museum** (☎ 74289; Bomb House Lane; adult £2; ☺ 10am-6pm Mon-Fri, 10am-2pm Sat) is worth a peek.

The large **Upper Rock Nature Reserve** (☎ 74950; adult/vehicle £7/1.50; ☺ 9.30am-7pm) has spectacular views and several interesting spots to visit. The rock's most famous inhabitants are its colony of **Barbary macaques**, the only wild primates in Europe. Some of these hang around the **Apes' Den** near the middle cable-car station. Other attractions include **St Michael's Cave**, a large natural grotto renowned for its stalagmites and stalactites and the **Great Siege Tunnels**, a series of galleries hewn from the rock by the British during the Great Siege (1779–1783) to provide new gun emplacements. A **cable car** (adult return trip £6.50) leaves from Red Sands Rd every few minutes from 10am to 6pm Monday to Saturday.

Sleeping & Eating

Compared to Spain, expect to pay through the nose. The cheapest place is the privately run **Emile Youth Hostel** (☎ 51106; Montagu Bastion, Line Wall Rd; dm incl breakfast £15) with fairly soul-less dorms.

Cannon Hotel (☎ 51711; www.cannonhotel.gi; 9 Cannon Lane; s/d £24.50/36.50, d with bathroom £45) This friendly hotel is in the heart of town with a bar, pretty patio and airy rooms. Rates include an English breakfast.

The Lord Nelson (☎ 50009; 10 Casemates Sq; mains £5-8; ☺ 10am-2am) Decked out as Nelson's ship, with painted clouds on a ceiling crossed with beams and sails, this brasserie is an excellent choice. The mussels in white wine, garlic and cream are particularly good. Live music at weekends.

Star Bar (☎ 75924; Parliament Ln; mains £6-7; ⏲ 7am-11pm) Gibraltar's oldest pub.

Clipper (☎ 79791; Irish Town; mains £3-5; ⏲ 9.30am-11pm) Has sport on the TV and does the best English breakfast in town.

Getting There & Around

There are no regular buses to Gibraltar, but La Línea bus station is only a five-minute walk from the border. Bus Nos 3, 9 and 10 run frequently, direct from the border into the town. All of Gibraltar can be easily covered on foot.

EXTREMADURA

A sparsely populated land of vast skies and open plains, Extremadura's distance from most tourist trails offers a genuine sense of exploration, something that *Extremeños* themselves have a flair for. Many epic 16th-century conquistadors arose from here.

The remarkable old towns of Trujillo and Cáceres are so perfectly preserved that they are often used as film sets. In Mérida, some of Spain's most spectacular Roman ruins scatter the city.

TRUJILLO
pop 9564

Trujillo is a delightful little town that can't be much bigger now than in 1529, when its most famous son Francisco Pizarro set off for an expedition that culminated in the bloody conquest of the Incan empire.

From the broad Plaza Mayor, rises a remarkably preserved old town. There's a **tourist office** (☎ 927 32 26 77; ofitur@ayto-trujillo.com; Plaza Mayor; ⏲ 9.30am-2pm & 4.30-7.30pm) and you can connect to the Internet at **Ciberalia** (Calle Tiendas 18; per hr €2; ⏲ 10.30am-2am).

Sights

A **statue of Pizarro** dominates the Plaza Mayor. On the plaza's southern side, the façade of the **Palacio de la Conquista** sports the carved images of Pizarro and the Inca princess Inés Yupanqui.

Two noble mansions open to visitors are the 16th-century **Palacio de los Duques de San Carlos** (Plaza Mayor; admission €1.30; ⏲ 9.30am-1pm & 4.30-6.30pm Mon-Sat, 10am-12.30pm Sun) and **Palacio de Juan-Pizarro de Orellana** (admission free; ⏲ 10am-1pm & 4-6pm Mon-Fri, 11am-2pm & 4.30-7pm Sat & Sun), down alley at the plaza's southwestern corner.

Up the hill, the **Iglesia de Santa María la Mayor** (admission €1.20; ⏲ 10am-2pm & 4.30-8pm) is an interesting hotchpotch of 13th- to 16th-century styles, with some fine paintings. Higher up, the **Casa-Museo de Pizarro** (admission €1.30; ⏲ 10am-2pm & 4-7pm) has displays (in Spanish) on the lives and adventures of the Pizarro family. At the top of the hill, Trujillo's impressive **castillo** (admission €1.30; ⏲ 10am-2pm & 4.30-7.30pm) is of Moorish origin with a **hermitage** within.

Sleeping & Eating

Pensión Roque (☎ 927 32 23 13; Calle Domingo de Ramos 30; d with/without bathroom €24/18) Pleasant and quiet with lots of communal space.

Hostal La Cadena (☎ 927 32 14 63; Plaza Mayor 8; d €37.30; 🖧) In a tastefully restored 16th-century building, it has a handy tapas bar and restaurant.

Restaurante La Troya (☎ 927 23 13 64; Plaza Mayor 10; menú €17) Carnivores shouldn't miss out on this place. The food isn't cheap, but portions are gigantic and it will save you from eating much else for the next few days. There are great tapas here, too.

Getting There & Away

From the **bus station** (☎ 927 32 12 02; Carretera de Mérida), 500m south of Plaza Mayor, buses run to/from Cáceres (€3, 45 minutes, eight daily), Mérida (€7.50, 1¼ hours, four daily) and Madrid (€17, four hours, 10 daily).

CÁCERES
pop 87,088

Cáceres' perfectly preserved Ciudad Monumental (Old Town), built in the 15th and 16th centuries, is worth two visits – one by day to look around and one by night to soak up the atmosphere of the accumulated ages.

There is a **tourist office** (☎ 927 01 08 34; otcaceres@eco.juntaex.es; Plaza Mayor 3; ⏲ 9am-2pm & 4-6pm Mon-Fri Oct-May, 9am-2pm & 5-7pm Jun-Sep, 9.30am-2pm Sat & Sun year-round). **Ciberjust** (Calle Diego Maria Crehuet 7; per hr €2; ⏲ 10am-2.30pm & 4.30pm-midnight Mon-Sat, 5pm-midnight Sun) has Internet access.

The Old Town is still surrounded by walls and towers raised by the Almohads in the 12th century. Arriving from Plaza Mayor, ahead you'll see the fine 15th-century **Concatedral de Santa María** (⏲ 10am-1pm).

Sights

Many of the old city's churches and imposing medieval mansions can be admired only from outside, but you can climb up the **Torre de Bujaco** (☾ 10am-2pm & 4.30-7.30pm Tue-Sun) and enter the **Museo Provincial de Cáceres** (☎ 927 24 72 34; Plaza de Veletas; non-EU/EU citizens €2/free; ☾ 9.30am-2.30pm & 4-7pm Tue-Sat, 10.15am-2.30pm Sun), housed in a 16th-century mansion built over a 12th-century Moorish *aljibe* (cistern).

Sleeping & Eating

The best area to stay is around the pretty Plaza Mayor.

Pensión Carretera (☎ 927 247 482; pens_carretero@ yahoo.es; Plaza Mayor 22; s/d €13/22) An old-fashioned, crumbling building, it has rooms with high ceilings overlooking the plaza.

Albergue Turístico Las Veletas (☎ 927 21 12 10; www.alberguesturisticos.com; Calle Margallo 36; dm incl breakfast €20) Charming and privately run, with sparkling rooms in a recently restored mansion.

The bars and cafés on Plaza Mayor are perfect for watching the world go by over a coffee or beer but the food is overpriced. Your best bet is to nip up one of the side streets for a bite to eat.

Croissanterie (Calle Pintores 4; ☾ 10am-11pm; bocadillos €1.50) This hole-in-the-wall has a range of freshly baked, filled baguettes and croissants.

Café-Bar Adarve (☎ 927 24 48 74; Calle Sánchez Garrido 4; raciónes €6-8; ☾ 7.30am-1am) Does a roaring trade with locals who flock here to eat €6 platefuls of *riñones* (kidneys) and the bar's famous *gambas rebozadas* (deep-fried and battered prawns).

El Corral de las Cigüeñas (Cuesta de Aldana; breakfast/milkshakes/cocktails €2/3/5; ☾ 8am-3am) The fabulous ivy-clad courtyard is chock-a-block with cool young things and hosts regular live gigs.

Getting There & Away

From the **bus station** (☎ 927 23 25 50; Carretera Gijón-Sevilla), 1.5km southwest of Plaza Mayor, services run to/from Trujillo (€3, 45 minutes, eight daily), Mérida (€6, 1¼ hours, six daily), Madrid (€16, 3½ hours, eight daily) and Seville (€27, four hours, six daily). The **train station** (Av de Alemania) has services to/from Madrid (€22.50, 3½ to five hours, five daily) and Mérida (€3.30 to €11.50, one

hour, four daily). The single daily train to Lisbon (€35, 5¼ hours) leaves at 3am.

MÉRIDA

pop 52,110

Once the biggest city in Roman Spain, Mérida is home to more Roman-era ruins than anywhere else in the country. The **tourist office** (☎ 924 00 97 30; otmerida@eco.juntaex.es; Av de José Álvarez Saenz de Buruaga s/n; ☾ 9am-2pm & 4-6.30pm Mon-Sat, 9.30am-2pm Sun) is by the gates to the Roman theatre. **Cibersala** (Calle Camilo Cela 28; per hr €1.50; ☾ 10am-2pm & 5pm-midnight) is a dingy Internet hang-out.

The opening hours for all of Mérida's sights are 9.30am to 1.45pm and 4pm to 6.15pm October to May, 9.30am to 1.45pm and 5pm to 7.15pm June to September. A combined ticket for entry into all of them costs €8/4/4 per adult/student/over 65.

The awesome ruins of Mérida's **Teatro Romano & Anfiteatro** (☎ 924 31 25 30) shouldn't be missed. The theatre was built in 15 BC and the gladiators' ring, or Anfiteatro, seven years later. Combined they could hold 20,000 spectators. Other monuments of interest are the **Casa del Anfiteatro** (☎ 924 31 85 09), the **Casa Romana del Mithraeo** (☎ 924 30 15 04) the **Alcazaba** (☎ 924 31 73 09), the **Basílica de Santa Eulalia** (☎ 924 30 34 07) and the **Arqueológica de Moreria**.

Simple **Hostal Bueno** (☎ 924 30 29 77; hbueno@ eresmas.com; Calle Calvario 9; s/d €15/18) is on a noisy street near the centre. Bright and quirky **Hostal El Alfarero** (☎ 924 30 31 83; www.hostalelalfarero.com; Calle Sagasta 40; d €40) is owned by a family of potters and has a lovely patio.

Walk through the busy tapas bar at the front of **Bar-Restaurante Briz** (☎ 924 31 93 07; Calle Felix Valverde Lillo 7; menú €9.60; ☾ 7am-midnight) to get to the glaringly lit, windowless *comedor* (dining room). Don't let the décor put you off – this place is fantastic value for money and serves up huge portions (the steak is particularly good).

From the **bus station** (☎ 924 37 14 04; Av de la Libertad) buses run to/from Seville (€10, three hours, seven daily), Madrid (€20, four hours, seven daily), Cáceres (€6, 1¼ hours, six daily) and Trujillo (€7.50, 1¼ hours, four daily).

The **train station** (Calle Cardero) has services to/from Cáceres (€3.30, one hour, four daily), Seville (€11, 4¾ hours, one daily) and Madrid (€19.20, six hours, four daily).

ARAGÓN, BASQUE COUNTRY & NAVARRA

The Basque Country (País Vasco) is a privileged region, with a rugged coast dotted with fishing villages and surfing beaches, and a lusciously green interior. The grand city of San Sebastián crowns the coast, and nearby Bilbao can claim one of the world's greatest museums as its own.

Navarra, linked historically with the Basque Country, is a fantastic wine region, though it's probably known most for being the home of the wild San Fermín festival. Aragón differs culturally and geographically from its two northern neighbours; a proud, stern land, it has fascinating mountain scenery and an interesting capital in Zaragoza.

ZARAGOZA

Founded by the 'modest' Caesar Agustus as the Roman city 'Caesaragusta', Zaragoza later became a Muslim stronghold, and their influence is present in the abundant use of brick as a building material and in the number of *Mudéjar*-style architecture.

These days Zaragoza, the proud capital of once-mighty Aragón, is a largely industrial city. Its shining light is the Basílica del Pilar, a fairy-tale creation beside the Río Ebro.

Orientation

The new Las Delicias train station and the main bus terminal both lie west of the centre. From the Agreda bus station, take Av de César Augusto into town (15 minutes). From Las Delicias, it's a 10-minute walk east into town. You can also catch a bus; several run by regularly.

Information

Conecta-T (☎ 976 20 59 79; Calle Murallas Romanas 4; per hr €1.20; 🕑 10am-11pm Mon-Fri, 11am-11pm Sat & Sun) Internet access.

Main tourist office (☎ 976 20 12 1200 or 902 20 12 1212; www.turismozaragoza.com; Plaza del Pilar; 🕑 10am-8pm) Housed in a futuristic glass cube.

Police (☎ 091)

Post office (☎ 976 23 68 68; Paseo de la Independencia 33; 🕑 8.30am-8.30pm Mon-Fri, 9.30am-2pm Sat)

Torreón de la Zuda Tourist Office (☎ 902 20 12 1212; 🕑 10am-2pm & 4.30-8pm) Climb to the top for a small exhibition about Zaragoza and a view of the river bank.

Sights

Roman, *Mudéjar* and baroque architecture are beautifully combined in Zaragoza. Towering over the city is the **Basílica de Nuestra Señora del Pilar** (Plaza del Pilar; 🕑 5.45am-8.30pm, to 9.30pm Jul-Aug), a 17th-century baroque basilica of epic proportions. The spiritual heart of Zaragoza, the basilica crowns the sprawling plaza of the same name. People flock to the Capilla Santa to kiss a piece of marble pillar believed to have been left by the Virgin Mary when she visited St James here in AD 40.

At the plaza's southeastern end is Zaragoza's brooding 12th- to 16th-century cathedral, **La Seo** (Plaza de La Seo; admission €2; 🕑 10am-2pm & 4-6pm Tue-Fri, 10am-1pm & 4-6pm Sat, 10am-noon & 4-6pm Sun, open 1 hr later in summer) Its northwestern façade is a *Mudéjar* masterpiece, and inside is a striking 15th-century main altarpiece in coloured alabaster.

The odd trapezoid structure in front of La Seo is similar to the Louvre, but it's the entrance to the **Museo del Foro de Caesaraugusto** (☎ 976 39 97 52; Plaza de La Seo; admission €2; 🕑 10am-2pm & 5-8pm Tue-Sat, 10am-2pm Sun), an interesting museum about Roman life. Some 70m below lie the remains of Roman shops, porticoes and a great sewerage system, all brought to life by an audiovisual show.

Sleeping

Many cheap rooms are found near the Plaza del Pilar.

Try **Hostal Santiago** (☎ 976 39 45 50; Calle de Santiago 3-5; s €20-25, d €30-36; 🛇) Neon-green walls add an original touch to an otherwise standard *hostal*. The 26 rooms are cheerful and comparatively spacious.

Hotel Las Torres (☎ 976 39 42 50; torres@able.es; Plaza del Pilar 11; s/d from €41/55) Go here for comfort and great basilica views. The lovely chimes of the basilica will wake you bright and early. Rooms are dated but spic 'n' span.

Eating & Drinking

Casa Juanica (☎ 976 39 72 52; Calle de Santa Cruz 21; menú €9) Can't be beat for cheap tapas and a friendly atmosphere, and the summer terrace is ideal.

Other good tapas bars are scattered around **El Tubo**, especially around Plaza de Santa Marta, and in **La Zona**, a trendy district south of the centre.

El Prior (☎ 976 20 11 48; Calle de Santa Cruz 7; mains €4-8; 🕑 closed Wed) Inside a 16th-century palace,

SPAIN

this eatery serves tasty Aragonés meals, like *ternasco* (lamb's ribs) and *migas* (fried bread-crumbs) and has a pub downstairs.

Il Pastificcio (☎ 976 23 66 62; Calle de Zurita 15; mains €9-10; ✆ 1-4pm & 8pm-midnight) Vegetarians will find plenty at this Italian bistro where dishes are always tasty and big enough to share.

Getting There & Away

Zaragoza's brand-new train station, Las Delicias offers connections throughout Spain. The high-speed AVE train connects Zaragoza with Madrid in under two hours (€43, four daily, 11 non-AVE) and with Lleida in one hour (€24, four daily, 15 non-AVE). Other trains head to Barcelona (€34, three hours, 15 daily), Valencia via Teruel (€16.45, six hours, three daily) and San Sebastián via Pamplona (€26.50, four hours, three daily).

Bus stations are scattered all over town. **Agreda Company** (☎ 976 22 93 43; www.agredasa.com; Paseo de María Agustín 7) runs to most major Spanish cities, including Madrid (€12.09, four hours, 18 daily).

SAN SEBASTIÁN

San Sebastián ('Donostia' in Basque) is a grand old dame, a trendy seaside resort that looks good and knows it. The clean-swept footpaths and orderly boulevards hug the Bahía de la Concha, where the perfectly shell-shaped Playa de la Concha shimmers. The hip Parte Vieja (Old Quarter) is crammed with tempting tapas bars and restaurants boasting the best of Basque cuisine.

Orientation

The bus station is a 20-minute walk south of the Parte Vieja, and the train station is just across the river. Cross the bridge and you're in the centre.

Information

Donosti-Net (☎ 943 42 94 97; Calle Embeltrán 2; per hr €3; ✆ 9am-11pm) A one-stop travellers' stop, with email, office services and even a spot to leave your luggage (per day €9).

Police (☎ 091)

Tourist office (☎ 943 48 11 66; www.sansebastianturismo.com; Reina Regente 3; ✆ 8am-8pm Jun-Sep, 9am-1.30pm & 3.30-7pm Mon-Sat, 10am-2pm Sun Oct-May)

Sights & Activities

In summer, most people head straight for the shore. **Playa de la Concha** and **Playa de Ondarreta** are among the most beautiful city beaches in Spain, and beyond them is **Isla de Santa Clara**, an island in the middle of the bay; you can reach it by **boat** (adult return trip €2.60; ✆ 10am-8pm Jun-Sep) from the harbour. To beat the crowds, head to the **Playa de la Zurriola** (also known as 'Playa de Gros'), east of the Río Urumea, which is popular with surfers.

For views over the bay, head up to **Monte Urgull**, topped by low castle walls and a statue of Christ. It takes 30 minutes to walk up – a stairway starts from Plaza de Zuloaga in the Parte Vieja.

Even better are the views from **Monte Igueldo**. Drive or catch the **funicular** (☎ 943 21 05 64; return trip €1.60; ✆ 11am-6pm Mon-Fri, 11am-8pm Sat & Sun Nov-Mar, closed Wed Nov-Mar & Jan, to 8pm daily Apr-Jun & Sep 15-Oct, 10am-10pm Jul-Aug) to the **Parque de Atracciones**, an old-timey funfair. At the foot of the hill is Eduardo Chillida's abstract iron sculpture *Peine de los Vientos* (Comb of the Winds).

San Sebastián's **Aquarium** (☎ 943 44 00 99; www.aquariumss.com; Paseo del Muelle 34; admission €9; ✆ 10am-8pm Sep, May-Jun, 10am-7pm Mon-Fri, 11am-8pm Sat & Sun Oct-Apr, 10am-9pm Jul-Aug) has 10 large tanks teeming with tropical fish, morays, sharks and other finned creatures.

Sleeping & Eating

Budget *pensiónes* and *hostales* are huddled in the Parte Vieja. There are lots of options, but they fill quickly and get pricey in summer.

Pensión Balerid (☎ 943 42 68 14; Calle San Juan 1; s €18-30, d €35-50) Cheerful, charming sunny rooms and quirky décor.

Pensión Urkia (☎ 943 42 44 36; Calle de Urbieta 12; s €23-30, d €33-45) Just as nice, Urkia boasts impeccable rooms with elegant furnishings.

Pensión San Lorenzo (☎ 943 42 55 16; www.infonegocio.com/pensionsanlorenzo; Calle San Lorenzo 2; r €20-45) In this category, San Lorenzo is another good choice.

San Sebastián's gastronomy is one of its major draws, and its tapas, here called *pinxos*, are famous. Nibble your way through the Parte Vieja, especially along and around Calle de Fermín Calbetón, which is crammed with bars. You can't go wrong at **Bar Sport** (☎ 943 42 68 88; Calle de Fermín Calbetón) or **Egosari** (☎ 943 42 82 10; Calle de Fermín Calbetón 15).

Caravanserai (☎ 943 47 54 18; Calle de San Bartolome 1; mains €5-8), Sit-down fare is cheap and abundant at Caravanserai, which offers a 'vegetarians' corner' and outdoor dining.

Alderdi-Zahar (☎ 943 42 52 54; Calle de Fermín Calbetón 9; mains €9-15, menú €11) This simple restaurant serves local seafood and hearty Basque fare and offers a good-value lunch *menú*.

Sidreria Donostiarra (☎ 943 42 04 21; Calle Embeltran 5; mains €5.50-17), For a memorable meal head here, where local hard cider is served from the barrel.

Drinking

The **Parte Vieja** is a fun place to be nearly every night of the week. Around 8pm the tapas bars start hopping as people make a predinner round of pinxos, and the revelry lasts until midnight midweek and until the cock crows on weekends.

Getting There & Away

From the airport catch the CIA Interbus (€1.40, every 20 to 30 minutes), which runs to Plaza Gipuzkoa in town.

Renfe runs daily trains to Madrid (€33, eight hours, four daily), Barcelona (€33.50 to €42.50, eight to 10 hours, two daily) and Pamplona (€16, two hours, three daily). Eusko Tren is a private company (international passes not valid) running trains around the region.

Buses leave from Plaza de Pío XII for places all over Spain. **PESA** (☎ 902 10 12 10) has services to Bilbao (€7.75, up to one hour, 27 daily), while La Roncalesa goes to Pamplona (€5.60, 1¼ hours, eight daily). Ticket offices are on the streets just north of the station.

BILBAO

Straddling the Ría de Bilbao and encircled by green mountains, Bilbao is a spirited city in the midst of the beautiful Basque countryside. Most visitors limit their focus to one thing: the Guggenheim Museum – Frank Ghery's masterpiece of modern architecture and one of the world's best modern art museums. But this evocative city has a lot more to offer. The Casco Viejo, or Old Quarter, is full of funky shops and traditional cafés, and smaller museums scattered about town are worth visiting too.

Orientation

From the airport, bus No 3247 leaves every half-hour from 6.30am to 10.30pm for the central Plaza Moyúa, where there's a metro stop. The Renfe and FEVE train stations both sit by the river, in the heart of town

near the Casco Viejo. The main bus station (Termibús) is west of town just next to the San Mamés metro stop, a five-minute ride from the centre.

Information

Guggenheim tourist office branch (Alameda Mazarredo; ☾ 11am-2.30pm & 3.30-6pm Mon-Fri, 11am-3pm & 4-7pm Sat, 11am-2pm Sun)

Police (☎ 092 or 944 205 000; Calle Luis Briñas 14)

Postal Transfer (☎ 944 15 3042; Calle Santa María 5; per hr €1.50; ☾ 10am-11pm Mon-Fri, 11am-midnight Sat, noon-11pm Sun) Internet access and post.

Tourist office (☎ 944 79 57 60; www.bilbao.net; Teatro Arriaga; ☾ 9.30am-2pm & 4-7.30pm Mon-Sat, 9.30am-2pm Sun) Just across the river from the train station.

Sights

Designed by Frank Gehry, the spectacular **Guggenheim Museum** (☎ 944 35 90 80; www .guggenheim-bilbao.es; Abandoibarra Et 2; admission €10; ☾ 10am-8pm Tue-Sun, daily Jul & Aug) is an experience not soon forgotten. The building itself, undulating forms covered in titanium scales, was inspired by the shapes of ships and fish, two of Bilbao's traditional industries. Inside, the guts of the building are exposed, as few columns, ugly support beams or for that matter floors and walls obstruct the view. Many credit this creation with revitalising modern architecture and creating a new standard in vanguard design.

To dig further into the local culture, head to the **Euskal Museoa** (Basque Museum; ☎ 944 15 54 23; http://euskal-museoa.org; Plaza de Miguel de Unamuno 4; adult €3; ☾ 11am-5pm Tue-Sat, 11am-2pm Sun), documenting the history and lifestyle of the Basque people.

Sleeping & Eating

Hostal-Residencia La Estrella (☎ 944 16 40 66; Calle de María Muñoz 6; s €30-39, d €48-57) The spiral staircase prepares you for grandeur, and this sparkling *hostal* doesn't disappoint, with spotless, freshly painted rooms.

Iturrienea Ostatua (☎ 944 16 15 00; Calle de Santa María 14; s €45, d €54-60) For unbeatable charm, head to this B&B decorated with museum-worthy Basque artefacts and rustic elegance.

Codfish and local stews are Bilbao's star meals. Try some of both at **Rio-Oja** (☎ 944 15 08 71; Calle del Perro 4; mains €4-12), great for wallet-friendly fare. Don't pay too much attention to its unappetising English translations, like 'beef-face stew' or 'lamb-insides stew'.

SPAIN

Harrobia (☎ 946 79 00 90; Calle del Perro 2; mains €15-20, menú €9.90) A sleek restaurant that's pricey at night but has a great-value midday lunch *menú*. Specialities are local seafood and, in season, game dishes.

Zuretzat (☎ 944 24 85 05; Calle de Iparraguirre 7; menú €8.50) Near the Guggenheim, stop for pinxos or, downstairs, the tasty fixed-price *menú*.

Getting There & Around

Renfe offers services to Madrid (€30 to €38, six to eight hours, two daily) and Barcelona (€34.50, seven hours, two daily).

FEVE (www.feve.es) has trains heading westward to Cantabria and beyond. Often these bumpy rides take considerably longer than the bus trip to the same destinations.

Regular buses come and go from San Sebastián (€7.75, one hour, up to 27 daily), Santander (€5.40 to €9.65, 1½ hours, up to 27 daily) and Zaragoza (€16.14 to €26.75, three to four hours, up to 10 daily).

Bilbao has an outstanding public transportation system, with an easy to follow web of metros, trams and buses crisscrossing the city and heading in to the countryside.

PAMPLONA

Immortalised by Ernest Hemingway in *The Sun Also Rises*, the busy city of Pamplona ('Iruña' in Basque) is of course the home of the wild **fiestas de San Fermín** (aka Encierro, or 'Running of the Bulls'), but it's also an extremely walkable city that mixes the charm of old plazas and buildings with modern shops and a lively nightlife.

This is the capital of Navarra, but there are few noteworthy sights in town, which means you can party all night and not feel guilty whiling the day away in the street cafés. Make an exception for the **cathedral** (☎ 948 21 08 27; adult €3.85; 🕑 10am-1.30pm & 4-7pm Mon-Fri, 10am-1.30pm Sat), a 14th-century Gothic creation with a neoclassical façade.

To get to town from the train station, which is northwest of the centre, hop on bus No 9. The main bus station is in the centre of town, a 10-minute walk from the Plaza de Castilla.

Information

Kuria.net (☎ 948 22 30 77; Calle Curia 15; per hr €3; 🕑 10am-10pm Mon-Sat, noon-10pm Sun)

Police (☎ 092)

Tourist office (☎ 948 42 04 20; www.navarra.es; Calle de Eslava 1; 🕑 10am-2pm & 4-6pm Mon-Sat, 10am-2pm Sun Sep-Jun, 9am-8pm Mon-Sat, 10am-2pm Sun Jul & Aug, 8am-8pm during fiestas de San Fermín) Don't expect this otherwise-helpful office to provide much guidance during San Fermíns.

Sleeping

Accommodation is expensive and hard to come by during San Fermín; you'll need to book months in advance. Prices below don't reflect the huge (up to 300%) markup you'll find in mid-July.

La Viña (☎ 948 21 32 50; Calle de Jarauta 8; s/d from €15/25) In town, it offers cheerful rooms with sky-blue walls and clean shared bathrooms.

Also try **Hostal Dom Luis** (☎ 948 22 17 31; Calle de San Nicolás 24; s €30-35, d €35-45), which is highly recommended, **Pensión Lambertini** (☎ 948 21 03 03; Calle Mercaderes 17; s €20, d €30-50) and **Pensión Pamplona** (☎ 948 22 99 63; Calle Tudela 5; s/d €30/42), near the bus station.

The nearest camping ground, **Camping Ezcaba** (☎ 948 33 03 15; N-125; camp site per person €7), is 7km north of the city. Regular buses head to Pamplona.

Eating & Drinking

Central streets like Calle de San Nicolás, and Calle Estafeta are lined with tapas bars, many of which morph into nightspots on weekends. Get great tapas at **Bar Baserri** (☎ 948 22 20 21; www.restaurantebaserri.com; Calle de San Nicolás 32; pinxo menú €17), **Otano** (☎ 948 22 50 95; Calle de San Nicolás 5; pinxos from €2) and **Cervecería La Estafeta** (☎ 948 22 79 77; Calle Estafeta 54).

Restaurant Saraste (☎ 948 22 57 27; Calle de San Nicolás 19-21; menú €10 or €16) A vegetarian haven.

Café Iruña (☎ 948 22 20 64; Plaza de Castillo 44; menú €10-21) This old Hemingway haunt is great for coffee, breakfast or a quick meal.

SURVIVING SAN FERMIN

The madcap fiestas de San Fermín runs from 6 to 14 July, when the city is overrun with thrill-seekers, curious onlookers and, oh yeah, bulls. The Encierro (Running of the Bulls) begins at 8am, when bulls are let loose from the Coralillos de Santo Domingo. The race lasts just three minutes, so don't be late. The safest place to watch the Encierro is on TV. If that's too tame for you, try to sweet-talk your way onto a balcony or book a room in a hotel with views.

Getting There & Away

Up to four trains arrive daily from Madrid (four hours). Bus No 9 connects the station with the centre.

Several companies operate out of Pamplona's central bus station near Plaza de Castilla. **Conda** (☎ 948 22 10 26) runs up to seven daily buses each way between Madrid and Pamplona. Up to 10 buses come and go daily from Zaragoza.

CANTABRIA, ASTURIAS & GALICIA

'Green Spain' has little in common with the dry, sun-baked regions of the rest of the country. You'll think you're in Scotland with the lush green hills and wet Atlantic climate. Yet this area of hard-working people provides a fascinating contrast to the rest of Spain.

SANTIAGO DE COMPOSTELA

The supposed burial place of St James (Santiago in Castilian), this beautiful city is the end of the **Camino de Santiago** and one of the Christian world's most important pilgrimage sites. Santiago's compact Old Town is a work of art, and a walk around the cathedral will take you through some of its most inviting squares.

Orientation

From the airport, regular **Freire buses** (☎ 981 54 24 16) go to the bus station and to República de El Salvador about once an hour. From the train station, it's a 15-minute walk uphill on the Rúa do Hórreo to central Plaza de Galicia. From the bus station west of town, hop on bus No 10 for Plaza de Galicia.

Information

Camino de Santiago Information (Xacobeo; ☎ 981 57 20 04; www.xacobeo.es; Av da Coruña 6; ☺ 8.30am-2.30pm & 4.30-6.30pm Mon-Fri)

Cyber Nova 50 (☎ 981 57 51 88; Rúa Nova 50; per hr €1.20; ☺ 9am-1am Mon-Sat, 10am-1am Sun) Internet access.

Municipal tourist office (☎ 981 55 51 29; Rúa Vilar 63; ☺ 10am-3pm & 5-8pm Oct-May, 9am-9pm Jun-Sep)

Police (☎ 092; Rúa de Trindade)

Post office (☎ 981 58 12 52; Travesía de Fonesca; ☺ 8.30am-8.30pm Mon-Fri, 9.30am-2pm Sat)

Sights

The **cathedral** (☎ 981 56 05 27; Plaza de Obradoiro; ☺ museum: 10am-1.30pm & 4-6.30pm Mon-Sat, 10am-1.30pm Sun, Mass: noon & 6pm), a superb Romanesque work of the 11th to 13th centuries, is the heart and soul of Santiago. It's said that St James' remains were buried here in the 1st century AD and rediscovered in 813. Today visitors line up to kiss his statue, which sits behind the main altar.

To get a grasp on local culture, visit the **Museo do Pobo Galego** (☎ 981 58 36 20; www.museodopobo.es; San Domingos de Bonaval; admission free; ☺ 10am-2pm & 4-8pm Tue-Sat), which has exhibits on items from boating and fishing to music and pottery. The **Museo de los Peregrinos** (☎ 981 58 15 58; www.mdperegrinacions.com; Rúa San Miguel 4; adult €2.40; ☺ 10am-8pm Tue-Fri, 10.30am-1.30pm & 5-8pm Sat) explores the pilgrim culture that has so shaped Santiago.

Santiago's university is one of Spain's oldest and most emblematic. The 16th-century **Colegio de Fonesca** (Fonesca College; ☎ 981 56 31 00; Plaza de Fonesca; ☺ 11am-2pm & 5-8.30pm Tue-Sat, 11am-2pm Sun) is one of the prettiest university buildings and now houses the university library. There are usually exhibits held in the two ornate rooms at the front.

Sleeping & Eating

Hostal Girasol (☎ 981 56 62 87; www.hgirasol.com; Porta de Pena 4; s €15-20, d €26-32, d with bathroom €33-39) With wrought-iron beds, wooden floors and country charm, the clean, bright Girasol is a great choice.

Hostal Suso (☎ 981 58 66 11; Rúa do Vilar 65; s €15-18, d €30-36) Also excellent value, this *hostal* boasts fashionable décor, parquet floors and rooms with small balconies.

Seafood is the local speciality, and you'll find tasty delights from the ocean just about everywhere, especially along central streets like Calle Franco and Calle Raiña. Also try **Casa Manolo** (☎ 981 58 29 50; Plaza Cervantes; menú €6) where everything is served as part of a super cheap €6 fixed-price *menú*.

El Asesino (The Killer; ☎ 981 58 15 68; Plaza Universidad 16; mains €8-12, menú €12-15) This homey places has been serving local specialities for 127 years.

Entre-Rúas (☎ 981 58 61 08; Callejón de Entre-Rúas 2; raciónes €2.50-8, menú €8) Have seafood alfresco at this place sitting on a tiny plaza in the middle of the thinnest street in all Santiago.

A Tulla (☎ 981 50 08 89; Entre-Rúas 1; menú €8.50-10.50) Next door, it has a vegetarian *menú*.

Drinking

The old quarter is home to atmospheric bars and pubs popular with the city's large student population. Some of the best spots are around Rúa da Congo, Rúa San Paio de Antealtares and Plaza de Cervantes. At **Acarimo** (Preguntoiro 2) you'll find a laid-back atmosphere.

Getting There & Away

There are regular trains to/from La Coruña (€3.30 to €11.50, one hour, hourly), Vigo (€5.10, 1½ hours, hourly) and other regional destinations. Two trains (€38.50, eight hours) come in from Madrid.

Buses come in from León (€22.52, 6½ hours, one daily) and Oviedo (€22.18, five hours, three daily) to the **bus station** (☎ 981 58 77 00; San Caetano).

LA CORUÑA

La Coruña ('A Coruña' in Gallego) is a breezy ocean-side city with a stylish centre and pretty historic quarter. A mushroom-shaped peninsula jutting into the wild Atlantic, it's surrounded by water and boasts great urban beaches and a lively port.

The train station is on the waterfront and near the city centre. To reach the bulk of sights, *hostales* and restaurants, turn right out of the station and walk along the waterfront.

Information

Ciber Zalaet@.Net (☎ 981 20 38 41; Calle Zalaeta 7; per hr €1.20; ☽ 10am-2am)

Municipal tourist office (☎ 981 18 43 44; www.turis mocoruna.com; Plaza de María Pita; ☽ 10am-2pm & 4-8pm Mon-Sat, 10am-2pm Sun) Housed in a glass cube on the plaza, the office has loads of great information.

Sights

With so much ocean around, beaches are naturally a major part of La Coruña's attraction. The main beach, **Playa del Orzán**, runs along the western border of the town centre. Across town is the busy **marina**, lined with iconic balconied houses, and to the north is the pretty **Ciudad Vieja**.

The city's best-known and best-loved monument is the **Torre de Hércules** (☎ 981 22 37 30; Av de Navarra; admission €2; ☽ 10am-5.45pm Oct-Mar, 10am-6.45pm Apr-Jun & Sep, 10am-8.45pm Sun-Thu, 10am-11.45pm Fri-Sat Jul & Aug), the oldest functioning lighthouse in the world. The 18th-century,

neoclassical tower that stands today completely masks the Roman foundations lying underneath. The tower is a 20-minute walk from town, but you can hop on bus No 3 or the **tram** that runs around the waterfront, both of which stop nearby.

Sleeping & Eating

La Coruña has a solid selection of budget and mid-range lodgings. Most are clustered around Rúa Nueva and Calle Real.

Hostal-Residencia Carbonara (☎ 981 20 14 29; fax 981 22 52 51; Rúa Nueva 16; s €18-26.50, d €25-40) Rooms here are spacious, sunny and a great deal. There's no elevator, so rooms are cheaper on higher floors.

Hostal Linar (☎ 981 22 78 37; Calle del General Mola 7; s €20-25, d €30-45) You'll find sophisticated rooms with shiny ceramic floors and bathrooms worthy of a three-star hotel.

La Coruña is one of the best places in Spain to eat fresh seafood and shellfish. Stroll along streets like Calle de la Franja, Calle Olmos and Calle Estrella for endless dining options. Try **Mesón do Pulpo** (☎ 981 20 24 44; Calle de la Franja 9-11; mains €8-10), a rustic tavern where you can get excellent shellfish *raciónes*, or **Mesón el Virira** (☎ 981 22 01 09; Calle de la Galera 28; menú €6.60), offering one of the cheapest fixed-price lunches in town.

Getting There & Away

Trains from Santiago (€3.30 to €11.50, one hour, hourly), Vigo (from €8.25, up to three hours, hourly) and elsewhere in Galicia come and go regularly. Numerous bus companies operate in the **bus station** (☎ 981 18 43 35; Calle Caballeros 21). **Castromil** (www.castromil.com) offers services from cities like Santiago and Vigo, and **Alsa** (www.alsa.es) heads to Madrid (€34 to €49, six to eight hours, seven daily).

SANTANDER

Stylish Santander has a pretty Old Town, but it's mostly known for its upscale beach, **El Sardinero**. Many beachside shops, eateries and hotels are open in summer only, but surfers abound year-round, braving the cold to ride winter's powerful waves.

Near Santander is the fascinating **Cueva de Altamira** (☎ 942 81 80 05; www.cultura.mecd.es ☽ 9.30am-7.30pm Tue-Sat 9.30am-3pm Sun Jun-Sep 9.30am-5pm Tue-Sat 9.30am-3pm Sun Oct-May), a cave with prehistoric paintings called the 'Sistine Chapel' of the prehistoric world. The 270m cave is 2km southwest of Santillana de Mar. The waiting list to get into the cave itself is years long, but you can visit an excellent on-site museum with replicas of the cave art.

There is a **municipal tourist office** (☎ 942 20 30 00; www.ayto-santander.es; Jardines de Pereda; ☺ 9.30am-1.30pm & 4-7pm Mon-Fri, 9am-1.30pm Sat).

Sleeping & Eating

Pensión La Corza (☎ 942 21 29 50; Calle de Hernán Cortés 25; s €20-30, d €35-50) Offers the best value in town, with spotless, coordinated rooms, some with their own tidy bathroom.

Old Santander is full of traditional-style bodegas and *mesones* (wine bars) that serve as both pubs and sit-down restaurants. One of the better-priced is **Cervecería Apsy** (☎ 942 31 45 95; Calle de Hernán Cortés 22; mains €5.40-13), with lots of seafood dishes on the menu.

Getting There & Away

Santander is loaded with public transport options. Its ferry port is one of Spain's largest, and regular ferries arrive here from the UK. Trains come from Madrid (from €23.75, six hours, four daily) and Valladolid (€12.80 to €22.50, three to four hours, six daily). The jostling FEVE trains are usually slower than the bus, but this is a scenic way to get to and from Bilbao (€6.25, 2½ hours, three daily).

The excellent **bus station** (☎ 942 21 19 95; Plaza de las Estaciones) is home to a half-dozen companies offering service to destinations throughout Cantabria and further afield.

SPAIN DIRECTORY

ACCOMMODATION

Spain's camping sites vary enormously and grounds are officially rated from 1st class to 3rd class. You can expect to pay around €4 each per person, car and tent. Quite a few close from around October to Easter. With certain exceptions (such as on many beaches and in environmentally protected areas) it is legal to camp outside camping grounds. You'll need permission to camp on private land.

Albergues juveniles (youth hostels), are often the cheapest places to stay for solo travellers. Prices often depend on whether you're aged under 26; typically you pay €12 or more. Many youth hostels have curfews

and are often heavily booked by school groups. Most are members of the country's Hostelling International (HI) organisation **Red Española de Albergues Juveniles** (REAJ; Map pp1064-5; ☎ 9152 2 70 07; www.reaj.com; Calle de José Ortega y Gasset 71, 28006 Madrid). Some hostels require HI membership; others may charge more if you're not a member. You can buy HI cards for €11 at virtually all hostels.

Officially, other establishments are either hotels (from one to five stars), *hostales* (one to two stars) or *pensiónes*. In practice, there are all sorts of overlapping categories, especially at the budget end of the market. In broad terms, the cheapest are usually *fondas* (inns) and *casas de huéspedes* (guesthouses), followed by *pensiónes*. All these normally have shared bathrooms and singles/doubles for €10/15 to €20/30. Some *hostales* come in the same price range, but others have rooms with private bathrooms costing anywhere up to €60 or so for a double.

ACTIVITIES

The Basque Country has good surf spots, including San Sebastián (p1116), Zarauz and the legendary left at Mundaca. Tarifa (p1111), with its long, empty beaches and ceaseless wind, is generally considered to be the windsurfing and kite-surfing capital of Europe.

Skiing is cheap, and facilities and conditions are good but queuing at lifts can be a mad scramble. The season runs from December to May. The most accessible resorts are in the Sierra Nevada, close to Granada and the Pyrenees, north of Barcelona. Contact tourist offices in these cities for information.

Bike touring isn't nearly as prevalent as in other parts of Europe because of the often-mountainous terrain and summer heat. It's a more viable option on the Balearic Islands, although plenty of people get on their bikes in spring and autumn in the south. Mountain biking is increasingly popular, and areas such as Andalucía and Catalonia have many good tracks.

Spain is a trekker's paradise, so much so that Lonely Planet has published a guide to some of the best treks in the country, *Walking in Spain*. Walking country roads and paths, between settlements, can also be highly enjoyable and a great way to meet the locals. Useful for hiking and exploring some areas are the *Guía Cartográfica* and *Guía Excursionista y Turística* series published by Editorial Alpina. The series combines information booklets in Spanish (or sometimes Catalan) with detailed maps at scales ranging from 1:25,000 to 1:50,000, well worth their price (around €8).

If you fancy a really long walk, there's the Camino de Santiago. This route, which has been followed by Christian pilgrims for centuries, can be commenced at various places in France. It then crosses the Pyrenees and runs via Pamplona, Logroño and León all the way to Santiago de Compostela (p1119).

BUSINESS HOURS

Banks generally open from 8.30am to 2pm Monday to Friday and 8.30am to 1pm Saturday. Main post offices in provincial capitals are usually open from about 8.30am to 8.30pm Monday to Friday and about 9am to 1.30pm Saturday. Generally, people work Monday to Friday from 9am to 2pm and then again from 4.30pm or 5pm to about 8pm. Shops and travel agencies are usually open these hours on Saturday, too, though some may skip the evening session. Museums all have their own opening hours; major ones tend to open for something like normal business hours (with or without the afternoon break), but often have their weekly closing day on Monday, not Sunday.

COURSES

The best place to take a language course in Spain is generally at a university. There are also hundreds of private language colleges throughout the country; the **Instituto Cervantes** (Map pp1064-5; Spain ☎ 914 36 76 00; informa@cervantes.es; Palacio de la Trinidad, Calle Francisco Silvela 82, Madrid; London ☎ 020-7235 0353; cenlon@cervantes.es; 102 Eaton Square, London SW1 W9AN) can send you lists of these and of universities that run courses. Have a look at the excellent website www .spanish-in-spain.biz.

EMBASSIES & CONSULATES
Embassies & Consulates in Spain

The following embassies are based in Madrid:

Australia (☎ 914 41 93 00; Plaza del Descubridor Diego de Ordás 3-28003, Edificio Santa Engrácia 120)
Canada (Map pp1064-5; ☎ 914 31 43 00; Calle de Núñez de Balboa 35)
France (☎ 914 23 89 00; Calle de Salustiano Olózaga 9)
Germany (☎ 915 57 90 00; Calle de Fortuny 8)

Ireland (Map pp1064-5; ☎ 915 76 35 00; Paseo de la Castellana 36)
Netherlands (☎ 915 35 75 00; Av del Comandante Franco 32)
New Zealand (Map pp1064-5; ☎ 915 23 02 26; Plaza de la Lealtad 3)
Portugal (☎ 917 82 49 60; Calle de Pinar 1)
UK (Map pp1064-5; ☎ 917 00 82 00; Calle de Fernando el Santo 16)
USA (Map pp1064-5; ☎ 915 87 22 00; Calle de Serrano 75)

Spanish Embassies & Consulates Abroad

Australia Canberra (☎ 02-6273 3555; embespau@mail .mae.es; 15 Arkana St, Yarralumla, ACT 2600)
Canada Ontario (☎ 613-747 2252; embespca@mail.mae.es; 74 Stanley Ave, Ottawa, Ontario K1M 1P4)
France (☎ 01 44 43 18 00; ambespfr@mail.mae.es; 22 Ave Marceau, 75381 Paris, Cedex 08)
Germany (☎ 030-254 0070; embespde@correo.mae.es; Lichtensteinallee 1, 10787 Berlin)
Ireland (☎ 269-16 40; embespie@mail.mae.es; 17A Merlyn Park, Ballsbridge, Dublin 4)
Netherlands (☎ 302-49 99; ambespni@correo.mae.es; Lange Voorhout 50, Den Haag 2514EG)
Portugal (☎ 01-347 2381; embesppt@mail.mae.es; Rua do Salitre 1, 1250 Lisbon)
UK London (☎ 020-7235 5555; embespuk@mail.mae.es; 39 Chesham Place, London SW1X 8SB)
USA Washington (☎ 202-452 0100; embespus@mail.mae.es; 2375 Pennsylvania Ave NW, Washington, DC 20037)

FESTIVALS & EVENTS

Spaniards indulge their love of colour, noise, crowds and partying at innumerable local fiestas and ferias, or fairs. Many fiestas are based on religion. Local tourist offices can supply detailed information. Among festivals to look out for are:

La Tamborada (20 January) In San Sebastián, the whole town dresses up and goes berserk.
Carnaval A time of fancy-dress parades and merrymaking celebrated around the country about seven weeks before Easter (wildest in Cádiz and Sitges).
Las Fallas de San José Valencia's week-long party, held in mid-March, with all-night dancing and drinking, first-class fireworks and processions
Semana Santa (Easter week) Parades of holy images and huge crowds, notably in Seville.
Feria de Abril A week-long party in Seville in late April.
Fiestas de San Fermín (July) Includes the Running of the Bulls, in Pamplona.
Semana Grande Another week of heavy drinking and hangovers, all along the northern coast; held in the first half of August.

La Tomatina More than 20,000 revellers throw tomatoes at each other in Buñol in late August (see p43).

Festes de la Mercè (around 24 September) Barcelona's week-long party.

FOOD & DRINK

Think of Spanish food and you will probably come up with paella, gazpacho and tortilla. As good as these old staples are they only scratch the surface of Spanish cuisine, which is as varied as it is delicious.

Meat is the mainstay of most dishes and is often cooked up in *cocidos* (rich stews with beans). *Jamon* (cured ham) is also wildly popular throughout the country. In a nation of seafood addicts, most Spanish bars and restaurants also offer up a dazzling array of fresh fish and shellfish. Needless to say vegetarians struggle.

Spain is fuelled by alcohol and coffee, sometimes at the same time – brandy and *carajillo* (coffee) is a favourite. Wines are superb (Rioja and Ribero de Duero are among the best), beer is plentiful and the spirits are poured in knockout measures. Most regions have their own tipple, such as Asturian *sidra* (cider) and agua de Valencia, a beguiling mix of orange juice and sparkling wine, presumably named to jolt your memory of your whereabouts when staggering from the bar.

Eating out in Spain is as much an experience as the food itself and there's a long tradition of propping up a crowded bar with a glass of wine or beer and artfully crafted snacks, or tapas. Each region, town and even bar has it's own variation of tapas but most agree that San Sebastián offers the finest.

HOLIDAYS

Spain has at least 14 official holidays a year, some observed nationwide, some local. When a holiday falls close to a weekend, Spaniards like to make a *puente* (bridge), taking the intervening day off, too. The following holidays are observed virtually everywhere:

New Year's Day 1 January

Epiphany or **Three Kings' Day** 6 January (when children receive presents)

Good Friday before Easter Sunday

Labour Day 1 May

Feast of the Assumption 15 August

National Day 12 October

All Saints' Day 1 November

Feast of the Immaculate Conception 8 December

Christmas 25 December

The two main periods when Spaniards take holidays are Semana Santa (the week before Easter Sunday) and the month of August. At these times accommodation in resorts can be scarce and transport heavily booked, but other cities are often half-empty.

LEGAL MATTERS

Spaniards no longer enjoy liberal drug laws. No matter what anyone tells you, it is not legal to smoke dope in public bars. There is a reasonable degree of tolerance when it comes to people having a smoke in their own home, but not in hotel rooms or guesthouses.

If arrested in Spain you have the right to an attorney and to know the reason you are being held. You may also request to make a phone call.

MONEY

Spain's currency is the euro (€). Banks tend to give better exchange rates than currency-exchange offices.

Consumer Taxes & Refunds

In Spain, VAT (value-added tax) is called *impuesto sobre el valor añadido* (IVA). On accommodation and restaurant prices, there's a flat IVA of 7%, which is usually, but not always, included in quoted prices.

On retail goods, alcohol, electrical appliances etc IVA is 16%. Visitors are entitled to a refund of IVA on any item costing more than €90 that they are taking out of the EU. Ask the shop for a Europe Tax-Free Shopping Cheque when you buy, then present the goods and cheque to customs when you leave. If the shop can't offer a cheque, get an official receipt with the business's address and a description of the item purchased.

Costs

Spain is one of Western Europe's more affordable countries. If you are particularly frugal, it's possible to scrape by on €20 to €30 a day. This would involve staying in the cheapest possible accommodation, avoiding eating in restaurants or going to museums, and not moving around too much. Places such as Madrid, Barcelona, Seville and San Sebastián will place a greater strain on your moneybelt.

A more reasonable budget would be €50 a day. This would allow you €20 for accommodation, €20 for meals, €2 for public transport and €5 for entry fees to museums, sights or entertainment…and a bit left over for a drink or two and intercity travel.

Students (and sometimes seniors) are entitled to discounts of up to 50% on entry fees and about 30% on transportation.

Tipping & Bargaining

In restaurants, prices include a service charge, and tipping is a matter of personal choice – most people leave some small change, and 5% is plenty. It's common to leave small change in bars and cafés. The only places where you are likely to bargain are markets and, occasionally, cheap hotels, particularly if you're staying for a few days.

POST

Stamps are also sold at *estancos* (tobacco shops with the 'Tabacos' sign in yellow letters on a maroon background). A standard airmail letter or card costs €0.27 within Spain, €0.50 to the rest of Europe, and €0.77 to the rest of the world.

Mail to/from Europe normally takes up to a week, and to North America, Australia or New Zealand around 10 days, but there may be unaccountable long delays.

Poste-restante mail can be addressed to you at either *poste restante* or *lista de correos* at the city in question. It's a fairly reliable system, although mail may well arrive late.

TELEPHONE & FAX

Blue public payphones are common and easy to use. They accept coins, phonecards and, in some cases, credit cards.

A three-minute call from a payphone costs about €0.15 within a local area, €0.35 to other places in the same province, €0.45 to other provinces, or €1 to another EU country or the USA. A three-minute call to Australia and Asia is about €4.50.

Provincial and interprovincial calls, except those to mobile phones, are around 50% cheaper between 8pm and 8am weekdays and all day Saturday and Sunday; local

and international calls are around 10% cheaper between 6pm and 8am and all day Saturday and Sunday.

International reverse-charge (collect) calls are simple to make: from a payphone or private phone, dial ☎ 900 99 00 followed by the country code.

Fax

Most main post offices have a fax service, but you'll often find cheaper rates at shops or offices with 'Fax Público' signs.

Mobile Phones

Mobile phone numbers in Spain start with the number 6. Calls to mobiles vary but a three-minute call should cost about €1.20.

Phone Codes

Area codes in Spain are an integral part of the phone number. All numbers are nine digits and you just dial that nine-digit number, anywhere in the country.

Phonecards

Tarjetas telefónicas (phonecards) come in denominations of €6 and €12 and are available at main post offices and estancos.

VISAS

EU, Norway, Iceland and Lichtenstein citizens do not need a visa. Nationals of Australia, Canada, Israel, Japan, New Zealand, Switzerland and the USA do not need a visa for stays of up to 90 days. South Africans are among nationalities that do need a visa. See p1112 for information on visa requirements for Gibraltar. Obtaining a multiple-entry visa will save you a lot of time and trouble if you plan to leave Spain (say to Gibraltar or Morocco), then re-enter it.

For stays of longer than 90 days you're supposed to get a residence card. This is a nightmarish process, starting with a residence visa issued by a Spanish consulate in your country of residence; start the process well in advance.

Sweden

HIGHLIGHTS

- **Stockholm** Exploring gorgeous Gamla Stan, cycling around Djurgården and taking in some Nordic nightlife (p1133)
- **Ice Hotel** Chilling out at this unique, ultra-cool attraction in the far north (p1154)
- **Malmö** Eating and drinking alfresco style as well as people-watching on Lilla Torg or Möllevångstorget (p1144)
- **Best journey** Taking a boat trip out of Stockholm (the destination is irrelevant!) to enjoy postcard-perfect city panoramas from the water (p1142)
- **Off-the-beaten track** Letting your hair down with holidaying Swedes on Gotland, perfect for cycling and camping (p1152)

FAST FACTS

- **Area** 449,964 sq km (about 10 Denmarks)
- **ATMs** Widespread
- **Budget** Skr600-700 per day
- **Capital** Stockholm
- **Country code** ☎ 46
- **Famous for** Vikings, Volvos, blondes, ABBA, meatballs, IKEA
- **Head of State** King Carl XVI Gustav, Prime Minister Goran Persson
- **Language** Swedish, English widely spoken
- **Money** Swedish krona; (A$1 = Skr5.27, CA$1 = Skr5.77, €1 = Skr9.02, ¥100 = Skr6.63, NZ$1 = 4.93Skr, UK£1 = Skr12.98; US$1 = Skr7.07)
- **Phrases** *Hej* (hello), *hej då* (goodbye), *ja* (yes), *nej* (no), *tack* (thanks)

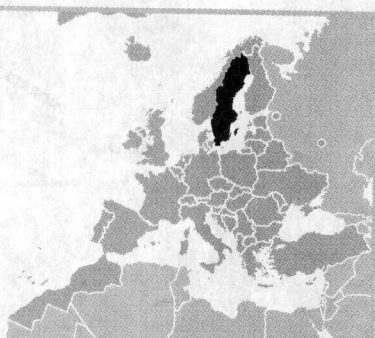

- **Population** 8.9 million
- **Time** GMT/UTC + 1 hour
- **Visas** Not needed for most visitors for stays of up to three months.

TRAVEL HINTS

Eat out at lunch time, buy your alcohol duty-free, take advantage of Sweden's fab network of hostels.

ROAMING SWEDEN

Succumb to Stockholm's charms, visit Uppsala, Gothenburg and Malmö, take in some islands – big (Gotland) or small (Stockholm archipelago).

Some way off the well-worn European backpacker trail, in the continent's northern reaches, is this beacon of style and civility. If you're coming straight from Eastern or Southern Europe, you'll be blown away by the order and cleanliness, the way everything runs on time and how almost every hostel resembles an IKEA showroom. The stereotype of a wholesome blonde populace enjoying a fabulously high standard of living is not too far from the truth.

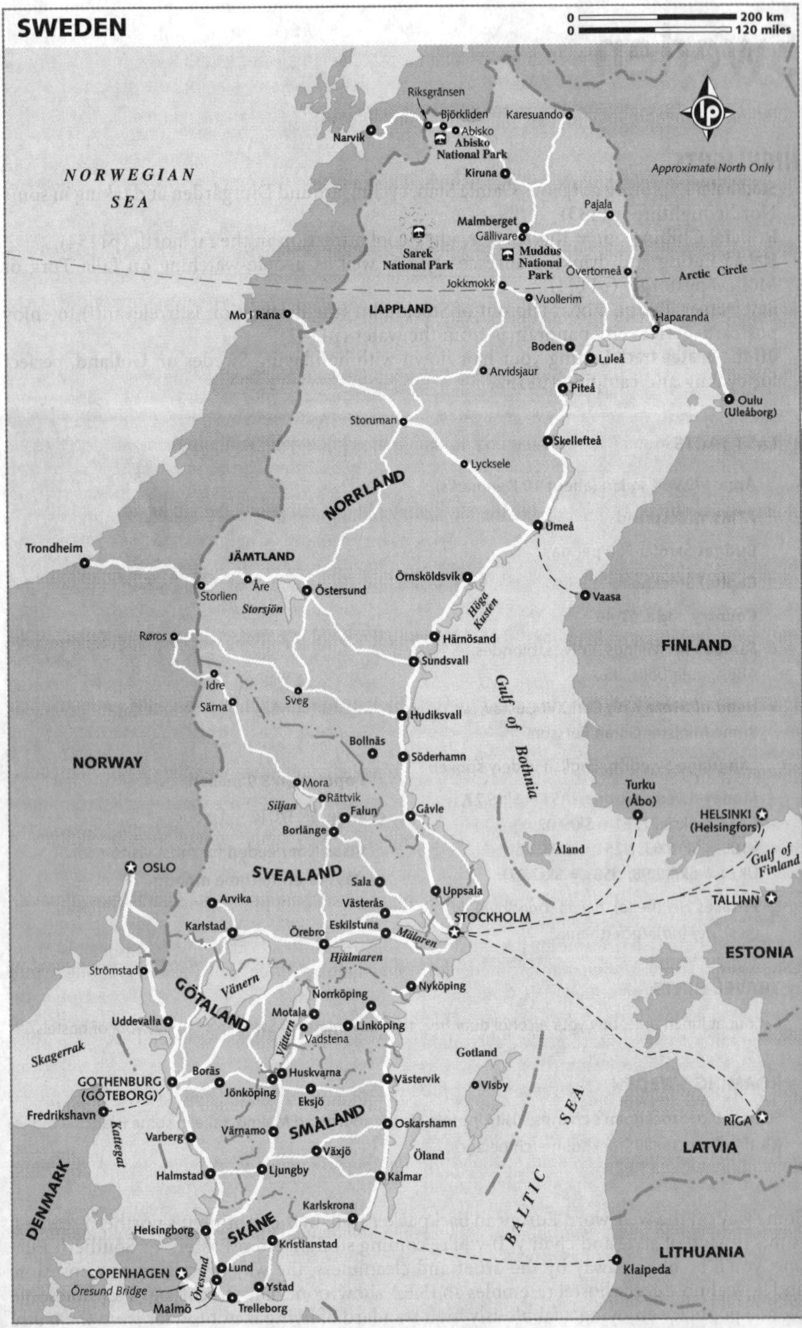
SWEDEN
0 200 km
0 120 miles
Approximate North Only
NORWEGIAN SEA
Riksgränsen
Björkliden
Abisko
Abisko National Park
Narvik
Karesuando
Kiruna
Pajala
Malmberget
Gällivare
Sarek National Park
Muddus National Park
Övertorneå
Arctic Circle
Jokkmokk
Vuollerim
LAPPLAND
Mo I Rana
Haparanda
Boden
Luleå
Arvidsjaur
Piteå
Oulu (Uleåborg)
Storuman
Skellefteå
Lycksele
NORRLAND
Umeå
Trondheim
JÄMTLAND
Örnsköldsvik
Vaasa
Storlien
Åre
Storsjön
Östersund
Höga Kusten
Røros
Härnösand
FINLAND
Sundsvall
Idre
Särna
Sveg
Gulf of Bothnia
Hudiksvall
Bollnäs
Söderhamn
NORWAY
Mora
Rättvik
Siljan
Falun
Gävle
Turku (Åbo)
HELSINKI (Helsingfors)
Borlänge
Åland
Gulf of Finland
OSLO
SVEALAND
Sala
Uppsala
Arvika
Västerås
TALLINN
STOCKHOLM
Karlstad
Örebro
Eskilstuna
Mälaren
Hjälmaren
ESTONIA
Strömstad
Vänern
GÖTALAND
Nyköping
Norrköping
Motala
Uddevalla
Linköping
Vadstena
Vättern
Skagerrak
Gotland
Borås
Huskvarna
GOTHENBURG (GÖTEBORG)
Västervik
Jönköping
Eksjö
Visby
Fredrikshavn
Kattegat
SMÅLAND
SEA
RIGA
Värnamo
Oskarshamn
Varberg
Växjö
LATVIA
Öland
Halmstad
Ljungby
Kalmar
DENMARK
BALTIC
Karlskrona
Helsingborg
SKÅNE
LITHUANIA
Kristianstad
Klaipeda
Lund
COPENHAGEN
Öresund
Öresund Bridge
Ystad
Malmö
Trelleborg

SWEDEN

Dig below the glossy surface and you'll find more to be impressed by: the stunning capital, Stockholm, offers a smorgasbord of sights, while Gothenburg and Malmö also beckon with urban delights. Picture-perfect towns like Uppsala, Visby and Lund are dripping with history. Away from the cities, Sweden also takes in vast areas of scenic coastline and idyllic islands, plus forested and lake-studded landscapes.

Sweden's other reputation – that of notoriously high prices – is also fairly accurate, but don't let that put you off. Although Sweden may pack a punch to your pursestrings, its endless delights will knock you out even more effectively.

HISTORY

Early cultural life is eloquently expressed by *hällristningar* (rock paintings) that survive in many parts of Sweden. The Viking Age was getting underway by the 9th century; Vikings made their mark in Russia, as well as trading with (and pillaging) Byzantine territories. Pagan gods and slightly more earthly kings held sway over the domestic population, with Christianity only taking root in the 11th century. Sweden avoided feudalism, but a privileged aristocracy owed its allegiance to the king. Danish monarchs held the Swedish throne for a while, tolerating a national assembly. A century of Swedish nationalist grumblings erupted in rebellion under the young nobleman Gustaf Vasa, who was crowned Gustaf I in 1523. A period of expansion resulted in Sweden's control over much of Finland and the Baltic countries.

The year 1809 saw the loss of Finland to Russia as well as the introduction of a constitution that divided legislative powers between king and Parliament. Sweden also negotiated with Denmark to exchange Swedish Pomerania for Norway. The enforcement of the 1814 union with Norway was Sweden's last military action.

By 1900 almost one in four Swedes lived in cities, and the level of industry was increasing. In this environment, the working class was radicalised. Sweden declared itself neutral at the outbreak of WWI. The Social Democrats introduced a welfare state after the war and progress was scarcely interrupted by Sweden's ambiguous approach to WWII. The 1950s and '60s saw the rapid rise in the standard of living for ordinary Swedes.

Serious current-account problems in the early 1990s provoked frenzied speculation against the Swedish krona, forcing a massive devaluation of the currency. With both economy and national confidence shaken, Swedes voted in favour of joining the EU, effective in 1995. Since then, Sweden's welfare state has undergone major reforms and the economy has improved considerably. The country has remained outside the single European currency; a 2003 referendum on adopting the euro resulted in a 'no' vote.

PEOPLE & CULTURE

Around 8.9 million people call Sweden home, making it Scandinavia's most populous country. There are 17,000 Sami (formerly known as Lapps) in Sweden, largely concentrated in the north.

Close to 550,000 foreign citizens (mostly from neighbouring Nordic countries) live in Sweden. The largest non-Nordic group of immigrants is from Iraq (with 36,000), followed by Yugoslavs and Bosnians.

ARTS

The best-known members of Sweden's artistic community have been writers, chiefly the influential dramatist and author August Strindberg and the widely translated children's writer Astrid Lindgren (creator of Pippi Longstocking). Vilhelm Moberg, a representative of 20th-century proletarian literature, won acclaim with *The Immigrants* and *The Emigrants*. Ingmar Bergman remains one of the greatest cinema directors of all time.

The most eminent Swedish cultural figure has been scientist Carl von Linné, the 18th-century botanist who pioneered plant taxonomy under Latin classifications, which are still used. Also, there is Alfred Nobel, the inventor of dynamite, whose will founded the Nobel Institute and the Noble Prize in 1901.

Sweden's modern music industry is one of the Europe's strongest. About 120 music

READING UP

The History of Sweden (2002) is an easily digested history of the country by Byron J Nordstrom. Chart Sweden's progress from the Viking age to today's ordered, peaceful welfare state.

TOP FIVE SWEDEN

- **Festival** Midsummer (the first Saturday after 21 June) anywhere in the country
- **Walk** Wander the beautiful streets of Gamla Stan (p1133)
- **Bar/Club** A bar-crawl along buzzing Kungsportsavenyn, Gothenburg (p1150)
- **Impressive sight** The walled medieval town of Visby on Gotland (p1152)
- **Idyllic islands** Visit anywhere in the Stockholm archipelago (p1142)

festivals are staged annually, covering medieval, baroque, folk, jazz and rock. You can't go past ABBA as one of Sweden's chief exports, and the 1980s and '90s saw mainstream bands like Roxette, The Cardigans and Ace of Base gain an overseas profile. More recently, a diverse bunch of music-makers has gained attention, led by punk rockers The Hives plus bands such as Sahara Hotnights and Soundtrack of Our Lives.

ENVIRONMENT

Sweden covers an area of 449,964 sq km and its maximum north–south extent is 1574km. Flat and open Skåne in the south is similar to Denmark, but further north the landscape is hillier and heavily forested. The coastline is notable for its small fjords and skerries.

Nature-loving Swedes led Europe in setting up national parks in the early 20th century; there are now 28 in Sweden (the biggest and best are in Lappland).

Many elk (moose) and deer live in the forests, while in Norrland there are large herds of reindeer (no longer truly wild, as each animal belongs to a local Sami community).

Ecological consciousness in Sweden is very high. Swedes are fervent believers in sorting and recycling household waste (paper, glass, plastic etc) – you'll be expected to do the same in hostels and camping grounds.

TRANSPORT

GETTING THERE & AWAY
Air
The major international airport is Stockholm's **Arlanda airport** (☎ 08-797 6000; www.lfv.se),

with direct flights linking the country to major Scandinavian towns, and European and North American cities. Gothenburg's **Landvetter airport** (☎ 031-941000) and Malmö's **Sturup airport** (☎ 040-613 1000), as well as a few other minor airports, also have direct international flights.

The national carrier is **SAS** (SK; ☎ 0770-727727; www.scandinavian.net).

Boat
FROM THE BALTIC COUNTRIES
Tallink (☎ 08-666 6001; www.tallink.ee) sails daily between Sweden and Estonia on two routes: Stockholm–Tallinn (from Skr285, 15 hours) and Kapellskär–Paldiski (from Skr205, 10 to 11 hours).

Riga Sea Line (☎ 08-510 015 00; www.rigasealine.lv) sails between Stockholm and Riga in Latvia (from Skr310, 17½ hours, three weekly).

Lisco Line (☎ 0454-33680; www.shipping.lt) sails between Klaipeda in Lithuania and Karlshamn, near Karlskrona in southern Sweden (from Skr400, 14 hours, three to six weekly).

FROM DENMARK
The quickest and most frequent services are between Helsingør and Helsingborg (Skr20 to Skr22, 20 minutes). Three companies operate on this busy route.

Stena Line (☎ 031-704 0000; www.stenaline.se) has five to 10 sailings daily between Gothenburg and Frederikshavn (from Skr100, 3¼ hours). Stena Line also sails three or four times daily between Grenå and Varberg (from Skr100, four hours). It's cheaper to travel between 10pm and 6am, or from Monday to Thursday. Prices also increase in summer.

BornholmsTrafikken (☎ 0411-558700; www.bornholmstrafikken.dk) sails from Ystad to Rønne (Bornholm) from Skr188. There are conventional (2½ hours) and fast (70 minutes) services, two to nine times daily.

FROM FINLAND
Daily services go year-round on Stockholm–Turku and Stockholm–Helsinki routes (all via the Åland islands). Note that Helsinki is called Helsingfors in Swedish, and Turku is known as Åbo. There are two main operators, and it costs more to travel from Thursday to Saturday, and in summer periods. Both companies offer bus services to and from ports.

Silja Line (☎ 08-222140; www.silja.com) sails daily (overnight) from Stockholm to Helsinki from Skr395, around 15 hours) and to Turku (from Skr180/330 day/night crossing, 11 hours).

Viking Line (☎ 08-452 4000; www.vikingline.fi) operates daily on the same routes. Overnight from Stockholm to Helsinki costs from Skr284. Stockholm to Turku sailings cost from Skr126/162 for a day/night crossing.

There are inexpensive connections to the Åland islands from Kapellskär and Grisslehamn, small towns north of Stockholm.

Further north, **RG Line** (☎ 090-185200; www.rgline.com) operates a connection from Umeå to Vaasa (Skr270 to Skr450, four hours, daily).

FROM GERMANY

Trelleborg is the main gateway. **TT-Line** (☎ 0410-56200; www.ttline.se) sails between Trelleborg and Travemünde (seven hours) and Trelleborg and Rostock (5½ hours). Fares for both start at Skr180. **Scandlines** (☎ 0410-65000; www.scandlines.se) is cheaper and sails between Trelleborg and Rostock (from Skr170, 5¾ hours) and Trelleborg and Sassnitz (from Skr100, 3¾ hours).

Stena Line (☎ 031-704 0000; www.stenaline.se) has overnight cruises between Gothenburg and Kiel (from Skr340, 13½ hours, daily).

FROM NORWAY

Color Line (☎ 0526-62000; www.colorline.com) operates ferries between Strömstad and Sandefjord (Skr150 to Skr180, 2½ hours, two to six daily).

DFDS Seaways (www.dfdsseaways.com; Gothenburg ☎ 031-650650; Helsingborg ☎ 042-266000) runs overnight ferries between Copenhagen and Oslo, via Helsingborg. Fares between Helsingborg and Oslo (14 hours) vary according to the season and day of the week, and range from Skr725 to Skr1025. It also sails from Gothenburg to Kristiansand (Skr98 to Skr248, seven hours, three weekly).

FROM POLAND

Polferries (☎ 040-121700; www.polferries.se) operates between Świnoujście and Ystad (from Skr465, seven to nine hours, daily) and also between Gdańsk and Nynäshamn (from

Skr510, 18 hours, three weekly). **Unity Line** (☎ 0411-556900; www.unityline.pl) also operates on the Świnoujście–Ystad route (from Skr450, nine hours, daily). **Stena Line** (☎ 0455-366300; www.stenaline.se) sails between Gdynia and Karlskrona (from Skr290, 10½ to 12 hours, one or two daily).

FROM THE UK

DFDS Seaways (☎ 031-650650; www.dfdsseaways.com) sails from Gothenburg to Newcastle (from Skr198/698 low/high season, 25 hours, twice weekly) via Kristiansand (Norway).

Bus

Direct access to Sweden by land is possible from Norway, Finland and Denmark (from Denmark via the Öresund toll bridge). Train and bus journeys are also possible between Sweden and the Continent – these vehicles go directly to ferries.

Eurolines (☎ 031-100240; www.eurolines.com), the long-distance bus operator, has an office located inside the bus terminals in Stockholm, Gothenburg and Malmö.

All fares are one way unless specified.

FROM THE CONTINENT

Eurolines services run between Sweden and several European cities. The Stockholm to London service (from Skr1318 or £105, approximately 30 hours, two to five weekly) goes via Malmö, Copenhagen, Hamburg and Amsterdam or Brussels. There are services from Gothenburg to Berlin (Skr573, approx 12 hours, two daily).

Berlin Night Express (www.berlin-night-express.com) is a direct night train from Berlin and Malmö (Skr750/1100 or €85/120 for a couchette/bed, 8½ hours, three to seven weekly).

FROM DENMARK

Eurolines runs buses between Stockholm and Copenhagen (Skr460 or Dkr370, nine hours, two to four daily), and between Gothenburg and Copenhagen (Skr285 or Dkr230, 4½ hours, three to five daily). **Swebus Express** (☎ 0200-218218; www.swebusexpress.se) and **Säfflebussen** (☎ 0771-151515; www.safflebussen.se) both run regular buses on the same routes, and have discount fares for travel from Monday to Thursday. All companies offer student, youth (under 26) and senior discounts.

Trains are the quickest option, especially from southern Sweden, and run between

Copenhagen and Malmö (Skr85, 35 minutes, every 20 minutes) via the Öresund bridge.

X2000 trains run regularly between Copenhagen and Stockholm (five hours, up to 14 a day) via Norrköping, Linköping, Lund and Malmö. Three high-speed services operate between Copenhagen and Gothenburg (3½ hours) via Helsingborg, Lund and Malmö (slower InterCity trains take 4½ hours, seven daily). Prices vary dramatically depending on when you buy your ticket – for best prices, purchase at least one day before departure. Contact the Swedish national rail company, **Sveriges Järnväg** (SJ; ☎ 0771-757575; www.sj.se), for more information.

FROM FINLAND

There are seven crossing points along the river border. Bus services on the Swedish side are run by **Länstrafiken Norrbotten** (☎ 020-470047), who also run the 'Bothnian Arc X-press', a daily bus service along the northern coast into Finland, from Skellefteå or Luleå on to Haparanda, Tornio and Kemi, finishing in Oulu. One-way fares from Luleå to Kemi cost Skr155, to Oulu is Skr260.

Tapanis Buss (☎ 0922-12955, 08-153300) runs overnight coaches between Stockholm and Tornio via Haparanda (Skr480 or €55, 15 hours, twice weekly).

Train passengers going to Finland can only reach Boden or Luleå in northern Sweden – from there it's essential to go by bus.

FROM NORWAY

The major bus companies operate on routes connecting Stockholm and Oslo, and Gothenburg and Oslo (many of the services from Oslo to Gothenburg continue on to Malmö and Copenhagen).

Eurolines has regular daily services between Oslo and Copenhagen via Gothenburg, Helsingborg and Malmö. Gothenburg to Oslo costs Skr225/Nkr205 (4¼ hours).

Swebus Express (☎ 0200-218218; www.swebus express.se) runs services between Stockholm and Oslo (from Skr265, 7½ hours, three daily) and between Gothenburg and Oslo (from Skr160, four hours, up to six daily).
Säfflebussen (☎ 0771-151515; www.safflebussen.se) runs the Stockholm–Oslo route (five daily), and Gothenburg to Oslo (10 daily), charging slightly cheaper prices than Swebus Express.

Many regional transport networks (*lästra-fiken*) run buses to within a few kilometres

of Norway's border. **Länstrafiken Norrbotten** (☎ 020-470047) operates services between Kiruna and Narvik in summer (Skr191, 2½ hours, one or two daily).

The main rail links run from Stockholm to Oslo, from Gothenburg to Oslo, from Stockholm to Östersund and Storlien (Norwegian trains go to Trondheim), and from Luleå to Kiruna and Narvik in the far north.

GETTING AROUND

Public transport is well organised using 24 different *länstrafik* (regional networks). The confusion of so many operators is partly alleviated by the **Resplus system** (☎ 0771-878787; www.resplus.se), where one ticket is valid on trains and on *länstrafik* buses. The website has timetables for all trains, boats and buses in Sweden.

Bicycle

Skåne and Gotland are ideal for cycling. The best season is May to September in the south, and July and August in the north. You'll find bike-rental outlets in most major towns. Some country areas, towns and cities have special cycle routes – check with local tourist offices for information and maps.

Boat

An extensive boat network opens up the Stockholm archipelago and boat services on Lake Mälaren, west of Stockholm, are busy in summer. Gotland is served by regular ferries from Nynäshamn and Oskarshamn and there are summer services to many small islands off the coast.

Bus

Sweden has a safe, reliable and extensive bus network. Travellers to the north of the country, in particular, will rely heavily on buses. If you're under 26, a student or senior, it's worth asking for a discount. Advance bookings are required for all but Swebus Express.
Säfflebussen (☎ 0771-151515; www.safflebussen .se) Smaller network, running daily on major routes (eg Stockholm-Malmö, Stockholm-Gothenburg, Gothenburg-Malmö). Also serves Oslo, Copenhagen and Berlin. Fares are 30% cheaper from Monday to Thursday.
Svenska Buss (☎ 0771-676767; www.svenskabuss.se) Network connects many southern towns with Stockholm.
Swebus Express (☎ 0200-218218; www.swebusexpress .se) Has the largest 'national network' of buses, but only serves the southern half of the country (as far north as

Mora in Dalarna). Fares for journeys over 100km are 30% cheaper between Monday and Thursday most weeks (not public or school holidays).

Ybuss (☎ 0771-334444; www.ybuss.se) Daily journeys from Stockholm north along the coast as far as Umeå (via Uppsala, Gävle, Sundsvall), and to Östersund.

Car & Motorcycle

Sweden has good roads and there are no public toll roads or bridges. You usually only need a recognised full driving licence, even for car rental. If bringing your own car, you'll need vehicle registration documents. Insurance Green Cards are recommended.

The Swedish national motoring association is **Motormännens Riksförbund** (☎ 020-911111, 08-690 3800; www.motormannen.se; Sveavägen 159, SE-10435 Stockholm).

International rental chains are expensive, starting at around Skr600 per day for smaller models, but shop around, as weekend or summer packages may be offered at discount rates. All the major firms (eg Avis, Hertz, Europcar) have offices in major cities.

Mabi Hyrbilar (☎ 020-110 1000; www.mabirent.se) is a national company with competitive rates and branches in major cities. Cars can also be hired from many large petrol stations (look for 'hyrbilar' or 'biluthyrning' signs) at reasonable rates.

Local Transport

In Sweden, local transport is always linked with the regional *länstrafik* – rules and prices for city buses may differ slightly from long-distance transport, but a regional pass is valid both in the city and on the rural routes. There's usually a flat fare of around Skr15 to Skr20 in towns.

Stockholm has an extensive underground metro system, and Gothenburg runs a good tram network and a city ferry service.

Train

Trains are the fastest way to get around, although many destinations in the northern half of the country can't be reached by train alone.

The national network **Sveriges Järnväg** (SJ; ☎ 0771-757575; www.sj.se) covers most main lines, especially in the country's southern half. Its flag carriers are the X2000 trains going at speeds of up to 200km/h, with services from Stockholm to major destinations. InterCity trains also run on a lot of these routes; InterCity fares are cheaper and journey times longer. **Connex** (☎ 0771-260000; www.connex.se) runs in the far north and offers services from Stockholm and Gothenburg north as far as Kiruna and across to Narvik in Norway. Several counties run small regional train networks as part of their *länstrafik* service.

There are huge variations on fares depending on time of travel, type of service and how far in advance you book. Full-price tickets are pricey, you'll receive a big discount for booking at least a day before departure (ask for the *'just nu'* fare). People aged under 26 get up to 30% discount on the standard adult fare. All SJ ticket prices are reduced in summer, from late June to mid-August, and during off-peak travel times (10am to 2pm from Monday to Thursday and after 7pm, Friday and Sunday until noon, all day Saturday).

TRAIN PASSES

The Sweden Rail Pass, Eurodomino tickets and InterRail, Eurail and ScanRail passes are accepted on SJ services and most other operators, such as regional trains. Not so for the local Storstockholms Lokaltrafik (SL) *pendeltåg* (commuter) trains around Stockholm.

X2000 and overnight trains require all pass-holders to pay a supplement of Skr50 (including obligatory seat reservation). The reservation supplements for non-X2000 (ie, InterCity) trains (Skr50) aren't obligatory, and there are no supplements for regional *länstrafik* trains.

STOCKHOLM

☎ 08 / pop 760,000

Scattered across a series of islands, Stockholm is one of the world's most beautiful capitals. It's a compact city and has remained a manageable size even while its status as a cultural centre has grown rapidly. It's a mecca for lovers of architecture, museums, shopping and design, but everyone will enjoy simply strolling and taking in its loveliness. The city is best seen from the water but you can also explore the parklands of Djurgården or the alleys of Gamla Stan on foot.

Stockholm has Scandinavia's broadest selection of budget accommodation plus a great café and restaurant scene. Around 1.8 million people live in greater Stockholm

SWEDEN

and over 15% of them are immigrants, making for a lively, international atmosphere.

ORIENTATION

Stockholm is built on 14 islands. The modern centre (Norrmalm) is focused on the square known as Sergels Torg. This business and shopping hub is linked by a network of subways to Centralstationen (the central train station); these subways also link with the *tunnelbana* (metro; or T) stations. The large, busy tourist office is in the eastern part of Norrmalm; the popular garden, Kungsträdgården, is almost next door.

Smack in the middle of Stockholm is Gamla Stan, the historic Old Town. To the east of Gamla Stan is the island of Djurgården, home to many of Stockholm's better-known museums. The small island of Skeppsholmen sits between Djurgården and Gamla Stan. Södermalm, the city's funky, bohemian area, inhabits the large island to the south of Gamla Stan. It's linked by the car-and-pedestrian bridge Centralbron.

INFORMATION

Discount Cards

SL Public Transport Pass (Skr95/180 for 24/72 hr) Covers transport only.

Stockholm Card (Skr260/390/540 for 24/48/72 hr) Gives free entry to over 75 attractions, free sightseeing by boat and free travel on public transport. Available from tourist offices, many camping grounds, hostels and hotels, and SL centres.

Emergency

Police stations (Kungsholmen Map pp1134-5; ☎ 401 1300; Kungsholmsgatan 37; Södermalm Map pp1138-9; ☎ 401 0100; Torkel Knutssonsgatan 20) Both stations open 24 hours.

Internet Access

Café Access IT (Map pp1138-9; Kulturhuset, Sergels Torg; per 30min/hr Skr25/45; ☺ 11am-7pm Tue-Fri, 11am-5pm Sat & Sun) At the lower level in Kulturhuset.

Nine (Map pp1134-5; Odengatan 44; per min Skr0.75; ☺ 10am-1am)

Sidewalk Express (www.sidewalkexpress.se; per hr Skr19) A chain of Internet kiosks at central locations (Centralstationen, Cityterminalen, Arlanda and Bromma airports, inside some 7-Eleven stores); vouchers are purchased from vending machines.

Laundry

Tvättomat (Map pp1134-5; ☎ 346 480; Västmannagatan 61; Ⓜ T-Odenplan; ☺ 8.30am-6.30pm Mon-Fri, 9.30am-3pm Sat) Laundrette; Skr70 to wash and dry.

Left Luggage

In the lower level at Centralstationen, different-sized lockers cost Skr25 to Skr70 for 24hr. Similar facilities at the neighbouring bus station and major ferry terminals.

Medical Services

CW Scheele Apotek (Map pp1138-9; ☎ 454 8130; Klarabergsgatan 64; ☺ 24hr) Central pharmacy near Centralstationen.

St Eriks Sjukhus (Map pp1134-5; ☎ 654 1117; Flemminggatan 22; ☺ 8am-8.30pm) Emergency dental treatment is available here.

Södersjukhuset (Map pp1134-5; ☎ 616 1000; Ringvägen 52; ☺ 24hr) Large hospital in Södermalm handling casualties from central city area.

Money

There are ATMs all over town, including few inside Centralstationen. There are banks around Sergels Torg and along Hamngatan.

The exchange company **Forex** (www.forex.se; Centralstationen (Map pp1138-9; ☺ 7am-9pm); Cityterminalen (Map pp1138-9; ☺ 7am-8pm Mon-Fri, 8am-5pm Sat & Sun); Vasagatan 14 (Map pp1138-9; ☺ 10am-7pm Mon-Fri, 9am-3pm Sat) charges Skr15 per travellers cheque.

Post

Post office (Map pp1138-9; Centralstationen; ☺ 7am-10pm Mon-Fri, 10am-7pm Sat & Sun) By Hotelcentrallen.

Tourist Information

Sweden House (Sverigehuset; Map pp1138-9; ☎ 789 2490; www.stockholmtown.com; Hamngatan 27; ☺ 9am-7pm Mon-Fri, 9am-5pm Sat, 10am-4pm Sun Jun-Aug;

9am-6pm Mon-Fri, 10am-4pm Sat & Sun May & Sep; 9am-6pm Mon-Fri, 10am-3pm Sat & Sun Oct-Apr) Main tourist office, by Kungsträdgården. Lots of good brochures. Staff can book accommodation and packages such as trips to the archipelago. **Hotellcentralen** (Map pp1138-9; ☎ 789 2456; hotels@svb .stockholm.se; Centralstationen; ⏰ 8am-8pm Jun-Aug; 9am-6pm Mon-Sat, noon-4pm Sun Sep-May) More convenient for arriving travellers, inside the train station. Can book accommodation and sightseeing tours, plus sells the Stockholm Card, SL Public Transport Pass, maps and souvenirs.

SIGHTS

Arm yourself with your Stockholm Card (opposite) and head to the following sights, most of which are open daily in summer but are closed Monday the rest of the year. Students and seniors usually pay a discounted entrance fee.

Gamla Stan

The oldest part of Stockholm is also its most beautiful, containing cobblestone streets, vaulted cellar restaurants and the royal palace. The city emerged here in the 13th century and adopted the trade and, partly, the accents of its German Hanseatic guests. It grew with Sweden's power until the 17th century, when the castle of Tre Kronor, symbol of that power, burned to the ground.

The 'new' royal palace, **Kungliga Slottet** (Map pp1138-9; ☎ 402 6130; www.royalcourt.se; Slottsbacken; adult per attraction Skr70, combined ticket Skr110; ⏰ 10am-4pm mid-May–Aug, noon-3pm Tue-Sun Sep–mid-May, closed Jan), is constructed on the ruins of Tre Kronor and is one of Stockholm's highlights. Its 608 rooms make it the largest royal palace in the world. The **Changing of the Guard** (⏰ 12.15pm Mon-Sat, 1.15pm Sun & public holidays) takes place in the outer courtyard.

Near the palace, **Storkyrkan** (Map pp1138-9; ☎ 723 3021; adult Skr20 mid-May–Aug, otherwise free; ⏰ daily) is the Royal Cathedral of Sweden, consecrated in 1306. On the lovely square Stortorget is **Nobelmuseet** (Map pp1138-9; ☎ 232506; Stortorget; adult Skr50; ⏰ daily mid-May–mid-Sep, Tue-Sun mid-Sep–mid-May), presenting the history of the Nobel Prize and its recipients.

The site of **Medeltidsmuseet** (Map pp1138-9; ☎ 5083 1790; Strömparterren; adult Skr60; ⏰ daily July-Aug, Tue-Sun Sep-Jun), the museum of medieval Stockholm, had been allocated as parking space for members of the nearby **Riksdagshuset** (Parliament House; Map pp1138-9; ☎ 786 4872; Riksgatan 3A; free guided tours Jun-Aug),

but excavations in the late 1970s revealed foundations of the medieval town and it's now a museum.

Djurgården

Leafy, attraction-rich Djurgården is a must-see. Take bus No 47 from Centralstationen or the regular Djurgården ferry services from Nybroplan or Slussen. By the bridge you can rent bikes – the best way to explore the area. Beyond Djurgården's large tourist haunts are plenty of small gems, including some excellent art collections.

You could easily spend all day at **Skansen** (Map pp1134-5; ☎ 442 8000; www.skansen.se; adult Skr50-80; ⏰ 10am-8pm May, 10am-10pm Jun-Aug, 10am-5pm Sep, 10am-4pm Oct-Apr). This 'Sweden in miniature' was the world's first open-air museum (it opened in 1891); today over 150 traditional houses and exhibits from all over Sweden occupy the attractive hill top.

The acclaimed **Vasamuseet** (Map pp1134-5; ☎ 5195 4800; adult Skr70; ⏰ 9.30am-7pm mid-Jun–late Aug, 10am-5pm late Aug–mid-Jun) allows you to look into the lives of 17th-century sailors plus appreciate a brilliant achievement in marine archaeology. The flagship *Wasa* sank within minutes of being launched in 1628 and guides explain the extraordinary and controversial 300-year story of the ship's death and resurrection.

Nordiska Museet (National Museum of Cultural History; Map pp1134-5; ☎ 5195 6000; Djurgårdordsvägen 6-16; adult Skr75; ⏰ daily) is housed in an enormous Renaissance-style castle, with notable temporary exhibitions and vast Swedish collections.

Gröna Lund Tivoli (Map pp1134-5; ☎ 5875 0100; adult Skr60; ⏰ May–mid-Sep) is a fun park with dozens of rides and amusements – the Åkbandet day pass (Skr235) gives unlimited rides.

Central Stockholm

Near Centralstationen is **Sergels Torg**, a severely modern public square bordered on one side by the giant, boxy **Kulturhuset** (Map pp1138-9; ☎ 5083 1508; Sergels Torg; ⏰ closed Mon), which houses temporary exhibitions, a theatre, bookshop, design store, reading room, several cafés, comics library and Internet café.

Not far away is the beloved public park **Kungsträdgården** (Map pp1138–9), where locals gather in all weather. There's an outdoor stage, winter ice-skating rink and restaurants, cafés and kiosks.

STOCKHOLM

INFORMATION		
British Embassy	1	G2
Finnish Embassy	2	G2
German Embassy	3	G2
Irish Embassy	4	E2
Nine Internet Café	5	C1
Norwegian Embassy	6	G2
Police Station	7	B3
RFSL (Gay & Lesbian Organisation)	8	C1
St Eriks Sjukhus	9	B2
Södersjukhuset	10	C5
Tvättomat	11	C1
US Embassy	12	G2

SIGHTS & ACTIVITIES	(pp1133–6)	
Gröna Lund Tivoli	13	F3
Historiska Museet	14	F2
Nordiska Museet	15	F3
Skansen Main Entrance	16	F3
Vasamuseet	17	F3

SLEEPING	(pp1136–7)	
Columbus Hotell	18	E4
Hostel Bed & Breakfast	19	C1
Hotel Tre Små Rum	20	D5
Oden Pensionat Vasastan	21	C1
STF Vandrarhem Fridhemsplan	22	B3
STF Vandrarhem Långholmen	23	B4

EATING	(pp1137–40)	
Hermans	24	E4
Indian Curry House	25	C3
Jerusalem Royal Kebab	26	E5
Mamas & Tapas	27	C3
Sirap	28	B3
Söderhallarna	29	D5

DRINKING	(p1140)	
Cliff Barnes	30	C1
Djurgårdsbrons Sjöcafe	31	F3
Tvillingarnas	32	F2

ENTERTAINMENT	(p1141)	
Kvarnen	33	E5
La Habana	34	C1

TRANSPORT	(pp1141–2)	
Djurgårdsbrons Sjöcafé Bike Rental	(see 31)	
Viking Line Terminal	35	F4

SWEDEN

0   600 m
0   0.4 miles

To Östermalms Citycamping (500m)

Olaus Petriparken

Gärdet

Askrikegatan

Tessinparken

To Silja Line Terminal (500m)

Tallink & Riga Sea Line Terminal

Frihamnen

Stadion

Valhallavägen

Erik Dahlbergsgatan

Hedinsgatan

De Geersgatan

Värtavägen

Fågelberget

Lindarängsvägen

Storgatan

Sturegatan

Runtunegatan

Nobelgatan

Östermalmsgatan

Karlaplan

Wittstocksgatan

Gieve von Essens Väg

Ladugårdsgärdet

Grev Turegatan

Kommendörsgatan

Karlaplan

Gustav Adolfsparken

Karlavägen

Östermalmstorg

Brahegatan

Karlavägen

Nybergsgatan

Linnégatan

Oxenstiernsgatan

2

3

1

6

Djurgårdsbrunnsvägen

Käknäsvägen

Hunduddsvägen

Artillerigatan

Skeppargatan

Grevgatan

Styrmansgatan

Narvavägen

Storgatan

14

12

Dag Hammarskjölds Väg

Nybroplan

Riddargatan

Strandvägen

Djurgårdsbron

Folke Bernadottes Väg

Nobelparken

Djurgårds brunnskanalen

Nybroviken

Styrmansgatan

Djurgårdsbrunnsviken

Nobelvägen

De Besches Väg

Prins Carl Väg

Djurgårdsfärjan Ferry (Summer Only)

Ladugårdslandsviken

32

31

Nordiska Museet - Vasamuseet

Fredrik Bloms Väg

Nybroken

Galärparken

15

Skansen

Söndbacken

Sirishovsvägen

DJURGÅRDEN

Strömkajen

Norrström

17

Hazeliusporten

Galärkyrkogården

Skansen

Solidbacken

Bellmans Väg

Djurgården

Djurgårdsvägen

To Thielska Galleriet (1.2km)

Svensksundsvägen

Konsthallen - Grönalund

16

Singelbacken

Bellmansro

Bergsjölundsvägen

Skeppsbron

Skeppsholmen

Gröna Lunden

13

Skansen

Tram Line 7

Prins Eugens Väg

Strömmen

Kastellholmen

Djurgårdsfärjan Ferry (All Year)

Waldermarsudde

Kastellparken

Beckholmen

Waldemarsviken

Saltsjön

Stadsgårdsleden

Katarinavägen

Högbergsgatan

Nytorgsgatan

Fjällgatan

24

Stadsgårdshamnen

35

Masthamnen

Finnbodavägen

18

Folkungagatan

Södermannagatan

Danviks Kanalen

Kvarnholmsvägen

33

Medborgarplatsen

26

Åsögatan

Bondegatan

Skånegatan

Alsnögatan

Hästholmsvägen

Svinderviken

Katarina Bangata

Tegelviksgatan

NACKA

Värmdöleden

5

Götgatan

Gotlandsgatan

Malmgårdsvägen

Vita Bergen

Barnängsgatan

Alphyddevägen

Svindersviksvägen

Nacka Station

Lilla Blecktornsparken

Metargatan

Vintertullsparken

Kanalvägen

Värmdövägen

Sickla Station

Skanstull

Stora Blecktornsparken

Hammarby sjö

Båtbyggargatan

Fabriksvägen

Sickla

Östgötagatan

Tulgårdsgatan

Norra Hammarbyhamnen

Sickla Kanalväg

Sickla Allé

Tvärbanan

Järlaleden

Atlasvägen

Sickla Strand

Gillevägen

Swedenborgsgatan

Hammarbyleden

Hammarby Fabriksväg

Södra Hammarbyhamnen

Virkesgatan

Sicklasjön

6

Johannshovsbron

Hammarbybacken

Renhammarbyvägen

Hammarbyvägen

Kalmgatan

Hammarby Fabriksväg

Simlångsvägen

SWEDEN

Sweden's largest art museum, the **National-museum** (Map pp1138-9; ☎ 5195 4300; Södra Blasieholmshamnen; adult Skr75; ☉ Tues-Sun) has the national painting and sculpture collection.

The main national historical collection is at **Historiska Museet** (Museum of National Antiquities; Map pp1134-5; ☎ 5195 5600; Narvavägen 13; adult Skr60; ☉ daily mid-May–mid-Sep, Tue-Sun rest of year). Displays cover prehistoric, Viking and medieval archaeology and culture.

Kungsholmen

The **Stadshuset** (Town Hall; Map pp1138-9; ☎ 5082 9058; Hantverkargatan; tours adult Skr50; ☉ 10am-3pm Jun-Aug, 10am & noon Sep-May) resembles a large church, although its size is deceptive. It has two internal courtyards. The interior has the Blue Hall, where the annual Nobel Prize banquet is held. Entry is by 45-minute tour only.

Climb Stadhuset's 106m-high **Stadshustorn** (Tower; Map pp1138-9; ☎ 5082 9058; adult Skr20; ☉ daily May-Sep, Sat & Sun Apr), with 365 steps, for a great view of the city.

Other Areas

Södermalm is Stockholm's most striking neighbourhood. Home to many city's artists, Söder (as it's called) has a bohemian feel, and alternative youth culture scarcely ventures beyond the borders of this island. There are many funky shops and art galleries, plus hip nightlife. For evening walks, go to the northern cliffs for streetscapes of old houses and fine panoramas. There are great views from **Katarinahissen** (Slussen; adult Skr5; ☉ daily), an old lift that goes to the heights from Slussen.

Fjäderholmarna are wee islands that offer an easy escape from the city. They're 25 minutes away by boat (off the east coast of Djurgården) and are a popular local swimming spot. Take a boat (Skr80 return trip, buy tickets on board) that leave from either Nybroplan (half-hourly) or from Slussen (hourly) from May to early September. There are eateries here and the last boats leave at about midnight, making the islands a perfect spot to enjoy the long daylight hours.

ACTIVITIES

In summer locals and visitors flock to the coast and the archipelago islands or have picnics in the parks. From **Djurgårdsbrons Sjöcafé** (Map pp1134-5; ☎ 660 5757; ☉ May-Sep), by the bridge reaching Djurgården, you can rent bikes, inline skates, kayaks, canoes and boats

(from Skr60/200 per hour/day for inline skates, Skr65/250 per hour/day for bikes).

SLEEPING

Budget options are spread out all over th city, and all are accessible by transport and close to a neighbourhood of bars and cafés

Hostels

For a Skr25 fee, Hotelcentrallen (p1133) ca find you a bed in a hostel.

All hostels listed here are open year-round Many have options for single, double or fam ily rooms, breakfast is usually available, and linen costs extra. A few hostels have 24-hou reception (a rarity elsewhere in Sweden), and all are non-smoking.

City Backpackers (Map pp1138-9; ☎ 206920; ww .citybackpackers.se; Upplandsgatan 2A; dm Skr180-220, Skr490; 🖳) About 500m from Centralstatio and deservedly popular with backpackers. has clean rooms, friendly staff and facilitie including kitchen, sauna, laundry, locker and courtyard, plus free Internet access. N breakfast offered.

Hostel Bed & Breakfast (Map pp1134-5; ☎ 15283 www.hostelbedandbreakfast.com; Rehnsgatan 21; Ⓜ T-Rå mansgatan; dm/s/d Skr190/375/500; 🖳) Cosy, warr basement hostel, with breakfast include Good facilities including kitchen and laun dry. Also a large, cheap summer annexe her with 40 beds (June to August, Skr125), bu it's not for the privacy-conscious!

Mälaren den Röda Båten (Map pp1138-9; ☎ 64 4385; www.theredboat.com; Söder Mälarstrand, Kajplats dm/s/d Skr195/430/490, cabins s/d from Skr675/915; Ⓟ This red-painted boat in northern Söder malm is probably the cosiest of Stockholm' handful of floating hostels. It features a rusti interior and a good summer restaurant (bu no self-catering facilities). It also has pleasar cabins, with private bathroom.

STF Vandrarhem Zinkensdamm (Map pp1134- ☎ 616 8100; www.zinkensdamm.com; Zinkens väg 2 Ⓜ T-Zinkendamm; dm/s/d Skr220/485/560; 🖳 Ⓟ) large, well equipped and warm STF (Svensk Turistföreningen; part of Hostelling Interna tional) hostel complex (with hotel) in a quie locale at the Södermalm's green western en It has on-site café, sauna and bike rental.

STF Vandrarhem af Chapman & Skeppsholme (Map pp1138-9; ☎ 463 2266; info@chapman.stfturist.s Skeppsholmen; dm/d Skr230/510; 🖳 Ⓟ) Anchore off Skeppsholmen (bus No 65), this bo is a popular hostel, with bunks below an great views from on deck. On dry land beside the boat, with the same reception and prices, is Skeppsholmen Hostel, with kitchen and laundry facilities. From autumn 2004, af Chapman will be closed for an estimated nine months while it undergoes renovation. The land-based hostel will be open as usual.

STF Vandrarhem Fridhemsplan (Map pp1134-5; ☎ 653 8800; info@fridhemsplan.se; St Eriksgatan 20; Ⓜ T-Fridhemsplan; dm/s/d Skr240/435/675; 🖳 P) Brandnew, 150-room STF hostel on Kungsholmen. From its smart lobby to rooftop breakfast area, this place epitomises the Swedish approach to hostelling (ie, good facilities, great décor, excellent value).

STF Vandrarhem Långholmen (Map pp1134-5; ☎ 720 8500; www.langholmen.com; Långholmsmuren; Ⓜ Hornstull; dm/d Skr240/585; P) Off the northwestern corner of Södermalm is the small island of Långholmen, home to this complex (formerly a prison). Hostel beds are in former cells. Hotel-standard rooms are also available, plus there's an on-site café and restaurant and even a prison museum. Take the metro to Hornstull, walk north along Långholmsgatan and turn left onto Högalidsgatan, then north across the footbridge.

Hotels

Most Stockholm hotels give discount rates at weekends and in summer (Midsummer's day to mid-August). Discounts can reach 50% off the normal price, making some hotels surprisingly affordable. Most hotel prices include breakfast; there are always non-smoking rooms available (many places are entirely non-smoking).

Hotellcentralen (see p1133) can find suitable hotel accommodation for a Skr60 fee.

Hotel Tre Små Rum (Map pp1134-5; ☎ 641 2371; www.tresmarum.se; Högbergsgatan 81; Ⓜ T-Mariatorget; r Skr695) In a quiet part of Södermalm, this cute, cosy place has small but comfortable rooms, shared bathroom facilities and rental bikes. Hard to beat for value and location.

Oden Pensionat (☎ 796 9600; www.pensionat.nu; City Map pp1138-9; Kammakargatan 62, Södermalm Map pp1138-9; Hornsgatan 66, Vasastan Map pp1134-5; Odengatan 38; s Skr600-950, d Skr740-1295) A chain of affordable *pension* in character-rich old buildings with attractive rooms. Prices vary according to season, room size and facilities.

Columbus Hotell (Map pp1134-5; ☎ 5031 1200; www.columbus.se; Tjärhovsgatan 11; Ⓜ T-Medborgarplatsen; budget s/d Skr695/895; P) A Södermalm option

set around a cobblestone courtyard and by a park, close to nightlife. The excellent budget rooms are on the third floor (no lift) and have phone, TV and shared bathroom.

Camping

Östermalms Citycamping (Map pp1134-5; ☎ 102903; Östermalms Idrottsplats, Fiskartorpsvägen; Ⓜ T-Stadion; camping Skr100; ☼ mid-Jun–mid-Aug) Stockholm's most central camping ground (1.5km from the city centre) is open only in summer. Take the metro or bus No 55.

Bredäng Camping (☎ 977071; bredangcamping@telia.com; Stora Sällskapets väg; Ⓜ T-Bredäng; camping Skr170-205, 4-bed cabin Skr650-850, hostel dm/d Skr150/440; ☼ Apr-late Oct) In a pleasant lakeside location 10km southwest of the city centre. Cabins and hostel beds also available.

EATING

Stockholm has thousands of eateries to cater to all tastes and budgets, ranging from old-style *konditori* (bakery cafés) to gourmet restaurants; the city is also home to some wonderful market halls.

Most cafés and restaurants serve a daily lunch special called *dagens rätt* or *dagens lunch* at a fixed price (usually Skr60 to Skr70) between 11.30am and 2pm. The price usually includes main course, salad, bread, cold drink and coffee, and it's one of the most economical ways to sample upscale Swedish cooking.

For a quick, inexpensive snack, it's hard to beat a *grillad korv med bröd* – a basic grilled hotdog on a bun (Skr12 to Skr25, available from countless stands and carts). Variations include *kokt korv* (boiled hotdog) and several types of *rulle*, hotdogs wrapped up with *mos* (mashed potatoes), onions, shrimp salad and other unlikely things in pitta-style bread.

Gamla Stan

Café Art (Map pp1138-9; ☎ 411 7661; Västerlånggatan 60; snacks Skr35-65) A barrel-vaulted cellar-café that's an atmospheric retreat from the Gamla Stan souvenir-grab on Västerlånggatan.

Hermitage (Map pp1138-9; ☎ 411 9500; Stora Nygatan 11; meals Skr65-85) One for the herbivores: Hermitage rustles up fine vegetarian fare from around the world. The lunch deal (Skr65 weekdays) is great value.

Chokladkoppen (Map pp1138-9; ☎ 203170; Stortorget 18; snacks & sweets Skr40-70; ☼ daily until 11pm) In a pair of gorgeous Renaissance buildings from the 1650s you'll find the gay-friendly café

CENTRAL STOCKHOLM

0 _____ 300 m
0 _____ 0.2 miles

A   **B**   **C**   **D**

Rådmansgatan
Tegnérlunden
Tegnérgatan
Tegnérgatan
Saltmätargatan
Luntmakargatan
Döbelnsgatan
Johannesgatan
Birger Jarlsgatan
Jutas Backe
Regeringsgatan
Humlegården
Brahegatan
Kommendörsgatan
Sibyllegatan
6

Upplandsgatan
Kammakargatan
Holländargatan
Drottninggatan
Adolf Fredriks Kyrkogata
Olofsgatan
Smala Gränd
Linnégatan
21

Wallingatan
Barnhusgatan
Humlegårdsgatan
19
Brunnsgatan
Östermalmstorg
Östermalmstorg
35

Norra Bantorget
Apelbergsgatan
42
40
50
52
Storgatan
Kungsgatan
Oxtorget
Hötorget
Stureplan
Östermalmstorg
Olof Palmes Gata
33
44
Oxtorgsgatan
Lästmakargatan
Nybrogatan

32
Malmskillnadsgatan
Jakobsbergsgatan
Klaratunneln
36
Riddargatan

43
Sveavägen
Sergelgatan
Smålandsgatan
Normalmstorg
Normalmstorg
Hamngatan
45
Väpnargatan

Vasaplan
54
55
Vasagatan
Klarabergsgatan
39
37
60
Mäster Samuelsgatan
Sergels Torg
T-Centralen
12
10
Kungsträdgården
Berzelii Park
Nybroplan
58
56
Strandvägen

T-Centralen
Centralplan
Klara Östra Kyrkogatan
Klarabergsgatan
Kungsträdgården
Kåkstorget
Brunkebergstorg
Jakobs Torg
27
Wahrendorffsgatan
Arsenalsgatan
Stallgatan
Nybroviken
Nybrokajen
Djurgårdsfärjan Ferry (Summer Only)

Stockholm Centralstationen
5
Vattugatan
Herkulesgatan
4
25
61
46
Karl XII:s Torg
59
63
62
Strömgatan
Museiparken
14
Strömkajen
Hovslagargatan

Klarabergsviadukten T-Centralen
Jakobsgatan
Gustav Adolfs Torg
Strömstorg
Klarabergsgatan
Rödbodtorget
2
Fredsgatan
Strömparterren
13

Blekholmsfaret
Klara Sjö
Klarabergsviadukten
Tegelbacken
Mälarstrand
Vasabron
Norrström
Helgeandsholmen
16
Slottskajen
Kungliga Slottet
Slottsbacken
18
48
Skeppar Karls Gränd

Kungsholmen
17
Ragnar Östbergs Plan
Norra Järnvägsbron
Akvägatan
Strömsborg
Bankkajen
Yttre Borggården
Gamla Stan
Batteriparken
Amiralitetsparken
24
23

Myntgatan
Birger Jarls Torg
51
30
41
15
28
Stortorget
Nygränd
Strömmen

Evert Taubes Terrass
Wrangelska Backen
Riddarholmen
Södra Riddarholmshamnen
Lilla Nygatan
Stora Nygatan
Prästgatan
Västerlånggatan
Svartmangatan
Köpmangatan
Skeppsbrokajen

Riddarfjärden
Munkbrogatan
Gamla Stan
53
26
Tyska Brinken
Järntorget
Köpmanbrinken
Kornhamnstorg

Södra Järnvägsbron
Centralbron
Sjöbergsplan
Djurgårdsfärjan Ferry (All Year)

20
Mariaberget
Pustegränd
Guldfjärdsplan
Södermalmstorg
Saltsjöbanans Station
11
57
47
Stadsgårdshamnen
Stadsgårdsleden

Axel Knutssonsgatan
Prysgränd
Blecktornsgränd
Brännkyrkagatan
Bellmansgatan
8
34
Slussen
Katarinavägen
49
Klevgränd
Fiskargränd
Mosebacketorg

Södermalm
Ludvigsbergsgatan
Bastugatan
Tavastgatan
22
Timmermansgatan
Mariatorget
Hökens Gata
Högbergsgatan
Katarina Östra Kyrkogatan

Hornsgatan
9
Sankt Paulsgatan
Mariatorget
Kvarngatan
Repslagargatan
Götgatan
Svartensgatan
29
Mosebacke
Kapellgränd

Krukmakargatan
Rosenlundsgatan
Wollmar Yxkullsgatan
Maria Prästgårdsgata
Fatbursparken
38

SWEDEN

Chokladkoppen and its next-door sibling, Kaffekoppen. Service can be slow, but the food is good and the outdoor area is one of the best hang-outs in Gamla Stan.

City

Hötorgshallen (Hötorget; Map opposite) has many Mediterranean food stalls and good specialist shops, while **Kungshallen** (Hötorget; Map opposite), opposite, has an enormous selection of food stalls where you can eat anything you fancy from Tex-Mex to Indian or Cajun at budget prices. In between, on Hötorget itself, is a colourful open-air market with vendors selling fresh fruit, vegies and flowers.

Perfect for night owls and close to Centralstationen, **Kebab House** (Map opposite; cnr Vasagatan & Kungsgatan; snacks from Skr19; ☻ until 5am daily) offers cheap kebabs and burgers.

Head to the stalls along the edge of Kungsträdgården for a range of quick bites. A park favourite is **Café Piccolino** (Map opposite; Kungsträdgården), a long and lean café with large windows to capture the sun (and the passing parade).

Bakfickan (Map opposite; ☎ 676 5808; mains Skr95-200; ☻ Mon-Sat) Kungliga Operan (Stockholm's opera house) houses one of our Stockholm favourites. This intimate little restaurant features great service, Art Nouveau décor and gourmet-quality home-cooking at moderate prices.

Sirap (Map pp1134–5; ☎ 612 9419; Surbrunnsgatan 31A; meals Skr30-95) A brunch hotspot, with a huge menu of breakfast dishes (great pancakes), sandwiches and salads.

Östermalm

Sturekatten (Map opposite; ☎ 611 1612; Riddargatan 4; sandwiches Skr35-70) A traditional café, full of old-world charm and antiques. Having afternoon tea here is like visiting your posh great-aunt's house.

Östermalms Saluhall (Map opposite; Östermalmstorg; ☻ Mon-Sat) Beautiful covered market hall, now home to gourmet food stalls. It offers the chance for excellent eat-in meals, and is the perfect place to fill a picnic basket.

Södermalm

Söderhallarna (Map pp1134–5; Medborgarplatsen; ☻ Mon-Sat) A modern food hall, but not the most atmospheric place, so plan on enjoying your lunch outdoors on Medborgarplatsen.

Crêperie Fyra Knop (Map opposite; ☎ 640 7727; Svartensgatan 4; crepes Skr36-74; ☻ nightly) An intimate little place with lots of small rooms. Serves delicious crepes (savoury from Skr60, sweet from Skr36).

Hermans (Map pp1134–5; ☎ 643 9480; Fjällgatan 23A; lunch Skr68/98) A great place where you'll get gigantic portions of vegetarian food, plus summer veranda seating with a million-dollar view.

For a quick fix, find **Jerusalem Royal Kebab** (Map pp1134–5; Götgatan 61; ☻ 24hr), with kebabs and felafels from Skr25. A fast-food option with a more Swedish slant, is the **Nystekt**

Strömming (Map p1138-9; Södermalmstorg) van outside metro T-Slussen; it sells some of the best fried herring in Stockholm.

Kungsholmen

Indian Curry House (Map pp1134-5; ☎ 650 2024; Scheelegatan 6; dishes Skr65-120) Basic restaurant serving Stockholm's cheapest Indian food (all the favourites, and good veg options).

Mamas & Tapas (Map pp1134-5; ☎ 653 5390; Scheelegatan 3; tapas Skr35, mains Skr98-158) A fun, bright and busy tapas joint with a great range of snacks to wash down with sangria or vino.

Self-Catering

Ask at your accommodation for the location of the nearest food store, or mosey along to one of the food halls. The handiest central supermarket is **Hemköp** (Map pp1138-9; Klarabergsgatan 50; ☺ 8am-9pm Mon-Fri, 10am-9pm Sat & Sun), in the basement of the Åhlens department store, and there's a **Systembolaget** (Map pp1138-9; Klarabergsgatan 62; ☺ 10am-8pm Mon-Fri, 10am-3pm Sat) nearby for buying alcohol.

DRINKING

It seems that almost every decent restaurant in Stockholm has a cool bar attached, and many cafés bring in a DJ of an evening and, *voila*, another groovy bar is born.

Nightlife focusses on neighbourhoods that have pubs and bars within walking distance. In Södermalm, see the Götgatan, Östgötagatan and Skånegatan area, and near Medborgarplatsen. In Kungsholmen, visit Scheelegatan, and in the northern area try the Tegnérgatan and Rörstrandsgatan areas. For fashionable late-night bars and clubs brimful of the beautiful people, go to Stureplan.

The outdoor restaurant-bars on either side of the bridge leading across to Djurgården, **Tvillingarnas** (Map pp1134-5; ☎ 663 3714; Strandvägskajen 27) and **Djurgårdsbrons Sjöcafé** (Map pp1134-5; ☎ 660 5757; Djurgårdsbron), also do a roaring trade on fine summer days; come here for long leisurely drinks and good people-watching.

Cliff Barnes (Map pp1134-5; ☎ 318070; Nortullsgatan 45) Join the locals to get sozzled and dance on the tables. This is a rowdy, popular beerhall-type place with an outdoor bar in summer.

Loft (Map pp1138-9; ☎ 411 1991; Regeringsgatan 66) An unpretentious Irish pub with a full restaurant menu. The mostly Irish staff are everyone's best friend, and you can't go in without meeting 10 new people.

Mosebacke Etablissement (Map pp1138-9; ☎ 5560 9890; www.mosebacke.se; Mosebacketorg 3) Even if you're not partaking in Mosebacke's many cool club nights, its terrace bar in summertime is a fantastic place to relax.

Fenix (Map pp1138-9; ☎ 640 4506; Götgatan 40) Eclectically decorated bar-restaurant; grab a seat at the window and watch the action on Götgatan.

Wirströms Irish Pub (Map pp1138-9; ☎ 212874; Stora Nygatan 13) This Gamla Stan place feels more like a medieval dungeon than an Irish pub – the dark, brick-vaulted cellar here goes on forever.

Ice Bar (Map pp1138-9; ☎ 5056 3000; Vasaplan; ☺ 4.30pm-midnight Mon-Fri, 3pm-midnight Sat) Head inside the Nordic Sea Hotel for a taste of the Ice Hotel in the country's far north (see p1154). It's not cheap, but it is unique. For an entry charge of Skr125 you get to play inside a bar filled with ice sculptures where the temperature is a constant -5°C (spunky silver poncho provided) and drink vodka from a glass made of ice.

CLUBBING

Östermalm's Stureplan is the pinnacle of chic, trendy clubs in Stockholm. The door policy at many places in this area is strict, and a number of places have high entry charges (Skr100 is not uncommon). And remember, the longer the queue, the more prestigious the bar and the higher the drink prices.

Super-cool **Spy Bar** (Map pp1138-9; ☎ 5450 3704; Birger Jarlsgatan 20; admission Skr125; ☺ Wed-Sat night) is Stureplan's crown jewel. Nearby **Sturecompagniet** (Map pp1138-9; ☎ 611 7800; Sturegatan 4), with several rooms over three floors, is usually slightly more welcoming.

For more down-to-earth options, head to **La Habana** (Map pp1134-5; ☎ 166465; Sveavägen 108), a Cuban restaurant-bar featuring cigars, rum and lots of salsa-ing, or **Kvarnen** (Map pp1134-5; ☎ 643 0380; Tjärhovsgatan 4) in Södermalm – beyond the traditional beerhall is a hot dance party, with DJ nights ranging from reggae to house. Queues are constant.

Gay & Lesbian Venues

The gay scene is well established in Stockholm, although Sweden's famous open-mindedness means that non-heteros are welcome in almost all bars and clubs, and there is no real 'gay district'. The tourist office publishes a brochure listing gay venues, but the best source of local information is the free, monthly newspaper *QX* (see p1157).

There are popular gay restaurant-bars on Gamla Stan, including **Mandus** (Map pp1138-9; ☎ 206055; Österlånggatan 7) and **Torget** (Map pp1138-9; ☎ 205560; Mälartorget 13), while **Chokladkoppen** (☎ 203170; Stortorget 18) is a cheery café-bar staffed by pretty young things.

Lady Patricia (☎ 743 0570; www.ladypatricia.se; Stadsgårdskajen 152) is a fabulous nightclub on board a ship with a unique history. It's moored near Slussen and is known for its gay nights (complete with drag shows) that draw partiers of all persuasions every Sunday.

ENTERTAINMENT
Concerts & Theatre
Stockholm is a theatre city, with outstanding dance, opera and music performances; for an overview, pick up the free *Teater Guide* from tourist offices. For tickets, contact the tourist office, theatre box offices or **Biljett Direkt** (☎ 0771-707070; www.ticnet.se). Operas are usually performed in their original language; theatre performances are invariably in Swedish. Major theatres include:

Konserthuset (Map pp1138-9; ☎ 5066 7788; www.konser thuset.se; Hötorget) Features classical concerts and other musical events, including the Royal Philharmonic Orchestra.

Kungliga Dramatiska Teatern (Map pp1138-9; ☎ 667 0680; www.dramaten.se; Nybroplan) The Royal Theatre (aka Dramaten) stages a range of plays in a fantastic Art Nouveau environment.

Kungliga Operan (Map pp1138-9; ☎ 248240; www .operan.se; Gustav Adolfs Torg) The place to go for opera and classical ballet.

Live Music
Live jazz is popular in the capital and the **Stockholm Jazz Festival** (www.stockholmjazz.com) is held annually in mid-July. The intimate **Glenn Miller Café** (Map pp1138-9; ☎ 100322; Brunns gatan 21) has live jazz shows several nights a week, and the larger **Jazzclub Fasching** (Map pp1138-9; ☎ 5348 2960; www.fasching.se; Kungsgatan 63) is one of Stockholm's main jazz venues, attracting acts from around the world.

In Gamla Stan, **Stampen** (Map pp1138-9; ☎ 205793; Stora Nygatan 5) provides live blues and jazz performances. **Mosebacke Etablisse ment** (Map pp1138-9; ☎ 5560 9890; www.mosebacke. se; Mosebacketorg 3), located in Södermalm, is a cool bar, nightclub and concert venue, which features a broad assortment of music and performers.

GETTING THERE & AWAY
Air
Stockholm's main airport, **Arlanda** (☎ 797 6000), is 45km north of the city centre. **Bromma airport** (☎ 797 6874), 8km west of Stockholm, is a minor airport used for some domestic flights. Two airports are used by some low-cost carriers and sometimes labelled as 'Stockholm', despite being a fair distance from the capital: **Skavsta airport** (☎ 0155-280400) is 100km south of Stockholm, near Nyköping, and **Västerås airport** (☎ 021-805600) is near the town of Västerås, about 105km northwest of Stockholm. Transport connects all airports to Stockholm (see p1142).

Land
BUS
Cityterminalen (⏱ 3.30am-midnight) is above and next door to Centralstationen (follow the signs inside the main station hall, or use the street entrance on Klarabergsviadukten). From Cityterminalen there are long-distance buses to most major towns in Sweden (see p1130) as well as international destinations (see p1129), airport buses and buses to ferry ports. Cityterminalen has good facilities, including ATMs, foreign exchange, cafés, lockers and Internet access.

TRAIN
Stockholm is the centre for SJ's national services (see p1128). Direct trains to/from Copenhagen, Oslo, Storlien (for Trondheim) and Narvik arrive and depart from Centralstationen (Stockholm C), as do the SL *pendeltåg* (commuter) services that operate within Stockholm county.

The central hall at **Centralstationen** (⏱ 5am-12.30am) has restaurants, shops, lockers, ATMs, Internet access, public toilets as well as showers. Rail ticket offices are open:
Domestic (⏱ 7.30am-8pm Mon-Fri, 8.30am-6pm Sat, 9.30am-7pm Sun)
International (⏱ 10am-6pm Mon-Fri)

Sea
See p1128 for details of ferry connections from Stockholm to Finland (Helsinki and Turku), Estonia (Tallinn) and Latvia (Riga).

Frihamnen is the arrival and departure point for both **Tallink** (☎ 666 6001; www.tallink .ee; Klarabergsgatan 31) ferries to/from Tallinn, and **Riga Sea Line** (☎ 510 015 00; www.rigasealine.lv;

SWEDEN

Frihamnen) services to/from Riga. To get to Frihamnen, take a bus from Cityterminalen operated by the ferry company, or town bus No 1, 72 or 76.

Silja Line (☎ 222140; www.silja.com; Kungsgatan 2) ferries depart for Helsinki and Turku from Värtahamnen – take the connecting bus, walk from T-Gärdet or take local bus No 76 from T-Ropsten.

Viking Line (☎ 452 4000; www.vikingline.fi; inside Cityterminalen) ferries sail to Turku and Helsinki from the terminal in northeast Södermalm. Take the connecting bus (Skr30) from Cityterminalen, or walk 1.5km east of T-Slussen.

GETTING AROUND
To/From the Airports
The **Arlanda Express** (☎ 020-222224) train travels between Arlanda and Centralstationen (Skr180, 22 minutes) at regular intervals from around 5am to midnight. A cheaper option is the **Flygbussarna** (☎ 600 1000; www.flygbussarna.se) bus service to/from Cityterminalen (Skr89, 40 minutes).

There are also Flygbussarna services from Cityterminalen to Bromma airport (Skr69, 15 to 20 minutes), Skavsta airport (Skr130, 80 minutes), and Västerås airport (Skr130, 75 minutes).

Bicycle
Stockholm has an extensive network of bicycle paths, and top day trips include Djurgården; a loop going from Gamla Stan to Södermalm, Långholmen and Kungsholmen (on lakeside paths); and Drottningholm.

Djurgårdsbrons Sjöcafé (☎ 660 5757; Djurgårdsbron; Skr65/250 per hour/day), by the bridge to Djurgården, rents bikes and has options for longer rentals.

Boat
Djurgårdsfärjan city ferries link Djurgården with Nybroplan and Slussen; ferries cost from Skr25 and run every 20 minutes in summer (less often in the low season).

Public Transport
Storstockholms Lokaltrafik (SL; ☎ 600 1000; www.sl.se) runs all *tunnelbana* (T or T-bana) metro trains, local trains and buses within Stockholm county. At T-Centralen there are SL information offices in the lower level of the station hall (🕑 6.30am-11.15pm Mon-Sat, 7am-11.15pm Sun) and at the Sergels Torg entrance

(🕑 7am-6.30pm Mon-Fri, 10am-5pm Sat & Sun). Both offices issue timetables plus sell SL transport passes and the Stockholm Card.

The Stockholm Card (see p1132) covers travel in greater Stockholm, as well as entry to many attractions. A cheaper alternative is the SL Public Transport Pass (Skr95/180 24/72 hours), covering transport only.

On Stockholm's public transport system the lowest fare costs two coupons, and each extra zone costs another coupon. Coupons are available individually for Skr15; it's best to buy a 10/20-coupon discount ticket for Skr80/145. Coupons are valid for an hour and must be stamped at the ride's start. International rail passes aren't valid on SL trains.

BUS
Check where the regional bus hub is for different outlying areas. Buses to Vaxholm (No 670) and the Åland ferries (bus No 640 to Norrtälje then No 637 to Grisslehamn or No 631 to Kapellskär) depart from T-Tekniska Högskolan.

METRO
The most useful mode of transport in Stockholm is the *tunnelbana*, which has three lines and converges on T-Centralen (connected by an underground walkway to Centralstationen).

Taxi
There's usually no problem finding a taxi in Stockholm; costs are about Skr35 flagfall, then Skr8 to Skr9 per kilometre (more costly on Friday and Saturday nights). A trip within the city shouldn't be more than Skr200. Reputable firms include the following:
Taxi Kurir (☎ 300000)
Taxi Stockholm (☎ 150000)
Taxi 020 (☎ 020-939393)

AROUND STOCKHOLM

As gorgeous as the capital is, some of Sweden's loveliest areas are just outside of it and can easily be reached on a day trip or overnight excursion.

STOCKHOLM ARCHIPELAGO
☎ 08
The Stockholm archipelago and its 24,000 islands is the favourite time-off destination

for locals. The website www.stockholm town.com has a large section devoted to the archipelago, and www.skargardsstiftelsen.se is another great resource.

The main boat operator to the archipelago is **Waxholmsbolaget** (☎ 679 5830; www.waxholms bolaget.se); timetables are located at offices outside the Grand Hôtel on Strömkajen in Stockholm, and at the harbour in Vaxholm. Its Båtluffarkortet (Skr490) is a pass valid for 16-day unlimited rides plus an island map. Bikes can be taken on the ferries for a fee, but it's best to hire them on arrival.

It's also worth checking what **Cinderella Båtarna** (☎ 5871 4000; www.cinderellabatarna.com) has to offer. Its boats go to many of the most interesting islands from Stockholm.

Each island has its character, and while many can be visited on a day trip, staying overnight is a recommended experience.

Chi-chi **Sandhamn** on Sandön is popular with sailors and day-trippers; accommodation here is expensive, so this island is best as a day trip.

Finnhamn has excellent swimming spots; book in advance to stay at the **STF hostel** (☎ 5424 6212; www.finnhamn.se; dm/s/d Skr275/410/550; ☺ year-round), the largest hostel in the archipelago with 80 beds.

Utö, far out in the southern archipelago, is popular among cyclists; here there's an **STF hostel** (☎ 5042 0315; www.uto-vardshus.se; dm/s/d Skr325/325/650; ☺ May-Sep), with its reception at the nearby **Utö Värdshus**, ranked among the best restaurants in the archipelago.

UPPSALA
☎ 018 / pop 191,100
Uppsala, about 70km from Stockholm, is the fourth-largest city in Sweden, and one of its oldest. It's a good excursion from the capital and has decent budget accommodation. You can soak up the history and academic genteel air, or party with the city's 40,000 students.

Gamla (Old) Uppsala flourished as early as the 6th century. The cathedral was consecrated in 1435 after 175 years of construction and the castle was first built in the 1540s, although today's edifice belongs to the 18th century. The city's university was founded in 1477 and is Scandinavia's oldest.

Information
The **tourist office** (☎ 727 4800; www.uppsalatourism.se; Fyristorg 8; ☺ 10am-6pm Mon-Fri, 10am-3pm Sat year-round;

also noon-4pm Sun late Jun–mid-Aug) is close to the cathedral.

The **public library** (cnr St Olofsgatan & Svartbäcksgatan; ☺ Mon-Sat) has free Internet access, but expect long waits. Other options include **Sidewalk Express** (St Persgatan & Dragarbrunnsgatan; per hr Skr19) inside McDonald's (purchase voucher from vending machine). Sidewalk Express also has Internet access inside Uppsala Centralstation.

Sights & Activities
Uppsala began at the three great grave mounds at **Gamla Uppsala** (free; ☺ 24hr), 4km north of the modern city and well signposted (bus No 2 from Stora Torget). The mounds are said to be the graves of pre-Viking kings and lie in a cemetery with about 300 smaller mounds and a great heathen temple. The modern **Gamla Uppsala Historical Centre** (☎ 239300; www .raa.se/olduppsala; adult Skr50; ☺ 11am-5pm daily May-Aug, noon-3pm Sun Sep-Apr) has museum-style exhibits of ancient artefacts excavated from Gamla Uppsala and the nearby archaeological sites, and has guided tours of Gamla Uppsala from May to August (included in the entry fee).

Originally constructed by Gustav Vasa in the mid-16th century, **Uppsala Slott** (Castle; ☎ 727 2485; adult Skr60; ☺ tours 1pm & 3pm Jun-Aug) features the state hall where kings were enthroned and a queen abdicated. It's open by guided tour only. The tour price includes entry to **Uppsala Konstmuseum** (Art Museum; ☎ 727 0000; adult Skr30; ☺ Tues-Sun), housed in the southern wing of the castle.

The Gothic **Domkyrka** (Cathedral; free; Domkyrkoplan; ☺ 8am-6pm) dominates the city, just as some of those buried here dominated their country, including St Erik, Gustav Vasa, Johan III and Carl von Linné. Inside, visit the **treasury** (☎ 187201; adult Skr30; ☺ daily May-Sep, Tue-Sun Oct-Apr) in the north tower.

Gustavianum Museum (☎ 471 7571; Akademigatan 3; adult Skr40; ☺ Tues-Sun), the university museum, has an excellent antiquities collection. **Uppland Museum** (☎ 169100; Sankt Eriks Torg; adult Skr30; ☺ Tues-Sun), in an 18th-century mill, houses county collections from the Middle Ages.

Carolina Rediviva (☎ 471 3900; Dag Hammarskjöldsväg 1; adult Skr20; ☺ daily mid-May–mid-Sep, Mon-Sat rest of year) is the old university library and has a display hall with maps and historical and scientific literature, the pride of which is the surviving half of the 6th-century *Codex Argentus* (Silver Bible).

The lovely **Botanic Gardens** (free; ☼ 7am-9pm May-Aug, 7am-7pm Sep-Apr) are below the castle hill.

Sleeping
STF Vandrarhem Sunnersta Herrgård (☎ 324220; Sunnerstavägen 24; dm/s/d Skr235/385/470) An old manor house 6km south of the centre in a beautiful setting. Bike rental is available. Take bus No 20 or 50.

Hotel Uppsala (☎ 480 5000; www.profilhotels.se; Kungsgatan 27; hostel dm/s/d Skr235/415/590, hotel s/d from Skr1050/1275, both discounted to Skr700 at the weekend and in summer) A huge hotel offering rooms for all budgets. It has a good hostel section (affiliated with STF), plus modern hotel rooms, with some cooking facilities.

Fyrishov Camping (☎ 727 4960; www.fyrishov.se; Idrottsgatan 2; camping Skr115-130, 4-bed cabins from Skr450) Well equipped, pro-family ground 2km north of the city. Take bus No 4, 6, 25 or 50.

Eating & Drinking
There are several eateries on and around the pedestrian mall and Stora Torget, and around the cathedral. Try Sysslomangatan for more good choices.

The **Hemköp supermarket** (Stora Torget; ☼ until 10pm) is in Åhlens's basement. The great indoor market, **Saluhallen** (Sankt Eriks Torg; ☼ Mon-Sat), is between the cathedral and the river.

Saffet's (☎ 124125; Stora Torget 1; meals Skr59) When it comes to quick sustenance and cheap food, Saffet's has the works – burgers, enchiladas, baked potatoes, fish and chips, and kebabs.

O'Connor's (☎ 144010; Stora Torget 1; mains Skr59-180) Upstairs from Saffet's, O'Connor's is the quinessential Irish pub – crowded, lively, friendly, and well stocked with Guinness. There's live music most nights.

Uppsala has excellent cafés keeping students well supplied with caffeine. **Ofvandahls** (☎ 132404; Sysslomansgatan 3-5) is a classy konditori full of old-world charm; in contrast is stylish and modern **Wayne's Coffee** (☎ 710012; Smedsgränd 4).

Getting There & Away
The bus station is outside the train station, on Kungsgatan. Bus No 801 departs at least twice an hour for nearby Arlanda airport (Skr80). Swebus Express runs regularly to Stockholm (Skr55), as do SJ trains (Skr47 to Skr62).

A local bus ticket costs from Skr20 and gives unlimited two-hour travel – enough for a visit to Gamla Uppsala. Take a city bus from Stora Torget or on Dragarbrunnsgatan.

SOUTHERN SWEDEN

MALMÖ
☎ 040 / pop 265,000
Malmö is a vibrant place, perhaps due to the influence of Copenhagen across the Öresund; the relatively large immigrant population adds a multicultural feel. The amazing 16km Öresund bridge and tunnel link, which includes Europe's longest bridge (7.8km), has made Copenhagen and Malmö even closer.

Information
Cyberspace Café (Engelbrektsgatan 13; per hr Skr30-44; ☼ daily) Internet café open until late; cheaper rates after 6pm.
Dot.Spot (Kalendegatan 13; per hr Skr25; ☼ noon-6am) Central Internet café.
Forex (inside Centralstationen; ☼ 7am-9pm) One of a handful of Forex branches in Malmö; all offer currency exchange.
Malmö Card (Skr130/160/190 for one/two/three days) Allows free bus transport, free entry to several museums and discounts at other attractions; available from the tourist office.
Post office (Skeppsbron 1; 7am-7pm Mon-Fri) Near the train station.
Tourist office (☎ 341200; www.malmo.se; Centralstationen; ☼ 9am-7pm Mon-Fri, 10am-5pm Sat & Sun Jun-Aug; 9am-6pm Mon-Fri, 10am-3pm Sat & Sun May & Sep; 9am-5pm Mon-Fri, 10am-2pm Sat Oct-Apr) Inside the train station. Pick up the useful, free booklet Malmö This Month.

Sights & Activities
The cobblestone streets and appealing buildings around **Lilla Torg** are restored parts of the late-medieval town. The houses are now galleries, boutiques and restaurants.

The main museums of Malmö are based in and around **Malmöhus** (☎ 344437; Malmöhusvägen; adult Skr40; ☼ 10am-4pm Jun-Aug, noon-4pm Sep-May). You can walk through the royal apartments, and see the **Stadsmuseum** with its Malmö collection, and the art of **Konstmuseum**. Especially interesting are the **aquarium** and the **Naturmuseum**.

Ribersborg is a long sandy beach backed by parkland about 2km west of the town centre. Out in Öresund, reached by a 200m-long pier, is the naturist **Ribersborgs Kallbadhus** (☎ 260366; admission Skr45; ☼ daily), dating from 1898. There's a cold, open-air saltwater pool and wood-fired sauna, and separate sections for men and women. Take bus No 20 or 22.

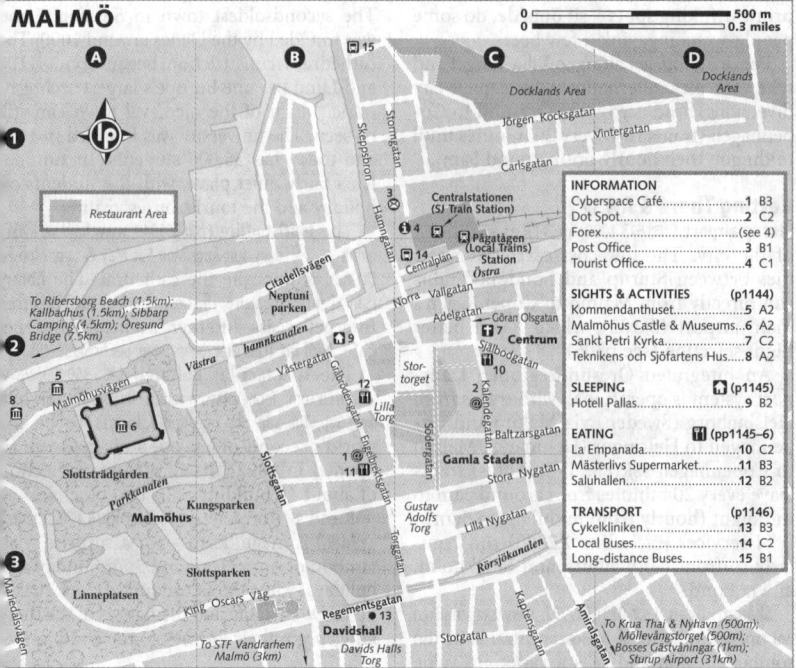

MALMÖ

INFORMATION
Cyberspace Café.........................1 B3
Dot Spot..................................2 C2
Forex......................................(see 4)
Post Office...............................3 B1
Tourist Office...........................4 C1

SIGHTS & ACTIVITIES   (p1144)
Kommendanthuset.......................5 A2
Malmöhus Castle & Museums...6 A2
Sankt Petri Kyrka......................7 C2
Teknikens och Sjöfartens Hus....8 A2

SLEEPING   (p1145)
Hotell Pallas..............................9 B2

EATING   (pp1145–6)
La Empanada...........................10 C2
Mästerlivs Supermarket...........11 B3
Saluhallen..............................12 B2

TRANSPORT   (p1146)
Cykelkliniken...........................13 B3
Local Buses............................14 C2
Long-distance Buses...............15 B1

Sleeping

STF Vandrarhem Malmö (☎ 82220; www.malmo
ostel.com; Backavägen 18; dm/s/d from Skr175/315/410)
Well hidden, about 3.5km south of the city
entre (get a map before setting off), but
worth seeking out, as it's big, bright, clean
and well equipped. Catch bus No 21 from
n front of Centralstationen.

Bosses Gästvåningar (☎ 326250; www.bosses
se; Södra Förstadsgatan 110B; s/d/tr Skr295/495/495) A
pleasant guesthouse in a regular apartment
block, close to the cheap eateries on Möl-
evångstorget. Shared bathrooms and guest
kitchens.

Hotel Pallas (☎ 611 5077; home.swipnet.se/Hotell
Pallas/; Norra Vallgatan 74; s Skr395, d Skr455-535) An
affordable budget hotel close to the train
tation, with shared bathrooms and break-
ast for Skr30. Opt for a 'large' double room,
s these are huge.

Sibbarp Camping (☎ 155165; Strandgatan 101;
amping Skr150-190, cabins from Skr280) By the beach
about 5km southwest of the town centre,
with a great view of the Öresund bridge. It's
a large, well-equipped ground with cabins.
Catch bus No 12B or 12G.

Eating & Drinking

Lilla Torget is a picturesque cobblestone
square lined with restaurant-bars and often
teeming with people. The area around Möllevångstorget reflects the city's interesting
ethnic mix, and there's cheap food here from
a mix of stalls, grocers, restaurants and bars.

Buy your groceries at central **Mästerlivs supermarket** (Engelbrektsgatan; ⏲ 7am-9pm). The best
produce market is on Möllevångstorget.

Saluhallen (Lilla Torg; ⏲ Mon-Sat) One of the
best lunchtime pit stops, with an excellent
range of food stalls offering something to
appeal to every taste, including pasta, sushi,
kebabs and Vietnamese.

La Empanada (☎ 120262; Själbodgatan 10; dishes
Skr29-59; ⏲ 11am-9pm Mon-Sat) Recommended
cheap and cheerful cafeteria, with a huge
menu of mainly Mexican dishes, plus pasta,
and even Swedish meatballs.

Krua Thai (☎ 122287; Möllevångstorget 14; lunch
Skr55, mains Skr75-95) Long-standing Thai eatery
with cheap, popular meals (curries, soups
and noodle dishes) to eat in or take away.

Nyhavn (☎ 128830; Möllevångstorget; mains Skr55-
109) This has to be one of Möllevångstorget's

prime drinking spots – sit outside, do some people-watching, sink a few beers.

For drinking, get along to Lilla Torget and take your pick; alternatively, for capital-city diversions, head across the Öresund to Copenhagen (trains run every 20 minutes until midnight, then hourly until around 5am).

Getting There & Away

Sturup airport (☎ 613 1000) is 31km southeast of the city. The low-cost carrier Ryanair flies between Sturup and London. Trains run directly from Malmö to Copenhagen's main airport (Skr85), which has a better flight selection (see p306).

An integrated Öresundregionen transport system is operational, with trains from Helsingborg (Sweden) via Malmö and Copenhagen to Helsingør (Denmark). Malmö to Copenhagen (Skr85, 35 minutes) trains leave every 20 minutes from around 5am to midnight (hourly from midnight to 5am).

SJ services (including X2000) run regularly to/from Gothenburg and Stockholm, all via Lund.

Skånetrafiken (☎ 0771-777777; www.skanetrafiken .se) operates the local buses and trains in the southern region and sells a variety of value cards and passes. Local (purple) trains run to Helsingborg (Skr84), Lund (Skr36), Ystad (Skr72) and other nearby destinations. The platform is at the eastern end of Centralstationen; you buy tickets from a machine. International rail passes are accepted.

Long-distance buses depart from a terminal at the end of Skeppsbron, about 500m north of the train station. Swebus Express runs daily to Stockholm, Gothenburg and Oslo. Trains are best for trips across the Öresund bridge.

Getting Around

Malmö Lokaltrafik information kiosks are at main bus hubs, including Centralplan and Gustav Adolfs Torg. Local buses are green (regional buses are yellow); tickets cost Skr15 for one hour's travel. Bicycles can be rented from **Cykelkliniken** (☎ 611 6666; Regementsgatan 12; Skr120/600 per day/week).

LUND

☎ 046 / pop 99,600

As in Uppsala, visitors to Lund can soak up an historic academic atmosphere or hang-out in cafés catering to thousands of students.

The second-oldest town in Sweden, Lund was founded by the Danes around 1000. The cathedral's construction began about 1100 and Lund became Europe's largest archbishopric. Much of the medieval town can still be seen. The university was founded in 1666 and today has 35,000 students. In summer it's a fairly quiet place, with the students on holiday and the tourist buses visiting.

The **tourist office** (☎ 355040; www.lund.se; Kyrkogatan 11; ☺ daily Jun-Aug; Mon-Sat May & Sep; Mon-Fri Oct-Apr) is opposite the cathedral. The **library** (Sankt Petri Kyrkogatan 6; ☺ closed Sun May-Aug) has free Internet access, and there's a nearby Internet café, **Noll Ett** (Lilla Gråbrödersgatan; per hr Skr39-49).

The spectacular **Kulturen** (☎ 350400; www .kulturen.com; Tegnerplatsen; adult Skr50; ☺ daily mid Apr–Sep, Tue-Sun Oct–mid-Apr) claims to be the world's second-oldest open-air museum (it opened in 1892). Its impressive collection of about 40 buildings fills two blocks.

Lund's Romanesque **Domkyrka** (Cathedral; ☺ daily) is magnificent – for a surprise, visit at noon or 3pm (1pm and 3pm Sunday and holidays) when the astronomical clock strikes up *In Dulci Jubilo* and the figures of the three kings begin their journey to the child Jesus.

Sleeping & Eating

STF Vandrarhem Tåget (☎ 142820; www.trainhostel .com; dm Skr175) Take the overpass from the bus station to access this unusual hostel. Guests sleep in railway carriages set in parkland with three bunks to a room.

Private rooms can be booked at the tourist office from around Skr250 per person plus a Skr50 fee.

Saluhallen (Mårtenstorget; ☺ Mon-Sat) A good place for reasonably priced food, from pasta to Thai dishes and kebabs.

Ebbas Skafferi (☎ 134156; Bytaregatan 5; meals Skr38-55) This courtyard café, with a great lunchtime selection, is one of the most appealing places in town. A breakfast buffet is also available (Skr50).

There's an **ICA supermarket** (Bangatan; ☺ 8am-10pm) opposite the train station.

Getting There & Away

There are frequent SJ and local train departures from Lund to Malmö (Skr36, 15 minutes); some trains continue to Copenhagen (Skr110). All long-distance trains between Stockholm and Malmö stop in Lund. Buses leave from outside the train station.

HELSINGBORG

☎ 042 / pop 84,500

The busy port of Helsingborg is perched on the Öresund coastline, with Denmark only 20 minutes away by ferry. Too many travellers leave town without seeing any more than the train station, but it's an appealing place with seaside character, quality budget accommodation and great parkland.

The **tourist office** (☎ 104350; www.helsingborgsguiden.com; Stortorget; ⊙ daily May-Aug, Mon-Sat Sep-Apr) can help with inquiries. **First Stop Sweden** (☎ 104130; Bredgatan 2; ⊙ daily Jun-Aug, Mon-Fri Sep-May), near the car-ferry ticket booths, gives advice for new arrivals from Denmark.

Most other travel-related needs are met inside the vast Knutpunkten complex at the seafront, including ATMs and **Forex** (⊙ 7am-9pm; 1st level) for currency exchange.

The eye-catchingly modern **Dunkers Kulturhus** (☎ 107400; www.dunkerskulturhus.com; Kungsgatan 11; admission free; ⊙ 10am-5pm Tue-Sun), just north of the transport terminals, houses the **town museum** and **art museum** (combined entry adult Skr70), plus a concert hall, restaurant and café. Take a stroll along the northern waterfront from here to admire the sleek apartment buildings and restaurants, all part of a successful harbour redevelopment project.

You can access the square medieval tower **Kärnan** (☎ 105991; adult Skr20; ⊙ daily Jun-Aug, Tue-Sun Sep-May) from steps near the tourist office. The tower is all that remains of a 14th-century castle; the view from the top (34m) overlooks Öresund to the Danish heartland.

North of town, the **Pålsjö area** houses a fine park, a 16th-century castle (closed to the public) and a nature reserve.

Sleeping & Eating

Villa Thalassa (☎ 380660; www.villathalassa.com; Dag Hammarskjöldsväg; dm Skr170, d Skr400-480) This recommended hostel, 3km north of the city centre, is 500m from the bus stop at Pålsjöbaden. The villa and gardens are a delight; there are three sleeping options in modern annexes and wooden huts. Take bus No 219.

Helsingborgs Vandrarhem (☎ 145850; www.hbgturist.com; Järnvägsgatan 39; dm/s/d Skr165/245/370) A central hostel, inside a nondescript building, about 200m from Knutpunkten. It has high-quality rooms and good facilities.

Fahlmans Café (☎ 213060; Stortorget 11) is the most traditional of the town's cafés; in contrast is fashionable **Wayne's Coffee** (☎ 149696;

Stortorget), opposite, serving the usual modern café fare (bagels, salads, muffins). Unique **Ebbas Fik** (☎ 281440; Bruksgatan 20; ⊙ Mon-Sat) is styled in 1950s retro with superb results.

Self-caterers should head to the **ICA supermarket** (Drottninggatan 48; ⊙ daily).

Getting There & Away

The main transport centre is Knutpunkten; the underground platforms serve SJ trains bound for Stockholm, Gothenburg, Copenhagen and Oslo, plus regional trains. At ground level and a little south, but still inside the same complex, is the bus terminal. Daily long-distance services run to destinations including Gothenburg and Oslo.

Knutpunkten is the terminal for frequent ferries across to Helsingborg in Denmark, and there are regular ferries to/from Oslo; see p1128.

GOTHENBURG (GÖTEBORG)

☎ 031 / pop 475,000

There's a lot more to Gothenburg than the showpiece Kungsportsavenyn boulevard and myriad of museums, plus its industrial and architectural heritage and lovely gardens. The Liseberg fun park is Scandinavia's largest amusement park, with about 3.2 million annual visitors. Gothenburg (the Swedish name, Göteborg, sounds like 'yoo-te-bor') is Sweden's second-largest city and has a more continental outlook than Stockholm.

From the centre of the city, Kungsportsavenyn crosses the canal and heads for Götaplatsen. 'Avenyn' is the city's heart with boutiques, restaurants, theatres and cafés.

Information

DISCOUNT CARDS

Göteborg Pass (Skr175/295 for 24/48 hours) Gives free entry to Liseberg and some city attractions, city tours and public transport. Collect it at tourist offices, hotels and hostels.

EMERGENCY

Police station (☎ 739 2000; Ernst Fontells Plats) Off Skånegatan, near Nya Ullevi stadium.

INTERNET ACCESS

IT-Grottan (Chalmersgatan 27; per hr Skr38-43; ⊙ daily until midnight) Cheaper hourly rate before 6pm.

Sidewalk Express (www.sidewalkexpress.se; per hr Skr19) A chain of Internet kiosks at central locations (Centralstationen, Landvetter airport, inside the 7-Eleven store at Vasaplatsen); vouchers are purchased from vending machines.

SWEDEN

GOTHENBURG (GÖTEBORG)

SWEDEN

To Östra
Sjukhuset
Hospital (4km)

To Marstrand
(50km)

To Gothenburg City
Airport (10km)

To Lisebergs
Camping (4km);
Slottsskogen Karralund (4km);
Landvetter Airport (25km)

To Liseberg

To Botanic
Gardens (600m)

Fabriksgatan
Åvägen
Vallhallagatan
Örgrytevägen
Södra Vägen
Skånegatan
Tampegatan
Ugnsgatan
Skänegatan
Ullevigatan
Sten Sturegatan
Heden
Korsvägen
Götaplatsen
Kristinelundsgatan
Parkgatan
Ny Alléy
Kungsportsavenyn
Södra
Chalmersgatan
Götabergsgatan
Vasagatan
Engelbrektsgatan
Viktoriagatan
Gibraltargatan
Södra Allégatan
Rosenlundsgatan
Hagakyrkan
Haga
Skansen
Kronan
Linnégatan
Skanstorget
Vegagatan
Slottsskogsparken
August Kobbs gatan
Bangatan
Masthuggskyrkan
Oscar Fredriks
Kyrka
Masthuggstorget
Andréegatan
Stigbergslidet
Masthamnsgatan
Oscarsleden
Klippan
Eriksberg
Ostindiefararen

Central Train
Station
Nils
Ericsson
Platsen
Drottningtorget
Frälsnings-
foreningen
Nordstan
Complex
Kronhusgatan
Kanaltorgsgatan
Ubiken Tower
Lilla
Bommen
Götaalvbron
Götaleden
Torggatan
Skeppsbron
Älv-Snabben
Lundby Strand
Rosenlund
Lindholm
Göta älv
Lundby Hamngata
Hisingen

Hamngatan
Drottninggatan
Kyrkog
Västra Hamngatan
Magasinsgatan
Södra Hamngatan
Vallgatan S
Domkyrkan

See Enlargement

0   0.5 miles
0   1 km

500 m
0.3 miles

INFORMATION		Göteborgs Vandrarhem	..................14 F4	DRINKING	(p1140)
Apoteket Vasan	...........................(see 1)	Hotel Flora	..............................15 A2	O'Leary's	...................................28 B1
Branch Tourist Office	................(see 1)	Masthuggsterrassens Vandrarhem	...16 C3	Ölhallen 7:an	..............................29 B2
Forex	....1 E2	STF Vandrarhem		The Dubliner	...............................30 B1
Forex	....2 E3	Slottsskogen	...........................17 C4		
IT-Grottan	................................3 E3	STF Vandrarhem		ENTERTAINMENT	(pp1140–1)
Main Tourist Office	....................4 B2	Stigbergsliden	........................18 B3	Avenyn 10	...................................31 E3
Police Station	...........................5 F2			Bubbles	....32 E3
Post Office	............................(see 1)	EATING	(pp1137–40)	Göteborgs Konserthus	...............33 E3
Sidewalk Express	......................6 E3	Aldardo	....19 B2	Göteborgs Stadsteatern	............34 F3
		Alexandras	..............................(see 26)	GöteborgsOperan	.......................35 D1
SIGHTS & ACTIVITIES	(pp1133–6)	Café Publik	..............................20 E3	Nya Ullevi	..................................36 F2
Göteborgs Maritima Centrum	.....7 D2	Chopsticks	..............................(see 24)	Scandinavium	............................37 F3
Konstmuseet	.............................8 F3	Crepe Van	.................................21 D4	Valand	....38 E3
Liseberg Main Entrance	..............9 F3	Cyrano	....22 C3		
Röhsska Museet	......................10 E3	Den Lilla Taverna	....................23 C4	TRANSPORT	(pp1141–2)
Stadsmuseum	..........................11 A1	Espresso House	........................24 D3	Cykelkungen Bike Rental	...........39 E3
Universeum	.............................12 F4	Eva's Paley	...............................25 E3	Nils Ericsson Bus Terminal	........40 E1
		Hemköp supermarket	...............(see 1)	SeaCat Terminal	.........................41 B3
SLEEPING	(pp1136–7)	Saluhallen	.................................26 B2	Stena Line Denmark Terminal	.....42 C3
City Hotel	...............................13 E3	Smaka	....27 E3	Stena Line Germany Terminal	.....43 A4

MEDICAL SERVICES

Apoteket Vasan (☎ 802 0532; Nordstan complex; 🕑 8am-10pm)

Östra Sjukhuset (☎ 343 4000) Large hospital near tram terminus No 1, northeast of town.

MONEY

Banks with ATMs can be found all over town, including inside the Nordstan complex and train station. Forex has branches throughout Gothenburg, including inside Centralstationen.

TOURIST INFORMATION

Tourist offices (☎ 612500; www.goteborg.com) Kungsportsplatsen 2 (Main tourist office; 🕑 9am-6pm daily Jun-Aug; 9am-5pm Mon-Fri, 10am-2pm Sat Sep-May); Nordstan (🕑 10am-6pm Mon-Fri, 10am-4pm Sat, noon-3pm Sun)

Sights

Liseberg (☎ 400100; www.liseberg.se; tram No 5; admission Skr50; 🕑 late Apr-early Oct) fun park is dominated by its spaceport-like tower. The ride to the top, some 83m above the ground, climaxes in a spinning dance and a breathtaking view of the city. You can buy a pass for Skr255 that allows you to ride the attractions all day. Opening hours are complex – call ahead or check the website.

By Liseberg is the striking **Universeum** (☎ 335 6450; www.universeum.se; Södra Vägen; admission Skr110-135; 🕑 Tues-Sun mid-Aug–Apr, daily May–mid-Aug), a huge and impressive 'science discovery centre' featuring everything from rainforests to a shark tank. It has great displays and hands-on experiments, but it's not cheap to visit (use the Göteborg Pass).

The **Stadsmuseum** (☎ 612770; Norra Hamngata 12; adult Skr40; 🕑 daily May-Aug, Tue-Sun Sep-Apr)

has archaeological, local and historical collections, including Sweden's only original Viking ship.

The main art collections are at **Konstmuseet** (☎ 611000; Götaplatsen; adult Skr40; 🕑 Tues-Sun), with impressive collections of Nordic and European masters (notable for works by Rubens, Van Gogh, Rembrandt and Picasso).

The excellent **Röhsska Museet** (☎ 613850; Vasagatan 37; adult Skr40; 🕑 noon-5pm Tue-Sun) covers modern Scandinavian design and decorative arts.

Göteborgs Maritima Centrum (☎ 105950; Packhuskajen; adult Skr70; 🕑 daily Mar-Oct), by the opera house north of the centre, claims to be the largest floating ship museum in the world and usually displays 13 historical ships, including the submarine *Nordkaparen*.

There are some great green oases, including **Trädgårdsföreningen** (entry on Nya Allén; adult Skr15 May-Aug, otherwise free; 🕑 daily), laid out in 1842 and home to pretty cafés, a rosarium and palm house. In Gothenburg's southwest is **Slottsskogsparken**, the 'lungs' of the city, and the **Botanic Gardens** – the largest in Sweden.

Sleeping

Gothenburg offers several exceptional hostels; most are clustered in the central southwest area, in apartment buildings that inspire little confidence from the outside. All are open year-round.

STF Vandrarhem Slottsskogen (☎ 426520; www .sov.nu; Vegagatan 21; dm/s/d from Skr155/285/390; 🖳) Regarded as one of Sweden's best hostels, so book early. It's a friendly, social place with facilities such as 24-hour reception, breakfast buffet, bike hire, laundry, sauna and lounge. Take tram No 1 or 2 to Olivedalsgatan.

SWEDEN

Masthuggsterrassens Vandrarhem (☎ 424820; www.mastenvandrarhem.com; Masthuggsterrassen 10H; dm/ s/d Skr160/290/400) A clean, well-run spot near the ferries to/from Denmark. Take tram No 3, 9 or 11 to Masthuggstorget and check the signs (upstairs, behind the supermarket).

STF Vandrarhem Stigbergsliden (☎ 241620; www .hostel-gothenburg.com; Stigbergsliden 10; dm/s/d Skr165/ 295/390) Another welcoming, well-run STF hostel, this time in a renovated 19th-century seaman's house. It has a good kitchen, laundry, TV room and garden, plus bike hire. Take tram No 3, 9 or 11 to Stigbergstorget.

Göteborgs Vandrarhem (☎ 401050; www.gote borgsvandrarhem.se; Mölndalsvägen 23; dm/s/d Skr170/ 400/450) A well-equipped, well-run place, just south of Liseberg, which is convenient for the big attractions. Take tram No 4 to Getebergsäng.

Hotel Flora (☎ 138616; www.hotelflora.se; Grönsak storget 2; s/d with shared bathroom Skr415/575, s/d with private bathroom Skr890/1070, discounted to Skr650/850) Not far from the tourist office and Saluhallen. Flora is a fine, affordable option, with budget and standard rooms plus a stylish ground-level restaurant-café.

City Hotel (☎ 708 4000; www.cityhotelgbg.se; Lorens bergsgatan 6; s/d with shared bathroom from Skr495/595, with private bathroom from Skr795/995) If you want to taste the nightlife, this is for you – it's within stumbling distance of Kungsportsavenyn. Weekend and summer discounts see rates reduced by Skr100 to Skr200.

Lisebergs Camping & Stugbyar Kärralund (☎ 840200; www.liseberg.se; Olbergsgatan; camping Skr100-325) The closest camping ground to town. It's geared for families and has a wide range of cabins, cottages and hostel beds for rent. Prices for all options have a ridiculously complex schedule of rates. Take tram No 5 to Welandergatan.

Eating

Kungsportsavenyn is lined with restaurants, cafés and bars (although prices along here can be higher than in other parts of town). Vasagatan is close to the student heartland and has excellent cafés, Linnégatan (close to most of the hostels) has more good options.

RESTAURANTS & CAFÉS

Cyrano (☎ 143010; Prinsgatan 7; mains Skr65-190) A highly regarded French bistro-style restaurant, where three-course set menus cost from as little as Skr135. There's also a selection of good French á la carte dishes, and simpler pizzas (Skr65 to Skr85).

Smaka (☎ 132247; Vasaplatsen 3; mains Skr89-195; 🕐 nightly) Smaka (meaning 'taste') serves traditional Swedish *husmanskost* (home cooking) including classics such as herring, meatballs, or *gravad lax* (cured salmon).

Den Lilla Taverna (☎ 128805; Olivedalsgatan 17; mezes Skr29-60, mains Skr69-99) A welcoming place with authentic Greek dishes, plus a great array of *mezes* (starters) perfect for sharing.

The cosy **Café Garbo** (☎ 774 1925; Vasagatan 40) and the sleek **Espresso House** (☎ 39750; Vasagatan 22) are two of several places along the leafy Vasagatan boulevard, both offering outdoor seating and good people-watching.

Eva's Paley (☎ 163070; Kungsportsavenyn 39; meals Skr40-60; 🕐 until 11pm) A huge place open until late and serving good-value dishes including panini, baked potatoes, pasta, salads and seriously good muffins – an institution on Avenyn.

QUICK EATS

Aldardo (☎ 132300; Kungstorget 12; snacks Skr25-55; 🕐 Mon-Sat) Right by the tourist office, this busy deli sells authentic Italian fast food – pizza *al taglio* (by the slice) and pasta dishes.

Saluhallen (Kungstorget; 🕐 Mon-Sat) You can buy a huge range of deli foods at this classic old market hall. There are also great budget eateries where a meal costs under Skr40: **Alexandras** is renowned for its Greek soups and stews.

Chopsticks (☎ 133600; Vasagatan 24; meals Skr55-65) A cool little spot, offering quick rice or noodle dishes.

Crepe Van (Linnégatan; crepes Skr20-40 🕐 4-10pm Mon-Thu, 4pm-3.30am Fri & Sat) This takeaway van near McDonald's offers sweet and savoury crepes.

SELF-CATERING

Head to the **Hemköp supermarket** (🕐 8am-10pm daily) in the Nordstan complex, or central **Saluhallen** (Kungstorget; 🕐 Mon-Sat) for fresh-produce stalls and food vans.

Drinking

Swedish licensing laws mean that bars must have a restaurant section – in most cases, it's vice versa. Stroll down Kungsportsavenyn and take your pick.

The **Dubliner** (☎ 139020; Östra Hamngatan 50B) is as authentic an Irish pub as you'll find on the Continent and has live music nightly in summer. Almost opposite is **O'Leary's** (☎ 711 5519; Östra Hamngatan 36), an American-style sports bar with TV screens and bar snacks.

Ölhallen 7:an (☎ 136079; Kungstorget 7) is well worth seeking out. This gem is a well-worn Swedish beerhall that hasn't changed in about 100 years. There's no food, wine or pretension – just beer, and plenty of choices.

Clubbing

Kungsportsavenyn is the place to go for nightlife. Popular nightclubs include **Bubbles** (Kungsportsavenyn 8), downstairs next to Brasserie Lipp; vintage **Valand** (cnr Kungsportsavenyn & Vasagatan), drawing a mixed crowd of partiers; and **Avenyn 10** (Kungsportsavenyn 10-12), one of the biggest clubs in town.

Entertainment

For culture-vultures, facing each other at the end of Avenyn are **Göteborgs Stadsteatern** (City Theatre; ☎ 615050; Götaplatsen), with dramatic performances (usually in Swedish), and **Göteborgs Konserthus** (Concert Hall; ☎ 726 5300; Götaplatsen), home to the local symphony orchestra. It's worth investigating what's on at the striking **GöteborgsOperan** (☎ 131300; Christina Nilssons gata), at Lilla Bommen harbour, which stages ballet, opera and assorted musical performances.

Gothenburghers are avid sports fans. The city has outdoor stadiums such as **Nya Ullevi**, hosting football matches, and the indoor **Scandinavium**, where ice hockey is played in front of enthusiastic crowds.

Getting There & Away

AIR

Landvetter airport (☎ 941000) is 25km east of the city. There are many services to many European cities. **Gothenburg City Airport** (☎ 926060; www.goteborgcityairport.se) is a minor airport 10km northwest of the city, used by Ryanair.

BOAT

Gothenburg is a major entry point for ferries, with several terminals. For more details of ferry services and fares to Denmark, Germany and the UK, see p1128.

Nearest the city centre, the Stena Line Denmark terminal on Masthuggstorget (tram No 3, 9 or 11) has regular departures for Frederikshavn. Faster and more pricey catamarans to Frederikshavn leave from near Sjöfartsmuseet (tram No 3, 9 or 11 to Stigbergstorget).

Further west is the Stena Line terminal for the daily ferry to Kiel (in Germany). Take tram No 3 or 9 to Chapmans Torg.

DFDS Seaways sails twice weekly to Newcastle from Frihamnen on Hisingen (tram No 5, 6 or 10 to Frihamnen, then a 10-minute walk).

BUS

The modern bus station, Nils Ericson Terminalen, is next to the train station. Eurolines and Swebus Express share an office here.

Swebus Express (☎ 0200-218218; www.swebusexpress.se) operates frequent buses to/from most major towns. There are services to/from Stockholm (Skr250/360 discount/full price, six hours, up to 10 daily) and Oslo (Skr160/225 discount/full price, 3½ hours, up to six daily).

Svenska Buss (☎ 0771-676767; www.svenskabuss.se) and **Säfflebussen** (☎ 0771-151515; www.safflebussen.se) also run on the major routes.

There's a **Tidpunkten office** (☎ 0771-414300; ☾ daily) which gives advice and sells tickets for city and regional public transport.

TRAIN

Centralstationen serves SJ and regional trains, with direct trains to Malmö, Copenhagen, Oslo and Stockholm, plus other destinations in the southern half of Sweden. Connex night trains travel to the far north. Direct train services to Stockholm depart approximately hourly.

Getting Around

Buses, trams and ferries make up the city public transport system; there are Tidpunkten information booths inside Nils Ericson Terminalen, on Drottningtorget and at Brunnsparken. An individual transport ticket costs Skr20. Cheaper and easy-to-use 'value cards' cost Skr100 and reduce the cost considerably. A 24-hour *Dagkort* (day pass) for the city area costs Skr50. Holders of the Göteborg Pass travel free.

The easiest way to cover lengthy distances in Gothenburg is by tram. There are 11 lines, all converging near Brunnsparken, one block from the train station. Also convenient and a good way to see the city are the Älvsnabben ferries, which run between Lilla Bommen and Klippan every 30 minutes or so.

Cykelkungen (☎ 184300; Chalmersgatan 19; Skr120/500 per day/week) offers bike rental.

SWEDEN

GOTLAND

☎ 0498 / pop 57,400
Gotland, the largest of the Baltic islands, is the top budget travel destination in Sweden; bicycle travel is the best option, free camping in forests is easy and legal, many attractions are free and there are more than 30 hostels around the island. The island is jam-packed with holidaying Swedes in July and August, and is *the* summer party spot for young Swedes, who come not for the history but for beaches and booze.

Gotland is also one of the most historical regions in Sweden – there are more than 100 medieval churches and numerous prehistoric sites. Other attractions include the beautiful walled, medieval trading town of Visby, on Unesco's World Heritage List. You could easily pass a week here seeing the highlights and/or relaxing on a beach.

Getting There & Away

Destination Gotland (☎ 0771-223300; www.destination gotland.se) operates car ferries year-round between Visby and both Nynäshamn and Oskarshamn. Departures from Nynäshamn are from two to six times daily (five hours, or three by high-speed catamaran). From Oskarshamn there are one or two daily departures (three hours).

Regular one-way adult tickets cost from Skr218/290 for the ferry/catamaran, but from mid-June to mid-August most crossings cost from Skr304/496 (some overnight, evening and early-morning sailings in the middle of the week retain the cheaper fares).

Getting Around

Gotlands Cykeluthyrning (☎ 214133; info@gotlands cykeluthyrning.com; ☉ mid-May–Aug), behind Saluhall not far from Visby harbour, rents bikes from Skr65/325 per day/week. It also offers rental of a three-man tent (Skr100/400 per day/week), or for Skr250/1250 you can hire its 'camping package' – two bikes, a tent, camping stove and two sleeping mats.

Kollektiv Trafiken (☎ 214112) runs buses to all corners of the island. A one-way ticket costs between Skr12 (for a short journey less than 4km) to Skr59 (for journeys of more than 51km). Taking a bike on board costs an additional Skr40.

VISBY

☎ 0498 / pop 21,400
The narrow cobblestone streets and impressive town walls of the medieval port of Visby attest to the town's former Hanseatic glories. The place is heaving with tourists in summer, and from mid-May to mid-August cars are banned in the old town.

The **tourist office** (☎ 201700; www.gotland.info; Hamngatan 4; ☉ daily May-Sep, Mon-Fri Oct-Apr) can help with maps and information, but doesn't book accommodation. The **library** (Cramérgatan; ☉ Mon-Sat) offers free Internet access.

The town is a noble sight, with its **13th-century wall** of 40 towers. Set aside enough time to stroll the perimeter (3.5km), and meander around the town's narrow roads and pretty lanes. The ruins of 10 medieval churches are all within the town walls and contrast with the old but sound **Cathedral** (☉ daily), north of Stortorget. **Gotlands Fornsal** (☎ 292700; Strandgatan 14; adult Skr60; ☉ daily May–mid-Sep, Tue-Sun mid-Sep–Apr) is one of the largest and best regional museums in Sweden. The nearby **Konstmuseum** (☎ 292775; Sankt Hansgatan 21; adult Skr40; ☉ daily May–mid-Sep, Tue-Sun mid-Sep–Apr) displays varying art exhibitions.

Sleeping

Moderately priced accommodation in and around Visby is in demand; book well in advance.

Gotlands Resor (☎ 201260; www.gotlandsresor.se; s Skr300-350, d Skr440-480) This travel agency books private rooms in Visby; you'll pay marginally more for a room inside the city walls.

Rosas (☎ 213514; St Hansgatan 22; d Skr440) Above Rosas café, simple rooms with shared facilities are on offer (see opposite).

STF Vandrarhem Visby (☎ 269842; carl.tholin@ tjelvar.org; Fältgata 30; dm/d from Skr160/440; ☉ mid-Jun–mid-Aug) This hostel is southeast of the town centre, off Lännavägen, in a school residence

Fängelse Vandrarhem (☎ 206050; Skeppsbron 1; dm Skr200-300; ☉ May-Sep) Not far from the harbour, it's an interesting option, with beds in the converted cells of an old jail. Facilities include kitchen, TV-room and sauna.

Norderstrands Camping (☎ 212157; www.norder strandscamping.se; camping Skr100-175, 4-bed cabins Skr450-650; ☉ mid-Apr–mid-Sep) By the sea, 800m north of the ring wall (connected by a walking/cycling path), this is the closest camping ground to Visby.

Eating & Drinking

There's no shortage of restaurants, cafés and bars around the old town squares, on Adelsgatan or at the harbour.

Rosas (☎ 213514; St Hansgatan 22; light meals Skr30-70) In a pretty half-timbered house with sunny courtyard, Rosas makes a wonderful lunch spot.

Vinäger Café (☎ 211160; cnr Hästgatan & Mellansgatan; lunch buffet Skr59) This unsigned café is frequented by the cool crowd.

Effes Bar (☎ 215111; Adelsgatan 2; mains Skr60-130; ☺ closed Tue) A unique pub-bar that's built into the town wall. It's a great place for a laid-back meal or drink; there's a bar menu, outdoor courtyard, pool tables and regular live music.

There's a central **ICA supermarket** (Stora Torget; ☺ 8am-8pm Mon-Sat, 10am-8pm Sun), or large supermarkets outside the town walls (head to Österväg, through Österport gate).

Do as the locals do and stop by **Saluhall 1** (Skeppsbron) for ice cream.

NORTHERN SWEDEN

Norrland, the northern half of Sweden, has always been considered a world apart. It's associated with the pioneers' struggle to produce the timber and iron ore necessary for the construction of the railways that opened up the region. Areas along the Norwegian border are known for their great natural beauty and attract walkers, skiers and canoeists.

ÖSTERSUND

☎ 063 / pop 58,400

This pleasant town by Lake Storsjön, in whose chilly waters is said to lurk a rarely sighted monster, has good budget accommodation and is a relaxed and scenic place. The **tourist office** (☎ 144001; www.turist.ostersund.se; Rådhusgatan 44; ☺ daily Jun-Aug, Mon-Fri Sep-May) is opposite the town hall, one block from the bus station. The **library** (Rådhusgatan; ☺ Mon-Sat) has free Internet access.

Don't miss **Jamtli** (☎ 150100; www.jamtli.com; admission Skr60-90; ☺ daily Jun-Aug; Tue-Sun Sep-May), 1 km north of the town centre. It combines the lively exhibitions of the regional museum and a large museum village.

Some attractions lie on the adjacent island of Frösön, reached by road or footbridge from the middle of Östersund (the footbridge is from Badhusparken – nearby you can rent bikes, inline skates and canoes).

Monster-spotting lake cruises run from June to mid-September and cost Skr65 to Skr95.

Sleeping & Eating

STF Vandrarhem Jamtli (☎ 122060; vandrarhemmet@ jamtli.com; dm/s/d Skr185/280/380) Take the chance to live amongst Östersund's major attraction: this small, quaint hostel is inside the Jamtli museum precinct. Catch bus No 2.

STF Vandrarhem (☎ 34130; micke2@algonet.se; Södra Gröngatan 36; dm/s/d 210/375/420; ☺ late Jun-early Aug) Excellent apartments not far from the train station are available.

Vandrarhemmet Rallaren (☎ 132232; rallaren@ hotmail.com; Bangårdsgatan 6; dm/s/d Skr150/200/340) A small, clean and modern hostel, next to the train station.

Brunkullans Krog & Bar (☎ 101454; Postgränd 5; lunch Skr65, dinner mains Skr140-200; ☺ lunch Mon-Fri, dinner Tue-Sat) A classy eatery with friendly staff. The lunch buffet is excellent value.

Getting There & Away

The train station is a short walk south of the town centre, but the main regional bus station is central on Gustav III Torg.

Bus No 156 runs west to Åre (Skr115); and bus No 63 runs northeast to Umeå (Skr287, two daily).

Direct trains run from Stockholm via Uppsala and Gävle, and some continue west to Storlien (from where you can catch trains to Trondheim, Norway).

ÅRE & AROUND

☎ 0647 / pop 9600

Sweden's top mountain-sports destination, the Åre area (www.skistar.com/are) has 40 ski lifts that serve 100 pistes and 1000 vertical metres of skiable slopes (day pass Skr305). The season is from November to early May, but conditions are best from February, when daylight hours increase, and Easter is hugely busy. There are cross-country tracks in the area, a big *aprés-ski* scene, and winter activities such as dog-sledding and snowmobile safaris. When the snow melts and the weather warms up, Åre offers hiking, kayaking, rafting, fishing and mountain biking.

The **tourist office** (☎ 17720; ☺ daily) is in the train station. Most facilities are around the main square, reached by walking through the park opposite the station.

SWEDEN

In winter it's best to book accommodation and skiing packages via **Åre Resor** (☎ 17700; www.skistar.com/are); the same company also organises summer packages, but independent travellers at this time of year shouldn't have problems finding accommodation.

Åre Ski Lodge (☎ 51029; summer s/d/tr Skr190/290/390) On the E14 above the town, next to the fire station, is this Austrian-style ski lodge. Great summer prices and facilities, such as sauna and kitchen, are available.

You'll have no trouble finding supermarkets or eating and drinking options – they're all clustered around the main square.

Regional bus No 156 runs from Östersund to Åre (Skr115). Regular trains between Stockholm and Storlien, via Östersund, stop at Åre. Storlien is the terminus for SJ trains; change here for Norwegian trains to Hell and Trondheim.

UMEÅ
☎ 090 / pop 105,000

Umeå has a large university and a port with ferry connections to Finland. It's among the fastest-growing towns in Sweden and has some 22,000 students, making it an agreeable place to hang out en route north. The **tourist office** (☎ 161616; www.umea.se/turism; Renmarkstorget 15; ☼ daily mid-Jun–mid-Aug, Mon-Fri rest of year) has free Internet access. The **Gammlia** (☎ 171800; free; ☼ daily Jun-Aug, Tue-Sun rest of year) complex, 2km east of the town centre, is home to several good museums.

STF Vandrarhem Umeå (☎ 771650; info@vandrarhem met.se; Västra Esplanaden 10; dm/d Skr210/420) is everything you need from a hostel – clean, central and well run. **Wayne's Coffee** (☎ 701700; Storgatan 50; meals Skr30-60) offers good food and an outdoor area for soaking up the long daylight hours.

Getting There & Away
The long-distance bus station is opposite the train station on Järnvägsallén, just north of the centre. Umeå is the main centre for **Länstrafiken Västerbotten** (☎ 020-910019), the regional bus network that covers over 55,000 sq km. Direct buses run to Mo i Rana in Norway (Skr232, daily); other daily destinations include Östersund (Skr287) and Luleå (Skr252). Connex trains leave daily from Umeå to connect with the north–south trains between Stockholm and Luleå.

There are daily ferries between Umeå and Vaasa in Finland (see p1128).

KIRUNA
☎ 0980 / pop 23,900

The region around Kiruna includes Sweden's highest peak (Kebnekaise, 2111m), a hotel made from ice, and several fine national parks and trekking routes. It's worth making the effort to get up there! This far north, the midnight sun lasts from 27 May to 14 July and there's a bluish darkness throughout December and the New Year.

The helpful **tourist office** (☎ 18880; www.lap land.se; Lars Janssonsgatan 17; ☼ daily summer, Mon-Sat rest of year) has loads of detailed brochures. Staff can arrange various activities including Sami experiences year-round; rafting, hiking, horse riding, rock-climbing and fishing in warmer weather; and dog-sledging and snowmobile safaris in winter.

The **library** (Biblioteksgatan), behind the bus station, offers free Internet access.

The highlight of a trip this far north is a visit to the **Ice Hotel** (☎ 66800; www.icehotel.com; Marknadsvägen, Jukkasjärvi; day visit adult Skr120; Skr2800), a unique and super-cool experience (if you'll pardon the pun). Every winter at Jukkasjärvi, 18km east of Kiruna, a structure is built from tonnes of ice taken from the frozen local river. This huge, custom-built 'igloo' has a chapel, a bar and exhibitions of ice sculpture. It also has more than 60 'hotel rooms', where guests sleep on beds covered with reindeer skins and in side sleeping bags guaranteed to keep them warm despite the -5°C to -8°C temperature (and in winter that's nothing – outside the hotel it can be as low as -30°C!). The hotel is normally open mid-December to late April (weather permitting). Staying at the hotel might prove too expensive for most shoe stringers, but anyone can pay for a day visit. Take bus No 501.

In summer (from June), after the Ice Hotel has melted away, day visitors can still experience a little of the magic. Inside a giant freezer warehouse called the **Ice Hotel Art Center** (adult Skr100; ☼ 10am-5pm Jun–mid-Aug), at a temperature of -5°C, some features of the Ice Hotel remain, including a bar and ice sculptures; entry fee includes warm clothing.

Sleeping & Eating
STF Vandrarhem Kiruna (☎ 17195; Bergmästaregatan 7; dm/s/d Skr195/315/450) In a central location, it has good facilities (including sauna) and an adjacent Chinese restaurant.

Yellow House (☎ 13750; www.yellowhouse.nu; Hantverkaregatan 25; dm/s/d Skr120/300/400) Another good budget option, with facilities including sauna, kitchen, laundry and TV in each room.

Gullriset Lägenhetshotellet (☎ 10937; Bromsgatan 12; apartments Skr400-700) About 1.5km from the tourist office is this bargain option. Rent an apartment sleeping up to four people, with kitchen, bathroom and cable-TV.

Easily the nicest café is **Café Safari** (☎ 17460; Geologsgatan 4; light meals Skr20-60). **3nd Baren** (☎ 66380; Föreningsgatan 11; lunch Skr65, mains Skr69-89) is a moderately priced restaurant and lively drinking spot; you can try local specialties like reindeer, or play it safe with teak or pasta.

There's an **ICA supermarket** (Föreningsgatan; ☺ daily) next to 3nd Baren.

Getting There & Away

The small **airport** (☎ 68000), 9km east of the town, has flights to/from Stockholm.

Regional buses in this vast region are operated by **Länstrafiken Norrbotten** (☎ 020-70047) from the bus station on Hjalmar Lundbohmsvägen, opposite the town hall. Buses serve all major settlements. Bus No 91 runs to Riksgränsen (Skr117, two or three daily) on the Norwegian border.

Regular trains connect Kiruna with Luleå, Stockholm (overnight) and Narvik (Norway).

SWEDEN DIRECTORY

ACCOMMODATION

Camping

Sweden has hundreds of camping grounds; the best time for camping is from May to August. Prices vary with facilities, from Skr80 for a basic site to Skr200 for the highest standards. Most camping grounds have kitchens and laundry facilities, and many are popular family holiday spots with the works – swimming pool, minigolf, bike and/or canoe rental, restaurant etc.

Visit www.camping.se for information. See also p1156 for advice on free camping in Sweden.

Cabins & Chalets

Daily rates for *stugor* (cabins and chalets, often found at camping grounds or in the countryside) offer good value for small groups and families and range in both facilities and price (Skr200 to Skr800). Some cabins are simple, with bunk beds and little else (you share the bathroom and kitchen facilities with campers), others are fully equipped with kitchen, bathroom and living room. See www.stuga.nu for information.

Hostels

Sweden has over 475 hostels (*vandrarhem*), the vast majority are excellent. Some 315 hostels are affiliated with **Svenska Turistföreningen** (STF; ☎ 08-463 2100; www.svenskaturistforeningen.se), part of Hostelling International (HI). Holders of HI cards stay at STF hostels for between Skr80 and Skr280. Nonmembers pay Skr45 extra per night or can join up at hostels (membership costs Skr285 for adults, Skr110 for those aged 16 to 25). In this chapter we list prices at STF hostels for nonmembers.

Around 160 hostels belong to the 'rival' **Sveriges Vandrarhem i Förening** (SVIF; ☎ 0413-553 450). No membership is required; rates and facilities are similar to those of the STF. Also look out for other hostels that are not affiliated with either STF or SVIF, and note that some camping grounds have hostels.

Hostels in Sweden are difficult to get into outside reception opening times. The secret is to phone and make a reservation during the (usually short) reception hours; they'll provide you with an entry code. Reception hours vary, but are generally from 5pm to 7pm.

Breakfast is often available (Skr40 to Skr60); linen is available for rent, but bring your own from home to save money. You'll be expected to clean your room upon departure.

There are numerous mountain huts and lodges, especially in Lappland, run by STF. These are popular with hikers and outdoor enthusiasts; more information is available on STF's website.

Hotels

There are few budget accommodation options in Sweden. However, practically all of the hotels provide good-value weekend and summer (midsummer to mid-August) rates, often below Skr800 for a luxurious double (up to 50% cheaper than regular prices).

ACTIVITIES

The image of wholesome, outdoorsy Swedes is pretty spot-on (well, except for all the coffee they consume and cigarettes they smoke). The Swedes are huge nature-lovers and are active year-round, on bike paths, forest jogging tracks, rivers and lakes, mountain trails and the snow and ice.

The right of public access to the countryside (called 'allemansrätten') means that in Sweden, by law, you're allowed to walk, boat, ski or swim on private land as long as you stay at least 70m from houses and keep out of gardens, fenced areas and cultivated land. You can camp for more than one night in the same place, and fires may be set where safe (not on bare rocks) with fallen wood. Cars may not be driven across open land or on private roads. Close all gates. Do not disturb farm animals or reindeer.

Countless activities exist, including horse riding, cycling, canoeing, rock-climbing, fishing, golf, sailing and rafting in summer, and skating, ice-fishing, ice-climbing, snowmobile safaris and dog-sledging in winter. Tourist offices can provide information.

Hiking

Hiking is popular everywhere in Sweden and the mountain challenge of the northern national parks is compelling. However, these parks are rarely snow-free and the jewel, Sarek, is only for experienced hikers. Good equipment is vital.

Easy walking trails are common. The best hiking time is between late June and mid-September, but conditions are better after early August, when the mosquitoes have gone.

For information on organised group walks and STF mountain huts, which are placed at intervals averaging about 20km along popular trails like Kungsleden, contact STF (see p1155).

Skiing

Cross-country (nordic) skiing opportunities vary depending on snow and temperatures, but the northwest usually has plenty of snow from December to April (but not a lot of daylight in December and January). Practically all town areas (except the far south) have marked skiing tracks, often illuminated. There are large ski resorts catering mainly for downhill skiing in the west –

Åre (p1153) is the biggest. The websites www.goski.com and www.thealps.com have useful reviews of the Swedish ski fields.

DISCOUNT CARDS

A Hostelling International (HI) membership card means discounts at STF hostels (non-members pay an additional Skr45 per night, or can join in Sweden). Students should bring an ISIC card, although some discounts only apply to people with a Swedish student card. Seniors normally receive discounts.

There are discount cards available in the major cities of Stockholm, Gothenburg and Malmö, which cover all local transport and most sightseeing needs. See the Information sections under each city for details.

EMBASSIES & CONSULATES
Embassies & Consulates in Sweden

The diplomatic missions listed here are in Stockholm.

Australia (Map pp1138-9; ☎ 08-613 2900; 11th fl, Sergels Torg 12)
Canada (Map pp1138-9; ☎ 08-453 3000; 7th fl, Tegelbacken 4)
Denmark (Map pp1138-9; ☎ 08-406 7500; Jakobs Torg 1)
Finland (Map pp1134-5; ☎ 08-676 6700; Gärdesgatan 9-11)
France (Map pp1138-9; ☎ 08-459 5300; Kommendörsgatan 13)
Germany (Map pp1134-5; ☎ 08-670 1500; Skarpögatan 9)
Ireland (Map pp1134-5; ☎ 08-661 8005; Östermalmsgatan 97)
Netherlands (Map pp1138-9; ☎ 08-556 933 00; Götgatan 16A)
Norway (Map pp1134-5; ☎ 08-665 6340; Skarpögatan 4)
UK (Map pp1134-5; ☎ 08-671 3000; Skarpögatan 6-8)
USA (Map pp1134-5; ☎ 08-783 5300; Dag Hammarskjöldsväg 31)

Swedish Embassies & Consulates Abroad

Australia (☎ 02-6270 2700; www.embassyofsweden .org.au; 5 Turrana St, Yarralumla ACT 2600)
Canada (☎ 613-241 8553; www.swedishembassy.ca; 377 Dalhousie St, Ottawa ON K1N 9N8)
Denmark (☎ 33 36 03 70; www.swedenabroad.com /copenhagen; Sankt Annæ Plads 15A, DK-1250 Copenhagen K
Finland (☎ 09-6877 660; www.swedenabroad.com /helsinki; Pohjoisesplanadi 7B, 00170 Helsinki)
France (☎ 01 44 18 88 00; www.swedenabroad.com /paris; 17 rue Barbet-de-Jouy, F-75007 Paris)

Germany (☎ 030-505060; www.swedenabroad.com /berlin; Rauchstrasse 1, 10787 Berlin)
Ireland (☎ 01-474 4400; www.swedenabroad.com /dublin; 13–17 Dawson St; Dublin 2)
Netherlands (☎ 070-412 0200; www.swedenabroad. :om/thehague; Jan Willem Frisolaan 3, 2517 JS Den Haag)
New Zealand (☎ 04-499 9895; sweden@xtra.co.nz; 13th floor, Vogel Bldg, Aitken St, Wellington)
Norway (☎ 24 11 42 00, www.swedenabroad.com/oslo; Nobels gate 16, NO-0244 Oslo)
UK (☎ 020-7917 6400, www.swedish-embassy.org.uk; 11 Montagu Place, London W1H 2AL)
USA (☎ 202-467 2600, www.swedenabroad.com /washington; Suite 900, 1501 M St NW, Washington DC 20005)

GAY & LESBIAN TRAVELLERS

Sweden is famous for its liberal attitudes and there are laws allowing same-sex 'registered partnerships', which grant most marriage rights. The organisation concerned with equality for lesbians and gays is **Riksförbundet för Sexuellt Likaberättigande** (RFSL; ☎ 08-457 1300; Sveavägen 57-59, Stockholm).

A good source of information is the free, monthly newspaper *QX*, giving gay and lesbian information and listings (only in Swedish). You can pick it up at many clubs, stores and restaurants, mainly in Stockholm, Gothenborg, Malmö and Copenhagen. Its website (www.qx.se) has great information and recommendations in English.

HOLIDAYS

Public holidays in Sweden are:
New Year's Day 1 January
Epiphany 6 January
Good Friday to Easter Monday March/April
Labour Day 1 May
Ascension Day May/June (39th day after Easter)
Whit Sunday & Monday late May or early June
Midsummer's Day first Saturday after 21 June
All Saints' Day Saturday, late October or early November
Christmas Day 25 December
Boxing Day 26 December

Christmas Eve, New Year's Eve and Midsummer's Eve are not official holidays, but are generally non-working days for most of the population. Midsummer is *the* festival of the year. If you're in Stockholm for Midsummer or any other holiday, participate in the festivities at Skansen (p1133).

MONEY

You should encounter few problems if you carry cash in any convertible currency or internationally recognised travellers cheques. The national ATM networks provided by Swedish banks usually accept international Visa, Plus, EC, Eurocard, MasterCard or Cirrus cards.

Forex, with branches in the biggest cities and most airports and ferry terminals, is the easiest place to exchange money and charges Skr15 per cheque. Banks charge up to Skr60 per cheque. You can buy foreign notes for no fee at Forex.

TELEPHONE

About 70% of Swedes own a mobile phone, so the number of public phones has dwindled. There are no coin phones; public telephones take Telia phonecards (widely available). Many Telia booths accept credit cards (with pricey rates). You can buy a wide range of phonecards that give cheap rates for calls abroad from tobacconists.

For international directory assistance dial ☎ 118119 (not a freecall). For international calls dial ☎ 00 followed by the country code and the local area code. To place a collect call, dial ☎ 020-0018.

VISAS

Citizens of the EU, Norway and Iceland can enter Sweden with a passport or a national identification card. Nationals of Nordic countries can stay and work indefinitely but others require residence permits for stays of between three months and five years.

Passport-holders from Australia, New Zealand, Canada and the US can enter and stay in Sweden without a visa for up to three months. Young Australian and New Zealand passport-holders can also qualify for a one-year working holiday visa. Citizens of South Africa and other African, Asian and some Eastern European countries require tourist visas for entry; these are only available in advance from Swedish embassies (allow at least two months).

Migrationsverket (☎ 011-156000; www.migration sverket.se; SE-60170 Norrköping) handles all applications for visas and work or residency permits. Its website is full of useful information.

SWEDEN

Switzerland

HIGHLIGHTS

- **Interlaken** Gargantuan mountain vistas and white knuckle adrenalin adventures abound in this backpackers mecca, part of the off-the-charts gorgeous Jungfrau region (p1177)
- **Zermatt** Moody alpine scenery and ski slopes at the base of the mighty Matterhorn (p1170)
- **Zürich** Buzzing with an electricity found nowhere else in the country, this city is elegant and sedate during the day and a positive party at night (p1172)
- **Best journey** Ride the rails to the top of the Jungfraujoch, one of the best train trips in Europe (p1180)
- **Off-the-beaten track** The country's best-kept secret, the tiny hamlet of Gimmelwald, is the Switzerland you thought existed only in the picture books (p1179)

FAST FACTS

- **Area** 41,285 sq km (similar to the Netherlands)
- **ATMs** Available everywhere
- **Budget** Sfr40-60 per day
- **Capital** Bern
- **Country Code** ☎ 41
- **Famous for** The Matterhorn, cheese, clocks, banking
- **Languages** French, German, Italian and Romansch
- **Money** Swiss franc (A$1 = Sfr0.90, CA$1 = Sfr0.98, €1 = Sfr1.54, ¥100 = Sfr1.13, NZ$1 = Sfr0.85, UK£1 = Sfr2.22, US$1 = Sfr1.23)
- **Population** 7.4 million
- **Phrases** Guten tag (good day), danke

(thanks), *auf wiedersehen* (goodbye), *sprechen sie Englisch?* (do you speak English?)

- **Time** GMT/UTC + 1
- **Visas** None required for passport holders of the EU, the USA, Canada, Australia, New Zealand and South Africa.

TRAVEL HINT

Drinking before a toast is unforgivable and will lead to seven years of bad sex... or so the superstition goes.

ROAMING SWITZERLAND

Start at Château de Chillon near Montreux, then hit Zermatt, Interlaken and the Jungfrau region, Lucerne and Zürich. Extra time? Explore Ticino.

Chocolate, cheese and clocks; strait-laced bankers, big business and neutrality – the clichés associated with this small, fiercely independent nation are likely implanted in your mind before you arrive. Look beyond the stereotypes, however, and you just might be stupefied. There's more to the story than Heidi and the Matterhorn, than goat herders and cowbells

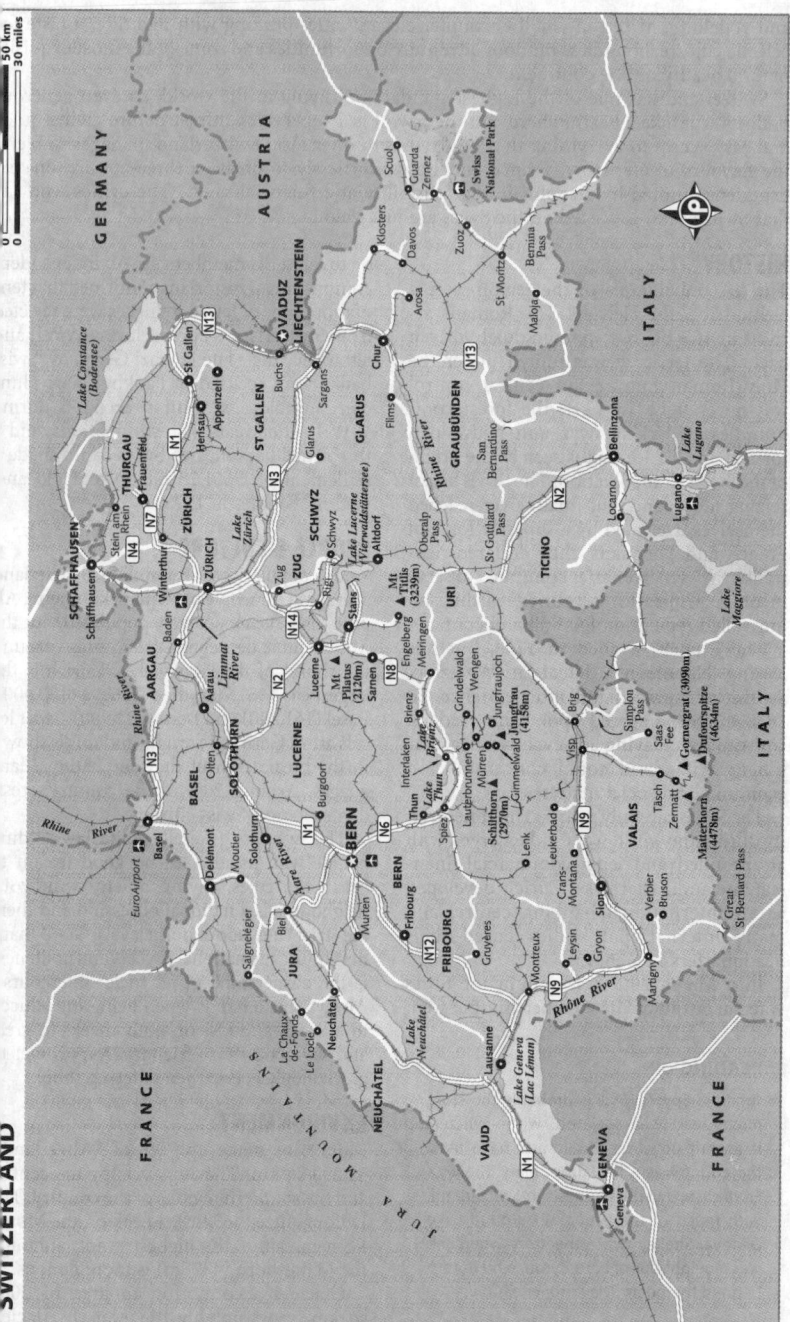

SWITZERLAND

and yodelling. Mixed in you'll encounter elegant cities buzzing with nightlife, a taste fo eclectic culture, boundless outdoor adventure opportunities and some of the most exquisite natural beauty on the continent.

Switzerland has one of the highest standards of living in the world, so even generous budgets will take a beating here, but the payoff is a super-slick infrastructure giving quick and easy access to everything the country has to offer. And Switzerland manages to blend the flavours of Germany, France and Italy effortlessly to create a three-cultures-in-one experience united by a sophisticated sensibility and financial savvy. The cynics who say that Switzerland is wasted on the Swiss are just jealous.

HISTORY

The first inhabitants of the region were a Celtic tribe, the Helvetii. The Romans arrived in 107 BC but were gradually driven back. The territory was united under the Holy Roman Empire but central control was never tight. In 1291, the forest communities of Uri, Schwyz and Nidwalden formed an alliance that is seen as the origin of the Swiss Confederation. The Swiss began seizing more land, but finally over-reached themselves. Defeated by a superior force of French and Venetians, they declared neutrality. Swiss mercenaries continued to serve in other armies for centuries, earning an unrivalled reputation for skill and courage.

The French invaded in 1798, but following Napoleon's defeat at Waterloo, Switzerland gained full independence. In 1848 the Swiss agreed upon a new federal constitution. Having achieved political stability, Switzerland could concentrate on economic and social matters.

The Swiss carefully guarded their neutrality during the world wars and emerged with an expanded (and rising) commercial, financial and industrial base. Zürich developed as an international banking centre, and many international bodies based their headquarters in Geneva.

In a March 2002 referendum the Swiss voted in favour of UN membership, but went on to reject EU membership. An independent commission of historians confirmed that ten of thousands of Jewish refugees were rejected from Switzerland's border during WWII and left to face their fate in Nazi Germany. Swiss banks were accused of banking Nazi plunder and holocaust victims' accounts during WWII. After years of recriminations, and threatened lawsuit, two Swiss banks made settlement of US$1.25 billion to Holocaust victims' families in 1998.

PEOPLE & CULTURE

With a population of 7.4 million, Switzerland averages 174 people per square kilometre. Alpine districts are sparsely populated, but the Mittelland is densely settled, moreso around the shores of the larger lakes. Zürich is the largest city (351,700) then Geneva (180,400), Basel (161,800) and Bern (122,900). Most locals are of Germanic origin, and this is shown in the breakdown of the four national languages. Around 20% of the country's residents are non-Swiss citizens.

The Swiss are generally polite, law-abiding people who usually see no good reason to break the rules. Living quietly with your neighbours is a national obsession and there are strict rules about noise levels. Good manners infuse the national psyche, and politeness is the cornerstone of all social intercourse. Always shake hands when being introduced to a Swiss, and kiss on both cheeks to greet and say goodbye to friends. Don't forget to greet shopkeepers when entering shops.

ENVIRONMENT

Mountains make up 70% of Switzerland's 41,290 sq km. The Alps occupy the central and the southern regions of the country. The Dufourspitze (4634m), a peak on the Monte Rosa massif, is the highest point, although the Matterhorn (4478m) is more famous.

Glaciers account for an area of 2000 sq km, most notably the Aletsch Glacier

> **READING UP**
>
> Johanna Spyri's *Heidi* is probably the story most readily associated with Switzerland, but novelists of all sorts have used the country as a backdrop. Mary Shelley's *Frankenstein* had its genesis in Switzerland, with much of the action set around Lake Geneva. Shelley wrote the story when she was a neighbour of Lord Byron, who in turn penned the poem *The Prisoner of Chillon*.

which at 169 sq km is the largest valley glacier in Europe. The St Gotthard Massif, in the centre of Switzerland, is the source of many lakes and rivers, such as the Rhine and the Rhône. The Jura Mountains straddle the border with France, and peak at around 1700m. Between the two mountain systems is the Mittelland, a region of hills crisscrossed by rivers, ravines and winding valleys.

The most distinctive Alpine animal in Switzerland is the ibex, a mountain goat that has huge curved and ridged horns. There are about 12,000 of them left in the country.

Switzerland has just one national park, the Swiss National Park. At just 169 sq km it is quite small, but offers opportunities for walking and ibex viewing.

Switzerland has long been an environmentally aware nation. Its citizens diligently recycle household waste and cities encourage the use of public transport.

TRANSPORT

GETTING THERE & AWAY
Air
Most international airlines fly into Switzerland. Zürich and Geneva are the two busiest international airports. Budget airline **Easyjet** (☎ 0848 888 222; www.easyjet.com) offers regular services between London and Zürich and Geneva. Switzerland's international carrier

> **DEPARTURE TAX**
>
> Airport departure taxes for international flights are always included in the ticket price.

is **Swiss International Air Lines** (☎ 0848 853 00 00; www.swiss.com).

Bus
Eurolines (☎ 0900 573 747; www.eurolines.com) has bus services to Eastern Europe, Austria, Spain, Germany and Portugal, but distances are long. The UK-based **Busabout** (☎ 020 7950 1661; www.busabout.com) operates summer services from Bern to Paris, and from Lauterbrunnen (for Interlaken) to Paris and Venice.

Car & Motorcycle
Roads into Switzerland are good, but special care is needed to negotiate mountain passes. To use the Swiss motorways you will need to purchase a *vignette* for Sfr40. The sticker is valid for one year and must be displayed on the windscreen.

Train
Switzerland is a hub for train travel to the rest of the continent. Zürich is the busiest international terminus with trains to Austria, Germany and Italy, among other destinations. There are several trains daily to Geneva and Lausanne from Paris.

> **PASSES & DISCOUNTS**
>
> Swiss public transport is highly efficient and incorporates trains, buses, boats and funiculars. If you're planning on travelling extensively in the country, especially if you don't have a European rail pass, it's best to invest in a local discount pass. In any case, while Eurail passes allow you to travel on Swiss national railways at no extra cost, they are not valid on the postbuses, city transport, some private rail lines or the cable cars.
>
> The Swiss Pass offers unlimited travel on Swiss federal railways, boats, most alpine postbuses, and trams and buses in 35 towns. Reductions of 25% apply to funiculars and mountain railways. These passes are available for four days (Sfr240), eight days (Sfr340), 15 days (Sfr410), 22 days (Sfr475) and one month (Sfr525). The Swiss Flexi Pass allows free, unlimited trips for three (Sfr230) to eight days (Sfr420) within a month. With either pass, two people travelling together get 15% off.
>
> The Swiss Card (one month Sfr165) allows a free round-trip from your arrival point to any destination in Switzerland, 50% off rail, boat and bus excursions, and reductions on mountain railways. The Half-Fare Card (one month Sfr99) is a similar deal minus the free round-trip.
>
> Except for the Half-Fare Card, these passes are best purchased before arrival in Switzerland from Switzerland Tourism (www.myswitzerland.com).
>
> There are also passes valid for any four days of unlimited travel in Switzerland and Austria (Sfr391) or Switzerland and France (Sfr391) within two months.

SWITZERLAND

GETTING AROUND
Bicycle
You can hire bikes from most train stations (adult/child Sfr30/25 per day) and return them to any station with a rental office for an extra Sfr6. Bikes can be transported on most trains; SBB rentals travel free. If you have your own wheels you'll need a bike pass (one day Sfr15, with Swiss travel pass Sfr10).

Bus
Yellow postbuses are a supplement to the rail network and link the more inaccessible regions. Services are regular, and departures tie in with train arrivals. Postbus stations are next to train stations.

Car
You do not need an International Driver's Licence to operate a vehicle in Switzerland. For the best deals on car hire you have to pre-book. Some of the lowest rates are found through **Auto Europe** (www.autoeurope.com). One-way drop-offs are often free, but collision-damage waiver costs extra.

Train
Trains are clean, reliable, frequent and as fast as the terrain allows. They're costly: if you plan on taking more than one or two trips, and don't have a European rail pass, it's best to purchase a travel pass (p1161). All major stations are linked by hourly departures, but services stop from around midnight to 6am. For train information, consult **Schweizerische Bundesbahnen** (SBB; www.sbb.ch) or call ☎ 0900-300 300 (Sfr1.19 per minute).

BERN

pop 122,900
Switzerland's capital is a captivating place to lose oneself for an afternoon. Curving, cobbled streets lined with 15th-century terraced buildings, covered arcades, historic fountains and the deep-green Aare River amplify the medieval old town's persona. Founded in 1191 by Berchtold V, Bern was named for the unfortunate bear (*Bärn* in local dialect) that was Berchtold's first hunting victim. Today the bear remains the heraldic mascot of the city. In 1983 Unesco declared Bern a World Heritage Site, a fact the city is immensely proud of.

EMERGENCY NUMBERS

- Police ☎ 117
- Fire brigade ☎ 118
- Ambulance ☎ 144
- Motoring breakdown service ☎ 140
- REGA air rescue ☎ 1414

INFORMATION
Bookshops
Stauffacher (☎ 031 311 24 11; Neuengasse 25; ⏰ 8am-6.30pm Mon-Fri, 8am-4pm Sat) English language bookstore.

Emergency
Police (☎ 031 321 21 21)

Internet Access
Internet Pub (☎ 031 313 81 91; Aarbergergasse 46; per hr Sfr7.50; ⏰ 9am-11pm) Fully stocked bar and a groovy atmosphere.

Medical Services
Contact ☎ 0900 57 67 47 for help locating a doctor or dentist.
University Hospital (☎ 031 632 21 11; Freiburgstrasse)

Money
SBB exchange office (Lower level of train station; ⏰ 6.30am-9pm)

Post
Main post office (Schanzenstrasse; ⏰ 7.30am-6.30pm Mon-Fri, 8am-noon Sat)

Tourist Information
Bern Tourismus (☎ 031 328 12 28; www.berne tourism.ch; inside train station; ⏰ 9am-8.30pm Jun-Sep, 9am-6.30pm Mon-Sat & 10am-5pm Sun Oct-May).
There is another **tourist office** (⏰ 9am-6pm Jun-Sep, 10am-4pm Mar-May & Oct, 11am-4pm Nov-Feb) across the river by the bear pits.

GETTING INTO TOWN

A bus links Belp airport to the train station (Sfr14, 20 minutes) and is coordinated with flight arrivals and departures. The train station is on the western edge of the old town and just a few minutes walk from all the main sights.

Travel Agencies
STA Travel (☎ 031 302 03 12; Falkenplatz 9;
🕑 9.30am-6pm Mon-Fri, 10am-1pm Sat) Budget and
student travel agency.

SIGHTS & ACTIVITIES
Bern is a great city to explore on a budget –
a lot of impressive stuff is free.

Old Town
Make sure to check out the **ogre fountain** in
Kornhausplatz, depicting a giant enjoying a
meal of wriggling children, and the **Zeitglockenturm** dividing Marktgasse and Kramgasse,
a colourful clock tower with revolving figures that herald the chiming hour.

The unmistakably Gothic, 15th-century
Münster (cathedral; 🕑 10am-5pm Tue-Sat, 11.30am-5pm
Sun) is worth stepping into. It features impos-
ing, 12m-high, stained-glass windows.

Across the Aare River are the **Bärengraben**
(bear pits). Though bears have been the entertainment at this site since 1857, it's sad to
see such majestic beasts doing tricks for treats
in a cramped, concrete environment.

Bundeshäuser
The 1902 **Houses of Parliament** (☎ 031 332 85 22;
www.parliament.ch; Bundesplatz; admission free; 🕑 tours
on the hour 9-11am & 2-4pm Mon-Fri, 11am Sat), home of
the Swiss Federal Assembly, are impressively
ornate, with statues of the nation's founding fathers, a stained-glass dome adorned
with cantonal emblems and a huge, 214-bulb
chandelier. Bring a passport to gain entry.

Swimming
The open-air **Marzili pools** (admission free; 🕑 May-
Sep) are an excellent budget option on a hot
summer day. You can also follow the local
lead and walk upriver, fling yourself into the
swift current of the Aare, then float back to
Marzili. You need to be a very strong swim-
mer, however.

SLEEPING
Bern has budget options in stumbling distance of its eateries and bars. Please be mindful that prices listed in this chapter for SYHA
hostels do not include the guest fee.

Hotel Glocke Backpackers (☎ 031 311 37 71; www
.bernbackpackers.com; Rathausgasse 75; dm Sfr27, s/d with
shared bathroom Sfr65/110; 🖳) The lounge area
with pool tables and TV give this place
its flavour. Dorms are simple with lockers

IT ALL HAPPENED IN SWITZERLAND

- Albert Einstein came up with his theories of relativity, including the 'E=MC2'
  formula, while working in Bern.

- Switzerland gave birth to the Worldwide Web at the acclaimed CERN
  research institute outside Geneva.

- Val de Travers, near Neuchâtel, claims to
  be the birthplace of the mythical green
  alcohol, absinthe.

- Carl Gustav Jung (1875–1961), founder
  of the analytical school of psychology,
  was born in the small Swiss village of
  Kesswil.

- Chemist Albert Hofmann was using
  LSD to conduct migraine cure tests
  in Basel in 1943 when he accidentally
  absorbed the compound through his
  fingertips and became the first man to
  trip on acid. He liked the psychedelic
  hallucinations so much he tried the
  drug again. And again. He once told a
  British newspaper he hoped LSD would
  become part of mainstream culture,
  with the same acceptance as alcohol.

---

and sinks. Self-caterers will appreciate the
kitchen.

Landhaus Hotel (☎ 031 331 41 66; www.landhaus
bern.ch; Altenbergstrasse 4; dm Sfr30, d with shared
bathroom from Sfr110; 🖳) Modern minimalist
rooms and a slick restaurant/bar downstairs (live jazz Thursday evenings) make
this place a viable option. Dorm dwellers
pay extra for bedding and breakfast. There's
a kitchen and TVs upon request.

Hotel National (☎ 031 381 19 88; www.nation
albern.ch; Hirschengraben 24; s with shared bathroom
Sfr60, s/d with private bathroom Sfr100/150; 🅿 🖳) A
grand, old-world family-run hotel kept in
the style of 100 years ago; don't miss the
old-fashioned lift. There's free Internet for
guests. Excellent value.

SYHA Hostel (☎ 031 311 63 16; www.jugibern.ch;
Weihergasse 4; dm Sfr30, s/d with shared bathroom Sfr43/
76; 🖳) Not as well maintained as other SYHA
facilities, the showers are less than spotless, but
it does occupy a scenic spot on the river and is
a cheap back-up if other places are full.

Camping Eichholz (☎ 031 961 26 02; Strandweg 49;
per adult/tent Sfr7/5, bungalows Sfr15 plus per adult Sfr7;

SWITZERLAND

BERN

0 ———— 400 m
0 ———— 0.2 miles

INFORMATION
Bern Tourismus...........................1 C2
British Embassy............................2 F4
Canadian Embassy.......................3 F4
Internet Pub................................4 D2
Irish Embassy...............................5 F4
Italian Embassy............................6 F4
Main Post Office..........................7 C2
SBB Exchange Office..............(see 1)
STA Travel....................................8 C1
Stauffacher Bookshop..................9 D2
Tourist Office.............................10 F2

SIGHTS & ACTIVITIES   (p1163)
Bärengraben (Bear Pits)............11 F2
Bundeshäuser (Parliament).......12 D3
Kornhausplatz...........................13 D2
Marzili Pools..............................14 D4
Münster (Cathedral)..................15 E3
Ogre Fountain......................(see 13)
Zeitglockenturm (Clock Tower)..16 D2

SLEEPING   (pp1163-5)
Hotel Glocke Backpackers.........17 E2
Hotel National............................18 C3
Landhaus Hotel...........................19 F2
SYHA Hostel...............................20 D3

EATING   (p1165)
Coop..21 D2
Greenhouse.................................22 E2
Le Mazot.....................................23 D2
Manora..24 C2
Menuetto....................................25 E3
Migros...26 D2

DRINKING   (p1165)
Altes Tramdepot.........................27 F2
Kornhauskeller............................28 D2

ENTERTAINMENT   (p1165)
Quasimodo............................(see 7)
Reitschule...................................29 C1
Wasserwerk.................................30 F3

TRANSPORT   (p1165)
Bus Station.................................31 C2

May-Sep) It's nestled by the river, 2.5km from the centre; take tram No 9 to Wabern.

EATING

Wall-to-wall cafés and restaurants line the popular meeting places of Bärenplatz and Theaterplatz. Restaurants open in the morning and generally do not close between meals. Self-caterers can buy up at **Coop** (Neuengasse) and **Migros** (Marktgasse 46), which also have cheap self-service restaurants serving everything from cheese to salad and chicken in the Sfr3-7 range.

Le Cultina (☎ 031 376 13 70; Seftigenstrasse 1; mains from Sfr11; �%️ closed Sat & Sun) A rotating list of daily dishes and gigantic portions are found at this spacious restaurant. If you're on a tight budget, you won't regret the 10-minute ride southwest on tram No 9 to get here.

Le Mazot (☎ 031 311 70 88; Bärenplatz 5; mains Sfr11-30) Very cosy with dark wood panels, Le Mazot is a well-known specialist in Swiss food such as rösti, raclette and fondue. Half-portions are available. Sit outside in the glassed-in patio on warm days.

Menuetto (☎ 031 311 14 48; Münstergasse 47; mains Sfr22; �%️ 11.15am-2.15pm & 5.30-10pm Mon-Sat) A big draw for vegetarians, Menuetto produces mouth-wateringly fragrant and wholesome food in a congenial atmosphere.

Manora (☎ 031 311 37 55; Bubenbergplatz 5a; mains Sfr5-15) Delicious fresh food and a funky atmosphere are served in equal portions at this busy, two-level buffet-style restaurant.

Greenhouse (☎ 031 311 65 44; Münstergasse 68; mains Sfr17) With a distinct Parisian café vibe, the varied menu features rösti, potatoes and spaghetti. Portions are decent.

DRINKING & CLUBBING

Bern has a hip nightlife, with lots of bars and clubs to choose from. See the website www.bernbynight.ch for a full list. Bars open in the early afternoon and stay open past midnight. Clubs get going after 10pm.

Reitschule (☎ 031 306 69 69; www.reitschule.ch in German; Schützenmattstrasse) Perhaps the Swiss capital's most famous nightlife option, this centre for alternative arts is sprawled throughout several graffiti-splattered, derelict-looking buildings under the railway line. It attracts a diverse crowd looking for dance, theatre and live music.

Wasserwerk (☎ 031 312 12 31; www.wasserwerk.ch in German; Wasserwerkgasse 5; admission free-Sfr30) In a converted riverside warehouse, this is a favourite among pool-players and clubbers. International DJs spin regularly.

Altes Tramdepot (☎ 031 368 14 15; Am Bärengraben) Beer is still made on the premises at Bern's first microbrewery in a cavernous converted tram depot. The place serves snacks, monster meals and sweeping views across the river.

Kornhauskeller (☎ 031 327 72 72; Kornhausplatz 18) This is a magnificent underground gallery bar and restaurant with vaulted ceilings, frescoes and comfy sofas. Drinks are dear, but worth it to soak up the atmosphere.

Quasimodo (☎ 031 311 13 81; Rathausgasse 75) Backpackers staying at Hotel Glocke will like the convenience of this techno bar/club downstairs. At night it pumps out a hard electronic pulse.

GETTING THERE & AROUND

Postbuses depart from the western side of the train station. There are train connections to most Swiss cities and major towns, including Geneva (Sfr47, 1¾ hours, hourly), Basel (Sfr34, 70 minutes, hourly), Interlaken (Sfr23, 50 minutes, hourly) and Zürich (Sfr45, 70 minutes, hourly).

Bus and tram tickets cost Sfr1.70 (maximum six stops) or Sfr2.60. A day pass for the city and regional network is Sfr9.

From May to October there are free daily loans of city bikes outside the train station. Bring ID and Sfr20 deposit.

TOP FIVE SWITZERLAND

- **Festival** Zürich's techno Street Parade (p1173) – has even recently overtaken Berlin's Love Parade in size

- **Walk** Anywhere in the Berner Oberland – picking a favourite is hard, but we really liked the hike from Stechelberg up to magical little Gimmelwald (p1179)

- **Bar/Club** Zürich's Hotel Otter (p1175) and Wüste bar (p1176) – no contest

- **Impressive sight** Lausanne's Musée de L'Art Brut (p1169) – criminals and the mentally insane created the artwork

- **Mountain** The Matterhorn (p1170) – in a country of mountains it is still the A-list star

SWITZERLAND

LAKE GENEVA REGION

Stretching like a liquid mirror east from Geneva and south to France is Western Europe's largest lake, known to most as Lake Geneva, and to Francophones as Lac Léman. Cosmopolitan Geneva, as well as the elegant city of Lausanne and the Swiss Riviera town of Montreux line the lake's shores.

GENEVA (GENÈVE, GENF, GINEVRA)
pop 180,400

International Geneva had a key place on the world stage for most of last century. The European Headquarters of the UN are here, plus the International Red Cross and the World Health Organization, among 250 other international groups. Tidy and aesthetic Geneva belongs less to Switzerland than to the world. More than 40% of residents are non-Swiss, and this city of bankers, diplomats and transients has a seriously worldly flavour.

GETTING INTO TOWN

From the airport there are regular trains into Gare de Cornavin (Sfr2.60, six minutes), the main train station in the heart of the old town.

Information
EMERGENCY
Police station (☎ 117; Rue de Berne 6)

INTERNET ACCESS
Video Club (☎ 022 731 47 48; Rue des Alpes 19; ⏰ 11am-midnight Mon-Thu, 11-2am Fri-Sat, noon-midnight Sun; per hr Sfr5)

MEDICAL SERVICES
Cantonal Hospital (☎ 022 372 33 11; Rue Micheli-du-Crest 24)
Medical Information (☎ 111)
Servette Clinique (☎ 022 733 98 00; Ave Wendt 60) Emergency dental treatment.

MONEY
Exchange office (Gare de Cornavin; ⏰ 6.50am-7.40pm Mon-Sat, 6.50am-6.40pm Sun)

POST
Main post office (Rue du Mont-Blanc 18; ⏰ 7.30am-6pm Mon-Fri, 8.30am-noon Sat)

TOURIST INFORMATION
Genève Tourism (☎ 022 909 70 00; www.geneve -tourism.ch; Rue du Mont-Blanc 18; ⏰ 10am-6pm Mon, 9am-6pm Tue-Sat) Grab a copy of the free *Vélo-Cité* map or the budget-conscious brochure *Genève info-jeunes*.

Sights & Activities
OLD TOWN
Start a scenic walk through the old town at the **Île Rousseau**, home to a statue honouring the celebrated free thinker, then follow the narrow, cobbled Rue de la Cité just until it becomes Grand-Rue. **Rousseau's birthplace** is at No 40. A short detour off the Grand-Rue takes you to the part-Romanesque, part-Gothic **Cathédrale St Pierre**, where John Calvin preached from 1536 to 1564. Take Rue de la Fontaine to reach the lakeside where you'll find Geneva's most visible landmark – the **Jet d'Eau**. Calling this a fountain is an understatement. The water shoots up with incredible force to create a 140m-high plume.

UNITED NATIONS
At the Art-Deco **Palais des Nations** (☎ 022 907 48 96; Ave de la Paix 9-14; adult/student Sfr8.50/6.50; ⏰ 9am-6pm Jul-Aug, 10am-noon & 2-4pm Apr-Jun & Sep-Oct, 10am-noon & 2-4pm Mon-Fri Nov-Mar), the European arm of the UN, you can see where decisions about world affairs are made on the hour-long tour (bring your passport). Afterwards don't miss the extensive gardens and the towering grey titanium monument donated by the USSR to commemorate the conquest of space. Get there by catching bus No 5 or 8.

INTERNATIONAL RED CROSS & RED CRESCENT MUSEUM
This **museum** (☎ 022 748 95 25; Ave de la Paix 17; adult/student Sfr10/5; ⏰ 10am-5pm Wed-Mon) is a compelling multimedia trawl through atrocities perpetuated by humanity in recent history. Against the long litany of war and nastiness, documented in films, photos, sculptures and soundtracks, the noble aims of the organisation are set. Catch bus No 5 or 8.

Sleeping
Hotels in Geneva are pricey, but there are centrally located backpackers.

Hôme St Pierre (☎ 022 310 37 07; www.homest pierre.ch; Cour St-Pierre 4; dm Sfr24, s/d with shared bathroom Sfr46/62; 💻) It's women only in the singles and doubles at this hostel, but there is a men's dorm. A long time favourite, it's a

GENEVA (GENÈVE)

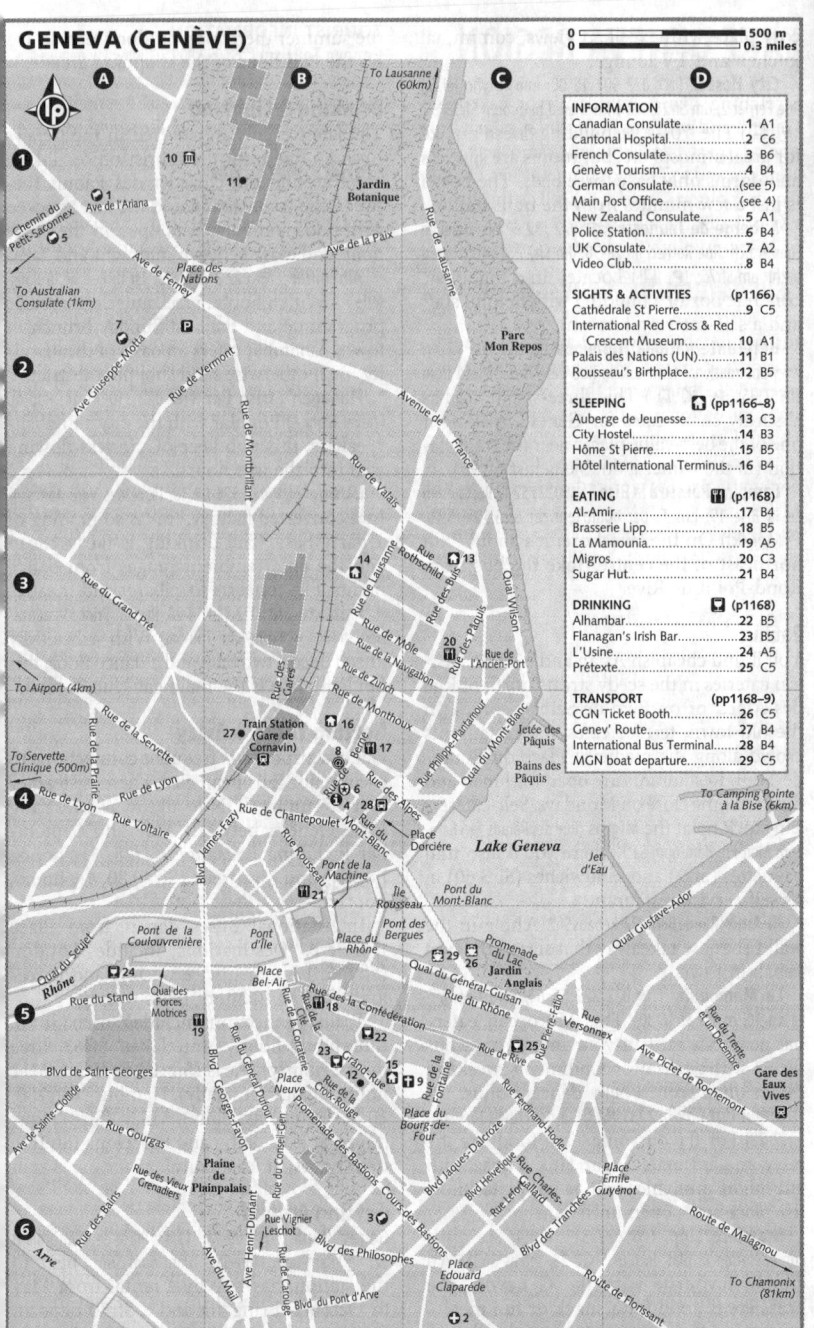

0		500 m
0		0.3 miles

INFORMATION
Canadian Consulate................1 A1
Cantonal Hospital...................2 C6
French Consulate.....................3 B6
Genève Tourism.......................4 B4
German Consulate.............(see 5)
Main Post Office...............(see 4)
New Zealand Consulate.........5 A1
Police Station...........................6 B4
UK Consulate............................7 A2
Video Club................................8 B4

SIGHTS & ACTIVITIES (p1166)
Cathédrale St Pierre................9 C5
International Red Cross & Red
  Crescent Museum................10 A1
Palais des Nations (UN)..........11 B1
Rousseau's Birthplace............12 B5

SLEEPING (pp1166–8)
Auberge de Jeunesse..............13 C3
City Hostel..............................14 B3
Hôme St Pierre......................15 B5
Hôtel International Terminus..16 B4

EATING (p1168)
Al-Amir...................................17 B4
Brasserie Lipp.........................18 B5
La Mamounia.........................19 A5
Migros....................................20 C3
Sugar Hut...............................21 B4

DRINKING (p1168)
Alhambar................................22 B5
Flanagan's Irish Bar................23 B5
L'Usine....................................24 A5
Prétexte..................................25 C5

TRANSPORT (pp1168–9)
CGN Ticket Booth...................26 C5
Genev' Route..........................27 B4
International Bus Terminal......28 B4
MGN boat departure..............29 C5

cosy place with excellent views, communal kitchen and TV lounge.

City Hostel (☎ 022 901 15 00; info@cityhostel.ch; Rue Ferrier 2; dm Sfr28, s/d with shared bathroom Sfr58/85; 🅿 🖳) The '70s-style building doesn't make for great atmosphere, but rooms are spotless and dorms only have three beds. The hostel is just a few minutes from the train station.

Auberge de Jeunesse (☎ 022 732 62 60; www.yh -geneva.ch; Rue Rothschild 28-30; dm Sfr25, d with shared bathroom Sfr75; 🅿 🖳) Located in a big, busy, concrete box of a building with helpful staff and a self-catering kitchen.

Hôtel International Terminus ☎ 022 906 97 77; www.international-terminus.ch; Rue des Alpes 20; s/d from Sfr95/135; 🅿 ❌ 🖳) This three-star hotel has absurdly cheap rates for Geneva, making it one of the best-value places near the train station (in the winter a double is just Sfr95).

Camping Pointe á la Bise (☎ 022 752 12 96; Chemin de la Bise 19; bus E; per adult/tent/car Sfr6.50/6/5.50; 🕙 Apr-Oct) On the lakeshore, it's about 7km northeast of the centre. Take the bus from Rond-Point de Rive.

Eating

You'll find cheapish Asian and Middle Eastern eateries in the seedy streets north of Rue des Alpes, or on Blvd de Saint-Georges. In the old town, terrace cafés and restaurants crowd along the medieval Place du Bourg-de-Four. Restaurants are open for lunch and dinner. Some close on Mondays. Self-caterers can stock up at the **Migros** (Rue des Pâquis 🕙 8am-7pm Mon-Fri, 8am-6pm Sat) where you'll also find baguettes (Sfr2) and sandwiches (Sfr3.60) in its self-service restaurant.

Al-Amir (Rue de Berne 22; kebabs Sfr8) A hole-in-the-wall Lebanese takeaway that serves the best kebab in town.

La Mamounia (☎ 022 329 55 61; Blvd Georges-Favon 10; mains Sfr16-30) This Moroccan eatery has generous melt-in-your-mouth couscous dishes with an array of condiments; weekend diners often score a belly-dancer bonus.

Sugar Hut (☎ 022 731 4613; Rue des Etuves 16; mains Sfr22-28) For flavoursome Thai food, try the busy and intimate Sugar Hut. Those with late-night munchies will be happy to know the place stays open until 2am.

Brassiere Lipp (☎ 022 311 10 11; Rue des la Confédération 8; plat du jour Sfr20-28, mains Sfr35) An eternal favourite with the Genevois, the brassiere is good for a snack or full meal – everything from oysters to a perch fillet. In the summer there is an outdoor terrace. It's on the 2nd floor of the shopping arcade.

Drinking & Clubbing

The latest events are covered in the *Genève Agenda*, free from the tourist office. Take a stroll around the Quartier des Pâquis (between the train station and the lake) packed with pubs and bars. Bars open in the afternoon and close between midnight and 2am.

Alhambar (☎ 022 314 13 13; 1st fl, Rue de la Rôtisserie 10) With a hubbub feel, an eclectic music programme and the best Sunday brunch in town, Alhambar offers an oasis of theatricality in an otherwise staid shopping district.

Flanagan's Irish Bar (☎ 022 310 13 14; Rue du Cheval-Blanc 4) Popular with the city's English-speakers, this pub keeps Guinness flowing well into the wee hours.

L'Usine (☎ 022 328 08 18; Place des Volontaires 4) In a converted factory, this is something of a party base. The drinking is fairly cheap and the entertainment ranges from dance nights and concerts to cabaret and theatre.

Prétexte (☎ 022 310 14 28; Rue du Prince 9; admission Sfr10; 🕙 11pm-5am Thu-Sat) With a healthily kitsch décor, two bars and a dance floor, this opulent place is the main gay club in town.

Getting There & Away

Geneva airport has frequent connections to each major European city. There is steamer service run by CGN to all towns bordering Lake Geneva between May and September including Lausanne (Sfr28, 3½ hours, hourly) and Montreux (Sfr40.80, 4½ hours, hourly).

International buses depart from Place Dorcière. Destinations include London (Sfr145, 17 hours, twice weekly) and Barcelona (Sfr100, 10 hours, twice weekly).

Trains connections include Zürich (Sfr76, three hours, hourly), Interlaken (Sfr63, three hours, hourly), Paris (Sfr103 by TGV, 31/2 hours, eight times daily), Hamburg (Sfr280, 10 hours, at least daily), Milan (Sfr81, four hours, at least daily) and Barcelona (Sfr100, nine hours, at least daily).

Getting Around

Genev' Roule (☎ 022 740 13 43; Place de Montbrillant 17; 🕙 8am-6pm Mon-Sat, 10am-6pm Sun), next to the station, has free bike rental from May to October. Bring ID and a Sfr50 deposit. Public transport is excellent, and ticket dispensers are found at all bus, boat or tram stops. A day pass costs Sfr6.

LAUSANNE
pop 118,200

This beautiful hillside city overlooking Lake Geneva has several distinct personalities. There's relaxed former fishing village Ouchy, stylish cobblestoned Place St-François, and the warehouse district of Flon, filled with bars, galleries and boutiques.

The main train station is south of Place St François and the old town. The **tourist office** (☎ 021 613 73 21; www.lausanne-tourisme.ch; Place de la Navigation 4; ☺ 9am-6pm) is next door to the Ouchy metro station.

The **Musée de L'Art Brut** (☎ 021 647 54 35; www .artbrut.ch in German; Ave de Bergiéres 11; adult/student Sfr6/4; ☺ 11am-1pm & 2-6pm Tue-Fri, 11am-6pm Sat & Sun) is maybe the country's most alluring museum. It has a fascinating amalgam of 15,000 works of art created by psychiatric patients, eccentrics and incarcerated criminals.

Another must-see is the Gothic **Cathédrale de Notre Dame** (☺ 7am-7pm Mon-Fri, 8am-7pm Sat & Sun Apr-Sep; closes 5.30pm Oct-Mar) in central Lausanne, arguably the finest in Switzerland.

Sleeping

You will need to catch a bus from Place St François to reach much of the budget accommodation.

Lausanne Guesthouse & Backpacker (☎ 021 601 80 00; www.lausanne-guesthouse.ch; Chemin des Epinettes 4; dm Sfr29, s/d with shared bathroom Sfr80/86; ✗) Stunning views of the lake and Alps are on offer at this tastefully renovated 1894 townhouse high on a hill; a stroll from the train station.

Jeunotel SA (☎ 021 626 02 22; www.jeunotel.ch; Chemin du Bois-de-Vaux 36; bus No 2; dm Sfr30, s/d with shared bathroom Sfr60/80; P 🖳) The cheaper rooms feel rather dismal with exposed cinderblock walls, but the place caters to young Swiss and the bar can become lively.

Camping de Vidy (☎ 021 622 50 00; info@ campinglausannevidy.ch; Chemin du Camping 3; bus No 2; per person/tent Sfr7.80/12) Lakeside camping is available year-round.

Eating & Drinking

Le Mix Snack Bar (☎ 078 808 7968; Rue Central 29; mains from Sfr4.50; ☺ 7am-8.30pm) This low-key place fills up at lunch when locals flock inside for a sandwich, kebab, burger or coffee. It's small and smoky with cheery orange walls.

Café de L'Evêché (☎ 021 323 93 23; Rue Louis-Auguste Curtat 4; mains Sfr15-25; ☺ closed Sun) The pasta and fondues are said to be the best in town, and the restaurant has a lovely back garden perfect for a late summer night drink.

Pinte Besson (☎ 021 312 72 27; Rue de l'Ale 4; ☺ closed 6pm Sat & all day Sun) The city's oldest tavern has been serving local wines to Lausannois punters since 1780, and exudes the atmosphere of a time past.

Mad – Moulin a Danse (☎ 021 312 11 22; www .mad.ch; Rue de Genéve 23; admission Sfr20 Thu-Sun; ☺ Wed-Sun) This large club relies on music theme nights to keep things interesting. The downstairs bar has free admission weeknights. On Sunday the club hosts Trixx Club for gays and lesbians.

Getting There & Around

There are trains to Geneva (Sfr18.80, 50 minutes, three hourly), Bern (Sfr30, 70 minutes, one or two hourly) and Interlaken Ost (Sfr52, two hours, two hourly). For boat services, see p1168 in the Geneva section.

MONTREUX
pop 22,800

Centrepiece of the 'Swiss Riviera', Montreux is an affluent town with stunning views of the French Alps, excellent lakeside walks and well maintained pastel buildings.

The extraordinary oval-shaped **Château de Chillon** (☎ 021 966 89 10; www.chillon.ch; adult/student/child Sfr8.50/6.50/4; ☺ 9am-7pm daily Apr-Sep, 9.30am-5pm Mar & Oct, 10am-4pm Nov-Feb) fairly receives more visitors than any other historical building in Switzerland. The 11th-century fortress caught the public imagination when Lord Byron wrote *The Prisoner of Chillon* about Bonivard, a prior chained in the dungeons for almost four years in the 16th century. The castle is a pleasant 45-minute walk along the lakefront from Montreux. Otherwise take trolley bus No 1 (Sfr2.60; Veytaux stop).

Auberge de Jeunesse (☎ 021 963 49 34; fax 021 963 27 29; Passage de l'Auberge 8, Territet; bus No 1; dm Sfr32, d with shared bathroom Sfr76; ☺ mid-Feb–mid-Nov) is a simple hostel on the waterfront a 30-minute walk from the centre. **Hostellerie du Lac** (☎ 021 963 32 71; fax 021 963 18 35; Rue du Quai 12; s/d with shared bathroom Sfr50/85; ☺ Mar-Nov) offers faded grandeur and a prime lakeside position.

Inexpensive sandwiches, croissants, quiches and a mouth-watering chocolate selection make **La Rose des Sables** (☎ 021 961 15 46; Ave des

Alps 42; mains from Sfr3; ⊗ lunch) a lovely lunch option.

Brasserie des Alpes (☎ 021 963 21 20; Ave des Alpes 23; mains Sfr15-30; ⊗ closed Sun) is a cosy and quaintly decorated spot that serves heaps of pizza and pasta.

There are trains to Geneva (Sfr26, 70 minutes, hourly), Lausanne (Sfr9.80, 25 minutes, hourly) and Interlaken (Sfr54, three hours, daily).

GRYON

To get off the beaten track consider quiet **Gryon**, 30km southeast of Montreux. It's near the ski fields of Villars, and home to one of Switzerland's best backpackers' dens – the **Swiss Alp Retreat** (☎ 024 498 33 21; www.gryon.com; Chalet Martin; dm/d from Sfr18/52; P 🖳). In a funky wooden chalet, you can make new friends over an après ski beer by the log fire or on the sundeck. The hostel has a laid-back vibe and gets rave reviews from travellers. Ask about the ski and stay packages.

From Lausanne go via train to Bex (Sfr17, 40 minutes, hourly), then the cogwheel train to the village (Sfr5.80, 30 minutes, hourly).

VALAIS (WALLIS)

Welcome to Matterhorn country – the place where they shoot the postcards. An area of extraordinary natural beauty, the Valais boasts the 10 highest mountains in Switzerland – all over 4000m.

ZERMATT

pop 5500

One word says it all: Matterhorn. Synonymous with Switzerland, the most famous peak in the Alps keeps solitary vigil over this skiing, mountaineering and hiking hotspot.

Zermatt is small and car-free, but tiny electric taxis and vans whisk guests about. Bahnhofstrasse is the main street, but street names aren't used. **Zermatt Tourismus** (☎ 027 966 81 00; www.zermatt.ch; ⊗ 8.30am-noon & 1.30-6pm Mon-Fri, 8.30am-noon Sat) is beside the train station.

Activities

Arguably perhaps the country's best ski resort, **Zermatt Bergbahnen** (☎ 027 966 01 01; http://bergbahnen.zermatt.ch/e; lift ticket winter/summer Sfr72/60; ski & boot rental Sfr45) caters mainly to intermediate and expert riders. One ski region,

the Klein Matterhorn, provides access to the most extensive summer ski region in Switzerland and the highest skiing on the continent.

In summer, Zermatt is a hiker's paradise with 400km of trails offering spectacular views. Take a cable car up and hike or bike down the slopes. A day lift pass for cyclists costs Sfr54. To climb the Matterhorn you'll need prior climbing experience, a week's preparation and a staggering Sfr1120 per person. The ascent and descent takes eight hours. For more detals visit the **Alpin Center** (☎ 027 966 24 60; www.zermatt.ch/alpincenter; Bahnhofstrasse; ⊗ 8.30am-noon & 4-7pm Jul-Sep, 5-7pm Jan–midMay) near the post office. It arranges a myriad of other adventure sports.

Sleeping, Eating & Drinking

Be warned that many hotels and restaurants close between seasons.

Matterhorn Hostel (☎ 027 968 19 19; www.matterhornhostel.com; Schluhmattstrasse 32; dm from Sfr29, d with shared bathroom Sf78; 🖳) In a Swiss chalet, a short walk from the station, this place has its own restaurant and après-ski bar.

Hotel Bahnhof (☎ 027 967 24 06; www.hotelbahnhof.com; dm Sfr30, s/d with shared bathroom from Sfr64/84) A long-time mountaineers' mecca, the hotel has an impressive kitchen, large dorms, and doubles with balconies facing the Matterhorn. It's directly opposite the station.

Brown Cow (Hotel de la Poste; ☎ 027 967 19 32; Bahnhofstrasse 41; mains Sfr6-14) Great music, hearty food and cowhide décor make the Brown Cow a favourite with resort workers. Don't miss the monster burgers (including veggie) with chunky chips.

North Wall Bar (☎ 027 967 28 63; pizzas from Sfr13; ⊗ 6.30pm-midnight) Cheap beer, inspirational ski videos, 'the best pizza in town' and folks from all over the world (it's another resort workers' favourite') all co-exist at this cheery place. It's just off the Bahnhofstrasse.

Restaurant Weisshorn (☎ 027 967 11 12; Bahnhofstrasse; mains Sfr16-30) Offering Valais specialties as well as raclette, rösti and fondue, Weisshorn is beyond the church on the main street.

Getting There & Around

Trains depart from Brig, stopping at Visp en route (one-way/round-trip Sfr37/65, 80 minutes, hourly). Swiss Passes are valid, but there is no discount for Eurail Pass holders. Zermatt is car-free. You need to park at

Täsch (from Sfr5.50 per day) and take the train (Sfr8.60). Parking is free near the Visp station if you take the Zermatt train.

TICINO (TESSIN)

The Mediterranean air is hot and spicy, the attitude laid-back, with cafés in the colourful piazzas buzzing under a brilliant blue sky. Melodic notes and lots of hand gestures, steaming plates of pasta, creamy gelatos. Did you cross the border into Italy? No, this is just the Switzerland that defies the stereotypes.

South of the Alps, Ticino (Tessin in German) enjoys an unmistakable Italian flavour, and Italian is the official language. Although not technically in Ticino, we've included the resort town of St Moritz in this section because of its proximity.

LOCARNO
pop 14,400
A rambling red enclave of Mediterranean-style houses, piazzas and arcades ending at the northern end of Lake Maggiore, Locarno enjoys more hours of sunshine than anywhere else in Switzerland.

Piazza Grande is the town's centre. Gulp shots, smoke Cuban cigars and check emails at the **Pardo Bar** (☎ 091 752 21 23; Via della Motta 3; per hr Sfr20; ☼ 11-1am). The **tourist office** (☎ 091 751 03 33; locarno@ticino.com; ☼ 9am-6pm Mon-Fri, 10am-5pm Sat, 10am-2pm Sun) is in the casino complex.

Don't miss the formidable **Madonna del Sasso**, with its panoramic views of the lake and town. It features a church with 15th-century paintings, a small museum and several distinctive statues.

Make sure to stroll around the lake to **Giardini Jean Arp**, off Lungolago Motta, where sculptures by the surrealist artist are scattered among palm trees and springtime tulips.

Pensione Cittá Vecchia (☎ 091 751 45 54; citta vecchia@datacomm.ch; Via Toretta 13; dm Sfr25, s/d Sfr36/72; ☼ Mar-Nov; ✗) has basic dorms, smiley staff and a non-smoking environment. It's uphill from Piazza Grande via a lane next to the Manor department store.

The radio station and music school at **SYHA Palagiovani Hostel** (☎ 091 756 15 00; locarno@ youthhostel.ch; Via Varenna 18; dm/d with shared bathroom from Sfr33/66) allow for the chance to interact with locals. Otherwise it's a rather charmless place 500m west of Piazza Grande.

If you're looking for great views and easy access to lake swimming, then head to **Delta Camping** (☎ 091 751 60 81; Via Respini 7; per adult/tent from Sfr11/21; ☼ Mar-Oct).

Lake Maggiore has a great range of fresh and tasty fish. Check out *persico* (perch) and *corigone* (whitefish). For self-caterers there's a **Coop supermarket** and a **Migros De Gustibus** snack bar on Pizza Grande. Young residents flock to the popular **Lungolago** (☎ 091 923 12 33; Via Nassa 11; mains Sfr10-25), which has outside tables overlooking the lake and a range of pizzas to sop up the cheap beer.

There are trains from Brig (Sfr50, 2½ hours, hourly).

LUGANO
pop 26,100
Switzerland's southernmost tourist town is a sophisticated slice of Italian life, with vibrant markets, fancy shops, pedestrian-only piazzas and lakeside parks. Resting on the shore of Lake Lugano with Montes San Salvatore and Bré rising on either side, it's also a great base for lake trips, water sports and hillside hikes.

The old town is a 10-minute walk down the hill to the east from the train station. Internet access is at **City Disc** (Via P Peri; per hr Sfr11). On the lake side of the Municipio building is the **tourist office** (☎ 091 913 32 32; info@lugano-tourism .ch; Riva Albertolli; ☼ 9am-6.30pm Mon-Fri, 9am-12.30pm & 1.30-5pm Sat, 10am-3pm Sun; closed weekends in winter).

Sights & Activities
Stroll through the winding alleyways of Lugano's old town, go window-shopping along the stylish arcade-lined **Via Nassa** (street of fishing nets), then pop into the **Santa Maria degli Angioli Church** (Piazza Luini), featuring a vivid 1529 fresco of the *Crucifixion* by Bernardino Luini.

Waterbabies will love the **Lido** (admission Sfr8; ☼ 9.30am-6pm May-Sep), east of the Cassarate River, with a swimming pool and sandy beaches. Or take a **boat trip** to one of the photogenic villages hugging Lake Lugano's shoreline. One of the most popular is **Gandria**, a tiny hillside village with historic homes and shops and narrow winding alleyways right down to the water.

Sleeping & Eating
The **Hotel Backpackers Montarina** (☎ 091 966 72 72; www.montarina.ch; Via Montarina 1; dm Sfr25, s/d

Sfr70/100; P ☎) In a 19th-century villa, Montarina is a summer haven with a large pool, a garden with plenty of palm trees and a kitchen. Ask about the array of adventure activities that can be arranged.

SYHA hostel (☎ 091 966 27 28; fax 091 968 23 63; Via Cantonale 13; dm/d Sfr31/72; ☾ mid-Mar–Nov; ☎) Warm and laid-back, this family-run hostel has a swimming pool that is a great place to meet other travellers. It's a hard 20-minute walk uphill from the train station (signposted), or take bus No 5 to Crocifisso.

Tempt the tastebuds with panini (Sfr5) and gelati (Sfr3) from street stalls in the pedestrian-only piazzas.

Sayonara (☎ 091 922 01 70; Via Soave 10; pasta from Sfr10, pizza from Sfr15.50) With delicious Italian cuisine and a good wine list (try the Ticinese white Merlot), this restaurant is a popular venue.

Panino Gusto (☎ 091 922 51 51; Via Motta 7a; panini Sfr9-19) Panini with smoked meats, salmon and cheeses are the favourite options at this casual spot.

La Tinéra (Via dei Gorini; mains Sfr11-27; ☾ closed Sun) This critically acclaimed restaurant in a tiny cellar off Piazza della Reformat serves local specialities to a jam-packed crowd.

Getting There & Around

Postbuses run to St Moritz (Sfr74, four hours; daily summer, Friday, Saturday and Sunday winter). Swiss pass holders pay Sfr11. Everyone needs to reserve seats the day before by visiting or phoning the **bus station** (☎ 091 807 85 20; Via Serafino Balestra).

Trains run to Locarno (Sfr15, one hour) and from Locarno to Brig (Sfr50, two and a half hours).

ST MORITZ

pop 4900

St Moritz has built its reputation as the playground of the international jet set for more than a century. The plush main town, St Moritz Dorf, is above the train station. Two kilometres southwest around the lake is the more downmarket St Moritz Bad; buses run between the two. St Moritz is seasonal and becomes a ghost town during November and late April to early June.

The **tourist office** (☎ 081 837 33 33; www.stmoritz.ch; Via Maistra 12; ☾ 9am-noon & 2-6pm Mon-Fri, 9am-noon Sat) is in St Moritz Dorf.

Bobby's Pub (☎ 081 834 42 83; Via dal Bagn 50a; per hr Sfr12; ☾ 10-1am) is where to surf the Web.

In winter 350km of superb slopes draw skiers and snowboarders to **Corviglia-Marguns** (☎ 081 830 00 00; www.bergbahnenengadin.ch; lift ticket Sfr63, ski & boot rental Sfr43). The choice for beginners is limited. There are also 160km of **crosscountry trails** (equipment rental Sfr20). In summer check out the 120km of marked **hiking paths**.

Backing onto the forest and nordic ski course is the **Youth Hostel St Moritz Bad** (☎ 081 833 39 69; www.youthhostel.ch/st.moritz; Via Surpunt 60; dm with half-board Sfr45.50; 💻). Large and modern, it has excellent facilities including mountain bike rental, compulsory half-board and a TV lounge. Take a bus towards Maloja from the train station and get off at the Hotel Sonne, then walk half a kilometer.

Sporthotel Stille (☎ 081 833 69 48; hotel.stille@bluewin.ch; Via Surpunt 58; s/d Sfr72/144; P) is next to the hostel and attracts a young, sporty crowd. In the winter it has a bar and occasionally a disco; in summer, prices drop.

For a romantic candlelit dining experience and delicious pasta dishes in St Moritz Bad, try **La Fontana** (☎ 081 833 12 66; Via dal Bagn 16; mains Sfr12-28; 9am-midnight Mon-Sat, 11am-midnight Sun).

If you're craving fondue, **Engiadina** (☎ 081 833 3265; Plazza da Sculoda 2; fondue from Sfr28; ☾ closed Sun), in the Dorf, is famous for the dish. Make a romantic dinner of it by ordering fondue and champagne for Sfr34.

Next to La Fontana is a **Coop supermarket** for self-caterers.

Two postbuses run to/from Lugano. See p1172 for details.

Trains link St Moritz and Tirano, Italy (Sfr52, two and a half hours, nine daily). From Tirano you can connect to Milan.

ZÜRICH

pop 351,700

There's an electricity in the air in Switzerland's most populous city, which is not found anywhere else in the country. Banks, art galleries and trendy bars greet you, and the city will charm the most jaded traveller. During the day it is a relatively sedate place, where hours pass easily wandering the graceful old town. When darkness falls, the city kicks it up a notch as the pinstripe brigade yields the streets to bar-hoppers and clubbers in Switzerland's most happening scene.

GETTING INTO TOWN

Regular trains make the 10-minute trip from the airport to the main train station (Sfr5.40) on the western bank of the river and the edge of the old town.

ORIENTATION

Compact and easy to navigate, Zürich is at the northern end of Lake Zürich. The Limmat River splits the city centre.

INFORMATION

Bookshops

Orell Füssli Bookshop (☎ 01 211 04 44; Bahnhofstrasse 70) Fiction and travel books in English.

Emergency

Medical and dental help (☎ 01 269 69 69)
Police (☎ 01216 71 11; Bahnhofquai 3)

Internet Resources

Quanta (☎ 01 260 72 66; cnr Niederdorfstrasse & Mühlegasse; per hr Sfr10)

Medical Services

Cantonal University Hospital (☎ 01 255 11 11; Rämistrasse 100)
Bellevue Apotheke (☎ 01 252 56 00; Theaterstrasse 14) 24-hour chemist.

Money

There's no shortage of choice when exchanging money in this banking city. Banks are open 8.15am to 4.30pm Monday to Friday (until 6pm Thursday).

Post

Main post office (☎ 01 296 21 11; Kasernenstrasse 95-97; ☼ 7.30am-8pm Mon-Fri, 8am-4pm Sat)

Tourist Information

Zürich Tourism (☎ 01 215 30 00; www.zurichtourism.ch; ☼ 8.30am-8.30pm Mon-Fri, 8.30am-6.30pm Sat & Sun) Inside the train station; arranges hotels, car rentals and tours.

Travel Agencies

STA Travel (☎ 01 261 97 57; Leonhardstrasse 10; ☼ 10am -6pm Mon-Wed & Fri, 10am-8pm Thu, 10am-1pm Sat)

SIGHTS

Old Town & Lakeside

Stroll down elegant **Bahnhofstrasse**, the city's infamous shopping street, where the bank vaults underneath are said to be crammed with gold and silver. Above ground you'll find luxury shops selling the best Switzerland can offer. Perfect for window-shopping.

On Sundays it seems as if all of Zürich takes an afternoon stroll around the lake; make sure to join in. There are human traffic jams at times, but it is a worthwhile cultural experience. On the eastern bank, the **Zürichhorn Park** has sculptures and a Chinese Garden. In summer it buzzes with food stalls and entertainment. There is a roped-off swimming area with a slide and diving board.

Churches

The 13th-century **Fraumünster** (cathedral; Münsterplatz; ☼ 9am-6pm May-Sep, 10am-5pm Oct-Apr) has some of the world's most distinctive stained-glass windows (designed by 20th-century surrealist Marc Chagall), while the 13th-century tower of **St Peterskirche** (St Peter's Church; St.-Peter-hofstatt; ☼ 8am-6pm Mon-Fri, 8am-3pm Sat) has Europe's largest clock face (8.7m in diameter). The dual-towered **Grossmünster** (Grossmünsterplatz; ☼ 9am-6pm mid-Mar–Oct, 10am-5pm Nov–mid-Mar) is notable too. From here, Protestant preacher Huldrych Zwingli had spread the word to 'pray and work' during the Reformation.

Kunsthaus

The **museum of fine arts** (☎ 01 253 84 84; www .kunsthaus.ch; Heimplatz 1; adult/student Sfr12/7, free Sun; ☼ 10am-9pm Tue-Thu, 10am-5pm Fri-Sun) has one of the best collections in the country. Don't miss the Alberto Giacometti paintings and stick-figure sculptures.

Zoo Zürich & Masoala Rainforest

About 2000 animals are on exhibit at the **Zoo Zürich** (☎ 01 254 25 00; www.zoo.ch in German; Zürichberg-strasse 221; adult/student Sfr14/7; ☼ 8am-6pm Mar-Oct, 8am-5pm Nov-Feb), one of the best in Europe. The zoo was creating a Madagascan rainforest on 10,000 sq metres of parkland at the time of research. To get there, take tram No 6.

FESTIVALS & EVENTS

Zürich lets its hair down in August with the techno **Street Parade**. It attracts well over half a million ravers. All-night parties around the city follow a three-hour parade.

SLEEPING

Zürich has a bizarre love affair with theme hotels – everything from rock to animal

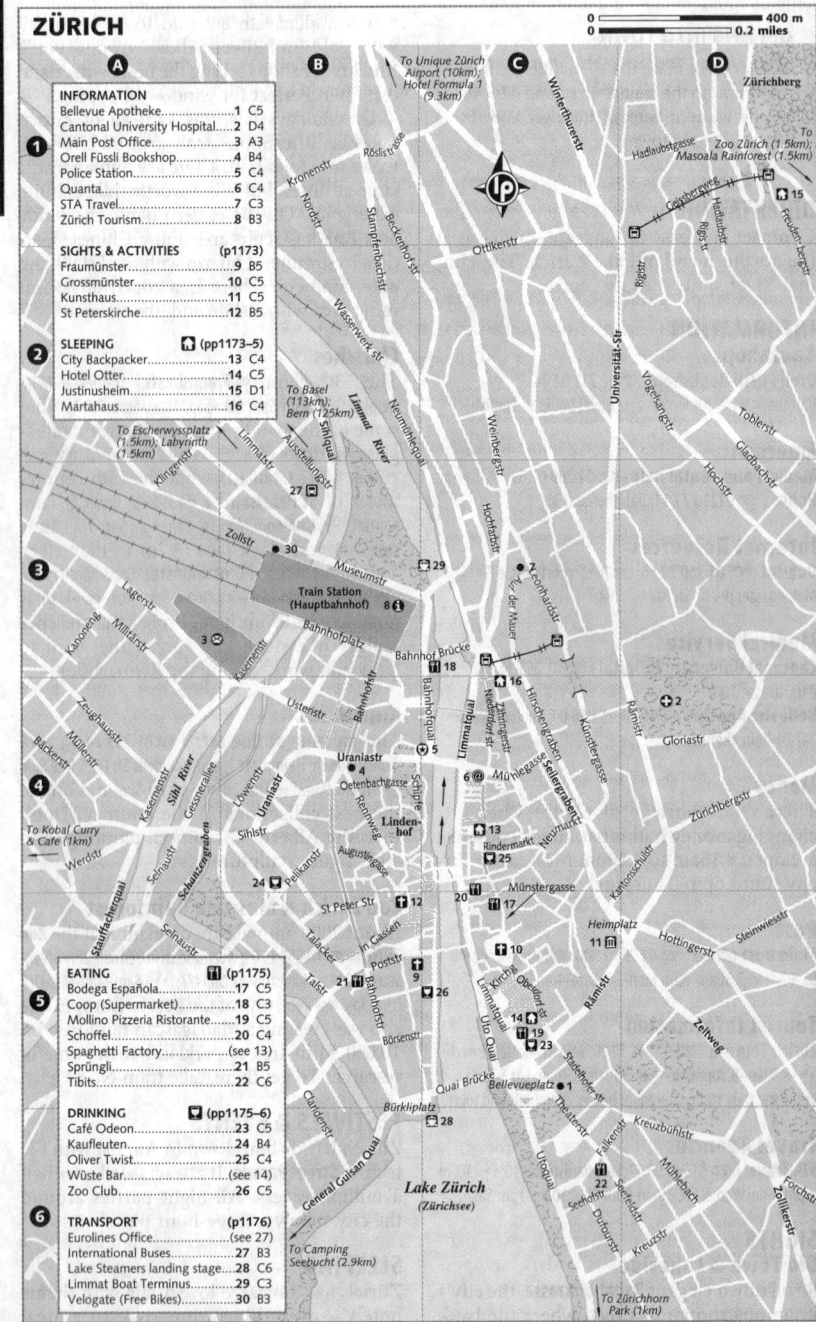

ZÜRICH

0 — 400 m
0 — 0.2 miles

INFORMATION
Bellevue Apotheke................1 C5
Cantonal University Hospital...2 D4
Main Post Office..................3 A3
Orell Füssli Bookshop...........4 B4
Police Station.....................5 C4
Quanta...............................6 C4
STA Travel..........................7 C3
Zürich Tourism....................8 B3

SIGHTS & ACTIVITIES (p1173)
Fraumünster........................9 B5
Grossmünster.....................10 C5
Kunsthaus.........................11 C5
St Peterskirche...................12 B5

SLEEPING (pp1173–5)
City Backpacker..................13 C4
Hotel Otter........................14 C5
Justinusheim......................15 D1
Martahaus.........................16 C4

EATING (p1175)
Bodega Española.................17 C5
Coop (Supermarket)............18 C3
Mollino Pizzeria Ristorante...19 C5
Schoffel...........................20 C4
Spaghetti Factory.........(see 13)
Sprüngli............................21 B5
Tibits...............................22 C6

DRINKING (pp1175–6)
Café Odeon........................23 C5
Kaufleuten.........................24 B4
Oliver Twist.......................25 C4
Wüste Bar....................(see 14)
Zoo Club...........................26 C5

TRANSPORT (p1176)
Eurolines Office..............(see 27)
International Buses...............27 B3
Lake Steamers landing stage...28 C6
Limmat Boat Terminus..........29 C3
Velogate (Free Bikes)...........30 B3

To Unique Zürich Airport (10km); Hotel Formula 1 (9.3km)

Zürichberg

To Zoo Zürich (1.5km); Masoala Rainforest (1.5km)

Winterthurerstr
Hadlaubstrasse
Rösslistr
Kronenstr
Nordstr
Stampfenbachstr
Beckenhofstr
Ottikerstr
Universität-Str
Voglerstr
Gladbachstr
Toblerstr
Hochstr
Rigistr
Freudenbergstr
Seilergraben

Wasserwerk str
Weinbergstr
Hochstr

To Basel (113km); Bern (125km)
Limmat River
Neumühlequai

To Escherwyssplatz (1.5km); Labyrinth (1.5km)
Limmatstr
Ausstellungsstr
Klingenstr
Sihlquai

Zollstr
Museumstr
29
27

30
Train Station (Hauptbahnhof)
8
Bahnhofplatz
3
Lagerstr
Milltärstr
Kasernenstr
Kanonenstr

Bahnhofstr
Bahnhof Brücke
18
Bahnhofquai
16

Zeughausstr
Müllerstr
Sihl River
Uraniastr
5
Uraniastr
4
Oetenbachgasse
Schipfe
6
Mühlegasse
Niederdorfstr

Lindenhof
13
Rindermarkt
25

Backerstr
Kasernenstr
Gessneralles
Sihlstr
Lowenstr
Renweg
Augustinerg
St Peter Str
12
17
Münstergasse
20
11
Heimplatz
Hottingerstr

To Kobal Curry & Cafe (1km)
Werdstr
Selnaustr
Stauffacherquai
Schanzengraben
24
Pelikanstr
In Gassen
10
Kirchg
9
Oberdorfstr
14
19
23

Talacker
Poststr
21
26
Limmatquai

Börsenstr
Quai Brücke
Bellevueplatz
1

Gen General Guisan Quai
Bürkliplatz
28

Lake Zürich (Zürichsee)

To Camping Seebucht (2.9km)

To Zürichhorn Park (1km)

2
Gloriastr
Zürichbergstr
Rämistr
Kantonsschulstr
Neumarkt

Zelbelg
Seefeldstr
Stadelhofer
22
Kreuzbühlstr
Theaterstr
Falkenstr
Seehofstr
Dufourstr
Kreuzstr
Forchstr
Zollikerstr
Mühlebach

print to Dada and in-bed-with Ronald-McDonald rooms. Despite the plethora of rooms in the city, it's best to book ahead, especially between April and October.

Martahaus (☎ 01 251 45 50; www.martahaus.ch; Zähringerstrasse 36; dm Sfr37, s/d with shared bathroom from Sfr75/98; 🖳) The best budget option in town, just a five-minute walk from the station. Privacy prevails in the six-bed dorms with individual cubicles fashioned from partitions and curtains. There's a bar and a great lounge with TV, pool table and best of all – a free Internet station.

City Backpacker (☎ 01 251 90 15; backpacker@access .ch; Niederdorfstrasse 5; dm 31, s/d with shared bathroom Sfr66/92; 🖳) Centrally located for bar hopping, the roof-top terrace has great views of the city and is a perfect spot for hanging out in summer. There's a self-catering kitchen and laundry machines.

Justinusheim (☎ 01 361 38 06; fax 01 362 29 82; Freudenbergstrasse 146; s/d with shared bathroom Sfr50/85) This tranquil student home has lake and city views, spacious rooms and always a few places for travellers. Take tram No 10 to Rigiblik, then the frequent Seilbahn to the top station.

Hotel Formule 1 (☎ 01 307 48 00; www.hotelformule 1.com; Heidi Abel-Weg 7; s, d & tr Sfr59) You can't beat the price for clean, modern, in-room facilities with TV, even if it's slightly lacking in charm. It is just minutes from the airport.

Camping Seebucht (☎ 01 482 16 12; Seestrasse 559; bus No 161 or 165 from Bürkliplatz; per adult/tent/car Sfr9.50/12/5; 🕑 May-Sep) On the west shore of the lake, 4km from the centre (signposted), this camp site has a shop and café.

EATING

Niederdorfstrasse has a string of snack bars offering bratwurst, kebabs and Asian food for about Sfr9. The nearby backstreets are filled with wall-to-wall cafés, restaurants and bars. Cheap eats also abound around the train station, especially in the underground Shopville. By the station there is a large Coop supermarket. Most restaurants stay open from early morning to late evening.

Spaghetti Factory (☎ 012 51 94 00; Niederdorfstrasse 5; pasta Sfr15-22) With a fun, buzzing atmosphere, this restaurant serves big, delicious bowls of its namesake dish (22 choices).

Mollino Pizzeria Ristorante (☎ 01 261 01 17; Limmatquai 16; mains Sfr18-25) Head to this lively restaurant for mouth-watering pizzas, delicious cappuccinos and exquisite lake views. Sit outside when it's warm.

Kobal Curry & Café (☎ 01 241 26 19; Kanzleistrasse 78; tram No 8 to Helvetiaplatz; mains Sfr20; 🕑 lunch & dinner Mon-Fri, dinner only Sat & Sun) Tiny, low-key Kobal is a favourite with the media and students. Try the melt-in-your mouth chicken korma or vegetarian roti. It's well worth the walk through the red-light district to get there.

Bodega Española (☎ 01 251 23 10; Münstergasse 15; mains downstairs from Sfr15) This popular restaurant fulfils Iberian cravings with sumptuous Spanish staples such as paella. Eat in the cheaper, wood-tabled downstairs restaurant.

Tibits (☎ 01 260 32 22; Seefeldstrasse 2; buffet Sfr3.50 per 100g) Creative vegetarian options are served in a very cool, very modern, very red atmosphere. Choose from 30 different items at the hot and cold salad bar. A big plate costs about Sfr14.

Schoffel (☎ 01 261 20 70; Schoffelgasse 7; mains Sfr8-16) Locals crowd this café on weekend mornings searching for a leisurely coffee and newspaper read. Soups, salads and big bowls of yoghurt and fruit are on the menu.

Sprüngli (☎ 01 244 47 11; Bahnhofstrasse 21; chocolates from Sfr2, mains Sfr19-28) The mother of all chocolate shops, it's a Zürich legacy and must for chocoholics. There's a huge range of truffles and cakes from downstairs, or mingle with the well-heeled crowd in the elegant 1st-floor tearooms for a rather special experience.

DRINKING & CLUBBING

Late-night pubs, clubs and discos clutter Niederdorfstrasse and its adjoining streets. Factories in the industrial quarter, west of the train station, are being taken over by a wave of hip bars and clubs. Head to Escherwyssplatz (tram No 4 or 13) and follow your ears. Bars are open all day; clubs get started after 11pm and stay open until at least 4am.

Oliver Twist (☎ 01 252 47 10; Rindermarkt 6) English speakers gravitate towards this pub, which serves Irish, British, Australian and South African beers. It's smoky, noisy, somewhat of a meat market and often standing room only.

Café Odeon (☎ 01 251 16 50; Am Bellevue) Lenin and James Joyce once downed drinks at this swish, smoky bar with marble walls and chandeliers and packed with an arty crowd.

Wüste Bar (☎ 01 251 22 07; Oberdorfstrasse 7) One of our favourites, located underneath the Hotel Otter, it's small and groovy with plush red seats and a cowhide bar. There's sometimes live music.

Labyrinth (☎ 01 440 59 80; Pfingstweidstrasse 70) Zürich's top gay club features half-naked pole-dancing narcissists flaunting their six packs and lots of eye-candy at the bar. Take the tram No 4 to Förrlibuckstrasse to get there.

Zoo (☎ 01 211 57 52; www.zooclub.ch in German; Stadthausquai 13; tram No 2/3/8/9/11 to Bürkliplatz) Dance the night away to pounding house music in an über-stylish setting – although you'll pay royally for the privilege to party with Zürich's pretty people. It was one of the city's *in* clubs at the time of research.

Kaufleuten (☎ 01 225 33 22; www.kaufleuten.com; Pelikanstrasse 18; tram No 2/9 to Sihlstrasse) A club with a long history and hot reputation at the top end of the market. Dress to impress as everyone in here looks like they walked out of a model shoot. The place boasts that Prince and Madonna were once guests.

GETTING THERE & AROUND

Unique Zürich Airport (☎ 043 816 22 11; www.zurich -airport.com) is 10km north of the city centre.

Trains go to Stuttgart (Sfr61, three hours, daily), Munich (Sfr86, 4½ hours, daily), Innsbruck (Sfr66, four hours, daily), Milan (Sfr72, four hours, daily), Lucerne (Sfr22, 50 minutes, hourly), Bern (Sfr48, 70 minutes, hourly) and Basel (Sfr32, 65 minutes, hourly).

City bikes are free at **Velogate** (platform 18, main train station; ☉ 7.30am-9.30pm). Bring photo ID and a Sfr20 deposit.

There's a comprehensive bus, tram, boat and S-Bahn service. Short trips under five stops are Sfr2.30. A 24-hour pass including travel to/from the airport is Sfr10.80.

Various buses head east to Budapest, Belgrade, Dubrovnik and other destinations. The bus station is behind the train station. **Eurolines** (☎ 01 272 40 42) has an office here.

CENTRAL SWITZERLAND & BERNER OBERLAND

Mountains and lakes, tinkling cowbells and alpine villages – this is the land of Heidi, an area of such breathtaking beauty it defies description. If you're only going to visit one region of Switzerland, make this it.

LUCERNE
pop 58,600

Photogenic Lucerne has everything a Swiss city needs – a lake, a medieval cobbled old-town and some snow-capped mountains. Without a doubt it's one of the most beautiful cities in the country.

The mostly pedestrian-only old town is on the northern bank of the Reuss River. The train station is minutes away on the southern bank. The **Internet Shop** (☎ 041 211 21 31; cnr Pilatusstrasse & Seebrücke; per hr Sfr10; ☉ 9am-10pm Mon-Sat, 9am-8pm Sun) is across from the train station. **Luzern Tourismus** (☎ 041 227 17 17; www .luzern.org; Zentralstrasse 5; ☉ 8.30am-7.30pm Mon-Fri, 9am-7.30pm Sat & Sun Apr-Oct; closes 6pm Nov-Mar) is in the train station.

Sights

Don't miss the medieval old town with ancient rampart walls and towers and 15th-century buildings with painted facades. **Kapellbrücke** (Chapel Bridge), dating from 1333, is Lucerne's best-known landmark. Also check out the rather dark and dour *Dance of Death* panels under the roofline of **Spreuerbrücke** (Spreuer Bridge).

At the **Picasso Museum** (☎ 041 410 35 33; Furrengasse 21; adult/student Sfr6/3; ☉ 10am-6pm Apr-Oct, 11am-1pm & 2-4pm Nov-Mar), nearly 200 photographs show an impish Picasso at work and play in his Cannes home during the last 17 years of his life.

Space rockets, simulators, a planetarium and an IMAX theatre all make the huge **Verkehrshaus** (Transport Museum; ☎ 041 370 44 44; Lidostrasse 5; bus No 6, 8 or 24 from Bahnhofplatz; adult/student/child Sfr21/19/12; ☉ 10am-6pm Apr-Oct, 10am-5pm Nov-Mar) one of Switzerland's most popular.

Sleeping

Lucerne's budget options are spread out around the city.

Backpackers Lucerne (☎ 041 360 04 20; fax 041 360 04 42; Alpenquai 42; dm Sfr27, d with shared bathroom Sfr66) Friendly and comfy, the backpackers borders parkland and a scrap of lakefront beach. Dorms only have four beds and there is a kitchen. It's a 15-minute walk southeast of the station.

SYHA hostel (☎ 041 420 88 00; luzern@youthhostel .ch; Sedelstrasse 12; dm Sfr31.50, s/d with shared bathroom Sfr64/78, with private bathroom Sfr70/90) A large, modern, reliable option about 1km north of the city walls. To get here, catch bus No 18 to Goplismoos, or bus No 1 to Schlossberg in the evening.

Hotel Löwengraben (☎ 041 417 12 12; www.loewen graben.ch; Löwengraben 18; s/d with shared bathroom Sfr110/160; (P) (X) (🖵)) In a converted prison with whitewashed, 'cell-like' rooms and some fancier suites (albeit with bars on the windows), the hotel is good for novelty value. There's also a trendy bar and nightclub. In winter, prices drop by about Sfr20.

Camping Lido (☎ 041 370 21 46; Lidostrasse 8; per adult/tent/car Sfr7.70/3/5, cabin dm Sfr13; (Y) mid-Mar–Oct) The tranquil spot makes for happy camping. Catch bus No 6, 8 or 24.

Eating & Drinking

Many restaurants double as bars. Self-caterers should head to Hertensteinstrasse, where cheap eats are plentiful and there's a Coop supermarket. The places listed here usually open around 8am and stay open until at least midnight.

Manora (5th fl, Weggisgasse 5; mains Sfr5-15) Mountain vistas are plentiful from the small rooftop terrace at this reliable buffet-style inexpensive eatery.

Cafeteria Emilio (☎ 041 410 28 10; Ledergasse 8; mains Sfr6-14) You'll be rubbing shoulders with other diners at this tiny place, but it has a certain charm and you won't find cheaper pizzas, pastas and salads.

Rathaus Brauerei (☎ 041 410 52 57; Unter der Egg 2; mains Sfr8-30) Sit outside by the water or inside among the shiny copper beer tanks at this atmospheric restaurant. It serves big home brews and some of the most delicious and varied food in town.

Hotel Bar Schiff (☎ 041 418 52 52; Unter der Egg 8; soups & sandwiches Sfr8-12, mains Sfr20-40) Come for the daily happy hour when a drink and appetizer costs Sfr12.50. Try the local speciality, *Kügelipastetli* – vol-au-vents stuffed with meat and mushrooms and topped with a rich sauce – at this esteemed restaurant.

Mr Pickwick Pub (☎ 041 410 59 27; Rathausquai 6; sandwiches Sfr6.50, mains Sfr10-23) For Brit beer, food and footy stop at this congenial spot. The pub sandwiches are a real steal and there's outdoor seating right on the river.

Jazzkantine (☎ 041 410 73 73; Grabengasse 8; mains from Sfr15) A funky, arty and rather smoky haunt of the young and creative. There's cool music, counter meals, Saturday-night gigs and weeknight jazz workshops.

Getting There & Around

Trains connect Lucerne to Zürich (Sfr19, 50 minutes, hourly), Interlaken (Sfr26, two hours, hourly), Bern (Sfr30, 1½ hours, hourly), Lugano (Sfr56, 2½ hours) and Geneva (Sfr70, 3¼ hours, hourly).

INTERLAKEN
pop 15,000

Flanked by the stunning Lakes Thun and Brienz is ever-popular Interlaken – a great base for exploring the delights of the Jungfrau region. Catering to backpackers like nowhere else in Switzerland, many budget travellers make this their main stop in the country. Solo travellers hoping to meet like-minded individuals will have a field day here. Interlaken is a mecca for thrillseekers, and many a traveller leaves with a much lighter wallet after blowing mind-boggling amounts of cash on a range of white-knuckle, high-adrenalin sports. Most are not disappointed.

Even if you don't have tons of money to spend, you won't be bored. Instead check out the myriad hiking trails in the area - the views are amazing and free!

Orientation & Information

Most of Interlaken lies between its two train stations, Interlaken Ost and West. Both offer bike rental and daily money-exchange facilities. The main shopping street, Höheweg, runs between the stations, and you can walk from one to the other in 20 minutes.

Near Interlaken West is **Interlaken Tourismus** (☎ 033 826 53 00; www.interlakentourism.ch; Höheweg 37; (Y) 8am-6.30pm Mon-Fri, 8am-5pm Sat, 10am-noon & 4-6pm Sun Jul-Aug; 8am-noon & 1.30-6pm Mon-Fri, 8am-noon Sat Sep-Jun).

Activities

Some say leaping from an aeroplane over the Swiss Alps is a life-changing experience. Others argue the canyoning is superior, while some swear by night sledding. Whatever your tastes, most adventure sports are offered from Interlaken. The town's two major adventure companies, **Outdoor Interlaken** (☎ 033 826 77 19; www.outdoor-interlaken.com; Hauptstrasse 16) and **Alpin Raft** (☎ 033 823 41 00; www.alpinraft.ch; Hauptstrasse 7), are linked with the town's two major hostels, Balmer's Herberge and Funny Farm. Both offer the same activities at the same prices and have offices in the hostels. Options are sky-diving (Sfr380), snowshoe trekking (Sfr80), night sledding past frozen waterfalls prior to a fondue dinner (Sfr95), and skiing or snow-boarding including transport, lift ticket and ski clothing and gear rental (Sfr160). You can also fly-in, drink some champagne, then hit the virgin power glacier skiing (Sfr250). In summer there's canyoning, where you jump, slide and rappel down rocks and waterfalls (from Sfr110) and rafting on the class III-IV Lütschine River (Sfr95).

Those without huge amounts of cash should check out the **hiking trails**, all with signposts giving average walking times, that dot the area.

Hostels can suggest good hikes and provide maps. You can also check with the tourist office, or just set off on foot and look for the signs. For more on hiking in the region, see p1179.

Sleeping

The most popular budget accommodation is on Hauptstrasse, a 15-minute signposted walk from either train station.

Balmer's Herberge (☎ 033 822 19 61; www.balmers .ch; Hauptstrasse 23; dm Sfr24, s/d with shared bathroom Sfr40/68; 🖳) Young Americans have flocked to this cosy Swiss chalet with a raucous summer-camp feel for more than 50 years. There's a bar, a restaurant and even a night-club. On the negative side you're locked out of your room (even the doubles) from 9.30am to 4.30pm, you'll be constantly harassed to partake in the adventure sports and they even charge you to use the kitchen. Still travellers love the place, and it's a great spot to meet people and party the night away.

Funny Farm (☎ 033 828 12 81; www.funny-farm.ch; Hauptstrasse 36; dm from Sfr25; 🖳 🖳) The town's other budget powerhouse has a similarly raucous feel and draws in hordes of Australians. It revels in its anarchic, ramshackle premises – the banana tree by the swimming pool, the floating surfboard. The unspoken mantra? Party, party, *party*!

Backpackers Villa Sonnenhof (☎ 033 826 71 71; www.villa.ch; Alpenstrasse 16; dm Sfr29, d Sfr82) The town's quieter and more genteel option, it has spacious renovated rooms with steamer trunks and balconies, some with mountain views. In a corner, though, someone is bound to be hyped up after their latest skydive.

Sackgut (☎ 033 822 44 34; sackgut@swisscamps.ch; Brienzstrasse; per adult/car/tent from Sfr7.50/3/6.50, 🕑 mid-May–Oct) Behind Interlaken Ost station, this is the only in-town camping option. The shower blocks are rather outdated.

Eating & Drinking

Balmer's has the town's hottest after-dark scene, especially when its club is open, and guests rarely venture out at night. Funny Farm is a close second. Neither hostel appears to care if non-guests drink at their bars. Drinks are pricey, so stock up on beer (and food) at the **Coop Pronto** (Höheweg 11; 🕑 10am-10pm Mon-Sat) with the rest of the town.

Buddy's Pub & Restaurant Splendid (☎ 033 822 30 51; Höheweg 33; snacks Sfr3-7, mains Sfr22-30; 🕑 lunch & dinner) A popular watering hole, you can fill up on beer and cheap sandwiches or chilli at Buddy's. The attached restaurant serves a range of fondues and raclettes.

Top o'Met (☎ 033 828 66 66; 18th fl, Metropole Hotel, Höheweg 37; buffet from Sfr10.50, mains from Sfr18 🕑 11.30am-2pm & 6.30-11pm) Sip on a cocktail and enjoy the sweeping mountain views, or stop by for an ice-cream sundae, meal or coffee.

Restaurant Chalet Interlaken (☎ 033 827 87 87 Kirchgasse 37; mains Sfr15-40; 🕑 lunch & dinner) Fake trees and candles add to the ambience inside this chalet. It's a popular place serving Swiss cuisine, including rather sumptuous fondue and sausage dishes. There are a few vegetarian options.

Getting There & Away

Trains to Lucerne (Sfr30, two hours, hourly) Grindelwald (Sfr9.80, 40 minutes, hourly) and Lauterbrunnen (Sfr6.60, 30 minutes hourly) depart from Interlaken Ost. Trains to Brig (Sfr38, 1½ hours, hourly) and Montreux via Bern (Sfr91, two hours, hourly) depart from Interlaken West or Ost.

JUNGFRAU REGION

The views get better the further south you go from Interlaken. In winter the Jungfrau is a magnet for skiers and snowboarders with 200km of pistes. A one-day ski pass for regional resorts costs Sfr55.

The Lauterbrunnen Valley branches out from Interlaken with sheer rock faces and towering mountains on either side, attracting an army of hikers and mountain bikers. Cowbells echo in the valley and every house and hostel has a postcard-worthy view. Many visitors choose to visit the valley on a daytrip from Interlaken.

Grindelwald

Picturesque Grindelwald was once a simple farming village. Today it's the largest ski resort in the Jungfrau, nestled in a valley under the north face of the Eiger.

Grindelwald Tourism (☎ 033 854 12 12; www .grindelwald.ch in German; ☺ 8am-7pm Mon-Fri, 8am-6pm Sat, 9am-noon & 2-5pm Sun Jul-Sep; shorter hours & closed Sun between seasons) is in the centre at the Sportzentrum, 200m from the train station.

The First is the main **skiing area** in winter. In summer there are 90km of **hiking trails** above 1200m. You can catch the longest **cable car** in Europe from Grindelwald-Grund to Männlichen, where there are more extraordinary views and hikes (one-way/round-trip Sfr29/46).

There are magnificent vistas from the cosy wooden chalet housing the **SYHA hostel** (☎ 033 853 10 09; grindelwald@youthhostel.ch; Terrassenweg; dm from Sfr29.50). Take the Terrassenweg-bound bus to the Gaggi Säge stop.

Near the Mälichen cable-car station, the big, blue **Mountain Hostel** (☎ 033 853 39 00; www.mountainhostel.ch; dm/d with shared bathroom from Sfr34/88) is a good base for sports junkies. An array of rather unique activities centred on hiking (there's a hiking and painting seminar) can be arranged.

Most hotels in town have their own attached restaurants. Some also have bars and clubs. Self-caterers can stock up at **Coop supermarket** opposite the tourist office. For tasty traditional food and staggering Eiger views, try **Rendez-vous Restaurant** (☎ 033 853 11 81; mains Sfr13.50-27; ☺ closed Tue) on the main street.

There is a train that connects to Interlaken Ost (Sfr9.40, 40 minutes, hourly) as well as other locations.

Lauterbrunnen

Tiny Lauterbrunnen, with an appealing main street cluttered with Swiss chalet architecture, is friendly and genuine. You'll find the impressive **Trümmelbach Falls** (admission Sfr10; ☺ 9am-5pm Apr-Nov), 4km out of town. A bus from the train station (Sfr3) reaches there.

Camping Jungfrau (☎ 033 856 20 10; end of Main St; per adult/tent Sfr9/6, cabins per adult Sfr25) has excellent facilities and views of towering peaks and sheer cliffs. Another option is the **Valley Hostel** (☎ 033 855 20 08; www.valleyhostel.ch; dm Sfr21, d Sfr52; ☒ ⌨), which offers comfy rooms (many with balconies), a communal kitchen and a mellow environment.

Stock up on food at the **Coop**, near the tourist office; or try the restaurant at the **Hotel Oberland** (☎ 033 855 12 41; Main St through town; mains from Sfr17). It has a big menu of rösti, pasta and salads.

Gimmelwald

When the sun is out, Gimmelwald will take your breath away. The hamlet is particularly enchanting in winter when the weathered wooden chalets peep out from a thick blanket of snow and the mountains seem to envelope you. Really, the place is Switzerland's best-kept secret.

Jaw-dropping views, snacks and beer are available at the simple, rustic **Mountain Hostel** (☎ 033 855 17 04; www.mountainhostel.com; dm Sfr20; ⌨). At **Esther's Guesthouse** (☎ 033 855 54 88; www .esthersguesthouse.ch; barn accommodation Sfr21, s/d with shared bathroom Sfr40/80), you can sleep on beds of straw in a big barn (June to October). A generous breakfast of organic food and a shower are included in the price. Even if you don't stay, stop by to pick up homemade beef jerky (some of the best we've ever tasted), cheeses and other organic products.

Restaurant-Pension Gimmelwald (☎ 033 855 17 30; mains Sfr18) has hearty home cooking, including fondue and farmers' barley soup. Don't miss the 'Gimmelwalder Horse-Shit Balls' for Sfr4. You'll have to visit to find out what they're made out of.

To reach Gimmelwald you can hike up a steep trail from Stechelberg for about 1½ hours (it's sometimes closed in winter due to avalanches) or take the cable car (one-way Sfr8). A great way to get to Stechelberg from Lauterbrunnen is to hike along a flat path past dramatic scenery for about 1½ hours. From Mürren, Gimmelwald is a pleasant 40-minute walk downhill, or you can catch the cable car (one-way Sfr8).

Mürren

Arrive in Mürren on a clear evening, when the sun hangs low on the horizon and the peaks feel close enough to touch, and you just might think you've died and gone to heaven. Mürren is a skiing and hiking destination with some 50km of prepared ski runs nearby.

The **Eiger Guesthouse** (☎ 033 855 35 35; eiger guesthouse@muerren.ch; dm from Sfr50, d with shared bathroom Sfr110), by the train station, has a bar, restaurant and game room, and is the only budget option. **Kandahar** (Sportzentrum; salads & sandwiches from Sfr6) serves big, thick sandwiches, tasty muffins and healthy salads.

Schilthorn

There's a fantastic 360° panorama from the top of the 2970m Schilthorn. On a good day you can see from Titlis around to Mont Blanc and across to the German Black Forest. If you never miss a James Bond film and the scenery looks familiar it's because this is where Bond performed his stunts in *On Her Majesty's Secret Service*. Schilthorn can be reached by the Stechelberg cable car for Sfr94 round-trip (Half-Fare Card/Swiss Pass/Eurail Pass Sfr47/48/81).

Jungfraujoch

The trip to Jungfraujoch (3454m) by train is something you do because a) it's generally a once-in-a-lifetime experience and b) you have to see it for yourself. If it's a clear day the outlook at Europe's highest train station is indisputably spectacular. The track up powers through both the Eiger as well as the Mönch and pauses briefly for travellers to take happy snaps of views from two windows blasted in the mountainside.

From Interlaken Ost the journey is 2½ hours each way (Sfr169 round-trip). There's a cheaper 'good morning ticket' of Sfr145 if you take the early train (6.35am from Interlaken) and leave the summit by noon. From 1 November to 30 April the reduction is also valid for the 7.35am train and the noon restriction does not apply. Eurail passholders get 25% off, and Swisspass holders slightly more.

Good weather is essential so call ☎ 033 855 10 22 for taped forecasts before leaving.

NORTHERN SWITZERLAND

This region is important for industry and commerce, yet by no means lacks tourist attractions. Take time to explore the tiny rural towns set among green rolling hills.

BASEL (BÂLE)

pop 161,800

Basel is an affluent city squeezed into the top left corner of the country, bordering France and Germany. The famous Renaissance humanist, Erasmus of Rotterdam, was associated with the city and his tomb rests in the cathedral.

The old town, train station and most popular sights are all within walking distance of each other on the south bank in Grossbasel (Greater Basel). The **Internet Pub** (☎ 0844 89 19 91; Steinentorstrasse 11; per hr Sfr8; ☺ 9am-10pm Mon-Thu, 9am-8pm Fri, 9am-5pm Sat) is a smoky joint where you can down a beer and surf the Web.

Basel Tourismus (☎ 061 268 68 68; www.base tourismus.ch in German; Schifflände 5; ☺ 7.30am-6.30pm Mon-Fri, 10am-5pm Sat, 10am-4pm Sun) has all the usual information.

Sights & Activities

With its cobbled streets, colourful fountains, Middle Age churches and stately buildings, the old town is a wonderful place to wander. In Marktplatz check out the impressive rust-coloured **Rathaus** (town hall) with frescoed courtyard. The 12th-century **Münster** (cathedral) is another highlight with Gothic spires and Romanesque St Gallus doorway. Theaterplatz is a crowd-pleaser, with a curious **fountain** designed by Swiss sculptor Jean Tinguely. His madcap scrap-metal machines perform a peculiar water dance.

The **Kunstmuseum** (Art Museum; ☎ 061 206 62 62; www.kunstmuseumbasel.ch; St Albangraben 16; adult, student Sfr8/5, free 1st Sun of month; ☺ 10am-5pm Tue-Sun) holds the largest art collection in Switzerland, including Klees and Picassos and the world's largest Holbein collection.

If you arrive on a hot summer day, join the locals for a swim in the Rhine. It's spectacular, popular and free. Look for clusters of bobbing bodies.

Festivals & Events

If you're fortunate to be in town on the Monday after Ash Wednesday you'll experience **Fasnacht**, a three-day spectacle of parades, masks, music and costumes, starting at 4am. The largest celebration of it's kind in Switzerland, it makes for a great night.

Sleeping

Basel's hostels are easily accessible to the town's nightlife.

Basel Backpack (☎ 061 333 00 37; www.baselback pack.ch; Dornacherstrasse 192; dm Sfr37, s/d with shared bathroom Sfr80/94; ✗) Enormous attention has gone into refitting this former factory, and the results are pleasing. Dorms are cheerful and colour coded, each housing eight beds.

SYHA Hostel (☎ 061 272 05 72; basel@youthhostel .ch; St Alban Kirchrain 10; tram No 3 to St Alban Tor; dm from Sfr31; 🖳) In a converted textiles factory in St Alban, a quiet, leafy, old money part of town, it has small spick-and-span rooms.

Eating & Drinking

For a cheap bite, the daily **market** on Marktplatz has tasty bratwurst (Sfr5) and delicious breads (Sfr3 to Sfr7). Also, there's pedestrian-only Steinenvorstadt, with its myriad of fast-food outlets, cafés and restaurants. For self-caterers, there's the local **Migros** (Sternengasse 17). Or for a huge range of organic local produce (and 200 different cheeses), try the **Bell Centralhalle** (cnr Streitgasse & Weisse Gasse). Restaurants don't close between meals. Bars are open until at least midnight.

Rossarios (☎ 061 261 03 76; Spalenberg 10; mains Sfr15-30) A charming Italian wine bar, Rossarios has frescoes on the cheerful red walls, big wooden tables and a sky-coloured ceiling. It serves heaping portions of pasta.

Aladin (☎ 061 261 57 31; Barfüsserplatz 17; mains from Sfr10) This Lebanese restaurant has cheap vegetarian options like hummus as well as more substantial meat dishes. In case you were worried, the flamboyant **Don't Worry Be Happy Bar** is upstairs.

Papa Joe's (☎ 061 274 04 04; am Barfi; mains Sfr22) A rather over-the-top Tex-Mex-style restaurant serving burgers, ribs and nachos to appreciative locals. Its adjoining bar, with terracotta tiles, plastic toucans and American paraphernalia, attracts a cocktail-quaffing crowd.

Paddy Reilly's Irish Pub (☎ 061 281 33 36; Steinentorstrasse 45; mains Sfr5-12.50) This pub entices expats with Brit beers and big-screen TV.

It's a cosy spot to kick back with a Guinness and watch the sport.

Cafe des Arts (☎ 061 273 57 37; Am Barfüsserplatz 6) Modern art graces the walls and a piano player tickles the ivories at this stylish and spacious place with a Parisian feel and an extensive drinks menu (happy hour 5-7pm).

Getting There & Around

Basel is a major European rail hub. Trains to France leave from the SNCF section of SBB station. Destinations include Paris (Sfr69, five hours, seven times daily). Germany-bound trains stop at Badischer Bahnhof (BBF) on the northern bank. Main routes are Frankfurt (Sfr80, three hours, daily) and Hamburg (Sfr198, 6½ hours, daily). There are fast trains to Geneva (Sfr71, three hours; twice hourly) and Zürich (Sfr30, 70 minutes, twice hourly) from the SBB.

City buses and trams cost Sfr1.80 for four or fewer stops, Sfr2.80 for the central zone or Sfr8 for a day pass.

ST GALLEN

pop 70,500

It all started with a bush, a bear and a monk. In AD 612. That was when Gallus, an itinerant Irish monk, fell into a briar and instead of believing it was a mere stumble, interpreted the mishap as a sign from God. He decided to stay put and build a hermitage with a little help from a passing bear (or so the legend goes). From this inauspicious beginning the town of St Gallen evolved.

St Gallen-Bodensee Tourismus (☎ 071 227 37 37; www.st.gallen-bodensee.ch; Bahnhofplatz 1a; ⊙ 9am-noon & 1-6pm Mon-Fri, 9am-noon Sat) is near the train station.

St Gallen has a pedestrian-only **old town** straight out of Hans Christian Anderson. Many buildings have colourful murals and the balconies are sculpted with the loving care of a master craftsman. Bookworms will treasure the nearby **Stiftsbibliothek** (Abbey Library; ☎ 071 227 34 16; adult/student Sfr8/6; ⊙ 9am-noon & 1.30-5pm Mon-Sat, 10.30am-noon & 1.30-4pm Sun Apr-Oct, closed Sun Dec-Mar, closed Nov), adjoining the cathedral. It's one of the oldest libraries of the Western world and contains some rare manuscripts from the Middle Ages.

SYHA Hostel (☎ 071 245 47 77; fax 071 245 49 83; Jüchstrasse 25; dm Sfr27, s/d with shared bathroom Sfr46.50/72; ⊙ Mar–mid-Dec) is a modern hostel. It's a signposted 15-minute walk east of the old town or take the Trogenerbahn from the station to 'Schülerhaus' (Sfr2.40).

Central, good value rooms and a mellow bistro-bar are found at **Weisses Kreuz** (☎ /fax 071 223 28 43; Engelgasse 9; s/d with shared bathroom from Sfr45/80).

Fast-food stalls selling St Gallen sausage and bread for around Sfr6 proliferate around the old town. Otherwise **Restaurant Marktplatz** (☎ 071 222 36 41; Neugasse 2; mains Sfr14-19) is a rowdy beer-hall-style restaurant serving pizza and local meaty dishes.

There are regular trains to Zürich (Sfr26, 70 minutes, hourly).

SWITZERLAND DIRECTORY

ACCOMMODATION

Compared to other parts of Europe, prices might seem steep at even the most inexpensive places. Hostels and hotels usually include breakfast in their price. Switzerland has two types of hostels: official Swiss Youth Hostels (SYHA), affiliated with Hostelling International (HI), where non-members pay an additional 'guest fee' of Sfr6; and the independent hostels. Independent hostels tend to be more charismatic and better bets for solo travellers, or anyone wanting to meet other backpackers. Prices listed in this chapter for SYHA hostels do not include the guest fee. On average a dorm bed in either type of hostel costs between Sfr20 and Sfr40.

When their cows are out to pasture, Swiss farmers often allow travellers to sleep in their barns for a fee of about Sfr20. It's a unique experience that disappoints few. A booklet listing participating farmers is available from **Aventure sur la paille** (☎ 024 445 16 31; www.aventure-sur-la-paille.ch).

ACTIVITIES

There are dozens of ski resorts throughout Switzerland and some 200 ski schools. Equipment hire is available at resorts, and ski passes allow unlimited use of mountain transport.

There's no better way to enjoy Switzerland's spectacular scenery than to walk through it. There are 50,000km of designated paths, often with a convenient inn or café en route. Yellow trail signs make it difficult to get lost, and each

gives an average walking time to the next destination. Slightly more strenuous mountain paths have white-red-white markers. You can water-ski, sail and windsurf on most lakes, and there are over 350 lake beaches. Rafting is possible on many alpine rivers, including the Rhine and the Rhône.

Bungy-jumping, paragliding, canyoning and other high-adrenalin sports are available throughout Switzerland, especially in the Interlaken area.

Embassies & Consulates in Switzerland

All embassies are in Bern. Consulates can be found in several other cities, particularly Zürich and Geneva. Australia and New Zealand don't have embassies in Switzerland, but each has a consulate in Geneva.

Australia Geneva (☎ 022 799 91 00; Chemin des Fins 2)
Canada Bern (☎ 031 357 32 00; Kirchenfeldstrasse 88); Geneva (☎ 022 919 92 00; Ave de l'Ariana 5)
France Bern (☎ 031 359 21 11; Schosshaldenstrasse 46); Geneva (☎ 022 319 00 00; Rue Imbert Galloix 11)
Germany Bern (☎ 031 359 41 11; Willadingweg 83); Geneva (☎ 022 730 11 11; Chemin du Petit-Saconnex 28C)
Ireland Bern (☎ 031 352 14 42; Kirchenfeldstrasse 68)
Italy Bern (☎ 031 350 07 77; Elfenstrasse 14)
New Zealand Geneva (☎ 022 734 95 30; Chemin du Petit-Saconnex 28A)
UK Bern (☎ 031 359 77 00; Thunstrasse 50); Geneva (☎ 022 918 24 00; Rue de Vermont 37-39)
USA Bern (☎ 031 357 70 11; Jubiläumsstrasse 93); Geneva (☎ 022 840 51 60; Rue Versonnex 7); Zürich (☎ 01 422 25 66 ; Dufourstrasse 101)

EMBASSIES & CONSULATES
Swiss Embassies & Consulates Abroad

Swiss embassies can be located in plenty of countries:

Australia (☎ 02-6273 3977; vertretung@can.rep.admin .ch; 7 Melbourne Ave, Forrest, Canberra, ACT 2603)
Canada (☎ 613-235 1837; vertretung@ott.rep.admin .ch; 5 Marlborough Ave, Ottawa, Ontario K1N 8E6)
France (☎ 041-31 359 21 11; vertretung@par.rep .admin.ch; Rue de Grenelle 142, Paris)
Germany (☎ 030-390 40 00; www.botschaft-schweiz .de in German; Otto-von-Bismarck-Allee 4a, Berlin)
Ireland (☎ 01-218 6382; vertretung@dub.rep.admin.ch; 6 Ailesbury Rd, Ballsbridge, Dublin 4)
Netherlands (☎ 070-364 28 31; www.eda.admin.ch /denhaag_emb; Lange Voorhout 42, Den Haag)
UK (☎ 020-7616 6000; swissembassy@lon.rep.admin.ch; 16-18 Montague Place, London W1H 2BQ)
USA (☎ 202-745 7900; www.swissemb.org; 2900 Cathedral Ave NW, Washington, DC 20008-3499)

New Zealand (☎ 04-472 1593; vertretung@wel.rep
.admin.ch; 22 Panama St, Wellington)

FESTIVALS & EVENTS

Many events take place at a local level
throughout the year (check with the local
tourist offices). Dates often vary from year
to year. This is just a brief selection:

Fasnacht In February, a lively spring carnival of wild
parties and parades is celebrated countrywide, but with
particular enthusiasm in Basel and Lucerne.

Combats de Reines From March to October, the lower
Valais stages traditional cow fights.

Montreux Jazz Festival Big-name rock/jazz acts hit
town in July for this famous festival.

National Day On 1 August, celebrations and fireworks
mark the country's National Day.

Street Parade In early August, Zürich lets its hair down
with an enormous techno parade with 30 lovemobiles and
more than half a million ravers (see p1173).

Vintage Festivals You can down a couple in wine-
growing regions such as Neuchâtel and Lugano in October.

Onion Market In late November, Bern takes on a carnival
atmosphere for a unique market day.

Escalade Festival This historical festival held in Geneva
on 11 December celebrates deliverance from would-be
conquerors.

HOLIDAYS

New Year's Day 1 January
Easter March/April – Good Friday, Easter Sunday & Monday
Ascension Day 40th Day after Easter
Whit Sunday & Monday 7th week after Easter
National Day 1 August
Christmas Day 25 December
St Stephen's Day 26 December

MONEY

Swiss francs (Sfr, written CHF locally) are
divided into 100 centimes (called *rappen* in
German-speaking Switzerland). There are
notes for 10, 20, 50, 100, 500 and 1000 francs,
and coins for five, 10, 20 and 50 centimes,
and one, two and five francs.

All major travellers cheques and credit
cards are accepted. Virtually all train stations
have money-exchange facilities open daily.
Commission is not usually charged for changing cash or cheques but it's gradually creeping
in. Shop around for the best exchange rates.
Hotels usually have the worst rates.

POST

Postcards and letters to Europe cost Sfr1.30/1.20
priority/economy; to other places they cost

Sfr1.80/1.40. The term poste restante is used
nationwide or you could use the German term,
Postlagernde Briefe. Mail can be sent to any
town with a post office and is held for 30 days;
show your passport to collect mail. American
Express also retains mail for one month for
people who use its cheques or cards.

Post office opening times can change but
typically are 7.30am to noon and 2pm to
6.30pm Monday to Friday and until 11am
Saturday.

TELEPHONE

The privatised Swisscom is the main telecommunications provider. The minimum
charge in Swisscom payphones is Sfr0.60,
though per-minute rates are low. Swisscom
charges the same rate for national or local
calls. During the day it's Sfr0.08 per minute,
and during evenings and weekends it drops
to Sfr0.04.

The country code for Switzerland is ☎ 41.
Regional codes are no longer required in
Switzerland. Although the numbers for a
particular city or town all commence with
the same two or three digits (for example Zurich ☎ 01, Geneva ☎ 022), numbers always must be dialled in full, even
when you're calling from within the same
town.

International call prices have dropped
substantially in recent years. A standard-rate
call to the USA/Australia/UK costs Sfr0.12/
0.25/0.12 per minute. Standard rates apply
on weekdays (day or night), and there are
reduced rates on weekends and public holidays. Many telephone boxes no longer take
coins; the prepaid *taxcard* comes in values
of Sfr5, Sfr10 and Sfr20, and is sold in post
offices, kiosks and train stations.

You can purchase a SIM card from Swisscom for your mobile phone as well as prepaid cards. Calls are not cheap, however.
The SIM card costs about Sfr40 and calls are
almost Sfr1 per minute, although cheaper
at night and on weekends. Mobile service in Switzerland is generally excellent –
even in the mountains.

VISAS

Visas are not required for passport holders
of the EU, USA, Canada, Australia, New
Zealand or South Africa. A maximum three-
month stay applies although passports are
rarely stamped.

Turkey

HIGHLIGHTS

- **Istanbul** Sights, sounds and carpet touts: the irresistible mystique of the old Ottoman capital (p1188)
- **Cappadocia** Fairy chimneys, underground chambers and cave houses in Turkey's top natural attraction (p1209)
- **Selçuk** The best *pensions* on the coast, with the best Roman ruins down the road (p1199)
- **Best journey** Blue cruising: sailing the Med from Fethiye to Olympos, or Marmaris, or wherever … (p1204)
- **Off-the-beaten track** Mt Nemrut, in the recesses of eastern Turkey; keep your head where the gods lost theirs (p1212)

TURKEY

FAST FACTS

- **Area** 788,695 sq m (six times the size of Greece)
- **ATMs** Available everywhere
- **Budget** €15-20 per day
- **Capital** Ankara
- **Country codes** ☎ 90, international access code 00
- **Famous for** Turkish Delight, baths, coffee, moustaches, ancient history
- **Head of State** President Ahmet Necdet Sezer
- **Language** Turkish
- **Money** Turkish lira ($A1 = 1,115,671TL, €1 = 1.9 millionTL, UK£1 = 2,300,000 TL, US$1 = 1.4 millionTL)
- **Phrases** *Merhaba* (hello), *tamam* (OK),

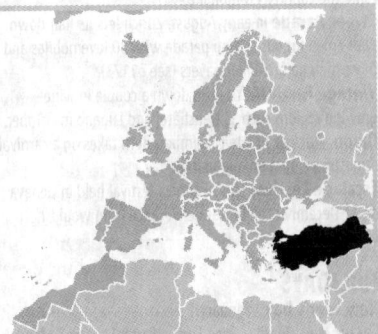

teşekkürler (thank you), *bu akşam olmaz* (not tonight, thanks)
- **Population** 68 million
- **Time** GMT + 2
- **Visas** Available on entry.

TRAVEL HINTS

Take buses rather than trains – they're faster and provide drinks. Mosquitoes can be a pain in watery areas like Dalyan.

ROAMING TURKEY

Head anticlockwise from Istanbul: Gallipoli, Efes (Ephesus), Fethiye, Kaş, Olympos, Antalya, Konya, Cappadocia and Ankara make a neat circle.

Given Turkey's unique position, bridging the vast physical and cultural gap between Europe and Islamic Asia, it's hardly surprising that a distinctive culture has developed here.

In fact, without Turkey East might never have met West in the first place. For centuries Istanbul was the seat of the Roman, Byzantine and Ottoman empires, exerting influence as far afield as Iran and the Balkans, and a host of familiar figures, from Achilles to St Paul, once strode through these very lands. Hundreds of ancient sites here illustrate the triumphs and defeats of some truly epoch-making generations.

Modern Turkey somehow manages to handle its many contradictions: secular but Muslim, Mediterranean but not European, rich but underproducing, traditional but ever-modernising. Your experiences as a traveller might vary wildly from town to town, but it takes a hard heart to resist the charms of this legendary country and its genuinely friendly people.

HISTORY

The greatest early Anatolian civilisation was the Hittites, a force to be reckoned with from 2000 to 1200 BC. After the collapse of the Hittite empire, parts of the country were not reunited until the Greco-Roman period.

In AD 330 the Roman emperor Constantine founded an imperial city at Byzantium. Renamed Constantinople, it became the capital of the Eastern Roman Empire and was the the Byzantine Empire's heart for a thousand years. But invasion by the Seljuk Turks heavily reduced the empire's territory, and the Fourth Crusade (1202–04) basically ruined Constantinople. The Byzantines eventually regained the ravaged city in 1261.

In 1453 Constantinople fell to Ottoman Turk Sultan Mehmet II (the Conqueror) and was renamed Istanbul. A century later, under Süleyman the Magnificent, the Ottoman Empire reached its zenith, spreading deep into Europe, Asia and North Africa.

By the 20th century, European nationalism had led to widespread independence movements, and the Turks emerged from WWI stripped of their last non-Turkish provinces. Most of Anatolia itself was divided among the victorious Europeans, leaving virtually nothing for Turkey.

At this low point, Mustafa Kemal (later Atatürk), the father of modern Turkey, took over. Under him, the Turks won their War of Independence by repelling the Greeks at Smyrna (İzmir), founding a new secular Turkish republic.

Since Atatürk's death in 1938, and the introduction of full democracy in 1950, Turkey has experienced three military coups and considerable political turbulence, including the execution of Democratic Party leader Adnan Menderes. The army became a key force in national politics, stepping in roughly once a decade to restore order and repair imbalances of power. The occupation and division of Cyprus became the major issue of the 1970s, while 1980 was marked by widespread civil unrest, a deadlocked parliament and yet another military intervention.

During the 1980s and '90s it was wracked by conflict with the PKK (Kurdistan Workers Party), which wanted the creation of a Kurdish state in the southeast.

In February 2001 the Turkish economy collapsed spectacularly, and the events of 11 September hit the previously resilient tourist sector hard. The IMF (International Monetary Fund) quickly pumped in funds to refloat the economy, but the slump hindered Turkey's bid to enter the European Union. Tourism suffered another major blow in 2004 when bombs exploded in Istanbul and Ankara, apparently a terrorist reaction to the occupation of Iraq.

Despite setbacks, joining Europe remains a key priority, and in 2002 the death penalty was abolished to meet EU criteria. With member countries ambivalent, however, it could be some time before accession talks begin.

PEOPLE & CULTURE

Turkey's population consists predominantly of Turks, with a large Kurdish minority (perhaps 12 million) and much smaller groups of Laz, Hemsin, Arabs, Jews, Greeks and Armenians. Arab influence is strongest in the Hatay (Antakya) area bordering Syria. Southeastern Turkey is solidly Kurdish.

Republican Turkey has predominantly adopted a Westernised lifestyle, at least on the surface. In smaller towns and villages, particularly in the east, you might encounter people more conservative.

READING UP

Lords of the Horizons (Jason Godwin) describes the rise and fall of the Ottoman empire; *Gallipoli* (Alan Moorehead) is an account of the tragic battle for the Dardanelles; *A Fez of the Heart* (Jeremy Seal) is a personal perspective on modern Turkey; and *Crescent & Star* (Stephen Kinzer) gives an insightful new examination of Turkish history and contemporary society.

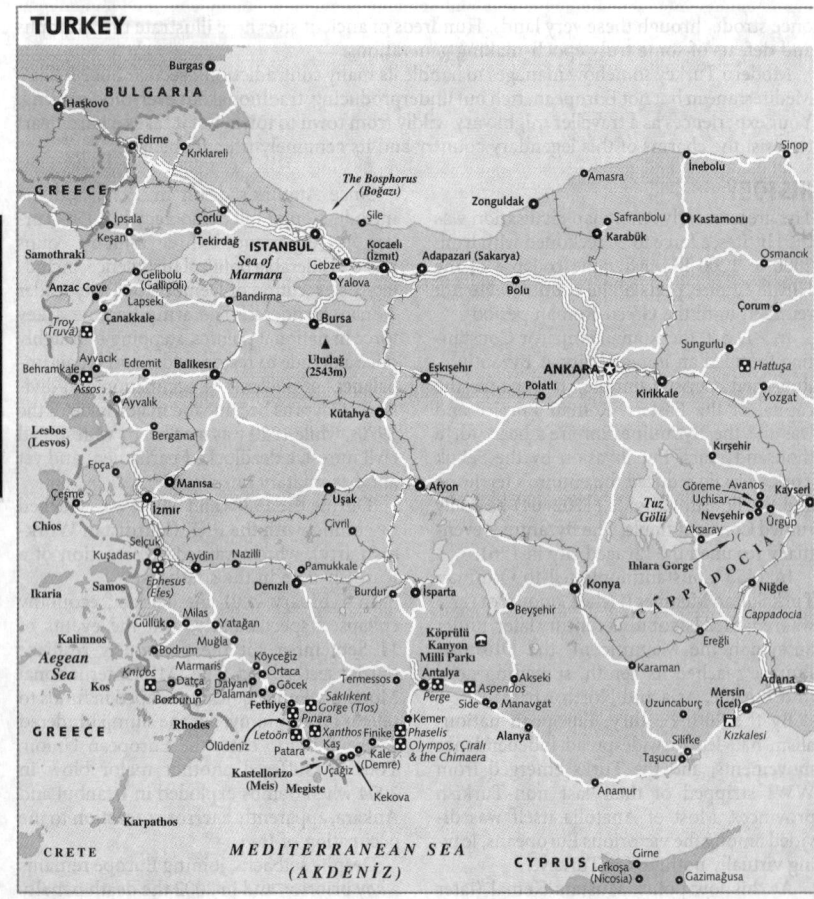

ENVIRONMENT

The Dardanelles, Sea of Marmara and Bosphorus strait divide Turkey between Asia and Europe, but Eastern Thrace (European Turkey) makes up only 3% of the land area. The remaining 97% is Anatolia, a vast plateau rising eastward towards the Caucasus Mountains. Large parts of Turkey's 6000km-long coastline are given over to tourism.

The Aegean and Mediterranean coasts have mild, rainy winters and hot, dry summers. The Anatolian plateau can be boiling in summer and freezing in winter. The Black Sea coast is mild and humid in summer, chilly and wet in winter.

Mountainous eastern Turkey is icy cold and snowy in winter, and only pleasantly warm during high summer. The southeastern parts are dry and mild in winter and baking hot during summer.

TRANSPORT

GETTING THERE & AWAY
Air

The cheapest fares are almost always to Istanbul. Turkish Airlines (THY), Onur Air and European carriers fly to Istanbul from most major European cities; a return ticket from London starts around UK£185. If you're planning a two- or three-week stay, it's also worth inquiring about charter flights.

Land

No direct trains run between Western Europe and Turkey. Instead, one train a day heads from Istanbul to Bucharest (15½ hours) and then on to Budapest (32 hours), with connections to elsewhere in Europe. There have been reports of long delays and pestering (especially women) at the Bulgarian border.

Long-distance buses are often a better option. Turkish lines such as Ulusoy and Varan offer reliable, comfortable services between Istanbul and major European cities.

If you're travelling to mainland Greece, you should note that the daily Istanbul-Thessaloniki train takes 16 to 18 hours, with a train change at the border. The bus gets there (more comfortably) in about 10 hours.

Sea

Turkish Maritime Lines (TML) runs weekly car ferries from İzmir to Venice in summer. Fares start at €150.

Private ferries link Turkey's Aegean coast and the many Greek islands. Services are usually daily in summer, several times a week in spring and autumn, and perhaps once a week in winter.

There are daily services to Turkish Cyprus from Taşucu (near Silifke) and less frequent services from Alanya.

GETTING AROUND
Bicycle

Bike hire is often available in tourist areas, and road surfaces are acceptable, if a touch bumpy. Turkish drivers, however, don't have much time for cyclists.

Bus

Turkish buses go almost everywhere, cheaply, frequently, comfortably and free of smoke. Kamil Koç, Metro, Ulusoy and Varan are the better companies, offering greater speed and comfort for slightly higher fares (plus better safety records than many rivals).

A town's *otogar* (bus terminal) is often outside the centre, but the bigger bus companies usually offer a *servis* (free minibus) to the centre.

Local routes are usually operated by midibuses or *dolmuşes* (minibuses), which might run to a timetable or set off when full.

Fez Travel (Map p1193; ☎ 0212-516 9024; www .feztravel.com; Aybıyık Caddesi, Sultanahmet, Istanbul) is a hop-on, hop-off bus service linking the main resorts of the Aegean and the Mediterranean with Istanbul and Cappadocia.

Car & Motorcycle

Car hire in Turkey is pricey (around €35 a day), and driving can be hazardous. **Türkiye Turing ve Otomobil Kurumu** (TTOK, Turkish Touring & Automobile Association; ☎ 0212-282 8140) can help with questions and problems. An International Driving Permit could be handy.

Hitching

Hitching is possible but not common in Turkey, and works better over short distances. Commercial vehicles are most likely to pick you up, but will expect payment. Women should never hitchhike alone.

Train

Turkish State Railways (TCDD) has a hard time competing with the long-distance buses – trains are usually marginally cheaper, but only special express services, such as the *Fatih* and *Başkent*, are faster. With *yolcu* and *posta* trains you might be quicker jogging.

The sleeper trains linking Istanbul, İzmir and Ankara can be good value.

ISTANBUL

☎ 0212/0216 / pop 12 million

On arrival in Istanbul you'll quickly see just what a sprawling mammoth city the former Ottoman capital is. Straddling the Bospho-

---

TOP FIVE TURKEY

▪ **Festival** Mevlana Festival, Konya (p1208)

▪ **Walk** Lycian Way (p1213)

▪ **Bar/Club** Babylon, Istanbul (p1195)

▪ **Impressive sight** Ephesus ruins (p1199)

▪ **Beach** Pamucak, near Selçuk (p1199)

---

rus with a foot in both Europe and Asia, the city embodies the head-on collision of ancient and modern, exotic and prosaic: minarets jostle for space with banks and housing developments, Western chic competes with Oriental kitsch, and the beer flows as freely as the *çay*. Istanbul's tourist sites might emphasise tradition, but its inhabitants are set firmly on the cutting edge of everything that is modern Turkey.

HISTORY

Late in the 2nd century AD, the Roman Empire conquered the small city-state of Byzantium, which was renamed Constantinople in AD 330 after Emperor Constantine moved his capital there. The city walls kept out barbarians for centuries while the western part of the Roman Empire collapsed. When the city fell for the first time in 1204, it was ransacked by the loot-hungry Europeans of the misguided Fourth Crusade.

Istanbul regained its former glory only after 1453, when it was captured by Mehmet the Conqueror and made capital of the Ottoman Empire. During the glittering reign of Süleyman the Magnificent (1520–66) the city was graced with many beautiful new buildings, and retained much of its charm even during the empire's long decline.

Occupied by Allied forces after WWI, the city came to be regarded as the decadent playpen of the sultans, and when the Turkish Republic was proclaimed in 1923 Ankara became the new capital. Nevertheless, Istanbul remains a commercial and financial centre, and is still Turkey's number one city in all but name.

Perhaps because of this reputation and its conspicuous westernisation, Istanbul was the target of terrorist attacks in 2004, when car bombs exploded near the British Consulate and the headquarters of the British-owned HSBC bank.

ORIENTATION
The Bosphorus strait, between the Black and Marmara Seas, divides European Istanbul from its Asian half. The European side is divided by the Haliç (Golden Horn) estuary into the 'newer' quarter of Beyoğlu in the north and Old Istanbul in the south; the Galata Bridge spans the two. Istanbul's *otogar* is at Esenler, about 10km west of the city.

Sultanahmet, Old Istanbul's heart, has most of the tourist sites, exchange offices, cheap hotels and eateries. Divan Yolu runs west through Sultanahmet past the Grand Bazaar to Aksaray, a major transport hub.

Eminönü, at the southern end of Galata Bridge, is the terminus for a tram line as well as many buses and ferries. Sirkeci train station is 100m east.

Karaköy, on the other side of the bridge, is another ferry terminus. Up the hill is the southern end of Beyoğlu's shopping strip, İstiklal Caddesi; at its northern end is Taksim Square, heart of 'modern' Istanbul.

INFORMATION
Emergency
Tourist police (Map p1193; ☎ 527 4503; Yerebatan Caddesi 6, Sultanahmet)

Internet Access
Café Turka (Map p1193; ☎ 514 6551; Divan Yolu 22/2, Sultanahmet; per hr €1.50)
SKM (Map p1193; ☎ 518 1075; Şehit Mehmetpaşa Sokak 21, Sultanahmet; per hr €1.25)
Taksim Internet (Map pp1190–1; ☎ 243 9567; Zombak Sokak 10, Taksim; per hr €0.60–0.75)

GETTING INTO TOWN
The Aksaray Metro serves the airport and the *otogar*; change at Aksaray and board the tram from Yusufpaşa for Sultanahmet and Eminönü (€1.25, up to 80 minutes).

From the airport, the fastest way into town is by taxi. During the day (*gündüz*) it costs around €10 to Sultanahmet (20 minutes), €12 to Taksim (30 minutes) and €8 to the *otogar* at Esenler (20 minutes).

Several shuttle buses also operate, including the Havaş airport bus (€4.50, 35 to 60 minutes, every 30 minutes), which goes to Taksim Square via Aksaray. Sultanahmet travel agents and hostels book minibuses in the other direction for around €3 a head.

EMERGENCY NUMBERS
Most emergency services have only Turkish-speaking operators, so your best bet is to find an English-speaking local to help.

- **Ambulance** ☎ 112
- **Doctor** (after hours) ☎ 141
- **Fire** ☎ 110
- **Jandarma (Gendarmerie)** ☎ 156 (a branch of the military)
- **Police** ☎ 155

Internet Resources
www.biletix.com Entertainment listings and tickets.
www.Istanbulguide.net
www.sultanahmetnews.com

Medical Services
American Hospital (Map pp1190–1; ☎ 231 4050; Güzelbahçe Sokak 20, Nişantaşı)
German Hospital (Alman Hastanesi; Map pp1190–1; ☎ 293 2150; Sıraselviler Caddesi 119, Taksim)

Money
There are banks, ATMs and exchange offices all over Istanbul.
Yapı Kredi (Map pp1190–1; ☎ 252 4700; İstiklal Caddesi 285, Beyoğlu)

Post
PTT Sirkeci (Map p1193; Büyük Postane Caddesi, Eminönü); Taksim (Map pp1190–1; Cumhuriyet Caddesi)

Telephone
Istanbul has two area codes: 0212 for the European side, 0216 for the Asian zone. All numbers listed here use the 0212 code unless otherwise indicated.

Tourist Information
Atatürk airport (☎ 573 4136; international arrivals)
Eminönü (Map p1193; ☎ 511 5888; Sirkeci station, Sirkeci)
Sultanahmet (Map p1193; ☎ 518 8754; Divan Yolu, Sultanahmet)

Travel Agencies
Backpackers Travel (Map p1193; ☎ 638 6343; www.backpackerstravel.net; Yeni Akbıyık Caddesi 22, Sultanahmet)
Setur (Map pp1190–1; ☎ 230 0336; www.setur.com.tr; Cumhuriyet Caddesi 107, Elmadağ)
Turkish Airlines (Map pp1190–1; ☎ 225 0556; Cumhuriyet Caddesi 199-201, Taksim)

TURKEY

TURKEY

ISTANBUL

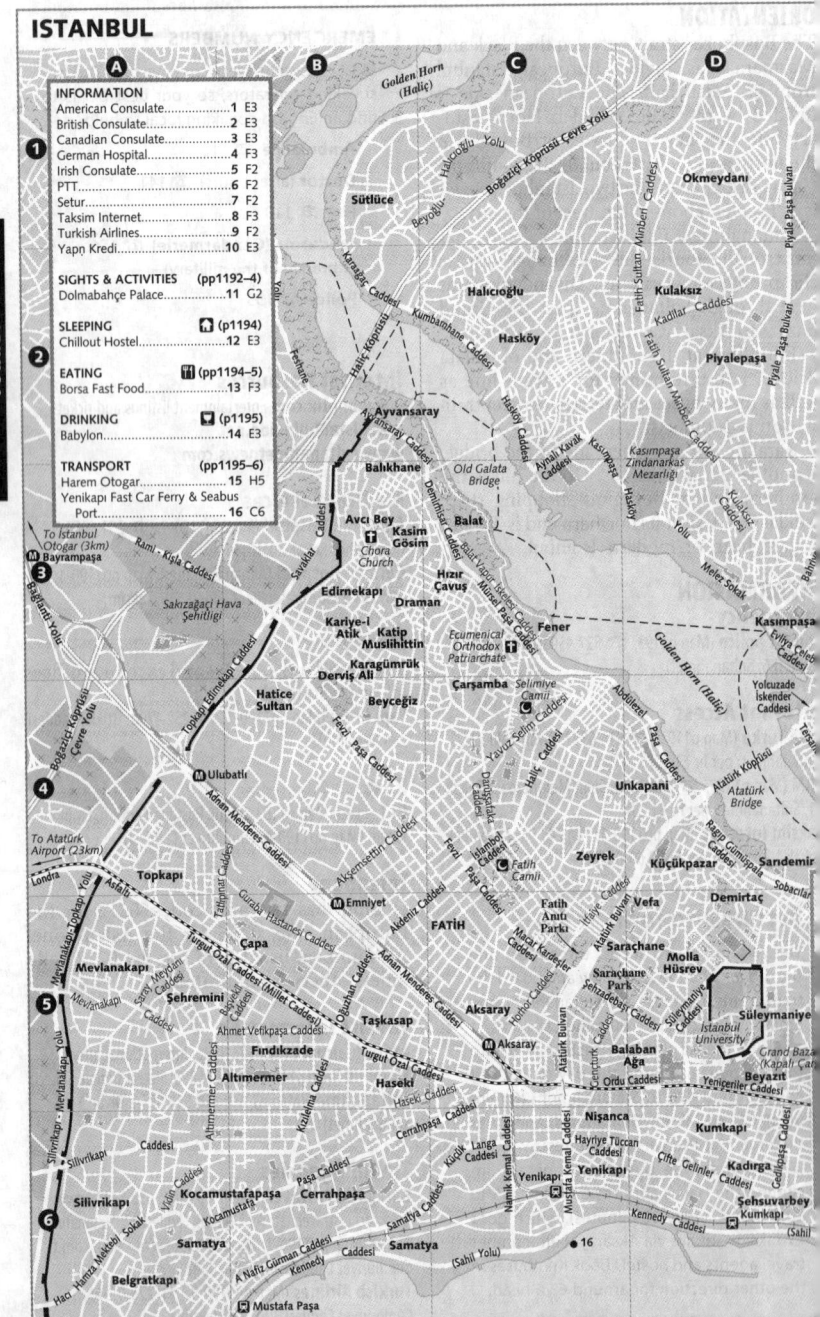

INFORMATION
American Consulate..................1 E3
British Consulate......................2 E3
Canadian Consulate..................3 E3
German Hospital.......................4 F3
Irish Consulate.........................5 F2
PTT...6 F2
Setur.......................................7 F2
Taksim Internet........................8 F3
Turkish Airlines........................9 F2
Yapı Kredi..............................10 E3

SIGHTS & ACTIVITIES   (pp1192–4)
Dolmabahçe Palace.................11 G2

SLEEPING   (p1194)
Chillout Hostel........................12 E3

EATING   (pp1194–5)
Borsa Fast Food......................13 F3

DRINKING   (p1195)
Babylon..................................14 E3

TRANSPORT   (pp1195–6)
Harem Otogar.........................15 H5
Yenikapı Fast Car Ferry & Seabus
    Port..................................16 C6

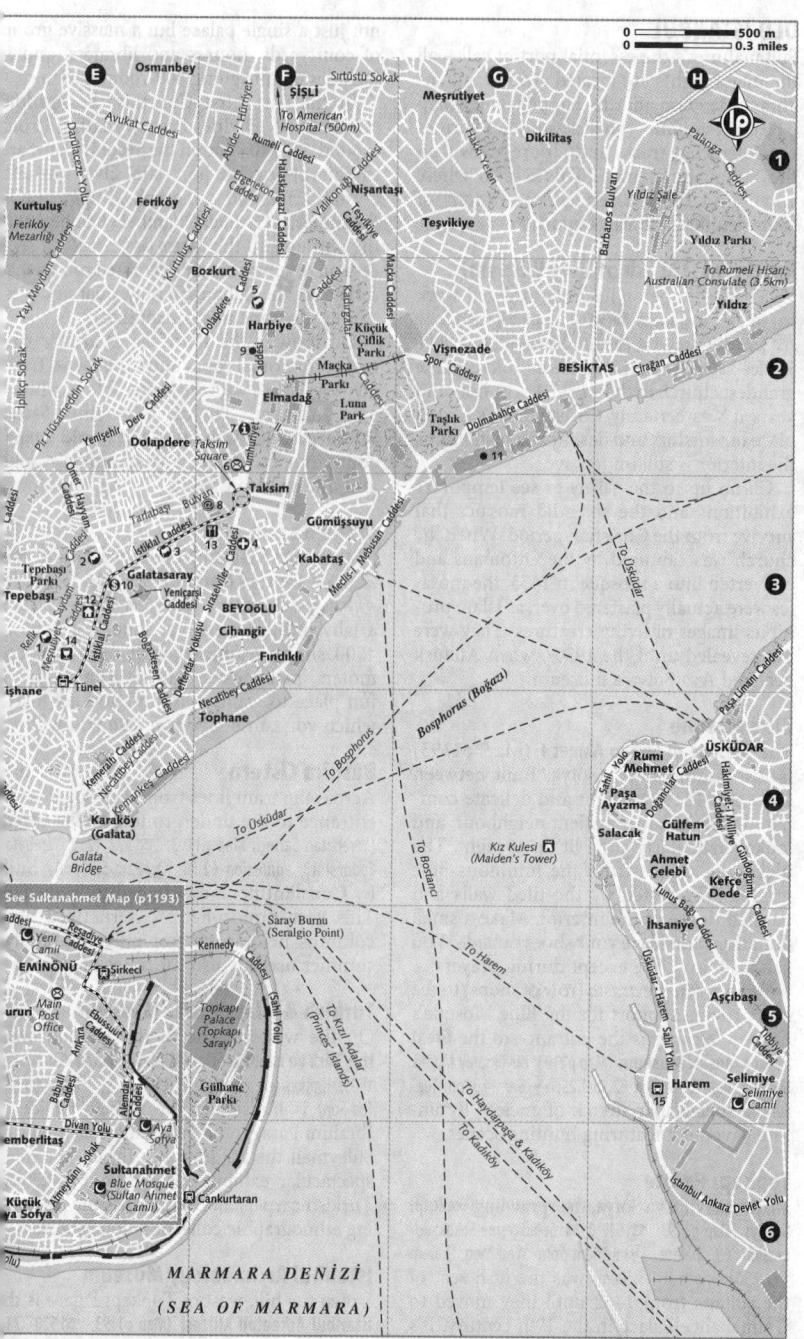

OLD ISTANBUL

Sultanahmet's essential port of call – all the major sights are located around Sultanahmet Meydanı and the Hippodrome (Map p1193), Istanbul's obelisk-studded former chariot-racing track, and all are shown on the Sultanahmet map. This is also where you'll find the greatest concentrations of touts, 'guides' and carpet pushers.

Aya Sofya (Church of Holy Wisdom)

When the Emperor Justinian ordered work to start on **Sancta Sofya** (Map p1193; Hagia Sofia; ☎ 522 0989; Aya Sofya Meydanı; admission €9; ☒ 9am-5pm Tue-Sun) in 532 AD, he meant to create the grandest church in the world. For a thousand years it was certainly Christendom's largest place of worship, and despite the scaffolding, the interior is still impressive.

Climb up to the **gallery** to see temporary exhibitions and the splendid mosaics that survive from the Christian period. When the church was captured by the Ottomans and converted into a mosque in 1453, the mosaics were actually plastered over, as Islam prohibits images of living creatures. They were not revealed until the 1930s, when Atatürk declared Aya Sofya a museum.

Blue Mosque

The **Mosque of Sultan Ahmet I** (Map p1193) is just south of Aya Sofya. Built between 1609 and 1619, it's light and delicate compared with its squat ancient neighbour, and looks particularly good lit up at night. The nickname comes from the luminous blue impression created by the tiled walls and painted dome of the interior. Make a small donation, and leave your shoes outside. You can visit any time except during prayers.

Rents from the *arasta* (row of shops) to the east provide support for the Blue Mosque's upkeep. Nearby is the entrance to the **Great Palace Mosaic Museum** (Map p1193; Büyüksaray Mozaik Müzesi; adult/concession €2.50/1.25; ☒ 9am-4.30pm Tue-Sun), a spectacular stretch of ancient Byzantine pavement featuring hunting scenes.

Topkapı Palace

Northeast of Aya Sofya, the sprawling **Topkapı Sarayı** (Map p1193; ☎ 512 0480; Soğukçeşme Sokak; admission €9; palace ☒ 9.30am-5pm Wed-Mon, harem ☒ 9.30am-noon & 1-3.30pm) was the lush seat of the sultans from 1462 until they moved to Dolmabahçe Palace in the 19th century. It's not just a single palace but a massive group of courtyards, houses and libraries, and i includes an intriguing 400-room harem.

In the vast First Court is the **Aya İrin** (Church of Divine Peace), dating from around AD 540. Within the Second Court are exhibits of priceless porcelain, silverware an crystal, arms and calligraphy. Right beside the Imperial Council Chamber (Kubbealtı) i the entrance to the **harem** (admission €9), a succession of sumptuously decorated rooms tha served as the sultan's family quarters (yes 'family' does include concubines).

On show in the Third Court are the sultan's ceremonial robes and the **Imperial Treasury** (admission €9) with its incredible wealth of gold and gems. The catchily named **Sacre Safekeeping Rooms** hold a solid gold caske containing the Prophet Mohammed's cloa and other Islamic relics.

Grand Bazaar

Just north of Divan Yolu is the Grand Bazaar or **Covered Market** (Map p1193; Kapalı Çarş www.mygrandbazaar.net; ☒ 8.30am-6.30pm Mon-Sat) a labyrinthine medieval shopping mall c 4500 shops crammed with punters, pro moters, pickpockets and policemen. It's fun place to wander around and get lost which you can bet your *arasta* you will!

Basilica Cistern

Across the tram lines from Aya Sofya is th entrance to the underground **Basilica Cister** (Yerebatan Sarnıcı; Map p1193; ☎ 522 1259; Yerebata Caddesi 13; admission €2.50; ☒ 9am-5.30pm), bui by Constantine and enlarged by Justinia This vast, atmospheric cistern filled wit columns held water not only for regula summer use but also for times of siege.

Turkish & Islamic Arts Museum

On the western side of the Hippodrom the **Türk ve İslam Eserleri Müzesi** (Map p1193; ☎ 5 1805; Hippodrome; admission €1.75; ☒ 9.30am-4.30p Tue-Sun) is housed in the former palace İbrahim Paşa, grand vizier and son-in-law Süleyman the Magnificent. Inside, the mo spectacular exhibits are the floor-to-ceilir Turkish carpets, but don't miss the fascina ing ethnographic collection downstairs.

Istanbul Archaeology Museum

Down the hill, west of Topkapı Palace is th **Istanbul Arkeoloji Müzesi** (Map p1193; ☎ 520 774

SULTANAHMET

0   200 m
0   0.1 miles

TURKEY

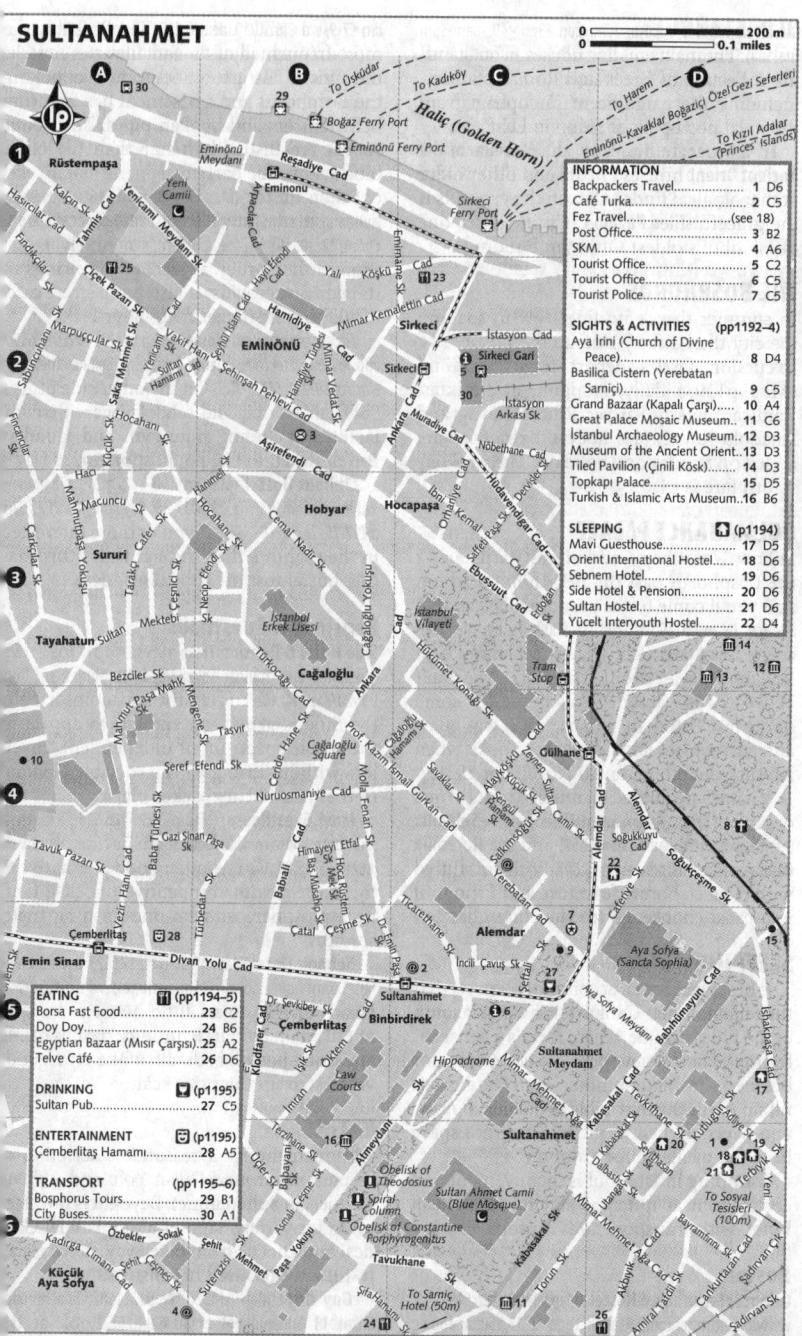

INFORMATION
Backpackers Travel....................	**1** D6
Café Turka...............................	**2** C5
Fez Travel.............................	(see **18**)
Post Office..............................	**3** B2
SKM......................................	**4** A6
Tourist Office..........................	**5** C2
Tourist Office..........................	**6** C5
Tourist Police..........................	**7** C5

SIGHTS & ACTIVITIES   (pp1192–4)
Aya İrini (Church of Divine Peace)................................	**8** D4
Basilica Cistern (Yerebatan Sarnıçı)............................	**9** C5
Grand Bazaar (Kapalı Çarşı)..	**10** A4
Great Palace Mosaic Museum..	**11** C6
İstanbul Archaeology Museum..	**12** D3
Museum of the Ancient Orient..	**13** D3
Tiled Pavilion (Çinili Köşk)..	**14** D3
Topkapı Palace.......................	**15** D3
Turkish & Islamic Arts Museum..	**16** B6

SLEEPING   (p1194)
Mavi Guesthouse.....................	**17** D5
Orient International Hostel......	**18** D6
Şebnem Hotel.........................	**19** D6
Side Hotel & Pension.............	**20** D6
Sultan Hostel.........................	**21** D6
Yücelt Interyouth Hostel.........	**22** D4

EATING   (pp1194–5)
Borsa Fast Food.......................	**23** C2
Doy Doy................................	**24** B6
Egyptian Bazaar (Mısır Çarşısı)..	**25** A2
Telve Café.............................	**26** D6

DRINKING   (p1195)
Sultan Pub..............................	**27** C5

ENTERTAINMENT   (p1195)
Çemberlitaş Hamamı..................	**28** A5

TRANSPORT   (pp1195–6)
Bosphorus Tours.......................	**29** B1
City Buses..............................	**30** A1

Osman Hamdi Bey Yokuşu; admission €3; 🕒 9.30am-5pm Tue-Sun). The main building houses an outstanding collection of Greek and Roman statuary, including the magnificent sarcophagi from the royal necropolis at Sidon in Lebanon.

In a separate building, the **Museum of the Ancient Orient** houses Hittite and other older archaeological finds. Also on the grounds is the graceful **Tiled Pavilion** (Çinili Köşk), one of Istanbul's oldest Ottoman buildings.

THE BOSPHORUS

In summer there's no finer way to soak up the city than a ferry ride up the Bosphorus. Excursion ferries depart from Eminönü (Map p1193) daily, stopping at Beşiktaş, Kanlıca, Yeniköy, Sarıyer, Rumeli Kavağı and Anadolu Kavağı (1¾ hours). Extra trips are added on Sunday and holidays. The weekday return fare is €4.

DOLMABAHÇE PALACE

Follow Necatibey Caddesi eastwards along the Bosphorus past the BJK Inönü Stadium and you'll come to the grandiose **Dolmabahçe Palace** (Map pp1190-1; ☎ 236 9000; Dolmabahçe Caddesi; combined ticket €6.25; 🕒 9am-3pm Tue-Wed & Fri-Sun), on the waterfront. The palace was built between 1843 and 1856 as home for some of the last Ottoman sultans, but it was guaranteed its place in the history books when Atatürk died there on 10 November 1938.

Visitors are guided on hurried tours of one or both of the two main buildings: the **Selamlik** (men's apartments; admission €3.50) and the **Haremlik** (family apartments; admission €3.50). Both are stuffed with over-elaborate furniture and fittings; if you must choose, go for the Haremlik.

SLEEPING

The best place for all accommodation types is the Sultanahmet–Cankurtaran district south of the Blue Mosque, where there's a dense selection of hostels and *pensions* competing for business. In high summer even the hostels fill up (with the inevitable problems of noise and overstretched facilities), and roof space becomes available for around €5.

Camping in Istanbul is inconvenient and costs about as much as staying in a cheap hotel, with transport fares on top.

Hostels

Orient International Hostel (Map p1193; ☎ 518 0789; www.orienthostel.com; Akbıyık Caddesi 13, Sultanahmet;

dm €7-9, s/d €16.50/19, deluxe €35; 💻) Probably the most-frequented of the Sultanahmet hostels, the Orient has a top-floor café overlooking the Bosphorus and a basement bar featuring belly dancers and hookah pipes. The newer rooms are distinctly better than the older block above the bar.

Sultan Hostel (Map p1193; ☎ 516 9260; www.sultanhostel.com; Terbıyık Sokak 3, Sultanahmet; dm/s/d/t €8/16/22/30; 💻) The Orient's main rival, just around the corner, is smaller but brings in the Fez Bus crowds. It also has a street café something its bigger neighbour lacks.

Yücelt Interyouth Hostel (Map p1193; ☎ 513 6150; info@yucelthostel.com; Caferiye Sokak 6/1, Sultanahmet; dm, s/d/tr US$9/22/26/33; 💻) On the other side of Aya Sofya, this is a big, old-school place with many facilities including mini-gym and laundry. Prices switch to UK pounds for Anzac Day!

Chillout Hostel (Map pp1190-1; ☎ 249 4784; www.chillouthc.com; Balyoz Sokak 17-19, Beyoğlu; dm/s €7.75/8, d €17.75-23.50; 🅿 💻) If you're more interested in the nightlife than the sights, try this chaotic hostel just off İstiklal Caddesi.

Pensions & Guesthouses

Side Hotel & Pension (Map p1193; ☎ 517 6590; www.sidehotel.com; Utangaç Sokak 20, Sultanahmet; s/d from US$20/35; ✂) Friendly and comfortable the Side is grown-up enough to appeal to the whole spectrum of independent travellers without losing all the sociable element of the 'youth' backpacker places.

Mavi Guesthouse (Map p1193; ☎ 516 5878; www.maviguesthouse.com; Kutluğün Sokak 3, Sultanahmet; dm/s €6/10.75/15.50; 💻) Another good alternative to the hostels, with competitive prices, a family atmosphere and no-one pushing travel services!

Sebnem Hotel (Map p1193; ☎ 5176623; www.sebnemhotel.com; Adliye Sokak 1, Sultanahmet; s/d €35/55; ✂) Head for this smart little house for a spot of Ottoman colour. Paintings, dashes of silk and four-poster beds all make it a good value step up the price scale.

EATING

Although there's a reasonable selection of restaurants around Divan Yolu and Akbıyık Caddesi in Sultanahmet, Beyoğlu is the place to go for variety Saunter along İstiklal Caddesi and choose from takeaway *döner* places to fully westernised bar-bistros.

Doy Doy (Map p1193; ☎ 517 1588; Şifa Hamam Sokak 13, Sultanahmet; mains €2-4.75) Look at the fading photos upstairs to see just how long this pide and kebab place has been a travellers' (and locals') favourite.

Telve Café (Map p1193; Akbıyık Caddesi, Sultanahmet; mains €2.50-6) At the far western end of the backpacker strip, this vaguely authentic-looking patio restaurant serves up traditional meals and hookah pipes (€4.25) away from the crowds.

Borsa Fast Food (Map pp1190-1; stiklal Caddesi 89, Beyoğlu; mains €1.50-4.50) All the standard Turkish dishes, plus ice cream and, unusually, alcohol. Also in **Eminönü** (Map p1193; Yalı Köşkü Caddesi).

Hard-up fish fans can grab a dirt-cheap treat direct from the boat along the Eminönü waterfront, where wave-tossed fishermen cook and sell their catch for around €1.

For fresh produce, hit the **street market** (Map p1193; Akbıyık Caddesi, Sultanahmet) every Wednesday or head for the **Egyptian Bazaar** (Map p1193; Mısır Çarşısı) for dried fruit, pulses, fish and more.

DRINKING

The Sultanahmet bar scene is concentrated on Akbıyık Caddesi, catering mainly for the denizens of the surrounding hostels. Dedicated club kids should head to the sidestreets of Beyoğlu, where the flashier local hipsters drink and groove to cutting-edge electronic music. Check *Time Out Istanbul* (€1.50) for monthly listings. There are also plenty of more traditional *meyhanes* and Turkish bars off İstiklal Caddesi.

Beyoğlu can be pretty seedy. Ignore friendly' locals who try to lure you into trouble with promises of free drinks etc.

Babylon (Map pp1190-1; ☎ 292 7368; www.babylon.com.tr; Şehbender Sokak 3, Beyoğlu) An essential stop on the Taksim circuit, with regular film screenings and more than its fair share of big-name DJs and bands.

Sultan Pub (Map p1193; Divan Yolu, Sultanahmet) A popular pub-restaurant opposite Sultanahmet Meydanı, the Sultan has a less rowdy atmosphere than some of the backpacker bars.

ENTERTAINMENT

Istanbul's historical *hammams* (Turkish baths) are pretty touristy, with prices to reflect their foreign clientele. The best for first-timers is the beautiful **Çemberlitaş Hamamı** (Map p193; ☎ 522 7974; Vezirhan Caddesi 8; wash & massage €18; ☑ 6am-midnight), just off Divan Yolu.

GETTING THERE & AWAY
Air

Most people fly into Istanbul's Atatürk International Airport, Turkey's flight hub. Most foreign airlines have their offices around Taksim.

Boat

Yenikapı (Map pp1190-1), south of Aksaray Square, is the dock for *hızlı feribot* (fast car-ferries) across the Sea of Marmara.

Bus

Istanbul Otogar, at Esenler, about 10km west of the city, is a monster of a place, with 168 ticket offices and buses leaving for all parts of Turkey and beyond. Buses depart for Ankara (€12 to €21, six hours) roughly every 15 minutes, day and night; buses for most other cities depart at least every hour.

Coming from or heading to Anatolia, you could also use the smaller Harem Otogar on the Asian shore, which is accessible by ferry (€0.60) and saves you crossing town twice.

Train

Sirkeci is the station for services to Edirne, Greece and Eastern Europe. The nightly *Bosfor Expresi* goes to Bucharest (€26, 15½ hours) and Budapest (€95, 32 hours).

Haydarpaşa, on the Asian shore, is the terminus for trains to Anatolia, Syria and Iran. Seven express trains a day run to Ankara (€10 to €28, seven to 10 hours), the fastest being sleeper only.

GETTING AROUND
Boat

The cheapest and nicest way to travel any distance in Istanbul is by ferry. Short ferry hops cost €0.60, longer ones €1.20. The main ferry docks are located at the mouth of the Golden Horn (Eminönü, Sirkeci and Karaköy) and at Kabataş, just before Dolmabahçe Palace.

Bus

City buses are crowded but can be useful. On most routes you must have a ticket (€0.60) before boarding. Stock up from the white booths near major stops, or nearby shops.

Taxi

Istanbul has 60,000 yellow taxis, all of them with meters (although not every driver

TURKEY

wants to run them). A trip from Sultanahmet to Taksim costs around €5.

Train

To get to Sirkeci station, take the *tramvay* (tram) from Aksaray or Sultanahmet, or any bus for Eminönü. Haydarpaşa station is connected by ferry to Karaköy (€0.60, at least every 30 minutes).

Suburban trains from Sirkeci (€0.60) run along the southern walls of Old Istanbul and the Marmara shore at least twice an hour.

Tram

The useful *hızlı tramvay* (fast tram) or Metro network has three lines. The first runs between Eminönü and Aksaray via Divan Yolu and Sultanahmet; the second runs west from Aksaray to the airport. A third line runs from Taksim to 4 Levent, while a separate restored tram also trundles along İstiklal Caddesi to Taksim. All tram tickets cost €0.60.

Underground

The Tünel, Istanbul's old underground train, hill-climbs from Karaköy to Tünel Meydanı and İstiklal Caddesi (€0.60, 7am to 9pm).

AROUND ISTANBUL

Since Istanbul is such a vast city, few places are within easy day-trip reach. The fast ferry link means that you can just about make Bursa and back in a day, although it's much better to plan on an overnight stay.

Bursa

☎ 0224 / pop 1.2 million

Sprawling at the base of Uludağ, Turkey's biggest winter sports centre, Bursa was the original centre of the Ottoman Empire. It retains several fine mosques from those early days, as well as some popular thermal springs in the suburb of Çekirge. Bursa's wonderful covered market makes a good visitor-friendly alternative to Istanbul's efforts.

The city's heart is along Atatürk Caddesi, with the Ulu Cami (Grand Mosque) to the west and the main square, Cumhuriyet Alanı (commonly called Heykel), to the east. The *otogar* is 10km north of the centre. Çekirge is about 6km west of Heykel.

SIGHTS & ACTIVITIES

The grandest of Bursa's beautiful mosques is the 20-domed **Ulu Cami** (Grand Mosque; Atatürk

Caddesi), built in 1399. Northeast of Ulu Cami is the **bedesten** (covered bazaar), where you'll find, among other things, the **Karagöz shop** (☎ 221 8727; Eski Aynalı Çarşı 4), which has details on traditional shadow-puppet shows.

Northwest of Ulu Cami is the **Muradiye Complex**, which has decorated tombs dating from the 14th and 15th centuries. The **mineral baths** in Çekirge are further along the road.

East of Heykel, the **Yeşil Cami** (Green Mosque; Emir Sultan Caddesi) is widely considered Bursa's finest building. It marks the transition from Seljuk to true Ottoman architecture.

SLEEPING

Central hotels are convenient but not exactly great value. Alternatively, for a bit more money you can stay in Çekirge, where you'll also get free mineral baths.

Otel Güneş (☎ 222 1404; Tahtakale Mahallesi 75; s/d tr €9/14.75/17.75) A traditional(ish) family-run hotel, you'll find basic but serviceable rooms here, although not always much English.

Hotel Çamlıbel (☎ 221 5565; İnebey Caddesi 71; s/d €13.50/19, with bathroom €17.75/26.50; P) Ignore the scabby tiling and odd wiring: this is the closest it gets to a bargain in the centre.

EATING

Bursa was the birthplace of the İskender kebab, although these days quality isn't always what it was. Head for the bazaar area or east of Heykel for the best selection.

Çiçek Izgara (Belediye Caddesi 15; mains €1.25-6.50) Although outdoor seating would be better, the 1st-floor restaurant here is great for catching the flower market action on the street.

Turan (☎ 221 2025; Sönmez Rş Sarayı 120; cakes from €0.60) Those with a sweet tooth should sink them into the tasty profiteroles at this long-running *pastane* (patisserie).

GETTING THERE & AROUND

If you time it right, the fastest way to get to Istanbul is to take the hourly bus to Yalova (€, one hour), then a catamaran or fast car-ferry to Istanbul's Yenikapı docks (€4.25, one hour, at least seven a day). Get a bus at least 1 hours before the scheduled boat departure.

There are also regular direct buses to Istanbul (€6). Those designated *feribot ile* (by ferry) are quicker and much more pleasant than the *karayolu ile* (by road) services.

There are no *servis* buses between the *otogar* and the centre; take an ordinary bus (€0.30, 45 minutes).

AEGEAN COAST

Turkey's Aegean coast is seen as poor cousin to the Med at times in scenic terms, and hence it doesn't have as many resort developments – a definite plus for independent travellers. The area also makes up for what it lacks in natural drama with historical weight, boasting some of the country's best-preserved classical ruins at Ephesus and Bergama, as well as the more recent resonance of the Gallipoli battlefields.

GALLIPOLI (GELİBOLU)

For most Europeans, Gallipoli is little more than a footnote in the events of WWI, but to generations of Australians, New Zealanders and Turks the battle for the Dardanelles represents one of the most poignant moments of their history. On 25 April 1915, Anzac (Australia and New Zealand Army Corps) and British troops landed on the Gallipoli peninsula, hoping for a quick victory against inferior Turkish defences. However, strategic blunders turned the operation into a protracted stalemate, and after nine months of horrendous casualties the Allied forces withdrew.

The Turkish officer responsible for the defence of Gallipoli was none other than Mustafa Kemal, later Atatürk, and his success is commemmorated in Turkey on 18 March. The big draw for visitors, however, is Anzac Day on 25 April, when a dawn service commemorates the anniversary of the Allied landings. The service attracts thousands of travellers from Down Under and beyond.

The scenic peninsula is now a national park, scattered with moving memorials to the dead of the various nations that fought here. If time is tight, the easiest way to see the sights is on a minibus tour from Çanakkale with **Hassle Free Tours** (☎ 213 5969) or **Troyanzac Tours** (☎ 217 5849) for about €20 per person. If you're less pressed for time, it's cheaper to take a ferry from Çanakkale to Eceabat and a *dolmuş* to Kabatepe, then follow the heritage trail. It's a pretty long circuit – taking at least a day or two to cover the whole peninsula on foot.

You could also stay at Eceabat, on the Thracian (European) side of the strait. **TJs Hostel** (☎ 814 3122; www.anzacgallipolitours.com; Cumhuriyet Caddesi 5; dm/s/d €4/7.50/11.50; 🖳) gets fond reviews from its guests, and also runs its own highly rated tours.

Hourly car ferries cross the strait from Çanakkale to Eceabat and from Lapseki to Gallipoli (€0.60).

TROY

Troy (Truva) is one of the most evocative names in legend, conjuring up images from Homer's great saga of the Trojan War. According to the *Odyssey*, the Greeks besieged Troy for 10 years trying to win back King Menelaus' wife Helen, who had been lured away by the charms of Prince Paris. Eventually victory was secured by retreating and hiding soldiers inside a wooden horse, giving the world a new phrase and Hollywood a new Brad Pitt movie.

However, even hardcore Homer (or Brad) fans might be disappointed at the actual **site** (admission €6; 🕙 8.30am-5pm Nov-May, 8am-7.30pm Jun-Oct), as there's little drama about it apart from the playground-style 'reconstruction' Trojan Horse. Excavations illustrate parts of nine successive cities built on this site: Troy I goes right back to the Bronze Age; legendary Troy could be Troy VI or VII; and most of the visible ruins are Roman ones from Troy IX. Unless you're well up on archaeological matters, it's worth taking a guided tour from Çanakkale (around €15) to get the most out of a visit here.

In summer, frequent *dolmuşes* run from Çanakkale (€1.25).

ÇANAKKALE
☎ 0286 / pop 60,000

Although it's used mainly as a base for outward excursions, there's enough to the town of Çanakkale itself to keep you busy in between tours, although it can get pretty crowded at peak times. The slightly touristy centre, with all the cheap hotels, a range of restaurants and even a couple of bars, is close to the ferry pier, around the small clock tower. The harbour area is full of tea gardens (informal outdoor cafés serving a basic range of drinks and snacks) and more expensive eateries.

Built by Sultan Mehmet the Conqueror in 1452, the **Ottoman castle** at the southern end of the waterfront now houses a **Naval**

Museum (adult/student €1.25/0.50; ⌚ 9am-noon & 1.30-5pm Tue-Wed & Fri-Sun). Just over 2km south of the ferry pier, on the road to Troy, the **Archaeological Museum** (admission €1.25; ⌚ 9am-5pm) holds artefacts found at Troy and Assos.

Information

Tourist information (☎ 217 1187; Rıhtım Caddesi)
Uğur Internet (☎ 214 0634; Kemalyeri Sokak; per hr €0.50)

Sleeping & Eating

Çanakkale usually has plenty of accommodation. Unfortunately the mass influx of visitors around Anzac Day results in shortages, price hikes and more complaints about Çanakkale hotels than just about anywhere else in the country. Always check prices carefully.

Yellow Rose Pension (☎ 217 3343; www.yellowrose.4mg.com; Yeni Sokak 5; dm/s/d €4/9/14.75; 💻) Popular with travellers, this appealing guesthouse has a quiet location and many extras, from laundry and book exchange to a video library. It's the TJs Tours's local agent.

Anzac House (☎ 213 5969; www.anzachouse.com; Cumhuriyet Bulvarı; dm/s/d €4/7.50/11.75; 💻) Not to be confused with the pricier Anzac Hotel around the corner, Anzac House is the first place most backpackers head for. It's big and cheap, and it's the base for Hassle Free Tours. Unfortunately many of the rooms are little more than cupboards.

Papağan (Tekke Sokak 6; mains €0.60-1.75) Bright and eerily clean, this new fast-food and patisserie chain has several branches in town, pulling in young locals who've outgrown McDonald's.

Truva 2001 (Fetvane Sokak; mains €0.60-2.50) The usual staple grills and casseroles are on offer here, with the added bonus of a student set menu for €1.75.

Getting There & Away

Hourly buses run to Istanbul (€11.75, five hours) and İzmir (€7, five hours). Minibuses also run to Lapseki (€1.75, 30 minutes) every half hour.

BEHRAMKALE (ASSOS)

☎ 0286 / pop 500

Behramkale, 19km southwest of Ayvacık, is a beautiful hilltop village with a pre-Ottoman **mosque** and the ruins of a **Temple of Athena** (admission €3; ⌚ 8am-5pm Tue-Sun) looking across the water to Lesvos in Greece. Two kilometres further on, on the other side of the hill, is a small *iskele* (port), packed with waterfront restaurants and several camp sites. Both become overcrowded in summer, especially at weekends, so visit in the low season if possible.

With freshly spruced-up decking and solar power, **Tekin Pension** (☎ 721 7099; s/d €9/18) is among the best of the many cheap options on the hillside.

Infrequent *dolmuşes* come here from Ayvacık (€1.75), which is linked by bus to Çanakkale and Ayvalık.

AYVALIK

☎ 0266 / pop 30,000

Inhabited by Ottoman Greeks until 1923, this small modern fishing port and beach resort is the point of departure for ferries to Lesvos. Also offshore is **Alibey Island** (Cunda), which is lined with open-air fish restaurants and linked by ferries and a causeway to the mainland. The *otogar* is 1.5km north of the town centre. The **tourist office** (☎ 312 2122) is 1km south, opposite the marina.

Bonjour Pansiyon (☎ 312 8085; Çeşme Sokak 5; s/d €12/20; ⌚ May-Sep) This fine restored house once accommodated a French ambassador to the sultan (take a peek at the grand salon) and now caters for more humble travellers. It serves an excellent local breakfast.

There are frequent direct buses from İzmir to Ayvalık (€3, three hours). Coming from Çanakkale (€4, 3½ hours), buses drop you off at the OPET station on the main highway to take a *servis*.

Boats to Lesvos (€40/50 one way/return) run daily from late May to September and up to three times a week at other times.

BERGAMA

☎ 0232 / pop 50,000

From the 3rd century BC to the 1st century AD, Bergama (formerly Pergamum) was a powerful and cultured kingdom. A line of rulers beginning with one of Alexander the Great's generals reigned over this small but wealthy kingdom; it's now a charming, old-fashioned town famous for its extensive ruins. The **tourist office** (☎ 633 1862; İzmir Caddesi 54) is midway between the *otogar* and the market.

The **Acropolis** (admission €6; ⌚ 8.30am-5pm), a windswept hilltop site 6km from the city centre, is the part everyone comes to see with its commanding location, reconstructed columns and spectacular sloping theatre. You can follow the pretty path marked by dots down through the ruins to get back to town. The **Asclepion** (Temple of Asclepios; admission €6; 🕑 8.30am-5pm), 3.5km from the city centre, is the remains of a famous medical school with a library that rivalled that of Alexandria in Egypt.

The excellent **Archaeology Museum** (admission €2.50; 🕑 8.30am-5pm) contains finds from both these sites, although the stunning Altar of Zeus was whisked away to Berlin (see p454) by the German excavators.

Pension Athena (🕿 633 3420; İmam Çıkmazı 5; s/d €4.50/9, with bathroom €6/12) At the Acropolis end of town, this old Ottoman house is arguably the best place if you want to stay overnight. Breakfast is extra (but worth it).

Buses run between Bergama and İzmir every half-hour in summer (€3.50, two hours). Fairly regular buses and *dolmuşes* also link Bergama with Ayvalık (€3, one hour).

İZMİR
🕿 0232 / pop 2.5 million

If you've been pottering around smaller Aegean towns like Assos and Bergama, İzmir might come as a shock. Turkey's third-largest city is a vast, cosmopolitan sprawl with an aspiring Riviera feel. Many people choose to skip it, as prices are relatively high, little remains of the historic town and the sheer size of the place can be offputting.

Those who do stick around could check out the ruins of the extensive 2nd-century AD Roman **agora** (admission €1.25; 🕑 8.30am-noon & 1-5pm) on the eastern edge of the chaotic, atmospheric bazaar. It's also worth taking a bus to the hilltop **Kadifekale** fortress, where women still weave traditional kilims (rugs) on horizontal looms.

Information
İpeksan Internet (857 Sokak 6; per hr €0.90)
Tourist information (🕿 484 2147; Gaziosmanpaşa Bulvarı 1/C)
Turkish Airlines (🕿 489 2881; Akdeniz Caddesi 14)

Sleeping & Eating
The cheapest places to stay are along Anafartalar Caddesi, between Basmane station and the bazaar area, although standards aren't exactly stellar.

Hotel Alav (🕿 484 9925; Anafartalar Caddesi 749; s/d €4.25/8.50, with bathroom & TV €12/15) Favoured by Turkish businessmen, the Alav is not as

dubious as some of its budget counterparts, and it has a good location near the station.

Alican Otel (🕿 484 2768; Favzi Paşa Bulvarı 157; s/d €18/30; 🞰) In the thick of the hotel quarter around the Dokuz Eylül Meydanı roundabout, this is a good bet in value-for-money terms, despite some street noise. The unfancy house restaurant is also worth a try.

For bargain basement meals, head either towards the bazaar or to Kıbrısşehitleri Caddesi in the trendy northern district of Alsancak. The waterfront Kordon strip provides upmarket alternatives.

Getting There & Around
Many bus companies have ticket offices around Dokuz Eylül Meydanı, near Basmane station. They usually provide a *servis* to the *otogar*, 6.5km from the centre. Frequent buses serve Selçuk (€4.50, one hour), Çanakkale (€7, five hours), Pamukkale (€3.50, four hours) and many other destinations.

For details of summer-only ferry services from Venice, see p1187.

Local bus tickets cost €0.75; buy from kiosks and newsstands before boarding. Bus 33 goes to Kadifekale, and Nos 601, 603 and 605 go to the *otogar*.

SELÇUK
🕿 0232 / pop 23,100

Selçuk is a pleasant, generally easy-going town best known for its population of storks and for the splendid Roman ruins of Efes (Ephesus), once Rome's capital in the province of Asia. In its heyday only Athens was more magnificent, and the site is one of Turkey's major attractions.

Although the town is undeniably touristy, most bus tours skip it so you avoid the resort mentality you'll find elsewhere. The western side of Atatürk Caddesi, behind the museum, is the quieter part of town, and it contains some of the best *pensions*. The eastern side holds the *otogar* and plenty of shops and restaurants. The **tourist office** (🕿 892 1328) is in the park across from the *otogar*.

Efes is a 3km, 35-minute walk west. Frequent *dolmuşes* to Pamucak and Kuşadası pass the turn-off (€0.90, five minutes).

Efes
The city of **Ephesus** (admission €9; 🕑 8am-5pm, to 7pm in summer) initially flourished as a centre for worship of the Anatolian goddess later

identified with Diana/Artemis, and it quickly became an important port, although the harbour has long since silted up. Wandering down the former main street, you'll see the well-preserved (or restored) remains of structures such as the Temple of Hadrian, Marble Way (where the rich lived) and the Fountain of Trajan. The real photo opportunities, however, are the reconstructed façade of the monumental Library of Celsus and the immense Great Theatre, which could hold 24,000 people. An audio guide with brain-addling amounts of information can be hired for €3 (€1.25 for students).

Town Centre

In Selçuk itself, the main attraction is the excellent **Ephesus Museum** (admission €2.50; ☒ 8.30am-noon & 12.30-4.30pm), with its priceless array of artefacts from the Roman period. On the hill above Atatürk Caddesi, the **Basilica of St John** (admission €2.50; ☒ 8am-6pm) is said to have been built over the apostle's tomb, and is another common coach party stop. Between Ephesus and Selçuk, the foundations and one solitary pillar of the **Temple of Artemis** (☒ 8.30am-5.30pm) are all that remain of one of the Seven Wonders of the Ancient World.

On Saturdays a lively and mostly untouristy **market** is held on the main square.

Sleeping

Hospitality is a serious business in Selçuk, with dozens of small *pensions* competing for backpacker trade. As a result standards and services are pretty high, and the best places put a lot of effort into making sure you won't want to leave (even if you've just come to look around).

Homeros Pension (☎ 892 3995; homerospension@ yahoo.com; Asmali Sokak 17; s €7.50-10.25, d €14.75-20.75; ☒ 🖳) A consistent standard-setter, Homeros will positively shower you with extras. The superb rooms show the owner's carpentry skills to great effect, and ambitious expansion plans are in the offing, including a swimming pool.

Australia & New Zealand Guesthouse (☎ 892 6050; www.anzguesthouse.com; 1064 Sokak 12; dm €6, r per person €9; 🖳) This sociable multilevel backpacker favourite has plenty of communal terrace and lounging space, plus a room with Jacuzzi (€30) for those who fancy a soak.

Artemis Guest House (☎ 892 6191; www.artemis guesthouse.com; 1012 Sokak 2; dm/s/d €6/9/15.25; ☒ 🖳 🖳) On the more modern eastern side of town, 'Jimmy's Place' is another paradise for frill-seekers, with everything from balconies and satellite TV to Turkish nights, wall paintings and swimming pool. Deluxe rooms are also available (€30).

Eating

If you can dismiss the friendly pressure to eat at your pension, there's no shortage of cheap restaurants in Selçuk. Those at the eastern end of Cengiz Topel Caddesi have neat views of the town's Byzantine aqueduct.

Belediye Restaurant (Municipal swimming pool) When it's open, this restaurant is a local favourite – ask for directions.

Zefk'ü Sefa (☎ 892 9443; 1066 Sokak 1; mains €2.50-5.25) You'll find a decent menu and friendly service at this place below the town's chamber of commerce. It also has a great rear courtyard set away from the central hubbub.

Getting There & Away

Buses from İzmir (€4.50, one hour) usually drop you on the main highway nearby. Frequent minibuses head for Kuşadası (€1.25, 30 minutes) and the excellent beach at Pamucak (€0.90, 10 minutes).

KUŞADASI

☎ 0256 / pop 50,000
Kuşadası is an unabashed resort town, with everything that entails, and it is effectively the start of Turkey's coastal package holiday strip. Many independent travellers just dash through to catch a boat out to Samos (Greece). If you're up for a big, messy night out, however, you can practically guarantee it on Bar St here.

Apart from the 16th-century **castle** in the harbour, which opens irregularly, Kuşadası is short of sights. However, it does make a good base for visits to the ancient cities of **Priene**, **Miletus** and **Didyma** to the south. Admission to each site is €0.85.

Most cheap accommodation is near the harbour. **Hotel Liman** (☎ 614 7770; Buyral Sokak 4; dm/s/d €5/14.75/20.75; ☒ 🖳) is an average place distinguished by its fantastically nutty owner. **Stella Travellers Inn** (☎ 614 1632; www.stellahostel .com; Bezirgan Sokak 44; dm/s/d/tr €9/20/30/36; 🖳 🖳) is a big backpackers' den with great sea views and unusual extras like a basketball court.

If you don't fancy paying €10 for roast beef and Yorkshires, there are plenty of cheaper Turkish options away from the tourist joints; try the bright new **Ismail Usta** (☎ 612 9454; Cephane Sokak 1/1; mains €1.25-3.50) for ide, grills and casseroles.

Kuşadası's *otogar* is 1.5km southeast of he centre. Off season you'll need to change t İzmir (€5, 1½ hours) or Söke (€1.25, 30 minutes) for most places. In summer there re regular buses to Bodrum (€6, two hours) nd Denizli (for Pamukkale; €7, three hours). 'or Selçuk (€1.25, 30 minutes) and Söke, take minibus on Adnan Menderes Bulvarı.

In summer three boats daily sail to Samos €45 open return). In winter there might be nly one or two boats a week.

PAMUKKALE
☎ 0258 / pop 4000

Renowned for its brilliant white ledges and ools (travertines), the Pamukkale plateau an disappoint as well as delight. In recent ears the water supply has dried up, you can o longer swim in most of the pools, and ru-nour has it that some of the famous calcium idges have been uplifted with whitewash. 's still an impressive site and if you're not onvinced there's the bonus of the extensive Hierapolis ruins.

Climb the hill above Pamukkale village, nd pay to enter the **travertines and Hierapolis** admission €2.50, valid next day; ☺ 9am-10am). The Hierapolis ruins, including a theatre, a col-nnaded street (with public toilet) and a ast necropolis, are very spread out; at least alf a day will do them justice.

Later, swim amid sunken Roman columns t **Pamukkale Termal** (€9.50), on the ridge's top, nd visit **Hierapolis Archaeology Museum** (admis-on €1; ☺ 9am-noon & 1-5pm Tue-Sun), which has ome spectacular sarcophagi and friezes.

Regular buses run from hub Denizli to zmir (€4, four hours) and Konya (€10, seven ours). A full-day tour costs about €30 from ost Aegean towns. Buses and *dolmuşes* huttle between Denizli and Pamukkale each alf hour (€0.50, 30 minutes).

BODRUM
☎ 0252 / pop 25,000

nce known as Halicarnassus, Bodrum as gone through various incarnations in s long history but is now hardcore resort rritory and is crammed with (mainly Brit-

ish) tourists every summer. Fortunately the town has resisted rampant modernisation and retains a charming element in the wind-ing streets of its old town and bazaar area. Only the pricey restaurants and the persist-ent bass beats from waterfront clubs belie the illusion of a fishing village lifestyle.

The Adliye Camii, a small mosque on the castle promontory, marks the centre, sep-arating the town's two main bays. The *otogar* is 500m inland, along Cevat Sakir Caddesi.

Information
Doğuş Internet (Türkuyusu Caddesi 175A; per hr €0.90)
PTT (☎ 316 1212; Cevat Sakir Caddesi)
Tourist information (☎ 316 1091; Kale Meydanı 48)

Sights
You'll see the **Castle of St Peter** on about every brochure, postcard and flyer in Bodrum, and it's still an essential stop plus a scenic asset. Built in 1402 and rebuilt in 1522 by the Crusaders, the castle has the **Museum of Underwater Archaeology** (admission €6; ☺ 9am-noon & 1-5pm Tue-Sun), containing the oldest Medi-terranean shipwreck's finds ever discovered and a model of a Carian princess's **tomb** (admission €1.75). Ignore the poor excuse for a 'Trojan horse' in the courtyard.

Sleeping
The narrow streets around the harbour have plenty of *pensions*, although few places stay open out of season, and breakfast, air-con and other 'extras' are seldom included in the price. The western bay tends to be quieter.

Sevin Pansiyon (☎ 316 7682; Türkkuyusu Sokak 5; s/d €9/12, with air-con & TV €12/17.75; ❄ 🖳) The Sevin's extras are a bit perfunctory, but the rooms are a decent size and it's well placed for just about everything.

Emiko Pension (☎ 316 5560; Uslu Sokak 11; s/d €9/18) This Japanese-run guesthouse, just off Atatürk Caddesi, has simple rooms with paved floors and a leafy courtyard setting – not exactly feng shui, but it works.

Bodrum Backpackers (☎ 313 2762; www.bodrum backpackers.com; Atatürk Caddesi 31/B; dm €3; 🖳) If you've arrived from Selçuk the standards here might come as a shock, but it's the town's cheapest choice by quite a margin.

Eating
The small streets east of the Adliye Camii have some cheap eateries where döner can be

bought for less than €2 (€3 for an İskender). Or, go eastward to Kilise Meydanı, a plaza filled with open-air eateries. Check out Meyhaneler Sokak (Taverna St), where wall-to-wall tavernas offer food, drink and live music for €6 to €15.

Mantı Evi (☎ 316 7925; Sanatokulu Caddesi 14; mains €1.50-2.50; ☾ dinner only) Nip off Atatürk Caddesi to this family-run and convincingly traditional place for a proper dose of homemade *mantı* (Turkish ravioli).

Getting There & Away

There are frequent bus services from Bodrum to Antalya (€14.75, eight hours), Fethiye (€6, 4½ hours), İzmir (€7.75, four hours), Kuşadası and Selçuk (€6, two hours) and Marmaris (€6, three hours).

In summer daily hydrofoils and boats link Bodrum with Kos (€20, one hour). In winter services are cut to three times weekly, but prices fall accordingly.

MEDITERRANEAN COAST

With 1200km of coastline stretching between Marmaris and Antakya, Turkey's Mediterranean front is the beacon of the national tourist industry. The stunning scenery just begs to be sailed, trekked or explored, and ruins abound to keep the classicists happy. The main centres of activity are Fethiye, at the busy western end, and Antalya, start of the less resorty eastern strip.

MARMARİS

☎ 0252 / pop 22,700

A firm favourite with UK and Dutch package companies, Marmaris has suffered from

some haphazard town planning and lack the endearing qualities of Bodrum, despit having a very similar setting. However, i you steer clear of the tackier Brit-swampe parts you'll find the atmosphere ain't al bad, and it's a good place to board a boa or chug a few beers.

İskele Meydanı, the main square, is b the ferry pier northeast of the castle; Ha Mustafa Sokak, also known as Bar St, run east from here. The *otogar* is 2km north o town, off the road to Bodrum.

Information

Galaxie Internet (☎ 413 4082; 44 Sokak 30/1; per hr €1.25)
PTT (☎ 412 1212; Fevzipaşa Caddesi 14)
Tourist information (☎ 412 1035; İskele Meydanı)
Turkish Airlines (☎ 412 3750; Atatürk Caddesi 26-B)

Boat Excursions

Wooden boats along the waterfront offe tours of outlying beaches and island Check carefully exactly what you pay an what you get for it. A day's outing usual costs around €20 per person.

The most popular excursions are to **Daly** and **Kaunos** or to the bays around Marmari but you can also take longer, more seriou trips to **Datça** and the ruins at **Knidos**. It also worth asking about boats heading fo **Cleopatra's Island**, which offers silky-soft san and water as warm as a Jacuzzi.

Sleeping & Eating

Dominated by package hotels, Marmaris ha few central cheap options, and those that d survive can be noisy and uninspiring.

Barış Motel (☎ 413 0652; www.barismotel.com; € Sokak 10; s/d €9/12, with bathroom €18/23.50) There no attempt at flashiness in this family-ru establishment, but the rooms are a pristin

---

A MIR TRIFLE

Wandering around the edge of Marmaris harbour, you might see a statue of what appears to be an old-fashioned diver. If you take a closer look, however, you'll find that it actually depicts an American astronaut. So what's the story?

As the plaque underneath explains, the space-hopper concerned is one James Reilly, a Texan, who took the Turkish flag into space in 1998 at the request of the Turkish government. The flag, along with a Marmaris pennant, was presented at a special ceremony, and flew in the Mir space station for five days before being returned home to serve as a museum piece.

So far no live Turks have made it into space, but who knows – with a successful Eurovision Song Contest behind them and the drive for the EU gaining momentum, anything seems possible!

shade of whiter-than-white and the staff are utterly obliging.

Interyouth Hostel (☎ 412 7823; interyouth@turk .net; 42 Sokak 45; dm €6, r per person €15; 🖳) In the depths of the bazaar, the local HI outpost can be sociable when it's full but is little more than functional out of season.

Azmakbası Restaurant (Hacı Mustafa Sokak; mains €1.50-9) At the eastern end of Bar St, opposite the marina, this deceptively smart place serves up cheap *mantı* and *gözleme* as well as the tourist standards.

For the cheapest food, head through the bazaar; the whole waterfront heaves with pricier but more varied restaurants. Self-caterers can stock up at the huge **Tansaş supermarket** (☎ 413 9100; Ugusal Egemenlık Bulvarı).

Getting There & Away

Frequent buses and minibuses serve Fethiye (€4.75, three hours, hourly), Bodrum (€6, three hours) and Dalyan (via Ortaca; €4, two hours), plus several daily services to Antalya (€13, seven hours). Car ferries run to Rhodes daily in summer, less frequently in winter (open return €65).

DATÇA

☎ 0252 / pop 6100

The small, relatively peaceful town of Datça is a good place to sidestep the summer resort crowds, with enough restaurants and bars to keep busy but a much smaller tourist capacity than its nearest neighbours. Don't miss the charming **old quarter**, which overlooks the harbour, the beach and the small Esenada peninsula.

Regular buses shuttle to and from Marmaris (€4, 1¾ hours). You can also catch boats to Bodrum (€9) and Rhodes (€40).

KÖYCEĞIZ

☎ 0252 / pop 7600

Taking its name from the tranquil lake that laps its shore, Köyceğiz takes the yearly influxes of German and Dutch tourists well in its stride and still gives the impression of a town where life doesn't stop out of season. It has a thriving agricultural community. Many people prefer it to Dalyan as a base for visiting Kaunos and İztuzu beach.

Of the places catering specifically to the backpacker market, **Fulya Pension** (☎ 262 2301; Ali İhsan Kalmaz Caddesi; s/d €7/14; 🖳 🖳), refitted in 2004, and **Flora Hotel** (☎ 262 4976; www.florahotel.info; Kordon Boyu 96; s/d €9/18; 🖳), a Dutch favourite, are arguably the best. Both offer a range of services and excursions.

For slightly more money **Hotel Alila** (☎ 262 1150; Emeksiz Caddesi; s/d €15/21; 🅿 🖳) is even better value, and it has a well-frequented waterfront restaurant.

To eat, head for the market or the Atapark area by the lake shore, which has several restaurants and tea gardens.

Hourly buses connect to Ortaca (€0.90, 25 minutes) from the *otogar*, 2km up the main road.

DALYAN

☎ 0252 / pop 4000

Independent travellers might have trouble knowing what to make of Dalyan. In summer the crowds, facilities and coloured lights virtually scream 'tourist trap'. However, the setting, right on the Dalyan River and overlooked by Lycian rock tombs, is hard to write off completely.

In any event, the major activity here is boating out of town, and there is a variety of excursions on offer. **İztuzu beach**, a short paddle away, is a gorgeous place to sun yourself as well as being one of the few remaining nesting grounds of the sea turtle *(Carretta carretta)*. The same trips (€5) usually take in a visit to the ruined city of **Kaunos** (admission €1.75; ⏰ 8.30am-5.30pm) and the **Sultaniye hot springs** (admission €0.60) on the shores of Köyceğiz Lake, possibly with a mud bath thrown in.

The roof terrace and swimming pool set the family-run guesthouse, **Kristal Pansiyon** (☎ 284 2263; Erkul Sokak; s/d €12/18; 🖳 🖳), apart from many of its counterparts, although the lack of river frontage is a major minus.

Dalyan Camping (☎ 0532-700 6565; tent/caravan €7/14.75, bungalows s/d €11.75/17.75) is tucked away amid the many *pensions* around the southern reaches of Maraş Caddesi. It is a passable site with few facilities.

Bistro Clou (☎ 284 3452; mains €3-7) is just north of the market and the *dolmuş* stand. It's a friendly place with atmospheric gourd lanterns, a notch above the bog-standard tourist fare elsewhere.

To connect to any other location from Dalyan you have to catch a minibus to Ortaca (€0.75, 30 minutes) and tranfer to another bus there.

TURKEY

FETHİYE

☎ 0252 / pop 48,200

Thanks to the popular 'blue cruises' that leave from here, Fethiye has much more of a backpacker vibe than resort towns such as Marmaris, although it still becomes very hot and crowded in summer. The picture-perfect harbour and mountain backdrop are irresistible at any time, and the town also makes a good base for visiting the beautiful **Saklıkent Gorge** and the ruins at **Tlos** and **Pınara**.

Fethiye's *otogar* is 2km east of the centre. Karagözler *dolmuşes* ply the main street, taking you past government buildings, PTT and banks before skirting the bazaar district, curving round the bay and cutting up by the marina on the western side of the town.

Information

Madlife Travel (☎ 612 1564; www.blueyachtcruise .com; Atatürk Caddesi)
Tourist office (☎ 614 1527; İskele Meydanı)
Trend Internet (Ishane Caddesi; per hr €2)

Sights & Activities

Over the mountains to the south of Fethiye, lovely **Ölüdeniz** (Dead Sea) is a textbook case of a good thing spoiled by progress, with incessant paragliders overhead and more than 50 hotels nudging the small beach. The famous **lagoon** (adult/student €1.25/0.60; ☾ 8am-8pm) remains tranquillity incarnate, and you can also catch a boat to the beautiful **Butterfly Valley** (€8 return).

In Fethiye, little remains of the original town of Telmessos besides the ruins of a Roman theatre and some Lycian sarcophagi dating from about 400 BC. The cliffs backing the centre hold picturesque Lycian tombs, including the **Tomb of Amyntas** (admission €1.75; 117 Sokak; ☾ 8am-7pm), ideal for gazing out over the harbour and pondering ancient times.

Most people succumb to, and enjoy, the well-promoted **12 Island boat tours**, a populist mix of swimming, cruising and sightseeing. Prices are typically around €15 per person, or UK£75 for a three-day, two-night trip.

Dolmuşes run to the nearby evocative Ottoman Greek 'ghost town' of **Kayaköy** (admission €1.75), abandoned after the population exchange of 1923.

Sleeping & Eating

Most of the nicer *pensions* are uphill from the marina, off Fevzi Çakmak Caddesi.

Ferah Pension (Monica's Place; ☎ 614 2816; www .ferahpension.com; Ordu Caddesi 2; dm €6, d €14.75-17.75; ☐) Ferah is well known locally and consistently popular with backpackers. The shady terrace is a real plus in a hot summer.

Paradise Guest House (Cennet Hostel; ☎ 614 2230; Fevzi Çakmak Caddesi; dm €6-9, d €17.75) One for the younger budget crowd, this lackadaisical place is essentially the sideline project of a boat company, but can be good fun. Try speaking German to the staff.

Café Oley (Eski Meğri Sokak 4; mains €2-6; ☐) A homesick traveller's paradise, offering sandwiches, cakes, muffins, Thai curry and other rare treats in inviting, homy surrounds.

Şark Sofrası (☎ 612 0233; Çarşın Caddesi; mains €0.90-3) Dig into more prosaic grill fare here, near the bazaar, or try the intriguing 'sensitive meatball'.

Getting There & Away

Heading for Antalya, the *yayla* (inland) route (€6, four hours) is shorter and cheaper, although less scenic, than the *sahil* (coastal) route (€8, seven hours), which also serves Patara (€1.75, 1½ hours) and Kaş (€3, 2½ hours). Minibuses to local destinations leave from behind the Yeni Cami in the centre.

A summer hydrofoil service links Rhodes (Greece) and Fethiye on Tuesday and Thursday (€50).

The 'blue cruise' has become a travellers' institution, and is still the nicest way to get between Fethiye and Olympos or Marmaris. You travel on a *gület* (wooden yacht), calling in at bays along the way for swimming, sunbathing and variable amounts of boozing. Prices for three-day cruises start around UK£99 or €135.

PATARA

☎ 0242

Patara's main claim to fame is its superb 20km-long beach, one of Turkey's best. It's also a turtle breeding ground, so most of the sandy expanse is out of bounds between 8pm and 8am in summer. A secondary attraction are the extensive but overgrown **ruins** (admission €6; ☾ 8.30am-7pm May-Oct, 9am-5.30pm Nov-Apr), which are good for a scramble.

Near Patara are two Unesco World Heritage sites: the **Letoön** (admission €1.75), which has excellent mosaics and a sacred pool, and impressive **Xanthos** (admission €1.75), which boasts a Roman theatre and Lycian pillar tombs.

Midibuses plying the Fethiye-Antalya main road will drop you at Gelemiş, 3.5km from the beach.

KAŞ
☎ 0242 / pop 8000

Of all Turkey's popular coastal towns, Kaş has perhaps the most convincing small-town feel to it, with some wonderful winding streets in its old quarter and a waterfront area that retains enough character to be charming even at the height of the tourist season. Even the drive here is a treat, strewn with mountain views all the way from Fethiye.

Apart from enjoying the town's ambience and few small pebble beaches, you can also walk west a couple of hundred metres to the well-preserved Roman **theatre**. Lycian **sarcophagi** are dotted about the streets, and the **tombs** cut into the cliffs above the town are beautifully lit at night.

The most popular boat trips head round **Kekova island** and out to beautiful **Kaleköy** (Simena), passing over Lycian ruins beneath the sea. You'll pay around €10 per person in a glass-bottomed boat.

Information
Bougainville Travel (☎ 836 3737; www.bougainville -turkey.com; İbrahim Selin Caddesi 10)
Nethouse Internet (☎ 836 2845; Çukurbağlı Sokak 16; per hr €0.90)
Tourist office (☎ 836 1238; Cumhuriyet Meydanı)

Sleeping & Eating
Kaş's quietest places to stay are all on the western side of town and rise in price (and quality) the nearer they are to the sea. There are lots of small *pensions* south of the *otogar*.

Anı Motel (☎ 836 1791; Recep Bilgin Caddesi 12; www.motelani.com; s €6, d €11.75-14.75; ✕ 🖳) Some effort has actually been put into the décor of this backpacker haunt, which boasts spacious rooms, nice windows and a large roof terrace, complete with hammocks.

Kaş Camping (☎ 836 1050; Hastane Caddesi; tent €5) A popular and pleasant camping ground in an olive grove west of town.

Türkmen Sofrası (PTT Caddesi; mains €1.50-3) It's not exactly the most atmospheric place in town, but the Türkmen's set menus (€3.25 to €5) are top value.

İkbal (Süleyman Sandıklı Sokak; mains €4.75-10.75) If you're going to splash out at any of the touristy restaurants in town, the stepped stone terrace here must be about the coolest setting around.

Getting There & Away
Midibuses depart from Kaş's convenient central *otogar* for all local destinations. Regular services include Fethiye (€3, 2½ hours), Olympos (€4.25, 2½ hours) and Antalya (€4.25, four hours).

OLYMPOS
☎ 0242

Long beloved of hippies and New Age types, **ancient Olympos** (adult/concession €6/1.75; 🕑 8am-7pm) was once a major port city; now it's a fantastically wild, abandoned place where ruins peek out from forest copses, rock outcrops and riverbanks. You also have to pay the admission fee to reach the extensive **beach**, although your ticket should be valid for at least two days.

According to legend, the nearby **Chimaera** (Yanartaş), a natural eternal flame, was the hot breath of a subterranean monster. Easily sighted by ancient mariners, it is now a mere glimmer of its former fiery self, but no less exotic. To find the Chimaera, follow the signs 3km east down a neighbouring valley. A half-hour climb leads to the flames.

Sleeping & Eating
Most visitors come here to stay in the treehouse camps, a motley assortment of wooden huts, restaurants and bars lining the 3.5km road from the beach to Olympos village. If that's not your thing, there are normal *pensions* and hotels at neighbouring Çıralı. All prices listed here are for half-board.

Kadir's (☎ 892 1250; dm €9, r per person €11.75-18; ✕ 🖳) The place that started it all is still a good bet. It's daubed colourfully throughout and staffed by a range of seasoned Antipodeans. The bar-disco is throbbing in every sense, but it's the furthest treehouse camp from the beach.

Türkmen (☎ 892 1249; www.olymposturkmentree houses.com; dm US$8, r per person US$10-14; 🖳) Another place in the same mould, with real treehouses and the full range of facilities.

Getting There & Away
Fethiye–Antalya buses will drop you at the highway turn-off, where *dolmuşes* wait to run you down to Olympos village and the camps (€1.50).

ANTALYA

☎ 0242 / pop 509,000

A bustling, modern town, Antalya's unspectacular beaches are pure tourist zones, but the city itself has much more to it. Kaleiçi, the restored Ottoman old town, is a charming hilltop village of winding lanes, characterful buildings and souvenir shops, and cliffside vantage points on either side of the harbour provide superb views over a beautiful marina and the sea-facing Karaalioğlu Parkı.

The *otogar* is 4km north of the centre; a minibus into town costs €0.45. The city centre is at Kalekapısı, a major intersection marked by a landmark clock tower.

Information

Natural Internet (☎ 243 8763; Tophane Parkı; per hr €0.75)
Owl Bookshop (☎ 243 5718; Akarçeşme Sokak 21)
PTT (Güllük Caddesi)
Tourist office (☎ 241 1747; Cumhuriyet Caddesi 91)

Sights & Activities

About 2km from the centre is the **Antalya Museum** (Cumhuriyet Caddesi; admission €6; ✆ 9am-6pm Tue-Sun), which houses spectacular finds from nearby Perge, Aspendos and Side, as well as a wonderful ethnographical collection. Hop on the *tramvay* (tram; €0.50) to the Müze stop.

To get into **Kaleiçi**, head south down the hill from the clock tower. You'll pass the **Yivli Minare** (Grooved Minaret), which rises above an old mosque. Further into Kaleiçi the **Kesik Minare** (Truncated Minaret) is built on the site of a ruined Roman temple. The monumental **Hadriyanüs Kapısı** (Hadrian's Gate), just off Atatürk Caddesi, was built for the Roman emperor's visit in AD 130. The **Suna & İnan Kıraç Kaleiçi Museum** (☎ 243 4274; Kocatepe Sokak; admission €0.90; ✆ 9am-noon & 1-6pm Thu-Tue Oct-May, 9am-noon & 2-7.30pm Jun-Sep) houses a fine collection of pottery together with rooms showing important events in Ottoman family life.

Park life is a key feature of the Antalyan daily grind, and you'd have to be in a real rush not to make time for a relaxed tea, coffee or *nargileh* (water pipe) at the viewpoint cafés in **Tophane** or **Karaalioğlu Parkı**.

Sleeping

Kaleiçi is substantially a pension district, and it provides an ever-changing selection of accommodation.

Sabah Pansiyon (☎ 247 5345; www.sabahpansiyon .8m.com; Hesapçı Sokak 60; s/d €6/12, with bathroom €9/14.75; ⚅ 💻) Antalya's most popular backpackers' haven offers tours, car hire and decent evening meals, with plenty of lounging space to boot.

Pansiyon White Garden (☎ 241 9115; Hesapçı Geçidi 9; s/d €9/14.75; ⚅) Floral motifs and spotless rooms give the White Garden a dash of homely charm, and the shady rear courtyard is a real selling point.

Dedehan Pansiyon (☎ 248 3787; Mescit Sokak 29 s/d €17.75/20; Ⓟ ⚅) How could you dislike a place with heart-shaped pillows? The décor might not be urban chic, but this is another good family place.

Eating

Eski Sebzeciler İçi Sokak, a covered passage near the junction of Cumhuriyet and Atatürk Caddesis, is lined with open-air eateries, where a *tandır kebap* (mutton cooked in earthenware), salad and drink can cost as little as €4. The bazaar's a good starting point but avoid the rip-off kebab shops without marked prices around the clock tower.

Chang-Qing (☎ 247 6587; İmaret Sokak; mains €4-17.50) Wok chicks and lychee lads should grab the opportunity to chow down on chow mein or do some dim sum at this bright-red Szechuan place.

Getting There & Away

From the *otogar*, buses head for Göreme (€10.50, 10 hours), Konya (€10.50, six hours) and Olympos (€2, 1½ hours).

CENTRAL ANATOLIA

Away from the resorts and the tourist-saturated coast, the Anatolian plateau is Turkey's true heartland. It's halfway between the European sophistication of Istanbul and the quasi-Arabic flavour of the remote east.

ANKARA

☎ 0312 / pop 4 million

Ankara has never enjoyed a great reputation either as a tourist hotspot or as a dynamic capital, but it's a much more manageable size than Istanbul and no less cosmopolitan in its outlook. With its key position at the heart of the country, transport links here are unbeatable, and it's worth checking out the citadel area and the city's excellent museum before you hop aboard a bus.

Ankara's *hisar*, or citadel, crowns a hill km east of Ulus Meydanı (Ulus Square), he epicentre of Old Ankara. The more nodern Ankara is situated further south. It s located around Kızılay Meydanı (Kızılay square).

Atatürk Bulvarı is the city's main north–outh axis. Ankara's mammoth *otogar* is .5km southwest of Ulus Meydanı. Ankara Garı (train station) is 1.4km southwest of Jlus Meydanı

nformation

Emirhan Internet (☎ 311 5771; Plevnı Sokak 9/1; er hr €0.90)
PTT (Atatürk Bulvarı)
Tourist office (☎ 231 5572; Gazi Mustafa Kemal Bulvarı 121)

Sights & Activities

The **Anatolian Civilisations Museum** (Anadolu Medeniyetleri Müzesi; ☎ 329 3160; Hisarparkı Caddesi; admission €4.75; ⏱ 8.30am-5pm Tue-Sun), next to the citadel, holds the world's richest collection of Hittite artefacts, an essential supplement to visiting central Turkey's Hittite sites. However museum-fatigued you are, this place is a must. Besides, what else are you going to do in Ankara?

The **Anıt Kabir** (Mausoleum of Atatürk; ⏱ 9am-5pm), 2km west of Kızılay Meydanı, is the monumental tomb of modern Turkey's founder, Kemal Atatürk. It's tantamount to a place of pilgrimage for many Turks.

Various Roman ruins are scattered around town, including the **Column of Julian**, erected

in AD 363, and the **Temple of Augustus and Rome**. Nearby are remains of the **Roman Baths** (admission €1.25; ☾ 8.30am-12.30pm & 1.30-5.30pm).

After all this antiquity, take a break and see the lighter side of Ankara life by hanging out in **Genelik Parkı** and nipping into the **Luna Park** funfair (admission €0.15).

Sleeping

Ulus has numerous budget hotels, mostly concentrated around Opera Meydanı (Opera Square) and north of Ulus Meydanı.

Otel Mithat (☎ 311 5410; www.otelmithat.com.tr; Tavus Sokak 2; s/d €13/17.75) Minimalist décor in Turkey? The comfortably beige rooms here are proof that it can work. Breakfast is extra, however.

Mar & Si Hotel (☎ 310 8383; Eşdost Sokak 10; s/d €45/56) More beige, this time combined with tasteful blues to complement the three-star facilities. You'll rarely be expected to pay the full posted rates – €18/24 is normal out of season.

Otel Fuar (☎ 312 3288; Kosova Sokak 11; s/d €6/9) If you're strapped for cash this is about the cheapest option in town. Don't expect too many creature comforts.

Eating

Urfalı Hacı Mehmet (☎ 311 2636; www.urfalihacimehmet.com.tr; Kızılbey Sokak 3/A; mains €0.60-3.50) The next generation of family grill restaurants, this place is so shiny it's practically space age. The descriptions might not appeal – 'compacted sliced meat', anyone? – but the special Urfa kebabs (€5.75 to €22.50) will feed up to eight people.

Zenger Paşa Konağı (☎ 311 7070; www.zengerpasa.com; Doyran Sokak 13; mains €1.75-6; ☒) One of several atmospheric (if slightly touristy) restaurants up in the citadel, this restored old house is enlivened by wonderful ethnographic displays .

Getting There & Around

Ankara's enormous *otogar* (AŞTİ) dispatches passengers across the country all day and night. For Istanbul (€12 to €21, six hours) buses depart at least every 15 minutes. Useful services include Antalya (€12, eight hours), İzmir (€12, nine hours) and Göreme (€9, five hours), all at least hourly.

A taxi between the *otogar* and the train station costs €3.

KONYA

☎ 0332 / pop 680,000

An important Muslim town with a lingering reputation for conservatism, Konya was the capital of the Seljuk Turks, and it showcases some excellent Seljuk architecture. It was here that the 13th-century poet Mevlana Rumi founded the whirling dervishes, one of Islam's most important mystical orders. Their successors still perform during the **Mevlana Festival** every December.

The centre of town stretches from Alaettin Tepesi (Aladdin Hill) along Alaettin Caddesi and Mevlana Caddesi to the Mevlana Museum. The *otogar* is 10km northwest of the centre; minibuses run you into town, or you can catch the tram as far as Alaettin Tepesi (€0.30).

Information

PTT (Hükümet Meydanı)
Selale Internet (☎ 350 1061; Başaralı Caddesi; per hr €0.45)
Tourist office (☎ 351 1074; Mevlana Caddesi 67)

Sights & Activities

The **Mevlana Museum** (Mevlana Müsezi; adult/concession €2.50/1.25; ☾ 10am-5.30pm Mon, 9am-5.30pm Tue-Sun) holds the remains of the great Sufi saint and other important figures in the dervish order, all in coffins topped with turbans plus a casket supposedly holding Mohammed's beard. It's very popular with pilgrims, and visitors should show due respect here. The distinctive turquoise tower is an unofficial symbol of the city.

As a religious centre, Konya is also known for its Seljuk seminaries, of which there are several around town. **Büyük Karatay Museum** (admission €0.60; ☾ 9am-noon & 1.30-5.30pm) is now a ceramics museum, and **İnceminare Medresesi** (Seminary of the Slender Minaret; admission €0.60; ☾ 9am-noon & 1-5pm) contains a museum of wood- and stone-carving.

If you don't want to pay admission prices just exploring the town centre is a crash course in Seljuk architecture, as there are some spectacular specimens on show. Start at Alaettin Tepesi and wander at will.

Sleeping & Eating

Hotel Ulusan (☎ 351 5004; Kurşuncular Sokak 2; s/d €11.75/13.50, with bathroom €16.50/19; ☒) Tucked away behind the PTT, this impeccably renovated gem is as good as many twice

CAPPADOCIA •• Göreme **1209**

the price, with that all-important dash of character (teddy bears!).

Yeni Kök & Esra Otel (☎ 352 0671; Kadılar Sokak 28; s/tw/d €17.75/26.50/29.50; **P** 🅧 🖳) A bizarre subterranean tunnel links two separate buildings here, each with small but well-equipped rooms.

Şifa Restaurant (☎ 352 0519; Mevlana Caddesi 56; mains €1.25-4.50) Regional speciality *tandir kebap* (lamb baked in earthenware) tops the bill of standards at Şifa. Service can be pretty rushed when it's busy.

Samancılar (☎ 351 2243; Sırçalı Medrese Caddesi 39/A; mains €0.30-2) A super-cheap kebab'n'pide shacks south of the centre.

Getting There & Away

There are frequent buses from Konya to Cappadocia, via Nevşehir (€9, three hours), Ankara (€9, three hours) and Pamukkale (€10, seven hours).

CAPPADOCIA

Cappadocia (Kapadokya in Turkish), the central region between Ankara and Kayseri, is famous for its unique scenery, which is strewn with fantastic natural rock formations, cave houses and historical remnants of a semi-troglodyte population. Highlights include the Göreme valleys, Ihlara Gorge and some extraordinary underground cities.

GÖREME

☎ 0384 / pop 2000

The Göreme landscape is one of Turkey's most amazing sights. Over the centuries a thick layer of volcanic tufa has been eroded into fantastic, eerie shapes, dubbed 'fairy chimneys' by the locals. Into the chimneys early Christians carved chambers and vaults for use as churches, stables and homes.

Information

Flintstones Internet (☎ 271 2825; Belediye Caddesi; per hr €1.75)

Ötüken Voyage (☎ 271 2588; www.otukentravel.8m .com; Avanos Yolu 9)

Zemi Tours (☎ 271 2576; Kayseri Caddesi 28)

Sights & Activities

Ditch your bags on arrival and leg it straight to the **Göreme Open Air Museum** (adult/concession €7/1.75; ☯ 8.30am-5.30pm), Cappadocia's finest collection of rock-hewn cave churches, complete with medieval frescoes. The churches are tiny, so try to get in between the many bus tours. You can have your photo taken on a camel while you wait…

Don't miss the **Tokalı Church**, one of the largest here, or the **Dark Church** (Karanlık Kilise; admission €3), which has some of the most colourful frescoes.

Göreme is the main base for **tours** of Cappadocia's most popular sites (from €30), although every travel agent within 200km runs similar excursions. Stops usually include nearby Pigeon Valley, Ihlara Gorge, Ürgüp or Avanos, and one of the underground cities at **Kaymaklı** or **Derinkuyu** (adult/concession €6/1.75; ☯ 8am-5pm). Many companies also offer trips to Mt Nemrut (see p1212).

Sleeping

Clustered on the hilly southern side of town are dozens of charismatic *pensions*, many offering rooms carved out of the natural rock itself. A small information office in the *otogar* displays details of most options.

Elif Star Caves (☎ 271 2479; www.elifstar.com.tr.tc; Uzundere Caddesi; dm €6, r per person €10.75) The latest expat operation to enter the fray offers excellent en-suite cave rooms and a family-friendly atmosphere.

ShoeString Cave Pansion (☎ 271 2450; shoestring@ superonline.com; dm US$4, r per person US$5-7; 🖳) Over the other side of the hill, the ShoeString tempts shoestringers with simple cave rooms set around a pleasant courtyard.

Köse Pension (☎ 271 2294; www.kosepension.com; Ragıp Üner Caddesi; dm €4, d from €11; 🖳 🕾) Staying in a modern building instead of a cave might seem dull, but you'll really appreciate the difference in winter. Even in summer the lovely pool and home-cooked food make this a popular choice.

You can camp at **Dilek** or **Berlin camping grounds** (tent €5.50), on the road leading to the open-air museum.

Eating

Most of Göreme's eating options are lined up on the main street, although there are some good 'uns further afield.

Fırın Express (Cami Sokak; mains €0.60-2.50) Seek out this little local place for excellent pide at rock-bottom (sorry) prices.

Orient (Adnan Menderes Caddesi; mains €2.50-8.50) Widely reputed as the ultimate in town, the

TURKEY

Orient does a good line in steak as well as the Turkish staples.

Cappı (Kayseri Caddesi; mains €2.50-8) Vegetarians will find this a good port of call on the main strip.

Getting There & Away

As well as regular services to Ankara (€9, five hours) and Konya (€9, 3½ hours), overnight buses run to Istanbul (€17.75, 11 hours) and Antalya (€10.50, 10 hours). Half-hourly *dolmuşes* connect Göreme with Nevşehir (€0.60, 30 minutes), a bigger transport hub.

ÜRGÜP

☎ 0384 / pop 13,500

Lacking the spectacular setting of Göreme, Ürgüp used to be a quieter alternative base but now attracts huge numbers of Turkish visitors thanks to the massive popularity of the *Asmali Konak* TV series, which was filmed here and in nearby Mustafapaşa. Even if you're not a fan, it's worth a visit to see the restored houses and try some local wine.

The helpful **tourist office** (☎ 341 4059; Kayseri Caddesi) is in the park.

Vaulted stone rooms, big beds and small bathrooms all contribute to the charm of **Hotel Elvan** (☎ 341 4191; Barbaros Hayrettin Sokak 11; s/d US$15/25), a family-run pension-hotel.

With most of Ürgüp's best eateries set around the main square, **Sömine Restaurant** (mains €3-8) goes one better and occupies the square itself. Ürgüp-style kebabs, baked on tiles, are a speciality.

Buses run hourly to Nevşehir and every two hours to Göreme (€0.60).

IHLARA GORGE

☎ 0382

A beautiful canyon full of rock-cut churches dating back to Byzantine times, Ihlara is now a mainstay of the excursions run out of Göreme. If you have time on your hands, you're better off staying and walking the entire 16km length of the gorge.

There are four main entrances to the gorge; admission costs €3. The most inviting camp sites and restaurants are in the gorge itself, near the village of Belisırma.

KAYSERİ

☎ 0352 / pop 425,000

Despite its rapid modernisation, the former capital of Cappadocia continues to boast many ancient buildings. Don't listen to Turks who tell you to avoid the place completely. If nothing else, it's worth a stop to feast your eyes on the broadside views of Mt Erciyes, a winter ski centre.

Near the **tourist office** (☎ 222 3903) is the beautiful **Hunat Hatun** mosque, tomb and seminary. Opposite, behind the massive 6th-century city walls, are the **Ulu Cami** (Great Mosque), begun by the Seljuks in 1136, and **Vezirhanı**, once a caravanserai. The beautifully decorated **Güpgüpoğlu Konağı** (admission €1.25; ☽ 8am-5pm Tue-Sun), an 18th-century mansion, is beside the Ethnographic Museum.

Hunat Oteli (☎ 232 4319; Zengin Sokak 5; s/d/tr €5/8.25/10.75), behind the Hunat Mosque, is as cheap (and basic) as they come. Behind the city walls just opposite, **Hotel Sur** (☎ 222 4080; Talas Caddesi 12; s/d €14.75/23.50; P) has prison-style corridors but decent mod cons.

Sivas Caddesi, Millet Caddesi and Düvenönü Meydanı have more than enough restaurants to keep you fed and watered.

Buses serve all local destinations, including Ürgüp (€3, 1¼ hours) and Göreme (€4, 1½ hours).

BLACK SEA COAST

Turkey's Black Sea coast is steep and craggy, damp and lush, and is isolated behind the Pontic Mountains for most of its length. Heavy industry around Zonguldak keeps most people off the coast between Sinop and the Bosphorus, although the fishing port of Amasra, with its Roman and Byzantine ruins, is worth a look. Sinop, three hours northwest of Samsun, is a fine small backwater, with beaches on both sides of the peninsula.

Samsun itself makes a good starting point for coastal travel, although there's little of interest in the town itself. There are excellent beaches around the cheerful resort of Ünye, on a wide bay 85km east.

TRABZON

☎ 0462 / pop 240,000

Trabzon is by far the most interesting place along the Black Sea coast, with lots of old Byzantine buildings and the amazing Sumela Monastery right on its doorstep. It held out against the Seljuks and Mongols and was the last town to fall to the Ottoman Turks.

Today it still feels very different from other Turkish towns, not least because its trading focus is on Russia and the Caucasus.

Modern Trabzon is centred on Atatürk Square, upon a steep hill above the harbour. The **tourist office** (☎ 321 4659) is off the square's southern side. Minibuses plying the coastal highway wait at the foot of a hill. To reach Atatürk Square, just take the steepest climb up. The *otogar* is about 3km to the east.

Sights

Many travellers come to Trabzon solely to visit **Sumela Monastery** (admission €2.50; ☒ 9am-6pm), which is built into a cliff face like a swallow's nest and dates back to Byzantine times. Newly restored, it boasts fine murals (damaged by vandals) and amazing views. Ulusoy buses (€6, 45 minutes) depart for Sumela from a small terminal on Taksim Caddesi. You can also visit on a tour or by taking a shared taxi.

A 20-minute walk west of Atatürk Square are the dark walls of the Byzantine metropolis. The **old town**, with its timber houses and stone bridges, still looks medieval.

Sleeping & Eating

Sadly, traders and prostitutes from former Soviet states often fill the cheapest hotels, so you might have trouble finding somewhere affordable and tolerable. The cheapest rooms are east of Atatürk Square on Güzelhisar Caddesi and surrounding streets.

Sankta Maria Katolik Kilisesi (☎ 321 2192; Sümer Sokak 26) The Catholic church a few blocks downhill from Atatürk Square has an excellent, welcoming hostel. Don't forget to leave a realistic donation.

Hotel Nur (☎ 323 0445; Cami Sokak 4; s/d €12/20) A good bet for single women, Hotel Nur's only nuisance is the noise from the mosque right opposite.

Lots of cheap food is available around Atatürk Square.

Getting There & Around

Westbound *dolmuşes* run from the minibus yard on the highway below the bazaar. Eastbound transport leaves from the yard east of Atatürk Square, near the ferry terminal. A dozen buses a day head for Erzurum (€8, five hours).

Dolmuşes connect the *otogar* with Atatürk Square (€0.30).

EASTERN TURKEY

Like a challenge? Eastern Turkey – vast, remote and culturally very Middle Eastern – is the toughest part of Turkey to travel in but probably the most exotic, and certainly the part that feels least affected by mass tourism. Winter here can be bitterly cold and snowy. Brass monkeys should avoid the region between January and April.

PKK activity in southeastern Turkey has largely faded out, making the area much safer to travel, but with the situation in Iraq still volatile we wouldn't recommend going anywhere near the borders.

ERZURUM

☎ 0442 / pop 400,000

Erzurum is famous mainly for its harsh climate, but it does have some striking Seljuk buildings that justify sleeping over. All the main sites are within walking distance of each other.

The well-preserved walls of the 5th-century **citadel** loom over a maze of narrow streets and offer good views of the town's layout and the bleak surrounding plains.

The beautifully symmetrical **Çifte Minareli Medrese** (p1253) is a famous example of Seljuk architecture. Its classic carved portal is flanked by twin minarets, framing the conical dome behind.

Further west along Cumhuriyet Caddesi is a square with an Ottoman **mosque** and, at the western corner, another seminary, the **Yakutiye Medresesi**, built by the local Mongol emir in 1310. It's now a **museum** (admission €0.75; ☒ 8.30am-5pm Tue-Sun).

The area around Kazım Karabekir Caddesi has lots of cheap hotels, although some are dismal. There are several reasonable restaurants along Cumhuriyet Caddesi near the Yakutiye Medresesi.

Erzurum is an important transport hub, with frequent buses to most big towns in eastern Turkey, including Doğubayazıt (€6, four hours). The *Yeni Doğu Ekspresi* offers good rail connections with Istanbul and Ankara via Kayseri.

KARS

☎ 0474 / pop 90,000

The massive fortress and fine old Russian houses are worth a look, but most people come to Kars to visit the dramatic, romantic ruins of **Ani** (admission €3.50; ☾ 8.30am-5pm), 45km east of town. Formerly the capital of the Urartian and Armenian kingdoms, Ani was completely deserted in 1239 after a Mongol invasion. The ghost city, fronted by a hefty wall, now lies in fields overlooking the Arpaçay River, which forms the border with Armenia.

To visit Ani you must first get a permit and ticket from the **tourist office** (☎ 223 2300; Milli Eğitim Müd, Atatürk Caddesi) in Kars. Owing to tensions with Armenia, photography might not be permitted at the site.

Güngören Oteli (☎ 212 5630; Millet Sokak 4; s/d €15/25), with its own *hammam* and restaurant, is the most popular with travellers.

Kars is not well served by transport, although there are a few daily bus services to Erzurum (€5, 3½ hours) and Doğubayazıt (€4, three hours).

DOĞUBAYAZIT
☎ 0472 / pop 66,000
Turkey's last outpost on the road to Iran is a drab little town in a dramatic setting. The dormant snowcapped cone of **Mt Ararat** is an impressive sight across the surrounding plain. This is the mountain where Noah and his two-by-twos are said to have gone forth and multiplied – a story that innumerable mountaineers (ark-aeologists?) have failed to confirm. It is once again possible to climb the mountain and check for yourself, although you need to pick your dates carefully and come equipped with suitable gear. For more information, inquire at a travel agency.

Bus services to Doğubayazıt are fairly limited and usually go via Erzurum (€4, four hours) or Iğdır (€1.50, 45 minutes). Minibuses to Gürbülak for Iran cost €1.

MT NEMRUT
Mt Nemrut (Nemrut Dağı) is one of the great must-see attractions of eastern Turkey. Two thousand years ago, an obscure Commagene king chose to erect his own **memorial sanctuary** right on top of the mountain, creating an artificial summit crammed with portentous sculpture. The fallen heads of the gigantic statues of gods and kings, toppled by earthquakes, form one of Turkey's most enduring images.

There are several possible bases for visiting Mt Nemrut. To the north is fast-modernising

Malatya, where the **tourist office** (☎ 323 3025) organises daily minibus tours (€30, April to mid-October). The tours take in a sunset visit to the heads, a night at a hotel near the summit and a second visit at dawn. Alternatively you can visit the mountain from the south via the oil-prospecting town of Kahta.

Because of the transport difficulties, many people prefer to take tours from Göreme in Cappadocia (p1209).

In high summer the nicest places to stay, especially with your own transport, are on the slopes of the mountain near Kahta in the village guesthouses.

VAN
☎ 0432 / pop 315,000
On the southeastern shore of vast Lake Van, Van boasts the 3000-year-old **Rock of Van citadel** (admission €0.75) and an interesting **museum** (admission €0.75; ☾ 9am-6pm). The 10th-century church on **Akdamar Island** in the lake is a fascinating piece of Armenian architecture in a beautiful setting. It has biblical frescoes and reliefs. To get there you need to take a *dolmuş* from Beş Yol in Van to the harbour or at least to Gevaş (€1) and then pick up a ferry from the harbour. An inclusive ticket for the crossing and admission should cost no more than €4.50.

Accommodation in the bazaar to the west of Cumhuriyet Caddesi tends to be the cheapest. To the east it's slightly more expensive but also cleaner and more comfortable.

There are several *dolmuşes* a day to Doğubayazıt (€3, 2½ hours).

TURKEY DIRECTORY

ACCOMMODATION
HI-type hostels are a rarity in Turkey, although Istanbul and other tourist areas have a few backpacker institutions with dorms (from €3) and extensive services. Otherwise, small family-run *pensions* take in most of the traveller traffic and generally offer excellent value for money, with singles/doubles starting at €6/9.

There are many budget hotels, but the cheapest are basic and not really suitable for women travelling alone. The rates shown in most receptions are those fixed by local authorities. If you're not given a cheaper price immediately it's worth bargaining, especially out of season. TVs and phones are found even in one-star places.

Camping facilities are dotted around Turkey, although not as frequently as you might hope. Some hotels and *pensions* will also let you camp in their grounds for a small fee (€2 to €4).

ACTIVITIES

Hiking and trekking, particularly in national parks, are a great way to get to grips with the country. So far Turkey has two waymarked national routes: the Lycian Way (Fethiye to Antalya) and St Paul's Trail (Perge/Aspendos to Lake Egirdir), both around 500km long.

Water sports from diving to kayaking are available in the Aegean and Mediterranean resorts. Skiing is becoming more popular, and the best facilities are at Uludağ, near Bursa, and Mt Erciyes, near Kayseri. Those of a lazier (or drunker) disposition can take an extended boat trip along the coast.

BUSINESS HOURS

Most banks, businesses and offices are open 8.30am to noon and 1pm to 5pm Monday to Friday, and Saturday opening is common in cities. Many museums close on Monday. In tourist areas food and souvenir shops are often open virtually around the clock.

CUSTOMS

It's strictly illegal to buy or sell antiquities or to export them from Turkey.

DANGERS & ANNOYANCES

Turkey counts as one of the safer countries in Europe, but tourists are not exempt from hassle. Wear a moneybelt under your clothing, and be wary in crowded places and when using ATMs.

In Istanbul, single men are sometimes lured to bars by new Turkish 'friends', then made to pay an outrageous bill. Drugging is also a serious risk. Be a tad wary whom you befriend, especially when you're new to the country.

After the 2004 bomb attacks in Istanbul and Ankara, visitors, especially British and American citizens, should be aware of the risk of terrorism. Security has been stepped up at major hotels, metro and bus stations, and tourist sites, so a repeat is unlikely but can't be discounted.

EMBASSIES & CONSULATES

Most countries have consulates in Istanbul (listed below) and embassies in Ankara. For entry requirements, see Visas (p1215).

Consulates in Turkey

Australia (Map pp1190-1; ☎ 257 7050; Tepecik Yolu 58, Etiler)

Canada (Map pp1190-1; ☎ 251 9838; İstiklal Caddesi 373-5, Beyoğlu)

Ireland (Map pp1190-1; ☎ 246 6025; Cumhuriyet Caddesi 26/A, Harbiye)

New Zealand (☎ 327 2211; Yeşilgimen Sokak 75, Ihlamur)

UK (Map pp1190-1; ☎ 334 6400; Meşrutiyet Caddesi 34, Beyoğlu)

USA (Map pp1190-1; ☎ 335 9000; Kaplıcalar Mevkii 2, İstinye)

Turkish Embassies & Consulates Abroad

Australia (☎ 02-6295 0227; 60 Mugga Way, Red Hill ACT 2603)

Canada (☎ 613-789 4044; 197 Wurtemburg St, Ottawa, Ontario KIN 8L9)

Ireland (☎ 1-668 5240; 11 Clyde Rd, Ballsbridge, Dublin 4)

New Zealand (☎ 4-472 1290; Level 8, 15-17 Murphy St, Wellington)

UK (☎ 020-7393 0202; 43 Belgrave Square, London SW1X 8PA)

USA (☎ 202-659 8200; 1714 Massachusetts Ave NW, Washington, DC 20036)

FESTIVALS & EVENTS

APRIL

Istanbul International Film Festival

Anzac Day Held at Gallipoli

JUNE

Oil-wrestling Championships Held at Kırkpınar, near Edirne

International Istanbul Music Festival Held late June/early July

DECEMBER

Mevlana Festival Held in Konya

FOOD & DRINKS

The infamous *döner kebap* (kebab) is the mainstay of the Turkish diet, and you'll find *lokantas* (basic restaurants) everywhere selling a wide range of lamb and chicken kebabs. Try the *dürüm kebap* (sliced lamb rolled up in flatbread), or the *İskender kebap* (lamb slices, yogurt and tomato puree drizzled with melted butter). Pide (Turkish pizza), topped with cheese or meat, is almost always the cheapest sit-down option. For vegetarians, a selection of *mezes* (hors d'oeuvres) can be an excellent way to ensure a varied diet.

The national drink is *çay* (tea), grown on the Black Sea coast and served in tiny tulip-shaped glasses. The milder but wholly chemical *elma çay* (apple tea) is also popular. Traditional Turkish *kahve* (coffee) is like espresso, served *sade* (no sugar), *orta* (medium-sweet) or *çok şekerli* (very sweet). The Turkish liquor of choice is *rakı*, a potent aniseed spirit traditionally cut with water and accompanied by *mezes*. Turkish wine is worth the occasional splurge.

GAY & LESBIAN TRAVELLERS

Overt homosexuality is socially acceptable only in certain parts of Istanbul and some resorts. Laws prohibiting 'lewd behaviour' can be turned against homosexuals, so be discreet.

For more information, contact Turkey's own gay and lesbian support group, **Lambda Istanbul** (www.lambdaistanbul.org).

HOLIDAYS

Public holidays include New Year's Day (1 January), Children's Day (23 April), Youth and Sports Day (19 May), Victory Day (30 August), Republic Day (29 October) and Atatürk's Death (10 November).

Turkey also celebrates all major Islamic festivals and holidays. The most important are Şeker Bayramı, at the end of Ramazan, and Kurban Bayramı, two months later.

INTERNET RESOURCES

www.letsgoturkey.com Information and travel resources.

www.mymerhaba.com Information site aimed at foreign expats.

www.neredennereye.com Public transport information.

www.turkey.org News, arts, upcoming events and links.

www.turkishdailynews.com Newspaper home page.

LANGUAGE

Turkish is the official language, spoken nationwide. Many locals speak passable English, French, German or Japanese. See p1298 for pronunciation guidelines and useful words and phrases.

MONEY

As the Turkish lira remains unstable, prices in this chapter are in euros, except where they are quoted in another hard currency (US$ or UK£) by the establishment concerned.

Credit Cards

A surprising number of places take plastic, from kebab shacks to carpet emporiums; Visa and MasterCard are the most widely recognised. Widespread ATMs dispense cash for most international credit and debit cards.

Exchanging Money

It's easy to change major currencies in most exchange offices, post offices (PTTs), shops and hotels. Foreign currencies are widely accepted in the main tourist areas, and prices are increasingly being quoted in euros as the US dollar loses favour. Exchange rates fluctuate daily – check shortly before your visit.

Cashing travellers cheques is harder (try post offices in tourist areas), and the exchange rate is usually worse. Places that don't charge commission generally offer poor rates.

Taxes & Refunds

Value-added tax (*KDV*) is included in the price of most items and services. If you buy an expensive item, ask the shopkeeper for a *KDV iade özel fatura* (special VAT-refund receipt). Get it stamped as you clear customs, then try to get a refund at a bank in the departure lounge, you are entitled to it but it can be more pain than it's worth.

Tipping & Bargaining

Waiters and bath attendants expect around 10% of the bill. You can also round up taxi fares if you wish. Hotel, food and transport prices might or might not be negotiable, but you should always bargain for souvenirs, even if prices are 'fixed'.

POST

The Turkish postal service is known as the PTT. Turkish *postanes* (post offices) are indicated by black-on-yellow 'PTT' signs.

RESPONSIBLE TOURISM

Respecting Muslim sensibilities should be a point of principle, even when you're surrounded by half-naked sunseekers. Women should keep their legs, upper arms and neckline covered, except on the beach. When entering a mosque, women should cover their heads and shoulders, and everyone should cover their legs and remove their shoes.

TELEPHONE

Phoning home from Turkey is surprisingly expensive, mainly because of taxes. The cheapest rates are at night and on Sunday. Wherever possible, try to make reverse-charge (collect) calls.

Almost all public telephones require phonecards, which can be bought from telephone centres, shops and street vendors. If you're going to make only one call, it's easier to look for signs saying *köntörlü telefon*, where the cost of your call will be metered. Post offices often have the best rates.

TOURIST INFORMATION

Local tourist offices can rarely do more than hand out glossy brochures and sketch maps. That said, some staff do make a real effort to help with specific queries.

VISAS

Citizens of Belgium, Denmark, Finland, France, Germany, Japan, the Netherlands, New Zealand, Norway, Sweden and Switzerland don't need a visa for visits of up to three months. Although other nationalities require a visa, it is just a sticker you buy on arrival; join the queue before passport control. British citizens pay UK£10, Australians, Canadians and Americans US$20, and Irish nationals US$10, payable in hard currency. The standard visa is valid for three months and allows multiple entries.

WOMEN TRAVELLERS

Turkish society is still sexually segregated, especially once you get away from the big cities and resorts. Foreign women find themselves being hassled – it's mostly just catcalls and dubious remarks, but serious assaults do occasionally occur. Travelling with companions usually improves matters.

Turkish women ignore men who speak to them in the street. Wearing a long skirt and a wedding ring might make you less conspicuous. Away from beach resorts you should avoid skimpy tops and brief shorts. Take your cue from hip locals rather than Turkish music videos!

TURKEY

Ukraine

HIGHLIGHTS

- **Kyiv** Mummified monks, glorious cathedrals, and all the restaurants, nightclubs and bar any huge capital city can offer (p1220)
- **Lviv** Winding cobblestone alleys packed with haunting architecture and large square circled with busy outdoor cafés (p1223)
- **Best journey** Boarding a night train in frenetic Kyiv and waking up in elegant Lviv, completely different Ukrainian world

FAST FACTS

- **Area** The biggest in Europe at 603,700 sq km (that's 3773 Liechtensteins)
- **ATMs** Widespread
- **Budget** 212 hryvnia per day
- **Capital** Kyiv
- **Country code** ☎ 380
- **Famous for** A nuclear nightmare and freakishly talented gymnasts
- **Head of State** President Leonid Kuchma; elections were being held at the time of writing
- **Languages** Ukrainian, Russian
- **Money** Ukrainian hryvnia (A$1 = 3.97hry, CA$1 = 4.46, ¥100 = 4.98hry, NZ$1 = 3.70hry, €1 = 6.79hry, UK£1 = 9.78hry, US$1 = 5.32hry)
- **Phrases** *Doh-brih dyen* (hello), *ya nih rah-zoo-mee-yu* (I don't understand), *dya-koo-yoo* (thanks)

- **Population** 48.4 million
- **Time** GMT/UTC +2
- **Visas** Required for most visitors; arrange in advance.

TRAVEL HINTS

When travelling on trains, it's customary to share your snacks and cigarettes with neighbouring passengers. Join the spirit and share your food, but avoid offering junk – stick to fruits, bread, cheese and sausage (and beer if the feeling is right).

ROAMING UKRAINE

Kyiv (p1220) needs at least two days of your lovin', and Lviv (p1223) just as much, if not more.

There's no 'the' in 'Ukraine' any more, just in case you hadn't noticed. And a lot of othe things have changed since the country dropped the USSR like an overly possessive boyfrien and started batting her eyes at the West.

Frenetic, cosmopolitan Kyiv has gone through major reconstructive surgery (and has been almost completely deloused of Lenin statues), but the city's classic charm is accentuated b

UKRAINE

its age, with sparkling onion-dome cathedrals and a fascinating monastery (with mummified monks!).

Lviv – the capital of Ukrainian nationalism, religion and pride – is more demure than her popular sister but is so much easier to talk to and deserves just as much attention as the official capital. Here, everything slows down, and cafés, cobblestone streets and smudgy old architecture all create a charming, central European atmosphere.

Sure, the face of Ukraine is still spotted with blemishes of Soviet mentality and architecture – but these throwbacks only highlight how much the rest has changed since then. Besides, soon those anachronisms will be gone – and who knows, you might regret you missed your chance to experience them.

HISTORY

The name Ukraine means 'borderland', which accounts for its sort of Wild West history. Before the 13th century, the land was yanked back and forth by nogoodniks such as the Huns and Mongols before it settled into the hands of Russian princes. By the 15th century, groups of fierce, wild fighters calling themselves Cossacks (sort of like punks on horseback) fought anyone who encroached upon their borders or belief system (Orthodoxy).

Then came the Soviet Union. The 1930s saw the evil of Stalin, who engineered a famine in 1932–33, killing millions in Ukraine. In WWII, which left most of the country's cities in ruin, an estimated six million Ukrainians died.

Both the strong religious sentiments in the western region and the disastrous Chornobyl event (and its cover-up) were catalysts for Ukraine's declaring of independence from the USSR in August 1991. Leonid Kuchma has been the president since the mid-1990s; he is legally not allowed to occupy the presidential role again, so he has been scheming to make constitutional changes that would diminish the power of the next president and boost the power of parliament, to which his puppet strings are still firmly attached. Naughty.

PEOPLE & CULTURE

The Ukrainian population is 78% Ukrainian and 17% Russian. The remainder includes Belarusians, Moldovans, Bulgarians, Poles, Hungarians, Romanians, Tatars and Jews. Almost all of the country's Tatar population (about 250,000) lives in Crimea.

Although most Ukrainians speak Russian, many people in Lviv will not use the language, and the number of English-language speakers is growing.

RELIGION

Nearly 97% of Ukrainians are Christian. Complex historical reasons mean central and southern Ukraine mostly follow the Moscow-based Ukrainian Orthodox Church, while the rest of the country follows either the Kyiv-based Ukrainian Autocephalous Orthodox Church or the Uniate Church (also known as the Ukrainian Catholic or Greek Catholic Church and under the jurisdiction of the Vatican). There are some small Jewish minorities in all cities, while Muslim communities, primarily Tatars, live in Crimea.

ENVIRONMENT

On 26 April 1986, reactor No 4 at Chornobyl (Chernobyl in Russian) nuclear power station, 100km north of Kyiv, exploded and almost 9 tonnes of radioactive matter (90 times as much as released by the Hiroshima bomb) spewed into the sky. Roughly 4.9 million people living in northern Ukraine, southern Belarus and southwestern Russia were affected. Western monitors now figure that radioactivity levels at Chornobyl are negligible, so organised site tours and surrounding 'ghost' villages occur, if you dare. A web search will reveal some agencies offering tours.

READING UP

Everything Is Illuminated, by Jonathan Safran Foer, is the unforgettable, mostly fictional story of the author's trip to western Ukraine to find the woman who saved his grandfather from the Nazis. Nineteenth-century writer Nikolai Gogol wrote *Taras Bulba,* a tale of the lives of Cossacks; he's written other stories about his native Ukraine as well.

Borderland: A Journey Through the History of Ukraine, by Anna Reid, is a captivating and creatively presented account of the country's past.

UKRAINE

TRANSPORT

GETTING THERE & AWAY
Air
AeroSvit, Ukrainian International Airlines and major European airlines fly to and from Kyiv. See also the boxed text, p1220.
Boryspil Airport (☎ 296 72 43; www.airport-borispol .kiev.ua) Some domestic and short international flights; 35km from centre.
Zhulyany Airport (☎ 242 23 08; Povitroflotskii praspekt 92) Domestic and short international flights; 4km from Kyiv.

Boat
See www.eugeniatours.com.ua for details on boat travel in the Black Sea.

Bus
Train travel is far more comfortable than the bouncy, pungent experience of public long-distance buses, but **Autolux** (www.autolux .ua) is a private company that provides comfortable buses around the country. To get to Kyiv **Central Bus Station** (☎ 265 57 74; ploshcha Moskovska 3) you can catch trolleybus No 1, 4 or 11 (or walk 20 minutes) from the Lybidska metro station.

Train
Passports are required for ticket purchase in Kyiv. **Kyiv Train Station** (☎ 223 11 11; Vokzalna 2) is modern, with English signs. Advance tickets are sold at the **train ticket office** (☎ 050; bulvar Tarasa Shevchenka 38/40; ⏰ 8am-8pm).

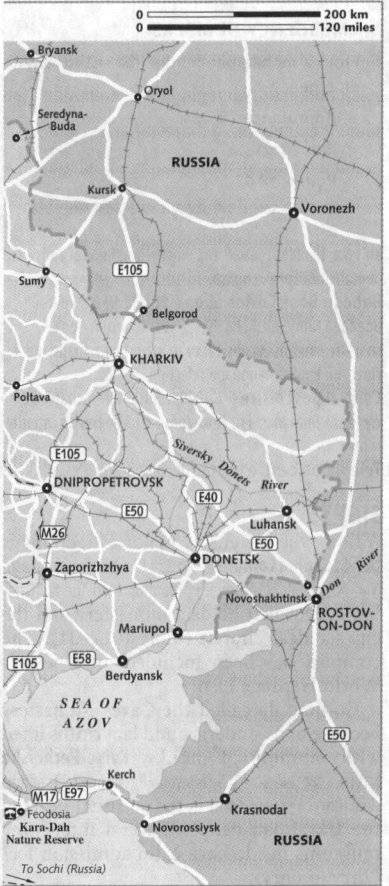

IN A BIG COUNTRY

Ukraine is the largest country wholly within Europe. And that's not all. Leonid Stadnyk is said to be the tallest man in the world, at 2.53m. He lives in a village in the Zhytomyr region, and, like the giants in fairy tales, he suffers from loneliness and physical pain.

The grandiose city planning of the Soviet era made its superior mark on the country. In Crimea, go on the longest trolleybus ride in the world from Simferopol to Yalta (117km, 2½ hours). The longest, steepest escalators in the world used to be in Kyiv's central metro stations, and although those days are long gone, the city's 1931 record for the longest face-slapping contest (30 hours) still holds.

GETTING AROUND

Tickets for the metro (Kyiv), buses, trolleybuses and trams (50 kopeks) are sold on board and must be punched. *Marshrutka* (marsh-*root*-kee) are minivans that run as private buses and are often a more costly than a regular bus. They usually leave when full. Kyiv transport runs from 5.45am to 11pm.

Taxis are easy to find (many are unmarked private cars), but drivers rarely use their meter – set a price beforehand. You can hail one by gesturing as if you're dribbling a basketball. When someone pulls over, state your destination, and then agree on a price (the less you speak the language, the higher the price).

From the boat passenger terminal in Kyiv, boats go up and down the Dnipro River, and as far as Odesa (Odessa in Russian); contact www.eugeniatours.com.ua.

Drivers: police cannot issue on-the-spot fines, so some people stash a 20hry note in their car's documents, which is miraculously gone when the docs are handed back and the officer waves them on. No level of alcohol in the blood is legal. Rentals (Avis, Hertz and Europcar) are available in Kyiv and Lviv but sometimes only allow driving in the city.

DEPARTURE TAX

Airport departure taxes for international flights are always included in the ticket price.

Prices are shown as *kupeyny/platskartny* (see p1258), but many only have *kupeyny* cabins. International points are Prague (*kupeyny* 567hry, 11 hours, daily), Minsk (*kupeyny/platskartny* 102/64hry, 12 hours, daily), Moscow (134/86hry, 15 hours, dozens daily), Kraków (*kupeyny* 388hry, 16 hours, three weekly), Warsaw (*kupeyny* 313hry, 18 hours, daily), St Petersburg (175/113hry, 26 hours, daily), Belgrade (*kupeyny* 671hry, 34 hours, daily) and Berlin (694hry, 24 hours, daily).

Within Ukraine, destinations include Lviv (36/32hry, 11 hours, five or six daily), Odesa (40/27hry, 11 hours, four to six daily), Sevastopol (52/39hry, 17 hours, twice daily) and Simferopol (48/30hry, 17 hours, one or two daily).

KYIV

☎ 044 / pop 2.6 million

Fans of big cities will love Kyiv (Kiev in Russian). In comparison with its Russian cousin Moscow, it's got almost as much to offer but with a softer touch and a lower price tag. It's vast and vivacious, with quaint old sectors, as well as busy modern areas humming with activity. There are dozens of lovely public parks and gardens, museums and almost every kind of restaurant you could wish to try, from casual cafeterias to Indian buffets and pricey sushi joints. Every weekend, the main street (Khreshchatyk) is closed to traffic, and the wide boulevard fills up with friends, family and lovers strolling, eating ice cream, drinking beer and listening to buskers. It's the kind of city that's cosmopolitan enough to satisfy virtually any desire, but historic enough to provide a fulfilling cultural experience as well.

ORIENTATION

The main street, closed to motor traffic on weekends and so swarming with peds and buskers, is Khreshchatyk. The Dnipro River flows north–south a bit east of the centre. Although there are some sandy beach areas along the east side of the river (called the Left Bank), the area is generally devoid of interest and somewhat dangerous at night.

INFORMATION

Just around the corner from the post office (walk towards the McDonald's on the square) is an **Internet centre** (10hry per hr; ☉ 24hr). ATMs, currency exchanges and Western Union branches are easily found. There are no tourist offices in town.

American Medical Center (☎ 490 76 00; www.am centers.com; vulitsa Berdychivsta 1) Near metro Luki-

EMERGENCY NUMBERS

From a mobile phone, dial ☎ 112 for any emergency.

- Ambulance ☎ 03
- Fire ☎ 01
- Police ☎ 02

anivska; handles routine and emergency medical and dental. Staff speak English.

Baboon Book Coffee Shop (☎ 235 59 80; vulitsa Bogdana Khmelnitskoho 39; ☉ 9am-2am) A bookshop–restaurant (mains 12hry to 36hry) with maps and a clued-up English-language selection.

Central post office (☎ 065; vulitsa Khreshchatyk 22; ☉ 8am-9pm Mon-Fri, 8am-7pm Sat) Also has an Internet centre.

Telephone centre (next to the post office; ☉ 24hr)

SIGHTS

Among the dozens of major attractions is the **St Sophia Complex** (☎ 228 61 52; Sofiyivska ploshcha; adult/child 11/4hry; ☉ 10am-6pm Fri-Tue & 10am-5pm Wed), which holds a monastery and the city's oldest church (built 1017–31). The complex has been included on Unesco's World Heritage List.

Commonly called the Caves Monastery because of its underground labyrinths lined with mummified monks, **Kyivo-Pecherska Lavra** (☎ 290 30 71; Sichnevoho Povstannya 21; admission 10hry; ☉ 9am-6pm) is the spiritual heart of the Ukrainian people. Several interesting museums inside have extra admission fees (2hry to 6hry).

Your visit – and your souvenir shopping – wouldn't be complete without a walk along steep, cobblestoned **Andriyivsky uzviz** (Andrew's Descent), one of the oldest and definitely the quaintest street in town. It's lined with tables where people sell crafts and gifts both desirable and bizarre (small ceramic cats?). Avoid the incline by taking the **funicular** (metro Ploshcha Poshtova; admission 50 kopeks; ☉ 6.30am-11pm) to the top of the street, where you'll find **St Michael's Monastery**, and further down the *uzviz*, the gorgeous baroque **St Andrew's Church** (☎ 228 58 61; Andriyivsky uzviz 23; admission 4hry; ☉ 10am-6pm), built in 1754. From there, you can spend an hour or two shopping down the *uzviz* or stop to loiter in a café or restaurant. Views during the funicular ride are obstructed by trees, so go to the **Monument to the Unification of Russia &**

Ukraine, which looks like a metallic rainbow arch, for excellent vistas of the city along the Dnipro.

Erected in 1037, the **Golden Gate** (☎ 224 70 68; vulitsa Volodymyrska 40a; admission 5hry; ⊙ 10am-5pm Fri-Wed) was the original entrance into Old Kyiv. It was under reconstruction during research, but it's still worth a glimpse from the street. Notice the chapel at the top.

Arguably the most interesting museums for foreigners are the following (nothing's in English):

Bulgakov House-Museum (☎ 416 31 88; Andriyivsky uzviz 13; admission 3hry; ⊙ 10am-5pm Thu-Tue) The author of *The Master & Margarita* lived here in the early 20th century.

Chornobyl Museum (☎ 470 54 22; prov Khoryva; admission 5hry; ⊙ 10am-6pm Mon-Sat, closed last Mon of month) Extremely artistic and moving presentations; the signs above the stairs represent the 'ghost' cities in the area of the disaster.

Museum of the Great Patriotic War (☎ 295 94 52; Sichnevoho Povstannya 44; admission 4hry; ⊙ 10am-4pm Tue-Sun) Triumphant displays of Soviet heroism and many a WWII monument.

Russian Art Museum(☎ 224 62 18; vulitsa Tereshchenkivska 9; admission 7hry; ⊙ 10am-6pm Fri-Sun, 11am-6pm Mon & Tue, closed last Mon of month) One of the largest collections of Russian artwork.

SLEEPING

Although Ukraine's tourist infrastructure is developing well, at the time of writing there was still a poor selection of good-value budget accommodations, and no real youth hostels. For updates, check the Thorn Tree at www.lonelyplanet.com before your trip.

Rostick Gavrilov of www.come2ukraine .com can help find central apartments for US$20 to US$45 a day, and can arrange for cheaper airport or train station pick-ups.

Hotel Ukraina (☎ 229 02 66; www.ukraine-hotel .kiev.ua; vulitsa Instytutska 4; s 210-395hry, d 330-430hry; P ▣) Like a kinder, gentler big brother watching over the people and activities of the thriving main square, the slowly improving but still Soviet-style Ukraina is perched on a hillside above maydan Nezalezhnosti. The views and awesome location make it worth the extra cash.

Hotel Andreyevskiy (☎ 416 22 56; vulitsa Vozdvizhenskaya 60; s 180-408hry, d 300-408hry) Pro: right off cute-as-a-button Andriyivsky *uzviz* (opposite). Con: all hallways are dark and

ATTACK OF THE 108M WOMAN

If you visit the Museum of the Great Patriotic War, or even approach that area, it won't be long before you see on the horizon the huge metal Soviet woman that is Rodina Mat, or the Defence of the Motherland Monument.

For decades, she has been affectionately known as 'Tin Tits' among expats.

spooky; some bathrooms dank and stinky. There is only one cheap single, but the five cheap doubles are good value. Its semi-suite (588hry) could fit four backpackers.

Other options are **St Petersburg Hotel** (☎ 229 73 64; s-peter@i.kiev.ua; bulvar Tarasa Shevchenka 4; s 129-343hry, d 182-572hry, tr 213hry) and its illiterate buck-toothed stepsister, **St Petersburg Hotel 2** (☎ 229 59 43; s-peter@i.kiev.ua; vulitsa Volodymyrska 36; s 73-127hry, d 206-314hry, tr 150hry, q 172hry), which is depressing and only for the desperately low on funds. The triples and quads are supercheap but supergrim.

EATING & DRINKING

Kyiv is a modern capital now, and so you can get virtually any cuisine at any price.

Puzata Khata (☎ 246 72 45; vulitsa Baseina 1/2; mains 10-15hry) Costumed girls ladle out fresh old-fashioned Ukrainian goodness in this popular cafeteria-style eatery.

Himalaya (☎ 462 04 37; vulitsa Khreshchatyk 23; mains 25-52hry) Indian food apparently hasn't caught on with *kyivlany* (citizens of Kyiv) but the place is good and has vegetarian food. The curries and samosas are tasty, but the spinach sauce is not. During the week, the set lunch (noon to 3.30pm) is only 40hry.

Gurme (☎ 227 73 63; vulitsa Chervonoarmiyska 12; mains 4.50-9.50hry) Colourful, slightly spicier regional foods displayed in the window will catch your eye as you walk past this cafeteria-style place.

Two Irish-style pubs with lots of beer and proper brekkies are **Golden Gate** (☎ 235 51 88; vulitsa Volodymyrska 40/2; ⊙ 11am-1am) and **O'Brien's Pub** (☎ 229 15 84; vulitsa Mykhaylivska 17a; ⊙ 8am-2am).

ENTERTAINMENT

Extensive lists of performances are featured in *What's On* and the *Kyiv Post*, available at the Baboon Book Coffee Shop (opposite).

UKRAINE

KYIV

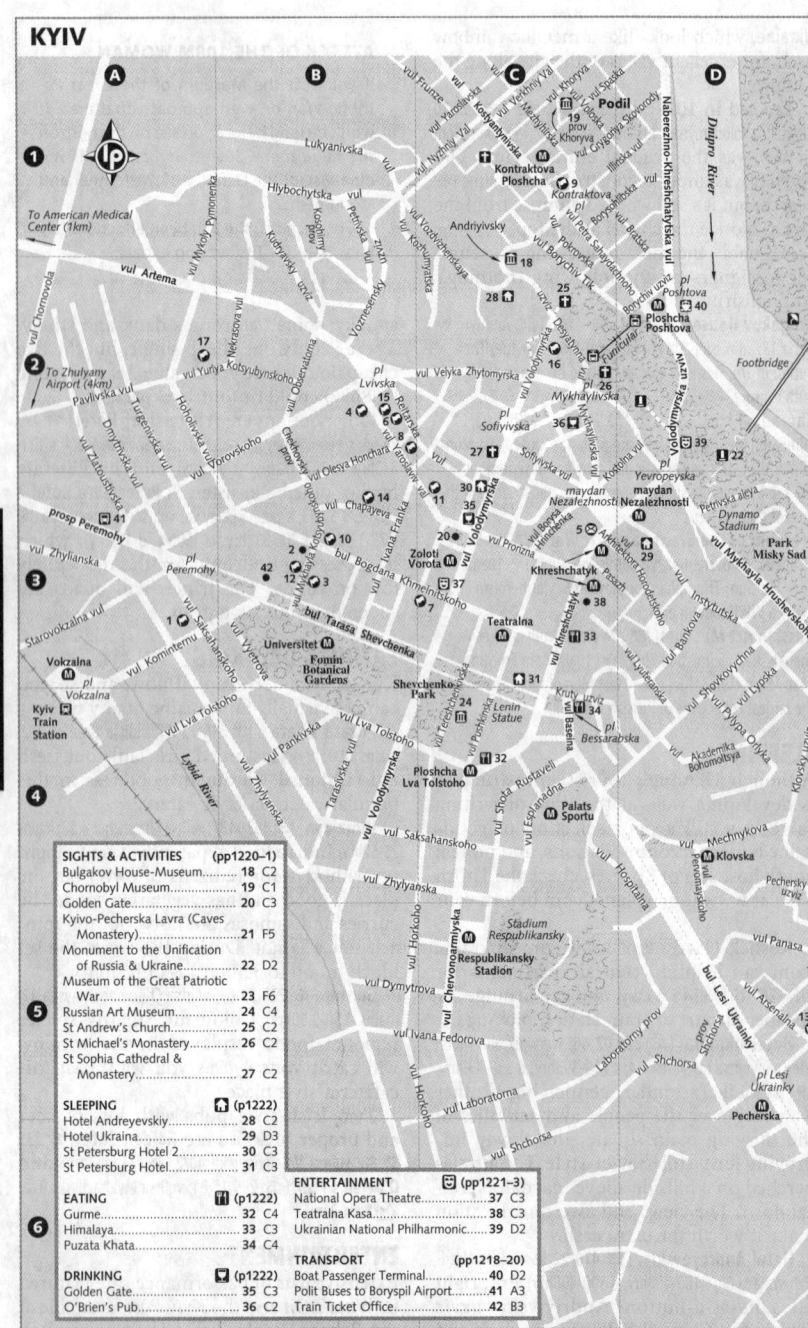

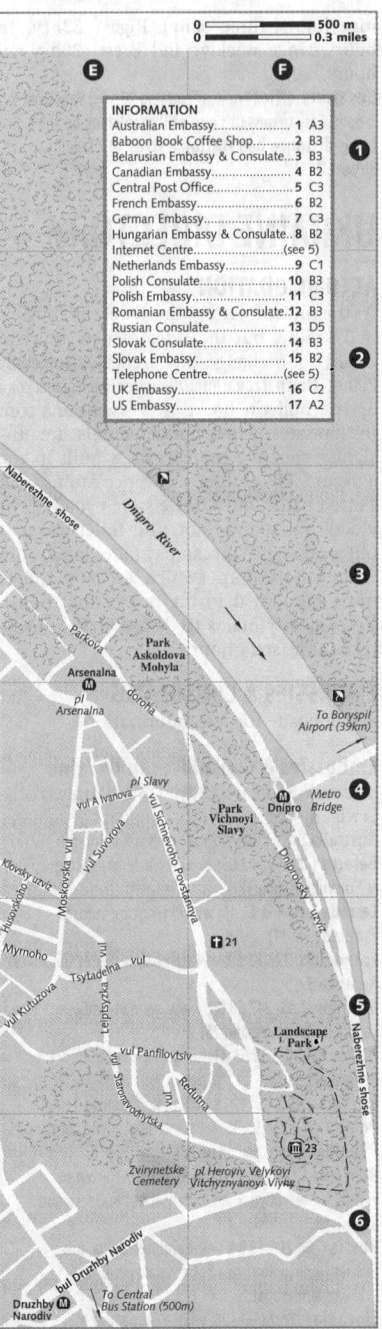

INFORMATION
Australian Embassy.......................1   A3
Baboon Book Coffee Shop...............2   B3
Belarusian Embassy & Consulate...3   B3
Canadian Embassy........................4   B2
Central Post Office.......................5   C3
French Embassy...........................6   B2
German Embassy..........................7   C3
Hungarian Embassy & Consulate..8   B2
Internet Centre...........................(see 5)
Netherlands Embassy.....................9   C1
Polish Consulate..........................10 B3
Polish Embassy............................11 B3
Romanian Embassy & Consulate.12 B3
Russian Consulate........................13 D5
Slovak Consulate.........................14 B3
Slovak Embassy...........................15 B2
Telephone Centre........................(see 5)
UK Embassy................................16 C2
US Embassy................................17 A2

Schedules and advance tickets (cheeeeap!) are available at the **teatralna kasa** (vulitsa Khreshchatyk 21); same-day tickets are available at the venues.

National Opera Theatre (☎ 229 11 69; vulitsa Volodymyrska 50) A night here is a grandiose affair, but not as pricey as you might think.

Ukrainian National Philharmonic (☎ 228 16 97; Volodymyrska uzviz 2) Looks great on the outside and sounds great on the inside.

LVIV

☎ 032 / pop 758,000

Lviv (Lvov in Russian) is one of those rare Ukrainian cities that managed to avoid being bombed during WWII. Now, old Lviv is an unforgettable vision of Gothic, Renaissance, baroque and neoclassical buildings and churches smudged black with age (it's so beautiful that it was included on Unesco's World Heritage List in 1998). Its quiet alleys and mesmerising façades make it the type of place you can get happily lost in by day and enjoy a good meal over coffee at night.

Widely considered to be the capital of Ukrainian nationalism, Lviv has almost completely disassociated from Russia and really looks westward, which means that traveller information, restaurants and coffee (that true indicator of Western civilisation) are generally better than anywhere else in the country.

INFORMATION

Good websites are www.about.lviv.ua and www.tourism.lviv.ua. Maps are available at kiosks, and ATMs, currency exchanges and Western Union offices abound.

The **Tourist Information Centre** (☎ 297 57 67; www.tourism.lviv.ua; vulitsa Pidvalna 3; ☽ 10am-1pm & 2-6pm Mon-Fri) has English-speaking staff who can arrange tours and give out free information.

SIGHTS

Apart from wandering around the gorgeous **old town** and ogling the architecture, you can head to the **High Castle** for hilltop views. **Lychakiv Cemetery** (vulitsa Mechnikova; admission 3hry, more for cameras; ☽ 9am-5pm) is one of the most beautiful in Eastern Europe. Take tram No 7 five stops from vulitsa Pidvalna (by the outdoor book market) to Lychakivska

Kladovyshche. About 2.5km east is the open-air **Museum of Folk Architecture & Rural Life** (☎ 71 80 17; vulitsa Chernecha Hora 1; admission 1.50hry; 🕑 11am-5pm Tue-Sun), where about 100 old wooden buildings dot 50 hectares. Unfortunately, picnics are not allowed. Take tram No 7 four stops from the same stop suggested for the cemetery (earlier). Then follow the signs uphill on foot (1.25km).

There are lots of other museums in the Old Town, but nothing's in English.

SLEEPING & EATING

Hotel Lviv (☎ 72 86 51; praspekt Vyacheslava Chornovola 7; s/d without bathroom 40/50hry, s with bathroom 00-120hry d with bathroom140-240hry) OK, it does the job for kopek-pinchers, but the building is ugly and at any given time, the staff is nonexistent.

Hotel George (☎ 72 59 52; www.georgehotel.ukrbiz.net; ploshcha Mitskevycha 1; s without bathroom 105-121hry, d without bathroom 109-124hry, s with bathroom 283-411hry, d with bathroom 316-415hry) The George is worth the extra hryvnia. Housed in an elegant 100-year-old building and staffed by friendly people, you'll find huge rooms – and the rooms with shared toilet and shower are a great deal. Breakfast is 20 hryvnia more.

Hotel George has an acceptable restaurant, and there are some good sidewalk cafés along praspekt Svabody, the main street.

GETTING THERE & AWAY

The **Lviv airport** (☎ 69 21 12) is at the end of vulitsa Lyubinska, which turns into vulitsa Horodotska closer to town. **Lviv Airlines** (☎ 72 78 18; www.avia.lviv.ua; ploshcha Grigorenka 5) offers flights every day from Lviv to Kyiv and Moscow, and less regularly to Odesa and Simferopol (May to September only).

The **train station** (☎ 35 33 60) is about 2km west from the centre; a taxi costs about 20hry, or take tram No 9 or No 1 (45 kopeks) or *marshrutka* No 66, 67 or 68 (80 kopeks). Buy tickets at the **railway booking office** (☎ 005, 748 20 68; vulitsa Hnatyuka 20). Train destinations include Kyiv (*kupeyny/platskartny* 53/32hry, 10 hours, several daily), Brest (62/39hry, 11 hours, daily), Moscow (205/135hry, 25 hours, daily) St Petersburg (205/135hry, 31 hours, daily), Warsaw (*kupeyny* 210hry, 11 hours, three a day) and Prague (*kupeyny* 390hry, 24 hours, daily).

Bus journeys include Ivano-Frankivsk (11hry, three hours, hourly), Kyiv (52hry, nine hours, three daily), Rīga (233hry, 18 hours, twice weekly) and Brest (20hry, 19 hours, daily).

Bus ticket office (vulitsa Teatralna 26; 🕑 9am-2pm & 3-6pm) Easy to miss (it's also a CD shop); look for the sign.

Long-distance bus station (☎ 63 24 73; vulitsa Stryiska 189)

UKRAINE DIRECTORY

ACCOMMODATION

At the time of writing there were no hostels in Ukraine, but the tides of new tourism might soon change this – check the **Lonely Planet Thorn Tree** (http://thorntree.lonelyplanet.com) or the bulletin board at www.brama.com for updates. Most budget hotels are unsightly concrete monstrosities built in the '60s and '70s and have cheaper rooms with shared bathroom – towels are usually provided, but soap is not, and toilet paper is often missing. You can pay more for a room with a bathroom (which are sometimes more modern than the rest of the room). You can pay maids to do laundry, but this takes at least 24 hours.

EMBASSIES & CONSULATES

See opposite for visa information.

Embassies & Consulates in Ukraine

The following are in **Kyiv** (☎ 044) unless otherwise noted.

Australia (☎ /fax 235 75 86; vulitsa Kominternu 18/137)

Belarus (☎ 537 52 03; ukraine@belembassy.org; vulitsa M Kotsyubynskoho 3)

Canada (☎ 464 11 44; www.kyiv.gc.ca; vulitsa Yaroslaviv val 31)

France (☎ 228 73 69; www.ambafrance.kiev.ua; vulitsa Reitarska 39)

Germany (☎ 247 68 00; www.german-embassy.kiev.ua; vulitsa B Khmelnitskoho 25)

Hungary (☎ 238 63 81; hungary@kiev.farlep.net; vulitsa Reitarska 33)

Netherlands (☎ 490 82 00; pl Kontraktova 7)

Poland (☎ 234 92 36; consulate@svitonline.com; vulitsa B Khmelnitskoho) Consulate in Lviv.

Romania (☎ 234 52 61; romania@iptelecom.net.ua; vulitsa M Kotsyubynskoho 8) Consulates in Odesa and Chernivtsi.

Russia (☎ 296 45 04; www.embrus.org.ua, in Russian; vulitsa Kutuzova 8) Consulates in Odesa, Lviv and Simferopol.

Slovakia (☎ 234 06 06; vulitsa Chapayeva 4)

K (☎ 490 36 00; vulitsa Desyatynna 9)

JSA (☎ 490 00 00; www.usemb.kiev.ua; vulitsa Yuriya
otsyubynskoho 10)

Ukrainian Embassies & Consulates Abroad

Australia (☎ 02-6230 5789; fax 02-6230 7298; Level 12,
George Centre, 60 Marcus Clarke St, Canberra)

Belarus (☎ 017-283 1980; fax 017-283 1990; vulitsa
taravilenska 51, Minsk)

Canada (☎ 613-230 2961; fax 613-230 2400; 310
Somerset St West, Ottawa) Consulate in Toronto.

France (☎ 01 43 06 07 37; fax 01 43 06 02 94; 21 ave
e Saxe, Paris)

Germany (☎ 030-288 871 16; fax 030-288 871 63;
Albrechtsrasse 26, Berlin) Consulate in Munich.

Hungary (☎ 1-422 4120; fax 1-220 9873; 77 Stefania St;
Magyarorszag, Budapest)

Netherlands (☎ 070-362 60 95; fax 070-361 55 65; 26
root Hertoginnelaan, Den Haag)

Poland (☎ 022-622 4797; fax 629 8103; 7 Aleja Szucha,
Warsaw)

Romania (☎ 021-201 69 86; fax 01 211 69 49; Calea
Dorobantilor nr 16, Bucharest)

Russia (☎ 095-229 1079; fax 095-924 8469; Leontevsky
ereulok 18, Moscow)

Slovakia (☎ 02-5920 2811; fax 5441 2651; Radvanska
5, Bratislava)

JK (☎ 020-7727 6312; fax 020-7792 1708; 60 Holland
ark, London)

SA (☎ 202-333 0606; fax 202-333 0817; 3350 M St NW,
Washington DC) Consulates in New York & Chicago.

FESTIVALS & EVENTS

Kyiv will host the 2005 Eurovision song
contest. On the last weekend of May, the
apital celebrates Kyiv Days with fireworks,
olk festivals and a big beauty contest. In
October, Kyiv holds both its International
Music Festival and its International Film
estival.

HOLIDAYS

New Year's Day 1 January

Orthodox Christmas 7 January

Women's Day 8 March

Orthodox Easter April/May

International Labour Day 1 May

Victory Day 9 May

Constitution Day 28 June

Independence Day 24 August

LANGUAGE

Ukrainian was adopted as the sole official
language at independence. However, apart

from in the west, many Ukrainians (especially in the south), prefer to speak Russian. A
hybrid of the two languages, called Surzhyk,
is spoken in Kyiv and other major cities.

MONEY

One hryvnia equals 100 kopeks. Coins come
in denominations of one, two, five, 10, 25
and 50 kopeks and there are new one-hryvnia
coins; notes come in denominations of one,
two, five, 10, 20, 50, 100 and 200. The only
things you can legally pay for in US dollars are
international flights and foreign visas. ATMs,
currency exchanges and Western Unions will
never be hard to find in the cities.

POST

Cities have DHL and FedEx offices, although
regular mail is pretty reliable, if slow. You
can pay more for air mail (*ah*-via) or for
certified (za-kaz-*noi*).

TELEPHONE

Long-distance calls and faxes can be completed from the (usually 24-hour) telephone
offices located in each city (normally near
the post office). To call, pay in advance, go
to your assigned booth and hit the button
when the person you're calling answers.

To dial within Ukraine, dial ☎ 8, (wait for
tone) + city code + number. To dial abroad,
dial ☎ 8 (wait for tone) + 10 + country code
+ city code + number. To phone Ukraine
from abroad, dial ☎ 380 followed by the city
code and number.

VISAS

With the exception of citizens of the Commonwealth of Independent States (CIS)
and a few other countries, all visitors need
a visa (US$40 to US$100). Always get your
visa in advance and disregard anything you
read that tells you that you can get any kind
of visa (including transit) upon arrival.

Visas are not difficult to obtain, but regulations are in disarray. Technically, the visa that
applies to most visitors – the tourist visa –
requires a 'support letter' (invitation) from
a hotel or tourist agency or proof of prebooked accommodation for at least the first
night. However, many readers (including the
author) have recently received a tourist visa
without having to do this. The requirements
seem to vary not only from consulate to consulate, but even from visa application to visa

UKRAINE

application within a single consulate. To save time and money, contact your consulate before applying.

People whose consulate needs an invitation have reported that they have had no trouble if they apply for a private visa instead, inventing a place they'll be staying on the form. If your consulate for some reason does request a 'support letter', you can get one from online agencies (US$30 to $US50); search under 'Ukraine tourist visa'.

Transit visas are required (a Russian visa doesn't cut it), are *not issued* on arrival (get yours in advance) and cannot be extended (they are valid for up to five days).

For more information, see the following websites:

www.ukraineinfo.us

www.usemb.kiev.ua

http://thorntree.lonelyplanet.com Eastern Europe branch.

www.brama.com Travel bulletin board for Ukraine.

Europe Directory

CONTENTS

This chapter includes general information about the region; for country-specific information refer to the individual country chapters. Please note: Prices mentioned in this chapter are usually given in the currency quoted by the source.

ACCOMMODATION

The cheapest places to stay in Europe are camping grounds, followed by hostels and student dormitories. Cheap hotels are less common in the northern half of Europe, but variations on renting a room from a private residence fill the upper-budget gap. Self-catering flats and cottages are worth considering with a group, especially if you plan to stay somewhere for a while.

Accommodation is listed for each relevant city or town by preference or budget type with worthwhile options for splurging. The hotels recommended in this book will generally range from no stars to one or two stars.

See the Directory sections in the individual country chapters for an overview of local accommodation options. During peak holiday periods, accommodation, even camping grounds, can be hard to find and it's advisable to book ahead.

The online resource **Couch Surfing.com** (www.couchsurfing.com) links travellers with travel-friendly residents all over the world who have a couch or a room to spare (for free). Visit the website for details on becoming a member. Similar schemes include **Globalfreeloaders** (www.globalfreeloaders.com) and **Stay4free** (www.stay4free.com), but in these instances you must be able to offer a couch or room in return at some point.

Cheap hotels fill up quickly in popular destinations (eg Paris, London, Rome), especially well-run hotels in desirable or central neighbourhoods. It's a good idea to make your reservations as far ahead as possible.

Tourist offices often have extensive accommodation lists, and the more helpful ones will go out of their way to find something suitable. In most countries, the fee for this service is very low, and if accommodation is tight, it can save you a lot of running around. This is also an easy way to get around any language problems. Agencies offering private rooms can also be good value. Remember that while staying with a local family doesn't always mean you'll lack privacy, you won't be able to bring the after-party back to your place.

In many destinations, particularly further east in Europe, you might be approached by people in the train station at a commission-paying hostel or rented room. Be sure that such accommodation isn't in a far-flung suburb that requires an expensive taxi ride to and from town. Also make sure that both parties are clear on the price. Always be careful when someone offers to carry your luggage: they might carry it away altogether.

B&Bs, Guesthouses & Hotels

Occupying the upper-budget and mid-range level are guesthouses and hotels. Private accommodation goes under various names: pension, guesthouse, *Gasthaus, Zimmer frei* ('rooms available'), *chambre d'hôte* and so on. Although most guesthouses are simple affairs, there are more expensive ones, with en suite bathrooms and other luxuries.

Owner-occupied B&Bs (bed and breakfasts) in the UK and Ireland, don't generally fall into the category of budget accommodation. You might strike it lucky, but even the most lowly tend to have mid-range prices. Recent years have also seen the growth of 'boutique' or 'designer' B&Bs, which are at the top end of the market.

Budget hotels might be only marginally more expensive than guesthouses. You'll often find inexpensive hotels clustered around the bus and train station areas, which can be convenient for late-night or early morning arrivals and departures. But some hotels are no-tell, pay-by-the-hour numbers.

Ask to see a room, checking the bed, bedsheets and bathroom for cleanliness and security, before you agree to pay, and make sure you know the price. Discounts are often available for groups or longer stays. Ask about breakfast: sometimes it's included, but other times it may be obligatory and you'll have to pay extra.

If you think a hotel room is too expensive, ask if there's anything cheaper. Often hotel owners may try to steer you into more expensive rooms. In southern Europe in particular, hotel owners may be open to a little bargaining if times are slack. In France and the UK it is common practice for business hotels (usually more than two stars) to slash their rates by up to 40% on slow Friday and Saturday nights.

Two budget hotel chains to keep an eye out for across the Continent are **Etap** (www .etaphotel.com; s/d/tr from €35/40/45) and **Formule 1** (www.hotelformule1.com; s/d/tr from €30). Both follow the McDonald's model of convenience first; their garish interior décor could never be described as anything tasteful and they have zero personality. However, if you need a break from hostels, they do make useful bolt-holes.

Camping

Camping is immensely popular in Europe (especially among Germans, Dutch, Czechs and Poles) and provides the cheapest accommodation available. There's usually a charge per tent or site, per person and per vehicle. National tourist offices provide lists of camping grounds all over their country.

In large cities, most camping grounds will be some distance from the centre. Hence, people who have their own transport are those who camp, and is not an economical option otherwise due to commuting expenses to and from the centre. You will also need to arrive in the country with the required gear: a tent, sleeping bag and cooking equipment. As camping isn't always realistic for many budget travellers, this book lists camping grounds only in areas where camping is easily accessible from the interesting parts of a city, or where it's common for travellers to bed down en masse under the stars (for example, on some Greek islands).

Camping other than in designated camping grounds is difficult in Western Europe where it's hard to find a suitable spot to pitch a tent away from prying eyes. Camping is also illegal without permission from the local authorities (the police or local council office) or from the owner of the land (don't be shy about asking – you may be pleasantly surprised by the response).

In some countries, such as Austria, the UK, France and Germany, free camping is illegal on all but private land, and in Greece it's illegal altogether but not enforced. This doesn't prevent hikers from occasionally pitching their tent, and you'll usually get away with it if you have only a small tent are discreet, stay only one or two nights take the tent down during the day and do not light a campfire or leave rubbish. At worst, you'll be woken up by the police and asked to move on.

Hostels

Hostels offer the cheapest (secure) roof over your head in Europe, and you don't have to be a youngster to use them. (Only southern German hostels enforce a strict age limit o

26 years old.) Most hostels are part of the national youth hostel association (YHA), which is affiliated to **Hostelling International** (HI; www.hihostels.com).

Most hostels have dorm rooms sleeping four to five people, although larger ones do exist. There are self-catering facilities or kitchens at many. Hostel rules vary per facility and country, but most ask that guests vacate the rooms for cleaning purposes and some impose a curfew. Many offer a complimentary breakfast of toast, cereal, coffee and tea.

Technically, you're supposed to be a YHA or HI member to use affiliated hostels, but you can often stay by paying an extra charge, which will then be set against future membership. Stay enough nights and you automatically become a member. To join, ask at any hostel, contact your local or national hostelling office, or follow online directions provided at www.hihostels.com under the 'Membership' page.

HI also publishes an annual Europe hostel guide available through local chapters or bookshops. Below is a list of national HI organisations and their websites, which list addresses and telephone numbers for the in-country travel centres.

An Óige (www.anoige.ie) Covers Ireland.
Australian Youth Hostels Association (www.yha.com.au)
England & Wales Youth Hostels Association (www.yha.org.uk)
Hostelling International Canada (www.hihostels.ca)
Hostelling International Northern Ireland (www.yha.org.nz)
Hostelling International South Africa (www.hisa.org.za)
Hostelling International/American Youth Hostels (www.hiayh.org)
Scottish Youth Hostels Association (www.syha.org.uk)
Youth Hostels Association of New Zealand (☎ 03-379 9970; www.yha.org.nz)

There are also some privately run hostelling organisations in Europe and hundreds of unaffiliated hostels. Private hostels have fewer rules (eg no curfew, no daytime lockout) and are often booked by small groups of independent travellers rather than large and noisy groups of European school children. The main drawback is that the facilities often vary greatly (unlike HI hostels, which must meet minimum safety and cleanliness standards).

University Accommodation

Some university towns rent out their student accommodation during the holiday periods. This is a very popular practice in France, the UK and many Eastern European countries (see individual country chapters for more details). University accommodation will sometimes be in single rooms (although it's more commonly in doubles or triples) and may have cooking facilities. For details inquire at the college or university itself, at the student information services or at local tourist offices.

ACTIVITIES

Europe offers countless opportunities to indulge in more active pursuits than sightseeing. The varied geography and climate support the full range of outdoor pursuits, which include windsurfing, skiing, fishing, trekking, cycling, mountaineering and adventure sports. For local information see the individual country chapters.

Adventure Sports

New Zealand might boast that it's the world's leading adventure-sports destination, but when it comes to bungee jumping, canyoning, ice-climbing, paragliding and skydiving, Interlaken in Switzerland (see p1177) gives the Kiwis a thrill-per-minute run for their money. Here, you'll also find dog-sledding, and zorbing (where you're strapped inside an inflated ball, inside another inflated ball and then propelled head-over-heels down a hill). Hydrospeed is a little like canyoning, where you're kitted out in a helmet and wetsuit and ride the wild river, but this time you lie on your stomach, on top of a specially designed, surfboard-like 'raft'. For operators see **Swissraft** (www.swissraft.ch) or the companies mentioned in the Switzerland chapter.

Another burgeoning, and more reasonably priced, adventure-sports destination is Bovec in Slovenia (see p1051). Bungee jumping, paragliding, rafting – you name it – they all take place against a wonderful alpine backdrop.

In Switzerland, you'll pay the equivalent of €125 to go paragliding, €125 to €255 for a bungee jump, and €75 to €125 to go rafting or canyoning. In Slovenia, prices are more like €90 for paragliding or bungee jumping and €35 for rafting or canyoning.

Cycling

Much of Europe is ideally suited to cycling. In the northwest, the flat terrain ensures that bicycles are a popular form of everyday transport, though rampant headwinds often spoil the fun. In the rest of the region, hills and mountains can make for tough going, but this is offset by the dense concentration of things to see. Cycling is a great way to explore many of the Mediterranean islands.

Popular cycling areas among holiday-makers include the Belgian Ardennes, the west of Ireland, the upper reaches of the Danube in southern Germany, anywhere in the Alps and the south of France. Exploring the small villages of Turkey and Eastern Europe also provides up-close access to areas otherwise seen from a train window.

If you are arriving from outside Europe, you can often bring your own bicycle on the plane (see p1249).

Hiking

Keen hikers could spend a lifetime exploring Europe's many exciting trails. Probably the most spectacular are in the Alps and Italian Dolomites, which are crisscrossed with well-marked trails. In season, food and accommodation are available along the way. The equally sensational Pyrenees are less developed, which can add to the experience as you often rely on remote mountain villages for rest and sustenance. Hiking areas that are less well known, but nothing short of stunning, are also in Sardinia, northern Portugal, Turkey, Morocco, Slovakia, Poland, Romania and Bulgaria. One trend that has been sweeping Alpine countries such as Austria and Switzerland in recent years is so-called 'Nordic walking', which is basically skiing without the snow. If you see people rhythmically swinging themselves between two walking poles, don't be taken aback; they're simply working their upper bodies more and giving themselves a better cardio workout. You might even want to try it yourself.

The **Ramblers' Association** (☎ 020-7339 8500; www.ramblers.org.uk; 87-90 Albert Embankment, Camelford House, 2nd fl, London SE1 7TW, UK) promotes long-distance walking in the UK and can help with maps and information.

Skiing & Snowboarding

In winter, Europeans descend on the hundreds of resorts in the Alps and Pyrenees for downhill skiing and snowboarding. Cross-country skiing is popular in some areas.

A skiing holiday can be expensive due to the costs of ski lifts, accommodation and the inevitable après-ski drinking sessions. Equipment hire (or even purchase), on the other hand, can be relatively cheap and avoids the hassle of bringing your own skis. As a rule, a skiing holiday in Europe will work out to be twice as expensive as a summer holiday of the same length. Cross-country skiing costs less than downhill, since you don't rely as much on ski lifts.

The skiing season used to last from early December to late March, but the season has got off to a slow start in recent years. This has largely been due to poor snow-falls, which is perceived as a result of global warming. Snow conditions can vary greatly from one year to the next and from region to region, but January and February tend to be the best (and busiest) months. During the ski season, travel sections of newspapers across the country will give details on conditions in various resorts.

Ski resorts in the French and Swiss Alps offer challenging slopes and great facilities, but they're also the most expensive. Expect high prices in the German Alps, but less so in the less popular Black Forest and Harz Mountains. Austria is generally slightly cheaper than France and Switzerland. Prices in the Italian Alps are similar to Austria (with some up-market exceptions like Cortina d'Ampezzo), and can work out relatively cheaply with the right package.

Possibly the cheapest skiing (and best for beginners) in Western Europe is found in the Pyrenees and Andorra, and in the Sierra Nevada range in the south of Spain. Eastern Europe (Bulgaria, Romania, Slovakia, Czech Republic and Poland) is the most inexpensive of all but facilities are limited.

Many Alpine resorts are just as attractive to snowboarders. One popular destination with boarders is the Stubai Glacier, south of Innsbruck in Austria (see p91), where you can board (and ski) all year round.

Windsurfing & Surfing

After swimming and fishing, windsurfing could well be the most popular of the many water sports on offer in Europe. It's easy to rent sailboards in many tourist centres, and courses are usually available for beginners.

Believe it or not, you can also go surfing in Europe. Forget the shallow North Sea and Mediterranean and the calm Baltic, but there can be excellent surf, and an accompanying surfer scene, in southwest England and west Scotland (wetsuit advisable), along Ireland's northwest coast, on the Atlantic coast of France and Portugal, and along the north and southwest coasts of Spain. The area around Agadir, Morocco, also has great surf from late autumn to early spring.

BOOKS

Lonely Planet produces a wide range of travel guides and other books to complement the information provided here. This guide is tailored for travellers on a budget who wish to cover a lot of Europe, while other books provide more in-depth information on specific areas and cater to a wider range of budgets.

As well as more detailed regional titles to Western, Mediterranean, Eastern, Central and Scandinavian Europe, Lonely Planet publishes individual guides to most of the countries in this book, as well as to regions within some countries. Lonely Planet also publishes city guides to some of Europe's great capitals (London, Paris, Rome, Berlin, Amsterdam, etc) and walking guides to Britain, Italy, Turkey, Switzerland and more.

For cyclists, there are cycling guides to Britain and France, and for foodies the Lonely Planet World Food series covers Ireland, Italy, Morocco, Spain and Turkey. Budding photographers can improve their technique with a copy of Lonely Planet's *Travel Photography: A Guide to Taking Better Pictures*.

Travel Literature

Comic travel writing has been in vogue in recent years, and three of the best examples of the genre recount pan-European journeys. In *Neither Here nor There: Travels in Europe*, Bill Bryson retraces his youthful 1970s European tour some 20 years later as an older, less agile, more sober adult. Tim Moore reaches further back into history with *Continental Drifter*. Here, he muses on the origins of the 17th-century European 'Grand Tour', by which well-to-do young English men sought to educate themselves – all the while recreating it himself, sleeping rough in a vintage Rolls Royce and velvet suit.

Peter Moore (no relation to Tim) makes life even more difficult for himself in *The Wrong Way Home*. The 'wrong way' turns out to be without a plane journey, from London to Sydney. Although the travelogue naturally ventures into Asia, it does have some sterling episodes in Europe.

If you don't get yourself into hair-raising situations at every turn, and want to read something more akin with your own experience, try *Rite of Passage: Tales of Backpacking 'Round Europe*. Edited by Lisa Johnson, this is a group of stories by young travellers conquering the continent for the first time. From crowded hostels to heated flings, this book taps into the seemingly insignificant events that fuel life-long memories.

Last, but by no means least, is Mark Twain's *A Tramp Abroad*. With his usual wit, Twain chronicles a 15-month 'walking tour' (by train and coach) through central Europe and the Alps in the 19th century.

BUSINESS HOURS

In most of Europe businesses are open 9am to 6pm Monday to Friday, and 9am to 1pm or 5pm on Saturday. In smaller towns there may be a one- to two-hour closure for lunch. Some shops close on Sunday. National holidays and local feast days are also cause for business closings.

Banks are the most liberal with their closing times, keeping an inconvenient 9am to 12.30pm or 1pm and 1.30pm to 3pm or 4pm Monday to Friday; on Thursdays, banks have extended hours until 5.30pm. Museums usually close on Monday or Tuesday.

Restaurants typically open around noon until midnight and bars around 6pm.

CLIMATE

The climate in Western Europe is generally temperate and mild except in mountainous areas.

The weather in Eastern Europe can be fairly extreme at times, but never enough to prevent travel. It's a fascinating place to visit any time of year – even during the icy winter (and that's particularly icy in the Baltic countries, Russia and Ukraine) the cities take on a magical frosty charm.

In the Mediterranean the weather generally follows a predictable pattern: in the summer the sun shines and it's hot; in autumn it gets colder and rains, often in short,

DIRECTORY

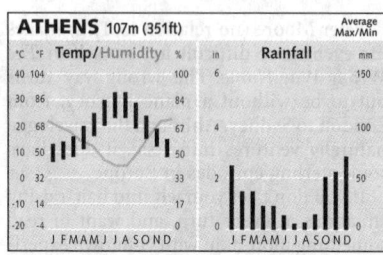

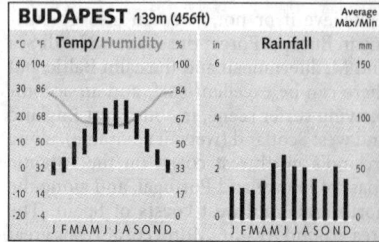

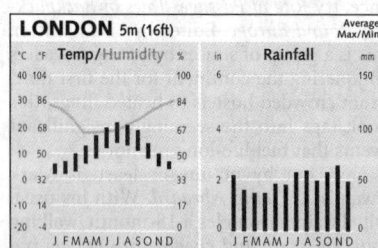

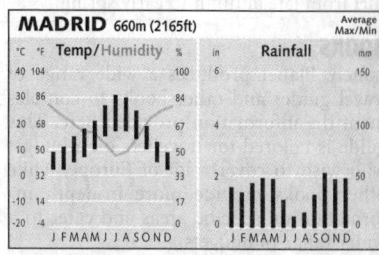

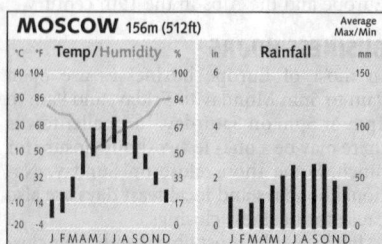

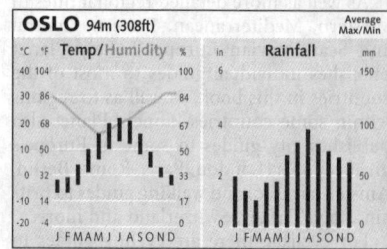

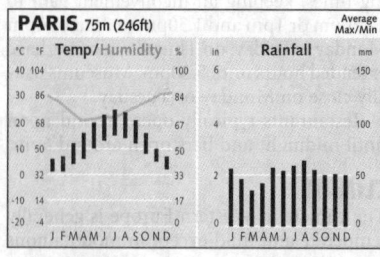

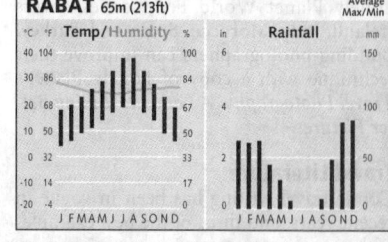

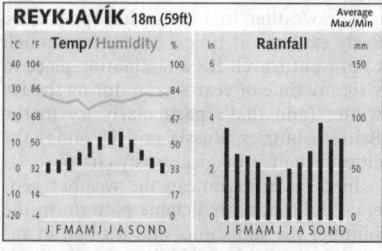

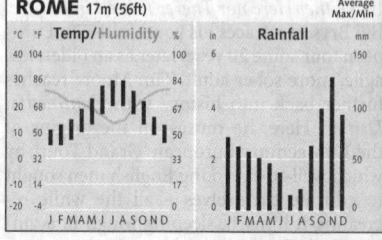

very sharp bursts; in winter temperatures drop considerably.

The following climate charts provide a snapshot of Europe's weather patterns.

CUSTOMS

Duty-free goods are no longer sold to those travelling from one EU country to another.

Travellers to Europe can transport these goods for their own personal use: 800 cigarettes, 200 cigars or 1kg of loose tobacco; 10L of spirits (more than 22% alcohol by volume), 20L of fortified wine or aperitif, 90L of wine or 110L of beer; unlimited quantities of perfume.

Non-EU countries might have different customs regulations. Many countries forbid the exportation of antiquities and cultural treasures. See the individual country chapters for more information.

DANGERS & ANNOYANCES

Travelling in Europe is usually safe. Violent crime is rare; the main threats facing travellers are pickpockets and scam artists. Specific country perils are covered in the Dangers & Annoyances sections of the individual country chapters. The following outlines a range of general guidelines that all travellers should keep in mind. Visit the 'Postcards' section of the Lonely Planet website (www.lonelyplanet.com) for reports from travellers about ever-evolving scams.

Druggings

Although rare, some drugging of travellers does occur in Europe. Travellers are especially vulnerable on trains and buses where a new 'friend' may offer you food or drink that will knock you out, giving them time to fleece you of your belongings.

Gassings have also been reported on a handful of overnight international trains. The usual scenario involves the release of a sleep-inducing gas into a sleeping compartment in the middle of the night. The best protection is to lock the door of your sleeping compartment (use your own lock if there isn't one) and to lock your bags to luggage racks.

If you can help it, never sleep alone in a train compartment.

Illegal Drugs

Narcotics are sometimes quite openly available in Europe, but that doesn't mean they're legal. The Netherlands is most famed for its liberal attitudes to cannabis, mainly because the police there even turn a blind eye to the selling of the drug in coffee shops. However, even in the Netherlands the possession of cannabis is only decriminalised not legalised (apart from medicinal use). Don't take this relaxed attitude as an invitation to buy harder drugs; if you get caught, you will be punished.

In Belgium, the possession of up to 5g of cannabis has been legal since March 2003; but the selling of the drug is still illegal, so if you get caught at the point of sale, you could be in trouble. In Portugal, the possession of *all* drugs has been decriminalised, from cannabis to cocaine and heroin. Once again, however, selling is illegal.

Britain has downgraded cannabis from a Class B to a Class C drug, but many police are unhappy with the decision. In theory, if you're caught with a small quantity of cannabis, all that should happen is confiscation. But if police decide to take a more heavy-handed approach, you don't have a lot of legal back-up.

Moves to decriminalise cannabis in Switzerland were abandoned in October 2003. Many Swiss still act as if decriminalisation were just around the corner, but it's not really advisable to follow suit. If police decide to enforce the law, you'll face a fine of up to Sfr400.

Getting caught with drugs in other parts of Europe, particularly countries such as Tunisia, Turkey and Morocco can have very unpleasant consequences.

For your own safety, don't even think about taking drugs across international borders.

Phoney Cops

'Can I see some ID?' In some countries, especially in Eastern Europe, you may encounter people claiming to be from the tourist police, the special police, the super-secret police, whatever. Unless they're wearing a uniform and have good reason for accosting you (eg you're robbing a bank), treat their claims with suspicion.

One common scam runs like this: a random person asks you to change money. You say no, and seconds later an 'undercover' police officer 'arrests' the moneychanger. The undercover agent then asks to check your passport and money, in case it's counterfeit. Something will then invariably go missing or be confiscated when the alleged undercover officer handles your valuables.

Needless to say, never show your passport or cash to anyone on the street. Simply walk away. If they flash a badge, offer to accompany them to the nearest police station.

Pickpockets & Thieves

Theft is definitely a problem across large parts of Europe and nowadays you also have to be aware of other travellers. Train station lockers or luggage storage counters are useful places to store your bags (but never valuables) while you wander around and get your bearings in a new town. Be very suspicious about people who offer to help you operate your locker. Carry your own padlock for hostel lockers.

Cameras or shoulder bags are an open invitation for snatch thieves, who sometimes operate from motorcycles or scooters and expertly slash the strap before you have a chance to react. A small day-pack is better.

Pickpockets are most active in dense crowds, especially in busy train stations and on public transport during peak hours. A common ploy is for one person to distract you while another zips through your pockets. Beware of gangs of kids waving newspapers and demanding attention. In the blink of an eye, a wallet or camera can go missing.

Be careful even in hotels; don't leave valuables lying around in your room. Parked cars containing luggage and other bags are prime targets for petty criminals in most cities.

You can deter most pickpockets by wearing a moneybelt with your essentials (passport, cash, credit cards, airline tickets). Be aware that crafty thieves can cut the thin strap of a neck pouch without the wearer noticing; be discreet about your moneybelt.

For a little piece of mind, small zipper locks are handy for securing backpacks and day-packs. On trains and buses it's wise to lock your bags to a luggage rack, preferably with a sturdy combination cable.

On overnight trains, be extra vigilant about your belongings. Always keep your money and passport well hidden on your person.

Carry less than 10% to 15% of your total trip money in cash. The rest could be in travellers cheques, which can be replaced if lost or stolen. More useful are ATM cards that are linked to a cheque or savings account back home (see also p1237).

Flaunting cameras, portable CD players and other expensive electronic goods is only asking for trouble. Keep all valuables in a day-pack or backpack when they're not being used. Never leave them sitting in the open on trains or buses.

Have at least one contingency plan in the unlikely event that your moneybelt is stolen. Some travellers walk around with €100 in their shoe; others stash €50 in their aspirin bottle.

Hassles created by having your passport stolen can be considerably reduced if you have a record of its number and issue date; even better are photocopies of the relevant data pages. Also add the serial numbers of your travellers cheques (cross them off as you cash them) and photocopies of your credit cards, airline tickets and other travel documents. If you do lose your passport, notify the police immediately to get a statement, and contact your nearest consulate.

All this said, there's no need to fret about theft constantly, just be sensible and take precautions with your possessions.

DISABLED TRAVELLERS

If you have a physical disability, contact your national support organisation and ask about the countries you plan to visit. Such organisations often have libraries devoted to travel, and can put you in touch with travel agents who specialise in tours for the disabled.

Global Access (www.geocities.com/paris/1502) Operates a site for accessible holidays with travel and hotel suggestions.

Lonely Planet message board (thorntree.lonely planet.com) Has a branch called Travellers With Disabilities, where first-hand experience is shared.

Mobility International USA (☎ 541-343-1284; www.miusa.org; PO Box 10767, Eugene, OR 97440) Publishes guides to travelling internationally, advises disabled travellers on mobility issues and runs education programmes.

Royal Association for Disability & Rehabilitation (Radar; ☎ 020-7250 3222; www.radar.org.uk; 12 City Forum, 250 City Rd, London EC1V 8AF) The British-based association publishes a useful guide entitled *Holidays in Britain & Ireland 2004 – A Guide for Disabled People*, which gives a good overview of facilities available in these countries.

Society for the Advancement of Travelers with Handicaps (☎ 212-447-7284; www.sath.org; 347 5th Ave Suite 610, New York 10016) Publishes *Open World*, a magazine for disabled travellers.

DISCOUNT CARDS

Consider getting an ISIC (International Student Identity Card; isiccard.com), if eligible, ITIC (International Teacher Identity Card; isiccard.com), IYTC (International Youth Travel Card; isiccard.com) or Euro26 card (www.euro26.org). In some nations, these may get you a discount on accommodation.

Hostelling & Camping Cards

A hostelling card is useful – if not always mandatory – for those staying at HI hostels. Many hostels issue one on the spot or after a few stays, though this might cost a bit more than getting it in your home country. Visit www.hihostels.com for more information.

The Camping Card International (CCI; formerly the Camping Carnet) is a camping ground ID that can be used instead of a passport when checking into a camp site and includes third-party insurance. Many camping grounds offer a small discount if you sign in with one. CCIs are issued by automobile associations, camping federations and, sometimes, at camping grounds.

Rail Passes

If you plan to visit more than a few countries, you will save money with a rail pass. The most used passes are Inter-Rail (for European citizens) and Eurail (for non-Europeans), both of which offer unlimited travel within a set number of days in many (but not all) European countries. For a complete rundown, see International Rail Passes (p1256).

Students Cards

Registered students can save a pile of money with an International Student Identification Card (ISIC; www.istc.org). Discounts vary from country to country – at best you'll save up to 50% on museum entry fees and 10% to 30% on some buses, trains and ferries, and inexpensive meals in some student caféterias and restaurants.

If you're under 26 but not a student, you can apply for a GO25 card issued by the Federation of International Youth Travel Organisations (FIYTO) or the Euro26 card, both of which go under different names in various countries. Both give much the same discounts and benefits as an ISIC.

All these cards are issued by student unions, hostelling organisations or youth-oriented travel agencies such as STA and Council Travel.

DISCRIMINATION

Frustration with immigration issues is increasing in Europe, and travellers of African or Arab descent might encounter unpleasant attitudes that are unrelated to them personally. In rural areas, travellers whose skin colour marks them as foreigners might experience unwanted attention. Some travellers have reported negative encounters because locals mistook them as Roma (Gypsies). Attitudes vary per country and tend to be more accepting in cities than in the country.

DRIVING LICENCE

Many non-European driving licences are valid in Europe, but it's still a good idea to get an International Driving Permit (IDP) if you intend to drive. This document (basically a translation of the vehicle class and personal details noted on your own driver's licence) can make life much simpler when hiring cars and motorcycles. An IDP is not valid unless accompanied by your original licence. One can be obtained for a small fee from your local automobile association – bring along a passport photo and a valid licence.

EMBASSIES & CONSULATES

It's important to realise what your own embassy – the embassy of the country of which you are a citizen – can and can't do to help you if you get into trouble.

Generally speaking, it won't be much help in emergencies if the trouble you're in is remotely your own fault. Remember that you are bound by the laws of the country you are in. Your embassy will not be sympathetic if you end up in jail after committing a crime locally, even if such actions are legal in your own country.

In genuine emergencies you might get some assistance, but only if other channels have been exhausted. For example, if you need to get home urgently, a free ticket is exceedingly unlikely – the embassy would expect you to have insurance. If you have all your money and documents stolen, it might assist with getting a new passport, but a loan for onward travel is out of the question.

See the individual country chapters for contact information for foreign embassies.

FESTIVALS & EVENTS

Many European festivals are tied to the religious calendar or to significant events in the nation's history. Both religious and national holidays are observed by public institutions and some restaurants. Depending on the size and importance of the holiday, travel or lodging might be difficult to secure. See the individual country chapters about major holidays that might interfere with your plans. See the Festivals chapter (p41) for events of interest to backpackers.

GAY & LESBIAN TRAVELLERS

In cosmopolitan centres, especially in Western Europe, you'll find accepting attitudes toward homosexuality. The Netherlands and Belgium have legalised same-sex marriages. London, Paris, Berlin, Amsterdam, Madrid and even Lisbon enjoy thriving gay communities and pride events. The Greek islands of Mykonos and Lesvos are popular gay beach destinations.

Outside of the big cities, attitudes become more conservative and discretion is advised.

The *Spartacus International Gay Guide* (www.spartacusworld.com) is a good male-only international directory of gay entertainment venues in Europe plus other places. It's best when used in conjunction with listings in local gay papers, usually distributed for free at gay bars and clubs.

The USA's leading gay publisher, **Damron** (www.damron.com) publishes several guides targeted to women, men and specific European cities.

International Lesbian and Gay Association (ILGA; ☎ 32-2-5022471; www.ilga.org; 81 rue Marché-au-Charbon, B-1000, Brussels, Belgium) is a good resource for country-specific political information on homosexual issues.

See the individual country chapters for contact addresses of useful organisations, as well as gay and lesbian venues.

INSURANCE

A travel-insurance policy to cover theft, loss and medical problems is a good idea. The policies handled by STA Travel and other student travel organisations are usually good value. There is a wide variety of policies available, so check the small print.

Some policies specifically exclude 'dangerous activities', which can include scuba diving, motorcycling and even trekking. A locally acquired motorcycle licence is not valid under some policies.

You may prefer a policy that pays doctors or hospitals directly rather than having you pay on the spot and claim later. If you have to claim later, make sure you keep all documentation. Some policies ask you to call back (reverse charges) to a centre in your home country, where an immediate assessment of your problem is made. Check that the policy covers ambulances or an emergency flight home.

For health insurance see p1259; see p1251 for details on car insurance.

INTERNET ACCESS

You'll find Internet cafés throughout Europe. Check the individual country chapters for more details or visit www.netcaféguide.com for an up-to-date list. You may also find public Internet access in post offices, libraries, hostels, hotels, universities and so on.

INTERNET RESOURCES

The Internet is a rich resource for travellers. You can research your trip, hunt for bargain air fares, book hotels, check on weather conditions or chat with locals and other travellers about the best places to visit (or avoid!).

The following websites offer useful information about Europe, its cities, transport systems, currencies etc. Country-specific websites are listed in the country chapters.

Budget Travellers Guide to Sleeping in Airports (www.sleepinginairports.net) Indispensable for the backpacker flying stand-by. First-hand accounts describe the search for a good-night's sleep in airports throughout Europe.

Currency Conversions (www.xe.net/ucc) Up-to-the-second exchange rates for hundreds of currencies worldwide.

Guide for Europe (www.guideforeurope.com) With a handy hostel review page posted by recent visitors.

Lonely Planet (www.lonelyplanet.com) Succinct summaries on travelling to most places on earth, postcards from other travellers and the Thorn Tree bulletin board, where you can link up with a community of thousands of fellow travellers to ask questions before you go or dispense advice when you get back. You can also find travel news and updates to many of our most popular guidebooks, while the subWWWay section links you to the most useful travel resources elsewhere on the Web.

The Man in Seat 61 (www.seat61.com) How to travel by rail from London to almost anywhere in Europe by rail with rail company contact information, descriptions of routes and what to expect. It is a personal website that makes a modest commission on selling rail and youth passes.

Tourist offices (www.towd.com) List of tourist offices at home and around the world for most countries.

LEGAL MATTERS

Police in most of Europe are friendly and helpful, especially if you have been a victim of a crime. You are required by law to prove your identity if asked by the police, so always carry your passport, or an identity card if you're an EU citizen. Please note that drugs in the Netherlands are decriminalised rather than being legal, meaning that small amounts of certain drugs are not prosecuted. See The Netherlands chapter (p865) for details.

MAPS

Good maps are easy to find once you're in Europe, but you might want to buy some region-wide maps for planning. Lonely Planet publishes plastic-coated full-colour maps to certain Europe's greatest cities – Amsterdam, Barcelona, Berlin, Brussels, Budapest, Dublin, Istanbul, London, Paris, Prague and Rome plus a full index of streets, sights and transit routes and walking tours.

Proper road maps are essential if you're driving or cycling. You can't go wrong with Michelin maps. Some people prefer the maps meticulously produced by Freytag & Berndt, Kümmerly + Frey and Hallwag. As a rule, maps published by European automobile associations (the AA in Britain, the ADAC in Germany etc) are excellent and sometimes free if membership of your local association gives you reciprocal rights. Tourist offices are often another good source for (usually free and fairly basic) maps.

MONEY
Black Market

Black-market, or illegal exchanges, are rare these days in Europe, although you find them still in some nations, such as Albania. Changing money on the street is extremely risky, not only because it is illegal, but also because many of the people offering to change are professional thieves with years of experience in cheating tourists.

Cash

Nothing beats cash for convenience…or risk. If you lose it, it's gone forever and very few travel insurers will come to your rescue. Those that do will limit the amount to somewhere around €300. For tips on carrying your money safely, see p1234.

It's still a good idea, though, to bring some local currency in cash, if only to cover you until you get to an exchange facility or find an ATM. The equivalent of, say, €50 or €100 should usually be enough. Some extra cash in an easily exchanged currency is also a good idea, especially in Eastern Europe. Many travellers stash a small amount of emergency funds in their sock or into a special, difficult-to-access pocket.

Credit Cards & ATMs

Bank-issued ATM cards connected to the Visa/Plus, Eurocard and MasterCard/Cirrus networks are widely accepted in European countries. This will let you draw cash directly from your home account, but it's worth having a back-up option, as some travellers have reported inexplicable glitches with ATMs in individual countries, even when their card worked fine elsewhere across Europe. (Sometimes the network will not recognise your card if it's very early in the morning back in your home country, when banks sometimes back up their systems. If your card is rejected, try again in a few hours' time.)

When you do get money from an ATM, the amounts are converted and dispensed in the local currency, and a small fee (about €2) will be levied for each withdrawal.

Credit cards also allow you to draw cash at foreign ATMs, provided you have a four-digit PIN number for the card. For this, your credit-card company will normally levy a slightly larger fee, and interest on cash advances is normally higher than for normal purchases.

If you are unfamiliar with the options available, ask your bank to explain the workings, and the relative merits of credit, credit/debit, debit, charge and cash cards. Also inquire about charges for using non-home bank ATMs and for currency conversion.

Credit cards are a blessing on the road, allowing you to make major purchases, such as air or rail tickets, without having to carry large amounts of cash, and offering a lifeline in certain emergencies.

Visa and MasterCard/Eurocard are more widely accepted in Europe than AmEx and Diners Club; Visa (sometimes called Carte Bleue) is particularly strong in France and Spain. There are, however, regional differences in the general acceptability of credit cards. In the UK, for example, you can usually flash your plastic in the most humble of budget restaurants; in Germany few

DIRECTORY

restaurants take credit cards. Cards are not widely accepted off the beaten track.

Of course, you need to be aware of possible fraud. You will lessen the chances of someone getting hold of your number and making purchases against your account if you don't let the credit card out of your sight when making transactions and you keep records of all transaction. Check your statements, either when you return home, or set up your account for online browsing, and check your statements while on the road. For the really punctilious traveller, letting your credit-card company know that you are travelling in Europe lessens the chance of it cutting off the card when it sees unusual spending on your account.

For security and flexibility, diversify your source of funds. Carry an ATM card, credit card, travellers cheques and cash. Always keep these on your person.

Exchanging Money

In 2002, 12 EU members adopted a common currency, the euro. The countries making this so-called 'euro-zone' are Austria, Belgium, Luxembourg, France, Finland, Germany, Greece, Ireland, Italy, the Netherlands, Portugal and Spain. The three then-remaining EU member states, Denmark, Britain and Sweden, have held out against adopting the euro for political reasons. New EU member states in Eastern Europe will probably join the euro zone in 2007 or 2008. Non-EU members, such as Norway, Russia, Switzerland and Ukraine, still have local currencies in place. See individual country chapters for details.The euro is divided into 100 cents.

In general, US dollars, UK pounds and euros are the most easily exchanged currencies in Europe. The major local European currencies are fully convertible, but you may have trouble exchanging some of the lesser-known ones at small banks. The importation and exportation of certain currencies (eg Moroccan dirham) is restricted or banned entirely, so try to get rid of any local currency before you leave the country. Get rid of Scottish pounds before leaving the UK; nobody outside Britain will touch them. The same goes for Latvian currency and small denominations (only) of Czech crowns.

Most airports, central train stations, big hotels and many border posts have banking facilities outside regular business hours, at times on a 24-hour basis. You'll often find automatic exchange machines outside banks or tourist offices that accept the currencies of up to two dozen countries. Post offices in Europe often perform banking tasks, tend to be open longer hours, and outnumber banks in remote places. Be aware, though, that while they always exchange cash, they might baulk at handling travellers cheques unless they're denominated in the local currency.

The best exchange rates are usually at banks. *Bureaux de change* usually – but not always – offer worse rates or charge higher commissions. Hotels are almost always the worst places to change money. American Express (AmEx) and Thomas Cook offices usually do not charge commission for changing their own cheques, but might offer a less favourable exchange rate than banks.

International Transfers

Telegraphic transfers can occasionally be ridiculously expensive. Despite their name they can also be quite slow. Be sure to specify the name of the bank and the name and address of the branch where you'd like to pick up your money.

It's quicker and easier to have money wired via an AmEx office (US$60 for US$1000). Western Union's Money Transfer system (available at post offices in some countries) and Thomas Cook's Money Gram service are also popular.

Taxes & Refunds

A kind of sales tax called value-added tax (VAT) applies to many goods and services in Europe. VAT will add anywhere between 10% to 20% to the price of goods, and if you spend more than a certain amount (usually around €75) and you're not an EU resident shopping in another EU state, you can usually claim that money back when you leave the country.

The procedure for making a tax-back claim is fairly straightforward. First of all make sure the shop offers duty-free sales. (Often a sign will be displayed reading 'Tax-Free Shopping'.) When making your purchase ask the shop attendant for a VAT-refund voucher, filled in with the correct amount and the date. This can be used either to claim a refund directly at international airports, or stamped at ferry ports or border crossings and mailed back for a refund.

None of this applies if you live in the EU and buy goods in another EU country. Even an American citizen living in London is not entitled to rebate on items bought in Paris. On the other hand, an EU passport holder living in New York is.

Tipping & Bargaining

Tipping has become more complicated in recent years, with 'service charges' increasingly added to bills. In theory, this means you're not obliged to tip. In practice, that money often doesn't go to the server and they might make it clear they still expect a gratuity.

Don't pay twice. If the service charge is optional, remove it from the bill and pay a tip. If it's not, don't tip.

Generally, waiters in Western Europe tend to be paid decent wages. For more details, see the individual country chapters.

Bargaining is common in Turkey and Morocco; see those chapters for more information.

Travellers Cheques

The main idea of carrying travellers cheques rather than cash is the protection they offer from theft, though they are losing their popularity as more travellers – including those on a tight budget – deposit their money in their bank at home and withdraw it as they go along using ATMs.

AmEx, Visa and Thomas Cook travellers cheques are widely accepted and have efficient replacement policies. If you're going to remote places, it's worth sticking to AmEx, since small local banks may not always accept other brands.

When you change cheques, don't look at just the exchange rate; ask about fees and commissions as well. There may be a service fee per cheque, a flat transaction fee or a percentage of the total amount irrespective of the number of cheques. Some banks charge fees (often exorbitant) to cash cheques and not cash; others do the reverse.

Cheques are available in various currencies, but ones denominated in US dollars, British pounds or euros are the easiest to cash.

Keeping a record of the cheque numbers and those you have used is vital when it comes to replacing lost travellers cheques. You should keep this separate from the cheques themselves.

MEDIA

Many UK newspapers, such as the *Guardian* and *The Financial Times* (see p222) have international editions, which are circulated across large parts of Europe. These aside, perhaps the best-known English-language newspaper is the *International Herald Tribune*, produced in Paris by a US publisher for expats. International news weeklies such as *The Economist, Newsweek* and *Time* are also widely available.

In addition, many European capitals have their own English-language newspapers. The most famous are probably the *Prague Post* and *Moscow Times*. For others, see individual country chapters.

Serbia's well-known B92 radio station has a Web-based English-language service and Radio Free Europe/Radio Liberty, once largely an American Cold-War propaganda tool, survives across several countries in Eastern Europe as a station for both locals and expats.

The BBC World Service is available across Europe. See www.bbc.co.uk/world service for how to tune in depending on which country you're in.

PASSPORT

Your most important travel document is your passport. Many countries require that your passport remain valid for at least six month after you *leave*. If your passport is just about to expire, renew it before you go. This may not be easy to do overseas.

Applying for or renewing a passport can take anything from a few days to several months, so don't leave it till the last minute. Bureaucratic wheels usually turn faster if you do everything in person rather than relying on the post or agents, but check first what you need to take with you (photos of a certain size, birth certificate, signed statements, exact payment in cash etc).

US citizens must apply in person (but may renew by mail) at a US Passport Agency office or at some courthouses and post offices. Australian citizens can apply at a post office or the passport office in their state capital; Britons can pick up application forms from major post offices, and the passport is issued by the regional passport office; Canadians can apply at regional passport offices; New Zealanders can apply at any district office of the Department of Internal Affairs.

Once you start travelling, carry your passport on your person at all times and guard it carefully. Camping grounds and hotels sometimes ask that you hand over your passport for the duration of your stay. If you're worried about this, a driving licence, HI membership card or Camping Card International usually suffices.

EU citizens and those from certain other European countries (eg Switzerland) don't need a valid passport to travel to another EU country or even some non-EU countries; a national identity card is sufficient. If you want to exercise this option, check with your travel agent or the embassies of the countries you plan to visit.

PHOTOGRAPHY & VIDEO

Both where you'll be travelling and the weather will dictate what film to take or buy locally. In places like Ireland and Britain, where the sky is often overcast, photographers should bring high-speed film (eg 200 to 400 ASA). For southern Europe (or northern Europe under snow and sunny skies) slower film is the answer (eg 100 to 200 ASA).

Film and camera equipment is available all over Europe, but obviously shops in the larger cities and towns have a wider range. Avoid buying film at major tourist centres (eg at kiosks below the Eiffel Tower or at the Tower of London). It may have been stored badly or have exceeded its sell-by date and will be very expensive.

If you want to record or buy video tapes to play back home, you won't get a picture if the image registration systems are different. Europe generally uses PAL (France uses Secam), which is incompatible with the North American and Japanese NTSC system. Australia also uses PAL.

POST

From major European centres, airmail typically takes about five days to North America and about a week to Australasian destinations, although mail from such countries as Greece is much slower. Postage costs vary from country to country, as does post office efficiency.

You can collect mail from poste restante sections at major post offices. Ask people writing to you to print your name clearly and capitalise and underline your surname. When collecting mail, your passport may be required for identification and you may have to pay a small fee. If an expected letter is not awaiting you, ask to check under your given name; letters are commonly misfiled. Post offices usually hold mail for about a month, but sometimes less (in Germany, for instance, they hold mail for two weeks only). Unless the sender specifies otherwise, mail will always be sent to the city's main post office.

SOCIAL PROBLEMS

Some parts of Europe are still subject to random violence by separatist groups, such as FLNC (a Corsican group in France). In the past, ETA has often bombed targets in its campaign for Basque independence in southern France and Spain. Whether it will continue to do so after the public outcry surrounding the al-Qaeda–linked Madrid bombings in March 2004 remains to be seen.

Tension continues across the Greek-Turkish divide in Cyprus. Northern Ireland usually experiences some civil unrest in July (partly around the 12th) during marching season. Peace and stability are still tender and vulnerable in the Balkans (Bosnia-Hercegovina, Serbia, Montenegro, Albania and Macedonia). Russia has experienced attacks on civilians allegedly orchestrated by Chechen rebels.

Travel advisories on individual countries are available from your own government or from:

Department of Foreign Affairs and Trade (www.smartraveller.gov.au)
Foreign and Commonwealth Office (www.fco.gov.uk)
State Department (http://travel.state.gov)

Note that Australia's Department of Foreign Affairs and Trade and the US State Department both tend to be more conservative than the Foreign and Commonwealth Office.

STUDYING

If your interests are more cerebral, you can enrol in courses in Europe on anything from language to alternative medicine. Of course, the best way to learn a language is to immerse yourself in its home culture. Language courses are available to foreigners through universities or private schools, and are justifiably popular. **Cactus Education** (www.cactuseducation.com) help students find educational opportunities at topnotch universities in Europe and the UK.

Major cultural and language teaching institutes include:

Alliance Française (www.alliancefr.org) The Parisian school's website has details of all Alliances worldwide, under 'Alliances Network'.

Goethe Institut (www.goethe.de) Learn *Deutsch* all across Europe, including in Germany itself.

Instituto Cervantes (www.cervantes.es) Bizarrely the website is in Spanish only. Either click on 'IC en el Mundo', then 'Red de Centros Asociades' and the relevant map, or email informa@cervantes.es.

You can also take courses in art, literature, architecture, drama, music, cooking, alternative energy, photography and organic farming, among other subjects.

The best sources of information are the cultural institutes maintained by many European countries around the world; or, try their national tourist offices or embassies. Student exchange organisations, student travel agencies such as STA and Council Travel, and organisations like YMCA/YWCA and HI can also put you on the right track. Ask about special holiday packages that include a course.

TELEPHONE

You can ring abroad from almost any phone box in Europe. Public telephones accepting stored-value phonecards (available from post offices, telephone centres, newsstands or retail outlets) are virtually the norm now; in some countries, France for example, coin-operated phones are almost impossible to find.

Without a phonecard, you can ring from a telephone booth inside a post office or telephone centre and settle your bill at the counter. Reverse-charge (collect) calls are often possible, but not always. From many countries, however, the Country Direct system lets you phone home by billing the long-distance carrier you use at home. These numbers can often be dialled from public phones without even inserting a phonecard.

TIME

The standard international time measurements, GMT and UTC, are identical, and both are calibrated to the prime meridian, which passes through Greenwich in London. For the sake of comparison, if it's noon in Britain (GMT/UTC) it's 4am on the US west coast (GMT/UTC minus eight hours), 7am on the US east coast (GMT/UTC minus five

hours), 1pm in Paris (GMT/UTC plus one hour; also called Central European Time), 2pm in Greece (GMT/UTC plus two hours) and 10pm in Sydney (GMT/UTC plus 10 hours).

In most European countries, clocks are turned one hour ahead for daylight-saving time on the last Sunday in March, and turned back again on the last Sunday in October. During daylight-saving time, Britain and Ireland are GMT/UTC plus one hour, Central European Time is GMT/UTC plus two hours and Greece is GMT/UTC plus three hours.

TOILETS

Many public toilets in Europe require a small fee either deposited in a box or given to the attendant.

TOURIST INFORMATION

Tourist offices in larger cities tend to be better organised and more helpful than in small towns. Western and Central Europe tend to have better tourism infrastructure and tourist outreach than Eastern Europe. Some tourism offices can help make lodging reservations, especially if you arrive in town during a peak period without arrangements.

TOURS

Package tours cater to all tastes, interests and ages. See your travel agent or look in the small ads in newspaper travel pages. A bit of Internet surfing can yield excellent results for those seeking unusual tours. For walking, skiing and other outdoor adventures, contact **Ramblers Holidays** (☎ 01707-331 133; www.ramblersholidays.co.uk) in Britain, and **CBT Tours** (☎ 800 736 2453; www.cbttours.com) in the USA for bicycle trips.

Young revellers can party on Europe-wide bus tours. **Contiki** (☎ 020-8290 6777; www.contiki .com) and **Top Deck** (☎ 020-7370 4555; www.topdeck travel.co.uk) offer camping or hotel-based bus tours for the 18-to-35 age group. Contiki's tours last from five to 46 days. Both companies have London offices plus offices or company representatives in Europe, North America, Australasia and South Africa.

A British company highly experienced in booking travel to Eastern Europe is **Regent Holidays** (☎ 0117-9211711; www.regent-holidays.co.uk; 15 John St, Bristol BS1 2HR).

National tourist offices in most countries offer organised trips to points of interest.

These may range from one-hour city tours to several-day excursions. They often work out more expensive than going it alone but are sometimes worth it if you are really pressed for time.

VISAS

Citizens of the USA, Australia, New Zealand, Canada and the UK need only a valid passport to enter most members of the EU. Eastern European countries, including Belarus, Moldova, Russia and Ukraine, require a prearranged visa before arrival and some require an 'invitation' from (or booking with) a tour operator or hotel. See the respective countries for specific information on prearranged travel visas or check first with the embassies or consulates of the countries you plan to visit. Visas to these countries are seldom available at the border, and then not reliably.

There's a wide variety of visas, including tourist, transit and business permits. Transit visas are usually cheaper than tourist or business visas, but they only allow a very short stay (one or two days) and can be difficult to extend.

Austria, Belgium, Denmark, Finland, France, Germany, Iceland, Italy, Greece, Luxembourg, the Netherlands, Norway, Portugal, Spain and Sweden are signatories to the Schengen Agreement, which dismantled border controls, and an identity card for EU members is typically all that is required to pass between these countries. But to be on the safe side, travel with your passport. All non-EU citizens visiting a Schengen country and intending to stay for longer than three days or to visit another Schengen country are supposed to obtain an official entry stamp in their passport either at the point of entry or from the local police within 72 hours. This is very loosely enforced, however, and in general registering at a hotel will be sufficient.

For those who do require visas, it's important to remember that these will have a 'use-by' date, and you'll be refused entry after that period has elapsed. It may not be checked when entering these countries overland, but major problems can arise if it is requested during your stay or on departure and you can't produce it.

Visa requirements can change, and you should check with the individual embassies or a respected travel agent before travelling.

In some cases it's easier to get your visas as you go along, rather than arranging them all beforehand. Carry spare passport photos (you may need from one to four every time you apply for a visa).

Visas are usually issued immediately by consulates in Eastern Europe, although some may levy a 50% to 100% surcharge for 'express service'. Russia, Belarus and Ukraine have more confusing regulations that can be simplified by obtaining a visa before arrival. Visas are often cheaper in your home country anyway.

Consulates are generally open weekday mornings (if there's both an embassy and a consulate, you want the consulate). Consulates in countries not neighbouring the one you want to visit are far less crowded. Take your own pen and be sure to have a good supply of passport photos that actually look like you (if such things exist).

Be aware that if you're visiting both Turkish-controlled North Cyprus and mainland Greece, you should get your Cypriot immigration stamp on a separate piece of paper, rather than in the pages of your passport. Otherwise, due to political tension over the divided island, you will have difficulty trying to get into Greece.

VOLUNTEERING

To gain more insight into a culture, consider breaking up a train-hopping tour with a short-term volunteer stint. Volunteer positions range from being a farm hand to teaching English and can vary from a one-week to a year-long commitment.

Adriatic Dolphin Project (www.blue-world.org) A Croatia-based programme that unites paying volunteers to work with researchers on a two-week expedition. Volunteers assist scientists by counting dolphins, recording data and even working in the mess hall.

British Trust for Conservation Volunteers (www .btcv.org) BTCV's activities range from monitoring wolf populations in Slovakia to building roads in Iceland. Volunteers pay from UK£300 to UK£700, which covers air fares, food and lodging.

Global Volunteers (www.globalvolunteers.org) Has one- to three-week volunteer programmes, including English-teaching positions, in Poland, Hungary, Italy, Ukraine and Greece; programme fees range from $1500 to $2000 for placement and lodging.

Idealist.org (www.idealist.org) This database lists nonprofit, nongovernmental organisations throughout Europe that are looking for volunteers with specific skills.

WWOOF International (www.wwoof.org) Helps link volunteers with organic farms in Germany, Slovenia, Czech Republic, Denmark, the UK, Austria and Switzerland. A small membership fee is required to join the national chapter and begin receiving newsletters about farms looking for additional hands. In exchange for your labour, you receive food and lodging.

WOMEN TRAVELLERS

Women possibly will attract unwanted notice in rural Spain and southern Italy, especially Sicily, where many men view whistling and cat-calling as flattery. Conservative dress can help to deter lascivious gazes and wolf-whistles, dark sunglasses help avoid unwanted eye contact. Marriage is highly respected in southern Europe, and a wedding ring (on the left ring finger) can help, along with talk about 'my husband'. Women travelling with male friends or boyfriends may find that hotel operators in southern Europe would prefer to hear that the couple is married. Hitchhiking alone in southern Europe is not recommended.

Female readers have reported assaults at Turkish hotels with shared bathrooms; women travelling to Turkey should consider opting for a more expensive room with a private bathroom to avoid vulnerability.

Journeywoman (www.journeywoman.com) maintains an online newsletter about solo female travels all over the world.

WORKING

Working in Europe is not always straightforward. Officially, an EU citizen is allowed to work in any other EU country, but the paperwork is sometimes quite complicated for long-term employment. Other country/nationality combinations require special work permits that can be almost impossible to arrange, especially for temporary work.

However, that doesn't prevent enterprising travellers from topping up their funds occasionally by working in the hotel or restaurant trades at beach or ski resorts or teaching a little English – and they don't always have to do this illegally.

The UK, for example, issues special 'working holiday' visas to Commonwealth citizens who are aged between 17 and 30, valid for two years. Your national student exchange organisation might be able to arrange temporary work permits to several countries through special programmes.

If you have a grandparent or parent who was born in an EU country, you may have certain rights of residency or citizenship. Get in touch with that country's embassy and ask about dual citizenship and work permits (if you go for citizenship, also ask about any obligations, such as military service and residency). Be aware that your home country may not recognise dual citizenship.

If you do find a temporary job, the pay might be less than that offered to locals. Typical tourist jobs (picking grapes in France, washing dishes in Alpine resorts, working at a bar in Greece) often come with board and lodging, and the pay is little more than pocket money, but you'll have a good time partying with other travellers. Visit **Resort Jobs.com** (www.resortjobs.com) for leads.

Teaching English is sometimes a viable option, although most schools prefer a bachelor's degree and a TEFL-type certificate. It is easier to find English-teaching jobs in Eastern Europe than in Western or Central Europe. **Dave's ESL Café** (www.eslcafé.com) is a good first stop for an overseas position. The site contains job postings from schools in Turkey, Poland and Slovakia.

Work Your Way Around the World, by Susan Griffith, gives practical advice primarily to UK residents on being a hobo worker. Its publisher, Vacation Work, has many other useful titles, including *Summer Jobs Abroad,* edited by David Woodworth. *Working Holidays,* published by the Central Bureau for Educational Visits & Exchanges in London, is another good source.

If you play an instrument or have other artistic talents, you could try busking. As every Peruvian pipe player knows, busking is fairly common in major European cities such as Amsterdam and Paris. However, it's illegal in some parts of Switzerland and Austria; in Belgium and Germany, where it has been more or less tolerated in the past, crackdowns are not unknown. Most other countries require municipal permits that can be hard to obtain. Talk to other buskers first.

Selling goods on the street is generally frowned upon and can be tantamount to vagrancy, apart from at flea markets. It's also a hard way to make money if you're not selling something special. Most countries require permits for this sort of thing. It's fairly common, though officially illegal, in the UK, Germany and Spain.

Transport

GETTING THERE & AWAY

Planes, trains and automobiles, the mode of transport that dominates in bringing intercontinental travellers to Europe is inevitably the one with wings.

A few hardy souls do still arrive overland from Asia and the Middle East, while some adventurers drive north across Africa before taking a ferry. Yet even with these rarer alternatives, there tend to be certain well-trodden 'gateways' through which you enter Europe.

AIR

If travelling from another continent, your air ticket to Europe will be your single biggest expense. To save money, it's best to book off-season, that's to say outside of mid-June to early September, Easter and Christmas.

Regardless of your ultimate destination, it's best to pick a recognised transport 'hub' as your initial port of entry, where high traffic volumes help keep prices down. The busiest, and therefore most obvious, airports are London Heathrow and Frankfurt; Barcelona, Paris and Shannon (Ireland) are other consistently cheaper destinations. Sometimes tickets to Amsterdam, Athens, Rome and Vienna are worth investigating, but

long-haul airfares to Eastern Europe are rarely a bargain.

Most of the above gateway cities are also well serviced by low-cost carriers that fly to other parts of Continental Europe. London gives the most obvious choice; see p1247.

Most airlines no longer ask you to reconfirm onward or return bookings 72 hours before departure on international flights. If yours does, do.

Tickets

STUDENT & YOUTH FARES

Full-time students and people aged under 26 have access to better deals than other travellers. This might not mean cheaper fares but could offer greater flexibility to change flights or routes or both. You have to show written proof of your date of birth or a valid International Student Identity Card (ISIC) when buying your ticket and boarding the plane. It's not unknown for nonstudents to get fake student cards, but if you get caught using a falsified card you could have your ticket confiscated and face other penalties.

ROUND-THE-WORLD TICKETS

RTW tickets can work out to be as cheap as, or even cheaper than, an ordinary return ticket. Official RTW tickets are usually put together by a combination of two or more partner airlines and permit you to fly anywhere you want on their route systems as long as you don't backtrack.

Two airline alliances dominate the global market: **Oneworld** (www.oneworld.com) and the **Star Alliance** (www.staralliance.com).

Oneworld members Aer Lingus, American Airlines, British Airways, Cathay Pacific, Finnair, Iberia, LAN Chile and Qantas can piece together a journey using any of their partners' routes.

The same goes for the Star Alliance, which groups Air Canada, Air New Zealand, Asiana Airlines, Austrian Airlines, BMI (British Midland), LOT (Polish Airlines), Lufthansa, SAS (Scandinavian Airlines), Singapore Airlines, Spanair, Thai, United Airlines and US Airways.

While you cannot backtrack on your route with a RTW ticket, there are other restrictions, too. You must (usually) book the first sector in advance and cancellation penalties apply. There may be restrictions on how many stops (or kilometres) you are permitted. Many RTW routes originate in the USA, stop in London and continue on to Southeast Asian destinations.

An alternative type of RTW ticket is one put together by a travel agent using a combination of discounted tickets. These can be much cheaper than the official ones, but usually carry a lot of restrictions.

Independent travellers' forum **BootsnAll** (www.bootsnall.com) publishes a regular newsletter of current RTW offers and goes through the pros and cons of buying a RTW ticket.

OPEN-JAW TICKETS

So-called 'open-jaw' returns, where you land in one city and exit from another, are worth considering if you're pressed for time, but open-jaws can at times work out to be more costly than simple returns. Most travel agents will sell multicity flights, but before paying up compare the extra charge of the third city to the overland price of returning to your original destination. Open-jaws are especially convenient if you plan on traipsing across the Continent, say from London to Istanbul.

COURIER FLIGHTS

Most courier flights have been discontinued because of heightened airline security after 11 September 2001. They've never been brilliant for anything but a short trip. Couriers can't check in a suitcase – important documents for hand delivery and carry-on baggage are all that's allowed – and ticket restrictions often mean they must be home in two weeks.

From Africa & Asia

Nairobi in Kenya and Johannesburg in South Africa, are probably the best places in Africa to buy tickets to Europe, thanks to myriad discount shops and lively competition. **Africa Travel Centre** (☎ 021-423 4530; www .backpackers.co.za) in Cape Town is worth trying for cheap tickets. **STA Travel** (☎ 051-444 6062; www.statravel.co.za) is a reliable option.

Several West African countries, for example, Senegal and The Gambia, offer cheap charter flights to France and Britain. Charter fares to Morocco can be quite cheap if you're lucky enough to find a seat.

Singapore and Bangkok are the discount-airfare capitals of Asia. Shop around and ask the advice of other travellers before handing over any money to ground-level travel agents. **STA Travel** (www.sta.com) has branches in cities as far-flung as Hong Kong, Tokyo, Singapore, Bangkok, Manila, Jakarta and Kuala Lumpur.

In India, tickets may be even cheaper from the discount shops around Delhi's Connaught Place. Check with other travellers about their current trustworthiness.

From Australia & New Zealand

Some travellers might be completing RTW trips and choose to fly via the USA. However, the cheapest flights from Australia and New Zealand to Europe generally go through Southeast Asian or Middle Eastern capitals, involving stopovers in Kuala Lumpur, Bangkok, Singapore or Dubai. Large Italian- and Greek-Australian communities culminate in efficient services to Rome and Athens, as an alternative to London and Frankfurt.

Airlines such as Thai, Malaysian, Qantas, Singapore Airlines and Emirates all have frequent promotional fares, so it pays to check daily newspapers. Some travel agencies, particularly smaller ones, also advertise, so check the travel sections of weekend newspapers, such as the *Age* in Melbourne and the *Sydney Morning Herald*.

Flights from Perth are often a couple of hundred dollars cheaper than those originating in other Australian cities.

In Australia, the best-known agencies for cheap fares are **STA Travel** (☎ 1300 733 035; www.statravel.com.au) and **Flight Centre** (☎ 133 133; www.flightcentre.com.au). Both have dozens of offices throughout the country.

These two operators are also the most popular in New Zealand. For info there, contact **STA Travel** (☎ 0508-782 872; www.statravel .co.nz) or **Flight Centre** (☎ 800 243 544; www.flight centre.co.nz).

From the USA & Canada

If you're flexible with your flight dates, contact discount travel agencies (known as consolidators) that serve as clearing houses for unsold seats on flights departing from major cities, including San Francisco, Los Angeles, New York, Montreal and Toronto. If you're adaptable with your destination city, scan major newspapers, such as the *New York Times*, *LA Times*, *Chicago Tribune*, *San Francisco Chronicle*, *Boston Globe*, *Globe & Mail*, *Toronto Star*, *Montreal Gazette* and *Vancouver Sun*, for seasonal sales. Several websites, including www.travelzoo.com, www.smarter living.com and www.johnnyjet.com, post sales fares for large and small airlines.

STA Travel (☎ 800 781 4040; www.sta.com) specialises in youth and student fares and has offices in major cities in the USA. **Travel CUTS** (☎ 866-246 9762; www.travelcuts.com) is Canada's national student travel agency and has offices in all major cities.

New York–based **Airhitch** (☎ 212-864 2000; www.airhitch.org) sells stand-by tickets from US cities and Montreal to several European cities. Travel dates are not set but are based on availability of open seats. To reduce the time you spend waiting at the airport on stand-by, try to avoid travel during seasonal spikes, such as popular international events (the World Cup, Olympic Games etc).

Courier agencies that now offer consolidated tickets include **International Association of Air Travel Couriers** (IAATC; ☎ 308-632 3273; www.courier.org; PO Box 847, Scottsbluff, NE 69363, USA) and **Now Voyager Travel** (☎ 212-459 1616; www .nowvoyagertravel.com; 45 W 21st St, Suite 5A, New York, NY 10010, USA).

Icelandair (☎ 800 223 5500; www.icelandair.com) flies from some North American cities via Reykjavík to several Scandinavian and Western European cities. All of its transatlantic flights stop over in Reykjavík – a great excuse to spend a few days in Iceland.

For those planning on flying within Scandinavian and Baltic Europe, **Scandinavian Airlines** (☎ 800 221 2350; www.scandinavian.net) has regional air passes available to passengers who fly on their transatlantic flights.

LAND

For details covering travel from Britain to continental Europe see pp1248-9 in Getting Around as well as the individual country chapters.

From Africa & Asia

Getting to Europe from Africa probably will involve a Mediterranean ferry crossing (see Sea on p1250) The only feasible overland route to Europe is via Egypt, Jordon, Syria and on to Turkey. Most overland routes through Africa have all but closed down.

It is possible to get to Western Europe by rail from Central and Eastern Asia, though count on spending at least eight days doing it. You can choose from these different routes to Moscow:

The Trans-Siberian (9297km from Vladivostok)
The Trans-Mongolian (7860km from Beijing)
The Trans-Manchurian (9001km from Beijing)

Lonely Planet's *Trans-Siberian Railway* is a comprehensive guide to the route with details of costs, travel agencies who specialise in the trip and highlights. There are countless travel options onwards between Moscow and the rest of Europe. Most people will opt for the train, usually to/from Berlin, Helsinki, Munich, Budapest or Vienna.

The situation in Iraq means only the most seasoned traveller (some would say foolhardy), with an ear for news on places he/she is going to would want to cross this way between East/South Asia and Europe; but it is possible to travel from Pakistan, through Iran and on to Turkey. However, travel from Central Asia, especially the former Soviet republics, remains feasible. For details on this route (think plenty of paperwork and mounds of dust), see Lonely Planet's *Central Asia*.

SEA

There are numerous ferry routes between Europe and Africa. For details on services within Europe, including the English Channel and the Baltic and North Seas, see (p1250), as well as the individual country chapters.

Mediterranean Ferries

Ferries ply routes between Africa and Europe, including from Spain to Morocco, Italy to Tunisia, France to Morocco and France to Tunisia. There are also ferries between Greece and Israel via Cyprus. Ferries are often filled to capacity in summer, especially to and from Tunisia, so book well in advance if you're taking a vehicle across. See the relevant country chapters for details.

Passenger Ships & Freighters

Regular long-distance passenger ships disappeared with the advent of cheap air travel and were replaced by a small number of luxury cruise ships. Even passenger freighters (typically carrying up to 12 passengers) aren't nearly as competitively priced as airlines. The journey also takes time; however, if you've got your heart set on a transatlantic or trans-pacific journey, **Travltips Cruise & Freighter** (www.travltips.com) has a downloadable freighter directory.

GETTING AROUND

Travel within the EU, whether by air, rail or car, was made easier by the Schengen Agreement, which abolished border controls between most member states (see below).

In most European countries, the train is the best option for internal transport. Check the websites of national rail systems as they often offer fare specials and national passes that are significantly cheaper than point-to-point tickets.

AIR
Air Passes

Various travel agencies and airlines offer air passes for non-European citizens. Check with your travel agent for current promotions. The **Europebyair FlightPass** (www.europebyair.com) costs US$100 per flight for hundreds of European cities. The most economic routes would be long hops from one region of Europe to another, such as St Petersburg to London, rather than shorter routes serviced by low-cost carriers (see later).

British Midlands (☎ 800 788 0555; www.flybmi.com) offers a Discover Europe Pass available to US residents for flights within its network for US$109 to US$159.

Scandinavian Airline's **Visit Scandinavia/Europe Air Pass** (☎ 08-797 0000; www.scandinavian.net; Frösundaviks Allé 1, 195 87 Stockholm) connects visitors to Scandinavian cities for US$75 to US$80 per flight.

Charter Flights

Charter flights, arranged by tour operators, typically fly from Britain to holiday destinations in Europe, Asia and the USA. Tour organisers typically sell spare seats to fill out the flight at discounts that can work out as a cheaper alternative to scheduled flights, especially if you are aged over 26 and not a student. Travel agencies to contact include **Bridge the World** (☎ 0870 444 7474; www.bridgetheworld.com; 4 Regent Pl, London W1R 5FB); and **ebookers** (☎ 0870 010 7000; www.ebookers.com; 177-178 Tottenham Court Rd, London W1P 9LF).

Low-cost Airlines

Low-cost carriers have revolutionised European transport in recent years. Indeed, with some hour-long flights offered in the UK

BORDER CROSSINGS

Border formalities have been relaxed in most of the EU, but still exist in all their bureaucratic former glory in parts of Eastern Europe.

In line with the Schengen Agreement, there are no passport controls at the borders between Austria, Belgium, Denmark, Finland, France, Germany, Greece, Iceland, Italy, Luxembourg, the Netherlands, Norway, Portugal, Spain and Sweden; an identity card for EU members should suffice, but it's always safest to carry your passport. The other western EU countries (Britain and Ireland) are not members of Schengen and still maintain low-key border controls over traffic from other EU countries. Travellers should also have few border hassles crossing from EU countries into the Czech Republic, Estonia, Hungary, Latvia, Lithuania, Poland, Slovakia and Slovenia, all of which are now also in the EU.

Most borders in Eastern Europe will be crossed via train where border guards board the train and go through the compartments checking passengers' papers. It is rare to get hit up for bribes, but Belarus still seems to be clinging to the habit. Travelling between Turkey and Bulgaria typically requires a change of trains and is subject to a lengthy border procedure. For information on visas, see p1242 .

for as little as £30, £5 or even £1 (and €30, €5 and €2 fares in Ireland), plus taxes, it has reached the point where even the most avid fliers have to admit it's not sustainable, either financially or environmentally. Some low-cost carriers – Ryanair being the perfect example – have made a habit of flying to smaller, less convenient airports on the outskirts of their destination city, and the EU competition authorities have objected to various issues surrounding this.

All this means change is probably in the offing. While the following details were correct at the time of going to press, both routes and prices might have altered. It's recommended you check on the individual websites. Sample fares were based on bookings made on a high-season (summer) weekday, two weeks before the flight was due to leave. Fares will be cheaper during low season, during special offers and if you book sooner. Shop around; you might find the picture is totally different at the time you come to book. Indeed, a couple of carriers plan to introduce charges for checked-in luggage, which might make them a less attractive proposition for backpackers.

Departure tax is included in the final price of your ticket – by the end of the online booking process – but it's usually excluded from the price flashed on the website's front page. Departing from London, you'll pay about £16 extra, from many other European airports it's €15 (£10).

The highest-profile low-cost carriers are Ryanair, easyJet, Air Berlin and SkyEurope. You can find details at **LowCostAirlinesEurope. org** (www.discountairfares.com/lcosteur.htm). **BMIBaby** (www.bmibaby.com) and **MyTravelLite** (www.mytrav-ellite.com) offer good services from UK regional airports.

Ryanair (www.ryanair.com) is an Irish carrier, with major hubs at Dublin and, above all, London Stansted. Most of its flights are routed over the Irish Sea or the English Channel. However, recently it began adding Continental routes. Direct journeys are now possible from Stockholm to Paris, Frankfurt, Milan and Rome, from Oslo to Frankfurt and from Hamburg-Lübeck (the airport is actually an hour away from Hamburg in Lübeck) to Milan and Pisa.

Included among its 84 destinations, Ryanair counts many provincial airports; some are so remote that even extensively travelled

customers joke they have to look them up on a map! Even when flying to larger cities, Ryanair sometimes uses smaller, outlying airports, so study the information on the website carefully.

Some sample fares, without taxes:
London-Berlin £25-100
London-Carcassonne £20-130
London-Mälmo Sturrup (southern Sweden) £50-90
London-Rome £15-70
London-Salzburg £30-40
London-Tours £6-25

Award-winning **easyJet** (www.easyjet.com), run by a UK-based, Greek-born scion of a millionaire shipping family, started flights across the Continent, instead of just across the English Channel, quite early on. You can fly from Amsterdam, Athens, Barcelona and Geneva to other European destinations. The company also has car rental and Internet cafés.

Some sample fares, without taxes:
Amsterdam-Barcelona €95-125
Athens-Berlin €66-82
London-Amsterdam £17-32
London-Barcelona £32-67
London-Geneva £32-67
London-Prague £32-67

As its name suggests, **Air Berlin** (www.airberlin .com) is a German operation, run mainly out of the national capital. It caters principally to German holidaymakers heading for Spain, Italy or Greece, but it does have 'city shuttle' flights to capitals such as London, Vienna, Warsaw and similar places. Booking just two weeks ahead, Air Berlin looks to be more expensive than other low-cost carriers. To get good prices with this airline – and with fares starting at €29 it really does have some – you need to plan about two months ahead. Air Berlin sometimes flies to subsidiary airports.

Some sample fares, this time including taxes:
Berlin-London €50-130
Berlin-Rome €80-120
Berlin-Seville €190-240
Berlin-Vienna €40-50
Berlin-Warsaw €80-100
Hamburg-Iraklio (Greece) €150-200

The newest of the large low-cost carriers, **SkyEurope** (www.skyeurope.com) is interesting for some of the unusual destinations it serves, including Bratislava, Dubrovnik, Split and Zadar. Its fleet is new and based at Budapest's Ferihegy 1 airport. While it advertises airfares from only €25 (£17), you'll find the entry price to be more like €70 if you're booking two weeks in advance. Be warned that the 'Vienna (Bratislava)' airport is pretty far, and across the Slovakian border, from Vienna.

Some sample fares, excluding taxes:

Budapest-Amsterdam €70-100
Budapest-Dubrovnik €100-180
Budapest-Rome €70-100
London-Budapest £50-70
London-Warsaw £35-50
Venice-Bratislava €70-120

National Airlines

In the face of competition from low-cost airlines, many national carriers have decided to drop their prices and/or offer special deals. Some, such as British Airways, have even adopted the low-cost model of online booking, where the customer can opt to buy just a one-way flight, or can piece together their own return journey from two one-way legs.

For details of national airlines, see individual country chapters.

BICYCLE

France is the most frequently cycled country in Europe thanks to its network of minor highways and roads. Germany, Italy, Portugal, Ireland and Norway are other strong contenders. A primary consideration on a cycling tour is to travel light, but you should take a few tools and spare parts, including a puncture-repair kit and an extra inner tube. Panniers are essential to balance your possessions on either side of the bike frame. A bike helmet is also a very good idea. Take a good lock and *always* use it when you leave your bike unattended.

Michelin maps indicate scenic routes, which can help you plan good cycling itineraries. Seasoned cyclists can average 80km a day, but there's no point in overdoing it. The slower you travel, the more locals you are likely to meet.

If you get tired of pedalling or simply want to skip a boring section, you can put your feet up on the train. On slower trains, bikes can usually be transported as luggage, subject to a small supplementary fee. Some cyclists have reported that Italian and French train attendants have refused bikes on slow trains, so be prepared that regulations may be interpreted differently by indifferent civil servants. Fast trains can rarely accommodate bikes; they might need to be sent as registered luggage and may end up on a different train from the one you take. This is often the case in France and Spain. Eurostar (the train service through the Channel Tunnel) charges £20 to send a bike as registered luggage on its routes. You can also transport your bicycle with you on Eurotunnel through the Channel Tunnel. With a bit of tinkering and dismantling (eg removing wheels), you might be able to get your bike into a bag or sack and take it on a train as hand luggage.

The **European Bike Express** (☎ 01642-308 800; www.bike-express.co.uk) is a coach service based in the UK where cyclists can travel with their bicycles to various cycling destinations on the Continent. It runs in the summer from northeastern England to France, Italy and Spain, with pick-up/drop-off points en route.

The **Cyclists' Touring Club** (CTC; ☎ 0870 873 0060; www.ctc.org.uk; Cotterell House, 69 Meadrow, Godalming, Surrey GU7 3HS) provides resources for cycling conditions in Europe as well as detailed routes, itineraries and maps to members. Membership includes specialised insurance and costs £30/18.75/11 annually for adults aged 26 and over/seniors/under 26s.

Rental & Purchase

It is easy to hire bikes throughout most of Europe on an hourly, half-day, daily or weekly basis. Many train stations have bike-rental counters. Long-term rentals are easier to arrange in Ireland than in other countries. See the country chapters for more details. It is sometimes possible to return the bike at a different outlet so you don't have to retrace your route.

There are plenty of places to buy bikes in Europe (shops sell new and second-hand bicycles, or you can check local papers for private vendors), but you'll need a specialist bicycle shop for a bike capable of withstanding a European tour. CTC can provide a leaflet on purchasing. Cycling is very popular in the Netherlands and Germany, and those countries are good places to pick up a well-equipped touring bicycle. European prices

TRANSPORT

are quite high (certainly higher than in North America), however non-Europeans should be able to claim back VAT on the purchase.

Transporting a Bicycle

For major cycling tours, it's best to have a bike you're familiar with, so consider bringing your own rather than buying on arrival. Ask about the airline's bike policy before purchasing your ticket. Most airlines require you to package your bike in a box so that it can be considered checked luggage. Because bike boxes won't fit in X-ray machines, you'll be required to open the box for hand inspection. Airlines have varying requirements for how much of your bike should be dismantled, so contact the customer service office for details. If your bicycle and other luggage exceed your weight allowance, ask about alternatives or you may suddenly find yourself being charged for excess baggage. Some airlines also levy a surcharge on bicycles.

Be aware that most bike tools will not be allowed in carry-on luggage. It is probably wise to pack these separately from your bicycle to discourage theft.

BOAT

Several different ferry companies compete on the main ferry routes, resulting in a comprehensive but complicated service. The same ferry company can have a host of different prices for the same route, depending on the time of day or year, validity of the ticket, and length of your vehicle. Vehicle tickets include the driver and often up to five passengers free of charge. It's worth planning (and booking) ahead where possible as there may be special reductions on off-peak crossings and advance-purchase tickets. On English Channel routes, apart from one-day or short-term excursion returns, there is little price advantage in buying a return ticket versus two singles.

Rail-pass holders are entitled to discounts or free travel on some lines, and most ferry companies give discounts to disabled drivers. Food on ferries is often expensive (and lousy), so it is worth bringing your own. Also be aware that if you take your vehicle on board, you are usually denied access to it during the voyage.

P&O Ferries (www.poferries.com) is one of the world's main ferry companies, serving Britain, Ireland, Scandinavia, the Netherlands, Poland and Spain. Ferries sail from England to France (Dover–Calais, Portsmouth–Le Havre), to the Netherlands (Hull–Rotterdam), to Belgium (Hull–Zeebrugge) and to Ireland (Liverpool–Dublin), among many other routes.

Although there is now great competition from the Channel Tunnel, **Hoverspeed** (www.hoverspeed.co.uk) operates high-speed services from Dover–Calais and Newhaven–Dieppe. **Brittany Ferries** (www.brittany-ferries.co.uk) operates services from England to France or Spain.

You can also go by ferry from Ireland to France.

Blue Star Ferries (www.bluestarferries.com) and **Hellenic Mediterranean** (www.hml.gr) travel from Italy (Ancona, Brindisi or Bari) to Greece (Corfu, Igoumenitsa and Patras). The Greek islands are connected to the mainland and each other by a spider web of routes; see p526 for more information.

Northern Germany port towns are connected by ferry to the UK and Scandinavia. Regularly scheduled services include a 2½-hour crossing from Kiel to Bagenkop (on the Danish island of Langeland), to Gothenburg in Sweden (14 hours) and all the way to Oslo (19½ hours). Start with **Stena Line** (www.stenaline.de) and **Color Line** (☎ 730 00; www.colorline.com) or look in the individual country chapter for further details.

There are also ferries going to Denmark, Sweden and/or Finland from the eastern German ports of Travemünde and Sassnitz on Rügen Island.

Lake services operate in many countries, Austria and Switzerland being just two. For more details, see the individual country chapters.

BUS
International Buses

International bus travel tends to take third place to train travel, and now low-cost air travel, in Europe. Buses are often cheaper than trains, sometimes substantially so, but also generally slower and less comfortable. While they are generally more expensive and take much longer than low-cost airlines (a double whammy), they do cover many routes low-cost airlines don't. In Portugal, Greece, parts of Spain and Turkey, buses are a better option than trains.

Europe's biggest organisation of international buses operates under the name **Eurolines** (www.eurolines.com). The various national companies that create this group can be accessed through their website, and more details are given in individual country chapters.

The group's network covers cities as far afield as Edinburgh, Stockholm, Rīga, Bucharest, Rome and Madrid. A Eurolines Pass is offered for extensive travel, allowing passengers to visit 35 cities over 15/30/60 days. In the high season, the pass costs €240/345/380 for those aged under 26, or €285/425/490 for those 26 and over. The Eurolines Pass is cheaper from mid-September to the end of March, when the youth option costs €185/250/310, and the adult pass €220/310/390. See p150 for discount round-trips from London.

On ordinary one-way trips, sample fares and times, including stopovers, include the following:

Amsterdam-Barcelona €97/107 under 26/26 & over, 25¼ hours

Basel-Zagreb Sfr99/110 under 26/26 & over, 15½ hours

Berlin–St Petersburg €80/87 under 26/26 & over, 36 hours

Hamburg-Warsaw €44/48 under 26/26 & over, 15 hours

London-Rome £82/89 under 26/26 & over, 32 hours

Paris-Madrid €72/79 under 26/26 & over, 19 hours

Another popular option is **Busabout** (☎ 020-7950 1661; www.busabout.com; 258 Vauxhall Bridge Rd, Victoria, London SW1V 1BS), whose buses do complete circuits around Europe, stopping at major cities. You get unlimited travel per sector and can 'hop off' at any scheduled stop, then 'hop on' a later bus. Buses are often oversubscribed, so book each sector to avoid being stranded. It departs every two days from April to the end of October (May to September for Spain and Portugal). The circuits cover all countries in continental Western Europe, and you pay extra to add on Greece, Scandinavia or a London–Paris link.

Busabout's Unlimited Pass allows unlimited travel within a given time period (two-week increments up to two months) for £219 to £619 for those under 26, and from £269 to £699 for those 26 and over. The Flexipass allows you to select a number of travel days and destination cities. You can travel for eight to 20 days, for £249 to £519 if you're under 26, or £279 to £579 if you're 26 and over.

Busabout is a great deal for teachers, nurses and students who are all entitled to the lower fare with the relevant ID.

National Buses

Domestic buses provide a viable alternative to trains in most countries. Again, they are usually slightly cheaper and somewhat slower. Buses are generally best for shorter hops such as getting around cities and reaching remote villages. They are often the only option in mountainous regions. Reservations are rarely necessary. On many city buses you usually buy your ticket in advance from a kiosk or machine and validate it on entering the bus. See the individual country chapters for more details on local buses.

CAR & MOTORCYCLE

Travelling with your own vehicle gives flexibility and is the best way to reach remote places. However, the independence does isolate you from the local people. Also, cars can be a target for theft and are often impractical in city centres, where it's worth ditching your vehicle and using public transport. Various car-carrying trains can help you avoid long, tiring drives.

Eurotunnel (in Britain ☎ 08705 353535; www.eurotunnel.com) transports motor vehicles and bicycles between Folkestone in England and Coquelles in France (near Calais) through the Channel Tunnel. Services run up to every 15 minutes (up to two-hourly from midnight to 6am). Normal fares are more advantageous for those going on day trips than for travellers on long jaunts, although you should keep an eye out for special deals. While a day return for a car and passengers normally costs £40 to £100, a one-way ticket costs £160. An open-ended return costs £295. The company takes a very dim view of passengers buying a day return and only using the outgoing leg, and has legal remedies open to it in such instances.

Camper Van

One popular way to tour Europe is for a group of three or four people to band together and buy or rent a camper van. London is the usual embarkation point. Look at the advertisements in London's free magazine **TNT** (www.tntmagazine.com) if you wish to form or join a group. *TNT* is also a good source for purchasing a van, as is the **Loot** (www.loot.com) newspaper.

Some second-hand dealers offer a 'buy-back' scheme for when you return from the Continent, but we've received warnings that some dealers don't fully honour their refund commitments. Anyway, buying and reselling privately should be more advantageous if you have the time. In the UK, **Downunder Insurance** (☎ 020-7402 9211; www.downunder insurance.co.uk) offers a Camper Van policy.

Camper vans usually feature a fixed hightop or elevating roof and two to five bunk beds. Apart from the essential camping gas cooker, you may get a sink, fridge and built-in cupboards. Prices vary considerably, and it's worth getting advice from a mechanic to determine whether you're being offered a fair price. Once on the road you should be able to keep budgets lower than backpackers using trains, but don't forget to set money aside for emergency repairs.

The main advantage of going by camper van is flexibility; with transport, eating and sleeping requirements all taken care of in one unit, you are tied to nobody's timetable but your own. It's also easier to set up at night than if you rely on a car and tent.

A disadvantage of camper vans is that you are in a confined space for much of the time. Four adults in a small van can soon get on each other's nerves, particularly if the group has been formed at short notice. You might also miss out on experiences in the world outside your van. Other negatives are that vans are not very manoeuvrable around town, and you'll often have to leave your gear unattended inside (many people bolt extra locks onto the van). They're also expensive to buy in spring and hard to sell in autumn.

Fuel

Fuel prices can vary enormously (though it's always more expensive than in North America or Australia). Refuelling in Luxembourg or Andorra is about 30% cheaper than in neighbouring countries. The Netherlands, France and Italy have Europe's most expensive petrol; Gibraltar and Andorra are by far the cheapest in Western Europe. Greece, Spain and Switzerland are also reasonably cheap.

Petrol is unleaded-only through much of Europe, although not in Romania, Albania, Slovakia, or Serbia and Montenegro. Diesel is usually significantly cheaper, though the difference is marginal in Britain, Ireland and Switzerland.

For up-to-date prices across Europe, see www.theaa.com/allaboutcars/fuel.

Leasing

Leasing a vehicle involves fewer hassles than purchasing and can work out considerably cheaper than hiring for longer than 17 days. This programme is limited to certain types of new cars, including Renault and Peugeot, but you save money because leasing is exempt from VAT, and inclusive insurance plans are cheaper than daily insurance rates. Leasing is also open to people as young as 18 years old. Your permanent address must be outside the EU. In the USA, contact **Renault Eurodrive** (☎ 800 221 1052; www .renaultusa.com) or **AutoEurope** (☎ 888-223 5555; www.autoeurope.com) for more information.

Motorcycle Touring

Europe is made for motorcycle touring, with quality winding roads, stunning scenery, and an active motorcycling scene. Just ensure your wet-weather gear is up to scratch.

Rider and passenger crash helmets are compulsory everywhere in Europe. Austria, Belgium, France, Germany, Luxembourg, Portugal and Spain also require that motorcyclists use headlights during the day; in other countries it is recommended.

On ferries, motorcyclists rarely have to book ahead as they can generally be squeezed in. Take note of the local custom about parking motorcycles on pavements (sidewalks). Though this is illegal in some countries, the police often turn a blind eye provided the vehicle doesn't obstruct pedestrians. Don't try this in Britain, however.

Preparations

Always carry proof of ownership of your vehicle (Vehicle Registration Document for British-registered cars) when touring Europe. An EU driving licence is acceptable for those driving throughout Europe. If you have any other type of licence, you should obtain an International Driving Permit (IDP) from your motoring organisation (see p1235). Check what type of licence is required in your destination prior to departure.

Third-party motor insurance is compulsory. Most UK policies automatically provide this for EU countries. Get your insurer to issue a Green Card (which may cost extra), an internationally recognised proof of insurance, and check that it lists all the countries you intend to visit. You'll need this in the event of an accident outside the country where the vehicle is insured. Also ask your insurer for a European Accident Statement form, which can simplify things if worst comes to worst. Never sign statements that you can't read or understand – insist on a translation and sign that only if it's acceptable. For non-EU countries, check the requirements with your insurer. Travellers from the UK can obtain additional advice and information from the **Association of British Insurers** (☎ 020-7600 3333; www.abi.org.uk).

Taking out a European motoring assistance policy – such as AA Five Star Service or RAC Eurocover Motoring Assistance – is a good investment. Expect to pay about £50 for 14 days' coverage, with a 10% discount for association members. Non-Europeans might find it cheaper to arrange international coverage with their national motoring organisation before leaving home. Ask your motoring organisation for details about the free services offered by affiliated organisations around Europe.

Every vehicle that travels across an international border should display a sticker indicating its country of registration. A warning triangle, to be used in the event of breakdown, is compulsory almost everywhere. Some recommended accessories include a first-aid kit (compulsory in Austria, Slovenia, Croatia, Serbia and Montenegro, and Greece), a spare bulb kit (compulsory in Spain), and a fire extinguisher (compulsory in Greece and Turkey). Bail bonds are no longer required for Spain. Residents in the UK should contact the **RAC** (☎ 0800 550 055; www.rac.co.uk) or the **AA** (☎ 08705-500 600; www.theaa.com) for more information. In the USA, contact **AAA** (www.aaa.com).

Purchase

The purchase of vehicles in some European countries is illegal for non-nationals or non-EU residents. Britain is probably the best place to buy; second-hand prices are good and, whether buying privately or from a dealer, the absence of language difficulties will help you establish exactly what you are getting and what guarantees you can expect if you break down.

However, bear in mind that British cars have steering wheels on the right-hand side. If you wish to have left-hand drive and can afford to buy a new car, prices are generally reasonable in Greece, France, Germany,

Belgium, Luxembourg and the Netherlands. Paperwork can be tricky wherever you buy, and many countries have compulsory roadworthiness checks on older vehicles.

Rental

Renting a car is ideal for people who will need cars for 16 days or less. Anything more, it's better to lease; see opposite. Big international rental firms will give you reliable service and good vehicles. Usually you will have the option of returning the car to a different outlet at the end of the rental period, but inquire about extra charges for noncircular itineraries. Prebook for the lowest rates and compare rates in different cities. Prices in Brussels tend to be cheaper than in Paris. Taxes range from 15% to 20% and surcharges apply if rented from an airport.

One operator worth bearing in mind if you're renting a car in the UK, Spain, Greece or Cyprus is **Easycar** (www.easycar.com), which has rentals from €35 a day in high season in popular summer destinations such as Ibiza and Crete.

Otherwise, check the sites of the following major operators, from which you can make reservations online: **Alamo** (www.alamo.com), **Avis** (www.avis.com), **Budget** (www.budget.com), **Europcar** (www.europcar.com) and **Hertz** (www.hertz.com). Sample fares for an economy car:

Frankfurt €30/150
London £40/140 day/week
Madrid €60/200
Paris €85/300

Please note that if you rent a car outside of the EU, you will only be able to drive within the EU for eight days. Ask at the rental agencies for other EU-specific regulations.

Brokers can sometimes cut costs over quoted rates. In the UK **Holiday Autos** (☎ 0870 400 0099; www.holidayautos.com) has low rates and either offices or representatives in over 20 countries. In the USA call **Kemwel Holiday Autos** (☎ 877 820 0668; www.kemwel.com).

If you want to rent a car and haven't prebooked, look for national or local firms, which can often undercut the big companies by up to 40%. Nevertheless, you need to be wary of dodgy operations that take your money and point you towards some clapped-out wreck, or where the rental agreement is bad news if you have an accident or the car is stolen. Read before you sign.

TRANSPORT

No matter where you rent, make sure you understand what is included in the price (unlimited or paid kilometres, tax, injury insurance, collision damage waiver etc) and what your liabilities are. We recommend taking the collision damage waiver, though you can probably skip the injury insurance if you and your passengers have decent travel insurance. Ask in advance if you can drive a rented car across borders from a country where hire prices are low to another where they're high.

The minimum rental age is usually 21 years or even 25, and you'll probably need a credit card. Motorcycle and moped rental is common in some countries, such as Italy, Spain, Greece and southern France. Sadly, it's also common for inexperienced riders to leap on rented bikes and very quickly fall off them again, leaving a layer or two of skin on the road in the process.

Road Conditions & Road Rules

Conditions and types of roads vary across Europe. The fastest routes are generally four- or six-lane dual carriageways/highways (two or three lanes either side) called 'autoroutes', *autostrade* etc. These tend to skirt cities and plough through the countryside in straight lines, often avoiding the most scenic bits. Some incur tolls, which are often quite hefty (eg in Italy, France and Spain), but there will always be an alternative route. Motorways and other primary routes are generally in good condition.

Road surfaces on minor routes are unreliable in some countries (eg Romania, Ireland, Morocco and Greece), although normally they will be more than adequate. These roads are narrower and progress is generally much slower. However, to compensate this, you can expect much better scenery and plenty of interesting villages along the way.

Except in Britain and Ireland, drive on the right. Vehicles brought to the Continent from either of these locales should have their headlights adjusted to avoid blinding oncoming traffic (a simple solution on older headlight lenses is to cover up a triangular section of the lens with tape). Priority is often given to traffic approaching from the right in countries that drive on the right-hand side.

Speed limits vary from country to country. You may be surprised at the apparent disregard for traffic regulations in some places

(particularly in Italy and Greece), but as a visitor it is always best to be cautious. Many driving infringements are subject to an on-the-spot fine. Always ask for a receipt.

European drink-driving laws are particularly strict. The blood-alcohol concentration (BAC) limit when driving is usually between 0.05% and 0.08%, but in certain areas (such as Gibraltar and some Eastern European countries such as Bulgaria) it can be 0%.

HITCHING

Hitching is never entirely safe in any country in the world, and we cannot recommend it. Travellers who decide to hitch should understand that they are taking a small but potentially serious risk. People who do choose to hitch will be safer if they travel in pairs and let someone know where they plan to go.

Hitching can be the most rewarding and frustrating way of getting around. You get to meet and interact with local people and can have unplanned detours that may yield unexpected highlights off-the-beaten track. But you might get stuck on the side of the road to nowhere with nowhere (or nowhere cheap) to stay. Then it begins to rain.

That said, hitchers can end up making good time, but obviously your plans need to be flexible in case you're invisible to passing motorists. A man and woman travelling together is probably the best combination. Two or more men should expect some delays; two women together will make good time and be relatively safe. A woman hitching on her own is taking a big risk, particularly in parts of southern Europe.

Don't try to hitch from city centres; take public transport to the suburban exit routes. Hitching is usually illegal on motorways (freeways) – stand on the slip roads, or approach drivers at petrol stations and truck stops. Look presentable and cheerful, and make a cardboard sign indicating your intended destination in the local language. Never hitch where drivers can't stop in good time or without causing an obstruction. At dusk, give up and find somewhere to stay. If your itinerary includes a ferry crossing (for instance, across the Channel), it might be worth trying to score a ride before the ferry rather than after, since vehicle tickets sometimes include a number of passengers free of charge. This applies to Eurotunnel via the Channel Tunnel.

It is sometimes possible to arrange a lift in advance. Scan student notice boards in colleges.

If you're considering hitching around Europe, check out www.bugeurope.com and www.hitchhikers.org.

LOCAL TRANSPORT

High-density populations mean European towns and cities have excellent local transport systems, often encompassing trams as well as buses and metro/subway/underground rail networks. Be sure to remove your pack on public transport and hold it in front of you to avoid battering your neighbour and deter pickpockets. Also give up your seat to the elderly, infirm or pregnant women.

Most travellers will find European cities to be easily traversed by foot or bicycle. In Greece and in Italy, travellers sometimes rent mopeds and motorcycles for scooting around a city or island.

TAXI

Taxis in Europe are metered and rates are usually high. There might also be supplements for things such as luggage, time of day, location of pick-up and extra passengers. Good bus, rail and underground-railway networks often render taxis unnecessary, but if you need one in a hurry they can be found idling near train stations or outside big hotels. Lower fares make taxis more viable in some countries, such as Spain, Greece, Portugal and Turkey.

TRAIN

Comfortable, frequent and reliable, trains are *the* way of getting around Europe. Indeed, it's safe to say that Europe has some of the most efficient and comprehensive rail services in the world, particularly in Switzerland, Austria and Germany (but not Britain!). Trains are a great way to meet people, see the countryside, get into the heart of cities and to scribble furiously into that sacred journal.

If you plan to travel extensively by train, it is worth obtaining the *Thomas Cook European Timetable,* giving a complete listing of train schedules and indicating where supplementary fares apply or where reservations are necessary. It is updated monthly and is available from Thomas Cook outlets in the UK or online at www.railpass.com.

If you are planning to travel in just a few countries, look online. Many state railways now have interactive websites publishing their timetables and fares. The *European Planning & Rail Guide* is also an informative annual magazine. To get a copy, contact the US-based **Budget Europe Travel Service** (☎ 800 441 2387; www.budgeteuropetravel.com).

Paris, Milan and Vienna are important hubs for international rail connections. See the relevant city sections for details. Note that European trains sometimes split in route to service two destinations, so even if you're on the right train, make sure you're also in the correct carriage.

A rail journey to almost every station in Europe can be booked via **Rail Europe** (☎ 0870 584 8848; www.raileurope.co.uk; 178 Piccadilly London W1), which also sells Inter-Rail and other passes; see p1257 . Sample single fares:

Amsterdam-Barcelona €220
London-Marseilles £165
Madrid-Milan €210
Paris-Berlin €140
Paris-Lisbon £175
Zurich-Salzburg €75

Express Trains

Europeans are normally avid fliers, but they're less likely to catch a plane between London and Paris or Brussels. That's because those routes are conveniently served by the high-speed passenger rail service **Eurostar** (www.eurostar.com) in Britain (☎ 0870 518 6186, 01233-617575); in France (☎ 08 92 35 35 39); in Belgium (☎ 02 528 28 28).

Eurostar links London's Waterloo station, via the Channel Tunnel, with Paris' Gare du Nord (2¾ hours, up to 25 a day) and Brussels' international terminal (2½ hours, up to 12 a day). Some trains also stop at Lille and Calais in France. The train stations at London Waterloo, Paris and Brussels are all much more central than the cities' airports. So, overall, the journey takes as little time as the equivalent flight, with less hassle.

From London to Paris or Brussels fares start at £59 for a return, to Calais or Lille it's £55. These fares are widely available, but at times you might pay a higher price (up to £119). A return fare is only valid for six months. If you're going for longer you'll need a single ticket, from £40.

Eurostar in London also sells tickets onwards to some Continental destinations,

TRANSPORT

although its list is much less comprehensive than Rail Europe's (see earlier). Sample return fares:

London-Avignon (or anywhere in France zone D) £109
London-Belgium (any station) £59
London-Bordeaux (or anywhere in France zone C) £99
London-Strasbourg (or anywhere in France zone B) £89
London–The Netherlands (any major station) £79
London-Tours (or anywhere in France zone A) £79

Look on the website for French zones. Eurostar passengers aged under 26 are entitled to change their booking once. Holders of Eurail and Inter-Rail passes are offered discounts on some Eurostar services; check when booking.

Within Europe, express trains are identified by the symbols 'EC' (EuroCity) or 'IC' (InterCity). The French TGV, Spanish AVE and German ICE trains are even faster, reaching up to 300km/h. Supplementary fares can apply on fast trains (which you often have to pay when travelling on a rail pass), and it is a good idea (sometimes obligatory) to reserve seats at peak times and on certain lines. The same applies for branded express trains, such as the Thalys (between Paris and Brussels, Bruges, Amsterdam and Cologne), and the Eurostar Italia (between Rome and Naples, Florence, Milan and Venice).

If you don't have a seat reservation, you can still obtain a seat that doesn't have a reservation ticket attached to it. Be sure to check which destination a seat is reserved for – you might be able to use the unused portion.

International Rail Passes

If you're covering lots of ground, you should get a rail pass. But do some price comparisons of point-to-point ticket charges and rail passes to determine that you'll break even. Also shop around for rail-pass prices as they do vary per outlet. When weighing up options, look into cheap ticket deals that include advance-purchase reductions, one-off promotions or special circular-route tickets. Normal point-to-point tickets are valid for two months, and you can make as many stops as you like en route; make your intentions known when purchasing, and inform train conductors how far you're going before they punch your ticket.

Supplementary charges (eg for some express and overnights trains) and seat reservation fees (mandatory on some trains, a good

idea on others) are not covered by rail passes. Always ask. Note that European rail passes also give reductions on Eurostar through the Channel Tunnel and on certain ferries.

Pass-holders must always carry their passport with them for identification purposes. The railways' policy is that passes cannot be replaced or refunded if lost or stolen. However, with some sales outlets (ie www.raileurope.com) you can buy insurance that will reimburse you for any days not used at the point a pass is stolen.

NON-EUROPEAN RESIDENTS
Eurail Passes

Eurail (www.eurail.com) passes are valid for unlimited travel on national railways within 17 countries, namely Austria, Belgium, Denmark, Finland, France (including Monaco), Germany, Greece, Hungary, Ireland, Italy, Luxembourg, the Netherlands, Norway, Portugal, Spain, Sweden and Switzerland (including Liechtenstein). Some private rail lines in the region are also covered. If you plan to travel extensively in Switzerland, be warned that the many private rail networks and cable cars, especially in the Jungfrau region around Interlaken, don't give Eurail discounts. A Swiss Pass or Half-Fare Card (see p1161) might be an alternative or necessary addition.

While the UK is not covered by any Eurail pass (sometimes known as a Eurorail pass), you can use it on some Italy-Greece, Denmark-Sweden, Germany-Sweden and Sweden-Finland ferries. Reductions are given on some other ferry routes and on river/lake steamer services in various countries.

Eurail can be bought only by residents of non-European countries and should be purchased before arriving in Europe.

For those under 26 years old, a continuous Eurail Youth pass will cost US$414/534/664/938/1160 for 15 days/21 days/one month/two months/three months. Holders of youth passes must travel in 2nd-class compartments.

Those aged 26 and over must purchase the full-fare Eurail pass. This costs US$588/762/946/1338/1654 for the periods outlined above. However, this full-fare pass entitles you to travel 1st class.

Many permutations of the pass are available, both in the youth (under 26s) and full-fare 'adult' versions. A Flexipass is valid for either 10 or 15 days of travel within a two-month period (US$488/642 for a youth pass, US$694/914 for a pass for adults). With a Selectpass you nominate three, four or five countries in which you wish to travel, and then buy a pass allowing five, six, eight, 10 or 15 travel days in a two-month period. Prices start at US$250/356 per youth/adult. The five- and six-day passes offer an attractive price break, but as the Selectpass continues up its pricing ladder, the continuous pass becomes better value.

A range of three Eurail Two-Country Passes is also offered, but you might want to ensure that they have good value given your travel plans. The first two offer five- to 10-days' travel within two months, within Germany and Benelux countries (starting at US$199/246 per youth/adult) or Romania and Hungary (starting at US$140/200 per youth/adult). The France and Switzerland pass offers four days in two months (US$209/300 per youth/adult), with an extra day costing US$27/36 per youth/adult.

Two to five people travelling together can get a Saver version of all Eurail passes for a 15% to 25% discount.

The traveller must fill out (in ink) the relevant box in the calendar before starting a day's travel.

European East Pass
The European East Pass provides five days of travel in Austria, Czech Republic, Hungary, Poland and Slovakia for US$226/160 for 1st/2nd class; extra rail days (maximum five) cost US$26/19 each. There are discounts for children but not for persons aged under 26. This pass is sold in North America, Australia and the UK. In the USA you can try purchase the pass with **Rail Europe** (☎ 800 257-2887; www.raileurope.com).

EUROPEAN RESIDENTS
Inter-Rail
Rail Europe (☎ 0870 584 8848; www.raileurope.co.uk; 178 Piccadilly London W1) sells Inter-Rail passes to European residents for unlimited 2nd- and 3rd-class rail travel through 29 European and North African countries (excluding the pass-holder's country of residence). To qualify as a resident in this sense, you must have lived in a European country for six months.

The countries in the Inter-Rail community are split into zones. Zone A is Ireland and the UK; B is Sweden, Norway and Finland; C is Denmark, Germany, Switzerland and Austria; D is the Czech Republic, Slovakia, Poland, Hungary and Croatia; E is France, Belgium, the Netherlands and Luxembourg; F is Spain, Portugal and Morocco; G is Italy, Greece, Turkey, Slovenia and Italy–Greece ferries; and H is Bulgaria, Romania, Serbia and Montenegro, and Macedonia.

Inter-Rail passes for any one zone and 16 days of travel costs £159/223 for under 26s/26 and over, two zones and 22 days of travel costs £215/303 and an all-zone global pass for one month is £295/415.

While an Inter-Rail pass will get you further than a Eurail pass along the private rail networks of Switzerland's Jungfrau region (near Interlaken), its benefits are limited. A Swiss Pass or Half-Fare Card (see p1161) might be a necessary addition if you plan to travel extensively in that region.

Euro Domino
The Euro Domino pass, also offered by Rail Europe, allows European residents unlimited travel in any one of the Inter-Rail countries for three to eight days. Prices vary depending on the country, the number of travel days and the train class. A three-day Euro Domino pass for France will cost £100 for 2nd class for people aged under 26 and £183/138 for 1st/2nd class for those aged 26 and over. A three-day pass for Spain costs £71 for under 26s, £110/84 for those aged 26 and over.

Railplus Card
For a small fee, European residents can buy a Railplus Card, entitling the holder to a 25% discount on international train journeys. In most countries, it's sold only to those aged 60 and over. However, some national rail networks may make the Railplus Card available to young people or other travellers. It is available from counters in main train stations.

ALL NATIONALITIES
Scan-Rail
This pass is best purchased outside Scandinavia and is valid for travel within Denmark, Finland, Norway and Sweden. Five-days' travel in a two-month period costs £119/171 per youth/adult, a 10-day pass costs £160/229. A 21-day consecutive-days pass will set you back £185/266. Contact Rail Europe for more information.

National Rail Passes

If you intend to travel extensively within one country, national rail passes can sometimes save you a lot of money. Look for details in the Getting Around sections of the country chapters or www.raileurope.com. Plan ahead if you intend to take this option, as some passes can only be purchased prior to arrival in the country.

Overnight Trains

Want to do the whirlwind tour without wasting a day? Use your sleeping hours to traverse territory. On overnight trains, there are usually two types of sleeping accommodations: dozing off upright in your seat or stretching out in a sleeper. Again, reservations are advisable, as sleeping options are allocated on a first-come, first-served basis.

Couchette bunks are comfortable enough, if lacking in privacy. There are four per compartment in 1st class, six in 2nd class. A bunk costs a fixed price of around US$20 for most international trains, irrespective of the length of the journey.

Sleepers are the most comfortable option, offering beds for one or two passengers in 1st class, or two or three passengers in 2nd class. Charges vary depending upon the journey, but they are significantly more costly than couchettes. Most long-distance trains have a dining (buffet) car or an attendant who wheels a snack trolley through carriages. Prices tend to be steep.

In the few FSU (Former Soviet Union) countries explored in this guide, the most common options are either 2nd-class *kupeyny* compartments – which have four bunks – or the cheaper *platskartny*, which are open-plan compartments with reserved bunks. This 3rd-class equivalent is not great for those who value privacy, and theft might be a problem. Other options include the very basic bench seats in *obshchiy* (*zahalney* in Ukrainian) class and 1st-class, two-person sleeping carriages (*myagki/spalney* in Russian/Ukrainian). This last option is not available on every train.

Security

Stories sometimes surface about passengers being gassed or drugged and then robbed, but bag-snatching is much more of a worry. Sensible security measures include always keeping your bags in sight (especially at stations), chaining them to the luggage rack, and locking compartment doors overnight. For more information, see p1233.

Health Dr Caroline Evans

CONTENTS

Prevention is the key to staying healthy in Europe. Travellers who take the necessary precautions and adopt a common-sense approach to their health usually suffer nothing more than a little diarrhoea.

BEFORE YOU GO

Bring medications in their original, clearly labelled containers. A signed and dated letter from your physician describing your medical conditions and medications, including generic names, is a good idea. If carrying syringes or needles, be sure to have a physician's letter documenting their medical necessity.

INSURANCE

If you're an EU citizen, an E111 form (which is gradually being replaced by the European Health Insurance Card over the next few years) covers you for most medical care. The form is available from health centres or, in the UK, post offices. The E111 will not cover you for nonemergencies or emergency repatriation, though. Citizens from other countries should find out if there is a reciprocal arrangement for free medical care between their country and the country

visited. If you do need health insurance, strongly consider a policy that covers you for the worst possible scenario, such as an accident requiring an emergency flight home. Find out in advance if your insurance plan will make payments directly to providers or reimburse you later for overseas health expenditures. The former option is generally preferable, as it doesn't require you to pay out of pocket in a foreign country.

RECOMMENDED VACCINATIONS

No jabs are necessary for Europe. However, the World Health Organization (WHO) recommends that all travellers should be covered for diphtheria, tetanus, measles, mumps, rubella and polio, regardless of their destination. Since most vaccines don't produce immunity until at least two weeks after they're given, visit a physician at least six weeks before departure.

ONLINE RESOURCES

There is a wealth of travel health advice on the Internet. For further information, the Lonely Planet website (www.lonelyplanet.com) is a good place to start. The World Health Organization (www.who.int/ith) also publishes a superb book called *International Travel and Health*, which is revised annually and available online at no cost. Another useful website is MD Travel Health (www.mdtravelhealth.com), which provides travel health recommendations for every country; information is updated daily.

It's usually a good idea to consult your government's website before departure, if one is available:

Australia www.smartraveller.gov.au
Canada www.travelhealth.gc.ca
UK www.dh.gov.uk
USA www.cdc.gov/travel

FURTHER READING

Health Advice for Travellers (currently called the 'T6' leaflet) is an annually updated leaflet by the Department of Health in the UK available free in post offices. It contains some general information, legally required and recommended vaccines for different countries, reciprocal health agreements and an E111 application form. Recommended references include *Traveller's Health* by Dr Richard Dawood and *The Traveller's Good Health Guide* by Ted Lankester.

IN TRANSIT

DEEP VEIN THROMBOSIS (DVT)

Blood clots may form in the legs during plane flights, chiefly because of prolonged immobility. The chief symptom of DVT is swelling or pain of the foot, ankle or calf, usually but not always on just one side. If a blood clot travels to the lungs, it may cause chest pain and breathing difficulties. Travellers with any of these symptoms should immediately seek medical attention.

To prevent the development of DVT on long flights you should walk about the cabin, contract the leg muscles while sitting, drink plenty of fluids and avoid alcohol.

JET LAG & MOTION SICKNESS

To avoid jet lag (common when crossing more than five time zones), try to drink plenty of nonalcoholic fluids and eat light meals. Upon arrival, get exposure to natural sunlight and readjust your schedule (for meals, sleep and so on) as soon as possible.

Antihistamines such as dimenhydrinate (Dramamine) and meclizine (Antivert, Bonine) are usually the first choice for treating motion sickness. A herbal alternative is ginger.

IN EUROPE

AVAILABILITY OF HEALTH CARE

Good health care is readily available for most of Europe and, for minor illnesses, pharmacists can give valuable advice and sell over-the-counter medication. They can also advise when more specialised help is required and point you in the right direction. The standard of dental care is usually good.

In Eastern Europe, medical care is not always readily available outside of major cities but embassies, consulates and five-star hotels can usually recommend doctors or clinics. In some cases, medical supplies required in hospital may need to be bought from a pharmacy and nursing care may be limited. Note that there can be an increased risk of hepatitis B and HIV transmission via poorly sterilised equipment.

INFECTIOUS DISEASES
Poliomyelitis

Poliomyelitis is spread through contaminated food and water. It is one of the vaccines given in childhood and should be boosted every 10 years, either orally (a drop on the tongue) or as an injection.

Rabies

Rabies is spread through bites or licks on broken skin from an infected animal. It is always fatal unless treated promptly. Animal handlers should be vaccinated, as should those travelling to remote areas where reliable source of post-bite vaccine is not available within 24 hours. Three preventive injections are needed over a month. If you have not been vaccinated, you will need course of five injections starting 24 hours or as soon as possible after the injury. If you have been vaccinated, you will need fewer injections and have more time to seek medical help.

MEDICAL CHECKLIST

- Acetaminophen/paracetamol or aspirin
- Adhesive or paper tape
- Antibacterial ointment (eg Bactroban) for cuts and abrasions
- Antibiotics
- Antidiarrhoeal drugs
- Antihistamines (for hay fever and allergic reactions)
- Anti-inflammatory drugs (eg ibuprofen)
- Bandages, gauze, gauze rolls
- Insect repellent containing DEET, for the skin
- Insect spray containing permethrin, for clothing, tents, and bed nets
- Pocket knife
- Scissors, safety pins, tweezers
- Thermometer
- Steroid cream or cortisone (for poison ivy and other allergic rashes)
- Sun block

Tickborne Encephalitis

This disease is transmitted by tick bites. It is a serious infection of the brain and vaccination is advised for those in risk areas who are unable to avoid tick bites (such as campers, forestry workers and walkers). Two doses of vaccine will give a year's protection, three doses up to three years'.

Typhoid & Hepatitis A

These diseases are distributed through contaminated food (particularly shellfish) and water. Typhoid can cause septicaemia (blood poisoning); hepatitis A causes liver inflammation and jaundice. Neither is fatal but recovery can be prolonged. Typhoid vaccine (Typhim Vi, Typherix) will give protection for three years. In some countries, the oral vaccine Vivotif is also available. Hepatitis A vaccine (Avaxim, VAQTA, Havrix) is given as an injection; a single dose will give protection for up to a year, and a booster after a year gives 10 years' protection. Hepatitis A and typhoid vaccines can also be given as a single-dose vaccine (Hepatyrix, Viatim).

TRAVELLER'S DIARRHOEA

If you develop diarrhoea, be sure to drink plenty of fluids, preferably an oral rehydration solution such as Dioralyte. If diarrhoea is bloody, persists for more than 72 hours or is accompanied by a fever, shaking, chills or severe abdominal pain, you should seek medical attention.

ENVIRONMENTAL HAZARDS
Altitude Sickness

Lack of oxygen at high altitudes (over 2500m) affects most people to some extent. Symptoms of Acute Mountain Sickness (AMS) usually develop during the first 24 hours at altitude but may be delayed up to three weeks. Mild symptoms include headache, lethargy, dizziness, difficulty sleeping and loss of appetite. AMS may become more severe without warning and can be fatal. Severe symptoms include breathlessness, a dry, irritative cough (which may progress to the production of pink, frothy sputum), severe headache, lack of coordination and balance, confusion, irrational behaviour, vomiting, drowsiness and unconsciousness. There is no hard-and-fast rule as to what is too high: AMS has been fatal at 3000m, although 3500m to 4500m is the usual range.

> **WARNING**
>
> Codeine, which is commonly found in headache preparations, is banned in Greece; check labels carefully or risk prosecution. There are strict rules applying to the importation of medicines into Greece, so obtain a certificate from your doctor that outlines any medication you may have to carry into the country with you.

Treat mild symptoms by resting at the same altitude until recovery, usually a day or two. Paracetamol or aspirin can be taken for headaches. If symptoms persist or become worse, however, *immediate descent is necessary*; even 500m can help. Drug treatments should never be used to avoid descent or to enable further ascent.

Diamox (acetazolamide) reduces the headache of AMS and helps the body acclimatise to the lack of oxygen. It is only available on prescription and those who are allergic to the sulfonamide antibiotics may also be allergic to Diamox.

In the UK, fact sheets are available from **British Mountaineering Council** (177–179 Burton Rd, Manchester, M20 2BB).

The risk of getting AMS can be reduced by ascending slowly and spending two to three nights at each rise of 1000m. It is always wise to sleep at a lower altitude than the greatest height reached during the day if possible.

Bites & Stings

Mosquitoes are found in most parts of Europe. They may not carry malaria but can cause irritation and infected bites. Use a DEET-based insect repellent.

Sand flies are found around the Mediterranean beaches. They usually cause only a nasty itchy bite but can carry a rare skin disorder called cutaneous leishmaniasis.

Bees and wasps cause real problems only to those with a severe allergy (anaphylaxis). If you have a severe allergy to bee or wasp stings carry an 'epipen' or similar adrenaline injection.

Bedbugs lead to very itchy, lumpy bites. Spraying the mattress with insect killer after changing bedding will get rid of them.

Scabies are tiny mites that live in the skin, particularly between the fingers. They cause an intensely itchy rash. Scabies is easily treated with lotion from a pharmacy; other members of the household also need treating to avoid spreading scabies between asymptomatic carriers.

Scorpions can also be found in a number of European countries but although their sting can be distressingly painful, it is not considered fatal.

Check for ticks if you have been walking where sheep and goats graze: they can cause skin infections and other more serious diseases.

Snakes can be found in Europe and to avoid being bitten do not walk barefoot or stick your hand into holes or cracks. If bitten, do not panic. Immobilise the bitten limb with a splint (eg a stick) and apply a bandage over the site firmly, similar to a bandage over a sprain. Do not apply a tourniquet, or cut or suck the bite. Get the victim to medical help as soon as possible so that antivenin can be given if necessary.

Different varieties of jellyfish can be found throughout southern European waters. However they generally occur in large numbers or hardly at all, so it's fairly easy to know when not to go in the sea. Heed local warnings.

Heat Exhaustion & Heat Stroke
Heat exhaustion occurs following excessive fluid loss with inadequate replacement of fluids and salt. Symptoms include headache, dizziness and tiredness. Dehydration has already started by the time you're thirsty – aim to drink sufficient water to produce pale, diluted urine. Replace lost fluids by drinking water and/or fruit juice, and cool the body with cold water and fans. Treat salt loss with salty fluids such as soup or add a little more table salt to foods than usual.

Heat stroke is much more serious, resulting in irrational and hyperactive behaviour and eventually loss of consciousness and death. Rapid cooling by spraying the body with

water and fanning is ideal. Emergency fluid and electrolyte replacement by intravenous drip may be required.

Hypothermia
The weather in mountainous regions can be extremely changeable at any time of year. Proper preparation will reduce the risks of getting hypothermia. Even on a hot day the weather can change rapidly; carry waterproof garments and warm layers, and inform others of your route.

Hypothermia starts with shivering, loss of judgment and clumsiness. Unless rewarming occurs, the sufferer deteriorates into apathy, confusion and eventually coma. Prevent further heat loss by seeking shelter, warm dry clothing, hot sweet drinks and shared bodily warmth.

Water
Tap water is generally safe to drink in Europe but bottled or purified water is a better option in Eastern Europe. Do not drink water from rivers or lakes as it may contain bacteria or viruses that can cause diarrhoea or vomiting.

WOMEN'S HEALTH
Travelling during pregnancy is usually possible but always seek a medical check-up before planning your trip. The most risky times for travel are during the first 12 weeks of pregnancy and after 30 weeks.

SEXUAL HEALTH
Condoms are widely available in Europe, however emergency contraception may not be, so take the necessary precautions. The **International Planned Parent Federation** (www .ippf.org) can advise about the availability of contraception in different countries.

When buying condoms, look for a European CE mark, which means they have passed quality tests. Remember to keep them in a cool, dry place.

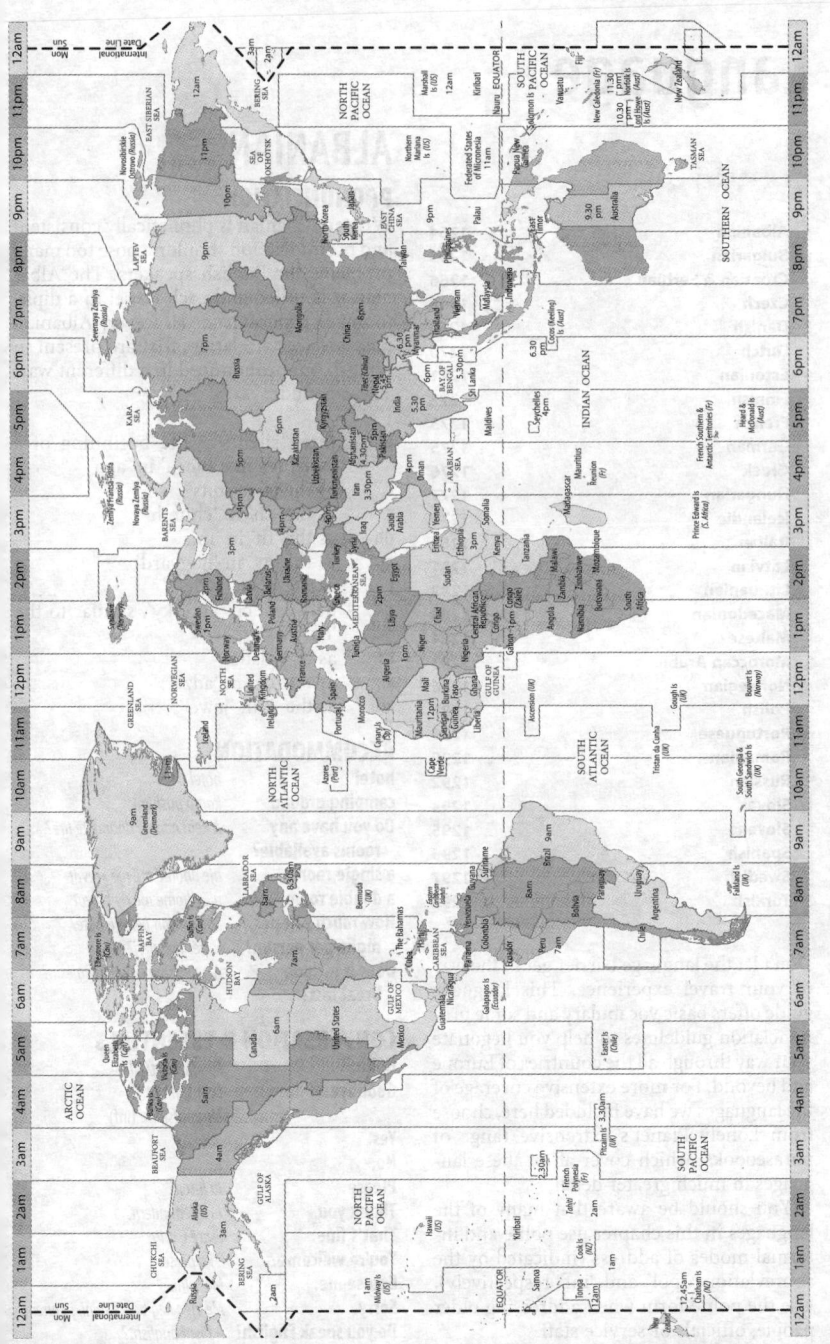

Language

CONTENTS

Don't let the language barrier get in the way of your travel experience. This language guide offers basic vocabulary and some pronunciation guidelines to help you negotiate your way through all the countries of Europe and beyond. For more extensive coverage of the languages we have included here, choose from Lonely Planet's extensive range of phrasebooks, which cover all of these languages in much greater detail.

You should be aware that many of the languages in this chapter use polite and informal modes of address (indicated by the abbreviations 'pol' and 'inf' respectively). Use the polite form when addressing older people, officials or service staff.

ALBANIAN

PRONUNCIATION

Written Albanian is phonetically consistent and pronunciation shouldn't pose too many problems for English speakers. The Albanian **rr** is rolled and each vowel in a diphthong is pronounced. However, Albanian possesses certain letters that are present in English but pronounced in a different way. These include:

ë	often silent; at the beginning of a word it's like the 'a' in 'ago'
c	as the 'ts' in 'bits'
ç	as the 'ch' in 'church'
dh	as the 'th' in 'this'
gj	as the 'gy' in 'hogyard'
j	as the 'y' in 'yellow'
q	between 'ch' and 'ky', similar to the 'cu' in 'cure'
th	as in 'thistle'
x	as the 'dz' in 'adze'
xh	as the 'j' in 'jewel'

ACCOMMODATION

hotel	hotel
camping ground	kamp pushimi
Do you have any rooms available?	A keni ndonjë dhomë të lirë?
a single room	një dhomë më një krevat
a double room	një dhomë më dy krevat
How much is it per night/per person?	Sa kushton për një natë/për një njeri?
Does it include breakfast?	A e përfshin edhe mëngjesin?

CONVERSATION & ESSENTIALS

Hello.	Tungjatjeta/Allo.
Goodbye.	Lamtumirë.
	Mirupafshim. (inf)
Yes.	Po.
No.	Jo.
Please.	Ju lutem.
Thank you.	Ju falem nderit.
That's fine.	Eshtë e mirë.
You're welcome.	S'ka përse.
Excuse me.	Me falni.
Sorry.	Më vjen keq or Më falni, ju lutem.
Do you speak English?	A flisni anglisht?

How much is it?	Sa kushton?
What's your name?	Si quheni ju lutem?
My name is ...	Unë quhem .../Mua më quajnë ...

SHOPPING & SERVICES

a bank	një bankë
chemist/pharmacy	farmaci
the ... embassy	... ambasadën
my hotel	hotelin tim
the market	pazarin
newsagency	agjensia e lajmeve
the post office	postën
the telephone centre	centralin telefonik
the tourist office	zyrën e informimeve turistike
What time does it open/close?	Në ç'ore hapet/mbyllet?

TIME, DAYS & NUMBERS

What time is it?	Sa është ora?
today	sot
tomorrow	nesër
yesterday	dje
in the morning	në mëngjes
in the afternoon	pas dreke

Monday	e hënë
Tuesday	e martë
Wednesday	e mërkurë
Thursday	e ënjte
Friday	e premte
Saturday	e shtunë
Sunday	e diel

1	një	7	shtatë
2	dy	8	tetë
3	tre	9	nëntë
4	katër	10	dhjetë
5	pesë	100	njëqind
6	gjashtë	1000	njëmijë

TRANSPORT & DIRECTIONS

What time does the ... leave/arrive?	Në ç'orë niset/arrin ...?
boat	barka/lundra
bus	autobusi
tram	tramvaji
train	treni

I'd like ...	Dëshiroj ...
a one-way ticket	një biletë vajtje
a return ticket	një biletë kthimi

1st/2nd class	klas i parë/i dytë
timetable	orar
bus stop	stacion autobusi

Where is ...?	Ku është ...?
Go straight ahead.	Shko drejt.
Turn left.	Kthehu majtas.
Turn right.	Kthehu djathtas.
near/far	afër/larg

BULGARIAN

ALPHABET

Bulgarian uses the Cyrillic alphabet (see The Cyrillic Alphabet boxed text in the Russian section of this chapter.)

ACCOMMODATION

Do you have any rooms available?
imateh li svobodni stai?
How much is it?
kolko struva?
Does it include breakfast?
zakuskata vklyuchena li e?

camping ground	kâmpinguvane
youth hostel	obshtezhitie
guesthouse	pansion
hotel	khotel
private room	stoya v chastna kvartira
single room	edinichna staya
double room	dvoyna staya

CONVERSATION & ESSENTIALS

Hello.	zdraveyte/zdrasti (pol/inf)
Goodbye.	dovizhdane/chao (pol/inf)
Yes.	da

No.	*ne*
Please.	*molya*
Thank you.	*blagodarya/mersi* (pol/inf)
I'm sorry.	*sâzhalyavam*
Excuse me.	*izvinete me*
Do you speak English?	*govorite li angliski?*
I don't understand.	*az ne razbiram*
What's it called?	*kak se kazva tova?*
How much is it?	*kolko struva?*

SIGNS – BULGARIAN

Вход	Entrance
Изход	Exit
Информация	Information
Отворено	Open
Затворено	Closed
Забранено	Prohibited
Тоалетни	Toilets
Мъже	Men
Жени	Women

EMERGENCIES – BULGARIAN

Help!	*pomosh!*
Call a doctor!	*povikayte lekar!*
Call the police!	*povikayte politsiya!*
Go away!	*mahayte se!*
I'm lost.	*zagubih se*

SHOPPING & SERVICES

the bank	*bankata*
the hospital	*bolnitsata*
the market	*pazara*
the museum	*muzeya*
the post office	*poshtata*
the tourist office	*byuroto za turisticheska informatsiya*

TIME, DAYS & NUMBERS

What time is it?	*kolko e chasât?*
today	*dnes*
tonight	*dovechera*
tomorrow	*utre*
yesterday	*vchera*
in the morning	*sutrinta*
in the evening	*vecherta*

Monday	*ponedelnik*
Tuesday	*vtornik*
Wednesday	*sryada*
Thursday	*chetvârtâk*
Friday	*petâk*
Saturday	*sâbota*
Sunday	*nedelya*

1	*edno*	7	*sedem*
2	*dve*	8	*osem*
3	*tri*	9	*devet*
4	*chetiri*	10	*deset*
5	*pet*	100	*sto*
6	*shest*	1000	*hilyada*

TRANSPORT & DIRECTIONS

What time does the ... leave/arrive?
v kolko chasa zaminava/pristiga ...?

city bus	*gradskiyat avtobus*
intercity bus	*mezhdugradskiyat avtobus*
plane	*samolehtât*
train	*vlakât*
tram	*tramvayat*
arrival	*pristigane*
departure	*zaminavane*
timetable	*razpisanie*

Where is the bus stop?
kâde e avtobusnata spirka?
Where is the train station?
kâde e zhelezopâtnata gara?
Where is the left-luggage room?
kâde e garderobât?
Please show me on the map.
molya pokazhete mi na kartata

straight ahead	*napravo*
left	*lyavo*
right	*dyasno*

CROATIAN & SERBIAN

Serbian uses the Cyrillic alphabet and it's worth familiarising yourself with it (see The Cyrillic Alphabet in the Russian section of this chapter on p1293). Croatian uses a Roman alphabet and many letters are pronounced as in English. Note the following exceptions:

c	as the 'ts' in 'cats'
ć	as the 'tch' sound in 'future'
č	as the 'ch' in 'chop'
đ	as the 'dy' sound in 'verdure'
dž	as the 'j' in 'just'
j	as the 'y' in 'young'
lj	as the 'lli' in 'million'
nj	as the 'ny' in 'canyon'
š	as the 'sh' in 'hush'
ž	as the 's' in 'pleasure'

Croatian and Serbian are very similar. In the following phrase list, any variations in vocabulary between the two languages are indicated by 'C' and 'S' respectively.

ACCOMMODATION

hotel	*hotel*
guesthouse	*privatno prenočište*
youth hostel	*omladinsko prenočište*
camping ground	*kamping*
Do you have any rooms available?	*Imate li slobodne sobe?*
How much is it per night/per person?	*Koliko košta za jednu noč/ po osobi?*
Is breakfast included?	*Da li je u cijenu uključen i doručak?*
I'd like a (single/ double) room.	*Želim sobu sa (jednim/ duplim) krevetom.*

EMERGENCIES – CROATIAN & SERBIAN

Help!	*Upomoć!*
Call a doctor!	*Pozovite liječnika/lekara!* (C/S)
Call the police!	*Pozovite policiju!*
Go away!	*Idite!*
I'm lost.	*Izgubljen/Izgubljena sam.* (m/f)

CONVERSATION & ESSENTIALS

Hello.	*Zdravo.*
Goodbye.	*Doviđenja.*
Yes.	*Da.*
No.	*Ne.*
Please.	*Molim.*
Thank you.	*Hvala.*
That's fine/You're welcome.	*U redu je/Nema na čemu.*
Excuse me.	*Pardon.*
Sorry.	*Oprostite.*
Do you speak English?	*Govorite li engleski?*
How much is it ...?	*Koliko košta ...?*

SHOPPING & SERVICES

I'm looking for ...	*Tražim ...*
a bank	*banku*
the ... embassy	*... ambasadu*
the market	*pijacu*
the post office	*poštu*
the tourist office	*turistički biro*

TIME, DAYS & NUMBERS

What time is it?	*Koliko je sati?*
today	*danas*
tomorrow	*sutra*
yesterday	*jučer*
in the morning	*ujutro*
in the afternoon	*popodne*

SIGNS – CROATIAN & SERBIAN

Ulaz/Izlaz Улаз/Излаз	Entrance/Exit
Otvoreno/Zatvoreno Отворено/Затворено	Open/Closed
Informacije Информације	Information
Zabranjeno Забрањено	Prohibited
Toaleti/WC Тоалети/WC	Toilets

Monday	*ponedeljak*
Tuesday	*utorak*
Wednesday	*srijeda*
Thursday	*četvrtak*
Friday	*petak*
Saturday	*subota*
Sunday	*nedjelja*

1	*jedan*	**7**	*sedam*
2	*dva*	**8**	*osam*
3	*tri*	**9**	*devet*
4	*četiri*	**10**	*deset*
5	*pet*	**100**	*sto*
6	*šest*	**1000**	*tisuću* (C)/*hiljada* (S)

TRANSPORT & DIRECTIONS

What time does the ... leave/arrive?	*Kada ... polazi/dolazi?*
boat	*brod*
city bus	*gradski autobus*
intercity bus	*međugradski autobus*
train	*vlak* (C)/*voz* (S)
tram	*tramvaj*

one-way ticket	*kartu u jednom pravcu*
return ticket	*povratnu kartu*
1st class	*prvu klasu*
2nd class	*drugu klasu*

Where is the bus/tram stop?
Gdje je autobuska/tramvajska postaja?
Can you show me (on the map)?
Možete li mi pokazati (na karti)?
Go straight ahead.
Idite pravo naprijed.
Turn left.
Skrenite lijevo.
Turn right.
Skrenite desno.
near/far
blizu/daleko

LANGUAGE

CZECH

PRONUNCIATION

Many Czech letters are pronounced as per their English counterparts. An accent over a vowel lengthens its pronunciation and the stress is always on the first syllable. Words are pronounced as written, so if you follow the guidelines below you should have no trouble being understood. When consulting indexes on Czech maps, be aware that **ch** comes after **h**.

c	as the 'ts' in 'bits'
č	as the 'ch' in 'church'
ch	as in Scottish *loch*
ď	as the 'd' in 'duty'
ě	as the 'ye' in 'yet'
j	as the 'y' in 'you'
ň	as the 'ni' in 'onion'
ř	as the sound 'rzh'
š	as the 'sh' in 'ship'
ť	as the 'te' in 'stew'
ž	as the 's' in 'pleasure'

ACCOMMODATION

hotel	hotel
guesthouse	penzión
youth hostel	ubytovna
camping ground	kemping
private room	privát
single room	jednolůžkový pokoj
double room	dvoulůžkový pokoj
Do you have any rooms available?	Máte volné pokoje?
How much is it?	Kolik to je?

CONVERSATION & ESSENTIALS

Hello/Good day.	Dobrý den. (pol)
Hi.	Ahoj. (inf)
Goodbye.	Na shledanou.
Yes.	Ano.
No.	Ne.
Please.	Prosím.
Thank you.	Děkuji.
That's fine/You're welcome.	Není zač/Prosím.
Excuse me/Sorry.	Promiňte.
Do you speak English?	Mluvíte anglicky?
I don't understand.	Nerozumím.
How much is it?	Kolik to stojí?

SHOPPING & SERVICES

Where is it?	Kde je to?
the bank	banka

EMERGENCIES – CZECH	
Help!	Pomoc!
Go away!	Běžte pryč!
I'm lost.	Zabloudil jsem. (m)
	Zabloudila jsem. (f)
Call ...!	Zavolejte ...!
a doctor	doktora
an ambulance	sanitku
the police	policii

---

the chemist	lékárna
the market	trh
the museum	muzeum
the post office	pošta
the tourist office	turistické informační centrum (středisko)

TIME, DAYS & NUMBERS

What time is it?	Kolik je hodin?
today	dnes
tonight	dnes večer
tomorrow	zítra
yesterday	včera
in the morning	ráno
in the evening	večer
Monday	pondělí
Tuesday	úterý
Wednesday	středa
Thursday	čtvrtek
Friday	pátek
Saturday	sobota
Sunday	neděle

1	jeden	7	sedm
2	dva	8	osm
3	tři	9	devět
4	čtyři	10	deset
5	pět	100	sto
6	šest	1000	tisíc

TRANSPORT & DIRECTIONS

What time does the ... leave/arrive?	Kdy odjíždí/přijíždí ...?
boat	loď
city bus	městský autobus
intercity bus	meziměstský autobus
train	vlak
tram	tramvaj
arrival	příjezdy
departure	odjezdy
timetable	jízdní řád

Where is the ...?	Kde je ...?
bus stop	autobusová zastávka
station	nádraží
left-luggage room	úschovna zavazadel

Please show me on the map.	Prosím, ukažte mi to na mapě.
left/right	vlevo/vpravo
straight ahead	rovně

DANISH

PRONUNCIATION

a	as in 'father'
a/æ	as in 'act'
o/å/	a long rounded 'a' as in 'walk'
u(n)	
e(g)	as in 'eye'
e, i	as the 'e' in 'bet'
i	as the 'e' in 'theme'
ø	as the 'er' in 'fern'
o, u	as the 'oo' in 'cool'
o	as in 'pot'
o(v)	as the 'ou' in 'out'
o(r)	as the 'or' in 'for' with less emphasis on the 'r'
u	as in 'pull'
y	say 'ee' while pursing your lips
sj	as in 'ship'
c	as in 'celery'
(o)d	a flat 'dh' sound, as the 'th' in 'these'
r	a rolling 'r' abruptly cut short
j	as the 'y' in 'yet'

ACCOMMODATION

hotel	hotel
guesthouse	gæstgiveri
hostel	vandrerhjem
camping ground	campingplads
Do you have any rooms available?	Har I ledige værelser?
How much is it per night/person?	Hvor meget koster det per nat/person?

| one day/two days | en nat/to nætter |

I'd like ...	Jeg ønsker ...
a single room	et enkeltværelse
a double room	et dobbeltværelse

CONVERSATION & ESSENTIALS

Hello.	Hallo.
	Hej. (informal)
Goodbye.	Farvel.
Yes.	Ja.
No.	Nej.
Please.	Må jeg bede/Værsgo.
Thank you.	Tak.
That's fine/ You're welcome.	Det er i orden/Selv tak.
Excuse me/Sorry.	Undskyld.
Do you speak English?	Taler De engelsk?
How much is it?	Hvor meget koster det?

SHOPPING & SERVICES

a bank	en bank
a chemist/pharmacy	et apotek
the ... embassy	den ... ambassade
the market	ma rkedet
a newsagent	en aviskiosk
the post office	postkontoret
the tourist office	turistinformationen

| What time does it open/close? | Hvornår åbner/lukker det? |

TIME, DAYS & NUMBERS

What time is it?	Hvad er klokken?
today	i dag
tomorrow	i morgen
yesterday	i går
morning	morgenen
afternoon	eftermiddagen

Monday	mandag
Tuesday	tirsdag
Wednesday	onsdag
Thursday	torsdag
Friday	fredag
Saturday	lørdag
Sunday	søndag

0	*nul*	7	*syv*
1	*en*	8	*otte*
2	*to*	9	*ni*
3	*tre*	10	*ti*
4	*fire*	11	*elve*
5	*fem*	100	*hundrede*
6	*seks*	1000	*tusind*

TRANSPORT & DIRECTIONS

What time does ... leave/arrive?	*Hvornår går/ankommer ...?*
the boat	*båden*
the bus (city)	*bussen*
the bus (intercity)	*rutebilen*
the tram	*sporvognen*
the train	*toget*

I'd like ...	*Jeg vil gerne have ...*
a one-way ticket	*en enkeltbillet*
a return ticket	*en tur-retur billet*
1st/2nd class	*første/anden klasse*

left-luggage office	*reisegodsoppbevaringen*
timetable	*køreplan*
bus stop	*bus holdeplads*
tram stop	*sporvogn holdeplads*
train station	*jernbanestation (banegård)*

Where can I hire a car/bicycle?	*Hvor kan jeg leje en bil/cykel?*
Where is ...?	*Hvor er ...?*
Go straight ahead.	*Gå ligefrem.*
Turn left/right.	*Drej til venstre/højre.*
near/far	*nær/fjern*

DUTCH

PRONUNCIATION

au/ou	pronounced somewhere between the 'ow' in 'how' and the 'ow' in 'glow'
eu	a tricky one; try saying 'eh' with rounded lips and the tongue forward, then slide the tongue back and down to make an 'oo' sound; it's similar to the 'eu' in French *couleur*
i/ie	long, as the 'ee' in 'meet'
ij	as the 'ey' in 'they'
oe	as the 'oo' in 'zoo'
ui	a very tricky one; pronounced somewhere between au/ou and eu; it's similar to the 'eui' in French *fauteuil*, without the slide to the 'i'
ch/g	in the north, a hard 'kh' sound as in the Scottish *loch*; in the south, a softer, lisping sound
j	as the 'y' in 'yes'; also as the 'j' in 'jam' or 'zh' 'pleasure'
r	in the south, a rolled sound; in the north it varies, often guttural

ACCOMMODATION

hotel	*hotel*
guesthouse	*pension*
youth hostel	*jeugdherberg*
camping ground	*camping*

Do you have any rooms available?	*Heeft U kamers vrij?*
single/double room	*eenpersoons/twee-persoons kamer*
one/two nights	*één nacht/twee nachten*
How much is it per night/ per person?	*Hoeveel is het per nacht/ per persoon?*

CONVERSATION & ESSENTIALS

Hello.	*Dag/Hallo.*
Goodbye.	*Dag.*
Yes.	*Ja.*
No.	*Nee.*
Please.	*Alstublieft/Alsjeblieft.*
Thank you.	*Dank U/je (wel).*
You're welcome.	*Geen dank.*
Excuse me.	*Pardon.*
Sorry.	*Sorry.*
Do you speak English?	*Spreekt U/spreek je Engels?*
How much is it?	*Hoeveel kost het?*

SHOPPING & SERVICES

a bank	een bank
the ... embassy	de ... ambassade
the market	de markt
the pharmacy	de drogist
the newsagent/	de krantenwinkel/
stationer	kantoorboekhandel
the post office	het postkantoor
the tourist office	de VVV/het toeristenbureau
What time does it open/close?	Hoe laat opent/sluit het?

TIME, DAYS & NUMBERS

What time is it?	Hoe laat is het?
today	vandaag
tomorrow	morgen
in the morning	's-morgens
in the afternoon	's-middags
Monday	maandag
Tuesday	dinsdag
Wednesday	woensdag
Thursday	donderdag
Friday	vrijdag
Saturday	zaterdag
Sunday	zondag

0	nul	7	zeven
1	één	8	acht
2	twee	9	negen
3	drie	10	tien
4	vier	11	elf
5	vijf	100	honderd
6	zes	1000	duizend

TRANSPORT & DIRECTIONS

What time does the ... leave/arrive?	Hoe laat vertrekt/ arriveert de ...?
(next)	(volgende)
boat	boot
bus	bus
train	trein
tram	tram
I'd like to hire a car/bicycle.	Ik wil graag een auto/fiets huren.
I'd like a one-way/ return ticket.	Ik wil graag een enkele reis/een retour.
1st/2nd class	eerste/tweede klas
left-luggage locker	bagagekluis
bus/tram stop	bushalte/tramhalte
train station/ ferry terminal	treinstation/veerhaven

Where is the ...?	Waar is de ...?
Go straight ahead.	Ga rechtdoor.
Turn left/right.	Ga linksaf/rechtsaf.
far/near	ver/dichtbij

ESTONIAN

ALPHABET & PRONUNCIATION

The letters of the Estonian alphabet are: **a b d e f g h i j k l m n o p r s š z ž t u v õ ä ö ü**.

a	as the 'u' in 'cut'
b	similar to English 'p'
g	similar to English 'k'
j	as the 'y' in 'yes'
š	as 'sh'
ž	as the 's' in 'pleasure'
õ	somewhere between the 'e' in 'bed' and the 'u' in 'fur'
ä	as the 'a' in 'cat'
ö	as the 'u' in 'fur' but with rounded lips
ü	as a short 'you'
ai	as the 'i' in 'pine'
ei	as in 'vein'
oo	as the 'a' in 'water'
uu	as the 'oo' in 'boot'
öö	as the 'u' in 'fur'

CONVERSATION & ESSENTIALS

Hello.	Tere.
Goodbye.	Head aega/Nägemiseni.
Yes.	Jah.
No.	Ei.
Excuse me.	Vabandage.
Please.	Palun.
Thank you.	Tänan/Aitäh. (thanks)
Do you speak English?	Kas te räägite inglise keelt?

SHOPPING & SERVICES

bank	pank
chemist	apteek

currency exchange	valuutavahetus
market	turg
toilet	tualett

Where?	Kus?
How much?	Kui palju?

TIME, DAYS & NUMBERS

today	täna
tomorrow	homme
yesterday	eile

Monday	esmaspäev
Tuesday	teisipäev
Wednesday	kolmapäev
Thursday	neljapäev
Friday	reede
Saturday	laupäev
Sunday	pühapäev

1	üks	7	seitse
2	kaks	8	kaheksa
3	kolm	9	üheksa
4	neli	10	kümme
5	viis	100	sada
6	kuus	1000	tuhat

SIGNS – ESTONIAN

Sissepääs	Entrance
Väljapääs	Exit
Avatud/Lahti	Open
Suletud/Kinni	Closed
Mitte Suitsetada	No Smoking
WC	Public Toilet
Meestele	Women
Naistele	Men

TRANSPORT & DIRECTIONS

airport	lennujaam
bus station	bussijaam
port	sadam

stop (eg bus stop)	peatus
train station	raudteejaam

bus	buss
taxi	takso
train	rong
tram	tramm
trolleybus	trollibuss

ticket	pilet
ticket office	piletikassa/kassa
soft class/deluxe	luksus
sleeping carriage	magamisvagun
compartment (class)	kupee

FINNISH

PRONUNCIATION

The final letters of the alphabet are **å**, **ä** and **ö** (important to know when looking for something in a telephone directory).

y	as the 'u' in 'pull' but with the lips stretched back (like the German 'ü')
å	as the 'oo' in 'poor'
ä	as the 'a' in 'act'
ö	as the 'e' in 'summer'
z	pronounced (and sometimes written) as 'ts'
v/w	as the 'v' in 'vain'
h	a weak sound, except at the end of a syllable, when it is almost like 'ch' in German *ich*
j	as the 'y' in 'yellow'
r	a rolled 'r'

ACCOMMODATION

hotel	hotelli
guesthouse	matkustajakoti
youth hostel	retkeilymaja
campground	leirintäalue

Do you have any rooms available?	Onko teillä vapaata huonetta?
one day	yhden päivän
two days	kaksi päivää

How much is it ...?	Paljonko se on ...?
per night	yöltä
per person	hengeltä

I'd like ...	Haluaisin ...
a single room	yhden hengen huoneen
a double room	kahden hengen huoneen

CONVERSATION & ESSENTIALS

Hello.	Hei/Terve.
	Moi. (inf)
Goodbye.	Näkemiin/Moi. (inf)
Yes.	Kyllä/Joo.
No.	Ei. (pronounced 'ay')
Please.	Kiitos.
Thank you.	Kiitos.
That's fine/You're welcome.	Ole hyvä/Eipä kestä. (inf)
Excuse me/Sorry.	Anteeksi.
Do you speak English?	Puhutko englantia?
How much is it?	Paljonko se maksaa?

SHOPPING & SERVICES

bank	pankkia
chemist/pharmacy	apteekki
... embassy	... -n suurlähetystöä
market	toria
newsagent	lehtikioski
post office	postia
tourist office	matkailutoimistoa/ matkailutoimisto
What time does it open/close?	Milloin se aukeaan/sul jetaan?

TIME, DAYS & NUMBERS

What time is it?	Paljonko kello on?
today	tänään
tomorrow	huomenna
yesterday	eilen
morning	aamulla
afternoon	iltapäivällä
Monday	maanantai
Tuesday	tiistai
Wednesday	keskiviikko
Thursday	torstai
Friday	perjantai
Saturday	lauantai
Sunday	sunnuntai

0	nolla	7	seitsemän
1	yksi	8	kahdeksan
2	kaksi	9	yhdeksän
3	kolme	10	kymmenen
4	neljä	11	yksitoista
5	viisi	100	sata
6	kuusi	1000	tuhat

TRANSPORT & DIRECTIONS

What time does ... leave/arrive?	Mihin aikaan ... lähtee/saapuu?
the boat	laiva
the bus (city)	bussi
the bus (intercity)	bussi/linja-auto
the train	juna
the tram	raitiovaunu/raitikka
I'd like a one-way/ return ticket.	Saanko menolipun/ menopaluulipun.
Where can I hire a car?	Mistä mina voisin vuokrata auton?
Where can I hire a bicycle?	Mistä mina voin vuokrata polkupyörän?

1st class	ensimmäinen luokka
2nd class	toinen luokka
left luggage	säilytys
timetable	aikataulu
bus/tram stop	pysäkki
train station	rautatieasema
ferry terminal	satamaterminaali

Where is ...?	Missä on ...?
Go straight ahead.	Kulje suoraan.
Turn left.	Käänny vasempaan.
Turn right.	Käänny oikeaan.
near/far	lähellä/kaukana

FRENCH

ACCOMMODATION

the hotel	l'hôtel
the youth hostel	l'auberge de jeunesse
the camping ground	le camping
Do you have any rooms available?	Est-ce que vous avez des chambres libres?

for one person	*pour une personne*
for two people	*deux personnes*
How much is it ...?	*Quel est le prix ...?*
per night	*par nuit*
per person	*par personne*

CONVERSATION & ESSENTIALS

Hello.	*Bonjour.*
Goodbye.	*Au revoir.*
Yes.	*Oui.*
No.	*Non.*
Please.	*S'il vous plaît.*
Thank you.	*Merci.*
That's fine/You're welcome.	*Je vous en prie.*
Excuse me.	*Excusez-moi*
Sorry.	*Pardon*
Do you speak English?	*Parlez-vous anglais?*
How much is it?	*C'est combien?*

> **EMERGENCIES – FRENCH**
>
> | | |
> |---|---|
> | **Help!** | *Au secours!* |
> | **Call a doctor!** | *Appelez un médecin!* |
> | **Call the police!** | *Appelez la police!* |
> | **Leave me alone!** | *Fichez-moi la paix!* |
> | **I'm lost.** | *Je me suis égaré/e.* |

SHOPPING & SERVICES

a bank	*une banque*
chemist/pharmacy	*la pharmacie*
the ... embassy	*l'ambassade de ...*
market	*le marché*
newsagent	*l'agence de presse*
post office	*le bureau de poste*
the tourist office	*l'office de tourisme*
What time does it open/close?	*Quelle est l'heure de ouverture/fermeture?*

TIME, DAYS & NUMBERS

What time is it?	*Quelle heure est-il?*
today	*aujourd'hui*
tomorrow	*demain*
yesterday	*hier*
morning	*matin*
afternoon	*après-midi*
Monday	*lundi*
Tuesday	*mardi*
Wednesday	*mercredi*
Thursday	*jeudi*

> **SIGNS – FRENCH**
>
> | | |
> |---|---|
> | **Entrée** | Entrance |
> | **Sortie** | Exit |
> | **Renseignements** | Information |
> | **Ouvert** | Open |
> | **Fermée** | Closed |
> | **Interdit** | Prohibited |
> | **Toilettes, WC** | Toilets |
> | **Hommes** | Men |
> | **Femmes** | Women |

Friday	*vendredi*
Saturday	*samedi*
Sunday	*dimanche*

1	*un*	**7**	*sept*
2	*deux*	**8**	*huit*
3	*trois*	**9**	*neuf*
4	*quatre*	**10**	*dix*
5	*cinq*	**100**	*cent*
6	*six*	**1000**	*mille*

TRANSPORT & DIRECTIONS

When does the next ... leave/arrive?	*À quelle heure part/ arrive le prochain ...?*
boat	*bateau*
bus (city)	*bus*
bus (intercity)	*car*
train	*train*
tram	*tramway*
left-luggage office	*consigne*
timetable	*horaire*
bus stop	*arrêt d'autobus*
tram stop	*arrêt de tramway*
train station	*gare*
ferry terminal	*gare maritime*
I'd like a ... ticket.	*Je voudrais un billet ...*
one-way	*aller simple*
return	*aller retour*
1st class	*de première classe*
2nd class	*de deuxième classe*
I'd like to hire a car/bicycle.	*Je voudrais louer une voiture/un vélo.*
Where is ...?	*Où est ...?*
Go straight ahead.	*Continuez tout droit.*
Turn left.	*Tournez à gauche.*
Turn right.	*Tournez à droite.*
near	*proche*
far	*loin*

GERMAN

PRONUNCIATION
Vowels

As a rule, German vowels are long before one consonant and short before two consonants, eg the **o** is long in the word *Dom* (cathedral), but short in the word *doch* (after all).

au	as the 'ow' in 'vow'
ä	short, as in 'cat' or long, as in 'care'
äu	as the 'oy' in 'boy'
ei	as the 'ai' in 'aisle'
eu	as the 'oy' in 'boy'
ie	as the 'brief'
ö	as the 'er' in 'fern'
ü	similar to the 'u' in 'pull' but with lips stretched back

Consonants

The consonants **b**, **d** and **g** sound like 'p', 't' and 'k', respectively, when word-final.

ch	as in Scottish *loch*
j	as the 'y' in 'yet'
qu	as 'k' plus 'v'
r	can be rolled or guttural, depending on the region
s	as in 'sun'; as the 'z' in 'zoo' when followed by a vowel
sch	as the 'sh' in 'ship'
sp, st	as 'shp' and 'sht' when word-initial
tion	the 't' is pronounced as the 'ts' in 'its'
v	as the 'f' in 'fan'
w	as the 'v' in 'van'
z	as the 'ts' in 'its'

ACCOMMODATION

hotel	*Hotel*
guesthouse	*Pension, Gästehaus*
youth hostel	*Jugendherberge*
camping ground	*Campingplatz*
Do you have any rooms available?	*Haben Sie noch freie Zimmer?*
a single room	*ein Einzelzimmer*
a double room	*ein Doppelzimmer*
How much is it ...?	*Wieviel kostet es ...?*
per night	*pro Nacht*
per person	*pro Person*

CONVERSATION & ESSENTIALS

Good day.	*Guten Tag.*
Hello. (in Bavaria and Austria)	*Grüss Gott.*
Goodbye.	*Auf Wiedersehen.*
Bye.	*Tschüss.* (informal)
Yes.	*Ja.*
No.	*Nein.*
Please.	*Bitte.*
Thank you.	*Danke.*
You're welcome.	*Bitte sehr.*
Excuse me/Sorry.	*Entschuldigung.*
What's your name?	*Wie heissen Sie?*
My name is ...	*Ich heisse ...*
Do you speak English?	*Sprechen Sie Englisch?*
How much is it?	*Wieviel kostet es?*

EMERGENCIES – GERMAN

Help!	*Hilfe!*
Call a doctor!	*Holen Sie einen Arzt!*
Call the police!	*Rufen Sie die Polizei!*
Go away!	*Gehen Sie weg!*
I'm lost.	*Ich habe mich verirrt.*

SHOPPING & SERVICES

I'm looking for ...	*Ich suche ...*
a bank	*eine Bank*
the ... embassy	*die ... Botschaft*
the market	*der Markt*
the newsagency	*der Zeitungshändler*
the pharmacy	*die Apotheke*
the post office	*das Postamt*
the stationers	*der Schreibwarengeschäft*
the tourist office	*das Verkehrsamt*
What time does it open/close?	*Um wieviel Uhr macht es auf/zu?*

TIME, DAYS & NUMBERS

What time is it?	*Wie spät ist es?*
today	*heute*
tomorrow	*morgen*
yesterday	*gestern*
in the morning	*morgens*
in the afternoon	*nachmittags*
Monday	*Montag*
Tuesday	*Dienstag*
Wednesday	*Mittwoch*
Thursday	*Donnerstag*
Friday	*Freitag*
Saturday	*Samstag/Sonnabend*
Sunday	*Sonntag*

LANGUAGE

SIGNS – GERMAN

Eingang	Entrance
Ausgang	Exit
Auskunft	Information
Offen	Open
Geschlossen	Closed
Verboten	Prohibited
Toiletten (WC)	Toilets
Herren	Men
Damen	Women

0	null	**8**	acht
1	eins	**9**	neun
2	zwei/zwo	**10**	zehn
3	drei	**11**	elf
4	vier	**12**	zwölf
5	fünf	**13**	dreizehn
6	sechs	**100**	hundert
7	sieben	**1000**	tausend

TRANSPORT & DIRECTIONS

What time does ... leave/arrive?	Wann (fährt ... ab/kommt ... an)?
the boat	das Boot
the (intercity) bus	der (überland) Bus
the train	der Zug
the tram	die Strassenbahn
I'd like to hire a car/bicycle.	Ich möchte ein Auto/ Fahrrad mieten.
I'd like a one-way/ return ticket.	Ich möchte eine Einzelkarte/ Rückfahrkarte.
1st/2nd class	erste/zweite Klasse
left-luggage lockers	Schliessfächer
timetable	Fahrplan
bus stop	Bushaltestelle
tram stop	Strassenbahnhaltestelle
train station	Bahnhof (Bf)
ferry terminal	Fährhafen
Where is the ...?	Wo ist die ...?
Go straight ahead.	Gehen Sie geradeaus.
Turn left.	Biegen Sie links ab.
Turn right.	Biegen Sie rechts ab.
near/far	nahe/weit

GREEK

ACCOMMODATION

a hotel	ena xenotohohio
a youth hostel	enas xenonas neoitos
a camping ground	ena kamping

I'd like a ... room.	thelo ena dhomatio ...
single	ya ena atomo
double	ya dhio atoma
How much is it per night/person?	poso kostizi ya ena vradhi/atomo?

CONVERSATION & ESSENTIALS

Hello.	yasu (informal)
	yasas (polite/plural)
Goodbye.	andio
Yes.	ne
No.	okhi
Please.	sas parakalo
Thank you.	sas efharisto
That's fine/You're welcome.	ine endaksi/parakalo
Excuse me/Sorry.	signomi
Do you speak English?	milate anglika?
How much is it?	poso kani?

EMERGENCIES – GREEK

Help!	voithia!
Call a doctor!	fonakste ena yatro!
Call the police!	tilefoniste tin astinomia!
Go away!	fighe/dhromo!
I'm lost.	eho hathi

SHOPPING & SERVICES

a bank	mia trapeza
the ... embassy	i ... presvia
the market	i aghora
newsagent	efimeridhon
pharmacy	farmakio
the post office	to takhidhromio
the tourist office	to ghrafio turistikon pliroforion
What time does it open/close?	ti ora aniyi/klini?

TIME, DAYS & NUMBERS

What time is it?	ti ora ine?
today	simera
tomorrow	avrio
yesterday	hthes
in the morning	to proi
in the afternoon	to apoyevma
Monday	dheftera
Tuesday	triti
Wednesday	tetarti
Thursday	pempti
Friday	paraskevi
Saturday	savato
Sunday	kiryaki

THE GREEK ALPHABET

Greek	English	Pronunciation
Α α	a	as in 'father'
Β β	v	as the 'v' in 'vine'
Γ γ	gh/y	like a rough 'g', or as the 'y' in 'yes'
Δ δ	dh	as the 'th' in 'then'
Ε ε	e	as in 'egg'
Ζ ζ	z	as in 'zoo'
Η η	i	as the 'ee' in 'feet'
Θ θ	th	as the 'th' in 'throw'
Ι ι	i	as the 'ee' in 'feet'
Κ κ	k	as in 'kite'
Λ λ	l	as in 'leg'
Μ μ	m	as in 'man'
Ν ν	n	as in 'net'
Ξ ξ	x	as in 'taxi'
Ο ο	o	as in 'hot'
Π π	p	as in 'pup'
Ρ ρ	r	slightly trilled 'r'
Σ σ/ς	s	as in 'sand' (ς at the end of a word)
Τ τ	t	as in 'to'
Υ υ	i	as the 'ee' in 'feet'
Φ φ	f	as in 'fee'
Χ χ	kh/h	as the 'ch' in Scottish *loch*, or as a rough 'h'
Ψ ψ	ps	as the 'ps' in 'lapse'
Ω ω	o	as in 'lot'

1	*ena*	7	*epta*
2	*dhio*	8	*okhto*
3	*tria*	9	*enea*
4	*tesera*	10	*dheka*
5	*pende*	100	*ekato*
6	*eksi*	1000	*khilya*

TRANSPORT & DIRECTIONS

What time does the ... leave/arrive?	*ti ora fevyi/apo horito ...?*
boat	*to plio*
bus (city/intercity)	*to leoforio (ya tin boli/ya ta proastia)*
train	*to treno*
tram	*to tram*
I'd like a ... ticket.	*tha ithela isitirio ...*
one-way	*horis epistrofi*
return	*met epistrois*
1st class	*proti thesi*
2nd class	*dhefteri thesi*

SIGNS – GREEK

Εισοδος	Entrance
Εξοδος	Exit
Πληροφοριες	Information
Ανοικτο	Open
Κλειστο	Closed
Απαγορευεται	Prohibited
Τουαλετες	Toilets
Ανδρων	Men
Γυναικων	Women

left luggage	*horos aspokevon*
timetable	*dhromologhio*
bus stop	*i stasi tu leoforiu*
Go straight ahead.	*pighenete efthia*
Turn left.	*stripste aristera*
Turn right.	*stripste dheksya*

HUNGARIAN

PRONUNCIATION

The letters **cs**, **dz**, **dzs**, **gy**, **ly**, **ny**, **sz**, **ty**, and **zs** (consonant clusters) are separate letters in Hungarian and appear that way in telephone books and other alphabetical listings, eg *cukor* (sugar) appears in the dictionary before *csak* (only).

c	as the 'ts' in 'hats'
cs	as the 'ch' in 'church'
dz	as in 'adze'
dzs	as the 'j' in 'jet'
gy	as the 'du' in 'endure'
j	as the 'y' in 'yes'
ly	as the 'y' in 'yes'
ny	as the 'ni' in 'onion'
r	like a slightly rolled Scottish 'r'
s	as the 'sh' in 'ship'
sz	as the 'sh' in 'set'
ty	as the 'tu' in British English 'tube'
w	as 'v' (found in foreign words only)
zs	as the 's' in 'pleasure'

The meaning of words with **a**, **e** or **o** with and without an accent mark is great. For example, *hát* means 'back' while *hat* means 'six'.

a	as the 'o' in hot
á	as in 'father'
e	a short 'e' as in 'set'

é	as the 'e' in 'they' with no 'y' sound
i	as in 'hit' but shorter
í	as the 'i' in 'police'
o	as in 'open'
ó	a longer version of **o** above
ö	as the 'u' in 'fur' with no 'r' sound
ő	a longer version of **ö** above
u	as in 'pull'
ú	as the 'ue' in 'blue'
ü	similar to the 'u' in 'flute'; purse your lips tightly and say 'ee'
ű	a longer, breathier version of **ü** above

ACCOMMODATION

hotel	szálloda
guesthouse	panzió
youth hostel	ifjúsági szálló
camping ground	kemping
private room	fizetővendégszoba

Do you have rooms available?	Van szabad szobájuk?

How much is it ...?	Mennyibe kerül ...?
per night	éjszakánként
per person	személyenként

single room	egyágyas szoba
double room	kétágyas szoba

EMERGENCIES – HUNGARIAN

Help!	Segítség!
Call a doctor!	Hívjon orvost!
Call an ambulance!	Hívja a mentőket!
Call the police!	Hívja a rendőrséget!
Go away!	Menjen innen!
I'm lost.	Eltévedtem.

CONVERSATION & ESSENTIALS

Hello.	Jó napot kivánok. (pol)
	Szia/Szervusz. (inf)
Goodbye.	Viszontlátásra. (pol)
	Szia/Szervusz. (inf)
Yes.	Igen.
No.	Nem.
Please.	Kérem.
Thank you.	Köszönöm.
Excuse me.	Bocsánat.
Sorry.	Elnézést.
What's your name?	Mi a neve?/Mi a neved? (pol/inf)
My name is ...	A nevem ...
I don't understand.	Nem értem.
Do you speak English?	Beszél angolul?
How much is it?	Mennyibe kerül?

SHOPPING & SERVICES

Where is ...?	Hol van ...?
a bank	bank
a chemist	gyógyszertár
the market	a piac
the museum	a múzeum
the post office	a posta
a tourist office	turistairoda

What time does it (open/close)?	Mikor (nyit ki/zár be)?

TIME, DAYS & NUMBERS

What time is it?	Hány óra?
today	ma
tonight	ma este
tomorrow	holnap
yesterday	tegnap
in the morning	reggel
in the evening	este

Monday	hétfő
Tuesday	kedd
Wednesday	szerda
Thursday	csütörtök
Friday	péntek
Saturday	szombat
Sunday	vasárnap

1	egy		7	hét
2	kettő		8	nyolc
3	három		9	kilenc
4	négy		10	tíz
5	öt		100	száz
6	hat		1000	ezer

TRANSPORT & DIRECTIONS

What time does the ... leave/arrive?	Mikor indul/érkezik a ...?
boat/ferry	hajó/komp
city bus	város
intercity bus	varosközi
plane	repülőgép
train	vonat
tram	villamos

arrival	érkezés
departure	indulás
timetable	menetrend

Where is ...?	Hol van ...?
the bus stop	az autóbuszmegálló
the station	az állomás
the left-luggage office	a csomagmegőrző

SIGNS – HUNGARIAN

Bejárat	Entrance
Kijárat	Exit
Információ	Information
Nyitva	Open
Zárva	Closed
Tilos	Prohibited
Toalett/WC	Toilets
Férfiak	Men
Nők	Women

Turn left.	Forduljon balra.
Turn right.	Forduljon jobbra.
Go straight ahead.	Menyen egyenesen elore.
near/far	közel/messze

ICELANDIC

PRONUNCIATION

i, y	as the 'e' in 'pretty'
í, ý	as the 'e' in 'evil'
ú	as the 'o' in 'moon', or as the 'o' in 'woman'
ö	as the 'er' in 'fern', but without a trace of 'r'
á	as the 'ou' in 'out'
ei, ey	as the 'ay' in 'day'
ó	as the word 'owe'
æ	as the word 'eye'
au	as 'er' + 'ee' (as in French *oeil*)
é	as the 'y' in 'yet'
ð	as the 'th' in 'lather'
j	as the 'y' in 'yellow'
þ	as the 'th' in 'thin' or 'three'

ACCOMMODATION

hotel	hótel
guesthouse	gistiheimili
youth hostel	farfuglaheimili
camping ground	tjaldsvæði
Do you have any rooms available?	Eru herbergi laus?
How much is it per night/per person?	Hvað kostar nóttin/fyrir manninn?
one day	einn dag
two days	tvo daga
I'd like ...	Gæti ég fengið ...
a single room	einstaklingsherbergi
a double room	tveggjamannaherbergi

CONVERSATION & ESSENTIALS

Hello.	Halló.
Goodbye.	Bless.
Yes.	Já.
No.	Nei.
Please.	Gjörðu svo vel.
Thank you.	Takk fyrir.
That's fine/You're welcome.	Allt í lagi/Ekkert að þakka.
Excuse me/Sorry.	Afsakið.
Do you speak English?	Talar þú ensku?
How much is it?	Hvað kostar tað

EMERGENCIES – ICELANDIC

Help!	Hjálp!
Call a doctor!	Náið í lækni!
Call the police!	Náið í lögregluna!
Go away!	Farðu!
I'm lost	Ég er villtur/villt. (m/f)

SHOPPING & SERVICES

bank	banka
chemist/pharmacy	apótek
... embassy	... sendiráðinu
market	markaðnum
newsagent/stationer	blaðasala/bókabúð
post office	pósthúsinu
tourist office	upplýsingaþjónustu fyrir ferðafólk

TIME, DAYS & NUMBERS

What time is it?	Hvað er klukkan?
today	í dag
tomorrow	á morgun
yesterday	í gær
in the morning	að morgni
in the afternoon	eftir hádegi

Monday	mánudagur
Tuesday	þriðjudagur
Wednesday	miðvikudagur
Thursday	fimmtudagur
Friday	föstudagur
Saturday	laugardagur
Sunday	sunnudagur

0	núll	**7**	sjö	
1	einn	**8**	átta	
2	tveir	**9**	níu	
3	þrír	**10**	tíu	
4	fjórir	**20**	tuttugu	
5	fimm	**100**	eitt hundrað	
6	sex	**1000**	eitt þúsund	

LANGUAGE

SIGNS – ICELANDIC

Inngangur/Inn	Entrance
Útgangur/Út	Exit
Opið	Open
Lokað	Closed
Bannað	Prohibited
Upplýsingar	Information
Snyrting	Toilets
Karlar	Men
Konur	Women

TRANSPORT & DIRECTIONS

What time does ... leave/arrive?	Hvenær fer/kemur ...?
the boat	báturinn
the bus (city)	vagninn
the tram	sporvagninn

I'd like ...	Gæti ég fengid ...
a one-way ticket	miða/aðra leiðina
a return ticket	miða/báðar leiðir
1st-class	fyrsta farrými
2nd-class	annað farrými

timetable	tímaáætlun
bus stop	biðstöð
ferry terminal	ferjuhöfn
I'd like to hire a car/bicycle.	Ég vil leigia bíl/reiðhjól.

Where is ...?	Hvar er ...?
Go straight ahead.	Farðu beint af áfram.
Turn left.	Beygðu til vinstri.
Turn right.	Beygðu til hægri.
near/far	nálægt/langt í burtu

ITALIAN

Many older Italians expect to be addressed in the second person formal – *Lei* instead of *tu*. It isn't polite to use *ciao* when addressing strangers, unless they use it first; use *buongiorno* and *arrivederci*.

PRONUNCIATION

c	as 'k' before **a**, **o** and **u**; as the 'ch' in 'choose' before **e** and **i**
ch	a hard 'k' sound
g	as in 'get' before **a**, **o** and **u**; as in 'gem' before **e** and **i**
gh	as in 'get'
gli	as the 'lli' in 'million'
gn	as the 'ny' in 'canyon'
h	always silent
r	a rolled 'rrr' sound
sc	as the 'sh' in 'sheep' before **e** and **i**; a hard sound as in 'school' before **h**, **a**, **o** and **u**
z	as the 'ts' in 'lights' or the 'ds' in 'beds'

ACCOMMODATION

hotel	albergo
guesthouse	pensione
youth hostel	ostello per la gioventù
camping ground	campeggio

Do you have any rooms available?	Ha delle camere libere/ C'è una camera libera?
How much is it per (night/person)?	Quanto costa per (la notte/ciascuno)?

a single room	una camera singola
a twin room	una camera doppia
a double-bed room	una camera matrimoniale
for one night	per una notte
for two nights	per due notti

EMERGENCIES – ITALIAN

Help!	Aiuto!
Call a doctor!	Chiama un dottore/medico!
Call the police!	Chiama la polizia!
Go away!	Vai via!
I'm lost.	Mi sono perso/a (m/f)

CONVERSATION & ESSENTIALS

Hello.	Buongiorno. (pol)
	Ciao. (inf)
Goodbye.	Arrivederci. (pol)
	Ciao. (inf)
Yes.	Sì.
No.	No.
Please.	Per favore/Per piacere.
Thank you.	Grazie.
That's fine/You're welcome.	Prego.
Excuse me.	Mi scusi.
Sorry.	Mi scusi/Mi perdoni.
Do you speak English?	Parla inglese?
How much is it?	Quanto costa?

SHOPPING & SERVICES

a bank	una banca
chemist/pharmacy	la farmacia

```
SIGNS – ITALIAN
Ingresso/Entrata        Entrance
Uscita                  Exit
Informazione            Information
Aperto                  Open
Chiuso                  Closed
Proibito/Vietato        Prohibited
Gabinetti/Bagni         Toilets
    Uomini              Men
    Donne               Women
```

the market	il mercato
newsagent	l'edicola
post office	la posta
the tourist office	l'ufficio di turismo

What time does it open/close?	A che ora (si) apre/chiude?

TIME, DAYS & NUMBERS

What time is it?	Che (ora è?/ore sono)?
today	oggi
tomorrow	domani
yesterday	ieri
morning	mattina
afternoon	pomeriggio

Monday	lunedì
Tuesday	martedì
Wednesday	mercoledì
Thursday	giovedì
Friday	venerdì
Saturday	sabato
Sunday	domenica

1	uno	7	sette
2	due	8	otto
3	tre	9	nove
4	quattro	10	dieci
5	cinque	100	cento
6	sei	1000	mille

TRANSPORT & DIRECTIONS

When does the ... leave/arrive?	A che ora parte/ arriva ...?
boat	la barca
bus	l'autobus
ferry	il traghetto
train	il treno

bus stop	fermata dell'autobus
train station	stazione
ferry terminal	stazione marittima

1st/2nd class	prima/seconda classe
left luggage	deposito bagagli
timetable	orario

I'd like a one-way/ return ticket.	Vorrei un biglietto di solo andata/ di andata e ritorno.
I'd like to hire a car/bicycle.	Vorrei noleggiare una macchina/bicicletta.

Where is ...?	Dov'è ...?
Go straight ahead.	Si va sempre diritto.
Turn left/right.	Giri a sinistra/destra.
far/near	lontano/vicino

LATVIAN

ALPHABET & PRONUNCIATION

The letters of the Latvian alphabet are: **a b c č d e f g ģ (Ģ) h i j k ķ l ļ m n ņ o p r s š t u v z ž.**

c	as the 'ts' in 'bits'
č	as the 'ch' in 'church'
ģ	as the 'j' in 'jet'
j	as the 'y' in 'yes'
ķ	as 'tu' in 'tune'
ļ	as the 'lli' in 'billiards'
ņ	as the 'ni' in 'onion'
o	as the 'a' in 'water'
š	as the 'sh' in 'ship'
ž	as the 's' in 'pleasure'
ai	as in 'aisle'
ei	as in 'vein'
aa	as the 'a' in 'barn'
ē	as the 'e' in 'where'
oo	as the 'oo' in 'boot'

CONVERSATION & ESSENTIALS

Hello.	Labdien or Sveiki.
Goodbye.	Uz redzēšanos or Ataa.
Yes.	Jaa.
No.	Nē.
Excuse me.	Atvainojiet.
Please.	Loodzu.
Thank you.	Paldies.
Do you speak English?	Vai joos runaajat angliski?

```
EMERGENCIES – LATVIAN
Help!              Palīgā!
I'm ill.           Es esmu slims/slima. (m/f)
I'm lost.          Es esmu apmaldijies/
                   apmaldijusies. (m/f)
Go away!           Ejiet projam!
```

LANGUAGE

SIGNS – LATVIAN

Ieeja	Entrance
Izeja	Exit
Informācija	Information
Atvērts	Open
Slēgts	Closed
Smēķet Aizliegts	No Smoking
Maksas Tualetes	Public Toilets
Sieviešu	Women
Vīriešu	Men

SHOPPING & SERVICES

bank	banka
chemist	aptieka
currency exchange	valootas maiņa
hotel	viesneeca
market	tirgus
post office	pasts
toilet	tualete
Where?	Kur?
How much?	Cik?

TIME, DAYS & NUMBERS

today	šodien
yesterday	vakar
tomorrow	reet
Sunday	svētdiena
Monday	pirmdiena
Tuesday	otrdiena
Wednesday	trešdiena
Thursday	ceturtdiena
Friday	piektdiena
Saturday	sestdiena

1	viens	7	septiņi
2	divi	8	astoņi
3	trees	9	deviņi
4	četri	10	desmit
5	pieci	100	simts
6	seši	1000	tookstots

TRANSPORT & DIRECTIONS

airport	lidosta
train station	dzelzceļa stacija
train	vilciens
bus station	autoosta
bus	autobuss
port	osta
taxi	taksometrs
tram	tramvajs
stop (eg bus stop)	pietura

departure time	atiešanas laiks
arrival time	pienaakšanas laiks
ticket	biļete
ticket office	kase

LITHUANIAN

ALPHABET & PRONUNCIATION

The letters of the Lithuanian alphabet are:
a b c č d e f g h i/j y j k l m n o p r s š t u v z ž. The **i**
and **y** are very similar.

c	as 'ts'
č	as 'ch'
y	between the 'i' in 'tin' and the 'ee' in 'feet'
j	as the 'y' in 'yes'
š	as 'sh'
ž	as the 's' in 'pleasure'
ei	as the 'ai' in 'pain'
ie	as the 'ye' in 'yet'
ui	as the 'wi' in 'win'

Accent marks above and below vowels (eg
aa, **ė** and **į**) all have the general effect of
lengthening the vowel:

aa	as the 'a' in 'father'
ę	as the 'ai' in 'air'
į	as the 'ee' in 'feet'
ų	as the 'oo' in 'boot'
oo	as the 'oo' in 'boot'
ė	as the 'a' in 'late'

CONVERSATION & ESSENTIALS

Hello.	Labas/Sveikas.
Goodbye.	Sudie or Viso gero.
Yes.	Taip.
No.	Ne.
Excuse me.	Atsiprašau.
Please.	Prašau.
Thank you.	Ačioo.
Do you speak English?	Ar kalbate angliškai?

EMERGENCIES – LITHUANIAN

Help!	Gelėbkite!
I'm ill.	Aš sergu.
I'm lost.	Aš paklydęs/paklydusi. (m/f)
Go away!	Eik šalin!
Call ...!	Iššaukite ...!
a doctor	gydytoją
an ambulance	greitąją
the police	policiją

SHOPPING & SERVICES

bank	bankas
chemist	vaistinė
currency exchange	valiutos keitykla
hotel	viešbutis
market	turgus
post office	paštas
toilet	tualetas
Where?	Kur?
How much?	Kiek?

TIMES, DAYS & NUMBERS

today	šiandien
tomorrow	rytoj
yesterday	vakar

Monday	pirmadienis
Tuesday	antradienis
Wednesday	trečiadienis
Thursday	ketvirtadienis
Friday	penktadienis
Saturday	šeštadienis
Sunday	sekmadienis

1	vienas	7	septyni
2	du	8	aštuoni
3	trys	9	devyni
4	keturi	10	dešimt
5	penki	100	šimtas
6	šeši	1000	tookstantis

TRANSPORT & DIRECTIONS

airport	oro uostas
bus station	autobusų stotis
port	uostas
train station	geležinkelio stotis
stop (eg bus stop)	stotelė
bus	autobusas
taxi	taksi
train	traukinys
tram	tramvajus
departure time	išvykimo laikas
arrival time	atvykimo laikas
ticket	bilietas
ticket office	kasa

MACEDONIAN

PRONUNCIATION

There are 31 letters in the Macedonian Cyrillic alphabet (see p1293).

ACCOMMODATION

hotel	hotel
guesthouse	privatno smetuvanje
youth hostel	mladinsko prenocjishte
camping ground	kamping

Do you have any rooms available?	dali imate slobodni sobi?
How much is it per night/per person?	koja e cenata po nocj/po osoba?

a single room	soba so eden krevet
a double room	soba so brachen krevet
for one/two nights	za edna/dva vecheri

CONVERSATION & ESSENTIALS

Hello.	zdravo
Goodbye.	priatno
Yes.	da
No.	ne
Please.	molam
Thank you.	blagodaram
You're welcome.	nema zoshto/milo mi e
Excuse me.	izvinete
Sorry.	oprostete ve molam
Do you speak English?	zboruvate li angliski?
What's your name?	kako se vikate?
My name is ...	jas se vikam ...
How much is it?	kolku chini toa?

SHOPPING & SERVICES

bank	banka
chemist/pharmacy	apteka
my hotel	mojot hotel
the market	pazarot
newsagent	kiosk za vesnici
the post office	poshtata
the tourist office	turistichkoto biro
What time does it open/close?	koga se otvora/zatvora?

SIGNS – MACEDONIAN

Влез	Entrance
Излез	Exit
Отворено	Open
Затворено	Closed
Информации	Information
Забрането	Prohibited
Клозети	Toilets
Машки	Men
Женски	Women

TIME, DAYS & NUMBERS

What time is it?	kolku e chasot?
today	denes
tomorrow	utre
yesterday	vchera
morning	utro
afternoon	popladne
Monday	ponedelnik
Tuesday	vtornik
Wednesday	sreda
Thursday	chetvrtok
Friday	petok
Saturday	sabota
Sunday	nedela

1	eden	7	sedum
2	dva	8	osum
3	tri	9	devet
4	chetiri	10	deset
5	pet	100	sto
6	shest	1000	hiljada

TRANSPORT & DIRECTIONS

What time does the next ... leave/arrive?	koga doagja/zaminuva idniot ...?
boat	brod
city bus	avtobus gradski
intercity bus	avtobus megjugradski
train	voz
tram	tramvaj
I'd like ...	sakam ...
a one-way ticket	bilet vo eden pravec
a return ticket	povraten bilet
1st class	prva klasa
2nd class	vtora klasa
timetable	vozen red
bus stop	avtobuska stanica
train station	zheleznichka stanica

I'd like to hire a car/bicycle.	sakam da iznajmam kola/tochak
Where is ...?	kade je ...?
Go straight ahead.	odete pravo napred
Turn left/right.	svrtete levo/desno
near/far	blisku/daleku

MALTESE

PRONUNCIATION

ċ	as the 'ch' in 'child'
g	as in 'good'
ġ	as the 'j' in 'job'
għ	silent; lengthens the preceding or following vowel
h	silent, as in 'hour'
ħ	as the 'h' in 'hand'
j	as the 'y' in 'yellow'
ij	as the 'igh' in 'high'
ej	as the 'ay' in 'day'
q	a glottal stop; like the missing 't' between the two syllables in 'bottle'
x	as the 'sh' in 'shop'
z	as the 'ts' in 'bits'
ż	soft as in 'buzz'

ACCOMMODATION

Do you have a room available?	Għandek kamra jekk jogħġobok?
Do you have a room for one person/two people?	Għandek kamra għal wieħed/tnejn?
Do you have a room for one/two nights?	Għandek kamra għal lejl/żewgt iljieli?

EMERGENCIES – MALTESE

Help!	Ajjut!
Call a doctor.	Qibgħad ghat-tabib.
Police!	Pulizija!
I'm lost.	Ninsab mitluf.
hospital	sptar
ambulance	ambulans

CONVERSATION & ESSENTIALS

Hello.	Merħba.
Good morning/day.	Bonġu.
Goodbye.	Saħħa.
Yes.	Iva.
No.	Le.
Please.	Jekk jogħġobok.
Thank you.	Grazzi.
Excuse me.	Skużani.
Do you speak English?	Titkellem bl-ingliż?
How much is it?	Kemm?

SHOPPING & SERVICES

the bank	il-bank
chemist/pharmacy	l-ispiżerija
the ... embassy	l'ambaxxata ...
the market	is-suq
the post office	il-posta
shop	ħanut

What time does it open/close?	Fix'ħin jiftaħ/jagħlaq?

TIME, DAYS & NUMBERS

What's the time?	X'ħin hu?
today	illum
tomorrow	għada
yesterday	il-bieraħ
morning	fil-għodu
afternoon	nofs in-nhar

Monday	it-tnejn
Tuesday	it-tlieta
Wednesday	l-erbgħa
Thursday	il-ħamis
Friday	il-gimgħa
Saturday	is-sibt
Sunday	il-ħadd

xejn		7	sebgħa
wieħed		8	tmienja
tnejn		9	disgħa
tlieta		10	għaxra
erbgħa		11	ħdax
ħamsa		100	mija
sitta		1000	elf

TRANSPORT & DIRECTIONS

When does the boat leave/arrive?	Meta jitlaq/jasal il-vapur?
When does the bus leave/arrive?	Meta titlaq/jasal il-karozza?

I'd like a ... ticket.	Nixtieq biljett ...
one-way/return	'one-way/return'
1st-/2nd-class	'1st/2nd class'

left luggage	ħallejt il-bagalji
bus/trolleybus stop	xarabank/coach

I'd like to hire a car/ bicycle.	Nixtieq nikri karozza/rota.
Where is a/the ...?	Fejn hu ...?
Go straight ahead.	Mur dritt.
Turn left.	Dur fuq il-lemin.
Turn right.	Dur fuq ix-xellug.
near/far	il-viċin/-boghod

MOROCCAN ARABIC

PRONUNCIATION

a	as in 'had' (sometimes very short)
aa	as the 'a' in 'father'
e	as in 'bet' (sometimes very short)
ee	as in 'beet'
i	as in 'hit'
o	as in 'hot'
oo	as in 'cool'
u	as the 'oo' in 'book'
aw	as the 'ow' in 'how'
ai	as the 'i' in 'high'
ei/ay	as the 'a' in 'cake'
j	more or less as the 'j' in 'John'
H	a strongly whispered 'h', almost like a sigh of relief
q	a strong guttural 'k' sound
kh	a slightly gurgling sound, like the 'ch' in Scottish 'loch'
sh	as in 'she'
z	as the 's' in pleasure
gh	called 'ghayn', similar to the French 'r', but more guttural

GLOTTAL STOP (')

The glottal stop is the sound you hear between the vowels in the expression 'oh oh!'. When it occurs before a vowel (eg 'ayn), the vowel is 'growled' from the back of the throat. Before a consonant or at the end of a word, it sounds like a glottal stop.

ACCOMMODATION

hotel	al-otēl
youth hostel	dar shabbab
camp site	mukhaym

Is there a room available?	wash kayn shee beet xaweeya?
How much is this room per night?	bshaHal al-bayt liyal?

CONVERSATION & ESSENTIALS

Hello.	as-salaam 'alaykum
Goodbye.	ma' as-salaama
Yes.	eeyeh
No.	la
Please.	'afak
Thank you (very much).	shukran (jazilan)
You're welcome.	la shukran, 'ala wajib
Excuse me.	smeH leeya
Do you speak English?	wash kat'ref negleezeeya?
I understand.	fhemt
I don't understand.	mafhemtsh
How much (is it)?	bish-hal?

SHOPPING & SERVICES

the bank	al-banka
the embassy	as-sifaara
the market	as-sooq
the police station	al-bolees
the post office	al-boosta, maktab al-bareed
a toilet	bayt al-ma, mirHad

TIME, DATES & NUMBERS

What time is it?	shHal fessa'a?
today	al-yoom
tomorrow	ghaddan
yesterday	al-bareh
in the morning	fis-sabaH
in the evening	fil-masa'

Monday	(nhar) al-itnēn
Tuesday	(nhar) at-talata
Wednesday	(nhar) al-arba'
Thursday	(nhar) al-khamees
Friday	(nhar) al-juma'
Saturday	(nhar) as-sabt
Sunday	(nhar) al-ahad

1	waaHid	7	saba'a
2	jooj/itneen	8	tamanya
3	talata	9	tissa'
4	arba'a	10	'ashara
5	khamsa	100	miyya
6	sitta	1000	alf

TRANSPORT & DIRECTIONS

What time does the ... leave/arrive?	emta qiyam/wusool ...
boat	al-baboor
bus (city)	al-otobees
bus (intercity)	al-kar
train	al-masheena

1st class	ddarazha lloola
2nd class	ddarazha ttaneeya
train station	maHattat al-masheena/al-qitar
bus stop	mawqif al-otobis
Where can I hire a car/bicycle?	fein yimkin ana akra tomobeel/beshkleeta?
Where is (the) ...?	fein ...?
Go straight ahead.	seer neeshan
Turn right.	dor 'al leemen
Turn left.	dor 'al leeser

NORWEGIAN

PRONUNCIATION

å	as the 'aw' in 'paw'
æ	as the 'a' in 'act'
ø	long, as the 'er' in 'fern'; short, as th 'a' in 'ago'
u, y	say 'ee' while pursing your lips
ai	as the word 'eye'
ei	as the 'ay' in 'day'
au	as the 'o' in 'note'
øy	as the 'oy' in 'toy'
d	at the end of a word, or between tw vowels, it's often silent
g	as the 'g' in 'get'; as the 'y' in 'yar before **ei, i, j, øy, y**
j	as the 'y' in 'yard'
k	as in 'kin'; as the 'ch' in 'chin' befo **ei, i, j, øy**, and **y**
r	a rolled 'r'
rs	as the 'sh' in 'fish'
s	as in 'so'; as the 'sh' in 'ship' befo **ei, i, j, øy** and **y**

ACCOMMODATION

hotel	hotell
guesthouse	gjestgiveri/pensionat
youth hostel	vandrerhjem
camping ground	kamping/leirplass
Do you have any rooms available?	Har du ledige rom?
How much is it per night/person?	Hvor mye er det pr dag/person
one day/two days	en dag/to dager

SIGNS – NORWEGIAN

Inngang	Entrance
Utgang	Exit
Åpen	Open
Stengt	Closed
Forbudt	Prohibited
Toaletter	Toilets
Herrer	Men
Damer	Women

I'd like ...	Jeg vil gjerne ha ...
a single room	et enkeltrom
a double room	et dobbeltrom

CONVERSATION & ESSENTIALS

Hello.	Goddag.
Goodbye.	Ha det.
Yes.	Ja.
No.	Nei.
Please.	Vær så snill.
Thank you.	Takk.
That's fine/You're welcome.	Ingen årsak.
Excuse me/Sorry.	Unnskyld.
Do you speak English?	Snakker du engelsk?
How much is it?	Hvor mye koster det?

EMERGENCIES – NORWEGIAN

Help!	Hjelp!
Call a doctor!	Ring en lege!
Call the police!	Ring politiet!
Go away!	Forsvinn!
I'm lost.	Jeg har gått meg vill.

SHOPPING & SERVICES

bank	banken
chemist/pharmacy	apotek
... embassy	... ambassade
market	torget
newsagent	kiosk
post office	postkontoret
telephone centre	televerket
tourist office	turistinformasjon

TIME, DAYS & NUMBERS

What time is it?	Hva er klokka?
today	i dag
tomorrow	i morgen
yesterday	i går
in the morning	om formiddagen
in the afternoon	om ettermiddagen

Monday	mandag
Tuesday	tirsdag
Wednesday	onsdag
Thursday	torsdag
Friday	fredag
Saturday	lørdag
Sunday	søndag

0	null		7	sju
1	en		8	åtte
2	to		9	ni
3	tre		10	ti
4	fire		11	elleve
5	fem		100	hundre
6	seks		1000	tusen

TRANSPORT & DIRECTIONS

What time does ... leave/arrive?	Når går/kommer ...?
the boat	båten
the (city) bus	(by)bussen
the intercity bus	linjebussen
the tram	trikken
the train	toget

I'd like ...	Jeg vil gjerne ha ...
a one-way ticket	enkeltbillett
a return ticket	tur-retur
1st class	første klasse
2nd class	annen klasse

left luggage	reisegods
timetable	ruteplan
bus stop	bussholdeplass
tram stop	trikkholdeplass
train station	jernbanestasjon
ferry terminal	ferjeleiet

Where can I rent a car/bicycle?	Hvor kan jeg leie en bil/sykkel?
Where is ...?	Hvor er ...?
Go straight ahead.	Det er rett fram.
Turn left.	Ta til venstre.
Turn right.	Ta til høyre.
near/far	nær/langt

POLISH

PRONUNCIATION

Written Polish is phonetically consistent, which means that the pronunciation of letters or clusters of letters doesn't vary from word to word. The stress almost always goes on the second-last syllable.

Vowels

a	as the 'u' in 'cut'
e	as in 'ten'
i	as the 'ee' in 'feet' but shorter
o	as in 'lot'
u	as the 'oo' in 'book' but shorter
y	similar to the 'i' in 'bit'

There are three vowels unique to Polish:

ą	a nasal vowel sound like the French *un*, similar to 'own' in 'sown'
ę	also nasalised, like the French *un*, but pronounced as 'e' when word-final
ó	similar to Polish **u**

CONSONANTS

In Polish, the consonants **b**, **d**, **f**, **k**, **l**, **m**, **n**, **p**, **t**, **v** and **z** are pronounced more or less as they are in English. The following consonants and clusters of consonants sound distinctly different to their English counterparts:

c	as the 'ts' in 'its'
ch	similar to the 'ch' in the Scottish *loch*
cz	as the 'ch' in 'church'
ć	much softer than Polish **c** (as 'tsi' before vowels)
dz	as the 'ds' in 'suds' but shorter
dź	a soft **dz** (as 'dzi' before vowels)
dż	as the 'j' in 'jam'
g	as in 'get'
h	as **ch**
j	as the 'y' in 'yet'
ł	as the 'w' in 'wine'
ń	as the 'ny' in 'canyon' (as 'ni' before vowels)
r	always rolled
rz	as the 's' in 'pleasure'
s	as in 'set'
sz	as the 'sh' in 'show'
ś	as **s** but softer (as 'si' before vowels)
w	as the 'v' in 'van'
ź	softer version of **z** (as 'zi' before vowels)
ż	as **rz**

ACCOMMODATION

hotel	hotel
youth hostel	schronisko młodzieżowe
camping ground	kemping
private room	kwatera prywatna
Do you have any rooms available?	Czy są wolne pokoje?
How much is it?	Ile to kosztuje?
Does it include breakfast?	Czy śniadanie jest wliczone?
single room	pokój jednoosobowy
double room	pokój dwuosobowy

CONVERSATION & ESSENTIALS

Hello/Good morning.	Dzień dobry.
Hello.	Cześć. (informal)
Goodbye.	Do widzenia.
Yes/No.	Tak/Nie.
Please.	Proszę.
Thank you.	Dziękuję.
Excuse me/Sorry.	Przepraszam.
Do you speak English?	Czy pan/pani mówi po angielsku? (m/f)
I don't understand.	Nie rozumiem.
What is it called?	Jak się nazywa?
How much is it?	Ile to kosztuje?

EMERGENCIES – POLISH

Help!	Pomocy!/Ratunku!
Call a doctor!	Proszę wezwać lekarza!
Call the police!	Proszę wezwać policję!
I'm lost.	Zgubiłem się. (m)
	Zgubiłam się. (f)

SHOPPING & SERVICES

the bank	bank
the chemist	apteka
the church	kościół
the city centre	centrum miasta
the market	targ/bazar
the museum	muzeum
the post office	poczta
the tourist office	informacja turystyczna
What time does it open/close?	O której otwierają/ zamykają?

TIME, DAYS & NUMBERS

What time is it?	Która jest godzina?
today	dzisiaj
tonight	dzisiaj wieczorem
tomorrow	jutro
yesterday	wczoraj
in the morning	rano
in the evening	wieczorem
Monday	poniedziałek
Tuesday	wtorek
Wednesday	środa

SIGNS – POLISH

Wejście	Entrance
Wyjście	Exit
Informacja	Information
Otwarte	Open
Zamknięte	Closed
Wzbroniony	Prohibited
Toalety	Toilets
Panowie	Men
Panie	Women

Thursday	czwartek
Friday	piątek
Saturday	sobota
Sunday	niedziela

1	jeden	**7**	siedem
2	dwa	**8**	osiem
3	trzy	**9**	dziewięć
4	cztery	**10**	dziesięć
5	pięć	**100**	sto
6	sześć	**1000**	tysiąc

TRANSPORT & DIRECTIONS

What time does the ... leave/arrive?	O której godzinie przychodzi/odchodzi ...?
plane	samolot
boat	statek
bus	autobus
train	pociąg
tram	tramwaj
arrival	przyjazd
departure	odjazd
timetable	rozkład jazdy
Where is the bus stop?	Gdzie jest przystanek autobusowy?
Where is the station?	Gdzie jest stacja kolejowa?
Where is the left-luggage office?	Gdzie jest przechowalnia bagażu?
Please show me on the map.	Proszę pokazać mi to na mapie.
straight ahead	prosto
left	lewo
right	prawo

PORTUGUESE

Note that Portugese uses masculine and feminine word endings, usually '-o' and '-a' respectively – to say 'thank you', a man will therefore use *obrigado*, a woman, *obrigada*.

NASAL VOWELS

Nasalisation is represented by an 'n' or an 'm' after the vowel, or by a tilde over it, eg **ã**. The nasal 'i' exists in English as the 'ing' in 'sing'.

ão	nasal 'ow' (owng)
ãe	nasal 'ay' (eing)
õe	nasal 'oy' (oing)
ui	similar to the 'uing' in 'ensuing'
é	short, as in 'bet'
ê	long, as the 'a' in 'gate'
ô	long, as in 'note'
c	as in 'cat' before **a**, **o** or **u**; as the 's' in 'sin' before **e** or **i**
ç	as the 'c' in 'celery'
g	as in 'go' before **a**, **o** or **u**; as the 's' in 'treasure' before **e** or **i**
h	never pronounced when word-initial
nh	as the 'ni' in 'onion'
lh	as the 'lli' in 'million'
j	as the 's' in 'treasure'
m	not pronounced when word-final – it simply nasalises the previous vowel, eg *um* (oong), *bom* (bõ)
x	as the 'sh' in 'ship', as the 'z' in 'zeal', or as the 'x' in 'taxi'
z	as the 's' in 'treasure' before a consonant or at the end of a word

ACCOMMODATION

hotel	hotel
guesthouse	pensão
youth hostel	pousada da juventude
camping ground	parque de campismo
Do you have any rooms available?	Tem quartos livres?
How much is it per night/per person?	Quanto é por noite/por pessoa?
a single room	um quarto individual
a twin room	um quarto duplo
a double bed room	um quarto de casal
for one night	para uma noite
for two nights	para duas noites

CONVERSATION & ESSENTIALS

Hello.	Olá.
Goodbye.	Adeus/Ciao. (informal)
Yes.	Sim.
No.	Não.
Please.	Se faz favor.
Thank you.	Obrigado/a. (m/f)

You're welcome.	De nada.
Excuse me.	Com licença.
Sorry.	Desculpe.
Do you speak English?	Fala Inglês?
How much is it?	Quanto custa?

EMERGENCIES – PORTUGUESE

Help!	Socorro!
Call a doctor!	Chame um médico!
Call the police!	Chame a polícia!
Go away!	Deixe-me em paz! (pol)
	Vai-te embora! (inf)
I'm lost.	Estou perdido/a. (m/f)

SHOPPING & SERVICES

a bank	um banco
the chemist/ pharmacy	a farmácia
the ... embassy	a embaixada de ...
the market	o mercado
the newsagent	a papelaria
the post office	os correios
the tourist office	o (posto de) turismo
What time does it open/close?	A que horas abre/fecha?

TIME, DAYS & NUMBERS

What time is it?	Que horas são?
today	hoje
tomorrow	amanhã
yesterday	ontem
morning	manhã
afternoon	tarde

Monday	segunda-feira
Tuesday	terça-feira
Wednesday	quarta-feira
Thursday	quinta-feira
Friday	sexta-feira
Saturday	sábado
Sunday	domingo

0	zero	7	sete
1	um/uma	8	oito
2	dois/duas	9	nove
3	três	10	dez
4	quatro	11	onze
5	cinco	100	cem
6	seis	1000	mil

TRANSPORT & DIRECTIONS

What time does the ... leave/arrive?	A que horas parte/chega ...?

SIGNS – PORTUGUESE

Entrada	Entrance
Saída	Exit
Informações	Information
Aberto	Open
Fechado	Closed
Proíbido	Prohibited
Empurre/Puxe	Push/Pull
Lavabos/WC	Toilets
Homens (h)	Men
Senhoras (s)	Women

boat	o barco
bus (city)	o autocarro
bus (intercity)	a camioneta
tram	o eléctrico
train	o combóio

bus stop	paragem de autocarro
train station	estação ferroviária
timetable	horário

I'd like a ... ticket.	Queria um bilhete ...
one-way	simples/de ida
return	de ida e volta
1st class	de primeira classe
2nd class	de segunda classe

I'd like to hire ...	Queria alugar ...
a car	um carro
a bicycle	uma bicicleta

Where is ...?	Onde é ...?
Go straight ahead.	Siga sempre a direito/ Siga sempre em frente.
Turn left.	Vire à esquerda.
Turn right.	Vire à direita.
near/far	perto/longe

ROMANIAN

PRONUNCIATION

Until the mid-19th century, Romanian was written in the Cyrillic script. Today Romanian employs 28 Latin letters, some of which bear accents. At the beginning of a word, e and i are pronounced 'ye' and 'yi' while at the end of a word i is almost silent. At the end of a word ii is pronounced 'ee'. Word stress usually falls on the penultimate syllable.

ă	as the 'er' in 'brother'
î	as the 'i' in 'river'
c	as 'k', except before **e** and **i**, when it's as the 'ch' in 'chip'
ch	always as the 'k' in 'king'
g	as in 'go', except before **e** and **i**, when it's as in 'gentle'
gh	always as the 'g' in 'get'
ş	as 'sh'
ţ	as the 'tz'in 'tzar'

ACCOMMODATION

hotel	hotel
guesthouse	casa de oaspeţi
youth hostel	camin studentesc
camping ground	camping
private room	cameră particulară
single room	o cameră pentru o persoană
double room	o cameră pentru două persoane
Do you have any rooms available?	Aveţi camere libere?
How much is it?	Cît costă?
Does it include breakfast?	Include micul dejun?

CONVERSATION & ESSENTIALS

Hello.	Bună.
Goodbye.	La revedere.
Yes.	Da.
No.	Nu.
Please.	Vă rog.
Thank you.	Mulţumesc.
Excuse me.	Scuzaţi-mă.
Sorry.	Iertaţi-mă.
Do you speak English?	Vorbiţi engleza?
I don't understand.	Nu înţeleg.
What is it called?	Cum se cheamă?
How much is it?	Cît costă?

SHOPPING & SERVICES

the bank	banca
the chemist/ pharmacy	farmacistul
the city centre	centrum oraşului
the ... embassy	ambasada ...

SIGNS – ROMANIAN

Intrare	Entrance
Ieşire	Exit
Informaţii	Information
Deschis	Open
Inchis	Closed
Nu Intraţi	No Entry
Toaleta	Toilets

the market	piaţa
the museum	muzeu
the post office	poşta
the tourist office	birou de informatii turistice

TIME, DAYS & NUMBERS

What time is it?	Ce oră este?
today	azi
tonight	deseară
tomorrow	mîine
yesterday	ieri
in the morning	dimineaţa
in the evening	seară
Monday	luni
Tuesday	marţi
Wednesday	miercuri
Thursday	joi
Friday	vineri
Saturday	sîmbătă
Sunday	duminică

1	unu	7	şapte
2	doi	8	opt
3	trei	9	nouă
4	patru	10	zece
5	cinci	100	o sută
6	şase	1000	o mie

TRANSPORT & DIRECTIONS

What time does the ... leave/arrive?	La ce oră pleacă/soseşte ...?
boat	vaporul
bus	autobusul
train	trenul
tram	tramvaiul
plane	avionul
arrival	sosire
departure	plecare
timetable	mersul/orar
Where is the bus stop?	Unde este staţia de autobuz?
Where is the station?	Unde este gară?

Where is the left-luggage office?	Unde este biroul pentru bagaje de mînă?
Please show me on the map.	Vă rog arătați-mi pe hartă.

straight ahead	drept înainte
left	stînga
right	dreapta

RUSSIAN

Russian uses the Cyrillic alphabet. The table on p1293 shows all the characters used in the Cyrillic alphabets of Bulgarian, Macedonian, Russian and Serbian. It's well worth familiarising yourself with them.

ACCOMMODATION

hotel	gastinitsa
room	nomer
breakfast	zaftrak

How much is a room?	skol'ka stoit nomer?

CONVERSATION & ESSENTIALS

Hello.	zdrastvuyte
Good morning.	dobraye utra
Good afternoon.	dobryy den'
Good evening.	dobryy vecher
Goodbye.	da svidaniya
Bye!	paka! (inf)
How are you?	kak dila?
Yes.	dat
No.	net
Please.	pazhalsta
Thank you (very much).	(bal'shoye) spasiba
Pardon me.	prastite/pazhalsta
No problem/Never mind.	nichevo (literally, 'nothing')
Do you speak English?	vy gavarite pa angliyski?
What's your name?	kak vas zavut?
My name is ...	minya zavut ...
How much is it?	skol'ka stoit?

SHOPPING & SERVICES

bank	bank
market	rynak
pharmacy	apteka
post office	pochta
telephone booth	tilifonnaya budka
open	otkryta
closed	zakryta

TIME, DATE & NUMBERS

What time is it?	katoryy chas
today	sivodnya
yesterday	vchira
tomorrow	zaftra
am/in the morning	utra
pm/in the afternoon	dnya
in the evening	vechira

Monday	panidel'nik
Tuesday	ftornik
Wednesday	srida
Thursday	chitverk
Friday	pyatnitsa
Saturday	subota
Sunday	vaskrisen'e

0	nol'	7	sem'
1	adin	8	vosim'
2	dva	9	devit'
3	tri	10	desit'
4	chityri	11	adinatsat'
5	pyat'	100	sto
6	shest'	1000	tysyacha

TRANSPORT & DIRECTIONS

What time does the ... leave?	f katoram chasu pribyvaet ...?
What time does the ... arrive?	f katoram chasu atpravlyaetsa ...?

THE CYRILLIC ALPHABET

CYRILLIC	ROMAN	PRONUNCIATION
А а	a	as in 'father'; also as in 'ago' when unstressed in Russian
Б б	b	as in 'but'
В в	v	as in 'van'
Г г	g	as in 'go'
Ѓ ѓ	gj	as the 'gu' in 'legume' (Macedonian only)
Д д	d	as the 'd' in 'dog'
Е е	ye	as in 'yet' when stressed; as in 'year' when un-stressed (Russian)
	e	as in 'bet' (Bulgarian); as in 'there' (Macedonian)
Ё ё	yo	as in 'yore' (Russian only)
Ж ж	zh	as the 's' in 'measure'
З з	z	as in 'zoo'
Ѕ ѕ	zj	as the 'ds' in 'suds' (Macedonian only)
И и	i	as the 'ee' in 'meet'
Й й	y	as in 'boy'
Ј ј	j	as the 'y' in 'young' (Macedonian only)
К к	k	as in 'kind'
Ќ ќ	kj	as the 'cu' in 'cure' (Macedonian only)
Л л	l	as in 'lamp'
Љ љ	lj	as the 'lli' in 'million' (Macedonian only)
М м	m	as in 'mat'
Н н	n	as in 'not'
Њ њ	nj	as the 'ny' in 'canyon' (Macedonian only)

CYRILLIC	ROMAN	PRONUNCIATION
О о	o	as the 'a' in 'water' when stressed; as the 'a' in 'ago' when un-stressed (Russian); as in 'hot' (Bulgarian & Macedonian)
П п	p	as in 'pick'
Р р	r	as in 'rub' (but rolled)
С с	s	as in 'sing'
Т т	t	as in 'ten'
У у	u	as in 'rule'
Ф ф	f	as in 'fan'
Х х	kh	as the 'ch' in 'Bach' (Russian)
	h	as in 'hot' (Macedonian)
Ц ц	ts	as in 'bits'
Џ џ	dz	as the 'j' in 'judge' (Macedonian only)
Ч ч	ch	as in 'chat'
Ш ш	sh	as in 'shop'
Щ щ	shch	as 'shch' in 'fresh chips' (Russian)
	sht	as the '-shed' in pushed' (Bulgarian)
Ъ ъ	â	as the 'a' in 'ago' (Bulgarian only)
ъ		'hard' sign (Russian only)
ы ы	y	as the 'i' in 'ill' (Russian only)
ь		'soft' sign (Russian only)
Э э	e	as in 'end' (Russian only)
Ю ю	yu	as the word 'you'
Я я	ya	as in 'yard'

bus	aftobus
fixed-route minibus	marshrutnaye taksi
steamship	parakhot
train	poyezt
tram	tramvay
trolleybus	traleybus
pier/quay	prichal/pristan'
train station	zhilezna darozhnyy vagzal
stop (bus/trolleybus/ tram)	astanofka
one-way ticket	bilet v adin kanets
return ticket	bilet v oba kantsa
two tickets	dva bilety
soft/1st-class	myahkiy
hard/2nd-class	kupeyny
3rd-class	platskartny

Where is ...?	gde ...?
to (on) the left	naleva
to (on) the right	naprava
straight on	pryama

SLOVAK

PRONUNCIATION

In words of three syllables or less the stress falls on the first syllable. Longer words generally also have a secondary accent on the third or fifth syllable. There are thirteen vowels (a, á, ä, e, é, i, í, o, ó, u, ú, y, ý), three semi-vowels (l, ľ, r) and five diphthongs (ia, ie, iu, ou, ô).

c	as the 'ts' in 'its'
č	as the 'ch' in 'church'
dz	as the 'ds' in 'suds'
dž	as the 'j' in 'judge'
ia	as the 'yo' in 'yonder'
ie	as the 'ye' in 'yes'
iu	as the word 'you'
j	as the 'y' in 'yet'
ň	as the 'ni' in 'onion'
ô	as the 'wo' in 'won't'
ou	as the 'ow' in 'know'
š	as the 'sh' in 'show'
y	as the 'i' in 'machine'
ž	as the 'z' in 'azure'

ACCOMMODATION

hotel	hotel
guesthouse	penzión
youth hostel	mládežnícka ubytovňa
camping ground	kemping
private room	privat
Do you have any rooms available?	Máte voľné izby?
How much is it?	Koľko to stojí?
Does it include breakfast?	Sú raňajky zahrnuté v cene?
single room	jednolôžková izba
double room	dvojlôžková izba

CONVERSATION & ESSENTIALS

Hello.	Ahoj.
Goodbye.	Dovidenia.
Yes.	Áno.
No.	Nie.
Please.	Prosím.
Thank you.	Ďakujem.
Excuse me.	Prepáčte mi.
Sorry.	Odpuste mi.
Do you speak English?	Hovoríte anglicky?
I don't understand.	Nerozumiem.
What is it called?	Ako sa do volá?
How much is it?	Koľko to stojí?

EMERGENCIES – SLOVAK

Help!	Pomoc!
Call a doctor!	Zavolajte doktora/lekára!
Call an ambulance!	Zavolajte záchranku!
Call the police!	Zavolajte políciu!
Go away!	Chod preč! (sg)/
	Chodte preč! (pl)
I'm lost.	Nevyznám sa tu.

SHOPPING & SERVICES

the bank	banka
the chemist	lekárnik
the market	trh
the post office	pošta
the telephone centre	telefónnu centrálu
the tourist office	turistické informačné centrum

TIME, DAYS & NUMBERS

What time is it?	Koľko je hodín?
today	dnes
tonight	dnes večer
tomorrow	zajtra
yesterday	včera
in the morning	ráno
in the evening	večer
Monday	pondelok
Tuesday	utorok
Wednesday	streda
Thursday	štvrtok
Friday	piatok
Saturday	sobota
Sunday	nedeľa

1	jeden	7	sedem
2	dva	8	osem
3	tri	9	deväť
4	štyri	10	desať
5	päť	100	sto
6	šesť	1000	tisíc

TRANSPORT & DIRECTIONS

What time does the ... leave/arrive?	Kedy odchádza/prichádza ...?
boat	loč
city bus	mestský autobus
intercity bus	medzimestský autobus
plane	lietadlo
train	vlak
tram	električka
arrival	príchod
departure	odchod
timetable	cestovný poriadok
Where is the bus stop?	Kde je autobusová zastávka?
Where is the station?	Kde je vlaková stanica?
Where is the left luggage room?	Kde je úschovňa batožín?
Please show me on the map.	Prosím, ukážte mi to na mape.
left	vľavo
right	vpravo
straight ahead	rovno

SIGNS – SLOVAK	
Vchod	Entrance
Východ	Exit
Informácie	Information
Otvorené	Open
Zatvorené	Closed
Zakázané	Prohibited
Telefón	Telephone
Záchody/WC/Toalety	Toilets

SLOVENE

PRONUNCIATION

The letters **l** and **v** are both pronounced like the English 'w' when they occur at the end of syllables and before vowels. Though words like *trn* (thorn) look unpronounceable, most Slovenes (depending on dialect) add a short vowel like an 'a' or the German 'ö' in front of the 'r' to give a Scot's pronunciation of 'tern' or 'tarn'.

c	as the 'ts' in 'its'
č	as the 'ch' in 'church'
ê	as the 'a' in 'apple'
e	as the 'a' in 'ago' (when unstressed)
é	as the 'ay' in 'day'
j	as the 'y' in 'yellow'
ó	as the 'o' in 'more'
ò	as the 'o' in 'soft'
r	a rolled 'r' sound
š	as the 'sh' in 'ship'
u	as the 'oo' in 'good'
ž	as the 's' in 'treasure'

ACCOMMODATION

hotel	hotel
guesthouse	gostišče
camping ground	kamping

Do you have a ...?	Ali imate prosto ...?
bed	posteljo
cheap room	poceni sobo
single room	enoposteljno sobo
double room	dvoposteljno sobo

How much is it per night?	Koliko stane za eno noč?
How much is it per person?	Koliko stane za eno osebo?
for one/two nights	za eno noč/za dve noči
Is breakfast included?	Ali je zajtrk vključen?

CONVERSATION & ESSENTIALS

Hello.	Pozdravljeni. (pol)
	Zdravo/Živio. (inf)
Good day.	Dober dan!
Goodbye.	Nasvidenje!
Yes.	Da or Ja. (inf)
No.	Ne.
Please.	Prosim.
Thank you (very much).	Hvala (lepa).
You're welcome.	Prosim/Ni za kaj!
Excuse me.	Oprostite.
Do you speak English?	Govorite angleško?
What's your name?	Kako vam je ime?
My name is ...	Jaz sem ...

EMERGENCIES – SLOVENE	
Help!	Na pomoč!
Call a doctor!	Pokličite zdravnika!
Call the police!	Pokličite policijo!
Go away!	Pojdite stran!

SHOPPING & SERVICES

Where is the/a ...?	Kje je ...?
bank/exchange	banka/menjalnica
post office	pošta
telephone centre	telefonska centrala
tourist office	turistični informacijski urad

TIME, DAYS & NUMBERS

today	danes
tonight	nocoj
tomorrow	jutri
in the morning	zjutraj
in the evening	zvečer

Monday	ponedeljek
Tuesday	torek
Wednesday	sreda
Thursday	četrtek
Friday	petek
Saturday	sobota
Sunday	nedelja

1	ena	**7**	sedem
2	dve	**8**	osem
3	tri	**9**	devet
4	štiri	**10**	deset
5	pet	**100**	sto
6	šest	**1000**	tisoč

TRANSPORT & DIRECTIONS

What time does the ... leave/arrive?	Kdaj odpelje/pripelje ...?

LANGUAGE

SIGNS – SLOVENE

Vhod	Entrance
Izhod	Exit
Informacije	Information
Odprto	Open
Zaprto	Closed
Prepovedano	Prohibited
Stranišče	Toilets

boat/ferry	ladja/trajekt
bus	avtobus
train	vlak

timetable	spored
train station	železniška postaja
bus station	avtobusno postajališče
one-way ticket	enosmerna vozovnica
return ticket	povratna vozovnica

Can you show me on the map?	A mi lahko pokažete na mapi?

SPANISH

ACCOMMODATION

hotel	hotel
guesthouse	pensión/casa de huéspedes
youth hostel	albergue juvenil
camping ground	camping

Do you have any rooms available?	¿Tiene habitaciones libres?
How much is it per night/per person?	¿Cuánto cuesta por noche/ por persona?

a single room	una habitación individual
a double room	una habitación doble
a room with a double bed	una habitación con cama de matrimonio
for one night	para una noche
for two nights	para dos noches

CONVERSATION & ESSENTIALS

Hello/Goodbye.	¡Hola!/¡Adiós!
Yes.	Sí.
No.	No.
Please.	Por favor.
Thank you.	Gracias.
You're welcome.	De nada.
Excuse me.	Perdón/Perdoneme.
Sorry.	Lo siento/Discúlpeme.
Do you speak English?	¿Habla inglés?
How much is it?	¿Cuánto cuesta/vale?

EMERGENCIES – SPANISH

Help!	¡Socorro!/¡Auxilio!
Call a doctor!	¡Llame a un doctor!
Call the police!	¡Llame a la policía!
Go away!	¡Váyase!
I'm lost.	Estoy perdido/a. (m/f)

SHOPPING & SERVICES

a bank	un banco
the chemist	la farmacia
the ... embassy	la embajada ...
the market	el mercado
newsagent/stationer	papelería
the post office	los correos
the tourist office	la oficina de turismo

What time does it open/close?	¿A qué hora abren/cierran?

TIME, DAYS & NUMBERS

What time is it?	¿Qué hora es?
today	hoy
tomorrow	mañana
yesterday	ayer
morning	mañana
afternoon	tarde

Monday	lunes
Tuesday	martes
Wednesday	miércoles
Thursday	jueves
Friday	viernes
Saturday	sábado
Sunday	domingo

1	uno/una	10	diez
2	dos	11	once
3	tres	12	doce
4	cuatro	13	trece
5	cinco	14	catorce
6	seis	15	quince
7	siete	16	dieciéis
8	ocho	100	cien/ciento
9	nueve	1000	mil

TRANSPORT & DIRECTIONS

What time does the next ... leave/arrive?	¿A qué hora sale/llega el próximo ...?
boat	barco
bus (city)	autobús, bus
bus (intercity)	autocar
train	tranvía

I'd like a ... ticket.	*Quisiera un billete ...*
one-way	*sencillo/de sólo ida*
return	*de ida y vuelta*
1st class	*de primera clase*
2nd class	*de segunda clase*
left luggage	*consigna*
timetable	*horario*
bus stop	*parada de autobus*
train station	*estación de ferrocarril*
I'd like to hire ...	*Quisiera alquilar ...*
a car	*un coche*
a bicycle	*una bicicleta*
Where is ...?	*¿Dónde está ...?*
Go straight ahead.	*Siga/Vaya todo derecho.*
Turn left.	*Gire a la izquierda.*
Turn right.	*Gire a la derecha/recto.*
near/far	*cerca/lejos*

SWEDISH

PRONUNCIATION

å	long, as the word 'awe'; short as the 'o' in 'pot'
ä	as the 'a' in 'act'
ö	as the 'er' in 'fern', but without the 'r' sound
y	like 'ee' while pursing your lips
c	as the 's' in 'sit'
ck	as a double 'k'; shortens the preceding vowel
tj/rs	as the 'sh' in 'ship'
sj/ch	similar to the 'ch' in Scottish *loch*
g	as in 'get', but also as the 'y' in 'yet'
lj	as the 'y' in 'yet'

ACCOMMODATION

hotel	*hotell*
guesthouse	*gästhus*
youth hostel	*vandrarhem*
camping ground	*campingplats*
Do you have any rooms available?	*Finns det några lediga rum?*
How much is it per night/person?	*Hur mycket kostar det per natt/person?*
for one night	*i en natt*
for two nights	*i två nätter*
I'd like ...	*Jag skulle vilja ha ...*
a single room	*ett enkelrum*
a double room	*ett dubbelrum*

CONVERSATION & ESSENTIALS

Hello.	*Hej.*
Goodbye.	*Adjö/Hej då.*
Yes.	*Ja.*
No.	*Nej.*
Please.	*Snälla/Vänligen.*
Thank you.	*Tack.*
That's fine/You're welcome.	*Det är bra/Varsågod.*
Excuse me.	*Ursäkta mig.*
Sorry.	*Förlåt.*
Do you speak English?	*Talar du engelska?*
How much is it?	*Hur mycket kostar den?*

TIME, DAYS & NUMBERS

What time is it?	*Vad är klockan?*
today	*idag*
tomorrow	*imorgon*
yesterday	*igår*
morning	*morgonen*
afternoon	*efter middagen*

Monday	*måndag*			
Tuesday	*tisdag*			
Wednesday	*onsdag*			
Thursday	*torsdag*			
Friday	*fredag*			
Saturday	*lördag*			
Sunday	*söndag*			

0	*noll*	7	*sju*
1	*ett*	8	*åtta*
2	*två*	9	*nio*
3	*tre*	10	*tio*
4	*fyra*	11	*elva*
5	*fem*	100	*ett hundra*
6	*sex*	1000	*ett tusen*

SHOPPING & SERVICES

bank	*bank*
chemist/pharmacy	*apotek*
... embassy	*... ambassaden*
market	*marknaden*
newsagent/	*nyhetsbyrå/*
stationer	*pappers handel*
post office	*postkontoret*
tourist office	*turistinformation*
What time does it open/close?	*När öppnar/stänger de?*

TRANSPORT & DIRECTIONS

What time does ... leave/arrive?	*När avgår/kommer ...?*
the boat	*båten*
the city bus	*stadsbussen*
the intercity bus	*landsortsbussen*
the tram	*spårvagnen*
the train	*tåget*
I'd like ...	*Jag skulle vilja ha ...*
a one-way ticket	*en enkelbiljett*
a return ticket	*en returbiljett*
1st class	*första klass*
2nd class	*andra klass*
left luggage	*effektförvaring*
timetable	*tidtabell*
bus stop	*busshållplats*
train station	*tågstation*
Where can I hire a car/bicycle?	*Var kan jag hyra en bil/cykel?*
Where is ...?	*Var är ...?*
Go straight ahead.	*Gå rakt fram.*
Turn left.	*Sväng till vänster.*
Turn right.	*Sväng till höger.*
near/far	*nära/långt*

TURKISH

PRONUNCIATION

A, a	as the 'ar' in 'art' or 'bar'
E, e	as in 'fell'
İ, i	as 'ee'
I, ı	as 'uh'
O, o	as in 'hot'
U, u	as the 'oo' in 'moo'
Ö, ö	as the 'ur' in 'fur'
Ü, ü	as the 'ew' in 'few'

Note that both **ö** and **ü** are pronounced with pursed lips.

Ç, ç	as the 'ch' in 'church'
C, c	as English 'j'
Ğ, ğ	not pronounced; draws out the preceding vowel a bit – ignore it!
J, j	as the 's' in 'treasure'
S, s	hard, as in 'stress'
Ş, ş	as the 'sh' in 'shoe'
V, v	as the 'w' in 'weather'

ACCOMMODATION

hotel	*otel(i)*
guesthouse	*pansiyon*
student hostel	*öğrenci yurdu*
camping ground	*kampink*
Do you have any rooms available?	*Boş oda var mı?*
How much is it per night/per person?	*Bir gecelik/Kişibaşına kaç para?*
a single room	*tek kişilik oda*
a double room	*iki kişilik oda*

EMERGENCIES – TURKISH

Help!/Emergency!	*İmdat!*
Call a doctor!	*Doktor çağırın!*
Call the police!	*Polis çağırın!*
Go away!	*Gidin/Git!/Defol!*
I'm lost.	*Kayboldum.*

CONVERSATION & ESSENTIALS

Hello.	*Merhaba.*
Goodbye.	*Allahaısmarladık/Güle güle.*
Yes.	*Evet.*
No.	*Hayır.*
Please.	*Lütfen.*
Thank you.	*Teşekkür ederim.*

That's fine/You're welcome.	*Bir şey değil.*	Friday	*Cuma*
		Saturday	*Cumartesi*
Excuse me.	*Affedersiniz.*	Sunday	*Pazar*
Sorry/Pardon.	*Pardon.*		
Do you speak English?	*İngilizce biliyor musunuz?*	1	*bir*	8	*sekiz*
How much is it?	*Ne kadar?*	2	*iki*	9	*dokuz*

1	*bir*
2	*iki*
3	*üç*
4	*dört*
5	*beş*
6	*altı*
7	*yedi*

8	*sekiz*
9	*dokuz*
10	*on*
11	*on bir*
12	*on iki*
100	*yüz*
1000	*bin*

one million   *bir milyon*

SIGNS – TURKISH

Giriş	Entrance
Çıkış	Exit
Danışma	Information
Açık	Open
Kapali	Closed
Yasak(tir)	Prohibited
Tuvalet	Toilets

SHOPPING & SERVICES

a bank	*bir banka*
a chemist/pharmacy	*bir eczane*
the ... embassy	*... büyükelçiliği*
the post office	*postane*
the market	*çarşı*
the tourist office	*turizm danışma bürosu*
What time does it open/close?	*Ne zamam açılır/kapanır?*

TIME, DAYS & NUMBERS

What time is it?	*Saat kaç?*
today	*bugün*
tomorrow	*yarın*
yesterday	*dün*
morning	*sabah*
afternoon	*öğleden sonra*
Monday	*Pazartesi*
Tuesday	*Salı*
Wednesday	*Çarşamba*
Thursday	*Perşembe*

TRANSPORT & DIRECTIONS

What time does the next ... leave/arrive?	*Gelecek ... ne zaman kalkar/gelir?*
ferry/boat	*feribot/vapur*
bus (city)	*şehir otobüsü*
bus (intercity)	*otobüs*
tram	*tramvay*
train	*tren*
I'd like ...	*... istiyorum*
a one-way ticket	*gidiş bileti*
a return ticket	*gidiş-dönüş bileti*
1st/2nd class	*birinci/ikinci mevkii*
left luggage	*emanetçi*
timetable	*tarife*
bus/tram stop	*otobüs/tramvay durağı*
train station	*gar/istasyon*
boat/ship dock	*iskele*
I'd like to hire a car/bicycle.	*Araba/bisiklet kirala mak istiyorum.*
Where is a/the ...?	*... nerede?*
Go straight ahead.	*Doğru gidin.*
Turn left.	*Sola dönün.*
Turn right.	*Sağa dönün.*
near/far	*yakın/uzak*

Behind the Scenes

THIS BOOK

Many people have helped to create this 4th edition of *Europe on a Shoestring*. *Europe on a Shoestring* is part of Lonely Planet's Europe series, which includes *Eastern Europe, Mediterranean Europe, Central Europe, Scandinavian Europe* and *Western Europe*. Lonely Planet also publishes phrasebooks for these regions.

THANKS FROM THE AUTHORS

Reuben Acciano Thanks to my frustrated, tolerant family in Perth, the Italian people, incredible Leonardo & Maria Theresa in Venice, inspirational Livio, Paolo Vallelonga for *sgropino*, warmth and being the Most Incredible Guide, George and the Siena boys *(acaniamo c'e'?')*, enchanting Melissa Rosati in Bologna/Brescia, the Brits in Florence & Milan, the incomparable hospitality of the mixindex.com/ Mansion gang, gorgemouse Zoe Rose (shenaniganarchy!), Clancy the Perpetual and beloved pip-spitting 'Bella, forgiver/forgetter.

Fiona Adams Thanks to all the staff in the tourist offices throughout southern Spain, particularly Caty Serra and Rita Hunziker in Ibiza. A special thanks to Salvador and his charming family in Marbella, Felicity in the hostal in Valencia, Joe and Lucy in Tarifa (may the *poniente* be with you), Frans de Man, Sarah Andrews, my co-author on the Spain chapter and to the LP staff who worked on this edition, Loli Cabarcos and Juan Balan (*besos y abrazos* for your help and friendship). And Mum, thank you so much for looking after Gaucho while I was away (again). Most of all I would like to thank my husband Jamie, the biggest star of them all. I couldn't have done it without you.

Sarah Andrews I owe so much to friends, old and new. This Spain chapter wouldn't have been the same without the awesome advice of people like Nuria Pardina, Fede Alvarez and Ana Maeso in Madrid, Theresa Coryn and Dani Muñoz in Aragón, and Courtney Edwards in Santiago de Compostela. The biggest thanks of all goes to my wonderful husband Miquel, who helped me in every way on the road and back at home base. And a big hand for the rest of the LP crew, who made my job much easier!

Carolyn Bain Various locals, expats and tourists in Malta gave their time and shared their local knowledge, for which I am grateful, especially Charmaine Saliba, Tony, Jean Paul, Charlie and Joseph. In Sweden, I'm indebted to Magnus Welin for his friendship and assistance. *Tack så mycket* goes to Per Hellsten, Amy Archer & Jesper Neilsen, and Danni Überfeld. Huge thanks to Sally O'Brien for making work seem so much fun in Stockholm, Malmö and Copenhagen. Finally, for making it to both destinations, warm thanks to Kelvin Adams, place-dropper extraordinaire.

Joe Bindloss My thanks as always to Linda Nylind for putting up with me going away so much. In the Republic of Cyprus, my thanks to the Cyprus Tourism Organisation, Liz and Dimitri in Lefkosia and Efthymia at Cyprus Antiquities. In the north, my thanks to the staff at Sun Car Hire in Lefkoşa and the helpful people of Karpasia. Credit to the people on both sides of the line who are striving for peaceful reunification and a fair settlement for refugees.

Becca Blond I'd like to dedicate my part of this book to my cousin Lynn Seidler, who passed away on 18 March 2004 in the Turks & Caicos Islands: her love of travel always inspired me. Big thanks to the folks at Switzerland Tourism, especially Erika Loser, who offered so much advice, Heather Dickson, who joined me for three days in Zurich (you survived the trams and the mapping!), the travellers I met in Interlaken, Christine and Ashley for spending the day with me in Gimmelwald. As always I'm grateful for the love and support of my family and friends: David, Patricia, Jessica, Jennie, John, Vera and Lani. To Aaron – thanks for waiting.

Michael Grosberg Special thanks to Yvonne Seidel for her generosity and extensive network of friends across southern Germany, including Achim Becker in Constance, and Anna Linder in Munich. Thanks to Nathalie Weber, Christian and his parents, Christina and Alex von Hoffmeister for their hospitality, Gabi Daikeler-Meurer and Karl-Heinz Herse in Freiburg, Luci Westphal-Solary for advice about Hamburg and the Frisian Islands, Martyn Leder and Inga Scheffler for their expertise in Hamburg, Ulrich Plass and Ilona Ryvkin for their general impressions about the country, Margaret Lydecker and Jane Stewart for their advice about Bonn and Cologne, Peter Guryan, Lara and Shirly Daniel for their help on Frankfurt, Glenn Yeck for tips on Stuttgart, Andrea Mohr for the drink in Nurmberg. And thanks to the professional staff at tourist offices across the country for making my job easier. And finally thanks to Orly Isaccson, my brother Joel and my parents, Sheldon and Judy Grosberg.

Paul Harding Thanks to everyone who made my Finland trip an enjoyable and fruitful one, especially Markku in Savonlinna, Jussi, Mikko, Paula and Mari in Oulu, Seija in Helsinki, Valur for company in Lapland and Kaisa. Thanks as always to the movers and shakers at Lonely Planet: Amanda Canning, Fiona Christie, Alan Murphy, Mark Griffiths and my fellow authors. And to Cath Graham in Melbourne: thanks for the travels.

Amy Karafin Infinite gratitude to Virginia Tevendale, queen of wonderment, who opened up her house, her heart, and showed me how to explore ruins and eat dandelions. Big thanks to Mum and Dad for the neverending supply of love and support, my Dhamma brothers and sisters in Ireland, especially Frances, Kate, Michael and Rachel, Beverly and Wally Serkin for the ghost stories and the perfect evening, John Connolly for the calls and Andy McKay for the toasties, the folks at Fáilte Ireland, Tourism Ireland and the Northern Ireland Tourist Board, Joan and Dr. Peter Pyne, Mary Pierse, Trevor Storey, and Carmel and Mattie Shannon, Erik Vickstrom for reading everything and for helping with my cabin fever. *Tous mes remerciements à Maïmouna Ciss pour son aide pendant la période de 'chambre–café–chambre–café' et également à Lucien Mbengue pour les appels.* And finally, apologies to those who I almost killed driving on the wrong side of the road.

Steve Kokker Thanks goes to Misha and Albert at Baltma tours in Kaliningrad, Rodion, Sasha and Andrei for all their help and fun times, the customs officers in Sovetsk for a unique experience, Dmitry Podcovyrin at Komsomolskaya Pravda and Henri Kaasik-Aaslav in Estonia.

John Lee Thanks to VisitScotland and VisitBritain (particularly Val in the Toronto office) for their sterling assistance, my parents in St Albans for feeding me whenever I turned up unannounced (which was often), my brother Michael for including me in his pub crawl of Glasgow and my nephew Christopher for planning to use this book on his own upcoming travels.

Alex Leviton I must profusely thank my travelling companion and driver/sherpa, Len Amaral. Thanks also to Maha Shamiyeh, who left her honeymoon early to hike the Glastonbury tor with me. Props, y'all. Thanks to Paul Spurr in Bristol, Dave Jones in Liverpool, Dean Hoskins in Shrewsbury, Alex Watts in Newquay, Paul Chibeba at Visit Britain, Vicki and Hannah in Oxford, Gabriel in Windermere, Chris in Wales, Sarah Singfield in London, and countless other locals, travellers and tourist personnel and the British people, for continuously and vociferously pointing out the flaws of my imperialist government.

Leanne Logan & Geert Cole Thanks for the enthusiastic help from Els Maes at Toerisme Vlaanderen and Sabine Rosen at the Office de Promotion de Tourisme in Brussels, Anne De Meerleer at Toerisme Brugge in Brugge, Jean-Claude Conter from the Luxembourg National Tourist Office, Roos and Bert Cole for their boundless Belgian hospitality, our ever-keen road mates, Sixy and Bluey, and Eleonor, our daughter, for loving life on the road. Thanks also to those readers who provided insights and the travellers we met on the road for spot-on suggestions. And *bedankt* to all those at LP who were involved with this book's production.

Craig McLachlan I'd like to thank my exceptionally beautiful wife, Yuriko, for not squeezing too hard and breaking any of my ribs while petrified on the back of the countless scooters we hired to get around. Thanks also to our sons for letting us go. The team at Lonely Planet was exceptional. I'll be back to Greece sometime to buy a Mythos for Jonathon, Stamati, Panos, Sofi, Rena, Yiannis, Dimitri, Francesco, Stelios, 'Professor' Yiannis, Kim, Prokopis, Katerina, Alexis, Sonya, Mikaelis, Sandy, Stelios, Betty, Georgina and her lovely sisters. Thanks also to the team at Wilderness Adventures in Queenstown for keeping things going while we were away.

Vesna Maric A million thanks goes to Rafael (*!gracias amor!*) who led me to enjoy every moment of the journey. Big thanks goes to Gabriel for his grammar fascism, patience and kindness, Tom for being a friend and for answering all my boring questions, Balina for showing us her country and taking care, Blerina and Andi for being so kind, Beni Andoni in Tirana, Koli and his scary driving, Ines, Gianfranco and Annalisa for all their care in Bari. My eternal thanks to my mama.

Tom Masters Thanks goes to Clem Cecil and Malinka for letting me stay with them in Moscow, Alex

Tampokopolous for great company and the inimitable Dima Makarov for comic value, Simon Patterson, Marc de Mauny, Dmitry Dzhafarov, Galina Stolyarova, Rosemary Masters and Gillian Argyle in St Petersburg for all their good company and support.

Tom Parkinson Thanks simply to everyone who's helped me out, put me up or met me on the road in Germany and Turkey. Extra credit is due to Anne and Annika in Berlin for repeated hospitality, Tarun and Dan for some top tips, Hasan, Anthea and Catherine for a good night out (Elvis lives!), Pat Yale for extra info, Jen Rigby for her fine editorial work (though not on this book), and Nina K, for all the usual.

Fran Parnell Huge thanks to everyone who assisted on the road, including tourist officers, fellow travellers, random passers-by and the smiley people at Reykjavík City Hostel, *Grapevine* bods Valur Gunnarsson and Jón Trausti Sigurðurson who answered endless questions on the *runtur*, Svanhvít Helga Runarsdóttir, stalwart aid at the BSÍ bus station and Jón Þór Eyþórsson at Reykjavík tourist information centre for streams of spot-on information. A big thank you to Heather Murphy for making this first assignment such a painless experience, Mark Griffiths for mapping help, and William J 'Billabong' Frugal: big love.

Josephine Quintero I'd like to thank Robin Chapman for sharing my enthusiasm for Portuguese wines and custard tarts, Terry and Colin Geary for their invaluable input, Heather Dickson for encouraging me while on the road, and all the helpful staff of the local tourist associations. Thanks also to Kevin Hawthorn in Silves for his spare bed and insight into the nightlife nuances of the Algarve.

Robert Reid Big thanks go to George Kamen and Hristo Georgiev, the Bulgarian tutor, for helping me prepare my trip from New York City, and to Lonely Planet's Imogen Franks and Fiona Christie for sending me in the first place. Also to Anne Mulvaney for editing. Scores of folks went out of their way to help me get info. Notable thanks goes to Assen Davidov in Sofia (for introducing me to his Roma friends and much more), former Prime Minister Philip Dimitrov for getting me Dunkin' Donuts coffee, Stefan of Veliko for bringing me along the all-night birthday party in the forest, Emil Svetan of Vidin (and family) for putting me up when the Belogradchik bus didn't show, Maria Tutundjian of Plovdiv for the canal walk, Tony Paskov for last-second info, all the Peace Corps folks (Dave Elmstrom, Jennifer Nikolaeff, Nellie Goddard), Dobrich

TV for putting me on the airways of northeastern Bulgaria and countless folks like the Shumen bus-station clerk for showing me photos of her family as the line stacked up behind her.

Miles Roddis A packful of thanks to Ingrid, who regaled me daily with tales of her skiing exploits as I explored the inner recesses of Andorra's hotels and restaurant kitchens. Thank you too to the always cheerful and helpful team in Canillo's tourist office, Lourdes and Meritxell (Andorra la Vella), Laura (La Massana), Xesca (Ordino), Sylvia and Jordi (Pas de la Casa) and Anna Gascón in the Centre d'Interpretació de la Natura, Ordino.

Simon Sellars Thanks to Michelle Farley, Kate James, Daniel New, Rachel Thorpe and Tasmin McNaughtan for their help and encouragement during the research and write-up for this Netherlands chapter. Thanks also to *Europe on a Shoestring*'s Commissioning Editor, Heather Dickson, Coordinating Author, Sarah Johnstone, Coordinating Editor, Melissa Faulkner, and Managing Cartographer, Mark Griffiths.

Lisa Steer-Guérard Thanks to the London, Southeast and East England tourist offices. Much gratitude to Mum, Mike and Matthew for fortitudal talks with cups of tea and choccy biscuits while I was researching London. Also to Gilles for his numerous words of encouragement, and for putting up with my unsociability while I was writing.

Wendy Taylor A huge thanks to my friends in Minsk: Robert Heuer, Goran Subotic, Ilija 'Ika' Todorovic, Tatsiana Aliakseyeva and, Inna Bukshtynovich – St Inna is now deemed the patron saint of travel guidebook writers. In Ukraine, the Lviv Tourist Board and Eugenia Travel supplied me with lots of facts, and, in Kyiv, Rostick Gavrilov of Come2Ukraine.com set me up with everything I needed. So much preparatory information came from Lonely Planet author Steve Kokker. Brian Vitunic and Alexis Menten were indispensable: they gave me a bed, a dial-up connection and plenty of cosmopolitans. And Matthew Wood, my dearest friend and partner, provided all those necessary intangibles – laughter, inspiration and motivation.

Richard Watkins Many thanks are due to Aneta, Warsaw tourist office, for guiding me around her city and whose inside knowledge of the Polish capital was invaluable, the helpful and professional staff at tourist offices in Łódź, Lublin, Wrocław, Premyśl, Sanok and Toruń, Jan Piotrowski, Gosia

Graczyk and the staff at the Polish Embassy in London for their kind assistance with my research.

Neil Wilson *Mockrat děkuji* to tourist office staff around the Czech Republic and to Richard Nebeský and Tomáš Harabís for their insights into Czech society. And, as always, a big thank you to Carol for helping with the restaurants and shops in Prague.

CREDITS

Europe on a Shoestring was commissioned and developed in Lonely Planet's UK office by Heather Dickson, and assessed by Susie Ashworth, Heather Dickson, Sam Trafford and Stefanie di Trocchio. Imogen Franks assisted in a commissioning role. The book was coordinated by Melissa Faulkner (editorial), Csanad Csutoros (cartography) and David Kemp (layout). Susie Ashworth, Sarah Bailey, Sasha Baskett, Andrea Baster, Yvonne Byron, Dan Caleo, Emily Coles, Kate Daly, Kate Evans, Cathryn Game, Charlotte Harrison, Nancy Ianni, Evan Jones, Craig Kilburn (who also assisted with the book's coordination), Katie Lynch, Anne Mulvaney, Stephanie Pearson, Sally Steward and Katrina Webb assisted with editing and proofing. Barbara Benson, Marion Byass, Piotr Czajkowski, Jovan Djukanovic, Daniel Fennessey, Tadhgh Knaggs, Valentina Kremenchutskaya, Kim McDonald, Emma McNicol, Laurie Mikkelson, Adrian Persoglia, Jolyon Philcox, Charles Rawlings-Way, Helen Rowley, Jacqui Saunders, Amanda Sierp, Lyndell Stringer, Chris Thomas, Simon Tillema, Natasha Velleley assisted with cartography. David Kemp and Jenny Jones laid the book out, Yvonne Bischofberger designed the colour content and Maria Vallianos designed the cover. Kaitlin Beckett, Adam Bextream, Steven Cann, Pablo Gastar, Laura Jane, Margie Jung, Indra Kilfoyle, Katherine Marsh and John Shippick assisted with layout. Adrianna Mammarella and Kate McDonald assisted with layout checking. Quentin Frayne prepared the Language chapter, and Gabbi Wilson and Melissa Faulkner prepared the index. Overseeing production were Ray Thomson (Project Manager), Bruce Evans (Managing Editor), Martin Heng (Managing Editor) and Mark Griffiths (Managing Cartographer). The series was designed by James Hardy, with mapping development by Paul Piaia.

THANKS FROM LONELY PLANET

Many thanks to the travellers who used the last edition and wrote to us with helpful hints, useful advice and interesting anecdotes:

A Chloe Adams, E Adams, Ryan Adserias, Christopher Allsop, Esteban Altamirano, Phil & Hilary Andre, Pippa Andre, Hugh Anand **B** Peter Baker, Bronwyn Batchelor, Sylvia Bator, Alessandro Bavila, Miriam Baxter, Daniel Belavy, Chris Bell, Jesse Bergman, Jim Berry, Mary Bickmore, Roger Bielec, Owen Billing, Burke Bindbeutel, Kate Black, Brian W Boag, Julie Branaghan, David Breen, Joan Brown, Malcolm & Joan Brown, Dr John D Brunton, Deborah Burnett, Timothy Burrows **C** Norman Cain, Sonia Cairns, Juan Manuel Perez Campo-Cossio, Maria Castillo-Stone, Cherie Chasling, Nikitas Chondroyannos, William Christ, Shelia Christos, Mona Clark, Martin Clohessy, Beryl Coe, Loyola Colebeck, Krista Coleman, Polly Cook, Ron & Sheila Corbett, Lynne Corcoran, James Costello, Peter Coville, John and Elizabeth Cox, Kate Crane, Rebecca Cutri-Kohart **D** Leanne Danelisky, Kate Darwent, Bob & Pat Davis, Roger Davis, Lynn Dawson, Rosemarijn & Joost Dekker, Janet Denye, Mirka Doubravova, David Doughan, Linda Drath **E** Jim Edwards, Keith Ellis, Pippa Ellwood, John Else, Aaron Epstein, Tan Ergen, Hanne Espolin Johnson, Rich Esteves **F** Rachel Faggetter, Emmanuel Fankhauser, Olivia Faul, Sarah Feigh, Dr Med Lars Floter, Lyall Ford, Joanne Fox, Max Francis, Sarah French, Michael Fust, Mr & Mrs Fyvie **G** Laura Galimberti, Natasha George, Megan Gibbs, Douglas & Isolde Gibson, Z Gillies, Planet Glassberg, Helen Graham, Maggie & Hugh Gravelle, Jim Green, Charles V Greenless, Romualdo Grillo, Stephanie Guilbert, Olena Guseva **H** Alex Hall, Alison Harris, Edward Haughney, Patricia Havekost, Megan Heim, Sandi Heimlich, Ian Hellen, David Henderson, Jim Hendrickson, John Hesketh, Georgina Hewes, Francis Higbie, N Hill, Adam Hobill, Leigh Hopkinson, Tina Hough, Henri Hovine, Margaret Huggett, Denis Hughes, Gareth Hughes, Lynn W Humeston, Christopher Hunt, Geoff Hutcheison **I** John Iaquinto, Claudia Immisch, Shamin Islam **J** Erine Jackson, Neil Jackson, Emma Jacobs, Cameron Jacotine, Chad Jansen, Barry Johnston, Jo Johnston, M D Jones, Ronaele Jones **K** Kapka Kassabova, Naja Kastanje, Karen, Lisa Keeley, Kathryn Kerridge, M J Kinrade, Madame Mary Ellen Kitler, Claudine Knobel, Ivana Kotalova, Ann Kramer, Anatoliy Kurmanaev **L** Ruud Lampf, M Langham, Donald & Nancy Lareau, Jane Larew, Mick Lauson Jr, Tram Anh Le, Margaret Lee, James Leitzell, Frances & Andrea Lench, Michael Leonard, Stephen Leong, Phil Linz, Ynyr Lloyd, Ute Loeffelsend, Paul Lyddon **M** Rebecca Mair, Victoria Martinez, Jacek Matwiejczyk, Ross McAlpine, Jamie McBride, Richard McBride, ALastair McCall, Dr J S McLintock, Ricardo Medeiros, Helene Mercier, John Meredith, John & Lynn Midgley, Tiziana Milizia, Alan Millward, Joe Milum, Tina Mizgalski, Mark Mocicka, Heather Monell, Kay Mould, Don Munro, Allison Murray **N** Stephen Burke Nau, Ian Nelder, Emma Newton, John & Anne Nield **O** Geordie Oakes, Catherine O'Neill, Agnes Ong, Tim Ottevanger **P** Gregory Palermo, Erlandas Paplauskis, Lance Patford, Shalom S Paul, Stjepan Perkovic, Lea Ann Pestotnik, Carl Pickerill, Gemma Purves **Q** Janet Quilter **R** Karlmarx Rajangam, Kent Raju, Emanuele Ramella, Marc Ramsbottom, William Reeves, Maria Katja Ressel, Peter & Yumiko Riley, Terry Rolleri, Amber Rowland **S** Robert Sanders, Vivienne Sandy, C T Sartain, Alan Schneider, Harvey Schwartz, Nigel Sewell, Matt Sharpe, Linda Shaw, Nicole Sheldon, Maria Sherry, Susan & James Shields, Aneta Singh, Andrea Sita, Clyde and Elva Slonaker, Amanda Smith, David K. Smith, Richard Smith, Richard & B Smith, Ian Southwell, Bonnie Spoales, Alistair Staton, Ann Stewart, Wesley Streeting, Anna Swindells, Thor & Mary Swope, David Szylit **T** Peter Taylor, Laura

Theng, James Thomas, Michael Thompson, Paul Tiebosch, Bobby Tim, Marcelo Trasel, Nicole Trombley **U** Gregory Ulrich **V** Camille Van Wessem, Theijs Van Wlij, Wim Vandenbussche **W** Raoul Wainwright, Catherine Waldby, Terry Walker, E-J Walsh, Loes Walsteijn, Alan & Liz Walter, Kate Walters, Jennifer Wang, Andy Ward, Sabine Wehinger, Gail Weinkauf, Andrew Wenrick, John & Deborah Wheaton, Ada Whitaker, James Wilbrot, Chad Williams, Kathleen A Williams, Maggie Willsher, Isobel Wilson, Joseph and Elaine Wojtowicz, Caroline Woodgate, David Woodhouse, Christopher Woods, Susan Wuchter-Stein, Frankas Wurft, D S Wyber, Collier Wylie **Y** Andrew Yale

ACKNOWLEDGMENTS

Many thanks to the following for the use of their content:

Globe on back cover – Mountain High Maps®
© 1993 Digital Wisdom, Inc

Index

000 Map pages
000 Location of colour photographs

000 Map pages
000 Location of colour photographs

000 Map pages
000 Location of colour photographs

INDEX

THE LONELY PLANET STORY

The story begins with a classic travel adventure: Tony and Maureen Wheeler's 1972 journey across Europe and Asia to Australia. There was no useful information about the overland trail then, so Tony and Maureen published the first Lonely Planet guidebook to meet a growing need.

From a kitchen table, Lonely Planet has grown to become the largest independent travel publisher in the world, with offices in Melbourne (Australia), Oakland (USA) and London (UK). Today Lonely Planet guidebooks cover the globe. There is an ever-growing list of books and information in a variety of media. Some things haven't changed. The main aim is still to make it possible for adventurous travellers to get out there – to explore and better understand the world.

At Lonely Planet we believe travellers can make a positive contribution to the countries they visit – if they respect their host communities and spend their money wisely. Every year 5% of company profit is donated to charities around the world.

SEND US YOUR FEEDBACK

We love to hear from travellers – your comments keep us on our toes and help make our books better. Our well-travelled team reads every word on what you loved or loathed about this book. Although we cannot reply individually to postal submissions, we always guarantee that your feedback goes straight to the appropriate authors, in time for the next edition. Each person who sends us information is thanked in the next edition – and the most useful submissions are rewarded with a free book. See the Behind the Scenes section.

To send us your updates – and find out about Lonely Planet events, newsletters and travel news – visit our award-winning website: **www.lonelyplanet.com/feedback**

Note: We may edit, reproduce and incorporate your comments in Lonely Planet products such as guidebooks, websites and digital products, so let us know if you don't want your comments reproduced or your name acknowledged. For a copy of our privacy policy, go to www.lonelyplanet.com/privacy

Published by Lonely Planet Publications Pty Ltd
ABN 36 005 607 983

© Lonely Planet 2005

© photographers as indicated 2005
Cover montage by Maria Vallianos. Cover photographs by Lonely Planet Images: Jon Davison, Lee Foster, Christopher Groenhout, Chris Mellor, Richard Nebeský, Nicholas Reuss, Neil Setchfield; back cover: Corsican beach, France, Jean-Bernard Carillet. Many of the images in this guide are available for licensing from Lonely Planet Images: www.lonelyplanetimages.com

Printed through SNP SPrint Singapore Pte Ltd at
KHL Printing Co Sdn Bhd, Malaysia

LONELY PLANET OFFICES

Australia
Head Office
Locked Bag 1, Footscray, Victoria 3011
☎ 03 8379 8000, fax 03 8379 8111
talk2us@lonelyplanet.com.au

USA
150 Linden St, Oakland, CA 94607
☎ 510 893 8555, toll free 800 275 8555
fax 510 893 8572, info@lonelyplanet.com

UK
72–82 Rosebery Ave,
Clerkenwell, London EC1R 4RW
☎ 020 7841 9000, fax 020 7841 9001
go@lonelyplanet.co.uk